CONTENTS

Major Leagues
2002 In Review............................... 4
World Series................................... 25
American League 31
National League 43

Organizations
Club-by-Club Statistics 55

Minor Leagues
2002 In Review............................. 274

Prospects
Rankings...................................... 327

Independent Leagues
2002 In Review............................. 348

Foreign Leagues
2002 In Review............................. 371

Winter Leagues
2002 In Review............................. 380

College Baseball
2002 In Review............................. 389

High School Baseball
2002 In Review............................. 428

Amateur Baseball
2002 In Review............................. 435

Draft
2002 In Review............................. 454

Appendix
Obituaries 473
Index 479

4

LARRY GOREN

274

JEFFREY CAMARATI

389

BOB LIBBY

MAJOR
LEAGUES

2002 IN REVIEW
Threat of work stoppage casts shadow over season

BY JOHN PERROTTO

It hung over the game from the time spring training began through the beginning of the regular season and all the way through the summer months.

The 2002 major league baseball season began without a collective bargaining agreement between the owners and Major League Baseball Players Association after the previous one expired Nov. 7, 2001.

Baseball history insisted the season could not be played to completion without interruption. The labor agreement had expired eight times since 1972. All eight times, there were work stoppages—five strikes by the players and three lockouts by the owners.

For much of the 2002 season, it did appear a strike was imminent.

Though the owners promised on March 26 that they would not lock out the players until at least after the World Series, management also did not agree to waive its right to declare an impasse in the negotiations at the end of the year and impose new working conditions in 2004. Those new conditions could have included a salary cap, something in effect in the NFL and NBA but staunchly opposed by the players.

What followed was eight sometimes contentious months of negotiations before both sides finally made some positive labor history.

Bud Selig

On Aug. 30, just three hours before the players planned to walk out before an afternoon game between the St. Louis Cardinals and Chicago Cubs at Wrigley Field, the game's long history of labor contentiousness ended. The sides agreed to a four-year contract that enabled the season to be played to completion. The contract was officially ratified on Oct. 1.

"All streaks come to an end and this was one that was overdue to come to an end," MLBPA executive director Donald Fehr said.

Don Fehr

"It came down to us playing baseball or having our reputations and life ripped by the fans," said Cardinals pitcher Steve Kline, the club's player representative to the MLBPA. "Baseball would have never been the same if we had walked out."

After a round-the-clock negotiation session in New York that started on Aug. 29, Commissioner Bud Selig and Fehr, longtime mortal enemies, struck a deal that will run through 2006 and penalize big spending on player salaries while giving poorer teams a greater share of the wealth.

The players also agreed to be tested for drugs while the owners gave a guarantee that they would not contract any teams until the labor agreement expires in 2006.

"I think a lot of people thought they'd never live long enough to see these two parties come together with a very meaningful deal and do it without one game of work stoppage," Selig said.

Walkout Had Dire Implications

A potential walkout threatened the final 31 days and 438 games of the regular season. Some observers believed the entire postseason would also be wiped out if an agreement was not reached, mirroring the 1994 strike that stretched all the way through spring training in 1995.

"I really believe if we would have gone on strike then we would have stayed on strike for a long, long time," Atlanta Braves second baseman Keith Lockhart said. "Once that line would have been crossed then both sides would have been dug in. That's why it was so important to get a deal done. As much damage as the last strike did, another one could have been even worse for everyone involved."

The final hours of talks involved plenty of intrigue as lawyers continually shuttled the short distance between the commissioner's office and the union headquarters in Manhattan.

Two lawyers from each side bargained until 2 a.m. then both sides broke for caucuses. Players gave owners a proposal during a 20-minute meeting that began at 4 a.m. and owners responded with a counteroffer at 6:30 a.m. The union returned with a response at 9:15 a.m.

The final meeting between Selig and Fehr lasted three hours.

"That was going to be the make-or-break meeting," said Gene Orza, Fehr's top assistant with the MLBPA. "If that meeting had ended poorly, it seemed to me there would have been a breakdown and each party would do what they had to do."

However, both sides put aside their acrimonious histo-

PLAYER OF THE YEAR

It was mid-March in Port Charlotte, Fla., an hour or so after yet another spring training game. Rangers players had already showered and changed and zipped off in their tinted SUVs for the evening. The minor league managers and hitting coaches, meanwhile, gathered in one of the batting cages with assistant general manager Grady Fuson for an organizational pow-wow.

The dozen or so staff members spoke about teaching farmhands plate discipline. Getting a good pitch to hit. Taking pitches to force the bullpen. About 40 minutes in, Rudy Jaramillo, the major league club's hitting coach, walked by with a player he'd been throwing BP to in another cage. The two quietly sat down to listen in. The player was Alex Rodriguez.

Alex Rodriguez: Humble, but carries a big stick

He sat his $252 million behind on the ground—"With the rest of the $30,000 grunts," Fuson recalls in amazement—and just listened, without a word, for a half hour. Only then did he literally raise his hand, as if a deferential schoolboy, and ask if he could share his outlook and theories. He spoke about pitch selection, about grinding starters down. About the difference between first-pitch hacking and first-pitch swinging. He squatted there for the rest of the two-hour meeting, speaking only when spoken to, just another Rangers employee.

Fuson shook his head and wondered, "How good is this?"

How good is it? Good enough to become one of the many reasons why Baseball America chose Alex Rodriguez as its 2002 Major League Player of the Year. Needless to say, he's got the stats: 57 home runs and 142 RBIs to lead the major leagues, with a .300 average to boot. All as a shortstop, one whose offense often overshadows just what an asset he is defensively, as well.

For all the hoo-ha surrounding his contract, Rodriguez, still only 27 and probably just entering his prime, has become all the major leagues could ask from a star player: performance, preparation, personality. Perfect? No. To validate his overall package he probably must lead his team to a World Series, something that doesn't seem particularly imminent for the last-place Rangers.

But Rodriguez is doing more than most recognize, a

great deal of it behind the scenes, to help that happen. "He's a baseball guy," former Rangers manager Jerry Narron says, "who just happens to be the most talented player in the world."

Knowing he has little wiggle room between arrogance and diffidence, Rodriguez tries to describe his efforts as what any high-profile player would do. "I don't do things to make a splash about my work ethic or what people may think," he says. Splash no, but ripple yes: Since he was 17, Rodriguez has savvily honed his public image and brand awareness by saying all the right things at all the right times. Nonetheless, he has played the role of Big Deal about as well as could be asked, and often better.

"My biggest pride is when kids—it's funny, they're like two years younger than me—when they come to me and ask a question, because that means they have the comfort level to ask me anything about anything," Rodriguez says. "I think for your teammates to have the confidence to ask you a question, or kid you or razz you, I think that's the best part of leadership—when they can feel like we're all one."

Rodriguez puts an optimistic face on the Rangers' current direction, despite two last-place finishes, and he could be correct. Texas did go 52-52 against teams outside the ridiculously strong AL West. The Rangers farm system, highlighted by slugger Mark Teixeira and a promising group of arms, should make an impact by 2004. The rebuilding should be hastened by the hiring of manager Buck Showalter, who helped develop the mid-1990s Yankees clubs and the quickly contending Diamondbacks.

"I look at myself like Bernie Williams was in the early 1990s with the Yankees," Rodriguez says. "He didn't win for a while. They had a very active owner. He had the financial commitment. Once they were able to turn the page and do what they did with Gene Michael and Mark Newman and who they started listening to, that's how they turned it around. I hope that's where we are."

—ALAN SCHWARZ

PREVIOUS WINNERS

1998—Mark McGwire, 1b, Cardinals
1999—Pedro Martinez, rhp, Red Sox
2000—Alex Rodriguez, ss, Mariners
2001—Barry Bonds, of, Giants

TOP 10 PLAYERS

1. Alex Rodriguez, ss, Rangers
2. Barry Bonds, of, Giants
3. Alfonso Soriano, 2b, Yankees
4. Vladimir Guerrero, of, Expos
5. Miguel Tejada, ss, Athletics
6. Randy Johnson, lhp, Diamondbacks
7. Barry Zito, lhp, Athletics
8. Curt Schilling, rhp, Diamondbacks
9. Pedro Martinez, rhp, Red Sox
10. Jim Thome, 1b, Indians

ry and got the deal done.

"It was workmanlike," Orza said. "There was no great argument that was necessary to shake somebody out of the doldrums. There was no dramatic, 'OK, OK, I give up' from either side. It proceeded in a logical way."

The agreement culminated 17 months worth of bargaining that started in March 2001 when MLB chief operating officer Paul Beeston and the MLBPA held two dozen secret and informal talks.

After believing progress had been made, the MLBPA was angered when Selig began taking power away from Beeston and declared two days after the 2001 World Series ended that the owners planned to fold two teams—most likely the Minnesota Twins and Montreal Expos—in what the commissioner called "contraction." The climate got testier Jan. 9 when the owners proposed a 50 percent luxury tax on the portions of payrolls above $98 million and increasing the percentage of shared locally-generated revenue from 20 percent to 50 percent.

The owners replaced Beeston, whom they felt was too soft with the MLBPA, on March 8 with Bob DuPuy, Selig's longtime lawyer and a hardline negotiator. The negotiations then made slow progress until the players voted Aug. 16 to set their Aug. 30 strike date.

"It came down to the last three hours to get an agreement but why wouldn't it come down to the last minute?" Orza said. "Why should the clubs believe anything we say until they're facing the threat of a strike and why should the players believe anything they say until the players are facing having to go on strike?"

Revenue Sharing At The Core

The most important aspect of the agreement, which guarantees 11 consecutive uninterrupted seasons, was that teams are required to share 34 percent of their locally generated revenues, an increase from the 20 percent of the previous agreement. That money will be divided evenly among the 30 franchises and is intended to help middle-market teams. While owners are not required to use all of the money on player salaries, Selig has the power to impose sanctions if clubs try to pocket their revenue-sharing payments without improving the franchise.

Furthermore, a luxury tax will be imposed on high-payroll teams to try to curb increases in player salaries. Teams will pay a tax ranging from 17.5 percent to 40 percent of the portions of salaries, including benefits, above $117 million in 2003, $120.5 million in 2004, $128 million in 2005 and $136.5 million in 2006. The money generated by a luxury tax will be used for player benefits and various development programs.

Another major part of the deal is that players convicted of drug possession face automatic suspensions. The drug prevention program, the first one agreed to by the

TOP 10 MAJOR LEAGUE STORIES OF 2002

1 **Disaster averted.** The mere threat of a strike was enough to temper enthusiasm for the season, but the leaders of the game at least avoided a fatal misstep by reaching a labor deal before any games were missed. Whether the new deal leads to a new age for baseball remains to be seen, but labor peace without a work stoppage was a good first step. As a fringe benefit, the new labor deal also silenced talk about contraction, which dominated hot-stove conversations following the 2001 World Series and leading up to spring training.

2 **End of 41 years of futility.** In a West Coast World Series, the Angels prevailed in a seven-game series that wasn't an absolute classic but did provide plenty of gripping moments, from the emergence of Francisco Rodriguez, to the drama of every Barry Bonds at-bat, to the Angels' amazing comeback in Game Six and win in Game Seven. And yes, there was the Rally Monkey too.

3 **Steroid hysteria.** Former National League MVP Ken Caminiti admitted in a Sports Illustrated cover story that he used steroids, prompting calls to test major league players. The new labor deal included a provision for some random testing, but skeptics said it didn't go far enough.

4 **Another amazing season for Bonds.** As an encore to setting a new single-season home run record, Barry Bonds put together a season that may have been even better, and finally got to a World Series. In other notable statistical accomplishments, Alex Rodriguez broke his own shortstop home run record with 57, and Vladimir Guerrero and Alfonso Soriano both came up just short in their pursuit of 40 home run/40 stolen base seasons.

5 **Cardinals persevere.** If an assortment of injuries and the death of franchise icon Jack Buck weren't enough, the Cardinals received a shock in June when pitcher Darryl Kile died. But they stuck together and made it to the NLCS.

6 **Expos become a ward of the state.** As it became clear contraction wasn't going to happen, Major League Baseball took the unprecedented step of buying the Expos from Jeffrey Loria and allowing him to buy another team. Loria bought the Marlins, whose owner John Henry in turn bought the Red Sox in a bizarre three-way franchise swap. In spite of the chaos, the Expos finished 83-79 and second in the NL East under Omar Minaya and Frank Robinson.

7 **Ugliness follows death of a legend.** Ted Williams died in July after years of declining health. But amid the remembrances of Williams' accomplishments, his family staged an ugly battle over what do with his remains.

8 **All-Star Game ends in a tie.** In what was supposed to be a big moment for Bud Selig and the Brewers, the All-Star Game in Milwaukee ended in a 7-7 tie after 11 innings, bringing a hail of criticism from fans and the media.

9 **Athletics win 20 straight.** After a slow start, the A's charged back to take the AL West title, spurred by an AL-record 20-game winning streak. Perhaps even more amazing, the Angels hung in the race during the streak.

10 **Managers go on endangered list.** After a year of managerial stability, teams didn't hesitate to pull the trigger in 2002. Starting in spring training through the aftermath of the World Series, 16 teams made changes.

players and owners since 1985, calls for suspensions of 15-30 days for a first offense, 30-90 days for a second conviction, an automatic one-year penalty for a third and a two-year suspension for the fourth.

Players convicted of the sale or distribution of prohibited substances face suspensions of 60-90 days and $100,000 fines for a first offense and two years for a second offense.

A player who has not been in the drug program who voluntarily admits to a problem is put into treatment without penalty.

"If you get caught, you're given a grace period, a chance to rectify the problem," Anaheim Angeles pitcher Scott Schoeneweis said. "I think that's a good thing."

Marijuana use and possession is covered separately in the agreement, with players facing fines of up to $15,000 but no suspensions.

Also, penalties for illegal steroid use are less severe as a first positive test would result in treatment and a second in a 15-day suspension or fine up to $10,000. The length of the suspensions, all without pay, would increase to 25 days for a third positive test, 50 days for a fourth and one year for a fifth.

Each player will be given two announced tests for steroids in 2003 during spring training or the regular season as part of a survey and both tests will take place within a week. If more than five percent test positive, "program" testing starts the following year and continues until less than 2.5 percent test positive in two consecutive years combined. If there is program testing in 2004, owners can conduct up to 240 additional random tests.

Over-the-counter supplements such as androstenedione are not banned but if more than 10 percent of players in a year test positive for them on the first test but negative on the follow-up, a joint MLBPA-management health committee may prohibit their use.

Minnesota, Montreal Spared

The deal also saved the Twins and Expos until at least 2006. Owners had tried to fold both franchises in a contraction plan announced by Selig two days after the 2001 World Series ended.

"It will give us a chance to play baseball," Twins manager Ron Gardenhire said. "If there had been a work stoppage, who knows what would have happened to this ballclub?"

The basic agreement also boosts the minimum salary for players from $200,000 to $300,000.

Selig and many owners had been lobbying hard for economic reform since the previous strike in 1994-95, claiming the game had lost its competitive balance and at least as many as half the 30 clubs went to spring training each year believing they had no chance to reach the postseason.

"We still have a lot of internal issues," Selig said. "We have a lot of work to be done. But I really believe what we need to have now is peace and stability. We need to get everybody's focus back on the field. Every day that goes by where the focus is on the field means I've had a good day and that baseball has had a good day."

Even though a strike was averted, the negative labor talk had an effect on attendance. It dropped 6.1 percent in 2002, its second straight decline and the biggest decrease since the season after the 1994-95 strike. In 2002, the average crowd fell to 28,168 from 30,012.

COLLECTIVE BARGAINING AGREEMENT: IN A NUTSHELL

Highlights of the Collective Bargaining Agreement reached between baseball players and owners on Aug. 30, 2002, that runs through Dec. 19, 2006:

REVENUE SHARING

$258 million each year phased in over four years. A $175-billion base to be distributed to each club on a straight-pool basis with the remainder split by the commissioner out of the central and discretionary funds. It phases in at $230 million in 2003, $243 million in 2004, $258 million in 2005 and $301 million in 2006.

LUXURY/COMPETITIVE BALANCE TAX

Thresholds of $117 million in 2003, $120 million in 2004, $128 million in 2005 and $136.5 million in 2006. The percentage for all teams being penalized the first time is 17.5 percent throughout the agreement with second-timers being penalized as high as 40 percent.

CONTRACTION

Tabled for the length of the agreement. Owners can unilaterally contract at the start of the next agreement. Grievance case filed by the players in November, 2001 was dropped.

WORLDWIDE DRAFT

Provision to discuss during new agreement. June first-year player draft remains the same until changed.

SALARY ARBITRATION

Language remains the same as in the 1996 collective bargaining agreement. Any player with three years of service (and some with two-plus) and less than six years of service at the major-league level can file. An arbitrator either picks the dollar figure submitted by the player or the club. The decision is binding.

DRUG TESTING

Testing for anabolic androgenic steroids only throughout the agreement. No testing for recreational drugs.

MINIMUM SALARY

Increase from $200,000 to $300,000 in 2003 for all major-league players. Those on split major-league/minor-league contracts go from $40,500 to $50,000 for the minor-league portion in 2003.

DEBT

A team may not have more debt than 10 times EBIDTA (earnings before interest, depreciation, taxes and amortization), except that a team that has moved into a newly constructed ballpark within the past 10 years may not have more debt than 15 times EBIDTA. There will be a three-year grace period, during which the commissioner has the right to retain the debt service rule, fully implemented. If he so elects, the commissioner must revoke the 60-40 assests-to-debt ratio rule. If he doesn't want to revoke the 60-40 rule, the debt-service rule becomes fully implemented.

INTERLEAGUE PLAY

Games between American and National league clubs, agreed to on a test basis in the 1997-2001 agreement, continue for the length of the new contract.

FREE AGENT DRAFT PICK COMPENSATION

Draft-pick compensation for losing Type A, B and C free agents is eliminated.

BENEFITS PLAN

The clubs' contributions will be $114 million-$115 million annually, up from $70 million in 2002.

ALLOWANCES

Spring training and in-season allowances will be increased at the rate of the Consumer Price Index.

WAIVERS

Each year will be divided into four waiver periods instead of three. The new periods will be Nov. 11-Feb. 15, Feb. 16-30th day of the season, 31st day of the season-July 31 and Aug. 1-Nov. 10.

INJURY REHABILITATION

Players with less than five years of major-league service can be directed for no more than 20 days to undergo baseball-related rehabilitation at a team's spring training facility. However, starting with the 11th day, each day at the spring training site would be deducted from the limit on a rehabilitation assignment to the minor leagues for the player, a maximum of 30 days for pitchers and 20 days for others.

SECOND MEDICAL OPINIONS

A provision that divided the United States into three regions and required a player to pay for his transportation if he went out of his region is eliminated.

TENDERS

All contract tenders to unsigned players on 40-man rosters will be made by the commissioner's office instead of individual teams.

CLIFF WELCH

LARRY GOREN

Jose Canseco, left, and Ken Caminiti talked about steroid use in the game

Pitchers Curt Schilling of the Arizona Diamondbacks and Kenny Rogers of the Texas Rangers said in the Sports Illustrated report they felt steroid use had tainted baseball's record book.

"I'm not sure how it snuck in so quickly but it's become a prominent thing very quickly," Schilling said. "It's widely known in the game. When you add in steroids and strength training, you're seeing records not just being broken but completely shattered."

"Basically, steroids can jump you a level or two," Rogers said. "The average player can become a star and the star player can become a superstar. And the superstar? Forget it. He can do things we've never seen before."

"The bottom line is the fans want to see us play," said Detroit second baseman Damion Easley, the Tigers' player rep. "And they don't care about the labor stuff that goes on.

"You're talking about a lot of money that we make, that the game makes. They just want to see us play baseball. They don't want to hear about us bickering over this and that."

Steroids A Hot Topic

The labor situation wasn't baseball's only dark cloud for most of the 2002 season. Sitting right beside it was the issue of steroids in the game.

It had long been suspected steroids had become more prevalent in recent seasons as scoring continued to rise and new home run records kept being set. While most talk about potential steroid use had been hushed, former players Jose Canseco and Ken Caminiti brought the issue to the forefront in May.

A few days after announcing his retirement from the Chicago White Sox' Triple-A Charlotte farm club in the International League, Canseco, the former all-star slugger, claimed in an interview with Fox Sports Net that 85 percent of major league players were taking steroids.

"There would be no baseball left if they drug-tested everyone today," said Canseco, who refused to say if he took steroids. "It's completely restructured the game as we know it. That's why guys are hitting 50 or 60 or 75 home runs."

Canseco's statements were just the beginning.

A few days later, Caminiti, the retired third baseman, told Sports Illustrated he was on steroids in 1996 when he won the National League Most Valuable Player award while playing for the San Diego Padres. Caminiti estimated that 50 percent of major leaguers used steroids. He also showed no remorse for using the performance-enhancing drugs, which had been banned by the NFL and NBA but not by baseball until the new collective bargaining agreement was put in place later in the season.

Anabolic steroids elevate the body's testosterone, increasing muscle mass. They are illegal in the United States unless prescribed by a physician for medical reasons.

"I've made a ton of mistakes," Caminiti told S.I. "I don't think using steroids is one of them.

"It's no secret what's going on in baseball. At least half the guys are using steroids. They joke about it with each other."

San Francisco Giants left fielder Barry Bonds set the single-season home run record with 73 in 2001. However, Bonds, whose homer count dropped to 46 in 2002, bristled at the suggestion his longball prowess had been chemically aided and said he was clean.

"Doctors ought to quit worrying about what ballplayers are taking," Bonds said. "What players take doesn't matter. It's nobody else's business. The doctors should spend their time looking for cures for cancer. It takes more than muscles to hit homers. If all those guys were using stuff, how come they're not all hitting homers?"

The estimates being thrown around—ranging from Canseco's 85 percent to Caminiti's 50 percent—had clubhouses buzzing around the major leagues.

Braves pitcher Tom Glavine, long one of the most active MLBPA members, and New York Mets manager Bobby Valentine doubted the problem was so widespread.

"Fifty percent is a lot and if I'm going to sit here and look at 25 guys on my ballclub and think 12 or 13 are on steroids then, no, I don't believe it," Glavine said. "But if I look at 700 players overall, there might be some teams who have more than 13. I don't know."

"The only way 85 percent of major league players are on steroids is if it's in the water or there's some way players are ingesting them without knowing," Valentine said. "I think it's a total exaggeration unless you're saying some of the stuff like MetRx mix and the blender stuff is a steroid instead of a supplement; then I stand corrected.

"As far as something injected or prescribed, I think it's preposterous to say 85 percent."

White Sox first baseman Frank Thomas was glad to see steroid testing, even in what critics felt was a somewhat watered-down version, be made part of the collective bargaining agreement.

LARRY GOREN

Bobby Valentine

"I don't know who's on and who's not on," Thomas said. "There is definitely more activity in the weight room nowadays. I was hoping that it was just old guys working hard in the weight room. I really think it's time for testing.

"I know what I put into the game day in and day out. I'd feel cheated if everyone's on steroids because I know how I've worked to get to this level and try to maintain it."

2002 MAJOR LEAGUE ALL-STARS

Curt Schilling: Won 23, walked 33 for Diamondbacks

Barry Zito: AL Cy Young winner went 23-5, 2.75 for A's

Selected by Baseball America

FIRST TEAM

Pos.	Player, Team	B-T	Ht.	Wt.	Age	AVG	AB	R	H	2B	3B	HR	RBI	SB
C	Jorge Posada, Yankees	B-R	6-2	200	30	.268	511	79	137	40	1	20	99	1
1B	Jim Thome, Indians	L-R	6-4	240	31	.304	480	101	146	19	2	52	118	1
2B	Alfonso Soriano, Yankees	R-R	6-1	180	24	.300	696	128	209	51	2	39	102	41
3B	Eric Chavez, Athletics	L-R	6-1	206	24	.275	585	87	161	31	3	34	109	8
SS	Alex Rodriguez, Rangers	R-R	6-3	195	26	.300	624	125	187	27	2	57	142	9
OF	Barry Bonds, Giants	L-L	6-1	206	37	.370	403	117	149	31	2	46	110	9
OF	Vladimir Guerrero, Expos	R-R	6-3	210	26	.336	614	106	206	37	2	39	111	40
OF	Magglio Ordonez, White Sox	R-R	6-0	200	28	.320	590	116	189	47	1	38	135	7
DH	Garret Anderson, Angels	L-L	6-3	220	30	.306	638	93	195	56	3	29	123	6

Pos.	Player, Team	B-T	Ht.	Wt.	Age	W	L	ERA	G	SV	IP	H	BB	SO
SP	Randy Johnson, D'backs	R-L	6-10	230	38	24	5	2.32	35	0	260	197	71	334
	Pedro Martinez, Red Sox	R-R	5-11	170	30	20	4	2.26	30	0	199	144	40	239
	Curt Schilling, D'backs	R-R	6-4	231	35	23	7	3.23	36	0	259	218	33	316
	Barry Zito, Athletics	L-L	6-4	210	24	23	5	2.75	35	0	229	182	78	182
RP	Eric Gagne, Dodgers	R-R	6-2	195	26	4	1	1.97	77	52	82	55	16	114

SECOND TEAM

Pos.	Player, Team	B-T	Ht.	Wt.	Age	AVG	AB	R	H	2B	3B	HR	RBI	SB
C	Mike Piazza, Mets	R-R	6-3	223	33	.280	478	69	134	23	2	33	98	0
1B	Jason Giambi, Yankees	L-R	6-3	235	31	.314	560	120	176	34	1	41	122	2
2B	Jeff Kent, Giants	R-R	6-1	205	34	.313	623	102	195	42	2	37	108	5
3B	Scott Rolen, Phillies/Cardinals	R-R	6-4	226	27	.266	580	89	154	29	8	31	110	8
SS	Miguel Tejada, Athletics	R-R	5-9	196	26	.308	662	108	204	30	0	34	131	7
OF	Lance Berkman, Astros	B-L	6-1	205	26	.292	578	106	169	35	2	42	128	8
OF	Shawn Green, Dodgers	L-L	6-4	200	29	.285	582	110	166	31	1	42	114	8
OF	Albert Pujols, Cardinals	R-R	6-3	210	22	.314	590	118	185	40	2	34	127	2
DH	Manny Ramirez, Red Sox	R-R	6-0	205	30	.349	436	84	152	31	0	33	107	0

Pos.	Player, Team	B-T	Ht.	Wt.	Age	W	L	ERA	G	SV	IP	H	BB	SO
SP	Bartolo Colon, Indians/Expos	R-R	6-0	225	29	20	8	2.94	33	0	233	219	70	149
	Derek Lowe, Red Sox	R-R	6-6	200	29	21	8	2.58	32	0	220	166	48	127
	Roy Oswalt, Astros	R-R	6-0	170	24	19	9	3.01	35	0	233	215	86	208
	Jarrod Washburn, Angels	L-L	6-1	198	27	18	6	3.15	32	0	206	183	59	139
RP	John Smoltz, Braves	R-R	6-3	220	35	3	2	3.25	75	55	80	59	24	85

Ages as of July 1, 2002

Player of the Year: Alex Rodriguez, ss, Rangers. **Pitcher of the Year:** Randy Johnson, lhp, Diamondbacks. **Rookie of the Year:** Eric Hinske, 3b, Blue Jays. **Manager of the Year:** Mike Scioscia, Angels. **Executive of the Year:** Billy Beane, Athletics.

Colorado Rockies outfielder Jay Payton took the opposite tack. He didn't understand all the fuss about steroids.

"Who's to say steroids should be illegal?" Payton said. "There's plenty of legal stuff to take to serve that purpose. If they did test, it might even the playing field and it might not. If you take steroids, it doesn't mean you can hit a 95 mph fastball."

Steroids have been clinically proven to cause a multitude of health problems with side effects including heart and liver damage, endocrine-system imbalance, elevated cholesterol levels, strokes, aggressive behavior and genitalia dysfunction. However, Cleveland Indians infielder John McDonald understands why a player might use them and why the issue may not go away soon.

"It's a great debate," McDonald said. "Do you do it? Do you not do it? If you had the opportunity to play in the big leagues and you only had a small window of opportunity to do it in, what would you do?"

Three Teams Win 100

While Selig and the owners continually complained about the lack of competitive balance throughout the collective bargaining negotiations, their point looked valid during the regular season because there was clearly

a stratification of teams in 2002.

The Braves, New York Yankees, Oakland Athletics all won at least 100 games and the other five playoffs teams—the Twins, Anaheim Angels, Cardinals, Diamondbacks and Giants—all had at least 94 victories. In all, there were 11 90-win teams as the Boston Red Sox, Seattle Mariners and Los Angeles Dodgers also reached that plateau.

The major leagues had not had three 100-win teams since 1998. The Braves also extended their major American professional sports record with an 11th straight division title.

Conversely, the Tampa Bay Devil Rays, Tigers, Milwaukee Brewers and Kansas City Royals were 100-game losers. It was the first time in baseball history four teams lost 100 games in the same season.

There were eight members of the 90-loss club as the Baltimore Orioles, Rangers, Cubs and Padres fell to that level. Therefore, only 11 of the 30 major league clubs had win totals between 73 and 89.

However, everything became wide open once postseason play began as the wild-card winners, the Angels and Giants, wound up meeting in the World Series for the first time since MLB began allowing the best second-place finish in each league into the playoffs in 1995. In the end, the Angels wound up winning a thrilling World Series in seven games for their first championship since entering the AL as an expansion team in 1961.

The Angels won their crown in dramatic fashion. Faced with elimination in Game Six and trailing 5-0 in the seventh, the Angels rallied for a 6-5 win. They then won 4-1 in Game Seven as left fielder Garret Anderson's three-run double in the third inning broke a 1-1 tie and made a winner of John Lackey, the first rookie starter to win a Game Seven since the Pittsburgh Pirates' Babe Adams in 1909.

Angels third baseman Troy Glaus was named the Series' Most Valuable Player despite a monster series by Bonds. Glaus hit .385 (10-for-26) with three homers and eight RBIs, including a two-run double that capped the Angels' amazing comeback in Game Six. Bonds batted .471 with four homers, six RBIs and 13 walks.

Also for the first time since the division playoffs started in '95, all four teams with home-field advantage lost in the first round. Both wild-card teams beat division champions as the Angels (99-63) knocked off the defending AL

Carlos Delgado

Kevin Brown

champion Yankees (103-58) in four games in the best-of-five series, while the Giants (95-66) beat the Braves (101-59) in five games in the NL.

In the other opening-round series, the Twins (94-67) defeated the Athletics (103-59) in five games in the AL, and the Cardinals (97-65) swept the defending World Series champion Diamondbacks (97-65).

By the end of the first round, the teams with the nine-highest payrolls at the start of the season were no longer playing. San Francisco, which ranked No. 10, was the highest-priced team standing.

The Angels polished off the Twins in five games in the American League Championship Series. Second baseman Adam Kennedy became only the fifth player in major league history to belt three home runs in a postseason game as he led the Angels to a 13-5 win in the decisive Game 5. The three-homer game was enough for Kennedy, who had hit only 23 homers in 1,652 regular-season at bats, to win the series MVP award despite going 1-for-10 in the first four games.

The Giants beat the Cardinals in five games in the National League Championship Series with ageless catcher Benito Santiago leading the way. The 37-year-old was the series MVP as he hit .300 (6-for-20) with two homers, including a game-winning shot in Game 4, and six RBIs.

Bonds Enjoys Another Big Year

Bonds' home run total might have dropped by 27 in 2002, but that did not prevent him from having one of the great offensive seasons in history.

After 17 years in the major leagues, the 38-year-old Giants left fielder became the oldest player ever to win his first batting title as he paced the NL with a .370 average. He won the crown by 32 points over Rockies outfielder Larry Walker (.338) and became the first Giants player to lead the league in hitting since Willie Mays in 1954 when the franchise was still in New York. The only major league champion older than Bonds was Ted Williams, who led the AL with a .328 average for the Red Sox at age 40 in 1958.

Bonds earned the distinction of being only the third major leaguer to lead his league in hitting one year after leading in homers. Hank Aaron did it with the Milwaukee Braves in 1956-57 and Walker pulled off the feat for the Rockies in 1997-98.

"I'm very happy about it," Bonds said. "I never thought I could do it. (Eight-time NL batting champion) Tony Gwynn always thought I could do it because I'm a contact

400-HOME RUN CLUB

Barry Bonds

No.	Player	Home Runs
1.	Hank Aaron	755
2.	Babe Ruth	714
3.	Willie Mays	660
4.	**Barry Bonds**	**613**
5.	Frank Robinson	586
6.	Mark McGwire	583
7.	Harmon Killebrew	573
8.	Reggie Jackson	563
9.	Mike Schmidt	548
10.	Mickey Mantle	536
11.	Jimmie Foxx	534
12.	Ted Williams	521
	Willie McCovey	521
14.	Eddie Mathews	512
	Ernie Banks	512
16.	Mel Ott	511
17.	Eddie Murray	504
18.	**Sammy Sosa**	**499**
19.	Lou Gehrig	493
20.	**Rafael Palmeiro**	**480**
21.	**Fred McGriff**	**478**
22.	Stan Musial	475
	Willie Stargell	475
24.	**Ken Griffey**	**468**
25.	Dave Winfield	465
26.	Jose Canseco	462
27.	Carl Yastrzemski	452
28.	Dave Kingman	442
29.	Andre Dawson	438
30.	Cal Ripken	431
31.	Billy Williams	426
32.	Darrell Evans	414
33.	Duke Snider	407
34.	**Juan Gonzalez**	**405**

Bold indicates active player

Waiting in the Wings

No.	Player	Home Runs
40.	Andres Galarraga	386
46.	Jeff Bagwell	380
t50.	Frank Thomas	376
t52.	Matt Williams	374
61.	Greg Vaughn	352

hitter with power but it's never been something I tried for."

Bonds began the season as a .292 career hitter but finished 34 points higher than his previous best of .336 in 1993.

Perhaps Bonds' most impressive feat was his .582 on base percentage, which easily established a major league record. The old mark of .553 had been set in 1941 by Williams.

Bonds' on-base percentage was bolstered by 198 walks, which broke the major league record of 177 he set in 2001. He also shattered the major league record for intentional walks with 68—23 more than Willie McCovey drew for the Giants in 1969.

Bonds also became the fourth player in history to hit 600 home runs, joining Aaron, Babe Ruth and Mays on Aug. 9 when he connected off the Pittsburgh Pirates' Kip Wells in front of the home fans at Pacific Bell Park. Bonds finished the season with 613 homers and needs only six steals to become the first player in history to reach the 500-500 club.

"I'll wait until next year and do something different," Bonds said. "A home run record last year, the batting title this year and my 500th stolen base next year. Then I'll think of something else to do."

Bonds wasn't the only player or team to pull off outstanding feats.

■ The Athletics set the AL record by winning 20 straight games from Aug. 13-Sept. 4. The Florida Marlins' Luis Castillo was also a streaker, setting a major league record for second basemen by hitting in 35 straight games from May 8-June 21.

■ Diamondbacks lefthander Randy Johnson became the first major league pitcher since the Red Sox' Pedro Martinez in 1999 and the first NL pitcher since the Mets' Dwight Gooden in 1984 to win the pitching triple crown. Johnson went 24-5 with a 2.37 ERA and 334 strikeouts.

Johnson passed Walter Johnson, Gaylord Perry, Don Sutton, Tom Seaver and Bert Blyleven to move from ninth to fourth on the career strikeouts list with 3,746. Johnson and Schilling (23-7) became the first teammates to have back-to-back 20-win seasons since Jim Palmer, Mike Cuellar and Dave McNally for the Orioles in 1970-71.

■ Cubs first baseman Fred McGriff became the first player to hit 30 home runs with five different teams. He also reached that level with the Toronto Blue Jays, Padres, Braves and Devil Rays.

■ Yankees first baseman Jason Giambi (41) and Philadelphia Phillies first baseman Jeremy Giambi (20) set a record for home runs by brothers in the same season with 61. The old mark of 59 was set in 1937 by Joe DiMaggio (46) and Vince DiMaggio (13).

■ For the first time ever, there were two four-home run games in the same season and they came in a three-week span. Mariners center fielder Mike Cameron accomplished the feat May 2 against the White Sox and Dodgers right fielder Shawn Green matched it May 23 against the Brewers while going 6-for-6 with a major league record 19 total bases.

■ Mariners right fielder Ichiro Suzuki had 208 hits after collecting 242 in his rookie season of 2001. He became the first player since Harvey Kuenn in 1953-54 to reach 200 in each of his first two major league seasons.

■ Yankees shortstop Derek Jeter (124) and center fielder Bernie Williams (102) became just the second set of teammates with 100 runs scored in seven straight seasons. The others were the Yankees' Ruth, Lou Gehrig and Earle Combs from 1926-32.

■ The Cubs led the major leagues in strikeouts by batters (1,269) and pitchers (1,333), the first team to accomplish the feat since Boston of the defunct Union Association in 1884.

■ The Braves' Greg Maddux went 16-6 and became the first pitch to win 15 or more games in 15 consecutive seasons since Cy Young from 1891-1905.

John Smoltz, in his first full season as the Braves' closer, set the NL record for saves with 55, topping the mark shared by Randy Myers (1993) and Trevor Hoffman (1998).

■ The Braves' Bobby Cox became the first NL manager with five seasons of 100 or more wins.

■ The Red Sox' Derek Lowe became the third pitcher to throw a no-hitter and have 20-win and 40-save seasons, joining Dennis Eckersley and Dave Righetti. Lowe went 21-8 and threw the majors' only no-hitter of the year on April 27 when he dominated the Devil Rays in a home game at Fenway Park.

■ The Orioles' Mike Bordick set major league records for consecutive errorless games (110) and chances (543) by a shortstop.

■ Cardinals outfielder Albert Pujols, the 2001 NL Rookie of the Year, hit .314 with 118 runs scored, 34 home runs and 127 RBIs in his sophomore season. He became the first player to begin his career with back-to-back seasons batting at least .300 with 30 homers, 100 runs and 100 RBIs.

Albert Pujols

Williams' Death Turns Controversial

The 2002 season was also tainted by loss and tragedy.

Ted Williams, the Red Sox' larger-than-life hitting star and war hero died July 5 at age 83 due to cardiac arrest in Crystal River, Fla. That came soon after the Cardinals lost Hall of Fame broadcaster Jack Buck and pitcher Darryl

---

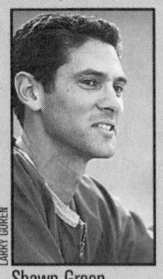
Kile within a week in June.

Williams often said he wanted people to remember him as the greatest hitter who ever lived and he could stake a strong claim to that title. He finished his 19-year career, interrupted for nearly five full seasons as he served in the military in World War II and Korean War, with a .344 batting average, 521 home runs and 1,839 RBIs in 19 seasons with the Red Sox (1939-42, 1946-1960).

Williams is the last player to hit .400 in a season as he batted .406 in 1941. He reached that mark by going 6-for-8 in a doubleheader against the Philadelphia Athletics on the final day of the season even though his batting average at the time was .3996. The average rounds up to .400, meaning Williams could have sat out the twinbill but he refused.

"He killed the ball, just killed it," said Pete Suder, who played second base for the Athletics that day. "He hit one into the loudspeaker horns. He hit another over the fence."

Williams also won two triple crowns—Rogers Hornsby is the only other player to accomplish that feat—six AL batting titles and four AL home run crowns.

Williams was singled out in an era when the press handed out freely colorful monikers. While many players had one nickname, Williams was called "The Splendid Splinter," "The Thumper," "Teddy Ballgame" and "The Kid."

"I think he was the best hitter that baseball has had," said Hall of Famer Bobby Doerr, Williams' teammate with the Red Sox for 10 seasons. "He wanted to be the greatest hitter of all time and he worked hard at that but he was also a great teammate. He patted everyone on the back."

Williams flew 39 combat missions as a Marine fighter pilot in the Korean War and received fire three times. Former senator and astronaut John Glenn had Williams as his wingman on combat missions in Korea.

"There was no one more dedicated to this country and more proud to serve his country than Ted Williams," Glenn said.

In recent years, Williams battled a series of strokes and congestive heart failure and got around in a wheelchair. However, anyone who saw Williams or knew of his accomplishments knew he was one of very best.

"He is the premier measuring stick for all hitters," said Frank Howard, the feared slugger who played for Washington from 1969-71 when Williams managed the Senators. "The country lost a great American."

Sadly, four months after his death, there was still no resolution on what to do with Williams' remains.

Williams said in his will that he wanted to be cremated and his ashes scattered off Florida's Gulf Coast, where he lived in his later years. Williams' oldest daughter, Bobby

ORGANIZATION OF THE YEAR

The three Rs of Minnesota baseball are not reading, 'riting and 'rithmetic. They are Ryan, Rantz and Radcliff. And around here, where Homer Hankys once again created an autumn breeze under a Teflon sky, they are the front-office equivalent of Tinker to Evers to Chance.

General manager Terry Ryan, farm director Jim Rantz and scouting director Mike Radcliff combine for more than 80 years with the Twins. All that longevity and all that experience—in scouting, developing, winnowing, nurturing, signing, trading and everything else having to do with ballplayers—paid off again in 2002, when the Twins advanced to the American League Championship Series.

Terry Ryan

It was a breakthrough season for the organization, and it's no surprise the Twins were Baseball America's Organization of the Year.

"It's not so much me, Jim or Mike; it's the people who work for this organization and have been loyal and accountable," Ryan says. "And they produce things that help get these types of awards, which is very flattering. It's a heck of a thing for us to experience."

Jim Rantz

The reasons for the Twins' success in 2002 were many. A strong bullpen, a solid rotation and a group of rapidly maturing youngsters helped Minnesota reach the heights. But it all goes back to this: finding, drafting, signing and developing players. And that's where Ryan, Rantz and Radcliff come in.

Ryan: 30 years with the Twins. Rantz: 42 years. Radcliff: 15 years. It seems like they've been in Minnesota longer than some of those 10,000 lakes. And don't be surprised if Rantz tries to convince you that he once scouted a great big local kid who could really swing the lumber. He would be listed in the old scouting files as Bunyan, Paul.

Radcliff, like Rantz, talks about the tremendous stability of the front office, even through the changeover from Andy MacPhail to Ryan.

"There was hardly any transition from Andy over to Terry," he says. "Terry worked under Andy, so there were a lot of the same people in the key positions and not a whole lot of change at all."

Among the current Twins drafted by Radcliff and his staff are third baseman Corey Koskie (1994), first baseman Doug Mientkiewicz (1995) and outfielder Jacque Jones (1996). In 1997 the Twins drafted infielder/outfielder Michael Cuddyer and catcher Matt LeCroy in the first round, outfielder Michael Restovich in the second round and pitcher J.C. Romero in the 21st round.

There is a comparison to be made between the big league lineup and the scouting staff, Radcliff says.

"Our scouting staff has basically gained experience just like that major league team," he says. "The (players) got there and took some bumps for a couple of years. We signed a bunch of young (scouts), and now they're all veterans."

Ryan says, "I think that helps make any organization successful. If you have people in place that are talented and everybody is on the same page all the time, that's vital to any organization."

Ryan is famous for deflecting praise away from himself and spreading it around the organization. Radcliff, more than most, knows how Ryan goes about his business.

"Terry's obviously the guy that all of us look up to," Radcliff says. "I ran into Terry when he was an area scout. I've seen how he works forever. He sets high standards. We have high accountability, and sometimes it's very difficult to walk behind him, but it makes us do everything the right way. We do things professionally, correct, thorough, complete, and

Mike Radcliff

that goes a long way toward why we've finally built up to where we've got some success going."

And now, after all the tribulations of 2002—contraction, the threat of a strike, the shaky future of the franchise—the Twins stand as AL Central champions, the light of the future shining bright. There's plenty of credit to go around, and everyone shares in it.

"All of us understand and realize how many other people are involved here," Radcliff says. "To get where we are right now is a tremendous team effort and a tremendous team experience. That's what we all have pride in.

"It is something to see, all the players that you go out and watch and then draft and then sign and then develop, and then they get to the big leagues. That is very rewarding."

—JOHN MILLEA

PREVIOUS WINNERS	
1982	Oakland Athletics
1983	New York Mets
1984	New York Mets
1985	Milwaukee Brewers
1986	Milwaukee Brewers
1987	Milwaukee Brewers
1988	Montreal Expos
1989	Texas Rangers
1990	Montreal Expos
1991	Atlanta Braves
1992	Cleveland Indians
1993	Toronto Blue Jays
1994	Kansas City Royals
1995	New York Mets
1996	Atlanta Braves
1997	Detroit Tigers
1998	New York Yankees
1999	Oakland Athletics
2000	Chicago White Sox
2001	Houston Astros

Jo Williams Ferrell, vowed to fulfill that wish. However, his youngest children, John Henry Williams and Claudia Williams, maintain they signed a handwritten pact with their father in November 2000 agreeing their bodies would be frozen.

John Henry Williams had his father's body moved to a Scottsdale, Ariz., cryogenics labs shortly after his death. Cryogenic supporters say frozen bodies might one day be thawed and brought back to life, although most experts say that is highly unlikely.

Traumatic Week For Cardinals

The Cardinals suffered a devastating week as Buck died at 77 on June 18 in a St. Louis hospital after a long hospital stay. Four days later, Kile, the 33-year-old pitcher, died in his sleep in his Chicago hotel room with an 80-90 percent blockage of his coronary artery

The Cardinals were getting ready to play the Cubs in an afternoon game when they realized Kile, not scheduled to pitch that day, had still not arrived at Wrigley Field just two hours before game time. Kile was customarily one of the first Cardinals at the ballpark each day.

The Cardinals then called the hotel to ask that Kile be checked on. Workers at the Westin Hotel found his body after forcing their way into Kile's 11th-floor room because of the safety latch on the door.

"Our club is just totally staggered," Cardinals manager Tony La Russa said. "Everyone knows what a pro he is. There was no bigger leader on our ballclub, in every way."

"We're thankful for how he touched each of our lives," Cardinals catcher Mike Matheny said. "Some saw him as a baseball player. Others were fortunate enough to call him friend."

Kile left behind a wife and three children.

"He's a great competitor, a great leader on our club," Cardinals general manager Walt Jocketty said. "He's one of the players I've grown close to over the years. He's a great father, and you could see with his wife, they were very much in love."

Once word came that Kile had died, officials quickly called off that day's game, which was to have been nationally televised.

Shortly after the scheduled starting time, La Russa came out of the dugout and walked across the field to meet with Chicago president and general manager Andy MacPhail

TYLER BOLDEN

Jack Buck

and catcher Joe Girardi, the Cubs' player representative. Then all the Cubs came out of the dugout and stood behind Girardi.

Speaking in front of the dugout on a microphone, Girardi told the crowd there had been a "tragedy in the Cardinals' family" and asked fans for their prayers.

Kile compiled a 133-119 lifetime record with a 4.12 ERA in 12 seasons with the Houston Astros (1991-97), Rockies (1998-99) and Cardinals (2000-02).

Kile died a day after Buck, who began broadcasting Cardinals games in 1954, was buried following a lengthy illness.

Buck underwent lung cancer surgery Dec. 5 then returned to the hospital Jan. 3 to have an intestinal blockage removed. Buck then spent the last 5½ months of his life hospitalized and went in and out of a coma several times in his last few weeks.

Controversy swirled around Hall of Famer Ted Williams' death

"He had a great life," said Joe Buck, who joined his father in the Cardinals' radio booth in 1991 and is also the lead television baseball play-by-play man for Fox. "He didn't waste one minute of one day. He packed two lifetimes into one lifetime. He went from poor to wealthy in his lifetime yet he never changed."

In addition to Williams, two other Hall of Famers passed away in 2002: Enos "Country" Slaughter and Hoyt Wilhelm.

Slaughter died on Aug. 12 at age 86 of cancer in a Durham, N.C. hospital after colon surgery July 25 and an operation to repair perforated stomach ulcers July 29. He was diagnosed with non-Hodgkins lymphoma a month earlier.

Slaughter hit .300 with 169 homers and 1,304 RBIs in 19 seasons with the Cardinals (1938-42, 1946-53), Yankees (1954-59), Kansas City Athletics (1955-56) and Milwaukee Braves (1959). He is best remembered for his "Mad Dash" in the 1946 World Series, scoring the winning run all the way from first base on Harry Walker's single in the bottom of the eighth inning to break a 3-3 tie against the Red Sox in the decisive seventh game.

"He was one of the great hustlers of baseball," said Hall of Famer Stan Musial, Slaughter's longtime teammate with the Cardinals. "He loved baseball. He always ran hard and played hard."

Wilhelm died Aug. 23 at age 80 in Sarasota, Fla., from an undisclosed illness. He became the first relief pitcher to make the Hall of Fame when he was inducted in 1985.

Using a knuckleball that baffled hitters, Wilhelm compiled a 143-122 lifetime record with 227 saves in a 21-year career with the New York Giants (1952-56), Cardinals (1957), Indians (1957-58), Orioles (1958-62), White Sox (1963-68), Angels (1969), Braves (1969-71), Cubs (1970) and Dodgers (1971-72).

Wilhelm, who won a Purple Heart during the Battle of the Bulge in World War II, also started on occasion and

ROOKIE OF THE YEAR

When J.P. Ricciardi took over as general manager of the Blue Jays, much was made of how he was expected to overhaul the organization from top to bottom and roust it out of a decade-long slumber.

And that's exactly what Billy Beane's former right-hand man with the Athletics did. But Ricciardi's broom wisely avoided baseball lifer Bobby Mattick, and it was Mattick who looked out at Eric Hinske working out one day in spring training and pronounced him a keeper.

"You could tell he had a helluva makeup," says Mattick, the Blue Jays vice president of baseball who has served in several capacities with the Blue Jays since 1976 and spent the previous 30 years as an administrator or scout with 10 other organizations. "He's going to be a good player for us for a long time."

While that remains to be seen, Hinske, 25, was good enough in his rookie season (.279-24-84 with 38 doubles in 566 at-bats) to garner the Baseball America Rookie of the Year award.

Hinske, Ricciardi's first significant acquisition, became a cornerstone of a suddenly promising team that closed out with a 19-8 September sprint. His 24 homers were the most by an AL rookie since Nomar Garciaparra belted 30 in 1997.

"You don't say, 'Oh my God, I love this guy,' " says Ricciardi, who acquired Hinske and righthander Justin Miller from the A's for Billy Koch. "You have to see him day in and day out to appreciate him.

Eric Hinske: Hit 24 homers for improving Blue Jays

LARRY GOREN

Sometimes you'll find that scouts hide behind numbers, but to me it's whether a guy can play the game—whether he has instincts—that's important. Not some number that tells you how fast he runs."

Ricciardi brought the Athletics mantra of on-base percentage with him when he went north of the border, and described the third baseman as "an on-base freak." But Hinske's offense was not often a source of worry, not even in the mixed scouting reports Ricciardi inherited from the regime of his predecessor, Gord Ash.

The same cannot be said about Hinske's defense. But by the end of the season, it was that part of his game to which Hinske pointed with pride. He committed 20 errors, but just four in his last 70 games.

And it was from that point on that Hinske was fully able to appreciate his rookie experience. "You watch players like Manny Ramirez and A-Rod (Alex Rodriguez), and they hit the ball hard consistently," Hinske says. "I mean, they don't take bad swings, never mind have bad at-bats. You see these guys on television and you're impressed. But in person? They're just so much better than anybody else. It's kind of cool to see that first hand."

Hinske grew up in a family of three children in Menasha, Wis. He

is very much a product of his era, passing his spare time playing X-Box and sprinkling the word "cool" into sentences during interviews—as he did when his first career big league homer landed in Monument Park at Yankee Stadium. "Near Yogi (Berra)," Hinske said later, smiling. "And that's cool."

Ricciardi was not surprised by Hinske's success.

"Guys like Hinske and Vernon Wells have stopped at every level," Ricciardi says. "They've played A-ball and Double-A and Triple-A. They have had a lot of at-bats and honed their craft. If Hinske were in another organization, someone would have had to get him in camp and give him a chance. It's not like we're taking an A-ball guy and saying he could be our everyday third baseman. Eric has done what he's needed to do to play complete seasons in the minors, and he's carried it over, here."

TOP 10 ROOKIES

1.	Eric Hinske, 3b, Blue Jays
2.	Austin Kearns, of, Reds
3.	Rodrigo Lopez, rhp, Orioles
4.	Mark Prior, rhp, Cubs
5.	Brad Wilkerson, of/1b, Expos
6.	Jason Jennings, rhp, Rockies
7.	Damian Moss, lhp, Braves
8.	Josh Phelps, dh/1b, Blue Jays
9.	Jorge Julio, rhp, Orioles
10.	John Lackey, rhp, Angels

Blue Jays ace Roy Halladay isn't worried about a sophomore jinx settling in for Hinske or other young Blue Jays such as Josh Phelps. "I know people say the second time around can be tough for young players, but guys like Hinske and Phelps did what they did for months," says Halladay. "They've already seen pitchers they've faced before, and they've adapted to whatever changes those pitchers made. They've had their second and third time around. As a team, that has to give you confidence.

"I think we came in thinking we had a four- to five-year plan. The way things have gone, we'd like to be there a little sooner."

—JEFF BLAIR

PREVIOUS WINNERS

1989—Gregg Olson, rhp, Orioles
1990—Sandy Alomar, c, Indians
1991—Jeff Bagwell, 1b, Astros
1992—Pat Listach, ss, Brewers
1993—Mike Piazza, c, Dodgers
1994—Raul Mondesi, of, Dodgers
1995—Hideo Nomo, rhp, Dodgers
1996—Derek Jeter, ss, Yankees
1997—Nomar Garciaparra, ss, Red Sox
1998—Kerry Wood, rhp, Cubs
1999—Carlos Beltran, of, Royals
2000—Rafael Furcal, ss/2b, Braves
2001—Albert Pujols, of/3b/1b, Cardinals

pitched a no-hitter for the Orioles in 1958 against the Yankees.

"Wilhelm's knuckleball did more than anyone else's," former White Sox general manager Roland Hemond said. "No one could predict where it was going to go. There was so much action on it."

Kile was one of two active players to meet a tragic demise in 2002. On the eve of the opening of spring training, Padres outfielder Mike Darr was killed in an automobile accident in Peoria, Ariz.

Darr's childhood friend, Duane Johnson, also died in the crash. Padres rookie pitcher Ben Howard, sitting in the backseat of Darr's sport utility vehicle and the only passenger wearing a seatbelt, escaped with just scrapes and bruises.

"We've lost a special teammate, a special person," said Trevor Hoffman, the Padres' relief ace. "There are a lot of heavy hearts in the locker room. You don't want to believe it."

Darr, 25, broke into the major leagues with the Padres in 1999 and hit .273 with five homers and 67 RBIs in 188 career games.

"He could run, he could throw, he could hit," Padres manager Bruce Bochy said. "He was a fun-loving guy who played the game like it was supposed to be played. He had his future ahead of him and it's a shame it happened."

Feel-Good Story Of The Year

One of baseball's best stories in 2002 was the Twins rolling to the AL Central championship. They made their first playoff appearance since 1991.

What made the Twins' run remarkable is they were nearly eliminated in the previous offseason as part of Commissioner Bud Selig's contraction plan. Thanks to a court injunction in Minnesota, the Twins were spared from being folded.

On Nov. 16, 2001, just 10 days after Selig and the owners targeted the Twins and Expos for elimination, judge Harry Seymour Crump issued an injunction in Hennepin County District Court that forced the team to honor its 2002 lease at the Metrodome.

Frank Robinson: Led MLB-owned Expos to 83-79 record

Crump was upheld Jan. 22 by the Minnesota Court of Appeals, and baseball abandoned its contraction plan for 2002 on Feb. 5, a day after Minnesota's Supreme Court refused to hear the case. A little more than six months later, baseball's new labor contract ensured no teams would be eliminated until at least 2007.

After sweating out an offseason of severe doubt, winning a division championship and advancing to the American League Championship Series before losing to the Anaheim Angles was sweet for the Twins.

"A lot of people with the Twins are happy we have the chance to keep playing for at least a few more years," general manager Terry Ryan said. "The roots run so deep with this organization that a lot of us don't want to consider anything but working for the Twins. We're all in this together."

MLB Takes Over Expos

While the Twins were spared from being sentenced to oblivion, so were the Expos. Instead, Major League Baseball took over operations of the Expos in February as part of a complicated three-way ownership swap.

On Feb. 12, just three days before the start of spring training, MLB took the unprecedented step of buying a club.

The 29 other owners bought the Expos from Jeffrey Loria for $120 million as he purchased the Marlins from John Henry for $158.5 million. The owners also granted Loria a $38.5 million loan to make up the difference between the selling price of the Expos and purchase price of the Marlins.

On Feb. 27, a group led by Henry and including former Padres owner Tom Werner, bought the Red Sox for a record $660 million.

MLB installed a four-man management club to oversee the Expos. Former Angels president Tony Tavares took over the same post in Montreal while longtime Expos executive Claude Delorme was named executive vice president. Mets assistant general manager Omar Minaya was installed as GM and MLB's Vice President of On Field Operations Frank Robinson, a Hall of Fame player and former major league manager, was chosen as the field skipper.

Despite having less than a week to get ready for spring training and put together a coaching staff, Robinson led the Expos to a surprising 83-79 finish. The Expos had lost at least 94 games in each of the previous four seasons.

With Montreal in the NL East and wild-card races in late June and early July, Minaya reversed the Expos' long-standing trend of dealing veteran stars for minor leaguers. Instead, Minaya packaged prospects to acquire Bartolo Colon, the 20-game winner, from the Indians and slugging outfielder Cliff Floyd from the Marlins.

While the Expos eventually faded from contention and dealt Floyd to the Red Sox in late July, their turnaround under such odd circumstances was fairly amazing. Though the Expos knew they wouldn't be contracted in 2003, they were still unsure at the end of the season if they would return to Montreal or if MLB would sell them to a group that would relocate the franchise to Washington, D.C., Northern Virginia, Portland, Ore., or possibly even San Juan, Puerto Rico.

"People said it would be a miracle if I could get this team over .500 when I took the job but I don't think what we did was a miracle," Robinson said. "We played well and we should have played even better. We didn't worry about contraction or relocation or any of that stuff."

EXECUTIVE OF THE YEAR

One year after standing pat—and having been proven correct, with Oakland surging to a 94-45 record the rest of the way to reach the playoffs—Billy Beane could have done the same when in May 2002 his team stood 19-24. But this time Beane moved, with stunning decisiveness: He shipped the right side of his Opening Day infield (Carlos Pena and Frank Menechino) to Triple-A Sacramento, and the next day traded his lead-off hitter, Jeremy Giambi, whose take-and-rake approach made him the offense's poster boy.

Once again the team responded, finishing a blistering 84-35 to win its second American League West title in three years.

For a general manager who builds his team with a single-minded resolution he describes himself as "draconian," Beane demonstrated an ability to adapt. He didn't just wait for the club's established engine—pitchers Mark Mulder, Barry Zito and Tim Hudson, and young sluggers Eric Chavez and Miguel Tejada—to kick in once again. He didn't allow his offseason replacements for three vital free agents to get comfortable. He showed that he knew exactly what his club needed and how to get it, once more.

In a season with many deserving candidates for Baseball America's Executive of the Year award, Beane earned the nod. As long as the A's stay in contention despite some of the paltriest financial resources in baseball, Beane will be regarded as an elite GM. To address the departures of former MVP Jason Giambi, center fielder Johnny Damon and closer Jason Isringhausen—the largest talent hit any club took last offseason—Beane traded for Pena and signed Scott Hatteberg;

Billy Beane: Pushed all the right buttons for A's

moved Terrence Long to center field and installed Giambi in left, while trading for David Justice; and dealt for the Blue Jays' Billy Koch.

Those moves didn't appear to be working in May, but the Sacramento Sendoff and Giambi deal slapped awake the team. Beane then made three trades in July: for lefthander Ted Lilly, second baseman Ray Durham and reliever Ricardo Rincon. Oakland finished the regular season with 103 wins, one more than 2001 and tying with the Yankees for the most in baseball.

"This job is like steering a boat in the ocean," Beane says, "in that you can't change direction fast, but you do things to make sure the direction is still right." With Beane at the helm, the A's shouldn't drift very far.

–ALAN SCHWARZ

PREVIOUS WINNERS

1998—Doug Melvin, Rangers	
1999—Jim Bowden, Reds	
2000—Walt Jocketty, Cardinals	
2001—Pat Gillick, Mariners	

MANAGER OF THE YEAR

Cut loose by the Dodgers after spending nearly his entire professional life with the organization, Mike Scioscia has made a nice home for himself just down the freeway in Southern California.

In his third season as manager of the Anaheim Angels, Scioscia took a team that had underachieved in 2001 and not only put them back into the playoffs, but also captured the franchise's first World Series championship.

Scioscia and his staff sold the players on the idea of putting the team above the individual, and that it wasn't stars and huge payrolls that led to championships.

"It starts at the top," outfielder Darin Erstad said. "It starts with

Mike Scioscia

Scioscia. That's just the way he is, the example he sets. We don't quit.

PREVIOUS WINNERS

1998—Larry Dierker, Astros	
1999—Jimy Williams, Red Sox	
2000—Dusty Baker, Giants	
2001—Lou Piniella, Mariners	

We keep playing. And it becomes infectious. The greatest feeling you can have as a team is when every single guy is on the same page. And that's us."

That much was clear throughout the season, and particularly in the playoffs, as the Angels continually fought back from deficits to stage improbable comebacks.

After awhile the comebacks weren't so improbable, the Angels had a title, and Scioscia was BA's Manager of the Year.

Also hanging over the Expos as the season ended was a lawsuit, filed July 16 in federal court in Miami, on behalf of 14 leading Canadian corporations alleging violations of the 1970 Racketeering Influenced and Corrupt Organizations Act. The group was seeking trebled compensatory damages and punitive damages of $100 million.

Meanwhile, the $660 million price tag for the Red Sox more than doubled the previous record for a baseball franchise—the $323 million paid by Larry Dolan for the Indians in 2000. The purchase also included 80 percent of the New England Sports Network plus $40 million in assumed debt.

The deal closed an often difficult 16-month sale process.

The Red Sox announced the agreement with Henry's group on Dec. 20, 2001 but the deal was held up as losing bidders tried to restart the auction and Massachusetts attorney general Thomas Reilly investigated whether the Jean R. Yawkey Trust, which owned 53 percent of the team, would receive fair value. Reilly later withdrew his objections.

"It seemed like a good baseball game," Henry said. "It was always in doubt up until the end."

The Mets also had a strained ownership shift as Fred Wilpon took over 100 percent control of the franchise by buying out Nelson Doubleday's share. They became 50-50 owners of the team in 1986 and agreed that if either partner wanted to sell, he would offer his half to the other, with a price set by an appraiser.

However, Doubleday sued Wilpon when the value of the club was appraised at $391 million in April by Bob Starkey, a former Arthur Andersen LLP partner who left in 1999 to form his own company, one that had done previous consulting work regarding MLB.

When Wilpon agreed in September to increase his up-front payment to Doubleday from $27 million to $100 million, the suit was dropped.

Omar Minaya

3,000-STRIKEOUT CLUB		
No.	Player	Strikeouts
1.	Nolan Ryan	5,714
2.	Steve Carlton	4,136
3.	**Roger Clemens**	**3,909**
4.	**Randy Johnson**	**3,746**
5.	Bert Blyleven	3,701
6.	Tom Seaver	3,640
7.	Don Sutton	3,574
8.	Gaylord Perry	3,534
9.	Walter Johnson	3,508
10.	Phil Niekro	3,342
11.	Ferguson Jenkins	3,192
12.	Bob Gibson	3,117

Randy Johnson

Active players in bold type

MAJOR LEAGUES

Front-Office Shakeup

Omar Minaya broke new ground when he accepted his post with the Expos. The Dominican Republic native, who grew up in Elmhurst, N.Y., became the first Hispanic general manager in baseball history.

Minaya admitted he made a risky move by taking the job. At the time, he was secure in his assistant GM job with the Mets and there were no guarantees the Expos wouldn't be folded at the end of the season or sold by MLB to another owner who would move them and bring in his own front office personnel.

"I've interviewed for other general manager jobs and, as a baseball man that's been involved since 1985, this is a dream come true," Minaya said. "I had a good job with the Mets, a secure job. I was working for my hometown team.

It's a situation, though, that replaces the guarantees I have with the Mets. It's a challenge. But to become the first Hispanic general manager, the implications are beyond my selfish interest of comfort and I overcame my fears."

Minaya became so entrenched with the Expos that he turned down the chance to interview for the Red Sox' GM vacancy at the end of the season.

Once Henry took over the Red Sox in the early stages of spring training, he fired GM Dan Duquette and manager Joe Kerrigan while promoting assistant GM Mike Port on an interim basis and hired Indians bench coach Grady Little as skipper.

In addition to the Expos and Red Sox, three other teams changed GMs in 2002.

When Loria sold the Expos and bought the Marlins, he brought Larry Beinfest along from Montreal. The Marlins had been without a GM after Dave Dombrowski left the previous offseason to become president of the Tigers.

Dombrowski added the title of GM with the Tigers on April 9 when he fired Randy Smith and manager Phil Garner after an 0-6 start and 145-185 record in three seasons. Bench coach Luis Pujols replaced Garner but was also fired the day after the season ended after the Tigers finished 55-106.

The Tigers then hired Padres

MANAGERIAL CHANGES

Sixteen teams made managerial changes before, during or after the 2002 major league season. Here are the changes and new managers for the 2003 season:

Team	Original Manager	In-Season Change(s)	Post-Season Change
Boston	Joe Kerrigan	*Grady Little	
Chicago (NL)	Don Baylor	Bruce Kimm	Dusty Baker
Cleveland	Charlie Manuel	Joel Skinner	Eric Wedge
Colorado	Buddy Bell	Clint Hurdle	
Detroit	Phil Garner	Luis Pujols	Alan Trammell
Florida	Open	*Jeff Torborg	
Kansas City	Tony Muser	John Mizerock/Tony Pena	
Milwaukee	Jerry Royster		Ned Yost
Montreal	Jeff Torborg	*Frank Robinson	
New York (NL)	Bobby Valentine		Art Howe
Oakland	Art Howe		Ken Macha
San Francisco	Dusty Baker		Felipe Alou
Seattle	Lou Piniella		Bob Melvin
Tampa Bay	Hal McRae		Lou Piniella
Texas	Jerry Narron		Buck Showalter
Toronto	Buck Martinez	Carlos Tosca	

*Change made before 2002 season

first base coach Alan Trammell as manager. Trammell played shortstop for the Tigers for 20 seasons from 1977-96.

While Dombrowski added the GM title, MacPhail dropped his on July 5 when he reshuffled the Cubs' brain trust. MacPhail decided to concentrate just on his club president role as he promoted assistant GM Jim Hendry.

At the same time, with Chicago struggling with a 34-49 record, MacPhail fired manager Don Baylor and replaced him with Bruce Kimm, skipper of the Cubs' Triple-A Iowa farm club in the Pacific Coast League. Baylor guided the Cubs to a 187-220 mark in four seasons.

Kimm was then fired on the last day of the season as the Cubs wound up going 67-95, including 33-46 during his tenure.

Brewers GM Dean Taylor was axed Sept. 25 as his club was in its final stages of a 56-106 season, the worst in franchise history. Former Rangers GM Doug Melvin was hired as Taylor's replacement.

On the day Taylor was fired, the Brewers also made history by hiring the first African-American club president in baseball history as Ulice Payne replaced Wendy Selig-Prieb. The daughter of the commissioner decided to take a reduced role of chairman of the board following the Brewers' 10th straight losing season and under heat from the board of directors.

Payne is a former state securities commissioner and a member of the Greater Milwaukee Committee, a civic organization that lobbied for the construction of the Brewers' Miller Park. He is also a member of the Milwaukee office of Foley & Lardner, whose partners include Bob DuPuy, baseball's COO and commissioner Bud Selig's personal lawyer.

"I'm going to bring my efforts and my experience as a businessperson to the business of the club," Payne said. "We're in last place now but you might as well take a picture because that's probably the last time you're going to see that."

A most interesting managerial shuffle took place the day after the World Series ended as Lou Piniella left the Mariners for the Devil Rays and a four-year, $13 million contract while Art Howe bolted the Athletics for the Mets and a four-year, $9.4 million deal.

Lou Piniella

Two weeks after the season ended, Piniella surprised the Mariners by saying he wanted out of the final year of his contract for 2003 because he wanted to work closer to his Tampa, Fla., home. Piniella was then traded to the Devil Rays with shortstop prospect Antonio Perez in a trade for all-star outfielder Randy Winn. Piniella compiled an 840-711 record in 10 seasons with the Mariners, including a 116-46 mark in 2001 that tied the major league record for most victories in a season.

Howe led the Athletics to three straight playoff appearances from 2000-02 and had a 600-533 record in seven seasons with Oakland. Bench coach Ken Macha was promoted to take Howe's place.

Many other managers also lost their jobs in 2002.

■ The Brewers fired Davey Lopes on April 18 following a 3-12 start and 144-195 record in three seasons. Bench coach Jerry Royster replaced him but was axed two days

11th-Inning Tie Results In Black Eye For Baseball

It was supposed to be one of the crowning moments of Bud Selig's tenure as commissioner.

The 2002 All-Star Game was coming to Milwaukee, Selig's native city and the town where he brought back Major League Baseball in 1970 after buying the Seattle Pilots out of bankruptcy court during spring training and transforming them into the Brewers.

The All-Star Game was also coming to Miller Park, the shiny $400-million facility that opened in 2001, financed after some shaky wee-hours maneuvering in the Wisconsin state legislature.

However, many things went awry for Selig during the festivities. Miller Park's retractable roof was closed during the latter stages of the home run derby on the eve of the All-Star Game

Torii Hunter

with rain approaching. However, the roof sprung some leaks, causing embarrassment for the Brewers.

That was small stuff compared to what happened when the All-Star Game went into extra innings with the National and American leagues tied at 7-7.

By the time the 10th inning started, NL manager Bob Brenly of the Diamondbacks and AL skipper Joe Torre of the Yankees had used all 30 players on their rosters, the first time that had ever happened in an All-Star Game.

When the game reached the middle of the 11th still knotted at 7-7, Selig huddled with both managers, the umpires, Major League Baseball executive vice president Sandy Alderson and Fox Sports president Ed Goren in his box beside the NL dugout. Just as the bottom half of the inning began, the public address announcer told the crowd of 41,871 the game would be called at the end of the inning if the NL didn't score.

Suddenly, Selig became about as popular in his beloved Milwaukee as Budweiser. His decision to declare a tie didn't sit well with Milwaukeeans who had waited 27 years since their last All-Star Game at County Stadium.

Selig was clearly shaken by the fan reaction. When he met with the media moments after the game ended, he was ashen.

"I feel very badly about it," Selig said. "Frankly, I couldn't feel any worse. In your wildest dreams, you would not have conceived that this game would end in a tie. As much as I hated to do it, and with all of the reluctance in the world, given the people here in the stadium and the people watching on television, I really, really had no choice at the end but to end the game at the end of the 11th inning."

Neither Brenly nor Torre wanted to extend their last two pitchers, the Phillies' Vicente Padilla and the

Mariners' Freddy Garcia.

"The last thing I want to do is get a pitcher hurt and send Freddy Garcia back to (Mariners manager) Lou Piniella saying he can't pitch," Torre said.

The game itself was exciting until the unfilled finish.

The AL tied the game at 7-7 in the eighth inning on a run-scoring triple by the Indians' Omar Vizquel into the right-field corner off Giants reliever Robb Nen after the lead changed hands twice in the seventh.

The AL had turned a 5-2 deficit into a 6-5 lead with four runs in the top of the seventh. The Angels' Garret Anderson drove in a run with a ground out, and pinch hitter Tony Batista of the Orioles had an RBI single before the White Sox' Paul Konerko ripped a two-run double into the gap in left-center. The AL lead didn't last long, though, as the Astros' Lance Berkman hit a two-run single up the middle with two outs in the bottom of the seventh to give the NL a 7-6 advantage.

The play of the game came in the first inning, when AL center fielder Torii Hunter robbed the Giants' Barry Bonds of a home run by getting his glove high above the fence in right-center to make the catch.

"I've seen Torii do that so many times on TV," said Red Sox pitcher Derek Lowe, on the mound at the time. "It was amazing. That's what people come here to see, and it was just a great play."

—JOHN PERROTTO

TOP VOTE-GETTERS

NATIONAL LEAGUE

CATCHER: 1. Mike Piazza, Mets, 1,966,940; 2. Benito Santiago, Giants, 707,275; 3. Michael Barrett, Expos, 569,607.

FIRST BASE: 1. Todd Helton, Rockies, 1,161,376; 2. Jeff Bagwell, Astros, 831,403; 3. Tino Martinez, Cardinals, 626,041.

SECOND BASE: 1. Jose Vidro, Expos, 1,106,097; 2. Roberto Alomar, Mets, 1,064,644; 3. Luis Castillo, Marlins, 554,992.

THIRD BASE: 1. Scott Rolen, Phillies, 799,364; 2. Mike Lowell, Marlins, 719,893; 3. David Bell, Giants, 461,807.

SHORTSTOP: 1. Jimmy Rollins, Phillies, 718,682; 2. Rafael Furcal, Braves, 588,670; 3. Rich Aurilia, Giants, 562,059.

OUTFIELD: 1. Sammy Sosa, Cubs, 2,062,038; 2. Barry Bonds, Giants, 2,056,743; 3. Vladimir Guerrero, Expos, 1,307,622; 4. Tsuyoshi Shinjo, Giants, 1,053,352; 5. Ken Griffey Jr., Reds, 731,677; 6. Lance Berkman, Astros, 696,478; 7. Jim Edmonds, Cardinals, 582,726; 8. Luis Gonzalez, Diamondbacks, 580,555; 9. Chipper Jones, Braves, 541,219.

AMERICAN LEAGUE

CATCHER: 1. Jorge Posada, Yankees, 1,160,795; 2. Ivan Rodriguez, Rangers, 1,142,276; 3. A.J. Pierzynski, Twins, 636,649.

FIRST BASE: 1. Jason Giambi, Yankees, 1,332,607; 2. John Olerud, Mariners, 719,073; 3. Doug Mientkiewicz, Twins, 637,554.

SECOND BASE: 1. Alfonso Soriano, Yankees, 1,681,510; 2. Bret Boone, Mariners, 1,315,320; 3. Luis Rivas, Twins, 598,941.

THIRD BASE: 1. Shea Hillenbrand, Red Sox, 863,779; 2. Robin Ventura, Yankees, 830,037; 3. Corey Koskie, Twins, 686,039.

SHORTSTOP: 1. Alex Rodriguez, Rangers, 1,316,645; 2. Nomar Garciaparra, Red Sox, 991,331; 3. Derek Jeter, Yankees, 907,719.

OUTFIELD: 1. Ichiro Suzuki, Mariners, 2,516,016; 2. Manny Ramirez, Red Sox, 1,228,449; 3. Torii Hunter, Twins, 1,118,980; 4. Mike Cameron, Mariners, 1,014,881; 5. Bernie Williams, Yankees, 971,447; 6. Johnny Damon, Red Sox, 721,576; 7. Kenny Lofton, White Sox, 657,803; 8. Jacque Jones, Twins, 601,855; 9. Magglio Ordonez, White Sox, 555,867.

ROSTERS

NATIONAL LEAGUE

MANAGER: Bob Brenly, Diamondbacks.

PITCHERS: Eric Gagne, Dodgers; x-Tom Glavine, Braves; Trevor Hoffman, Padres; x-Randy Johnson, Diamondbacks; Byung-Hyun Kim, Diamondbacks; x-Matt Morris, Cardinals; Robb Nen, Giants; Vicente Padilla, Phillies; Odalis Perez, Dodgers; Mike Remlinger, Braves; **Curt Schilling, Diamondbacks**; John Smoltz, Braves; Mike Williams, Pirates.

CATCHERS: Damian Miller, Diamondbacks; **Mike Piazza, Mets**; Benito Santiago, Giants.

INFIELDERS: Luis Castillo, Marlins; **Todd Helton, Rockies (1b)**; Jose Hernandez, Brewers; Mike Lowell, Marlins; **Scott Rolen, Phillies (3b)**; **Jimmy Rollins, Phillies (ss)**; Richie Sexson, Brewers; Junior Spivey, Diamondbacks; **Jose Vidro, Expos (2b)**;

OUTFIELDERS: Lance Berkman, Astros; **Barry Bonds, Giants (lf)**; Adam Dunn, Reds; Luis Gonzalez, Diamondbacks; Shawn Green, Dodgers; **Vladimir Guerrero, Expos (cf)**; Andruw Jones, Braves; **Sammy Sosa, Cubs (rf)**.

AMERICAN LEAGUE

MANAGER: Joe Torre, Yankees.

PITCHERS: Mark Buehrle, White Sox; Freddy Garcia, Mariners; Eddie Guardado, Twins; Roy Halladay, Blue Jays; **Derek Lowe, Red Sox**; x-Pedro Martinez, Red Sox; Mariano Rivera, Yankees; Kazuhiro Sasaki, Mariners; Ugueth Urbina, Red Sox; Barry Zito, Athletics.

CATCHERS: A.J. Pierzynski, Twins; **Jorge Posada, Yankees.**

INFIELDERS: Tony Batista, Orioles; Nomar Garciaparra, Red Sox; **Jason Giambi, Yankees (1b)**; **Shea Hillenbrand, Red Sox (3b)**; Derek Jeter, Yankees; Paul Konerko, White Sox; **Alex Rodriguez, Rangers (ss)**; **Alfonso Soriano, Yankees (2b)**; Mike Sweeney, Royals; Miguel Tejada, Athletics; Robin Ventura, Yankees; Omar Vizquel, Indians.

OUTFIELDERS: Garret Anderson, Angels; Johnny Damon, Red Sox; Robert Fick, Tigers; **Torii Hunter, Twins (cf)**; **Manny Ramirez, Red Sox (lf)**; **Ichiro Suzuki, Mariners (rf)**; Randy Winn, Devil Rays.

Starters in **boldface**.

x-injured, did not play.

July 9 in Milwaukee
American League 7, National League 7

AMERICAN	ab	r	h	bi	NATIONAL	ab	r	h	bi
Suzuki, rf	2	0	0	0	**Vidro, 2b**	2	0	0	0
Winn, rf	2	1	1	0	Spivey, 2b	2	0	0	0
Urbina, p	0	0	0	0	Nen, p	0	0	0	0
Rivera, p	0	0	0	0	Smoltz, p	0	0	0	0
Garcia, p	1	0	0	0	Santiago, ph-c	2	0	1	0
Hillenbrand, 3b	2	0	0	0	**Helton, 1b**	2	1	1	1
Ventura, 3b	1	0	0	0	Berkman, lf-1b	3	0	1	2
Batista, ph-3b	3	1	1	1	**Bonds, lf**	2	1	1	2
Rodriguez, ss	2	0	0	0	Sexson, 1b	1	0	0	0
Tejada, ss	2	1	1	0	Dunn, lf	1	0	0	0
Garciaparra, ph-ss	1	0	0	0	**Sosa, rf**	2	0	1	0
Giambi, 1b	2	1	1	0	Green, rf	3	0	1	0
Konerko, 1b	2	0	2	2	**Guerrero, cf**	2	1	1	0
Sweeney, 1b	1	0	0	0	Jones, ph-cf	3	0	0	0
Ramirez, lf	2	0	2	1	**Piazza, c**	2	0	0	1
Buehrle, p	0	0	0	0	Gagne, p	0	0	0	0
Pierzynski, ph-c	3	0	0	0	Hernandez, ss	3	0	0	0
Posada, c	3	0	0	0	**Rolen, 3b**	3	0	0	0
Zito, p	0	0	0	0	Castillo, 2b	2	0	0	0
Guardado, p	0	0	0	0	**Rollins, ss**	2	2	2	0
Sasaki, p	0	0	0	0	Hoffman, p	0	0	0	0
Fick, ph-rf	2	1	1	0	Remlinger, p	0	0	0	0
Hunter, cf	2	0	0	0	Kim, p	0	0	0	0
Damon, cf	3	1	1	0	Lowell, ph-3b	3	1	2	0
Soriano, 2b	2	1	1	1	**Schilling, p**	0	0	0	0
Vizquel, 2b	2	0	1	1	Williams, p	0	0	0	0
Lowe, p	0	0	0	0	Gonzalez, ph	1	0	0	0
Jeter, ph	1	0	0	0	Perez, p	0	0	0	0
Halladay, p	0	0	0	0	Miller, c	3	1	2	1
Anderson, lf	4	0	0	1	Padilla, p	1	0	0	0
Totals	**45**	**7**	**12**	**7**	**Totals**	**45**	**7**	**13**	**7**

American	**000 110 410 00—7**
National	**013 010 020 00—7**

LOB—American 7, National 6. **2B**—Winn, Konerko 2, Miller 2. **3B**—Vizquel. **HR**—Soriano, Bonds. **SB**—Damon, Winn, Fick, Berkman, Green.

National	ip	h	r	er	bb	so	American	ip	h	r	er	bb	so
Lowe	2	2	1	1	0	0	Schilling	2	1	0	0	0	3
Halladay	1	3	3	3	0	1	Williams	1	0	0	0	0	2
Buehrle	2	2	1	1	0	2	Perez	1	2	1	0	0	2
Zito	⅓	0	0	0	0	0	Gagne	1	2	1	1	0	1
Guardado	⅔	0	0	0	0	2	Hoffman	1	1	0	0	0	1
Sasaki	1	3	2	2	1	2	Remlinger	⅔	1	2	2	1	0
Urbina	1	0	0	0	0	1	Kim	⅓	3	2	2	0	0
Rivera	1	1	0	0	0	0	Nen	1	2	1	1	0	2
Garcia	2	2	0	0	0	3	Smoltz	1	0	0	0	0	1
							Padilla	2	0	0	0	1	0

PB—Piazza. **BK**—Lowe.

Umpires: HP—Gerry Davis; **1B**—Tim Tschida; **2B**—Chuck Meriwether; **3B**—Jerry Meals; **LF**—Marty Foster; **RF**—Paul Emmel.

T—3:29. **A**—41,871.

after the season ended as he led the Brewers to only a 53-94 mark.

■ Before the first month of the season was over, the ax fell on two more managers as the Rockies fired Buddy Bell on April 26 after a 6-16 start and the Royals jettisoned Tony Muser on April 29 after an 8-15 start.

Bell, 161-185 in three seasons, was replaced by hitting coach Clint Hurdle. Later in the season, Hurdle received a two-year contract extension.

Muser, 317-431 in six seasons, was replaced by bullpen coach John Mizerock on an interim basis. The Royals then hired Tony Pena, manager of the Houston Astros' Triple-A New Orleans farm club, on a permanent basis May 15.

■ The Blue Jays fired Buck Martinez on June 3, a day after he won his 100th game, and replaced him with third base coach Carlos Tosca. Martinez was 100-115 in

Travis Fryman

his two seasons but the Blue Jays were only 20-33 at the time he was let go. Tosca's contract was extended two years later in the season.

■ As the second half of the season began July 11, the Indians and Charlie Manuel parted ways. The Indians began trading veterans for youngsters a few weeks earlier and Manuel wanted assurances he would be around to oversee the rebuilding. When general manager Mark Shapiro couldn't make any promises, the sides made a mutual split.

Cleveland went 220-190 in three years with Manuel at the helm but only 39-47 in the first half of 2002. Third base coach Joel Skinner finished out the season as interim manager, going 35-41, before being replaced by Eric Wedge, manager of the Indians' Triple-A Buffalo farm club in the International League.

■ The Devil Rays' Hal McRae, the Mets' Bobby Valentine and the Rangers' Jerry Narron all were given pink slips when the season ended.

The Devil Rays finished 55-106 and were 113-196 in McRae's two seasons.

Valentine guided to the Mets to a 536-467 record in seven seasons but went only 75-86 in 2002.

Narron went 134-162 in two seasons, including 72-90 in 2002. The Rangers hired former Diamondbacks and Yankees manager Buck Showalter to replace Narron.

Canseco, Raines, Fryman Hang 'Em Up

Following a 2001 season in which sure first-ballot Hall of Famers Cal Ripken Jr., Mark McGwire and Tony Gwynn retired, the list of luminaries leaving the game in 2002 wasn't as bright.

However, one of the more colorful and controversial characters of recent years decided to hang them up on May 14. Outfielder Jose Canseco, released by the Expos in spring training, walked away from the White Sox' Triple-A Charlotte farm club in May after hitting just .172 in 18 games against International League pitching with five home runs and nine RBIs.

Not surprisingly, the 37-year-old Canseco did not leave quietly as he lived up to his controversial reputation by claiming he should still be in the major leagues.

"I've had a lot of athletes in different sports and I

know a lot of people in the acting field that all told me I've been exiled, basically, blackballed," Canseco said.

Canseco became the first player to hit 40 home runs and steal 40 bases in the same season, performing the feat with the Athletics in 1988. However, his performance level slipped from there as he ran into a string of injuries and off-field problems.

For the second time in his illustrious career, Marlins outfielder Tim Raines retired. He announced his retirement before the 2000 season after being diagnosed with lupus but returned to play in 2001 and 2002.

Raines, 43, was one of the best leadoff hitters in history as he batted .294 with 170 homers, 980 RBIs and 808 stolen bases during 23 seasons with the Expos (1979-90, 2001), White Sox (1991-95), Yankees (1996-98), Athletics (1999), Orioles (2001) and Marlins (2002).

"A lot of players play a long time and don't really know when to quit," Raines said. "I actually feel real good about it. I've reached the maximum, it's time to close the book on my career as a player."

Indians third baseman Travis Fryman decided to close the book on his 13-season career at the relative young age of 33 after battling shoulder and elbow injuries for many seasons. Fryman hit .274 with 223 homers and 1,022 RBIs with the Tigers (1990-97) and Indians (1998-2002).

Athletics infielder Randy Velarde called an end to his 15-year career. He batted .276 with 100 homers and 444 RBIs with the Yankees (1987-95, 2001), Angels (1996-99), Athletics (1999-2000, 2002) and Rangers (2001).

Infielder Luis Sojo decided to retire from the Yankees when they offered the job of managing their Double-A Norwich farm club in the Eastern League. Sojo, 36, batted .261 with 36 homers and 261 RBIs in 12 seasons with the Blue Jays (1990, 1993), Angels (1991-92), Mariners (1994-96), Yankees (1996-2001) and Pirates (2000). He then guided Norwich to the league title as a rookie manager.

Ozzie Smith: Lone Hall of Fame inductee in 2002

Righthander Mark Gardner retired one victory short of 100 for his 13-year career just before spring training began. The 40-year-old went 99-93 with a 4.56 ERA with the Expos (1989-92), Royals (1993), Marlins (1994-95) and Giants (1996-2001).

Broadcasting giant Ernie Harwell also retired after 55 years behind the mike, including 42 with the Tigers. Harwell signed off following the Tigers' season finale with the Blue Jays on Sept. 29.

"Thank you for letting me be part of my family," Harwell told listeners in his goodbye. "Thank you for taking me with you to that cottage up north, to the beach, the picnic, your work place and your backyard. Thank you for sneaking your transistor under the pillow as you grew up loving the Tigers.

"I might have been a small part of your life but you have been a very large part of mine. And it's my privilege and honor to share with you the greatest game of all."

Cincinnati's Riverfront Stadium makes way for the Great American Ball Park in 2003

Smith Walks In Alone

While Canseco's chances of getting to Cooperstown are iffy, defensive whiz Ozzie Smith was the only player inducted into the Hall of Fame in 2002.

Smith hit just .260 with 28 home runs and 793 RBIs while stealing 580 bases in 19 seasons with the Padres (1978-81) and Cardinals (1982-96). However, he redefined the art of shortstop defense.

The acrobatic Smith, nicknamed "The Wizard of Oz", won 13 Gold Glove awards and played in 15 All-Star Games. He set all-time records for double plays (1,590) and assists (8,375) by a shortstop.

Despite his subpar offensive number, Smith received 91.74 percent of the Baseball Writers Association of America vote when he was elected on his first try. The congenial Smith also was one of the most popular players of his era.

"I sincerely believe that there is nothing truly great in any man or woman, except their character," Smith said. "Giving back is the ultimate talent in life. That is the great trophy on my mantel."

Smith spent most of his 28-minute speech comparing his career journey to that of Dorothy in the Wizard of Oz. With brains from the Scarecrow, love and faith from the Tin Man and determination from the Cowardly Lion, Smith turned L. Frank Baum's classic children's book into a metaphor for success.

"My glove has given me so much," Smith said. "But most importantly, it's given me the ability to give back."

Detroit News columnist Joe Falls accepted the J.G. Taylor Spink Award for writers and longtime Phillies voice Harry Kalas received the Ford C. Frick Award for broadcasters.

Changing Of The Guard

Baseball bid farewell to another one of the cookie-cutter stadiums built in the early 1970s as the Reds played their final game at Cinergy Field on Sept. 22, losing 4-3 to the Phillies.

The ballpark opened with a Reds' loss in 1970 as Riverfront Stadium and closed with another loss under a different name. However, a postgame ceremony which included 52 Reds' greats of the Riverfront/Cinergy Era that included the Big Red Machine championship teams of the 1970s and the World Series winners in 1990 helped offset the sting of losing.

"There was so much history," said Reds center fielder Ken Griffey Jr., whose father also called Riverfront home from 1973-81 as Cincinnati's right fielder. "When you see all the guys who came before us walking around the stadium and doing all the fun things that means something."

Riverfront Stadium had the first wall-to-wall artificial turf and sliding pits when it opened. Three Rivers Stadium opened later in 1970 and Philadelphia christened Veterans Stadium in 1971.

Three Rivers Stadium was torn down after the 2000 season and the Phillies will play their final season at "The Vet" in 2003. Meanwhile, the Reds will move into Great American Ball Park for '03.

"I know what a lot of fans think and how they'd like to see these stadiums blown up but a lot of sentimental things have gone on in those stadiums" Phillies manager Larry Bowa said.

Hall of Fame manager Sparky Anderson threw out the ceremonial first pitch and remembered back to the time when Riverfront Stadium was the place to be.

"If you didn't play in Cincinnati, you didn't play in the major leagues," Anderson said. "The people supported these players like you've never seen. There was excitement every night."

Missing from the closing festivities was Reds great Pete Rose, who got his record-setting hit No. 4,192 at the stadium in 1985 but is banned from baseball for life for gambling.

Tom Browning, who pitched a perfect game for the Reds at Riverfront Stadium in 1988, got a can of red spray paint and put Rose's No. 14 on the mound after the game. The crowd of 40,964 chanted "Pete! Pete!"

"You could sense the crowd wanted some sort of acknowledgement of Pete," Browning said.

Somehow, it was fitting for the crowd to clamor for someone who wasn't there. After all, the 2002 season will be remembered for something that didn't happen.

MAJOR LEAGUE DEBUTS, 2002

AMERICAN LEAGUE

Anaheim Angels

Alfredo Amezaga, ss	April 24
Brendan Donnelly, rhp	April 9
Chone Figgins, 2b	Aug. 25
John Lackey, rhp	June 24
Francisco Rodriguez, rhp	Sept. 18

Baltimore Orioles

Steve Bechler, rhp	Sept. 6
Erik Bedard, lhp	April 17
Howie Clark, dh	July 16
Travis Driskill, rhp	April 26
Eric DuBose, lhp	Sept. 19
Luis Garcia, of	April 10
Jose Leon, 1b	June 16
Mike Moriarty, ss	April 11
Ed Rogers, ss	Sept. 5
John Stephens, rhp	July 30

Boston Red Sox

Juan Diaz, 1b	June 12
Josh Hancock, rhp	Sept. 10
Bryant Nelson, 2b	May 14
Freddy Sanchez, 2b	Sept. 10

Chicago White Sox

Joe Borchard, of	Sept. 2
Miguel Olivo, c	Sept. 15
Jon Rauch, rhp	April 2

Cleveland Indians

Josh Bard, c	Aug. 23
Jason Beverlin, rhp	July 29
Ben Broussard, of	June 22
Covelli Crisp, of	Aug. 15
Jason Davis, rhp	Sept. 9
Dave Elder, rhp	July 24
Alex Herrera, lhp	Sept. 13
Cliff Lee, lhp	Sept. 15
Victor Martinez, c	Sept. 10
Brandon Phillips, 2b	Sept. 13
Ricardo Rodriguez, rhp	Aug. 21
Carl Sadler, lhp	July 31
Earl Snyder, 1b	April 28
Brian Tallet, lhp	Sept. 16

Detroit Tigers

Eric Eckenstahler, lhp	Sept. 9
Jeff Farnsworth, rhp	April 3
Franklyn German, rhp	Sept. 7
Omar Infante, ss	Sept. 7
Kris Keller, rhp	May 24
Shane Loux, rhp	Sept. 10
Mike Maroth, lhp	June 8
Terry Pearson, rhp	April 4
Fernando Rodney, rhp	May 4
Oscar Salazar, 2b	April 10
Ramon Santiago, ss	May 17
Andres Torres, of	April 7
Andy Van Hekken, lhp	Sept. 3

Kansas City Royals

Jeremy Affeldt, lhp	April 6
Miguel Asencio, rhp	April 6
Juan Brito, c	May 3
Ryan Bukvich, rhp	July 12
Nate Field, rhp	April 12
Alexis Gomez, of	June 16
Aaron Guiel, of	June 22
Runelvys Hernandez, rhp	July 15
Jeremy Hill, rhp	Sept. 7
Wes Obermueller, rhp	Sept. 20
Kit Pellow, 3b	Aug. 14
Shawn Sedlacek, rhp	June 18
Dusty Wathan, c	Sept. 24

Minnesota Twins

Kevin Frederick, rhp	July 15
Michael Restovich, of	Sept. 18
Mike Ryan, of	Sept. 20
Todd Sears, 1b	Sept. 17

New York Yankees

Drew Henson, 3b	Sept. 5
Marcus Thames, of	June 10

Oakland Athletics

Mark Ellis, 2b	April 9
Jose Flores, 2b	Sept. 7
Esteban German, 2b	May 21
Jason Grabowski, of	Sept. 22
Aaron Harang, rhp	May 25
Cody McKay, c	Sept. 22

Seattle Mariners

Willie Bloomquist, of	Sept. 1
Brian Fitzgerald, lhp	April 17
Justin Kaye, rhp	May 9
Julio Mateo, rhp	May 7
Chris Snelling, of	May 25
Rafael Soriano, rhp	May 10
Aaron Taylor, rhp	Sept. 9
Luis Ugueto, ss	April 3
Ron Wright, 1b	April 14

Tampa Bay Devil Rays

Brandon Backe, rhp	July 19
Dewon Brazelton, rhp	Sept. 13
Carl Crawford, of	July 20
Luis de los Santos, rhp	July 20
Felix Escalona, ss	April 4
Lee Gardner, rhp	May 24
Delvin James, rhp	April 16
Jason Jimenez, lhp	June 3
Steven Kent, lhp	April 4
Juan Sosa, rhp	April 4

Texas Rangers

Hank Blalock, 3b	April 1
Randy Flores, lhp	April 23
Reynaldo Garcia, rhp	July 19
Travis Hafner, 1b	Aug. 6
Jason Hart, of	Aug. 18
Ben Kozlowski, lhp	Sept. 19
Colby Lewis, rhp	April 1
Ryan Ludwick, of	June 5
Kevin Mench, of	April 9
Jason Romano, of	April 17

Toronto Blue Jays

Kevin Cash, c	Sept. 6
Scott Cassidy, rhp	April 1
Mark Hendrickson, lhp	Aug. 6
Eric Hinske, 3b	April 1
Orlando Hudson, 2b	July 24
Joe Lawrence, 2b	April 8
Justin Miller, rhp	April 12
Mike Smith, rhp	April 26
Corey Thurman, rhp	April 5
Jayson Werth, of	Sept. 1
Scott Wiggins, rhp	Sept. 11

NATIONAL LEAGUE

Arizona Diamondbacks

John Patterson, rhp	July 20

Atlanta Braves

Jung Bong, lhp	April 23
Joey Dawley, rhp	Sept. 29
John Ennis, rhp	April 10
John Foster, lhp	April 24
Kevin Gryboski, rhp	April 13
Trey Hodges, rhp	Sept. 10
Ryan Langerhans, of	April 28
Andy Pratt, lhp	Sept. 28

Chicago Cubs

Francis Beltran, rhp	June 28
Hee Seop Choi, 1b	Sept. 3
Bobby Hill, 2b	May 10
Mark Prior, rhp	May 22
Steve Smyth, lhp	Aug. 6

Cincinnati Reds

Luke Hudson, rhp	July 1
Austin Kearns, of	April 17
Wily Mo Pena, of	Sept. 10

Colorado Rockies

Aaron Cook, rhp	Aug. 10
Cory Vance, lhp	Sept. 21

Florida Marlins

Hansel Izquierdo, rhp	April 21
Abraham Nunez, of	Sept. 3
Nate Robertson, lhp	Sept. 7
Nate Teut, lhp	May 4
Justin Wayne, rhp	Sept. 3

Houston Astros

Jason Lane, of	May 10
Brad Lidge, rhp	April 26
Brandon Puffer, rhp	April 17
Jeriome Robertson, lhp	Sept. 2
Kirk Saarloos, rhp	June 18
Barry Wesson, of	July 15
Alan Zinter, 1b	June 18

Los Angeles Dodgers

Luke Allen, of	Sept. 10
Victor Alvarez, lhp	July 30
Chin-Feng Chen, of	Sept. 14
Kazuhisa Ishii, lhp	April 6
David Ross, c	June 29
Wilkin Ruan, of	Sept. 1
Joe Thurston, 2b	Sept. 2

Milwaukee Brewers

Matt Childers, rhp	Aug. 3
Ben Diggins, rhp	Sept. 2
Jayson Durocher, rhp	June 11
Bill Hall, ss	Sept. 1
Brian Mallette, rhp	April 12
Shane Nance, lhp	Aug. 24
Takahito Nomura, lhp	April 3
Dave Pember, rhp	Sept. 3
Jim Rushford, of	Sept. 3

Montreal Expos

Jamey Carroll, 3b	Sept. 11
Matt Cepicky, of	July 31
Zach Day, rhp	June 15

New York Mets

Jaime Cerda, lhp	June 28
Pedro Feliciano, lhp	Sept. 4
Satoru Komiyama, rhp	April 4
Marco Scutaro, 2b	July 21
Jae Seo, rhp	July 21
Esix Snead, of	Sept. 3
Pat Strange, rhp	Sept. 13
Tyler Walker, rhp	July 2
Ty Wigginton, 3b	May 16

Philadelphia Phillies

Marlon Byrd, of	Sept. 8
Eric Junge, rhp	Sept. 11
Brett Myers, rhp	July 24
Carlos Silva, rhp	April 1

Pittsburgh Pirates

Tony Alvarez, of	Sept. 4
J.J. Davis, of	Sept. 4
Duaner Sanchez, rhp	June 14

St. Louis Cardinals

Mike Crudale, rhp	April 10
Matt Duff, rhp	July 30
Kevin Joseph, rhp	Aug. 1
Josh Pearce, rhp	April 20
Jason Simontacchi, rhp	May 4
So Taguchi, of	June 10

San Diego Padres

Sean Burroughs, 3b	April 2
Mike Bynum, rhp	Aug. 17
Clay Condrey, rhp	Aug. 28
Eric Cyr, lhp	June 23
Ben Howard, rhp	April 28
Jason Kershner, lhp	July 25
Julius Matos, 2b	May 31
Wil Nieves, c	July 21
Jason Pearson, lhp	June 4
Jake Peavy, rhp	June 22
Alex Pelaez, 1b	May 16
Oliver Perez, lhp	June 16
Kevin Pickford, lhp	May 16
Jason Shiell, rhp	Sept. 8
Dennis Tankersley, rhp	May 10
J.J. Trujillo, rhp	June 11

San Francisco Giants

Trey Lunsford, c	Sept. 12
Tony Torcato, of	July 26

BY JOHN PERROTTO

When the Anaheim Angels convened for spring training at Tempe, Ariz., in 2002, no one outside their clubhouse gave them a chance of hoisting the World Series trophy eight months later.

The Angels had gone 75-87 the year before, finishing a whopping 41 games behind the Seattle Mariners in the American League West. And they hadn't received an offseason overhaul, as their only significant moves were to trade disgruntled first baseman Mo Vaughn to the Mets for righthander Kevin Appier and sign righthander Aaron Sele as a free agent.

The Angels had a star-crossed history since joining the AL as an expansion team in 1961. In addition to a string of tragic off-field events, the Angels had two more name changes than pennants—going from the Los Angeles Angels to the California Angels to the Anaheim Angels.

The only two times the Angels had even reached the postseason, their dreams of a title ended in heartbreaking fashion in the AL Championship Series. The Angels won the first two games in 1982 in a best-of-five affair only to see the Brewers win the next three and the pennant.

Four years later, the Angels were one strike away from the pennant in Game Five when closer Donnie Moore surrendered the game-tying home run to the Red Sox' Dave Henderson in the bottom of the ninth. The Red Sox won in 11 innings, then went home to Boston

Heaven on Earth
The Anaheim Angels pulled off one of the biggest surprises in baseball history

and captured the final two games of ALCS to move into the World Series. Moore committed suicide three years later.

The Angels were shut out of the postseason the next 15 seasons and became known in recent years more for bad uniforms and the Rally Monkey than their play on the field. The Angels' scoreboard crew would play a video of the little primate jumping up and down in late innings of games when the home team trailed as a means of inspiration.

But when the 2002 season ended with a Game Seven of a fascinating World Series, long-suffering right fielder Tim Salmon was clutching the championship trophy and leading his Angels teammates in a victory lap around Edison International Field. The Angels had pulled off the improbable, rallying from a 3-2 series deficit to beat the San Francisco Giants and record their first-ever World Series title.

One For The Cowboy

Forty-one years after singing cowboy Gene Autry brought the Angels into existence primarily to provide summer programming for his Los Angeles radio station, the franchise was on top of the baseball world.

"It's an incredible lift to this whole community," Angels manager Mike Scioscia said. "The Angels have had championships here. They've won divisions. But they've never gotten to the level we have.

"I don't look at not winning in the past as demons as much as the pieces of a puzzles finally falling into place. This organization has a tremendous player-development

WORLD SERIES YEAR-BY-YEAR

Year	Winner	Manager	Loser	Manager	Result	MVP
1903	Boston (AL)	Jimmy Collins	Pittsburgh (NL)	Fred Clarke	5-3	None Selected
1904	NO SERIES					
1905	New York (NL)	John McGraw	Philadelphia (AL)	Connie Mack	4-1	None Selected
1906	Chicago (AL)	Fielder Jones	Chicago (NL)	Frank Chance	4-2	None Selected
1907	Chicago (NL)	Frank Chance	Detroit (AL)	Hugh Jennings	4-0	None Selected
1908	Chicago (NL)	Frank Chance	Detroit (AL)	Hugh Jennings	4-1	None Selected
1909	Pittsburgh (NL)	Fred Clarke	Detroit (AL)	Hugh Jennings	4-3	None Selected
1910	Philadelphia (AL)	Connie Mack	Chicago (NL)	Frank Chance	4-1	None Selected
1911	Philadelphia (AL)	Connie Mack	New York (NL)	John McGraw	4-2	None Selected
1912	Boston (AL)	Jake Stahl	New York (NL)	John McGraw	4-3-1	None Selected
1913	Philadelphia (AL)	Connie Mack	New York (NL)	John McGraw	4-1	None Selected
1914	Boston (NL)	George Stallings	Philadelphia (AL)	Connie Mack	4-0	None Selected
1915	Boston (AL)	Bill Carrigan	Philadelphia (NL)	Pat Moran	4-1	None Selected
1916	Boston (AL)	Bill Carrigan	Brooklyn (NL)	Wilbert Robinson	4-1	None Selected
1917	Chicago (AL)	Pants Rowland	New York (NL)	John McGraw	4-2	None Selected
1918	Boston (AL)	Ed Barrow	Chicago (NL)	Fred Mitchell	4-2	None Selected
1919	Cincinnati (NL)	Pat Moran	Chicago (AL)	Kid Gleason	5-3	None Selected
1920	Cleveland (AL)	Tris Speaker	Brooklyn (NL)	Wilbert Robinson	5-2	None Selected
1921	New York (NL)	John McGraw	New York (AL)	Miller Huggins	5-3	None Selected
1922	New York (NL)	John McGraw	New York (AL)	Miller Huggins	4-0	None Selected
1923	New York (AL)	Miller Huggins	New York (NL)	John McGraw	4-2	None Selected
1924	Washington (AL)	Bucky Harris	New York (NL)	John McGraw	4-3	None Selected
1925	Pittsburgh (NL)	Bill McKechnie	Washington (AL)	Bucky Harris	4-3	None Selected
1926	St. Louis (NL)	Rogers Hornsby	New York (AL)	Miller Huggins	4-3	None Selected
1927	New York (AL)	Miller Huggins	Pittsburgh (NL)	Donie Bush	4-0	None Selected
1928	New York (AL)	Miller Huggins	St. Louis (NL)	Bill McKechnie	4-0	None Selected
1929	Philadelphia (AL)	Connie Mack	Chicago (NL)	Joe McCarthy	4-1	None Selected
1930	Philadelphia (AL)	Connie Mack	St. Louis (NL)	Gabby Street	4-2	None Selected
1931	St. Louis (NL)	Gabby Street	Philadelphia (AL)	Connie Mack	4-3	None Selected
1932	New York (AL)	Joe McCarthy	Chicago (NL)	Charlie Grimm	4-0	None Selected
1933	New York (NL)	Bill Terry	Washington (AL)	Joe Cronin	4-1	None Selected
1934	St. Louis (NL)	Frankie Frisch	Detroit (AL)	Mickey Cochrane	4-3	None Selected
1935	Detroit (AL)	Mickey Cochrane	Chicago (NL)	Charlie Grimm	4-2	None Selected
1936	New York (AL)	Joe McCarthy	New York (NL)	Bill Terry	4-2	None Selected
1937	New York (AL)	Joe McCarthy	New York (NL)	Bill Terry	4-1	None Selected
1938	New York (AL)	Joe McCarthy	Chicago (NL)	Gabby Hartnett	4-0	None Selected
1939	New York (AL)	Joe McCarthy	Cincinnati (NL)	Bill McKechnie	4-0	None Selected
1940	Cincinnati (NL)	Bill McKechnie	Detroit (AL)	Del Baker	4-3	None Selected
1941	New York (AL)	Joe McCarthy	Brooklyn (NL)	Leo Durocher	4-1	None Selected
1942	St. Louis (NL)	Billy Southworth	New York (AL)	Joe McCarthy	4-1	None Selected
1943	New York (AL)	Joe McCarthy	St. Louis (NL)	Billy Southworth	4-1	None Selected
1944	St. Louis (NL)	Billy Southworth	St. Louis (AL)	Luke Sewell	4-2	None Selected
1945	Detroit (AL)	Steve O'Neill	Chicago (NL)	Charlie Grimm	4-3	None Selected
1946	St. Louis (NL)	Eddie Dyer	Boston (AL)	Joe Cronin	4-3	None Selected
1947	New York (AL)	Bucky Harris	Brooklyn (NL)	Burt Shotton	4-3	None Selected
1948	Cleveland (AL)	Lou Boudreau	Boston (NL)	Billy Southworth	4-2	None Selected
1949	New York (AL)	Casey Stengel	Brooklyn (NL)	Burt Shotton	4-1	None Selected
1950	New York (AL)	Casey Stengel	Philadelphia (NL)	Eddie Sawyer	4-0	None Selected
1951	New York (AL)	Casey Stengel	New York (NL)	Leo Durocher	4-2	None Selected
1952	New York (AL)	Casey Stengel	Brooklyn (NL)	Chuck Dressen	4-3	None Selected
1953	New York (AL)	Casey Stengel	Brooklyn (NL)	Chuck Dressen	4-2	None Selected
1954	New York (NL)	Leo Durocher	Cleveland (AL)	Al Lopez	4-0	None Selected
1955	Brooklyn (NL)	Walter Alston	New York (AL)	Casey Stengel	4-3	Johnny Podres, p, Brooklyn
1956	New York (AL)	Casey Stengel	Brooklyn (NL)	Walter Alston	4-3	Don Larsen, p, New York
1957	Milwaukee (NL)	Fred Haney	New York (AL)	Casey Stengel	4-3	Lew Burdette, p, Milwaukee
1958	New York (AL)	Casey Stengel	Milwaukee (NL)	Fred Haney	4-3	Bob Turley, p, New York
1959	Los Angeles (NL)	Walter Alston	Chicago (AL)	Al Lopez	4-2	Larry Sherry, p, Los Angeles
1960	Pittsburgh (NL)	Danny Murtaugh	New York (AL)	Casey Stengel	4-3	Bobby Richardson, 2b, New York
1961	New York (AL)	Ralph Houk	Cincinnati (NL)	Fred Hutchinson	4-1	Whitey Ford, p, New York
1962	New York (AL)	Ralph Houk	San Francisco (NL)	Alvin Dark	4-3	Ralph Terry, p, New York
1963	Los Angeles (NL)	Walter Alston	New York (AL)	Ralph Houk	4-0	Sandy Koufax, p, Los Angeles
1964	St. Louis (NL)	Johnny Keene	New York (AL)	Yogi Berra	4-3	Bob Gibson, p, St. Louis
1965	Los Angeles (NL)	Walter Alston	Minnesota (AL)	Sam Mele	4-3	Sandy Koufax, p, Los Angeles
1966	Baltimore (AL)	Hank Bauer	Los Angeles (NL)	Walter Alston	4-0	Frank Robinson, of, Baltimore
1967	St. Louis (NL)	Red Schoendienst	Boston (AL)	Dick Williams	4-3	Bob Gibson, p, St. Louis
1968	Detroit (AL)	Mayo Smith	St. Louis (NL)	Red Schoendienst	4-3	Mickey Lolich, p, Detroit
1969	New York (NL)	Gil Hodges	Baltimore (AL)	Earl Weaver	4-1	Donn Clendenon, 1b, New York
1970	Baltimore (AL)	Earl Weaver	Cincinnati (NL)	Sparky Anderson	4-1	Brooks Robinson, 3b, Baltimore
1971	Pittsburgh (NL)	Danny Murtaugh	Baltimore (AL)	Earl Weaver	4-3	Roberto Clemente, of, Pittsburgh
1972	Oakland (AL)	Dick Williams	Cincinnati (NL)	Sparky Anderson	4-3	Gene Tenace, c, Oakland
1973	Oakland (AL)	Dick Williams	New York (NL)	Yogi Berra	4-3	Reggie Jackson, of, Oakland
1974	Oakland (AL)	Alvin Dark	Los Angeles (NL)	Walter Alston	4-1	Rollie Fingers, p, Oakland
1975	Cincinnati (NL)	Sparky Anderson	Boston (AL)	Darrell Johnson	4-3	Pete Rose, 3b, Cincinnati
1976	Cincinnati (NL)	Sparky Anderson	New York (AL)	Billy Martin	4-0	Johnny Bench, c, Cincinnati
1977	New York (AL)	Billy Martin	Los Angeles (NL)	Tom Lasorda	4-2	Reggie Jackson, of, New York
1978	New York (AL)	Bob Lemon	Los Angeles (NL)	Tom Lasorda	4-2	Bucky Dent, ss, New York
1979	Pittsburgh (NL)	Chuck Tanner	Baltimore (AL)	Earl Weaver	4-3	Willie Stargell, 1b, Pittsburgh
1980	Philadelphia (NL)	Dallas Green	Kansas City (AL)	Jim Frey	4-2	Mike Schmidt, 3b, Philadelphia
1981	Los Angeles (NL)	Tom Lasorda	New York (AL)	Bob Lemon	4-2	Cey/Guerrero/Yeager, L.A.
1982	St. Louis (NL)	Whitey Herzog	Milwaukee (AL)	Harvey Kuenn	4-3	Darrell Porter, c, St. Louis
1983	Baltimore (AL)	Joe Altobelli	Philadelphia (NL)	Paul Owens	4-1	Rick Dempsey, c, Baltimore
1984	Detroit (AL)	Sparky Anderson	San Diego (NL)	Dick Williams	4-1	Alan Trammell, ss, Detroit
1985	Kansas City (AL)	Dick Howser	St. Louis (NL)	Whitey Herzog	4-3	Bret Saberhagen, p, Kansas City
1986	New York (NL)	Dave Johnson	Boston (AL)	John McNamara	4-3	Ray Knight, 3b, New York
1987	Minnesota (AL)	Tom Kelly	St. Louis (NL)	Whitey Herzog	4-3	Frank Viola, p, Minnesota
1988	Los Angeles (NL)	Tom Lasorda	Oakland (AL)	Tony La Russa	4-1	Orel Hershiser, p, Los Angeles
1989	Oakland (AL)	Tony La Russa	San Francisco (NL)	Roger Craig	4-0	Dave Stewart, p, Oakland
1990	Cincinnati (NL)	Lou Piniella	Oakland (AL)	Tony La Russa	4-0	Jose Rijo, p, Cincinnati
1991	Minnesota (AL)	Tom Kelly	Atlanta (NL)	Bobby Cox	4-3	Jack Morris, p, Minnesota
1992	Toronto (AL)	Cito Gaston	Atlanta (NL)	Bobby Cox	4-2	Pat Borders, c, Toronto
1993	Toronto (AL)	Cito Gaston	Philadelphia (NL)	Jim Fregosi	4-2	Paul Molitor, dh, Toronto
1994	NO SERIES					
1995	Atlanta (NL)	Bobby Cox	Cleveland (AL)	Mike Hargrove	4-2	Tom Glavine, p, Atlanta
1996	New York (AL)	Joe Torre	Atlanta (NL)	Bobby Cox	4-2	John Wetteland, p, New York
1997	Florida (NL)	Jim Leyland	Cleveland (AL)	Mike Hargrove	4-3	Livan Hernandez, p, Florida
1998	New York (AL)	Joe Torre	San Diego (NL)	Bruce Bochy	4-0	Scott Brosius, 3b, New York
1999	New York (AL)	Joe Torre	Atlanta (NL)	Bobby Cox	4-0	Mariano Rivera, p, New York
2000	New York (AL)	Joe Torre	New York (NL)	Bobby Valentine	4-1	Derek Jeter, ss, New York
2001	Arizona (NL)	Bob Brenly	New York (AL)	Joe Torre	4-3	Johnson, p/Schilling, p, Arizona
2002	Anaheim (AL)	Mike Scioscia	San Francisco (NL)	Dusty Baker	4-3	Troy Glaus, 3b, Anaheim

system. They get guys to the major leagues, but they never put it together at the major league level until now.

"Everyone talks about a curse or demons or 40 years to get here. All I know is we won the World Series and to get to this level is incredible and very, very rewarding."

Salmon found it particularly rewarding. He had been with the Angels since 1992, when he received a September callup after being named Baseball America's Minor League Player of the Year. Salmon played in 1,388 regular season games before finally getting into a playoff game, more than any other active player.

"Every October, I would sit at home and wonder what it would be like to be in a situation where you could win a World Series," Salmon said. "Now I know, and it's the greatest feeling in the world."

While Salmon finally won a World Series ring, Barry Bonds' long wait continued.

The Giants left fielder almost singlehandedly brought his club its first title since 1954, when the franchise was still in New York and four years away from moving to San Francisco. Bonds was left still searching for his first ring, though, having played 17 seasons since breaking into the major leagues with the Pittsburgh Pirates in 1986.

Bonds had one of the finest performances in World Series history. He went 8-for-17 (.471) with four home runs, a .700 on-base percentage and a 1.294 slugging percentage. Bonds also set World Series records for most walks in a series (13), most intentional walks in a series (seven) and most intentional walks in a game (three in Game Four).

Bonds didn't show emotion during a brief session with the media after Game Seven.

"You want the results to be different," Bonds said. "They outplayed us, they deserve it. They beat us. They're world champions."

If nothing else, Bonds put to rest the idea he could not perform on the postseason stage, as he hit .356 with eight

Francisco Rodriguez shone with a dominating playoff performance

homers, 16 RBIs and 27 walks in the Giants' 17 playoff games. In five previous Octobers, Bonds' teams had been eliminated in the first round as he hit .196 with one homer and six RBIs in 97 at-bats.

The 38-year-old got testy, however, when asked if he felt his best chance to win a World Series had slipped away. "Stupid question. Next question," he said.

A Total Team Effort

While Bonds was the dominant force in this World Series, the MVP award went to Angels third baseman Troy Glaus. He batted .385 (10-for-26) with three homers and eight RBIs, hitting safely in every game but the finale.

It was Glaus who provided the biggest hit of the series with his two-run double into the left-center gap in Game Six. Glaus' hit capped a three-run eighth inning and propelled the Angels to a 6-5 win in a game they trailed 5-0 going into the bottom of the seventh.

"Troy Glaus stepped up and did what big-game players do in a series like this," Scioscia said. "The hits he got for us were just incredible. Although, it was a team effort, I think he absolutely brought his A-game to the series. You can see how talented he is."

Glaus was humbled by the award and tried to deflect the attention to his teammates.

"This is why you play, why we put in all the time and effort," Glaus said. "This is what all the swings against the garage door when you were a kid were for, to bring you to this point.

"It's a great honor obviously to be MVP but we play for the big trophy with the pennants on it, not for the MVP. No one guy on this team has carried us through to this point. It's been a team effort all the way through, 25 guys contributing and understanding what we are supposed to do."

The Angels needed contributions from everyone as the World Series was a slugfest until their 4-1 win in Game

Barry Bonds' first World Series championship was within his sight

MEL BAILEY

Troy Glaus capped his playoff power surge with Series MVP honors

Seven. This marked the first World Series between two wild-card teams, and it was wild as the Angels and Giants combined to set World Series records for home runs (21), total bases (231), extra-base hits (45) and runs scored (85). The Giants' 14 homers were also a record.

Glaus was one of many offensive standouts for the Angels. Salmon hit .346 with two homers and five RBIs, first baseman Scott Spiezio drove in eight runs, second baseman and leadoff hitter David Eckstein batted .310 and center fielder Darin Erstad had a .300 average.

Left fielder Garrett Anderson added six RBIs and delivered the big blow in Game Seven. His three-run double in the bottom of the third inning off losing pitcher Livan Hernandez snapped a 1-1 tie and made a winner of John Lackey, who worked five innings to become the first rookie starter to win in Game Seven since the Pirates' Babe Adams in 1909.

Troy Percival recorded the save, escaping a two-on, one-out jam in the ninth by striking out Tsuyoshi Shinjo and getting Kenny Lofton to fly out to Erstad in right-center. The Angels became the eighth straight home team to win a Game Seven.

"This team has worked as hard as any team ever," Percival said. "We deserve it after what we went through."

Indeed, the Angels had to make a most improbable comeback just to get to the final game, as they trailed 5-0 late in Game Six with the Giants holding a 3-2 lead in the series.

Spiezio's three-run homer in the seventh off reliever Felix Rodriguez drew the Angels within two runs, 5-3. They won it an inning later as Erstad hit a leadoff homer off Tim Worrell and Glaus belted his two-run double off closer Robb Nen.

"The turning point was basically when they came back in Game Six," Giants manager Dusty Baker said. "It's tough to overcome something like that, very tough."

"I'm sure we'll all remember Game Six," Giants shortstop Rich Aurilia said. "We lost Game Six. They beat us in Game Seven."

Homer-Fest In First Six Games

The Giants got started on the right foot, winning the series opener 4-3 in Anaheim with home runs from Bonds, Reggie Sanders and J.T. Snow, who hit .407 in the series. Jason Schmidt pitched 5⅔ innings for the win, beating Jarrod Washburn.

The Angels then blew a 5-0 lead but posted an 11-10 win in a wild Game Two to even the series. Salmon hit a two-run homer in the eighth to snap a 9-9 tie and cap a 4-for-4 night with two homers, three runs and four RBIs.

Rookie Francisco Rodriguez, at age 20 and with just 5⅔ innings of regular season experience, became the youngest pitcher to win a World Series game with three perfect innings of relief as he beat Felix Rodriguez. Percival got the save.

The series moved to San Francisco for Game Three and the Angels took a 10-4 victory. Erstad sparked a 16-hit attack with three hits, while Spiezio drove in three runs and Ramon Ortiz got the win, beating Hernandez.

The momentum shifted back to the Giants as they rallied from a 3-0 deficit to post a 4-3 win in Game Four, deadlocking the series at two games apiece. An RBI single by David Bell, who hit .304 in the series, in the eighth off Francisco Rodriguez broke a 3-3 tie as Worrell got the win and Nen notched the save.

The Giants took the series lead with a 16-4 rout in Game Five. Jeff Kent led the way by going 3-for-5 with two homers, four runs scored and four RBIs, while Lofton had three hits and scored three runs and Aurilia and Benito Santiago each had three RBIs. Chad Zerbe was the winner and Washburn took his second loss.

The Giants looked to have the title in their hip pocket with a 5-0 lead in Game Six. In the end, though, nothing could stop the Angels as they made the kind of comeback worthy of a Disney movie.

The rights fee for a movie would be cheap since the Disney Co. bought into the Angels in 1996 and then bought controlling interest from Autry's widow Jackie a year after he died in 1999. Disney put the club up for sale before the 2002 season and was still looking for a buyer when Salmon and his teammates took possession of the championship trophy.

"Wherever he is, my husband is smiling down at these ballplayers and he's having a wonderful time watching me

MEL BAILEY

A coup for MLB merchandisers

get drowned in champagne," Jackie Autry said during the postgame celebration.

And where did the Angels go after winning their first World Series? Three miles down the street to Disneyland, of course, where the victory parade was held.

WORLD SERIES
BOX SCORES

GAME ONE: October 19
San Francisco 4, Anaheim 3

San Francisco	ab	r	h	bi	bb	so	Anaheim	ab	r	h	bi	bb	so
Lofton, cf	3	0	0	0	0	1	Eckstein, ss	5	0	1	0	0	1
Aurilia, ss	4	0	0	0	0	0	Erstad, cf	5	0	1	0	0	2
Kent, 2b	4	0	0	0	0	1	Salmon, rf	4	0	0	0	0	1
Bonds, lf	3	1	1	1	1	1	Anderson, lf	4	0	1	0	0	2
Santiago, c	4	0	1	0	0	1	Glaus, 3b	4	2	2	2	0	1
Sanders, rf	3	2	2	1	1	1	Fullmer, dh	3	1	1	0	1	1
Snow, 1b	3	1	1	2	1	0	Spiezio, 1b	3	0	1	0	1	0
Bell, 3b	4	0	0	0	0	1	Figgins, pr	0	0	0	0	0	0
Shinjo, dh	3	0	1	0	0	1	Wooten, 1b	0	0	0	0	0	0
Goodwin, dh	1	0	0	0	0	0	B. Molina, c	3	0	0	0	0	0
							Palmeiro, ph	1	0	0	0	0	0
							J. Molina, c	0	0	0	0	0	0
							Kennedy, 2b	4	0	2	1	0	1
Totals	32	4	6	4	3	7	**Totals**	36	3	9	3	2	9

San Francisco	**020 002 000— 4**
Anaheim	**010 002 000— 3**

LOB—San Francisco 5, Anaheim 8. **2B**—Kennedy (1), Spiezio (1). **HR**—Bonds (1), Sanders (1), Snow (1), Glaus 2 (2). **SB**—Fullmer (1). **SH**—Lofton.

San Fran.	ip	h	r	er	bb	so	Anaheim	ip	h	r	er	bb	so
Schmidt W	5⅔	9	3	3	1	6	Washburn L	5⅔	6	4	4	2	5
Fe. Rodriguez	1⅓	0	0	0	0	1	Donnelly	1⅓	0	0	0	0	0
Worrell	1	0	0	0	1	1	Schoeneweis	0	0	0	0	1	0
Nen S	1	0	0	0	0	1	Weber	1⅔	0	0	0	0	2

Schoeneweis pitched to one batter in 8th.

Umpires: HP—Crawford; **1B**—Hernandez; **2B**—Tschida; **3B**—Winters; **LF**—Reilly; **RF**—McClelland.

T—3:44. **A**—44,603.

GAME TWO: October 20
Anaheim 11, San Francisco 10

San Francisco	ab	r	h	bi	bb	so	Anaheim	ab	r	h	bi	bb	so
Lofton, cf	5	0	1	0	0	1	Eckstein, ss	5	3	3	0	0	0
Aurilia, ss	5	1	1	0	0	2	Erstad, cf	5	2	2	1	0	0
Kent, 2b	5	1	1	1	0	2	Salmon, rf	4	3	4	4	1	0
Bonds, lf	2	3	1	1	3	0	Ochoa, rf	0	0	0	0	0	0
Santiago, c	5	1	1	0	0	1	Anderson, lf	5	1	2	2	0	0
Snow, 1b	4	2	2	2	0	0	Glaus, 3b	4	1	2	0	0	0
Sanders, rf	4	1	2	3	0	2	Fullmer, dh	3	1	2	1	1	0
Bell, 3b	4	1	2	2	0	0	Spiezio, 1b	3	0	1	2	0	0
Dunston, dh	4	0	1	1	0	0	B. Molina, c	4	0	0	0	0	0
							Kennedy, 2b	4	0	0	0	0	0
Totals	38	10	12	10	3	8	**Totals**	37	11	16	10	2	0

San Francisco	**041 040 001—10**
Anaheim	**520 011 02x—11**

E—Lofton (1), Anderson (1). **DP**—San Francisco 1, Anaheim 1. **LOB**—San Francisco 4, Anaheim 5. **2B**—Aurilia (1), Erstad 2 (2), Glaus (1). **HR**—Sanders (2), Bell (1), Kent (1), Bonds (2), Salmon 2 (2). **SB**—Sanders (1), Spiezio (1), Fullmer (2). **SF**—Spiezio. **PB**—Santiago.

San Fran.	ip	h	r	er	bb	so	Anaheim	ip	h	r	er	bb	so
Ru. Ortiz	1⅔	9	7	7	0	0	Appier	2	5	5	5	2	2
Zerbe	4	4	2	1	0	0	Lackey	2⅓	2	2	2	1	1
Witasick	0	0	0	0	1	0	Weber	⅔	4	2	2	0	1
Fultz	⅓	1	0	0	0	0	Fr. Rodriguez W	3	0	0	0	0	4
Fe. Rodriguez L	1⅔	2	2	2	1	0	Percival S	1	1	1	1	0	0
Worrell	⅓	0	0	0	0	0							

Appier pitched to two batters in 3rd. Witasick pitched to one batter in 6th.

IBB—Bonds (by Lackey).

Umpires: HP—Hernandez; **1B**—Tschida; **2B**—Winters; **3B**—Reilly; **LF**—McClelland; **RF**—Crawford.

T—3:57. **A**—44,584.

GAME THREE: October 22
Anaheim 10, San Francisco 4

Anaheim	ab	r	h	bi	bb	so	San Francisco	ab	r	h	bi	bb	so
Eckstein, ss	5	1	2	1	1	0	Lofton, cf	4	1	0	0	1	0
Erstad, cf	6	2	3	0	0	0	Aurilia, ss	5	1	2	1	0	2
Salmon, rf	4	2	1	1	2	1	Kent, 2b	4	1	2	0	0	0
Schoeneweis, p	0	0	0	0	0	0	Bonds, lf	2	1	1	2	2	1
Anderson, lf	6	0	1	1	0	0	Santiago, c	4	0	0	1	0	0
Glaus, 3b	5	2	2	1	1	0	Snow, 1b	4	0	1	0	0	0
Spiezio, 1b	5	1	2	3	1	0	Sanders, rf	4	0	0	0	0	1
Kennedy, 2b	5	1	2	1	0	2	Bell, 3b	1	0	0	0	3	0
B. Molina, c	2	1	2	1	3	0	Hernandez, p	0	0	0	0	0	0
Ra. Ortiz, p	3	0	0	0	0	2	Witasick, p	0	0	0	0	0	0
Wooten, ph	1	0	0	0	0	0	Feliz, ph	1	0	0	0	0	0
Donnelly, p	0	0	0	0	0	0	Fultz, p	0	0	0	0	0	0
Gil, ph	1	0	1	0	0	0	Dunston, ph	1	0	0	0	0	0
Ochoa, rf	0	0	0	0	0	0	Fe. Rodriguez, p	0	0	0	0	0	0
							Eyre, p	0	0	0	0	0	0
							Martinez, ph	1	0	0	0	0	1
Totals	43	10	16	9	8	5	**Totals**	31	4	6	4	6	5

Anaheim	**004 401 010—10**
San Francisco	**100 030 000— 4**

E—Bell (1), Santiago (1). **DP**—Anaheim 1, San Francisco 1. **LOB**—Anaheim 15, San Francisco 7. **2B**—Kennedy (2), Erstad (3), Salmon (1). **3B**—Spiezio. **HR**—Aurilia (1), Bonds (3). **SB**—Salmon (1), Erstad (1), Lofton (1). **SH**—Hernandez.

Anaheim	ip	h	r	er	bb	so	San Fran.	ip	h	r	er	bb	so
Ra. Ortiz W	5	5	4	4	4	3	Hernandez L	3⅔	5	6	5	5	3
Donnelly	2	0	0	0	2	0	Witasick	⅓	3	2	2	1	1
Schoeneweis	2	1	0	0	0	2	Fultz	2	3	1	1	1	0
							Rodriguez	1	1	0	0	0	0
							Eyre	2	4	1	0	1	1

IBB—Bonds (by Ra. Ortiz), B. Molina 2 (by Hernandez 2), Salmon (by Eyre). **HBP**—Kennedy (by Fultz).

Umpires: HP—Tschida; **1B**—Winters; **2B**—Reilly; **3B**—McClelland; **LF**—Crawford; **RF**—Hernandez.

T—3:37. **A**—42,707.

GAME FOUR: October 23
San Francisco 4, Anaheim 3

Anaheim	ab	r	h	bi	bb	so	San Francisco	ab	r	h	bi	bb	so
Eckstein, ss	3	0	0	1	0	0	Lofton, cf	4	1	3	0	0	0
Erstad, cf	4	0	0	0	0	0	Aurilia, ss	4	1	3	1	0	0
Salmon, rf	4	0	1	0	0	1	Kent, 2b	3	0	0	1	0	2
Anderson, lf	4	1	2	0	0	0	Bonds, lf	1	0	0	0	3	0
Glaus, 3b	4	1	1	2	0	0	Santiago, c	4	0	1	1	0	0
Spiezio, 1b	4	0	1	0	0	0	Snow, 1b	4	1	1	0	0	0
Gil, 2b	3	1	2	0	0	1	Sanders, rf	4	0	1	0	0	1
A. Kennedy, ph	1	0	1	0	0	0	Bell, 3b	4	0	2	1	0	0
B. Molina, c	3	0	1	0	0	0	Rueter, p	2	1	1	0	0	0
Fullmer, ph	1	0	0	0	0	0	Goodwin, ph	0	0	0	0	1	0
Lackey, p	2	0	1	0	0	0	Fe. Rodriguez, p	0	0	0	0	0	0
Weber, p	0	0	0	0	0	0	Worrell, p	0	0	0	0	0	0
Palmeiro, ph	1	0	0	0	0	1	Martinez, ph	1	0	0	0	0	1
Fr. Rodriguez, p	0	0	0	0	0	0	Nen, p	0	0	0	0	0	0
Totals	34	3	10	3	0	3	**Totals**	31	4	12	4	4	4

Anaheim	**012 000 000— 3**
San Francisco	**000 030 010— 4**

E—Salmon (1), Bell (2). **DP**—Anaheim 5, San Francisco 3. **LOB**—Anaheim 5, San Francisco 8. **2B**—Aurilia (2). **HR**—Glaus (3). **SB**—Goodwin (1). **CS**—Bell. **SF**—Eckstein, Kent. **PB**—B. Molina.

Anaheim	ip	h	r	er	bb	so	San Fran.	ip	h	r	er	bb	so
Lackey	5	9	3	3	3	2	Rueter	6	9	3	3	0	2
Weber	1	1	0	0	1	0	Fe. Rodriguez	1	0	0	0	0	1
Fr. Rodriguez L	2	2	1	0	0	2	Worrell W	1	0	0	0	0	0
							Nen S	1	1	0	0	0	0

IBB—Bonds 3 (by Lackey 3).

Umpires: HP—Winters; **1B**—Reilly; **2B**—McClelland; **3B**—Crawford; **LF**—Hernandez; **RF**—Tschida.

T—3:02. **A**—42,703.

GAME FIVE: October 24
San Francisco 16, Anaheim 4

Anaheim	ab	r	h	bi	bb	so	San Francisco	ab	r	h	bi	bb	so
Eckstein, ss	4	1	2	1	1	1	Lofton, cf	6	3	3	2	0	0
Erstad, cf	4	0	1	1	0	1	Eyre, p	0	0	0	0	0	0
Salmon, rf	4	1	1	0	0	2	Aurilia, ss	6	2	2	3	0	1
Ochoa, rf	1	0	0	0	0	0	Kent, 2b	5	4	3	4	1	0
Anderson, lf	5	0	1	0	0	1	Bonds, lf	4	2	3	1	1	0
Glaus, 3b	4	0	1	1	0	3	Santiago, c	3	0	1	3	1	0
Spiezio, 1b	2	0	0	0	2	1	Sanders, rf	1	0	0	1	1	1
Shields, p	0	0	0	0	0	0	Fe. Rodriguez, p	0	0	0	0	0	0
Kennedy, 2b	4	0	0	0	0	1	Dunston, ph	1	0	0	0	0	1
B. Molina, c	4	1	1	0	0	1	Worrell, p	0	0	0	0	0	0
J. Molina, c	0	0	0	0	0	0	Feliz, ph	1	0	0	0	0	0
Washburn, p	1	0	0	0	0	0	Goodwin, rf	0	0	0	0	0	0
Palmeiro, ph	1	1	1	0	0	0	Snow, 1b	4	2	2	0	1	1
Donnelly, p	0	0	0	0	0	0	Bell, 3b	3	2	2	1	1	0
Gil, ph	1	0	1	0	0	0	Schmidt, p	1	0	0	0	0	1
Weber, p	0	0	0	0	0	0	Zerbe, p	0	0	0	0	0	0
Wooten, 1b	1	0	1	0	0	0	Shinjo, rf-cf	2	1	0	0	0	1
Totals	36	4	10	3	3	11	**Totals**	37	16	16	15	6	6

Anaheim	**000 031 000— 4**
San Francisco	**330 002 44x—16**

E—Erstad (1), Glaus (1). **LOB**—Anaheim 9, San Francisco 8. **2B**—

Palmeiro (1), Glaus (2), Gil (1), Bonds 2 (2), Kent (1). **3B**—Lofton (1) **HR**—Kent 2 (2), Aurilia (2). **SB**—Eckstein (1). **SH**—Schmidt, Shinjo. **SF**—Erstad, Santiago, Sanders.

Anaheim	ip	h	r	er	bb	so	San Fran.	ip	h	r	er	bb	so
Washburn L	4	6	6	6	5	1	Schmidt	4⅓	7	3	3	3	8
Donnelly	1	0	0	0	0	2	Zerbe W	1	2	1	1	0	0
Weber	1⅓	5	5	5	1	2	Fe. Rodriguez	⅓	0	0	0	0	0
Shields	1⅔	5	5	1	0	1	Worrell	2	1	0	0	0	2
							Eyre	1	0	0	0	0	1

WP—Schmidt. **IBB**—Sanders (by Washburn), Bonds (by Washburn), Santiago (by Weber). **HBP**—Bell (by Weber). **Umpires:** HP—Reilly; 1B—McClelland; 2B—Crawford; 3B—Hernandez; LF—Tschida; RF—Winters.
T—3:53. **A**—42,713.

GAME SIX: October 26
Anaheim 6, San Francisco 5

San Francisco	ab	r	h	bi	bb	so	Anaheim	ab	r	h	bi	bb	so
Lofton, cf	5	2	2	0	0	0	Eckstein, ss	4	0	0	0	0	0
Aurilia, ss	4	0	0	1	0	2	Erstad, cf	3	1	1	1	1	0
Kent, 2b	4	0	2	1	0	0	Salmon, rf	4	0	2	0	0	1
Bonds, lf	2	1	1	1	2	1	Figgins, pr	0	1	0	0	0	0
Santiago, c	3	0	0	1	1	0	Ochoa, rf	0	0	0	0	0	0
Snow, 1b	4	0	1	0	0	0	Anderson, lf	4	1	1	0	0	0
Sanders, rf	4	0	0	0	0	3	Glaus, 3b	3	1	2	2	1	0
Bell, 3b	4	1	1	0	0	2	Fullmer, dh	4	1	1	0	0	1
Dunston, dh	3	1	1	2	0	0	Spiezio, 1b	3	1	1	3	1	0
Goodwin, dh	1	0	0	0	0	1	B.Molina, c	2	0	0	0	0	0
							Palmeiro, ph	1	0	0	0	0	1
							J.Molina, c	0	0	0	0	0	0
							Kennedy, 2b	4	0	2	0	0	2
Totals	34	5	8	4	4	10	**Totals**	32	6	10	6	3	5

San Francisco	000	031	100	—	5
Anaheim	000	000	33x	—	6

E—Bonds (1), B. Molina (1). **DP**—San Francisco 1, Anaheim 1. **LOB**—San Francisco 6, Anaheim 6. **2B**—Lofton (1), Glaus (3). **HR**—Dunston (1), Bonds (4), Spiezio (1), Erstad (1). **SB**—Lofton 2 (3). **SH**—J. Molina.

San Fran.	ip	h	r	er	bb	so	Anaheim	ip	h	r	er	bb	so
Ru.Ortiz	6⅓	4	2	2	2	2	Appier	4⅓	4	3	3	2	2
Fe. Rodriguez	⅓	1	1	1	0	1	Fr. Rodriguez	2⅔	4	2	2	0	4
Eyre	0	1	0	0	0	0	Donnelly W	1	0	0	0	1	2
Worrell L	⅓	3	3	2	0	0	Percival S	1	0	0	0	0	2
Nen	1	1	0	0	1	2							

Eyre pitched to one batter in 7th. Worrell pitched to three batters in 8th.
WP—Fr. Rodriguez. **IBB**—Bonds (by Appier), Spiezio (by Nen).
Umpires: HP—McClelland; 1B—Crawford; 2B—Hernandez; 3B—Tschida; LF—Winters; RF—Reilly.
T—3:48. **A**—44,506.

GAME SEVEN: October 27
Anaheim 4, San Francisco 1

San Francisco	ab	r	h	bi	bb	so	Anaheim	ab	r	h	bi	bb	so
Lofton, cf	4	0	0	0	1	0	Eckstein, ss	3	1	1	0	1	0
Aurilia, ss	4	0	0	0	0	2	Erstad, cf	3	1	1	0	1	0
Kent, 2b	4	0	0	0	0	2	Salmon, rf	2	1	0	0	1	1
Bonds, lf	3	0	1	0	1	0	Ochoa, rf	0	0	0	0	0	0
Santiago, c	3	1	2	1	1	1	Anderson, lf	4	0	1	3	0	0
Snow, 1b	4	0	3	0	0	0	Glaus, 3b	2	0	0	0	2	2
Sanders, rf	1	0	0	1	0	0	Fullmer, dh	4	0	0	0	0	0
Goodwin, ph-rf	2	0	0	0	0	0	Spiezio, 1b	3	1	0	0	1	0
Bell, 3b	3	0	0	0	1	1	B. Molina, c	3	0	2	1	0	0
Feliz, dh	3	0	0	0	0	2	Kennedy, 2b	3	0	0	0	0	1
Shinjo, dh	1	0	0	0	0	1							
Totals	32	1	6	1	4	10	**Totals**	27	4	5	4	5	5

San Francisco	010	000	000	—	1
Anaheim	013	000	00x	—	4

DP—San Francisco 1. **LOB**—San Francisco 9, Anaheim 6. **2B**—Snow (1), B. Molina 2 (2), Anderson (1). **SH**—Erstad. **SF**—Sanders.

San Fran.	ip	h	r	er	bb	so	Anaheim	ip	h	r	er	bb	so
Hernandez L	2	4	4	4	4	1	Lackey W	5	4	1	1	1	4
Zerbe	1	0	0	0	0	0	Donnelly	2	1	0	0	1	2
Rueter	4	1	0	0	1	3	Fr. Rodriguez	1	0	0	0	1	3
Worrell	1	0	0	0	0	1	Percival S	1	1	0	0	1	1

Hernandez pitched to five batters in 3rd.
IBB—Glaus (by Hernandez). **HBP**—Salmon (by Hernandez).
Umpires: HP—Crawford; 1B—Hernandez; 2B—Tschida; 3B—Winters; LF—Reilly; RF—McClelland.
T—3:16. **A**—44,598.

SAN FRANCISCO

Player, Pos.	AVG	G	AB	R	H	2B	3B	HR	RBI	BB	SO	SB
Kirk Rueter, p	.500	1	2	1	1	0	0	0	0	0	0	0
Barry Bonds, lf	.471	7	17	8	8	2	0	4	6	13	3	0
J.T. Snow, 1b	.407	7	27	6	11	1	0	1	4	2	1	0
David Bell, 3b	.304	7	23	4	7	0	0	1	4	5	4	0
Kenny Lofton, cf	.290	7	31	7	9	1	1	0	2	2	2	3
Jeff Kent, 2b	.276	7	29	6	8	1	0	3	7	1	7	0
Rich Aurilia, ss	.250	7	32	5	8	2	0	2	5	1	9	0
Reggie Sanders, rf	.238	7	21	3	5	0	0	2	6	2	9	1
Benito Santiago, c	.231	7	26	2	6	0	0	0	5	3	4	0
Shawon Dunston, dh-ph	.222	4	9	1	2	0	0	1	3	0	1	0
Tsuyoshi Shinjo, dh-ph	.167	3	6	1	1	0	0	0	0	0	3	0
Tom Goodwin, ph-dh-rf	.000	5	4	0	0	0	0	0	1	2	1	0
Jason Schmidt, p	.000	1	1	0	0	0	0	0	0	0	1	0
Livan Hernandez, p	.000	1	0	0	0	0	0	0	0	0	0	0
Ramon Martinez, ph	.000	2	2	0	0	0	0	0	0	0	2	0
Pedro Feliz, ph-dh	.000	2	3	0	0	0	0	0	0	0	2	0
Totals	.281	7	235	44	66	7	1	14	42	30	50	5

Pitcher	W	L	ERA	G	GS	SV	IP	H	R	ER	BB	SO
Robb Nen	0	0	0.00	3	0	2	3	2	0	0	1	3
Scott Eyre	0	0	0.00	3	0	0	3	5	1	0	1	2
Kirk Rueter	0	0	2.70	2	1	0	10	10	3	3	1	5
Chad Zerbe	1	0	3.00	3	0	0	6	6	3	2	0	0
Tim Worrell	1	1	3.18	6	0	0	6	4	3	2	1	4
Aaron Fultz	0	0	3.86	2	0	0	2	4	1	1	1	0
Felix Rodriguez	0	0	4.76	6	0	0	6	8	4	3	1	3
Jason Schmidt	1	0	5.23	2	2	0	10	16	6	6	4	14
Russ Ortiz	0	0	10.13	2	2	0	8	13	9	9	2	2
Livan Hernandez	0	2	14.29	2	2	0	6	9	10	9	9	4
Jay Witasick	0	0	54.00	1	0	0	3	2	2	2	2	1
Totals	3	4	5.55	7	7	2	60	76	41	37	23	38

ANAHEIM

Player, Pos.	AVG	G	AB	R	H	2B	3B	HR	RBI	BB	SO	SB
Benji Gil, ph-2b	.800	3	5	1	4	1	0	0	0	0	1	0
Shawn Wooten, 1b-ph	.500	3	2	0	1	0	0	0	0	0	0	0
John Lackey, p	.500	1	2	0	1	0	0	0	0	0	0	0
Troy Glaus, 3b	.385	7	26	7	10	3	0	3	8	4	6	0
Tim Salmon, rf	.346	7	26	7	9	1	0	2	5	4	7	1
David Eckstein, ss	.310	7	29	6	9	0	0	0	3	3	2	1
Darin Erstad, cf	.300	7	30	6	9	3	0	1	3	1	4	1
Bengie Molina, c	.286	7	21	2	6	2	0	0	2	3	1	0
Garret Anderson, lf	.281	7	32	3	9	1	0	0	6	0	3	0
Adam Kennedy, 2b	.280	7	25	1	7	2	0	0	2	0	7	0
Brad Fullmer, dh-ph	.267	5	15	3	4	0	0	0	1	2	2	2
Scott Spiezio, 1b	.261	7	23	6	1	1	1	8	6	1	1	0
Orlando Palmeiro, ph	.250	4	4	1	1	1	0	0	0	2	0	0
Alex Ochoa, rf	.000	5	1	0	0	0	0	0	0	0	0	0
Jarrod Washburn, p	.000	1	1	0	0	0	0	0	0	0	0	0
Ramon Ortiz, p	.000	1	3	0	0	0	0	0	0	0	2	0
Jose Molina, c	.000	1	0	0	0	0	0	0	0	0	0	0
Chone Figgins, pr	.000	2	0	1	0	0	0	0	0	0	0	0
Totals	.310	7	245	41	76	15	1	7	38	23	38	6

Pitcher	W	L	ERA	G	GS	SV	IP	H	R	ER	BB	SO
Scott Schoeneweis	0	0	0.00	2	0	0	2	1	0	0	1	2
Brendan Donnelly	1	0	0.00	5	0	0	6	3	0	0	4	6
Francisco Rodriguez	1	1	2.08	4	0	0	9	6	3	2	1	13
Troy Percival	0	0	3.00	3	0	3	3	2	1	1	1	3
John Lackey	1	0	4.38	3	2	0	12	15	6	6	5	7
Scot Shields	0	0	5.40	1	0	0	2	5	5	1	0	1
Ramon Ortiz	0	0	7.20	1	1	0	5	5	4	4	3	1
Jarrod Washburn	0	2	9.31	2	2	0	10	12	10	10	7	6
Kevin Appier	0	0	11.37	2	2	0	6	9	8	8	5	4
Ben Weber	0	0	13.50	4	0	0	5	10	7	7	2	5
Totals	4	3	5.75	7	7	3	61	66	44	39	30	50

SCORE BY INNINGS

San Francisco	4(10)1	0(13)5	551	—44
Anaheim	559	445	360	—41

E—Lofton, Bell 2, Santiago, Bonds, Anderson, Salmon, Erstad, Glaus, B. Molina. **DP**—San Francisco 7, Anaheim 6. **LOB**—San Francisco 47, Anaheim 54. **SH**—Lofton, Shinjo, Schmidt, Hernandez, Erstad, J. Molina. **SF**—Sanders 2, Kent, Santiago, Eckstein, Erstad, Spiezio. **IBB**—Bonds 6 (4 by Lackey, by Ra. Ortiz, by Appier), Sanders (by Washburn), Santiago (by Weber), B. Molina 2 (by Washburn), Salmon (by Eyre), Spiezio (by Nen), Glaus (by Hernandez). **HBP**—Bell (by Weber), Kennedy (by Fultz), Salmon (by Hernandez). **WP**—Schmidt, Fr. Rodriguez. **PB**—Santiago, B. Molina.

BY J.J. COOPER

For the American League, 2002 was the year when baseball went retro and unconventional wisdom proved to be inspired.

Free agents? Who needs 'em?

Blockbuster deals at the trade deadline? Won't do you any good.

Putting together a team through player development and a couple of trades, the way teams did in the days before free agency? Call it a prescription for a pennant.

After five years when the big-budget, money-is-no-object Yankees dominated the American League, player development and fiscal frugality proved to be a winning combination in 2002.

When Anaheim and Minnesota faced off in the AL Championship Series, they did it with lineups filled with homegrown players and plenty of patience. The Angels were in the middle of the pack in team payroll, while the Twins fielded one of the least expensive teams in baseball. And the team the Twins beat in an AL Division Series, the Athletics, got 103 wins on their usual shoe-string budget.

The Yankees, featuring former A's slugger Jason Giambi and baseball's biggest budget? Slayed by the Angels' offense and a healthy dose of rookie reliever Francisco Rodriguez and the rest of the Angels' bullpen.

The result was an unexpected ALCS that brought together two teams that hadn't made the playoffs in more than a decade.

When Twins righthander Joe Mays shut down the Angels for a 2-1 Game One victory, it appeared the string of bad luck that had doomed the Angels for 42 seasons might still be around.

But Anaheim erased those concerns by finding every way possible to finish off the Twins.

There was a workmanlike 6-3 win in Game Two, as outfielder Darin Erstad and DH Brad Fullmer homered to spot Anaheim a six-run lead in a game it hung on to win.

There was the pitcher's duel win in Game Three, as third baseman Troy Glaus hit a tie-breaking home run off lefthander J.C. Romero in the eighth inning. The Angels

LARRY GOREN

John Lackey

had some nervous moments in the ninth, but right fielder Alex Ochoa made a diving catch for the first out of the inning, and left fielder Garret Anderson snatched catcher A.J. Pierzynski's liner inches from the turf for the third out.

"They were both fantastic catches," Angels closer Troy Percival said. "That last one, I thought there was no chance in the world at it."

There was the rookie hero in Game Four, as rookie righthander John Lackey threw seven shutout innings of a 7-1 victory. Lackey, making his first postseason start, allowed three singles while never allowing a Twin to reach second base.

And then there was the Rally Monkey/Adam Kennedy-inspired Game Five victory that sent the Angels to their

Adam Kennedy: Three homers in ALCS championship game

JOHN WILLIAMSON

first World Series appearance.

Kennedy kept the Angels in the game early with a homer in the third and a two-run shot in the fifth that tied the game, 3-3. But it was his seventh-inning homer that will be remembered in Anaheim for years.

With the Angels trailing 5-3 and the Rally Monkey dancing on the big screen in center, Kennedy came up with two men on. Despite his earlier pair of homers, manager Mike Scioscia initially signaled for Kennedy to bunt. But after the second baseman fouled off his first bunt attempt, Scioscia took the bunt off and let Kennedy swing away.

The decision ended up earning Kennedy the series MVP award and put the Angels in the World Series, as Kennedy cracked a three-run homer off lefthander Johan Santana, starting a 10-run seventh-inning onslaught. Kennedy's three-homer game was only the sixth in playoff history.

"It's the biggest game of my life," said Kennedy, a Southern California native.

The Twins had reason to be stunned by Kennedy's heroics—he had hit only seven home runs in the regular season.

Unlikely Heroes

Kennedy's unlikely night in the spotlight was a fitting story in a season when the Angels surprised a lot of people.

Anaheim was picked by most experts to finish last in the AL West. It was almost impossible to picture the Angels as a playoff team after they finished 12 games under .500 and 41 games behind the Mariners in 2001. And they were playing in baseball's toughest division.

MAJOR LEAGUES

Year	PENNANT	PCT	GA
1901	Chicago	.610	4
1902	Philadelphia	.610	5
1903	Boston	.659	14½
1904	Boston	.617	1½
1905	Philadelphia	.622	2
1906	Chicago	.616	3
1907	Detroit	.613	1½
1908	Detroit	.588	½
1909	Detroit	.645	3½
1910	Philadelphia	.680	14½
1911	Philadelphia	.669	13½
1912	Boston	.691	14
1913	Philadelphia	.627	6½
1914	Philadelphia	.651	8½
1915	Boston	.669	2½
1916	Boston	.591	2
1917	Chicago	.649	9
1918	Boston	.595	2½
1919	Chicago	.629	3½
1920	Cleveland	.636	2
1921	New York	.641	4½
1922	New York	.610	1
1923	New York	.645	16
1924	Washington	.597	2
1925	Washington	.636	8½
1926	New York	.591	3
1927	New York	.714	19
1928	New York	.656	2½
1929	Philadelphia	.693	18
1930	Philadelphia	.662	8
1931	Philadelphia	.704	13½
1932	New York	.695	13
1933	Washington	.651	7
1934	Detroit	.656	7

Year	PENNANT	PCT	GA	MVP
1935	Detroit	.616	3	Hank Greenberg, 1b, Detroit
1936	New York	.667	19½	Lou Gehrig, 1b, New York
1937	New York	.662	13	Charlie Gehringer, 2b, Detroit
1938	New York	.651	9½	Jimmie Foxx, 1b, Boston
1939	New York	.702	17	Joe DiMaggio, of, New York
1940	Detroit	.584	1	Hank Greenberg, 1b, Detroit
1941	New York	.656	17	Joe DiMaggio, of, New York
1942	New York	.669	9	Joe Gordon, 2b, New York
1943	New York	.636	13½	Spud Chandler, rhp, New York
1944	St. Louis	.578	1	Hal Newhouser, lhp, Detroit
1945	Detroit	.575	1½	Hal Newhouser, lhp, Detroit
1946	Boston	.675	12	Ted Williams, of, Boston
1947	New York	.630	12	Joe DiMaggio, of, New York
1948	Cleveland	.626	1	Lou Boudreau, ss, Cleveland
1949	New York	.630	1	Ted Williams, of, Boston
1950	New York	.636	3	Phil Rizzuto, ss, New York
1951	New York	.636	5	Yogi Berra, c, New York
1952	New York	.617	2	Bobby Shantz, lhp, Philadelphia
1953	New York	.656	8½	Al Rosen, 3b, Cleveland
1954	Cleveland	.721	8	Yogi Berra, c, New York
1955	New York	.623	3	Yogi Berra, c, New York
1956	New York	.630	9	Mickey Mantle, of, New York
1957	New York	.636	8	Mickey Mantle, of, New York
1958	New York	.597	10	Jackie Jensen, of, Boston
1959	Chicago	.610	5	Nellie Fox, 2b, Chicago
1960	New York	.630	8	Roger Maris, of, New York
1961	New York	.673	8	Roger Maris, of, New York
1962	New York	.593	5	Mickey Mantle, of, New York
1963	New York	.646	10½	Elston Howard, c, New York
1964	New York	.611	1	Brooks Robinson, 3b, Baltimore
1965	Minnesota	.630	7	Zoilo Versalles, ss, Minnesota
1966	Baltimore	.606	9	Frank Robinson, of, Baltimore
1967	Boston	.568	1	Carl Yastrzemski, of, Boston
1968	Detroit	.636	12	Denny McLain, rhp, Detroit

Year	EAST	PCT	GA	WEST	PCT	GA	PENNANT		MVP
1969	Baltimore	.673	19	Minnesota	.599	9	Baltimore	3-0	Harmon Killebrew, 1b-3b, Minnesota
1970	Baltimore	.667	15	Minnesota	.605	9	Baltimore	3-0	Boog Powell, 1b, Baltimore
1971	Baltimore	.639	12	Oakland	.627	16	Baltimore	3-0	Vida Blue, lhp, Oakland
1972	Detroit	.551	½	Oakland	.600	5½	Oakland	3-2	Dick Allen, 1b, Chicago
1973	Baltimore	.599	8	Oakland	.580	6	Oakland	3-2	Reggie Jackson, of, Oakland
1974	Baltimore	.562	2	Oakland	.556	5	Oakland	3-1	Jeff Burroughs, of, Texas
1975	Boston	.594	4½	Oakland	.605	7	Boston	3-0	Fred Lynn, of, Boston
1976	New York	.610	10½	Kansas City	.556	2½	New York	3-2	Thurman Munson, c, New York
1977	New York	.617	2½	Kansas City	.630	8	New York	3-2	Rod Carew, 1b, Minnesota
1978	New York	.613	1	Kansas City	.568	5	New York	3-1	Jim Rice, of, Boston
1979	Baltimore	.642	8	California	.543	3	Baltimore	3-1	Don Baylor, dh, California
1980	New York	.636	3	Kansas City	.599	14	Kansas City	3-0	George Brett, 3b, Kansas City
1981	New York*	.607	2	Oakland**	.587	—	New York	3-0	Rollie Fingers, rhp, Milwaukee
	Milwaukee	.585	1½	Kansas City	.566	1			
1982	Milwaukee	.586	1	California	.574	3	Milwaukee	3-2	Robin Yount, ss, Milwaukee
1983	Baltimore	.605	6	Chicago	.611	20	Baltimore	3-1	Cal Ripken, ss, Baltimore
1984	Detroit	.642	15	Kansas City	.519	3	Detroit	3-0	Willie Hernandez, lhp, Detroit
1985	Toronto	.615	2	Kansas City	.562	1	Kansas City	4-3	Don Mattingly, 1b, New York
1986	Boston	.590	5½	California	.568	5	Boston	4-3	Roger Clemens, rhp, Boston
1987	Detroit	.605	2	Minnesota	.525	2	Minnesota	4-1	George Bell, of, Toronto
1988	Boston	.549	1	Oakland	.642	13	Oakland	4-0	Jose Canseco, of, Oakland
1989	Toronto	.549	2	Oakland	.611	7	Oakland	4-1	Robin Yount, of, Milwaukee
1990	Boston	.543	2	Oakland	.636	9	Oakland	4-0	Rickey Henderson, of, Oakland
1991	Toronto	.562	7	Minnesota	.586	8	Minnesota	4-1	Cal Ripken, ss, Baltimore
1992	Toronto	.593	4	Oakland	.593	6	Toronto	4-2	Dennis Eckersley, rhp, Oakland
1993	Toronto	.586	7	Chicago	.580	2	Toronto	4-2	Frank Thomas, 1b, Chicago

* Won first half; defeated Milwaukee 3-2 in best-of-5 playoff.   ** Won first half; defeated Kansas City 3-0 in best-of-5 playoff.

Year	EAST	PCT	GA	CENTRAL	PCT	GA	WEST	PCT	GA	WILD CARD	PCT
1994	New York	.619	6½	Chicago	.593	1	Texas	.456	1	None	
	PENNANT: None (season incomplete)						MVP: Frank Thomas, 1b, Chicago				
1995	Boston	.597	7	Cleveland	.694	30	Seattle	.545	1	New York (East)	.549
	PENNANT: Cleveland def. Seattle 4-2						MVP: Mo Vaughn, 1b, Boston				
1996	New York	.568	4	Cleveland	.615	14½	Texas	.556	4	Baltimore (East)	.543
	PENNANT: New York def. Baltimore 4-1						MVP: Juan Gonzalez, of, Texas				
1997	Baltimore	.605	2	Cleveland	.534	6	Seattle	.556	6	New York (East)	.593
	PENNANT: Cleveland def. Baltimore 4-2						MVP: Ken Griffey, of, Seattle				
1998	New York	.704	22	Cleveland	.549	9	Texas	.543	3	Boston (East)	.568
	PENNANT: New York def. Cleveland 4-2						MVP: Juan Gonzalez, of, Texas				
1999	New York	.605	4	Cleveland	.599	21½	Texas	.586	8	Boston (East)	.580
	PENNANT: New York def. Boston 4-1						MVP: Ivan Rodriguez, c, Texas				
2000	New York	.540	2½	Chicago	.586	5	Oakland	.565	½	Seattle (West)	.562
	PENNANT: New York def. Seattle 4-2						MVP: Jason Giambi, 1b, Oakland				
2001	New York	.594	13½	Cleveland	.562	6	Seattle	.716	14	Oakland (West)	.630
	PENNANT: New York def. Seattle 4-1						MVP: Ichiro Suzuki, of, Seattle				
2002	New York	.640	10½	Minnesota	.584	13½	Oakland	.636	4	Anaheim (West)	.611
	PENNANT: Anaheim def. Minnesota 4-1						MVP: Miguel Tejada, ss, Oakland				

Page	EAST	W	L	PCT	GB	Manager(s)	General Manager	Attendance	Avg.	Last Penn.
187	New York Yankees	103	58	.640	—	Joe Torre	Brian Cashman	3,465,807	43,322	2001
86	Boston Red Sox	93	69	.574	10½	Grady Little	Mike Port	2,650,862	32,726	1986
268	Toronto Blue Jays	78	84	.481	25½	B. Martinez/C. Tosca	J.P. Ricciardi	1,637,900	20,220	1993
78	Baltimore Orioles	67	95	.414	36½	Mike Hargrove	Syd Thrift	2,682,439	33,116	1983
253	Tampa Bay Devil Rays	55	106	.342	48	Hal McRae	Chuck LaMar	1,065,742	13,157	None
Page	CENTRAL	W	L	PCT	GB	Manager(s)	General Manager	Attendance	Avg.	Last Penn.
172	Minnesota Twins	94	67	.584	—	Ron Gardenhire	Terry Ryan	1,924,473	23,758	1991
93	Chicago White Sox	81	81	.500	13½	Jerry Manuel	Ken Williams	1,676,911	20,702	1959
115	Cleveland Indians	74	88	.457	20½	C. Manuel/J. Skinner	Mark Shapiro	2,616,940	32,307	1997
151	Kansas City Royals	62	100	.383	32½	T. Muser/T. Pena	Allard Baird	1,323,036	17,182	1985
130	Detroit Tigers	55	106	.342	39	P. Garner/L. Pujols	R. Smith/D. Dombrowski	1,503,623	18,795	1984
Page	WEST	W	L	PCT	GB	Manager	General Manager	Attendance	Avg.	Last Penn.
203	Oakland Athletics	103	59	.636	—	Art Howe	Billy Beane	2,169,811	26,787	1990
57	*Anaheim Angels	99	63	.611	4	Mike Scioscia	Bill Stoneman	2,305,547	28,463	2002
246	Seattle Mariners	93	69	.574	10	Lou Piniella	Pat Gillick	3,542,938	43,739	None
260	Texas Rangers	72	90	.444	31	Jerry Narron	John Hart	2,352,397	29,404	None

*Won wild-card playoff berth
NOTE: Team's individual batting, pitching and fielding statistics can be found on page indicated in lefthand column.

Despite having the sixth-worst record in the American League in 2001, the Angels didn't make wholesale changes. They tweaked a line-up that scored the third-fewest runs in the league, sending first baseman Mo Vaughn, who didn't play a game in 2001, to the Mets for righthander Kevin Appier, and adding Fullmer as a lefthanded-hitting DH. Signing righthander Aaron Sele was the lone big free-agent move.

The Angels decided the core of the offense—a strong outfield and third baseman Troy Glaus—was enough to win, especially if some younger players continued to show improvement.

Patience paid off as left-hander Jarrod Washburn (18-6, 3.15) developed into an ace, and Lackey (9-4, 3.66) pitched well after a midseason callup to replace the injured Sele, turning the Angels rotation into an asset. Former independent leaguers Ben Weber (7-2, 2.54) and Brendan Donnelly (1-1, 2.17) proved to be solid set-up men for Percival (1.92 ERA, 40 saves).

The offense also turned itself around. The development of Kennedy (.312-7-52) and Anderson (.306-29-123) and the resurgence of outfielder Tim Salmon (.286-22-88) gave Anaheim a top-notch offense despite the lack of overwhelming power. While Anaheim's 152 homers were 10th in the league, the Angels finished fourth in runs, thanks to a league-best .282 batting average.

It was good enough that the Angels didn't make any major deals at the trade deadline, adding only Ochoa, a backup outfielder. With the team playing well, general manager Bill Stoneman was afraid of hurting team chemistry.

"We didn't have a glaring weakness," Percival said at the time. "How about asking, 'What did we do in the off-

JOHN WILLIAMSON

Torii Hunter: Inspired underdog Twins

season?' That's when we did our work."

One final move proved to be a key to the Angels' playoff success. After dominating at Double-A and Triple-A, Rodriguez was called up in September. He proceeded to strike out 13 in his 5⅔ innings of big league work. A loophole in the roster rules allowed the Angels to place Steve Green (who hadn't thrown a pitch all season) on the playoff roster and select Rodriguez as an injury replacement.

It was a decision that helped earn the Angels the title. Rodriguez went 5-1 through the playoffs with a 1.93 ERA and 28 strikeouts in 19 innings.

Wild, Wild West

The Angels' biggest challenge may have been simply making it out of the AL West. While they brought home the World Series title, Oakland won the AL West, with Anaheim making the playoffs as a wild card.

For the second consecutive season, the A's drifted through April, seemingly getting in an impossible hole. But after his team struggled to a 20-25 record in the first two months, GM Billy Beane pulled off another deal, sending leadoff hitter Jeremy Giambi to Philadelphia for journeyman first baseman/outfielder John Mabry.

The Giambi-Mabry deal seemed counter to Beane's sabermetric methods. Giambi was getting on base at nearly a 40 percent clip, while Mabry was going to be a bench player at best for Oakland.

But the deal worked. Oakland's season was slipping away at the time, and after the trade the A's won 24 of 30 games to get back into the race. Then they ran off an AL-record 20-game winning streak to take the division lead. While Mabry didn't become a star, his 11 homers as a part-time player sure didn't hurt.

As the trade deadline arrived, Beane picked up left-hander Ted Lilly from the Yankees in a three-way deal that sent prospects Jeremy Bonderman, Franklyn German

MAJOR LEAGUES

AL YEAR-BY-YEAR BATTING LEADERS

Year	Batting Average		Home Runs		RBIs	
1901	Nap Lajoie, Philadelphia	.422	Nap Lajoie, Philadelphia	14	Nap Lajoie, Philadelphia	125
1902	Ed Delahanty, Washington	.376	Socks Seybold, Philadelphia	16	Buck Freeman, Boston	121
1903	Nap Lajoie, Cleveland	.355	Buck Freeman, Boston	13	Buck Freeman, Boston	104
1904	Nap Lajoie, Cleveland	.381	Harry Davis, Philadelphia	10	Nap Lajoie, Cleveland	102
1905	Elmer Flick, Cleveland	.306	Harry Davis, Philadelphia	8	Harry Davis, Philadelphia	83
1906	George Stone, St. Louis	.358	Harry Davis, Philadelphia	12	Harry Davis, Philadelphia	96
1907	Ty Cobb, Detroit	.350	Harry Davis, Philadelphia	8	Ty Cobb, Detroit	116
1908	Ty Cobb, Detroit	.324	Sam Crawford, Detroit	7	Ty Cobb, Detroit	108
1909	Ty Cobb, Detroit	.377	Ty Cobb, Detroit	9	Ty Cobb, Detroit	115
1910	Ty Cobb, Detroit	.385	Jake Stahl, Boston	10	Sam Crawford, Detroit	120
1911	Ty Cobb, Detroit	.420	Frank Baker, Philadelphia	11	Ty Cobb, Detroit	144
1912	Ty Cobb, Detroit	.410	Two tied at	10	Frank Baker, Philadelphia	133
1913	Ty Cobb, Detroit	.390	Frank Baker, Philadelphia	12	Frank Baker, Philadelphia	126
1914	Ty Cobb, Detroit	.368	Frank Baker, Philadelphia	9	Sam Crawford, Detroit	112
1915	Ty Cobb, Detroit	.370	Braggo Roth, Cleveland	7	Sam Crawford, Detroit	116
1916	Tris Speaker, Cleveland	.386	Wally Pipp, New York	12	Wally Pipp, New York	99
1917	Ty Cobb, Detroit	.383	Wally Pipp, New York	9	Bobby Veach, Detroit	115
1918	Ty Cobb, Detroit	.382	Two tied at	11	Bobby Veach, Detroit	74
1919	Ty Cobb, Detroit	.384	Babe Ruth, Boston	29	Babe Ruth, Boston	114
1920	George Sisler, St. Louis	.407	Babe Ruth, New York	54	Babe Ruth, New York	137
1921	Harry Heilmann, Detroit	.394	Babe Ruth, New York	59	Babe Ruth, New York	171
1922	George Sisler, St. Louis	.420	Kenny Williams, St. Louis	39	Kenny Williams, St. Louis	155
1923	Harry Heilmann, Detroit	.403	Babe Ruth, New York	41	Babe Ruth, New York	131
1924	Babe Ruth, New York	.378	Babe Ruth, New York	46	Goose Goslin, Washington	129
1925	Harry Heilmann, Detroit	.393	Bob Meusel, New York	33	Bob Meusel, New York	138
1926	Heinie Manush, Detroit	.377	Babe Ruth, New York	47	Babe Ruth, New York	145
1927	Harry Heilmann, Detroit	.398	Babe Ruth, New York	60	Lou Gehrig, New York	175
1928	Goose Goslin, Washington	.379	Babe Ruth, New York	54	Two tied at	142
1929	Lew Fonseca, Cleveland	.369	Babe Ruth, New York	46	Al Simmons, Philadelphia	157
1930	Al Simmons, Philadelphia	.381	Babe Ruth, New York	49	Lou Gehrig, New York	174
1931	Al Simmons, Philadelphia	.390	Two tied at	46	Lou Gehrig, New York	184
1932	Dale Alexander, Det.-Bos.	.367	Jimmie Foxx, Philadelphia	58	Jimmie Foxx, Philadelphia	169
1933	Jimmie Foxx, Philadelphia	.356	Jimmie Foxx, Philadelphia	48	Jimmie Foxx, Philadelphia	163
1934	Lou Gehrig, New York	.363	Lou Gehrig, New York	49	Lou Gehrig, New York	165
1935	Buddy Myer, Washington	.349	Two tied at	36	Hank Greenberg, Detroit	170
1936	Luke Appling, Chicago	.388	Lou Gehrig, New York	49	Hal Trosky, Cleveland	162
1937	Charlie Gehringer, Detroit	.371	Joe DiMaggio, New York	46	Hank Greenberg, Detroit	183
1938	Jimmie Foxx, Boston	.356	Hank Greenberg, Detroit	58	Jimmie Foxx, Boston	175
1939	Joe DiMaggio, New York	.381	Jimmie Foxx, Boston	35	Ted Williams, Boston	145
1940	Joe DiMaggio, New York	.352	Hank Greenberg, Detroit	41	Hank Greenberg, Detroit	150
1941	Ted Williams, Boston	.406	Ted Williams, Boston	37	Joe DiMaggio, New York	125
1942	Ted Williams, Boston	.356	Ted Williams, Boston	36	Ted Williams, Boston	137
1943	Luke Appling, Chicago	.328	Rudy York, Detroit	34	Rudy York, Detroit	118
1944	Lou Boudreau, Cleveland	.327	Nick Etten, New York	22	Vern Stephens, St. Louis	109
1945	Snuffy Stirnweiss, New York	.309	Vern Stephens, St. Louis	24	Nick Etten, New York	111
1946	Mickey Vernon, Wash.	.352	Hank Greenberg, Detroit	44	Hank Greenberg, Detroit	127
1947	Ted Williams, Boston	.343	Ted Williams, Boston	32	Ted Williams, Boston	114
1948	Ted Williams, Boston	.369	Joe DiMaggio, New York	39	Joe DiMaggio, New York	155
1949	George Kell, Detroit	.343	Ted Williams, Boston	43	Two tied at	159
1950	Billy Goodman, Boston	.354	Al Rosen, Cleveland	37	Two tied at	144
1951	Ferris Fain, Philadelphia	.344	Gus Zernial, Chi.-Phil.	33	Gus Zernial, Chi.-Phil.	129

Year	Batting Average		Home Runs		RBIs	
1952	Ferris Fain, Philadelphia	.327	Larry Doby, Cleveland	32	Al Rosen, Cleveland	105
1953	Mickey Vernon, Washington	.337	Al Rosen, Cleveland	43	Al Rosen, Cleveland	145
1954	Bobby Avila, Cleveland	.341	Larry Doby, Cleveland	32	Larry Doby, Cleveland	126
1955	Al Kaline, Detroit	.340	Mickey Mantle, New York	37	Two tied at	116
1956	Mickey Mantle, New York	.353	Mickey Mantle, New York	52	Mickey Mantle, New York	130
1957	Ted Williams, Boston	.388	Roy Sievers, Washington	42	Roy Sievers, Washington	114
1958	Ted Williams, Boston	.328	Mickey Mantle, New York	42	Jackie Jensen, Boston	122
1959	Harvey Kuenn, Detroit	.353	Two tied at	42	Jackie Jensen, Boston	112
1960	Pete Runnels, Boston	.320	Mickey Mantle, New York	40	Roger Maris, New York	112
1961	Norm Cash, Detroit	.361	Roger Maris, New York	61	Roger Maris, New York	142
1962	Pete Runnels, Boston	.326	Harmon Killebrew, Minnesota	48	Harmon Killebrew, Minnesota	126
1963	Carl Yastrzemski, Boston	.321	Harmon Killebrew, Minnesota	45	Dick Stuart, Boston	118
1964	Tony Oliva, Minnesota	.323	Harmon Killebrew, Minnesota	49	Brooks Robinson, Baltimore	118
1965	Tony Oliva, Minnesota	.321	Tony Conigliaro, Boston	32	Rocky Colavito, Cleveland	108
1966	Frank Robinson, Baltimore	.316	Frank Robinson, Baltimore	49	Frank Robinson, Baltimore	122
1967	Carl Yastrzemski, Boston	.326	Two tied at	44	Carl Yastrzemski, Boston	121
1968	Carl Yastrzemski, Boston	.301	Frank Howard, Washington	44	Ken Harrelson, Boston	109
1969	Rod Carew, Minnesota	.332	Harmon Killebrew, Minnesota	49	Harmon Killebrew, Minnesota	140
1970	Alex Johnson, California	.329	Frank Howard, Washington	44	Frank Howard, Washington	126
1971	Tony Oliva, Minnesota	.337	Bill Melton, Chicago	33	Harmon Killebrew, Minnesota	119
1972	Rod Carew, Minnesota	.318	Dick Allen, Chicago	37	Dick Allen, Chicago	113
1973	Rod Carew, Minnesota	.350	Reggie Jackson, Oakland	32	Reggie Jackson, Oakland	117
1974	Rod Carew, Minnesota	.364	Dick Allen, Chicago	32	Jeff Burroughs, Texas	118
1975	Rod Carew, Minnesota	.359	George Scott, Milwaukee	36	George Scott, Milwaukee	109
1976	George Brett, Kansas City	.333	Graig Nettles, New York	32	Lee May, Baltimore	109
1977	Rod Carew, Minnesota	.388	Jim Rice, Boston	39	Larry Hisle, Minnesota	119
1978	Rod Carew, Minnesota	.333	Jim Rice, Boston	46	Jim Rice, Boston	139
1979	Fred Lynn, Boston	.333	Gorman Thomas, Milwaukee	45	Don Baylor, California	139
1980	George Brett, Kansas City	.390	Two tied at	41	Cecil Cooper, Milwaukee	122
1981	Carney Lansford, Boston	.336	Four tied at	22	Eddie Murray, Baltimore	78
1982	Willie Wilson, Kansas City	.332	Two tied at	39	Hal McRae, Kansas City	133
1983	Wade Boggs, Boston	.361	Jim Rice, Boston	39	Two tied at	126
1984	Don Mattingly, New York	.343	Tony Armas, Boston	43	Tony Armas, Boston	123
1985	Wade Boggs, Boston	.368	Darrell Evans, Detroit	40	Don Mattingly, New York	145
1986	Wade Boggs, Boston	.357	Jesse Barfield, Toronto	40	Joe Carter, Cleveland	121
1987	Wade Boggs, Boston	.363	Mark McGwire, Oakland	49	George Bell, Toronto	134
1988	Wade Boggs, Boston	.366	Jose Canseco, Oakland	42	Jose Canseco, Oakland	124
1989	Kirby Puckett, Minnesota	.339	Fred McGriff, Toronto	36	Ruben Sierra, Texas	119
1990	George Brett, Kansas City	.329	Cecil Fielder, Detroit	51	Cecil Fielder, Detroit	132
1991	Julio Franco, Texas	.341	Two tied at	44	Cecil Fielder, Detroit	133
1992	Edgar Martinez, Seattle	.343	Juan Gonzalez, Texas	43	Cecil Fielder, Detroit	124
1993	John Olerud, Toronto	.363	Juan Gonzalez, Texas	46	Albert Belle, Cleveland	129
1994	Paul O'Neill, New York	.359	Ken Griffey, Seattle	40	Kirby Puckett, Minnesota	112
1995	Edgar Martinez, Seattle	.356	Albert Belle, Cleveland	50	Albert Belle, Cleveland	126
1996	Alex Rodriguez, Seattle	.358	Mark McGwire, Oakland	52	Albert Belle, Cleveland	148
1997	Frank Thomas, Chicago	.347	Ken Griffey, Seattle	56	Ken Griffey, Seattle	147
1998	Bernie Williams, New York	.339	Ken Griffey, Seattle	56	Juan Gonzalez, Texas	157
1999	Nomar Garciaparra, Boston	.357	Ken Griffey, Seattle	48	Manny Ramirez, Cleveland	165
2000	Nomar Garciaparra, Boston	.372	Troy Glaus, Anaheim	47	Edgar Martinez, Seattle	145
2001	Ichiro Suzuki, Seattle	.350	Alex Rodriguez, Texas	52	Bret Boone, Seattle	141
2002	Manny Ramirez, Boston	.349	Alex Rodriguez, Texas	57	Alex Rodriguez, Texas	142

and Carlos Pena to the Tigers. Pena—picked up in an off-season deal with the Rangers—came into the season as the heir apparent to Jason Giambi at first base, but he was sent to Triple-A after a poor first month of the season.

"Originally, we intended to have Pena here for a long time," A's manager Art Howe said. "He just didn't take advantage of the opportunity. That's not to say he won't be a great player. He just needs a little time."

The formula added up to a 103-59 record for the A's, a half-game behind the Yankees for the best record in baseball. Oakland was able to make up for Jason Giambi's departure because of the continued improvement of shortstop Miguel Tejada (.308-34-131) and third baseman Eric Chavez (.275-34-109). The rotation of Barry Zito (23-5, 2.75), Tim Hudson (15-9, 2.98), Mark Mulder (19-7, 3.47) and Cory Lidle (8-10, 3.89) was clearly the league's best.

But all of that couldn't bring Oakland its first playoff series victory in a decade. Minnesota won the battle of small-budget teams, winning a thrilling Game Five of their Division Series with a three-run ninth for a 5-4 victory.

Even so, the Mariners would have gladly traded places with Oakland.

It wasn't long ago that the AL West was the weakest division in the league. In 1998, the Rangers took the division with 89 wins. In 2002, Seattle won 93 games and finished third.

For most teams, 93 wins would be a great season. But for a Mariners team that won 116 in 2001, it was a sharp decline. Seattle was in front of the AL West for most of the first half, but as Oakland and Anaheim showed they would be factors in the playoff chase all season, Seattle faltered.

After everything went the Mariners' way in 2001, they were not nearly as fortunate in 2002. Staff ace Freddy Garcia saw his ERA jump by more than a run, while DH Edgar Martinez was limited by a multitude of injuries. Third baseman Jeff Cirillo's .249 average was more than 50 points worse than his career average, and while Bret Boone (.278-24-107) was solid, he didn't come close to his 2001 numbers (.331-37-141).

Despite the struggles, the Mariners were in the chase when August arrived. Hamstrung by ownership that was not willing to add significantly to its payroll, they didn't swing any deals, with the exception of a mid-August pickup of righthander Ismael Valdes from Texas and a waiver claim on second baseman Jose Offerman.

"If you don't operate as a business, all sorts of bad things happen," team president Howard Lincoln said. "I'd like to think of us as being like the Atlanta Braves. It is inevitable that we will have swings in performance, but the goal is to keep them at a minimum."

While not swinging any deadline deals didn't hurt Anaheim or Minnesota, it seemed to doom Seattle. After taking a 66-42 record into August, Seattle went 27-27 down the stretch and finished out of the playoffs.

LARRY GOREN

Magglio Ordonez

Texas was out of the race by the end of April again, despite trying to shore up its pitching problems again. The Rangers were busy in the offseason, bringing in Chan Ho Park and several relievers in a bid to try to fix the worst pitching staff in the majors.

LARRY GOREN

Miguel Tejada: Had breakout season for A's, with 34 HRs, 131 RBIs

They didn't do enough. A 5.15 team ERA overshadowed another amazing season by shortstop Alex Rodriguez, Baseball America's Major League Player of the Year. Playing in all 162 games for the second straight season, Rodriguez broke his own record for homers by a shortstop with a .300-57-142 season and excelled defensively.

Central Changes

While the West was once again wild, the AL Central saw a changing of the guard. After the Indians won six of the last seven Central titles, the Twins established themselves as the new force in the Central, not only for 2002 but probably for years to come.

The Twins made it to the ALCS with a team that was almost entirely homegrown. Outfielders Jacque Jones (.300-27-85) and Torii Hunter (.289-29-94) led an offense that had seven hitters with 10 or more home runs. While several of the Twins starters slumped, they were rescued by a deep, talented bullpen led by J.C. Romero (9-2, 1.89), LaTroy Hawkins (6-0, 2.13), Eddie Guardado (2.93 ERA, 45 saves) and Tony Fiore (10-3, 3.16).

Cleveland signaled its switch into rebuilding mode when it shipped Roberto Alomar to the Mets in a deal that brought outfielder Matt Lawton and prospects Billy Traber and Alex Escobar in return.

The Indians did get another outstanding season from first baseman Jim Thome, as the lefthanded slugger hit .304-52-118. But even with Thome's slugging, the Indians slipped under .500, prodding them to undertake wholesale rebuilding as the season went along.

Ace righthander Bartolo Colon went to the Expos midway through the season, bringing in another nice haul of prospects (Brandon Phillips, Cliff Lee and Grady Sizemore). The club turned the final month of the season into a tryout for their prospects, and it was an encouraging preview as the Indians attempt to repeat the formula that brought them success in the 1990s.

AL YEAR-BY-YEAR PITCHING LEADERS

Year	Wins		ERA		Strikeouts	
1901	Cy Young, Boston	33	Cy Young, Boston	1.63	Cy Young, Boston	158
1902	Cy Young, Boston	32	Ed Siever, Detroit	1.91	Rube Waddell, Philadelphia	210
1903	Cy Young, Boston	28	Earl Moore, Cleveland	1.77	Rube Waddell, Philadelphia	302
1904	Jack Chesbro, New York	41	Addie Joss, Cleveland	1.59	Rube Waddell, Philadelphia	349
1905	Rube Waddell, Philadelphia	26	Rube Waddell, Philadelphia	1.48	Rube Waddell, Philadelphia	287
1906	Al Orth, New York	27	Doc White, Chicago	1.52	Rube Waddell, Philadelphia	196
1907	Two tied at	27	Ed Walsh, Chicago	1.60	Rube Waddell, Philadelphia	232
1908	Ed Walsh, Chicago	40	Addie Joss, Cleveland	1.16	Ed Walsh, Chicago	269
1909	George Mullin, Detroit	29	Harry Krause, Philadelphia	1.39	Frank Smith, Chicago	177
1910	Jack Coombs, Philadelphia	31	Ed Walsh, Chicago	1.27	Walter Johnson, Washington	313
1911	Jack Coombs, Philadelphia	28	Vean Gregg, Cleveland	1.81	Ed Walsh, Chicago	255
1912	Joe Wood, Boston	34	Walter Johnson, Washington	1.39	Walter Johnson, Washington	303
1913	Walter Johnson, Washington	36	Walter Johnson, Washington	1.14	Walter Johnson, Washington	243
1914	Walter Johnson, Washington	28	Dutch Leonard, Boston	1.00	Walter Johnson, Washington	225
1915	Walter Johnson, Washington	27	Joe Wood, Boston	1.49	Walter Johnson, Washington	203
1916	Walter Johnson, Washington	25	Babe Ruth, Boston	1.75	Walter Johnson, Washington	228
1917	Ed Cicotte, Chicago	28	Ed Cicotte, Chicago	1.53	Walter Johnson, Washington	188
1918	Walter Johnson, Washington	23	Walter Johnson, Washington	1.27	Walter Johnson, Washington	162
1919	Ed Cicotte, Chicago	29	Walter Johnson, Washington	1.49	Walter Johnson, Washington	147
1920	Jim Bagby, Cleveland	31	Bob Shawkey, New York	2.45	Stan Coveleski, Cleveland	133
1921	Two tied at	27	Red Faber, Chicago	2.48	Walter Johnson, Washington	143
1922	Eddie Rommel, Phil.	27	Red Faber, Chicago	2.80	Urban Shocker, St. Louis	149
1923	George Uhle, Cleveland	26	Stan Coveleski, Cleveland	2.76	Walter Johnson, Washington	130
1924	Walter Johnson, Washington	23	Walter Johnson, Washington	2.72	Walter Johnson, Washington	158
1925	Two tied at	21	Stan Coveleski, Washington	2.84	Stan Coveleski, Washington	116
1926	George Uhle, Cleveland	27	Lefty Grove, Philadelphia	2.51	Lefty Grove, Philadelphia	194
1927	Two tied at	22	Wilcy Moore, New York	2.28	Lefty Grove, Philadelphia	174
1928	Two tied at	24	Garland Braxton, Washington	2.52	Lefty Grove, Philadelphia	183
1929	George Earnshaw, Philadelphia	24	Lefty Grove, Philadelphia	2.82	Lefty Grove, Philadelphia	170
1930	Lefty Grove, Philadelphia	28	Lefty Grove, Philadelphia	2.54	Lefty Grove, Philadelphia	209
1931	Lefty Grove, Philadelphia	31	Lefty Grove, Philadelphia	2.05	Lefty Grove, Philadelphia	175
1932	General Crowder, Washington	26	Lefty Grove, Philadelphia	2.84	Red Ruffing, New York	190
1933	Two tied at	24	Monte Pearson, Cleveland	2.33	Lefty Gomez, New York	163
1934	Lefty Gomez, New York	26	Lefty Grove, Boston	2.33	Lefty Gomez, New York	158
1935	Wes Ferrell, Boston	25	Lefty Grove, Boston	2.70	Tommy Bridges, Detroit	163
1936	Tommy Bridges, Detroit	23	Lefty Grove, Boston	2.81	Tommy Bridges, Detroit	175
1937	Lefty Gomez, New York	21	Lefty Gomez, New York	2.33	Lefty Gomez, New York	194
1938	Red Ruffing, New York	21	Lefty Grove, Boston	3.07	Bob Feller, Cleveland	240
1939	Bob Feller, Cleveland	24	Lefty Grove, Philadelphia	2.54	Bob Feller, Cleveland	246
1940	Bob Feller, Cleveland	27	Bob Feller, Cleveland	2.62	Bob Feller, Cleveland	261
1941	Bob Feller, Cleveland	25	Thornton Lee, Chicago	2.37	Bob Feller, Cleveland	260
1942	Tex Hughson, Boston	22	Ted Lyons, Chicago	2.10	Two tied at	113
1943	Two tied at	20	Spud Chandler, New York	1.64	Allie Reynolds, Cleveland	151
1944	Hal Newhouser, Detroit	29	Dizzy Trout, Detroit	2.12	Hal Newhouser, Detroit	187
1945	Hal Newhouser, Detroit	25	Hal Newhouser, Detroit	1.81	Hal Newhouser, Detroit	212
1946	Two tied at	26	Hal Newhouser, Detroit	1.94	Bob Feller, Cleveland	348
1947	Bob Feller, Cleveland	20	Spud Chandler, New York	2.46	Bob Feller, Cleveland	196
1948	Hal Newhouser, Detroit	21	Gene Bearden, Cleveland	2.43	Bob Feller, Cleveland	164
1949	Mel Parnell, Boston	25	Mel Parnell, Boston	2.78	Virgil Trucks, Detroit	153
1950	Bob Lemon, Cleveland	23	Early Wynn, Cleveland	3.20	Bob Lemon, Cleveland	170
1951	Bob Feller, Cleveland	22	Saul Rogovin, Det.-Chi.	2.78	Vic Raschi, New York	164
1952	Bobby Shantz, Philadelphia	24	Allie Reynolds, New York	2.07	Allie Reynolds, New York	160
1953	Bob Porterfield, Washington	22	Eddie Lopat, New York	2.43	Billy Pierce, Chicago	186
1954	Three tied at	23	Mike Garcia, Cleveland	2.64	Bob Turley, Baltimore	185
1955	Three tied at	18	Billy Pierce, Chicago	1.97	Herb Score, Cleveland	245
1956	Frank Lary, Detroit	21	Whitey Ford, New York	2.47	Herb Score, Cleveland	263
1957	Two tied at	20	Bobby Shantz, New York	2.45	Early Wynn, Cleveland	184
1958	Bob Turley, New York	21	Whitey Ford, New York	2.01	Early Wynn, Chicago	179
1959	Early Wynn, Chicago	22	Hoyt Wilhelm, Baltimore	2.19	Jim Bunning, Detroit	201
1960	Two tied at	18	Frank Baumann, Chicago	2.68	Jim Bunning, Detroit	201
1961	Whitey Ford, New York	25	Dick Donovan, Washington	2.40	Camilo Pascual, Minnesota	221
1962	Ralph Terry, New York	23	Hank Aguirre, Detroit	2.21	Camilo Pascual, Minnesota	206
1963	Whitey Ford, New York	24	Gary Peters, Chicago	2.33	Camilo Pascual, Minnesota	202
1964	Two tied at	20	Dean Chance, L.A.	1.65	Al Downing, New York	217
1965	Mudcat Grant, Minnesota	21	Sam McDowell, Cleveland	2.18	Sam McDowell, Cleveland	325
1966	Jim Kaat, Minnesota	25	Gary Peters, Chicago	1.98	Sam McDowell, Cleveland	225
1967	Two tied at	22	Joel Horlen, Chicago	2.06	Jim Lonborg, Boston	246
1968	Denny McLain, Detroit	31	Luis Tiant, Cleveland	1.60	Sam McDowell, Cleveland	283
1969	Denny McLain, Detroit	24	Dick Bosman, Washington	2.19	Sam McDowell, Cleveland	279
1970	Three tied at	24	Diego Segui, Oakland	2.56	Sam McDowell, Cleveland	304
1971	Mickey Lolich, Detroit	25	Vida Blue, Oakland	1.82	Mickey Lolich, Detroit	308
1972	Two tied at	24	Luis Tiant, Boston	1.91	Nolan Ryan, California	329
1973	Wilbur Wood, Chicago	24	Jim Palmer, Baltimore	2.40	Nolan Ryan, California	383
1974	Two tied at	25	Catfish Hunter, Oakland	2.49	Nolan Ryan, California	367
1975	Jim Palmer, Baltimore	23	Jim Palmer, Baltimore	2.09	Frank Tanana, California	269
1976	Jim Palmer, Baltimore	22	Mark Fidrych, Detroit	2.34	Nolan Ryan, California	327
1977	Two tied at	20	Frank Tanana, California	2.54	Nolan Ryan, California	341
1978	Ron Guidry, New York	25	Ron Guidry, New York	1.74	Nolan Ryan, California	260
1979	Two tied at	23	Ron Guidry, New York	2.78	Nolan Ryan, California	223
1980	Steve Stone, Baltimore	25	Rudy May, New York	2.47	Len Barker, Cleveland	187
1981	LaMarr Hoyt, Oakland	14	Steve McCatty, Oak.	2.32	Len Barker, Cleveland	127
1982	LaMarr Hoyt, Chicago	19	Rick Sutcliffe, Cleveland	2.96	Floyd Bannister, Seattle	209
1983	LaMarr Hoyt, Chicago	24	Rick Honeycutt, Texas	2.42	Jack Morris, Detroit	232
1984	Mike Boddicker, Baltimore	20	Mike Boddicker, Baltimore	2.79	Mark Langston, Seattle	204
1985	Ron Guidry, New York	22	Dave Stieb, Toronto	2.48	Bert Blyleven, Cleve.-Minn.	206
1986	Roger Clemens, Boston	24	Roger Clemens, Boston	2.48	Mark Langston, Seattle	245
1987	Two tied at	20	Jimmy Key, Toronto	2.76	Mark Langston, Seattle	262
1988	Frank Viola, Minnesota	24	Allan Anderson, Minnesota	2.45	Roger Clemens, Boston	291
1989	Bret Saberhagen, Kansas City	23	Bret Saberhagen, Kansas City	2.16	Nolan Ryan, Texas	301
1990	Bob Welch, Oakland	27	Roger Clemens, Boston	1.93	Nolan Ryan, Texas	232
1991	Roger Clemens, Boston	20	Roger Clemens, Boston	2.62	Roger Clemens, Boston	241
1992	Roger Clemens, Boston	21	Roger Clemens, Boston	2.41	Randy Johnson, Seattle	241
1993	Jack McDowell, Chicago	22	Kevin Appier, Kansas City	2.56	Randy Johnson, Seattle	308
1994	Jimmy Key, New York	17	Steve Ontiveros, Oakland	2.65	Randy Johnson, Seattle	204
1995	Mike Mussina, Baltimore	19	Randy Johnson, Seattle	2.48	Randy Johnson, Seattle	294
1996	Andy Pettitte, New York	21	Juan Guzman, Toronto	2.93	Roger Clemens, Boston	257
1997	Roger Clemens, Toronto	21	Roger Clemens, Toronto	2.05	Roger Clemens, Boston	292
1998	Three tied at	20	Roger Clemens, Toronto	2.65	Roger Clemens, Toronto	271
1999	Pedro Martinez, Boston	23	Pedro Martinez, Boston	2.07	Pedro Martinez, Boston	313
2000	Two tied at	20	Pedro Martinez, Boston	1.74	Pedro Martinez, Boston	284
2001	Mark Mulder, Oakland	21	Freddy Garcia, Seattle	3.05	Hideo Nomo, Boston	220
2002	Barry Zito, Oakland	23	Pedro Martinez, Boston	2.26	Pedro Martinez, Boston	239

The youth movement was supposed to pay off for the White Sox. But while Magglio Ordonez, Paul Konerko and Mark Buehrle are three of the best players in baseball, the pitching didn't come together as hoped in 2002 (hurt in part by a trade of Sean Lowe, Josh Fogg and Kip Wells for Todd Ritchie) and the club finished 81-81. By the end of the season, the White Sox showed signs of hope again as third baseman Joe Crede (.285-12-35 in 200 at-bats) and shortstop D'Angelo Jimenez (.384 on-base percentage in 108 at-bats) played well in their auditions.

Still The East's Beast

By now Red Sox fans have learned to treat April and May as a cruel joke.

Once again, the Red Sox challenged the Yankees for AL East supremacy for a while, only to falter in the second half of the season.

LARRY GOREN

Alfonso Soriano: 39 homers, 41 steals

Despite having ERA leader Pedro Martinez (20-4, 2.26), a second 20-game winner in Derek Lowe (21-8, 2.58) and batting leader Manny Ramirez (.349-33-107), the Red Sox faltered down the stretch, while the Yankees got better as the season moved on. Boston was 23 games above .500 by June 6 but 53-52 for the rest of the season, allowing the Yankees to pull away in the East.

While the Yankees didn't return to the World Series, they did finish with the best record in baseball (103-58). The offense benefited from the development of second baseman Alfonso Soriano (.300-39-102), who set an AL record for homers by a second baseman while also stealing 41 bases. Jason Giambi earned the money from his big new contract with a .314-41-122 season.

But the Yankees' starting pitching, the strength of the team during their five-year reign over the AL, was a problem in 2002. The rotation of Roger Clemens, Andy Pettitte, Mike Mussina and David Wells was blitzed for a 10.38 ERA in the four-game Division Series loss to the Angels.

The postseason problems were foreshadowed by the rotation's struggles with inconsistency and injuries during the regular season. While the overall staff was still strong, Clemens (13-6, 4.35) and Mussina (18-10, 4.05) failed to match their performances of 2001.

The Blue Jays weren't a factor in the East, but they did appear

STEVE MOORE

Derek Lowe

to finally turn a corner in their attempts to rebuild. Third baseman Eric Hinske, picked up in a trade with Oakland before the season, became BA's Rookie of the Year with a .279-24-84 season, while DH Josh Phelps (.309-15-58), center fielder Vernon Wells (.275-23-100), shortstop Chris

Woodward (.273-13-45) and second baseman Orlando Hudson (.276-4-23) all established themselves.

The Devil Rays had another season to forget, but they at least could point to one minor stat: After finishing alone with the worst record in the AL for the previous two seasons, the Devil Rays shared the honor with the Tigers as both teams finished 55-106. The 55 wins were the fewest by any team since Florida won 54 in 1998.

Around The AL

■ Seattle center fielder Mike Cameron became the 13th player to hit four home runs in a game when he did it in four consecutive at-bats against the White Sox on May 22.

■ With 13 wins in 2002, Clemens now has 293 wins, good for 21st place on the career wins list.

■ Boston left fielder Rickey Henderson continued his rise though the record books. Henderson already holds the career runs scored, walks and stolen base records. His 10,889 career at-bats passed Willie Mays for 10th place. Henderson also leaped five spots to fourth for games played (3,051).

BATTING

GAMES
Carlos Beltran, Royals 162
Terence Long, Athletics 162
Alex Rodriguez, Rangers 162
Miguel Tejada, Athletics 162
Tony Batista, Orioles 161

AT-BATS
Alfonso Soriano, Yankees 696
Miguel Tejada, Athletics 662
Ichiro Suzuki, Mariners 647
Derek Jeter, Yankees 644
Garret Anderson, Angels 638

RUNS
Alfonso Soriano, Yankees 128
Alex Rodriguez, Rangers 125
Derek Jeter, Yankees 124
Jason Giambi, Yankees 120
Johnny Damon, Red Sox 118

HITS
Alfonso Soriano, Yankees 209
Ichiro Suzuki, Mariners 208
Miguel Tejada, Athletics 204
Bernie Williams, Yankees 204
Nomar Garciaparra, Red Sox 197

TOTAL BASES
Alex Rodriguez, Rangers 389
Alfonso Soriano, Yankees 381
Magglio Ordonez, White Sox 352
Garret Anderson, Angels 344
Miguel Tejada, Athletics 336

EXTRA-BASE HITS
Alfonso Soriano, Yankees 92
Garret Anderson, Angels 88
Magglio Ordonez, White Sox 86
Alex Rodriguez, Rangers 86
Nomar Garciaparra, Red Sox 85

SINGLES
Ichiro Suzuki, Mariners 165
Derek Jeter, Yankees 147
Bernie Williams, Yankees 146
David Eckstein, Angels 142
Miguel Tejada, Athletics 140

DOUBLES
Garret Anderson, Angels 56
Nomar Garciaparra, Red Sox 56
Alfonso Soriano, Yankees 51

Johnny Damon: 11 triples, 31 stolen bases

Magglio Ordonez, White Sox 47
Carlos Beltran, Royals 44

TRIPLES
Johnny Damon, Red Sox 11
Randy Winn, Devil Rays 9
Ichiro Suzuki, Mariners 8
Mike Young, Rangers 8
Carlos Beltran, Royals 7

HOME RUNS
Alex Rodriguez, Rangers 57
Jim Thome, Indians.................................. 52
Rafael Palmeiro, Rangers 43
Jason Giambi, Yankees 41
Alfonso Soriano, Yankees 39

HOME RUN RATIO
(At-Bats per Home Run)
Jim Thome, Indians 9.2
Alex Rodriguez, Rangers 10.9
Rafael Palmeiro, Rangers 12.7
Manny Ramirez, Red Sox 13.2
Jason Giambi, Yankees 13.7

RUNS BATTED IN
Alex Rodriguez, Rangers 142
Magglio Ordonez, White Sox 135
Miguel Tejada, Athletics 131
Garret Anderson, Angels 123
Jason Giambi, Yankees 122

SACRIFICE BUNTS
David Eckstein, Angels 14
Jeff Cirillo, Mariners 13
Mike Young, Rangers 13
Aaron Rowand, White Sox 9
Six tied at 8

SACRIFICE FLIES
John Olerud, Mariners 12
Nomar Garciaparra, Red Sox 11
Joe Randa, Royals 11
Garret Anderson, Angels 10
Jeff Conine, Orioles 10
Frank Thomas, White Sox 10
Omar Vizquel, Indians 10

HIT BY PITCH
David Eckstein, Angels 27
Melvin Mora, Orioles 20
Brad Fullmer, Angels 15
Jason Giambi, Yankees 15
Alfonso Soriano, Yankees 14

WALKS
Jim Thome, Indians 122
Jason Giambi, Yankees 109
Rafael Palmeiro, Rangers 104
Carlos Delgado, Blue Jays 102
John Olerud, Mariners 98

INTENTIONAL WALKS
Ichiro Suzuki, Mariners 27
Carlos Delgado, Blue Jays 18
Jim Thome, Indians 18
Rafael Palmeiro, Rangers 16
Manny Ramirez, Red Sox 14

STRIKEOUTS
Mike Cameron, Mariners 176
Alfonso Soriano, Yankees 157
Troy Glaus, Angels 144
Jorge Posada, Yankees 143
Jared Sandberg, Devil Rays 139
Jim Thome, Indians 139

TOUGHEST TO STRIKE OUT
(Plate Appearances per SO)
Randall Simon, Tigers 16.9
David Eckstein, Angels 16.0
Mike Sweeney, Royals 11.8

Jim Thome: 52 home runs, 122 walks

Ichiro Suzuki, Mariners 11.7
Bobby Higginson, Tigers 11.1

STOLEN BASES
Alfonso Soriano, Yankees 41
Carlos Beltran, Royals 35
Derek Jeter, Yankees 32
Mike Cameron, Mariners 31
Johnny Damon, Red Sox 31
Ichiro Suzuki, Mariners 31

CAUGHT STEALING
Ichiro Suzuki, Mariners 15
David Eckstein, Angels 13
Cristian Guzman, Twins 13
Alfonso Soriano, Yankees 13
Corey Koskie, Twins 11

GIDP
Jorge Posada, Yankees 23
Magglio Ordonez, White Sox 21
Miguel Tejada, Athletics 21
John Olerud, Mariners 19
Bernie Williams, Yankees 19

HITTING STREAKS
Miguel Tejada, Athletics 24
Cristian Guzman, Twins 23
David Ortiz, Twins 19
Bernie Williams, Yankees 19
Five tied at 18

MULTIPLE-HIT GAMES
Alfonso Soriano, Yankees 69
Bernie Williams, Yankees 65
Ichiro Suzuki, Mariners 63
Garret Anderson, Angels 60
Derek Jeter, Yankees 58

SLUGGING PERCENTAGE
Jim Thome, Indians .... .677
Manny Ramirez, Red Sox .... .647
Alex Rodriguez, Rangers .... .623
Jason Giambi, Yankees .... .598
Magglio Ordonez, White Sox .... .597

ON-BASE PERCENTAGE
Manny Ramirez, Red Sox .... .450
Jim Thome, Indians .... .445
Jason Giambi, Yankees .... .435
Mike Sweeney, Royals .... .417
Bernie Williams, Yankees .... .415

PITCHING

WINS
Barry Zito, Athletics 23

Derek Lowe, Red Sox 21
Pedro Martinez, Red Sox 20
Mark Buehrle, White Sox 19
Roy Halladay, Blue Jays 19
Mark Mulder, Athletics 19
David Wells, Yankees 19

LOSSES
Tanyon Sturtze, Devil Rays 18
Steve Sparks, Tigers 16
Jeff Suppan, Royals 16
Frank Castillo, Red Sox 15
Mark Redman, Tigers 15
Todd Ritchie, White Sox 15

WINNING PERCENTAGE
Pedro Martinez, Red Sox .... .833
Barry Zito, Athletics .... .821
Jarrod Washburn, Angels .... .750
Roy Halladay, Blue Jays .... .731
Mark Mulder, Athletics .... .731
David Wells, Yankees .... .731

GAMES
Billy Koch, Athletics 84
J.C. Romero, Twins 81
Mike Stanton, Yankees 79
Steve Karsay, Yankees 78
Kelvim Escobar, Blue Jays 76

GAMES STARTED
Barry Zito, Athletics 35
Mark Buehrle, White Sox 34
Freddy Garcia, Mariners 34
Roy Halladay, Blue Jays 34
Tim Hudson, Athletics 34
Jamie Moyer, Mariners 34

COMPLETE GAMES
Paul Byrd, Royals 7
Mark Buehrle, White Sox 5
Joe Kennedy, Devil Rays 5
Five tied at 4

SHUTOUTS
Jeff Weaver, Tigers/Yankees 3
Seven tied at 2

GAMES FINISHED
Billy Koch, Athletics 74
Kelvim Escobar, Blue Jays 67
Eddie Guardado, Twins 57
Jorge Julio, Orioles 55
Ugueth Urbina, Red Sox 54

SAVES
Eddie Guardado, Twins 45
Billy Koch, Athletics 44
Troy Percival, Angels 40
Ugueth Urbina, Red Sox 40
Kelvim Escobar, Blue Jays 38

INNINGS PITCHED
Roy Halladay, Blue Jays 239
Mark Buehrle, White Sox 239
Tim Hudson, Athletics 238
Jamie Moyer, Mariners 231
Barry Zito, Athletics 229

HITS ALLOWED
Tanyon Sturtze, Devil Rays 271
Steve Sparks, Tigers 238
Tim Hudson, Athletics 237
Mark Buehrle, White Sox 236
Jeff Suppan, Royals 229

RUNS ALLOWED
Tanyon Sturtze, Devil Rays 141
Steve Sparks, Tigers 134
Jeff Suppan, Royals 134
Dan Wright, White Sox 124
Joe Kennedy, Devil Rays 114

HOME RUNS ALLOWED
Ramon Ortiz, Angels 40
Paul Byrd, Royals 36
Tanyon Sturtze, Devil Rays 33
Rick Reed, Twins 32
Jeff Suppan, Royals 32
Dan Wright, White Sox 32

Paul Byrd: Seven complete games

WALKS
Tanyon Sturtze, Devil Rays 89
C.C. Sabathia, Indians 88
Jon Garland, White Sox 83
Danys Baez, Indians 83
Chan Ho Park, Rangers 78
Barry Zito, Athletics 78

FEWEST WALKS PER 9 INNINGS
Rick Reed, Twins 1.24
Paul Byrd, Royals 1.50
Brad Radke, Twins 1.52
Eric Milton, Twins 1.58
Ryan Franklin, Mariners 1.67

HIT BATSMEN
Chan Ho Park, Rangers 17
Joe Kennedy, Devil Rays 16
Pedro Martinez, Red Sox 15
Paul Wilson, Devil Rays 13
Derek Lowe, Red Sox 12
Steve Sparks, Tigers 12

STRIKEOUTS
Pedro Martinez, Red Sox 239
Roger Clemens, Yankees 192
Mike Mussina, Yankees 182
Barry Zito, Athletics 182
Freddy Garcia, Mariners 181

STRIKEOUTS PER 9 INNINGS
Pedro Martinez, Red Sox 10.79
Roger Clemens, Yankees 9.60
Casey Fossum, Red Sox 8.52
Chuck Finley, Indians 7.78
Mike Mussina, Yankees 7.60

PICKOFFS
Mark Buehrle, White Sox 7
Joe Kennedy, Devil Rays 7
Andy Pettitte, Yankees 6
Mark Mulder, Athletics 5
Five tied at 4

WILD PITCHES
Johan Santana, Twins 15
Roger Clemens, Yankees 14
Ryan Drese, Indians 11
Mark Redman, Tigers 11
Four tied at 10

BALKS
Steve Kent, Devil Rays 3
Ramon Ortiz, Angels 3
C.C. Sabathia, Indians 3
Ten tied at 2

OPPONENTS BATTING AVERAGE
Pedro Martinez, Red Sox .... .198
Tim Wakefield, Red Sox .... .204
Derek Lowe, Red Sox .... .211
Barry Zito, Athletics .... .218

Jamie Moyer, Mariners .... .230
Ramon Ortiz, Angels .... .230

FIELDING

PITCHER
PCT	Tim Hudson, Athletics	1.000
PO	Tim Hudson, Athletics	26
A	Mark Buehrle, White Sox	46
E	Joe Kennedy, Devil Rays	10
TC	Roy Halladay, Blue Jays	65
	Kenny Rogers, Rangers	65
DP	Three tied at	5

CATCHER
PCT	Bengie Molina, Angels	.999
PO	Jorge Posada, Yankees	965
A	Einar Diaz, Indians	75
E	Jorge Posada, Yankees	12
TC	Jorge Posada, Yankees	1043
DP	Geronimo Gil, Orioles	14
PB	Geronimo Gil, Orioles	19

FIRST BASE
PCT	Scott Spiezio, Angels	.997
PO	Carlos Delgado, Blue Jays	1232
A	John Olerud, Mariners	105
E	Carlos Delgado, Blue Jays	12
TC	Carlos Delgado, Blue Jays	1339
DP	John Olerud, Mariners	122

SECOND BASE
PCT	Rey Sanchez, Red Sox	.991
PO	Alfonso Soriano, Yankees	300
A	Mike Young, Rangers	420
E	Alfonso Soriano, Yankees	23
TC	Alfonso Soriano, Yankees	725
DP	Adam Kennedy, Angels	90

THIRD BASE
PCT	Jeff Cirillo, Mariners	.973
PO	Eric Chavez, Athletics	120
A	Eric Chavez, Athletics	301
E	Shea Hillenbrand, Red Sox	23
	Robin Ventura, Yankees	23
TC	Eric Chavez, Athletics	438
DP	Tony Batista, Orioles	35

SHORTSTOP
PCT	Mike Bordick, Orioles	.998
PO	Alex Rodriguez, Rangers	259
A	Miguel Tejada, Athletics	504
E	Nomar Garciaparra, Red Sox	25
TC	Miguel Tejada, Athletics	752
DP	Alex Rodriguez, Rangers	108

OUTFIELD
PCT	Rondell White, Yankees	1.000
PO	Darin Erstad, Angels	452
A	Robert Fick, Tigers	21
E	Robert Fick, Tigers	12
TC	Darin Erstad, Angels	464
DP	Robert Fick, Tigers	5
	Melvin Mora, Orioles	5

Eddie Guardado: 45 saves

2002 AMERICAN LEAGUE STATISTICS

CLUB BATTING

	AVG	G	AB	R	H	2B	3B	HR	BB	SO	SB
New York	.275	161	5601	897	1540	314	12	223	640	1171	100
Boston	.277	162	5640	859	1560	348	33	177	545	944	80
Chicago	.268	162	5502	856	1475	289	29	217	555	952	75
Anaheim	.282	162	5678	851	1603	333	32	152	462	805	117
Texas	.269	162	5618	843	1510	304	27	230	554	1055	62
Seattle	.275	162	5569	814	1531	285	31	152	629	1003	137
Toronto	.261	162	5581	813	1457	305	38	187	522	1142	71
Oakland	.261	162	5558	800	1450	279	28	205	609	1008	46
Minnesota	.272	161	5582	768	1518	348	36	167	472	1089	79
Cleveland	.249	162	5423	739	1349	255	26	192	542	1000	52
Kansas City	.256	162	5535	737	1415	285	42	140	524	921	140
Tampa Bay	.253	161	5604	673	1418	297	35	133	456	1115	102
Baltimore	.246	162	5491	667	1353	311	27	165	452	993	110
Detroit	.248	161	5406	575	1340	265	37	124	363	1035	65

CLUB PITCHING

	ERA	G	CG	SHO	SV	IP	H	R	ER	BB	SO
Oakland	3.68	162	9	19	48	1452	1391	654	593	474	1021
Anaheim	3.69	162	7	14	54	1452	1345	644	595	509	999
Boston	3.75	162	5	17	51	1446	1339	665	603	430	1157
New York	3.87	161	9	11	53	1452	1441	697	625	403	1135
Seattle	4.07	162	8	12	43	1445	1422	699	654	441	1063
Minnesota	4.12	161	8	9	47	1444	1454	712	662	439	1026
Baltimore	4.46	162	8	3	31	1450	1491	773	719	549	967
Chicago	4.53	162	7	7	35	1423	1422	798	716	528	945
Toronto	4.80	162	6	6	41	1438	1504	828	767	590	991
Cleveland	4.91	162	9	4	34	1424	1508	837	777	603	1058
Detroit	4.93	161	11	7	33	1414	1593	864	774	463	794
Texas	5.15	162	4	4	33	1439	1528	882	824	669	1030
Kansas City	5.21	162	12	6	30	1441	1587	891	834	572	909
Tampa Bay	5.29	161	12	3	25	1440	1567	918	846	620	925

CLUB FIELDING

	PCT	PO	A	E	DP		PCT	PO	A	E	DP
Minnesota	.987	4334	1422	74	124	Boston	.983	4338	1645	104	140
Anaheim	.986	4357	1571	87	151	Toronto	.982	4315	1616	107	159
Baltimore	.985	4352	1721	91	173	Cleveland	.981	4274	1664	113	161
Seattle	.985	4336	1516	88	134	Tampa Bay	.979	4321	1569	126	168
Texas	.984	4319	1684	99	152	Kansas City	.979	4323	1705	130	153
Chicago	.984	4269	1596	97	157	New York	.979	4356	1524	127	117
Oakland	.984	4356	1798	102	144	Detroit	.977	4242	1720	142	148

INDIVIDUAL BATTING LEADERS

(Minimum 502 Plate Appearances)

	AVG	G	AB	R	H	2B	3B	HR	RBI	BB	SO	SB
Ramirez, Manny, Boston	.349	120	436	84	152	31	0	33	107	73	85	0
Sweeney, Mike, Kansas City	.340	126	471	81	160	31	1	24	86	61	46	9
Williams, Bernie, New York	.333	154	612	102	204	37	2	19	102	83	97	8
Suzuki, Ichiro, Seattle	.321	157	647	111	208	27	8	8	51	68	62	31
Ordonez, Magglio, Chicago	.320	153	590	116	189	47	1	38	135	53	77	7
Giambi, Jason, New York	.314	155	560	120	176	34	1	41	122	109	112	2
Kennedy, Adam, Anaheim	.312	144	474	65	148	32	6	7	52	19	80	17
Garciaparra, Nomar, Boston	.310	156	635	101	197	56	5	24	120	41	63	5
Tejada, Miguel, Oakland	.308	162	662	108	204	30	0	34	131	38	84	7
Anderson, Garret, Anaheim	.306	158	638	93	195	56	3	29	123	30	80	6

INDIVIDUAL PITCHING LEADERS

(Minimum 162 Innings)

	W	L	ERA	G	GS	CG	SV	IP	H	R	ER	BB	SO
Martinez, Pedro, Boston	20	4	2.26	30	30	2	0	199	144	62	50	40	239
Lowe, Derek, Boston	21	8	2.58	32	32	1	0	220	166	65	63	48	127
Zito, Barry, Oakland	23	5	2.75	35	35	1	0	229	182	79	70	78	182
Wakefield, Tim, Boston	11	5	2.81	45	15	0	3	163	121	57	51	51	134
Halladay, Roy, Toronto	19	7	2.93	34	34	2	0	239	223	93	78	62	168
Hudson, Tim, Oakland	15	9	2.98	34	34	4	0	238	237	87	79	62	152
Washburn, Jarrod, Anaheim	18	6	3.15	32	32	1	0	206	183	75	72	59	139
Pineiro, Joel, Seattle	14	7	3.24	37	28	2	0	194	189	75	70	54	136
Moyer, Jamie, Seattle	13	8	3.32	34	34	4	0	231	198	89	85	50	147
Mulder, Mark, Oakland	19	7	3.47	30	30	2	0	207	182	88	80	55	159

AWARD WINNERS

Selected by Baseball Writers Association of America

MVP

Player, Team	1st	2nd	3rd	Total
Miguel Tejada, Oak.	21	6	1	356
Alex Rodriguez, Texas	5	7	11	254
Alfonso Soriano, N.Y.	2	11	9	234
Garret Anderson, Ana.	0	4	5	184
Jason Giambi, N.Y.	0	0	2	162
Torii Hunter, Minn.	0	0	0	132
Jim Thome, Cleve.	0	0	0	69
Magglio Ordonez, Chi.	0	0	0	59
Manny Ramirez, Bos.	0	0	0	39
Bernie Williams, N.Y.	0	0	0	32
David Eckstein, Ana.	0	0	0	24
Nomar Garciaparra, Bos.	0	0	0	24
Barry Zito, Oakland	0	0	0	22
Eric Chavez, Oak.	0	0	0	14
Troy Percival, Ana.	0	0	0	12
Eddie Guardado, Minn.	0	0	0	12
Ichiro Suzuki, Sea.	0	0	0	10
Billy Koch, Oakland	0	0	0	8
Derek Lowe, Boston	0	0	0	3
Pedro Martinez, Bos.	0	0	0	1
Mike Sweeney, K.C.	0	0	0	1

CY YOUNG AWARD

Player, Team	1st	2nd	3rd	Total
Barry Zito, Oakland	17	9	2	114
Pedro Martinez, Bos.	11	12	5	96
Derek Lowe, Boston	0	7	20	41
Jarrod Washburn, Ana.	0	0	1	1

ROOKIE OF THE YEAR

Player, Team	1st	2nd	3rd	Total
Eric Hinske, Toronto	19	9	0	122
Rodrigo Lopez, Balt.	9	17	1	97
Jorge Julio, Balt.	0	1	11	14
Bobby Kielty, Minn.	0	1	2	5
John Lackey, Ana.	0	0	5	5
Josh Phelps, Tor.	0	0	3	3
Kevin Mench, Texas	0	0	2	2
Mark Ellis, Oakland	0	0	1	1
Tony Fiore, Minn.	0	0	1	1
Dustan Mohr, Minn.	0	0	1	1
Carlos Pena, Oak./Det.	0	0	1	1

MANAGER OF THE YEAR

Manager, Team	1st	2nd	3rd	Total
Mike Scioscia, Ana.	17	10	1	116
Art Howe, Oakland	9	5	14	74
Ron Gardenhire, Minn.	2	13	10	59
Joe Torre, N.Y.	0	0	3	3

NOTE: MVP balloting based on 14 points for first-place vote, nine for second, eight for third, etc.; Cy Young Award, Rookie of the Year and Manager of the Year balloting based on five points for first-place vote, three for second and one for third.

GOLD GLOVE AWARDS

Selected by AL managers

C—Bengie Molina, Anaheim. 1B—John Olerud, Seattle. 2B—Bret Boone, Seattle. 3B—Eric Chavez, Oakland. SS—Alex Rodriguez, Texas. OF—Darin Erstad, Anaheim; Torii Hunter, Minnesota; Ichiro Suzuki, Seattle. P—Kenny Rogers, Texas.

ANAHEIM VS. NEW YORK

COMPOSITE BOX

ANAHEIM

Player, Pos.	AVG	G	AB	R	H	2B	3B	HR	RBI	BB	SO	SB
Benji Gil, 2b	.800	2	5	1	4	0	0	0	1	0	0	0
Shawn Wooten, dh-ph	.667	3	9	4	6	0	0	1	2	0	1	0
Adam Kennedy, 2b-ph	.500	4	8	4	4	1	0	1	3	1	2	1
Darin Erstad, cf	.421	4	19	4	8	2	0	0	2	0	1	1
Scott Spiezio, 1b	.400	4	15	2	6	1	0	1	6	2	1	0
Garret Anderson, lf	.389	4	18	5	7	2	0	1	4	1	3	0
Troy Glaus, 3b	.313	4	16	4	5	0	0	3	3	1	3	0
Brad Fullmer, dh-ph	.286	3	7	1	2	1	0	0	0	1	1	0
David Eckstein, ss	.278	4	18	2	5	0	0	0	1	0	0	1
Bengie Molina, c	.267	4	15	0	4	2	0	0	2	0	1	0
Tim Salmon, rf	.263	4	19	3	5	1	0	2	7	1	5	0
Alex Ochoa, rf	.000	3	0	0	0	0	0	0	0	0	0	0
Chone Figgins, pr	.000	1	0	1	0	0	0	0	0	0	0	1
Totals	.376	4	149	31	56	10	0	9	31	7	18	4

Pitcher	W	L	ERA	G	GS	SV	IP	H	R	ER	BB	SO
John Lackey	0	0	0.00	1	0	0	3	3	0	0	1	3
Francisco Rodriguez	2	0	3.18	3	0	0	6	2	2	2	8	
Jarrod Washburn	1	0	3.75	2	2	0	12	12	6	5	3	4
Kevin Appier	0	0	5.40	1	1	0	5	5	3	3	3	3
Troy Percival	0	0	5.40	3	0	2	3	6	2	2	0	4
Brendan Donnelly	0	0	13.50	3	0	0	2	3	3	3	1	2
Ben Weber	0	1	18.00	2	0	0	1	2	2	2	2	0
Ramon Ortiz	0	0	20.25	1	1	0	3	6	6	6	4	1
Scott Schoeneweis	0	0	27.00	3	0	0	2	1	1	0	0	
Totals	3	1	6.17	4	4	2	35	38	25	24	16	25

NEW YORK

Player, Pos.	AVG	G	AB	R	H	2B	3B	HR	RBI	BB	SO	SB
Ron Coomer, dh	.500	1	2	0	1	0	0	0	0	0	0	0
Derek Jeter, ss	.500	4	16	6	8	0	0	2	3	2	3	0
Jason Giambi, 1b-dh	.357	4	14	5	5	0	0	1	3	4	1	0
Bernie Williams, cf	.333	4	15	4	5	1	0	1	3	3	2	0
Rondell White, dh	.333	3	3	1	1	0	0	1	1	0	0	0
Robin Ventura, 3b	.286	4	14	1	4	2	0	0	4	1	2	0
Raul Mondesi, rf	.250	4	12	1	3	0	0	0	1	3	1	0
Juan Rivera, lf	.250	4	12	2	3	0	0	0	3	1	3	0
Jorge Posada, c	.235	4	17	2	4	0	0	1	3	0	3	0
Nick Johnson, 1b-dh-ph	.182	3	11	1	2	0	0	0	1	1	5	0
Alfonso Soriano, 2b	.118	4	17	2	2	1	0	1	2	1	4	1
John Vander Wal, ph-lf	.000	2	2	0	0	0	0	0	0	0	1	0
Shane Spencer, lf	.000	1	0	0	0	0	0	0	0	0	0	0
Enrique Wilson, pr	.000	1	0	0	0	0	0	0	0	0	0	0
Totals	.281	4	135	25	38	4	0	7	24	16	25	1

Pitcher	W	L	ERA	G	GS	SV	IP	H	R	ER	BB	SO
Mariano Rivera	0	0	0.00	1	0	1	1	0	0	0	0	0
Orlando Hernandez	0	1	2.84	2	0	0	6	5	2	2	0	7
Roger Clemens	0	0	6.35	1	1	0	6	8	4	4	3	5
Steve Karsay	1	0	6.75	4	0	0	3	3	2	2	0	1
Jeff Weaver	0	0	6.75	2	0	0	3	4	2	2	3	1
Mike Mussina	0	0	9.00	1	1	0	4	6	4	4	0	2
Mike Stanton	0	1	10.13	3	0	0	3	6	3	3	1	1
Andy Pettitte	0	0	12.00	1	1	0	3	8	4	4	0	1
Ramiro Mendoza	0	0	13.50	2	0	0	1	5	2	2	0	0
David Wells	0	1	15.43	1	1	0	5	10	8	8	0	0
Totals	1	3	8.21	4	4	1	34	56	31	31	7	18

SCORE BY INNINGS

Anaheim	135 1(10)2 171	—31
New York	414 423 142	—25

E—Gil, Glaus, Jeter, Posada, Wells. **DP**—Anaheim 6, New York 9. **LOB**—Anaheim 31, New York 28. **SH**—Molina 2, Eckstein, Erstad. **HBP**—Eckstein (by Weaver), Glaus (by Mussina), Mondesi 2 (by Appier, by Ortiz), Giambi (by Washburn), Soriano (by Percival). **IBB**—Fullmer (by Weaver), Glaus (by Stanton). **WP**—Ortiz, Rodriguez.

MINNESOTA VS. OAKLAND

COMPOSITE BOX

MINNESOTA

Player, Pos.	AVG	G	AB	R	H	2B	3B	HR	RBI	BB	SO	SB
Dustan Mohr, rf-lf	1.000	4	2	1	2	1	0	0	0	1	0	0
Denny Hocking, rf-ph	.500	3	6	1	3	1	0	0	1	0	1	0
Matt LeCroy, ph-dh	.444	3	9	1	4	0	0	0	1	0	3	0
A.J. Pierzynski, c	.438	5	16	4	7	0	1	1	4	2	2	0

Derek Jeter: .500 average, two homers didn't inspire Yankees

Player, Pos.	AVG	G	AB	R	H	2B	3B	HR	RBI	BB	SO	SB
Michael Cuddyer, rf	.385	5	13	1	5	1	0	0	1	3	3	0
Torii Hunter, cf	.300	5	20	4	6	4	0	0	2	1	4	0
Cristian Guzman, ss	.286	5	21	5	6	2	0	1	2	2	4	2
Doug Mientkiewicz, 1b	.250	5	20	3	5	0	0	2	4	1	1	0
Jacque Jones, lf	.250	5	20	3	5	3	0	0	1	1	8	0
Luis Rivas, 2b	.250	4	12	2	3	1	0	0	0	1	2	0
David Ortiz, dh-ph	.231	4	13	0	3	2	0	0	2	0	5	0
Corey Koskie, 3b	.143	5	21	3	3	0	1	1	5	2	6	0
Tom Prince, c	.000	1	2	0	0	0	0	0	0	0	2	0
Bobby Kielty, ph-of	.000	3	4	0	0	0	0	0	0	0	1	0
Totals	.291	5	179	27	52	15	2	5	23	14	42	2

Pitcher	W	L	ERA	G	GS	SV	IP	H	R	ER	BB	SO
Mike Jackson	0	0	0.00	1	0	0	1	1	0	0	0	0
LaTroy Hawkins	0	0	0.00	3	0	0	2	0	0	0	0	5
J.C. Romero	0	0	0.00	3	0	0	3	3	0	0	1	2
Kyle Lohse	0	0	0.00	2	0	0	4	2	0	0	0	5
Brad Radke	2	0	1.54	2	2	0	12	14	6	2	1	7
Eric Milton	1	0	2.57	1	1	0	7	6	2	2	1	3
Johan Santana	0	0	6.00	2	0	0	3	3	2	2	2	2
Rick Reed	0	1	7.20	1	1	0	5	6	4	4	2	8
Eddie Guardado	0	0	13.50	2	0	1	2	5	3	3	1	1
Joe Mays	0	1	14.73	1	1	0	4	9	6	6	2	1
Tony Fiore	0	0	20.25	1	0	0	1	4	3	3	2	0
Totals	3	2	4.50	5	5	1	44	53	26	22	12	34

OAKLAND

Player, Pos.	AVG	G	AB	R	H	2B	3B	HR	RBI	BB	SO	SB
Randy Velarde, ph-1b	.600	4	5	1	3	1	0	0	1	0	1	0
Scott Hatteberg, 1b	.500	5	14	5	7	2	0	1	3	3	0	0
Jermaine Dye, rf	.400	5	20	3	8	2	0	1	1	1	5	0
Eric Chavez, 3b	.381	5	21	3	8	0	0	1	5	2	1	0
Mark Ellis, 2b	.368	5	19	1	7	2	0	1	4	1	2	0
Ray Durham, dh	.333	5	21	7	7	3	0	2	2	2	4	1
Adam Piatt, ph-lf	.333	3	3	0	1	0	0	0	0	1	0	0
David Justice, lf	.238	5	21	2	5	1	1	0	4	0	4	0
Terrence Long, cf	.167	5	18	1	3	0	0	1	1	2	0	
Miguel Tejada, ss	.143	5	21	3	3	1	0	1	4	1	7	0
Ramon Hernandez, c	.059	5	17	0	1	0	0	0	0	0	4	0
Greg Myers, c	.000	2	1	0	0	0	0	0	0	0	1	0
John Mabry, ph-1b-rf	.000	2	2	0	0	0	0	0	0	0	1	0
Olmedo Saenz, ph-1b	.000	1	0	0	0	0	0	0	0	0	1	0
Eric Byrnes, lf-ph	.000	2	1	0	0	0	0	0	0	0	1	0
Totals	.288	5	184	26	53	13	1	8	25	12	34	1

Pitcher	W	L	ERA	G	GS	SV	IP	H	R	ER	BB	SO
Jim Mecir	0	0	0.00	1	0	0	1	0	0	0	0	2
Ricardo Rincon	0	0	0.00	2	0	0	3	2	0	0	0	1
Chad Bradford	0	0	0.00	2	0	0	3	1	0	0	1	0
Micah Bowie	0	0	0.00	1	0	1	0	0	0	0	0	3
Mark Mulder	1	1	2.08	2	2	0	13	14	3	3	3	12

Darin Erstad: Topped Angels with .364 average in ALCS

JOHN WILLIAMSON

Player, Pos.		AVG	G	AB	R	H	2B	3B	HR	RBI	BB	SO	SB
Scott Spiezio, 1b	.353	5	17	5	6	2	0	1	5	2	1	0
Brad Fullmer, dh	.333	4	12	2	4	2	0	1	4	0	2	0
Troy Glaus, 3b	.316	5	19	4	6	0	1	1	2	2	5	0
David Eckstein, ss	.286	5	21	1	6	0	0	0	2	2	2	0
Garret Anderson, lf	.250	5	20	3	5	1	0	1	3	1	0	0
Shawn Wooten, ph-dh	.250	3	8	1	2	0	0	0	1	0	3	0
Tim Salmon, rf	.214	5	14	0	3	0	0	0	0	3	1	0
Bengie Molina, c	.214	5	14	0	3	0	1	0	2	1	2	0
Benji Gil, 1b	.000	1	2	0	0	0	0	0	0	0	1	0
Orlando Palmeiro, ph-rf	.000	2	2	0	0	0	0	0	0	0	1	0
Alex Ochoa, ph-rf	.000	4	4	2	0	0	0	0	0	0	3	0
Jose Molina, c	.000	3	1	0	0	0	0	0	0	0	0	0
Totals	.287	5	171	29	49	5	2	8	26	9	26	1

Pitcher	W	L	ERA	G	GS	SV	IP	H	R	ER	BB	SO
Troy Percival	0	0	0.00	3	0	2	3	0	0	0	0	3
Scott Schoeneweis	0	0	0.00	1	0	0	1	0	0	0	0	0
John Lackey	1	0	0.00	1	1	0	7	3	0	0	0	7
Felix Rodriguez	2	0	0.00	4	0	0	4	2	0	0	2	7
Jarrod Washburn	0	0	1.29	1	1	0	7	6	1	1	0	7
Ben Weber	0	0	3.38	3	0	0	3	3	1	1	0	3
Kevin Appier	0	1	3.48	2	2	0	10	10	4	4	4	3
Ramon Ortiz	1	0	5.06	1	1	0	5	10	3	3	1	3
Brendan Donnelly	0	0	8.10	3	0	0	3	3	3	3	0	5
Totals	4	1	2.45	5	5	2	44	37	12	12	7	38

MINNESOTA

Player, Pos.	AVG	G	AB	R	H	2B	3B	HR	RBI	BB	SO	SB
Dustan Mohr, rf-ph	.417	5	12	3	5	1	0	0	0	0	4	1
Matt LeCroy, dh	.333	1	3	0	1	0	0	0	0	1	0	0
David Ortiz, dh-ph	.313	5	16	0	5	1	0	0	2	0	5	0
Corey Koskie, 3b	.278	5	18	3	5	2	0	0	2	2	8	0
Doug Mientkiewicz, 1b	.278	5	18	1	5	1	0	0	2	1	2	0
A.J. Pierzynski, c	.250	5	16	1	4	0	0	0	2	0	2	0
Luis Rivas, 2b	.250	5	12	1	3	0	0	0	0	1	3	0
Michael Cuddyer, rf	.200	3	5	0	1	0	0	0	0	1	1	0
Torii Hunter, cf	.167	5	18	2	3	2	0	0	0	1	3	0
Cristian Guzman, ss	.167	5	18	1	3	1	0	0	0	0	3	0
Jacque Jones, lf	.100	5	20	0	2	1	0	0	2	0	4	0
Tom Prince, c	.000	1	1	0	0	0	0	0	0	0	0	0
David Lamb, 2b	.000	2	0	0	0	0	0	0	0	0	0	0
Bobby Kielty, ph-rf	.000	4	3	0	0	0	0	0	0	1	1	0
Totals	.231	5	160	12	37	9	0	0	11	7	38	1

Pitcher	W	L	ERA	G	GS	SV	IP	H	R	ER	BB	SO
Eddie Guardado	0	0	0.00	1	0	1	1	0	0	0	1	2
Kyle Lohse	0	0	0.00	1	0	0	1	0	0	0	0	1
Eric Milton	0	0	1.50	1	1	0	6	5	1	1	2	4
Joe Mays	1	0	2.03	2	2	0	13	12	4	3	0	8
Brad Radke	0	1	2.70	1	1	0	7	5	2	2	1	4
Rick Reed	0	1	6.75	1	1	0	5	8	6	4	0	0
Bob Wells	0	0	9.00	2	0	0	1	2	1	1	0	2
Johan Santana	0	1	10.80	4	0	0	3	4	4	4	0	4
LaTroy Hawkins	0	0	20.25	4	0	0	1	4	3	3	1	1
J.C. Romero	0	1	22.50	4	0	0	2	4	5	5	2	3
Mike Jackson	0	0	27.00	3	0	0	1	5	3	3	2	2
Totals	1	4	5.57	5	5	1	42	49	29	26	9	26

SCORE BY INNINGS

Anaheim	142	022	(12)60—29
Minnesota	120	013	401—12

E—Eckstein, Guzman. DP—Anaheim 4, Minnesota 4. LOB—Anaheim 29, Minnesota 28. CS—Spiezio, Anderson, Pierzynski. SH— Gil, Kennedy, Hunter, Guzman. SF—Pierzynski, Jones. HBP—Eckstein (by Wells), B. Molina (by Radke), Guzman (by Donnelly). IBB—Spiezio (by Jackson). WP—Appier 2, Donnelly, Rodriguez, Santana 2, Romero.

	W	L	ERA	G	GS	SV	IP	H	R	ER	BB	SO
Barry Zito	1	0	4.50	1	1	0	6	5	3	3	4	8
Tim Hudson	0	1	6.23	2	2	0	9	13	11	6	4	8
Cory Lidle	0	0	9.00	1	0	0	1	2	1	1	0	0
Billy Koch	0	0	9.00	3	0	1	3	5	3	3	2	3
Ted Lilly	0	1	13.50	2	0	0	4	10	6	6	1	3
Totals	2	3	4.50	5	5	1	44	52	27	22	14	42

SCORE BY INNINGS

Minnesota	025	824	303—27
Oakland	823	611	203—26

E—Guzman, Koskie, Jones, Pierzynski, Ellis, Hatteberg, Tejada. DP—Minnesota 1, Oakland 4. LOB—Minnesota 39, Oakland 39. SH—Guzman, Rivas. SF—Tejada. HBP—Jones (by Hudson), Koskie (by Bradford), Durham (by Mays). IBB—Cuddyer (by Mulder), Chavez (by Mays). WP—Fiore, Hudson, Lilly, Mulder, Zito.

CHAMPIONSHIP SERIES

ANAHEIM VS. MINNESOTA

COMPOSITE BOX

ANAHEIM

Player, Pos.	AVG	G	AB	R	H	2B	3B	HR	RBI	BB	SO	SB
Chone Figgins, pr	1.000	3	1	2	1	0	0	0	0	0	0	0
Darin Erstad, cf	.364	5	22	4	8	0	0	1	2	0	3	1
Adam Kennedy, 2b	.357	4	14	5	5	0	0	3	5	0	2	0

BY GEOFF WILSON

Sure, Barry Bonds set the single-season home run mark in 2001. Sure, he'll be in the Hall of Fame. But there were still plenty of things he hadn't accomplished.

Like Ted Williams, he hadn't managed to have a successful postseason. Unlike the Splendid Splinter, he hadn't won a batting title. And after one of the best offensive seasons ever to go with his 73 bombs in 2001— all coming as he became a free agent—the hometown Giants were the only team that showed interest in him.

Such were the knocks on Barry Bonds coming into the '02 season. But after his performance, his résumé is almost complete. Bonds set three more major league records and posted an even better season in San Francisco, leading the Giants to their first World Series appearance in 13 years.

Bonds was back in San Francisco after no other teams showed serious interest in signing the 37-year-old left fielder during the offseason. After signing for four more years and $72 million, Bonds carried the Giants offensively yet again in 2002.

By hitting a career-best .370, Bonds became the oldest player to win his first batting title and shattered the major league marks for single-season on-base percentage (.582), walks (198) and intentional walks (68). And he followed up his 500th homer in 2001 with his 600th in 2002, adding nine more steals to get within six of becoming the first player ever with 500 homers and 500 steals.

No Ring, But A Pennant

To top it off, the Giants became just the second National League wild card winner, after the Marlins in 1997, to make it to the World Series. They dispatched the Braves in five games in the first round, ending what may have been Atlanta's most successful regular season during its 11-year run at the top of its division. And in the NL Championship Series, they steamrolled the Cardinals, who had knocked off the defending World Series champ Diamondbacks in their NL Division Series and were the sentimental favorites after their tragic summer.

As during the regular season, it was Bonds who set the pace—even if that pace was a leisurely stroll to first base.

Benito Santiago

In San Francisco's 10 games against Atlanta and St. Louis, opposing pitchers walked Bonds intentionally five times. When they didn't, he was hitting balls out of various parts of the park, clubbing three home runs in the series against the Braves and one against the Cardinals. Including the World Series, he hit .356 with eight homers, 16 RBIs and 27 walks (13 intentional).

But while Bonds shined individually, it was a team effort that put the Giants in the Fall Classic. Unheralded players like NLCS MVP Benito Santiago and leadoff man Kenny Lofton—acquired from the White Sox in a trade deadline deal—helped spur the Giants' playoff run.

"When you play this game long enough, you realize personal things don't mean as much," said first baseman

Barry Bonds: Set three major league records in 2002

J.T. Snow, who had a better postseason than regular season at the plate. "It's all about winning. People are going to remember championships. They're not going to know 10 or 15 years down the road what your batting average was or how many home runs you had. We played like champions against the Braves, and we played like champions against the Cardinals."

A Long Season

St. Louis ran out of gas by the middle of October, but not before making a magical run to the NLCS. Injuries decimated the Cardinals pitching staff from spring training, when troubled lefthander Rick Ankiel's return from control problems was derailed by an arm injury that kept him out the entire season. But that was just the beginning.

Longtime Cardinals announcer Jack Buck, who had been fighting cancer for several years and was hospitalized for several months, died on June 18. The loss clearly affected the team, which held a brief ceremony at Busch Stadium a few days after Buck's death before heading to Chicago for a series against the Cubs.

NATIONAL LEAGUE CHAMPIONS, 1901-2002

Year	PENNANT	PCT	GA		Year	PENNANT	PCT	GA	MVP
1901	Pittsburgh	.647	1½		1935	Chicago	.649	4	Gabby Hartnett, c, Chicago
1902	Pittsburgh	.741	27½		1936	New York	.597	5	Carl Hubbell, lhp, New York
1903	Pittsburgh	.650	6½		1937	New York	.625	3	Joe Medwick, of, St. Louis
1904	New York	.693	13		1938	Chicago	.586	2	Ernie Lombardi, c, Cincinnati
1905	New York	.686	9		1939	Cincinnati	.630	4½	Bucky Walters, rhp, Cincinnati
1906	Chicago	.763	20		1940	Cincinnati	.654	12	Frank McCormick, 1b, Cincinnati
1907	Chicago	.704	17		1941	Brooklyn	.649	2½	Dolf Camilli, 1b, Brooklyn
1908	Chicago	.643	1		1942	St. Louis	.688	2	Mort Cooper, rhp, St. Louis
1909	Pittsburgh	.724	6½		1943	St. Louis	.682	18	Stan Musial, of, St. Louis
1910	Chicago	.675	13		1944	St. Louis	.682	14½	Marty Marion, ss, St. Louis
1911	New York	.647	7½		1945	Chicago	.636	3	Phil Cavarretta, 1b, Chicago
1912	New York	.682	10		1946	St. Louis	.628	2	Stan Musial, 1b, St. Louis
1913	New York	.664	12½		1947	Brooklyn	.610	5	Bob Elliott, 3b, Boston
1914	Boston	.614	10½		1948	Boston	.595	6½	Stan Musial, of, St. Louis
1915	Philadelphia	.592	7		1949	Brooklyn	.630	1	Jackie Robinson, 2b, Brooklyn
1916	Brooklyn	.610	2½		1950	Philadelphia	.591	2	Jim Konstanty, rhp, Philadelphia
1917	New York	.636	10		1951	New York	.624	1	Roy Campanella, c, Brooklyn
1918	Chicago	.651	10½		1952	Brooklyn	.627	4½	Hank Sauer, of, Chicago
1919	Cincinnati	.686	9		1953	Brooklyn	.682	13	Roy Campanella, c, Brooklyn
1920	Brooklyn	.604	7		1954	New York	.630	5	Willie Mays, of, New York
1921	New York	.614	4		1955	Brooklyn	.641	13½	Roy Campanella, c, Brooklyn
1922	New York	.604	7		1956	Brooklyn	.604	1	Don Newcombe, rhp, Brooklyn
1923	New York	.621	4½		1957	Milwaukee	.617	8	Hank Aaron, of, Milwaukee
1924	New York	.608	1½		1958	Milwaukee	.597	8	Ernie Banks, ss, Chicago
1925	Pittsburgh	.621	8½		1959	Los Angeles	.564	2	Ernie Banks, ss, Chicago
1926	St. Louis	.578	2		1960	Pittsburgh	.617	7	Dick Groat, ss, Pittsburgh
1927	Pittsburgh	.610	1½		1961	Cincinnati	.604	4	Frank Robinson, of, Cincinnati
1928	St. Louis	.617	2		1962	San Francisco	.624	1	Maury Wills, ss, Los Angeles
1929	Chicago	.645	10½		1963	Los Angeles	.611	6	Sandy Koufax, lhp, Los Angeles
1930	St. Louis	.597	2		1964	St. Louis	.574	1	Ken Boyer, 3b, St. Louis
1931	St. Louis	.656	13		1965	Los Angeles	.599	2	Willie Mays, of, San Francisco
1932	Chicago	.584	4		1966	Los Angeles	.586	1½	Roberto Clemente, of, Pittsburgh
1933	New York	.599	5		1967	St. Louis	.627	10½	Orlando Cepeda, 1b, St. Louis
1934	St. Louis	.621	2		1968	St. Louis	.599	9	Bob Gibson, rhp, St. Louis

Year	EAST	PCT	GA	WEST	PCT	GA	PENNANT		MVP
1969	New York	.617	8	Atlanta	.574	3	New York	3-0	Willie McCovey, 1b, San Francisco
1970	Pittsburgh	.549	5	Cincinnati	.630	14½	Cincinnati	3-0	Johnny Bench, c, Cincinnati
1971	Pittsburgh	.599	7	San Francisco	.556	1	Pittsburgh	3-1	Joe Torre, 3b, St. Louis
1972	Pittsburgh	.619	11	Cincinnati	.617	10½	Cincinnati	3-2	Johnny Bench, c, Cincinnati
1973	New York	.509	1½	Cincinnati	.611	3½	New York	3-2	Pete Rose, of, Cincinnati
1974	Pittsburgh	.543	1½	Los Angeles	.630	4	Los Angeles	3-1	Steve Garvey, 1b, Los Angeles
1975	Pittsburgh	.571	6½	Cincinnati	.667	20	Cincinnati	3-0	Joe Morgan, 2b, Cincinnati
1976	Philadelphia	.623	9	Cincinnati	.630	10	Cincinnati	3-0	Joe Morgan, 2b, Cincinnati
1977	Philadelphia	.623	5	Los Angeles	.605	10	Los Angeles	3-1	George Foster, of, Cincinnati
1978	Philadelphia	.556	1½	Los Angeles	.586	2½	Los Angeles	3-1	Dave Parker, of, Pittsburgh
1979	Pittsburgh	.605	2	Cincinnati	.559	1½	Pittsburgh	3-0	Hernandez, St. Louis; Stargell, Pittsburgh
1980	Philadelphia	.562	1	Houston	.571	1	Philadelphia	3-2	Mike Schmidt, 3b, Philadelphia
1981	Montreal*	.566	½	Los Angeles**	.632	½	Los Angeles	3-2	Mike Schmidt, 3b, Philadelphia
	Philadelphia	.618	1½	Houston	.623	1			
1982	St. Louis	.568	3	Atlanta	.549	1	St. Louis	3-0	Dale Murphy, of, Atlanta
1983	Philadelphia	.556	6	Los Angeles	.562	3	Philadelphia	3-1	Dale Murphy, of, Atlanta
1984	Chicago	.596	6½	San Diego	.568	12	San Diego	3-2	Ryne Sandberg, 2b, Chicago
1985	St. Louis	.623	3	Los Angeles	.586	5½	St. Louis	4-2	Willie McGee, of, St. Louis
1986	New York	.667	21½	Houston	.593	10	New York	4-2	Mike Schmidt, 3b, Philadelphia
1987	St. Louis	.586	3	San Francisco	.556	6	St. Louis	4-3	Andre Dawson, of, Chicago
1988	New York	.625	15	Los Angeles	.584	7	Los Angeles	4-3	Kirk Gibson, of, Los Angeles
1989	Chicago	.571	6	San Francisco	.568	3	San Francisco	4-1	Kevin Mitchell, of, San Francisco
1990	Pittsburgh	.586	4	Cincinnati	.562	5	Cincinnati	4-2	Barry Bonds, of, Pittsburgh
1991	Pittsburgh	.605	14	Atlanta	.580	1	Atlanta	4-3	Terry Pendleton, 3b, Atlanta
1992	Pittsburgh	.593	9	Atlanta	.605	8	Atlanta	4-3	Barry Bonds, of, Pittsburgh
1993	Philadelphia	.599	3	Atlanta	.642	1	Philadelphia	4-2	Barry Bonds, of, San Francisco

* Won second half; defeated Philadelphia 3-2 in best-of-5 playoff. ** Won first half; defeated Houston 3-2 in best-of-5 playoff.

Year	EAST	PCT	GA	CENTRAL	PCT	GA	WEST	PCT	GA	WILD CARD	PCT
1994	Montreal	.649	6	Cincinnati	.593	½	Los Angeles	.509	3½	None	
	PENNANT: None (season incomplete)						MVP: Jeff Bagwell, 1b, Houston				
1995	Atlanta	.625	21	Cincinnati	.590	9	Los Angeles	.542	1	Colorado (West)	.535
	PENNANT: Atlanta def. Cincinnati, 4-2						MVP: Barry Larkin, ss, Cincinnati				
1996	Atlanta	.593	8	St. Louis	.543	6	San Diego	.562	1	L.A. (West)	.556
	PENNANT: Atlanta def. St. Louis 4-3						MVP: Ken Caminiti, 3b, Houston				
1997	Atlanta	.623	9	Houston	.519	5	San Francisco	.556	2	Florida (East)	.568
	PENNANT: Florida def. Atlanta 4-2						MVP: Larry Walker, of, Colorado				
1998	Atlanta	.654	18	Houston	.630	12½	San Diego	.605	9½	Chicago (Central)	.552
	PENNANT: San Diego def. Atlanta 4-2						MVP: Sammy Sosa, of, Chicago				
1999	Atlanta	.636	6½	Houston	.599	1½	Arizona	.617	14	New York (East)	.595
	PENNANT: Atlanta def. New York 4-2						MVP: Chipper Jones, 3b, Atlanta				
2000	Atlanta	.586	1	St. Louis	.586	10	San Francisco	.599	11	New York (East)	.580
	PENNANT: New York def. St. Louis 4-1						MVP: Jeff Kent, 2b, San Francisco				
2001	Atlanta	.543	2	Houston	.574	—	Arizona	.599	11	St. Louis (Central)	.574
	PENNANT: Arizona def. Atlanta 4-1						MVP: Barry Bonds, of, San Francisco				
2002	Atlanta	.631	19	St. Louis	.599	13	Arizona	.605	2½	San Francisco (West)	.590
	PENNANT: San Francisco def. St. Louis 4-1						MVP: Barry Bonds, of, San Francisco				

STANDINGS

Page	EAST	W	L	PCT	GB	Manager	General Manager	Attendance	Avg.	Last Penn.
64	Atlanta Braves	101	59	.631	—	Bobby Cox	John Schuerholz	2,603,484	32,141	1999
179	Montreal Expos	83	79	.512	19	Frank Robinson	Omar Minaya	812,045	10,025	None
210	Philadelphia Phillies	80	81	.497	21½	Larry Bowa	Ed Wade	1,618,467	20,486	1993
138	Florida Marlins	79	83	.488	23	Jeff Torborg	Larry Beinfest	813,118	10,038	1997
195	New York Mets	75	86	.466	26½	Bobby Valentine	Steve Phillips	2,804,838	35,959	2000
Page	**CENTRAL**	**W**	**L**	**PCT**	**GB**	**Manager(s)**	**General Manager**	**Attendance**	**Avg.**	**Last Penn.**
224	St. Louis Cardinals	97	65	.599	—	Tony La Russa	Walt Jocketty	3,011,756	37,182	1987
145	Houston Astros	84	78	.519	13	Jimy Williams	Gerry Hunsicker	2,517,357	31,078	None
107	Cincinnati Reds	78	84	.481	19	Bob Boone	Jim Bowden	1,855,787	23,197	1990
217	Pittsburgh Pirates	72	89	.447	24½	Lloyd McClendon	Dave Littlefield	1,784,988	22,594	1979
100	Chicago Cubs	67	95	.414	30	D. Baylor/B. Kimm	A. MacPhail/J. Hendry	2,693,096	34,526	1945
165	Milwaukee Brewers	56	106	.346	41	D. Lopes/J. Royster	Dean Taylor	1,969,153	24,310	None
Page	**WEST**	**W**	**L**	**PCT**	**GB**	**Manager(s)**	**General Manager**	**Attendance**	**Avg.**	**Last Penn.**
64	Arizona Diamondbacks	98	64	.605	—	Bob Brenly	Joe Garagiola Jr.	3,198,977	39,493	2001
239	*San Francisco Giants	95	66	.590	2½	Dusty Baker	Brian Sabean	3,253,203	40,163	2002
158	Los Angeles Dodgers	92	70	.568	6	Jim Tracy	Dan Evans	3,131,255	38,657	1988
123	Colorado Rockies	73	89	.451	25	B. Bell/C. Hurdle	Dan O'Dowd	2,737,838	33,800	None
231	San Diego Padres	66	96	.407	32	Bruce Bochy	Kevin Towers	2,220,601	27,414	1998

*Won wild-card playoff berth

NOTE: Team's individual batting, pitching and fielding statistics can be found on page indicated in lefthand column.

Then, before a Saturday afternoon game at Wrigley Field, righthander Darryl Kile didn't show up. When hotel workers at the Westin Hotel forced their way into Kile's room, they found the 33-year-old had died in his sleep.

"He made sure he gave something back," said former teammate Doug Drabek. "And if he gave something first, he didn't want anything back."

"The losses that we've had are never going to leave us," outfielder Jim Edmonds said. "It's not every day stuff like that happens. There's definitely some bittersweet to it."

In a testament to the Cardinals' resilience, they trudged through the Sunday game—which Kile had been scheduled to start—and did their best to regroup for the stretch run in the NL Central. And despite having to use 26 pitchers during the season, Tony La Russa's troops help up and held off the Astros and Reds in the division race.

Behind the improved command and hammer curve from righthander Matt Morris—who learned his hook from Kile—as well as the deadline deal for third baseman Scott Rolen, St. Louis avenged its loss to the Diamondbacks in the 2001 playoffs, beating Randy Johnson and Curt Schilling in the first two games. Rolen's shoulder injury in Game Two, however sidelined him for the NLCS, and the team's star-crossed season ended at Pac Bell Park.

"We came to play every day," catcher Mike Matheny said. "We never made excuses, when even fans and media in St. Louis and around the nation were willing to put those excuses on a platter for us. We never ran from what happened to us. Our response was to compete as hard as we could."

Dominance, Disappointment In Desert

Through the regular season, the Diamondbacks looked more than prepared to defend their World Series title. Behind the incomparable one-two punch of Johnson (24-5, 2.32 with 334 strikeouts in a league-leading 260 innings) and Schilling (23-7, 3.23 with a jaw-dropping 316-33 strikeout-to-walk ratio in 259 innings), Arizona overtook Los Angeles shortly after the all-star break and held off San Francisco in the West.

Johnson's and Schilling's dominance—at one point, Schilling had 21 wins and just 20 walks—evoked memories of another NL West dynamic duo from pitching's

Darryle Kile: His death, at age 33, stunned baseball

LARRY GOREN

golden age.

"I played with Sandy Koufax and Don Drysdale, and I have to say Curt and Randy are comparable," Arizona manager Bob Brenly said. "I mean it. They both work and prepare so hard it amazes me."

"The man throws strikes and is a model of mechanics," Reds manager Bob Boone said of Schilling. "You want to learn how to pitch perfectly? Put in a tape of him and there it is."

Johnson wasn't too shabby either, registering 300-plus strikeouts for the fifth straight season and the sixth time in his career. He also won the NL pitching triple crown, but he grew tired of all the talk about strikeouts.

"It's an indicator of dominance, but what's (more)

NL YEAR-BY-YEAR BATTING LEADERS

Year	Batting Average	Home Runs	RBIs
1901	Jesse Burkett, St. Louis .382	Sam Crawford, Cincinnati 16	Honus Wagner, Pittsburgh 126
1902	Ginger Beaumont, Pitt. .357	Tom Leach, Pittsburgh 6	Honus Wagner, Pittsburgh 91
1903	Honus Wagner, Pittsburgh .355	Jim Sheckard, Brooklyn 9	Sam Mertes, New York 104
1904	Honus Wagner, Pittsburgh .349	Harry Lumley, Brooklyn 9	Bill Dahlen, New York 80
1905	Cy Seymour, Cincinnati .377	Fred Odwell, Cincinnati 9	Cy Seymour, Cincinnati 121
1906	Honus Wagner, Pittsburgh .339	Tim Jordan, Brooklyn 12	Two tied at 83
1907	Honus Wagner, Pittsburgh .350	Dave Brain, Boston 10	Sherry Magee, Philadelphia 85
1908	Honus Wagner, Pittsburgh .354	Tim Jordan, Brooklyn 12	Honus Wagner, Pittsburgh 109
1909	Honus Wagner, Pittsburgh .339	Red Murray, New York 7	Honus Wagner, Pittsburgh 100
1910	Sherry Magee, Phil. .331	Two tied at 10	Sherry Magee, Philadelphia 123
1911	Honus Wagner, Pittsburgh .334	Wildfire Schulte, Chicago 21	Wildfire Schulte, Chicago 121
1912	Heinie Zimmerman, Chi. .372	Heinie Zimmerman, Chicago 14	Heinie Zimmerman, Chicago 103
1913	Jake Daubert, Brooklyn .350	Gavvy Cravath, Philadelphia 19	Gavvy Cravath, Philadelphia 128
1914	Jake Daubert, Brooklyn .329	Gavvy Cravath, Philadelphia 19	Sherry Magee, Philadelphia 103
1915	Larry Doyle, New York .320	Gavvy Cravath, Philadelphia 24	Gavvy Cravath, Philadelphia 115
1916	Hal Chase, Cincinnati .339	Two tied at 12	Heinie Zimmerman, Chi.-N.Y. 83
1917	Edd Roush, Cincinnati .341	Gavvy Cravath, Philadelphia 12	Heinie Zimmerman, N.Y. 102
1918	Zack Wheat, Brooklyn .335	Gavvy Cravath, Philadelphia 8	Sherry Magee, Cincinnati 76
1919	Edd Roush, Cincinnati .321	Gavvy Cravath, Philadelphia 12	Hy Myers, Brooklyn 73
1920	Rogers Hornsby, St. Louis .370	Cy Williams, Philadelphia 15	Rogers Hornsby, St. Louis 94
1921	Rogers Hornsby, St. Louis .397	George Kelly, New York 23	Rogers Hornsby, St. Louis 126
1922	Rogers Hornsby, St. Louis .401	Rogers Hornsby, St. Louis 42	Rogers Hornsby, St. Louis 155
1923	Rogers Hornsby, St. Louis .384	Cy Williams, Philadelphia 41	Emil Meusel, New York 125
1924	Rogers Hornsby, St. Louis .424	Jack Fournier, Brooklyn 27	George Kelly, New York 136
1925	Rogers Hornsby, St. Louis .403	Rogers Hornsby, St. Louis 39	Rogers Hornsby, St. Louis 143
1926	Bubbles Hargrave, Cin. .353	Hack Wilson, Chicago 21	Jim Bottomley, St. Louis 121
1927	Paul Waner, Pittsburgh .380	Two tied at 30	Paul Waner, Pittsburgh 131
1928	Rogers Hornsby, St. Louis .370	Two tied at 31	Jim Bottomley, St. Louis 136
1929	Lefty O'Doul, Philadelphia .398	Chuck Klein, Chicago 43	Hack Wilson, Chicago 159
1930	Bill Terry, New York .401	Hack Wilson, Chicago 56	Hack Wilson, Chicago 190
1931	Chick Hafey, St. Louis .349	Chuck Klein, Philadelphia 31	Chuck Klein, Philadelphia 121
1932	Lefty O'Doul, Brooklyn .368	Two tied at 38	Frank Hurst, Philadelphia 143
1933	Chuck Klein, Philadelphia .368	Chuck Klein, Philadelphia 28	Chuck Klein, Philadelphia 120
1934	Paul Waner, Pittsburgh .362	Mel Ott, New York 35	Mel Ott, New York 135
1935	Arky Vaughan, Pittsburgh .385	Wally Berger, Boston 34	Wally Berger, Boston 130
1936	Paul Waner, Pittsburgh .373	Mel Ott, New York 33	Joe Medwick, St. Louis 138
1937	Joe Medwick, St. Louis .374	Two tied at 31	Joe Medwick, St. Louis 154
1938	Ernie Lombardi, Cincinnati .342	Mel Ott, New York 36	Frank McCormick, Cincinnati 122
1939	Johnny Mize, St. Louis .349	Johnny Mize, St. Louis 28	Frank McCormick, Cincinnati 128
1940	Debs Garms, Pittsburgh .355	Johnny Mize, St. Louis 43	Johnny Mize, St. Louis 137
1941	Pete Reiser, Brooklyn .343	Dolf Camilli, Brooklyn 34	Dolf Camilli, Brooklyn 120
1942	Ernie Lombardi, Boston .330	Mel Ott, New York 30	Johnny Mize, New York 110
1943	Stan Musial, St. Louis .357	Bill Nicholson, Chicago 29	Bill Nicholson, Chicago 128
1944	Dixie Walker, Brooklyn .357	Bill Nicholson, Chicago 33	Bill Nicholson, Chicago 122
1945	Phil Cavarretta, Chicago .355	Tommy Holmes, Boston 28	Dixie Walker, Brooklyn 124
1946	Stan Musial, St. Louis .365	Ralph Kiner, Pittsburgh 23	Enos Slaughter, St. Louis 130
1947	Harry Walker, St.L.-Phil. .363	Two tied at 51	Johnny Mize, New York 138
1948	Stan Musial, St. Louis .376	Two tied at 40	Two tied at 131
1949	Jackie Robinson, Brooklyn .342	Ralph Kiner, Pittsburgh 54	Ralph Kiner, Pittsburgh 127
1950	Stan Musial, St. Louis .346	Ralph Kiner, Pittsburgh 47	Del Ennis, Philadelphia 126
1951	Stan Musial, St. Louis .355	Ralph Kiner, Pittsburgh 42	Monte Irvin, New York 121
1952	Stan Musial, St. Louis .336	Two tied at 37	Hank Sauer, Chicago 121
1953	Carl Furillo, Brooklyn .344	Eddie Mathews, Milwaukee 47	Roy Campanella, Brooklyn 142
1954	Willie Mays, New York .345	Ted Kluszewski, Cincinnati 49	Ted Kluszewski, Cincinnati 141
1955	Richie Ashburn, Phil. .338	Willie Mays, New York 51	Duke Snider, Brooklyn 136
1956	Hank Aaron, Milwaukee .328	Duke Snider, Brooklyn 43	Stan Musial, St. Louis 109
1957	Stan Musial, St. Louis .351	Hank Aaron, Milwaukee 44	Hank Aaron, Milwaukee 132
1958	Richie Ashburn, Phil. .350	Ernie Banks, Chicago 47	Ernie Banks, Chicago 129
1959	Hank Aaron, Milwaukee .355	Eddie Mathews, Milwaukee 46	Ernie Banks, Chicago 143
1960	Dick Groat, Pittsburgh .325	Ernie Banks, Chicago 41	Hank Aaron, Milwaukee 126
1961	Roberto Clemente, Pitt. .351	Orlando Cepeda, S.F. 46	Orlando Cepeda, S.F. 142
1962	Tommy Davis, L.A. .346	Willie Mays, San Francisco 49	Tommy Davis, Los Angeles 153
1963	Tommy Davis, L.A. .326	Hank Aaron, Milwaukee 44	Hank Aaron, Milwaukee 130
1964	Roberto Clemente, Pitt. .339	Willie Mays, San Francisco 47	Ken Boyer, St. Louis 119
1965	Roberto Clemente, Pitt. .329	Willie Mays, San Francisco 52	Deron Johnson, Cincinnati 130
1966	Matty Alou, Pittsburgh .342	Hank Aaron, Atlanta 44	Hank Aaron, Atlanta 127
1967	Roberto Clemente, Pitt. .357	Hank Aaron, Atlanta 39	Orlando Cepeda, S.F. 111
1968	Pete Rose, Cincinnati .335	Willie McCovey, S.F. 36	Willie McCovey, S.F. 105
1969	Pete Rose, Cincinnati .348	Willie McCovey, S.F. 45	Willie McCovey, S.F. 126
1970	Rico Carty, Atlanta .366	Johnny Bench, Cincinnati 45	Johnny Bench, Cincinnati 148
1971	Joe Torre, St. Louis .363	Willie Stargell, Pittsburgh 48	Joe Torre, St. Louis 137
1972	Billy Williams, Chicago .333	Johnny Bench, Cincinnati 40	Johnny Bench, Cincinnati 125
1973	Pete Rose, Cincinnati .338	Willie Stargell, Pittsburgh 44	Willie Stargell, Pittsburgh 119
1974	Ralph Garr, Atlanta .353	Mike Schmidt, Philadelphia 36	Johnny Bench, Cincinnati 129
1975	Bill Madlock, Chicago .354	Mike Schmidt, Philadelphia 38	Greg Luzinski, Philadelphia 120
1976	Bill Madlock, Chicago .339	Mike Schmidt, Philadelphia 38	George Foster, Cincinnati 121
1977	Dave Parker, Pittsburgh .338	George Foster, Cincinnati 52	George Foster, Cincinnati 149
1978	Dave Parker, Pittsburgh .334	George Foster, Cincinnati 40	George Foster, Cincinnati 120
1979	Keith Hernandez, St. Louis .344	Dave Kingman, Chicago 48	Dave Winfield, San Diego 118
1980	Bill Buckner, Chicago .324	Mike Schmidt, Philadelphia 48	Mike Schmidt, Philadelphia 121
1981	Bill Madlock, Pittsburgh .341	Mike Schmidt, Philadelphia 31	Mike Schmidt, Philadelphia 91
1982	Al Oliver, Montreal .331	Dave Kingman, New York 37	Dale Murphy, Atlanta 109
1983	Bill Madlock, Pittsburgh .323	Mike Schmidt, Philadelphia 40	Dale Murphy, Atlanta 121
1984	Tony Gwynn, San Diego .351	Dale Murphy, Atlanta 36	Two tied at 106
1985	Willie McGee, St. Louis .353	Dale Murphy, Atlanta 37	Dave Parker, Cincinnati 125
1986	Tim Raines, Montreal .334	Mike Schmidt, Philadelphia 37	Mike Schmidt, Philadelphia 119
1987	Tony Gwynn, San Diego .370	Andre Dawson, Chicago 49	Andre Dawson, Chicago 137
1988	Tony Gwynn, San Diego .313	Darryl Strawberry, New York 39	Will Clark, San Francisco 109
1989	Tony Gwynn, San Diego .336	Kevin Mitchell, San Francisco 47	Kevin Mitchell, S.F. 125
1990	Willie McGee, St. Louis .335	Ryne Sandberg, Chicago 40	Matt Williams, S.F. 122
1991	Terry Pendleton, Atlanta .319	Howard Johnson, New York 38	Howard Johnson, New York 117
1992	Gary Sheffield, San Diego .330	Fred McGriff, San Diego 35	Darren Daulton, Philadelphia 109
1993	Andres Galarraga, Colo. .370	Barry Bonds, San Francisco 46	Barry Bonds, San Francisco 123
1994	Tony Gwynn, San Diego .394	Matt Williams, San Francisco 43	Jeff Bagwell, Houston 116
1995	Tony Gwynn, San Diego .368	Dante Bichette, Colorado 40	Dante Bichette, Colorado 128
1996	Tony Gwynn, San Diego .353	Andres Galarraga, Colorado 47	Andres Galarraga, Colorado 150
1997	Tony Gwynn, San Diego .372	Larry Walker, Colorado 49	Andres Galarraga, Colorado 140
1998	Larry Walker, Colorado .363	Mark McGwire, St. Louis 70	Sammy Sosa, Chicago 158
1999	Larry Walker, Colorado .379	Mark McGwire, St. Louis 65	Mark McGwire, St. Louis 147
2000	Todd Helton, Colorado .372	Sammy Sosa, Chicago 50	Todd Helton, Colorado 147
2001	Larry Walker, Colorado .350	Barry Bonds, San Francisco 73	Sammy Sosa, Chicago 160
2002	Barry Bonds, San Francisco .370	Sammy Sosa, Chicago 49	Lance Berkman, Houston 128

dominating?" Johnson asked early in the season. "Striking out 300, or striking out 200 and winning 20 or 25 games?" Somehow, he managed to do both and establish a new personal high in wins.

He was tagged for six runs (five earned) in six innings during Game One of the Division Series, though, and Schilling couldn't get the win in a close Game Two. In truth, Arizona's chances at a repeat probably disappeared when No. 3 hitter Luis Gonzalez separated his shoulder in an outfield collision Sept. 23. The Diamondbacks managed just six runs in their three playoff games against the Cardinals.

11th Heaven . . . And Hell

Arizona wasn't the only favorite to go out in the first round. The Braves posted the NL's best record and dusted off their nearest NL East competitor (the surprising Expos) by 19 games on the way to an unprecedented 11th consecutive division title.

But in the end, the 2002 season will be remembered in Atlanta more for blowing a 2-1 Division Series lead against San Francisco. It was reminiscent of 1996, when the Braves led the Yankees 2-1 in the World Series and 6-3 in Game Four before Jim Leyritz' homer off Mark Wohlers began a remarkable New York comeback.

"This is right up there," Chipper Jones said after the Division Series loss. "It's right up there with '96 for me. We had a team we were all confident in, and we found ways to win this sort of game all year."

Aside from the usual contributors, the Braves' 2002 success stemmed largely from Jones' transition from third base to left field, Gary Sheffield's arrival in right field and a healthy John Smoltz' move from the rotation to the bullpen.

Sheffield, who came over from the Dodgers for lefthander Odalis Perez and outfielder Brian Jordan, hit .307-25-84. Not only was he productive, but he also fit in better in the clubhouse than he had in any of his previous four stops in the majors.

"After tough losses or big wins, I don't have to take all the credit or all the blame," Sheffield said. "They've got superstars here. I just want to be part of the puzzle."

Smoltz, who came out of the bullpen in 2001 while recovering from Tommy John surgery, agreed to spend the first season of his new three-year, $30 million contract as the closer. That decision resulted in an NL-record 55 saves—just two shy of Bobby Thigpen's major league-record 57 in 1990.

And of course, there was Atlanta's answer to great pitching pairs in the form of lefthander Tom Glavine (18-11, 2.96) and righthander Greg Maddux (16-6, 2.62). Whether the Braves make it a dozen titles in 2003 will depend largely on whether Glavine and Maddux—both free agents—

Randy Johnson: Led NL in wins, ERA and strikeouts

John Smoltz: NL-record 55 saves

returned to Turner Field.

"I don't want them to go anywhere," manager Bobby Cox said of his dynastic duo. "We'd go from geniuses to idiots real quick."

"I think this team can do anything it wants to do," Glavine said. "They've got a budget they try to stick by, and I respect that. But they've always found a way to sign the people they want to sign. And whatever happens, I think it's safe to say Greg and I will be pitching somewhere next year."

Wild, Wild . . . East

As the 2002 season approached, the commissioner's office kept saying the NL East might be reduced from five teams to four, because the Expos could become a victim of contraction as baseball shrunk from 30 to 28 teams. Such talk proved to be merely wind whistling between commissioner Bud Selig's lips, but it set the stage for an unusual set of circumstances that saw several franchise swaps on the eve of spring training.

Just two days before pitchers and catchers were to report, Major League Baseball announced it had purchased the Expos from Jeffrey Loria and would keep them in Montreal for the 2002 season. Loria, in turn, bought the Marlins from John Henry, who in turn bought the Red Sox and divested himself of his minority interest in the Yankees.

It didn't seem to bother the Expos and Marlins—at least on the field. Before the Braves set a torrid pace beginning in June, all five teams in the East hovered around .500. The Marlins and Expos sat one-two in the division as late as mid-May.

From there, the Marlins struggled more—both on and off the field. While no one expected Montreal to post great results in the standings or at the turnstiles, Florida had an exciting young team with speed (second baseman Luis Castillo), emerging power (third baseman Mike Lowell and outfielder Cliff Floyd) and strong young

NL YEAR-BY-YEAR PITCHING LEADERS

Year	Wins	W	ERA	ERA	Strikeouts	SO
1901	Bill Donovan, Brooklyn	25	Jesse Tannehill, Pittsburgh	2.18	Noodles Hahn, Cincinnati	233
1902	Jack Chesbro, Pittsburgh	28	Jack Taylor, Chicago	1.33	Vic Willis, Boston	226
1903	Joe McGinnity, New York	31	Sam Leever, Pittsburgh	2.06	Christy Mathewson, N.Y.	267
1904	Joe McGinnity, New York	35	Joe McGinnity, New York	1.61	Christy Mathewson, N.Y.	212
1905	Christy Mathewson, N.Y.	32	Christy Mathewson, N.Y.	1.27	Christy Mathewson, N.Y.	206
1906	Joe McGinnity, New York	27	Mordecai Brown, Chicago	1.04	Fred Beebe, Chi.-St.L.	171
1907	Christy Mathewson, New York	24	Jack Pfiester, Chicago	1.15	Christy Mathewson, N.Y.	178
1908	Christy Mathewson, N.Y.	37	Christy Mathewson, N.Y.	1.43	Christy Mathewson, N.Y.	259
1909	Mordecai Brown, Chicago	27	Christy Mathewson, N.Y.	1.14	Orval Overall, Chicago	205
1910	Christy Mathewson, N.Y.	27	George McQuillan, Phil.	1.60	Christy Mathewson, N.Y.	190
1911	Grover Alexander, Phil.	28	Christy Mathewson, N.Y.	1.99	Rube Marquard, New York	237
1912	Two tied at	26	Jeff Tesreau, New York	1.96	Grover Alexander, Phil.	195
1913	Tom Seaton, Philadelphia	27	Christy Mathewson, N.Y.	2.06	Tom Seaton, Philadelphia	168
1914	Two tied at	27	Bill Doak, St. Louis	1.72	Grover Alexander, Phil.	214
1915	Grover Alexander, Phil.	31	Grover Alexander, Phil.	1.22	Grover Alexander, Phil.	241
1916	Grover Alexander, Phil.	33	Grover Alexander, Phil.	1.55	Grover Alexander, Phil.	167
1917	Grover Alexander, Phil.	30	Grover Alexander, Phil.	1.85	Grover Alexander, Phil.	200
1918	Hippo Vaughn, Chicago	22	Hippo Vaughn, Chicago	1.74	Hippo Vaughn, Chicago	148
1919	Jesse Barnes, New York	25	Grover Alexander, Chicago	1.72	Hippo Vaughn, Chicago	141
1920	Grover Alexander, Chicago	27	Grover Alexander, Chicago	1.91	Grover Alexander, Chicago	173
1921	Two tied at	22	Bill Doak, St. Louis	2.58	Burleigh Grimes, Brooklyn	136
1922	Eppa Rixey, Cincinnati	25	Rosy Ryan, New York	3.00	Dazzy Vance, Brooklyn	134
1923	Dolf Luque, Cincinnati	27	Dolf Luque, Cincinnati	1.93	Dazzy Vance, Brooklyn	197
1924	Dazzy Vance, Brooklyn	28	Dazzy Vance, Brooklyn	2.16	Dazzy Vance, Brooklyn	262
1925	Dazzy Vance, Brooklyn	22	Dolf Luque, Cincinnati	2.63	Dazzy Vance, Brooklyn	221
1926	Four tied at	20	Ray Kremer, Pittsburgh	2.61	Dazzy Vance, Brooklyn	140
1927	Charlie Root, Chicago	26	Ray Kremer, Pittsburgh	2.47	Dazzy Vance, Brooklyn	184
1928	Two tied at	25	Dazzy Vance, Brooklyn	2.09	Dazzy Vance, Brooklyn	200
1929	Pat Malone, Chicago	22	Bill Walker, New York	3.08	Pat Malone, Chicago	166
1930	Two tied at	20	Dazzy Vance, Brooklyn	2.61	Bill Hallahan, St. Louis	177
1931	Three tied at	19	Bill Walker, New York	2.26	Bill Hallahan, St. Louis	159
1932	Lon Warneke, Chicago	22	Lon Warneke, Chicago	2.37	Dizzy Dean, St. Louis	191
1933	Carl Hubbell, New York	23	Carl Hubbell, New York	1.66	Dizzy Dean, St. Louis	199
1934	Dizzy Dean, St. Louis	30	Carl Hubbell, New York	2.30	Dizzy Dean, St. Louis	195
1935	Dizzy Dean, St. Louis	28	Cy Blanton, Pittsburgh	2.59	Dizzy Dean, St. Louis	182
1936	Carl Hubbell, New York	26	Carl Hubbell, New York	2.31	Van Lingle Mungo, Brooklyn	238
1937	Carl Hubbell, New York	22	Jim Turner, Boston	2.38	Carl Hubbell, New York	159
1938	Bill Lee, Chicago	22	Bill Lee, Chicago	2.66	Clay Bryant, Chicago	135
1939	Bucky Walters, Cincinnati	27	Bucky Walters, Cincinnati	2.29	Two tied at	137
1940	Bucky Walters, Cincinnati	22	Bucky Walters, Cincinnati	2.48	Kirby Higbe, Philadelphia	137
1941	Two tied at	22	Elmer Riddle, Cincinnati	2.24	Johnny Vander Meer, Cin.	202
1942	Mort Cooper, St. Louis	22	Mort Cooper, St. Louis	1.77	Johnny Vander Meer, Cin.	186
1943	Three tied at	21	Howie Pollet, St. Louis	1.75	Johnny Vander Meer, Cin.	174
1944	Bucky Walters, Cincinnati	23	Ed Heusser, Cincinnati	2.38	Bill Voiselle, New York	161
1945	Red Barrett, Bos.-St.L.	23	Hank Borowy, Chicago	2.14	Preacher Roe, Pittsburgh	148
1946	Howie Pollet, St. Louis	21	Howie Pollet, St. Louis	2.10	John Schmitz, Chicago	135
1947	Ewell Blackwell, Cincinnati	22	Warren Spahn, Boston	2.33	Ewell Blackwell, Cincinnati	193
1948	Johnny Sain, Boston	24	Harry Brecheen, St. Louis	2.24	Harry Brecheen, St. Louis	149
1949	Warren Spahn, Boston	21	Dave Koslo, New York	2.50	Warren Spahn, Boston	151
1950	Warren Spahn, Boston	21	Jim Hearn, St.L.-N.Y.	2.49	Warren Spahn, Boston	191
1951	Two tied at	23	Chet Nichols, Boston	2.88	Two tied at	164
1952	Robin Roberts, Philadelphia	28	Hoyt Wilhelm, New York	2.43	Warren Spahn, Boston	183
1953	Two tied at	23	Warren Spahn, Milwaukee	2.10	Robin Roberts, Philadelphia	198
1954	Robin Roberts, Philadelphia	23	John Antonelli, New York	2.29	Robin Roberts, Philadelphia	185
1955	Robin Roberts, Philadelphia	23	Bob Friend, Pittsburgh	2.84	Sam Jones, Chicago	198
1956	Don Newcombe, Brooklyn	27	Lew Burdette, Milwaukee	2.71	Sam Jones, Chicago	176
1957	Warren Spahn, Milwaukee	21	Johnny Podres, Brooklyn	2.66	Jack Sanford, Philadelphia	188
1958	Two tied at	22	Stu Miller, San Francisco	2.47	Sam Jones, St. Louis	225
1959	Three tied at	21	Sam Jones, San Francisco	2.82	Don Drysdale, Los Angeles	242
1960	Two tied at	21	Mike McCormick, S.F.	2.70	Don Drysdale, Los Angeles	246
1961	Two tied at	21	Warren Spahn, Milwaukee	3.01	Sandy Koufax, Los Angeles	269
1962	Don Drysdale, Los Angeles	25	Sandy Koufax, Los Angeles	2.54	Don Drysdale, Los Angeles	232
1963	Sandy Koufax, Los Angeles	25	Sandy Koufax, Los Angeles	1.88	Sandy Koufax, Los Angeles	306
1964	Larry Jackson, Chicago	24	Sandy Koufax, Los Angeles	1.74	Bob Veale, Pittsburgh	250
1965	Sandy Koufax, Los Angeles	26	Sandy Koufax, Los Angeles	2.04	Sandy Koufax, Los Angeles	382
1966	Sandy Koufax, Los Angeles	27	Sandy Koufax, Los Angeles	1.73	Sandy Koufax, Los Angeles	317
1967	Mike McCormick, S.F.	22	Phil Niekro, Atlanta	1.87	Jim Bunning, Philadelphia	253
1968	Juan Marichal, S.F.	26	Bob Gibson, St. Louis	1.12	Bob Gibson, St. Louis	268
1969	Tom Seaver, New York	25	Juan Marichal, S.F.	2.10	Ferguson Jenkins, Chicago	273
1970	Two tied at	23	Tom Seaver, New York	2.81	Tom Seaver, New York	283
1971	Ferguson Jenkins, Chicago	24	Tom Seaver, New York	1.76	Tom Seaver, New York	289
1972	Steve Carlton, Philadelphia	27	Steve Carlton, Philadelphia	1.98	Steve Carlton, Philadelphia	310
1973	Ron Bryant, San Francisco	24	Tom Seaver, New York	2.08	Tom Seaver, New York	251
1974	Two tied at	20	Buzz Capra, Atlanta	2.28	Steve Carlton, Philadelphia	240
1975	Tom Seaver, New York	23	Randy Jones, San Diego	2.24	Tom Seaver, New York	243
1976	Randy Jones, San Diego	22	John Denny, St. Louis	2.52	Tom Seaver, New York	235
1977	Steve Carlton, Philadelphia	23	John Candelaria, Pittsburgh	2.34	Phil Niekro, Atlanta	252
1978	Gaylord Perry, San Diego	21	Craig Swan, New York	2.43	J.R. Richard, Houston	303
1979	Two tied at	21	J.R. Richard, Houston	2.71	J.R. Richard, Houston	313
1980	Steve Carlton, Philadelphia	24	Don Sutton, Los Angeles	2.21	Steve Carlton, Philadelphia	286
1981	Tom Seaver, Cincinnati	14	Nolan Ryan, Houston	1.69	Fernando Valenzuela, L.A.	180
1982	Steve Carlton, Philadelphia	23	Steve Rogers, Montreal	2.40	Steve Carlton, Philadelphia	286
1983	John Denny, Philadelphia	19	Atlee Hammaker, S.F.	2.25	Steve Carlton, Philadelphia	275
1984	Joaquin Andujar, St. Louis	20	Alejandro Pena, Los Angeles	2.48	Dwight Gooden, New York	276
1985	Dwight Gooden, New York	24	Dwight Gooden, New York	1.53	Dwight Gooden, New York	268
1986	Fernando Valenzuela, L.A.	21	Mike Scott, Houston	2.22	Mike Scott, Houston	306
1987	Rick Sutcliffe, Chicago	18	Nolan Ryan, Houston	2.76	Nolan Ryan, Houston	270
1988	Two tied at	23	Joe Magrane, St. Louis	2.18	Nolan Ryan, Houston	228
1989	Mike Scott, Houston	20	Scott Garrelts, S.F.	2.28	Jose DeLeon, St. Louis	201
1990	Doug Drabek, Pittsburgh	22	Danny Darwin, Houston	2.21	David Cone, New York	233
1991	Two tied at	20	Dennis Martinez, Montreal	2.39	David Cone, New York	241
1992	Two tied at	20	Bill Swift, San Francisco	2.08	John Smoltz, Atlanta	215
1993	Two tied at	22	Greg Maddux, Atlanta	2.36	Jose Rijo, Cincinnati	227
1994	Two tied at	16	Greg Maddux, Atlanta	1.56	Andy Benes, San Diego	189
1995	Greg Maddux, Atlanta	19	Greg Maddux, Atlanta	1.63	Hideo Nomo, Los Angeles	236
1996	John Smoltz, Atlanta	24	Kevin Brown, Florida	1.89	John Smoltz, Atlanta	276
1997	Denny Neagle, Atlanta	20	Pedro Martinez, Montreal	1.90	Curt Schilling, Philadelphia	319
1998	Greg Maddux, Atlanta	20	Greg Maddux, Atlanta	2.22	Curt Schilling, Philadelphia	300
1999	Mike Hampton, Houston	22	Randy Johnson, Arizona	2.48	Randy Johnson, Arizona	364
2000	Tom Glavine, Atlanta	21	Kevin Brown, Los Angeles	2.58	Randy Johnson, Arizona	347
2001	Two tied at	22	Randy Johnson, Arizona	2.49	Randy Johnson, Arizona	372
2002	Randy Johnson, Arizona	24	Randy Johnson, Arizona	2.32	Randy Johnson, Arizona	334

Vladimir Guerrero: Missed a 40-40 season by one homer

NL: BEST TOOLS

A Baseball America survey of National League managers, conducted at midseason 2002, ranked NL players with the best tools:

BEST HITTER
1. Todd Helton, Rockies
2. Barry Bonds, Giants
3. Larry Walker, Rockies

BEST POWER
1. Barry Bonds, Giants
2. Sammy Sosa, Cubs
3. Vladimir Guerrero, Expos

BEST BUNTER
1. Luis Castillo, Marlins
2. Fernando Vina, Cardinals
3. Juan Pierre, Rockies

BEST HIT-AND-RUN BATTER
1. Placido Polanco, Cardinals/Phillies
2. Craig Counsell, Diamondbacks
3. Edgar Renteria, Cardinals

BEST BASERUNNER
1. Larry Walker, Rockies
2. Luis Castillo, Marlins
3. Jimmy Rollins, Phillies

FASTEST BASERUNNER
1. Luis Castillo, Marlins
2. Juan Pierre, Rockies
3. Rafael Furcal, Braves

BEST PITCHER
1. Curt Schilling, Diamondbacks
2. Randy Johnson, Diamondbacks
3. Tom Glavine, Braves

BEST FASTBALL
1. Randy Johnson, Diamondbacks
2. Curt Schilling, Diamondbacks
3. Billy Wagner, Astros

BEST CURVEBALL
1. Kerry Wood, Cubs
2. Matt Morris, Cardinals
3. Roy Oswalt, Astros

BEST SLIDER
1. Randy Johnson, Diamondbacks
2. Robb Nen, Giants
3. John Smoltz, Braves

BEST CHANGEUP
1. Trevor Hoffman, Padres
2. Tom Glavine, Braves
3. Greg Maddux, Braves

BEST CONTROL
1. Greg Maddux, Braves
2. Curt Schilling, Diamondbacks
3. Jon Lieber, Cubs

BEST PICKOFF MOVE
1. Brian Anderson, Diamondbacks
2. Terry Mulholland, Dodgers
3. Jamey Wright, Brewers

BEST RELIEVER
1. John Smoltz, Braves
2. Eric Gagne, Dodgers
3. Trevor Hoffman, Padres

BEST DEFENSIVE C
1. Mike Matheny, Cardinals
2. Damian Miller, Diamondbacks
3. Brad Ausmus, Astros

BEST DEFENSIVE 1B
1. J.T. Snow, Giants
2. Todd Helton, Rockies
3. Derrek Lee, Marlins

BEST DEFENSIVE 2B
1. Roberto Alomar, Mets
2. Fernando Vina, Cardinals
3. Pokey Reese, Reds

BEST DEFENSIVE 3B
1. Scott Rolen, Phillies/Cardinals
2. Mike Lowell, Marlins
3. Aaron Boone, Reds

BEST DEFENSIVE SS
1. Jimmy Rollins, Phillies
2. Rey Ordonez, Mets
3. Orlando Cabrera, Expos

BEST INFIELD ARM
1. Rafael Furcal, Braves
2. Scott Rolen, Phillies/Cardinals
3. Adrian Beltre, Dodgers

BEST DEFENSIVE OF
1. Andruw Jones, Braves
2. Jim Edmonds, Cardinals
3. Larry Walker, Rockies

BEST OUTFIELD ARM
1. Vladimir Guerrero, Expos
2. Andruw Jones, Braves
3. Larry Walker, Rockies

MOST EXCITING PLAYER
1. Vladimir Guerrero, Expos
2. Barry Bonds, Giants
3. Sammy Sosa, Cubs

BEST MANAGER
1. Bobby Cox, Braves
2. Dusty Baker, Giants
3. Tony La Russa, Cardinals

pitching (righthanders A.J. Burnett, Ryan Dempster and Josh Beckett).

But by the time the trading deadline passed, Floyd had been dealt to the Expos, Dempster was shipped off to the Reds and Beckett had missed time with a blister on his throwing hand. Castillo provided the brightest spot with a 35-game hitting streak that had people talking about whether he could reach Joe DiMaggio's immortal 56-game record.

"During the streak, when I got my first at-bat, I'd bunt sometimes just to take the pressure off," Castillo said. "That would make me more relaxed, and I'd end up with two or three hits. When I'm relaxed, I hit better."

In Montreal, Vladimir Guerrero continued to produce at a superstar level despite a dearth of media attention. With 39 homers and 40 steals to go with his .336 average, he narrowly missed becoming the fourth major leaguer to reach the 40-homer, 40-stolen base plateau.

General manager Omar Minaya, uncertain that his organization would even exist until a new labor agreement was signed, wheeled and dealed for the first half of the season. He brought in righthander Bartolo Colon (10-4, 3.31 with the Expos) from the Indians and Floyd from the Marlins before shipping Floyd to the Red Sox a few weeks later when the team's shot at the NL wild card faded. And regardless of the outcome, he got people talking baseball instead of contraction.

"We wanted to make sure we played well enough so that we got a lot of questions about what was happening on the field, not off," manager Frank Robinson said in August. "We still get those questions, but less than we thought."

The moves made by GM Steve Phillips in New York didn't help the Mets, as they sank to 11 games below .500 and a last-place finish despite a payroll in excess of $100 million.

"Any time you have a lot of changes in your personnel, it takes time to come together," catcher Mike Piazza said before the season. Despite Piazza's 33 homers and 99 RBIs—a down year for him—new additions Mo Vaughn (.259, just 10 of his 26 homers before the all-star break), Jeromy Burnitz (.215, 135 strikeouts) and Roberto Alomar (a career-low .266 average) all struggled and made the new edition of the Mets a flop.

Odds And Ends

■ It was a rough season for managers, as two were fired before the season was a month old, and a third found himself without a job by the all-star break. The Brewers were the first NL team to act, firing Davey Lopes April 18 after Milwaukee began the season 3-12. Interim manager Jerry Royster didn't fare much better: The Brewers ended the season 56-106, the franchise's worst season ever, and Royster got the boot at the end of the season in favor of Braves coach Ned Yost.

Rockies manager Buddy Bell was the next to go, losing his job April 26 after Colorado's 6-16 start. The Rockies responded by winning 24 of their first 34 games under

NATIONAL LEAGUE
DEPARTMENT LEADERS

BATTING

GAMES
Aaron Boone, Reds 162
Derrek Lee, Marlins 162
Vladimir Guerrero, Expos 161
Mike Lowell, Marlins 160
Adrian Beltre, Dodgers 159

AT-BATS
Jimmy Rollins, Phillies 637
Rafael Furcal, Braves 636
Jeff Kent, Giants 623
Fernando Vina, Cardinals 622
Vladimir Guerrero, Expos 614

RUNS
Sammy Sosa, Cubs 122
Albert Pujols, Cardinals 118
Barry Bonds, Giants 117
Shawn Green, Dodgers 110
Todd Helton, Rockies 107

HITS
Vladimir Guerrero, Expos 206
Jeff Kent, Giants 195
Jose Vidro, Expos 190
Luis Castillo, Marlins 185
Albert Pujols, Cardinals 185

TOTAL BASES
Vladimir Guerrero, Expos 364
Jeff Kent, Giants 352
Lance Berkman, Astros 334
Albert Pujols, Cardinals 331
Sammy Sosa, Cubs 330

EXTRA-BASE HITS
Jeff Kent, Giants 81
Brian Giles, Pirates 80
Lance Berkman, Astros 79
Barry Bonds, Giants 79
Pat Burrell, Phillies 78
Vladimir Guerrero, Expos 78

SINGLES
Luis Castillo, Marlins 160
Juan Pierre, Rockies 144
Fernando Vina, Cardinals 133
Rafael Furcal, Braves 128
Vladimir Guerrero, Expos 128

DOUBLES
Bobby Abreu, Phillies 50

Bobby Abreu: Topped NL with 50 doubles

Mike Lowell, Marlins 44
Orlando Cabrera, Expos 43
Jose Vidro, Expos 43
Jeff Kent, Giants 42
Todd Walker, Reds 42

TRIPLES
Jimmy Rollins, Phillies 10
Rafael Furcal, Braves 8
Quinton McCracken, Diamondbacks 8
Scott Rolen, Phillies/Cardinals 8
Brad Wilkerson, Expos 8

HOME RUNS
Sammy Sosa, Cubs 49
Barry Bonds, Giants 46
Lance Berkman, Astros 42
Shawn Green, Dodgers 42
Vladimir Guerrero, Expos 39

HOME RUN RATIO
(At-Bats per Home Run)
Barry Bonds, Giants 8.8
Sammy Sosa, Cubs 11.3
Brian Giles, Pirates 13.1
Lance Berkman, Astros 13.8
Shawn Green, Dodgers 13.9

RUNS BATTED IN
Lance Berkman, Astros 128
Albert Pujols, Cardinals 127
Pat Burrell, Phillies 116
Shawn Green, Dodgers 114
Vladimir Guerrero, Expos 111

SACRIFICE BUNTS
Jack Wilson, Pirates 17
Glendon Rusch, Brewers 14
Tom Glavine, Braves 13
Quinton McCracken, Diamondbacks 13
Placido Polanco, Cardinals/Phillies 13
Kirk Rueter, Giants 13
Kip Wells, Pirates 13

SACRIFICE FLIES
Mike Lowell, Marlins 11
Aramis Ramirez, Pirates 11
Todd Helton, Rockies 10
Jeff Bagwell, Astros 9
Ten tied at 7

HIT BY PITCH
Craig Wilson, Pirates 21
Fernando Vina, Cardinals 18
Craig Biggio, Astros 17
Junior Spivey, Diamondbacks 16
Mike Lieberthal, Phillies 14

WALKS
Barry Bonds, Giants 198
Brian Giles, Pirates 135
Adam Dunn, Reds 128
Lance Berkman, Astros 107
Chipper Jones, Braves 107

INTENTIONAL WALKS
Barry Bonds, Giants 68
Vladimir Guerrero, Expos 32
Brian Giles, Pirates 24
Chipper Jones, Braves 23
Shawn Green, Dodgers 22

STRIKEOUTS
Jose Hernandez, Brewers 188
Adam Dunn, Reds 170
Derrek Lee, Marlins 164
Brad Wilkerson, Expos 161
Pat Burrell, Phillies 153

TOUGHEST TO STRIKE OUT
(Plate Appearances per SO)
Jason Kendall, Pirates 20.9
Paul Lo Duca, Dodgers 20.4

Luis Castillo: 48 steals led NL

MORRIS FOSTOFF

Fernando Vina, Cardinals 19.2
Eric Young, Brewers 14.6
Placido Polanco, Cardinals/Phillies 14.5

STOLEN BASES
Luis Castillo, Marlins 48
Juan Pierre, Rockies 47
Dave Roberts, Dodgers 45
Vladimir Guerrero, Expos 40
Alex Sanchez, Brewers 37

CAUGHT STEALING
Vladimir Guerrero, Expos 20
Luis Castillo, Marlins 15
Rafael Furcal, Braves 15
Alex Sanchez, Brewers 14
Jimmy Rollins, Phillies 13

GIDP
Brad Ausmus, Astros 30
Todd Zeile, Rockies 27
Shawn Green, Dodgers 26
Mike Piazza, Mets 26
Vinny Castilla, Braves 22
Scott Rolen, Phillies/Cardinals 22

HITTING STREAKS
Luis Castillo, Marlins 35
Vladimir Guerrero, Expos 26
Kevin Millar, Marlins 25
Jose Vidro, Expos 21
Kevin Millar, Marlins 18
Junior Spivey, Diamondbacks 18

MULTIPLE-HIT GAMES
Jeff Kent, Giants 63
Vladimir Guerrero, Expos 60
Todd Helton, Rockies 57
Jose Vidro, Expos 54
Albert Pujols, Cardinals 53

SLUGGING PERCENTAGE
Barry Bonds, Giants .... .799
Brian Giles, Pirates .... .622
Larry Walker, Rockies .... .602
Sammy Sosa, Cubs .... .594
Vladimir Guerrero, Expos .... .593

ON-BASE PERCENTAGE
Barry Bonds, Giants .... .582
Brian Giles, Pirates .... .450
Chipper Jones, Braves .... .435
Todd Helton, Rockies .... .429
Larry Walker, Rockies .... .421

LARRY GOREN

PITCHING

WINS
Randy Johnson, Diamondbacks 24
Curt Schilling, Diamondbacks 23
Roy Oswalt, Astros 19
Tom Glavine, Braves 18
Kevin Millwood, Braves 18

LOSSES
Livan Hernandez, Giants 16
Glendon Rusch, Brewers 16
Ben Sheets, Brewers 16
Mike Hampton, Rockies 15
John Thomson, Rockies/Mets 14
Kip Wells, Pirates 14

WINNING PERCENTAGE
Randy Johnson, Diamondbacks .... .828
Wade Miller, Astros .... .789
Curt Schilling, Diamondbacks .... .767
Denny Stark, Rockies .... .733
Greg Maddux, Braves .... .727

GAMES
Paul Quantrill, Dodgers 86
Octavio Dotel, Astros 83
Todd Worrell, Giants 80
Todd Jones, Rockies 79
Braden Looper, Marlins 78
Scott Sauerbeck, Pirates 78
Ricky Stone, Astros 78

GAMES STARTED
Tom Glavine, Braves 36
Randy Johnson, Diamondbacks 35
Curt Schilling, Diamondbacks 35
Eight tied at 34

COMPLETE GAMES
Randy Johnson, Diamondbacks 8
A.J. Burnett, Marlins 7
Livan Hernandez, Giants 5
Curt Schilling, Diamondbacks 5
Five tied at 4

SHUTOUTS
A.J. Burnett, Marlins 5
Randy Johnson, Diamondbacks 4
Livan Hernandez, Giants 3
Six tied at 2

GAMES FINISHED
John Smoltz, Braves 65
Eric Gagne, Dodgers 64
Jose Jimenez, Rockies 64
Byung-Hyun Kim, Diamondbacks 62
Jose Mesa, Phillies 61
Robb Nen, Giants 61

SAVES
John Smoltz, Braves 55
Eric Gagne, Dodgers 52
Mike Williams, Pirates 46
Jose Mesa, Phillies 45
Robb Nen, Giants 43

INNINGS PITCHED
Randy Johnson, Diamondbacks 260
Curt Schilling, Diamondbacks 259
Roy Oswalt, Astros 233
Javier Vazquez, Expos 230
Tom Glavine, Braves 225

HITS ALLOWED
Javier Vazquez, Expos 243
Ben Sheets, Brewers 237
Livan Hernandez, Giants 233
Brian Lawrence, Padres 230
Ryan Dempster, Marlins/Reds 228
Mike Hampton, Rockies 228

RUNS ALLOWED
Mike Hampton, Rockies 135
Ryan Dempster, Marlins/Reds 127
Glendon Rusch, Brewers 118
John Thomson, Rockies/Mets 116
Livan Hernandez, Giants 113

HOME RUNS ALLOWED
Pedro Astacio, Mets 32
Rick Helling, Diamondbacks 31

Tom Glavine: NL's best fielding pitcher

Brett Tomko, Padres 31
Glendon Rusch, Brewers 30
Curt Schilling, Diamondbacks 29

WALKS
Kazuhisa Ishii, Dodgers 106
Hideo Nomo, Dodgers 101
Kerry Wood, Cubs 97
Russ Ortiz, Giants 94
Ryan Dempster, Marlins/Reds 93

FEWEST WALKS PER 9 INNINGS
Curt Schilling, Diamondbacks 1.15
Odalis Perez, Dodgers 1.54
Brian Anderson, Diamondbacks 1.85
Javier Vazquez, Expos 1.91
Greg Maddux, Braves 2.03

HIT BATSMEN
Pedro Astacio, Mets 16
Kerry Wood, Cubs 16
Vicente Padilla, Phillies 15
Julian Tavarez, Marlins 15
Randy Johnson, Diamondbacks 13

STRIKEOUTS
Randy Johnson, Diamondbacks 334
Curt Schilling, Diamondbacks 316
Kerry Wood, Cubs 217
Matt Clement, Cubs 215
Roy Oswalt, Astros 208

STRIKEOUTS PER 9 INNINGS
Randy Johnson, Diamondbacks 11.56
Mark Prior, Cubs 11.34
Curt Schilling, Diamondbacks 10.97
Jason Schmidt, Giants 9.52
Josh Beckett, Marlins 9.45

PICKOFFS
Brian Anderson, Diamondbacks 8
Damian Moss, Braves 8
Odalis Perez, Dodgers 8
Jimmy Anderson, Pirates 6
Mike Fetters, Pirates/Diamondbacks 5

WILD PITCHES
Tony Armas, Expos 14
A.J. Burnett, Marlins 14
Damian Moss, Braves 13
Jason Schmidt, Giants 12
David Coggin, Phillies 11

BALKS
Brian Anderson, Diamondbacks 5
Odalis Perez, Dodgers 3
Fourteen tied at 2

OPPONENTS BATTING AVERAGE
Randy Johnson, Diamondbacks .... .208
A.J. Burnett, Marlins .... .209
Matt Clement, Cubs .... .215
Odalis Perez, Dodgers .... .218
Jason Schmidt, Giants .... .218

FIELDING

PITCHER
PCT	Tom Glavine, Braves	1.000
PO	Ben Sheets, Brewers	28
A	Livan Hernandez, Giants	53
E	T.J. Tucker, Expos	5
TC	Odalis Perez, Dodgers	76
DP	Livan Hernandez, Giants	7

CATCHER
PCT	Brad Ausmus, Astros	.997
PO	Paul Lo Duca, Dodgers	965
A	Paul Lo Duca, Dodgers	76
E	Mike Piazza, Mets	12
TC	Paul Lo Duca, Dodgers	1049
DP	Jason Kendall, Pirates	13
PB	Jason LaRue, Reds	20

FIRST BASE
PCT	Eric Karros, Dodgers	.997
PO	Todd Helton, Rockies	1357
A	Derrek Lee, Marlins	121
E	Mo Vaughn, Mets	18
TC	Todd Helton, Rockies	1477
DP	Todd Helton, Rockies	138
	Derrek Lee, Marlins	138

SECOND BASE
PCT	Todd Walker, Reds	.989
PO	Jose Vidro, Expos	314
	Todd Walker, Reds	314
A	Jose Vidro, Expos	448
E	Marlon Anderson, Phillies	20
TC	Jose Vidro, Expos	773
DP	Jeff Kent, Giants	113

THIRD BASE
PCT	Vinny Castilla, Braves	.982
PO	Mike Lowell, Marlins	150
A	Scott Rolen, Phillies/Cards	335
E	Todd Zeile, Rockies	21
TC	Scott Rolen, Phillies/Cards	484
DP	Aaron Boone, Reds	42

SHORTSTOP
PCT	Jimmy Rollins, Phillies	.980
PO	Rafael Furcal, Braves	245
A	Juan Uribe, Rockies	504
E	Orlando Cabrera, Expos	29
TC	Juan Uribe, Rockies	792
DP	Juan Uribe, Rockies	118

OUTFIELD
PCT	Doug Glanville, Phillies	1.000
PO	Andruw Jones, Braves	404
A	Vladimir Guerrero, Expos	14
	Larry Walker, Rockies	14
E	Vladimir Guerrero, Expos	10
TC	Andruw Jones, Braves	412
DP	Juan Encarnacion, Reds/Marlins	6

Paul Quantrill: 86 appearances

2002 NATIONAL LEAGUE STATISTICS

TEAM BATTING

	AVG	G	AB	R	H	2B	3B	HR	BB	SO	SB
Colorado	.274	162	5512	778	1508	283	41	152	497	1043	103
St. Louis	.268	162	5505	787	1475	285	26	175	542	927	86
Arizona	.267	162	5508	819	1471	283	41	165	643	1016	92
San Francisco	.267	162	5497	783	1465	300	35	198	616	961	74
Los Angeles	.264	162	5554	713	1464	286	29	155	428	940	96
Houston	.262	162	5503	749	1441	291	32	167	589	1120	71
Montreal	.261	162	5479	735	1432	300	36	162	575	1104	118
Florida	.261	162	5496	699	1433	280	32	146	595	1130	177
Atlanta	.260	161	5495	708	1428	280	25	164	558	1028	76
Philadelphia	.259	161	5523	710	1428	325	41	165	640	1095	104
New York	.256	161	5496	690	1409	238	22	160	486	1044	87
Cincinnati	.253	162	5470	709	1386	297	21	169	583	1188	116
Milwaukee	.253	162	5415	627	1369	269	29	139	500	1125	94
San Diego	.253	162	5515	662	1393	243	29	136	547	1062	71
Chicago	.246	162	5496	706	1351	259	29	200	585	1269	63
Pittsburgh	.244	161	5330	641	1300	263	20	142	537	1109	86

TEAM PITCHING

	ERA	G	CG	SHO	SV	IP	H	R	ER	BB	SO
Atlanta	3.13	161	3	15	57	1467	1302	565	511	554	1058
San Francisco	3.54	162	10	13	43	1437	1349	616	566	523	992
Los Angeles	3.69	162	4	15	56	1457	1311	643	598	555	1132
St. Louis	3.70	162	4	9	42	1446	1355	648	595	547	1009
New York	3.89	161	9	10	36	1442	1408	703	624	543	1107
Arizona	3.92	162	14	10	40	1446	1361	674	630	421	1303
Montreal	3.97	162	9	3	39	1453	1475	718	641	508	1088
Houston	4.00	162	2	11	43	1445	1423	695	643	546	1219
Philadelphia	4.17	161	5	9	47	1449	1381	724	671	570	1075
Pittsburgh	4.23	161	2	7	47	1412	1447	730	664	572	920
Cincinnati	4.27	162	2	8	42	1453	1502	774	690	550	980
Chicago	4.29	162	11	9	23	1441	1373	759	687	606	1333
Florida	4.36	162	11	12	36	1456	1449	763	706	631	1104
San Diego	4.62	162	5	10	40	1436	1522	815	737	582	1108
Milwaukee	4.73	162	7	4	32	1432	1468	821	752	666	1026
Colorado	5.20	162	1	8	43	1426	1554	898	825	582	920

TEAM FIELDING

TEAM	PCT	PO	A	E	DP	TEAM	PCT	PO	A	E	DP
Houston	.986	4335	1663	83	149	Atlanta	.982	4402	1822	114	170
Philadelphia	.986	4349	1700	88	156	Pittsburgh	.982	4238	1899	115	177
Arizona	.985	4340	1506	89	117	Colorado	.982	4280	1701	112	158
Los Angeles	.985	4373	1686	90	134	Chicago	.981	4324	1500	114	144
San Francisco	.985	4312	1630	90	166	Cincinnati	.981	4361	1773	120	169
Florida	.983	4369	1636	106	163	San Diego	.979	4309	1681	128	162
St. Louis	.983	4339	1674	103	168	Montreal	.978	4359	1799	139	160
Milwaukee	.983	4297	1633	103	154	New York	.976	4328	1628	144	138

INDIVIDUAL BATTING LEADERS
(Minimum 502 Plate Appearances)

	AVG	G	AB	R	H	2B	3B	HR	RBI	BB	SO	SB
Bonds, Barry, San Francisco	.370	143	403	117	149	31	2	46	110	198	47	9
Walker, Larry, Colorado	.338	136	477	95	161	40	4	26	104	65	73	6
Guerrero, Vladimir, Montreal	.336	161	614	106	206	37	2	39	111	84	70	40
Helton, Todd, Colorado	.329	156	553	107	182	39	4	30	109	99	91	5
Jones, Chipper, Atlanta	.327	158	548	90	179	35	1	26	100	107	89	8
Vidro, Jose, Montreal	.315	152	604	103	190	43	3	19	96	60	70	2
Pujols, Albert, St. Louis	.314	157	590	118	185	40	2	34	127	72	69	2
Kent, Jeff, San Francisco	.313	152	623	102	195	42	2	37	108	52	101	5
Edmonds, Jim, St. Louis	.311	144	476	96	148	31	2	28	83	86	134	4
Alfonzo, Edgardo, New York	.308	135	490	78	151	26	0	16	56	62	55	6

INDIVIDUAL PITCHING LEADERS
(Minimum 162 Innings)

	W	L	ERA	G	GS	CG	SV	IP	H	R	ER	BB	SO
Johnson, Randy, Arizona	24	5	2.32	35	35	8	0	260	197	78	67	71	334
Maddux, Greg, Atlanta	16	6	2.62	34	34	0	0	199	194	67	58	45	118
Glavine, Tom, Atlanta	18	11	2.96	36	36	2	0	225	210	85	74	78	127
Perez, Odalis, Los Angeles	15	10	3.00	32	32	4	0	222	182	76	74	38	155
Oswalt, Roy, Houston	19	9	3.01	35	34	0	0	233	215	86	78	62	208
Dessens, Elmer, Cincinnati	7	8	3.03	30	30	0	0	178	173	70	60	49	103
Ohka, Tomo, Montreal	13	8	3.18	32	31	2	0	193	194	83	68	45	118
Wolf, Randy, Philadelphia	11	9	3.20	31	31	3	0	211	172	77	75	63	172
Rueter, Kirk, San Francisco	14	8	3.23	33	33	0	0	204	204	83	73	54	76
Schilling, Curt, Arizona	23	7	3.23	36	35	5	0	259	218	95	93	33	316

AWARD WINNERS

Selected by Baseball Writers Association of America

MVP

Player, Team	1st	2nd	3rd	Total
Barry Bonds, S.F.	32	2	0	448
Albert Pujols, St.L.	0	26	4	276
Lance Berkman, Hou.	0	1	7	181
Vladimir Guerrero, Mon.	0	4	5	168
Shawn Green, L.A.	0	0	3	146
Jeff Kent, S.F.	0	0	3	135
Randy Johnson, Ariz.	0	0	5	127
John Smoltz, Atlanta	0	1	3	124
Sammy Sosa, Chicago	0	0	0	63
Curt Schilling, Ariz.	0	0	0	53
Chipper Jones, Atlanta	0	0	2	50
Eric Gagne, L.A.	0	0	0	44
Brian Giles, Pittsburgh	0	0	0	27
Junior Spivey, Ariz.	0	0	0	8
Pat Burrell, Phil.	0	0	0	8
Andruw Jones, Atlanta	0	0	0	7
Gary Sheffield, Atlanta	0	0	0	6
Jim Edmonds, St.L.	0	0	0	6
Todd Helton, Colo.	0	0	0	3
Benito Santiago, S.F.	0	0	0	2
Edgar Renteria, St.L.	0	0	0	2
Larry Walker, Colo.	0	0	0	2
Roy Oswalt, Houston	0	0	0	1
Jose Vidro, Montreal	0	0	0	1

CY YOUNG AWARD

Player, Team	1st	2nd	3rd	Total
Randy Johnson, Ariz.	32	0	0	160
Curt Schilling, Ariz.	0	29	3	90
John Smoltz, Atl.	0	1	18	21
Eric Gagne, L.A.	0	2	2	8
Roy Oswalt, Houston	0	0	8	8
Bartolo Colon, Mon.	0	0	1	1

ROOKIE OF THE YEAR

Player, Team	1st	2nd	3rd	Total
Jason Jennings, Colo.	27	5	0	150
Brad Wilkerson, Mon.	2	14	5	57
Austin Kearns, Cin.	2	8	6	40
Kazuhisa Ishii, L.A.	1	2	5	16
Damian Moss, Atl.	0	2	6	12
Ryan Jensen, S.F.	0	0	4	4
Mark Prior, Chicago	0	1	0	3
Josh Fogg, Pittsburgh	0	0	3	3
Alex Sanchez, Mil.	0	0	1	1
Jason Simontacchi, St.L.	0	0	1	1
Denny Stark, Colo.	0	0	1	1

MANAGER OF THE YEAR

Manager, Team	1st	2nd	3rd	Total
Tony La Russa, St.L.	22	6	1	129
Bobby Cox, Atlanta	9	14	6	93
Frank Robinson, Mon.	0	6	5	23
Jim Tracy, L.A.	0	4	10	22
Dusty Baker, S.F.	1	2	7	18
Bob Brenly, Arizona	0	0	2	2
Bob Boone, Cincinnati	0	0	1	1

NOTE: MVP balloting based on 14 points for first place vote, nine for second, eight for third, etc.; Cy Young Award, Rookie of the Year and Manager of the Year balloting based on five points for first-place vote, three for second and one for third.

GOLD GLOVE AWARDS

Selected by NL managers

C—Brad Ausmus, Houston. 1B—Todd Helton, Colorado. 2B—Fernando Vina, St. Louis. 3B—Scott Rolen, Philadelphia/St. Louis. SS—Edgar Renteria, St. Louis. OF—Jim Edmonds, St. Louis; Andruw Jones, Atlanta; Larry Walker, Colorado. P—Greg Maddux, Atlanta.

hitting coach Clint Hurdle, but he couldn't maintain the momentum and finished six games under .500 (67-73) for the season. However, he did manage to keep his job for 2003.

Cubs skipper Don Baylor, suffering under the higher-than-normal expectations brought on by a successful 2001 campaign, was replaced by Triple-A Iowa manager Bruce Kimm July 5. Kimm didn't fare any better—the club finished 67-95—and was also let go after the season.

■ In the NL Central, the Astros made another run at the postseason but came up short despite a breakout season from center fielder Lance Berkman. Berkman hit .292-42-128 to lead the NL in RBIs. He also made one of the best defensive plays of the season when he ran down a ball on the hill in center field of the Astros' Minute Maid Park.

Lance Berkman

The Reds overachieved in the Central as well, leading the division for a good chunk of the season and staying in wild card contention until their lack of starting pitching finally caught up with them in the dog days of August. Outfielder Adam Dunn went from Futures Game participant in 2001 to major league all-star in 2002, and the next bright star in the system, outfielder Austin Kearns, hit .315-13-56 to establish himself as part of the outfield picture when Cincinnati moves into the Great American Ballpark in 2003. "We brought him up for a cup of coffee," said Reds GM Jim Bowden of Kearns. "He's been a whole pot. And he may be a Starbucks franchise."

■ The Dodgers' run at the NL West title and the wild card may have fallen short, but it wasn't from a lack of outstanding individual performances. Outfielder Shawn Green clubbed four home runs in a game against the Brewers May 23 at Miller Park, and had another stretch of four homers in four at-bats later in the season, ending up with 42 bombs and 114 RBIs to go with a .285 average.

Brian Giles

And Eric Gagne, like the Braves' Smoltz, moved from the rotation to the bullpen and became nearly automatic as the closer, notching 52 saves.

"Having Gagne out there, you're not worried," said Green near midseason. "And there are only a few teams in baseball that can feel like that."

■ Attendance woes beset the league, as both the Marlins and Expos finished below the 1 million mark, and 12 of the league's 16 teams saw overall declines from 2001 numbers. The Rockies failed to draw 3 million for the first time in franchise history.

■ Though they played on teams out of contention, several players turned in strong offensive seasons. Cubs outfielder Sammy Sosa led the NL in home runs again with 49, though he failed to reach at least 50 for the first time in five seasons, leaving him with 499 for his career. Pirates outfielder Brian Giles hit .298-38-103 and finished second in the league in on-base (.450) and slugging (.622) percentages, walks (135) and extra-base hits (80).

Rockies outfielder Larry Walker finished second to Bonds in the batting race at .338 and topped 100 RBIs for

the fifth time in his career. Brewers shortstop Jose Hernandez enjoyed an all-star season (.288-24-73), but some of his enjoyment was tempered by the controversy surrounding his approaching the single-season strikeout mark. Hernandez sat out most of the season's final week and finished with 188 whiffs, one short of Bobby Bonds' record.

NATIONAL LEAGUE
DIVISION SERIES

SAN FRANCISCO VS. ATLANTA
COMPOSITE BOX

SAN FRANCISCO

Player, Pos.	AVG	G	AB	R	H	2B	3B	HR	RBI	BB	SO	SB
Kenny Lofton, cf	.350	5	20	5	7	1	0	0	2	2	3	1
J.T. Snow, 1b	.316	5	19	3	6	2	0	1	3	1	5	0
Barry Bonds, lf	.294	5	17	5	5	0	0	3	4	4	1	0
Jeff Kent, 2b	.263	5	19	1	5	2	0	0	1	2	7	0
Benito Santiago, c	.238	5	21	1	5	2	0	0	5	1	5	0
Rich Aurilia, ss	.238	5	21	4	5	1	0	2	7	1	5	0
Reggie Sanders, rf	.222	5	18	1	4	1	0	0	1	3	5	0
David Bell, 3b	.188	5	16	3	3	0	0	0	1	3	4	0
Russ Ortiz, p	.167	2	6	1	1	0	0	0	0	0	4	0
Shawon Dunston, ph	.000	2	1	0	0	0	0	0	0	0	1	0
Tom Goodwin, ph	.000	2	2	0	0	0	0	0	0	0	2	0
Kirk Rueter, p	.000	1	1	0	0	0	0	0	0	0	1	0
Jason Schmidt, p	.000	1	2	0	0	0	0	0	0	0	1	0
Livan Hernandez, p	.000	1	2	0	0	0	0	0	0	0	0	0
Ramon Martinez, ph	.000	1	0	0	0	0	0	0	0	1	0	0
Pedro Feliz, ph	.000	1	1	0	0	0	0	0	0	0	1	0
Totals	.247	5	166	24	41	9	0	6	24	18	45	1

Pitcher	W	L	ERA	G	GS	SV	IP	H	R	ER	BB	SO
Robb Nen	0	0	0.00	4	0	2	3	4	0	0	1	1
Felix Rodriguez	0	0	0.00	3	0	0	3	1	0	0	2	2
Jay Witasick	0	0	0.00	2	0	0	2	0	0	0	0	1
Scott Eyre	0	0	0.00	3	0	0	1	1	0	0	0	0
Russ Ortiz	2	0	2.19	2	2	0	12	9	3	3	8	8
Livan Hernandez	1	0	3.24	1	1	0	8	8	3	3	2	6
Jason Schmidt	0	1	6.75	1	1	0	5	3	4	4	4	5
Manny Aybar	0	0	6.75	2	0	0	3	2	2	2	1	3
Tim Worrell	0	0	12.00	3	0	0	3	7	6	4	2	3
Kirk Rueter	0	1	18.00	1	1	0	3	7	7	6	2	1
Aaron Fultz	0	0	inf	2	0	0	0	2	1	1	0	0
Totals	3	2	4.70	5	5	2	44	44	26	23	22	30

ATLANTA

Player, Pos.	AVG	G	AB	R	H	2B	3B	HR	RBI	BB	SO	SB
Tom Glavine, p	.500	2	2	0	1	0	0	0	2	0	1	0
Marcus Giles, ph	.500	3	2	0	1	0	0	0	0	0	0	0
Mark DeRosa, ph-2b	.429	4	7	2	3	1	1	0	3	1	1	0
Vinny Castilla, 3b	.389	5	18	5	7	0	0	1	4	2	2	0
Javy Lopez, c	.333	4	15	4	5	1	0	2	4	1	3	0
Keith Lockhart, 2b	.333	5	12	1	4	0	0	1	4	2	4	0
Andruw Jones, cf	.316	5	19	4	6	1	0	0	2	2	3	0
Chipper Jones, lf	.294	5	17	3	5	0	0	0	2	5	2	0
Rafael Furcal, ss	.250	5	24	2	6	1	1	0	2	0	5	1
Julio Franco, 1b	.182	5	22	2	4	0	0	0	1	2	3	1
Henry Blanco, c	.167	2	6	0	1	0	0	0	0	0	2	0
Gary Sheffield, lf	.063	5	16	3	1	0	0	1	1	7	3	0
Greg Maddux, p	.000	1	3	0	0	0	0	0	0	0	1	0
Darren Bragg, ph-lf	.000	4	3	0	0	0	0	0	0	0	0	0
Matt Franco, ph	.000	4	2	0	0	0	0	0	0	0	1	0
Kevin Millwood, p	.000	2	2	0	0	0	0	0	0	0	0	0
Totals	.259	5	170	26	44	4	2	5	25	22	30	2

Pitcher	W	L	ERA	G	GS	SV	IP	H	R	ER	BB	SO
Darren Holmes	0	0	0.00	3	0	0	3	1	0	0	0	5
Kerry Ligtenberg	0	0	0.00	1	0	0	2	0	0	0	0	1
Kevin Gryboski	0	0	0.00	3	0	0	4	2	0	0	2	3
John Smoltz	0	0	2.70	2	0	0	3	2	1	1	2	7
Greg Maddux	1	0	3.00	1	1	0	6	5	2	2	1	3
Damian Moss	0	0	3.00	2	0	0	3	2	1	1	1	3
Kevin Millwood	1	1	3.27	2	2	0	11	7	4	4	0	14
Mike Remlinger	0	0	4.50	3	0	0	2	3	1	1	2	3
Chris Hammond	0	0	6.75	3	0	0	3	2	2	2	3	3
Tom Glavine	0	2	15.26	2	2	0	8	17	13	13	7	4
Totals	2	3	4.91	5	5	0	44	41	24	24	18	45

SCORE BY INNINGS

San Francisco	373	414	101—24
Atlanta	151	318	034—26

E—Bell, Bonds, Kent, Santiago. **DP**—San Francisco 5, Atlanta 2. **LOB**—San Francisco 33, Atlanta 36. **CS**—Bonds, Furcal. **SH**—Hernandez 2, Millwood. **HBP**—Kent (by Maddux), Lockhart (by Hernandez). **IBB**—Bell (by Glavine), Bonds 2 (by Hammond, by Maddux), Lockhart (by Ortiz), C. Jones (by Schmidt). **WP**—Ortiz 2, Millwood. **PB**—Santiago.

ST. LOUIS VS. ARIZONA
COMPOSITE BOX

ST. LOUIS

Player, Pos.	AVG	G	AB	R	H	2B	3B	HR	RBI	BB	SO	SB
Miguel Cairo, ph-3b	1.000	2	4	2	4	1	0	0	3	0	0	0
Fernando Vina, 2b	.600	3	15	3	9	0	0	0	1	1	0	0
Kerry Robinson, ph	.500	2	2	0	1	0	0	0	1	0	0	0
Mike Matheny, c	.444	3	9	3	4	1	0	0	2	2	1	0
Scott Rolen, 3b	.429	2	7	1	3	0	0	1	2	0	2	0
Albert Pujols, lf-3b-1b	.300	3	10	3	3	0	1	0	3	3	1	0
Jim Edmonds, cf	.273	3	11	1	3	0	0	1	2	2	4	0
Edgar Renteria, ss	.250	3	12	3	3	0	0	0	0	1	1	2
Matt Morris, p	.250	1	4	1	1	0	0	0	2	0	2	0
J.D. Drew, rf	.222	2	9	1	2	0	0	1	1	1	2	0
Chuck Finley, p	.000	1	3	0	0	0	0	0	0	0	2	0
Andy Benes, p	.000	1	1	0	0	0	0	0	0	1	0	0
Tino Martinez, 1b	.000	3	11	2	0	0	0	0	0	2	1	0
Eduardo Perez, ph	.000	1	1	0	0	0	0	0	0	0	0	0
Eli Marrero, pf-lf-rf	.000	2	6	0	0	0	0	0	1	0	1	0
Totals	.314	3	105	20	33	2	1	3	19	12	17	2

Pitcher	W	L	ERA	G	GS	SV	IP	H	R	ER	BB	SO
Chuck Finley	0	0	0.00	1	1	0	6	4	0	0	2	7
Jeff Fassero	2	0	0.00	3	0	0	3	3	0	0	0	2
Rick White	0	0	0.00	2	0	0	2	1	1	0	1	1
Jason Isringhausen	0	0	0.00	2	0	2	2	0	0	0	0	1
Steve Kline	0	0	0.00	2	0	0	1	1	0	0	1	0
Mike Crudale	0	0	0.00	1	0	0	1	0	0	0	1	2
Matt Morris	1	0	1.29	1	1	0	7	7	2	1	2	3
Andy Benes	0	0	5.79	1	1	0	5	2	3	3	4	5
Totals	3	0	1.33	3	3	2	27	18	6	4	11	21

ARIZONA

Player, Pos.	AVG	G	AB	R	H	2B	3B	HR	RBI	BB	SO	SB
Damian Miller, c	.500	1	2	0	1	0	0	0	0	2	0	0
Chad Moeller, c-ph	.400	3	5	0	2	0	0	0	0	0	1	0
Quinton McCracken, rf	.364	3	11	1	4	1	0	0	2	1	2	0
David Dellucci, lf	.286	3	7	1	2	0	0	1	2	0	1	0
Mark Grace, 1b-ph	.250	2	4	0	1	0	0	0	0	1	0	0
Rod Barajas, c	.250	2	4	1	1	0	0	1	1	0	1	0
Steve Finley, cf	.222	3	9	1	2	0	0	0	1	2	2	1
Tony Womack, ss	.154	3	13	1	2	0	0	0	0	1	1	0
Junior Spivey, 2b	.154	3	13	0	2	0	0	0	0	1	3	0
Matt Williams, 3b	.083	3	12	0	1	0	0	0	0	0	3	0
Curt Schilling, p	.000	1	2	0	0	0	0	0	0	0	1	0
Randy Johnson, p	.000	1	2	0	0	0	0	0	0	0	2	0
Chris Donnels, ph	.000	2	2	0	0	0	0	0	0	1	0	0
Miguel Batista, p	.000	1	1	0	0	0	0	0	0	0	1	0
Greg Colbrunn, 1b	.000	1	3	1	0	0	0	0	0	0	1	0
Mark Little, ph-lf	.000	2	4	0	0	0	0	0	0	0	2	0
Erubiel Durazo, ph-1b	.000	2	4	0	0	0	0	0	0	1	1	0
Alex Cintron, pr-3b	.000	2	0	0	0	0	0	0	0	0	0	0
Totals	.184	3	98	6	18	2	0	2	6	11	21	1

Pitcher	W	L	ERA	G	GS	SV	IP	H	R	ER	BB	SO
Mike Fetters	0	0	0.00	1	0	0	1	1	0	0	1	1
Rick Helling	0	0	0.00	2	0	0	4	1	0	0	0	2
Mike Myers	0	0	0.00	2	0	0	2	2	0	0	1	0
Curt Schilling	0	0	1.29	1	1	0	7	7	1	1	1	7
Mike Koplove	0	1	6.75	1	0	0	1	2	1	1	0	1
Randy Johnson	0	1	7.50	1	1	0	6	10	6	5	2	4
Miguel Batista	0	1	9.82	1	1	0	4	5	4	4	3	1
Byung-Hyun Kim	0	0	18.00	1	0	0	1	2	2	2	3	0
Greg Swindell	0	0	27.00	1	0	0	0	2	4	1	1	0
Matt Mantei	0	0	54.00	1	0	0	0	1	2	2	1	0
Totals	0	3	5.54	3	3	0	26	33	20	16	12	17

SCORE BY INNINGS
St. Louis	212 501	621—20
Arizona	121 010	010—6

E—Pujols, Renteria, Swindell, Womack. **DP**—Arizona 1. **LOB**—St. Louis 25, Arizona 23. **CS**—Cairo, Vina, Edmonds. **SH**—Matheny 2, Benes. **SF**—Marrero, Finley. **HBP**—Cairo (by Batista), Renteria (by Johnson), Rolen (by Schilling). **IBB**—Renteria (by Johnson). **BK**—Benes.

CHAMPIONSHIP SERIES
ST. LOUIS VS. SAN FRANCISCO
COMPOSITE BOX

ST. LOUIS

Player, Pos.	AVG	G	AB	R	H	2B	3B	HR	RBI	BB	SO	SB
Jim Edmonds, cf	.400	5	20	2	8	2	0	1	4	2	5	0
Miguel Cairo, 3b	.385	3	13	2	5	0	0	1	2	0	2	0
J.D. Drew, rf-ph	.385	5	13	1	5	0	0	1	1	1	2	0
Mike Matheny, c	.316	5	19	2	6	2	0	1	1	0	2	0
Albert Pujols, lf-1b	.263	5	19	2	5	1	0	1	2	2	5	0
Fernando Vina, 2b	.261	5	23	2	6	2	0	0	2	0	0	0
Eduardo Perez, pf-lf	.250	3	4	1	1	0	0	1	1	1	0	0
Eli Marrero, lf-rf	.188	4	16	1	3	1	0	0	1	1	1	0
Edgar Renteria, ss	.158	5	19	0	3	0	0	0	1	0	2	0
Tino Martinez, 1b	.143	4	14	1	2	0	0	0	1	2	1	1
Matt Morris, p	.000	2	4	0	0	0	0	0	0	0	0	0
Andy Benes, p	.000	1	2	0	0	0	0	0	0	0	0	0
Chuck Finley, p	.000	1	2	1	0	0	0	0	0	0	0	0
Kerry Robinson, ph-lf	.000	3	2	1	0	0	0	0	0	1	1	0
Mike DiFelice, ph	.000	1	1	0	0	0	0	0	0	0	0	0
Totals	.257	5	171	16	44	8	0	7	16	10	23	1

Pitcher	W	L	ERA	G	GS	SV	IP	H	R	ER	BB	SO
Dave Veres	0	0	0.00	2	0	0	4	2	0	0	1	5
Steve Kline	0	0	0.00	4	0	0	2	2	0	0	0	1
Jeff Fassero	0	0	0.00	1	0	0	1	0	0	0	0	0
Andy Benes	0	0	3.38	1	1	0	5	2	2	2	4	5
Woody Williams	0	1	4.50	1	1	0	6	6	3	3	1	7
Rick White	0	1	4.50	3	0	0	4	2	2	2	1	3
Jason Isringhausen	0	0	4.50	2	0	1	2	1	1	1	3	3
Matt Morris	0	2	6.23	2	2	0	13	16	9	9	6	6
Chuck Finley	0	0	7.20	1	1	0	5	7	4	4	3	1
Mike Crudale	0	0	10.80	1	0	0	2	1	2	2	1	2
Totals	1	4	5.01	5	5	1	44	39	23	23	21	36

SAN FRANCISCO

Player, Pos.	AVG	G	AB	R	H	2B	3B	HR	RBI	BB	SO	SB
Russ Ortiz, p	1.000	1	1	0	1	0	0	0	0	0	0	0
Shawon Dunston, ph-rf	.500	2	2	0	1	0	0	0	0	0	1	0
David Bell, 3b	.412	5	17	4	7	1	0	1	1	2	3	0
Rich Aurilia, ss	.333	5	15	4	5	1	0	2	5	2	2	0
Benito Santiago, c	.300	5	20	2	6	0	0	2	6	2	4	0
Barry Bonds, lf	.273	5	11	5	3	0	1	1	6	10	2	0
Jeff Kent, 2b	.263	5	19	3	5	0	0	0	2	0	4	0
J.T. Snow, 1b	.250	5	20	1	5	1	0	2	1	4	0	0
Kenny Lofton, cf	.238	5	21	4	5	0	0	1	2	2	4	1
Reggie Sanders, rf	.063	4	16	0	1	0	0	0	0	4	0	0
Kirk Rueter, p	.000	2	5	0	0	0	0	0	0	0	1	0
Tom Goodwin, ph-rf	.000	2	3	0	0	0	0	0	0	0	2	0
Jason Schmidt, p	.000	1	2	0	0	0	0	0	0	0	2	0
Pedro Feliz, ph	.000	1	1	0	0	0	0	0	0	0	0	0
Livan Hernandez, p	.000	1	1	0	0	0	0	0	0	0	1	0
Ramon Martinez, ph-ss	.000	2	1	0	0	0	0	0	0	1	0	0
Robb Nen, p	.000	3	1	0	0	0	0	0	0	0	0	0
Felix Rodriguez, p	.000	4	1	0	0	0	0	0	0	0	1	0
Tsuyoshi Shinjo, rf	.000	1	1	0	0	0	0	0	0	0	0	0
Totals	.247	5	158	23	39	3	2	7	23	21	36	1

Pitcher	W	L	ERA	G	GS	SV	IP	H	R	ER	BB	SO
Scott Eyre	0	0	0.00	4	0	0	2	2	0	0	0	0
Aaron Fultz	0	0	0.00	1	0	0	0	0	0	0	1	0
Jason Schmidt	1	0	1.17	1	1	0	8	4	1	1	1	8
Felix Rodriguez	0	0	1.93	4	0	0	5	3	1	1	2	2
Kirk Rueter	1	0	4.09	2	2	0	11	15	5	5	2	3
Livan Hernandez	0	0	2.84	1	1	0	6	9	2	2	1	0
Russ Ortiz	0	0	7.71	1	1	0	5	5	4	4	3	3
Tim Worrell	2	0	2.08	4	0	0	4	2	1	1	0	3
Robb Nen	0	0	2.70	3	0	3	3	3	1	1	1	4
Jay Witasick	0	1	9.00	1	0	0	1	1	1	1	0	0
Totals	4	1	3.20	5	5	3	45	44	16	16	10	23

SCORE BY INNINGS
St. Louis	212 133	121—16
San Francisco	251 064	032—23

E—Renteria, Aurilia. **DP**—St. Louis 3, San Francisco 4. **LOB**—St. Louis 34, San Francisco 38. **CS**—Robinson. **SH**— Morris 2, Renteria, Benes, Aurilia 3, Schmidt, R. Martinez, Williams, Dunston, Ortiz, Hernandez. **SF**—Renteria, Vina, Aurilia, Bonds. **HBP**—Renteria (by Rueter), Pujols (by Hernandez), Lofton (by Morris), Aurilia (by Morris), Kent (by Morris). **IBB**—Bell (by Isringhausen), Lofton (by Isringhausen), Bonds 3 (by Veres, by White, by Morris).

Anaheim 56
Arizona 63
Atlanta 70
Baltimore 77
Boston 85
Chicago (AL) 92
Chicago (NL) 99
Cincinnati 106
Cleveland 114
Colorado 122
Detroit 129
Florida 137
Houston 144
Kansas City 150
Los Angeles 157

Milwaukee 164
Minnesota 171
Montreal 178
New York (AL) 186
New York (NL) 194
Oakland 202
Philadelphia 209
Pittsburgh 216
St. Louis 223
San Diego 230
San Francisco 238
Seattle 245
Tampa Bay 252
Texas 259
Toronto 267

ORGANIZATION
STATISTICS

ANAHEIM ANGELS

BY BILL SHAIKIN

As fireworks ascended toward the heavens and streamers descended onto the field, as the Angels celebrated their first World Series championship, a camera crew rushed out of the dugout and into the bedlam.

For the first time in any sport, a Disney team was a champion. For the first time, that traditional perk of victory—the delirious shouting of "I'm going to Disneyland!" into the camera—would be hollered by a Disney star.

But third baseman Troy Glaus, the World Series MVP, wouldn't do it by himself. Glaus and first baseman Scott Spiezio, who tied a major league record by driving in 19 postseason runs, wouldn't do it by themselves. So the camera crew settled for a chorus of shouts from a group hug of Glaus, Spiezio, outfielder Alex Ochoa and infielders Benji Gil and Adam Kennedy.

Ochoa batted once in the World Series. Gil started one game. The commercial was entirely fitting.

A team without a superstar accomplished what so many all-stars and Hall of Famers passing through Anaheim could not. There are no individual honors so great, closer Troy Percival suggested, as the honor conferred upon the Angels in 2002.

"Angel immortality," Percival said, "for this entire team."

Once and for all, the Angels cast aside their image as bumblers and stumblers, losers and choke artists. After four decades of frustration and humiliation, the Angels were champions, no longer distinguished solely by an awful history, by sorrows known to longtime fans in shorthand—one strike away, one win away, 11-game lead.

"Good things always happened to someone else," said coach Joe Maddon, whose Angels career started as a minor league catcher in 1975. "It's so wonderful to lay our negative history to rest and build a new history."

The Angels rallied from a 6-14 start, the worst start in franchise history. They won a club-record 99 games after finishing 41 games out of first place in 2001.

Garret Anderson

Robb Quinlan

JOHN SPEAR

PLAYERS OF THE YEAR

MAJOR LEAGUE: Garret Anderson, of
Anderson reached a career-high in 2002 with 195 hits, leading the Angels in that category as well as RBIs (123), doubles (53), total bases (344) and slugging percentage (.539).

MINOR LEAGUE: Robb Quinlan, of
Quinlan wasn't on the Angels' 40-man roster after the 2001 season, but earned a spot after slugging .555 at Triple-A Salt Lake and ranking second in the minors with 112 RBIs and 293 total bases.

For the first time in the 42-year history of a star-crossed franchise, they won a postseason series, tripping the mighty Yankees in four games in the division series. They dispatched the Twins in five games in the American League Championship Series, stomping upon whatever curses, hexes and jinxes had allegedly barred the Angels from entry into the World Series.

And they won, defeating the Giants in seven games and offering hope to fans across America that championships could be won without unlimited spending. The Angels won with a roster assembled from the farm system and the scrap heap. A core—Glaus, Percival, 18-game winner Jarrod Washburn, 15-game winner Ramon Ortiz and outfielders Garret Anderson, Darin Erstad and Tim Salmon—remained from the previous administration.

Under the current regime of GM Bill Stoneman, assistants Gary Sutherland and Ken Forsch and scouting director Donny Rowland, the Angels traded for Kennedy, Appier and DH Brad Fullmer, signed Spiezio as a free agent utilityman and claimed shortstop David Eckstein and reliever Ben Weber on waivers. The playoff roster included more independent league refugees (Weber, reliever Brendan Donnelly and DH Shawn Wooten) than players drafted by the Angels in the first round (Erstad, Glaus).

The farm system prospered too, with three affiliates—Triple-A Salt Lake, low Class A Cedar Rapids and Rookie-level Provo—advancing to the playoffs. Reliever Francisco Rodriguez dazzled the world after his September callup, earning five of the Angels' 11 postseason victories, striking out 28 in 19 playoff innings and, at 20, becoming the youngest player to win a World Series game. And John Lackey, promoted in June, became the first rookie starter in 93 years to win Game Seven of the World Series.

ORGANIZATION LEADERS

BATTING

*AVG	Rick Short, Salt Lake	.356
R	Chone Figgins, Salt Lake	100
H	Robb Quinlan, Salt Lake	176
TB	Robb Quinlan, Salt Lake	293
2B	Jeff Mathis, Cedar Rapids	41
3B	Chone Figgins, Salt Lake	18
HR	Michael O'Keefe, Arkansas	21
	Carlos Duncan, Arkansas/Rancho Cucamonga	21
RBI	Robb Quinlan, Salt Lake	112
BB	Dallas McPherson, Cedar Rapids	78
SO	Brian Specht, Arkansas	129
SB	Kenny James, Arkansas	40

PITCHING

W	Johan Santana, Cedar Rapids	14
L	Three tied at.	14
#ERA	Francisco Rodriguez, Salt Lake/Arkansas	2.27
G	Bart Miadich, Salt Lake	59
CG	Rich Fischer, Rancho Cucamonga/Arkansas.	5
SV	Joel Peralta, Arkansas/Cedar Rapids	27
IP	Rich Fischer, Arkansas/Rancho Cucamonga	176
BB	Bobby Jenks, Arkansas/Rancho Cucamonga	90
SO	Pedro Liriano, Rancho Cucamonga.	176

*Minimum 250 At-Bats #Minimum 75 Innings

ANAHEIM
ANGELS

Manager: Mike Scioscia

2002 Record: 99-63, .611 (2nd, AL West)

BATTING	AVG	G	AB	R	H	2B	3B	HR	RBI	BB	SO	SB	CS	SLG	OBP	B	T	HT	WT	DOB	1st Yr	Resides
Amezaga, Alfredo	.538	12	13	3	7	2	0	0	2	0	1	1	0	.692	.538	S	R	5-10	160	1-16-78	1999	Obregon, Mexico
Anderson, Garret	.306	158	638	93	195	56	3	29	123	30	80	6	4	.539	.332	L	L	6-3	220	6-30-72	1990	Tustin Ranch, Calif.
Bellinger, Clay	.000	2	1	0	0	0	0	0	0	0	1	0	0	.000	.000	R	R	6-3	190	11-18-68	1989	Chandler, Ariz.
DaVanon, Jeff	.167	16	30	3	5	3	0	1	4	2	6	1	0	.367	.219	S	R	6-0	180	12-8-73	1995	Scottsdale, Ariz.
Eckstein, David	.293	152	608	107	178	22	6	8	63	45	44	21	13	.388	.363	R	R	5-8	170	1-20-75	1997	Sanford, Fla.
Erstad, Darin	.283	150	625	99	177	28	4	10	73	27	67	23	3	.389	.313	L	L	6-2	220	6-4-74	1995	Fargo, N.D.
Fabregas, Jorge	.193	35	88	8	17	1	0	0	8	6	6	0	0	.205	.245	L	R	6-3	220	3-13-70	1991	Miami Beach, Fla.
Fasano, Sal	.000	2	1	0	0	0	0	0	0	0	1	0	0	.000	.000	R	R	6-2	250	8-10-71	1993	Overland Park, Kan.
Figgins, Chone	.167	15	12	6	2	1	0	0	1	0	5	2	1	.250	.167	S	R	5-9	150	1-22-78	1997	Seffner, Fla.
Fullmer, Brad	.289	130	429	75	124	35	6	19	59	32	44	10	3	.531	.357	L	R	6-0	220	1-17-75	1994	Henderson, Nev.
Gil, Benji	.285	61	130	11	37	8	1	3	20	5	33	2	1	.431	.307	R	R	6-2	210	10-6-72	1991	Grapevine, Texas
Glaus, Troy	.250	156	569	99	142	24	1	30	111	88	144	10	3	.453	.352	R	R	6-5	240	8-3-76	1997	Norco, Calif.
Kennedy, Adam	.312	144	474	65	148	32	6	7	52	19	80	17	4	.449	.345	L	R	6-1	190	1-10-76	1997	Newport Beach, Calif.
Molina, Bengie	.245	122	428	34	105	18	0	5	47	15	34	0	0	.322	.274	R	R	5-11	210	7-20-74	1993	Yuma, Ariz.
Molina, Jose	.271	29	70	5	19	3	0	0	5	5	15	0	2	.314	.312	R	R	6-2	210	6-3-75	1993	Vega Alta, P.R.
Nieves, Jose	.289	45	97	17	28	2	0	6	2	14	1	1	.309	.303	R	R	6-0	180	6-16-75	1992	Carabobo, Venez.
Ochoa, Alex	.277	37	65	8	18	7	0	2	10	10	5	2	2	.477	.373	R	R	6-0	200	3-29-72	1991	Miami, Fla.
Palmeiro, Orlando	.300	110	263	35	79	12	1	0	31	30	22	7	2	.354	.368	L	R	5-11	180	1-19-69	1991	Miami, Fla.
Ramirez, Julio	.281	29	32	6	9	0	1	1	7	2	14	0	2	.438	.343	R	R	5-11	170	8-10-77	1994	Santo Domingo, D.R.
Salmon, Tim	.286	138	483	84	138	37	1	22	88	71	102	6	3	.503	.380	R	R	6-3	220	8-24-68	1989	Scottsdale, Ariz.
Spiezio, Scott	.285	153	491	80	140	34	2	12	82	67	52	6	7	.436	.371	S	R	6-2	220	9-21-72	1993	Morris, Ill.
Wooten, Shawn	.292	49	113	13	33	8	0	3	19	6	24	2	0	.442	.331	R	R	5-10	220	7-24-72	1993	Covina, Calif.

PITCHING	W	L	ERA	G	GS	CG	SV	IP	H	R	ER	BB	SO	AVG	B	T	HT	WT	DOB	1st Yr	Resides
Appier, Kevin	14	12	3.92	32	32	0	0	188	191	89	82	64	132	.267	R	R	6-2	200	12-6-67	1987	Paola, Kan.
Callaway, Mickey	2	1	4.19	6	6	0	0	34	31	20	16	11	23	.234	R	R	6-2	200	5-13-75	1996	Memphis, Tenn.
Cook, Dennis	1	1	3.38	37	0	0	0	24	21	9	9	10	13	.241	L	L	6-3	190	10-4-62	1985	Austin, Texas
Donnelly, Brendan	1	1	2.17	46	0	0	1	50	32	13	12	19	54	.183	R	R	6-3	200	7-4-71	1992	Hilton Head, S.C.
Lackey, John	9	4	3.66	18	18	1	0	108	113	52	44	33	69	.266	R	R	6-6	200	10-23-78	1999	Abilene, Texas
Levine, Alan	4	4	4.24	52	0	0	5	64	61	35	30	34	40	.253	L	R	6-3	190	5-22-68	1991	Gilbert, Ariz.
Lukasiewicz, Mark	2	0	3.86	17	0	0	0	14	17	6	6	9	15	.298	L	L	6-5	240	3-8-73	1994	Clay, N.Y.
Ortiz, Ramon	15	9	3.77	32	32	4	0	217	188	97	91	68	162	.230	R	R	6-0	170	3-23-73	1995	Cotui, D.R.
Percival, Troy	4	1	1.92	58	0	0	40	56	38	12	12	25	68	.188	R	R	6-3	230	8-9-69	1990	Riverside, Calif.
Pote, Lou	0	2	3.22	31	0	0	0	50	33	20	18	26	32	.194	R	R	6-3	200	8-27-71	1991	Phoenix, Ariz.
Rodriguez, Francisco	0	0	0.00	5	0	0	0	6	3	0	0	2	13	.166	R	R	6-0	170	1-7-82	1999	Caracas, Venez.
Schoeneweis, Scott	9	8	4.88	54	15	0	1	118	119	68	64	49	65	.264	L	L	6-0	180	10-2-73	1996	Fountain Hills, Ariz.
Sele, Aaron	8	9	4.89	26	26	1	0	160	190	92	87	49	82	.299	R	R	6-5	220	6-25-70	1991	Bellevue, Wash.
Shields, Scot	5	3	2.20	29	1	0	0	49	31	13	12	21	30	.187	R	R	6-1	170	7-22-75	1997	Livonia, Mich.
Wall, Donne	0	0	6.43	17	0	0	0	21	17	15	15	7	13	.220	R	R	6-1	200	7-11-67	1989	Pearland, Texas
Washburn, Jarrod	18	6	3.15	32	32	1	0	206	183	75	72	59	139	.234	L	L	6-1	180	8-13-74	1995	Danbury, Wis.
Weber, Ben	7	2	2.54	63	0	0	7	78	70	25	22	22	43	.249	R	R	6-4	210	11-17-69	1991	Beaumont, Texas
Wise, Matt	0	0	3.24	7	0	0	0	8	7	3	3	1	6	.233	R	R	6-4	190	11-18-75	1997	Yorba Linda, Calif.

FIELDING

Catcher	PCT	G	PO	A	E	DP	PB
Fabregas	.994	32	156	8	1	1	1
Fasano	1.000	2	10	2	0	0	0
Figgins	.000	1	0	0	0	0	0
B. Molina	.999	121	707	60	1	6	5
J. Molina	.983	29	154	16	3	3	1
Palmeiro	.000	1	0	0	0	0	0
Wooten	1.000	2	2	1	0	0	0

First Base	PCT	G	PO	A	E	DP
Bellinger	1.000	2	2	0	0	0
Erstad	1.000	5	9	0	0	2
Fullmer	.995	29	176	8	1	22
Gil	.973	10	33	3	1	6
Nieves	1.000	3	16	1	0	3
Spiezio	.997	143	1078	59	3	101
Wooten	1.000	16	62	4	0	3

Second Base	PCT	G	PO	A	E	DP
Figgins	.941	8	7	9	1	2
Gil	.990	26	41	58	1	11
Kennedy	.983	139	273	367	11	90
Nieves	.938	18	30	31	4	8
Spiezio	.000	1	0	0	0	0
Wooten	.000	1	0	0	0	0

Third Base	PCT	G	PO	A	E	DP
Glaus	.950	156	101	281	20	30
Nieves	1.000	5	0	5	0	0
Spiezio	.943	20	14	19	2	2
Wooten	.000	1	0	0	0	0

Shortstop	PCT	G	PO	A	E	DP
Amezaga	1.000	5	7	11	0	1
Eckstein	.977	147	205	397	14	91
Gil	.960	14	16	32	2	5
Glaus	1.000	2	1	1	0	1
Nieves	.939	13	11	20	2	4

Outfield	PCT	G	PO	A	E	DP
Anderson	.994	147	302	7	2	3
DaVanon	1.000	10	13	0	0	0
Erstad	.998	143	452	11	1	3
Kennedy	.000	1	0	0	0	0
Nieves	.500	2	1	0	1	0
Ochoa	.975	36	37	2	1	1
Palmeiro	.993	86	146	3	1	1
Ramirez	1.000	23	26	1	0	0
Salmon	.986	111	201	4	3	0
Spiezio	1.000	10	3	0	0	0

Troy Glaus

LARRY GOREN

FARM SYSTEM

Player Development: Tony Reagins

Class	Farm Team	League	W	L	Pct.	Finish*	Manager	First Yr.
AAA	SaltLake (Utah) Stingers	Pacific Coast	78	66	.542	3rd (16)	Mike Brumley	2001
AA	Arkansas Travelers	Texas	51	89	.364	8th (8)	Doug Sisson	2001
High A	Rancho Cucamonga (Calif.) Quakes	California	52	88	.371	10th (10)	Bobby Meacham	2001
Low A	Cedar Rapids (Iowa) Kernels	Midwest	81	58	.583	3rd (14)	Todd Claus	1993
Rookie	Provo (Utah) Angels	Pioneer	38	38	.500	4th (8)	Tom Kotchman	2001
Rookie	Mesa (Ariz.) Angels	Arizona	28	28	.500	t-3rd (7)	Brian Harper	2001

*Finish in overall standings (No. of teams in league)

SALT LAKE STINGERS · Class AAA

PACIFIC COAST LEAGUE

BATTING	AVG	G	AB	R	H	2B	3B	HR	RBI	BB	SO	SB	CS	SLG	OBP	B	T	HT	WT	DOB	1st Yr	Resides
Amezaga, Alfredo	.251	128	518	77	130	25	7	6	51	45	100	23	14	.361	.317	S	R	5-10	160	1-16-78	1999	Obregon, Mexico
Barnes, Larry	.314	114	452	71	142	29	11	20	95	28	90	8	1	.560	.354	L	L	6-1	190	7-23-74	1995	Bakersfield, Calif.
Bellinger, Clay	.256	89	324	45	83	17	5	13	41	13	87	4	2	.460	.289	R	R	6-3	190	11-18-68	1989	Chandler, Ariz.
Burke, Jamie	.304	88	316	47	96	12	4	8	44	20	37	1	3	.443	.350	R	R	6-0	190	9-24-71	1993	Roseburg, Ore.
DaVanon, Jeff	.330	25	100	21	33	10	1	5	18	17	24	5	3	.600	.429	S	R	6-0	180	12-8-73	1995	Scottsdale, Ariz.
Durrington, Trent	.206	19	68	6	14	3	1	3	10	3	15	2	1	.412	.260	R	R	5-10	190	8-27-75	1994	Broadbeach Waters, Australia
Fasano, Sal	.276	22	76	13	21	3	0	5	10	7	24	1	0	.513	.349	R	R	6-2	250	8-10-71	1993	Overland Park, Kan.
Figgins, Chone	.305	125	511	100	156	25	18	7	62	53	83	39	8	.466	.364	S	R	5-9	150	1-22-78	1997	Seffner, Fla.
Gil, Benji	.417	6	24	4	10	5	1	2	6	1	4	0	2	.958	.440	R	R	6-2	210	10-6-72	1991	Grapevine, Texas
Gregorio, Tom	.255	15	51	7	13	4	0	1	3	2	9	0	0	.392	.309	R	R	6-2	200	5-5-77	1999	Staten Island, N.Y.
Guiel, Jeff	.253	95	316	51	80	22	4	12	45	43	72	6	3	.462	.350	L	R	5-11	190	1-12-74	1997	Langley, B.C.
Haynes, Nathan	.283	67	283	37	80	14	6	2	12	12	53	10	10	.396	.313	L	L	5-9	170	9-7-79	1997	Vallejo, Calif.
Johnson, Gary	.266	40	143	30	38	9	3	5	35	15	49	1	1	.476	.341	L	L	6-3	210	10-29-75	1999	Atherton, Calif.
Johnson, Keith	.281	98	367	55	103	22	3	15	56	11	65	6	3	.480	.312	R	R	5-11	200	4-17-71	1992	Las Vegas, Nev.
Molina, Jose	.307	79	290	30	89	14	2	4	43	12	60	0	3	.410	.341	R	R	6-2	210	6-3-75	1993	Vega Alta, P.R.
Nieves, Jose	.286	15	63	12	18	3	1	4	13	4	6	2	1	.556	.328	R	R	6-0	180	6-16-75	1992	Carabobo, Venez.
Quinlan, Robb	.333	136	528	95	176	31	13	20	112	41	93	8	2	.555	.376	R	R	6-1	200	3-17-77	1999	Maplewood, Minn.
Ramirez, Julio	.273	39	139	17	38	3	5	2	10	4	31	8	3	.410	.299	R	R	5-11	170	8-10-77	1994	Santo Domingo, D.R.
Short, Rick	.356	105	410	71	146	29	2	7	68	23	43	3	2	.488	.399	R	R	6-0	200	12-6-72	1994	Peoria, Ill.
Urquhart, Derick	.222	14	54	6	12	2	1	1	6	5	11	0	2	.352	.288	L	L	5-8	170	12-20-75	1998	Florence, S.C.
Wooten, Shawn	.262	10	42	2	11	2	0	0	7	0	11	0	0	.310	.279	R	R	5-10	220	7-24-72	1993	Covina, Calif.

PITCHING	W	L	ERA	G	GS	CG	SV	IP	H	R	ER	BB	SO	AVG	B	T	HT	WT	DOB	1st Yr	Resides
Bergman, Dusty	1	1	6.44	21	0	0	1	29	34	25	21	9	26	.290	L	L	6-4	200	2-1-78	1999	Carson City, Nev.
Bootcheck, Chris	4	3	3.88	9	9	1	0	58	64	29	25	16	38	.283	R	R	6-5	200	10-24-78	2001	La Porte, Ind.
Callaway, Mickey	9	2	1.68	17	14	1	0	91	79	26	17	22	75	.228	R	R	6-2	220	6-3-76	1997	Memphis, Tenn.
Cummings, Ryan	3	2	3.80	22	0	0	0	24	24	11	10	6	13	.266	R	R	6-2	220	6-3-76	1997	Marietta, Ga.
Dillinger, John	3	0	6.64	8	6	0	0	42	56	33	31	7	26	.323	R	R	6-5	260	8-28-73	1992	Dawson, Pa.
Donnelly, Brendan	4	0	3.48	25	0	0	6	34	27	13	13	11	42	.212	R	R	6-3	200	7-4-71	1992	Hilton Head, S.C.
Emanuel, Brandon	2	3	7.25	7	7	0	0	36	59	29	29	11	27	.375	R	R	6-3	210	4-9-76	1998	Tampa, Fla.
Hensley, Matt	7	5	4.97	19	18	1	0	118	132	76	65	39	106	.287	R	R	6-2	230	8-18-78	2000	San Diego, Calif.
Hundley, Jeff	0	1	9.28	4	2	0	0	11	16	13	11	7	8	.333	L	L	6-2	200	2-19-77	1998	Warren, Ohio
Janzen, Marty	2	2	4.40	11	6	0	0	29	34	17	14	9	16	.314	R	R	6-3	190	5-31-73	1991	Gainesville, Fla.
Jones, Greg	7	4	4.31	39	0	0	2	63	68	35	30	22	55	.273	R	R	6-2	190	11-15-76	1997	Seminole, Fla.
Kelley, Rich	6	5	4.08	40	15	1	0	119	128	64	54	40	72	.276	L	L	6-3	210	5-27-70	1991	Lakeland, Fla.
Lackey, John	8	2	2.57	16	16	2	0	102	89	35	29	28	82	.234	R	R	6-6	200	10-23-78	1999	Abilene, Texas
Levine, Alan	0	0	3.00	2	0	0	0	3	5	1	1	0	0	.384	L	R	6-3	190	5-22-68	1991	Gilbert, Ariz.
Lukasiewicz, Mark	3	2	3.98	35	0	0	0	43	46	26	19	17	48	.277	L	L	6-5	240	3-8-73	1994	Clay, N.Y.
Mendoza, Mario	0	1	10.29	3	0	0	1	7	13	11	8	4	7	.393	R	R	6-3	200	1-19-79	1999	Navojoa, Mexico
Miadich, Bart	4	3	3.68	59	0	0	14	81	60	43	33	64	92	.200	R	R	6-4	200	2-3-76	1997	Lake Oswego, Ore.
Nina, Elvin	5	9	4.64	26	15	0	0	109	115	75	56	50	68	.273	R	R	6-0	180	11-25-75	1997	Tempe, Ariz.
Pine, Chris	1	6	5.40	19	6	0	0	42	56	30	25	23	21	.329	R	R	6-2	200	9-25-76	1998	Tigard, Ore.
Pote, Lou	2	1	6.00	7	7	0	0	39	42	29	26	10	43	.267	R	R	6-0	170	8-27-71	1991	Phoenix, Ariz.
Rodriguez, Francisco	2	3	2.57	27	0	0	6	42	30	13	12	13	59	.204	R	R	6-0	170	1-7-82	1999	Caracas, Venez.
Shields, Scot	2	2	3.06	28	1	0	1	47	39	18	16	6	50	.222	R	R	6-1	170	7-22-75	1997	Livonia, Mich.
Stephens, Jason	0	4	6.91	5	5	0	0	27	37	25	21	7	14	.310	R	R	6-3	190	9-10-75	1996	Springhill, La.
Wall, Donne	0	1	5.40	1	1	0	0	2	1	1	1	0	2	.166	R	R	6-1	200	7-11-67	1989	Pearland, Texas
Wise, Matt	3	4	5.42	16	16	0	0	78	102	51	47	15	76	.323	R	R	6-4	190	11-18-75	1997	Yorba Linda, Calif.

FIELDING

Catcher	PCT	G	PO	A	E	DP	PB
Bellinger	1.000	3	14	1	0	0	1
Burke	.980	35	225	20	5	1	3
Durrington	1.000	2	16	0	0	0	2
Fasano	.978	22	168	14	4	3	2
Gregorio	1.000	13	59	9	0	0	4
Guiel	.000	1	0	0	0	0	0
Molina	.994	76	582	62	4	1	5
Wooten	1.000	1	3	0	0	0	0

First Base	PCT	G	PO	A	E	DP
Barnes	.991	80	693	56	7	78
Bellinger	.989	20	170	7	2	14
Burke	1.000	19	147	12	0	16

	PCT	G	PO	A	E	DP
Gil	.889	1	8	0	1	0
Guiel	1.000	2	13	0	0	1
K. Johnson	1.000	1	9	3	0	1
Nieves	.900	1	9	0	1	2
Quinlan	1.000	7	66	4	0	6
Short	.993	17	130	17	1	11
Wooten	.973	5	35	1	1	2

Second Base	PCT	G	PO	A	E	DP
Amezaga	1.000	1	1	2	0	1
Durrington	1.000	4	3	12	0	3
Figgins	.966	117	214	380	21	81
Gil	1.000	2	8	2	0	1
K. Johnson	1.000	8	13	26	0	7

	PCT	G	PO	A	E	DP
Nieves	.917	4	3	8	1	1
Short	.950	9	18	20	2	5

Third Base	PCT	G	PO	A	E	DP
Bellinger	.943	26	13	37	3	0
Burke	.916	31	23	64	8	5
Durrington	1.000	4	0	6	0	1
Guiel	.500	1	0	1	1	0
K. Johnson	.952	78	47	151	10	11
Nieves	.917	6	1	10	1	1
Short	.909	5	3	7	1	0
Wooten	1.000	1	1	1	0	0

Shortstop	PCT	G	PO	A	E	DP
Amezaga	.962	126	207	397	24	90
Figgins	.933	6	8	20	2	3
Gil	1.000	2	3	10	0	1
K. Johnson	.917	8	11	22	3	11
Nieves	.750	2	2	1	1	0

Outfield	PCT	G	PO	A	E	DP
Barnes	.973	22	36	0	1	0
Bellinger	.985	36	59	5	1	0
DaVanon	.962	25	49	2	2	0
Durrington	.960	10	21	3	1	0
Guiel	.980	81	144	6	3	1
Haynes	.974	66	147	5	4	1

	PCT	G	PO	A	E	DP
G. Johnson	1.000	37	67	0	0	0
K. Johnson	.000	1	0	0	0	0
Nieves	1.000	2	4	0	0	0
Quinlan	.984	108	177	7	3	0
Ramirez	.976	37	80	1	2	0
Short	.917	9	11	0	1	0
Urquhart	1.000	14	23	0	0	0

ARKANSAS TRAVELERS
Class AA

TEXAS LEAGUE

BATTING

BATTING	AVG	G	AB	R	H	2B	3B	HR	RBI	BB	SO	SB	CS	SLG	OBP	B	T	HT	WT	DOB	1st Yr	Resides
Budde, Ryan	.111	3	9	1	1	0	0	1	1	1	2	0	0	.444	.200	R	R	5-11	200	8-15-79	2001	Midwest City, Okla.
Burns, Kevin	.178	56	169	20	30	11	1	4	21	34	49	1	0	.325	.322	L	L	6-5	220	9-9-75	1995	El Dorado, Ark.
Camilli, Jason	.225	112	338	39	76	13	1	4	28	37	64	6	5	.305	.306	R	R	6-0	190	10-18-75	1994	Phoenix, Ariz.
Christensen, Brian	.223	122	413	33	92	18	2	5	35	15	98	1	2	.312	.253	R	R	6-2	190	5-24-76	1998	Naples, Fla.
Del Chiaro, Brent	.000	3	8	0	0	0	0	0	0	0	3	0	0	.000	.000	R	R	6-3	210	6-26-79	2001	Oakley, Calif.
Duncan, Carlos	.274	60	215	31	59	11	1	6	23	11	44	15	5	.419	.336	R	R	6-1	200	6-30-77	1995	San Pedro de Macoris, D.R.
Durrington, Trent	.246	107	382	59	94	18	4	9	47	39	71	25	14	.385	.328	R	R	5-10	190	8-27-75	1994	Broadbeach, Australia
Gregorio, Tom	.250	56	188	18	47	10	1	3	15	9	33	2	0	.362	.291	R	R	6-2	200	5-5-77	1999	Staten Island, NY
Guiel, Jeff	.286	5	14	2	4	0	0	1	4	4	2	1	0	.500	.450	L	R	5-11	190	1-12-74	1997	Langley, BC, Canada
Guzman, Elpidio	.247	124	454	57	112	15	9	4	41	40	91	21	11	.346	.309	R	R	6-0	160	2-24-77	1996	Santo Domingo, D.R.
Hill, Jason	.271	118	431	41	117	21	2	6	54	14	63	2	4	.371	.302	R	R	6-3	200	3-17-77	1998	Danville, Calif.
Huisman, Jason	.243	77	263	41	64	15	1	5	36	13	33	11	6	.365	.301	R	R	6-3	190	4-16-76	1998	Thornton, Ill.
James, Kenny	.268	96	380	48	102	17	1	3	32	21	58	40	13	.342	.319	S	R	6-0	190	10-9-76	1995	Ocala, Fla.
McKinley, Dan	.240	26	100	10	24	7	0	0	9	2	15	2	1	.310	.245	R	R	5-10	190	5-15-76	1997	Chandler, Ariz.
O'Keefe, Mike	.280	132	468	72	131	34	7	21	78	62	73	10	3	.517	.367	L	L	5-10	190	6-28-78	1999	Hamden, Conn.
Rogers, Brandon	.091	6	11	0	1	0	0	0	2	2	0	0	0	.091	.231	R	R	6-0	200	3-1-78	2000	El Cajon, Calif.
Specht, Brian	.248	126	476	64	118	24	4	13	60	49	129	18	4	.397	.321	S	R	5-11	170	10-19-80	1999	Colorado Springs, Colo.
Urquhart, Derick	.206	82	233	25	48	10	2	2	17	26	31	6	4	.292	.289	L	L	5-8	170	12-20-75	1998	Florence, S.C.
Warriax, Brandon	.264	18	53	5	14	2	1	1	2	3	9	0	0	.396	.304	R	R	6-0	160	6-23-79	1997	Maxton, N.C.
2-team (88 Tulsa)	.187	106	316	32	59	9	3	6	20	31	91	3	2	.291	.264							

PITCHING

PITCHING	W	L	ERA	G	GS	CG	SV	IP	H	R	ER	BB	SO	AVG	B	T	HT	WT	DOB	1st Yr	Resides
Bergman, Dusty	5	0	2.41	35	0	0	3	56	48	21	15	8	38	.229	L	L	6-4	200	2-1-78	1999	Carson City, Nev.
Bootcheck, Chris	8	7	4.81	19	19	3	0	116	130	68	62	35	90	.276	R	R	6-5	200	10-24-78	2001	La Porte, Ind.
Camilli, Jason	0	0	6.75	2	0	0	0	1	2	2	1	0	1	1.000	R	R	6-0	190	10-18-75	1994	Phoenix, Ariz.
Cummings, Ryan	4	3	3.49	21	0	0	1	39	42	20	15	22	21	.274	R	R	6-2	220	6-3-76	1997	Marietta, Ga.
Dillinger, John	2	1	4.24	5	5	0	0	34	45	22	16	14	25	.314	R	R	6-5	260	8-28-73	1992	Dawson, Pa.
Emanuel, Brandon	5	3	2.81	14	14	1	0	83	76	32	26	18	47	.243	R	R	6-3	210	4-9-76	1998	Tampa, Fla.
Fischer, Rich	1	3	4.23	7	7	0	0	45	40	22	21	10	36	.232	R	R	6-3	180	10-21-80	2000	Riverside, Calif.
Grezlovski, Ben	0	2	5.13	38	2	0	1	60	70	41	34	34	29	.286	R	R	5-11	180	11-22-76	1999	Miami, Fla.
Hundley, Jeff	1	4	3.38	38	0	0	1	59	53	24	22	19	38	.244	L	L	6-2	200	2-19-77	1998	Warren, Ohio
Jackson, Dan	1	0	9.00	8	0	0	0	12	25	15	12	6	7	.431	R	R	5-11	210	7-12-78	2000	Lyons, Ill.
Jenks, Bobby	3	6	4.66	10	10	1	0	58	49	34	30	44	58	.234	R	R	6-3	240	3-14-81	2000	Bothell, Wash.
McClain, Kevin	1	1	4.63	8	0	0	1	12	11	8	6	3	8	.229	R	R	6-4	180	2-22-78	1998	Grant, Fla.
Mendoza, Hatuey	3	10	5.58	29	14	2	0	90	113	68	56	36	45	.304	R	R	6-1	170	3-16-78	1997	Santo Domingo, D.R.
Mendoza, Mario	0	4	3.80	10	8	2	0	47	55	23	20	16	30	.298	R	R	6-3	200	1-19-79	1999	Navojoa, Mexico
Milo, Tony	2	4	7.92	15	9	0	0	44	57	43	39	24	35	.314	L	L	6-5	200	5-5-78	2000	Laguna Hills, Calif.
Nickoli, Mike	3	10	6.12	17	17	0	0	82	116	64	56	45	32	.347	R	R	6-5	200	3-6-80	2001	Hoover, Ala.
O'Neal, Brandon	0	0	6.75	2	0	0	0	4	6	3	3	4	3	.352	S	R	6-1	210	10-17-78	2000	Olathe, Kan.
Peralta, Joel	0	0	6.62	12	0	0	0	18	25	15	13	10	11	.337	R	R	5-11	160	3-23-76	1996	Bonao, D.R.
Pine, Chris	1	3	6.39	17	4	1	1	38	38	29	27	15	16	.263	R	R	6-2	200	9-25-76	1998	Tigard, Ore.
Rodriguez, Francisco	3	3	1.96	23	0	0	9	41	32	13	9	15	61	.206	R	R	6-0	170	1-7-82	1999	Caracas, Venez.
Stephens, Jason	1	4	4.85	5	5	0	0	30	37	20	16	8	18	.303	R	R	6-0	180	9-10-75	1996	Springhill, La.
Stokley, Billy	4	14	4.33	38	19	4	1	131	156	77	63	34	41	.304	L	R	6-4	200	5-13-77	2000	Pasadena, Texas
Thames, Charlie	1	3	5.03	38	0	0	4	54	45	34	30	35	42	.234	R	R	6-1	190	5-23-79	2000	Humble, Texas
Wilson, Phil	2	4	7.17	7	7	0	0	43	57	37	34	14	15	.314	R	R	6-8	220	4-1-81	1999	Ramona, Calif.

FIELDING

Catcher	PCT	G	PO	A	E	DP	PB
Budde	1.000	2	15	2	0	0	0
Del Chiaro	1.000	2	13	0	0	0	2
Durrington	.988	41	207	30	3	0	9
Gregorio	.977	43	213	44	6	3	7
Hill	.994	58	310	38	2	2	5
Rogers	1.000	3	5	2	0	0	0

First Base	PCT	G	PO	A	E	DP
Burns	.988	36	302	25	4	30
Camilli	1.000	1	1	0	0	1
Christensen	1.000	5	23	0	0	3
Hill	.986	23	191	20	3	23
Huisman	1.000	1	10	0	0	1
O'Keefe	.991	89	714	65	7	70

Second Base	PCT	G	PO	A	E	DP
Camilli	.972	52	92	155	7	39
Duncan	.960	50	98	142	10	38
Durrington	.964	30	60	74	5	11
Huisman	.971	20	27	40	2	8
Warriax	1.000	2	1	0	0	0

Third Base	PCT	G	PO	A	E	DP
Camilli	.878	17	8	28	5	1
Christensen	.941	117	74	263	21	24
Durrington	.850	11	9	8	3	0
Huisman	1.000	1	0	1	0	0
Warriax	.818	4	3	6	2	1

Shortstop	PCT	G	PO	A	E	DP
Camilli	.938	29	60	62	8	15
Duncan	.727	3	2	6	3	0

	PCT	G	PO	A	E	DP
Durrington	.842	4	5	11	3	3
Specht	.932	95	179	301	35	61
Warriax	.949	12	13	43	3	6

Outfield	PCT	G	PO	A	E	DP
Camilli	1.000	7	5	1	0	0
Duncan	1.000	8	15	0	0	0
Durrington	1.000	16	27	1	0	1
Guiel	1.000	5	11	0	0	0
Guzman	.970	121	247	15	8	4
Huisman	.943	60	94	6	6	1
James	.982	90	217	2	4	1
McKinley	.979	23	43	4	1	1
O'Keefe	.986	44	65	4	1	0
Urquhart	.992	72	123	3	1	1

RANCHO CUCAMONGA QUAKES
High Class A

CALIFORNIA LEAGUE

BATTING

BATTING	AVG	G	AB	R	H	2B	3B	HR	RBI	BB	SO	SB	CS	SLG	OBP	B	T	HT	WT	DOB	1st Yr	Resides
Abruzzo, Jared	.244	101	385	53	94	27	0	16	53	30	124	1	1	.439	.300	S	R	6-3	220	11-15-81	2000	La Mesa, Calif.
Adames, Epidaro	.000	1	1	0	0	0	0	0	0	0	1	0	0	.000	.000	R	R	6-1	190	3-29-79	1996	Santo Domingo, D.R.

BATTING	AVG	G	AB	R	H	2B	3B	HR	RBI	BB	SO	SB	CS	SLG	OBP	B	T	HT	WT	DOB	1st Yr	Resides
Budde, Ryan	.241	87	307	40	74	17	1	5	39	27	60	2	1	.352	.305	R	R	5-11	200	8-15-79	2001	Midwest City, Okla.
Campo, Mike	.313	126	450	86	141	35	6	9	53	75	127	18	10	.478	.451	L	R	5-10	180	11-14-76	2000	Absecon, N.J.
Contreras, Sergio	.271	81	291	44	79	17	3	5	35	24	58	4	3	.402	.335	L	L	5-11	195	4-30-80	1999	Esperanza, Mexico
Corbeil, Al	.252	105	373	46	94	23	1	9	58	35	95	1	2	.391	.325	L	R	6-0	190	12-16-78	2001	Margate, Fla.
Coulie, Jason	.249	91	365	53	91	25	3	12	58	15	82	8	8	.433	.284	R	R	6-2	200	4-13-78	2000	Manchester, N.H.
Duncan, Carlos	.263	70	274	45	72	19	4	15	68	30	80	20	5	.526	.342	R	R	6-1	200	6-30-77	1995	San Pedro de Macoris, D.R.
Haynes, Nathan	.280	11	50	6	14	0	0	0	2	4	8	6	2	.280	.345	L	L	5-9	170	9-7-79	1997	Vallejo, Calif.
Maher, Caleb	.444	3	9	0	4	1	0	0	0	2	2	0	0	.556	.545	R	R	6-2	190	3-22-83	2002	Ceres, Calif.
Mathis, Jake	.222	5	18	3	4	1	0	0	2	1	8	0	0	.278	.263	L	R	6-3	200	1-24-80	2002	Marianna, Fla.
Melgarejo, Ransel	.200	4	15	0	3	0	0	3	1	0	0	0	0	.200	.235	R	R	6-0	180	8-28-81	2001	Miami, Fla.
Molina, Bengie	.500	1	2	0	1	0	0	0	0	1	0	0	0	.500	.750	R	R	5-11	210	7-20-74	1993	Yuma, Ariz.
Nunez, Felix	.143	5	14	3	2	0	0	0	0	4	5	0	0	.143	.333	R	R	6-1	170	10-9-82	2001	El Tigre, Venez.
Pichardo, Maximo	.250	51	168	15	42	6	1	1	14	6	27	7	5	.315	.277	R	R	6-0	150	6-27-79	1999	Santo Domingo, D.R.
Raburn, Johnny	.292	115	448	71	131	20	5	1	36	77	88	35	19	.366	.397	S	R	6-1	160	2-16-79	2000	Plant City, Fla.
Rodriguez, Javy	.254	59	213	23	54	6	4	1	22	15	44	19	11	.333	.299	R	R	5-11	170	1-16-79	2002	Miami, Fla.
Roper, Zach	.242	69	252	36	61	16	0	7	34	32	47	1	1	.389	.338	R	R	6-2	200	9-26-77	2000	Pompano Beach, Fla.
Selmo, Wilson	.200	4	10	1	2	0	0	0	0	1	2	0	0	.200	.273	S	R	5-11	160	9-27-82	2000	Santo Domingo, D.R.
Smith, Casey	.248	112	408	40	101	9	4	2	35	30	56	9	8	.304	.306	R	R	6-2	200	3-18-79	2001	Ashford, Ala.
Swenson, Sam	.233	80	283	49	66	16	2	9	40	26	105	4	5	.399	.321	R	R	6-0	190	2-28-78	2001	South Jordan, Utah
Urquhart, Derick	.000	2	7	0	0	0	0	0	0	1	0	0	0	.000	.125	L	L	5-8	170	12-20-75	1998	Florence, S.C.
Warriax, Brandon	.161	18	56	4	9	3	0	1	5	4	19	0	0	.268	.217	R	R	6-0	160	6-23-79	1997	Maxton, N.C.
Webb, Ryan	.249	82	241	23	60	11	2	0	26	21	63	10	7	.311	.313	R	R	6-3	190	5-30-78	2001	Upland, Calif.
Wooten, Shawn	.222	6	18	2	4	3	0	0	3	4	4	0	0	.389	.348	R	R	5-10	220	7-24-72	1993	Covina, Calif.
Zamora, Junior	.269	30	119	12	32	10	0	3	14	1	31	0	1	.429	.293	R	R	6-2	190	5-3-76	1994	San Pedro de Macoris, D.R.

PITCHING	W	L	ERA	G	GS	CG	SV	IP	H	R	ER	BB	SO	AVG	B	T	HT	WT	DOB	1st Yr	Resides
Andujar, Jesse	0	3	6.64	32	1	0	1	60	68	48	44	24	53	.285	R	R	6-1	170	7-23-79	1996	San Pedro de Macoris, D.R.
Balser, Jeff	0	0	8.22	4	0	0	0	8	16	8	7	6	6	.400	R	R	6-1	210	12-31-80	2001	Venice, Fla.
Brunet, Rich	0	1	3.57	39	0	0	16	40	39	16	16	11	50	.251	R	R	6-2	160	3-5-77	1997	Land O'Lakes, Fla.
Bukowski, Stan	1	6	5.89	14	12	1	0	73	92	54	48	22	53	.309	R	R	6-4	220	9-16-81	1999	Clearwater, Fla.
Cook, Dennis	0	1	17.18	4	3	0	0	4	8	7	7	1	5	.421	L	L	6-3	190	10-4-62	1985	Austin, Texas
Dennis, Jason	2	3	3.75	28	0	0	0	36	29	15	15	17	22	.230	L	L	6-0	190	8-12-78	2001	Concord, Calif.
Fischer, Rich	7	8	3.50	19	19	5	0	131	118	61	51	29	138	.239	R	R	6-3	180	10-21-80	2000	Riverside, Calif.
Hensley, Matt	1	1	5.40	12	2	0	0	32	42	21	19	11	27	.318	R	R	6-2	220	8-18-78	2000	San Diego, Calif.
Jackson, Dan	9	4	4.22	31	9	0	4	98	96	58	46	34	111	.248	R	R	5-11	210	7-12-78	2000	Lyons, Ill.
Jenks, Bobby	3	5	4.82	11	10	1	0	65	50	42	35	46	64	.211	R	R	6-3	240	3-14-81	2000	Bothell, Wash.
Liriano, Pedro	10	14	3.60	28	28	1	0	167	129	86	67	74	176	.212	R	R	6-2	160	10-23-80	1999	Fantino, D.R.
Marquez, Jeff	0	0	3.00	2	0	0	0	3	4	1	1	0	1	.235	L	R	6-0	200	11-5-81	2002	Hialeah, Fla.
McClain, Kevin	0	4	6.00	40	0	0	1	54	60	37	36	18	52	.287	R	R	6-4	180	2-22-78	1998	Grant, Fla.
Mendoza, Mario	0	2	4.79	21	0	0	0	41	51	27	22	14	33	.301	R	R	6-3	200	1-19-79	1999	Navojoa, Mexico
Milo, Tony	1	0	0.00	4	0	0	0	8	4	0	0	1	9	.148	L	L	6-5	220	5-5-78	2000	Laguna Hills, Calif.
Morris, Will	0	0	5.79	4	0	0	0	9	10	7	6	7	5	.303	L	R	6-0	180	3-26-78	2000	Rancho Cucamonga, Calif.
Mozingo, Dan	2	3	5.18	9	7	0	0	42	52	33	24	21	28	.307	L	L	6-2	190	6-3-80	1998	Ashtabula, Ohio
O'Neal, Brandon	5	14	5.24	24	22	0	0	124	132	113	72	69	81	.273	S	R	6-1	210	10-17-78	2000	Olathe, Kan.
Smith, Cliff	3	8	4.81	36	3	0	0	79	95	57	42	35	77	.296	R	R	6-0	190	10-13-79	2001	Haverhill, Mass.
Thomas, Adam	0	3	14.58	5	3	0	0	17	36	29	27	9	18	.423	R	R	6-4	190	5-22-79	2000	North Miami, Fla.
Toledo, Jean	0	1	8.00	3	2	0	0	9	12	9	8	6	8	.333	R	R	6-1	180	3-6-83	2001	Barcelona, Venez.
Turnbow, Derrick	0	0	5.25	13	0	0	0	12	16	11	7	9	14	.320	R	R	6-3	218	1-25-78	1997	Scottsdale, Ariz.
Wawrzyniak, Alan	0	2	7.67	10	5	0	1	29	35	32	25	20	29	.277	R	R	6-3	200	9-14-77	1999	Blandon, Pa.
Wilson, Phil	5	5	5.53	14	14	1	0	86	93	62	53	29	71	.268	R	R	6-8	220	4-1-81	1999	Ramona, Calif.

FIELDING

Catcher	PCT	G	PO	A	E	DP	PB
Abruzzo	.976	59	438	53	12	3	17
Budde	.985	77	615	84	11	7	6
Corbeil	.982	9	45	9	1	0	0
Molina	1.000	1	8	1	0	0	0

First Base	PCT	G	PO	A	E	DP
Contreras	.977	23	165	8	4	17
Corbeil	.988	97	784	45	10	70
Roper	.983	24	215	12	4	16
Wooten	1.000	3	29	2	0	2
Zamora	.966	7	51	5	2	4

Second Base	PCT	G	PO	A	E	DP
Pichardo	.983	24	51	62	2	19
Raburn	.978	45	99	121	5	27
Rodriguez	.967	9	10	19	1	2

	PCT	G	PO	A	E	DP
Smith	.955	66	114	182	14	34

Third Base	PCT	G	PO	A	E	DP
Duncan	.868	50	35	110	22	9
Mathis	.905	5	5	14	2	2
Pichardo	.857	17	8	28	6	4
Raburn	.929	10	9	17	2	2
Rodriguez	.000	1	0	0	0	0
Roper	.964	12	3	24	1	1
Smith	.976	34	23	60	2	2
Zamora	.918	21	10	46	5	2

Shortstop	PCT	G	PO	A	E	DP
Pichardo	.875	6	12	23	5	6
Raburn	.910	57	94	160	25	34
Rodriguez	.939	51	58	141	13	27
Selmo	.923	4	4	8	1	1

	PCT	G	PO	A	E	DP
Smith	.889	13	18	30	6	5
Warriax	.917	17	25	52	7	7

Outfield	PCT	G	PO	A	E	DP
Campo	.952	96	115	4	6	1
Contreras	.959	53	91	3	4	0
Coulie	.963	90	146	8	6	3
Duncan	.913	14	20	1	2	0
Haynes	.955	11	21	0	1	0
Maher	1.000	2	3	0	0	0
Melgarejo	1.000	4	9	0	0	0
Nunez	1.000	5	14	0	0	0
Raburn	1.000	3	10	0	0	0
Swenson	.975	77	113	6	3	1
Urquhart	1.000	2	3	0	0	0
Webb	.957	76	152	3	7	0

CEDAR RAPIDS KERNELS — Low Class A

MIDWEST LEAGUE

BATTING	AVG	G	AB	R	H	2B	3B	HR	RBI	BB	SO	SB	CS	SLG	OBP	B	T	HT	WT	DOB	1st Yr	Resides
Cahill, Jon	.208	72	221	26	46	8	1	1	28	27	42	4	3	.267	.295	R	R	6-0	180	2-21-78	2001	Peabody, Mass.
Del Chiaro, Brent	.213	37	94	12	20	1	0	0	9	10	38	0	0	.223	.292	R	R	6-3	210	6-26-79	2001	Oakley, Calif.
Eylward, Mike	.263	98	350	55	92	22	4	8	43	31	55	2	3	.417	.340	R	R	6-2	210	9-28-79	2001	Clearwater, Fla.
Gates, David	.220	29	82	13	18	1	1	2	9	17	21	2	0	.329	.379	R	R	6-1	200	9-23-80	2001	Huntsville, Ala.
Gorneault, Nick	.289	103	346	60	100	17	7	10	53	30	106	12	5	.465	.346	R	R	6-3	200	4-19-79	2001	Springfield, Mass.
Kimpton, Nick	.262	93	302	51	79	12	4	0	26	42	61	20	12	.328	.345	L	L	6-1	170	10-27-83	2001	Canberra, Australia
Kotchman, Casey	.281	81	288	42	81	30	1	5	50	48	37	2	1	.444	.390	L	L	6-3	210	2-22-83	2001	Seminole, Fla.
Mathis, Jeff	.287	128	491	75	141	41	3	10	73	40	75	7	4	.444	.346	R	R	6-0	180	3-31-83	2001	Marianna, Fla.
McPherson, Dallas	.277	132	499	71	138	24	3	15	88	78	128	30	6	.427	.381	L	R	6-4	210	7-23-80	2001	Randleman, N.C.
Melgarejo, Ransel	.237	118	427	63	101	14	5	2	37	53	71	19	12	.307	.333	R	R	6-0	180	8-28-81	2001	Miami, Fla.

BATTING	AVG	G	AB	R	H	2B	3B	HR	RBI	BB	SO	SB	CS	SLG	OBP	B	T	HT	WT	DOB	1st Yr	Resides
Murphy, Tommy	.270	128	485	72	131	20	2	3	48	40	115	31	11	.338	.324	R	R	6-0	180	8-27-79	2000	Boynton Beach, Fla.
Napoli, Mike	.251	106	362	57	91	19	1	10	50	62	104	6	5	.392	.362	R	R	6-0	200	10-31-81	2000	Cooper City, Fla.
Nevins, Ryan	.200	19	50	5	10	2	0	0	4	0	0	0	0	.240	.305	L	R	5-11	170	12-29-78	2001	Flushing, N.Y.
Porter, Greg	.229	77	266	29	61	14	1	1	38	28	69	2	4	.301	.307	L	R	6-4	220	8-15-80	2001	Keller, Texas
Turner, Justin	.256	111	379	63	97	23	2	11	61	47	118	7	8	.414	.339	R	R	6-1	190	12-19-79	2001	Cape Coral, Fla.
Welch, Ed	.143	18	35	4	5	0	0	0	2	2	17	2	1	.143	.189	R	R	6-0	190	2-22-80	1998	Vancouver, B.C.

PITCHING	W	L	ERA	G	GS	CG	SV	IP	H	R	ER	BB	SO	AVG	B	T	HT	WT	DOB	1st Yr	Resides
Andrade, Stephen	1	1	1.16	46	0	0	11	54	30	7	7	16	93	.162	R	R	6-1	220	2-6-78	2001	Woodland, Calif.
Cahill, Jon	0	0	0.00	2	0	0	0	2	2	0	0	0	0	.000	R	R	6-0	180	2-21-78	2001	Peabody, Mass.
Dennis, Jason	2	0	2.92	8	0	0	0	12	10	4	4	3	14	.208	L	L	6-0	190	8-12-78	2001	Concord, Calif.
Griffith, Dustin	5	4	3.91	45	0	0	2	74	68	36	32	25	52	.242	R	R	6-4	190	9-16-80	2001	Littleton, Colo.
Mozingo, Dan	3	2	4.24	22	3	0	1	47	44	28	22	22	41	.245	L	L	6-2	190	6-3-80	1998	Ashtabula, Ohio
Nickoli, Mike	0	1	5.19	2	2	0	0	9	10	5	5	3	6	.285	R	R	6-5	200	3-6-80	2001	Hoover, Ala.
O'Sullivan, Mark	5	9	5.47	42	3	0	1	76	94	53	46	46	80	.308	R	R	6-2	200	10-24-78	2001	Andover, Mass.
Pawelczyk, Kyle	1	2	4.62	7	6	0	0	25	20	13	13	27	28	.217	L	L	6-5	180	11-18-81	2002	Elkins, W.Va.
Peralta, Joel	5	0	0.95	41	0	0	21	47	28	7	5	11	53	.163	R	R	5-11	160	3-23-76	1996	Bonao, D.R.
Rouwenhorst, Jonathon	4	2	1.26	44	3	0	1	86	54	15	12	29	78	.182	L	L	6-1	190	9-25-79	2001	Anaheim, Calif.
Santana, Johan	14	8	4.16	27	27	0	0	147	133	75	68	48	146	.239	R	R	6-2	150	11-28-83	2001	San Cristobal, D.R.
Saunders, Joe	3	1	1.88	5	5	0	0	29	16	7	6	9	27	.168	L	L	6-2	190	6-16-81	2002	Springfield, Va.
Shell, Steven	11	4	3.72	22	21	1	0	121	119	59	50	26	86	.254	R	R	6-3	190	3-10-83	2001	Cleburne, Texas
Steward, Jaime	6	6	3.66	26	11	0	0	93	80	49	38	33	71	.236	L	L	6-0	180	1-26-79	2001	Blackwood, N.J.
Thomas, Adam	4	4	5.02	32	0	0	2	52	63	35	29	15	39	.295	R	R	6-4	190	5-22-79	2000	North Miami, Fla.
Torres, Joe	11	8	3.52	25	25	0	0	133	125	73	52	66	87	.250	L	L	6-2	180	9-3-82	2000	Kissimmee, Fla.
Wolensky, Dave	0	1	3.15	30	6	0	1	69	66	31	24	41	58	.255	R	R	6-0	190	1-15-80	2000	Atlanta, Ga.
Woods, Jake	10	5	3.05	27	27	1	0	153	128	66	52	54	121	.228	L	L	6-1	190	9-3-81	2001	Kingsburg, Calif.

FIELDING

Catcher	PCT	G	PO	A	E	DP	PB
Cahill	1.000	1	1	0	0	0	0
Del Chiaro	.986	35	194	16	3	2	1
Mathis	.994	80	606	70	4	2	6
Napoli	.987	37	275	35	4	5	8

First Base	PCT	G	PO	A	E	DP
Cahill	1.000	1	1	0	0	0
Eylward	.983	59	488	32	9	53
Kotchman	.992	75	596	48	5	57
Napoli	.955	9	60	4	3	9
Turner	1.000	2	16	2	0	1

Second Base	PCT	G	PO	A	E	DP
Cahill	.994	44	67	108	1	31
Turner	.952	107	184	248	22	60

Third Base	PCT	G	PO	A	E	DP
Cahill	.909	12	8	12	2	4
Eylward	.931	14	6	21	2	4
McPherson	.898	123	70	204	31	20
Murphy	.000	1	0	0	0	0
Napoli	1.000	1	1	1	0	0
Turner	1.000	1	0	2	0	0

Shortstop	PCT	G	PO	A	E	DP
Cahill	.972	18	30	39	2	11

Murphy	.942	126	203	329	33	74

Outfield	PCT	G	PO	A	E	DP
Cahill	1.000	1	1	0	0	0
Del Chiaro	.000	1	0	0	0	0
Eylward	.967	22	28	1	1	0
Gates	.958	27	45	1	2	0
Gorneault	.979	101	183	4	4	0
Kimpton	.990	92	186	4	2	1
Melgarejo	.978	116	255	6	6	0
Nevins	1.000	13	15	1	0	0
Porter	.982	72	105	3	2	0
Welch	1.000	17	14	0	0	0

PROVO ANGELS — Rookie

PIONEER LEAGUE

BATTING	AVG	G	AB	R	H	2B	3B	HR	RBI	BB	SO	SB	CS	SLG	OBP	B	T	HT	WT	DOB	1st Yr	Resides
Aybar, Eric	.326	67	273	64	89	15	6	4	29	21	43	15	10	.469	.395	S	R	5-11	160	1-14-84	2002	Bani, D.R.
Brown, Matt	.296	32	108	14	32	5	1	0	11	15	21	3	3	.361	.406	R	R	6-0	180	8-8-82	2001	Hayden, Idaho
Callaspo, Alberto	.338	70	299	70	101	16	10	3	60	17	14	13	4	.488	.374	R	R	5-10	150	4-19-83	2001	Maracay, Venez.
Cosby, Quan	.302	76	291	66	88	9	4	0	29	45	62	22	4	.361	.404	S	R	5-10	180	12-23-82	2001	Mart, Texas
Duenas, Tommy	1.000	1	1	0	1	0	0	0	1	0	0	0	0	0.1000	1.000	R	R	5-11	200	7-16-81	2002	Miami, Fla.
Dvorsky, Alex	.321	65	234	48	75	15	0	9	52	47	36	2	0	.500	.453	R	R	6-2	200	8-8-79	2002	Marion, Iowa
Gates, David	.286	9	35	7	10	2	0	1	6	8	4	1	1	.429	.444	R	R	6-1	200	9-23-80	2001	Huntsville, Ala.
Gray, Josh	.186	51	183	22	34	8	0	0	21	8	43	0	0	.230	.235	R	R	6-3	210	2-22-81	2000	Durant, Okla.
Guzman, Junior	.256	57	215	22	55	13	4	4	28	10	45	0	1	.409	.293	R	R	5-11	180	8-10-82	2000	Bonao, D.R.
Hancock, Justin	.249	61	189	21	47	10	2	2	30	20	35	5	3	.354	.327	R	R	6-2	190	3-10-80	2001	Valrico, Fla.
Jenkins, Kevin	.179	13	28	10	5	0	1	0	3	13	12	0	0	.250	.452	L	L	6-0	200	4-6-82	2000	Miami, Fla.
Kenning, Ryan	.207	33	87	20	18	8	1	2	10	33	42	0	0	.391	.426	L	L	6-0	190	11-10-80	2002	North Vancouver, B.C.
Mathis, Jake	.262	41	145	23	38	8	4	4	28	14	45	0	2	.455	.331	L	R	6-3	200	1-24-80	2002	Marianna, Fla.
Nunez, Felix	.348	15	46	11	16	4	1	1	13	7	8	4	0	.543	.426	R	R	6-1	170	10-9-82	2001	El Tigre, Venez.
Perdomo, Mike	.270	56	204	33	55	16	3	4	39	35	71	4	1	.436	.381	R	R	6-2	190	6-29-81	2002	Miami, Fla.
Selmo, Wilson	.188	31	80	9	15	0	0	3	5	15	2	1	.188	.233	S	R	5-11	160	9-27-82	2001	Santo Domingo, D.R.
Sugden, Jason	.299	65	224	37	67	7	3	1	42	22	43	7	4	.371	.366	R	R	6-3	180	10-11-81	2002	Harrisburg, Pa.

GAMES BY POSITION: C—Dvorsky 48, Guzman 29. **1B**—Gray 39, Kenning 30, Mathis 16. **2B**—Brown 6, Callaspo 68, Selmo 9. **3B**—Brown 30, Hancock 32, Mathis 22, Selmo 6. **SS**—Aybar 67, Callaspo 1, Selmo 15, Sugden 1. **OF**—Cosby 76, Gates 8, Hancock 30, Jenkins 11, Kenning 1, Nunez 5, Perdomo 54, Sugden 55.

PITCHING	W	L	ERA	G	GS	CG	SV	IP	H	R	ER	BB	SO	AVG	B	T	HT	WT	DOB	1st Yr	Resides
Allen, Blakely	0	1	15.43	1	0	0	0	2	5	4	4	3	1	.454	R	R	6-4	190	7-12-79	2001	Alexander City, Ala.
Arias, Daniel	0	1	4.26	4	0	0	0	6	7	3	3	1	4	.333	R	R	6-1	200	6-19-82	2000	Bani, D.R.
Astacio, Hector	6	3	4.72	17	6	0	0	61	77	38	32	17	56	.313	R	R	6-0	160	10-8-83	2000	Yerba Buena, D.R.
Bailey, Ryan	1	21.00		4	0	0	0	3	4	8	7	5	4	.333	R	R	6-2	210	5-10-80	2001	Chula Vista, Calif.
Balser, Jeff	0	0	4.76	4	0	0	0	6	3	3	3	4	6	.157	R	R	6-1	210	12-31-80	2001	Venice, Fla.
Barnett, Brian	0	0	0.00	1	0	0	0	1	0	0	0	0	1	.000	R	R	6-1	200	3-31-80	2002	Scottsdale, Ariz.
Bilke, Austin	2	2	4.93	28	0	0	6	35	42	19	19	11	28	.302	R	R	6-2	220	8-13-79	2002	Beaver Dam, Wis.
Burden, Randy	0	0	7.45	10	0	0	0	12	12	8	12	9	.324		R	R	6-3	210	11-8-79	2002	Suffolk, Va.
Cimorelli, Brett	1	1	3.52	10	0	0	0	15	13	7	6	12	4	.245	R	R	6-4	210	2-22-82	2000	Zephyrhills, Fla.
D'Amico, Leonardo	3	0	3.57	14	14	0	0	63	58	27	25	14	54	.242	R	R	6-2	170	12-14-81	1999	Mariara, Venez.
Delgadillo, Ambiroix	0	10	8.00	2	0	0	0	8	8	5	1	.714			L	L	5-11	160	8-7-83	2001	San Pedro de Macoris, D.R.
Fuller, Justin	3	1	4.22	26	0	1	0	43	32	22	20	12	58	.202	L	L	6-1	190	6-20-80	2002	South Windsor, Conn.
Goas, Adrian	1	3	3.91	20	0	0	1	23	21	13	10	12	13	.250	R	R	6-7	210	11-24-79	2001	San Juan, P.R.
Hindman, Scott	0	1	9.00	3	0	0	0	4	4	2	0	2	.363		L	L	6-4	210	3-6-81	2002	Inverness, Ill.
Holcomb, James	2	1	3.38	12	12	0	0	53	62	27	20	10	55	.289	R	R	6-1	190	11-28-80	2000	Reno, Nev.

PITCHING	W	L	ERA	G	GS	CG	SV	IP	H	R	ER	BB	SO	AVG	B	T	HT	WT	DOB	1st Yr	Resides
Lugo, Osvaldo	0	2	4.28	17	0	0	0	27	41	23	13	13	23	.359	R	R	6-0	230	12-22-80	2002	Miami, Fla.
Luther, Heath	0	2	6.75	23	0	0	0	32	44	25	24	9	23	.330	L	L	5-11	180	1-7-79	2001	Fort Wayne, Ind.
Marquez, Jeff	4	2	4.22	14	10	0	0	60	69	36	28	34	43	.292	L	R	6-0	200	11-5-81	2002	Hialeah, Fla.
McCarthy, Matt	0	1	6.92	15	3	0	0	26	40	26	20	19	16	.357	L	L	6-1	190	7-16-80	2002	Winter Springs, Fla.
Ramirez, Edward	1	0	9.31	2	1	0	0	10	14	10	10	4	4	.368	R	R	6-3	150	3-28-84	2001	San Juan, D.R.
Reed, Anthony	4	7	5.83	29	0	0	10	29	40	27	19	19	24	.327	R	R	6-2	210	6-18-79	2002	Walters, Okla.
Rodriguez , Rafael	1	1	5.96	6	6	0	0	26	26	17	17	14	25	.268	R	R	6-1	170	9-24-84	2001	Santo Domingo, D.R.
Saunders, Joe	2	1	3.62	8	8	0	0	32	40	19	13	11	21	.305	L	L	6-2	190	6-16-81	2002	Springfield, Va.
Sisco, Kelly	1	0	22.50	2	0	0	0	2	4	7	5	4	2	.400	L	L	6-4	190	10-25-81	2002	Westville, Okla.
Steward, Jaime	1	0	8.10	4	2	0	0	17	25	17	15	4	15	.342	L	L	6-0	180	1-26-79	2001	Blackwood, N.J.
Torres, Jose	0	0	6.00	5	0	0	0	6	8	6	4	5	4	.285	R	R	6-6	230	2-9-81	2001	Puerto Plata, D.R.
Williams, Bryan	5	7	4.93	16	14	0	0	66	72	41	36	23	71	.270	R	R	5-11	170	1-26-80	2002	Orlando, Fla.

MESA ANGELS · Rookie

ARIZONA LEAGUE

BATTING	AVG	G	AB	R	H	2B	3B	HR	RBI	BB	SO	SB	CS	SLG	OBP	B	T	HT	WT	DOB	1st Yr	Resides
Abad, Noel	.188	24	64	9	12	2	1	0	2	4	26	3	0	.250	.257	R	R	6-1	160	11-9-82	2000	Santo Domingo, D.R.
Batista, Christian	.241	29	79	11	19	4	0	1	8	11	13	2	1	.329	.326	R	R	6-1	200	6-5-82	2000	Santo Domingo, D.R.
Batista, Juan	.238	48	143	23	34	2	3	0	5	14	50	7	4	.294	.319	S	R	6-0	160	7-14-84	2001	Santo Domingo, D.R.
Brown, Matt	.361	28	97	16	35	7	0	2	22	15	14	3	1	.495	.443	R	R	6-0	180	8-8-82	2001	Hayden, Idaho
Collins, Mike	.275	43	153	23	42	10	1	0	22	14	31	7	3	.353	.353	R	R	6-2	190	7-18-84	2001	Canberra, Australia
Coulie, Jason	.462	4	13	0	6	1	0	0	4	0	3	1	0	.538	.429	R	R	6-2	200	4-13-78	2002	Manchester, N.H.
DaVanon, Jeff	.667	5	15	5	10	6	1	0	4	5	2	2	0	1.200	.714	S	R	6-0	180	12-8-73	1995	Scottsdale, Ariz.
Duenas, Tommy	.234	45	137	15	32	12	3	0	23	21	35	2	2	.365	.352	R	R	5-11	200	7-16-81	2002	Miami, Fla.
Jones, Joshua	.225	23	71	10	16	3	0	0	8	2	11	0	0	.268	.257	R	R	6-4	200	6-29-83	2001	Houston, Texas
Kendrick, Howard	.318	42	157	24	50	6	4	0	13	7	11	12	6	.408	.368	R	R	5-10	170	7-12-83	2002	Callahan, Fla.
Kenning, Ryan	.318	6	22	4	7	4	0	0	4	4	8	0	0	.500	.423	L	L	6-0	190	11-10-80	2002	North Vancouver, B.C.
Maher, Caleb	.299	48	194	22	58	11	2	2	31	9	51	3	3	.407	.338	R	R	6-2	190	3-22-83	2002	Ceres, Calif.
Nunez, Felix	.133	4	15	2	2	0	0	0	2	1	6	1	0	.133	.188	R	R	6-1	170	10-9-82	2001	El Tigre, Venez.
Peel, Aaron	.252	43	147	13	37	10	1	0	15	9	35	4	2	.333	.288	R	R	6-1	190	2-8-83	2002	Seminole, Texas
Renz, Jordan	.214	42	145	16	31	5	1	0	10	20	51	1	1	.262	.337	S	R	6-2	200	7-21-83	2002	Broken Arrow, Okla.
Seijas, Luis	.323	16	31	5	10	3	0	0	6	0	6	1	0	.419	.313	S	R	5-11	190	1-17-84	2002	Baul, Venez.
Soto, Maximo	.211	22	76	6	16	4	0	1	13	7	35	1	2	.303	.271	R	R	6-3	200	7-16-82	2002	San Pedro de Macoris, D.R.
Soto, Wilber	.217	52	189	35	41	4	4	0	15	34	36	28	10	.280	.346	R	R	5-11	150	2-21-84	2001	San Pedro de Macoris, D.R.
Walston, Chris	.207	41	150	16	31	6	1	0	10	8	67	0	1	.260	.256	R	R	6-6	230	10-1-84	2002	Lakeside, Calif.

GAMES BY POSITION: C—Collins 11, Duenas 44, Seijas 13. **1B**—Batista 1, Collins 12, Kenning 2, Maher 1, Soto 15, Walston 28. **2B**—Abad 1, Batista 1, Brown 1, Kendrick 34, Soto 23. **3B**—Abad 7, Batista 23, Brown 23, Duenas 1, Soto 14. **SS**—Abad 2, Batista 44, Brown 1, Soto 16. **OF**—Abad 16, Arias 1, Coulie 2, DaVanon 3, Jones 21, Kenning 1, Maher 43, Nunez 4, Peel 42, Renz 40, Soto 1, Walston 11.

PITCHING	W	L	ERA	G	GS	CG	SV	IP	H	R	ER	BB	SO	AVG	B	T	HT	WT	DOB	1st Yr	Resides
Arias, Daniel	1	2	1.20	27	0	0	15	30	24	6	4	3	38	.216	R	R	6-1	200	6-19-82	2000	Bani, D.R.
Arnold, Mitchell	0	1	7.54	15	2	0	0	23	29	34	19	29	19	.311	R	R	6-9	230	1-31-82	2002	Saratoga, Wyo.
Balser, Jeff	1	0	4.35	8	0	0	0	10	12	8	5	6	11	.300	R	R	6-1	210	12-31-80	2001	Venice, Fla.
Delgadillo, Ambiroix	5	1	3.86	21	1	0	1	35	19	16	15	24	44	.162	L	L	5-11	160	8-7-83	2001	San Pedro de Macoris, D.R.
Jepsen, Kevin	1	3	6.84	8	5	0	0	26	29	22	20	12	19	.273	R	R	6-3	200	7-26-84	2002	Sparks, Nev.
Mena, Juan	0	1	7.71	5	0	0	0	5	5	5	4	4	5	.238	R	R	5-11	160	1-1-85	2002	San Pedro de Macoris, D.R.
Morban, Carlos	2	0	5.19	17	0	0	1	26	26	19	15	15	35	.257	R	R	6-6	180	1-29-83	2001	Nigua, D.R.
Moreno, Abel	2	3	3.00	13	7	0	0	45	44	27	15	10	47	.257	R	R	6-2	180	6-15-83	2001	Santo Domingo, D.R.
Pawelczyk, Kyle	0	0	0.00	1	1	0	0	3	2	0	0	2	2	.200	L	L	6-5	180	11-18-81	2002	Elkins, W.Va.
Ramirez, Edward	2	5	3.69	13	7	0	0	46	47	22	19	13	45	.262	R	R	6-3	150	3-28-84	2001	San Juan, D.R.
Ray, Ronnie	4	4	4.91	16	7	0	0	59	59	34	32	22	65	.257	R	R	6-3	190	5-11-84	2002	Pacific, Mo.
Reyes, Julio	3	1	7.58	16	0	0	0	19	35	21	16	4	14	.380	L	L	5-10	160	11-21-79	2001	San Pedro de Macoris, D.R.
Rodriguez , Rafael	2	1	3.99	8	8	0	0	38	37	19	17	20	50	.255	R	R	6-1	170	9-24-84	2001	Santo Domingo, D.R.
Shull, Johnathan	0	0	6.25	16	5	0	0	40	56	43	28	24	25	.345	R	R	6-3	200	6-23-82	2001	Butler, Ind.
Sisco, Kelly	0	0	0.00	2	0	0	0	2	2	0	0	1	3	.222	L	L	6-4	190	10-25-81	2002	Westville, Okla.
Thompson, Richard	2	0	2.70	15	0	0	1	23	14	12	7	9	29	.166	R	R	6-1	170	7-1-84	2002	Sydney, Australia
Toledo, Jean	3	5	4.47	11	10	0	0	56	60	33	28	26	42	.276	R	R	6-1	180	3-6-83	2001	Barcelona, Venez.
Turnbow, Derrick	0	1	4.50	3	3	0	0	8	5	5	4	3	12	.161	R	R	6-3	218	1-25-78	1997	Scottsdale, Ariz.

BY JACK MAGRUDER

The Diamondbacks continued their run as the most successful expansion franchise in major league history—pro sports history, for that matter—by winning their third National League West title in four seasons behind dominating power pitchers Randy Johnson and Curt Schilling.

While Johnson and Schilling combined for 47 victories and 650 strikeouts, they could not rekindle their 2001 postseason magic, when they combined for nine victories in raising Arizona to the World Series title. The Diamondbacks were swept by the Cardinals in 2002 after losing top offensive components Luis Gonzalez and Craig Counsell to late-season injuries.

The absence of leading run producer Gonzalez (28 home runs, 103 RBIs) and the clutch-hitting Counsell (career-high 51 RBIs, .364 with runners in scoring position) showed in the playoffs, when the Diamondbacks scored six runs and had only four extra-base hits in three games. Gonzalez suffered a grade-three left shoulder separation in the final week of the regular season, while Counsell went out Aug. 9 with a neck injury that required disk fusion. Both are expected to be at full strength in 2003.

Despite the sour taste left after the postseason, Arizona had 98 victories to give it 375 over the last four years. Only the Braves (387), Yankees (383), Athletics (383) and Mariners (379) have more since 1999, when the Diamondbacks became the first expansion team to make the postseason in its second year.

"Every year in spring training, what is the most important thing? To stay healthy," general manager Joe Garagiola Jr. said. "People say, 'Can't you come up with a new cliché?' Well, no. That's always number one, keeping your key players healthy."

Johnson and Schilling stayed fit to continue their run as the most dominant power tandem in baseball history by becoming the first teammates to record 300 strikeouts in the same season. Johnson had 334 strikeouts while

Randy Johnson   Scott Hairston

RODGER WOOD

PLAYERS OF THE YEAR

MAJOR LEAGUE: Randy Johnson, lhp

Curt Schilling's fast start might have given him an early edge for the National League Cy Young Award, but Johnson closed fast and ended up winning the National League's pitching triple crown: wins, ERA and strikeouts.

MINOR LEAGUE: Scott Hairston, 2b

Hairston's season was split between Class A South Bend and Lancaster. His bat speed and power drew comparisons to Gary Sheffield as he ranked second in the minors in doubles, extra-base hits and slugging percentage.

winning a career-high 24 games.

Johnson, who turned 39 in September, passed Hall of Famers Walter Johnson, Gaylord Perry, Don Sutton and Tom Seaver and nominee Bert Blyleven to claim fourth place in career strikeouts with 3,746. He trails only Nolan Ryan, Steve Carlton and Roger Clemens.

Schilling won 23 while striking out 316 and walking just 35, a marvelous display of control. He went from May 3-June 8 without issuing a walk, a span of 165 batters, and had other stretches of 88, 73, 49, 48, 47 (twice) and 45 batters without a walk. His strikeout-to-walk ratio (9.02-to-1) was second in history among qualifiers behind Bret Saberhgen in 1994 (11-to-1).

Veteran Matt Williams suffered torn ankle ligaments in spring training and was out until July 11, but Junior Spivey had a breakout season at second base after Counsell moved to third to compensate. Spivey, who had two five-hit games as a rookie in 2001, set career highs in all offensive categories and showed great range while making his first all-star team.

In the minors, first baseman Lyle Overbay set franchise records for batting average (.340) and RBIs (109) while making the midseason and postseason Pacific Coast League all-star teams at Triple-A Tucson. Third baseman Chad Tracy, a seventh-round pick in 2001, was invited to the showcase Futures Games and was the Texas League player of the year while leading the league in average (.344), hits (177) and doubles (39).

Scott Hairston, whose baseball roots run deep, hit a composite .340-22-98 at two Class A stops with 46 doubles and five triples while being named the organization's player of the year. His 73 extra-base hits tied for best among all minor leaguers.

ORGANIZATION LEADERS

BATTING

*AVG	Scott Hairston, Lancaster/South Bend	.345
R	Scott Hairston, Lancaster/South Bend	99
H	Lyle Overbay, Tucson	180
TB	Scott Hairston, Lancaster/South Bend	285
2B	Scott Hairston, Lancaster/South Bend	46
3B	Victor Hall, El Paso/Lancaster	13
HR	Scott Hairston, Lancaster/South Bend	22
RBI	Lyle Overbay, Tucson	109
BB	Andy Green, Tucson/Lancaster	69
SO	Josh Kroeger, Lancaster	136
SB	Marland Williams, Yakima	51

PITCHING

W	Steve Randolph, Tucson	15
L	Ryan Holsten, South Bend	13
#ERA	Edgar Gonzalez, Lancaster/South Bend	2.63
G	Javier Lopez, El Paso	61
CG	Edgar Gonzalez, Lancaster/South Bend	4
SV	Bret Prinz, Tucson/Lancaster	18
IP	Andrew Good, El Paso	178
BB	Steve Randolph, Tucson	81
SO	Edgar Gonzalez, Lancaster/South Bend	131

*Minimum 250 At-Bats #Minimum 75 Innings

ARIZONA
DIAMONDBACKS

Manager: Bob Brenly

2002 Record: 98-64, .605 (1st, NL West)

BATTING	AVG	G	AB	R	H	2B	3B	HR	RBI	BB	SO	SB	CS	SLG	OBP	B	T	HT	WT	DOB	1st Yr	Resides
Barajas, Rod	.234	70	154	12	36	10	0	3	23	10	25	1	0	.357	.288	R	R	6-2	220	9-5-75	1996	Phoenix, Ariz.
Bautista, Danny	.325	40	154	22	50	5	2	6	23	11	21	4	2	.500	.367	R	R	5-11	200	5-24-72	1989	Santo Domingo, D.R.
Bell, Jay	.163	32	49	3	8	1	0	2	11	5	9	0	0	.306	.250	R	R	6-0	180	12-11-65	1984	Phoenix, Ariz.
Cintron, Alex	.213	38	75	11	16	6	0	0	4	12	13	0	0	.293	.322	S	R	6-2	180	12-17-78	1997	Yabucoa, P.R.
Colbrunn, Greg	.333	72	171	30	57	16	2	10	27	13	19	0	0	.626	.378	R	R	6-0	210	7-26-69	1988	Mount Pleasant, S.C.
Counsell, Craig	.282	112	436	63	123	22	1	2	51	45	52	7	5	.351	.348	L	R	6-0	170	8-21-70	1992	Mequon, Wis.
Dellucci, David	.245	97	229	34	56	11	2	7	29	28	55	2	4	.402	.326	L	L	5-11	190	10-31-73	1995	Baton Rouge, La.
Donnels, Chris	.238	74	80	5	19	4	1	3	16	10	14	0	0	.425	.312	L	R	6-0	180	4-21-66	1987	Coto de Caza, Calif.
Durazo, Erubiel	.261	76	222	46	58	12	2	16	48	49	60	0	1	.550	.395	L	L	6-3	240	1-23-75	1997	Hermosillo, Mexico
Finley, Steve	.287	150	505	82	145	24	4	25	89	65	73	16	4	.499	.370	L	L	6-2	190	3-12-65	1987	Del Mar, Calif.
Gonzalez, Luis	.288	148	524	90	151	19	3	28	103	97	76	9	2	.496	.400	L	R	6-2	190	9-3-67	1988	Scottsdale, Ariz.
Grace, Mark	.252	124	298	43	75	19	0	7	48	46	30	2	0	.386	.351	L	L	6-2	200	6-28-64	1986	Paradise Valley, Ariz.
Guillen, Jose	.229	54	131	13	30	4	0	4	15	7	25	3	4	.351	.277	R	R	5-11	190	5-17-76	1993	San Cristobal, D.R.
Jose, Felix	.263	13	19	5	5	0	0	2	4	4	8	0	0	.579	.360	S	R	6-1	220	5-8-65	1984	Boca Raton, Fla.
Klassen, Danny	.333	4	3	0	1	0	0	0	0	0	1	0	0	.333	.333	R	R	6-0	190	9-22-75	1993	Stuart, Fla.
Little, Mark	.273	15	22	8	6	0	1	0	2	2	5	0	0	.364	.429	R	R	6-0	190	7-11-72	1994	Edwardsville, Ill.
3-team (3 Mets, 61 Colorado)	.208	79	130	28	27	5	3	0	7	15	34	2	2	.292	.327							
McCracken, Quinton	.309	123	349	60	108	27	8	3	40	32	68	5	4	.458	.367	S	R	5-7	170	3-16-70	1992	Scottsdale, Ariz.
Miller, Damian	.249	101	297	40	74	22	0	11	42	38	88	0	0	.434	.340	R	R	6-3	210	10-13-69	1990	La Crosse, Wis.
Moeller, Chad	.286	37	105	10	30	11	1	2	16	17	23	0	1	.467	.385	R	R	6-3	210	2-18-75	1996	Manhattan Beach, Calif.
Overbay, Lyle	.100	10	10	0	1	0	0	0	1	0	5	0	0	.100	.100	L	L	6-2	210	1-28-77	1999	Centralia, Wash.
Spivey, Junior	.301	143	538	103	162	34	6	16	78	65	100	11	6	.476	.389	R	R	6-2	210	1-28-75	1996	Oklahoma City, Okla.
Williams, Matt	.260	60	215	29	56	7	2	12	40	21	41	3	1	.479	.324	R	R	6-2	210	11-28-65	1986	Scottsdale, Ariz.
Womack, Tony	.271	153	590	90	160	23	5	5	57	46	80	29	12	.353	.325	L	R	5-9	170	9-25-69	1991	Greensboro, N.C.

PITCHING	W	L	ERA	G	GS	CG	SV	IP	H	R	ER	BB	SO	AVG	B	T	HT	WT	DOB	1st Yr	Resides
Anderson, Brian	6	11	4.79	35	24	0	0	156	174	86	83	32	81	.284	R	L	6-1	180	4-26-72	1993	Bratenahl, Ohio
Batista, Miguel	8	9	4.29	36	29	1	0	185	172	99	88	70	112	.245	R	R	6-0	190	2-19-71	1988	Santo Domingo, D.R.
Fetters, Mike	2	3	5.11	33	0	0	0	25	28	18	14	19	24	.291	R	R	6-4	230	12-19-64	1986	Gilbert, Ariz.
2-team (32 Pittsburgh)	.3	3	4.09	65	0	0	0	55	53	31	25	37	53	.252							
Helling, Rick	10	12	4.51	30	30	0	0	176	180	94	88	48	120	.264	R	R	6-3	220	12-15-70	1992	Southlake, Texas
Johnson, Randy	24	5	2.32	35	35	8	0	260	197	78	67	71	334	.208	R	L	6-10	230	9-10-63	1985	Scottsdale, Ariz.
Kim, Byung-Hyun	8	3	2.04	72	0	0	36	84	64	20	19	26	92	.207	R	R	5-11	180	1-21-79	1999	Kwangsan-Ku, Korea
Koplove, Mike	6	1	3.36	55	0	0	0	62	47	24	23	23	46	.212	R	R	6-0	170	8-30-76	1998	Philadelphia, Pa.
Mantei, Matt	2	2	4.73	31	0	0	0	27	28	15	14	12	26	.256	R	R	6-1	210	7-7-73	1991	Pembroke Pines, Fla.
Morgan, Mike	1	1	5.29	29	0	0	0	34	41	22	20	9	13	.288	R	R	6-2	220	10-8-59	1978	Park City, Utah
Myers, Mike	4	3	4.38	69	0	0	4	37	39	18	18	17	31	.274	L	L	6-4	210	6-26-69	1990	St. Lucie, Fla.
Oropesa, Eddie	2	0	10.30	32	0	0	0	25	39	30	29	15	18	.348	L	L	6-3	210	11-23-71	1993	Conoga Park, Calif.
Parra, Jose	0	1	3.21	16	0	0	0	14	13	5	5	11	8	.254	R	R	5-11	170	11-28-72	1990	Santiago, D.R.
Patterson, John	2	0	3.23	7	5	0	0	31	27	11	11	7	31	.234	R	R	6-5	180	1-30-78	1996	Orange, Texas
Prinz, Bret	0	2	9.45	20	0	0	0	13	23	14	14	10	10	.403	R	R	6-3	210	6-15-77	1998	Peoria, Ariz.
Reynoso, Armando	0	0	10.80	2	0	0	0	2	3	2	2	1	2	.375	R	R	6-0	210	5-1-66	1989	Chandler, Ariz.
Sanchez, Duaner	0	0	4.91	6	0	0	0	4	3	2	2	5	4	.214	R	R	6-0	190	10-14-79	1996	Cotui, D.R.
Schilling, Curt	23	7	3.23	36	35	5	0	259	218	95	93	33	316	.223	R	R	6-5	230	11-14-66	1986	Kennett Square, Pa.
Stottlemyre, Todd	0	2	7.52	5	4	0	0	20	26	17	17	7	12	.313	L	R	6-3	210	5-20-65	1986	Paradise Valley, Ariz.
Swindell, Greg	0	2	6.27	34	0	0	0	33	38	23	23	5	23	.279	L	L	6-3	230	1-2-65	1986	Paradise Valley, Ariz.

FIELDING

Catcher	PCT	G	PO	A	E	DP	PB
Barajas	.997	69	293	18	1	1	4
Grace	.000	1	0	0	0	0	0
Miller	.997	100	716	49	2	8	8
Moeller	.997	35	310	7	1	0	1

First Base	PCT	G	PO	A	E	DP
Barajas	1.000	1	2	0	0	0
Bell	1.000	5	16	0	0	0
Colbrunn	.993	40	260	12	2	16
Donnels	1.000	1	1	0	0	0
Durazo	.984	56	409	26	7	29
Grace	.990	98	649	34	7	58

Second Base	PCT	G	PO	A	E	DP
Bell	1.000	2	1	2	0	0
Cintron	1.000	18	27	31	0	9
Counsell	1.000	13	24	20	0	5
Spivey	.977	143	288	358	15	64

Third Base	PCT	G	PO	A	E	DP
Bell	1.000	6	4	8	0	2
Cintron	1.000	9	2	7	0	1
Colbrunn	1.000	5	1	3	0	0

	PCT	G	PO	A	E	DP	PB
Counsell	.974	94	66	194	7	13	
Donnels	1.000	26	10	16	0	0	
Klassen	1.000	2	0	1	0	0	
Williams	.969	56	29	94	4	7	

Shortstop	PCT	G	PO	A	E	DP
Bell	1.000	2	1	4	0	0
Cintron	.962	8	7	18	1	5
Counsell	.984	22	23	37	1	8
Klassen	.000	1	0	0	0	0
Womack	.964	149	175	364	20	66

Outfield	PCT	G	PO	A	E	DP
Bautista	.985	39	65	0	1	0
Dellucci	.967	64	85	2	3	2
Durazo	1.000	2	3	0	0	0
Finley	.994	144	319	4	2	2
Gonzalez	.985	146	252	4	4	1
Guillen	1.000	37	54	2	0	0
Jose	1.000	5	5	0	0	0
Little	1.000	12	14	0	0	0
McCracken	.995	97	182	5	1	1
Womack	.000	1	0	0	0	0

Junior Spivey

LARRY GOREN

FARM SYSTEM

Director, Minor League Operations: Tommy Jones

Class	Farm Team	League	W	L	Pct.	Finish*	Manager(s)	First Yr.
AAA	Tucson (Ariz.) Sidewinders	Pacific Coast	73	68	.518	7th (16)	Al Pedrique	1998
AA	El Paso (Texas) Diablos	Texas	76	62	.551	2nd (8)	Chip Hale	1999
High A	Lancaster (Calif.) Jet Hawks	California	63	77	.450	8th (10)	Steve Scarsone/Bill Plummer	2001
Low A	South Bend (Ind.) Silver Hawks	Midwest	52	87	.374	14th (14)	Dick Schofield	1997
SS A	Yakima (Wash.) Bears	Northwest	23	53	.303	8th (8)	Mike Aldrete	2001
Rookie	Missoula (Mont.) Osprey	Pioneer	35	41	.461	t-6th (8)	Jerry Hairston	1999

*Finish in overall standings (No. of teams in league)

TUCSON SIDEWINDERS   Class AAA

PACIFIC COAST LEAGUE

BATTING	AVG	G	AB	R	H	2B	3B	HR	RBI	BB	SO	SB	CS	SLG	OBP	B	T	HT	WT	DOB	1st Yr	Resides
Barajas, Rod	.438	5	16	2	7	1	0	1	1	1	2	0	0	.688	.471	R	R	6-2	220	9-5-75	1996	Phoenix, Ariz.
Bell, Jay	.227	7	22	4	5	3	0	0	2	4	1	0	0	.364	.346	R	R	6-0	180	12-11-65	1984	Phoenix, Ariz.
Cintron, Alex	.322	85	351	53	113	22	3	4	26	11	33	9	5	.436	.345	S	R	6-2	180	12-17-78	1997	Yabucoa, P.R.
Colbrunn, Greg	.360	6	25	6	9	3	0	2	7	3	3	0	0	.720	.429	R	R	6-0	210	7-26-69	1988	Mount Pleasant, S.C.
Cresse, Brad	.270	36	126	23	34	10	0	2	14	4	38	0	0	.397	.306	R	R	6-1	210	7-31-78	2000	Rancho Mirage, Calif.
Dallimore, Brian	.294	122	419	62	123	26	2	6	50	28	72	13	4	.408	.346	R	R	6-1	180	11-15-73	1996	Las Vegas, Nev.
Dellucci, David	.133	4	15	2	2	1	0	0	1	2	4	0	0	.200	.235	L	L	5-11	190	10-31-73	1995	Baton Rouge, La.
Devore, Doug	.261	125	436	58	114	20	6	14	59	27	103	9	6	.431	.311	L	L	6-4	200	12-14-77	1999	Dublin, Ohio
Donnels, Chris	.300	4	10	3	3	1	0	0	2	3	0	0	0	.400	.500	L	R	6-0	180	4-21-66	1987	Coto de Caza, Calif.
Durazo, Erubiel	.318	7	22	5	7	2	1	1	3	0	2	0	0	.636	.348	L	L	6-3	240	1-23-75	1997	Hermosillo, Mexico
Franklin, Micah	.286	89	311	63	89	19	0	17	60	47	73	5	3	.511	.396	S	R	6-0	200	4-25-72	1990	San Francisco, Calif.
Frias, Hanley	.269	90	331	53	89	18	7	3	33	27	45	4	2	.393	.324	S	R	6-0	170	12-5-73	1991	Villa Ariagracia, D.R.
Green, Andy	.222	27	99	13	22	8	0	1	9	9	17	2	1	.333	.294	R	R	5-9	170	7-7-77	2000	Lexington, Ky.
Klassen, Danny	.230	103	361	41	83	20	5	2	42	22	106	6	1	.330	.277	R	R	6-0	190	9-22-75	1993	Stuart, Fla.
Little, Mark	.315	13	54	6	17	3	1	2	8	0	11	2	1	.519	.304	R	R	6-0	190	7-11-72	1994	Edwardsville, Ill.
Mashore, Damon	.196	21	56	3	11	3	0	0	10	7	13	0	1	.250	.281	R	R	5-11	190	10-31-69	1991	Concord, Calif.
McCool, Lee	.333	2	6	1	2	0	0	0	1	0	1	0	0	.333	.333	R	R	5-11	180	3-5-79	2000	Palatka, Fla.
Miller, Damian	.333	3	9	1	3	0	0	0	1	0	0	0	0	.444	.333	R	R	6-3	210	10-13-69	1990	La Crosse, Wis.
Moeller, Chad	.318	60	211	37	67	8	2	10	48	29	46	1	0	.517	.401	R	R	6-3	210	2-18-75	1996	Manhattan Beach, Calif.
Morales, Willie	.311	93	315	44	98	24	0	6	53	15	57	4	4	.444	.342	R	R	5-10	180	9-7-72	1993	Tucson, Ariz.
Mouton, James	.285	75	263	50	75	21	3	7	36	23	79	7	6	.468	.349	R	R	5-9	170	12-29-68	1991	Missouri City, Texas
Murphy, Nate	.278	84	245	41	68	13	5	10	32	35	60	8	4	.494	.379	L	L	6-0	190	4-15-75	1996	Tucson, Ariz.
Overbay, Lyle	.343	134	525	83	180	40	4	19	109	42	86	0	0	.528	.396	L	L	6-2	210	1-28-77	1999	Centralia, Wash.
Ramirez, Dan	.301	85	236	32	71	6	4	1	20	17	49	7	9	.373	.352	R	R	6-1	180	2-22-74	1992	San Pedro de Macoris, D.R.
Saba, Donnie	.000	1	3	1	0	0	0	0	0	2	0	0	0	.000	.400	L	R	6-0	200	3-2-81	2002	Sandy, Utah
Santora, Jack	.095	16	21	3	2	0	0	0	3	7	0	0	0	.095	.208	S	R	5-9	160	10-6-76	1999	Monterey, Calif.
Waldron, Jeff	.400	1	5	0	2	0	0	0	0	0	1	0	0	.400	.400	L	R	6-1	200	10-4-76	1999	Lynn, Mass.
Williams, Matt	.200	5	15	1	3	0	0	1	3	0	0	0	0	.400	.200	R	R	6-2	210	11-28-65	1986	Scottsdale, Ariz.
Young, Ernie	.325	48	160	29	52	9	1	14	48	24	33	0	3	.656	.426	R	R	6-1	230	7-8-69	1990	Mesa, Ariz.

PITCHING	W	L	ERA	G	GS	CG	SV	IP	H	R	ER	BB	SO	AVG	B	T	HT	WT	DOB	1st Yr	Resides
Capuano, Chris	4	1	2.72	6	6	0	0	36	30	12	11	11	29	.227	L	L	6-3	210	8-19-78	1999	West Springfield, Mass.
Chavez, Anthony	2	2	6.67	21	0	0	1	30	42	24	22	17	24	.330	R	R	5-11	180	10-22-70	1992	Scottsdale, Ariz.
Cortes, David	0	0	0.00	3	0	0	0	4	3	0	0	0	1	.187	R	R	5-11	190	10-15-73	1996	El Centro, Calif.
Estrada, Horacio	8	7	3.90	29	25	2	1	164	167	75	71	40	107	.268	L	L	6-0	160	10-19-75	1992	San Joaquin, Venez.
Gray, Mike	0	0	8.44	6	0	0	0	11	19	11	10	3	8	.387	L	L	6-1	170	12-6-76	1999	Paso Robles, Calif.
Helling, Rick	1	0	1.29	1	1	0	0	7	4	1	1	1	7	.166	R	R	6-3	220	12-15-70	1992	Southlake, Texas
Holzemer, Mark	2	3	5.29	51	0	0	2	34	36	23	20	20	33	.283	L	L	6-0	180	8-20-69	1988	Highland Ranch, Colo.
Johnson, Jonathan	0	3	9.41	14	5	0	0	36	48	41	38	14	27	.320	R	R	6-0	180	7-16-74	1995	Irmo, S.C.
Knott, Eric	8	10	4.86	31	23	1	0	150	188	91	81	23	96	.306	L	L	6-0	180	9-23-74	1997	Sebring, Fla.
Koplove, Mike	1	2	1.17	23	0	0	3	31	21	5	4	4	31	.196	R	R	6-0	170	8-30-76	1998	Philadelphia, Pa.
Mantei, Matt	1	0	0.00	9	0	0	0	10	8	1	0	4	9	.210	R	R	6-1	210	7-7-73	1991	Pembroke Pines, Fla.
Mayo, Blake	1	4	6.89	8	8	0	0	33	44	27	25	20	21	.323	R	R	6-2	210	12-18-72	1996	Gadsden, Ala.
Morgan, Mike	0	0	0.00	2	0	0	0	3	3	1	0	0	2	.300	R	R	6-2	220	10-8-59	1978	Park City, Utah
Oropesa, Eddie	1	0	3.86	29	0	0	0	26	23	11	11	13	26	.242	L	L	6-3	210	11-23-71	1993	Canoga Park, Calif.
Parra, Jose	0	0	0.00	7	0	0	1	9	3	0	0	2	10	.093	R	R	5-11	170	11-28-72	1990	Santiago, D.R.
Patterson, John	10	5	4.23	19	18	0	0	113	117	59	53	45	104	.265	R	R	6-5	180	1-30-78	1996	Orange, Texas
Prinz, Bret	2	2	2.97	37	0	0	18	39	42	14	13	9	34	.269	R	R	6-3	210	6-15-77	1996	Peoria, Ariz.
Randolph, Steve	15	7	3.47	28	27	1	0	163	151	70	63	81	129	.250	L	L	6-3	180	5-1-74	1995	Austin, Texas
Reynoso, Armando	1	2	5.20	6	6	0	0	28	29	16	16	9	16	.276	R	R	6-0	210	5-1-66	1989	Chandler, Ariz.
Sabel, Erik	4	5	4.32	25	7	0	1	67	67	37	32	19	46	.261	R	R	6-3	190	10-14-74	1996	Indianapolis, Ind.
Sanchez, Duaner	1	1	6.75	4	0	0	1	5	6	4	4	1	9	.260	R	R	6-0	190	10-14-79	1996	Cotui, D.R.
Sollecito, Gabe	1	0	2.40	13	0	0	0	15	9	6	4	5	13	.169	S	R	6-1	190	3-3-72	1993	Monterey, Calif.
2-team (7 Iowa)	2	1	2.95	20	0	0	0	21	16	9	7	8	16	.202							
Steenstra, Kennie	1	1	3.86	9	2	0	0	21	20	9	9	7	12	.259	R	R	6-5	210	10-13-70	1992	Liberty, Mo.
2-team (9 Calgary)	2	3	8.27	18	6	0	0	53	84	50	49	18	31	.360							
Stottlemyre, Todd	1	1	3.45	11	0	0	1	16	13	6	6	4	12	.213	L	R	6-2	210	5-20-65	1986	Paradise Valley, Ariz.
Swindell, Greg	0	0	0.00	1	1	0	0	1	0	0	0	0	0	.000	L	L	6-3	230	1-2-65	1986	Paradise Valley, Ariz.
Valverde, Jose	2	4	5.85	49	0	0	5	48	45	33	31	23	65	.250	R	R	6-4	220	7-24-79	1997	El Seibo, D.R.
Villarreal, Oscar	3	3	4.36	10	10	0	0	64	68	33	31	22	40	.277	L	R	6-0	170	11-22-81	1999	Nuevo Leon, Mexico
Ward, Jeremy	4	6	4.31	54	0	0	1	63	68	35	30	14	40	.278	R	R	6-3	220	2-24-78	1999	Rocky Mount, N.C.
Webb, Brandon	0	1	3.86	1	1	0	0	7	5	3	3	4	5	.200	R	R	6-3	190	5-9-79	2000	Ashland, Ky.

ORGANIZATION STATISTICS

FIELDING

Catcher	PCT	G	PO	A	E	DP	PB
Barajas	1.000	3	26	2	0	0	0
Cresse	.992	35	219	20	2	2	1
Miller	1.000	1	5	0	0	0	0
Moeller	.994	59	431	29	3	0	1
Morales	.994	50	297	28	2	3	4
Waldron	1.000	1	4	0	0	0	0

First Base	PCT	G	PO	A	E	DP
Barajas	1.000	1	8	0	0	2
Colbrunn	.958	3	23	0	1	3
Durazo	.971	5	32	2	1	5
Franklin	.938	4	27	3	2	3
Morales	.969	7	57	5	2	3
Overbay	.991	127	997	87	10	89

Second Base	PCT	G	PO	A	E	DP
Cintron	.961	35	60	87	6	22
Dallimore	.949	19	28	28	3	4

Catcher (cont.)	PCT	G	PO	A	E	DP	PB
Frias	.983	68	111	175	5	35	
Green	.980	26	37	61	2	12	
Klassen	.875	2	1	6	1	1	
McCool	1.000	2	6	3	0	2	
Santora	1.000	7	4	8	0	0	

Third Base	PCT	G	PO	A	E	DP
Bell	.833	7	1	9	2	0
Colbrunn	1.000	1	0	1	0	0
Dallimore	.957	99	65	157	10	9
Donnels	1.000	4	1	3	0	0
Franklin	1.000	4	1	0	0	0
Klassen	1.000	24	18	51	0	8
Morales	.927	24	11	40	4	5
Santora	1.000	2	0	1	0	0
Williams	.875	4	2	5	1	1

Shortstop	PCT	G	PO	A	E	DP
Cintron	.960	53	73	119	8	30

(cont.)	PCT	G	PO	A	E	DP
Dallimore	1.000	2	5	5	0	2
Frias	.978	15	17	27	1	5
Klassen	.971	79	125	214	10	43
Santora	1.000	3	2	3	0	0

Outfield	PCT	G	PO	A	E	DP
Dallimore	1.000	8	10	1	0	0
Dellucci	1.000	4	11	0	0	0
Devore	.968	119	233	6	8	1
Franklin	.966	71	107	5	4	0
Little	.976	13	38	3	1	3
Mashore	.938	12	15	0	1	0
Morales	1.000	8	11	0	0	0
Mouton	.989	53	90	0	1	0
Murphy	.994	74	176	4	1	1
Ramirez	.981	73	155	4	3	0
Saba	1.000	1	1	0	0	0
Young	.988	41	83	2	1	0

BATTING	AVG	G	AB	R	H	2B	3B	HR	RBI	BB	SO	SB	CS	SLG	OBP	B	T	HT	WT	DOB	1st Yr	Resides
Ansman, Craig	.226	19	53	6	12	3	0	3	9	6	7	0	0	.453	.311	R	R	6-3	220	3-10-78	2000	West Islip, N.Y.
Burns, Kevan	.326	58	187	36	61	9	5	3	26	22	25	2	5	.476	.400	L	L	6-0	180	11-10-76	1999	Beloit, Wis.
Ceriani, Matt	.143	3	7	1	1	0	0	0	0	2	2	0	0	.143	.333	R	R	6-2	220	10-9-76	1998	Vacaville, Calif.
Cresse, Brad	.229	66	240	25	55	15	0	3	24	16	74	1	0	.329	.282	R	R	6-2	210	7-31-78	2000	Rancho Mirage, Calif.
Durazo, Erubiel	.500	5	14	5	7	3	0	2	7	4	1	0	0	1.143	.611	L	L	6-3	240	1-23-75	1997	Hermosillo, Mexico
Gordon, Brian	.287	130	477	73	137	32	9	10	67	36	111	2	6	.455	.343	L	R	6-0	170	8-16-78	1997	Round Rock, Texas
Hall, Victor	.286	38	161	18	46	4	5	0	12	6	23	7	4	.373	.322	L	L	5-11	178	9-16-80	1998	Arleta, Calif.
Hammock, Rob	.290	122	441	68	128	28	4	11	73	43	68	5	4	.447	.358	R	R	5-11	180	5-13-77	1998	Dacula, Ga.
Harris, Cedrick	.268	36	82	10	22	3	1	2	8	2	19	2	1	.402	.286	R	R	6-2	190	11-14-77	2000	Ashdown, Ark.
Kata, Matt	.298	136	578	95	172	33	9	11	57	37	79	12	7	.443	.341	S	R	6-1	180	3-14-78	1999	Willoughby Hills, Ohio
Klassen, Danny	.231	18	65	11	15	4	0	2	7	7	24	0	0	.385	.306	R	R	6-0	190	9-22-75	1993	Stuart, Fla.
Martin, Billy	.216	83	264	34	57	16	0	7	38	32	92	0	0	.356	.301	R	R	6-2	200	6-10-76	1998	Abilene, Texas
Mashore, Damon	.375	4	16	4	6	0	0	1	4	1	3	0	0	.563	.412	R	R	5-11	190	10-31-69	1991	Concord, Calif.
Neal, Steve	.283	122	407	57	115	29	0	16	75	63	106	3	1	.472	.383	L	L	6-2	260	2-14-77	1998	Pine Bluff, Ark.
Olson, Tim	.273	126	433	61	118	24	2	10	64	27	91	9	11	.406	.337	R	R	6-2	200	8-1-78	2000	Bismarck, N.D.
Santora, Jack	.213	69	169	23	36	3	3	1	8	18	28	3	4	.284	.304	S	R	5-9	160	10-6-76	1999	Monterey, Calif.
Terrero, Luis	.286	104	360	49	103	20	6	8	54	23	89	18	22	.442	.342	R	R	6-2	190	5-18-80	1997	Barahona, D.R.
Tracy, Chad	.344	129	514	80	177	39	5	8	74	38	51	2	3	.486	.389	L	R	6-2	190	5-22-80	2001	Charlotte, N.C.
Waldron, Jeff	.301	83	209	23	63	11	0	1	27	29	39	0	2	.368	.390	L	R	6-1	200	10-4-76	1999	Lynn, Mass.
Williams, Jason	.111	7	9	3	1	1	0	0	1	1	0	0	0	.222	.200	R	R	5-11	170	12-6-78	2000	Fairfield, Calif.

PITCHING	W	L	ERA	G	GS	CG	SV	IP	H	R	ER	BB	SO	AVG	B	T	HT	WT	DOB	1st Yr	Resides
Belflower, Jay	5	3	4.04	36	0	0	2	56	67	29	25	14	53	.303	R	R	6-4	210	11-12-79	2001	Sebring, Fla.
Bevis, P.J.	4	5	2.83	49	0	0	11	64	50	22	20	29	62	.220	R	R	6-3	170	7-28-80	1998	Capalaba, Australia
Bruney, Brian	0	2	2.92	10	0	0	0	12	11	5	4	4	14	.268	R	R	6-2	220	2-17-82	2000	Warrenton, Ore.
Cervantes, Chris	6	4	3.33	33	12	0	0	122	131	56	45	23	88	.271	L	L	6-1	150	2-4-79	1998	Tucson, Ariz.
Daigle, Casey	3	2	3.25	7	7	2	0	44	46	19	16	9	29	.275	R	R	6-7	210	4-4-81	1999	Vinton, La.
Gann, Jamie	1	2	6.14	19	2	0	1	29	41	25	20	15	22	.317	R	R	6-1	190	5-1-75	1996	Norman, Okla.
Good, Andrew	13	6	3.54	28	27	2	0	178	170	89	70	26	127	.247	R	R	6-3	170	9-19-79	1998	Rochester Hills, Mich.
Gosling, Mike	14	5	3.13	27	27	2	0	167	149	66	58	62	115	.238	L	L	6-2	210	9-23-80	2001	Las Vegas, Nev.
Gray, Mike	3	2	3.46	19	1	0	0	26	39	15	10	12	20	.333	L	L	6-1	170	12-6-76	1999	Paso Robles, Calif.
Henthorne, Kevin	1	1	11.32	5	2	0	0	10	20	13	13	1	8	.416	S	R	6-2	190	12-9-69	1994	La Crosse, Wis.
Johnson, Jonathan	0	1	5.56	3	1	0	0	11	14	7	7	3	9	.304	R	R	6-0	180	7-16-74	1995	Irmo, S.C.
Lopez, Javier	2	2	2.72	61	0	0	6	46	34	16	14	16	47	.203	L	L	6-4	200	7-11-77	1998	Fairfax, Va.
Mantei, Matt	0	1	2.25	4	3	0	0	4	3	3	1	1	5	.200	R	R	6-1	210	7-7-73	1991	Pembroke Pines, Fla.
Martines, Jason	2	1	4.69	27	0	0	2	40	45	22	21	13	25	.281	L	R	6-2	190	1-21-76	1997	Hanover, Mich.
Mayo, Phil	0	1	5.96	11	1	0	0	23	25	17	15	10	19	.280	R	R	6-2	210	12-18-72	1996	Gadsden, Ala.
Perez, Beltran	3	8	5.47	20	19	1	0	97	114	70	59	33	77	.291	R	R	6-2	150	10-24-81	1999	San Francisco de Macoris, D.R.
Sanchez, Duaner	4	3	3.03	31	0	0	13	36	31	16	12	13	37	.223	R	R	6-0	190	10-14-79	1996	Cotui, D.R.
Sikaras, Pete	0	1	6.75	4	0	0	0	4	7	3	3	2	4	.388	R	R	6-2	200	5-5-79	2000	Niles, Ill.
Silva, Jesus	1	3	5.01	21	0	0	3	23	29	17	13	10	22	.298	R	R	6-0	182	12-24-82	1999	Maracay, Venez.
Villarreal, Oscar	6	3	3.74	14	12	1	0	84	73	36	35	26	85	.233	L	R	6-0	170	11-22-81	1999	Nuevo Leon, Mexico
Webb, Brandon	10	6	3.14	26	25	1	0	152	141	66	53	59	122	.247	R	R	6-3	190	5-9-79	2000	Ashland, Ky.

FIELDING

Catcher	PCT	G	PO	A	E	DP	PB
Ansman	1.000	9	73	7	0	0	2
Ceriani	1.000	3	17	3	0	0	1
Cresse	.991	45	298	43	3	2	4
Hammock	.989	56	397	36	5	2	3
Waldron	1.000	39	224	23	0	1	6

First Base	PCT	G	PO	A	E	DP
Durazo	1.000	4	35	4	0	4
Martin	1.000	24	175	10	0	22
Neal	.985	118	969	69	16	75
Tracy	.980	6	46	3	1	7

Second Base	PCT	G	PO	A	E	DP
Kata	.974	127	235	361	16	66

(cont.)	PCT	G	PO	A	E	DP
Klassen	1.000	1	3	1	0	0
Olson	.800	1	2	2	1	0
Santora	.967	14	29	30	2	9
Williams	1.000	5	7	9	0	2

Third Base	PCT	G	PO	A	E	DP
Hammock	.929	11	8	18	2	0
Kata	1.000	3	1	2	0	0
Klassen	.923	4	6	6	1	0
Santora	.914	20	4	28	3	0
Tracy	.924	113	84	218	25	13
Williams	.000	1	0	0	0	0

Shortstop	PCT	G	PO	A	E	DP
Kata	.941	9	13	19	2	7

(cont.)	PCT	G	PO	A	E	DP
Klassen	.919	13	18	50	6	8
Olson	.943	107	158	301	28	62
Santora	.950	25	39	57	5	9

Outfield	PCT	G	PO	A	E	DP
Burns	1.000	48	64	1	0	0
Gann	.000	1	0	0	0	0
Gordon	.971	119	226	10	7	2
Hall	.964	38	53	0	2	0
Hammock	.989	55	80	7	1	3
Harris	1.000	32	39	2	0	0
Martin	.909	39	36	4	4	0
Mashore	1.000	4	3	0	0	0
Olson	.951	21	37	2	2	0
Terrero	.973	100	243	11	7	3

ORGANIZATION STATISTICS

CALIFORNIA LEAGUE

BATTING	AVG	G	AB	R	H	2B	3B	HR	RBI	BB	SO	SB	CS	SLG	OBP	B	T	HT	WT	DOB	1st Yr	Resides
Ansman, Craig	.305	100	374	67	114	21	7	18	55	34	113	3	3	.543	.385	R	R	6-3	220	3-10-78	2000	West Islip, N.Y.
Barden, Brian	.335	64	269	58	90	19	1	8	46	16	63	3	1	.502	.370	R	R	5-11	190	4-2-81	2002	San Diego, Calif.
Bell, Jay	.200	7	20	4	4	1	0	1	7	4	6	0	0	.400	.333	R	R	6-0	180	12-11-65	1984	Phoenix, Ariz.
Berroa, Joandry	.231	85	251	27	58	7	1	1	17	12	49	4	5	.279	.274	R	R	5-11	158	9-26-84	2001	La Romana, D.R.
Bevins, Andy	.125	6	24	1	3	0	0	0	2	1	9	0	0	.125	.160	R	R	6-3	210	10-10-75	1997	Port Coquitlam, B.C.
Cota, Jesus	.280	135	540	73	151	33	3	16	101	38	121	0	1	.441	.325	L	R	6-3	220	11-7-81	2001	Tucson, Ariz.
Edge, Dwight	.279	131	451	56	126	15	2	0	44	35	103	10	8	.322	.343	R	R	6-7	230	7-7-78	2001	St. Cloud, Fla.
Epke, Brian	.250	9	28	2	7	0	0	1	2	9	0	1	0	.250	.323	R	R	6-0	190	5-2-77	2001	Waco, Neb.
Firlit, Dan	.257	23	74	13	19	4	1	0	13	5	18	0	1	.338	.321	R	R	6-1	190	11-22-78	2000	Orland Park, Ill.
Foreman, JuJu	.235	40	132	15	31	2	0	0	7	19	13	5	3	.250	.329	L	R	5-8	165	2-18-79	2000	Girard, Ga.
Garthwaite, Jay	.364	7	11	2	4	0	0	1	3	2	7	0	0	.636	.462	R	R	6-2	210	11-26-80	2002	Kent, Wash.
Gil, Jerry	.216	10	37	4	8	0	0	1	4	1	11	1	1	.297	.237	R	R	6-3	180	10-14-82	1999	Santo Domingo, D.R.
Green, Andy	.309	102	401	74	124	36	4	6	50	60	59	15	10	.464	.401	R	R	5-9	170	7-7-77	2000	Lexington, Ky.
Hairston, Scott	.405	18	79	20	32	11	1	6	26	6	16	1	0	.797	.442	R	R	6-1	190	5-25-80	2001	Oro Valley, Ariz.
Hall, Victor	.278	91	352	72	98	10	8	3	32	47	72	26	15	.378	.373	L	L	5-11	178	9-16-80	1998	Arleta, Calif.
Kroeger, Josh	.235	133	497	63	117	20	7	5	58	23	136	2	4	.346	.274	L	L	6-3	210	8-31-82	2000	San Diego, Calif.
Macha, Erick	.221	64	172	23	38	5	2	1	18	9	22	3	1	.291	.259	R	R	6-1	180	12-13-79	2001	Victoria, Texas
Mashore, Damon	.200	9	15	1	3	0	0	0	2	1	4	0	0	.200	.235	R	R	5-11	190	10-31-69	1991	Concord, Calif.
Murphy, Nate	.243	10	37	6	9	3	0	1	5	4	10	0	1	.405	.326	L	L	6-0	190	4-15-75	1996	Tucson, Ariz.
Myers, Corey	.290	130	497	63	144	33	4	13	84	41	129	1	3	.451	.342	R	R	6-2	220	6-5-80	1999	Henderson, Nev.
Simpson, Bodie	.097	9	31	3	3	1	0	0	4	3	11	0	0	.129	.176	R	R	6-2	195	12-13-77	2001	Lubbock, Texas
Snyder, Chris	.258	60	217	31	56	16	0	9	44	25	54	0	0	.456	.337	R	R	6-3	220	2-12-81	2002	Houston, Texas
Sprowl, Jon-Mark	.278	76	230	39	64	12	1	6	27	43	42	2	4	.417	.404	L	R	6-1	200	8-1-80	1999	Panama City, Fla.
Symonds, Grady	.200	6	10	1	2	0	0	0	1	4	0	0	0	.200	.273	R	R	6-2	180	1-15-81	2002	Buffalo Grove, Ill.
Uggla, Dan	.228	54	184	21	42	7	2	3	16	21	51	3	2	.337	.311	R	R	5-11	180	3-11-80	2001	Columbia, Tenn.
Williams, Matt	.333	4	12	2	4	1	0	1	5	2	1	0	0	.667	.429	R	R	6-2	210	11-28-65	1986	Scottsdale, Ariz.

PITCHING	W	L	ERA	G	GS	CG	SV	IP	H	R	ER	BB	SO	AVG	B	T	HT	WT	DOB	1st Yr	Resides
Aquino, Greg	4	1	3.67	8	8	0	0	49	50	20	20	18	50	.267	R	R	6-1	150	1-11-79	1996	Palenque, D.R.
Barber, Scott	7	3	4.25	32	9	0	0	110	118	57	52	24	81	.273	R	R	6-4	200	12-17-78	2000	Belton, S.C.
Belflower, Jay	0	1	3.86	16	0	0	1	19	17	8	8	3	14	.229	R	R	6-4	210	11-12-79	2001	Sebring, Fla.
Belson, Greg	5	4	6.88	40	2	0	0	71	88	56	54	25	59	.307	R	R	5-10	170	8-16-78	2000	Staten Island, N.Y.
Biggs, Billy	1	0	3.48	8	0	0	1	10	12	6	4	1	9	.300	R	L	6-1	190	9-9-79	2002	Scott Depot, W.Va.
Bulger, Jason	1	1	5.40	2	2	0	0	10	11	7	6	3	12	.289	R	R	6-4	200	12-6-78	2002	Snellville, Ga.
Cramblitt, Joey	3	7	3.92	48	4	0	2	83	98	46	36	28	74	.297	R	R	6-3	230	7-27-78	2000	Meridian, Miss.
Daigle, Casey	4	10	5.09	21	21	0	0	122	137	82	69	42	85	.284	R	R	6-7	210	4-4-81	1999	Vinton, La.
Gonzalez, Edgar	3	0	0.78	4	4	0	0	23	24	7	2	3	21	.263	R	R	6-0	220	2-23-83	2000	San Nicolas, Mexico
Gonzalez, Enrique	1	4	12.27	5	5	0	0	18	34	27	25	14	11	.409	R	R	5-10	195	7-14-82	1999	Bolivar, Venez.
Gray, Mike	2	0	0.93	18	0	0	0	19	18	4	2	7	25	.243	L	L	6-1	170	12-6-76	1999	Paso Robles, Calif.
Henrie, Matt	0	1	3.91	16	0	0	1	25	27	11	11	4	14	.275	L	R	6-3	200	11-28-79	2002	Jupiter, Fla.
Henthorne, Kevin	0	1	3.72	2	2	0	0	10	13	8	4	3	6	.325	S	R	6-2	190	12-9-69	1994	La Crosse, Wis.
Matzenbacher, Brian	2	0	4.56	38	1	0	1	79	89	43	40	32	65	.279	R	R	6-3	210	3-23-77	1999	Marissa, Ill.
Mayo, Blake	0	1	4.50	2	2	0	0	12	13	8	6	5	12	.260	R	R	6-2	210	12-18-72	1996	Gadsden, Ala.
McMachen, Cliff	0	1	13.50	5	0	0	0	5	7	8	8	9	4	.323	L	L	6-2	195	1-14-81	2001	North Las Vegas, Nev.
Medders, Brandon	3	6	5.38	43	12	0	15	99	111	73	59	36	104	.282	R	R	6-2	205	1-26-80	2001	Duncanville, Ala.
Perez, Beltran	3	2	2.51	5	5	0	0	32	31	11	9	3	30	.262	R	R	6-2	150	10-24-81	1999	San Francisco de Macoris, D.R.
Prinz, Bret	1	0	0.00	5	0	0	0	7	2	0	0	1	6	.083	R	R	6-3	210	6-15-77	1998	Peoria, Ariz.
Ramirez, Joslin	0	0	9.82	5	0	0	0	11	13	12	12	6	4	.288	R	R	5-11	190	11-19-79	1998	Sabana Perdida, D.R.
Shabansky, Rob	0	0	7.16	11	0	0	0	16	22	16	13	13	11	.323	L	L	5-10	180	2-27-77	2000	Tucson, Ariz.
Silva, Jesus	2	3	2.08	34	0	0	12	43	50	12	10	5	51	.194	R	R	6-0	182	12-24-82	1999	Maracay, Venez.
Slaten, Doug	1	6	9.00	8	8	0	0	35	59	43	35	12	23	.359	L	L	6-5	190	2-4-80	2000	Venice, Calif.
Stockman, Phil	7	5	4.40	20	20	0	0	108	91	58	53	58	108	.231	R	R	6-7	225	1-25-80	1997	Brisbane, Australia
Taulli, Sam	5	4	6.02	14	12	0	0	55	52	41	37	33	25	.271	L	L	6-2	190	9-19-79	2001	Marianna, Fla.
Trejo, Francisco	4	10	6.91	28	14	0	0	86	107	75	66	68	78	.305	L	L	5-11	150	3-6-80	1997	Santo Domingo, D.R.
Wells, Carlton	3	1	3.99	37	3	0	2	70	77	35	31	23	54	.276	L	L	6-2	210	3-26-80	2000	Tampa, Fla.
White, Bill	0	3	10.24	6	6	0	0	19	31	23	22	16	15	.369	L	L	6-4	215	11-20-78	2000	Alexander City, Ala.

FIELDING

Catcher	PCT	G	PO	A	E	DP	PB
Ansman	.991	70	517	54	5	0	7
Epke	1.000	5	32	4	0	1	2
Myers	1.000	1	3	0	0	0	0
Snyder	.992	43	355	32	3	1	6
Sprowl	1.000	28	140	13	0	0	5
Symonds	.889	3	8	0	1	0	0

First Base	PCT	G	PO	A	E	DP
Ansman	1.000	4	33	2	0	1
Bevins	1.000	1	3	0	0	0
Cota	.989	72	601	54	7	50
Myers	.988	67	545	38	7	49
Sprowl	.971	6	33	0	1	2

Second Base	PCT	G	PO	A	E	DP
Green	.979	95	206	253	10	61

	PCT	G	PO	A	E	DP
Hairston	.970	9	11	21	1	3
Macha	.946	11	18	17	2	2
Uggla	.950	34	59	73	7	13

Third Base	PCT	G	PO	A	E	DP
Barden	.946	57	37	121	9	16
Epke	.000	1	0	0	0	0
Hairston	.889	4	4	4	1	1
Macha	.889	7	3	5	1	0
Myers	.906	58	31	133	17	7
Sprowl	.833	3	2	3	1	0
Uggla	.870	16	15	25	6	3
Williams	.889	4	3	5	1	0

Shortstop	PCT	G	PO	A	E	DP
Bell	1.000	7	8	17	0	3
Berroa	.925	85	113	208	26	37

	PCT	G	PO	A	E	DP
Firlit	.989	23	31	62	1	11
Gil	.917	10	19	36	5	6
Macha	.878	41	54	90	20	15

Outfield	PCT	G	PO	A	E	DP
Bevins	1.000	1	3	0	0	0
Cota	.962	56	74	2	3	0
Edge	.968	126	231	10	8	2
Foreman	1.000	25	27	5	0	1
Garthwaite	1.000	7	5	0	0	0
Hall	.975	84	188	6	5	0
Kroeger	.978	118	213	9	5	0
Macha	.000	2	0	0	0	0
Mashore	1.000	5	7	0	0	0
Murphy	1.000	8	8	0	0	0
Simpson	1.000	9	16	0	0	0
Sprowl	1.000	18	18	5	0	0

MIDWEST LEAGUE

BATTING	AVG	G	AB	R	H	2B	3B	HR	RBI	BB	SO	SB	CS	SLG	OBP	B	T	HT	WT	DOB	1st Yr	Resides
Ball, Jarred	.240	87	321	48	77	13	4	2	23	42	85	12	1	.324	.338	S	R	6-0	170	4-18-83	2001	Tomball, Texas

BATTING

BATTING	AVG	G	AB	R	H	2B	3B	HR	RBI	BB	SO	SB	CS	SLG	OBP	B	T	HT	WT	DOB	1st Yr	Resides
Barrett, Rich	.225	54	178	17	40	10	1	1	14	11	60	12	2	.309	.287	R	R	6-6	200	8-20-79	2001	Hartsville, Pa.
Brand, Kevin	.250	28	92	7	23	1	0	0	4	8	18	3	1	.261	.307	S	R	5-10	170	1-24-80	2001	Mesa, Ariz.
Callahan, Dan	.293	50	181	21	53	4	2	0	11	8	36	2	1	.337	.321	L	L	6-4	190	11-5-79	2002	Medfield, Mass.
DiRosa, Michael	.220	67	205	23	45	12	0	4	21	44	81	1	1	.337	.368	R	R	5-11	190	1-17-80	2001	Miami, Fla.
Foreman, JuJu	.129	9	31	0	4	1	0	0	2	1	8	1	0	.161	.182	L	R	5-8	165	2-18-79	2000	Girard, Ga.
Garcia, Lino	.185	67	232	28	43	9	0	4	18	17	69	4	4	.276	.258	R	R	6-3	180	10-12-83	2001	San Fernando, Venez.
Garthwaite, Jay	.247	46	162	21	40	10	2	2	18	11	62	2	2	.370	.301	R	R	6-2	210	11-26-80	2002	Kent, Wash.
Hairston, Scott	.332	109	394	79	131	35	4	16	72	58	74	9	3	.563	.426	R	R	6-1	190	5-25-80	2001	Oro Valley, Ariz.
Haydel, Rick	.194	124	413	45	80	10	1	5	40	35	119	14	9	.259	.265	R	R	6-1	180	8-26-78	2001	Prairieville, La.
Hilinski, Scott	.136	43	125	10	17	2	0	0	6	12	52	0	3	.152	.206	R	R	6-0	170	12-17-79	2001	Lake Mary, Fla.
Honeycutt, Heath	.244	22	82	9	20	2	1	1	7	9	22	3	1	.329	.330	R	R	6-4	210	7-30-76	1998	Alpharetta, Ga.
Hutchinson, Burney	.239	38	117	11	28	5	1	3	13	14	17	0	3	.376	.321	L	R	6-1	180	10-12-78	2002	Tupelo, Miss.
Jacobo, Kervin	.163	29	98	9	16	4	0	1	7	14	42	3	2	.235	.268	S	R	6-2	160	9-26-82	1999	Haina, D.R.
Janz, Jeramy	.212	31	113	11	24	6	0	1	8	8	23	0	1	.292	.276	L	R	6-3	190	8-5-79	2001	Fresno, Calif.
Loeb, Bryan	.229	98	362	44	83	23	2	4	46	24	71	4	4	.337	.290	R	R	6-2	190	4-8-78	2000	Sugar Land, Texas
Lopez, Mike	.171	29	105	10	18	7	0	0	5	7	19	4	0	.238	.221	R	R	5-10	190	9-19-77	2001	Glendale, Ariz.
Luellwitz, Sean	.216	48	162	15	35	9	2	1	21	22	35	0	1	.315	.323	R	R	6-5	230	11-16-79	2002	Brookfield, Wis.
Mace, Clark	.095	8	21	1	2	1	0	0	0	0	5	1	0	.143	.095	L	L	6-4	190	4-21-79	2001	London, Ohio
McCool, Lee	.186	18	70	10	13	2	1	1	4	7	12	1	1	.286	.256	R	R	5-11	180	3-5-79	2000	Palatka, Fla.
2-team (36 Fort Wayne)	.204	54	196	26	40	7	3	2	13	12	47	2	2	.301	.258							
Montilla, Sam	.133	5	15	0	2	1	0	0	3	0	2	0	0	.200	.125	R	R	5-11	170	2-7-82	1998	Santo Domingo, D.R.
Nichols, Kyle	.245	122	453	44	111	35	0	12	72	56	101	0	1	.402	.327	R	R	6-2	210	3-29-78	2001	Southport, Fla.
Paredes, Jeison	.233	40	172	17	40	6	4	1	14	6	47	9	3	.331	.263	R	R	6-2	180	6-25-80	2001	Haina, D.R.
Uggla, Dan	.199	53	171	16	34	5	1	2	10	23	34	0	2	.275	.291	R	R	5-11	190	3-11-80	2001	Columbia, Tenn.
Urueta, Luis	.121	9	33	1	4	1	0	0	0	0	11	0	0	.152	.121	S	R	6-2	180	1-9-81	1998	Barranquilla, Colombia
Vugteveen, Dustin	.214	84	285	29	61	9	3	2	31	17	77	5	5	.288	.274	R	R	6-1	200	8-26-79	2001	Grandville, Mich.

PITCHING

PITCHING	W	L	ERA	G	GS	CG	SV	IP	H	R	ER	BB	SO	AVG	B	T	HT	WT	DOB	1st Yr	Resides
Bruney, Brian	4	3	1.68	37	0	0	10	48	37	15	9	17	54	.210	R	R	6-3	220	2-17-82	2000	Warrenton, Ore.
Bulger, Jason	4	9	4.94	20	20	1	0	95	111	65	52	39	84	.291	R	R	6-4	200	12-6-78	2002	Snellville, Ga.
Castellanos, Jon	4	10	4.36	28	20	1	0	130	134	73	63	42	84	.269	R	R	6-0	190	9-17-81	2000	San Nicolas, Mexico
Cormier, Lance	3	0	2.93	11	3	0	1	28	29	9	9	9	2	17	.258	R	R	6-1	190	8-19-80	2002	Lafayette, La.
Ferns, Robert	1	0	0.00	1	0	0	0	3	0	0	0	1	2	.000	R	R	6-4	230	1-4-81	2002	Troy, Mich.
Garber, Mike	0	1	2.93	15	0	0	0	31	41	15	10	10	20	.328	L	L	6-2	190	1-9-81	2001	Palos Heights, Ill.
Gonzalez, Edgar	11	8	2.91	23	23	4	0	151	141	66	49	34	110	.246	R	R	6-0	220	2-23-83	2000	San Nicolas, Mexico
Gonzalez, Enrique	1	2	3.74	4	4	0	0	22	23	16	9	9	20	.270	R	R	5-10	195	7-14-82	1999	Bolivar, Venez.
Heiberger, Heath	0	4	4.39	36	0	0	2	55	62	30	27	27	46	.283	L	L	6-4	200	6-20-80	2001	Hennepin, Ill.
Holsten, Ryan	6	13	3.30	28	28	1	0	174	180	83	64	42	83	.266	R	R	6-4	220	5-5-79	2001	Wilmington, Del.
McMachen, Cliff	5	3	2.63	37	2	1	0	68	52	32	20	27	64	.210	L	L	6-2	195	1-14-81	2001	North Las Vegas, Nev.
Medlin, Corbey	2	7	5.03	45	0	0	6	59	60	41	33	33	54	.264	R	R	6-3	180	8-4-81	2001	Katy, Texas
Perkin, Greg	2	6	6.18	12	12	1	0	63	77	48	43	22	61	.299	R	R	6-2	200	4-15-81	1999	Kingwood, Texas
Ricciardi, Joe	0	1	6.10	8	0	0	0	10	16	11	7	7	7	.333	R	R	6-2	200	8-2-79	2000	Tampa, Fla.
Sikaras, Pete	2	4	1.95	37	0	0	4	60	52	19	13	23	42	.229	R	R	6-2	200	5-5-79	2000	Niles, Ill.
Slaten, Doug	0	0	4.40	7	0	0	0	14	18	8	7	4	5	.310	L	L	6-5	190	2-4-80	2001	Venice, Calif.
Wechsler, Justin	7	12	4.01	26	25	0	0	141	165	87	63	37	96	.291	R	R	6-2	230	4-6-80	2001	Pendleton, Ind.
Wilkinson, Matt	0	4	3.72	36	2	0	2	68	71	32	28	9	79	.259	L	R	6-3	190	10-25-77	2001	Chicago, Ill.

FIELDING

Catcher	PCT	G	PO	A	E	DP	PB
DiRosa	.995	59	390	40	2	0	12
Loeb	.978	78	528	59	13	0	8
Montilla	.968	5	26	4	1	1	2

First Base	PCT	G	PO	A	E	DP
Loeb	.974	9	66	8	2	6
Lopez	.974	5	35	2	1	4
Luellwitz	.994	48	435	39	3	35
Nichols	.986	69	598	44	9	58
Urueta	1.000	9	73	2	0	7

Second Base	PCT	G	PO	A	E	DP
Brand	.882	4	5	10	2	3
Hairston	.949	95	171	277	24	56
Haydel	.971	5	13	21	1	4
Hilinski	.962	14	33	42	3	11

	PCT	G	PO	A	E	DP
Jacobo	.958	6	9	14	1	5
McCool	.951	12	17	22	2	3
Uggla	.969	6	11	20	1	6

Third Base	PCT	G	PO	A	E	DP
Brand	.926	9	6	19	2	2
Hairston	.862	10	8	17	4	2
Hilinski	.833	3	3	2	1	0
Honeycutt	.934	22	20	37	4	5
Jacobo	.898	21	13	40	6	3
Lopez	.930	24	23	30	4	1
McCool	.941	6	4	12	1	3
Uggla	.923	46	37	94	11	9

Shortstop	PCT	G	PO	A	E	DP
Brand	1.000	4	2	4	0	0
Haydel	.934	119	163	357	37	71

	PCT	G	PO	A	E	DP
Hilinski	.933	23	29	68	7	13

Outfield	PCT	G	PO	A	E	DP
Ball	.981	83	158	1	3	0
Barrett	.990	49	89	7	1	1
Callahan	.963	43	76	1	3	0
Foreman	.846	8	10	1	2	0
Garcia	.974	65	149	3	4	0
Garthwaite	.980	45	98	0	2	0
Hutchinson	1.000	26	41	1	0	0
Janz	.939	22	43	3	3	0
Loeb	1.000	6	9	1	0	0
Mace	1.000	5	6	0	0	0
Paredes	.988	33	79	4	1	0
Vugteveen	.963	48	98	7	4	4

YAKIMA BEARS
Short-Season A

NORTHWEST LEAGUE

BATTING	AVG	G	AB	R	H	2B	3B	HR	RBI	BB	SO	SB	CS	SLG	OBP	B	T	HT	WT	DOB	1st Yr	Resides
Barden, Brian	.333	4	15	5	5	1	0	0	2	1	1	0	0	.400	.412	R	R	5-11	190	4-2-81	2002	San Diego, Calif.
Barrett, Rich	.198	56	172	22	34	5	1	1	11	18	44	14	4	.256	.302	R	R	6-6	200	8-20-79	2001	Hartsville, Pa.
Berroa, Angel	.227	25	88	7	20	5	1	0	9	6	21	0	3	.307	.274	R	R	5-11	150	9-26-84	2001	La Romana, D.R.
Brown, Nebasett	.185	63	173	20	32	9	0	0	13	18	38	5	1	.237	.262	L	R	6-0	180	11-7-79	2002	Stillwater, Okla.
Callahan, Dan	.333	8	15	2	5	1	0	0	3	3	1	0	0	.400	.421	L	L	6-4	190	11-5-79	2002	Medfield, Mass.
Garcia, Lino	.194	25	62	8	12	2	1	1	6	6	15	3	0	.306	.296	R	R	6-3	180	10-12-83	2001	San Fernando, Venez.
Garthwaite, Jay	.176	14	51	9	9	5	0	1	3	3	12	0	0	.333	.236	R	R	6-2	210	11-26-80	2002	Kent, Wash.
Gates, Bookie	.233	61	223	20	52	4	3	0	23	9	42	12	6	.278	.271	R	R	6-2	200	1-31-80	2001	Seattle, Wash.
Gil, Jerry	.250	65	224	21	56	11	2	2	28	6	47	14	1	.344	.274	R	R	6-3	180	10-14-82	1999	Santo Domingo, D.R.
Gorman, Jason	.128	44	94	1	12	0	0	0	3	9	25	1	2	.128	.219	R	R	6-0	190	9-9-80	2002	Palmdale, Calif.
Haley, Adam	.111	6	9	1	1	0	0	0	0	2	0	0	0	.111	.200	L	R	6-0	170	9-4-80	2002	Louisville, Ky.
Huff, Ken	.194	35	103	9	20	3	1	2	11	13	22	0	1	.301	.297	L	L	5-11	210	9-17-79	2001	Phoenix, Ariz.
Hutchinson, Burney	.133	7	15	0	2	1	0	0	3	1	3	0	0	.200	.167	L	R	6-1	180	10-12-78	2002	Tupelo, Miss.
Johnson, Bryan	.231	72	238	24	55	12	1	1	22	42	54	0	3	.303	.354	S	R	6-1	200	2-23-81	2002	Ephrata, Wash.

BATTING	AVG	G	AB	R	H	2B	3B	HR	RBI	BB	SO	SB	CS	SLG	OBP	B	T	HT	WT	DOB	1st Yr	Resides
Luellwitz, Sean	.317	13	41	6	13	2	0	0	3	5	8	0	0	.366	.391	R	R	6-5	230	11-16-79	2002	Brookfield, Wis.
McCool, Lee	.205	15	44	4	9	2	1	0	5	5	8	1	0	.295	.314	R	R	5-11	180	3-5-79	2000	Palatka, Fla.
Montilla, Sam	.191	42	131	9	25	5	0	1	12	8	23	1	1	.252	.236	R	R	5-11	170	2-7-82	1998	Santo Domingo, D.R.
Paredes, Jeison	.209	37	110	12	23	5	0	1	9	2	25	4	1	.282	.237	R	R	6-2	180	6-25-80	2001	Haina, D.R.
Saba, Donnie	.229	60	157	22	36	6	0	1	15	22	63	5	3	.287	.341	L	R	6-0	200	3-2-81	2002	Sandy, Utah
Tiesing, Tyler	.186	44	113	10	21	3	1	1	15	8	33	0	0	.257	.260	R	R	6-3	200	8-15-79	2001	Pratt, Kan.
Wilkins, Joe	.254	49	138	13	35	4	0	0	14	15	23	2	3	.283	.329	S	R	6-1	200	8-8-79	2002	Grove City, Ohio
Williams, Marland	.246	70	280	46	69	4	8	3	17	27	86	51	7	.350	.311	R	R	5-9	170	6-22-81	2002	Williston, Fla.

GAMES BY POSITION: C—Montilla 35, Tiesing 13, Wilkins 37. **1B**—Huff 13, Johnson 57, Luellwitz 6, Tiesing 6. **2B**—Berroa 11, Brown 46, Gates 2, Gorman 21, Haley 3, McCool 13, Tiesing 2. **3B**—Barden 4, Brown 12, Gates 56, Gil 1, Gorman 15, Luellwitz 1. **SS**—Berroa 17, Gil 60, Gorman 7, Haley 3. **OF**—Barrett 55, Callahan 7, Garcia 24, Garthwaite 14, Gates 1, Gorman 1, Huff 9, Hutchinson 3, Luellwitz 1, Paredes 31, Saba 43, Wilkins 2, Williams 67.

PITCHING	W	L	ERA	G	GS	CG	SV	IP	H	R	ER	BB	SO	AVG	B	T	HT	WT	DOB	1st Yr	Resides
Aquino, Greg	1	1	2.06	6	6	0	0	35	26	9	8	17	34	.213	R	R	6-1	150	1-11-79	1996	Palenque, D.R.
Biggs, Billy	1	2	2.42	20	0	0	8	26	18	9	7	8	19	.197	R	R	6-1	190	9-9-79	2002	Scott Depot, W.Va.
Bonnell, Jared	1	1	5.06	19	1	0	0	32	36	21	18	22	31	.292	R	R	6-2	210	12-9-80	2002	Las Vegas, Nev.
Corley, Klent	0	5	7.55	19	5	0	0	39	57	44	33	32	19	.333	R	R	6-5	200	6-26-81	2002	Phoenix, Ariz.
Cormier, Lance	0	0	27.00	1	0	0	0	1	4	4	3	0	3	.500	R	R	6-2	190	8-19-80	2002	Lafayette, La.
Davis, Mike	3	4	4.38	22	1	0	0	51	46	31	25	26	46	.239	R	R	6-4	180	7-6-80	1999	Eddyville, Ky.
Douglas, Mitch	0	0	10.13	3	0	0	0	3	4	3	3	5	3	.333	L	L	5-10	190	1-22-81	2002	Douglas, Ga.
Doyle, Jared	4	4	2.87	16	8	0	1	63	44	24	20	29	70	.198	L	L	6-0	190	1-30-81	2002	Wilmington, N.C.
Garber, Mike	1	6	2.54	9	7	0	0	46	49	27	13	14	31	.257	L	L	6-2	190	1-9-81	2001	Palos Heights, Ill.
Gonzalez, Enrique	5	2	2.45	11	11	0	0	66	53	27	18	18	57	.219	R	R	5-10	195	7-14-82	1999	Bolivar, Venez.
Gorman, Jason	0	0	0.00	2	0	0	0	2	2	0	0	0	0	.000	R	R	6-0	190	9-9-80	2002	Palmdale, Calif.
Lizarraga, Sergio	4	8	4.05	16	13	0	0	91	90	48	41	19	86	.261	R	R	6-4	170	7-23-81	2001	Mazatlan, Mexico
Medina, Franklin	0	3	6.08	9	4	0	0	27	33	25	18	22	34	.300	R	R	6-2	180	3-25-82	1998	San Cristobal, D.R.
Medina, Roberto	1	2	4.05	26	0	0	0	33	39	30	15	30	28	.284	L	L	6-0	160	8-6-80	2001	Hermosillo, Mexico
Mercedes, Gabriel	0	5	4.11	20	4	0	2	46	48	26	21	32	31	.284	R	R	6-2	160	11-30-82	1999	Villa Mella, D.R.
Perez, Edwin	0	0	7.71	2	0	0	0	2	1	2	2	1	3	.142	R	R	5-10	200	6-12-80	2001	San Cristobal, D.R.
Silva, Erick	1	0	5.40	6	0	0	0	12	11	7	7	9	12	.255	R	R	6-1	150	11-20-82	1999	Maracay, Venez.
Taulli, Sam	0	2	3.91	5	5	0	0	23	22	14	10	8	19	.244	L	L	6-2	190	9-19-79	2001	Marianna, Fla.
Waroff, Shane	0	0	4.31	24	8	0	1	63	69	36	30	24	45	.277	R	R	6-5	220	8-19-80	2001	Walnut, Calif.
White, Bill	0	1	9.35	3	3	0	0	9	10	9	9	10	11	.277	L	L	6-4	215	11-20-78	2000	Alexander City, Ala.

MISSOULA OSPREY — Rookie

PIONEER LEAGUE

BATTING	AVG	G	AB	R	H	2B	3B	HR	RBI	BB	SO	SB	CS	SLG	OBP	B	T	HT	WT	DOB	1st Yr	Resides
Avlas, Phil	.276	50	152	22	42	13	2	0	19	21	37	3	1	.388	.371	R	R	5-11	170	12-17-82	2001	North Hills, Calif.
Boll, Javier	.222	7	27	1	6	0	0	0	2	0	2	0	0	.222	.214	R	R	6-2	170	3-18-82	1999	Caracas, Venez.
Frazier, Alex	.260	65	235	32	61	11	3	8	35	17	51	1	2	.434	.338	R	R	6-4	210	12-21-80	2002	Dunnellon, Fla.
Garcia, Lino	.233	23	73	15	17	5	0	0	9	14	20	4	2	.301	.383	R	R	6-3	180	10-12-83	2001	San Fernando, Venez.
Heath, Matt	.169	25	71	9	12	3	0	0	3	11	30	2	1	.211	.277	S	R	6-0	190	3-21-79	2002	Live Oak, Fla.
Jacobo, Kervin	.213	47	164	23	35	8	2	4	26	16	51	7	3	.360	.287	S	R	6-2	160	9-26-82	1999	Haina, D.R.
Montero, Danilo	.208	35	101	11	21	1	2	0	6	3	23	4	1	.257	.245	S	R	6-2	160	1-28-83	1999	Santo Domingo, D.R.
Montero, Miguel	.263	50	152	21	40	10	1	3	14	17	26	2	1	.401	.343	L	R	5-11	180	7-9-83	2001	Caracas, Venez.
Moreno, Juan J.	.214	40	103	17	22	3	2	0	8	13	34	5	0	.282	.299	L	R	5-9	160	8-16-81	1999	Santo Domingo, D.R.
Morgan, Matt	.261	71	253	39	66	12	2	3	30	38	42	6	4	.360	.354	R	R	6-2	190	8-10-81	2002	Orsini, Calif.
Raposo, Angel	.111	6	9	0	1	0	0	0	0	3	5	0	0	.111	.333	R	R	6-3	210	10-8-82	2002	San Pedro de Macoris, D.R.
Sanchez, Braulio	.200	21	45	6	9	3	0	0	5	5	12	0	0	.267	.280	L	L	6-1	180	5-25-82	1999	Santo Domingo, D.R.
Santana, Mayobanex	.307	53	202	24	62	11	2	3	35	13	32	3	3	.426	.353	R	R	6-3	190	8-23-81	1999	Santo Domingo, D.R.
Santiago, Ricardo	.254	64	228	39	58	6	5	2	28	17	54	8	2	.351	.306	L	R	6-1	180	12-23-82	1999	Santo Domingo, D.R.
Santos, Sergio	.272	54	202	38	55	19	2	9	37	29	49	6	3	.520	.367	R	R	6-3	190	7-4-83	2002	Hacienda Heights, Calif.
Simon, Brandon	.215	60	191	46	41	3	1	0	16	21	46	30	16	.241	.362	L	L	6-0	170	9-9-80	2002	Fresno, Calif.
Stanek, Jeff	.306	71	232	41	71	16	1	9	51	68	66	2	0	.500	.457	L	R	6-3	220	8-18-80	2002	Lockport, Ill.
Symonds, Grady	.280	11	25	3	7	2	0	0	2	2	6	0	0	.360	.333	R	R	6-2	180	1-15-81	2002	Buffalo Grove, Ill.
Urueta, Luis	.176	41	102	10	18	5	0	2	9	5	41	0	1	.284	.229	L	R	5-8	180	1-9-81	1998	Barranquilla, Colombia

GAMES BY POSITION: C—Avlas 40, Montero 40, Symonds 9, Urueta 1. **1B**—Avlas 1, Heath 3, Montero 1, Santana 7, Simon 1, Stanek 66, Urueta 11. **2B**—Jacobo 29, Moreno 16, Morgan 37, Santana 4. **3B**—Jacobo 9, Montero 4, Moreno 22, Morgan 10, Raposo 5, Santana 42, Urueta 1. **SS**—Moreno 2, Morgan 24, Santana 1, Santos 52. **OF**—Boll 7, Frazier 50, Garcia 23, Heath 19, Montero 30, Sanchez 7, Santiago 63, Simon 56, Urueta 2.

PITCHING	W	L	ERA	G	GS	CG	SV	IP	H	R	ER	BB	SO	AVG	B	T	HT	WT	DOB	1st Yr	Resides
Allender, John	1	1	8.49	21	0	0	0	35	43	39	33	34	21	.300	R	R	6-4	180	2-18-85	2002	Gowrie, Australia
Coffin, Ryan	2	5	2.61	22	8	0	3	62	55	25	18	12	54	.229	R	R	6-4	180	8-5-81	2002	Tempe, Ariz.
Ferns, Robert	0	2	6.57	8	2	0	0	12	19	16	9	5	15	.333	R	R	6-4	230	1-4-81	2002	Troy, Mich.
Garcia, Kelvin	2	4	4.96	18	11	0	1	65	86	46	36	16	56	.309	L	L	6-3	150	9-8-82	1999	San Pedro de Macoris, D.R.
Gilliam, Wes	1	0	6.43	8	0	0	1	7	6	8	5	7	8	.200	L	L	6-5	220	7-31-79	2002	New Lenox, Ill.
Incinelli, Matt	2	2	2.98	27	0	0	0	42	46	19	14	11	38	.278	R	R	6-2	180	2-2-80	2002	Orlando, Fla.
Juarez, William	6	2	2.43	16	11	1	0	81	85	30	22	12	56	.272	R	R	6-2	180	4-22-81	2000	Chinandega, Nicaragua
Kranawetter, Josh	4	3	2.42	30	0	0	3	45	41	26	12	14	41	.239	R	R	5-10	180	5-21-80	2002	Jacob, Ill.
Nippert, Dustin	4	2	1.65	17	11	0	0	55	42	12	10	9	77	.207	R	R	6-7	210	5-6-81	2002	Beallsville, Ohio
Perez, Edwin	2	4	4.41	8	7	0	0	33	33	23	16	10	28	.257	R	R	5-10	200	6-12-80	2001	San Cristobal, D.R.
Rosario, Adriano	1	2	6.30	4	4	0	0	20	26	15	14	3	14	.320	R	R	6-2	190	5-16-85	2002	San Francisco de Macoris, D.R.
Rosen, Mark	1	1	3.93	13	1	0	0	18	15	11	8	12	15	.220	L	L	5-11	200	6-30-84	2002	Randolph, Mass.
Sierra, Jairo	0	3	10.12	6	6	0	0	21	34	29	24	21	9	.350	R	R	6-2	150	10-5-83	1999	San Pedro de Macoris, D.R.
Silva, Erick	0	3	9.77	11	6	0	0	31	40	41	34	28	27	.305	R	R	6-1	150	11-20-82	1999	Maracay, Venez.
Smith, Sam	1	4	2.59	27	0	0	8	42	41	18	12	8	45	.244	R	R	6-4	210	8-23-79	2002	Rio Rancho, N.M.
Whatley, Keith	7	2	2.85	22	9	0	0	66	56	25	21	14	75	.224	L	L	6-2	210	4-23-80	2002	Atlanta, Texas
Yamaguchi, Tetsuya	1	1	3.94	21	0	0	0	32	35	21	14	21	39	.265	L	L	6-0	170	11-83	2002	Yokohama, Japan

ATLANTA BRAVES

BY BILL BALLEW

For the 10th time in 11 championship campaigns, the Atlanta Braves ended a season wondering how something so right could wind up so wrong.

In what has become a most unwelcome tradition just south of the Georgia capitol, the Braves were eliminated from the playoffs at Turner Field after posting the National League's best record in 2002. Atlanta overcame its annual bumpy start to go 60-20 from mid-May to mid-August and cruise to the NL East crown, topping second-place Montreal by 19 games.

With the help of offseason acquisition Gary Sheffield and a dominant bullpen, the Braves went 101-59, enabling Bobby Cox to become the first NL manager to have five 100-win seasons and extending the Braves' playoff string to 11 straight division titles, the longest run in professional sports history.

Yet such accomplishments meant little when the Braves fell in five games to the Giants in the Division Series after leading two games to one. Most everyone in the organization believed Atlanta fielded its strongest overall team in its current run, which only intensified the pain when the season came to a sudden halt.

"I don't know if it's as bad as '96 (when the Braves lost the World Series to the Yankees after leading two games to none), but it's right up there," said Chipper Jones, who made a seamless move from third base to left field and became just the fourth player in major league history to post at least 100 RBIs in seven straight seasons.

Jones had some offensive support, though the consistency was lacking at times. Sheffield was limited to 135 games due to assorted nagging ailments and provided Jones with some protection as the cleanup hitter before going 1-for-16 in the NLDS. Center fielder Andruw Jones equaled his three-year norm of 35 home runs, while

John Smoltz   Trey Hodges

PLAYERS OF THE YEAR

MAJOR LEAGUE: John Smoltz, rhp

Smoltz completed his conversion from feared starter to feared closer by registering a National League record 55 saves in 59 chances. Overall, he went 3-2, 3.25 with 85 strikeouts in 80 innings.

MINOR LEAGUE: Trey Hodges, rhp

Hodges led all Braves farmhands in wins for the second straight season, going 15-9, 3.19 in 172 innings for Triple-A Richmond. He could get a chance as Atlanta's fifth starter in 2003.

shortstop Rafael Furcal slumped early in the year defensively before regaining his consistency.

There were disappointments, headed by the offensive output of third baseman Vinny Castilla. A free-agent acquisition prior to the season, Castilla endured the least productive year of his career that included a combined no home runs and eight RBIs in July and August.

Not surprisingly, pitching was again the Braves' calling card. Tom Glavine won 18 games—a total matched by Kevin Millwood, who regained his dominating form after back-to-back disappointing campaigns. Greg Maddux tied Cy Young's major league mark by winning at least 15 games for the 15th straight season.

Once the bane of the Braves, the bullpen served as a major reason the team led the big leagues with a 3.13 ERA. The relief corps' 2.60 was the best in the majors, and six relievers threw 50 innings or more. Former starter John Smoltz reluctantly took over the closer's role and registered an NL-record 55 saves. Atlanta also caught lightning in a bottle with Chris Hammond and Darren Holmes, after both pitchers were considered retired before making impressive comebacks.

Pitching also served as the strength of the Atlanta farm system, which went a combined 350-334 after cutting from seven to six teams in March by allowing Jamestown in the New York-Penn League to affiliate with the Marlins. Class A Myrtle Beach was the only club to reach postseason play.

Individually, righthander Bubba Nelson led the minors with a 1.72 ERA at Myrtle Beach. Righthander Trey Hodges topped the International League with 15 wins, and Macon lefty Macay McBride, the Braves' first-round draft pick in 2001, was named the South Atlantic League's pitcher of the year.

ORGANIZATION LEADERS

BATTING
*AVG	Adam LaRoche, Greenville/Myrtle Beach	.317
R	Gregor Blanco, Macon	87
H	Carlos Duran, Macon	144
TB	Andy Marte, Macon	240
2B	Scott Thorman, Macon	38
3B	Adam Stern, Myrtle Beach	10
	Carlos Duran, Macon	10
HR	Mike Hessman, Richmond	26
RBI	Andy Marte, Macon	105
BB	Gregor Blanco, Macon	85
SO	Gregor Blanco, Macon	120
SB	Adam Stern, Myrtle Beach	40
	Gregor Blanco, Macon	40

PITCHING
W	Trey Hodges, Richmond	15
L	Brett Evert, Greenville/Myrtle Beach	13
ERA	Ray Aguilar, Myrtle Beach/Danville	1.57
G	Ray Beasley, Richmond	64
CG	Daniel Curtis, Greenville/Myrtle Beach	4
SV	Kevin Barry, Myrtle Beach	26
	Billy Sylvester, Richmond/Greenville	26
IP	Chris Waters, Myrtle Beach	183
BB	Adam Wainwright, Myrtle Beach	66
SO	Adam Wainwright, Myrtle Beach	167

*Minimum 250 At-Bats #Minimum 75 Innings

ORGANIZATION STATISTICS

ATLANTA BRAVES

Manager: Bobby Cox

2002 Record: 101-59, .631 (1st, NL East)

BATTING	AVG	G	AB	R	H	2B	3B	HR	RBI	BB	SO	SB	CS	SLG	OBP	B	T	HT	WT	DOB	1st Yr	Resides
Blanco, Henry	.204	81	221	17	45	9	1	6	22	20	51	0	2	.335	.267	R	R	5-11	220	8-29-71	1990	Guarenas, Venez.
Bragg, Darren	.269	109	212	34	57	15	2	3	15	24	52	5	2	.401	.347	L	R	5-9	180	9-7-69	1991	Roswell, Ga.
Castilla, Vinny	.232	143	543	56	126	23	2	12	61	22	69	4	1	.348	.268	R	R	6-1	200	7-4-67	1990	Littleton, Colo.
DeRosa, Mark	.297	72	212	24	63	9	2	5	23	12	24	2	3	.429	.339	R	R	6-1	200	2-2-75	1996	Atlanta, Ga.
Franco, Julio	.284	125	338	51	96	13	1	6	30	39	75	5	1	.382	.357	R	R	6-1	180	8-23-61	1978	San Pedro de Macoris, D.R.
Franco, Matt	.317	81	205	25	65	15	4	6	30	27	31	1	0	.517	.395	L	R	6-1	210	8-19-69	1987	Thousand Oaks, Calif.
Furcal, Rafael	.275	154	636	95	175	31	8	8	47	43	114	27	15	.387	.323	S	R	5-10	160	10-24-77	1997	Loma de Cabrera, D.R.
Garcia, Jesse	.197	39	61	6	12	1	0	0	5	0	14	0	1	.213	.197	R	R	5-10	170	9-24-73	1993	Robstown, Texas
Giles, Marcus	.230	68	213	27	49	10	1	8	23	25	41	1	1	.399	.315	R	R	5-8	180	5-18-78	1997	El Cajon, Calif.
Helms, Wes	.243	85	210	20	51	16	0	6	22	11	57	1	1	.405	.283	R	R	6-4	230	5-12-76	1994	Gastonia, N.C.
Jones, Andruw	.264	154	560	91	148	34	0	35	94	83	135	8	3	.513	.366	R	R	6-1	180	4-23-77	1994	Willemstad, Curacao
Jones, Chipper	.327	158	548	90	179	35	1	26	100	107	89	8	2	.536	.435	S	R	6-4	210	4-24-72	1990	Alpharetta, Ga.
Langerhans, Ryan	.000	1	1	0	0	0	0	0	0	0	0	0	0	.000	.000	L	L	6-3	190	2-20-80	1998	Round Rock, Texas
Lockhart, Keith	.216	128	296	34	64	13	3	5	32	27	50	0	1	.331	.282	L	R	5-10	170	11-10-64	1986	Overland Park, Kan.
Lopez, Javy	.233	109	347	31	81	15	0	11	52	26	63	0	1	.372	.299	R	R	6-3	220	11-5-70	1988	Ponce, P.R.
Sheffield, Gary	.307	135	492	82	151	26	0	25	84	72	53	12	2	.512	.404	R	R	6-0	200	11-18-68	1986	St. Petersburg, Fla.
Surhoff, B.J.	.293	25	75	5	22	5	0	0	9	9	5	1	3	.360	.369	L	R	6-1	200	8-4-64	1985	Cockeysville, Md.
Torrealba, Steve	.059	13	17	1	1	0	0	0	1	3	4	0	0	.059	.200	R	R	6-0	170	2-24-78	1995	Barquisimeto, Venez.

PITCHING	W	L	ERA	G	GS	CG	SV	IP	H	R	ER	BB	SO	AVG	B	T	HT	WT	DOB	1st Yr	Resides
Bong, Jung	0	1	7.50	1	1	0	0	6	8	5	5	2	4	.320	L	L	6-3	170	7-15-80	1997	Norcross, Ga.
Dawley, Joey	0	0	0.00	1	0	0	0	0	0	0	0	0	1	.000	R	R	6-4	205	9-19-71	1993	Moreno Valley, Calif.
Ennis, John	0	0	4.50	1	1	0	0	4	5	2	2	3	1	.384	R	R	6-5	220	10-17-79	1998	Panorama, Calif.
Foster, John	1	0	10.80	5	0	0	0	5	6	6	6	6	6	.285	L	L	6-0	200	5-17-78	1999	Stockton, Calif.
Glavine, Tom	18	11	2.96	36	36	2	0	225	210	85	74	78	127	.252	L	L	6-0	180	3-25-66	1984	Alpharetta, Ga.
Gryboski, Kevin	2	3	3.48	57	0	0	0	52	50	20	20	37	33	.256	R	R	6-5	230	11-15-73	1995	Plains, Pa.
Hammond, Chris	7	2	0.95	63	0	0	0	76	53	15	8	31	63	.194	L	L	6-1	190	1-21-66	1986	Hallandale, Fla.
Hodges, Trey	2	0	5.40	4	0	0	0	12	16	7	7	2	6	.347	R	R	6-3	180	6-29-78	2000	Spring, Texas
Holmes, Darren	2	2	1.81	55	0	0	1	55	41	12	11	12	47	.210	R	R	6-0	200	4-25-66	1987	Fletcher, N.C.
Ligtenberg, Kerry	3	4	2.97	52	0	0	0	67	52	23	22	33	51	.213	R	R	6-2	210	5-11-71	1994	Cottage Grove, Minn.
Lopez, Albie	1	4	4.37	30	4	0	0	56	66	29	27	18	39	.300	R	R	6-2	240	8-18-71	1991	Gilbert, Ariz.
Maddux, Greg	16	6	2.62	34	34	0	0	199	194	67	58	45	118	.257	R	R	6-0	180	4-14-66	1984	Las Vegas, Nev.
Marquis, Jason	8	9	5.04	22	22	0	0	114	127	66	64	49	84	.283	L	R	6-1	210	8-21-78	1996	Staten Island, N.Y.
Millwood, Kevin	18	8	3.24	35	34	1	0	217	186	83	78	65	178	.229	R	R	6-4	220	12-24-74	1993	Duluth, Ga.
Moss, Damian	12	6	3.42	33	29	0	0	179	140	80	68	89	111	.221	L	L	6-0	180	11-24-76	1994	Dublin, Ga.
Pratt, Andy	0	0	6.75	1	0	0	0	1	1	1	1	4	1	.200	L	L	6-0	180	8-27-79	1998	Chino Valley, Ariz.
Remlinger, Mike	7	3	1.99	73	0	0	0	68	48	17	15	28	69	.198	L	L	6-1	210	3-23-66	1987	Alpharetta, Ga.
Small, Aaron	0	0	27.00	1	0	0	0	2	2	1	1	2	1	.666	R	R	6-5	220	11-23-71	1989	Loudon, Tenn.
Smoltz, John	3	2	3.25	75	0	0	55	80	59	30	29	24	85	.205	R	R	6-3	220	5-15-67	1986	Duluth, Ga.
Spooneybarger, Tim	1	0	2.63	51	0	0	1	51	38	16	15	26	33	.206	R	R	6-3	190	10-21-79	1999	Pensacola, Fla.

FIELDING

Catcher	PCT	G	PO	A	E	DP	PB
Blanco	.993	79	417	38	3	1	6
J. Lopez	.986	103	635	54	10	8	5
Torrealba	1.000	12	40	2	0	1	1

First Base	PCT	G	PO	A	E	DP
J. Franco	.990	95	717	59	8	79
M. Franco	.990	51	353	30	4	31
Helms	.987	45	285	27	4	34
Surhoff	1.000	11	72	7	0	12

Second Base	PCT	G	PO	A	E	DP
DeRosa	.974	32	59	89	4	23
Furcal	1.000	4	7	12	0	5
Garcia	.986	21	28	42	1	10
Giles	.977	52	118	139	6	35
Lockhart	.979	89	141	230	8	46

Third Base	PCT	G	PO	A	E	DP
Castilla	.982	139	75	256	6	23
DeRosa	1.000	4	1	4	0	0

	PCT	G	PO	A	E	DP
Giles	.905	8	6	13	2	2
Helms	.970	24	8	24	1	0
Lockhart	1.000	1	1	0	0	0

Shortstop	PCT	G	PO	A	E	DP
DeRosa	.976	19	30	52	2	17
Furcal	.963	150	245	466	27	111
Garcia	1.000	5	4	7	0	4

Outfield	PCT	G	PO	A	E	DP
Bragg	.971	63	98	2	3	0
DeRosa	1.000	7	4	0	0	0
M. Franco	1.000	4	3	0	0	0
Garcia	1.000	4	6	0	0	0
Helms	1.000	9	15	1	0	0
A. Jones	.993	154	404	5	3	1
C. Jones	.975	152	268	8	7	0
Langerhans	.000	1	0	0	0	0
Sheffield	.984	127	232	7	4	0
Surhoff	1.000	9	27	2	0	0

Bobby Cox

LARRY GOREN

Tom Glavine: 18-11, 2.96 on the mound

Gary Sheffield: Hit .307-25-84 in first season in Atlanta

FARM SYSTEM

Directors, Player Development: Dick Balderson/Dayton Moore

Class	Farm Team	League	W	L	Pct.	Finish*	Manager	First Yr.
AAA	Richmond (Va.) Braves	International	75	67	.528	7th (14)	Fredi Gonzalez	1966
AA	Greenville (S.C.) Braves	Southern	65	69	.485	7th (10)	Brian Snitker	1984
High A	Myrtle Beach (S.C.) Pelicans	Carolina	79	61	.564	3rd (8)	Randy Ingle	1999
Low A	Macon (Ga.) Braves	South Atlantic	66	74	.471	t-10th (16)	Lynn Jones	1991
Rookie	Danville (Va.) Braves	Appalachian	37	31	.544	5th (10)	Ralph Henriquez	1993
Rookie	Kissimmee (Fla.) Braves	Gulf Coast	28	32	.467	t-8th (14)	Rick Albert	1998

*Finish in overall standings (No. of teams in league)

RICHMOND BRAVES   Class AAA

INTERNATIONAL LEAGUE

BATTING	AVG	G	AB	R	H	2B	3B	HR	RBI	BB	SO	SB	CS	SLG	OBP	B	T	HT	WT	DOB	1st Yr	Resides
Betemit, Wilson	.245	93	343	43	84	17	1	8	34	34	82	8	5	.370	.312	S	R	6-3	190	11-2-81	1996	Santo Domingo, D.R.
Boscan, Jean	.167	2	6	0	1	0	0	0	0	1	2	0	1	.167	.286	R	R	6-2	160	12-26-79	1996	Maracaibo, Venez.
Bragg, Darren	.293	22	75	15	22	5	0	1	8	20	15	4	2	.400	.442	L	R	5-9	180	9-7-69	1991	Roswell, Ga.
Castro, Ramon	.231	39	121	22	28	7	1	6	14	14	22	4	3	.455	.340	R	R	6-0	190	10-23-79	1996	Valencia, Venez.
DeRosa, Mark	.255	16	55	9	14	3	0	0	6	5	2	2	0	.309	.339	R	R	6-1	200	2-2-75	1996	Atlanta, Ga.
Franco, Matt	.289	47	173	24	50	11	0	6	28	14	19	1	0	.457	.349	L	R	6-1	210	8-19-69	1987	Thousand Oaks, Calif.
Garcia, Jesse	.300	58	230	29	69	12	1	6	17	16	32	9	5	.439	.349	R	R	5-10	170	9-24-73	1993	Robstown, Texas
Giles, Marcus	.322	31	115	25	37	6	0	3	16	13	15	3	0	.452	.385	R	R	5-8	180	5-18-78	1997	El Cajon, Calif.
Hessman, Mike	.262	134	484	67	127	28	1	26	77	34	107	1	5	.486	.321	R	R	6-5	210	3-5-78	1996	Westminster, Calif.
Hollins, Damon	.279	128	498	66	139	34	1	12	59	35	77	10	2	.424	.326	R	L	5-11	180	6-12-74	1992	Fairfield, Calif.
Lombard, George	.308	11	39	10	12	4	1	1	5	5	12	2	0	.538	.400	L	R	6-0	210	9-14-75	1994	Atlanta, Ga.
Lopez, Rafael	.348	7	23	4	8	1	0	0	1	1	4	0	1	.391	.375	R	R	6-0	200	10-22-76	1996	Miami, Fla.
Martinez, Lou	.125	6	8	1	1	0	0	0	0	0	0	0	0	.125	.125	R	R	6-0	170	11-1-76	1999	Tampa, Fla.
Norris, Dax	.260	79	262	29	68	14	0	4	25	15	28	1	1	.359	.299	R	R	5-10	190	1-14-73	1996	La Grange, Ga.
Petersen, Chris	.229	76	223	29	51	6	2	0	15	18	40	0	2	.274	.287	R	R	5-11	170	11-6-70	1992	Southington, Conn.
Porter, Bo	.296	108	392	55	116	26	2	8	52	50	113	18	9	.434	.374	R	R	6-2	190	7-5-72	1994	Fresno, Texas
Smothers, Stewart	.222	17	18	3	4	0	0	0	2	3	5	0	0	.222	.333	R	R	5-10	180	4-29-76	1997	Los Angeles, Calif.
Timmons, Ozzie	.258	131	496	55	128	23	1	15	76	39	90	6	1	.399	.309	R	R	6-2	220	9-18-70	1991	Tampa, Fla.
Torrealba, Steve	.236	61	191	19	45	11	0	3	18	19	31	0	0	.340	.313	R	R	6-0	170	2-24-78	1995	Barquisimeto, Venez.
Unroe, Tim	.242	94	264	33	64	13	1	10	40	28	86	1	2	.413	.332	R	R	6-3	200	10-7-70	1992	Mesa, Ariz.
Wilson, Travis	.263	133	494	59	130	23	5	13	71	13	106	10	3	.409	.287	R	R	6-2	180	7-10-77	1996	Christ Church, New Zealand
Zapp, A.J.	.185	34	92	9	17	3	0	4	7	10	27	1	0	.348	.286	L	R	6-3	190	4-24-78	1996	Greenwood, Ind.

PITCHING	W	L	ERA	G	GS	CG	SV	IP	H	R	ER	BB	SO	AVG	B	T	HT	WT	DOB	1st Yr	Resides
Beasley, Ray	6	5	2.59	64	0	0	4	56	55	24	16	16	45	.261	R	L	5-11	160	10-26-76	1996	Lake City, Fla.
Dawley, Joe	9	7	2.63	24	23	1	0	140	113	44	41	36	136	.219	R	R	6-4	200	9-19-71	1993	Moreno Valley, Calif.

PITCHING

	W	L	ERA	G	GS	CG	SV	IP	H	R	ER	BB	SO	AVG	B	T	HT	WT	DOB	1st Yr	Resides
Foster, John	8	4	4.21	55	0	0	8	62	67	30	29	28	48	.275	L	L	6-0	200	5-17-78	1999	Stockton, Calif.
Gryboski, Kevin	1	0	1.29	7	0	0	3	7	7	1	1	5	5	.250	R	R	6-5	230	11-15-73	1995	Plains, Pa.
Hodges, Trey	15	9	3.19	28	28	1	0	172	158	66	61	56	116	.247	R	R	6-3	180	6-29-78	2000	Spring, Texas
Keller, Kris	1	0	3.60	29	0	0	2	35	26	16	14	13	20	.208	R	R	6-2	260	3-1-78	1996	Atlantic Beach, Fla.
2-team (17 Toledo)	3	0	2.95	46	0	0	2	61	46	26	20	30	40	.209							
Lee, Garrett	0	0	5.19	5	1	0	0	9	15	7	5	2	2	.365	R	R	6-5	210	8-17-76	1996	Montrose, Calif.
Lewis, Derrick	3	5	4.56	18	13	0	0	77	77	49	39	34	52	.261	R	R	6-5	210	5-7-76	1997	Montgomery, Ala.
Linton, Doug	9	11	2.53	28	28	1	0	174	167	63	49	26	160	.249	R	R	6-1	190	9-2-65	1987	Overland Park, Kan.
Marquis, Jason	0	1	3.60	1	1	0	0	5	5	2	2	1	6	.263	L	R	6-1	190	8-21-78	1996	Staten Island, N.Y.
Pratt, Andy	4	2	3.10	6	6	1	0	41	35	15	14	9	36	.231	L	L	6-0	180	8-27-79	1998	Chino Valley, Ariz.
Robbins, Jake	1	4	4.76	47	0	0	3	57	59	36	30	43	37	.269	R	R	6-5	190	5-23-76	1994	Charlotte, N.C.
Saipe, Mike	4	6	3.83	42	12	0	1	94	107	49	40	26	63	.284	R	R	6-5	220	11-23-71	1989	San Diego, Calif.
Small, Aaron	0	3	6.39	14	4	0	0	31	48	27	22	14	19	.363	R	R	6-5	220	11-23-71	1989	Loudon, Tenn.
Sobkowiak, Scott	2	0	3.18	5	1	0	0	11	8	5	4	8	11	.200	R	R	6-5	230	10-26-77	1998	Orlando, Fla.
Spooneybarger, Tim	1	0	0.90	18	0	0	11	20	13	2	2	8	21	.178	R	R	6-3	190	10-21-79	1999	Pensacola, Fla.
Sylvester, Billy	0	0	3.86	7	0	0	1	9	10	4	4	5	5	.277	R	R	6-5	210	10-1-76	1997	Florence, S.C.
Takeoka, Kazuhiro	1	0	2.32	23	0	0	0	31	31	12	8	12	16	.267	R	R	6-4	190	1-25-75	2001	Shiga-Kan, Japan
Wheeler, Dan	9	6	4.65	27	25	0	0	155	163	87	80	42	110	.267	R	R	6-3	220	12-10-77	1997	Warwick, R.I.
Winkelsas, Joe	1	2	2.10	16	0	0	2	26	25	6	6	9	13	.265	R	R	6-3	180	9-14-73	1996	Buffalo, N.Y.
Yankosky, L.J.	0	2	4.97	23	0	0	0	29	40	17	16	14	27	.325	R	R	6-2	200	2-1-75	1998	Springfield, Va.

FIELDING

Catcher	PCT	G	PO	A	E	DP	PB
Boscan	.955	2	21	0	1	0	0
Lopez	1.000	7	41	2	0	0	3
Norris	.987	76	498	45	7	4	5
Torrealba	.979	61	393	33	9	0	7
DeRosa	.947	10	16	20	2	4	
Garcia	.980	43	80	118	4	21	
Giles	.968	15	26	34	2	9	
Petersen	.995	41	70	121	1	20	
Wilson	.976	29	51	71	3	25	
Castro	.985	18	20	46	1	5	
DeRosa	.958	6	11	12	1	2	
Garcia	.907	11	21	28	5	10	
Martinez	1.000	5	3	7	0	3	
Petersen	.958	20	33	59	4	15	

First Base	PCT	G	PO	A	E	DP
Franco	.993	32	274	21	2	25
Hessman	.991	14	99	8	1	11
Timmons	.933	2	13	1	1	5
Unroe	.990	46	350	41	4	41
Wilson	.989	45	322	23	4	28
Zapp	.986	17	134	10	2	10

Second Base	PCT	G	PO	A	E	DP
Castro	.957	20	30	58	4	17

Third Base	PCT	G	PO	A	E	DP
Franco	1.000	6	2	8	0	1
Garcia	1.000	2	0	8	0	0
Giles	.974	13	9	28	1	4
Hessman	.941	116	72	200	17	12
Petersen	1.000	4	2	5	0	1
Wilson	.833	5	2	8	2	0

Shortstop	PCT	G	PO	A	E	DP
Betemit	.946	92	139	227	21	51

Outfield	PCT	G	PO	A	E	DP
Bragg	1.000	21	46	3	0	0
Garcia	1.000	2	3	0	0	0
Hollins	.988	125	308	8	4	0
Lombard	1.000	10	17	0	0	0
Porter	.972	107	235	7	7	1
Smothers	1.000	6	5	0	0	0
Timmons	.995	109	185	5	1	3
Unroe	1.000	3	3	0	0	0
Wilson	.991	57	110	1	1	0

GREENVILLE BRAVES
Class AA

SOUTHERN LEAGUE

BATTING

	AVG	G	AB	R	H	2B	3B	HR	RBI	BB	SO	SB	CS	SLG	OBP	B	T	HT	WT	DOB	1st Yr	Resides
Allensworth, Jermaine	.281	77	270	46	76	18	3	1	36	48	48	8	2	.381	.383	R	R	6-0	190	1-11-72	1993	Anderson, Ind.
Boscan, Jean	.259	10	27	2	7	1	0	1	3	4	10	0	0	.407	.355	R	R	6-2	160	12-26-79	1996	Maracaibo, Venez.
Burrows, Angelo	.213	14	47	3	10	3	1	0	1	2	6	5	2	.319	.245	L	R	5-11	170	7-2-80	1999	Freeport, Bahamas
Castro, Ramon	.324	56	210	47	68	17	2	5	22	39	44	14	8	.495	.446	R	R	6-0	190	10-23-79	1996	Valencia, Venez.
De Renne, Keoni	.275	107	320	51	88	25	3	3	47	41	39	2	4	.400	.355	R	R	5-7	160	4-30-79	2000	Honolulu, Hawaii
Fiore, Curtis	.276	99	319	41	88	21	1	9	40	39	48	3	0	.433	.369	R	R	6-2	190	7-28-77	1999	San Juan Capistrano, Calif.
Green, Nick	.239	94	355	49	85	16	2	15	50	36	92	2	5	.423	.321	R	R	6-0	170	9-10-78	1999	Duluth, Ga.
Gutierrez, Vic	.212	13	33	4	7	1	1	0	1	1	2	1	0	.303	.235	R	R	5-9	170	12-23-77	1994	Santo Domingo, D.R.
Haas, Chris	.118	31	76	6	9	4	1	1	5	16	31	0	0	.237	.272	L	R	6-1	200	10-15-76	1995	Paducah, Ky.
Jones, Damian	.218	66	211	21	46	8	1	1	12	23	55	9	5	.280	.295	L	L	6-2	200	7-10-79	1998	Mobile, Ala.
Langerhans, Ryan	.251	109	391	57	98	23	2	9	62	68	83	10	5	.389	.366	L	L	6-3	180	2-20-80	1998	Round Rock, Texas
LaRoche, Adam	.289	45	173	17	50	9	0	4	19	19	38	1	1	.410	.363	L	L	6-3	180	11-6-79	2000	Fort Scott, Kan.
Lombard, George	.280	8	25	4	7	0	0	3	5	5	6	2	0	.640	.419	L	R	6-0	210	9-14-75	1994	Atlanta, Ga.
McNamara, Rusty	.270	126	448	54	121	19	2	6	52	34	47	7	1	.362	.337	R	R	5-9	190	1-23-75	1997	Riverside, Calif.
Munoz, Adan	.264	16	53	4	14	4	0	2	6	4	12	0	0	.453	.328	L	R	6-1	180	3-9-77	1999	Empalme, Mexico
Orr, Pete	.249	89	305	36	76	10	2	2	36	21	47	23	4	.315	.302	L	R	6-1	170	6-8-79	1999	Newmarket, Ontario
Porter, Bo	.500	2	8	2	4	1	1	1	7	2	0	0	1	1.250	.600	R	R	6-2	190	7-5-72	1994	Fresno, Texas
Serrano, Ray	.246	20	65	7	16	3	0	2	7	5	9	0	0	.385	.315	R	R	5-9	180	1-19-81	1999	Ponce, P.R.
Smothers, Stewart	.149	29	87	7	13	1	0	2	7	14	31	0	3	.230	.299	R	R	5-10	180	4-29-76	1997	Los Angeles, Calif.
Taveras, Luis	.256	45	156	11	40	10	1	5	25	18	25	5	1	.429	.337	R	R	5-10	180	8-1-75	1995	Santiago, D.R.
Terveen, Bryce	.215	55	172	23	37	8	0	3	13	28	42	0	2	.314	.338	L	R	6-1	200	3-1-78	1999	Modesto, Calif.
Thomas, Chuck	.231	71	229	40	53	8	2	3	18	28	43	5	3	.293	.322	L	L	6-0	190	12-26-78	2000	Asheville, N.C.
Zapp, A.J.	.237	85	300	37	71	15	0	14	46	31	81	0	0	.427	.312	L	R	6-3	220	4-24-78	1996	Greenwood, Ind.

PITCHING

	W	L	ERA	G	GS	CG	SV	IP	H	R	ER	BB	SO	AVG	B	T	HT	WT	DOB	1st Yr	Resides
Baker, Ryan	1	0	5.06	5	0	0	0	5	4	3	3	4	2	.222	R	R	6-0	200	3-20-78	2000	Linthicum, Md.
Belisle, Matt	5	9	4.35	26	26	1	0	159	162	91	77	39	123	.260	S	R	6-3	190	6-6-80	1998	Austin, Texas
Bong, Jung	7	8	3.25	27	17	0	2	122	136	59	44	45	107	.286	L	L	6-3	170	7-15-80	1997	Norcross, Ga.
Collazo, Willie	4	2	3.47	51	0	0	4	73	70	34	28	27	74	.252	L	L	5-9	170	11-7-79	2001	Miami, Fla.
Curtis, Daniel	4	4	4.80	10	10	1	0	54	61	29	29	19	29	.303	R	R	6-3	210	11-3-79	1998	Chattanooga, Tenn.
Emiliano, Jamie	3	1	1.66	42	0	0	3	54	34	16	10	24	39	.186	R	R	5-10	210	8-2-74	1995	Andrews, Texas
Ennis, John	9	9	4.18	26	26	0	0	149	131	79	69	62	103	.242	R	R	6-5	220	10-17-79	1998	Panorama, Calif.
Evert, Brett	5	8	4.90	16	15	1	0	94	94	59	51	35	84	.262	L	R	6-4	200	10-23-80	1999	Salem, Ore.
Gawer, Matt	0	1	7.00	6	0	0	0	9	6	7	7	5	8	.181	L	L	6-4	230	4-15-78	1999	Sullivan, Mo.
Hernandez, Buddy	4	0	1.22	40	0	0	1	59	36	13	8	23	81	.175	R	R	5-9	170	3-3-79	2000	Birdsboro, Pa.
Kent, Nathan	1	6	6.00	1	1	0	0	3	3	2	2	3	2	.250	R	R	6-6	210	8-16-78	1999	Frankfort, Ky.
Lee, Garrett	3	2	3.52	19	2	0	0	46	47	21	18	10	26	.268	R	R	6-5	210	8-17-76	1996	Montrose, Calif.
Lewis, Derrick	1	0	0.00	1	1	0	0	6	3	0	0	3	2	.150	R	R	6-5	210	5-7-76	1997	Montgomery, Ala.
Lopez, Albie	0	0	4.50	1	1	0	0	4	4	2	2	2	4	.142	R	R	6-2	240	8-18-71	1991	Gilbert, Ariz.
Pratt, Andy	4	9	4.26	20	18	1	0	93	92	54	44	44	67	.262	L	L	6-0	180	8-27-79	1998	Chino Valley, Ariz.
Ramirez, Horacio	9	5	3.03	16	16	0	0	92	85	41	31	32	64	.252	L	L	6-1	170	11-24-79	1997	Inglewood, Calif.
Sobkowiak, Scott	1	2	4.50	12	1	0	0	28	22	14	14	23	32	.215	R	R	6-5	230	10-26-77	1998	Orlando, Fla.

PITCHING	W	L	ERA	G	GS	CG	SV	IP	H	R	ER	BB	SO	AVG	B	T	HT	WT	DOB	1st Yr	Resides
Sylvester, Billy	2	3	3.47	51	0	0	25	49	31	20	19	32	48	.181	R	R	6-5	210	10-1-76	1997	Florence, S.C.
Takeoka, Kazuhiro	1	3	5.82	21	0	0	4	34	33	25	22	19	26	.251	R	R	6-4	190	1-25-75	2001	Shiga-Kan, Japan
Veronie, Shanin	2	2	3.93	29	0	0	0	53	54	27	23	22	32	.260	R	R	6-1	190	8-18-76	1999	W. Sacramento, Calif.
Winkelsas, Joe	0	0	0.00	2	0	0	2	2	1	0	0	1	0	.142	R	R	6-3	180	9-14-73	1996	Buffalo, N.Y.

FIELDING

Catcher	PCT	G	PO	A	E	DP	PB
Boscan	.969	9	58	5	2	0	4
Munoz	1.000	15	113	8	0	2	1
Serrano	.993	20	143	9	1	1	1
Taveras	.975	45	320	24	9	1	15
Terveen	.992	54	337	47	3	4	3

First Base	PCT	G	PO	A	E	DP
Fiore	.972	12	65	4	2	10
Haas	1.000	14	85	4	0	9
LaRoche	.998	45	408	32	1	33
Terveen	1.000	1	1	0	0	1
Zapp	.982	77	611	51	12	41

Second Base	PCT	G	PO	A	E	DP
De Renne	.960	59	109	131	10	27

Fiore	.875	2	2	5	1	0
Green	.964	76	145	199	13	48
McNamara	.000	1	0	0	0	0
Orr	1.000	4	7	11	0	2

Third Base	PCT	G	PO	A	E	DP
Castro	.962	13	3	22	1	1
Fiore	.967	14	5	24	1	2
Haas	.964	9	8	19	1	2
McNamara	.927	104	84	220	24	12
Orr	1.000	2	1	1	0	0

Shortstop	PCT	G	PO	A	E	DP
Castro	.974	44	66	125	5	21
De Renne	.917	12	9	24	3	4
Green	.889	3	2	6	1	2

	PCT	G	PO	A	E	DP
Gutierrez	.917	9	9	24	3	2
Orr	.974	79	88	251	9	43

Outfield	PCT	G	PO	A	E	DP
Allensworth	.963	74	127	2	5	0
Burrows	.960	14	23	1	1	0
Fiore	.966	58	81	3	3	2
Jones	.960	57	92	4	4	1
Langerhans	.992	109	247	9	2	2
Lombard	1.000	8	19	1	0	0
Orr	1.000	3	4	1	0	0
Porter	.833	2	5	0	1	0
Smothers	.964	28	50	3	2	1
Thomas	.987	70	153	3	2	0

MYRTLE BEACH PELICANS — High Class A

CAROLINA LEAGUE

BATTING	AVG	G	AB	R	H	2B	3B	HR	RBI	BB	SO	SB	CS	SLG	OBP	B	T	HT	WT	DOB	1st Yr	Resides
Anderson, Travis	.267	40	120	19	32	4	0	3	12	14	26	0	4	.375	.369	R	R	6-0	190	8-29-79	2001	Burney, Calif.
Boscan, Jean	.217	86	276	21	60	19	0	2	27	28	71	3	1	.308	.294	R	R	6-2	160	12-26-79	1996	Maracaibo, Venez.
Brown, Kevin	.165	48	133	11	22	5	0	1	11	13	36	0	0	.226	.253	R	R	6-4	230	4-11-79	2001	North Fort Myers, Fla.
Coleman, Alph	.209	120	407	40	85	9	1	2	29	23	68	15	13	.251	.254	R	R	6-3	180	4-8-79	2000	Houston, Texas
DeRosa, Mark	.000	2	7	0	0	0	0	0	0	1	1	0	0	.000	.125	R	R	6-1	200	2-2-75	1996	Atlanta, Ga.
Forbes, Mike	.204	34	98	14	20	5	0	2	6	17	32	4	2	.316	.322	L	R	6-1	170	5-27-80	1998	West Lakes, Australia
Jeffcoat, Bryon	.227	67	225	24	51	15	0	5	30	14	48	5	1	.360	.278	L	R	6-1	190	5-14-79	2001	West Columbia, S.C.
Johnson, Kelly	.255	126	482	62	123	21	5	12	49	51	105	12	15	.394	.325	L	R	6-1	180	2-22-82	2000	Austin, Texas
Jones, Damien	.262	23	61	8	16	2	1	0	1	6	22	3	0	.328	.328	L	L	6-2	190	7-10-79	1998	Mobile, Ala.
Jurries, James	.290	48	176	23	51	9	3	5	30	17	26	2	2	.460	.352	R	R	6-0	190	4-13-79	2002	Lake Jackson, Texas
Kent, Mailon	.246	105	337	34	83	14	2	0	20	47	50	8	8	.300	.343	R	R	6-0	180	9-2-78	2001	Birmingham, Ala.
LaRoche, Adam	.336	69	250	30	84	17	0	9	53	27	37	0	2	.512	.406	L	L	6-3	180	11-6-79	2000	Fort Scott, Kan.
Lewis, Richard	.279	130	484	82	135	23	4	2	51	55	80	31	10	.355	.359	R	R	6-1	190	6-29-80	2001	Marietta, Ga.
Manning, Pat	.196	29	97	13	19	4	0	4	8	11	18	1	1	.412	.297	R	R	6-1	180	2-27-80	1999	Anaheim Hills, Calif.
Martinez, Lou	.250	72	252	21	63	10	0	1	30	11	19	0	3	.302	.277	R	R	6-0	170	11-1-76	1998	Tampa, Fla.
McCarthy, Bill	.305	128	442	52	135	26	4	11	65	38	88	6	5	.457	.386	R	R	6-2	200	12-2-79	2001	Sewell, N.J.
Orr, Pete	.392	17	51	8	20	0	2	0	8	3	6	3	0	.471	.436	L	R	6-1	170	6-8-79	1999	Newmarket, Ontario
Pena, Brayan	.211	6	19	3	4	1	0	0	1	3	4	0	0	.263	.318	S	R	5-11	210	1-7-82	2001	San Jose, Costa Rica
Rodriguez , Ricardo	.200	5	15	1	3	0	0	0	0	4	1	0	0	.200	.200	R	R	6-0	140	4-28-81	1998	Caracas, Venez.
Serrano, Ray	.202	37	114	11	23	4	0	2	18	6	21	0	1	.289	.240	R	R	5-9	180	1-19-81	1999	Ponce, P.R.
Stern, Adam	.253	119	462	65	117	22	10	3	47	27	89	40	8	.364	.298	L	R	5-11	180	2-12-80	2001	London, Ontario
Terveen, Bryce	.289	16	45	13	13	3	0	2	5	7	6	2	0	.489	.439	L	R	6-1	200	3-1-78	1999	Modesto, Calif.
Thomas, Chuck	.286	2	7	0	2	0	0	0	0	0	0	0	0	.286	.286	L	L	6-0	190	12-26-78	2000	Asheville, N.C.

PITCHING	W	L	ERA	G	GS	CG	SV	IP	H	R	ER	BB	SO	AVG	B	T	HT	WT	DOB	1st Yr	Resides
Aguilar, Ray	8	1	1.60	35	6	0	2	107	82	25	19	28	114	.208	S	L	5-11	200	1-18-80	2000	South El Monte, Calif.
Baker, Ryan	3	4	3.72	36	0	0	6	39	40	17	16	20	44	.268	R	R	6-0	200	3-20-78	2000	Linthicum, Md.
Barry, Kevin	4	2	2.52	47	0	0	26	50	37	14	14	17	67	.215	R	R	6-2	210	8-18-78	2001	Princeton Junction, N.J.
Colon, Roman	9	8	3.53	26	26	1	0	163	170	81	64	38	94	.269	R	R	6-3	170	8-13-79	1996	Monte Cristi, D.R.
Curtis, Daniel	7	7	2.53	17	17	3	0	117	106	37	33	18	99	.241	R	R	6-3	210	11-3-79	1998	Chattanooga, Tenn.
David, Brad	0	1	14.29	5	0	0	0	6	10	9	9	6	7	.400	L	L	6-0	190	5-26-80	2002	Baton Rouge, La.
Evert, Brett	3	5	3.75	10	10	1	0	58	53	30	24	21	51	.240	L	R	6-4	200	10-23-80	1999	Salem, Ore.
Kozlowski, Ben	0	1	4.50	1	1	0	0	4	4	5	2	3	3	.235	L	L	6-6	220	8-16-80	1999	Seminole, Fla.
McClendon, Matt	2	4	8.66	17	1	0	0	18	10	20	17	28	12	.163	R	R	6-6	220	10-13-77	1999	Orlando, Fla.
Miller, Matt	2	2	4.84	36	0	0	1	45	54	29	24	17	35	.301	L	L	6-2	200	6-6-78	2000	Devon, Pa.
Nelson, Kenny	11	5	1.72	23	23	0	0	136	98	37	26	44	105	.201	R	R	6-2	200	8-26-81	2000	Fort Washington, Md.
Sobkowiak, Scott	5	1	2.83	16	0	0	0	29	25	9	9	7	32	.240	R	R	6-5	230	10-26-77	1998	Orlando, Fla.
Tillery, Josh	2	3	4.11	37	0	0	0	57	53	26	26	18	41	.246	R	R	6-2	250	8-2-78	2000	Laverne, Okla.
Veronie, Shanin	0	1	7.36	5	0	0	1	11	16	9	9	1	12	.347	R	R	6-1	190	8-18-76	1999	West Sacramento, Calif.
Wainwright, Adam	9	6	3.31	28	28	1	0	163	149	67	60	66	167	.240	R	R	6-6	200	8-30-81	2000	St. Simons, Ga.
Waters, Chris	13	7	2.76	28	28	2	0	183	154	63	56	43	103	.229	L	L	6-0	170	8-17-80	2000	Lakeland, Fla.
Watkins, Dave	1	0	0.00	4	0	0	0	4	2	0	0	4	3	.181	R	R	6-1	190	8-18-81	1999	Leitchfield, Ky.
Yankosky, L.J.	0	0	0.00	1	0	0	0	1	2	1	0	0	0	.500	R	R	6-2	200	2-1-75	1998	Springfield, Va.
Zumwalt, Alec	0	3	8.63	21	0	0	0	24	33	25	23	13	21	.323	R	R	6-2	190	1-20-81	1999	Kernersville, N.C.

FIELDING

Catcher	PCT	G	PO	A	E	DP	PB
Anderson	.971	25	151	15	5	0	5
Boscan	.992	83	666	56	6	3	15
Pena	1.000	6	35	5	0	0	2
Serrano	1.000	19	117	12	0	2	0
Terveen	.989	12	74	16	1	0	3

First Base	PCT	G	PO	A	E	DP
Brown	.986	38	269	21	4	28
Forbes	1.000	8	58	3	0	0
Jeffcoat	.964	4	26	1	1	3
Jurries	.988	30	225	17	3	27

LaRoche	.991	64	518	38	5	45
Martinez	1.000	3	20	0	0	1

Second Base	PCT	G	PO	A	E	DP
DeRosa	.889	2	5	3	1	1
Jeffcoat	.944	6	3	14	1	3
Lewis	.985	124	207	314	8	78
Manning	1.000	8	6	18	0	3
Orr	1.000	1	3	1	0	0
Rodriguez	.933	2	3	11	1	3

Third Base	PCT	G	PO	A	E	DP
Forbes	.871	14	7	20	4	0

	PCT	G	PO	A	E	DP
Jeffcoat	.877	35	20	44	9	7
Johnson	1.000	4	5	2	0	0
Jurries	.625	6	2	3	3	1
Manning	.938	28	19	42	4	1
Martinez	.964	51	40	93	5	11
Orr	.929	3	6	10	1	1
Rodriguez	1.000	3	1	4	0	0

Shortstop	PCT	G	PO	A	E	DP
Jeffcoat	.972	12	19	16	1	5
Johnson	.952	118	168	313	24	72
Martinez	.889	5	8	16	3	2

Orr	.964	7	12	15	1	4
Outfield	**PCT**	**G**	**PO**	**A**	**E**	**DP**
Coleman	.991	115	216	7	2	0

Forbes	1.000	1	2	0	0	0
Jeffcoat	1.000	1	1	0	0	0
Jones	1.000	11	12	0	0	0
Kent	.984	95	172	7	3	1

McCarthy	.994	94	173	4	1	0
Orr	1.000	1	4	0	0	0
Stern	.990	117	280	3	3	0
Thomas	1.000	2	4	1	0	0

MACON BRAVES — Low Class A

SOUTH ATLANTIC LEAGUE

BATTING	AVG	G	AB	R	H	2B	3B	HR	RBI	BB	SO	SB	CS	SLG	OBP	B	T	HT	WT	DOB	1st Yr	Resides
Albert, Luke	.333	2	6	1	2	0	0	0	1	0	2	0	0	.333	.333	S	R	6-2	200	4-25-79	2001	Hollywood, Fla.
Bernard, Miguel	.214	55	182	12	39	8	0	3	15	9	33	2	2	.308	.258	R	R	5-11	170	1-1-81	1997	San Pedro de Macoris, D.R.
Blanco, Gregor	.271	132	468	87	127	14	9	7	36	85	120	40	16	.385	.392	L	L	5-11	170	12-12-83	2000	Cua, Venez.
Brown, Kevin	.222	37	117	17	26	7	1	6	17	21	39	0	1	.453	.357	R	R	6-4	230	4-11-79	2001	North Fort Myers, Fla.
Burrows, Angelo	.239	96	314	31	75	15	4	4	24	10	35	1	4	.350	.265	L	R	5-11	170	7-2-80	1999	Freeport, Bahamas
Duran, Carlos	.270	132	534	86	144	22	10	7	50	29	80	23	17	.388	.312	L	L	6-1	160	12-27-82	1999	Barquisimeto, Venez.
Guzman, Carlos	.100	7	20	4	2	0	0	0	3	10	0	0	0	.100	.217	R	R	6-3	180	7-5-83	1999	La Vega, D.R.
Herr, Aaron	.248	82	290	31	72	16	0	6	34	14	64	3	1	.366	.283	R	R	5-11	180	3-7-81	2000	Lancaster, Pa.
Jeffcoat, Bryon	.258	48	159	24	41	6	1	5	13	18	35	8	2	.403	.343	R	R	6-1	190	5-14-79	2001	West Columbia, S.C.
Marte, Andy	.281	126	488	69	137	32	4	21	105	41	114	2	1	.492	.339	R	R	6-1	180	10-21-83	2001	Villa Tapia, D.R.
Miller, Greg	.313	103	361	46	113	14	1	0	34	38	66	17	4	.357	.383	R	R	6-0	180	1-9-79	2001	Sterling, Va.
Morales, Mike	.231	10	26	3	6	3	0	0	5	1	4	0	0	.346	.355	R	R	6-1	180	4-4-79	2001	West Palm Beach, Fla.
Pena, Brayan	.229	81	271	26	62	10	0	3	25	22	37	0	3	.299	.290	S	R	5-11	210	1-7-82	2001	San Jose, Costa Rica
Pena, Tony	.249	118	405	42	101	9	5	2	36	14	68	11	15	.311	.282	R	R	6-1	160	3-23-81	1999	Santiago, D.R.
Rodriguez , Ricardo	.291	26	79	11	23	1	1	3	4	14	2	1	1	.367	.364	R	R	6-0	140	4-28-81	1998	Caracas, Venez.
Salas, Jose	.229	80	293	22	67	14	0	7	39	13	81	0	1	.348	.269	S	R	6-3	210	2-16-82	1998	Caracas, Venez.
Schuerholz, Jonathan	.167	2	6	1	1	0	1	0	0	1	1	0	0	.500	.167	R	R	5-11	180	6-25-80	2002	Atlanta, Ga.
Thorman, Scott	.294	127	470	57	138	38	3	16	82	51	83	2	2	.489	.367	L	R	6-3	200	1-6-82	2000	Cambridge, Ontario
Timmons, Wes	.283	40	120	17	34	4	1	1	14	19	10	6	3	.358	.423	R	R	6-0	190	7-12-79	2002	Jacksonville Beach, Fla.

PITCHING	W	L	ERA	G	GS	CG	SV	IP	H	R	ER	BB	SO	AVG	B	T	HT	WT	DOB	1st Yr	Resides
Albertus, Roberto	2	3	6.10	26	2	0	1	62	63	45	42	28	50	.256	L	L	6-4	190	11-14-81	1998	San Nicholas, Aruba
Alvarez, Juan	2	5	6.79	12	11	0	0	52	71	43	39	27	45	.341	L	L	6-0	170	5-6-82	1999	Monclova, Mexico
Boyer, Blaine	5	9	3.07	43	0	0	1	70	52	30	24	39	73	.207	R	R	6-3	190	7-11-81	2000	Marietta, Ga.
Davies, Kyle	0	1	6.00	2	1	0	0	6	6	4	4	4	4	.272	R	R	6-2	190	9-9-83	2001	Dover, Fla.
Digby, Bryan	1	2	6.20	7	3	0	0	20	25	16	14	16	16	.312	R	R	6-2	190	12-31-81	2000	Peachtree City, Ga.
Gryboski, Kevin	0	0	0.00	2	1	0	0	2	1	0	0	1	2	.166	R	R	6-5	230	11-15-73	1995	Plains, Pa.
Herndon, Eric	0	1	6.00	5	0	0	0	6	12	6	4	1	6	.428	R	R	6-1	190	10-4-76	1998	Upper Marlboro, Md.
Lewis, Derrick	0	0	1.80	1	1	0	0	5	5	1	1	0	7	.263	R	R	6-5	210	5-7-76	1997	Montgomery, Ala.
Lopez, Gonzalo	7	10	3.10	28	27	1	0	157	134	72	54	51	130	.233	R	R	6-2	170	10-6-83	2000	Managua, Nicaragua
Mabry, Barry	0	1	3.86	1	0	0	0	2	3	1	1	0	1	.300	R	R	6-5	180	11-2-81	2000	Spartanburg, S.C.
McBride, Macay	12	8	2.12	25	25	2	0	157	119	49	37	48	138	.208	L	L	5-11	180	10-24-82	2001	Sylvania, Ga.
Merricks, Matt	5	5	5.12	19	14	0	0	83	82	54	47	51	60	.256	L	L	5-11	180	8-6-82	2000	Oxnard, Calif.
Miner, Zach	8	9	3.28	29	28	1	0	159	143	73	58	51	131	.242	R	R	6-3	190	3-12-82	2001	Jupiter, Fla.
Padilla, Nick	1	5	3.74	16	1	0	1	34	38	21	14	12	15	.299	R	R	6-3	200	1-11-79	2002	Whittier, Calif.
Ramirez, Horacio	0	2	6.00	2	1	0	0	6	11	10	4	2	5	.354	L	L	6-1	170	11-24-79	1997	Inglewood, Calif.
Roberts, Ralph	4	3	2.30	49	0	0	19	55	37	16	14	14	58	.185	R	R	6-2	200	3-28-80	2001	Cherryville, N.C.
Rodriguez, Jose	2	0	6.46	32	0	0	0	47	51	45	34	41	34	.277	R	R	6-0	170	1-15-82	1998	Carora, Venez.
Staveland, Toby	2	1	7.43	12	0	0	0	23	27	21	19	10	19	.306	R	R	6-3	220	3-27-80	2000	Juneau, Alaska
Vianna, Marcel	3	0	1.48	29	0	0	2	49	29	9	8	20	53	.171	R	R	6-2	170	3-23-81	1997	Sao Paulo, Brazil
Watkins, Dave	0	0	0.00	7	0	0	1	12	3	2	0	6	4	.069	R	R	6-1	190	8-18-81	1999	Leitchfield, Ky.
Wright, Matt	10	8	3.18	26	25	0	0	153	135	68	54	60	146	.235	R	R	6-2	220	3-13-82	2000	Lorena, Texas
Zumwalt, Alec	2	1	4.31	24	0	0	0	40	39	25	19	16	34	.250	R	R	6-2	190	1-20-81	1999	Kernersville, N.C.

FIELDING

Catcher	PCT	G	PO	A	E	DP	PB
Bernard	.981	47	302	50	7	2	14
B. Pena	.990	65	466	42	5	3	10
Salas	.988	40	276	44	4	7	15

First Base	PCT	G	PO	A	E	DP
Albert	.857	1	6	0	1	1
Brown	.990	12	93	9	1	6
Jeffcoat	1.000	1	1	0	0	0
Salas	.979	6	44	2	1	4
Thorman	.986	122	976	44	14	88

Second Base	PCT	G	PO	A	E	DP
Herr	.960	79	155	204	15	56
Jeffcoat	.943	29	49	84	8	10
Morales	.909	10	15	15	3	5
Rodriguez	.967	15	26	32	2	6
Timmons	1.000	9	13	24	0	5

Third Base	PCT	G	PO	A	E	DP
Jeffcoat	.885	10	4	19	3	3
Marte	.917	121	93	207	27	25
Timmons	.963	9	7	19	1	5

Shortstop	PCT	G	PO	A	E	DP
Jeffcoat	1.000	7	11	20	0	1

T. Pena	.940	117	186	311	32	58
Rodriguez	.880	6	8	14	3	2
Schuerholz	.500	1	1	2	3	1
Timmons	.981	10	16	35	1	7

Outfield	PCT	G	PO	A	E	DP
Blanco	.946	123	219	7	13	0
Burrows	.984	89	177	13	3	4
Duran	.964	125	264	7	10	1
Guzman	1.000	7	6	1	0	0
Miller	.993	83	133	8	1	1

DANVILLE BRAVES — Rookie

APPALACHIAN LEAGUE

BATTING	AVG	G	AB	R	H	2B	3B	HR	RBI	BB	SO	SB	CS	SLG	OBP	B	T	HT	WT	DOB	1st Yr	Resides
Albert, Luke	.308	4	13	1	4	1	0	0	1	0	1	0	0	.385	.357	S	R	6-2	200	4-25-79	2001	Hollywood, Fla.
Bessa, Laumin	.288	39	111	15	32	6	2	1	24	5	27	4	2	.405	.322	R	R	6-3	170	1-23-83	1999	Caracas, Venez.
Burrus, Josh	.236	68	263	34	62	13	1	0	23	35	60	16	7	.293	.338	R	R	5-11	180	8-20-83	2001	Marietta, Ga.
Esquivel, Matt	.278	61	227	38	63	13	2	5	41	21	67	2	0	.419	.345	R	R	6-2	220	12-17-82	2001	San Antonio, Texas
Francoeur, Jeff	.327	38	147	31	48	12	1	8	31	15	34	8	5	.585	.395	R	R	6-4	200	1-8-84	2002	Panama City Beach, Fla.
Grasso, Mike	.201	61	169	22	34	2	0	0	11	21	42	22	4	.213	.303	R	R	6-0	170	12-25-79	2002	Albany, N.Y.
Guzman, Carlos	.283	51	166	21	47	12	1	2	22	21	54	2	0	.404	.363	R	R	6-3	180	7-5-83	1999	La Vega, D.R.
Infante, Franklin	.157	23	51	7	8	3	0	1	6	2	23	0	0	.275	.214	R	R	6-0	170	2-11-83	2000	Santiago, D.R.
Jansen, Ardley	.295	62	207	33	61	8	3	10	44	13	44	9	2	.507	.341	R	R	6-2	160	2-16-83	1999	Willemstad, Curacao
Jurries, James	.333	4	15	4	5	1	0	1	4	2	2	0	0	.600	.412	R	R	6-0	190	4-13-79	2002	Lake Jackson, Texas
Peters, Yaron	.243	50	177	32	43	10	2	7	30	21	41	1	1	.441	.330	R	R	6-2	220	7-30-79	2002	Sherman Oaks, Calif.

BATTING	AVG	G	AB	R	H	2B	3B	HR	RBI	BB	SO	SB	CS	SLG	OBP	B	T	HT	WT	DOB	1st Yr	Resides
Roat, Kyle	.298	36	124	16	37	6	0	4	22	10	16	0	0	.444	.351	R	R	5-10	180	5-14-80	2001	Coweta, Okla.
Ruelas, Alonzo	.331	35	121	17	40	6	0	2	13	9	8	1	1	.430	.383	R	R	6-1	190	4-2-81	2001	El Paso, Texas
Ruiz, Daniel	.230	49	135	19	31	8	0	1	6	20	30	1	0	.311	.342	R	R	6-4	180	1-1-80	2001	Yuma, Ariz.
Schuerholz, Jonathan	.237	66	245	40	58	7	3	0	14	38	47	11	4	.290	.345	R	R	5-11	180	6-25-80	2002	Atlanta, Ga.
Woods, Ahmad	.177	31	79	11	14	2	2	1	12	5	31	1	1	.291	.244	R	R	6-2	180	11-27-81	2000	Stone Mountain, Ga.

GAMES BY POSITION: C—Roat 36, Ruelas 34. **1B**—Albert 4, Bessa 4, Jurries 4, Peters 39, Ruiz 26. **2B**—Grasso 59, Infante 18, Ruiz 8. **3B**—Burrus 68, Infante 1. **SS**—Infante 2, Schuerholz 66. **OF**—Bessa 27, Esquivel 58, Francoeur 36, Guzman 34, Jansen 59, Woods 16.

PITCHING	W	L	ERA	G	GS	CG	SV	IP	H	R	ER	BB	SO	AVG	B	T	HT	WT	DOB	1st Yr	Resides
Acosta, Jasiel	2	2	4.83	7	6	0	0	32	37	21	17	6	28	.286	L	L	5-10	160	7-30-82	2001	Guasave, Mexico
Adams, Josh	1	5	3.62	20	0	0	0	37	32	19	15	9	37	.233	L	L	6-5	190	1-12-80	2002	New Palestine, Ind.
Aguilar, Ray	0	0	0.00	1	0	0	0	2	1	1	0	2	0	.142	S	L	5-11	200	1-18-80	1999	South El Monte, Calif.
Almeida, Brian	0	1	3.91	13	1	0	0	23	22	13	10	15	17	.241	L	R	6-5	210	7-26-81	2000	Englewood, Fla.
Alvarez, Juan	3	5	3.46	13	13	0	0	65	61	35	25	27	71	.255	L	L	6-0	170	5-6-82	1999	Monclova, Mexico
Arteaga, Francisco	4	4	3.48	21	0	0	2	34	36	19	13	10	43	.257	R	R	6-1	170	10-4-81	2001	Los Angeles, Calif.
Bush, Paul	4	1	2.35	20	2	0	0	46	39	19	12	14	48	.225	R	R	6-1	190	10-5-79	2002	Titusville, Fla.
David, Brad	3	1	3.00	13	3	0	2	24	20	9	8	7	27	.232	L	L	6-0	190	5-26-80	2002	Baton Rouge, La.
Davies, Kyle	5	3	3.50	14	14	0	0	69	73	39	27	23	62	.262	R	R	6-2	190	9-9-83	2001	Dover, Fla.
Furnald, Donnie	0	0	8.31	4	0	0	0	4	1	4	4	7	1	.100	R	R	6-3	210	12-2-79	2001	Alta Loma, Calif.
Lerew, Anthony	8	3	1.73	14	14	0	0	83	60	23	16	25	75	.205	L	R	6-3	210	10-28-82	2001	Wellsville, Pa.
Mason, Robert	1	1	3.24	3	1	0	0	8	11	4	3	2	3	.323	L	L	5-11	190	9-5-83	2001	Walnut, Calif.
Meyer, Dan	3	3	2.74	13	13	1	0	66	47	22	20	18	77	.198	R	L	6-3	190	7-3-81	2002	Mickleton, N.J.
Mueller, Mike	3	2	4.80	20	0	0	0	30	33	22	16	18	27	.279	R	R	6-5	220	8-22-80	2002	West Bend, Wis.
Parker, Aaron	1	0	5.66	18	1	0	1	35	37	26	22	18	39	.264	R	R	6-2	190	2-11-80	2002	Stockton, Calif.
Tadefa, Fernando	0	0	2.45	23	0	0	16	26	21	8	7	8	29	.218	L	L	6-0	200	11-2-79	2002	San Antonio, Texas

KISSIMMEE BRAVES — Rookie

GULF COAST LEAGUE

BATTING	AVG	G	AB	R	H	2B	3B	HR	RBI	BB	SO	SB	CS	SLG	OBP	B	T	HT	WT	DOB	1st Yr	Resides
Aldridge, Cory	.288	17	59	10	17	5	3	3	13	11	17	0	0	.627	.394	L	R	6-1	220	6-13-79	1997	Abilene, Texas
Barthel, Cole	.277	52	177	24	49	6	1	5	15	23	27	11	1	.407	.380	R	R	6-2	200	8-11-82	2001	Decatur, Ala.
Betemit, Wilson	.263	7	19	2	5	4	0	0	2	5	2	1	0	.474	.417	S	R	6-3	190	11-2-81	1996	Santo Domingo, D.R.
Castro, Ramon	.250	9	32	3	8	0	0	1	4	3	6	2	0	.344	.333	R	R	6-0	190	10-23-79	1996	Valencia, Venez.
Cruz, Ramon	.136	24	66	2	9	0	0	1	6	4	26	0	0	.182	.183	R	R	6-1	180	10-22-83	2001	Santo Domingo, D.R.
Donato, Greg	.200	5	15	1	3	0	0	0	1	2	3	0	1	.200	.333	R	R	6-0	180	11-10-80	1998	Clovis, Calif.
Foskey, Will	.175	18	40	1	7	2	0	0	6	9	14	0	4	.225	.333	R	R	6-0	200	8-19-80	2002	Dublin, Ga.
Hernandez, Luis	.254	53	201	34	51	8	4	0	20	19	29	11	6	.333	.330	S	R	5-10	140	6-26-84	2001	Quibor, Venez.
James, Willie	.230	39	126	20	29	5	0	0	5	10	21	5	3	.270	.297	S	R	5-8	160	4-30-81	2002	Moreno Valley, Calif.
Martinez, Edwin	.286	19	42	5	12	3	0	1	9	1	4	0	0	.429	.295	S	R	5-11	170	10-12-82	2001	Caracas, Venez.
Maybin, Neal	.196	19	51	5	10	3	0	1	9	9	20	1	1	.314	.328	R	R	6-5	220	10-5-79	2002	Casselberry, Fla.
McCann, Brian	.220	29	100	9	22	5	0	2	11	10	22	0	0	.330	.295	L	R	6-3	190	2-20-84	2002	Satellite Beach, Fla.
Moreta, Carlos	.190	39	126	9	24	5	0	5	19	6	38	0	0	.349	.259	R	R	6-2	180	1-5-83	1999	Barahona, D.R.
Mota, Miguel	.305	58	213	27	65	8	4	3	28	14	39	12	8	.423	.353	R	R	6-1	150	2-9-83	2000	San Pedro de Macoris, D.R.
Ortega, Pedro	.133	22	60	6	8	3	1	0	4	9	14	6	0	.217	.250	S	R	5-10	140	3-12-84	2001	Santiago, D.R.
Partridge, Dominique	.270	58	185	27	50	5	3	0	8	21	40	2	4	.330	.358	R	R	6-2	210	7-28-83	2001	Palmetto, Ga.
Santana, Roberto	.231	47	130	14	30	4	0	0	10	7	7	1	0	.262	.268	L	R	5-11	180	3-2-83	2001	Las Piedras, P.R.
Timmons, Wes	.500	2	4	1	2	1	0	0	1	3	0	0	0	.750	.750	R	R	6-0	190	7-12-79	2002	Jacksonville Beach, Fla.
White, Dean	.185	50	168	23	31	5	2	2	17	9	48	10	1	.274	.299	R	R	6-2	180	2-12-83	2001	Perth, Australia
Wilson, Vontrez	.229	24	83	12	19	5	0	0	7	5	20	3	1	.289	.289	S	R	6-1	190	9-18-80	2001	Aurora, Colo.

GAMES BY POSITION: C—Cruz 21, Foskey 15, Martinez 14, McCann 17, Moreta 5. **1B**—Moreta 29, Santana 38. **2B**—Castro 1, Hernandez 6, James 31, Maybin 1, Ortega 17, Timmons 1, White 12. **3B**—Barthel 24, Castro 8, Santana 2, white 30. **SS**—Betemit 6, Castro 1, Hernandez 47, James 5, White 6. **OF**—Barthel 27, Donato 4, Maybin 8, Mota 51, Ortega 1, Partridge 58, Santana 4, Wilson 22.

PITCHING	W	L	ERA	G	GS	CG	SV	IP	H	R	ER	BB	SO	AVG	B	T	HT	WT	DOB	1st Yr	Resides
Aguilar, Rick	1	0	2.20	9	0	0	5	16	10	5	4	4	17	.175	R	L	5-11	210	8-19-83	2002	Lompoc, Calif.
Arteaga, Francisco	0	1	1.80	3	0	0	0	5	7	1	1	1	7	.333	R	R	6-1	170	10-4-81	2001	Los Angeles, Calif.
Colton, Kyle	0	1	3.38	4	2	0	0	8	5	3	3	5	7	.192	R	R	6-2	170	11-16-80	1999	Longwood, Fla.
Cooper, Dexter	4	4	3.12	11	7	0	0	58	43	24	20	22	36	.210	R	R	6-2	210	7-14-82	2001	Acworth, Ga.
Dewar, Andrew	0	0	4.50	1	0	0	0	2	2	1	1	0	2	.250	L	L	6-0	190	3-9-84	2001	Melbourne, Australia
Digby, Bryan	0	0	7.50	3	2	0	0	6	9	5	5	5	5	.360	R	R	6-2	190	12-31-81	2000	Peachtree City, Ga.
Ewin, Ryan	1	1	1.65	6	3	0	0	16	10	4	3	7	18	.175	R	R	6-7	180	10-31-81	1999	Spring Valley, Calif.
Farr, Whitt	3	0	4.50	7	0	0	2	16	18	8	8	3	17	.285	R	R	6-2	180	5-15-81	2002	Danville, Va.
Herndon, Eric	0	0	0.00	3	1	0	0	4	2	0	0	0	5	.142	L	R	6-1	190	10-4-76	1998	Upper Marlboro, Md.
Jung, Sung	0	0	0.00	2	0	0	0	2	0	0	0	0	2	.000	R	R	5-10	160	8-6-79	2002	Yee Soo, Korea
Lee, Garrett	0	0	0.00	1	0	0	0	3	2	0	0	1	3	.200	R	R	6-5	210	8-17-76	1996	Montrose, Calif.
Mason, Robert	1	2	3.71	4	3	0	0	17	20	8	7	3	12	.290	L	L	5-11	190	9-5-83	2001	Walnut, Calif.
Mateo, Manuel	7	3	1.98	12	8	1	0	68	47	18	15	12	76	.193	R	R	6-3	170	8-26-82	1999	San Cristobal, D.R.
McClendon, Matt	0	0	3.00	3	0	0	0	3	2	1	1	2	2	.181	R	R	6-6	220	10-13-77	1999	Orlando, Fla.
Mead, Dan	2	7	7.03	15	0	0	1	32	30	28	25	33	23	.243	R	L	6-4	190	8-4-81	2002	Worthington, Ohio
Morton, Charles	1	7	4.54	11	5	0	0	40	37	34	20	30	32	.243	R	R	6-4	190	10-12-83	2002	Redding, Conn.
Nelson, Kenny	0	0	0.00	3	3	0	0	5	1	0	0	1	7	.062	R	R	6-2	200	8-26-81	2000	Fort Washington, Md.
Nieves, Roberto	0	3	5.30	5	4	0	0	19	18	14	11	9	19	.257	S	R	6-2	170	12-25-82	2002	Vega Alta, P.R.
Padilla, Nick	0	0	0.00	1	0	0	0	2	1	0	0	0	1	.142	R	R	6-3	200	1-11-79	2002	Whittier, Calif.
Parker, Justin	2	1	1.32	8	0	0	1	14	12	3	2	8	17	.240	L	L	6-0	180	1-19-79	2002	Nesbit, MS
Peralta, Efigenio	6	2	1.78	14	5	0	0	56	32	13	11	18	44	.165	R	R	6-2	180	4-18-82	1999	San Cristobal, D.R.
Reiss, Mike	1	1	14.67	13	0	0	1	15	16	34	25	35	9	.253	R	R	6-5	190	7-30-82	2001	Thornhill, Ontario
Reiss, Steve	0	2	9.13	13	0	0	0	23	26	29	23	31	12	.298	R	R	6-5	190	7-30-82	2001	Thornhill, Ontario
Russell, Steve	1	3	5.68	11	6	0	0	44	43	30	28	29	42	.265	R	R	6-0	180	12-20-83	2002	Las Vegas, Nev.
Santana, Roberto	0	0	3.38	2	0	0	0	2	2	1	1	0	1	.000	L	R	5-11	180	3-2-83	2001	Las Piedras, P.R.
Simpson, Brian	0	0	10.66	8	1	0	0	13	10	19	15	20	9	.212	R	R	6-3	170	1-25-83	2001	Jackson, Tenn.
Small, Aaron	0	0	6.00	5	0	0	0	6	9	4	4	0	3	.360	R	R	6-5	220	11-23-71	1989	Loudon, Calif.
Yankosky, L.J.	0	0	0.00	6	6	0	0	8	3	0	0	3	7	.115	R	R	6-2	200	2-1-75	1998	Springfield, Va.

BALTIMORE ORIOLES

BY ROCH KUBATKO

On Aug. 23, the Orioles defeated the Blue Jays to reach .500 after several failed attempts. But with their record at 63-63, they seemed to hit a wall in 2002.

At least they hit something. Opposing pitchers weren't as easy a target.

The Orioles scuffled for runs, fielding lineups each night that lacked a true leadoff, No. 3, cleanup or No. 5 batter. Their ace, rookie Rodrigo Lopez, grew fatigued and less effective. Their rookie closer, Jorge Julio, became invisible with no late-inning leads to protect. And an entire season crumbled to the ground, which for the Orioles was fourth place in the American League East.

They lost 32 of their last 36 games to finish at 67-95, with only the Devil Rays keeping them in fourth place for the fifth consecutive year. The Orioles rose one game above .500 four times, the last coming May 10 when they were 18-17. They dropped their last 12 games, the longest season-ending streak since the 1899 Cleveland Spiders lost their last 16.

The Orioles' skid matched the third longest in club history, and was their worst since losing 21 in a row to open the 1988 season. By going 4-32, the Orioles endured their worst 36-game stretch in franchise history. The 24 losses in September were the most in a single month since they lost a club-record 25 in August 1954. They were 36½ games behind the Yankees in the AL East, the furthest they've been out of first place since the conclusion of the 1955 season.

The Orioles batted .212 and posted a 5.31 team ERA in September. The slump left their season average at .246, the second straight year they finished last in the AL. It was all or nothing for the Orioles, who batted .296 and scored 6.7 runs per game in their 67 wins, compared to .208 and 2.3 runs per game in their 95 losses.

Predictably, attendance suffered as the losing continued. The Orioles, no longer able to rely on Cal Ripken's drawing power after his retirement, attracted 2,682,917 fans—the lowest total for a full season in the 11-year his-

Rodrigo Lopez — John Stephens

PLAYERS OF THE YEAR

MAJOR LEAGUE: Rodrigo Lopez, rhp

Signed in late 2001 as a minor league free agent, Lopez stunned the baseball world in 2002 by going 15-9, 3.57 for a club that won just 67 games. It marked the most wins for an Oriole since Mike Mussina won 18 in 1999.

MINOR LEAGUE: John Stephens, rhp

The Aussie used three speeds—slow, slower and slowest—to strike out 126 batters in 143 innings while compiling an 11-5, 3.03 mark at Triple-A Rochester before a late July promotion to Baltimore.

tory of Camden Yards.

"The last month took the luster off the season," manager Mike Hargrove said, "but 80 percent of it was very successful. We'll try to build on the progress we made in the first 80 percent. I don't think that has been lost or destroyed. It's just been tough to find."

Injuries again conspired against the team. David Segui (wrist), Jeff Conine (hamstring), Gary Matthews (wrist) and Mike Bordick (knee) spent considerable time on the disabled list, with Segui appearing in just 26 games. Starters Jason Johnson and Sidney Ponson also went on the DL, and Scott Erickson was shut down over the final month.

The rotation would have been in much worse shape if not for Lopez, a minor league free agent who was named most valuable Oriole after going 15-9, 3.57 in 197 innings. Lopez went 6-0, 2.57 in July to earn the league's rookie of the month award, and was 14-5, 3.14 before tiring.

In the final year of his contract, Bordick set major league records for most consecutive errorless games (110) and chances (543) by a shortstop. He hinted at retirement if the Orioles didn't resign him. And lefthander Buddy Groom made 70 appearances for the seventh straight season, also a major league record.

The minor league system didn't bring much relief from all the losing. The Orioles' top three affiliates—Triple-A Rochester, Double-A Bowie and high Class A Frederick— combined to finish 109 games below .500. Rochester filed for free agency and joined the Twins' organization, leaving the Orioles with Ottawa as their new affiliate.

Two of the Orioles' lower-level affiliates made the playoffs, but low Class A Delmarva and Rookie-level Bluefield came up short of winning a championship. Short-season Aberdeen of the New York-Penn League, owned by Ripken, went 30-45 in its first season.

ORGANIZATION LEADERS

BATTING

*AVG	Neal Stephenson, Aberdeen	.310
R	Tripper Johnson, Delmarva	73
H	Darryl Brinkley, Rochester	145
TB	Darnell McDonald, Rochester/Bowie	212
2B	Tripper Johnson, Delmarva	32
3B	Three tied at	7
HR	Alex Gordon, Frederick/Delmarva	18
RBI	Doug Gredvig, Bowie	80
BB	Tripper Johnson Delmarva	62
SO	Bryan Bass, Delmarva	146
SB	Napolean Calzado, Bowie	42

PITCHING

W	Rich Bartlett, Frederick/Delmarva	12
L	Jay Spurgeon, Rochester	14
#ERA	Dave Farren, Delmarva/Aberdeen	2.95
G	Lesli Brea, Rochester	60
CG	Kurt Birkins, Delware	3
SV	Rommie Lewis, Delmarva	25
IP	Steve Bechler, Rochester/Bowie	173
BB	Cory Morris, Frederick/Delmarva	67
SO	Jancy Andrade, Frederick/Delmarva	152

*Minimum 250 At-Bats #Minimum 75 Innings

BALTIMORE ORIOLES

Manager: Mike Hargrove

2002 Record: 67-95, .414 (4th, AL East)

BATTING	AVG	G	AB	R	H	2B	3B	HR	RBI	BB	SO	SB	CS	SLG	OBP	B	T	HT	WT	DOB	1st Yr	Resides
Batista, Tony	.244	161	615	90	150	36	1	31	87	50	107	5	4	.457	.309	R	R	6-0	200	12-9-73	1992	Mao Valverde, D.R.
Bigbie, Larry	.176	16	34	1	6	1	0	0	3	1	11	1	0	.206	.194	L	L	6-4	200	11-4-77	1999	Hobart, Ind.
Bordick, Mike	.232	117	367	37	85	19	3	8	36	35	63	7	4	.365	.302	R	R	5-11	170	7-21-65	1986	Ruxton, Md.
Casanova, Raul	.000	2	1	0	0	0	0	0	0	0	1	0	0	.000	.000	S	R	6-0	210	8-23-72	1990	Ponce, P.R.
Clark, Howie	.302	14	53	3	16	5	0	0	4	3	6	0	0	.396	.362	L	R	5-10	190	2-13-74	1992	Lake Charles, La.
Conine, Jeff	.273	116	451	44	123	26	4	15	63	25	66	8	0	.448	.307	R	R	6-1	210	6-27-66	1988	Weston, Fla.
Cordova, Marty	.253	131	458	55	116	25	2	18	64	47	111	1	6	.434	.325	R	R	6-0	200	7-10-69	1989	Las Vegas, Nev.
Fordyce, Brook	.231	56	130	7	30	8	0	1	8	9	19	1	0	.315	.301	R	R	6-0	190	5-7-70	1989	Stuart, Fla.
Garcia, Luis	.333	6	3	0	1	0	0	0	0	0	1	0	0	.333	.333	R	R	6-3	200	9-22-75	1995	Hermosillo, Mexico
Gibbons, Jay	.247	136	490	71	121	29	1	28	69	45	66	1	3	.482	.311	L	L	6-0	190	3-2-77	1998	Lakewood, Calif.
Gil, Geronimo	.232	125	422	33	98	19	0	12	45	21	88	2	2	.363	.270	R	R	6-2	220	8-7-75	1996	Oaxaca, Mexico
Hairston, Jerry	.268	122	426	55	114	25	3	5	32	34	55	21	6	.376	.329	R	R	5-10	170	5-29-76	1997	Pikesville, Md.
Leon, Jose	.247	36	89	8	22	2	0	3	10	3	20	1	0	.371	.280	R	R	6-0	210	12-8-76	1994	Cayey, P.R.
Lopez, Luis	.211	52	109	10	23	6	0	2	9	3	20	1	0	.321	.232	S	R	5-11	170	9-4-70	1988	Cidra, P.R.
Lunar, Fernando	.000	1	0	0	0	0	0	0	0	0	0	0	0	.000	.000	R	R	6-1	230	5-25-77	1994	Alamogordo, N.M.
Matos, Luis	.129	17	31	0	4	1	0	0	1	1	6	1	0	.161	.156	R	R	6-0	200	10-30-78	1996	Bayamon, P.R.
Matthews, Gary	.276	109	344	54	95	25	3	7	38	43	69	15	5	.427	.355	S	R	6-3	210	8-25-74	1994	Canoga Park, Calif.
McGuire, Ryan	.077	17	26	0	2	1	0	0	2	2	7	0	0	.115	.143	L	L	6-0	210	11-23-71	1993	Coto de Caza, Calif.
Molina, Izzy	.333	1	3	1	1	0	0	0	0	0	0	0	0	.333	.333	R	R	6-1	220	6-3-71	1990	Miami, Fla.
Mora, Melvin	.233	149	557	86	130	30	4	19	64	70	108	16	10	.404	.338	R	R	5-11	190	2-2-72	1991	Bel Air, Md.
Moriarty, Mike	.188	8	16	0	3	1	0	0	3	0	2	0	1	.250	.188	R	R	6-0	180	3-8-74	1995	Mount Laurel, N.J.
Richard, Chris	.232	50	155	15	36	11	0	4	21	12	30	0	3	.381	.292	L	L	6-2	200	6-7-74	1995	San Diego, Calif.
Roberts, Brian	.227	38	128	18	29	6	0	1	11	15	21	9	2	.297	.308	S	R	5-9	170	10-9-77	1999	Chapel Hill, N.C.
Rogers, Ed	.000	5	3	0	0	0	0	0	0	0	0	0	0	.000	.000	R	R	6-1	170	8-29-78	1997	San Pedro de Macoris, D.R.
Segui, David	.263	26	95	10	25	4	0	2	16	11	22	0	0	.368	.336	S	L	6-1	220	7-19-66	1988	Kansas City, Kan.
Singleton, Chris	.262	136	466	67	122	30	6	9	50	21	83	20	2	.410	.296	L	L	6-2	210	8-15-72	1993	Atlanta, Ga.

PITCHING	W	L	ERA	G	GS	CG	SV	IP	H	R	ER	BB	SO	AVG	B	T	HT	WT	DOB	1st Yr	Resides
Bauer, Rick	6	7	3.98	56	1	0	1	84	84	41	37	36	45	.267	R	R	6-6	200	1-10-77	1997	Eagle, Idaho
Bechler, Steve	0	0	13.50	3	0	0	0	5	6	7	7	4	3	.300	R	R	6-2	230	11-18-79	1998	Medford, Ore.
Bedard, Erik	0	0	13.50	2	0	0	0	1	2	1	1	0	1	.500	L	L	6-1	180	3-6-79	1999	Naum, Ontario
Brock, Chris	2	1	4.70	22	0	0	0	44	52	24	23	14	21	.297	R	R	6-1	180	2-5-71	1992	Altamonte Springs, Fla.
Douglass, Sean	0	5	6.08	15	8	0	0	53	58	41	36	35	44	.282	R	R	6-6	210	4-28-79	1997	Lancaster, Calif.
Driskill, Travis	8	8	4.95	29	19	0	0	133	150	78	73	48	78	.283	R	R	6-0	220	8-1-71	1993	Austin, Texas
DuBose, Eric	0	0	3.00	4	0	0	0	6	7	2	2	1	4	.304	L	L	6-3	230	5-15-76	1997	Nashville, Tenn.
Erickson, Scott	5	12	5.55	29	28	3	0	161	192	109	99	68	74	.303	R	R	6-4	220	2-2-68	1989	Stateline, Nev.
Groom, Buddy	3	2	1.60	70	0	0	2	62	44	11	11	12	48	.196	L	L	6-2	200	7-10-65	1987	Red Oak, Texas
Hentgen, Pat	0	4	7.77	4	4	0	0	22	31	20	19	10	11	.336	R	R	6-3	230	11-13-68	1986	Tarpon Springs, Fla.
Johnson, Jason	5	14	4.59	22	22	1	0	131	141	68	67	41	97	.275	R	R	6-6	210	10-27-73	1992	Henderson, Nev.
Julio, Jorge	5	6	1.99	67	0	0	25	68	55	22	15	27	55	.213	R	R	6-1	210	3-3-79	1996	Caracas, Venez.
Lopez, Rodrigo	15	9	3.57	33	28	1	0	197	172	83	78	62	136	.233	R	R	6-1	180	12-14-75	1995	Mexico City, Mexico
Maduro, Calvin	2	5	5.56	12	10	0	0	57	64	37	35	22	29	.279	R	R	6-0	200	9-5-74	1992	Santa Cruz, Aruba
Perez, Yorkis	0	0	3.29	23	0	0	1	27	21	12	10	14	25	.198	S	L	6-0	210	9-30-67	1983	Bajos de Haina, D.R.
Ponson, Sidney	7	9	4.09	28	28	3	0	176	172	84	80	63	120	.258	R	R	6-1	230	11-2-76	1994	Baltimore, Md.
Roberts, Willis	5	4	3.36	66	0	0	1	75	79	34	28	32	51	.269	R	R	6-3	240	6-19-75	1992	San Cristobal, D.R.
Ryan, B.J.	2	1	4.68	67	0	0	1	58	51	31	30	33	56	.240	L	L	6-6	240	12-28-75	1998	Benton, La.
Stephens, John	2	5	6.09	12	11	0	0	65	68	44	44	22	56	.270	R	R	6-1	200	11-15-79	1996	Berala, Australia
Towers, Josh	0	3	7.90	5	3	0	0	27	42	24	24	5	13	.362	R	R	6-1	180	2-26-77	1996	Owings Mills, Md.

FIELDING

Catcher	PCT	G	PO	A	E	DP	PB
Casanova	1.000	2	3	0	0	0	0
Fordyce	.986	55	267	8	4	1	3
Gil	.995	125	740	60	4	14	19
Lunar	1.000	2	2	0	0	0	0
Molina	1.000	1	7	1	0	0	0
Richard	.000	1	0	0	0	0	0

First Base	PCT	G	PO	A	E	DP
Clark	1.000	1	7	0	0	2
Conine	.990	103	947	58	10	99
Gibbons	.996	30	208	17	1	26
Leon	1.000	17	135	9	0	15
Lopez	1.000	1	5	0	0	0
McGuire	1.000	7	36	3	0	4
Richard	1.000	9	63	3	0	0
Segui	1.000	7	61	5	0	12

Second Base	PCT	G	PO	A	E	DP
Hairston	.982	119	232	365	11	75
Lopez	.969	12	12	19	1	3
Mora	.969	12	22	41	2	10
Moriarty	1.000	2	4	10	0	4
Roberts	.976	25	43	80	3	19

Third Base	PCT	G	PO	A	E	DP
Batista	.962	154	111	290	16	35
Leon	1.000	12	7	16	0	2
Moriarty	1.000	1	0	1	0	0

Shortstop	PCT	G	PO	A	E	DP
Bordick	.998	117	197	372	1	92
Lopez	.967	22	18	41	2	5
Mora	.959	41	57	108	7	17
Moriarty	1.000	4	2	6	0	0
Rogers	1.000	4	2	5	0	1

Outfield	PCT	G	PO	A	E	DP
Bigbie	1.000	12	19	0	0	0
Clark	1.000	4	10	0	0	0
Conine	1.000	6	8	0	0	0
Cordova	.971	72	132	2	4	1
Garcia	1.000	2	1	0	0	0
Gibbons	.994	92	174	6	1	2
Leon	.800	2	4	0	1	0
Matos	1.000	14	17	0	0	0
Matthews	.969	100	179	6	6	1
Mora	.989	104	251	9	3	5
Singleton	.986	126	274	3	4	0

Jorge Julio

LARRY GOREN

Jeff Conine: fought through injuries to hit .273-15-63

Tony Batista: led Orioles in homers, RBIs

FARM SYSTEM

Director, Minor League Operations: Don Buford

Class	Farm Team	League	W	L	Pct.	Finish*	Manager(s)	First Yr.
AAA	Rochester (N.Y.) Red Wings	International	55	89	.382	14th (14)	Andy Etchebarren	1961
AA	Bowie (Md.) Baysox	Eastern	55	85	.393	11th (12)	Dave Cash/Dave Stockstill	1993
High A	Frederick (Md.) Keys	Carolina	47	92	.338	8th (8)	Jack Voigt	1989
Low A	Delmarva (Md.) Shorebirds	South Atlantic	76	64	.543	4th (16)	Joe Ferguson	1997
SS A	Aberdeen (Md.) IronBirds	New York-Penn	31	45	.408	11th (14)	Joe Almaraz	2002
Rookie	Bluefield (W.Va.) Orioles	Appalachian	45	23	.662	1st (10)	Bien Figueroa	1958
Rookie	Sarasota (Fla.) Orioles	Gulf Coast	24	36	.400	12th (14)	Jesus Alfaro	1991

*Finish in overall standings (No. of teams in league)

ROCHESTER RED WINGS
Class AAA

INTERNATIONAL LEAGUE

BATTING	AVG	G	AB	R	H	2B	3B	HR	RBI	BB	SO	SB	CS	SLG	OBP	B	T	HT	WT	DOB	1st Yr	Resides
Allen, Chad	.219	8	32	1	7	2	1	0	1	0	6	0	0	.344	.219	R	R	6-1	190	2-6-75	1996	Dallas, Texas
Arias, Alex	.135	16	52	2	7	2	0	0	3	5	11	0	0	.173	.211	R	R	6-3	200	11-20-67	1987	Hollywood, Fla.
Bigbie, Larry	.302	98	348	42	105	23	2	2	35	35	79	7	3	.397	.363	L	L	6-4	200	11-4-77	1999	Hobart, Ind.
Brinkley, Darryl	.285	128	509	58	145	31	3	8	73	25	67	19	5	.405	.317	R	R	5-11	200	12-23-68	1995	Norwalk, Conn.
Clark, Howie	.309	108	418	57	129	21	4	7	43	41	28	3	4	.428	.369	L	R	5-10	190	2-13-74	1992	Lake Charles, La.
De los Santos, Luis	.267	50	187	21	50	8	1	6	16	14	43	0	0	.417	.318	R	R	6-5	220	12-29-66	1984	New York, N.Y.
Diaz, Maikell	.000	4	10	1	0	0	0	0	0	0	2	0	0	.000	.000	R	R	5-11	160	9-29-78	1996	Estado Miranda, Venez.
Figueroa, Franky	.266	57	207	27	55	8	1	4	31	10	45	0	0	.372	.300	R	R	6-6	240	2-9-77	1996	Hialeah, Fla.
Frias, Hanley	.198	25	96	9	19	1	0	2	4	6	16	3	0	.271	.245	S	R	6-0	170	12-5-73	1991	Villa Ariagracia, D.R.
Garabito, Eddy	.258	110	434	52	112	20	4	4	32	24	48	11	8	.350	.300	S	R	5-10	170	12-2-76	2000	Manrreza, D.R.
Garcia, Luis	.242	89	339	23	82	14	2	4	31	7	45	1	1	.330	.260	R	R	6-3	200	9-22-75	1995	Hermosillo, Mexico
Hammond, Joey	.248	35	109	13	27	2	1	1	8	14	14	1	1	.312	.336	R	R	6-1	180	10-27-77	1998	Frederick, Md.
Hubbard, Mike	.280	60	211	26	59	11	0	4	30	19	24	1	2	.389	.338	R	R	6-2	200	2-16-71	1992	Madison Heights, Va.
Leon, Jose	.279	83	312	39	87	16	1	8	40	18	54	0	0	.413	.319	R	R	6-0	210	12-8-76	1994	Cayey, P.R.
Lopez, Luis	.324	17	68	12	22	6	0	3	8	3	11	0	0	.544	.361	S	R	5-11	170	9-4-70	1988	Cidra, P.R.
2-team (6 Indianapolis)	.300	23	90	14	27	6	0	3	8	3	15	0	0	.467	.337							
Lunar, Fernando	.193	42	145	7	28	1	0	2	8	4	27	1	0	.241	.234	R	R	6-1	230	5-25-77	1994	Alamogordo, N.M.
McDonald, Darnell	.289	91	332	43	96	21	6	6	35	32	78	11	3	.443	.353	R	R	5-11	210	11-17-78	1997	Glendale, Colo.
McGuire, Ryan	.286	81	315	44	90	15	2	11	46	29	69	0	1	.451	.343	L	L	6-0	210	11-23-71	1993	Coto de Caza, Calif.
Molina, Izzy	.171	42	146	11	25	4	0	2	15	9	24	1	1	.240	.231	R	R	6-1	220	6-3-71	1990	Miami, Fla.
Moriarty, Mike	.277	90	311	48	86	18	1	4	26	37	50	4	1	.379	.357	R	R	6-0	180	3-8-74	1995	Mount Laurel, N.J.
Richard, Chris	.321	14	53	10	17	6	0	6	18	6	14	0	0	.774	.397	L	L	6-2	200	6-7-74	1995	San Diego, Calif.
Roberts, Brian	.275	78	313	49	86	9	7	3	30	40	46	22	4	.377	.361	S	R	5-9	170	10-9-77	1999	Chapel Hill, N.C.
Salinas, Trey	.074	12	27	1	2	0	0	1	2	2	10	0	0	.185	.167	R	R	6-1	190	6-29-75	1996	Corpus Christi, Texas

PITCHING	W	L	ERA	G	GS	CG	SV	IP	H	R	ER	BB	SO	AVG	B	T	HT	WT	DOB	1st Yr	Resides
Atchley, Justin	1	0	8.68	10	0	0	1	9	17	10	9	2	5	.386	L	L	6-3	210	9-5-73	1995	Mt. Vernon, Wash.
2-team (7 Louisville)	2	0	8.00	17	0	0	1	18	30	18	16	5	12	.365							
Bauer, Rick	0	1	6.75	1	1	0	0	4	4	4	3	2	1	.266	R	R	6-6	200	1-10-77	1997	Eagle, ID
Bechler, Steve	6	11	4.09	24	24	2	0	150	154	78	68	52	77	.264	R	R	6-2	230	11-18-79	1998	Medford, Ore.
Brea, Lesli	3	7	3.22	60	0	0	3	87	81	37	31	37	75	.244	R	R	5-11	210	10-12-78	1996	Phoenix, Ariz.
Douglass, Sean	4	6	4.73	14	13	0	0	67	66	39	35	35	71	.255	R	R	6-6	210	4-28-79	1997	Lancaster, Calif.
Driskill, Travis	2	2	1.64	4	4	1	0	22	17	8	4	1	15	.202	R	R	6-0	220	8-1-71	1993	Austin, Texas
Drumright, Mike	5	7	3.46	23	21	0	0	125	121	67	48	42	89	.248	L	R	6-4	210	4-19-74	1995	Valley Center, Kan.
2-team (7 Pawtucket)	6	8	4.01	30	24	0	0	150	156	92	67	50	109	.260							
Dubose, Eric	0	0	27.00	1	0	0	0	0	1	2	1	2	0	.333	L	L	6-3	230	5-15-76	1997	Nashville, Tenn.
Espina, Rendy	1	2	4.44	18	0	0	0	24	27	12	12	10	11	.293	L	L	6-0	180	5-11-78	1995	Cabimas, Venez.
2-team (27 Syracuse)	2		6.75	45	0	0	0	53	65	43	40	31	38	.300							
Foster, Kris	0	1	7.71	14	0	0	1	19	22	16	16	10	14	.301	R	R	6-1	210	8-30-74	1992	Lehigh Acres, Fla.
Garcia, Mike	1	0	0.00	9	0	0	2	10	7	0	0	1	9	.189	R	R	6-2	220	5-11-68	1989	Moreno Valley, Calif.
Looney, Brian	1	4	4.73	9	0	0	0	13	12	7	7	7	14	.240	L	L	5-10	180	6-26-69	1991	Cheshire, Conn.
Marshall, Lee	4	6	4.85	59	0	0	4	78	101	47	42	32	36	.314	R	R	6-5	230	9-25-76	1995	Ariton, Ala.
McDill, Allen	1	1	7.90	15	0	0	0	14	17	12	12	7	6	.309	L	L	6-0	170	8-23-71	1992	Arkadelphia, Ark.
Mohler, Mike	1	2	2.76	34	0	0	1	49	51	16	15	15	44	.268	R	L	6-2	200	7-26-68	1990	Gonzales, La.
Nussbeck, Mark	1	2	6.39	11	3	0	0	25	30	20	18	8	6	.303	L	R	6-4	200	5-25-74	1996	Kansas City, Mo.
Perez, Yorkis	1	1	3.79	28	0	0	0	40	42	20	17	20	44	.265	S	L	6-0	210	9-30-67	1983	Bajos de Haina, D.R.
Pina, Rafael	6	5	3.49	50	0	0	10	111	117	53	43	31	74	.273	R	R	6-1	170	8-16-71	1991	Alta Loma, Calif.
Rosario, Juan	0	0	11.57	2	0	0	0	2	4	3	3	1	1	.363	R	R	6-4	210	11-17-75	1993	Perth Amboy, NJ
Runyan, Sean	0	0	9.00	3	0	0	0	3	3	3	3	1	5	.250	L	L	6-3	220	6-21-74	1992	Haines City, Fla.
Sequea, Jacobo	1	4	5.27	5	5	0	0	27	26	16	16	11	16	.245	R	R	6-1	190	8-31-81	1997	Anaco, Venez.
Spurgeon, Jay	4	14	5.38	29	26	1	0	154	184	104	92	42	84	.292	R	R	6-6	230	7-5-76	1997	Coarsegold, Calif.
Steenstra, Kennie	1	2	4.76	6	4	0	0	23	31	15	12	7	4	.316	R	R	6-5	210	10-13-70	1992	Liberty, Mo.
Stephens, John	11	5	3.03	21	21	1	0	143	126	51	48	23	118	.236	R	R	6-1	200	11-15-79	1996	Berala, Australia
Towers, Josh	0	9	7.57	15	13	1	0	69	109	65	58	14	43	.352	R	R	6-1	180	2-26-77	1996	Owings Mills, Md.

FIELDING

Catcher	PCT	G	PO	A	E	DP	PB
Hubbard	.989	57	349	25	4	1	1
Lunar	.982	42	246	32	5	3	1
Molina	.978	40	243	19	6	0	0
Salinas	.982	12	48	6	1	0	1

	PCT	G	PO	A	E	DP
Garabito	.962	37	64	87	6	18
Hammond	.981	11	19	33	1	7
Lopez	.987	14	30	45	1	9
Moriarty	1.000	2	5	6	0	2
Roberts	.978	71	125	180	7	35

	PCT	G	PO	A	E	DP
Diaz	.947	3	8	10	1	2
Frias	.966	24	33	53	3	7
Garabito	.955	65	93	163	12	28
Lopez	1.000	1	1	3	0	1
Moriarty	.958	51	64	139	9	22

First Base	PCT	G	PO	A	E	DP
Arias	.923	2	12	0	1	0
Clark	.993	16	134	8	1	5
De Los Santos	.993	32	255	21	2	16
Figueroa	.977	49	394	36	10	32
Hubbard	1.000	1	6	1	0	0
McGuire	.990	50	358	42	4	37

Third Base	PCT	G	PO	A	E	DP
Arias	1.000	3	1	4	0	0
Clark	.500	1	1	0	1	0
Frias	1.000	1	0	1	0	0
Garabito	.875	5	2	5	1	0
Hammond	.981	23	23	30	1	3
Leon	.957	79	66	157	10	14
Moriarty	.950	38	35	80	6	5

Outfield	PCT	G	PO	A	E	DP
Allen	1.000	3	5	0	0	0
Bigbie	.990	69	184	5	2	0
Brinkley	.986	106	202	6	3	2
Clark	.973	68	140	4	4	1
Garabito	1.000	2	3	0	0	0
Garcia	.991	77	206	7	2	2
McDonald	.983	90	277	6	5	1
McGuire	1.000	23	48	0	0	0

Second Base	PCT	G	PO	A	E	DP
Arias	1.000	3	10	4	0	1
Clark	.957	11	21	24	2	3

Shortstop	PCT	G	PO	A	E	DP
Arias	.833	3	1	4	1	0

BOWIE BAYSOX — Class AA

EASTERN LEAGUE

BATTING	AVG	G	AB	R	H	2B	3B	HR	RBI	BB	SO	SB	CS	SLG	OBP	B	T	HT	WT	DOB	1st Yr	Resides
Cabrera, Ray	.276	61	243	26	67	21	0	4	29	7	29	6	5	.412	.304	R	R	6-3	220	11-10-78	1996	Upata, Venez.
Calzado, Napolean	.276	130	482	71	133	20	3	3	42	34	50	42	11	.349	.332	R	R	6-3	180	2-9-76	1996	Santo Domingo, D.R.
Cates, Gary	.333	7	18	1	6	0	0	0	2	3	0	2	1	.333	.455	R	R	5-7	160	7-3-81	1999	Brandon, Fla.
Diaz, Maikell	.175	48	143	12	25	3	3	0	11	6	29	2	1	.238	.213	R	R	5-11	160	9-29-78	1996	Estado Miranda, Venez.
Figueroa, Franky	.367	8	30	6	11	2	1	0	3	1	7	0	0	.500	.387	R	R	6-6	240	2-9-77	1996	Hialeah, Fla.
Gibbs, Mark	.167	2	6	1	1	0	0	0	2	0	3	0	0	.333	.167	R	R	6-0	190	8-16-77	2000	Davidsonville, Md.
Gredvig, Doug	.275	129	465	48	128	22	1	14	80	46	94	2	3	.417	.345	R	R	6-3	230	8-25-79	2000	Sacramento, Calif.
Hammond, Joey	.256	52	176	25	45	9	1	0	13	30	32	3	1	.318	.359	R	R	6-1	180	10-27-77	1998	Frederick, Md.
Hoffpauir, Josh	.268	86	302	31	81	12	3	1	25	21	28	10	6	.338	.321	L	R	5-11	188	9-21-77	2000	Vidalia, La.
Hunter, Scott	.226	84	340	26	77	20	0	5	31	16	55	4	3	.343	.291	R	R	6-1	210	12-17-75	1994	Philadelphia, Pa.
2-team (24 Binghamton)	.228	108	386	49	88	24	0	7	43	24	73	10	5	.345	.279							
Martinez, Octavio	.217	7	23	4	5	0	0	0	1	0	3	0	0	.217	.250	R	R	6-0	180	7-30-79	1999	Bakersfield, Calif.
Matos, Luis	.275	62	218	34	60	14	2	9	40	32	45	14	4	.482	.370	R	R	6-0	200	10-30-78	1996	Bayamon, P.R.
McDonald, Darnell	.292	37	144	21	42	9	1	4	15	22	27	9	3	.451	.393	R	R	5-11	210	11-17-78	1997	Glendale, Colo.
McGee, Tom	.154	15	39	1	6	1	0	0	4	1	5	0	0	.179	.171	R	R	5-11	200	1-29-75	1997	Frederick, Md.
Molina, Izzy	.260	57	196	23	51	7	0	5	18	19	34	1	0	.372	.327	R	R	6-1	220	6-3-71	1990	Miami, Fla.
Rachels, Wes	.201	69	199	19	40	6	1	0	19	21	33	4	0	.241	.279	R	R	5-9	185	1-19-76	1998	Las Vegas, Nev.
Raines, Tim	.261	123	491	66	128	17	4	5	25	34	101	33	15	.342	.310	S	R	5-10	180	8-31-79	1998	Heathrow, Fla.
Reed, Keith	.246	137	488	57	120	20	1	15	64	40	107	3	10	.383	.314	R	R	6-2	210	10-8-78	1997	Yarmouth Port, Mass.
Richard, Chris	.333	2	6	0	2	0	0	0	1	1	2	0	0	.500	.375	L	L	6-2	200	6-7-74	1995	San Diego, Calif.
Rogers, Ed	.261	112	422	59	110	26	2	11	57	16	70	14	4	.410	.300	R	R	6-1	170	8-29-78	1997	San Pedro de Macoris, D.R.
Salinas, Trey	.154	8	26	2	4	1	0	0	3	3	4	0	0	.192	.267	R	R	6-2	195	5-25-76	1996	Corpus Christi, Texas
Seestedt, Mike	.000	1	3	0	0	0	0	0	0	0	0	0	0	.000	.000	R	R	6-0	200	11-10-77	1999	Mt. Pleasant, Mich.
Ullery, Dave	.189	38	106	12	20	5	0	1	6	15	32	0	0	.264	.289	L	R	6-3	220	12-16-74	1997	Brazil, Ind.
Whiteside, Eli	.263	27	99	11	26	5	0	2	11	4	18	0	1	.374	.311	R	R	6-2	200	10-22-79	2001	New Albany, Miss.

PITCHING	W	L	ERA	G	GS	CG	SV	IP	H	R	ER	BB	SO	AVG	B	T	HT	WT	DOB	1st Yr	Resides
Andrade, Jancy	0	1	162.00	1	0	0	0	0	5	6	6	3	1	.833	R	R	6-2	230	6-29-78	1995	Cumana, Venez.
Babula, Shaun	0	1	4.32	7	0	0	0	8	12	4	4	1	12	.324	S	L	6-1	180	5-21-77	1999	Burlington, N.J.
Bechler, Steve	2	1	3.42	4	4	0	0	24	28	11	9	6	13	.304	R	R	6-2	230	11-18-79	1998	Medford, Ore.
Bedard, Erik	6	3	1.97	13	12	0	0	69	43	18	15	30	66	.176	L	L	6-1	180	3-6-79	1999	Navan, Ontario
Brock, Chris	0	0	3.60	1	1	0	0	5	6	2	2	0	2	.300	R	R	6-1	180	2-5-71	1992	Altamonte Springs, Fla.

PITCHING	W	L	ERA	G	GS	CG	SV	IP	H	R	ER	BB	SO	AVG	B	T	HT	WT	DOB	1st Yr	Resides
Brown, Derek	3	6	5.07	41	3	0	0	87	116	62	49	25	53	.309	R	R	6-1	180	7-23-76	1994	Clear Spring, Md.
Brownson, Mark	0	0	6.75	3	0	0	0	7	10	5	5	2	3	.357	L	R	6-2	180	6-17-75	1994	Sun Lakes, Ariz.
Corcoran, Tim	0	5	3.67	35	0	0	1	49	61	31	20	29	48	.308	R	R	6-2	200	4-15-78	1997	Slaughter, La.
DuBose, Eric	5	3	2.51	41	0	0	3	65	46	21	18	21	66	.198	L	L	6-3	230	5-15-76	1997	Nashville, Tenn.
Figueroa, Juan	1	6	5.06	24	11	0	1	89	100	51	50	26	68	.278	R	R	6-3	240	6-24-75	1996	Santo Domingo, D.R.
Hale, Beau	2	0	0.84	2	2	0	0	11	11	2	1	3	6	.255	R	R	6-2	200	12-1-78	2000	Mauriceville, Texas
Hentgen, Pat	0	0	1.50	1	1	0	0	6	5	2	1	2	3	.227	R	R	6-2	200	11-13-68	1986	Tarpon Springs, Fla.
Johnson, Jason	1	0	0.00	1	1	0	0	5	4	0	0	1	6	.210	R	R	6-6	210	10-27-73	1992	Henderson, Nev.
Paradis, Mike	8	13	5.64	27	27	1	0	152	174	108	95	66	94	.290	R	R	6-3	199	5-18-79	1999	Clemson, S.C.
Rakers, Aaron	5	1	2.06	36	0	0	10	48	39	12	11	12	45	.232	R	R	6-3	200	1-22-77	1999	Trenton, Ill.
Riley, Matt	4	10	6.34	22	22	0	0	109	136	84	77	48	105	.306	L	L	6-1	200	8-2-79	1998	Oakley, Calif.
Rodriguez, Eddy	0	0	5.63	6	0	0	1	8	6	6	5	7	7	.200	R	R	6-1	190	8-8-81	1999	San Pedro de Macoris, D.R.
Rosario, Juan	4	10	5.01	25	20	0	0	128	144	88	71	54	88	.282	R	R	6-4	210	11-17-75	1993	Perth Amboy, N.J.
Salazar, Richard	0	0	4.32	8	0	0	0	17	15	8	8	15	19	.238	L	L	5-11	200	1-6-81	2001	Miami, Fla.
Sequea, Jacobo	1	6	5.40	15	14	0	0	73	69	53	44	35	37	.251	R	R	6-1	180	8-31-81	1997	Anaco, Venez.
Serrano, Willy	4	4	7.58	27	2	0	0	49	75	44	41	30	28	.353	R	R	6-1	180	3-13-77	1997	Santo Domingo, D.R.
Sims, Kenny	5	11	5.62	28	18	0	0	107	131	82	67	40	52	.303	R	R	6-4	210	7-24-75	1996	Union, S.C.
Wilson, Jeff	4	4	2.18	50	2	0	10	91	72	29	22	31	79	.215	R	L	6-2	190	5-30-76	1977	Greensboro, N.C.

FIELDING

Catcher	PCT	G	PO	A	E	DP	PB
Martinez	.986	7	68	3	1	2	0
McGee	.953	15	75	7	4	1	2
Molina	.988	56	362	39	5	3	7
Salinas	1.000	5	26	4	0	1	2
Seestedt	1.000	1	6	1	0	1	3
Ullery	.988	38	240	17	3	3	5
Whiteside	.972	25	160	14	5	0	2

First Base	PCT	G	PO	A	E	DP
Figueroa	1.000	5	26	2	0	2
Gredvig	.990	125	1014	85	11	80
Hammond	1.000	1	1	1	0	0
Rachels	.971	15	93	7	3	7

Second Base	PCT	G	PO	A	E	DP
Cates	1.000	5	10	8	0	1
Diaz	.971	17	29	37	2	9
Gibbs	.909	2	4	6	1	0
Hammond	.986	27	61	76	2	13
Hoffpauir	.963	78	146	194	13	34
Rachels	.953	19	41	40	4	8

Third Base	PCT	G	PO	A	E	DP
Calzado	.938	127	133	227	24	15
Diaz	.933	7	2	12	1	1
Hammond	.778	5	3	4	2	0
Hoffpauir	.800	4	2	6	2	0

Shortstop	PCT	G	PO	A	E	DP
Cates	.667	2	1	1	1	0
Diaz	.989	22	23	65	1	15
Hammond	1.000	1	4	1	0	0
·Hoffpauir	.846	6	8	14	4	4
Rogers	.958	111	153	301	20	47

Outfield	PCT	G	PO	A	E	DP
Cabrera	.980	52	93	5	2	2
Hunter	.973	69	103	4	3	0
Matos	.992	57	121	4	1	1
McDonald	.984	24	58	2	1	0
Rachels	.905	12	17	2	2	0
Raines	.978	114	254	8	6	1
Reed	.976	97	193	14	5	5

FREDERICK KEYS — High Class A

CAROLINA LEAGUE

BATTING	AVG	G	AB	R	H	2B	3B	HR	RBI	BB	SO	SB	CS	SLG	OBP	B	T	HT	WT	DOB	1st Yr	Resides
Cates, Gary	.198	32	126	12	25	6	0	0	7	7	18	2	2	.246	.239	R	R	5-7	160	7-3-81	1999	Brandon, Fla.
Cox, George	.238	6	21	3	5	1	0	1	5	0	4	0	0	.429	.238	R	R	6-0	190	5-11-80	2002	Melbourne, Fla.
Del Rosario, Manny	.150	8	20	2	3	1	0	0	0	3	0	0	0	.200	.150	S	R	5-11	150	7-8-81	1997	Hato Mayor del Rey, D.R.
Figueroa, Franky	.257	48	191	16	49	9	0	3	29	14	49	0	0	.351	.309	R	R	6-6	240	2-9-77	1996	Hialeah, Fla.
Fontenot, Mike	.264	122	481	61	127	16	4	8	53	42	117	13	9	.364	.333	L	R	5-8	160	6-9-80	2002	Slidell, La.
Garcia, Nick	.253	58	198	13	50	6	0	1	21	4	18	1	0	.298	.271	R	R	5-11	180	5-2-80	1999	Obregon, Mexico
Gordon, Alex	.203	49	158	19	32	5	0	5	16	10	67	1	1	.329	.253	L	L	6-4	230	3-3-80	1998	Seattle, Wash.
Kessick, Jon	.219	10	32	6	7	1	1	0	4	6	17	0	0	.313	.342	R	R	6-5	210	1-9-78	1999	Charleston, S.C.
Keylor, Cory	.258	132	497	70	128	26	1	5	47	57	109	14	3	.344	.337	L	R	6-3	190	8-25-79	2001	Westerville, Ohio
Leon, Alfredo	.264	74	235	24	62	7	0	0	28	15	23	2	2	.294	.320	R	R	6-0	190	3-14-80	1996	Puerto Ordaz, Venez.
Littleton, B.J.	.171	45	152	21	26	3	3	0	8	12	33	5	2	.230	.236	S	L	5-10	160	10-3-79	2000	Arlington, Texas
Mack, Tony	.254	82	236	31	60	13	0	0	14	18	50	7	4	.309	.313	S	R	5-11	200	3-19-79	1998	Orlando, Fla.
Matos, Luis	.333	3	12	2	4	1	0	0	1	2	3	0	0	.417	.429	R	R	6-0	200	10-30-78	1996	Bayamon, P.R.
Ndungidi, Ntema	.222	55	189	29	42	7	2	4	17	29	40	6	5	.344	.335	L	R	6-2	190	3-18-80	1997	Montreal, Quebec
Oropeza, Asdrubal	.203	91	315	33	64	13	0	7	43	33	58	1	1	.311	.287	R	R	6-2	170	7-3-80	1996	Barquisimeto, Venez.
Seestedt, Mike	.206	53	141	16	29	4	0	0	11	28	16	1	2	.234	.343	R	R	6-0	200	11-10-77	1999	Mt. Pleasant, Mich.
Shanks, Eric	.269	57	186	22	50	9	0	0	26	21	23	2	2	.317	.367	R	R	5-11	180	7-7-78	2002	Charlotte, N.C.
Shier, Peter	.340	35	97	21	33	5	1	1	9	22	24	0	4	.443	.467	R	R	6-2	160	3-16-81	1999	Columbus, Ohio
Tucker, Mamon	.300	127	473	62	142	16	4	4	55	33	75	9	8	.376	.348	R	R	6-3	180	10-18-79	1998	Austin, Texas
Webster, Kevin	.232	22	82	7	19	1	0	0	6	4	12	0	0	.244	.297	R	R	5-9	220	2-7-78	2001	New Caney, Texas
Whiteside, Eli	.259	80	313	34	81	19	0	8	42	14	57	0	0	.396	.296	R	R	6-2	200	10-22-79	2001	New Albany, Miss.
Wilken, Kris	.259	131	506	58	131	24	3	6	61	39	84	1	1	.354	.312	S	R	5-11	190	4-11-79	2000	Albuquerque, N.M.

PITCHING	W	L	ERA	G	GS	CG	SV	IP	H	R	ER	BB	SO	AVG	B	T	HT	WT	DOB	1st Yr	Resides
Andrade, Jancy	5	11	3.84	30	22	1	0	145	133	73	62	52	151	.247	R	R	6-2	230	6-29-78	1995	Cumana, Venez.
Bartlett, Richard	6	10	5.35	18	18	1	0	99	116	72	59	29	57	.292	R	R	6-3	210	10-6-81	2000	Kennewick, Wash.
Cierlik, Jason	0	0	3.00	4	0	0	0	6	3	2	2	2	1	.166	L	L	6-0	200	2-21-81	2002	Brooklyn Park, Minn.
Figueroa, Juan	4	1	2.28	9	9	1	0	59	47	16	15	7	53	.214	R	R	6-3	240	6-24-75	1996	Santo Domingo, D.R.
Ford, Tom	2	3	4.85	46	0	0	0	65	75	38	35	32	55	.291	L	L	6-0	210	11-8-76	2000	Santa Rosa, Calif.
Forystek, Brian	1	4	4.50	43	1	0	3	70	71	47	35	36	79	.258	L	L	6-1	170	10-30-78	2000	Palos Park, Ill.
Guzman, Juan	0	4	7.85	5	5	0	0	18	23	20	16	12	11	.310	R	R	6-2	190	3-4-77	1995	San Pedro de Macoris, D.R.
Hale, Beau	8	8	5.02	22	22	0	0	131	157	83	73	27	79	.296	R	R	6-2	200	12-1-78	2000	Mauriceville, Texas
Hentgen, Pat	1	0	2.57	1	1	1	0	7	5	2	2	2	5	.208	R	R	6-2	200	11-13-68	1986	Tarpon Springs, Fla.
Jones, Sean	4	5	3.44	32	1	0	3	55	62	27	21	17	35	.278	R	R	6-7	210	4-12-77	1997	Hamilton, Ontario
Mejia, Francisco	0	0	0.00	1	1	0	0	3	2	0	0	3		.200	L	L	6-1	180	12-20-80	1996	San Rafael de Yuma, D.R.
Montilla, Elvis	0	3	12.74	10	3	0	1	18	40	30	25	6	10	.449	R	R	6-3	200	7-16-78	1997	Ramon Santana, D.R.
Morris, Cory	1	10	6.32	16	16	0	0	73	84	58	51	47	59	.298	R	R	6-2	180	6-2-79	2001	Beckville, Texas
Ormond, Rodney	1	2	2.25	46	0	0	6	72	62	24	18	20	61	.229	R	R	6-4	210	6-17-77	1999	Princeton, N.C.
Ramirez, Enrique	3	4	4.04	32	0	0	1	62	50	32	28	37	47	.224	R	R	6-2	210	8-15-76	1996	El Seibo, D.R.
Reilly, Chris	1	1	9.45	14	0	0	0	13	24	14	14	8	10	.369	R	R	6-6	220	11-17-80	2002	Bound Brook, N.J.
Rodriguez, Eddy	0	3	2.23	38	0	0	11	48	28	14	12	20	58	.168	R	R	6-1	190	8-8-81	1999	San Pedro de Macoris, D.R.
Roque, Darryl	3	10	5.45	32	12	0	1	102	116	69	62	35	87	.283	S	R	6-4	210	4-20-77	1999	Nashville, Tenn.
Schwager, Matt	7	13	6.04	28	28	0	0	149	185	124	100	53	108	.303	R	R	6-2	220	10-10-77	1998	Orchard, Neb.
Sperring, Jayme	0	0	6.43	18	0	0	1	21	27	15	15	11	21	.300	R	R	6-2	200	4-26-79	1998	Cypress, Texas

FIELDING

Catcher
Catcher	PCT	G	PO	A	E	DP	PB
Cox	1.000	6	36	1	0	0	1
Seestedt	.985	51	360	36	6	1	5
Webster	.985	19	113	16	2	1	7
Whiteside	.975	70	516	58	15	3	17

First Base
First Base	PCT	G	PO	A	E	DP
Figueroa	.987	35	280	24	4	21
Gordon	1.000	6	39	0	0	2
Leon	.985	41	309	16	5	22
Oropeza	.000	1	0	0	0	0
Seestedt	1.000	1	11	0	0	1
Wilken	.989	66	503	39	6	43

Second Base
Second Base	PCT	G	PO	A	E	DP
Cates	.947	9	14	22	2	5
Del Rosario	1.000	2	3	5	0	0
Fontenot	.955	116	199	327	25	59
Shanks	1.000	5	7	12	0	0
Wilken	.969	14	27	35	2	10

Third Base
Third Base	PCT	G	PO	A	E	DP
Cates	.906	12	4	25	3	2
Leon	.850	7	4	13	3	1
Oropeza	.922	88	82	153	20	14
Shanks	.500	4	1	0	1	0
Wilken	.950	37	26	50	4	0

Shortstop
Shortstop	PCT	G	PO	A	E	DP
Cates	.878	7	14	22	5	2
Del Rosario	.875	4	4	3	1	0
Garcia	.931	57	97	146	18	33
Shanks	.912	44	66	99	16	18
Shier	.969	34	57	68	4	12
Wilken	1.000	2	3	2	0	0

Outfield
Outfield	PCT	G	PO	A	E	DP
Gordon	.929	16	23	3	2	0
Keylor	.956	127	229	9	11	1
Littleton	.979	43	88	4	2	1
Mack	.974	72	177	7	5	2
Matos	1.000	3	8	0	0	0
Ndungidi	.964	51	104	2	4	0
Tucker	.960	121	188	6	8	0
Wilken	1.000	1	2	0	0	0

DELMARVA SHOREBIRDS — Low Class A
SOUTH ATLANTIC LEAGUE

BATTING
BATTING	AVG	G	AB	R	H	2B	3B	HR	RBI	BB	SO	SB	CS	SLG	OBP	B	T	HT	WT	DOB	1st Yr	Resides
Arko, Tommy	.127	22	63	5	8	3	0	0	0	7	28	0	0	.175	.236	R	R	6-1	190	7-28-82	2000	Abilene, Texas
Ascencion, Quincy	.195	23	87	9	17	2	0	0	6	3	24	3	0	.218	.226	R	R	6-0	210	11-1-82	1999	Willemstad, Curacao
Bass, Bryan	.221	130	457	60	101	20	7	6	59	40	146	15	2	.335	.299	S	R	6-1	180	4-12-82	2001	Seminole, Fla.
Cates, Gary	.284	82	317	50	90	18	1	2	28	16	36	12	6	.366	.324	R	R	5-7	160	7-3-81	1999	Brandon, Fla.
Cliffords, Woody	.264	87	314	50	83	21	1	1	20	53	57	15	5	.347	.385	L	R	6-2	190	12-2-80	2001	West Hills, Calif.
Del Rosario, Manny	.215	36	107	11	23	1	0	0	6	7	16	5	1	.224	.271	S	R	5-11	150	7-8-81	1997	Hato Mayor del Rey, D.R.
Francisco, Ruben	.215	54	163	16	35	8	2	2	14	6	29	3	5	.325	.253	L	L	6-0	180	7-13-77	1997	San Pedro de Macoris, D.R.
Gibbs, Mark	.180	39	100	10	18	4	0	1	8	4	20	2	1	.250	.219	R	R	6-0	190	8-16-77	2000	Davidsonville, Md.
Gordon, Alex	.233	60	206	32	48	11	1	13	33	14	76	1	0	.485	.291	L	L	6-4	230	3-3-80	1998	Seattle, Wash.
Hackett, Richard	.186	64	172	11	32	3	1	0	5	10	48	4	1	.215	.235	R	R	6-1	200	4-30-79	2001	Stockton, Calif.
Johnson, Tripper	.260	136	493	73	128	32	6	11	71	62	88	19	6	.416	.349	R	R	6-1	200	4-28-82	2000	Bellevue, Wash.
Jordan, Eddie	.170	45	112	15	19	6	1	1	9	20	35	4	2	.268	.299	R	R	6-1	170	11-18-80	2001	Falls Church, Va.
Lehr, Ryan	.290	51	186	22	54	13	0	2	38	19	26	3	2	.392	.354	R	R	5-11	200	2-15-79	1997	La Mesa, Calif.
Littleton, B.J.	.257	64	206	29	53	7	3	0	19	22	42	14	3	.320	.332	S	L	5-10	160	10-3-79	2000	Arlington, Texas
Majewski, Val	.118	7	17	2	2	0	0	1	3	1	1	0	0	.294	.158	R	L	6-2	200	6-19-81	2002	Freehold, N.J.
Manley, Adam	.262	133	462	58	121	29	5	9	57	38	133	9	4	.405	.326	L	L	6-2	190	7-18-78	2001	Lakewood, Wash.
Martin, Kyle	.253	52	146	17	37	6	0	5	19	20	36	1	1	.397	.345	R	R	5-11	210	6-12-80	1999	Yakima, Wash.
Martinez, Octavio	.284	20	81	9	23	3	0	0	11	3	5	3	2	.321	.326	R	R	6-0	180	7-30-79	1999	Bakersfield, Calif.
McGee, Tom	.249	68	193	16	48	8	0	6	18	17	45	0	1	.383	.315	R	R	5-11	200	1-29-75	1997	Frederick, Md.
Rogers, Omar	.276	78	297	47	82	21	1	3	27	26	53	3	1	.384	.349	R	R	6-0	180	8-12-82	1999	San Pedro de Macoris, D.R.
Salinas, Trey	.283	70	251	31	71	21	1	8	45	24	45	2	0	.470	.361	R	R	6-0	190	5-25-76	1996	Corpus Christi, Texas
Seestedt, Mike	.136	9	22	2	3	2	0	0	2	3	2	0	0	.227	.240	R	R	6-0	200	11-10-77	1999	Mt. Pleasant, Mich.
Shanks, Eric	.205	14	39	3	8	4	0	0	4	3	9	1	1	.308	.326	R	R	5-11	180	7-7-78	2002	Charlotte, N.C.
Soriano, Jairo	.234	15	47	5	11	2	1	1	5	0	16	1	0	.383	.234	S	R	6-1	160	12-13-80	1999	Villa Mella, D.R.
Webster, Kevin	.289	13	38	3	11	0	0	1	7	4	6	1	0	.368	.386	R	R	5-9	220	2-7-78	2001	New Caney, Texas

PITCHING
PITCHING	W	L	ERA	G	GS	CG	SV	IP	H	R	ER	BB	SO	AVG	B	T	HT	WT	DOB	1st Yr	Resides
Bartlett, Richard	6	0	2.63	9	8	0	0	48	45	16	14	16	33	.243	R	R	6-3	210	10-6-81	2000	Kennewick, Wash.
Birkins, Kurt	9	7	3.51	27	25	3	0	144	140	66	56	46	102	.257	L	L	6-2	180	8-11-80	2001	Canoga Park, Calif.
Boughner, Anthony	4	2	4.32	18	8	0	0	50	57	29	24	14	37	.289	L	L	6-3	210	11-1-78	2002	Beallsville, Ohio
Crouthers, Dave	8	6	3.34	25	25	1	0	129	117	66	48	58	108	.243	R	R	6-3	200	12-18-79	2001	Edwardsville, Ill.
Deza, Fredy	0	5	4.38	12	12	0	0	49	50	26	24	15	38	.260	R	R	6-2	160	12-11-82	1999	La Romana, D.R.
Farren, Dave	3	2	3.15	21	2	0	0	40	32	17	14	8	43	.213	R	R	6-1	180	3-20-81	1999	Texarkana, Texas
Hentgen, Pat	0	1	1.80	1	1	0	0	5	4	1	1	1	4	.235	R	R	6-2	200	11-13-68	1986	Tarpon Springs, Fla.
Jones, D.J.	4	2	3.42	26	5	0	1	50	53	24	19	18	32	.270	L	L	6-0	180	6-3-78	2001	Forney, Texas
Keefer, Ryan	2	3	3.44	22	1	0	0	37	36	15	14	11	29	.257	L	R	6-3	200	8-10-81	2000	Catawissa, Pa.
Knapp, Ben	8	11	3.18	26	26	1	0	153	154	67	54	36	125	.265	R	R	6-7	210	11-8-79	1998	Oviedo, Fla.
LaCorte, Vince	2	4	4.32	20	5	0	1	42	26	14	18	23	23	.277	R	R	6-3	200	9-10-78	1999	Gilroy, Calif.
Lewis, Rommie	1	2	2.15	53	0	0	25	71	50	19	17	20	77	.197	L	L	6-6	200	9-2-82	2001	Bellevue, Wash.
Maine, John	1	1	1.36	6	5	0	0	33	21	8	5	4	39	.177	R	R	6-4	190	5-8-81	2002	Hartwood, Va.
Marchetti, Dan	5	4	2.67	39	0	0	3	57	48	21	17	24	40	.234	R	R	6-1	180	7-20-78	2000	Gaithersburg, Md.
Mejia, Francisco	5	2	5.00	37	1	0	0	63	76	44	35	23	51	.295	L	L	6-1	180	12-20-80	1996	San Rafael de Yuma, D.R.
Mitchell, Andy	5	1	2.36	27	0	0	0	42	34	16	11	17	20	.219	R	R	6-3	210	9-10-78	2001	Conyers, Ga.
Montilla, Elvis	0	0	18.00	1	0	0	0	1	4	2	2	0	0	.571	R	R	6-3	200	7-16-78	1997	Ramon Santana, D.R.
Morris, Cory	3	1	2.88	10	10	0	0	56	44	20	18	20	50	.210	R	R	6-2	180	6-2-79	2001	Beckville, Texas
Rice, Scott	0	6	5.40	18	3	0	0	40	45	26	24	21	22	.288	L	L	6-6	210	9-21-81	1999	Simi Valley, Calif.
Rleal, Sendy	1	0	6.10	28	1	0	1	41	53	28	28	15	34	.317	R	R	6-1	160	8-26-80	1999	San Pedro de Macoris, D.R.
Rogers, Brad	1	0	7.36	13	0	0	0	15	26	13	12	5	11	.388	R	R	6-4	190	12-6-81	1999	Nanaimo, B.C.
Sperring, Jayme	7	3	1.73	33	0	0	6	52	47	15	10	15	55	.237	R	R	6-4	200	11-16-78	2000	Cypress, Texas
Stahl, Richard	1	1	5.59	2	2	0	0	10	10	8	6	5	9	.277	R	L	6-7	220	4-11-81	1999	Covington, Ga.

FIELDING

Catcher
Catcher	PCT	G	PO	A	E	DP	PB
Arko	.987	22	143	14	2	1	5
Martin	.987	15	72	6	1	0	1
Martinez	1.000	11	75	6	0	0	2
McGee	.991	61	386	38	4	0	9
Salinas	.983	32	199	27	4	0	5
Seestedt	1.000	8	50	5	0	0	1
Webster	.979	12	79	13	2	0	3

First Base
First Base	PCT	G	PO	A	E	DP
Gibbs	1.000	19	139	9	0	6
Lehr	1.000	3	23	0	0	2
Manley	.979	76	619	48	14	46
McGee	.938	2	14	1	1	1
Rogers	.988	43	375	33	5	28
Salinas	1.000	10	78	8	0	11

Second Base
Second Base	PCT	G	PO	A	E	DP
Cates	.963	77	167	196	14	32
Del Rosario	.938	33	49	71	8	12
Gibbs	.850	7	9	8	3	1
Rogers	.990	25	47	52	1	14
Shanks	1.000	2	2	4	0	1
Soriano	.970	7	10	22	1	2

Third Base
Third Base	PCT	G	PO	A	E	DP
Cates	1.000	3	3	2	0	0
Gibbs	.895	8	0	17	2	1
Johnson	.968	133	117	276	13	23
Lehr	.000	1	0	0	0	0
Shanks	1.000	1	1	3	0	0

Shortstop
Shortstop	PCT	G	PO	A	E	DP
Bass	.937	129	194	374	38	56

ORGANIZATION STATISTICS

Cates	1.000	2	1	4	0	1	Cliffords	.994	81	155	4	1	0	Lehr	.986	46	71	1	1	0

Cates	1.000	2	1	4	0	1	Cliffords	.994	81	155	4	1	0	Lehr	.986	46	71	1	1	0
Shanks	.977	12	11	31	1	6	Francisco	.955	51	79	6	4	1	Littleton	.989	47	92	2	1	0
Soriano	1.000	2	6	4	0	1	Gordon	.968	54	86	5	3	1	Majewski	1.000	7	10	0	0	0
Outfield	**PCT**	**G**	**PO**	**A**	**E**	**DP**	Hackett	.984	51	62	1	1	0	Manley	.981	59	101	2	2	0
Ascencion	.960	21	23	1	1	0	Jordan	1.000	36	63	2	0	0	Martin	1.000	4	3	1	0	0

ABERDEEN IRONBIRDS — Short-Season A

NEW YORK-PENN LEAGUE

BATTING	AVG	G	AB	R	H	2B	3B	HR	RBI	BB	SO	SB	CS	SLG	OBP	B	T	HT	WT	DOB	1st Yr	Resides
Combs, Will	.247	30	93	10	23	5	0	0	14	8	21	2	1	.301	.308	L	L	6-3	210	2-3-79	2002	Statesville, N.C.
Cox, George	.130	11	23	2	3	0	0	0	2	8	0	0	3	.130	.231	R	R	6-0	190	5-11-80	2002	Melbourne, Fla.
Davies, Gregg	.224	69	228	21	51	13	0	0	22	28	45	4	5	.281	.309	L	L	6-1	200	1-8-80	2002	Olney, MD
Del Rosario, Manny	.250	67	252	23	63	10	3	1	24	16	22	15	2	.325	.294	S	R	5-11	150	7-8-81	1997	Hato Mayor Del Rey, D.R.
Fahey, Brandon	.281	63	253	31	71	10	6	0	15	20	34	5	8	.368	.333	L	R	6-2	180	1-18-81	2002	Dallas, Texas
Gilhooly, Tim	.197	61	203	16	40	6	0	3	22	15	79	8	3	.271	.252	R	R	6-3	210	8-31-81	2002	Danville, Calif.
Gonzalez, Patrick	.204	61	142	18	29	3	1	0	12	23	30	3	3	.239	.325	R	R	5-10	170	11-21-79	2002	Ontario, Calif.
Hubele, Ryan	.206	50	155	11	32	3	1	2	12	16	35	2	3	.277	.282	R	R	5-11	180	9-9-80	2002	Paradise Valley, Ariz.
Huggins, Mike	.262	76	271	32	71	15	2	1	27	31	55	9	4	.343	.340	R	R	6-3	210	8-29-80	2002	San Antonio, Texas
Jordan, Eddie	.237	37	93	14	22	3	0	0	7	11	27	3	1	.269	.343	R	R	6-1	170	11-18-78	2001	Falls Church, VA
Kessick, Jon	.196	17	56	9	11	4	0	0	7	4	23	0	1	.268	.286	R	R	6-5	210	1-9-78	1999	Charleston, S.C.
Majewski, Val	.300	31	110	22	33	7	4	1	15	13	14	8	4	.464	.376	R	L	6-2	200	6-19-81	2002	Freehold, NJ
Recio, Bolivar	.258	10	31	2	8	0	0	0	3	1	5	1	1	.258	.273	R	R	6-2	180	1-14-81	1999	San Francisco de Macoris, D.R.
Richard, Chris	.600	1	5	2	3	1	0	1	3	0	*1	0	0	1.400	.667	L	L	6-2	200	6-7-74	1995	San Diego, Calif.
Robinson-Pierce, Whitney	.149	15	47	1	7	2	0	0	0	2	12	0	0	.191	.184	R	R	6-3	210	3-4-82	2002	Fresno, Calif.
Rodriguez, Raul	.000	2	0	1	0	0	0	0	0	2	0	2	0	.000	1.000	S	R	5-10	180	11-23-79	2000	Cayey, P.R.
Russell, Mike	.273	59	183	26	50	3	1	4	29	19	56	4	0	.366	.352	R	R	6-0	190	8-14-81	2000	Bothell, Wash.
Shier, Peter	.196	12	46	4	9	1	1	0	4	5	11	0	1	.261	.283	R	R	6-2	160	3-16-81	1999	Columbus, Ohio
Soriano, Jairo	.200	33	75	8	15	1	0	0	2	9	21	4	1	.213	.294	S	R	6-1	160	12-13-80	1999	Villa Mella, D.R.
Stephenson, Neal	.310	70	255	30	79	17	6	3	40	13	50	4	4	.459	.349	L	R	6-1	200	1-15-80	2002	Bryan, Texas
Webster, Kevin	.000	1	0	0	0	0	0	0	0	1	0	0	0	.000	1.000	R	R	5-9	220	2-7-78	2001	New Caney, Texas

GAMES BY POSITION: C—Cox 9, Hubele 33, Kessick 15, Robinson-Pierce 14, Russell 12. **1B**—Combs 2, Cox 1, Davies 3, Huggins 72. **2B**—Del Rosario 64, Gonzalez 14, Rodriguez 1, Soriano 4. **3B**—Del Rosario 3, Fahey 12, Gonzalez 35, Hubele 9, Recio 10, Russell 7, Soriano 22. **SS**—Fahey 55, Gonzalez 16, Shier 12, Soriano 5. **OF**—Combs 19, Davies 53, Gilhooly 56, Hubele 3, Jordan 34, Majewski 30, Stephenson 55.

PITCHING	W	L	ERA	G	GS	CG	SV	IP	H	R	ER	BB	SO	AVG	B	T	HT	WT	DOB	1st Yr	Resides
Berube, Martin	2	4	3.75	17	9	0	1	62	53	27	26	20	48	.226	L	R	6-1	190	9-12-81	1999	Montreal, Quebec
Cierlik, Jason	0	0	3.21	12	0	0	2	14	12	5	5	6	16	.218	L	L	6-0	200	2-21-81	2002	Brooklyn Park, Minn.
Cooney, Jim	3	1	1.36	25	0	0	4	33	17	11	5	13	27	.157	L	L	6-0	170	4-6-80	2002	Boca Raton, Fla.
Edwards, Brad	0	0	4.98	17	1	0	0	22	20	14	12	9	24	.250	L	L	6-3	180	4-10-80	2001	Dumfries, Va.
Farren, Dave	5	5	2.86	14	14	1	0	85	74	31	27	28	58	.241	R	R	6-1	180	3-20-81	1999	Texarkana, Texas
Hentgen, Pat	1	1	3.09	2	2	0	0	12	16	8	4	0	10	.313	R	R	6-2	200	11-13-68	1986	Tarpon Springs, Fla.
Keefer, Ryan	3	7	3.91	13	13	0	0	69	77	38	30	18	64	.280	L	R	6-3	200	8-10-81	2000	Catawissa, Pa.
Maine, John	1	1	1.74	4	2	0	0	10	6	2	2	3	21	.153	R	R	6-4	190	5-8-81	2002	Hartwood, Va.
Makowsky, Carl	5	3	3.45	23	0	0	1	31	26	13	12	20	32	.232	R	R	6-1	200	12-13-79	2002	Conroe, Texas
McCurdy, Nick	4	7	3.55	13	12	1	1	71	67	29	28	16	45	.251	R	R	6-1	180	1-24-80	2002	Thomasville, Ala.
Mincey, T.W.	1	2	4.76	18	4	0	0	45	54	29	24	21	30	.295	L	L	6-3	190	5-17-80	2001	Winston, Ga.
Phillips, Chase	2	1	4.22	17	1	0	1	32	34	16	15	8	24	.274	R	R	6-2	180	10-24-80	1999	Zanesville, Ohio
Rice, Scott	1	7	4.47	11	10	0	1	56	66	40	28	24	41	.297	L	L	6-6	210	9-21-81	1999	Simi Valley, Calif.
Rogers, Brad	1	0	5.17	17	0	0	2	31	32	24	18	11	21	.260	R	R	6-4	190	12-6-81	1999	Nanaimo, B.C.
Rohr, Matt	0	1	12.64	14	0	0	0	16	30	24	22	11	12	.400	S	L	6-1	180	4-16-80	2002	Upland, Calif.
Spivey, Melvin	0	0	5.82	14	0	0	1	17	22	12	11	8	19	.314	R	R	6-3	210	12-6-79	2002	Orange Beach, Ala.
Sutton, Zach	0	1	2.08	14	0	0	7	17	12	4	4	4	15	.210	R	R	6-1	180	1-6-79	2002	Lake Wales, Fla.
Tate, Matt	1	4	5.64	6	6	0	0	30	34	27	19	4	22	.278	R	R	6-2	180	9-21-80	1999	Bonifay, Fla.
Teeter, Travis	1	0	3.00	2	2	0	0	12	14	6	4	2	8	.285	R	R	6-1	210	7-13-80	2002	Cohoes, N.Y.

BLUEFIELD ORIOLES — Rookie

APPALACHIAN LEAGUE

BATTING	AVG	G	AB	R	H	2B	3B	HR	RBI	BB	SO	SB	CS	SLG	OBP	B	T	HT	WT	DOB	1st Yr	Resides
Alvarez, Gera	.263	58	175	34	46	11	0	2	31	22	29	6	4	.360	.348	R	R	5-10	180	10-31-79	2002	Vista, Calif.
Arko, Tommy	.265	57	181	41	48	11	0	14	37	35	58	0	1	.558	.387	R	R	6-1	190	7-28-82	2000	Abilene, Texas
Ascencion, Quincy	.236	54	199	28	47	11	0	2	30	13	29	7	2	.322	.299	R	R	6-0	210	11-1-82	1999	Willemstad, Curacao
Bera, Roberto	.194	28	72	7	14	5	0	2	8	1	20	1	1	.347	.197	R	R	6-1	160	9-17-81	1998	San Pedro de Macoris, D.R.
Done, Robert	.316	58	193	46	61	12	1	6	39	54	37	6	3	.482	.473	R	R	5-11	190	7-27-79	2002	Aurora, Colo.
Jimenez, Luis	.375	51	176	40	66	13	1	8	42	33	33	9	1	.597	.474	L	L	6-4	200	5-7-82	1999	Bobure, Venez.
Joyce, Tom	.277	44	141	35	39	11	4	3	15	30	34	4	2	.475	.407	L	L	5-11	160	3-20-80	2002	Macon, Ga.
Martinez, Raul	.172	33	64	8	11	3	0	1	8	14	23	2	0	.266	.338	R	R	6-0	190	10-7-79	2000	San Lorenzo, P.R.
Morales, Porfirio	.122	20	41	6	5	1	0	0	2	0	10	0	0	.146	.196	R	R	6-2	170	3-14-81	1999	Hato Mayor del Rey, D.R.
Rijo, Carlos	.311	64	238	39	74	22	0	3	45	12	40	9	3	.441	.355	R	R	6-0	180	9-11-82	1999	La Romana, D.R.
Rivas, Arturo	.272	55	213	45	58	11	1	8	34	19	47	11	4	.446	.342	R	R	6-0	180	2-2-84	2001	San Francisco, Venez.
Robinson-Pierce, Whitney	.211	18	38	3	8	1	0	0	2	8	0	0	2	.237	.231	R	R	6-3	210	3-4-82	2002	Fresno, Calif.
Robinson, Levi	.280	50	143	42	40	12	0	2	10	33	30	18	4	.406	.429	R	R	6-0	180	3-28-80	2002	Anchorage, Alaska
Smallwood, Erik	.215	53	186	36	40	10	0	10	37	37	62	4	1	.430	.344	L	R	5-10	180	9-5-79	2002	Robertsdale, Ala.
Yount, Dustin	.241	61	203	38	49	9	0	14	51	35	44	3	0	.493	.350	L	R	6-1	200	10-27-82	2001	Scottsdale, Ariz.

GAMES BY POSITION: C—Arko 39, Martinez 28, Morales 13, Robinson-Pierce 9. **1B**—Jimenez 16, Yount 53. **2B**—Alvarez 19, Done 45, Robinson 13. **3B**—Done 9, Rijo 64, Yount 1. **SS**—Alvarez 37, Rijo 1, Robinson 35. **OF**—Ascencion 43, Bera 24, Jimenez 21, Joyce 36, Rivas 52, Robinson 2, Smallwood 43.

PITCHING	W	L	ERA	G	GS	CG	SV	IP	H	R	ER	BB	SO	AVG	B	T	HT	WT	DOB	1st Yr	Resides
Acosta, Richal	1	1	6.39	3	3	0	0	13	19	10	9	2	12	.345	R	R	6-1	140	2-5-84	2001	San Rafael de Yuma, D.R.
Britton, Chris	3	0	4.54	9	8	0	0	36	30	21	18	10	27	.227	R	R	6-3	220	12-16-82	2001	Plantation, Fla.
Cabrera, Daniel	5	2	3.28	12	12	0	0	60	52	25	22	25	69	.234	R	R	6-7	170	5-28-81	1999	San Pedro de Macoris, D.R.

ORGANIZATION STATISTICS

PITCHING	W	L	ERA	G	GS	CG	SV	IP	H	R	ER	BB	SO	AVG	B	T	HT	WT	DOB	1st Yr	Resides
Coppinger, Joe	5	2	4.38	12	12	0	0	64	68	39	31	20	49	.269	R	R	6-3	210	7-23-82	2001	El Paso, Texas
Crump, Joel	1	0	2.49	15	0	0	0	22	23	13	6	10	25	.261	R	L	6-2	210	8-20-81	2000	Yuma, Ariz.
Henry, Paul	2	1	4.71	16	0	0	3	21	25	11	11	9	31	.290	R	R	6-3	190	6-27-81	2002	Chattanooga, Tenn.
Johnson, James	4	2	4.37	11	9	0	0	56	52	36	27	16	36	.250	R	R	6-5	210	6-27-83	2001	Endicott, N.Y.
Jones, Alvin	0	0	5.79	18	0	0	0	19	18	14	12	17	18	.243	R	R	6-1	210	5-21-82	2000	Seguin, Texas
Machen, Mike	4	0	7.20	21	1	0	0	30	31	30	24	28	22	.260	R	R	6-4	190	10-5-81	2000	Mobile, Ala.
Montani, Jeff	3	3	2.34	30	0	0	15	35	30	12	9	15	34	.238	R	R	5-11	170	11-22-80	2001	Liverpool, N.Y.
Nash, Justin	0	3	5.18	16	7	0	1	49	58	35	28	16	39	.284	R	R	6-3	200	9-22-80	2002	Hunt Valley, Md.
Patitucci, Mike	4	0	1.44	24	0	0	1	31	26	7	5	16	38	.230	L	L	6-0	190	11-6-80	2002	Uniontown, Pa.
Sala, Marino	3	0	5.40	27	0	0	0	37	44	31	22	21	34	.291	R	R	6-0	180	2-2-81	1998	Hato Mayor, D.R.
Salazar, Richard	1	0	0.82	7	0	0	0	11	3	1	1	5	15	.088	L	L	5-11	200	1-6-81	2001	Miami, Fla.
Smith, Chris	0	3	11.45	5	5	0	0	11	12	14	14	21	4	.300	L	L	5-11	210	12-10-79	2001	Wantagh, N.Y.
Spillers, Larry	4	1	5.40	21	0	0	0	33	43	23	20	28	24	.328	R	L	6-3	210	3-12-82	2000	Roberta, Ga.
Tiller, James	4	5	4.82	12	11	1	0	65	74	44	35	16	43	.284	R	R	6-5	190	4-13-83	2001	Elysian Fields, Texas

SARASOTA ORIOLES — Rookie

GULF COAST LEAGUE

BATTING	AVG	G	AB	R	H	2B	3B	HR	RBI	BB	SO	SB	CS	SLG	OBP	B	T	HT	WT	DOB	1st Yr	Resides
Blanton, Stephen	.193	40	119	11	23	4	1	0	8	16	18	1	1	.244	.295	L	R	6-4	210	10-14-82	2002	Brooksville, Fla.
Brown, Darrius	.111	22	18	2	2	1	0	0	2	2	0	0	0	.167	.200	L	L	5-11	190	9-10-79	2002	Biloxi, Miss.
Carbonara, William	.264	52	174	27	46	10	1	2	19	6	32	7	2	.368	.303	R	R	6-3	210	3-9-79	2002	Cuero, Texas
Colbert, Eddie	.207	47	169	22	35	5	1	0	17	9	52	8	2	.249	.244	S	R	6-3	200	12-3-81	2002	Baltimore, Md.
Davis, Zach	.176	48	170	17	30	5	2	0	11	22	56	13	1	.229	.277	L	L	6-0	170	2-20-84	2002	Little Rock, Ark.
Garcia, Nick	.217	7	23	2	5	1	0	0	3	1	4	1	0	.261	.308	R	R	5-11	180	5-2-80	1999	Obregon, Mexico
Guerrero, Henry	.290	35	93	16	27	8	0	2	9	14	15	0	0	.441	.394	R	R	6-0	180	4-4-82	2000	Valencia, Venez.
Hadad, Jorge	.299	39	127	10	38	6	2	1	16	15	25	0	2	.402	.371	R	R	6-2	180	5-4-82	2001	Mexico City, Mexico
Howerton, Matthew	.205	40	122	21	25	2	1	0	9	24	35	6	2	.238	.351	R	R	5-11	170	8-29-84	2002	Fort Myers, Fla.
Leon, Alfredo	.087	8	23	2	2	0	0	0	2	2	3	0	0	.087	.222	R	R	6-0	190	3-14-80	1996	Puerto Ordaz, Venez.
Marmolejos, Hector	.143	2	7	2	1	0	0	0	1	0	1	1	0	.143	.250	R	R	6-4	200	7-29-83	2001	Santo Domingo, D.R.
Martinez, Octavio	.353	10	34	4	12	1	0	0	3	3	0	2	1	.382	.476	R	R	6-0	180	7-30-79	1999	Bakersfield, Calif.
Morales, Porfirio	.200	3	10	0	2	0	0	0	2	0	4	0	0	.200	.200	R	R	6-2	170	3-14-81	1999	Hato Mayor del Rey, D.R.
Opel, Chad	.174	49	144	19	25	4	2	1	10	17	23	6	0	.250	.302	R	R	5-9	170	12-19-79	2002	Edwardsville, Ill.
Piste, Carlos	.188	47	133	15	25	2	2	1	8	13	37	1	0	.256	.280	S	R	6-1	160	3-8-85	2002	Merida, Mexico
Richard, Chris	1.000	1	1	1	1	0	0	0	0	1	0	0	0	1.000	1.000	L	L	6-2	200	6-7-74	1995	San Diego, Calif.
Thurman, Tim	.236	56	199	14	47	9	1	1	18	15	58	0	0	.307	.289	R	R	6-7	250	12-31-79	2002	Corona Del Mar, Calif.
Wahl, Mark	.240	33	96	5	23	2	0	0	9	14	14	0	0	.260	.351	L	R	6-0	200	9-17-80	2002	Dale, Ind.
Zapata, Jose	.196	52	148	16	29	6	0	0	12	19	28	1	4	.236	.296	R	R	6-3	150	4-4-84	2001	San Pedro de Macoris, D.R.

GAMES BY POSITION: C—Guerrero 24, Hadad 10, Martinez 6, Morales 2, Wahl 24. 1B—Blanton 6, Carbonara 4, Hadad 2, Leon 1, Thurman 52, Wahl 1. 2B—Carbonara 1, Opel 41, Piste 19, Zapata 5. 3B—Blanton 1, Carbonara 29, Leon 7, Opel 10, Thurman 1, Zapata 20. SS—Garcia 7, Hadad 1, Leon 1, Opel 1, Piste 28, Zapata 28. OF—Blanton 21, Brown 6, Carbonara 23, Colbert 47, Davis 48, Guerrero 2, Hadad 5, Howerton 40, Marmolejos 2, Teeter 1.

PITCHING	W	L	ERA	G	GS	CG	SV	IP	H	R	ER	BB	SO	AVG	B	T	HT	WT	DOB	1st Yr	Resides
Acosta, Richal	1	1	1.93	10	9	0	0	47	44	13	10	12	30	.251	R	R	6-1	140	2-5-84	2001	San Rafael de Yuma, D.R.
Bolander, Matt	0	7	8.16	9	8	0	0	29	40	39	26	28	12	.338	R	R	6-2	180	11-2-83	2002	Anderson, Ind.
Brown, Darrius	1	1	5.76	16	1	0	1	25	24	21	16	25	23	.000	L	L	5-11	190	9-10-79	2002	Biloxi, Miss.
Brubaker, Doug	2	3	2.51	11	10	0	0	43	29	17	12	17	38	.188	R	R	6-2	200	1-15-82	2002	Shelton, Wash.
Cahill, Casey	0	3	5.14	22	0	0	2	35	43	32	20	20	27	.302	R	R	6-3	180	3-15-82	2000	New Brunswick, N.J.
Caughey, Trevor	1	4	4.87	10	9	0	0	41	50	27	22	13	45	.303	L	L	6-1	160	11-23-82	2002	San Luis Obispo, Calif.
Cierlik, Jason	0	0	6.00	3	0	0	0	3	4	4	2	5	2	.307	L	L	6-0	200	2-21-81	2002	Brooklyn Park, Minn.
Gorman, Pat	1	1	4.91	4	0	0	0	7	8	4	4	3	7	.275	R	R	6-2	250	8-16-77	1997	Valley Cottage, N.Y.
Hentgen, Pat	0	0	0.00	1	1	0	0	3	2	0	0	0	3	.181	R	R	6-2	200	11-13-68	1986	Tarpon Springs, Fla.
Mendez, Wimer	3	1	2.70	20	0	0	3	37	29	17	11	12	44	.219	R	R	6-2	150	1-5-84	2001	Santo Domingo, D.R.
Meque, Jacobo	2	4	2.86	12	12	0	0	50	41	26	16	33	56	.227	L	L	6-2	200	10-1-83	2000	Villa Altagracia, D.R.
Perez, Carlos	2	2	2.63	12	5	0	0	38	35	18	11	17	32	.257	L	L	6-1	180	5-20-82	2000	San Pedro de Macoris, D.R.
Plank, Terry	0	0	9.00	7	0	0	1	8	9	8	8	6	4	.281	L	R	6-5	210	4-19-78	1999	Hampton, Va.
Potter, Josh	3	3	2.98	19	1	0	0	42	48	20	14	17	22	.290	R	R	6-4	170	4-8-83	2001	Philipsburg, Pa.
Ramirez, Luis	2	1	4.44	19	0	0	2	26	17	13	13	17	46	.184	R	R	6-4	180	6-9-82	2000	Barcelona, Venez.
Reilly, Chris	1	1	7.50	3	1	0	0	6	4	6	5	9	7	.173	R	R	6-6	220	11-17-80	2002	Bound Brook, N.J.
Teeter, Travis	5	4	3.72	16	3	1	2	46	40	21	19	10	51	.000	R	R	6-1	210	7-13-80	2002	Cohoes, N.Y.

BOSTON RED SOX

BY JOHN TOMASE

Enthusiastic new owners. Same old story.

The Red Sox began 2002 under the auspices of former Marlins owner John Henry, who bought the team in January, ending 69 years of stewardship under the Yawkey family name.

Henry fired general manager Dan Duquette and manager Joe Kerrigan during spring training, naming Mike Port interim GM and Grady Little manager. They inherited a team full of questions, beginning with the health of Pedro Martinez, Nomar Garciaparra and Jason Varitek.

The Red Sox seemed like longshots in the American League East, especially after four straight second-place finishes to the Yankees, who had retooled by signing AL MVP Jason Giambi.

But a 40-17 start—spearheaded by new ace Derek Lowe, the return of Martinez and Garciaparra and the leadoff skills of free agent Johnny Damon—had Sox fans thinking World Series.

Then it all fell apart. Boston endured a soberingly average stretch from June 6-Sept. 6, going 38-44 and never winning or losing more than five in a row. The Yankees, Angels and Athletics streaked past, and Boston's 93-69 record left it six games out of the wild card.

It was a depressing finish to a season that saw so much go right. The Red Sox finished second in batting (.277) in the American League, and third in ERA (3.75) and run differential (plus-194). In addition to batting champion Manny Ramirez, they boasted seven all-stars, a pair of 20-game winners and a 40-save closer.

But none of it could lift a team that went 13-23 in one run games, 5-13 in interleague play, and 77-66 against everyone not named the Tampa Bay Devil Rays.

A faulty bullpen sat atop the list of culprits. The formerly reliable Rich Garces pitched himself into unemployment. Tim Wakefield and Casey Fossum moved to the rotation. Rolando Arrojo looked disinterested, Willie

Pedro Martinez   Kevin Youkilis

PLAYERS OF THE YEAR

MAJOR LEAGUE: Pedro Martinez, rhp

Red Sox fans wondered whether Pedro's period of dominance was over after two ugly starts early in the 2002 season. Winning the major league ERA and America League strikeout titles answered that with a resounding "No".

MINOR LEAGUE: Kevin Youkilis, 3b

Youkilis doesn't ooze tools, but he always seems to be on base—ranking fifth in the minors in on-base percentage and second among Red Sox farmhands in average and RBIs.

Banks and Wayne Gomes appeared chiefly in blowouts, and $6 million acquisition Dustin Hermanson owned a relief ERA of 9.00.

The lone reliable setup arm belonged to lefty Alan Embree, acquired from the Padres in June. Embree's effectiveness led to overuse. He began his Red Sox career by pitching seven times in 10 days, landing on the disabled list with a sore elbow. Closer Ugueth Urbina posted a 1-6 record but saved 40 games and generally proved reliable.

The team remained relatively injury free, with the major exception being Ramirez, who missed 40 games after breaking his left index finger with an ill-advised headfirst slide into home against the Mariners May 11.

There were plenty of individual highlights. Lowe recovered from a disastrous 2001 as closer to blossom as a starter. He no-hit the Devil Rays April 27, started the All-Star Game and won 11 games after losses.

Martinez rebounded as well. His career in doubt after a partially torn rotator cuff, he went 20-4 and led the American League in ERA and strikeouts. He also proved durable, making 30 starts.

Garciaparra returned from wrist surgery to hit .310, co-lead the league in doubles, and drive in a team-best 120 runs.

Ramirez won his first batting title, but ignited a firestorm when he didn't leave the batter's box after hitting a comebacker against the Devil Rays in September. The play summed up the Red Sox' season, which was full of individual success, but short on team achievement.

Two developments highlighted the minor league season. The Red Sox traded six pitchers in deals for Floyd, Embree and Bobby Howry, including top prospect Seung Song. On the plus side, shortstop Hanley Ramirez earned the top prospect nod in two leagues, catapulting himself to a place among the game's most exciting youngsters.

ORGANIZATION LEADERS

BATTING

*AVG	Hanley Ramirez, GCL Red Sox/Lowell	.352
R	Freddy Sanchez, Pawtucket/Trenton	85
H	Freddy Sanchez, Pawtucket/Trenton	157
TB	Freddy Sanchez, Pawtucket/Trenton	215
2B	Kelly Shoppach, Sarasota	35
3B	Tonayne Brown, Trenton	9
HR	Shane Andrews, Pawtucket	22
RBI	Wilton Veras, Pawtucket/Trenton	83
BB	Kevin Youkilis, Trenton/Sarsota	93
SO	Steve Lomasney, Pawtucket/Trenton	148
SB	Freddy Sanchez, Pawtucket/Trenton	24

PITCHING

W	Isauro Pineda, Trenton	9
	Alex Solano, Sarasota	9
L	Matt Thompson, Trenton	14
#ERA	Brian Adams, Trenton/Sarasota	2.11
G	Tim Young, Pawtucket	57
CG	Four tied at	2
SV	Jason Howell, Augusta	16
IP	Don Wengert, Pawtucket	169
BB	Anastacio Martinez, Trenton	75
SO	Manny Delcarmen, Augusta	136

*Minimum 250 At-Bats #Minimum 75 Innings

BOSTON
RED SOX

Manager: Grady Little

2002 Record: 93-69, .574 (2nd, AL East).

BATTING	AVG	G	AB	R	H	2B	3B	HR	RBI	BB	SO	SB	CS	SLG	OBP	B	T	HT	WT	DOB	1st Yr	Resides
Agbayani, Benny	.297	13	37	5	11	1	0	0	8	6	5	0	0	.324	.395	R	R	6-0	220	12-28-71	1993	Aiea, Hawaii
Andrews, Shane	.077	7	13	2	1	1	0	0	1	3	0	0	0	.154	.200	R	R	6-1	220	8-28-71	1990	Carlsbad, N.M.
Baerga, Carlos	.286	73	182	17	52	11	0	2	19	7	20	6	0	.379	.316	S	R	5-11	210	11-4-68	1986	Toa Alda, P.R.
Brown, Kevin	.000	2	1	0	0	0	0	0	0	0	0	0	0	.000	.000	R	R	6-2	230	4-21-73	1994	Mt. Vernon, Ind.
Clark, Tony	.207	90	275	25	57	12	1	3	29	21	57	0	0	.291	.265	S	R	6-7	240	6-15-72	1990	Glendale, Ariz.
Damon, Johnny	.286	154	623	118	178	34	11	14	63	65	70	31	6	.443	.356	L	L	6-2	190	11-5-73	1992	Overland Park, Kan.
Daubach, Brian	.266	137	444	62	118	24	2	20	78	51	126	2	1	.464	.348	L	R	6-1	230	2-11-72	1990	Belleville, Ill.
Diaz, Juan	.286	4	7	2	2	1	0	1	2	1	2	0	0	.857	.375	R	R	6-2	260	2-19-74	1996	Santo Domingo, D.R.
Floyd, Cliff	.316	47	171	30	54	21	0	7	18	15	28	4	0	.561	.374	L	R	6-4	230	12-5-72	1991	Weston, Ill.
Garciaparra, Nomar	.310	156	635	101	197	56	5	24	120	41	63	5	2	.528	.352	R	R	6-0	190	7-23-73	1994	Boston, Mass.
Henderson, Ricky	.223	72	179	40	40	6	1	5	16	38	47	8	2	.352	.369	R	L	5-10	190	12-25-58	1976	Hillsborough, Calif.
Hillenbrand, Shea	.293	156	634	94	186	43	4	18	83	25	95	4	2	.459	.330	R	R	6-1	210	7-27-75	1996	Toluca Lake, Calif.
Merloni, Lou	.247	84	194	28	48	12	2	4	18	20	35	1	2	.392	.332	R	R	5-11	200	4-6-71	1993	Framingham, Mass.
Mirabelli, Doug	.225	57	151	17	34	7	0	7	25	17	33	0	0	.411	.312	R	R	6-1	220	10-18-70	1992	Orlando, Fla.
Nelson, Bryant	.265	25	34	6	9	3	0	0	2	4	1	1	1	.353	.342	S	R	5-10	200	1-27-74	1994	Crossett, Ark.
Nixon, Trot	.256	152	532	81	136	36	3	24	94	65	109	4	2	.470	.338	L	L	6-2	210	4-11-74	1993	Wilmington, N.C.
Offerman, Jose	.232	72	237	39	55	10	0	4	27	33	29	8	5	.325	.325	S	R	6-0	190	11-11-68	1988	Toluca Lake, Calif.
Ramirez, Manny	.349	120	436	84	152	31	0	33	107	73	85	0	0	.647	.450	R	R	6-0	200	5-30-72	1991	Fort Lauderdale, Fla.
Sanchez, Freddy	.188	12	16	3	3	0	0	0	2	2	3	0	0	.188	.278	R	R	5-11	180	12-21-77	2000	Burbank, Calif.
Sanchez, Rey	.286	107	357	46	102	12	3	1	38	17	31	2	2	.345	.318	R	R	5-9	170	10-5-67	1986	Trujillo Alto, P.R.
Varitek, Jason	.266	132	467	58	124	27	1	10	61	41	95	4	3	.392	.332	S	R	6-2	230	4-11-72	1995	Suwanee, Ga.

PITCHING	W	L	ERA	G	GS	CG	SV	IP	H	R	ER	BB	SO	AVG	B	T	HT	WT	DOB	1st Yr	Resides
Arrojo, Rolando	4	3	4.98	29	8	0	1	81	83	47	45	27	51	.269	R	R	6-4	230	7-18-68	1997	St. Petersburg, Fla.
Banks, Willie	2	1	3.23	29	0	0	1	39	32	15	14	14	26	.222	R	R	6-1	200	2-27-69	1987	Miami, Fla.
Burkett, John	13	8	4.53	29	29	1	0	173	199	93	87	50	124	.287	R	R	6-3	210	11-28-64	1983	Southlake, Texas
Castillo, Frank	6	15	5.07	36	23	0	1	163	174	101	92	58	112	.274	R	R	6-1	200	4-1-69	1987	Cave Creek, Ariz.
Embree, Alan	1	2	2.97	32	0	0	2	33	24	12	11	11	43	.203	L	L	6-2	190	1-23-70	1990	Vancouver, Wash.
Fossum, Casey	5	4	3.46	43	12	0	1	107	113	56	41	30	101	.268	S	L	6-1	160	1-9-78	1999	Waco, Texas
Garces, Rich	0	1	7.59	26	0	0	0	21	21	20	18	12	16	.272	R	R	6-0	250	5-18-71	1988	Maracay, Venez.
Gomes, Wayne	1	2	4.64	20	0	0	1	21	20	11	11	12	15	.240	R	R	6-2	220	1-15-73	1993	Cherry Hill, N.J.
Hancock, Josh	0	1	3.68	3	1	0	0	7	5	3	3	2	6	.200	R	R	6-3	210	4-11-78	1998	Tupelo, Miss.
Haney, Chris	0	0	4.20	24	0	0	1	30	32	14	14	10	15	.273	L	L	6-3	210	11-16-68	1990	Keswick, Mass.
Hermanson, Dustin	1	1	7.77	12	1	0	0	22	35	19	19	7	13	.353	R	R	6-2	200	12-21-72	1994	Phoenix, Ariz.
Howry, Bob	1	3	5.00	20	0	0	0	18	22	15	10	4	14	.305	L	R	6-5	220	8-4-73	1994	Glendale, Ariz.
2-team (47 Chicago)	3	5	4.19	67	0	0	0	69	67	37	32	21	45	.261							
Kim, Sun-Woo	2	0	7.45	15	2	0	0	29	34	24	24	7	18	.288	R	R	6-2	180	9-4-77	1997	Seoul, Korea
Lowe, Derek	21	8	2.58	32	32	1	0	220	166	65	63	48	127	.210	R	R	6-6	210	6-1-73	1991	Fort Myers, Fla.
Martinez, Pedro	20	4	2.26	30	30	2	0	199	144	62	50	40	239	.198	R	R	5-11	180	10-25-71	1988	Santo Domingo, D.R.
Oliver, Darren	4	5	4.66	14	9	1	0	58	70	30	30	27	32	.316	R	L	6-2	220	10-6-70	1988	Southlake, Texas
Urbina, Ugueth	1	6	3.00	61	0	0	40	60	44	21	20	20	71	.201	R	R	6-0	200	2-15-74	1991	Ocumare Del Tuy, Venez.
Wakefield, Tim	11	5	2.81	45	15	0	3	163	121	57	51	51	134	.204	R	R	6-2	210	8-2-66	1988	Melbourne, Fla.

FIELDING

Catcher	PCT	G	PO	A	E	DP	PB
Brown	1.000	2	1	0	0	0	0
Mirabelli	1.000	50	285	30	0	3	10
Varitek	.996	127	912	54	4	8	10

First Base	PCT	G	PO	A	E	DP
Andrews	1.000	2	6	1	0	1
Clark	.992	85	653	58	6	54
Daubach	.990	60	443	30	5	37
Diaz	1.000	1	8	0	0	0
Merloni	1.000	3	1	0	0	0
Offerman	.994	41	309	29	2	35

Second Base	PCT	G	PO	A	E	DP
Baerga	.983	17	25	32	1	4
Merloni	.988	66	99	142	3	28
Nelson	.964	11	11	16	1	2
F. Sanchez	1.000	5	4	9	0	1
R. Sanchez	.991	100	151	272	4	61

Third Base	PCT	G	PO	A	E	DP
Andrews	1.000	4	3	6	0	1
Baerga	.000	1	0	0	0	0

Hillenbrand	.943	156	100	283	23	27
Merloni	.967	8	5	24	1	1

Shortstop	PCT	G	PO	A	E	DP
Garciaparra	.965	154	220	467	25	92
Merloni	.857	5	2	4	1	1
F. Sanchez	1.000	5	5	3	0	1
Sanchez	.972	10	9	26	1	3

Outfield	PCT	G	PO	A	E	DP
Agbayani	.962	13	24	1	1	0
Andrews	.000	1	0	0	0	0
Damon	.997	151	352	7	1	2
Daubach	1.000	48	64	3	0	0
Floyd	.977	26	41	1	1	1
Henderson	.946	54	83	4	5	0
Merloni	.000	2	0	0	0	0
Nelson	1.000	11	14	1	0	0
Nixon	.984	152	293	7	5	3
Offerman	.667	2	2	0	1	0
Ramirez	.959	68	110	6	5	1

LARRY GOREN

Nomar Garciaparra

Director, Player Development: Kent Qualls.

Class	Farm Team	League	W	L	Pct.	Finish*	Manager	First Yr.
AAA	Pawtucket (R.I.) Red Sox	International	60	84	.417	11th(14)	Buddy Bailey	1973
AA	Trenton (N.J.) Thunder	Eastern	63	77	.450	t-9th (12)	Ron Johnson	1995
High A	Sarasota (Fla.) Red Sox	Florida State	62	74	.456	10th (12)	Billy Gardner	1994
Low A	Augusta (Ga.) GreenJackets	South Atlantic	69	67	.507	8th (16)	Arnie Beyeler	1999
SS A	Lowell (Mass.) Spinners	New York-Penn	34	41	.453	8th (14)	Mike Boulanger	1996
Rookie	Fort Myers (Fla.) Red Sox	Gulf Coast	26	34	.433	11th (14)	John Sanders	1993

*Finish in overall standings (No. of teams in league)

PAWTUCKET RED SOX — Class AAA

INTERNATIONAL LEAGUE

BATTING	AVG	G	AB	R	H	2B	3B	HR	RBI	BB	SO	SB	CS	SLG	OBP	B	T	HT	WT	DOB	1st Yr	Resides
Abbott, Jeff	.283	100	367	47	104	28	1	10	41	25	44	4	2	.447	.331	R	L	6-2	200	8-17-72	1994	Dunwoody, Ga.
Agbayani, Benny	.176	5	17	1	3	1	0	0	2	3	6	0	0	.235	.300	R	R	6-0	220	12-28-71	1993	Aiea, Hawaii
Andrews, Shane	.256	116	390	61	100	19	1	22	63	52	123	1	1	.479	.346	R	R	6-1	220	8-28-71	1990	Carlsbad, N.M.
Barker, Glen	.163	15	43	6	7	3	0	0	1	5	10	1	1	.233	.265	S	R	5-10	180	5-10-71	1993	Albany, N.Y.
Betts, Todd	.291	121	416	60	121	16	2	14	45	63	58	3	5	.440	.392	L	R	6-0	180	6-24-73	1993	Scarborough, Ontario
Brown, Kevin	.243	70	226	29	55	13	1	6	21	18	60	0	0	.389	.299	R	R	6-2	230	4-21-73	1994	Mt. Vernon, Ind.
2-team (6 Durham)	.236	76	246	33	58	13	1	8	25	20	66	0	0	.394	.293							
Buford, Damon	.161	10	31	5	5	1	0	1	2	4	5	1	0	.290	.257	R	R	5-10	180	6-12-70	1990	Dallas, Texas
Clemente, Edgard	.264	63	231	28	61	12	0	7	31	14	63	5	0	.407	.309	R	R	5-11	180	12-15-75	1993	Bayamon, P.R.
Coleman, Michael	.235	65	204	27	48	7	1	9	22	29	56	0	0	.412	.332	R	R	5-11	210	8-16-75	1994	Antioch, Tenn.
Diaz, Juan	.260	104	389	47	101	14	0	20	53	24	105	0	0	.450	.305	R	R	6-2	260	2-19-74	1996	Santo Domingo, D.R.
DiSarcina, Gary	.243	35	144	23	35	11	2	1	9	8	15	0	1	.368	.297	R	R	6-2	200	11-19-67	1988	East Sandwich, Mass.
Lofton, James	.251	81	299	32	75	6	2	4	27	13	54	9	3	.324	.287	S	R	5-10	200	3-6-74	1993	Los Angeles, Calif.
Lomasney, Steve	.067	12	30	1	2	1	0	0	1	2	15	0	0	.100	.152	R	R	6-0	190	8-29-77	1995	Peabody, Mass.
Merloni, Lou	.200	8	25	1	5	2	0	0	2	1	3	0	0	.280	.250	R	R	5-10	200	4-6-71	1993	Framingham, Mass.
Morris, Warren	.305	43	164	21	50	11	2	3	21	11	22	2	1	.451	.352	L	R	5-11	180	1-11-74	1996	Alexandria, La.
Nelson, Bryant	.296	60	223	25	66	8	3	8	24	14	19	1	5	.466	.340	S	R	5-10	200	1-27-74	1994	Crossett, Ark.
Ramirez, Manny	.100	11	30	2	3	1	0	1	2	8	9	0	0	.233	.308	R	R	6-0	200	5-30-72	1991	Fort Lauderdale, Fla.
Rodriguez, Luis	.228	82	259	24	59	12	5	7	31	12	62	0	3	.394	.264	R	R	5-11	180	1-3-74	1991	Tampa, Fla.
Ryan, Rob	.266	63	233	44	62	16	3	10	31	36	39	4	1	.489	.375	L	L	5-11	190	6-24-73	1996	Renton, Wash.
Salzano, Jerry	.250	2	8	1	2	0	0	1	1	0	3	0	0	.625	.250	R	R	6-0	170	10-27-74	1992	Trenton, N.J.
Sanchez, Freddy	.301	45	183	25	55	10	1	4	28	12	21	5	3	.432	.350	R	R	5-11	170	12-21-77	2000	Burbank, Calif.
Santos, Angel	.260	102	350	40	91	15	2	10	50	38	70	12	8	.400	.332	S	R	5-11	170	8-14-79	1997	Cayey, P.R.
Sergio, Tom	.000	1	4	0	0	0	0	0	0	0	0	0	0	.000	.000	L	R	5-9	170	6-27-75	1997	Norristown, Pa.
Stenson, Dernell	.250	107	368	44	92	20	1	9	36	37	96	4	3	.383	.321	L	L	6-1	230	6-17-78	1996	La Grange, Ga.
Veras, Wilton	.255	57	200	13	51	10	1	0	28	11	11	0	0	.315	.294	R	R	6-2	200	1-19-78	1995	Santo Domingo, D.R.

PITCHING	W	L	ERA	G	GS	CG	SV	IP	H	R	ER	BB	SO	AVG	B	T	HT	WT	DOB	1st Yr	Resides
Banks, Willie	1	2	4.50	6	4	0	1	26	20	14	13	9	15	.215	R	R	6-1	200	2-27-69	1987	Miami, Fla.
Boyd, Jason	1	0	3.94	9	0	0	1	16	13	7	7	9	15	.213	R	R	6-3	170	2-23-73	1994	Edwardsville, Ill.
Brewington, Jamie	5	6	4.43	18	16	0	0	91	86	55	45	35	61	.244	R	R	6-4	190	9-28-71	1992	Phoenix, Ariz.
Brownson, Mark	0	1	4.50	3	1	0	0	6	4	3	3	4	2	.200	L	R	6-2	180	6-17-75	1994	Sun Lakes, Ariz.
Burkett, John	0	1	11.57	1	1	0	0	2	4	3	3	1	2	.400	R	R	6-3	210	11-28-64	1983	Southlake, Texas
Cho, Jin Ho	3	6	5.63	20	8	0	2	54	74	37	34	12	20	.331	R	R	6-3	220	8-16-75	1998	Yeok, South Korea
Crawford, Paxton	2	3	5.55	9	9	0	0	47	61	33	29	19	22	.317	R	R	6-3	210	8-4-77	1995	Morrilton, Ark.
Drumright, Mike	1	1	6.75	7	3	0	0	25	35	25	19	8	20	.309	L	R	6-4	210	4-19-74	1995	Valley Center, Kan.
Elmore, Chris	0	3	6.37	7	7	0	0	30	43	25	21	12	30	.335	L	L	6-1	190	4-28-77	2000	Virginia Beach, Va.
Erdos, Todd	4	4	3.22	52	2	0	10	78	87	31	28	21	48	.279	R	R	6-1	200	11-21-73	1992	Meadville, Pa.
Fossum, Casey	0	3	3.96	5	3	1	0	25	34	15	11	6	28	.336	S	L	6-1	160	1-9-78	1999	Waco, Texas
Gomes, Wayne	5	2	2.64	42	0	0	4	72	61	30	21	28	54	.229	R	R	6-2	220	1-15-73	1993	Cherry Hill, N.J.
Hancock, Josh	4	2	3.45	8	8	0	0	44	39	20	17	26	34	.234	R	R	6-3	210	4-11-78	1998	Tupelo, Miss.
Haney, Chris	2	0	2.79	25	0	0	4	29	27	9	9	10	31	.241	L	L	6-3	210	11-16-68	1990	Keswick, Mass.
Hasselhoff, Derek	0	4	5.04	39	0	0	11	45	47	29	25	8	30	.268	L	L	6-2	180	10-10-73	1995	Pasadena, Md.
Hazlett, Andy	1	0	1.59	5	0	0	0	11	6	2	2	2	6	.153	L	L	6-3	180	8-27-75	1997	The Dalles, Ore.
Heams, Shane	1	0	5.52	11	0	0	0	15	14	9	9	12	8	.245	R	R	6-1	210	9-29-75	1994	Lambertville, Mich.
Hermanson, Dustin	0	1	2.63	5	3	0	0	14	9	5	4	7	11	.191	R	R	6-2	200	12-21-72	1994	Phoenix, Ariz.
Kim, Sun-Woo	4	2	3.18	8	8	1	0	45	34	18	16	16	37	.206	R	R	6-2	180	9-4-77	1997	Seoul, Korea
Kusiewicz, Mike	2	5	4.99	10	10	0	0	49	52	31	27	21	42	.261	R	L	6-2	180	11-1-76	1995	Nepean, Ontario
McLeary, Marty	1	1	7.32	18	1	0	0	36	44	30	29	23	19	.312	R	R	6-5	220	10-26-74	1997	Mansfield, Ohio
Michalak, Chris	5	9	5.77	17	16	0	0	94	125	68	60	31	52	.322	L	L	6-2	190	1-4-71	1993	Keller, Texas
Moreno, Juan	0	0	10.13	3	0	0	0	3	2	4	3	3	1	.200	L	L	6-1	200	2-28-75	1994	Cagua, Venez.
Pena, Juan	4	11	5.33	17	16	1	0	83	84	51	49	36	59	.264	R	R	6-5	210	6-27-77	1995	Carol City, Fla.
Shibilo, Andy	0	1	5.19	6	0	0	0	9	9	7	5	2	9	.264	R	R	6-7	220	9-16-76	1998	Belleville, N.J.
Spencer, Corey	0	0	5.81	15	0	0	0	26	29	18	17	15	23	.271	L	L	6-1	200	9-4-76	1999	Shrewsbury, Mass.
Viera, Rolando	0	0	2.70	3	0	0	0	7	6	2	2	4	6	.230	L	L	5-10	180	8-1-73	2001	Tampa, Fla.
Wallace, Jeff	0	1	6.57	23	0	0	0	25	30	20	18	14	19	.303	L	L	6-2	240	4-12-76	1995	Louisville, Ohio
Wengert, Don	8	12	4.53	29	28	1	0	169	218	95	85	33	74	.313	R	R	6-3	200	11-6-69	1992	Des Moines, Iowa
Young, Tim	5	3	3.59	57	0	0	4	73	56	34	29	37	63	.215	L	L	5-9	170	10-15-73	1996	Bristol, Fla.

FIELDING

Catcher	PCT	G	PO	A	E	DP	PB
Brown	.991	67	395	35	4	1	1
Lomasney	.966	12	57	0	2	0	3
Rodriguez	.987	77	408	38	6	4	14

First Base	PCT	G	PO	A	E	DP
Andrews	1.000	14	113	9	0	9
Betts	.991	86	714	65	7	55
Diaz	.986	51	401	22	6	42

Second Base	PCT	G	PO	A	E	DP
Andrews	1.000	1	0	1	0	0
DiSarcina	.981	30	72	79	3	18
Morris	.989	24	38	53	1	19
Nelson	.937	19	34	40	5	9

Sanchez .... .945 11 17 35 3 7
Santos .... .967 67 147 179 11 37

Third Base	PCT	G	PO	A	E	DP
Andrews	.951	79	54	141	10	10
Merloni	1.000	1	3	1	6	0
Nelson	.826	9	10	9	4	1
Rodriguez	.000	1	0	0	0	0
Santos	1.000	5	2	12	0	2
Veras	.930	54	34	99	10	11

Shortstop	PCT	G	PO	A	E	DP
Lofton	.986	77	120	232	5	41

Merloni 1.000 3 6 7 0 3
Nelson .... .935 6 12 17 2 3
Sanchez .... .942 37 53 108 10 16
Santos .... .952 29 43 97 7 17

Outfield	PCT	G	PO	A	E	DP
Abbott	.994	85	173	2	1	2
Agbayani	1.000	4	7	0	0	0
Andrews	1.000	8	15	0	0	0
Barker	.970	15	32	0	1	0
Buford	.967	10	28	1	1	1
Clemente	1.000	60	124	7	0	0

Coleman .... .977 58 121 5 3 0
Lofton 1.000 4 10 0 0 0
Merloni 1.000 1 2 0 0 0
Morris 1.000 11 11 0 0 0
Nelson .... .968 25 59 2 2 0
Ramirez 1.000 4 3 0 0 0
Rodriguez 1.000 4 1 0 0 0
Ryan 1.000 62 145 1 0 0
Salzano 1.000 2 3 0 0 0
Sergio 1.000 1 2 0 0 0
Stenson .... .957 101 191 10 9 0

TRENTON THUNDER — Class AA

EASTERN LEAGUE

BATTING	AVG	G	AB	R	H	2B	3B	HR	RBI	BB	SO	SB	CS	SLG	OBP	B	T	HT	WT	DOB	1st Yr	Resides
Ahumada, Alex	.243	66	185	31	45	4	3	1	19	16	42	10	3	.314	.312	R	R	6-1	170	1-20-79	1996	Culiacan, Mexico
Brown, Tonayne	.265	125	472	70	125	22	9	12	59	35	86	12	16	.426	.319	R	L	5-11	190	8-24-77	1998	Tallahassee, Fla.
Capista, Aaron	.247	56	174	22	43	10	2	2	10	15	26	5	2	.362	.311	S	R	6-2	180	5-31-79	1997	Shorewood, Ill.
Dominique, Andy	.271	103	361	40	98	21	1	8	51	36	60	2	1	.402	.347	R	R	6-0	220	10-30-75	1997	Granada Hills, Calif.
Fischer, Mark	.145	43	131	17	19	5	0	3	9	12	44	2	1	.252	.215	R	R	6-1	200	4-15-76	1997	Marietta, Ga.
French, Anton	.247	20	85	15	21	2	1	7	5	24	13	6	.353	.297	S	R	5-11	170	7-25-75	1993	St. Louis, Mo.
Hage, Tom	.250	27	64	7	16	3	0	1	9	12	16	0	1	.344	.372	L	R	6-4	220	8-2-74	1996	Bronx, N.Y.
Headley, Justin	.268	112	377	60	101	23	1	11	56	43	61	4	7	.422	.350	L	L	6-2	200	4-27-76	1998	Memphis, Tenn.
Larned, Drew	.250	1	4	1	1	0	1	1	0	1	1	0	0	1.000	.250	R	R	6-0	190	11-13-75	1998	Concord, Ohio
Leon, Carlos	.279	81	265	44	74	11	2	1	20	27	31	15	9	.347	.353	S	R	5-10	160	8-31-79	1997	Cabimas, Venez.
Lofton, James	.236	35	127	15	30	9	0	0	11	12	28	1	2	.307	.307	S	R	5-10	200	3-6-74	1993	Los Angeles, Calif.
Lomasney, Steve	.210	109	338	43	71	17	3	8	56	55	133	5	5	.349	.333	R	R	6-0	190	8-29-77	1995	Peabody, Mass.
Mooney, Dan	.113	23	62	4	7	1	0	0	4	0	21	0	0	.129	.127	R	R	6-1	200	2-14-77	2000	Forked River, N.J.
Morales, Andy	.231	16	39	2	9	2	0	2	7	7	2	1	.282	.348	R	R	6-1	200	12-3-74	2001	Lima, Peru
Nieves, Raul	.265	13	34	2	9	2	0	0	3	4	6	0	1	.324	.342	S	R	6-2	180	1-1-79	2000	Barranquitas, P.R.
Ramos, Kelly	.138	10	29	0	4	0	0	0	3	2	8	0	0	.138	.194	R	R	6-0	210	10-15-76	1994	San Pedro de Macoris, D.R.
Rose, Mike	.103	10	29	1	3	1	1	0	0	5	7	0	0	.207	.235	S	R	6-1	180	8-25-76	1995	Elk Grove, Calif.
Salzano, Jerry	.252	121	437	70	110	27	0	11	66	53	74	19	5	.389	.338	R	R	6-0	170	10-27-74	1992	Trenton, N.J.
Sanchez, Freddy	.328	80	311	60	102	23	1	3	38	37	45	19	3	.437	.403	R	R	5-11	180	12-21-77	2000	Burbank, Calif.
Sergio, Tom	.272	123	482	77	131	28	3	14	75	46	82	6	6	.429	.345	L	R	5-9	170	6-27-75	1997	Norristown, Pa.
Sherrod, Justin	.255	70	243	37	62	19	1	9	47	29	81	8	4	.453	.343	R	R	6-2	200	1-11-78	2000	Boynton Beach, Fla.
Smith, Will	.000	2	5	0	0	0	0	0	0	2	0	0	.000	.000	R	R	5-11	180	5-7-77	2000	Prattville, Ala.
Veras, Wilton	.336	68	271	40	91	22	1	6	55	23	29	0	2	.491	.390	R	R	6-2	200	1-19-78	1995	Santo Domingo, D.R.
Youkilis, Kevin	.344	44	160	34	55	10	0	6	26	31	18	5	4	.500	.462	R	R	6-1	220	3-15-79	2001	Cincinnati, Ohio

PITCHING	W	L	ERA	G	GS	CG	SV	IP	H	R	ER	BB	SO	AVG	B	T	HT	WT	DOB	1st Yr	Resides
Adams, Brian	1	0	2.90	16	1	0	1	31	29	15	10	18	17	.245	L	L	6-3	190	10-2-77	2000	Bishopville, S.C.
Ambrose, John	2	2	7.08	10	3	0	0	20	26	18	16	17	25	.298	R	R	6-5	180	11-1-74	1994	Evansville, Ind.
Crawford, Paxton	1	0	0.00	1	1	0	0	6	3	1	0	1	6	.136	R	R	6-3	210	8-4-77	1995	Morrilton, Ark.
De La Rosa, Jorge	4	4	5.50	4	4	0	0	18	17	12	11	9	15	.239	L	L	6-1	190	4-5-81	1998	San Nicolas, Mexico
Dickinson, Rodney	0	1	7.20	4	0	0	0	5	7	5	4	4	4	.304	R	R	5-10	170	11-9-75	1998	Jonesboro, Ga.
Elmore, Chris	8	2	2.34	14	13	2	0	85	76	27	22	22	57	.242	L	L	6-1	190	4-28-77	2000	Virginia Beach, Va.
Fontana, Tony	2	2	6.23	11	0	0	0	22	26	16	15	5	15	.295	R	R	6-2	170	5-21-79	2000	Parma Heights, Ohio
Francisco, Frank	2	2	5.63	9	0	0	0	16	10	13	10	16	18	.172	R	R	6-2	170	9-11-79	1997	Santo Domingo, D.R.
Giese, Dan	1	2	3.83	23	0	0	3	49	53	24	21	9	39	.281	R	R	6-3	200	5-19-77	1999	San Clemente, Calif.
Glaser, Eric	2	9	5.70	33	12	0	1	114	145	80	72	32	80	.310	R	R	6-6	230	1-23-78	1997	Fort Thomas, Ky.
Hancock, Josh	3	4	3.61	15	14	2	1	85	82	40	34	18	69	.250	R	R	6-3	210	4-11-78	1998	Tupelo, Miss.
Heams, Shane	4	2	4.02	14	0	0	0	16	12	8	7	16	17	.222	R	R	6-1	210	9-29-75	1994	Lambertville, Mich.
Hill, Terry	6	5	5.96	45	0	0	3	83	108	62	55	36	86	.313	L	L	5-10	170	10-17-75	1998	Thibodaux, La.
Kusiewicz, Mike	5	3	3.29	13	11	0	0	66	58	28	24	12	44	.227	R	L	6-2	180	11-1-76	1995	Nepean, Ontario
Martinez, Anastacio	5	12	5.31	27	27	0	0	139	152	98	82	75	127	.276	R	R	6-2	180	11-3-78	1998	Santo Domingo, D.R.
McLeary, Marty	0	2	4.86	11	0	0	0	17	20	12	9	8	10	.312	R	R	6-5	220	10-26-74	1997	Mansfield, Ohio
Nelson, Joe	0	0	14.54	4	0	0	0	4	9	8	7	2	3	.409	R	R	6-2	180	10-25-74	1996	Alameda, Calif.
Pineda, Isauro	9	13	5.65	28	28	2	0	156	172	109	98	68	121	.288	R	R	6-0	160	11-10-78	1997	Mazatlan, Mexico
Shibilo, Andy	0	1	3.19	21	0	0	6	31	27	11	11	7	34	.232	R	R	6-2	220	9-16-76	1998	Belleville, N.J.
Song, Seung	7	7	4.39	21	21	0	0	109	106	61	53	37	116	.256	R	R	6-1	190	6-29-80	1999	Pusan, South Korea
Spencer, Corey	2	4	5.59	32	2	0	7	48	60	34	30	25	49	.301	L	L	6-1	220	9-4-76	1999	Shrewsbury, Mass.
Viera, Rolando	5	1	4.89	45	3	0	10	77	87	50	42	34	44	.287	L	L	5-10	180	6-1-73	2001	Tampa, Fla.
Villegas, Felix	1	2	3.20	12	0	0	0	20	16	9	7	13	12	.228	R	R	6-2	200	8-8-78	2000	San Juan, P.R.

FIELDING

Catcher	PCT	G	PO	A	E	DP	PB
Dominique	1.000	14	83	9	0	0	1
Larned	1.000	1	9	1	0	0	0
Lomasney	.983	100	675	66	13	7	12
Mooney	.983	20	96	19	2	1	3
Ramos	.953	10	80	2	4	0	1
Rose	1.000	10	71	14	0	2	0

First Base	PCT	G	PO	A	E	DP
Capista	1.000	9	50	6	0	8
Dominique	.990	81	604	59	7	54
Hage	.994	24	150	8	1	7
Headley	.966	8	55	2	2	6
Salzano	1.000	37	264	20	0	31
Sergio	1.000	1	9	1	0	1

Second Base	PCT	G	PO	A	E	DP
Ahumada	.956	21	36	51	4	11

	PCT	G	PO	A	E	DP
Capista	.957	37	65	70	6	17
Leon	.964	69	129	168	11	54
Nieves	.976	12	12	28	1	4
Salzano	1.000	1	1	1	0	0
Sanchez	.963	11	25	27	2	7

Third Base	PCT	G	PO	A	E	DP
Ahumada	1.000	2	2	4	0	1
Capista	1.000	5	2	10	0	1
Morales	.833	15	7	23	6	5
Salzano	.957	10	6	16	1	0
Veras	.957	67	43	157	9	10
Youkilis	.916	44	34	86	11	7

Shortstop	PCT	G	PO	A	E	DP
Ahumada	.933	28	41	70	8	11
Capista	.750	3	3	6	3	3
Leon	.860	9	14	23	6	4

	PCT	G	PO	A	E	DP
Lofton	.961	35	54	92	6	19
Sanchez	.953	69	121	165	14	38

Outfield	PCT	G	PO	A	E	DP
Ahumada	.947	12	17	1	1	0
Brown	.985	124	261	3	4	1
Fischer	.942	39	47	2	3	1
French	.944	20	51	0	3	0
Headley	1.000	99	188	4	0	0
Lomasney	1.000	1	1	0	0	0
Mooney	1.000	2	5	0	0	0
Salzano	.978	57	89	2	2	0
Sergio	1.000	22	33	1	0	1
Sherrod	.939	69	128	10	9	1
Smith	.000	2	0	0	0	0

FLORIDA STATE LEAGUE

BATTING	AVG	G	AB	R	H	2B	3B	HR	RBI	BB	SO	SB	CS	SLG	OBP	B	T	HT	WT	DOB	1st Yr	Resides
Ahumada, Alex	.247	24	73	11	18	1	0	1	9	9	18	3	2	.301	.356	R	R	6-1	170	1-20-79	1996	Culiacan, Mexico
Bailie, Stefan	.258	43	159	16	41	8	2	2	26	16	33	1	0	.371	.330	R	R	6-0	210	5-16-80	2001	Mesa, Wash.
Blanco, Tony	.221	65	244	22	54	13	2	6	32	6	70	2	0	.365	.250	R	R	6-1	170	11-10-81	1998	Haina, D.R.
Blasi, Blake	.230	37	139	9	32	4	0	1	9	17	31	5	0	.281	.323	S	R	5-8	160	3-23-79	2000	Wichita, Kan.
2-team (3 Daytona)	.240	40	150	11	36	4	0	1	10	17	33	6	0	.287	.325							
Bowman, Addison	.130	6	23	1	3	1	0	0	2	2	6	0	0	.174	.200	R	R	6-2	200	8-31-79	2002	Dayton, Va.
Brisson, Dustin	.286	34	119	15	34	9	1	5	19	16	20	0	0	.504	.370	L	R	6-2	210	3-18-78	2000	West Palm Beach, Fla.
Catalanotte, Greg	.174	30	92	9	16	3	0	2	4	9	34	1	0	.272	.255	S	R	6-3	210	6-18-77	1999	Glendale, Ariz.
Coleman, Michael	.333	1	3	0	1	0	0	0	0	0	0	0	0	.333	.333	R	R	5-11	210	8-16-75	1994	Antioch, Tenn.
Crespo, Manny	.241	51	158	12	38	7	0	3	18	17	30	0	0	.342	.311	R	R	5-10	180	1-4-79	2000	Miami, Fla.
Dorta, Melvin	.257	99	378	46	97	8	1	0	31	49	54	9	10	.283	.342	R	R	5-11	160	1-15-82	1999	Guscara, Venez.
Durazo, William	.053	7	19	0	1	0	0	0	0	1	3	0	0	.053	.100	S	R	6-1	210	2-15-79	2002	Los Angeles, Calif.
Esposito, Brian	.162	31	99	8	16	5	0	2	7	5	20	0	0	.273	.208	R	R	6-1	190	2-24-79	2000	Willington, Conn.
Garcia, Nick	.143	7	14	1	2	0	0	0	2	0	1	0	1	.143	.250	R	R	5-11	180	5-2-80	1999	Obregon, Mexico
Hattig, John	.247	24	85	6	21	6	0	0	6	7	16	0	0	.318	.301	S	R	6-2	210	2-27-80	1999	Dededo, Guam
Money, Freddie	.234	120	397	56	93	6	1	0	34	35	74	22	9	.254	.306	R	R	5-11	160	1-11-79	2000	Cowarts, Ala.
Mooney, Dan	.194	20	67	3	13	3	0	0	7	0	16	0	0	.239	.225	R	R	6-1	190	2-14-77	2000	Forked River, N.J.
Nieves, Raul	.254	93	299	36	76	11	0	0	19	23	36	5	4	.291	.310	R	R	6-2	180	1-1-79	2000	Barranquitas, P.R.
Perez, Kenny	.251	121	447	53	112	12	4	2	28	51	58	16	5	.309	.329	S	R	6-2	190	9-28-81	2000	Miami, Fla.
Petersen, Ryan	.000	1	0	0	0	0	0	0	0	0	0	0	0	.000	.000	R	R	5-9	170	10-21-77	2001	Plantsville, Conn.
Rodriguez, Carlos	.220	127	472	59	104	27	3	13	59	26	129	6	5	.373	.275	R	R	6-2	210	6-12-77	1998	Louisville, Ky.
Santoro, Pat	.221	27	95	15	21	7	0	4	17	11	34	1	2	.421	.315	R	R	6-0	170	11-9-78	1998	River Forest, Ill.
Shoppach, Kelly	.271	116	414	54	112	35	1	10	66	59	112	2	1	.432	.369	R	R	5-11	210	4-29-80	2001	Fort Worth, Texas
Smith, Will	.256	80	277	51	71	12	5	2	23	63	55	14	5	.357	.413	R	R	5-11	180	5-7-77	2000	Prattville, Ala.
Tarbett, Brent	.091	3	11	1	1	1	0	0	0	1	3	0	0	.182	.167	R	R	6-2	220	11-30-80	2001	Las Vegas, Nev.
Warren, Chris	.146	13	41	1	6	1	1	0	4	5	13	0	0	.220	.271	R	R	6-3	200	9-30-76	1998	Newton Grove, N.C.
Wright, Corey	.180	14	50	0	9	1	1	0	2	4	10	0	1	.240	.255	L	L	5-11	160	11-26-79	1997	La Puente, Calif.
2-team (56 Charlotte)	.189	70	233	25	44	7	3	2	18	27	62	4	1	.270	.286							
Youkilis, Kevin	.295	76	268	45	79	16	0	3	48	49	37	0	2	.388	.422	R	R	6-1	220	3-15-79	2001	Cincinnati, Ohio

PITCHING	W	L	ERA	G	GS	CG	SV	IP	H	R	ER	BB	SO	AVG	B	T	HT	WT	DOB	1st Yr	Resides
Adams, Brian	0	2	1.58	21	0	0	1	46	27	8	8	25	28	.182	L	L	6-3	190	10-2-77	2000	Bishopville, S.C.
An, Byeong	4	7	5.33	25	12	0	0	98	102	64	58	33	58	.267	L	L	6-2	190	7-1-80	2001	Bu Chun City, Korea
Arrojo, Rolando	0	0	0.00	1	0	0	0	2	2	0	0	0	2	.285	R	R	6-4	230	7-18-68	1997	St. Petersburg, Fla.
Baker, Brad	7	1	2.79	12	12	1	0	61	53	22	19	25	65	.233	R	R	6-2	180	11-6-80	1999	Leyden, Mass.
Benitez, Fabricio	1	0	4.94	10	0	0	1	24	32	14	13	4	10	.329	R	R	6-3	170	5-10-78	1997	Santo Domingo, D.R.
Blaney, Matthew	0	0	9.00	1	0	0	0	1	1	2	1	1	1	.250	S	R	5-11	180	5-7-79	2001	Oxnard, Calif.
Byron, Terry	1	1	2.51	8	0	0	0	14	12	4	4	2	20	.244	R	R	6-0	200	3-28-79	1999	St. Croix, VI
2-team (31 Jupiter)	4	3	5.14	39	0	0	0	61	64	37	35	30	49	.275							
Crawford, Paxton	1	0	0.00	1	1	0	0	6	1	0	0	1	5	.055	R	R	6-3	200	8-4-77	1995	Morrilton, Ark.
De la Rosa, Jorge	7	7	3.65	23	23	0	0	121	105	53	49	52	95	.231	L	L	6-1	190	4-5-81	1998	San Nicolas, Mexico
Dumatrait, Phil	0	2	3.86	4	4	0	0	14	10	9	6	15	16	.192	R	L	6-1	170	7-12-81	2000	Bakersfield, Calif.
Fontana, Tony	4	2	2.70	31	4	0	2	73	79	34	22	17	68	.274	R	R	6-3	170	5-21-79	2000	Parma Heights, Ohio
Francisco, Frank	1	5	2.55	16	10	0	0	53	33	19	15	27	58	.185	R	R	6-2	190	9-11-79	1997	Santo Domingo, D.R.
Heams, Shane	0	0	6.75	2	0	0	0	3	2	2	2	4	1	.200	R	R	6-1	210	9-29-75	1994	Lambertville, Mich.
Kumagai, Ryo	2	1	4.50	21	0	0	5	32	29	18	16	17	27	.235	R	R	6-1	180	8-22-79	2002	Tokyo, Japan
Lara, Mauricio	4	2	4.35	23	4	0	0	62	74	36	30	27	43	.310	S	L	5-11	180	4-2-79	1999	Hermosillo, Mexico
Miniel, Rene	7	10	4.51	26	26	0	0	128	125	72	64	39	78	.257	R	R	6-2	170	4-26-79	1998	Santo Domingo, D.R.
Perez, Juan	6	3	3.78	16	14	0	0	67	71	34	28	19	39	.274	R	L	6-0	150	2-10-81	1999	Villa Rivas, D.R.
Perez, Michelandy	0	1	6.00	2	0	0	0	3	2	2	2	3	1	.222	R	R	6-2	200	5-14-79	2001	Hialeah, Fla.
Solano, Alex	9	3	5.33	45	1	0	4	79	83	55	47	35	52	.266	R	R	6-1	150	8-22-78	1997	La Romana, D.R.
Thompson, Matt	6	14	4.21	25	24	0	0	120	131	70	56	44	64	.275	R	R	6-2	200	8-28-81	1999	Boise, Idaho
Valle, Yoiset	7	4	4.37	37	0	0	2	80	98	53	39	24	34	.294	L	L	6-3	200	6-9-78	1996	Miami Lakes, Fla.
Villegas, Felix	1	1	2.52	29	0	0	7	39	24	11	11	13	30	.175	R	R	6-2	200	8-8-78	2000	San Juan, P.R.
Wallace, Jeff	0	1	9.00	1	1	0	0	2	1	2	2	1	1	.142	L	L	6-2	240	4-12-76	1995	Louisville, Ohio
Weatherby, Charles	0	3	4.57	17	0	0	9	22	23	15	11	5	17	.267	R	R	6-0	200	12-23-78	2001	Beaufort, N.C.
Yennaco, Jay	0	1	11.25	4	0	0	0	8	12	10	10	3	10	.333	R	R	6-2	230	11-17-75	1996	Windham, N.H.
Yoo, Byung Mok	0	0	5.87	5	0	0	0	8	10	7	5	3	2	.303	R	R	6-2	180	11-21-79	2001	Seoul, Korea
Zink, Charlie	0	0	.00	4	0	0	0	9	2	1	0	3	11	.071	R	R	6-1	190	8-26-79	2001	El Dorado Hills, Calif.

FIELDING

Catcher	PCT	G	PO	A	E	DP	PB
Crespo	1.000	1	11	1	0	0	2
Durazo	.947	6	36	0	2	0	2
Esposito	.969	21	111	14	4	2	5
Mooney	.992	20	116	10	1	1	4
Shoppach	.986	92	573	62	9	6	15

First Base	PCT	G	PO	A	E	DP
Bailie	.978	39	318	33	8	32
Bowman	.963	3	24	2	1	1
Brisson	.993	33	259	16	2	24
Crespo	1.000	9	56	3	0	6
Durazo	.923	1	11	1	1	1
Esposito	.966	9	52	4	2	6
Hattig	.985	9	62	3	1	8
Youkilis	.984	40	334	27	6	22

Second Base	PCT	G	PO	A	E	DP
Ahumada	.833	2	3	2	1	0
Blasi	.977	28	56	69	3	19
Dorta	.969	99	228	273	16	57
Nieves	.980	11	24	25	1	10

Third Base	PCT	G	PO	A	E	DP
Ahumada	.917	12	7	26	3	1
Blanco	.828	61	32	112	30	9
Blasi	.000	1	0	0	1	0
Crespo	.000	1	0	0	0	0
Hattig	1.000	5	0	14	0	2
Nieves	.886	31	10	52	8	4
Youkilis	.936	33	19	69	6	6

Shortstop	PCT	G	PO	A	E	DP
Blasi	.900	2	6	3	1	2
Garcia	.905	6	7	12	2	3

	PCT	G	PO	A	E	DP
Nieves	.964	33	51	109	6	19
Perez	.948	101	157	277	24	48
Outfield	PCT	G	PO	A	E	DP
Bailie	.000	1	0	0	0	0
Blasi	1.000	1	2	0	0	0
Bowman	1.000	3	7	0	0	0
Catalanotte	1.000	29	51	2	0	0
Crespo	.909	5	10	0	1	0
Money	.984	117	294	6	5	1
Nieves	.972	16	34	1	1	1
Rodriguez	.968	123	252	18	9	4
Santoro	1.000	24	39	1	0	0
Smith	1.000	77	156	5	0	1
Tarbett	1.000	1	0	0	0	0
Warren	.944	10	17	0	1	0
Wright	1.000	14	25	0	0	0

ORGANIZATION STATISTICS

SOUTH ATLANTIC LEAGUE

BATTING	AVG	G	AB	R	H	2B	3B	HR	RBI	BB	SO	SB	CS	SLG	OBP	B	T	HT	WT	DOB	1st Yr	Resides
Aleman, Carlos	.222	6	18	1	4	0	0	0	2	2	4	3	0	.222	.300	R	R	5-11	170	12-21-79	1998	Mao Valverde, D.R.
Barnowski, Bryan	.187	67	235	33	44	14	0	8	32	26	93	0	1	.349	.299	R	R	6-2	200	9-3-80	1999	Granville, Mass.
Bowman, Addison	.500	3	8	1	4	2	0	1	2	2	0	1	0	1.125	.600	R	R	6-2	200	8-31-79	2002	Dayton, Va.
Brackley, Carlos	.061	12	33	1	2	1	0	0	3	10	0	1	.091	.139	R	R	6-2	220	10-10-79	2001	Hamilton, N.J.
Brunner, Ryan	.212	123	424	49	90	22	3	5	45	50	101	0	1	.314	.312	L	L	6-0	220	1-20-79	2001	Charles City, Iowa
Bryan, Jason	.218	16	55	6	12	3	0	2	8	7	23	1	1	.382	.302	R	R	6-2	190	11-18-81	1999	Brooklyn, N.Y.
2-team (1 Savannah)	.220	17	59	6	13	3	0	2	8	7	24	1	1	.373	.299							
Castillo, Osmar	.205	37	117	22	24	1	0	0	7	22	28	4	3	.214	.331	S	R	5-10	170	1-3-79	2002	Manhattan, Kan.
Coffey, Kris	.220	107	368	46	81	4	1	0	18	39	62	15	10	.236	.302	R	R	5-9	170	4-27-79	2001	Newark, Calif.
Cooper, Matt	.238	99	320	41	76	14	0	12	47	42	99	5	2	.394	.362	R	R	6-3	200	10-10-80	2000	Stillwater, Okla.
Cruz, Luis	.188	58	202	16	38	7	1	3	15	9	30	0	2	.277	.221	R	R	6-1	180	2-10-84	2000	Sonora, Mexico
Esposito, Brian	.253	40	154	20	39	5	0	5	15	7	32	0	0	.383	.307	R	R	6-2	190	2-24-79	2000	Willington, Conn.
Figueroa, Daniel	.236	107	377	33	89	20	7	7	51	33	122	2	1	.382	.313	L	L	6-2	170	1-7-79	1998	Santo Domingo, D.R.
Hattig, John	.282	93	347	46	98	20	7	0	56	52	73	1	2	.401	.377	S	R	6-2	210	2-27-80	1999	Dededo, Guam
Kent, Bryan	.239	91	318	35	76	18	1	2	27	17	57	4	2	.321	.293	R	R	6-0	190	6-27-78	2001	Waco, Texas
Lewis, Russell	.283	63	223	24	63	13	2	7	37	12	48	1	1	.453	.322	L	R	5-8	170	3-3-78	2000	Blue Ridge, Texas
Martinez, Edgar	.249	77	265	30	66	13	1	2	29	19	34	1	1	.328	.314	R	R	6-0	160	10-23-81	1998	Guigue, Venez.
Minami, Yasumichi	.000	4	10	1	0	0	0	0	1	5	0	0	.000	.091	R	R	5-11	180	11-20-78	2001	Tokyo, Japan
Nathans, John	.182	20	55	9	10	3	0	0	6	7	13	3	0	.236	.286	R	R	6-1	210	6-10-79	2001	Warwick, N.Y.
Petersen, Ryan	.213	43	127	14	27	4	2	1	10	6	38	12	3	.299	.254	R	R	5-9	170	10-21-77	2001	Plantsville, Conn.
Salazar, Juan	.197	112	350	36	69	5	2	0	22	33	54	11	10	.223	.300	S	R	5-11	150	10-17-81	1999	Barquisimeto, Venez.
Seiber, Antron	.298	76	309	46	92	15	4	2	22	18	68	10	9	.392	.339	R	R	6-1	180	5-19-80	1999	Independence, La.
Youkilis, Kevin	.283	15	53	5	15	5	0	0	6	13	8	0	0	.377	.433	R	R	6-1	220	3-15-79	2001	Cincinnati, Ohio

PITCHING	W	L	ERA	G	GS	CG	SV	IP	H	R	ER	BB	SO	AVG	B	T	HT	WT	DOB	1st Yr	Resides
Benitez, Fabricio		1	0	2.08	3	0	0	0	.4	4	1	1	0	0	.235	R	R	6-3	170	5-18-79	1997	Santo Domingo, D.R.
Delcarmen, Manny	7	8	4.10	26	24	0	0	136	124	77	62	56	136	.241	R	R	6-2	190	2-16-82	2000	Boston, Mass.
Dumatrait, Phil	8	5	2.77	22	22	1	0	120	109	44	37	47	108	.248	R	L	6-2	170	7-12-81	2000	Bakersfield, Calif.
Gabbard, Kason	0	4	1.89	7	7	0	0	38	31	14	8	7	31	.221	L	L	6-4	200	4-8-82	2001	Royal Palm Beach, Fla.
Gamble, Jerome	1	2	1.82	14	14	0	0	49	34	12	10	22	42	.192	R	R	6-2	200	4-5-80	1998	Alexander City, Ala.
Generelli, Dan	1	3	4.30	39	1	0	5	73	86	43	35	32	65	.286	R	R	6-2	200	8-25-80	1999	Hubbardston, Mass.
Hall, Shane	0	1	13.50	6	0	0	0	11	17	16	16	9	3	.386	R	R	6-5	220	6-14-80	2000	Herford, Ariz.
Howell, Jason	7	3	2.11	40	0	0	16	77	73	30	18	16	47	.244	L	L	6-2	190	5-25-79	2001	Millers Creek, N.C.
Huang, Jun-Chung	6	2	5.06	29	1	0	4	59	53	34	33	19	56	.233	R	R	6-0	170	4-25-82	2001	Chau Chou, Taiwan
Kumagai, Ryo	1	1	3.82	21	0	0	0	31	33	18	13	16	21	.277	R	R	6-1	180	8-22-79	2002	Tokyo, Japan
Ledezma, Wil	2	2	3.80	5	5	0	0	24	23	10	10	8	38	.250	L	L	6-3	150	1-21-81	1998	Maracay, Venez.
Pahucki, David	2	1	4.15	4	4	0	0	22	24	10	10	7	15	.285	R	R	6-2	210	10-17-80	2002	New Hampton, N.Y.
Rhodes, Shane	9	6	3.09	31	20	0	0	134	117	57	46	62	97	.244	L	L	6-2	200	1-19-80	2001	Monkton, Md.
Rudrude, Brett	6	7	3.43	34	7	0	3	94	98	47	36	26	73	.272	R	R	6-3	190	1-23-79	2001	Alta Loma, Calif.
Sanchez, Rafael	7	12	5.15	29	22	0	1	129	152	85	74	63	109	.302	R	R	6-2	190	5-24-82	1999	Higuey, D.R.
Thigpen, Josh	6	3	3.92	25	9	0	2	83	76	45	36	45	87	.252	R	R	6-4	190	6-27-82	2000	Killen, Ala.
Weatherby, Charles	4	0	2.92	17	0	0	4	25	20	8	8	5	23	.212	R	R	6-0	200	12-23-78	2001	Beaufort, N.C.
Yoo, Byung Mok	0	2	6.94	8	0	0	1	12	16	10	9	15	8	.347	R	R	6-2	180	11-21-79	2001	Seoul, Korea
Zink, Charlie	1	2	1.68	26	0	0	0	48	42	17	9	16	48	.240	R	R	6-1	190	8-26-79	2002	El Dorado Hills, Calif.

FIELDING

Catcher	PCT	G	PO	A	E	DP	PB
Aleman	1.000	5	28	2	0	0	1
Barnowski	1.000	2	15	1	0	0	1
Bowman	1.000	2	8	4	0	0	0
Esposito	.980	39	307	41	7	4	3
Martinez	.979	71	537	78	13	1	12
Nathans	.986	19	125	14	2	0	4

First Base	PCT	G	PO	A	E	DP
Barnowski	.975	9	74	4	2	8
Brunner	.996	34	259	9	1	23
Cooper	.981	88	673	60	14	69
Hattig	.987	9	68	6	1	7

Second Base	PCT	G	PO	A	E	DP
Castillo	1.000	25	53	68	0	16
Kent	1.000	1	1	1	0	1

	PCT	G	PO	A	E	DP
Lewis	.977	8	12	31	1	6
Minami	1.000	1	1	2	0	0
Petersen	.991	22	45	62	1	8
Salazar	.976	84	166	233	10	56

Third Base	PCT	G	PO	A	E	DP
Castillo	1.000	5	3	9	0	1
Hattig	.929	83	44	153	15	17
Kent	.910	30	20	41	6	2
Lewis	.857	5	4	8	2	0
Minami	.500	1	0	1	1	0
Petersen	1.000	1	0	1	0	0
Youkilis	.913	15	11	31	4	3

Shortstop	PCT	G	PO	A	E	DP
Castillo	.857	1	4	2	1	0
Cruz	.934	58	103	150	18	34

	PCT	G	PO	A	E	DP
Kent	.964	56	95	120	8	25
Minami	1.000	1	1	7	0	2
Petersen	.800	1	2	2	1	1
Salazar	.956	21	32	55	4	11

Outfield	PCT	G	PO	A	E	DP
Brackley	.941	8	14	2	1	0
Brunner	.974	87	138	11	4	1
Bryan	.935	16	29	0	2	0
Coffey	.969	104	181	4	6	1
Figueroa	.942	74	159	3	10	0
Lewis	1.000	41	56	2	0	0
Petersen	1.000	16	21	4	0	0
Seiber	.982	76	163	5	3	1

NEW YORK-PENN LEAGUE

BATTING	AVG	G	AB	R	H	2B	3B	HR	RBI	BB	SO	SB	CS	SLG	OBP	B	T	HT	WT	DOB	1st Yr	Resides
Alcala, Arian	.197	51	178	16	35	5	1	1	18	14	41	0	0	.253	.271	R	R	6-2	200	10-7-79	2002	Hialeah, Fla.
Aleman, Carlos	.243	39	136	19	33	9	0	1	15	16	30	5	1	.331	.316	R	R	5-11	170	12-21-79	1998	Mao Valverde, D.R.
Barclay, Mike	.250	7	16	1	4	1	0	1	3	1	6	0	0	.500	.333	R	R	6-3	170	8-6-79	2002	Tampa, Fla.
Benson, Donald	.169	44	142	16	24	5	0	0	9	21	43	0	2	.204	.285	R	R	5-11	190	9-22-80	2001	Murrieta, Calif.
Boran, Pat	.262	53	191	39	50	9	1	3	22	23	36	8	6	.366	.347	S	R	6-2	200	8-8-80	2002	Pottsville, Pa.
Bowman, Addison	.257	71	272	28	70	16	1	3	22	23	73	3	3	.357	.336	R	R	6-2	200	8-31-79	2002	Dayton, Va.
Brackley, Carlos	.200	4	15	1	3	0	0	1	1	4	0	0	.400	.250	R	R	6-2	220	10-10-79	2001	Hamilton, N.J.
Brown, Dustin	.282	21	78	12	22	3	1	0	12	8	20	1	0	.346	.371	R	R	6-0	180	6-19-82	2001	Fort Collins, Colo.
Buckley, Jim	.197	41	132	15	26	8	1	1	11	12	49	0	0	.295	.269	R	R	6-1	230	9-14-79	2002	Ocean City, N.J.
Campos, Mario	.210	59	229	21	48	15	1	6	29	13	71	2	3	.362	.255	R	R	6-6	230	11-24-78	2001	Miami, Fla.
Castillo, Osmar	.217	8	23	4	5	1	0	0	4	9	2	0	1	.261	.424	S	R	5-10	170	1-3-79	2002	Manhattan, Kan.
Concepcion, Alberto	.225	56	209	29	47	8	4	4	39	31	51	3	1	.359	.354	R	R	6-1	200	4-18-81	2002	El Segundo, Calif.
Goss, Michael	.398	21	83	9	33	2	1	0	10	4	15	14	4	.446	.438	L	L	5-11	210	9-26-80	2002	Louisville, Miss.

BATTING	AVG	G	AB	R	H	2B	3B	HR	RBI	BB	SO	SB	CS	SLG	OBP	B	T	HT	WT	DOB	1st Yr	Resides
Ontiveros, Jeff	.247	58	227	28	56	9	0	7	46	21	39	3	0	.379	.322	R	R	6-0	220	4-26-79	2002	Round Rock, Texas
Ramirez, Hanley	.371	22	97	17	36	9	2	1	19	4	14	4	3	.536	.400	S	R	6-0	170	12-23-83	2000	Santo Domingo, D.R.
Stone, Greg	.243	71	267	45	65	5	1	0	22	29	42	14	5	.270	.319	L	R	5-11	170	2-19-81	2002	Claremore, Okla.
Tarbett, Brent	.158	5	19	2	3	1	0	0	2	2	6	0	0	.211	.304	R	R	6-2	220	11-30-80	2001	Las Vegas, Nev.
West, Eric	.240	64	225	35	54	6	1	1	14	34	48	11	9	.289	.348	R	R	6-1	160	3-24-83	2001	Southside, Ala.

GAMES BY POSITION: C—Aleman 32, Brown 1, Buckley 21, Concepcion 25. **1B**—Bowman 15, Buckley 2, Concepcion 1, Ontiveros 57, Tarbett 2. **2B**—Boran 12, Castillo 8, Stone 35, West 20. **3B**—Alcala 30, Boran 24, Bowman 1, Concepcion 22. **SS**—Boran 8, Ramirez 22, Stone 3, West 44. **OF**—Aleman 1, Barclay 5, Benson 38, Boran 7, Bowman 56, Brackley 4, Brown 15, Campos 52, Gross 21, Stone 32.

PITCHING	W	L	ERA	G	GS	CG	SV	IP	H	R	ER	BB	SO	AVG	B	T	HT	WT	DOB	1st Yr	Resides
Balan, Ryan	0	0	1.35	4	0	0	0	7	4	1	1	4	10	.173	L	L	6-0	190	6-26-79	2002	Whitby, Ontario
Galvez, Willy	2	6	6.42	15	12	0	0	55	68	49	39	30	41	.299	R	R	6-4	160	4-1-80	1998	Cotuy, D.R.
Gonzalez, Jose	1	1	3.70	12	1	0	0	24	16	10	10	21	13	.188	R	R	6-2	170	9-19-78	1997	Santo Domingo, D.R.
Grant, Michael	6	5	3.81	22	3	0	0	57	51	29	24	26	59	.253	R	R	6-1	190	11-12-79	2001	Beech Grove, Ind.
Hall, Shane	1	1	5.40	22	0	0	1	35	39	21	21	10	18	.272	R	R	6-5	200	6-14-80	2000	Herford, Ariz.
Heagen, Doug	1	0	4.32	4	0	0	0	8	10	4	4	2	6	.312	L	L	6-3	180	6-20-80	2002	Herndon, Va.
MacLane, Tom	3	2	1.54	19	0	0	1	41	36	15	7	19	38	.235	L	L	6-0	170	2-2-80	2002	Riverside, R.I.
Mateo, Aneudis	2	0	1.45	3	3	0	0	19	8	3	3	2	13	.133	R	R	6-4	180	10-3-82	2000	San Pedro de Macoris, D.R.
Mims, Brandon	0	2	9.00	10	3	0	0	23	40	27	23	8	15	.370	L	L	6-2	180	12-2-81	2000	Prattville, Ala.
Pahucki, David	1	2	1.84	9	9	0	0	44	31	11	9	8	48	.193	R	R	6-2	210	10-17-80	2002	New Hampton, N.Y.
Priola, Andy	3	0	2.54	27	0	0	13	46	36	15	13	5	33	.226	R	R	6-3	190	9-30-79	2002	Jemison, Ala.
Rodriguez, Hector	2	6	5.43	15	13	0	0	66	79	48	40	28	54	.307	R	R	5-10	170	12-24-78	2000	Santo Domingo, D.R.
Simon, Billy	0	1	1.64	3	0	0	0	11	10	6	2	6	12	.238	R	R	6-6	220	11-11-82	2001	Wellington, Fla.
Smith, Brandon	0	3	8.82	7	5	0	0	16	21	19	16	4	7	.323	R	R	6-2	200	2-18-80	2002	Ballwin, Mo.
Smith, Chris	3	3	4.13	14	14	0	0	57	54	29	26	14	50	.245	R	R	6-2	200	4-9-81	2002	Hesperia, Calif.
Vaquedano, Jose	1	3	4.35	22	0	0	0	39	46	33	19	18	35	.292	R	R	6-4	170	7-9-81	2002	San Antonio, Texas
Villarreal, Luis	4	3	4.45	16	9	0	0	63	68	33	31	14	47	.274	L	L	6-1	210	12-20-79	2002	San Antonio, Texas
Wells, Clint	4	1	2.78	16	0	0	0	36	27	17	11	13	23	.198	L	L	6-3	200	10-24-79	2002	Cooper City, Fla.
Yoo, Byung Mok	1	0	5.18	19	0	0	0	24	26	14	14	16	29	.279	R	R	6-2	180	11-21-79	2001	Seoul, Korea

FORT MYERS RED SOX — Rookie

GULF COAST LEAGUE

BATTING	AVG	G	AB	R	H	2B	3B	HR	RBI	BB	SO	SB	CS	SLG	OBP	B	T	HT	WT	DOB	1st Yr	Resides
Bailie, Stefan	.143	2	7	1	1	1	0	0	1	0	2	0	0	.286	.143	R	R	6-0	210	5-16-80	2001	Mesa, Wash.
Bianucci, Anthony	.089	38	79	16	7	1	1	0	1	13	37	6	1	.127	.234	S	R	5-11	180	4-25-81	2002	Annandale, Va.
Blasi, Blake	.435	7	23	8	10	2	0	0	2	2	4	4	0	.522	.480	S	R	5-8	160	3-23-79	2000	Wichita, Kan.
Bonvechio, Brett	.291	30	103	19	30	11	1	3	24	14	24	0	0	.505	.373	L	R	6-1	190	11-13-82	2001	Santa Clara, Calif.
Brown, Dustin	.321	45	159	28	51	12	2	1	20	23	24	11	4	.440	.404	R	R	6-0	180	6-19-82	2001	Fort Collins, Colo.
Ciofrone, Peter	.243	35	111	20	27	5	1	2	18	11	11	3	2	.360	.333	L	R	5-11	190	9-28-83	2002	Nesconset, N.Y.
Cronkhite, Ian	.193	52	171	11	33	8	2	0	13	14	53	3	5	.263	.253	L	L	6-1	180	8-11-83	2002	Edmond, Okla.
Cruz, Luis	.292	21	72	10	21	4	0	0	9	3	6	2	2	.347	.329	R	R	6-1	180	2-10-84	2000	Sonora, Mexico
De la Cruz, Carlos	.168	42	143	20	24	2	1	1	9	13	31	3	1	.217	.234	S	L	6-0	160	7-2-84	2001	Santo Domingo, D.R.
DeVries, Jon	.185	43	119	13	22	3	0	1	11	30	31	3	0	.235	.368	R	R	6-3	200	8-22-82	2001	Fort Myers, Fla.
Durazo, William	.190	18	42	7	8	3	1	0	7	4	11	2	0	.310	.294	S	R	6-1	210	2-15-79	2002	Los Angeles, Calif.
Guzman, Heriberto	.182	47	143	11	26	3	0	1	9	17	53	5	4	.224	.287	R	R	6-1	180	1-26-84	2001	Bajo de Haina, D.R.
Minami, Yasumichi	.280	8	25	3	7	1	0	1	5	1	4	1	1	.440	.308	R	R	5-11	180	11-20-78	2001	Tokyo, Japan
Moss, Brandon	.204	42	113	10	23	6	2	0	6	13	40	1	2	.292	.295	L	R	6-0	180	9-16-83	2002	Monroe, Ga.
Perez, Koby	.000	4	5	0	0	0	0	0	0	3	0	0	0	.000	.000	R	R	6-2	220	9-26-82	2001	Santo Domingo, D.R.
Ramirez, Hanley	.341	45	164	29	56	11	3	6	26	16	15	8	6	.555	.402	S	R	6-1	170	12-23-83	2000	Santo Domingo, D.R.
Santoro, Pat	.240	8	25	1	6	1	0	0	3	1	6	0	0	.280	.269	R	R	6-0	170	11-9-78	1998	River Forest, Ill.
Spann, Chad	.222	57	203	20	45	8	3	6	28	12	37	1	2	.379	.271	R	R	6-1	190	10-25-83	2002	Buena Vista, Ga.
Williams, Devoris	.093	44	129	19	12	1	1	1	7	29	68	6	2	.140	.272	S	R	5-10	180	8-8-83	2002	Greensboro, Ala.
Williams, John	.000	2	6	0	0	0	0	0	0	0	3	0	0	.000	.143	R	R	6-5	220	8-26-68	2002	Hernando, Fla.

GAMES BY POSITION: C—Brown 16, DeVries 39, Durazo 6, Perez 4. **1B**—Bonvechio 29, Durazo 12, Guzman 23, Williams 1. **2B**—Blasi 7, Ciofrone 15, Minami 6, Moss 31, Ramirez 5, Spann 1, Williams 7. **3B**—Bonvechio 1, Ciofrone 5, Guzman 17, Minami 2, Moss 1, Ramirez 2, Spann 36, Williams 1. **SS**—Cruz 21, Ramirez 40, Spann 3, Williams 1. **OF**—Bianucci 33, Brown 28, Cronkhite 49, De la Cruz 41, Santoro 8, Spann 1, Williams 35.

PITCHING	W	L	ERA	G	GS	CG	SV	IP	H	R	ER	BB	SO	AVG	B	T	HT	WT	DOB	1st Yr	Resides
Arrojo, Rolando	0	0	0.00	1	1	0	0	3	1	0	0	0	1	.272	R	R	6-4	230	7-18-68	1997	St. Petersburg, Fla.
Astacio, Olivo	0	2	6.35	6	3	0	0	17	26	17	12	15	7	.376	R	R	6-5	190	7-28-84	2002	Santo Domingo, D.R.
Balan, Ryan	3	2	3.38	13	0	0	0	21	23	12	8	17	10	.291	L	L	6-0	190	6-26-79	2002	Whitby, Ontario
Batista, Antonio	3	3	3.60	22	0	0	7	35	33	20	14	14	47	.237	R	R	6-2	160	11-17-81	1999	San Pedro de Macoris, D.R.
Benitez, Fabricio	1	1	2.45	3	0	0	0	7	5	2	2	0	4	.192	R	R	6-3	170	5-10-78	1997	Santo Domingo, D.R.
Blaney, Matthew	2	2	15.15	21	1	0	0	27	54	49	46	19	14	.435	S	R	5-11	180	5-7-79	2001	Oxnard, Calif.
Cedeno, Juan	2	5	4.19	11	7	0	0	43	55	31	20	12	32	.297	L	L	6-1	160	8-19-83	2001	Higuey, D.R.
Elmore, Chris	0	1	14.73	1	0	0	0	4	8	6	6	0	3	.421	L	L	6-1	190	4-28-77	2000	Virginia Beach, Va.
Farley, Chris	2	3	4.40	12	6	0	0	43	34	28	21	29	38	.217	R	R	6-2	180	2-24-83	2001	Orange, Mass.
Frias, Junior	2	3	5.83	12	4	0	1	42	59	34	27	13	21	.327	R	R	6-3	200	8-26-84	2002	Santo Domingo, D.R.
Garces, Rich	0	0	0.00	2	2	0	0	4	1	1	0	0	5	.076	R	R	6-0	250	5-18-71	1988	Maracay, Venez.
Hermanson, Dustin	0	0	9.00	1	1	0	0	2	5	3	2	0	1	.500	R	R	6-2	200	12-21-72	1994	Phoenix, Ariz.
Jackson, Kyle	0	0	0.00	1	1	0	0	2	0	0	0	0	1	.000	R	R	6-3	180	4-9-83	2002	Litchfield, N.H.
Lane, Josh	0	0	9.95	13	0	0	0	13	17	16	14	21	9	.333	L	L	6-5	240	10-1-79	2002	Fort Pierce, Fla.
Leach, B.J.	0	0	4.76	5	0	0	1	6	5	3	3	2	3	.238	R	R	5-11	190	8-3-77	1999	Seminole, Fla.
Ledezma, Wil	0	0	6.00	1	0	0	0	3	4	2	2	0	3	.307	L	L	6-3	150	1-21-81	1998	Maracay, Venez.
Lester, Jon	0	1	13.50	1	1	0	0	1	5	6	1	1	1	.714	L	L	6-3	200	1-7-84	2002	Puyallup, Wash.
Mateo, Aneudis	4	3	1.76	11	11	2	0	51	45	14	10	11	45	.231	R	R	6-4	180	10-3-82	2000	San Pedro de Macoris, D.R.
Mendoza, Luis	3	4	4.21	13	10	0	1	58	76	36	27	8	21	.329	R	R	6-3	180	10-31-83	2000	Mexico City, Mexico
Moreno, Juan	0	1	1.80	3	3	0	0	5	4	2	1	0	10	.210	L	L	6-1	200	2-28-75	1994	Cagua, Venez.
Pena, Juan	0	0	0.00	1	1	0	0	4	4	0	0	2	4	.250	R	R	6-1	190	7-18-84	2002	Santiago, D.R.
Simon, Billy	1	1	1.64	9	0	0	2	22	12	6	4	5	24	.155	R	R	6-6	220	11-11-82	2001	Wellington, Fla.
Suarez, Pedro	0	0	3.14	15	0	0	1	29	33	11	10	10	21	.286	R	R	6-3	190	10-22-83	2001	Spring Valley, Calif.
Tussen, Denny	2	2	2.60	12	3	0	0	52	48	28	15	15	37	.246	R	R	6-4	140	4-25-83	1999	San Pedro de Macoris, D.R.
Wells, Clint	1	0	5.79	2	0	0	0	5	3	3	3	5	1	.166	L	L	6-3	200	10-24-79	2002	Cooper City, Fla.

ORGANIZATION STATISTICS

CHICAGO WHITE SOX

BY PHIL ROGERS

For the White Sox, it's back to the drawing board. Again.

No ceremony or press release was necessary to mark the occasion. But with a series of trades made before the 2002 deadline, the Sox signaled they had overestimated the staying power of the team that had captured a Central Division title in 2000.

For the second year in a row, Jerry Manuel's team spent spring training talking about how they were the best team in the American League Central, only to fall flat on their faces before Memorial Day. A stretch of 9-19 from May 9-June 8 dropped the division favorites six games behind the Twins. They slid to 7½ back by the all-star break, 10 by July 17 and never again cut the deficit to single digits.

General manager Ken Williams, who added a number of veterans to the young nucleus that had won 95 games in 2000, kept the faith longer than almost anyone. But even his patience reached its limit in late July.

In a one-week span, Williams traded second baseman Ray Durham, center fielder Kenny Lofton, catcher Sandy Alomar and righthander Bob Howry. Manuel benched shortstop Royce Clayton, who would be released in September.

Suddenly the team that had been 47-56 began to show a pulse. With third baseman Joe Crede, center fielder Aaron Rowand and other youngsters taking advantage of the chance to play, the Sox put together a 14-13 August and a 16-11 September. They lost the final two games of the season to finish at 81-81.

Lefthander Mark Buehrle and right fielder Magglio Ordonez were once again the two biggest contributors for the Sox. Buehrle earned a spot on the all-star team and won 19 games. Ordonez failed to make the All-Star Game for the first time since 1998 but generated career highs with 38 homers and 135 RBIs.

Magglio Ordonez   Joe Crede

PLAYERS OF THE YEAR

MAJOR LEAGUE: Magglio Ordonez, of

Ordonez consistently—and quietly—produces year after year. He finished among the top 10 American Leaguers in eight offensive categories in 2002, including average (.320), doubles (47) and homers (38). He was second in RBIs, with 135.

MINOR LEAGUE: Joe Crede, 3b

Crede led the International League in slugging in 2002 while improving his offensive numbers across the board in Triple-A before smacking 12 homers in 200 major league at-bats after a promotion to Chicago in late July.

While Buehrle matched up with any ace in the AL Central, the White Sox failed in Williams' attempt to improve their pitching depth. Righthander Todd Ritchie was ineffective after being added in a deal that sent starters Kip Wells and Josh Fogg to the Pirates, and the seven pitchers other than Buehrle to start games wound up 42-52, 6.13.

Closer Keith Foulke lost his job after getting hit hard during May. Even though Foulke put up a 0.74 ERA in the second half, Manuel continued to give save opportunities to young lefty Damaso Marte and veteran righthander Antonio Osuna.

It wasn't a banner yet for player development, either. While top prospect Joe Borchard played well during a September cameo with the Sox, he had a somewhat underwhelming season at Triple-A Charlotte, striking out 139 times in 117 games. Righthander Jon Rauch bombed after Manuel let him sit for two weeks in the bullpen during April. Lefty Corwin Malone, impressive with the Sox in spring training, experienced control problems with Double-A Birmingham and had to be shut down with a sore elbow.

Birmingham, managed by Wally Backman, was the farm system's saving grace. With catcher Miguel Olivo the lone top-10 prospect in the lineup, the Barons rolled to a Southern League title. Second baseman Aaron Miles, acquired from the Astros as a minor league pick in the Rule 5 draft two years earlier, earned MVP honors during the regular season. Olivo, who homered four times in nine games, was the playoff MVP.

Rookie-level Bristol won a title in the Appalachian League. The Sox were led by outfielders Anthony Webster and Darren Ciraco, and shortstop Andy Gonzalez.

ORGANIZATION LEADERS

BATTING

*AVG	Aaron Miles, Birmingham	.322
R	Danny Sandoval, Birmingham	86
H	Aaron Miles, Birmingham	171
TB	Aaron Miles, Birmingham	239
2B	Aaron Miles, Birmingham	39
3B	Miguel Olivo, Birmingham	10
HR	Joe Crede, Charlotte	24
RBI	Ryan Hankins, Birmingham	72
BB	Scott Bikowski, Birmingham	58
	Eric Storey, Kannapolis	58
SO	Darron Ingram, Charlotte/Birmingham	162
SB	Edwin Yan, Winston-Salem	88

PITCHING

W	Ryan Wing, Kannapolis	12
L	Heath Phillips, Winston-Salem	16
#ERA	Josh Fields, Winston-Salem/Kannapolis	2.51
G	Gary Majewski, Birmingham	57
	Josh Fields, Winston-Salem/Kannapolis	57
CG	Heath Phillips, Winston-Salem	5
SV	Joe Valentine, Birmingham	36
IP	Heath Phillips, Winston-Salem	179
BB	Corwin Malone, Birmingham	89
SO	Kris Honel, Winston-Salem/Kannapolis	160

*Minimum 250 At-Bats #Minimum 75 Innings

Manager: Jerry Manuel

2002 Record: 81-81, .500 (2nd, AL Central)

ORGANIZATION STATISTICS

BATTING	AVG	G	AB	R	H	2B	3B	HR	RBI	BB	SO	SB	CS	SLG	OBP	B	T	HT	WT	DOB	1st Yr	Resides
Alomar, Sandy	.287	51	167	21	48	10	1	7	25	5	14	0	0	.485	.309	R	R	6-5	230	6-18-66	1984	Chicago, Ill.
Borchard, Joe	.222	16	36	5	8	0	0	2	5	1	14	0	0	.389	.243	S	R	6-5	220	11-25-78	2000	Camarillo, Calif.
Clayton, Royce	.251	112	342	51	86	14	2	7	35	20	67	5	1	.365	.295	R	R	6-0	180	1-2-70	1988	Scottsdale, Ariz.
Crede, Joe	.285	53	200	28	57	10	0	12	35	8	40	0	2	.515	.311	R	R	6-2	190	4-26-78	1996	Westphalia, Mo.
Durham, Ray	.299	96	345	71	103	20	2	9	48	49	59	20	5	.446	.390	S	R	5-8	180	11-30-71	1990	Charlotte, N.C.
Graffanino, Tony	.262	70	229	35	60	12	4	6	31	22	38	2	1	.428	.329	R	R	6-1	190	6-6-72	1990	Marietta, Ga.
Harris, Willie	.233	49	163	14	38	4	0	2	12	9	21	8	0	.294	.270	L	R	5-9	170	6-22-78	1999	Cairo, Ga.
Jimenez, D'Angelo	.287	48	167	21	48	4	3	1	11	16	10	2	1	.407	.384	S	R	6-0	190	12-21-77	1995	Santo Domingo, D.R.
Johnson, Mark	.209	86	263	31	55	8	1	4	18	30	52	0	0	.293	.297	L	R	6-0	180	9-12-75	1994	Warner Robins, Ga.
Konerko, Paul	.304	151	570	81	173	30	0	27	104	44	72	0	0	.498	.359	R	R	6-2	210	3-5-76	1994	Scottsdale, Ariz.
Lee, Carlos	.264	140	492	82	130	26	2	26	80	75	73	1	4	.484	.359	R	R	6-2	230	6-20-76	1994	Aguadulce, Panama
Liefer, Jeff	.230	76	204	28	47	8	0	7	26	16	60	0	0	.373	.295	L	R	6-3	210	8-17-74	1996	Upland, Calif.
Lofton, Kenny	.259	93	352	68	91	20	6	8	42	49	51	22	8	.418	.348	L	L	6-0	180	5-31-67	1988	Tucson, Ariz.
Olivo, Miguel	.211	6	19	2	4	1	0	1	5	2	5	0	0	.421	.286	R	R	6-0	180	7-15-78	1996	Villa Vasquez, D.R.
Ordonez, Magglio	.320	153	590	116	189	47	1	38	135	53	77	7	5	.597	.381	R	R	6-0	210	1-28-74	1991	Coro Falcon, Venez.
Paul, Josh	.240	33	104	11	25	4	0	0	11	9	22	2	0	.279	.302	R	R	6-1	200	5-19-75	1996	Buffalo Grove, Ill.
Rowand, Aaron	.258	126	302	41	78	16	2	7	29	12	54	0	1	.394	.298	R	R	6-1	200	8-29-77	1998	Glendora, Calif.
Thomas, Frank	.252	148	523	77	132	29	1	28	92	88	115	3	0	.472	.361	R	R	6-5	270	5-27-68	1989	Chicago, Ill.
Valentin, Jose	.249	135	474	70	118	26	4	25	75	43	99	3	3	.479	.311	S	R	5-10	180	10-12-69	1987	Manati, P.R.

PITCHING	W	L	ERA	G	GS	CG	SV	IP	H	R	ER	BB	SO	AVG	B	T	HT	WT	DOB	1st Yr	Resides
Barcelo, Lorenzo	0	1	9.00	4	0	0	0	6	9	6	6	1	1	.333	R	R	6-4	230	8-10-77	1994	San Pedro de Macoris, D.R.
Biddle, Rocky	3	4	4.06	44	7	0	1	78	72	42	35	39	64	.244	R	R	6-3	230	5-21-76	1997	Arcadia, Calif.
Buehrle, Mark	19	12	3.58	34	34	5	0	239	236	102	95	61	134	.259	L	L	6-2	200	3-23-79	1999	St. Charles, Mo.
Foulke, Keith	2	4	2.90	65	0	0	11	78	65	26	25	13	58	.224	R	R	6-0	210	10-19-72	1994	Huffman, Texas
Garland, Jon	12	12	4.58	33	33	1	0	193	188	109	98	83	112	.258	R	R	6-6	200	9-27-79	1997	Granada Hills, Calif.
Ginter, Matt	1	0	4.47	33	0	0	1	54	59	34	27	21	37	.278	R	R	6-1	220	12-24-77	1999	Winchester, Ky.
Glover, Gary	7	8	5.20	41	22	0	1	138	136	86	80	52	70	.253	R	R	6-5	200	12-3-76	1994	Deland, Fla.
Howry, Bob	2	2	3.91	47	0	0	0	51	45	22	22	17	31	.244	L	R	6-5	220	8-4-73	1994	Glendale, Ariz.
Marte, Damaso	1	1	2.83	68	0	0	10	60	44	19	19	18	72	.203	L	L	6-2	200	2-14-75	1993	Santo Domingo, D.R.
Osuna, Antonio	8	2	3.86	59	0	0	11	68	64	32	29	28	66	.250	R	R	5-11	200	4-12-73	1991	Sinaloa, Mexico
Parque, Jim	1	4	9.95	8	4	0	0	25	34	29	28	16	13	.317	L	L	5-11	170	2-8-76	1997	Puyallup, Wash.
Porzio, Mike	2	2	4.81	32	0	0	0	43	40	25	23	23	33	.248	L	L	6-3	190	8-20-72	1993	Norwalk, Conn.
Rauch, Jon	2	1	6.59	8	6	0	0	29	28	26	21	14	19	.247	R	R	6-11	230	9-27-78	1999	Westport, Ky.
Ritchie, Todd	5	15	6.06	26	23	0	0	134	176	104	90	52	77	.318	R	R	6-3	210	11-7-71	1990	Kerens, Texas
Wright, Danny	14	12	5.18	33	33	1	0	196	200	124	113	71	136	.262	R	R	6-5	220	12-14-77	1999	Batesville, Ark.
Wunsch, Kelly	2	1	3.41	50	0	0	0	32	26	12	12	19	22	.230	L	L	6-5	220	7-12-72	1993	Houston, Texas

FIELDING

Catcher	PCT	G	PO	A	E	DP	PB
Alomar	.994	50	293	14	2	3	2
Johnson	.994	85	484	27	3	3	3
Olivo	1.000	6	31	1	0	0	2
Paul	.990	32	200	6	2	1	2

First Base	PCT	G	PO	A	E	DP
Konerko	.993	140	1146	75	8	113
Liefer	.990	31	187	10	2	23
Thomas	.955	4	38	4	2	5

Second Base	PCT	G	PO	A	E	DP
Durham	.968	92	188	261	15	61
Graffanino	.948	25	33	58	5	17
Harris	.985	38	87	104	3	21
Jimenez	.988	17	30	53	1	16

Third Base	PCT	G	PO	A	E	DP
Crede	.938	53	33	87	8	12
Graffanino	.952	35	19	61	4	5

Jimenez	1.000	1	0	2	0	0
Valentin	.952	83	65	152	11	14

Shortstop	PCT	G	PO	A	E	DP
Clayton	.989	109	166	292	5	72
Graffanino	.970	8	13	19	1	1
Jimenez	.978	10	13	31	1	8
Valentin	.962	50	81	124	8	38

Outfield	PCT	G	PO	A	E	DP
Borchard	1.000	15	21	0	0	0
Harris	1.000	6	19	1	0	0
Konerko	.000	1	0	0	0	0
Lee	.996	137	249	8	1	1
Liefer	1.000	36	54	1	0	0
Lofton	1.000	92	229	3	0	0
Ordonez	.986	150	283	8	4	0
Paul	1.000	1	3	0	0	0
Rowand	.983	120	224	5	4	3

Carlos Lee

Mark Buehrle: led Chicago with 19 wins, 239 innings

Paul Konerko: .304-27-104 for White Sox

FARM SYSTEM

Director, Player Development: Bob Fontaine.

Class	Farm Team	League	W	L	Pct.	Finish*	Manager	First Yr.
AAA	Charlotte (N.C.) Knights	International	55	88	.385	13th (14)	Nick Capra	1999
AA	Birmingham (Ala.) Barons	Southern	79	61	.564	+1st (10)	Wally Backman	1986
High A	Winston-Salem (N.C.) Warthogs	Carolina	50	90	.357	7th (8)	Razor Shines	1997
Low A	Kannapolis (N.C.) Intimidators	South Atlantic	66	74	.471	t-11th (16)	John Orton	1999
Rookie	Bristol (Va.) Sox	Appalachian	43	25	.632	+2nd (10)	Nick Leyva	1995
Rookie	Phoenix (Ariz.) White Sox	Arizona	27	29	.482	5th (7)	Jerry Hairston	1998

*Finish in overall standings (No. of teams in league)   +League champion

CHARLOTTE KNIGHTS
Class AAA

INTERNATIONAL LEAGUE

BATTING	AVG	G	AB	R	H	2B	3B	HR	RBI	BB	SO	SB	CS	SLG	OBP	B	T	HT	WT	DOB	1st Yr	Resides
Acevas, Jon	.000	1	1	0	0	0	0	0	0	0	1	0	0	.000	.000	R	R	6-2	180	3-7-78	1997	Sonora, Mexico
Alomar, Sandy	.125	3	8	0	1	0	0	0	0	0	0	0	0	.125	.125	R	R	6-5	230	6-18-66	1984	Chicago, Ill.
Battersby, Eric	.251	55	183	14	46	8	0	2	17	17	30	1	1	.328	.313	R	L	6-1	200	2-28-76	1998	Corpus Christi, Texas
Baughman, Justin	.229	124	420	57	96	12	6	6	37	31	75	31	9	.300	.295	R	R	5-11	180	8-1-74	1995	Portland, Ore.
Borchard, Joe	.272	117	438	62	119	35	2	20	59	49	139	2	4	.498	.349	S	R	6-5	220	11-25-78	2000	Camarillo, Calif.
Buford, Damon	.246	41	138	20	34	8	0	2	10	12	22	6	1	.348	.314	R	R	5-10	180	6-12-70	1990	Dallas, Texas
2-team (10 Pawtucket)	.231	51	169	25	39	9	0	3	12	16	27	7	1	.337	.303							
Canseco, Jose	.172	18	64	11	11	1	0	5	9	9	21	1	0	.422	.280	R	R	6-4	240	7-2-64	1982	Westin, Fla.
Caradonna, Brett	.000	2	3	0	0	0	0	0	0	1	1	0	0	.000	.250	L	R	6-1	180	12-3-78	1997	San Diego, Calif.
Crede, Joe	.312	95	359	57	112	21	0	24	65	26	48	0	1	.571	.359	R	R	6-2	190	4-26-78	1996	Westphalia, Mo.
Dalesandro, Mark	.225	46	160	12	36	8	0	2	10	5	13	0	0	.313	.254	R	R	6-0	190	5-14-68	1990	Chicago, Ill.
Dellaero, Jason	.244	28	82	10	20	6	0	4	10	0	27	0	0	.463	.241	R	R	6-2	190	12-17-76	1997	Brewster, N.Y.
Evans, Lee	.243	72	243	27	59	18	2	4	22	16	74	4	1	.383	.295	S	R	6-1	180	7-20-77	1996	Northport, Ala.
Harris, Willie	.283	89	360	54	102	16	5	5	33	33	61	32	14	.397	.345	L	R	5-9	170	6-22-78	1999	Cairo, Ga.
Hummel, Tim	.260	142	523	55	136	33	0	4	41	51	95	6	5	.346	.332	R	R	6-2	190	11-18-78	2000	Montgomery, N.Y.
Inglin, Jeff	.276	39	152	18	42	4	0	6	22	8	22	2	2	.421	.305	R	R	5-11	180	10-8-75	1996	Petaluma, Calif.
Ingram, Darron	.153	16	59	5	9	2	0	3	6	6	22	0	1	.339	.227	R	R	6-3	220	6-7-76	1994	Lexington, Ky.
Jimenez, D'Angelo	.280	42	157	24	44	11	1	6	18	24	14	6	2	.478	.372	S	R	6-0	190	12-21-77	1995	Santo Domingo, D.R.
Kieschnick, Brooks	.275	69	189	32	52	11	0	13	40	14	46	0	0	.540	.320	L	R	6-4	220	6-6-72	1993	Caldwell, Texas
McKee, Scott	.000	1	1	0	0	0	0	0	0	0	1	0	0	.000	.000	S	R	6-1	200	5-6-77	1999	Bowie, Md.
Morgan, Scott	.269	84	309	33	83	15	0	9	34	14	81	3	1	.405	.303	R	R	6-7	230	7-19-73	1995	Lompoc, Calif.
Paul, Josh	.273	65	231	18	63	15	2	0	17	17	45	10	4	.355	.323	R	R	6-1	200	5-19-75	1996	Buffalo Grove, Ill.
Quintero, Humberto	.220	15	41	2	9	1	0	0	5	3	8	0	0	.244	.273	R	R	5-9	190	8-2-79	1997	Maracaibo, Venez.
Reyes, Guillermo	.308	4	13	1	4	0	0	0	0	1	2	0	.308	.308	S	R	5-9	160	12-29-81	1999	Villa Vasquez, D.R.
Sanders, Anthony	.232	58	211	20	49	9	2	6	24	10	64	3	2	.379	.266	R	R	6-2	200	3-2-74	1993	Tucson, Ariz.
2-team (33 Louisville)	.239	91	335	32	80	15	3	12	48	17	95	7	3	.409	.275							
Saunders, Chris	.218	81	285	23	62	16	0	5	33	17	70	0	0	.326	.264	R	R	6-1	200	7-19-70	1992	Clovis, Calif.
Zywica, Mike	.221	39	140	17	31	6	0	5	16	10	39	1	0	.371	.288	R	R	6-4	200	9-14-74	1996	Richton Park, Ill.

PITCHING

	W	L	ERA	G	GS	CG	SV	IP	H	R	ER	BB	SO	AVG	B	T	HT	WT	DOB	1st Yr	Resides
Adkins, Jon	4	2	3.69	8	7	1	0	46	47	20	19	12	31	.259	L	R	6-0	200	8-30-77	1998	Wayne, W.Va.
Allen, Wyatt	0	1	9.00	1	1	0	0	5	6	5	5	6	2	.300	R	R	6-4	200	4-12-80	2001	Brentwood, Tenn.
Almonte, Ed	2	3	2.24	50	0	0	26	60	52	16	15	12	56	.236	R	R	6-3	200	12-17-76	1998	New York, N.Y.
Barcelo, Lorenzo	0	0	6.75	2	1	0	0	5	5	4	4	1	1	.227	R	R	6-4	230	8-10-77	1994	San Pedro de Macoris, D.R.
Biddle, Rocky	0	0	1.29	2	2	0	0	7	4	1	1	1	9	.160	R	R	6-3	230	5-21-76	1997	Arcadia, Calif.
Chantres, Carlos	4	6	4.90	15	15	0	0	86	99	51	47	49	45	.299	R	R	6-3	190	4-1-76	1994	Miami, Fla.
2-team (10 Durham)	8	9	4.53	25	23	0	0	139	153	78	70	67	74	.288							
Eason, Clay	0	0	4.43	11	0	0	0	20	22	11	10	9	14	.275	R	R	5-11	190	9-28-75	1997	Dunn, N.C.
Freeman, Kai	0	0	18.00	1	0	0	0	1	3	2	2	0	0	.500	R	R	6-2	180	3-11-77	1998	Shorewood, Ill.
Ginter, Matt	1	0	3.94	13	0	0	0	16	20	8	7	10	9	.312	R	R	6-1	220	12-24-77	1999	Winchester, Ky.
Jacquez, Tom	0	7	6.75	14	7	1	0	61	79	48	46	21	45	.325	L	L	6-2	190	12-29-75	1997	Stockton, Calif.
Kane, Kyle	0	0	4.26	4	0	0	0	6	7	3	3	3	9	.269	L	R	6-3	210	2-4-76	1997	Reno, Nev.
Kieschnick, Brooks	0	1	2.59	25	0	0	0	31	30	9	9	10	30	.000	L	R	6-4	220	6-6-72	1993	Caldwell, Texas
Kohlmeier, Ryan	2	1	4.96	38	1	0	0	65	65	42	36	20	58	.258	R	R	6-2	220	6-25-77	1996	Cottonwood Falls, Kan.
Lantigua, Delvis	1	5	5.85	15	8	0	0	52	46	36	34	29	41	.238	R	R	6-0	170	1-5-80	1998	La Carmelita, D.R.
Lee, Corey	7	6	3.89	38	12	1	0	111	130	54	48	37	92	.299	S	L	6-2	180	12-26-74	1996	Raleigh, N.C.
McWhirter, Kris	0	1	4.09	2	2	0	0	11	13	6	5	1	5	.288	L	R	6-4	190	5-11-79	1999	Goodlettsville, Tenn.
Mendoza, Geronimo	1	9	8.15	11	10	0	0	53	68	52	48	25	36	.311	L	R	6-4	180	3-23-80	1995	Santo Domingo, D.R.
Meyer, Jake	0	0	1.17	4	0	0	0	8	1	1	1	0	9	.043	R	R	6-1	190	1-7-75	1997	San Diego, Calif.
Parque, Jim	7	9	6.47	20	20	0	0	106	131	80	76	38	63	.309	L	L	5-11	170	2-8-76	1997	Puyallup, Wash.
Parrish, Wade	5	5	4.67	15	14	0	0	89	105	49	46	26	28	.301	L	L	6-4	190	11-13-77	1999	Othello, Wash.
Porzio, Mike	6	5	4.52	14	13	0	0	76	83	43	38	29	59	.285	L	L	6-3	190	8-20-72	1993	Norwalk, Conn.
Rauch, Jon	7	8	4.28	19	19	1	0	109	91	60	52	42	97	.225	R	R	6-11	230	9-27-78	1999	Westport, Ky.
Schrenk, Steve	2	7	4.06	38	3	0	0	78	74	36	35	25	44	.251	R	R	6-1	190	11-20-68	1987	Parrish, Fla.
Simas, Bill	1	3	3.60	28	0	0	2	40	46	22	16	8	22	.294	L	R	6-3	230	11-28-71	1992	Fresno, Calif.
Vining, Ken	2	5	2.87	44	0	0	1	47	37	15	15	25	35	.220	L	L	6-0	180	12-5-74	1996	Hopkins, S.C.
Wagner, Denny	0	1	3.00	2	0	0	0	3	2	1	1	1	1	.200	R	R	6-0	200	11-8-76	1997	Castlewood, Va.
Wunsch, Kelly	1	0	2.25	10	2	0	0	12	13	3	3	5	9	.295	L	L	6-5	220	7-12-72	1993	Houston, Texas
Wylie, Mitch	2	3	4.76	6	6	0	0	34	43	22	18	5	23	.307	R	R	6-3	190	1-14-77	1998	Princeton, Iowa

FIELDING

Catcher	PCT	G	PO	A	E	DP	PB
Acevas	1.000	1	5	0	0	0	
Alomar	1.000	3	15	0	0	0	
Dalesandro	.978	33	211	8	5	0	4
Evans	.984	39	229	18	4	0	6
Paul	.993	61	377	25	3	4	3
Quintero	.964	15	66	15	3	1	3

First Base	PCT	G	PO	A	E	DP
Battersby	.994	42	337	19	2	31
Baughman	.990	15	90	14	1	8
Dalesandro	1.000	13	79	4	0	9
Evans	1.000	28	215	17	0	23
Hummel	1.000	5	34	1	0	3
Morgan	.980	10	90	10	2	12
Paul	1.000	4	40	5	0	10
Saunders	.988	37	298	18	4	31

Second Base	PCT	G	PO	A	E	DP
Baughman	.966	8	26	30	2	9
Harris	.986	82	192	220	6	64
Hummel	.981	54	112	141	5	37

Third Base	PCT	G	PO	A	E	DP
Baughman	.903	16	4	24	3	4
Crede	.944	94	67	185	15	21
Dellaero	.927	16	15	36	4	4
Hummel	1.000	5	6	4	0	1
Reyes	1.000	1	0	1	0	1
Saunders	.981	19	11	41	1	2

Shortstop	PCT	G	PO	A	E	DP
Baughman	.980	13	21	29	1	7
Dellaero	.952	8	13	27	2	4
Hummel	.980	78	113	222	7	56
Jimenez	.966	42	65	106	6	17

	PCT	G	PO	A	E	DP
Reyes	1.000	3	7	9	0	2

Outfield	PCT	G	PO	A	E	DP
Battersby	.963	16	24	2	1	0
Baughman	1.000	77	166	7	0	0
Borchard	.990	116	290	12	3	2
Buford	.972	38	66	3	2	0
Dellaero	1.000	1	2	0	0	0
Evans	.889	3	8	0	1	0
Harris	1.000	7	18	0	0	0
Inglin	.982	31	52	4	1	0
Ingram	1.000	5	11	1	0	1
Kieschnick	1.000	1	1	0	0	0
Morgan	.958	68	157	1	7	0
Paul	1.000	1	1	0	0	0
Sanders	.978	50	84	6	2	1
Zywica	.978	26	41	3	1	0

BIRMINGHAM BARONS

Class AA

SOUTHERN LEAGUE

BATTING	AVG	G	AB	R	H	2B	3B	HR	RBI	BB	SO	SB	CS	SLG	OBP	B	T	HT	WT	DOB	1st Yr	Resides
Acevas, Jon	.232	60	164	26	38	8	1	3	16	21	35	0	1	.348	.321	R	R	6-2	180	3-7-78	1997	Sonora, Mexico
Battersby, Eric	.233	63	202	23	47	9	2	4	19	16	38	3	3	.356	.291	R	L	6-1	200	2-28-76	1998	Corpus Christi, Texas
Bikowski, Scott	.256	125	395	46	101	16	2	4	35	58	68	17	11	.337	.355	L	L	6-0	180	2-12-77	1999	Suffield, Conn.
Bravo, Danny	.239	46	138	17	33	8	0	1	15	15	20	7	5	.319	.316	S	R	5-11	170	5-27-77	1996	Maracaibo, Venez.
Dellaero, Jason	.209	63	182	20	38	7	1	5	20	11	53	6	4	.341	.255	R	R	6-2	190	12-17-76	1997	Brewster, N.Y.
Durham, Chad	.276	119	366	62	101	11	2	0	35	36	72	39	18	.317	.341	R	R	5-8	170	6-23-78	1997	Charlotte, N.C.
Evans, Lee	.277	22	65	13	18	3	1	4	7	5	19	0	0	.538	.329	S	R	6-4	180	7-20-77	1996	Northport, Ala.
Fernandez, Alex	.292	87	343	34	100	15	0	7	52	8	60	20	7	.397	.304	L	L	6-1	200	5-15-81	1998	Cotui, D.R.
Hankins, Ryan	.280	115	422	51	118	28	1	7	72	45	74	8	6	.400	.349	R	R	5-11	200	6-30-76	1997	Simi Valley, Calif.
Harris, Blair	.000	2	5	0	0	0	0	0	0	0	1	0	0	.000	.000	R	R	6-2	210	6-6-79	2002	Oklahoma City, Okla.
Ingram, Darron	.240	107	375	50	90	20	2	17	64	48	140	9	6	.440	.329	R	R	6-3	220	6-7-76	1994	Lexington, Ky.
Lebron, Francisco	.167	4	12	1	2	0	0	1	1	4	0	0	0	.167	.231	R	R	6-6	230	5-10-75	1999	Bayamon, P.R.
Miles, Aaron	.322	138	531	67	171	39	1	9	68	40	45	25	16	.450	.369	S	R	5-8	170	12-15-76	1995	Antioch, Calif.
Olivo, Miguel	.306	106	359	51	110	24	10	6	49	40	66	29	13	.479	.381	R	R	6-0	180	7-15-78	1996	Villa Vasquez, D.R.
Piniella, Juan	.307	55	153	22	47	9	0	1	12	18	34	12	7	.386	.386	R	R	5-10	180	3-13-78	1996	Stafford, Va.
Quintero, Humberto	.500	4	12	1	6	0	0	0	3	0	1	1	0	.500	.538	R	R	6-1	190	8-2-79	1997	Maracaibo, Venez.
Sandoval, Danny	.264	135	546	86	133	30	2	5	45	45	56	39	24	.361	.329	R	R	5-11	180	4-7-79	1997	Lara, Venez.
Saunders, Chris	.239	19	67	9	16	2	0	0	10	6	10	0	1	.269	.297	R	R	6-1	200	7-19-70	1992	Clovis, Calif.
Shaffer, Josh	.229	78	210	25	48	7	1	0	17	33	59	1	5	.271	.329	L	R	6-1	180	6-26-80	1999	Yorba Linda, Calif.
Zywica, Mike	.204	18	49	6	10	1	0	1	8	6	8	4	0	.286	.288	R	R	6-4	200	9-14-74	1996	Richton Park, Ill.

PITCHING	W	L	ERA	G	GS	CG	SV	IP	H	R	ER	BB	SO	AVG	B	T	HT	WT	DOB	1st Yr	Resides
Bohannan, Brad	0	1	7.71	8	0	0	0	12	18	14	10	2	7	.346	R	R	6-3	170	9-2-77	2000	Springdale, Ark.
Bullard, Jim	0	3	4.50	3	3	0	0	20	21	10	10	4	12	.269	L	L	6-7	190	12-29-79	2001	West Covina, Calif.
Dellaero, Jason	2	3	9.00	13	0	0	0	16	23	16	16	10	16	.000	R	R	6-2	190	12-17-76	1997	Brewster, N.Y.
Diaz, Felix	4	0	3.48	7	6	0	0	31	25	14	12	8	30	.206	R	R	6-1	170	7-20-80	1998	Las Mata de Farfan, D.R.
Eason, Clay	5	2	2.00	29	3	0	4	68	48	16	15	26	60	.206	R	R	5-11	190	9-28-75	1997	Dunn, N.C.
Lantigua, Delvis	6	2	3.48	16	15	0	0	85	67	36	33	35	66	.217	R	R	6-0	170	1-5-80	1998	La Carmelita, D.R.
Majewski, Gary	5	3	2.65	57	1	0	3	75	61	31	22	34	75	.221	R	R	6-2	200	2-26-80	1999	Houston, Texas
Malone, Corwin	10	7	4.71	22	22	0	0	124	116	77	65	89	89	.248	R	L	6-3	200	7-3-80	1999	Thomasville, Ala.

PITCHING	W	L	ERA	G	GS	CG	SV	IP	H	R	ER	BB	SO	AVG	B	T	HT	WT	DOB	1st Yr	Resides
Meyer, Jake	2	0	3.38	23	0	0	0	40	35	15	15	20	31	.244	R	R	6-1	190	1-7-75	1997	San Diego, Calif.
Munoz, Arnaldo	6	0	2.61	51	0	0	6	72	62	29	21	29	78	.231	L	L	5-9	170	6-21-82	1999	Mao, D.R.
Parrish, Wade	4	4	3.38	13	13	0	0	72	75	31	27	31	43	.279	L	L	6-1	190	11-13-77	1999	Othello, Wash.
Purvis, Rob	1	1	5.40	9	0	0	0	17	17	13	10	15	9	.261	R	R	6-2	200	8-11-77	1999	Tipton, Ind.
Sanders, Dave	3	1	1.84	47	0	0	0	64	56	17	13	28	61	.234	L	L	6-0	200	8-29-79	1999	Derby, Kan.
Smith, Matt	1	0	1.74	8	0	0	1	10	2	2	2	9	12	.060	R	R	6-5	240	8-14-78	1999	Godfrey, Ill.
Stewart, Josh	11	7	3.53	26	26	1	0	150	145	65	59	56	92	.254	L	L	6-3	200	12-5-78	1999	Ledbetter, Ky.
Ulacia, Dennis	6	14	4.82	28	25	0	1	146	173	95	78	51	88	.298	L	L	6-1	180	4-2-81	1999	Hialeah, Fla.
Valentine, Joe	4	1	1.97	55	0	0	36	59	36	16	13	30	63	.173	R	R	6-2	200	12-24-79	1999	Pensacola, Fla.
Wagner, Denny	0	1	12.75	9	0	0	1	12	19	17	17	4	4	.358	R	R	6-0	200	11-8-76	1997	Castlewood, Va.
West, Brian	9	11	4.34	27	26	0	0	149	129	91	72	71	91	.236	R	R	6-4	230	8-4-80	1999	West Monroe, La.

FIELDING

Catcher	PCT	G	PO	A	E	DP	PB
Acevas	.978	39	236	32	6	1	9
Evans	1.000	2	17	1	0	0	0
Olivo	.983	102	674	87	13	10	21
Quintero	1.000	4	32	0	0	0	1

First Base	PCT	G	PO	A	E	DP
Acevas	.987	12	74	3	1	9
Battersby	.993	54	422	22	3	35
Eason	1.000	1	0	0	0	0
Evans	1.000	4	40	0	0	4
Hankins	.988	66	527	34	7	39
Lebron	.962	4	22	3	1	2
Sandoval	1.000	4	29	6	0	3
Zywica	.984	9	58	5	1	7

Second Base	PCT	G	PO	A	E	DP
Bravo	1.000	5	8	15	0	5
Miles	.955	129	243	314	26	56
Sandoval	.978	11	21	23	1	6
Shaffer	.000	1	0	0	4	0

Third Base	PCT	G	PO	A	E	DP
Bravo	.946	34	19	68	5	2
Evans	.923	8	6	6	1	1
Hankins	.926	13	4	21	2	0
Miles	1.000	1	1	1	0	0
Sandoval	.885	35	24	53	10	4
Saunders	.939	11	6	25	2	3
Shaffer	.919	62	35	102	12	10

Shortstop	PCT	G	PO	A	E	DP
Bravo	.889	3	5	3	1	1
Dellaero	.972	55	105	174	8	35
Sandoval	.967	82	130	223	12	44
Shaffer	.828	12	15	33	10	3

Outfield	PCT	G	PO	A	E	DP
Battersby	.950	9	18	1	1	0
Bikowski	.977	119	235	15	6	1
Bravo	1.000	4	2	0	0	0
Durham	.978	116	262	10	6	1
Fernandez	.981	85	146	9	3	1
Ingram	1.000	48	91	1	0	0
Piniella	.989	53	90	3	1	0
Sandoval	1.000	10	13	1	0	0
Zywica	1.000	8	12	2	0	0

WINSTON-SALEM WARTHOGS — High Class A

CAROLINA LEAGUE

BATTING	AVG	G	AB	R	H	2B	3B	HR	RBI	BB	SO	SB	CS	SLG	OBP	B	T	HT	WT	DOB	1st Yr	Resides
Aspito, Jason	.253	102	316	40	80	14	2	6	36	26	83	2	5	.367	.325	R	R	6-0	200	1-3-79	2000	Itasca, Ill.
Borchard, Joe	.000	2	3	1	0	0	0	0	0	6	0	0	0	.000	.667	S	R	6-5	220	11-25-78	2000	Camarillo, Calif.
Buford, Damon	.286	7	28	2	8	2	0	0	2	4	4	1	1	.357	.375	R	R	5-10	180	6-12-70	1990	Dallas, Texas
Caradonna, Brett	.269	110	390	42	105	16	1	7	55	25	47	10	4	.369	.314	L	R	6-1	180	12-3-78	1997	San Diego, Calif.
Ciraco, Darren	.151	17	53	4	8	1	0	1	3	4	18	1	1	.226	.211	R	R	6-2	200	4-6-81	2000	New Rochelle, N.Y.
Gillikin, Joe	.500	2	4	1	2	1	0	0	1	0	1	0	0	.750	.400	R	R	5-10	170	3-17-77	2000	Yukon, Okla.
Harris, Blair	.400	2	5	1	2	0	0	1	4	0	0	0	0	1.00	.400	R	R	6-2	210	6-6-79	2002	Oklahoma City, Okla.
Hickman, Brian	.094	28	64	9	6	0	0	0	2	10	21	1	2	.094	.293	R	R	6-2	200	2-7-78	2001	Yuba City, Calif.
Koslowski, Kasey	.111	5	9	1	1	0	0	0	0	3	2	0	1	.111	.385	R	R	5-11	190	5-8-79	2001	Ozone Park, N.Y.
Lebron, Francisco	.266	56	203	22	54	15	0	8	27	15	54	3	0	.458	.320	R	R	6-6	230	5-10-75	1999	Bayamon, P.R.
Lisk, Charles	.185	18	54	5	10	3	0	1	9	3	19	2	0	.296	.241	R	R	6-1	190	1-3-83	2001	Fort Mill, S.C.
Martel, Normand	.232	81	254	33	59	15	2	3	29	29	58	12	2	.343	.313	L	R	6-0	180	8-4-78	2001	Newport News, Va.
Muro, Robert	.208	34	101	12	21	4	0	1	10	18	21	2	0	.277	.341	R	R	5-9	180	1-16-76	1998	Apple Valley, Calif.
Nicholson, Tommy	.245	122	428	41	105	25	0	1	34	41	82	8	5	.311	.313	L	R	6-3	190	8-23-79	2000	Anaheim, Calif.
Oborn, Spencer	.227	94	273	34	62	11	2	2	29	24	59	5	4	.304	.294	R	R	6-3	190	8-27-77	1999	Diamond Bar, Calif.
Piniella, Juan	.246	55	187	13	46	5	1	2	12	22	47	8	2	.316	.332	R	R	5-10	160	3-13-78	1996	Stafford, Va.
Quintero, Humberto	.194	52	160	13	31	1	1	0	12	8	23	2	3	.213	.247	R	R	6-1	190	8-2-79	1997	Maracaibo, Venez.
Reyes, Guillermo	.279	122	455	51	127	20	1	4	49	35	71	30	15	.354	.335	S	R	5-9	160	12-29-81	1999	Villa Vasquez, D.R.
Rogowski, Casey	.255	55	184	27	47	5	0	3	23	28	46	16	3	.332	.358	L	L	6-3	230	5-1-81	1999	Livonia, Mich.
Rosa, Wally	.243	33	107	8	26	4	0	1	8	9	21	2	1	.308	.314	R	R	6-1	180	11-28-81	2000	Hialeah, Fla.
Salvo, Andrew	.326	31	89	8	29	5	1	0	7	14	16	3	4	.404	.417	L	R	5-10	170	8-27-79	2001	East Islip, N.Y.
Sienko, Ryan	.211	34	114	18	24	8	0	5	17	9	40	1	1	.412	.311	R	R	6-4	220	9-16-75	1997	Elgin, Ill.
Welsh, Eric	.233	126	464	61	108	25	0	23	71	36	159	9	2	.435	.294	L	L	6-0	160	9-17-76	1997	Tinley Park, Ill.
Yan, Edwin	.253	132	490	78	124	6	7	4	35	42	57	88	19	.318	.312	S	R	6-0	160	2-18-82	1999	Santo Domingo, D.R.
Zywica, Mike	.203	48	172	25	35	7	1	7	18	9	53	4	1	.378	.279	R	R	6-4	200	9-14-74	1996	Richton Park, Ill.

PITCHING	W	L	ERA	G	GS	CG	SV	IP	H	R	ER	BB	SO	AVG	B	T	HT	WT	DOB	1st Yr	Resides
Allen, Wyatt	8	9	4.45	28	28	1	0	162	163	91	80	80	110	.263	R	R	6-4	200	4-12-80	2001	Brentwood, Tenn.
An, Byeong	2	0	3.80	11	1	0	0	21	29	10	9	7	11	.333	L	L	6-2	190	7-1-80	2001	Bu Chun City, Korea
Bullard, Jim	9	8	3.32	23	23	0	0	144	147	64	53	46	89	.268	L	L	6-7	190	12-29-79	2001	West Covina, Calif.
Curreri, Joe	0	0	12.71	5	0	0	0	6	14	8	8	0	3	.466	R	R	6-1	190	6-29-77	1999	Pomona, N.Y.
Ferrand, Dario	2	13	4.36	27	20	0	1	122	116	67	59	43	60	.260	R	R	6-1	160	1-19-81	1998	Santo Domingo, D.R.
Fields, Josh	2	2	2.96	36	0	0	4	46	45	23	15	19	50	.257	R	R	6-1	170	1-20-80	2001	Hungry Horse, Mont.
Francisco, Frank	0	4	8.06	6	6	0	0	26	31	23	23	18	25	.310	R	R	6-2	190	9-11-79	1997	Santo Domingo, D.R.
Freeman, Kai	0	0	18.00	1	0	0	0	1	3	2	2	1	1	.500	R	R	6-2	180	3-11-77	1998	Shorewood, Ill.
Garza, Rolando	0	1	8.04	14	0	0	1	16	14	15	14	18	9	.254	R	R	6-4	210	12-14-79	1997	Coachella, Calif.
Honel, Kris	0	1	1.69	1	1	0	0	5	3	2	1	3	6	.150	R	R	6-5	190	11-7-82	2001	Bourbonnais, Ill.
Kirkland, Aaron	3	5	3.68	34	0	0	2	44	41	24	18	23	34	.251	R	R	6-4	200	3-1-79	2001	Chatom, Ala.
Madril, Steve	2	2	5.82	36	0	0	2	39	50	27	25	16	27	.316	L	L	5-11	180	6-20-78	2000	Riverside, Calif.
McWhirter, Kris	2	14	5.46	24	22	0	0	125	147	84	76	55	76	.303	L	R	6-4	190	5-11-79	1999	Goodlettsville, Tenn.
Murray, Brad	4	2	3.82	53	0	0	1	66	62	31	28	23	42	.255	L	L	5-11	170	8-20-78	2000	La Belle, Fla.
Olivo, Rigal	1	3	5.54	15	1	0	0	26	27	18	16	9	20	.254	R	R	6-0	170	10-28-81	2001	Monte Cristi, D.R.
Pacheco, Enemencio	1	4	4.74	8	4	0	0	25	31	17	13	8	24	.298	R	R	6-1	170	8-31-78	1997	Santo Domingo, D.R.
2-team (41 Salem)	3	3	3.67	49	4	0	6	76	83	39	31	34	55	.274							
Pena, Ed	1	0	2.16	11	0	0	1	17	15	6	4	5	10	.230	L	L	5-10	170	8-12-79	2001	Caguas, P.R.
Phillips, Heath	6	16	3.52	28	25	0	8	179	184	82	70	10	112	.267	L	L	6-3	200	3-24-82	2001	Evansville, Ind.
Ring, Royce	2	0	3.91	21	0	0	5	23	20	11	10	11	22	.246	L	L	6-0	220	12-21-80	2002	La Mesa, Calif.
Rupp, Mike	1	2	4.50	11	0	0	0	14	12	11	7	6	14	.240	R	R	6-3	200	2-21-78	1997	La Mesa, Calif.
Smith, Matt	3	3	4.30	47	0	0	4	69	65	35	33	36	50	.248	R	R	6-5	240	8-14-78	1999	Godfrey, Ill.
Wagner, Denny	1	5	5.82	21	6	0	1	43	48	35	28	35	13	.292	R	R	6-0	200	11-8-76	1997	Castlewood, Va.

Catcher	PCT	G	PO	A	E	DP	PB
Harris	1.000	1	5	1	0	0	0
Hickman	.993	26	117	16	1	0	5
Koslowski	.909	3	10	0	1	0	1
Lisk	.991	18	98	12	1	1	7
Quintero	.990	52	310	67	4	2	4
Rosa	.986	31	184	31	3	0	4
Sienko	.985	22	119	12	2	3	2

First Base	PCT	G	PO	A	E	DP
Lebron	.984	32	285	23	5	33
Oborn	1.000	1	1	0	0	1
Rogowski	.991	42	411	19	4	38
Welsh	.992	66	625	29	5	58

Second Base	PCT	G	PO	A	E	DP
Nicholson	.981	14	25	27	1	8

	PCT	G	PO	A	E	DP
Reyes	1.000	1	2	2	0	0
Salvo	1.000	4	6	9	0	3
Yan	.957	130	270	381	29	88

Third Base	PCT	G	PO	A	E	DP
Koslowski	.750	1	1	2	1	0
Muro	.897	28	23	47	8	4
Nicholson	.959	104	77	248	14	30
Oborn	.963	7	6	20	1	3
Salvo	.810	9	4	13	4	2
Yan	.000	1	0	0	0	0

Shortstop	PCT	G	PO	A	E	DP
Nicholson	.889	6	6	18	3	2
Reyes	.957	121	189	367	25	85
Salvo	.984	16	23	40	1	6

Outfield	PCT	G	PO	A	E	DP
Aspito	.970	93	158	4	5	0
Borchard	1.000	2	3	0	0	0
Buford	1.000	7	16	2	0	0
Caradonna	.991	73	103	10	1	1
Ciraco	1.000	17	22	1	0	0
Hickman	.000	1	0	0	0	0
Martel	.980	78	141	5	3	0
Oborn	.982	84	165	2	3	0
Piniella	.985	54	126	5	2	3
Rosa	1.000	1	1	0	0	0
Sienko	.000	1	0	0	0	0
Welsh	.917	10	10	1	1	0
Zywica	.939	40	58	4	4	0

KANNAPOLIS INTIMIDATORS — Low Class A

SOUTH ATLANTIC LEAGUE

BATTING	AVG	G	AB	R	H	2B	3B	HR	RBI	BB	SO	SB	CS	SLG	OBP	B	T	HT	WT	DOB	1st Yr	Resides
Amador, Chris	.201	124	418	60	84	5	4	3	26	38	142	56	15	.254	.279	R	R	5-10	160	12-14-82	2000	Camuy, P.R.
Barnett, Dan	.244	18	45	8	11	2	2	0	8	4	12	0	0	.378	.308	R	R	5-10	180	3-31-80	2002	Wauchula, Fla.
Cavin, Jonathan	.253	94	300	33	76	18	1	2	29	41	71	2	4	.340	.350	L	R	6-3	220	3-19-80	2000	Stilwell, Okla.
Ciraco, Darren	.189	44	159	15	30	4	0	0	11	16	39	3	1	.214	.261	R	R	6-2	200	4-6-81	2000	New Rochelle, N.Y.
Harris, Blair	.250	15	52	4	13	4	0	1	6	4	12	0	0	.385	.304	R	R	6-2	210	6-6-79	2002	Oklahoma City, Okla.
Lee, Carlos	.286	10	35	2	10	2	0	0	6	1	6	0	0	.343	.306	R	R	6-1	220	9-29-81	2000	Provincia, Panama
Martel, Normand	.267	34	135	14	36	6	3	0	13	6	32	3	4	.356	.303	L	R	6-0	180	8-4-78	2001	Newport News, Va.
McKee, Scott	.271	119	439	47	119	26	0	11	65	45	81	0	2	.405	.340	S	R	6-1	200	5-6-77	1999	Bowie, Md.
Molina, Gustavo	.226	94	310	37	70	13	1	2	34	27	61	7	2	.294	.301	R	R	6-2	180	2-24-82	2000	La Guaira, Venez.
Monegan, Anthony	.130	23	77	8	10	0	0	0	3	1	17	5	1	.130	.141	L	R	6-1	170	5-11-79	2000	Flossmoor, Ill.
Morse, Michael	.257	113	417	43	107	30	4	2	56	25	73	7	6	.362	.310	R	R	6-4	180	3-22-82	2000	Plantation, Fla.
Reed, Jeremy	.319	57	210	37	67	15	0	4	32	11	24	17	5	.448	.377	L	L	6-0	180	6-15-81	2002	La Verne, Calif.
Reyes, Julio	.287	55	195	25	56	14	2	7	24	6	35	2	1	.487	.319	L	R	6-2	180	6-30-80	1999	San Luis, Mexico
Rosa, Wally	.273	57	198	21	54	7	1	0	18	21	42	4	1	.318	.360	R	R	6-1	180	11-28-81	2000	Hialeah, Fla.
Salvo, Andrew	.252	57	202	24	51	7	2	2	23	33	29	10	6	.337	.360	L	R	5-10	170	8-27-79	2001	East Islip, N.Y.
Santamarina, Juan	.271	93	332	31	90	18	4	3	29	32	62	3	2	.377	.335	L	R	6-1	180	10-3-79	1998	Miami, Fla.
Spidale, Mike	.291	93	357	57	104	11	1	0	30	34	50	37	25	.328	.372	L	R	6-1	180	3-12-82	2000	Broadview, Ill.
Storey, Eric	.260	110	388	65	101	19	1	9	42	58	136	4	0	.384	.358	R	R	6-0	170	10-12-77	2000	Indianapolis, Ind.
Wigginton, Derek	.231	110	398	32	92	14	2	4	47	29	89	10	8	.307	.283	L	L	6-1	210	4-20-79	2000	Antioch, Tenn.

PITCHING	W	L	ERA	G	GS	CG	SV	IP	H	R	ER	BB	SO	AVG	B	T	HT	WT	DOB	1st Yr	Resides
Bittner, Tim	5	13	4.58	29	29	0	0	157	166	98	80	67	123	.273	L	L	6-2	200	6-9-80	2001	Wilmington, Del.
Castro, Julio	5	2	4.21	43	0	0	4	58	52	29	27	28	61	.250	R	R	6-1	160	6-30-81	1998	San Pedro de Macoris, D.R.
Dobyns, Heath	1	2	4.12	23	0	0	0	44	50	30	20	13	23	.280	R	R	6-4	190	1-16-79	2001	Fountain, Colo.
Fields, Josh	2	0	1.82	21	0	0	7	30	22	13	6	3	35	.198	R	R	6-1	170	1-20-80	2001	Hungry Horse, Mont.
Fryson, Andrew	5	7	5.03	17	16	0	0	82	100	62	46	24	54	.297	R	R	6-7	200	10-13-80	2001	Tallahassee, Fla.
Honel, Kris	9	8	2.82	26	26	0	0	153	128	57	48	52	152	.227	R	R	6-5	190	11-7-82	2001	Bourbonnais, Ill.
Lubisich, Nik	9	3	2.79	34	13	2	0	123	123	45	38	26	81	.265	L	L	6-2	190	4-19-79	2001	Portland, Ore.
Meaux, Ryan	0	2	1.35	10	0	0	6	13	19	10	2	0	13	.322	R	L	5-11	170	10-5-78	2001	Lamar, Colo.
2-team (44 Hagerstown)	4	5	2.38	54	0	0	23	68	60	32	18	12	57	.229							
Olivo, Rigal	2	6	4.55	30	2	0	2	57	53	31	29	18	45	.245	R	R	6-0	170	10-28-81	2001	Monte Cristi, D.R.
Patten, Scott	4	4	2.50	49	0	0	10	72	61	27	20	40	50	.226	R	R	6-3	210	11-26-80	1999	Tecumseh, Okla.
Reynoso, Paulino	6	8	4.24	33	14	1	2	102	96	61	48	65	73	.253	L	L	6-3	190	8-10-80	1999	Santiago, D.R.
Stumm, Jason	0	1	2.25	22	0	0	5	40	37	10	10	12	45	.245	R	R	6-2	210	4-13-81	1999	Centralia, Wash.
Szado, Craig	5	9	3.40	30	19	0	0	127	124	63	48	51	88	.259	L	L	6-3	180	3-19-79	2001	Monson, Mass.
Williams, Mike	1	0	1.54	22	0	0	1	41	28	15	7	23	37	.177	R	R	6-3	190	8-9-78	1998	Cypress, Texas
Wing, Ryan	12	7	3.78	25	21	0	0	124	111	64	52	60	109	.239	L	L	6-2	170	2-1-82	2001	Murrieta, Calif.
Young, Curtis	0	2	15.00	7	0	0	0	9	15	15	15	6	11	.384	R	R	6-2	170	1-30-80	2000	Grand Junction, Colo.

FIELDING

Catcher	PCT	G	PO	A	E	DP	PB
Barnett	1.000	18	109	8	0	0	2
Harris	.933	4	27	1	2	0	1
Lee	1.000	1	1	0	0	0	2
Molina	.984	75	527	86	10	2	14
Rosa	.985	50	349	42	6	4	7

First Base	PCT	G	PO	A	E	DP
Lee	.875	1	7	0	1	0
McKee	.983	100	785	49	14	57
Molina	.982	19	150	10	3	13
Reyes	1.000	7	44	0	0	3
Santamarina	.944	4	32	2	2	4
Storey	.993	20	135	6	1	14

Second Base	PCT	G	PO	A	E	DP
Amador	.960	115	239	288	22	54
Salvo	.965	23	51	58	4	23
Storey	.938	9	10	20	2	2

Third Base	PCT	G	PO	A	E	DP
Lee	.909	5	4	6	1	0
Morse	.937	23	10	49	4	3
Santamarina	.917	59	44	99	13	8
Storey	.945	59	35	102	8	8

Shortstop	PCT	G	PO	A	E	DP
Amador	.923	8	12	24	3	4
Morse	.934	91	145	250	28	43

	PCT	G	PO	A	E	DP
Salvo	.922	22	40	54	8	6
Storey	.926	23	39	74	9	14

Outfield	PCT	G	PO	A	E	DP
Cavin	.975	77	112	5	3	0
Ciraco	.976	42	81	0	2	0
Martel	1.000	30	68	2	0	0
Monegan	1.000	20	33	1	0	0
Reed	1.000	55	119	5	0	0
Reyes	1.000	20	19	2	0	0
Rosa	.000	1	0	0	0	0
Spidale	1.000	91	232	3	0	1
Wigginton	.970	103	189	6	6	0

BRISTOL SOX — Rookie

APPALACHIAN LEAGUE

BATTING	AVG	G	AB	R	H	2B	3B	HR	RBI	BB	SO	SB	CS	SLG	OBP	B	T	HT	WT	DOB	1st Yr	Resides
Bohlander, Michael	.161	23	62	4	10	2	0	1	7	2	20	1	1	.242	.197	L	R	6-1	230	11-8-80	2002	Katonah, N.Y.
Bounds, Brandon	.285	55	193	34	55	14	2	9	38	36	48	0	0	.518	.401	L	R	6-6	190	8-10-81	2001	Arlington, Texas

BATTING	AVG	G	AB	R	H	2B	3B	HR	RBI	BB	SO	SB	CS	SLG	OBP	B	T	HT	WT	DOB	1st Yr	Resides
Brice, Thomas	.327	29	98	11	32	4	1	0	20	10	11	1	0	.388	.395	L	L	6-5	210	8-24-81	2002	Mile End, Australia
Ciraco, Darren	.329	56	219	47	72	15	0	10	51	27	39	2	0	.534	.398	R	R	6-2	200	4-6-81	2000	New Rochelle, N.Y.
Ford, Mark	.232	25	69	13	16	1	0	1	10	10	14	1	2	.290	.346	R	R	5-9	160	3-23-79	2002	Charlotte, N.C.
Gonzalez, Andy	.280	66	254	48	71	17	0	1	45	32	43	5	4	.358	.358	R	R	6-2	180	12-15-81	2001	Rio Piedras, P.R.
Huson, Tim	.265	42	132	19	35	7	2	4	12	11	45	3	1	.439	.322	L	R	6-2	200	4-8-80	2001	Cottonwood, Ark.
Ivy, Bjorn	.272	53	162	37	44	2	1	1	14	33	43	15	5	.315	.407	R	R	5-10	170	9-20-81	2000	Shannon, Miss.
Koslowski, Kasey	.067	5	15	2	1	0	0	0	1	1	3	0	0	.067	.222	R	R	5-11	190	5-8-79	2001	Ozone Park, N.Y.
Lee, Carlos	.293	15	41	6	12	5	0	0	7	5	5	1	0	.415	.388	R	R	6-1	220	5-29-80	2001	Provincia, Panama
Lisk, Charles	.202	28	104	9	21	4	0	3	16	3	32	0	0	.327	.227	R	R	6-3	200	1-3-83	2001	Fort Mill, S.C.
Lopez, Pedro	.319	63	260	42	83	11	0	0	35	20	27	22	8	.362	.370	R	R	6-1	160	4-28-84	2001	Moca, D.R.
Morris,	.219	54	183	27	40	10	2	5	28	18	73	2	0	.377	.289	R	R	6-2	200	8-25-80	2002	Hamilton, Ohio
Stewart, Chris	.278	42	158	25	44	9	0	1	12	14	23	0	0	.354	.350	R	R	6-4	200	2-19-82	2001	Moreno Valley, Calif.
Varela, Edgar	.330	55	188	30	62	11	1	8	40	13	29	0	1	.527	.395	L	R	6-1	200	8-9-80	2002	Rancho Dominguez, Calif.
Webster, Anthony	.352	61	244	58	86	7	3	1	30	38	38	16	7	.418	.448	L	L	5-10	190	4-10-83	2001	Parsons, Tenn.

GAMES BY POSITION: C—Kowlowski 2, Lee 1, Lisk 27, Stewart 39. **1B**—Bohlander 11, Bounds 46, Huson 18. **2B**—Ford 16, Huson 3, Lopez 53. **3B**—Ford 8, Huson 6, Koslowski 2, Lee 11, Varela 53. **SS**—Gonzalez 62, Lopez 8. **OF**—Brice 12, Ciraco 50, Huson 7, Ivy 46, Morris 46, Webster 58.

PITCHING	W	L	ERA	G	GS	CG	SV	IP	H	R	ER	BB	SO	AVG	B	T	HT	WT	DOB	1st Yr	Resides
Curreri, Joe	2	0	2.00	9	0	0	2	18	11	6	4	5	18	.161	R	R	6-1	190	6-29-77	1999	Pomona, N.Y.
Deininger, Todd	0	1	1.38	19	0	0	1	39	26	9	6	20	41	.189	R	R	6-3	200	9-4-81	2002	Joliet, Ill.
Dowdy, Justin	6	4	3.72	13	11	0	0	58	61	29	24	21	47	.268	L	L	6-1	160	8-13-83	2001	San Diego, Calif.
Fryson, Andrew	0	0	4.50	3	1	0	0	4	5	2	2	0	2	.294	R	R	6-7	200	10-13-80	2001	Tallahassee, Fla.
Hummel, Rick	1	1	2.59	24	0	0	5	31	24	10	9	10	26	.212	R	R	6-2	190	9-12-80	2002	Wonder Lake, Ill.
Larson, Adam	2	1	3.06	26	0	0	8	35	35	16	12	9	34	.253	R	R	6-3	230	12-6-79	2002	Terre Haute, Ind.
LaMura, B.J.	1	2	4.50	11	0	0	0	18	21	11	9	7	20	.283	R	R	6-1	200	1-1-81	2002	Ronkonkoma, N.Y.
McGary, Gerron	2	3	5.90	20	0	0	0	29	29	25	19	24	34	.266	L	L	5-11	180	2-14-82	2002	Texarkana, Texas
Miller, Brian	7	3	4.30	13	13	0	0	61	57	32	29	30	63	.251	R	R	6-3	200	10-18-82	2001	Charlotte, Mich.
Morales, Ruddy	6	0	3.15	13	13	0	0	66	62	26	23	21	45	.255	R	R	6-5	180	1-20-82	1999	La Romana, D.R.
Nowlen, Jake	0	1	9.00	2	0	0	0	2	2	2	2	2	1	.285	R	R	6-2	190	9-8-80	2002	Monticello, Ark.
Payne, Matt	0	2	4.30	20	0	0	1	23	21	14	11	14	27	.238	R	R	6-2	190	12-25-78	2002	San Francisco, Calif.
Perez, Armando	5	1	3.55	19	4	0	0	51	48	22	20	19	39	.247	L	L	6-2	190	12-26-80	2000	San Ysidro, Calif.
Reed, Rylan	3	0	2.44	12	12	0	0	55	38	23	15	37	44	.195	R	R	6-7	260	11-18-81	2000	Round Rock, Texas
Rupe, Josh	3	3	5.26	17	2	0	0	38	38	23	22	22	40	.260	R	R	6-3	180	8-18-82	2002	Chesapeake, Va.
Sager, Brian	0	1	12.46	6	0	0	0	9	15	12	11		8	.257	R	R	6-5	230	10-30-79	2002	Branford, Conn.
Tracey, Sean	5	2	3.02	13	12	0	0	66	57	27	22	19	50	.240	L	R	6-3	210	11-14-80	2002	Upland, Calif.

PHOENIX WHITE SOX — Rookie

ARIZONA LEAGUE

BATTING	AVG	G	AB	R	H	2B	3B	HR	RBI	BB	SO	SB	CS	SLG	OBP	B	T	HT	WT	DOB	1st Yr	Resides
Arias, Angel	.083	6	12	2	1	1	0	0	1	0	3	0	0	.167	.154	R	R	5-11	170	9-8-82	1999	Azua, D.R.
Barnett, Dan	.389	9	36	10	14	3	1	0	2	4	6	2	1	.528	.450	R	R	5-10	180	3-31-80	2002	Wauchula, Fla.
Bohlander, Michael	.250	15	48	5	12	3	0	0	4	1	10	0	0	.313	.265	L	R	6-1	230	11-8-80	2002	Katonah, N.Y.
Castillo, Cesar	.293	18	58	9	17	3	2	0	7	14	12	2	1	.414	.432	R	R	5-10	180	6-26-79	2002	Yuma, Ariz.
Collaro, Thomas	.213	39	127	22	27	4	3	7	29	14	45	3	0	.457	.292	R	R	6-4	210	4-4-83	2002	Sunrise, Fla.
Harris, Blair	.174	9	23	4	4	1	0	0	0	3	10	0	0	.217	.269	R	R	6-2	210	6-6-79	2002	Oklahoma City, Okla.
Herring, Matt	.200	12	25	4	5	1	0	0	4	6	9	0	0	.240	.412	L	L	6-2	210	9-24-80	2002	Valdosta, Ga.
Ido, Nobutoshi	.245	21	49	11	12	2	2	1	7	4	10	2	1	.429	.327	R	R	6-0	180	12-28-76	2002	Osaka, Japan
Keefner, Eric	.228	36	127	15	29	8	1	2	16	10	41	2	1	.354	.288	R	R	6-3	220	12-8-81	2002	Chicago, Ill.
Lebron, Freddie	.279	41	147	30	41	7	3	0	17	18	18	10	4	.367	.359	S	R	5-9	170	1-23-82	2001	Humacao, P.R.
Luna, Leonardo	.335	50	221	38	74	13	6	1	30	3	13	8	4	.462	.341	R	R	6-0	160	2-14-82	1999	Santiago, D.R.
Myers, Mike	.333	44	165	34	55	12	3	0	23	24	24	18	1	.442	.422	R	R	6-1	190	12-11-79	2002	St. Petersburg, Fla.
Perez, Melvin	.244	44	135	18	33	7	3	0	13	9	36	0	4	.341	.286	R	R	6-1	170	2-2-84	2001	Santo Domingo, D.R.
Rivera, Jhonny	.268	46	153	26	41	10	4	0	21	12	31	7	4	.386	.339	R	R	6-0	170	7-4-83	2000	Miranda, Venez.
Rogowski, Casey	.484	8	31	4	15	6	0	2	8	1	5	2	1	.871	.485	L	L	6-3	230	5-1-81	1999	Livonia, Mich.
Schnurstein, Micah	.332	50	205	28	68	26	1	3	48	12	34	1	2	.512	.373	R	R	6-1	200	7-18-84	2002	Henderson, Nev.
Scoville, Shane	.278	32	108	16	30	8	0	1	13	8	19	1	1	.380	.336	R	R	6-1	180	2-19-80	2002	Basking Ridge, N.J.
Young, Chris	.217	55	184	26	40	13	1	5	17	19	54	7	8	.380	.308	R	R	6-2	170	9-5-83	2001	Houston, Texas
Young, Eddie	.256	45	156	31	40	2	3	1	22	10	37	10	4	.327	.306	R	R	6-2	190	2-6-82	2000	Macon, Ga.

GAMES BY POSITION: C—Arias 5, Barnett 9, Castillo 18, Harris 6, Scoville 26. **1B**—Barnett 1, Bohlander 9, Harris 2, Herring 10, Keefner 22, Perez 15, Rogowski 8. **2B**—Lebron 13, Luna 37, Perez 12. **3B**—Collaro 1, Lebron 4, Myers 1, Perez 10, Schnurstein 42. **SS**—Lebron 26, Luna 11, Myers 23. **OF**—Bohlander 1, Collaro 25, Ido 16, Rivera 45, C. Young 55, E. Young 45.

PITCHING	W	L	ERA	G	GS	CG	SV	IP	H	R	ER	BB	SO	AVG	B	T	HT	WT	DOB	1st Yr	Resides
Banks, Demetrius	0	0	5.40	8	0	0	0	10	12	10	6	8	10	.300	L	L	6-1	160	5-23-83	2002	Austell, Ga.
Curreri, Joe	0	0	5.40	3	0	0	0	5	5	3	3	0	7	.227	R	R	6-1	190	6-29-77	1999	Pomona, N.Y.
Freeman, Kai	0	0	2.00	8	0	0	0	9	9	2	2	1	8	.264	R	R	6-1	180	3-11-77	1998	Shorewood, Ill.
Gomez, Rafael	1	1	3.46	14	0	0	0	13	13	5	5	7	12	.236	R	R	6-1	190	9-26-83	2001	Miami, Fla.
Haeger, Charles	1	4	4.17	15	0	0	6	41	46	25	19	13	24	.294	R	R	6-1	190	9-19-83	2001	Plymouth, Mich.
Haigwood, Daniel	8	4	2.28	14	14	0	0	75	69	31	19	26	74	.243	R	L	6-2	200	11-19-83	2002	Pleasant Plains, Ark.
Huchingson, Jamin	0	0	3.86	6	0	0	0	7	5	3	3	1	5	.192	R	R	6-7	180	2-2-84	2002	Fayetteville, Ark.
Johnson, J.D.	1	1	4.58	16	0	0	2	18	15	9	9	8	17	.227	R	R	6-5	180	12-10-82	2002	Moriarty, N.M.
Lopez, Orionny	1	4	3.97	17	3	0	3	34	31	15	15	11	38	.244	R	R	6-2	170	4-1-84	2002	West Palm Beach, Fla.
McCarthy, Brandon	4	4	2.76	14	14	0	0	78	78	40	24	15	79	.254	R	R	6-7	180	7-7-83	2002	Colorado Springs, Colo.
McCurdy, Jason	2	0	3.38	17	0	0	0	21	17	8	8	7	15	.220	L	L	6-3	170	12-14-82	2002	Miami, Fla.
Ortiz, Dario	3	5	4.87	14	12	1	0	61	55	46	33	32	49	.230	R	R	6-5	200	12-19-82	2002	Santo Domingo, D.R.
Ring, Royce	0	0	0.00	3	0	0	0	5	2	0	0	0	9	.117	L	L	6-0	220	12-21-80	2002	La Mesa, Calif.
Rodriguez, Ryan	2	3	2.76	14	12	0	0	69	69	36	29	16	47	.262	L	L	6-4	210	7-10-84	2002	Keller, Texas
Rupp, Mike	1	1	7.50	11	0	0	0	12	15	13	10	8	15	.306	R	R	6-3	200	2-21-78	1997	La Mesa, Calif.
Sager, Brian	0	0	4.50	2	0	0	0	2	2	1	1	0	2	.250	R	R	6-5	230	10-30-79	2002	Branford, Conn.
Saint Hilaire, Reynaldo	0	0	2.42	15	1	0	1	22	28	16	6	9	9	.321	R	R	6-6	190	12-7-81	1999	San Pedro de Macoris, D.R.
Tisch, Timothy	0	3	4.50	17	0	0	0	22	30	13	11	14	14	.315	L	L	6-5	190	4-11-80	2002	Santee, Calif.

BY JEFF VORVA

About the only interest the Cubs provided their fans during the last homestand of the 2002 season came in the form of Sammy Sosa's quest for 500 career home runs. He needed two in the final six games.

He came up one short. And the way the season went, it was quite fitting that Sosa missed his mark.

"I guess I'll have to wait 'til next year," Sosa said, echoing an often-made remark of Cubs fans for decades.

It was a year of high expectations and higher disappointments. The Cubs entered 2002 armed with a strong starting pitching staff and a beefed up offense ready to improve on an 88-win season from 2001. Instead, the Cubs started out slow and never picked up enough steam, finishing 67-95. It marked the fourth time in six years they lost 90 or more. In the process, they lost two managers: Don Baylor and interim skipper Bruce Kimm both picked up pink slips.

A team that was supposed to be a contender turned into a major disappointment full of excuses. At times, the players complained it was too cold. Then it was too hot. Then there were too many day games.

At one point, a disgusted Cubs official said: "We have to stop making so many excuses. We lead the league in excuses. Look in the box score. There is no category for 'excuses.' "

If anyone deserved to whine and make excuses, it would be the starting pitching staff. Kerry Wood had a 12-11 mark and left seven games with the lead only to have the bullpen blow those leads. He was saddled with seven no-decisions. Matt Clement (12-11, 217 strikeouts), Mark Prior (6-6), Carlos Zambrano (4-8) and Jason Bere (1-10 before a groin injury sidelined him) all could make cases that their records should be better.

But either a lack of offense, a porous or indifferent defense or an abysmal bullpen wasted many sparkling starts for Cubs hurlers. An offense that featured a 3-4-5

Sammy Sosa | Hee Seop Choi

PLAYERS OF THE YEAR

MAJOR LEAGUE: Sammy Sosa, of

Sosa just missed out on his fifth consecutive 50-homer season and reaching the 500-career homer mark. But his 49 blasts led the National League, as did his 122 runs scored.

MINOR LEAGUE: Hee Seop Choi, 1b

Choi, 23, rebounded from wrist and hand injuries in 2001 to enjoy a breakout season. He batted .287-26-97 at Triple-A to make his case for becoming the Cubs starting first baseman in 2003.

ORGANIZATION STATISTICS

combination of Sosa, Fred McGriff and Moises Alou hit just .246 on the season. Sosa (.288-49-108) was the only player to hit well early, but McGriff (.273-30-103) didn't heat up until after May and Alou (.275-15-61) battled slumps and injuries all year.

And the bullpen, which was rock-solid in 2001, faltered as closer Antonio Alfonseca blew nine save opportunities and setup men Kyle Farnsworth (7.33 ERA) and Jeff Fassero (6.18 before he was dealt to the Cardinals) struggled mightily.

"It's unfortunate the way things happened," said Jim Hendry, who took over from Andy MacPhail as general manager during the season. "If we would have won early, I think we would have been a whole different ballclub. If we hadn't gotten out of the gates so poorly, I think we could have maintained (a winning record) and maybe added (players) in July instead of subtracted.

"Some of the guys on this team have character and have had a history of winning. But they got off to bad starts and didn't play as well, and it didn't work out."

The Cubs did get a glimpse of the future with some of their heralded homegrown young talent. Prior, their top draft pick in 2001, breezed through Double-A West Tenn and Triple-A Iowa to make 19 starts in Chicago, striking out 147 batters in 117 innings.

On the minor league level, lefthander Andy Sisco was named the top prospect in the Northwest League by league managers, while outfielder Felix Pie picked up the same recognition in the Rookie-level Arizona League. Though none of the top three farm clubs made the postseason, low Class A Lansing (lost in the Midwest League finals), short-season Boise (swept Everett in the Northwest league championship) and the AZL Cubs (won a one-game playoff over the Giants) all did well in the playoffs.

ORGANIZATION LEADERS

BATTING

*AVG	Brendan Harris, West Tenn/Daytona	.328
R	Hee Seop Choi, Iowa	94
H	Brendan Harris, West Tenn/Daytona	157
TB	Brendan Harris, West Tenn/Daytona	255
2B	Brendan Harris, West Tenn/Daytona	39
3B	Felix Pie, Boise/AZL Cubs	13
HR	Julio Zuleta, Iowa	31
RBI	Julio Zuleta, Iowa	104
BB	Hee Seop Choi, Iowa	95
SO	Dave Kelton, West Tenn	129
SB	Ryan Theriot, Lansing	32
	Ray Sadler, West Tenn/Daytona	32

PITCHING

W	Angel Guzman, Daytona/Lansing	11
L	Chris Gissell, Iowa	12
#ERA	Angel Guzman, Daytona/Lansing	2.19
G	Dave Hooten, West Tenn	65
CG	Three tied at	2
SV	Francis Beltran, West Tenn	23
IP	Matt Bruback, West Tenn	174
BB	Ben Ford, Iowa	73
SO	Matt Bruback, West Tenn	158

*Minimum 250 At-Bats #Minimum 75 Innings

CHICAGO
CUBS

Managers: Don Baylor, Bruce Kimm

2002 Record: 67-95, .414 (5th, NL Central)

BATTING	AVG	G	AB	R	H	2B	3B	HR	RBI	BB	SO	SB	CS	SLG	OBP	B	T	HT	WT	DOB	1st Yr	Resides
Alou, Moises	.275	132	484	50	133	23	1	15	61	47	61	8	0	.419	.337	R	R	6-3	190	7-3-66	1986	Santo Domingo, D.R.
Bellhorn, Mark	.258	146	445	86	115	24	4	27	56	76	144	7	5	.512	.374	S	R	6-1	200	8-23-74	1995	Oviedo, Fla.
Brown, Roosevelt	.211	111	204	14	43	12	0	3	23	23	50	2	2	.314	.299	L	R	5-10	200	8-3-75	1993	Midland, Ga.
Choi, Hee Seop	.180	24	50	6	9	1	0	2	4	7	15	0	0	.320	.281	L	L	6-5	240	3-16-79	1999	Mesa, Ariz.
DeShields, Delino	.192	67	146	20	28	6	1	3	10	21	38	10	1	.308	.292	L	R	6-1	180	1-15-69	1987	Fairburn, Ga.
Echevarria, Angel	.306	50	98	14	30	7	0	3	21	8	17	0	0	.469	.351	R	R	6-2	230	5-25-71	1992	Bridgeport, Conn.
Encarnacion, Mario	.000	3	7	0	0	0	0	0	0	2	3	0	0	.000	.222	R	R	6-2	210	9-24-75	1994	Bani, D.R.
Girardi, Joe	.226	90	234	19	53	10	1	1	13	16	35	1	0	.291	.275	R	R	5-11	200	10-14-64	1986	Chicago, Ill.
Gonzalez, Alex	.248	142	513	58	127	27	5	18	61	46	136	5	3	.425	.312	R	R	6-0	200	4-8-73	1991	Coral Gables, Fla.
Hermansen, Chad	.209	35	43	3	9	3	0	1	3	5	14	0	0	.349	.292	R	R	6-2	190	9-10-77	1995	Henderson, Nev.
2-team (65 Pittsburgh) ...	.207	100	237	25	49	14	1	8	18	22	82	7	5	.376	.276							
Hill, Bobby	.253	59	190	26	48	7	2	4	20	17	42	6	1	.374	.327	S	R	5-10	190	4-3-78	2000	San Jose, Calif.
Hundley, Todd	.211	92	266	32	56	8	0	16	35	32	80	0	0	.421	.301	S	R	5-11	200	5-27-69	1987	Port St. Lucie, Fla.
Lewis, Darren	.241	58	79	7	19	3	1	0	7	7	11	1	3	.304	.326	R	R	6-0	200	8-28-67	1988	Hillsborough, Calif.
Machado, Robert	.276	22	58	5	16	4	0	1	5	5	11	0	0	.397	.333	R	R	6-1	210	6-3-73	1989	Caracas, Venez.
Mahoney, Mike	.207	16	29	2	6	3	0	0	3	1	10	0	0	.310	.233	R	R	6-1	200	12-5-72	1995	Raleigh, N.C.
McGriff, Fred	.273	146	523	67	143	27	2	30	103	63	99	1	2	.505	.353	L	L	6-3	220	10-31-63	1981	Tampa, Fla.
Mueller, Bill	.266	103	353	51	94	19	4	7	37	51	41	0	0	.402	.355	S	R	5-10	180	3-17-71	1993	Maryland Heights, Mo.
Ojeda, Augie	.186	30	70	4	13	4	0	0	4	5	5	1	0	.243	.247	S	R	5-8	170	12-20-74	1996	South Gate, Calif.
Orie, Kevin	.281	13	32	4	9	3	0	0	5	1	4	0	0	.375	.306	R	R	6-4	220	9-1-72	1993	Pittsburgh, Pa.
Patterson, Corey	.253	153	592	71	150	30	5	14	54	19	142	18	3	.392	.284	L	R	5-9	170	8-13-79	1999	Kennesaw, Ga.
Sosa, Sammy	.288	150	556	122	160	19	2	49	108	103	144	2	0	.594	.399	R	R	6-0	220	11-12-68	1986	San Pedro de Macoris, D.R.
Stynes, Chris	.241	98	195	25	47	9	1	5	26	21	29	1	1	.374	.314	R	R	5-10	200	1-19-73	1991	Deerfield Beach, Fla.

PITCHING	W	L	ERA	G	GS	CG	SV	IP	H	R	ER	BB	SO	AVG	B	T	HT	WT	DOB	1st Yr	Resides
Alfonseca, Antonio	2	5	4.00	66	0	0	19	74	73	34	33	36	61	.257	R	R	6-5	230	4-16-72	1990	La Romana, D.R.
Beltran, Francis	0	0	7.50	11	0	0	0	12	14	11	10	16	11	.311	R	R	6-5	220	11-29-79	1997	Santo Domingo, D.R.
Benes, Alan	2	2	4.35	7	7	0	0	39	42	22	19	12	32	.276	R	R	6-5	240	1-21-72	1993	St. Louis, Mo.
Bere, Jason	1	10	5.67	16	16	0	0	86	98	63	54	28	65	.289	R	R	6-3	220	5-26-71	1990	North Andover, Mass.
Borowski, Joe	4	4	2.73	73	0	0	2	96	84	31	29	29	97	.237	R	R	6-2	240	5-4-71	1989	Bayonne, N.J.
Chiasson, Scott	0	0	23.14	4	0	0	0	5	11	12	12	6	3	.440	R	R	6-3	200	8-14-77	1998	Norwich, Conn.
Clement, Matt	12	11	3.60	32	32	3	0	205	162	84	82	85	215	.215	R	R	6-3	190	8-12-74	1994	Butler, Pa.
Cruz, Juan	3	11	3.98	45	9	0	1	97	84	56	43	59	81	.240	R	R	6-2	160	10-15-78	1997	Bonao, D.R.
Cunnane, Will	1	1	5.47	16	0	0	0	26	27	16	16	13	30	.270	R	R	6-1	200	4-24-74	1993	Rockland, N.Y.
Duncan, Courtney	0	0	0.00	2	0	0	0	2	2	0	0	1	1	.250	L	R	6-0	190	10-9-74	1996	Huntsville, Ala.
Farnsworth, Kyle	4	6	7.33	45	0	0	1	47	53	47	38	24	46	.292	R	R	6-4	230	4-14-76	1995	Canton, Ga.
Fassero, Jeff	5	6	6.18	57	0	0	1	51	65	37	35	22	44	.312	L	L	6-1	200	1-5-63	1984	Paradise Valley, Ariz.
Gordon, Tom	1	1	3.42	19	0	0	0	24	27	12	9	10	31	.293	R	R	5-9	190	11-18-67	1986	Avon Park, Fla.
Lieber, Jon	6	8	3.70	21	21	3	0	141	153	64	58	12	87	.276	R	R	6-2	230	4-2-70	1992	Mobile, Ala.
Mahay, Ron	2	0	8.59	11	0	0	0	15	13	14	14	8	14	.228	L	L	6-2	190	6-28-71	1991	Manalapan, N.J.
Mahomes, Pat	1	1	3.86	16	2	0	0	33	36	15	14	17	23	.285	R	R	6-4	210	8-9-70	1988	Lindale, Texas
Osborne, Donovan	0	1	6.19	11	0	0	0	16	19	11	11	10	13	.296	L	L	6-2	190	6-21-69	1990	Carson City, Nev.
Prior, Mark	6	6	3.32	19	19	1	0	117	98	45	43	38	147	.225	R	R	6-5	220	9-7-80	2002	Bonita, Calif.
Sanchez, Jesus	0	0	12.96	8	0	0	0	8	15	12	12	10	6	.394	L	L	5-11	170	10-11-74	1992	Nizao Bani, D.R.
Smyth, Steve	1	3	9.35	8	7	0	0	26	34	28	27	10	16	.320	L	L	6-1	200	6-3-78	1999	Temecula, Calif.
Wood, Kerry	12	11	3.66	33	33	4	0	214	169	92	87	97	217	.221	R	R	6-5	230	6-16-77	1995	Scottsdale, Ariz.
Zambrano, Carlos	4	8	3.66	32	16	0	0	108	94	53	44	63	93	.235	S	R	6-5	250	6-1-81	1997	Puerto Cabello, Venez.

FIELDING

Catcher	PCT	G	PO	A	E	DP	PB
Girardi	.990	88	554	43	6	6	6
Hundley	.984	79	622	40	11	8	7
Machado	.985	21	110	25	2	2	1
Mahoney	1.000	16	76	7	0	0	1

First Base	PCT	G	PO	A	E	DP
Bellhorn	.989	22	90	3	1	10
Choi	.983	22	106	8	2	16
Echevarria	.985	13	61	4	1	12
Machado	.000	1	0	0	0	0
McGriff	.993	137	1005	60	7	84

Second Base	PCT	G	PO	A	E	DP
Bellhorn	.980	77	121	175	6	42
DeShields	.970	41	65	98	5	15
Hill	.991	55	96	117	2	31
Ojeda	.969	10	18	13	1	4
Stynes	1.000	20	22	33	0	12

Third Base	PCT	G	PO	A	E	DP
Bellhorn	.942	36	16	33	3	3

Mueller	.973	101	60	156	6	19
Ojeda	1.000	5	1	5	0	0
Orie	.895	12	4	13	2	1
Stynes	.921	40	15	43	5	3

Shortstop	PCT	G	PO	A	E	DP
Bellhorn	.974	12	15	22	1	7
Gonzalez	.965	142	220	360	21	84
Hill	.000	1	0	0	0	0
Ojeda	.966	16	15	41	2	4

Outfield	PCT	G	PO	A	E	DP
Alou	.991	124	203	6	2	1
Bellhorn	.000	1	0	0	0	0
Brown	.975	64	78	1	2	1
DeShields	1.000	1	2	0	0	0
Echevarria	.971	19	33	1	1	1
Encarnacion	1.000	2	5	0	0	0
Hermansen	.895	21	17	0	2	0
Lewis	1.000	47	46	2	0	1
Patterson	.990	147	303	5	3	1
Sosa	.980	150	284	7	6	1

Matt Clement

LARRY GOREN

Director, Player Development: Oneri Fleita.

Class	Farm Team	League	W	L	Pct.	Finish*	Manager(s)	First Yr.
AAA	Iowa Cubs	Pacific Coast	71	73	.493	11th (16)	Bruce Kimm/Pat Listach	1981
AA	West Tenn Diamond Jaxx	Southern	73	67	.521	4th (10)	Bobby Dickerson	1998
High A	Daytona (Fla.) Cubs	Florida State	64	73	.467	8th (12)	Dave Trembley	1993
Low A	Lansing (Mich.) Lugnuts	Midwest	74	65	.532	5th (14)	Julio Garcia	1999
SS A	Boise (Idaho) Hawks	Northwest	49	27	.645	+1st (8)	Steve McFarland	2001
Rookie	Mesa (Ariz.) Cubs	Arizona	35	21	.625	+1st (7)	Carmelo Martinez	1997

*Finish in overall standings (No. of teams in league)   +League champion

IOWA CUBS — Triple-A

PACIFIC COAST LEAGUE

ORGANIZATION STATISTICS

BATTING	AVG	G	AB	R	H	2B	3B	HR	RBI	BB	SO	SB	CS	SLG	OBP	B	T	HT	WT	DOB	1st Yr	Resides
Amrhein, Mike	.294	29	85	13	25	5	0	0	11	6	12	0	0	.353	.371	R	R	6-2	220	6-14-75	1997	Oak Park, Ill.
Bartee, Kimera	.253	133	419	59	106	27	2	10	64	41	111	25	13	.399	.318	R	R	6-1	190	7-21-72	1993	Peoria, Ariz.
Bass, Jayson	.286	124	419	78	120	14	3	21	79	52	90	13	7	.484	.365	L	L	6-3	220	6-22-74	1993	Seattle, Wash.
Budzinski, Mark	.281	12	32	6	9	2	1	0	4	3	5	1	0	.406	.343	L	L	6-2	180	8-26-73	1995	Richmond, Va.
Choi, Hee Seop	.287	135	478	94	137	24	3	26	97	95	119	3	2	.513	.406	L	L	6-5	240	3-16-79	1999	Mesa, Ariz.
Coffie, Ivanon	.239	124	373	55	89	32	5	7	51	41	65	2	5	.408	.318	L	R	6-1	190	5-16-77	1995	Curacao, Neth. Antilles
Curry, Chris	.105	7	19	0	2	1	0	0	0	1	8	0	0	.158	.190	L	R	6-1	190	11-17-77	1999	Conway, Ark.
Echevarria, Angel	.295	63	217	40	64	12	3	13	45	17	48	0	0	.558	.357	R	R	6-4	230	5-25-71	1992	Bridgeport, Conn.
Encarnacion, Mario	.280	61	200	24	56	9	0	7	28	17	61	0	2	.430	.342	R	R	6-2	210	9-24-75	1994	Bani, D.R.
Gissell, Chris	.222	29	36	5	8	2	0	3	11	1	13	0	0	.528	.243	R	R	6-5	210	1-4-78	1996	Vancouver, Wash.
Hill, Bobby	.280	92	354	80	99	23	3	8	39	49	66	29	5	.429	.382	S	R	5-10	190	4-3-78	2000	San Jose, Calif.
Hundley, Todd	.222	3	9	1	2	0	0	1	4	1	2	0	0	.556	.300	S	R	5-11	200	5-27-69	1987	Port St. Lucie, Fla.
Lopez, Mickey	.263	107	338	48	89	25	1	5	39	39	45	8	5	.388	.340	S	R	5-10	160	11-17-73	1995	Miami, Fla.
Mahoney, Mike	.256	78	223	33	57	12	1	2	18	17	44	1	1	.345	.311	R	R	6-1	200	12-5-72	1995	Raleigh, N.C.
Melhuse, Adam	.292	72	226	33	66	19	0	7	39	28	47	2	3	.469	.370	S	R	6-2	200	3-27-72	1993	San Luis Obispo, Calif.
Mueller, Bill	.375	6	16	2	6	1	0	1	5	3	1	0	1	.625	.474	S	R	5-10	180	3-17-71	1993	Maryland Heights, Mo.
Ojeda, Augie	.230	73	291	54	67	20	4	1	27	31	30	5	3	.337	.318	S	R	5-8	170	12-20-74	1996	South Gate, Calif.
Ordaz, Luis	.273	61	194	22	53	10	0	1	14	9	21	5	2	.340	.309	R	R	5-11	170	8-12-75	1993	Maracaibo, Venez.
Orie, Kevin	.299	86	294	51	88	16	3	20	63	25	40	0	1	.578	.358	R	R	6-4	220	9-1-72	1993	Pittsburgh, Pa.
Ramsey, Brad	.000	2	4	1	0	0	0	0	1	0	0	0	0	.000	.000	R	R	6-4	220	11-7-76	1997	West Monroe, La.
Weekly, Chris	.250	7	12	2	3	1	0	0	2	3	0	0	0	.333	.357	L	R	6-2	190	12-4-76	1999	Mesa, Ariz.
Zuleta, Julio	.293	120	444	80	130	21	0	31	104	43	106	0	1	.550	.362	R	R	6-5	230	3-28-75	1993	Chandler, Ariz.

PITCHING	W	L	ERA	G	GS	CG	SV	IP	H	R	ER	BB	SO	AVG	B	T	HT	WT	DOB	1st Yr	Resides
Agosto, Stevenson	2	1	6.41	4	4	0	0	20	28	16	14	9	16	.329	L	L	5-11	200	9-2-76	1994	Rio Grande, P.R.
Benes, Alan	10	9	5.65	28	19	0	0	113	130	79	71	53	85	.292	R	R	6-5	240	1-21-72	1993	St. Louis, Mo.
Bere, Jason	1	0	1.80	1	1	0	0	5	2	1	1	3	3	.117	R	R	6-3	220	5-26-71	1990	North Andover, Mass.
Brown, Eric	0	0	0.00	1	0	0	0	1	0	0	0	0	2	.000	R	R	6-3	210	12-5-78	2001	Basking Ridge, N.J.
Chiasson, Scott	1	4	7.94	27	0	0	7	28	34	26	25	13	26	.303	R	R	6-3	200	8-14-77	1998	Norwich, Conn.
Cunnane, Will	4	1	2.20	43	0	0	2	74	67	23	18	23	69	.244	R	R	6-1	200	4-24-74	1993	Rockland, N.Y.
Deschenes, Marc	0	1	7.20	4	0	0	0	5	5	4	4	4	3	.277	R	R	6-0	200	1-6-73	1995	Dracut, Mass.
Duncan, Courtney	3	5	3.99	55	0	0	6	68	67	35	30	33	64	.261	L	R	6-0	190	10-9-74	1996	Huntsville, Ala.
Estrella, Leo	0	0	5.91	8	0	0	1	11	10	8	7	7	9	.238	R	R	6-1	180	2-20-75	1994	Port St. Lucie, Fla.
Farnsworth, Kyle	0	1	6.00	2	0	0	0	3	3	2	2	0	2	.272	R	R	6-4	230	4-14-76	1995	Canton, Ga.
Ford, Ben	6	11	4.88	32	23	0	0	142	157	91	77	73	84	.284	R	R	6-7	240	8-15-75	1994	Cedar Rapids, Iowa
Gissell, Chris	8	12	6.12	28	27	2	0	154	177	108	105	61	133	.289	R	R	6-5	210	1-4-78	1996	Vancouver, Wash.
Gordon, Tom	0	0	16.20	2	0	0	1	2	1	4	3	3	0	.166	R	R	5-10	190	11-18-67	1986	Avon Park, Fla.
Kolb, Brandon	0	1	6.75	13	0	0	0	17	20	17	13	10	14	.289	R	R	6-1	200	11-20-73	1995	Scottsdale, Ariz.
Lopez, Mickey	0	0	0.00	2	0	0	0	2	3	0	0	1	0	.000	S	R	5-10	160	11-17-73	1995	Miami, Fla.
Mahay, Ron	0	1	1.93	39	1	0	2	47	32	11	10	15	50	.189	L	L	6-2	190	6-28-71	1991	Manalapan, N.J.
Mahomes, Pat	4	5	3.48	44	5	0	14	72	57	30	28	20	70	.214	R	R	6-4	210	8-9-70	1988	Lindale, Texas
Miller, Travis	0	1	6.17	9	0	0	0	12	13	8	8	5	8	.309	R	L	6-3	210	11-2-72	1994	Eaton, Ohio
2-team (24 Edmonton)	0	2	4.61	33	0	0	1	41	48	23	21	10	32	.301							
Palma, Rick	0	0	6.00	2	0	0	0	3	3	2	2	1	2	.300	L	L	6-1	160	9-26-79	1996	Maracay, Venez.
Prior, Mark	1	1	1.65	3	3	0	0	16	13	10	3	8	24	.203	R	R	6-5	220	9-7-80	2002	Bonita, Calif.
Sanchez, Jesus	8	9	5.90	26	24	0	0	125	144	90	82	65	94	.293	L	L	5-11	170	10-11-74	1992	Nizao Bani, D.R.
Sinclair, Steve	6	2	3.91	52	1	0	1	74	71	33	32	33	59	.255	L	L	6-2	190	8-2-71	1991	Victoria, B.C.
Smyth, Steve	3	2	5.81	6	6	0	0	31	35	21	20	10	25	.286	L	L	6-1	200	6-3-78	1999	Temecula, Calif.
Sollecito, Gabe	1	1	4.26	7	0	0	0	6	7	3	3	3	3	.269	S	R	6-1	190	3-3-72	1993	Monterey, Calif.
Watson, Mark	4	0	4.30	28	0	0	1	38	35	22	18	19	25	.255	R	L	6-4	230	1-23-74	1996	Dunwoody, Ga.
Wilkins, Marc	0	0	0.79	8	0	0	0	11	6	3	1	3	6	.153	R	R	5-11	210	10-21-70	1992	Palmetto, Fla.
Wuertz, Mike	9	5	5.55	28	27	0	0	154	185	109	95	69	131	.294	R	R	6-3	200	12-15-78	1997	Austin, Minn.
Zambrano, Carlos	0	0	0.00	3	3	0	0	9	2	0	0	6	11	.068	S	R	6-5	250	6-1-81	1997	Puerto Cabello, Venez.

FIELDING

Catcher	PCT	G	PO	A	E	DP	PB
Amrhein	.984	26	168	16	3	1	2
Curry	1.000	6	27	1	0	0	0
Hundley	1.000	3	18	0	0	0	0
Mahoney	.978	74	499	45	12	7	5
Melhuse	.991	55	322	24	3	1	5

First Base	PCT	G	PO	A	E	DP
Choi	.990	128	1074	75	12	105

	PCT	G	PO	A	E	DP
Echevarria	1.000	4	21	1	0	3
Melhuse	1.000	4	28	1	0	2
Ramsey	.900	2	9	0	1	0
Zuleta	1.000	10	84	5	0	6

Second Base	PCT	G	PO	A	E	DP
Coffie	.929	3	6	7	1	3
Hill	.986	91	170	245	6	67
Lopez	.978	46	84	137	5	29

		PCT	G	PO	A	E	DP
Ordaz		.970	6	15	17	1	3
Weekly		.750	2	1	2	1	1
Third Base	PCT	G	PO	A	E	DP	
Coffie	.922	58	26	92	10	13	
Encarnacion	.000	1	0	0	0	0	
Lopez	1.000	14	5	18	0	4	
Melhuse	.867	13	5	21	4	1	
Mueller	.909	5	0	10	1	0	

	PCT	G	PO	A	E	DP
Ojeda	1.000	5	1	4	0	0
Orie	.954	75	43	144	9	9
Weekly	.500	3	0	1	1	0

Shortstop	PCT	G	PO	A	E	DP
Coffie	.931	17	17	37	4	10
Lopez	.934	22	28	43	5	10

Melhuse	.000	1	0	0	0	0
Ojeda	.983	68	94	204	5	41
Ordaz	.944	52	73	112	11	24

Outfield	PCT	G	PO	A	E	DP
Bartee	.992	121	252	9	2	3
Bass	.971	117	218	15	7	2

Budzinski	1.000	11	9	0	0	0
Coffie	.989	39	84	4	1	1
Echevarria	1.000	54	90	6	0	0
Encarnacion	.969	57	93	2	3	1
Lopez	1.000	18	27	0	0	0
Melhuse	1.000	4	1	0	0	0
Zuleta	.931	57	66	1	5	1

WEST TENN DIAMOND JAXX · Class AA

SOUTHERN LEAGUE

BATTING	AVG	G	AB	R	H	2B	3B	HR	RBI	BB	SO	SB	CS	SLG	OBP	B	T	HT	WT	DOB	1st Yr	Resides
Abreu, Dennis	.286	122	402	45	115	17	4	7	51	24	102	18	14	.400	.328	R	R	6-0	180	4-22-78	1995	Tumero, Venez.
Amrhein, Mike	.302	63	232	26	70	13	2	5	30	20	24	4	3	.440	.373	R	R	6-2	220	6-14-75	1997	Oak Park, Ill.
Balfe, Ryan	.200	23	85	5	17	3	0	1	7	4	15	0	0	.271	.244	S	R	6-1	180	11-11-75	1994	Cornwall, N.Y.
Budzinski, Mark	.297	114	427	68	127	19	6	4	36	51	85	21	7	.398	.377	L	L	6-2	180	8-26-73	1995	Richmond, Va.
Curry, Chris	.171	12	35	4	6	2	0	0	2	1	10	0	0	.229	.216	R	R	6-1	190	11-17-77	1999	Conway, Ark.
Dzurilla, Mike	.250	6	16	3	4	1	0	0	2	1	3	0	0	.313	.294	R	R	6-0	190	5-4-78	1999	Bayside, N.Y.
Frese, Nate	.226	70	230	24	52	10	1	2	18	23	59	4	3	.304	.301	R	R	6-3	200	7-10-77	1998	Norway, Iowa
Gibralter, Dave	.235	55	166	22	39	8	0	2	18	12	28	1	1	.319	.293	R	R	6-1	210	6-19-75	1993	Duncanville, Texas
Gripp, Ryan	.232	116	380	51	88	24	2	10	49	46	85	4	2	.384	.319	R	R	6-1	210	4-20-78	1999	Indianola, Iowa
Hamilton, Jon	.277	66	238	35	66	13	5	4	32	19	47	4	3	.424	.331	L	L	6-1	190	10-23-77	1997	San Ramon, Calif.
Harris, Brendan	.321	13	53	8	17	4	1	2	11	2	5	1	1	.547	.345	R	R	6-1	190	8-26-80	2001	Queensbury, N.Y.
Jackson, Nic	.290	32	131	18	38	9	1	3	20	6	23	8	2	.443	.329	L	R	6-3	200	9-25-79	2000	Richmond, Va.
Johnson, Mike	.257	121	389	48	100	15	2	6	45	50	77	13	8	.352	.356	R	R	6-4	210	9-6-76	1997	Rancho Cucamonga, Calif.
Johnstone, Ben	.750	6	4	1	3	1	0	0	2	1	0	3	0	1.000	.800	R	R	6-0	190	2-5-78	1999	Atlanta, Ga.
Kelton, Dave	.261	129	498	68	130	28	6	20	79	52	129	12	6	.462	.332	R	R	6-3	200	12-17-79	1998	La Grange, Ga.
Kopitzke, Casey	.221	76	244	16	54	6	0	0	20	13	34	2	3	.246	.270	R	R	6-2	210	5-31-78	1999	Appleton, Wis.
Lopez, Mickey	.274	17	62	11	17	2	0	0	7	5	9	5	2	.306	.324	S	R	5-10	160	11-17-73	1995	Miami, Fla.
McKnight, Lukas	.143	2	7	1	1	0	0	0	1	1	0	1	0	.143	.250	L	R	6-0	190	2-19-80	2000	Libertyville, Ill.
Melian, Jackson	.308	71	234	25	72	17	0	4	26	17	62	10	6	.432	.375	R	R	6-2	190	1-7-80	1996	Barcelona, Venez.
2-team (56 Huntsville)	.270	127	418	59	113	23	1	10	50	52	125	20	9	.402	.369							
Piedra, Jorge	.167	23	60	5	10	3	1	0	4	3	11	2	0	.250	.219	L	L	6-0	190	4-17-79	1997	Van Nuys, Calif.
Powers, John	.298	68	198	33	59	9	2	6	23	30	30	8	2	.455	.394	L	R	5-9	170	6-2-74	1996	Scottsdale, Ariz.
Reyes, Jose	.400	1	5	0	2	0	0	0	0	3	0	0	0	.400	.400	S	R	5-11	170	2-26-84	1999	Barahona, D.R.
Sadler, Ray	.067	10	30	4	2	1	0	0	1	5	5	2	0	.100	.263	R	R	6-1	200	9-19-80	2000	Waco, Texas
Schrager, Tony	.229	117	350	57	80	23	4	10	48	78	93	9	3	.403	.378	R	R	6-1	180	6-14-77	1998	Omaha, Neb.
Weekly, Chris	.194	18	36	4	7	3	0	4	5	5	12	0	2	.278	.293	L	R	6-2	190	12-4-76	1999	Mesa, Ariz.

PITCHING	W	L	ERA	G	GS	CG	SV	IP	H	R	ER	BB	SO	AVG	B	T	HT	WT	DOB	1st Yr	Resides
Abreu, Winston	1	0	7.20	11	0	0	0	15	9	12	12	20	20	.169	R	R	6-2	150	4-5-77	1994	Cotui, D.R.
Achilles, Matt	8	7	3.90	41	11	0	1	115	125	58	50	38	70	.287	R	R	6-3	180	2-18-76	1996	East Moline, Ill.
Beltran, Francis	2	2	2.59	39	0	0	23	42	28	14	12	19	43	.191	R	R	6-5	220	11-29-79	1997	Santo Domingo, D.R.
Brown, Eric	1	0	0.00	4	0	0	0	3	1	0	0	0	3	.090	R	R	6-3	210	12-5-78	2001	Basking Ridge, N.J.
Bruback, Matt	9	7	3.16	28	28	0	0	174	157	70	61	48	158	.243	R	R	6-7	210	1-12-79	1998	Sarasota, Fla.
Chavez, Wilton	8	5	3.76	18	18	0	0	103	97	48	43	39	86	.255	R	R	6-3	200	6-13-78	1998	Monte Cristi, D.R.
Chiasson, Scott	0	0	3.00	3	0	0	0	3	5	2	1	1	5	.312	R	R	6-3	200	8-14-77	1998	Norwich, Conn.
Christensen, Ben	2	6	6.33	12	12	0	0	64	73	49	45	35	36	.293	R	R	6-4	210	2-7-78	1999	Wichita, Kan.
Estrella, Leo	2	2	3.28	10	3	0	0	25	23	13	9	8	18	.250	R	R	6-1	180	2-20-75	1994	Port St. Lucie, Fla.
Freed, Mark	9	11	5.16	29	24	0	0	133	159	88	76	58	106	.306	L	L	6-5	210	8-10-78	2000	Pennsville, N.J.
Gross, Rafael	0	0	6.00	1	1	0	0	3	4	2	2	3	1	.307	R	R	5-11	200	8-8-74	1993	Port St. Lucie, Fla.
Hazlett, Andy	0	0	1.38	9	0	0	0	13	7	3	2	3	12	.159	L	L	6-3	180	8-27-75	1997	The Dalles, Ore.
Hooten, Dave	5	1	1.30	65	0	0	9	76	49	13	11	19	66	.184	R	R	6-0	180	5-8-75	1996	Shreveport, La.
Jongejan, Ferenc	3	4	3.34	62	3	0	2	67	59	26	25	28	51	.244	L	L	6-2	170	10-20-78	2001	Houten, Netherlands
Leicester, Jon	2	2	4.61	5	4	0	0	27	24	16	14	13	18	.230	R	R	6-2	220	2-7-79	2000	Huntington Beach, Calif.
Noyce, Dave	3	2	2.72	53	0	0	0	76	64	25	23	36	55	.238	L	L	6-5	220	3-2-77	1998	North Augusta, S.C.
Palma, Rick	1	2	1.71	43	0	0	0	58	52	14	11	17	56	.244	L	L	6-1	160	9-26-79	1996	Maracay, Venez.
Prior, Mark	4	1	2.60	6	6	0	0	35	26	16	10	10	55	.198	R	R	6-5	200	9-7-80	2002	Bonita, Calif.
Smyth, Steve	4	4	3.58	11	11	0	0	73	62	34	29	18	74	.227	L	L	6-1	200	6-3-78	1999	Temecula, Calif.
Sollecito, Gabe	1	2	3.60	30	0	0	6	30	28	15	12	5	24	.239	R	R	6-1	190	3-3-72	1993	Monterey, Calif.
Webb, John	4	5	4.52	11	11	0	0	62	52	33	31	22	45	.231	R	R	6-3	200	5-23-79	1999	Pensacola, Fla.
Wellemeyer, Todd	3	3	4.70	8	8	1	0	46	33	25	24	18	37	.203	R	R	6-3	200	8-30-78	2000	Louisville, Ky.

FIELDING

Catcher	PCT	G	PO	A	E	DP	PB
Amrhein	.982	57	428	53	9	3	5
Curry	.987	12	70	7	1	1	7
Kopitzke	.994	73	545	68	4	3	7
McKnight	.938	2	14	1	1	0	0
Reyes	1.000	1	10	0	0	0	0

First Base	PCT	G	PO	A	E	DP
Amrhein	1.000	3	21	1	0	3
Balfe	1.000	1	1	0	0	0
Dzurilla	1.000	3	22	1	0	1
Gibralter	.965	8	52	3	2	2
Gripp	.942	9	59	6	4	10
Kelton	.990	121	965	72	10	78

Second Base	PCT	G	PO	A	E	DP
Abreu	.977	36	76	91	4	20
Harris	1.000	6	9	14	0	2

	PCT	G	PO	A	E	DP
Lopez	.889	2	3	5	1	2
Powers	.982	49	91	123	4	24
Schrager	.962	59	127	129	10	27
Weekly	1.000	2	3	3	0	1

Third Base	PCT	G	PO	A	E	DP
Abreu	.930	35	23	70	7	8
Balfe	.000	1	0	0	0	0
Gripp	.944	87	52	151	12	12
Harris	1.000	7	3	11	0	0
Kelton	.769	6	5	5	3	0
Schrager	.882	5	1	14	2	0
Weekly	.938	8	6	9	1	1

Shortstop	PCT	G	PO	A	E	DP
Abreu	.938	35	42	79	8	15
Frese	.973	65	89	162	7	35
Lopez	.849	12	21	24	8	7

	PCT	G	PO	A	E	DP
Schrager	.933	43	60	93	11	15

Outfield	PCT	G	PO	A	E	DP
Abreu	1.000	4	7	0	0	0
Balfe	1.000	17	13	3	0	0
Budzinski	.987	109	234	2	3	0
Gibralter	.952	27	37	3	2	0
Hamilton	.992	60	108	11	1	0
Jackson	.967	31	57	1	2	0
Johnson	.989	107	248	11	3	2
Johnstone	1.000	3	5	0	0	0
Kelton	.000	1	0	0	0	0
Lopez	1.000	4	6	0	0	0
Melian	.967	56	111	5	4	2
Piedra	.971	17	32	1	1	0
Sadler	1.000	8	16	0	0	0

FLORIDA STATE LEAGUE

BATTING

BATTING	AVG	G	AB	R	H	2B	3B	HR	RBI	BB	SO	SB	CS	SLG	OBP	B	T	HT	WT	DOB	1st Yr	Resides
Alou, Moises	.625	2	8	0	5	1	0	0	2	1	1	0	0	.750	.667	R	R	6-3	190	7-3-66	1986	Santo Domingo, D.R.
Arteaga, Josh	.190	29	79	8	15	1	1	0	4	3	19	0	2	.228	.229	R	R	5-9	170	3-14-80	2001	Homestead, Fla.
Barbier, Blair	.234	95	351	43	82	19	0	11	49	32	66	7	5	.382	.302	R	R	5-10	200	2-13-78	2000	Harvey, La.
Blasi, Blake	.364	3	11	2	4	0	0	0	1	0	2	1	0	.364	.364	S	R	5-8	160	3-23-79	2000	Wichita, Kan.
Butler, Keith	.211	27	90	15	19	3	0	1	9	7	11	6	1	.278	.290	R	R	5-10	180	8-11-80	2002	Marietta, Ga.
Cameron, Antoine	.167	41	132	11	22	5	1	0	12	15	35	0	0	.220	.265	L	L	6-1	210	3-17-80	2000	Sun City, Calif.
Cerminaro, Mike	.209	16	43	6	9	0	0	0	1	6	12	3	0	.209	.306	R	R	5-11	170	4-1-79	2001	Howell, N.J.
Curry, Chris	.245	44	155	16	38	12	0	0	13	15	43	2	0	.323	.310	R	R	6-1	190	11-17-77	1999	Conway, Ark.
DuBois, Jason	.321	99	361	64	116	25	1	20	85	57	95	6	2	.562	.422	R	R	6-5	220	3-26-79	2000	Virginia Beach, Va.
Dzurilla, Mike	.259	104	363	51	94	21	5	9	48	37	44	12	6	.419	.330	R	R	6-0	190	5-4-78	1999	Bayside, N.Y.
Garcia, Tony	.250	97	292	36	73	15	1	3	37	28	38	16	8	.339	.330	R	R	5-10	160	6-17-80	2001	Temecula, Calif.
Goldbach, Jeff	.261	76	272	40	71	17	0	11	47	30	43	0	0	.445	.340	R	R	6-0	190	12-20-79	1998	Princeton, Ind.
Greenberg, Adam	.384	21	73	20	28	5	3	1	9	14	18	15	2	.575	.500	L	L	5-9	170	2-21-81	2002	Sparta, N.J.
Harris, Brendan	.329	110	425	82	140	35	6	13	54	43	57	16	4	.532	.395	R	R	6-0	190	8-26-80	2001	Queensbury, N.Y.
Johnstone, Ben	.233	81	240	32	56	6	0	0	22	13	34	18	13	.258	.278	R	R	6-0	190	2-5-78	1999	Atlanta, Ga.
Kweon, Yoon-Min	.220	88	300	32	66	11	0	5	36	23	34	1	4	.307	.286	R	R	6-2	210	1-22-79	1999	Inchon, Korea
McKnight, Lukas	.500	1	2	1	1	0	0	0	1	0	1	0	0	.500	.500	L	R	6-0	190	2-19-80	2000	Libertyville, Ill.
Montanez, Luis	.265	124	487	69	129	21	5	4	59	44	89	14	8	.353	.333	R	R	6-2	180	12-15-81	2000	Miami, Fla.
Navarro, Mandy	.130	11	23	7	3	1	0	0	3	1	4	7	2	1	.174	.459	S	R	6-0	170	4-24-81	2001	Miami, Fla.
Sadler, Ray	.286	112	462	81	132	31	1	11	47	27	91	30	12	.429	.333	R	R	6-2	200	9-19-80	2000	Waco, Texas
Sing, Brandon	.248	125	440	65	109	18	5	18	64	64	96	5	7	.434	.348	R	R	6-4	210	3-13-81	1999	Joliet, Ill.
Slavik, Corey	.257	10	35	1	9	3	1	0	3	3	5	0	1	.400	.325	L	R	6-0	190	3-24-81	2001	South River, N.J.

PITCHING

PITCHING	W	L	ERA	G	GS	CG	SV	IP	H	R	ER	BB	SO	AVG	B	T	HT	WT	DOB	1st Yr	Resides
Albright, Eric	0	0	7.94	12	0	0	2	17	27	17	15	10	14	.355	R	R	6-2	190	10-4-77	2000	Long Beach, Calif.
Alvarez, Larry	1	0	0.00	1	0	0	0	2	1	0	0	1	0	.166	R	R	6-3	210	9-24-79	1998	Walnut, Calif.
Benik, B.J.	2	2	7.99	5	5	0	0	24	37	23	21	3	14	.362	R	R	6-1	190	9-13-78	2001	Delray Beach, Fla.
Blanton, Jason	2	2	2.29	20	0	0	2	39	25	14	10	11	32	.179	R	R	6-4	230	9-10-79	2001	Titusville, Fla.
Brown, Eric	1	0	0.93	25	0	0	9	29	16	7	3	4	39	.150	R	R	6-3	210	12-5-78	2001	Basking Ridge, N.J.
Carter, Mark	3	5	5.52	24	2	0	1	44	42	28	27	17	40	.248	L	L	6-4	220	8-27-80	2001	Oneonta, Ala.
Chavez, Wilton	0	3	4.74	8	6	0	0	25	30	18	13	12	25	.300	R	R	6-2	170	6-13-78	1998	Monte Cristi, D.R.
Corbin, John	0	2	7.31	5	2	0	0	16	25	14	13	8	14	.362	R	R	6-3	200	6-18-77	2000	Hollywood, Fla.
Diaz, Eddy	2	4	7.93	25	2	0	1	36	47	37	32	21	30	.299	R	R	6-3	210	10-26-77	1998	Azua, D.R.
Ellis, Steve	2	2	8.40	10	0	0	0	15	17	14	14	14	19	.288	R	R	6-2	200	2-4-79	2001	Elsah, Ill.
Fisher, Marc	1	1	1.23	6	0	0	0	15	12	5	2	4	9	.214	R	R	6-4	200	5-17-79	2001	Conshohocken, Pa.
Fries, Scott	3	1	4.43	13	0	0	0	20	29	10	10	13	12	.349	L	L	6-1	190	12-3-77	2000	Dannebrog, Neb.
Gordon, Tom	0	0	3.38	2	2	0	0	3	1	1	1	2	3	.100	R	R	5-10	190	11-18-67	1986	Avon Park, Fla.
Guzman, Angel	6	2	2.39	16	15	1	0	94	99	34	25	33	74	.268	R	R	6-2	180	12-14-81	1999	Caracas, Venez.
Krawiec, Aaron	7	10	4.09	28	28	0	0	169	159	89	77	48	128	.249	L	L	6-6	210	3-17-79	2000	Lakeland, Fla.
Lavery, Tim	5	6	2.98	29	8	1	1	99	99	37	30	14	56	.275	L	L	6-3	210	11-16-78	1999	Naperville, Ill.
Leicester, Jon	2	3	3.97	20	14	0	0	82	77	43	36	48	57	.247	R	R	6-2	220	2-7-79	2000	Huntington Beach, Calif.
Martin, Nick	1	1	3.20	4	4	0	0	20	18	15	7	6	16	.230	L	L	6-3	190	3-5-80	2001	Houston, Texas
McMullen, Jeremy	0	0	8.22	3	1	0	0	8	11	7	7	6	8	.354	R	R	6-2	190	7-23-80	2002	Carl Junction, Mo.
Montero, Oscar	5	7	4.39	51	0	0	9	70	64	41	34	40	79	.245	R	R	6-4	210	5-9-78	1997	Caracas, Venez.
Murphy, Matt	7	5	4.13	48	0	0	0	70	76	37	32	26	69	.266	L	L	6-3	200	10-31-78	1998	Delano, Tenn.
Pinto, Renyel	3	3	5.51	7	7	0	0	33	45	23	20	11	24	.338	L	L	6-4	190	7-8-82	1999	Cupira, Miranda, Venez.
Reyes, Luis	0	1	4.15	2	0	0	0	6	2	2	2	2	2	.300	R	R	6-0	200	6-26-81	2001	Toabaja, P.R.
Szuminski, Jason	5	2	5.12	39	7	0	1	91	95	61	52	41	53	.260	R	R	6-4	220	12-11-78	2000	San Antonio, Texas
Webb, John	5	5	3.43	10	10	1	0	58	43	23	22	13	65	.206	R	R	6-3	200	5-23-79	1999	Pensacola, Fla.
Wellemeyer, Todd	2	4	3.79	14	14	0	0	74	63	33	31	19	87	.229	R	R	6-3	200	8-30-78	2000	Louisville, Ky.
Wynegar, Adam	1	4	6.66	13	10	0	0	51	59	49	38	46	28	.289	L	L	6-1	180	9-11-80	2001	Centreville, Va.

FIELDING

Catcher

Catcher	PCT	G	PO	A	E	DP	PB
Curry	.989	37	226	30	3	3	11
Dzurilla	1.000	4	14	0	0	3	
Goldbach	.976	35	225	20	6	1	6
Kweon	.995	69	528	47	3	3	9
McKnight	1.000	1	1	0	0	0	

First Base

First Base	PCT	G	PO	A	E	DP
Barbier	.980	29	227	12	5	21
Curry	1.000	2	5	0	0	0
Dzurilla	.994	94	747	60	5	76
Goldbach	1.000	5	27	1	0	2
Sing	.984	16	112	8	2	8

Second Base

Second Base	PCT	G	PO	A	E	DP
Arteaga	.927	13	15	23	3	5
Blasi	1.000	3	6	9	0	0

	PCT	G	PO	A	E	DP
Cerminaro	.931	15	30	37	5	10
Dzurilla	1.000	5	13	6	0	1
Garcia	.961	32	72	77	6	18
Harris	.972	54	119	163	8	37
Montanez	.945	22	41	62	6	16
Navarro	.960	8	10	14	1	4

Third Base

Third Base	PCT	G	PO	A	E	DP
Arteaga	1.000	1	0	1	0	0
Barbier	.926	44	19	68	7	8
Garcia	.926	36	16	59	6	6
Harris	.951	59	43	112	8	19
Slavik	.913	10	9	12	2	1

Shortstop

Shortstop	PCT	G	PO	A	E	DP
Arteaga	.891	12	18	39	7	6
Cerminaro	.500	1	0	1	1	0

	PCT	G	PO	A	E	DP
Garcia	.888	26	29	66	12	12
Montanez	.928	101	162	250	32	52
Navarro	1.000	3	5	10	0	2

Outfield

Outfield	PCT	G	PO	A	E	DP
Alou	1.000	1	1	0	0	0
Barbier	.750	3	3	0	1	0
Butler	.921	20	34	1	3	1
Cameron	1.000	29	32	3	0	2
Dubois	.975	88	151	6	4	1
Garcia	1.000	3	1	0	0	0
Greenberg	.943	21	45	5	3	1
Johnstone	.986	80	142	3	2	0
Sadler	.971	110	236	2	7	0
Sing	.965	91	132	4	5	0

MIDWEST LEAGUE

BATTING

BATTING	AVG	G	AB	R	H	2B	3B	HR	RBI	BB	SO	SB	CS	SLG	OBP	B	T	HT	WT	DOB	1st Yr	Resides
Arteaga, Josh	.252	45	143	16	36	9	1	1	12	14	15	1	2	.350	.321	R	R	5-9	170	3-14-80	2001	Homestead, Fla.
Bouras, Brad	.271	127	457	54	124	30	1	16	71	54	72	1	2	.446	.356	R	R	6-3	230	8-10-79	2001	Lilburn, Ga.
Cameron, Antoine	.273	34	128	22	35	14	0	5	22	17	39	2	2	.500	.363	L	L	6-1	210	3-17-80	2000	Sun City, Calif.
Cedeno, Ronny	.213	98	376	44	80	17	4	2	31	22	74	14	10	.295	.269	R	R	6-0	180	2-2-83	1999	Carabobo, Venez.
Coats, Buck	.257	133	501	65	129	21	4	4	47	31	67	14	3	.339	.303	L	R	6-3	190	6-6-82	2000	Valdosta, Ga.

BATTING

BATTING	AVG	G	AB	R	H	2B	3B	HR	RBI	BB	SO	SB	CS	SLG	OBP	B	T	HT	WT	DOB	1st Yr	Resides
Creighton, Matt	.167	2	6	0	1	0	0	0	1	1	1	0	0	.167	.375	R	R	6-1	200	2-22-79	2002	Weldon, Calif.
Esterlin, Yban	.227	53	154	23	35	3	2	3	22	15	30	3	5	.331	.294	L	L	6-2	190	11-24-80	1997	San Pedro de Macoris, D.R.
Francisco, Alfredo	.000	2	7	0	0	0	0	0	0	0	2	0	0	.000	.000	R	R	6-3	180	8-27-84	2002	San Pedro de Macoris, D.R.
Greenberg, Adam	.224	35	116	20	26	7	2	1	11	15	22	2	1	.345	.331	L	L	5-9	170	2-21-81	2002	Sparta, N.J.
Hanna, Warren	.187	57	182	16	34	11	1	2	17	12	36	1	1	.291	.241	R	R	6-1	200	9-12-79	2001	Pensacola, Fla.
Johnson, J.J.	.240	112	420	58	101	25	2	2	56	38	89	7	7	.324	.308	R	R	6-2	190	11-3-81	2000	Appling, Ga.
Mallory, Mike	.265	131	495	60	131	34	5	16	65	24	119	6	6	.451	.313	R	R	6-4	210	12-8-80	1999	Dinwiddie, Va.
Marmol, Carlos	.149	15	47	2	7	0	1	0	4	1	7	0	2	.191	.167	R	R	6-2	190	10-14-82	1999	Bonao, D.R.
McKnight, Lukas	.295	53	173	20	51	8	0	3	22	18	27	3	1	.393	.366	L	R	6-0	190	2-19-80	2000	Libertyville, Ill.
Miliano, Hector	.219	31	105	10	23	4	1	0	4	4	26	1	4	.276	.255	R	R	6-2	170	3-26-80	1998	Santo Domingo, D.R.
Miller, Chris	.143	5	14	0	2	0	0	0	1	3	1	0	0	.143	.368	R	R	6-2	210	9-12-80	2002	Long Beach, Calif.
Monahan, Joey	.225	25	89	9	20	3	0	1	6	4	21	4	0	.292	.286	R	R	6-0	180	1-14-81	2002	Marietta, Ga.
O'Toole, Paul	.209	25	67	9	14	5	0	0	8	10	2	0	.284	.312	L	R	6-1	220	2-24-80	2002	Lakewood, Ohio
Salas, Francisco	.270	12	37	5	10	4	0	1	9	3	3	0	1	.459	.349	R	R	5-9	170	7-25-82	2001	Tijuana, Mexico
Silver, Travis	.203	23	69	5	14	1	2	2	9	4	17	0	0	.362	.267	R	R	6-3	210	6-11-78	2001	Weaverville, N.C.
Slavik, Corey	.218	90	308	33	67	14	4	4	34	34	49	4	6	.328	.302	L	R	6-0	190	3-24-80	2001	South River, N.J.
Theriot, Ryan	.252	130	489	75	123	19	4	1	37	59	77	32	8	.313	.335	S	R	5-11	170	12-7-79	2001	Baton Rouge, La.
Thornton-Murray, Jandin	.063	8	16	2	1	0	0	0	3	3	0	0	.063	.250	S	R	6-0	190	6-24-81	1999	Ewa Beach, Hawaii
Welsch, Travis	.207	40	116	14	24	4	0	1	9	11	25	1	3	.267	.295	R	R	5-10	170	11-30-79	2002	Muscatine, Iowa
Weston, Aron	.260	28	96	10	25	4	1	2	14	13	23	5	2	.385	.366	L	L	6-3	190	11-5-80	1999	Solon, Ohio

PITCHING

PITCHING	W	L	ERA	G	GS	CG	SV	IP	H	R	ER	BB	SO	AVG	B	T	HT	WT	DOB	1st Yr	Resides
Alvarez, Larry	1	0	5.14	9	0	0	0	14	16	8	8	4	12	.280	R	R	6-3	210	9-24-79	1998	Walnut, Calif.
Atlee, Thomas	0	0	4.91	3	0	0	0	4	5	3	2	2	1	.312	R	R	5-10	200	8-6-79	2002	Houston, Texas
Benik, B.J.	6	2	1.34	27	8	1	1	101	67	18	15	17	69	.190	R	R	6-1	190	9-13-78	2001	Delray Beach, Fla.
Brown, Eric	3	1	0.98	23	0	0	9	28	16	4	3	5	23	.170	R	R	6-3	210	12-5-78	2001	Basking Ridge, N.J.
Carlsen, Jeff	1	0	12.00	2	0	0	0	3	3	4	4	2	3	.250	R	R	6-6	230	3-6-79	2001	Seattle, Wash.
Carter, Mark	1	0	3.38	13	0	0	2	16	14	7	6	10	18	.233	L	L	6-4	220	8-27-80	2001	Oneonta, Ala.
Diaz, Eddy	1	0	2.25	6	0	0	0	12	5	4	3	9	9	.238	R	R	6-3	210	10-26-77	1998	Azua, D.R.
Ellis, Steve	5	3	1.90	37	0	0	16	47	31	13	10	29	70	.185	R	R	6-2	200	2-4-79	2001	Elsah, Ill.
Ferreras, Yorkin	3	6	2.78	51	0	0	1	65	50	24	20	45	67	.216	L	L	6-1	180	1-28-81	1998	Santo Domingo, D.R.
Foli, Daniel	3	3	3.16	32	2	0	1	57	51	21	20	25	44	.248	R	R	6-1	180	3-30-81	2001	Kodak, Tenn.
Guzman, Angel	5	2	1.89	9	9	1	0	62	42	18	13	16	49	.185	R	R	6-2	180	12-14-81	1999	Caracas, Venez.
Hines, Matthew	2	0	5.79	11	0	0	0	19	21	13	12	7	15	.291	R	R	6-7	220	5-13-81	2002	Coal City, Ill.
Martin, Nick	2	7	3.92	19	14	0	0	85	79	46	37	34	55	.250	L	L	6-3	190	3-5-80	2001	Houston, Texas
Martinez, Dionnar	2	0	4.58	13	0	0	1	18	14	9	9	11	10	.222	R	R	6-5	180	1-15-81	1998	Barcelona, Venez.
McMullen, Jeremy	0	0	0.00	1	0	0	0	1	0	0	0	0	1	.000	R	R	6-2	190	7-23-80	2002	Carl Junction, Mo.
Mitre, Sergio	8	10	2.83	27	27	2	0	169	166	72	53	27	96	.261	R	R	6-4	210	2-16-81	2001	San Ysidro, Calif.
Olivero, Pedro	3	3	3.54	48	0	0	3	56	52	28	22	34	54	.247	R	R	6-3	190	3-26-82	1999	Santo Domingo, D.R.
Pignatiello, Carmen	9	11	3.17	27	27	1	0	167	152	76	59	51	139	.240	R	L	6-0	170	9-12-82	2000	Mokena, Ill.
Pinto, Renyel	7	5	3.31	17	16	0	0	98	79	39	36	28	92	.220	L	L	6-4	190	7-8-82	1999	Cupira, Venez.
Rohlicek, Russ	0	2	6.92	2	0	0	0	13	12	10	10	6	11	.250	R	L	6-5	220	12-26-79	2001	Pleasant Hill, Calif.
2-team (25 Michigan)	9	7	3.29	27	27	0	0	164	160	68	60	42	106	.256							
Ryu, Jae-kuk	1	2	7.11	5	4	0	0	19	26	15	15	8	21	.333	R	R	6-3	180	5-30-83	2001	Seoul, Korea
Sanchez, Felix	6	6	4.15	26	21	0	2	119	130	67	55	44	101	.286	R	L	6-3	180	3-29-81	1999	Puerto Plata, D.R.
Wynegar, Adam	5	2	3.11	13	9	0	0	55	46	24	19	24	37	.226	L	L	6-1	180	9-11-80	2001	Centreville, Va.

FIELDING

Catcher	PCT	G	PO	A	E	DP	PB
Hanna	.991	57	389	37	4	2	10
Marmol	.961	14	88	10	4	1	3
McKnight	.973	40	259	25	8	1	9
Miller	1.000	3	21	2	0	0	1
O'Toole	.986	17	132	8	2	0	3
Silver	.986	19	130	11	2	1	2

First Base	PCT	G	PO	A	E	DP
Bouras	.989	111	992	43	11	122
Esterlin	.972	35	223	19	7	20
McKnight	1.000	4	10	0	0	1
O'Toole	1.000	1	2	0	0	0
Slavik	.986	7	65	4	1	8

Second Base	PCT	G	PO	A	E	DP
Arteaga	1.000	10	13	24	0	7

	PCT	G	PO	A	E	DP
Cedeno	.968	32	63	90	5	20
Creighton	1.000	2	3	9	0	1
Monahan	.960	16	26	46	3	10
Salas	.962	5	8	17	1	6
Theriot	.959	66	146	202	15	57
Thornton-Murray	1.000	1	2	2	0	2
Welsch	.966	12	30	27	2	6

Third Base	PCT	G	PO	A	E	DP
Arteaga	.951	26	15	62	4	12
Francisco	1.000	2	3	5	0	2
O'Toole	.875	3	4	10	2	3
Salas	.762	7	5	11	5	0
Slavik	.922	82	65	182	21	22
Welsch	.957	26	8	58	3	3

Shortstop	PCT	G	PO	A	E	DP
Cedeno	.935	66	92	209	21	48
Monahan	.886	9	11	20	4	3
Theriot	.956	66	81	223	14	41
Thornton-Murray	.000	1	0	0	0	0
Welsch	1.000	3	0	4	0	1

Outfield	PCT	G	PO	A	E	DP
Cameron	1.000	19	26	1	0	0
Coats	.955	118	179	11	9	0
Esterlin	.909	9	9	1	1	0
Greenberg	1.000	22	36	1	0	0
Johnson	.973	94	169	10	5	3
Mallory	.992	116	231	7	2	0
Miliano	.931	20	26	1	2	0
O'Toole	.875	3	7	0	1	0
Weston	.930	24	39	1	3	0

BOISE HAWKS — Short-Season A

NORTHWEST LEAGUE

BATTING	AVG	G	AB	R	H	2B	3B	HR	RBI	BB	SO	SB	CS	SLG	OBP	B	T	HT	WT	DOB	1st Yr	Resides
Bacon, Dwaine	.225	64	218	46	49	8	2	5	20	27	67	31	6	.349	.319	S	R	6-0	180	4-11-79	2001	Fort Washington, Md.
Banks, Gary	.241	60	199	26	48	8	1	0	20	15	56	7	6	.291	.303	S	R	6-1	190	11-4-81	2000	Gilbertown, Ala.
Butler, Keith	.318	30	110	16	35	9	1	3	17	7	8	9	4	.500	.353	R	R	5-10	180	8-11-80	2002	Marietta, Ga.
Cedeno, Ronny	.218	29	110	17	24	5	2	0	6	9	25	8	2	.300	.275	R	R	6-0	180	2-2-83	1999	Carabobo, Venez.
Chirinos, Robinson	.247	62	231	35	57	15	2	8	38	16	66	5	2	.433	.311	R	R	6-1	180	6-5-84	2000	Punto Fijo, Venez.
Collins, Kevin	.342	52	187	39	64	18	2	13	37	14	52	0	2	.668	.399	L	L	6-2	210	5-6-81	2000	Land O' Lakes, Fla.
Craig, Matt	.193	37	140	19	27	2	0	5	20	12	28	0	0	.314	.252	S	R	6-2	200	4-16-81	2002	Dallas, Texas
Fransz, Jason	.285	59	221	44	63	19	1	8	40	21	52	2	1	.489	.352	R	R	6-3	210	2-5-81	2002	Corona, Calif.
Hoffpauir, Micah	.301	60	216	35	65	10	3	10	41	7	35	2	6	.514	.330	L	L	6-3	190	3-1-80	2002	Jacksonville, Texas
Hood, Donnie	.279	49	172	36	48	13	1	12	42	11	42	2	0	.576	.340	R	R	6-1	180	12-30-78	2002	Jasper, Ga.
Medlin, C.J.	.216	42	134	10	29	8	0	1	14	9	34	0	0	.299	.279	R	R	6-2	210	3-3-82	2002	Broken Arrow, Okla.
Miller, Chris	.250	29	104	16	26	7	0	5	23	6	20	0	0	.462	.319	R	R	6-2	210	9-12-80	2002	Long Beach, Calif.
Monahan, Joey	.270	41	159	31	43	10	3	3	26	19	45	10	1	.428	.350	R	R	6-0	180	1-14-81	2002	Marietta, Ga.

BATTING	AVG	G	AB	R	H	2B	3B	HR	RBI	BB	SO	SB	CS	SLG	OBP	B	T	HT	WT	DOB	1st Yr	Resides
Navarro, Mandy	.086	15	35	3	3	0	0	0	2	9	14	0	2	.086	.273	S	R	6-0	170	4-24-81	2001	Miami, Fla.
O'Sullivan, Steve	.333	5	9	2	3	0	0	0	1	0	1	0	0	.333	.333	R	R	6-0	180	3-8-80	2002	Bronx, N.Y.
O'Toole, Paul	.000	2	7	0	0	0	0	0	1	0	1	0	0	.000	.000	L	R	6-1	220	2-24-80	2002	Lakewood, Ohio
Pie, Felix	.125	2	8	1	1	0	0	0	1	1	1	0	0	.250	.222	L	L	6-2	160	2-8-85	2001	Romana, D.R.
Servais, Eric	.299	40	87	13	26	8	0	3	16	11	20	0	1	.494	.378	L	R	6-1	180	11-15-79	2001	La Crosse, Wis.
Soto, Geovany	.400	1	5	1	2	0	0	0	0	1	1	0	0	.400	.400	R	R	6-1	190	1-20-83	2001	San Juan, P.R.
Spearman, Jemel	.273	3	11	1	3	0	0	0	0	1	1	1	0	.273	.333	R	R	6-0	190	12-27-80	2002	Lawrenceville, Ga.
Walker, Chris	.247	60	231	33	57	7	1	1	18	17	52	25	11	.299	.303	R	R	5-8	180	7-3-80	2002	Alpharetta, Ga.
Wells, Randy	.188	9	16	0	3	1	0	0	0	0	9	0	0	.250	.235	R	R	6-3	200	8-28-82	2002	Lebanon, Ill.

GAMES BY POSITION: C—Medlin 42, Miller 29, Servais 8, Soto 1, Wells 8. **1B**—Collins 26, Hoffpauir 58. **2B**—Cedeno 1, Chirinos 61, Hood 6, Monahan 1, Navarro 9, O'Sullivan 4, Spearman 1. **3B**—Craig 30, Hood 40, Navarro 3, O'Sullivan 1, O'Toole 2, Sevais 7. **SS**—Cedeno 28, Chirinos 2, Craig 1, Hood 3, Monahan 40, Navarro 3, Spearman 2. **OF**—Bacon 61, Banks 59, Fransz 55, Pie 2, Walker 58.

PITCHING	W	L	ERA	G	GS	CG	SV	IP	H	R	ER	BB	SO	AVG	B	T	HT	WT	DOB	1st Yr	Resides
Atlee, Thomas	1	2	1.65	19	0	0	5	27	26	8	5	4	21	.250	R	R	5-10	200	8-6-79	2002	Houston, Texas
Baez, Federico	0	0	0.00	1	0	0	0	2	0	0	0	1	0	.000	R	R	6-2	170	8-4-81	2001	Dorado, P.R.
Burnau, Ryan	3	1	2.95	25	0	0	0	43	39	15	14	19	46	.245	R	R	6-4	190	12-10-81	2000	Markle, Ind.
Clanton, Matt	1	0	9.00	1	0	0	0	2	1	2	2	1	1	.200	S	R	6-3	220	4-16-81	2002	Fountain Valley, Calif.
Flanagan, Jeremy	1	0	3.16	22	0	0	1	31	28	18	11	11	25	.224	R	R	6-3	210	4-14-81	2000	Richmond, Calif.
Hagerty, Luke	5	3	1.13	10	10	0	0	48	32	15	6	15	50	.189	R	L	6-7	230	4-1-81	2002	Defiance, Ohio
Hill, Rich	2	0	8.36	6	0	0	0	14	15	19	13	14	12	.267	L	L	6-4	180	3-11-80	2002	Milton, Mass.
Hines, Matthew	0	0	0.00	3	0	0	0	5	2	1	0	2	2	.111	R	R	6-7	220	5-13-81	2002	Coal City, Ill.
Jones, Justin	0	1	1.80	1	1	0	0	5	4	1	1	3	4	.210	L	L	6-4	180	9-25-84	2002	Virginia Beach, Va.
Martinez, Dionnar	0	0	0.00	2	0	0	0	2	0	0	0	1	2	.000	S	R	6-5	180	1-15-81	1998	Barcelona, Venez.
Nolasco, Ricky	7	2	2.48	15	15	0	0	91	72	32	25	25	92	.214	R	R	6-2	220	12-13-82	2001	Rialto, Calif.
O'Brien, Weston	3	3	2.89	23	1	0	2	44	34	15	14	15	51	.211	R	R	6-6	220	10-4-82	2001	Chino Hills, Calif.
O'Malley, Ryan	3	1	2.52	23	0	0	1	39	32	16	11	15	26	.226	R	L	6-1	190	4-9-80	2002	Springfield, Ill.
Rapada, Clayton	0	0	1.50	12	0	0	1	18	18	7	3	8	12	.250	R	L	6-5	180	3-9-81	2002	Chesapeake, Va.
Reyes, Luis	0	4	2.95	20	0	0	0	37	33	20	12	17	29	.237	R	R	6-0	200	6-26-81	2001	Toa Baja, P.R.
Ryu, Jae-kuk	6	1	3.57	10	10	0	0	53	45	28	21	25	56	.222	R	R	6-3	180	5-30-83	2001	Seoul, Korea
Sisco, Andy	7	2	2.43	14	14	0	0	78	51	23	21	39	101	.188	L	L	6-9	250	1-13-83	2001	Seattle, Wash.
Urrutia, Carlos	1	3	11.69	12	5	0	0	22	34	32	29	22	18	.336	R	R	6-3	210	9-3-81	1999	Mariara, Venez.
Vasquez, Carlos	5	6	4.26	15	15	0	0	80	77	45	38	33	68	.248	L	L	6-2	180	12-6-82	2000	Sucre, Venez.
Wylie, Jason	1	1	1.99	24	0	0	11	41	26	9	9	7	44	.187	R	R	6-5	220	5-27-81	2002	West Jordan, Utah

MESA CUBS · Rookie

ARIZONA LEAGUE

BATTING	AVG	G	AB	R	H	2B	3B	HR	RBI	BB	SO	SB	CS	SLG	OBP	B	T	HT	WT	DOB	1st Yr	Resides
Agustin, Pedro	.208	30	77	16	3	1	0	1	1	22	1	2	.273	.218		R	R	6-1	160	8-27-81	2002	Santo Domingo, D.R.
Creighton, Matt	.361	50	169	43	61	14	1	8	39	31	27	12	7	.598	.502	R	R	6-1	200	2-22-79	2002	Weldon, Calif.
De Vinney, Rick	.500	3	4	0	2	1	0	1	1	0	0	0	.750	.500		R	R	6-2	190	11-21-83	2001	Fullerton, Calif.
Dopirak, Brian	.253	21	79	10	20	4	0	6	6	23	0	0	.304	.306		R	R	6-4	220	12-20-83	2002	Crystal Beach, Fla.
Francisco, Alfredo	.266	48	188	23	50	6	1	1	24	9	58	1	3	.324	.296	R	R	6-3	180	8-27-84	2002	San Pedro de Macoris, D.R.
Marmol, Carlos	.258	47	186	22	48	6	3	1	16	3	35	10	4	.339	.271	R	R	6-2	190	10-14-82	1999	Bonao, D.R.
O'Toole, Paul	.444	3	9	2	4	1	0	1	1	0	1	0	0	.556	.583	L	R	6-1	220	2-24-80	2002	Lakewood, Ohio
Pie, Felix	.321	55	218	42	70	16	13	4	37	21	47	17	8	.569	.385	L	L	6-2	160	2-8-85	2001	La Romana, D.R.
Reyes, Jose	.180	19	50	4	9	0	1	0	7	6	13	3	1	.220	.276	S	R	5-11	170	2-26-84	1999	Barahona, D.R.
Rick, Alan	.232	23	69	11	16	2	0	0	4	11	16	1	2	.261	.353	L	R	6-3	200	9-8-83	2002	Palatka, Fla.
Salas, Francisco	.311	34	122	33	38	2	2	5	24	9	14	4	1	.484	.391	R	R	5-9	170	7-25-82	2001	Tijuana, Mexico
Soto, Geovany	.269	44	156	24	42	10	2	3	24	13	35	0	2	.417	.333	R	R	6-1	190	1-20-81	2001	San Juan, P.R.
Spearman, Jemel	.313	54	208	46	65	7	5	1	21	28	22	29	1	.409	.397	R	R	6-0	190	12-27-80	2002	Lawrenceville, Ga.
Summerall, Dennis	.262	49	187	22	49	9	4	4	27	11	54	1	1	.417	.319	L	L	6-0	180	4-14-81	2002	Seffner, Fla.
Thornton-Murray, Jandin	.205	10	39	7	8	3	1	0	7	2	6	0	1	.333	.244	S	R	6-0	190	6-24-81	1999	Ewa Beach, Hawaii
Vazquez, Rafael	.283	36	138	13	39	9	1	0	20	2	16	0	4	.362	.306	R	R	6-3	180	4-2-82	1999	Barquisimeto, Venez.
Wells, Randy	.146	14	41	6	6	1	0	0	4	3	16	0	0	.171	.234	R	R	6-3	200	8-28-82	2002	Lebanon, Ill.

GAMES BY POSITION: C—DeVinney 2, O'Toole 1, Reyes 19, Rick 19, Soto 10, Wells 14. **1B**—Creighton 25, Dopirak 10, Rick 2, Soto 7, Valdez 1, Vazquez 17. **2B**—Creighton 26, Salas 26, Spearman 1, Thornton-Murray 7. **3B**—Francisco 46, O'Toole 1, Salas 3, Vazquez 8. **SS**—Francisco 2, Salas 3, Spearman 52, Thornton-Murray 1. **OF**—Agustin 24, Dopirak 4, Marmol 46, Pie 54, Salas 2, Summerall 47.

PITCHING	W	L	ERA	G	GS	CG	SV	IP	H	R	ER	BB	SO	AVG	B	T	HT	WT	DOB	1st Yr	Resides
Albright, Eric	0	0	1.50	2	2	0	0	6	7	1	1	1	2	.280	R	R	6-2	190	10-4-77	2000	Long Beach, Calif.
Alvarez, Larry	0	0	5.06	5	3	0	0	11	11	6	6	2	12	.261	R	R	6-3	210	9-24-79	1998	Walnut, Calif.
Baez, Federico	0	1	0.95	18	0	0	9	28	22	7	6	8	19	.222	R	R	6-2	170	8-4-81	2001	Dorado, P.R.
Dominguez, Carlos	1	0	2.76	7	0	0	1	16	11	7	5	6	16	.180	R	R	6-5	210	5-16-83	1999	Caracas, Venez.
Hines, Matthew	0	0	0.00	4	0	0	2	7	4	0	0	1	6	.173	R	R	6-7	220	5-13-81	2002	Coal City, Ill.
Jones, Justin	3	1	1.80	11	11	0	0	50	31	12	10	18	63	.181	L	L	6-4	180	9-25-84	2002	Virginia Beach, Va.
Martinez, Jose	1	0	2.84	3	0	0	0	6	4	2	2	1	4	.181	L	L	6-4	180			Higuerote, Venez.
McMullen, Jeremy	1	1	1.65	10	0	0	1	16	11	6	3	13	18	.186	R	R	6-2	190	7-23-80	2002	Carl Junction, Mo.
Mejia, Andy	7	3	6.04	15	10	0	1	54	60	48	36	24	28	.277	R	R	6-2	170	6-15-82	1999	Hato Mayor, D.R.
Mitchell, Nathan	2	1	2.53	14	0	0	5	21	25	6	6	7	22	.316	R	R	5-11	200	5-2-80	2002	Houston, Texas
Petrick, Billy	2	1	1.71	6	6	0	0	32	21	8	6	6	35	.189	R	R	6-6	220	4-29-84	2002	Morris, Ill.
Ramos, Jonathan	3	0	0.95	4	2	0	0	19	10	2	2	6	25	.147	L	L	6-2	180	8-31-81	1999	Haina, D.R.
Rodriguez, Pedro	1	2	6.38	16	1	0	1	37	53	34	26	16	27	.344	R	R	6-6	180	11-20-84	2001	Anzoategui, Venez.
Santana, Candido	2	3	3.79	15	2	0	1	40	39	29	17	28	36	.248	L	L	6-3	170	11-3-83	2000	San Pedro de Macoris, D.R.
Tavarez, Carlos	7	4	3.64	14	13	0	0	72	65	39	29	16	71	.232	R	R	6-1	170	10-24-83	2001	Santiago, D.R.
Toribio, Auri	3	3	6.44	14	4	0	1	43	48	37	31	21	36	.277	R	R	6-1	160	11-2-82	1999	Azua, D.R.
Valdez, Richard	2	2	4.01	14	2	0	1	42	39	19	19	18	34	.000	R	R	6-3	160	7-11-81	2001	Nizao Bani, D.R.

ORGANIZATION STATISTICS

CINCINNATI REDS

BY CHRIS HAFT

The Reds are definitely on the move. They learned during the 2002 season they must take definite steps to keep moving up.

Having resided in Cinergy Field (nee Riverfront Stadium) since mid-1970, the Reds will begin the 2003 season literally next door, at 42,000-seat Great American Ball Park. The new yard is billed as an intimate place, where spectators will get a closer look at the action.

To make the view worthwhile for their fans, the Reds must improve in several areas: pitching, keeping top players healthy and situational hitting.

The Reds were a curiosity for much of the 2002 season. Their offense underachieved, they lacked a decent starting rotation and they frequently operated with patchwork lineups. Yet they spent 106 consecutive days in first or second place from April 20-Aug. 6, leading the National League Central for 51 of those days. The Reds were just two games out of first place as late as Aug. 11 before they sagged and St. Louis surged.

That Cincinnati remained competitive for so long was a testament to their admirable talent, embodied in outfielders Austin Kearns and Adam Dunn, infielders Sean Casey and Aaron Boone and pitchers Danny Graves, Scott Williamson and John Riedling.

"We feel like we have a pretty good core here," said Boone, who became the seventh player in franchise history to reach or exceed 25 homers and 25 stolen bases in the same season. "Hopefully we can make a move or two in the offseason to help bolster that."

The presence of general manager Jim Bowden, one of baseball's most creative deal-makers, guarantees the Reds will try to upgrade themselves. But the club's reluctance to increase the payroll could limit Bowden's efforts.

Bowden has spoken for years of developing and acquiring young, skilled (and low-salaried) players to prime the Reds for the advent of GABP in 2003. In Dunn and

Danny Graves   Brandon Larson

PLAYERS OF THE YEAR

MAJOR LEAGUE: Danny Graves, rhp

Graves joined John Franco as the only Reds pitchers to compile 30 saves in three straight seasons. He also made four starts at the end of the 2002 season, winning his only decision. Overall, he went 7-3, 3.19 with 32 saves.

MINOR LEAGUE: Brandon Larson, 3b

Laser eye surgery helped Larson see the ball better in 2002 and bumped his numbers at Triple-A from .255-14-55 in 2001 to .340-25-69 in 2002—in 154 fewer at-bats. It also earned him a July promotion to Cincinnati.

Kearns, both only 22, Cincinnati may have minted players who can anchor the outfield corners and serve as franchise cornerstones through the rest of the decade.

Dunn plummeted into a horrific slump after making the midseason all-star team, hitting .190-9-17 after the break. The left fielder established a club record with 170 strikeouts, reflecting his futility at the plate. But the Reds believe Dunn will find consistency through experience. He did enhance his production (.249-26-71) with 128 walks, four shy of Joe Morgan's 1975 club record.

Kearns looked instantly polished upon joining the team from Double-A Chattanooga in mid-April. He hit .400 in his first 24 games, played a solid right field, ran the bases expertly and generally behaved like a 10-year veteran.

Though deals for Kenny Rogers and Chuck Finley were nixed, the Reds acquired starters Ryan Dempster, Brian Moehler and Shawn Estes in separate trades when the team remained in postseason contention. While all struggled to various degrees and failed to help push Cincinnati past the Cardinals or Astros, the trades demonstrated the front office's recognition of the need for pitching and the depth of the organization's farm system, which provided the prospects to facilitate these moves.

That farm system didn't quite match its overwhelming success of 2001, when five of the six teams reached the postseason. But with Cincinnati ranking third in the majors in player-days lost to the disabled list in 2002, the system was forced to provide reinforcement just as much as development.

Nevertheless, three of Cincinnati's teams—high Class A Stockton, low Class A Dayton and Rookie-level Billings—earned playoff spots, while Triple-A Louisville barely missed qualifying. Stockton captured the California League championship, defeating Lake Elsinore in four games.

ORGANIZATION LEADERS

BATTING

*AVG	Brandon Larson, Louisville	.340
R	Raul Gonzalez, Louisville	91
	Andrew Beattie, Chattanooga/Stockton	91
H	Noochie Varner, Dayton	160
TB	Stephen Smitherman, Stockton	246
2B	Stephen Smitherman, Stockton	36
3B	Noochie Varner, Dayton	12
HR	Brandon Larson, Louisville	25
RBI	Kevin Witt, Louisville	107
BB	Andrew Beattie, Chattanooga/Stockton	71
SO	Kevin Witt, Louisville	140
SB	Noochie Varner, Dayton	37

PITCHING

W	Three tied at	13
L	Three tied at	10
#ERA	Andy Boutwell, Stockton/Dayton	2.28
G	Trever Miller, Louisville	65
CG	Bobby Basham, Dayton	4
SV	Nathan Cotton, Dayton	34
IP	Ryan Mottl, Stockton	180
BB	John Koronka, Chattanooga/Stockton	87
SO	Josh Hall, Chattanooga/Stockton	167

*Minimum 250 At-Bats #Minimum 75 Innings

CINCINNATI REDS

Manager: Bob Boone

BATTING	AVG	G	AB	R	H	2B	3B	HR	RBI	BB	SO	SB	CS	SLG	OBP	B	T	HT	WT	DOB	1st Yr	Resides
Boone, Aaron	.241	162	606	83	146	38	2	26	87	56	111	32	8	.439	.314	R	R	6-2	200	3-9-73	1994	Villa Park, Calif.
Branyan, Russell	.244	84	217	34	53	9	1	16	39	34	86	3	1	.516	.349	L	R	6-3	190	12-19-75	1994	Warner Robins, Ga.
Casey, Sean	.261	120	425	56	111	25	0	6	42	43	47	2	1	.362	.334	L	R	6-4	220	7-2-74	1995	Jupiter, Fla.
Castro, Juan	.220	54	82	5	18	3	0	2	11	7	18	0	0	.329	.278	R	R	5-11	190	6-20-72	1991	Glendale, Ariz.
Clark, Brady	.152	51	66	6	10	3	0	0	9	6	9	1	2	.197	.233	R	R	6-2	190	4-18-73	1996	Beaverton, Ore.
Dawkins, Gookie	.125	31	48	2	6	2	0	0	6	21	2	1	.167	.222	R	R	6-1	180	5-12-79	1997	Chappells, S.C.
Dunn, Adam	.249	158	535	84	133	28	2	26	71	128	170	19	9	.454	.400	L	R	6-6	240	11-9-79	1998	Porter, Texas
Encarnacion, Juan	.277	83	321	43	89	11	2	16	51	26	63	9	4	.474	.330	R	R	6-3	210	3-8-76	1992	Las Matas de Farfan, D.R.
Gonzalez, Raul	.261	10	23	4	6	1	0	0	1	2	5	2	0	.304	.320	R	R	5-9	190	12-27-73	1991	Carolina, P.R.
Griffey, Ken	.264	70	197	17	52	8	0	8	23	28	39	1	2	.426	.358	L	L	6-3	200	11-21-69	1987	Orlando, Fla.
Guerrero, Wilton	.244	59	78	9	19	1	1	0	4	6	13	2	1	.282	.298	S	R	6-0	170	10-24-74	1992	Nizao, D.R.
Guillen, Jose	.248	31	109	12	27	3	0	4	16	7	18	1	1	.385	.299	R	R	5-11	190	5-17-76	1993	San Cristobal, D.R.
2-team (54 Arizona)	.238	85	240	25	57	7	0	8	31	14	43	4	5	.367	.287							
Kearns, Austin	.315	107	372	66	117	24	3	13	56	54	81	6	3	.500	.407	R	R	6-3	220	5-20-80	1998	Lexington, Ky.
Larkin, Barry	.245	145	507	72	124	37	2	7	47	44	57	13	4	.367	.305	R	R	6-0	180	4-28-64	1985	Orlando, Fla.
Larson, Brandon	.275	23	51	8	14	2	0	4	13	6	10	1	0	.549	.362	R	R	6-0	210	5-24-76	1997	San Antonio, Texas
LaRue, Jason	.249	113	353	42	88	17	1	12	52	27	117	1	2	.405	.324	R	R	5-11	200	3-19-74	1995	Boerne, Texas
Mateo, Ruben	.256	46	86	11	22	6	0	2	7	6	20	0	0	.395	.319	R	R	6-0	180	2-10-78	1995	San Cristobal, D.R.
Miller, Corky	.254	39	114	9	29	10	0	3	15	9	20	0	0	.421	.328	R	R	6-1	210	3-18-76	1998	Calimesa, Calif.
Pena, Wily Mo	.222	13	18	1	4	0	0	1	1	0	11	0	0	.389	.222	R	R	6-3	210	1-23-82	1998	Laguna Salada, D.R.
Stinnett, Kelly	.226	34	93	10	21	5	0	3	13	15	25	2	0	.376	.333	R	R	5-11	220	2-4-70	1990	Mesa, Ariz.
Taylor, Reggie	.254	135	287	41	73	15	4	9	38	14	79	11	8	.429	.291	L	R	6-1	170	1-12-77	1995	Newberry, S.C.
Walker, Todd	.299	155	612	79	183	42	3	11	64	50	81	8	5	.431	.353	L	R	6-0	190	5-25-73	1994	Castle Rock, Colo.

PITCHING	W	L	ERA	G	GS	CG	SV	IP	H	R	ER	BB	SO	AVG	B	T	HT	WT	DOB	1st Yr	Resides
Acevedo, Jose	4	2	7.23	6	5	0	0	24	28	21	19	12	14	.291	R	R	6-0	180	12-18-77	1997	Santiago, D.R.
Almanzar, Carlos	0	1	2.31	8	1	0	0	12	6	4	3	5	7	.157	R	R	6-2	200	11-6-73	1991	Santo Domingo, D.R.
Brower, Jim	2	0	3.89	22	0	0	0	39	38	18	17	10	24	.260	R	R	6-3	210	12-29-72	1994	Solana Beach, Calif.
Chen, Bruce	2	4	4.31	39	1	0	0	40	37	24	19	20	37	.243	L	L	6-1	210	6-19-77	1994	Panama City, Panama
3-team (1 N.Y./15 Phil.)	2	5	5.56	55	6	0	0	78	85	53	48	43	80	.274							
Dempster, Ryan	5	5	6.19	15	15	1	0	89	102	61	61	38	66	.293	R	R	6-1	200	5-3-77	1995	Gibsons, B.C.
2-team (18 Florida)	10	13	5.38	33	33	4	0	209	228	127	125	93	153	.286							
Dessens, Elmer	7	8	3.03	30	30	0	0	178	173	70	60	49	93	.257	R	R	6-0	180	1-13-72	1993	Hermosillo, Mexico
Estes, Shawn	1	3	7.71	6	6	0	0	28	38	24	24	17	17	.345	R	L	6-2	200	2-18-73	1991	San Francisco, Calif.
2-team (23 New York)	5	12	5.10	29	29	1	0	161	171	94	91	83	109	.281							
Fernandez, Jared	1	3	4.44	14	8	0	0	51	59	31	25	24	36	.293	R	R	6-1	220	2-2-72	1994	Ogden, Utah
Graves, Danny	7	3	3.19	68	4	0	32	99	99	37	35	25	58	.264	R	R	6-0	180	8-7-73	1995	Lake Mary, Fla.
Hamilton, Joey	4	10	5.27	39	17	0	1	125	136	78	73	50	85	.278	R	R	6-4	240	9-9-70	1991	Norcross, Ga.
Haynes, Jimmy	15	10	4.12	34	34	0	0	197	210	97	90	81	126	.278	R	R	6-4	210	9-5-72	1991	La Grange, Ga.
Hudson, Luke	0	0	4.50	3	0	0	0	6	5	5	3	6	7	.227	R	R	6-3	190	5-2-77	1998	Fountain Valley, Calif.
Moehler, Brian	2	4	6.02	10	9	0	0	43	61	34	29	11	18	.329	R	R	6-3	230	12-31-71	1993	Marietta, Ga.
Pineda, Luis	1	3	4.18	26	2	0	0	32	25	16	15	24	31	.221	R	R	6-1	170	10-17-74	1995	San Cristobal, D.R.
Reitsma, Chris	6	12	3.64	32	21	1	0	138	144	73	56	45	84	.266	R	R	6-5	210	12-31-77	1996	Calgary, Alberta
Riedling, John	2	4	2.70	33	0	0	0	47	39	16	14	26	30	.233	R	R	5-11	190	8-29-75	1994	Pompano Beach, Fla.
Rijo, Jose	5	4	5.14	31	9	0	0	77	89	48	44	20	38	.282	R	R	6-3	200	5-13-65	1981	Parkland, Fla.
Silva, Jose	1	0	4.24	12	0	0	0	23	25	11	11	10	6	.294	R	R	6-6	230	12-19-73	1991	Tijuana, Mexico
Sullivan, Scott	6	5	6.06	71	0	0	1	79	93	60	53	31	78	.294	R	R	6-3	210	3-13-71	1993	Livingston, Ala.
White, Gabe	6	1	2.98	62	0	0	0	54	49	19	18	10	41	.237	L	L	6-2	200	11-20-71	1990	Sebring, Fla.
Williamson, Scott	3	4	2.92	63	0	0	8	74	46	27	24	36	84	.181	R	R	6-0	180	2-17-76	1997	Friendswood, Texas

FIELDING

Catcher	PCT	G	PO	A	E	DP	PB
LaRue	.994	110	626	56	4	5	20
Miller	.992	38	220	23	2	4	1
Stinnett	.990	30	189	14	2	3	7

First Base	PCT	G	PO	A	E	DP
Branyan	.995	18	170	14	1	23
Casey	.993	108	927	70	7	93
Castro	1.000	1	0	1	0	0
Dunn	.985	44	360	22	6	30
Larson	1.000	2	5	0	0	1

Second Base	PCT	G	PO	A	E	DP
Castro	1.000	17	15	24	0	7
Dawkins	.000	3	0	0	1	0
Guerrero	1.000	10	11	22	0	5
Walker	.989	154	314	438	8	93

Third Base	PCT	G	PO	A	E	DP
Boone	.954	154	90	324	20	42
Branyan	.912	16	10	21	3	1
Castro	.857	1	2	4	1	1
Guerrero	.750	3	1	2	1	0

Larson	1.000	5	2	10	0	3

Shortstop	PCT	G	PO	A	E	DP
Boone	.967	16	23	35	2	6
Branyan	.000	1	0	0	0	0
Castro	.964	25	20	33	2	10
Dawkins	.944	21	18	33	3	6
Larkin	.979	135	191	370	12	89

Outfield	PCT	G	PO	A	E	DP
Branyan	.951	25	36	3	2	0
Clark	.938	22	15	0	1	0
Dunn	.959	118	201	10	9	2
Encarnacion	.977	82	211	5	5	4
Gonzalez	1.000	6	11	1	0	0
Griffey	.971	55	96	4	3	1
Guillen	.980	27	45	3	1	0
Kearns	.983	103	223	8	4	2
Larson	1.000	9	13	0	0	0
Mateo	1.000	24	33	1	0	0
Pena	1.000	4	4	0	0	0
Taylor	.973	103	177	2	5	0

Aaron Boone

Adam Dunn: team-high 128 walks, tied for lead with 26 homers

Jimmy Haynes: led staff with 15 victories

LARRY GOREN

MORRIS FOSTOFF

FARM SYSTEM

Director, Player Development: Mark Naehring.

Class	Farm Team	League	W	L	Pct.	Finish*	Manager	First Yr.
AAA	Louisville (Ky.) RiverBats	International	79	65	.549	6th (14)	Dave Miley	2000
AA	Chattanooga (Tenn.) Lookouts	Southern	60	80	.429	9th (10)	Phillip Wellman	1988
High A	Stockton (Calif.) Ports	California	89	51	.636	+1st (10)	Jayhawk Owens	2001
Low A	Dayton (Ohio) Dragons	Midwest	73	67	.521	7th (14)	Donnie Scott	2000
Rookie	Billings (Mont.) Mustangs	Pioneer	38	37	.507	3rd (8)	Rick Burleson	1974
Rookie	Sarasota (Fla.) Reds	Gulf Coast	30	30	.500	7th (14)	Edgar Caceras	1999

*Finish in overall standings (No. of teams in league)   +League champion

LOUISVILLE RIVERBATS   Class AAA

INTERNATIONAL LEAGUE

BATTING	AVG	G	AB	R	H	2B	3B	HR	RBI	BB	SO	SB	CS	SLG	OBP	B	T	HT	WT	DOB	1st Yr	Resides
Broussard, Ben	.273	57	187	31	51	14	1	11	30	31	50	4	1	.535	.396	L	L	6-3	220	9-24-76	1999	Beaumont, Texas
Casey, Sean	.500	2	8	2	4	0	0	1	3	1	0	0	0	.875	.556	L	R	6-4	220	7-2-74	1995	Jupiter, Fla.
Castro, Juan	.176	5	17	2	3	0	0	0	2	1	3	0	0	.176	.222	R	R	5-11	190	6-20-72	1991	Glendale, Ariz.
Clark, Brady	.303	25	109	17	33	7	0	1	17	3	9	0	2	.394	.328	R	R	6-2	190	4-18-73	1996	Beaverton, Ore.
Darula, Bobby	.245	23	49	6	12	1	0	0	5	7	4	0	0	.265	.333	L	R	5-10	170	10-29-74	1996	New York, N.Y.
Dawkins, Gookie	.251	47	167	14	42	5	2	0	8	12	34	2	3	.305	.302	R	R	6-1	180	5-12-79	1997	Chappells, S.C.
Edwards, Mike	.404	15	57	7	23	5	1	2	8	6	9	0	0	.632	.460	R	R	6-1	180	11-24-76	1995	Mechanicsburg, Pa.
Frye, Jeff	.297	93	357	44	106	13	0	1	24	29	34	4	3	.342	.349	R	R	5-9	170	8-31-66	1988	Mansfield, Texas
Gonzalez, Raul	.333	114	432	91	144	27	2	13	69	61	59	9	8	.495	.416	R	R	5-9	190	12-27-73	1991	Carolina, P.R.
Guillen, Jose	.310	8	29	4	9	4	0	2	8	0	5	0	0	.655	.310	R	R	5-11	190	5-17-76	1993	San Cristobal, D.R.
Hernandez, Alex	.238	10	21	1	5	1	0	0	3	3	7	0	0	.286	.333	L	L	6-4	180	5-28-77	1995	Levittown, P.R.
Jennings, Robin	.222	107	351	29	78	21	0	4	48	27	56	4	4	.316	.282	L	L	6-2	210	4-11-72	1992	Springfield, Va.
Jordan, Kevin	.220	25	82	14	18	4	0	0	8	10	11	0	0	.268	.313	R	R	6-1	200	10-9-69	1990	Birkdale, Australia
Kearns, Austin	.750	1	4	3	3	2	0	0	2	1	0	0	0	1.250	.800	R	R	6-3	220	5-20-80	1998	Lexington, Ky.
Larson, Brandon	.340	80	297	47	101	20	1	25	69	24	70	1	1	.667	.393	R	R	6-0	210	5-24-76	1997	San Antonio, Texas
Leon, Donny	.250	18	68	9	17	5	0	3	13	2	10	0	0	.456	.278	S	R	6-2	180	5-7-76	1995	Ponce, P.R.
Levis, Jesse	.283	84	254	24	72	11	1	3	25	31	19	1	1	.370	.369	L	R	5-9	200	4-14-68	1989	Elkins Park, Pa.
Malloy, Marty	.244	56	180	25	44	7	1	4	16	21	24	7	4	.361	.330	R	R	5-10	160	7-6-72	1992	Trenton, Fla.
Mateo, Ruben	.301	52	209	37	63	14	0	9	23	11	40	6	2	.498	.342	R	R	6-0	180	2-10-78	1995	San Cristobal, D.R.
Maxwell, Jason	.301	80	269	44	81	21	3	2	31	36	45	5	4	.424	.381	R	R	6-1	180	3-26-72	1993	Lewisburg, Tenn.
Miller, Corky	.231	43	134	14	31	5	0	6	21	16	21	1	2	.403	.340	R	R	6-1	210	3-18-76	1998	Calimesa, Calif.
Mitchell, Derek	.164	23	55	6	9	0	0	0	6	9	19	0	0	.164	.277	R	R	6-2	170	3-9-75	1995	Gurnee, Ill.
Patchett, Gary	.286	7	7	0	2	2	0	0	3	0	2	0	0	.571	.286	R	R	6-2	180	9-25-78	2000	Gardena, Calif.
Sanders, Anthony	.250	33	124	12	31	6	1	6	24	7	31	4	1	.460	.289	R	R	6-2	200	3-2-74	1993	Tucson, Ariz.
Sexton, Chris	.316	108	414	79	131	29	5	6	49	42	41	3	2	.454	.378	R	R	5-11	180	8-3-71	1993	Cincinnati, Ohio
Stefanski, Mike	.281	73	203	23	57	8	1	7	23	13	26	0	0	.433	.326	R	R	6-2	190	9-12-69	1991	Redford, Mich.

BATTING	AVG	G	AB	R	H	2B	3B	HR	RBI	BB	SO	SB	CS	SLG	OBP	B	T	HT	WT	DOB	1st Yr	Resides
Stinnett, Kelly	.198	30	86	6	17	6	0	0	5	3	24	0	0	.267	.225	R	R	5-11	220	2-4-70	1990	Mesa, Ariz.
Williams, Gerald	.263	48	205	29	54	10	3	2	12	11	36	6	4	.371	.307	R	R	6-2	180	8-10-66	1987	Tampa, Fla.
Witt, Kevin	.263	131	509	77	134	32	1	24	107	34	140	0	1	.472	.314	L	R	6-4	210	1-5-76	1994	Jacksonville, Fla.

PITCHING	W	L	ERA	G	GS	CG	SV	IP	H	R	ER	BB	SO	AVG	B	T	HT	WT	DOB	1st Yr	Resides
Acevedo, Jose	12	7	3.20	23	23	0	0	155	146	61	55	34	128	.250	R	R	6-0	180	12-18-77	1997	Santiago, D.R.
Almanzar, Carlos	1	0	2.74	21	0	0	11	23	21	7	7	5	19	.247	R	R	6-2	200	11-6-73	1991	Santo Domingo, D.R.
Atchley, Justin	1	0	7.27	7	0	0	0	9	13	8	7	3	7	.342	L	L	6-3	210	9-5-73	1995	Mt. Vernon, Wash.
Bohanon, Brian	3	0	4.87	14	7	0	0	44	52	25	24	20	24	.300	L	L	6-2	250	8-1-68	1987	Houston, Texas
Cordova, Jorge	1	0	4.50	2	0	0	0	2	1	1	1	0	2	.125	R	R	6-0	200	1-13-78	1998	La Asuncion, Venez.
D'Amico, Jeff	3	6	3.69	11	6	0	0	38	43	28	28	12	26	.286	R	R	6-3	200	11-9-74	1993	Seattle, Wash.
3-team (2 Buff./14 Scranton)	6	10	4.94	27	21	0	1	118	130	80	65	39	73	.276							
Darnell, Paul	0	3	3.67	12	3	0	0	27	27	11	11	14	14	.270	R	L	6-6	200	6-4-76	1999	Hubbard, Texas
Davis, Lance	3	4	4.50	11	11	0	0	62	78	32	31	17	27	.317	L	L	6-0	170	9-1-76	1995	Polk City, Fla.
Dingman, Craig	0	1	4.15	22	0	0	0	26	20	12	12	13	26	.215	R	R	6-4	210	3-12-74	1994	Wichita, Kan.
Etherton, Seth	0	1	8.22	5	5	0	0	15	21	16	14	6	10	.328	R	R	6-1	200	10-17-76	1998	Monarch Beach, Calif.
Feliciano, Pedro	1	1	3.04	20	0	0	0	27	35	10	9	4	19	.328	L	L	5-10	180	8-25-76	1995	Dorado, P.R.
Fernandez, Jared	12	5	3.93	26	18	1	0	128	151	63	56	31	80	.297	R	R	6-1	220	2-2-72	1994	Ogden, Utah
Foster, Kevin	0	0	2.08	3	0	0	0	4	3	1	1	4	4	.187	R	R	6-1	170	1-13-69	1988	Evanston, Ill.
Gil, David	2	3	8.86	9	4	0	0	21	29	21	21	11	18	.329	R	R	6-4	210	10-1-78	2000	Miami, Fla.
Hamilton, Joey	1	0	2.57	3	3	0	0	14	10	4	4	6	10	.196	R	R	6-4	240	9-9-70	1991	Norcross, Ga.
Hudson, Luke	5	9	4.51	30	17	0	3	118	102	64	59	57	129	.233	R	R	6-3	190	5-2-77	1998	Fountain Valley, Calif.
Kolb, Brandon	3	2	5.06	41	0	0	1	48	54	33	27	28	39	.288	R	R	6-1	200	11-20-73	1995	Scottsdale, Ariz.
Lira, Felipe	3	2	4.83	11	10	0	0	60	63	33	32	17	35	.272	R	R	6-1	210	4-26-72	1990	Miranda, Venez.
2-team (21 Norfolk)	4	6	4.91	32	11	0	1	99	108	55	54	30	57	.287							
MacRae, Scott	4	2	3.34	49	0	0	2	73	74	39	27	28	54	.256	R	R	6-3	220	8-13-74	1995	Marietta, Ga.
Miller, Trever	9	5	3.18	65	1	0	0	82	76	30	29	23	80	.242	R	L	6-3	200	5-29-73	1991	Mt. Washington, Ky.
Neu, Mike	2	3	4.02	40	0	0	16	40	35	19	18	18	47	.231	S	R	5-10	190	3-9-78	1999	Napa, Calif.
Pineda, Luis	1	1	4.26	3	3	0	0	13	9	6	6	4	12	.200	R	R	6-1	170	10-17-74	1995	San Cristobal, D.R.
Reith, Brian	8	9	4.75	23	22	0	0	133	137	76	70	46	99	.267	R	R	6-5	220	2-28-78	1996	Fort Wayne, Ind.
Reitsma, Chris	2	0	3.86	3	3	1	0	21	17	10	9	8	13	.223	R	R	6-5	210	12-31-77	1996	Calgary, Alberta
Riedling, John	1	0	4.66	7	0	0	0	10	10	6	5	4	10	.256	R	R	5-11	190	8-29-75	1994	Pompano Beach, Fla.
Ruffin, Johnny	0	0	3.86	3	0	0	0	2	1	1	1	1	3	.142	R	R	6-3	170	7-29-71	1988	Tampa, Fla.
Silva, Jose	1	2	2.27	20	3	0	1	36	41	15	9	4	28	.284	R	R	6-6	230	12-19-73	1991	Tijuana, Mexico
Thompson, Mark	1	1	4.64	9	0	0	0	21	27	11	11	9	17	.321	R	R	6-2	210	4-7-71	1992	Russellville, Ky.
Thompson, Travis	2	0	6.06	8	5	0	0	33	39	23	22	4	23	.297	R	R	6-5	210	7-3-77	1999	Matthews, N.C.

FIELDING

Catcher	PCT	G	PO	A	E	DP	PB
Levis	.998	59	395	29	1	2	4
Miller	.993	41	279	26	2	2	8
Stefanski	.996	36	205	23	1	2	6
Stinnett	.988	23	160	11	2	1	1

First Base	PCT	G	PO	A	E	DP
Broussard	.995	45	364	26	2	38
Edwards	.955	2	19	2	1	1
Hernandez	1.000	1	11	2	0	1
Jennings	1.000	15	112	6	0	14
Jordan	.978	4	41	3	1	4
Stefanski	.958	22	123	13	6	5
Witt	.986	69	518	49	8	60

Second Base	PCT	G	PO	A	E	DP
Castro	.933	2	7	7	1	3
Dawkins	1.000	1	4	2	0	0
Frye	.980	54	106	142	5	34
Jordan	1.000	2	7	6	0	1
Malloy	.965	41	86	80	6	19

	PCT	G	PO	A	E	DP
Maxwell	.961	24	41	57	4	12
Mitchell	.966	6	14	14	1	6
Sexton	.986	26	50	90	2	21

Third Base	PCT	G	PO	A	E	DP
Clark	.000	1	0	0	0	0
Jordan	.900	12	10	26	4	3
Larson	.912	64	38	138	17	11
Leon	1.000	10	9	19	0	2
Malloy	1.000	1	2	0	0	0
Mitchell	1.000	4	2	5	0	0
Sexton	.964	44	33	74	4	4
Witt	1.000	12	5	24	0	1

Shortstop	PCT	G	PO	A	E	DP
Castro	1.000	3	4	7	0	0
Dawkins	.982	46	69	151	4	27
Frye	.889	3	2	14	2	0
Malloy	1.000	3	7	9	0	3
Maxwell	.975	52	85	152	6	46
Mitchell	1.000	10	12	24	0	6

	PCT	G	PO	A	E	DP
Patchett	.000	1	0	0	0	0
Sexton	.981	36	56	99	3	21

Outfield	PCT	G	PO	A	E	DP
Clark	.955	25	60	4	3	0
Darula	1.000	14	22	1	0	0
Edwards	1.000	9	19	1	0	0
Frye	1.000	31	46	3	0	0
Gonzalez	.970	109	250	10	8	1
Guillen	1.000	8	15	1	0	0
Hernandez	.923	8	12	0	1	0
Jennings	.957	76	126	8	6	3
Kearns	1.000	1	1	0	0	0
Larson	1.000	6	11	1	0	0
Leon	1.000	4	7	1	0	0
Mateo	.967	49	86	1	3	1
Sanders	1.000	33	77	2	0	0
Sexton	1.000	1	1	0	0	0
Williams	.992	48	122	1	1	1
Witt	.985	39	60	6	1	0

CHATTANOOGA LOOKOUTS — Class AA

SOUTHERN LEAGUE

BATTING	AVG	G	AB	R	H	2B	3B	HR	RBI	BB	SO	SB	CS	SLG	OBP	B	T	HT	WT	DOB	1st Yr	Resides
Beattie, Andy	.247	43	166	23	41	9	1	6	19	18	30	2	2	.422	.319	S	R	5-10	170	2-28-78	1998	Clearwater, Fla.
Caruso, Mike	.357	3	14	4	5	0	0	1	4	1	0	1	0	.571	.400	L	R	6-0	170	5-27-77	1996	Coral Springs, Fla.
Curry, Mike	.194	26	72	12	14	0	0	3	15	18	5	1	.194	.333	L	R	5-10	190	2-15-77	1998	Jacksonville, Fla.
Darula, Bobby	.325	96	323	48	105	17	4	4	36	43	27	10	3	.440	.413	L	R	5-10	170	10-29-74	1996	New York, N.Y.
Dawkins, Gookie	.271	40	155	21	42	10	1	1	12	25	28	5	5	.368	.372	R	R	6-1	180	5-12-79	1997	Chappells, S.C.
Denorfia, Chris	.429	3	7	3	3	2	1	0	0	2	1	0	0	1.000	.556	R	R	6-1	180	7-15-80	2002	Norton, Mass.
Diaz, Alejandro	.227	52	150	13	34	7	3	1	18	12	32	6	2	.333	.280	R	R	5-9	190	7-9-78	1999	Constanza, D.R.
Edwards, Mike	.307	119	424	57	130	19	2	11	60	41	57	9	11	.439	.377	R	R	6-1	180	11-24-76	1995	Mechanicsburg, Pa.
Espino, Damaso	.333	6	12	0	4	0	0	0	1	0	1	0	0	.333	.333	S	R	6-0	160	5-8-83	1999	Panama City, Panama
Hall, Noah	.167	11	42	8	7	1	0	0	3	2	5	2	0	.190	.213	R	R	5-11	200	6-9-77	1996	Aptos, Calif.
Hernandez, Alex	.255	89	286	38	73	19	1	5	31	33	79	6	0	.381	.332	L	L	6-4	180	5-28-77	1995	Levittown, P.R.
Kearns, Austin	.268	12	41	10	11	2	0	5	13	9	9	1	0	.683	.434	R	R	6-3	220	5-20-80	1998	Lexington, Ky.
King, Cesar	.206	12	34	4	7	1	1	1	3	3	10	0	0	.382	.289	R	R	6-0	210	2-28-78	1995	La Romana, D.R.
Leon, Donny	.284	111	408	61	116	29	1	19	67	46	97	14	8	.500	.362	S	R	6-2	180	5-7-76	1995	Ponce, P.R.
Miller, David	.500	3	2	1	0	0	0	0	2	0	0	0	0	.500	.750	L	L	6-3	180	12-9-73	1996	Wyndmoor, Pa.
Mitchell, Derek	.209	64	129	19	27	6	0	3	19	22	35	5	3	.326	.331	R	R	6-2	170	3-9-75	1995	Gurnee, Ill.
Nevers, Tom	.313	126	444	58	139	26	2	13	77	37	77	9	6	.468	.369	R	R	6-1	190	9-13-71	1990	Edina, Minn.
Olmedo, Rainer	.247	132	478	62	118	21	1	3	30	33	86	15	16	.314	.301	R	R	5-11	150	5-31-81	1999	Maracay, Venez.
Pena, Wily Mo	.255	105	388	49	99	23	1	11	47	36	126	8	0	.405	.330	R	R	6-3	210	1-23-82	1998	Laguna Salada, D.R.
Peterson, Brian	.286	9	28	6	8	1	1	1	3	3	5	0	1	.500	.355	R	R	6-2	220	10-22-78	1999	Greencastle, Pa.
Rose, Pete	.226	9	31	1	7	0	0	0	3	5	5	0	0	.226	.333	L	R	6-1	220	11-16-69	1989	Cincinnati, Ohio

BATTING

BATTING	AVG	G	AB	R	H	2B	3B	HR	RBI	BB	SO	SB	CS	SLG	OBP	B	T	HT	WT	DOB	1st Yr	Resides
Santana, Pedro	.280	121	350	39	98	17	3	6	29	25	79	12	9	.397	.328	R	R	5-11	160	12-21-74	1994	San Pedro de Macoris, D.R.
Sapp, Damian	.234	45	137	19	32	10	0	3	12	24	45	0	1	.372	.376	R	R	6-3	240	5-20-76	1994	Pleasant Grove, Utah
Sardinha, Dane	.206	106	394	34	81	20	0	4	40	14	114	0	2	.287	.234	R	R	6-0	210	4-8-79	2001	Gulfport, Fla.

PITCHING

PITCHING	W	L	ERA	G	GS	CG	SV	IP	H	R	ER	BB	SO	AVG	B	T	HT	WT	DOB	1st Yr	Resides
Andrews, Clayton	0	3	7.23	4	4	0	0	19	33	20	15	8	8	.392	R	L	6-0	170	5-15-78	1996	Largo, Fla.
Aramboles, Ricardo	1	0	3.13	4	4	0	0	23	22	8	8	8	22	.268	R	R	6-4	220	12-4-81	1996	Santo Domingo, D.R.
Atchley, Justin	0	1	19.29	2	0	0	0	2	5	5	5	2	1	.454	L	L	6-3	210	9-5-73	1995	Mt. Vernon, Wash.
Cordova, Jorge	4	2	3.99	35	0	0	13	38	38	21	17	14	30	.255	R	R	6-0	200	1-13-78	1998	La Asuncion, Venez.
Darnell, Paul	3	1	3.27	27	0	0	0	41	33	20	15	18	47	.234	R	L	6-0	200	6-4-76	1999	Hubbard, Texas
Davis, Lance	1	6	3.58	12	11	1	0	65	72	38	26	17	51	.285	R	L	6-0	170	9-1-76	1995	Polk City, Fla.
DeHart, Casey	3	6	6.53	21	0	0	1	30	32	23	22	15	24	.283	L	L	6-1	180	11-1-77	1998	Burleson, Texas
Dunn, Scott	5	7	3.92	37	12	0	1	110	99	57	48	54	114	.245	R	R	6-3	180	5-23-78	1999	San Antonio, Texas
Etherton, Seth	0	1	0.96	3	3	0	0	9	5	1	1	2	4	.166	R	R	6-1	200	10-17-76	1998	Monarch Beach, Calif.
Feliciano, Pedro	2	1	2.56	28	0	0	4	39	33	14	11	11	26	.234	L	L	5-10	180	8-25-76	1995	Dorado, P.R.
German, Rafael	0	0	1.80	1	1	0	0	5	5	1	1	1	3	.263	R	R	6-1	160	11-15-82	1999	Nizao, D.R.
Gil, David	10	4	3.66	18	18	2	0	111	102	49	45	36	103	.245	R	R	6-4	210	10-1-78	2000	Miami, Fla.
Gooch, Arnie	3	3	6.21	7	7	0	0	38	45	30	26	16	27	.286	R	R	6-2	190	11-12-76	1994	Doylestown, Pa.
Gray, Brett	6	6	2.78	48	3	0	0	94	88	37	29	21	60	.250	R	R	6-0	180	8-19-76	1998	Wyoming, Ontario
Hall, Josh	7	8	3.75	22	22	1	0	132	140	76	55	50	116	.275	R	R	6-2	190	12-16-80	1998	Lynchburg, Va.
Howington, Ty	1	5	5.12	15	15	1	0	65	65	39	37	33	51	.261	S	L	6-5	220	11-4-80	1999	Vancouver, Wash.
Knoff, Justin	0	0	0.00	1	0	0	0	1	0	0	0	0	0	.000	R	R	6-4	190	6-22-81	2002	Burlington, N.J.
Koronka, John	2	8	4.99	16	15	0	0	96	109	56	53	52	69	.297	L	L	6-1	180	7-3-80	1998	Orlando, Fla.
Lowe, Benny	1	1	5.93	9	0	0	0	14	13	11	9	8	12	.245	L	L	5-10	200	6-13-74	1994	Key West, Fla.
Martinez, Javier	1	2	4.94	18	0	0	0	24	21	13	13	18	17	.247	R	R	6-2	230	2-5-77	1994	Toa Alta, P.R.
Martinez, Willie	1	0	3.38	4	1	0	0	13	12	5	5	4	6	.260	R	R	6-2	210	1-4-78	1995	Barquisimeto, Venez.
Moseley, Dustin	5	6	4.13	13	13	0	0	81	91	47	37	37	52	.292	R	R	6-4	205	12-26-81	2001	Texarkana, Ark.
Neu, Mike	1	0	1.33	21	0	0	7	27	22	4	4	9	38	.217	S	R	5-10	190	3-9-78	1999	Napa, Calif.
Ozias, Todd	1	0	4.12	15	0	0	1	20	23	9	9	7	20	.310	R	R	6-1	180	8-19-76	1998	Coral Springs, Fla.
Riedling, John	1	1	11.05	6	0	0	0	7	13	11	9	5	5	.382	R	R	5-11	190	8-29-75	1994	Pompano Beach, Fla.
Ruhl, Nathan	0	1	2.08	4	0	0	0	4	4	2	1	3	2	.222	R	R	6-4	230	7-16-76	1996	Lee's Summit, Mo.
2-team (40 Orlando)	1	5	4.88	44	0	0	19	48	47	32	26	34	40	.246							
Smith, Cam	0	0	27.00	6	0	0	0	4	5	14	13	13	5	.294	R	R	6-3	190	9-20-73	1993	Selkirk, N.Y.
Snare, Ryan	0	0	3.00	5	0	0	0	6	5	3	2	3	4	.263	L	L	6-0	190	2-8-79	2000	Palm Harbor, Fla.
Taglienti, Jeff	2	0	3.52	24	0	0	0	31	37	14	12	7	18	.293	R	R	6-0	210	11-13-79	1997	Walpole, Mass.
Thompson, Mark	0	3	1.42	3	3	0	0	19	21	6	3	3	11	.283	R	R	6-2	210	4-7-71	1992	Russellville, Ky.
Thompson, Travis	0	7	4.99	15	8	0	0	49	67	34	27	18	43	.343	R	R	6-5	210	7-3-77	1999	Matthews, N.C.
Wells, Mark	0	0	6.00	2	0	0	0	3	4	3	2	0	1	.285	R	R	6-4	190	6-14-80	2002	Charlotte, N.C.

FIELDING

Catcher	PCT	G	PO	A	E	DP	PB
King	.946	7	27	8	2	1	2
Peterson	.985	8	52	15	1	1	1
Sapp	.995	27	178	10	1	0	3
Sardinha	.990	100	751	100	9	6	3

First Base	PCT	G	PO	A	E	DP
Edwards	1.000	46	353	15	0	35
Hernandez	.991	25	210	20	2	23
King	1.000	4	17	1	0	2
Mitchell	.889	3	14	2	2	2
Nevers	.985	53	386	20	6	45
Rose	1.000	7	63	2	0	5
Sapp	.991	14	105	8	1	13

Second Base	PCT	G	PO	A	E	DP
Beattie	.950	6	10	9	1	3
Caruso	.909	2	5	5	1	1
Darula	.000	1	0	0	0	0

Dawkins	.947	14	39	32	4	10
Espino	.941	3	7	9	1	3
Mitchell	.973	20	32	41	2	11
Nevers	.966	20	40	46	3	12
Olmedo	.965	21	50	59	4	18
Santana	.974	67	142	163	8	41

Third Base	PCT	G	PO	A	E	DP
Edwards	.889	18	10	38	6	6
Leon	.910	103	74	189	26	18
Mitchell	.926	9	9	16	2	3
Nevers	.953	15	15	26	2	3
Rose	1.000	1	2	1	0	1

Shortstop	PCT	G	PO	A	E	DP
Dawkins	.982	26	39	70	2	17
Espino	1.000	1	0	3	0	0
Mitchell	.971	7	13	21	1	6
Nevers	1.000	1	0	4	0	1

Olmedo	.960	107	195	305	21	65

Outfield	PCT	G	PO	A	E	DP
Beattie	.974	38	70	4	2	0
Caruso	.833	1	4	1	1	1
Curry	1.000	22	45	2	0	1
Darula	.977	85	126	2	3	0
Denorfia	1.000	3	4	1	0	0
Diaz	.961	40	93	5	4	0
Edwards	.965	56	103	6	4	0
Hall	.957	11	21	1	1	0
Hernandez	.974	50	108	6	3	1
Kearns	1.000	12	15	2	0	0
Miller	1.000	3	1	0	0	0
Mitchell	.000	1	0	0	0	0
Pena	.979	100	171	14	4	2
Santana	.977	21	42	1	1	0

STOCKTON PORTS
High Class A

CALIFORNIA LEAGUE

BATTING	AVG	G	AB	R	H	2B	3B	HR	RBI	BB	SO	SB	CS	SLG	OBP	B	T	HT	WT	DOB	1st Yr	Resides
Anderson, Bryan	.271	104	369	44	100	18	3	3	47	38	94	6	6	.360	.349	R	R	6-2	170	7-10-78	2000	San Antonio, Texas
Bannon, Jeff	.260	131	481	71	125	28	2	7	41	34	106	12	7	.370	.309	R	R	6-4	190	8-21-78	2001	Camarillo, Calif.
Beattie, Andy	.289	92	350	68	101	21	2	15	62	53	88	26	5	.489	.384	S	R	5-10	170	2-28-78	1998	Clearwater, Fla.
Bonilla, Clemente	.274	19	62	13	17	5	0	1	4	15	11	0	2	.403	.416	R	R	5-9	170	2-6-80	2002	Trabuco Canyon, Calif.
Calitri, Mike	.260	104	331	63	86	24	0	11	58	48	105	3	2	.432	.359	R	R	6-3	210	3-14-78	2000	Canton, Mass.
Curry, Mike	.330	28	106	24	35	7	3	1	13	16	16	5	4	.481	.411	L	R	5-10	190	2-15-77	1998	Jacksonville, Fla.
Espinosa, David	.245	95	367	71	90	13	7	7	44	62	104	26	17	.376	.356	S	R	6-2	190	12-16-81	2001	Miami, Fla.
Hall, Noah	.278	27	90	17	25	5	1	3	6	17	16	6	5	.456	.409	R	R	5-11	200	6-9-77	1996	Aptos, Calif.
Lundquist, Ryan	.252	95	341	41	86	12	3	2	51	41	92	6	0	.326	.338	R	R	6-1	180	11-26-76	1999	Oklahoma City, Okla.
Martinez, Candido	.263	53	179	36	47	9	4	6	24	6	46	19	4	.458	.289	R	R	6-2	170	1-10-78	1996	Sabana Perdida, D.R.
Mercado, Onix	.000	3	10	0	0	0	0	0	0	5	1	0	0	.000	.000	R	R	5-11	190	6-15-80	1999	Isabela, P.R.
Peters, Samone	.198	73	257	32	51	9	0	17	52	13	106	0	0	.428	.251	R	R	6-8	265	7-30-78	1998	Santa Rosa, Calif.
Peterson, Brian	.239	77	272	28	65	16	2	2	31	14	54	2	1	.335	.280	R	R	6-2	220	10-22-78	1999	Greencastle, Pa.
Raymundo, G.J.	.278	60	205	30	57	9	0	5	29	25	36	1	0	.395	.365	R	R	6-1	190	3-3-77	1999	Clovis, Calif.
Rios, Fernando	.239	69	213	32	51	8	1	4	30	28	23	2	2	.343	.324	R	R	6-2	180	12-15-78	1997	Glendale, Calif.
Ruiz, Randy	.260	28	100	16	26	9	0	3	17	13	29	0	3	.440	.357	R	R	6-3	220	10-19-77	1999	Bronx, N.Y.
Ruiz, Willy	.111	5	9	1	1	0	0	0	0	1	0	1	0	.111	.111	R	R	5-11	150	10-15-76	1996	Nagua, D.R.
Sapp, Damian	.238	45	160	34	38	5	1	13	35	23	64	1	0	.525	.351	R	R	6-3	240	5-20-76	1994	Pleasant Grove, Utah
Senjem, Guye	.275	102	338	61	93	17	2	14	57	50	59	2	3	.462	.378	L	R	6-3	220	5-2-75	1997	Kenyon, Minn.
Smitherman, Stephen	.313	128	482	78	151	36	1	19	99	39	126	17	2	.510	.362	R	R	6-4	230	9-1-78	2000	Hartshorne, Okla.

PITCHING

PITCHING	W	L	ERA	G	GS	CG	SV	IP	H	R	ER	BB	SO	AVG	B	T	HT	WT	DOB	1st Yr	Resides
Arroyo, Luis	1	0	0.63	10	1	0	0	14	10	1	1	7	18	.185	L	L	6-0	170	9-29-73	1992	Bajadero, P.R.
Berry, Jon	5	3	4.59	19	0	0	0	33	27	23	17	16	33	.219	R	R	6-1	190	11-17-77	1999	Branchville, S.C.
Bludau, Frank	3	3	1.91	43	0	0	22	42	42	13	10	12	48	.230	R	R	6-0	200	11-19-76	2000	Hallettsville, Texas
Boutwell, Andy	3	2	3.83	7	7	0	0	42	35	18	18	24	39	.225	L	R	6-1	180	7-24-79	2000	Valdosta, Ga.
Brannon, Nick	0	1	3.68	22	0	0	0	37	39	18	15	18	52	.267	L	L	6-4	190	4-23-78	2001	Sevierville, Tenn.
Carter, Justin	2	3	2.94	23	0	0	1	49	47	24	16	20	44	.251	R	L	6-2	180	3-8-77	1998	Birmingham, Ala.
Cordova, Jorge	4	0	0.40	14	0	0	0	22	11	2	1	6	27	.146	R	R	6-0	200	1-13-78	1998	La Asuncion, Venez.
Culp, Brandon	5	3	2.50	35	8	0	3	101	73	34	28	47	104	.198	R	R	6-6	240	8-27-77	2000	Jemison, Ala.
DeHart, Casey	5	7	3.66	16	16	0	0	96	87	44	39	38	57	.243	L	L	6-1	180	11-1-77	1998	Burleson, Texas
Eusebio, Mike	1	0	1.80	4	0	0	0	5	5	1	1	2	3	.285	R	R	5-10	150	1-17-79	2002	Hoboken, N.J.
Hall, Josh	4	0	2.27	7	7	1	0	44	31	13	11	13	51	.193	R	R	6-2	190	12-16-80	2000	Lynchburg, Va.
Howington, Ty	1	1	3.09	2	2	0	0	12	7	6	4	4	9	.170	S	L	6-5	220	11-4-80	1999	Vancouver, Wash.
Kelly, Steve	6	3	4.09	19	19	0	0	106	119	63	48	32	80	.280	R	R	6-1	190	9-30-79	2001	Hamilton, Ohio
Koronka, John	11	0	3.07	12	12	0	0	73	59	36	25	35	69	.213	L	L	6-1	180	7-3-80	1998	Orlando, Fla.
Light, Scott	0	1	22.50	1	0	0	0	2	6	5	5	2	5	.500	R	R	6-1	200	1-25-77	1995	Danville, Va.
Martin, Jeff	4	5	3.23	33	8	0	2	98	97	42	35	34	82	.262	R	R	6-2	230	2-5-77	1994	Las Vegas, Nev.
Martinez, Javier	0	1	6.75	5	0	0	3	5	4	4	4	4	7	.222	R	R	6-2	205	12-26-81	2001	Toa Alta, P.R.
Moseley, Dustin	6	3	2.74	14	14	2	0	89	60	28	27	21	80	.188	R	R	6-4	205	12-26-81	2001	Texarkana, Ark.
Mottl, Ryan	13	6	3.50	27	27	2	0	180	169	84	70	39	148	.248	S	R	6-3	190	12-9-77	2000	Florissant, Mo.
Snare, Ryan	8	2	3.07	13	13	0	0	82	74	36	28	18	81	.237	L	L	6-0	190	2-8-79	2000	Palm Harbor, Fla.
Stanton, Kyle	1	0	2.08	9	0	0	0	13	9	3	3	4	14	.187	R	R	6-2	200	2-19-77	2000	Coshocton, Ohio
Therneau, Dave	6	7	3.44	29	7	0	4	89	96	39	34	24	88	.271	R	R	6-5	190	12-23-75	1998	Denton, Texas

FIELDING

Catcher	PCT	G	PO	A	E	DP	PB
Mercado	.972	3	31	4	1	0	0
Peterson	.985	76	590	74	10	4	11
Sapp	.990	43	359	37	4	1	7
Senjem	.994	22	164	7	1	1	10

First Base	PCT	G	PO	A	E	DP
Calitri	.994	73	591	46	4	43
Peters	.979	54	449	22	10	27
Ruiz	.944	17	143	8	9	8
Sapp	1.000	1	10	0	0	0

Second Base	PCT	G	PO	A	E	DP
Anderson	.976	28	53	70	3	13

	PCT	G	PO	A	E	DP
Beattie	1.000	6	12	14	0	2
Bonilla	.970	16	29	36	2	5
Espinosa	.942	95	159	263	26	40

Third Base	PCT	G	PO	A	E	DP
Anderson	.925	56	34	89	10	9
Beattie	.815	9	8	14	5	1
Calitri	.874	31	17	59	11	2
Raymundo	.954	52	31	113	7	7
Ruiz	.000	1	0	0	0	0

Shortstop	PCT	G	PO	A	E	DP
Anderson	.909	13	18	32	5	8
Bannon	.928	130	183	355	42	51

Outfield	PCT	G	PO	A	E	DP
Anderson	1.000	10	18	0	0	0
Beattie	.982	78	156	5	3	0
Curry	.971	27	67	0	2	0
Hall	.980	25	47	1	1	0
Lundquist	.981	82	148	9	3	1
Martinez	.957	18	20	2	1	0
Raymundo	1.000	1	0	0	0	0
Rios	.949	63	106	6	6	0
Ruiz	1.000	1	1	0	0	0
Senjem	1.000	9	16	1	0	0
Smitherman	.975	125	187	11	5	1

DAYTON DRAGONS — Low Class A

MIDWEST LEAGUE

BATTING	AVG	G	AB	R	H	2B	3B	HR	RBI	BB	SO	SB	CS	SLG	OBP	B	T	HT	WT	DOB	1st Yr	Resides
Bassett, Mike	.250	12	44	5	11	1	0	0	2	2	7	0	0	.273	.283	L	L	6-2	200	2-10-80	2002	Paramus, N.J.
Bergolla, William	.248	68	274	38	68	13	1	3	23	16	36	13	2	.336	.291	R	R	6-0	150	2-4-83	1999	Valencia, Venez.
Boone, Matt	.190	33	121	13	23	6	0	3	19	9	37	1	1	.314	.267	R	R	6-2	170	7-18-79	1997	Villa Park, Calif.
Campana, Wandel	.280	115	432	68	121	23	3	6	44	20	40	15	13	.384	.313	R	R	6-0	170	6-6-78	1998	Santo Domingo, D.R.
Davis, Justin	.277	114	354	45	98	25	4	3	36	54	56	5	6	.395	.370	L	L	6-3	190	7-17-78	2001	Chino, Calif.
Denorfia, Chris	.000	3	10	2	0	0	0	0	0	0	3	0	0	.000	.000	R	R	6-1	180	7-15-80	2002	Norton, Mass.
Encarnacion, Edwin	.282	136	518	80	146	32	4	17	73	40	108	25	7	.458	.338	R	R	6-1	170	1-7-83	2000	Caguas, P.R.
Gutierrez, Jesse	.273	123	458	51	125	28	1	13	66	32	78	2	2	.424	.324	R	R	6-1	180	6-16-78	2001	McAllen, Texas
Hanigan, Ryan	.273	6	11	1	3	1	0	0	1	2	0	0	0	.364	.333	R	R	6-1	180	8-16-80	2002	Andover, Mass.
Hawes, B.J.	.257	55	191	17	49	11	2	0	27	9	32	10	7	.335	.298	R	R	6-0	170	6-2-79	1999	Appling, Ga.
Huguet, J.C.	.139	20	36	4	5	0	0	0	2	11	12	1	0	.139	.367	L	L	6-2	210	5-18-78	2000	Miami, Fla.
Humphries, Jared	.300	32	70	14	21	2	0	0	8	7	10	1	0	.329	.364	L	L	6-2	180	3-24-79	2002	La Grange, Ga.
Hurtado, Omar	.225	56	187	15	42	8	1	3	17	11	45	5	2	.326	.271	R	R	6-0	180	10-24-78	1996	Caracas, Venez.
Lewis, Domonique	.245	62	151	23	37	5	4	1	12	18	36	10	4	.351	.320	R	R	5-9	170	8-6-79	2001	Channelview, Texas
Mercado, Onix	.218	19	55	5	12	2	0	2	7	2	18	0	0	.364	.246	R	R	5-11	190	6-15-80	1999	Isabela, P.R.
Nina, Amaurys	.228	29	92	12	21	5	0	1	10	5	24	7	1	.315	.283	R	R	5-11	150	8-10-77	1995	Santo Damingo, D.R.
Patchett, Gary	.227	94	278	42	63	15	0	4	30	20	73	5	3	.324	.308	R	R	6-2	180	9-25-78	2000	Gardena, Calif.
Prince, Bryan	.201	83	239	31	48	12	0	4	22	32	43	2	0	.301	.314	R	R	6-2	200	11-4-78	2001	Fort Oglethorpe, Ga.
Ruiz, Junior	.222	23	63	11	14	4	0	0	4	14	7	1	0	.286	.375	L	R	5-10	180	6-7-80	2001	Manteca, Calif.
Ruiz, Randy	.302	78	285	47	86	17	4	8	49	36	88	9	3	.474	.390	R	R	6-3	220	10-19-77	1999	Bronx, N.Y.
Varner, Noochie	.309	129	517	82	160	27	12	10	69	32	117	37	4	.466	.354	R	R	6-0	180	12-7-80	2000	Cynthiana, Ky.
Williamson, Chris	.240	99	333	57	80	17	1	22	73	50	116	2	6	.495	.354	L	L	6-5	220	8-21-78	2000	Houston, Texas

PITCHING	W	L	ERA	G	GS	CG	SV	IP	H	R	ER	BB	SO	AVG	B	T	HT	WT	DOB	1st Yr	Resides
Basham, Bobby	6	4	1.64	13	13	4	0	88	64	25	16	9	97	.195	R	R	6-3	200	3-7-80	2001	Hardy, Va.
Batista, Gorky	0	3	7.86	11	3	0	1	26	37	27	23	15	23	.321	R	R	6-0	180	3-20-81	2000	Barahona, D.R.
Boutwell, Andy	6	0	1.46	16	11	1	0	80	44	19	13	37	98	.160	L	R	6-1	180	7-24-79	2000	Valdosta, Ga.
Brannon, Nick	1	0	3.00	3	0	0	0	3	2	1	1	4	6	.200	L	L	6-4	190	4-23-78	2001	Sevierville, Tenn.
Carter, Justin	0	1	2.70	8	3	0	0	20	19	11	6	7	16	.256	R	L	6-2	180	3-8-77	1998	Birmingham, Ala.
Childress, Daylan	9	10	3.51	28	27	1	0	169	147	82	66	68	152	.233	R	R	6-1	200	7-31-78	2001	Floresville, Texas
Coffey, Todd	6	4	3.59	38	5	0	2	80	78	34	32	25	62	.260	R	R	6-5	240	9-9-80	1998	Caroleen, N.C.
Cotton, Nathan	2	5	1.96	53	0	0	34	64	49	17	14	18	65	.213	L	R	6-2	190	7-19-79	2000	Southside, Ala.
Detillion, Jamie	0	0	5.63	6	0	0	0	8	10	5	5	5	8	.312	L	L	6-1	200	10-17-76	1998	Monarch Beach, Calif.
Etherton, Seth	0	0	0.00	1	1	0	0	1	1	0	0	0	2	.250	R	R	6-1	210	7-5-77	1998	Manteca, Calif.
Eusebio, Mike	2	0	5.50	13	0	0	0	18	18	18	11	19	13	.260	R	R	5-10	150	1-17-79	2002	Hoboken, N.J.
Gemmell, Don	0	0	0.00	1	0	0	0	0	5	5	2	0	0	1.000	R	R	6-1	210	7-15-79	2002	Manteca, Calif.
Gillman, Justin	1	3	3.49	7	7	0	0	39	29	17	15	17	30	.208	R	R	6-2	180	6-27-83	2001	Panama City, Fla.
Granado, Jan	0	0	1.80	3	0	0	0	5	3	1	1	2	7	.176	L	L	6-0	180	9-26-82	1999	Anzoategui, Venez.
Gruler, Chris	0	1	5.60	7	7	0	0	27	23	19	17	16	31	.227	R	R	6-3	200	9-11-83	2002	Brentwood, Calif.
Keelin, Chris	3	2	2.76	22	0	0	3	33	24	12	10	15	48	.201	R	R	6-2	190	3-3-77	1999	Sussex, N.J.
Kelly, Steve	4	1	3.15	7	7	1	0	46	42	16	16	7	35	.242	R	R	6-1	190	9-30-79	2001	Hamilton, Ohio
King, O.J.	2	2	3.70	8	6	0	0	41	44	23	17	14	37	.276	R	R	6-3	210	9-12-79	2002	Tahlequah, Okla.

PITCHING

PITCHING	W	L	ERA	G	GS	CG	SV	IP	H	R	ER	BB	SO	AVG	B	T	HT	WT	DOB	1st Yr	Resides
Mancha, Tony	0	1	5.03	14	0	0	1	20	20	13	11	7	15	.259	S	R	6-2	200	10-9-78	1997	Las Cruces, N.M.
McMurray, Heath	5	5	4.04	14	13	0	0	76	75	42	34	33	57	.260	R	R	6-3	200	5-22-79	2000	Splendora, Texas
Moak, Curtus	3	4	3.65	43	0	0	1	49	46	24	20	23	33	.248	L	L	6-0	180	11-19-78	2001	Hamilton, Ohio
Patchett, Gary	0	0	0.00	2	0	0	0	2	1	0	0	1	1	.000	R	R	6-2	200	9-25-78	2000	Gardena, Calif.
Powers, Joe	1	5	6.02	36	1	0	2	49	61	44	33	30	55	.299	R	R	6-3	220	8-5-78	2001	Cincinnati, Ohio
Salmon, Brad	12	9	4.46	29	27	1	0	159	165	94	79	48	117	.261	R	R	6-4	210	1-3-80	1999	Pensacola, Fla.
Severino, Cleris	6	6	4.43	16	9	0	0	63	81	37	31	25	37	.325	L	L	5-11	160	12-23-81	1999	Santo Domingo, D.R.
Stanton, Kyle	4	0	5.47	33	0	0	1	54	56	37	33	20	43	.269	R	R	6-2	200	2-19-77	2000	Coshocton, Ohio
Valera, Luis	0	1	2.84	8	0	0	0	13	12	4	4	9	15	.255	R	R	5-11	170	1-30-82	1999	Maracaibo, Venez.

FIELDING

Catcher	PCT	G	PO	A	E	DP	PB
Davis	.000	1	0	0	0	0	0
Gutierrez	1.000	33	256	31	0	1	4
Hanigan	.952	6	37	3	2	0	1
Huguet	.963	20	114	16	5	2	0
Mercado	.984	19	105	19	2	1	4
Prince	.986	82	587	70	9	1	5

First Base	PCT	G	PO	A	E	DP
Gutierrez	.991	70	580	49	6	36
Patchett	1.000	1	5	1	0	1
J. Ruiz	1.000	4	24	2	0	3
R. Ruiz	.982	45	374	14	7	30
Williamson	.979	29	209	20	5	20

Second Base	PCT	G	PO	A	E	DP
Bergolla	.960	50	83	135	9	15
Campana	.959	68	130	173	13	40
Lewis	.960	33	46	74	5	20
Patchett	1.000	4	8	10	0	2

Third Base	PCT	G	PO	A	E	DP
Boone	.935	19	9	34	3	3
Campana	1.000	8	6	15	0	1
Encarnacion	.901	116	89	211	33	15
Varner	1.000	3	0	1	0	0

Shortstop	PCT	G	PO	A	E	DP
Bergolla	.953	16	25	36	3	12
Campana	.926	38	48	65	9	10

	PCT	G	PO	A	E	DP
Encarnacion	.894	17	22	37	7	10
Patchett	.955	89	132	227	17	38

Outfield	PCT	G	PO	A	E	DP
Bassett	1.000	9	10	0	0	0
Davis	.933	71	93	4	7	0
Denorfia	1.000	3	6	0	0	0
Hawes	.981	53	99	6	2	0
Humphries	.929	23	24	2	2	0
Hurtado	.978	54	85	5	2	1
Lewis	.952	21	19	1	1	0
Nina	.974	26	38	0	1	0
R. Ruiz	.941	7	16	0	1	0
Varner	.986	125	261	11	4	2
Williamson	.968	66	87	3	3	0

BILLINGS MUSTANGS

Rookie

PIONEER LEAGUE

BATTING

BATTING	AVG	G	AB	R	H	2B	3B	HR	RBI	BB	SO	SB	CS	SLG	OBP	B	T	HT	WT	DOB	1st Yr	Resides
Andujar, Elvin	.286	40	140	23	40	3	2	5	20	12	49	2	1	.443	.365	R	R	6-3	190	1-19-81	1999	San Cristobal, D.R.
Bassett, Mike	.301	50	183	35	55	12	0	8	44	22	38	2	2	.497	.387	L	L	6-2	200	2-10-80	2002	Paramus, N.J.
Bergolla, William	.352	53	210	35	74	9	1	3	29	24	26	16	5	.448	.408	R	R	6-0	150	2-4-83	1999	Valencia, Venez.
Booth, Steve	.216	48	148	23	32	6	0	3	14	7	45	0	0	.318	.278	R	R	6-1	190	8-14-79	2002	San Jose, Calif.
Cairns, Troy	.324	39	145	19	47	7	0	0	9	9	13	8	1	.372	.365	R	R	6-0	160	9-29-80	2002	Blue Springs, Mo.
Campos, Tiago	.357	18	56	9	20	5	0	1	14	6	11	6	1	.500	.446	R	R	6-2	170	3-18-81	2000	Sao Paulo, Brazil
Colina, Yinner	.059	6	17	0	1	0	0	0	0	4	0	0	0	.059	.059	R	R	6-3	180	8-29-81	1999	Maracaibo, Venez.
Correll, Richard	.286	56	224	34	64	11	3	5	41	17	41	2	2	.429	.339	R	R	6-2	200	6-17-81	2002	Gastonia, N.C.
Fry, Ryan	.195	21	82	11	16	5	0	4	17	7	32	0	0	.402	.258	R	R	6-1	190	5-11-80	2001	Stockertown, Pa.
Ghutzman, Phillip	.400	2	5	0	2	1	0	0	1	0	0	0	0	.600	.400	R	R	6-2	200	10-1-78	2001	Spring, Texas
Humphries, Jared	.300	6	20	4	6	2	0	0	3	3	3	1	0	.400	.391	L	L	6-2	180	3-24-79	2002	La Grange, Ga.
Ison, Jeremy	.188	8	16	3	3	2	0	0	2	4	7	1	0	.313	.350	R	R	6-0	190	9-5-78	2001	Hudson, Ohio
Krimmel, Matt	.348	21	69	14	24	5	1	2	16	13	19	0	1	.536	.483	L	R	6-4	200	9-26-80	2002	Schnecksville, Pa.
Lewis, Domonique	.326	11	46	9	15	3	0	1	3	2	10	3	0	.457	.354	R	R	5-9	170	8-6-79	2001	Channelview, Texas
Mateo, Dan	.259	48	185	33	48	7	3	2	14	17	39	16	4	.362	.324	S	R	6-0	150	10-27-82	1999	San Cristobal, D.R.
Mercado, Onix	.310	8	29	6	9	2	0	1	5	0	6	0	0	.483	.333	R	R	5-11	190	6-15-80	1999	Isabela, P.R.
Motooka, Rafael	.226	30	84	7	19	4	0	0	12	8	12	0	1	.274	.293	R	R	6-0	170	8-18-82	2000	Guarulhos, Brazil
Moye, Alan	.261	43	157	20	41	6	4	5	22	9	47	3	1	.446	.324	R	R	6-2	180	10-8-82	2001	Longview, Texas
Olmstead, Walter	.189	44	164	29	31	3	0	6	19	20	65	2	4	.317	.289	S	R	6-6	230	12-5-80	2002	San Antonio, Texas
Paula, Manuel	.228	38	127	14	29	4	0	1	9	6	39	9	4	.283	.283	R	R	6-2	190	1-25-81	1999	Bonao, D.R.
Petersen, Ryan	.267	5	15	3	4	2	0	1	1	2	2	0	0	.600	.353	R	R	6-2	190	9-23-79	2002	Portland, Ore.
Ruiz, Junior	.304	56	181	40	55	5	1	2	23	37	19	10	1	.376	.430	L	R	5-10	180	6-7-80	2001	Manteca, Calif.
Schmidt, Jarrod	.281	35	121	14	34	4	1	2	16	15	35	4	3	.380	.369	R	R	6-2	200	10-2-80	2002	Marietta, Ga.
Vavao, Jason	.323	51	189	35	64	17	0	8	35	26	51	3	3	.502	.323	R	R	6-2	220	5-5-81	2001	Carson, Calif.

GAMES BY POSITION: C—Booth 47, Ghutzman 2, Mercado 7, Motooka 30. **1B**—Colina 4, Olmstead 22, Ruiz 10, Vavao 41. **2B**—Bergolla 50, Cairns 9, Ison 1, Lewis 10, Mateo 1, Ruiz 9. **3B**—Correll 34, Fry 20, Ison 4, Krimmel 18, Ruiz 1. **SS**—Bergolla 1, Cairns 28, Correll 2, Humphries 5, Moye 41, Olmstead 4, Paula 36, Petersen 3, Ruiz 15, Schmidt 31.

PITCHING

PITCHING	W	L	ERA	G	GS	CG	SV	IP	H	R	ER	BB	SO	AVG	B	T	HT	WT	DOB	1st Yr	Resides
Batista, Gorky	2	0	4.91	2	2	0	0	11	14	6	6	0	8	.311	R	R	6-0	180	3-20-81	2000	Barahona, D.R.
Bell, Chris	2	2	10.13	7	0	0	0	8	9	19	9	19	5	.281	R	R	6-3	200	9-24-80	2002	Miami, Fla.
Curran, Joe	2	2	4.96	20	0	0	0	33	34	25	18	14	28	.257	L	L	6-7	210	8-27-79	2002	Quincy, Wash.
Escorcha, Orlando	1	3	6.07	11	2	0	0	30	35	25	20	17	24	.307	L	L	6-2	170	1-20-82	1999	Valencia, Venez.
Gemmell, Don	1	3	3.14	25	0	0	12	29	27	15	10	4	41	.247	R	R	6-1	210	7-15-79	2002	Manteca, Calif.
George, Brad	2	2	5.36	9	9	0	0	47	62	34	28	11	33	.324	R	R	6-5	200	5-31-82	2000	New Braunfels, Texas
Gomez, Jose	2	3	3.06	13	13	0	0	71	52	29	24	23	58	.204	R	R	6-2	180	11-27-81	1999	Parral, Mexico
Groeger, Jeff	1	0	1.62	10	0	0	0	17	11	7	3	4	19	.180	R	R	6-5	220	9-5-80	2002	Diamond Bar, Calif.
Gruler, Chris	0	0	1.08	4	4	0	0	17	11	3	2	6	11	.183	R	R	6-3	200	9-11-83	2002	Brentwood, Calif.
Jumelles, Victor	2	4	3.45	22	0	0	2	31	23	14	12	20	29	.205	R	R	6-4	190	3-6-80	1998	Santo Domingo, D.R.
Keller, Frankie	1	4	4.15	14	14	0	0	74	72	43	34	45	61	.261	L	L	6-2	220	1-12-80	2002	Midland, Texas
King, O.J.	2	0	2.08	4	4	1	0	26	19	6	6	5	28	.202	R	R	6-3	210	9-12-79	2002	Tahlequah, Okla.
Lane, Brian	0	2	4.07	13	2	0	0	24	27	18	11	14	23	.270	R	R	6-3	220	12-5-80	2001	Crofton, Md.
Light, Scott	1	1	5.09	4	0	0	0	23	26	16	13	6	14	.285	R	R	6-1	180	2-22-80	2001	Danville, Va.
Lucas, Chris	2	0	1.93	10	3	0	0	19	27	11	4	5	17	.337	R	R	6-5	210	8-31-79	2002	Lancaster, S.C.
McWilliams, Matt	0	0	6.35	3	0	0	0	6	7	5	4	3	6	.318	L	L	6-3	210	4-27-79	2001	Lawrenceburg, Ky.
Quintero, Mayque	2	1	4.11	7	6	0	0	31	33	17	14	8	25	.268	R	R	6-2	220	4-19-78	2001	Miami, Fla.
Rincon, Carlos	4	3	4.45	23	0	0	1	30	29	17	15	21	30	.261	L	L	5-11	160	3-11-82	2001	San Pedro de Macoris, D.R.
Severino, Cleris	7	1	0.96	10	10	0	0	66	56	17	7	14	63	.229	L	L	5-11	160	12-23-81	1999	Santo Domingo, D.R.
Shafer, David	5	2	1.72	19	0	0	4	31	30	14	6	11	30	.241	R	R	6-3	170	3-7-82	2002	Flagstaff, Ariz.
Valera, Luis	0	1	13.50	2	0	0	0	1	3	3	2	1	1	.428	R	R	5-11	170	1-30-82	1999	Maracaibo, Venez.
Wachman, Corey	1	3	6.18	17	2	0	2	39	45	31	27	17	38	.286	R	R	6-0	180	10-16-80	2002	Valdosta, Ga.

GULF COAST LEAGUE

BATTING	AVG	G	AB	R	H	2B	3B	HR	RBI	BB	SO	SB	CS	SLG	OBP	B	T	HT	WT	DOB	1st Yr	Resides
Araque, Tulio	.222	53	171	20	38	10	2	1	23	4	48	4	2	.322	.260	R	R	6-2	170	10-17-81	1999	Maracaibo, Venez.
Bolivar, Luis	.306	50	186	39	57	17	1	4	24	8	37	13	6	.473	.369	S	R	6-1	150	2-15-81	1999	Estado Aragua, Venez.
Campos, Tiago	.233	8	30	2	7	1	0	0	2	1	10	1	1	.267	.258	R	R	6-2	170	3-18-81	2000	Sao Paulo, Brazil
Colina, Yinner	.235	31	85	12	20	5	3	0	6	12	16	2	2	.365	.353	R	R	6-2	200	8-29-81	1999	Maracaibo, Venez.
Correll, Richard	.111	5	18	1	2	0	0	0	0	0	3	1	0	.111	.111	R	R	6-2	200	6-17-81	2002	Gastonia, N.C.
Delacruz, Jose	.303	12	33	3	10	3	0	1	6	1	4	0	0	.485	.343	R	R	5-10	160	12-22-82	2000	Santo Domingo, D.R.
Dennis, Billy	.000	1	1	0	0	0	0	0	0	0	0	0	0	.000	.000	L	L	6-2	180	9-29-80	2002	Bigfoot, Texas
Denorfia, Chris	.340	57	200	38	68	9	2	0	19	31	23	18	8	.405	.425	R	R	6-1	180	7-15-80	2002	Norton, Mass.
Diaz, Juan	.235	27	98	11	23	5	1	1	11	1	19	2	1	.337	.257	R	R	6-0	170	1-31-83	2000	Bonao, D.R.
Esparragoza, Eyoxy	.189	18	53	6	10	4	0	1	5	5	22	1	4	.321	.259	R	R	6-0	180	9-9-84	2002	El Sombrero, Venez.
Espino, Damaso	.332	58	223	35	74	22	0	0	32	16	30	8	1	.430	.381	S	R	6-0	160	5-8-83	1999	Panama City, Panama
Fry, Ryan	.167	8	24	3	4	2	0	0	0	0	8	0	0	.250	.167	R	R	6-1	190	5-11-80	2001	Stockertown, Pa.
Galan, Jorman	.160	35	50	14	8	0	1	2	6	11	12	2	1	.320	.323	R	R	6-2	160	9-8-81	1999	Maracaibo, Venez.
Ghutzman, Phillip	.167	3	6	2	1	0	0	0	0	3	1	0	0	.167	.444	R	R	6-0	200	10-1-78	2001	Spring, Texas
Hall, Noah	.261	8	23	4	6	2	0	1	3	3	2	4	0	.478	.346	R	R	5-11	200	6-9-77	1996	Aptos, Calif.
Hawes, Don	.237	36	93	13	22	8	0	1	9	11	20	4	0	.355	.321	R	R	5-11	180	2-11-80	2002	Tremonton, Utah
Mateo, Dan	.240	9	25	6	6	1	0	0	1	2	3	2	3	.280	.321	S	R	6-0	150	10-27-82	1999	San Cristobal, D.R.
Mosby, Robert	.212	39	118	11	25	5	0	1	14	15	36	0	1	.280	.299	R	R	6-3	240	4-9-82	2002	Belleville, Ill.
Perez, Miguel	.360	26	86	12	31	1	0	0	11	2	9	3	0	.372	.396	R	R	6-3	190	9-25-83	2001	Guatire, Venez.
Soto, Melvin	.119	26	59	5	7	1	0	0	3	11	33	1	1	.136	.268	S	R	6-0	150	10-31-84	2002	Bani, D.R.
Votto, Joey	.269	50	175	29	47	13	3	9	33	21	45	7	2	.531	.342	L	R	6-3	200	9-10-83	2002	Toronto, Ontario
Wong, Travis	.317	52	180	27	57	10	0	10	45	12	23	4	2	.539	.381	R	R	6-6	230	8-28-81	2002	Boise, Idaho

GAMES BY POSITION: C—Delacruz 6, Fry 7, Ghutzman 3, Hawes 28, Perez 21, Votto 7. **1B**—Colina 7, Mosby 14, Perez 2, Wong 41. **2B**—Bolivar 23, Diaz 25, Espino 16, Mateo 1. **3B**—Correll 4, Diaz 1, Espindo 37, Perez 2, Soto 1, Votto 19, Wong 1. **SS**—Bolivar 30, Diaz 1, Espino 8, Mateo 7, Soto 23. **OF**—Araque 51, Campos 8, Colina 17, Dennis 1, Denorfia 57, Esparragoza 18, Galan 28, Hall 8, Hawes 3, Mosby 10, Perez 1, Votto 3.

PITCHING	W	L	ERA	G	GS	CG	SV	IP	H	R	ER	BB	SO	AVG	B	T	HT	WT	DOB	1st Yr	Resides
Aichele, Shawn	0	4	5.70	11	5	0	0	36	49	28	23	14	28	.326	R	R	6-1	210	10-27-82	2002	Cincinnati, Ohio
Bartel, Richard	1	1	3.14	7	0	0	0	14	19	8	5	4	9	.327	R	R	6-5	190	2-3-83	2001	Grapevine, Texas
Bell, Chris	0	0	10.80	3	0	0	0	5	6	6	6	4	3	.315	R	R	6-3	200	9-24-80	2002	Miami, Fla.
Bohorquez, Carlos	0	0	2.70	4	0	0	0	7	5	2	2	1	5	.208	R	R	5-11	160	10-6-81	1999	Maracaibo, Venez.
Brock, Tanner	0	0	0.00	1	0	0	0	2	2	0	0	0	2	.250	R	R	6-3	190	12-21-78	2002	Longwood, Fla.
Carpenter, Miles	0	4	7.71	9	4	0	0	23	35	23	20	16	12	.350	R	R	6-4	200	3-1-83	2002	Jasper, Ga.
Carswell, Jeffery	0	4	4.80	12	0	0	2	15	13	10	8	6	16	.228	R	R	6-1	210	5-28-80	2002	Albany, Ga.
Escorcha, Orlando	1	0	0.00	2	1	0	0	7	2	0	0	0	6	.090	L	L	6-2	170	1-20-82	1999	Valencia, Venez.
Eusebio, Mike	2	1	4.08	9	0	0	0	18	15	13	8	14	19	.241	R	R	5-10	150	1-17-79	2002	Hoboken, N.J.
Farfan, Alexander	3	4	5.18	20	5	0	4	40	28	28	23	20	31	.194	R	R	6-3	170	1-6-83	2000	Maracay, Venez.
Galan, Jorman	0	0	6.00	4	0	0	0	6	6	5	4	4	5	.000	R	R	6-2	160	9-8-81	1999	Maracaibo, Venez.
Gault, Tim	1	0	5.84	8	0	0	0	12	15	9	8	8	9	.306	L	L	6-0	200	5-10-81	2002	Scottsdale, Ariz.
George, Brad	1	2	2.49	5	0	0	0	22	16	10	6	6	13	.200	R	R	6-5	200	5-31-82	2002	New Braunfels, Texas
George, Jonathan	1	1	5.14	10	8	0	1	35	31	28	20	16	27	.226	R	R	6-3	210	7-6-84	2002	Pennsauken, N.J.
German, Rafael	6	2	2.04	10	10	0	0	53	39	21	12	12	39	.206	R	R	6-1	160	11-15-82	1999	Nizao, D.R.
Granado, Jan	4	2	2.91	13	12	0	0	56	45	23	18	22	45	.218	L	L	6-0	180	9-26-82	1999	Anzoategui, Venez.
Huguet, J.C.	0	0	4.76	6	0	0	1	11	16	7	6	5	10	.340	R	R	6-4	190	5-18-78	2000	Miami, Fla.
Knoff, Justin	4	1	3.38	13	2	0	1	32	27	15	12	13	21	.238	R	R	6-4	190	6-22-81	2002	Burlington, N.J.
Locklear, Joseph	2	1	2.96	16	0	0	2	27	18	11	9	20	16	.195	R	R	6-2	190	10-5-80	2002	Greensboro, N.C.
O'Donnell, Tony	0	0	15.43	2	0	0	0	2	4	4	4	2	1	.400	L	L	6-4	200	2-21-79	2002	Covington, Ky.
Shafer, David	1	0	1.29	3	0	0	1	7	3	2	1	2	7	.125	R	R	6-3	170	3-7-82	2002	Flagstaff, Ariz.
Speir, Zach	0	0	4.74	10	0	0	0	19	24	13	10	7	13	.303	R	R	6-5	200	9-16-82	2002	Buford, Ga.
Wagnon, Dwayne	1	3	2.78	10	8	0	0	36	28	23	11	24	39	.218	R	R	6-4	210	12-27-81	2001	Corpus Christi, Texas
Wells, Mark	2	0	1.93	5	0	0	2	9	7	4	2	0	5	.212	R	R	6-4	190	6-14-80	2002	Charlotte, N.C.

CLEVELAND INDIANS

BY JIM INGRAHAM

General manager Mark Shapiro's rookie season couldn't have been more tumultuous. Or controversial.

In his first year on the job, replacing the highly successful John Hart, Shapiro was in the driver's seat for one of the most eventful, and disappointing seasons in franchise history.

The Indians began the 2002 season feeling they could contend for still another American League Central Division title. An 11-1 start, which included a 10-game winning streak, fueled the early excitement. But then the roof caved in. A collapse of such proportions followed that by midseason Shapiro was overseeing a full-blown rebuilding project.

To his credit, Shapiro acted decisively and dramatically. In one frenetic four-week period between late June and late July, Shapiro orchestrated five different trades with four different organizations, involving 16 players, 10 of whom came to Cleveland.

Those trades, which included two of the club's top starters—Bartolo Colon and Chuck Finley—plus two of the top relievers—Paul Shuey and Ricardo Rincon—were the climax of a cataclysmic first few months on the job for Shapiro.

It started with the controversial trade of a future Hall of Famer (Roberto Alomar) in Shapiro's first official trade as GM. It also included a gunshot wound suffered by a player while fending off a failed car-jacking attempt (Jolbert Cabrera), two emergency appendectomies (John McDonald and Milton Bradley), an arrest for spousal abuse (Finley's wife), a pitcher being robbed at gunpoint (C.C. Sabathia), a managerial firing (Charlie Manuel), the sudden death of one of the most beloved members of the organization (longtime trainer Jimmy Warfield), disastrous seasons by key veterans (Travis Fryman and Einar Diaz), a banged-up veteran being forced to retire (Fryman), several season-ending surgeries (Bob Wickman, Matt Lawton, Ricky Gutierrez), and, of course, that cluster of midseason, season-conceding, franchise-rocking trades.

Jim Thome

Victor Martinez

PLAYERS OF THE YEAR

MAJOR LEAGUE: Jim Thome, 1b

Thome put up another Thome-like season, despite trade rumors and the Indians undergoing a major rebuilding process. He ranked second in the majors to Barry Bonds in on-base plus slugging (1.122) and second to Alex Rodriguez in home runs (52).

MINOR LEAGUE: Victor Martinez, c

Another year, another batting title, another league MVP award for Martinez, who hit .336-22-85 at Double-A Akron in 2002. The 23-year-old has become the Indians most decorated minor leaguer since Manny Ramirez.

When the dust had cleared, the Indians, playing under interim manager Joel Skinner in the second half, finished in third place in the AL Central, 20 games behind the division-winning Twins. The Indians' record of 74-88 was their first losing season since 1993, and it was their worst record since 1991, when they lost a franchise-record 105 games.

Amidst the wreckage, Jim Thome produced one of the greatest offensive seasons in franchise history. Thome set a franchise single-season record with 52 home runs, breaking the previous mark of 50 held by Albert Belle. Thome hit .304-52-118, with 101 runs scored.

The end of the season saw the end of the road for Fryman, who decided to retire at age 33, after two injury-plagued seasons. The Indians also said goodbye to veteran pitcher Charles Nagy, whose career spanned the rebirth of the organization. Nagy spent 12 years in an Indians uniform, starting in 1990. Eric Wedge, 34, who managed Triple-A Buffalo in 2002, was named the Tribe's new manager, replacing Skinner.

As the Indians were saying goodbye to their past, they were also saying hello to some of the players who will be their future. The midseason trades helped replenish a depleted minor league system.

The roster's season-long revolving door resulted in the Indians using a franchise-record 59 players in 2002, with 15 different players making their major league debuts. Further help may also arrive eventually from a Double-A Akron team that had a record of 93-48, a winning percentage of .660—tops in all the minor leagues—and was selected as Baseball America's Minor League Team of the Year.

ORGANIZATION LEADERS

BATTING

*AVG	Victor Martinez, Akron	.336
R	Victor Martinez, Akron	84
H	Chris Coste, Buffalo	152
TB	Victor Martinez, Akron	255
2B	Victor Martinez, Akron	40
3B	Zach Sorensen, Buffalo	12
HR	Victor Martinez, Akron	22
RBI	Victor Martinez, Akron	85
BB	J.J. Sherrill, Columbus	65
SO	Corey Smith, Kinston	141
SB	Alex Requena, Kinston	72

PITCHING

W	Billy Traber, Buffalo/Akron	17
L	Jake Dittler, Columbus	11
#ERA	Marcos Mendoza, Akron/Kinston	1.61
G	Ryan Larson, Buffalo/Akron/Kinston	56
CG	Three tied at	2
SV	Lee Gronkiewicz, Columbus	27
IP	Billy Traber, Buffalo/Akron	162
BB	Dan Denham, Columbus	65
SO	Travis Foley, Columbus	138

*Minimum 250 At-Bats #Minimum 75 Innings

CLEVELAND INDIANS

Managers: Charlie Manuel, Joel Skinner

2002 Record: 74-88, .457 (3rd, AL Central)

BATTING	AVG	G	AB	R	H	2B	3B	HR	RBI	BB	SO	SB	CS	SLG	OBP	B	T	HT	WT	DOB	1st Yr	Resides
Allen, Chad	.100	5	10	0	1	1	0	0	0	0	2	0	0	.200	.100	R	R	6-1	190	2-6-75	1996	Dallas, Texas
Anderson, Brady	.163	34	80	4	13	4	0	1	5	18	23	4	0	.250	.327	L	L	6-1	200	1-18-64	1985	Lake Tahoe, Nev.
Aven, Bruce	.118	7	17	1	2	0	0	0	0	4	4	1	0	.118	.286	R	R	5-9	180	3-4-72	1994	Orange, Texas
Bard, Josh	.222	24	90	9	20	5	0	3	12	4	13	0	0	.378	.255	S	R	6-3	200	3-30-78	1999	Englewood, Colo.
Bradley, Milton	.249	98	325	48	81	18	3	9	38	32	58	6	3	.406	.317	S	R	6-0	190	4-15-78	1996	Long Beach, Calif.
Branyan, Russell	.205	50	161	16	33	4	0	8	17	17	65	1	2	.379	.278	L	R	6-3	190	12-19-75	1994	Warner Robins, Ga.
Broussard, Ben	.241	39	112	10	27	4	0	4	9	7	25	0	0	.384	.292	L	L	6-3	220	9-24-76	1999	Beaumont, Texas
Burks, Ellis	.301	138	518	92	156	28	0	32	91	44	108	2	3	.541	.362	R	R	6-2	200	9-11-64	1983	Denver, Colo.
Cabrera, Jolbert	.111	38	72	5	8	1	0	0	7	5	13	1	1	.125	.177	R	R	6-0	170	12-8-72	1991	Cartagena, Colombia
Cordero, Wil	.222	6	18	1	4	0	0	0	1	0	3	0	0	.222	.222	R	R	6-2	200	10-3-71	1988	Mayaguez, P.R.
Crisp, Covelli	.260	32	127	16	33	9	2	1	9	11	19	4	1	.386	.314	S	R	6-0	180	11-1-79	1999	Desert Hot Springs, Calif.
Diaz, Einar	.206	102	320	34	66	19	0	2	16	17	27	0	1	.284	.258	R	R	5-10	160	12-28-72	1991	Chesnee, S.C.
Dunwoody, Todd	.000	2	6	0	0	0	0	0	0	0	3	0	0	.000	.000	L	L	6-1	210	4-11-75	1993	West Lafayette, Ind.
Fryman, Travis	.217	118	397	42	86	14	3	11	55	40	82	0	0	.350	.292	R	R	6-1	190	3-25-69	1987	Pensacola, Fla.
Garcia, Karim	.299	51	197	29	59	8	0	16	52	6	40	0	3	.584	.317	L	L	6-0	180	10-29-75	1992	Ciudad Obregon, Mexico
2-team (2 New York)	.297	53	202	30	60	8	0	16	52	6	41	0	3	.574	.314							
Gutierrez, Ricky	.275	94	353	38	97	13	0	4	38	20	48	0	1	.346	.325	R	R	6-1	190	5-23-70	1988	Pembroke Pines, Fla.
LaRocca, Greg	.269	21	52	12	14	3	1	0	4	6	6	1	0	.365	.367	R	R	5-11	180	11-10-72	1994	Bedford, N.H.
Lawton, Matt	.236	114	416	71	98	19	2	15	57	59	34	8	9	.399	.342	L	R	5-10	180	11-3-71	1991	Saucier, Miss.
Magruder, Chris	.217	87	258	34	56	15	1	6	29	15	55	2	0	.353	.261	S	R	5-11	200	4-26-77	1998	Yakima, Wash.
Martinez, Victor	.281	12	32	2	9	1	0	1	5	3	2	0	0	.406	.333	S	R	6-2	190	12-23-78	1997	Ciudad Bolivar, Venez.
McDonald, John	.250	93	264	35	66	11	3	1	12	10	50	3	0	.326	.288	R	R	5-11	170	9-24-74	1996	East Lyme, Conn.
Perez, Eddie	.214	42	117	6	25	9	0	0	4	5	25	0	0	.291	.252	R	R	6-1	220	5-4-68	1987	Duluth, Ga.
Phillips, Brandon	.258	11	31	5	8	3	1	0	4	3	6	0	0	.419	.343	R	R	5-11	180	6-28-81	1999	Stone Mountain, Ga.
Selby, Bill	.214	65	159	15	34	7	2	6	21	15	27	0	1	.396	.278	L	R	5-9	190	6-11-70	1992	Walls, Miss.
Snyder, Earl	.200	18	55	5	11	2	0	1	4	6	21	0	0	.291	.279	R	R	6-0	200	5-6-76	1998	Plainville, Conn.
Stevens, Lee	.222	53	153	22	34	7	1	5	26	15	32	0	0	.379	.285	L	L	6-4	230	10-3-67	1986	Highland Ranch, Colo.
Thome, Jim	.304	147	480	101	146	19	2	52	118	122	139	1	0	.677	.445	L	R	6-4	220	8-27-70	1989	Aurora, Ohio
Vizquel, Omar	.275	151	582	85	160	31	5	14	72	56	64	18	10	.418	.341	S	R	5-9	170	4-24-67	1984	Issaquah, Wash.

PITCHING	W	L	ERA	G	GS	CG	SV	IP	H	R	ER	BB	SO	AVG	B	T	HT	WT	DOB	1st Yr	Resides
Baez, Danny	10	11	4.41	39	26	1	6	165	160	84	81	82	130	.256	R	R	6-4	220	9-10-77	2000	Miami, Fla.
Beverlin, Jason	0	0	7.36	4	0	0	0	7	9	7	6	4	9	.290	L	R	6-5	220	11-27-73	1994	Royal Oak, Mich.
Burba, Dave	1	0	4.50	12	3	0	0	34	30	20	17	17	25	.236	R	R	6-4	240	7-7-66	1987	Gilbert, Ariz.
2-team (23 Texas)	5	5	5.20	35	21	1	0	145	155	91	84	57	95	.269							
Colon, Bartolo	10	4	2.55	16	16	4	0	116	104	37	33	31	75	.244	R	R	6-0	220	5-24-73	1994	Westlake, Ohio
Davis, Jason	1	0	1.84	3	2	0	0	15	12	3	3	4	11	.218	R	R	6-6	190	5-8-80	2000	Cleveland, Tenn.
DePaula, Sean	1	1	12.79	5	0	0	0	6	11	9	9	3	8	.366	R	R	6-4	210	11-7-73	1996	Derry, N.H.
Drese, Ryan	10	9	6.55	26	26	1	0	137	176	104	100	62	102	.317	R	R	6-3	220	4-5-76	1998	Oakland, Calif.
Elder, Dave	0	2	3.13	15	0	0	0	23	18	10	8	14	23	.219	R	R	6-0	180	9-23-75	1997	Conyers, Ga.
Finley, Chuck	4	11	4.44	18	18	1	0	105	114	56	52	48	91	.283	L	L	6-6	220	11-26-62	1985	Newport Beach, Calif.
Herrera, Alex	0	0	0.00	5	0	0	0	5	3	0	0	1	5	.157	L	L	5-11	170	11-5-76	1997	Maracaibo, Venez.
Lee, Cliff	0	1	1.74	2	2	0	0	10	6	2	2	8	6	.171	L	L	6-3	190	8-30-78	2000	Benton, Ark.
Maurer, Dave	0	1	13.50	2	0	0	0	1	3	2	2	0	0	.428	R	L	6-2	200	2-23-75	1997	Burnsville, Minn.
Mulholland, Terry	3	2	4.60	16	3	0	0	47	56	27	24	14	21	.301	R	L	6-3	200	3-9-63	1984	Scottsdale, Ariz.
Murray, Heath	0	2	7.50	9	0	0	0	12	12	10	10	7	11	.266	L	L	6-4	210	4-19-73	1994	Troy, Ohio
Nagy, Charles	1	4	8.88	19	7	0	0	49	76	51	48	13	22	.360	L	R	6-3	200	5-5-67	1989	Westlake, Ohio
Paronto, Chad	0	2	4.04	29	0	0	0	36	34	19	16	11	23	.248	R	R	6-5	250	7-28-75	1996	North Haverhill, N.H.
Phillips, Jason	1	3	4.97	8	6	0	0	42	41	24	23	20	23	.259	R	R	6-6	220	3-22-74	1992	Hughesville, Pa.
Riggan, Jerrod	2	1	7.64	29	0	0	0	33	53	28	28	18	22	.373	R	R	6-3	190	5-16-74	1996	Brewster, Wash.
Rincon, Ricardo	1	4	4.79	46	0	0	0	36	36	21	19	8	30	.262	L	L	5-10	180	4-13-70	1997	Veracruz, Mexico
Riske, David	2	2	5.26	51	0	0	1	51	49	32	30	35	65	.256	R	R	6-2	170	10-23-76	1997	Kent, Wash.
Rodriguez, Nerio	0	0	0.00	1	0	0	0	0	0	0	0	0	0	.000	R	R	6-1	200	3-4-71	1991	San Pedro de Macoris, D.R.
Rodriguez, Ricardo	2	2	5.66	7	7	0	0	41	40	27	26	18	24	.254	R	R	6-3	160	5-21-78	1996	Guayubin, D.R.
Sabathia, C.C.	13	11	4.37	33	33	2	0	210	198	109	102	88	149	.251	L	L	6-7	230	7-21-80	1998	Vallejo, Calif.
Sadler, Carl	1	2	4.43	24	0	0	0	20	15	10	10	11	23	.211	L	L	6-2	180	10-11-76	1996	Perry, Fla.
Shuey, Paul	3	0	2.41	39	0	0	0	37	31	11	10	10	39	.224	R	R	6-3	210	9-16-70	1992	Wake Forest, N.C.
Smith, Roy	0	0	3.00	4	1	0	0	6	9	4	2	5	2	.310	R	R	6-6	230	5-18-76	1994	Pinellas Park, Fla.
Tallet, Brian	1	0	1.50	2	2	0	0	12	9	3	2	4	5	.214	L	L	6-7	200	9-21-77	2000	Bethany, Okla.
Westbrook, Jake	1	3	5.83	11	4	0	0	42	50	30	27	12	20	.295	R	R	6-3	180	9-29-77	1996	Danielsville, Ga.
Wickman, Bob	1	3	4.46	36	0	0	20	34	42	22	17	10	36	.283	R	R	6-1	230	2-6-69	1990	Wausaukee, Wis.
Wohlers, Mark	3	4	4.79	64	0	0	7	71	71	41	38	26	46	.261	R	R	6-4	200	1-23-70	1988	Alpharetta, Ga.
Wright, Jaret	2	3	15.71	8	6	0	0	18	40	34	32	19	12	.434	R	R	6-2	230	12-29-75	1994	Newport Beach, Calif.

FIELDING

Catcher	PCT	G	PO	A	E	DP	PB
Bard	.988	24	153	13	2	4	2
Diaz	.989	100	640	75	8	4	8
Martinez	.983	9	55	2	1	0	1
Perez	.988	42	235	19	3	7	4
Selby	.000	1	0	0	0	0	0

First Base	PCT	G	PO	A	E	DP
Broussard	1.000	4	27	1	0	2
Cordero	1.000	1	1	0	0	0
Snyder	.981	12	98	8	2	3
Stevens	.987	25	216	8	3	19
Thome	.991	128	1063	75	10	118

Second Base	PCT	G	PO	A	E	DP
Cabrera	1.000	3	3	7	0	2
Gutierrez	.976	93	167	277	11	66
La Rocca	1.000	3	3	4	0	1
McDonald	.986	64	93	184	4	42
Phillips	.957	11	16	28	2	4

	PCT	G	PO	A	E	DP
Selby	1.000	6	5	10	0	3
Third Base	**PCT**	**G**	**PO**	**A**	**E**	**DP**
Branyan	.929	8	3	10	1	1
Fryman	.960	113	53	185	10	27
La Rocca	.800	15	9	15	6	1
Martinez	.000	1	0	0	0	0
McDonald	.882	10	4	11	2	0
Selby	.933	33	20	50	5	3
Snyder	1.000	2	1	4	0	0

Shortstop	PCT	G	PO	A	E	DP
McDonald	.973	21	31	42	2	10
Vizquel	.990	150	239	431	7	98
Outfield	**PCT**	**G**	**PO**	**A**	**E**	**DP**
Allen	1.000	4	4	0	0	0
Anderson	.981	29	52	0	1	0
Aven	1.000	7	12	0	0	0
Bradley	.982	94	214	9	4	2
Branyan	.986	42	66	4	1	1
Broussard	.960	32	47	1	2	0

	PCT	G	PO	A	E	DP
Burks	1.000	6	6	0	0	0
Cabrera	1.000	34	42	0	0	0
Cordero	1.000	4	8	2	0	1
Crisp	.988	32	83	1	1	1
Dunwoody	1.000	2	1	0	0	0
Garcia	.990	51	98	2	1	0
Lawton	.975	108	229	6	6	2
Magruder	.987	83	146	2	2	0
Selby	1.000	18	15	0	0	0
Stevens	1.000	16	32	1	0	0

Ellis Burks: second on team with 32 homers, 91 RBIs

C.C. Sabathia: 13 wins led Tribe staff

FARM SYSTEM

Director, Player Development: John Farrell.

Class	Farm Team	League	W	L	Pct.	Finish*	Manager	First Yr.
AAA	Buffalo (N.Y.) Bisons	International	87	57	.604	2nd (14)	Eric Wedge	1995
AA	Akron (Ohio) Aeros	Eastern	93	48	.660	1st (12)	Brad Komminsk	1997
High A	Kinston (N.C.) Indians	Carolina	74	65	.532	4th (8)	Ted Kubiak	1987
Low A	Columbus (Ga.) RedStixx	South Atlantic	79	60	.568	3rd (16)	Torey Lovullo	1991
SS A	Mahoning Valley (Ohio) Indians	New York-Penn	46	30	.605	5th (14)	Chris Bando	1999
Rookie	Burlington (N.C.) Indians	Appalachian	29	39	.426	8th (10)	Rouglas Odor	1986

*Finish in overall standings (No. of teams in league)

BUFFALO BISONS · Class AAA

INTERNATIONAL LEAGUE

BATTING	AVG	G	AB	R	H	2B	3B	HR	RBI	BB	SO	SB	CS	SLG	OBP	B	T	HT	WT	DOB	1st Yr	Resides
Allen, Chad	.301	70	279	45	84	20	1	10	62	15	34	0	1	.487	.340	R	R	6-1	190	2-6-75	1996	Dallas, Texas
2-team (8 Rochester)	.293	78	311	46	91	22	2	10	63	15	40	0	1	.473	.328							
Aven, Bruce	.286	35	119	17	34	5	0	5	16	14	21	1	0	.454	.375	R	R	5-9	180	3-4-72	1994	Orange, Texas
Bard, Josh	.297	94	344	36	102	26	2	6	53	20	45	0	0	.436	.332	S	R	6-3	200	3-30-78	1999	Englewood, Colo.
Bradley, Milton	.261	6	23	3	6	0	0	0	3	3	5	2	1	.261	.321	S	R	6-0	190	4-15-78	1996	Long Beach, Calif.
Broussard, Ben	.242	42	153	30	37	8	0	5	21	24	30	0	0	.392	.354	L	L	6-3	220	9-24-76	1999	Beaumont, Texas
2-team (57 Louisville)	.259	99	340	61	88	22	1	16	51	55	80	4	1	.471	.377							
Cabrera, Jolbert	.286	23	91	16	26	5	0	0	7	9	10	4	2	.341	.353	R	R	6-0	170	12-8-72	1991	Cartagena, Colombia
Coste, Chris	.318	124	478	59	152	32	1	8	67	34	54	0	0	.439	.377	R	R	6-1	200	2-4-73	1995	Fargo, N.D.
Crisp, Covelli	.238	4	21	3	5	1	0	0	2	0	2	1	0	.286	.238	S	R	6-0	180	11-1-79	1999	Desert Hot Springs, Calif.
Davis, Tommy	.252	36	147	9	37	9	0	3	17	1	37	0	1	.374	.265	R	R	6-1	210	5-21-73	1994	Semmes, Ala.
Dunwoody, Todd	.267	102	363	57	97	31	4	7	29	12	62	8	3	.433	.298	L	L	6-1	210	4-11-75	1993	West Lafayette, Ind.
Fitzgerald, Jason	.385	4	13	2	5	2	0	0	2	0	6	1	1	.538	.385	L	L	6-1	190	9-16-75	1997	Belle Chasse, La.
Garcia, Karim	.396	23	91	16	36	7	2	3	22	9	14	0	1	.615	.450	L	L	6-0	180	10-29-75	1992	Ciudad Obregon, Mexico
2-team (74 Columbus)	.301	97	379	60	114	23	5	15	71	29	62	1	6	.507	.349							
Gerut, Jody	.322	55	183	31	59	7	2	1	21	23	20	3	5	.399	.401	L	L	6-0	190	9-18-77	1998	Lombard, Ill.

BATTING	AVG	G	AB	R	H	2B	3B	HR	RBI	BB	SO	SB	CS	SLG	OBP	B	T	HT	WT	DOB	1st Yr	Resides
Goelz, Jim	.308	4	13	0	4	0	1	0	4	0	1	0	0	.462	.357	R	R	5-10	170	2-13-76	1998	St. James, N.Y.
Gonzalez, Luis	.105	6	19	0	2	0	0	0	1	1	4	0	0	.105	.190	R	R	5-11	170	6-26-79	1997	El Tigre, Venez.
Laker, Tim	.227	62	216	23	49	10	0	4	28	21	52	2	0	.329	.303	R	R	6-3	220	11-27-69	1988	Simi Valley, Calif.
Lansing, Mike	.245	24	94	9	23	4	2	2	8	6	7	2	1	.394	.297	R	R	6-0	190	4-3-68	1990	Palm Beach Gardens, Fla.
LaRocca, Greg	.293	107	382	70	112	28	2	7	41	48	48	17	4	.432	.402	R	R	5-11	180	11-10-72	1994	Bedford, N.H.
Magruder, Chris	.267	54	191	28	51	10	2	5	16	26	34	3	2	.419	.364	S	R	5-11	200	4-26-77	1998	Yakima, Wash.
Medrano, Tony	.220	74	264	28	58	10	2	1	30	20	25	7	1	.284	.284	R	R	5-10	170	12-8-74	1993	Long Beach, Calif.
Myers, Kenton	.000	1	1	0	0	0	0	0	0	0	1	0	0	.000	.000	R	R	6-1	200	4-14-80	2001	Albuquerque, NM
Phillips, Brandon	.283	55	223	30	63	14	0	8	27	14	39	8	2	.453	.321	R	R	5-11	180	6-28-81	1999	Stone Mountain, Ga.
2-team (10 Ottawa)	.279	65	258	31	72	18	0	9	32	16	45	8	2	.453	.318							
Pratt, Scott	.250	4	20	2	5	1	0	0	3	1	2	0	1	.300	.286	L	R	5-10	180	2-4-77	1998	Tooele, Utah
Selby, Bill	.299	51	184	28	55	14	2	5	22	20	33	4	1	.478	.364	L	R	5-9	190	6-11-70	1992	Walls, Miss.
Snyder, Earl	.263	110	400	69	105	29	1	19	66	43	96	0	1	.483	.341	R	R	6-0	200	5-6-76	1998	Plainville, Conn.
Sorensen, Zach	.264	120	455	55	120	12	12	7	54	24	72	13	6	.389	.300	S	R	6-0	190	1-3-77	1998	Mesquite, Nev.
Ware, Jeremy	.296	42	135	18	40	10	0	1	17	6	23	2	1	.393	.326	R	R	6-0	200	10-23-75	1995	Guelph, Ontario

PITCHING	W	L	ERA	G	GS	CG	SV	IP	H	R	ER	BB	SO	AVG	B	T	HT	WT	DOB	1st Yr	Resides
Beverlin, Jason	10	8	3.87	23	20	1	0	119	107	55	51	39	106	.243	L	R	6-5	220	11-27-73	1994	Royal Oak, Mich.
Caraccioli, Lance	4	0	3.05	8	6	0	1	44	45	16	15	19	33	.272	L	L	6-4	190	12-14-77	1998	Walker, La.
Coste, Chris	1	1	3.60	2	0	0	0	5	3	2	2	0	3	.000	R	R	6-1	200	2-4-73	1995	Fargo, N.D.
D'Amico, Jeff	0	1	4.15	2	1	0	1	9	10	6	4	2	2	.285	R	R	6-3	200	11-9-74	1993	Seattle, Wash.
De Paula, Sean	2	3	3.95	34	0	0	9	57	55	26	25	18	53	.252	R	R	6-4	210	11-7-73	1996	Derry, N.H.
Drese, Ryan	1	0	1.64	3	3	0	0	22	16	4	4	4	16	.200	R	R	6-3	220	4-5-76	1998	Oakland, Calif.
Drew, Tim	8	4	3.27	15	15	2	0	96	96	43	35	23	43	.260	R	R	6-1	190	8-31-78	1997	Hahira, Ga.
Elder, Dave	3	1	2.65	22	1	0	5	34	32	11	10	14	42	.248	R	R	6-0	190	9-23-75	1997	Conyers, Ga.
Herrera, Alex	0	1	11.57	5	0	0	0	7	10	9	9	8	5	.344	L	L	5-11	170	11-5-76	1997	Maracaibo, Venez.
Larson, Ryan	0	0	10.80	1	0	0	0	3	2	2	2	1	1	.375	R	R	5-10	150	5-13-79	2000	Rocklin, Calif.
Lee, Cliff	3	2	3.77	8	8	0	0	43	36	18	18	22	30	.229	L	L	6-3	190	8-30-78	2000	Benton, Ark.
Matheny, Brandon	0	0	9.00	1	0	0	0	4	7	4	4	1	1	.368	L	L	6-3	200	10-22-78	2000	Damascus, Va.
Maurer, Dave	5	1	2.90	36	3	0	5	68	50	27	22	24	73	.204	R	L	6-2	200	2-23-75	1997	Burnsville, Minn.
Mercedes, Jose	2	0	3.49	5	5	0	0	28	32	11	11	6	13	.283	R	R	6-1	180	3-5-71	1992	La Romano, D.R.
Miller, Travis	1	1	2.45	7	0	0	0	15	15	9	4	8	5	.277	R	L	6-3	210	11-2-72	1994	Eaton, Ohio
Murray, Heath	1	2	3.03	21	2	0	5	30	23	10	10	6	32	.221	L	L	6-4	210	4-19-73	1994	Troy, Ohio
Nagy, Charles	1	2	3.19	5	5	2	0	37	38	18	13	4	18	.267	L	R	6-3	200	5-5-67	1989	Westlake, Ohio
Olivares, Omar	0	2	4.66	2	2	0	0	10	18	10	5	3	8	.382	R	R	6-1	210	7-6-67	1987	San German, P.R.
Paronto, Chad	0	0	0.00	8	0	0	1	13	10	0	0	1	7	.212	R	R	6-5	250	7-28-75	1996	North Haverhill, N.H.
Phillips, Jason	7	4	3.39	16	16	1	0	98	88	37	37	17	71	.242	R	R	6-6	220	3-22-74	1992	Hughesville, Pa.
Riggan, Jerrod	4	1	2.38	27	0	0	3	45	40	12	12	11	37	.246	R	R	6-3	190	5-16-74	1996	Brewster, Wash.
Riske, David	1	1	3.72	9	0	0	3	10	6	4	4	4	17	.181	R	R	6-2	170	10-23-76	1997	Kent, Wash.
Rodriguez, Nerio	4	2	1.82	13	10	1	0	74	55	20	15	12	44	.202	R	R	6-1	200	3-4-71	1991	San Pedro de Macoris, D.R.
Rodriguez, Ricardo	1	3	3.60	4	4	0	0	25	26	10	10	7	14	.270	R	R	6-3	160	5-21-78	1996	Guayubin, D.R.
Rose, Ted	2	1	2.93	5	5	0	0	28	26	9	9	11	13	.247	L	R	6-1	180	8-23-73	1996	St. Clairsville, Ohio
Sadler, Carl	1	1	1.93	12	0	0	1	19	19	7	4	8	13	.267	L	L	6-2	180	10-1-76	1996	Perry, Fla.
Smith, Roy	5	4	3.84	36	3	0	1	70	65	37	30	29	65	.246	R	R	6-5	230	5-18-76	1994	Pinellas Park, Fla.
Spiegel, Mike	0	0	9.00	1	1	0	0	5	9	5	5	4	1	.409	L	L	6-5	200	11-24-75	1996	Carmichael, Calif.
Stanford, Jason	3	1	2.78	6	5	0	0	36	33	12	11	11	23	.244	L	L	6-2	200	1-23-77	1999	Lawrence, Kan.
Tallet, Brian	2	3	3.07	8	7	0	0	44	47	17	15	16	25	.283	L	L	6-7	200	9-21-77	2000	Bethany, Okla.
Thoms, Hank	0	1	5.40	1	1	0	0	5	7	5	3	1	2	.333	R	R	6-4	210	6-7-76	1999	Newton, Miss.
Traber, Billy	4	3	3.29	9	9	0	0	55	58	22	20	12	33	.276	L	L	6-5	200	9-18-79	2001	El Segundo, Calif.
Vargas, Jason	3	2	2.31	22	0	0	8	35	36	15	9	11	18	.270	R	R	6-0	150	2-22-77	1996	San Pedro de Macoris, D.R.
Westbrook, Jake	1	0	6.00	1	1	0	0	6	8	4	4	0	2	.333	R	R	6-3	195	9-29-77	1996	Danielsville, Ga.
White, Matt	0	0	4.76	7	1	0	0	17	23	13	9	6	12	.319	R	L	6-1	180	8-19-77	1998	Windsor, Mass.
Wright, Jaret	5	3	3.88	10	10	1	0	56	57	27	24	24	43	.267	R	R	6-2	230	12-29-75	1994	Newport Beach, Calif.

FIELDING

Catcher	PCT	G	PO	A	E	DP	PB
Bard	.984	93	609	60	11	2	1
Coste	.992	20	118	9	1	3	1
Davis	1.000	2	12	0	0	0	0
Laker	.991	31	198	16	2	1	1
Myers	1.000	1	3	0	0	0	0

First Base	PCT	G	PO	A	E	DP
Broussard	1.000	9	43	2	0	3
Cabrera	1.000	2	20	0	0	3
Coste	.988	65	543	43	7	69
Davis	1.000	10	101	6	0	11
Laker	.994	20	147	14	1	15
Lansing	.971	4	30	3	1	3
Snyder	.989	40	334	22	4	30

Second Base	PCT	G	PO	A	E	DP
Cabrera	1.000	1	1	3	0	0
Gonzalez	.967	6	17	12	1	3
Lansing	.953	8	22	19	2	6
LaRocca	.993	29	61	78	1	26
Medrano	.990	10	24	24	1	3

Phillips	.961	11	37	37	3	10
Pratt	1.000	1	2	2	0	1
Selby	.972	17	25	44	2	10
Sorensen	.984	62	126	190	5	45

Third Base	PCT	G	PO	A	E	DP
Cabrera	1.000	2	3	3	0	0
Coste	.950	16	4	34	2	5
Davis	1.000	5	3	7	0	1
Goelz	1.000	3	1	5	0	1
Lansing	.500	1	0	1	1	0
LaRocca	.958	51	36	82	5	11
Selby	.870	10	5	15	3	3
Snyder	.911	62	45	109	15	11

Shortstop	PCT	G	PO	A	E	DP
Cabrera	1.000	3	11	13	0	1
Goelz	1.000	1	2	6	0	1
Lansing	.833	2	5	5	2	3
LaRocca	.909	4	3	7	1	1
Medrano	.976	37	45	116	4	12
Phillips	.949	44	72	153	12	34

Sorensen	.970	55	85	170	8	42

Outfield	PCT	G	PO	A	E	DP
Allen	1.000	45	92	3	0	1
Aven	1.000	28	48	5	0	1
Bradley	1.000	5	10	1	0	0
Broussard	.959	34	69	1	3	0
Cabrera	1.000	14	31	1	0	0
Crisp	1.000	4	8	0	0	0
Davis	1.000	6	12	0	0	0
Dunwoody	.983	83	175	2	3	0
Fitzgerald	.909	4	10	0	1	0
Garcia	1.000	18	38	0	0	0
Gerut	.993	53	137	3	1	1
Lansing	.917	8	11	0	1	0
LaRocca	.880	13	21	1	3	0
Magruder	.991	49	112	0	1	0
Medrano	1.000	26	62	3	0	1
Pratt	1.000	3	7	0	0	0
Selby	1.000	18	37	1	0	0
Snyder	1.000	5	9	0	0	0
Ware	1.000	34	55	3	0	0

AKRON AEROS — Double-A

EASTERN LEAGUE

BATTING	AVG	G	AB	R	H	2B	3B	HR	RBI	BB	SO	SB	CS	SLG	OBP	B	T	HT	WT	DOB	1st Yr	Resides
Bradley, Milton	.273	3	11	1	3	1	0	0	1	1	1	0	1	.364	.333	S	R	6-0	190	4-15-78	1996	Long Beach, Calif.

BATTING

BATTING	AVG	G	AB	R	H	2B	3B	HR	RBI	BB	SO	SB	CS	SLG	OBP	B	T	HT	WT	DOB	1st Yr	Resides
Cameron, Troy	.222	71	230	26	51	12	1	4	24	22	71	0	1	.335	.301	S	R	5-11	180	8-31-78	1997	Plantation, Fla.
Church, Ryan	.296	71	291	39	86	17	4	12	51	12	58	1	0	.505	.325	L	L	6-1	190	10-14-78	2000	Lompoc, Calif.
Crisp, Covelli	.406	7	32	9	13	1	0	1	4	3	3	4	0	.531	.457	S	R	6-0	180	11-1-79	1999	Desert Hot Springs, Calif.
2-team (89 New Haven)	.310	96	387	70	120	17	1	10	51	39	59	30	10	.437	.372							
Crozier, Eric	.296	43	142	19	42	8	1	1	13	21	50	1	0	.387	.398	L	L	6-4	200	8-11-78	2000	Columbus, Ohio
Erickson, Corey	.232	99	345	49	80	21	3	20	64	34	101	3	3	.484	.309	R	R	5-11	190	1-10-77	1995	Springfield, Ill.
Fitzgerald, Jason	.255	106	392	43	100	23	0	11	57	41	80	21	6	.398	.324	L	L	6-1	190	9-16-75	1997	Belle Chasse, La.
Garcia, Luis	.289	39	166	24	48	9	0	6	21	13	27	1	0	.452	.343	R	R	6-4	180	11-5-78	1997	Guadalajara, Mexico
2-team (88 New Haven)	.274	127	474	66	130	25	1	18	58	45	86	4	2	.445	.338							
Gerut, Jody	.281	65	256	44	72	15	2	9	39	34	30	17	8	.461	.368	L	L	6-0	190	9-18-77	1998	Lombard, Ill.
Goelz, Jim	.122	17	49	7	6	3	0	0	4	2	6	0	1	.184	.173	R	R	5-10	170	2-13-76	1998	St. James, N.Y.
Gonzalez, Luis	.266	73	263	42	70	10	3	6	24	12	37	4	0	.395	.304	R	R	5-11	170	6-26-79	1997	El Tigre, Venez.
Grindell, Nate	.283	119	435	73	123	24	8	11	60	33	61	4	3	.451	.335	R	R	6-1	180	4-9-77	1998	Carrollton, Texas
Hamilton, Jon	.230	43	148	24	34	7	3	6	22	16	33	5	1	.439	.305	L	L	6-1	190	10-23-77	1997	San Ramon, Calif.
Izturis, Maicer	.277	67	253	34	70	12	7	0	32	17	28	8	4	.379	.326	S	R	5-8	150	9-12-80	1998	Barquisimeto, Venez.
Lawton, Matt	.000	3	10	1	0	0	0	0	0	3	1	0	0	.000	.231	L	R	5-10	180	11-3-71	1991	Saucier, Miss.
Luderer, Brian	.245	50	155	29	38	11	1	3	17	11	32	0	0	.387	.308	R	R	5-11	160	8-19-78	1996	Tarzana, Calif.
Martinez, Victor	.336	121	443	84	149	40	0	22	85	58	62	3	3	.576	.417	S	R	6-2	160	12-23-78	1997	Ciudad Bolivar, Venez.
McDougall, Marshall	.389	7	18	6	7	2	0	1	4	6	2	0	0	.667	.542	R	R	6-1	200	12-19-78	2000	Valrico, Fla.
Munoz, Billy	.250	74	248	37	62	22	1	5	44	41	47	0	1	.407	.353	L	L	6-2	220	6-30-75	1998	Mesa, Ark.
Peralta, John	.281	130	470	62	132	28	5	15	62	45	87	4	2	.457	.343	R	R	6-1	180	5-28-82	1999	Santiago, D.R.
Pratt, Scott	.267	115	446	81	119	17	4	17	54	62	88	19	4	.437	.363	L	R	5-10	180	2-4-77	1998	Tooele, Utah

PITCHING

PITCHING	W	L	ERA	G	GS	CG	SV	IP	H	R	ER	BB	SO	AVG	B	T	HT	WT	DOB	1st Yr	Resides
Brown, Jamie	9	5	2.78	18	17	0	0	104	98	41	32	17	72	.249	R	R	6-2	200	3-31-77	1997	Collinsville, Miss.
Burba, Dave	0	0	0.00	1	1	0	0	5	2	0	0	1	1	.133	R	R	6-4	240	7-7-66	1987	Gilbert, Ark.
Byrdak, Tim	0	0	6.23	9	0	0	1	13	16	12	9	11	8	.307	L	L	5-11	180	10-31-73	1994	Oak Forest, Ill.
Cabrera, Fernando	1	2	5.33	7	4	0	1	27	26	16	16	12	29	.252	R	R	6-4	170	11-16-81	1999	Toa Baja, P.R.
Colon, Jose	5	4	2.37	46	2	0	5	76	72	21	20	8	43	.251	R	R	6-0	170	11-24-74	1993	Puerto Plata, D.R.
Davis, Jason	6	2	3.51	10	10	0	0	59	63	26	23	16	45	.277	R	R	6-6	190	5-8-80	2000	Cleveland, Tenn.
Denney, Kyle	3	1	1.56	6	5	0	0	35	23	7	6	5	32	.182	R	R	6-2	190	7-27-77	1999	Prague, Okla.
Edmondson, Brian	2	0	0.00	5	0	0	1	7	2	1	0	1	6	.086	R	R	6-2	170	1-29-73	1991	Riverside, Calif.
Elder, Dave	2	1	2.00	23	1	0	9	36	19	8	8	18	42	.154	R	R	6-0	180	9-23-75	1997	Conyers, Ga.
Evans, Kyle	1	0	4.09	2	2	0	0	11	9	5	5	6	9	.219	R	R	6-3	190	10-10-78	2000	Albuquerque, N.M.
Garza, Alberto	2	0	1.72	20	0	0	1	37	15	7	7	29	45	.131	R	R	5-11	180	5-25-77	1996	Wapato, Wash.
Guillory, Dan	3	3	1.11	19	0	0	2	32	20	11	4	20	35	.181	R	R	6-3	200	5-12-76	1998	Baton Rouge, La.
Herrera, Alex	0	2	3.38	30	0	0	5	61	47	24	23	30	65	.211	L	L	5-11	170	11-5-76	1997	Maracaibo, Venez.
Johnson, James	0	0	4.50	5	0	0	0	6	3	3	3	4	6	.181	S	L	6-1	170	8-7-76	1998	San Diego, Calif.
Larson, Ryan	2	3	1.78	32	0	0	8	35	37	10	7	6	30	.264	R	R	5-10	190	5-13-79	2000	Rocklin, Calif.
Lee, Cliff	2	1	5.40	3	3	0	0	17	11	11	10	10	18	.180	L	L	6-3	190	8-30-78	2000	Benton, Ark.
2-team (15 Harrisburg)	.9	3	3.58	18	18	0	0	103	72	42	41	33	123	.194							
Mendoza, Marcos	2	3	2.41	21	0	0	0	37	30	17	10	24	27	.220	L	L	5-10	180	10-31-80	2001	Santee, Calif.
Montano, Ignacio	0	0	8.10	2	0	0	0	3	3	3	3	2	6	.250	L	L	5-8	150	3-8-80	2001	Veracruz, Mexico
Paronto, Chad	0	0	27.00	1	1	0	0	1	1	1	1	1	0	.500	R	R	6-5	250	7-28-75	1996	North Haverhill, N.H.
Rakers, Jason	0	0	6.00	1	1	0	0	3	4	2	2	1	0	.333	R	R	6-2	200	6-29-73	1995	Pittsburgh, Pa.
Riske, David	0	0	3.00	4	2	0	0	6	5	2	2	1	10	.217	R	R	6-2	170	10-23-76	1997	Kent, Wash.
Rose, Ted	2	2	4.60	6	6	0	0	29	29	17	15	6	18	.250	L	R	6-1	180	8-23-73	1996	St. Clairsville, Ohio
Sadler, Carl	4	1	2.33	21	0	0	2	46	39	12	12	12	37	.229	L	L	6-2	180	10-11-76	1996	Perry, Fla.
Shuey, Paul	0	0	4.50	2	2	0	0	2	2	1	1	0	3	.250	R	R	6-3	210	9-16-70	1992	Wake Forest, N.C.
Sido, Wilson	0	0	4.50	1	1	0	0	4	5	3	2	2	1	.294	R	R	6-2	170	8-16-78	1998	Barahona, D.R.
Spiegel, Mike	7	3	3.08	25	17	0	0	91	63	37	31	51	87	.193	L	L	6-5	200	11-24-75	1996	Carmichael, Calif.
Stanford, Jason	7	6	3.43	18	18	1	0	102	108	44	39	33	86	.275	L	L	6-2	200	1-23-77	1999	Lawrence, Kan.
Tallet, Brian	10	1	3.08	18	18	1	0	102	93	41	35	32	73	.243	L	L	6-7	190	9-21-77	2000	Bethany, Okla.
Traber, Billy	13	2	2.76	18	17	2	0	108	99	38	33	20	82	.243	L	L	6-5	200	9-18-79	2001	El Segundo, Calif.
Vargas, Jose	4	1	4.31	18	1	0	2	40	42	21	19	16	33	.270	R	R	6-0	170	3-25-77	1998	Barahona, D.R.
Westbrook, Jake	0	1	4.80	3	3	0	0	15	13	8	8	1	8	.228	R	R	6-3	180	9-29-77	1996	Danielsville, Ga.
White, Matt	6	2	3.93	27	11	0	1	89	97	42	39	39	63	.279	R	L	6-1	180	8-19-77	1998	Windsor, Mass.

FIELDING

Catcher	PCT	G	PO	A	E	DP	PB
Luderer	.981	44	290	20	6	2	5
Martinez	.988	101	770	66	10	4	8

First Base	PCT	G	PO	A	E	DP
Crozier	.997	38	326	19	1	27
Erickson	.996	30	229	13	1	18
Garcia	.984	7	59	3	1	3
Gonzalez	1.000	2	12	1	0	1
Grindell	1.000	2	22	1	0	2
Luderer	1.000	1	3	0	0	1
Munoz	.982	70	556	41	11	50

Second Base	PCT	G	PO	A	E	DP
Erickson	1.000	5	11	6	0	1
Goelz	1.000	6	8	11	0	1
Gonzalez	.972	31	59	81	4	23

Third Base	PCT	G	PO	A	E	DP
Cameron	.906	61	35	109	15	5
Erickson	.941	59	33	111	9	12
Goelz	1.000	3	0	3	0	0
Gonzalez	.882	11	5	25	4	1
Grindell	.000	1	0	0	0	0
McDougall	.917	7	1	10	1	0
Pratt	.912	10	7	24	3	2

Shortstop	PCT	G	PO	A	E	DP
Goelz	.964	7	10	17	1	4
Gonzalez	1.000	4	2	10	0	0
Peralta	.965	130	201	374	21	73
Pratt	1.000	5	8	12	0	1

Izturis	.961	65	118	155	11	41
Pratt	.970	39	70	89	5	17

Outfield	PCT	G	PO	A	E	DP
Bradley	1.000	2	3	1	0	0
Church	.993	67	139	12	1	3
Crisp	1.000	6	9	0	0	0
Crozier	1.000	3	4	0	0	0
Erickson	1.000	2	3	0	0	0
Fitzgerald	.994	83	169	3	1	0
Garcia	.978	22	41	3	1	0
Gerut	.979	64	142	1	3	0
Goelz	1.000	1	5	0	0	0
Gonzalez	1.000	3	6	0	0	0
Grindell	.974	96	141	6	4	1
Hamilton	.975	38	72	5	2	0
Lawton	1.000	3	9	0	0	0
Luderer	.000	1	0	0	0	0
Pratt	.978	43	89	1	2	0

KINSTON INDIANS — High Class A

CAROLINA LEAGUE

BATTING	AVG	G	AB	R	H	2B	3B	HR	RBI	BB	SO	SB	CS	SLG	OBP	B	T	HT	WT	DOB	1st Yr	Resides
Bastardo, Angel	.222	16	54	10	12	4	0	1	11	2	8	1	0	.352	.283	R	R	6-0	170	4-2-77	1997	Miraflores, Venez.
Church, Ryan	.326	53	181	30	59	12	1	10	30	31	51	4	4	.569	.433	L	L	6-1	190	10-14-78	2000	Lompoc, Calif.

BATTING

BATTING	AVG	G	AB	R	H	2B	3B	HR	RBI	BB	SO	SB	CS	SLG	OBP	B	T	HT	WT	DOB	1st Yr	Resides
Colmenter, Jesus	.000	2	2	0	0	0	0	0	0	1	2	0	0	.000	.333	S	R	5-10	150	12-1-81	1998	Cabudare, Venez.
Crozier, Eric	.326	72	258	40	84	16	2	9	55	42	57	4	3	.508	.423	L	L	6-4	200	8-11-78	2000	Columbus, Ohio
Dempsey, Nick	.129	9	31	2	4	0	0	0	1	0	8	0	2	.129	.156	R	R	6-5	210	12-15-78	1997	Durban, South Africa
DePippo, Jeff	.242	48	149	11	36	4	0	4	15	10	35	1	2	.349	.307	R	R	5-7	170	4-29-76	1998	Garden Grove, Calif.
Inglett, Joe	.282	66	238	24	67	12	0	0	29	29	38	5	2	.332	.362	L	R	5-10	170	6-29-78	2000	Citrus Heights, Calif.
Izturis, Maicer	.262	58	233	28	61	13	1	1	30	24	26	24	6	.339	.332	S	R	5-8	150	9-12-80	1998	Barquisimeto, Venez.
Janowicz, Nate	.265	44	151	12	40	7	1	1	20	17	28	1	0	.344	.339	L	L	5-10	180	5-16-78	2000	Atascadero, Calif.
Luna, Hector	.276	128	468	67	129	15	6	11	51	39	79	32	11	.404	.334	R	R	6-1	170	2-1-80	1999	Monte Cristi, D.R.
Minges, Tyler	.231	113	394	65	91	20	5	16	58	32	71	8	10	.429	.292	R	R	6-0	180	11-15-79	1998	Hamilton, Ohio
Moreno, Jorge	.206	82	267	31	55	8	5	3	20	24	75	2	1	.307	.283	R	R	6-0	170	10-26-79	1998	Ciudad Ojeda, Venez.
Morton, Rickie	.239	95	339	45	81	13	4	13	39	30	100	1	1	.416	.302	R	R	6-3	200	9-15-78	2001	Citrus Heights, Calif.
Peguero, Miguel	.150	7	20	2	3	0	0	0	2	0	3	0	0	.150	.150	S	R	6-0	160	9-29-79	1997	Santo Domingo, D.R.
Pichardo, Henry	.214	74	248	23	53	10	2	3	37	8	64	4	3	.306	.238	R	R	5-10	140	1-15-77	1996	Tamboril, D.R.
Requena, Alex	.230	128	512	66	118	13	4	2	21	57	132	72	19	.283	.312	S	R	5-11	150	8-13-80	1998	Maracay, Venez.
Scott, Luke	.239	48	163	22	39	7	1	8	30	16	47	2	1	.442	.326	L	R	6-0	210	6-25-78	2001	Deleon Springs, Fla.
Sizemore, Grady	.343	47	172	31	59	9	3	3	20	33	30	14	7	.483	.451	L	L	6-2	200	8-2-82	2000	Mill Creek, Wash.
Smith, Corey	.255	134	505	71	129	29	2	13	67	59	141	7	2	.398	.341	R	R	6-1	200	4-15-82	2000	Piscataway, N.J.
Wilson, Heath	.185	80	260	18	48	6	1	1	18	28	106	2	1	.227	.271	R	R	6-2	190	8-9-78	1996	Torquay, Australia

PITCHING

PITCHING	W	L	ERA	G	GS	CG	SV	IP	H	R	ER	BB	SO	AVG	B	T	HT	WT	DOB	1st Yr	Resides
Byrdak, Tim	1	0	4.50	2	0	0	0	4	3	2	2	4	3	.214	L	L	5-11	180	10-31-73	1994	Oak Forest, Ill.
Cabrera, Fernando	6	8	3.52	21	21	0	0	110	83	48	43	40	107	.206	R	R	6-4	170	11-16-81	1999	Toa Baja, P.R.
Cooper, Chris	0	1	1.93	8	0	0	1	14	9	4	3	7	9	.191	L	L	5-11	190	10-31-79	2000	Sewickley, Pa.
Cruceta, Alberto	2	0	2.50	7	7	0	0	40	31	13	11	25	37	.216	R	R	6-2	170	7-4-81	1999	La Vega, D.R.
Davis, Jason	3	6	4.15	17	17	1	0	100	107	64	46	31	68	.272	R	R	6-6	190	5-8-80	2000	Cleveland, Tenn.
De la Cruz, Carlos	2	2	5.59	6	6	0	0	29	33	23	18	11	23	.289	R	R	6-1	160	1-14-82	1999	Santo Domingo, D.R.
Denney, Kyle	7	6	3.60	15	14	0	0	85	76	37	34	41	68	.242	R	R	6-2	190	7-27-77	1999	Prague, Okla.
Evans, Kyle	4	4	3.36	11	11	0	0	70	66	30	26	26	42	.255	R	R	6-3	190	10-10-78	2000	Albuquerque, N.M.
Fernley, Nate	3	1	1.17	15	0	0	3	23	19	3	3	6	15	.234	R	R	6-3	160	1-13-77	2001	Orem, Utah
Field, Luke	1	0	5.79	6	0	0	1	9	13	6	6	4	8	.325	R	R	5-11	170	1-27-79	2000	Tempe, Ariz.
Fitch, Steve	0	4	6.39	15	1	0	0	31	50	31	22	6	19	.364	R	R	6-1	180	2-15-78	2000	West Chester, Pa.
Jackson, Brian	2	1	3.18	11	0	0	3	11	11	4	4	9	5	.255	R	R	6-4	190	8-12-77	1998	Tiburon, Calif.
Lantz, Doug	4	2	5.40	11	0	0	0	23	25	15	14	9	19	.271	R	R	6-1	180	8-26-79	2001	Southlake, Texas
Larson, Ryan	1	3	3.05	23	0	0	8	38	35	14	13	15	33	.246	R	R	5-10	190	5-3-79	2000	Rocklin, Calif.
Matheny, Brandon	4	3	3.35	30	12	0	4	75	69	28	28	42	41	.249	L	L	6-3	200	10-22-78	2000	Damascus, Va.
Mendoza, Marcos	4	0	0.97	22	0	0	4	46	37	7	5	18	36	.221	L	L	5-10	180	10-31-80	2001	Santee, Calif.
Moran, Nick	2	3	4.73	9	9	0	0	51	51	33	27	17	46	.256	R	R	6-5	190	1-3-80	2001	Elk Grove, Calif.
Neil, Dan	1	1	4.19	7	0	0	0	19	20	10	9	9	18	.251	L	L	6-0	180	8-8-78	1999	Bardonia, N.Y.
Pinales, Aquiles	3	4	2.67	48	0	0	14	61	48	23	18	20	63	.214	R	R	5-11	190	9-5-74	1996	La Romana, D.R.
Powalski, Rick	0	0	7.94	3	0	0	0	6	7	5	5	5	6	.304	L	L	6-11	190	5-9-78	1997	Clearwater, Fla.
Prahm, Ryan	2	2	5.40	4	0	0	0	20	22	12	12	9	16	.278	R	R	6-5	210	5-17-79	2000	Cedar Rapids, Iowa
Reinike, Chris	0	0	0.00	1	0	0	0	2	0	0	0	0	2	.000	R	R	6-0	190	11-16-76	1998	Gulfport, Miss.
Sturkie, Scott	3	1	3.41	30	0	0	2	63	68	26	24	15	30	.284	R	R	6-3	210	6-12-79	2001	West Columbia, S.C.
Thompson, Derek	2	3	3.87	13	13	0	0	74	72	36	32	32	41	.258	L	L	6-2	180	1-8-81	2000	Land O' Lakes, Fla.
Thoms, Hank	5	2	2.43	17	7	0	0	63	57	25	17	15	50	.244	R	R	6-4	210	6-7-76	1999	Newton, Miss.
Vargas, Jose	4	0	0.61	19	0	0	0	44	35	9	3	11	50	.213	R	R	6-0	170	3-25-77	1998	Barahona, D.R.
Wade, Matt	3	0	5.51	20	1	0	1	33	34	24	20	13	15	.261	R	R	6-2	190	1-14-80	1997	Lilburn, Ga.
Wallace, Shane	3	4	4.21	9	9	0	0	51	54	28	24	28	24	.278	L	L	6-2	200	12-29-80	1999	Carrollton, Texas
Warden, Jim Ed	2	4	6.61	7	7	0	0	33	38	27	24	30	29	.290	R	R	6-7	190	5-7-79	2001	Murfreesboro, Tenn.

FIELDING

Catcher	PCT	G	PO	A	E	DP	PB
Bastardo	.967	16	108	8	4	0	1
DePippo	.982	48	290	34	6	1	6
Wilson	.989	80	542	72	7	4	18

First Base	PCT	G	PO	A	E	DP
Crozier	.995	49	400	35	2	33
Dempsey	.984	6	60	2	1	9
Morton	.999	79	710	61	1	54
Pichardo	1.000	6	50	2	0	4
Scott	1.000	4	21	2	0	1
Wilson	.000	1	0	0	0	0

Second Base	PCT	G	PO	A	E	DP
Colmenter	1.000	1	1	3	0	1

Second Base	PCT	G	PO	A	E	DP
Inglett	.970	54	86	174	8	31
Izturis	.967	57	96	142	8	22
Peguero	.960	6	8	16	1	2
Pichardo	.985	26	57	72	2	18

Third Base	PCT	G	PO	A	E	DP
Morton	1.000	2	1	1	0	0
Pichardo	.905	12	5	14	2	0
Smith	.911	130	111	235	34	13
Wilson	.000	1	0	0	0	0

Shortstop	PCT	G	PO	A	E	DP
Colmenter	1.000	1	0	1	0	0
Luna	.947	126	226	348	32	74
Peguero	1.000	1	2	3	0	0

	PCT	G	PO	A	E	DP
Pichardo	.962	19	29	46	3	8
Smith	1.000	2	1	0	0	0

Outfield	PCT	G	PO	A	E	DP
Church	.965	48	79	3	3	1
Crozier	1.000	3	9	0	0	0
Janowicz	.970	15	32	0	1	0
Minges	.977	104	205	6	5	0
Moreno	.969	65	119	5	4	3
Pichardo	1.000	5	3	0	0	0
Requena	.981	123	246	11	5	1
Scott	.961	29	48	1	2	0
Sizemore	.949	42	73	1	4	0

COLUMBUS REDSTIXX — Low Class A

SOUTH ATLANTIC LEAGUE

BATTING	AVG	G	AB	R	H	2B	3B	HR	RBI	BB	SO	SB	CS	SLG	OBP	B	T	HT	WT	DOB	1st Yr	Resides
Bastardo, Angel	.167	23	72	7	12	4	1	0	7	4	26	1	1	.250	.211	R	R	6-0	170	4-2-77	1997	Miraflores, Venez.
Camacaro, Armando	.218	91	303	27	66	8	0	2	33	20	56	11	6	.264	.287	R	R	5-11	170	4-6-79	1998	Guarenas, Venez.
Choy Foo, Rodney	.264	103	386	63	102	14	8	8	44	36	75	16	3	.404	.326	S	R	6-1	180	12-12-81	2000	Waimanalo, Hawaii
Colmenter, Jesus	.223	33	103	10	23	4	0	1	8	7	17	2	1	.291	.268	S	R	5-10	150	12-1-81	1998	Cabudare, Venez.
Cooper, Jason	.255	17	55	9	14	5	0	4	17	6	17	0	0	.564	.339	L	L	6-2	220	12-6-80	2002	Moses Lake, Wash.
Folsom, Mark	.196	91	311	38	61	10	2	8	26	31	120	6	1	.318	.270	R	R	6-5	210	6-7-81	2000	Winter Garden, Fla.
Inglett, Joe	.311	60	235	44	73	18	5	2	46	28	25	5	3	.455	.389	L	R	5-10	170	6-29-78	2000	Citrus Heights, Calif.
Kirby, Brian	.246	99	337	48	83	15	2	14	48	47	123	2	2	.427	.337	L	R	6-2	190	8-3-79	2001	North Little Rock, Ariz.
Knox, Matt	.277	50	191	22	53	13	0	6	26	6	25	1	1	.440	.300	R	R	6-4	210	12-29-79	2001	Lebanon, Pa.
Laker, Tim	.289	11	38	5	11	1	0	2	13	10	6	0	0	.474	.440	R	R	6-3	220	11-27-69	1988	Simi Valley, Calif.
Malave, Dennis	.246	90	301	35	74	8	3	4	37	25	56	32	11	.332	.336	L	L	5-9	180	1-6-80	1997	Caracas, Venez.
Ochoa, Ivan	.217	125	391	54	85	9	3	0	28	54	87	47	10	.256	.324	R	R	5-10	140	12-16-82	2000	Guacara, Venez.
Peshke, Chad	.266	97	327	42	87	11	1	3	37	47	40	16	5	.333	.369	R	R	5-9	180	9-10-79	2001	Redondo Beach, Calif.

BATTING	AVG	G	AB	R	H	2B	3B	HR	RBI	BB	SO	SB	CS	SLG	OBP	B	T	HT	WT	DOB	1st Yr	Resides
Quintana, Miguel	.261	71	238	22	62	12	0	4	29	21	41	4	6	.361	.323	L	R	6-1	190	6-29-79	2001	Miami, Fla.
Scott, Luke	.257	49	171	28	44	15	4	7	32	21	58	9	1	.515	.345	L	R	6-0	210	6-25-78	2001	Deleon Springs, Fla.
Sherrill, J.J.	.236	107	365	61	86	18	1	13	56	65	126	23	14	.397	.373	R	R	5-7	170	8-11-80	1999	Seaside, Calif.
Swedlow, Sean	.232	76	285	32	66	9	1	6	36	25	89	5	1	.333	.299	L	R	6-3	220	5-25-82	2000	Glendora, Calif.
Taveras, Willy	.265	85	313	68	83	14	1	4	27	45	68	54	12	.355	.385	R	R	6-0	160	12-25-81	1999	Tenares, D.R.
Van Every, Jon	.140	15	43	10	6	0	1	3	4	13	25	1	0	.395	.362	L	L	6-3	200	11-27-79	2001	Brandon, Miss.
Whitney, Matthew	.111	6	18	0	2	0	0	0	3	4	0	0	0	.111	.238	R	R	6-4	190	2-13-84	2002	Palm Beach Gardens, Fla.

PITCHING	W	L	ERA	G	GS	CG	SV	IP	H	R	ER	BB	SO	AVG	B	T	HT	WT	DOB	1st Yr	Resides
Alvarez, Oscar	2	6	3.45	33	5	0	2	78	88	42	30	34	61	.286	L	L	6-0	160	9-17-80	1997	Anzoategui, Venez.
Arthurs, Shane	1	1	1.53	6	1	0	0	18	7	3	3	2	15	.125	R	R	6-5	180	8-30-79	1997	Oklahoma City, Okla.
Blethen, Matt	2	0	8.80	11	0	0	0	15	24	18	15	8	13	.342	L	L	6-3	210	2-23-80	2001	Havre de Grace, Md.
Cooper, Chris	3	6	3.36	38	0	0	5	62	51	33	23	21	69	.219	L	L	5-11	190	10-31-78	2001	Sewickley, Pa.
Cox, Adam	0	1	5.40	4	0	0	0	5	5	3	3	5	5	.294	L	L	6-4	160	6-27-80	2000	Thomasville, Ga.
De la Cruz, Carlos	5	2	2.75	30	1	0	2	69	59	30	21	29	63	.236	R	R	6-1	180	1-14-82	1999	Santo Domingo, D.R.
Denham, Dan	9	8	4.76	28	28	0	0	125	123	76	66	65	109	.265	R	R	6-2	190	12-24-82	2001	Stateline, Nev.
Dittler, Jake	5	11	4.28	25	25	0	0	128	127	77	61	51	108	.257	R	R	6-4	220	11-24-82	2001	Henderson, Nev.
Douglas, Shea	0	0	0.00	1	0	0	0	2	2	1	0	2	2	.285	L	L	6-1	190	2-3-81	2002	Vicksburg, Miss.
Fernley, Nate	1	1	1.61	15	0	0	1	28	17	10	5	8	25	.171	R	R	6-3	160	1-13-77	2001	Orem, Utah
Foley, Travis	13	4	2.82	26	26	1	0	137	108	47	43	44	138	.215	R	R	6-1	180	3-11-83	2001	Louisville, Ky.
Gomez, Mariano	8	2	2.75	34	13	0	1	111	106	44	34	40	98	.246	L	L	6-6	170	9-12-82	1999	San Pedro Sula, Honduras
Gronkiewicz, Lee	4	2	2.35	50	0	0	27	61	58	19	16	27	72	.252	R	R	5-11	180	8-21-78	2001	Lancaster, S.C.
Lantz, Doug	2	2	2.93	26	0	0	4	58	53	23	19	12	51	.230	R	R	6-1	180	8-26-79	2001	Southlake, Texas
Martin, J.D.	14	5	3.90	27	26	0	0	138	141	76	60	46	131	.266	R	R	6-4	170	1-2-83	2001	Las Vegas, Nev.
Montano, Ignacio	0	0	0.52	8	0	0	1	17	10	1	1	2	9	.161	L	L	5-8	150	3-8-80	2001	Veracruz, Mexico
Pennington, Todd	1	1	1.75	16	0	0	2	26	15	5	5	12	32	.170	R	R	6-2	210	4-6-80	2001	McClure, Ill.
Pereyra, Honeudis	1	2	9.00	8	0	0	0	11	10	12	11	10	9	.250	R	R	5-11	160	3-3-81	2001	Santo Domingo, D.R.
Shouse, Dan	1	1	8.53	11	0	0	0	19	28	19	18	11	8	.358	L	L	6-3	200	9-21-78	2001	Wildwood, Mo.
Sturkie, Scott	3	0	0.99	10	0	0	0	27	17	5	3	4	29	.177	R	R	6-3	210	6-12-79	2001	West Columbia, S.C.
Thompson, Derek	3	4	3.42	14	14	0	0	74	71	39	28	27	50	.252	L	L	6-2	180	1-8-81	2000	Land O' Lakes, Fla.

FIELDING

Catcher	PCT	G	PO	A	E	DP	PB
Bastardo	.973	21	155	23	5	0	3
Camacaro	.991	90	713	67	7	11	
Kirby	.986	25	191	13	3	1	8
Laker	1.000	6	52	6	0	0	1

First Base	PCT	G	PO	A	E	DP
Bastardo	1.000	1	3	0	0	0
Kirby	.996	31	206	19	1	18
Knox	.989	40	335	32	4	28
Peshke	.944	2	16	1	1	3
Swedlow	.960	71	559	43	25	44

Second Base	PCT	G	PO	A	E	DP
Choy Foo	.984	81	146	215	6	43

	PCT	G	PO	A	E	DP
Colmenter	.933	7	5	9	1	2
Inglett	.901	13	28	36	7	7
Peshke	.750	2	2	1	1	1
Sherrill	.907	41	88	87	18	18

Third Base	PCT	G	PO	A	E	DP
Choy Foo	.909	9	5	15	2	1
Colmenter	1.000	7	0	11	0	1
Inglett	.940	33	27	67	6	6
Knox	1.000	9	2	13	0	0
Peshke	.901	81	56	144	22	8
Whitney	.818	6	1	8	2	0

Shortstop	PCT	G	PO	A	E	DP
Choy Foo	1.000	3	7	5	0	3

	PCT	G	PO	A	E	DP
Colmenter	.974	13	14	23	1	6
Knox	1.000	1	1	2	0	0
Ochoa	.959	125	218	394	26	69

Outfield	PCT	G	PO	A	E	DP
Colmenter	1.000	1	2	0	0	0
Folsom	.939	80	113	11	8	2
Kirby	.977	20	40	3	1	0
Malave	.975	88	147	9	4	2
Quintana	1.000	56	96	9	0	2
Scott	.971	32	32	2	1	0
Sherrill	.982	59	103	5	2	1
Taveras	.944	84	157	11	10	1
Van Every	1.000	15	34	3	0	2

MAHONING VALLEY SCRAPPERS — Short-Season A

NEW YORK-PENN LEAGUE

BATTING	AVG	G	AB	R	H	2B	3B	HR	RBI	BB	SO	SB	CS	SLG	OBP	B	T	HT	WT	DOB	1st Yr	Resides
Abreu, Angel	.205	14	39	2	8	0	0	0	3	1	4	0	1	.205	.225	S	R	6-2	160	1-7-82	2000	Santo Domingo, D.R.
Baxter, Andy	.252	64	218	34	55	14	3	4	32	26	52	13	3	.399	.339	L	R	6-4	210	4-8-79	2001	Erwin, Tenn.
Conroy, Mike	.186	56	188	22	35	5	3	0	18	13	43	1	2	.245	.241	L	L	6-3	190	10-3-82	2001	Scituate, Mass.
Diaz, Einar	.385	3	13	2	5	2	0	0	5	0	1	0	0	.538	.429	R	R	5-10	160	12-28-72	1991	Chesnee, S.C.
Francisco, Ben	.349	58	235	55	82	23	2	3	23	22	28	22	6	.502	.416	R	R	6-1	180	10-23-81	2002	Anaheim, Calif.
Gomez, Hose	.145	37	62	10	9	2	0	1	3	8	14	3	0	.226	.264	S	R	5-11	170	12-22-80	1999	Oranjestad, Aruba
Guglielmelli, Brad	.200	5	15	1	3	1	0	0	2	1	5	0	0	.267	.250	R	R	6-1	190	10-31-79	2001	San Luis Obispo, Calif.
Haase, Jeff	.277	48	148	29	41	3	1	8	29	18	26	6	1	.473	.374	R	R	6-2	200	5-15-78	2000	Eastlake, Ohio
Knox, Matt	.319	14	47	4	15	2	2	0	6	1	7	1	1	.447	.333	R	R	6-4	210	12-29-79	2001	Lebanon, Pa.
Larkin, Shaun	.226	71	235	35	53	8	2	9	38	42	40	5	3	.391	.345	L	R	5-9	170	9-7-79	2002	Cypress, Calif.
Manfredonia, Sean	.238	8	21	4	5	0	0	2	1	7	0	0	.238	.273	R	R	6-1	190	3-22-79	2002	Independence, Ohio
McDougall, Marshall	.200	2	5	0	1	0	0	0	1	0	0	.200	.333	R	R	6-1	200	12-19-78	2000	Valrico, Fla.
Myers, Kenton	.240	10	25	4	6	0	0	0	4	0	6	0	0	.360	.240	R	R	6-3	210	2-27-81	2002	Gainesville, Fla.
Osborn, Pat	.242	52	194	28	47	8	2	1	29	24	42	4	0	.320	.330	L	R	6-0	190	4-14-80	2001	Albuquerque, N.M.
Peavey, Bill	.279	71	247	33	69	14	0	6	41	31	37	1	0	.409	.371	L	L	6-4	250	1-16-79	2002	Brisbane, Calif.
Peguero, Miguel	.200	25	65	7	13	2	0	4	7	16	6	2	.231	.293	S	R	6-0	160	9-29-79	1997	Santo Domingo, D.R.
Rojas, Ricardo	.318	6	22	4	7	0	1	0	5	1	5	5	0	.409	.375	R	R	6-0	160	2-2-83	2001	Puerto Plata, D.R.
Simoneaux, Neil	.200	26	65	12	13	1	0	0	5	5	19	0	1	.215	.257	R	R	6-1	180	3-16-80	2001	Lake Charles, La.
2-team (12 New Jersey)	.239	38	109	17	26	4	2	0	15	5	27	3	3	.312	.270							
Torres, Eider	.307	19	75	9	23	5	0	0	8	3	9	3	3	.373	.342	S	R	5-9	157	1-16-83	2000	Maracaibo, Venez.
Uegawachi, Bryce	.261	42	88	13	23	5	0	0	10	8	13	0	0	.318	.323	S	R	5-6	150	4-28-79	2001	Honolulu, Hawaii
Van Every, Jon	.257	42	140	31	36	7	6	6	26	20	45	6	0	.521	.350	L	L	6-3	200	11-27-79	2001	Brandon, Miss.
Wallace, Dave	.255	45	145	22	37	5	0	3	17	11	48	3	0	.352	.345	R	R	6-4	220	10-17-79	2001	Brentwood, Tenn.
Wright, Brian	.285	67	235	40	67	9	3	4	47	38	35	7	0	.413	.375	L	R	6-1	200	4-6-80	2002	Ramseur, N.C.

GAMES BY POSITION: C—Diaz 3, Haase 31, Myers 9, Rickon 1, Wallace 42. **1B**—Baxter 44, Gomez 1, Knox 1, Manfredonia 4, Peavey 35, Simoneaux 1. **2B**—Abreu 4, Larkin 70, Simoneaux 6, Uegawachi 9. **3B**—Abreu 1, Guglielmelli 5, Haase 4, Knox 13, McDougall 1, Osborn 52, Peguero 9, Simoneaux 5. **SS**—Abreu 9, Peguero 19, Simoneaux 14, Torres 19, Uegawachi 34. **OF**—Conroy 55, Francisco 57, Gomez 22, Guglielmelli 1, Rojas 6, Simoneaux 1, Van Every 38, Wright 63.

PITCHING	W	L	ERA	G	GS	CG	SV	IP	H	R	ER	BB	SO	AVG	B	T	HT	WT	DOB	1st Yr	Resides
Allen, Blake	5	5	4.82	15	15	0	0	80	94	50	43	17	62	.284	L	L	6-2	200	7-17-81	2002	Humboldt, Tenn.
Blethen, Matt	1	2	5.23	16	0	0	0	31	32	22	18	19	19	.258	L	L	6-3	210	2-23-80	2001	Havre de Grace, Md.

PITCHING	W	L	ERA	G	GS	CG	SV	IP	H	R	ER	BB	SO	AVG	B	T	HT	WT	DOB	1st Yr	Resides
Carmona, Fausto	0	0	0.00	3	0	0	0	4	2	0	0	1	0	.181	R	R	6-4	180	12-7-83	2001	Santo Domingo, D.R.
Culp, Todd	0	0	5.23	18	0	0	0	21	20	14	12	27	27	.250	R	R	6-4	210	8-7-78	2001	Sacramento, Calif.
Evans, Kyle	1	0	1.59	3	3	0	0	17	16	3	3	7	18	.266	R	R	6-3	190	10-10-78	2000	Albuquerque, N.M.
George, Jahseam	0	0	6.75	1	0	0	0	1	1	1	1	1	3	.200	L	L	6-4	220	5-11-79	2002	Clovis, Calif.
Hernandez, Michael	3	1	2.78	22	0	0	2	45	37	20	14	28	58	.216	L	L	6-4	190	4-8-81	2002	Fresno, Calif.
Kleine, Victor	9	3	3.80	15	15	0	0	73	73	33	31	40	48	.257	L	L	6-4	180	9-12-79	2000	Florence, Ky.
Martin, Kevin	1	2	4.08	26	0	0	5	46	43	23	21	13	37	.244	R	R	6-2	180	1-3-79	2001	Las Vegas, Nev.
Montano, Ignacio	1	1	2.70	12	0	0	3	17	13	5	5	2	17	.209	L	L	5-8	150	3-8-80	2001	Veracruz, Mexico
Pennington, Todd	1	1	0.59	8	0	0	2	15	6	1	1	6	23	.125	R	R	6-2	210	4-6-80	2001	McClure, Ill.
Ramsey, Keith	6	3	2.04	13	10	0	0	62	43	16	14	10	71	.191	L	L	5-11	170	3-5-80	2002	Los Angeles, Calif.
Rich, Dan	1	0	2.70	21	0	0	4	23	18	7	7	8	20	.211	L	L	6-2	230	8-31-79	2002	Rocky River, Ohio
Rogers, Michael	5	4	3.60	15	15	0	0	75	70	33	30	31	64	.245	R	R	6-3	200	7-9-79	2002	Tulsa, Okla.
Slocum, Brian	5	2	2.60	11	11	0	0	55	47	19	16	14	48	.230	R	R	6-4	190	3-27-81	2002	East Chester, N.Y.
Southerland, Chip	0	0	5.63	5	0	0	0	8	7	5	5	3	8	.241	R	R	6-3	230	5-3-82	2002	Eugene, Ore.
Wallace, Shane	2	2	3.42	5	5	0	0	26	31	12	10	6	15	.298	L	L	6-2	200	12-29-80	1999	Carrollton, Texas
White, Chris	0	2	5.00	14	0	0	0	18	19	15	10	11	12	.263	L	L	6-1	190	9-11-80	2002	Frankfort, Ohio
Young, Simon	0	2	4.25	19	2	0	2	49	44	31	23	22	39	.251	L	L	6-4	240	9-14-77	1999	Flowery Branch, Ga.

BURLINGTON INDIANS — Rookie

APPALACHIAN LEAGUE

BATTING	AVG	G	AB	R	H	2B	3B	HR	RBI	BB	SO	SB	CS	SLG	OBP	B	T	HT	WT	DOB	1st Yr	Resides
Abreu, Angel	.283	30	106	14	30	1	0	1	8	10	22	4	3	.321	.339	S	R	6-2	160	1-7-82	2000	Santo Domingo, D.R.
Cruz, Jose	.225	51	178	25	40	7	0	2	18	23	38	7	2	.298	.314	S	R	6-1	180	10-21-82	2001	Rio Piedras, P.R.
Davidson, Aaron	.180	15	50	6	9	0	2	3	3	3	15	1	2	.440	.226	R	R	5-9	160	6-5-79	2002	Atascadero, Calif.
De la Cruz, Chris	.367	43	180	33	66	7	6	1	12	17	27	13	4	.489	.422	R	R	6-0	160	5-3-82	2001	Monte Plata, D.R.
Encarnacion, Teodoro	.236	39	148	18	35	4	4	2	13	17	51	5	0	.358	.319	R	R	6-2	190	3-26-83	2001	Santo Domingo, D.R.
Hodge, Luis	.269	60	234	31	63	9	2	1	19	12	52	1	3	.338	.318	R	R	6-1	170	2-13-82	2000	San Pedro de Macoris, D.R.
McCullough, Clayton	.278	20	54	5	15	3	0	0	8	18	8	1	0	.333	.459	L	R	5-10	180	12-27-79	2002	Greenville, N.C.
Myers, Kenton	.429	4	7	0	3	1	0	0	0	3	3	1	0	.571	.636	R	R	6-1	200	4-14-80	2001	Albuquerque, N.M.
Nixon, Jason	.151	18	53	7	8	0	1	1	5	3	18	1	1	.245	.196	R	R	6-2	220	11-24-81	2000	Coeburn, Va.
Noviskey, Josh	.224	33	98	4	22	5	0	2	15	19	27	1	0	.337	.345	S	R	6-4	210	3-15-83	2001	Newton, N.J.
Pacheco, Fernando	.188	41	133	16	25	5	0	3	10	21	57	1	0	.293	.295	L	L	6-1	190	10-1-84	2002	San Diego, Calif.
Panther, Nathan	.240	34	125	17	30	7	4	2	21	16	22	3	2	.408	.324	L	L	6-2	180	7-12-81	2002	Muscatine, Iowa
Parra, Carlos	.253	26	95	11	24	6	1	4	18	5	26	0	1	.463	.304	R	R	6-1	170	3-16-83	2001	Santiago, D.R.
Rojas, Ricardo	.262	55	202	23	53	5	0	3	26	12	54	13	5	.332	.309	R	R	6-0	160	2-2-83	2000	Puerto Plata, D.R.
Schilling, Micah	.206	33	126	13	26	6	1	0	10	15	39	5	2	.270	.303	L	R	5-11	180	12-27-82	2001	Clinton, La.
Threinen, Scott	.273	7	22	5	6	2	0	1	1	4	2	0	0	.500	.429	R	R	6-0	190	8-23-81	2001	Mantorville, Minn.
Torres, Eider	.320	45	194	26	62	6	1	0	13	15	22	28	3	.361	.371	S	R	5-9	157	1-16-83	2000	Maracaibo, Venez.
Vasquez, Domingo	.198	51	187	17	37	7	0	4	18	5	48	2	1	.299	.215	R	R	6-1	200	9-6-83	2000	Guarcara, Venez.
Whitney, Matt	.286	45	175	33	50	12	1	10	33	18	49	5	1	.537	.359	R	R	6-4	190	2-13-84	2002	Palm Beach Gardens, Fla.

GAMES BY POSITION: C—McCullough 18, Myers 3, Noviskey 30, Parra 24. **1B**—Cruz 2, Noviskey 2, Pacheco 39, Parra 1, Vasquez 31. **2B**—Abreu 8, Cruz 1, Davidson 8, Schilling 29, Torres 23, Vasquez 2. **3B**—Abreu 11, Threinen 7, Vasquez 14, Whitney 37. **SS**—Abreu 9, De la Cruz 42, Rojas 2, Torres 17. **OF**—Cruz 41, Davidson 3, Encarnacion 33, Hodge 54, Nixon 11, Panther 22, Rojas 49.

PITCHING	W	L	ERA	G	GS	CG	SV	IP	H	R	ER	BB	SO	AVG	B	T	HT	WT	DOB	1st Yr	Resides
Alvarado, Luis	4	1	2.12	18	0	0	2	34	29	11	8	18	29	.232	L	L	5-11	160	9-11-82	2001	Bayamon, P.R.
Burton, T.J.	1	4	7.36	12	12	0	0	44	56	39	36	24	29	.311	R	R	6-3	170	7-30-83	2001	Ottawa, Ontario
Carmona, Fausto	2	4	3.30	13	11	0	1	76	89	36	28	10	42	.294	R	R	6-4	180	12-7-83	2001	Santo Domingo, D.R.
Casey, Reid	2	4	3.46	17	1	0	1	42	38	22	16	14	46	.230	R	R	6-1	170	2-1-80	2002	Kingsport, Tenn.
Cevette, Dan	2	4	4.67	13	13	0	0	52	52	32	27	31	36	.270	L	L	6-3	180	10-19-83	2002	Elkland, Pa.
Davis, Jeff	0	0	6.00	2	0	0	0	3	5	2	2	1	1	.416	R	R	6-3	210	8-7-80	2002	Lawrence, Kan.
Douglas, Shea	3	1	1.36	12	0	0	1	33	26	13	5	10	49	.203	L	L	6-1	190	2-3-81	2002	Vicksburg, Miss.
George, Jahseam	2	2	4.86	15	0	0	1	33	40	23	18	16	29	.305	L	L	6-4	220	5-11-79	2002	Clovis, Calif.
Haynes, Matthew	3	3	3.93	13	8	0	0	50	40	28	22	33	48	.218	L	L	6-3	180	4-18-83	2002	Maroochydore, Australia
Lara, Juan	2	6	4.98	14	14	0	0	65	67	42	36	28	50	.274	R	L	6-2	150	1-26-81	1999	Bani, D.R.
Martinez, Paul	2	1	3.50	16	0	0	0	36	35	23	14	25	32	.259	L	L	5-10	150	9-28-81	1999	Navarrete, D.R.
Pereyra, Honeudis	4	2	2.73	10	0	0	1	26	9	10	8	22	46	.107	R	R	5-11	160	3-3-81	2001	Santo Domingo, D.R.
Santana, Hector	0	1	8.27	12	0	0	0	21	22	22	19	15	14	.271	R	R	6-0	160	7-13-82	2000	San Pedro de Macoris, D.R.
Schultz, Jimmy	1	2	6.51	13	0	0	0	28	34	28	20	23	10	.300	R	R	6-3	170	9-12-82	2001	Houston, Texas
Smith, Sean	1	1	3.24	10	9	0	0	33	29	14	12	12	29	.235	R	R	6-4	180	10-13-83	2002	Pleasant Hill, Calif.
Spaulding, Richard	0	1	9.00	4	0	0	0	8	10	8	8	13	8	.312	L	L	6-3	160	10-27-80	2001	Lexington, Ky.
Taylor, Blake	0	2	2.78	19	0	0	6	23	25	11	7	9	23	.280	R	R	6-2	160	3-5-80	2002	Columbus, Ga.

BY BARNEY HUTCHINSON

In the 10th season for the Rockies, there was another first the organization never wanted to see: they fired a manager during the season for the first time.

Buddy Bell became a casualty of a 6-16 start, and long-time hitting coach Clint Hurdle became the Rockies' fourth manager April 26. Any time a club has to fire a manager during the season, it's a sign of trouble.

The 2002 Rockies had more than their share of trouble. They relied on a key core of young players up the middle to have breakout seasons, but each struggled to varying degrees.

The club once again attempted to lean on a veteran duo of starting lefthanders, but both Mike Hampton and Denny Neagle struggled to a combined 15-26 record. A rebuilt bullpen had trouble keeping the team close when behind. And offensively, while the Rockies led the National League in hitting, they had their weakest team at the plate since they moved to Coors Field.

The Rockies rallied around Hurdle, going 24-10 in the first five weeks after the managerial change. But from a 30-26 record, they ran into a tough interleague schedule featuring the Yankees, Indians and Mariners. Another June swoon dropped the team to 42-46 at the all-star break, and they finished 67-73 under Hurdle.

An eight-game losing streak followed at the end of July, then a nine-game losing streak at the end of August. Their 26-55 record on the road was the worst in club history.

Rockies general manager Dan O'Dowd instituted a hands-off policy on player personnel through the first half of the season, then made a flurry of trades near the end of July to try new people in the outfield and behind the plate.

Todd Helton (.329-30-109) and Larry Walker (.338-26-104) turned in solid offensive seasons. Jose Jimenez set a club record with 41 saves, and the Rockies found a strong

Larry Walker   Brad Hawpe

PLAYERS OF THE YEAR

MAJOR LEAGUE: Larry Walker, of

Walker's .338 batting average ranked second in the National League behind Barry Bonds and fourth in the majors. He also compiled the majors' sixth-best OPS (on-base plus slugging percentage), one spot better than Alex Rodriguez.

MINOR LEAGUE: Brad Hawpe, 1b

In addition to winning league MVP honors, Hawpe led the triple crown race in the Class A Carolina League most of the season before being passed in homers and RBIs. Overall, he hit .347-22-97.

three-man combination in Justin Speier, Todd Jones and Jimenez to preserve leads going into the seventh inning.

Rockies starting pitchers contributed with the bat, hitting .257 as a unit. Mike Hampton batted .344 with three home runs, even going 1-for-4 as a pinch hitter. Jason Jennings hit .306 and became the first rookie pitcher to hit more than .300 since Jim Perry in 1959 for the Indians.

The Rockies uncovered two outstanding rookie starters in Jennings and Denny Stark. Both solved Coors Field, with Jennings going 9-4 and Stark 8-1 at home.

Hampton and Neagle failed to anchor the rotation. Hampton lost his first three starts of the season and won back-to-back starts only once. Neagle pitched poorly enough to get banished to the bullpen during July. He came back to put together seven solid starts, then struggled with floating bone chips in his left elbow.

Jose Ortiz, given the starting job at second at the start of the year, hit just .244 in his first 53 games, with only one home run. He lost his starting job and went to the minors on a minor league rehab assignment.

After a fast start in April, shortstop Juan Uribe hit just .194 from May through August, leading the Rockies to question his offensive output.

Attendance also fell for the sixth consecutive season and went under 3 million for the first time in club history, to 2,737,838.

The Rockies fell short of their goal of .500 or better for the minor league system, going a collective 336-374 (.473). Only two teams had seasons of .500 or better in Class A Salem (73-66) and short-season Tri-City (40-36). Only Double-A Carolina, which won the first half of the Southern League's Eastern Division but finished in the cellar in the second half, qualified for postseason play.

ORGANIZATION LEADERS

BATTING

*AVG	Brad Hawpe, Salem	.347
R	Tony Miller, Asheville	109
H	Cory Sullivan, Salem	161
TB	Brad Hawpe, Salem	264
2B	Cory Sullivan, Salem	42
3B	Jorge Piedra, Salem	13
HR	Jack Cust, Colorado Springs	23
RBI	Brad Hawpe, Salem	97
BB	Tony Miller, Asheville	88
SO	Justin Lincoln, Salem	145
SB	Tony Miller, Asheville	50

PITCHING

W	Zach Parker, Asheville	16
L	Gerrit Simpson, Salem/Asheville	15
#ERA	Aaron Cook, Colo. Springs/Carolina	2.37
G	Matt Whiteside, Colorado Springs	60
CG	Aaron Cook, Colo. Springs/Carolina	3
SV	Matt Whiteside, Colorado Springs	26
IP	Scott Dohmann, Salem	170
BB	Cory Vance, Carolina	76
SO	Jason Young, Colo. Springs/Carolina	150

*Minimum 250 At-Bats #Minimum 75 Innings

COLORADO ROCKIES

Managers: Buddy Bell, Clint Hurdle

2002 Record: 73-89, .451 (4th, NL West)

BATTING	AVG	G	AB	R	H	2B	3B	HR	RBI	BB	SO	SB	CS	SLG	OBP	B	T	HT	WT	DOB	1st Yr	Resides
Agbayani, Benny	.205	48	117	10	24	5	0	4	19	10	35	1	0	.350	.266	R	R	6-0	220	12-28-71	1993	Aiea, Hawaii
Alomar, Sandy	.267	38	116	8	31	4	0	0	12	4	19	0	0	.302	.292	R	R	6-5	230	6-18-66	1984	Chicago, Ill.
Bennett, Gary	.265	90	291	26	77	10	2	4	26	15	45	1	3	.354	.314	R	R	6-0	200	4-17-72	1990	Waukegan, Ill.
Butler, Brent	.259	113	344	55	89	18	4	9	42	10	40	2	6	.413	.287	R	R	6-0	180	2-11-78	1996	Laurinburg, N.C.
Cust, Jack	.169	35	65	8	11	2	0	1	8	12	32	0	1	.246	.295	L	R	6-1	200	1-16-79	1997	Flemington, N.J.
Estalella, Bobby	.205	38	112	17	23	8	0	8	25	14	33	0	1	.491	.285	R	R	6-1	210	8-23-74	1993	Weston, Fla.
Gload, Ross	.258	26	31	4	8	1	0	1	4	3	7	0	0	.387	.324	L	L	6-0	180	4-5-76	1997	East Hampton, N.Y.
Hampton, Mike	.344	36	64	9	22	2	0	3	5	1	13	1	1	.516	.354	R	L	5-10	180	9-9-72	1990	Evergreen, Colo.
Helton, Todd	.329	156	553	107	182	39	4	30	109	99	91	5	1	.577	.429	L	L	6-2	200	8-20-73	1995	Thornton, Colo.
Hollandsworth, Todd	.295	95	298	39	88	21	1	11	48	26	71	7	8	.483	.352	L	L	6-2	210	4-20-73	1991	Castle Rock, Colo.
Kapler, Gabe	.311	40	119	12	37	4	3	2	17	8	23	6	2	.445	.359	R	R	6-2	200	8-31-75	1995	Sherman Oaks, Calif.
Little, Mark	.200	61	105	20	21	5	2	0	5	13	28	2	1	.286	.311	R	R	6-0	190	7-11-72	1994	Edwardsville, Ill.
McKeel, Walt	.308	5	13	1	4	0	0	0	0	0	3	0	0	.308	.308	R	R	6-2	200	1-17-72	1990	Stantonsburg, N.C.
Norton, Greg	.220	113	168	19	37	8	1	7	37	24	52	2	3	.405	.314	S	R	6-1	200	7-6-72	1993	Denver, Colo.
Ortiz, Jose	.250	65	192	22	48	7	1	1	12	16	30	2	0	.313	.315	R	R	5-10	180	6-13-77	1995	Santo Domingo, D.R.
Payton, Jay	.335	47	170	36	57	14	4	8	28	8	20	3	3	.606	.376	R	R	5-10	180	11-22-72	1994	Zanesville, Ohio
2-team (87 New York)	.303	134	445	69	135	20	7	16	59	29	54	7	4	.488	.351							
Petrick, Ben	.211	38	95	10	20	3	1	5	11	9	33	0	1	.421	.283	R	R	6-0	200	4-7-77	1996	Hillsboro, Ore.
Pierre, Juan	.287	152	592	90	170	20	5	1	35	31	52	47	12	.343	.332	L	L	6-0	180	8-14-77	1998	Alexandria, La.
Romano, Jason	.324	18	37	9	12	0	1	0	1	3	11	4	1	.378	.375	R	R	6-0	180	6-24-79	1997	Tampa, Fla.
Shumpert, Terry	.235	106	234	30	55	12	1	6	21	21	41	4	1	.372	.304	R	R	6-0	190	8-16-66	1987	Lone Tree, Colo.
Uribe, Juan	.240	155	566	69	136	25	7	6	49	34	120	9	2	.341	.286	R	R	5-11	170	7-22-79	1997	Palenque, D.R.
Walker, Larry	.338	136	477	95	161	40	4	26	104	65	73	6	5	.602	.421	L	R	6-3	230	12-1-66	1985	Evergreen, Colo.
Zeile, Todd	.273	144	506	61	138	23	0	18	87	66	92	1	1	.425	.353	R	R	6-1	200	9-9-65	1986	Thousand Oaks, Calif.

PITCHING	W	L	ERA	G	GS	CG	SV	IP	H	R	ER	BB	SO	AVG	B	T	HT	WT	DOB	1st Yr	Resides
Chacon, Shawn	5	11	5.73	21	21	0	0	119	122	84	76	60	67	.263	R	R	6-3	210	12-23-77	1996	Greeley, Colo.
Cook, Aaron	2	1	4.54	9	5	0	0	36	41	18	18	13	14	.294	R	R	6-3	170	2-8-79	1997	Loveland, Ohio
Corey, Mark	0	0	12.00	14	0	0	0	12	22	16	16	8	12	.400	R	R	6-3	200	11-16-74	1995	Austin, Pa.
2-team (12 New York)	0	3	8.59	26	0	0	0	22	32	23	21	16	21	.336							
Flores, Randy	0	2	9.53	8	2	0	0	17	29	19	18	8	7	.381	L	L	6-0	180	7-31-75	1997	Pico Rivera, Calif.
Fuentes, Brian	2	0	4.73	31	0	0	0	27	25	14	14	13	38	.250	L	L	6-4	220	8-9-75	1996	Merced, Calif.
Hampton, Mike	7	15	6.15	30	30	0	0	179	228	135	122	91	74	.312	R	L	5-10	180	9-9-72	1990	Evergreen, Colo.
James, Mike	0	0	5.56	13	0	0	0	11	12	9	7	5	10	.266	R	R	6-3	200	8-15-67	1988	Mary Esther, Fla.
Jennings, Jason	16	8	4.52	32	32	0	0	185	201	102	93	70	127	.279	L	R	6-2	240	7-17-78	1999	Rockwall, Texas
Jimenez, Jose	2	10	3.56	74	0	0	41	73	76	34	29	11	47	.264	R	R	6-3	230	7-7-73	1992	Boca China, D.R.
Jones, Todd	1	4	4.70	79	0	0	1	82	84	43	43	28	73	.269	R	R	6-3	230	4-24-68	1989	Pell City, Ala.
Lowe, Sean	1	1	8.71	8	0	0	0	16	16	13	10	7	7	.347	R	R	6-2	220	3-29-71	1992	Royse City, Texas
2-team (43 Pittsburgh)	5	3	5.79	51	1	0	0	79	101	58	51	41	64	.312							
Mercker, Kent	3	1	6.14	58	0	0	44	55	33	30	22	37	.298	L	L	6-2	190	2-1-68	1986	Dublin, Ohio
Neagle, Denny	8	11	5.26	35	28	1	0	164	170	101	96	63	111	.265	L	L	6-3	220	9-13-68	1989	Morrison, Colo.
Nichting, Chris	1	1	4.46	29	0	0	0	36	40	18	18	5	25	.279	R	R	6-1	200	5-13-66	1988	Cincinnati, Ohio
Reyes, Dennys	0	1	4.24	43	0	0	0	40	43	19	19	24	30	.279	R	L	6-3	240	4-19-77	1994	Zaragoza, Mexico
Santos, Victor	0	4	10.38	24	2	0	0	26	41	30	30	22	25	.359	R	R	6-3	190	10-2-76	1995	San Pedro de Macoris, D.R.
Speier, Justin	5	1	4.33	63	0	0	1	62	51	31	30	19	47	.216	R	R	6-4	200	11-6-73	1995	Paradise Valley, Ariz.
Stark, Dennis	11	4	4.00	32	20	0	0	128	108	69	57	64	64	.225	R	R	6-2	210	10-27-74	1996	Edgerton, Ohio
Thomson, John	7	8	4.88	21	21	0	0	127	136	77	69	27	76	.268	R	R	6-3	190	10-1-73	1993	Sulphur, La.
Vance, Cory	0	0	6.75	2	1	0	0	4	4	3	3	4	1	.266	L	L	6-1	190	6-20-79	2000	Vandalia, Ohio
White, Rick	2	6	6.20	41	0	0	0	41	49	30	28	18	27	.310	R	R	6-4	230	12-23-68	1990	Springfield, Ohio

FIELDING

Catcher	PCT	G	PO	A	E	DP	PB
Alomar	1.000	38	190	8	0	1	3
Bennett	.992	90	453	32	4	5	6
Estalella	.995	38	203	9	1	0	2
McKeel	1.000	5	22	0	0	0	1
Petrick	.979	14	89	3	2	0	0
Walker	.000	1	0	0	0	0	0

First Base	PCT	G	PO	A	E	DP
Gload	1.000	4	20	3	0	1
Helton	.995	156	1357	113	7	138
Norton	1.000	15	55	3	0	5

Second Base	PCT	G	PO	A	E	DP
Butler	.974	72	121	178	8	46
Ortiz	.987	53	103	133	3	24
Romano	.952	12	6	14	1	2

	PCT	G	PO	A	E	DP
Shumpert	.974	60	95	126	6	30

Third Base	PCT	G	PO	A	E	DP
Butler	1.000	33	4	16	0	0
Helton	.000	1	0	0	0	0
Norton	.896	22	16	27	5	4
Ortiz	1.000	1	1	1	0	0
Romano	.000	1	0	0	0	0
Shumpert	1.000	1	0	2	0	0
Zeile	.942	139	87	257	21	23

Shortstop	PCT	G	PO	A	E	DP
Butler	.975	13	15	24	1	5
Norton	.000	1	0	0	0	0
Romano	.786	5	6	5	3	1
Shumpert	1.000	3	2	4	0	0
Uribe	.966	155	261	504	27	118

Outfield	PCT	G	PO	A	E	DP
Agbayani	1.000	37	53	1	0	0
Cust	.960	18	24	1	1	0
Gload	1.000	2	0	1	0	0
Hollandsworth	.973	90	138	7	4	0
Kapler	1.000	38	62	3	0	0
Little	.970	36	62	2	2	1
Norton	1.000	2	4	0	0	0
Payton	1.000	44	88	3	0	1
Petrick	.952	16	20	0	1	0
Pierre	.995	149	363	2	2	1
Romano	1.000	3	7	1	0	0
Shumpert	1.000	8	10	0	0	0
Walker	.984	123	229	14	4	5

Director, Player Development: Michael Hill.

Class	Farm Team	League	W	L	Pct.	Finish*	Manager	First Yr.
AAA	Colo. Springs (Colo.) Sky Sox	Pacific Coast	58	86	.403	15th (16)	Chris Cron	1993
AA	Carolina (Zebulon, N.C.) Mudcats	Southern	65	71	.478	8th (10)	P.J. Carey	1999
High A	Salem (Va.) Avalanche	Carolina	74	66	.529	5th (8)	Stu Cole	1995
Low A	Asheville (N.C.) Tourists	South Atlantic	64	74	.464	12th (16)	Joe Mikulik	1994
SS A	Tri-City (Wash.) Dust Devils	Northwest	40	36	.526	5th (8)	Ron Gideon	2001
Rookie	Casper (Wyo.) Rockies	Pioneer	35	41	.461	t-6th (8)	Darron Cox	2001

*Finish in overall standings (No. of teams in league)

COLORADO SPRINGS SKY SOX — Class AAA

PACIFIC COAST LEAGUE

BATTING	AVG	G	AB	R	H	2B	3B	HR	RBI	BB	SO	SB	CS	SLG	OBP	B	T	HT	WT	DOB	1st Yr	Resides
Agbayani, Benny	.272	43	147	28	40	8	1	11	32	28	32	1	0	.565	.391	R	R	6-0	220	12-28-71	1993	Aiea, Hawaii
Alviso, Jerome	.313	112	304	32	95	14	0	1	26	12	29	4	1	.368	.338	S	R	6-1	150	9-4-75	1997	Livermore, Calif.
Bair, Rod	.267	89	258	33	69	18	2	4	37	19	49	14	5	.399	.338	R	R	5-11	190	10-29-74	1996	Tempe, Ariz.
Barnes, John	.286	67	269	46	77	20	2	6	30	18	16	5	4	.442	.340	R	R	6-2	200	4-24-76	1996	El Cajon, Calif.
Bell, Mike	.283	64	240	33	68	19	2	3	35	16	42	4	4	.417	.340	R	R	6-2	190	12-7-74	1993	Cincinnati, Ohio
Bogar, Tim	.163	13	43	2	7	1	0	0	1	1	6	0	2	.186	.182	R	R	6-2	190	10-28-66	1987	Normal, Ill.
Brumbaugh, Cliff	.293	136	505	85	148	36	2	16	81	57	107	6	2	.467	.362	R	R	6-2	200	4-21-74	1995	New Castle, Del.
Butler, Brent	.333	24	105	20	35	9	1	2	17	6	12	0	0	.495	.375	R	R	6-0	180	2-11-78	1996	Laurinburg, N.C.
Colina, Javier	.245	95	322	40	79	23	3	4	30	22	53	0	2	.373	.295	R	R	6-1	190	2-15-79	1997	Cocorote, Venez.
Cust, Jack	.265	105	359	74	95	24	0	23	55	83	121	6	3	.524	.407	L	R	6-1	200	1-16-79	1997	Flemington, N.J.
Dewey, Jason	.194	36	103	7	20	3	0	4	20	4	27	0	0	.340	.220	R	R	6-2	190	4-18-77	1997	Valrico, Fla.
Estalella, Bobby	.291	23	79	16	23	9	0	6	20	11	20	0	0	.633	.374	R	R	6-1	210	8-23-74	1993	Weston, Fla.
Gload, Ross	.314	104	442	69	139	28	6	16	71	18	59	9	4	.514	.338	L	L	6-0	180	4-5-76	1997	East Hampton, N.Y.
Guillen, Jose	.412	5	17	2	7	3	0	0	5	1	2	0	1	.588	.474	R	R	5-11	190	5-17-76	1993	San Cristobal, D.R.
Hernandez, Carlos	.321	48	159	22	51	7	3	0	13	10	25	8	6	.403	.364	R	R	5-9	170	12-7-75	1993	Caracas, Venez.
Keck, Brian	.160	11	25	0	4	2	0	0	2	0	3	1	0	.240	.160	R	R	6-3	190	1-15-74	1996	Dodge City, Kan.
Lopez, Rafael	.143	3	7	1	1	0	0	0	1	1	1	0	0	.143	.250	R	R	6-0	200	10-22-76	1996	Miami, Fla.
2-team (15 Las Vegas)	.264	18	53	7	14	2	0	2	6	5	13	1	0	.415	.350							
McKeel, Walt	.246	49	130	10	32	7	0	2	11	16	27	0	0	.346	.327	R	R	6-2	200	1-17-72	1990	Stantonsburg, N.C.
Melhuse, Adam	.348	34	115	25	40	10	1	6	20	16	23	2	1	.609	.424	S	R	6-2	200	3-27-72	1993	San Luis Obispo, Calif.
2-team (72 Iowa)	.311	106	341	58	106	29	1	13	59	44	70	4	4	.516	.389							
Merrill, Ronnie	.190	19	63	9	12	2	1	1	2	4	12	0	0	.302	.239	S	R	6-1	180	11-13-78	2000	Seffner, Fla.
Nicholson, Kevin	.083	18	36	1	3	1	0	0	1	5	11	0	0	.111	.195	S	R	5-10	190	3-29-76	1997	Surrey, B.C.
Norton, Greg	.083	3	12	2	1	0	0	0	0	3	5	0	0	.083	.267	S	R	6-1	200	7-6-72	1993	Denver, Colo.
Ortiz, Jose	.333	26	111	23	37	9	2	6	18	4	13	1	1	.613	.353	R	R	5-10	180	6-13-77	1995	Santo Domingo, D.R.
Owens, Ryan	.260	70	227	24	59	11	2	6	41	24	74	8	3	.405	.329	R	R	6-2	200	3-18-78	1999	Anaheim Hills, Calif.
Petrick, Ben	.321	79	265	51	85	18	4	16	54	40	77	10	6	.600	.406	R	R	6-0	200	4-7-77	1996	Hillsboro, Ore.
Porter, Bo	.170	14	47	5	8	2	0	1	7	3	16	3	1	.277	.235	R	R	6-2	190	7-5-72	1994	Fresno, Texas
Romano, Jason	.310	31	129	20	40	7	2	0	9	6	27	8	3	.395	.338	R	R	6-0	180	6-24-79	1997	Tampa, Fla.
2-team (48 Oklahoma)	.286	79	325	48	93	15	3	4	37	25	68	18	6	.388	.332							
Servais, Scott	.281	39	128	21	36	12	0	1	26	6	22	0	0	.398	.322	R	R	6-2	210	6-4-67	1989	Castle Rock, Colo.
2-team (4 Fresno)	.287	43	136	22	39	12	0	1	26	7	22	0	0	.397	.333							
Stratton, Rob	.213	23	80	13	17	2	1	7	14	6	42	0	1	.525	.308	R	R	6-2	250	10-7-77	1996	Santa Barbara, Calif.

PITCHING	W	L	ERA	G	GS	CG	SV	IP	H	R	ER	BB	SO	AVG	B	T	HT	WT	DOB	1st Yr	Resides
Alviso, Jerome	0	0	6.75	4	0	0	0	5	9	4	4	1	0	.000	S	R	6-1	150	9-4-75	1997	Livermore, Calif.
Belitz, Todd	1	3	5.11	22	5	0	2	44	53	33	25	20	29	.296	L	L	6-3	200	10-23-75	1997	Spokane, Wash.
Brittan, Corey	3	6	5.64	35	12	0	0	97	122	79	61	46	70	.305	R	R	6-6	200	2-23-75	1996	Scott City, Kan.
Cameron, John	1	108.00	1	1	0	0	1	4	8	8	3	1	.666	R	R	6-1	170	9-13-77	1998	Williamstown, Mass.
Chacon, Shawn	2	0	4.79	4	4	0	0	21	23	12	11	10	15	.291	R	R	6-3	210	12-23-77	1996	Greeley, Colo.
Chouinard, Bobby	1	0	4.35	9	0	0	0	10	13	5	5	5	5	.309	R	R	6-1	180	5-1-72	1990	Forest Grove, Ore.
Cook, Aaron	4	4	3.78	10	10	1	0	64	67	40	27	18	32	.263	R	R	6-3	200	2-8-79	1997	Loveland, Ohio
Esslinger, Cam	0	1	6.19	29	0	0	0	32	30	27	22	17	23	.243	R	R	5-11	180	12-28-76	1999	Hewitt, N.J.
Fitzgerald, Brian	1	1	4.00	7	0	0	0	9	8	4	4	3	4	.242	L	L	5-11	170	12-26-74	1996	Woodbridge, Va.
2-team (29 Tacoma)	3	4	5.34	36	0	0	2	57	65	40	34	26	31	.283							
Flores, Randy	2	2	3.28	7	7	0	0	36	36	15	13	18	27	.268	L	L	6-0	180	7-31-75	1997	Pico Rivera, Calif.
2-team (15 Oklahoma)	3	3	4.18	22	7	0	1	56	58	28	26	23	43	.268							
Fuentes, Brian	3	3	3.70	41	0	0	1	49	44	25	20	32	61	.246	L	L	6-4	220	8-9-75	1996	Merced, Calif.
Heams, Shane	0	1	18.90	9	1	0	0	10	14	23	21	23	7	.341	R	R	6-1	210	9-29-75	1994	Lambertville, Mich.
Holt, Chris	6	3	3.71	12	11	0	1	70	68	34	29	16	53	.251	R	R	6-4	200	9-18-71	1992	Dallas, Texas
James, Mike	1	1	8.13	24	0	0	1	31	38	31	28	16	21	.301	R	R	6-3	200	8-15-67	1988	Mary Esther, Fla.
Martin, Chandler	1	4	7.07	8	6	0	0	28	39	24	22	21	14	.348	R	R	6-1	190	10-23-73	1995	Salem, Ore.
Mercker, Kent	0	0	21.60	2	0	0	0	2	3	4	4	2	0	.428	L	L	6-2	190	2-1-68	1986	Dublin, Ohio
Munoz, Bobby	4	8	8.46	15	6	0	0	45	69	48	42	25	42	.370	R	R	6-7	210	3-3-68	1989	Irving, Texas
Nichting, Chris	1	4	10.19	23	0	0	1	33	53	40	37	22	23	.368	R	R	6-1	200	5-13-66	1988	Cincinnati, Ohio
Rekar, Bryan	7	10	5.93	20	20	0	0	123	173	91	81	35	88	.331	R	R	6-3	220	6-3-72	1993	Lutz, Fla.
2-team (5 Omaha)	7	10	5.69	25	24	0	0	147	203	107	93	40	108	.327							
Robbins, Jake	1	2	12.00	11	0	0	0	12	17	18	16	13	15	.326	R	R	6-5	190	5-23-76	1994	Charlotte, N.C.
Santos, Victor	4	9	5.72	21	21	1	0	118	147	81	75	43	134	.306	R	R	6-3	190	10-2-76	1995	San Pedro de Macoris, D.R.
Scanlan, Bob	2	4	2.13	17	0	0	2	34	34	14	11	9	6	.336	R	R	6-7	210	8-9-66	1984	Beverly Hills, Calif.
Seifert, Ryan	1	5	7.04	9	1	0	0	63	80	52	49	28	35	.310	R	R	6-5	220	8-14-75	1997	Chaska, Minn.
Smith, Chuck	1	0	1.02	4	4	0	0	18	16	2	2	9	18	.250	R	R	6-1	180	10-21-69	1991	Hillside, Ill.
Speier, Justin	2	0	3.86	12	0	0	2	14	20	7	6	3	14	.333	R	R	6-4	200	11-6-73	1995	Paradise Valley, Ark.
Stark, Dennis	1	2	3.82	7	7	0	0	38	35	20	16	14	38	.246	R	R	6-2	210	10-27-74	1996	Edgerton, Ohio

PITCHING	W	L	ERA	G	GS	CG	SV	IP	H	R	ER	BB	SO	AVG	B	T	HT	WT	DOB	1st Yr	Resides
Thompson, Mark	0	0	11.00	8	1	0	0	18	33	27	22	3	12	.392	R	R	6-2	210	4-7-71	1992	Russellville, Ky.
Wall, Donne	1	2	5.19	14	0	0	0	17	16	10	10	4	11	.262	R	R	6-1	200	7-11-67	1989	Pearland, Texas
2-team (1 Salt Lake)	1	3	5.21	15	1	0	0	19	17	11	11	4	13	.253							
Ward, Bryan	1	2	4.97	6	6	0	0	38	37	22	21	15	26	.258	L	L	6-2	200	1-25-72	1993	Mt. Holly, N.J.
Watson, Mark	0	0	16.03	10	0	0	0	11	22	19	19	11	10	.423	R	L	6-4	230	1-23-74	1996	Dunwoody, Ga.
3-team (28 Iowa, 6 Tacoma)	6	0	5.64	44	0	0	0	61	67	43	38	33	43	.368							
White, Rick	0	1	9.00	2	0	0	0	2	3	2	2	0	2	.333	R	R	6-4	230	12-23-68	1990	Springfield, Ohio
Whiteside, Matt	4	7	5.50	60	0	0	26	70	85	50	43	15	79	.292	R	R	6-0	200	8-8-67	1990	Arlington, Texas
Wrigley, Jase	0	1	5.79	9	0	0	0	14	23	13	9	7	8	.348	R	R	6-3	210	11-6-75	1998	Atlanta, Ga.
Young, Jason	6	5	4.97	13	13	0	0	80	87	52	44	38	74	.271	R	R	6-5	210	9-28-79	2001	Bodega, Calif.

FIELDING

Catcher	PCT	G	PO	A	E	DP	PB
Dewey	.966	35	181	18	7	1	6
Estalella	.995	20	182	10	1	3	1
Lopez	1.000	2	10	2	0	0	0
McKeel	.988	40	235	19	3	1	4
Melhuse	.990	26	175	19	2	2	2
Petrick	.977	8	39	3	1	0	6
Servais	.995	29	201	15	1	2	1

	PCT	G	PO	A	E	DP
Bell	.989	17	39	49	1	16
Bogar	1.000	2	4	7	0	3
Butler	1.000	8	11	18	0	3
Colina	.973	66	137	187	9	37
Hernandez	.968	9	14	16	1	7
Nicholson	.929	10	15	24	3	8
Ortiz	.967	5	8	21	1	3
Romano	.979	10	23	24	1	5

	PCT	G	PO	A	E	DP
Butler	.953	16	27	55	4	18
Hernandez	.947	34	51	93	8	18
Keck	.900	3	7	11	2	2
Merrill	.967	17	31	56	3	15
Nicholson	1.000	1	2	3	0	0
Ortiz	.975	14	26	53	2	14
Owens	.865	12	10	22	5	3
Romano	.952	6	9	11	1	4

First Base	PCT	G	PO	A	E	DP
Alviso	.989	13	79	7	1	11
Bell	.987	12	72	5	1	10
Brumbaugh	.983	34	267	27	5	31
Gload	.987	88	738	69	11	81
Keck	1.000	2	1	0	0	1
McKeel	1.000	1	5	1	0	1
Melhuse	.920	4	22	1	2	1
Norton	1.000	2	19	2	0	4
Owens	1.000	1	7	2	0	1
Petrick	.933	1	12	2	1	1
Servais	1.000	1	8	0	0	0

Third Base	PCT	G	PO	A	E	DP
Alviso	.909	10	3	7	1	0
Bell	.943	41	22	78	6	6
Brumbaugh	.938	22	14	46	4	6
Colina	.898	22	8	45	6	5
Hernandez	1.000	2	2	1	0	0
Keck	1.000	2	1	4	0	0
Nicholson	1.000	1	1	0	0	0
Norton	1.000	1	1	1	0	1
Ortiz	.950	7	4	15	1	4
Owens	.893	58	28	80	13	6

Outfield	PCT	G	PO	A	E	DP
Agbayani	1.000	27	45	1	0	0
Bair	.973	69	105	5	3	2
Barnes	.985	60	126	3	2	1
Brumbaugh	.947	83	115	9	7	2
Cust	.961	89	143	6	6	0
Gload	1.000	19	25	1	0	0
Guillen	1.000	4	7	0	0	0
Petrick	.971	59	92	7	3	0
Porter	.923	13	23	1	2	0
Romano	.976	18	39	1	1	0
Stratton	1.000	22	38	1	0	0

Second Base	PCT	G	PO	A	E	DP
Alviso	.977	35	57	72	3	21

Shortstop	PCT	G	PO	A	E	DP
Alviso	.920	46	61	122	16	26
Bogar	.950	10	11	27	2	10

CAROLINA MUDCATS   Class AA

SOUTHERN LEAGUE

BATTING	AVG	G	AB	R	H	2B	3B	HR	RBI	BB	SO	SB	CS	SLG	OBP	B	T	HT	WT	DOB	1st Yr	Resides
Atkins, Garrett	.271	128	510	71	138	27	3	12	61	59	77	6	6	.406	.345	R	R	6-2	190	12-12-79	2000	Irvine, Calif.
Barmes, Clint	.272	103	438	62	119	23	2	15	60	31	72	15	11	.436	.329	R	R	6-0	170	3-6-79	2000	Vincennes, Ind.
Burford, Kevin	.282	77	266	44	75	23	1	3	33	48	51	2	6	.410	.397	L	L	6-1	210	11-7-77	1997	Westminster, Calif.
Cameron, Troy	.232	28	95	11	22	3	1	5	17	7	24	0	0	.442	.282	S	R	5-11	180	8-31-78	1997	Plantation, Fla.
Closser, J.D.	.283	95	315	43	89	27	1	13	62	44	69	9	3	.498	.369	S	R	5-10	170	1-15-80	1998	Alexandria, Ind.
Colina, Javier	.272	35	136	17	37	6	1	1	17	7	21	4	3	.353	.310	R	R	6-1	190	2-15-79	1997	Cocorote, Venez.
Dewey, Jason	.259	73	255	42	66	22	0	9	44	24	75	5	4	.451	.322	R	R	6-1	200	4-18-77	1997	Valrico, Fla.
Freeman, Ashley	.667	2	6	2	4	1	0	0	1	1	1	2	0	.833	.750	R	R	6-1	190	1-27-79	2001	Town Creek, Ala.
Freeman, Choo	.291	124	430	81	125	18	6	12	64	64	101	16	13	.444	.400	R	R	6-2	200	10-20-79	1998	Dallas, Texas
Holliday, Matt	.276	130	463	79	128	19	2	10	64	67	102	16	2	.391	.375	R	R	6-4	230	1-10-80	1998	Chico, Texas
Keck, Brian	.129	24	62	6	8	3	0	0	3	9	8	4	0	.177	.250	R	R	6-3	190	1-15-74	1996	Dodge City, Kan.
Lambert, Casey	.200	3	10	1	2	1	0	0	3	2	3	0	0	.300	.333	R	R	5-9	160	8-31-79	2001	St. Amant, La.
Owens, Ryan	.255	39	110	18	28	11	0	4	14	21	35	0	1	.464	.393	R	R	6-2	200	3-18-78	1999	Anaheim Hills, Calif.
Phillips, Dan	.220	86	287	27	63	10	5	2	24	13	70	9	7	.310	.269	R	R	6-3	180	8-23-78	1999	Northridge, Calif.
Reyes, Rene	.292	123	455	64	133	33	4	14	54	29	69	11	10	.475	.339	S	R	5-11	210	2-21-78	1996	Margarita, Venez.
Sanchez, Tino	.283	89	272	32	77	16	1	3	27	43	28	11	4	.382	.379	R	R	6-0	150	2-2-79	1997	Yauco, P.R.
Sullivan, Kevin	.182	5	11	0	2	0	0	0	2	1	2	0	0	.182	.250	R	R	6-1	210	10-4-77	2000	Stevens Point, Wis.
Taylor, Seth	.261	49	161	19	42	14	0	3	27	14	33	1	1	.404	.324	R	R	6-1	180	8-23-77	1999	Cantonment, Fla.
Tejada, Mike	.250	2	8	1	2	0	0	0	0	0	2	0	0	.250	.250	R	R	6-1	210	3-8-79	2000	Provo, Utah
Tena, Hector	.125	2	8	0	1	0	0	0	0	0	3	0	0	.125	.125	R	R	6-0	150	6-20-82	1999	San Cristobal, D.R.
Warren, Chris	.215	65	205	31	44	6	1	7	23	23	60	2	2	.356	.299	R	R	6-0	160	11-24-76	1999	Athens, Ga.

PITCHING	W	L	ERA	G	GS	CG	SV	IP	H	R	ER	BB	SO	AVG	B	T	HT	WT	DOB	1st Yr	Resides
Averette, Robert	1	6	7.15	11	11	1	0	62	90	58	49	22	33	.347	R	R	6-2	190	9-30-76	1997	Sylacauga, Ala.
Bradley, Ryan	1	2	12.38	5	0	0	0	8	13	14	11	6	7	.351	R	R	6-4	220	10-26-75	1997	Chino Hills, Calif.
Brantley, Ryan	2	3	4.56	17	0	0	0	24	25	12	12	12	11	.265	R	R	6-4	160	4-23-76	1998	Chesapeake, Va.
Brueggemann, Dean	6	3	6.97	34	0	0	0	52	61	49	40	33	36	.299	L	L	6-2	180	3-11-76	1998	Smithton, Ill.
Cameron, Ryan	5	7	3.26	37	15	0	0	119	84	55	43	55	139	.200	R	R	6-1	170	9-13-77	1998	Williamstown, Mass.
Cercy, Rick	3	4	5.12	47	0	0	1	65	70	55	37	47	75	.275	R	R	6-0	180	10-10-76	1999	Ormond Beach, Fla.
Chouinard, Bobby	0	0	0.00	5	0	0	1	7	4	3	0	3	10	.153	R	R	6-1	180	5-1-72	1990	Forest Grove, Ore.
Cook, Aaron	7	2	1.42	14	14	2	0	95	73	24	15	19	58	.213	R	R	6-3	170	2-8-79	1997	Loveland, Ohio
Crowder, Chuck	2	0	12.27	11	0	0	1	15	18	22	20	16	9	.305	L	L	6-1	190	9-30-76	1999	Mantua, Ohio
De la Cruz, Fernando	2	5	5.45	31	0	0	6	33	39	25	20	15	15	.291	R	R	6-0	170	1-25-71	1993	La Romana, D.R.
Esslinger, Cam	0	1	2.57	6	0	0	2	7	6	2	2	3	6	.240	R	R	5-11	180	12-28-76	1999	Hewitt, N.J.
Huisman, Justin	0	3	6.66	18	0	0	2	24	30	22	18	12	10	.291	R	R	6-1	190	4-6-78	2000	Thornton, Ill.
Kibler, Ryan	7	8	4.91	25	25	0	0	143	158	98	78	64	59	.280	R	R	6-2	180	9-17-80	1999	Tampa, Fla.
Martin, Chandler	7	4	3.18	19	19	1	0	113	109	48	40	34	82	.260	R	R	6-1	190	10-23-73	1995	Salem, Ore.
Roney, Matt	3	6	6.11	13	13	0	0	71	73	52	48	33	61	.265	R	R	6-3	230	1-10-80	1998	Edmond, Okla.
Thompson, Doug	6	2	4.09	50	0	0	6	70	62	39	32	25	68	.234	R	R	6-0	180	7-22-76	1998	Biloxi, Miss.
Vance, Cory	10	8	3.77	25	25	1	0	150	142	73	63	76	114	.256	L	L	6-1	190	6-20-79	2000	Vandalia, Ohio
Wrigley, Jase	2	2	2.18	44	0	0	10	58	48	15	14	28	31	.242	R	R	6-3	210	11-6-75	1998	Atlanta, Ga.
Young, Colin	0	1	1.98	15	0	0	0	14	14	5	3	10	14	.264	L	L	6-0	180	8-1-77	1999	West Newbury, Mass.
Young, Jason	7	4	2.64	14	14	1	0	89	71	30	26	30	76	.219	R	R	6-5	210	9-28-79	2001	Bodega, Calif.

FIELDING

Catcher	PCT	G	PO	A	E	DP	PB
Closser	.977	64	456	56	12	7	10
Dewey	.973	53	320	38	10	3	4
Sanchez	.976	24	149	17	4	1	1
Sullivan	1.000	4	16	3	0	1	0

First Base	PCT	G	PO	A	E	DP
Atkins	.985	7	62	2	1	7
Burford	.984	72	728	57	13	68
Keck	.993	17	138	13	1	9
Reyes	.985	41	372	30	6	40
Taylor	1.000	9	66	4	0	1

Second Base	PCT	G	PO	A	E	DP
Cameron	.972	25	56	83	4	17

	PCT	G	PO	A	E	DP
Colina	.989	33	60	116	2	29
Lambert	1.000	1	0	6	0	0
Owens	.921	15	26	44	6	5
Sanchez	.968	4	15	15	1	5
Taylor	.968	26	49	72	4	18
Warren	.946	38	65	128	11	25

Third Base	PCT	G	PO	A	E	DP
Atkins	.945	119	70	238	18	24
Freeman	.833	2	1	4	1	0
Owens	1.000	11	3	13	0	2
Sanchez	.500	1	0	1	1	0
Taylor	.929	4	2	11	1	1
Warren	.333	1	0	1	2	0

Shortstop	PCT	G	PO	A	E	DP
Barmes	.940	102	162	359	33	76
Lambert	1.000	1	1	7	0	1
Owens	.926	8	10	15	2	3
Taylor	.955	5	4	17	1	5
Tena	.889	2	2	6	1	1
Warren	.913	22	40	75	11	14

Outfield	PCT	G	PO	A	E	DP
Freeman	.977	117	244	9	6	3
Holliday	.961	117	166	6	7	0
Keck	1.000	1	1	0	0	0
Phillips	.941	77	121	7	8	1
Reyes	.955	70	100	7	5	1
Sanchez	.970	41	59	5	2	0

SALEM AVALANCHE — High Class A

CAROLINA LEAGUE

BATTING	AVG	G	AB	R	H	2B	3B	HR	RBI	BB	SO	SB	CS	SLG	OBP	B	T	HT	WT	DOB	1st Yr	Resides
Berroa, Cristian	.273	91	326	40	89	21	1	1	29	12	48	6	0	.353	.313	S	R	5-11	150	4-29-79	1996	Haina, D.R.
Catalanotte, Greg	.252	37	119	18	30	6	0	5	21	17	47	0	1	.429	.350	S	R	6-3	210	6-18-77	1999	Glendale, Ariz.
Conway, Dan	.230	41	135	19	31	10	0	5	14	15	33	0	2	.415	.318	R	R	6-2	190	10-13-79	2000	Delmar, N.Y.
Hawpe, Brad	.347	122	450	87	156	38	2	22	97	81	84	1	1	.587	.447	L	L	6-3	190	6-22-79	2000	Fort Worth, Texas
Lambert, Casey	.233	69	240	34	56	10	0	0	24	25	36	1	1	.275	.326	R	R	5-9	160	8-31-79	2001	St. Amant, La.
Lincoln, Justin	.226	126	429	53	97	19	0	14	52	32	145	1	1	.368	.287	R	R	6-2	200	4-4-79	1999	Sarasota, Fla.
Merrill, Ronnie	.282	76	280	48	79	13	5	6	27	41	36	2	3	.429	.378	R	R	6-1	180	11-13-78	2000	Seffner, Fla.
Moore, Chris	.224	61	214	20	48	10	1	2	29	27	39	1	1	.308	.311	L	R	5-11	180	11-16-76	1999	Wilmington, N.C.
Muth, Edmund	.225	72	262	29	59	16	2	3	28	21	87	1	2	.336	.289	L	L	6-0	190	12-1-77	2000	Long Beach, Calif.
Ortega, Sixto	.250	2	4	0	1	0	0	0	0	0	0	0	0	.250	.250	R	R	5-10	190	12-24-76	1997	Santo Domingo, D.R.
Peck, Bryan	.251	62	235	34	59	10	0	4	30	19	30	2	1	.345	.318	R	R	5-11	190	8-9-77	2000	Athens, Tenn.
Phillips, Dan	.340	12	47	4	16	1	0	2	7	0	11	3	1	.489	.380	R	R	6-3	180	8-23-78	1999	Northridge, Calif.
Piedra, Jorge	.301	104	392	64	118	37	12	13	64	37	55	10	2	.556	.366	L	L	6-0	190	4-17-79	1997	Van Nuys, Calif.
Reyes, Ambiorix	.207	19	58	7	12	1	0	0	5	0	6	1	0	.224	.220	S	R	5-11	160	2-6-78	1996	La Vega, D.R.
Rosario, Melvin	.213	79	216	26	46	10	2	1	17	12	69	3	4	.292	.261	L	L	6-2	170	9-22-78	1998	Carolina, P.R.
Sullivan, Cory	.288	138	560	90	161	42	6	12	67	36	70	26	5	.448	.340	L	L	6-0	180	8-20-79	2001	Evanston, Wyo.
Sullivan, Kevin	.264	77	280	29	74	24	1	3	37	11	49	3	0	.389	.294	R	R	6-1	210	10-4-77	2000	Stevens Point, Wis.
Vilorio, Miguel	.247	48	170	18	42	6	1	0	10	7	25	2	8	.294	.295	R	R	5-10	150	7-22-79	1997	La Romana, D.R.
Winchester, Jeff	.246	97	357	36	88	21	1	3	36	15	59	2	2	.336	.282	R	R	5-11	210	1-21-80	1998	Metairie, La.

PITCHING	W	L	ERA	G	GS	CG	SV	IP	H	R	ER	BB	SO	AVG	B	T	HT	WT	DOB	1st Yr	Resides
Bouknight, Kip	14	7	3.35	27	27	2	0	167	156	74	62	48	120	.249	R	R	6-0	190	11-16-78	2001	Gaston, S.C.
Brantley, Brian	0	0	5.23	6	0	0	0	10	19	14	6	10	9	.380	R	R	6-4	160	4-23-76	1998	Chesapeake, Va.
Buglovsky, Chris	9	9	3.12	27	27	1	0	165	161	68	57	58	126	.258	R	L	6-2	160	11-22-79	2000	Iselin, N.J.
Crowder, Chuck	1	2	5.13	23	1	0	1	40	49	27	23	24	36	.296	L	L	6-1	190	9-30-76	1999	Mantua, Ohio
Difelice, Mark	3	0	2.80	6	6	0	0	35	40	12	11	5	21	.289	R	R	6-1	180	8-23-76	1998	Havertown, Pa.
Dohmann, Scott	13	5	4.23	28	28	0	0	170	149	85	80	53	131	.232	R	R	6-1	180	2-13-78	2000	Morgan City, La.
Dotel, Melido	2	3	5.70	37	0	0	0	54	63	41	34	28	28	.298	R	R	6-3	210	4-20-77	1993	San Cristobal, D.R.
Gallagher, Buddy	4	4	3.76	15	12	0	0	65	66	42	27	30	37	.261	L	L	5-11	170	1-3-79	2001	Billings, Mont.
Gomez, Diogenes	0	0	9.00	6	0	0	1	6	10	6	6	1	4	.400	R	R	5-11	160	3-27-79	1997	Chorrera, Panama
Green, Sean	2	5	3.90	52	0	0	2	67	92	41	29	31	26	.332	R	R	6-6	230	4-20-79	2000	Louisville, Ky.
Huisman, Justin	3	4	1.57	41	0	0	20	52	47	11	9	14	24	.250	R	R	6-1	190	4-16-79	2000	Thornton, Ill.
Pacheco, Enemencio	2	2	3.16	41	0	0	6	51	52	22	18	26	31	.262	R	R	6-1	170	8-31-78	1997	Santo Domingo, D.R.
Price, Ryan	0	4	11.30	21	2	0	0	29	30	40	36	43	19	.280	R	R	6-3	190	1-31-78	1997	Roswell, N.M.
Simpson, Gerrit	0	3	7.16	5	2	0	0	16	16	15	13	12	12	.246	R	R	6-3	200	12-18-79	2001	Austin, Texas
Speier, Ryan	2	2	3.94	24	0	0	4	32	35	21	14	11	33	.284	R	R	6-7	200	7-24-79	2001	Springfield, Va.
Stepka, Tom	5	4	2.97	45	3	0	5	100	96	35	33	23	54	.256	R	R	6-1	190	11-25-79	1996	Williamsville, N.Y.
Tsao, Chin-Hui	4	2	2.09	9	9	0	0	47	34	13	11	12	45	.203	R	R	6-2	170	6-2-81	1999	Hualien, Taiwan
Webb, Nicholas	10	10	5.05	26	23	2	0	134	145	80	75	37	90	.277	L	L	6-3	200	7-8-79	2000	Houston, Texas

FIELDING

Catcher	PCT	G	PO	A	E	DP	PB
Conway	.985	32	174	20	3	2	4
Ortega	1.000	1	2	0	0	0	0
Peck	.983	8	55	2	1	0	2
Sullivan	.993	22	128	15	1	1	1
Winchester	.980	82	523	61	12	3	18

First Base	PCT	G	PO	A	E	DP
Hawpe	.994	120	1136	116	8	103
Lincoln	.974	4	35	2	1	3
Moore	.988	16	152	10	2	12

Second Base	PCT	G	PO	A	E	DP
Berroa	.961	40	68	105	7	22
Lambert	.971	40	54	112	5	18

	PCT	G	PO	A	E	DP
Merrill	.000	1	0	0	0	0
Moore	.967	15	21	37	2	7
Reyes	.949	13	22	34	3	6
Vilorio	.969	45	81	141	7	31

Third Base	PCT	G	PO	A	E	DP
Berroa	1.000	8	6	14	0	3
Lambert	1.000	11	9	20	0	3
Lincoln	.949	117	73	208	15	18
Moore	1.000	3	1	6	0	0
Peck	.893	10	12	13	3	1

Shortstop	PCT	G	PO	A	E	DP
Berroa	.924	42	59	112	14	21
Lambert	.966	21	32	53	3	11

	PCT	G	PO	A	E	DP
Lincoln	1.000	6	10	13	0	2
Merrill	.959	76	133	220	15	49
Reyes	1.000	4	6	10	0	1

Outfield	PCT	G	PO	A	E	DP
Catalanotte	.945	28	49	3	3	0
Lambert	1.000	1	0	1	0	0
Muth	.970	42	62	2	2	0
Peck	.939	26	43	3	3	0
Phillips	1.000	6	10	1	0	1
Piedra	.975	100	183	11	5	1
Rosario	.987	73	143	4	2	0
Sullivan	.987	137	278	16	4	4
Sullivan	.983	32	56	1	1	0

ASHEVILLE TOURISTS — Low Class A

SOUTH ATLANTIC LEAGUE

BATTING	AVG	G	AB	R	H	2B	3B	HR	RBI	BB	SO	SB	CS	SLG	OBP	B	T	HT	WT	DOB	1st Yr	Resides
Bird, T.J.	.245	94	327	36	80	16	3	10	42	23	99	1	0	.404	.305	L	L	5-11	200	6-20-79	2000	Cloverdale, Calif.
Brand, Kevin	.189	30	95	6	18	3	1	0	8	13	22	2	1	.242	.294	S	R	5-10	170	1-24-80	2001	Mesa, Arikz.
Colina, Alvin	.236	59	212	22	50	8	0	7	36	20	57	1	0	.373	.312	R	R	6-3	200	12-26-81	1999	Puerto Cabello, Venez.

BATTING

BATTING	AVG	G	AB	R	H	2B	3B	HR	RBI	BB	SO	SB	CS	SLG	OBP	B	T	HT	WT	DOB	1st Yr	Resides
Diaz, Eduardo	.204	43	108	11	22	2	0	1	10	8	43	3	0	.250	.256	R	R	5-11	160	12-18-77	1998	Santo Domingo, D.R.
Freeman, Ashley	.261	131	479	59	125	36	1	10	55	42	92	13	9	.403	.335	R	R	6-1	190	1-27-79	2001	Town Creek, Ala.
Frome, Jason	.254	37	142	22	36	10	1	1	13	11	45	6	3	.359	.307	L	L	6-0	190	7-3-79	2001	Appleton, Wis.
Gretz, Nick	.316	104	383	52	121	18	0	5	70	55	72	1	1	.402	.405	L	R	5-11	200	1-26-78	2001	Apple Valley, Minn.
Lambert, Casey	.208	19	53	7	11	3	0	0	3	6	11	2	1	.264	.300	R	R	5-9	160	8-31-79	2001	St. Amant, La.
Miller, Tony	.283	129	501	109	142	23	4	17	48	88	129	50	19	.447	.396	R	R	5-9	180	8-18-80	2001	Lorain, Ohio
Nix, Jayson	.246	132	487	73	120	29	2	14	79	62	105	14	5	.400	.340	R	R	5-11	180	8-26-82	2001	Midland, Texas
Ortega, Sixto	.130	17	54	1	7	0	0	0	2	1	12	0	0	.130	.145	R	R	5-10	190	12-24-76	1997	Santo Domingo, D.R.
Peck, Bryan	.363	55	212	32	77	14	2	9	49	17	32	1	2	.575	.409	R	R	5-11	190	8-9-77	2000	Athens, Tenn.
Reyes, Ambiorix	.182	27	99	7	18	1	0	0	5	0	14	1	2	.192	.182	S	R	5-11	160	2-6-78	1996	La Vega, D.R.
Tejada, Jesus	.228	91	325	37	74	17	0	10	40	28	54	0	3	.372	.291	S	R	6-1	210	3-8-79	2000	Provo, Utah
Tena, Hector	.191	131	435	55	83	16	1	7	39	29	129	0	5	.280	.263	R	R	6-0	150	6-20-82	1999	San Cristobal, D.R.
Testa, Chris	.253	124	463	66	117	24	0	8	56	48	98	5	4	.356	.336	L	L	6-2	180	5-23-81	1999	Palmdale, Calif.
Vasquez, Jose	.223	93	319	44	71	20	2	6	36	30	122	4	5	.354	.302	L	L	6-3	220	12-28-82	2000	Sarasota, Fla.

PITCHING

PITCHING	W	L	ERA	G	GS	CG	SV	IP	H	R	ER	BB	SO	AVG	B	T	HT	WT	DOB	1st Yr	Resides
Abell, Joe	0	0	10.80	7	0	0	0	7	10	10	8	8	4	.344	R	R	6-2	180	3-7-78	2000	Boulder, Colo.
Crockett, Ben	2	3	7.36	6	6	0	0	29	51	25	24	6	18	.372	R	R	6-3	200	12-19-79	2002	Topsfield, Mass.
Cruz, Jeff	0	0	2.89	6	0	0	0	9	11	6	3	6	4	.289	L	L	6-0	190	3-14-79	2001	Fullerton, Calif.
Dannemiller, Beau	1	8	4.65	19	10	0	1	60	76	40	31	23	40	.314	R	R	6-0	210	12-26-79	2001	Munroe Falls, Ohio
Francis, Jeff	0	0	1.80	4	4	0	0	20	16	6	4	4	23	.231	L	L	6-5	200	1-8-81	2002	Sammamish, Wash.
Hampson, Justin	9	8	3.83	27	27	1	0	164	162	87	70	58	123	.260	L	L	6-1	180	5-24-80	2000	Mordes, Ill.
Lorenzo, Javier	4	3	5.98	39	0	0	0	62	64	43	41	50	75	.267	R	R	6-0	160	12-26-78	1999	Hialeah, Fla.
Merricks, Charles	7	5	6.70	29	10	0	0	83	109	73	62	48	42	.317	L	L	6-0	200	12-6-78	2000	Camarillo, Calif.
Moore, Greg	0	1	9.64	7	0	0	0	14	26	15	15	6	12	.400	R	R	6-6	210	5-23-79	1999	San Ramon, Calif.
Parker, Zach	16	7	4.01	28	28	1	0	168	174	89	75	64	119	.273	R	L	6-2	200	8-19-81	2001	Austin, Texas
Roney, Matt	4	6	3.48	14	14	1	0	83	82	39	32	25	88	.261	R	R	6-3	230	1-10-80	1998	Edmond, Okla.
Serrano, Alex	5	5	4.96	48	0	0	8	62	61	37	34	14	61	.325	R	R	6-1	200	2-18-81	1998	Barcelona, Venez.
Simpson, Andre	0	2	3.72	24	0	0	1	29	30	12	12	14	21	.267	R	R	6-3	180	7-1-80	1998	Lemon Grove, Calif.
2-team (4 So. Georgia)	0	4	4.46	28	2	0	1	36	40	20	18	19	26	.277							
Simpson, Gerrit	3	12	4.28	22	21	0	0	132	136	76	63	40	120	.263	R	R	6-3	200	12-18-79	2001	Austin, Texas
Songster, Judson	1	2	2.81	47	0	0	12	64	65	27	20	21	57	.270	R	R	6-3	190	12-26-79	2001	North Platte, Neb.
Speier, Ryan	3	1	3.93	28	0	0	1	37	32	21	16	13	39	.235	R	R	6-7	200	7-24-79	2001	Springfield, Va.
Van Buren, Jermaine	6	9	4.96	30	17	0	0	107	115	71	59	44	88	.276	R	R	6-1	200	7-2-80	1998	Hattiesburg, Miss.
Vazquez, Will	2	2	4.21	48	0	0	11	62	73	34	29	16	65	.286	R	R	6-0	140	12-26-79	2000	Guayama, P.R.
Villacis, Eduardo	1	0	1.89	11	1	0	0	19	12	4	4	2	17	.173	R	R	6-2	170	8-29-79	1998	Mirando, Venez.

FIELDING

Catcher	PCT	G	PO	A	E	DP	PB
Colina	.980	54	395	55	9	3	11
Freeman	.923	4	10	2	1	0	1
Ortega	.992	17	104	13	1	0	5
Peck	.970	12	88	10	3	2	5
Tejada	.981	59	426	36	9	3	12

First Base	PCT	G	PO	A	E	DP
Bird	1.000	2	11	1	0	0
Freeman	1.000	4	14	0	0	3
Gretz	.989	99	844	73	10	88
Peck	1.000	4	34	2	0	2
Tejada	.935	6	40	3	3	1
Testa	.979	34	299	22	7	20

Second Base	PCT	G	PO	A	E	DP
Brand	.857	1	2	4	1	0

	PCT	G	PO	A	E	DP	
Diaz	1.000	10	13	14	0	1	
Lambert	1.000	3	9	5	0	1	
Nix	.942	131	236	351	36	77	
Reyes	1.000	1	0	2	0	0	

Third Base	PCT	G	PO	A	E	DP
Brand	.941	7	5	11	1	0
Diaz	.917	12	7	15	2	2
Freeman	.891	98	74	156	28	9
Gretz	1.000	1	1	0	0	0
Lambert	1.000	5	3	7	0	0
Peck	.938	6	6	9	1	1
Reyes	.916	26	26	50	7	2

Shortstop	PCT	G	PO	A	E	DP
Brand	.941	3	4	12	1	5
Diaz	.000	1	0	0	0	0

	PCT	G	PO	A	E	DP
Freeman	.000	2	0	0	0	0
Lambert	.964	8	10	17	1	0
Reyes	.929	3	5	8	1	1
Tena	.948	131	201	400	33	86

Outfield	PCT	G	PO	A	E	DP
Bird	.938	55	78	12	6	0
Brand	1.000	7	10	1	0	1
Diaz	.800	5	4	0	1	0
Freeman	.957	32	38	6	2	0
Frome	.984	28	58	4	1	0
Lambert	1.000	4	8	0	0	0
Miller	.952	129	246	13	13	3
Peck	.986	29	66	2	1	0
Testa	.963	91	122	8	5	1
Vasquez	.952	52	75	5	4	1

TRI-CITY DUST DEVILS · Short-Season A

NORTHWEST LEAGUE

BATTING	AVG	G	AB	R	H	2B	3B	HR	RBI	BB	SO	SB	CS	SLG	OBP	B	T	HT	WT	DOB	1st Yr	Resides
Barker, Sean	.223	45	166	21	37	9	1	1	15	12	38	4	2	.307	.283	R	R	6-3	220	5-26-80	2002	Bakersfield, Calif.
Bernier, Doug	.197	64	208	26	41	5	0	1	24	58	55	3	4	.236	.380	S	R	5-11	170	6-24-80	2002	Santa Maria, Calif.
Bibee, Hal	.198	33	106	8	21	4	0	1	8	15	25	0	2	.264	.304	R	R	6-0	190	5-8-79	2002	Knoxville, Tenn.
Bushey, Andrew	.190	49	163	9	31	4	0	0	12	14	24	2	0	.215	.253	L	R	5-11	190	8-30-79	2002	Boardman, Ohio
Delgado, Jorge	.167	4	12	2	2	0	0	0	1	2	4	0	0	.167	.375	R	R	6-1	190	12-13-79	1999	Jackson, Miss.
Gearlds, Aaron	.000	2	7	1	0	0	0	0	0	1	6	0	0	.000	.125	R	R	6-1	190	4-19-80	2002	Mt. Pleasant, Pa.
Glessner, Jeremiah	.000	2	8	0	0	0	0	0	0	1	3	0	0	.000	.111	R	R	6-0	220	4-19-80	2002	Mt. Pleasant, Pa.
Gonzalez, Bernie	.283	66	265	34	75	14	3	3	36	15	67	7	3	.392	.326	R	R	6-2	200	5-10-80	2002	Miami, Fla.
Guance, Walkill	.266	65	241	31	64	13	1	3	23	33	49	7	5	.365	.355	R	R	5-9	160	3-6-82	1999	Sabana Grande, D.R.
Materano, Oscar	.259	68	270	38	70	14	0	9	40	11	61	7	5	.411	.293	R	R	6-1	170	11-18-81	1998	Valera, Venez.
Riley, Kenny	.043	9	23	0	1	0	0	0	0	4	0	0	0	.043	.083	R	R	6-2	200	4-15-80	2002	Sparks, Nev.
Salazar, Jeff	.235	72	268	38	63	5	4	4	21	47	43	10	6	.328	.351	L	L	6-0	180	11-24-80	2002	Port Bolivar, Texas
Smith, Sam	.157	55	185	19	29	9	0	4	16	22	50	2	0	.270	.282	R	R	6-0	190	3-21-79	1997	Jasper, Texas
Spilborghs, Ryan	.230	71	261	34	60	11	1	4	34	29	61	11	7	.326	.313	R	R	6-1	190	9-5-79	2002	Santa Barbara, Calif.
Street, Dan	.203	46	153	13	31	6	1	0	12	17	44	3	1	.255	.311	R	R	6-2	200	10-27-80	2002	Purcellville, Va.
Sweeney, James	.111	19	54	5	6	2	0	1	5	11	22	2	1	.204	.262	R	R	6-1	190	6-13-83	2001	Austin, Texas
Ventura, Juan	.286	4	14	0	4	0	0	0	2	2	4	2	0	.286	.375	R	R	6-1	160	12-10-78	1997	Puerto Plata, D.R.
White, Carson	.269	27	93	9	25	8	0	3	11	12	23	0	0	.452	.352	R	R	5-8	170	10-20-79	2002	Clovis, Calif.

GAMES BY POSITION: C—Bibee 25, Bushey 36, Glessner 2, Riley 8, Sweeney 11. **1B**—Bernier 2, Smith 47, Street 26, Ventura 3. **2B**—Bernier 6, Guance 61, White 14. **3B**—Bernier 48, Bushey 10, Street 22. **SS**—Bernier 10, Materano 67. **OF**—Barker 35, Gearlds 1, Gonzalez 52, Salazar 71, Spilborghs 64, Ventura 1, White 4.

PITCHING	W	L	ERA	G	GS	CG	SV	IP	H	R	ER	BB	SO	AVG	B	T	HT	WT	DOB	1st Yr	Resides
Averette, Robert	0	1	1.29	3	3	0	0	14	11	2	2	0	13	.211	R	R	6-2	190	9-30-76	1997	Sylacauga, Ala.
Beckstead, Jentry	1	3	1.21	29	0	0	19	30	12	6	4	18	37	.121	R	R	6-4	201	6-9-80	2001	Sandy, Utah

PITCHING	W	L	ERA	G	GS	CG	SV	IP	H	R	ER	BB	SO	AVG	B	T	HT	WT	DOB	1st Yr	Resides
Clarke, Darren	4	3	6.98	12	9	0	0	40	51	34	31	19	38	.305	R	R	6-8	230	3-19-81	2001	Tampa, Fla.
Collado, Jerry	0	1	11.42	8	0	0	0	9	15	17	11	7	4	.365	R	R	6-3	210	5-16-79	1997	Santiago, D.R.
Crockett, Ben	0	1	2.88	7	6	0	0	25	26	8	8	3	21	.262	R	R	6-3	200	12-19-79	2002	Topsfield, Mass.
Cruz, Jeff	1	0	4.57	15	0	0	1	22	26	14	11	12	19	.302	L	L	6-0	190	3-14-79	2001	Fullerton, Calif.
Davies, Michael	5	0	2.75	16	9	0	0	69	55	25	21	18	72	.222	L	L	6-3	180	3-29-81	2000	Beaverton, Ore.
Difelice, Mark	0	0	5.29	6	1	0	0	17	18	12	10	0	13	.246	R	R	6-1	170	8-23-76	1998	Havertown, Pa.
Dooley, Jason	3	3	3.59	19	0	0	1	48	45	21	19	17	42	.250	R	R	6-3	170	2-4-80	2002	Danville, Va.
Dunkle, Peter	4	2	2.91	20	0	0	1	43	22	17	14	19	27	.148	R	R	6-5	210	8-7-80	2002	Alamo, Calif.
Francis, Jeff	0	0	0.00	4	3	0	0	11	5	0	0	4	16	.142	L	L	6-5	200	1-8-81	2002	Sammamish, Wash.
Johnson, Doug	5	3	3.47	15	15	0	0	70	63	33	27	24	43	.243	R	R	6-1	180	12-1-80	2002	Pelham, N.H.
Nicholson, Scott	0	3	4.91	9	4	0	0	29	36	20	16	8	20	.300	L	L	6-0	170	8-24-79	2001	Longview, Wash.
Pavlik, Isaac	5	1	1.13	27	0	0	1	32	26	6	4	10	32	.232	R	L	5-8	170	5-19-80	2002	Rutherford, N.J.
Ponder, Steven	0	0	18.00	1	0	0	0	3	5	7	6	3	5	.384	S	L	6-0	200	11-16-79	2002	Austin, Texas
Reba, Steve	1	1	1.66	14	2	0	3	38	28	8	7	4	47	.204	R	R	6-3	190	3-23-80	2002	Fort Wayne, Ind.
Shartzer, Bryan	0	1	2.57	9	0	0	0	14	12	4	4	6	16	.226	R	R	6-0	180	6-17-80	2002	Louisville, Ky.
Tetuan, John	2	6	5.58	15	15	0	0	60	61	40	37	27	39	.257	R	R	6-0	200	9-16-80	2002	Topeka, Kan.
Tsao, Chin-Hui	0	0	0.00	3	3	0	0	11	6	2	0	2	16	.150	R	R	6-2	170	6-2-81	1999	Hualien, Taiwan
Watson, Mike	4	3	3.43	18	0	0	0	42	37	19	16	15	39	.237	R	R	6-1	180	9-28-80	2002	Altoona, Pa.
Young, Chris	5	5	2.34	17	6	0	0	62	45	20	16	23	47	.202	R	R	6-4	210	4-19-81	2002	Stow, Ohio

CASPER ROCKIES — Rookie

PIONEER LEAGUE

BATTING	AVG	G	AB	R	H	2B	3B	HR	RBI	BB	SO	SB	CS	SLG	OBP	B	T	HT	WT	DOB	1st Yr	Resides
Almonte, Sandy	.295	54	217	46	64	13	3	5	32	23	46	11	6	.452	.361	S	R	5-11	150	11-16-82	2002	Puerto Plata, D.R.
Barre, Brian	.300	62	227	60	68	12	5	9	35	40	55	11	0	.515	.412	L	L	5-9	180	6-23-80	2002	Garden Grove, Calif.
Bello, Vladimir	.279	59	226	39	63	7	7	2	29	13	45	17	2	.398	.322	R	R	5-11	160	1-2-82	2000	Santo Domingo, D.R.
Bibee, Hal	.250	1	4	0	1	0	0	0	0	0	1	0	0	.250	.250	R	R	6-0	190	5-8-79	2002	Knoxville, Tenn.
Fuller, Casey	.225	50	187	22	42	8	5	1	27	15	50	0	0	.337	.284	L	L	6-6	210	2-9-79	2002	Marysville, Calif.
George, Trey	.287	67	261	35	75	15	1	0	39	25	43	1	1	.352	.346	R	R	6-0	200	1-26-83	2001	Houston, Texas
Hendricks, K.J.	.314	64	258	51	81	11	1	1	32	36	24	21	3	.376	.399	S	R	5-7	160	2-20-81	2002	Killeen, Texas
Mills, Rock	.250	48	196	24	49	13	2	7	41	12	49	0	1	.444	.312	R	R	6-1	210	7-11-80	2002	Westlake, Ohio
Morel, Robinson	.255	41	137	31	35	3	0	4	11	6	40	4	5	.365	.290	R	R	5-10	160	2-5-82	1999	Esperanza Mao, D.R.
Nunez, Florentino	.295	52	193	32	57	15	5	2	23	19	41	2	1	.456	.367	S	R	6-0	190	6-4-82	2002	Villa Mella, D.R.
Ortega, Sixto	.188	4	16	2	3	0	0	1	1	1	2	0	0	.375	.278	R	R	5-10	190	12-24-76	1997	Santo Domingo, D.R.
Robledo, Nelson	.231	38	134	13	31	2	1	0	13	16	27	0	1	.261	.327	R	R	6-1	180	6-13-84	2001	Panama City, Panama
Sardinha, Duke	.248	41	137	21	34	8	1	1	16	19	49	2	1	.343	.360	R	R	6-0	200	12-9-80	2002	Kailua, Hawaii
Shealy, Ryan	.368	69	231	55	85	21	1	19	70	50	52	0	0	.714	.497	R	R	6-5	240	8-29-79	2002	Fort Lauderdale, Fla.
Tejeda, Francisco	.221	25	77	12	17	1	2	0	8	1	22	3	1	.286	.231	R	R	6-1	150	12-19-80	2002	Santo Domingo, D.R.
Wilson, Neil	.239	37	134	18	32	2	3	2	17	10	30	0	0	.343	.296	R	R	6-1	190	12-7-83	2002	Vero Beach, Fla.

GAMES BY POSITION: C—Mills 21, Ortega 4, Robledo 25, Wilson 28. **1B**—Robledo 10, Sardinha 2, Shealy 65. **2B**—Almonte 13, Hendricks 21, Morel 32, Tejeda 12. **3B**—Almonte 16, Hendricks 1, Morel 4, Nunez 28, Sardinha 23, Tejeda 5. **SS**—Almonte 20, Hendricks 40, Nunez 13, Tejeda 6. **OF**—Almonte 3, Barre 62, Bello 58, Fuller 42, George 65, Morel 1.

PITCHING	W	L	ERA	G	GS	CG	SV	IP	H	R	ER	BB	SO	AVG	B	T	HT	WT	DOB	1st Yr	Resides
Cartier, Richard	5	3	4.28	29	0	0	6	34	35	19	16	6	33	.257	R	R	6-1	180	10-9-79	2002	Simi Valley, Calif.
Chivilli, Pedro	2	4	5.66	14	13	0	0	70	84	50	44	20	72	.294	R	R	6-0	150	2-21-83	2001	Santo Domingo, D.R.
Corpas, Manuel	2	4	5.73	29	0	0	2	33	37	24	21	18	42	.274	R	R	6-3	170	12-3-82	1999	Panama City, Panama
Diaz, Pedro	1	2	5.10	18	0	0	1	30	35	22	17	11	23	.275	R	R	6-0	190	9-9-82	2002	Gurabo, P.R.
Fardella, Jason	1	5	5.68	21	3	0	0	59	78	44	37	17	47	.313	R	R	6-4	190	10-24-80	2001	South Ozone Park, N.Y.
Garcia, Rurik	0	0	12.86	11	0	0	0	7	11	12	10	19	4	.366	L	L	5-11	160	6-13-82	1999	Valencia, Venez.
Hernandez, Santos	8	1	3.50	14	14	0	0	72	65	30	28	32	39	.238	R	R	6-1	180	1-19-84	2001	Santo Domingo, D.R.
Jimenez, Ubaldo	3	5	6.53	14	14	0	0	62	72	46	45	29	65	.288	R	R	6-2	160	1-22-84	2001	San Cristobal, D.R.
Lo, Ching-Lung	2	4	3.20	14	9	0	0	45	44	22	16	22	21	.245	R	R	6-4	160	8-20-85	2002	Tainan, Taiwan
Mitchell, Jay	5	4	4.95	16	16	0	0	73	85	50	40	34	46	.290	R	R	6-7	200	1-5-83	2001	La Grange, Ga.
Ponder, Steven	1	0	6.54	16	5	0	0	32	24	27	23	38	28	.205	S	L	6-0	200	11-16-79	2002	Austin, Texas
Reba, Steve	0	0	5.87	2	1	0	0	8	11	7	5	3	6	.314	R	R	6-3	190	3-23-80	2002	Fort Wayne, Ind.
Salas, Pedro	0	1	4.11	13	0	0	0	15	18	7	7	2	8	.295	R	R	6-3	170	7-14-82	1999	Barinas, Venez.
Santiago, Tomas	0	1	4.50	19	0	0	0	34	41	24	17	20	24	.303	R	R	6-4	210	10-30-81	2002	Cidra, P.R.
Shartzer, Bryan	0	3	5.29	12	1	0	1	17	17	10	10	5	20	.242	R	R	6-0	180	6-17-80	2002	Louisville, Ky.
Valcarcel, Jonathan	2	0	3.71	21	0	0	1	27	32	17	11	8	26	.290	L	L	6-3	180	11-23-83	2002	Bayamon, P.R.
Vargas, Reynardo	3	3	3.61	26	0	0	1	42	38	24	17	22	45	.234	R	R	6-1	160	11-13-82	1999	Santo Domingo, D.R.

DETROIT TIGERS

BY PAT CAPUTO

The 2002 season started out poorly for the Tigers and only got worse.

After the Tigers lost their first six games to open the season, team president Dave Dombrowski—who had  signed a five-year, $10 million contract during the off season—fired manager Phil Garner and general manager Randy Smith.

Dombrowski then hired Luis Pujols, who had been Garner's bench coach, as interim manager, and appointed himself as general manager.

The Tigers promptly lost their next five games, making it 11 straight losses to begin the season. They never recovered. The Tigers' final record was 55-106, tying the Devil Rays for the worst in the major leagues. It was the Tigers' ninth straight losing season, and fifth time in the last seven seasons they have lost at least 90 games.

It is difficult to pinpoint any particular area which ailed the Tigers beyond others. Offensively, the Tigers were last in the American League in runs, home runs, on-base percentage, slugging percentage, hits and walks. In the field, the Tigers committed a league-leading 142 errors. On the mound, Detroit ranked 11th with a 4.92 ERA despite playing its home games in the most spacious stadium in the major leagues, Comerica Park.

The Tigers' most productive hitter was first baseman Randall Simon, who batted .301-19-82. But typical of the team's problems, he walked just 13 times in 505 plate appearances.

Detroit's best player was outfielder Bobby Higginson. A .300-30-102 hitter as recently as 2000, Higginson's production fell to .282-10-63 in 2002, his first year of a five-year, $35.5 million contract extension.

The Tigers were boxed in with several expensive contracts for veteran players they would have loved to unload once the losing snowballed but couldn't because there were no takers. Higginson, second baseman Damion Easley, infielder Shane Halter, utilityman Craig Paquette, reliever Danny Patterson, third baseman Dean

Randall Simon

Eric Munson

PLAYERS OF THE YEAR

MAJOR LEAGUE: Randall Simon, 1b

After spending parts of five seasons in Triple-A with four different organizations, Simon made good on his first full season in the majors in 2002. He led the Tigers in the triple crown categories (.301-19-82).

MINOR LEAGUE: Eric Munson, 1b

Munson hit .192 through May, but broke out of his 2002 slump in a big way, finishing second in the International League in extra-base hits (58). Overall, Munson hit .262-24-84. He will fight for time in Detroit's first base/DH logjam in 2003.

Palmer, reliever Matt Anderson, righthander Steve Sparks and first baseman Dmitri Young all fell into that category. That Palmer and Patterson missed all of the season, and Anderson most of it, with injuries hurt their trade value.

That's why the Tigers' most significant trade under Dombrowski involved their best pitcher, Jeff Weaver, the organization's first-round draft choice in 1998. He was moved to the Yankees in a three-way trade with the Athletics which yielded first baseman Carlos Pena, hard-throwing reliever Franklyn German and pitching prospect Jeremy Bonderman in return.

At the minor league level, the Tigers continued to make progress in 2002. With key prospects such as first baseman Eric Munson, shortstop Omar Infante, righthanders Nate Cornejo and Shane Loux and left-hander Andy Van Hekken keying the effort, Triple-A Toledo made the playoffs.

On the downside, Detroit's first-round choices in 2000 and 2001, righthanders Matt Wheatland and Kenny Baugh, both missed the entire 2002 season because of surgery on their throwing shoulders. Infielder Scott Moore and outfielder Brent Clevlen, Detroit's first two selection's in June's draft, both performed well in the Rookie-level Gulf Coast League.

A day after the Tigers' season was thankfully put out of its misery, Pujols was fired. Alan Trammell, the Tigers' shortstop for two decades and an integral part of their last World Series title in 1984, was hired to replace him. Trammell had been a coach with the Padres the last three years and brought with him from the '84 championship team Kirk Gibson and Lance Parrish to be part of his coaching staff. His first message to his players was a simple one: professionalism.

ORGANIZATION LEADERS

BATTING

*AVG	Craig Monroe, Toledo	.321
R	Juan Francia, West Michigan	94
H	Juan Tejeda, West Michigan	157
TB	Juan Tejeda, West Michigan	236
2B	Ryan Jackson, Toledo	35
3B	David Mattle, West Michigan	10
HR	Eric Munson, Toledo	24
RBI	Juan Tejeda, West Michigan	106
BB	Eric Munson, Toledo	77
SO	Jason Knoedler, West Michigan	145
SB	Nook Logan, Lakeland	55

PITCHING

W	Chad Petty, West Michigan	15
L	Kevin Lidle, Erie/Lakeland	14
#ERA	Homero Rivera, Toledo/Erie	3.07
G	Jason Birtwell, West Michigan	58
CG	Shane Loux, Toledo	5
SV	Mike Kobow, West Michigan	31
IP	Andy Van Hekken, Toledo/Erie	183
BB	Tommy Marx, Lakeland	83
SO	Matt Coenen, West Michigan	141

*Minimum 250 At-Bats #Minimum 75 Innings

DETROIT TIGERS

Managers: Phil Garner, Luis Pujols

2002 Record: 55-106, .342 (5th, AL Central)

BATTING	AVG	G	AB	R	H	2B	3B	HR	RBI	BB	SO	SB	CS	SLG	OBP	B	T	HT	WT	DOB	1st Yr	Resides
Bocachica, Hiram	.223	34	103	14	23	4	0	4	8	5	22	2	2	.379	.259	R	R	5-11	160	3-4-76	1994	Toa Alta, P.R.
Cruz, Jacob	.273	35	88	12	24	3	1	2	6	13	20	3	1	.398	.377	L	L	6-0	210	1-28-73	1994	Gilbert, Ariz.
Easley, Damion	.224	85	304	29	68	14	1	8	30	27	43	1	3	.355	.307	R	R	5-11	180	11-11-69	1988	Glendale, Ariz.
Fick, Robert	.270	148	556	66	150	36	2	17	63	46	90	0	1	.433	.331	L	R	6-1	200	3-15-74	1996	Manhattan Beach, Calif.
Halter, Shane	.239	122	410	46	98	22	6	10	39	39	92	0	4	.395	.309	R	R	6-0	180	11-8-69	1991	Overland Park, Kan.
Higginson, Bob	.282	119	444	50	125	24	3	10	63	41	45	12	5	.417	.345	L	R	5-11	200	8-18-70	1992	Bloomfield Hills, Mich.
Infante, Omar	.333	18	72	4	24	3	0	1	6	3	10	0	1	.417	.360	R	R	6-0	150	12-26-81	1999	Guanta, Venez.
Inge, Brandon	.202	95	321	27	65	15	3	7	24	24	101	1	3	.333	.266	R	R	5-11	180	5-19-77	1998	Ann Arbor, Mich.
Jackson, Damian	.257	81	245	31	63	20	1	1	25	21	36	12	3	.359	.320	R	R	5-11	180	8-16-73	1992	Concord, Calif.
Jackson, Ryan	.333	4	6	0	2	1	1	0	0	1	2	0	0	.833	.429	L	L	6-2	200	11-15-71	1994	Sarasota, Fla.
Lombard, George	.241	72	241	34	58	11	3	5	13	20	78	13	2	.373	.300	L	R	6-0	210	9-14-75	1994	Atlanta, Ga.
Macias, Jose	.234	33	107	10	25	4	0	0	6	8	13	3	2	.271	.291	S	R	5-10	180	1-25-72	1992	Panama City, Panama
Magee, Wendell	.271	97	347	34	94	19	1	6	35	10	64	2	4	.383	.289	R	R	6-0	220	8-3-72	1994	Hattiesburg, Miss.
Meluskey, Mitch	.222	8	27	3	6	0	0	0	1	5	3	0	0	.222	.353	S	R	6-0	200	9-18-73	1992	Yakima, Wash.
Monroe, Craig	.120	13	25	3	3	1	0	1	1	0	5	0	2	.280	.154	R	R	6-1	190	2-27-77	1995	Texarkana, Texas
Munson, Eric	.186	18	59	3	11	0	0	2	5	6	11	0	0	.288	.269	L	R	6-3	220	10-3-77	1999	San Diego, Calif.
Palmer, Dean	.000	4	12	0	0	0	0	0	0	1	5	0	0	.000	.077	R	R	6-1	210	12-27-68	1986	Tallahassee, Fla.
Paquette, Craig	.194	72	252	20	49	14	1	4	20	10	53	1	0	.306	.223	R	R	6-0	190	3-28-69	1989	Chesterfield, Mo.
Pena, Carlos	.253	75	273	31	69	13	4	12	36	26	73	2	2	.462	.321	L	L	6-2	210	5-17-78	1998	Haverhill, Mass.
2-team (40 Oakland)	.242	115	397	43	96	17	4	19	52	41	111	2	2	.448	.316							
Rivera, Mike	.227	39	132	11	30	8	1	1	11	4	35	0	0	.326	.254	R	R	6-0	210	9-8-76	1997	Bayamon, P.R.
Salazar, Oscar	.190	8	21	2	4	1	0	1	3	1	2	0	0	.381	.227	R	R	5-11	170	6-27-78	1994	Maracay, Venez.
Santiago, Ramon	.243	65	222	33	54	5	5	4	20	13	48	8	5	.365	.306	S	R	5-11	150	8-31-79	1998	Las Matas de Farfan, D.R.
Simon, Randall	.301	130	482	51	145	17	1	19	82	13	30	0	1	.459	.320	L	L	6-0	230	5-26-75	1993	Willemstad, Curacao
Torres, Andres	.200	19	70	7	14	1	1	0	3	6	16	2	2	.243	.266	S	R	5-10	180	1-26-78	1998	Aguada, P.R.
Truby, Chris	.199	89	277	23	55	13	2	2	15	5	71	1	1	.282	.215	R	R	6-2	210	12-9-73	1993	Noblesville, Ind.
Walbeck, Matt	.235	27	85	4	20	2	0	0	3	3	14	0	0	.259	.258	S	R	5-11	180	10-2-69	1987	Sacramento, Calif.
Young, Dmitri	.284	54	201	25	57	14	0	7	27	12	39	2	0	.458	.329	S	R	6-2	230	10-11-73	1991	Parkland, Fla.

PITCHING	W	L	ERA	G	GS	CG	SV	IP	H	R	ER	BB	SO	AVG	B	T	HT	WT	DOB	1st Yr	Resides
Acevedo, Juan	1	5	2.65	65	0	0	28	75	68	33	22	23	43	.246	R	R	6-2	220	5-5-70	1992	Algonguin, Il
Anderson, Matt	2	1	9.00	12	0	0	0	11	17	13	11	8	8	.377	R	R	6-4	190	8-17-76	1997	Louisville, Ky.
Bernero, Adam	4	7	6.20	28	11	0	0	102	128	74	70	31	69	.309	R	R	6-4	210	11-28-76	1999	Elk Grove, Calif.
Beverlin, Jason	0	3	9.49	3	3	0	0	12	18	15	13	5	7	.327	L	R	6-5	220	11-27-73	1994	Royal Oak, Mich.
2-team (4 Cleveland)	0	3	8.69	7	3	0	0	20	27	22	19	9	16	.313							
Cornejo, Nate	1	5	5.04	9	9	1	0	50	63	33	28	18	23	.302	R	R	6-5	240	9-24-79	1998	Wellington, Kan.
Eckenstahler, Eric	1	0	5.63	7	0	0	0	8	14	5	5	2	13	.378	L	L	6-7	210	12-17-76	2000	Lake Villa, Ill.
Farnsworth, Jeff	2	3	5.79	44	0	0	0	70	100	47	45	29	28	.337	R	R	6-0	190	10-6-75	1996	Pensacola, Fla.
German, Franklyn	1	0	0.00	7	0	0	1	7	3	0	0	2	6	.150	R	R	6-4	260	1-20-80	1996	San Cristobal, D.R.
Greisinger, Seth	2	2	6.21	8	8	0	0	38	46	26	26	13	14	.302	R	R	6-3	190	7-29-75	1996	Falls Church, Va.
Henriquez, Oscar	1	1	4.50	30	0	0	2	28	19	14	14	15	23	.195	R	R	6-6	220	1-28-74	1991	La Guaira, Venez.
Jimenez, Jason	0	0	27.00	1	0	0	0	1	3	4	2	1	0	.500	R	L	6-2	200	1-10-76	1997	Elk Grove, Calif.
2-team (5 Tampa Bay)	0	0	7.36	6	0	0	0	7	12	8	6	2	5	.363							
Keller, Kris	0	0	27.00	1	0	0	0	1	2	3	3	3	1	.400	R	R	6-2	260	3-1-78	1996	Atlantic Beach, Fla.
Lima, Jose	4	6	7.77	20	12	0	0	68	86	60	59	21	33	.313	R	R	6-2	200	9-30-72	1989	Houston, Texas
Loux, Shane	0	3	9.00	3	3	0	0	14	19	16	14	3	7	.316	R	R	6-2	230	8-31-79	1997	Gilbert, Ariz.
Maroth, Mike	6	10	4.48	21	21	0	0	129	136	68	64	36	58	.276	L	L	6-0	180	8-17-77	1998	Orlando, Fla.
Miller, Matt	0	0	13.50	2	0	0	0	1	4	2	1	1	1	.571	L	L	6-3	190	8-2-74	1996	Lubbock, Texas
Moehler, Brian	1	1	2.29	3	3	0	0	20	17	5	5	2	13	.232	R	R	6-3	230	12-31-71	1993	Marietta, Ga.
Paniagua, Jose	0	1	5.83	41	0	0	1	42	50	30	27	15	34	.294	R	R	6-2	190	8-20-73	1991	Santo Domingo, D.R.
Patterson, Danny	0	2	15.00	6	0	0	0	7	15	5	5	2	1	.357	R	R	6-0	180	2-17-71	1989	Colleyville, Texas
Pearson, Terry	0	0	10.50	4	0	0	0	6	8	7	7	2	4	.320	R	R	6-0	200	11-10-71	1995	Carrollton, Ala.
Perisho, Matt	0	0	8.71	5	0	0	0	10	16	11	10	6	3	.372	L	L	6-0	190	6-8-75	1993	Chandler, Ariz.
Powell, Brian	1	5	4.84	13	9	0	0	58	64	34	31	21	30	.278	R	R	6-2	200	10-10-73	1995	Bainbridge, Ga.
Redman, Mark	8	15	4.21	30	30	3	0	203	211	107	95	51	109	.267	L	L	6-5	240	1-5-74	1995	Catoosa, Okla.
Rodney, Fernando	1	3	6.00	20	0	0	0	18	25	15	12	10	10	.328	R	R	5-11	170	3-18-77	1997	Santo Domingo, D.R.
Sabel, Erik	0	0	0.00	1	0	0	0	2	2	2	0	1	0	1.000	R	R	6-3	190	10-14-74	1996	Indianapolis, Ind.
Santana, Julio	3	5	2.84	9	9	0	0	57	49	19	18	28	38	.237	R	R	6-2	200	1-20-73	1992	Santo Domingo, D.R.
Sparks, Steve	8	16	5.52	32	30	3	0	189	238	134	116	67	98	.305	R	R	6-0	190	7-2-65	1987	Sugar Land, Texas
Van Hekken, Andy	1	3	3.00	5	5	1	0	30	38	13	10	6	5	.311	R	L	6-3	170	7-31-79	1998	Holland, Mich.
Walker, Jamie	1	1	3.71	57	0	0	1	44	32	19	18	9	40	.198	L	L	6-2	190	7-1-71	1992	Overland Park, Kan.
Weaver, Jeff	6	8	3.18	17	17	3	0	122	112	50	43	33	75	.242	R	R	6-5	200	8-22-76	1998	Simi Valley, Calif.

FIELDING

Catcher	PCT	G	PO	A	E	DP	PB
Inge	.998	94	484	46	1	3	10
Meluskey	1.000	8	34	3	0	0	1
Rivera	.990	37	189	19	2	1	10
Walbeck	.993	27	127	8	1	2	2

First Base	PCT	G	PO	A	E	DP
Cruz	1.000	4	26	2	0	1

	PCT	G	PO	A	E	DP	
Halter	1.000	1	8	1	0	0	
Munson	.970	4	29	3	1	3	
Paquette	.991	14	96	9	1	5	
Pena	.996	73	659	29	3	71	
Simon	.988	59	541	27	7	48	
Young	.971	15	117	16	4	5	

Second Base	PCT	G	PO	A	E	DP
Bocachica	1.000	2	1	4	0	0
Easley	.980	84	181	253	9	54
Halter	.875	6	8	2	2	2
Infante	1.000	2	5	9	0	4
D. Jackson	.981	56	110	146	5	37
Macias	.964	17	26	54	3	5
Salazar	.938	6	7	8	1	3

Third Base	PCT	G	PO	A	E	DP
Halter	.943	30	21	45	4	9
D. Jackson	1.000	2	0	3	0	0
Macias	.857	8	4	8	2	0
Paquette	.936	49	35	82	8	5
Salazar	1.000	1	0	3	0	0
Truby	.958	89	71	181	11	22
Young	1.000	1	2	2	0	0

Shortstop	PCT	G	PO	A	E	DP
Halter	.962	81	122	253	15	37

Infante	.935	16	18	54	5	10
D. Jackson	.882	6	4	11	2	0
Salazar	1.000	1	1	1	0	0
Santiago	.977	63	97	205	7	41

Outfield	PCT	G	PO	A	E	DP
Bocachica	.966	32	54	3	2	0
Cruz	.929	12	13	0	1	0
Fick	.963	140	288	21	12	5
Halter	1.000	8	15	2	0	1
Higginson	.973	117	241	15	7	3

D. Jackson	.889	6	8	0	1	0
R. Jackson	1.000	3	2	0	0	0
Lombard	.982	69	158	2	3	0
Macias	1.000	10	24	0	0	0
Magee	.982	91	262	6	5	1
Monroe	.950	9	18	1	1	0
Paquette	1.000	8	15	0	0	0
Torres	.981	19	51	0	1	0
Young	1.000	1	1	0	0	0

Robert Fick: lone Detroit representative at All-Star Game

Randall Simon: hit .301 to lead Tigers in average

FARM SYSTEM

Director, Player Development: Greg Smith.

Class	Farm Team	League	W	L	Pct.	Finish*	Manager	First Yr.
AAA	Toledo (Ohio) Mud Hens	International	81	63	.563	4th (14)	Bruce Fields	1987
AA	Erie (Pa.) Sea Wolves	Eastern	52	89	.369	12th (12)	Kevin Bradshaw	2001
High A	Lakeland (Fla.) Tigers	Florida State	69	70	.496	7th (12)	Gary Green	1960
Low A	West Michigan Whitecaps	Midwest	83	57	.593	2nd (14)	Phil Regan	1997
SS A	Oneonta (N.Y.) Tigers	New York-Penn	47	27	.635	2nd (14)	Randy Ready	1999
Rookie	Lakeland (Fla.) Tigers	Gulf Coast	23	37	.383	13th (14)	Howard Bushong	1995

*Finish in overall standings (No. of teams in league)

TOLEDO MUD HENS — Class AAA

INTERNATIONAL LEAGUE

BATTING	AVG	G	AB	R	H	2B	3B	HR	RBI	BB	SO	SB	CS	SLG	OBP	B	T	HT	WT	DOB	1st Yr	Resides
Alexander, Chad	.275	97	313	36	86	23	3	7	34	20	58	2	4	.435	.316	R	R	6-1	190	5-22-74	1995	Norfolk, Va.
Cruz, Jacob	.163	11	43	6	7	1	1	0	5	8	14	1	0	.233	.302	L	L	6-0	210	1-28-73	1994	Gilbert, Ariz.
Easley, Damion	.115	8	26	5	3	1	0	0	0	5	0	0	2	.154	.281	R	R	5-11	180	11-11-69	1988	Glendale, Ariz.
Infante, Omar	.268	120	436	49	117	16	8	4	51	28	49	19	15	.369	.309	R	R	6-0	150	12-26-81	1999	Guanta, Venez.
Inge, Brandon	.262	21	65	10	17	2	4	3	13	11	16	1	3	.554	.380	R	R	5-11	180	5-19-77	1998	Ann Arbor, Mich.
Jackson, Ryan	.271	104	420	40	114	35	1	8	50	13	84	5	3	.417	.297	L	L	6-2	200	11-15-71	1994	Sarasota, Fla.
Lindsey, Rodney	.226	11	31	2	7	1	0	0	2	2	4	5	1	.258	.273	R	R	5-8	170	1-28-76	1994	Opelika, Ala.
Meran, Jorge	.167	3	12	1	2	0	0	0	0	0	2	0	0	.167	.167	R	R	6-1	160	6-18-74	1993	Santo Domingo, D.R.
Monroe, Craig	.321	99	358	61	115	30	4	10	49	35	57	7	3	.511	.379	R	R	6-1	190	2-27-77	1995	Texarkana, Texas
Munson, Eric	.262	136	477	77	125	30	4	24	84	77	114	1	3	.493	.367	L	R	6-3	220	10-3-77	1999	San Diego, Calif.
Nicholson, Derek	.288	89	292	46	84	22	3	6	58	50	71	1	0	.445	.387	L	R	6-0	200	6-17-76	1998	Redondo Beach, Calif.
Patterson, Jarrod	.295	117	447	66	132	34	6	13	70	46	71	3	1	.485	.364	L	R	6-1	190	9-7-73	1993	Clanton, Ala.
Rios, Brian	.263	80	262	28	69	12	3	3	28	18	45	0	2	.366	.314	R	R	6-3	190	7-25-74	1996	Corona, Calif.

BATTING

BATTING	AVG	G	AB	R	H	2B	3B	HR	RBI	BB	SO	SB	CS	SLG	OBP	B	T	HT	WT	DOB	1st Yr	Resides
Rivera, Mike	.249	74	265	43	66	11	1	20	53	35	64	0	1	.525	.341	R	R	6-0	210	9-8-76	1997	Bayamon, P.R.
Salazar, Oscar	.316	8	19	0	6	0	0	0	1	3	1	0	1	.316	.409	R	R	5-11	170	6-27-78	1994	Maracay, Venez.
Santiago, Ramon	.429	9	28	8	12	1	0	2	6	3	4	0	2	.679	.515	S	R	5-11	150	8-31-79	1998	Las Matas de Farfan, D.R.
St. Pierre, Maxim	.000	1	2	0	0	0	0	0	1	0	0	0	0	.000	.000	R	R	6-0	170	4-17-80	1997	Montreal, Quebec
Torres, Andres	.266	115	462	80	123	17	8	4	42	53	116	42	12	.364	.345	S	R	5-10	180	1-26-78	1998	Aguada, P.R.
Truby, Chris	.333	3	12	2	4	0	2	1	1	2	1	0	0	.917	.429	R	R	6-2	210	12-9-73	1993	Noblesville, Ind.
Valera, Yohanny	.252	44	131	15	33	8	1	1	6	7	36	0	0	.351	.310	R	R	6-1	200	8-17-76	1993	San Cristobal, D.R.
Wakeland, Chris	.242	90	297	38	72	11	1	10	32	24	106	5	3	.387	.302	L	L	6-0	190	6-15-74	1996	St. Helens, Ore.
Walbeck, Matt	.213	21	75	4	16	3	0	1	6	4	10	0	0	.293	.250	S	R	5-11	180	10-2-69	1987	Sacramento, Calif.
Wilson, Craig	.263	119	415	48	109	21	2	2	46	45	39	2	2	.337	.340	R	R	6-0	180	9-3-70	1992	Phoenix, Ariz.

PITCHING

PITCHING	W	L	ERA	G	GS	CG	SV	IP	H	R	ER	BB	SO	AVG	B	T	HT	WT	DOB	1st Yr	Resides
Adkins, Tim	2	2	4.06	31	8	0	0	69	66	34	31	34	54	.256	L	L	6-0	190	5-12-74	1992	Huntington, W.Va.
Ahearne, Pat	5	4	3.16	12	12	1	0	83	78	32	29	13	48	.256	R	R	6-3	190	12-10-69	1992	Atascadero, Calif.
Bernero, Adam	2	2	1.58	9	9	2	0	57	46	13	10	13	49	.223	R	R	6-4	210	11-28-76	1999	Elk Grove, Calif.
Beverlin, Jason	3	0	1.93	4	3	0	0	19	17	5	4	5	13	.242	L	R	6-5	220	11-27-73	1994	Royal Oak, Mich.
2-team (23 Buffalo)	13	8	3.60	27	23	1	0	137	124	60	55	45	119	.243							
Cornejo, Nate	9	8	4.42	21	20	1	0	132	163	72	65	31	86	.306	R	R	6-5	240	9-24-79	1998	Wellington, Kan.
Eckstahler, Eric	2	4	4.43	52	0	0	6	67	57	37	33	35	69	.233	L	L	6-7	210	12-17-76	2000	Lake Villa, Ill.
Farmer, Tom	0	0	6.00	1	1	0	0	6	7	4	4	2	3	.291	R	R	6-2	190	7-27-79	2001	Crestwood, Ill.
German, Franklyn	1	1	1.59	23	0	0	13	23	15	4	4	7	31	.187	R	R	6-4	260	1-20-80	1996	San Cristobal, D.R.
Greisinger, Seth	1	1	4.11	3	3	0	0	15	15	8	7	1	11	.277	R	R	6-3	190	7-29-75	1996	Falls Church, Va.
Henriquez, Oscar	2	1	3.31	33	0	0	17	33	30	13	12	14	39	.243	R	R	6-6	220	1-28-74	1991	La Guaira, Venez.
Johnson, Mark	3	0	2.31	8	2	0	0	23	24	9	6	5	15	.272	R	R	6-3	220	5-2-75	1997	Leesburg, Fla.
2-team (4 Indianapolis)	4	1	4.95	12	6	0	0	44	50	27	24	17	23	.297							
Kalita, Tim	1	9	4.93	15	15	0	0	88	93	56	48	22	47	.268	R	L	6-2	220	11-21-78	1999	Oak Park, Ill.
Keller, Kris	2	0	2.08	17	0	0	0	26	20	10	6	17	20	.210	R	R	6-2	260	3-1-78	1996	Atlantic Beach, Fla.
Loux, Shane	11	10	4.72	26	26	5	0	158	196	94	83	38	87	.306	R	R	6-2	230	8-31-79	1997	Gilbert, Ariz.
Maroth, Mike	8	1	2.82	11	11	1	0	73	53	25	23	22	51	.200	L	L	6-0	180	8-17-77	1998	Orlando, Fla.
Moehler, Brian	2	1	4.88	4	4	0	0	24	28	15	13	3	7	.277	R	R	6-3	230	12-31-71	1993	Marietta, Ga.
Paniagua, Jose	2	0	1.15	12	0	0	1	16	10	2	2	4	13	.188	R	R	6-2	190	8-20-73	1991	Santo Domingo, D.R.
Patterson, Danny	0	0	0.00	5	1	0	0	5	1	0	0	0	3	.066	R	R	6-0	180	2-17-71	1989	Colleyville, Texas
Pearson, Terry	3	8	4.79	40	0	0	2	47	52	29	25	18	30	.282	R	R	6-0	200	11-10-71	1995	Carrollton, Ala.
Perisho, Matt	4	4	2.45	51	2	0	1	66	62	20	18	19	44	.246	L	L	6-0	200	6-8-75	1993	Chandler, Ariz.
Powell, Brian	10	3	3.92	20	20	0	0	119	127	54	52	26	82	.270	R	R	6-2	200	10-10-73	1995	Bainbridge, Ga.
Rivera, Homero	1	1	6.10	12	0	0	0	21	26	17	14	8	10	.309	R	L	5-10	160	8-13-77	1995	Nizao, D.R.
Rodney, Fernando	1	1	0.81	20	0	0	4	22	13	4	2	9	25	.171	R	R	5-11	170	3-18-77	1997	Santo Domingo, D.R.
Sabel, Erik	1	0	6.55	14	0	0	0	11	15	8	8	4	7	.319	R	R	6-3	190	10-14-74	1996	Indianapolis, Ind.
Santana, Julio	0	1	2.13	7	0	0	1	13	12	5	3	3	12	.250	R	R	6-0	220	1-20-73	1992	Santo Domingo, D.R.
Van Hekken, Andy	5	0	1.82	7	7	1	0	49	41	14	10	11	19	.227	R	L	6-3	170	7-31-79	1998	Holland, Mich.
Walker, Jamie	0	1	1.98	10	0	0	1	14	7	3	3	3	9	.155	L	L	6-2	190	7-1-71	1992	Overland Park, Kan.

FIELDING

Catcher	PCT	G	PO	A	E	DP	PB
Inge	.978	21	157	19	4	1	2
Meran	.968	3	29	1	1	0	1
Rivera	.993	67	381	35	3	3	6
St. Pierre	1.000	1	6	0	0	0	0
Valera	.988	43	218	24	3	2	5
Walbeck	.986	20	134	6	2	2	1

First Base	PCT	G	PO	A	E	DP
Jackson	1.000	13	124	7	0	11
Munson	.990	129	1159	89	12	118
Nicholson	.900	3	9	0	1	3
Walbeck	.900	1	8	1	1	1

Second Base	PCT	G	PO	A	E	DP
Easley	.949	8	13	24	2	3
Patterson	.952	47	68	109	9	25
Salazar	1.000	3	7	6	0	4
Wilson	.978	94	204	275	11	73

Third Base	PCT	G	PO	A	E	DP
Nicholson	.000	1	0	0	0	0
Patterson	.938	72	34	149	12	14
Rios	.951	52	27	110	7	10
Truby	.818	3	4	5	2	2
Wilson	.955	24	11	53	3	3

Shortstop	PCT	G	PO	A	E	DP
Infante	.959	120	191	416	26	91

	PCT	G	PO	A	E	DP
Rios	.971	16	18	49	2	12
Salazar	.933	4	5	9	1	3
Santiago	.956	9	14	29	2	4
Wilson	.000	1	0	0	0	0

Outfield	PCT	G	PO	A	E	DP
Alexander	.993	78	140	11	1	4
Cruz	1.000	6	12	0	0	0
Jackson	.986	62	131	5	2	1
Lindsey	1.000	10	13	0	0	0
Monroe	.983	79	161	8	3	0
Nicholson	.978	45	88	3	2	0
Rios	1.000	3	6	0	0	0
Torres	.967	115	289	3	10	0
Wakeland	.964	48	99	7	4	1

ERIE SEAWOLVES — Class AA

EASTERN LEAGUE

BATTING	AVG	G	AB	R	H	2B	3B	HR	RBI	BB	SO	SB	CS	SLG	OBP	B	T	HT	WT	DOB	1st Yr	Resides
Airoso, Kurt	.288	109	386	76	111	18	0	20	63	57	107	6	3	.490	.385	R	R	6-2	190	2-12-75	1996	Tulare, Calif.
Bautista, Rayner	.265	89	302	35	80	20	2	4	33	22	72	5	2	.384	.319	R	R	5-11	150	9-17-78	1995	Nizao, D.R.
Camilo, Juan	.205	45	156	17	32	7	4	5	21	16	49	5	0	.397	.274	L	R	6-0	190	6-24-76	1996	Santo Domingo, D.R.
Carter, Charley	.280	135	492	61	138	32	1	21	92	51	91	1	0	.478	.349	R	R	6-2	200	12-11-75	1998	Mt. Pleasant, Texas
Castillo, Carlos	.214	35	112	7	24	5	2	0	6	3	35	1	1	.295	.235	S	R	5-10	170	1-26-80	2002	San Jose, Costa Rica
Cleveland, Russ	.255	16	51	3	13	2	1	0	1	5	17	0	0	.333	.321	R	R	6-3	200	12-26-79	1998	Las Vegas, Nev.
Garland, Ross	.333	1	6	0	2	0	0	0	0	2	0	0	0	.333	.333	R	R	6-0	190	2-27-80	2000	Johnson City, Tenn.
Hannahan, Jack	.239	65	226	17	54	12	1	3	20	21	50	2	1	.341	.309	L	R	6-2	200	3-4-80	2001	St. Paul, Minn.
Kropf, Andy	.270	23	74	6	20	6	0	1	9	7	15	0	0	.392	.333	S	R	6-1	190	7-19-78	2000	Roswell, Ga.
Lindsey, Rodney	.261	99	371	45	97	14	6	2	20	28	94	27	9	.348	.321	R	R	5-8	170	1-28-76	1994	Opelika, Ala.
Meran, Jorge	.250	56	184	18	46	5	3	5	17	16	55	1	0	.391	.315	R	R	6-1	160	6-18-74	1993	Santo Domingo, D.R.
Neill, Ryan	.189	11	37	4	7	2	0	1	3	4	13	1	1	.324	.286	R	R	6-2	200	10-23-77	2000	Broken Arrow, Okla.
Nicholson, Derek	.294	10	34	9	10	5	1	2	7	6	11	0	1	.676	.415	L	R	6-0	200	6-17-76	1998	Redondo Beach, Calif.
Oakes, Matty	.185	9	27	1	5	1	0	0	2	0	6	0	0	.222	.185	R	R	5-11	180	8-30-79	2002	Taloga, Okla.
Perez, Jhonny	.306	94	343	45	105	14	2	3	47	30	51	8	6	.385	.361	R	R	5-10	180	10-23-76	1994	Santo Domingo, D.R.
Richardson, Corey	.255	109	377	53	96	13	1	2	22	60	80	30	5	.310	.358	S	R	6-0	160	3-9-77	1999	Lone Star, Texas
Ross, Cody	.280	105	400	73	112	28	3	19	72	44	86	16	2	.508	.352	R	L	5-11	180	12-23-80	1999	Carlsbad, N.M.
Salazar, Oscar	.215	53	191	16	41	18	1	6	26	14	36	2	1	.414	.239	R	R	5-11	170	6-27-78	1994	Maracay, Venez.
Santiago, Ramon	.280	22	75	9	21	0	2	1	7	3	12	6	0	.373	.329	S	R	5-11	150	8-31-79	1998	Las Matas de Farfan, D.R.
Sequea, Jorge	.267	112	397	55	106	24	3	5	39	41	79	13	2	.380	.343	S	R	5-10	160	10-1-80	1998	Anaco, Venez.

BATTING	AVG	G	AB	R	H	2B	3B	HR	RBI	BB	SO	SB	CS	SLG	OBP	B	T	HT	WT	DOB	1st Yr	Resides
St. Pierre, Maxim	.266	60	207	24	55	9	0	3	28	17	31	0	1	.353	.320	R	R	6-0	170	4-17-80	1997	Montreal, Quebec
Ust, Brant	.201	60	209	28	42	11	1	9	20	20	55	0	1	.392	.284	R	R	6-2	200	7-17-78	1999	Redmond, Wash.
Valera, Yohanny	.133	4	15	0	2	1	0	0	1	0	5	0	0	.200	.133	R	R	6-1	200	8-17-76	1993	San Cristobal, D.R.

PITCHING	W	L	ERA	G	GS	CG	SV	IP	H	R	ER	BB	SO	AVG	B	T	HT	WT	DOB	1st Yr	Resides
Adkins, Tim	0	1	15.88	3	0	0	0	6	11	10	10	4	6	.392	L	L	6-0	190	5-12-74	1992	Huntington, W.Va.
Arias, Pablo	5	8	6.86	29	15	0	0	106	138	94	81	60	53	.317	R	R	6-2	160	1-9-79	1996	Bani, D.R.
Borkowski, Dave	0	2	7.56	2	2	0	0	8	12	7	7	2	6	.342	R	R	6-1	220	2-7-77	1995	Monroe, Mich.
Camp, Jared	0	2	10.13	6	0	0	0	8	12	11	9	5	4	.324	R	R	6-2	190	5-4-75	1995	Huntington, W.Va.
Chipperfield, Calvin	0	1	5.79	1	1	0	0	5	5	3	3	5	5	.294	R	R	6-1	170	3-7-78	1998	Adelaide, Australia
Edmondson, Brian	3	2	4.00	38	0	0	5	45	52	27	20	12	36	.293	R	R	6-2	170	1-29-73	1991	Riverside, Calif.
2-team (5 Akron)	5	2	3.46	43	0	0	6	52	54	28	20	13	42	.270							
Farmer, Tom	6	8	5.33	18	18	1	0	103	122	68	61	32	51	.293	R	R	6-2	190	7-27-79	2001	Crestwood, Ill.
Graves, Bobby	1	2	7.62	11	0	0	0	13	18	13	11	17	14	.352	L	L	5-10	170	1-20-80	2001	Las Vegas, Nev.
Greisinger, Seth	2	0	1.29	4	4	0	0	21	12	4	3	9	21	.160	R	R	6-3	190	7-29-75	1996	Falls Church, Va.
Johnson, Jeremy	6	1	3.88	8	8	0	0	49	51	24	21	15	26	.260	R	R	6-3	170	7-19-82	2000	Mooresville, N.C.
Johnson, Mark	0	1	3.00	5	1	0	0	9	10	4	3	1	8	.277	R	R	6-3	220	5-2-75	1997	Leesburg, Fla.
Keelin, Chris	0	0	32.40	2	0	0	0	2	6	6	6	1	0	.545	R	R	6-2	190	3-3-77	1999	Sussex, N.J.
Kirsten, Rick	1	0	4.50	3	1	0	0	8	11	7	4	4	8	.323	R	R	6-0	160	7-23-78	1996	Rolling Meadows, Ill.
Lidle, Kevin	2	11	5.84	23	13	1	0	91	121	63	59	29	45	.327	S	R	5-11	170	3-22-72	1992	West Covina, Calif.
Marquetti, Agustin	0	2	6.75	8	4	0	0	19	24	20	14	17	10	.307	S	R	6-6	220	2-24-78	2002	Caracas, Venez.
Pearsall, J.J.	2	2	3.00	24	0	0	1	33	26	12	11	15	33	.213	L	L	6-2	200	9-9-73	1995	Burnt Hills, N.Y.
2-team (12 Portland)	2	3	3.06	36	0	0	1	50	44	20	17	23	51	.236							
Pearson, Terry	0	0	3.68	15	0	0	4	15	25	7	6	2	11	.373	R	R	6-0	200	11-10-71	1995	Carrollton, Ala.
Perez, Frank	0	7	5.35	31	7	0	1	72	76	48	43	36	53	.265	R	R	5-11	160	5-11-75	1998	San Francisco de Macoris, D.R.
Peters, Chris	3	3	4.73	43	0	0	0	59	70	36	31	25	56	.304	L	L	6-1	170	1-28-72	1993	Bethel Park, Pa.
Ramirez, Jose	0	3	6.00	28	0	0	0	45	54	30	30	28	37	.306	L	L	6-1	170	9-1-75	1994	Santo Domingo, D.R.
Rivera, Jimmy	5	3	2.05	40	0	0	8	61	48	17	14	16	35	.293	R	L	5-10	160	8-13-77	1995	Nizao, D.R.
Rodney, Fernando	1	0	1.33	21	0	0	11	20	14	4	3	5	18	.194	R	R	5-11	170	3-18-77	1997	Santo Domingo, D.R.
Smith, Clint	5	13	6.19	38	19	1	0	121	169	92	83	59	76	.336	R	R	6-4	180	9-4-76	1998	Claremore, Okla.
Tekavec, Nate	6	9	7.09	27	27	0	0	141	196	123	111	53	56	.333	R	R	6-5	200	5-2-79	2000	Concord, Ohio
Van Hekken, Andy	4	7	3.83	21	21	1	0	134	138	69	57	34	97	.270	R	L	6-3	170	7-31-79	1998	Holland, Mich.
Watson, Greg	0	1	6.23	7	0	0	0	9	13	6	6	2	8	.361	R	R	6-2	160	1-8-77	1999	Tampa, Fla.

FIELDING

Catcher	PCT	G	PO	A	E	DP	PB
Cleveland	.979	16	84	9	2	1	3
Garland	.952	1	17	3	1	2	2
Kropf	.952	17	68	11	4	1	0
Meran	.984	48	285	32	5	4	5
Oakes	.971	6	32	1	1	0	0
St. Pierre	.991	58	299	35	3	2	7
Valera	1.000	4	25	3	0	0	2

First Base	PCT	G	PO	A	E	DP
Carter	.989	128	1073	52	13	113
Kropf	.938	2	15	0	1	3
Meran	1.000	7	25	2	0	2
Nicholson	1.000	1	6	0	0	0
Oakes	.800	2	4	0	1	0
Perez	1.000	10	66	5	0	5
Salazar	1.000	1	6	0	0	1

Second Base	PCT	G	PO	A	E	DP
Castillo	.966	7	10	18	1	4
Kropf	1.000	1	0	1	0	0
Perez	.970	26	48	83	4	16
Salazar	.990	20	56	48	1	21
Sequea	.982	95	179	247	8	58

Third Base	PCT	G	PO	A	E	DP
Bautista	1.000	3	4	3	0	0
Castillo	.000	1	0	0	0	0
Hannahan	.958	64	42	163	9	13
Nicholson	.818	3	2	7	2	0
Perez	.949	51	14	23	2	1
Ust	.944	58	44	140	11	23

Shortstop	PCT	G	PO	A	E	DP
Bautista	.934	78	119	205	23	54
Castillo	.882	26	44	61	14	11
Perez	.846	8	7	15	4	1
Salazar	1.000	15	16	24	0	6
Santiago	.966	21	26	58	3	7

Outfield	PCT	G	PO	A	E	DP
Airoso	.983	51	111	4	2	1
Arias	.000	1	0	0	0	0
Camilo	.966	37	55	2	2	1
Edmondson	.000	1	0	0	0	0
Lindsey	.978	97	214	10	5	2
Meran	1.000	1	2	1	0	0
Neill	1.000	6	10	1	0	0
Perez	.946	21	33	2	2	1
Richardson	.993	106	272	14	2	3
Ross	.975	102	216	16	6	2
Salazar	.920	15	21	2	2	0

LAKELAND TIGERS — High Class A

FLORIDA STATE LEAGUE

BATTING	AVG	G	AB	R	H	2B	3B	HR	RBI	BB	SO	SB	CS	SLG	OBP	B	T	HT	WT	DOB	1st Yr	Resides
Allec, Jason	.667	1	3	0	2	2	0	0	0	0	1	0	0	1.333	.667	R	R	6-3	200	3-19-81	2002	Palmdale, Calif.
Bautista, Rayner	.231	9	39	8	9	1	1	0	2	4	10	1	0	.308	.302	R	R	5-11	150	9-17-78	1995	Nizao, D.R.
Boone, Matt	.246	51	195	24	48	5	1	3	19	11	51	3	3	.328	.293	R	R	6-2	170	7-18-79	1997	Villa Park, Calif.
Camilo, Juan	.293	81	283	48	83	24	5	8	53	45	73	25	8	.498	.393	L	R	6-0	200	6-24-76	1996	Santo Domingo, D.R.
Castillo, Carlos	.190	5	21	0	4	0	0	0	0	3	0	0	0	.190	.190	S	R	5-10	170	1-26-80	2002	San Jose, Costa Rica
Cleveland, Russ	.221	25	86	7	19	7	0	4	13	3	18	1	1	.442	.264	R	R	6-3	200	12-26-79	1998	Las Vegas, Nev.
Daigle, Leo	.258	129	466	75	120	23	0	23	85	49	99	3	1	.455	.346	R	R	6-3	220	9-18-79	1997	Spring Valley, Calif.
Flamont, Sam	.156	16	45	3	7	1	0	0	7	5	14	0	1	.178	.235	L	R	6-0	210	3-17-80	2002	Interlochen, Mich.
Garland, Ross	.207	31	87	11	18	3	0	1	10	7	19	0	0	.276	.296	R	R	6-0	190	2-27-80	2000	Johnson City, Tenn.
Hannahan, Jack	.272	66	246	28	67	11	1	6	42	36	44	9	3	.398	.362	L	R	6-2	200	3-4-80	2001	St. Paul, Minn.
Heath, Demetrius	.258	37	128	15	33	5	2	1	13	6	22	8	3	.352	.294	R	R	5-10	170	1-23-81	2001	Bethel, N.C.
Hernandez, Anderson	.259	123	410	52	106	13	7	2	42	33	102	16	14	.339	.314	S	R	5-9	150	10-30-82	2001	Santo Domingo, D.R.
Jenkins, Neil	.241	56	228	27	55	9	2	10	34	9	87	3	0	.430	.276	R	R	6-5	200	7-17-80	1999	Jupiter, Fla.
Johnson, Forrest	.191	12	47	4	9	1	0	1	2	2	8	0	1	.277	.269	R	R	6-2	190	3-21-79	2000	Rialto, Calif.
Kropf, Andy	.474	5	19	2	9	1	0	0	3	1	2	0	0	.526	.524	S	R	6-1	190	7-19-78	2000	Roswell, Ga.
Logan, Nook	.269	124	506	75	136	14	7	2	26	40	111	55	16	.336	.321	S	R	6-2	180	11-28-79	2000	Nashville, Tenn.
Neill, Ryan	.196	43	143	24	28	6	0	3	13	20	43	8	1	.301	.301	R	R	6-2	200	10-23-77	2000	Broken Arrow, Okla.
Quattlebaum, Hugh	.155	20	58	8	9	2	0	0	1	10	16	0	1	.190	.299	R	R	6-4	200	6-26-78	2000	Andover, Mass.
Sanchez, Danilo	.177	34	96	10	17	2	0	3	12	13	18	0	0	.292	.295	S	R	5-11	180	10-25-80	1997	Santo Domingo, D.R.
St. Pierre, Maxim	.256	55	195	20	50	12	0	4	27	13	30	2	4	.379	.324	R	R	6-0	170	4-17-80	1997	Montreal, Quebec
Tousa, Scott	.215	117	395	55	85	14	0	3	33	68	75	14	4	.273	.337	L	R	5-11	180	8-3-79	2001	St. George, Utah
Ust, Brant	.236	61	216	26	51	12	2	5	29	21	47	9	0	.380	.310	R	R	6-2	200	7-17-78	1999	Redmond, Wash.
Walker, Matt	.244	112	409	66	100	23	0	13	53	29	94	10	1	.396	.301	R	R	6-2	200	12-3-77	2000	Gibsonia, Pa.
Woods, Michael	.225	33	111	20	25	6	4	2	11	28	25	7	5	.405	.385	R	R	6-1	200	9-11-80	2001	Baton Rouge, La.
Yount, Andy	.154	39	123	10	19	3	1	2	15	23	56	1	3	.244	.311	R	R	6-2	180	2-14-77	1995	Kingwood, Texas

PITCHING	W	L	ERA	G	GS	CG	SV	IP	H	R	ER	BB	SO	AVG	B	T	HT	WT	DOB	1st Yr	Resides
Bonderman, Jeremy	0	1	6.00	2	2	1	0	12	11	8	8	4	10	.261	R	R	6-2	210	10-28-82	2001	Pasco, Wash.
Chipperfield, Calvin	9	10	3.29	27	20	3	0	126	97	57	46	74	114	.216	R	R	6-1	170	3-7-78	1998	Adelaide, Australia
Clark, Wade	0	2	8.14	5	5	0	0	21	33	22	19	14	9	.383	R	R	6-7	230	7-1-80	2002	Los Olivos, Calif.
Corrado, Matt	4	2	4.87	37	4	0	3	94	102	52	51	36	58	.280	L	R	6-6	200	8-4-78	2001	Sevierville, Tenn.
Detillion, Jamie	4	0	1.50	7	0	0	0	12	8	2	2	5		.195	L	L	6-2	216	6-22-78	2000	Tiffin, Ohio
Frasor, Jason	5	6	3.54	24	24	0	0	117	112	54	46	46	87	.256	R	R	5-10	170	8-9-77	1999	Oak Forest, Ill.
Gerk, Jordan	0	1	4.96	8	0	0	0	16	20	10	9	3	14	.298	L	L	6-1	180	7-6-79	2000	Kelowna, B.C.
Hamman, Corey	1	0	0.49	16	0	0	4	18	11	1	1	3	18	.166	L	L	6-2	190	4-12-80	2002	Flanders, N.J.
Howell, Michael	0	2	5.46	6	6	0	0	30	32	21	18	10	28	.285	R	R	6-4	200	11-9-79	2001	Binghamton, N.Y.
Johnson, Jeremy	7	1	3.10	15	7	0	1	58	50	20	20	21	42	.231	R	R	6-3	170	7-19-82	2000	Mooresville, N.C.
Keelin, Chris	1	2	2.92	19	0	0	8	25	18	9	8	20	30	.211	R	R	6-2	190	3-3-77	1999	Sussex, N.J.
Koenig, Ross	2	0	9.69	8	0	0	0	13	12	17	14	10	9	.266	R	R	6-3	170	5-4-80	2001	Festus, Mo.
Larrison, Preston	10	5	2.39	21	19	3	0	120	86	39	32	45	92	.199	R	R	6-4	210	11-19-80	2001	Aurora, Ill.
Leuenberger, Jeff	0	0	5.40	3	0	0	0	5	6	3	3	4	3	.304	R	R	5-11	180	10-15-78	2002	Orange, Calif.
Lidle, Kevin	1	3	2.79	9	6	0	1	48	37	17	15	6	31	.211	S	R	5-11	170	3-22-72	1992	West Covina, Calif.
Marx, Tommy	6	8	5.04	30	19	2	0	123	115	84	69	83	64	.254	R	L	6-7	200	9-5-79	1998	West Bloomfield, Mich.
Matthews, Barry	1	2	7.46	12	5	0	0	35	42	29	29	14	32	.297	L	L	6-0	180	4-6-78	2001	Northridge, Calif.
Moehler, Brian	1	1	2.92	2	2	0	0	12	10	9	4	1	7	.208	R	R	6-3	230	12-31-71	1993	Marietta, Ga.
Ostlund, Ian	2	3	2.89	29	0	0	3	37	30	13	12	8	30	.215	R	L	6-1	200	10-17-78	2001	Singers Glen, Va.
Perez, Frank	2	2	5.71	8	0	0	0	17	13	11	11	5	24	.196	R	R	5-11	180	5-11-75	1998	San Francisco de Macoris, D.R.
Pineda, Jairo	2	5	3.32	33	0	0	5	57	59	26	21	26	30	.270	R	R	6-3	180	9-25-76	1997	Granada, Nicaragua
Ramirez, Jose	0	1	5.48	13	0	0	0	23	26	18	14	6	20	.273	L	L	6-1	170	9-1-75	1994	Santo Domingo, D.R.
Rodney, Lee	6	4	3.74	22	13	0	0	84	79	40	35	40	60	.250	R	R	6-2	180	11-6-77	2000	Dacula, Ga.
Smith, Dan	0	0	1.29	9	0	0	0	14	10	3	2	5	13	.204	R	R	6-4	210	11-29-78	2001	Bonne Terre, Mo.
Watson, Greg	3	1	4.87	16	0	0	5	20	25	16	11	8	15	.290	R	R	6-2	160	1-8-77	1999	Tampa, Fla.
Woodyard, Mark	2	8	7.64	17	7	0	2	66	81	62	56	32	22	.302	R	R	6-2	180	12-19-78	2000	Grand Bay, Ala.

FIELDING

Catcher	PCT	G	PO	A	E	DP	PB
Allec	1.000	1	8	0	0	0	0
Cleveland	.986	24	127	9	2	1	6
Garland	.978	31	167	11	4	1	7
Kropf	1.000	4	20	1	0	0	0
Sanchez	.966	34	196	29	8	3	5
St. Pierre	.988	55	366	54	5	8	10

First Base	PCT	G	PO	A	E	DP
Daigle	.987	126	1046	74	15	115
Johnson	.938	3	29	1	2	4
Neill	1.000	5	44	3	0	5
Quattlebaum	1.000	2	8	0	0	0
Ust	.974	5	33	4	1	5
Walker	1.000	1	13	2	0	0

Second Base	PCT	G	PO	A	E	DP
Flamont	.000	1	0	0	0	0
Heath	.951	25	46	51	5	16
Tousa	.983	90	169	241	7	68
Woods	.962	31	51	75	5	14

Third Base	PCT	G	PO	A	E	DP
Hannahan	.942	66	44	150	12	21
Neill	.500	1	0	1	1	0
Quattlebaum	.667	1	1	1	1	0
Tousa	.910	18	17	44	6	4
Ust	.933	57	45	135	13	13

Shortstop	PCT	G	PO	A	E	DP
Bautista	.947	9	12	24	2	3

	PCT	G	PO	A	E	DP
Castillo	1.000	4	2	12	0	1
Hernandez	.953	121	209	334	27	88
Tousa	1.000	9	10	22	0	6

Outfield	PCT	G	PO	A	E	DP
Boone	.964	36	51	2	2	1
Camilo	.986	74	132	7	2	0
Daigle	1.000	1	2	0	0	0
Flamont	1.000	6	3	3	0	1
Jenkins	.969	55	118	5	4	2
Logan	.970	122	316	7	10	1
Neill	.946	13	35	0	2	0
Walker	.979	90	187	2	4	0
Yount	.917	26	40	4	4	1

WEST MICHIGAN WHITECAPS — Low Class A

MIDWEST LEAGUE

BATTING	AVG	G	AB	R	H	2B	3B	HR	RBI	BB	SO	SB	CS	SLG	OBP	B	T	HT	WT	DOB	1st Yr	Resides
Allec, Jason	.000	3	7	0	0	0	0	0	0	0	3	0	0	.000	.000	R	R	6-3	200	3-19-81	2002	Palmdale, Calif.
Anderson, Sam	.163	16	43	1	7	0	0	0	5	2	12	0	0	.163	.200	R	R	5-11	180	3-23-79	2001	Mesquite, Texas
Brostrom, Jeremy	.256	42	125	9	32	10	1	0	13	13	24	1	0	.352	.324	L	L	6-3	190	1-19-78	2001	Peachtree City, Ga.
Durham, Miles	.222	4	18	1	4	2	0	0	0	0	3	0	0	.333	.222	L	R	6-3	190	8-19-78	2000	Dallas, Texas
Francia, Juan	.270	128	503	94	136	13	5	2	41	53	94	53	14	.328	.346	S	R	5-9	140	1-4-82	1998	San Antonio, Venez.
Gonzalez, Juan	.252	120	444	71	112	17	8	5	50	64	104	21	11	.360	.353	S	R	6-0	160	2-23-82	1999	Valencia, Venez.
Kelly, Donald	.286	128	455	72	130	21	5	1	59	59	40	9	6	.360	.368	L	R	6-4	190	2-15-80	2001	Pittsburgh, Pa.
Kennedy, Jason	.252	41	131	15	33	8	1	0	16	19	36	0	1	.328	.388	R	R	6-3	200	7-14-79	2002	Minneapolis, Minn.
Knoedler, Jason	.209	135	417	63	87	14	6	5	33	68	145	18	8	.307	.324	S	R	6-1	190	7-17-80	2001	Springfield, Ill.
Kolodzey, Chris	.225	66	151	16	34	10	2	1	18	12	41	2	0	.338	.290	R	R	6-0	200	7-15-79	2001	Cherry Hill, N.J.
Lugo, Alfredo	.289	89	235	25	68	14	1	0	31	25	50	1	2	.357	.357	R	R	6-2	190	7-18-79	2001	Caracas, Venez.
Mattle, David	.272	136	511	62	139	26	10	7	68	46	110	9	4	.403	.334	L	R	6-2	200	12-21-79	2001	Barberton, Ohio
Mejia, Gilberto	.246	19	69	17	17	4	2	2	15	11	23	4	2	.449	.341	S	R	5-9	160	9-1-82	2000	Bani, D.R.
Neill, Ryan	.225	62	204	25	46	8	1	4	20	21	61	15	1	.333	.300	S	R	6-2	200	10-23-77	2000	Broken Arrow, Okla.
Peguero, Miguel	.069	14	29	1	2	0	0	0	2	0	9	0	0	.069	.097	S	R	6-0	160	9-29-79	1997	Santo Domingo, D.R.
Rabelo, Mike	.195	123	410	32	80	13	1	2	41	42	91	3	1	.246	.281	S	R	6-1	190	1-17-80	2001	New Port Richey, Fla.
Raburn, Ryan	.220	40	150	27	33	10	1	6	28	16	46	0	2	.420	.306	R	R	6-1	180	4-17-81	2001	Plant City, Fla.
Scott, Mike	.221	45	113	15	25	4	0	1	11	15	21	4	1	.283	.318	L	L	5-10	170	11-17-78	2001	Darien, Conn.
Stringham, Jed	.167	13	36	5	6	2	0	1	6	6	13	0	0	.306	.273	R	R	6-3	210	12-28-77	2001	Provo, Utah
Tejeda, Juan	.300	137	524	68	157	34	6	11	106	60	89	5	1	.450	.372	R	R	6-2	190	1-26-82	1999	Santiago, D.R.
Trezza, Alex	.211	18	38	2	8	4	0	0	5	3	11	0	0	.316	.268	L	R	6-3	210	9-1-80	2001	Middletown, N.Y.
Varner, Noochie	.176	4	17	1	3	1	1	0	1	0	4	0	0	.353	.176	R	R	6-0	180	12-7-80	2001	Cynthiana, Ky.
2-team (128 Dayton)	.305	133	534	83	163	28	13	10	70	32	121	37	4	.463	.349							
Yount, Andy	.128	18	47	2	6	1	0	0	4	6	32	1	0	.149	.232	R	R	6-2	180	2-14-77	1995	Kingwood, Texas

PITCHING	W	L	ERA	G	GS	CG	SV	IP	H	R	ER	BB	SO	AVG	B	T	HT	WT	DOB	1st Yr	Resides
Badgley, Daniel	0	1	3.09	21	0	0	0	32	32	18	11	22	19	.266	R	R	6-5	220	1-22-78	2002	McHenry, Ill.
Birtwell, John	7	2	1.59	58	0	0	0	79	48	19	14	18	101	.175	R	R	6-1	190	9-4-79	2001	Walpole, Mass.
Coenen, Matt	14	8	3.38	28	28	2	0	165	148	69	62	65	141	.239	L	L	6-6	230	3-13-80	2001	St. Michael's, Md.
Diaz, Luis	2	1	10.13	7	2	0	0	19	30	23	21	8	19	.330	S	R	6-0	160	4-16-78	1997	Nizao, D.R.
Dunn, Jay	1	5	4.89	9	9	0	0	46	51	33	25	20	32	.274	R	R	6-4	210	6-30-81	2001	Charlotte, N.C.
Fuell, Jerrod	5	4	2.34	51	0	0	2	77	68	25	20	20	63	.238	R	R	6-4	210	10-3-80	1999	Tucson, Ariz.
Gerk, Jordan	0	0	7.30	8	0	0	0	12	19	10	10	6	8	.380	L	L	6-1	180	7-6-79	2000	Kelowna, B.C.
Gonzales, James	2	3	6.92	21	2	0	1	39	45	35	30	22	30	.281	R	R	6-1	180	8-4-79	2001	Las Vegas, Nev.
Johnson, Jeremy	1	0	4.26	6	0	0	0	13	14	6	6	2	11	.274	R	R	6-3	170	7-19-82	2000	Mooresville, N.C.

PITCHING

PITCHING	W	L	ERA	G	GS	CG	SV	IP	H	R	ER	BB	SO	AVG	B	T	HT	WT	DOB	1st Yr	Resides
Kobow, Mike	2	2	1.99	55	0	0	31	59	41	13	13	23	50	.194	R	R	6-4	190	4-9-79	2001	Hutchinson, Minn.
Leu, Trevor	2	0	4.53	37	0	0	0	58	53	31	29	49	79	.237	L	L	6-2	200	12-29-78	2001	Bartlesville, Okla.
Lewis, Jeremy	2	3	5.27	6	6	0	0	27	31	21	16	11	15	.274	R	L	6-4	180	9-12-80	1999	Concord, N.C.
McDowell, Kevin	11	6	2.60	27	27	0	0	166	156	63	48	64	123	.250	L	L	6-2	200	11-20-78	2001	Cheswick, Pa.
Moates, Jason	11	5	3.82	28	25	0	0	148	140	70	63	68	103	.252	R	R	6-2	210	8-22-78	2001	Columbia, Tenn.
Myers, Damien	0	0	4.70	11	0	0	0	8	8	6	4	5	9	.242	L	L	6-0	180	11-3-80	2002	New York, N.Y.
Petty, Chad	15	10	3.24	28	28	3	0	161	155	73	58	77	119	.254	L	L	6-4	200	2-17-82	2000	West Farmington, Ohio
Smith, Dan	0	0	1.50	5	0	0	1	12	9	3	2	5	4	.214	R	R	6-4	210	11-29-78	2001	Bonne Terre, Mo.
Stockman, Landon	3	5	3.97	43	0	0	4	57	55	29	25	27	53	.251	R	R	6-2	190	8-28-79	2001	Dickson, Tenn.
Warren, Andy	5	2	2.45	13	13	0	0	70	69	24	19	35	29	.266	R	R	6-4	190	6-11-78	2000	Conroe, Texas

FIELDING

Catcher	PCT	G	PO	A	E	DP	PB
Allec	.917	3	21	1	2	0	1
Anderson	1.000	15	90	15	0	1	2
Rabelo	.984	122	813	102	15	5	16
Trezza	.977	15	81	4	2	1	4

First Base	PCT	G	PO	A	E	DP
Gonzalez	1.000	1	1	0	0	0
Lugo	.967	6	27	2	1	2
Neill	1.000	6	22	1	0	1
Tejeda	.988	136	1187	84	16	118

Second Base	PCT	G	PO	A	E	DP
Francia	.947	125	312	351	37	91

	PCT	G	PO	A	E	DP
Gonzalez	.966	13	31	26	2	11
Mejia	.968	6	15	15	1	5
Peguero	1.000	2	5	3	0	3

Third Base	PCT	G	PO	A	E	DP
Gonzalez	.910	77	49	153	20	18
Lugo	.936	61	29	102	9	12
Peguero	.947	7	3	15	1	1
Raburn	.786	17	9	35	12	4

Shortstop	PCT	G	PO	A	E	DP
Gonzalez	.966	33	38	103	5	15
Kelly	.951	111	168	374	28	72
Lugo	1.000	1	0	1	0	1

Outfield	PCT	G	PO	A	E	DP
Brostrom	.938	16	15	0	1	0
Durham	1.000	4	8	1	0	0
Kennedy	.955	38	41	1	2	0
Knoedler	.977	134	299	5	7	2
Kolodzey	.968	51	60	0	2	0
Lugo	1.000	1	1	0	0	0
Mattle	.970	133	224	5	7	1
Neill	.985	43	63	3	1	0
Scott	.946	32	49	4	3	0
Stringham	1.000	1	1	0	0	0
Varner	1.000	4	13	0	0	0
Yount	.857	9	10	2	2	0

ONEONTA TIGERS — Short-Season A

NEW YORK-PENN LEAGUE

BATTING	AVG	G	AB	R	H	2B	3B	HR	RBI	BB	SO	SB	CS	SLG	OBP	B	T	HT	WT	DOB	1st Yr	Resides
Allec, Jason	.333	7	24	2	8	1	0	0	5	2	6	0	0	.375	.407	R	R	6-3	200	3-19-81	2002	Palmdale, Calif.
Caravella, Drew	.210	45	167	19	35	5	1	0	16	17	17	0	1	.251	.294	L	L	6-2	210	6-16-80	2002	Columbus, Ohio
Carlin, Luke	.227	45	150	23	34	5	2	0	10	34	28	0	2	.287	.371	S	R	5-11	180	12-20-80	2002	Aylmer, Quebec
De Leon, Virgilio	.223	42	157	22	35	5	1	4	16	8	52	10	3	.344	.268	R	R	6-2	170	4-3-80	1998	San Pedro de Macoris, D.R.
Dean, Herman	.140	35	107	17	15	1	1	1	7	7	35	3	5	.196	.197	R	R	6-3	190	11-25-80	2001	Monrovia, Calif.
Garcia, David	.224	18	58	5	13	2	0	1	9	2	14	0	0	.310	.286	S	R	6-0	160	2-24-82	2002	Temecula, Calif.
Granderson, Curtis	.344	52	212	45	73	15	4	3	34	20	35	9	2	.495	.417	L	R	6-1	180	3-16-81	2002	Lynwood, Ill.
Heath, Demetrius	.259	35	143	25	37	8	3	0	9	12	13	9	3	.357	.327	R	R	5-10	170	1-23-81	2001	Bethel, N.C.
Kennedy, Jason	.225	13	40	10	9	1	2	0	7	15	11	1	1	.350	.446	R	R	6-3	200	7-14-79	2002	Minneapolis, Minn.
Loomis, Corey	.218	32	110	18	24	4	3	0	17	13	39	2	1	.309	.304	L	R	6-1	180	10-23-80	2002	Pemberville, Ohio
Maples, Chris	.200	31	115	17	23	6	2	2	16	10	23	1	0	.339	.262	R	R	5-10	180	10-31-79	2002	Hillsborough, N.C.
McDonald, Kevin	.237	30	93	13	22	5	0	2	10	11	17	0	0	.355	.317	L	R	6-1	210	3-8-80	2002	Rockaway, N.J.
Mendez, Victor	.282	59	241	36	68	11	5	3	31	20	50	16	5	.407	.338	S	R	5-11	180	6-28-80	1998	Las Matas de Farfan, D.R.
Reynolds, Wilton	.232	69	272	41	63	7	6	9	57	29	75	10	3	.401	.319	R	R	6-4	190	3-5-80	2002	Sacramento, Calif.
Romprey, Ed	.259	52	174	25	45	7	0	2	20	21	40	2	3	.333	.352	R	R	6-0	180	4-13-80	2002	Victorville, Calif.
Roughton, Jody	.308	54	208	30	64	10	1	3	38	19	43	0	1	.409	.374	L	R	6-1	190	5-6-81	2002	Carthage, Mo.
Trezza, Alex	.353	12	34	3	12	2	0	0	4	4	6	0	0	.412	.410	L	R	6-3	210	9-1-80	2001	Middletown, N.Y.
Watson, Rob	.280	62	232	38	65	22	3	1	37	29	32	2	0	.414	.371	R	R	5-10	180	12-31-79	2002	Riverside, Calif.

GAMES BY POSITION: C—Allec 3, Carlin 44, McDonald 30. **1B**—Caravella 45, Loomis 1, Roughton 20, Trezza 12. **2B**—Heath 33, Loomis 19, Watson 22. **3B**—Garcia, Loomis, Maples 31, Roughton 8, Watson 31. **SS**—Garcia 12, Loomis 8, Romprey 52, Watson 4. **OF**—De Leon 18, Dean 27, Granderson 51, Kennedy 13, Mendez 59, Reynolds 61.

PITCHING	W	L	ERA	G	GS	CG	SV	IP	H	R	ER	BB	SO	AVG	B	T	HT	WT	DOB	1st Yr	Resides
Barrios, Rafael	1	0	0.00	2	0	0	0	3	1	0	0	1	3	.100	R	R	6-3	170	7-10-81	1998	Zaraza, Venez.
Campbell, Dayle	5	1	3.35	20	1	0	0	38	33	16	14	28	28	.237	R	R	6-7	190	9-30-78	1999	Carson, Calif.
Carlson, Jesse	2	2	1.66	19	0	0	0	38	19	8	7	10	47	.146	L	L	6-1	160	12-31-80	2002	Kensington, Conn.
Connolly, Jon	5	3	4.01	14	14	0	0	85	102	46	38	10	50	.293	R	L	6-0	200	8-24-83	2001	Oneonta, N.Y.
Delacruz, Eulogio	0	0	23.14	2	0	0	0	2	7	8	6	4	4	.500	R	R	5-11	160	3-12-84	2002	Santo Domingo, D.R.
Diaz, Luis	4	1	3.24	9	6	0	0	42	31	19	15	15	45	.202	S	R	6-0	160	4-16-78	1997	Nizao, D.R.
Dunn, Jay	4	0	0.67	5	5	0	0	27	17	4	2	5	14	.180	R	R	6-4	210	6-30-81	2001	Charlotte, N.C.
Figueroa, Juan	0	2	3.81	28	0	0	21	28	23	14	12	13	34	.219	R	R	6-0	180	10-8-81	2001	Carolina, P.R.
Gerk, Jordan	1	0	1.86	10	0	0	0	10	9	3	2	2	11	.243	L	L	6-1	180	7-6-79	2000	Kelowna, B.C.
Gonzales, James	1	0	5.30	7	1	0	0	19	18	12	11	10	10	.250	R	R	6-1	180	8-4-79	2001	Las Vegas, Nev.
Graham, Jason	1	1	3.20	14	0	0	1	20	15	11	7	9	12	.200	R	R	6-3	190	9-24-79	2002	Atlantis, Fla.
Hamman, Corey	0	0	0.00	3	0	0	1	7	2	0	0	0	8	.095	L	L	6-2	190	4-12-80	2002	Flanders, N.J.
Hancock, Everett	0	1	4.61	13	0	0	0	14	24	8	7	7	6	.406	L	L	6-0	180	2-27-80	2002	Havelock, N.C.
Johnston, Rikki	8	2	3.17	15	12	0	0	82	79	37	29	29	60	.251	L	L	6-1	180	4-2-81	1998	Victoria, Australia
Kieninger, Billy	1	2	2.90	16	0	0	3	31	32	12	10	7	22	.264	R	R	6-4	200	12-31-79	2002	Xenia, Ohio
Koenig, Ross	2	3	1.67	18	0	0	0	32	18	9	6	16	33	.159	R	R	6-3	170	5-4-80	2001	Festus, Mo.
Lewis, Jeremy	4	3	4.09	16	11	0	1	70	76	42	32	26	45	.273	R	L	6-4	180	9-12-80	1999	Concord, N.C.
Myers, Damien	1	0	0.00	7	0	0	0	16	6	0	0	3	15	.113	L	L	6-0	180	11-3-80	2002	New York, N.Y.
Parris, Matt	1	1	5.00	2	2	0	0	9	9	5	5	3	8	.257	R	R	6-3	190	10-4-82	2000	Ventura, Calif.
Pender, Matt	2	2	2.31	9	9	0	0	39	34	16	10	12	35	.234	R	R	6-5	210	6-11-81	2002	Kathleen, Ga.
Pickford, Troy	2	0	0.98	4	4	0	0	18	10	2	2	5	14	.153	R	R	6-8	220	8-9-79	2002	Fresno, Calif.
Sanchez, Humberto	2	2	3.62	9	9	0	0	32	29	18	13	21	26	.243	R	R	6-6	230	5-28-83	2001	Bronx, N.Y.
Steinborn, Chris	0	1	3.38	2	0	0	1	3	3	1	1	2	4	.300	L	L	6-4	210	3-23-82	2002	Akron, Ohio

LAKELAND TIGERS — Rookie

GULF COAST LEAGUE

BATTING	AVG	G	AB	R	H	2B	3B	HR	RBI	BB	SO	SB	CS	SLG	OBP	B	T	HT	WT	DOB	1st Yr	Resides
Allec, Jason	.333	6	21	2	7	3	0	0	1	1	4	0	0	.476	.364	R	R	6-3	200	3-19-81	2002	Palmdale, Calif.

BATTING	AVG	G	AB	R	H	2B	3B	HR	RBI	BB	SO	SB	CS	SLG	OBP	B	T	HT	WT	DOB	1st Yr	Resides
Assael, Samuel	.184	16	38	4	7	1	0	0	4	4	8	0	0	.211	.283	R	R	6-0	190	4-18-80	2002	Glendora, Calif.
Blue, Vincent	.219	56	183	20	40	5	4	0	7	17	38	20	3	.290	.282	L	R	6-2	180	2-8-83	2001	Houston, Texas
Boone, Matt	.333	4	15	1	5	1	0	0	3	1	5	0	0	.400	.375	R	R	6-2	170	7-18-79	1997	Villa Park, Calif.
Castillo, Carlos	.263	6	19	3	5	2	0	1	2	0	4	0	2	.526	.300	S	R	5-10	170	1-26-80	2002	San Jose, Costa Rica
Clevlen, Brent	.330	28	103	14	34	2	3	3	21	8	24	2	1	.495	.372	R	R	6-2	190	10-27-83	2002	Cedar Park, Texas
Cotto, Pedro	.200	13	45	4	9	2	0	0	1	0	4	3	0	.244	.200	L	L	5-11	170	5-26-82	2002	San Juan, P.R.
Flamont, Sam	.331	40	130	26	43	4	1	1	17	24	12	5	5	.400	.436	L	R	6-0	210	3-17-80	2002	Interlochen, Mich.
Flowers, Bo	.278	26	97	18	27	4	1	0	7	3	24	8	1	.340	.320	R	R	6-0	180	11-12-83	2002	Maywood, Ill.
Garland, Ross	.133	6	15	0	2	0	0	0	2	0	1	0	0	.133	.133	R	R	6-0	190	2-27-80	2000	Johnson City, Tenn.
Gonzalez, Jose	.237	45	139	22	33	3	4	0	8	19	28	7	2	.317	.327	S	R	5-9	140	3-29-84	2001	San Cristobal, D.R.
Long, Robert	.000	3	2	0	0	0	0	0	0	0	2	0	0	.000	.000	R	R	6-0	200	1-30-80	2002	Holland, Mich.
Maples, Chris	.412	4	17	6	7	3	0	1	4	0	1	0	0	.765	.444	R	R	5-10	180	10-31-79	2002	Hillsborough, N.C.
McKinney, Garth	.276	11	29	3	8	1	0	0	3	4	10	2	2	.310	.364	R	R	6-3	210	5-7-82	2002	Johnson City, Tenn.
Mendez, Rafael	.136	25	59	3	8	1	0	2	5	9	24	0	0	.254	.257	R	R	6-0	190	4-24-84	2002	Caguas, P.R.
Moore, Scott	.293	40	133	18	39	6	2	4	25	10	31	1	2	.459	.349	L	R	6-2	180	11-17-83	2002	Stateline, Nev.
Oakes, Matty	.223	37	121	12	27	7	0	0	16	9	23	0	0	.281	.286	R	R	5-11	180	8-30-79	2002	Taloga, Okla.
Ortiz, Edgar	.248	34	113	10	28	8	0	2	10	8	23	2	2	.372	.331	R	R	6-3	220	2-1-79	2002	Lakewood, Calif.
Raburn, Ryan	.300	8	30	4	9	3	1	1	5	3	7	0	0	.567	.364	R	R	6-0	180	4-17-81	2001	Plant City, Fla.
Reyes, Angel	.200	37	100	8	20	5	0	1	6	5	34	0	0	.280	.245	R	R	6-3	180	1-9-84	2002	Santo Domingo, D.R.
Roa, Joel	.250	14	40	1	10	2	0	0	2	3	9	0	1	.300	.318	R	R	6-0	170	1-2-84	2001	Santo Domingo, D.R.
Roughton, Jody	.400	5	10	1	4	1	0	2	4	6	2	1	0	.680	.516	L	R	6-1	190	5-6-81	2002	Carthage, Mo.
Sanchez, Danilo	.111	11	27	2	3	0	1	1	3	2	5	0	0	.296	.172	R	R	5-11	180	10-25-80	1997	Santo Domingo, D.R.
Sovie, Robbie	.188	24	80	9	15	1	0	0	7	2	24	3	2	.200	.207	R	R	6-0	200	11-24-83	2002	Macon, Ga.
Williams, Edwin	.261	31	92	4	24	1	2	0	8	7	12	6	3	.315	.343	L	L	6-1	170	1-16-83	2001	San Pedro de Macoris, D.R.
Williams, Matt	.181	55	160	15	29	3	2	0	10	11	37	3	8	.225	.250	S	R	6-2	170	11-18-83	2001	Los Angeles, Calif.
Wise, Brad	.177	20	62	2	11	1	0	0	6	6	11	0	1	.194	.254	L	R	6-2	170	1-18-84	2000	Parkwood, Australia

GAMES BY POSITION: C—Allec 6, Garland 6, Long 3, Oakes 33, Roa 14, Sanchez 10. **1B**—Cotto 11, McKinney 1, Oakes 5, Ortiz 29, Wise 18. **2B**—Blue 1, Castillo 1, Flamont 1, Gonzalez 45, M. Williams 12, Woods 7. **3B**—Castillo 3, Flamont 4, Flowers 1, Maples 4, Mendez 24, Raburn 6, Reyes 18, M. Williams 12. **SS**—Castillo 2, Moore 35, Reyes 20, Roughton 1, M. Williams 10. **OF**—Blue 55, Clevlen 25, Cotto 1, Flamont 33, Flowers 23, McKinney 8, Ortiz 1, Sovie 7, E. Williams 22, M. Williams 25.

PITCHING	W	L	ERA	G	GS	CG	SV	IP	H	R	ER	BB	SO	AVG	B	T	HT	WT	DOB	1st Yr	Resides
Arias, Javier	1	5	7.92	15	4	0	0	31	46	34	27	17	33	.345	R	R	6-0	160	10-30-83	2001	Altamira, D.R.
Barrios, Rafael	0	3	5.40	20	0	0	4	20	28	15	12	13	13	.325	R	R	6-3	170	7-10-81	1998	Zaraza, Venez.
Borkowski, Dave	0	0	8.44	3	2	0	0	5	9	5	5	0	4	.360	R	R	6-1	220	2-7-77	1995	Monroe, Mich.
Clark, Wade	3	0	1.39	7	5	1	0	32	23	8	5	9	33	.196	R	R	6-7	230	7-1-80	2002	Los Olivos, Calif.
Delacruz, Eulogio	1	1	2.63	20	0	0	1	38	40	24	11	21	46	.259	R	R	5-11	160	3-12-84	2002	Santo Domingo, D.R.
Feliz, Welinton	2	6	2.76	20	3	0	4	49	50	18	15	17	36	.268	R	R	6-0	170	5-11-82	1998	Barahona, D.R.
Gonzalez, Jose	2	2	4.08	17	1	0	0	35	31	24	16	29	28	.236	R	R	6-3	190	4-9-83	1999	Barahona, D.R.
Graham, Jason	0	0	3.00	2	0	0	0	3	2	1	1	1	3	.181	R	R	6-3	190	9-24-79	2002	Atlantis, Fla.
Hernandez, Marcos	0	4	6.75	11	7	0	0	31	41	27	23	18	12	.325	L	L	6-4	200	5-25-84	2002	Sabana Hoyos, P.R.
Lyons, Thomas	2	2	2.97	7	6	0	0	30	29	10	10	11	36	.245	L	R	6-2	200	3-22-83	2001	Downers Grove, Ill.
Marquetti, Agustin	0	0	0.00	1	1	0	0	3	3	1	0	1	1	.272	S	R	6-6	220	2-24-78	2002	Caracas, Venez.
Mena, Amaurys	0	2	4.79	5	0	0	0	21	25	20	11	18	17	.284	R	R	6-0	200	7-31-82	2000	Santo Domingo, D.R.
Myers, Damien	0	1	3.38	2	0	0	0	5	6	6	2	1	3	.272	L	L	6-0	180	11-3-80	2002	New York, N.Y.
Parris, Matt	5	4	3.34	11	10	0	0	62	70	35	23	11	45	.278	R	R	6-3	190	10-4-82	2000	Ventura, Calif.
Rivas, Gabriel	1	1	5.61	15	0	0	0	26	22	19	16	22	14	.241	R	R	6-1	170	5-24-82	1999	Ciudad Bolivar, Venez.
Smith, Dan	0	0	0.00	2	0	0	0	4	2	0	0	0	3	.153	R	R	6-4	210	11-29-78	2001	Bonne Terre, Mo.
Smith, Michael	3	2	1.93	18	0	0	0	23	17	6	5	18	28	.200	L	L	6-5	205	7-8-81	2002	Valdosta, Ga.
Steinborn, Chris	1	3	3.02	10	8	0	0	51	50	30	17	15	47	.242	L	L	6-4	210	3-23-82	2002	Akron, Ohio
Zumaya, Joel	2	1	1.93	9	8	0	0	37	21	9	8	11	46	.162	R	R	6-3	210	11-9-84	2002	Chula Vista, Calif.

FLORIDA MARLINS

BY MIKE BERARDINO

If the Marlins' 2002 season seemed to have a slapdash quality, there were plenty of reasons for that.

They spent the previous winter in organizational limbo, courtesy of Major League Baseball's franchise shell  game. At one point privately targeted for contraction, the Marlins survived—but barely.

Former owner John Henry, frustrated in his efforts to secure a new baseball-only facility, sold the team back to MLB for $158 million, which was what he paid for it three years earlier. While Henry landed in Boston atop a new Red Sox ownership group, the Marlins fell into the hands of former Expos owner Jeffrey Loria.

Loria, after two controversial seasons in Montreal, received $120 million for the failing franchise, plus another $38 million in loans from baseball's Central Fund. The official transfer wasn't complete until the week spring training opened, and the resulting chaos hovered over the organization all year.

Dozens of loyal Marlins workers were displaced, scattered throughout the game and, in some cases, into the unemployment line as Loria brought virtually his entire Expos infrastructure south. Only a handful of employees on the baseball side were retained. Meanwhile, Loria faced a lawsuit under federal anti-racketeering statutes from his former limited partners in Montreal.

Unable to market the club in conventional fashion, the Marlins saw their season-ticket base sag to 4,000 and attendance plummet to 813,118, both franchise lows. They finished 29th in per-game attendance, just ahead of the MLB-operated Expos, and even that required the purchase of 15,000 tickets on the final day of the season by an anonymous "friend of the Marlins."

Loria, despite a $40 million payroll that ranked among the game's lowest, claimed losses of $20 million in his first year of ownership. The losses piled up on the field as well, where new manager Jeff Torborg, who came down

A.J. Burnett

Jason Stokes

PLAYERS OF THE YEAR

MAJOR LEAGUE: A.J. Burnett, rhp
Despite spending a few weeks on the disabled list with an elbow injury, Burnett still threw seven complete games and recorded a major league-high five shutouts. He also ranked sixth in the National League with 206 strikeouts.

MINOR LEAGUE: Jason Stokes, 1b
Stokes, Florida's second-round draft pick in 2000, led the Midwest League with a .341 average and 27 home runs in 2002, earning league MVP honors. He also earned an appearance in the Futures Game in Milwaukee.

from Montreal, guided the club to a 79-83 mark amid a summer marked by injuries and controversial trades.

The Marlins spent nine days in first place in the middle of May, but their downward spiral to a fourth-place finish began around the time shortstop Alex Gonzalez wrecked his left shoulder on a freak play in San Francisco (May 18) and was lost for the season.

Young righthander Josh Beckett, expected to contend for National League rookie of the year, instead landed on the disabled list several times with nagging blister problems on his pitching hand. Beckett won just six games.

Fellow starters Brad Penny and A.J. Burnett also landed on the DL, though the season was a rousing success in all for Burnett. He went 12-9 and ranked among league leaders in strikeouts and complete games.

Some felt the club could have done more if new management hadn't dealt closer Antonio Alfonseca and righthander Matt Clement to the Cubs six days before the season opener. The Marlins received Julian Tavarez and three prospects in return, including lefty Dontrelle Willis, who became their minor league pitcher of the year.

More controversy followed the July 11 trades that sent prospective free agent Cliff Floyd to the Expos and two-time Opening Day starter Ryan Dempster to the Reds.

In the minors, Class A Kane County slugger Jason Stokes was named organizational player of the year after batting .341-27-75. Class A Jupiter, which boasted third-base prospect Miguel Cabrera and later Willis, was eliminated in the semifinals of the Florida State League playoffs.

An affiliate shuffle saw the Marlins' Triple-A franchise move from Calgary to Albuquerque, their Double-A affiliation switch from Portland (Eastern) to Carolina (Southern) and their low Class A affiliation go from Kane County (Midwest) to Greensboro (South Atlantic).

ORGANIZATION LEADERS

BATTING

*AVG	Jason Stokes, Kane County	.341
R	Brian Banks, Calgary	90
H	Will Smith, Jupiter	164
TB	Will Smith, Jupiter	260
2B	Miguel Cabrera, Jupiter	43
3B	Will Smith, Jupiter	12
HR	Jason Stokes, Kane County	27
RBI	Adrian Gonzalez, Portland	96
BB	Jesus Medrano, Portland	79
	Pat Magness, Jupiter	79
SO	Matt Padgett, Portland	131
SB	Charles Frazier, Jupiter/Kane County	48

PITCHING

W	Rob Henkel, Portland/Jupiter	13
L	Phil Akens, Kane County	15
#ERA	Dontrelle Willis, Jupiter/Kane County	1.83
G	Mike Flannery, Jupiter	58
CG	Three tied at	3
SV	Mike Flannery, Jupiter	26
IP	Nate Robertson, Portland	163
BB	Omar Ortiz, Portland	70
SO	Rob Henkel, Portland/Jupiter	150

*Minimum 250 At-Bats #Minimum 75 Innings

FLORIDA MARLINS

Manager: Jeff Torborg

2002 Record: 79-83, .488 (4th, NL East)

BATTING	AVG	G	AB	R	H	2B	3B	HR	RBI	BB	SO	SB	CS	SLG	OBP	B	T	HT	WT	DOB	1st Yr	Resides
Banks, Brian	.321	20	28	3	9	1	0	1	4	1	6	0	0	.464	.345	S	R	6-3	210	9-28-70	1993	Mesa, Ariz.
Bush, Homer	.222	40	54	7	12	0	0	0	5	3	13	2	1	.222	.263	R	R	5-10	180	11-12-72	1991	Keller, Texas
Castillo, Luis	.305	146	606	86	185	18	5	2	39	55	76	48	15	.361	.364	S	R	5-11	170	9-12-75	1993	Roseville, Calif.
Castro, Ramon	.238	54	101	11	24	4	0	6	18	14	24	0	0	.455	.322	R	R	6-3	220	3-1-76	1994	Vega Baja, P.R.
Encarnacion, Juan	.262	69	263	34	69	11	3	8	34	20	50	12	5	.418	.317	R	R	6-3	210	3-8-76	1992	Las Matas de Farfan, D.R.
2-team (83 Cincinnati)	.271	152	584	77	158	22	5	24	85	46	113	21	9	.449	.324							
Floyd, Cliff	.287	44	296	49	85	20	0	18	57	58	68	10	5	.537	.414	L	R	6-4	230	12-5-72	1991	Weston, Ill.
Fox, Andy	.251	133	435	55	109	14	5	4	41	49	94	31	7	.333	.338	L	R	6-4	180	1-12-71	1989	Sacramento, Calif.
Gonzalez, Alex	.225	42	151	15	34	7	1	2	18	12	32	3	1	.325	.296	R	R	6-0	170	2-15-77	1994	Turmero, Venez.
Johnson, Charles	.217	83	244	18	53	19	0	6	36	31	61	0	0	.369	.301	R	R	6-2	220	7-20-71	1992	Pembroke Pines, Fla.
Lee, Derrek	.270	162	581	95	157	35	7	27	86	98	164	19	9	.494	.378	R	R	6-5	220	9-6-75	1993	Folsom, Calif.
Lowell, Mike	.276	160	597	88	165	44	0	24	92	65	92	4	3	.471	.346	R	R	6-4	200	2-24-74	1995	Coral Gables, Fla.
Malloy, Marty	.120	24	25	1	3	0	0	0	1	2	8	0	0	.120	.185	R	R	5-10	160	7-6-72	1992	Trenton, Fla.
Millar, Kevin	.306	126	438	58	134	41	0	16	57	40	74	0	2	.509	.366	R	R	6-0	210	9-24-71	1993	Encino, Calif.
Mordecai, Mike	.286	38	77	10	22	4	0	0	7	5	13	1	1	.338	.337	R	R	5-10	180	12-13-67	1989	Kennesaw, Ga.
2-team (55 Montreal)	.245	93	151	19	37	8	0	0	11	13	27	2	2	.298	.313							
Nunez, Abraham	.118	19	17	2	2	0	0	0	1	0	5	0	1	.118	.118	S	R	6-2	180	2-5-77	1996	Haina, D.R.
Owens, Eric	.270	131	385	44	104	15	5	4	37	31	33	26	9	.366	.324	R	R	6-1	180	2-3-71	1992	Rocky Mount, Va.
Ozuna, Pablo	.277	34	47	4	13	2	2	0	3	1	3	1	1	.404	.300	R	R	6-0	160	8-25-74	1996	Santo Domingo, D.R.
Raines, Tim Sr.	.191	98	89	9	17	3	0	1	7	22	19	0	0	.258	.351	S	R	5-8	190	9-16-59	1977	Heathrow, Fla.
Redmond, Mike	.305	89	256	19	78	15	0	2	28	21	34	0	2	.387	.372	R	R	6-1	180	5-5-71	1993	Spokane, Wash.
Wilson, Preston	.243	141	510	80	124	22	2	23	65	58	140	20	11	.429	.329	R	R	6-2	190	7-19-74	1993	Eastover, S.C.

PITCHING	W	L	ERA	G	GS	CG	SV	IP	H	R	ER	BB	SO	AVG	B	T	HT	WT	DOB	1st Yr	Resides
Almanza, Armando	3	2	4.34	51	0	0	2	46	36	22	22	23	57	.223	L	L	6-3	200	10-26-72	1993	El Paso, Texas
Beckett, Josh	6	7	4.10	23	21	0	0	108	93	56	49	44	113	.231	R	R	6-4	190	5-15-80	2000	Spring, Texas
Borland, Toby	1	0	5.27	15	0	0	0	14	14	8	8	5	11	.269	R	R	6-6	200	5-29-69	1989	Quitman, La.
Burnett, A.J.	12	9	3.30	31	29	7	0	204	153	84	75	90	203	.209	R	R	6-5	200	1-3-77	1995	North Little Rock, Ark.
Darensbourg, Vic	1	2	6.14	42	0	0	0	48	61	34	33	26	33	.305	L	L	5-10	160	11-13-70	1992	Las Vegas, Nev.
Dempster, Ryan	5	8	4.79	18	18	3	0	120	126	66	64	55	87	.280	R	R	6-1	200	5-3-77	1995	Gibsons, B.C.
Izquierdo, Hansel	2	0	4.55	20	2	0	0	30	33	17	15	21	20	.289	R	R	6-2	200	1-2-77	1995	Miami, Fla.
Knotts, Gary	3	1	4.40	28	0	0	0	31	21	15	15	14	21	.192	R	R	6-4	200	2-12-77	1996	Decatur, Ala.
Lloyd, Graeme	2	2	4.44	25	0	0	0	26	26	13	13	11	20	.262	L	L	6-7	220	4-9-67	1988	Gnarwarre, Australia
2-team (41 Montreal)	4	5	5.21	66	0	0	5	57	67	34	33	19	37	.297							
Looper, Braden	2	5	3.14	78	0	0	13	86	73	31	30	28	55	.230	R	R	6-5	220	10-28-74	1996	Palm Beach Gardens, Fla.
Mairena, Ozwaldo	2	3	5.35	31	0	0	0	34	38	21	20	12	21	.287	L	L	5-11	160	6-30-74	1996	Chinandega, Nicaragua
Neal, Blaine	3	0	2.73	32	0	0	0	33	32	12	10	14	33	.248	R	R	6-4	220	4-6-78	1996	Haddon Heights, N.J.
Nunez, Vladimir	6	5	3.41	77	0	0	20	98	80	38	37	37	73	.224	R	R	6-4	220	3-15-75	1996	Miramar, Fla.
Olsen, Kevin	0	5	4.53	17	8	0	0	56	57	31	28	31	38	.270	R	R	6-2	200	7-26-76	1998	Norco, Calif.
Pavano, Carl	3	2	3.79	22	8	0	0	62	76	33	26	14	41	.306	R	R	6-5	230	1-8-76	1994	Palm Beach Gardens, Fla.
2-team (15 Montreal)	6	10	5.16	37	22	0	0	136	174	88	78	45	92	.312							
Penny, Brad	8	7	4.66	24	24	1	0	129	148	76	67	50	93	.288	R	R	6-4	200	5-24-78	1996	Broken Arrow, Okla.
Robertson, Nate	0	1	11.88	6	1	0	0	8	15	11	11	4	3	.375	R	L	6-2	210	9-3-77	1999	Valley Center, Kan.
Tavarez, Julian	10	12	5.39	29	27	0	0	154	188	100	92	74	67	.308	L	R	6-2	190	5-22-73	1990	Broadview, Ohio
Tejera, Michael	8	8	4.45	47	18	0	1	140	144	71	69	60	95	.268	L	L	5-9	170	10-18-76	1995	Miami, Fla.
Teut, Nate	0	1	9.82	2	1	0	0	7	13	8	8	3	4	.393	R	L	6-7	220	3-11-76	1997	Des Moines, Iowa
Wayne, Justin	2	3	5.32	5	5	0	0	24	22	16	14	13	16	.244	R	R	6-3	200	4-16-79	2000	Honolulu, Hawaii

FIELDING

Catcher	PCT	G	PO	A	E	DP	PB
Castro	1.000	37	148	12	0	0	0
Johnson	.994	82	488	49	3	9	5
Redmond	.993	80	492	50	4	9	1

First Base	PCT	G	PO	A	E	DP
Banks	.667	1	2	0	1	1
Lee	.992	162	1312	121	12	138
Millar	1.000	2	6	1	0	0
Mordecai	1.000	1	1	0	0	0
Redmond	1.000	2	4	0	0	0

Second Base	PCT	G	PO	A	E	DP
Bush	.962	12	11	14	1	2
Castillo	.981	144	269	391	13	93
Fox	.976	7	18	23	1	7
Malloy	1.000	3	5	3	0	1
Mordecai	.857	4	6	6	2	2
Ozuna	.967	10	13	16	1	3

Third Base	PCT	G	PO	A	E	DP
Banks	1.000	1	1	1	0	0
Fox	1.000	4	2	1	0	0

	PCT	G	PO	A	E	DP	PB
Lowell	.969	159	150	286	14	36	
Malloy	1.000	2	0	1	0	0	
Millar	.857	2	1	5	1	0	
Mordecai	1.000	7	5	4	0	2	

Shortstop	PCT	G	PO	A	E	DP
Bush	.000	4	0	0	0	0
Fox	.965	112	187	279	17	73
Gonzalez	.984	42	72	113	3	32
Mordecai	.988	24	26	53	1	11

Outfield	PCT	G	PO	A	E	DP
Banks	1.000	8	8	0	0	0
Encarnacion	.993	67	135	4	1	2
Floyd	.983	80	173	5	3	1
Fox	.000	1	0	0	0	0
Millar	.985	108	187	6	3	1
Mordecai	.000	1	0	0	0	0
Nunez	1.000	15	12	0	0	0
Owens	.975	121	223	10	6	1
Ozuna	.000	1	0	0	0	0
Raines	.917	14	10	1	1	0
Wilson	.981	138	301	8	6	2

Preston Wilson

FARM SYSTEM

Director, Player Development: Jim Fleming.

Class	Farm Team	League	W	L	Pct.	Finish*	Manager	First Yr.
AAA	Calgary (Alberta) Cannons	Pacific Coast	67	71	.486	12th (16)	Dean Treanor	1999
AA	Portland (Maine) Sea Dogs	Eastern	63	77	.450	t-9th (12)	Eric Fox	1994
High A	Jupiter (Fla.) Hammerheads	Florida State	81	57	.587	2nd (14)	Luis Dorante	2002
Low A	Kane County (Ill.) Cougars	Midwest	64	75	.460	10th (14)	Steve Phillips	1993
SS A	Jamestown (N.Y.) Jammers	New York-Penn	32	42	.432	10th (14)	Johnny Rodriguez	2002
Rookie	Jupiter (Fla.) Marlins	Gulf Coast	31	29	.517	6th (14)	Jesus Campos	1992

*Finish in overall standings (No. of teams in league)

CALGARY CANNONS — Class AAA

PACIFIC COAST LEAGUE

BATTING	AVG	G	AB	R	H	2B	3B	HR	RBI	BB	SO	SB	CS	SLG	OBP	B	T	HT	WT	DOB	1st Yr	Resides
Abad, Andy	.301	111	352	50	106	28	2	11	70	57	44	0	3	.486	.402	L	L	6-1	180	8-25-72	1993	Jupiter, Fla.
Banks, Brian	.310	130	439	90	136	38	3	19	89	73	77	10	5	.540	.410	S	R	6-3	210	9-28-70	1993	Mesa, Ariz.
Candelaria, Ben	.240	11	25	3	6	2	0	1	6	1	4	0	0	.440	.259	L	R	5-11	160	1-29-75	1992	Hatillo, P.R.
Erickson, Matt	.288	108	379	63	109	30	2	1	27	31	63	15	4	.385	.359	L	R	5-11	190	7-30-75	1997	Appleton, Wis.
Greene, Charlie	.250	99	320	34	80	24	0	7	41	11	53	0	0	.391	.283	R	R	6-2	170	1-23-71	1991	Miami, Fla.
Hooper, Kevin	.288	117	452	70	130	21	3	2	38	34	51	17	10	.361	.341	R	R	5-10	160	12-7-76	1999	Lawrence, Kan.
Nunez, Abraham	.250	129	428	68	107	24	5	21	60	51	112	31	6	.477	.329	S	R	6-2	180	2-5-77	1996	Haina, D.R.
Ozuna, Pablo	.326	77	261	37	85	16	1	7	33	17	37	16	3	.475	.371	R	R	6-0	160	8-25-74	1996	Santo Domingo, D.R.
Peeples, Mike	.260	75	231	32	60	14	2	7	36	12	41	8	4	.429	.300	R	R	6-0	170	9-3-76	1994	Green Cove Springs, Fla.
Rolison, Nate	.254	37	126	22	32	7	0	9	21	14	45	0	0	.524	.329	L	R	6-6	240	3-27-77	1995	Petal, Miss.
Roneberg, Brett	.400	3	5	1	2	0	0	0	2	0	0	0	1	.400	.571	L	L	6-2	200	2-5-79	1996	Cairns, Australia
Rumfield, Toby	.287	56	157	15	45	7	0	1	20	15	25	0	2	.350	.347	R	R	6-3	190	9-4-72	1991	Belton, Texas
Smith, Mark	.290	115	389	60	113	30	0	12	55	41	79	5	2	.460	.369	R	R	6-3	220	5-7-70	1991	Arcadia, Calif.
Treanor, Matt	.284	36	95	10	27	8	0	1	18	12	13	1	1	.400	.393	R	R	6-2	220	3-3-76	1994	Anaheim, Calif.
Wathan, Derek	.280	102	329	43	92	18	7	5	41	23	44	7	11	.422	.330	S	R	6-3	190	12-13-76	1998	Blue Springs, Mo.
Wood, Jason	.315	121	457	78	144	37	2	15	70	38	92	3	0	.503	.370	R	R	6-1	200	12-16-69	1991	Fresno, Calif.

PITCHING	W	L	ERA	G	GS	CG	SV	IP	H	R	ER	BB	SO	B	T	HT	WT	DOB	1st Yr	Resides
Abad, Andy	0	0	9.00	2	0	0	0	3	4	3	3	0	1	L	L	6-1	180	8-25-72	1993	Jupiter, Fla.
Arnold, Jamie	3	8	7.39	16	10	1	0	67	82	59	55	29	25	R	R	6-2	200	3-24-74	1992	Belton, Texas
Borland, Toby	5	2	2.96	56	0	0	14	70	55	24	23	30	75	R	R	6-6	200	5-29-69	1989	Quitman, La.
Christman, Tim	2	1	7.07	11	0	0	0	14	16	11	11	9	11	L	L	6-0	190	3-31-75	1996	Oneonta, N.Y.
Glynn, Ryan	5	5	6.00	14	14	0	0	78	102	58	52	27	48	R	R	6-3	200	11-1-74	1995	Grand Prairie, Texas
Grilli, Jason	0	1	1.59	1	1	0	0	6	3	1	1	3	8	R	R	6-4	180	11-11-76	1997	Orlando, Fla.
Izquierdo, Hansel	4	5	5.32	13	13	0	0	71	90	55	42	23	36	R	R	6-2	200	1-2-77	1995	Miami, Fla.
Judd, Mike	8	6	5.24	23	23	0	0	125	137	80	73	51	100	R	R	6-1	210	6-30-75	1995	La Mesa, Calif.
Knotts, Gary	5	3	4.25	42	0	0	3	53	53	29	25	32	44	R	R	6-4	200	2-12-77	1996	Decatur, Ala.
Mairena, Ozwaldo	3	0	4.97	25	0	0	1	29	39	20	16	13	19	L	L	5-11	200	6-30-74	1996	Chinandega, Nicaragua
Neal, Blaine	3	1	2.90	29	0	0	11	31	27	11	10	15	26	L	R	6-5	200	4-6-78	1996	Haddon Heights, N.J.
Olsen, Kevin	2	5	3.86	8	1	0	0	49	45	22	21	14	25	R	R	6-2	200	7-26-76	1998	Norco, Calif.
Pearsall, J.J.	1	0	7.43	9	0	0	0	13	15	11	11	6	14	L	L	6-2	200	9-9-73	1995	Burnt Hills, N.Y.
Phelps, Tommy	4	2	3.15	51	0	0	2	74	76	27	26	21	62	L	L	6-3	190	3-4-74	1993	Tampa, Fla.
Radinsky, Scott	0	3	6.86	18	0	0	1	21	27	18	16	13	13	L	L	6-3	210	3-3-68	1986	Simi Valley, Calif.
Ratliff, Jon	0	1	0.00	1	1	0	0	0	5	6	6	1	0	R	R	6-5	200	12-22-71	1993	Pittsford, N.Y.
Rodgers, Bobby	5	5	5.72	25	17	0	1	94	105	62	60	54	67	R	R	6-3	220	7-22-74	1996	St. Charles, Mo.
Secoda, Jason	6	3	4.47	35	10	1	0	117	107	60	58	41	64	R	R	6-2	200	9-24-74	1995	Fullerton, Calif.
Sloan, Brandon	0	0	12.00	2	0	0	0	3	6	4	4	1	2	S	R	6-2	190	10-26-77	2000	Wichita, Kan.
Steenstra, Kennie	1	2	11.13	9	4	0	0	32	64	41	40	11	19	R	R	6-5	210	10-13-70	1992	Liberty, Mo.
Teut, Nate	5	6	5.28	27	19	0	0	116	132	81	68	52	82	R	L	6-7	220	3-11-76	1997	Des Moines, Iowa
Vargas, Claudio	4	11	6.72	17	16	1	0	76	88	63	57	35	61	R	R	6-3	200	5-19-79	1996	Santiago, D.R.
Wayne, Justin	0	1	6.35	2	2	0	0	11	8	8	8	6	10	R	R	6-3	200	4-16-79	2000	Honolulu, Hawaii
Woodards, Orlando	1	0	0.00	1	0	0	0	1	2	0	0	1	0	R	R	6-2	200	1-2-78	1997	Sacramento, Calif.

FIELDING

Catcher	PCT	G	PO	A	E	DP	PB
Banks	.981	9	49	3	1	0	2
Greene	.989	92	560	49	7	8	8
Rumfield	.988	18	84	1	1	0	3
Treanor	.983	30	159	14	3	1	0

First Base	PCT	G	PO	A	E	DP
Abad	.984	23	177	13	3	14
Banks	.989	67	563	43	7	62
Erickson	.000	1	0	0	0	0
Rolison	.993	35	273	14	2	24
Rumfield	1.000	17	117	15	0	14
Treanor	1.000	2	14	0	0	0
Wood	.857	3	6	0	1	0

Second Base	PCT	G	PO	A	E	DP
Erickson	.978	62	92	180	6	36
Hooper	.985	43	73	126	3	28
Ozuna	.963	40	79	104	7	19

Third Base	PCT	G	PO	A	E	DP
Banks	1.000	1	1	1	0	0
Erickson	.955	29	24	60	4	5
Wathan	1.000	2	2	3	0	0
Wood	.962	112	85	192	11	22

Shortstop	PCT	G	PO	A	E	DP
Erickson	1.000	3	1	6	0	1
Hooper	.971	72	100	206	9	45
Wathan	.977	68	83	174	6	36

Wood	.882	4	4	11	2	2

Outfield	PCT	G	PO	A	E	DP
Abad	1.000	74	130	4	0	2
Banks	.990	43	93	3	1	0
Candelaria	1.000	8	9	0	0	0
Erickson	1.000	4	1	0	0	0
Nunez	.978	125	306	10	7	1
Ozuna	.952	23	40	0	2	0
Peeples	.979	54	90	2	2	0
Roneberg	1.000	2	5	0	0	0
Rumfield	1.000	2	4	0	0	0
Smith	.980	88	145	3	3	0
Wathan	.941	18	30	2	2	0

PORTLAND SEA DOGS — Class AA

EASTERN LEAGUE

BATTING	AVG	G	AB	R	H	2B	3B	HR	RBI	BB	SO	SB	CS	SLG	OBP	B	T	HT	WT	DOB	1st Yr	Resides
Aguila, Chris	.294	130	429	62	126	28	4	6	46	48	101	14	8	.420	.369	R	R	5-11	180	2-23-79	1997	Reno, Nev.

BATTING	AVG	G	AB	R	H	2B	3B	HR	RBI	BB	SO	SB	CS	SLG	OBP	B	T	HT	WT	DOB	1st Yr	Resides
Candelaria, Ben	.291	29	103	9	30	9	0	0	13	7	19	2	2	.379	.336	L	R	5-11	160	1-29-75	1992	Hatillo, P.R.
Coquillette, Trace	.208	43	144	24	30	7	2	4	20	22	45	1	3	.368	.333	R	R	5-11	180	6-4-74	1993	Orangevale, Calif.
Dina, Mike	.258	51	182	34	47	15	1	6	20	8	32	5	3	.451	.288	R	R	5-10	190	9-28-73	1998	Stratford, Conn.
Foster, Quincy	.243	23	74	6	18	2	0	2	14	5	13	10	4	.351	.293	L	R	6-2	170	10-30-74	1996	Hendersonville, N.C.
Gonzalez, Adrian	.266	138	508	70	135	34	1	17	96	54	112	6	3	.437	.344	L	L	6-2	190	5-8-82	2000	Bonita, Calif.
Honeycutt, Heath	.136	12	44	7	6	3	0	2	6	3	15	1	0	.341	.188	R	R	6-4	210	7-30-76	1998	Alpharetta, Ga.
Iapoce, Anthony	.286	75	280	42	80	15	2	2	30	28	46	20	3	.375	.366	R	L	5-10	170	8-23-73	1994	Ridgewood, N.Y.
Jorgensen, Ryan	.222	41	144	15	32	4	0	2	14	12	33	3	1	.292	.287	R	R	6-2	200	5-4-79	2000	Kingwood, Texas
Kelly, Heath	.200	69	180	25	36	8	1	7	24	16	74	3	0	.372	.271	R	R	6-1	180	2-16-76	1998	Pensacola, Fla.
Lopez, Angel	.353	5	17	2	6	1	0	1	2	0	6	0	0	.588	.353	R	R	5-11	180	4-17-73	2002	Miami Beach, Fla.
Medrano, Jesus	.297	116	414	77	123	27	6	3	32	79	82	39	18	.413	.411	R	R	6-0	180	9-11-78	1997	La Puente, Calif.
Millar, Kevin	.083	3	12	1	1	0	0	1	3	0	5	0	0	.333	.077	R	R	6-0	210	9-24-71	1993	Encino, Calif.
Morales, Steve	.262	51	164	16	43	10	0	5	25	5	22	0	1	.415	.292	S	R	5-10	190	5-4-78	1996	Mayaguez, P.R.
Niles, Drew	.224	86	259	27	58	10	8	0	16	14	69	3	2	.324	.269	S	R	6-1	170	3-17-77	1998	Irmo, S.C.
Padgett, Mike	.234	117	406	52	95	26	1	16	63	43	131	6	5	.421	.310	L	L	6-2	210	7-22-77	1998	Lexington, S.C.
Peeples, Mike	.205	24	83	11	17	5	1	1	8	10	21	1	2	.325	.281	R	R	6-0	170	9-3-76	1994	Green Cove Springs, Fla.
Rigsby, Randy	.250	53	156	10	39	10	0	5	21	9	47	5	2	.410	.304	L	L	6-0	190	8-7-76	1998	Goldsboro, N.C.
Santos, Jose	.210	68	214	24	45	8	1	3	33	23	57	3	3	.299	.289	R	R	5-10	190	3-1-74	1995	Santiago, D.R.
Treanor, Matt	.250	50	156	24	39	5	1	9	28	28	33	3	0	.468	.387	R	R	6-2	220	3-3-76	1994	Anaheim, Calif.
Valdez, Wilson	.261	114	375	51	98	19	5	1	30	15	47	18	6	.347	.294	R	R	5-11	160	5-20-78	1997	Nizao, D.R.
Wilson, Josh	.341	12	41	5	14	3	0	2	5	2	6	0	1	.561	.372	R	R	6-1	160	3-26-81	1999	Pittsburgh, Pa.

PITCHING	W	L	ERA	G	GS	CG	SV	IP	H	R	ER	BB	SO	AVG	B	T	HT	WT	DOB	1st Yr	Resides
Bowe, Brandon	6	4	3.72	45	3	0	4	75	89	37	31	23	53	.287	R	R	6-3	210	3-13-76	1999	Stockton, Calif.
Bridges, Donnie	0	4	13.21	6	3	0	0	16	29	26	23	18	6	.414	R	R	6-4	220	12-10-78	1997	Purvis, Miss.
2-team (14 Harrisburg)	4	8	7.55	20	16	0	0	79	92	74	66	60	55	.294							
Bump, Nate	7	6	3.38	20	20	3	0	128	110	56	48	29	81	.227	R	R	6-2	180	7-24-76	1998	Monroeton, Pa.
Chavez, Chris	1	0	5.24	15	0	0	2	22	22	18	13	21	19	.255	R	R	6-0	180	7-23-75	1999	Tallahassee, Fla.
Christman, Tim	1	1	5.52	11	0	0	2	15	17	12	9	5	10	.274	L	L	6-0	190	3-31-75	1996	Oneonta, N.Y.
Clark, Chris	2	9	9.00	10	0	0	0	15	14	15	15	17	7	.254	R	R	6-1	180	10-29-74	1994	Tucson, Ariz.
Cueto, Jose	1	4	3.92	9	9	0	0	44	34	21	19	21	47	.217	R	R	6-2	170	9-13-76	1996	San Pedro de Macoris, D.R.
Fesh, Sean	1	1	4.22	24	0	0	5	43	35	23	20	22	49	.224	L	L	6-2	180	11-3-72	1991	Bethel, Conn.
Goetz, Geoff	1	3	3.86	2	2	0	0	7	5	4	3	7	9	.208	L	L	5-11	160	4-3-79	1997	Lutz, Fla.
Hamulack, Tim	8	4	2.88	38	1	0	6	78	73	32	25	29	53	.251	L	L	6-4	210	11-14-76	1996	Edgewood, Md.
Henkel, Rob	5	4	3.86	13	13	0	0	70	54	31	30	27	68	.211	R	L	6-2	210	8-3-78	2001	La Mesa, Calif.
Izquierdo, Hansel	0	1	1.29	1	1	0	0	7	5	2	1	1	4	.192	R	R	6-2	200	1-2-77	1995	Miami, Fla.
Klepacki, Ed	2	1	3.22	13	0	0	1	22	16	10	8	14	17	.202	R	R	6-5	180	4-26-78	1998	Midwest City, Okla.
2-team (6 Harrisburg)	2	1	3.51	19	0	0	2	33	23	15	13	23	21	.196							
Lopez, Gustavo	0	0	13.50	2	2	0	0	3	6	5	5	1	5	.352	R	R	5-9	180	8-12-75	1996	Santiago, D.R.
Massingale, Matt	1	0	9.00	6	0	0	0	10	9	10	10	9	6	.225	R	R	6-1	200	5-14-79	2000	Kennewick, Wash.
Ortiz, Omar	4	8	5.38	33	16	0	3	104	107	69	62	70	74	.273	S	R	6-1	210	9-11-77	1999	Brownsville, Texas
Pearsall, J.J.	0	1	3.18	12	0	0	0	17	18	8	6	8	18	.281	L	L	6-2	200	9-9-73	1995	Burnt Hills, N.Y.
Robertson, Nate	10	9	3.42	27	27	3	0	163	156	77	62	50	109	.260	R	L	6-2	210	9-3-77	1999	Valley Center, Kan.
Rodgers, Bobby	0	0	0.90	3	0	0	1	10	6	1	1	3	15	.176	R	R	6-3	220	7-22-74	1996	St. Charles, Mo.
Sergent, Joe	3	6	6.43	20	12	1	0	70	85	61	50	22	41	.302	L	L	6-2	180	8-29-78	1999	Manteca, Calif.
Skinner, John	0	0	2.25	2	0	0	0	4	2	1	1	3	0	.181	R	R	6-1	180	6-15-77	2001	Dublin, Calif.
Sloan, Brandon	2	6	4.08	43	0	0	8	71	76	38	32	32	45	.273	S	R	6-2	190	10-26-77	2000	Wichita, Kan.
Snare, Ryan	4	2	3.44	11	9	0	0	55	46	25	21	19	52	.224	L	L	6-0	190	2-8-79	2000	Palm Harbor, Fla.
Wayne, Justin	3	3	4.85	7	7	1	0	43	43	26	23	13	30	.268	R	R	6-3	200	4-16-79	2000	Honolulu, Hawaii
2-team (17 Harrisburg)	8	5	3.12	24	24	1	0	141	117	67	49	45	77	.230							
Woodards, Orlando	4	9	3.52	28	15	2	1	102	106	52	40	35	61	.271	R	R	6-2	200	1-2-78	1999	Sacramento, Calif.

FIELDING

Catcher	PCT	G	PO	A	E	DP	PB
Jorgensen	.983	41	256	41	5	4	3
Lopez	1.000	5	28	3	0	0	0
Morales	.982	49	285	36	6	4	5
Treanor	.977	48	339	39	9	5	2

First Base	PCT	G	PO	A	E	DP
Gonzalez	.987	136	1127	89	16	107
Kelly	1.000	8	27	3	0	4
Peeples	1.000	1	2	0	0	0
Santos	1.000	1	7	0	0	2

Second Base	PCT	G	PO	A	E	DP
Kelly	.826	5	9	10	4	1

	PCT	G	PO	A	E	DP
Medrano	.973	114	220	282	14	72
Niles	.979	24	53	41	2	13
Third Base	**PCT**	**G**	**PO**	**A**	**E**	**DP**
Coquillette	.903	34	22	71	10	5
Honeycutt	.976	11	11	29	1	3
Kelly	.919	27	13	67	7	6
Niles	.940	34	23	71	6	6
Peeples	.667	2	1	1	1	0
Santos	.887	42	29	97	16	6
Shortstop	**PCT**	**G**	**PO**	**A**	**E**	**DP**
Niles	.979	24	33	60	2	11
Valdez	.944	113	171	304	28	67

	PCT	G	PO	A	E	DP
Wilson	.967	12	25	33	2	14
Outfield	**PCT**	**G**	**PO**	**A**	**E**	**DP**
Aguila	.988	122	233	15	3	0
Candelaria	.970	21	32	0	1	0
Coquillette	1.000	11	17	1	0	0
Dina	.978	43	85	4	2	0
Foster	.979	20	45	1	1	0
Iapoce	.989	73	170	6	2	0
Kelly	1.000	2	4	0	0	0
Millar	1.000	3	2	0	0	0
Padgett	.961	81	145	4	6	1
Peeples	.957	15	22	0	1	0
Rigsby	.949	41	73	2	4	0

JUPITER HAMMERHEADS — High Class A

FLORIDA STATE LEAGUE

BATTING	AVG	G	AB	R	H	2B	3B	HR	RBI	BB	SO	SB	CS	SLG	OBP	B	T	HT	WT	DOB	1st Yr	Resides
Ambres, Chip	.236	123	509	88	120	25	7	9	37	57	98	23	8	.365	.323	R	R	6-1	190	12-19-79	1998	Beaumont, Texas
Anderson, Dennis	.310	42	126	13	39	6	1	6	16	23	23	1	0	.397	.437	S	R	6-0	200	2-1-78	1999	Tucson, Ariz.
Cabrera, Miguel	.274	124	489	77	134	43	1	9	75	38	85	10	1	.421	.333	R	R	6-2	180	4-18-83	1999	Maracay, Venez.
DeMarco, Matt	.266	109	368	41	98	13	0	3	46	21	36	5	2	.318	.311	L	R	5-10	160	1-24-80	1999	Clayton, N.J.
Easterday, Matt	.228	81	254	42	58	9	5	1	30	38	41	13	4	.315	.339	R	R	6-1	180	5-3-79	2000	Covington, Ga.
Ferrand, Frank	.121	31	99	8	12	0	0	0	7	5	19	2	0	.121	.170	L	L	5-10	170	5-20-73	1997	Santo Domingo, D.R.
Frazier, Charles	.276	8	29	8	8	1	0	0	3	4	8	0	1	.310	.364	R	R	6-3	180	7-6-80	1999	Toms River, N.J.
Garcia, Juan-Carlos	.033	10	30	2	1	0	0	0	1	14	0	0	.033	.065	R	R	6-1	180	10-10-82	1998	Santiago-Caballero, D.R.
Helps, Jay	.232	25	56	8	13	3	1	0	7	5	13	2	0	.321	.317	S	R	6-0	180	12-20-78	2001	Wyoming, Ontario
Johnson, Charles	.438	5	16	5	7	0	0	3	9	2	4	0	0	1.000	.500	R	R	6-2	220	7-20-71	1992	Pembroke Pines, Fla.
Jorgensen, Ryan	.260	60	223	26	58	16	0	3	35	24	38	4	1	.372	.335	R	R	6-2	200	5-4-79	2000	Kingwood, Texas

BATTING	AVG	G	AB	R	H	2B	3B	HR	RBI	BB	SO	SB	CS	SLG	OBP	B	T	HT	WT	DOB	1st Yr	Resides
Kavourias, Jim	.214	97	337	42	72	17	2	7	35	41	90	7	4	.338	.313	R	R	6-4	230	10-4-79	2000	Strongsville, Ohio
Kelly, Heath	.000	1	4	0	0	0	0	0	0	0	1	0	0	.000	.000	R	R	6-1	180	2-16-76	1998	Pensacola, Fla.
Lepine, Olivier	.000	1	0	1	0	0	0	0	0	0	0	0	0	.000	1.000	R	R	5-11	190	11-2-78	2002	
Lopez, Angel	.225	45	142	20	32	7	1	8	21	13	42	1	0	.458	.293	R	R	5-11	200	4-17-73	2002	Miami Beach, Fla.
Lynam, Guy	.000	4	11	0	0	0	0	0	0	0	7	0	0	.000	.000	R	R	5-11	190	10-27-80	2001	Williamstown, N.J.
Magness, Pat	.292	111	390	73	114	26	1	16	73	79	86	2	1	.487	.413	L	R	6-3	230	1-19-78	2000	Overland Park, Kan.
Rigsby, Randy	.272	27	103	11	28	4	1	1	15	5	25	3	1	.359	.309	L	L	6-0	190	8-7-76	1998	Goldsboro, N.C.
Roneberg, Brett	.211	15	57	4	12	1	1	0	7	7	11	1	1	.263	.297	L	L	6-2	200	2-5-79	1996	Cairns, Australia
Santos, Jose	.235	29	98	14	23	5	4	0	5	9	33	2	0	.367	.315	R	R	5-10	190	3-1-74	1995	Santiago, D.R.
Smith, Will	.299	133	549	84	164	30	12	14	73	31	75	8	3	.474	.336	L	R	6-1	180	10-23-81	2000	Tucson, Ariz.
Willingham, Josh	.274	107	376	72	103	21	4	17	69	63	88	18	5	.487	.394	R	R	6-1	200	2-17-79	2000	Florence, Ala.
Wilson, Josh	.256	111	398	51	102	17	1	11	50	28	67	7	10	.387	.318	R	R	6-1	160	3-26-81	1999	Pittsburgh, Pa.
Zapey, Winton	.136	6	22	1	3	0	0	1	3	0	8	0	0	.273	.136	R	R	5-11	170	3-21-78	1997	Santo Domingo, D.R.

PITCHING	W	L	ERA	G	GS	CG	SV	IP	H	R	ER	BB	SO	AVG	B	T	HT	WT	DOB	1st Yr	Resides
Almanza, Armando	0	0	0.00	6	5	0	0	7	1	0	0	3	6	.050	L	L	6-3	200	10-26-72	1993	El Paso, Texas
Bautista, Denny	4	6	4.99	19	15	0	0	88	80	52	49	40	79	.242	R	R	6-5	170	10-23-82	2000	Santo Domingo, D.R.
Beckett, Josh	1	0	0.00	1	1	0	0	6	4	0	0	1	12	.173	R	R	6-4	190	5-15-80	2000	Spring, Texas
Blalock, Casey	0	1	1.50	4	0	0	0	6	7	1	1	2	6	.304	R	R	5-11	180	1-25-80	2002	Shreveport, La.
Byron, Terry	3	2	5.94	31	0	0	0	47	52	33	31	28	29	.284	R	R	6-0	200	3-28-79	1999	St. Croix, V.I.
Campos, David	0	1	5.19	24	0	0	0	35	38	26	20	22	27	.273	L	L	5-11	170	8-31-77	1998	Kerman, Calif.
Chavez, Chris	0	0	2.91	12	0	0	1	22	24	14	7	7	24	.263	R	R	6-0	180	7-23-75	1999	Tallahassee, Fla.
Esquivia, Manuel	2	2	11.25	3	3	0	0	8	5	12	10	12	8	.185	R	R	6-6	180	5-30-80	1997	Cartagena, Colombia
Flannery, Mike	2	5	2.21	58	0	0	26	61	58	20	15	10	44	.250	R	R	6-1	190	9-20-79	2000	Collings Lakes, N.J.
Harber, Ryan	0	0	4.12	15	0	0	1	20	24	9	9	4	7	.311	L	L	6-4	210	9-25-76	1998	Fort Wayne, IN
Henkel, Rob	8	3	2.51	14	12	0	0	75	55	22	21	22	82	.205	R	L	6-2	210	8-3-78	2001	La Mesa, Calif.
Key, Chris	6	2	1.63	47	0	0	4	94	84	20	17	7	54	.240	R	R	6-3	210	10-30-77	2000	Reno, Nev.
Klepacki, Ed	0	0	7.94	5	0	0	0	6	5	7	5	4	3	.217	R	R	6-5	180	4-26-78	1998	Midwest City, Okla.
2-team (3 Brevard)	0	0	7.53	8	1	0	0	14	15	15	12	8	7	.250							
Lopez, Gustavo	8	3	2.33	18	17	0	0	89	70	23	23	24	73	.219	R	R	5-9	180	8-12-75	1996	Santiago, D.R.
Massingale, Matt	0	0	3.86	4	0	0	1	7	8	3	3	1	6	.275	R	R	6-1	200	5-14-79	2000	Kennewick, Wash.
McNutt, Mike	12	8	3.17	27	23	0	0	145	138	66	51	33	102	.250	R	R	6-2	190	10-18-79	2000	Cincinnati, Ohio
Messenger, Randy	11	8	4.37	28	27	1	0	157	178	94	76	58	96	.284	R	R	6-0	220	8-13-81	1999	Sparks, Nev.
Moser, Todd	7	4	3.59	17	12	0	0	78	73	33	31	12	70	.247	L	L	6-5	180	10-28-76	1999	Davie, Fla.
Penny, Brad	0	0	0.00	2	2	0	0	8	5	0	0	0	9	.178	R	R	6-4	200	5-24-78	1996	Broken Arrow, Okla.
Ratliff, Jon	0	0	3.38	2	2	0	0	5	4	2	2	1	4	.222	R	R	6-5	200	12-22-71	1993	Pittsford, N.Y.
Russell, Eddie	0	0	9.00	4	0	0	0	6	5	6	6	10	7	.217	R	R	6-2	190	6-20-78	2001	San Francisco, Calif.
Sauer, Marc	4	1	2.26	30	0	0	0	52	32	14	13	7	31	.173	R	R	6-2	190	6-30-80	1999	Gloucester, N.J.
Sawyer, Steve	6	4	4.38	46	0	0	1	76	77	43	37	39	77	.263	R	R	6-1	190	7-31-78	2000	Hammond, La.
Sergent, Joe	4	3	2.15	12	10	0	0	63	61	26	15	13	34	.256	L	L	6-0	180	8-29-78	1999	Manteca, Calif.
Skinner, John	1	1	4.50	11	0	0	0	14	18	7	7	6	10	.321	R	R	6-1	180	6-15-77	2001	Dublin, Calif.
Sloan, Brandon	1	0	1.17	6	0	0	2	8	9	1	1	1	3	.310	S	R	6-2	190	10-26-77	2000	Wichita, Kan.
Ungs, Nick	1	3	4.34	4	4	0	0	19	20	9	9	4	14	.277	R	R	6-1	220	9-3-79	2001	Dyersville, Iowa
Willis, Dontrelle	2	0	1.80	5	5	0	0	30	24	7	6	3	27	.216	L	L	6-4	200	1-12-82	2000	Alameda, Calif.

FIELDING

Catcher	PCT	G	PO	A	E	DP	PB
Anderson	.992	38	234	22	2	2	5
Johnson	1.000	5	30	3	0	1	0
Jorgensen	.990	59	367	40	4	2	4
Lepine	.750	1	3	0	1	0	0
Lopez	.987	40	275	25	4	2	5
Lynam	1.000	3	8	1	0	0	0
Zapey	.969	4	30	1	1	0	2

First Base	PCT	G	PO	A	E	DP
Anderson	1.000	1	1	0	0	0
DeMarco	1.000	3	3	1	0	0
Garcia	1.000	3	25	2	0	2
Magness	.985	96	823	33	13	81
Rigsby	.750	1	3	0	1	0
Roneberg	1.000	11	90	9	0	9
Willingham	.989	32	254	18	3	30

Second Base	PCT	G	PO	A	E	DP
DeMarco	.984	81	151	207	6	60
Easterday	.966	62	116	165	10	33
Helps	.960	7	8	16	1	5
Wilson	1.000	3	4	6	0	0

Third Base	PCT	G	PO	A	E	DP
Cabrera	.936	88	58	177	16	16
DeMarco	.933	9	3	11	1	1
Easterday	1.000	1	1	2	0	0
Garcia	.929	7	5	8	1	2
Helps	1.000	1	0	1	0	0
Kelly	1.000	1	1	1	0	0
Santos	.885	20	16	30	6	2
Willingham	.931	20	15	39	4	2
Wilson	.000	1	0	0	0	0

Shortstop	PCT	G	PO	A	E	DP
Cabrera	.972	9	10	25	1	9
Demarco	.949	17	28	46	4	10
Easterday	.000	1	0	0	0	0
Helps	.951	11	19	39	3	7
Wilson	.963	107	168	305	18	68

Outfield	PCT	G	PO	A	E	DP
Ambres	.987	122	292	8	4	3
DeMarco	1.000	1	2	0	0	0
Easterday	1.000	11	26	0	0	0
Ferrand	.917	31	43	1	4	0
Frazier	1.000	7	14	0	0	0
Kavourias	.970	89	191	6	6	1
Rigsby	1.000	25	51	1	0	0
Roneberg	1.000	5	10	1	0	0
Smith	.967	126	221	10	8	2
Willingham	.935	10	27	2	2	1

KANE COUNTY COUGARS — Low Class A

MIDWEST LEAGUE

BATTING	AVG	G	AB	R	H	2B	3B	HR	RBI	BB	SO	SB	CS	SLG	OBP	B	T	HT	WT	DOB	1st Yr	Resides
Anderson, Dennis	.247	47	166	17	41	7	3	4	19	18	23	4	2	.398	.337	S	R	6-0	200	2-1-78	1999	Tucson, Ariz.
Arnott, George	.208	89	308	29	64	16	0	8	36	26	96	4	2	.338	.279	R	R	6-1	200	9-3-77	2000	Santa Cruz, Calif.
Arroyo, William	.238	72	223	30	53	5	2	0	22	48	38	11	10	.278	.375	S	R	5-10	170	11-8-81	1999	Cabudare, Venez.
Blackburn, Franco	.154	17	52	4	8	1	0	0	3	6	8	1	0	.173	.241	L	R	6-1	180	2-18-79	2001	Huntsville, Ala.
Brewer, Anthony	.198	119	405	52	80	14	5	3	32	52	112	22	12	.279	.298	R	R	6-0	160	8-2-82	2000	Chicago, Ill.
Clute, Kris	.241	91	328	49	79	20	2	0	24	38	73	22	8	.314	.327	R	R	5-9	170	4-20-79	2001	Miami, Fla.
Ferrand, Frank	.306	17	62	5	19	2	2	1	9	6	11	0	1	.452	.368	L	L	5-10	170	5-20-73	1997	Santo Domingo, D.R.
Frazier, Charles	.250	114	440	63	110	18	2	2	38	59	111	48	16	.314	.344	R	R	6-3	180	7-6-80	1999	Toms River, N.J.
Garcia, Juan-Carlos	.182	5	11	0	2	2	0	0	0	4	4	0	2	.364	.400	S	R	6-1	180	10-10-82	1998	Santiago-Caballero, D.R.
Hartig, Phil	.188	12	48	5	9	5	0	0	2	3	8	0	1	.292	.245	R	R	6-3	210	12-18-77	2001	Asheville, N.C.
Helps, Jay	.180	21	61	12	11	2	0	1	4	10	22	0	0	.262	.333	S	R	6-0	180	12-20-78	2001	Wyoming, Ontario
Hicks, Scott	.228	124	452	44	103	11	3	1	58	53	107	5	6	.272	.311	L	R	6-4	210	6-6-80	2000	Altamonte Springs, Fla.
Kelly, Heath	.224	24	76	9	17	1	1	1	7	10	28	1	1	.303	.322	R	R	5-11	190	2-16-76	1998	Pensacola, Fla.
Lynam, Guy	.200	6	20	1	4	2	0	0	1	0	5	0	1	.300	.238	R	R	5-11	190	10-27-80	2001	Williamstown, N.J.

BATTING	AVG	G	AB	R	H	2B	3B	HR	RBI	BB	SO	SB	CS	SLG	OBP	B	T	HT	WT	DOB	1st Yr	Resides
Molina, Angel	.254	35	122	16	31	3	1	6	25	11	41	0	0	.443	.324	R	R	6-2	200	11-4-81	2000	Santa Isabel, P.R.
Ortiz, Daniel	.154	14	52	6	8	2	0	0	4	6	23	0	1	.192	.262	R	R	6-5	200	12-19-80	1999	Nuevo, Calif.
Reed, Eric	.360	12	50	11	18	1	0	0	2	3	11	7	1	.380	.396	L	L	5-11	170	12-2-80	2002	College Station, Texas
Rundgren, Rex	.230	122	426	33	98	11	2	2	40	24	84	6	3	.279	.273	R	R	6-1	170	11-20-80	2001	Princeville, Hawaii
Stokes, Jason	.341	97	349	73	119	25	0	27	75	47	96	1	1	.645	.421	R	R	6-4	220	1-23-82	2000	Coppell, Texas
Tucker, Michael	.244	121	435	53	106	20	3	6	61	53	100	6	2	.345	.329	R	R	6-3	200	11-7-79	2001	Lakeland, Fla.
Wyant, Hunter	.211	56	209	25	44	8	1	1	17	15	39	7	0	.273	.264	R	R	6-2	190	10-4-78	2001	Whitehall, Va.
Zapey, Winton	.246	67	252	22	62	14	0	3	21	14	55	1	1	.337	.296	R	R	5-11	170	3-21-78	1997	Santo Domingo, D.R.

PITCHING	W	L	ERA	G	GS	CG	SV	IP	H	R	ER	BB	SO	AVG	B	T	HT	WT	DOB	1st Yr	Resides
Akens, Phil	6	15	4.89	28	26	1	0	160	180	101	87	47	109	.283	R	R	6-6	200	8-9-82	2000	Bel Air, Md.
Asahina, Jon	8	7	4.02	27	16	0	0	112	102	65	50	50	87	.237	S	R	6-1	190	12-31-80	2001	Fresno, Calif.
Banks, Tyler	1	1	7.78	13	0	0	0	20	27	20	17	9	21	.313	R	R	6-2	200	2-9-81	2001	Palm Harbor, Fla.
Baxter, Allen	0	2	3.06	4	4	0	0	18	19	9	6	8	15	.287	R	R	6-4	210	7-6-83	2001	Sandston, Va.
Belizario, Ronald	6	5	3.46	23	22	1	0	140	143	67	54	56	98	.247	R	R	6-2	140	12-31-82	1999	Aragua, Venez.
Cave, Kevin	3	7	4.58	41	0	0	10	55	53	32	28	21	60	.258	R	R	6-3	210	5-25-80	2001	Levittown, Pa.
DeJesus, Elvis	3	3	4.01	29	0	0	3	43	38	19	19	20	40	.237	R	R	6-3	150	7-12-78	1999	Moca, D.R.
Esquivia, Manny	0	2	2.77	13	1	0	2	26	12	10	8	18	31	.133	R	R	6-0	160	5-30-80	1997	Cartagena, Colombia
Evans, Louis	0	1	27.00	4	0	0	0	3	8	11	9	5	2	.500	L	L	6-5	210	10-5-80	2001	San Jose, Calif.
Farizo, Brad	1	0	6.00	2	2	0	0	9	12	6	6	4	7	.342	R	R	6-4	190	11-3-78	1996	Marrero, La.
Fulchino, Jeff	5	5	3.87	24	22	0	0	133	114	67	57	51	94	.230	R	R	6-5	240	11-26-79	2001	Hollis, N.H.
Holdzkom, Lincoln	1	5	2.53	30	0	0	11	32	21	11	9	29	42	.181	R	R	6-4	240	3-23-82	2001	Lacey, Wash.
Johnston, Dave	0	1	7.71	10	0	0	1	14	20	19	12	11	13	.333	R	R	6-3	190	4-27-81	1999	Marshalltown, Iowa
McCrotty, Wes	4	1	6.44	19	0	0	0	36	53	32	26	10	31	.339	L	L	6-2	190	6-22-79	2001	Russellville, Ark.
Russell, Eddie	1	0	5.25	9	0	0	0	12	12	9	7	5	10	.260	R	R	6-2	190	6-20-78	2001	San Francisco, Calif.
Schilling, Tim	1	4	6.34	26	2	0	1	61	71	53	43	33	33	.299	L	L	5-11	180	1-15-79	2000	High Point, N.C.
Skinner, John	5	3	2.11	22	0	0	2	47	28	11	11	10	49	.167	R	R	6-1	180	6-15-77	2001	Dublin, Calif.
Tejada, Frailyn	1	5	3.61	9	9	0	0	52	56	26	21	18	24	.267	L	L	6-2	170	7-25-82	1999	Santiago, D.R.
Ungs, Nick	7	7	3.73	24	16	0	1	118	116	55	49	19	84	.255	R	R	6-1	220	9-3-79	2001	Dyersville, Iowa
Willis, Dontrelle	10	2	1.83	19	19	3	0	128	91	29	26	21	101	.200	L	L	6-4	200	1-12-82	2000	Alameda, Calif.

FIELDING

Catcher	PCT	G	PO	A	E	DP	PB
Anderson	.986	47	321	38	5	3	5
Arnott	1.000	2	13	1	0	0	0
Lynam	.930	6	51	2	4	0	1
Molina	.986	21	128	16	2	1	8
Zapey	.984	64	458	32	8	2	19

First Base	PCT	G	PO	A	E	DP
Arnott	1.000	1	2	0	0	0
Garcia	1.000	3	30	2	0	5
Hartig	.993	12	131	4	1	5
Hicks	.997	35	317	11	1	32
Kelly	1.000	1	10	0	0	0
Ortiz	1.000	3	29	1	0	3
Stokes	.992	87	779	74	7	59

Second Base	PCT	G	PO	A	E	DP
Arroyo	.942	43	73	122	12	21
Clute	.955	72	103	217	15	38
Helps	1.000	2	1	2	0	0
Kelly	.981	9	18	34	1	7
Wyant	.941	18	28	52	5	7

Third Base	PCT	G	PO	A	E	DP
Arroyo	.833	7	3	7	2	1
Garcia	.600	2	1	2	2	0
Helps	1.000	7	4	21	0	2
Kelly	1.000	4	2	7	0	1
Tucker	.921	116	64	216	24	13
Wyant	.895	7	4	13	2	3

Shortstop	PCT	G	PO	A	E	DP
Arroyo	.667	1	1	3	2	1

	PCT	G	PO	A	E	DP
Clute	.909	3	2	8	1	1
Helps	.977	8	15	28	1	8
Kelly	.857	2	2	4	1	0
Rundgren	.959	122	199	364	24	64
Wyant	1.000	4	4	7	0	1

Outfield	PCT	G	PO	A	E	DP
Arnott	.967	73	112	5	4	1
Blackburn	.952	16	19	1	1	0
Brewer	.978	119	269	3	6	1
Ferrand	.950	8	19	0	1	0
Frazier	.970	113	218	6	7	3
Helps	.000	1	0	0	0	0
Hicks	.969	79	117	7	4	0
Reed	1.000	12	25	0	0	0
Wyant	1.000	6	9	0	0	0

JAMESTOWN JAMMERS — Short-Season A

NEW YORK-PENN LEAGUE

BATTING	AVG	G	AB	R	H	2B	3B	HR	RBI	BB	SO	SB	CS	SLG	OBP	B	T	HT	WT	DOB	1st Yr	Resides
Andino, Robert	.167	9	36	2	6	1	1	0	3	1	9	1	0	.250	.189	R	R	6-0	170	4-25-84	2002	Miami, Fla.
Apotheker, Joe	.282	55	181	19	51	9	1	2	20	9	22	2	2	.376	.333	L	R	6-1	220	2-13-80	2002	Stoughton, Mass.
Arlis, Patrick	.270	47	148	17	40	9	0	3	25	22	40	0	1	.392	.366	R	R	6-0	210	12-18-80	2002	Glendale Heights, Ill.
Blackburn, Franco	.217	31	69	12	15	2	0	1	8	14	11	1	1	.290	.341	L	R	6-1	180	2-18-79	2001	Huntsville, Ala.
Grzecka, Casey	.304	18	46	8	14	4	1	0	2	9	9	1	0	.435	.439	R	R	6-2	200	11-12-79	2002	Laguna Niguel, Calif.
Guerrero, Jorge	.167	6	18	1	3	1	0	1	1	0	12	1	0	.389	.167	R	R	6-0	150	8-13-80	1997	Sabana Grande, D.R.
Hartig, Phil	.260	52	196	29	51	5	0	6	35	16	39	8	1	.378	.319	R	R	6-3	210	12-18-77	2001	Asheville, N.C.
Helps, Jay	.158	9	19	0	3	1	0	0	0	1	8	0	0	.211	.200	S	R	6-0	180	12-20-78	2001	Wyoming, Ontario
Hermida, Jeremy	.319	13	47	8	15	2	1	0	7	7	10	1	3	.404	.407	L	R	6-4	200	1-30-84	2002	Marietta, Ga.
Laidlaw, Jacob	.205	64	205	28	42	13	1	3	27	12	51	0	1	.322	.258	R	R	6-2	190	10-5-81	1999	North Las Vegas, Nev.
Lepine, Olivier	.343	35	108	16	37	10	1	1	21	10	13	0	0	.481	.403	R	R	5-11	190	11-2-78	2002	
Merkle, Tom	.222	12	45	7	10	2	0	3	4	2	14	1	0	.467	.255	R	R	6-1	190	8-4-80	2002	East Meadow, N.Y.
Molina, Angel	.222	3	9	1	2	1	0	1	2	1	5	0	0	.667	.300	R	R	6-2	200	11-4-81	2000	Santa Isabel, P.R.
Ordorica, Eric	.234	65	248	34	58	7	1	5	29	21	35	10	4	.331	.295	R	R	5-9	170	5-28-80	2002	West Covina, Calif.
Ortiz, Daniel	.188	18	48	7	9	1	0	1	4	6	25	0	0	.271	.278	R	R	6-5	200	12-19-80	1999	Nuevo, Calif.
Puccinelli, John	.207	38	92	4	19	7	0	0	8	13	21	0	0	.283	.302	R	R	6-4	180	3-5-81	1999	North Hollywood, Calif.
Randel, Kevin	.277	69	253	34	70	11	5	7	27	49	56	13	3	.443	.404	L	R	6-1	180	6-11-81	2002	Montclair, Calif.
Reed, Eric	.308	60	250	35	77	5	1	0	17	17	30	19	10	.336	.348	L	L	5-11	170	12-2-80	2002	College Station, Texas
Rohleder, Andy	.308	65	182	29	56	12	4	3	26	28	37	2	3	.467	.409	R	R	6-0	190	2-27-80	2002	Ferdinand, Ind.
Word, Robert	.214	58	192	22	41	10	1	3	25	18	72	1	0	.323	.291	L	L	6-2	200	9-16-80	2002	Charlottesville, Va.
Wyant, Hunter	.196	53	184	16	36	6	1	2	17	10	31	3	4	.272	.240	R	R	6-2	190	10-4-78	2001	Whitehall, Va.

GAMES BY POSITION: C—Arlis 45, Grzecka 13, Lepine 19, Molina 3. 1B—Hartig 33, Ortiz 10, Word 36. 2B—Blackburn 3, Guerrero 3, Helps 1, Ordorica 23, Randel 24, Wyant 25. 3B—Blackburn 1, Guerrero 2, Helps 1, Lepine 4, Merkle 12, Ordorica 19, Ortiz 1, Puccinelli 37, Wyant 20. SS—Andino 9, Helps 7, Ordorica 22, Randel 33, Wyant 9. OF—Apotheker 33, Blackburn 24, Hermida 13, Laidlaw 62, Ortiz 3, Reed 60, Rohleder 64, Word 12.

PITCHING	W	L	ERA	G	GS	CG	SV	IP	H	R	ER	BB	SO	AVG	B	T	HT	WT	DOB	1st Yr	Resides
Banks, Tyler	2	1	4.97	13	0	0	0	25	29	16	14	9	26	.284	R	R	6-2	200	2-9-81	2001	Palm Harbor, Fla.
Bazardo, Yorman	5	0	2.72	25	0	0	6	36	39	11	11	6	26	.274	R	R	6-2	170	7-11-84	2000	Maracay, Venez.
Blalock, Casey	3	2	1.64	23	0	0	2	33	17	10	6	9	30	.153	R	R	5-11	180	1-25-80	2002	Shreveport, La.
Bush, Jason	1	1	7.32	9	0	0	0	20	29	18	16	5	13	.345	R	R	6-3	190	5-19-80	2002	Richmond, Va.
Byers, Waylon	0	0	7.71	4	0	0	0	5	5	4	4	4	7	.263	R	L	5-11	180	5-6-80	2002	Milo, Iowa

PITCHING	W	L	ERA	G	GS	CG	SV	IP	H	R	ER	BB	SO	AVG	B	T	HT	WT	DOB	1st Yr	Resides
Crohan, Thomas	3	2	5.64	7	5	0	0	30	38	20	19	11	15	.316	R	L	6-1	200	9-2-80	2002	New Brunswick, N.J.
Davis, Lance	2	3	6.04	11	10	2	0	48	60	36	32	10	26	.298	R	R	6-3	190	1-18-83	2001	Lucedale, Miss.
Demontel, Jimmy	2	6	7.69	15	7	0	0	48	72	50	41	27	35	.336	R	R	6-4	240	6-7-80	2002	Wichita Falls, Texas
Evans, Louis	1	0	2.70	5	0	0	0	13	15	5	4	5	13	.277	L	L	6-5	210	10-5-80	2001	San Jose, Calif.
Greusel, Evan	1	2	5.06	8	7	0	0	32	29	18	18	15	38	.233	R	R	6-3	210	8-22-79	2002	Norman, Okla.
Johnston, Dave	2	3	11.09	10	2	0	0	19	34	29	23	13	16	.386	R	R	6-3	190	4-27-81	1999	Marshalltown, Iowa
Kupper, Dustin	2	7	5.68	16	14	1	0	76	84	54	48	21	39	.282	R	R	6-6	190	2-22-81	2001	Tucson, Ariz.
Mildren, Paul	0	3	5.54	3	3	0	0	13	16	10	8	9	6	.313	R	L	6-1	160	5-3-84	2001	Melbourne, Australia
Naylor, Kody	3	3	4.60	25	0	0	0	47	52	28	24	24	33	.282	R	R	6-2	200	3-8-80	2001	Jackson, Mich.
Primus, Carl	0	1	7.71	24	1	0	0	49	69	47	42	27	27	.334	R	R	6-3	180	7-1-80	2002	Pride, La.
Selmo, Santo	0	0	5.87	8	0	0	0	15	21	11	10	5	10	.318	R	R	6-4	180	11-21-78	1999	Santo Domingo, D.R.
Treanor, Bryan	1	0	8.17	17	0	0	0	25	42	25	23	11	22	.362	R	R	5-11	180	2-11-80	2002	San Luis Obispo, Calif.
Warpinski, Ryan	2	4	2.48	15	15	0	0	76	70	31	21	29	61	.240	R	R	6-3	210	6-30-81	2002	Maribel, Wis.
Wolf, Ross	2	4	4.66	11	11	0	0	46	56	30	24	12	18	.294	R	R	6-0	180	10-18-82	2002	Wheeler, Ill.
Wyrick, Patrick	0	0	9.00	4	0	0	0	7	11	7	7	3	7	.379	L	R	6-4	190	3-11-81	2002	Norman, Okla.

JUPITER MARLINS — Rookie

GULF COAST LEAGUE

BATTING	AVG	G	AB	R	H	2B	3B	HR	RBI	BB	SO	SB	CS	SLG	OBP	B	T	HT	WT	DOB	1st Yr	Resides
Anderson, Rondon	.208	45	120	20	25	1	1	3	14	30	35	4	2	.308	.368	L	R	5-10	190	9-29-79	2002	La Place, La.
Andino, Robert	.259	9	27	2	7	0	0	0	2	5	6	3	0	.259	.364	R	R	6-0	170	4-25-84	2002	Miami, Fla.
Aponte, Jose	.285	53	165	35	47	3	7	4	18	24	31	10	1	.461	.371	L	R	5-10	160	1-4-83	2000	Aragua, Venez.
Arroyo, Xavier	.158	27	76	8	12	4	0	0	6	23	22	5	3	.211	.360	S	R	6-1	170	8-9-84	2002	San Juan, P.R.
Baker, Jordan	.178	30	73	7	13	1	0	0	8	10	30	1	3	.192	.274	L	L	6-1	170	9-15-83	2002	Chillicothe, Ohio
Bastardo, Frederick	.231	54	173	27	40	14	0	3	23	20	31	6	3	.364	.314	R	R	5-11	160	8-8-81	1998	Maracay, Venez.
Berkenbosch, Kenny	.333	4	9	1	3	0	0	1	1	2	0	0	0	.444	.455	R	R	6-2	200	3-17-85	2002	Flevoland, Netherlands
Carofiles, Bladimir	.254	41	126	12	32	3	1	1	16	9	24	7	3	.317	.309	R	R	5-11	160	8-11-81	1999	Panama City, Panama
Coffey, Josh	.160	19	50	3	8	0	0	0	2	6	10	0	0	.160	.263	R	R	6-2	180	8-4-83	2001	Mechanicsville, Va.
Garcia, Juan-Carlos	.150	34	107	16	16	4	0	0	8	21	36	4	2	.187	.300	S	R	6-1	180	10-10-82	1998	Santiago-Caballero, D.R.
Gerlits, Gooby	.224	24	76	12	17	8	1	1	11	1	11	0	0	.395	.244	R	R	6-0	200	11-17-82	2001	Parkland, Fla.
Gonzalez, Alex	.167	5	12	0	2	1	0	0	1	0	5	0	0	.250	.154	R	R	6-3	210	1-12-83	2001	Gastonia, N.C.
Graham, Tyson	.350	6	20	2	7	3	0	0	2	3	0	0	0	.500	.409	R	R	6-2	200	11-12-79	2002	Laguna Niguel, Calif.
Grzecka, Casey	.233	9	30	1	7	1	0	0	5	1	5	0	0	.267	.273	R	R	6-2	200	11-12-79	2002	Marietta, Ga.
Hermida, Jeremy	.224	38	134	15	30	7	3	0	14	15	25	5	0	.321	.316	L	R	6-4	190	1-30-84	2002	Marietta, Ga.
Lynam, Guy	.200	11	30	2	6	2	0	0	6	6	6	1	0	.267	.351	R	R	5-11	190	10-27-80	2001	Williamstown, N.J.
Rengifo, Amado	.221	33	77	14	17	4	1	0	5	10	18	6	0	.299	.318	R	R	5-10	160	12-7-81	1998	Yaracuy, Venez.
Resop, Chris	.264	28	91	7	24	5	2	0	11	5	21	1	2	.363	.323	R	R	6-3	200	11-4-82	2001	Naples, Fla.
Spano, Robert	.117	41	103	14	12	1	0	0	4	27	39	4	3	.126	.321	S	R	5-10	170	10-20-79	2002	Naples, Fla.
Wells, Dan	.224	28	85	13	19	3	0	1	8	7	29	2	0	.294	.313	R	R	6-2	210	9-3-79	2002	Littleton, Colo.
Yepez, Marcos	.286	58	192	29	55	16	3	0	22	35	41	19	8	.401	.397	S	R	5-10	160	12-29-81	1999	Caracas, Venez.

GAMES BY POSITION: C—Coffey 14, Gerlits 24, Grzecka 7, Lynam 11, Wells 12. **1B**—Baker 11, Bastardo 6, Carofiles 13, Coffey 1, Garcia 23, Spano 2, Wells 14. **2B**—Anderson 31, Bastardo 4, Spano 17, Yepez 18. **3B**—Bastardo 38, Garcia 8, Spano 16. **SS**—Andino 9, Carofiles 8, Gonzalez 4, Spano 5, Yepez 39. **OF**—Anderson 1, Aponte 50, Arroyo 27, Baker 16, Bastardo 5, Berkenbosch 1, Carofiles 16, Graham 5, Hermida 27, Rengifo 31, Resop 19.

PITCHING	W	L	ERA	G	GS	CG	SV	IP	H	R	ER	BB	SO	AVG	B	T	HT	WT	DOB	1st Yr	Resides
Anderson, Wes	0	1	3.00	4	4	0	0	15	15	6	5	3	7	.267	R	R	6-4	170	9-10-79	1997	Pine Bluff, Ark.
Baez, Benito	0	0	3.86	5	3	0	0		3	2	2	2	5	.187	L	L	6-0	160	5-6-77	1994	Bonao, D.R.
Beckett, Josh	0	0	4.50	1	1	0	0	4	5	2	2	1	7	.294	R	R	6-3	190	5-15-80	2000	Spring, Texas
Birk, Ben	0	0	0.00	1	1	0	0	4	0	0	0	0	2	.000	L	L	6-5	210	11-6-77	2001	St. Paul, Minn.
Bush, Jason	0	0	9.00	2	0	0	0	4	7	4	4	1	1	.411	R	R	6-3	190	5-19-80	2002	Richmond, Va.
Chick, Travis	3	2	2.76	12	8	0	1	46	40	16	14	19	39	.227	R	R	6-3	220	6-10-84	2002	Whitehouse, Texas
Eazor, Kyle	2	0	3.72	16	0	0	3	29	27	17	12	15	24	.245	L	L	6-0	200	8-17-81	2002	Phoenix, Ariz.
Esquivia, Manny	1	0	1.00	2	1	0	0	9	3	1	1	3	11	.103	R	R	6-0	160	5-30-80	1997	Cartagena, Colombia
Farizo, Brad	1	0	2.03	3	3	0	0	13	10	3	3	1	14	.196	R	R	6-2	190	11-3-78	1996	Marrero, La.
Gabriel, Chris	2	2	3.60	17	0	0	0	35	36	26	14	19	18	.260	R	R	6-1	190	10-6-82	2002	Rancho Cucamonga, Calif.
Iehl, Jason	2	3	3.00	7	5	0	0	24	18	10	8	6	16	.195	R	R	6-2	180	4-23-84	2002	Woodridge, Ill.
Johnson, Josh	2	0	6.60	4	3	0	0	15	8	3	1	3	11	.153	L	R	6-7	220	1-31-84	2002	Tulsa, Okla.
Mairena, Ozwaldo	0	0	0.00	1	1	0	0	1	1	0	0	0	1	.200	L	L	5-11	160	6-30-74	1996	Chinandega, Nicaragua
Mildren, Paul	3	4	1.97	11	10	2	0	59	52	16	13	17	38	.233	R	L	6-1	160	5-3-84	2001	Melbourne, Australia
Nova, Juan	2	1	1.11	22	0	0	7	32	26	8	4	6	32	.216	R	R	6-3	190	3-11-84	2001	Villa Vasquez, D.R.
O'Connor, Shaun	0	1	7.36	3	0	0	0	4	1	3	3	3	1	.100	R	R	6-10	260	5-6-79	2002	Stafford, Va.
Olsen, Scott	2	3	2.96	13	11	0	0	52	39	18	17	17	50	.204	L	L	6-4	170	1-12-84	2002	Lake in the Hills, Ill.
Prieto, Victor	4	2	3.16	8	7	1	0	31	14	17	11	19	21	.134	R	R	6-2	190	4-24-83	1999	Aragua, Venez.
Russell, Eddie	2	0	0.00	2	0	0	0	3	0	0	0	0	7	.000	R	R	6-2	190	6-20-78	2001	San Francisco, Calif.
Selmo, Santo	1	4	1.50	14	1	0	1	30	19	16	5	6	18	.172	R	R	6-4	180	11-21-78	1999	Santo Domingo, D.R.
Sosa, Alexis	0	0	5.14	3	0	0	0	7	9	5	4	7	3	.310	S	L	6-1	160	6-25-83	2001	Santo Domingo, D.R.
Sterrett, Adam	0	0	7.31	15	0	0	0	28	29	29	23	30	14	.284	S	R	6-2	190	8-11-82	2000	Staunton, Va.
Taki, Yusuke	0	2	3.48	6	0	0	0	10	11	4	4	4	5	.297	R	R	6-2	190	3-22-83	2002	Tokyo, Japan
Targac, Matthew	0	1	6.00	1	0	0	0	3	4	2	2	1	2	.250	S	L	6-3	210	6-25-80	1998	Delano, Calif.
Tejada, Frailyn	0	0	4.50	1	0	0	0	2	1	1	1	1	2	.142	L	L	6-1	180	7-25-82	1999	Santiago, D.R.
Treanor, Bryan	1	1	0.00	3	1	0	0	12	11	1	0	0	14	.250	R	R	5-11	180	2-11-80	2002	San Luis Obispo, Calif.
Wyrick, Patrick	3	1	2.70	10	0	0	0	20	17	9	6	5	22	.220	L	R	6-4	190	3-11-81	2002	Norman, Okla.

HOUSTON ASTROS

BY TOM HALLIBURTON

A mild second-half improvement could not bail out the 2002 Astros from a 41-45 start, causing Houston to finish 84-78 and miss the playoffs for the second time in the last six years.

Under first-year manager Jimy Williams, the Astros finished 13 games behind the National League Central champion Cardinals and never reached first place after the season's opening week.

The Astros won 27 of 38 games during their season's warmest stretch, from June 25-Aug. 7. That enabled Houston to move within one game of St. Louis. But the Astros lost three of their next four games and never seriously challenged the Cardinals during the final month.

Other than all-star outfielder Lance Berkman, the Astros lacked enough offensive production. They scored 100 fewer runs than in 2001. The noteworthy exception, Berkman won the NL RBI crown with 128 and tied for third in home runs with 42.

Jeff Bagwell (.291-31-98) competed bravely despite experiencing considerable pain from offseason shoulder surgery. Craig Biggio (.253-15-58) dipped 30 points below his career batting average.

"I believe this club had the ability to play better and compete for a championship," Gerry Hunsicker said after his sixth year as general manager. "It was just a matter of too many guys having subpar years offensively. We didn't hit with the power that I expected, and that was a big part of our offense."

Injuries prevented veteran righthanders Shane Reynolds and Dave Mlicki from steadily contributing to the Astros starting rotation. Reynolds (3-6, 4.86) underwent season-ending back surgery in June. Mlicki (4-10, 5.34) missed nearly two months with an abdominal

Lance Berkman | Kirk Saarloos

PLAYERS OF THE YEAR

MAJOR LEAGUE: Lance Berkman, of

A year after hitting .331-34-126, Berkman proved his success was no fluke by batting .292-42-128. He led the National League in RBIs while serving as Houston's everyday center fielder.

MINOR LEAGUE: Kirk Saarloos, rhp

A third-round draft pick in 2001, Saarloos went 12-1, 1.54 in 99 innings between New Orleans and Round Rock. He allowed just two earned runs in his last 68 Double-A innings on his way to becoming the second player from the Class of '01 to reach the majors.

injury and never regained top form.

Those losses placed the staff's leadership on the able shoulders of an outstanding righthanded tandem of Roy Oswalt and Wade Miller.

Oswalt (19-9, 3.01) and Miller (15-4, 3.28) produced numbers that matched any major league team's 1-2 combo after the all-star break. But Houston lacked the depth and consistency necessary from other starting pitchers in order to win the division.

Promising lefthander Carlos Hernandez went 7-5, 4.38 but would miss two extended segments due to shoulder problems. Minor league sensation Kirk Saarloos earned Texas League all-star accolades before he struggled to 6-7, 6.01 numbers in Houston.

If Oswalt and Miller impressed, so did the Astros' bullpen, though it struggled during the club's 17-21 start. Octavio Dotel (6-4, 1.85, six saves) and Billy Wagner (4-2, 2.52, 35 saves) continued to remain one of the league's premier setup-closer duos.

Houston's top four farm clubs combined for a .547 winning percentage in 2002. Two teams—Triple-A New Orleans and Class A Lexington—led their respective leagues in pitching.

Outfielder Jason Lane became an encouraging September callup after he won his fourth MVP award in the Astros organization. The righthanded-hitting Southern California product compiled a .484 slugging percentage at New Orleans.

As the only team in the game with no high Class A clubs and two low A clubs in 2000-01, the Astros opted to return to the high Class A Carolina League in 2003 for the first time since 1968 by reaching a four-year working agreement with Salem.

ORGANIZATION LEADERS

BATTING

*AVG	Royce Huffman, Round Rock	.322
R	Brooks Conrad, Michigan	94
	Mike Rodriguez, Michigan	94
H	Royce Huffman, Round Rock	168
TB	Henri Stanley, Round Rock	247
2B	Five tied at	36
3B	Brooks Conrad, Michigan	14
HR	Three tied at	16
RBI	Brooks Conrad, Michigan	94
	Todd Self, Michigan	94
BB	Henri Stanley, Round Rock	72
SO	Charlton Jimerson, Lexington	168
SB	Eric Bruntlett, New Orleans/Round Rock	36

PITCHING

W	Mike Burns, Michigan	14
	D.J. Houlton, Michigan	14
L	Anthony Pluta, Michigan	13
	Chad Qualls, Round Rock	13
#ERA	Kirk Saarloos, New Orleans/Round Rock	1.54
G	Tom Shearn, New Orleans	57
CG	Mike Burns, Michigan	3
SV	Miguel Saladin, New Orleans/Round Rock	24
IP	Mike Burns, Michigan	181
BB	Anthony Pluta, Michigan	83
SO	Chad Qualls, Round Rock	142

*Minimum 250 At-Bats #Minimum 75 Innings

HOUSTON ASTROS

Manager: Jimy Williams

BATTING	AVG	G	AB	R	H	2B	3B	HR	RBI	BB	SO	SB	CS	SLG	OBP	B	T	HT	WT	DOB	1st Yr	Resides
Ausmus, Brad	.257	130	447	57	115	19	3	6	50	38	71	2	3	.353	.322	R	R	5-11	200	4-14-69	1987	San Diego, Calif.
Bagwell, Jeff	.291	158	571	94	166	33	2	31	98	101	130	7	3	.518	.401	R	R	6-0	210	5-27-68	1989	Houston, Texas
Berkman, Lance	.292	158	578	106	169	35	2	42	128	107	118	8	4	.578	.405	S	L	6-1	220	2-10-76	1997	Houston, Texas
Biggio, Craig	.253	145	577	96	146	36	3	15	58	50	111	16	2	.404	.330	R	R	5-11	180	12-14-65	1987	Houston, Texas
Blum, Geoff	.283	130	368	45	104	20	4	10	52	49	70	2	0	.440	.367	S	R	6-3	200	4-26-73	1994	Los Angeles, Calif.
Chavez, Raul	.250	2	4	1	1	0	0	0	1	0	0	0	0	.500	.500	R	R	5-11	210	3-18-74	1990	Valencia, Venez.
Ensberg, Morgan	.242	49	132	14	32	7	2	3	19	18	25	2	0	.394	.346	R	R	6-2	210	8-26-75	1998	Orlando, Fla.
Everett, Adam	.193	40	88	11	17	3	0	0	4	12	19	3	0	.227	.297	R	R	6-0	160	2-2-77	1998	Kennesaw, Ga.
Ginter, Keith	.200	7	5	1	1	1	0	0	0	2	1	0	0	.400	.500	R	R	5-10	190	5-5-76	1998	Fullerton, Calif.
Hidalgo, Richard	.235	114	388	54	91	17	4	15	48	43	85	6	2	.415	.319	R	R	6-3	220	7-2-75	1991	Guarenas, Venez.
Hunter, Brian	.269	98	201	32	54	16	3	3	20	16	39	5	0	.423	.329	R	R	6-3	180	3-25-71	1989	Vancouver, Wash.
Lane, Jason	.290	44	69	12	20	3	1	4	10	10	12	1	1	.536	.375	R	L	6-2	210	12-22-76	1999	Sebastopol, Calif.
Loretta, Mark	.424	21	66	10	28	4	0	2	8	9	5	1	1	.576	.481	R	R	6-0	180	8-14-71	1993	Scottsdale, Ariz.
2-team (86 Milwaukee)	.304	107	283	33	86	18	0	4	27	32	37	1	1	.410	.381							
Lugo, Julio	.261	88	322	45	84	15	1	8	35	28	74	9	3	.388	.322	R	R	6-1	190	11-16-75	1995	Brooklyn, N.Y.
Merced, Orlando	.287	123	251	35	72	13	3	6	30	26	50	4	0	.434	.350	L	R	6-1	190	11-2-66	1985	Orlando, Fla.
Vizcaino, Jose	.303	125	406	53	123	19	2	5	37	24	40	3	5	.397	.342	S	R	6-1	180	3-26-68	1986	Jamul, Calif.
Ward, Daryle	.276	136	453	41	125	31	0	12	72	33	82	1	3	.424	.324	L	L	6-2	240	6-27-75	1994	Riverside, Calif.
Wesson, Barry	.200	15	20	1	4	0	1	0	1	1	5	0	0	.300	.238	R	R	6-2	210	4-6-77	1995	Glen Allan, Miss.
Zaun, Gregg	.222	76	185	18	41	7	1	3	24	12	36	1	0	.319	.275	S	R	5-10	190	4-14-71	1989	Colleyville, Texas
Zinter, Alan	.136	39	44	5	6	2	0	2	3	0	19	0	0	.318	.136	S	R	6-2	200	5-19-68	1989	Oro Valley, Ariz.

PITCHING	W	L	ERA	G	GS	CG	SV	IP	H	R	ER	BB	SO	AVG	B	T	HT	WT	DOB	1st Yr	Resides
Borbon, Pedro	3	2	5.50	56	0	0	1	38	41	24	23	19	39	.286	L	L	6-1	230	11-15-67	1988	Houston, Texas
Cruz, Nelson	2	6	4.48	43	5	0	0	78	90	44	39	29	61	.283	R	R	6-1	180	9-13-72	1989	Washington, DC
Dotel, Octavio	6	4	1.85	83	0	0	6	97	58	21	20	27	118	.173	R	R	6-0	200	11-25-73	1993	Santo Domingo, D.R.
Gordon, Tom	0	2	3.32	15	0	0	0	19	15	7	7	6	17	.217	R	R	5-10	190	11-18-67	1986	Avon Park, Fla.
2-team (19 Chicago)	1	3	3.38	34	0	0	0	43	42	19	16	16	48	.260							
Hernandez, Carlos	7	5	4.38	23	21	0	0	111	112	56	54	61	93	.261	S	L	5-10	180	4-22-80	1997	Yagua, Venez.
Lidge, Brad	1	0	6.23	6	1	0	0	9	12	6	6	9	12	.333	R	R	6-5	200	12-23-76	1998	Englewood, Colo.
Linebrink, Scott	0	0	7.03	22	0	0	0	24	31	21	19	13	24	.298	R	R	6-2	200	8-4-76	1997	Taylor, Texas
Mann, Jim	0	1	4.09	17	0	0	0	22	19	10	10	7	19	.234	R	R	6-3	220	11-17-74	1994	Holbrook, Mass.
Mathews, T.J.	0	0	3.44	12	0	0	0	18	19	7	7	5	13	.271	R	R	6-1	220	1-19-70	1992	Las Vegas, Nev.
Miller, Wade	15	4	3.28	26	26	1	0	165	151	63	60	62	144	.248	R	R	6-2	200	9-13-76	1996	Reading, Pa.
Mlicki, Dave	4	10	5.34	22	16	0	0	86	101	57	51	34	57	.290	R	R	6-4	200	6-8-68	1989	Columbus, Ohio
Munro, Peter	5	5	3.57	19	14	0	0	81	89	37	32	23	45	.283	R	R	6-3	210	6-14-75	1994	Windham, N.H.
Oswalt, Roy	19	9	3.01	35	34	0	0	233	215	86	78	62	208	.247	R	R	6-0	170	8-29-77	1997	Weir, Miss.
Pichardo, Hipolito	0	1	81.00	1	0	0	0	3	3	3	2	0	.750	R	R	6-1	190	8-22-69	1988	Esperanza, D.R.
Puffer, Brandon	3	3	4.43	55	0	0	0	69	67	37	34	38	48	.257	R	R	6-3	190	10-5-75	1994	Round Rock, Texas
Redding, Tim	3	6	5.40	18	14	0	0	73	78	49	44	35	63	.275	R	R	6-0	190	2-12-78	1998	Churchville, N.Y.
Reynolds, Shane	3	6	4.86	13	13	0	0	74	80	43	40	26	47	.273	R	R	6-3	210	3-26-68	1989	Houston, Texas
Robertson, Jeriome	0	2	6.52	11	1	0	0	10	13	8	7	5	6	.393	L	L	6-1	190	3-30-77	1996	Exeter, Calif.
Saarloos, Kirk	6	7	6.01	17	17	1	0	85	100	59	57	27	54	.301	R	R	6-0	180	5-23-79	2001	Long Beach, Calif.
Stone, Ricky	3	3	3.61	78	0	0	1	77	78	36	31	34	63	.266	R	R	6-1	190	2-28-75	1994	Hamilton, Ohio
Wagner, Billy	4	2	2.52	70	0	0	35	75	51	21	21	22	88	.196	L	L	5-11	190	7-25-71	1993	Charlottesville, Va.

FIELDING

Catcher	PCT	G	PO	A	E	DP	PB
Ausmus	.997	129	942	65	3	9	2
Chavez	1.000	2	10	0	0	0	0
Zaun	.985	44	307	18	5	3	3
Zinter	1.000	1	2	0	0	0	0

First Base	PCT	G	PO	A	E	DP
Bagwell	.995	153	1254	112	7	119
Blum	1.000	1	1	0	0	1
Loretta	1.000	5	20	1	0	2
Merced	1.000	7	53	3	0	8
Vizcaino	1.000	5	10	1	0	2
Zinter	1.000	8	24	2	0	3

Second Base	PCT	G	PO	A	E	DP
Biggio	.988	142	313	352	8	88
Blum	1.000	1	2	2	0	0
Loretta	1.000	3	7	8	0	2
Vizcaino	1.000	25	38	57	0	5

Third Base	PCT	G	PO	A	E	DP
Blum	.971	104	69	199	8	27
Ensberg	.929	43	28	76	8	5

	PCT	G	PO	A	E	DP
Ginter	.875	4	3	4	1	1
Loretta	.944	10	6	11	1	1
Merced	1.000	1	0	1	0	0
Vizcaino	1.000	30	18	44	0	3

Shortstop	PCT	G	PO	A	E	DP
Blum	.000	2	0	0	0	0
Everett	.962	34	34	93	5	22
Loretta	.957	6	6	16	1	2
Lugo	.976	84	121	205	8	32
Vizcaino	.980	58	58	135	4	35

Outfield	PCT	G	PO	A	E	DP
Berkman	.977	156	293	6	7	1
Biggio	1.000	1	1	0	0	0
Blum	1.000	10	8	0	0	0
Hidalgo	.995	110	210	6	1	3
Hunter	1.000	88	121	4	0	1
Lane	.980	38	47	3	1	1
Merced	.980	56	89	7	2	1
Ward	.981	122	146	9	3	3
Wesson	1.000	15	11	0	0	0

Craig Biggio

RON VESELY

Director, Player Development: Tim Purpura

Class	Farm Team	League	W	L	Pct.	Finish*	Manager	First Yr.
AAA	New Orleans (La.) Zephyrs	Pacific Coast	75	69	.521	t-5th(16)	Chris Maloney	1997
AA	Round Rock (Texas) Express	Texas	75	65	.536	4th (8)	Jackie Moore	2000
Low A	Michigan Battle Cats	Midwest	79	61	.564	4th (14)	John Massarelli	1999
Low A	Lexington (Ky.) Legends	South Atlantic	81	59	.579	2nd (16)	J.J. Cannon	2001
SS A	Tri-City (Troy, N.Y.) Valley Cats	New York-Penn	27	48	.360	13th (14)	Ivan DeJesus	2001
Rookie	Martinsville (Va.) Astros	Appalachian	41	26	.612	3rd (10)	Jorge Orta	1999

*Finish in overall standings (No. of teams in league)

NEW ORLEANS ZEPHYRS — Class AAA

PACIFIC COAST LEAGUE

BATTING

	AVG	G	AB	R	H	2B	3B	HR	RBI	BB	SO	SB	CS	SLG	OBP	B	T	HT	WT	DOB	1st Yr	Resides
Bruntlett, Eric	.206	18	68	9	14	3	0	0	1	10	10	1	1	.250	.308	R	R	6-0	200	3-29-78	2000	Lafayette, Ind.
Charles, Frank	.265	105	332	30	88	10	2	6	49	17	83	1	3	.361	.306	R	R	6-4	210	2-23-69	1991	San Diego, Calif.
Chavez, Raul	.228	111	373	24	85	10	2	3	36	21	50	3	4	.279	.278	R	R	5-11	210	3-18-74	1990	Valencia, Venez.
Cromer, Tripp	.257	77	265	31	68	13	2	7	26	9	42	0	0	.400	.289	R	R	6-2	160	11-21-67	1989	Columbia, S.C.
Ensberg, Morgan	.288	83	292	50	84	12	3	7	37	50	56	9	5	.421	.401	R	R	6-2	210	8-26-75	1998	Orlando, Fla.
Everett, Adam	.275	88	345	51	95	16	7	2	25	24	59	12	3	.380	.331	R	R	6-0	160	2-2-77	1998	Kennesaw, Ga.
Frye, Jeff	.200	15	40	1	8	1	0	0	4	3	0	1	.225	.273	R	R	5-9	170	8-31-66	1988	Mansfield, Texas
Ginter, Keith	.264	121	435	70	115	28	1	12	54	56	97	3	4	.416	.362	R	R	5-10	190	5-5-76	1998	Fullerton, Calif.
Hunter, Brian L.	.158	5	19	4	3	0	1	0	0	2	7	2	0	.263	.238	R	R	6-3	180	3-25-71	1989	Vancouver, Wash.
Lane, Jason	.272	111	426	65	116	36	2	15	83	31	90	13	3	.472	.328	R	L	6-2	210	12-22-76	1999	Sebastopol, Calif.
Logan, Kyle	.299	94	335	54	100	20	3	12	46	24	48	22	8	.484	.357	L	R	6-0	200	7-11-75	1997	Hattiesburg, Miss.
Maldonado, Carlos	.172	12	29	1	5	0	0	0	2	1	7	0	0	.172	.200	R	R	6-2	180	1-3-79	1996	Maracaibo, Venez.
Matranga, Dave	.273	101	300	47	82	15	3	7	40	27	79	7	2	.413	.342	R	R	6-0	170	1-8-77	1998	Aloso Viejo, Calif.
Murphy, Mike	.179	15	39	0	7	0	0	0	1	2	10	0	0	.179	.220	R	R	6-2	180	1-23-72	1990	Martinez, Calif.
Porter, Colin	.265	134	461	59	122	30	5	6	38	46	127	28	7	.390	.331	L	L	6-2	200	11-23-75	1998	Tucson, Ariz.
Prieto, Chris	.198	21	86	10	17	2	0	0	1	8	11	0	1	.221	.274	L	L	5-11	180	8-24-72	1993	Fontana, Calif.
Saylor, Jamie	.224	100	237	23	53	7	3	3	12	21	60	4	1	.316	.287	L	R	5-11	180	9-11-74	1994	Garland, Texas
Wesson, Barry	.293	111	413	43	121	25	5	11	61	16	100	4	7	.458	.325	R	R	6-2	210	4-6-77	1995	Glen Allan, Miss.
Zinter, Alan	.231	63	225	30	52	14	0	11	39	22	64	2	0	.440	.298	S	R	6-2	200	5-19-68	1989	Oro Valley, Ariz.

PITCHING

	W	L	ERA	G	GS	CG	SV	IP	H	R	ER	BB	SO	AVG	B	T	HT	WT	DOB	1st Yr	Resides
Arteaga, J.D.	9	10	4.29	42	15	0	3	120	135	70	57	40	77	.284	L	L	6-3	220	8-2-74	1997	Miami, Fla.
Bullinger, Kirk	4	1	2.75	55	1	0	4	75	61	25	23	11	46	.222	R	R	6-2	170	10-28-69	1992	Gretna, La.
Cruz, Nelson	0	1	4.50	6	0	0	1	8	4	4	4	8	.148	R	R	6-1	180	9-13-72	1989	Washington, D.C.
Franklin, Wayne	13	9	3.12	29	27	1	0	179	153	68	62	59	141	.235	L	L	6-2	200	3-9-74	1996	North East, Md.
Guerra, Mark	6	11	4.01	28	28	1	0	173	183	88	77	35	89	.274	R	R	6-2	200	11-4-71	1994	Pensacola Beach, Fla.
Hernandez, Carlos	0	0	0.00	1	1	0	0	3	1	0	0	1	2	.100	S	L	5-10	180	4-22-80	1997	Yagua, Venez.
Lidge, Brad	5	5	3.39	24	19	0	0	112	83	47	42	47	110	.206	R	R	6-5	200	12-23-76	1998	Englewood, Colo.
Linebrink, Scott	1	1	6.00	13	0	0	0	15	17	11	10	11	16	.293	R	R	6-2	200	8-4-76	1997	Taylor, Texas
Mann, Jim	0	3	4.15	33	0	0	22	35	33	20	16	8	29	.253	R	R	6-3	220	11-17-74	1994	Holbrook, Mass.
Mathews, T.J.	0	0	1.80	4	0	0	0	5	3	1	1	1	3	.157	R	R	6-1	200	1-19-70	1992	Las Vegas, Nev.
Miller, Wade	0	0	2.25	2	2	0	0	8	10	4	2	1	9	.322	R	R	6-2	200	9-13-76	1996	Reading, Pa.
Mlicki, Dave	0	0	0.00	1	1	0	0	3	2	0	0	1	2	.200	R	R	6-4	200	6-8-68	1989	Columbus, Ohio
Munro, Peter	7	1	2.39	19	13	1	0	94	68	30	25	15	73	.200	R	R	6-3	210	6-14-75	1994	Windham, N.H.
Nitkowski, C.J.	1	2	2.78	24	0	0	2	23	21	7	7	7	20	.244	L	L	6-3	200	3-9-73	1994	Houston, Texas
Pichardo, Hipolito	0	0	0.00	5	1	0	0	7	6	0	0	1	4	.260	R	R	6-1	190	8-22-69	1988	Esperanza, D.R.
Puffer, Brandon	2	1	1.80	11	0	0	0	15	8	3	3	4	13	.156	R	R	6-3	190	10-5-75	1994	Round Rock, Texas
Ramirez, Santiago	2	0	3.38	18	0	0	1	21	17	8	8	11	15	.220	R	R	5-11	180	8-15-78	1997	Bonao, D.R.
Redding, Tim	3	3	5.21	11	7	0	0	38	32	22	22	13	50	.225	R	R	6-0	190	2-12-78	1998	Churchville, N.Y.
Robertson, Jeriome	12	8	2.55	27	27	2	0	180	160	59	51	45	114	.238	L	L	6-1	190	3-30-77	1996	Exeter, Calif.
Saarloos, Kirk	2	0	2.25	4	2	0	0	16	12	4	4	2	19	.210	R	R	6-0	180	5-23-79	2001	Long Beach, Calif.
Saladin, Miguel	0	0	4.50	2	0	0	0	2	3	1	1	1	2	.375	R	R	5-11	190	5-22-75	1996	San Pedro de Macoris, D.R.
Sessions, Doug	0	1	6.57	11	0	0	0	12	15	9	9	3	4	.319	R	R	6-1	200	9-28-76	1998	Orange Park, Fla.
Shearn, Tom	4	6	2.92	57	0	0	8	83	77	29	27	41	80	.250	R	R	6-4	200	8-28-77	1994	Columbus, Ohio
Shouse, Brian	1	0	3.43	19	0	0	0	21	17	10	8	3	20	.215	L	L	5-11	180	9-26-68	1990	Peoria, Ill.
2-team (5 Omaha)	1	0	4.24	24	0	0	0	23	24	13	11	4	22	.260							
Wade, Travis	3	6	6.32	27	0	0	0	37	44	26	26	18	22	.299	R	R	6-3	210	7-8-75	1997	Climax, Mich.

FIELDING

Catcher	PCT	G	PO	A	E	DP	PB
Charles	.974	37	211	11	6	1	5
Chavez	.991	107	734	77	7	9	4
Maldonado	1.000	10	43	6	0	1	1

First Base	PCT	G	PO	A	E	DP
Charles	.985	47	372	16	6	37
Cromer	.994	38	305	18	2	36
Ensberg	.967	4	26	3	1	2
Lane	1.000	10	63	7	0	6
Zinter	.998	58	502	54	1	53

Second Base	PCT	G	PO	A	E	DP
Bruntlett	.900	2	4	5	1	3
Cromer	.973	22	39	71	3	17
Ginter	.965	61	126	151	10	36

Third Base	PCT	G	PO	A	E	DP
Charles	1.000	1	0	1	0	0
Cromer	1.000	1	1	0	0	0
Ensberg	.920	79	45	163	18	12
Frye	.875	4	2	5	1	0
Ginter	.929	53	30	128	12	12
Matranga	.000	1	0	0	0	0
Saylor	.957	11	10	12	1	1

Shortstop	PCT	G	PO	A	E	DP
Bruntlett	.946	16	30	57	5	12
Cromer	.960	7	11	13	1	4
Everett	.984	86	144	285	7	66

Matranga	.981	64	107	156	5	40
Saylor	.982	14	22	33	1	6

Frye	.900	3	2	7	1	1
Matranga	.986	17	26	45	1	9
Saylor	.939	25	50	57	7	19

Outfield	PCT	G	PO	A	E	DP
Frye	1.000	1	2	0	0	0
Ginter	1.000	1	1	0	0	0
Hunter	1.000	4	11	0	0	0
Lane	.991	103	230	2	2	0
Logan	.980	76	146	3	3	0
Murphy	1.000	12	30	0	0	0
Porter	.965	124	204	15	8	2
Prieto	.939	19	29	2	2	0
Saylor	1.000	7	5	1	0	0
Wesson	.996	109	217	10	1	2

ORGANIZATION STATISTICS

TEXAS LEAGUE

BATTING

BATTING	AVG	G	AB	R	H	2B	3B	HR	RBI	BB	SO	SB	CS	SLG	OBP	B	T	HT	WT	DOB	1st Yr	Resides
Alfaro, Jason	.314	124	455	71	143	36	2	16	74	50	75	11	9	.508	.393	R	R	5-10	190	11-29-77	1997	Fort Worth, Texas
Bruntlett, Eric	.265	116	464	81	123	21	2	2	48	56	61	35	12	.332	.351	R	R	6-0	200	3-29-78	2000	Lafayette, Ind.
Buck, John	.263	120	448	48	118	29	3	12	89	31	93	2	3	.422	.314	R	R	6-3	210	7-7-80	1998	Salt Lake City, Utah
Burke, Chris	.264	136	481	66	127	19	8	3	37	39	61	16	15	.356	.330	R	R	5-11	180	3-11-80	2001	Knoxville, Tenn.
Fatheree, Danny	.172	10	29	3	5	1	0	0	3	1	8	0	0	.207	.200	R	R	5-11	210	8-25-78	1997	Grand Prairie, Texas
Hill, Mike	.283	135	527	75	149	30	6	14	61	39	105	14	8	.442	.337	R	R	6-4	200	9-30-76	1999	Lawton, Okla.
Huffman, Royce	.322	132	522	79	168	36	3	12	91	41	70	13	6	.471	.381	R	R	6-0	200	1-11-77	1999	Missouri City, Texas
Maldonado, Carlos	.252	47	123	13	31	8	0	4	20	22	23	0	0	.415	.356	R	R	6-2	180	1-3-79	1996	Maracaibo, Venez.
Maule, Jason	.263	76	171	33	45	3	0	2	15	19	27	13	4	.316	.347	L	R	6-0	170	7-1-77	1999	East Berlin, Conn.
Rosamond, Mike	.230	118	422	48	97	22	4	13	49	28	120	6	9	.393	.281	R	R	6-5	210	4-18-78	1999	Madison, Miss.
Soto, T.J.	.154	14	39	3	6	1	0	0	3	2	20	1	0	.179	.190	R	R	5-11	200	8-31-77	2000	Ruston, La.
Stanley, Henri	.314	127	456	90	143	36	10	16	72	72	85	14	9	.542	.408	L	L	5-10	190	12-15-77	2000	Columbia, S.C.
Topolski, Jon	.237	102	300	41	71	6	2	9	34	48	88	3	6	.360	.343	L	R	5-10	180	12-28-76	1999	Houston, Texas
Tremie, Chris	.231	50	134	16	31	3	0	2	19	13	18	0	1	.299	.295	R	R	6-2	210	10-17-69	1992	New Waverly, Texas
Whiteman, Tommy	.179	15	56	3	10	2	1	0	5	4	17	1	1	.250	.246	R	R	6-3	170	7-14-79	2000	Edmond, Okla.
Wright, Gavin	.333	2	9	2	3	0	0	0	2	0	2	0	0	.333	.364	R	R	6-2	180	5-6-79	1999	Lufkin, Texas

PITCHING

PITCHING	W	L	ERA	G	GS	CG	SV	IP	H	R	ER	BB	SO	AVG	B	T	HT	WT	DOB	1st Yr	Resides
Coughenour, Jory	3	2	3.52	32	4	0	3	61	72	32	24	26	46	.298	R	R	6-0	200	6-17-78	2000	Dunbar, Pa.
Gallo, Mike	0	0	6.75	1	0	0	0	1	1	1	1	0	0	.200	L	L	6-0	170	4-2-77	1999	Long Beach, Calif.
Hernandez, Carlos	0	0	4.15	2	2	0	0	9	4	4	4	4	10	.137	S	L	5-10	180	4-22-80	1997	Yagua, Venez.
Ireland, Eric	1	0	1.00	4	0	0	0	9	6	1	1	1	6	.187	R	R	6-1	170	3-11-77	1996	Long Beach, Calif.
Jamison, Ryan	3	2	3.77	31	1	0	1	57	63	31	24	23	57	.278	R	R	6-3	180	1-5-78	1999	El Cajon, Calif.
Lidge, Brad	1	1	2.45	5	0	0	0	11	9	4	3	3	18	.219	R	R	6-5	200	12-23-76	1998	Englewood, Colo.
Linebrink, Scott	0	0	0.00	2	2	0	0	2	2	0	0	2	1	.285	R	R	6-2	200	8-4-76	1997	Taylor, Texas
Lira, James	3	4	3.35	28	0	0	3	43	35	18	16	17	30	.220	R	R	6-1	160	5-19-78	1998	Bishop, Texas
Mann, Jim	0	0	4.50	1	0	0	0	2	1	1	1	0	2	.142	R	R	6-3	220	11-17-74	1994	Holbrook, Mass.
Mathews, T.J.	0	0	0.00	1	0	0	0	1	1	0	0	0	1	.250	R	R	6-2	220	1-19-70	1992	Las Vegas, Nev.
Miller, Greg	3	6	5.00	14	12	0	0	68	77	44	38	20	51	.274	L	L	6-5	210	9-30-79	1997	Aurora, Ill.
Mlicki, Dave	1	1	3.00	2	2	0	0	9	8	3	3	2	7	.235	R	R	6-4	200	6-8-68	1989	Columbus, Ohio
Nannini, Mike	7	10	5.81	29	24	1	0	141	151	97	91	64	120	.273	R	R	5-11	190	8-9-80	1998	Las Vegas, Nev.
Peguero, Darwin	3	2	4.48	54	0	0	1	60	66	42	30	28	41	.277	R	L	6-0	190	12-5-78	1996	Hato Mayor, D.R.
Qualls, Chad	6	13	4.36	29	29	0	0	163	174	92	79	67	142	.273	R	R	6-5	200	8-17-78	2000	Reno, Nev.
Ramirez, Santiago	5	2	2.56	33	0	0	4	63	45	19	18	26	73	.199	R	R	5-11	180	8-15-78	1997	Bonao, D.R.
Roberts, Nick	12	7	4.34	28	27	2	0	172	195	102	83	42	98	.283	R	R	6-2	180	11-6-76	1999	Annabella, Utah
Rosario, Rodrigo	11	6	3.11	26	23	0	0	130	106	56	45	59	94	.222	R	R	6-2	160	12-14-77	1996	La Romana, D.R.
Saarloos, Kirk	10	1	1.04	13	13	1	0	83	48	17	13	21	82	.168	R	R	6-0	180	5-23-79	2001	Long Beach, Calif.
Saladin, Miguel	4	5	2.06	53	0	0	24	57	36	18	13	25	46	.184	R	R	5-11	190	5-22-75	1996	San Pedro de Macoris, D.R.
Sessions, Doug	2	1	5.44	30	1	0	0	46	48	28	28	20	39	.271	R	R	6-1	200	9-28-76	1998	Orange Park, Fla.
Tremblay, Max	0	0	1.59	3	0	0	0	6	7	1	1	0	5	.304	L	L	6-0	190	6-18-76	1998	San Dimas, Calif.
Wade, Travis	0	2	3.77	21	0	0	1	31	31	13	13	12	24	.269	R	R	6-3	210	7-8-75	1997	Climax, Mich.

FIELDING

Catcher	PCT	G	PO	A	E	DP	PB
Buck	.990	104	727	64	8	4	14
Fatheree	1.000	9	58	4	0	0	1
Maldonado	.976	18	116	7	3	0	5
Tremie	.993	20	125	10	1	2	0

First Base	PCT	G	PO	A	E	DP
Huffman	.989	129	1067	63	13	93
Maldonado	1.000	3	17	3	0	0
Soto	1.000	6	29	4	0	4
Tremie	1.000	6	43	4	0	7

Second Base	PCT	G	PO	A	E	DP
Alfaro	1.000	1	2	0	0	0

Third Base	PCT	G	PO	A	E	DP
Bruntlett	.988	33	71	89	2	21
Burke	.976	94	173	280	11	62
Maule	.894	15	20	22	5	3
Alfaro	.963	113	87	196	11	18
Maule	.907	25	12	27	4	2
Soto	1.000	1	0	1	0	0
Tremie	.941	12	2	14	1	0

Shortstop	PCT	G	PO	A	E	DP
Alfaro	1.000	1	2	3	0	1
Bruntlett	.957	83	147	230	17	55
Burke	.938	43	72	108	12	17

Outfield	PCT	G	PO	A	E	DP
Whiteman	.875	15	25	31	8	11
Alfaro	1.000	5	5	0	0	0
Hill	.975	133	261	13	7	2
Huffman	.000	1	0	0	0	0
Maule	1.000	1	1	0	0	0
Rosamond	.974	113	254	9	7	1
Stanley	.984	98	177	6	3	1
Topolski	.964	85	125	10	5	1
Wright	1.000	2	3	0	0	0

MIDWEST LEAGUE

BATTING

BATTING	AVG	G	AB	R	H	2B	3B	HR	RBI	BB	SO	SB	CS	SLG	OBP	B	T	HT	WT	DOB	1st Yr	Resides
Checksfield, Steven	.218	122	440	59	96	21	4	16	87	40	113	4	5	.393	.281	R	R	6-3	230	6-11-79	2001	Hurley, N.Y.
Conrad, Brooks	.287	133	499	94	143	25	14	14	94	62	102	18	8	.477	.368	S	R	5-11	180	1-16-80	2001	Spring Valley, Calif.
Hodges, Kerry	.251	84	243	35	61	13	3	1	17	20	74	11	7	.342	.319	R	R	6-0	180	8-12-77	2001	Glendale, Ariz.
Lentini, Fehlandt	.289	71	246	41	71	12	3	1	35	29	35	25	5	.374	.362	R	R	6-0	180	8-12-77	2001	Santa Rosa, Calif.
Likely, Cameron	.273	100	315	56	86	10	5	0	28	50	49	26	7	.333	.386	R	R	5-10	170	2-2-78	2001	Port St. Joe, Fla.
Lucas, Matt	.190	65	189	19	36	11	0	1	13	3	39	3	0	.265	.221	R	R	6-1	180	11-21-78	2000	Fullerton, Calif.
Lydic, Joe	.218	70	234	36	51	16	1	5	27	12	57	3	0	.359	.257	R	R	6-4	190	2-20-79	2000	Bethel Park, Pa.
Mote, Trevor	.277	130	480	66	133	25	1	9	70	43	89	7	9	.390	.339	S	R	6-1	190	7-22-79	2001	Kingman, Ariz.
Obradovich, Mark	.225	108	356	43	80	15	1	3	36	55	96	8	7	.298	.331	R	R	6-0	180	10-26-80	2001	Tuscaloosa, Ala.
Pines, Greg	.133	13	15	1	2	0	0	0	2	4	0	0	.133	.235	R	R	6-0	180	8-3-78	1999	Garden Grove, Calif.
Rodriguez, Mike	.253	133	499	94	126	23	4	4	46	65	85	35	11	.333	.338	L	L	5-10	160	10-15-80	2001	Cooper City, Fla.
Rojas, Randy	.210	71	181	33	38	7	0	2	29	23	22	19	7	.282	.305	R	R	6-1	170	3-12-80	2001	Brooklyn, N.Y.
Self, Todd	.310	136	491	81	152	36	5	12	94	65	104	10	1	.477	.394	L	R	6-5	210	11-9-78	2000	Stonewall, La.
Stegall, Ryan	.238	122	408	45	97	25	3	4	44	42	75	6	3	.336	.322	R	R	6-1	190	11-13-79	2001	Liberty, Mo.

PITCHING

PITCHING	W	L	ERA	G	GS	CG	SV	IP	H	R	ER	BB	SO	AVG	B	T	HT	WT	DOB	1st Yr	Resides
Burns, Mike	14	9	2.49	28	28	3	0	181	146	59	50	29	126	.217	R	R	6-1	190	7-14-78	2000	Diamond Bar, Calif.

PITCHING	W	L	ERA	G	GS	CG	SV	IP	H	R	ER	BB	SO	AVG	B	T	HT	WT	DOB	1st Yr	Resides
Campos, Juan	3	2	2.01	36	0	0	9	58	50	19	13	8	63	.225	R	R	6-0	180	3-28-80	1997	Edo Monagas, Venez.
Coughenour, Jory	1	0	1.46	5	0	0	3	12	10	2	2	0	8	.217	R	R	6-1	200	6-17-78	2000	Dunbar, Pa.
Dorn, Grant	0	4	3.57	39	0	0	3	58	62	26	23	11	57	.271	R	R	6-4	210	2-26-78	1999	New Alexandria, Pa.
Doyne, Cory	9	8	4.26	27	26	0	0	142	131	76	67	63	101	.243	R	R	6-2	180	8-13-81	2000	Lutz, Fla.
Hamilton, Mark	2	0	2.63	11	2	0	0	24	22	11	7	5	14	.244	L	L	6-2	200	4-23-78	2000	Hurst, Texas
Houlton, D.J.	14	5	3.14	35	16	0	2	141	120	57	49	30	138	.223	R	R	6-4	220	8-12-79	2001	Yorba Linda, Calif.
Mansfield, Monte	4	4	5.30	20	13	0	0	71	64	53	42	56	65	.237	R	R	6-4	210	3-22-81	2000	Hesperia, Calif.
Pluta, Anthony	11	13	5.92	28	28	1	0	143	155	100	94	83	120	.276	R	R	6-2	190	10-28-82	2000	Las Vegas, Nev.
Powell, Greg	5	5	2.78	48	1	0	7	81	75	28	25	13	41	.246	R	R	6-4	200	8-26-78	2001	Holland, Pa.
Rodaway, Brian	2	2	4.00	23	1	0	1	45	50	26	20	14	32	.295	L	L	6-3	190	9-11-78	2001	Lincoln, Neb.
Rohlicek, Russ	9	5	2.98	25	25	0	0	151	148	58	50	36	95	.256	R	L	6-5	220	12-26-79	2001	Pleasant Hill, Calif.
Tremblay, Max	3	3	1.26	41	0	0	14	57	39	14	8	20	61	.187	L	L	6-0	190	6-18-76	1998	San Dimas, Calif.
Wood, Brandon	2	1	2.55	34	0	0	4	53	45	21	15	19	46	.225	R	R	6-0	200	2-20-79	1999	Nacogdoches, Texas

FIELDING

Catcher	PCT	G	PO	A	E	DP	PB
Lucas	.993	62	411	27	3	1	2
Obradovich	.994	90	569	48	4	1	10
Pines	.889	6	8	0	1	0	0

First Base	PCT	G	PO	A	E	DP
Checksfield	.988	54	463	34	6	38
Lydic	.997	36	327	13	1	25
Mote	1.000	1	7	0	0	0
Obradovich	1.000	1	9	1	0	1
Self	.994	57	472	30	3	41

Second Base	PCT	G	PO	A	E	DP
Conrad	.971	121	207	335	16	59
Mote	1.000	2	5	5	0	2
Rojas	.980	21	38	59	2	11

Third Base	PCT	G	PO	A	E	DP
Lydic	.880	11	7	15	3	1
Mote	.913	121	69	257	31	18
Stegall	.917	18	7	26	3	1

Shortstop	PCT	G	PO	A	E	DP
Rojas	.949	39	53	97	8	22

	PCT	G	PO	A	E	DP
Stegall	.957	111	165	345	23	56

Outfield	PCT	G	PO	A	E	DP
Checksfield	.973	43	70	2	2	0
Hodges	.987	61	76	0	1	0
Lentini	.962	64	93	8	4	3
Likely	.969	91	156	2	5	0
Rodriguez	.984	124	237	5	4	1
Self	.986	65	127	10	2	0

LEXINGTON LEGENDS

Low Class A

SOUTH ATLANTIC LEAGUE

BATTING	AVG	G	AB	R	H	2B	3B	HR	RBI	BB	SO	SB	CS	SLG	OBP	B	T	HT	WT	DOB	1st Yr	Resides
Acevedo, Anthony	.302	116	437	89	132	28	0	12	80	62	89	11	8	.449	.386	L	L	6-5	200	5-5-78	2000	Bakersfield, Calif.
Caraway, Brandon	.304	89	332	62	101	25	1	7	30	32	53	22	10	.449	.372	S	R	6-0	180	10-6-77	2000	Houston, Texas
Cuevas, Aneudi	.355	8	31	4	11	2	1	0	5	3	7	1	1	.484	.412	R	R	6-1	160	10-6-81	1999	Nizao, D.R.
Downing, Lance	.265	16	49	9	13	1	0	2	6	4	17	0	0	.408	.321	L	R	5-10	180	3-9-79	1997	Pine Bluff, Ark.
Fatheree, Danny	.211	39	109	12	23	7	0	1	11	17	17	0	0	.303	.326	R	R	5-11	210	8-25-79	1997	Grand Prairie, Texas
German, Ramon	.241	86	328	46	79	15	1	11	49	43	77	15	4	.393	.328	S	R	5-11	160	1-15-80	1997	Santo Domingo, D.R.
Gimenez, Hector	.263	85	297	41	78	16	1	11	42	25	78	2	3	.434	.320	S	R	5-10	180	9-28-82	1999	San Felipe, Venez.
Helquist, Jon	.254	105	346	47	88	15	4	5	38	37	87	17	4	.364	.338	R	R	6-0	170	8-17-80	1999	Jacksonville, Fla.
Jimerson, Charlton	.228	125	439	65	100	22	4	14	57	36	168	34	9	.392	.295	R	R	6-3	200	9-22-79	2001	Hayward, Calif.
Kochen, Ryan	.243	10	37	6	9	1	0	1	4	2	6	0	0	.351	.300	R	R	6-2	190	6-13-79	2001	Batavia, Ill.
Lockhart, Paul	.223	87	296	30	66	20	2	9	29	32	64	5	3	.395	.303	S	L	6-0	190	4-12-78	2000	Bellingham, Wash.
McKee, Mickey	.229	79	258	34	59	15	1	5	30	23	55	0	3	.353	.308	R	R	6-0	180	1-21-78	2000	Houston, Texas
Ruiz, Reinaldo	.188	29	96	15	18	6	0	0	14	12	16	1	3	.250	.277	R	R	6-0	170	2-4-80	1996	Falcon, Venez.
Schmitt, Brian	.256	121	386	46	99	24	3	5	61	32	113	6	4	.373	.323	L	L	6-2	190	5-16-79	1999	Kerrville, Texas
Soto, T.J.	.244	66	197	24	48	9	0	8	33	21	75	11	3	.411	.311	R	R	5-11	200	8-31-77	2000	Ruston, La.
Toven, John	.283	70	244	34	69	12	0	1	23	14	30	19	11	.344	.317	R	R	5-8	160	11-10-74	1998	Los Angeles, Calif.
Whiteman, Tommy	.303	90	350	50	106	29	2	10	49	36	66	6	6	.483	.374	R	R	6-3	170	7-14-79	2000	Edmond, Okla.
Wright, Gavin	.296	128	517	73	153	23	6	8	57	40	92	21	18	.410	.346	R	R	6-2	180	5-6-79	1999	Lufkin, Texas

PITCHING	W	L	ERA	G	GS	CG	SV	IP	H	R	ER	BB	SO	AVG	B	T	HT	WT	DOB	1st Yr	Resides
Anderson, Travis	4	5	4.46	48	2	0	8	85	81	45	42	31	81	.253	R	R	6-4	240	3-18-78	1999	Bellevue, Wash.
Barrett, Jimmy	9	5	2.81	27	22	0	1	134	112	53	42	40	131	.229	R	R	6-2	190	6-7-81	1999	Cumberland, Md.
Barrios, Angel	0	0	0.00	1	0	0	0	2	0	0	0	0	3	.000	R	R	6-2	160	8-6-81	1998	Ciudad Bolivar, Venez.
Barzilla, Philip	6	9	3.26	43	0	0	4	86	66	39	31	34	62	.214	L	L	6-0	180	1-25-79	2001	Sugar Land, Texas
Bayrer, Thomas	0	2	4.13	12	0	0	2	24	24	12	11	12	21	.266	R	R	6-4	200	1-2-80	2001	Roanoke, Va.
Bobbitt, Seth	7	4	3.08	14	14	0	0	85	79	31	29	21	63	.244	R	R	6-1	180	3-24-79	2001	Alabaster, Ala.
Cabreja, Eny	11	4	3.78	28	28	0	0	159	167	74	67	44	137	.275	S	L	5-11	160	8-18-81	1999	Santiago Rodriguez, D.R.
Campos, Juan	2	0	2.70	4	0	0	0	7	3	2	2	1	5	.130	R	R	6-0	180	3-28-80	1997	Edo Monagas, Venez.
Gallo, Mike	4	4	1.83	42	2	0	8	88	69	29	18	26	93	.211	L	L	6-0	170	4-2-77	1999	Long Beach, Calif.
Lira, James	2	1	0.00	15	0	0	6	19	7	2	0	3	27	.111	R	R	6-1	160	5-19-78	1998	Bishop, Texas
McNair, Pat	1	2	3.21	37	0	0	5	70	60	37	25	34	57	.229	R	R	6-4	200	5-15-79	2001	Arlington, Va.
Nieve, Fernando	0	1	6.00	1	1	0	0	3	6	5	2	0	2	.352	R	R	6-0	170	7-15-82	1999	San Felipe, Venez.
Pena, Francisco	7	6	4.30	36	7	0	1	73	61	44	35	57	68	.223	R	R	5-11	180	3-9-79	1997	Bonao, D.R.
Roberson, Brandon	8	5	2.40	23	18	0	0	112	105	34	30	22	115	.247	R	R	6-3	190	4-26-78	2001	Aledo, Texas
Rodaway, Brian	6	3	2.13	14	13	0	0	85	66	22	20	13	63	.214	L	L	6-3	190	9-11-78	2001	Lincoln, Neb.
Santillan, Manny	5	5	2.06	14	14	1	0	96	73	27	22	28	76	.210	R	R	6-0	200	8-20-79	1996	La Romana, D.R.
Sinclair, Ernnie	9	3	3.38	25	19	0	1	123	112	66	46	47	109	.243	R	R	6-0	160	4-2-80	1998	Bluefields, Nicaragua

FIELDING

Catcher	PCT	G	PO	A	E	DP	PB
Fatheree	.993	38	250	24	2	2	8
Gimenez	.993	85	665	67	5	6	19
McKee	1.000	1	2	0	0	0	0
Ruiz	.976	29	223	21	6	1	3

First Base	PCT	G	PO	A	E	DP
German	1.000	1	2	0	0	0
McKee	.981	15	93	8	2	10
Schmitt	.986	120	1028	80	16	83
Soto	.986	23	201	12	3	19

Second Base	PCT	G	PO	A	E	DP
Downing	.984	15	25	36	1	4

	PCT	G	PO	A	E	DP
Helquist	.964	102	160	290	17	61
McKee	1.000	2	4	2	0	1
Soto	1.000	8	19	22	0	5
Toven	.979	24	37	55	2	10

Third Base	PCT	G	PO	A	E	DP
Downing	1.000	1	1	0	0	
German	.917	84	46	153	18	14
McKee	.916	42	38	82	11	5
Soto	.875	16	4	17	3	0
Toven	.800	2	1	3	1	1

Shortstop	PCT	G	PO	A	E	DP
Cuevas	.946	8	9	26	2	7

	PCT	G	PO	A	E	DP
Helquist	.941	4	6	10	1	4
Kochen	.966	7	9	19	1	4
Toven	.952	41	70	110	9	22
Whiteman	.957	86	112	268	17	42

Outfield	PCT	G	PO	A	E	DP
Acevedo	.969	84	91	4	3	0
Caraway	.982	64	101	6	2	1
Jimerson	.970	122	250	5	8	1
Lockhart	.960	37	46	2	2	0
Soto	1.000	1	1	0	0	0
Wright	.971	124	187	14	6	3

NEW YORK-PENN LEAGUE

BATTING	AVG	G	AB	R	H	2B	3B	HR	RBI	BB	SO	SB	CS	SLG	OBP	B	T	HT	WT	DOB	1st Yr	Resides
Cespedes, Robinson	.266	69	274	25	73	12	4	1	23	13	34	10	3	.350	.314	R	R	6-0	150	7-30-82	1998	Palmarejo, Venez.
Covarrubias, Nick	.210	57	200	13	42	10	1	0	21	12	36	7	1	.270	.277	R	R	6-2	200	6-12-80	2002	West Covina, Calif.
Cuevas, Aneudi	.250	36	116	17	29	1	1	3	13	9	42	3	3	.353	.310	R	R	6-1	160	10-6-81	1999	Nizao, D.R.
Fernando, Osvaldo	.077	4	13	1	1	0	0	0	1	0	2	0	0	.077	.077	S	R	6-0	170	10-15-80	2000	San Pedro de Macoris, D.R.
Harrington, Jesse	.209	30	67	8	14	1	0	0	7	9	12	4	0	.224	.325	R	R	6-1	170	12-22-79	2002	Vancouver, Wash.
Hoover, Clint	.250	8	24	2	6	1	0	0	3	1	10	0	0	.292	.269	R	R	6-2	190	3-26-79	2001	Moraga, Calif.
Jones, Kendall	.298	21	57	12	17	2	0	0	4	11	11	1	3	.333	.406	R	R	6-3	210	12-14-80	2001	Broken Arrow, Okla.
Larson, Ryan	.100	5	10	1	1	0	0	0	1	4	5	0	0	.100	.400	R	R	6-3	210	2-19-80	2002	Carlsbad, Calif.
Macchi, Brandon	.278	68	255	30	71	8	1	6	31	31	53	3	2	.388	.355	S	L	6-0	180	9-23-79	2001	Santa Clara, Calif.
Mackor, Jeff	.200	32	90	13	18	5	0	1	9	11	19	3	0	.289	.314	R	R	6-1	210	6-17-80	2002	Salem, N.H.
McGarvey, Randy	.259	41	108	13	28	4	0	0	7	14	27	1	0	.296	.362	L	R	6-3	200	2-6-79	2002	Hilton Head, S.C.
Peavey, Pat	.236	57	208	30	49	9	0	6	27	13	37	2	2	.365	.285	R	R	6-1	200	5-5-80	2002	Brisbane, Calif.
Reuss, Jason	.194	31	93	11	18	3	1	3	9	9	41	1	1	.344	.276	R	R	6-6	210	11-2-79	2002	Anaheim, Calif.
Salmela, Andy	.190	68	221	23	42	6	1	4	26	23	57	2	3	.281	.272	R	R	6-1	210	2-14-80	2002	Cottage Grove, Minn.
Sandoval, Jjalil	.242	57	190	21	46	6	0	0	17	27	39	12	7	.274	.342	R	R	5-9	160	12-17-79	2001	Montebello, Calif.
Seuss, Adam	.218	69	243	29	53	10	2	4	28	22	32	3	3	.325	.289	L	R	6-0	190	8-31-80	2002	La Quinta, Calif.
Topham, Andrew	.232	47	181	22	42	8	1	2	16	7	45	5	2	.320	.270	R	R	6-0	190	8-31-80	2002	Carmichael, Calif.
Whitesides, Jake	.222	45	126	13	28	5	4	0	6	12	21	3	2	.325	.295	L	R	5-11	190	6-23-81	2000	Columbia, Mo.

GAMES BY POSITION: C—Jones 19, Mackor 29, McGarvey 39. **1B**—Hoover 8, Mackor 1, Salmela 68. **2B**—Harrington 26, Sandoval 55, Whitesides 1. **3B**—Covarrubias 36, Larson 3, Peavey 38. **SS**—Cuevas 36, Fernando 3, Harrington 1, Sandoval 1, Topham 38. **OF**—Cespedes 69, Covarrubias 14, Macchi 38, Reuss 23, Seuss 61, Whitesides 38.

PITCHING	W	L	ERA	G	GS	CG	SV	IP	H	R	ER	BB	SO	AVG	B	T	HT	WT	DOB	1st Yr	Resides
Ally, Ben	1	1	3.72	9	3	0	0	29	31	12	12	5	23	.264	R	R	6-2	200	2-9-79	2001	Lakeland, Fla.
Bayrer, Thomas	0	0	3.57	11	0	0	1	23	21	9	9	9	17	.256	R	R	6-4	200	1-2-80	2001	Roanoke, Va.
Deleon, Joey	4	10	4.35	16	16	0	0	81	66	49	39	34	63	.225	R	R	5-11	180	10-21-82	2001	Nixon, Texas
Duran, J.P.	1	2	4.65	20	0	0	2	31	24	17	16	21	30	.216	R	R	5-10	180	9-13-79	2002	San Marcos, Texas
Flores, Manuel	3	2	2.59	15	9	0	1	56	37	16	16	19	63	.192	R	R	5-11	160	6-5-84	2001	La Victoria, D.R.
Gothreaux, Jared	2	3	2.72	28	0	0	4	46	55	23	14	12	53	.287	R	R	6-0	200	1-27-80	2002	Lake Charles, La.
Hamilton, Mark	6	4	4.12	13	13	0	0	68	69	35	31	25	64	.263	L	L	6-0	200	4-23-78	2000	Hurst, Texas
Hansack, Devorn	3	4	3.60	12	10	0	0	50	44	21	20	17	37	.240	R	R	6-2	170	8-5-82	1999	Pearl Lagoon, Nicaragua
Heitzman, Aaron	3	4	3.05	23	3	0	0	59	58	25	20	22	34	.262	L	L	6-0	180	11-21-79	2002	New Ulm, Minn.
Kramer, Sean	0	0	4.58	21	0	0	2	37	35	22	19	16	31	.238	R	R	6-3	220	4-25-81	2002	Albuquerque, N.M.
McLemore, Mark	1	5	14.09	9	6	0	0	23	42	37	36	17	16	.392	L	L	6-2	210	10-9-80	2002	Granite Bay, Calif.
Peguero, Jailen	1	1	3.44	25	3	0	6	50	49	20	19	17	42	.260	R	R	6-0	160	1-4-81	2000	Azua, D.R.
Tomaszewski, Eliot	0	3	4.85	17	2	0	0	43	47	26	23	23	31	.274	R	R	6-4	190	1-13-80	1998	Albuquerque, N.M.
Westhoff, Billy	2	9	6.19	18	10	0	0	64	72	49	44	21	43	.289	L	R	6-0	190	1-18-80	2002	Frisco, Texas

APPALACHIAN LEAGUE

BATTING	AVG	G	AB	R	H	2B	3B	HR	RBI	BB	SO	SB	CS	SLG	OBP	B	T	HT	WT	DOB	1st Yr	Resides
Acevedo, Freddy	.284	53	208	39	59	11	4	9	44	18	67	11	1	.476	.352	R	R	6-2	200	8-23-81	1999	La Romana, D.R.
Babilonia, Edgar	.273	38	128	22	35	2	1	0	14	10	28	18	1	.305	.329	R	R	5-10	160	8-5-83	1999	Cartagena, Colombia
Batista, Ariel	.227	52	211	38	48	5	3	1	15	23	68	12	4	.294	.314	R	R	6-0	170	8-28-80	1999	Chitre, Panama
Davidson, Kevin	.221	28	95	11	21	7	0	1	10	19	25	1	1	.326	.350	R	R	5-9	190	7-21-80	2002	Winter Park, Fla.
Fagan, John	.291	26	86	29	25	7	0	3	26	24	21	1	2	.477	.449	R	R	6-5	200	8-8-79	2001	Mill Creek, Wash.
Fernando, Osvaldo	.287	57	216	42	62	6	1	0	25	16	35	8	5	.324	.356	S	R	6-0	170	10-15-80	2000	San Pedro de Macoris, D.R.
Hawkins, Dustin	.288	31	118	26	34	7	1	1	22	18	17	9	1	.390	.382	L	L	6-0	180	11-22-79	2002	Ogden, Utah
Humphries, Justin	.265	51	185	30	49	11	0	5	28	15	49	0	2	.405	.325	R	R	6-4	220	2-24-83	2001	Richmond, Texas
Larson, Ryan	.238	31	105	11	25	5	0	1	16	18	21	1	0	.314	.370	R	R	6-3	210	2-19-80	2002	Carlsbad, Calif.
Lorsbach, Michael	.275	43	142	26	39	7	1	2	28	31	32	2	0	.380	.395	L	R	6-6	220	10-12-79	2002	Omaha, Neb.
Melendez, German	.291	38	141	23	41	6	0	1	21	17	27	7	5	.355	.362	R	R	6-0	160	9-13-81	1998	Mariara, Venez.
Mendez, Valentin	.307	52	199	26	61	14	0	1	38	27	24	8	6	.392	.396	R	R	6-0	160	2-14-81	1999	San Pedro de Macoris, D.R.
Sarabia, Hamilton	.282	64	238	50	67	9	1	2	32	34	44	18	4	.353	.382	L	R	5-11	180	6-11-82	1999	Cartagena, Colombia
Torres, Saul	.271	54	192	46	52	10	2	2	28	36	35	4	1	.375	.390	R	R	6-3	200	2-18-82	1999	Curarigua, Venez.

GAMES BY POSITION: C—Davidson 28, Humphries 1, Melendez 38. **1B**—Fagan 26, Humphries 39, Larson 3, Torres 1. **2B**—Babilonia 23, Mendez 46. **3B**—Babilonia 1, Larson 18, Torres 48. **SS**—Babilonia 11, Fernando 57. **OF**— Acevedo 52, Babilonoia 1, Batista 49, Hawkins 25, Larson 2, Lorsbach 14, Sarabia 61.

PITCHING	W	L	ERA	G	GS	CG	SV	IP	H	R	ER	BB	SO	AVG	B	T	HT	WT	DOB	1st Yr	Resides
Albers, Matthew	2	3	5.13	13	13	0	0	60	61	38	34	38	72	.273	L	R	6-0	190	1-20-83	2002	Sugar Land, Texas
Ally, Ben	4	3	2.72	13	0	0	2	40	35	21	12	10	36	.228	R	R	6-2	200	2-9-79	2001	Lakeland, Fla.
Barrios, Angel	1	0	1.40	7	0	0	0	19	13	3	3	7	26	.185	R	R	6-2	160	8-6-81	1998	Ciudad Bolivar, Venez.
Beltre, Juan	3	4	3.89	24	0	0	6	42	41	20	18	16	52	.254	L	L	6-0	160	12-6-81	2000	Azua, D.R.
Douglass, Chance	2	1	3.65	12	9	0	0	44	45	19	18	23	34	.254	R	R	6-1	190	2-24-84	2002	Amarillo, Texas
Escobar, Rodrigo	6	2	3.12	16	10	0	0	78	71	33	27	18	64	.238	R	R	5-11	180	2-11-83	1999	Cartagena, Colombia
Estrada, Paul	2	2	11.65	14	6	0	0	32	45	45	41	36	42	.326	R	R	6-1	190	9-10-82	1999	Ciudad Bolivar, Venez.
Fischer, Sam	3	2	4.50	8	8	0	0	38	37	23	19	23	27	.258	R	R	6-0	180	9-20-80	2002	Orland Park, Ill.
Freeman, Daniel	9	1	2.96	20	0	0	6	46	47	23	15	18	50	.254	R	R	6-2	210	8-3-82	2002	Jonesboro, La.
Long, Brent	1	3	7.99	17	0	0	0	24	24	27	21	38	18	.263	R	R	6-3	180	6-23-80	2002	Blountville, Tenn.
McLemore, Mark	0	1	1.80	4	2	0	0	10	9	3	2	5	11	.234	L	L	6-2	210	10-9-80	2002	Granite Bay, Calif.
Nieve, Fernando	4	1	2.39	13	13	0	0	68	46	23	18	27	60	.185	R	R	6-0	170	7-15-82	1999	San Felipe, Venez.
Soler, Jose	2	1	5.29	18	6	0	0	48	49	32	28	23	43	.264	R	R	6-3	180	8-25-82	1998	La Romana, D.R.
Stander, Mark	2	2	5.63	19	0	0	1	38	49	29	24	10	34	.296	R	R	6-2	210	6-19-79	2002	Littleton, Colo.

KANSAS CITY ROYALS

BY ALAN ESKEW

Just when it was thought the Royals had hit rock bottom with 97 losses in 2001, they dropped a franchise-record 100 games in 2002. In the process, the Royals went through three managers and a club-record 51 players, including 13 players making their major league debut, and 14 starting pitchers.

Manager Tony Muser, who replaced Bob Boone during the 1997 all-star break, was fired April 29 when the Royals started 8-15. Muser's overall record with Kansas City, 317-431, gave him the worst winning percentage (.423) of any Royals skipper who managed at least one season.

John Mizerock, Baseball America's minor league manager of the year in 1999, was named interim manager. Mizerock had a 5-8 record before Tony Pena, the Astros' bench coach, was hired on May 15 as the club's 13th full-time manager. The Royals went 49-77 under Pena.

The Royals began the season with three key players on the disabled list: outfielder Mark Quinn (fractured rib from a Ku-Fu fighting accident with his brother), closer Roberto Hernandez (strained elbow) and left-hander Darrell May (pulled left groin). Quinn tore his left hamstring during the season and was restricted to 23 games.

In July, the Royals seemed to be headed in the right direction, piecing together a nine-game winning streak—their longest since a 14-game streak in 1994. The streak, however, turned out to be an aberration, not the norm.

After winning 10 of 11 to end a homestand, the Royals went on the road and promptly lost six straight at Detroit and Chicago and 12 of their next 13 games. They lost 45 of their final 64 games and have not had a winning month since August 2000.

Righthander Paul Byrd was a godsend to the rotation. He won a career-high 17 games, 27.4 percent of the club's total victories. His 17 wins were the most by a Royals

Mike Sweeney   Ian Ferguson

PLAYERS OF THE YEAR

MAJOR LEAGUE: Mike Sweeney, 1b

Sweeney made a run at the American League batting title in 2002. He was hitting a league-best .355 mark in August, when he went on the disabled list and missed 30 games. He finished at .340—nine points behind Boston's Manny Ramirez.

MINOR LEAGUE: Ian Ferguson, rhp

Ferguson led the minor leagues in 2002 with 18 wins, accumulated between Class A Wilmington and Double-A Wichita. His 185 innings ranked second in the minors. The 23-year-old won 18 games combined over his previous two pro seasons.

pitcher since Kevin Appier won 18 in 1993. Byrd also set career highs with 228 innings, 129 strikeouts and an American League-leading seven complete games.

The rest of the rotation combined for a 23-58 record, while the bullpen again proved to be a weak link. Kansas City relievers had 30 saves and a 5.21 ERA, which ranked next-to-last in the league. Pitching coach Al Nipper was fired during the season and replaced by John Cumberland. And after a .256 batting average and a .323 on-base percentage for the season, the club also fired hitting coach Lamar Johnson.

There were a few offensive plusses, but not nearly enough. Carlos Beltran, who played in all 162 games, led the club with 44 doubles, 29 homers, 105 RBIs and 114 runs. He became the first player in club history to score 100 runs and drive in more than 100 runs in three different seasons.

Mike Sweeney's .340 average ranked second in the league, but he missed a month with a bad back. Raul Ibanez, who was twice designated for assignment in 2001 but not picked up, had a career year at .294-24-103. Joe Randa had another steady season—.282-11-80 with 36 doubles.

The Royals' minor league system produced three playoff teams in 2002: Burlington in the Midwest League, Wilmington in the Carolina League and Wichita in the Texas League, but none advanced beyond the first round.

There are plenty of pitching prospects in the system, including Ian Ferguson, who led all minor leaguers with 18 victories; Runelvys Hernandez, who went 4-4 in 12 big league starts; and hard-throwing relievers Ryan Bukvich and Jeremy Hill. Hernandez, however, turned out to be 2 1/2 years older than he claimed and will turn 25 in April.

ORGANIZATION LEADERS

BATTING

*AVG	Chan Perry, Wichita	.316
R	Ruben Gotay, Burlington	87
	Tydus Meadows, Wichita/Wilmington	87
H	James Shanks, Burlington	152
TB	Ruben Gotay, Burlington	232
2B	Ruben Gotay, Burlington	42
3B	Donzell McDonald, Omaha	15
HR	Kit Pellow, Omaha	27
RBI	Ruben Gotay, Burlington	83
BB	Richard Paz, Wichita	81
SO	Jon Guzman, Burlington	159
SB	Patrick Hallmark, Wichita	42

PITCHING

W	Ian Ferguson, Wichita/Wilmington	18
L	Mike Stodolka, Burlington	14
	Chris Tierney, Burlington	14
#ERA	Kris Wilson, Omaha/Wich./Wilmington	2.08
G	Jeremy Hill, Wichita	56
CG	Three tied at	2
SV	Jeremy Hill, Wichita	19
IP	Ian Ferguson, Wichita/Wilmington	185
BB	Colt Griffin, Wilmington/Burlington	87
SO	Ian Ferguson, Wichita/Wilmington	141

*Minimum 250 At-Bats #Minimum 75 Innings

KANSAS CITY ROYALS

Managers: Tony Muser, John Mizerock, Tony Pena

2002 Record: 62-100, .383 (4th, AL Central)

BATTING	AVG	G	AB	R	H	2B	3B	HR	RBI	BB	SO	SB	CS	SLG	OBP	B	T	HT	WT	DOB	1st Yr	Resides
Alicea, Luis	.228	94	237	28	54	8	2	1	23	32	34	2	3	.291	.322	S	R	5-9	170	7-29-65	1988	Loxahatchie, Fla.
Beltran, Carlos	.273	162	637	114	174	44	7	29	105	71	135	35	7	.501	.346	S	R	6-1	190	4-24-77	1995	Manati, P.R.
Berger, Brandon	.201	51	134	16	27	5	1	6	17	8	32	1	0	.388	.255	R	R	5-11	200	2-21-75	1996	Ft. Mitchell, Ky.
Berroa, Angel	.227	20	75	8	17	7	1	0	5	7	10	3	0	.347	.301	R	R	6-0	170	1-27-78	1997	Santo Domingo, D.R.
Brito, Juan	.304	9	23	1	7	2	0	0	1	0	3	0	0	.391	.304	R	R	5-11	200	11-7-79	1996	Santiago Rodriguez, D.R.
Brown, Dee	.235	16	51	5	12	3	1	1	7	4	20	0	0	.392	.291	L	R	6-0	220	3-27-78	1996	Orlando, Fla.
Caruso, Mike	.100	12	20	3	2	0	0	0	1	2	0	0	0	.100	.143	L	R	5-27-77	170	5-27-77	1996	Coral Springs, Fla.
Febles, Carlos	.245	119	351	44	86	16	4	4	26	41	63	16	5	.348	.336	R	R	5-11	180	5-24-76	1994	La Romana, D.R.
Gomez, Alexis	.200	5	10	0	2	0	0	0	0	2	0	0	0	.200	.200	L	L	6-2	180	8-6-80	1997	Loma de Cabrera, D.R.
Guiel, Aaron	.233	70	240	30	56	13	0	4	38	19	61	1	5	.338	.296	L	R	5-10	200	10-5-72	1993	Langley, BC, Canada
Hinch, A.J.	.249	72	197	25	49	7	1	7	27	18	35	3	3	.401	.321	R	R	6-1	200	5-15-74	1996	Scottsdale, Ariz.
Ibanez, Raul	.294	137	497	70	146	37	6	24	103	40	76	5	3	.537	.346	L	R	6-2	200	6-2-72	1992	Miami, Fla.
Knoblauch, Chuck	.210	80	300	41	63	9	0	6	22	28	32	19	3	.300	.284	R	R	5-9	170	7-7-68	1989	Houston, Texas
Mayne, Brent	.236	101	326	35	77	8	2	4	30	34	54	4	4	.310	.309	L	R	6-1	190	4-19-68	1989	Corona Del Mar, Calif.
McCarty, Dave	.094	13	32	3	3	1	0	1	2	2	10	0	0	.219	.147	R	L	6-5	210	11-23-69	1991	Menlo Park, Calif.
McDonald, Donzell	.182	10	22	3	4	2	0	0	1	4	5	1	0	.273	.296	S	R	5-11	180	2-20-75	1995	Glendale, Colo.
Ordaz, Luis	.223	33	94	11	21	2	0	0	4	12	13	2	3	.245	.308	R	R	5-11	170	8-12-75	1993	Maracaibo, Venez.
Pellow, Kit	.238	29	63	6	15	1	0	1	5	9	21	1	1	.302	.342	R	R	6-1	200	8-28-73	1996	Olathe, Kan.
Perez, Neifi	.236	145	554	65	131	20	4	3	37	20	53	8	9	.303	.260	S	R	6-0	170	6-2-73	1993	Santo Domingo, D.R.
Perry, Chan	.091	5	11	0	1	0	0	0	3	0	1	0	0	.091	.091	R	R	6-2	200	9-13-72	1994	Mayo, Fla.
Quinn, Mark	.237	23	76	9	18	4	0	2	11	5	15	2	1	.368	.301	R	R	6-1	190	5-21-74	1995	West Covina, Calif.
Randa, Joe	.282	151	549	63	155	36	5	11	80	46	69	2	1	.426	.341	R	R	5-11	190	12-18-69	1991	Overland Park, Kan.
Sadler, Donnie	.191	35	68	10	13	1	1	0	5	4	12	3	1	.235	.233	R	R	5-6	170	6-17-75	1994	Valley Mills, Texas
Sweeney, Mike	.340	126	471	81	160	31	1	24	86	61	46	9	7	.563	.417	R	R	6-3	220	7-22-73	1991	Overland Park, Kan.
Tucker, Michael	.248	144	475	65	118	27	6	12	56	56	105	23	9	.406	.330	L	R	6-2	190	6-25-71	1992	Chase City, Va.
Wathan, Dusty	.600	5	5	1	3	0	0	0	3	0	0	0	0	.800	.667	R	R	6-4	210	8-22-73	1994	Peoria, Ariz.

PITCHING	W	L	ERA	G	GS	CG	SV	IP	H	R	ER	BB	SO	AVG	B	T	HT	WT	DOB	1st Yr	Resides
Affeldt, Jeremy	3	4	4.64	34	7	0	0	78	85	41	40	37	67	.274	L	L	6-4	210	6-6-79	1997	Medical Lake, Wash.
Asencio, Miguel	4	7	5.11	31	21	0	0	123	136	73	70	64	58	.282	R	R	6-2	190	9-29-80	1998	La Victoria, D.R.
Austin, Jeff	0	0	4.91	10	0	0	0	11	14	6	6	6	6	.318	R	R	6-0	180	10-19-76	1999	Kingwood, Texas
Bailey, Cory	3	4	4.11	37	0	0	1	46	53	24	21	31	24	.306	R	R	6-1	210	1-24-71	1991	El Cajon, Calif.
Bukvich, Ryan	1	0	6.12	26	0	0	0	25	26	19	17	19	20	.276	R	R	6-2	250	5-13-78	2000	Brandon, Miss.
Byrd, Paul	17	11	3.90	33	33	7	0	228	224	111	99	38	129	.256	R	R	6-1	180	12-3-70	1991	Louisville, Ky.
Durbin, Chad	0	1	11.88	2	2	0	0	8	13	11	11	4	5	.342	R	R	6-2	200	12-3-77	1996	Baton Rouge, La.
Field, Nathan	0	0	9.00	5	5	0	0	5	8	5	5	3	3	.364	R	R	6-2	185	12-11-75	1998	Littleton, Colo.
George, Chris	0	4	5.60	6	6	0	0	27	37	17	17	8	13	.324	L	L	6-2	200	9-16-79	1998	Spring, Texas
Grimsley, Jason	4	7	3.91	70	0	0	1	71	64	32	31	37	59	.236	R	R	6-3	200	8-7-67	1985	Lafayette, La.
Hernandez, Roberto	1	3	4.33	53	0	0	26	52	62	29	25	12	39	.299	R	R	6-4	250	11-11-64	1986	Largo, Fla.
Hernandez, Runelvys	4	4	4.36	12	12	0	0	74	79	36	36	22	45	.273	R	R	6-1	200	4-27-78	1998	Santo Domingo, D.R.
Hill, Jeremy	0	1	3.86	10	0	0	0	9	8	4	4	8	7	.235	R	R	5-11	200	8-8-77	1996	Dallas, Texas
MacDougal, Mike	0	1	5.00	6	0	0	0	9	5	5	5	7	10	.161	S	R	6-4	190	3-5-77	1999	Marco Island, Fla.
May, Darrell	4	10	5.35	30	21	2	0	131	144	83	78	50	95	.276	L	L	6-2	180	6-13-72	1992	Rogue River, Ore.
Mullen, Scott	4	5	3.15	44	0	0	0	40	40	16	14	13	21	.266	R	L	6-2	190	1-17-75	1996	Beaufort, S.C.
Obermueller, Wes	0	2	11.74	2	2	0	0	8	14	10	10	2	5	.378	R	R	6-2	190	12-22-76	1999	North Liberty, Iowa
Reichert, Dan	3	5	5.32	30	6	0	0	66	77	48	39	25	36	.306	R	R	6-3	175	7-12-76	1997	Turlock, Calif.
Rekar, Bryan	0	2	15.43	2	2	0	0	7	12	12	12	6	2	.387	R	R	6-3	220	6-3-72	1993	Lutz, Fla.
Sedlacek, Shawn	3	5	6.72	16	14	0	0	84	99	64	63	36	52	.302	R	R	6-2	200	6-29-77	1998	Cedar Rapids, Iowa
Shouse, Brian	0	0	6.14	23	0	0	0	15	15	10	10	9	11	.258	L	L	5-11	180	9-26-68	1990	Peoria, Ill.
Stein, Blake	0	4	7.91	27	2	0	1	47	59	41	41	27	42	.305	R	R	6-7	240	8-3-73	1994	Folsom, La.
Suppan, Jeff	9	16	5.32	33	33	3	0	208	229	134	123	68	109	.278	R	R	6-2	210	1-2-75	1993	West Hills, Calif.
Suzuki, Mac	2	9	9.00	7	1	0	0	21	24	21	21	17	15	.296	R	R	6-3	200	5-31-75	1992	Kobe, Japan
Voyles, Brad	0	2	6.51	22	0	0	1	28	31	21	20	18	26	.284	R	R	6-1	190	12-30-76	1998	Green Bay, Wis.
Wilson, Kris	2	0	8.20	12	0	0	0	19	29	18	17	5	10	.353	R	R	6-4	220	8-6-76	1997	Palm Harbor, Fla.

FIELDING

Catcher	PCT	G	PO	A	E	DP	PB
Brito	.978	9	42	3	1	1	1
Hinch	.989	68	349	23	4	2	2
Mayne	.993	99	552	39	4	4	5
Wathan	1.000	3	14	0	0	0	0

First Base	PCT	G	PO	A	E	DP
Alicea	1.000	2	8	0	0	0
Berger	1.000	1	1	0	0	0
Ibanez	.995	49	362	30	2	36
Pellow	1.000	10	36	3	0	5
Perry	1.000	5	35	2	0	2
Sweeney	.991	102	838	105	9	94
Tucker	.962	5	22	3	1	2

Second Base	PCT	G	PO	A	E	DP
Alicea	.986	32	56	90	2	21
Caruso	.933	4	10	4	1	1

	PCT	G	PO	A	E	DP	PB
Febles	.971	116	193	312	15	76	
Ordaz	.982	28	43	68	2	14	
Perez	.964	5	14	13	1	2	
Sadler	1.000	4	9	5	0	0	
Tucker	.833	2	2	3	1	1	

Third Base	PCT	G	PO	A	E	DP
Alicea	.887	32	8	39	6	1
Caruso	1.000	2	1	0	0	0
Ordaz	1.000	6	0	2	0	0
Pellow	.844	12	5	22	5	3
Randa	.972	129	108	234	10	12
Sadler	.909	11	4	6	1	0

Shortstop	PCT	G	PO	A	E	DP
Alicea	.000	1	0	0	0	0
Berroa	.964	20	41	67	4	13
Caruso	1.000	5	4	10	0	0

	PCT	G	PO	A	E	DP
Febles	.000	1	0	0	0	0
Ordaz	1.000	2	4	5	0	2
Perez	.972	139	251	400	19	107
Sadler	.800	4	2	2	1	0

Outfield	PCT	G	PO	A	E	DP
Alicea	.000	1	0	0	0	0
Beltran	.983	149	398	12	7	0
Berger	1.000	36	60	4	0	1
Brown	.923	8	12	0	1	0
Gomez	1.000	2	4	1	0	1
Guiel	.952	61	114	5	6	1
Ibanez	.989	55	88	3	1	0
Knoblauch	.980	74	145	5	3	0
McDonald	1.000	7	3	0	0	0
Quinn	1.000	15	25	0	0	0
Sadler	.957	15	22	0	1	0
Tucker	.991	108	224	9	2	1

FARM SYSTEM

Director, Minor League Operations: Bob Hegman

Class	Farm Team	League	W	L	Pct.	Finish*	Manager	First Yr.
AAA	Omaha (Neb.) Royals	Pacific Coast	76	68	.528	4th (16)	Bucky Dent	1969
AA	Wichita (Kan.) Wranglers	Texas	80	59	.576	1st (8)	Keith Bodie	1995
High A	Wilmington (Del.) Blue Rocks	Carolina	89	51	.636	1st (8)	Jeff Garber	1993
Low A	Burlington (Iowa) Bees	Midwest	68	71	.489	9th (16)	Joe Szekely	2001
SS A	Spokane (Wash.) Indians	Northwest	29	47	.382	7th (8)	Tom Poquette	1995
Rookie	Baseball City (Fla.) Royals	Gulf Coast	22	38	.367	14th (14)	Lloyd Simmons	1993

*Finish in overall standings (No. of teams in league)

OMAHA ROYALS — Class AAA

PACIFIC COAST LEAGUE

BATTING	AVG	G	AB	R	H	2B	3B	HR	RBI	BB	SO	SB	CS	SLG	OBP	B	T	HT	WT	DOB	1st Yr	Resides
Ardoin, Danny	.208	25	77	10	16	3	0	3	10	11	25	1	0	.364	.297	R	R	6-0	220	7-8-74	1995	Ville Platte, La.
Berger, Brandon	.291	68	261	34	76	16	1	13	47	25	43	11	2	.510	.363	R	R	5-11	200	2-21-75	1996	Fort Mitchell, Ky.
Berroa, Angel	.215	77	297	37	64	11	4	8	35	15	84	6	4	.360	.277	R	R	6-0	170	1-27-78	1997	Santo Domingo, D.R.
Brito, Juan	.222	3	9	1	2	1	0	0	1	1	0	0	0	.333	.300	R	R	5-11	200	11-7-79	1996	Santiago Rodriguez, D.R.
Brown, Dee	.275	121	458	66	126	23	1	17	75	44	111	10	4	.441	.344	L	R	6-0	220	3-27-78	1996	Orlando, Fla.
Caruso, Joe	.192	14	52	4	10	4	0	0	5	4	10	0	0	.269	.263	R	R	5-9	190	12-30-74	1997	South Williamsport, Pa.
Caruso, Mike	.306	60	219	28	67	3	2	3	23	12	14	10	3	.379	.350	L	R	6-0	170	5-27-77	1996	Coral Springs, Fla.
Espada, Joe	.224	74	223	18	50	12	0	0	23	19	26	14	4	.278	.289	R	R	5-10	170	8-30-75	1996	Carolina, P.R.
Febles, Carlos	.222	13	54	10	12	2	1	1	5	4	5	2	1	.352	.283	R	R	5-11	180	5-24-76	1994	La Romana, D.R.
Guiel, Aaron	.353	61	215	44	76	11	1	9	50	29	34	8	1	.540	.443	L	R	5-10	200	10-5-72	1993	Langley, B.C.
Hansen, Jed	.263	102	339	63	89	18	3	15	49	53	85	17	5	.466	.363	R	R	6-1	190	8-19-72	1994	Olympia, Wash.
Hart, Corey	.100	11	30	1	3	0	0	0	3	6	4	1	0	.100	.250	S	R	6-0	190	9-5-75	1998	Oklahoma City, Okla.
Harvey, Ken	.277	128	488	75	135	30	1	20	75	42	87	8	3	.463	.342	R	R	6-2	240	3-1-78	1999	Cerritos, Calif.
Hatcher, Chris	.182	12	44	3	8	1	0	1	5	3	9	1	0	.273	.245	R	R	6-3	230	1-7-69	1990	Council Bluffs, Iowa
Johnson, Rontrez	.300	109	403	71	121	27	4	9	53	50	51	31	11	.454	.397	R	R	5-10	160	12-8-76	1995	Marshall, Texas
McDonald, Donzell	.261	112	452	63	118	15	15	7	35	56	102	30	6	.407	.346	S	R	5-11	180	2-20-75	1995	Glendale, Colo.
Metcalfe, Mike	.248	44	149	27	37	7	0	1	15	11	11	10	2	.315	.301	L	R	5-10	190	1-2-73	1994	Orlando, Fla.
Nunnally, Jon	.241	20	58	12	14	5	0	3	12	8	19	1	3	.483	.343	L	R	5-10	190	11-9-71	1992	Keeling, Va.
Ordaz, Luis	.309	35	136	25	42	11	4	2	19	9	16	4	1	.493	.351	R	R	5-11	170	8-12-75	1993	Maracaibo, Venez.
2-team (61 Iowa)	.288	96	330	47	95	21	4	3	33	18	37	9	3	.403	.327							
Ortiz, Hector	.253	35	99	10	25	5	0	1	5	11	15	1	0	.333	.339	R	R	6-0	200	10-14-69	1988	Canovanas, P.R.
2-team (25 Oklahoma)	.232	60	181	13	42	7	0	1	12	22	31	1	1	.287	.320							
Pellow, Kit	.289	105	402	63	116	25	2	27	76	21	82	4	2	.562	.350	R	R	6-1	200	8-28-73	1996	Olathe, Kan.
Quinn, Mark	.179	12	39	4	7	2	1	0	2	4	7	0	0	.282	.289	R	R	6-1	190	5-21-74	1995	West Covina, Calif.
Rose, Mike	.260	52	177	22	46	12	2	3	17	28	40	2	3	.401	.364	S	R	6-1	180	8-25-76	1995	Elk Grove, Calif.
Sadler, Donnie	.333	5	21	6	7	0	0	0	2	3	0	2	0	.333	.417	R	R	5-6	170	6-17-75	1994	Valley Mills, Texas
Sweeney, Mike	.250	3	12	2	3	1	0	1	4	1	2	0	0	.583	.286	R	R	6-3	220	7-22-73	1991	Overland Park, Kan.
Wathan, Dusty	.288	49	160	22	46	9	1	1	26	16	36	1	1	.375	.385	R	R	6-4	210	8-22-73	1994	Peoria, Ariz.

PITCHING	W	L	ERA	G	GS	CG	SV	IP	H	R	ER	BB	SO	AVG	B	T	HT	WT	DOB	1st Yr	Resides
Austin, Jeff	4	0	3.27	39	0	0	2	52	54	24	19	15	44	.263	R	R	6-0	180	10-19-76	1999	Kingwood, Texas
Baerlocher, Ryan	5	2	4.41	13	7	0	0	49	50	31	24	22	37	.270	R	R	6-5	220	8-6-77	1999	Lewiston, Idaho
Bailey, Cory	1	0	1.83	18	0	0	9	20	13	4	4	10	17	.194	R	R	6-1	210	1-24-71	1991	EL Cajon, Calif.
Bukvich, Ryan	1	0	0.00	12	0	0	8	14	4	0	0	7	17	.093	R	R	6-2	250	5-13-78	2000	Brandon, Miss.
Calero, Kiko	7	7	3.44	20	18	0	0	126	112	52	48	35	109	.244	R	R	6-1	180	1-9-75	1996	Rio Piedras, P.R.
DeHart, Rick	1	0	3.90	49	0	0	1	58	55	25	25	21	46	.246	L	L	6-1	180	3-21-70	1992	Topeka, Kan.
Durbin, Chad	0	1	10.80	1	1	0	0	2	4	2	2	0	2	.444	R	R	6-2	200	12-3-77	1996	Baton Rouge, La.
Field, Nathan	0	1	3.31	18	0	0	7	16	22	10	6	8	13	.301	R	R	6-2	200	12-11-75	1998	Littleton, Colo.
Fussell, Chris	12	6	4.43	28	27	0	0	165	165	97	81	71	103	.263	R	R	6-2	200	5-19-76	1994	Oregon, Ohio
George, Chris	6	12	5.87	22	21	1	0	127	145	86	83	65	94	.286	L	L	6-2	200	9-16-79	1998	Spring, Texas
Gilfillan, Jason	2	2	3.69	33	0	0	4	39	32	16	16	14	28	.231	R	R	6-5	220	8-31-76	1997	Blacksburg, S.C.
Hernandez, Roberto	0	0	0.00	2	0	0	0	2	0	1	0	3	3	.000	R	R	6-4	250	11-11-64	1986	Lugo, P.R.
Hurtado, Edwin	4	4	4.50	11	10	0	0	60	69	36	30	19	46	.283	R	R	6-2	210	2-1-70	1991	Naguanagua, Venez.
Laxton, Brett	9	13	4.94	29	28	1	0	157	182	97	86	49	104	.294	R	R	6-1	210	10-5-73	1996	Audubon, N.J.
MacDougal, Mike	3	5	5.60	12	10	0	0	53	52	42	33	55	30	.265	S	R	6-4	190	3-5-77	1999	Marco Island, Fla.
May, Darrell	1	0	0.75	2	2	0	0	12	8	1	1	0	9	.200	L	L	6-2	190	6-13-72	1992	Rogue River, Ore.
Mullen, Scott	1	2	2.61	19	1	0	0	31	32	12	9	9	21	.273	L	L	6-2	190	1-17-75	1996	Beaufort, S.C.
Reichert, Dan	0	0	5.40	5	0	0	0	5	6	3	3	4	3	.352	R	R	6-3	170	7-12-76	1997	Turlock, Calif.
Rekar, Bryan	0	0	4.50	5	4	0	0	24	30	16	12	5	20	.306	R	R	6-3	220	6-3-72	1993	Lutz, Fla.
Sedlacek, Shawn	6	5	3.70	11	11	2	0	80	67	37	33	15	66	.221	R	R	6-4	200	6-29-77	1998	Cedar Rapids, Iowa
Shouse, Brian	0	0	11.57	5	0	0	0	2	7	3	3	1	2	.500	L	L	5-11	180	9-26-68	1990	Peoria, Ill.
Skrmetta, Matt	8	0	2.51	40	0	0	1	61	48	21	17	34	58	.216	S	R	6-3	200	11-6-72	1993	Satellite Beach, Fla.
Suzuki, Mac	0	4	4.53	29	1	0	0	54	63	30	27	21	46	.301	R	R	6-3	200	5-31-75	1992	Kobe, Japan
Voyles, Brad	3	4	4.18	26	0	0	5	32	29	15	15	22	34	.247	R	R	6-1	190	12-30-76	1998	Green Bay, Wis.
Wilson, Kris	2	0	3.08	8	3	0	1	26	38	9	9	1	17	.342	R	R	6-4	200	8-6-76	1997	Palm Harbor, Fla.
Zimmerman, Jordan	0	0	40.50	1	0	0	0	1	3	3	4	1	.333		R	L	6-0	200	4-28-75	1995	Brenham, Texas

FIELDING

Catcher	PCT	G	PO	A	E	DP	PB
Ardoin	.983	24	167	10	3	2	3
Brito	1.000	3	14	3	0	0	0
Ortiz	.979	34	221	11	5	1	1
Rose	.981	42	298	12	6	1	4
Wathan	.988	46	306	24	4	3	1

First Base	PCT	G	PO	A	E	DP
Ardoin	1.000	2	8	0	0	3
Berger	1.000	1	4	0	0	1
Hansen	.953	10	53	8	3	6
Harvey	.984	110	851	78	15	124
Hatcher	1.000	4	16	2	0	1

	PCT	G	PO	A	E	DP
Nunnally	.000	1	0	0	0	0
Pellow	.984	24	172	17	3	17
Sweeney	1.000	1	7	1	0	1

Second Base	PCT	G	PO	A	E	DP
J. Caruso	1.000	1	1	2	0	0
M. Caruso	.966	12	17	40	2	7

	PCT	G	PO	A	E	DP
Espada	.977	61	109	150	6	46
Febles	.982	13	20	35	1	10
Hansen	.947	17	25	46	4	14
Metcalfe	.991	22	44	62	1	21
Ordaz	.992	26	55	75	1	20
Sadler	1.000	1	5	5	0	2

Third Base	PCT	G	PO	A	E	DP
J. Caruso	.900	11	14	22	4	5
M. Caruso	.923	12	5	19	2	3
Espada	1.000	2	1	0	0	0
Hansen	.920	46	25	55	7	5

	PCT	G	PO	A	E	DP
Pellow	.914	80	44	127	16	16
Sadler	1.000	2	3	2	0	0

Shortstop	PCT	G	PO	A	E	DP
Berroa	.956	77	133	212	16	54
M. Caruso	.943	34	56	77	8	17
Espada	.857	4	8	4	2	1
Hansen	.941	7	4	12	1	6
Hart	.977	11	18	24	1	8
Metcalfe	.870	4	8	12	3	6
Ordaz	.956	11	20	23	2	12
Sadler	1.000	2	4	9	0	2

Outfield	PCT	G	PO	A	E	DP
Berger	.974	52	108	6	3	3
Brown	.968	80	149	4	5	0
J. Caruso	1.000	2	1	0	0	0
Guiel	.977	54	120	9	3	2
Hansen	.977	22	39	3	1	0
Johnson	.979	104	274	7	6	5
McDonald	.979	108	268	10	6	0
Metcalfe	.900	4	9	1	0	0
Nunnally	1.000	8	9	0	0	0
Quinn	1.000	7	9	0	0	0

WICHITA WRANGLERS Class AA

TEXAS LEAGUE

BATTING	AVG	G	AB	R	H	2B	3B	HR	RBI	BB	SO	SB	CS	SLG	OBP	B	T	HT	WT	DOB	1st Yr	Resides
Brito, Juan	.255	89	302	40	77	11	0	7	38	21	46	1	1	.361	.303	R	R	5-11	200	11-7-79	1996	Santiago Rodriguez, D.R.
Calderon, Henry	.143	18	49	3	7	0	0	0	4	3	8	0	1	.143	.208	R	R	6-0	180	9-3-77	1996	Santo Domingo, D.R.
Caruso, Joe	.279	46	154	19	43	7	3	2	22	11	25	1	1	.403	.329	R	R	5-9	190	12-30-74	1997	South Williamsport, Pa.
Cotto, Luis	.000	1	1	0	0	0	0	0	0	2	0	0	0	.000	.667	R	R	5-10	180	7-9-81	2000	Rio Piedras, P.R.
Cunningham, Marco	.186	77	215	39	40	7	0	4	29	37	39	13	8	.274	.335	R	R	5-10	180	8-3-77	2000	Lubbock, Texas
DeJesus, David	.253	25	79	7	20	5	2	2	15	8	10	3	1	.443	.347	L	L	6-0	170	12-20-79	2000	Manalapan, N.J.
Glendenning, Mike	.220	22	59	7	13	3	0	2	4	13	16	1	1	.373	.378	R	R	6-0	200	8-26-76	1996	West Hills, Calif.
Gomez, Alexis	.295	114	461	72	136	21	8	14	75	45	84	36	24	.466	.359	L	L	6-2	180	8-6-80	1997	Loma de Cabrera, D.R.
Hallmark, Pat	.254	98	362	55	92	14	1	2	33	35	63	42	12	.315	.334	R	R	6-0	170	12-31-73	1995	Houston, Texas
Harris, Brian	.278	133	490	82	136	23	8	3	47	52	76	10	5	.376	.352	S	R	5-10	170	4-28-75	1997	Carmel, Ind.
Hart, Corey	.238	79	252	32	60	13	2	1	33	41	49	4	5	.317	.340	S	R	6-0	190	9-5-75	1998	Oklahoma City, Okla.
Johnson, Brian	.248	37	109	15	27	5	0	1	13	6	16	3	0	.321	.314	R	R	6-1	200	4-20-77	1999	Derby, Kan.
Knoblauch, Chuck	.313	5	16	3	5	2	0	0	6	4	1	0	0	.438	.500	R	R	5-9	170	7-7-68	1989	Houston, Texas
Martinez, Felix	.260	85	304	44	79	11	4	3	34	25	51	6	4	.352	.333	S	R	6-0	180	5-18-74	1993	Nagua, D.R.
Mayne, Brent	.500	2	4	0	2	0	0	0	1	1	0	0	0	.500	.600	L	R	6-1	190	4-19-68	1989	Corona Del Mar, Calif.
Meadows, Tydus	.345	33	119	24	41	12	3	4	20	14	23	4	2	.597	.421	R	R	6-2	210	9-5-77	1998	Evans, Ga.
Monahan, Shane	.307	97	391	55	120	27	3	10	59	18	53	11	10	.468	.341	L	R	6-0	190	8-12-74	1995	Marietta, Ga.
Nelson, Eric	.227	12	22	2	5	1	0	0	1	4	2	1	1	.273	.346	S	R	5-11	180	5-7-79	1999	Missouri City, Texas
Paz, Rich	.284	137	479	83	136	27	0	5	74	81	80	5	6	.372	.390	R	R	5-8	170	7-30-77	1994	Los Teques, Venez.
Perry, Chan	.316	105	399	59	126	20	2	14	73	29	44	6	5	.481	.359	R	R	6-2	200	9-13-72	1994	Mayo, Fla.
Quinn, Mark	.250	2	8	0	2	1	0	0	1	0	1	0	0	.375	.250	R	R	6-1	190	5-21-74	1995	West Covina, Calif.
Rose, Mike	.305	14	59	13	18	5	0	2	14	7	11	0	1	.492	.379	S	R	6-1	180	8-25-76	1995	Elk Grove, Calif.
Shackelford, Brian	.217	86	244	29	53	10		6	31	23	42	3	4	.332	.288	L	L	6-1	190	8-30-76	1998	Norman, Okla.
Walter, Scott	.197	32	71	6	14	2	0	1	7	10	23	1	0	.268	.256	R	R	6-2	190	12-28-78	2000	Manhattan Beach, Calif.

PITCHING	W	L	ERA	G	GS	CG	SV	IP	H	R	ER	BB	SO	AVG	B	T	HT	WT	DOB	1st Yr	Resides
Abreu, Winston	3	0	3.32	23	1	0	2	41	29	16	15	21	52	.198	R	R	6-2	150	4-5-77	1994	Cotui, D.R.
Affeldt, Jeremy	0	0	1.50	3	3	0	0	6	1	1	1	3	3	.058	L	L	6-4	210	6-6-79	1997	Medical Lake, Wash.
Baerlocher, Ryan	3	2	3.79	11	9	0	0	62	55	30	26	24	40	.237	R	R	6-5	220	8-6-77	1999	Lewiston, Idaho
Bukvich, Ryan	1	1	1.31	23	0	0	8	34	17	8	5	15	47	.145	R	R	6-2	250	5-13-78	2000	Brandon, Miss.
Burch, Matt	1	1	5.28	6	5	0	0	29	33	19	17	12	13	.284	R	R	6-2	190	12-21-76	1998	Horseheads, N.Y.
Calero, Kiko	1	0	2.25	5	2	0	0	16	10	5	4	5	15	.172	R	R	6-1	180	1-9-75	1996	Rio Piedras, P.R.
Cogan, Tony	4	6	3.47	17	16	0	0	91	92	48	35	26	62	.263	L	L	6-2	200	12-24-77	1999	Highland Park, Ill.
Durbin, Chad	0	0	5.06	3	1	0	0	5	5	4	3	4	6	.238	R	R	6-2	200	12-3-77	1996	Baton Rouge, La.
Ferguson, Ian	6	2	2.61	11	11	2	0	76	60	24	22	17	60	.218	R	R	6-4	220	8-23-79	2000	Bellingham, Wash.
Gilfillan, Jason	2	2	2.63	21	1	0	0	38	35	16	11	27	31	.250	R	R	6-5	220	8-31-76	1997	Blacksburg, S.C.
Gobble, Jimmy	5	7	3.38	13	13	0	0	69	71	29	26	19	52	.266	L	L	6-3	190	7-19-81	1999	Bristol, Va.
Gooding, Jason	2	1	3.60	20	0	0	2	25	28	14	10	18	26	.294	R	L	5-11	190	7-29-74	1997	Cambridge, Ontario
Grimsley, Jason	0	0	9.00	1	1	0	0	1	1	1	1	1	0	.250	R	R	6-3	200	8-7-67	1985	Lafayette, La.
Guerrero, Junior	0	0	3.38	11	0	0	0	19	17	10	7	3	9	.236	R	R	6-2	210	8-21-77	1996	Santo Domingo, D.R.
Hernandez, Runelvys	8	3	2.71	16	14	2	0	106	96	38	32	24	86	.248	R	R	6-1	200	4-27-78	1998	Santo Domingo, D.R.
Hill, Jeremy	4	7	2.36	56	0	0	19	76	61	26	20	32	80	.221	R	R	5-11	200	8-8-77	1996	Dallas, Texas
Lee, Garrett	5	0	1.69	13	3	0	2	37	30	8	7	7	19	.212	R	R	6-5	210	8-17-76	1996	Montrose, Calif.
MacDougal, Mike	1	1	3.06	4	4	1	0	18	11	12	6	24	14	.192	S	R	6-4	190	3-5-77	1999	Marco Island, Fla.
Mangrum, Micah	1	2	3.55	23	0	0	1	38	46	18	15	9	19	.315	R	R	6-2	170	9-11-77	2000	Sandy, Utah
May, Darrell	0	0	2.08	1	1	0	0	4	4	1	1	1	5	.235	L	L	6-2	180	6-13-72	1992	Rogue River, Ore.
Morrison, Robbie	0	1	4.50	12	0	0	0	18	20	12	9	7	11	.286	R	R	6-0	210	12-7-76	1998	Valrico, Fla.
Natale, Mike	4	3	5.21	24	2	0	0	48	39	33	28	44	52	.225	R	R	6-0	190	9-2-79	2000	Whittier, Calif.
Obermueller, Wes	9	5	2.90	17	17	0	0	106	98	39	34	40	65	.250	R	R	6-2	190	12-22-76	1999	North Liberty, Iowa
Reichert, Dan	0	1	11.45	8	0	0	0	11	16	15	14	9	11	.340	R	R	6-3	170	7-12-76	1997	Turlock, Calif.
Sanches, Brian	10	6	4.40	33	15	0	0	117	111	60	57	43	101	.251	R	R	6-0	190	8-8-78	1999	Nederland, Texas
Sedlacek, Shawn	2	1	1.47	3	3	0	0	18	14	6	3	4	16	.202	R	R	6-4	200	6-29-77	1998	Cedar Rapids, Iowa
Shackelford, Brian	3	1	3.51	22	0	0	0	25	23	12	10	26	15	.000	L	L	6-1	190	8-30-76	1998	Norman, Okla.
Snyder, Kyle	2	2	4.21	6	6	0	0	26	21	12	12	7	18	.225	R	R	6-8	220	9-9-77	1999	Sarasota, Fla.
Stein, Blake	0	1	3.48	6	3	0	0	10	11	4	4	7	7	.282	R	R	6-7	240	8-3-73	1994	Folsom, La.
Suzuki, Mac	0	0	0.00	1	1	0	0	5	0	0	0	2	3	.000	R	R	6-3	200	5-31-75	1992	Kobe, Japan
Wilson, Kris	3	3	1.88	13	7	1	0	48	47	17	10	4	33	.259	R	R	6-4	220	8-6-76	1997	Palm Harbor, Fla.

FIELDING

Catcher	PCT	G	PO	A	E	DP	PB
Brito	.992	85	583	72	5	5	3
Johnson	.986	34	184	31	3	2	4
Mayne	1.000	2	10	0	0	1	0
Rose	.977	7	37	6	1	0	1
Walter	1.000	22	166	13	0	3	3

First Base	PCT	G	PO	A	E	DP
Caruso	1.000	6	37	6	0	3

	PCT	G	PO	A	E	DP
Glendenning	.857	2	17	1	3	1
Hallmark	.955	6	37	5	2	3
Hart	.989	19	166	11	2	15
Perry	.998	100	885	56	2	98
Shackelford	.981	12	90	14	2	18

Second Base	PCT	G	PO	A	E	DP
Harris	.976	129	256	393	16	104
Hart	1.000	9	10	21	0	2

	PCT	G	PO	A	E	DP
Martinez	.667	1	0	2	1	1
Nelson	.950	5	9	10	1	5

Third Base	PCT	G	PO	A	E	DP
Calderon	.936	18	15	29	3	1
Caruso	.909	18	14	26	4	0
Hallmark	1.000	4	3	10	0	2
Harris	.750	2	1	3	1	0
Hart	.842	25	13	35	9	5

Nelson	.778	5	1	6	2	0
Paz	.912	77	57	129	18	16

Shortstop	PCT	G	PO	A	E	DP
Cotto	.571	1	1	3	3	0
Harris	1.000	1	2	4	0	1
Martinez	.932	79	133	211	25	59
Paz	.962	62	99	183	11	48

Outfield	PCT	G	PO	A	E	DP
Caruso	1.000	23	26	1	0	0
Cunningham	.993	75	133	8	1	2
DeJesus	.976	24	40	0	1	0
Gomez	.967	112	228	6	8	0
Hallmark	.985	76	125	5	2	1
Hart	.000	2	0	0	0	0

Johnson	.000	1	0	0	1	0
Knoblauch	1.000	4	11	0	0	0
Meadows	.968	17	30	0	1	0
Monahan	.993	87	141	2	1	0
Quinn	.000	2	0	0	1	0
Rose	.000	1	0	0	0	0
Shackelford	.974	20	37	1	1	0

WILMINGTON BLUE ROCKS — High Class A

CAROLINA LEAGUE

BATTING	AVG	G	AB	R	H	2B	3B	HR	RBI	BB	SO	SB	CS	SLG	OBP	B	T	HT	WT	DOB	1st Yr	Resides
Arnerich, Tony	.273	73	278	28	76	11	0	2	43	17	44	2	2	.335	.317	R	R	6-0	190	12-14-79	2001	Santa Rosa, Calif.
Blanco, Andres	.308	5	13	2	4	1	0	0	0	1	4	0	0	.385	.357	S	R	5-10	150	4-11-84	2000	Moron, Venez.
Cotto, Luis	.167	14	36	3	6	0	0	0	2	3	11	0	0	.167	.231	R	R	5-10	180	7-9-81	2000	Rio Piedras, P.R.
Cowan, Justin	.300	92	323	53	97	24	1	5	43	28	58	4	0	.427	.370	R	R	5-10	190	11-24-77	2000	Canon City, Colo.
Cunningham, Marco	.320	29	103	13	33	4	0	4	17	18	21	5	2	.476	.449	R	R	5-10	180	8-3-77	2000	Lubbock, Texas
DeJesus, David	.296	87	334	69	99	22	6	4	41	48	42	15	6	.434	.400	L	L	6-0	170	12-20-79	2000	Manalapan, N.J.
Fenster, Darren	.245	74	245	25	60	5	0	1	28	33	32	1	3	.278	.336	R	R	5-9	170	9-11-78	2000	Middletown, N.J.
Gemoll, Justin	.310	93	335	56	104	20	2	1	49	40	55	0	3	.391	.395	R	R	6-2	200	11-19-77	2000	San Jose, Calif.
Gettis, Byron	.283	120	449	76	127	33	2	8	70	48	103	10	5	.419	.364	R	R	6-0	240	3-13-80	1998	East St. Louis, Ill.
Hopper, Norris	.272	125	514	78	140	12	3	1	46	31	55	22	9	.313	.323	R	R	5-9	200	3-24-79	1998	Passaic, N.Y.
Keppinger, Billy	.182	5	11	1	2	0	0	0	1	3	4	0	0	.182	.357	L	L	6-0	180	12-15-78	2000	Auburn, Ga.
Lora, Tom	.265	97	328	47	87	18	2	1	32	27	62	8	6	.341	.325	S	R	5-10	180	10-14-77	1997	Monte Cristi, D.R.
Machado, Alejandro	.314	101	325	53	102	9	1	2	29	27	43	20	6	.366	.381	R	R	6-0	160	4-26-82	1998	Caracas, Venez.
Meadows, Tydus	.295	94	339	63	100	19	4	11	55	54	83	13	3	.472	.402	R	R	6-2	210	9-5-77	1998	Evans, Ga.
Nelson, Eric	.208	80	255	28	53	11	2	2	32	26	76	2	3	.290	.285	S	R	5-11	180	5-2-77	1999	Missouri City, Texas
Ross, Don	.200	38	125	19	25	7	2	3	21	23	39	1	2	.360	.333	L	R	6-1	220	8-1-77	1999	Mt. Juliet, Tenn.
Ruiz, Willy	.283	15	60	8	17	2	1	0	5	5	4	4	1	.350	.338	R	R	5-11	150	10-15-76	1996	Nagua, D.R.
Santos, Chad	.240	110	379	46	91	21	0	9	54	46	122	0	0	.367	.330	L	L	5-11	220	4-28-81	1999	Kaneohe, Hawaii
Walter, Scott	.261	60	222	21	58	19	0	4	35	16	46	1	0	.401	.317	R	R	6-2	200	12-28-78	2000	Manhattan Beach, Calif.

PITCHING	W	L	ERA	G	GS	CG	SV	IP	H	R	ER	BB	SO	AVG	B	T	HT	WT	DOB	1st Yr	Resides
DePaula, Freddy	0	0	5.17	33	0	0	2	56	57	35	32	46	55	.268	L	L	6-3	170	12-9-77	1997	Santo Domingo, D.R.
Douglass, Ryan	11	6	3.22	27	19	0	1	145	144	60	52	35	98	.261	R	R	6-3	210	12-3-78	1997	Pittsburgh, Pa.
Eppeneder, Jamie	1	1	5.00	16	0	0	1	18	18	11	10	9	9	.276	L	L	6-3	210	11-17-78	1999	Antioch, Calif.
Ferguson, Ian	12	1	2.39	17	17	0	0	109	100	36	29	20	81	.247	R	R	6-4	220	8-23-79	2000	Bellingham, Wash.
Gooding, Jason	3	2	3.60	17	0	0	0	30	21	12	12	7	15	.198	R	L	5-11	190	7-29-74	1997	Cambridge, Ontario
Greinke, Zack	0	0	0.00	1	0	0	0	2	1	0	0	0	0	.166	R	R	6-2	190	10-21-83	2002	Apopka, Fla.
Griffin, Colt	0	1	3.86	3	0	0	0	5	3	2	2	5	3	.214	R	R	6-4	200	9-29-82	2001	Marshall, Texas
Guerrero, Junior	6	8	4.55	36	1	0	4	65	74	42	33	17	45	.287	R	R	6-2	210	8-21-77	1996	Santo Domingo, D.R.
Hernandez, Runelvys	1	1	3.50	2	2	0	0	12	12	6	5	1	9	.272	R	R	6-1	200	4-27-78	1998	Santo Domingo, D.R.
MacDougal, Mike	0	1	1.08	5	0	0	2	8	3	4	1	5	10	.107	S	R	6-3	190	3-5-77	1999	Marco Island, Fla.
Mangrum, Micah	1	0	2.39	16	0	0	6	26	21	7	7	2	24	.218	R	R	6-2	170	9-11-77	2000	Sandy, Utah
McClellan, Zach	7	9	4.03	28	27	0	0	145	162	76	65	43	45	.287	R	R	6-5	190	11-25-78	2000	Toledo, Ohio
Morrison, Robbie	2	3	2.42	32	0	0	9	48	34	15	13	19	53	.193	R	R	6-0	170	12-7-76	1998	Valrico, Fla.
Natale, Mike	2	2	2.48	13	2	0	4	29	20	10	8	9	41	.192	R	R	6-0	190	9-2-79	2000	Whittier, Calif.
Obermueller, Wes	5	0	2.76	8	4	0	0	46	38	14	14	14	44	.227	R	R	6-2	190	12-22-76	1999	North Liberty, Iowa
Snyder, Kyle	2	2	2.98	15	15	0	0	48	49	19	16	11	48	.260	S	R	6-8	220	9-9-77	1999	Sarasota, Fla.
Stiles, Brad	4	0	3.40	38	0	0	4	50	44	21	19	21	49	.236	L	L	6-5	230	2-9-81	1999	Lamar, Colo.
Tamayo, Danny	14	4	2.77	23	20	0	0	123	121	48	38	32	108	.259	R	R	6-1	240	6-3-79	2001	Miami, Fla.
Vasquez, Jorge	0	0	4.91	10	0	0	0	11	12	6	6	3	17	.255	R	R	6-1	160	7-16-78	1999	Nagua, D.R.
Villacis, Eduardo	2	1	2.25	17	0	0	1	28	19	8	7	10	15	.190	R	R	6-2	170	8-29-79	1998	Mirando, Venez.
Wilkerson, Wes	9	5	3.14	20	20	0	0	112	98	49	39	34	65	.236	R	R	6-3	200	9-11-76	2000	Nashville, Tenn.
Wilson, Kris	0	0	0.00	4	3	0	0	8	3	0	0	1	10	.107	R	R	6-4	220	8-6-76	1997	Palm Harbor, Fla.
Wrightsman, Dusty	9	4	2.38	39	10	0	5	106	99	36	28	18	85	.239	R	R	6-4	220	12-7-79	2000	Terre Haute, Ind.

FIELDING

Catcher	PCT	G	PO	A	E	DP	PB
Arnerich	.984	66	442	48	8	8	11
Cowan	.975	25	140	14	4	1	3
Walter	.979	55	406	23	9	1	6

First Base	PCT	G	PO	A	E	DP
Cowan	.994	21	171	7	1	15
Gemoll	1.000	5	34	3	0	1
Ross	.982	16	102	10	2	10
Santos	.989	106	914	65	11	76

Second Base	PCT	G	PO	A	E	DP
Fenster	.982	12	17	37	1	7
Lora	.974	77	159	261	11	51

Machado	1.000	3	4	11	0	0
Nelson	.964	61	106	162	10	33
Ruiz	1.000	1	1	5	0	1

Third Base	PCT	G	PO	A	E	DP
Cotto	.500	1	0	1	1	1
Fenster	.901	48	20	71	10	7
Gemoll	.919	78	67	115	16	10
Nelson	.818	7	6	3	2	2
Ruiz	.839	14	6	20	5	0

Shortstop	PCT	G	PO	A	E	DP
Blanco	.926	5	13	12	2	5
Cotto	.909	11	7	23	3	4

Fenster	.971	17	26	42	2	8
Lora	.967	22	30	57	3	20
Machado	.954	98	130	243	18	46

Outfield	PCT	G	PO	A	E	DP
Cowan	1.000	13	14	0	0	0
Cunningham	1.000	29	66	3	0	1
DeJesus	.994	75	162	5	1	2
Gettis	.981	110	196	8	4	1
Hopper	.985	122	245	15	4	3
Keppinger	.889	4	7	1	1	0
Lora	.750	4	6	0	2	0
Meadows	.969	68	123	4	4	1
Ross	.000	1	0	0	0	0

BURLINGTON BEES — Low Class A

MIDWEST LEAGUE

BATTING	AVG	G	AB	R	H	2B	3B	HR	RBI	BB	SO	SB	CS	SLG	OBP	B	T	HT	WT	DOB	1st Yr	Resides
Alleva, J.D.	.225	58	187	15	42	6	0	0	18	20	24	0	0	.257	.303	L	R	5-11	190	11-2-78	2001	Durham, N.C.
Arnerich, Tony	.231	11	39	5	9	1	0	0	3	4	9	0	0	.256	.295	R	R	6-0	190	12-14-79	2001	Santa Rosa, Calif.
Ayala, Odannys	.297	114	401	68	119	22	7	6	61	61	70	5	3	.431	.393	R	R	5-11	170	7-2-80	2001	Carolina, P.R.
Cleveland, Matt	.181	55	160	19	29	6	2	0	14	14	45	2	2	.244	.263	R	R	5-10	190	6-18-79	2001	Fort Lauderdale, Fla.
Cordova, Ben	.258	70	229	26	59	8	1	4	27	33	36	1	0	.354	.352	L	L	5-10	200	12-3-79	1998	Chula Vista, Calif.
Dean, Erik	.243	21	70	11	17	5	1	0	8	3	9	0	0	.343	.289	L	R	6-0	190	2-7-82	2001	Santa Clara, Calif.

BATTING	AVG	G	AB	R	H	2B	3B	HR	RBI	BB	SO	SB	CS	SLG	OBP	B	T	HT	WT	DOB	1st Yr	Resides
Draper, John	.278	94	317	45	88	12	4	1	23	17	38	2	2	.350	.323	R	R	6-2	190	8-11-80	2001	Whittier, Calif.
Fallon, Chris	.294	125	463	58	136	33	6	7	67	91	0	4	.417	.381	L	R	6-2	180	3-9-79	2001	Bayonne, N.J.
Figuereo, Anibal	.221	68	258	22	57	11	2	3	24	10	77	2	1	.314	.263	R	R	6-1	170	1-21-82	1999	Barahona, D.R.
Gomez, Galinda	.236	95	326	42	77	18	1	7	43	37	75	1	4	.362	.327	R	R	6-2	190	7-27-80	2001	Puerto Plata, D.R.
Gotay, Ruben	.285	133	509	87	145	42	9	9	83	73	110	5	4	.456	.377	S	R	5-11	160	12-25-82	2001	Fajardo, P.R.
Groves, Brett	.254	112	413	64	105	22	0	1	38	62	86	15	18	.315	.360	R	R	6-0	180	10-1-78	2002	Tampa, Fla.
Guzman, Jon	.220	123	423	56	93	18	5	10	57	55	159	17	7	.357	.319	R	R	6-1	170	8-28-78	1998	Santiago, D.R.
Keim, Adam	.148	7	27	3	4	3	0	0	5	3	8	0	0	.259	.226	R	R	6-0	180	1-5-81	2002	Lebanon, Pa.
Murphy, Don	.225	33	120	12	27	6	3	0	15	11	31	0	2	.325	.300	R	R	5-10	180	3-10-83	2002	Anaheim, Calif.
Pereyra, Joel	.000	7	12	0	0	0	0	0	0	0	7	0	0	.000	.000	R	R	5-11	181	10-1-80	1999	Nagua, D.R.
Rodriguez, Alex	.224	21	58	8	13	0	0	0	4	5	13	0	0	.224	.308	S	R	5-11	150	9-2-82	1999	La Romana, D.R.
Rosario, Victor	.264	36	125	32	33	5	0	1	14	20	22	3	1	.328	.372	L	R	5-8	170	12-26-80	2001	Poinciana, Fla.
Shanks, James	.295	126	515	81	152	26	4	6	53	51	94	26	11	.396	.362	R	R	6-0	180	1-26-79	1998	Appling, Ga.

PITCHING	W	L	ERA	G	GS	CG	SV	IP	H	R	ER	BB	SO	AVG	B	T	HT	WT	DOB	1st Yr	Resides
Ackerman, Eric	0	1	11.72	7	2	0	1	18	24	23	23	10	10	.315	L	L	6-0	190	10-19-79	2002	Denver, Pa.
Armitage, Barry	5	2	2.04	38	3	0	10	75	51	23	17	38	79	.188	R	R	6-4	250	5-11-79	2000	Durban, South Africa
Bass, Brian	5	7	3.83	20	20	1	0	110	103	57	47	31	60	.245	R	R	6-0	190	1-6-82	2000	Montgomery, Ala.
Douglass, Ryan	0	0	3.48	4	0	0	0	10	10	4	4	3	7	.277	R	R	6-3	210	12-3-78	1997	Pittsburgh, Pa.
Eppender, Jamie	1	1	1.06	8	0	0	0	3	17	7	2	2	15	.118	L	L	6-3	210	11-17-78	1999	Antioch, Calif.
Fallon, Chris	0	0	0.00	2	0	0	0	2	1	0	0	1	0	.000	L	R	6-2	180	3-9-79	2001	Bayonne, N.J.
Griffin, Colt	6	6	5.36	19	9	0	0	91	75	60	54	82	66	.232	R	R	6-4	200	9-29-82	2001	Marshall, Texas
Kaanoi, Jason	1	9	5.07	29	15	0	0	121	151	89	68	38	76	.304	R	L	5-11	170	8-19-82	2000	Kaneohe, Hawaii
Keppinger, Billy	0	0	0.00	1	0	0	0	1	0	0	0	0	2	.000	L	L	6-0	180	12-15-78	2000	Auburn, Ga.
Leclair, Aric	1	0	0.00	10	0	0	3	17	6	0	0	6	25	.107	L	L	6-0	190	4-12-78	2000	Swanzey, N.H.
Melnyk, Brian	1	1	2.93	10	0	0	0	15	15	7	5	4	18	.250	L	L	6-2	200	8-2-80	2001	Colliers, N.J.
Middleton, Kyle	14	5	3.74	29	17	0	1	125	124	67	52	31	64	.254	R	R	6-6	230	6-13-80	2000	Pensacola, Fla.
Pace, Adam	3	2	4.94	23	2	0	2	51	47	33	28	25	30	.241	L	L	6-1	190	9-20-79	2000	Brooklyn, N.Y.
Palmer, Lucas	0	1	8.22	3	1	0	0	8	9	7	7	5	8	.281	R	R	6-3	200	5-7-83	2002	Baker, Ore.
Rosado, Hector	2	2	7.50	31	0	0	0	54	77	49	45	34	28	.334	L	L	5-11	170	3-13-81	2000	Dorado, P.R.
Sanchez, Jason	1	2	8.82	28	0	0	1	34	41	38	33	31	26	.299	R	R	6-0	170	1-9-80	2001	Chicago, Ill.
Stodolka, Mike	8	14	5.27	27	27	1	0	149	173	109	87	51	105	.290	L	L	6-2	210	9-24-81	2000	Corona, Calif.
Tierney, Chris	9	14	3.25	27	27	2	0	166	179	86	60	41	89	.271	L	L	6-6	200	9-1-83	2001	Lockport, Ill.
Vasquez, Jorge	2	1	1.57	22	0	0	6	46	22	8	8	15	55	.141	R	R	6-1	160	7-16-78	1999	Nagua, D.R.
Wilkerson, Wes	2	3	4.99	6	0	0	0	31	37	22	17	11	19	.305	R	R	6-3	200	9-11-76	2000	Nashville, Tenn.
Zary, Richard	4	0	5.94	20	0	0	1	33	44	30	22	6	25	.305	R	R	6-3	200	6-18-78	2001	Mt. Holly Springs, Pa.
Zurita, Tom	3	0	4.46	26	0	0	1	36	37	20	18	19	15	.258	R	R	5-11	160	6-28-80	1999	Anzoategui, Venez.

FIELDING

Catcher	PCT	G	PO	A	E	DP	PB
Alleva	.996	44	244	30	1	2	6
Arnerich	1.000	5	33	8	0	0	0
Draper	.989	91	549	58	7	7	11
Pereyra	1.000	3	3	0	0	0	0

First Base	PCT	G	PO	A	E	DP
Fallon	.995	80	658	68	4	62
Figuereo	.986	61	524	47	8	50
Gomez	1.000	1	2	0	0	0

Second Base	PCT	G	PO	A	E	DP
Cleveland	.968	19	38	53	3	6

	PCT	G	PO	A	E	DP
Gotay	.973	115	266	338	17	88
Rodriguez	.968	7	15	15	1	4

Third Base	PCT	G	PO	A	E	DP
Cleveland	.786	6	3	8	3	0
Dean	.750	4	0	6	2	0
Gomez	.858	90	75	167	40	17
Gotay	1.000	10	7	15	0	3
Groves	.889	25	18	46	8	5
Keim	.917	7	3	8	1	0
Pereyra	.000	1	0	0	0	0

Shortstop	PCT	G	PO	A	E	DP
Cleveland	.800	6	10	18	7	3
Dean	.897	6	8	18	3	1
Groves	.923	83	146	235	32	53
Murphy	.934	33	41	101	10	17
Rodriguez	.891	14	27	30	7	7

Outfield	PCT	G	PO	A	E	DP
Ayala	.964	92	157	5	6	1
Cordova	.982	62	108	3	2	0
Guzman	.939	122	218	11	15	4
Rosario	.982	24	53	3	1	0
Shanks	.978	126	316	2	7	0

SPOKANE INDIANS — Short-Season A

NORTHWEST LEAGUE

BATTING	AVG	G	AB	R	H	2B	3B	HR	RBI	BB	SO	SB	CS	SLG	OBP	B	T	HT	WT	DOB	1st Yr	Resides
Alexander, Alexis	.258	48	124	14	32	6	0	1	11	10	34	6	2	.331	.343	R	R	5-11	200	11-18-82	2001	Spokane, Wash.
Dean, Erik	.290	12	31	5	9	2	0	0	2	7	5	0	0	.355	.436	L	R	6-0	190	2-7-82	2001	Santa Clara, Calif.
Dyson, Trey	.236	48	174	15	41	9	0	6	36	8	30	2	1	.391	.280	R	R	6-4	220	3-11-80	2002	Blythewood, S.C.
Ferrara, Matt	.048	6	21	2	1	1	0	0	2	2	7	0	0	.095	.130	R	R	6-0	190	9-27-82	2001	Miramar, Fla.
Frend, Tim	.326	65	242	36	79	19	2	2	34	33	34	5	3	.446	.412	R	R	6-2	180	5-20-80	2002	Charlotte, N.C.
Guzman, Jacob	.187	26	75	10	14	3	0	3	10	9	16	0	0	.347	.295	R	R	6-0	190	8-2-82	2001	Santee, Calif.
Jensen, David	.258	70	267	41	69	10	2	3	34	30	63	8	1	.345	.345	L	L	6-3	210	12-16-79	2002	Henderson, Nev.
Keim, Adam	.231	55	195	18	45	14	2	4	30	19	57	5	1	.385	.297	R	R	6-0	180	1-5-81	2002	Lebanon, Pa.
Legendre, Curtis	.209	43	148	10	31	11	0	3	19	9	37	1	0	.345	.287	R	R	6-1	180	9-1-81	2001	Port Neches, Texas
Lonnquist, Eric	.203	55	202	33	41	6	1	0	14	33	50	11	2	.243	.324	R	R	6-0	180	6-20-80	2002	Rosemount, Minn.
Lytle, Derrik	.250	31	88	7	22	3	0	0	8	9	25	2	2	.284	.340	L	L	6-2	180	12-1-81	2002	Mesa, Ariz.
Meyer, Rusty	.095	7	21	2	2	1	0	0	1	7	6	0	0	.143	.321	R	R	6-0	180	2-8-81	2002	Grain Valley, Mo.
Murphy, Don	.303	28	109	20	33	10	2	0	15	6	17	0	0	.431	.356	R	R	5-10	180	3-10-83	2002	Anaheim, Calif.
Rodriguez, Alex	.197	62	178	20	35	4	0	0	10	14	49	8	2	.219	.273	S	R	5-11	150	9-2-82	1999	La Romana, D.R.
Rosario, Victor	.229	25	83	5	19	2	3	0	7	7	21	2	1	.325	.286	L	R	5-8	170	12-26-80	2001	Poinciana, Fla.
Stephens, Bernard	.238	64	206	35	49	7	3	1	19	36	61	15	10	.316	.367	L	R	6-0	190	11-11-79	2002	North Augusta, S.C.
Stocker, Mel	.224	61	210	48	47	7	2	4	14	27	35	26	12	.305	.340	S	R	5-10	160	8-15-80	2001	Tucson, Ariz.
Tupman, Matt	.271	51	170	26	46	7	0	2	23	22	22	3	0	.347	.364	L	R	5-11	180	11-25-79	2002	Concord, N.H.
Valles, Jake	.143	10	21	1	3	0	0	1	2	1	2	0	0	.286	.182	R	R	6-0	190	6-12-80	2002	El Paso, Texas

GAMES BY POSITION: C—Guzman 21, Meyer 6, Tupman 50, Valles 8. **1B**—Dyson 7, Guzman 1, Jensen 66, Legendre 4. **2B**—Dean 11, Keim 11, Lonnquist 53, Rodriguez 13. **3B**—Dean 1, Ferrara 4, Keim 42, Legendre 36, Lonnquist 2. **SS**—Keim 7, Lonnquist 6, Murphy 26, Rodriguez 47. **OF**—Alexander 40, Frend 41, Lytle 27, Rosario 63, Stephens 62, Stocker 58.

PITCHING	W	L	ERA	G	GS	CG	SV	IP	H	R	ER	BB	SO	AVG	B	T	HT	WT	DOB	1st Yr	Resides
Ackerman, Eric	4	1	3.10	8	8	0	0	41	33	14	14	13	36	.226	L	L	6-0	190	10-19-79	2002	Denver, Pa.
Atencio, Greg	4	7	6.07	14	12	0	0	59	70	45	40	16	35	.296	R	R	6-3	210	7-15-81	2002	Albuquerque, N.M.

PITCHING	W	L	ERA	G	GS	CG	SV	IP	H	R	ER	BB	SO	AVG	B	T	HT	WT	DOB	1st Yr	Resides
Barnett, John	0	0	7.07	7	0	0	0	14	26	22	11	6	6	.376	R	R	6-0	210	6-26-82	2001	Moreno Valley, Calif.
Bartz, Jason	0	2	5.68	7	1	0	0	19	22	16	12	6	12	.289	R	R	6-2	200	11-25-79	2002	Bradenton, Fla.
Bayliss, Jonah	4	8	5.35	15	15	0	0	71	70	46	42	29	38	.264	R	R	6-2	200	8-13-80	2002	Williamstown, Mass.
Brown, Ira	2	5	5.43	16	14	0	1	60	47	47	36	58	42	.212	R	R	6-4	210	8-3-82	2001	Conroe, Texas
Carter, Ramsey	0	0	3.76	20	1	0	1	41	37	19	17	18	40	.245	S	R	6-2	190	11-26-80	2001	El Paso, Texas
Chamberlain, Steve	0	2	5.06	7	4	0	0	16	16	11	9	8	11	.258	L	R	6-3	200	7-20-80	2002	Pullman, Wash.
Christensen, Danny	0	2	1.10	6	6	0	0	33	24	6	4	14	23	.198	L	L	6-2	200	8-10-83	2002	Vero Beach, Fla.
Dodson, Jeremy	0	2	16.50	8	0	0	0	6	9	14	11	10	3	.346	L	R	6-2	200	5-3-77	1998	Sherman, Texas
Dossett, Dusty	0	1	2.49	15	0	0	0	25	21	8	7	10	11	.225	R	R	6-2	170	4-11-80	2001	Athens, Texas
Encarnacion, Alexis	0	0	2.86	11	0	0	0	22	19	7	7	3	14	.223	R	R	6-0	160	9-26-82	1999	Santo Domingo, D.R.
Endicott, Drew	7	3	3.06	19	6	0	0	68	62	28	23	25	44	.243	R	R	6-3	180	3-30-81	2002	Carthage, Mo.
Greinke, Zack	0	0	7.71	2	2	0	0	5	9	4	4	0	5	.391	R	R	6-2	190	10-21-83	2002	Apopka, Fla.
Keppinger, Billy	0	2	1.29	28	0	0	16	42	29	9	6	10	39	.193	L	L	6-0	180	12-15-78	2000	Auburn, Ga.
McDonnell, Matt	1	1	4.29	21	0	0	2	36	30	17	17	16	17	.240	R	R	6-4	210	8-7-79	2002	Oak Hill, Va.
Nunez, Kelvin	1	7	9.19	10	7	0	0	32	57	37	33	15	17	.404	R	R	6-5	210	3-18-83	1999	La Romana, D.R.
Stefani, Jason	1	1	6.14	12	0	0	0	15	16	11	10	6	11	.271	L	L	6-4	190	4-11-79	2001	Sacramento, Calif.
Suarez, Victor	1	0	10.57	7	0	0	0	8	14	16	9	8	3	.368	S	R	6-1	180	11-23-79	1999	Santo Domingo, D.R.
Taylor, Justin	1	2	6.69	18	0	0	0	35	50	34	26	7	28	.326	R	R	6-2	200	12-8-79	2002	Duncanville, Texas
Zettler, Nate	1	3	7.16	22	0	0	2	28	43	28	22	19	14	.344	R	R	6-2	190	3-26-80	2002	Hamilton, Ohio

BASEBALL CITY ROYALS — Rookie

GULF COAST LEAGUE

BATTING	AVG	G	AB	R	H	2B	3B	HR	RBI	BB	SO	SB	CS	SLG	OBP	B	T	HT	WT	DOB	1st Yr	Resides
Batista, Alexander	.210	50	181	15	38	7	1	1	25	16	36	9	6	.276	.285	R	R	5-10	180	8-11-83	2001	Puerto Plata, D.R.
Blanco, Andres	.249	52	193	27	48	8	0	0	14	15	29	16	4	.290	.315	S	R	5-10	150	4-11-84	2000	Moron, Venez.
Cotto, Luis	.158	5	19	2	3	0	0	0	2	1	7	0	0	.158	.200	R	R	5-10	180	7-9-81	2000	Rio Piedras, P.R.
Donachie, Adam	.206	21	68	7	14	3	0	0	3	9	12	0	0	.250	.304	R	R	6-2	170	3-3-84	2002	Orlando, Fla.
Ferrara, Matt	.186	45	140	15	26	5	0	3	14	23	44	2	0	.286	.297	R	R	6-0	190	9-27-82	2001	Miramar, Fla.
Figueroo, Anibal	.309	14	55	10	17	2	0	0	3	3	9	0	0	.345	.345	R	R	6-1	200	11-21-82	1999	Barahona, D.R.
Gonzalez, Luis	.259	37	116	11	30	6	0	2	17	4	22	1	0	.362	.317	R	R	6-1	200	11-8-82	1999	Guanta, Venez.
Kaaihue, Kila	.259	43	139	15	36	8	0	3	21	26	35	0	0	.381	.381	L	R	6-3	210	3-29-84	2002	Kailua, Hawaii
Lisson, Mario	.200	6	10	2	2	0	0	0	4	4	0	1	0	.200	.467	R	R	5-11	170	5-31-84	2002	Caracas, Venez.
McDonald, Chamar	.204	44	137	17	28	5	1	1	16	23	39	1	0	.277	.347	R	R	6-4	200	6-18-83	2001	Madison, Miss.
Oriental, Rene	.214	44	140	19	30	7	3	0	16	14	43	2	5	.307	.288	R	R	6-2	190	5-4-84	2001	San Pedro de Macoris, D.R.
Pereyra, Joel	.105	7	19	1	2	0	0	0	1	3	0	0	0	.105	.190	R	R	5-11	181	10-1-80	1999	Nagua, D.R.
Salazar, Darwinson	.218	35	101	11	22	5	1	0	6	14	32	3	0	.287	.331	R	R	6-3	195	12-12-82	2000	Higuerote, Venez.
Sanchez, Angel	.251	49	175	21	44	4	0	0	12	10	24	9	2	.274	.302	R	R	6-0	170	9-20-83	2001	Las Piedras, P.R.
Springer, Kenard	.189	38	95	11	18	2	0	0	2	9	13	5	1	.211	.280	R	R	5-11	200	9-18-83	2002	Nettleton, Miss.
Tonis, Mike	.176	6	17	2	3	0	0	1	3	2	3	0	0	.353	.300	R	R	6-3	220	2-9-79	2000	Elk Grove, Calif.
Valles, Jake	.147	10	34	0	5	1	0	0	1	0	9	0	1	.176	.147	R	R	6-0	190	6-12-80	2002	El Paso, Texas
Watkins, Cedric	.160	40	106	12	17	4	0	3	12	20	35	0	1	.283	.299	R	R	5-11	215	5-25-83	2001	Bassett, Va.
Weitz, Konrad	.160	16	25	1	4	0	0	0	2	10	0	0	0	.160	.222	R	R	6-2	180	7-16-85	2001	Capetown, South Africa
Willemburg, Brett	.160	16	25	2	4	0	1	0	2	6	5	0	1	.240	.323	R	R	6-0	180	7-2-84	2000	Capetown, South Africa
Williams, Mervin	.180	38	89	6	16	1	0	0	3	9	26	6	2	.191	.250	L	R	5-10	180	9-1-83	2001	Garyville, La.

GAMES BY POSITION: C—Donachie 19, Gonzalez 30, Lisson 2, Pereyra 7, Valles 5, Weitz 13. **1B**—Ferrara 7, Figueroo 12, Gonzalez 4, Kaaihue 14, Lisson 4, McDonald 23. **2B**—Batista 20, Sanchez 39, Willemburg 9. **3B**—Batista 27, Ferrara 36, Sanchez 1, Springer 3, Willemburg 3. **SS**—Blanco 50, Cotto 5, Sanchez 8, Willemburg 5. **OF**—McDonald 19, Oriental 44, Salazar 32, Springer 31, Watkins 40, Weitz 2, Williams 35.

PITCHING	W	L	ERA	G	GS	CG	SV	IP	H	R	ER	BB	SO	AVG	B	T	HT	WT	DOB	1st Yr	Resides
Bays, Leonard	0	0	11.57	2	0	0	0	2	2	3	3	2	6	.200	R	R	5-11	180	12-15-79	2002	Bellevue, Ky.
Bryan, Robert	0	2	2.31	7	0	0	0	12	9	5	3	4	10	.209	R	R	6-0	190	5-31-80	2002	Richmond, Texas
Chen, Jose	0	2	6.48	2	1	0	0	8	12	10	6	4	8	.307	R	R	6-5	200	9-15-81	2002	Panama City, Panama
Christensen, Danny	1	3	3.10	7	6	0	0	29	20	13	10	14	28	.196	L	L	6-2	200	8-10-83	2002	Vero Beach, Fla.
Dodson, Jeremy	1	2	7.50	8	0	0	0	12	17	14	10	8	4	.340	L	R	6-2	200	5-3-77	1998	Sherman, Texas
Dossett, Dusty	0	0	9.00	1	0	0	0	1	2	1	1	0	0	.400	R	R	6-2	170	4-11-80	2001	Athens, Texas
Durbin, Chad	0	0	0.00	3	3	0	0	6	4	0	0	1	5	.200	R	R	6-2	200	12-3-77	1996	Baton Rouge, La.
Encarnacion, Alexis	1	0	3.60	6	0	0	1	15	15	6	6	4	13	.263	R	R	6-0	160	9-26-82	1999	Santo Domingo, D.R.
Gore, Kirk	0	0	1.23	5	0	0	0	7	6	1	1	2	4	.214	R	R	5-11	180	11-8-79	2002	Taloga, Okla.
Greinke, Zack	0	0	1.93	3	3	0	0	5	3	1	1	3	4	.200	R	R	6-2	190	10-21-83	2002	Apopka, Fla.
Hoelscher, Nate	2	2	1.60	9	2	1	0	34	28	10	6	7	27	.225	L	L	6-2	190	11-11-79	2002	St. Joseph, Minn.
Lowery, Devon	0	3	3.86	15	0	0	4	26	25	13	11	11	26	.255	R	R	6-1	190	3-24-83	2001	Belmont, N.C.
MacDougal, Mike	0	0	3.00	1	1	0	0	3	3	1	1	0	3	.272	S	R	6-4	190	3-5-77	1999	Marco Island, Fla.
Mattison, Kieran	1	1	1.80	13	0	0	1	20	13	4	4	3	19	.188	R	R	6-0	190	6-21-80	2002	Greenville, N.C.
Melnyk, Brian	0	1	4.66	7	1	0	1	10	10	5	5	7	8	.277	L	L	6-2	200	8-2-80	2001	Colliers, N.J.
Moreno, Orber	0	0	0.00	2	2	0	0	2	1	0	0	0	3	.142	R	R	6-3	200	4-27-77	1994	Los Altos, Venez.
Nelson, David	6	2	3.32	16	1	0	1	43	47	17	16	15	29	.281	L	L	6-5	210	9-13-80	2002	Walkertown, N.C.
Nelson, Justin	1	7	4.30	12	9	0	0	59	67	37	28	25	23	.288	L	L	6-4	180	12-15-82	2001	Kersey, Colo.
Nunez, Kelvin	3	1	1.32	5	0	0	0	27	20	6	4	15	15	.208	R	R	6-5	210	3-18-83	1999	La Romana, D.R.
Palmer, Lucas	2	4	4.31	13	8	1	0	56	68	31	27	13	32	.302	R	R	6-3	200	5-7-83	2002	Baker, Ore.
Poles, Donnie	0	0	8.03	9	0	0	0	12	10	13	11	13	12	.222	R	R	6-0	200	11-17-82	2002	Charlotte, N.C.
Rosa, Carlos	0	4	6.19	10	9	0	0	32	52	32	22	12	11	.361	R	R	6-0	160	9-21-84	2002	San Francisco de Macoris, D.R.
Rose, Brian	0	1	9.00	2	2	0	0	3	6	3	3	1	1	.461	R	R	6-3	210	2-13-76	1995	Dartmouth, Mass.
Runyon, Roy	1	1	2.03	11	2	0	0	31	22	9	7	3	28	.194	R	R	6-2	190	9-27-80	2002	Suffolk, Va.
Sanchez, Elby	3	2	1.80	15	5	0	2	50	49	18	10	7	36	.250	R	R	6-1	170	2-6-83	1999	Dajabon, D.R.

LOS ANGELES DODGERS

BY CHRIS COCOLES

In many ways, the 2002 Dodgers were a big hit. In others, they were a bitter disappointment.

They won 92 games, the franchise's most since 1991. But they also let a good opportunity at making the play-

offs slip away. It's now a six-year postseason drought. Dodger Blue hasn't tasted victory in October's party since Game Five of the 1988 World Series.

But maybe the Dodgers shouldn't have been so close, finishing just 3½ games behind the Giants for the National League wild card and six behind the National League West-champion Diamondbacks. After all, their two big-money pitchers, Kevin Brown and Darren Dreifort, were shut down for most or all of the season with injuries in a repeat of 2001. The Dodgers were a near-miss playoff team then too.

The Dodgers were a tease throughout the 2002 season. They led the West at the all-star break but were rattled by losing three of four to Arizona to open the second half. As late as Sept. 16, they were in the wild card spot, again fading.

General manager Dan Evans made some shrewd dealing in his first full season at the helm. An essentially new starting rotation was brought in. Odalis Perez was something of a throw-in to complement Brian Jordan in the Gary Sheffield trade with the Braves, but Perez blossomed into a 15-10, 3.00 lefthanded stopper.

If Perez was a pleasant surprise, the 16-6, 3.39 performance by former Dodger cult hero-turned-journeyman Hideo Nomo was a shocking one. Brown was supposed to be the staff ace, but Perez, Nomo and another Evans acquisition—Kazuhisa Ishii (14-10, 4.27 before his season ended because of a fractured skull off a line drive) provided a strong trio.

And then there was Eric Gagne, so ineffective as a starter he was booed off the Dodger Stadium mound many times

Eric Gagne   Joe Thurston

PLAYERS OF THE YEAR

MAJOR LEAGUE: Eric Gagne, rhp

Gagne went from a question mark in the Los Angeles rotation in 2001 to the rock of the Dodgers bullpen by converting 52 of 56 saves in 2002. He allowed more than one run just once all season while posting a 1.97 ERA.

MINOR LEAGUE: Joe Thurston, 2b

Traditionally, sluggers top the total bases charts. But Thurston led the minor leagues with 297 in 2002, while also topping the list with 196 hits. That offensive outburst earned Thurston, 23, his first September promotion to Los Angeles.

in 2001. Converting the Canadian to a closer made him one of baseball's best—Gagne's 52 saves were a club record.

The Dodgers were probably two bats short of overtaking the Diamondbacks and Giants in the West. If only Jordan's torrid September (30 RBIs, but just 80 for the season) was more typical of his whole season, he would have looked far better as Sheffield's replacement.

Shawn Green (.285-42-114) made an MVP bid, including a four-homer game at Milwaukee, but he was the lone 100-RBI man in the lineup.

And not all was so rosy for Evans, whose trade deadline moves to get a setup reliever (Paul Shuey) and a utility infielder (Tyler Houston) not only didn't push Los Angeles into the playoffs but were costly for the future. And the Dodgers have a sizable chunk of payroll money invested in the gimpy bodies of Dreifort and Brown.

Hope rests in an improving farm system, though the Houston and Shuey trades lost the organization's No. 1 pitching prospect in Ricardo Rodriguez, former first-rounder Ben Diggins and yet another young arm, Francisco Cruceta. But first-year farm director Bill Bavasi and scouting director Logan White, another newcomer, made strides towards rebuilding a once proud minor league system that had crumbled amid questionable drafts.

Triple-A Las Vegas won its Pacific Coast League division title and boasted possibly the club's future right side of the infield in first baseman Chin-Feng Chen and second baseman Joe Thurston. Both should have a chance at unseating incumbents Eric Karros and Mark Grudzielanek.

That Rookie-level Great Falls won the Pioneer League title suggests White's first draft was a smashing success. Great Falls featured 2002 picks James Loney, Greg Miller, Mike Nixon, and Jonathan Broxton, all high schoolers plucked out of the early rounds.

ORGANIZATION LEADERS

BATTING

*AVG	Mike Kinkade, Las Vegas	.341
R	Joe Thurston, Las Vegas	106
H	Joe Thurston, Las Vegas	196
TB	Joe Thurston, Las Vegas	297
2B	Joe Thurston, Las Vegas	39
3B	Joe Thurston, Las Vegas	13
	Reggie Abercrombie, Jacksonville/Vero Beach	13
HR	Chin-Feng Chen, Las Vegas	26
RBI	Chin-Feng Chen, Las Vegas	84
BB	Koyie Hill, Jacksonville	76
SO	Chin-Feng Chen, Las Vegas	160
SB	Shane Victorino, Jacksonville	45

PITCHING

W	Heath Totten, Jacksonville/Vero Beach	12
L	Ben Diggins, Vero Beach	10
	Andrew Brown, Vero Beach	10
#ERA	Jonathan Figueroa, South Georgia/Great Falls	1.42
G	Steve Coyler, Jacksonville	59
CG	Francisco Cruceta, South Georgia	3
SV	Lino Urdaneta, Jacksonville/Vero Beach	32
IP	Robert Ellis, Las Vegas	173
BB	Scott Proctor, Jacksonville	85
SO	Joel Hanrahan, Jacksonville/Vero Beach	149

*Minimum 250 At-Bats #Minimum 75 Innings

LOS ANGELES DODGERS

Manager: Jim Tracy

2002 Record: 92-70, .568 (2nd, NL West)

BATTING	AVG	G	AB	R	H	2B	3B	HR	RBI	BB	SO	SB	CS	SLG	OBP	B	T	HT	WT	DOB	1st Yr	Resides
Allen, Luke	.143	6	7	2	1	1	0	0	0	2	3	0	0	.286	.333	L	R	6-2	220	8-4-78	1996	Covington, Ga.
Beltre, Adrian	.257	159	587	70	151	26	5	21	75	37	96	7	5	.426	.303	R	R	5-11	200	4-7-79	1994	Santo Domingo, D.R.
Bocachica, Hiram	.215	49	65	12	14	3	0	4	9	5	19	1	1	.446	.271	R	R	5-11	160	3-4-76	1994	Toa Alta, P.R.
Cabrera, Jolbert	.333	10	12	3	4	1	0	0	1	2	2	0	0	.417	.429	R	R	6-0	170	12-8-72	1991	Cartagena, Colombia
Chen, Chin-Feng	.000	3	5	1	0	0	0	0	0	1	3	0	0	.000	.167	R	R	6-1	180	10-28-77	1999	Tainan City, Taiwan
Cora, Alex	.291	115	258	37	75	14	4	5	28	26	38	7	2	.434	.371	L	R	6-0	180	10-18-75	1996	Caguas, P.R.
Green, Shawn	.285	158	582	110	166	31	1	42	114	93	112	8	5	.558	.385	L	L	6-4	200	11-10-72	1991	Newport Beach, Calif.
Grissom, Marquis	.277	111	343	57	95	21	4	17	60	22	68	5	1	.510	.321	R	R	5-11	180	4-17-67	1988	Atlanta, Ga.
Grudzielanek, Mark	.271	150	536	56	145	23	0	9	50	22	89	4	1	.364	.301	R	R	6-1	180	6-30-70	1991	West Palm Beach, Fla.
Hansen, Dave	.292	96	120	15	35	6	0	2	17	14	22	1	0	.392	.363	L	R	6-0	190	11-24-68	1986	San Juan Capistrano, Calif.
Houston, Tyler	.200	35	65	9	13	5	1	0	7	2	21	0	0	.308	.224	L	R	6-1	210	1-17-71	1989	Henderson, Nev.
2-team (76 Milwaukee)	.281	111	320	34	90	20	3	7	40	16	62	1	0	.428	.323							
Izturis, Cesar	.232	135	439	43	102	24	2	1	31	14	39	7	7	.303	.253	S	R	5-9	170	2-10-80	1996	Barquisimeto, Venez.
Jordan, Brian	.285	128	471	65	134	27	3	18	80	34	86	2	2	.469	.338	R	R	6-1	205	3-29-67	1988	Alpharetta, Ga.
Karros, Eric	.271	142	524	52	142	26	1	13	73	37	74	4	2	.399	.323	R	R	6-4	220	11-4-67	1988	Los Angeles, Calif.
Kinkade, Mike	.380	37	50	7	19	5	0	2	11	4	10	1	0	.600	.483	R	R	6-1	210	5-6-73	1995	Pullman, Wash.
Kreuter, Chad	.263	41	95	8	25	5	0	2	12	10	31	1	0	.379	.333	S	R	6-2	200	8-26-64	1985	La Quinta, Calif.
LoDuca, Paul	.281	149	580	74	163	38	1	10	64	34	31	3	1	.402	.330	R	R	5-10	180	4-12-72	1993	Peoria, Ariz.
Reboulet, Jeff	.208	38	48	3	10	3	0	0	2	6	13	0	0	.271	.291	R	R	6-0	170	4-30-64	1986	Dayton, Ohio
Roberts, Dave	.277	127	422	63	117	14	7	3	34	48	51	45	10	.365	.353	L	L	5-10	180	5-31-72	1994	Oceanside, Calif.
Ross, Dave	.200	8	10	2	2	1	0	1	2	2	4	0	0	.600	.385	R	R	6-2	200	3-19-77	1998	Tallahassee, Fla.
Ruan, Wilkin	.273	12	11	2	3	1	0	0	3	0	2	0	0	.364	.273	R	R	6-0	170	9-18-78	1996	Guaymate, D.R.
Thurston, Joe	.462	8	13	1	6	1	0	0	1	0	1	0	0	.538	.429	L	R	5-11	170	9-29-79	1999	Vallejo, Calif.

PITCHING	W	L	ERA	G	GS	CG	SV	IP	H	R	ER	BB	SO	AVG	B	T	HT	WT	DOB	1st Yr	Resides
Alvarez, Victor	0	1	4.35	4	1	0	0	10	9	5	5	2	7	.236	L	L	5-10	150	11-8-76	1997	Culiacan, Mexico
Ashby, Andy	9	13	3.91	30	30	0	0	182	179	85	79	65	107	.261	R	R	6-1	200	7-11-67	1986	Pittston, Pa.
Beirne, Kevin	2	0	3.41	12	3	0	0	29	26	11	11	17	17	.245	L	R	6-4	210	1-1-74	1995	The Woodlands, Texas
Brown, Kevin	3	4	4.81	17	10	0	0	64	68	36	34	23	58	.274	R	R	6-4	200	3-15-65	1986	Macon, Ga.
Carrara, Giovanni	6	3	3.28	63	1	0	1	91	83	34	33	32	56	.243	R	R	6-2	230	3-4-68	1990	Edo Anzoategui, Venez.
Corey, Bryan	0	0	0.00	1	0	0	0	1	0	0	0	0	0	.000	R	R	6-0	170	10-21-73	1993	Phoenix, Ariz.
Daal, Omar	11	9	3.90	39	23	0	0	161	142	73	70	54	105	.238	L	L	6-3	200	3-1-72	1990	Valencia, Venez.
Ellis, Robert	0	1	10.13	3	0	0	0	3	6	3	3	0	0	.461	R	R	6-5	220	12-15-70	1991	Carthage, Texas
Gagne, Eric	4	1	1.97	77	0	0	52	82	55	18	18	16	114	.189	R	R	6-2	190	1-7-76	1995	Montreal, Quebec
Ishii, Kazuhisa	14	10	4.27	28	28	0	0	154	137	82	73	106	143	.231	L	L	6-0	190	9-9-73	2002	Chiba, Japan
Mota, Guillermo	1	3	4.15	43	0	0	0	61	45	30	28	27	49	.201	R	R	6-4	200	7-25-73	1991	San Pedro de Macoris, D.R.
Mulholland, Terry	0	0	7.31	21	0	0	0	32	45	29	26	7	17	.330	R	L	6-3	220	3-9-63	1984	Scottsdale, Ariz.
Nomo, Hideo	16	6	3.39	34	34	0	0	220	189	92	83	101	193	.235	R	R	6-2	200	8-31-68	1995	Tokyo, Japan
Orosco, Jesse	1	2	3.00	56	0	0	1	27	24	10	9	12	22	.228	R	L	6-2	190	4-21-57	1978	San Diego, Calif.
Perez, Odalis	15	10	3.00	32	32	4	0	222	182	76	74	38	155	.225	L	L	6-0	190	6-11-77	1994	Las Matas de Farfan, D.R.
Quantrill, Paul	5	5	2.70	86	0	0	1	77	80	27	23	25	55	.266	L	R	6-1	190	11-3-68	1989	Tarpon Springs, Fla.
Shuey, Paul	5	2	4.40	28	0	0	1	31	25	18	15	21	24	.217	R	R	6-3	210	9-16-70	1992	Wake Forest, N.C.
Springer, Dennis	0	1	6.75	1	0	0	0	1	1	1	1	2	1	.200	R	R	5-10	180	2-12-65	1987	Fresno, Calif.
Williams, Jeff	0	0	11.70	10	0	0	0	10	15	13	13	7	11	.333	R	L	6-0	180	6-6-72	1996	Page, Australia

FIELDING

Catcher	PCT	G	PO	A	E	DP	PB
Chen	.000	1	0	0	0	0	0
Kreuter	.986	41	197	16	3	1	0
LoDuca	.992	137	965	76	8	9	12
Ross	1.000	6	19	2	0	0	0

First Base	PCT	G	PO	A	E	DP
Hansen	1.000	27	76	5	0	3
Houston	.981	12	98	3	2	9
Karros	.997	142	1175	106	4	101
Kinkade	1.000	11	39	4	0	3
LoDuca	.979	18	45	1	1	3

Second Base	PCT	G	PO	A	E	DP
Cabrera	1.000	1	2	1	0	0
Cora	.976	40	30	53	2	11
Grudzielanek	.989	147	253	366	7	76
Izturis	1.000	1	1	3	0	0
Reboulet	.933	11	6	22	2	2
Thurston	1.000	4	4	6	0	3

Third Base	PCT	G	PO	A	E	DP
Beltre	.954	157	120	294	20	18

	PCT	G	PO	A	E	DP
Cabrera	1.000	3	2	4	0	1
Hansen	.895	11	4	13	2	0
Houston	.800	2	0	4	1	0
Reboulet	.000	3	0	0	0	0

Shortstop	PCT	G	PO	A	E	DP
Cora	.977	61	67	144	5	32
Izturis	.979	128	155	306	10	69
Reboulet	.714	5	3	2	2	0

Outfield	PCT	G	PO	A	E	DP
Allen	1.000	3	4	0	0	0
Bocachica	.960	22	24	0	1	0
Cabrera	1.000	4	4	0	0	0
Chen	1.000	1	3	0	0	0
Green	.994	156	333	7	2	3
Grissom	.978	102	169	5	4	0
Jordan	.982	125	213	10	4	4
Kinkade	1.000	8	4	0	0	0
LoDuca	1.000	9	4	1	0	0
Roberts	1.000	117	253	4	0	1
Ruan	1.000	5	5	0	0	0

Shawn Green

LARRY GOREN

FARM SYSTEM

Director, Player Development: Bill Bavasi

Class	Farm Team	League	W	L	Pct.	Finish*	Manager(s)	First Yr.
AAA	Las Vegas (Nev.) 51s	Pacific Coast	85	59	.590	1st (16)	Brad Mills	2001
AA	Jacksonville (Fla.) Suns	Southern	77	62	.554	2nd (10)	Dino Ebel	2001
High A	Vero Beach (Fla.) Dodgers	Florida State	72	63	.533	4th (12)	Juan Bustabad	1980
Low A	South Georgia (Albany, Ga.) Waves	South Atlantic	75	63	.543	5th (16)	Scott Little	2001
Rookie	Great Falls (Mont.) Dodgers	Pioneer	47	28	.627	+1st (8)	Dann Bilardello	1984
Rookie	Vero Beach (Fla.) Dodgers	Gulf Coast	33	27	.550	5th (14)	Luis Salazar	2001

*Finish in overall standings (No. of teams in league)   +League champion

LAS VEGAS 51s — Class AAA
PACIFIC COAST LEAGUE

BATTING	AVG	G	AB	R	H	2B	3B	HR	RBI	BB	SO	SB	CS	SLG	OBP	B	T	HT	WT	DOB	1st Yr	Resides
Allen, Luke	.329	137	501	85	165	28	3	12	78	56	77	4	6	.469	.395	L	R	6-2	220	8-4-78	1996	Covington, Ga.
Bell, Rick	.270	122	448	60	121	26	4	13	77	16	75	0	1	.433	.293	R	R	6-2	180	4-5-79	1997	Cincinnati, Ohio
Branson, Jeff	.245	88	233	30	57	15	1	3	26	20	53	0	1	.356	.310	L	R	6-0	180	1-26-67	1989	Union, Ky.
Cabrera, Jolbert	.343	27	102	22	35	8	1	2	11	14	18	2	3	.500	.417	R	R	6-0	170	12-8-72	1991	Cartagena, Colombia
Canales, Josh	.000	1	1	0	0	0	0	0	0	1	0	0	0	.000	.000	R	R	5-11	170	1-15-79	2001	Carson, Calif.
Chen, Chin-Feng	.284	137	511	90	145	26	4	26	84	58	160	1	0	.503	.352	R	R	6-1	180	10-28-77	1999	Tainan City, Taiwan
Clapinski, Chris	.295	102	342	58	101	25	3	12	57	39	52	2	0	.491	.373	S	R	6-0	170	8-20-71	1992	Cape Canaveral, Fla.
Crosby, Bubba	.262	73	279	26	73	12	1	9	36	19	47	3	1	.409	.312	L	L	5-11	180	8-11-76	1998	Bellaire, Texas
Davis, Tommy	.269	15	52	8	14	2	1	3	13	0	14	0	0	.519	.283	R	R	6-1	210	5-21-73	1994	Semmes, Ala.
2-team (28 Memphis)	.275	43	142	17	39	6	1	7	33	5	33	0	0	.479	.302							
Greene, Todd	.352	32	125	27	44	12	0	11	41	3	21	0	0	.712	.373	R	R	5-10	200	5-8-71	1993	Alpharetta, Ga.
Gutierrez, Franklin	.300	2	10	2	3	2	0	0	2	1	4	0	0	.500	.364	R	R	6-2	170	2-21-83	2001	Caracas, Venez.
Hiatt, Phil	.304	95	355	70	108	14	2	23	82	42	88	1	2	.549	.375	R	R	6-3	200	5-1-69	1990	Pensacola, Fla.
Ingram, Garey	.317	25	63	9	20	3	0	1	10	6	14	0	0	.413	.394	R	R	5-11	190	7-25-70	1990	Columbus, Ga.
Kellner, Ryan	.400	11	35	3	14	4	0	3	11	0	6	0	0	.514	.462	R	R	6-2	200	12-9-77	1997	Morganton, N.C.
Kinkade, Mike	.341	74	287	63	98	22	6	11	50	29	49	6	2	.575	.433	R	R	6-1	210	5-6-73	1995	Pullman, Wash.
Lopez, Rafael	.283	15	46	6	13	2	0	2	5	4	12	1	0	.457	.365	R	R	6-0	200	10-22-76	1996	Miami, Fla.
Martinez, Felix	.195	24	82	13	16	4	0	2	9	5	19	0	0	.317	.256	S	R	6-0	180	5-18-74	1993	Nagua, D.R.
Pose, Scott	.203	23	74	11	15	3	0	0	6	14	6	5	3	.243	.337	L	R	5-11	190	2-11-67	1989	Raleigh, N.C.
Reboulet, Jeff	.254	18	63	10	16	2	0	1	3	6	9	2	0	.333	.314	R	R	6-0	170	4-30-64	1986	Dayton, Ohio
Ross, David	.297	92	293	48	87	16	2	15	68	35	86	1	1	.519	.384	R	R	6-2	200	3-19-77	1998	Tallahassee, Fla.
Ruan, Wilkin	.327	40	153	18	50	7	3	0	29	2	17	12	0	.412	.335	R	R	6-0	170	9-18-78	1996	Guaymate, D.R.
Socarras, Tony	.333	1	3	1	1	0	0	0	2	0	1	0	0	.333	.500	L	R	6-0	200	11-8-78	2000	Miami, Fla.
Theodorou, Nick	.600	2	5	1	3	0	0	0	1	0	0	0	0	.600	.667	S	R	5-11	180	6-7-75	1998	Rialto, Calif.
Thurston, Joe	.334	136	587	106	196	39	13	12	55	25	60	22	9	.506	.372	L	R	5-11	170	9-29-79	1999	Vallejo, Calif.
Tyler, Brad	.243	66	148	34	36	9	3	2	13	41	37	0	2	.385	.408	L	R	6-2	180	3-3-69	1990	Aurora, Ind.
Whiten, Mark	.160	8	25	3	4	1	0	1	2	2	4	1	0	.320	.250	S	R	6-3	230	11-25-66	1986	Clearwater, Fla.

PITCHING	W	L	ERA	G	GS	CG	SV	IP	H	R	ER	BB	SO	AVG	B	T	HT	WT	DOB	1st Yr	Resides
Aldred, Scott	2	2	4.43	42	0	0	2	45	50	22	22	19	48	.284	L	L	6-4	190	6-12-68	1987	Fenton, Mich.
Alvarez, Victor	10	7	4.70	34	15	0	3	123	132	69	64	39	106	.277	L	L	5-10	150	11-8-76	1997	Culiacan, Mexico
Beirne, Kevin	10	3	4.15	22	22	0	0	126	129	64	58	41	88	.268	L	R	6-4	210	1-1-74	1995	The Woodlands, Texas
Bones, Ricky	0	2	3.86	30	0	0	9	30	34	19	13	12	15	.276	R	R	6-0	200	4-6-69	1986	Guayama, P.R.
Brown, Kevin	1	0	1.86	2	2	0	0	10	6	2	2	3	7	.181	R	R	6-4	200	3-15-65	1986	Macon, Ga.
Caraccioli, Lance	2	4	4.14	10	10	0	0	59	58	30	27	28	39	.267	L	L	6-4	190	12-14-77	1998	Walker, La.
Corey, Bryan	5	4	4.36	37	0	0	1	54	79	31	26	18	33	.348	R	R	6-0	170	10-21-73	1993	Phoenix, Ariz.
Devey, Phil	2	4	5.83	26	10	0	0	76	115	54	49	29	34	.360	L	L	6-0	170	5-31-77	1999	Lachute, Quebec
Ellis, Robert	9	7	4.17	29	28	1	0	173	195	100	80	37	110	.283	R	R	6-5	220	12-15-70	1991	Carthage, Texas
Falteisek, Steve	0	2	10.69	13	0	0	0	16	21	20	19	7	12	.308	R	R	6-2	200	1-28-72	1992	Floral Park, N.Y.
Gonzalez, Alfredo	2	3	2.91	14	0	0	1	22	23	10	7	9	23	.280	R	R	5-11	160	9-17-79	1997	Nagua, D.R.
Gulin, Lindsay	1	4	4.14	14	14	0	0	69	80	42	32	26	70	.293	L	L	6-3	170	11-22-76	1995	Issaquah, Wash.
House, Craig	0	0	7.40	19	0	0	0	21	25	19	17	16	25	.297	R	R	6-2	220	7-8-77	1999	Nashville, Tenn.
Johnson, Mike	2	1	4.09	8	8	0	0	44	54	24	20	18	35	.312	L	R	6-2	180	10-3-75	1993	Jupiter, Fla.
Magnante, Mike	1	3	3.00	7	0	0	0	6	5	3	2	2	4	.208	L	L	6-2	210	6-17-65	1988	Burbank, Calif.
Mota, Guillermo	1	3	2.95	20	0	0	1	37	34	13	12	8	38	.259	R	R	6-4	200	7-25-73	1991	San Pedro de Macoris, D.R.
Nance, Shane	11	3	4.17	37	0	0	1	58	58	32	27	26	53	.260	L	L	5-8	180	9-7-77	2000	Houston, Texas
Rodriguez, Ricardo	1	0	3.86	2	2	0	0	12	13	5	5	5	7	.295	R	R	6-3	160	5-21-78	1996	Guayubin, D.R.
Simon, Ben	4	0	5.70	23	10	0	1	73	84	49	46	28	47	.296	R	R	6-1	180	11-12-74	1996	Berlin Heights, Ohio
Skrmetta, Matt	1	1	9.82	7	0	0	0	7	14	9	8	2	6	.424	S	R	6-3	220	11-6-72	1993	Satellite Beach, Fla.
2-team (40 Omaha)	9	1	3.29	47	0	0	1	68	62	30	25	36	64	.243							
Spencer, Stan	1	0	0.00	3	1	0	0	8	5	1	0	1	5	.172	R	R	6-4	220	8-7-69	1991	Battle Ground, Wash.
Springer, Dennis	7	8	5.85	26	22	1	1	143	203	100	93	37	38	.344	R	R	5-10	180	2-12-65	1987	Fresno, Calif.
Williams, Jeff	6	4	2.60	56	0	0	28	80	80	25	23	22	75	.264	L	L	6-0	180	6-6-72	1996	Page, Australia

FIELDING

Catcher	PCT	G	PO	A	E	DP	PB
Davis	1.000	12	60	7	0	0	1
Greene	.988	25	160	11	2	3	2
Kellner	.987	11	73	4	1	1	1
Kinkade	.857	2	6	0	1	0	1
Lopez	.987	15	68	10	1	0	0
Ross	.989	90	589	59	7	5	10
Socarras	1.000	1	5	0	0	0	0

First Base	PCT	G	PO	A	E	DP
Bell	1.000	9	58	4	0	6
Chen	.987	97	799	68	11	78
Davis	1.000	2	17	0	0	2
Greene	1.000	1	4	0	0	1
Hiatt	.993	45	269	27	2	28
Kinkade	.988	9	76	5	1	7

Second Base	PCT	G	PO	A	E	DP
Branson	.958	9	19	27	2	8

	PCT	G	PO	A	E	DP
Cabrera	.000	1	0	0	0	0
Canales	1.000	1	0	2	0	0
Clapinski	.917	6	16	17	3	4
Reboulet	.959	11	18	29	2	6
Thurston	.972	118	285	378	19	77

Third Base	PCT	G	PO	A	E	DP
Bell	.920	108	61	192	22	13
Branson	.948	29	10	45	3	2
Cabrera	.800	3	3	1	1	0

ORGANIZATION STATISTICS

Hiatt	.857	5	1	5	1	1		Theodorou	1.000	1	3	4	0	2		Gutierrez	1.000	2	9	0	0	0
Kinkade	.964	11	7	20	1	0		Thurston	.976	17	35	46	2	11		Hiatt	1.000	47	63	1	0	1
Reboulet	1.000	3	0	2	0	0										Ingram	.963	16	26	0	1	0

Outfield PCT G PO A E DP — Allen .969 132 257 23 9 7; Cabrera .980 24 47 1 1 0; Chen 1.000 1 2 0 0 0; Clapinski .000 1 0 0 0 0; Crosby .989 71 182 5 2 2; Greene 1.000 1 1 0 0 0

Kinkade .979 53 87 5 2 0; Pose 1.000 21 48 2 0 1; Ruan 1.000 39 97 3 0 0; Theodorou 1.000 1 1 0 0 0; Tyler .968 49 84 7 3 0; Whiten 1.000 5 12 0 0 0

Shortstop	PCT	G	PO	A	E	DP
Branson	.958	26	33	81	5	14
Cabrera	1.000	2	4	6	0	1
Clapinski	.977	80	131	206	8	47
Martinez	.938	22	43	78	8	21
Reboulet	1.000	2	3	4	0	1

JACKSONVILLE SUNS — Class AA

SOUTHERN LEAGUE

BATTING	AVG	G	AB	R	H	2B	3B	HR	RBI	BB	SO	SB	CS	SLG	OBP	B	T	HT	WT	DOB	1st Yr	Resides
Abercrombie, Reggie	.250	1	4	1	1	0	0	0	0	1	1	0		.250	.250	R	R	6-3	210	7-15-80	2000	Damascus, Ga.
Bledsoe, Hunter	.279	110	348	39	97	18	2	4	38	54	42	3	4	.376	.381	R	R	6-4	210	1-24-76	1999	Nashville, Tenn.
Brock, Tarrik	.265	111	325	59	86	16	2	9	47	72	93	8	8	.409	.401	L	L	6-2	180	12-25-73	1991	Reseda, Calif.
Collins, Mike	.313	117	384	40	120	14	1	0	45	44	36	7	1	.354	.383	R	R	5-9	160	1-29-77	1998	Phoenix, Ariz.
Crosby, Bubba	.260	38	150	14	39	6	2	2	20	11	23	7	3	.367	.317	L	L	5-11	180	8-11-76	1998	Bellaire, Texas
Detienne, Dave	.000	2	8	0	0	0	0	0	0	0	2	0	0	.000	.000	R	R	6-3	190	8-16-79	1997	Dartmouth, N.S.
Diaz, Victor	.211	42	152	22	32	7	0	4	24	7	42	7	5	.336	.258	R	R	6-0	200	12-10-81	2001	Chicago, Ill.
Duplissea, Bill	.286	8	14	2	4	1	0	0	2	4	7	0	0	.357	.444	R	R	6-0	200	9-27-77	1999	San Carlos, Calif.
Feliciano, Jesus	.237	100	245	32	58	5	1	0	13	13	28	10	10	.265	.281	L	L	5-11	160	6-6-79	1997	Bayamon, P.R.
Hill, Koyie	.271	130	468	57	127	25	1	11	64	76	88	5	3	.400	.368	S	R	6-0	190	3-9-79	2000	Lawton, Okla.
Kellner, Ryan	.162	16	37	1	6	1	0	0	3	3	12	0	0	.189	.244	R	R	6-2	200	12-9-77	1997	Morganton, N.C.
King, Brennan	.271	127	435	62	118	19	2	7	63	58	48	1	1	.372	.361	R	R	6-3	180	1-20-81	1999	Murfreesboro, Tenn.
Langill, Eric	.150	8	20	1	3	0	0	0	1	1	9	0	0	.150	.190	R	R	5-9	190	4-4-79	2000	Kirkland, Quebec
Lopez, Rafael	.137	20	51	4	7	0	0	1	9	7	6	0	0	.196	.241	R	R	6-0	200	10-22-76	1996	Miami, Fla.
Matthews, Lamont	.192	112	317	41	61	17	1	9	33	67	98	3	3	.338	.336	L	L	6-2	210	6-15-78	1999	Petersburg, Va.
Riggs, Eric	.248	128	455	69	113	36	2	7	69	62	74	4	4	.382	.341	S	R	6-2	190	8-19-76	1998	Miami, Fla.
Ruan, Wilkin	.253	78	324	44	82	16	6	3	34	17	33	23	3	.367	.306	R	R	6-0	170	9-18-78	1996	Guaymate, D.R.
Theodorou, Nick	.223	75	193	20	43	9	0	0	25	38	29	5	0	.269	.349	S	R	5-11	180	6-7-75	1998	Rialto, Calif.
Victorino, Shane	.258	122	481	61	124	15	1	4	34	47	49	45	16	.318	.328	R	R	5-9	160	11-30-80	1999	Wailuku, Hawaii

PITCHING	W	L	ERA	G	GS	CG	SV	IP	H	R	ER	BB	SO	AVG	B	T	HT	WT	DOB	1st Yr	Resides
Bauer, Greg	2	4	2.83	38	3	0	1	70	62	35	22	30	38	.233	R	R	6-1	190	11-30-77	2000	Tulsa, Okla.
Caraccioli, Lance	4	2	3.06	10	10	1	0	62	53	21	21	25	48	.235	L	L	6-4	190	12-14-77	1998	Walker, La.
Castillo, Marcos	0	0	7.71	2	2	0	0	2	3	2	2	1	0	.333	R	R	6-2	170	2-15-79	1995	Edo Bolivar, Venez.
Colyer, Steve	5	4	3.45	59	0	0	21	63	50	29	24	40	68	.213	L	L	6-4	200	2-22-79	1998	St. Peters, Mo.
Devey, Phil	3	1	1.91	8	7	0	0	47	44	12	10	12	20	.258	L	L	6-0	175	5-31-77	1999	Lachute, Quebec
Dunning, Justin	0	0	4.82	8	0	0	0	9	5	7	5	11	8	.161	R	R	6-3	210	2-16-77	1998	Tustin, Calif.
Falteisek, Steve	0	0	0.00	1	0	0	0	1	0	0	0	0	1	1.000	R	R	6-2	200	1-28-72	1992	Floral Park, N.Y.
Farmer, Tom	3	1	3.19	6	6	0	0	37	36	13	13	9	26	.262	R	R	6-2	190	7-27-79	2001	Crestwood, Ill.
Gonzalez, Alfredo	0	1	1.35	13	0	0	3	20	13	4	3	2	18	.191	R	R	5-11	160	9-17-79	1997	Nagua, D.R.
Gulin, Lindsay	5	2	2.64	19	3	0	3	61	54	21	18	17	67	.234	L	L	6-3	170	11-22-76	1995	Issaquah, Wash.
Hanrahan, Joel	1	1	10.64	3	3	0	0	11	15	14	13	7	10	.326	R	R	6-4	210	10-31-75	1998	Weaverville, N.C.
Harrell, Tim	3	1	7.07	8	1	0	0	14	12	11	11	7	9	.235	R	R	6-2	220	7-8-77	1999	Nashville, Tenn.
House, Craig	0	0	4.50	3	0	0	0	4	3	2	2	2	1	.214	R	R	6-2	200	1-12-78	2000	Reading, Mass.
Langone, Steve	2	2	1.38	14	0	0	1	33	21	7	5	12	17	.185	R	R	6-0	170	11-4-77	1999	Levittown, N.Y.
Leek, Randy	7	5	2.16	15	14	1	0	96	94	30	23	11	56	.263	L	L	6-0	190	5-22-80	1999	Brooklyn, N.Y.
Lugo, Ruddy	3	1	4.05	11	0	2	0	33	34	15	15	13	23	.274	R	R	6-0	190	6-23-79	1997	Russellville, Ark.
McCrotty, Will	1	4	2.39	43	0	0	6	53	37	16	14	30	57	.202	R	R	6-2	180	8-26-77	1995	San Pedro de Macoris, D.R.
Montero, Agustin	1	3	3.95	31	0	0	0	41	38	21	18	29	25	.260	R	R	6-1	190	1-2-77	1998	Jensen Beach, Fla.
Proctor, Scott	7	9	3.51	26	25	0	0	133	111	63	52	85	131	.227	R	R	5-11	150	11-15-77	1995	La Romana, D.R.
Rijo, Fernando	8	8	3.74	27	27	1	0	142	130	62	59	72	106	.245	L	L	6-1	180	5-20-79	1997	Summer Hill, Pa.
Roberts, Rick	8	2	3.18	51	0	0	2	88	66	34	31	42	85	.208	R	R	6-3	160	5-21-78	1996	Guayubin, D.R.
Rodriguez, Ricardo	5	4	1.99	11	11	2	0	68	56	21	15	13	44	.224	R	R	5-10	160	3-20-82	1999	San Pedro de Macoris, D.R.
Rojas, Jose	3	4	4.83	10	10	0	0	54	56	29	29	30	40	.280	R	R	6-1	180	11-12-74	1996	Berlin Heights, Ohio
Simon, Ben	3	0	0.83	15	6	1	0	43	31	7	4	18	31	.194	L	L	6-3	210	12-9-79	2002	Argos, Ind.
Stults, Eric	0	0	0.00	1	0	0	0	1	0	0	0	1	0	.000	R	R	6-3	210	9-30-78	2000	Groves, Texas
Totten, Heath	3	3	2.94	9	9	0	0	49	45	16	16	14	30	.250	R	R	6-1	160	11-20-79	1996	Guarenas, Venez.
Urdaneta, Lino	0	0	0.00	1	0	0	0	1	3	0	0	1	1	.600							

FIELDING

Catcher	PCT	G	PO	A	E	DP	PB
Duplissea	1.000	5	42	2	0	1	2
Hill	.981	117	815	81	17	7	11
Kellner	1.000	12	55	7	0	0	2
Langill	1.000	6	27	3	0	0	0
Lopez	.968	7	59	1	2	0	1

First Base	PCT	G	PO	A	E	DP
Bledsoe	.999	79	669	72	1	50
Brock	.987	39	282	15	4	23
Diaz	.991	28	220	12	2	25

Second Base	PCT	G	PO	A	E	DP
Collins	.988	95	207	277	6	56

	PCT	G	PO	A	E	DP
Detienne	1.000	1	2	5	0	2
Diaz	1.000	2	5	4	0	1
Riggs	.955	7	9	12	1	1
Theodorou	.961	45	54	94	6	18

Third Base	PCT	G	PO	A	E	DP
Collins	1.000	5	2	3	0	1
Diaz	.947	9	5	13	1	2
King	.945	124	77	216	17	18
Lopez	1.000	2	3	9	0	1
Theodorou	1.000	4	1	7	0	1

Shortstop	PCT	G	PO	A	E	DP
Collins	.972	20	21	49	2	5

	PCT	G	PO	A	E	DP
Detienne	1.000	1	1	2	0	2
Riggs	.958	121	193	338	23	67
Theodorou	1.000	1	1	5	0	1

Outfield	PCT	G	PO	A	E	DP
Abercrombie	1.000	1	2	0	0	0
Brock	.989	41	81	5	1	2
Crosby	1.000	34	68	2	0	1
Feliciano	.991	61	106	7	1	0
Matthews	.977	88	156	12	4	1
Ruan	.979	77	182	4	4	2
Theodorou	1.000	15	20	1	0	0
Victorino	.986	120	259	14	4	2

VERO BEACH DODGERS — High Class A

FLORIDA STATE LEAGUE

BATTING	AVG	G	AB	R	H	2B	3B	HR	RBI	BB	SO	SB	CS	SLG	OBP	B	T	HT	WT	DOB	1st Yr	Resides
Abercrombie, Reggie	.276	132	526	80	145	23	13	10	56	27	158	41	17	.426	.321	R	R	6-3	210	7-15-80	2000	Damascus, Ga.
Alvarez, Nick	.226	55	195	22	44	4	0	4	23	13	34	7	2	.308	.296	R	R	6-3	200	2-8-77	2000	Miami, Fla.

BATTING	AVG	G	AB	R	H	2B	3B	HR	RBI	BB	SO	SB	CS	SLG	OBP	B	T	HT	WT	DOB	1st Yr	Resides
Aracena, Sandy	.196	70	224	19	44	3	0	1	15	20	50	2	0	.223	.264	R	R	6-0	180	1-3-78	1998	La Vega, D.R.
Aybar, Willy	.215	108	372	56	80	18	2	11	65	69	54	15	8	.363	.339	S	R	6-0	170	3-9-83	2000	Bani, D.R.
Canales, Josh	.189	71	185	23	35	6	2	0	16	10	38	5	9	.243	.242	R	R	5-11	170	1-15-79	2001	Carson, Calif.
Dacey, Ryan	.171	28	76	6	13	3	0	2	9	17	0	0	0	.211	.292	R	R	6-3	200	5-31-78	2000	Edgewater, Md.
Detienne, Dave	.249	103	342	34	85	20	1	5	40	23	96	10	4	.357	.301	R	R	6-3	190	8-16-79	1997	Dartmouth, N.S.
Diaz, Jose	.200	3	10	3	2	0	0	1	3	1	3	0	0	.500	.333	R	R	6-0	170	4-13-80	1996	San Pedro de Macoris, D.R.
Duplissea, Bill	.186	25	70	10	13	1	0	0	7	14	20	0	0	.200	.329	R	R	6-0	200	9-27-77	1999	San Carlos, Calif.
Herrera, Christian	.173	27	81	10	14	1	0	0	5	10	23	1	0	.185	.269	R	R	5-11	160	4-9-82	2001	Aguascalientes, Mexico
Kellner, Ryan	.202	25	89	9	18	1	0	1	7	5	14	0	1	.247	.276	R	R	6-2	200	12-9-77	1997	Morganton, N.C.
Langs, Ronte	.205	50	190	21	39	3	2	2	17	14	50	7	5	.274	.261	R	R	5-10	200	1-29-79	2000	Memphis, Tenn.
Loney, James	.299	17	67	6	20	6	0	0	5	6	10	0	0	.388	.356	L	L	6-3	200	5-7-84	2002	Missouri City, Texas
Martinez, Candido	.193	24	88	11	17	2	1	2	14	9	27	6	3	.307	.280	R	R	6-2	170	1-10-78	1996	Sabana Perdida, D.R.
Michaelis, Derek	.265	122	426	59	113	30	4	17	58	44	114	0	0	.474	.333	L	L	6-7	230	12-2-78	2000	Waco, Texas
Montague, Ed	.213	28	89	5	19	4	0	2	14	10	18	1	3	.326	.300	L	R	6-0	190	3-23-80	2002	San Mateo, Calif.
Price, Jared	.200	12	35	0	7	1	0	0	1	6	16	0	0	.229	.333	R	R	6-1	190	3-18-82	2000	Rupert, Idaho
Radwan, Jason	.216	11	37	4	8	1	0	1	4	3	7	0	0	.324	.275	R	R	6-1	210	11-11-77	2000	Laguna Hills, Calif.
Repko, Jason	.272	120	470	73	128	29	5	9	53	25	92	29	13	.413	.319	R	R	5-11	170	12-27-80	1999	West Richland, Wash.
Socarras, Tony	.290	21	62	8	18	5	0	3	11	9	16	0	0	.516	.392	L	R	6-0	200	11-8-78	2000	Miami, Fla.
2-team (46 Brevard)	.200	67	175	21	35	11	0	8	30	20	56	0	0	.400	.286							
Thomas, C.J.	.244	80	266	31	65	13	2	4	37	22	69	10	5	.353	.305	R	R	6-0	190	6-10-80	1998	Fresno, Calif.
Van Buizen, Rodney	.280	131	497	74	139	24	4	8	51	22	59	17	8	.392	.330	R	R	6-0	190	9-25-80	1998	Sydney, Australia

PITCHING	W	L	ERA	G	GS	CG	SV	IP	H	R	ER	BB	SO	AVG	B	T	HT	WT	DOB	1st Yr	Resides
Alvarez, Gabriel	0	0	11.81	3	0	0	0	5	12	7	7	4	4	.444	R	R	5-11	170	8-10-84	2002	Nuevo Leon, Mexico
Andrews, Aron	1	5	4.70	25	0	0	0	38	44	21	20	7	31	.285	R	R	6-0	170	8-24-77	2000	Tuscaloosa, Ala.
Bauer, Greg	2	0	2.08	9	0	0	1	26	16	9	6	3	27	.164	R	R	6-1	190	11-30-77	2000	Tulsa, Okla.
Beirne, Kevin	0	0	0.00	1	0	0	0	2	1	0	0	0	2	.142	L	R	6-4	210	1-1-74	1995	The Woodlands, Texas
Berry, Jon	2	4	5.84	13	11	0	0	49	56	35	32	33	32	.287	R	R	6-1	190	11-17-77	1999	Branchville, S.C.
Brown, Andrew	10	10	4.11	25	24	1	0	127	97	63	58	62	129	.215	R	R	6-6	230	2-17-81	1999	Deltona, Fla.
Castillo, Marcos	0	1	3.07	17	1	0	0	29	25	13	10	8	27	.229	R	R	6-2	170	2-15-79	1995	Edo Bolivar, Venez.
Chavez, Carlos	0	1	6.66	11	2	0	0	24	29	20	18	5	16	.295	R	R	6-1	210	8-25-72	1997	El Paso, Texas
Crabtree, Tim	1	0	8.53	4	1	0	0	6	10	6	6	4	6	.370	R	R	6-4	220	10-13-69	1992	Colleyville, Texas
Diggins, Ben	6	10	3.63	20	19	0	0	114	103	54	46	41	101	.238	R	R	6-7	230	6-13-79	2000	Tucson, Ariz.
Dunning, Justin	4	5	5.14	26	9	0	1	70	68	48	40	46	46	.263	R	R	6-3	210	2-16-77	1998	Tustin, Calif.
Gonzalez, Alfredo	2	1	1.57	17	0	0	6	34	20	6	6	11	47	.170	R	R	5-11	160	9-17-79	1997	Nagua, D.R.
Hanrahan, Joel	10	6	4.20	25	25	2	0	144	129	74	67	51	139	.242	R	R	6-3	210	10-6-81	2000	Norwalk, Iowa
Johansen, Ryan	1	3	5.04	16	0	0	0	25	30	21	14	9	21	.288	R	R	6-0	180	6-19-80	2001	Jensen Beach, Fla.
Keirstead, Michael	0	1	7.71	2	0	0	0	2	4	3	2	2	1	.400	R	R	6-0	180	1-26-81	2000	Musquash, N.B.
Kuo, Hong-Chih	0	1	6.75	4	4	0	0	8	11	6	6	2	8	.323	L	L	6-0	200	7-23-81	1999	Tainan City, Taiwan
Lizarraga, Edgar	4	0	1.04	12	0	0	0	17	12	3	2	2	19	.190	R	R	6-1	190	1-27-80	2000	Culiacan, Mexico
Lopez, Arturo	0	0	54.00	1	0	0	0		2	4	2	3	0	.500	L	L	5-10	160	2-22-83	2001	Sinaloa, Mexico
Lugo, Ruddy	8	2	2.38	22	9	1	1	87	68	28	23	26	77	.216	R	R	6-0	190	5-22-80	1999	Brooklyn, N.Y.
Montero, Agustin	1	0	3.46	7	0	0	0	13	10	5	5	4	14	.217	R	R	6-2	180	8-26-77	1995	San Pedro de Macoris, D.R.
Nall, T.J.	2	1	4.17	17	2	0	1	37	42	19	17	13	30	.293	R	R	6-1	170	11-4-80	1999	Schaumburg, Ill.
Newman, Eric	1	1	3.86	7	0	0	0	14	12	6	6	8	13	.240	R	R	6-4	200	8-27-72	1995	Phoenix, Ariz.
Olson, Jason	1	0	2.66	10	0	0	0	20	21	7	6	8	16	.256	R	R	6-2	180	6-12-78	2000	Chino Valley, Ariz.
Osoria, Franquelis	0	1	2.45	3	0	0	0	7	4	2	2	2	10	.153	R	R	6-0	160	9-12-81	2000	Santiago, D.R.
Pilkington, Brian	2	1	2.37	3	3	0	0	19	16	7	5	3	10	.235	R	R	6-5	210	9-17-82	2001	Garden Grove, Calif.
Reina, Dimas	0	0	23.63	3	0	0	0	3	4	7	7	5	0	.333	R	R	6-0	170	2-23-82	1998	Caracas, Venez.
Rodriguez, Orlando	0	0	0.00	7	0	0	0	7	6	0	0	3	10	.240	L	L	5-10	150	11-28-80	2000	Santiago, D.R.
Santiago, Victor	1	0	6.75	4	1	0	0	8	15	6	6	3	5	.405	R	R	5-11	170	8-10-81	1998	Santiago, D.R.
Simpson, Andre	0	0	16.20	4	0	0	0	3	7	6	6	4	2	.437	R	R	6-3	180	7-1-80	1998	Lemon Grove, Calif.
Stefani, Jason	0	0	1.93	8	0	0	0	14	14	5	3	4	8	.259	L	L	6-1	190	4-11-79	2001	Sacramento, Calif.
Steffek, Brian	0	0	2.45	2	0	0	0	7	8	2	2	1	5	.296	R	R	6-2	190	3-2-78	2000	Stafford, Texas
Stults, Eric	3	1	3.00	13	6	0	0	42	39	19	14	20	40	.243	L	L	6-3	210	12-9-79	2002	Argos, Ind.
Totten, Heath	9	5	3.63	18	18	2	0	109	115	47	44	20	83	.270	R	R	6-1	200	9-30-78	2000	Groves, Texas
Urdaneta, Lino	2	2	2.41	52	0	0	32	52	39	15	14	17	30	.207	R	R	6-1	160	10-29-79	1996	Guarenas, Venez.

FIELDING

Catcher	PCT	G	PO	A	E	DP	PB
Aracena	.982	66	495	56	10	3	11
Diaz	1.000	3	25	1	0	0	3
Duplissea	.989	25	162	22	2	3	5
Kellner	.996	25	221	15	1	0	6
Price	1.000	12	80	4	0	0	3
Socarras	.982	7	50	5	1	0	1

First Base	PCT	G	PO	A	E	DP
Alvarez	1.000	10	69	7	0	7
Dacey	.989	10	87	6	1	4
Detienne	1.000	9	24	1	0	3
Loney	1.000	13	100	6	0	16
Michaelis	.987	101	740	64	11	57
Radwan	1.000	3	23	1	0	1

Second Base	PCT	G	PO	A	E	DP
Socarras	.976	5	39	2	1	5
Canales	.990	21	34	61	1	13
Van Buizen	.976	118	217	322	13	61

Third Base	PCT	G	PO	A	E	DP
Aybar	.943	107	71	178	15	20
Canales	1.000	2	1	0	0	0
Dacey	1.000	2	1	2	0	0
Detienne	.912	16	10	21	3	1
Van Buizen	.969	13	3	28	1	1

Shortstop	PCT	G	PO	A	E	DP
Alvarez	.667	1	1	1	1	0
Canales	.930	38	39	67	8	14

	PCT	G	PO	A	E	DP
Detienne	.948	78	121	205	18	43
Herrera	.925	26	36	75	9	7
Van Buizen	.000	1	0	0	0	0

Outfield	PCT	G	PO	A	E	DP
Abercrombie	.957	125	229	15	11	5
Alvarez	.982	26	52	4	1	1
Canales	1.000	1	2	0	0	0
Dacey	1.000	2	1	0	0	0
Langs	.989	42	83	4	1	0
Martinez	1.000	16	34	1	0	0
Michaelis	.500	5	1	0	1	0
Montague	.957	26	41	3	2	0
Repko	.973	120	245	10	7	3
Thomas	.978	47	84	3	2	0

SOUTH GEORGIA WAVES — Low Class A

SOUTH ATLANTIC LEAGUE

BATTING	AVG	G	AB	R	H	2B	3B	HR	RBI	BB	SO	SB	CS	SLG	OBP	B	T	HT	WT	DOB	1st Yr	Resides
Bellorin, Edwin	.280	92	318	28	89	13	1	0	38	19	39	4	2	.327	.331	R	R	5-11	170	2-21-82	1998	Edo Bolivar, Venez.
Dacey, Ryan	.274	32	113	14	31	6	0	2	19	17	25	1	3	.381	.381	R	R	6-3	200	5-31-78	2000	Edgewater, Md.
De los Santos, Omar	.204	46	147	12	30	4	0	1	15	14	45	6	2	.252	.291	R	R	6-0	160	8-13-81	1998	San Pedro de Macoris, D.R.
Diaz, Victor	.350	91	349	64	122	26	2	10	58	27	69	20	6	.521	.407	R	R	6-0	200	12-10-81	2001	Chicago, Ill.
Escalera, Jose	.269	60	193	18	52	6	1	2	15	3	25	3	1	.342	.291	R	R	6-3	230	10-21-80	1999	Loiza, P.R.

BATTING	AVG	G	AB	R	H	2B	3B	HR	RBI	BB	SO	SB	CS	SLG	OBP	B	T	HT	WT	DOB	1st Yr	Resides
Essian, Jim	.181	27	72	13	13	1	0	0	8	18	25	9	4	.194	.379	S	R	6-3	210	11-8-79	1998	Troy, Mich.
Ezi, Travis	.233	70	227	31	53	0	4	2	23	24	75	19	7	.295	.311	S	L	6-0	170	9-5-81	2000	Baltimore, Md.
Garcia, Jose	.261	128	468	59	122	24	7	3	59	37	110	25	5	.361	.318	R	R	6-1	190	8-22-80	1996	Santo Domingo, D.R.
Gillitzer, Scott	.287	123	474	47	136	20	4	2	70	36	51	15	7	.359	.338	R	R	6-1	180	6-11-79	2001	Prairie du Chien, Wis.
Gutierrez, Franklin	.283	92	361	61	102	18	4	12	45	31	88	13	4	.454	.344	R	R	6-2	170	2-21-83	2001	Caracas, Venez.
Herrera, Christian	.248	75	218	35	54	6	0	1	19	35	57	7	4	.289	.363	R	R	5-11	160	4-9-82	2001	Aguascalientes, Mexico
Langill, Eric	.154	7	13	0	2	0	0	0	0	0	4	0	0	.154	.154	R	R	5-9	190	4-4-79	2000	Kirkland, Quebec
Mann, Derek	.309	101	350	55	108	13	2	0	36	64	64	17	11	.357	.418	L	R	6-0	160	3-8-78	1996	Columbus, Ga.
Nunez, Manuel	.160	46	125	22	20	2	0	0	6	14	44	12	4	.176	.255	R	R	5-11	160	3-9-79	1997	Santiago, D.R.
Pacheco, Julio	.281	40	135	16	38	6	0	2	12	8	22	3	5	.370	.322	L	L	6-0	170	12-22-81	1998	San Pedro de Macoris, D.R.
Pierce, Sean	.265	88	291	57	77	10	2	6	38	44	67	18	5	.375	.367	R	R	5-9	190	11-26-78	2001	Covina, Calif.
Price, Jared	.214	69	210	31	45	12	1	9	34	35	83	5	4	.410	.360	R	R	6-1	190	3-18-82	2000	Rupert, Idaho
Radwan, Jason	.143	22	70	12	10	2	0	4	8	7	34	1	1	.343	.256	R	R	6-1	210	11-11-77	2000	Laguna Hills, Calif.
Story-Harden, Thomari	.285	114	393	57	112	18	2	11	56	46	109	4	3	.425	.376	R	R	6-0	200	4-6-80	1998	Richmond, Calif.

PITCHING	W	L	ERA	G	GS	CG	SV	IP	H	R	ER	BB	SO	AVG	B	T	HT	WT	DOB	1st Yr	Resides
Arellan, Felix	4	5	9.53	35	4	0	0	45	53	58	48	41	32	.286	L	L	6-2	170	2-23-81	1997	Maracay, Venez.
Astacio, Andres	5	5	3.87	31	10	0	1	93	98	50	40	26	67	.272	R	R	6-2	160	8-5-80	1999	La Romana, D.R.
Castillo, Albenis	0	0	0.00	2	1	0	0	8	5	0	0	1	2	.178	R	R	6-4	170	12-24-83	2001	Cocle, Panama
Cruceta, Alberto	8	5	2.80	20	20	3	0	113	98	42	35	34	111	.230	R	R	6-2	170	7-4-81	1999	La Vega, D.R.
Diaz, Jose	3	1	4.21	19	0	0	1	26	14	12	12	25	33	.162	R	R	6-0	170	4-13-80	1996	San Pedro de Macoris, D.R.
Diaz, Jose R.	1	1	3.94	3	3	0	0	16	16	7	7	10	7	.280	R	R	6-4	230	2-27-84	2001	La Romana, D.R.
Figueroa, Jonathan	5	2	1.42	8	8	0	0	44	22	10	7	20	57	.147	L	L	6-2	170	9-15-83	2002	Acarigua, Venez.
Garcia, Carlos	0	1	4.26	1	1	0	0	6	6	3	3	3	1	.272	R	R	6-1	170	9-23-78	1996	Empalme, Mexico
Hawley, Ross	1	2	5.61	18	1	0	0	26	28	20	16	17	17	.271	R	R	6-0	180	12-14-79	2002	Wentworth, S.D.
Hosford, Clint	1	1	3.60	6	6	0	0	25	24	13	10	3	23	.263	R	R	6-2	180	8-8-80	1998	Vancouver, B.C.
Hull, Eric	1	0	2.05	13	0	0	1	22	22	6	5	6	13	.271	R	R	5-11	180	12-3-79	2002	Selah, Wash.
Jackson, Edwin	5	2	1.98	19	19	0	0	105	79	34	23	33	85	.206	R	R	6-3	190	9-9-83	2001	Columbus, Ga.
Johansen, Ryan	4	2	2.88	27	0	0	6	34	27	14	11	16	31	.221	R	R	6-0	180	6-19-80	2001	Jensen Beach, Fla.
Keirstead, Michael	4	5	3.93	14	14	1	0	69	77	35	30	20	43	.288	R	R	6-0	180	1-26-81	2000	Musquash, N.B.
Leek, Randy	2	0	0.68	2	2	0	0	13	8	1	1	1	8	.213	L	L	6-0	170	4-18-77	1999	Levittown, N.Y.
Lizarraga, Edgar	5	3	2.79	19	0	0	1	42	35	16	13	10	37	.224	R	R	6-1	190	1-27-80	2000	Culiacan, Mexico
McCracken, Vance	2	4	3.62	8	0	0	0	32	33	21	13	11	23	.257	R	R	6-7	220	4-16-79	2001	St. Albans, W.Va.
Nall, T.J.	3	1	0.63	21	0	0	3	43	28	7	3	12	39	.193	R	R	6-1	170	11-4-80	1999	Schaumburg, Ill.
Nelson, Steve	3	1	5.27	18	1	0	0	41	41	27	24	9	32	.253	L	R	6-3	200	11-10-82	2001	Dartmouth, N.S.
Neuage, Leigh	1	2	3.07	8	8	0	0	41	35	17	14	13	35	.231	R	R	6-4	210	7-6-83	2001	Adelaide, Australia
Osoria, Franquelis	2	2	3.32	21	1	0	1	43	40	22	16	13	30	.225	R	R	6-0	160	9-12-81	2000	Santiago, D.R.
Ott, Thom	3	4	3.27	45	0	0	7	63	67	25	23	20	33	.271	R	R	6-3	190	3-28-80	2001	Lincoln, Neb.
Pilkington, Brian	8	4	3.45	20	18	1	0	112	129	61	43	13	78	.282	R	R	6-5	210	9-17-82	2001	Garden Grove, Calif.
Rodriguez, Orlando	3	0	0.00	20	0	0	5	28	12	0	0	10	42	.134	L	L	5-10	150	11-28-80	2000	Santiago, D.R.
Santiago, Victor	0	1	7.56	5	0	0	0	8	14	12	7	6	2	.358	R	R	5-11	170	8-10-81	1998	Santiago, D.R.
Simpson, Andre	0	2	7.36	4	2	0	0	7	10	8	6	5	5	.312	R	R	6-3	180	7-1-80	1998	Lemon Grove, Calif.
Strayhorn, Kole	1	7	4.24	31	13	0	4	93	99	61	44	38	50	.272	R	R	6-1	180	10-1-82	2001	Shawnee, Okla.

FIELDING

Catcher	PCT	G	PO	A	E	DP	PB
Bellorin	.978	79	539	50	13	1	12
Langill	1.000	5	23	5	0	0	3
Price	.985	62	405	45	7	2	8
Radwan	1.000	2	1	0	0	0	1

First Base	PCT	G	PO	A	E	DP
Dacey	1.000	5	33	2	0	4
V. Diaz	1.000	3	21	3	0	0
Escalera	1.000	5	26	3	0	4
Gillitzer	.988	46	306	34	4	32
Radwan	.976	9	80	2	2	6
Story-Harden	.976	85	688	45	18	58

Second Base	PCT	G	PO	A	E	DP
De Los Santos	.964	31	53	108	6	24
V. Diaz	.981	15	21	31	1	7
Gillitzer	.946	35	71	104	10	19
Herrera	.000	1	0	0	0	0
Mann	.949	59	115	147	14	34
Nunez	.912	6	19	12	3	2
Story-Harden	1.000	1	2	5	0	2

Third Base	PCT	G	PO	A	E	DP
Dacey	.922	29	18	29	4	4
De Los Santos	.889	15	9	23	4	3
V. Diaz	.863	67	31	108	22	13
Gillitzer	.884	24	14	47	8	0
Nunez	.920	17	11	35	4	3

Shortstop	PCT	G	PO	A	E	DP
Gillitzer	.897	18	24	46	8	9
Herrera	.951	74	119	212	17	39
Mann	.907	39	68	78	15	16
Nunez	.911	22	39	53	9	8

Outfield	PCT	G	PO	A	E	DP
Escalera	1.000	16	11	2	0	0
Essian	1.000	21	40	1	0	0
Ezi	.968	69	122	0	4	0
Garcia	.960	122	222	16	10	0
Gutierrez	.986	91	200	5	3	1
Pacheco	.952	38	75	4	4	0
Pierce	.952	70	93	6	5	0

GREAT FALLS DODGERS · Rookie

PIONEER LEAGUE

BATTING	AVG	G	AB	R	H	2B	3B	HR	RBI	BB	SO	SB	CS	SLG	OBP	B	T	HT	WT	DOB	1st Yr	Resides
Bagley, David	.337	51	175	39	59	7	0	5	31	21	37	2	2	.463	.442	R	R	6-2	200	12-26-80	2002	Poway, Calif.
Bok, Matt	.213	26	75	11	16	3	0	1	13	18	19	1	2	.293	.378	L	R	5-11	200	10-5-79	2001	Akron, Ohio
Cardona, David	.216	35	116	11	25	5	1	0	19	13	42	2	3	.276	.298	R	R	6-0	170	11-7-82	2001	San Juan, P.R.
Carter, Ryan	.236	18	55	11	13	3	1	2	8	5	14	1	0	.436	.311	R	R	6-2	170	1-4-83	2001	Fort Myers, Fla.
De los Santos, Omar	.260	33	123	29	32	5	4	1	14	12	41	3	4	.390	.333	R	R	6-0	160	8-13-81	1998	San Pedro de Macoris, D.R.
Ezi, Travis	.283	54	219	36	62	6	3	1	16	26	70	12	6	.352	.369	S	L	6-0	170	9-5-81	2000	Baltimore, Md.
Farmer, John	.436	17	39	12	17	2	0	0	7	7	13	3	1	.487	.577	R	R	6-0	170	3-30-79	2001	Eugene, Ore.
Goelz, Bryan	.278	42	133	27	37	6	2	0	20	31	22	8	4	.353	.422	L	L	6-1	180	4-10-80	2002	St. James, N.Y.
Gonzalez, Juan	.244	47	131	27	32	4	0	0	12	8	23	2	0	.275	.291	R	R	5-9	160	8-21-82	2001	Carolina, P.R.
Guzman, Joel	.252	43	151	19	38	8	2	3	27	18	54	5	3	.391	.331	R	R	6-4	190	11-24-84	2001	San Pedro de Macoris, D.R.
Hoorelbeke, Jesse	.309	47	152	29	47	8	0	8	34	17	37	0	0	.520	.383	R	R	6-3	250	10-13-77	2002	Hansen, Idaho
Jacobo, Dioscar	.242	44	161	22	39	6	1	5	16	6	48	2	0	.385	.289	R	R	5-11	160	12-25-80	1999	La Romana, D.R.
Langill, Eric	.400	4	15	5	6	2	0	0	6	0	0	1	0	.533	.375	R	R	5-9	190	4-4-79	2000	Kirkland, Quebec
Loney, James	.371	47	170	33	63	22	3	5	30	25	18	5	4	.624	.457	L	L	6-3	200	5-7-84	2002	Missouri City, Texas
Montague, Ed	.277	15	47	8	13	3	0	1	8	6	14	1	0	.404	.358	L	R	6-0	190	3-23-80	2002	San Mateo, Calif.
Nixon, Mike	.311	55	219	38	68	10	0	1	31	11	36	7	2	.370	.355	R	R	6-3	210	8-17-83	2002	Phoenix, Ariz.
Owen, Ryan	.141	23	64	9	9	2	1	1	7	15	24	5	0	.250	.368	R	R	6-0	200	9-15-80	2002	Wichita, Kan.
Pacheco, Julio	.305	14	59	6	18	2	1	0	11	3	8	1	4	.373	.349	L	L	6-0	170	12-22-81	1998	San Pedro de Macoris, D.R.

BATTING	AVG	G	AB	R	H	2B	3B	HR	RBI	BB	SO	SB	CS	SLG	OBP	B	T	HT	WT	DOB	1st Yr	Resides
Perozo, Hector	.255	56	192	30	49	11	1	6	32	19	63	3	1	.417	.360	R	R	6-2	190	9-20-83	2000	Caracas, Venez.
Solis, Ricky	.243	13	37	5	9	1	0	0	1	3	9	1	0	.270	.300	R	R	6-0	160	7-22-80	2002	El Paso, Texas
Young, Delwyn	.300	59	240	42	72	18	1	10	41	27	60	4	2	.508	.380	S	R	5-10	180	6-30-82	2002	Santa Barbara, Calif.

GAMES BY POSITION: C—Bok 4, Langill 4, Nixon 51, Owen 21. **1B**—Bok 3, Hoorelbeke 31, Loney 42, Nixon 2, Young. **2B**—De los Santos 13, Farmer 11, Gonzalez 4, Hoorelbeke 1, Solis 8, Young 46. **3B**—De Los Santos 16, Farmer 1, Gonzalez 11, Perozo 54. **SS**—De los Santos 8, Farmer 4, Gonzalez 21, Guzman 43, Solis 6. **OF**—Bok 19, Cardona 34, Carter 16, Ezi 54, Goelz 42, Gonzalez 8, Hoorelbeke 1, Jacobo 41, Montague 12, Nixon 4, Owen 1, Pacheco 14.

PITCHING	W	L	ERA	G	GS	CG	SV	IP	H	R	ER	BB	SO	AVG	B	T	HT	WT	DOB	1st Yr	Resides
Aquino, Juan	0	0	5.40	2	0	0	0	2	2	1	1	3	1	.285	R	R	6-0	160	4-2-80	1997	Higuey, D.R.
Broxton, Jonathan	2	0	2.76	11	6	0	2	29	22	9	9	16	33	.211	R	R	6-4	240	6-16-84	2002	Waynesboro, Ga.
Cuen, David	2	3	4.07	10	9	0	0	42	48	23	19	13	42	.284	L	L	6-4	180	8-4-83	2001	Somerton, Ariz.
Diaz, Jose	1	1	3.65	3	3	0	0	12	11	6	5	6	14	.224	R	R	6-4	230	2-27-84	2001	La Romana, D.R.
Escobedo, Edgar	1	1	4.62	18	0	0	0	37	39	20	19	22	28	.268	R	R	6-4	170	2-6-83	2000	Tijuana, Mexico
Figueroa, Jonathan	2	1	1.42	7	7	0	0	32	16	7	5	19	48	.146	L	L	6-5	200	9-15-83	2002	Acarigua, Venez.
Gonzalez, Luis	0	1	7.71	4	3	0	0	12	18	12	10	5	15	.346	L	L	6-0	190	2-27-83	2001	Carolina, P.R.
Hawley, Ross	1	0	0.00	3	0	0	0	7	2	0	0	2	5	.083	R	R	6-0	180	12-14-79	2002	Wentworth, S.D.
Hull, Eric	0	1	0.00	11	0	0	5	12	4	1	0	4	17	.108	R	R	5-11	180	12-3-79	2002	Selah, Wash.
LaSalle, Julio	3	0	1.74	17	0	0	2	31	20	15	6	13	49	.170	R	R	6-3	210	9-14-81	2002	Brooklyn, N.Y.
Lopez, Arturo	7	3	3.66	15	15	0	0	76	79	44	31	21	72	.265	L	L	5-10	160	2-22-83	2001	Sinaloa, Mexico
Miller, Greg	3	2	2.37	11	7	0	0	38	27	14	10	13	37	.198	L	L	6-5	190	11-3-84	2002	Yorba Linda, Calif.
Nelson, Steve	6	5	3.99	14	14	0	0	70	79	39	31	23	44	.279	L	R	6-3	200	11-10-82	2001	Dartmouth, N.S.
Plummer, Jarod	1	0	0.00	1	0	0	0	2	1	0	0	1	1	.125	R	R	6-5	200	1-27-84	2002	Garland, Texas
Reina, Dimas	5	1	3.35	31	0	0	7	40	29	22	15	21	36	.195	R	R	6-0	170	2-23-82	1998	Caracas, Venez.
Rodriguez, Mike	3	2	4.17	18	4	0	1	41	35	21	19	25	52	.231	R	R	6-1	180	8-31-82	2002	Roseville, Calif.
Stewart, James	5	3	3.78	19	6	0	0	50	47	30	21	9	33	.243	R	R	6-3	170	5-9-82	2001	Vail, Ariz.
Stults, Eric	1	0	2.25	5	0	0	1	8	6	4	2	3	9	.200	L	L	6-3	210	12-9-79	2002	Argos, Ind.
Tibbs, Jeff	3	1	5.92	24	1	0	3	49	64	40	32	26	25	.315	R	R	6-2	170	12-11-81	2000	Farmington, Utah
White, Michael	0	2	5.93	20	0	0	0	27	46	29	18	10	22	.370	L	L	6-2	210	9-12-82	2002	Clearwater, Fla.
Williams, Ryan	1	1	4.66	18	0	0	2	37	42	21	19	11	28	.287	R	R	6-4	210	11-10-80	2002	Virginia Beach, Va.

VERO BEACH DODGERS — Rookie

GULF COAST LEAGUE

BATTING	AVG	G	AB	R	H	2B	3B	HR	RBI	BB	SO	SB	CS	SLG	OBP	B	T	HT	WT	DOB	1st Yr	Resides
Andujar, Pedro	.218	38	119	10	26	7	0	0	19	9	13	5	1	.277	.284	R	R	5-11	190	9-20-82	2000	Bani, D.R.
Benson, Cedric	.200	9	25	1	5	3	2	0	2	7	10	2	3	.480	.412	R	R	6-0	200	12-28-82	2001	Midland, Texas
Cabrera, Ruben	.133	8	15	0	2	1	0	0	1	1	5	0	0	.200	.188	R	R	5-10	170	7-7-81	2000	Edo Carabobo, Venez.
Comfort, Geoff	.213	29	89	13	19	7	0	2	14	18	17	4	0	.360	.366	R	R	6-0	210	3-27-80	2002	Burlingame, Calif.
De Aza, Alejandro	.227	38	128	27	29	6	1	1	14	22	17	16	2	.313	.346	L	L	6-0	170	4-11-84	2001	La Romana, D.R.
Ferrer, Simon	.175	37	103	18	18	5	0	1	13	16	23	3	0	.252	.309	R	R	5-10	170	6-24-80	2002	Santa Ynez, Calif.
Garcia, Sergio	.274	47	157	29	43	8	0	1	9	23	18	12	3	.344	.383	R	R	5-9	170	3-29-80	2002	Paramount, Calif.
Guzman, Joel	.212	10	33	4	7	2	0	0	2	5	8	1	0	.273	.316	R	R	6-4	190	11-24-84	2001	San Pedro de Macoris, D.R.
Hatton, Vern	.225	23	71	13	16	4	1	0	13	11	14	4	3	.310	.371	R	R	6-1	200	4-4-80	2002	Chicago, Ill.
Hernandez, Miguel	.246	56	199	28	49	10	1	2	21	17	36	11	4	.337	.311	R	R	6-2	220	3-19-83	2001	San Pedro de Macoris, D.R.
Jordan, Mickey	.182	33	99	9	18	0	0	0	6	11	25	2	2	.182	.270	L	L	5-10	160	1-20-79	2002	Sarasota, Fla.
Lynch, Michael	.312	33	109	19	34	4	0	0	11	16	14	2	0	.349	.400	R	R	6-3	220	10-31-82	2002	Oak Forest, Ill.
Martin, Russell	.286	41	126	22	36	3	3	0	10	23	18	7	1	.357	.412	R	R	5-11	200	2-15-83	2002	Chelsea, Quebec
Milons, Jereme	.243	45	152	28	37	8	1	1	23	10	24	9	1	.329	.297	R	R	6-2	200	2-5-83	2002	Starkville, Miss.
Montague, Ed	.147	10	34	3	5	0	1	0	3	3	7	3	0	.206	.211	L	R	6-0	190	3-23-80	2002	San Mateo, Calif.
Perez, Jesus	.226	33	93	15	21	5	0	0	11	7	23	3	0	.280	.302	R	R	6-1	180	12-19-83	2001	Caracas, Venez.
Radwan, Jason	.321	25	78	16	25	3	0	4	13	14	14	0	0	.513	.439	R	R	6-1	210	11-11-77	2000	Laguna Hills, Calif.
Rohan, James	.268	14	41	4	11	0	0	0	4	6	2	1	1	.268	.360	R	R	6-1	190	5-13-84	2002	Valencia, Calif.
Wayne, Brett	.209	43	139	9	29	3	1	0	13	14	26	4	2	.245	.286	R	R	6-0	170	4-28-80	2002	Simi Valley, Calif.

GAMES BY POSITION: C—Andujar 33, Cabrera 7, Lynch 26. **1B**—Hernandez 45, Lynch 5, Radwan 11. **2B**—Ferrer 25, Garcia 35, Wayne 3. **3B**—Ferrer 10, Martin 40, Wayne 11. **SS**—Ferrer 1, Garcia 11, Guzman 10, Martin 1, Rohan 11, Wayne 29. **OF**—Benson 7, Comfort 16, DeAza 37, Hatton 23, Jordan 22, Milons 43, Montague 10, Perez 28.

PITCHING	W	L	ERA	G	GS	CG	SV	IP	H	R	ER	BB	SO	AVG	B	T	HT	WT	DOB	1st Yr	Resides
Ahumada, Edgar	1	0	2.08	9	2	0	2	26	22	8	6	12	13	.231	L	L	6-1	180	11-17-82	2002	Culiacan, Mexico
Alvarez, Gabriel	2	1	5.49	15	0	0	4	20	14	13	12	16	17	.194	R	R	5-11	170	8-10-84	2002	Nuevo Leon, Mexico
Carvajal, Marcos	3	2	1.71	13	5	0	0	42	30	12	8	15	35	.201	R	R	6-4	170	8-19-84	2001	Edo Bolivar, Venez.
Cerrillo, Francisco	0	1	2.84	5	0	0	0	6	6	3	2	2	4	.250	R	R	6-4	190	10-6-83	2001	Sinaloa, Mexico
Cuen, David	1	0	0.00	3	2	0	0	16	8	1	0	2	11	.160	L	L	6-4	180	8-4-83	2001	Somerton, Ariz.
Diaz, Jose	3	1	1.95	10	6	0	0	32	19	11	7	12	26	.174	R	R	6-4	230	2-27-84	2001	La Romana, D.R.
Dumesnil, Bryan	5	1	2.87	20	0	0	0	31	28	15	10	24	30	.245	R	L	6-3	210	9-19-83	2002	Nanaimo, B.C.
Garcia, Carlos	1	1	1.42	5	5	0	0	19	20	8	3	4	7	.263	R	R	6-1	170	9-23-78	1996	Empalme, Mexico
Gonzalez, Luis	1	1	3.07	6	2	0	0	15	13	5	5	6	9	.245	L	L	6-0	190	2-27-83	2001	Carolina, P.R.
Hamilton, Jamaal	3	2	4.50	10	3	0	0	28	33	15	14	7	21	.294	L	L	6-3	220	9-13-83	2002	Lubbock, Texas
Hammes, Zach	2	2	3.27	10	8	0	0	33	26	14	12	15	27	.216	R	R	6-6	220	5-15-84	2002	Iowa City, Iowa
Hosford, Clint	0	1	4.50	2	2	0	0	4	4	2	2	0	3	.266	R	R	6-2	180	8-8-80	1998	Vancouver, B.C.
Kennedy, Dajuan	0	2	3.60	16	0	0	0	25	20	15	10	22	27	.215	R	R	6-2	190	6-8-82	2002	Las Vegas, Nev.
Kuo, Hong-Chih	0	0	4.50	3	3	0	0	6	4	3	3	1	9	.200	L	L	6-0	200	7-23-81	1999	Tainan City, Taiwan
Looney, Marshall	2	0	0.42	8	5	0	0	21	13	2	1	1	17	.173	L	L	6-4	250	3-23-84	2002	Lapine, Ore.
Megrew, Mike	1	1	2.03	5	4	0	0	13	8	4	3	3	12	.177	L	L	6-6	210	1-29-84	2002	Hope Valley, R.I.
Neuage, Leigh	0	2	4.68	7	6	0	0	25	30	14	13	4	15	.303	R	R	6-4	210	7-6-83	2001	Adelaide, Australia
Parker, David	2	2	3.18	20	0	0	6	34	32	13	12	14	24	.258	R	R	6-4	180	4-18-83	2002	Winnipeg, Manitoba
Plummer, Jarod	2	2	2.94	16	2	0	0	34	28	17	11	7	41	.220	R	R	6-5	200	1-27-84	2002	Garland, Texas
Potoczny, Robert	3	3	5.91	11	2	0	0	21	20	15	14	14	21	.256	R	R	6-1	190	12-27-83	2002	Worthington, W.Va.
Santiago, Victor	1	1	1.35	10	0	0	1	13	7	3	2	4	12	.166	R	R	5-11	170	8-10-81	1998	Santiago, D.R.
Silva, Efrain	0	0	3.86	5	0	0	0	9	8	4	4	6	6	.242	R	R	6-7	240	7-25-78	2002	Elk Grove, Calif.
Soria, Joakim	0	0	3.60	4	0	0	0	5	6	2	2	0	6	.285	R	R	6-3	180	5-18-84	2002	Monclova, Mexico
Steffek, Brian	0	1	2.84	3	3	0	0	6	4	2	2	2	6	.181	R	R	6-2	190	3-2-78	2000	Stafford, Texas
White, Michael	0	0	0.00	2	0	0	0	4	3	0	0	1	3	.214	L	L	6-2	210	9-12-82	2002	Clearwater, Fla.

BY DREW OLSON

The 2002 season did not have a happy ending for the Brewers. Then again, the beginning and the middle weren't exactly joyful, either.

In their second season at Miller Park, the Brewers bum-

bled and stumbled to their 10th consecutive losing season—a 56-106 mark that registered as the worst record in franchise history and prompted an attendance drop of more than 800,000.

The end of the season was marked by both controversy and change. The controversy came when shortstop Jose Hernandez sat out the final week of the season to avoid breaking the all-time record for strikeouts in a season.

As Hernandez approached the record, frustrated fans at Miller Park began cheering his strikeouts and booing each time he put the ball in play. Manager Jerry Royster, who took over the team when Davey Lopes was fired after a 3-12 start, responded by keeping Hernandez on the bench for the final four home games. After playing three games in Houston without a strikeout, Hernandez sat out a season-ending four-game series in St. Louis and finished with 188 punchouts, one short of Bobby Bonds' record.

Royster was trying to protect Hernandez from ridicule and criticism and shift focus to the successful season he enjoyed—one of the rare bright spots in a dismal season. Royster's intentions may have been good, but his decision had the opposite effect.

Hernandez's season-ending sabbatical was quickly overshadowed, though. Going into the final weekend of the season, the Brewers' front office underwent a major shakeup. Team president Wendy Selig-Prieb, the daughter of commissioner Bud Selig, relinquished control of the team's day-to-day operations.

Selig-Prieb, who had basically been running the team since her father took over as acting commissioner in 1992, became chairman of the board of directors. At the same time Payne's appointment was announced, general

Jose Hernandez

Brad Nelson

PLAYERS OF THE YEAR

MAJOR LEAGUE: Jose Hernandez, ss

Hernandez struck out 188 times—one short of Bobby Bonds' season record—but also hit .288-24-73, the best offensive numbers of any National League shortstop. He represented the host Brewers in the All-Star Game.

MINOR LEAGUE: Brad Nelson, 1b

The 19-year-old Nelson, in his first full season after being drafted in the fourth round in 2001, led the minor leagues in doubles (49) and RBIs (116). He split the season between Class A Beloit and High Desert.

manager Dean Taylor—whose teams got progressively worse at the big league level—was fired with one year left on his contract.

Taylor, who began a rebuilding process at midseason by dealing Alex Ochoa, Tyler Houston, Mark Loretta and Jamey Wright for prospects, was replaced by former Rangers GM Doug Melvin. Shortly after the season ended, Melvin fired Royster. The Brewers' new regime began the process of rebuilding the club's tattered public image by hiring ex-Brewer Ned Yost, most recently a coach with the Braves.

Sparked by the lure of the All-Star Game, which ended in a frustrating tie, more than 1.8 million fans attended Brewers home games in 2002. Generally speaking, what they saw was far from entertaining.

The offense failed to function correctly all season. Veteran second baseman Eric Young was signed to make the Brewers more dynamic on offense, but he was a flop in the leadoff spot and was replaced by rookie center fielder Alex Sanchez. Jeffrey Hammonds, the team's most expensive player at $7 million per season, had another unproductive season amid questions about his health.

Victimized by inconsistency and a lack of run support, second-year righthander Ben Sheets scuffled most of the year, though he was able to pitch 200 innings. Lefty Glendon Rusch continued his hit-or-miss pattern of previous years, and rookie Nick Neugebauer missed most of the season due to injury.

Things on the farm weren't much better. Of the four full-season teams, only Double-A Huntsville (70-69) posted a winning record, and Rookie-level Ogden—the only team to make the playoffs—was bounced in the first round. On the bright side, first base prospect Brad Nelson led the minor leagues in RBIs, combining for 116 between low Class A Beloit and high Class A High Desert.

ORGANIZATION LEADERS

BATTING

*AVG	Callix Crabbe, Ogden	.328
R	Brad Nelson, High Desert/Beloit	94
H	Brad Nelson, High Desert/Beloit	150
TB	Brad Nelson, High Desert/Beloit	263
2B	Brad Nelson, High Desert/Beloit	49
3B	Dave Krynzel, Huntsville/High Desert	15
HR	Israel Alcantara, Indianapolis	27
RBI	Brad Nelson, High Desert/Beloit	116
BB	Three tied at	68
SO	Jeff Deardorff, Huntsville	131
SB	Dave Krynzel, Huntsville/High Desert	42

PITCHING

W	Paul Stewart, Huntsville	12
	Dan Hall, Beloit	12
L	Gerry Oakes, Beloit	14
#ERA	Ben Hendrickson, Huntsville/High Desert	2.74
G	Jack Krawczyk, Indianapolis/Huntsville	52
CG	Jimmy Osting, Indianapolis	3
SV	Brian Mallette, Indianapolis	25
IP	Pete Smart, High Desert	180
BB	Gerry Oakes, Beloit	84
SO	Mike Jones, Beloit	132

*Minimum 250 At-Bats #Minimum 75 Innings

MILWAUKEE BREWERS

Managers: Davey Lopes, Jerry Royster

2002 Record: 56-106, .346 (6th, NL Central)

BATTING	AVG	G	AB	R	H	2B	3B	HR	RBI	BB	SO	SB	CS	SLG	OBP	B	T	HT	WT	DOB	1st Yr	Resides
Alcantara, Izzy	.250	16	32	3	8	1	0	2	5	0	6	0	1	.469	.250	R	R	6-2	210	5-6-71	1991	Santo Domingo, D.R.
Bako, Paul	.235	87	234	24	55	8	1	4	20	20	46	0	2	.329	.295	L	R	6-2	200	6-20-72	1993	Lafayette, La.
Belliard, Ronnie	.211	104	289	30	61	13	0	3	26	18	46	2	3	.287	.257	R	R	5-8	190	4-7-75	1994	Miami, Fla.
Casanova, Raul	.184	31	87	3	16	1	0	1	8	10	18	0	0	.230	.273	S	R	6-0	210	8-23-72	1990	Ponce, P.R.
Christenson, Ryan	.155	22	58	5	9	4	0	1	3	5	13	0	0	.276	.222	R	R	6-0	190	3-28-74	1995	Apple Valley, Calif.
Fabregas, Jorge	.164	30	67	5	11	3	0	3	14	2	7	0	0	.343	.178	L	R	6-3	220	3-13-70	1991	Miami Beach, Fla.
Ginter, Keith	.237	21	76	6	18	8	0	1	8	15	14	0	0	.382	.363	R	R	5-10	190	5-5-76	1998	Fullerton, Calif.
2-team (7 Houston)	.235	28	81	7	19	9	0	1	8	17	15	0	0	.383	.374							
Hall, Bill	.194	19	36	3	7	1	1	1	5	3	13	0	1	.361	.256	R	R	6-0	170	12-28-79	1998	Nettleton, Miss.
Hammonds, Jeffrey	.257	128	448	47	115	26	5	9	41	52	86	4	5	.397	.332	R	R	6-0	200	3-5-71	1992	Cincinnati, Ohio
Harris, Lenny	.305	122	197	23	60	8	2	3	17	14	17	4	1	.411	.355	L	R	5-10	220	10-28-64	1983	Miami, Fla.
Hernandez, Jose	.288	152	525	72	151	24	2	24	73	52	188	3	5	.478	.356	R	R	6-1	180	7-14-69	1987	Dorado, P.R.
Houston, Tyler	.302	76	255	25	77	15	2	7	33	14	41	1	0	.459	.347	L	R	6-1	210	1-17-71	1989	Henderson, Nev.
Jenkins, Geoff	.243	67	243	35	59	17	1	10	29	22	60	1	2	.444	.320	L	R	6-1	210	7-21-74	1996	Scottsdale, Ariz.
Jensen, Marcus	.114	16	35	2	4	0	0	1	4	4	11	0	0	.200	.200	S	R	6-4	200	12-14-72	1990	Scottsdale, Ariz.
Lopez, Luis	.000	6	8	1	0	0	0	0	1	2	1	0	0	.000	.200	S	R	5-11	170	9-4-70	1988	Cidra, P.R.
Loretta, Mark	.267	86	217	23	58	14	0	2	19	23	32	0	0	.359	.350	R	R	6-0	180	8-14-71	1993	Scottsdale, Ariz.
Machado, Robert	.255	51	153	14	39	10	1	2	17	12	30	0	0	.373	.310	R	R	6-1	210	6-3-73	1989	Caracas, Venez.
2-team (22 Chicago)	.261	73	211	19	55	14	1	3	22	17	41	0	0	.379	.316							
Ochoa, Alex	.256	85	215	32	55	9	0	6	21	32	30	8	5	.381	.357	R	R	6-0	200	3-29-72	1991	Miami, Fla.
Rushford, Jim	.143	23	77	8	11	2	0	1	6	6	9	0	0	.208	.214	L	L	6-1	190	3-24-74	1996	San Diego, Calif.
Sanchez, Alex	.289	112	394	55	114	10	7	1	33	31	62	37	14	.358	.343	L	L	5-10	150	8-26-76	1996	Coral Gables, Fla.
Sexson, Richie	.279	157	570	86	159	37	2	29	102	70	136	0	0	.504	.363	R	R	6-8	220	12-29-74	1993	Vancouver, Wash.
Stairs, Matt	.244	107	270	41	66	15	0	16	41	36	50	2	0	.478	.349	L	R	5-9	210	2-27-68	1989	Bangor, Maine
Thompson, Ryan	.248	62	137	16	34	9	2	8	24	7	38	1	0	.518	.295	R	R	6-3	210	11-4-67	1987	Edesville, Md.
Young, Eric	.280	138	496	57	139	29	3	3	28	39	38	31	11	.369	.338	R	R	5-8	180	5-18-67	1989	Aventura, Fla.

PITCHING	W	L	ERA	G	GS	CG	SV	IP	H	R	ER	BB	SO	AVG	B	T	HT	WT	DOB	1st Yr	Resides
Buddie, Mike	1	2	4.54	25	0	0	0	40	46	23	20	21	28	.292	R	R	6-3	210	12-12-70	1992	Lutz, Fla.
Cabrera, Jose	6	10	6.79	50	11	0	0	103	131	84	78	36	61	.314	R	R	6-0	180	3-24-72	1991	Santiago, D.R.
Childers, Matt	0	0	12.00	8	0	0	0	9	13	12	12	8	4	.342	R	R	6-5	190	12-3-78	1997	Augusta, Ga.
De Jean, Mike	1	5	3.12	68	0	0	27	75	66	28	26	39	65	.236	R	R	6-4	210	9-28-70	1992	Castle Rock, Colo.
De los Santos, Valerio	2	3	3.12	51	0	0	0	58	42	21	20	26	38	.211	L	L	6-2	200	10-6-72	1993	Santo Domingo, D.R.
Diggins, Ben	0	4	8.63	5	5	0	0	24	28	24	23	18	15	.297	R	R	6-7	230	6-13-79	2000	Tucson, Ariz.
Durocher, Jayson	1	1	1.88	19	0	0	0	48	27	13	10	21	44	.163	R	R	6-3	190	8-18-74	1993	Scottsdale, Ariz.
Figueroa, Nelson	1	7	5.03	30	11	0	0	93	96	59	52	37	51	.270	S	R	6-1	150	5-18-74	1995	Voorhees, N.J.
Fox, Chad	1	0	5.79	3	0	0	0	5	6	3	3	5	3	.315	R	R	6-3	200	9-3-70	1992	Houston, Texas
Franklin, Wayne	2	1	2.63	4	4	0	0	24	16	8	7	17	17	.188	L	L	6-2	200	3-9-74	1996	North East, Md.
King, Ray	3	2	3.05	76	0	0	0	65	61	24	22	24	50	.255	L	L	6-1	240	1-15-74	1995	Franklin, Wis.
Lorraine, Andrew	0	1	11.25	5	1	0	0	12	22	18	15	6	10	.379	L	L	6-3	200	8-11-72	1993	Scottsdale, Ariz.
Mallette, Brian	0	0	10.80	5	0	0	0	5	7	6	6	3	5	.304	R	R	6-0	180	1-19-75	1997	Glenwood, Ga.
Matthews, Mike	0	0	4.50	4	0	0	0	4	3	2	2	7	2	.214	L	L	6-2	170	10-24-73	1992	Woodbridge, Va.
2-team (43 St. Louis)	2	1	3.94	47	0	0	0	46	43	23	20	29	34	.255							
Nance, Shane	0	0	4.26	4	0	0	0	6	4	3	3	4	5	.173	L	L	5-8	180	9-7-77	2000	Houston, Texas
Neugebauer, Nick	1	7	4.72	12	12	0	0	55	56	33	29	44	47	.264	R	R	6-3	230	7-15-80	1999	Riverside, Calif.
Nomura, Takahito	0	0	8.56	21	0	0	0	14	11	14	13	18	9	.224	L	L	5-7	170	1-10-69	2002	Koochi, Japan
Osting, Jimmy	0	2	7.50	3	3	0	0	12	18	11	10	10	7	.333	R	L	6-5	190	4-7-77	1995	Louisville, Ky.
Pember, David	0	1	5.19	4	1	0	0	9	7	6	5	6	5	.218	R	R	6-5	220	5-24-78	1999	Knoxville, Tenn.
Quevedo, Ruben	6	11	5.76	26	25	1	0	139	159	100	89	68	93	.287	R	R	6-1	250	1-5-79	1996	Valencia, Venez.
Rusch, Glendon	10	16	4.70	34	34	4	0	211	227	116	110	76	140	.279	L	L	6-1	200	11-7-74	1993	Seattle, Wash.
Sheets, Ben	11	16	4.15	34	34	1	0	217	237	105	100	70	170	.280	R	R	6-1	200	7-18-78	1999	Baton Rouge, La.
Stull, Everett	0	1	6.30	2	2	0	0	10	15	7	7	9	7	.357	R	R	6-3	200	8-24-71	1992	Stone Mountain, Ga.
Vizcaino, Luis	5	3	2.99	76	0	0	5	81	55	27	27	30	79	.191	R	R	5-11	190	8-6-74	1995	Bani, D.R.
Wright, Jamey	5	13	5.35	19	19	1	0	114	115	72	68	63	69	.269	R	R	6-5	230	12-24-74	1993	Oklahoma City, Okla.

FIELDING

Catcher	PCT	G	PO	A	E	DP	PB
Alcantara	.000	1	0	0	0	0	0
Bako	.991	76	420	33	4	2	5
Casanova	.994	28	166	13	1	0	2
Fabregas	.992	20	118	9	1	0	1
Jensen	.976	15	73	9	2	1	2
Machado	.987	48	277	31	4	5	2

First Base	PCT	G	PO	A	E	DP
Alcantara	.929	2	13	0	1	1
Harris	1.000	12	49	7	0	1
Houston	1.000	1	4	0	0	0
Machado	1.000	2	8	1	0	1
Sexson	.995	155	1224	119	7	134

Second Base	PCT	G	PO	A	E	DP
Belliard	.975	49	86	107	5	27
Loretta	1.000	3	7	6	0	2
Young	.979	123	249	323	12	79

Third Base	PCT	G	PO	A	E	DP
Belliard	.929	42	22	43	5	5
Ginter	.961	21	18	31	2	3
Hall	1.000	2	2	0	0	0
Harris	1.000	14	7	14	0	3
Houston	.947	72	43	101	8	8
Loretta	.991	47	37	73	1	6

Shortstop	PCT	G	PO	A	E	DP
Ginter	1.000	1	2	1	0	0
Hall	.947	13	15	21	2	5

Hernandez	.973	149	244	451	19	107
Lopez	1.000	4	3	1	0	0
Loretta	.923	12	14	10	2	3

Outfield	PCT	G	PO	A	E	DP
Alcantara	1.000	7	7	0	0	0
Christenson	1.000	21	38	0	0	0
Hammonds	.992	125	247	3	2	1
Harris	1.000	16	26	0	0	0
Jenkins	.992	66	124	7	1	1
Ochoa	.993	72	135	5	1	1
Rushford	.956	22	43	0	2	0
Sanchez	.982	100	271	1	5	0
Stairs	.993	84	129	6	1	1
Thompson	.985	51	62	2	1	0
Young	1.000	2	1	0	0	0

Director, Player Development: Greg Riddoch

Class	Farm Team	League	W	L	Pct.	Finish*	Manager(s)	First Yr.
AAA	Indianapolis (Ind.) Indians	International	67	76	.469	9th (14)	Ed Romero	2000
AA	Huntsville (Ala.) Stars	Southern	70	69	.509	5th (10)	Frank Kremblas	1999
High A	High Desert (Calif.) Mavericks	California	60	80	.429	9th (10)	Mike Caldwell	2001
Low A	Beloit (Wis.) Snappers	Midwest	57	82	.410	12th (14)	Don Money	1982
Rookie	Ogden (Utah) Raptors	Pioneer	40	35	.533	2nd (8)	Wendell Kim	1996
Rookie	Phoenix (Ariz.) Brewers	Arizona	26	30	.464	6th (7)	Carlos Lezcano	2001

*Finish in overall standings (No. of teams in league)

INDIANAPOLIS INDIANS — Class AAA

INTERNATIONAL LEAGUE

BATTING	AVG	G	AB	R	H	2B	3B	HR	RBI	BB	SO	SB	CS	SLG	OBP	B	T	HT	WT	DOB	1st Yr	Resides
Alcantara, Izzy	.268	110	410	61	110	21	2	27	65	51	88	9	3	.527	.350	R	R	6-2	210	5-6-71	1991	Santo Domingo, D.R.
Alexander, Manny	.294	22	85	11	25	6	1	1	7	4	17	5	3	.424	.326	R	R	5-10	180	3-20-71	1988	San Pedro de Macoris, D.R.
Burkhart, Lance	.145	27	69	3	10	2	0	1	2	10	23	0	0	.217	.263	R	R	5-9	220	12-16-74	1997	Florissant, Mo.
Casanova, Raul	.279	14	43	2	12	4	0	0	8	3	8	0	0	.372	.313	S	R	6-0	210	8-23-72	1990	Ponce, P.R.
Cesar, Dionys	.257	133	479	52	123	22	3	6	38	30	75	8	7	.353	.301	S	R	5-10	150	9-27-76	1994	Santo Domingo, D.R.
Christenson, Ryan	.254	67	260	38	66	17	2	5	30	18	28	11	5	.392	.306	R	R	6-0	190	3-28-74	1995	Apple Valley, Calif.
Clemente, Edgard	.204	40	142	10	29	7	2	1	9	9	37	1	1	.303	.265	R	R	5-11	180	12-15-75	1993	Bayamon, P.R.
2-team (63 Pawtucket)	.241	103	373	38	90	19	2	8	40	23	100	6	1	.367	.292							
Cummings, Midre	.308	11	39	7	12	2	0	3	8	2	4	1	1	.590	.341	L	R	6-0	190	10-14-71	1990	Tarpon Springs, Fla.
Fasano, Sal	.206	34	97	5	20	9	0	1	11	3	24	0	0	.330	.271	R	R	6-2	250	8-10-71	1993	Overland Park, Kan.
2-team (31 Durham)	.232	65	198	16	46	15	0	7	20	15	53	0	1	.414	.332							
Hall, Bill	.228	134	465	35	106	20	1	4	31	25	105	17	10	.301	.272	R	R	6-0	170	12-28-79	1998	Nettleton, Miss.
Jensen, Marcus	.230	70	183	24	42	7	0	4	25	33	39	0	0	.333	.347	S	R	6-4	200	12-14-72	1990	Scottsdale, Ariz.
Jones, Chris	.282	78	273	34	77	13	5	3	30	25	50	5	6	.399	.343	R	R	6-2	210	11-16-65	1984	Utica, N.Y.
Lopez, Luis	.227	6	22	2	5	0	0	0	0	0	4	0	0	.227	.261	S	R	5-11	170	9-4-70	1988	Cidra, P.R.
Luuloa, Keith	.189	31	53	7	10	0	0	0	3	7	11	0	2	.189	.283	R	R	6-0	180	12-24-74	1994	Canyon Lake, Calif.
Moon, Brian	.242	39	99	8	24	5	0	0	7	12	24	1	0	.293	.324	S	R	6-0	190	7-15-77	1997	Mansfield, Ga.
Pena, Elvis	.258	34	97	17	25	4	1	1	6	10	19	7	3	.351	.351	S	R	5-11	160	8-15-74	1994	Santo Domingo, D.R.
Perez, Robert	.197	43	122	7	24	6	0	3	13	2	21	2	3	.320	.208	R	R	6-3	230	6-4-69	1990	Bolivar, Venez.
Rushford, Jim	.316	117	405	54	128	33	3	7	68	45	41	0	2	.464	.391	L	L	6-1	190	3-24-74	1996	San Diego, Calif.
Sasser, Rob	.227	72	185	19	42	9	0	3	18	19	30	7	0	.324	.306	R	R	6-3	200	3-9-75	1993	Oakland, Calif.
Scarborough, Steve	.216	39	116	9	25	7	1	2	12	10	30	2	1	.345	.295	R	R	6-0	160	3-10-78	1999	Carrollton, Texas
Smith, Bobby	.239	80	293	26	70	21	0	7	31	25	57	11	2	.382	.307	R	R	6-3	190	4-10-74	1992	Oakland, Calif.
Thompson, Ryan	.293	70	273	36	80	12	3	12	40	11	46	0	4	.491	.324	R	R	6-3	210	11-4-67	1987	Edesville, Md.
Zuber, Jon	.239	130	385	54	92	13	3	2	25	68	50	5	2	.304	.355	L	L	6-0	190	12-10-69	1992	San Ramon, Calif.

PITCHING	W	L	ERA	G	GS	CG	SV	IP	H	R	ER	BB	SO	AVG	B	T	HT	WT	DOB	1st Yr	Resides
Campos, Francisco	3	0	2.05	4	2	0	0	22	15	6	5	1	14	.180	R	R	6-0	160	8-12-72	1991	Guaymas, Mexico
Childers, Jason	2	3	4.61	28	2	0	0	53	57	31	27	30	29	.275	R	R	6-0	160	1-13-75	1997	Douglas, Ga.
Childers, Matt	0	0	0.00	3	0	0	0	5	1	0	0	2	4	.062	R	R	6-5	190	12-3-78	1997	Augusta, Ga.
De los Santos, Valerio	1	0	0.00	2	0	0	0	2	1	0	0	1	5	.142	L	L	6-2	200	10-6-72	1993	Santo Domingo, D.R.
Durocher, Jayson	1	0	2.73	20	0	0	2	26	19	9	8	15	39	.193	R	R	6-3	190	8-18-74	1993	Scottsdale, Ariz.
Ebert, Derrin	6	4	3.50	50	1	0	4	75	66	33	29	25	46	.240	L	L	6-3	190	8-21-76	1994	Hesperia, Calif.
Figueroa, Nelson	5	0	3.63	6	6	0	0	40	39	18	16	13	25	.253	S	R	6-1	150	5-18-74	1995	Voorhees, N.J.
Gandarillas, Gus	0	0	18.00	2	0	0	0	2	4	4	4	1	3	.400	R	R	6-0	190	7-19-71	1992	Miami, Fla.
Garcia, Jose	0	7	5.70	17	13	0	0	84	96	56	53	37	43	.300	R	R	6-3	190	4-29-78	1996	Las Vegas, Nev.
Giron, Roberto	0	0	6.75	15	0	0	1	17	19	14	13	9	26	.263	R	R	6-2	170	3-24-76	1994	Villa Mella, D.R.
Glynn, Ryan	3	6	5.23	12	11	0	0	64	75	48	37	26	36	.286	R	R	6-3	200	11-1-74	1995	Grand Prairie, Texas
Harikkala, Tim	8	10	3.50	31	20	1	1	162	172	76	63	23	90	.270	R	R	6-2	180	7-15-71	1992	Lake Worth, Fla.
Johnson, Mark	1	1	7.97	4	4	0	0	20	26	18	18	12	8	.325	R	R	6-3	220	5-2-75	1997	Leesburg, Fla.
King, Ray	0	0	0.00	1	1	0	0	1	1	0	0	1	1	.333	L	L	6-1	240	1-15-74	1995	Franklin, Wis.
Krawczyk, Jack	0	0	6.75	2	0	0	0	3	3	4	2	3	3	.333	R	R	6-4	190	8-12-75	1998	Scottsdale, Ariz.
Leskanic, Curt	0	0	1.35	5	1	0	0	7	5	1	1	1	7	.192	R	R	6-0	190	4-2-68	1990	Longwood, Fla.
Lorraine, Andrew	7	11	3.05	25	24	2	0	165	157	65	56	42	86	.253	L	L	6-3	200	8-11-72	1993	Scottsdale, Ariz.
Mallette, Brian	3	2	2.78	45	0	0	25	45	39	15	14	17	50	.234	R	R	6-0	180	1-19-75	1997	Glenwood, Ga.
Marquez, Rob	4	7	3.82	47	0	0	8	68	61	34	29	24	43	.239	R	R	6-0	200	4-21-73	1995	Houston, Texas
Nance, Shane	3	0	0.00	9	0	0	0	17	12	0	0	6	18	.206	L	L	5-8	180	9-7-77	2000	Houston, Texas
Neugebauer, Nick	0	3	5.12	5	5	0	0	19	20	13	11	12	18	.263	R	R	6-3	230	7-15-80	1999	Riverside, Calif.
Nomura, Takahito	1	2	5.73	31	0	0	0	33	38	24	21	11	23	.287	L	L	5-7	170	1-10-69	2002	Koochi, Japan
Osting, Jimmy	5	7	3.48	22	22	3	0	127	115	52	49	38	112	.242	R	L	6-5	190	4-7-77	1995	Louisville, Ky.
Quevedo, Ruben	0	0	0.00	1	1	0	0	2	1	0	0	1	3	.142	R	R	6-2	250	1-5-79	1996	Valencia, Venez.
Rigdon, Paul	0	1	5.06	3	3	0	0	11	11	6	6	2	6	.261	R	R	6-5	240	11-2-75	1996	Jacksonville, Fla.
Strong, Joe	0	0	4.19	15	0	0	1	19	23	9	9	8	7	.315	S	R	6-0	200	9-9-62	1984	Seattle, Wash.
Stull, Everett	11	11	3.87	24	24	0	0	151	149	72	65	49	119	.258	R	R	6-3	200	8-24-71	1992	Stone Mountain, Ga.
Wright, Jamey	1	1	4.11	4	4	0	0	15	16	7	7	5	13	.271	R	R	6-5	230	12-24-74	1993	Oklahoma City, Okla.

FIELDING

Catcher	PCT	G	PO	A	E	DP	PB
Burkhart	1.000	26	138	8	0	1	1
Casanova	1.000	11	44	5	0	0	1
Fasano	.983	25	150	19	3	2	1
Jensen	.986	67	389	21	6	2	3
Moon	.995	37	185	23	1	3	4

First Base	PCT	G	PO	A	E	DP
Alcantara	.989	19	165	12	2	8
Fasano	1.000	1	10	3	0	0
Smith	.977	17	116	12	3	8
Zuber	.995	125	971	72	5	102

Second Base	PCT	G	PO	A	E	DP
Cesar	.977	82	153	194	8	43

	PCT	G	PO	A	E	DP
Lopez	1.000	3	5	10	0	2
Luuloa	1.000	5	3	1	0	1
Pena	.951	26	48	50	5	13
Sasser	1.000	4	3	5	0	0
Scarborough	1.000	27	53	58	0	16
Smith	1.000	16	27	34	0	9

Third Base	PCT	G	PO	A	E	DP
Alcantara	1.000	1	1	0	0	0
Alexander	.952	17	12	28	2	1
Cesar	.915	40	30	88	11	10
Lopez	1.000	1	0	3	0	0
Luuloa	.839	13	4	22	5	2
Moon	1.000	1	2	2	0	0
Sasser	.927	58	30	109	11	7
Scarborough	1.000	4	3	11	0	0
Smith	.897	29	19	59	9	6

Shortstop	PCT	G	PO	A	E	DP
Alexander	.917	4	1	10	1	0
Cesar	1.000	3	4	7	0	2
Hall	.934	129	207	376	41	77
Lopez	1.000	2	3	9	0	2
Luuloa	.933	5	4	10	1	0
Scarborough	.946	10	9	26	2	8

Outfield	PCT	G	PO	A	E	DP
Alcantara	.974	62	109	2	3	0
Cesar	.875	4	7	0	1	0
Christenson	1.000	64	186	5	0	3
Clemente	.967	39	87	2	3	0
Cummings	1.000	2	6	0	0	0
Jones	.980	74	144	2	3	2
Perez	.967	34	58	1	2	0
Rushford	.988	91	161	6	2	1
Smith	.967	16	27	2	1	0
Thompson	.984	66	118	2	2	1

SOUTHERN LEAGUE

BATTING

	AVG	G	AB	R	H	2B	3B	HR	RBI	BB	SO	SB	CS	SLG	OBP	B	T	HT	WT	DOB	1st Yr	Resides
Alfonzo, Eliezer	.258	69	244	23	63	15	1	7	38	9	55	2	3	.414	.292	R	R	6-0	205	2-7-79	1996	Puerto la Cruz, Venez.
Alvarado, Joel	.250	15	32	4	8	0	0	0	1	2	2	1	1	.250	.314	R	R	6-2	190	6-30-80	2001	Cayey, P.R.
Alvarez, Gabe	.202	29	94	17	19	3	0	1	12	18	24	0	0	.266	.336	R	R	6-1	200	3-6-74	1995	San Gabriel, Calif.
Burkhart, Lance	.247	28	85	16	21	9	0	3	15	22	33	2	3	.459	.414	R	R	5-9	220	12-16-74	1997	Florissant, Mo.
Deardorff, Jeff	.254	131	425	69	108	23	1	19	61	60	131	13	6	.447	.353	R	R	6-3	220	8-14-78	1997	Clermont, Fla.
Foster, Brian	.242	11	33	2	8	3	0	0	6	0	16	1	2	.333	.265	R	R	6-2	205	8-21-81	1999	Burlington, N.C.
Fox, Jason	.191	41	131	9	25	6	2	0	13	6	32	2	1	.267	.243	S	R	6-2	180	3-30-77	1998	York, Pa.
Guerrero, Cristian	.223	111	394	47	88	17	1	8	48	26	101	21	9	.332	.274	R	R	6-5	200	7-12-80	1997	Bani, D.R.
Hardy, J.J.	.228	38	145	14	33	7	0	1	13	9	19	1	2	.297	.269	R	R	6-2	180	8-19-82	2001	Tucson, Ariz.
Hart, Corey	.266	28	94	16	25	3	0	2	15	7	16	3	2	.362	.340	R	R	6-6	205	3-24-82	2000	Bowling Green, Ky.
Jacobsen, Bucky	.253	61	198	31	50	9	2	11	39	22	41	2	2	.485	.336	R	R	6-4	220	8-30-75	1997	Hermiston, Ore.
Knox, Ryan	.212	66	217	26	46	8	1	0	9	24	44	17	7	.258	.304	R	R	6-1	190	6-28-77	1999	Peoria, Ill.
Krynzel, Dave	.240	31	129	13	31	2	3	2	13	4	30	13	5	.349	.269	L	L	6-1	180	11-7-81	2000	Henderson, Nev.
Luuloa, Keith	.254	80	287	52	73	12	4	9	39	52	42	5	1	.418	.367	R	R	6-0	180	12-24-74	1994	Canyon Lake, Calif.
Mathis, Jared	.232	82	203	23	47	6	3		18	9	26	5	5	.335	.270	R	R	5-10	180	8-8-75	1997	Port Orange, Fla.
Melian, Jackson	.223	56	184	34	41	6	1	6	24	35	63	10	3	.364	.362	R	R	6-2	190	1-7-80	1996	Barcelona, Venez.
Moon, Brian	.189	36	122	16	23	4	0	1	11	16	30	3	1	.246	.291	S	R	6-0	190	7-15-77	1997	Mansfield, Ga.
Pena, Elvis	.277	89	300	42	83	10	4	1	24	38	58	25	10	.347	.364	S	R	5-11	160	8-15-74	1994	Santo Domingo, D.R.
Randolph, Jaisen	.314	13	51	7	16	2	1	0	3	5	7	4	3	.392	.386	S	R	6-0	180	1-19-79	1997	Tampa, Fla.
Rushford, Jim	.211	8	19	2	4	1	0	0	1	2	5	1	0	.263	.286	L	L	6-1	190	3-24-74	1996	San Diego, Calif.
Scarborough, Steve	.283	88	322	50	91	29	1	7	40	48	66	8	8	.444	.380	R	R	6-0	160	3-10-78	1999	Carrollton, Texas
Scott, Bill	.237	80	249	16	59	9	0	3	27	15	62	4	2	.309	.282	R	R	6-1	210	4-8-79	2001	Granada Hills, Calif.
Wathan, Dusty	.160	9	25	2	4	0	0		2	2	4	0	0	.240	.276	R	R	6-4	210	8-22-73	1994	Peoria, Ariz.
West, Todd	.217	46	120	13	26	5	0		8	8	24	6	3	.258	.266	R	R	5-11	160	3-2-79	2000	El Paso, Texas
Zoccolillo, Peter	.295	75	227	43	67	12	1	12	45	40	50	6	7	.515	.399	L	R	6-2	200	2-6-77	1999	White Plains, N.Y.

PITCHING

	W	L	ERA	G	GS	CG	SV	IP	H	R	ER	BB	SO	AVG	B	T	HT	WT	DOB	1st Yr	Resides
Adams, Mike	1	0	3.38	13	0	0	1	19	14	11	7	12	17	.208	R	R	6-5	190	7-29-78	2001	Sinton, Texas
Allen, Rodney	0	0	3.10	15	0	0	0	20	17	9	7	17	15	.229	R	R	6-2	200	6-29-74	1996	Lewisburg, W.Va.
Altman, Gene	0	3	8.37	24	0	0	1	33	31	31	31	42	23	.260	R	R	6-7	230	9-1-78	1996	Lynchburg, S.C.
Childers, Jason	1	1	2.10	11	1	0	0	26	22	6	6	12	22	.244	R	R	6-0	160	1-13-75	1997	Douglas, Ga.
Childers, Matt	2	5	4.50	35	10	0	12	82	103	47	41	27	57	.308	R	R	6-5	190	12-3-78	1997	Augusta, Ga.
Dent, Doug	3	1	3.81	12	2	0	0	28	27	13	12	9	23	.252	R	R	6-8	210	3-23-77	1998	Gilbert, Ariz.
Diggins, Ben	2	1	1.91	7	7	0	0	38	26	13	8	15	34	.208	R	R	6-7	230	6-13-79	2000	Tucson, Ariz.
Fox, Chad	0	1	0.00	3	0	0	0	5	5	1	0	2	7	.263	R	R	6-3	200	9-3-70	1992	Houston, Texas
Gandarillas, Gus	0	0	0.00	1	1	0	0	2	2	0	0	3	4	.222	R	R	6-0	190	7-19-71	1992	Miami, Fla.
Garcia, Jose	3	4	2.37	11	11	0	0	61	47	19	16	31	37	.214	R	R	6-3	190	4-29-78	1996	Las Vegas, Nev.
Giron, Roberto	2	4	2.39	36	2	0	10	53	38	21	14	33	52	.203	R	R	6-2	170	3-24-76	1994	Villa Mella, D.R.
Hendrickson, Ben	4	2	2.97	13	13	0	0	70	57	31	23	35	50	.230	R	R	6-4	190	2-4-81	1999	Eden Prairie, Minn.
High, Andy	1	1	2.84	16	1	0	1	32	35	14	10	11	29	.291	L	L	6-4	190	5-22-74	1996	Chester, N.J.
Krawczyk, Jack	5	3	2.71	44	0	0	5	66	54	22	20	15	69	.212	R	R	6-4	190	8-12-75	1998	Scottsdale, Ariz.
Lee, Derek	5	10	3.04	34	16	0	0	127	138	59	43	45	104	.278	L	L	6-4	180	8-20-74	1997	Fort Worth, Texas
Leskanic, Curt	0	0	3.00	3	0	0	0	3	4	1	2	1	2	.333	R	R	6-0	190	4-2-68	1990	Longwood, Fla.
Martinez, Luis	8	8	5.20	29	18	0	1	109	114	70	63	65	106	.276	L	L	6-6	200	1-20-80	1997	Boca Chica, D.R.
Parker, Matt	4	4	3.84	40	3	0	2	77	73	39	33	34	80	.248	R	R	6-3	210	12-13-78	1999	Hartsfield, Ga.
Pember, David	10	6	3.17	27	27	2	0	156	157	69	55	53	111	.262	R	R	6-5	220	5-24-78	1999	Knoxville, Tenn.
Penney, Mike	7	4	2.34	37	0	0	3	58	53	15	15	22	37	.253	R	R	6-1	190	3-29-77	1998	Peoria, Ariz.
Stewart, Paul	12	9	3.28	27	27	2	0	162	147	69	59	42	124	.245	R	R	6-5	220	10-21-78	1996	Raleigh, N.C.

FIELDING

Catcher	PCT	G	PO	A	E	DP	PB
Alfonzo	.987	62	476	62	7	3	4
Alvarado	1.000	14	87	13	0	3	0
Burkhart	.992	17	114	11	1	0	3
Foster	.984	9	54	9	1	1	1
Moon	1.000	36	252	36	0	3	4
Wathan	.983	9	52	5	1	1	0

First Base	PCT	G	PO	A	E	DP
Alfonzo	1.000	1	13	0	0	2
Alvarado	1.000	1	2	0	0	0
Burkhart	1.000	7	47	10	0	7
Deardorff	.997	36	280	19	1	38
Foster	1.000	1	10	0	0	1
Hart	.980	5	48	2	1	3
Jacobsen	.988	46	381	27	5	34
Luuloa	1.000	6	28	2	0	2
Mathis	.968	13	28	2	1	4
Scott	.984	43	355	21	6	34
Zoccolillo	1.000	1	6	0	0	1

Second Base	PCT	G	PO	A	E	DP
Luuloa	.938	15	48	43	6	15
Mathis	.968	14	28	33	2	8
Pena	.974	82	173	209	10	48
Scarborough	.904	15	31	44	8	11
West	.979	20	44	49	2	18

Third Base	PCT	G	PO	A	E	DP
Alvarez	.806	27	13	45	14	6
Burkhart	1.000	1	1	0	0	0
Deardorff	.909	17	12	28	4	5
Hart	.836	21	9	37	9	5
Luuloa	.916	47	39	102	13	13
Mathis	.988	35	24	60	1	2
Pena	1.000	1	0	2	0	0
Scarborough	.889	4	3	5	1	1

Shortstop	PCT	G	PO	A	E	DP
Hardy	.948	37	54	127	10	30
Luuloa	1.000	16	26	45	0	10
Pena	.818	2	2	7	2	1
Scarborough	.936	70	107	214	22	34
West	.961	19	23	51	3	10

Outfield	PCT	G	PO	A	E	DP
Burkhart	.000	2	0	0	0	0
Deardorff	.990	66	92	3	1	0
Fox	.989	38	82	4	1	1
Guerrero	.970	102	190	6	6	2
Jacobsen	.800	3	3	1	1	0
Knox	1.000	61	103	6	0	1
Krynzel	.971	30	67	1	2	0
Luuloa	.000	1	0	0	0	0
Mathis	.857	4	6	0	1	0
Melian	.981	54	95	7	2	2
Randolph	.941	12	15	1	1	0
Rushford	1.000	5	5	0	1	0
West	.000	1	0	0	0	0
Zoccolillo	.990	59	93	5	1	0

ORGANIZATION STATISTICS

CALIFORNIA LEAGUE

BATTING	AVG	G	AB	R	H	2B	3B	HR	RBI	BB	SO	SB	CS	SLG	OBP	B	T	HT	WT	DOB	1st Yr	Resides
Alfonzo, Eliezer	.349	12	43	7	15	2	0	2	9	3	14	0	0	.535	.417	R	R	6-0	205	2-7-79	1996	Puerto la Cruz, Venez.
Ayala, Elio	.086	16	35	3	3	1	0	0	0	0	7	0	0	.114	.086	R	R	5-9	160	11-7-78	1998	Bronx, N.Y.
Barnwell, Chris	.242	35	132	19	32	7	0	1	14	8	14	1	1	.318	.294	R	R	5-10	180	3-1-79	2001	Jacksonville, Fla.
Boyd, Dan	.237	24	97	14	23	4	1	2	11	7	21	0	1	.361	.299	R	R	5-11	190	9-28-78	2001	Dade City, Fla.
Candelaria, Scott	.298	60	225	37	67	8	4	3	27	9	39	9	4	.409	.329	R	R	6-2	190	11-2-78	2000	Albuquerque, N.M.
Clark, Daryl	.244	93	340	57	83	18	2	19	78	58	117	4	5	.476	.352	L	R	6-2	210	9-25-79	2000	King of Prussia, Pa.
Derosso, Tony	.369	28	103	28	38	11	2	7	34	16	20	2	0	.718	.463	R	R	6-3	220	11-7-75	1994	Moultrie, Ga.
Foster, Brian	.235	67	230	36	54	9	1	14	34	20	87	5	0	.465	.298	R	R	6-2	205	8-21-81	1999	Burlington, N.C.
Fox, Jason	.245	59	151	25	37	4	3	1	15	11	29	9	2	.331	.294	S	R	6-2	180	3-30-77	1998	York, Pa.
Gemoll, Brandon	.280	46	175	29	49	12	3	2	27	16	33	2	1	.417	.344	L	L	6-2	210	9-15-80	2001	San Jose, Calif.
Hammond, Derry	.224	92	353	49	79	18	1	16	54	24	112	3	1	.416	.276	R	R	6-2	200	10-19-79	1998	West Point, Miss.
Hardy, J.J.	.293	84	335	53	98	19	1	6	48	19	38	9	3	.409	.327	R	R	6-2	180	8-19-82	2001	Tucson, Ariz.
Harris, Cedrick	.289	58	180	27	52	9	3	3	28	11	34	12	5	.422	.330	R	R	6-2	190	11-14-77	2000	Ashdown, Ark.
Hart, Corey	.288	100	393	76	113	26	10	22	84	37	101	24	11	.573	.356	R	R	6-6	205	3-24-82	2000	Bowling Green, Ky.
Johnson, Kade	.276	33	123	20	34	8	3	5	28	11	39	0	2	.512	.355	R	R	6-1	200	9-28-78	1998	Baytown, Texas
Knox, Ryan	.355	25	93	21	33	7	1	5	15	8	12	15	3	.613	.423	R	R	6-1	190	6-28-77	1999	Peoria, Ill.
Krynzel, Dave	.268	97	365	76	98	13	12	11	45	64	100	29	17	.460	.391	L	L	6-1	180	11-7-81	2000	Henderson, Nev.
Nelson, Brad	.255	26	102	24	26	11	0	3	17	12	28	0	0	.451	.333	L	R	6-2	220	12-23-82	2001	Algona, Iowa
Patterson, Derek	.200	21	65	8	13	2	0	2	10	10	12	1	0	.323	.321	R	R	5-11	190	6-3-78	2002	Valley Center, Calif.
Raburn, Johnny	.212	16	66	8	14	3	1	0	3	7	13	5	1	.288	.288	S	R	6-1	160	2-16-79	2000	Plant City, Fla.
2-team (115 R. Cucamonga)	.282	131	514	79	145	23	6	1	39	84	101	40	20	.356	.384							
Ramirez, Manuel	.269	62	193	30	52	10	0	3	22	23	55	3	0	.368	.352	R	R	6-0	202	9-7-82	2000	Acarigua, Venez.
Randolph, Jaisen	.321	26	106	16	34	5	0	0	9	10	15	11	3	.368	.379	S	R	6-0	180	1-19-79	1997	Tampa, Fla.
Rowan, Chris	.270	87	282	52	76	16	3	16	52	12	95	16	3	.518	.311	R	R	6-1	205	3-18-79	1997	South Ogden, Utah
Villanueva, Florian	.207	28	111	14	23	4	2	1	14	6	20	2	1	.306	.250	R	R	6-2	150	10-5-78	1997	Santo Domingo, D.R.
Voltz, Jude	.229	49	166	18	38	9	1	2	17	10	52	1	0	.331	.278	L	L	6-6	210	5-5-78	2000	Metairie, La.
West, Todd	.266	64	229	38	61	8	1	1	19	29	36	17	6	.323	.355	R	R	5-11	160	3-2-79	2000	El Paso, Texas
Zoccolillo, Peter	.342	44	161	31	55	10	0	8	37	28	24	2	1	.553	.436	L	R	6-2	200	2-6-77	1999	White Plains, N.Y.

PITCHING	W	L	ERA	G	GS	CG	SV	IP	H	R	ER	BB	SO	AVG	B	T	HT	WT	DOB	1st Yr	Resides
Adams, Mike	2	1	2.57	10	0	0	5	14	9	6	4	7	23	.173	R	R	6-5	190	7-29-78	2001	Sinton, Texas
Altman, Gene	0	1	14.59	11	0	0	0	12	20	25	20	16	8	.363	R	R	6-7	230	9-1-78	1996	Lynchburg, S.C.
Alvarado, Carlo	2	1	3.00	17	0	0	0	27	22	12	9	16	31	.217	R	R	6-4	210	1-24-78	1995	Arecibo, P.R.
Cordero, Victor	3	0	5.40	10	0	0	1	13	13	9	8	6	15	.260	R	R	6-2	180	9-7-78	1997	Santo Domingo, D.R.
Dent, Doug	4	3	4.01	13	12	0	0	67	64	35	30	36	62	.251	R	R	6-8	210	3-23-77	1998	Gilbert, Ariz.
Gold, J.M.	1	3	7.63	7	7	0	0	31	33	29	26	22	33	.292	R	R	6-5	245	4-10-80	1998	Toms River, N.J.
Gordon, Justin	4	9	7.58	25	20	0	0	127	172	128	107	77	86	.320	L	L	6-5	225	5-26-79	1999	Taunton, Mass.
Hendrickson, Ben	5	5	2.55	14	14	0	0	81	61	31	23	41	70	.208	R	R	6-4	190	2-4-81	1999	Eden Prairie, Minn.
High, Andy	1	5	4.11	12	6	0	0	50	60	24	23	9	39	.306	L	L	6-5	245	5-22-74	1996	Chester, N.J.
Krawczyk, Jack	0	2	6.52	6	0	0	2	10	13	10	7	3	12	.325	R	R	6-1	190	8-12-75	1998	Scottsdale, Ariz.
Lamattina, Ryan	3	6	6.12	41	1	0	3	60	77	49	41	32	30	.316	R	L	6-2	210	1-14-76	1998	Lake View, N.Y.
Maysonet, Roberto	3	2	9.48	35	5	0	0	82	97	93	86	80	61	.293	R	R	6-1	204	1-16-80	1998	Vega Baja, P.R.
McGee, Chris	1	2	7.54	39	0	0	4	51	62	49	43	30	48	.289	R	R	6-3	210	7-28-77	1999	Laceyville, Pa.
Miller, Ryan	6	5	5.11	36	9	0	1	107	106	73	61	57	100	.256	R	R	6-1	200	2-12-78	2000	Newburgh, Ind.
Parker, Matt	0	1	4.50	1	1	0	0	4	4	2	2	3	1	.266	R	R	6-3	210	12-13-78	1999	Hartsfield, Ga.
Perez, George	5	12	8.18	35	14	0	0	113	153	117	103	69	80	.324	R	R	6-4	200	3-20-79	1997	San Pedro de Macoris, D.R.
Poe, Ryan	1	1	3.95	3	0	0	0	14	18	8	6	3	6	.327	R	R	6-2	220	9-3-77	1998	Mission Viejo, Calif.
Robinson, Jeff	0	0	12.00	1	1	0	0	3	4	4	4	5	3	.307	R	R	6-5	220	6-2-77	1999	Broussard, La.
Sams, Aaron	3	3	7.07	9	9	0	0	50	65	48	39	18	36	.314	L	L	6-1	200	4-30-76	1998	Bedford, Pa.
Schaub, Greg	2	4	6.60	34	0	0	10	44	41	37	32	30	59	.239	R	R	6-1	200	3-30-77	1995	Kirkwood, Pa.
Shwam, Mike	1	0	6.43	5	0	0	0	7	11	8	5	3	4	.366	R	R	6-2	200	12-22-77	2000	Huntington Beach, Calif.
Sismondo, Bobby	4	5	6.57	38	4	0	3	75	89	62	55	34	69	.289	L	L	6-1	200	11-14-76	1998	Steubenville, Ohio
Smart, Pete	9	9	5.10	29	29	0	0	180	212	119	102	59	116	.295	R	L	6-7	200	11-22-77	2001	Lawrence, Kan.

FIELDING

Catcher	PCT	G	PO	A	E	DP	PB
Alfonzo	.976	12	72	11	2	1	2
Foster	.969	64	419	47	15	3	13
Patterson	.993	20	126	8	1	1	3
Ramirez	.978	32	201	23	5	3	9
Villanueva	.995	22	185	15	1	1	3

First Base	PCT	G	PO	A	E	DP
Candelaria	1.000	3	31	1	0	4
Clark	1.000	12	89	3	0	8
Derosso	1.000	1	7	2	0	0
Gemoll	.990	24	178	14	2	19
Hart	.995	43	350	31	2	34
Nelson	.987	26	204	26	3	30
Ramirez	.967	8	51	7	2	8
Rowan	1.000	2	2	1	0	0
Voltz	.992	32	220	16	2	17

Second Base	PCT	G	PO	A	E	DP
Ayala	.963	6	14	12	1	3

	PCT	G	PO	A	E	DP
Candelaria	.937	43	93	99	13	29
Clark	1.000	2	0	2	0	0
Raburn	.956	14	33	32	3	9
Rowan	.966	23	57	56	4	18
West	.975	60	118	160	7	38

Third Base	PCT	G	PO	A	E	DP
Ayala	1.000	6	1	2	0	0
Clark	.855	55	40	78	20	2
Derosso	.927	26	15	61	6	7
Hart	.866	47	31	98	20	8
Raburn	1.000	1	0	2	0	0
Rowan	.943	14	9	24	2	5
Villanueva	.500	1	0	2	2	1

Shortstop	PCT	G	PO	A	E	DP
Barnwell	.962	35	56	97	6	27
Candelaria	1.000	1	0	1	0	0
Hardy	.973	82	122	268	11	57
Rowan	.915	26	36	72	10	10

	PCT	G	PO	A	E	DP
West	.960	6	6	18	1	3

Outfield	PCT	G	PO	A	E	DP
Boyd	.923	23	22	2	2	0
Candelaria	1.000	1	3	0	0	0
Clark	.931	23	25	2	2	0
Derosso	.500	1	1	0	1	0
Foster	1.000	1	3	0	0	0
Fox	.973	49	103	4	3	1
Gemoll	.893	19	25	0	3	0
Hammond	.956	56	103	5	5	0
Harris	.976	55	116	5	3	0
Johnson	.921	24	33	2	3	1
Knox	.947	24	30	6	2	0
Krynzel	.971	96	223	11	7	1
Patterson	1.000	1	0	0	0	0
Randolph	.955	26	60	3	3	1
Rowan	.842	16	16	0	3	0
Villanueva	.800	4	8	0	2	0
Zoccolillo	.986	37	71	0	1	0

MIDWEST LEAGUE

BATTING	AVG	G	AB	R	H	2B	3B	HR	RBI	BB	SO	SB	CS	SLG	OBP	B	T	HT	WT	DOB	1st Yr	Resides
Ayala, Elio	.260	58	196	23	51	5	2	0	18	17	29	4	1	.306	.326	R	R	5-9	160	11-7-78	1998	Bronx, N.Y.

BATTING	AVG	G	AB	R	H	2B	3B	HR	RBI	BB	SO	SB	CS	SLG	OBP	B	T	HT	WT	DOB	1st Yr	Resides
Barnwell, Chris	.227	91	344	37	78	12	2	1	40	27	47	13	5	.282	.294	R	R	5-10	180	3-1-79	2001	Jacksonville, Fla.
Belcher, Jason	.261	98	348	44	91	19	0	6	38	45	42	3	1	.368	.348	L	R	6-1	190	1-13-82	2000	Walnut Ridge, Ark.
Bell, Paul	.186	19	59	3	11	3	0	1	4	7	23	0	0	.288	.273	R	R	5-10	170	6-24-80	2000	Kerwyn, South Africa
Boyd, Dan	.286	95	381	62	109	22	3	4	54	37	54	2	0	.391	.362	R	R	5-11	190	9-28-78	2001	Dade City, Fla.
Candelaria, Scott	.325	34	126	23	41	7	2	0	17	6	20	2	1	.413	.348	R	R	6-2	190	11-2-78	2000	Albuquerque, N.M.
Carrow, Tom	.263	75	270	30	71	11	0	7	35	15	51	2	2	.381	.314	R	R	6-2	180	7-31-81	2001	Lutz, Fla.
Chavez, Ozzie	.255	128	463	55	118	13	6	1	36	46	86	10	6	.315	.323	S	R	6-1	150	7-13-83	1999	Villa Mella, D.R.
Esparragoza, Pedro	.194	57	180	18	35	3	1	1	18	21	36	5	3	.239	.291	R	R	5-11	160	3-16-82	1999	Caracas, Venez.
Fielder, Prince	.241	32	112	15	27	7	0	3	11	10	27	0	0	.384	.320	L	R	5-11	280	5-9-84	2002	Melbourne, Fla.
Garcia, Hector	.231	107	359	38	83	15	0	4	38	8	88	8	3	.306	.254	R	R	6-3	160	12-19-78	1997	Haina, D.R.
Gemoll, Brandon	.283	47	173	31	49	8	0	4	23	22	34	0	3	.399	.367	L	L	6-2	210	9-15-80	2001	San Jose, Calif.
Hinton, Travis	.253	76	269	28	68	14	0	3	23	26	61	2	0	.338	.327	L	L	6-1	210	11-21-80	2001	Chandler, Ariz.
Mayo, Terry	.112	50	170	12	19	3	0	5	10	10	69	1	2	.218	.175	R	R	6-4	210	7-1-81	1999	Greensboro, N.C.
McClanahan, Jonah	.222	14	45	3	10	1	0	0	2	2	9	0	0	.244	.255	R	R	6-2	190	3-25-81	2000	Monterey, Calif.
Morris, Chris	.357	4	14	3	5	2	0	0	1	1	3	1	0	.500	.400	S	R	5-8	180	7-1-79	2000	Andrews, S.C.
Nelson, Brad	.297	106	417	70	124	38	2	17	99	34	86	4	1	.520	.353	L	R	6-2	220	12-23-82	2001	Algona, Iowa
Santana, Ralph	.261	107	387	58	101	10	6	0	29	37	58	31	14	.318	.329	L	R	6-1	170	9-30-80	2001	Leesburg, Fla.
Villanueva, Florian	.278	95	374	53	104	30	2	10	51	18	60	2	2	.449	.314	R	R	6-2	150	10-5-78	1997	Santo Domingo, D.R.

PITCHING	W	L	ERA	G	GS	CG	SV	IP	H	R	ER	BB	SO	AVG	B	T	HT	WT	DOB	1st Yr	Resides
Adams, Mike	0	0	2.93	11	0	0	5	15	13	6	5	2	21	.228	R	R	6-5	190	7-29-78	2001	Sinton, Texas
Artman, Dane	2	9	5.91	20	13	1	0	75	90	57	49	41	44	.302	L	L	6-3	210	6-3-82	2000	Key West, Fla.
Dishman, Richard	0	1	6.75	6	2	0	0	15	17	14	11	6	13	.298	R	R	6-5	220	4-26-75	1997	Roosevelt Island, N.Y.
Hall, Dan	12	3	2.92	41	6	0	0	99	86	38	32	35	87	.240	R	R	6-3	220	6-18-79	2000	Plymouth, N.C.
Henderson, Eric	1	3	6.75	6	6	0	0	28	35	24	21	12	17	.315	L	L	6-4	210	9-5-79	2000	Winter Park, Fla.
Jones, Mike	7	7	3.12	27	27	0	0	139	135	63	48	62	132	.255	R	R	6-4	200	4-23-83	2001	Phoenix, Ariz.
Kolb, Dan	8	9	4.00	32	15	0	1	119	125	67	53	38	114	.268	R	R	6-1	190	6-5-80	2001	Palmetto, Fla.
Michaels, Carl	0	3	3.57	19	0	0	5	40	39	17	16	9	37	.251	R	R	6-1	200	5-21-81	2001	Cape Town, South Africa
Nielsen, Brian	0	2	7.36	9	2	0	0	26	34	28	21	10	25	.323	L	L	6-2	190	9-8-81	2000	Sanford, Fla.
Nolasco, Dave	2	2	5.65	32	3	0	1	73	88	55	46	29	44	.294	R	R	6-2	200	4-3-79	2001	Rialto, Calif.
Oakes, Gerard	5	14	7.17	27	20	0	0	113	136	99	90	84	53	.314	L	R	6-4	170	4-29-82	2000	Westchester, Pa.
Richardson, Judd	0	2	7.13	5	5	0	0	18	25	23	14	14	15	.316	L	R	6-4	200	2-13-80	2001	Terra Cotta, Ontario
Saenz, Chris	3	5	3.51	37	0	0	8	74	59	31	29	32	99	.216	R	R	6-3	200	8-14-81	2001	Tucson, Ariz.
Stavros, Tony	5	2	1.68	42	0	0	17	70	50	16	13	25	72	.206	R	R	6-2	180	8-7-80	2001	Eugene, Ore.
Steitz, Jon	0	11	7.62	30	14	0	0	96	130	96	81	77	76	.332	R	R	6-3	200	9-5-80	2001	New Haven, Conn.
Trytten, Ryan	1	2	5.50	31	2	0	0	69	82	50	42	29	35	.297	R	R	6-3	200	5-10-81	2001	Agency, Iowa
Wheeler, James	0	0	2.00	4	0	0	0	9	12	6	2	3	4	.324	L	L	6-2	190	12-24-78	2001	Pigeon, Mich.
Yeatman, Matt	11	7	2.48	25	25	1	0	127	101	51	35	77	127	.219	R	R	6-4	200	8-2-82	2000	Tomball, Texas

FIELDING

Catcher	PCT	G	PO	A	E	DP	PB
Belcher	.981	34	243	16	5	1	6
Esparragoza	.985	57	445	74	8	3	12
Villanueva	.982	51	336	54	7	5	8

First Base	PCT	G	PO	A	E	DP
Fielder	.973	32	243	14	7	20
Garcia	1.000	5	35	2	0	3
Gemoll	1.000	2	13	0	0	2
Nelson	.988	103	835	70	11	75

Second Base	PCT	G	PO	A	E	DP
Ayala	1.000	11	28	30	0	4
Barnwell	.889	1	4	4	1	1
Bell	.833	5	3	12	3	3

	PCT	G	PO	A	E	DP
Candelaria	.945	24	39	81	7	14
Santana	.949	105	229	289	28	64

Third Base	PCT	G	PO	A	E	DP
Ayala	.846	46	45	59	19	6
Barnwell	.931	84	78	153	17	11
Bell	.833	5	2	3	1	0
Boyd	.000	1	0	0	0	0
Candelaria	1.000	4	4	9	0	0
Villanueva	.941	7	4	12	1	0

Shortstop	PCT	G	PO	A	E	DP
Barnwell	.951	8	15	24	2	5
Bell	1.000	5	7	13	0	2
Chavez	.950	128	202	351	29	70

Outfield	PCT	G	PO	A	E	DP
Ayala	1.000	2	4	0	0	0
Belcher	.965	33	52	3	2	0
Boyd	.970	85	121	7	4	2
Carrow	.962	66	122	6	5	1
Garcia	.964	102	175	11	7	2
Gemoll	.966	20	27	1	1	0
Hinton	.969	51	92	3	3	1
Mayo	.973	50	98	9	3	1
McClanahan	.931	12	26	1	2	0
Morris	.857	4	5	1	1	0
Villanueva	.857	16	15	3	3	0

OGDEN RAPTORS — Rookie

PIONEER LEAGUE

BATTING	AVG	G	AB	R	H	2B	3B	HR	RBI	BB	SO	SB	CS	SLG	OBP	B	T	HT	WT	DOB	1st Yr	Resides
Alvarado, Joel	.224	17	67	8	15	2	0	0	5	4	3	1	1	.254	.278	R	R	6-2	190	6-30-80	2001	Cayey, P.R.
Bell, Paul	.263	14	38	5	10	2	0	0	5	4	15	0	1	.316	.364	R	R	5-10	170	6-24-80	2000	Kerwyn, South Africa
Bibbs, Kennard	.243	64	235	53	57	3	3	0	18	44	31	22	11	.281	.371	L	L	5-9	160	3-5-80	2002	Houston, Texas
Bohanan, Keith	.194	54	170	27	33	2	2	0	14	20	39	2	3	.229	.307	R	R	6-2	190	3-25-81	2002	Fremont, Calif.
Carter, Nic	.278	53	209	27	58	10	3	2	30	11	53	8	7	.383	.321	R	R	6-3	190	9-17-80	2002	Parkersburg, W.Va.
Crabbe, Callix	.328	67	250	55	82	16	4	4	38	29	34	22	9	.472	.407	S	R	5-8	190	2-14-83	2002	Lithonia, Ga.
Eure, Jeffrey	.249	70	265	50	66	18	1	9	44	23	90	14	2	.426	.321	R	R	6-1	200	8-17-80	2001	Pillow, Pa.
Fielder, Prince	.390	41	146	35	57	12	0	10	40	37	27	3	4	.678	.531	L	R	5-11	280	5-9-84	2002	Melbourne, Fla.
Frost, Jeremy	.176	9	34	8	6	3	0	0	5	3	6	0	1	.265	.237	R	R	6-3	210	11-19-79	2002	Oviedo, Fla.
Gomez, Andri	.250	30	96	13	24	4	2	0	11	2	11	5	3	.333	.265	S	R	5-11	160	10-31-81	1999	Cabral, D.R.
Hunt, Stephen	.286	3	14	2	4	2	0	0	1	0	5	0	0	.429	.286	L	R	6-3	190	9-4-81	2002	Scottsdale, Ariz.
McClanahan, Jonah	.265	23	83	12	22	6	0	0	8	2	10	5	0	.337	.299	R	R	6-2	190	3-25-81	2000	Monterey, Calif.
Melo, Manuel	.274	32	84	16	23	1	1	1	6	7	18	15	2	.345	.330	S	R	6-1	160	9-28-81	1999	Guarico, Venez.
Mendez, Mario	.280	66	257	44	72	11	3	6	47	20	60	20	7	.416	.338	S	R	6-0	170	8-21-81	1999	Azua, D.R.
Moss, Steve	.500	5	8	3	4	2	1	0	3	1	1	0	1	1.000	.538	R	R	6-2	180	1-12-84	2002	Sherman Oaks, Calif.
Murray, Josh	.255	48	157	18	40	7	0	2	19	14	48	3	5	.338	.328	R	R	6-2	180	8-12-84	2002	Lutz, Fla.
Plasencia, Francisco	.183	34	104	15	19	3	1	0	9	11	29	7	0	.231	.261	L	L	6-2	150	6-19-84	2000	Baranitas, Venez.
Serafini, Matt	.270	39	141	14	38	6	1	2	21	13	30	0	2	.369	.335	R	R	6-1	230	3-4-80	2001	Lockport, Ill.
Soriano, Carlos	.300	3	10	3	3	1	0	0	3	1	4	2	0	.400	.364	R	R	5-11	170	9-19-78	1997	San Cristobal, D.R.
Vanden Berg, John	.295	59	224	38	66	15	1	7	52	17	40	4	1	.464	.353	R	R	6-2	210	2-5-80	2002	Cedarburg, Wis.

GAMES BY POSITION: C—Alvarado 17, Eure 3, Frost 9, Serafini 20, Vanden Berg 32. **1B**—Bell 1, Bohanan 1, Eure 29, Fielder 35, Melo 2, Mendez 1, Serafini 17. **2B**—Bell 5, Bohanan 9, Crabbe 63, Eure 1, Gomez 4. **3B**—Bell 4, Bohanan 20, Eure 35, Gomez 23, Murray 1. **SS**—Bell 3, Bohanan 28, Crabbe 2, Eure 1, Gomez 4, Murray 48. **OF**—Bibbs 59, Carter 42, Eure 5, Hunt 2, McClanahan 22, Melo 24, Mendez 56, Moss 5, Plasencia 29, Soriano 1.

PITCHING	W	L	ERA	G	GS	CG	SV	IP	H	R	ER	BB	SO	AVG	B	T	HT	WT	DOB	1st Yr	Resides
Alliston, Josh	3	0	4.76	6	0	0	1	11	11	6	6	2	10	.250	R	R	6-5	230	2-29-80	2002	Long Beach, Calif.
Baker, Jason	4	3	4.96	13	1	0	0	33	28	20	18	9	24	.235	R	R	6-0	200	9-18-80	2002	Accokeek, Md.
Ballouli, Khalid	4	0	4.37	15	12	0	0	60	78	31	29	11	65	.317	R	R	6-2	190	3-20-80	2002	Austin, Texas
Breslow, Craig	6	2	1.82	23	0	0	2	54	42	15	11	24	56	.217	L	L	6-1	180	8-8-80	2002	Trumbull, Conn.
Carpenter, Calvin	4	2	4.44	16	15	0	0	71	81	48	35	27	65	.278	R	R	6-2	190	9-23-82	2001	Natchitoches, La.
Desalme, Gene	0	0	5.68	14	1	0	0	25	25	17	16	12	28	.255	L	L	6-5	210	9-14-79	2001	Rolla, Mo.
Gabriel, Justin	2	2	3.93	12	1	0	1	18	18	11	8	8	12	.250	L	L	5-9	160	3-2-79	2002	Las Vegas, Nev.
Hall, Bo	2	6	3.82	16	9	0	0	66	53	29	28	21	58	.218	R	R	6-0	180	9-5-80	2002	Ormond Beach, Fla.
Housman, Jeff	1	3	8.07	16	5	0	0	32	55	38	29	12	23	.371	L	L	6-3	180	8-4-81	2002	Visalia, Calif.
Michaels, Carl	1	0	1.23	4	0	0	0	7	6	1	1	2	12	.222	R	R	6-1	200	5-21-81	2001	Cape Town, South Africa
Moreira, Greg	1	3	4.66	18	2	0	1	46	72	38	24	13	37	.352	R	R	6-5	210	5-29-83	2001	Apopka, Fla.
Parra, Manuel	3	1	3.21	11	10	0	0	48	59	30	17	10	51	.297	L	L	6-3	200	10-30-82	2002	Citrus Heights, Calif.
Perez, Melvin	4	3	3.55	26	0	0	2	33	25	14	13	21	34	.196	R	R	6-5	170	7-24-81	1999	Jimani, D.R.
Price, Matt	0	0	5.22	17	1	0	0	29	26	23	17	15	10	.234	R	R	6-4	230	4-14-79	2001	Monroe, N.C.
Robinson, Jeff	0	2	6.75	4	3	0	0	11	16	11	8	5	16	.347	R	R	6-5	220	6-2-77	1999	Broussard, La.
Sarfate, Dennis	0	0	9.00	1	0	0	0	1	2	1	1	1	2	.400	R	R	6-4	210	4-9-81	2001	Chandler, Ariz.
Shepple, Tyler	3	4	7.49	25	0	0	4	34	56	33	28	8	30	.363	R	R	6-2	220	8-2-80	2002	Arvada, Colo.
Stone, Jeff	0	0	10.80	3	0	0	0	5	8	6	6	3	1	.400	L	L	6-1	190	10-15-77	2002	Highland, Utah
Thomas, Eric A.	2	1	5.36	15	9	0	0	45	50	31	27	21	38	.279	R	R	6-4	210	8-7-79	2002	Tyrone, Ga.
Thomas, Eric M.	0	3	9.90	12	6	0	0	30	46	39	33	17	32	.340	R	R	6-9	230	3-24-81	2002	Orange, Mass.

PHOENIX BREWERS — Rookie

ARIZONA LEAGUE

BATTING	AVG	G	AB	R	H	2B	3B	HR	RBI	BB	SO	SB	CS	SLG	OBP	B	T	HT	WT	DOB	1st Yr	Resides
Acosta, Gilberto	.315	50	184	38	58	9	2	0	25	26	29	4	4	.386	.415	S	R	6-1	150	10-5-82	1999	Valencia, Venez.
Alvarado, Joel	.324	11	34	4	11	3	0	0	4	5	3	2	0	.412	.400	R	R	6-2	190	6-30-80	2001	Cayey, P.R.
Bates, Dallas	.250	51	204	23	51	2	1	0	25	18	50	4	1	.270	.326	L	L	5-8	170	7-20-84	2002	Chandler, Ariz.
Bravo, Arturo	.189	12	37	7	7	2	0	0	4	4	10	0	0	.243	.268	R	R	5-11	190	2-7-84	2002	San Ysidro, Calif.
Cavanaugh, Brian	.212	12	33	3	7	1	0	0	2	7	9	0	0	.242	.366	L	L	6-0	170	8-25-80	2002	Vero Beach, Fla.
Christenson, Ryan	.400	4	10	1	4	2	0	0	2	0	2	0	0	.600	.364	R	R	6-0	190	3-28-74	1995	Apple Valley, Calif.
Franke, Michael	.202	32	109	19	22	6	0	0	10	11	33	2	1	.257	.298	S	R	6-2	180	9-22-81	2001	Strausberg, Germany
Frost, Jeremy	.258	27	97	14	25	7	2	1	15	15	24	4	3	.402	.363	R	R	6-3	210	11-19-79	2002	Oviedo, Fla.
Gomez, Andri	.321	20	84	16	27	1	1	0	7	5	12	4	2	.357	.367	S	R	5-11	160	10-31-81	1999	Cabral, D.R.
Guhring, Simon	.238	25	80	11	19	4	0	0	15	6	15	0	2	.288	.295	R	R	6-1	200	7-14-83	2002	Leonberg, Germany
Hunt, Stephen	.290	48	186	32	54	10	5	5	42	23	45	6	0	.478	.369	L	R	6-3	190	9-4-81	2002	Scottsdale, Ariz.
January, Javerro	.067	5	15	3	1	0	0	1	4	2	3	0	0	.267	.176	R	R	6-1	180	10-31-80	1999	Jackson, Miss.
Johnson, Kade	.000	3	7	1	0	0	0	0	0	2	4	0	0	.000	.222	R	R	6-1	200	9-28-78	1999	Baytown, Texas
McCormack, Taylor	.257	42	152	24	39	5	3	3	28	10	42	2	3	.388	.310	R	R	6-2	190	10-20-82	2001	Palm Harbor, Fla.
Melo, Manuel	.359	20	78	13	28	3	0	0	12	7	17	14	1	.397	.402	S	R	6-1	160	9-28-81	1999	Guarico, Venez.
Moss, Steve	.292	30	106	20	31	8	2	1	20	22	32	3	1	.434	.414	R	R	6-2	180	1-12-84	2002	Sherman Oaks, Calif.
Patterson, Derek	.283	19	60	13	17	5	1	1	8	8	11	0	0	.450	.366	R	R	5-11	190	6-3-78	2002	Valley Center, Calif.
Plasencia, Francisco	.348	17	66	15	23	2	1	1	14	8	13	4	1	.455	.427	L	L	6-2	150	6-19-84	2000	Baranitas, Venez.
Randolph, Jaisen	.200	2	5	0	1	0	0	0	1	1	0	0	0	.200	.333	S	R	6-0	180	1-19-79	1997	Tampa, Fla.
Rodriguez, Guilder	.258	47	186	38	48	3	2	0	20	11	23	6	1	.296	.299	S	R	6-1	160	7-24-83	2001	Barquisimeto, Venez.
Serafini, Matt	.263	20	76	16	20	4	0	2	11	8	18	3	0	.395	.337	R	R	6-1	230	3-4-80	2001	Lockport, Ill.
Viera, Orlando	.143	5	7	1	1	0	0	0	1	1	3	1	0	.143	.250	L	L	6-0	170	9-14-83	2001	Gurabo, P.R.
Willis, Lendon	.277	44	159	28	44	13	1	0	23	15	41	3	0	.371	.356	R	R	6-1	170	10-17-82	2002	Millington, Tenn.

GAMES BY POSITION: C—Alvarado 7, Bravo 7, Frost 17, Guhring 19, Patterson 7, Serafini 5. **1B**—Alvarado 3, Franke 13, Frost 1, McCormack 27, Patterson 5, Serafini 11. **2B**—Franke 3, Gomez 12, Rodriguez 42. **3B**—Franke 6, Gomez 1, McCormack 1, Willis 42. **SS**—Acosta 49, Gomez 6, Rodriguez 3, Willis 1. **OF**—Bates 48, Cavanaugh 10, Christenson 2, Frost 1, Hunt 43, January 5, Johnson 3, Melo 20, Moss 30, Plasencia 16, Randolph 1.

PITCHING	W	L	ERA	G	GS	CG	SV	IP	H	R	ER	BB	SO	AVG	B	T	HT	WT	DOB	1st Yr	Resides
Alliston, Josh	0	1	2.45	4	0	0	0	7	6	4	2	2	8	.230	R	R	6-5	230	2-29-80	2002	Long Beach, Calif.
Cordero, Victor	1	1	6.10	6	0	0	0	10	7	8	7	7	10	.184	R	R	6-2	180	9-7-98	1997	Santo Domingo, D.R.
Correa, Alexander	2	0	3.71	15	0	0	1	44	40	20	18	23	49	.243	L	L	6-4	170	7-17-82	1999	Chaguarama, Venez.
Garcia, Miguel	1	2	10.38	10	0	0	0	26	48	34	30	12	7	.417	R	R	6-2	160	6-29-85	2001	Barinas, Venez.
Gelatka, Todd	0		1243.00	2	1	0	0		4	9	9	3	0	.800	L	R	6-3	180	8-21-81	2001	Lake Forest, Calif.
Gittings, Christopher	0	0	0.00	1	0	0	0	1	0	0	0	0	0	.000	R	R	6-3	190	11-1-82	2001	Louisville, Ky.
Hawkins, Al	1	3	5.95	6	6	0	0	20	30	20	13	5	12	.357	R	R	6-1	210	1-1-78	1996	Elizabeth, N.J.
Jimenez, Julio	0	2	4.98	16	0	0	3	34	34	23	19	24	22	.255	L	L	6-2	160	10-24-81	1999	San Pedro de Macoris, D.R.
Martinez Sosa, Alvaro	0	5	7.30	15	3	0	0	37	42	41	30	32	34	.285	R	R	6-6	190	7-29-85	2002	Caracas, Venez.
Mendoza, Gabriel	2	1	3.53	19	0	0	6	43	42	23	17	18	50	.250	L	L	6-2	160	1-13-82	1999	Varinitas, Venez.
Parra, Manuel	0	0	4.50	1	1	0	0	2	1	1	1	0	4	.142	L	L	6-3	200	10-30-82	2002	Citrus Heights, Calif.
Pena, Luismar	4	1	3.49	11	7	0	0	49	45	28	19	24	52	.239	R	R	6-5	160	1-10-83	1999	Aragua, Venez.
Pierre, Adolfo	3	2	7.84	17	0	0	2	31	39	31	27	24	26	.309	L	L	6-4	170	12-15-81	1998	San Pedro de Macoris, D.R.
Poe, Ryan	1	0	1.80	3	3	0	0	10	8	3	2	2	13	.205	R	R	6-2	220	9-3-77	1998	Mission Viejo, Calif.
Pruett, Hubert	4	1	4.91	11	5	0	0	40	44	26	22	17	36	.273	R	R	6-2	220	3-16-83	2001	Pearl City, Hawaii
Ramirez, Carlos	6	5	3.70	15	14	0	0	75	84	41	31	25	60	.281	L	L	6-3	160	8-12-84	2001	Azua, D.R.
Richardson, Judd	0	3	7.04	7	7	0	0	23	24	21	18	14	22	.265	L	R	6-4	200	2-13-80	2001	Terra Cotta, Ontario
Robinson, Jeff	0	1	10.80	3	3	0	0	8	13	10	10	3	9	.351	R	R	6-5	220	6-2-77	1999	Broussard, La.
Sarfate, Dennis	0	0	2.57	5	5	0	0	14	6	4	4	7	22	.125	R	R	6-4	210	4-9-81	2001	Chandler, Ariz.
Walker, Edwin	1	0	1.69	4	1	0	0	11	14	5	2	5	14	.304	R	L	6-3	190	10-26-83	2002	San Antonio, Texas

BY JOHN MILLEA

The Twins experienced a breakthrough season in 2002. They broke through constant talk of contraction over the winter, survived the dirty dance between owners and players until a strike was averted, then broke through the glass ceiling atop the American League Central Division by winning 94 games.

Their first-place division finish was surprising, but not as surprising as their first-round playoff victory over powerful Oakland. The Angels crunched the Twins in the AL Championship Series, but going that deep into the postseason surpassed anyone's expectations for the little team that could.

Obviously, a lot of things went right. The bullpen, expected to be a weakness, became a strength. Starting pitchers Brad Radke, Eric Milton and Joe Mays all missed time with injuries, but they were healthy when it mattered most. Center fielder Torii Hunter became an all-star after a dazzling first half of the season, although he tailed off in the second half.

The maturation of a young everyday lineup had the biggest impact of all. Catcher A.J. Pierzynski was another first-time all-star and his .300 batting average tied Jacque Jones for the club lead.

Middle infielders Luis Rivas and Cristian Guzman didn't have spectacular seasons, but their futures are clearly bright. Jones was solid in left field, and right field was platooned by Bobby Kielty and Dustan Mohr much of the season, with rookie Michael Cuddyer getting serious playing time late in the year and in the playoffs.

First baseman Doug Mientkiewicz and third baseman Corey Koskie had down years, numbers-wise, but another year of experience—including the valuable playoff games—can only be considered a positive for 2003 and beyond.

The bullpen was nothing short of spectacular. J.C. Romero had a career year and Eddie Guardado became

Torii Hunter   Lew Ford

PLAYERS OF THE YEAR

MAJOR LEAGUE: Torii Hunter, of

The superlative defender's 2002 season might best be remembered for robbing Barry Bonds of a home run at the All-Star Game, but he broke out offensively as well, posting career-bests in average (.289), doubles (37), home runs (29) and RBIs (94).

MINOR LEAGUE: Lew Ford, of

Splitting time between Triple-A Edmonton and Double-A New Britain, Ford enjoyed a breakthrough season in 2002. He led the minors with 121 runs, tied for second with 180 hits and ranked third with 286 total bases.

one of the best closers in the game. LaTroy Hawkins—former starter, former closer—was outstanding as a setup man.

But there were shortcomings. The Twins have no reliable home run hitter, as evidenced by this fact: nobody hit even 30 homers. The club also was very weak against lefthanded starters, with a 23-29 record in the regular season.

The reappearance of Homer Hankys inside the Metrodome in 2002 was a reminder of the franchise's glory days, when the Twins won the World Series in 1987 and 1991. Back then, of course, big sluggers like Kirby Puckett and Kent Hrbek were available to knock the ball around the park and give their teammates some coattails to ride. The 2002 Twins had no such standouts, but that should change.

Hunter had some moments, especially in the Oakland playoff series, when he barked at teammates to get going. As one of the highest-paid and most-decorated players on the club, Hunter should become even more of a leader in the future.

The Twins need more on-field and clubhouse leadership. More importantly, they will need more pop in the batting order in 2003. But if 2002 proved anything, it's that the Twins are definitely on the right track.

Down on the farm, the Edmonton Trappers won the Pacific Coast League playoff title under John Russell, Baseball America's minor league manager of the year. Soon after, the organization signed a Triple-A affiliation agreement with the Rochester Red Wings of the International League. The rest of the affiliates remained unchanged: Double-A New Britain, high Class A Fort Myers and low Class A Quad City.

ORGANIZATION LEADERS

BATTING

*AVG	Jason Kubel, Quad City	.321
R	Lew Ford, Edmonton/New Britain	121
H	Lew Ford, Edmonton/New Britain	180
TB	Lew Ford, Edmonton/New Britain	286
2B	Lew Ford, Edmonton/New Britain	38
3B	Michael Cuddyer, Edmonton	9
HR	Mike Ryan, Edmonton	31
RBI	Mike Ryan, Edmonton	101
BB	Lew Ford, Edmonton/New Britain	62
SO	Michael Restovich, Edmonton	151
SB	Lew Ford, Edmonton/New Britain	28

PITCHING

W	Scott Randall, Edmonton/New Britain	14
L	Brad Thomas, Edmonton	12
#ERA	Willie Eyre, New Britain/Fort Myers	2.90
G	Beau Kemp, Fort Myers	59
CG	Juan Rincon, Edmonton	3
SV	Juan Padilla, New Britain	29
	Beau Kemp, Fort Myers	29
IP	Brent Hoard, New Britain	161
	J.D. Durbin, Quad City	161
BB	Jon Pridie, New Britain/Fort Myers	76
SO	J.D. Durbin, Quad City	163

*Minimum 250 At-Bats #Minimum 75 Innings

MINNESOTA TWINS

Manager: Ron Gardenhire

2002 Record: 94-67, .584 (1st, AL Central)

BATTING	AVG	G	AB	R	H	2B	3B	HR	RBI	BB	SO	SB	CS	SLG	OBP	B	T	HT	WT	DOB	1st Yr	Resides
Blake, Casey	.200	9	20	2	4	1	0	0	1	2	7	0	0	.250	.273	R	R	6-2	210	8-23-73	1996	Indianola, Iowa
Buchanan, Brian	.252	44	135	19	34	5	1	5	15	6	33	2	1	.415	.294	R	R	6-4	230	7-21-73	1994	Fort Myers, Fla.
Canizaro, Jay	.214	38	112	14	24	8	1	0	11	10	22	0	1	.304	.280	R	R	5-9	190	7-4-73	1993	Spring, Texas
Cuddyer, Michael	.259	41	112	12	29	7	0	4	13	8	30	2	0	.429	.311	R	R	6-2	210	3-27-79	1997	Fort Myers, Fla.
Guzman, Cristian	.273	148	623	80	170	31	6	9	59	17	79	12	13	.385	.292	S	R	6-0	190	3-21-78	1995	Santo Domingo, D.R.
Hocking, Denny	.250	102	260	28	65	13	0	2	25	24	44	0	2	.323	.310	S	R	5-10	180	4-2-70	1989	Tustin, Calif.
Hunter, Torii	.289	148	561	89	162	37	4	29	94	35	118	23	8	.524	.334	R	R	6-2	210	7-18-75	1993	The Colony, Texas
Jones, Jacque	.300	149	577	96	173	37	2	27	85	37	129	6	7	.511	.341	L	L	5-10	200	4-25-75	1996	San Diego, Calif.
Kielty, Bobby	.291	112	289	49	84	14	3	12	46	52	66	4	1	.484	.405	S	R	6-1	220	8-5-76	1999	Fort Myers, Fla.
Koskie, Corey	.267	140	490	71	131	37	3	15	69	72	127	10	11	.447	.368	L	R	6-3	210	6-28-73	1994	White Rock, B.C.
Lamb, David	.100	7	10	0	1	0	0	0	0	0	2	0	0	.100	.100	S	R	6-2	200	6-6-75	1993	Newbury Park, Calif.
LeCroy, Matt	.260	63	181	19	47	11	1	7	27	13	38	0	2	.448	.306	R	R	6-2	220	12-13-75	1997	Belton, S.C.
Mientkiewicz, Doug	.261	143	467	60	122	29	1	10	64	74	69	1	2	.392	.365	L	R	6-2	200	6-19-74	1995	Estero, Fla.
Mohr, Dustan	.269	120	383	55	103	23	2	12	45	31	86	6	3	.433	.325	R	R	6-1	210	6-19-76	1997	Hattiesburg, Miss.
Morris, Warren	.000	4	7	0	0	0	0	0	0	0	1	0	0	.000	.000	L	R	5-11	180	1-11-74	1996	Alexandria, La.
Ortiz, David	.272	125	412	52	112	32	1	20	75	43	87	1	2	.500	.339	L	L	6-4	230	11-18-75	1993	Haina, D.R.
Pierzynski, A.J.	.300	130	440	54	132	31	6	6	49	13	61	1	2	.439	.334	L	R	6-3	220	12-30-76	1994	Fort Myers, Fla.
Prince, Tom	.224	51	125	14	28	7	1	4	16	14	26	1	3	.392	.317	R	R	5-11	200	8-13-64	1984	Bradenton, Fla.
Restovich, Michael	.308	8	13	3	4	0	0	1	1	1	4	1	0	.538	.357	R	R	6-4	240	1-3-79	1997	Fort Myers, Fla.
Rivas, Luis	.256	93	316	46	81	23	4	4	35	19	51	9	4	.392	.305	R	R	5-11	170	8-30-79	1995	La Guaira, Venez.
Ryan, Mike	.091	7	11	3	1	0	0	0	0	0	2	0	0	.091	.091	L	R	6-0	180	7-6-77	1996	Indiana, Pa.
Sears, Todd	.333	7	12	2	4	2	0	0	0	1	1	0	0	.500	.333	L	R	6-5	210	10-23-75	1997	Ankeny, Iowa
Valentin, Javier	.500	4	4	0	2	0	0	0	0	0	0	0	0	.500	.500	S	R	5-10	190	9-19-75	1993	Manati, P.R.

PITCHING	W	L	ERA	G	GS	CG	SV	IP	H	R	ER	BB	SO	AVG	B	T	HT	WT	DOB	1st Yr	Resides
Cressend, Jack	0	1	5.91	23	0	0	0	32	40	25	21	19	22	.305	R	R	6-1	190	5-13-75	1996	Mandeville, La.
Fiore, Tony	10	3	3.16	48	2	0	0	91	74	32	32	43	55	.223	R	R	6-4	220	10-12-71	1992	Tampa, Fla.
Frederick, Kevin	0	0	10.03	8	0	0	0	12	13	13	13	10	5	.282	L	R	6-1	210	11-4-76	1998	Prairie View, Ill.
Guardado, Eddie	1	3	2.93	68	0	0	45	68	53	22	22	18	70	.214	R	L	6-0	200	10-2-70	1990	Stockton, Calif.
Hawkins, LaTroy	6	0	2.13	65	0	0	0	80	63	23	19	15	63	.217	R	R	6-5	210	12-21-72	1991	Frisco, Texas
Jackson, Mike	2	3	3.27	58	0	0	0	55	59	20	20	13	29	.283	R	R	6-2	210	12-22-64	1984	Spring, Texas
Kinney, Matt	2	7	4.64	14	12	0	0	66	78	39	34	33	45	.295	R	R	6-5	220	12-16-76	1995	Bangor, Maine
Lohse, Kyle	13	8	4.23	32	31	1	0	181	181	92	85	70	124	.259	R	R	6-2	200	10-4-78	1997	Fort Myers, Fla.
Mays, Joe	4	8	5.38	17	17	1	0	95	113	60	57	25	38	.291	S	R	6-1	190	12-10-75	1995	Sarasota, Fla.
Miller, Travis	0	0	4.50	5	0	0	0	4	5	2	2	2	3	.294	R	L	6-3	210	11-2-72	1994	Eaton, Ohio
Milton, Eric	13	9	4.84	29	29	2	0	171	173	96	92	30	121	.258	L	L	6-3	220	8-4-75	1996	Fort Myers, Fla.
Radke, Brad	9	5	4.72	21	21	2	0	118	124	64	62	20	62	.271	R	R	6-2	180	10-27-72	1991	Largo, Fla.
Reed, Rick	15	7	3.78	33	32	2	0	188	192	89	79	26	121	.259	R	R	6-1	190	8-16-65	1986	Proctorville, Ohio
Rincon, Juan	0	2	6.28	10	3	0	0	29	44	23	20	9	21	.352	R	R	5-11	180	1-23-79	1996	Maracaibo, Venez.
Rodriguez, Jose	0	1	14.73	4	0	0	0	4	8	6	6	4	1	.421	L	L	6-1	200	12-18-74	1997	Cayey, P.R.
Romero, J.C.	9	2	1.89	81	0	0	1	81	62	17	17	36	76	.213	S	L	5-11	190	6-4-76	1997	San Juan, P.R.
Santana, Johan	8	6	2.99	27	14	0	1	108	84	41	36	49	137	.212	L	L	6-0	190	3-13-79	1996	Tovar, Venez.
Trombley, Mike	0	1	15.75	5	0	0	0	4	10	7	7	1	3	.454	R	R	6-2	200	4-14-67	1989	Fort Myers, Fla.
Wells, Bob	2	1	5.90	48	0	0	0	58	78	41	38	16	30	.325	R	R	6-0	200	11-1-66	1989	Cowiche, Wash.

FIELDING

Catcher	PCT	G	PO	A	E	DP	PB
LeCroy	1.000	6	20	1	0	0	2
Pierzynski	.996	124	757	41	3	3	2
Prince	.997	50	272	14	1	2	1
Valentin	1.000	4	14	1	0	0	0

First Base	PCT	G	PO	A	E	DP
Blake	1.000	3	12	0	0	0
Cuddyer	1.000	6	28	5	0	0
Hocking	1.000	7	9	0	0	0
Kielty	1.000	5	27	2	0	4
LeCroy	.976	8	39	1	1	8
Mientkiewicz	.996	143	1073	69	5	92
Ortiz	.990	15	90	6	1	8
Sears	1.000	6	26	2	0	3

Second Base	PCT	G	PO	A	E	DP
Canizaro	.990	30	39	62	1	13
Hocking	.963	56	69	115	7	22
Lamb	1.000	2	6	2	0	1
Morris	1.000	4	2	6	0	1
Rivas	.986	93	147	205	5	51

Third Base	PCT	G	PO	A	E	DP
Blake	.846	5	5	6	2	1
Canizaro	.905	8	3	16	2	3
Cuddyer	1.000	10	5	10	0	2
Hocking	1.000	16	10	20	0	2
Koskie	.969	138	117	254	12	16
Lamb	.000	1	0	0	0	0

Shortstop	PCT	G	PO	A	E	DP
Guzman	.981	147	247	360	12	84
Hocking	.962	25	32	43	3	8
Lamb	1.000	4	4	1	0	1

Outfield	PCT	G	PO	A	E	DP
Buchanan	1.000	24	48	0	0	0
Cuddyer	.980	25	47	1	1	0
Hocking	1.000	5	4	0	0	0
Hunter	.992	146	365	7	3	0
Jones	.986	143	330	11	5	1
Kielty	1.000	82	159	4	0	0
Mohr	.992	113	239	4	2	2
Restovich	1.000	5	7	0	0	0
Ryan	1.000	5	3	0	0	0

Brad Radke

RON WESELY

Doug Mientkiewicz: .261-10-64 for Twins

Jacque Jones: tied for team lead with 37 doubles

FARM SYSTEM

Director, Minor Leagues: Jim Rantz

Class	Farm Team	League	W	L	Pct.	Finish*	Manager	First Yr.
AAA	Edmonton (Alberta) Trappers	Pacific Coast	81	59	.579	+2nd (16)	John Russell	2001
AA	New Britain (Conn.) Rock Cats	Eastern	67	72	.482	8th (12)	Stan Cliburn	1995
High A	Fort Myers (Fla.) Miracle	Florida State	77	62	.554	3rd (12)	Jose Marzan	1993
Low A	Quad City (Iowa) River Bandits	Midwest	71	65	.522	6th (14)	Jeff Carter	1999
Rookie	Elizabethton (Tenn.) Twins	Appalachian	37	30	.552	4th (10)	Ray Smith	1974
Rookie	Fort Myers (Fla.) Twins	Gulf Coast	35	25	.583	4th (14)	Rudy Hernandez	1989

*Finish in overall standings (No. of teams in league)   +League champion

EDMONTON TRAPPERS

Class AAA

PACIFIC COAST LEAGUE

BATTING	AVG	G	AB	R	H	2B	3B	HR	RBI	BB	SO	SB	CS	SLG	OBP	B	T	HT	WT	DOB	1st Yr	Resides
Blake, Casey	.309	126	482	87	149	25	3	19	58	54	78	24	9	.492	.383	R	R	6-2	210	8-23-73	1996	Indianola, Iowa
Borrego, Ramon	.180	28	50	7	9	4	0	0	3	2	17	2	0	.260	.222	S	R	5-6	170	6-7-78	1995	Mariara, Venez.
Buchanan, Brian	.000	1	3	0	0	0	0	0	0	0	0	0	0	.000	.000	R	R	6-4	230	7-21-73	1994	Fort Myers, Fla.
Canizaro, Jay	.287	66	247	43	71	11	2	14	37	30	46	6	3	.518	.370	R	R	5-9	190	7-4-73	1993	Spring, Texas
Cuddyer, Michael	.309	86	330	70	102	16	9	20	53	36	79	12	7	.594	.379	R	R	6-2	210	3-27-79	1997	Fort Myers, Fla.
Dillon, Joe	.167	6	18	5	3	1	0	0	2	2	1	0	.222	.250	R	R	6-2	200	8-2-75	1997	Rocklin, Calif.
Ford, Lew	.332	47	193	40	64	11	2	5	24	13	21	11	1	.487	.390	R	R	6-0	190	8-12-76	1999	Lufkin, Texas
Green, Chad	.218	75	220	33	48	11	1	7	32	13	61	11	0	.373	.261	S	R	5-10	180	6-28-75	1996	Cincinnati, Ohio
Kielty, Bobby	.429	2	7	0	3	1	0	0	0	1	1	0	0	.571	.500	S	R	6-1	220	8-5-76	1999	Fort Myers, Fla.
Lamb, Dave	.309	123	440	72	136	25	3	10	72	45	57	2	6	.448	.377	S	R	6-2	200	6-6-75	1993	Newbury Park, Calif.
LeCroy, Matt	.351	46	174	36	61	7	1	12	50	17	34	2	0	.609	.412	R	R	6-2	220	12-13-75	1997	Belton, S.C.
Marsters, Brandon	.277	57	184	27	51	8	0	5	23	12	37	0	0	.402	.325	R	R	5-11	200	3-14-75	1996	Sarasota, Fla.
Morris, Warren	.261	27	92	15	24	6	2	2	10	3	16	2	1	.435	.281	L	R	5-11	180	1-11-74	1996	Alexandria, La.
Prieto, Alex	.264	80	276	38	73	14	1	7	29	19	47	4	4	.399	.315	R	R	5-10	200	6-19-76	1993	Derby, Kan.
Restovich, Michael	.286	138	518	95	148	32	7	29	98	53	151	11	7	.542	.353	R	R	6-4	240	1-3-79	1997	Fort Myers, Fla.
Ryan, Mike	.261	131	540	92	141	36	6	31	101	55	124	4	5	.522	.330	L	R	6-0	180	7-6-77	1996	Indiana, Pa.
Salazar, Ruben	.192	7	26	3	5	0	0	0	0	0	4	2	0	.192	.222	R	R	5-10	180	1-16-78	1997	San Felix, Venez.
Sears, Todd	.310	129	484	88	150	36	4	20	100	59	142	2	1	.525	.388	R	R	6-5	210	10-23-75	1997	Ankeny, Iowa
Smith, Jeff	.074	10	27	0	2	1	0	0	2	3	8	0	0	.111	.167	L	R	6-3	210	6-17-74	1995	Naples, Fla.
Valentin, Javier	.286	127	455	69	130	33	1	21	80	41	96	0	1	.501	.346	S	R	5-10	190	9-19-75	1993	Manati, P.R.

PITCHING	W	L	ERA	G	GS	CG	SV	IP	H	R	ER	BB	SO	AVG	B	T	HT	WT	DOB	1st Yr	Resides
Balfour, Grant	2	4	4.16	58	0	0	8	71	60	34	33	30	88	.230	R	R	6-2	170	12-30-77	1997	Sydney, Australia
Bochtler, Doug	7	4	3.68	34	9	1	0	88	71	41	36	44	79	.229	R	R	6-3	200	7-5-70	1989	West Palm Beach, Fla.
Carnes, Matt	4	3	6.61	21	12	0	0	80	104	62	59	29	42	.317	R	R	6-3	200	8-18-75	1997	Miami, Okla.

PITCHING	W	L	ERA	G	GS	CG	SV	IP	H	R	ER	BB	SO	AVG	B	T	HT	WT	DOB	1st Yr	Resides
Fiore, Tony	2	0	4.15	2	2	0	0	13	15	6	6	2	6	.294	R	R	6-4	220	10-12-71	1992	Tampa, Fla.
Frederick, Kevin	3	6	4.58	46	2	0	22	55	63	31	28	21	47	.288	L	R	6-1	210	11-4-76	1998	Prairie View, Ill.
Jerzembeck, Mike	1	2	11.70	3	2	0	0	16	14	16	14	3	4	.390	R	R	6-1	180	5-18-72	1993	Sanford, N.C.
Johnson, Adam	13	8	5.47	27	27	1	0	151	182	96	92	55	112	.304	R	R	6-2	210	7-12-79	2000	Fort Myers, Fla.
Kinney, Matt	2	1	8.89	5	5	0	0	27	42	27	27	4	21	.350	R	R	6-5	220	12-16-76	1995	Bangor, Maine
Lee, Dave	9	1	4.59	51	0	0	5	65	80	44	33	31	70	.296	R	R	6-1	200	3-12-73	1995	Pittsburgh, Pa.
Miller, Travis	0	1	3.99	24	0	0	1	29	35	15	13	5	24	.299	R	L	6-3	210	11-2-72	1994	Eaton, Ohio
Nakamura, Mike	4	3	4.74	46	4	0	2	87	85	51	46	22	80	.253	R	R	5-10	170	9-6-76	1997	Ferntree Gully, Australia
Palki, Jeromy	3	3	4.15	26	0	0	1	43	51	21	20	16	48	.293	R	R	6-0	200	4-14-76	1995	Oakland, Ore.
Randall, Scott	12	0	3.25	19	15	2	0	105	110	47	38	24	54	.266	R	R	6-3	200	10-29-75	1995	Goleta, Calif.
Rincon, Juan	7	4	4.78	19	16	3	0	102	111	56	54	35	75	.277	R	R	5-11	190	1-23-79	1996	Maracaibo, Venez.
Rodriguez, Jose	0	0	0.00	4	0	0	1	6	4	0	0	1	6	.200	L	L	6-1	200	12-18-74	1997	Cayey, P.R.
2-team (22 Memphis)	2	1	2.63	26	0	0	3	24	30	13	7	8	20	.312							
Sampson, Benj	3	1	7.01	13	8	0	0	51	69	41	40	19	19	.327	R	L	6-2	210	4-27-75	1993	Plymouth, Minn.
Santana, Johan	5	2	3.14	11	9	0	0	49	37	24	17	27	75	.202	L	L	6-0	190	3-13-79	1996	Tovar, Venez.
Sneed, John	0	0	0.00	1	0	0	0	1	0	0	0	2	1	.000	L	R	6-7	250	6-30-76	1997	Houston, Texas
Thomas, Brad	6	12	5.74	28	27	1	0	152	175	112	97	54	97	.291	L	L	6-4	220	10-22-77	1995	Sydney, Australia
Trombley, Mike	0	1	5.19	9	0	0	0	9	11	6	5	2	13	.314	R	R	6-2	200	4-14-67	1989	Fort Myers, Fla.
Wells, Bob	0	1	6.75	4	2	0	1	4	5	3	3	2	1	.312	R	R	6-0	200	11-1-66	1989	Cowiche, Wash.

FIELDING

Catcher	PCT	G	PO	A	E	DP	PB
LeCroy	.987	10	71	6	1	1	2
Marsters	.981	56	381	23	8	5	2
Smith	.984	10	59	3	1	1	2
Valentin	.990	71	482	39	5	5	6

First Base	PCT	G	PO	A	E	DP
Blake	1.000	6	49	3	0	4
Cuddyer	1.000	6	43	4	0	6
LeCroy	1.000	8	69	3	0	8
Sears	.997	121	931	52	3	93
Valentin	1.000	1	8	0	0	0

Second Base	PCT	G	PO	A	E	DP
Blake	1.000	7	6	19	0	2

	PCT	G	PO	A	E	DP
Borrego	.977	14	21	21	1	6
Canizaro	.971	58	101	136	7	32
Lamb	1.000	3	5	6	0	0
Morris	.948	25	37	55	5	14
Prieto	.983	32	64	111	3	25
Salazar	.926	7	7	18	2	2

Third Base	PCT	G	PO	A	E	DP
Blake	.961	111	76	216	12	14
Canizaro	1.000	4	1	8	0	0
Cuddyer	1.000	2	1	5	0	0
Dillon	1.000	2	0	1	0	0
Morris	.833	2	1	4	1	1
Prieto	.917	15	9	24	3	3
Valentin	.826	9	7	12	4	1

Shortstop	PCT	G	PO	A	E	DP
Lamb	.963	115	173	294	18	77
Morris	1.000	1	0	1	0	1
Prieto	.946	26	29	76	6	15

Outfield	PCT	G	PO	A	E	DP
Blake	1.000	6	4	1	0	0
Buchanan	1.000	1	1	0	0	0
Cuddyer	.960	74	160	10	7	2
Ford	.964	46	126	8	5	1
Green	1.000	69	169	0	0	0
Kielty	1.000	2	2	0	0	0
Restovich	.976	124	224	20	6	5
Ryan	.987	111	218	9	3	0

NEW BRITAIN ROCK CATS

Class AA

EASTERN LEAGUE

BATTING	AVG	G	AB	R	H	2B	3B	HR	RBI	BB	SO	SB	CS	SLG	OBP	B	T	HT	WT	DOB	1st Yr	Resides
Baron, Brian	.295	117	390	46	115	22	0	1	34	20	47	3	1	.359	.334	L	R	5-11	200	9-12-78	2001	Santa Clarita, Calif.
Bolivar, Papo	.278	137	547	78	152	35	2	13	87	47	98	18	5	.420	.332	R	R	5-9	200	10-18-78	1995	La Guaira, Venez.
Borrego, Ramon	.200	2	5	1	1	0	0	0	0	0	2	0	0	.200	.200	S	R	5-10	170	6-7-78	1995	Mariara, Venez.
Connacher, Kevin	.244	117	356	48	87	25	3	13	47	42	86	25	10	.441	.322	R	R	5-9	170	4-6-75	1997	West Palm Beach, Fla.
Dillon, Joe	.262	103	344	47	90	20	2	9	50	54	62	3	1	.410	.368	R	R	6-2	200	8-2-75	1997	Rocklin, Calif.
Ford, Lew	.311	93	373	81	116	27	2	15	51	49	47	17	5	.515	.401	R	R	6-0	190	8-12-76	1999	Lufkin, Texas
Green, Chad	.329	20	76	12	25	3	2	3	13	5	11	4	3	.539	.366	S	R	5-10	180	6-28-75	1996	Cincinnati, Ohio
Hodge, Kevin	.192	41	52	4	10	1	0	1	5	5	15	1	3	.269	.283	R	R	5-11	180	10-28-76	1998	Bryan, Texas
Lorenzo, Juan	.270	78	215	33	58	6	1	2	19	8	22	1	2	.335	.304	S	R	5-11	180	11-10-78	1995	Cambito Garabitos, D.R.
Marsters, Brandon	.237	22	76	12	18	8	0	2	13	7	18	0	0	.421	.310	R	R	5-11	200	3-14-75	1996	Sarasota, Fla.
Morneau, Justin	.298	126	494	72	147	31	4	16	80	42	88	7	0	.474	.356	L	R	6-4	200	5-15-81	1999	Fort Myers, Fla.
Rabe, Josh	.235	46	183	21	43	10	0	1	18	10	30	4	1	.306	.282	R	R	6-2	210	10-15-78	2000	Mendon, Ill.
Rodriguez, Luis	.257	129	455	60	117	18	2	8	40	61	44	3	2	.358	.349	S	R	5-9	170	6-27-80	1997	Cojedes, Venez.
Salazar, Ruben	.278	103	371	49	103	24	2	4	41	27	72	4	0	.385	.329	R	R	5-10	180	1-16-78	1997	San Felix, Venez.
Scanlon, Matt	.193	68	197	24	38	6	2	3	15	6	39	4	1	.289	.270	L	R	5-11	180	6-19-78	1999	Richfield, Minn.
Smith, Jeff	.296	90	297	40	88	15	0	11	48	21	47	1	2	.458	.348	L	R	6-3	210	6-17-74	1995	Naples, Fla.
Smith, Nestor	.000	5	9	2	0	0	0	0	1	0	5	1	0	.000	.000	S	R	5-11	200	1-21-78	1995	Maturin, Venez.
Sosa, Nick	.071	4	14	0	1	0	0	0	1	0	7	0	0	.071	.133	R	R	6-2	200	7-18-77	1996	Longwood, Fla.
Torres, Gabby	.272	73	191	21	52	13	1	2	24	28	26	0	2	.382	.371	R	R	5-10	200	3-22-78	1995	Acarigua, Venez.
Williams, Brady	.059	8	17	0	1	0	0	0	0	3	8	0	0	.059	.200	R	R	6-1	180	10-18-79	1999	Dunedin, Fla.

PITCHING	W	L	ERA	G	GS	CG	SV	IP	H	R	ER	BB	SO	AVG	B	T	HT	WT	DOB	1st Yr	Resides
Carnes, Matt	7	3	2.86	21	0	0	1	44	33	16	14	14	42	.210	R	R	6-3	200	8-18-75	1997	Miami, Okla.
Eyre, Willie	6	4	3.24	28	0	0	2	50	40	21	18	21	43	.219	R	R	6-1	190	7-21-78	1998	Magna, Utah
Fisher, Pete	0	4	8.06	6	4	0	0	22	38	25	20	12	15	.376	R	R	6-3	220	7-7-77	1998	Stoneham, Mass.
Flohr, Adam	4	5	2.40	43	7	0	0	82	83	35	22	19	47	.265	L	L	6-2	190	3-29-77	1998	Liberty Lake, Wash.
Hoard, Brent	11	8	3.69	31	26	2	0	161	153	80	66	52	126	.252	R	L	6-4	210	11-3-76	1998	San Francisco, Calif.
Hodge, Kevin	3	2	2.97	24	0	0	6	30	22	11	10	8	28	.000	R	R	5-11	180	10-28-76	1998	Bryan, Texas
Jerzembeck, Mike	1	0	2.25	3	2	0	0	8	4	2	2	2	7	.148	R	R	6-1	180	5-18-72	1993	Sanford, N.C.
Kinney, Matt	0	0	6.75	1	1	0	0	4	4	4	3	1	3	.250	R	R	6-5	220	12-16-76	1995	Bangor, Maine
Manning, David	3	3	4.62	11	10	0	0	62	69	37	32	27	38	.296	R	R	6-3	210	8-14-72	1992	West Palm Beach, Fla.
Mays, Joe	1	0	1.29	1	1	0	0	7	2	1	1	1	5	.086	S	R	6-1	190	12-10-75	1995	Sarasota, Fla.
McDonald, Jon	3	8	6.10	21	12	0	0	72	77	58	49	47	28	.275	R	R	6-3	190	10-16-77	2000	Orlando, Fla.
Mills, Ryan	3	11	5.37	26	21	0	0	106	117	80	63	68	68	.276	R	L	6-6	200	7-21-77	1998	Scottsdale, Ariz.
Padilla, Juan	3	5	3.31	54	0	0	29	65	69	30	24	18	52	.267	R	R	6-0	190	2-17-77	1998	Levittown, P.R.
Palki, Jeromy	3	3	3.17	30	0	0	2	48	45	19	17	17	52	.244	R	R	6-0	200	4-14-76	1995	Oakland, Ore.
Pridie, Jon	5	3	5.07	16	15	1	0	94	95	53	53	46	70	.266	R	R	6-4	220	12-7-79	1998	Prescott, Ariz.
Randall, Scott	2	0	3.48	5	5	0	0	31	25	13	12	4	19	.215	R	R	6-3	200	10-29-75	1995	Goleta, Calif.
Sampson, Benj	5	5	3.41	16	16	2	0	98	91	44	37	18	43	.256	R	L	6-2	210	4-27-75	1993	Plymouth, Minn.
Schoening, Brent	3	1	5.17	21	8	0	0	63	60	44	36	23	57	.250	R	R	6-1	190	4-7-78	1999	Houston, Texas
Silva, Doug	0	0	6.75	4	2	0	0	9	13	7	7	8	5	.333	R	R	6-3	190	7-8-79	1997	Miranda, Venez.
Sneed, John	3	7	5.04	39	9	0	1	91	96	57	51	43	80	.272	L	R	6-7	250	6-30-76	1997	Houston, Texas
Sturdy, Tim	1	0	6.37	35	0	0	0	54	63	49	38	29	21	.293	R	R	6-2	180	10-8-78	1997	Albuquerque, N.M.

FIELDING

Catcher	PCT	G	PO	A	E	DP	PB
Marsters	1.000	22	151	16	0	1	1
J. Smith	.986	80	493	58	8	4	3
Torres	.986	48	242	30	4	3	9

First Base	PCT	G	PO	A	E	DP
Dillon	1.000	8	71	3	0	7
Hodge	1.000	6	55	7	0	3
Morneau	.989	125	1061	96	13	98
Williams	1.000	3	12	0	0	0

Second Base	PCT	G	PO	A	E	DP
Connacher	.977	83	167	209	9	46
Hodge	1.000	1	1	2	0	0

Lorenzo	1.000	6	5	7	0	3
Rodriguez	.938	8	17	28	3	6
Salazar	.970	50	111	112	7	30

Third Base	PCT	G	PO	A	E	DP
Borrego	.778	2	2	5	2	0
Dillon	.929	76	63	184	19	15
Hodge	.944	6	3	14	1	1
Lorenzo	.853	32	26	61	15	3
Scanlon	.882	22	15	60	10	5
Williams	.947	5	5	13	1	0

Shortstop	PCT	G	PO	A	E	DP
Lorenzo	.989	35	34	56	1	10

Rodriguez	.973	119	203	375	16	74

Outfield	PCT	G	PO	A	E	DP
Baron	.986	109	200	6	3	1
Bolivar	.985	114	186	10	3	0
Connacher	.909	27	19	1	2	0
Ford	.986	93	202	6	3	3
Green	.976	20	38	3	1	0
Hodge	1.000	1	2	0	0	0
Lorenzo	.000	2	0	0	0	0
Rabe	1.000	46	97	5	0	1
Scanlon	1.000	24	28	1	0	1

FORT MYERS MIRACLE

FLORIDA STATE LEAGUE

BATTING	AVG	G	AB	R	H	2B	3B	HR	RBI	BB	SO	SB	CS	SLG	OBP	B	T	HT	WT	DOB	1st Yr	Resides
Bartlett, Jason	.262	39	145	24	38	7	0	2	9	17	24	11	2	.352	.341	R	R	6-0	170	10-30-79	2001	Lodi, Calif.
Boitel, Rafael	.240	81	254	28	61	10	3	1	28	15	48	11	3	.315	.284	S	L	6-1	170	1-21-81	1998	Lehigh Acres, Fla.
Bowen, Rob	.184	100	342	52	63	12	1	10	49	38	69	1	0	.313	.272	S	R	6-2	210	2-24-81	1999	Fort Myers, Fla.
Garbe, B.J.	.239	115	427	46	102	13	2	5	45	36	89	18	6	.314	.305	R	R	6-2	190	2-3-81	1999	Moses Lake, Wash.
Gulledge, Kelley	.269	76	242	29	65	9	0	6	34	20	60	0	2	.380	.349	R	R	6-1	210	1-25-79	2000	Arlington, Texas
Howarth, Jason	.136	8	22	1	3	0	0	0	2	2	7	0	0	.136	.208	R	R	5-11	180	3-13-80	2002	Germantown, Tenn.
Maza, Luis	.241	105	344	44	83	15	3	4	38	19	53	4	6	.337	.302	R	R	5-9	180	6-22-80	1997	Cumana, Venez.
Rabe, Josh	.340	85	297	60	101	23	2	5	40	44	36	16	4	.481	.427	R	R	6-2	210	10-15-78	2000	Mendon, Ill.
Renick, Josh	.272	107	368	61	100	14	1	1	26	44	58	10	10	.323	.359	R	R	5-9	180	12-28-78	2001	Sarasota, Fla.
Reyes, Deurys	.240	90	229	48	55	9	8	5	32	43	59	8	7	.415	.362	L	L	5-11	150	8-8-79	1996	Santo Domingo, D.R.
Rivas, Luis	.091	6	22	1	2	0	1	0	3	2	2	1	0	.182	.167	R	R	5-11	170	8-30-79	1995	La Guaira, Venez.
Sandberg, Eric	.231	19	65	5	15	5	0	0	8	6	13	0	0	.308	.306	L	L	6-1	210	8-15-79	1998	Spokane, Wash.
Scanlon, Matt	.323	47	164	28	53	8	2	6	37	19	11	1	1	.506	.398	L	R	5-11	180	6-19-78	1999	Richfield, Minn.
Sosa, Nick	.278	25	90	10	25	9	0	1	14	15	27	1	0	.411	.389	R	R	6-2	200	7-18-77	1996	Longwood, Fla.
Tiffee, Terry	.281	126	473	47	133	31	0	8	64	25	49	0	3	.397	.316	S	R	6-3	210	4-21-79	1999	N. Little Rock, Ark.
Torres, Digno	.174	48	138	9	24	3	0	0	11	17	36	0	2	.196	.270	L	L	6-4	190	8-27-79	1999	Morovis, P.R.
Watkins, Tommy	.234	94	269	38	63	10	2	2	24	29	46	10	5	.294	.314	R	R	5-7	180	6-18-80	1998	Fort Myers, Fla.
West, Kevin	.275	129	444	62	122	25	4	12	64	46	96	7	4	.430	.351	R	R	6-2	190	1-1-80	1999	Redwood Valley, Calif.
Williams, Brady	.234	50	141	26	33	7	0	7	26	27	49	2	0	.433	.351	R	R	6-1	180	10-18-79	1999	Dunedin, Fla.

PITCHING	W	L	ERA	G	GS	CG	SV	IP	H	R	ER	BB	SO	AVG	B	T	HT	WT	DOB	1st Yr	Resides
Bonilla, Henry	3	1	5.04	19	0	0	1	30	39	19	17	7	18	.309	R	R	6-0	190	8-16-79	2000	Reno, Nev.
Cento, Tony	2	3	3.74	15	2	0	1	34	32	14	14	14	23	.250	L	L	5-11	170	8-16-77	1999	Edgewood, Ky.
Contreras, J.C.	2	2	3.63	31	0	0	1	45	38	21	18	26	43	.231	L	L	6-0	150	4-24-82	1998	Caracas, Venez.
Corona, Ronnie	4	4	2.25	23	5	0	2	60	46	22	15	26	75	.206	R	R	6-0	180	1-27-79	2000	Apple Valley, Calif.
Cressend, Jack	1	0	3.60	3	1	0	0	5	4	2	2	2	5	.210	R	R	6-1	190	5-13-75	1996	Mandeville, La.
Daws, Josh	2	0	2.08	21	0	0	2	22	17	7	5	6	13	.212	R	R	5-10	190	12-8-78	2001	Palm Beach, Fla.
Eyre, Willie	4	1	2.41	19	0	0	2	34	28	9	9	13	25	.233	R	R	6-1	200	7-21-78	1999	Magna, Utah
Fisher, Pete	1	0	3.38	4	0	0	0	5	5	2	2	2	2	.277	R	R	6-3	220	7-7-77	1998	Stoneham, Mass.
Foote, Joe	12	7	3.11	26	23	2	0	145	141	64	50	35	92	.255	R	R	6-4	200	8-30-79	1997	Bradenton, Fla.
Hodge, Kevin	3	0	0.61	10	0	0	3	15	10	1	1	3	18	.192	R	R	5-11	180	10-28-79	1998	Bryan, Texas
Holubec, Ken	5	6	3.22	26	24	1	0	112	93	46	40	44	125	.227	L	L	6-0	220	9-1-78	2000	Houma, La.
Kemp, Beau	3	2	0.66	59	0	0	29	68	49	14	5	18	49	.202	R	R	6-0	180	10-31-80	2000	Tulsa, Okla.
Kinney, Matt	0	0	0.00	1	1	0	0	5	4	2	0	3	5	.222	R	R	6-5	220	12-16-76	1995	Bangor, Maine
Lamber, Justin	0	0	3.86	5	0	0	0	7	13	7	3	6	5	.419	R	L	6-0	210	5-22-76	1997	Hackensack, N.J.
Lincoln, Jeff	9	9	4.66	24	22	0	0	116	138	68	60	46	78	.302	R	R	6-2	180	4-30-78	2000	Citrus Heights, Calif.
Martin, Luke	0	0	12.71	3	0	0	0	6	8	8	5	7	7	.320	L	L	5-10	200	8-29-78	2000	Fort Myers, Fla.
Mays, Joe	1	2	2.08	3	3	0	0	9	9	2	2	3	7	.272	S	R	6-1	190	12-10-75	1995	Sarasota, Fla.
McDonald, Jon	1	0	4.66	2	2	0	0	10	13	7	5	3	5	.309	R	R	6-3	190	10-16-77	2000	Orlando, Fla.
Moseley, Marcus	2	2	5.16	35	2	0	1	61	64	39	35	51	47	.271	R	R	6-3	230	8-12-80	1998	Hohenwald, Tenn.
Murray, Steve	2	1	3.12	8	0	0	0	9	11	3	3	3	8	.305	L	L	6-1	200	6-29-80	1998	Ennismore, Ontario
Persby, Andy	3	2	8.24	25	0	0	0	44	54	40	40	33	33	.298	R	R	6-4	240	5-2-78	2000	North St. Paul, Minn.
Pridie, Jon	4	4	3.27	12	12	0	0	66	62	29	24	30	40	.248	R	R	6-4	220	12-7-79	1998	Prescott, Ariz.
Radke, Brad	0	1	3.12	2	2	0	0	9	11	6	3	0	6	.289	R	R	6-2	180	10-27-72	1991	Largo, Fla.
Romero, Josmir	6	3	4.20	18	13	1	0	79	78	43	37	25	52	.256	R	R	6-2	190	11-18-80	1997	Guarenas, Venez.
Schoening, Brent	0	2	7.30	4	3	0	0	12	14	12	10	10	10	.304	R	R	6-1	190	4-7-78	1999	Houston, Texas
Silva, Doug	1	2	1.74	17	1	0	0	31	19	6	6	7	26	.177	R	R	6-3	190	7-8-79	1997	Miranda, Venez.
Trombley, Mike	0	0	0.00	1	0	0	0	2	2	1	0	0	3	.250	R	R	6-2	200	4-14-67	1989	Fort Myers, Fla.
Weis, Brad	1	0	1.66	13	0	0	0	22	16	7	4	8	22	.205	L	L	6-1	190	11-29-77	1999	Winter Park, Fla.
Wolfe, Brian	6	9	4.64	25	23	0	0	132	160	84	68	34	85	.299	R	R	6-2	190	11-29-80	1999	Irvine, Calif.

FIELDING

Catcher	PCT	G	PO	A	E	DP	PB
Bowen	.981	88	554	68	12	8	12
Gulledge	.993	58	389	25	3	7	8

First Base	PCT	G	PO	A	E	DP
Bowen	1.000	1	1	0	0	0
Sandberg	.979	14	128	10	3	11
Scanlon	1.000	2	1	0	0	0
Sosa	.978	11	85	5	2	9
Tiffee	.991	77	641	58	6	70
Torres	.992	46	322	38	3	41
Williams	1.000	1	3	0	0	1

Second Base	PCT	G	PO	A	E	DP
Bartlett	.000	1	0	0	0	0

Maza	.950	24	34	62	5	7
Renick	.976	98	193	258	11	76
Rivas	.900	6	6	12	2	1
Scanlon	1.000	1	2	3	0	2
Watkins	.984	19	22	40	1	11
Williams	1.000	1	1	2	0	1

Third Base	PCT	G	PO	A	E	DP
Bartlett	1.000	2	1	3	0	0
Scanlon	.919	40	22	69	8	6
Tiffee	.912	39	19	64	8	5
Watkins	.907	33	20	48	7	9
Williams	.900	43	25	65	10	6

Shortstop	PCT	G	PO	A	E	DP
Bartlett	.948	29	52	75	7	22
Howarth	.923	7	8	16	2	2
Maza	.915	74	97	192	27	47
Watkins	.935	41	75	111	13	28

Outfield	PCT	G	PO	A	E	DP
Boitel	.987	73	147	3	2	0
Garbe	.987	104	225	10	3	3
Rabe	.983	73	112	5	2	0
Reyes	.983	75	106	7	2	4
Scanlon	1.000	1	3	0	0	0
Watkins	1.000	3	7	0	0	0
West	.970	117	118	13	6	4

MIDWEST LEAGUE

BATTING	AVG	G	AB	R	H	2B	3B	HR	RBI	BB	SO	SB	CS	SLG	OBP	B	T	HT	WT	DOB	1st Yr	Resides
Abram, Matt	.223	80	242	23	54	9	0	6	32	19	51	1	3	.335	.291	R	R	6-0	170	6-13-80	2001	Scottsdale, Ariz.
Agar, Cory	.151	15	53	4	8	2	0	0	3	14	0	0	0	.170	.224	R	R	5-10	210	4-9-81	2000	Palm Harbor, Fla.
Bowen, Rob	.190	5	21	1	4	1	0	0	2	4	0	0	0	.238	.261	S	R	6-2	210	2-24-81	1999	Fort Myers, Fla.
Davidson, Seth	.230	56	209	22	48	8	0	2	24	19	14	4	4	.297	.306	S	R	6-0	170	2-26-79	2001	San Diego, Calif.
Huff, Ken	.157	32	102	8	16	6	0	0	1	3	36	1	1	.216	.179	L	L	5-11	210	9-17-79	2001	Phoenix, Ariz.
Jones, Garrett	.202	63	223	21	45	8	0	10	32	11	82	3	1	.372	.238	L	L	6-4	200	6-21-81	1999	Tinley Park, Ill.
Kennedy, Bryan	.279	69	215	28	60	12	2	3	27	29	35	0	1	.395	.386	L	R	6-2	200	10-4-78	2001	Riverside, Calif.
Kubel, Jason	.321	115	424	60	136	26	4	17	69	41	48	3	5	.521	.380	L	R	5-11	190	5-25-82	2000	Palmdale, Calif.
Kuhaulua, Kaulana	.231	73	264	33	61	10	1	5	23	13	64	9	5	.333	.295	R	R	6-0	160	1-30-80	2001	Waianae, Hawaii
Manning, Ricky	.180	24	61	8	11	1	0	0	2	4	15	3	0	.197	.239	L	L	5-11	180	11-18-80	1999	Los Angeles, Calif.
Mauer, Jake	.226	84	252	37	57	9	0	0	20	26	25	2	0	.262	.334	R	R	6-2	170	12-20-78	2001	St. Paul, Minn.
Mauer, Joe	.302	110	411	58	124	23	1	4	62	61	42	0	0	.392	.393	L	R	6-4	220	4-19-83	2001	Fort Myers, Minn.
Merchan, Jesus	.279	92	308	47	86	18	1	3	31	22	35	8	0	.373	.336	R	R	5-11	170	3-26-81	1999	Maracay Venez.
Oeltjen, Trent	.240	10	25	4	6	1	0	0	1	3	2	1	0	.280	.321	L	L	6-1	180	2-28-83	2001	New South Wales, Australia
Quickstad, Barry	.140	42	107	12	15	1	0	0	3	20	47	5	2	.150	.292	L	R	6-1	190	7-20-80	2001	Waseca, Minn.
Sandoval, Michael	.260	119	438	64	114	23	2	9	60	39	62	2	2	.384	.343	R	R	5-10	200	7-8-81	1997	Puerto Cabello, Venez.
Tamburrino, Brett	.266	87	320	40	85	21	3	4	33	38	78	9	3	.388	.347	S	R	5-11	190	11-10-81	1998	Sunbury, Australia
Tomlin, James	.272	105	427	62	116	17	1	3	27	34	58	18	13	.337	.337	L	L	5-11	170	8-12-82	2000	Los Angeles, Calif.
Tope, Stephen	.258	72	260	42	67	16	1	10	47	22	76	2	0	.442	.333	R	R	6-0	190	1-12-82	1999	Perth, Australia
Torres, Digno	.274	52	186	18	51	12	3	3	31	15	36	0	1	.419	.327	L	L	5-11	190	8-27-79	1999	Morovis, P.R.

PITCHING	W	L	ERA	G	GS	CG	SV	IP	H	R	ER	BB	SO	AVG	B	T	HT	WT	DOB	1st Yr	Resides
Abbott, Jim	4	8	3.90	29	21	0	0	132	129	64	57	43	106	.255	R	R	6-3	190	10-12-79	1999	Caledonia, Mich.
Bowyer, Travis	4	4	2.16	39	9	0	3	92	74	28	22	46	90	.223	R	R	6-3	210	8-3-81	1999	Big Island, Va.
Contreras, J.C.	0	0	1.62	11	0	0	0	17	14	4	3	3	21	.218	L	L	6-0	150	4-24-82	1998	Caracas, Venez.
Crain, Jesse	1	1	1.50	9	0	0	1	12	6	3	2	4	11	.153	R	R	6-1	200	7-5-81	2002	Louisville, Colo.
Daws, Josh	1	3	2.43	26	0	0	17	30	26	14	8	13	36	.232	R	R	5-10	190	12-8-78	2001	Palm Beach, Fla.
Durbin, J.D.	13	4	3.19	27	27	0	0	161	144	66	57	51	163	.238	R	R	6-0	180	2-24-82	2000	Scottsdale, Ariz.
Gates, Brian	0	1	5.30	11	0	0	1	19	28	14	11	5	11	.358	R	R	6-0	190	9-25-79	2001	Granite Bay, Calif.
Gutierrez, Jannio	6	4	1.85	31	0	0	7	44	23	14	9	22	59	.154	R	R	5-10	190	5-3-82	2001	Maracaibo, Venez.
Hemus, Jared	0	1	7.06	14	0	0	1	22	25	18	17	24	10	.308	L	L	5-11	160	1-1-81	2001	Spring Valley, Calif.
Hill, Josh	0	0	0.00	2	0	0	0	3	2	0	0	0	3	.200	R	R	6-2	190	3-27-83	2001	Warilla, Australia
Lohse, Eric	2	3	3.67	11	1	0	1	27	29	17	11	7	26	.261	R	R	6-0	190	6-5-80	2001	Glenn, Calif.
Miller, Colby	10	11	3.78	27	27	1	0	155	143	75	65	67	139	.249	R	R	6-2	180	3-19-82	2000	Weatherford, Okla.
Miller, Jason	2	2	2.34	23	8	0	0	65	55	23	17	22	71	.223	L	L	6-1	200	7-20-82	2000	Sarasota, Fla.
Pylate, Chad	1	0	4.71	15	0	0	1	29	28	18	15	24	13	.274	R	R	6-1	200	10-4-80	2001	Vancleave, Miss.
Richardson, Jason	11	9	5.31	23	23	0	0	127	127	80	75	56	96	.261	R	R	6-3	210	6-11-80	1999	Lakeland, Fla.
Romero, Josmir	1	3	2.68	9	6	1	0	37	31	12	11	9	36	.224	R	R	6-2	190	11-18-80	1997	Guarenas, Venez.
Sandberg, Eric	0	1	13.50	2	0	0	0	1	3	3	2	0	0	.600	L	L	6-1	210	8-15-79	1998	Spokane, Wash.
Serafini, Vince	0	3	4.50	30	0	0	1	50	64	32	25	21	32	.318	R	R	6-1	230	3-4-80	2001	Lockport, Ill.
Smart, Richard	0	4	4.97	7	0	0	0	13	12	7	7	6	12	.279	L	L	6-4	190	10-15-79	2000	Panama City, Fla.
Tejada, Sandy	9	4	2.76	14	14	1	0	91	70	32	28	23	78	.210	R	R	6-1	190	4-16-82	1998	Puerto Plata, D.R.
Vorwald, Matt	5	3	2.33	46	0	0	6	66	43	20	17	28	77	.189	R	R	6-2	180	11-29-79	2001	Freeport, Ill.

FIELDING

Catcher	PCT	G	PO	A	E	DP	PB
Abram	1.000	2	1	0	0	0	0
Agar	1.000	2	17	2	0	0	0
Bowen	1.000	4	24	0	0	0	0
Kennedy	1.000	50	357	31	0	2	7
Joe Mauer	.994	81	723	71	5	5	7

First Base	PCT	G	PO	A	E	DP
Abram	.990	15	88	8	1	6
Agar	1.000	6	53	2	0	0
Huff	1.000	19	127	8	0	7
Jones	.991	40	313	29	3	38
Joe Mauer	.990	13	95	7	1	12
Sandoval	1.000	6	27	4	0	4
Tope	.977	31	239	17	6	24
Torres	.978	26	159	17	4	15

Second Base	PCT	G	PO	A	E	DP
Davidson	1.000	1	1	4	0	2
Kuhaulua	.989	15	40	49	1	11
Jake Mauer	.993	66	126	162	2	45
Merchan	.967	32	56	62	4	9
Tamburrino	.971	35	64	106	5	16

Third Base	PCT	G	PO	A	E	DP
Abram	.700	9	2	5	3	0
Kuhaulua	.000	1	0	0	0	0
Jake Mauer	.917	4	2	9	1	1
Merchan	.896	16	10	33	5	5
Sandoval	.899	111	75	183	29	16
Tope	.818	3	2	7	2	0

Shortstop	PCT	G	PO	A	E	DP
Davidson	.961	50	86	158	10	36

Kuhaulua	.897	47	64	118	21	18
Jake Mauer	.967	7	16	13	1	4
Merchan	.944	38	45	91	8	16

Outfield	PCT	G	PO	A	E	DP
Abram	.966	42	54	2	2	0
Jones	1.000	3	3	0	0	0
Kubel	.982	113	158	7	3	0
Kuhaulua	.000	1	0	0	0	0
Manning	.935	22	29	0	2	0
Merchan	.000	1	0	0	0	0
Oeltjen	.938	10	15	0	1	0
Quickstad	.952	40	58	1	3	0
Tamburrino	.986	55	67	5	1	1
Tomlin	.973	103	209	6	6	3
Tope	1.000	30	37	3	0	0
Torres	.957	22	43	2	2	0

APPALACHIAN LEAGUE

BATTING	AVG	G	AB	R	H	2B	3B	HR	RBI	BB	SO	SB	CS	SLG	OBP	B	T	HT	WT	DOB	1st Yr	Resides
Agar, Cory	.283	27	92	9	26	3	0	3	13	4	11	0	0	.413	.333	R	R	5-10	210	4-9-81	2000	Palm Harbor, Fla.
Deeds, Doug	.325	59	203	48	66	16	1	7	32	41	41	3	1	.517	.438	L	L	6-2	180	6-2-81	2002	Columbus, Ohio
Elliott, Justin	.172	8	29	1	5	0	0	0	1	2	6	0	0	.172	.226	R	R	5-11	190	4-27-82	2002	Lakeland, Fla.
Gomon, Dusty	.302	53	199	43	60	7	2	14	41	22	54	1	0	.568	.372	R	R	6-3	200	9-3-82	2001	Jacksonville, Fla.
Guzman, Garrett	.279	63	247	41	69	21	4	6	48	18	37	3	2	.470	.334	L	L	5-9	160	2-7-83	2001	Henderson, Nev.
Hiraldo, Sandy	.254	36	122	23	31	3	1	8	27	8	28	4	1	.492	.305	S	R	5-10	170	1-24-82	1999	Santiago, D.R.
Lebron, Edgardo	.201	61	219	31	44	10	0	4	29	10	66	3	1	.301	.231	S	R	6-1	180	8-16-82	2000	Las Piedras, P.R.
Marin, Daniel	.228	33	101	16	23	4	1	1	15	14	14	1	1	.317	.331	R	R	5-11	180	3-2-83	1999	Anzoategui, Venez.
Martinez, Peter	.202	35	114	15	23	4	1	3	14	9	39	7	4	.333	.272	S	R	5-11	180	11-20-81	1999	Santo Domingo, D.R.
Matienzo, Danny	.304	33	112	15	34	7	0	5	27	13	18	1	0	.500	.379	R	R	5-10	190	9-3-80	2002	Miami, Fla.
Molina, Felix	.263	50	175	31	46	9	2	3	21	18	21	6	1	.389	.340	S	R	5-7	160	5-5-83	2001	Mayaguez, P.R.
Oeltjen, Trent	.298	54	215	36	64	7	2	3	18	16	34	7	5	.391	.363	L	L	6-1	180	2-28-83	2001	New South Wales, Australia
Sims, Justin	.248	37	109	18	27	4	1	3	13	16	21	1	2	.358	.354	R	R	5-10	180	12-18-80	2002	Knoxville, Tenn.

BATTING	AVG	G	AB	R	H	2B	3B	HR	RBI	BB	SO	SB	CS	SLG	OBP	B	T	HT	WT	DOB	1st Yr	Resides
Taylor, Sam	.226	48	146	25	33	5	0	1	10	22	22	8	5	.281	.335	S	R	5-7	150	11-6-82	2001	San Leandro, Calif.
Whitrock, Scott	.300	48	160	27	48	10	2	7	23	11	50	12	2	.519	.354	R	R	6-0	180	12-18-80	2001	Wisconsin Rapids, Wis.

GAMES BY POSITION: C—Agar 6, Elliott 8, Marin 32, Matienzo 26. **1B**—Agar 11, Gomon 48, Lebron 11. **2B**—Martinez 30, Molina 45. **3B**—Hiraldo 15, Lebron 51, Molina 6. **SS**—Hiraldo 22, Lebron 1, Taylor 47. **OF**—Deeds 35, Guzman 45, Oeltjen 53, Sims 28, Whitrock 43.

PITCHING	W	L	ERA	G	GS	CG	SV	IP	H	R	ER	BB	SO	AVG	B	T	HT	WT	DOB	1st Yr	Resides
Barrett, Ricky	7	1	1.27	12	11	0	0	64	49	15	9	25	79	.217	L	L	5-11	190	3-9-81	2002	West Sacramento, Calif.
Blackburn, Nick	3	3	5.00	13	13	0	0	67	70	41	37	21	62	.261	R	R	6-3	220	2-24-82	2002	Norman, Okla.
Crain, Jesse	2	1	0.57	9	0	0	2	16	4	2	1	7	18	.081	R	R	6-1	200	7-5-81	2002	Louisville, Colo.
DePaula, Julio	0	2	9.13	5	5	0	0	24	40	25	24	9	15	.380	R	R	6-0	160	12-31-82	1999	Santo Domingo, D.R.
Hemus, Jared	0	0	2.70	4	0	0	1	10	11	7	3	2	11	.255	L	L	5-11	160	1-1-81	2001	Spring Valley, Calif.
Henkenjohann, Tim	2	3	6.82	10	6	0	0	33	34	33	25	31	34	.255	L	R	6-5	200	9-3-80	2001	Niedersachsen, Germany
Hill, Josh	2	1	2.18	10	0	0	0	21	12	6	5	13	23	.166	R	R	6-2	200	3-27-83	2001	Warilla, Australia
Keeling, Justin	3	1	6.16	22	0	0	0	31	37	24	21	16	34	.303	L	L	5-11	190	3-29-81	2002	Oceanside, Calif.
Lohse, Eric	2	2	5.35	8	7	0	0	37	39	23	22	14	20	.272	R	R	6-0	190	6-5-80	2001	Glenn, Calif.
Neshek, Pat	0	2	0.99	23	0	0	15	27	13	6	3	6	41	.141	S	R	6-3	200	9-4-80	2002	Brooklyn Park, Minn.
Niedbalski, Nick	2	4	4.95	22	0	0	0	36	37	23	20	19	41	.253	R	L	6-2	190	11-3-80	2001	St. Louis, Mo.
Prunty, T.J.	3	7	4.45	13	10	0	0	63	77	38	31	9	42	.311	R	R	6-1	200	10-4-80	2001	Inver Grove Heights, Minn.
Pylate, Chad	0	0	8.44	4	0	0	0	5	4	5	5	5	2	.210	R	R	6-1	200	10-4-80	2001	Vancleave, Miss.
Simon, Janewrys	0	0	8.47	13	0	0	0	17	24	16	19	14	14	.333	R	R	6-0	200	2-9-82	1998	Imberto, D.R.
Smith, Ryan	2	2	2.45	23	2	0	3	40	26	13	11	24	52	.185	S	R	6-1	210	10-21-80	2001	West Covina, Calif.
Streich, Isaac	1	0	8.05	14	0	0	0	19	22	22	17	19	14	.289	R	R	6-2	190	12-5-79	2000	Rogers City, Mich.
Tyler, Scott	8	1	2.93	14	13	0	0	68	37	23	22	46	92	.160	R	R	6-5	210	8-20-82	2001	Downingtown, Pa.

FORT MYERS TWINS — Rookie

GULF COAST LEAGUE

BATTING	AVG	G	AB	R	H	2B	3B	HR	RBI	BB	SO	SB	CS	SLG	OBP	B	T	HT	WT	DOB	1st Yr	Resides
Arneson, Justin	.344	37	125	37	43	7	3	1	17	15	22	16	3	.472	.423	R	R	5-11	170	12-17-81	2002	Fergus Falls, Minn.
Bernstine, David	.225	31	89	9	20	3	0	0	4	6	16	2	0	.258	.317	R	R	6-3	220	8-3-80	2002	Vallejo, Calif.
Burgos, Jose	.277	50	188	30	52	10	0	1	29	13	42	6	5	.346	.335	R	R	6-2	215	11-11-82	2000	Maturin, Venez.
Elliott, Justin	.224	29	76	8	17	2	0	0	6	6	10	0	1	.250	.291	R	R	5-11	190	4-27-82	2002	Lakeland, Fla.
Fermin, Angelo	.285	57	193	39	55	4	4	2	29	35	25	19	5	.378	.397	S	R	5-9	150	11-6-83	2000	Santo Domingo, D.R.
Howarth, Jason	.333	3	6	3	2	0	0	0	0	1	0	1	0	.333	.429	R	R	5-11	180	3-13-80	2002	Germantown, Tenn.
Huether, J.D.	.238	47	164	21	39	9	0	1	24	12	12	2	2	.311	.288	R	R	6-0	200	5-17-80	2002	Fort Myers, Fla.
Johnson, Josh	.224	27	58	11	13	3	0	2	10	13	15	0	1	.379	.392	R	R	5-10	180	11-3-82	2001	Ridgway, Pa.
Liz, Jose	.298	41	131	17	39	9	3	2	23	6	17	4	5	.458	.326	R	R	6-3	180	5-16-81	1999	Santo Domingo, D.R.
Lopez, Javier	.253	34	87	12	22	2	1	1	10	7	16	2	1	.333	.353	R	R	6-2	190	10-19-82	2002	Juana Diaz, P.R.
Mendez, Jose	.250	6	16	2	4	0	0	0	1	2	4	0	0	.250	.316	R	R	5-9	160	7-17-83	1999	Bejuma, Venez.
Morales, Jose	.309	53	175	26	54	7	2	0	28	7	28	3	1	.371	.347	S	R	5-11	170	2-20-83	2001	Rio Piedras, P.R.
Patterson, Tarrence	.349	27	43	8	15	2	1	0	3	5	16	5	3	.442	.417	R	R	5-8	170	6-12-84	2002	Bartow, Fla.
Perodin, Ron	.325	37	123	20	40	4	2	0	9	7	13	9	2	.390	.371	L	L	6-0	170	10-13-80	2002	Los Angeles, Calif.
Phillips, Kyle	.198	35	101	10	20	4	1	1	12	14	18	0	0	.287	.293	L	R	6-2	190	4-3-84	2002	El Cajon, Calif.
Romero, Alex	.333	56	186	31	62	13	2	2	42	29	14	16	6	.457	.423	L	R	6-0	160	9-9-83	2000	Maracaibo, Venez.
Rutgers, Paul	.244	31	86	11	21	2	0	0	9	1	18	0	0	.267	.270	R	R	5-9	180	1-17-84	2001	Melbourne, Australia
Spataro, Ryan	.333	53	189	36	63	3	2	0	19	28	34	12	6	.370	.420	L	R	5-10	180	9-1-82	2001	Barrie, Ontario

GAMES BY POSITION: C—Elliott 29, Huether 1, Johnson 25, Mendez 6, Morales 1, Phillips 19. **1B**—Bernstine 22, Burgos 1, Huether 29, Lopez 14, Patterson 1, Phillips 6, Romero 1. **2B**—Arneson 6, Burgos 1, Fermin 2, Morales 41, Rutgers 25. **3B**—Burgos 45, Huether 16, Lopez 1, Morales 8. **SS**—Burgos 6, Fermin 53, Howarth 2, Morales 4, Rutgers 2. **OF**—Arneson 21, Liz 37, Lopez 10, Patterson 14, Perodin 27, Romero 51, Spataro 47.

PITCHING	W	L	ERA	G	GS	CG	SV	IP	H	R	ER	BB	SO	AVG	B	T	HT	WT	DOB	1st Yr	Resides
Brown, Jeremy	0	0	6.00	4	0	0	0	3	1	2	2	1	5	.100	R	R	6-3	210	1-3-79	2001	London, Ky.
Cahill, John	0	1	6.35	14	0	0	0	17	13	14	12	17	9	.228	R	R	6-3	190	3-30-83	2002	Lakewood, Calif.
Crawford, Tristan	6	2	4.28	20	1	0	2	27	24	22	13	18	18	.250	R	R	6-3	180	7-22-82	2000	Brisbane, Australia
Cressend, Jack	0	0	7.11	3	3	0	0	6	10	7	5	1	8	.357	R	R	6-1	190	5-13-75	1996	Mandeville, La.
DePaula, Julio	3	2	1.82	7	6	1	0	40	39	16	8	5	21	.254	R	R	6-0	160	12-31-82	1999	Santo Domingo, D.R.
Fisher, Pete	0	2	2.95	7	3	0	0	21	16	10	7	7	13	.202	R	R	6-3	220	7-7-77	1998	Stoneham, Mass.
Garcia, Angel	4	4	3.40	13	7	0	0	53	44	24	20	31	63	.216	R	R	6-6	200	10-28-83	2001	Dorado, P.R.
Garcia, Edwin	0	0	7.64	16	1	0	0	18	18	18	15	30	14	.264	R	R	6-0	170	8-2-83	2000	Santo Domingo, D.R.
Hader, Ryan	2	1	2.60	11	9	0	0	45	31	15	13	25	47	.202	R	L	6-4	240	3-3-83	2002	Blue Springs, Mo.
Harben, Adam	4	1	3.20	12	3	0	0	25	27	11	9	8	27	.270	R	R	6-5	210	8-19-83	2002	Maumelle, Ark.
Hill, Josh	1	1	3.54	14	0	0	2	20	17	8	8	11	21	.226	R	R	6-2	200	3-27-83	2001	Warilla, Australia
Jerzembeck, Mike	0	1	1.93	2	0	0	0	5	4	2	1	2	8	.235	R	R	6-1	180	5-18-72	1993	Sanford, N.C.
Jones, K.C	0	1	3.10	12	3	0	0	29	20	15	10	21	21	.190	R	R	6-6	210	6-30-84	2002	Eatonville, Wash.
Kinney, Matt	0	0	3.00	2	2	0	0	6	2	2	2	4	7	.100	R	R	6-5	220	12-16-76	1995	Bangor, Maine
McDonald, Jon	2	0	0.00	3	2	0	0	11	6	1	0	2	9	.157	R	R	6-3	190	10-16-77	2000	Orlando, Fla.
Medina, Dennis	3	4	2.63	11	8	2	0	62	60	24	18	11	40	.256	R	R	6-3	160	1-17-83	2001	Cabimas, Venez.
Merricks, Alex	2	0	1.80	9	2	0	1	15	9	4	3	16	13	.183	L	L	5-11	180	12-23-83	2002	Oxnard, Calif.
Mutch, Paul	5	3	2.95	12	8	0	1	58	49	28	19	20	39	.228	R	R	6-3	200	1-15-83	2001	Chermside, Australia
Radke, Brad	0	0	0.00	1	1	0	0	3	2	0	0	0	4	.181	R	R	6-2	180	10-27-72	1991	Largo, Fla.
Randazzo, Jeff	0	0	6.00	3	0	0	0	3	6	4	2	0	2	.400	R	L	6-7	200	8-12-81	1999	Broomall, Pa.
Wheldon, Rhys	2	2	3.00	15	1	0	0	30	23	12	10	15	24	.219	R	R	6-2	190	2-12-84	2001	Perth, Australia
Williams, Aaron	1	3	4.03	25	0	0	9	29	34	15	13	4	19	.298	R	R	6-2	180	10-7-80	2002	Oakfield, N.Y.

MONTREAL EXPOS

BY MICHAEL LEVESQUE

After entering the 2002 season poised for contraction, baseball's new collective bargaining agreement has removed that threat from the Expos until at least 2006, but turmoil still lingers over the franchise. Major League Baseball bought the franchise from Jeffrey Loria, who owned the club for two seasons. With the offseason in full swing, questions about where the Expos would play in 2003 and its overall long-term future had yet to be answered.

Whether or not the team will be moved to Washington, D.C., Portland, Ore., or Puerto Rico—or returned for another lame-duck year at Olympic Stadium—remained to be seen. But if the team is kept intact, there appears to be sufficient talent on hand for it to have an opportunity to win the National League East.

In first place in the National League East Division as late as May 2—and as close as 1½ games out on May 29—the Expos stumbled in June. They were 8½ games behind the Braves by month's end and fell in July even though general manager Omar Minaya made two blockbuster trades for Bartolo Colon and Cliff Floyd to strengthen the club. But the Expos won four straight and 11 of 14 to end the season 83-79, claiming second place in the NL East—the team's best finish since 1996.

The club continued to be led on the field by quiet superstar Vladimir Guerrero, who had a fifth consecutive season with more than 100 runs and 100 RBIs. He batted .336-39-111 with 106 runs. Guerrero, going into the final season of a long-term contract in 2003, set a team record with an NL-leading 206 hits and fell just short of the 40-40 milestone—he had 39 homers and 40 stolen bases.

Second baseman Jose Vidro also had another stellar year hitting .315-19-96 with 43 doubles despite battling injuries.

It was also a season of reunions, as a number of former Expos returned to the club. Andres Galarraga, Wil Cordero, Floyd (who was traded to the Red Sox after

Vladimir Guerrero   Don Levinski

PLAYERS OF THE YEAR

MAJOR LEAGUE: Vladimir Guerrero, of

Like the Yankees' Alfonso Soriano, Guerrero fell one homer shy of the 40-40 club as he finished with 39 homers and 40 steals. He still was the only National Leaguer to top 200 hits and ranked third in batting average at .336.

MINOR LEAGUE: Don Levinski, rhp

In his professional debut, Levinski controlled Midwest League hitters with his sinking two-seamer, mid-90s four-seamer and slider. But he'll never reach the majors with the Expos—he was dealt to the Marlins in the Cliff Floyd trade.

three weeks), and Jose Macias all came back after beginning their careers with the Expos. Wilton Guerrero, Dan Smith and Joey Eischen also returned for another go-around.

Expos manager Frank Robinson got 49 wins out of the team at Olympic Stadium, but the team went just 34-47 on the road. Montreal made 139 errors, more than any NL team except the Mets. Two righthanders counted on to carry a big part of the load—Javier Vazquez and Tony Armas—got off to bad starts and for most of the season weren't up to par. Vazquez fell to 10-13 after going 16-11 in 2001, and Armas won his last four decisions to finish 12-12.

Colon, acquired in trade with the Indians, ended up going 10-4 with both Cleveland and Montreal—20-8 for the season, while Tomo Ohka blossomed in his first full season going 13-8, 3.18 in 31 starts.

If the team is kept together, payroll is expected to jump from about $38 million to $55 million in 2003. Guerrero, Vidro and third baseman Fernando Tatis all have salary increases guaranteed in their multi-year deals, and nine players were eligible for salary arbitration.

In the minors, Double-A Harrisburg returned to the Eastern League playoffs for the 10th time in 12 seasons as an Expos affiliate, while Triple-A Ottawa and the Expos parted ways after the club had its first winning season since 1995. Ottawa will be replaced by Edmonton for the 2003 season.

Righthander Josh Karp, who turned 23 in September, emerged as the organization's top prospect after going a combined 11-6, 3.07 between Class A Brevard County and Harrisburg. He gave up just 114 hits in 132 innings in his first professional season after signing too late to pitch in 2001.

ORGANIZATION LEADERS

BATTING		
*AVG	Endy Chavez, Ottawa	.343
R	Terrmel Sledge, Ottawa/Harrisburg	86
H	Scott Hodges, Harrisburg	143
TB	Joe Vitiello, Ottawa	224
2B	Luis Ortiz, Ottawa	38
3B	Terrmel Sledge, Ottawa/Harrisburg	8
HR	Val Pascucci, Harrisburg	27
RBI	Joe Vitiello, Ottawa	82
	Val Pascucci, Harrisburg	82
BB	Val Pascucci, Harrisburg	93
SO	Lorvin Louisa, Clinton/Vermont	121
SB	Danny Rombley, Brevard County/Clinton	28

PITCHING		
W	Julio Manon, Ottawa/Harrisburg	13
L	Ignacio Puello, Clinton	14
#ERA	Bryan Hebson, Ottawa/Harrisburg	2.00
G	David Maust, Brevard County/Clinton	49
CG	Julio Manon, Ottawa/Harrisburg	2
SV	Todd Williams, Ottawa	24
IP	Darwin Marrero, Harrisburg/Brevard County	160
BB	Ignacio Puello, Clinton	66
SO	Julio Manon, Ottawa/Harrisburg	132

*Minimum 250 At-Bats #Minimum 75 Innings

MONTREAL EXPOS

Manager: Frank Robinson

BATTING	AVG	G	AB	R	H	2B	3B	HR	RBI	BB	SO	SB	CS	SLG	OBP	B	T	HT	WT	DOB	1st Yr	Resides
Barrett, Michael	.263	117	376	41	99	20	1	12	49	40	65	6	3	.418	.332	R	R	6-2	200	10-22-76	1995	Alpharetta, Ga.
Bergeron, Peter	.187	31	123	24	23	3	2	0	7	22	44	10	3	.244	.310	L	R	6-0	190	11-9-77	1996	St. Petersburg, Fla.
Cabrera, Orlando	.263	153	563	64	148	43	1	7	56	48	53	25	7	.380	.321	R	R	5-10	180	11-2-74	1994	Cartagena, Colombia
Carroll, Jamey	.310	16	71	16	22	5	3	1	6	4	12	1	0	.507	.347	R	R	5-10	170	2-18-74	1996	St. Petersburg, Fla.
Cepicky, Matt	.216	32	74	7	16	3	0	3	15	4	21	0	0	.378	.256	L	R	6-2	210	11-10-77	1999	Sun City Center, Fla.
Chavez, Endy	.296	36	125	20	37	8	5	1	9	5	16	3	5	.464	.321	L	L	6-0	170	2-7-78	1996	Valencia, Venez.
Collier, Lou	.091	13	11	3	1	1	0	0	0	1	3	0	0	.182	.231	R	R	5-10	190	8-21-73	1993	Chicago, Ill.
Cordero, Wil	.273	66	143	21	39	9	0	6	29	17	26	2	0	.462	.349	R	R	6-2	200	10-3-71	1988	Mayaguez, P.R.
Floyd, Cliff	.208	15	53	7	11	2	0	3	4	3	10	1	0	.415	.263	L	R	6-4	230	12-5-72	1991	Weston, Ill.
2-team (84 Florida)	.275	99	349	56	96	22	0	21	61	61	78	11	5	.519	.394							
Galarraga, Andres	.260	104	292	30	76	12	0	9	40	30	81	2	2	.394	.344	R	R	6-3	230	6-18-61	1979	West Palm Beach, Fla.
Guerrero, Vladimir	.336	161	614	106	206	37	2	39	111	84	70	40	20	.593	.417	R	R	6-3	210	2-9-76	1993	Nizao Bani, D.R.
Guerrero, Wilton	.194	44	62	3	12	1	0	0	1	1	19	5	0	.210	.206	S	R	6-0	170	10-24-74	1992	Nizao, D.R.
2-team (59 Cincinnati)	.221	103	140	12	31	2	1	0	5	7	32	7	1	.250	.259							
Macias, Jose	.255	90	231	33	59	17	1	7	33	13	44	5	6	.429	.294	S	R	5-10	180	1-25-72	1992	Panama City, Panama
Mateo, Henry	.174	22	23	1	4	0	1	0	2	6	2	0	.261	.240	S	R	5-11	180	10-14-76	1995	Santo Domingo, D.R.
Mordecai, Mike	.203	55	74	9	15	4	0	0	4	8	14	1	1	.257	.289	R	R	5-10	180	12-13-67	1989	Kennesaw, Ga.
O'Leary, Troy	.286	97	273	27	78	12	2	3	37	34	47	1	2	.377	.371	L	L	6-0	200	8-4-69	1987	Phoenix, Ariz.
Rodriguez, Henry	.050	20	20	1	1	0	0	0	3	4	8	0	0	.050	.200	L	L	6-2	220	11-8-67	1986	Santo Domingo, D.R.
Schneider, Brian	.275	73	207	21	57	19	2	5	29	21	41	1	2	.459	.339	L	R	6-1	200	11-26-76	1995	West Palm Beach, Fla.
Stevens, Lee	.190	63	205	28	39	6	1	10	31	39	57	1	0	.376	.318	L	L	6-4	230	10-3-67	1986	Highland Ranch, Colo.
Tatis, Fernando	.228	114	381	43	87	18	1	15	55	35	90	2	2	.399	.303	R	R	5-10	180	1-1-75	1993	San Pedro de Macoris, D.R.
Truby, Chris	.257	35	105	12	27	5	2	7	5	27	1	1	.400	.297	R	R	6-2	210	12-9-73	1993	Noblesville, Ind.
Vidro, Jose	.315	152	604	103	190	43	3	19	96	60	70	2	1	.490	.378	S	R	5-11	190	8-27-74	1992	Sabana Grande, P.R.
Wilkerson, Brad	.266	153	507	92	135	27	8	20	59	81	161	7	8	.469	.370	L	L	6-0	200	6-1-77	1999	Owensboro, Ky.

PITCHING	W	L	ERA	G	GS	CG	SV	IP	H	R	ER	BB	SO	AVG	B	T	HT	WT	DOB	1st Yr	Resides
Armas, Tony	12	12	4.44	29	29	0	0	164	149	87	81	78	131	.243	R	R	6-4	210	4-29-78	1994	Puerto Piritu, Venez.
Brower, Jim	1	2	4.83	30	0	0	0	41	39	22	22	22	33	.245	R	R	6-3	210	12-29-72	1994	Solana Beach, Calif.
2-team (22 Cincinnati)	3	2	4.37	52	0	0	0	80	77	40	39	32	57	.252							
Chen, Bruce	2	3	6.99	15	5	0	0	37	47	29	29	23	43	.303	L	L	6-1	210	6-19-77	1994	Panama City, Panama
Colon, Bartolo	10	4	3.31	17	17	4	0	117	115	48	43	39	74	.259	R	R	6-0	220	5-24-73	1994	Westlake, Ohio
Day, Zach	4	1	3.62	19	2	0	1	37	28	18	15	15	25	.207	R	R	6-4	180	6-15-78	1996	West Harrison, Ind.
Drew, Tim	1	0	2.81	7	1	0	2	16	12	8	5	2	10	.200	R	R	6-1	190	8-31-78	1997	Hahira, Ga.
Eischen, Joey	6	1	1.34	59	0	0	2	54	43	11	8	18	51	.223	L	L	6-0	215	5-25-70	1989	Rotonda West, Fla.
Herges, Matt	2	5	4.04	62	0	0	6	65	80	33	29	26	50	.305	L	R	6-0	200	4-1-70	1992	Champaign, Ill.
Kim, Sun-Woo	1	0	0.89	4	3	0	0	20	18	2	2	7	11	.250	R	R	6-2	180	9-4-77	1997	Seoul, Korea
Lloyd, Graeme	2	3	5.87	41	0	0	5	31	41	21	20	8	17	.325	L	L	6-7	230	4-9-67	1988	Gnarwarre, Australia
Ohka, Tomo	13	8	3.18	32	31	2	0	193	194	83	68	45	118	.263	R	R	6-1	180	3-18-76	1999	Kyoto, Japan
Pavano, Carl	3	8	6.30	15	14	0	0	74	98	55	52	31	51	.318	R	R	6-5	230	1-8-76	1994	Palm Beach Gardens, Fla.
Reames, Britt	1	4	5.03	42	6	0	0	68	70	42	38	38	76	.269	R	R	5-11	170	8-19-73	1995	Seneca, S.C.
Smith, Dan	1	1	3.47	33	0	0	2	47	34	18	18	21	34	.209	R	R	6-3	210	9-15-75	1993	Girard, Kan.
Stewart, Scott	4	2	3.09	67	0	0	17	64	49	29	22	22	67	.206	R	L	6-2	220	8-14-75	1994	Stanley, N.C.
Strickland, Scott	0	0	0.00	1	0	0	0	1	0	0	0	2	0	.000	R	R	5-11	180	4-26-76	1997	Spring, Texas
Tucker, T.J.	6	3	4.11	57	0	0	4	61	69	32	28	31	42	.289	R	R	6-3	240	8-20-78	1997	New Port Richey, Fla.
Vazquez, Javier	10	13	3.91	34	34	2	0	230	243	111	100	49	179	.271	R	R	6-2	190	7-25-76	1994	Ponce, P.R.
Vosberg, Ed	0	0	18.00	4	0	0	0	1	3	3	2	1	0	.428	L	L	6-1	200	9-28-61	1983	Tucson, Ariz.
Yoshii, Masato	4	9	4.11	31	20	1	0	131	143	66	60	32	74	.281	R	R	6-2	210	4-20-65	1998	Tokyo, Japan

FIELDING

Catcher	PCT	G	PO	A	E	DP	PB
Barrett	.989	110	751	55	9	9	9
Schneider	.993	65	382	34	3	6	3

First Base	PCT	G	PO	A	E	DP
Barrett	1.000	6	27	1	0	4
Cordero	1.000	10	66	5	0	6
Galarraga	.981	89	629	59	13	55
Mordecai	1.000	3	20	2	0	1
Stevens	.993	58	512	47	4	47
Truby	1.000	2	10	0	0	2
Wilkerson	1.000	23	179	15	0	25

Second Base	PCT	G	PO	A	E	DP
Carroll	.000	1	0	0	0	0
Collier	1.000	2	1	1	0	0
W. Guerrero	1.000	7	9	12	0	2
Macias	1.000	6	13	15	0	5

Mateo	1.000	3	2	8	0	1
Vidro	.986	152	314	448	11	93

Third Base	PCT	G	PO	A	E	DP
Carroll	.917	13	7	26	3	2
Collier	.000	1	0	0	0	0
W. Guerrero	.800	2	1	3	1	0
Macias	.941	22	10	38	3	0
Mordecai	.931	28	6	21	2	3
Tatis	.948	99	59	180	13	17
Truby	.924	31	13	48	5	4

Shortstop	PCT	G	PO	A	E	DP
Cabrera	.962	153	237	498	29	102
Carroll	.941	3	6	10	1	2
W. Guerrero	.933	7	7	7	1	3
Macias	.941	4	3	13	1	2
Mateo	.900	2	2	7	1	0

Mordecai	1.000	3	3	9	0	1

Outfield	PCT	G	PO	A	E	DP
Bergeron	.974	31	76	0	2	0
Cepicky	1.000	17	21	0	0	0
Chavez	.989	35	82	7	1	2
Collier	1.000	7	6	0	0	0
Cordero	.958	28	45	1	2	0
Floyd	.941	13	14	2	1	0
V. Guerrero	.969	161	298	14	10	4
W. Guerrero	1.000	12	11	1	0	0
Macias	.978	49	83	4	2	1
O'Leary	.977	71	126	1	3	0
Rodriguez	.000	5	0	0	0	0
Schneider	.000	2	0	0	0	0
Truby	.000	1	0	0	0	0
Wilkerson	.972	129	226	13	7	3

LARRY GOREN

ANTHONY DeFALCO

Jose Vidro: second on club in RBIs, tied for lead in doubles

Tomo Ohka: 13 wins led pitching staff

FARM SYSTEM

Director, Player Development: Adam Wogan

Class	Farm Team	League	W	L	Pct.	Finish*	Manager(s)	First Yr.
AAA	Ottawa (Ontario) Lynx	International	80	61	.567	3rd (14)	Tim Leiper	1993
AA	Harrisburg (Pa.) Senators	Eastern	79	63	.556	2nd (12)	Dave Huppert	1991
High A	Brevard County (Fla.) Manatees	Florida State	50	85	.370	12th (12)	Bob Didier, Tony Torchia	2002
Low A	Clinton (Iowa) Lumber Kings	Midwest	61	75	.449	11th (14)	Dave Machemer	2001
SS A	Vermont Expos	New York-Penn	30	45	.400	12th (14)	Dave Barnett	1994
Rookie	Melbourne (Fla.) Expos	Gulf Coast	28	32	.467	t-8th (14)	Andy Skeels	1998

*Finish in overall standings (No. of teams in league)

OTTAWA LYNX · Class AAA

INTERNATIONAL LEAGUE

BATTING	AVG	G	AB	R	H	2B	3B	HR	RBI	BB	SO	SB	CS	SLG	OBP	B	T	HT	WT	DOB	1st Yr	Resides
Ackerman, Scott	.258	12	31	4	8	1	0	2	7	0	8	0	0	.484	.250	R	R	6-1	210	4-23-79	1997	Oregon City, Ore.
Andreopoulos, Alex	.300	6	20	4	6	2	0	0	1	2	3	0	0	.400	.364	L	R	5-10	200	8-19-72	1995	Toronto, Ontario
Battle, Howard	.238	56	193	20	46	11	0	4	18	10	28	0	1	.358	.276	R	R	6-0	190	3-25-72	1990	Ocean Springs, Miss.
Bergeron, Peter	.291	104	340	51	99	9	4	1	29	39	65	7	7	.350	.364	L	R	6-0	190	11-9-77	1996	St. Petersburg, Fla.
Calloway, Ron	.264	128	447	72	118	21	5	14	60	44	89	16	12	.427	.335	L	L	6-1	210	9-4-76	1997	Los Banos, Calif.
Carroll, Jamey	.280	117	421	57	118	19	2	8	49	37	39	6	10	.392	.342	R	R	5-10	170	2-18-74	1996	St. Petersburg, Fla.
Chavez, Endy	.343	103	405	67	139	28	5	4	41	33	37	21	13	.467	.392	L	L	6-0	170	2-7-78	1996	Valencia, Venez.
Collier, Lou	.316	89	307	48	97	26	6	6	52	37	69	5	2	.498	.394	R	R	5-10	190	8-21-73	1993	Chicago, Ill.
de la Rosa, Tomas	.000	2	3	0	0	0	0	0	0	2	0	1	0	.000	.400	R	R	5-10	170	1-28-78	1996	Santo Domingo, D.R.
Figueroa, Luis	.146	27	82	6	12	1	1	0	9	3	14	0	2	.220	.186	S	R	5-9	140	2-16-74	1997	Vega Alta, P.R.
2-team (2 Norfolk)	.140	29	86	6	12	1	1	1	9	3	15	0	2	.209	.178							
Knorr, Randy	.257	100	338	31	87	24	1	8	38	32	53	0	0	.405	.321	R	R	6-2	210	11-12-68	1986	Tampa, Fla.
Machado, Albenis	.244	15	41	10	10	2	0	1	5	9	9	1	1	.366	.370	S	R	6-0	170	3-20-79	1996	Caracas, Venez.
Martinez, Sandy	.226	39	133	12	30	3	1	3	18	10	41	2	0	.331	.288	L	R	6-2	210	10-8-70	1990	Santo Domingo, D.R.
Mateo, Henry	.256	74	285	35	73	10	6	5	25	18	53	15	6	.386	.306	S	R	5-11	180	10-14-76	1995	Santo Domingo, D.R.
McKinley, Dan	.120	17	25	2	3	1	0	0	3	1	6	0	1	.160	.179	R	R	6-0	180	5-15-76	1997	Chandler, Ariz.
Medrano, Anthony	.270	53	174	20	47	8	1	1	13	18	22	5	0	.345	.352	R	R	5-10	170	12-8-74	1993	Long Beach, Calif.
2-team (74 Buffalo)	.240	127	438	48	105	18	3	2	43	38	47	12	1	.308	.311							
Mouton, James	.271	29	70	10	19	3	0	1	7	12	17	3	0	.357	.378	R	R	5-9	170	12-29-68	1991	Missouri City, Texas
Nunez, Jorge	.291	91	282	42	82	9	4	0	20	12	43	27	7	.351	.322	R	R	5-10	150	3-5-75	1995	Villa Mella, D.R.
O'Leary, Troy	.337	23	86	11	29	6	0	3	16	7	15	0	1	.512	.387	L	L	6-0	200	8-4-69	1987	Phoenix, Ariz.
Ortiz, Luis	.291	106	382	47	111	38	0	5	63	22	35	1	0	.429	.329	R	R	6-0	180	5-25-70	1991	North Richland, Texas
Phillips, Brandon	.257	10	35	1	9	4	0	1	5	2	6	0	0	.457	.297	R	R	5-11	180	6-28-81	1999	Stone Mountain, Ga.
Sledge, Terrmel	.263	24	80	12	21	5	2	1	11	11	15	1	1	.413	.359	L	L	6-0	180	3-18-77	1999	Granada Hills, Calif.
Vitiello, Joe	.329	119	431	57	142	34	0	16	82	39	58	1	0	.520	.390	R	R	6-3	230	4-11-70	1991	Stoneham, Mass.

PITCHING	W	L	ERA	G	GS	CG	SV	IP	H	R	ER	BB	SO	AVG	B	T	HT	WT	DOB	1st Yr	Resides
Agamennone, Brandon	5	1	3.69	27	1	0	1	54	58	22	22	21	38	.277	R	R	6-2	190	11-6-75	1998	Crofton, Md.
Ayala, Luis	0	0	3.52	6	0	0	0	8	7	3	3	4	6	.250	R	R	6-2	170	1-12-78	1997	Los Mochis, Mexico
Billingsley, Brent	4	5	4.07	28	12	0	1	86	75	39	39	32	67	.236	L	L	6-2	200	4-19-75	1996	Chino Hills, Calif.
Blank, Matt	11	7	3.24	31	25	1	0	147	134	67	53	55	92	.241	L	L	6-2	190	4-5-76	1997	Arlington, Texas
Buddie, Mike	4	4	4.07	29	0	0	2	42	34	21	19	23	18	.223	R	R	6-3	210	12-12-70	1992	Lutz, Fla.
Crumpton, Chuck	0	2	5.40	19	0	0	0	25	26	15	15	8	11	.273	R	R	6-4	210	12-30-76	1999	Mesquite, Texas
Cubillan, Darwin	1	1	3.50	29	0	0	6	36	28	16	14	21	35	.218	R	R	6-2	170	11-15-72	1994	Tampa, Fla.
Day, Zach	5	6	3.50	17	16	1	0	90	77	38	35	32	68	.231	R	R	6-4	180	6-15-78	1996	West Harrison, Ind.
Downs, Scott	2	1	5.79	17	0	0	0	23	31	21	15	3	15	.319	L	L	6-2	190	3-17-76	1997	Lexington, Ky.
Drew, Tim	6	3	2.87	13	13	0	0	85	77	31	27	24	29	.247	R	R	6-1	190	8-31-78	1997	Hahira, Ga.
2-team (15 Buffalo)	14	7	3.08	28	28	2	0	181	173	74	62	47	72	.254							
Eischen, Joey	1	0	0.00	11	0	0	4	14	8	4	0	3	15	.166	L	L	6-0	210	5-25-70	1989	Rotonda West, Fla.
Evans, Keith	0	5	2.22	16	2	0	0	28	29	15	7	10	15	.263	R	R	6-5	220	11-2-75	1996	San Pedro, Calif.
Fernandez, Osvaldo	3	2	4.26	18	5	0	0	44	46	27	21	16	28	.272	R	R	6-2	190	11-4-68	1996	Miami, Fla.
Gonzalez, Dicky	8	3	3.76	22	22	0	0	120	137	59	50	33	72	.289	R	R	5-11	170	12-21-78	1996	Bayamon, P.R.
2-team (1 Norfolk)	8	5	3.75	23	23	0	0	125	143	61	52	35	79	.288							
Hebson, Bryan	1	0	4.82	5	0	0	0	9	8	5	5	3	11	.222	R	R	6-5	210	3-12-76	1997	Phenix City, Ala.
Kim, Sun-Woo	3	0	1.24	7	7	1	0	44	29	11	6	16	28	.194	R	R	6-2	180	9-4-77	1997	Seoul, Korea
2-team (8 Pawtucket)	7	2	2.22	15	15	2	0	89	63	29	22	32	65	.200							
Manon, Julio	8	6	3.50	28	13	2	2	105	83	42	41	45	81	.217	L	R	6-0	200	6-10-73	1992	St. Petersburg, Fla.
McAvoy, Jeff	1	0	1.80	1	1	0	0	5	5	1	1	1	2	.263	R	R	6-3	210	3-15-77	2000	Palmer, Mass.
Pavano, Carl	3	0	3.10	3	3	0	0	20	23	8	7	2	9	.294	R	R	6-5	230	1-8-76	1994	Palm Beach Gardens, Fla.
Reames, Britt	3	2	2.79	7	7	0	0	42	31	16	13	14	26	.206	R	R	5-11	170	8-19-73	1995	Seneca, S.C.
Seale, Dustin	0	0	4.50	1	0	0	0	2	4	1	1	0	1	.400	L	L	6-1	190	12-2-77	1997	Safford, Ariz.
Smith, Dan	5	4	3.24	14	14	1	0	83	71	30	30	18	61	.231	R	R	6-3	210	9-15-75	1993	Girard, Kan.
Spencer, Sean	1	0	5.14	16	0	0	0	21	24	13	12	8	15	.300	L	L	5-11	180	5-29-75	1996	Port Orchard, Wash.
Williams, Todd	3	5	3.75	46	0	0	24	48	56	26	20	12	21	.297	R	R	6-3	210	2-13-71	1991	Syracuse, N.Y.
Winchester, Scott	2	2	6.00	21	0	0	1	33	33	24	22	11	22	.255	R	R	6-2	210	4-20-73	1995	Midland, Mich.

FIELDING

Catcher	PCT	G	PO	A	E	DP	PB
Ackerman	1.000	12	53	5	0	0	0
Andreopoulos	1.000	6	31	2	0	0	0
Knorr	.983	97	504	28	9	4	5
Martinez	.996	34	219	14	1	1	3

First Base	PCT	G	PO	A	E	DP
Battle	1.000	6	16	1	0	0
Collier	1.000	3	11	1	0	3
Ortiz	.988	34	306	17	4	29
Sledge	1.000	5	35	6	0	6
Vitiello	.996	102	901	73	4	98

Second Base	PCT	G	PO	A	E	DP
Carroll	.993	29	57	90	1	24
Collier	.972	15	30	40	2	11
Machado	.983	12	25	33	1	8

Third Base	PCT	G	PO	A	E	DP
Mateo	.980	53	119	175	6	43
Nunez	.976	42	82	124	5	30
Battle	.950	47	24	90	6	5
Carroll	.976	83	58	181	6	26
Collier	.852	17	6	40	8	2
De La Rosa	1.000	1	0	1	0	0
Medrano	.833	2	1	4	1	1

Shortstop	PCT	G	PO	A	E	DP
Carroll	1.000	3	6	14	0	5
Collier	.778	6	5	9	4	1
De La Rosa	1.000	1	0	4	0	1
Figueroa	.975	26	42	75	3	25
Machado	1.000	2	3	7	0	1
Mateo	.941	22	33	62	6	12

	PCT	G	PO	A	E	DP
Medrano	.978	50	86	139	5	35
Nunez	.922	30	29	89	10	14
Phillips	1.000	10	12	20	0	6

Outfield	PCT	G	PO	A	E	DP
Bergeron	.984	100	170	9	3	0
Calloway	.988	123	243	10	3	5
Chavez	.985	101	253	9	4	1
Collier	1.000	26	49	1	0	0
McKinley	1.000	7	9	0	0	0
Medrano	1.000	2	3	2	0	0
Mouton	1.000	16	31	1	0	0
Nunez	1.000	2	2	0	0	0
O'Leary	.974	20	37	0	1	0
Ortiz	1.000	25	38	0	0	0
Sledge	.935	16	29	0	2	0

EASTERN LEAGUE

BATTING	AVG	G	AB	R	H	2B	3B	HR	RBI	BB	SO	SB	CS	SLG	OBP	B	T	HT	WT	DOB	1st Yr	Resides
Ackerman, Scott	.235	5	17	1	4	0	0	0	2	0	2	0	0	.235	.222	R	R	6-1	210	4-23-79	1997	Oregon City, Ore.
Bailey, Jeff	.282	99	309	45	87	17	1	13	52	63	78	3	4	.469	.416	R	R	6-2	200	11-19-78	1997	Kelso, Wash.
Brown, Jason	.237	20	59	6	14	2	0	2	8	4	21	0	0	.373	.303	R	R	6-2	200	5-22-74	1997	Rolling Hills Estates, Calif.
2-team (18 Altoona)	.208	38	106	9	22	7	0	2	13	9	42	0	0	.330	.275							
Carreno, Jose	.190	14	42	5	8	0	0	1	4	2	7	0	0	.262	.222	R	R	5-11	190	4-23-78	1996	El Tigre, Venez.
Carroll, Jamey	.444	3	9	1	4	0	0	0	1	3	0	0	0	.444	.583	R	R	5-10	170	2-18-74	1996	St. Petersburg, Fla.
Cepicky, Matt	.277	109	419	54	116	25	2	16	76	33	94	7	1	.461	.327	L	R	6-2	210	11-10-77	1999	Sun City Center, Fla.
Davis, Glenn	.275	27	91	23	25	2	0	6	17	13	29	1	0	.495	.362	S	L	6-2	200	11-25-75	1997	Aston, Pa.
2-team (7 Norwich)	.272	34	114	18	31	3	2	7	18	17	34	1	1	.518	.364							
Figueroa, Luis	.272	66	250	47	68	17	3	1	30	25	16	6	7	.376	.341	S	R	5-9	140	2-16-74	1997	Vega Alta, P.R.
Foster, Quincy	.300	57	190	35	57	7	5	2	18	14	30	16	8	.421	.353	L	R	6-2	170	10-30-74	1996	Hendersonville, N.C.
2-team (23 Portland)	.284	80	264	41	75	9	5	4	32	19	43	26	12	.402	.336							
Fox, Jason	.125	7	16	2	2	0	1	0	3	0	4	1	0	.250	.125	S	R	6-2	180	3-30-77	1998	York, Pa.
Gingrich, Troy	.333	1	3	0	1	0	0	0	0	0	0	0	0	.333	.333	L	L	5-10	170	1-17-77	2000	Apache Junction, Ariz.
Hodges, Scott	.272	135	526	79	143	35	2	9	68	63	102	2	2	.397	.351	L	R	6-0	190	12-26-78	1997	Lexington, Ky.
Machado, Albenis	.242	75	240	29	58	9	3	2	28	46	38	6	4	.329	.371	S	R	6-0	170	3-20-79	1996	Caracas, Venez.
McKinley, Dan	.225	52	169	20	38	5	4	3	20	11	35	3	2	.355	.277	L	R	6-0	180	5-15-76	1997	Chandler, Ariz.
McKinley, Josh	.234	103	325	40	76	17	0	7	33	42	81	2	4	.351	.321	S	R	6-2	200	9-14-79	1998	Windermere, Fla.
McNally, Sean	.136	9	22	1	3	0	0	0	0	6	0	0	0	.136	.120	R	R	6-4	210	12-14-72	1994	Rye, N.Y.
Pascucci, Val	.235	137	459	73	108	14	1	27	82	93	115	2	0	.447	.374	R	R	6-6	230	11-17-78	1999	Cerritos, Calif.
Phillips, Brandon	.327	60	245	40	80	13	2	9	35	16	33	6	3	.506	.380	R	R	5-11	180	6-28-81	1999	Stone Mountain, Ga.
Reding, Josh	.179	15	39	3	7	0	0	0	3	2	8	0	0	.179	.256	R	R	6-3	170	3-7-77	1997	Anaheim, Calif.
Roneberg, Brett	.294	63	214	36	63	15	2	4	36	27	38	2	1	.439	.374	L	L	6-2	200	2-5-79	1996	Cairns, Australia
Sandusky, Scott	.206	107	354	38	73	16	1	2	35	31	66	0	2	.274	.274	R	R	6-0	200	3-6-76	1998	Arvada, Colo.
Schnabel, Nick	.278	16	18	2	5	0	0	0	1	5	0	0	0	.278	.435	R	R	5-9	170	3-16-78	2000	Greenville, N.C.
Sledge, Terrmel	.301	102	396	74	119	18	6	8	43	55	70	11	8	.437	.401	L	L	6-0	180	3-18-77	1999	Granada Hills, Calif.
Ware, Jeremy	.263	24	95	13	25	6	1	6	18	7	17	0	0	.537	.320	R	R	6-0	200	10-23-75	1995	Guelph, Ontario
Watson, Brian	.333	2	6	2	2	0	0	0	0	1	0	0	0	.333	.429	L	R	6-1	170	9-30-81	1999	Inglewood, Calif.
Watson, Matt	.250	1	4	1	1	0	0	0	0	0	0	0	0	.250	.250	L	R	5-11	190	9-5-78	1999	Lancaster, Pa.
Wilson, Desi	.130	18	54	3	7	0	0	0	3	5	12	0	0	.130	.203	L	L	6-7	230	5-9-69	1991	Glen Cove, N.Y.

PITCHING

PITCHING	W	L	ERA	G	GS	CG	SV	IP	H	R	ER	BB	SO	AVG	B	T	HT	WT	DOB	1st Yr	Resides
Agamennone, Brandon	2	0	2.57	8	0	0	1	14	11	4	4	1	12	.220	R	R	6-2	190	11-6-75	1998	Crofton, Md.
Billingsley, Brent	0	4	10.23	6	4	0	0	22	37	28	25	9	26	.370	L	L	6-2	200	4-19-75	1996	Chino Hills, Calif.
Bridges, Donnie	4	4	6.14	14	13	0	0	63	63	48	43	42	49	.260	R	R	6-4	220	12-10-78	1997	Purvis, Miss.
Casadiego, Gerardo	1	3	6.88	9	7	0	0	35	46	35	27	15	25	.326	R	R	6-0	180	12-19-80	1998	Barquisimeto, Venez.
Chiavacci, Ron	6	9	4.27	35	10	0	0	112	105	70	53	65	98	.250	R	R	6-2	220	9-5-77	1998	Scranton, Pa.
Collins, Pat	3	0	1.78	29	0	0	7	51	42	11	10	19	51	.222	R	R	6-5	230	3-3-78	1999	Union, N.J.
Crumpton, Chuck	2	3	3.64	21	3	0	3	59	69	26	24	20	32	.286	R	R	6-4	210	12-30-76	1999	Mesquite, Texas
Davis, Allen	1	4	7.14	9	5	0	0	29	44	24	23	8	14	.354	L	L	6-4	190	10-1-75	1998	Ovilla, Texas
Ferrari, Anthony	7	4	4.06	44	0	0	6	75	79	35	34	34	53	.269	L	L	5-9	160	6-22-78	2000	Greenbrae, Calif.
Hebson, Bryan	10	1	1.72	38	3	0	7	94	60	20	18	24	75	.182	R	R	6-5	210	3-12-76	1997	Phenix City, Ala.
Karp, Josh	7	5	3.84	16	16	0	0	87	83	43	37	34	69	.256	R	R	6-5	210	9-21-79	2002	Bothell, Wash.
Klepacki, Ed	0	0	4.09	6	0	0	1	11	7	5	5	9	4	.184	R	R	6-5	180	4-26-78	1998	Midwest City, Okla.
Lee, Cliff	7	3	3.23	15	15	0	0	86	61	31	31	23	105	.196	L	L	6-3	190	8-30-78	2000	Benton, Ark.
Lewis, Craig	1	2	3.95	17	0	0	0	27	37	16	12	8	13	.316	R	R	6-5	220	12-30-76	1997	Carlingford, Australia
Mangum, Mark	7	5	4.16	18	11	0	2	80	85	41	37	25	40	.278	R	R	6-2	180	8-24-78	1997	Kingwood, Texas
Manon, Julio	5	1	3.00	6	6	0	0	39	37	13	13	4	51	.245	L	R	6-0	200	6-10-73	1992	St. Petersburg, Fla.
Marrero, Darwin	6	5	4.02	19	19	1	0	105	119	54	47	21	54	.281	R	R	6-1	190	2-9-81	1997	Valencia, Venez.
McAvoy, Jeff	2	3	6.23	16	1	0	3	35	40	25	24	11	21	.289	R	R	6-3	210	3-15-77	2000	Palmer, Mass.
Rivera, Saul	0	2	3.32	15	0	0	3	19	21	8	7	9	15	.287	R	R	5-11	150	12-7-77	1996	San Juan, P.R.
2-team (30 Binghamton)	2	5	3.12	45	0	0	16	58	46	26	20	32	47	.219							
Seale, Dustin	1	2	3.51	29	3	0	6	67	63	27	26	16	51	.242	L	L	6-1	190	12-27-77	1997	Safford, Ariz.
Song, Seung	0	0	0.00	1	1	0	0	5	5	2	0	0	5	.250	R	R	6-1	190	6-29-80	1999	Pusan, South Korea
2-team (21 Trenton)	7	7	4.20	22	22	0	0	114	111	63	53	37	121	.255							
Vargas, Claudio	2	2	4.64	8	8	0	0	33	38	17	17	9	34	.285	R	R	6-3	210	5-19-79	1996	Santiago, D.R.
Wayne, Justin	5	2	2.37	17	17	0	0	99	74	41	26	32	47	.212	R	R	6-3	200	4-16-79	2000	Honolulu, Hawaii

FIELDING

Catcher	PCT	G	PO	A	E	DP	PB
Ackerman	1.000	4	18	1	0	0	1
Bailey	.979	12	88	5	2	0	2
Brown	1.000	9	62	2	0	0	0
Carreno	1.000	13	85	8	0	2	3
Sandusky	.997	107	728	68	2	10	10

First Base	PCT	G	PO	A	E	DP
Bailey	.995	73	550	40	3	51
Brown	1.000	1	4	0	0	0
Davis	.991	25	188	21	2	16
McNally	1.000	1	4	0	0	0
Pascucci	.987	19	140	8	2	7
Roneberg	.995	25	180	9	1	24
Sledge	1.000	1	3	2	0	0
Wilson	1.000	8	62	4	0	2

Second Base	PCT	G	PO	A	E	DP
Carroll	1.000	3	5	9	0	2
Machado	.990	48	107	98	2	41
J. McKinley	.950	90	166	197	19	36
Reding	.918	10	19	26	4	0
Schnabel	.909	4	4	6	1	1

Third Base	PCT	G	PO	A	E	DP
Hodges	.931	130	81	256	25	24
Machado	1.000	9	5	10	0	1
McNally	1.000	3	3	3	0	0
Pascucci	.667	2	0	2	1	0
Schnabel	1.000	4	1	4	0	0

Shortstop	PCT	G	PO	A	E	DP
Figueroa	.981	66	114	192	6	49
Hodges	1.000	2	4	6	0	1
Machado	.928	19	30	47	6	9

	PCT	G	PO	A	E	DP
Phillips	.936	59	77	127	14	15
Reding	.889	3	2	6	1	1

Outfield	PCT	G	PO	A	E	DP
Cepicky	.988	84	153	5	2	1
Foster	.966	47	110	2	4	2
Fox	1.000	6	14	0	0	0
Gingrich	.500	1	1	0	1	0
D. McKinley	.979	41	92	1	2	0
Pascucci	.972	107	200	11	6	1
Reding	1.000	1	0	0	0	0
Roneberg	.972	35	68	2	2	1
Sledge	.996	93	231	8	1	4
Ware	.948	24	53	2	3	0
B. Watson	1.000	2	4	0	0	0
M. Watson	1.000	1	1	0	0	0
Wilson	1.000	2	3	0	0	0

BREVARD COUNTY MANATEES · High Class A

FLORIDA STATE LEAGUE

BATTING

BATTING	AVG	G	AB	R	H	2B	3B	HR	RBI	BB	SO	SB	CS	SLG	OBP	B	T	HT	WT	DOB	1st Yr	Resides
Ackerman, Scott	.295	61	217	24	64	11	2	7	35	14	39	1	0	.461	.336	R	R	6-1	210	4-23-79	1997	Oregon City, Ore.
Blum, Greg	.239	94	285	30	68	12	0	4	40	28	69	0	1	.354	.319	R	R	6-1	200	8-7-78	2000	Chino, Calif.
Boyer, Brett	.183	56	164	13	30	1	1	2	13	6	41	5	2	.238	.218	R	R	6-0	170	8-8-80	1999	Indian Rocks Beach, Fla.
Brown, Matt	.167	3	6	0	1	0	0	0	0	0	0	0	0	.167	.167	S	R	6-1	190	9-23-80	1999	Randleman, N.C.
Carreno, Jose	.225	36	102	9	23	5	1	2	8	6	10	0	0	.353	.282	R	R	5-11	190	4-23-78	1996	El Tigre, Venez.
Davis, Glenn	.256	11	43	2	11	5	0	1	5	1	12	0	0	.442	.273	S	L	6-1	200	11-25-75	1997	Aston, Pa.
Dempsey, Nick	.252	51	163	10	41	9	0	0	30	9	45	1	3	.307	.291	R	R	6-5	210	12-15-78	1997	Durban, South Africa
Desena, Francis	.111	8	9	0	1	0	0	0	0	0	4	0	0	.111	.111	R	R	6-1	150	5-30-83	2000	Mendoza, D.R.
Diaz, Frank	.226	10	31	3	7	2	0	0	1	6	4	3	0	.290	.351	R	R	6-2	180	10-6-83	2000	Yagua, Venez.
Downing, Phil	.241	59	170	22	41	11	2	3	14	17	65	0	5	.382	.314	L	L	6-1	190	8-22-78	2000	Sandy, Utah
Figueroa, Luis	.262	15	61	8	16	1	1	0	8	5	2	2	4	.311	.328	S	R	5-9	140	2-16-74	1997	Vega Alta, P.R.
Gingrich, Troy	.237	111	334	46	79	10	3	2	29	48	69	12	8	.302	.339	L	L	5-10	170	1-17-77	2000	Apache Junction, Ariz.
Hernandez, Vladimir	.278	36	108	12	30	2	0	0	10	7	16	5	3	.296	.314	R	R	5-11	180	2-2-77	2001	McAllen, Texas
Lane, Rich	.271	121	454	54	123	27	2	4	50	34	97	7	1	.366	.323	L	L	6-3	190	1-4-80	1999	Tustin, Calif.
Machado, Albenis	.278	5	18	3	5	1	0	0	3	1	0	0	0	.333	.381	S	R	6-0	170	3-20-79	1996	Caracas, Venez.
McMillan, Drew	.171	48	158	14	27	1	0	7	18	12	50	0	0	.310	.254	R	R	6-3	200	10-25-80	1999	Yorba Linda, Calif.
Miller, Eric	.256	129	472	49	121	19	3	1	38	28	62	8	8	.316	.300	R	R	6-2	170	12-9-77	2000	Tempe, Ariz.
Nicolas, Jose	.000	4	9	0	0	0	0	0	1	0	3	0	0	.000	.000	R	R	6-3	210	1-1-79	1997	Miami, Fla.
Piercy, Mike	.154	9	13	4	2	0	0	0	4	1	1	0	0	.154	.353	L	L	6-0	170	6-24-76	1999	Hillside, N.J.
Rombley, Danny	.293	54	191	26	56	6	3	1	16	13	36	15	7	.372	.341	R	R	6-1	180	11-26-79	1999	Amersfoort, Netherlands
Rooi, Vince	.193	118	367	38	71	11	1	4	38	52	86	7	5	.262	.295	R	R	6-1	190	12-13-81	1999	Amsterdam, Netherlands
Schnabel, Nick	.196	17	56	5	11	0	0	0	7	11	10	0	0	.196	.286	R	R	5-9	170	3-16-78	2000	Greenville, N.C.
Sizemore, Grady	.258	75	256	37	66	15	4	0	26	36	41	9	9	.348	.351	L	L	6-2	200	8-2-82	2000	Mill Creek, Wash.
Socarras, Tony	.150	46	113	13	17	6	0	5	19	11	40	0	0	.336	.227	L	R	6-0	200	11-8-78	2000	Miami, Fla.
Tatis, Fernando	.235	6	17	2	4	1	0	0	2	3	4	0	0	.294	.391	R	R	5-10	180	1-1-75	1993	San Pedro de Macoris, D.R.
Watson, Brandon	.267	111	424	57	113	16	2	0	24	27	53	22	13	.314	.314	L	L	6-1	170	9-30-81	1999	Inglewood, Calif.
Williams, Jason	.201	68	179	19	36	9	1	2	18	20	53	0	2	.296	.277	R	R	5-11	170	12-6-78	2000	Fairfield, Calif.

PITCHING

PITCHING	W	L	ERA	G	GS	CG	SV	IP	H	R	ER	BB	SO	AVG	B	T	HT	WT	DOB	1st Yr	Resides
Arthurs, Shane	0	10	5.13	23	10	0	0	72	87	55	41	40	42	.301	R	R	6-5	180	8-30-79	1997	Oklahoma City, Okla.
Bentz, Chad	0	1	3.64	23	0	0	5	30	30	14	12	14	34	.258	R	L	6-2	210	5-8-80	2001	Juneau, Alaska
Bye, Chris	2	5	4.50	38	0	0	2	68	58	43	34	32	45	.226	R	R	5-11	190	9-10-77	2000	Englewood, Colo.
Caputo, Rob	0	1	10.80	2	0	0	0	2	3	2	2	3	1	.375	R	R	6-6	200	11-7-79	2001	New Fairfield, Conn.
Casadiego, Gerardo	3	4	3.01	16	8	0	1	72	57	27	24	36	41	.216	R	R	6-0	180	12-19-80	1998	Barquisimeto, Venez.

PITCHING	W	L	ERA	G	GS	CG	SV	IP	H	R	ER	BB	SO	AVG	B	T	HT	WT	DOB	1st Yr	Resides
Collins, Pat	1	5	2.70	17	0	0	2	27	15	14	8	14	31	.157	R	R	6-5	230	3-3-78	1999	Union, N.J.
DeQuin, Benji	6	9	3.89	27	27	0	0	143	145	70	62	58	111	.262	R	L	5-10	170	6-2-80	2000	Gilroy, Calif.
Diaz, Eddie	0	0	1.59	4	0	0	0	6	3	1	1	2	9	.157	R	R	6-0	170	1-25-83	2001	Orlando, Fla.
Downs, Scott	0	0	3.00	7	0	0	1	9	7	3	3	2	7	.205	L	L	6-2	190	3-17-76	1997	Lexington, Ky.
Echols, Britt	0	0	5.40	1	1	0	0	5	6	3	3	3	3	.285	R	R	6-5	220	8-11-80	2002	Coal Township, Pa.
Karp, Josh	4	1	1.59	7	7	0	0	45	31	9	8	11	43	.190	R	R	6-5	210	9-21-79	2002	Bothell, Wash.
Klepacki, Ed	0	0	7.27	3	1	0	0	9	10	8	7	4	4	.270	R	R	6-5	180	4-26-78	1998	Midwest City, Okla.
Lewis, Craig	1	2	4.05	12	0	0	0	20	24	14	9	3	11	.289	R	R	6-5	220	12-30-76	1997	Carlingford, Australia
Lockwood, Luke	10	7	3.37	26	26	0	0	147	155	69	55	38	86	.274	L	L	6-3	170	7-21-81	1999	Victorville, Calif.
Marrero, Darwin	3	2	3.46	9	9	0	0	55	57	21	21	8	41	.268	R	R	6-1	190	2-9-81	1997	Valencia, Venez.
Martin, Greg	1	1	9.00	4	0	0	0	6	13	8	6	4	1	.433	L	L	6-1	190	4-10-80	2002	Scranton, Pa.
Mata, Gustavo	3	4	2.55	11	11	0	0	67	50	21	19	19	27	.210	R	R	6-1	190	5-20-83	2001	Carupano, Venez.
Maust, David	1	1	5.32	14	0	0	4	22	20	14	13	8	15	.238	L	L	6-2	200	11-6-78	2001	Morgantown, W.Va.
McAvoy, Jeff	3	3	5.40	12	6	1	0	47	55	28	28	8	22	.292	R	R	6-3	210	3-15-77	2000	Palmer, Mass.
Meyer, Todd	0	1	7.45	4	2	0	0	10	9	8	8	7	7	.257	R	R	6-3	180	8-2-79	2002	York, Pa.
Norderum, Jason	1	0	13.50	2	0	0	0	2	3	3	3	3	2	.333	L	L	6-3	220	11-21-81	2000	Redding, Calif.
Ortiz, Julio	0	0	0.00	2	0	0	0	1	1	0	0	2	1	.333	L	L	5-11	200	9-25-78	2002	Guayanilla, P.R.
Rengifo, Nohemar	0	0	7.71	1	0	0	0	2	1	3	2	5	0	.125	R	R	5-11	180	10-2-82	1999	Tucupido, Venez.
Rodriguez, Cristobal	2	3	1.62	11	0	0	2	17	11	4	3	4	21	.192	R	R	6-4	210	1-27-79	1996	Chichiriviche, Venez.
Rundles, Rich	2	7	4.08	12	11	0	0	57	66	34	26	16	31	.295	L	L	6-5	180	6-3-81	1999	Livingston, Ala.
Russo, Scott	0	0	4.67	11	0	0	0	17	19	9	9	6	11	.306	L	L	6-2	180	3-1-78	2000	Turnersville, N.J.
Schroder, Chris	2	2	1.52	23	0	0	6	30	13	6	5	19	36	.132	R	R	6-3	210	8-20-78	2001	Okarche, Okla.
Seale, Dustin	1	0	0.00	8	0	0	0	17	6	1	0	6	14	.107	L	L	6-1	190	12-2-77	1997	Safford, Ariz.
Spencer, Sean	0	0	0.00	3	0	0	4	1	0	0	0	4	3	.083	L	L	5-11	180	5-29-75	1996	Port Orchard, Wash.
Torres, Luis	4	8	4.97	16	15	1	0	87	99	56	48	28	46	.291	R	R	6-4	200	3-12-81	1999	Caracas, Venez.
Tucker, Julien	1	5	3.12	25	0	0	1	43	35	24	15	29	43	.217	L	R	6-7	200	4-19-73	1993	Chateauguay, Quebec
Washburn, Ben	0	3	7.41	19	2	0	0	38	52	41	31	13	25	.333	R	R	6-2	200	5-17-79	2000	Redlands, Calif.

FIELDING

Catcher	PCT	G	PO	A	E	DP	PB
Ackerman	.996	39	233	23	1	3	4
Blum	.985	43	254	15	4	3	11
Carreno	.977	13	77	7	2	1	3
McMillan	1.000	37	190	32	0	7	1
Socarras	.980	19	90	8	2	0	4

First Base	PCT	G	PO	A	E	DP
Blum	.983	22	159	11	3	16
Carreno	1.000	2	6	0	0	1
Davis	1.000	9	78	10	0	13
Dempsey	.973	28	205	11	6	13
Lane	.986	92	716	43	11	73

Second Base	PCT	G	PO	A	E	DP
Boyer	.936	52	98	136	16	30
Desena	1.000	3	2	4	0	1
Hernandez	.976	10	16	24	1	2
Machado	1.000	1	1	3	0	0
Miller	.963	39	83	101	7	23

	PCT	G	PO	A	E	DP
Schnabel	1.000	5	12	17	0	3
Socarras	1.000	1	1	0	0	0
Williams	.957	37	58	77	6	19
Third Base	**PCT**	**G**	**PO**	**A**	**E**	**DP**
Brown	.500	1	2	1	3	0
Machado	1.000	1	1	1	0	0
Miller	.913	8	12	9	2	0
Rooi	.922	118	77	230	26	24
Schnabel	1.000	5	1	7	0	0
Socarras	1.000	1	0	1	0	0
Tatis	.929	5	1	12	1	2
Williams	.938	7	2	13	1	1
Shortstop	**PCT**	**G**	**PO**	**A**	**E**	**DP**
Desena	.875	4	4	3	1	0
Figueroa	.918	15	29	38	6	9
Hernandez	.965	26	41	68	4	15
Machado	.950	3	7	12	1	8
Miller	.974	85	115	263	10	45

	PCT	G	PO	A	E	DP
Rooi	.000	1	0	0	0	0
Schnabel	1.000	7	13	28	0	9
Williams	.857	3	3	3	1	1
Outfield	**PCT**	**G**	**PO**	**A**	**E**	**DP**
Brown	1.000	1	2	0	0	0
Diaz	.941	10	14	2	1	0
Downing	.946	49	84	3	5	0
Gingrich	.975	98	187	11	5	3
Lane	.984	33	60	3	1	1
Nicolas	1.000	4	3	0	0	0
Piercy	1.000	4	3	0	0	0
Rombley	.983	54	108	7	2	3
Rooi	1.000	1	1	0	0	0
Sizemore	.977	71	126	4	3	1
Watson	.983	111	268	14	5	6
Williams	.923	10	9	3	1	0

CLINTON LUMBER KINGS

Low Class A

MIDWEST LEAGUE

BATTING	AVG	G	AB	R	H	2B	3B	HR	RBI	BB	SO	SB	CS	SLG	OBP	B	T	HT	WT	DOB	1st Yr	Resides
Ambrosini, Anthony	.216	70	199	21	43	7	1	0	20	19	31	0	0	.261	.284	R	R	5-9	180	9-22-78	2001	Ronkonkoma, N.Y.
Ambrosini, Dominick	.279	121	441	53	123	29	4	5	50	31	113	7	5	.397	.327	L	L	5-10	180	2-21-81	1999	Ronkonkoma, N.Y.
Boyer, Brett	.240	60	221	31	53	11	1	4	23	30	70	6	7	.353	.329	R	R	6-0	170	8-8-80	1999	Indian Rocks Beach, Fla.
Brown, Matt	.228	102	342	39	78	20	1	10	41	32	89	3	2	.380	.299	S	R	6-1	190	9-23-80	1999	Randleman, N.C.
Diaz, Felix	.251	52	191	34	48	7	4	12	30	19	63	1	1	.518	.324	S	R	6-2	200	8-1-80	1996	Bani, D.R.
Emmerick, Josh	.045	8	22	1	1	0	0	0	1	4	3	0	0	.045	.192	R	R	6-4	190	2-22-81	1999	Oceanside, Calif.
Encarnacion, Henry	.113	36	53	8	6	1	0	0	3	6	20	1	2	.132	.203	R	R	6-0	170	5-20-82	1999	Santo Domingo, D.R.
Guerrero, Pedro	.225	38	102	15	23	4	0	1	7	10	29	1	1	.294	.295	R	R	5-10	160	8-21-79	1996	Santo Domingo, D.R.
Hernandez, Vladimir	.000	4	9	0	0	0	0	0	1	0	0	0	0	.000	.100	R	R	5-11	180	2-2-77	2001	McAllen, Texas
Kerner, Craig	.265	40	117	15	31	6	2	2	12	8	18	8	4	.402	.313	L	L	6-1	190	11-13-78	2000	Whitesboro, N.Y.
Labandeira, John	.286	129	493	60	141	27	3	8	67	45	73	15	12	.402	.350	R	R	5-7	180	2-25-79	2001	Porterville, Calif.
Louisa, Lorvin	.177	41	124	16	22	4	0	2	8	9	55	1	0	.258	.248	R	R	6-4	200	2-7-83	1999	Willemstad, Curacao
Lutz, David	.193	58	176	16	34	6	1	3	17	17	36	1	2	.290	.268	L	L	6-3	190	9-25-81	1999	Spring Valley, Calif.
McMillan, Drew	.173	37	133	16	23	6	1	1	11	7	34	3	1	.256	.218	R	R	6-3	200	10-25-80	1999	Yorba Linda, Calif.
Norris, Shawn	.269	9	26	2	7	1	0	0	3	6	8	1	0	.308	.394	L	R	6-2	170	8-1-80	2001	Draper, Utah
Rombley, Danny	.272	72	279	49	76	14	4	2	23	21	62	13	7	.373	.337	R	R	6-1	180	11-26-79	1999	Amersfoort, Netherlands
Schnabel, Nick	.331	39	124	17	41	9	1	0	20	19	13	1	4	.419	.419	R	R	5-9	170	3-16-78	2000	Greenville, N.C.
Schneider, Michael	.233	11	30	3	7	2	0	0	2	3	10	0	0	.300	.303	R	R	6-4	210	8-20-79	2002	Northampton, Pa.
Sosa, Jovanny	.260	59	177	24	46	9	1	6	26	32	64	0	3	.424	.382	R	R	6-2	200	10-4-79	1997	Santo Domingo, D.R.
Swope, Matt	.215	45	135	19	29	5	0	2	8	21	23	2	1	.296	.321	R	R	6-0	190	6-1-80	2002	Brinklow, Md.
Thede, Matthew	.244	45	156	15	38	8	1	3	17	4	40	0	1	.365	.267	R	R	6-1	180	6-21-78	2001	Reinbeck, Iowa
Thissen, Greg	.255	129	486	69	124	27	1	13	68	48	101	3	6	.395	.327	R	R	6-4	180	6-1-81	2001	Davenport, Iowa
Williams, Clyde	.266	127	462	65	123	23	3	16	71	35	104	6	5	.433	.327	L	L	6-2	190	7-7-79	1998	Sanford, Fla.

PITCHING	W	L	ERA	G	GS	CG	SV	IP	H	R	ER	BB	SO	AVG	B	T	HT	WT	DOB	1st Yr	Resides
Barlow, Chris	2	5	3.76	9	9	1	0	53	64	27	22	11	23	.309	R	R	6-6	210	11-11-80	2002	Cazenovia, N.Y.
Bye, Chris	0	2	10.38	5	0	0	1	4	8	6	5	2	2	.400	R	R	5-11	190	9-10-77	2001	Englewood, Colo.
Caputo, Rob	3	0	2.63	21	6	0	1	48	32	15	14	36	69	.186	R	R	6-6	200	11-7-79	2001	New Fairfield, Conn.
Charron, Eric	0	0	5.26	32	0	0	0	63	73	49	37	22	36	.288	R	R	5-11	170	4-3-79	1999	Montreal, Quebec
Corcoran, Roy	3	4	4.16	48	1	0	11	80	82	51	37	24	106	.253	R	R	5-10	170	5-11-80	2001	Slaughter, La.

PITCHING

PITCHING	W	L	ERA	G	GS	CG	SV	IP	H	R	ER	BB	SO	AVG	B	T	HT	WT	DOB	1st Yr	Resides
Diaz, Eddie	2	0	3.53	6	0	0	0	13	9	6	5	13	15	.195	R	R	6-0	170	1-25-83	2001	Orlando, Fla.
Echols, Britt	1	0	1.80	1	1	0	0	5	6	3	1	1	6	.272	R	R	6-5	220	8-11-80	2002	Coal Township, Pa.
Girdley, Josh	0	3	6.85	7	5	0	1	24	33	19	18	13	14	.340	L	L	6-3	180	8-29-80	1999	Jasper, Texas
Hill, Shawn	12	7	3.44	25	25	0	0	147	149	75	56	35	99	.260	R	R	6-2	180	4-28-81	2000	Georgetown, Ontario
Levinski, Don	12	6	3.02	21	21	1	0	119	92	48	40	55	125	.211	R	R	6-4	200	10-20-82	2001	Weimar, Texas
Marceau, Pierre-Luc	1	3	6.52	12	4	0	0	29	31	21	21	28	13	.292	L	L	6-2	190	4-11-81	1999	Fleurimont, Quebec
Mata, Gustavo	1	3	4.11	8	5	0	0	31	36	19	14	9	15	.297	R	R	6-1	190	5-20-83	2001	Carupano, Venez.
Maust, David	1	1	1.87	35	0	0	5	58	45	13	12	10	57	.215	L	L	6-2	200	11-6-78	2001	Morgantown, W.Va.
Mitchell, Tom	0	6	6.11	22	15	1	0	96	120	73	65	59	42	.315	R	R	6-2	180	11-20-80	2000	Bladenboro, N.C.
Norderum, Jason	0	6	8.74	9	9	0	0	34	45	34	33	32	26	.323	L	L	6-3	220	11-21-81	2000	Redding, Calif.
Puello, Ignacio	7	14	4.77	27	26	0	0	140	155	95	74	66	91	.277	R	R	6-1	170	10-16-80	1998	San Pedro de Macoris, D.R.
Rodriguez, Jose	1	0	9.82	2	0	0	0	4	7	4	4	6	3	.437	R	R	6-2	180	2-9-81	1998	Santo Domingo, D.R.
Rueckel, Danny	3	1	4.15	14	0	0	0	26	23	12	12	10	25	.232	R	R	6-0	170	9-25-79	2002	Dunwoody, Ga.
Santana, Eddy	0	0	3.38	4	0	0	0	5	8	3	2	5	7	.347	R	R	6-2	160	10-12-80	1997	Santo Domingo, D.R.
Schroder, Chris	1	3	1.65	22	0	0	10	27	15	7	5	14	42	.156	R	R	6-2	210	8-20-78	2001	Okarche, Okla.
Stevenson, Jason	3	4	3.78	33	0	0	2	67	69	36	28	22	41	.270	L	L	6-1	170	8-8-81	2001	Redding, Calif.
Torres, Luis	5	1	3.73	7	7	0	0	41	29	17	17	14	41	.194	R	R	6-4	200	3-12-81	1999	Caracas, Venez.
Walker, Jason	0	1	7.04	12	1	0	0	15	15	17	12	25	11	.241	L	L	6-0	180	1-15-80	2001	Ontario, Calif.
Washburn, Ben	1	3	2.44	24	1	0	1	52	40	17	14	10	40	.216	R	R	6-2	200	5-17-79	2000	Redlands, Calif.

FIELDING

Catcher	PCT	G	PO	A	E	DP	PB
A. Ambrosini	.994	65	419	41	3	2	4
Emmerick	.917	7	41	3	4	0	1
Lutz	.982	32	208	15	4	0	9
McMillan	.982	31	200	23	4	1	5
Schneider	.969	10	53	9	2	1	1
Thede	1.000	5	31	4	0	0	0

First Base	PCT	G	PO	A	E	DP
D. Ambrosini	1.000	7	49	4	0	1
Lutz	1.000	2	17	2	0	2
Sosa	.964	5	26	1	1	0
Thede	.957	8	85	3	4	8
Williams	.978	120	1098	74	26	102

Second Base	PCT	G	PO	A	E	DP
Boyer	1.000	5	6	14	0	3
Encarnacion	.909	9	11	19	3	4
Guerrero	.969	5	8	23	1	2

	PCT	G	PO	A	E	DP
Hernandez	1.000	2	2	8	0	1
Schnabel	1.000	4	7	9	0	1
Thissen	.970	119	249	361	19	85

Third Base	PCT	G	PO	A	E	DP
A. Ambrosini	.000	1	0	0	0	0
Boyer	.500	2	0	3	3	0
Brown	.800	7	3	5	2	1
Diaz	.896	52	28	101	15	7
Encarnacion	.806	15	6	23	7	1
Guerrero	.909	7	1	9	1	1
Hernandez	1.000	1	3	2	0	0
Lutz	1.000	4	4	9	0	0
Norris	1.000	9	4	5	0	0
Schnabel	.908	33	20	59	8	6
Thede	.889	13	7	17	3	0
Thissen	.714	6	1	9	4	1

Shortstop	PCT	G	PO	A	E	DP
Encarnacion	.875	7	7	7	2	2
Guerrero	.800	4	2	2	1	0
Labandeira	.942	127	159	392	34	82
Schnabel	1.000	2	2	2	0	1
Thissen	.917	2	2	9	1	1

Outfield	PCT	G	PO	A	E	DP
D. Ambrosini	.925	112	169	17	15	2
Boyer	.972	51	101	4	3	2
Brown	.979	63	91	3	2	0
Guerrero	.968	15	30	0	1	0
Hernandez	.000	1	0	0	0	0
Kerner	.983	35	55	4	1	1
Louisa	.913	27	42	0	4	0
Rombley	.953	71	134	8	7	0
Sosa	.900	6	8	1	1	1
Swope	.964	43	78	2	3	1
Thede	1.000	5	5	0	0	0

VERMONT EXPOS — Short-Season A

NEW YORK-PENN LEAGUE

BATTING	AVG	G	AB	R	H	2B	3B	HR	RBI	BB	SO	SB	CS	SLG	OBP	B	T	HT	WT	DOB	1st Yr	Resides
Anderson, Brian	.176	39	125	10	22	6	0	1	11	6	30	0	0	.248	.211	L	R	6-2	180	6-11-80	2002	Chesapeake, Va.
Broadway, Larry	.315	35	127	13	40	3	0	4	23	13	33	0	0	.433	.379	L	L	6-4	230	12-17-80	2002	Scotts Hill, Tenn.
Brown, Anthony	.185	45	124	12	23	1	0	0	11	10	47	7	4	.194	.255	L	R	6-0	180	9-5-79	2002	Hockessin, Del.
Chop, Chad	.254	70	272	31	69	18	0	5	37	19	50	3	2	.375	.308	L	L	6-3	210	3-21-80	2002	Santa Ana, Calif.
Conlisk, Jason	.252	65	230	22	58	8	1	2	18	24	43	3	3	.322	.329	S	R	5-10	180	7-8-81	2002	Ridgewood, N.Y.
Ellerson, Brian	.191	15	47	4	9	1	0	2	3	1	11	0	0	.340	.224	R	R	6-1	190	9-18-79	2002	Bayonne, N.J.
Emmerick, Josh	.204	43	108	10	22	4	0	0	7	8	32	0	1	.241	.269	R	R	6-4	190	2-22-81	1999	Oceanside, Calif.
Encarnacion, Henry	.301	57	209	33	63	9	3	0	26	27	49	15	6	.373	.385	S	R	6-0	170	5-20-82	1999	Santo Domingo, D.R.
Fitzpatrick, Reggie	.237	71	270	34	64	10	0	2	16	27	59	15	10	.296	.310	L	L	5-11	180	2-28-83	2001	Atlanta, Ga.
Johnson, Seth	.150	39	127	14	19	0	0	2	10	15	35	0	1	.197	.252	R	R	6-4	190	6-3-82	2000	Longview, Wash.
Louisa, Lorvin	.145	48	159	10	23	3	2	1	13	8	66	2	1	.208	.199	R	R	6-4	200	2-7-83	1999	Willemstad, Curacao
Mancebo, Deni	.211	7	19	3	4	1	0	0	1	4	1	1	1	.263	.348	S	R	5-10	160	11-17-83	2001	Santo Domingo, D.R.
Mongeluzzo, Anthony	.178	16	45	6	8	2	0	0	3	5	17	0	0	.222	.288	R	R	6-1	210	11-23-78	2000	Huntington, N.Y.
Norris, Shawn	.287	42	157	22	45	5	2	4	14	22	23	2	0	.420	.376	L	R	6-2	190	8-1-80	2001	Draper, Utah
Rodriguez, Robert	.286	12	28	2	8	3	0	0	4	1	10	0	0	.393	.310	R	R	5-10	180	12-17-80	2002	Miami, Fla.
Schneider, Michael	.370	8	27	3	10	1	0	1	6	3	6	0	0	.519	.419	R	R	6-4	210	8-20-79	2002	Northampton, Pa.
Sweeney, Tim	.186	45	140	12	26	2	0	0	7	11	26	1	1	.200	.247	R	R	6-3	190	8-3-80	2002	Sparta, N.J.
Swope, Matt	.222	7	18	3	4	0	0	0	1	2	1	0	0	.222	.286	R	R	6-0	190	6-1-80	2002	Brinklow, Md.
Thede, Matthew	.353	9	34	8	12	5	0	4	9	1	6	0	0	.853	.361	R	R	6-1	180	6-21-78	2001	Reinbeck, Iowa
Urquhart, Adrian	.196	20	56	4	11	2	0	0	4	8	18	1	1	.232	.318	R	R	6-1	190	10-1-79	2002	Montgomery, Ala.
Weese, Nathan	.238	57	189	22	45	9	0	2	18	17	41	1	0	.317	.308	L	R	6-0	180	5-15-80	2002	West Bountiful, Utah

GAMES BY POSITION: C—Anderson 35, Emmerick 33, Rodriguez 9, Schneider 6. **1B**—Broadway 33, Chop 7, Johnson 18, Thede 5, Weese 19. **2B**—Conlisk 63, Encarnacion 7, Mancebo 6. **3B**—Ellerson 12, Johnson 2, Norris 40, Sweeney 11, Weese 14. **SS**—Encarnacion 50, Sweeney 28. **OF**—Brown 42, Chop 63, Fitzpatrick 68, Louisa 43, Mongeluzzo 3, Swope 7, Urquhart 13, Weese 2.

PITCHING	W	L	ERA	G	GS	CG	SV	IP	H	R	ER	BB	SO	AVG	B	T	HT	WT	DOB	1st Yr	Resides
Barlow, Chris	1	3	2.35	5	5	0	0	23	18	10	6	1	11	.195	R	R	6-6	210	11-11-80	2002	Cazenovia, N.Y.
Beck, Ken	0	0	5.29	14	0	0	1	17	28	17	10	7	14	.368	R	R	6-2	190	2-3-80	2002	Laurel, Md.
Bergmann, Jason	7	4	2.89	14	14	0	0	72	48	27	23	33	57	.193	R	R	6-4	180	9-25-81	2002	Manalpan, N.J.
Davis, Stockton	2	5	2.15	19	2	0	7	71	51	23	17	22	81	.196	R	R	6-3	210	9-8-79	2002	Owasso, Okla.
Diaz, Eddie	0	2	6.43	3	3	0	0	7	3	6	5	12	9	.130	R	R	6-0	170	1-25-83	2001	Orlando, Fla.
Felfoldi, Jonathan	2	3	3.38	3	3	0	0	8	10	6	3	2	6	.344	L	L	6-1	180	7-6-81	2002	San Diego, Calif.
Fiedler, Erik	0	3	4.68	10	0	0	0	25	30	19	13	9	19	.300	R	R	6-4	190	11-27-78	2002	Placerville, Calif.
Guerrero, Tomas	1	5	5.23	21	0	0	3	33	33	23	19	15	20	.255	R	R	6-0	160	1-6-82	1999	Nizao, D.R.
Hinckley, Mike	6	2	1.37	16	16	0	0	92	60	19	14	30	66	.188	R	L	6-3	170	10-5-82	2001	Moore, Okla.
Long, Nick	1	3	7.92	6	6	0	0	25	36	30	22	14	16	.336	R	R	6-3	180	11-24-82	2001	Columbus, Ga.
Marceau, Pierre-Luc	5	4	2.31	15	15	0	0	82	60	29	21	24	66	.202	L	L	6-2	190	4-11-81	1999	Fleurimont, Quebec
O'Connor, Mike	2	3	3.14	21	0	0	4	43	25	17	15	27	66	.173	L	L	6-3	170	8-17-80	2002	Ellicott City, Md.

PITCHING	W	L	ERA	G	GS	CG	SV	IP	H	R	ER	BB	SO	AVG	B	T	HT	WT	DOB	1st Yr	Resides

PITCHING	W	L	ERA	G	GS	CG	SV	IP	H	R	ER	BB	SO	AVG	B	T	HT	WT	DOB	1st Yr	Resides
Ortiz, Julio	1	2	3.82	15	1	0	0	33	28	18	14	16	28	.224	L	L	5-11	200	9-25-78	2002	Guayanilla, P.R.
Rasner, Darrell	2	5	4.33	10	10	0	0	44	44	27	21	18	49	.261	R	R	6-3	210	1-13-81	2002	Carson City, Nev.
Rengifo, Nohemar	1	1	5.40	12	0	0	0	20	19	15	12	20	13	.246	R	R	5-11	180	10-2-82	1999	Tucupido, Venez.
Rodriguez, Jose	1	2	5.97	17	0	0	0	32	29	28	21	27	40	.232	R	R	6-2	180	2-9-81	1998	Santo Domingo, D.R.
Rueckel, Danny	1	1	1.53	10	0	0	3	18	12	8	3	3	23	.187	R	R	6-0	170	9-25-79	2002	Dunwoody, Ga.
Santana, Eddy	0	0	3.00	4	0	0	0	6	5	2	2	3	1	.217	R	R	6-2	160	10-12-80	1997	Santo Domingo, D.R.
Walker, Jason	0	2	17.80	14	0	0	0	15	31	30	29	23	9	.436	L	L	6-0	180	1-15-80	2001	Ontario, Calif.

MELBOURNE EXPOS — Rookie

GULF COAST LEAGUE

BATTING	AVG	G	AB	R	H	2B	3B	HR	RBI	BB	SO	SB	CS	SLG	OBP	B	T	HT	WT	DOB	1st Yr	Resides
Apodaca, Luis	.231	12	39	4	9	1	0	0	2	7	7	1	0	.256	.348	R	R	5-11	170	7-15-82	1999	Caracas, Venez.
Bernadina, Rogearvin	.276	57	196	22	54	7	0	3	18	19	25	1	0	.357	.348	L	L	6-0	170	6-12-84	2002	Netherlands
Blanco, Luis	.230	45	148	17	34	12	0	3	17	7	55	0	0	.372	.303	R	R	6-3	200	7-6-81	1999	Caracas, Venez.
Broadway, Larry	.250	4	8	1	2	0	0	0	4	4	0	0	0	.250	.500	L	L	6-4	230	12-17-80	2002	Scotts Hill, Tenn.
Clanton, Ja'Mar	.158	56	190	23	30	6	0	0	10	21	30	7	4	.189	.245	R	R	6-0	170	7-14-81	2002	Bellwood, Ill.
Cobb, Maurice	.216	37	116	14	25	5	1	1	9	12	44	1	2	.302	.305	R	R	6-1	190	5-23-84	2002	Rocky Mount, N.C.
Desena, Francis	.232	29	99	10	23	5	1	0	13	5	18	3	0	.303	.267	R	R	6-1	150	5-30-83	2000	Mendoza, D.R.
Diaz, Frank	.277	51	173	33	48	8	2	5	24	19	28	8	5	.434	.370	R	R	6-2	180	10-6-83	2000	Yagua, Venez.
Ellerson, Brian	.150	8	20	3	3	0	1	0	0	3	2	0	1	.250	.292	R	R	6-1	190	9-18-79	2002	Bayonne, N.J.
Greene, Jason	.244	16	45	4	11	1	2	0	6	3	13	0	1	.356	.314	L	R	5-11	180	9-9-82	2001	Minford, Ohio
Honeycutt, Shedrick	.127	27	71	5	9	3	0	0	0	1	20	1	2	.169	.139	L	L	6-2	190	1-21-81	2001	Tallahassee, Fla.
Jenkins, Darryl	.000	1	1	0	0	0	0	0	0	0	0	0	0	.000	.000	L	R	6-2	180	6-13-81	2000	Plainfield, Ill.
Jimenez, Franklyn	.302	43	129	16	39	5	0	0	12	14	22	5	3	.341	.378	R	R	6-2	180	2-23-82	2002	Bayamon, P.R.
Kahr, Danny	.175	39	126	12	22	7	0	0	13	8	50	1	1	.230	.250	S	R	6-3	180	9-25-82	2001	Las Vegas, Nev.
Kerner, Craig	.240	8	25	3	6	1	1	0	4	5	4	2	0	.360	.375	L	R	6-1	190	11-13-78	2000	Whitesboro, N.Y.
Mancebo, Deni	.230	35	126	16	29	1	1	1	11	11	24	6	3	.278	.315	S	R	5-10	180	11-17-83	2001	Santo Domingo, D.R.
Manriquez, Salomon	.282	41	131	21	37	10	0	4	26	12	29	0	3	.450	.344	R	R	6-0	170	9-15-82	1999	Guacara, Venez.
Mujica, Jean	.600	2	5	0	3	1	0	0	1	0	0	0	0	.800	.600	R	R	6-1	180	8-15-82	2000	Carabobo, Venez.
Norris, Shawn	.206	9	34	1	7	1	0	0	3	3	3	0	0	.235	.270	L	R	6-2	170	8-1-80	2001	Draper, Utah
Rodriguez, Reynaldo	.000	2	2	0	0	0	0	0	0	1	0	0	0	.000	.333	R	R	6-0	160	7-23-82	2000	La Romana, D.R.
Rodriguez, Robert	.204	18	49	4	10	4	0	0	4	7	10	0	2	.286	.328	R	R	5-10	180	12-17-80	2002	Miami, Fla.
Sucre, Antonio	.272	37	114	12	31	6	1	2	17	12	28	3	2	.395	.349	R	R	6-1	190	8-13-83	2000	Anzoategui, Venez.
Urquhart, Adrian	.000	9	23	1	0	0	0	0	0	2	9	0	0	.000	.080	R	R	6-1	190	10-1-79	2002	Montgomery, Ala.

GAMES BY POSITION: C—Apodaca 9, Kahr 33, Manriquez 16, Reynaldo Rodriguez 1, Robert Rodriguez 5. **1B**—Blanco 39, Broadway 4, Jimenez 4, Manriquez 17, Mujica 1. **2B**—Clanton 8, Greene 8, Jimenez 35, Mancebo 10, Robert Rodriguez 4. **3B**—Clanton 3, Desena 15, Ellerson 8, Greene 1, Jimenez 1, Mancebo 23, Manriquez 1, Norris 9, Reynaldo Rodriguez 5, Robert Rodriguez 3. **SS**—Clanton 45, Desena 13, Greene 1, Mancebo 4. **OF**—Bernadina 45, Cobb 33, Diaz 49, Greene 1, Honeycutt 21, Jenkins 1, Jimenez 2, Kerner 8, Mujica 1, Sucre 29, Urquhart 7.

PITCHING	W	L	ERA	G	GS	CG	SV	IP	H	R	ER	BB	SO	AVG	B	T	HT	WT	DOB	1st Yr	Resides
Acuna, Jose	1	2	5.20	11	4	0	1	28	28	16	16	7	18	.259	R	R	6-2	180	8-15-81	1999	Cartagena, Colombia
Beck, Ken	0	2	6.75	5	0	0	2	8	8	6	6	3	6	.275	R	R	6-2	190	2-3-80	2002	Laurel, Md.
Casadiego, Gerardo	1	0	0.00	1	0	0	0	3	3	0	0	0	4	.250	R	R	6-0	180	12-19-80	1998	Barquisimeto, Venez.
Diaz, Eddie	0	3	4.56	9	3	0	0	26	24	16	13	8	26	.244	R	R	6-0	170	1-25-83	2001	Orlando, Fla.
Echols, Britt	4	2	2.82	11	10	0	0	51	54	22	16	9	24	.282	R	R	6-5	220	8-11-80	2002	Coal Township, Pa.
Evans, Keith	0	0	1.13	3	2	0	0	8	7	2	1	1	9	.225	R	R	6-5	220	11-2-75	1996	San Pedro, Calif.
Felfoldi, Jonathan	0	2	7.36	4	3	0	0	11	12	9	9	6	11	.292	L	L	6-1	180	7-6-81	2002	San Diego, Calif.
Figueroa, Williams	0	0	5.40	5	0	0	2	5	7	3	3	4	3	.318	R	R	6-1	190	1-5-84	2000	Caracas, Venez.
Galarraga, Armando	0	0	2.45	2	2	0	0	4	1	1	1	0	1	.083	R	R	6-3	170	1-15-82	1999	Caracas, Venez.
Gomez, Warmar	1	0	3.21	19	0	0	4	28	26	12	10	7	20	.247	R	R	6-2	210	5-8-83	2001	Rio Grande, P.R.
Imotichey, Tory	2	4	6.35	13	8	0	1	40	43	33	28	26	25	.288	L	L	6-3	180	8-20-82	2001	Purcell, Okla.
Kirkman, Tyler	2	1	5.14	7	3	0	0	21	23	14	12	5	6	.280	L	L	6-3	180	12-21-82	2001	Mt. Carmel, Ill.
Long, Nick	5	2	1.67	8	6	0	0	38	34	15	7	12	37	.234	R	R	6-3	180	11-24-82	2001	Columbus, Ga.
Marino, Nexcys	3	1	2.31	18	0	0	1	35	27	13	9	11	14	.219	R	R	6-3	170	12-11-83	2001	Monagas, Venez.
Martin, Greg	2	3	3.74	13	1	0	2	34	29	16	14	16	27	.230	L	L	6-1	190	4-10-80	2002	Scranton, Pa.
McAdam, Scott	1	1	3.29	19	0	0	2	27	32	13	10	6	11	.296	R	R	5-11	180	6-5-83	2001	Glenmore Park, Australia
Meyer, Todd	1	2	2.23	9	4	0	0	40	33	14	10	9	30	.222	R	R	6-3	180	8-2-79	2002	York, Pa.
Norderum, Jason	0	1	15.88	4	2	0	0	6	8	10	10	10	6	.363	L	L	6-3	220	11-21-81	2000	Redding, Calif.
Pearson, Anthony	0	1	8.22	4	2	0	0	8	11	8	7	6	4	.323	R	R	6-5	200	8-14-81	2002	Baton Rouge, La.
Pole, Hank	1	1	3.65	6	0	0	0	12	13	5	5	2	6	.276	R	R	6-1	180	7-22-82	2002	Trout Creek, Mich.
Thorne, David	3	2	1.50	9	9	0	0	42	33	12	7	19	45	.214	R	R	6-3	170	9-18-81	1999	Sydney, Australia
Torres, Luis	0	0	0.00	1	1	0	0	5	4	0	0	0	4	.235	R	R	6-4	200	3-12-81	1999	Caracas, Venez.
Wright, Isaiah	1	2	5.57	13	0	0	0	21	24	16	13	14	10	.303	R	R	6-1	170	7-21-83	2002	Dover, Del.

ORGANIZATION STATISTICS

NEW YORK YANKEES

BY GEORGE KING

The Yankees didn't win the 2002 World Series. Or make it there for the fifth straight year. Nor did they advance past the American League Division Series, where they were bounced hard by the Angels in four games.

So, 103 wins and a fifth straight AL East title meant very little to a team that is built for October by a demanding owner who looks at any season that doesn't include a World Series appearance as a downer.

As the Angels and Giants played in the Fall Classic, somewhere Yankee fans wrongly believe is their destiny to finish every season, the Yankees went about trying to fix what went wrong.

The vaunted pitching staff of Roger Clemens, Andy Pettitte, Mike Mussina and David Wells got shelled by an Angel lineup that put the bat on the ball. The best starting effort was a very pedestrian outing by Clemens, who allowed four runs and eight hits in 5⅔ innings in a Game One victory.

So, after a summer of answering questions about age (Clemens and Wells) and physical condition (Clemens, Wells and Pettitte), the Yankees watched the pillar of their latest dynasty crumble. It was so hard to watch that pitching coach Mel Stottlemyre decided to put off retirement plans and work one more year because he didn't want to go out on such a sour note.

Clemens became a free agent after the World Series, and the Yankees had an $11.5 million option on Pettitte, who missed two months before the all-star break with a balky left elbow. Clemens, Steinbrenner and Joe Torre wanted Clemens, seven victories shy of 300, back.

"This is a very good team that didn't play well for four days (in October)," general manager Brian Cashman said.

Whenever Steinbrenner was asked about his club during the season, he always delivered the same message in different words. "Cash and Joe assure me this is a team

Alfonso Soriano   Andy Phillips

RODGER WOOD

PLAYERS OF THE YEAR

MAJOR LEAGUE: Alfonso Soriano, 2b
Soriano fell one home run short from becoming just the fourth 40 homer-40 stolen base player in major league history. He led the American League with 41 stolen bases, 128 runs and 209 hits.

MINOR LEAGUE: Andy Phillips, 2b
An offensive second baseman like Soriano, Phillips led all Yankees minor leaguers with 28 home runs and 90 runs scored while ranking second with 87 RBIs and fourth with a .287 average.

that is good enough to get to the World Series," The Boss said countless times.

"I get paid a lot of money ($5 million a year) to sit here and make these decisions," Torre said after the ALDS. "Winning the World Series is something that you are supposed to do. I don't feel pressured. That's what makes this thing exciting. We know what George needs to have happen, and we certainly work toward that end."

With a $117 million salary threshold in place and clubs being taxed 17.5 cents on every dollar over the limit, Steinbrenner has vowed his payroll—$140 million at the end of the year—would be reduced. After the loss to the Angels, the Yankees explored ways to dump Raul Mondesi ($7 million), Sterling Hitchcock ($6 million) and Rondell White ($5 million).

In 2003, Juan Rivera will get a chance to be a regular outfielder, but immediate help for the rotation isn't expected from the minors after top pitching prospect Brandon Claussen had Tommy John surgery on his left elbow. Drew Henson is still a ways away from being ready to play third base in the big leagues.

Because the core—Derek Jeter, Jason Giambi, Bernie Williams, Jorge Posada, Alfonso Soriano and Mariano Rivera—is so good, the Yankees weren't in position to blow it all up and start over. However, they learned a hard lesson when their pitching melted.

Jeff Weaver, 26, will be in the 2003 rotation. That's why he was acquired in July from the Athletics via the Tigers. How he performs may dictate what type of season the Yankees have.

Of course, what kind of season the Yankees have will be also determined by how deep into October they play. But one thing's for sure: Not having won the title for two straight years chafes Steinbrenner's skin.

ORGANIZATION LEADERS

BATTING

*AVG	Juan Rivera, Columbus/GCL Yankees	.324
R	Andy Phillips, Columbus/Norwich	90
H	Robinson Cano, Greensboro/Staten Island	155
TB	Andy Phillips, Columbus/Norwich	262
2B	Mitch Jones, Norwich/Tampa	35
	Andy Phillips, Columbus/Norwich	35
3B	Robinson Cano, Greensboro/Staten Island	10
HR	Andy Phillips, Columbus/Norwich	28
RBI	Mike Cervenak, Norwich	91
BB	Brian Myrow, Norwich/Tampa	83
SO	Drew Henson, Columbus	151
	Andy Brown, Tampa	151
SB	Kevin Thompson, Tampa/Greensboro/SI	31

PITCHING

W	Julio DePaula, Norwich	14
L	Matt Smith, Norwich/Tampa	12
#ERA	Danny Borrell, Norwich/Tampa	2.32
G	Jay Tessmer, Columbus	63
CG	Julio DePaula, Norwich	6
SV	Mathew Brumit, Staten Island	22
IP	Javier Ortiz, Tampa/Greensboro	177
BB	Jeremy King, Greensboro	66
SO	Julio DePaula, Norwich	152

*Minimum 250 At-Bats #Minimum 75 Innings

NEW YORK YANKEES

Manager: Joe Torre

2002 Record: 103-58, .640 (1st, AL East)

ORGANIZATION STATISTICS

BATTING	AVG	G	AB	R	H	2B	3B	HR	RBI	BB	SO	SB	CS	SLG	OBP	B	T	HT	WT	DOB	1st Yr	Resides
Arias, Alex	.000	6	7	0	0	0	0	0	0	1	2	0	0	.000	.125	R	R	6-3	200	11-20-67	1987	Hollywood, Fla.
Castillo, Alberto	.135	15	37	3	5	1	1	0	4	1	12	0	0	.216	.158	R	R	6-0	200	2-10-70	1987	Port St. Lucie, Fla.
Coomer, Ron	.264	55	148	14	39	7	0	3	17	6	23	0	0	.372	.290	R	R	6-0	210	11-18-66	1987	Chicago, Ill.
Garcia, Karim	.200	2	5	1	1	0	0	0	0	0	1	0	0	.200	.200	L	L	6-0	180	10-29-75	1992	Ciudad Obregon, Mexico
Giambi, Jason	.314	155	560	120	176	34	1	41	122	109	112	2	2	.598	.435	L	R	6-3	230	1-8-71	1992	Covina, Calif.
Henson, Drew	.000	3	1	1	0	0	0	0	0	0	1	0	0	.000	.000	R	R	6-5	220	2-13-80	1998	Brighton, Mich.
Jeter, Derek	.297	157	644	124	191	26	0	18	75	73	114	32	3	.421	.373	R	R	6-3	190	6-26-74	1992	Tampa, Fla.
Johnson, Nick	.243	129	378	56	92	15	0	15	58	48	98	1	3	.402	.347	L	L	6-3	220	9-19-78	1996	Sacramento, Calif.
Mondesi, Raul	.241	71	270	39	65	18	0	11	43	28	46	6	4	.430	.315	R	R	5-11	230	3-2-71	1988	San Cristobal, D.R.
2-team (75 Toronto)	.232	146	569	90	132	34	1	26	88	59	103	15	6	.432	.308							
Posada, Jorge	.268	143	511	79	137	40	1	20	99	81	143	1	0	.468	.370	S	R	6-2	200	8-17-71	1991	Tampa, Fla.
Rivera, Juan	.265	28	83	9	22	5	0	1	6	6	10	1	1	.361	.311	R	R	6-2	170	7-3-78	1996	Guarenas, Venez.
Soriano, Alfonso	.300	156	696	128	209	51	2	39	102	23	157	41	13	.547	.332	R	R	6-1	180	1-7-78	1999	San Pedro de Macoris, D.R.
Spencer, Shane	.247	94	288	32	71	15	2	6	34	31	62	0	3	.375	.324	R	R	6-0	220	2-20-72	1990	Tampa, Fla.
Thames, Marcus	.231	7	13	2	3	1	0	1	2	0	4	0	0	.538	.231	R	R	6-2	200	3-6-77	1997	Louisville, Miss.
Vander Wal, John	.260	84	219	30	57	17	1	6	20	23	58	1	1	.429	.327	L	L	6-1	210	4-29-66	1987	Grand Rapids, Mich.
Ventura, Robin	.247	141	465	68	115	17	0	27	93	90	101	3	1	.458	.368	L	R	6-1	190	7-14-67	1989	Greenwich, Conn.
White, Rondell	.240	126	455	59	109	21	0	14	62	25	86	1	2	.378	.288	R	R	6-1	220	2-23-72	1990	Gray, Ga.
Widger, Chris	.297	21	64	4	19	5	0	0	5	2	9	0	0	.375	.338	R	R	6-2	210	5-21-71	1992	Pennsville, N.J.
Williams, Bernie	.333	154	612	102	204	37	2	19	102	83	97	8	4	.493	.415	S	R	6-2	200	9-13-68	1986	Armonk, N.Y.
Williams, Gerald	.000	30	6	0	0	0	0	0	2	0	4	2	0	.000	.105	R	R	6-2	180	8-10-66	1987	Tampa, Fla.
Wilson, Enrique	.181	60	105	17	19	2	2	2	11	8	22	1	1	.295	.239	S	R	5-11	190	7-27-73	1992	Santo Domingo, D.R.

PITCHING	W	L	ERA	G	GS	CG	SV	IP	H	R	ER	BB	SO	AVG	B	T	HT	WT	DOB	1st Yr	Resides
Choate, Randy	0	0	6.04	18	0	0	0	22	18	18	15	15	17	.216	L	L	6-2	190	9-5-75	1997	Tampa, Fla.
Clemens, Roger	13	6	4.35	29	29	0	0	180	172	94	87	63	192	.250	R	R	6-4	230	8-4-62	1983	Houston, Texas
Hernandez, Adrian	0	1	12.00	2	1	0	0	6	10	8	8	6	9	.357	R	R	6-1	180	3-25-75	2000	Tampa, Fla.
Hernandez, Orlando	8	5	3.64	24	22	0	1	146	131	63	59	36	113	.235	R	R	6-2	220	10-11-69	1998	Miami, Fla.
Hitchcock, Sterling	1	2	5.49	20	2	0	0	39	57	29	24	15	31	.325	L	L	6-0	200	4-29-71	1989	Tampa, Fla.
Karsay, Steve	6	4	3.26	78	0	0	12	88	87	33	32	30	65	.258	R	R	6-3	210	3-24-72	1990	Scottsdale, Ariz.
Knight, Brandon	0	0	11.42	7	0	0	0	9	11	12	11	5	7	.305	L	R	6-0	190	10-1-75	1995	Ventura, Calif.
Lilly, Ted	3	6	3.40	16	11	2	0	77	57	31	29	24	59	.202	L	L	6-1	190	1-4-76	1996	Oakhurst, Calif.
Mendoza, Ramiro	8	4	3.44	62	0	0	4	92	102	43	35	16	61	.274	R	R	6-2	190	6-15-72	1992	Los Santos, Panama
Mussina, Mike	18	10	4.05	33	33	2	0	216	208	103	97	48	182	.252	S	R	6-2	180	12-8-68	1990	Montoursville, Pa.
Pettitte, Andy	13	5	3.27	22	22	3	0	135	144	58	49	32	97	.272	L	L	6-5	220	6-15-72	1991	Deer Park, Texas
Rivera, Mariano	1	4	2.74	45	0	0	28	46	35	16	14	11	41	.203	R	R	6-2	180	11-29-69	1990	La Chorrera, Panama
Stanton, Mike	7	1	3.00	79	0	0	6	78	73	29	26	28	44	.256	L	L	6-1	210	6-2-67	1987	Magnolia, Texas
Tessmer, Jay	0	0	6.75	2	0	0	0	1	0	1	1	2	0	.000	R	R	6-3	180	12-26-71	1995	Port St. Lucie, Fla.
Thurman, Mike	1	0	5.18	12	2	0	0	33	45	21	19	12	23	.328	R	R	6-5	220	7-22-73	1994	West Palm Beach, Fla.
Weaver, Jeff	5	3	4.04	15	8	0	2	78	81	38	35	15	57	.260	R	R	6-5	200	8-22-76	1998	Simi Valley, Calif.
2-team (17 Detroit)	11	11	3.52	32	25	3	2	200	193	88	78	48	132	.250							
Wells, David	19	7	3.75	31	31	2	0	206	210	100	86	45	137	.258	L	L	6-4	230	5-20-63	1982	Clearwater, Fla.

FIELDING

Catcher	PCT	G	PO	A	E	DP	PB
Castillo	.990	14	93	9	1	0	2
Posada	.988	138	965	66	12	5	7
Widger	.983	21	111	6	2	1	1

First Base	PCT	G	PO	A	E	DP
Coomer	.985	11	60	6	1	5
Giambi	.995	92	761	35	4	53
Johnson	.988	78	519	44	7	46
Vander Wal	1.000	6	32	0	0	3
Ventura	1.000	5	19	2	0	1

Second Base	PCT	G	PO	A	E	DP
Soriano	.968	155	300	402	23	86
Wilson	1.000	7	15	18	0	5

Third Base	PCT	G	PO	A	E	DP
Arias	.750	4	0	3	1	1
Coomer	.882	26	12	33	6	2
Ventura	.941	137	109	261	23	22

Wilson	.932	26	15	26	3	1

Shortstop	PCT	G	PO	A	E	DP
Arias	1.000	1	0	3	0	0
Jeter	.977	156	219	367	14	69
Wilson	.941	14	11	21	2	5

Outfield	PCT	G	PO	A	E	DP
Garcia	1.000	2	1	0	0	0
Johnson	1.000	2	2	0	0	0
Mondesi	.969	70	121	4	4	0
Rivera	.966	28	54	2	2	1
Spencer	.975	91	152	5	4	1
Thames	1.000	7	7	0	0	0
Vander Wal	.978	57	87	0	2	0
White	1.000	113	246	3	0	0
B. Williams	.986	147	350	2	5	1
G. Williams	1.000	30	12	1	0	1
Wilson	.000	1	0	0	0	0

DIAMOND IMAGES

Jason Giambi

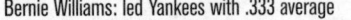
Bernie Williams: led Yankees with .333 average | David Wells: surprise staff leader with 19 wins

MICHAEL WALBY | LARRY GOREN

FARM SYSTEM

Director, Player Development: Rob Thomson

Class	Farm Team	League	W	L	Pct.	Finish*	Manager(s)	First Yr.
AAA	Columbus (Ohio) Clippers	International	59	83	.415	12th (14)	Brian Butterfield/Stump Merrill	1979
AA	Norwich (Conn.) Navigators	Eastern	76	64	.543	+3rd (12)	Stump Merrill/Luis Sojo	1995
High A	Tampa (Fla.) Yankees	Florida State	71	62	.534	5th (12)	Mitch Seoane	1994
Low A	Greensboro (N.C.) Bats	South Atlantic	75	65	.535	7th (16)	Bill Masse	1990
SS A	Staten Island (N.Y.) Yankees	New York-Penn	48	26	.649	+1st (14)	Derek Shelton	1999
Rookie	Tampa (Fla.) Yankees	Gulf Coast	36	24	.600	3rd (14)	Manny Crespo	1980

*Finish in overall standings (No. of teams in league)   +League champion

COLUMBUS CLIPPERS   Class AAA

INTERNATIONAL LEAGUE

BATTING	AVG	G	AB	R	H	2B	3B	HR	RBI	BB	SO	SB	CS	SLG	OBP	B	T	HT	WT	DOB	1st Yr	Resides
Abbott, Kurt	.273	3	11	2	3	1	0	0	1	1	1	0	0	.364	.333	R	R	6-0	200	6-2-69	1989	Davie, Fla.
Almonte, Erick	.235	66	221	25	52	10	1	9	28	15	60	2	1	.412	.282	R	R	6-2	180	2-1-78	1996	Santo Domingo, D.R.
Arias, Alex	.265	61	211	32	56	16	0	1	22	16	15	3	2	.355	.322	R	R	6-3	200	11-20-67	1987	Hollywood, Fla.
2-team (16 Rochester)	.240	77	263	34	63	18	0	1	25	21	26	3	2	.319	.300							
Bierek, Kurt	.218	51	147	13	32	8	0	2	12	12	29	1	1	.313	.294	L	R	6-4	220	9-13-72	1993	Tampa, Fla.
Bridges, Kary	.263	134	502	72	132	8	4	8	39	46	26	7	7	.343	.325	L	R	5-10	170	10-27-72	1993	Hattiesburg, Miss.
Castillo, Alberto	.275	30	91	7	25	7	0	0	8	9	8	1	0	.352	.350	R	R	6-0	150	5-30-84	2001	Santo Domingo, D.R.
Davidson, Cleatus	.000	1	1	0	0	0	0	0	0	0	1	0	0	.000	.000	S	R	5-10	180	11-1-76	1994	Haines City, Fla.
Garcia, Karim	.271	74	288	44	78	16	3	12	49	20	48	1	5	.472	.316	L	L	6-0	180	10-29-75	1992	Ciudad Obregon, Mexico
Gubanich, Creighton	.186	37	97	10	18	3	0	3	5	9	27	2	0	.309	.262	R	R	6-3	230	3-27-72	1991	Phoenixville, Pa.
Henson, Drew	.240	128	471	68	113	30	4	18	65	37	151	2	1	.435	.301	R	R	6-5	220	2-13-80	1998	Brighton, Mich.
Hernandez, Michel	.281	41	121	11	34	5	1	1	12	8	13	1	3	.364	.336	R	R	6-0	210	8-12-78	1998	Caracas, Venez.
Johnson, Nick	.091	3	11	1	1	0	0	0	0	1	4	0	0	.091	.167	L	L	6-3	220	9-19-78	1996	Sacramento, Calif.
Leach, Jalal	.251	92	287	35	72	14	5	7	28	19	49	6	4	.408	.297	L	L	6-2	220	3-14-69	1990	Novato, Calif.
McMillon, Billy	.301	115	442	72	133	32	3	8	46	59	71	2	5	.441	.388	L	L	5-11	170	11-17-71	1993	Indianapolis, Ind.
Nettles, Jeff	.242	24	62	4	15	5	1	0	5	6	16	1	2	.355	.304	R	R	6-2	200	8-20-78	1998	Encinitas, Calif.
Perez, Robert	.275	84	338	47	93	22	3	11	49	13	35	7	4	.456	.299	R	R	6-3	230	6-4-69	1990	Bolivar, Venez.
2-team (43 Indianapolis)	.254	127	460	54	117	28	3	14	62	15	56	9	7	.420	.276							
Phillips, Andy	.263	51	205	32	54	11	1	9	36	10	46	0	1	.459	.296	R	R	6-0	200	4-6-77	1999	Demopolis, Ala.
Polcovich, Kevin	.000	1	0	0	0	0	0	0	0	0	0	0	0	.000	.000	R	R	5-9	180	6-28-70	1992	Auburn, N.Y.
Rivera, Juan	.325	65	265	40	86	21	1	8	47	13	39	5	1	.502	.355	R	R	6-2	170	7-3-78	1996	Guarenas Miranda, Venez.
Santangelo, F.P.	.067	7	15	1	1	0	0	0	1	5	4	2	0	.067	.300	S	R	5-10	160	10-24-67	1989	El Dorado Hills, Calif.
Seabol, Scott	.259	121	428	56	111	29	1	15	68	29	89	3	3	.437	.309	R	R	6-4	200	5-17-75	1996	McKeesport, Pa.
Thames, Marcus	.207	107	386	51	80	21	3	13	45	43	71	5	4	.378	.297	R	R	6-2	200	3-6-77	1997	Louisville, Miss.
Widger, Chris	.244	61	217	26	53	14	1	10	39	17	31	0	3	.456	.300	R	R	6-2	210	5-21-71	1992	Pennsville, N.J.

PITCHING	W	L	ERA	G	GS	CG	SV	IP	H	R	ER	BB	SO	AVG	B	T	HT	WT	DOB	1st Yr	Resides
Anderson, Jason	5	1	3.15	26	0	0	7	34	26	13	12	11	28	.211	L	R	6-0	170	6-9-79	2000	Danville, Ill.
Beal, Andy	2	4	6.04	8	8	0	0	45	50	36	30	21	31	.289	L	L	6-2	180	10-31-78	2000	Paducah, Ky.
Beech, Matt	3	7	5.15	16	16	0	0	86	99	55	49	44	66	.290	L	L	6-2	190	1-20-72	1994	Clearwater, Fla.
Blevins, Jeremy	1	3	4.50	17	0	0	0	24	27	17	12	14	17	.287	R	R	6-2	210	10-5-77	1995	Bristol, Tenn.
Bradley, Ryan	0	0	18.00	1	0	0	0	1	4	2	2	0	1	.571	R	R	6-4	200	10-26-75	1997	Chino Hills, Calif.
Choate, Randy	3	2	1.72	31	0	0	1	37	25	8	7	15	32	.189	L	L	6-2	190	9-5-75	1997	Tampa, Fla.
Claussen, Brandon	2	8	3.28	15	15	0	0	93	85	47	34	46	73	.242	L	L	6-2	200	5-1-79	1999	Roswell, N.M.
Dillinger, Jon	0	1	7.89	9	2	0	0	22	24	22	19	12	24	.282	R	R	6-5	260	8-28-73	1992	Dawson, Pa.
Dingman, Craig	0	0	13.50	2	0	0	0	1	6	6	2	1	2	.545	R	R	6-4	210	3-12-74	1994	Wichita, Kan.
2-team (22 Louisville)	0	1	4.61	24	0	0	0	27	26	18	14	14	28	.250							
Donaldson, Bo	5	4	3.56	29	9	0	0	78	76	35	31	27	64	.256	R	R	6-0	200	10-10-74	1997	Tampa, Fla.
Field, Nathan	2	1	6.75	21	2	0	0	39	46	30	29	21	25	.304	R	R	6-2	200	12-11-75	1998	Littleton, Colo.
Graman, Alex	6	9	4.65	20	20	1	0	124	141	74	64	37	98	.283	L	L	6-4	200	11-17-77	1999	Huntingburg, Ind.
Hernandez, Adrian	6	7	5.25	20	20	0	0	110	114	67	64	45	109	.269	R	R	6-1	180	3-25-75	2000	Tampa, Fla.
Hernandez, Orlando	0	1	1.59	1	1	0	0	6	7	2	1	1	5	.280	R	R	6-2	220	10-11-69	1998	Miami, Fla.
Hitchcock, Sterling	0	0	13.50	2	2	0	0	7	19	11	11	3	3	.487	L	L	6-0	200	4-29-71	1989	Tampa, Fla.
Jean, Domingo	0	2	5.45	19	0	0	0	33	29	23	20	17	31	.230	R	R	6-2	170	1-9-69	1990	Coventry, Conn.
Jodie, Brett	1	1	5.40	6	2	0	0	18	24	14	11	7	7	.328	R	R	6-4	200	3-25-77	1998	Lexington, S.C.
Knight, Brandon	2	7	3.90	36	7	1	12	81	67	40	35	37	81	.219	L	R	6-0	190	10-1-75	1995	Ventura, Calif.
Lovingier, Kevin	0	2	6.37	21	1	0	1	30	41	30	21	28	19	.333	L	L	6-1	190	8-29-71	1994	Wichita, Kan.
McNichol, Brian	0	1	6.57	13	0	0	0	12	17	13	9	5	10	.320	L	L	6-5	220	5-20-74	1995	Woodbridge, Va.
Pacheco, Alex	0	1	2.03	14	0	0	2	13	13	5	3	6	15	.250	R	R	6-3	170	7-19-73	1990	Caracas, Venez.
Pulsipher, Bill	0	0	14.73	6	0	0	0	4	10	6	6	4	4	.500	S	L	6-3	200	10-9-73	1992	Port St. Lucie, Fla.
Rogers, Brian	6	6	5.68	14	13	0	0	71	80	49	45	27	51	.281	R	R	6-6	200	2-13-77	1998	Carthage, N.C.
Scanlan, Bob	0	1	4.86	34	0	0	1	46	66	34	25	14	25	.335	R	R	6-7	210	8-9-66	1984	Beverly Hills, Calif.
Shepard, David	0	1	7.20	1	1	0	0	5	6	5	4	2	2	.285	R	R	6-1	190	2-6-74	1996	Sarasota, Fla.
Tessmer, Jay	5	4	4.37	63	0	0	0	78	109	42	38	14	54	.327	R	R	6-3	180	12-26-71	1995	Port St. Lucie, Fla.
Thurman, Mike	7	3	3.52	12	12	0	0	77	83	34	30	14	51	.270	R	R	6-5	220	7-22-73	1994	West Palm Beach, Fla.
Walling, Dave	2	7	4.54	11	11	1	0	67	73	38	34	11	46	.270	R	R	6-6	220	11-12-78	1999	Norman, Okla.

FIELDING

Catcher	PCT	G	PO	A	E	DP	PB
Castillo	.984	30	230	15	4	2	1
Gubanich	.972	34	192	15	6	1	3
Hernandez	.966	37	208	16	8	1	3
Nettles	1.000	1	2	0	0	0	0
Widger	.990	55	367	19	4	1	3

First Base	PCT	G	PO	A	E	DP
Abbott	1.000	1	13	1	0	1
Bierek	.979	36	262	20	6	25
Bridges	1.000	11	83	7	0	12
Garcia	1.000	5	26	1	0	1
Johnson	1.000	3	21	4	0	3
McMillon	1.000	1	7	0	0	1
Nettles	.963	3	21	5	1	4
Perez	1.000	1	5	1	0	2
Phillips	1.000	2	14	1	0	1
Seabol	.984	89	695	58	12	51

Second Base	PCT	G	PO	A	E	DP
Abbott	1.000	2	3	8	0	0
Arias	.000	1	0	0	0	0
Bridges	.984	100	184	238	7	48
Nettles	1.000	5	2	8	0	1
Phillips	.984	41	74	105	3	28
Seabol	1.000	3	2	5	0	1
Tessmer	.000	1	0	0	0	0

Third Base	PCT	G	PO	A	E	DP
Arias	.938	7	3	12	1	2
Bierek	1.000	1	0	1	0	0
Gubanich	.000	1	0	0	0	0
Henson	.893	125	87	204	35	11
Nettles	.833	4	0	5	1	0
Seabol	1.000	9	7	18	0	2
Tessmer	.000	1	0	0	0	0

Shortstop	PCT	G	PO	A	E	DP
Almonte	.937	63	99	167	18	29

	PCT	G	PO	A	E	DP
Arias	.996	55	82	146	1	31
Bridges	.977	9	15	28	1	9
Nettles	.947	9	18	18	2	4
Polcovich	.000	1	0	0	1	0
Santangelo	.933	3	5	9	1	1
Seabol	.912	14	19	33	5	5

Outfield	PCT	G	PO	A	E	DP
Bierek	.833	3	5	0	1	0
Garcia	.984	51	122	3	2	2
Knight	.000	1	0	0	0	0
Leach	.970	56	96	3	3	0
McMillon	.993	75	131	2	1	1
Perez	.970	78	157	5	5	0
Rivera	.955	64	113	14	6	2
Seabol	1.000	5	0	0	0	0
Thames	.983	104	290	7	5	0
Widger	1.000	1	1	0	0	0

NORWICH NAVIGATORS — Class AA

EASTERN LEAGUE

BATTING	AVG	G	AB	R	H	2B	3B	HR	RBI	BB	SO	SB	CS	SLG	OBP	B	T	HT	WT	DOB	1st Yr	Resides
Almonte, Erick	.241	53	187	28	45	7	0	8	33	30	59	10	2	.406	.342	R	R	6-2	180	2-1-78	1996	Santo Domingo, D.R.
Brown, Rich	.253	23	83	9	21	7	0	1	8	6	14	1	1	.373	.311	L	L	6-1	190	4-28-77	1996	Plantation, Fla.
Calabrese, Tony	.357	8	14	2	5	1	0	0	1	1	5	0	0	.429	.400	R	R	6-4	190	11-5-78	2000	Riverside, Conn.
Cervenak, Mike	.276	134	492	74	136	34	1	21	91	30	78	5	2	.478	.330	R	R	5-11	180	8-17-76	1999	New Boston, Mich.
Cronin, Shane	.232	23	69	8	16	5	0	3	16	8	10	0	1	.435	.313	R	R	6-1	210	2-26-76	1996	Renton, Wash.
Davidson, Cleatus	.303	31	66	12	20	2	0	2	12	6	13	4	6	.394	.378	S	R	5-10	180	11-1-76	1994	Haines City, Fla.
2-team (23 New Haven)	.254	54	118	19	30	2	3	1	19	11	25	6	6	.347	.328							
Davis, Glenn	.261	7	23	5	6	1	2	1	1	4	5	0	1	.609	.370	S	L	6-1	200	11-25-75	1997	Aston, Pa.
Elwood, Brad	.000	1	1	0	0	0	0	0	0	0	0	0	0	.000	.000	R	R	6-1	190	10-22-75	1998	Clear Spring, Md.
Gibbs, Kevin	.295	63	217	36	64	8	3	2	18	21	32	20	8	.387	.357	S	R	6-2	180	4-3-74	1995	Davidsonville, Md.
Griffin, John-Ford	.328	18	67	17	22	3	0	5	10	8	13	0	1	.597	.400	L	L	6-2	210	11-19-79	2001	Sarasota, Fla.
Hernandez, Michel	.311	20	61	11	19	6	1	0	12	5	6	0	1	.459	.358	R	R	6-0	210	8-12-78	1998	Caracas, Venez.
Hooper, Clay	.233	77	236	32	55	6	1	2	16	21	34	0	6	.292	.305	R	R	6-1	190	4-9-77	2000	Greensboro, N.C.
Jackson, Brandon	.169	24	65	8	11	2	0	1	8	5	15	0	2	.246	.219	R	R	6-1	180	10-28-75	1998	House Springs, Mo.
Jones, Mitch	.218	61	216	31	47	16	0	10	27	18	59	1	4	.431	.290	R	R	6-2	210	10-15-77	2000	Orem, Utah
Kinchen, Jason	.236	41	123	14	29	5	1	7	19	15	27	1	1	.463	.317	L	R	6-0	210	7-30-75	1997	Baton Rouge, La.
Leach, Nick	.158	10	19	2	3	0	0	1	3	4	4	0	0	.316	.333	L	R	6-1	190	12-7-77	1996	Madera, Calif.
Loggins, Josh	.204	34	98	6	20	5	0	1	5	5	26	1	1	.286	.243	R	R	6-1	190	11-29-76	1998	West Lafayette, Ind.
Myrow, Brian	.303	61	188	37	57	16	0	3	30	41	42	5	0	.436	.441	L	R	5-11	190	9-4-76	1999	Fort Worth, Texas
Nettles, Jeff	.274	44	106	10	29	5	0	3	17	14	25	0	0	.406	.364	R	R	6-2	200	8-20-78	1998	Encinitas, Calif.
Olivares, Teuris	.261	40	142	22	37	6	1	2	15	13	30	4	3	.359	.327	R	R	6-0	160	12-15-78	1996	San Pedro de Macoris, D.R.
Parrish, Dave	.238	106	341	38	81	17	1	4	42	39	63	13	6	.328	.322	R	R	6-3	220	6-13-79	2000	Yorba Linda, Calif.
Phillips, Andy	.305	73	272	58	83	24	2	19	51	33	56	4	3	.618	.381	R	R	6-0	200	4-6-77	1999	Demopolis, Ala.
Reese, Kevin	.290	138	514	80	149	26	4	4	45	77	89	22	14	.383	.385	L	L	5-11	190	3-11-78	2000	San Diego, Calif.
Rifkin, Aaron	.251	70	235	40	59	13	1	4	34	28	64	5	3	.366	.337	L	L	6-3	220	3-12-79	2001	Upland, Calif.
Rodriguez, John	.215	103	354	51	76	18	3	15	63	35	94	13	3	.410	.302	L	L	6-0	180	1-20-78	1997	New York, N.Y.
Snusz, Chris	.146	15	41	3	6	2	0	1	3	2	13	0	0	.268	.205	R	R	6-0	190	11-8-72	1995	Buffalo, N.Y.

BATTING	AVG	G	AB	R	H	2B	3B	HR	RBI	BB	SO	SB	CS	SLG	OBP	B	T	HT	WT	DOB	1st Yr	Resides
Tyson, Torre	.171	15	35	6	6	0	0	0	3	5	8	1	2	.171	.293	S	R	5-10	180	12-31-75	1998	Columbia, Mo.
Vento, Mike	.238	64	227	29	54	16	2	4	26	25	49	3	3	.379	.314	R	R	6-0	190	5-25-78	1998	Corrales, N.M.

PITCHING	W	L	ERA	G	GS	CG	SV	IP	H	R	ER	BB	SO	AVG	B	T	HT	WT	DOB	1st Yr	Resides
Anderson, Jason	1	1	0.93	16	0	0	2	19	14	2	2	5	21	.212	L	R	6-0	170	6-9-79	2000	Danville, Ill.
Arnold, Jason	1	2	4.15	3	3	0	0	17	17	14	8	5	18	.253	R	R	6-3	210	5-2-79	2001	Palm Bay, Fla.
Beal, Andy	4	5	3.30	10	10	1	0	63	56	26	23	22	61	.240	L	L	6-2	180	10-31-78	2000	Paducah, Ky.
Bean, Colter	0	2	6.75	12	0	0	0	11	14	8	8	6	9	.318	R	R	6-6	250	1-16-77	2000	Anniston, Ala.
Beech, Matt	3	1	1.56	7	5	1	0	35	28	11	6	13	39	.220	L	L	6-2	210	1-20-72	1994	Clearwater, Fla.
Blevins, Jeremy	4	0	2.77	19	0	0	1	26	24	10	8	14	23	.233	L	L	6-2	210	10-5-77	1995	Bristol, Tenn.
Borrell, Danny	9	4	2.31	21	20	1	0	128	116	44	33	39	91	.238	L	L	6-3	200	1-24-79	2000	Sanford, N.C.
Buchanan, Brian	0	0	5.74	11	0	0	0	16	20	13	10	6	11	.307	L	L	6-4	230	4-23-77	1995	Oviedo, Fla.
Clemens, Roger	0	1	1.29	1	1	0	0	7	5	1	1	0	7	.200	R	R	6-4	230	8-4-62	1983	Houston, Texas
De Paula, Julio	14	6	3.45	27	26	6	0	175	141	74	67	52	152	.220	R	R	6-1	160	7-27-79	1997	Santo Domingo, D.R.
Donaldson, Bo	0	4	4.55	17	0	0	0	28	21	14	14	5	30	.207	R	R	6-0	200	10-10-74	1997	Tampa, Fla.
Einertson, Darrell	0	2	16.20	4	0	0	0	3	7	9	6	3	2	.388	R	R	6-2	190	9-4-72	1995	Urbandale, Iowa
Etherton, Seth	0	0	0.00	1	1	0	0	2	1	1	0	1	2	.142	R	R	6-1	200	10-17-76	1998	Monarch Beach, Calif.
Glick, David	3	1	2.57	8	4	0	0	28	23	12	8	11	24	.221	L	L	6-4	200	4-2-76	1995	Palmdale, Calif.
Graman, Alex	5	2	2.88	8	8	2	0	50	46	19	16	13	31	.242	L	L	6-4	200	11-17-77	1999	Huntingburg, Ind.
Jean, Domingo	0	4	3.38	36	0	0	19	37	38	16	14	8	26	.263	R	R	6-2	170	1-9-69	1990	Coventry, Conn.
Jodie, Brett	0	0	1.69	2	2	0	0	11	5	2	2	4	7	.147	R	R	6-4	200	3-25-77	1998	Lexington, S.C.
Lovingier, Kevin	0	2	1.96	19	0	0	0	18	21	5	4	7	12	.291	L	L	6-1	190	8-29-71	1994	Wichita, Kan.
Manning, Charlie	4	2	3.57	11	11	1	0	63	55	27	25	26	61	.235	L	L	6-2	180	3-31-79	2001	Winter Haven, Fla.
Marsonek, Sam	5	8	5.01	19	13	1	0	101	111	68	56	34	75	.276	R	R	6-5	220	7-10-78	1997	Tampa, Fla.
Pettitte, Andy	0	0	1.42	1	1	0	0	6	2	1	1	0	5	.095	L	L	6-5	220	6-15-72	1991	Deer Park, Texas
Pierson, Jason	0	0	7.71	11	0	0	0	14	22	12	12	3	12	.354	R	R	6-0	190	1-6-71	1992	Berwyn, Pa.
Rogers, Brian	7	2	2.77	13	11	1	0	68	69	29	21	16	48	.263	R	R	6-4	200	2-13-77	1998	Carthage, N.C.
Roller, Adam	2	1	3.27	21	0	0	9	22	19	10	8	13	20	.231	R	R	6-3	200	6-27-78	1997	Lakeland, Fla.
Shepard, David	8	7	4.43	42	0	0	1	87	87	47	43	24	66	.252	R	R	6-1	190	2-6-74	1996	Sarasota, Fla.
Smith, Matt	3	8	5.44	17	17	0	0	89	112	63	54	37	70	.305	L	L	6-5	220	6-15-79	2000	Henderson, Nev.
Stevens, Josh	1	1	3.83	24	0	0	0	40	50	21	17	8	33	.308	R	R	6-4	200	6-6-79	1998	Riverside, Calif.
Wiggins, Scott	2	1	2.28	24	0	0	0	28	19	8	7	9	26	.191	L	L	6-3	200	3-24-76	1997	Newport, Ky.

FIELDING

Catcher	PCT	G	PO	A	E	DP	PB
Cronin	1.000	19	99	8	0	1	3
Elwood	.000	1	0	0	0	0	0
Hernandez	.981	9	43	13	2	0	3
Parrish	.981	100	700	75	15	6	19
Snusz	.980	15	91	5	2	0	1

First Base	PCT	G	PO	A	E	DP
Cervenak	.990	63	458	28	5	33
Cronin	1.000	1	8	0	0	1
Davis	.981	6	50	3	1	3
Hooper	1.000	2	2	0	0	0
Kinchen	.957	6	44	0	2	6
Leach	1.000	9	49	3	0	2
Nettles	1.000	1	6	0	0	0
Rifkin	.992	63	467	22	4	48

Second Base	PCT	G	PO	A	E	DP
Calabrese	1.000	2	3	5	0	0
Cervenak	1.000	1	2	1	0	0
Davidson	.961	19	34	39	3	3

	PCT	G	PO	A	E	DP
Gibbs	1.000	1	2	0	0	0
Hooper	1.000	4	5	4	0	0
Jackson	1.000	6	9	10	0	4
Myrow	1.000	4	12	3	0	2
Nettles	.941	4	6	10	1	2
Olivares	.959	22	47	47	4	15
Phillips	.979	72	138	181	7	36
Tyson	.964	12	28	25	2	9

Third Base	PCT	G	PO	A	E	DP
Almonte	.000	2	0	0	0	0
Calabrese	.750	1	0	3	1	0
Cervenak	.913	16	10	32	4	1
Cronin	1.000	1	1	1	0	0
Davidson	.500	1	0	1	1	0
Hooper	.909	17	11	19	3	1
Jackson	1.000	3	1	6	0	1
Jones	.872	50	35	81	17	3
Myrow	.912	50	26	78	10	7
Nettles	.708	10	7	10	7	0

Shortstop	PCT	G	PO	A	E	DP
Almonte	.963	51	64	145	8	28
Calabrese	1.000	3	2	2	0	0
Davidson	1.000	1	1	1	0	1
Hooper	.929	51	73	123	15	19
Jackson	.947	13	16	38	3	5
Nettles	.864	12	13	25	6	9
Olivares	.974	18	25	50	2	7

Outfield	PCT	G	PO	A	E	DP
Brown	.962	15	25	0	1	0
Davidson	1.000	4	5	0	0	0
Gibbs	.974	59	149	1	4	0
Griffin	.935	18	27	2	2	1
Hooper	1.000	2	2	0	0	0
Jones	1.000	7	9	0	0	0
Loggins	.961	30	71	3	3	1
Myrow	1.000	2	1	0	0	0
Reese	.980	137	296	5	6	0
Rodriguez	.985	102	195	3	3	1
Vento	.977	61	123	3	3	2

TAMPA YANKEES

High Class A

FLORIDA STATE LEAGUE

BATTING	AVG	G	AB	R	H	2B	3B	HR	RBI	BB	SO	SB	CS	SLG	OBP	B	T	HT	WT	DOB	1st Yr	Resides
Boone, Doug	.219	14	32	6	7	4	0	0	4	9	13	0	0	.344	.390	R	R	6-1	200	5-16-79	2002	Sellersburg, Ind.
Bozanich, Sam	.279	102	365	44	102	26	3	6	47	41	58	4	6	.416	.355	R	R	5-9	190	11-10-78	2000	Bakersfield, Calif.
Brown, Andy	.215	121	438	59	94	15	4	14	59	51	151	12	4	.363	.297	L	L	6-6	190	4-14-80	1998	Richmond, Ind.
Calabrese, Tony	.230	28	100	8	23	4	2	3	15	7	24	1	1	.400	.278	R	R	6-4	190	11-5-78	2000	Riverside, Conn.
Cannizaro, Andy	.249	112	366	52	91	18	1	1	46	38	31	3	4	.311	.339	R	R	5-10	170	12-19-78	2001	Mandeville, La.
Corporan, Elvis	.262	108	378	46	99	19	3	7	45	48	74	10	3	.384	.347	S	R	6-3	200	6-9-80	1999	Catano, P.R.
Cronin, Shane	.136	18	44	7	6	1	0	0	1	8	10	0	0	.159	.296	R	R	6-1	210	2-26-76	1996	Renton, Wash.
Elwood, Brad	.191	64	204	23	39	5	0	2	12	20	55	1	0	.245	.273	R	R	6-3	190	10-22-75	1998	Clear Spring, Md.
Fowler, David	.197	67	173	24	34	4	2	0	14	21	61	3	3	.243	.289	R	R	6-3	190	10-17-79	1998	St. Louis, Mo.
Fuentes, Omar	.267	61	210	29	56	8	0	7	32	17	32	0	0	.405	.333	R	R	6-1	170	4-6-80	1996	Maracay, Venez.
Gibbs, Kevin	.200	2	5	2	1	0	0	0	3	2	0	1	.200	.500	S	R	6-2	180	4-3-74	1995	Davidsonville, Md.
Griffin, John-Ford	.267	65	255	32	68	15	1	3	31	29	45	1	0	.373	.344	L	L	6-2	210	11-19-79	2001	Sarasota, Fla.
Grove, Jason	.275	73	273	37	75	18	6	3	35	36	62	3	2	.418	.366	L	L	6-2	200	8-15-78	2000	Walla Walla, Wash.
Hooper, Clay	.278	16	54	9	15	3	0	0	9	9	0	3	.333	.391	R	R	6-1	190	4-9-77	2000	Greensboro, N.C.
Jackson, Brandon	.180	43	139	16	25	2	0	0	8	21	31	3	0	.194	.307	R	R	6-1	180	10-28-75	1998	House Springs, Mo.
Jones, Mitch	.266	61	229	36	61	19	0	13	49	20	71	0	0	.520	.329	R	R	6-2	210	10-15-77	2000	Orem, Utah
Kinchen, Jason	.200	7	25	1	5	0	0	0	3	1	4	0	0	.200	.259	L	R	6-0	210	7-30-75	1997	Baton Rouge, La.
Mendez, Deivi	.333	2	6	2	2	0	0	0	1	1	0	1	0	.833	.333	R	R	6-1	160	6-24-83	1999	Santo Domingo, D.R.
Myrow, Brian	.280	61	225	29	63	12	1	5	40	42	45	0	0	.409	.409	L	R	5-11	190	9-4-76	1999	Fort Worth, Texas
Navarro, Dioner	.500	1	2	1	1	0	0	0	0	0	0	0	0	.500	.500	S	R	5-10	180	2-9-84	2000	Caracas, Venez.
Rifkin, Aaron	.278	66	252	33	70	11	0	6	44	20	52	1	3	.393	.330	L	L	6-3	220	3-12-79	2001	Upland, Calif.
Segar, Jeff	.211	5	19	1	4	1	0	0	4	1	4	0	0	.263	.238	R	R	6-3	210	11-1-78	2000	Syracuse, N.Y.
Thompson, Kevin	.184	25	87	10	16	5	0	0	7	13	15	11	1	.241	.298	R	R	5-10	180	9-18-79	2000	Fort Worth, Texas

ORGANIZATION STATISTICS

BATTING

	AVG	G	AB	R	H	2B	3B	HR	RBI	BB	SO	SB	CS	SLG	OBP	B	T	HT	WT	DOB	1st Yr	Resides
Turner, Jason	.230	36	135	16	31	5	0	0	8	13	24	1	0	.267	.295	L	L	6-3	200	7-30-77	2000	Versailles, Ohio
Tyson, Torre	.217	85	309	58	67	12	4	3	26	56	42	10	4	.311	.344	S	R	5-10	180	12-31-75	1998	Columbia, Mo.
Vasquez, Wuillians	.000	2	8	0	0	0	0	0	0	0	2	0	0	.000	.111	S	R	6-0	150	7-26-83	1999	Piritu, Venez.

PITCHING

	W	L	ERA	G	GS	CG	SV	IP	H	R	ER	BB	SO	AVG	B	T	HT	WT	DOB	1st Yr	Resides
Anderson, Jason	4	2	4.07	12	3	0	1	24	27	13	11	3	22	.281	L	R	6-0	170	6-9-79	2000	Danville, Ill.
Arnold, Jason	7	1	2.48	13	13	0	0	80	64	27	22	22	83	.216	R	R	6-3	210	5-2-79	2001	Palm Bay, Fla.
Artiles, Carlos	2	0	7.91	17	0	0	0	19	20	22	17	20	12	.270	L	L	5-11	160	1-21-81	1997	Santo Domingo, D.R.
Beal, Andy	6	0	2.65	10	10	0	0	54	59	19	16	13	37	.273	L	L	6-2	180	10-31-78	2000	Paducah, Ky.
Bean, Colter	2	2	1.98	46	0	0	9	55	34	17	12	21	78	.174	R	R	6-6	250	1-16-77	2000	Anniston, Ala.
Blankenship, John	4	5	4.07	13	12	1	0	66	64	34	30	20	48	.250	L	L	6-3	180	11-6-78	2000	Logan, Ala.
Borrell, Danny	4	1	2.33	7	6	0	0	39	33	11	10	10	44	.239	L	L	6-3	200	1-24-79	2000	Sanford, N.C.
Bradley, Ryan	0	2	5.68	5	0	0	0	6	2	4	4	3	7	.105	R	R	6-4	220	10-26-75	1997	Chino Hills, Calif.
Buchanan, Brian	0	3	2.87	27	2	0	0	47	36	15	15	17	32	.209	L	L	6-3	190	4-23-77	1995	Oviedo, Fla.
Clark, Ryan	0	0	4.26	5	0	0	0	6	5	3	3	4		.227	L	L	6-3	210	8-3-79	2001	North Baltimore, Ohio
Clemens, Roger	1	0	5.40	1	1	0	0	5	5	3	3	2	6	.263	R	R	6-4	230	8-4-62	1983	Houston, Texas
Grace, Bryan	8	6	2.86	23	21	0	0	120	101	46	38	61	70	.231	R	R	6-1	190	4-1-76	1999	Baton Rouge, La.
Hitchcock, Sterling	0	0	1.50	1	1	0	0	6	3	1	1	0	3	.150	L	L	6-0	200	4-29-71	1989	Tampa, Fla.
Kennard, Jeff	0	2	3.92	12	0	0	0	21	18	9	9	14		.227	R	R	6-2	190	7-26-81	2001	Centerville, Ohio
Knowles, Mike	3	4	4.20	50	0	0	19	49	45	29	23	35	43	.236	R	R	6-5	210	7-15-79	1997	Daytona Beach, Fla.
Kremer, John	2	2	4.83	25	0	0	1	41	52	28	22	17	27	.309	R	R	6-1	220	11-19-76	1999	Indianapolis, Ind.
Lombardi, Justin	0	1	27.00	2	0	0	0	1	3	4	4	4	1	.428	L	L	6-4	210	8-21-79	2000	Taunton, Mass.
Manning, Charlie	6	4	3.24	17	16	0	0	100	82	48	36	31	85	.221	L	L	6-2	180	3-31-79	2001	Winter Haven, Fla.
Martinez, Oscar	1	3	7.54	25	0	0	0	37	45	38	31	17	33	.292	R	R	6-2	180	10-7-78	1996	Araura, Venez.
Mendoza, Cristian	0	0	6.75	1	1	0	0	3	1	2	2	2	2	.125	R	R	6-3	160	5-1-82	1998	Cartagena, Colombia
Ortiz, Javier	4	3	2.52	9	9	1	0	50	47	20	14	13	35	.250	R	R	6-0	150	11-28-79	1996	Cartagena, Colombia
Perez, Julio	1	1	3.00	6	0	0	0	9	15	3	3	2	7	.375	R	R	6-2	170	8-6-78	1997	Miami, Fla.
Pettitte, Andy	0	0	0.00	2	2	0	0	5	3	0	0	0	4	.166	L	L	6-5	220	6-15-72	1991	Deer Park, Texas
Pierson, Jason	0	2	5.11	11	0	0	0	12	16	7	7	6	9	.313	R	L	6-0	190	1-6-71	1992	Berwyn, Pa.
Pike, Matthew	0	0	5.91	6	1	0	0	11	11	10	7	4	10	.261	R	R	6-1	180	9-5-78	2000	White Lake, Mich.
Schmitt, Eric	6	6	2.36	19	19	0	0	91	75	30	24	32	97	.219	R	R	6-4	210	7-23-78	2000	Fairfax, Va.
Smith, Matt	0	4	6.59	8	6	0	0	27	37	23	20	17	20	.330	L	L	6-5	220	6-15-79	2000	Henderson, Nev.
Stevens, Josh	2	0	2.89	21	1	0	0	37	34	12	12	8	41	.237	R	R	6-4	200	6-6-79	1998	Riverside, Calif.
Strelitz, Brian	1	4	4.43	27	0	0	0	45	54	29	22	22	20	.301	R	R	6-2	200	1-8-80	2001	Temple City, Calif.
Witte, Lou	6	7	4.11	22	8	0	0	77	79	46	35	12	53	.262	R	R	6-0	180	10-30-76	1999	Richmond, Ind.
Wood, Bobby	0	0	10.80	1	1	0	0	5	11	7	6	2	7	.407	R	R	6-4	200	11-27-79	2001	Englewood, Colo.

FIELDING

Catcher	PCT	G	PO	A	E	DP	PB
Boone	.976	14	68	13	2	1	4
Cronin	1.000	9	32	2	0	0	1
Elwood	.992	64	459	37	4	2	23
Fuentes	.991	60	391	31	4	2	8
Navarro	1.000	1	3	0	0	0	0

First Base	PCT	G	PO	A	E	DP
Calabrese	1.000	1	1	1	0	1
Cronin	1.000	4	36	3	0	1
Jones	.992	27	225	14	2	21
Kinchen	.973	4	36	0	1	3
Rifkin	.991	66	593	39	6	47
Segar	1.000	2	22	0	0	0
Turner	.990	35	285	24	3	20

Second Base	PCT	G	PO	A	E	DP
Bozanich	.955	86	129	250	18	50

	PCT	G	PO	A	E	DP
Calabrese	.971	7	9	25	1	7
Cannizaro	.985	13	28	36	1	6
Jackson	.961	28	35	88	5	15
Tyson	1.000	1	1	0	0	0
Vasquez	.917	2	3	8	1	1

Third Base	PCT	G	PO	A	E	DP
Calabrese	1.000	1	2	2	0	0
Cannizaro	1.000	2	1	5	0	0
Corporan	.932	106	72	188	19	15
Jackson	.909	6	3	7	1	1
Myrow	.960	20	8	40	2	4

Shortstop	PCT	G	PO	A	E	DP
Calabrese	.957	13	14	30	2	5
Cannizaro	.952	98	131	290	21	56
Hooper	.988	16	24	60	1	8
Jackson	1.000	7	11	17	0	2

	PCT	G	PO	A	E	DP
Mendez	.889	2	3	5	1	2

Outfield	PCT	G	PO	A	E	DP
Brown	.960	111	182	9	8	0
Calabrese	1.000	1	4	0	0	0
Fowler	.979	60	133	6	3	0
Gibbs	1.000	2	5	0	0	0
Griffin	.959	50	70	0	3	0
Grove	.970	56	96	1	3	0
Jones	.959	23	45	2	2	1
Myrow	1.000	12	20	0	0	0
Segar	1.000	2	3	2	0	0
Thompson	.960	24	47	1	2	0
Tyson	.986	69	139	5	2	1

GREENSBORO BATS — Low Class A

SOUTH ATLANTIC LEAGUE

BATTING	AVG	G	AB	R	H	2B	3B	HR	RBI	BB	SO	SB	CS	SLG	OBP	B	T	HT	WT	DOB	1st Yr	Resides
Brazoban, Yhency	.242	69	252	33	61	11	2	3	28	15	74	0	0	.337	.290	R	R	6-1	170	6-11-80	1997	Santo Domingo, D.R.
Calabrese, Tony	.234	53	184	25	43	13	0	4	23	23	43	6	2	.370	.317	R	R	6-4	190	11-5-78	2000	Riverside, Conn.
Camacho, Juan	.241	124	478	51	115	16	0	1	59	28	85	0	0	.381	.284	S	R	6-2	170	1-13-81	1997	San Carlos, Venez.
Cano, Robinson	.276	113	474	67	131	20	9	14	66	29	78	2	1	.445	.321	L	R	6-0		10-22-82	2001	San Pedro de Macoris, D.R.
Christensen, Jeff	.236	78	237	36	56	9	4	4	30	34	76	8	4	.359	.332	L	L	6-1	200	10-12-78	2001	Knoxville, Tenn.
Corporan, Elvis	.278	14	54	10	15	2	0	3	9		19	0	0	.481	.391	S	R	6-3	200	6-9-80	1999	Catano, P.R.
Duncan, Shelley	.267	101	356	58	95	23	2	14	56	59	88	15	3	.461	.375	R	R	6-5	210	9-29-79	2001	Tucson, Ariz.
Fernandez, Alejandro	.238	51	160	17	38	10	0	7	27	13	56	1	0	.431	.305	R	R	6-2	170	12-19-80	1997	Maracaibo, Venez.
Lopez, Gabe	.279	17	61	11	17	1	1	0	7	9	4	5	1	.328	.366	R	R	5-8	170	3-11-80	2002	Pico Rivera, Calif.
Navarro, Dioner	.238	92	328	41	78	12	2	8	36	39	61	1	2	.360	.326	S	R	5-10	180	2-9-84	2000	Caracas, Venez.
O'Connor, Brian	.095	9	21	0	2	0	0	0	1	2	13	0	1	.095	.174	R	R	6-2	210	6-21-77	1999	Arlington Heights, Ill.
Pitney, Jared	.214	36	112	12	24	3	0	2	10	16	40	0	0	.295	.315	L	L	6-0	180	3-26-79	2001	Agoura, Calif.
Reyes, Ivan	.119	71	177	22	21	3	0	2	17	18	74	2	1	.169	.221	R	R	6-2	180	6-6-81	1999	Toa Baja, P.R.
Rosario, Carlos	.667	1	3	0	2	0	0	0	0	1	0			.667	.667	R	R	5-10	180	2-23-84	2001	Santo Domingo, D.R.
Santos, Omir	.233	23	73	7	17	2	1	1	8	2	15	0	0	.329	.275	R	R	5-10	194	4-29-81	2001	Toa Baja, P.R.
Sardinha, Bronson	.263	93	342	49	90	13	0	12	44	34	78	15	6	.406	.334	L	R	6-1	190	4-6-83	2001	Kahuku, Hawaii
Segar, Jeff	.277	103	382	63	106	17	2	19	60	40	74	16	7	.482	.347	R	R	6-3	210	11-1-78	2000	Syracuse, N.Y.
Summerville, Kaazim	.229	51	153	32	35	8	2	4	9	21	30	2	2	.386	.335	R	R	5-10	180	9-18-78	2001	Hayward, Calif.
Thompson, Kevin	.283	62	226	44	64	24	3	3	31	37	42	14	3	.456	.396	R	R	5-10	180	9-18-79	2000	Fort Worth, Texas
Turner, Jason	.300	72	257	36	77	16	1	3	31	31	37	8	3	.405	.381	L	L	6-3	200	7-30-77	2000	Versailles, Ohio
Verbryke, Eric	.231	30	108	10	25	6	0	2	9	11	31	2	3	.343	.308	L	L	6-2	220	8-6-81	2002	Santa Maria, Calif.
Winrow, Tommy	.234	73	239	29	56	12	1	5	27	10	52	4	3	.356	.273	L	L	6-2	180	7-12-80	1999	Fort Myers, Fla.

PITCHING	W	L	ERA	G	GS	CG	SV	IP	H	R	ER	BB	SO	AVG	B	T	HT	WT	DOB	1st Yr	Resides
Acosta, Manuel	2	5	6.40	13	10	0	0	52	65	47	37	44	35	.315	R	R	6-4	170	5-1-81	1998	Colon, Panama
Artiles, Carlos	3	3	2.38	34	0	0	12	45	37	17	12	34	46	.224	L	L	5-11	160	1-21-81	1997	Santo Domingo, D.R.
Blankenship, John	7	2	3.05	12	12	1	0	77	73	30	26	23	89	.246	L	L	5-10	180	11-6-78	2000	Logan, Ala.
Brian, Billy	1	3	4.75	7	7	0	0	36	37	21	19	13	14	.268	R	R	6-5	230	11-7-78	2002	Mandeville, La.
Caraballo, Angel	2	1	4.01	6	5	0	0	34	35	18	15	14	11	.284	R	R	6-4	170	6-5-80	1998	Anzoategui, Venez.
Carlson, Steve	6	1	2.44	43	0	0	1	66	45	26	18	31	75	.188	R	L	6-1	200	1-9-79	2001	Newark, Ill.
Cooksey, Wes	5	4	1.95	51	0	0	16	78	65	28	17	35	62	.221	L	R	6-3	210	5-22-78	2001	Port Arthur, Texas
Currier, Rik	3	4	3.92	24	2	0	2	39	41	19	17	24	41	.280	R	R	5-10	180	5-26-78	2001	Aliso Viejo, Calif.
DiFranco, Joseph	0	0	5.59	11	0	0	0	19	27	14	12	13	18	.321	R	R	6-1	180	10-10-78	2002	North Miami Beach, Fla.
Faigin, Jason	0	0	27.00	4	0	0	0	2	8	8	6	3	2	.571	R	R	6-2	190	9-20-78	1999	Marlboro, N.J.
Grace, Bryan	1	1	2.25	2	2	0	0	12	14	3	3	4	6	.297	R	R	6-1	190	4-1-76	1999	Baton Rouge, La.
Grinnell, Tyler	1	0	6.19	11	0	0	0	16	19	11	11	11	5	.316	R	R	6-3	230	4-28-79	2002	Lansing, Mich.
Joyce, Michael	0	0	5.84	11	0	0	1	12	17	9	8	4	10	.314	L	L	6-2	210	1-15-79	2002	Quaker Hill, Conn.
Kennard, Jeff	4	0	1.93	27	0	0	0	37	27	14	8	25	35	.200	R	R	6-2	190	7-26-81	2001	Centerville, Ohio
King, Jeremy	7	7	4.42	28	25	1	0	147	151	86	72	66	132	.267	R	R	6-2	210	11-12-81	2000	Nocatee, Fla.
Kremer, John	3	4	2.86	20	0	0	2	35	41	12	11	10	35	.290	R	R	6-2	220	11-19-76	1999	Indianapolis, Ind.
Landaeta, Argenis	0	2	12.86	2	2	0	0	7	15	10	10	2	2	.468	R	R	6-2	170	11-8-81	1998	Valencia, Venez.
Lombardi, Justin	0	0	6.43	6	0	0	0	7	10	10	5	10	8	.303	L	L	6-4	210	8-21-79	2000	Taunton, Mass.
Mosley, Eric	7	6	3.76	19	19	0	0	108	116	60	45	47	47	.279	R	R	6-3	180	5-27-81	2000	Tulsa, Okla.
Ortiz, Javier	9	5	4.11	18	18	3	0	127	128	66	58	25	63	.263	R	R	6-0	150	11-28-79	1996	Cartagena, Colombia
Picco, Jim	0	1	8.59	4	0	0	0	7	11	7	7	6	5	.343	L	L	6-1	190	7-9-83	2001	La Salle, Ontario
Reynolds, Eric	0	0	5.93	10	0	0	0	14	13	11	9	12	7	.276	L	L	6-3	210	4-20-80	2000	Guntown, Miss.
Russ, Chris	1	4	5.65	24	0	0	4	29	33	24	18	19	23	.294	R	R	5-11	180	3-27-79	2001	Comfort, Texas
Smith, Jason	5	5	3.47	17	16	1	0	96	94	44	37	21	46	.261	S	R	6-5	200	3-7-82	2000	Kennewick, Wash.
Strelitz, Brian	1	2	14.40	8	1	0	0	10	21	16	16	4	1	.446	R	R	6-2	200	1-8-80	2001	Temple City, Calif.
Wood, Bobby	7	5	4.24	21	21	3	0	117	120	59	55	43	99	.270	R	R	6-4	200	11-27-79	2001	Englewood, Colo.

FIELDING

Catcher	PCT	G	PO	A	E	DP	PB
Fernandez	.993	39	268	29	2	1	9
Navarro	.987	86	511	96	8	3	19
O'Connor	1.000	6	19	2	0	0	0
Rosario	1.000	1	6	0	0	0	0
Santos	.966	20	132	11	5	2	4

First Base	PCT	G	PO	A	E	DP
Calabrese	1.000	4	22	2	0	3
Pitney	.997	35	315	25	1	28
Segar	1.000	33	296	19	0	20
Turner	.993	72	655	62	5	56

Second Base	PCT	G	PO	A	E	DP
Calabrese	.968	36	63	116	6	20

	PCT	G	PO	A	E	DP
Cano	.950	54	112	152	14	33
Lopez	1.000	16	34	37	0	11
Reyes	.972	41	60	115	5	16
Sardinha	1.000	1	1	0	0	0
Segar	1.000	2	1	1	0	0

Third Base	PCT	G	PO	A	E	DP
Calabrese	.500	1	1	0	1	0
Camacho	.941	118	89	229	20	14
Corporan	.925	12	5	32	3	2
Reyes	.929	11	5	21	2	2

Shortstop	PCT	G	PO	A	E	DP
Calabrese	.978	11	13	32	1	8
Cano	.922	57	102	170	23	35

	PCT	G	PO	A	E	DP
Reyes	.886	10	14	17	4	2
Sardinha	.889	64	93	170	33	30

Outfield	PCT	G	PO	A	E	DP
Brazoban	.948	54	100	10	6	1
Christensen	.974	44	74	0	2	0
Duncan	.953	69	113	10	6	0
Sardinha	1.000	17	14	3	0	1
Segar	.986	62	131	8	2	1
Summerville	.959	45	91	2	4	0
Thompson	.951	61	129	8	7	0
Verbryke	.971	28	63	4	2	1
Winrow	.975	58	74	5	2	0

STATEN ISLAND YANKEES — Short-Season A

NEW YORK-PENN LEAGUE

BATTING	AVG	G	AB	R	H	2B	3B	HR	RBI	BB	SO	SB	CS	SLG	OBP	B	T	HT	WT	DOB	1st Yr	Resides
Blase, Blake	.159	21	44	5	7	2	0	1	6	5	25	1	0	.273	.245	L	R	6-3	220	1-31-81	2002	Columbia, Mo.
Bowden, Nathan	.200	17	50	6	10	3	0	0	3	6	18	1	1	.260	.286	R	R	6-3	200	9-23-79	2002	Pope, Miss.
Cano, Robinson	.276	22	87	11	24	5	1	1	15	4	8	6	1	.391	.308	L	R	6-0	170	10-22-82	2001	San Pedro de Macoris, D.R.
Carson, Matt	.203	48	177	19	36	8	4	1	11	11	48	4	1	.311	.264	R	R	6-2	190	7-1-81	2002	Yucaipa, Calif.
Drobiak, Jayson	.311	31	103	17	32	8	2	2	16	5	22	1	0	.485	.349	L	R	6-2	190	3-3-79	1999	Jewett, Conn.
Harris, Mike	.250	5	4	1	1	0	0	0	2	0	1	0	0	.250	.200	R	R	5-10	180	11-2-78	2002	Florence, Ky.
Koutnik, Jared	.133	14	45	2	6	2	0	0	3	5	14	0	0	.178	.226	R	R	6-3	190	11-9-79	2002	Milwaukee, Wis.
Lopez, Gabe	.213	46	164	28	35	8	1	0	18	14	15	7	2	.274	.303	R	R	5-8	170	3-11-80	2002	Pico Rivera, Calif.
Mamula, Matt	.225	52	182	20	41	8	0	3	25	16	52	0	0	.319	.287	L	R	6-2	210	2-10-80	2002	Hammond, Ind.
McClanahan, Scott	.222	45	162	16	36	7	0	2	17	14	35	4	3	.302	.288	R	R	6-3	225	8-29-80	2002	Tuscaloosa, Ala.
Meihls, Mike	.231	18	39	5	9	1	0	0	4	6	11	0	1	.256	.326	R	R	6-1	190	2-4-80	2002	North Ridgeville, Ohio
Pitney, Jared	.000	3	8	1	0	0	0	0	0	0	4	0	0	.000	.111	L	L	6-0	180	3-26-80	2002	Agoura, Calif.
Ramistella, John	.234	49	137	19	32	6	2	3	14	18	51	7	2	.372	.342	R	R	6-1	205	3-31-82	2001	Henderson, Nev.
Rojas, Tommy	.321	43	140	17	45	6	0	1	18	20	27	2	5	.386	.422	R	R	6-0	180	5-3-80	2002	Toa Baja, P.R.
Santos, Omir	.289	61	232	22	67	10	0	7	44	12	32	2	1	.422	.331	R	R	5-11	194	4-29-81	2001	Kahuku, Hawaii
Sardinha, Bronson	.323	36	124	25	40	8	1	6	16	24	36	4	1	.484	.433	L	R	6-2	190	4-6-83	2001	Honolulu, Hawaii
Sheaffer, Jon	.140	30	57	7	8	1	0	0	3	7	15	1	2	.158	.258	R	R	6-1	180	2-9-80	2000	Mesa, Ariz.
Tejeda, Ferdin	.276	47	181	29	50	7	2	0	18	11	33	11	3	.337	.316	R	R	5-11	178	9-15-82	2000	Santo Domingo, D.R.
Thompson, Kevin	.302	36	139	25	42	5	2	4	14	17	24	6	3	.453	.376	R	R	5-10	180	9-18-79	2000	Fort Worth, Texas
Treadway, Jared	.278	15	18	5	5	0	0	0	1	2	5	0	0	.278	.350	R	R	6-0	180	12-21-79	2002	Bay Village, Ohio
Vasquez, Wuillians	.234	50	175	22	41	8	1	3	22	15	46	0	3	.343	.299	S	R	6-0	150	7-26-83	1999	Piritu, Venez.
Verbryke, Eric	.219	30	114	8	25	6	1	0	9	14	31	3	0	.289	.305	L	L	6-2	220	8-6-81	2002	Santa Maria, Calif.
Zamora, Hector	.250	33	108	12	27	9	1	0	6	15	32	0	3	.352	.352	L	R	6-1	210	10-19-81	2002	Culver City, Calif.

GAMES BY POSITION: C—Meihls 5, Rojas 38, Santos 37. **1B**—Blasé 12, Drobiak 29, Mamula 41, Meihls 1, Pitney 3, Rojas 1. **2B**—Cano 20, Harris 3, Koutnik 2, Lopez 44, Vasquez 12. **3B**—Drobiak 1, Koutnik 11, Meihls 10, Vasquez 25, Zamora 32. **SS**—Bowden 15, Cano 2, Koutnik 1, Tejeda 47, Vasquez 12. **OF**—Carson 42, McClanahan 45, Ramistella 37, Sardinha 31, Sheaffer 23, Thompson 29, Treadway 9, Verbryke 29.

PITCHING	W	L	ERA	G	GS	CG	SV	IP	H	R	ER	BB	SO	AVG	B	T	HT	WT	DOB	1st Yr	Resides
Acosta, Manuel	2	1	4.11	3	3	0	0	15	20	9	7	8	12	.327	R	R	6-4	170	5-1-81	1998	Colon, Panama
Bell, Gary	1	0	2.63	6	5	0	0	24	23	9	7	6	23	.255	L	L	6-1	190	9-14-79	2002	Ponce Inlet, Fla.
Bicondoa, Ryan	6	4	1.90	14	14	3	0	85	64	25	18	7	94	.203	R	R	6-3	190	1-26-79	2002	Lovelock, Nev.
Bomer, Alan	0	0	4.05	2	2	0	0	7	8	3	3	1	2	.307	R	R	6-3	200	1-31-80	2002	Altoona, Iowa
Brumit, Mathew	1	2	2.21	33	0	0	22	37	32	11	9	8	40	.235	R	R	6-4	220	10-28-79	2002	Akron, Ohio
Clark, Ray	3	0	1.97	8	5	0	0	32	23	9	7	6	39	.207	R	R	6-2	185	10-27-80	2002	Grapevine, Texas
DiFranco, Joseph	0	1	2.84	6	0	0	0	6	5	2	2	4	9	.208	R	R	6-1	180	10-10-78	2002	North Miami Beach, Fla.
Halsey, Brad	6	1	1.93	11	10	0	0	56	39	15	12	17	53	.195	L	L	6-1	180	2-14-81	2002	Austin, Texas

PITCHING	W	L	ERA	G	GS	CG	SV	IP	H	R	ER	BB	SO	AVG	B	T	HT	WT	DOB	1st Yr	Resides
Isaacson, Charlie	5	3	2.54	14	12	0	0	74	57	25	21	21	76	.211	R	R	6-2	190	5-5-80	2002	Overland Park, Kan.
Joyce, Michael	0	0	3.00	4	0	0	0	6	9	3	2	0	4	.333	L	L	6-2	210	1-15-79	2002	Quaker Hill, Conn.
Kopp, Nathan	2	2	1.61	21	0	0	0	22	9	4	4	11	22	.121	R	L	6-0	200	3-26-80	2002	Huber Heights, Ohio
Meccage, Justin	2	2	3.11	19	3	0	2	46	36	21	16	19	45	.215	R	R	6-5	220	2-10-80	2002	San Antonio, Texas
Mieres, Alberto	0	0	5.91	6	1	0	0	11	9	8	7	7	7	.209	R	R	6-5	150	1-24-81	1999	Valencia, Venez.
Mosley, Eric	0	0	6.00	1	1	0	0	6	9	4	4	1	3	.346	R	R	6-3	180	5-27-81	2002	Tulsa, Okla.
Neitz, Josh	4	3	2.87	30	0	0	2	31	28	12	10	9	25	.245	R	R	6-1	180	7-2-79	2002	Tampa, Fla.
Rada, Gerald	1	1	4.34	21	0	0	0	29	26	15	14	12	22	.240	R	R	6-1	202	8-20-81	1998	Caracas, Venez.
Reynolds, Eric	6	0	1.22	14	1	0	0	37	23	8	5	10	43	.170	L	L	6-3	210	4-20-80	2000	Guntown, Miss.
Russ, Chris	0	0	4.70	4	0	0	0	8	7	4	4	2	6	.241	R	R	5-11	180	3-27-79	2001	Comfort, Texas
Thorp, Paul	0	1	3.60	1	1	0	0	5	8	4	2	3	1	.380	R	R	6-1	200	9-23-80	2002	Carrollton, Texas
Tribe, Phillip	2	1	3.16	15	0	0	0	26	26	12	9	10	27	.250	R	R	6-5	210	10-15-79	2002	Katy, Texas
Valdez, Jose	1	3	5.40	4	4	0	0	20	19	14	12	9	21	.250	R	R	6-4	180	1-23-83	2001	Santo Domingo, D.R.
Wang, Chien-ming	6	1	1.72	13	13	0	0	78	63	23	15	14	64	.218	R	R	6-3	200	3-31-80	2000	Tampa, Fla.

TAMPA YANKEES — Rookie

GULF COAST LEAGUE

BATTING	AVG	G	AB	R	H	2B	3B	HR	RBI	BB	SO	SB	CS	SLG	OBP	B	T	HT	WT	DOB	1st Yr	Resides
Andrus, Erold	.294	55	204	30	60	13	2	2	27	14	23	1	4	.407	.351	S	L	6-2	170	7-16-84	2000	Maracay, Venez.
Arias, Joaquin	.300	57	203	29	61	7	6	0	21	12	16	2	4	.394	.338	R	R	6-1	160	9-21-84	2001	Santo Domingo, D.R.
Boone, Doug	.300	3	10	0	3	0	0	0	2	1	3	0	0	.300	.364	R	R	6-1	200	5-16-79	2002	Sellersburg, Ind.
Boullon, Luis	.083	4	12	1	1	1	0	0	3	1	7	0	0	.167	.143	S	R	6-1	210	10-25-80	2002	Miami, Fla.
Brown, Rich	.273	7	22	4	6	1	0	0	4	3	5	0	0	.318	.360	L	L	6-1	190	4-28-77	1996	Plantation, Fla.
Davenport, Juston	.137	23	51	4	7	1	0	0	2	5	12	0	0	.157	.214	R	R	6-0	200	6-2-79	2002	Wheeler, Mich.
Fuentes, Omar	.182	4	11	0	2	0	0	0	2	2	3	0	0	.182	.308	R	R	6-1	170	4-6-80	1996	Maracay, Venez.
Gonzalez, Edwar	.275	19	51	7	14	2	1	1	8	0	11	0	0	.412	.283	R	R	5-10	200	1-1-83	2002	Maracaibo, Venez.
Guillen, Rudy	.306	59	219	38	67	7	2	3	35	14	39	7	2	.397	.351	R	R	6-3	180	11-23-83	2000	Santo Domingo, D.R.
Harris, Mike	.000	1	1	0	0	0	0	0	0	0	0	0	0	.000	.000	R	R	5-10	180	11-2-78	2002	Florence, Ky.
Koutnik, Jared	.311	28	90	16	28	7	0	0	15	10	15	3	1	.389	.375	R	R	6-3	190	11-9-79	2002	Milwaukee, Wis.
Mendez, Deivi	.233	31	90	9	21	6	0	2	11	10	16	1	1	.367	.324	R	R	6-1	160	6-24-83	1999	Santo Domingo, D.R.
Michelsen, Ross	.256	29	90	9	23	2	1	0	12	11	27	0	0	.300	.343	L	L	6-4	190	2-2-84	2002	Arlington, Texas
Nunez, Andres	.225	33	111	12	25	2	1	0	9	7	24	0	1	.261	.275	R	R	6-2	150	7-20-82	1999	Valencia, Venez.
Orlandos, Nicholas	.205	27	73	8	15	0	0	0	3	4	12	0	1	.205	.253	R	R	6-0	180	7-8-80	2002	Mission Viejo, Calif.
Pitney, Jared	.229	10	35	8	8	5	0	0	9	7	6	0	0	.371	.364	L	L	6-0	180	3-26-79	2001	Agoura Hills, Calif.
Rivera, Juan	.308	4	13	1	4	2	0	0	4	2	3	0	0	.462	.438	R	R	6-2	170	7-3-78	1996	Guarenas Venez.
Robles, Luis	.167	20	54	4	9	3	0	0	3	3	6	0	0	.222	.211	R	R	6-4	180	3-2-82	2002	Rialto, Calif.
Rosario, Carlos	.233	39	103	9	24	9	1	2	15	9	33	0	2	.398	.302	R	R	5-10	180	2-23-84	2001	Santo Domingo, D.R.
Santa, Alex	.227	54	198	34	45	2	2	0	7	28	54	12	6	.258	.329	L	L	6-0	170	12-27-82	1999	Santo Domingo, D.R.
Saunches, Michael	.306	48	157	13	48	12	0	2	29	11	44	0	2	.420	.345	L	L	6-3	250	7-6-81	2002	Decatur, Ill.
Schwab, Daniel	.053	13	19	3	1	0	0	0	1	10	12	0	0	.053	.379	L	L	6-5	220	7-14-83	2002	Arvada, Colo.
Tejeda, Ferdin	.300	16	60	13	18	3	0	0	2	10	9	3	1	.350	.394	R	R	5-11	178	9-15-82	2000	Santo Domingo, D.R.
Vasquez, Wuillians	.000	5	10	1	0	0	0	0	2	6	3	0	0	.000	.333	S	R	6-0	150	7-26-83	1999	Piritu, Venez.
Zamora, Hector	.241	11	29	5	7	2	0	2	5	5	7	0	1	.517	.371	L	R	6-1	210	10-19-81	2002	Culver City, Calif.

GAMES BY POSITION: C—Boone 3, Boullon 4, Fuentes 4, Robles 20, Rosario 39. **1B**—Davenport 1, Koutnik 7, Michelsen 25, Pitney 10, Saunches 19. **2B**—Arias 40, Mendez 1, Orlandos 20, Tejeda 1, Vasquez 4. **3B**—Arias 1, Davenport 1, Koutnik 21, Nunez 33, Orlandos 4, Vasquez 1, Zamora 3. **SS**—Arias 18, Koutnik 1, Mendez 31, Orlandos 2, Tejeda 16. **OF**—Andrus 51, Brown 2, Davenport 10, Guillen 56, Rivera 3, Santa 54.

PITCHING	W	L	ERA	G	GS	CG	SV	IP	H	R	ER	BB	SO	AVG	B	T	HT	WT	DOB	1st Yr	Resides
Brazoban, Yhency	0	0	4.50	6	0	0	0	6	3	3	3	4	11	.136	R	R	6-1	170	6-11-80	1997	Santo Domingo, D.R.
Garcia, Anderson	4	1	2.30	11	9	1	0	59	43	22	15	22	41	.203	R	R	6-2	170	3-23-81	2001	Santo Domingo, D.R.
Garcia, Randy	2	0	3.27	13	1	0	0	22	18	10	8	10	24	.225	L	L	6-1	180	10-9-82	2002	New York, N.Y.
Hacker, Eric	0	0	0.00	3	0	0	0	4	2	0	0	1	2	.166	S	R	6-1	210	3-26-83	2002	Duncanville, Texas
Harmsen, Brandon	4	5	3.59	12	10	0	0	58	51	29	23	17	46	.240	R	R	6-3	200	12-13-81	2002	Jenison, Mich.
Hitchcock, Sterling	0	0	0.00	2	2	0	0	3	0	0	0	0	6	.000	L	L	6-0	200	4-29-71	1989	Tampa, Fla.
Kemlo, Chris	1	0	4.19	11	0	0	1	19	18	10	9	9	13	.257	R	R	6-5	200	9-23-83	2002	Oshawa, Ontario
Kerschen, Josh	3	1	4.00	17	0	0	6	18	20	8	8	1	14	.281	R	R	6-4	180	11-21-81	2002	Merriam, Kan.
Klahs, Dave	3	1	3.90	14	0	0	1	28	29	13	12	6	21	.281	R	R	6-1	180	10-19-81	2002	High Ridge, Mo.
Landaeta, Argenis	2	1	3.65	10	0	0	1	25	21	11	10	7	26	.235	R	R	6-2	170	11-8-81	1998	Valencia, Venez.
Martinez, Dave	1	3	5.04	9	6	0	0	25	28	14	14	15	20	.294	L	L	6-1	160	6-7-80	1997	Ciudad, Venez.
Mendoza, Cristian	1	0	2.29	13	0	0	4	20	10	5	5	7	19	.151	R	R	6-1	180	5-1-82	1998	Cartagena, Colombia
Mieres, Alberto	2	0	0.00	4	0	0	0	8	4	1	0	3	6	.148	R	R	6-5	150	1-24-81	1999	Valencia, Venez.
Picco, John	4	5	5.58	11	8	0	0	50	53	33	31	27	39	.274	L	L	6-1	190	7-9-83	2001	La Salle, Ontario
Rivera, Mariano	0	0	0.00	1	1	0	0	2	2	0	0	1	2	.285	R	R	6-2	180	11-29-69	1990	La Chorrera, Panama
Russ, Chris	1	0	5.40	5	0	0	0	8	4	5	5	6	6	.129	R	R	5-11	180	3-27-79	2001	Comfort, Texas
Valdez, Jose	1	4	3.35	8	7	0	0	40	45	19	15	10	28	.283	R	R	6-4	180	1-23-83	2001	Santo Domingo, D.R.
Weeden, Brandon	2	1	2.86	11	7	0	1	35	29	13	11	16	30	.228	R	R	6-4	190	10-14-83	2002	Edmond, Okla.
Wheeler, Adam	0	0	1.35	3	2	0	0	7	6	1	1	4	8	.250	R	R	6-6	180	4-26-83	2001	Smyrna, Ga.
Wiseman, Steven	3	1	3.91	14	0	0	0	25	23	13	11	12	29	.252	R	R	5-11	170	4-23-80	2002	Winchester, Tenn.
Wright, Chase	2	3	3.43	10	7	0	0	42	32	19	16	39	23	.217	L	L	6-2	190	2-8-83	2001	Iowa Park, Texas

BY MARTY NOBLE

Two years after his failed tenure as Mets manager, Jeff Torborg returned to Shea Stadium in his new capacity as a radio announcer. As he walked through the Diamond Club, he noticed the bronze busts of those inducted into  the Mets Hall of Fame—Casey Stengel, Tom Seaver, Rusty Staub, et al. Torborg paused, smirked and spoke. "Ya know, I belong in here too," he said. "I was a bust when I was here."

Torborg had managed the Mets in 1992 and into May the following season. And though the 1993 season evolved into the franchise's worst, by record, in 28 years, the 1992 team bore the label "The Worst Team Money Could Buy."

The 2002 Mets were busts, too. Robbie Alomar, Jeromy Burnitz, Roger Cedeno and the rest produced a season that made the team's appearance in the 2000 World Series a distant memory and drew parallels to Torborg' terrible teams.

En route to a 75-86 record, the franchise's first last-place finish since 1993 and a deficit—26½ games—greater than those produced by all but five Mets teams, these underachievers ran the bases poorly, played abysmal defense and regularly stubbed their toes. Moreover, they often appeared lifeless.

The popular perception of these Mets was that they quit—despite late-season denials by their since-dismissed manager and their catcher. Bobby Valentine, discarded after two dismal seasons had stained his record and, in particular, Mike Piazza took issue with an internet critique by first baseman-turned-color commentator Keith Hernandez. From his vantage point in the booth, Hernandez concluded that, by mid-August, the Mets had conceded. Though he retracted his words and apologized for them, little in the Mets' subsequent performance suggested Hernandez had misspoken.

Owner Fred Wilpon said as late as Sept. 21 that Valentine

Edgardo Alfonzo   Jose Reyes

PLAYERS OF THE YEAR

MAJOR LEAGUE: Edgardo Alfonzo, 3b

With Mike Piazza posting his poorest statistical season as a major leaguer, Alfonzo gets the nod. He rebounded from a poor 2001 season to lead the team in average (.308), runs scored (78), walks (62) and on-base percentage (.391) while moving to third base to accommodate Roberto Alomar.

MINOR LEAGUE: Jose Reyes, ss

Reyes earned MVP honors at the Futures Game with a bases loaded triple, and his 19 three-baggers between Class A St. Lucie and Double-A Binghamton led the minors.

would return for 2003 and at least begin the final year of his three-year contract. But the team's lifelessness and the responses of veteran players to Wilpon's canvassing of the clubhouse persuaded the owner a change was essential even though a clear-cut successor wasn't apparent. Former A's Skipper Art Howe succeeded Valentine.

Players believed Valentine had lost his fire, and when he accused Al Leiter and Edgardo Alfonzo of losing focus because of contract considerations, he lost the team as well. His subsequent involvement in a newspaper report about marijuana use among the Mets ruptured the last strands of trust in the clubhouse.

The Mets had played poorly enough to that point to undermine the job security of any manager. Burnitz, before his too-little, too-late September renaissance, became the poster boy for the shortfall.

But Alomar's uneven performance—a .266 average, 40 points lower than his career average—and his detached manner also were primary, if more subtle components in the Mets' collapse.

Even Piazza wasn't faultless. His slugging, on-base and batting averages for '02 were 35, 32 and 45 points lower than his pre-'02 numbers, and for first time since strike-shortened seasons in 1994-95, he failed to drive in 100 runs in successive seasons. His throwing remains a liability.

Where the club goes from here is unclear. General manager Steve Phillips survived Valentine—in more ways that one. Though others are on the way—notably catcher Justin Huber and lefthnder Scott Kazmir, Phillips has just two minor league players in position to help at the major league level in 2003, shortstop Jose Reyes and righthander Aaron Heilman. And each needs at least a half-year more at Triple-A Norfolk.

ORGANIZATION LEADERS

BATTING

*AVG	Jeff Duncan, St. Lucie/Capital City	.373
R	Jose Reyes, Binghamton/St. Lucie	104
H	Jose Reyes, Binghamton/St. Lucie	162
TB	Craig Brazell, Binghamton/St. Lucie	252
2B	Prentice Redman, Binghamton	35
3B	Jose Reyes, Binghamton/St. Lucie	19
HR	Aaron McNeal, Norfolk/Binghamton	22
	Craig Brazell, Binghamton/St. Lucie	22
RBI	Craig Brazell, Binghamton/St. Lucie	101
BB	David Wright, Capital City	76
SO	Andy Tracy, Norfolk	123
SB	Wayne Lydon, Capital City	87

PITCHING

W	Harold Eckert, Capital City	13
L	Wayne Ough, Capital City/Brooklyn	11
#ERA	Jason Scobie, Capital City/Brooklyn	2.84
G	Jim Serrano, Norfolk	53
CG	Four tied at	2
SV	Tim Lavigne, Binghamton/St. Lucie	16
IP	Pat Stange, Norfolk	165
BB	Nick Maness, Norfolk/Binghamton	80
SO	Matt Peterson, St. Lucie/Capital City	158

*Minimum 250 At-Bats #Minimum 75 Innings

NEW YORK METS

Manager: Bobby Valentine

2002 Record: 75-85, .469 (5th, NL East)

BATTING	AVG	G	AB	R	H	2B	3B	HR	RBI	BB	SO	SB	CS	SLG	OBP	B	T	HT	WT	DOB	1st Yr	Resides
Alfonzo, Edgardo	.308	135	490	78	151	26	0	16	56	62	55	6	0	.459	.391	R	R	5-11	180	11-8-73	1991	St. Teresa, Venez.
Alomar, Roberto	.266	149	590	73	157	24	4	11	53	57	83	16	4	.376	.331	S	R	6-0	180	2-5-68	1985	Bradenton, Fla.
Burnitz, Jeromy	.215	154	479	65	103	15	0	19	54	58	135	10	7	.365	.311	L	R	6-0	210	4-14-69	1990	Poway, Calif.
Cedeno, Roger	.260	149	511	65	133	19	2	7	41	42	92	25	4	.346	.318	S	R	6-1	200	8-16-74	1992	Valencia, Venez.
Christensen, McKay	.333	4	3	1	1	0	0	0	0	1	1	0	0	.333	.500	L	L	5-11	180	8-14-75	1995	Alpine, Utah
Clark, Brady	.417	10	12	3	5	1	0	0	1	1	2	0	0	.500	.462	R	R	6-2	190	4-18-73	1996	Beaverton, Ore.
2-team (51 Cincinnati)	.192	61	78	9	15	4	0	0	10	7	11	1	2	.244	.267							
Gonzalez, Raul	.259	30	81	9	21	2	0	3	11	4	17	2	2	.395	.291	R	R	5-9	190	12-27-73	1991	Carolina, P.R.
2-team (10 Cincinnati)	.260	40	104	13	27	3	0	3	12	6	22	4	2	.375	.297							
Johnson, Mark	.137	42	51	5	7	4	0	1	4	9	18	0	0	.275	.267	L	L	6-4	230	10-17-67	1990	Rye, N.Y.
Little, Mark	.000	3	3	0	0	0	0	0	0	0	1	0	1	.000	.000	R	R	6-0	190	7-11-72	1994	Edwardsville, Ill.
Matthews, Gary	.000	2	1	0	0	0	0	0	0	0	0	0	0	.000	.000	S	R	6-3	210	8-25-74	1994	Canoga Park, Calif.
McEwing, Joe	.199	105	196	22	39	8	1	3	26	9	50	4	4	.296	.242	R	R	5-11	170	10-19-72	1992	Yardley, Pa.
Ordonez, Rey	.254	144	460	53	117	25	2	1	42	24	46	2	2	.324	.292	R	R	5-9	150	1-11-71	1993	Parkland, Fla.
Payton, Jay	.284	87	275	33	78	16	3	8	31	21	34	4	1	.415	.336	R	R	5-10	180	11-22-72	1994	Zanesville, Ohio
Perez, Timo	.295	136	444	52	131	27	6	8	47	23	36	10	6	.437	.331	L	L	5-9	160	4-8-75	2000	San Cristobal, D.R.
Phillips, Jason	.368	11	19	4	7	0	0	1	3	1	1	0	0	.526	.409	R	R	6-1	170	9-27-76	1997	El Cajon, Calif.
Piazza, Mike	.280	135	478	69	134	23	2	33	98	57	82	0	3	.544	.359	R	R	6-3	210	9-4-68	1989	Boynton Beach, Fla.
Scutaro, Marcos	.222	27	36	2	8	0	1	1	6	0	11	0	1	.361	.216	R	R	5-10	170	10-30-75	1995	San Fekipe, Venez.
Snead, Esix	.308	17	13	3	4	0	0	1	3	1	4	4	3	.538	.357	S	R	5-10	170	6-7-76	1998	Williston, Fla.
Tarasco, Tony	.250	60	96	15	24	5	0	6	15	8	13	2	1	.490	.305	L	R	6-1	200	12-9-70	1988	Miami, Fla.
Valentin, John	.240	114	208	18	50	15	0	3	30	22	37	0	0	.356	.339	R	R	6-0	180	2-18-67	1988	Homdel, N.J.
Vaughn, Mo	.259	139	487	67	126	18	0	26	72	59	145	0	1	.456	.349	L	R	6-1	270	12-15-67	1989	Columbus, Ohio
Wigginton, Ty	.302	46	116	18	35	8	0	6	18	8	19	2	1	.526	.354	R	R	6-0	200	10-11-77	1998	Chula Vista, Calif.
Wilson, Vance	.245	74	163	19	40	7	0	5	26	5	32	0	1	.380	.301	R	R	5-11	190	3-17-73	1994	Springdale, Ark.

PITCHING	W	L	ERA	G	GS	CG	SV	IP	H	R	ER	BB	SO	AVG	B	T	HT	WT	DOB	1st Yr	Resides
Astacio, Pedro	12	11	4.79	31	31	3	0	192	192	106	102	63	152	.261	R	R	6-2	210	11-28-69	1988	Hato Mayor, D.R.
Bacsik, Mike	3	2	4.37	11	9	1	0	56	63	29	27	19	30	.288	L	L	6-3	190	11-11-77	1996	Duncanville, Texas
Benitez, Armando	1	0	2.27	62	0	0	33	67	46	20	17	25	79	.190	R	R	6-4	220	11-3-72	1990	San Pedro de Macoris, D.R.
Cerda, Jaime	0	0	2.45	32	0	0	0	26	22	7	7	14	21	.231	L	L	6-0	170	10-26-78	1999	Selma, Calif.
Chen, Bruce	0	0	0.00	1	0	0	0	1	1	0	0	0	0	.333	L	L	6-1	210	6-19-77	1994	Panama City, Panama
Corey, Mark	0	3	4.50	12	0	0	0	10	10	7	5	8	9	.250	R	R	6-3	210	11-16-74	1995	Austin, Pa.
D'Amico, Jeff	6	10	4.94	29	22	1	0	146	152	84	80	37	101	.267	R	R	6-7	250	12-27-75	1993	Pinellas Park, Fla.
Davis, Kane	1	1	7.07	16	0	0	0	14	15	11	11	11	24	.272	R	R	6-3	190	6-25-75	1993	Reedy, W.Va.
Estes, Shawn	4	9	4.55	23	23	1	0	133	133	70	67	66	92	.267	R	L	6-2	200	2-18-73	1991	San Francisco, Calif.
Feliciano, Pedro	0	0	7.50	6	0	0	0	6	9	5	5	1	4	.360	L	L	5-10	180	8-25-76	1995	Dorado, P.R.
Guthrie, Mark	5	3	2.44	68	0	0	1	48	35	13	13	19	44	.207	R	L	6-4	210	9-22-65	1987	Bradenton, Fla.
Jones, Bobby M.	0	0	5.29	12	0	0	0	17	20	11	10	11	11	.298	R	L	6-0	170	4-11-72	1992	East Rutherford, N.J.
Komiyama, Saturo	0	3	5.61	25	0	0	0	43	53	29	27	12	33	.301	R	R	6-2	190	9-15-65	2002	Chiba, Japan
Leiter, Al	13	13	3.48	33	33	2	0	204	194	99	79	69	172	.249	L	L	6-3	220	10-23-65	1984	Weston, Fla.
Middlebrook, Jason	1	0	3.94	3	3	0	0	16	13	7	7	14	.220		R	R	6-3	210	6-26-75	1996	Austin, Texas
2-team (12 San Diego)	.2	3	4.73	15	5	0	0	51	44	27	27	22	42	.236							
Reed, Steve	0	1	2.08	24	0	0	0	26	23	6	6	4	14	.239	R	R	6-2	210	3-11-66	1988	Arvada, Colo.
2-team (40 San Diego)	.2	5	2.01	64	0	0	1	67	56	15	15	14	50	.232							
Roberts, Grant	3	1	2.20	34	0	0	0	45	43	12	11	16	31	.252	R	R	6-3	200	9-13-77	1995	El Cajon, Calif.
Seo, Jae	0	0	0.00	1	0	0	0	1	0	0	0	0	1	.000	R	R	6-1	210	5-24-77	1997	Naebang Dang, South Korea
Strange, Pat	0	0	1.13	5	0	0	0	8	6	1	1	1	4	.206	R	R	6-5	240	8-23-80	1998	Springfield, Mass.
Strickland, Scott	6	9	3.59	68	0	0	2	68	61	29	27	33	67	.236	R	R	5-11	180	4-26-76	1997	Spring, Texas
2-team (1 Montreal)	.6	9	3.54	69	0	0	2	69	61	29	27	33	69	.233							
Thomson, John	2	6	4.31	9	9	0	0	54	65	39	26	17	31	.290	R	R	6-3	190	10-1-73	1993	Sulphur, La.
2-team (21 Colorado)	.9	14	4.71	30	30	0	0	182	201	116	95	44	107	.274							
Trachsel, Steve	11	11	3.37	30	30	1	0	174	170	80	65	69	105	.257	R	R	6-4	200	10-31-70	1991	Mesa, Ariz.
Walker, Pete	0	0	9.00	1	0	0	0	1	2	1	1	0	0	.400	R	R	6-2	190	4-8-69	1990	Waterford, Conn.
Walker, Tyler	1	0	5.91	5	1	0	0	11	11	7	7	5	7	.250	R	R	6-3	230	5-15-76	1997	Ross, Calif.
Weathers, David	6	3	2.91	71	0	0	0	77	69	30	25	36	61	.244	R	R	6-3	230	9-25-69	1988	Loretto, Tenn.

FIELDING

Catcher	PCT	G	PO	A	E	DP	PB
Phillips	1.000	7	27	1	0	0	0
Piazza	.986	121	811	46	12	3	8
Wilson	.983	66	315	38	6	5	3

First Base	PCT	G	PO	A	E	DP
Guthrie	.000	1	0	0	0	0
Johnson	.989	15	84	6	1	7
McEwing	1.000	20	45	4	0	5
Tarasco	1.000	7	11	0	0	0
Valentin	.974	22	106	6	3	12
Vaughn	.984	134	1085	47	18	95
Wigginton	1.000	13	56	5	0	4
Wilson	1.000	1	2	0	0	0

Second Base	PCT	G	PO	A	E	DP
Alomar	.983	147	273	348	11	94
McEwing	1.000	13	15	14	0	2
Scutaro	1.000	12	4	7	0	0
Valentin	1.000	3	4	3	0	2
Wigginton	.966	12	22	34	2	4

Third Base	PCT	G	PO	A	E	DP
Alfonzo	.969	134	95	278	12	22
McEwing	.900	10	5	13	2	2
Scutaro	1.000	3	1	2	0	0
Valentin	.878	18	9	27	5	3
Wigginton	.900	14	7	20	3	3

Shortstop	PCT	G	PO	A	E	DP
McEwing	.921	21	18	40	5	4
Ordonez	.969	144	208	388	19	82
Scutaro	.941	6	5	11	1	3
Valentin	.971	24	20	48	2	9

Outfield	PCT	G	PO	A	E	DP
Burnitz	.966	140	249	7	9	0
Cedeno	.966	132	225	2	8	0
Christensen	1.000	3	3	0	0	0
Clark	1.000	6	4	0	0	0
Gonzalez	1.000	24	43	1	0	0
Johnson	.000	1	0	0	0	0
Little	.000	1	0	0	0	0

BASEBALL AMERICA 2003 ALMANAC • **195**

McEwing	1.000	35	48	0	0	1	Piazza	.000	1	0	0	0	0	Tarasco	.977	29	40	3	1	1
Payton	.994	82	164	6	1	0	Scutaro	.000	1	0	0	0	0	Wigginton	.000	2	0	0	0	0
Perez	.979	122	266	9	6	3	Snead	1.000	6	5	0	0	0							

Pedro Astacio: 12-11, 4.79 in New York

Mike Piazza: led Mets with 33 homers, 98 RBIs

FARM SYSTEM

Director, Player Development: Jim Duquette

Class	Farm Team	League	W	L	Pct.	Finish*	Manager	First Yr.
AAA	Norfolk (Va.) Tides	International	70	73	.490	8th (14)	Bobby Floyd	1969
AA	Binghamton (N.Y.) Mets	Eastern	73	68	.518	6th (12)	Howie Freiling	1992
High A	St. Lucie (Fla.) Mets	Florida State	71	69	.507	6th (12)	Ken Oberkfell	1988
Low A	Capital City (S.C.) Bombers	South Atlantic	75	64	.540	6th (16)	Tony Tijerina	1983
SS A	Brooklyn (N.Y.) Cyclones	New York-Penn	38	38	.500	7th (14)	Howard Johnson	2001
Rookie	Kingsport (Tenn.) Mets	Appalachian	23	44	.343	9th (10)	Joey Cora	1980

*Finish in overall standings (No. of teams in league)

NORFOLK TIDES   Class AAA

INTERNATIONAL LEAGUE

BATTING	AVG	G	AB	R	H	2B	3B	HR	RBI	BB	SO	SB	CS	SLG	OBP	B	T	HT	WT	DOB	1st Yr	Resides
Basak, Chris	.217	17	60	6	13	1	1	0	6	3	14	5	0	.267	.254	R	R	6-2	180	12-6-78	2000	Joliet, Ill.
Bates, Fletcher	.251	58	167	20	42	8	1	6	21	12	25	2	3	.419	.302	S	R	6-1	190	3-24-74	1994	Rocky Point, N.C.
Chevalier, Virgil	.300	19	60	5	18	1	0	2	8	10	7	1	1	.417	.408	R	R	6-2	240	10-31-73	1995	Ballston Lake, N.Y.
Christensen, McKay	.284	97	377	52	107	23	6	5	30	26	72	20	13	.416	.341	L	L	5-11	180	8-14-75	1995	Alpine, Utah
Curry, Mike	.293	26	92	12	27	4	0	0	4	15	18	4	4	.337	.394	L	R	5-10	190	2-15-77	1998	Jacksonville, Fla.
Depastino, Joe	.298	70	248	24	74	15	3	5	27	12	47	4	0	.444	.338	R	R	6-2	210	9-4-73	1992	Sarasota, Fla.
Figueroa, Luis	.000	2	4	0	0	0	0	0	0	0	1	0	0	.000	.000	S	R	5-9	140	2-16-74	1997	Vega Alta, P.R.
Hernandez, Carlos	.324	58	173	19	56	9	0	0	16	5	30	7	0	.376	.354	R	R	5-9	170	12-12-75	1993	Caracas, Venez.
Johnson, Mark	.259	77	270	45	70	17	1	14	37	32	53	1	0	.485	.343	L	L	6-4	230	10-17-67	1990	Rye, N.Y.
Latham, Chris	.232	117	405	60	94	22	6	6	43	62	103	26	9	.360	.338	S	R	6-0	200	5-26-73	1991	Las Vegas, Nev.
Little, Mark	.500	2	10	1	5	0	0	0	2	1	3	0	0	.500	.545	R	R	6-0	190	7-11-72	1994	Edwardsville, Ill.
Malave, Jaime	.333	4	3	0	1	0	0	0	0	1	0	0	0	.333	.500	R	R	6-0	210	3-22-75	1995	Yakima, Wash.
McNeal, Aaron	.186	25	86	7	16	2	0	3	8	6	23	0	0	.314	.237	R	R	6-3	230	4-28-78	1996	Castro Valley, Calif.
Perez, Timo	.571	5	21	5	12	2	1	1	5	2	2	3	1	.905	.609	L	L	5-9	160	4-8-75	2000	San Cristobal, D.R.
Phillips, Jason	.282	88	323	30	91	22	1	13	65	24	29	1	0	.477	.327	R	R	6-1	170	9-27-76	1997	El Cajon, Calif.
Scutaro, Marcos	.319	97	354	48	113	22	6	7	28	30	61	7	8	.475	.375	R	R	5-10	170	10-30-75	1995	San Felipe, Venez.
Soler, Ramon	.100	7	10	0	1	0	0	0	0	2	2	0	0	.100	.250	S	R	6-0	170	9-19-77	1997	Elias Pina, D.R.
Stratton, Rob	.246	73	256	44	63	8	0	20	46	18	84	6	3	.512	.305	R	R	6-2	250	10-7-77	1996	Santa Barbara, Calif.
Tamargo, John	.198	44	101	12	20	3	0	2	9	13	10	2	0	.287	.296	S	R	5-9	180	5-3-75	1996	Tampa, Fla.
Tarasco, Tony	.281	42	153	21	43	7	1	1	18	9	15	5	3	.359	.323	L	R	6-1	200	12-9-70	1988	Miami, Fla.
Toca, Jorge	.251	54	195	21	49	9	0	2	15	9	31	2	1	.328	.283	R	R	6-3	220	1-7-75	1999	Miami, Fla.
Tracy, Andy	.199	125	432	61	86	16	1	20	61	56	123	4	1	.380	.295	L	R	6-3	220	12-11-73	1996	Columbus, Ohio

ORGANIZATION STATISTICS

BATTING	AVG	G	AB	R	H	2B	3B	HR	RBI	BB	SO	SB	CS	SLG	OBP	B	T	HT	WT	DOB	1st Yr	Resides
Velandia, Jorge	.201	115	407	43	82	20	1	6	37	30	79	5	2	.300	.257	R	R	5-9	180	1-12-75	1992	Roadhouse, Ill.
Velazquez, Gil	.212	12	33	2	7	1	0	0	1	4	9	0	0	.242	.297	R	R	6-2	170	10-17-79	1998	Paramount, Calif.
Wigginton, Ty	.300	104	383	49	115	26	3	6	48	43	50	5	3	.431	.366	R	R	6-0	200	10-11-77	1998	Chula Vista, Calif.

PITCHING	W	L	ERA	G	GS	CG	SV	IP	H	R	ER	BB	SO	AVG	B	T	HT	WT	DOB	1st Yr	Resides
Bacsik, Mike	5	5	3.74	25	14	1	0	108	134	48	45	25	75	.311	L	L	6-3	190	11-11-77	1996	Duncanville, Texas
Bale, John	2	2	3.54	12	2	0	0	28	22	11	11	7	27	.220	L	L	6-4	210	5-22-74	1996	Crestview, Fla.
Bell, Heath	3	4	4.26	22	0	0	5	32	38	15	15	9	28	.301	R	R	6-2	240	9-29-77	1998	Tustin, Calif.
Brunette, Justin	2	2	4.09	45	0	0	2	77	77	40	35	20	42	.262	L	L	6-1	200	10-7-75	1997	Huntington Beach, Calif.
Cammack, Eric	0	2	13.50	11	0	0	0	10	13	15	15	12	6	.325	R	R	6-1	180	8-14-75	1997	Port Neches, Texas
Cerda, Jaime	0	0	0.43	12	0	0	1	21	10	2	1	7	17	.142	L	L	6-0	170	10-26-78	1999	Selma, Calif.
Cerros, Juan	1	3	3.35	25	3	0	2	38	40	21	14	11	23	.261	R	R	6-1	200	9-25-76	1996	Monterrey, Mexico
Cole, Joey	0	1	9.00	1	0	0	0	2	3	2	2	2	2	.375	R	R	6-7	240	9-15-77	1999	Nacogdoches, Texas
Corey, Mark	3	1	1.03	25	0	0	7	26	14	3	3	7	37	.157	R	R	6-3	210	11-16-74	1995	Austin, Pa.
Davis, Kane	0	0	0.00	1	0	0	0	1	1	0	0	0	2	.250	R	R	6-3	190	6-25-75	1993	Reedy, W.Va.
Feliciano, Pedro	0	0	7.00	5	0	0	2	9	14	7	7	1	11	.358	L	L	5-10	180	8-25-76	1995	Dorado, P.R.
2-team (20 Louisville)	1	1	4.04	25	0	0	2	36	49	17	16	5	30	.335							
Gonzalez, Dicky	0	0	3.60	1	1	0	0	5	6	2	2	2	7	.285	R	R	5-11	170	12-21-78	1996	Bayamon, P.R.
Heilman, Aaron	2	3	3.28	10	7	0	0	49	42	18	18	16	35	.240	R	R	6-5	220	11-12-78	2001	Logansport, Ind.
Jones, Bobby M.	1	4	4.02	13	6	0	0	40	42	25	18	15	35	.254	R	L	6-4	170	4-11-72	1992	East Rutherford, N.J.
Joseph, Jake	0	1	12.27	1	1	0	0	4	8	5	5	3	1	.421	R	R	6-1	210	1-24-78	1999	Citrus Heights, Calif.
Komiyama, Saturo	3	1	1.42	17	6	1	0	44	27	8	7	9	43	.176	R	R	6-2	190	9-15-65	2002	Chiba, Japan
Lira, Felipe	1	4	5.03	21	1	0	1	39	45	22	22	13	22	.310	R	R	6-1	210	4-26-72	1990	Miranda, Venez.
Maness, Nick	2	0	3.50	3	3	0	0	18	16	10	7	8	11	.238	R	R	6-4	210	10-17-78	1997	Robbins, N.C.
Middlebrook, Jason	2	1	2.66	5	5	0	0	24	13	7	7	1	22	.160	R	R	6-3	210	6-26-75	1996	Austin, Texas
Munoz, Bobby	0	0	30.86	3	0	0	0	2	9	8	8	4	3	.600	R	R	6-7	210	3-3-68	1989	Irving, Texas
Roach, Jason	6	6	2.79	19	17	0	0	106	117	41	33	31	64	.277	R	R	6-4	190	4-20-76	1997	Kinston, N.C.
Saenz, Jason	1	0	9.95	5	0	0	0	10	7	7	10	3	7	.357	L	L	6-2	190	2-13-77	1998	Santa Ana, Calif.
Seo, Jae	6	9	3.99	26	24	1	0	129	145	66	57	22	87	.284	R	R	6-1	210	5-24-77	1997	Naebang Dang, South Korea
Serrano, Jim	8	6	4.01	53	0	0	3	74	88	40	33	31	76	.293	R	R	5-10	170	5-9-76	1998	Grand Junction, Colo.
Strange, Pat	10	10	3.82	29	25	2	0	165	165	77	70	59	109	.264	R	R	6-5	240	8-23-80	1998	Springfield, Mass.
Walker, Adam	0	1	9.00	1	1	0	0	5	6	6	5	3	3	.285	L	L	6-7	200	5-28-76	1997	Albuquerque, N.M.
Walker, Pete	0	0	3.00	2	2	0	0	9	9	3	3	1	6	.243	R	R	6-2	190	4-8-69	1990	Waterford, Conn.
Walker, Tyler	10	5	3.99	28	25	1	1	142	152	65	63	38	109	.274	R	R	6-3	230	5-15-76	1997	Ross, Calif.
Williams, Matt	0	0	27.00	1	0	0	0	0	1	1	1	2	0	.500	S	L	6-0	170	4-12-71	1992	Atlanta, Ga.
Yates, Tyler	2	2	1.32	24	0	0	6	34	29	10	5	13	34	.226	R	R	6-4	220	8-7-77	1998	Koloa, Hawaii

FIELDING

Catcher	PCT	G	PO	A	E	DP	PB
Chevalier	1.000	8	50	4	0	0	2
Depastino	.988	57	376	32	5	4	3
Phillips	.993	82	552	31	4	6	2

First Base	PCT	G	PO	A	E	DP
Chevalier	1.000	3	19	0	0	2
Johnson	.997	41	368	28	1	28
McNeal	.987	19	144	10	2	13
Tamargo	1.000	1	1	0	0	0
Tarasco	1.000	2	6	1	0	0
Toca	.985	41	288	30	5	32
Tracy	.991	44	315	22	3	28
Wigginton	1.000	8	41	3	0	5

Second Base	PCT	G	PO	A	E	DP
Basak	1.000	17	29	28	0	5
Hernandez	.973	27	44	66	3	10
Scutaro	.978	50	100	119	5	30
Soler	1.000	5	7	3	0	1

Tamargo	1.000	14	15	18	0	2
Velandia	.962	9	18	33	2	9
Velazquez	.902	7	13	24	4	3
Wigginton	1.000	32	58	86	0	18

Third Base	PCT	G	PO	A	E	DP
Chevalier	1.000	1	1	2	0	0
Hernandez	1.000	9	7	13	0	3
Scutaro	1.000	7	4	3	0	0
Tamargo	.885	14	4	19	3	1
Tracy	.962	71	33	117	6	13
Velandia	1.000	8	3	15	0	0
Wigginton	.913	46	39	66	10	5

Shortstop	PCT	G	PO	A	E	DP
Basak	1.000	1	0	1	0	0
Figueroa	1.000	2	1	3	0	0
Hernandez	.976	13	12	28	1	4
Scutaro	.969	25	47	79	4	16

Tamargo	1.000	8	8	18	0	3
Velandia	.983	100	134	325	8	49
Velazquez	1.000	4	5	9	0	4

Outfield	PCT	G	PO	A	E	DP
Bates	.931	43	67	0	5	0
Chevalier	1.000	3	4	1	0	0
Christensen	.995	84	193	4	1	0
Curry	1.000	22	50	3	0	1
Hernandez	.000	1	0	0	0	0
Johnson	1.000	35	64	1	0	0
Latham	.974	107	249	10	7	1
Little	1.000	1	4	0	0	0
Perez	1.000	5	6	0	0	0
Scutaro	.957	11	21	1	1	0
Stratton	.988	70	155	4	2	0
Tarasco	1.000	36	62	3	0	1
Toca	1.000	11	21	1	0	0
Wigginton	.963	20	26	0	1	0

BINGHAMTON METS

Class AA

EASTERN LEAGUE

BATTING	AVG	G	AB	R	H	2B	3B	HR	RBI	BB	SO	SB	CS	SLG	OBP	B	T	HT	WT	DOB	1st Yr	Resides
Acuna, Ron	.208	10	24	3	5	2	2	0	3	2	5	1	1	.458	.250	R	R	5-11	200	6-30-79	1996	Guatire-Miranda, Venez.
Basak, Chris	.255	109	377	54	96	18	3	4	34	38	94	19	14	.350	.323	R	R	6-2	180	12-6-78	2000	Joliet, Ill.
Bates, Fletcher	.307	35	101	16	31	8	3	2	20	10	24	3	1	.505	.371	S	R	6-1	190	3-24-74	1994	Rocky Point, N.C.
Bay, Jason	.290	34	107	17	31	4	2	4	19	15	23	13	3	.477	.383	R	R	6-2	200	9-20-78	2000	Trail, B.C.
Brazell, Craig	.308	35	130	14	40	8	0	6	19	1	28	0	2	.508	.343	L	R	6-3	210	5-10-80	1998	Montgomery, Ala.
Chevalier, Virgil	.294	98	337	58	99	25	0	6	45	43	39	4	2	.421	.374	R	R	6-2	240	10-31-73	1995	Ballston Lake, N.Y.
Curry, Mike	.273	31	99	16	27	4	2	1	8	13	24	3	1	.384	.357	L	R	5-10	190	2-15-77	1998	Jacksonville, Fla.
Gonzalez, Jimmy	.241	96	299	33	72	10	2	6	38	45	51	3	3	.348	.352	R	R	6-3	230	3-8-73	1991	Hartford, Conn.
Hunter, Scott	.236	24	89	13	21	4	0	2	12	8	18	6	2	.348	.303	R	R	6-1	210	12-17-75	1994	Philadelphia, Pa.
Malave, Jaime	.222	13	36	2	8	0	0	1	5	2	10	0	0	.306	.263	R	R	6-3	210	3-22-75	1995	Yakima, Wash.
McEwing, Joe	.000	1	5	0	0	0	0	0	0	0	1	0	0	.000	.000	R	R	5-11	170	10-19-72	1992	Yardley, Pa.
McNeal, Aaron	.299	96	348	52	104	15	0	19	69	45	95	1	2	.506	.375	R	R	6-3	230	4-28-78	1996	Castro Valley, Calif.
Nye, Rodney	.236	121	394	51	93	17	0	13	53	55	99	4	2	.378	.346	R	R	6-4	200	12-2-76	1999	Cameron, Okla.
Redman, Prentice	.283	135	491	79	139	35	2	11	63	59	112	43	9	.430	.367	R	R	6-3	180	8-23-79	1999	Duncanville, Ala.
Reyes, Jose	.287	65	275	46	79	16	8	2	24	16	42	27	11	.425	.331	S	R	6-0	160	6-11-83	1999	Santiago, D.R.
Salazar, Oscar	.173	28	75	6	13	2	0	1	5	1	10	0	1	.240	.232	R	R	5-11	170	6-27-78	1994	Maracay, Venez.
2-team (53 Erie)	.203	81	266	22	54	20	1	7	31	19	55	2	2	.365	.266							
Shipp, Brian	.227	119	375	51	85	27	3	8	49	22	95	7	8	.379	.249	R	R	6-2	190	8-15-78	1999	Zachary, La.
Snead, Esix	.252	125	401	62	101	9	6	3	42	45	72	66	18	.327	.335	S	R	5-10	170	6-7-76	1998	Williston, Fla.
Soler, Ramon	.226	8	31	4	7	0	0	1	4	5	3	2	1	.226	.314	S	R	6-0	170	9-19-77	1997	Elias Pina, D.R.
Velazquez, Gil	.194	27	72	6	14	2	0	0	5	7	15	0	3	.222	.275	R	R	6-2	170	10-17-79	1998	Paramount, Calif.

BATTING	AVG	G	AB	R	H	2B	3B	HR	RBI	BB	SO	SB	CS	SLG	OBP	B	T	HT	WT	DOB	1st Yr	Resides
Watson, Matt	.279	127	437	55	122	26	2	10	67	39	52	12	8	.416	.339	L	R	5-11	190	9-5-78	1999	Lancaster, Pa.
2-team (1 Harrisburg)	.279	128	441	56	123	26	2	10	67	39	52	12	8	.415	.338							
Wilson, John	.208	10	24	0	5	1	0	0	1	1	8	0	0	.250	.296	R	R	6-1	210	9-29-78	2000	Newbury Park, Calif.

PITCHING	W	L	ERA	G	GS	CG	SV	IP	H	R	ER	BB	SO	AVG	B	T	HT	WT	DOB	1st Yr	Resides
Bell, Heath	1	0	1.18	24	0	0	6	38	22	6	5	6	49	.167	R	R	6-2	240	9-29-77	1998	Tustin, Calif.
Bevis, P.J.	1	0	1.29	4	0	0	0	7	5	1	1	3	14	.208	R	R	6-3	170	7-28-80	1998	Capalaba, Australia
Bland, Nate	4	2	2.55	15	0	0	0	25	16	9	7	8	19	.181	L	L	6-5	190	12-27-74	1993	Birmingham, Ala.
Braswell, Bryan	3	1	6.29	24	0	0	1	34	48	26	24	11	19	.322	L	L	6-1	200	6-30-75	1996	Springboro, Ohio
Brunette, Justin	1	0	0.00	3	0	0	0	4	3	0	0	1	3	.214	L	L	6-1	200	10-7-75	1997	Huntington Beach, Calif.
Cammack, Eric	3	2	3.98	36	0	0	5	54	44	28	24	43	64	.229	R	R	6-1	180	8-14-75	1997	Port Neches, Texas
Cerda, Jaime	5	1	2.27	14	0	0	0	32	21	8	8	10	33	.192	L	L	6-0	170	10-26-78	1999	Selma, Calif.
Cerros, Juan	0	0	0.00	3	0	0	0	3	0	0	0	0	3	.000	R	R	6-1	200	9-25-76	1996	Monterrey, Mexico
Cole, Joey	2	3	5.24	10	8	0	0	46	56	34	27	21	27	.302	L	R	6-7	240	9-15-77	1998	Nacogdoches, Texas
Cook, Andy	6	3	5.07	30	3	0	0	55	64	36	31	22	39	.290	R	R	6-5	190	2-26-77	1998	Danville, Va.
Griffiths, Jeremy	8	6	3.89	27	26	2	0	153	157	75	66	54	126	.271	R	R	6-6	240	3-22-78	1999	Avon Lakes, Ohio
Heilman, Aaron	4	4	3.82	17	17	0	0	97	85	43	41	28	97	.236	R	R	6-5	220	11-12-78	2001	Logansport, Ind.
Jamison, Ryan	0	4	4.34	11	6	0	0	37	41	19	18	16	33	.288	R	R	6-3	180	1-5-78	1999	El Cajon, Calif.
Joseph, Jake	6	4	2.91	14	14	0	0	87	79	37	28	24	42	.247	R	R	6-1	210	1-24-78	1999	Citrus Heights, Calif.
Lavigne, Tim	2	3	2.86	23	0	0	9	35	29	11	11	15	25	.235	R	R	5-11	180	7-4-78	2000	Virginia Beach, Va.
Maness, Nick	5	9	4.52	25	23	0	1	131	120	74	66	72	109	.246	R	R	6-4	210	10-17-78	1997	Robbins, N.C.
Ochoa, Pablo	0	2	9.00	8	4	0	0	20	31	21	20	8	13	.333	R	R	6-1	200	10-21-75	1996	Nuevo Leon, Mexico
Rivera, Saul	2	3	3.03	30	0	0	13	39	25	18	13	23	32	.182	R	R	5-11	180	12-7-77	1998	San Juan, P.R.
Roach, Jason	3	4	3.65	8	8	0	0	44	40	19	18	12	23	.251	R	R	6-4	190	4-20-76	1997	Kinston, N.C.
Roberts, Grant	0	0	0.00	1	1	0	0	1	0	0	0	0	1	.000	R	R	6-3	200	9-13-77	1995	El Cajon, Calif.
Saenz, Jason	1	0	5.10	36	1	0	2	72	69	48	41	55	47	.263	L	L	6-2	190	2-13-77	1998	Santa Ana, Calif.
Seibel, Phil	10	8	3.97	28	25	2	0	150	147	78	66	49	114	.263	L	L	6-1	190	1-28-79	2000	Cypress, Calif.
Seo, Jae	0	0	5.40	1	0	0	0	5	5	3	3	1	6	.250	R	R	6-1	215	5-24-77	1997	Naebang Dang, South Korea
Trachsel, Steve	1	0	0.00	1	1	0	0	6	3	1	0	4	5	.150	R	R	6-4	200	10-31-70	1991	Mesa, Ariz.
Vega, Rene	1	6	7.15	26	3	0	2	45	61	39	36	18	34	.322	L	L	5-10	170	8-4-76	1998	Bronx, N.Y.
Walker, Adam	0	0	1.93	1	1	0	0	5	4	1	1	1	5	.235	L	L	6-7	200	5-28-76	1997	Albuquerque, N.M.

FIELDING

Catcher	PCT	G	PO	A	E	DP	PB
Chevalier	.986	37	263	20	4	2	8
Gonzalez	.987	92	636	70	9	5	4
Malave	.985	11	60	4	1	0	0
Wilson	1.000	8	45	7	0	0	0

First Base	PCT	G	PO	A	E	DP
Brazell	.972	32	225	17	7	22
Chevalier	.990	18	93	8	1	8
McNeal	.991	94	810	70	8	87
Nye	.983	11	53	5	1	5

Second Base	PCT	G	PO	A	E	DP
Basak	1.000	17	23	46	0	8
McEwing	.000	1	0	0	0	0
Nye	1.000	3	3	2	0	1

	PCT	G	PO	A	E	DP
Salazar	.970	16	32	32	2	7
Shipp	.962	100	180	228	16	65
Soler	.969	8	17	14	1	4
Velazquez	.978	12	16	28	1	4

Third Base	PCT	G	PO	A	E	DP
Basak	.962	16	8	42	2	3
Chevalier	1.000	17	10	29	0	0
McEwing	1.000	1	0	1	0	0
Nye	.965	104	74	198	10	21
Salazar	.900	7	3	6	1	0
Shipp	.846	9	4	18	4	2
Velazquez	.900	4	2	7	1	0

Shortstop	PCT	G	PO	A	E	DP
Basak	.971	70	126	204	10	49

	PCT	G	PO	A	E	DP
Reyes	.940	65	92	176	17	37
Velazquez	.943	8	12	21	2	4

Outfield	PCT	G	PO	A	E	DP
Acuna	.875	7	6	1	1	0
Basak	1.000	3	6	0	0	0
Bates	1.000	21	23	1	0	0
Bay	.956	27	39	4	2	0
Chevalier	.944	16	16	1	1	0
Curry	1.000	21	27	1	0	0
Hunter	.968	20	29	1	1	0
Redman	.979	118	226	5	5	1
Snead	.985	119	259	11	4	1
Watson	.979	104	177	11	4	1

ST. LUCIE METS

FLORIDA STATE LEAGUE

BATTING	AVG	G	AB	R	H	2B	3B	HR	RBI	BB	SO	SB	CS	SLG	OBP	B	T	HT	WT	DOB	1st Yr	Resides
Acuna, Ron	.298	115	443	67	132	18	5	2	54	38	74	36	12	.375	.326	R	R	5-11	200	6-30-79	1996	Guatire-Miranda, Venez.
Bay, Jason	.272	69	261	48	71	12	2	9	54	34	54	22	2	.437	.363	R	R	6-2	200	9-20-78	2000	Trail, B.C.
Brazell, Craig	.266	100	402	38	107	25	3	16	82	13	78	2	1	.463	.292	L	R	6-3	210	5-10-80	1998	Montgomery, Ala.
Cruz, Enrique	.291	124	467	69	136	21	2	6	45	32	76	33	16	.383	.336	R	R	6-1	180	11-21-81	1998	Santo Domingo, D.R.
Deschenes, Pat	.298	75	248	33	74	15	1	1	28	30	34	0	2	.379	.373	L	R	6-0	190	4-26-78	1998	Quebec City, Quebec
Devarez, Noel	.262	34	122	18	32	9	0	4	21	9	41	2	0	.434	.326	R	R	6-0	190	12-24-78	1998	San Francisco de Macoris, D.R.
Duncan, Jeff	.343	29	102	20	35	5	0	2	10	24	15	10	1	.451	.472	L	L	6-2	180	12-9-78	2000	Frankfort, Ill.
Garcia, Daniel	.273	122	432	69	118	34	5	4	52	53	77	13	6	.403	.369	R	R	6-0	180	4-12-80	2001	Anaheim, Calif.
Harris, Cory	.277	26	83	10	23	4	0	1	15	7	8	4	2	.361	.358	R	R	5-10	180	12-7-79	1999	Davenport, Iowa
Huber, Justin	.270	28	100	15	27	2	1	3	15	11	18	0	0	.400	.370	R	R	6-2	190	7-1-82	2000	Emerald, Australia
Jacobs, Mike	.251	118	467	62	117	26	1	11	64	25	95	2	3	.381	.291	L	R	6-2	200	10-30-80	1999	San Diego, Calif.
Kay, Brett	.222	64	221	37	49	6	0	6	20	29	37	6	1	.330	.341	R	R	6-1	190	10-31-79	2001	Orange, Calif.
O'Sullivan, Patrick	.250	10	24	3	6	1	0	2	7	2	8	0	1	.542	.367	R	R	6-3	210	3-22-77	1999	Rockford, Ill.
Ochoa, Javier	.286	2	7	0	2	0	0	0	1	0	2	0	0	.286	.286	R	R	6-1	170	1-8-79	1996	Maracay, Venez.
Pagan, Angel	.343	16	67	12	23	2	1	1	7	7	9	10	2	.448	.405	S	R	6-1	180	7-2-81	2000	Rio Piedras, P.R.
Pittman, Sean	.255	44	129	11	33	9	1	1	16	16	36	2	1	.364	.333	S	R	5-10	180	4-24-78	2001	Lawrenceville, Ga.
Reyes, Jose	.288	69	288	58	83	10	11	6	38	30	35	31	13	.462	.353	S	R	6-0	160	6-11-83	1999	Santiago, D.R.
Rodriguez, Edgar	.207	8	29	3	6	1	2	2	8	2	9	0	1	.586	.258	R	R	5-11	150	11-29-79	1996	San Pedro de Macoris, D.R.
Seale, Marvin	.247	127	477	72	118	19	4	8	57	54	109	38	13	.354	.334	S	R	6-0	200	6-16-79	1998	La Canada, Calif.
Soler, Ramon	.203	21	64	11	13	4	0	0	4	7	13	10	2	.266	.292	S	R	6-0	170	9-19-77	1997	Elias Pina, D.R.
Velazquez, Gil	.212	33	118	13	25	6	0	0	16	6	30	2	0	.263	.250	R	R	6-2	170	10-17-79	1998	Paramount, Calif.
Wilson, John	.238	46	151	24	36	7	2	6	21	24	27	4	1	.430	.350	R	R	6-1	210	9-29-78	2000	Newbury Park, Calif.

PITCHING	W	L	ERA	G	GS	CG	SV	IP	H	R	ER	BB	SO	AVG	B	T	HT	WT	DOB	1st Yr	Resides
Bennett, Steve	5	5	1.97	41	0	0	7	69	43	19	15	37	73	.176	R	R	6-4	250	10-1-76	2000	Helena, Mont.
Brantley, Brian	1	2	4.81	12	4	0	1	39	48	25	21	7	34	.296	R	R	6-4	160	4-23-76	1998	Chesapeake, Va.
Chenard, Ken	2	4	3.72	13	13	0	0	56	42	27	23	25	39	.206	R	R	6-3	180	8-30-78	1999	Victorville, Calif.
Cole, Joey	8	2	3.20	18	18	1	0	107	93	46	38	25	74	.232	L	R	6-7	240	9-15-77	1998	Nacogdoches, Texas
Corey, Mark	0	0	0.00	1	0	0	0	2	0	0	0	0	3	.000	R	R	6-3	210	11-16-74	1995	Austin, Pa.
Cox, Mike	0	0	14.29	4	0	0	0	6	7	9	9	11	11	.304	L	L	5-11	190	11-3-78	2000	Pasadena, Texas

PITCHING	W	L	ERA	G	GS	CG	SV	IP	H	R	ER	BB	SO	AVG	B	T	HT	WT	DOB	1st Yr	Resides
Elliott, Chad	5	6	2.94	28	13	1	0	110	99	49	36	37	61	.240	R	L	6-1	180	1-28-78	2000	Yorba Linda, Calif.
Gahan, Matt	2	1	5.95	9	0	0	1	20	18	15	13	6	16	.230	R	R	6-0	180	11-26-75	2001	Goonellabah, Australia
Hee, Aaron	5	5	4.66	34	4	0	4	68	69	44	35	38	69	.259	L	L	6-0	190	3-4-79	1998	Las Vegas, Nev.
Joseph, Jake	3	3	3.59	13	13	0	0	73	75	33	29	13	47	.262	R	R	6-1	210	1-24-78	1999	Citrus Heights, Calif.
Keppel, Bob	9	7	4.32	27	26	0	0	152	162	83	73	43	109	.276	R	R	6-5	200	6-11-82	2000	Chesterfield, Mo.
Lavigne, Tim	2	3	3.76	22	0	0	7	26	21	11	11	9	25	.214	R	R	5-11	180	7-4-78	2000	Virginia Beach, Va.
Lohrman, Dave	1	0	2.35	8	0	0	0	15	8	5	4	13	22	.156	R	R	6-6	200	9-16-75	1997	East Amherst, N.Y.
Maberry, Mark	0	1	2.25	10	0	0	0	16	10	6	4	7	9	.178	R	R	6-3	200	7-31-74	1997	Cookeville, Tenn.
Mattioni, Nick	4	3	4.78	41	0	0	3	79	71	52	42	42	68	.238	R	R	6-3	200	3-14-79	2000	Deerfield Beach, Fla.
Mattox, David	4	4	2.82	9	9	2	0	51	46	21	16	24	34	.244	R	R	6-2	180	5-24-80	2001	Spartanburg, S.C.
McGinley, Blake	1	1	5.97	18	0	0	4	32	40	22	21	13	22	.298	R	L	6-1	170	8-2-78	2001	Bakersfield, Calif.
Musser, Neal	2	0	1.42	4	4	0	0	19	20	4	3	5	12	.273	L	L	6-2	200	8-25-80	1999	Otterbein, Ind.
Ochoa, Pablo	1	0	8.56	4	1	0	0	14	19	13	13	10	10	.339	R	R	6-1	200	10-21-75	1996	Nuevo Leon, Mexico
Peeples, Ross	2	3	5.59	6	6	0	0	29	33	24	18	13	26	.284	L	L	6-4	190	2-20-80	2000	Cordele, Ga.
Peterson, Matt	1	0	1.50	1	1	0	0	6	5	2	1	2	5	.217	R	R	6-5	210	2-11-82	2000	Alexandria, La.
Portobanco, Luz	0	2	8.18	2	2	1	0	11	12	10	10	9	6	.300	R	R	6-3	200	9-15-79	2000	Miami, Fla.
Reynolds, Josh	11	5	3.13	22	20	1	0	126	123	51	44	26	70	.254	R	R	6-4	190	9-27-79	2000	Holts Summit, Mo.
Vega, Rene	1	3	4.91	5	5	0	0	29	33	20	16	14	31	.275	L	L	5-10	170	8-4-76	1998	Bronx, N.Y.
Viole, Paul	3	9	5.99	40	0	0	5	68	76	67	45	54	64	.270	R	R	5-10	170	11-12-77	1999	Demarest, N.J.
Walker, Adam	0	1	9.00	1	1	0	0	2	3	2	2	0	3	.375	L	L	6-7	200	5-28-76	1997	Albuquerque, N.M.

FIELDING

Catcher	PCT	G	PO	A	E	DP	PB
Huber	.983	23	159	17	3	2	2
Jacobs	.988	56	397	29	5	2	7
Kay	.970	37	232	25	8	3	5
Ochoa	1.000	2	17	2	0	0	0
Wilson	.962	24	159	16	7	3	4

First Base	PCT	G	PO	A	E	DP
Brazell	.987	100	945	45	13	77
Deschenes	.990	35	294	16	3	22
Jacobs	.965	9	79	3	3	10

Second Base	PCT	G	PO	A	E	DP
Garcia	.972	105	184	300	14	57

	PCT	G	PO	A	E	DP
Pittman	.956	18	18	47	3	6
Soler	.947	20	40	50	5	11
Velazquez	1.000	1	2	1	0	1

Third Base	PCT	G	PO	A	E	DP
Cruz	.920	103	63	223	25	19
Deschenes	.968	21	18	43	2	1
Pittman	1.000	3	0	5	0	2
Velazquez	.976	15	7	33	1	3

Shortstop	PCT	G	PO	A	E	DP
Cruz	.918	21	28	61	8	10
Garcia	.907	18	23	45	7	9
Pittman	.890	18	29	44	9	7

	PCT	G	PO	A	E	DP
Reyes	.967	69	115	236	12	43
Velazquez	.943	16	27	55	5	9

Outfield	PCT	G	PO	A	E	DP
Acuna	.988	114	226	16	3	4
Bay	.950	68	106	9	6	2
Devarez	1.000	34	50	3	0	2
Duncan	.967	29	57	2	2	1
Garcia	.000	1	0	0	0	0
Harris	.962	25	47	3	2	0
O'Sullivan	1.000	3	4	0	0	0
Pagan	1.000	16	28	1	0	0
Rodriguez	1.000	8	10	0	0	0
Seale	.980	127	246	3	5	0

CAPITAL CITY BOMBERS — Low Class A

SOUTH ATLANTIC LEAGUE

BATTING	AVG	G	AB	R	H	2B	3B	HR	RBI	BB	SO	SB	CS	SLG	OBP	B	T	HT	WT	DOB	1st Yr	Resides
Bacani, David	.262	96	305	46	80	17	1	1	36	52	48	13	11	.334	.384	R	R	5-7	170	7-30-79	2001	Long Beach, Calif.
Beuerlein, Tyler	.182	22	66	7	12	0	0	2	4	5	24	0	1	.273	.239	S	R	6-2	200	5-29-79	2001	Cave Creek, Ariz.
Caligiuri, Jay	.235	62	221	25	52	13	0	5	38	22	40	0	4	.362	.309	R	R	6-0	190	3-29-80	2001	Camarillo, Calif.
Corr, Frank	.305	81	315	48	96	22	0	7	45	17	52	2	2	.441	.344	R	R	5-9	200	9-19-78	2001	Deltona, Fla.
Devarez, Noel	.242	17	62	8	15	5	1	0	7	3	17	4	1	.355	.288	R	R	6-0	190	12-24-78	1998	San Francisco de Macoris, D.R.
Duncan, Jeff	.393	40	150	33	59	13	3	4	17	18	34	15	3	.600	.468	L	L	6-2	180	12-9-78	2000	Frankfort, Ill.
Galante, Matt	.282	47	156	20	44	6	0	0	19	21	29	4	4	.321	.368	R	R	5-8	160	10-17-78	2000	Staten Island, N.Y.
Hietpas, Joe	.248	33	105	9	26	8	0	1	16	14	23	0	2	.352	.336	R	R	6-3	220	5-1-79	2001	Appleton, Wis.
Huber, Justin	.291	95	330	49	96	22	2	11	78	45	81	1	2	.470	.408	R	R	6-2	190	7-1-82	2000	Emerald, Australia
Jiannetti, Joe	.241	31	112	12	27	10	0	2	9	7	16	10	1	.384	.306	R	R	6-1	190	9-25-81	2001	St. Petersburg, Fla.
Kay, Brett	.239	38	117	14	28	5	0	1	7	14	22	1	3	.308	.346	R	R	6-1	190	10-31-79	2001	Orange, Calif.
Lawson, Forrest	.262	77	275	36	72	7	1	2	41	29	52	5	5	.316	.337	L	L	6-3	190	11-9-80	1999	Federal Way, Wash.
Lydon, Wayne	.294	127	473	93	139	9	5	0	46	54	104	87	13	.334	.368	R	R	6-2	190	4-17-81	1999	Jessup, Pa.
McIntyre, Robert	.252	98	345	46	87	16	3	5	50	16	102	10	6	.359	.291	R	R	5-10	180	12-8-80	1999	Tampa, Fla.
Ochoa, Javier	.235	32	85	13	20	1	0	2	10	11	15	0	0	.318	.343	R	R	6-1	170	1-8-79	1996	Maracay, Venez.
Pagan, Angel	.279	108	458	79	128	14	5	1	36	32	87	52	21	.338	.325	S	R	6-1	180	7-2-81	2000	Rio Piedras, P.R.
Pittman, Sean	.239	14	46	6	11	0	1	0	4	5	18	1	0	.283	.321	S	R	5-10	180	4-24-78	2001	Lawrenceville, Ga.
Ragsdale, Corey	.177	37	124	15	22	1	0	1	12	15	45	8	5	.210	.262	R	R	6-4	170	11-10-82	2001	Jonesboro, Ark.
Reynoso, Danilo	.167	3	6	0	1	0	0	0	1	1	1	0	0	.167	.375	R	R	5-10	160	4-5-82	1997	San Cristobal, D.R.
Rodriguez, Andres	.198	60	207	21	41	10	1	1	23	16	57	2	0	.271	.257	R	R	6-4	180	2-14-79	1998	San Cristobal, D.R.
Rodriguez, Edgar	.208	23	72	7	15	3	0	1	7	3	25	2	3	.292	.244	R	R	5-11	150	11-29-79	1996	San Pedro de Macoris, D.R.
Toner, John	.298	35	114	19	34	7	0	1	13	6	21	1	0	.377	.343	R	R	6-3	210	9-22-79	2001	St. Joseph, Mich.
Wright, David	.266	135	496	85	132	30	2	11	93	76	114	21	5	.401	.367	R	R	6-0	190	12-20-82	2001	Chesapeake, Va.

PITCHING	W	L	ERA	G	GS	CG	SV	IP	H	R	ER	BB	SO	AVG	B	T	HT	WT	DOB	1st Yr	Resides
Byard, David	7	4	3.57	45	0	0	5	68	55	32	27	43	48	.230	R	R	6-3	240	6-1-78	2000	Mt. Vernon, Ohio
Cabrera, Yunior	1	0	0.82	3	1	0	0	11	11	4	1	2	8	.261	L	L	6-0	160	10-25-79	1996	San Pedro de Macoris, D.R.
Cox, Mike	4	1	5.25	33	1	0	0	58	30	40	34	54	92	.166	L	L	5-11	190	11-3-78	2000	Pasadena, Texas
Dinardo, Lenny	5	5	4.35	24	19	0	1	101	106	60	49	56	103	.273	L	L	6-4	190	9-19-79	2001	High Springs, Fla.
Eckert, Harold	13	7	3.88	27	22	0	1	139	121	66	60	51	149	.233	R	R	6-3	210	7-18-77	1999	Edison, N.J.
Elliott, Adam	0	1	10.80	1	1	0	0	5	6	6	6	1	3	.333	S	R	6-2	200	3-27-84	2002	Concord, Calif.
Lohrman, Dave	1	0	2.79	1	0	0	2	10	9	3	3	7	10	.250	R	R	6-6	200	9-16-75	1997	East Amherst, N.Y.
Lopez, Rafael	1	3	4.02	22	0	0	1	40	49	22	18	20	35	.308	R	R	6-0	200	10-24-78	1997	Hato Mayor Del Rey, D.R.
Mattox, David	8	2	3.55	17	17	0	0	91	78	42	36	42	92	.234	R	R	6-2	180	5-24-80	2001	Spartanburg, S.C.
McGinley, Blake	1	1	1.80	26	0	0	10	35	19	9	7	6	53	.154	R	L	6-1	170	8-2-78	2001	Bakersfield, Calif.
Ogle, Rylie	0	0	0.56	9	0	0	0	16	17	2	1	3	15	.293	L	L	6-4	180	12-29-77	2001	Seal Beach, Calif.
Olson, Ryan	2	1	3.57	23	1	0	1	45	49	24	18	19	55	.273	S	L	6-5	190	1-16-80	2001	Oakhurst, Calif.
Osberg, Tanner	2	1	0.47	3	3	0	0	19	8	3	1	3	18	.121	L	L	6-4	180	9-10-82	2001	Red Deer, Alberta
Ough, Wayne	5	7	3.61	19	10	0	2	77	69	36	31	42	58	.242	R	R	6-2	180	11-27-78	2000	Queensland, Australia
Patterson, Quenten	1	1	1.95	17	0	0	1	28	26	13	6	20	14	.242	R	R	6-3	210	12-29-79	2000	Killeen, Texas
Peeples, Ross	7	7	2.43	20	19	0	1	115	104	49	31	25	98	.240	L	L	6-4	190	2-20-80	2000	Cordele, Ga.
Peterson, Matt	8	10	3.86	26	26	1	0	138	109	67	59	61	153	.220	R	R	6-5	210	2-11-82	2000	Alexandria, La.

PITCHING	W	L	ERA	G	GS	CG	SV	IP	H	R	ER	BB	SO	AVG	B	T	HT	WT	DOB	1st Yr	Resides
Portobanco, Luz	4	5	5.59	17	17	0	0	76	103	57	47	37	52	.334	R	R	6-3	200	9-15-79	2000	Miami, Fla.
Roman, Orlando	1	5	2.77	45	1	0	12	78	59	31	24	39	100	.210	R	R	6-2	210	11-28-78	1999	Vega Baja, P.R.
Scobie, Jason	2	2	2.57	16	1	0	4	35	29	16	10	12	33	.224	R	R	6-1	190	9-1-78	2001	Austin, Texas
Templet, Eric	2	1	4.87	13	0	0	0	20	19	11	11	9	19	.237	R	R	6-2	200	4-20-79	2001	Gonzales, La.

FIELDING

Catcher	PCT	G	PO	A	E	DP	PB
Beuerlein	1.000	1	3	3	0	0	1
Hietpas	1.000	28	212	29	0	3	5
Huber	.989	69	647	46	8	0	16
Kay	.972	24	196	9	6	0	10
Ochoa	.977	25	154	16	4	1	3
Reynoso	.950	3	19	0	1	0	1

First Base	PCT	G	PO	A	E	DP
Beuerlein	.984	17	115	11	2	13
Caligiuri	.992	57	466	49	4	30
Corr	.983	17	158	11	3	7
McIntyre	1.000	2	3	0	0	0
Ochoa	1.000	1	1	0	0	0
A. Rodriguez	.985	53	418	40	7	30

Second Base	PCT	G	PO	A	E	DP
Bacani	.976	66	121	208	8	30
Galante	.984	42	61	127	3	21
Jiannetti	.937	29	62	56	8	9
McIntyre	1.000	5	8	9	0	2
Pittman	1.000	3	4	4	0	0

Third Base	PCT	G	PO	A	E	DP
Bacani	.000	1	0	0	0	0
Galante	1.000	1	0	1	0	0
Kay	.000	1	0	0	0	0
McIntyre	.959	17	11	36	2	3
Pittman	1.000	3	0	3	0	0
Wright	.942	123	81	228	19	14

Shortstop	PCT	G	PO	A	E	DP
Bacani	.959	28	41	75	5	14

	PCT	G	PO	A	E	DP
Galante	.818	1	4	5	2	0
McIntyre	.916	75	108	197	28	25
Pittman	.733	5	4	7	4	2
Ragsdale	.932	37	56	121	13	17

Outfield	PCT	G	PO	A	E	DP
Corr	.922	46	55	4	5	0
Devarez	.926	15	25	0	2	0
Duncan	.882	28	26	4	4	0
Lawson	.963	74	95	8	4	1
Lydon	.967	117	166	8	6	2
McIntyre	1.000	5	5	2	0	0
Pagan	.951	103	168	7	9	0
E. Rodriguez	.913	18	21	0	2	0
Toner	.913	25	20	1	2	0

NEW YORK-PENN LEAGUE

BATTING	AVG	G	AB	R	H	2B	3B	HR	RBI	BB	SO	SB	CS	SLG	OBP	B	T	HT	WT	DOB	1st Yr	Resides
Anderson, Jimmy	.217	32	92	7	20	2	0	0	6	5	18	1	0	.239	.284	R	R	6-2	200	8-3-81	2002	Riverside, Calif.
Andujar, Elvin	.153	16	59	7	9	1	0	4	10	5	22	1	2	.373	.219	R	R	6-3	190	1-19-81	1999	San Cristobal, D.R.
Ayala, Abraham	.202	29	84	5	17	4	0	1	10	7	5	0	0	.286	.274	R	R	6-1	190	10-5-80	2000	Bayamon, P.R.
Baldiris, Aaron	.303	9	33	5	10	1	0	0	2	1	2	2	0	.333	.343	R	R	6-2	170	1-5-83	1999	St. Lucia Miranda, Venez.
Beuerlein, Tyler	.222	4	9	1	2	0	0	0	1	3	0	0	0	.222	.364	S	R	6-2	200	5-29-79	2001	Cave Creek, Ariz.
Caligiuri, Jay	.286	16	56	6	16	3	0	2	5	7	14	1	0	.446	.385	R	R	6-0	190	3-29-80	2001	Camarillo, Calif.
Chavez, Ender	.278	61	187	35	52	8	4	0	12	19	18	9	4	.364	.345	L	L	5-11	150	3-9-81	1999	Valencia, Venez.
Clements, Zachary	.048	6	21	1	1	0	0	0	1	0	6	0	0	.048	.048	R	R	6-2	210	4-17-80	2002	Memphis, Tenn.
Corr, Frank	.211	33	123	15	26	7	0	4	15	2	20	1	1	.366	.233	R	R	5-9	200	9-19-78	2001	Deltona, Fla.
Devarez, Noel	.200	8	5	2	7	0	0	1	2	1	8	0	0	.286	.222	R	R	6-0	190	12-24-78	1998	San Francisco de Macoris, D.R.
Harper, Brett	.279	53	183	21	51	6	1	4	20	14	37	2	2	.328	.333	L	R	6-4	180	7-31-81	2001	Scottsdale, Ariz.
Hietpas, Joe	.256	32	117	11	30	5	0	1	13	8	31	0	1	.325	.313	R	R	6-3	220	5-1-79	2001	Appleton, Wis.
Hudson, Will	.182	3	11	0	2	0	0	0	0	0	3	0	0	.182	.182	S	R	6-1	190	1-26-81	2002	Fountain Valley, Calif.
Jiannetti, Joe	.260	59	223	28	58	5	0	7	27	16	22	11	7	.377	.310	R	R	6-1	190	9-25-81	2001	St. Petersburg, Fla.
Lambin, Chase	.279	47	179	25	50	6	3	6	27	8	50	5	2	.447	.316	S	R	6-2	190	7-7-79	2002	Houston, Texas
Malek, Bobby	.207	28	111	7	23	3	1	0	10	3	20	4	0	.252	.235	L	R	6-1	200	7-6-81	2002	Canton, Mich.
Mannix, Brendan	.143	3	7	1	1	1	0	0	1	0	2	0	0	.286	.250	S	R	6-3	200	3-20-80	2002	Crofton, Md.
McEwing, Joe	.250	1	4	0	1	0	0	0	1	0	0	0	0	.250	.250	R	R	5-11	170	10-19-72	1992	Yardley, Pa.
Ragsdale, Corey	.183	66	224	35	41	7	2	2	19	23	72	26	3	.259	.277	R	R	6-4	170	11-10-82	2001	Jonesboro, Ark.
Reynoso, Danilo	.125	2	8	0	1	0	0	0	1	0	3	0	0	.125	.125	R	R	5-10	160	4-5-82	1997	San Cristobal, D.R.
Rodriguez, Andres	.181	21	72	9	13	0	1	1	3	9	17	2	1	.250	.280	R	R	6-4	180	2-14-79	1998	San Cristobal, D.R.
Rodriguez, Edgar	.256	11	39	3	10	2	0	2	5	4	10	0	1	.462	.326	R	R	5-11	150	11-29-79	1996	San Pedro de Macoris, D.R.
Slack, Jon	.245	47	147	16	36	8	1	1	11	20	47	5	5	.333	.341	L	L	5-11	180	12-4-81	2002	Henderson, Nev.
Toner, John	.286	53	196	27	56	7	0	8	24	11	40	4	1	.444	.343	R	R	6-3	210	9-22-79	2001	St. Joseph, Mich.
Turay, Alhaji	.327	40	153	21	50	10	1	4	19	11	48	7	3	.484	.380	R	R	6-0	200	9-22-82	2001	Auburn, Wash.
Watts, Derran	.154	10	26	2	4	1	0	0	2	14	0	1	1	.192	.267	R	R	6-2	180	6-28-80	2001	Brampton, Ontario
Whealy, Blake	.289	59	204	32	59	14	3	10	34	21	58	9	2	.534	.361	R	R	5-11	170	5-27-80	2002	River Forest, Ill.

GAMES BY POSITION: C—Anderson 27, Ayala 25, Clements 6, Hietpas 25, Reynoso 2. **1B**—Baldiris 5, Caligiuri 13, Corr 11, Harper 35, A. Rodriguez 19. **2B**—Jiannetti 49, Lambin 12, Whealy 20. **3B**—Baldiris 6, Harper 15, Lambin 24, Mannix 3, Rodriguez 8, Whealy 28, **SS**—Hudson 3, Lambin 8, Ragsdale 65. **OF**—Andujar 16, Chavez 55, Corr 18, Devarez 8, E. Rodriguez 3, Slack 41, Toner 50, Turay 38, Watts 9, Whealy 8.

PITCHING	W	L	ERA	G	GS	CG	SV	IP	H	R	ER	BB	SO	AVG	B	T	HT	WT	DOB	1st Yr	Resides
Acosta, Anthony	1	0	3.78	8	0	0	1	17	21	8	7	2	14	.300	R	R	6-1	180	10-5-80	2001	New York, N.Y.
Anez, Omar	4	4	3.88	19	5	0	2	53	53	30	23	19	34	.261	R	R	6-4	220	2-1-81	1997	Valencia, Venez.
Bowen, Chad	2	4	3.22	17	2	0	0	50	55	20	18	16	41	.291	R	R	6-4	200	4-28-82	2000	Hendersonville, Tenn.
Brewer, Jeff	0	0	9.00	2	0	0	0	2	3	2	2	2	1	.333	R	R	6-3	200	10-5-80	2002	Fredericton, New Brunswick
Cabrera, Yunior	3	4	2.89	8	8	0	0	37	31	18	12	15	39	.218	L	L	6-0	160	10-25-79	1996	San Pedro de Macoris, D.R.
Chenard, Ken	1	1	3.21	3	0	0	0	14	14	5	5	4	7	.264	R	R	6-3	180	8-30-78	1999	Victorville, Calif.
Cummings, Eric	2	1	2.61	5	0	0	0	10	12	3	3	3	5	.292	R	R	6-1	200	10-18-78	2002	Westminster, Colo.
Danly, Ryan	0	0	0.00	2	0	0	0	3	4	4	0	0	2	.307	L	L	6-7	190	6-23-81	2001	Cedar Rapids, Iowa
Deaton, Kevin	7	1	3.07	16	15	0	0	82	68	34	28	18	93	.227	R	R	6-4	260	8-7-81	2000	Merritt Island, Fla.
Elliott, Adam	0	0	1.50	3	0	0	0	6	3	2	1	1	6	.136	S	R	6-2	200	3-27-84	2002	Concord, Calif.
Kazmir, Scott	0	1	0.50	5	5	0	0	18	5	2	1	7	34	.089	L	L	6-1	170	1-24-84	2002	Houston, Texas
Kentner, Brandon	3	1	3.38	17	0	0	1	37	34	17	14	31	39	.237	R	R	6-3	210	8-7-81	2000	Benton, Ark.
King, Bryan	0	1	3.52	5	0	0	0	8	6	5	3	2	3	.200	R	R	6-1	180	5-20-81	2002	Englewood, Colo.
Lohrman, Dave	0	0	3.44	12	0	0	2	18	16	7	7	10	19	.231	R	R	6-6	200	9-16-75	1997	East Amherst, N.Y.
McNabb, Tim	2	2	3.44	17	0	0	2	34	33	16	13	12	30	.266	L	L	6-0	170	6-4-80	2002	Cooper City, Fla.
Musser, Neal	0	0	0.69	4	4	0	0	13	7	2	1	5	12	.162	L	L	6-2	200	8-25-80	1999	Otterbein, Ind.
Ogle, Rylie	1	2	5.49	13	0	0	3	20	25	14	12	4	19	.333	L	L	6-4	180	12-29-77	2001	Seal Beach, Calif.
Olson, Ryan	1	0	2.57	6	0	0	0	14	12	4	4	5	15	.226	S	L	6-5	190	1-16-80	2001	Oakhurst, Calif.
Osberg, Tanner	1	1	3.00	5	3	0	0	12	15	4	4	4	8	.333	L	R	6-4	180	9-10-82	2000	Red Deer, Alberta
Ough, Wayne	4	4	4.64	8	7	0	0	33	27	18	17	20	34	.228	R	R	6-2	180	11-27-78	2000	Queensland, Australia
Paulk, Robert	3	0	4.82	9	0	0	1	19	27	10	10	5	17	.341	R	R	5-11	180	3-14-81	2002	Madison, Fla.
Pinango, Miguel	2	7	3.59	16	15	1	0	80	85	39	32	14	64	.268	R	R	6-1	160	1-20-83	1999	St. Teresa, Venez.
Portobanco, Luz	0	1	6.00	2	2	0	0	12	12	8	8	2	9	.255	R	R	6-3	200	9-15-79	2000	Miami, Fla.
Scobie, Jason	2	2	3.07	8	7	1	0	41	36	16	14	12	34	.236	R	R	6-1	190	9-1-78	2001	Austin, Texas

PITCHING	W	L	ERA	G	GS	CG	SV	IP	H	R	ER	BB	SO	AVG	B	T	HT	WT	DOB	1st Yr	Resides
Sherman, Chris	1	1	3.35	19	0	0	2	38	32	15	14	13	28	.231	R	R	6-2	190	7-2-79	2001	Aptos, Calif.
Templet, Eric	1	0	3.72	7	0	0	1	10	14	5	4	5	12	.333	R	R	6-2	200	4-20-79	2001	Gonzales, La.
Weir, Jayson	0	0	4.91	2	0	0	0	4	8	3	2	2	1	.444	L	L	5-10	180	4-3-83	2001	Orlando, Fla.

KINGSPORT METS — Rookie

APPALACHIAN LEAGUE

BATTING	AVG	G	AB	R	H	2B	3B	HR	RBI	BB	SO	SB	CS	SLG	OBP	B	T	HT	WT	DOB	1st Yr	Resides
Baldiris, Aaron	.327	58	217	31	71	9	1	3	24	14	24	9	5	.419	.390	R	R	6-2	170	1-5-83	1999	St. Lucia Miranda, Venez.
Beuerlein, Tyler	.207	31	116	11	24	1	0	7	16	8	40	0	1	.397	.292	S	R	6-2	200	5-29-79	2001	Cave Creek, Ariz.
Camacho, Johan	.218	30	101	10	22	5	0	2	9	5	24	0	0	.327	.266	S	R	6-3	190	8-13-83	2000	Barquisimeto, Venez.
Clements, Zachary	.282	16	39	4	11	1	0	0	3	7	9	2	0	.308	.391	R	R	6-2	210	4-17-80	2002	Memphis, Tenn.
Garcia, Williams	.250	36	136	11	34	7	0	2	24	7	41	0	6	.346	.290	S	R	6-1	170	8-10-81	1999	Tucacas, Venez.
Garcia, Yunir	.233	33	90	15	21	3	0	3	15	27	17	2	1	.367	.423	R	R	6-0	170	8-3-82	1999	San Pablo, Venez.
Hill, Jamar	.295	56	200	34	59	14	2	8	31	22	48	7	4	.505	.374	R	R	6-3	200	9-20-82	2002	Juneau, Alaska
Housel, David	.248	36	117	15	29	6	1	1	7	7	33	2	4	.342	.302	S	R	6-2	160	9-6-81	2001	DeBary, Fla.
Hudson, Will	.250	34	96	9	24	4	1	2	7	16	18	3	2	.375	.354	S	R	6-1	190	1-26-81	2002	Fountain Valley, Calif.
Linares, Jesus	.254	38	138	27	35	4	2	3	17	16	31	3	4	.377	.329	R	R	6-0	170	6-7-82	1999	El Tocuyo, Venez.
Mannix, Brendan	.195	24	77	6	15	3	0	3	11	12	22	1	1	.351	.311	S	R	6-3	200	3-20-80	2002	Crofton, Md.
Martinez, Luis	.206	11	34	1	7	2	0	0	2	4	8	1	2	.265	.308	R	R	6-0	170	10-11-80	1998	Santiago, D.R.
Reynoso, Danilo	.190	15	42	8	8	2	0	0	1	7	12	1	1	.238	.320	R	R	5-10	160	4-5-82	1997	San Cristobal, D.R.
Solano, Roberto	.276	57	228	25	63	13	4	4	31	7	51	6	1	.421	.302	R	R	6-2	170	6-23-81	2001	Santo Domingo, D.R.
Soto, Yllysh	.279	33	122	18	34	3	1	2	12	12	17	2	3	.369	.353	S	R	5-11	170	8-18-78	1999	Caracas, Venez.
Watts, Derran	.257	49	179	33	46	15	3	2	20	30	50	18	6	.408	.378	L	R	6-2	180	6-28-80	2001	Brampton, Ontario
Wendt, Justin	.236	41	140	22	33	3	1	2	15	11	21	3	0	.314	.318	L	R	6-3	240	12-24-81	2000	Waterloo, Ontario
Wilson, Brandon	.252	35	139	11	35	7	0	2	12	8	35	0	2	.345	.293	R	R	6-4	190	9-1-82	2000	Baton Rouge, La.
Wilson, Laron	.216	13	37	4	8	1	0	1	2	0	11	1	0	.324	.237	R	R	6-0	200	9-2-81	2002	Mechanicsville, Va.

GAMES BY POSITION: C—Clements 8, Y. Garcia 19, Reynoso 12, B. Wilson 32. **1B**—Camacho 28, Mannix 5, Wendt 38, L. Wilson 3. **2B**—Housel 35, Hudson 6, Linares 19, Martinez 1, Soto 7. **3B**—Baldiris 58, Linares 4, Mannix 9, Martinez 2. **SS**—Hudson 24, Linares 16, Martinez 7, Soto 24. **OF**—Clements 6, W. Garcia 32, Y. Garcia 3, Hill 55, Mannix 7, Solano 57, Watts 47, L. Wilson 1.

PITCHING	W	L	ERA	G	GS	CG	SV	IP	H	R	ER	BB	SO	AVG	B	T	HT	WT	DOB	1st Yr	Resides
Acosta, Anthony	4	1	3.86	11	0	0	0	21	23	11	9	2	26	.273	R	R	6-1	180	10-5-80	2001	New York, N.Y.
Alfonzo, Edgar	0	0	1.13	6	0	0	0	8	9	2	1	3	5	.300	L	L	5-10	170	12-14-84	2002	Estado Miranda, Venez.
Brewer, Jeff	1	1	5.59	10	0	0	0	19	27	20	12	3	22	.306	R	R	6-3	200	10-5-80	2002	Fredericton, New Brunswick
Castro, Rafael	3	5	4.80	13	12	0	0	54	61	32	29	22	40	.286	R	R	6-0	160	2-5-81	2000	Cotui, D.R.
Danly, Ryan	2	3	5.03	13	8	0	0	54	61	34	30	17	27	.285	L	L	6-2	190	6-23-81	2001	Cedar Rapids, Iowa
DeLeon, Maikel	0	2	5.40	9	4	0	0	23	25	18	14	6	19	.274	R	R	6-3	150	10-26-79	1998	Azua, D.R.
Elliott, Adam	2	2	3.16	11	8	0	0	43	27	16	15	14	37	.182	S	R	6-2	200	3-27-84	2002	Concord, Calif.
Farrell, Sean	4	3	6.98	20	0	0	0	30	39	24	23	22	26	.319	L	L	6-4	220	10-24-81	2001	Huntington Station, N.Y.
Freites, Julio	1	4	12.00	17	1	0	0	30	40	43	40	24	28	.298	R	R	6-0	170	5-30-82	2000	Clarines, Venez.
Garay, Kelvin	0	0	6.48	6	0	0	0	8	8	6	6	5	7	.258	L	L	6-5	220	1-18-85	2002	Trujillo Alto, P.R.
George, Taylor	0	3	5.79	13	9	0	0	47	55	38	30	24	39	.289	R	R	6-2	190	8-14-82	2002	Long Beach, Calif.
King, Bryan	0	2	3.23	14	0	0	3	31	24	13	11	13	34	.224	R	R	6-1	180	10-23-80	2002	Englewood, Colo.
Lindstrom, Matt	0	6	4.84	12	11	0	0	48	56	45	26	21	39	.280	R	R	6-5	210	2-11-80	2002	Rexburg, Idaho
Maldonado, Ivan	0	0	3.86	3	0	0	0	7	9	6	3	0	5	.321	R	R	6-3	210	6-7-80	2002	Cayey, P.R.
Morban, Domingo	1	0	6.88	8	0	0	0	17	18	13	13	8	21	.272	L	L	6-2	190	8-22-81	1998	San Cristobal, D.R.
Osberg, Tanner	1	1	3.50	3	3	0	0	18	15	7	7	4	9	.238	L	R	6-4	180	9-10-82	2000	Red Deer, Alberta
Paulk, Robert	1	3	2.91	10	1	0	1	22	26	13	7	8	19	.313	R	R	5-11	170	12-13-84	2002	Madison, Fla.
Rondon, Celso	2	1	6.37	17	0	0	0	35	48	31	25	23	32	.335	R	R	6-0	160	4-7-84	2001	Cumana, Venez.
Weintraub, Jason	1	6	5.91	10	10	0	0	46	61	32	30	14	37	.317	R	R	6-3	160	8-13-82	2001	Tampa, Fla.
Weir, Jayson	0	0	1.56	10	0	0	3	17	14	4	3	1	20	.208	L	L	5-10	180	4-3-83	2001	Orlando, Fla.

OAKLAND ATHLETICS

BY CASEY TEFERTILLER

After a year crammed with so many highlights that the Athletics could not help believing they were bound for glory, the whole dream came crashing down in the 2002 American League Division Series against the Cinderella Twins. Threatened with contraction before the season began, the Twins won the final two games of the division series to advance to play the Angels in the ALCS. It was the third consecutive season Oakland lost in five games in the ALDS, the previous two to the Yankees.

Before the abrupt exit, the A's put together a remarkable regular season, winning 103 games and capturing the AL West title. After losing 17 games in May, Oakland finished the season with 78 wins in the final 109 games to take control of the division and tie the Yankees for the most wins in baseball. And after struggling through the beginning of the season, the A's inserted shortstop Miguel Tejada into the No. 3 spot in the batting order May 19. He hit .314-28-108 the rest of the way.

Engaged in a pennant race with the Angels and Mariners, the A's took off in August on a 20-game winning streak. By the time Brad Radke and the Twins broke the streak Sept. 6, Oakland had broken the AL record for consecutive victories, and put together the longest streak since the Cubs won 21 in 1931. No major league team had even won 17 straight since the 1953 Yankees. Oakland eclipsed the league record of 19 that had been shared by the 1947 Yankees and the 1906 White Sox.

The A's took the lead in the division and held off the charging Angels to win the title, only to meet the Twins in the first round. After winning two of the first three games, Minnesota came back to win Game Four, then Radke pitched the victory in Game Five that ended Oakland's season.

The individual highlights were numerous. Tejada finished at .308-34-131, mixed with dramatic moments and game-winning hits. At age 24, Eric Chavez put together

Miguel Tejada   Rich Harden

PLAYERS OF THE YEAR

MAJOR LEAGUE: Miguel Tejada, ss
Tejada inherited Jason Giambi's No. 3 slot in the batting order and rose to the challenge by playing in every game in 2002 for the Athletics and hitting .308-34-131, setting career bests in each category.

MINOR LEAGUE: Rich Harden, rhp
The 20-year-old Canadian mixed a 95-mph fastball with a changeup and slider to record 187 strikeouts, which ranked second in the minors. He went 12-6, 2.93 in 153 innings between Double-A Midland and Class A Visalia.

his second straight season over the 30-homer, 100-RBI mark, hitting .275-34-109.

The A's "Big Three" starting pitchers all had top-level seasons. Barry Zito finished at 23-5, 2.75 (leading the AL in wins), and Mark Mulder at 19-7, 3.47 despite missing nearly a month because of injury. Tim Hudson assembled 15-9, 2.98 numbers, but nine times left ahead only to have the bullpen blow the lead. Closer Billy Koch finished 11-4, 3.27 with 44 saves, the first pitcher in baseball history to save 40 and win 10 in the same season.

Rookie Mark Ellis took over the second base job in June and solidified the infield. He wound up hitting .272-6-35 in 98 games.

The big question of the offseason will be deciding how to replace retiring left fielder Dave Justice, who brought both a strong bat and a veteran presence to the Oakland clubhouse. Several players credited Justice's maturity and leadership with helping the team turn the season around.

At the minor league level, the results were not staggering, with only Double-A Midland (75-64) and Class A Modesto (78-62) finishing over the .500 mark. In the second half, Midland assembled a dominating pitching rotation with four arms that started the season in Class A. Rich Harden (8-3, 2.95), Mike Wood (11-3, 3.15), John Rheinecker (7-7, 3.38) and Jason Arnold (5-1. 2.33) combined to create a staff that had scouts' eyes flashing.

The draft took on a special meaning to the A's. After losing three free agents following the 2001 season, Oakland had seven picks before the second round, and chose center fielder Nick Swisher with the first of those seven. Supplemental first-rounder Jeremy Brown, a catcher from Alabama, had the most impressive debut, hitting .310-10-40 in the tough California League and drawing raves for his defensive skills.

ORGANIZATION LEADERS

BATTING
*AVG	Carlos Mendez, Sacramento	324
R	Caonabo Cosme, Modesto	90
H	Freddie Bynum, Visalia	165
TB	Daylan Holt, Midland/Visalia	244
2B	Larry Sutton, Sacramento	40
3B	Kirk Asche, Midland	10
HR	Jorge Soto, Visalia	31
RBI	Graham Koonce, Midland	96
BB	Graham Koonce, Midland	133
SO	Jorge Soto, Visalia	195
SB	Freddie Bynum, Visalia	41

PITCHING
W	Mike Wood, Midland/Modesto	14
L	Chris Enochs, Sacramento/Midland	13
#ERA	Brad Weis, Sacramento/Modesto	2.27
G	Claudio Galva, Midland	62
CG	Chris Enochs, Sacramento/Midland	3
SV	Mike Frick, Modesto	23
IP	John Rheinecker, Midland/Visalia	179
BB	Neal Cotts, Modesto	87
SO	Rich Harden, Midland/Visalia	187

*Minimum 250 At-Bats #Minimum 75 Innings

OAKLAND ATHLETICS

Manager: Art Howe

2002 Record: 103-59, .636 (1st, AL West)

BATTING	AVG	G	AB	R	H	2B	3B	HR	RBI	BB	SO	SB	CS	SLG	OBP	B	T	HT	WT	DOB	1st Yr	Resides
Byrnes, Eric	.245	90	94	24	23	4	2	3	11	4	17	3	0	.426	.291	R	R	6-2	210	2-16-76	1998	Woodside, Calif.
Chavez, Eric	.275	153	585	87	161	31	3	34	109	65	119	8	3	.513	.348	L	R	6-1	200	12-7-77	1996	Walnut Creek, Calif.
Colangelo, Mike	.174	20	23	2	4	1	0	0	0	1	2	0	0	.217	.240	R	R	6-1	180	10-22-76	1997	Dumfries, Va.
Durham, Ray	.274	54	219	43	60	14	4	6	22	24	34	6	2	.457	.350	S	R	5-8	180	11-30-71	1990	Charlotte, N.C.
2-team (96 Chicago)	.289	150	564	114	163	34	6	15	70	73	93	26	7	.450	.374							
Dye, Jermaine	.252	131	488	74	123	27	1	24	86	52	108	2	0	.459	.333	R	R	6-5	220	1-28-74	1993	Phoenix, Ariz.
Ellis, Mark	.272	98	345	58	94	16	4	6	35	44	54	4	2	.394	.359	R	R	5-11	180	6-6-77	1999	Rapid City, S.D.
Flores, Jose	.000	8	3	2	0	0	0	0	0	1	0	1	1	.000	.400	R	R	5-11	180	6-28-73	1994	Corpus Christi, Texas
German, Esteban	.200	9	35	4	7	0	0	0	4	11	1	0	.200	.300	R	R	5-9	160	1-26-78	1996	Santo Domingo, D.R.
Giambi, Jeremy	.274	42	157	26	43	7	0	8	17	27	40	0	0	.471	.390	L	L	5-11	210	9-30-74	1996	Las Vegas, Nev.
Grabowski, Jason	.375	4	8	3	3	1	1	0	1	3	1	0	0	.750	.545	L	R	6-3	200	5-24-76	1997	Clinton, Conn.
Hatteberg, Scott	.280	136	492	58	138	22	4	15	61	68	56	0	0	.433	.374	L	R	6-1	210	12-14-69	1991	Salem, Ore.
Hernandez, Ramon	.233	136	403	51	94	20	0	7	42	43	64	0	0	.335	.313	R	R	6-0	210	5-20-76	1994	Aragua, Venez.
Justice, Dave	.266	118	398	54	106	18	3	11	49	70	66	4	1	.410	.376	L	L	6-3	210	4-14-66	1985	Cincinnati, Ohio
Long, Terrence	.240	162	587	71	141	32	4	16	67	48	96	3	6	.390	.298	L	L	6-1	200	2-29-76	1994	Millbrook, Ala.
Mabry, John	.275	89	193	27	53	13	1	11	40	14	37	1	1	.523	.322	L	R	6-4	210	10-17-70	1991	St. Louis, Mo.
McKay, Cody	.667	2	3	0	2	0	0	0	2	0	1	0	0	.667	.500	L	R	6-0	200	1-11-74	1996	Scottsdale, Ariz.
Menechino, Frank	.205	38	132	22	27	7	0	3	15	20	32	0	0	.326	.312	R	R	5-8	190	1-7-71	1993	Staten Island, N.Y.
Myers, Greg	.222	65	144	15	32	5	0	6	21	26	36	0	0	.382	.341	L	R	6-2	220	4-14-66	1984	Riverside, Calif.
Pena, Carlos	.218	40	124	12	27	4	0	7	16	15	38	0	0	.419	.305	L	L	6-2	210	5-17-78	1998	Haverhill, Mass.
Piatt, Adam	.234	55	137	18	32	8	0	5	18	12	33	2	1	.401	.303	R	R	6-2	200	2-8-76	1997	Missouri City, Texas
Saenz, Olmedo	.276	68	156	15	43	10	1	6	18	13	31	1	1	.468	.354	R	R	5-11	220	10-8-70	1990	Chitre Herrera, Panama
Sutton, Larry	.105	7	19	3	2	0	0	1	3	1	8	0	0	.263	.150	L	L	6-0	180	5-14-70	1992	Overland Park, Kan.
Tejada, Miguel	.308	162	662	108	204	30	0	34	131	38	84	7	2	.508	.354	R	R	5-9	190	5-25-76	1994	Santo Domingo, D.R.
Velarde, Randy	.226	56	133	22	30	8	0	2	8	15	32	3	0	.331	.325	R	R	6-0	200	11-24-62	1985	Midland, Texas

PITCHING	W	L	ERA	G	GS	CG	SV	IP	H	R	ER	BB	SO	AVG	B	T	HT	WT	DOB	1st Yr	Resides
Bowie, Micah	2	0	1.50	13	0	0	0	12	12	2	2	8	8	.260	L	L	6-4	200	11-10-74	1993	New Braunfels, Texas
Bradford, Chad	4	2	3.11	75	0	0	2	75	73	29	26	14	56	.253	R	R	6-5	200	9-14-74	1996	Raymond, Miss.
Fyhrie, Mike	2	4	4.44	16	4	0	0	49	46	25	24	20	29	.245	R	R	6-2	200	12-9-69	1991	Coto de Caza, Calif.
Harang, Aaron	5	4	4.83	16	15	0	0	78	78	44	42	45	64	.260	R	R	6-7	240	5-9-78	1999	San Diego, Calif.
Hiljus, Erik	3	3	6.50	9	9	0	0	46	52	36	33	21	29	.284	R	R	6-6	220	12-25-72	1991	Northridge, Calif.
Holtz, Mike	0	0	6.43	16	0	0	0	14	24	11	10	9	7	.358	L	L	5-9	180	10-10-72	1994	Hollidaysburg, Pa.
Hudson, Tim	15	9	2.98	34	34	4	0	238	237	87	79	62	152	.262	R	R	6-1	160	7-14-75	1997	Auburn, Ala.
Koch, Billy	11	4	3.27	84	0	0	44	94	73	38	34	46	93	.214	R	R	6-3	210	12-14-74	1996	Clearwater, Fla.
Lidle, Cory	8	10	3.89	31	30	2	0	192	191	90	83	39	111	.258	R	R	5-11	190	3-22-72	1991	Las Vegas, Nev.
Lilly, Ted	2	1	4.63	6	5	0	0	23	23	12	12	7	18	.252	L	L	6-1	190	1-4-76	1996	Oakhurst, Calif.
2-team (16 New York)	5	7	3.69	22	16	2	0	100	80	43	41	31	77	.214							
Magnante, Mike	0	2	5.97	32	0	0	0	29	38	22	19	11	11	.316	L	L	6-2	210	6-17-65	1988	Burbank, Calif.
Mecir, Jim	6	4	4.26	61	0	0	1	68	68	36	32	29	53	.258	S	R	6-1	230	5-16-70	1991	Kildeer, Ill.
Mulder, Mark	19	7	3.47	30	30	2	0	207	182	88	80	55	159	.231	L	L	6-6	200	8-5-77	1999	Scottsdale, Calif.
Rincon, Ricardo	0	0	3.10	25	0	0	1	20	11	7	7	3	19	.164	L	L	5-10	180	4-13-70	1997	Veracruz, Mexico
2-team (46 Cleveland)	1	4	4.18	71	0	0	1	56	47	28	26	11	49	.230							
Tam, Jeff	1	2	5.13	40	0	0	0	40	56	26	23	13	14	.333	R	R	6-1	210	8-19-70	1993	Melbourne, Fla.
Venafro, Mike	2	2	4.62	47	0	0	0	37	45	22	19	14	16	.308	L	L	5-10	180	8-2-73	1995	Fort Myers, Fla.
Zito, Barry	23	5	2.75	35	35	1	0	229	182	79	70	78	182	.217	L	L	6-4	210	5-13-78	1999	Van Nuys, Calif.

FIELDING

Catcher	PCT	G	PO	A	E	DP	PB
Hernandez	.992	135	788	58	7	12	6
McKay	1.000	1	6	0	0	0	0
Myers	.997	53	264	21	1	0	3

First Base	PCT	G	PO	A	E	DP
Hatteberg	.994	91	768	74	5	77
Mabry	1.000	50	136	14	0	10
Pena	.997	40	351	42	1	25
Piatt	1.000	1	4	0	0	1
Saenz	1.000	34	190	12	0	17
Sutton	1.000	6	29	0	0	0
Velarde	.962	5	25	0	1	2

Second Base	PCT	G	PO	A	E	DP
Durham	.967	11	21	37	2	12
Ellis	.978	85	170	232	9	48
Flores	.000	2	0	0	0	0
German	.978	8	22	23	1	6
Mabry	.000	1	0	0	0	0
Menechino	.992	32	37	90	1	10
Velarde	.981	38	70	88	3	22

Third Base	PCT	G	PO	A	E	DP
Chavez	.961	143	120	301	17	24

	PCT	G	PO	A	E	DP
Ellis	.926	7	7	18	2	0
Menechino	.857	4	1	5	1	1
Saenz	.894	15	14	28	5	1
Velarde	1.000	1	0	1	0	0

Shortstop	PCT	G	PO	A	E	DP
Ellis	1.000	8	3	13	0	4
Flores	1.000	1	1	1	0	0
Menechino	1.000	2	2	1	0	1
Tejada	.975	162	229	504	19	106

Outfield	PCT	G	PO	A	E	DP
Byrnes	.982	79	53	1	1	0
Chavez	.000	1	0	0	0	0
Colangelo	1.000	19	17	0	0	0
Dye	.972	111	171	2	5	1
Giambi	.984	40	63	0	1	0
Grabowski	1.000	4	6	0	0	0
Justice	.985	75	125	3	2	0
Long	.980	162	382	5	8	1
Mabry	.978	53	87	1	2	0
Piatt	1.000	50	66	1	0	0
Sutton	1.000	3	5	1	0	0

Eric Chavez

LARRY GOREN

FARM SYSTEM

Director, Player Development: Keith Lieppman

Class	Farm Team	League	W	L	Pct.	Finish*	Manager	First Yr.
AAA	Sacramento (Calif.) RiverCats	Pacific Coast	66	78	.458	14th(16)	Bob Geren	2000
AA	Midland (Texas) RockHounds	Texas	75	64	.540	3rd (8)	Tony DeFrancesco	1999
High A	Modesto (Calif.) A's	California	78	62	.557	2nd (10)	Greg Sparks	1975
High A	Visalia (Calif.) Oaks	California	70	71	.496	5th (10)	Webster Garrison	1997
SS A	Vancouver (B.C.) Canadians	Northwest	37	39	.487	6th (8)	Orv Franchuk	2000
Rookie	Phoenix (Ariz.) Athletics	Arizona	28	28	.500	t-3rd (7)	Ruben Escalera	1988

*Finish in overall standings (No. of teams in league)

PACIFIC COAST LEAGUE

BATTING	AVG	G	AB	R	H	2B	3B	HR	RBI	BB	SO	SB	CS	SLG	OBP	B	T	HT	WT	DOB	1st Yr	Resides
Byrnes, Eric	.261	31	119	16	31	7	0	4	16	7	15	5	1	.420	.302	R	R	6-2	210	2-16-76	1998	Woodside, Calif.
Colangelo, Mike	.212	70	217	22	46	9	0	0	22	33	36	3	3	.253	.331	R	R	6-1	180	10-22-76	1997	Dumfries, Va.
Dye, Jermaine	.188	4	16	3	3	2	0	0	1	2	2	0	0	.313	.278	R	R	6-5	220	1-28-74	1993	Phoenix, Ariz.
Ellis, Mark	.298	21	84	14	25	10	1	0	5	6	13	4	0	.440	.372	R	R	5-11	180	6-6-77	1999	Rapid City, S.D.
Flores, Jose	.306	95	363	64	111	19	1	2	38	56	53	16	4	.380	.397	R	R	5-11	180	6-28-73	1994	Corpus Christi, Texas
German, Esteban	.275	121	458	72	126	16	4	2	43	78	66	26	14	.341	.390	R	R	5-9	160	1-26-78	1996	Santo Domingo, D.R.
Grabowski, Jason	.294	73	265	50	78	22	3	12	52	39	56	6	4	.536	.387	L	R	6-3	200	5-24-76	1997	Clinton, Conn.
Landry, Jacques	.243	57	185	24	45	8	1	7	35	26	68	5	3	.411	.332	R	R	6-3	200	8-15-73	1996	Lamarque, Texas
Lopez, Luis	.283	131	516	66	146	28	0	9	72	64	63	2	3	.390	.361	R	R	6-0	200	10-5-73	1996	Corpus Christi, Texas
McKay, Cody	.288	108	378	55	109	16	1	13	57	21	59	2	1	.439	.337	L	R	6-0	200	1-11-74	1996	Scottsdale, Ariz.
Mendez, Carlos	.324	103	404	58	131	26	1	12	74	12	52	3	1	.483	.348	R	R	6-0	210	6-18-74	1991	Caracas, Venez.
Menechino, Frank	.248	84	314	50	78	12	0	6	50	46	58	10	3	.344	.356	R	R	5-8	190	1-7-71	1993	Staten Island, N.Y.
Meyers, Chad	.204	18	54	11	11	0	0	1	2	12	10	0	0	.259	.358	R	R	5-11	190	8-8-75	1996	Omaha, Neb.
Pena, Carlos	.240	44	175	30	42	10	1	10	33	24	49	3	0	.480	.340	L	L	6-2	210	5-17-78	1998	Haverhill, Mass.
Piatt, Adam	.295	62	234	46	69	15	0	8	44	35	30	4	3	.462	.385	R	R	6-2	200	2-8-76	1997	Missouri City, Texas
Ryan, Rob	.249	61	209	34	52	14	1	7	27	24	40	0	0	.426	.332	L	L	5-11	190	6-24-73	1996	Renton, Wa.
Santangelo, F.P.	.174	44	86	10	15	4	0	1	4	13	19	1	3	.256	.324	S	R	5-10	160	10-24-67	1989	El Dorado Hills, Calif.
Sutton, Larry	.292	116	431	83	126	40	2	12	81	93	108	2	0	.478	.417	L	L	6-0	180	5-14-70	1992	Overland Park, Kan.
Thomas, Gary	.111	4	9	1	1	0	0	0	2	2	0	2	0	.111	.100	R	R	5-6	185	9-6-79	1997	Houma, La.
Valdez, Mario	.260	85	304	43	79	18	2	3	25	58	56	1	0	.362	.378	L	R	6-2	210	11-19-74	1994	Tamaulipas, Mexico
Velarde, Randy	.471	4	17	3	8	3	0	1	4	1	3	1	0	.824	.526	R	R	6-0	200	11-24-62	1985	Midland, Texas
Warner, Michael	.175	36	103	10	18	3	1	3	12	15	28	5	3	.311	.277	L	L	5-10	170	5-9-71	1992	Palm Beach Gardens, Fla.

PITCHING	W	L	ERA	G	GS	CG	SV	IP	H	R	ER	BB	SO	AVG	B	T	HT	WT	DOB	1st Yr	Resides
Adkins, Jon	7	6	6.03	20	20	0	0	97	139	74	65	33	76	.338	L	R	6-0	200	8-30-77	1998	Wayne, W.Va.
Bost, Heath	1	5	3.35	52	0	0	12	78	67	33	29	19	69	.229	R	R	6-3	200	10-13-74	1995	Taylorsville, N.C.
Bowie, Micah	3	2	3.13	46	0	0	4	55	40	21	19	24	64	.201	L	L	6-4	200	11-10-74	1993	New Braunfels, Texas
Coppinger, Rocky	0	1	6.75	2	2	0	0	8	3	7	6	13	5	.115	R	R	6-5	240	3-19-74	1994	El Paso, Texas
Crowell, Kyle	1	0	4.50	5	0	0	0	14	17	7	7	4	9	.293	R	R	6-0	190	6-16-79	2000	Webster, Texas
Duchscherer, Justin	2	4	5.57	14	11	0	0	63	73	45	39	17	52	.282	R	R	6-3	190	11-17-77	1996	Colleyville, Texas
Enochs, Chris	2	1	4.71	6	5	0	0	29	34	16	15	13	22	.300	R	R	6-3	220	10-11-75	1997	Newell, W.Va.
Florie, Bryce	4	6	5.08	18	16	0	0	83	90	55	47	38	69	.270	R	R	5-11	190	5-21-70	1988	Goose Creek, S.C.
Fyhrie, Mike	7	2	2.33	13	13	0	0	77	61	22	20	23	68	.212	R	R	6-2	190	12-9-69	1991	Coto de Caza, Calif.
Gregg, Kevin	2	5	7.52	16	8	0	0	59	82	56	49	23	45	.331	R	R	6-6	200	6-20-78	1996	Corvallis, Ore.
Harang, Aaron	3	3	3.26	8	8	0	0	39	41	17	14	9	39	.266	R	R	6-7	240	5-9-78	1999	San Diego, Calif.
Harville, Chad	1	2	5.40	24	0	0	5	30	32	19	18	13	26	.273	R	R	5-9	180	9-16-76	1997	Savannah, Tenn.
Hiljus, Erik	1	3	7.65	9	6	0	0	38	54	32	32	15	30	.341	R	R	6-6	220	12-25-72	1991	Northridge, Calif.
Lankford, Frank	6	6	4.59	46	0	0	0	80	91	43	41	22	56	.289	R	R	6-2	190	3-26-71	1993	Atlanta, Ga.
Levrault, Allen	7	8	6.39	24	23	0	0	111	145	91	79	45	81	.314	R	R	6-3	240	8-15-77	1996	Westport, Mass.
Lidle, Cory	0	0	2.25	1	1	0	0	4	2	1	1	3	3	.166	R	R	5-11	190	3-22-72	1991	Las Vegas, Nev.
Luebbers, Larry	11	11	4.91	28	28	0	0	169	201	108	92	55	80	.297	R	R	6-6	210	10-11-69	1990	Frankfort, Ky.
McClaskey, Tim	0	0	5.87	2	0	0	0	8	9	5	5	2	4	.283	R	R	5-10	170	1-11-76	1996	Melbourne, Fla.
McKay, Cody	0	0	0.00	3	0	0	0	2	4	0	0	0	2	.000	L	R	6-0	200	1-11-74	1996	Scottsdale, Ariz.
Miller, Matt	3	7	4.31	54	0	0	6	71	81	42	34	28	63	.286	R	R	6-3	210	11-23-71	1997	Greenville, Miss.
Pena, Juan	0	0	6.10	3	1	0	0	10	11	7	7	9	7	.282	L	L	6-4	200	12-4-77	1996	Santo Domingo, D.R.
Scheffer, Aaron	4	1	4.82	35	1	0	1	52	54	32	28	24	35	.271	R	R	6-2	170	10-15-75	1994	Westland, Mich.
Tam, Jeff	1	3	5.59	20	0	0	2	29	31	20	18	5	26	.276	R	R	6-1	210	8-19-70	1993	Melbourne, Fla.
Thompson, Eric	0	1	9.15	11	1	0	1	21	33	22	21	7	14	.351	R	R	6-2	190	9-7-77	1998	Fairborn, Ohio
Venafro, Mike	0	0	6.97	8	0	0	0	10	12	8	8	1	14	.292	L	L	5-10	180	8-2-73	1995	Fort Myers, Fla.
Villegas, Ismael	0	0	8.46	10	0	0	0	22	32	28	21	15	12	.329	R	R	6-0	180	8-12-76	1995	Caguas, P.R.
Weis, Brad	0	0	3.86	2	0	0	0	9	9	4	4	2	6	.257	L	L	6-1	190	11-29-77	1999	Winter Park, Fla.

FIELDING

Catcher	PCT	G	PO	A	E	DP	PB
Grabowski	.942	18	91	7	6	0	2
McKay	.991	77	497	41	5	4	9
Mendez	.991	63	419	24	4	1	7

First Base	PCT	G	PO	A	E	DP
Grabowski	1.000	5	25	3	0	5
McKay	1.000	2	11	0	0	2
Mendez	.992	16	119	11	1	10
Pena	.992	40	326	33	3	40
Piatt	1.000	3	19	0	0	1

	PCT	G	PO	A	E	DP
Sutton	.985	48	361	30	6	44
Valdez	.994	39	342	17	2	19

Second Base	PCT	G	PO	A	E	DP
Flores	1.000	3	10	6	0	2
German	.986	117	236	309	8	67
Landry	1.000	4	6	10	0	4
Menechino	.953	10	15	26	2	5
Meyers	1.000	7	14	22	0	6
Santangelo	.967	8	17	12	1	2
Velarde	.000	1	0	0	0	0

Third Base	PCT	G	PO	A	E	DP
Flores	.500	2	0	1	1	0
Grabowski	.923	6	1	11	1	1
Lopez	.957	131	87	227	14	21
McKay	1.000	4	2	9	0	1
Menechino	.500	2	0	1	1	0
Meyers	.750	3	1	2	1	0

Shortstop	PCT	G	PO	A	E	DP
Ellis	.974	21	44	68	3	18
Flores	.958	55	99	149	11	27

Menechino	.942	74	115	196	19	42
Meyers	.857	2	2	4	1	1
Santangelo	1.000	1	0	1	0	0

Outfield	PCT	G	PO	A	E	DP
Byrnes	.971	30	67	1	2	0
Colangelo	.986	68	145	1	2	0

Flores	.967	40	85	2	3	0
Grabowski	.984	38	60	3	1	1
Landry	.980	52	93	3	2	0
McKay	.000	2	0	0	0	0
Mendez	1.000	2	1	0	0	0
Meyers	1.000	2	2	0	0	0
Piatt	.976	55	81	1	2	0

Ryan	.941	49	75	5	5	2
Santangelo	1.000	30	43	0	0	0
Sutton	.950	46	93	3	5	0
Thomas	1.000	4	11	0	0	0
Valdez	.972	26	35	0	1	0
Warner	.964	33	79	1	3	0

MIDLAND ROCKHOUNDS — Class AA

TEXAS LEAGUE

BATTING	AVG	G	AB	R	H	2B	3B	HR	RBI	BB	SO	SB	CS	SLG	OBP	B	T	HT	WT	DOB	1st Yr	Resides
Asche, Kirk	.242	115	376	50	91	13	10	12	56	40	132	9	6	.426	.314	R	R	6-2	190	7-10-77	1999	Brandon, Fla.
Bowser, Matt	.206	19	63	12	13	2	2	7	6	14	1	0	.397	.286	L	L	6-3	200	3-8-79	2000	Palm Harbor, Fla.
Cancel, Robinson	.281	108	402	56	113	21	2	12	64	32	70	10	7	.433	.338	R	R	6-0	190	5-4-76	1994	Lajas, P.R.
Crosby, Bobby	.281	59	228	31	64	16	0	7	31	19	41	9	2	.443	.335	R	R	6-3	205	1-12-80	2001	Cypress, Calif.
DeCinces, Tim	.280	26	82	10	23	8	0	3	20	7	10	0	0	.488	.337	R	R	6-2	190	4-26-74	1996	Newport Beach, Calif.
Griffin, John-Ford	.143	2	7	0	1	0	0	0	0	0	3	0	0	.143	.250	L	L	6-2	210	11-19-79	2001	Sarasota, Fla.
Guevara, Giomar	.251	103	363	49	91	17	3	1	19	37	88	8	6	.322	.332	R	R	5-8	150	10-23-72	1990	Kirkland, Wash.
Hochgesang, Josh	.234	107	354	42	83	21	0	13	62	28	93	3	5	.404	.312	R	R	6-3	210	4-16-77	1999	Fullerton, Calif.
Holt, Daylan	.279	57	201	18	56	10	0	4	25	15	50	1	4	.388	.327	R	R	6-1	200	10-4-78	2000	Mesquite, Texas
Howe, Matt	.257	57	187	20	48	15	1	4	19	25	50	4	3	.412	.356	R	R	6-1	205	9-16-76	1998	Houston, Texas
Keith, Rusty	.265	95	358	52	95	16	0	1	22	26	44	7	4	.318	.320	R	R	6-0	200	9-18-77	1998	Brookings, Ore.
Koonce, Graham	.274	140	470	86	129	28	0	24	96	133	117	2	0	.487	.440	L	L	6-4	220	5-15-75	1994	Julian, Calif.
Kremblas, Mike	.199	51	141	15	28	2	0	0	7	17	35	1	2	.213	.311	R	R	6-0	190	10-1-75	1998	Sevierville, Tenn.
Landry, Jacques	.295	30	105	25	31	8	0	7	27	27	31	6	2	.571	.441	R	R	6-3	200	8-15-73	1996	Lamarque, Texas
Lockwood, Mike	.242	135	501	68	121	25	7	3	49	60	66	5	6	.337	.332	L	L	6-0	190	12-27-76	1999	Powell, Ohio
McDougall, Marshall	.303	84	323	60	98	22	5	9	56	38	57	7	4	.486	.374	R	R	6-0	200	12-19-78	2000	Valrico, Fla.
Mensik, Todd	.239	72	251	37	60	12	0	6	32	40	64	2	1	.359	.351	L	L	6-2	190	2-27-75	1996	Orland Park, Ill.
Morrissey, Adam	.235	90	302	39	71	15	1	2	22	38	71	4	2	.311	.323	R	R	5-11	185	6-8-81	1999	Ourimbah, Australia

PITCHING	W	L	ERA	G	GS	CG	SV	IP	H	R	ER	BB	SO	AVG	B	T	HT	WT	DOB	1st Yr	Resides
Arnold, Jason	5	1	2.33	10	10	0	0	58	42	22	15	24	53	.207	R	R	6-3	210	5-2-79	2001	Palm Bay, Fla.
Bazzell, Shane	5	7	4.61	39	12	0	3	98	101	59	50	47	88	.269	L	R	6-2	180	3-22-79	1998	Columbus, Miss.
Cotton, Joe	2	1	6.15	27	0	0	2	26	36	20	18	9	18	.333	R	R	6-2	180	3-25-75	1996	Union Town, Ohio
Enochs, Chris	5	12	5.19	23	23	3	0	135	151	89	78	61	91	.289	R	R	6-3	220	10-11-75	1997	Newell, W.Va.
Galva, Claudio	3	3	3.74	62	0	0	4	65	64	36	27	33	54	.257	L	L	6-3	210	3-28-77	1996	Santo Domingo, D.R.
Garcia, Sonny	4	3	3.94	21	7	0	1	59	68	27	26	19	38	.289	R	R	6-3	210	9-10-76	1998	Houston, Texas
German, Franklyn	1	1	3.05	37	0	0	16	41	28	14	14	27	59	.194	R	R	6-4	260	1-20-80	1996	San Cristobal, D.R.
Gregg, Kevin	3	3	4.30	11	4	0	0	38	31	20	18	18	45	.221	R	R	6-6	200	6-20-78	1996	Corvallis, Ore.
Harang, Aaron	2	0	1.08	3	3	0	0	17	12	3	2	7	21	.218	R	R	6-7	240	5-9-78	1999	San Diego, Calif.
Harden, Rich	8	3	2.95	16	16	1	0	85	67	33	28	52	102	.216	L	R	6-1	180	11-30-81	2001	Victoria, B.C.
Jones, Marcus	1	4	5.40	7	7	0	0	32	37	29	19	17	24	.296	R	R	6-5	230	3-29-75	1997	Yorba Linda, Calif.
Lehr, Justin	8	3	4.05	58	0	0	4	80	88	39	36	31	59	.290	R	R	6-1	200	8-3-77	1999	West Covina, Calif.
McClaskey, Tim	0	0	10.20	13	0	0	0	15	28	19	17	6	13	.394	R	R	5-10	170	1-11-76	1996	Melbourne, Fla.
O'Brien, Matt	1	3	2.98	54	0	0	2	63	47	29	21	20	49	.208	L	L	6-2	180	2-22-77	2000	Seattle, Wash.
Rheinecker, John	7	7	3.38	20	20	1	0	128	137	63	48	24	100	.274	L	L	6-2	210	5-29-79	2001	Waterloo, Ill.
Snow, Bert	0	3	4.98	24	0	0	8	22	21	12	12	11	29	.250	R	R	6-1	200	3-23-77	1998	Brooksville, Fla.
Surkont, Keith	2	3	3.86	27	5	0	1	65	70	36	28	35	36	.268	R	R	6-2	200	4-4-77	1999	Pawtucket, R.I.
Thompson, Eric	6	4	3.18	24	14	0	2	93	93	36	33	29	66	.261	R	R	6-2	190	9-7-77	1998	Fairborn, Ohio
Wood, Mike	11	3	3.15	17	17	0	0	106	103	41	37	29	63	.259	R	R	6-3	195	4-26-80	2001	West Palm Beach, Fla.
Ziegler, Mike	1	0	5.11	3	3	0	0	12	17	9	7	5	11	.346	R	R	6-3	220	7-25-79	2000	Glen Burnie, Md.

FIELDING

Catcher	PCT	G	PO	A	E	DP	PB
Cancel	.995	83	563	81	3	8	15
DeCinces	.989	22	156	16	2	3	2
Kremblas	.970	44	304	52	11	6	6

First Base	PCT	G	PO	A	E	DP
Bowser	1.000	2	2	0	0	0
Howe	1.000	7	40	4	0	4
Koonce	.987	119	1010	100	52	14	89
Kremblas	1.000	1	8	0	0	0
McDougall	.000	1	0	0	0	0
Mensik	.984	18	169	10	3	10

Second Base	PCT	G	PO	A	E	DP
Guevara	.986	31	61	81	2	15

	PCT	G	PO	A	E	DP
Howe	.961	14	24	25	2	7
McDougall	.970	16	31	34	2	12
Morrissey	.941	87	132	216	22	38

Third Base	PCT	G	PO	A	E	DP
Cancel	.000	1	0	0	0	0
Guevara	.935	11	6	23	2	1
Hochgesang	.907	87	52	144	20	10
Howe	.878	17	8	28	5	2
McDougall	.949	38	23	71	5	3

Shortstop	PCT	G	PO	A	E	DP
Crosby	.952	59	94	164	13	31
Guevara	.963	63	86	173	10	28
McDougall	.961	30	51	71	5	13

Outfield	PCT	G	PO	A	E	DP
Morrissey	1.000	1	0	1	0	0
Asche	.984	106	235	5	4	3
Bowser	1.000	16	24	3	0	1
Griffin	1.000	2	2	0	0	0
Guevara	1.000	2	1	0	0	0
Holt	.964	52	99	9	4	2
Howe	1.000	3	2	0	0	0
Keith	.981	89	143	10	3	4
Landry	.966	30	52	4	2	1
Lockwood	.996	135	252	6	1	3
Mensik	1.000	7	15	1	0	0

MODESTO A's — High Class A

CALIFORNIA LEAGUE

BATTING	AVG	G	AB	R	H	2B	3B	HR	RBI	BB	SO	SB	CS	SLG	OBP	B	T	HT	WT	DOB	1st Yr	Resides
Basil, Jason	.231	17	52	6	12	3	1	1	5	4	9	0	0	.385	.286	R	R	6-3	220	8-5-78	2001	Cincinnati, Ohio
Bowser, Matt	.233	84	305	34	71	13	1	4	36	38	54	0	1	.321	.325	L	L	6-3	200	3-8-79	2000	Palm Harbor, Fla.
Cosme, Caonabo	.291	131	529	90	154	33	6	11	68	46	113	19	14	.439	.353	R	R	6-2	200	3-18-79	1996	La Vega, D.R.
Craig, Beau	.209	87	273	30	57	10	3	0	26	29	71	3	1	.267	.282	S	R	5-10	190	2-12-79	2000	Santee, Calif.
Crosby, Bobby	.307	73	280	47	86	17	2	2	38	33	43	5	0	.404	.393	R	R	6-3	205	1-12-80	2001	Cypress, Calif.
Dye, Jermaine	.500	2	8	1	4	3	0	0	2	0	0	0	0	.875	.500	R	R	6-5	220	1-28-74	1993	Phoenix, Ariz.
Garcia, Isaac	.355	40	93	21	33	5	0	2	14	7	17	1	2	.473	.402	R	R	6-1	160	11-6-78	1998	Las Matas, Farfan, D.R.
2-team (34 Visalia)	.239	74	197	36	47	7	0	3	26	16	48	2	3	.320	.295							
Hoffpauir, Josh	.118	15	34	7	4	1	1	1	6	6	1	1	.294	.250	L	R	5-11	188	9-21-77	2000	Vidalia, La.
Howe, Matt	.256	71	277	42	71	17	1	11	53	31	66	8	1	.444	.340	R	R	6-1	205	9-16-76	1998	Houston, Texas
Jackson, Steve	.252	99	314	35	79	21	0	9	42	32	92	0	0	.404	.328	R	R	6-5	230	12-13-77	2000	Yakima, Wash.

BATTING

BATTING	AVG	G	AB	R	H	2B	3B	HR	RBI	BB	SO	SB	CS	SLG	OBP	B	T	HT	WT	DOB	1st Yr	Resides
Johnson, Dan	.293	126	426	56	125	23	1	21	85	57	87	4	1	.500	.371	L	R	6-2	220	8-10-79	2001	Coon Rapids, Minn.
Morrissey, Adam	.291	36	141	23	41	7	1	3	26	20	28	4	3	.418	.383	R	R	5-11	185	6-8-81	1999	Ourimbah, Australia
Myers, Casey	.247	60	219	23	54	16	0	4	30	24	33	1	2	.374	.328	R	R	5-11	210	10-23-78	2001	Phoenix, Ariz.
Nagle, Austin	.218	64	216	26	47	13	2	2	25	27	58	3	2	.324	.302	R	R	6-1	190	10-20-82	2001	Dallas, Texas
Neufeld, Andy	.261	39	111	22	29	5	1	1	8	19	26	3	2	.351	.369	L	R	5-11	170	2-21-79	2001	Winter Springs, Fla.
Sellier, Brian	.300	116	417	57	125	26	6	5	58	73	82	16	6	.427	.402	L	R	6-1	200	1-12-78	2000	Phoenix, Ariz.
Stanley, Steve	.286	63	262	48	75	11	1	1	17	39	46	4	6	.347	.382	L	L	5-8	150	12-23-79	2002	Columbus, Ohio
Teahen, Mark	.239	59	234	25	56	9	1	1	26	21	53	1	2	.299	.307	L	R	6-3	210	9-6-81	2002	Yucaipa, Calif.
Thomas, Gary	.257	118	428	74	110	18	6	5	49	45	77	31	11	.362	.340	R	R	5-6	185	9-6-79	1997	Houma, La.
Tritle, Chris	.197	51	178	20	35	9	0	4	23	11	55	3	1	.315	.242	R	R	6-3	218	6-22-82	2000	Center Point, Iowa
Valdez, Mario	.250	2	8	2	2	1	0	0	1	1	1	0	0	.375	.333	L	R	6-2	210	11-19-74	1994	Tamualipas, Mexico
Wayment, Kory	.179	16	39	0	7	2	0	0	5	4	15	1	0	.231	.244	R	R	6-1	175	2-18-81	2001	Ogden, Utah

PITCHING

PITCHING	W	L	ERA	G	GS	CG	SV	IP	H	R	ER	BB	SO	AVG	B	T	HT	WT	DOB	1st Yr	Resides
Adkins, Jon	0	1	8.10	1	1	0	0	7	11	7	6	1	4	.379	L	R	6-0	200	8-30-77	1998	Wayne, W.Va.
Beck, David	0	1	12.15	10	0	0	0	7	10	10	9	7	9	.322	L	L	6-5	230	2-23-78	2001	North Olmstead, Ohio
Blanton, Joe	0	1	7.50	2	1	0	0	6	8	6	5	6	6	.296	R	R	6-3	220	12-11-80	2002	Bowling Green, Ky.
Bonderman, Jeremy	9	8	3.61	25	25	1	0	145	129	77	58	55	160	.232	R	R	6-2	210	10-28-82	2001	Pasco, Wash.
Coppinger, Rocky	1	0	3.86	3	3	0	0	14	18	7	6	6	20	.310	R	R	6-5	240	3-19-74	1994	El Paso, Texas
Cotts, Neal	12	6	4.12	28	28	0	0	138	123	72	63	87	178	.238	L	L	6-2	200	3-25-80	2001	Lebanon, Ill.
Crowell, Kyle	9	3	2.99	42	0	0	3	72	64	24	24	20	89	.239	R	R	6-0	190	6-16-79	2000	Webster, Texas
Frick, Mike	7	6	2.89	50	0	0	23	62	54	26	20	21	66	.232	R	R	6-3	230	3-18-80	2001	Ventura, Calif.
Gilpatrick, T.Jay	1	3	6.91	16	0	0	1	29	39	24	22	12	25	.314	R	R	6-3	215	5-3-79	2000	Cody, Wyo.
Gwyn, Marc	1	3	5.97	8	7	0	0	35	40	27	23	20	30	.291	R	R	6-3	210	11-4-77	2000	The Woodlands, Texas
Mabeus, Chris	3	1	4.04	37	1	0	1	85	97	39	38	32	69	.289	R	R	6-3	210	2-11-79	2001	Soldotna, Alaska
McCall, Derell	8	5	3.32	25	23	1	0	133	140	54	49	50	82	.272	R	R	6-3	210	9-22-81	2000	Cantonment, Fla.
O'Brien, Matt	1	2	1.80	3	1	0	0	15	16	7	3	3	15	.271	L	L	6-0	180	2-22-77	2000	Seattle, Wash.
Pena, Juan	1	0	0.82	2	2	0	0	11	5	2	1	5	9	.135	L	L	6-4	200	12-4-77	1996	Santo Domingo, D.R.
Price, Brett	2	5	3.09	35	2	0	2	47	42	22	16	28	61	.234	L	L	5-10	170	12-7-79	2001	Leesville, S.C.
Ramos, Juan	0	0	6.00	4	0	0	0	3	5	4	2	2	6	.357	R	R	6-0	190	2-1-74	1995	Santo Domingo, D.R.
Robertson, Luke	6	5	4.23	29	15	0	1	121	106	61	57	34	144	.236	R	R	6-4	220	6-30-79	2001	Valley Center, Kan.
Simmering, Bryan	2	4	4.18	17	4	0	1	47	48	23	22	17	41	.269	R	R	6-0	160	11-11-80	2001	North East, Md.
Trosper, Tanner	2	2	2.60	25	0	0	1	45	40	21	13	22	39	.236	R	R	5-11	180	12-28-77	2000	West Hills, Calif.
Webb, Alan	0	1	6.23	2	2	0	0	9	11	7	6	6	9	.314	L	L	5-10	160	9-26-79	1997	Las Vegas, Nev.
Weis, Brad	5	2	2.24	32	0	0	2	52	40	16	13	23	51	.217	L	L	6-1	190	11-29-77	1999	Winter Park, Fla.
Withers, Darvin	7	3	3.46	30	16	1	1	125	116	53	48	33	106	.250	R	R	6-2	190	5-31-80	2000	Aiken, S.C.
Wood, Mike	3	3	3.48	7	7	0	0	41	41	17	16	6	50	.264	R	R	6-3	195	4-26-80	2001	West Palm Beach, Fla.

FIELDING

Catcher	PCT	G	PO	A	E	DP	PB
Basil	.986	8	64	8	1	0	4
Craig	.991	87	729	77	7	11	17
Jackson	.983	20	154	17	3	1	12
Myers	1.000	35	317	23	0	3	3

First Base	PCT	G	PO	A	E	DP
Cosme	1.000	3	7	0	0	0
Howe	1.000	1	2	0	0	0
Jackson	.996	69	463	43	2	34
Johnson	.990	89	603	62	7	53
Myers	1.000	1	5	0	0	0
Valdez	1.000	1	5	0	0	0

Second Base	PCT	G	PO	A	E	DP
Cosme	.968	68	136	139	9	35
Garcia	.980	18	21	28	1	6

	PCT	G	PO	A	E	DP
Hoffpauir	.973	6	18	18	1	3
Morrissey	.941	29	49	62	7	12
Neufeld	.955	28	40	44	4	10
Wayment	.833	4	5	5	2	0

Third Base	PCT	G	PO	A	E	DP
Garcia	.889	2	0	8	1	0
Hoffpauir	1.000	3	0	4	0	1
Howe	.918	70	38	108	13	7
Jackson	1.000	3	0	2	0	0
Neufeld	1.000	4	2	10	0	0
Teahen	.971	58	37	98	4	14
Wayment	.818	6	2	7	2	0

Shortstop	PCT	G	PO	A	E	DP
Cosme	.953	64	100	163	13	27
Crosby	.938	70	79	208	19	32

	PCT	G	PO	A	E	DP
Garcia	.950	6	7	12	1	3
Wayment	.917	4	1	10	1	2

Outfield	PCT	G	PO	A	E	DP
Bowser	.984	67	124	1	2	0
Dye	1.000	2	3	1	0	0
Hoffpauir	1.000	1	1	0	0	0
Jackson	1.000	2	1	0	0	0
Morrissey	1.000	3	6	0	0	0
Nagle	.920	51	68	1	6	0
Sellier	.985	86	127	3	2	0
Stanley	.988	63	158	2	2	1
Thomas	.966	114	192	9	7	4
Tritle	.976	46	78	2	2	0

VISALIA OAKS High Class A

CALIFORNIA LEAGUE

BATTING	AVG	G	AB	R	H	2B	3B	HR	RBI	BB	SO	SB	CS	SLG	OBP	B	T	HT	WT	DOB	1st Yr	Resides
Allegra, Matt	.281	125	494	74	139	35	3	20	93	47	160	9	9	.486	.352	R	R	6-3	210	7-10-81	2000	Lake Mary, Fla.
Basil, Jason	.248	95	351	42	87	10	1	10	60	47	84	0	0	.368	.346	R	R	6-3	220	8-5-78	2001	Cincinnati, Ohio
2-team (17 Modesto)	.246	112	403	48	99	13	2	11	65	51	93	0	0	.370	.338							
Brown, Jeremy	.310	55	187	36	58	14	0	10	40	44	49	1	1	.545	.444	R	R	5-10	210	10-25-79	2002	Hueytown, Ala.
Bynum, Freddie	.306	135	539	83	165	26	5	3	56	64	116	41	21	.390	.385	L	R	6-1	180	3-15-80	2000	Stantonsburg, N.C.
Christy, Jeff	.271	111	384	54	104	29	4	1	39	46	79	12	7	.375	.347	L	R	5-9	180	10-3-79	2001	Tampa, Fla.
Garcia, Isaac	.135	34	104	15	14	2	0	1	12	9	31	1	1	.183	.200	R	R	6-1	160	11-6-78	1998	Las Matas, D.R.
Gregg, Mitch	.137	63	197	33	27	4	1	7	24	34	87	0	1	.274	.270	L	R	6-7	260	7-7-76	1999	Scottsdale, Ariz.
Groff, Matt	.231	45	121	20	28	7	0	3	16	24	24	2	2	.364	.326	R	R	6-2	180	3-28-78	2001	Fort Myers, Fla.
Holt, Daylan	.291	77	309	48	90	26	1	16	63	29	75	3	5	.537	.355	R	R	6-1	200	10-4-78	2000	Mesquite, Texas
Kelly, Tripp	.176	20	68	6	12	6	0	0	11	7	27	0	0	.265	.250	R	R	6-1	210	5-27-79	2001	Florence, S.C.
Kremblas, John	.246	20	57	11	14	4	0	0	5	9	12	1	2	.316	.450	R	R	6-0	190	10-1-75	1998	Sevierville, Tenn.
McBeth, Marcus	.227	76	255	45	58	7	3	10	39	24	73	14	6	.396	.318	R	R	6-1	180	8-23-80	2001	Enoree, S.C.
Schmidt, J.P.	.272	65	217	32	59	9	6	3	23	28	50	13	3	.410	.355	L	R	6-3	185	1-4-80	1998	Palmdale, Calif.
Schneidmiller, Gary	.297	111	381	85	113	17	2	7	53	78	80	6	2	.407	.419	R	R	6-1	185	1-26-80	1998	Chino, Calif.
Soto, Jorge	.210	111	404	69	85	14	1	31	69	57	195	1	1	.480	.324	R	R	6-0	210	4-14-78	1999	Patillas, P.R.
Stotts, J.T.	.275	133	483	66	133	20	3	2	64	65	75	13	6	.342	.363	R	R	5-11	190	1-21-80	2001	Valencia, Calif.
Suomi, Richard	.214	20	70	9	15	6	0	1	10	7	13	1	0	.343	.295	L	R	5-11	180	10-5-80	2000	Toronto, Ontario
Swisher, Nick	.240	49	183	22	44	13	2	4	23	26	48	3	1	.399	.340	S	L	6-0	190	11-25-80	2002	Parkersburg, W.Va.

PITCHING	W	L	ERA	G	GS	CG	SV	IP	H	R	ER	BB	SO	AVG	B	T	HT	WT	DOB	1st Yr	Resides
Anderson, Jason	0	3	6.35	19	0	0	0	23	20	17	16	18	26	.227	L	L	6-2	195	4-6-76	1997	Abington, Va.
Bruksch, Jeff	8	11	4.65	27	27	0	0	149	143	98	77	63	163	.250	R	R	6-4	210	4-29-80	2002	Los Angeles, Calif.
Coleman, Jeff	5	1	3.99	45	0	0	0	65	78	37	29	14	52	.287	R	R	5-11	190	10-6-80	2001	San Dimas, Calif.

PITCHING

PITCHING	W	L	ERA	G	GS	CG	SV	IP	H	R	ER	BB	SO	AVG	B	T	HT	WT	DOB	1st Yr	Resides
Crider, J.R.	0	0	8.44	12	0	0	0	11	12	10	10	13	11	.300	R	R	6-1	190	12-7-79	2001	Phoenix, Ariz.
Cullen, Ryan	3	4	4.91	50	0	0	4	73	95	47	40	15	58	.309	L	L	6-4	200	1-20-80	1999	Melbourne, Fla.
Dickinson, Andy	1	1	3.38	4	4	0	0	24	32	9	9	6	14	.340	L	L	6-2	170	12-13-79	2002	Freeport, Ill.
Fischer, Steve	7	4	2.81	50	2	0	4	90	88	41	28	37	67	.264	R	R	6-0	200	6-20-78	2000	Benicia, Calif.
Flores, Ron	8	6	3.25	53	0	0	11	80	90	41	29	16	92	.281	L	L	5-11	190	8-9-79	2000	Pico Rivera, Calif.
Fritz, Ben	1	0	3.71	3	3	0	0	17	15	7	7	6	16	.241	R	R	6-4	220	3-29-81	2002	Clovis, Calif.
Garcia, Sonny	2	1	1.09	6	6	0	0	33	32	4	4	8	34	.253	R	R	6-3	210	9-10-76	1998	Houston, Texas
Gonzalez, Christian	5	7	4.95	29	11	0	0	107	127	76	59	29	72	.294	R	R	6-0	195	6-17-77	1996	Santo Domingo, D.R.
Gregg, Kevin	2	1	2.08	3	3	0	0	17	8	5	4	9	11	.140	R	R	6-6	200	6-20-78	1996	Corvallis, Ore.
Harden, Rich	4	3	2.93	12	12	1	0	68	49	27	22	24	85	.200	L	R	6-1	180	11-30-81	2001	Victoria, B.C.
Harriger, Mark	2	4	5.44	12	11	0	0	51	57	38	31	22	33	.278	R	R	6-2	190	4-29-75	1996	Lakewood, Calif.
Komine, Shane	3	6	5.96	18	0	0	0	26	23	20	17	20	22	.239	R	R	5-9	170	10-18-80	2002	Honolulu, Hawaii
McClaskey, Tim	4	6	4.31	19	17	2	0	102	131	59	49	21	64	.310	R	R	5-10	170	1-11-76	1996	Melbourne, Fla.
Minaya, Edwin	1	5	6.07	32	0	0	1	43	55	36	29	20	37	.300	R	R	6-2	185	6-20-76	1997	Monte Cristi, D.R.
Obenchain, Steve	2	0	3.00	4	4	0	0	24	23	8	8	3	10	.255	R	R	6-5	200	7-29-81	2002	Henderson, Ky.
Pena, Juan	0	5	7.83	7	7	0	0	23	40	36	20	12	18	.370	L	L	6-4	200	12-4-77	1996	Santo Domingo, D.R.
2-team (2 Modesto)	1	5	5.56	9	9	0	0	34	45	38	21	17	27	.310							
Rheinecker, John	3	0	2.31	9	9	0	0	51	41	16	13	10	62	.293	L	L	6-2	210	5-29-79	2001	Waterloo, Ill.
Snow, Bert	0	1	1.00	12	1	0	5	18	8	2	2	7	25	.131	R	R	6-1	200	3-23-77	1998	Brooksville, Fla.
Ziegler, Mike	11	6	4.21	25	24	1	0	152	169	80	71	20	139	.278	R	R	6-3	220	7-25-79	2000	Glen Burnie, Md.

FIELDING

Catcher	PCT	G	PO	A	E	DP	PB
Brown	.985	52	350	43	6	1	8
Kremblas	.988	17	153	18	2	1	2
Soto	.986	62	462	40	7	4	14
Suomi	.987	17	137	12	2	0	5

First Base	PCT	G	PO	A	E	DP
Basil	.982	51	396	36	8	29
Gregg	.975	59	469	36	13	40
Groff	1.000	2	2	1	0	0
Kelly	.992	15	121	5	1	3
Soto	.985	29	254	12	4	20

Second Base	PCT	G	PO	A	E	DP
Bynum	.948	134	288	364	36	73
Garcia	.957	8	9	13	1	2
Schmidt	1.000	5	6	9	0	0

Third Base	PCT	G	PO	A	E	DP
Basil	.837	20	12	29	8	0
Garcia	.825	21	9	38	10	5
Groff	.000	1	0	0	0	0
Schmidt	1.000	3	3	4	0	0
Schneidmiller	.916	104	69	214	26	20

Shortstop	PCT	G	PO	A	E	DP
Garcia	.857	4	2	4	1	1

	PCT	G	PO	A	E	DP
Schmidt	.848	8	8	20	5	5
Stotts	.943	133	150	398	33	55

Outfield	PCT	G	PO	A	E	DP
Allegra	.967	123	227	11	8	2
Basil	1.000	5	4	0	0	0
Christy	.970	89	124	6	4	0
Groff	.978	29	39	5	1	2
Holt	.985	71	123	8	2	0
McBeth	.971	50	96	6	3	0
Schmidt	.986	37	69	4	1	0
Swisher	.953	40	81	1	4	0

ORGANIZATION STATISTICS

VANCOUVER CANADIANS — Short-Season A

NORTHWEST LEAGUE

BATTING

BATTING	AVG	G	AB	R	H	2B	3B	HR	RBI	BB	SO	SB	CS	SLG	OBP	B	T	HT	WT	DOB	1st Yr	Resides
Baker, John	.235	39	115	15	27	5	0	1	13	22	37	2	0	.304	.389	L	R	6-1	210	1-20-81	2002	Walnut Creek, Calif.
Brown, Jeremy	.286	10	28	7	8	1	0	0	1	10	5	1	0	.321	.487	R	R	5-10	210	10-25-79	2002	Hueytown, Ala.
Colamarino, Brant	.259	67	228	30	59	6	2	6	41	27	54	3	1	.382	.348	L	L	5-11	200	12-4-80	2002	Pittsburgh, Pa.
Cruz, Nelson	.276	63	214	23	59	14	0	4	25	9	58	12	1	.397	.316	R	R	6-3	170	7-1-80	1998	Monte Cristi, D.R.
Gibbons, Daniel	.120	20	50	7	6	1	0	0	3	7	9	0	1	.140	.224	L	R	6-3	200	10-21-80	2002	Toronto, Ontario
Gomez, Francis	.265	21	68	15	18	8	0	1	9	8	10	1	0	.426	.338	R	R	6-1	160	9-2-81	1999	La Romana, D.R.
Harriman, David	.234	32	77	6	18	1	0	1	8	5	11	3	0	.286	.289	R	R	6-1	210	10-15-80	2002	Surrey, B.C.
Kelly, Tripp	.190	35	100	6	19	3	1	0	11	13	34	3	0	.240	.287	R	R	6-1	210	5-27-79	2001	Florence, S.C.
Kiger, Mark	.244	66	246	44	60	12	1	5	27	40	58	7	4	.362	.346	R	R	5-11	180	5-30-80	2002	San Diego, Calif.
Madera, Sandy	.222	9	9	2	2	0	0	0	1	0	0	0	0	.222	.222	R	R	6-2	170	8-11-80	1998	Santo Domingo, D.R.
McCurdy, John	.242	56	223	33	54	9	1	3	29	12	57	5	1	.332	.282	R	R	6-2	190	4-17-81	2002	Crofton, Md.
Morris, Jed	.264	31	87	6	23	7	0	1	16	13	20	1	1	.379	.394	L	R	5-11	190	3-4-80	2002	Ripon, Calif.
Nagle, Austin	.215	41	144	12	31	9	1	1	13	14	38	1	3	.313	.292	R	R	6-0	200	12-20-79	2002	Dallas, Texas
Nordness, Kirk	.227	12	44	8	10	4	0	0	5	5	7	0	0	.318	.314	R	R	6-3	210	10-4-79	2001	Beaverton, Ore.
Peirce, Justin	.000	1	1	0	0	0	0	0	0	0	0	0	0	.000	.000	R	R	6-3	200	8-8-79	2001	Wichita Falls, Texas
Rooke, Brian	.000	1	1	0	0	0	0	0	0	0	0	0	0	.000	.000	R	R	6-2	200	8-8-79	2001	Pacific Palisades, Calif.
Stavisky, Brian	.294	32	102	12	30	10	1	1	15	15	30	5	0	.441	.407	L	R	6-3	230	7-6-80	2002	Port Allegheny, Pa.
Suomi, Richard	.254	41	142	20	36	7	0	5	24	11	36	0	0	.408	.310	L	R	5-11	180	10-5-80	2000	Toronto, Ontario
Swisher, Nick	.250	13	44	10	11	3	0	2	12	13	11	3	0	.455	.433	S	L	6-0	190	11-25-80	2002	Parkersburg, W.Va.
Teahen, Mark	.404	13	57	10	23	5	1	0	6	5	9	4	1	.526	.444	L	R	6-3	210	9-6-81	2002	Yucaipa, Calif.
Tritle, Chris	.221	56	190	22	42	10	0	2	13	15	60	3	2	.305	.282	R	R	6-3	218	6-22-82	2002	Center Point, Iowa
Turner, Lloyd	.256	42	156	20	40	6	1	1	21	15	34	6	4	.327	.328	R	R	6-1	180	4-11-80	2002	Hephzibah, Ga.
Wayment, Kory	.203	60	182	26	37	1	1	1	10	40	52	3	2	.236	.355	R	R	6-1	175	2-18-81	2001	Ogden, Utah

GAMES BY POSITION: C—Baker 18, Brown 9, Harriman 22, Madera 1, Morris 17, Suomi 21. **1B**—Colamarino 63, Kelly 19. **2B**—Gomez 1, Kelly 1, Kiger 52, Turner 13, Wayment 13. **3B**—Gomez 12, Harriman 1, McCurdy 3, Suomi 1, Teahen 1, Turner 15, Wayment 37. **SS**—Gomez 9, Kiger 12, McCurdy 51, Wayment 9. **OF**—Cruz 62, Gibbons 19, Morris 1, Nordness 2, Peirce 1, Rooke 1, Stavisky 16, Suomi 15, Swisher 13, Tritle 56, Turner 14, Wayment 1.

PITCHING

PITCHING	W	L	ERA	G	GS	CG	SV	IP	H	R	ER	BB	SO	AVG	B	T	HT	WT	DOB	1st Yr	Resides
Atencio, Donald	0	0	18.00	1	0	0	0	1	1	2	2	0	1	.250	R	R	6-4	190	8-1-81	2000	Kirtland, N.M.
Beck, David	0	0	1.35	6	0	0	2	20	14	6	3	10	22	.200	L	L	6-5	230	2-23-78	2001	North Olmstead, Ohio
Blanton, Joe	1	1	3.14	4	2	0	0	14	11	5	5	2	15	.215	R	R	6-3	220	12-11-80	2002	Bowling Green, Ky.
Burton, Levi	0	4	3.58	13	5	0	1	38	32	22	15	14	38	.220	R	R	6-5	220	6-2-81	2002	Westminster, S.C.
Crider, J.R.	0	1	9.00	2	0	0	0	2	5	6	2	2	1	.454	R	R	6-1	190	12-7-79	2001	Phoenix, Ariz.
Crowder, Justin	2	3	2.25	17	3	0	2	40	31	12	10	3	50	.208	L	L	6-0	190	9-24-79	2002	Lewisville, Texas
Dickinson, Andy	4	0	2.06	11	10	0	0	48	37	11	11	12	40	.216	L	L	6-2	170	12-13-79	2002	Freeport, Ill.
Dunwell, Chris	1	5	6.46	14	9	0	0	47	47	36	34	20	38	.265	R	R	6-1	200	1-29-80	2002	El Cajon, Calif.
Fritz, Ben	1	4	2.95	9	9	0	0	40	29	16	13	14	33	.198	R	R	6-4	220	3-29-81	2002	Clovis, Calif.
Garcia, Jairo	0	3	7.30	3	0	0	0	12	15	11	10	7	16	.300	R	R	6-0	160	3-7-83	2000	Juan Baron, D.R.
Gill, Chris	4	2	4.13	20	0	0	0	28	30	15	13	17	24	.267	R	R	6-0	180	2-17-81	2001	Phoenix, Ariz.
Howay, Chris	0	0	2.37	11	0	0	0	19	14	5	5	12	12	.194	R	R	6-3	210	8-17-79	2002	New Westminster, B.C.
Johnson, Thad	1	0	3.14	5	2	0	0	14	9	5	5	4	12	.183	R	R	6-4	200	4-22-79	2001	Santa Rosa, Calif.
Kohn, Shawn	3	2	3.10	16	0	0	0	20	20	7	7	6	20	.263	R	R	6-2	190	1-28-80	2002	Snohomish, Wash.
Landeros, Leonard	6	1	3.28	21	1	0	0	49	53	25	18	14	39	.270	L	L	6-3	170	12-12-80	2001	Hanford, Calif.

PITCHING	W	L	ERA	G	GS	CG	SV	IP	H	R	ER	BB	SO	AVG	B	T	HT	WT	DOB	1st Yr	Resides
Leon, Brigmer	3	1	3.96	18	1	0	0	39	36	23	17	10	32	.244	R	R	6-3	160	4-7-81	1997	Cumana, Venez.
Muessig, Jeff	2	0	1.78	24	0	0	5	30	16	8	6	16	47	.152	R	R	6-2	180	2-27-82	2001	Mt. Sinai, N.Y.
Murphy, Bill	1	4	4.57	13	9	0	0	41	28	23	21	35	46	.191	L	L	6-0	190	5-9-81	2002	Riverside, Calif.
Obenchain, Steve	2	3	2.85	11	10	0	0	41	35	18	13	10	29	.225	R	R	6-5	200	7-29-81	2002	Henderson, Ky.
Pickens, J.R.	0	0	0.00	1	0	0	1	2	0	0	0	1	2	.000	L	R	6-1	210	6-22-80	2002	Liberty, Texas
Rodriguez, Manuel	5	0	1.91	21	0	0	1	38	27	9	8	15	26	.200	R	R	6-2	160	5-2-81	1999	Jusepin, Venez.
Schilsky, Steve	0	0	2.35	6	0	0	0	8	11	2	2	4	3	.343	R	R	6-2	210	1-3-81	2002	Springfield, Ill.
Shank, Chris	0	3	3.43	19	5	0	1	45	41	19	17	9	43	.235	R	R	6-2	180	1-31-81	2002	Westminster, Mich.
Sierra, Edwardo	0	2	6.11	9	7	0	0	28	42	24	19	17	23	.336	R	R	6-3	180	4-15-82	1999	San Cristobal, D.R.

PHOENIX ATHLETICS — Rookie

ARIZONA LEAGUE

BATTING	AVG	G	AB	R	H	2B	3B	HR	RBI	BB	SO	SB	CS	SLG	OBP	B	T	HT	WT	DOB	1st Yr	Resides
Bubalo, Ty	.217	32	115	16	25	6	0	2	14	15	37	0	2	.322	.336	R	R	6-3	200	8-8-83	2002	Beaverton, Ore.
De la Rosa, Isaias	.181	25	72	12	13	1	2	1	10	11	23	0	1	.292	.302	R	R	6-3	190	9-17-83	2001	Santo Domingo, D.R.
DeCinces, Tim	.000	1	2	0	0	0	0	0	0	1	0	0	0	.000	.000	L	R	6-2	190	4-26-74	1996	Newport Beach, Calif.
Francois, Francisco	.303	40	165	30	50	5	3	1	22	14	44	7	4	.388	.376	R	R	6-1	150	11-30-82	2000	La Romana, D.R.
Garcia, Eustaquio	.267	47	176	36	47	8	2	3	26	19	31	4	2	.386	.348	R	R	6-2	170	3-5-82	1999	El Bonito, D.R.
Garcia, Jairo	.462	16	13	4	6	2	1	0	5	1	1	1	0	.769	.500	R	R	6-0	160	3-7-83	2000	Juan Baron, D.R.
Gomez, Francis	.261	6	23	6	6	0	1	1	4	4	4	2	0	.478	.370	R	R	6-1	160	9-2-81	1999	La Romana, D.R.
Klippenstein, Tyler	.205	51	205	25	42	7	1	3	30	16	54	6	3	.293	.272	R	R	6-4	210	4-11-81	2002	Okotoks, Alberta
McBeth, Marcus	.333	4	9	5	3	0	0	0	3	0	3	0	0	.333	.500	R	R	6-1	180	8-23-80	2001	Enoree, S.C.
Mejia, Jorge	.240	35	129	19	31	4	0	0	14	10	33	4	1	.271	.303	R	R	6-1	160	8-15-82	1999	Santo Domingo, D.R.
Mejia, Lekis	.277	25	94	14	26	5	1	4	16	2	17	1	1	.479	.303	R	R	6-1	180	10-14-81	1999	Bani, D.R.
Metzger, Greg	.250	31	112	19	28	4	1	5	12	7	35	2	1	.438	.328	R	R	6-2	200	6-12-80	2002	Trumbull, Conn.
Morban, Franklin	.160	17	50	2	8	2	1	0	4	4	15	1	0	.240	.232	R	R	6-1	190	5-9-84	2001	San Cristobal, D.R.
Perez, Luis	.339	42	168	33	57	8	4	4	32	16	18	8	7	.506	.407	R	R	6-0	160	8-17-83	2000	Miranda, Venez.
Ramirez, Juan	.229	16	48	6	11	2	0	0	5	8	15	3	1	.271	.362	R	R	5-11	180	9-16-83	2001	Monte Plata, D.R.
Rodriguez, William	.217	38	120	22	26	6	2	1	12	30	46	3	1	.325	.399	L	L	6-0	170	5-8-84	2001	Santiago, D.R.
Rogers, Nick	.337	47	178	33	60	8	6	0	33	31	40	21	1	.449	.439	R	R	6-1	210	12-12-79	2002	Ponte Vedra Beach, Fla.
Trinidad, Edgar	.245	26	102	18	25	3	1	0	10	13	20	2	2	.294	.328	R	R	6-0	160	8-16-82	1999	Santo Domingo, D.R.
Valdez, Tommy	.188	43	149	26	28	5	2	6	18	21	57	3	2	.369	.288	R	R	6-2	170	3-27-82	1999	Santo Domingo, D.R.

GAMES BY POSITION: C—Bubalo 5, Metzger 25, Morban 16, Ramirez 16. **1B**—Bubalo 16, Klippenstein 41, McBeth 1, Valdez 1. **2B**—Francis 11, Garcia 1, J. Mejia 25, Perez 16, Trinidad 5. **3B**—Garcia 21, Klippenstein 1, J. Mejia 5, L. Mejia 23, Trinidad 12. **SS**—De la Rosa 21, E. Garcia 2, J. Garcia 3, McBeth 3, Perez 20, Rodriguez 36, Rogers 45, Valdez 41. **OF**—De la Rosa 21, E. Garcia 2, J. Garcia 3, McBeth 3, Perez 20, Rodriguez 36, Rogers 45, Valdez 41. J. Mejia 2.

PITCHING	W	L	ERA	G	GS	CG	SV	IP	H	R	ER	BB	SO	AVG	B	T	HT	WT	DOB	1st Yr	Resides
Avendano, Elvis	1	5	8.33	14	3	0	1	31	46	31	29	8	24	.328	R	R	6-1	160	2-8-83	1999	El Guayabo, Venez.
Baez, Hebel	1	1	9.00	5	1	0	0	10	17	11	10	3	8	.354	R	R	6-3	170	6-2-81	1997	San Cristobal, D.R.
Barnett, Daniel	0	2	6.08	13	4	0	2	37	50	33	25	17	30	.322	R	R	6-0	190	1-22-83	2002	Kearns, Utah
Burdette, Jason	5	3	2.52	15	8	0	1	61	59	26	17	17	59	.261	R	R	6-1	190	2-18-80	2002	Leesburg, Ga.
Cabaniel, Tomas	3	4	4.35	16	3	0	2	41	35	30	20	16	42	.228	R	R	6-1	160	2-10-83	2000	Caracas, Venez.
Corchado, Jose	3	1	2.44	14	6	0	1	48	54	23	13	12	38	.276	R	R	6-0	190	4-5-84	2002	Isabela, P.R.
Fyvie, Dan	3	1	2.92	19	0	0	2	25	24	18	8	12	16	.235	R	R	6-1	200	8-12-82	2002	Flint, Mich.
Garcia, Jairo	2	1	2.44	18	8	0	1	59	56	24	16	17	66	.200	R	R	6-0	160	3-7-83	2000	Juan Baron, D.R.
Gwyn, Marc	1	3	2.81	5	5	0	0	16	19	8	5	0	23	.283	R	R	6-3	210	11-4-77	2000	The Woodlands, Texas
Knox, Brad	2	3	4.17	10	7	0	0	41	44	28	19	9	42	.268	R	R	6-3	210	5-27-82	2002	Houston, Texas
Martinez, Pedro	2	0	4.64	10	2	0	1	21	22	15	11	7	19	.250	L	L	6-2	160	9-8-82	1999	Santo Domingo, D.R.
Reynoso, Anibal	1	0	12.54	10	2	0	0	19	38	32	26	9	9	.387	R	R	6-1	170	6-22-83	2001	Puerto Plata, D.R.
Sanchez, Adiel	1	2	5.76	16	1	0	0	30	35	25	19	9	22	.289	L	L	6-1	160	8-27-82	2000	Santo Domingo, D.R.
Santana, Roberto	1	0	9.45	11	0	0	0	13	18	21	14	10	11	.305	L	L	6-0	160	10-13-81	1999	Sabana Perdida, D.R.
Sierra, Edwardo	2	1	4.64	6	6	0	0	33	29	19	17	10	35	.239	R	R	6-3	180	4-15-82	1999	San Cristobal, D.R.
Stewart, Scott	0	1	4.05	9	0	0	0	13	17	7	6	3	7	.293	R	R	6-1	160	10-25-81	1999	Maturin, Venez.

PHILADELPHIA PHILLIES

BY PAUL HAGEN

A 2002 season that started with soaring hopes never got off the ground. The Phillies opened the schedule by losing 19 of their first 28 games and ended it with a losing record (80-81) for the 14th time in the last 16 years.

It was a huge disappointment for an organization that advertised itself as being ready to contend after winning 86 games and finishing second in the National League East in 2001.

Going into the season, general manager Ed Wade took a calculated risk by keeping third baseman Scott Rolen, a potential free agent who had given every indication he had no intention of remaining with the organization, rather than trading him at the Winter Meetings. That gamble backfired, and Rolen was sent to the Cardinals for third baseman Placido Polanco, righthander Mike Timlin and lefthander Bud Smith shortly before the July 31 trading deadline.

Fiery manager Larry Bowa continued to inspire fierce loyalty in some players, but his constant intensity also noticeably wore on others.

There were some positive developments. Left fielder Pat Burrell developed into one of the best young power hitters in baseball. In just his second full big league season he batted .281-37-116. Lefthander Randy Wolf showed signs of developing into a legitimate top-of-the-rotation starter. His final record of 11-9 was deceiving; in the nine defeats, the team scored a total of 14 runs.

Righthander Vicente Padilla was selected to the All-Star Game after coming into spring training as one of four candidates for the rotation. And righthander Carlos Silva made a smooth transition from Double-A starter to big league reliever.

That wasn't nearly enough to offset the areas that came up short, however. And the problems started at the top of the rotation.

Righthander Robert Person was the Opening Day starter. Coming off a strong second half (9-2, 3.41) in 2001 and going into his free agent season, it was hoped

Pat Burrell   Ryan Madson

PLAYERS OF THE YEAR

MAJOR LEAGUE: Pat Burrell, of

Burrell finally had the breakout year in 2002 that had been expected of him since the Phillies took him with the first overall pick in the 1998 draft. He hit .282-37-116, ranking third in the National League in RBIs.

MINOR LEAGUE: Ryan Madson, rhp

The 6-foot-6 Madson went 16-4, 3.20 at Double-A Reading in 2002, tying for the third most wins in the minors. Though his stuff sinks and has heavy run, Madson demonstrated great control by issuing 53 walks in 171 innings.

that he'd blossom further with a career year. Instead he struggled from the beginning, made just 16 starts before undergoing elbow surgery and finished at 4-5, 5.44.

Righthander Brandon Duckworth made an immediate impact after being called up for the stretch drive in 2001. He went 3-2, 3.52 in 11 starts. Counted on to be a contributing member of the rotation in 2002, he instead went 8-9, 5.41. And the biggest free agent acquisition—righthander Terry Adams, signed to be the No. 3 starter—was moved to the bullpen after 19 starts.

First baseman Travis Lee and second baseman Marlon Anderson had subpar seasons. Shortstop Jimmy Rollins was the NL's starter in the All-Star Game in just his second full year in the big leagues. But he struck out too much (103 times) and still hasn't learned to hit the ball on the ground to take advantage of his speed.

As a result, attendance at Veterans Stadium was third lowest in the National League, ahead of only the Marlins and Expos.

One highlight occurred June 24 at Chicago's Wrigley Field, when touted righthander Brett Myers made his major league debut by giving up just one run on two hits through eight innings to beat the Cubs. Myers had an up-and-down season after that but showed enough potential to compete for a spot in the rotation.

Going into 2003, the Phillies expect to get more help from their revived farm system. Center fielder Marlon Byrd has already been written into the lineup, and several young pitchers are in the pipeline, including Ryan Madson and Gavin Floyd.

With their new ballpark scheduled to be ready for Opening Day 2004, a sense of urgency has developed throughout the organization to do everything possible to insure another disappointment is avoided in 2003.

ORGANIZATION LEADERS

BATTING

*AVG	Troy McNaughton, Reading/Clearwater	.312
R	Marlon Byrd, Scranton	103
H	Dave Doster, Scranton	171
TB	Marlon Byrd, Scranton	256
2B	Chase Utley, Scanton	39
3B	Dave Doster, Scranton	10
HR	Ryan Howard, Lakewood	19
RBI	Dave Doster, Scranton	91
BB	Nick Punto, Scranton	76
SO	Ryan Howard, Lakewood	145
SB	Nick Punto, Scranton	42

PITCHING

W	Ryan Madson, Reading	16
L	Yoel Hernandez, Clearwater	16
#ERA	Seung Lee, Reading/Clearwater/Lakewood	2.77
G	Pete Zamora, Scranton	55
CG	Seung Lee, Reading/Clearwater/Lakewood	6
SV	Josh Miller, Lakewood	17
IP	Taylor Buchholz, Reading/Clearwater	182
BB	Keith Bucktrot, Clearwater	78
SO	Taylor Buchholz, Reading/Clearwater	146

*Minimum 250 At-Bats #Minimum 75 Innings

PHILADELPHIA
PHILLIES

Manager: Larry Bowa

2002 Record: 80-81, .497 (3rd, NL East)

ORGANIZATION STATISTICS

BATTING	AVG	G	AB	R	H	2B	3B	HR	RBI	BB	SO	SB	CS	SLG	OBP	B	T	HT	WT	DOB	1st Yr	Resides
Abreu, Bob	.308	157	572	102	176	50	6	20	85	104	117	31	12	.521	.413	L	R	6-0	190	3-11-74	1991	Aragua, Venez.
Anderson, Marlon	.258	145	539	64	139	30	6	8	48	42	71	5	1	.380	.315	L	R	5-11	200	1-6-74	1995	Prattville, Ala.
Burrell, Pat	.282	157	586	96	165	39	2	37	116	89	153	1	0	.544	.376	R	R	6-4	220	10-10-76	1998	Clearwater, Fla.
Byrd, Marlon	.229	10	35	2	8	2	0	1	1	1	8	0	2	.371	.250	R	R	6-0	220	8-30-77	1999	Marietta, Ga.
Estrada, Johnny	.118	10	17	0	2	1	0	0	2	2	2	0	0	.176	.211	S	R	5-11	200	6-27-76	1997	Salisbury, N.C.
Giambi, Jeremy	.244	82	156	32	38	10	0	12	28	52	54	0	1	.538	.435	L	L	5-11	210	9-30-74	1996	Las Vegas, Nev.
Glanville, Doug	.249	138	422	49	105	16	3	6	29	25	57	19	2	.344	.292	R	R	6-2	170	8-25-70	1991	Philadelphia, Pa.
Hollins, Dave	.118	14	17	1	2	0	0	0	0	0	3	0	1	.118	.167	S	R	6-1	210	5-25-66	1987	Orchard Park, N.Y.
Ledee, Ricky	.227	96	203	33	46	13	1	8	23	35	50	1	2	.419	.342	L	L	6-1	190	11-22-73	1990	Salinas, P.R.
Lee, Travis	.265	153	536	55	142	26	2	13	70	54	104	5	3	.394	.331	L	L	6-3	210	5-26-75	1997	Encinitas, Calif.
Lieberthal, Mike	.279	130	476	46	133	29	2	15	52	38	58	0	1	.443	.349	R	R	6-0	190	1-18-72	1990	Westlake Village, Calif.
Mabry, John	.286	21	21	1	6	0	0	0	3	1	5	0	0	.286	.304	L	R	6-4	210	10-17-70	1991	St. Louis, Mo.
Michaels, Jason	.267	81	105	16	28	10	3	2	11	13	33	1	1	.476	.347	R	R	6-0	200	5-4-76	1998	Tampa, Fla.
Perez, Tomas	.250	92	212	22	53	13	1	5	20	21	40	1	0	.392	.319	S	R	5-11	170	12-29-73	1991	Barquisimeto, Venez.
Polanco, Placido	.296	53	206	28	61	13	1	4	22	14	14	2	2	.427	.353	R	R	5-10	160	10-10-75	1994	Miami, Fla.
2-team (94 St. Louis)	.288	147	548	75	158	32	2	9	49	26	41	5	3	.403	.330							
Pratt, Todd	.311	39	106	14	33	11	0	3	16	24	28	2	0	.500	.449	R	R	6-3	230	2-9-67	1985	Deerfield, Fla.
Punto, Nick	.167	9	6	0	1	0	0	0	0	0	3	0	0	.167	.167	S	R	5-9	170	11-8-77	1998	Mission Viejo, Calif.
Rolen, Scott	.259	100	375	52	97	21	4	17	66	52	68	5	2	.472	.358	R	R	6-4	220	4-4-75	1993	Holmes Beach, Fla.
Rollins, Jimmy	.245	154	637	82	156	33	10	11	60	54	103	31	13	.380	.306	S	R	5-8	160	11-27-78	1996	Alameda, Calif.
Valent, Eric	.200	7	10	1	2	0	0	0	3	0	0	0	0	.200	.200	L	L	6-0	190	4-4-77	1998	Anaheim, Calif.
Wolf, Randy	.136	32	59	6	8	4	0	1	4	4	24	0	0	.254	.190	L	L	6-0	190	8-22-76	1997	West Hills, Calif.

PITCHING	W	L	ERA	G	GS	CG	SV	IP	H	R	ER	BB	SO	AVG	B	T	HT	WT	DOB	1st Yr	Resides
Adams, Terry	7	9	4.35	46	19	0	0	137	132	76	66	58	96	.255	R	R	6-3	210	3-6-73	1991	Semmes, Ala.
Bottalico, Ricky	0	3	4.61	30	0	0	0	27	33	16	14	13	24	.300	L	R	6-1	210	8-26-69	1991	Rocky Hill, Conn.
Coggin, Dave	2	5	4.68	38	7	0	0	75	65	42	40	51	64	.231	R	R	6-4	200	10-30-76	1995	Upland, Calif.
Cormier, Rheal	5	6	5.25	54	0	0	0	60	61	38	35	32	49	.265	L	L	5-10	180	4-23-67	1989	Vorhees, N.J.
Duckworth, Brandon	8	9	5.41	30	29	0	0	163	167	103	98	69	167	.261	S	R	6-2	180	1-23-76	1997	Kearns, Utah
Junge, Eric	2	0	1.42	4	1	0	0	13	14	3	2	5	11	.285	R	R	6-5	210	1-5-77	1999	Rye, N.Y.
Mercado, Hector	2	2	4.62	31	3	0	0	39	32	21	20	25	40	.223	L	L	6-3	200	4-29-74	1992	Dorado, P.R.
Mesa, Jose	4	6	2.97	74	0	0	45	76	65	26	25	39	64	.231	R	R	6-3	220	5-22-66	1982	West Lake, Ohio
Myers, Brett	4	5	4.25	12	12	1	0	72	73	38	34	29	34	.276	R	R	6-4	210	8-17-80	1999	Jacksonville, Fla.
Nickle, Doug	0	0	6.23	4	0	0	0	4	6	3	3	4	2	.315	R	R	6-4	230	10-2-74	1997	Sonoma, Calif.
Padilla, Vicente	14	11	3.28	32	32	1	0	206	198	83	75	53	128	.253	R	R	6-2	200	9-27-77	1998	Chinandega, Nicaragua
Person, Robert	4	5	5.44	16	16	0	0	88	79	58	53	51	61	.240	R	R	6-0	190	1-8-69	1989	Clearwater, Fla.
Plesac, Dan	2	1	4.70	41	0	0	1	23	16	12	12	12	27	.190	L	L	6-5	210	2-4-62	1983	Valparaiso, Ind.
Politte, Cliff	2	0	3.86	13	0	0	0	16	19	10	7	9	15	.287	R	R	5-11	180	2-27-74	1995	St. Louis, Mo.
Roa, Joe	4	4	4.04	14	11	0	0	71	78	33	32	13	35	.278	R	R	6-1	190	10-11-71	1989	Hazel Park, Mich.
Santiago, Jose	1	3	6.70	42	0	0	0	47	56	35	35	15	30	.290	R	R	6-3	210	11-5-74	1994	Loiza, P.R.
Silva, Carlos	5	0	3.21	68	0	0	1	84	88	34	30	22	41	.282	R	R	6-4	220	4-23-79	1996	Bolivar, Venez.
Timlin, Mike	3	3	3.79	30	0	0	0	36	27	16	15	7	15	.206	R	R	6-4	210	3-10-66	1987	Oldsmar, Fla.
2-team (42 St. Louis)	4	6	2.98	72	1	0	0	97	75	35	32	14	50	.211							
Wolf, Randy	11	9	3.20	31	31	3	0	211	172	77	75	63	172	.222	L	L	6-0	190	8-22-76	1997	West Hills, Calif.

FIELDING

Catcher	PCT	G	PO	A	E	DP	PB
Estrada	1.000	10	34	2	0	0	1
Lieberthal	.993	129	840	56	6	8	7
Perez	.000	1	0	0	0	0	0
Pratt	1.000	34	239	10	0	3	4

First Base	PCT	G	PO	A	E	DP
Giambi	.989	21	169	8	2	16
Hollins	1.000	5	37	1	0	4
Lee	.996	148	1262	75	6	120
Mabry	1.000	1	6	1	0	0
Perez	1.000	3	10	0	0	1
Pratt	1.000	2	19	1	0	1
Valent	.750	1	3	0	1	2

Second Base	PCT	G	PO	A	E	DP
Anderson	.970	143	272	382	20	90
Perez	.994	50	67	90	1	22
Polanco	.966	6	11	17	1	7
Punto	1.000	1	1	1	0	1
Rollins	.000	1	0	0	0	0

Third Base	PCT	G	PO	A	E	DP
Michaels	.000	1	0	0	2	0
Perez	.909	14	5	25	3	0
Polanco	.983	53	38	133	3	15
Rolen	.973	100	81	206	8	23

Shortstop	PCT	G	PO	A	E	DP
Perez	1.000	13	30	33	0	11
Polanco	1.000	13	19	24	0	7
Punto	.500	1	1	0	1	0
Rollins	.980	152	226	455	14	90

Outfield	PCT	G	PO	A	E	DP
Abreu	.983	154	282	10	5	2
Burrell	.979	157	273	8	6	1
Byrd	1.000	10	17	0	0	0
Giambi	.929	20	26	0	2	0
Glanville	1.000	117	220	7	0	4
Ledee	1.000	51	97	0	0	0
Mabry	1.000	1	1	0	0	0
Michaels	1.000	26	22	2	0	0
Valent	.000	2	0	0	0	0

LARRY GOREN

Vicente Padilla

Brett Myers: 4-5, 4.25 in rookie campaign

Bob Abreu: turned in another solid season (.308-20-85) in Philly

FARM SYSTEM

Director, Minor Leagues: Steve Noworyta

Class	Farm Team	League	W	L	Pct.	Finish*	Manager(s)	First Yr.
AAA	Scranton/W-B (Pa.) Red Barons	International	91	53	.632	1st (14)	Marc Bombard	1989
AA	Reading (Pa.) Phillies	Eastern	76	66	.535	4th (12)	Greg Legg	1967
High A	Clearwater (Fla.) Phillies	Florida State	57	79	.419	11th (12)	John Morris/Roly deArmas	1985
Low A	Lakewood (N.J.) Blue Claws	South Atlantic	69	70	.496	9th (16)	Jeff Manto	2001
SS A	Batavia (N.Y.) Muckdogs	New York-Penn	34	42	.447	8th (14)	Ron Ortegon	1988
Rookie	Clearwater (Fla.) Phillies	Gulf Coast	39	21	.650	+1st (14)	Ruben Amaro Sr.	1999

*Finish in overall standings (No. of teams in league)   +League champion

SCRANTON/WILKES-BARRE RED BARONS

Class AAA

INTERNATIONAL LEAGUE

BATTING	AVG	G	AB	R	H	2B	3B	HR	RBI	BB	SO	SB	CS	SLG	OBP	B	T	HT	WT	DOB	1st Yr	Resides
Aven, Bruce	.244	59	205	26	50	11	0	8	42	36	35	3	1	.415	.375	R	R	5-9	180	3-4-72	1994	Orange, Texas
2-team (35 Buffalo)	.259	94	324	43	84	16	0	13	58	50	56	4	1	.429	.375							
Byrd, Marlon	.297	136	538	103	160	37	7	15	63	46	98	15	1	.476	.362	R	R	6-0	220	8-30-77	1999	Marietta, Ga.
Casillas, Uriel	.429	9	21	4	9	1	0	1	3	2	3	0	0	.619	.478	R	R	5-11	180	8-22-75	1997	Downey, Calif.
Doster, Dave	.295	143	579	91	171	29	10	10	91	39	87	10	3	.432	.342	R	R	5-10	170	10-8-70	1993	New Haven, Ind.
Estrada, Johnny	.279	118	434	49	121	27	0	11	67	26	53	1	0	.417	.322	S	R	5-11	200	6-27-76	1997	Salisbury, N.C.
Forbes, P.J.	.273	91	355	45	97	18	1	1	42	22	47	4	1	.338	.313	R	R	5-10	160	9-22-67	1990	Wichita, Kan.
Francia, Dave	.214	48	117	13	25	7	1	1	10	5	19	4	2	.316	.254	L	L	6-0	160	4-16-75	1996	Mobile, Ala.
Hollins, Dave	.237	14	38	8	9	1	0	2	7	11	9	0	1	.421	.463	S	R	6-1	210	5-25-66	1987	Orchard Park, N.Y.
Knupfer, Jason	.270	77	259	42	70	11	2	0	28	36	64	10	3	.328	.358	R	R	6-0	180	9-21-74	1996	Redwood City, Calif.
Michaels, Jason	.281	9	32	3	9	2	0	0	7	5	5	1	3	.344	.359	R	R	6-0	200	5-4-76	1998	Tampa, Fla.
Punto, Nick	.271	115	443	74	120	12	5	1	29	76	84	42	8	.327	.378	S	R	5-9	170	11-8-77	1998	Mission Viejo, Calif.
Roberge, J.P.	.300	123	420	56	126	29	1	7	52	34	66	6	1	.424	.359	R	R	6-0	180	9-12-72	1994	Arcadia, Calif.
Salazar, Jeremy	.209	42	129	10	27	6	0	0	10	11	34	1	0	.256	.270	R	R	6-0	190	3-18-76	1998	Breaux Bridge, La.
Schall, Gene	.202	28	89	15	18	6	0	2	12	13	23	0	1	.337	.311	R	R	6-3	200	6-5-70	1991	Harleysville, Pa.
Utley, Chase	.263	125	464	73	122	39	1	17	70	46	89	8	3	.461	.352	L	R	6-1	170	12-17-78	2000	Las Vegas, Nev.
Valent, Eric	.251	140	546	69	137	34	2	9	84	49	94	0	2	.370	.311	L	L	6-0	190	4-4-77	1998	Anaheim, Calif.
Woods, Ken	.248	51	161	21	40	5	4	3	21	9	20	4	3	.385	.299	R	R	5-10	170	8-2-70	1992	Los Angeles, Calif.

PITCHING	W	L	ERA	G	GS	CG	SV	IP	H	R	ER	BB	SO	AVG	B	T	HT	WT	DOB	1st Yr	Resides
Cedeno, Blas	0	1	10.80	3	0	0	0	3	6	4	4	1	1	.400	R	R	6-0	160	11-15-72	1991	Campo Carabobo, Venez.
Crowell, Jim	2	0	2.52	4	4	0	0	25	20	7	7	11	19	.227	R	L	6-4	230	5-14-74	1995	Valparaiso, Ind.
D'Amico, Jeff	4	6	4.13	14	14	0	0	72	77	46	33	25	45	.270	R	R	6-3	200	11-9-74	1993	Seattle, Wash.
Geary, Geoff	4	2	3.03	38	8	0	1	101	108	46	34	32	82	.276	R	R	6-0	170	8-26-76	1998	El Cajon, Calif.
Hiles, Cary	4	3	3.81	26	2	0	1	52	51	24	22	21	27	.258	R	R	5-10	170	11-29-75	1998	Memphis, Tenn.
Junge, Eric	12	6	3.54	29	29	1	0	181	170	77	71	67	126	.249	R	R	6-5	210	1-5-77	1999	Rye, N.Y.
McConnell, Sam	3	3	3.53	7	7	0	0	36	41	17	14	16	23	.290	L	L	6-1	210	12-31-75	1997	Fairfield, Ohio
Mercado, Hector	3	1	1.62	26	0	0	3	33	22	6	6	12	43	.186	L	L	6-3	200	4-29-74	1992	Dorado, P.R.
Myers, Brett	9	6	3.59	19	19	4	0	128	121	54	51	20	97	.252	R	R	6-4	210	8-17-80	1999	Jacksonville, Fla.
Nickle, Doug	3	5	2.97	34	1	0	7	61	58	24	20	16	37	.258	R	R	6-4	230	10-2-74	1997	Sonoma, Calif.

PITCHING	W	L	ERA	G	GS	CG	SV	IP	H	R	ER	BB	SO	AVG	B	T	HT	WT	DOB	1st Yr	Resides
Nunez, Franklin	2	1	3.18	4	4	0	0	17	9	6	6	12	16	.157	R	R	6-0	170	1-18-77	1995	Rincon, D.R.
Person, Robert	0	1	4.32	2	2	0	0	8	8	4	4	1	7	.266	R	R	6-0	190	1-8-69	1989	Clearwater, Fla.
Pumphrey, Ken	4	2	4.01	8	8	1	0	52	54	25	23	12	34	.262	R	R	6-0	200	9-10-76	1994	Glen Burnie, Md.
Reith, Brian	0	4	7.00	4	0	0	0	18	26	18	14	11	13	.329	R	R	6-5	220	2-28-78	1996	Ft. Wayne, Ind.
2-team (23 Louisville)	8	13	5.02	27	26	0	0	151	163	94	84	57	112	.275							
Roa, Joe	14	0	1.86	17	17	1	0	111	83	24	23	16	74	.209	R	R	6-1	190	10-11-71	1989	Hazel Park, Mich.
Santiago, Jose	3	2	1.29	22	0	0	7	28	28	6	4	7	21	.264	R	R	6-3	210	11-5-74	1994	Loiza, P.R.
Serrano, Elio	1	3	2.92	43	0	0	5	71	64	28	23	17	45	.240	R	R	6-3	210	12-4-78	1996	Carabobo, Venez.
Smith, Bud	0	1	4.15	3	3	0	0	17	21	8	8	6	11	.313	L	L	6-0	170	10-23-79	1998	Lakewood, Calif.
Telemaco, Amaury	1	0	1.80	1	1	0	0	5	5	3	1	0	3	.263	R	R	6-3	220	1-19-74	1991	La Romana, D.R.
Thomas, Evan	10	2	3.90	22	20	0	0	113	106	53	49	37	75	.251	R	R	5-10	170	6-14-74	1996	Pembroke Pines, Fla.
Wedel, Jeremy	7	1	2.69	43	0	0	1	60	60	24	18	20	34	.262	R	R	6-0	190	11-27-76	1998	Wasco, Calif.
Woodard, Steve	3	1	2.16	15	1	0	0	25	17	6	6	6	13	.191	L	R	6-4	210	5-15-75	1994	Hartselle, Ala.
Zamora, Pete	5	2	3.48	55	0	0	15	62	63	25	24	29	32	.264	L	L	6-3	180	8-13-75	1997	Mission Viejo, Calif.

FIELDING

Catcher	PCT	G	PO	A	E	DP	PB
Estrada	.995	112	745	46	4	5	3
Salazar	.979	35	179	9	4	2	1

First Base	PCT	G	PO	A	E	DP
Casillas	1.000	1	1	0	0	0
Hollins	.990	10	96	6	1	9
Knupfer	.971	7	33	1	1	0
Roberge	.995	106	953	73	5	120
Schall	1.000	7	54	3	0	5
Valent	.977	23	197	11	5	22

Second Base	PCT	G	PO	A	E	DP
Casillas	1.000	3	4	10	0	2

Third Base	PCT	G	PO	A	E	DP
Casillas	1.000	2	1	3	0	1
Forbes	1.000	1	0	4	0	0
Knupfer	.962	19	12	38	2	2
Utley	.918	123	88	224	28	17

Shortstop	PCT	G	PO	A	E	DP
Doster	.975	27	33	84	3	14
Forbes	1.000	5	7	17	0	3
Punto	.967	115	158	401	19	101

	PCT	G	PO	A	E	DP
Doster	.987	81	189	284	6	80
Forbes	.993	32	50	88	1	20
Knupfer	.981	34	51	102	3	21

Outfield	PCT	G	PO	A	E	DP
Aven	1.000	8	12	0	0	0
Byrd	.975	136	298	8	8	1
Doster	.976	38	77	5	2	0
Forbes	.976	50	73	10	2	1
Francia	.984	29	57	3	1	1
Knupfer	1.000	9	17	2	0	1
Michaels	1.000	9	15	1	0	0
Valent	.982	118	260	14	5	4
Woods	.980	47	94	4	2	0

READING PHILLIES — Class AA

EASTERN LEAGUE

BATTING	AVG	G	AB	R	H	2B	3B	HR	RBI	BB	SO	SB	CS	SLG	OBP	B	T	HT	WT	DOB	1st Yr	Resides
Casillas, Uriel	.268	86	231	35	62	9	3	2	29	27	34	4	1	.359	.361	R	R	5-11	180	8-22-75	1997	Downey, Calif.
Chapman, Travis	.301	136	478	64	144	35	1	15	76	54	77	3	1	.473	.388	R	R	6-2	180	6-5-78	2000	Jacksonville, Fla.
Cruz, Edgar	.500	1	4	0	2	0	0	0	0	0	1	0	0	.500	.500	R	R	6-3	190	8-12-78	1997	Juncos, P.R.
Espy, Nate	.267	141	517	83	138	28	2	14	76	73	83	18	1	.410	.363	R	R	6-3	210	4-24-78	1998	Pensacola, Fla.
Gonzalez, Manny	.205	33	83	9	17	3	1	1	6	9	12	0	1	.301	.305	S	R	6-2	190	5-5-76	1994	Santo Domingo, D.R.
Hannahan, Buzz	.230	84	269	47	62	7	2	3	23	42	49	14	4	.305	.348	R	R	6-2	180	6-29-76	1998	St. Paul, Minn.
Hitchcox, Brian	.266	91	297	43	79	18	2	6	27	16	30	4	5	.401	.313	L	R	5-11	170	7-21-78	1999	Dayton, Tenn.
Jacobson, Russ	.195	86	282	20	55	15	0	3	34	18	78	1	0	.280	.263	R	R	6-3	210	10-14-77	1999	Scottsdale, Ariz.
Johnson, Jason	.285	113	411	40	117	16	0	0	45	16	76	19	10	.324	.322	R	R	6-1	170	8-21-77	1996	Collinsville, Va.
Knupfer, Jason	.225	10	40	9	9	2	0	3	4	6	8	4	0	.500	.326	R	R	6-0	185	9-21-74	1998	Redwood City, Calif.
Machado, Anderson	.251	126	450	71	113	24	3	12	77	72	118	40	11	.398	.353	S	R	5-11	160	1-25-81	1998	Caracas, Venez.
McNaughton, Troy	.158	18	57	7	9	2	0	2	7	5	19	0	0	.298	.226	L	L	6-0	190	1-27-75	1998	Tacoma, Wash.
Padilla, Jorge	.256	127	484	71	124	30	2	7	65	40	77	32	11	.370	.322	R	R	6-2	200	8-11-79	1998	Carolina, P.R.
Perez, Josue	.214	64	196	14	42	8	0	1	17	13	41	6	5	.270	.268	S	R	6-0	180	8-12-77	1998	Santo Domingo, D.R.
Perez, Tomas	.444	2	9	2	4	0	0	0	1	0	1	0	0	.444	.444	S	R	5-11	170	12-29-73	1991	Barquisimeto, Venez.
Roberge, J.P.	.182	3	11	2	2	0	0	1	3	0	0	1	0	.455	.250	R	R	6-0	190	9-12-72	1994	Arcadia, Calif.
Sitzman, Jay	.252	108	385	59	97	21	6	9	57	28	82	18	10	.408	.323	L	L	6-3	190	3-13-78	1999	Scottsdale, Ariz.
Van Iten, Bobby	.232	95	314	41	73	12	2	4	32	21	78	5	2	.322	.281	L	R	6-1	180	7-1-77	1996	Independence, Mo.
Woods, Ken	.338	19	80	18	27	7	0	2	8	2	9	3	1	.500	.345	R	R	5-10	170	8-2-70	1992	Los Angeles, Calif.

PITCHING	W	L	ERA	G	GS	CG	SV	IP	H	R	ER	BB	SO	AVG	B	T	HT	WT	DOB	1st Yr	Resides
Adams, Daniel	0	0	4.15	2	0	0	0	4	3	3	2	0	4	.166	R	R	6-0	200	2-21-78	2000	Burlington, Wash.
Bailie, Matt	0	1	2.91	12	3	0	0	22	18	8	7	9	15	.227	R	R	5-10	190	10-1-75	1998	Aloha, Ore.
Baisley, Brad	7	9	4.17	21	21	1	0	117	111	69	54	51	64	.252	R	R	6-9	200	8-24-79	1998	Tampa, Fla.
Brooks, Frank	1	1	3.10	17	1	0	2	29	29	11	10	12	23	.266	L	L	6-1	190	9-6-78	1999	Brooklyn, N.Y.
Buchholz, Taylor	0	2	7.43	4	4	0	0	23	29	19	19	6	17	.315	R	R	6-4	220	10-13-81	2000	Springfield, Pa.
Franco, Martire	4	8	5.76	16	16	2	0	89	109	62	57	25	50	.304	R	R	6-0	170	2-25-78	1998	Bani, D.R.
Hamilton, Jimmy	3	2	2.79	46	0	0	4	71	55	26	22	38	56	.215	R	L	6-3	200	8-1-75	1996	Weyers Cave, Va.
Hiles, Cary	1	5	4.55	21	0	0	7	32	43	20	16	12	23	.330	R	R	5-10	170	11-29-75	1998	Memphis, Tenn.
Kubes, Greg	13	7	3.46	28	27	0	0	174	177	74	67	45	106	.264	R	R	6-6	200	11-10-76	1998	East Bernard, Texas
Lee, Seung	0	1	0.00	1	1	0	0	6	5	2	0	0	6	.217	R	R	6-4	220	6-2-79	2001	Pusan, South Korea
Madson, Ryan	16	4	3.20	26	26	2	0	171	150	68	61	53	132	.242	L	R	6-6	180	8-28-80	1998	Moreno Valley, Calif.
McConnell, Sam	2	4	3.65	29	7	0	3	69	78	31	28	19	43	.289	L	L	6-1	210	12-31-75	1997	Fairfield, Ohio
Outlaw, Mark	6	2	4.44	41	0	0	2	51	45	30	25	34	29	.239	L	L	5-11	180	1-2-77	1999	Waco, Texas
Ozias, Todd	2	1	2.50	31	0	0	2	40	33	12	11	14	40	.224	R	R	6-1	188	8-19-76	1998	Coral Springs, Fla.
Pautz, Brad	4	6	3.06	43	3	0	3	79	70	36	27	26	59	.236	R	R	6-3	190	1-3-77	1999	Reedsville, Wis.
Perez, Frank	3	2	3.72	40	12	0	5	102	98	48	42	36	68	.255	R	R	6-2	170	6-10-78	1998	Bani, D.R.
Pumphrey, Ken	9	7	4.28	20	20	2	0	120	119	65	57	34	63	.262	R	R	6-0	200	9-10-76	1994	Glen Burnie, Md.
Silva, Carlos	0	0	0.00	2	0	0	1	3	0	0	0	0	1	.000	R	R	6-4	220	4-23-79	1998	Bolivar, Venez.
Telemaco, Amaury	0	0	9.00	1	1	0	0	1	1	1	1	0	1	.333	R	R	6-3	220	1-19-74	1991	La Romana, D.R.
Weaver, Eric	5	4	4.20	37	0	0	7	45	38	24	21	26	47	.226	R	R	6-5	230	8-4-73	1991	Springfield, Ill.

FIELDING

Catcher	PCT	G	PO	A	E	DP	PB
Estrada	.995	112	745	46	4	5	3
Salazar	.979	35	179	9	4	2	1

First Base	PCT	G	PO	A	E	DP
Casillas	1.000	1	1	0	0	0
Hollins	.990	10	96	6	1	9

	PCT	G	PO	A	E	DP
Knupfer	.971	7	33	1	1	0
Roberge	.995	106	953	73	5	120
Schall	1.000	7	54	3	0	5
Valent	.977	23	197	11	5	22

Second Base	PCT	G	PO	A	E	DP
Casillas	1.000	3	4	10	0	2

	PCT	G	PO	A	E	DP
Doster	.987	81	189	284	6	80
Forbes	.993	32	50	88	1	20
Knupfer	.981	34	51	102	3	21

Third Base	PCT	G	PO	A	E	DP
Casillas	1.000	2	1	3	0	1
Forbes	1.000	1	0	4	0	0

	PCT	G	PO	A	E	DP	
Knupfer	.962	19	12	38	2	2	
Utley	.918	123	88	224	28	17	
Shortstop	**PCT**	**G**	**PO**	**A**	**E**	**DP**	
Doster	.975	27	33	84	3	14	
Forbes	1.000	5	7	17	0	3	

	PCT	G	PO	A	E	DP
Punto	.967	115	158	401	19	101
Outfield	**PCT**	**G**	**PO**	**A**	**E**	**DP**
Aven	1.000	8	12	0	0	0
Byrd	.975	136	298	8	8	1
Doster	.976	38	77	5	2	0

	PCT	G	PO	A	E	DP
Forbes	.976	50	73	10	2	1
Francia	.984	29	57	3	1	1
Knupfer	1.000	9	17	2	0	1
Michaels	1.000	9	15	1	0	0
Valent	.982	118	260	14	5	4
Woods	.980	47	94	4	2	0

CLEARWATER PHILLIES — High Class A

FLORIDA STATE LEAGUE

BATTING	AVG	G	AB	R	H	2B	3B	HR	RBI	BB	SO	SB	CS	SLG	OBP	B	T	HT	WT	DOB	1st Yr	Resides
Abreu, Nielsen	.000	2	0	0	0	0	0	0	0	0	0	0	0	.000	.000	R	R	5-11	160	4-1-81	1999	Aragua, Venez.
Acevedo, Carlos	.217	32	115	8	25	6	0	0	6	6	19	0	2	.270	.268	R	R	6-0	160	1-31-79	1997	Santo Domingo, D.R.
Avila, Rob	.218	74	238	26	52	11	0	5	26	24	41	4	2	.328	.302	R	R	5-11	200	9-4-78	1999	Fresno, Calif.
Bennett, Kris	.218	30	110	13	24	3	0	0	10	10	11	5	1	.245	.295	R	R	5-10	180	10-23-78	2001	Huntingdon, Tenn.
Bush, Brian	.260	51	192	20	50	10	1	3	21	11	23	3	6	.370	.298	R	R	6-1	180	1-3-77	1999	Warren, Ohio
Carroll, Wes	.209	12	43	5	9	2	0	0	1	2	9	0	0	.256	.244	R	R	5-11	180	1-5-79	2001	Evansville, Ind.
Cruz, Edgar	.214	73	243	26	52	11	0	7	17	18	58	0	0	.346	.271	R	R	6-3	190	8-12-78	1997	Juncos, P.R.
Delgado, Mario	.203	51	187	16	38	9	0	4	14	7	47	0	0	.316	.239	L	L	6-0	220	8-5-79	2001	San Diego, Calif.
Dominique, Andy	.412	8	34	5	14	5	0	0	2	1	4	0	0	.559	.444	R	R	6-0	220	10-30-75	1997	Granada Hills, Calif.
Farnsworth, Troy	.232	97	358	35	83	18	2	12	50	28	85	1	0	.394	.294	R	R	6-2	200	2-4-76	1998	West Valley City, Utah
Giron, Alejandro	.225	41	142	11	32	1	2	2	15	10	24	2	1	.303	.277	R	R	6-2	180	4-21-79	1996	Santo Domingo, D.R.
Gomez, Ramon	.147	22	68	6	10	3	1	0	2	7	26	3	2	.221	.227	R	R	6-2	170	5-15-74	1994	San Pedro de Macoris, D.R.
Gonzalez, Manny	.229	76	280	20	64	15	2	1	24	21	48	1	5	.307	.288	S	R	6-2	190	5-5-76	1994	Santo Domingo, D.R.
Hensley, Anthony	.237	119	384	56	91	18	8	2	24	66	81	13	7	.341	.349	S	R	5-10	180	12-10-77	2000	College Station, Texas
Hitchcox, Brian	.248	32	121	17	30	4	0	1	12	12	17	4	3	.306	.324	L	L	5-11	170	7-21-78	1999	Dayton, Tenn.
McNaughton, Troy	.340	87	324	50	110	20	6	13	45	39	74	2	1	.559	.418	L	L	6-0	190	1-27-75	1998	Tacoma, Wash.
McRoberts, Mark	.000	1	2	0	0	0	0	0	0	0	1	0	0	.000	.000	R	R	6-2	190	1-15-82	2000	El Cajon, Calif.
Montas, Ricardo	.191	16	47	6	9	1	0	1	5	7	5	2	0	.277	.296	R	R	6-1	170	3-9-77	1994	Marietta, Ga.
Nunez, Alexis	.160	10	25	3	4	2	0	0	1	4	6	0	2	.240	.300	L	R	5-11	170	4-30-80	1999	Valencia, Venez.
Perry, Rod	.125	7	24	3	3	0	0	0	1	1	4	0	0	.125	.160	R	R	5-10	190	2-1-79	2001	Carlsbad, Calif.
Reyes, Ambiorix	.160	47	131	11	21	3	0	0	4	5	21	3	2	.183	.190	S	R	5-11	160	2-6-78	1996	La Vega, D.R.
Richardson, Juan	.257	122	456	52	117	21	2	18	83	44	122	0	6	.430	.339	R	R	6-1	170	1-27-79	1998	Bani, D.R.
Rivera, Eric	.125	4	16	1	2	1	0	0	1	1	2	0	0	.188	.176	R	R	6-2	200	5-22-81	1999	Utuado, P.R.
Ruiz, Carlos	.213	92	342	35	73	18	3	5	32	18	30	3	1	.327	.264	R	R	5-10	180	1-22-79	1999	Chiriqui, Panama
Sosa, Juan	.262	54	210	17	55	9	2	0	16	11	28	9	2	.324	.304	R	R	6-1	170	8-19-75	1993	San Francisco de Macoris, D.R.
Youngbauer, Scott	.236	106	406	60	96	25	7	9	47	38	78	3	4	.399	.302	S	R	6-1	170	1-14-79	2000	Powder Springs, Ga.

PITCHING	W	L	ERA	G	GS	CG	SV	IP	H	R	ER	BB	SO	AVG	B	T	HT	WT	DOB	1st Yr	Resides
Adams, Daniel	3	6	4.31	35	1	0	4	63	55	31	30	19	29	.237	R	R	6-0	200	2-21-78	2000	Burlington, Wash.
Brito, Eude	3	5	5.71	20	0	0	0	35	40	22	22	14	27	.291	L	L	6-0	160	8-19-78	1998	Sabana de la Mar, D.R.
Brooks, Frank	3	5	3.46	35	0	0	7	39	34	18	15	27	33	.232	L	L	6-1	190	9-6-78	1999	Brooklyn, N.Y.
Buchholz, Taylor	10	6	3.29	23	23	4	0	159	140	66	58	51	129	.232	R	R	6-4	220	10-13-81	2000	Springfield, Pa.
Bucktrot, Keith	8	9	4.88	27	24	2	0	160	167	101	87	78	84	.276	R	R	6-3	190	11-27-80	2000	Claremore, Okla.
Carter, Ryan	9	9	4.34	25	24	1	0	135	129	74	65	68	101	.252	L	L	6-7	240	8-1-79	2000	Riverbank, Calif.
Cedeno, Jesus	0	0	0.00	3	0	0	0	4	2	0	0	1	3	.181	R	R	6-0	160	11-15-72	1991	Campo Carabobo, Venez.
Cordero, Jesus	0	3	6.43	8	2	0	0	21	29	16	15	12	16	.333	R	R	6-1	170	5-25-78	2000	San Pedro de Macoris, D.R.
Dagley, Corey	0	2	6.60	15	2	0	0	30	46	33	22	4	7	.340	R	R	6-2	180	4-15-77	1998	Centralia, Ill.
Elskamp, Andy	3	0	4.47	26	0	0	0	44	44	26	22	21	35	.251	R	R	5-11	190	8-11-78	2000	Potosi, Wis.
Hernandez, Yoel	7	16	3.54	28	28	3	0	170	176	76	67	54	116	.271	R	R	6-1	170	4-15-82	1999	Ciudad Bolivar, Venez.
Hutchison, Ryan	1	2	3.51	29	0	0	0	51	56	26	20	20	37	.282	R	R	6-0	200	8-9-78	2001	Vincennes, Ind.
Lee, Seung	2	0	0.00	3	3	1	0	19	6	1	0	2	16	.095	R	R	6-4	220	6-27-79	2001	Pusan, South Korea
Mayfield, Brandon	0	0	3.07	7	0	0	1	15	14	9	5	1	12	.237	R	R	6-7	220	10-17-78	2000	Birmingham, Ala.
Miller, Josh	3	2	2.42	49	0	0	17	71	78	26	19	11	39	.277	R	R	6-1	200	2-7-79	2001	Melbourne, Fla.
Sadowski, Chad	0	0	0.00	2	0	0	0	2	1	0	0	0	0	.142	R	R	6-3	220	12-8-77	2000	West Allis, Wis.
Tejeda, Rob	4	8	3.97	17	17	1	0	100	73	48	44	48	87	.204	R	R	6-3	180	3-24-82	1999	Bani, D.R.
Telemaco, Amaury	0	1	1.50	3	3	0	0	12	15	5	2	3	10	.300	R	R	6-3	220	1-19-74	1991	La Romana, D.R.
Wilson, Mike	1	7	4.28	12	8	0	1	55	51	27	26	29	44	.251	R	R	6-6	220	6-12-80	1998	Las Vegas, Nev.
Wolf, Randy	0	0	0.00	1	1	0	0	5	1	0	0	1	8	.071	L	L	6-0	190	8-22-76	1997	West Hills, Calif.

FIELDING

Catcher	PCT	G	PO	A	E	DP	PB
Avila	1.000	18	118	9	0	1	4
Cruz	.987	61	396	43	6	3	4
McRoberts	1.000	1	0	1	0	0	0
Ruiz	.988	60	363	39	5	6	6

First Base	PCT	G	PO	A	E	DP
Avila	.994	21	155	15	1	14
Delgado	.986	45	397	22	6	41
Dominique	1.000	5	34	2	0	4
Farnsworth	.994	70	579	42	4	43

Second Base	PCT	G	PO	A	E	DP
Bennett	.955	4	6	15	1	1
Carroll	.889	11	15	25	5	6
Hitchcox	.969	29	58	97	5	23
Montas	.962	11	20	30	2	5

	PCT	G	PO	A	E	DP
Nunez	.941	9	19	13	2	6
Reyes	.965	15	30	52	3	8
Youngbauer	.953	61	109	196	15	34

Third Base	PCT	G	PO	A	E	DP
Bennett	.952	16	11	29	2	1
Farnsworth	.979	17	18	28	1	7
Montas	1.000	1	0	1	0	0
Reyes	.000	3	0	0	0	0
Richardson	.924	103	74	182	21	25

Shortstop	PCT	G	PO	A	E	DP
Bennett	.930	10	15	25	3	5
Carroll	1.000	1	1	1	0	0
Hitchcox	.714	2	4	1	2	0
Montas	.833	2	1	4	1	1
Reyes	.936	27	49	68	8	18

	PCT	G	PO	A	E	DP
Sosa	.963	54	96	163	10	25
Youngbauer	.901	44	64	118	20	23
Outfield	**PCT**	**G**	**PO**	**A**	**E**	**DP**
Acevedo	.969	29	58	4	2	1
Avila	.978	20	41	3	1	2
Bush	.975	49	115	3	3	1
Dominique	.000	1	0	0	0	0
Giron	1.000	33	52	2	0	0
Gomez	.938	15	29	1	2	0
Gonzalez	.964	62	129	5	5	1
Hensley	.992	116	255	7	2	1
McNaughton	.978	82	169	6	4	3
Perry	1.000	7	8	0	0	0
Rivera	1.000	2	3	0	0	0

LAKEWOOD BLUE CLAWS — Low Class A

SOUTH ATLANTIC LEAGUE

BATTING	AVG	G	AB	R	H	2B	3B	HR	RBI	BB	SO	SB	CS	SLG	OBP	B	T	HT	WT	DOB	1st Yr	Resides
Abreu, Nielsen	.000	2	1	1	0	0	0	0	0	0	0	0	0	.000	.000	R	R	5-11	160	4-1-81	1999	Aragua, Venez.
Bennett, Kris	.280	45	150	18	42	4	4	2	16	15	15	5	3	.400	.351	R	R	5-10	180	10-3-78	2001	Huntingdon, Tenn.

ORGANIZATION STATISTICS

BATTING	AVG	G	AB	R	H	2B	3B	HR	RBI	BB	SO	SB	CS	SLG	OBP	B	T	HT	WT	DOB	1st Yr	Resides
Cancio, Tony	.176	57	187	19	33	8	0	2	15	16	63	2	0	.251	.249	R	R	6-3	220	12-20-81	2000	Tampa, Fla.
Carroll, Wes	.228	81	294	33	67	16	0	1	29	16	36	8	1	.293	.274	R	R	5-11	180	1-5-79	2001	Evansville, Ind.
Delgado, Mario	.234	37	128	16	30	6	1	2	13	7	35	0	0	.344	.274	L	L	6-0	220	8-5-79	2001	San Diego, Calif.
Floyd, Mike	.246	69	248	29	61	11	3	1	19	23	59	13	5	.327	.320	R	R	6-0	200	1-15-80	2001	Severna Park, Md.
Foster, Gregg	.182	52	148	24	27	6	0	2	8	16	36	6	6	.264	.293	R	R	6-0	200	10-3-78	2000	Commack, N.Y.
Gonzalez, Daniel	.270	131	493	58	133	14	4	4	43	55	88	11	21	.339	.349	S	R	6-0	180	11-20-81	2001	Trujillo Alto, P.R.
Howard, Ryan	.280	135	493	56	138	20	6	19	87	66	145	5	4	.460	.367	L	L	6-4	230	11-19-79	2001	Wildwood, Mo.
Manfred, Brian	.053	8	19	1	1	0	0	0	0	2	6	0	0	.053	.182	R	R	6-2	210	4-11-79	2002	Newark, Calif.
Margalski, Ben	.211	79	266	25	56	11	2	3	27	23	65	6	4	.301	.282	L	R	6-2	210	9-2-79	2001	High Ridge, Mo.
Marshall, Andre	.226	56	186	30	42	8	0	1	10	23	72	13	5	.285	.318	S	R	6-5	200	10-2-80	2001	Oak Harbor, Wash.
Nunez, Alexis	.200	6	15	0	3	0	0	0	0	0	2	0	0	.200	.200	L	R	5-11	170	4-30-81	1999	Valencia, Venez.
Oliva, Chad	.260	31	96	8	25	4	0	2	10	12	22	2	2	.365	.349	R	R	5-11	210	8-27-80	2002	Riviera Beach, Fla.
Perry, Rod	.240	108	408	57	98	20	2	2	30	39	61	25	18	.314	.309	R	R	5-10	190	2-1-79	2001	Carlsbad, Calif.
Phelps, Jeff	.281	112	405	45	114	31	4	7	59	27	95	10	4	.430	.333	R	R	6-0	190	11-20-78	2001	Yuma, Ariz.
Rivera, Eric	.206	62	218	24	45	6	0	2	27	17	57	3	7	.261	.276	R	R	6-2	200	5-22-81	1999	Utuado, P.R.
Silvera, Andres	.200	21	55	5	11	2	1	2	8	5	11	0	1	.382	.267	R	R	6-0	170	7-23-81	1999	Caracas, Venez.
Tosca, Daniel	.239	71	234	26	56	19	2	5	29	19	56	2	2	.402	.304	L	R	6-0	180	11-1-80	1999	Seffner, Fla.
Vukovich, Vince	.245	59	184	20	45	11	1	0	9	21	34	5	5	.315	.327	L	R	6-0	170	5-6-80	2001	Voorhees, N.J.
Walsh, Sean	.259	90	274	34	71	9	1	1	28	31	58	26	4	.310	.358	L	R	6-4	220	11-15-79	2001	Aiken, S.C.
Youngbauer, Scott	.295	17	61	9	18	6	2	3	10	7	10	0	2	.607	.377	S	R	6-1	170	1-14-79	2000	Powder Springs, Ga.

PITCHING	W	L	ERA	G	GS	CG	SV	IP	H	R	ER	BB	SO	AVG	B	T	HT	WT	DOB	1st Yr	Resides
Astacio, Ezequiel	10	7	3.31	25	25	1	0	152	159	61	56	46	100	.275	R	R	6-3	150	11-4-79	1998	Hato Mayor, D.R.
Bernard, Jason	1	0	4.87	11	0	0	0	20	21	17	11	13	13	.265	R	R	6-5	220	8-14-78	2001	Panama City, Fla.
Brito, Eude	1	1	2.55	11	0	0	1	18	14	5	5	6	11	.225	L	L	6-0	160	8-19-78	1998	Sabana de la Mar, D.R.
Cable, Taft	11	10	3.76	27	27	5	0	177	174	84	74	24	115	.252	R	R	6-2	210	7-25-80	2001	Browns Summit, N.C.
Cordero, Jesus	0	0	3.00	6	0	0	0	6	5	2	2	3	1	.227	R	R	6-1	170	5-5-79	1998	San Pedro de Macoris, D.R.
Dagley, Corey	0	1	10.13	4	0	0	0	5	13	6	6	2	2	.500	R	R	6-4	180	4-15-77	1998	Centralia, Ill.
Davis, Tim	0	0	1.88	11	0	0	2	14	7	5	3	7	8	.140	L	L	6-4	230	4-8-79	2001	Lucedale, Miss.
Dawson, Layne	7	4	2.76	27	8	3	5	117	103	41	36	21	89	.235	R	R	6-2	180	9-13-79	2001	Somerville, Tenn.
DeChristofaro, Vinny	3	10	4.92	22	22	1	0	130	155	88	71	37	62	.295	L	L	6-2	160	4-2-82	2001	Richmond Hill, Ga.
Floyd, Gavin	11	10	2.77	27	27	3	0	166	119	59	51	64	140	.200	R	R	6-5	210	1-27-83	2001	Severna Park, Md.
Kim, Il	2	1	4.14	21	0	0	0	37	37	20	17	21	27	.255	R	R	6-3	220	2-15-80	2001	Taegu, Korea
Korecky, Bobby	2	2	3.00	8	4	2	1	27	25	10	9	3	15	.245	R	R	5-11	180	9-16-79	2002	Monmouth Junction, N.J.
Lee, Seung	7	10	3.24	23	22	5	1	147	132	64	53	46	112	.243	R	R	6-4	220	6-2-79	2001	Pusan, South Korea
Mayfield, Brandon	4	1	2.22	21	0	0	5	45	44	13	11	13	23	.258	R	R	6-7	220	10-17-78	2000	Birmingham, Ala.
Minor, Zach	0	1	7.36	4	0	0	0	4	5	3	3	1	1	.333	R	R	6-6	210	8-4-79	2002	Walnut Creek, Calif.
Moreno, Victor	1	0	0.00	7	0	0	1	10	5	0	0	4	13	.156	R	R	6-0	190	6-10-79	1997	Puerto Cabello, Venez.
Scott, Josh	0	1	7.71	3	0	0	0	5	7	5	4	5	2	.388	L	L	6-3	190	10-24-79	2001	Downey, Calif.
Silverio, Carlos	4	5	3.26	21	3	0	1	61	49	23	22	28	62	.228	R	R	6-2	180	4-1-79	1997	Puerto Plata, D.R.
Squires, Matt	5	6	3.82	36	1	0	8	66	62	34	28	40	71	.256	L	L	5-10	200	1-24-79	2001	Lewiston, Idaho
Wilson, Mike	0	0	0.00	5	0	0	3	8	3	0	0	0	7	.107	R	R	6-6	220	6-12-80	1998	Las Vegas, Nev.

FIELDING

Catcher	PCT	G	PO	A	E	DP	PB
Manfred	.957	6	40	5	2	0	1
Margalski	.988	72	444	58	6	2	15
Tosca	.983	65	418	37	8	2	7
Walsh	1.000	2	1	0	0	0	0

First Base	PCT	G	PO	A	E	DP
Cancio	1.000	14	109	4	0	8
Delgado	1.000	7	55	1	0	8
Howard	.985	118	1064	64	17	97
Walsh	1.000	7	26	4	0	2

Second Base	PCT	G	PO	A	E	DP
Abreu	.000	2	0	0	0	0

	PCT	G	PO	A	E	DP
Bennett	.980	35	60	85	3	23
Carroll	.976	74	130	201	8	37
Nunez	.941	5	5	11	1	3
Silvera	.975	21	31	46	2	15
Youngbauer	.937	15	28	46	5	3

Third Base	PCT	G	PO	A	E	DP
Bennett	1.000	3	1	0	0	0
Carroll	.000	1	0	0	0	0
Phelps	.923	93	60	192	21	11
Walsh	.922	49	31	88	10	5

Shortstop	PCT	G	PO	A	E	DP
Bennett	1.000	9	6	19	0	0

	PCT	G	PO	A	E	DP
Carroll	.935	10	4	25	2	3
Gonzalez	.962	128	213	387	24	88

Outfield	PCT	G	PO	A	E	DP
Delgado	.000	1	0	0	0	0
Floyd	.954	69	159	7	8	1
Foster	.975	42	76	2	2	0
Marshall	.993	55	133	4	1	0
Oliva	.909	25	48	2	5	0
Perry	.969	108	209	11	7	0
Rivera	.982	61	106	4	2	0
Vukovich	.975	57	112	3	3	0
Walsh	1.000	11	16	1	0	0

BATAVIA MUCKDOGS — Short-Season A

NEW YORK-PENN LEAGUE

BATTING	AVG	G	AB	R	H	2B	3B	HR	RBI	BB	SO	SB	CS	SLG	OBP	B	T	HT	WT	DOB	1st Yr	Resides
Abreu, Nielsen	.257	41	140	16	36	4	0	0	10	13	16	14	8	.286	.327	R	R	5-11	160	4-1-81	1999	Aragua, Venez.
Barthelemy, Ryan	.258	68	260	27	67	13	3	2	32	19	56	5	2	.354	.308	L	R	6-3	220	5-19-80	2002	Miami, Fla.
Cafiero, Rob	.222	60	225	22	50	6	0	6	35	16	59	0	2	.329	.273	R	R	6-4	230	5-1-80	2002	Massapequa Park, N.Y.
Dancy, Cliff	.200	47	155	12	31	2	2	1	3	7	45	10	2	.258	.242	R	R	6-1	180	2-7-80	2001	Casselberry, Fla.
Isenhower, Jeremy	.400	3	10	1	4	0	1	0	3	0	0	1	0	.600	.385	L	R	5-11	180	4-12-80	2002	Osawatomie, Kan.
Jones, Terry	.223	43	157	13	35	8	4	1	16	12	40	5	1	.344	.297	R	R	6-2	190	3-20-83	2001	Upland, Calif.
Manfred, Brian	.189	22	74	8	14	3	1	2	8	10	17	0	0	.338	.302	R	R	6-2	210	4-11-79	2002	Newark, Calif.
Marshall, Andre	.224	46	143	13	32	4	1	0	12	24	42	6	2	.266	.331	S	R	6-5	200	10-2-80	2001	Oak Harbor, Wash.
McRoberts, Mark	.295	46	166	27	49	12	2	4	17	21	40	6	1	.464	.383	R	R	6-2	190	1-15-82	2000	El Cajon, Calif.
Menocal, Victor	.100	22	10	2	1	0	0	0	1	1	3	0	0	.100	.182	R	R	6-4	210	8-7-79	2002	Gainesville, Ga.
Nunez, Alexis	.255	15	47	9	12	3	0	1	6	11	8	3	0	.383	.410	L	R	5-11	170	4-30-81	1999	Valencia, Venez.
Pratt, Trent	.237	39	118	10	28	7	0	0	12	19	33	0	1	.297	.352	R	R	6-2	210	8-25-79	2002	Tooele, Utah
Rivera, Eric	.249	49	181	19	45	11	1	2	19	13	40	10	4	.354	.312	R	R	6-2	200	5-22-81	1999	Utuado, P.R.
Rivero, Luis	.160	34	100	10	16	1	2	1	12	8	29	3	2	.240	.222	R	R	6-1	170	10-10-80	1998	Manicuare, Venez.
Roberson, Chris	.276	62	214	29	59	8	3	2	24	26	51	17	8	.369	.377	R	R	6-2	170	8-23-79	2001	San Pablo, Calif.
Rodriguez, Carlos	.290	61	248	29	72	7	3	0	15	19	48	21	11	.343	.351	S	R	6-0	170	10-4-83	2001	Santo Domingo, D.R.
Sato, G.G.	.306	20	72	16	22	5	0	3	8	8	25	2	1	.500	.381	R	R	6-2	220	8-9-78	2001	Chibu, Japan
Silvera, Andres	.230	31	113	13	26	6	1	4	12	12	40	10	5	.407	.318	R	R	6-0	170	7-23-81	1999	Caracas, Venez.
Wardinsky, Ryan	.262	26	84	8	22	2	0	1	7	8	24	2	2	.321	.347	S	R	6-1	180	11-28-79	2002	Kalispell, Mont.
Winegarden, Erik	.282	10	39	6	11	3	0	0	5	6	6	0	0	.359	.383	L	R	6-1	200	12-5-79	2002	Eden Prairie, Minn.

GAMES BY POSITION: C—Manfred 18, McRoberts 22, Pratt 34, Winegarden 7. 1B—Barthelemy 36, Cafiero 48, Rivero 1, Winegarden 1. 2B—Abreu 21, Isenhower 3, Nunez 14, Rodriguez 1, Silvera 28, Wardinsky 14. 3B—Abreu 3, Barthelemy 26, Jones 43, Menocal 3, Wardinsky 8. SS—Abreu 12, Menocal 1, Rodriguez 61, Wardinsky 6. OF—Dancy 42, Marshall 46, McRoberts 13, Rivera 48, Rivero 28, Roberson 60.

PITCHING	W	L	ERA	G	GS	CG	SV	IP	H	R	ER	BB	SO	AVG	B	T	HT	WT	DOB	1st Yr	Resides
Arteaga, Erick	3	1	2.79	12	12	0	0	81	61	27	25	21	44	.211	R	R	6-7	170	4-2-81	1999	Yaracuy, Venez.
Bourgeois, Nick	0	3	5.40	6	5	0	0	18	13	14	11	16	17	.200	L	L	6-4	200	10-26-80	2002	Lake Charles, La.
Brewster, Derek	0	0	0.00	4	0	0	1	7	1	0	0	1	3	.043	R	R	5-11	220	12-8-82	2002	Carthage, Texas
Bryant, Whit	1	5	5.40	16	6	0	1	43	43	29	26	40	36	.279	L	L	6-2	180	3-30-80	2002	Greenville, N.C.
Busbin, Brad	2	2	1.80	11	0	0	0	20	14	6	4	4	12	.189	R	R	6-3	210	8-29-80	2002	Orlando, Fla.
Cabrera, Carlos	9	2	3.59	15	14	0	0	90	79	44	36	46	77	.237	R	R	6-4	170	2-19-83	1999	Santiago, D.R.
Gwaltney, Lee	0	2	3.60	7	7	0	0	25	26	12	10	6	18	.276	R	R	6-5	210	5-6-80	2002	Willow Park, Texas
Harrand, Rob	1	5	4.17	8	8	0	0	41	44	20	19	13	25	.269	R	R	6-5	200	1-11-80	2002	Regina, Sask.
Korecky, Bobby	2	2	2.31	7	5	0	0	35	30	12	9	6	25	.241	R	R	5-11	180	9-16-79	2002	Monmouth Junction, N.J.
Menocal, Victor	2	1	3.45	19	0	0	2	31	36	13	12	13	16	.000	R	R	6-4	210	8-7-79	2002	Gainesville, Ga.
Minor, Zach	2	2	3.99	18	0	0	0	38	36	21	17	19	30	.255	R	R	6-6	210	8-4-79	2002	Walnut Creek, Calif.
Moreno, Victor	3	3	3.71	17	0	0	5	27	19	14	11	21	34	.197	R	R	6-0	190	6-10-79	1997	Puerto Cabello, Venez.
Naatjes, Darin	0	0	0.00	2	0	0	0	4	3	0	0	1	7	.200	L	R	6-9	240	7-27-80	2002	Sioux Falls, S.D.
Paddock, Josh	1	1	3.27	13	0	0	0	22	28	14	8	3	12	.307	R	R	6-2	190	10-15-80	2002	Covington, Ind.
Read, Robby	3	5	2.82	13	13	1	0	67	58	26	21	32	43	.241	R	R	6-1	190	7-12-81	2002	Tallahassee, Fla.
Reyes, Maximo	0	1	4.70	4	0	0	0	8	11	4	4	0	5	.333	R	R	5-9	170	9-24-81	2001	San Luis, Mexico
Richardson, Beau	5	4	3.54	16	6	0	1	61	68	29	24	18	35	.296	L	L	6-4	190	9-23-79	2002	San Francisco, Calif.
Rogelstad, Jeremy	0	3	3.77	24	0	0	2	45	39	19	19	15	30	.233	R	R	6-6	190	11-29-78	2002	Benicia, Calif.
Steen, Adam	0	0	2.45	12	0	0	0	22	19	6	6	5	15	.226	R	R	6-4	200	6-19-80	2002	Mankato, Minn.

CLEARWATER PHILLIES — Rookie

GULF COAST LEAGUE

BATTING	AVG	G	AB	R	H	2B	3B	HR	RBI	BB	SO	SB	CS	SLG	OBP	B	T	HT	WT	DOB	1st Yr	Resides
Blalock, Jake	.250	25	88	13	22	6	0	1	13	10	15	3	0	.352	.317	R	R	6-4	200	8-6-83	2002	San Diego, Calif.
Bramasco, Omar	.209	46	129	25	27	3	0	3	13	21	43	2	2	.302	.331	R	R	6-0	180	10-28-81	2002	Huntington Park, Calif.
Brito, Henry	.258	50	190	26	49	8	1	2	27	24	34	5	5	.342	.350	R	R	6-2	170	4-21-82	1999	Maiquetia Vargas, Venez.
Delos Santos, Esteban	.222	50	167	24	37	6	3	5	29	15	50	6	6	.383	.302	S	R	6-1	160	12-26-82	1999	Santo Domingo, D.R.
Diaz, Jeury	.328	21	61	12	20	5	0	0	5	9	11	4	0	.410	.414	S	R	6-1	170	2-16-81	1999	Bonao, D.R.
Fisher, Kiel	.229	35	105	9	24	4	1	3	20	13	34	1	2	.371	.322	L	R	6-4	190	9-29-83	2002	Riverside, Calif.
Gillies, Mike	.230	43	152	24	35	7	0	4	14	12	16	3	2	.355	.280	R	R	6-2	210	11-24-78	2002	Port Moody, B.C.
Gradoville, Tim	.267	37	101	16	27	6	0	0	4	8	19	14	2	.327	.327	R	R	6-3	190	1-30-80	2002	Aurora, Colo.
Hansen, Bryan	.306	54	180	21	55	16	4	1	28	14	26	3	3	.456	.362	L	L	6-2	190	5-8-83	2001	Coram, N.Y.
Isenhower, Jeremy	.308	27	91	16	28	8	1	1	10	10	21	6	3	.429	.385	L	R	5-11	180	4-12-80	2002	Osawatomie, Kan.
Moni-Erigbali, Timi	.098	18	41	4	4	0	0	0	3	1	25	1	0	.098	.140	R	R	6-1	205	6-11-82	2002	Irvington, N.J.
Nonemaker, Karl	.308	59	221	32	68	14	1	1	28	20	20	13	5	.394	.365	L	L	6-0	190	1-7-80	2002	Flanders, N.J.
Nunez, Alexis	.224	14	49	4	11	4	0	0	7	5	5	3	0	.306	.298	L	R	5-11	170	4-30-81	1999	Valencia, Venez.
Oliva, Chad	.211	28	90	10	19	1	1	1	8	12	21	4	1	.278	.301	R	R	5-11	210	8-27-80	2002	Riviera Beach, Fla.
Rivero, Luis	.333	4	6	1	2	0	0	1	3	1	0	0	0	.333	.556	R	R	6-1	170	10-10-80	1998	Manicuare, Venez.
Sato, G.G.	.267	17	60	5	16	4	1	0	1	7	10	4	1	.367	.343	R	R	6-2	220	8-9-78	2001	Chibu, Japan
Wardinsky, Ryan	.220	22	59	8	13	1	0	0	8	10	10	3	3	.237	.351	S	R	6-1	180	11-28-79	2002	Kalispell, Mont.
Winegarden, Erik	.211	32	90	14	19	6	1	2	16	17	19	5	0	.367	.333	L	R	6-1	200	12-5-79	2002	Eden Prairie, Minn.

GAMES BY POSITION: C—Diaz 20, Gradoville 33, Winegarden 13. 1B—Gillies 18, Hansen 42, Winegarden 6. 2B—Bramasco 29, De los Santos 1, Isenhower 18, Nunez 11, Wardinsky 8. 3B—Blalock 8, Bramasco 4, De los Santos 1, Fisher 33, Gillies 11, Wardinsky 10. SS—Bramasco 15, De los Santos 46, Wardinsky 5. OF—Blalock 15, Bramasco 1, Brito 55, Gillies 7, Gradoville 1, Isenhower 9, Moni-Erigbali 16, Nonemaker 58, Nunez 2, Oliva 25, Rivero 4.

PITCHING	W	L	ERA	G	GS	CG	SV	IP	H	R	ER	BB	SO	AVG	B	T	HT	WT	DOB	1st Yr	Resides
Butto, Francisco	7	2	2.31	12	9	3	1	62	37	18	16	20	52	.176	R	R	6-1	170	5-11-82	1999	Maturin, Venez.
De la Cruz, Julio	3	0	3.56	7	5	0	0	30	28	12	12	12	25	.250	R	R	6-1	160	10-7-80	2001	Cotui, D.R.
De la Cruz, Maximo	1	0	1.17	2	1	0	0	8	4	1	1	2	5	.160	R	R	6-1	160	5-29-85	2002	Santo Domingo, D.R.
Denison, Brandon	0	2	5.53	12	1	0	0	28	38	21	17	7	14	.308	L	R	6-3	210	12-2-80	2002	Paris, Texas
Dorsey, Brian	3	2	2.57	16	2	0	0	35	31	19	10	16	35	.242	R	R	6-0	180	4-5-80	2002	Smithtown, N.Y.
Machi, Jean	2	0	1.00	10	2	0	1	27	11	4	3	16	22	.129	R	R	6-0	160	2-1-83	2001	Guarico, Venez.
Mathieson, Scott	0	2	5.40	7	2	0	0	17	24	11	10	6	14	.338	R	R	6-3	190	2-27-84	2002	Aldergrove, B.C.
Nunez, Franklin	0	0	0.00	1	1	0	0	2	2	0	0	1	4	.250	R	R	6-0	170	1-18-77	1995	Rincon, D.R.
Paddock, Josh	2	1	2.16	6	2	0	0	25	16	7	6	5	13	.190	R	R	6-2	200	10-15-80	2002	Covington, Ind.
Ramirez, Elizardo	7	1	1.10	11	11	2	0	73	44	18	9	2	73	.165	R	R	6-0	140	1-28-83	1999	Santo Domingo, D.R.
Reyes, Maximo	2	0	0.35	22	0	0	12	26	12	2	1	3	29	.134	R	R	5-9	170	9-24-81	2001	San Luis, Mexico
Rupert, Chris	1	3	1.80	18	0	0	4	30	19	6	6	4	21	.186	S	L	6-0	180	6-19-80	2002	Bozeman, Mont.
Sanchez, Emilio	2	0	2.63	3	2	0	0	14	10	4	4	3	15	.200	R	R	6-3	180	7-20-80	1999	Puerto Plata, D.R.
Segovia, Zach	3	2	2.10	8	8	0	0	34	21	11	8	3	30	.173	R	R	6-1	220	4-11-83	2002	Forney, Texas
Steen, Adam	1	1	6.75	7	0	0	0	16	23	14	12	10	10	.333	R	R	6-4	200	6-19-80	2002	Mankato, Minn.
Sweeney, Matt	4	5	2.69	12	12	2	0	67	56	23	20	27	38	.232	R	R	6-2	180	2-25-83	2001	Yardville, N.J.
Telemaco, Amaury	1	0	1.64	2	2	0	0	11	4	2	2	2	5	.105	R	R	6-3	220	1-19-74	1991	La Romana, D.R.

ORGANIZATION STATISTICS

PITTSBURGH PIRATES

BY JOHN PERROTTO

The Pirates set a club record with their 10th straight losing season in 2002. However, Pittsburgh could take solace in the fact that it wasn't a laughingstock like in 2001.

After going 62-100 in 2001, the franchise's first season at PNC Park, the Pirates finished 72-89 in 2002 for a 10½-game improvement. While they didn't come close to challenging the Cardinals for the National League Central title, they did finish fourth in the division ahead of the Cubs and Brewers.

"Obviously, the record isn't what we want it to be, and we're not going to be satisfied with a fourth-place finish," said Pirates general manager Dave Littlefield, who replaced Cam Bonifay midway through the 2001 season. "The goal every year is to win the World Series. However, it takes time to reach that kind of goal when you come from where we are coming from.

"On the whole, I think this has been a good season because we showed improvement. We weren't a championship club or a contender, but we did take a good first step in getting things turned around."

The biggest area of improvement for the Pirates was in their pitching. They finished 10th in the NL with a 4.23 ERA after being 15th in 2001 with a 5.05 mark.

The Pirates went into spring training with 11 pitchers competing for five open rotation spots and their best hope for a No. 1 starter, Kris Benson, still recovering from reconstructive surgery. They headed home for the winter believing they had three quality young pitchers to build a rotation around.

Benson bounced back after going 0-4, 7.79 in his first eight starts to finish 9-6, 4.70 in 25 starts. Righthanders Kip Wells (12-14, 3.58) and Josh Fogg (12-12, 4.35), acquired from the White Sox in a five-player trade at the 2001 Winter Meetings, both moved into the top half of the rotation.

Brian Giles   Sean Burnett

PLAYERS OF THE YEAR

MAJOR LEAGUE: Brian Giles, of

The Pirates suffered through their 10th straight losing season in 2002, but Giles had another big year. He led his team in batting (.298), runs (95), doubles (37), home runs (38) and RBIs (103). He also drew 135 walks.

MINOR LEAGUE: Sean Burnett, lhp

Burnett was named the top prospect in the Class A Carolina League. He allowed more than three earned runs just twice and surrendered only four homers as he compiled a 13-4, 1.80 record.

After racking up 69 saves in 81 opportunities during his previous three seasons as a closer, Mike Williams emerged as a premier reliever in 2002 and anchored a solid bullpen. Williams shattered the club record for saves, notching 46 in 50 opportunities. The old save mark was 34 by Jim Gott in 1988.

The offense was a much different matter, as the Pirates finished last in the NL in average (.244) for a second straight year while also finishing at the bottom in on-base percentage (.319) and slugging percentage (.381).

The Pirates' only consistent threat was left fielder Brian Giles, who hit .298-38-103 with 15 steals in 153 games while again being one of the most underrated offensive players in the game. Giles' .450 on-base percentage, .622 slugging percentage, 135 walks and 80 extra-base hits were all second in the league, and his 13 outfield assists ranked third.

"In a lot of ways, this was my most satisfying season," Giles said. "I know teams pitched around me a lot, and I feel like I had a pretty good year number-wise considering most teams weren't going to let me beat them."

Meanwhile, the Pirates had plenty of success at the minor league level in Brian Graham's first season as player development director. Their six farms clubs went a combined 399-300 for a .571 winning percentage, second in baseball to the Indians' .577. That was a dramatic turnaround for an organization whose farm clubs had combined for one winning season the previous 33 years.

The Pirates were also one of only two organizations, along with the Dodgers, to have each of their six farm clubs with winning records. Four of the six made the playoffs, with the two full-season Class A clubs, Lynchburg (Carolina) and Hickory (South Atlantic), capturing league titles.

ORGANIZATION LEADERS

BATTING

*AVG	Chris Shelton, Hickory	.340
R	Chris Duffy, Lynchburg	85
H	Ray Navarrette, Lynchburg	169
TB	Walter Young, Hickory	277
2B	Ray Navarrette, Lynchburg	41
3B	Shawn Garrett, Altoona	8
HR	Josh Bonifay, Lynchburg	26
RBI	Walter Young, Hickory	103
BB	Jose Bautista, Hickory	67
SO	Humberto Cota, Nashville	106
SB	Manny Ravelo, Hickory	42

PITCHING

W	Sean Burnett, Lynchburg	13
	Jeff Miller, Hickory	13
L	Tony McKnight, Nashville	14
#ERA	Ben Shaffar, Nashville/Altoona	3.17
G	D.J. Carrasco, Lynchburg	55
CG	Bronson Arroyo, Nashville	3
SV	D.J. Carrasco, Lynchburg	29
IP	Tony McKnight, Nashville	175
BB	Adrian Burnside, Altoona	67
SO	Ian Oquendo, Hickory	149

*Minimum 250 At-Bats #Minimum 75 Innings

PITTSBURGH
PIRATES

Manager: Lloyd McClendon

2002 Record: 72-89, .447 (4th, NL Central)

BATTING	AVG	G	AB	R	H	2B	3B	HR	RBI	BB	SO	SB	CS	SLG	OBP	B	T	HT	WT	DOB	1st Yr	Resides
Alvarez, Tony	.308	14	26	6	8	2	0	1	2	3	5	1	0	.500	.379	R	R	6-1	200	5-10-78	1995	Los Teques, Venez.
Benjamin, Mike	.150	108	120	7	18	2	1	0	3	7	31	0	4	.183	.202	R	R	6-0	170	11-22-65	1987	Chandler, Ariz.
Brown, Adrian	.216	91	208	20	45	10	2	1	21	19	34	10	6	.298	.284	S	R	6-0	200	2-7-74	1992	Summit, Miss.
Cota, Humberto	.294	7	17	2	5	1	0	0	0	1	4	0	0	.353	.333	R	R	6-0	200	2-7-79	1995	San Luis, Mexico
Davis, J.J.	.100	9	10	1	1	0	0	0	0	0	4	0	0	.100	.182	R	R	6-5	250	10-25-78	1997	Pomona, Calif.
Giles, Brian	.298	153	497	95	148	37	5	38	103	135	74	15	6	.622	.450	L	L	5-10	200	1-20-71	1989	Pittsburgh, Pa.
Hermansen, Chad	.206	65	194	22	40	11	1	7	15	17	68	7	5	.381	.272	R	R	6-2	190	9-10-77	1995	Henderson, Nev.
Hyzdu, Adam	.232	59	155	24	36	6	0	11	34	21	44	0	0	.484	.324	R	R	6-2	220	12-6-71	1990	Mesa, Ariz.
Kendall, Jason	.283	145	545	59	154	25	3	3	44	49	29	15	8	.356	.350	R	R	6-0	190	6-26-74	1992	Manhattan Beach, Calif.
Lopez, Mendy	.000	3	3	0	0	0	0	0	0	0	3	0	0	.000	.000	R	R	6-2	200	10-15-73	1992	Santo Domingo, D.R.
Mackowiak, Rob	.244	136	385	57	94	22	0	16	48	42	120	9	3	.426	.328	L	R	5-10	190	6-20-76	1996	Lowell, Ind.
Nunez, Abraham	.233	112	253	28	59	14	1	2	15	27	44	3	4	.320	.311	S	R	5-11	190	3-16-76	1994	Santo Domingo, D.R.
Osik, Keith	.160	55	100	6	16	3	0	2	11	6	25	0	0	.250	.211	R	R	6-0	200	10-22-68	1990	Shoreham, N.Y.
Ramirez, Aramis	.234	142	522	51	122	26	0	18	71	29	95	2	0	.387	.279	R	R	6-1	210	6-25-78	1994	Santo Domingo, D.R.
Reese, Pokey	.264	119	421	46	111	25	0	4	50	41	81	12	1	.352	.330	R	R	5-11	180	6-10-73	1991	Columbia, S.C.
Rios, Armando	.264	76	208	20	55	11	0	1	24	16	39	1	1	.332	.319	L	L	5-9	180	9-13-71	1994	Pembroke Pines, Fla.
Wilson, Craig	.264	131	368	48	97	16	1	16	57	32	116	2	3	.443	.355	R	R	6-2	220	11-30-76	1995	Huntington Beach, Calif.
Wilson, Jack	.252	147	527	77	133	22	4	4	37	37	74	5	2	.332	.306	R	R	6-0	190	12-29-77	1998	Thousand Oaks, Calif.
Young, Kevin	.246	146	468	60	115	26	1	16	51	50	101	4	6	.408	.322	R	R	6-3	220	6-16-69	1990	Phoenix, Ariz.

PITCHING	W	L	ERA	G	GS	CG	SV	IP	H	R	ER	BB	SO	AVG	B	T	HT	WT	DOB	1st Yr	Resides
Anderson, Jimmy	8	13	5.44	28	25	1	0	141	167	91	85	63	47	.298	L	L	6-1	210	1-22-76	1994	Chesapeake, Va.
Arroyo, Bronson	2	1	4.00	9	4	0	0	27	30	14	12	15	22	.283	R	R	6-5	190	2-24-77	1995	Brooksville, Fla.
Beimel, Joe	2	5	4.64	53	8	0	0	85	88	49	44	45	53	.266	L	L	6-3	210	4-19-77	1998	St. Mary's, Pa.
Benson, Kris	9	6	4.70	25	25	0	0	130	152	76	68	50	79	.295	R	R	6-4	190	11-7-74	1996	Wexford, Pa.
Boehringer, Brian	4	4	3.39	70	0	0	1	80	65	30	30	33	65	.228	S	R	6-2	190	1-8-70	1991	Fenton, Mo.
Fetters, Mike	1	0	3.26	32	0	0	0	30	25	13	11	18	29	.219	R	R	6-4	230	12-19-64	1986	Gilbert, Ariz.
Fogg, Josh	12	12	4.35	33	33	0	0	194	199	102	94	69	113	.266	R	R	6-0	200	12-13-76	1998	Margate, Fla.
Lincoln, Mike	2	4	3.11	55	0	0	0	72	80	28	25	27	50	.289	R	R	6-2	200	4-10-75	1996	Citrus Heights, Calif.
Lowe, Sean	4	2	5.35	43	1	0	0	69	85	45	41	34	57	.306	R	R	6-2	220	3-29-71	1992	Royse City, Texas
Manzanillo, Josias	0	0	7.62	13	0	0	0	13	20	11	11	5	4	.363	R	R	6-0	190	10-16-67	1983	Hyde Park, Mass.
Meadows, Brian	1	6	3.88	11	11	0	0	63	62	29	27	14	31	.256	R	R	6-4	230	11-21-75	1994	Troy, Ala.
Reyes, Al	0	0	2.65	15	0	0	0	17	9	5	5	7	21	.160	R	R	6-1	200	4-10-71	1988	Santo Domingo, D.R.
Sanchez, Duaner	0	0	15.43	3	0	0	0	2	3	4	4	2	2	.300	R	R	6-0	190	10-14-79	1996	Cotui, D.R.
2-team (6 Arizona)	0	0	9.00	9	0	0	0	6	6	6	6	7	6	.250							
Sauerbeck, Scott	5	4	2.30	78	0	0	0	63	50	18	16	27	70	.220	R	L	6-3	190	11-9-71	1994	Cleaves, Ohio
Torres, Salomon	2	1	2.70	5	5	0	0	30	28	10	9	13	12	.256	R	R	5-11	190	3-11-72	1990	San Pedro de Macoris, D.R.
Villone, Ron	4	6	5.81	45	7	0	0	93	95	63	60	34	55	.256	L	L	6-3	230	1-16-70	1992	River Vale, N.J.
Wells, Kip	12	14	3.58	33	33	1	0	198	197	92	79	71	134	.260	R	R	6-3	200	4-21-77	1999	Missouri City, Texas
Williams, Dave	2	5	4.98	9	9	0	0	43	38	26	24	24	33	.231	L	L	6-2	190	3-12-79	1998	Douglasville, Ga.
Williams, Mike	2	6	2.93	59	0	0	46	61	54	24	20	21	43	.232	R	R	6-2	200	7-29-68	1990	Pembroke, Va.

FIELDING

Catcher	PCT	G	PO	A	E	DP	PB
Cota	1.000	7	33	1	0	1	0
Kendall	.990	143	797	64	9	13	8
Osik	.993	27	118	15	1	1	2
C. Wilson	1.000	5	10	0	0	0	2

First Base	PCT	G	PO	A	E	DP
Benjamin	1.000	1	4	0	0	1
Hyzdu	1.000	1	3	0	0	0
Osik	1.000	3	7	2	0	1
C. Wilson	.990	42	277	21	3	35
Young	.991	144	1277	89	13	119

Second Base	PCT	G	PO	A	E	DP
Benjamin	1.000	11	23	23	0	6
Mackowiak	.833	3	2	3	1	1
Nunez	.991	46	84	133	2	35
Osik	.000	1	0	0	0	0
Reese	.988	117	283	363	8	84

Third Base	PCT	G	PO	A	E	DP
Benjamin	.979	62	13	33	1	3
Mackowiak	.955	26	13	50	3	4

	PCT	G	PO	A	E	DP
Osik	1.000	4	2	16	0	1
Ramirez	.946	131	78	255	19	32

Shortstop	PCT	G	PO	A	E	DP
Benjamin	.981	15	18	35	1	5
Nunez	.938	24	19	57	5	15
J. Wilson	.977	143	187	463	15	90

Outfield	PCT	G	PO	A	E	DP
Alvarez	1.000	8	10	0	0	0
Benjamin	.000	1	0	0	0	0
Brown	.974	71	112	1	3	0
Davis	1.000	4	3	0	0	0
Giles	.973	151	244	13	7	5
Hermansen	.982	60	107	5	2	1
Hyzdu	1.000	50	85	2	0	0
Mackowiak	.988	106	151	7	2	3
Nunez	.000	1	0	0	0	0
Osik	.000	1	0	0	0	0
Rios	1.000	56	89	5	0	1
C. Wilson	.982	75	106	6	2	0

Jack Wilson

LARRY GOREN

Josh Fogg: 12-12, 4.35 in first season as a Pirate

LARRY GOREN

Mike Williams: set franchise record with 46 saves

LARRY GOREN

FARM SYSTEM

Director, Player Development: Brian Graham

Class	Farm Team	League	W	L	Pct.	Finish*	Manager	First Yr.
AAA	Nashville (Tenn.) Sounds	Pacific Coast	72	71	.503	t-8th (16)	Marty Brown	1998
AA	Altoona (Pa.) Curve	Eastern	72	69	.511	7th (12)	Dale Sveum	1999
High A	Lynchburg (Va.) Hillcats	Carolina	87	53	.621	+2nd (8)	Pete Mackanin	1995
Low A	Hickory (N.C.) Crawdads	South Atlantic	83	56	.597	+1st (16)	Tony Beasley	1999
SS A	Williamsport (Pa.) Crosscutters	New York-Penn	48	28	.632	3rd (14)	Andy Stewart	1999
Rookie	Bradenton (Fla.) Pirates	Gulf Coast	37	23	.617	2nd (14)	Woody Huyke	1967

*Finish in overall standings (No. of teams in league)   +League champion

NASHVILLE SOUNDS   Triple-A

PACIFIC COAST LEAGUE

BATTING	AVG	G	AB	R	H	2B	3B	HR	RBI	BB	SO	SB	CS	SLG	OBP	B	T	HT	WT	DOB	1st Yr	Resides
Brown, Adrian	.337	51	184	36	62	7	1	3	16	23	18	22	6	.435	.409	S	R	6-0	200	2-7-74	1992	Summit, Miss.
Coquillette, Trace	.209	40	110	13	23	5	0	2	14	7	31	1	1	.309	.287	R	R	5-11	180	6-4-74	1993	Orangevale, Calif.
Cota, Humberto	.267	118	404	51	108	27	1	9	54	31	106	5	8	.406	.321	R	R	6-0	200	2-7-79	1995	San Luis, Mexico
De la Rosa, Tomas	.224	105	348	38	78	17	2	3	33	24	52	9	5	.310	.279	R	R	5-10	170	1-28-78	1996	Santo Domingo, D.R.
Garcia, Luis	.213	69	188	16	40	11	1	2	19	9	33	2	0	.314	.253	R	R	6-0	170	5-25-72	1993	San Francisco de Macoris, D.R.
Gilbert, Shawn	.273	48	143	18	39	2	1	1	15	23	31	2	4	.322	.382	R	R	5-9	180	3-12-65	1987	Glendale, Ariz.
Haverbusch, Kevin	.277	37	94	8	26	5	1	2	11	3	18	3	1	.415	.324	R	R	6-3	200	6-16-76	1997	Massapequa, N.Y.
Hermansen, Chad	.196	16	56	11	11	2	0	4	9	8	23	1	0	.446	.318	R	R	6-2	190	9-10-77	1995	Henderson, Nev.
Hyzdu, Adam	.243	65	243	33	59	17	0	10	50	29	59	1	2	.436	.318	R	R	6-2	220	12-6-71	1990	Mesa, Ariz.
Landaeta, Luis	.200	2	5	1	1	0	0	0	1	0	1	0	0	.200	.167	L	L	6-0	180	3-4-77	1996	Valencia, Venez.
Lopez, Mendy	.252	101	385	60	97	26	0	11	72	34	99	4	1	.405	.309	R	R	6-2	200	10-15-73	1992	Santo Domingo, D.R.
Nunez, Abraham	.222	5	18	3	4	0	0	0	0	2	7	4	1	.222	.300	S	R	5-11	180	3-16-76	1994	Santo Domingo, D.R.
Post, David	.304	96	345	59	105	16	1	6	39	38	56	11	4	.409	.382	R	R	5-11	170	9-3-73	1992	Kingston, N.Y.
Pride, Curtis	.296	110	385	71	114	22	1	10	46	33	75	22	8	.436	.362	L	R	6-0	210	12-17-68	1986	West Palm Beach, Fla.
Pritchett, Chris	.292	118	397	53	116	15	2	9	60	46	95	3	0	.408	.367	L	R	6-4	210	1-31-70	1991	Carlsbad, Calif.
Radmanovich, Ryan	.225	93	271	35	61	16	0	7	27	30	58	2	4	.362	.310	L	R	6-2	200	8-9-71	1993	West Hartford, Conn.
Redman, Tike	.270	76	311	40	84	9	4	2	20	21	24	16	7	.344	.315	L	L	5-11	160	3-10-77	1996	Duncanville, Ala.
Rios, Armando	.250	15	52	6	13	2	0	0	6	5	10	1	2	.288	.322	L	L	5-9	180	9-13-71	1994	Pembroke Pines, Fla.
Romero, Mandy	.297	88	283	40	84	25	0	17	51	24	47	1	1	.565	.354	S	R	5-11	190	10-19-67	1988	Miami, Fla.
Secrist, Reed	.257	114	358	59	92	24	3	12	56	52	87	7	4	.441	.352	L	R	6-0	220	5-7-70	1992	Farmington, Utah

PITCHING	W	L	ERA	G	GS	CG	SV	IP	H	R	ER	BB	SO	AVG	B	T	HT	WT	DOB	1st Yr	Resides
Arroyo, Bronson	8	6	2.96	22	21	3	0	143	126	57	47	28	116	.235	R	R	6-5	190	2-24-77	1995	Brooksville, Fla.
Benson, Kris	0	2	1.53	4	4	0	0	18	8	4	3	8	25	.133	R	R	6-4	190	11-7-74	1996	Wexford, Pa.
Camp, Shawn	4	1	3.24	39	0	0	2	58	50	22	21	15	59	.239	R	R	6-1	200	11-18-75	1997	Fairfax, Va.
Cedeno, Blas	0	1	6.35	6	0	0	0	6	8	5	4	1	4	.347	R	R	6-0	160	11-15-72	1991	Campo Carabobo, Venez.
Dougherty, Jim	2	3	4.63	33	0	0	4	45	40	23	23	17	36	.240	R	R	6-2	230	3-8-68	1991	Kitty Hawk, N.C.

PITCHING	W	L	ERA	G	GS	CG	SV	IP	H	R	ER	BB	SO	AVG	B	T	HT	WT	DOB	1st Yr	Resides
Gomes, Wayne	0	2	15.43	6	1	0	0	9	21	16	16	12	7	.488	R	R	6-2	220	1-15-73	1993	Cherry Hill, N.J.
Guerrier, Matt	7	12	4.59	27	26	2	0	157	154	88	80	47	130	.253	R	R	6-3	180	8-2-78	1999	Shaker Heights, Ohio
Lincoln, Mike	0	0	1.23	10	0	0	2	15	14	2	2	2	15	.237	R	R	6-2	200	4-10-75	1996	Citrus Heights, Calif.
Looney, Brian	0	1	6.14	6	3	0	0	15	15	10	10	7	5	.267	L	L	5-10	180	6-26-69	1991	Cheshire, Conn.
Lowe, Sean	1	1	5.73	5	5	0	0	22	29	14	14	3	21	.318	R	R	6-2	220	3-29-71	1992	Royse City, Texas
Manzanillo, Josias	1	0	2.66	15	1	0	1	20	18	6	6	2	14	.233	R	R	6-0	190	10-16-67	1983	Hyde Park, Mass.
McKnight, Tony	11	14	5.24	30	28	1	0	175	198	108	102	45	120	.287	L	R	6-5	200	6-29-77	1995	Texarkana, Ark.
Meadows, Brian	9	8	4.27	23	22	1	0	126	132	69	60	26	98	.267	R	R	6-4	230	11-21-75	1994	Troy, Ala.
O'Connor, Brian	0	1	5.40	4	0	0	0	5	7	3	3	6	4	.318	L	L	6-2	190	1-4-77	1995	Pittsburgh, Pa.
Reyes, Al	7	3	2.70	43	0	0	1	67	40	21	20	22	90	.167	R	R	6-1	200	4-10-71	1988	Santo Domingo, D.R.
Sanchez, Duaner	0	3	4.76	20	0	0	6	23	23	12	12	11	20	.253	R	R	6-0	190	10-14-79	1996	Cotui, D.R.
2-team (4 Tucson)	1	4	5.14	24	0	0	7	28	29	16	16	12	29	.271							
Service, Scott	4	4	3.36	47	0	0	6	62	47	25	23	24	70	.208	R	R	6-6	250	2-26-67	1986	Cincinnati, Ohio
Shaffar, Ben	1	0	3.60	1	1	0	0	5	7	4	2	3	4	.318	S	R	6-3	190	9-28-77	1999	Leitchfield, Ky.
Smith, Brian	3	3	3.82	33	0	0	7	38	37	18	16	11	24	.258	R	R	5-10	190	7-19-72	1994	Toney, Ala.
Tolar, Kevin	6	1	2.54	44	7	1	1	78	66	23	22	27	82	.224	R	L	6-3	230	1-28-71	1989	Sarasota, Fla.
Torres, Salomon	8	5	3.83	26	24	2	0	162	169	78	69	39	136	.269	R	R	5-11	190	3-11-72	1990	San Pedro de Macoris, D.R.

FIELDING

Catcher	PCT	G	PO	A	E	DP	PB
Cota	.994	85	600	33	4	3	10
Romero	.998	51	417	28	1	3	8
Secrist	.987	12	72	5	1	1	3

First Base	PCT	G	PO	A	E	DP
Cota	1.000	1	1	0	0	0
Hyzdu	.953	5	39	2	2	6
Post	.980	7	43	5	1	3
Pritchett	.990	109	879	81	10	78
Romero	.988	19	153	16	2	24
Secrist	1.000	11	64	2	0	7

Second Base	PCT	G	PO	A	E	DP
Coquillette	1.000	8	14	19	0	3
De la Rosa	.967	33	61	84	5	16
Garcia	.988	20	34	46	1	14
Gilbert	1.000	10	10	22	0	7

	PCT	G	PO	A	E	DP
Lopez	1.000	6	13	9	0	3
Nunez	1.000	1	2	3	0	1
Post	.968	80	144	220	12	62

Third Base	PCT	G	PO	A	E	DP
Coquillette	.917	7	3	8	1	1
De la Rosa	.000	1	0	0	0	0
Garcia	.940	35	6	57	4	7
Gilbert	.919	14	7	27	3	3
Lopez	.953	40	25	76	5	7
Post	1.000	1	0	1	0	0
Secrist	.934	68	46	109	11	12

Shortstop	PCT	G	PO	A	E	DP
De la Rosa	.963	68	103	182	11	47
Gilbert	.965	14	21	34	2	11
Lopez	.984	62	103	151	4	28
Nunez	1.000	3	6	11	0	2

	PCT	G	PO	A	E	DP
Post	1.000	1	0	3	0	1
Outfield	PCT	G	PO	A	E	DP
Brown	.975	49	77	1	2	0
Coquillette	.978	26	44	0	1	0
Gilbert	.875	6	6	1	1	0
Haverbusch	.941	23	31	1	2	0
Hermansen	1.000	14	26	2	0	1
Hyzdu	.990	59	104	0	1	0
Landaeta	1.000	2	2	0	0	0
Nunez	1.000	1	1	0	0	0
Post	1.000	4	2	0	0	0
Pride	.968	93	177	5	6	0
Pritchett	1.000	1	0	0	0	0
Radmanovich	.991	72	108	5	1	1
Redman	.982	75	157	4	3	3
Rios	.923	12	12	0	1	0
Secrist	1.000	25	31	0	0	0

ALTOONA CURVE — Double-A

EASTERN LEAGUE

BATTING	AVG	G	AB	R	H	2B	3B	HR	RBI	BB	SO	SB	CS	SLG	OBP	B	T	HT	WT	DOB	1st Yr	Resides
Alvarez, Tony	.318	125	507	79	161	37	1	15	59	27	71	29	18	.483	.361	R	R	6-1	200	5-10-78	1995	Los Teques, Venez.
Brown, Jason	.170	18	47	3	8	5	0	0	5	5	21	0	0	.277	.241	R	R	6-2	200	5-22-74	1997	Rolling Hills Estates, Calif.
Caruso, Joe	.250	47	148	19	37	5	2	3	20	8	16	3	3	.372	.315	R	R	5-9	190	12-30-74	1997	South Williamsport, Pa.
Davis, J.J.	.287	101	348	51	100	17	3	20	62	33	101	7	4	.526	.351	R	R	6-5	250	10-25-78	1997	Pomona, Calif.
Derosso, Tony	.192	72	182	22	35	5	4	8	33	27	48	2	0	.396	.296	R	R	6-3	220	11-7-75	1994	Moultrie, Ga.
Garrett, Shawn	.290	131	489	71	142	24	8	11	73	33	88	19	6	.440	.342	S	R	6-3	190	11-2-78	1998	Kinmundy, Ill.
Haverbusch, Kevin	.292	35	130	18	38	7	0	5	16	4	21	4	2	.462	.319	R	R	6-3	190	6-16-76	1997	Massapequa, N.Y.
House, J.R.	.264	30	91	9	24	6	2	2	11	13	21	0	0	.396	.349	R	R	5-10	200	11-11-79	1999	Ormond Beach, Fla.
King, Brad	.264	45	129	28	34	4	0	3	12	30	24	1	1	.364	.407	R	R	6-2	200	12-3-74	1996	Boca Raton, Fla.
Lemonis, Chris	.000	6	17	1	0	0	0	0	2	1	1	0	0	.000	.105	L	R	5-11	180	8-21-73	1995	New York, N.Y.
Meadows, Randy	.126	48	111	16	14	2	0	2	8	6	29	2	1	.198	.190	R	R	6-0	190	8-15-76	1998	Nesbit, Miss.
Meier, Dan	.245	78	237	27	58	10	2	6	33	23	66	2	3	.380	.313	L	L	6-0	200	8-13-77	1998	Aurora, Colo.
Pachot, John	.262	94	321	31	84	29	0	3	44	6	31	1	0	.380	.277	R	R	6-2	210	11-11-74	1993	Ponce, P.R.
Rios, Armando	.000	1	2	0	0	0	0	0	0	1	0	0	0	.000	.333	L	L	5-9	180	9-13-71	1994	Pembroke Pines, Fla.
Rivera, Carlos	.302	128	494	67	149	28	2	22	84	27	75	1	1	.500	.345	L	L	5-11	230	6-10-78	1996	Rio Grande, P.R.
Rodriguez, Victor	.293	61	188	29	55	6	0	3	20	9	20	3	0	.372	.330	R	R	6-2	190	10-25-76	1994	Aguirre, P.R.
Sefcik, Kevin	.308	126	467	69	144	32	2	2	51	44	42	12	8	.398	.374	R	R	5-10	180	2-16-71	1993	Orland Park, Ill.
Skrehot, Shaun	.240	80	312	40	75	15	3	2	25	23	60	9	4	.327	.309	R	R	5-10	180	12-5-78	1998	Spring, Texas
Washington, Rico	.223	112	359	53	80	11	3	8	34	60	66	3	4	.337	.352	L	R	5-9	190	5-30-78	1997	Gray, Ga.
Weichard, Paul	.000	1	1	0	0	0	0	0	0	0	1	0	0	.000	.000	S	L	5-10	200	11-7-79	1997	Ringwood, Australia

PITCHING	W	L	ERA	G	GS	CG	SV	IP	H	R	ER	BB	SO	AVG	B	T	HT	WT	DOB	1st Yr	Resides
Benson, Kris	1	0	1.29	1	1	0	0	7	5	1	1	0	7	.208	R	R	6-4	190	11-7-74	1996	Wexford, Pa.
Burnside, Adrian	6	9	4.55	32	23	0	0	131	120	70	66	67	122	.242	R	L	6-3	210	3-15-77	1996	Alice Springs, Australia
Chrysler, Clint	3	3	3.97	51	0	0	3	57	55	29	25	21	26	.254	L	L	6-0	190	11-4-75	1997	St. Petersburg, Fla.
Deschenes, Marc	0	0	3.00	3	0	0	3	3	3	1	1	0	4	.272	R	R	6-0	200	1-6-73	1995	Dracut, Mass.
Dougherty, Jim	1	1	5.06	7	0	0	0	11	13	6	6	7	5	.317	R	R	6-2	230	3-8-68	1991	Kitty Hawk, N.C.
Gonzalez, Mike	8	4	3.80	16	16	0	0	85	77	38	36	47	82	.243	R	L	6-2	210	5-23-78	1997	Pasadena, Texas
Grabow, John	8	13	5.47	28	27	1	0	146	181	94	89	47	97	.307	L	L	6-2	190	11-4-78	1997	San Gabriel, Calif.
Gravelle, Nick	0	0	18.00	1	0	0	0	1	3	2	2	0	0	.500	L	L	6-4	190	2-14-80	2001	Kelso, Wash.
Guy, Brad	3	2	3.17	26	5	1	1	77	87	31	27	16	40	.290	R	R	6-2	190	10-25-75	1997	Eureka, Calif.
Looney, Brian	0	0	1.17	4	0	0	0	8	5	1	1	1	3	.192	L	L	5-10	180	6-26-69	1991	Cheshire, Conn.
Lopez, Jose	0	0	6.75	10	4	0	0	21	30	20	16	9	18	.326	R	R	5-11	200	1-28-76	1999	Corpus Christi, Texas
McDade, Neal	8	3	3.91	49	0	0	3	78	85	36	34	16	51	.275	R	R	6-2	180	6-16-76	1995	Orange Park, Fla.
Montgomery, Matt	3	0	4.21	44	0	0	3	66	62	32	31	26	50	.250	R	R	6-3	210	5-13-76	1997	Anaheim, Calif.
O'Connor, Brian	3	7	5.06	24	14	1	0	85	86	50	48	50	53	.263	L	L	6-2	190	1-4-77	1995	Pittsburgh, Pa.
Palma, Rick	1	1	1.80	10	0	0	0	10	12	2	2	3	10	.315	L	L	6-1	160	3-25-79	1996	Maracay, Venez.
Pavlovich, Tony	0	0	13.50	1	0	0	0	1	4	2	2	0	0	.571	R	R	6-0	190	8-23-74	1994	Pavo, Ga.
Reid, Justin	11	8	4.33	25	25	1	0	154	151	87	74	28	108	.253	R	R	6-5	210	6-30-77	1999	Folsom, Calif.
Shaffar, Ben	8	7	3.15	18	18	1	0	111	110	46	39	40	97	.256	S	R	6-3	190	9-28-77	1999	Leitchfield, Ky.
Spurling, Chris	4	3	2.19	51	0	0	20	70	54	18	17	12	60	.210	R	R	6-6	240	6-28-77	1998	Englewood, Ohio

PITCHING	W	L	ERA	G	GS	CG	SV	IP	H	R	ER	BB	SO	AVG	B	T	HT	WT	DOB	1st Yr	Resides
Vogelsong, Ryan	1	5	5.56	8	8	0	0	44	47	27	27	10	35	.278	R	R	6-3	200	7-22-77	1998	Carlisle, Pa.
Wimberly, Larry	1	2	4.05	26	0	0	1	53	49	25	24	18	36	.246	L	L	6-0	190	8-22-75	1994	Zellwood, Fla.

FIELDING

Catcher	PCT	G	PO	A	E	DP	PB
Brown	1.000	17	103	6	0	0	0
House	.994	20	147	11	1	1	1
King	.996	40	263	21	1	3	1
Pachot	.994	70	412	62	3	11	2

First Base	PCT	G	PO	A	E	DP
Caruso	1.000	1	14	2	0	2
Derosso	.982	7	56	0	1	3
King	1.000	2	5	0	0	1
Meier	1.000	10	94	0	0	7
Pachot	.980	12	87	12	2	7
Rivera	.993	119	974	56	7	88

Second Base	PCT	G	PO	A	E	DP
Haverbusch	.969	6	11	20	1	7

Lemonis	1.000	4	11	12	0	2
Meadows	1.000	8	14	11	0	6
Rodriguez	.989	40	80	108	2	20
Sefcik	.979	86	171	207	8	40
Washington	1.000	13	13	14	0	1

Third Base	PCT	G	PO	A	E	DP
Caruso	.929	35	32	85	9	9
Derosso	.960	29	21	51	3	7
Pachot	1.000	1	0	1	0	0
Rodriguez	1.000	2	0	1	0	0
Sefcik	1.000	2	1	3	0	1
Washington	.944	89	68	166	14	17

Shortstop	PCT	G	PO	A	E	DP
Caruso	.971	8	18	15	1	1

Lemonis	.714	2	2	3	2	0
Meadows	.963	36	48	83	5	22
Sefcik	.953	28	39	63	5	12
Skrehot	.956	80	126	198	15	36

Outfield	PCT	G	PO	A	E	DP
Alvarez	.978	124	253	11	6	1
Davis	.971	100	194	6	6	2
Derosso	1.000	10	9	1	0	0
Garrett	.979	128	220	8	5	1
Haverbusch	1.000	17	34	3	0	1
Meier	.963	50	75	3	3	0
Rios	1.000	1	2	0	0	0
Sefcik	.958	17	23	0	1	0
Weichard	.000	1	0	0	0	0

LYNCHBURG HILLCATS — High Class A

CAROLINA LEAGUE

BATTING	AVG	G	AB	R	H	2B	3B	HR	RBI	BB	SO	SB	CS	SLG	OBP	B	T	HT	WT	DOB	1st Yr	Resides
Asprilla, Avelino	.167	7	12	4	2	0	0	0	1	2	0	0	.167	.286	R	R	5-11	180	1-1-81	1998	Panama City, Panama
Barns, B.J.	.268	135	489	59	131	30	3	12	69	42	76	14	9	.415	.344	L	L	6-4	200	7-21-77	1999	Loysville, Pa.
Bonifay, Josh	.307	126	463	83	142	36	1	26	102	63	97	3	3	.557	.388	R	R	6-0	180	7-30-78	1999	Gibsonia, Pa.
Brown, Jason	.211	7	19	1	4	1	0	0	1	1	7	0	0	.263	.286	R	R	6-2	200	5-22-74	1997	Rolling Hills Estates, Calif.
Castillo, Jose	.300	134	503	82	151	25	2	16	81	49	95	27	14	.453	.370	R	R	6-1	190	3-19-81	1997	Las Mercedes, Venez.
Cockrell, Michael	.000	9	7	0	0	0	0	0	0	2	0	0	0	.000	.222	R	R	5-10	160	7-25-81	2001	Wilmington, Calif.
Cotten, Jeremy	.222	40	126	11	28	9	0	4	11	5	34	1	0	.389	.256	R	R	6-2	250	9-24-80	1998	Fuquay-Varina, N.C.
Cruz, Alex	.000	3	1	0	0	0	0	0	0	0	0	0	0	.000	.000	R	R	6-0	140	4-9-81	2000	Ridge Manor, Fla.
De Caster, Yurendell	.252	125	432	54	109	25	3	15	62	30	102	1	2	.428	.309	R	R	6-1	210	9-26-79	1996	Curacao, Neth. Antilles
Duffy, Chris	.301	132	539	85	162	27	5	10	52	33	101	22	7	.425	.353	S	L	5-10	180	4-20-80	2001	Glendale, Ariz.
Hill, Willy	.185	20	54	2	10	0	0	1	3	14	13	0	0	.185	.228	L	R	5-9	160	9-21-76	1998	Altadena, Calif.
Hudnall, Josh	.173	52	110	23	19	3	0	1	7	9	26	5	1	.227	.242	R	R	6-3	180	2-22-80	1999	Monroe, La.
Landaeta, Luis	.264	65	220	26	58	16	2	7	31	14	29	2	3	.450	.311	L	L	6-0	180	3-4-77	1996	Valencia, Venez.
Lopez-Cao, Mike	.302	70	212	33	64	16	1	8	20	18	35	0	0	.500	.365	L	R	5-9	180	8-14-75	1997	Miami, Fla.
McLouth, Nathan	.244	114	393	58	96	23	4	9	46	41	48	20	7	.392	.324	L	R	5-11	170	10-28-81	2000	Whitehall, Mich.
Meadows, Randy	.225	23	80	13	18	7	0	1	5	1	15	0	2	.350	.271	R	R	6-0	190	8-15-76	1998	Nesbit, Miss.
Meath, Matt	.500	5	10	5	5	0	0	0	2	8	2	0	0	.500	.737	S	R	6-0	190	6-6-79	2001	Boca Raton, Fla.
Meier, Dan	.278	22	79	15	22	6	0	3	13	13	18	1	1	.468	.383	L	L	6-0	200	8-13-77	1998	Aurora, Colo.
Mejia, Manuel	.500	2	2	1	1	0	0	1	1	0	0	0	0	2.000	.500	R	R	6-2	220	11-5-78	1996	Santo Domingo, D.R.
Navarrete, Ray	.318	134	532	75	169	41	2	6	69	38	48	8	3	.436	.373	R	R	6-3	210	5-20-78	2000	Colts Neck, N.J.
Paulino, Ronny	.262	119	442	63	116	26	2	12	55	39	87	2	1	.412	.321	R	R	6-3	210	4-21-81	1997	Santo Domingo, D.R.
Weichard, Paul	.196	21	51	7	10	2	0	0	4	4	13	0	0	.235	.311	S	L	5-10	180	11-7-79	1997	Ringwood, Australia

PITCHING	W	L	ERA	G	GS	CG	SV	IP	H	R	ER	BB	SO	AVG	B	T	HT	WT	DOB	1st Yr	Resides
Alcala, Jason	2	5	2.68	54	0	0	8	77	63	29	23	18	71	.220	R	R	6-2	210	9-18-80	1997	Cumana, Venez.
Bennett, Jeff	10	6	3.62	24	20	0	0	124	137	64	50	30	90	.280	R	R	6-3	190	6-10-80	1998	Brush Creek, Tenn.
Borner, Brady	9	4	2.00	37	9	0	1	95	84	32	21	12	81	.233	L	L	5-10	170	4-12-79	2001	Chaska, Minn.
Bumatay, Mike	5	2	3.24	52	0	0	2	67	50	27	24	31	79	.208	L	L	6-0	170	10-9-79	1998	Clovis, Calif.
Burnett, Sean	13	4	1.80	26	26	2	0	155	118	46	31	33	96	.210	L	L	6-1	170	9-17-82	2000	Wellington, Fla.
Carrasco, D.J.	4	4	1.61	55	0	0	29	73	52	18	13	18	83	.204	R	R	6-1	214	4-12-77	1997	Safford, Ariz.
Cedeno, Blas	0	0	2.08	9	0	0	0	13	11	3	3	7	11	.239	R	R	6-0	160	11-15-72	1991	Campo Carabobo, Venez.
Connolly, Mike	10	3	2.94	29	19	0	0	122	111	46	40	46	100	.250	L	L	6-0	160	6-2-82	2000	Oneonta, N.Y.
Dukeman, Greg	2	1	3.53	25	0	0	0	36	32	17	14	13	21	.242	R	R	6-7	220	12-6-78	1997	Costa Mesa, Calif.
Guzman, Wilson	1	2	3.42	22	2	0	0	47	47	22	18	23	34	.258	L	L	5-9	200	9-14-73	1994	Palo Verde, D.R.
Higgins, Josh	4	2	1.90	53	0	0	6	71	62	23	15	23	88	.228	R	R	6-5	180	6-16-79	2000	Santee, Calif.
Jackson, Brian	2	0	18.56	5	0	0	0	5	3	11	11	11	5	.166	R	R	6-8	190	8-12-77	1998	Tiburon, Calif.
2-team (11 Kinston)	4	1	8.10	16	0	0	3	17	14	15	15	20	10	.229							
Jacobsen, Landon	12	10	2.89	27	27	1	0	162	145	71	52	41	123	.242	R	R	6-3	180	5-4-79	1998	Canova, S.D.
Johnston, Mike	4	2	3.63	15	10	0	0	57	50	29	23	26	50	.230	L	L	6-3	190	3-30-79	1998	Colwyn, Pa.
Lavery, Tim	1	1	7.00	6	2	0	0	18	24	16	14	7	6	.324	L	L	6-3	210	11-16-78	1999	Naperville, Ill.
Sharber, Jason	7	6	3.71	22	21	0	0	104	109	52	43	37	96	.270	R	R	6-3	220	2-24-82	2000	Murfreesboro, Tenn.
Vogelsong, Ryan	1	1	8.04	4	4	0	0	16	19	14	14	7	20	.296	R	R	6-3	200	7-22-77	1998	Carlisle, Pa.

FIELDING

Catcher	PCT	G	PO	A	E	DP	PB
Brown	1.000	1	5	1	0	0	1
Lopez-Cao	.978	33	200	20	5	1	6
Mejia	1.000	1	1	0	0	0	0
Paulino	.981	111	854	88	18	5	17

First Base	PCT	G	PO	A	E	DP
Brown	.818	3	8	1	2	1
Cotten	.975	26	175	17	5	18
Lopez-Cao	1.000	3	10	3	0	3
Meier	.995	22	192	14	1	21
Navarrete	.988	99	801	52	10	81
Paulino	1.000	2	20	1	0	1

Second Base	PCT	G	PO	A	E	DP
Asprilla	.900	4	11	7	2	1
Bonifay	.941	75	114	190	19	55

Cockrell	.889	7	2	6	1	1
Cruz	1.000	2	0	1	0	0
Hudnall	.978	24	35	55	2	10
Meadows	.976	12	18	22	1	3
Navarrete	.945	34	42	62	6	15

Third Base	PCT	G	PO	A	E	DP
Cockrell	1.000	1	0	1	0	0
De Caster	.896	125	78	199	32	12
Hudnall	.938	9	3	12	1	1
Lopez-Cao	.800	3	0	4	1	0
Meadows	1.000	5	2	3	0	0
Navarrete	.909	5	1	9	1	1

Shortstop	PCT	G	PO	A	E	DP
Asprilla	1.000	1	1	3	0	0
Castillo	.951	132	245	402	33	92

Cockrell	1.000	1	0	1	0	0
Cruz	.000	1	0	0	0	0
Hudnall	1.000	10	6	15	0	5
Meadows	.941	6	13	19	2	5

Outfield	PCT	G	PO	A	E	DP
Barns	.976	131	269	12	7	3
Bonifay	1.000	21	31	1	0	0
Duffy	.989	130	274	6	3	0
Hill	.882	11	15	0	2	0
Hudnall	1.000	3	0	1	0	0
Landaeta	.971	20	34	0	1	0
Lopez-Cao	1.000	2	1	0	0	0
McLouth	.968	101	149	4	5	2
Meath	.875	5	6	1	1	0
Navarrete	1.000	4	4	0	0	0
Weichard	.833	10	15	0	2	0

SOUTH ATLANTIC LEAGUE

BATTING	AVG	G	AB	R	H	2B	3B	HR	RBI	BB	SO	SB	CS	SLG	OBP	B	T	HT	WT	DOB	1st Yr	Resides
Asprilla, Avelino	.250	54	176	27	44	4	1	3	21	12	47	7	2	.335	.305	R	R	5-11	180	1-1-81	1998	Panama City, Panama
Bautista, Jose	.301	129	438	72	132	26	3	14	57	67	104	3	2	.470	.402	R	R	6-0	180	10-19-80	2001	Santo Domingo, D.R.
Buttler, Vic	.285	124	460	77	131	15	3	7	64	45	65	30	11	.376	.353	L	L	6-0	160	8-12-80	2000	Hawthorne, Calif.
Chaves, Brandon	.248	105	335	56	83	18	2	4	44	40	89	10	7	.349	.337	S	R	6-3	160	8-5-79	2000	Hilo, Hawaii
Cortes, Jorge	.254	17	59	13	15	3	1	1	11	7	11	1	1	.390	.343	L	L	5-8	180	10-17-80	1997	Barranquilla, Colombia
Davis, Rajai	.429	6	14	4	6	0	0	0	3	6	2	2	2	.429	.619	S	R	5-11	170	10-19-80	2001	New London, Conn.
De la Cruz, Miguel	.212	56	151	15	32	9	1	3	14	11	40	0	0	.344	.274	R	R	6-2	180	10-18-79	1997	Santo Domingo, D.R.
Doumit, Ryan	.322	68	258	46	83	14	1	6	47	18	40	3	5	.453	.377	S	R	6-0	190	4-3-81	1999	Moses Lake, Wash.
Harts, Jeremy	.323	76	257	55	83	14	1	10	49	30	79	7	5	.502	.397	S	L	6-1	190	6-6-80	1998	Decatur, Ga.
Henley, Bob	.000	1	3	0	0	0	0	0	0	1	1	0	0	.000	.250	R	R	6-2	200	1-30-73	1993	Grand Bay, Ala.
Hernandez, Jose	.282	59	202	16	57	14	1	4	36	9	48	2	0	.421	.341	R	R	6-1	200	11-3-80	1998	Valencia, Venez.
Hill, Willy	.277	39	141	15	39	3	0	0	9	4	15	2	6	.298	.306	L	R	5-9	160	9-21-76	1998	Altadena, Calif.
Hudnall, Josh	.186	30	86	5	16	1	0	0	6	2	30	2	3	.198	.239	R	R	6-3	180	2-22-80	1999	Monroe, La.
Keppinger, Jeff	.276	126	478	75	132	23	4	10	73	47	33	6	2	.404	.344	R	R	6-0	180	4-21-80	2001	Auburn, Ga.
Landaeta, Luis	.267	9	30	3	8	0	0	0	4	4	2	0	1	.267	.353	L	L	6-0	180	3-4-77	1998	Valencia, Venez.
Meath, Matt	.125	15	40	8	5	0	0	0	2	8	13	2	0	.125	.271	S	R	6-0	170	10-6-79	2001	Boca Raton, Fla.
Ravelo, Manny	.238	92	341	48	81	10	1	2	22	38	80	42	18	.290	.325	R	R	5-10	150	8-8-79	1997	Santo Domingo, D.R.
Reyes, Milver	.214	4	14	2	3	2	0	0	2	1	2	0	0	.357	.267	R	R	5-11	180	9-3-82	1999	San Felipe, Venez.
Riera, Zack	.300	14	40	11	12	3	1	1	9	4	7	1	0	.500	.429	S	R	6-0	190	4-16-79	2000	Tallahassee, Fla.
Rogers, Brandon	.154	22	65	5	10	3	0	0	5	3	16	0	0	.200	.203	R	R	6-0	200	3-1-78	2000	El Cajon, Calif.
Scala, Mickey	.000	4	7	0	0	0	0	0	0	0	5	0	0	.000	.000	L	R	6-1	190	11-7-77	2002	Glenview, Ill.
Shelton, Chris	.340	93	332	72	113	27	2	17	65	47	74	0	0	.587	.425	R	R	6-0	200	6-26-80	2001	Salt Lake City, Utah
Weston, Aron	.239	67	226	38	54	10	2	4	30	25	49	20	5	.354	.337	L	L	6-3	190	11-5-80	1999	Solon, Ohio
Young, Walter	.333	132	492	84	164	34	2	25	103	36	102	2	6	.563	.390	L	R	6-5	290	2-18-80	1999	Purvis, Miss.

PITCHING	W	L	ERA	G	GS	CG	SV	IP	H	R	ER	BB	SO	AVG	B	T	HT	WT	DOB	1st Yr	Resides
Cedeno, Blas	0	0	0.00	7	0	0	3	14	6	0	0	5	13	.133	R	R	6-0	160	11-15-72	1991	Campo Carabobo, Venez.
De los Santos, Carlos	5	2	2.52	37	1	0	4	75	57	31	21	43	77	.210	R	R	6-0	180	4-11-78	1998	Santo Domingo, D.R.
DePriest, Derrick	0	1	5.14	5	0	0	0	7	9	5	4	2	3	.333	R	R	6-8	230	11-21-76	2000	Homestead, Fla.
Dukeman, Greg	0	1	3.13	11	0	0	1	23	22	11	8	7	17	.250	R	R	6-7	220	12-6-78	1997	Costa Mesa, Calif.
Fitch, Steve	2	2	2.87	14	2	0	1	31	22	13	10	11	21	.198	R	R	6-1	180	2-15-78	2000	West Chester, Pa.
Friedberg, Drew	2	2	3.80	37	0	0	2	45	43	24	19	18	34	.241	L	L	6-2	180	3-3-79	2001	Middleton, Wis.
Gravelle, Nick	2	0	3.38	6	4	0	1	27	25	12	10	9	24	.242	L	L	6-4	190	2-14-80	2001	Kelso, Wash.
Guerrero, Julio	7	3	3.66	31	1	0	2	71	72	39	29	12	49	.254	R	R	6-4	210	1-4-81	1999	San Pedro de Macoris, D.R.
Jackson, Brian	1	0	14.09	7	0	0	1	8	13	12	12	11	3	.406	R	R	6-4	190	8-12-77	1998	Tiburon, Calif.
Lissir, Alexander	0	2	4.35	16	0	0	1	31	30	16	15	13	18	.258	R	R	6-0	200	12-29-82	1999	Tucacas, Venez.
Lopez, Jose	1	0	0.00	2	0	0	0	6	3	0	0	0	6	.150	R	R	5-11	200	1-28-76	1999	Corpus Christi, Texas
Manzanillo, Josias	0	0	9.00	1	0	0	0	2	5	3	2	0	1	.416	R	R	6-0	190	10-16-67	1983	Hyde Park, Mass.
Miller, Jeff	13	5	3.75	31	15	0	4	103	100	44	43	28	75	.252	R	R	6-4	210	2-1-80	2001	Springfield, N.J.
Novoa, Roberto	1	5	5.48	10	10	0	0	43	61	30	26	15	29	.335	R	R	6-5	200	8-15-79	1999	Santo Domingo, D.R.
Nunez, Leo	0	0	0.00	1	1	0	0	4	5	0	0	3	1	.333	R	R	6-1	150	8-14-83	2000	Jamao Norte, D.R.
O'Brien, Pat	12	7	3.82	26	26	0	0	146	149	77	62	30	101	.259	R	R	6-5	190	11-20-80	1999	Bath, Ohio
Oquendo, Ian	11	6	2.71	24	22	0	0	140	127	49	42	45	149	.242	R	R	5-11	160	10-30-81	2000	Dover, Del.
Searles, Jon	2	3	5.81	31	4	0	1	79	86	59	51	34	53	.279	R	R	6-3	200	1-18-81	1999	Huntington, N.Y.
Shumaker, Casey	4	4	3.07	47	0	0	22	59	53	28	20	22	83	.233	R	R	6-3	190	7-12-80	2002	Jacksonville, Fla.
VanBenschoten, John	11	4	2.80	27	27	0	0	148	119	57	46	62	145	.218	R	R	6-4	210	4-14-80	2001	Milford, Ohio
Young, Chris	11	9	3.11	26	26	1	0	145	127	57	50	34	136	.233	R	R	6-10	250	5-25-79	2001	Dallas, Texas

FIELDING

Catcher	PCT	G	PO	A	E	DP	PB
Doumit	.968	31	199	15	7	0	6
Hernandez	.987	57	393	46	6	3	6
Reyes	.971	4	29	4	1	0	1
Riera	.944	11	78	6	5	0	3
Rogers	.988	22	156	7	2	0	4
Shelton	.995	25	189	7	1	1	5

First Base	PCT	G	PO	A	E	DP
De la Cruz	.982	17	106	5	2	8
Shelton	1.000	52	414	31	0	38
Young	.977	77	584	58	15	54

Second Base	PCT	G	PO	A	E	DP
Asprilla	.965	21	42	67	4	8
Hudnall	1.000	9	13	23	0	4

	PCT	G	PO	A	E	DP
Keppinger	.981	113	201	306	10	69
Third Base	**PCT**	**G**	**PO**	**A**	**E**	**DP**
Bautista	.916	124	74	187	24	12
Chaves	1.000	1	0	1	0	0
De la Cruz	.917	31	11	33	4	3
Hudnall	1.000	1	1	0	0	0
Shortstop	**PCT**	**G**	**PO**	**A**	**E**	**DP**
Asprilla	.962	31	45	82	5	20
Bautista	1.000	2	2	7	0	0
Chaves	.941	103	151	251	25	47
Hudnall	.894	12	12	30	5	8
Outfield	**PCT**	**G**	**PO**	**A**	**E**	**DP**
Asprilla	1.000	3	6	0	0	0

	PCT	G	PO	A	E	DP
Buttler	.989	120	253	7	3	0
Chaves	.667	1	2	0	1	0
Cortes	.912	17	28	3	3	1
Davis	1.000	6	15	0	0	0
De la Cruz	1.000	1	1	0	0	0
Harts	.931	75	142	7	11	0
Hill	1.000	39	66	1	0	1
Hudnall	.929	7	13	0	1	0
Landaeta	1.000	9	11	0	0	0
Meath	1.000	11	18	1	0	0
Ravelo	.960	87	162	5	7	0
Scala	1.000	4	4	0	0	0
Shelton	.000	1	0	0	1	0
Weston	.975	61	110	7	3	0

WILLIAMSPORT CROSSCUTTERS   Short-Season A

NEW YORK-PENN LEAGUE

BATTING	AVG	G	AB	R	H	2B	3B	HR	RBI	BB	SO	SB	CS	SLG	OBP	B	T	HT	WT	DOB	1st Yr	Resides
Aliendo, Humberto	.238	40	151	19	36	5	1	3	17	11	31	2	1	.344	.290	R	R	6-1	210	10-31-80	1998	Miranda, Venez.
Asprilla, Avelino	.224	24	85	14	19	1	2	3	6	5	18	0	2	.388	.261	R	R	5-11	180	1-1-81	1998	Panama City, Panama
Bass, Chris	.274	71	266	36	73	19	2	4	38	21	48	8	0	.406	.328	R	R	6-2	180	10-18-81	2000	Madison, Ind.
Bocchino, Anthony	.282	55	195	24	55	10	5	1	29	12	29	5	1	.400	.319	L	L	5-10	180	5-15-80	2002	Brooklyn, N.Y.
Chapman, Travis	.274	56	179	26	49	8	0	1	16	19	40	3	1	.335	.343	R	R	6-1	200	9-6-80	2001	Fort Walton Beach, Fla.
Christensen, Sam	.216	38	125	15	27	4	0	0	13	5	9	0	4	.248	.275	L	R	6-4	210	12-20-79	2002	Pocatello, Idaho
Cockrell, Michael	.421	8	38	11	16	4	2	1	8	1	5	5	1	.711	.415	R	R	5-10	160	7-25-81	2001	Wilmington, Calif.
Collum, Mike	.260	57	196	27	51	8	1	0	35	21	66	4	3	.311	.335	R	R	6-3	180	7-16-81	2001	Wellington, Fla.
Cortes, Jorge	.328	70	253	38	83	14	4	1	35	44	20	7	7	.427	.426	L	L	5-8	180	10-17-80	1997	Barranquilla, Colombia
Cruz, Alex	.217	7	23	1	5	0	0	0	1	2	4	0	1	.217	.280	R	R	6-0	140	4-9-81	2000	Ridge Manor, Fla.

BATTING	AVG	G	AB	R	H	2B	3B	HR	RBI	BB	SO	SB	CS	SLG	OBP	B	T	HT	WT	DOB	1st Yr	Resides
Cuello, Domingo	.273	11	44	13	12	2	2	1	5	1	3	7	1	.477	.304	R	R	5-11	170	4-12-83	1999	Santo Domingo, D.R.
Davis, Rajai	.000	1	4	0	0	0	0	0	0	1	0	0	0	.000	.000	S	R	5-11	170	10-19-80	2001	New London, Conn.
Devine, Dean	.154	4	13	1	2	0	0	1	0	0	4	0	0	.385	.214	R	R	6-0	170	10-4-79	2002	Seneca, Ill.
Eldred, Brad	.283	72	276	43	78	22	3	10	48	18	74	10	1	.493	.338	R	R	6-5	240	7-12-80	2002	Miami, Fla.
Kingsbury, Bobby	.267	39	131	17	35	10	3	1	12	8	20	6	1	.412	.312	L	L	6-1	180	8-30-80	2002	Lyndhurst, Ohio
Lee, Taber	.244	40	135	23	33	7	0	1	16	21	31	2	0	.319	.352	S	R	6-1	180	10-18-80	2002	Olympia, Wash.
Lytle, Chaz	.292	46	192	22	56	0	0	0	12	7	16	14	6	.302	.312	L	L	6-1	190	10-27-80	2002	Lake Mary, Fla.
Meath, Matt	.234	26	64	14	15	2	2	0	6	9	19	5	1	.328	.338	S	R	6-0	170	10-6-79	2001	Boca Raton, Fla.
Mejia, Manuel	.355	12	31	7	11	4	0	1	3	6	7	1	0	.581	.474	R	R	6-2	220	11-5-78	1996	Santo Domingo, D.R.
Newman, Ryan	.198	37	106	14	21	1	0	0	10	6	26	3	1	.208	.243	R	R	5-11	170	2-25-79	2002	Scottsdale, Ariz.
Ohtsuka, Yoshiyuki	.000	2	4	0	0	0	0	0	0	2	1	0	0	.000	.333	R	R	5-10	190	6-19-80	2002	Kanagawa, Japan
Ramos, Victor	.295	31	88	10	26	6	0	0	9	3	13	0	0	.364	.319	L	R	6-3	190	10-4-81	2000	Cayey, P.R.
Scala, Mickey	.333	5	6	1	2	0	0	0	1	3	1	0	0	.333	.556	R	R	6-1	190	11-7-77	2002	Glenview, Ill.

GAMES BY POSITION: C—Chapman 52, Devine 3, Mejia 8, Ramos 30. **1B**—Bass 3, Christensen 20, Eldred 60. **2B**—Asprilla 2, Cockrell 4, Collum 39, Cruz 5, Cuello 9, Newman 24. **3B**—Asprilla 4, Bass 67, Collum 1, Newman 7, Ohtsuka 2. **SS**—Asprilla 15, Cockrell 5, Collum 17, Cuello 1, Lee 40, Newman 4. **SS**—Aliendo 20, Bocchino 48, Cotes 66, Davis 1, Eldred 1, Kingsbury 35, Lytle 45, Meath 19, Ramos 1, Scala 3.

PITCHING	W	L	ERA	G	GS	CG	SV	IP	H	R	ER	BB	SO	AVG	B	T	HT	WT	DOB	1st Yr	Resides
Bayer, Russ	1	1	5.52	17	0	0	1	31	32	19	19	12	21	.264	L	L	6-4	210	12-19-79	2002	York, S.C.
Beigh, David	1	4	5.10	13	13	0	0	55	42	37	31	33	52	.205	R	R	6-5	240	2-2-81	2000	Battle Ground, Ind.
Davila, Marcus	0	2	1.71	15	0	0	0	26	19	6	5	7	20	.204	R	R	5-11	180	8-14-81	2002	Key West, Fla.
DeMaria, Chris	1	1	4.35	16	0	0	1	31	34	20	15	4	15	.272	R	R	6-3	210	9-28-80	2002	Torrance, Calif.
Gravelle, Nick	7	4	3.66	15	15	0	0	84	85	37	34	23	82	.265	L	L	6-4	190	2-14-80	2001	Kelso, Wash.
Hart, Alex	7	0	1.85	15	10	0	2	68	52	15	14	20	73	.210	R	R	6-6	220	1-10-80	2002	Indian Harbor Beach, Fla.
Holt, Chris	2	2	6.15	15	0	0	0	26	40	20	18	5	6	.350	R	R	6-0	190	4-19-79	2002	Portland, Maine
Lissir, Alexander	1	2	3.97	4	4	0	0	23	25	10	10	4	12	.294	R	R	6-0	200	12-29-82	1999	Tucacas, Venez.
Novoa, Roberto	8	3	3.65	12	12	0	0	67	62	32	27	8	56	.240	R	R	6-5	200	8-15-79	1999	Santo Domingo, D.R.
Owens, Henry	0	3	2.62	23	0	0	7	45	26	18	13	16	63	.165	R	R	6-3	230	4-23-79	2001	Miami, Fla.
Rodriguez, Juan	2	2	3.14	19	7	0	3	57	48	24	20	22	31	.227	R	R	5-11	190	6-10-81	1999	Monte Cristi, D.R.
Schneider, Jonathan	0	0	7.40	16	0	0	0	21	25	18	17	9	8	.294	R	R	6-7	210	10-28-79	2002	Springfield, Va.
Shafer, Kurt	4	0	0.84	10	2	1	2	32	22	5	3	4	19	.188	R	R	6-4	190	12-4-81	2000	Land O'Lakes, Fla.
Shortslef, Josh	10	4	3.33	14	13	0	0	76	84	36	28	18	37	.283	R	L	6-4	230	2-1-82	2000	Hannibal, N.Y.
Youman, Shane	4	0	1.45	20	0	0	5	37	25	7	6	8	48	.189	L	L	6-4	200	10-11-79	2001	New Iberia, La.

BRADENTON PIRATES Rookie

GULF COAST LEAGUE

BATTING	AVG	G	AB	R	H	2B	3B	HR	RBI	BB	SO	SB	CS	SLG	OBP	B	T	HT	WT	DOB	1st Yr	Resides
Acosta, Johe	.229	12	35	6	8	2	3	0	6	5	10	4	1	.457	.357	R	R	6-5	190	12-19-81	2000	Santo Domingo, D.R.
Arbinger, Mike	.327	59	214	32	70	11	2	2	46	25	22	4	4	.425	.393	L	R	5-10	180	4-21-80	2002	Toledo, Ohio
Arias, Garvi	.138	12	29	3	4	0	0	0	0	5	14	2	0	.138	.286	R	R	6-0	170	8-11-83	1999	Santo Domingo, D.R.
Brown, Tim	.240	42	129	14	31	7	1	2	25	18	32	1	2	.357	.331	L	L	6-3	220	2-21-83	2001	Eugene, Ore.
Cockrell, Michael	.302	47	159	32	48	11	1	1	22	29	13	7	4	.403	.408	R	R	5-10	160	7-25-81	2001	Wilmington, Calif.
Davis, Rajai	.384	58	224	38	86	16	5	4	35	20	25	24	6	.554	.436	S	R	5-11	170	10-19-80	2001	New London, Conn.
Guzman, Javier	.307	50	199	42	61	6	6	5	20	12	25	13	6	.472	.347	R	R	5-11	140	5-4-84	2001	Santo Domingo, D.R.
Hicks, Joseph	.106	22	47	4	5	2	0	0	3	5	17	1	1	.149	.189	R	R	5-11	180	4-22-84	2002	Houston, Texas
House, J.R.	.313	5	16	3	5	2	0	1	2	3	1	0	0	.625	.421	R	R	5-10	200	11-11-79	1999	Ormond Beach, Fla.
Kirkland, Kody	.306	46	157	22	48	10	2	0	18	14	39	2	1	.395	.373	R	R	6-2	200	6-9-83	2002	Pocatello, Idaho
Madrid, Mike	.200	29	90	12	18	5	1	2	12	9	8	1	1	.344	.291	L	L	6-0	220	6-8-80	2002	Silver City, N.M.
Mariot, Lino	.000	1	4	0	0	0	0	0	0	0	0	0	0	.000	.000	R	R	6-2	170	10-21-82	2001	Woodbridge, N.J.
McCuistion, Mike	.284	39	134	22	38	6	1	1	12	18	19	3	1	.366	.381	L	R	6-2	190	5-14-82	2001	Yucaipa, Calif.
Milauskas, Adam	.158	18	38	6	6	0	1	1	4	4	7	0	2	.289	.267	R	R	6-1	190	3-18-83	2001	St. Charles, Ill.
Nino, Denny	.192	11	26	3	5	1	0	0	3	7	5	0	0	.231	.382	R	R	6-1	170	6-4-83	2001	Caracas, Venez.
Ohtsuka, Yoshiyuki	.270	10	37	6	10	0	0	1	5	2	5	1	0	.351	.300	R	R	5-10	190	6-19-80	2002	Kanagawa, Japan
Reyes, Milver	.159	35	107	9	17	2	0	1	12	6	16	0	0	.206	.222	R	R	5-11	180	9-3-82	1999	San Felipe, Venez.
Smith, John	.228	35	127	22	29	7	3	1	14	18	19	2	3	.354	.327	L	R	5-10	180	1-18-82	2002	Hawkinsville, Ga.
Smith, Sean	.298	40	131	26	39	5	2	3	18	16	14	5	1	.435	.391	R	R	6-1	180	8-24-82	2000	Joliet, Ill.

GAMES BY POSITION: C—House 3, McCuistion 16, Nino 11, Reyes 35. **1B**—Brown 40, House 1, Madrid 23. **2B**—Cockrell 25, Kirkland 1, J. Smith 35. **3B**—Cockrell 5, Guzman 1, Kirkland 45, Ohtsuka 10. **SS**—Cockrell 15, Guzman 45, Mariot 1. **OF**—Acosta 11, Arbinger 42, Arias 11, Davis 54, Hicks 16, Milauskas 16, S. Smith 39.

PITCHING	W	L	ERA	G	GS	CG	SV	IP	H	R	ER	BB	SO	AVG	B	T	HT	WT	DOB	1st Yr	Resides
Albaladejo, Jonathan	3	2	2.40	12	10	0	0	60	71	20	16	6	37	.302	R	R	6-5	210	10-30-82	2001	Vega Alta, P.R.
Almonte, Henry	0	0	2.25	3	0	0	1	4	5	3	1	7	3	.333	R	R	6-2	200	2-22-80	1998	Hato Mayor, D.R.
Alvarez, Melvin	0	3	6.16	11	0	0	0	19	24	19	13	11	4	.333	L	L	6-3	190	11-24-81	1998	Puerto Plata, D.R.
Arias, Pedro	5	1	1.93	14	3	0	4	37	25	8	8	7	20	.187	R	R	5-11	160	8-30-83	2001	San Cristobal, D.R.
Bridwell, Jody	1	0	8.44	5	0	0	0	5	9	6	5	4	3	.409	S	L	5-11	180	9-5-80	2002	Vero Beach, Fla.
Burzynski, Cole	0	0	6.75	4	0	0	0	5	4	4	4	7	4	.190	R	R	6-4	200	9-3-81	2000	Navasota, Texas
Capps, Matt	1	0	0.69	7	0	0	1	13	13	2	1	6	8	.270	R	R	6-2	220	9-3-83	2002	Douglasville, Ga.
Cedeno, Blas	0	0	0.00	2	0	0	1	3	2	0	0	0	5	.200	R	R	6-0	160	11-15-72	1991	Campo Carabobo, Venez.
Contreras, Omar	2	3	4.35	11	0	0	2	21	27	16	10	5	13	.317	L	L	6-1	160	12-3-82	2000	Carabobo, Venez.
Duke, Zach	8	1	1.95	11	11	1	0	60	38	15	13	18	48	.185	L	L	6-2	210	4-19-83	2001	Waco, Texas
Gonzalez, Mike	0	0	0.00	2	2	0	0	13	5	1	0	3	14	.113	L	L	6-2	180	5-23-78	1997	Pasadena, Texas
Holliday, Brian	1	4	4.91	10	5	0	1	33	35	22	18	18	26	.282	L	L	6-2	180	6-1-84	2002	Moon Township, Pa.
Hummel, John	1	0	3.49	11	1	0	0	28	34	16	11	10	16	.309	L	L	6-2	210	4-18-84	2002	Hoffman Estates, Ill.
Johnson, Blair	0	1	8.10	2	1	0	0	3	4	6	3	3	4	.285	R	R	6-4	200	3-25-84	2002	Topeka, Kan.
Kiley, Jason	4	2	2.63	11	11	1	0	51	33	20	15	24	27	.185	R	R	6-4	220	10-15-82	2001	St. Charles, Ill.
Morel, Jhosandy	1	4	4.02	8	0	0	0	16	16	9	7	5	12	.266	L	L	6-1	150	1-9-82	2001	Union City, N.J.
Nunez, Leo	4	2	3.43	11	11	0	0	60	54	23	23	5	52	.237	R	R	6-1	150	8-14-83	2000	Jamao Norte, D.R.
Shafer, Kurt	3	2	6.00	5	5	0	0	27	30	21	18	3	15	.267	R	R	6-4	190	12-4-81	2000	Land O'Lakes, Fla.
Torrealba, Yoann	2	1	1.35	9	0	0	4	13	10	2	2	3	12	.263	R	R	5-11	170	6-24-82	2000	Veroe, Venez.
Tower, Scott	0	0	3.72	6	0	0	0	13	10	5	5	4	8	.277	L	L	6-0	160	8-19-81	2002	Lometa, Texas
White, Brian	0	1	5.00	11	0	0	1	18	18	10	10	12	8	.285	R	R	5-11	180	4-23-82	2002	Valrico, Fla.

BY DAVID WILHELM

The Cardinals' 2002 season was marked by tragedy and jubilation.

Despite the deaths of pitcher Darryl Kile and beloved broadcaster Jack Buck, the Cardinals (97-65) won 26 of their last 33 games to finish first in the National League Central. They stayed hot in the division series by sweeping the defending World Series champion Diamondbacks. And though they were the sentimental favorite to defeat the Giants in the NL Championship Series, the Cardinals were ousted in five games, largely because of their abysmal hitting with men in scoring position (3-for-39).

Kile, 33, died in his sleep of a heart attack June 22 in a Chicago hotel room before a scheduled game with the Cubs, stunning the Cardinals and the baseball world. Kile, one of the leaders on what was expected to be a deep and talented starting rotation, became a source of motivation for the Cardinals, who kept his jersey, shoes, glove and other personal belongings in his locker throughout the season.

Four days before Kile's death, Buck died after a seven-month illness at age 77. Buck's death wasn't totally unexpected, but he had become a St. Louis icon in his 48 years with the team.

Almost from Opening Day, the Cardinals had injury problems on their pitching staff. Ace Matt Morris (17-9, 3.42), Woody Williams (9-4, 2.53), Andy Benes (5-4, 2.78), Garrett Stephenson (2-5, 5.40), Bud Smith (1-5, 6.94) and Rick Ankiel all were injured.

That forced the Cardinals to use rookies Jason Simontacchi, Travis Smith and Josh Pearce in the rotation, along with reliever Luther Hackman. They were among 14 starting pitchers the Cardinals employed. Still, the Cardinals kept their heads above water.

Simontacchi, 28, was a pleasant surprise, going 11-5, 4.02 in 24 starts. Benes was rocked in an April start in Arizona and contemplated retirement. But he returned in July and was the Cardinals' best pitcher down the stretch.

Albert Pujols   Tyler Johnson

JOHN SPEAR

PLAYERS OF THE YEAR

MAJOR LEAGUE: Albert Pujols, 3b/of
By following his Rookie of the Year campaign with another MVP-worthy season, Pujols became the first player in major league history to hit .300 with 30 home runs, 100 RBIs and 100 runs scored in each of his first two seasons.

MINOR LEAGUE: Tyler Johnson, lhp
Johnson, 21, used his command of four pitches to blossom into a dominant pitcher in his first full season at Class A Peoria, going 15-3, 2.00 with 42 walks and 132 strikeouts in 121 innings.

Williams was bothered by a pulled muscle in his left side and missed more than a month in the early portion of the season. He returned in July, re-injured the side and returned in late August.

But Williams aggravated the injury again in the Cardinals' division-clinching victory over the Astros Sept. 20, and he missed the division series before making one start in the NLCS. Stephenson never was a factor in the rotation, and Smith was traded to the Phillies in July as part of the deal in which the Cardinals landed all-star third baseman Scott Rolen. Another July acquisition, Chuck Finley from the Indians, boosted the rotation. Finley was 7-4, 3.80 in 14 starts.

Left fielder Albert Pujols again led the offense, batting .314-34-127. Only Houston's Lance Berkman (128) had more RBIs. Rolen batted .266-31-110, but thrived in St. Louis with 13 homers and 42 RBIs in 53 games. Rolen, who signed an eight-year, $90 million contract in September, missed the NLCS with a left shoulder injury suffered in the division series, but he's expected to be healthy in 2003.

Shortstop Edgar Renteria (.305-11-83) had his best season and set a Cardinals record for shortstops with 82 RBIs, and center fielder Jim Edmonds (.311-28-83) was a mainstay in the middle of the batting order.

Four of the Cardinals' six minor league teams had records of .500 or better, and low Class A Peoria won the Midwest League championship. Left fielder Dee Haynes batted .312-21-98 at Double-A New Haven. First baseman-third baseman John Gall also shined at New Haven, batting .316-20-81 with 45 doubles.

Lefthander Tyler Johnson was the organization's brightest pitching prospect. He was 15-3, 2.00 in 18 starts at Peoria.

ORGANIZATION LEADERS

BATTING

*AVG	John Gall, New Haven	.316
R	Shaun Boyd, Peoria	91
H	John Gall, New Haven	166
TB	John Gall, New Haven	277
2B	John Gall, New Haven	45
3B	Reid Gorecki, New Jersey	13
HR	Ivan Cruz, Memphis	35
RBI	Ivan Cruz, Memphis	100
BB	Johnny Hernandez, Potomac	67
SO	Tim Lemon, Peoria	165
SB	Chris Morris, Potomac	55

PITCHING

W	Tyler Johnson, Peoria	15
L	B.R. Cook, New Haven	13
#ERA	Rich Burgess, Potomac/Peoria	2.72
G	Jason Karnuth, Memphis/New Haven	59
CG	Rhett Parrott, New Haven/Potomac	5
SV	Scotty Layfield, New Haven	24
IP	Dan Haren, Potomac/Peoria	194
BB	Les Walrond, Memphis/New Haven	73
SO	Dan Haren, Potomac/Peoria	171

*Minimum 250 At-Bats #Minimum 75 Innings

ST. LOUIS
CARDINALS

Manager: Tony La Russa

2002 Record: 97-55, .599 (1st, NL Central)

BATTING	AVG	G	AB	R	H	2B	3B	HR	RBI	BB	SO	SB	CS	SLG	OBP	B	T	HT	WT	DOB	1st Yr	Resides
Cairo, Miguel	.250	108	184	28	46	9	2	2	23	13	36	1	1	.353	.307	R	R	6-1	200	5-4-74	1991	Bakersfield, Calif.
Coolbaugh, Mike	.083	5	12	0	1	0	0	0	0	1	3	0	0	.083	.154	R	R	6-1	190	6-5-72	1990	San Antonio, Texas
Cruz, Ivan	.357	17	14	2	5	0	0	1	3	1	3	0	0	.571	.400	L	L	6-2	210	5-3-68	1989	Jacksonville, Fla.
Delgado, Wilson	.200	12	20	2	4	2	0	2	5	0	6	0	0	.600	.200	S	R	5-11	160	7-15-72	1993	San Cristobal, D.R.
DiFelice, Mike	.230	70	174	17	40	11	0	4	19	17	42	0	0	.362	.297	R	R	6-2	200	5-28-69	1991	Safety Harbor, Fla.
Drew, J.D.	.252	135	424	61	107	19	1	18	56	57	104	8	2	.429	.349	L	R	6-1	190	11-20-75	1997	Hahira, Ga.
Edmonds, Jim	.311	144	476	96	148	31	2	28	83	86	134	4	3	.561	.420	L	L	6-1	210	6-27-70	1988	Orange, Calif.
Marrero, Eli	.262	131	397	63	104	19	1	18	66	40	72	14	2	.451	.327	R	R	6-1	180	11-17-73	1993	Miami, Fla.
Martinez, Tino	.262	150	511	63	134	25	1	21	75	58	71	3	2	.438	.337	L	R	6-2	210	12-7-67	1989	Tampa, Fla.
Matheny, Mike	.244	110	315	31	77	12	1	3	35	32	49	1	3	.317	.313	R	R	6-3	200	9-22-70	1991	St. Charles, Mo.
Perez, Eduardo	.201	96	154	22	31	9	0	10	26	17	36	0	0	.455	.290	R	R	6-4	210	9-11-69	1991	Santurce, P.R.
Polanco, Placido	.284	94	342	47	97	19	1	5	27	12	27	5	3	.389	.316	R	R	5-10	160	10-10-75	1994	Miami, Fla.
Pujols, Albert	.314	157	590	118	185	40	2	34	127	72	69	2	4	.561	.394	R	R	6-3	210	1-16-80	1999	St. Louis, Mo.
Renteria, Edgar	.305	152	544	77	166	36	2	11	83	49	57	22	7	.439	.364	R	R	6-1	180	8-7-75	1992	Pembroke Pines, Fla.
Robinson, Kerry	.260	124	181	27	47	7	4	1	15	11	29	7	4	.359	.301	L	L	6-0	170	10-3-73	1994	Chesterfield, Mo.
Rolen, Scott	.278	55	205	37	57	8	4	14	44	20	34	3	2	.561	.354	R	R	6-4	220	4-4-75	1993	Holmes Beach, Fla.
2-team (100 Philadelphia)	.266	155	580	89	154	29	8	31	110	72	102	8	4	.503	.357							
Taguchi, So	.400	19	15	4	6	0	0	2	2	1	1	0		.400	.471	R	R	5-10	160	7-2-69	2002	Nishinomiya, Japan
Vina, Fernando	.270	150	622	75	168	29	5	1	54	44	36	17	11	.338	.333	L	R	5-9	170	4-16-69	1991	Stateline, Nev.

PITCHING	W	L	ERA	G	GS	CG	SV	IP	H	R	ER	BB	SO	AVG	B	T	HT	WT	DOB	1st Yr	Resides
Benes, Andy	5	4	2.78	18	17	1	0	97	80	39	30	51	64	.227	R	R	6-6	240	8-20-67	1989	Town and Country, Mo.
Crudale, Mike	3	0	1.88	49	1	0	0	53	43	11	11	14	47	.227	R	R	6-0	200	1-3-77	1999	Danville, Calif.
Duff, Matt	0	0	4.76	7	0	0	0	6	3	3	3	8	4	.150	R	R	6-1	190	10-6-74	1997	Alligator, Miss.
Fassero, Jeff	3	0	3.00	16	0	0	0	18	16	6	6	5	12	.231	L	L	6-1	200	1-5-63	1984	Paradise Valley, Ariz.
2-team (57 Chicago)	8	6	5.35	73	0	0	0	69	81	43	41	27	56	.292							
Finley, Chuck	7	4	3.80	14	14	1	0	85	69	41	36	30	83	.219	L	L	6-6	220	11-26-62	1985	Newport Beach, Calif.
Hackman, Luther	5	4	4.11	43	6	0	0	81	90	42	37	39	46	.286	R	R	6-4	190	10-10-74	1994	Columbus, Miss.
Isringhausen, Jason	3	2	2.48	60	0	0	32	65	46	22	18	18	68	.199	R	R	6-3	230	9-7-72	1992	Tarpon Springs, Fla.
Joseph, Kevin	0	1	4.91	11	0	0	0	11	16	7	6	6	2	.363	R	R	6-4	200	8-1-76	1997	Dallas, Texas
Kile, Darryl	5	4	3.72	14	14	0	0	109	82	36	35	28	50	.257	R	R	6-5	210	12-2-68	1988	Greenwood Village, Colo.
Kline, Steve	2	1	3.39	66	0	0	6	58	54	23	22	21	41	.251	L	L	6-1	210	8-22-72	1993	Winfield, Pa.
Matthews, Mike	2	1	3.89	43	0	0	0	42	40	21	18	22	32	.259	L	L	6-2	170	10-24-73	1992	Woodbridge, Va.
Molina, Gabe	1	0	1.59	12	0	0	0	11	6	2	2	6	4	.162	R	R	5-11	220	5-3-75	1996	Denver, Colo.
Morris, Matt	17	9	3.42	32	32	1	0	210	210	86	80	64	171	.260	R	R	6-5	210	8-9-74	1995	Jupiter, Fla.
Pearce, Josh	0	0	7.62	3	0	0	0	13	20	13	11	8	1	.377	R	R	6-3	210	8-20-77	1999	Yakima, Wa.
Rodriguez, Jose	0	0	54.00	2	0	0	0	0	4	2	2	2	0	.800	L	L	6-1	200	12-18-74	1997	Cayey, P.R.
Rodriguez, Nerio	0	0	4.15	2	0	0	0	4	4	3	2	1	2	.222	R	R	6-1	200	3-4-71	1991	San Pedro de Macoris, D.R.
Simontacchi, Jason	11	5	4.02	24	24	0	0	143	134	68	64	54	72	.252	R	R	6-2	180	11-13-73	1996	Santa Clara, Calif.
Smith, Bud	1	5	6.94	11	10	0	0	48	67	39	37	22	22	.338	L	L	6-0	170	10-23-79	1998	Lakewood, Calif.
Smith, Travis	4	2	7.17	12	10	0	0	54	69	44	43	20	32	.322	R	R	5-10	170	11-7-72	1995	Bend, Ore.
Stechschulte, Gene	6	2	4.78	29	0	0	0	32	27	19	17	17	21	.234	R	R	6-5	210	8-12-73	1996	Kalida, Ohio
Stephenson, Garrett	2	5	5.40	12	10	0	0	45	48	27	27	25	34	.282	R	R	6-5	200	1-2-72	1992	Kimberly, Idaho
Timlin, Mike	1	3	2.51	42	1	0	0	61	48	19	17	7	35	.215	R	R	6-4	210	3-10-66	1987	Oldsmar, Fla.
Veres, Dave	5	8	3.48	71	0	0	0	83	67	34	32	39	68	.224	R	R	6-2	220	10-19-66	1986	Castle Rock, Mo.
White, Rick	3	1	.82	20	0	0	0	22	13	3	2	3	14	.168	R	R	6-4	230	12-23-68	1990	Springfield, Ohio
2-team (41 Colorado)	5	7	4.31	61	0	0	0	63	62	33	30	21	41	.263							
Williams, Woody	9	4	2.53	17	17	1	0	103	84	30	29	25	76	.221	R	R	6-0	190	8-19-66	1988	Fresno, Texas
Wright, Jamey	2	0	4.80	4	3	0	0	15	15	8	8	12	8	.258	R	R	6-5	230	12-24-74	1993	Oklahoma City, Okla.
2-team (19 Milwaukee)	7	13	5.29	23	22	1	0	129	130	80	76	75	77	.268							

FIELDING

Catcher	PCT	G	PO	A	E	DP	PB
DiFelice	.991	61	313	32	3	5	2
Marrero	.976	44	151	9	4	2	2
Matheny	.994	106	562	64	4	6	5

First Base	PCT	G	PO	A	E	DP
Cairo	1.000	4	10	0	0	0
Cruz	1.000	7	12	1	0	0
Marrero	1.000	4	13	0	0	2
Martinez	.996	149	1220	86	5	119
Matheny	1.000	1	1	0	0	1
Perez	1.000	10	52	1	0	5
Pujols	.994	21	140	13	1	24

Second Base	PCT	G	PO	A	E	DP
Cairo	.982	18	25	31	1	8
DiFelice	.000	1	0	0	0	0
Vina	.981	150	287	401	13	104

Third Base	PCT	G	PO	A	E	DP
Cairo	.875	7	5	2	1	1

	PCT	G	PO	A	E	DP
Coolbaugh	1.000	4	0	8	0	3
Perez	.000	6	0	0	1	0
Polanco	.974	78	52	139	5	18
Pujols	.938	41	25	66	6	6
Rolen	.958	55	52	129	8	18

Shortstop	PCT	G	PO	A	E	DP
Cairo	1.000	6	7	6	0	3
Delgado	1.000		8	9	0	1
Pujols	.000	1	0	0	0	0
Renteria	.970	149	202	410	19	72

Outfield	PCT	G	PO	A	E	DP
Cairo	.905	24	19	0	2	0
Drew	.987	120	223	4	3	1
Edmonds	.986	139	347	11	5	4
Marrero	.985	106	186	9	3	4
Perez	.982	35	50	4	1	1
Pujols	.978	118	173	4	4	0
Robinson	.977	76	84	0	2	0
Taguchi	.929	14	11	2	1	0

LARRY GOREN

Matt Morris

Director, Player Development: Bruce Manno

Class	Farm Team	League	W	L	Pct.	Finish*	Manager	First Yr.
AAA	Memphis (Tenn.) Redbirds	Pacific Coast	71	71	.500	10th (16)	Gaylen Pitts	1998
AA	New Haven (Conn.) Ravens	Eastern	74	65	.532	5th (12)	Mark DeJohn	2001
High A	Potomac (Va.) Cannons	Carolina	59	81	.421	6th (8)	Joe Cunningham	1997
Low A	Peoria (Ill.) Chiefs	Midwest	85	53	.616	+1st (14)	Danny Sheaffer	1995
SS A	New Jersey Cardinals	New York-Penn	39	37	.513	6th (14)	Tommy Shields	1994
Rookie	Johnson City (Tenn.) Cardinals	Appalachian	29	38	.433	7th (10)	Brian Rupp	1975

*Finish in overall standings (No. of teams in league)   + League champion

MEMPHIS REDBIRDS   Class AAA

PACIFIC COAST LEAGUE

BATTING	AVG	G	AB	R	H	2B	3B	HR	RBI	BB	SO	SB	CS	SLG	OBP	B	T	HT	WT	DOB	1st Yr	Resides
Andreopoulos, Alex	.282	26	78	10	22	6	0	1	8	9	9	0	0	.397	.380	L	R	5-10	200	8-19-72	1995	Toronto, Ontario
Balfe, Ryan	.143	6	14	0	2	0	0	0	0	1	3	0	0	.143	.200	S	R	6-1	180	11-11-75	1994	Cornwall, N.Y.
Chamblee, Jim	.100	5	10	1	1	0	0	1	1	4	0	0	0	.100	.182	R	R	6-4	170	5-6-75	1995	Denton, Texas
Clapp, Stubby	.242	100	359	49	87	19	2	2	20	46	70	2	7	.323	.335	L	R	5-8	170	2-24-73	1996	Windsor, Ontario
Coolbaugh, Mike	.243	116	411	62	100	20	1	29	75	51	126	9	3	.509	.338	R	R	6-1	190	6-5-72	1990	San Antonio, Texas
Cruz, Ivan	.280	125	461	83	129	27	0	35	100	49	96	0	0	.566	.349	L	L	6-2	210	5-3-68	1989	Jacksonville, Fla.
Davis, Tommy	.278	28	90	9	25	4	0	4	20	5	19	0	4	.456	.313	R	R	6-1	210	5-21-73	1994	Semmes, Ala.
Delgado, Wilson	.260	98	365	31	95	19	2	7	35	23	54	2	5	.381	.309	S	R	5-11	160	7-15-72	1993	San Cristobal, D.R.
Frank, Mike	.275	88	262	29	72	13	1	6	39	18	21	9	2	.401	.336	L	L	6-2	190	1-14-75	1997	Upland, Calif.
Garrick, Matt	.220	27	82	9	18	7	0	2	8	10	28	0	1	.378	.312	R	R	6-0	180	8-19-75	1997	Duncanville, Texas
McDonald, Keith	.270	81	267	33	72	20	0	12	36	15	55	1	2	.479	.322	R	R	6-2	210	2-8-73	1994	Anaheim Hills, Calif.
Meyers, Chad	.268	100	358	56	96	19	1	8	35	51	54	43	9	.394	.387	R	R	5-11	190	8-8-75	1996	Omaha, Neb.
2-team (18 Sacramento)	.260	118	412	67	107	19	1	9	37	63	64	43	9	.376	.383							
Morris, Warren	.260	29	100	16	26	4	1	2	14	8	12	0	1	.380	.306	L	R	5-11	180	1-11-74	1996	Alexandria, La.
2-team (27 Edmonton)	.260	56	192	31	50	10	3	4	24	11	28	2	2	.406	.295							
Mota, Tony	.221	44	136	21	30	7	0	3	13	15	28	3	2	.338	.301	S	R	6-1	170	10-31-77	1995	Miami, Fla.
Newson, Warren	.267	20	30	6	8	4	0	1	5	3	10	0	0	.500	.333	L	L	5-7	200	7-3-64	1986	Southlake, Texas
Nicholson, Kevin	.256	39	125	12	32	8	2	1	19	14	21	2	3	.376	.326	S	R	5-10	190	3-29-76	1997	Surrey, B.C.
2-team (18 Colo. Spr.)	.217	57	161	13	35	9	2	1	20	19	32	2	3	.317	.297							
Nunnally, Jon	.242	87	302	44	73	14	1	14	46	34	82	13	1	.434	.322	L	R	5-10	190	11-9-71	1992	Keeling, Va.
2-team (20 Omaha)	.242	107	360	56	87	19	1	17	58	42	101	14	4	.442	.325							
Ortega, Bill	.253	96	293	46	74	17	2	7	35	36	43	1	4	.396	.339	R	R	6-4	200	7-24-75	1997	Miami, Fla.
Riggs, Adam	.230	43	122	26	28	9	0	2	11	23	27	5	1	.352	.347	R	R	6-0	190	10-4-72	1994	Andover, N.J.
Rumfelt, Chad	.244	13	41	6	10	1	0	2	7	2	6	0	0	.415	.279	R	R	6-3	190	9-4-72	1991	Belton, Texas
2-team (56 Calgary)	.278	69	198	21	55	8	0	3	27	17	31	0	2	.364	.333							
Saturria, Luis	.162	29	74	6	12	3	0	0	5	7	22	3	1	.203	.241	R	R	6-2	160	7-21-75	1994	Boca Chica, D.R.
Snopek, Chris	.261	33	92	15	24	6	0	3	13	11	13	4	1	.424	.343	R	R	6-1	190	9-20-70	1992	Madison, Ky.
Taguchi, So	.247	91	304	37	75	17	0	5	36	13	44	6	3	.352	.286	R	R	5-10	160	7-2-69	2002	Nishinomiya, Japan
Williams, Gerald	.151	21	73	11	11	3	0	1	3	3	8	2	0	.233	.195	R	R	6-2	180	8-10-66	1987	Tampa, Fla.

PITCHING	W	L	ERA	G	GS	CG	SV	IP	H	R	ER	BB	SO	AVG	B	T	HT	WT	DOB	1st Yr	Resides
Benes, Andy	1	1	3.12	4	4	0	0	17	17	7	6	4	8	.261	R	R	6-6	240	8-20-67	1989	Town and Country, Mo.
Coogan, Patrick	1	4	7.53	7	6	0	0	29	36	26	24	14	29	.302	R	R	6-3	190	9-12-75	1997	Baton Rouge, La.
Crudale, Mike	1	0	1.84	13	0	0	7	15	10	3	3	5	16	.192	R	R	6-0	200	1-3-77	1999	Danville, Calif.
Duff, Matt	0	0	1.93	4	0	0	1	5	2	1	1	4	3	.133	R	R	6-1	190	10-6-74	1997	Alligator, Miss.
Heiserman, Rick	1	1	4.93	22	0	0	1	38	42	21	21	10	15	.276	R	R	6-7	220	2-22-73	1994	Omaha, Neb.
Jacome, Jason	8	6	4.09	28	12	0	1	106	114	55	48	23	69	.275	L	L	6-1	160	11-24-70	1991	Tucson, Ariz.
Joseph, Kevin	1	1	1.77	31	0	0	2	36	37	10	7	11	14	.272	R	R	6-4	200	8-1-76	1997	Dallas, Texas
Journell, Jimmy	2	4	3.68	7	7	0	0	37	38	16	15	18	32	.263	R	R	6-4	200	12-29-77	1999	Springfield, Ohio
Karnuth, Jason	0	0	0.00	1	0	0	0	1	1	0	0	0	0	.250	R	R	6-2	190	5-15-76	1997	Glen Ellyn, Ill.
Lail, Denny	1	3	4.57	10	8	0	0	41	42	23	21	26	23	.259	R	R	6-1	170	9-10-74	1995	Taylorsville, N.C.
Mathews, T.J.	0	0	4.50	4	0	0	0	4	3	2	2	2	3	.200	R	R	6-1	220	1-19-70	1992	Las Vegas, Nev.
2-team (4 New Orleans)	0	0	3.00	8	0	0	0	9	6	3	3	3	6	.176							
Molina, Gabe	5	4	2.15	56	0	0	12	71	59	21	17	24	54	.223	R	R	5-11	220	5-3-75	1996	Denver, Colo.
Nickle, Doug	3	1	4.60	14	0	0	3	16	13	8	8	7	10	.224	R	R	6-4	230	10-2-74	1997	Sonoma, Calif.
Nitkowski, C.J.	1	2	9.82	16	1	0	0	15	24	18	16	9	12	.347	L	L	6-3	200	3-9-73	1994	Houston, Texas
2-team (24 New Orlens)	2	4	5.54	40	1	0	2	37	45	25	23	16	32	.290							
Ohme, Kevin	4	3	4.52	56	5	0	2	88	103	44	44	21	56	.304	L	L	6-1	180	4-13-71	1993	Brandon, Fla.
Oliver, Darren	0	2	7.88	5	5	0	0	16	17	16	14	17	9	.298	R	L	6-2	220	10-6-70	1988	Southlake, Texas
Pearce, Josh	0	4	7.65	4	4	0	0	20	28	18	17	3	17	.321	R	R	6-3	210	8-20-77	1999	Yakima, Wa.
Rodriguez, Jose	2	1	3.44	22	0	0	2	18	26	13	7	7	14	.342	L	L	6-1	200	12-18-74	1997	Cayey, P.R.
Rodriguez, Nerio	3	1	2.79	8	8	0	0	52	42	22	16	10	43	.218	R	R	6-1	200	3-4-71	1991	San Pedro de Macoris, D.R.
Sheredy, Kevin	1	2	4.75	35	0	0	2	42	42	25	22	22	35	.273	R	R	6-4	210	1-3-75	1996	Antioch, Calif.
Simontacchi, Jason	5	1	2.34	6	6	0	0	42	44	12	11	5	28	.273	R	R	6-2	180	11-13-73	1996	Santa Clara, Calif.
Smith, Bud	3	0	2.13	6	6	0	0	38	33	10	9	13	34	.232	L	L	6-0	170	10-23-79	1998	Lakewood, Calif.
Smith, Travis	4	7	2.31	16	13	1	0	86	76	24	22	14	62	.239	R	R	5-10	170	11-7-72	1995	Bend, Ore.
Sparks, Steve	0	0	10.80	2	0	0	0	3	1	4	4	6	2	.111	R	R	6-4	220	3-28-75	1998	Mobile, Ala.
Stechschulte, Gene	1	0	1.80	10	0	0	5	10	8	2	2	2	7	.210	R	R	6-5	210	8-12-73	1996	Kalida, Ohio
Stemle, Steve	3	4	3.65	20	11	0	0	94	97	41	38	23	55	.265	R	R	6-4	200	5-20-77	1998	New Albany, Ind.
Stephenson, Garrett	0	1	3.55	3	3	0	0	13	12	5	5	2	12	.260	R	R	6-5	200	1-2-72	1992	Kimberly, Idaho
Walrond, Les	8	7	4.98	28	18	0	0	123	127	75	68	63	111	.270	L	L	6-0	190	11-7-76	1998	Brentwood, Tenn.
Weibl, Clint	5	8	3.50	24	18	1	0	111	122	49	43	24	63	.283	R	R	6-3	180	3-17-75	1996	Dawson, Pa.
White, Rick	0	0	2.45	3	0	0	0	4	4	1	1	3	4	.285	R	R	6-4	230	12-23-68	1990	Springfield, Ohio
2-team (2 Colo. Spr.)	0	1	4.76	5	0	0	0	6	7	3	3	3	6	.304							

ORGANIZATION STATISTICS

PITCHING	W	L	ERA	G	GS	CG	SV	IP	H	R	ER	BB	SO	AVG	B	T	HT	WT	DOB	1st Yr	Resides
Williams, Woody	1	0	1.80	1	1	0	0	5	1	1	1	1	7	.066	R	R	6-0	190	8-19-66	1988	Fresno, Texas
Woodard, Steve	2	3	6.30	7	6	1	0	40	53	28	28	3	42	.319	L	R	6-4	210	5-15-75	1994	Hartselle, Ala.

FIELDING

Catcher	PCT	G	PO	A	E	DP	PB
Andreopoulos	.988	24	149	9	2	0	2
Coolbaugh	.000	1	0	0	0	0	0
Davis	1.000	19	81	4	0	2	0
Garrick	.980	24	143	7	3	1	0
McDonald	.995	78	516	37	3	7	2
Rumfield	.974	7	36	2	1	0	0

First Base	PCT	G	PO	A	E	DP
Balfe	1.000	1	9	1	0	1
Chamblee	1.000	1	5	0	0	0
Coolbaugh	1.000	1	11	0	0	2
Cruz	.995	122	1020	70	5	129
Davis	.975	6	38	1	1	5
Frank	.943	6	33	0	2	2
Riggs	.958	3	20	3	1	2
Rumfield	1.000	6	49	5	0	4
Snopek	1.000	2	12	0	0	3

Second Base	PCT	G	PO	A	E	DP
Chamblee	1.000	1	1	2	0	0
Clapp	.978	92	182	261	10	70
Meyers	.976	20	31	52	2	16
Morris	.990	24	42	62	1	17
Riggs	1.000	5	3	8	0	2
Snopek	.939	8	12	19	2	8

Third Base	PCT	G	PO	A	E	DP
Clapp	.857	6	3	9	2	0
Coolbaugh	.965	109	86	213	11	20
Davis	1.000	3	4	1	0	0
Meyers	1.000	2	1	1	0	0
Morris	.750	4	2	7	3	1
Riggs	.881	13	21	16	5	3
Snopek	.885	11	2	21	3	2

Shortstop	PCT	G	PO	A	E	DP
Coolbaugh	.958	5	10	13	1	5
Delgado	.977	97	142	285	10	69
Meyers	.963	7	5	21	1	3
Nicholson	.929	39	56	100	12	22
Snopek	.857	2	1	5	1	0

Outfield	PCT	G	PO	A	E	DP
Balfe	1.000	2	4	0	0	0
Chamblee	1.000	1	1	0	0	0
Clapp	1.000	3	6	1	0	0
Davis	1.000	1	1	0	0	0
Frank	.971	51	96	6	3	2
Meyers	.976	62	114	7	3	0
Mota	.986	35	66	2	1	1
Nunnally	.983	74	167	7	3	4
Ortega	.978	70	129	4	3	0
Riggs	.955	14	21	0	1	0
Saturria	.948	24	71	2	4	0
Snopek	.000	1	0	0	0	0
Taguchi	.990	88	196	11	2	1
Williams	1.000	18	33	1	0	0

NEW HAVEN RAVENS — Class AA

EASTERN LEAGUE

BATTING	AVG	G	AB	R	H	2B	3B	HR	RBI	BB	SO	SB	CS	SLG	OBP	B	T	HT	WT	DOB	1st Yr	Resides
Almonte, Wady	.188	17	48	3	9	1	0	0	3	1	11	1	0	.208	.220	R	R	6-0	200	4-20-75	1993	Higuey, D.R.
Bowers, Jason	.286	104	343	45	98	18	3	3	37	26	49	3	2	.382	.346	R	R	5-11	170	1-27-78	1998	Uniontown, Pa.
Burnett, Mark	.308	16	39	4	12	1	0	0	8	5	9	0	0	.333	.386	L	R	5-11	170	2-16-77	1999	Benton, Ark.
Chamblee, Jim	.274	122	434	77	119	32	3	17	72	48	92	8	2	.479	.355	R	R	6-4	170	5-6-75	1995	Denton, Texas
Crisp, Covelli	.301	89	355	61	107	16	1	9	47	36	56	26	10	.428	.365	S	R	6-0	180	11-1-79	1999	Desert Hot Springs, Calif.
Davidson, Cleatus	.192	23	52	7	10	0	1	1	7	5	12	2	0	.288	.263	S	R	5-10	180	11-1-76	1994	Haines City, Fla.
Farnsworth, Troy	.086	20	58	1	5	0	0	0	1	5	25	0	1	.086	.172	R	R	6-2	200	2-4-76	1998	West Valley City, Utah
Frank, Mike	.306	16	62	8	19	1	2	2	9	8	5	1	1	.484	.394	L	L	6-2	190	1-14-75	1997	Upland, Calif.
Gall, John	.316	135	526	82	166	45	3	20	81	38	75	4	1	.527	.362	R	R	6-0	190	4-2-78	2000	Portola Valley, Calif.
Garcia, Luis	.266	88	308	42	82	16	1	12	37	32	59	3	2	.442	.335	R	R	6-4	180	11-5-78	1997	Guadalajara, Mexico
Hart, Bo	.249	104	405	61	101	17	6	4	39	43	82	14	7	.351	.338	R	R	5-11	170	9-27-76	1999	Laselva Beach, Calif.
Haynes, Dee	.312	131	504	75	157	29	4	21	98	25	67	3	2	.510	.355	R	R	6-0	200	2-22-78	2000	Columbus, Miss.
Heintz, Chris	.314	105	373	40	117	29	1	7	45	19	61	1	0	.453	.349	R	R	6-1	200	8-6-74	1996	Clearwater, Fla.
Jacobsen, Bucky	.294	34	102	13	30	11	0	4	21	9	25	0	0	.520	.360	R	R	6-4	220	8-30-75	1997	Hermiston, Ore.
LeBron, Juan	.262	33	107	18	28	7	1	3	12	5	17	3	1	.430	.296	R	R	6-4	190	6-7-77	1995	Arroyo, P.R.
Martinez, Eddy	.213	24	80	8	17	4	0	0	3	4	17	1	1	.263	.284	R	R	6-2	170	10-23-77	1995	San Pedro de Macoris, D.R.
Nicholson, Kevin	.299	58	231	40	69	16	3	4	36	21	31	3	6	.446	.353	S	R	5-10	190	3-29-76	1997	Surrey, B.C.
Pogue, Jamie	.192	68	208	21	40	12	0	3	26	33	38	1	1	.293	.309	R	R	6-4	230	8-17-77	1999	Guelph, Ontario
Taguchi, So	.308	26	107	21	33	10	0	1	15	9	15	3	1	.430	.375	R	R	5-10	160	7-2-69	2002	Nishinomiya, Japan
Thompson, Andy	.000	2	5	1	0	0	0	0	1	2	4	0	0	.000	.250	R	R	6-3	220	8-28-75	1995	Cottage Grove, Wis.
Weber, Jake	.291	70	196	20	57	6	0	2	23	14	22	3	4	.352	.336	L	R	5-11	180	4-22-76	1998	Wappinger Falls, N.Y.
Weekly, Chris	.253	40	91	13	23	6	0	0	4	13	25	0	1	.319	.346	L	R	6-2	190	12-4-76	1999	Mesa, Ariz.

PITCHING	W	L	ERA	G	GS	CG	SV	IP	H	R	ER	BB	SO	AVG	B	T	HT	WT	DOB	1st Yr	Resides
Cook, B.R.	7	13	4.57	28	28	2	0	163	180	106	83	65	111	.281	R	R	6-4	200	3-2-78	1999	Salem, Ore.
Correa, Cristobal	6	9	4.53	26	26	0	0	137	143	77	69	58	76	.275	R	R	6-1	170	12-5-79	1998	Guarico, Venez.
Cummings, Jeremy	4	3	3.69	14	13	0	0	78	68	33	32	23	52	.242	R	R	6-2	210	11-7-76	1999	Hurricane, W.Va.
Duff, Matt	11	1	1.38	47	0	0	4	65	38	12	10	21	91	.167	R	R	6-1	190	10-6-74	1997	Alligator, Miss.
Estrella, Leo	2	2	4.81	14	5	0	0	39	46	30	21	20	23	.289	R	R	6-1	180	2-20-75	1994	Port St. Lucie, Fla.
Janke, Cheyenne	12	8	3.48	28	23	1	0	150	142	71	58	41	112	.246	R	R	6-5	230	2-16-77	1999	Elk Mound, Wis.
Journell, Jimmy	3	3	2.70	10	10	2	0	67	50	22	20	18	66	.205	R	R	6-4	200	12-29-77	1999	Springfield, Ohio
Karnuth, Jason	3	4	3.60	58	0	0	4	70	74	34	28	23	46	.265	R	R	6-2	190	5-15-76	1997	Glen Ellyn, Ill.
Kline, Steve	0	0	0.00	1	1	0	0	2	0	0	0	1	2	.000	S	L	6-1	210	8-22-72	1993	Winfield, Pa.
Lambert, Jeremy	1	1	6.16	18	0	0	0	19	24	13	13	11	21	.315	R	R	6-1	190	1-10-79	1997	Taylorsville, Utah
Langen, Brian	2	0	4.08	46	0	0	0	53	48	28	24	31	33	.240	L	L	6-7	210	3-13-78	1998	Farmersville, Ill.
Layfield, Scotty	6	4	2.35	58	0	0	24	65	54	22	17	24	63	.226	R	R	6-2	200	9-13-76	1999	Montezuma, Ga.
Padilla, Roy	0	1	7.71	3	0	0	0	2	3	2	2	5	2	.333	L	L	6-5	220	8-4-75	1993	Panama City, Panama
Pageler, Mick	0	0	9.00	3	0	0	0	2	5	2	2	1	3	.454	R	R	6-2	200	4-30-76	1996	Mesa, Ariz.
Parrott, Rhett	4	1	2.86	9	9	3	0	66	53	24	21	13	38	.222	R	R	6-2	190	11-12-79	2001	Dalton, Ga.
Ponce DeLeon, Damon	0	2	22.50	4	0	0	0	4	13	10	10	1	2	.619	R	R	5-11	180	11-2-77	2000	Demarest, N.J.
Prather, Scott	2	3	6.07	11	4	0	0	30	37	25	20	18	21	.296	L	L	6-2	180	10-8-76	1998	Atlanta, Ga.
Sansom, Trevor	4	4	4.07	47	1	0	0	80	78	39	36	29	51	.256	R	R	6-4	190	5-6-76	1999	Winfield, W.Va.
Schurman, Ryan	0	3	7.06	18	8	0	0	51	67	41	40	20	40	.314	R	R	6-3	180	8-28-76	1995	Tualatin, Ore.
Sprague, Kevin	0	0	6.75	6	0	0	0	4	5	3	3	2	1	.312	L	L	6-4	210	3-10-77	1999	Kansas City, Kan.
Stemle, Steve	5	2	4.36	8	7	0	0	43	45	24	21	15	26	.279	R	R	6-4	200	5-20-77	1998	New Albany, Ind.
Walrond, Les	2	1	2.42	4	4	0	0	22	19	8	6	10	31	.220	L	L	6-0	190	11-7-76	1998	Brentwood, Tenn.

FIELDING

Catcher	PCT	G	PO	A	E	DP	PB
Heintz	.986	82	504	65	8	4	17
Pogue	.985	64	397	53	7	0	6

First Base	PCT	G	PO	A	E	DP
Chamblee	.991	22	195	15	2	14
Farnsworth	.980	7	48	2	1	4
Gall	.990	95	862	40	9	77
Garcia	1.000	6	52	5	0	3
Heintz	.000	1	0	0	0	0
Jacobsen	.984	16	109	12	2	11

Second Base	PCT	G	PO	A	E	DP
Bowers	1.000	7	15	9	0	3
Burnett	.982	14	13	43	1	6
Chamblee	.875	3	3	4	1	0
Davidson	.923	2	6	6	1	1
Hart	.985	102	188	270	7	61
Martinez	.000	1	0	0	0	0
Nicholson	.967	13	17	41	2	8
Weekly	1.000	10	14	17	0	4

Third Base	PCT	G	PO	A	E	DP
Bowers	.964	9	7	20	1	0

Chamblee	.925	85	70	175	20	17					
Farnsworth	.900	8	1	17	2	1					
Gall	.870	18	15	32	7	2					
Heintz	.000	1	0	0	0	0					
Martinez	.875	4	2	5	1	0					
Nicholson	.891	16	12	29	5	5					
Weekly	.926	13	5	20	2	3					

Shortstop	PCT	G	PO	A	E	DP
Bowers	.953	86	153	230	19	55

Davidson	.976	9	11	29	1	3
Hart	1.000	1	0	1	0	1
Martinez	.926	19	26	49	6	10
Nicholson	.944	32	43	91	8	12

Outfield	PCT	G	PO	A	E	DP
Almonte	1.000	9	15	0	0	0
Chamblee	1.000	7	8	0	0	0
Crisp	.985	80	183	9	3	1
Frank	.975	16	38	1	1	0

Gall	1.000	8	10	0	0	0
Garcia	.972	80	132	6	4	0
Haynes	.946	122	213	14	13	0
Jacobsen	1.000	4	4	0	0	0
LeBron	.980	31	47	2	1	0
Taguchi	.970	26	64	1	2	0
Thompson	1.000	2	5	0	0	0
Weber	1.000	49	65	1	0	0
Weekly	1.000	6	7	1	0	0

POTOMAC CANNONS — High Class A

CAROLINA LEAGUE

BATTING	AVG	G	AB	R	H	2B	3B	HR	RBI	BB	SO	SB	CS	SLG	OBP	B	T	HT	WT	DOB	1st Yr	Resides
Araujo, Ramon	.214	59	173	22	37	6	0	0	11	6	34	7	3	.249	.239	S	R	5-10	150	3-4-81	1997	Bani, D.R.
Brisson, Dustin	.210	62	214	15	45	7	0	5	21	8	49	1	2	.313	.246	L	R	6-3	210	3-18-78	2000	West Palm Beach, Fla.
Burnett, Mark	.265	73	275	33	73	14	6	2	40	18	38	10	1	.382	.317	L	R	5-11	170	2-16-77	1999	Benton, Ark.
Canelliz, Chris	.259	15	27	2	7	0	0	0	3	6	7	0	0	.259	.394	R	R	6-0	180	1-2-81	2002	Brooklyn, N.Y.
Cordova, Ricardo	.168	34	95	9	16	2	0	3	9	7	25	0	1	.284	.223	S	R	5-11	160	7-5-81	1998	Aragua, Venez.
Davidson, Seth	.192	42	120	15	23	7	0	0	9	4	9	4	1	.250	.220	L	R	6-0	170	2-26-79	2001	San Diego, Calif.
Fera, Aaron	.258	70	252	34	65	15	1	12	36	22	61	4	1	.468	.324	R	R	6-2	220	11-13-77	1999	Sault Ste. Marie, Ontario
Fox, Mike	.059	8	17	0	1	0	0	0	0	1	4	0	1	.059	.111	R	R	6-1	190	8-13-79	2001	Coral Springs, Fla.
Garrick, Matt	.333	11	39	3	13	3	0	1	6	3	12	0	0	.487	.381	R	R	6-0	180	8-19-75	1997	Duncanville, Texas
Hamill, Ryan	.219	96	338	38	74	15	1	9	32	23	60	1	1	.349	.276	R	R	6-0	200	10-3-78	2000	Woodland Hills, Calif.
Hernandez, Johnny	.283	139	498	54	141	24	5	1	62	67	111	16	14	.357	.369	S	L	6-1	180	9-11-79	1999	Brooklyn, N.Y.
Jaramillo, Milko	.241	109	374	43	90	17	1	2	30	28	63	5	2	.307	.301	S	R	5-11	160	1-21-80	1996	Caracas, Venez.
Leach, Nick	.217	16	60	4	13	2	0	1	8	3	15	0	0	.300	.273	L	R	6-1	190	12-7-77	1996	Madera, Calif.
Lewis, Russell	.149	20	67	3	10	2	0	0	1	3	13	1	1	.179	.186	L	R	5-8	170	3-3-78	2000	Blue Ridge, Texas
Luster, Jeremy	.203	53	192	22	39	8	1	4	25	16	23	3	5	.318	.267	S	R	6-4	220	6-17-77	1999	Canton, Ga.
Morris, Chris	.249	114	422	68	105	17	2	0	38	58	92	55	19	.299	.348	S	R	5-8	180	7-1-79	2000	Andrews, S.C.
Moylan, Dan	.284	66	215	34	61	3	0	3	33	46	35	3	1	.340	.415	L	R	6-0	190	4-24-79	2000	Keene, N.H.
Munoz, Billy	.253	47	166	22	42	9	1	6	27	30	51	4	2	.428	.371	L	L	6-2	220	6-30-75	1998	Mesa, Ariz.
Netwall, Chris	.250	14	36	0	9	1	0	0	4	1	6	0	0	.278	.270	R	R	6-1	200	11-17-79	2001	Allentown, Pa.
Rodgers, Albert	.251	104	354	46	89	21	1	9	45	33	98	1	5	.393	.328	R	R	6-2	190	6-8-79	2000	Long Beach, Calif.
Schumaker, Skip	.287	136	551	71	158	22	4	2	44	45	84	26	16	.352	.342	L	R	5-10	170	2-3-80	2001	Laguna Niguel, Calif.
Williams, Matt	.242	47	157	17	38	9	1	5	17	22	45	2	0	.408	.353	R	R	6-1	210	3-24-79	2001	Signal Hill, Calif.

PITCHING	W	L	ERA	G	GS	CG	SV	IP	H	R	ER	BB	SO	AVG	B	T	HT	WT	DOB	1st Yr	Resides
Axelson, Josh	6	7	4.09	32	20	2	0	136	135	72	62	40	82	.259	R	R	6-1	200	12-4-78	2000	Brooklyn, Mich.
Benes, Andy	0	0	9.00	1	1	0	0	7	8	7	7	6	3	.307	R	R	6-6	240	8-20-67	1989	Town and Country, Mo.
Burgess, Richie	0	1	3.00	9	0	0	0	9	14	4	3	6	6	.368	R	R	6-4	210	10-9-79	2000	Redlands, Calif.
Cali, Carmen	2	2	4.11	29	0	0	0	35	31	18	16	21	24	.248	L	L	5-10	180	11-4-78	2000	Naples, Fla.
Cook, Jeremy	5	9	4.76	47	5	0	6	87	95	51	46	24	70	.274	R	R	6-6	230	5-11-78	2000	Yuba City, Calif.
Cummings, Jeremy	5	5	3.75	14	14	0	0	82	83	40	34	21	86	.262	R	R	6-2	210	11-7-76	1999	Hurricane, W.Va.
Duff, Matt	0	0	0.00	4	0	0	4	4	4	0	0	1	7	.235	R	R	6-1	190	10-6-74	1997	Alligator, Miss.
Ewasko, Tod	1	0	5.19	5	0	0	0	9	12	5	5	0	4	.315	R	R	6-2	230	6-1-78	2002	Orlando, Fla.
Graves, Don	2	7	3.81	14	13	0	0	80	87	42	34	33	50	.280	R	R	6-4	200	1-3-81	1999	Boonville, Mo.
Haren, Dan	3	6	3.62	14	14	1	0	92	90	43	37	19	82	.252	R	R	6-5	220	9-17-80	2001	West Covina, Calif.
Kinney, Josh	1	3	2.29	44	0	0	7	55	52	21	14	23	42	.247	R	R	6-1	190	3-31-79	2001	Port Allegheny, Pa.
Kohl, Doug	0	2	3.42	16	1	0	0	23	26	14	9	10	16	.000	R	R	6-3	200	7-9-79	1997	Henderson, Nev.
Martinez, Miguel	4	3	6.55	8	0	0	0	34	44	27	25	8	18	.323	R	R	6-1	160	9-29-81	1999	Monte Cristi, D.R.
Medlock, Chet	1	1	6.30	7	2	0	0	10	12	9	7	8	4	.292	R	R	6-1	170	10-23-78	2000	Brusly, La.
Mejia, Juan	6	7	3.09	23	16	3	0	119	121	50	41	41	49	.270	R	R	6-2	160	12-1-79	1996	Azua, D.R.
Merrigan, Josh	0	0	3.94	11	1	0	0	16	19	12	7	8	9	.287	L	L	6-4	220	6-30-78	2001	Yankton, S.D.
Meyer, Mike	0	1	7.71	13	0	0	0	21	34	22	18	4	9	.377	R	R	6-2	180	12-18-77	2000	Tucson, Ariz.
Novinsky, John	7	6	4.27	30	7	0	11	59	66	42	28	20	55	.279	R	R	6-3	190	4-25-79	2001	Hauppauge, N.Y.
Parrott, Rhett	8	5	2.71	19	19	2	0	113	91	42	34	41	82	.220	R	R	6-2	190	11-22-79	2001	Dalton, Ga.
Ponce DeLeon, Damon	2	3	6.42	27	0	0	0	41	54	33	29	11	35	.321	R	R	5-11	180	11-2-77	2000	Demarest, N.J.
Rawson, Anthony	1	4	3.63	48	0	0	0	52	46	28	21	31	47	.240	L	L	5-11	180	7-31-80	2001	Kosciusko, Miss.
Smith, Jared	0	0	11.57	6	0	0	0	7	5	9	9	10	9	.192	L	R	6-2	200	12-1-78	2001	Vestavia Hills, Ala.
Sprague, Kevin	5	2	5.89	28	9	0	1	65	65	30	21	25	46	.254	L	L	6-4	210	3-10-77	1999	Kansas City, Kan.
Stocks, Nick	0	2	5.74	3	3	0	0	16	18	13	10	6	11	.276	R	R	6-2	180	8-27-78	1999	Tampa, Fla.
Villalon, Julio	3	2	2.33	7	7	0	0	46	36	12	12	14	42	.208	R	R	6-2	180	5-11-78	2000	San Jose, Costa Rica

FIELDING

Catcher	PCT	G	PO	A	E	DP	PB
Garrick	.986	9	66	3	1	0	5
Hamill	.980	66	411	70	10	5	7
Moylan	.987	57	333	40	5	2	8
Netwall	.989	13	74	14	1	0	0

First Base	PCT	G	PO	A	E	DP
Brisson	.985	29	186	16	3	19
Canelliz	1.000	1	1	0	0	0
Hamill	.889	2	8	0	1	1
Kohl	1.000	1	6	0	0	1
Leach	.974	11	104	9	3	8
Luster	.980	24	179	17	4	25
Moylan	1.000	2	21	1	0	0
Munoz	.989	43	331	39	4	33
Rodgers	.985	33	244	22	4	21
Williams	.975	13	112	6	3	11

Second Base	PCT	G	PO	A	E	DP
Araujo	.980	45	115	126	5	27
Burnett	.959	65	131	176	13	41
Canelliz	1.000	3	15	14	0	3
Cordova	.909	10	26	24	5	8
Davidson	.957	18	28	38	3	3
Lewis	1.000	4	8	8	0	3

Third Base	PCT	G	PO	A	E	DP
Araujo	.923	11	3	9	1	0
Brisson	.933	8	7	21	2	2
Canelliz	1.000	2	1	5	0	0
Cordova	1.000	2	0	4	0	0
Davidson	.909	6	5	5	1	0
Fox	.941	7	3	13	1	1
Lewis	.967	12	6	23	1	2
Luster	.889	14	6	34	5	1
Rodgers	.943	70	54	128	11	12

Williams	.849	24	21	41	11	3

Shortstop	PCT	G	PO	A	E	DP
Araujo	1.000	1	0	2	0	0
Canelliz	.000	1	0	0	0	0
Cordova	.907	20	30	38	7	9
Davidson	.963	16	29	50	3	17
Jaramillo	.948	109	175	302	26	65

Outfield	PCT	G	PO	A	E	DP
Burnett	.929	10	13	0	1	0
Fera	.978	26	43	2	1	0
Hernandez	.982	139	266	9	5	2
Lewis	1.000	2	7	0	0	0
Morris	.986	113	284	5	4	2
Munoz	.000	1	0	0	2	0
Rodgers	1.000	5	6	0	0	0
Schumaker	.988	136	230	8	3	2

ORGANIZATION STATISTICS

MIDWEST LEAGUE

BATTING	AVG	G	AB	R	H	2B	3B	HR	RBI	BB	SO	SB	CS	SLG	OBP	B	T	HT	WT	DOB	1st Yr	Resides
Asadoorian, Rick	.265	137	445	70	118	12	11	8	55	44	96	14	8	.396	.340	R	R	6-2	180	7-23-80	1999	Whitinsville, Mass.
Boyd, Shaun	.313	129	520	91	163	36	5	12	60	54	78	32	7	.471	.379	R	R	5-10	170	8-15-81	2000	Las Vegas, Nev.
Chauncey, Clinton	.233	20	43	6	10	3	0	0	3	5	11	1	1	.302	.327	R	R	6-1	180	1-1-81	2000	Jacksonville, Fla.
Cordova, Ricardo	.324	24	37	11	12	2	1	1	6	0	8	2	0	.514	.324	S	R	5-11	160	7-5-81	1998	Edo Aragua, Venez.
Duncan, Chris	.271	129	487	58	132	25	4	16	75	44	118	5	5	.437	.337	L	R	6-5	210	5-5-81	1999	Tucson, Ariz.
Eickhorst, Chris	.194	16	36	3	7	4	0	0	1	13	0	0	0	.306	.216	R	R	6-3	200	12-29-79	2002	South Bound Brook, N.J.
Johnson, Gabe	.248	134	516	76	128	32	0	26	93	57	153	6	6	.461	.324	R	R	6-1	190	9-21-79	1998	Delray Beach, Fla.
Lafferty, Will	.111	17	36	1	4	0	0	0	4	3	9	0	1	.111	.190	R	R	6-2	200	4-18-79	2001	Pine Bluff, Alaska
Lemon, Tim	.236	133	500	67	118	36	3	11	78	53	165	17	6	.386	.315	R	R	6-1	180	9-23-80	1998	La Mirada, Calif.
Molina, Yadier	.280	112	393	39	110	20	0	7	50	21	36	2	7	.384	.331	R	R	5-11	180	7-13-82	2001	Vega Alta, P.R.
Moore, Bryan	.121	12	33	2	4	1	0	0	2	2	15	1	0	.152	.194	L	L	6-2	220	3-20-80	2001	Fort Lauderdale, Fla.
Nelson, John	.274	132	481	85	132	28	5	16	63	54	123	16	3	.453	.349	R	R	6-1	190	3-3-79	2001	Denton, Texas
Netwall, Chris	.250	2	4	1	1	0	0	0	0	1	0	0	0	.250	.400	R	R	6-1	200	11-17-79	2001	Allentown, Pa.
Robison, Jordan	.233	103	279	40	65	11	3	7	26	16	74	4	5	.369	.287	R	R	6-3	190	5-26-79	2001	Iona, Idaho
Roman, Jesse	.280	127	472	77	132	22	2	14	65	60	79	7	2	.424	.361	L	L	6-0	190	4-21-79	2001	Woodhaven, N.Y.
Santor, John	.000	1	4	0	0	0	0	0	0	0	1	0	0	.000	.000	S	R	6-1	210	11-16-81	2000	Palmdale, Calif.
Simoneaux, Neil	.161	19	56	4	9	0	0	1	4	4	16	2	1	.214	.230	R	R	6-1	180	3-16-80	2001	Lake Charles, La.
Voshell, Chase	.228	110	346	40	79	24	1	3	36	45	80	8	8	.329	.320	R	R	6-2	180	3-29-79	2000	Milford, Ohio

PITCHING	W	L	ERA	G	GS	CG	SV	IP	H	R	ER	BB	SO	AVG	B	T	HT	WT	DOB	1st Yr	Resides
Barreto, Joel	2	3	2.42	42	0	0	10	45	34	19	12	22	67	.208	R	R	5-10	170	10-14-80	1997	La Guaria, Venez.
Blasdell, Jared	6	2	1.37	53	0	0	23	66	34	11	10	14	79	.154	R	R	5-8	180	5-14-79	2001	Las Vegas, Nev.
Burgess, Richie	4	5	2.69	19	6	0	0	67	55	28	20	10	51	.210	R	R	6-4	210	10-9-79	2000	Redlands, Calif.
Cali, Carmen	1	1	1.78	24	0	0	2	35	36	17	7	14	27	.258	L	L	5-10	180	11-4-78	2000	Naples, Fla.
Caple, Chance	1	4	4.00	5	5	0	0	18	16	8	8	14	9	.242	R	R	6-6	210	8-9-78	1999	Southlake, Texas
Haren, Dan	7	3	1.95	14	14	1	0	102	89	32	22	12	89	.233	R	R	6-5	220	9-17-80	2001	West Covina, Calif.
Johnson, Kelly	0	1	4.30	16	0	0	0	23	27	17	11	10	15	.287	R	R	6-1	210	5-9-80	2000	Tucson, Ariz.
Johnson, Tyler	15	3	2.00	22	18	0	0	121	96	35	27	42	132	.217	S	L	6-2	180	6-7-81	2001	Newbury Park, Calif.
Julianel, Ben	8	3	3.50	38	0	1	0	100	106	49	39	32	96	.270	S	L	6-2	180	9-4-79	2001	Belmont, Calif.
Kline, Steve	0	0	0.00	2	1	0	0	2	1	0	0	1	5	.111	S	L	6-1	210	8-22-72	1993	Winfield, Pa.
Martinez, Miguel	3	0	0.79	5	5	0	0	23	16	2	2	5	10	.213	R	R	6-1	160	9-29-81	1999	Monte Cristi, D.R.
Merrigan, Josh	4	3	2.27	30	0	0	0	44	35	13	11	16	35	.220	L	L	6-4	220	6-30-78	2001	Yankton, S.D.
Narveson, Chris	2	1	4.46	9	9	0	0	42	49	24	21	8	36	.283	L	L	6-3	180	12-20-81	2000	Arden, N.C.
Plancich, Nick	1	5	6.26	19	8	0	0	46	62	35	32	15	27	.321	R	R	6-2	190	9-12-78	2001	Redondo Beach, Calif.
Pope, Justin	8	1	1.38	12	12	2	0	78	48	15	12	12	72	.173	S	R	6-0	180	11-8-79	2001	Lake Worth, Fla.
Rogers, Joe	0	0	2.21	25	0	0	0	41	32	11	10	6	38	.220	L	L	6-2	170	7-19-81	2001	Fullerton, Calif.
Russelburg, Aaron	8	8	3.38	26	24	1	0	147	148	70	55	48	120	.264	R	R	6-4	210	10-17-79	2001	Hawesville, Ky.
Shouse, Dan	1	1	2.19	17	0	0	0	25	20	10	6	7	16	.224	L	L	6-3	190	9-21-78	2001	Wildwood, Mo.
Smith, Jared	2	2	3.48	24	0	0	0	31	21	16	12	24	31	.194	R	R	6-2	200	12-1-78	2001	Vestavia Hills, Ala.
Stephenson, Garrett	0	0	0.00	2	2	0	0	9	0	0	0	1	11	.000	R	R	6-5	200	1-2-72	1992	Kimberly, Idaho
Stocks, Nick	0	0	2.25	1	1	0	0	8	6	2	2	1	3	.222	R	R	6-2	180	8-27-78	1999	Tampa, Fla.
Wodnicki, Mike	11	10	3.49	26	25	2	0	155	144	72	60	37	131	.244	R	R	6-3	210	1-17-80	2001	Southington, Conn.

FIELDING

Catcher	PCT	G	PO	A	E	DP	PB
Chauncey	1.000	19	75	11	0	1	1
Eickhorst	.988	13	72	8	1	0	1
Lafferty	1.000	17	102	11	0	0	1
Molina	.985	112	809	140	14	9	8
Netwall	1.000	2	13	1	0	0	1

First Base	PCT	G	PO	A	E	DP
Duncan	.982	117	983	53	19	80
Johnson	1.000	1	1	1	0	0
Moore	1.000	5	34	2	0	6
Roman	.994	23	145	21	1	15

	PCT	G	PO	A	E	DP
Santor	1.000	1	10	0	0	0
Voshell	1.000	1	2	0	0	0

Second Base	PCT	G	PO	A	E	DP
Boyd	.935	127	221	359	40	75
Chauncey	.000	1	0	0	0	0
Cordova	.700	7	3	4	3	1
Simoneaux	1.000	9	15	19	0	2

Third Base	PCT	G	PO	A	E	DP
Cordova	1.000	1	0	1	0	0
Johnson	.912	120	91	210	29	20
Voshell	.778	19	12	23	10	2

Shortstop	PCT	G	PO	A	E	DP
Cordova	.857	7	4	8	2	2
Nelson	.943	131	184	360	33	66
Simoneaux	.962	7	8	17	1	3

Outfield	PCT	G	PO	A	E	DP
Asadoorian	.979	137	352	18	8	5
Lemon	.988	131	238	11	3	4
Robison	.959	100	132	7	6	0
Roman	.956	84	105	3	5	0
Voshell	1.000	3	3	0	0	0

NEW YORK-PENN LEAGUE

BATTING	AVG	G	AB	R	H	2B	3B	HR	RBI	BB	SO	SB	CS	SLG	OBP	B	T	HT	WT	DOB	1st Yr	Resides
Boyer, Kyle	.292	49	178	27	52	10	3	0	19	14	49	20	4	.382	.357	R	R	6-0	180	3-5-80	2002	Ogden, Utah
Bridges, Josh	.133	8	15	0	2	0	0	0	0	0	5	0	0	.133	.133	R	R	6-0	200	10-21-79	2002	Centreville, Ala.
Chauncey, Clinton	.237	50	152	21	36	7	1	0	11	17	27	7	3	.296	.320	R	R	6-1	180	1-1-81	2000	Jacksonville, Fla.
Durham, Tyler	.224	57	196	19	44	5	0	1	20	13	51	10	5	.265	.292	R	R	6-0	190	10-8-79	2002	Fort Worth, Texas
Eickhorst, Chris	.176	6	17	2	3	1	0	0	2	3	0	0	0	.235	.263	R	R	6-3	200	12-29-79	2002	South Bound Brook, N.J.
Estrada, Rafael	.235	17	17	2	4	0	1	0	2	1	7	3	1	.353	.316	S	R	6-2	170	3-25-81	1999	Aragua, Venez.
Falu, Melvin	.221	49	145	12	32	9	1	1	12	7	22	1	5	.317	.269	S	R	6-0	180	8-28-80	2002	Carolina, P.R.
Gonce, Garris	.205	29	78	6	16	4	0	0	5	4	19	1	0	.256	.253	R	R	6-0	180	9-8-79	2002	Orange Park, Fla.
Gorecki, Reid	.281	73	274	55	77	8	13	8	52	20	57	22	11	.493	.327	R	R	6-1	180	12-22-80	2002	East Rockaway, N.Y.
Green, Steve	.217	7	23	2	5	0	0	1	2	3	0	0	0	.217	.280	L	R	6-1	180	7-22-78	2001	Monticello, Ark.
Hanson, Travis	.294	75	272	31	80	17	5	4	40	12	55	1	1	.438	.326	L	R	6-2	190	1-24-81	2002	Port Orchard, Wash.
Hileman, Jutt	.182	23	77	5	14	3	0	0	6	8	21	1	2	.221	.270	R	R	6-1	180	7-13-81	2000	Palmyra, Pa.
Monette, Daylon	.151	17	53	2	8	3	0	0	3	4	13	2	2	.208	.211	S	L	6-3	200	7-24-81	2002	Colton, Calif.
Moore, Bryan	.050	7	20	0	1	0	0	0	1	2	4	0	0	.050	.136	L	L	6-2	220	3-20-80	2001	Fort Lauderdale, Fla.
Parker, Tyler	.212	42	146	15	31	0	2	2	10	14	50	2	1	.281	.288	R	R	6-3	210	5-13-81	2002	Marietta, Ga.
Santor, John	.293	68	239	44	70	24	1	13	62	32	62	4	2	.565	.380	S	R	6-1	210	11-16-81	2000	Palmdale, Calif.
Schmitt, Billy	.244	52	164	19	40	8	0	2	9	9	35	5	2	.329	.283	R	R	6-1	200	8-16-82	2000	Henderson, Nev.
Simoneaux, Neil	.295	12	44	5	13	3	2	0	10	0	8	3	2	.455	.289	R	R	6-1	180	3-16-80	2001	Lake Charles, La.

BATTING	AVG	G	AB	R	H	2B	3B	HR	RBI	BB	SO	SB	CS	SLG	OBP	B	T	HT	WT	DOB	1st Yr	Resides
Tolotti, Jeff	.253	25	75	8	19	6	0	2	10	3	23	1	1	.413	.282	L	L	6-2	200	5-20-80	2002	Reno, Nev.
Vandever, Joey	.232	71	207	38	48	4	1	0	9	36	51	31	9	.261	.351	R	R	6-2	180	10-30-79	2002	Cincinnati, Ohio
Woodrow, Justin	.173	28	81	10	14	0	1	0	8	10	15	3	1	.198	.272	L	R	6-1	180	3-26-82	2000	Sarver, Pa.

GAMES BY POSITION: C—Bridges 8, Chauncey 46, Eickhorst 5, Parker 24. **1B**—Hileman 1, Moore 3, Parker 1, Santor 55, Schmitt 22. **2B**—Boyer 3, Durham 53, Falu 18, Simoneaux 6. **3B**—Falu 4, Hanson 63, Santor 1, Schmitt 14. **SS**—Boyer 43, Durham 3, Falu 19, Hanson 11, Simoneaux 6. **OF**—Estrada 13, Gonce 24, Gorecki 70, Green 7, Hileman 22, Monette 8, Moore 1, Santor 1, Tolotti 17, Vandever 68, Woodrow 28.

PITCHING	W	L	ERA	G	GS	CG	SV	IP	H	R	ER	BB	SO	AVG	B	T	HT	WT	DOB	1st Yr	Resides
Batista, Roberto	0	4	2.91	27	1	0	13	34	33	18	11	8	19	.250	R	R	6-1	160	3-10-82	1999	Guaymate, D.R.
Brockman, Dave	1	1	5.52	12	2	0	0	15	12	10	9	7	9	.214	R	R	6-1	210	6-14-80	2002	Phoenix, Ariz.
Ciprian, Wilson	7	5	3.32	15	15	2	0	89	78	43	33	22	71	.230	R	R	5-11	160	11-14-82	2000	Villa Mella, D.R.
Coleman, Kevin	1	0	2.00	14	0	0	0	18	12	4	4	7	13	.187	R	R	6-4	200	4-23-79	2002	Marietta, Ga.
D'Amato, Dan	1	1	1.27	23	0	0	1	28	29	8	4	6	23	.261	L	L	6-1	190	11-8-79	2001	Coatesville, Pa.
Davidson, Andy	5	3	2.63	15	6	0	0	65	50	22	19	19	51	.208	L	L	6-2	190	3-1-80	2002	Stevenson Ranch, Calif.
Ewasko, Tod	0	0	0.76	18	0	0	2	24	8	2	2	6	17	.102	R	R	6-2	230	6-1-78	2002	Orlando, Fla.
Flynn, Brian	5	3	2.96	18	4	1	1	52	47	19	17	12	41	.241	R	R	6-1	190	6-27-79	2002	Park Ridge, N.J.
Hawksworth, Blake	1	0	0.00	2	2	0	0	10	6	0	0	2	8	.171	R	R	6-3	190	3-1-83	2002	Sammamish, Wash.
Jaillet, Wes	3	2	2.27	22	1	0	0	36	33	11	9	12	30	.240	R	R	6-2	200	3-20-80	2002	Wildwood, Mo.
Johnson, Kelly	1	1	0.48	16	0	0	0	19	14	2	1	6	16	.202	R	R	6-1	210	5-9-80	2000	Tucson, Ariz.
Martinez, Wilmer	2	5	6.34	14	8	0	0	44	48	33	31	22	23	.274	R	R	6-3	150	4-3-81	1998	Miranda, Venez.
Plancich, Nick	3	2	2.37	7	7	0	0	38	31	12	10	11	18	.227	R	R	6-2	190	9-12-78	2001	Redondo Beach, Calif.
Schweitzer, Scott	2	1	2.93	23	0	0	1	31	20	10	10	23	34	.185	L	L	6-3	230	5-4-80	2002	Alexandria, Ky.
Stocks, Nick	0	2	5.73	7	7	0	0	22	28	14	14	13	24	.307	R	R	6-2	180	8-27-78	1999	Tampa, Fla.
Teekel, Josh	4	4	3.30	16	13	0	0	74	58	31	27	24	66	.218	R	R	6-5	200	9-18-80	1999	Greenwell Springs, La.
Van Gorder, Joe	1	0	2.70	2	2	0	0	10	12	3	3	1	8	.292	L	L	6-2	180	3-10-81	2002	Ithaca, N.Y.
Williams, Blake	0	1	1.69	2	2	0	0	5	2	1	1	1	8	.111	R	R	6-5	210	2-22-79	2000	San Marcos, Texas
Williamson, Willie	2	1	2.25	6	6	0	0	24	12	8	6	19	27	.151	L	L	6-1	180	5-13-80	2002	Manchester, N.H.
Withelder, Gregory	0	1	4.73	21	0	0	0	27	23	15	14	17	30	.234	R	L	6-3	200	5-11-79	2000	Wallingford, Pa.

JOHNSON CITY CARDINALS — Rookie

APPALACHIAN LEAGUE

BATTING	AVG	G	AB	R	H	2B	3B	HR	RBI	BB	SO	SB	CS	SLG	OBP	B	T	HT	WT	DOB	1st Yr	Resides
Belz, Tim	.167	15	36	1	6	0	0	0	1	3	14	1	0	.167	.231	R	R	6-4	210	4-7-80	2002	Westbury, N.Y.
Bridges, Josh	.238	7	21	1	5	1	0	0	3	1	8	0	0	.286	.304	R	R	6-3	200	10-21-79	2002	Centreville, Ala.
Capellan, Domingo	.280	33	100	13	28	8	0	2	9	1	20	5	1	.420	.308	R	R	5-10	180	12-12-82	1999	Cotui, D.R.
Cates, Zach	.206	53	170	28	35	8	2	7	22	27	36	3	3	.400	.322	L	R	6-3	210	9-21-79	2002	Tempe, Ariz.
Davie, Andrew	.219	45	169	18	37	9	2	6	23	8	63	6	1	.402	.263	L	R	6-5	230	1-5-83	2001	Little Rock, Ark.
Estrada, Rafael	.250	7	8	2	2	0	0	0	0	1	3	5	1	.250	.400	S	R	6-2	170	3-25-81	1999	Aragua, Venez.
Evans, Terry	.287	60	230	42	66	22	2	7	41	29	67	17	4	.491	.364	R	R	6-3	200	1-19-82	2002	Dublin, Ga.
Gunn, Cody	.244	29	86	8	21	6	0	2	11	9	22	1	2	.384	.343	L	R	6-0	180	3-9-82	2001	Brewster, Wa.
Hileman, Jutt	.187	26	91	14	17	3	0	2	9	8	27	1	0	.286	.275	R	R	6-1	180	7-13-81	2000	Palmyra, Pa.
Lemanczyk, Matt	.239	60	209	38	50	5	2	1	15	15	42	31	6	.297	.310	R	R	6-2	190	10-5-80	2002	Rockville Centre, N.Y.
Mather, Joe	.232	62	224	29	52	15	2	8	39	27	57	9	1	.424	.320	R	R	6-4	190	7-23-82	2001	Phoenix, Ariz.
McCoy, Mike	.312	50	154	46	48	9	1	4	22	42	23	18	7	.461	.465	R	R	5-9	170	4-2-81	2002	El Cajon, Calif.
Mojica, Robinson	.262	27	61	10	16	3	1	5	4	20	2	1	.393	.318	R	R	6-3	180	5-31-82	2000	Bani, D.R.
Monette, Daylon	.368	16	57	10	21	7	0	1	11	6	11	4	0	.544	.415	S	L	6-3	200	7-24-81	2002	Colton, Calif.
Nolasco, Jose	.271	52	188	25	51	11	3	6	32	5	36	13	4	.457	.292	S	R	6-2	160	6-20-81	1999	Santo Domingo, D.R.
Reyes, Eduardo	.309	29	94	20	29	4	2	4	12	6	26	6	1	.521	.356	R	R	5-11	150	1-14-82	2001	San Pedro de Macoris, D.R.
Rodriguez, Marcos	.214	18	56	7	12	3	2	0	9	3	20	0	1	.339	.267	L	L	6-1	180	4-7-83	2001	Lara, Venez.
Tolotti, Jeff	.289	31	114	14	33	5	6	0	10	10	37	1	0	.439	.344	L	L	6-2	200	5-20-80	2002	Reno, Nev.
Veloz, Gabe	.250	49	152	19	38	12	0	2	23	44	43	2	3	.368	.423	R	R	6-2	190	8-13-80	2002	Upland, Calif.

GAMES BY POSITION: C—Belz 11, Bridges 6, Capellan 33, Gunn 29. **1B**—Bridges 1, Cates 50, Davie 13, Mather 4, Rodriguez 8. **2B**—McCoy 25, Reyes 22, Veloz 29. **3B**—Mather 57, Nolasco 7, Reyes 5. **SS**—McCoy 27, Nolasco 45. **OF**—Estrada 2, Evans 58, Hileman 23, Lemanczyk 57, Mojica 19, Monette 15, Rodriguez 7, Tolotti 29.

PITCHING	W	L	ERA	G	GS	CG	SV	IP	H	R	ER	BB	SO	AVG	B	T	HT	WT	DOB	1st Yr	Resides
Adamczyk, Tyler	4	3	3.41	13	11	0	0	63	56	31	24	35	54	.232	R	R	6-6	190	11-9-82	2001	Westlake, Calif.
Aguero, Miguel	3	3	5.58	14	7	0	0	40	43	35	25	16	39	.268	R	R	6-3	180	5-19-82	2001	Lara, Venez.
Chafey, Hal	0	2	6.10	17	0	0	1	21	22	17	14	19	20	.275	L	L	6-4	210	5-7-80	2002	Moore, S.C.
Estes, Jonathan	4	1	3.38	11	5	0	0	43	55	20	16	6	25	.305	L	R	6-4	210	5-13-80	2002	St. Charles, Mo.
Galbraith, Jason	1	2	2.63	22	0	0	2	27	27	15	8	11	27	.250	L	L	6-3	210	7-18-80	2002	Lake Peekskill, N.Y.
Hawksworth, Blake	2	4	3.14	13	12	0	0	66	58	31	23	18	61	.232	R	R	6-3	190	3-1-83	2002	Sammamish, Wash.
Killalea, John	3	1	7.36	15	3	0	0	40	56	37	33	19	30	.333	L	L	6-1	180	2-23-83	2001	Seminole, Fla.
Ledbetter, Aaron	2	4	7.21	16	4	0	0	44	46	41	35	17	49	.264	R	R	6-5	210	6-28-81	2001	Fort Smith, Ark.
Maio, Mitch	1	3	2.67	24	0	0	0	34	29	12	10	7	35	.226	R	R	6-0	190	6-17-79	2002	Salt Lake City, Utah
McClellan, Kyle	0	2	11.25	7	3	0	0	12	17	17	15	7	8	.340	R	R	6-2	180	6-12-84	2002	Florissant, Mo.
Mondesir, James	1	6	8.26	14	9	0	0	40	60	46	37	21	27	.348	S	R	6-4	210	10-10-79	2002	Jamaica, N.Y.
Morales, Juan	0	2	4.24	30	0	0	6	34	36	19	16	15	42	.279	L	L	6-4	170	12-1-82	2000	Bonao, D.R.
Narveson, Chris	0	2	4.91	6	6	0	0	18	23	12	10	6	16	.306	L	L	6-3	180	12-20-81	2000	Arden, N.C.
Reedy, Shane	0	0	2.16	3	3	0	0	8	7	3	2	0	7	.212	R	R	6-2	200	6-2-82	2002	West Jordan, Utah
Scalamandre, Rich	7	1	4.67	25	0	0	6	27	34	19	14	15	20	.314	R	R	5-11	190	8-20-80	2002	Brooklyn, N.Y.
Van Gorder, Joe	1	2	7.36	6	4	0	0	18	25	16	15	5	17	.313	L	L	6-2	180	3-10-81	2002	Ithaca, N.Y.
Van Matre, Gary	0	0	9.00	7	0	0	0	8	16	10	8	6	7	.380	L	L	5-11	160	4-8-80	2002	St. Louis, Mo.
Wehrfritz, Brad	0	0	4.97	21	0	0	0	29	36	19	16	12	16	.302	R	R	6-1	180	6-25-80	2002	Chesterfield, Mo.

SAN DIEGO PADRES

BY JOHN MAFFEI

Nearly every prospect who was close to being ready—and quite honestly some who were not—got a chance to wear a Padres uniform in 2002. The results were a major league record-tying 59 players used and a 66-96 record.

But club officials learned a few things over the course of the season.

The pitching-rich farm system produced four potential stars—Oliver Perez, Jake Peavy, Brandon Villafuerte and Clay Condrey. Along the way, though, the team ran through 35 pitchers, 13 of whom made their major league debuts.

The 20-year-old Perez showed staff-ace stuff while going 4-5, 3.50 in 90 innings. And Peavy was brilliant at times while going 6-7, 4.52 over 98 innings. Villafuerte earned a spot as a setup man for closer Trevor Hoffman, posting a 1.41 ERA over 31 appearances. And Condrey was 1-2, 1.69 in nine games, three of them starts.

Throw in Brian Lawrence (12-12, 3.69), a potential No. 1 starter; Adam Eaton (1-1, 5.40), who bounced back from Tommy John surgery and was spectacular in his last three starts; and Brett Tomko (10-10, 4.49), and the rotation could be in good shape. Plus, Kevin Jarvis (2-4, 4.37) is expected back after an injury-plagued season.

On the down side, Dennis Tankersley (1-4, 8.06), Mike Bynum (1-0, 5.27), Ben Howard (1-2, 9.28) and Eric Cyr (0-1, 10.50) got chances and came up short. And Jeremy Fikac (4-7, 5.48) struggled after a brilliant rookie season.

There is a core of top-notch players—Mark Kotsay (.292-17-61), Ryan Klesko (.300-29-95) and Phil Nevin (.285-12-57)—around whom manager Bruce Bochy can build. But there's the question of where Nevin will play. A third baseman the last three seasons, he'll most likely move to left field to make room for Sean Burroughs (.271-1-11) at third.

After a slow start, Ramon Vazquez (.274-2-32) rallied to have a fine season. He'll play somewhere in the infield—maybe second, or maybe short. And he'll bat at the top of the order—maybe leadoff, or maybe second. So one infield spot must be filled.

After being claimed off waivers from the Mariners, outfielder Eugene Kingsale (.278-2-28) made an impact with his speed and defense, and he earned a shot to play right or center on a regular basis.

Ben Davis was traded away after the 2001 season, and Wiki Gonzalez (.220-1-20) was installed as the No. 1 catcher. But Gonzalez reported to camp out of shape, was hurt, didn't hustle most of the season and was a major disappointment.

On the minor league level, only Class A Lake Elsinore made it to the playoffs in 2002, with the Storm advancing to the California League finals before losing to Stockton. And while there are prospects at the lower levels, there is little immediate help in the minors.

Slugger Xavier Nady (.283-10-43) was being groomed as a left fielder at Triple-A Portland. But if Nevin moves to the outfield, where does Nady fit? Outfielder Jason Bay (.309-1-13) emerged as a prospect at Double-A Mobile after coming over from the Red Sox in a trade. First baseman Tagg Bozied (.214-9-32) struggled at Mobile after a brilliant first half at Lake Elsinore.

At second base, three prospects emerged. Bernie Castro (.260-0-32) had a fine season at Mobile with 43 stolen bases. Jake Gautreau (.286-10-62) was solid at Lake Elsinore, and Josh Barfield (.306-8-57) was brilliant at Class A Fort Wayne.

First baseman Jon Knott (.341-8-73) won the Cal League batting title, and first baseman Paul McAnulty (.379-8-51) won the Rookie-level Pioneer League batting title at Idaho Falls. Gabe Ribas (8-1, 1.97) had 16 saves at short-season Eugene and walked just five batters over 50 innings while striking out 66.

Ryan Klesko

Justin Germano

PLAYERS OF THE YEAR

MAJOR LEAGUE: Ryan Klesko, 1b/of

While the injury-riddled Padres used a major league-record 59 players, Klesko was one of the team's few constants. He led the club in the triple crown categories (.300-29-95) as well as doubles, runs scored, total bases and walks.

MINOR LEAGUE: Justin Germano, rhp

Germano led all Padres farmhands with 14 wins, while splitting the 2002 season between Class A Lake Elsinore and Fort Wayne. His 137 strikeouts and 2.94 ERA ranked third, and he walked just 24 batters in 175 innings.

ORGANIZATION LEADERS

BATTING

*AVG	John Knott, Lake Elsinore/Fort Wayne	.339
R	Marcus Nettles, Lake Elsinore	97
H	John Knott, Lake Elsinore/Fort Wayne	167
TB	John Knott, Lake Elsinore/Fort Wayne	267
2B	John Knott, Lake Elsinore/Fort Wayne	46
3B	Kory DeHaan, Portland	14
HR	Tagg Bozied, Mobile/Lake Elsinore	24
RBI	Tagg Bozied, Mobile/Lake Elsinore	92
BB	Marcus Nettles, Lake Elsinore	101
SO	Jeremy Owens, Portland/Lake Elsinore	157
SB	Pedro De los Santos, Lake Els./Ft. Wayne/Eug.	58

PITCHING

W	Justin Germano, Lake Elsinore/Fort Wayne	14
L	Junior Herndon, Portland	13
#ERA	Ian Harvey, Mobile/Lake Elsinore	2.65
G	Mike Nicolas, Lake Elsinore	65
CG	Junior Herndon, Portland	2
	Jon Huber, Fort Wayne	2
SV	Rusty Tucker, Lake Elsinore/Fort Wayne	27
IP	Justin Germano, Lake Elsinore/Fort Wayne	175
BB	Mark Phillips, Lake Elsinore	94
SO	Mark Phillips, Lake Elsinore	156

*Minimum 250 At-Bats #Minimum 75 Innings

ORGANIZATION STATISTICS

SAN DIEGO PADRES

Manager: Bruce Bochy

2002 Record: 66-96, .407 (5th, NL West)

ORGANIZATION STATISTICS

BATTING	AVG	G	AB	R	H	2B	3B	HR	RBI	BB	SO	SB	CS	SLG	OBP	B	T	HT	WT	DOB	1st Yr	Resides
Barker, Kevin	.158	7	19	0	3	0	0	0	0	1	6	1	0	.158	.200	L	L	6-3	200	7-26-75	1996	Mendota, Va.
Buchanan, Brian	.293	48	92	12	27	5	0	6	13	9	26	0	1	.543	.363	R	R	6-4	230	7-21-73	1994	Fort Myers, Fla.
Burroughs, Sean	.271	63	192	18	52	5	1	1	11	12	30	2	0	.323	.317	L	R	6-2	200	9-12-80	1999	Long Beach, Calif.
Cardona, Javier	.103	15	39	2	4	1	0	0	2	2	10	0	0	.128	.143	R	R	6-1	210	9-15-75	1994	Dorado, P.R.
Crespo, Cesar	.172	25	29	5	5	2	0	0	3	6	3	2	.241	.250	S	R	5-11	170	5-23-79	1997	Caguas, P.R.
Cruz, Deivi	.263	151	514	49	135	28	2	7	47	22	58	2	3	.366	.294	R	R	6-0	180	11-6-72	1993	Nizao, D.R.
De Haan, Kory	.091	12	11	1	1	0	0	0	0	0	6	0	0	.091	.091	L	R	6-2	180	7-16-76	1997	Pella, Iowa
Gant, Ron	.262	102	309	58	81	14	1	18	59	36	59	4	6	.489	.338	R	R	6-0	190	3-2-65	1983	Alpharetta, Ga.
Gonzalez, Wiki	.220	56	164	16	36	8	1	1	20	27	24	0	0	.299	.330	R	R	5-11	200	5-17-74	1992	Palo Negro, Venez.
Hubbard, Trenidad	.209	89	129	16	27	5	0	1	7	14	28	9	6	.271	.285	R	R	5-9	200	5-11-66	1986	Houston, Texas
Jimenez, D'Angelo	.240	87	321	39	77	11	4	3	33	34	63	4	2	.327	.311	S	R	6-0	190	12-21-77	1995	Santo Domingo, D.R.
Kingsale, Eugene	.278	89	216	27	60	10	3	2	28	20	47	9	2	.380	.346	S	R	6-3	190	8-20-76	1994	Oranjestad, Aruba
Klesko, Ryan	.300	146	540	90	162	39	1	29	95	76	86	6	2	.537	.388	L	L	6-3	220	6-12-71	1989	Couington, Ga.
Kotsay, Mark	.292	153	578	82	169	27	7	17	61	39	89	11	9	.452	.359	L	L	6-0	200	12-2-75	1996	Pembroke Pines, Fla.
Lampkin, Tom	.217	104	281	32	61	10	1	10	37	38	59	4	2	.367	.313	L	R	5-11	190	3-4-64	1986	Vancouver, Wash.
Lankford, Ray	.224	81	205	20	46	7	1	6	26	30	61	2	2	.356	.326	L	L	5-11	200	6-5-67	1987	St. Louis, Mo.
Matos, Julius	.238	76	185	19	44	3	0	2	19	9	33	1	1	.286	.279	R	R	5-11	170	12-12-74	1994	Racine, Wis.
Nevin, Phil	.285	107	407	53	116	16	0	12	57	38	87	4	0	.413	.344	R	R	6-2	230	1-19-71	1992	San Diego, Calif.
Nieves, Wil	.181	28	72	2	13	3	1	0	3	4	15	1	0	.250	.224	R	R	5-11	190	9-25-77	1996	Santurce, P.R.
Pelaez, Alex	.250	3	8	0	2	0	0	0	0	0	0	0	0	.250	.250	R	R	5-9	190	4-6-76	1998	Chula Vista, Calif.
Sweeney, Mark	.169	48	65	3	11	3	0	1	4	4	19	0	0	.262	.217	L	L	6-1	190	10-26-69	1991	Scottsdale, Ariz.
Trammell, Bubba	.243	133	403	54	98	16	1	17	56	53	71	1	3	.414	.333	R	R	6-2	220	11-6-71	1994	Clearwater, Fla.
Vazquez, Ramon	.274	128	423	50	116	21	5	2	32	45	79	7	2	.362	.344	L	R	5-11	170	8-21-76	1995	Cayey, P.R.

PITCHING	W	L	ERA	G	GS	CG	SV	IP	H	R	ER	BB	SO	AVG	B	T	HT	WT	DOB	1st Yr	Resides
Boyd, Jason	1	0	7.94	23	0	0	0	28	33	29	25	15	18	.300	R	R	6-3	170	2-23-73	1994	Edwardsville, Ill.
Bynum, Mike	1	0	5.27	14	3	0	0	27	33	16	16	15	17	.308	L	L	6-4	200	3-20-78	1999	Middleburg, Fla.
Condrey, Clay	1	2	1.69	9	3	0	0	27	20	7	5	8	16	.217	R	R	6-3	190	11-19-75	1998	Navasota, Texas
Cyr, Eric	0	1	10.50	5	0	0	0	6	6	7	7	6	4	.235	R	L	6-4	200	2-11-79	1999	Ada, Okla.
Davey, Tom	1	0	5.57	19	0	0	0	21	23	14	13	11	21	.287	R	R	6-7	230	9-11-73	1994	San Diego, Calif.
DeWitt, Matt	0	1	1.23	5	0	0	0	7	6	2	1	3	5	.230	R	R	6-3	220	9-4-77	1995	Las Vegas, Nev.
Eaton, Adam	1	1	5.40	6	6	0	0	33	28	20	20	17	25	.235	R	R	6-2	190	11-23-77	1996	Snohomish, Wash.
Embree, Alan	3	4	0.94	36	0	0	0	29	23	7	3	9	38	.211	L	L	6-2	190	1-23-70	1990	Vancouver, Wash.
Fikac, Jeremy	4	7	5.48	65	0	0	0	69	74	50	42	34	66	.267	R	R	6-2	180	4-8-75	1998	Shiner, Texas
Hoffman, Trevor	2	5	2.73	61	0	0	38	59	52	20	18	18	69	.234	R	R	6-0	210	10-13-67	1989	Del Mar, Calif.
Holtz, Mike	2	2	4.71	33	0	0	0	21	18	14	11	21	19	.236	L	L	5-9	180	10-10-72	1994	Hollidaysburg, Pa.
Howard, Ben	0	1	9.28	3	2	0	0	11	13	11	11	14	10	.302	R	R	6-2	190	1-15-79	1997	Jackson, Tenn.
Jarvis, Kevin	2	4	4.37	7	7	0	0	35	36	19	17	10	24	.268	R	R	6-2	200	8-1-69	1991	Lexington, Ky.
Johnson, Jonathan	1	2	4.11	16	0	0	0	15	15	8	7	5	21	.250	R	R	6-0	180	7-16-74	1995	Irmo, S.C.
Jones, Bobby J.	7	8	5.50	19	18	0	0	108	134	68	66	21	60	.299	R	R	6-4	220	2-10-70	1991	Fresno, Calif.
Jones, Bobby M.	0	0	6.52	4	2	0	0	10	10	7	7	7	7	.270	L	L	6-0	170	4-11-72	1992	East Rutherford, N.J.
2-team (12 New York)	0	0	5.74	16	2	0	0	27	30	18	17	18	18	.288							
Kershner, Jason	0	1	5.79	15	0	0	0	19	15	14	12	10	11	.217	L	L	6-2	160	12-19-76	1995	Scottsdale, Ariz.
Lawrence, Brian	12	12	3.69	35	31	2	0	210	230	97	86	52	149	.280	R	R	6-0	190	5-14-76	1998	Linden, Texas
Lundquist, Dave	0	0	16.88	3	0	0	0	3	8	5	5	5	0	.615	R	R	6-2	200	6-4-73	1993	Hickory, N.C.
Middlebrook, Jason	1	3	5.09	12	2	0	0	35	31	20	20	15	28	.244	R	R	6-3	210	6-26-75	1996	Austin, Texas
Moreno, Juan	0	0	7.50	4	0	0	0	6	6	6	5	10	3	.260	L	L	6-2	190	2-28-75	1994	Cagua, Venez.
Myers, Rodney	1	1	5.91	14	0	0	0	21	29	20	14	10	11	.333	R	R	6-1	200	6-26-69	1990	Chandler, Ariz.
Nickle, Doug	1	0	8.49	10	0	0	0	12	20	13	11	9	7	.357	R	R	6-4	230	10-2-74	1997	Sonoma, Calif.
2-team (4 Philadelphia)	1	0	7.88	14	0	0	0	16	26	16	14	13	9	.346							
Nunez, Jose	0	0	0.00	1	0	0	0	1	0	0	0	1	0	.000	L	L	6-2	170	3-14-79	1996	Monte Cristi, D.R.
Pearson, Jason	0	0	0.00	2	0	0	0	2	1	0	0	0	3	.125	L	L	6-0	195	12-29-75	1998	Cambridge, Mass.
Peavy, Jake	6	7	4.52	17	17	0	0	98	106	54	49	33	90	.273	R	R	6-1	180	5-31-81	1999	Semmes, Ala.
Perez, Oliver	4	5	3.50	16	15	0	0	90	71	37	35	48	94	.217	L	L	6-3	160	8-15-81	1999	Culiacan, Mexico
Pickford, Kevin	0	2	6.00	16	4	0	0	37	37	23	20	20	18	.313	L	L	6-4	200	3-12-75	1993	Fresno, Calif.
Reed, Steve	2	4	1.98	40	0	0	1	41	33	9	9	10	36	.227	R	R	6-2	210	3-11-66	1988	Arvada, Colo.
Shiell, Jason	0	0	27.00	3	0	0	0	1	7	4	4	3	1	.700	R	R	6-0	180	10-19-76	1995	Savannah, Ga.
Tankersley, Dennis	1	4	8.06	17	9	0	0	51	59	46	46	40	39	.304	R	R	6-2	180	2-24-79	1999	St. Charles, Mo.
Tollberg, Brian	5	6	6.13	12	11	0	0	62	88	47	42	19	33	.342	R	R	6-3	190	9-16-72	1994	Bradenton, Fla.
Tomko, Brett	10	10	4.49	32	32	3	0	204	212	107	102	60	126	.266	R	R	6-4	210	4-7-73	1995	San Diego, Calif.
Trujillo, J.J.	0	1	10.13	4	0	0	0	3	4	3	3	6	3	.363	R	R	6-0	180	10-9-75	1999	Corpus Christi, Texas
Villafuerte, Brandon	1	2	1.41	31	0	0	1	32	29	5	5	12	25	.247	R	R	5-11	160	12-17-75	1995	Morgan Hill, Calif.
Walker, Kevin	0	1	5.63	10	0	0	0	8	12	6	5	5	11	.333	L	L	6-4	190	9-20-76	1995	Glen Rose, Texas

FIELDING

Catcher	PCT	G	PO	A	E	DP	PB
Cardona	.976	14	76	5	2	2	0
Gonzalez	.985	54	367	27	6	4	6
Lampkin	.992	94	553	42	5	7	7
Nieves	.971	27	160	8	5	0	1

First Base	PCT	G	PO	A	E	DP
Barker	1.000	6	49	1	0	5

	PCT	G	PO	A	E	DP
Buchanan	1.000	15	74	6	0	6
Cruz	1.000	1	4	0	0	0
Klesko	.993	112	918	73	7	92
Matos	1.000	2	3	0	0	0
Nevin	.986	36	269	22	4	30
Pelaez	1.000	1	12	1	0	3
Sweeney	.946	11	32	3	2	5

Second Base	PCT	G	PO	A	E	DP
Burroughs	.980	13	26	23	1	8
Crespo	1.000	4	1	2	0	0
Hubbard	1.000	4	0	4	0	1
Jimenez	.975	54	116	159	7	44
Matos	.963	49	72	110	7	26
Pelaez	.000	1	0	0	0	0

Vazquez .... .985	81	131	190	5	46	

Third Base	PCT	G	PO	A	E	DP
Burroughs	.935	48	33	68	7	5
Crespo	.857	5	1	5	1	1
Hubbard	.900	6	4	5	1	1
Jimenez	.947	32	19	70	5	9
Matos	.931	17	9	18	2	3
Nevin	.928	71	49	131	14	17
Pelaez	1.000	1	1	1	0	0
Vazquez	1.000	20	7	27	0	5

Shortstop	PCT	G	PO	A	E	DP
Crespo	.000	1	0	0	0	0
Cruz	.973	147	169	372	15	83
Matos	1.000	4	3	3	0	1
Vazquez	.985	41	32	97	2	16

Outfield	PCT	G	PO	A	E	DP
Buchanan	.950	14	18	1	1	0
Crespo	1.000	7	2	1	0	0
De Haan	1.000	9	6	0	0	0
Gant	.980	80	142	6	3	0

Hubbard .... .981	57	49	2	1	0	
Kingsale 985	82	127	4	2	0	
Klesko 1.000	31	39	0	0	0	
Kotsay 989	147	349	11	4	3	
Lankford 953	59	98	4	5	1	
Matos 1.000	3	1	0	0	0	
Sweeney 1.000	5	8	0	0	0	
Trammell 973	122	174	4	5	1	

Mark Kotsay: second among Padres regulars with .292 average

Brian Lawrence: led staff with 12 wins

LARRY GOREN

FARM SYSTEM

Director, Player Development: Tye Waller

Class	Farm Team	League	W	L	Pct.	Finish*	Manager	First Yr.
AAA	Portland (Ore.) Beavers	Pacific Coast	72	71	.503	t-8th (16)	Rick Sweet	2001
AA	Mobile (Ala.) BayBears	Southern	76	63	.547	3rd (10)	Craig Colbert	1997
High A	Lake Elsinore (Calif.) Storm	California	75	65	.536	4th (10)	George Hendrick	2001
Low A	Fort Wayne (Ind.) Wizards	Midwest	69	68	.504	8th (14)	Tracy Woodson	1999
SS A	Eugene (Ore.) Emeralds	Northwest	41	35	.539	t-3rd (8)	Jeff Gardner	2001
Rookie	Idaho Falls (Idaho) Braves	Pioneer	32	44	.421	8th (8)	Don Werner	1995

*Finish in overall standings (No. of teams in league)

PORTLAND BEAVERS — Class AAA

PACIFIC COAST LEAGUE

BATTING	AVG	G	AB	R	H	2B	3B	HR	RBI	BB	SO	SB	CS	SLG	OBP	B	T	HT	WT	DOB	1st Yr	Resides
Amezcua, Adan	.312	43	138	17	43	9	2	2	19	11	14	0	0	.449	.377	R	R	6-1	190	3-9-74	1993	Mazatlan, Mexico
Barker, Kevin	.251	113	390	54	98	14	1	14	48	46	70	1	1	.400	.333	L	L	6-3	200	7-26-75	1996	Mendota, Va.
Benjamin, Al	.183	56	169	18	31	9	1	2	12	4	37	1	1	.284	.216	R	R	6-1	200	9-9-77	1996	Houston, Texas
Bitter, Jarrod	.333	1	3	1	1	0	0	0	2	0	0	0	0	.333	.333	R	R	6-1	220	10-16-78	2000	Tyler, Texas
Blakely, Darren	.133	4	15	3	2	0	0	2	3	1	3	0	0	.533	.188	S	R	6-0	190	3-14-77	1998	Pensacola, Fla.
Burroughs, Sean	.302	50	179	29	54	16	2	2	23	21	16	1	0	.447	.380	L	R	6-2	200	9-12-80	1999	Long Beach, Calif.
Cardona, Javier	.286	20	63	7	18	1	2	1	6	2	12	0	0	.413	.313	R	R	6-1	210	9-15-75	1994	Dorado, P.R.
Crespo, Cesar	.258	92	322	43	83	17	2	9	37	50	78	21	7	.407	.363	S	R	5-11	170	5-23-79	1997	Caguas, P.R.
DeHaan, Kory	.283	120	442	64	125	31	14	2	39	31	96	23	9	.430	.340	L	R	6-2	180	7-16-76	1997	Pella, Iowa
Eberwein, Kevin	.209	90	320	33	67	17	0	12	36	32	101	0	1	.375	.285	R	R	6-4	200	3-30-77	1998	Las Vegas, Nev.
Fernandez, Alex	.313	22	80	7	25	4	0	2	13	2	13	1	3	.438	.333	L	L	6-1	200	5-15-81	1998	Cotui, D.R.
Gomez, Rich	.237	113	334	43	79	15	2	11	53	25	74	13	5	.392	.297	R	R	5-11	190	7-19-76	1996	San Francisco de Macoris, D.R.
Hopper, Shane	.278	35	115	12	32	3	1	5	16	7	27	4	1	.452	.336	R	R	6-1	200	9-22-75	1999	Winder, Ga.

BATTING

BATTING	AVG	G	AB	R	H	2B	3B	HR	RBI	BB	SO	SB	CS	SLG	OBP	B	T	HT	WT	DOB	1st Yr	Resides
Hubbard, Trenidad	.379	8	29	9	11	2	0	3	6	2	3	2	2	.759	.406	R	R	5-9	200	5-11-66	1986	Houston, Texas
Incaviglia, Pete	.122	15	41	2	5	1	0	0	1	4	16	0	0	.146	.200	R	R	6-1	230	4-2-64	1986	Colleyville, Texas
Loyd, Brian	.169	24	83	10	14	2	0	2	9	5	14	0	0	.265	.216	R	R	6-2	200	12-3-73	1996	Yorba Linda, Calif.
Martinez, Thomas	.000	1	1	0	0	0	0	0	0	0	0	0	0	.000	.000	R	R	5-11	180	2-27-83	2000	Villa Alta Gracia, D.R.
Matos, Julius	.312	50	186	20	58	17	0	4	26	9	20	1	2	.468	.345	R	R	5-11	170	12-12-74	1994	Racine, Wis.
Mendez, Donaldo	.217	64	217	32	47	9	1	6	18	14	63	11	4	.350	.282	R	R	6-1	150	6-7-78	1996	Barquisimeto, Venez.
Morgan, Scott	.213	25	75	8	16	2	0	1	10	6	19	0	0	.280	.262	R	R	6-7	200	7-19-73	1995	Lompoc, Calif.
Nady, Xavier	.283	85	315	46	89	12	1	10	43	20	60	0	1	.422	.329	R	R	6-2	200	11-14-78	2001	Salinas, Calif.
Nieves, Wil	.308	70	237	24	73	20	2	7	29	5	40	0	0	.498	.321	R	R	5-11	190	9-25-77	1996	Santurce, P.R.
Owens, Jeremy	.174	13	23	4	4	0	1	2	7	3	9	1	1	.522	.259	R	R	6-1	200	12-9-76	1998	Johnson City, Tenn.
Pelaez, Alex	.309	112	411	47	127	31	1	11	64	20	40	0	1	.470	.339	R	R	5-9	190	4-6-76	1998	Chula Vista, Calif.
Selmo, Martin	.000	2	2	0	0	0	0	0	0	0	1	0	0	.000	.000	R	R	5-10	160	11-11-77	2000	Santo Domingo, D.R.
Sweeney, Mark	1.000	1	1	0	1	0	0	0	0	0	0	0	0	1.000	1.000	L	L	5-11	190	10-26-69	1991	Scottsdale, Ariz.
Thrower, Jake	.271	111	362	45	98	31	1	4	33	24	53	1	0	.395	.321	S	R	5-11	180	11-19-75	1997	Yuma, Ariz.

PITCHING

PITCHING	W	L	ERA	G	GS	CG	SV	IP	H	R	ER	BB	SO	AVG	B	T	HT	WT	DOB	1st Yr	Resides
Bausher, Andy	1	0	3.48	8	0	0	0	10	9	4	4	2	8	.230	R	L	6-2	200	8-17-76	1997	Bechtelsville, Pa.
Boyd, Jason	0	1	1.04	19	0	0	4	26	19	4	3	7	22	.200	R	R	6-3	170	2-3-73	1994	Edwardsville, Ill.
Bynum, Mike	3	2	3.51	7	7	0	0	41	36	19	16	7	35	.235	L	L	6-4	200	3-20-78	1999	Middleburg, Fla.
Condrey, Clay	10	4	3.50	25	23	0	0	134	128	55	52	40	73	.247	R	R	6-3	190	11-19-75	1998	Navasota, Texas
Cyr, Eric	0	0	3.14	9	2	0	0	14	14	6	5	10	11	.245	R	L	6-4	200	2-11-79	1999	Ada, Okla.
Davey, Tom	2	1	1.69	22	0	0	4	32	16	12	6	12	23	.149	R	R	6-7	230	9-11-73	1994	San Diego, Calif.
DeWitt, Matt	1	0	1.00	2	2	0	0	9	5	1	1	2	7	.166	R	R	6-3	220	9-4-77	1995	Las Vegas, Nev.
Eaton, Adam	1	1	2.92	2	2	0	0	12	9	9	4	3	6	.200	R	R	6-2	190	11-23-77	1996	Snohomish, Wash.
Hazlett, Andy	0	1	7.12	13	4	0	0	30	36	29	24	11	24	.295	L	L	6-3	180	8-27-75	1997	The Dalles, Ore.
Herbert, John	0	0	27.00	1	0	0	0	1	2	3	3	1	0	.500	R	R	6-8	230	10-23-77	2000	San Francisco, Calif.
Herndon, Junior	7	13	5.26	28	27	2	0	159	172	98	93	52	59	.276	R	R	6-1	190	9-11-78	1997	Craig, Colo.
Holtz, Mike	0	0	4.26	7	0	0	0	6	3	3	3	3	3	.136	L	L	5-9	180	10-10-72	1994	Hollidaysburg, Pa.
Howard, Ben	0	4	6.20	11	7	0	0	45	47	34	31	15	25	.265	R	R	6-2	190	1-15-79	1997	Jackson, Tenn.
Hunter, Johnny	1	1	7.27	12	3	0	1	26	26	22	21	16	17	.260	R	R	6-1	190	6-14-75	1997	Mansfield, Texas
Johnson, Jonathan	0	0	2.41	12	0	0	1	19	14	5	5	2	17	.215	R	R	6-0	180	7-16-74	1995	Irmo, S.C.
2-team (14 Tucson)	0	0	7.04	26	5	0	1	55	62	46	43	16	44	.288							
Kershner, Jason	7	2	3.03	31	12	0	0	86	65	30	29	26	83	.210	L	L	6-2	160	12-19-76	1995	Scottsdale, Ariz.
Lundquist, Dave	1	4	5.63	30	0	0	21	32	28	21	20	15	31	.235	R	R	6-2	200	6-4-73	1993	Hickory, N.C.
Middlebrook, Jason	2	5	5.65	10	7	0	0	37	42	27	23	13	32	.278	R	R	6-3	210	6-26-75	1996	Austin, Texas
Myers, Rodney	5	2	3.70	42	0	0	4	49	48	23	20	13	35	.259	R	R	6-1	200	6-26-69	1990	Chandler, Ariz.
Pearson, Jason	3	0	1.50	23	0	0	0	30	25	5	5	9	13	.219	L	L	6-0	190	12-29-75	1998	Freeport, Ill.
Pickford, Kevin	4	7	5.94	20	12	1	1	70	79	50	46	31	40	.290	L	L	6-4	200	3-12-75	1993	Fresno, Calif.
Shiell, Jason	4	3	2.78	56	0	0	6	74	62	26	23	29	74	.219	R	R	6-0	180	10-19-76	1995	Savannah, Ga.
Snyder, John	7	12	4.12	26	25	1	0	144	156	78	66	50	93	.274	R	R	6-3	200	8-16-74	1992	Joliet, Ill.
Soto, Darwin	1	0	0.00	2	0	0	1	0	0	0	0	1	1	.000	R	R	6-2	180	1-15-82	1998	Bani, D.R.
Tankersley, Dennis	3	4	3.88	9	9	0	0	51	43	29	22	30	51	.228	R	R	6-2	180	2-24-79	1999	St. Charles, Mo.
Trujillo, J.J.	2	0	4.33	18	1	0	0	27	30	14	13	8	28	.275	R	R	6-0	180	10-9-75	1998	Corpus Christi, Texas
Villafuerte, Brandon	8	4	2.02	47	0	0	1	58	43	17	13	22	54	.206	R	R	5-11	160	12-17-75	1995	Morgan Hill, Calif.
Walker, Kevin	0	0	3.00	3	0	0	0	3	1	1	1	0	4	.100	L	L	6-4	190	9-20-76	1995	Glen Rose, Texas

FIELDING

Catcher	PCT	G	PO	A	E	DP	PB
Amezcua	.976	37	227	15	6	3	2
Bitter	1.000	1	4	0	0	0	0
Cardona	1.000	19	110	8	0	2	1
Loyd	1.000	24	150	8	0	1	1
Nieves	.993	67	410	40	3	2	9
Selmo	1.000	2	5	0	0	0	0

First Base	PCT	G	PO	A	E	DP
Barker	.996	109	895	74	4	84
Eberwein	.995	21	167	19	1	15
Hopper	.929	3	22	4	2	1
Nieves	1.000	1	2	0	0	0
Pelaez	.991	16	108	7	1	7
Sweeney	.000	1	0	0	0	0

Second Base	PCT	G	PO	A	E	DP
Burroughs	.974	29	67	84	4	21

	PCT	G	PO	A	E	DP
Crespo	.978	34	84	97	4	24
Matos	1.000	1	3	4	0	1
Pelaez	1.000	19	34	52	0	11
Thrower	.970	71	120	174	9	27

Third Base	PCT	G	PO	A	E	DP
Burroughs	.946	16	10	25	2	1
Crespo	1.000	5	2	9	0	3
Eberwein	.906	40	23	64	9	4
Hopper	.900	11	6	12	2	0
Pelaez	.969	74	55	135	6	10
Thrower	.955	14	6	15	1	2

Shortstop	PCT	G	PO	A	E	DP
Crespo	.934	21	28	71	7	13
Matos	.959	49	67	121	8	28
Mendez	.969	62	84	162	8	27
Thrower	.972	21	20	49	2	12

Outfield	PCT	G	PO	A	E	DP
Barker	1.000	2	1	0	0	0
Benjamin	.961	46	71	2	3	1
Blakely	1.000	4	11	0	0	0
Crespo	.982	27	53	3	1	1
DeHaan	.990	117	297	6	3	2
Eberwein	1.000	29	43	3	0	1
Fernandez	1.000	22	43	4	0	2
Gomez	.960	93	183	8	8	0
Hopper	.971	22	32	2	1	0
Hubbard	1.000	7	12	1	0	0
Incaviglia	1.000	6	9	0	0	0
Morgan	1.000	20	27	0	0	0
Nady	.981	55	102	0	2	0
Owens	1.000	10	8	0	0	0

MOBILE BAYBEARS
Class AA

SOUTHERN LEAGUE

BATTING	AVG	G	AB	R	H	2B	3B	HR	RBI	BB	SO	SB	CS	SLG	OBP	B	T	HT	WT	DOB	1st Yr	Resides
Amezcua, Adan	.275	25	91	6	25	2	0	3	12	3	19	0	0	.396	.316	R	R	6-1	190	3-9-74	1993	Mazatlan, Mexico
Bay, Jason	.309	23	81	16	25	5	2	4	12	13	22	4	2	.568	.411	R	R	6-2	200	9-20-78	2000	Trail, B.C.
Benjamin, Al	.288	16	52	4	15	3	0	2	5	2	13	0	1	.462	.315	R	R	6-1	200	9-9-77	1996	Houston, Texas
Bitter, Jarrod	.200	8	25	1	5	2	0	0	2	7	0	0	0	.280	.259	R	R	6-1	220	10-16-78	2000	Tyler, Texas
Blakely, Darren	.217	123	424	63	92	22	4	8	57	70	132	10	4	.344	.339	S	R	6-0	190	3-14-77	1998	Pensacola, Fla.
Bozied, Tagg	.214	60	234	35	50	14	0	9	32	16	43	1	0	.389	.268	R	R	6-3	225	7-24-79	2001	Sioux Falls, S.D.
Castro, Bernie	.260	109	419	61	109	13	3	0	32	52	67	53	20	.305	.345	S	R	5-10	160	7-14-79	1997	Santo Domingo, D.R.
Donovan, Todd	.219	33	114	17	25	5	2	2	9	15	31	6	3	.351	.316	R	R	6-1	170	8-12-78	1999	East Lyme, Conn.
Duarte, Justin	.136	7	22	2	3	0	0	0	6	3	0	0	0	.136	.321	R	R	6-2	210	9-14-76	1999	Upland, Calif.
Faison, Vince	.253	100	359	40	91	23	5	7	44	39	103	5	1	.404	.339	L	R	6-0	190	1-22-81	1999	Lyons, Ga.
Fernandez, Alex	.273	16	66	8	18	4	0	1	8	3	8	6	1	.379	.296	L	L	6-1	200	5-15-81	1998	Cotui, D.R.
2-team (87 Birmingham)	.289	103	409	42	118	19	0	8	60	11	68	26	8	.394	.303							
Haad, Yamid	.283	18	53	6	15	1	0	1	13	5	8	1	0	.358	.333	R	R	6-2	210	9-2-77	1994	Cartagena, Colombia
2-team (29 Orlando)	.217	47	161	18	35	3	0	4	28	11	31	3	1	.311	.260							

BATTING

BATTING	AVG	G	AB	R	H	2B	3B	HR	RBI	BB	SO	SB	CS	SLG	OBP	B	T	HT	WT	DOB	1st Yr	Resides
Hopper, Shane	.241	19	58	5	14	5	2	0	9	5	19	1	0	.397	.313	R	R	6-1	200	9-22-75	1999	Winder, Ga.
Johnson, Ben	.241	131	456	58	110	23	4	10	55	65	127	11	9	.375	.337	R	R	6-1	200	6-18-81	1999	Memphis, Tenn.
Jones, Ryan	.211	89	266	39	56	10	2	13	53	30	56	2	1	.410	.294	R	R	6-2	220	11-5-74	1993	Irvine, Calif.
Lorenzana, Luis	.243	95	288	32	70	8	2	2	20	41	42	0	1	.306	.346	R	R	6-2	190	11-9-78	1996	San Diego, Calif.
Loyd, Brian	.276	53	174	19	48	8	0	3	22	9	26	0	1	.374	.319	R	R	6-2	200	12-3-73	1996	Yorba Linda, Calif.
Mendez, Donaldo	.219	56	224	36	49	16	0	4	18	19	53	15	5	.344	.297	R	R	6-1	150	6-7-78	1996	Barquisimeto, Venez.
Quintero, Humberto	.240	37	125	11	30	8	0	1	14	5	12	0	3	.328	.286	R	R	6-1	190	8-2-79	1997	Maracaibo, Venez.
2-team (4 Birmingham)	.263	41	137	12	36	8	0	1	17	5	13	1	3	.343	.308							
Reinking, Kevin	.000	1	2	0	0	0	0	0	0	2	1	0	0	.000	.500	R	R	6-1	195	1-25-79	2001	Long Beach, N.Y.
Risinger, Ben	.288	128	466	43	134	26	0	3	44	40	62	1	2	.363	.357	R	R	6-1	170	11-25-77	1999	Perth, Australia
Scales, Bobby	.276	97	250	40	69	13	3	4	27	27	56	6	3	.400	.356	S	R	6-0	170	10-4-77	1999	Roswell, Ga.
Scheschuk, John	.268	51	153	17	41	10	1	1	27	33	19	1	2	.366	.398	L	L	6-2	200	2-2-77	1999	Frisco, Texas

PITCHING

PITCHING	W	L	ERA	G	GS	CG	SV	IP	H	R	ER	BB	SO	AVG	B	T	HT	WT	DOB	1st Yr	Resides
Baker, Brad	4	4	4.48	12	12	1	0	64	47	33	32	45	57	.207	R	R	6-2	180	11-6-80	1999	Leyden, Mass.
Bartosh, Cliff	2	4	3.18	62	0	0	25	71	54	28	25	32	70	.210	L	L	6-2	170	9-5-79	1998	Duncanville, Texas
Bausher, Andy	4	1	3.11	34	1	0	0	64	70	27	22	17	40	.286	R	L	6-2	200	8-17-76	1997	Bechtelsville, Pa.
Bynum, Mike	4	0	0.82	6	5	0	0	33	17	5	3	7	29	.150	L	L	6-4	200	3-20-78	1999	Middleburg, Fla.
Cyr, Eric	4	6	3.24	14	14	0	0	72	62	37	26	34	65	.233	R	L	6-4	200	2-11-79	1999	Ada, Okla.
De Hart, Blair	2	3	4.45	7	7	0	0	32	44	21	16	9	29	.328	R	R	6-4	190	5-4-78	1999	Herndon, Va.
Fikac, Jeremy	1	0	3.00	3	0	0	1	3	5	1	1	0	0	.454	R	R	6-1	180	4-8-75	1998	Shiner, Texas
Gaal, Bryan	4	1	2.95	32	0	0	3	37	40	14	12	11	32	.279	R	R	6-4	200	12-17-76	1999	Syracuse, N.Y.
Garcia, Ariel	1	0	7.15	7	0	0	0	11	20	16	9	4	9	.370	R	R	6-5	200	10-3-75	1993	Panama City, Panama
Giese, Dan	4	5	2.91	32	0	0	0	53	56	24	17	13	51	.274	R	R	6-3	200	5-19-77	1999	San Clemente, Calif.
Gooris, Dan	0	1	9.00	1	0	0	0	2	5	3	2	0	0	.555	L	L	6-6	230	4-11-79	2002	Skokie, Ill.
Hampton, Matt	6	5	3.54	57	1	0	0	94	92	42	37	28	98	.250	R	L	6-4	200	6-20-77	2001	Wenatchee, Wash.
Harvey, Ian	6	1	1.89	12	9	0	0	57	54	14	12	15	44	.254	R	R	6-1	190	10-11-76	1999	Oakville, Ontario
Howard, Ben	3	1	2.18	6	6	0	0	33	26	10	8	16	30	.222	R	R	6-2	190	1-15-79	1997	Jackson, Tenn.
Hunter, Johnny	5	4	3.40	21	14	0	0	87	92	38	33	27	43	.277	R	R	6-1	190	6-14-75	1997	Mansfield, Texas
Jarvis, Kevin	0	0	0.00	1	1	0	0	3	2	0	0	0	3	.181	R	R	6-2	200	8-1-69	1991	Lexington, Ky.
Oxspring, Chris	0	0	1.26	6	1	0	0	14	13	3	2	8	21	.245	L	R	6-1	185	5-13-77	2000	Labrador, Australia
Peavy, Jake	4	5	2.80	14	14	0	0	80	65	26	25	30	89	.219	R	R	6-1	180	5-31-81	1999	Semmes, Ala.
Perez, Oliver	1	0	1.17	4	4	0	0	23	11	3	3	16	34	.146	L	L	6-3	160	8-15-81	1999	Culiacan, Mexico
Rojas, Chris	6	8	5.19	25	24	0	0	127	125	81	73	74	80	.264	R	R	6-2	180	3-30-77	1998	Glendale, N.Y.
Shibilo, Andy	4	3	4.89	29	0	0	0	42	49	26	23	16	42	.300	R	R	6-7	220	9-16-76	1998	Belleville, N.J.
Shiyuk, Todd	0	0	5.65	10	0	0	0	14	18	10	9	7	15	.300	L	L	6-0	190	3-1-77	1999	Delta, B.C.
Tankersley, Dennis	3	3	3.02	10	10	0	0	51	47	20	17	21	56	.244	R	R	6-2	180	2-24-79	1999	St. Charles, Mo.
Thompson, Mike	1	0	3.60	1	1	0	0	5	5	2	2	0	0	.263	R	R	6-4	205	11-6-80	1999	Lamar, Colo.
Trujillo, J.J.	3	0	0.66	31	0	0	20	41	25	3	3	12	49	.174	R	R	6-0	180	10-9-75	1999	Corpus Christi, Texas
Watkins, Steve	4	8	3.78	37	15	1	0	117	114	65	49	49	88	.280	R	R	6-4	190	7-19-78	1998	Lubbock, Texas

FIELDING

Catcher	PCT	G	PO	A	E	DP	PB
Amezcua	.991	23	207	12	2	1	2
Bitter	.964	7	47	7	2	0	0
Duarte	1.000	6	44	4	0	0	1
Haad	.957	17	98	14	5	1	1
Loyd	.987	48	357	29	5	3	3
Quintero	.983	37	247	42	5	8	2
Reinking	1.000	1	9	1	0	0	0
Risinger	.982	17	105	7	2	1	2

First Base	PCT	G	PO	A	E	DP
Bozied	.988	57	456	27	6	43
Fernandez	1.000	1	9	1	0	0
Jones	.994	41	316	28	2	25
Risinger	1.000	1	9	0	0	1

Second Base	PCT	G	PO	A	E	DP
Castro	.980	105	250	287	11	56
Risinger	.969	9	14	17	1	5
Scales	.969	29	54	72	4	10

Third Base	PCT	G	PO	A	E	DP
Bozied	1.000	1	3	2	0	0
Hopper	.844	11	7	20	5	1
Lorenzana	1.000	19	6	25	0	0
Risinger	.940	97	71	148	14	17
Scales	.841	19	5	32	7	4

Shortstop	PCT	G	PO	A	E	DP
Lorenzana	.945	76	103	221	19	42

	PCT	G	PO	A	E	DP
Mendez	.952	56	67	173	12	26
Risinger	.952	11	13	27	2	4

Outfield	PCT	G	PO	A	E	DP
Bay	1.000	22	34	1	0	0
Benjamin	1.000	10	11	1	0	0
Blakely	.981	117	298	9	6	2
Donovan	.973	31	32	4	1	0
Faison	.968	98	168	11	6	0
Fernandez	.966	14	23	5	1	1
Hopper	1.000	3	3	0	0	0
Johnson	.965	124	244	6	9	2
Jones	1.000	12	13	1	0	0
Risinger	1.000	1	2	0	0	0
Scales	1.000	4	1	0	0	0

LAKE ELSINORE STORM — High Class A

CALIFORNIA LEAGUE

BATTING	AVG	G	AB	R	H	2B	3B	HR	RBI	BB	SO	SB	CS	SLG	OBP	B	T	HT	WT	DOB	1st Yr	Resides
Arroyo, Abner	.190	16	58	2	11	3	0	0	6	8	19	0	0	.241	.290	L	L	6-0	180	12-16-79	2000	Maunabo, P.R.
Barfield, Josh	.087	6	23	2	2	0	0	0	4	1	4	0	0	.087	.120	R	R	6-0	180	12-17-82	2001	Spring, Texas
Bartlett, Jason	.250	75	308	57	77	14	4	1	33	32	53	24	5	.331	.329	R	R	6-0	170	10-30-79	2001	Lodi, Calif.
Benjamin, Al	.294	34	136	15	40	17	1	2	23	5	30	3	0	.478	.317	R	R	6-1	200	9-9-77	1996	Houston, Texas
Bozied, Tagg	.298	71	282	45	84	23	1	15	60	35	60	3	4	.546	.377	R	R	6-3	225	7-24-79	2001	Sioux Falls, S.D.
Bravo, Danny	.287	77	268	43	77	15	4	3	33	53	30	8	6	.407	.406	S	R	5-11	170	5-27-77	1996	Maracaibo, Venez.
Brooks, Jeff	.053	6	19	1	1	0	0	0	3	6	0	0	0	.053	.217	R	R	6-5	230	9-4-79	1997	Nottingham, Pa.
Davis, Mike	.122	28	90	10	11	5	0	1	8	9	27	4	0	.211	.200	R	R	5-8	190	10-10-76	2001	Chicago, Ill.
De los Santos, Pedro	.259	21	81	13	21	3	0	1	6	8	12	14	4	.333	.326	S	R	5-10	160	8-8-83	2000	Santo Domingo, D.R.
Donovan, Todd	.296	58	226	40	67	9	2	2	25	28	44	26	5	.381	.377	R	R	6-1	170	8-12-78	1999	East Lyme, Conn.
Duarte, Justin	.129	32	101	4	13	2	0	0	12	8	21	0	1	.149	.207	R	R	6-2	210	9-14-76	1999	Upland, Calif.
Eberwein, Kevin	.000	2	8	0	0	0	0	0	0	0	0	0	0	.000	.000	R	R	6-4	200	3-30-77	1998	Las Vegas, Nev.
Falcon, Omar	.000	2	5	0	0	0	0	0	2	4	0	0	.000	.286	R	R	6-0	190	9-1-82	2000	Miami, Fla.
Furmaniak, J.J.	.257	106	381	50	98	16	6	7	43	26	100	11	9	.386	.311	R	R	6-0	190	7-31-79	2000	Bolingbrook, Ill.
Gautreau, Jake	.286	93	350	43	100	20	1	10	62	42	86	2	3	.426	.358	L	R	6-0	180	11-14-79	2001	South Padre Island, Texas
Gomez, Andre	.163	56	184	29	30	5	2	3	15	10	56	6	3	.261	.258	R	R	6-2	180	9-6-78	2000	Playa del Rey, Calif.
Gonzalez, Wiki	.340	19	53	10	18	8	0	1	6	12	3	0	0	.547	.486	R	R	5-11	200	5-17-74	1992	Palo Negro, Venez.
Greene, Khalil	.317	46	183	33	58	9	1	9	32	12	33	0	0	.525	.368	R	R	5-11	210	10-21-79	2002	Key West, Fla.
Knott, Jon	.341	93	367	55	125	33	8	8	73	46	68	5	4	.540	.414	R	R	6-3	220	8-4-78	2002	Nokomis, Fla.
Nady, Xavier	.278	45	169	41	47	6	3	13	37	28	40	2	0	.580	.382	R	R	6-2	200	11-14-78	2001	Salinas, Calif.
Nettles, Marcus	.254	125	485	97	123	18	2	0	38	101	132	58	26	.299	.386	L	L	5-11	180	5-15-80	2001	Chicago, Ill.
Nevin, Phil	.333	2	6	2	2	1	0	1	6	1	2	0	0	1.000	.375	R	R	6-2	230	1-19-71	1992	San Diego, Calif.

BATTING	AVG	G	AB	R	H	2B	3B	HR	RBI	BB	SO	SB	CS	SLG	OBP	B	T	HT	WT	DOB	1st Yr	Resides
O'Donnell, Ryan	.198	24	86	5	17	3	0	0	5	2	11	2	0	.233	.225	L	R	6-0	180	8-21-78	2000	Tempe, Ariz.
Owens, Jeremy	.230	110	418	54	96	21	4	13	52	39	148	23	9	.392	.299	R	R	6-1	200	12-9-76	1998	Johnson City, Tenn.
Pagan, Andres	.217	71	258	16	56	9	1	0	18	8	74	1	3	.260	.241	R	R	6-4	180	3-18-81	1994	Yauco, P.R.
Pickens, Jordan	.000	3	10	0	0	0	0	0	0	1	6	0	0	.000	.091	R	R	6-2	190	6-10-81	2001	Atascadero, Calif.
Riggins, Auntwan	.266	73	259	35	69	10	4	0	20	12	77	14	12	.336	.298	S	R	6-1	180	6-17-76	1998	Houston, Texas

PITCHING	W	L	ERA	G	GS	CG	SV	IP	H	R	ER	BB	SO	AVG	B	T	HT	WT	DOB	1st Yr	Resides
Bumstead, Mike	10	10	4.82	27	26	0	0	146	164	100	78	61	108	.280	R	R	6-3	210	7-8-77	2001	Big Bear Lake, Calif.
Cassel, Jack	1	1	2.43	23	0	0	1	37	33	15	10	11	25	.237	R	R	6-2	190	8-8-79	2000	Northridge, Calif.
Davey, Tom	0	1	3.38	5	4	0	0	5	6	2	2	1	4	.315	R	R	6-7	230	9-11-73	1994	San Diego, Calif.
De Hart, Blair	3	1	2.70	5	5	0	0	30	29	10	9	5	32	.250	R	R	6-4	190	5-4-78	1999	Herndon, Va.
Eaton, Adam	0	0	2.70	3	3	0	0	13	10	7	4	3	19	.196	R	R	6-2	190	11-23-77	1996	Snohomish, Wash.
Gaal, Bryan	1	5	2.60	32	0	0	15	38	28	15	10	9	45	.210	R	R	6-4	200	12-17-76	1999	Syracuse, N.Y.
Germano, Justin	2	0	0.95	3	3	0	0	19	12	3	2	5	18	.173	R	R	6-3	200	8-6-82	2000	Claremont, Calif.
Gooris, Dan	3	0	4.08	24	0	0	0	40	36	20	18	25	27	.248	L	L	6-6	230	4-11-79	2002	Skokie, Ill.
Harvey, Ian	1	2	3.48	34	0	0	2	52	49	24	20	9	52	.239	R	R	6-1	190	10-11-76	1999	Oakville, Ontario
Herbert, John	5	3	5.21	42	0	0	1	66	69	46	38	33	54	.262	R	R	6-8	230	10-23-77	2000	San Francisco, Calif.
Jarvis, Kevin	1	0	0.00	1	1	0	0	5	2	0	0	1	1	.133	R	R	6-2	200	8-1-69	1991	Lexington, Ky.
Kozol, Anthony	0	0	2.25	3	0	0	0	4	3	1	1	0	3	.200	R	R	6-2	190	12-28-77	2000	Dudley, N.C.
McAdoo, Duncan	8	4	4.01	41	12	0	0	123	124	64	55	30	130	.257	R	R	6-1	200	4-15-78	2000	Houston, Texas
Nicolas, Mike	3	2	2.91	65	0	0	9	77	49	32	25	42	121	.180	R	R	6-3	225	9-5-79	2000	Santo Domingo, D.R.
Oxspring, Chris	0	1	4.78	15	1	0	0	26	24	16	14	8	30	.237	L	R	6-1	185	5-13-77	2000	Labrador, Australia
Perez, Oliver	3	3	1.85	9	8	0	0	49	36	13	10	24	66	.209	L	L	6-3	160	8-15-81	1999	Culiacan, Mexico
Phillips, Mark	10	8	4.19	28	26	0	0	148	123	81	69	94	156	.225	L	L	6-3	200	12-30-81	2000	Hanover, Pa.
Reynolds, Josh	3	2	8.82	7	3	0	0	16	30	18	16	3	16	.333	R	R	6-2	190	9-27-79	2000	Holts Summit, Mo.
Shiyuk, Todd	4	3	3.31	42	0	0	1	52	51	21	19	22	56	.262	L	L	6-0	190	3-1-77	1999	Delta, B.C.
Stewart, Cory	5	3	3.20	12	12	0	0	65	60	29	23	29	69	.251	L	L	6-4	180	11-14-79	1999	Boerne, Texas
Thompson, Mike	5	7	5.56	25	22	0	0	123	144	93	76	53	79	.283	R	R	6-4	205	11-6-80	1999	Lamar, Colo.
Tucker, Rusty	2	3	2.43	26	0	0	14	30	26	10	8	18	33	.226	R	L	6-1	190	7-15-80	2001	Gloucester, Mass.
Walker, Kevin	0	0	0.00	5	1	0	0	7	3	0	0	0	10	.136	L	L	6-4	190	9-20-76	1995	Glen Rose, Texas
Webster, Jeremy	1	0	4.11	8	0	0	0	15	16	8	7	10	15	.280	L	L	6-0	190	3-20-79	1999	Sandy, Utah
Wiedmeyer, Jason	4	5	4.74	14	13	0	0	76	81	48	40	29	57	.268	L	L	6-3	200	10-15-78	2001	West Bend, Wis.

FIELDING

Catcher	PCT	G	PO	A	E	DP	PB
Duarte	.989	19	160	14	2	1	3
Falcon	1.000	2	14	2	0	0	0
Gomez	.997	46	337	30	1	2	10
Gonzalez	.983	14	110	5	2	2	1
Pagan	.983	70	600	47	11	2	14

First Base	PCT	G	PO	A	E	DP
Bozied	.981	64	549	32	11	42
Bravo	1.000	2	17	2	0	0
Duarte	1.000	7	52	4	0	3
Gomez	1.000	4	18	1	0	0
Knott	.987	46	366	19	5	25
O'Donnell	.897	3	25	1	3	2
Pagan	1.000	1	14	1	0	0
Riggins	.983	18	150	19	3	18

Second Base	PCT	G	PO	A	E	DP
Barfield	.955	5	11	10	1	1
Bravo	.960	24	50	70	5	16

	PCT	G	PO	A	E	DP
Davis	1.000	2	6	4	0	2
De los Santos	.926	5	10	15	2	1
Furmaniak	1.000	14	28	42	0	8
Gautreau	.957	87	181	238	19	38
Greene	.900	3	4	14	2	4

Third Base	PCT	G	PO	A	E	DP
Bozied	.750	3	1	2	1	1
Bravo	.935	44	26	74	7	3
Davis	.902	19	8	29	4	1
De los Santos	.778	3	2	5	2	3
Eberwein	.900	2	4	5	1	0
Furmaniak	.927	69	48	143	15	15
Greene	1.000	3	3	5	0	2
Knott	.500	1	0	1	0	0
Nevin	.000	2	0	0	2	0

Shortstop	PCT	G	PO	A	E	DP
Bartlett	.929	75	90	197	22	33
Bravo	1.000	7	8	23	0	3

	PCT	G	PO	A	E	DP
Furmaniak	.920	21	25	56	7	5
Greene	.950	39	33	101	7	14

Outfield	PCT	G	PO	A	E	DP
Arroyo	1.000	6	8	0	0	0
Benjamin	.909	8	8	2	1	1
Bozied	1.000	2	1	0	0	0
De los Santos	.813	12	13	0	3	0
Donovan	.959	52	112	5	5	0
Duarte	1.000	5	5	0	0	0
Gomez	1.000	7	6	2	0	0
Knott	.963	41	71	8	3	0
Nady	1.000	1	1	0	0	0
Nettles	.966	122	193	4	7	0
O'Donnell	.946	21	30	5	2	0
Owens	.969	105	241	13	8	2
Riggins	.968	45	87	3	3	1

FORT WAYNE WIZARDS — Low Class A

MIDWEST LEAGUE

BATTING	AVG	G	AB	R	H	2B	3B	HR	RBI	BB	SO	SB	CS	SLG	OBP	B	T	HT	WT	DOB	1st Yr	Resides
Anderson, Keto	.281	88	310	32	87	11	8	1	28	10	34	11	9	.377	.302	L	R	5-11	180	2-12-79	1999	Prattville, Ala.
Aquino, Jackson	.206	101	320	33	66	12	1	1	25	28	70	12	10	.259	.276	S	R	5-8	150	2-26-83	2000	Santo Domingo, D.R.
Arroyo, Abner	.118	8	34	1	4	0	0	1	3	0	14	0	0	.206	.143	L	L	6-0	180	12-16-79	2000	Maunabo, P.R.
Barfield, Josh	.306	129	536	73	164	22	3	8	67	25	105	26	8	.403	.340	R	R	6-0	180	12-17-82	2001	Spring, Texas
Benick, Jon	.271	133	490	59	133	30	1	15	73	61	106	5	3	.429	.349	S	R	6-1	210	9-26-79	2001	Glen Lyon, Pa.
Biernbaum, L.J.	.258	42	132	20	34	7	0	1	17	24	24	5	2	.333	.373	L	L	6-3	200	7-30-79	2002	Newtown, Pa.
Brooks, Doc	.232	73	237	30	55	11	0	3	17	22	54	5	2	.316	.319	R	R	5-10	190	1-21-80	2001	Phenix City, Ala.
Carter, Josh	.268	77	272	28	73	10	1	2	21	11	33	5	2	.335	.304	R	R	6-2	210	11-5-80	2001	Fallbrook, Calif.
De los Santos, Pedro	.279	47	190	35	53	7	5	0	18	18	37	39	7	.368	.341	S	R	5-10	160	8-8-83	2000	Santo Domingo, D.R.
DiBetta, John	.200	17	50	7	10	0	0	0	5	8	5	2	0	.200	.317	R	R	6-1	190	10-19-80	2001	Las Vegas, Nev.
Ervin, Josh	.071	4	14	1	1	0	0	1	2	1	8	0	0	.286	.133	R	R	6-2	200	4-27-78	2002	Ephrata, Wash.
Hastings, Joseph	.262	118	451	51	118	38	0	11	69	42	124	3	1	.419	.327	L	R	6-3	200	6-25-78	2001	Connelly Springs, N.C.
Hellman, Matthew	.192	8	26	2	5	1	1	0	5	3	6	0	1	.308	.276	R	R	5-11	180	11-18-78	2001	Burbank, Calif.
Jones, Kennard	.286	20	77	15	22	4	0	0	5	11	21	3	4	.338	.382	L	L	5-11	180	9-8-81	2002	Beltsville, Md.
Knott, Jon	.333	37	126	19	42	12	3	3	18	17	33	2	1	.548	.411	R	R	6-3	220	8-4-78	2001	Nokomis, Fla.
McCool, Lee	.214	36	126	16	27	5	2	1	9	5	35	1	1	.310	.259	R	R	5-11	180	3-5-79	2000	Palatka, Fla.
Puccinelli, John	.000	5	14	0	0	0	0	0	1	1	6	0	0	.000	.067	R	R	6-4	180	3-5-81	1999	North Hollywood, Calif.
Reinking, Kevin	.241	43	145	8	35	6	0	1	15	7	34	0	0	.303	.295	R	R	6-1	190	1-25-79	2001	Long Beach, N.Y.
Sain, Greg	.245	105	387	54	95	29	0	13	57	35	77	2	0	.421	.323	R	R	6-2	200	12-26-79	2001	Torrance, Calif.
Serrano, Eddie	.220	74	218	24	48	10	0	4	28	14	50	1	2	.321	.267	R	R	6-0	170	10-26-81	2000	David, Panama
Stockton, Rick	.235	17	51	6	12	1	1	0	5	2	16	1	0	.294	.278	L	L	6-1	180	11-5-79	2001	Calabasas, Calif.
Trzesniak, Nick	.237	110	409	53	97	18	2	10	38	27	97	10	3	.364	.293	R	R	6-0	210	11-19-80	1999	Tinley Park, Ill.

PITCHING	W	L	ERA	G	GS	CG	SV	IP	H	R	ER	BB	SO	AVG	B	T	HT	WT	DOB	1st Yr	Resides
Cassel, Jack	4	1	3.02	27	0	0	0	51	58	22	17	11	34	.277	R	R	6-2	190	8-8-79	2000	Northridge, Calif.
Craker, Justin	4	5	3.51	54	0	0	1	59	66	28	23	29	51	.297	R	R	6-0	210	9-11-78	2002	Superior, Wis.

PITCHING

PITCHING	W	L	ERA	G	GS	CG	SV	IP	H	R	ER	BB	SO	AVG	B	T	HT	WT	DOB	1st Yr	Resides
De Hart, Blair	0	0	1.99	5	3	0	0	23	16	6	5	0	30	.188	R	R	6-4	190	5-4-78	1999	Herndon, Va.
Dulkowski, Marc	1	0	2.78	23	0	0	3	23	17	7	7	6	25	.207	S	R	6-0	190	5-28-82	2000	Tinley Park, Ill.
Earey, Ryan	3	4	2.94	47	0	0	1	67	71	30	22	16	41	.273	R	R	6-4	220	3-5-79	2000	Greensboro, N.C.
Fox, Ben	4	4	3.91	39	3	0	0	78	79	47	34	29	48	.259	S	L	5-11	180	6-22-81	2001	Las Vegas, Nev.
Garcia, Carlos	0	0	1.29	2	0	0	0	7	3	2	1	0	1	.125	R	R	6-1	170	9-23-78	1996	Empalme, Mexico
Germano, Justin	12	5	3.18	24	24	1	0	156	166	63	55	19	119	.269	R	R	6-3	200	8-6-82	2000	Claremont, Calif.
Gooris, Dan	4	3	2.60	22	0	0	0	28	25	10	8	8	20	.231	L	L	6-6	230	4-11-79	2002	Skokie, Ill.
Huber, Jon	8	12	5.12	28	26	2	0	146	168	99	83	59	86	.291	R	R	6-2	190	7-7-81	2000	North Fort Myers, Fla.
Jones, Geoffrey	1	5	3.60	18	9	0	1	65	59	29	26	17	63	.240	L	L	6-6	230	8-10-79	1999	Dolores, Colo.
Kozol, Anthony	1	3	3.21	41	0	0	21	42	43	18	15	5	43	.254	R	R	6-2	190	12-28-77	2000	Dudley, N.C.
Lipari, Tom	1	1	1.90	4	4	0	0	24	16	9	5	3	27	.192	L	L	6-5	180	4-23-79	2002	Omaha, Neb.
Martinez, Javier	6	4	3.38	12	12	0	0	69	55	28	26	19	69	.210	S	R	6-3	170	12-9-82	2000	Merida, Mexico
Percosky, Mark	1	5	4.85	14	14	0	0	65	74	45	35	18	47	.276	R	R	6-4	220	3-15-78	2000	Kent, Wash.
Richards, John	0	1	8.24	18	0	0	0	20	33	21	18	8	15	.362	L	L	6-4	200	11-12-78	2001	Coos Bay, Ore.
Siemon, David	0	1	3.68	3	2	0	0	7	9	4	3	3	4	.290	R	R	6-4	210	8-20-79	2002	West Palm Beach, Fla.
Soto, Darwin	2	0	1.76	13	0	0	0	15	8	4	3	3	17	.153	R	R	6-2	180	1-15-82	1998	Bani, D.R.
Stewart, Cory	6	3	2.39	17	11	0	0	64	46	21	17	18	86	.198	L	L	6-4	180	11-14-79	1999	Boerne, Texas
Tucker, Rusty	5	1	1.01	31	0	0	13	36	19	8	4	10	50	.149	R	L	6-1	190	7-15-80	2001	Gloucester, Mass.
Yoshida, Nobuaki	6	10	3.39	27	27	0	0	157	156	81	59	37	75	.256	L	L	6-1	170	8-10-81	2000	Sendai, Japan

FIELDING

Catcher	PCT	G	PO	A	E	DP	PB
Reinking	.988	40	324	15	4	1	7
Trzesniak	.990	101	672	56	7	0	8
Sain	1.000	1	1	0	0	0	
Serrano	.921	7	16	19	3	3	

First Base	PCT	G	PO	A	E	DP
Anderson	.667	1	2	0	1	0
Benick	.989	61	490	34	6	37
Hastings	.985	63	556	25	9	46
Knott	1.000	2	14	1	0	1
Sain	.986	16	130	6	2	9
Trzesniak	1.000	1	2	0	0	0

Second Base	PCT	G	PO	A	E	DP
Barfield	.962	129	241	364	24	66
McCool	.900	2	5	4	1	2

Third Base	PCT	G	PO	A	E	DP
Benick	.867	50	28	89	18	8
DiBetta	.956	16	9	34	2	2
Puccinelli	1.000	4	3	7	0	1
Sain	.933	55	45	108	11	9
Serrano	.887	20	12	35	6	4

Shortstop	PCT	G	PO	A	E	DP
Aquino	.907	99	127	275	41	42
Serrano	.901	47	58	105	18	17

Outfield	PCT	G	PO	A	E	DP
Anderson	.976	80	158	4	4	1
Barfield	1.000	1	1	0	0	0
Benick	1.000	1	1	0	0	0
Biernbaum	.989	41	84	6	1	1
Brooks	.964	66	100	6	4	0
Carter	.995	74	168	13	1	2
De los Santos	.950	46	107	6	6	0
DiBetta	.000	1	0	0	0	0
Hastings	1.000	17	28	0	0	0
Hellman	1.000	8	12	1	0	0
Jones	1.000	19	40	0	0	0
Knott	.948	35	51	4	3	2
McCool	.955	29	40	2	2	2
Serrano	.000	1	0	0	0	0
Stockton	1.000	10	14	0	0	0

EUGENE EMERALDS   Short-Season A

NORTHWEST LEAGUE

BATTING

BATTING	AVG	G	AB	R	H	2B	3B	HR	RBI	BB	SO	SB	CS	SLG	OBP	B	T	HT	WT	DOB	1st Yr	Resides
Agosto, Rolando	.281	65	235	32	66	14	3	0	19	31	47	4	9	.366	.383	R	R	6-0	180	1-10-81	2002	Bayamon, P.R.
Baker, Steve	.241	62	232	30	56	12	3	11	41	16	88	12	3	.461	.300	R	R	6-3	200	4-20-80	2002	Rome, N.Y.
Biernbaum, L.J.	.059	12	34	1	2	0	1	0	3	7	10	0	0	.118	.220	L	L	6-3	200	7-30-79	2002	Newtown, Pa.
Brooks, Jeff	.212	22	85	12	18	3	0	2	9	5	29	0	0	.318	.253	R	R	6-5	230	9-4-79	1997	Nottingham, Pa.
Burgamy, Brian	.268	70	261	44	70	17	1	9	43	38	64	14	4	.444	.361	S	R	5-10	190	6-27-81	2002	Lawton, Okla.
Carter, Josh	.351	9	37	5	13	3	1	3	9	3	7	1	0	.730	.390	R	R	6-2	190	11-5-80	2001	Fallbrook, Calif.
De los Santos, Pedro	.225	21	80	14	18	2	1	0	8	7	15	16	1	.275	.293	S	R	5-10	160	8-8-83	2000	Santo Domingo, D.R.
DiBetta, John	.238	67	239	29	57	8	0	1	29	28	40	10	3	.285	.320	R	R	6-1	190	10-19-80	2001	Las Vegas, Nev.
Ervin, Josh	.130	19	54	3	7	2	0	1	3	3	20	1	0	.222	.190	R	R	6-2	200	4-27-78	2002	Ephrata, Wash.
Giorgis, David	.248	37	133	9	33	9	2	2	24	8	46	1	1	.391	.289	R	R	6-1	190	8-14-81	2000	San Diego, Calif.
Greene, Khalil	.270	10	37	5	10	1	0	0	6	5	6	0	0	.297	.400	R	R	5-11	210	10-21-79	2002	Key West, Fla.
Jones, Kennard	.295	16	61	15	18	2	0	3	10	12	12	1	1	.328	.411	L	L	5-11	180	2-27-83	2002	Beltsville, Md.
Martinez, Thomas	.153	24	72	3	11	3	0	1	8	4	28	1	0	.236	.208	R	R	5-11	180	2-27-83	1999	Villa Alta Gracia, D.R.
Millan, Carlos	.219	24	64	9	14	5	0	1	7	6	20	4	3	.344	.282	R	R	5-11	170	9-25-81	1999	Ocumare, Venez.
Moore, Rusty	.091	5	11	0	1	0	0	0	2	4	0	0	0	.091	.231	R	R	6-2	210	10-11-80	2002	Windermere, Fla.
Mora, Ruben	.207	27	92	16	19	2	0	1	3	5	31	7	1	.261	.255	S	R	6-0	170	1-11-82	2000	Sabanitas, Panama
Nulton, Kevin	.235	47	153	22	36	3	1	1	13	15	25	5	2	.288	.302	R	R	6-0	170	8-16-82	2000	Lakeside, Calif.
Pickens, Jordan	.269	35	119	23	32	9	0	4	20	19	39	4	1	.445	.395	R	R	6-2	190	6-10-81	2001	Atascadero, Calif.
Richardson, Mike	.239	72	251	42	60	18	0	5	38	49	56	3	2	.371	.378	R	R	5-10	210	7-11-79	2002	Inverness, Calif.
Selmo, Martin	.097	9	31	1	3	0	0	0	2	5	2	0	0	.097	.152	R	R	5-10	160	11-11-77	2000	Santo Domingo, D.R.
Shorsher, Adam	.224	45	147	15	33	8	3	1	16	11	45	0	3	.340	.316	R	R	6-0	180	8-20-82	2000	San Jose, Calif.
Townsend, Rich	.253	29	91	18	23	5	3	1	11	7	29	2	0	.407	.320	R	R	6-0	180	7-30-80	2002	London, Ky.

GAMES BY POSITION: C—Ervin 17, Martinez 10, Richardson 2, Selmo 8, Shorsher 45. **1B**—Brooks, DiBetta 47, Martinez 14, Townsend 2. **2B**—Agosto 1, Burgamy 65, Nulton 13, Richardson 3. **3B**—Agosto 3, Brooks 4, DiBetta 21, Nulton 24, Richardson 4, Townsend 26. **SS**—Agosto 62, Burgamy 1, Greene 10, Nulton 8. **OF**—Baker 59, Biernbaum 9, Carter 6, De los Santos 20, Giorgis 21, Jones 16, Millan 19, Moore 4, Richardson 60.

PITCHING

PITCHING	W	L	ERA	G	GS	CG	SV	IP	H	R	ER	BB	SO	AVG	B	T	HT	WT	DOB	1st Yr	Resides
Beavers, Kevin	0	1	1.88	4	4	0	0	24	23	7	5	4	16	.261	L	L	6-5	190	10-22-79	2002	Irvine, Calif.
Bochy, Greg	0	0	3.13	17	0	0	0	23	10	11	8	24	23	.128	R	R	6-2	200	8-26-79	2002	Poway, Calif.
Bomar, Mike	1	1	5.65	12	0	0	0	14	14	11	9	12	7	.250	R	L	6-6	210	8-16-79	2002	Bush Prairie, Wash.
Coonrod, Aaron	3	3	5.54	15	12	0	0	65	75	48	40	24	45	.287	R	R	6-4	210	5-17-80	2002	Fremont, Ohio
Dulkowski, Marc	0	1	2.25	4	0	0	1	4	4	1	1	2	4	.266	S	R	6-0	190	5-28-82	2000	Tinley Park, Ill.
Ervin, Josh	0	0	0.00	2	0	0	0	1	1	0	0	1	0	.000	R	R	6-2	200	4-27-78	2002	Ephrata, Wash.
Jones, Geoffrey	0	0	5.40	1	1	0	0	5	4	3	3	1	5	.210	L	L	6-6	230	8-10-79	1999	Dolores, Colo.
Laratta, E.J.	3	1	1.33	12	0	0	0	20	16	8	3	10	13	.216	R	R	6-2	190	5-24-80	2002	Englewood, Colo.
Lipari, Tom	2	0	2.66	10	9	0	0	41	38	16	12	14	52	.238	L	L	6-5	180	4-23-79	2002	Omaha, Neb.
Martin, Scott	1	2	3.74	17	0	0	0	22	23	14	9	5	16	.261	R	L	6-2	210	5-10-78	2002	Long Island, N.Y.
Martinez, Javier	0	0	4.50	2	2	0	0	10	4	5	5	5	6	.121	S	R	5-11	170	4-24-72	1990	Levittown, P.R.
Modica, Greg	0	2	6.67	26	0	0	0	27	35	24	20	11	25	.309	R	R	6-0	200	5-28-80	2001	Glendale, N.Y.
Montarbo, Adam	0	2	8.00	12	0	0	1	9	10	8	8	5	8	.263	R	R	6-4	220	9-1-80	2002	Morgan Hill, Calif.
Morel, Eudy	6	0	2.54	23	0	0	1	28	26	13	8	5	27	.234	R	R	5-10	160	8-23-79	2000	Monte Cristi, D.R.
Pauley, David	6	1	2.81	15	15	0	0	80	81	32	25	18	62	.266	R	R	6-2	170	6-17-83	2001	Longmont, Colo.
Ribas, Gabe	8	1	1.97	32	1	0	16	50	36	14	11	5	66	.193	R	R	6-4	220	2-3-80	2002	Brunswick, Maine

PITCHING	W	L	ERA	G	GS	CG	SV	IP	H	R	ER	BB	SO	AVG	B	T	HT	WT	DOB	1st Yr	Resides
Richards, John	0	0	0.00	3	0	0	0	3	1	0	0	1	4	.125	L	L	6-4	200	11-12-78	2001	Coos Bay, Ore.
Ryan, Kevin	0	2	13.50	14	0	0	0	14	26	26	21	17	16	.400	R	R	6-3	200	1-23-79	2002	Elmhurst, Ill.
Soto, Darwin	1	0	2.00	7	0	0	0	9	6	2	2	2	17	.187	R	R	6-2	180	1-15-82	1998	Bani, D.R.
Steidlmayer, Luke	3	2	3.07	15	11	0	0	70	58	31	24	20	80	.223	R	R	6-5	190	8-13-80	2002	Colusa, Calif.
Villatoro, Wilmer	3	7	5.13	22	7	0	2	53	50	36	30	19	69	.245	R	R	6-0	140	6-27-83	2000	San Salvador, El Salvador
Whitaker, Brian	5	8	2.93	16	14	0	0	83	79	36	27	16	63	.250	R	R	6-4	200	11-5-79	2002	Salisbury, N.C.
Wykoff, Zach	0	1	12.46	8	0	0	0	9	16	12	12	4	6	.390	R	R	6-1	190	8-6-79	2001	Oxford, Ga.

IDAHO FALLS BRAVES   Rookie

PIONEER LEAGUE

BATTING	AVG	G	AB	R	H	2B	3B	HR	RBI	BB	SO	SB	CS	SLG	OBP	B	T	HT	WT	DOB	1st Yr	Resides
Antequera, Javier	.217	32	83	11	18	2	2	1	14	5	28	5	2	.325	.286	R	R	5-11	160	2-5-82	2000	Aragua, Venez.
Baez, Carlos	.276	49	199	24	55	5	0	0	19	7	43	9	7	.302	.318	R	R	6-1	160	2-20-83	1999	Palenque, D.R.
Dale, Lachlan	.233	38	133	12	31	4	1	1	14	13	36	0	1	.301	.315	R	R	6-3	190	6-22-83	2002	Kalamunda, Australia
Falcon, Omar	.227	55	185	32	42	12	0	9	34	36	100	1	1	.438	.363	R	R	6-0	190	9-1-82	2000	Miami, Fla.
Garcia, Angleidy	.308	26	91	14	28	3	0	1	11	12	21	1	2	.374	.406	R	R	5-11	170	5-6-84	2002	Santo Domingo, D.R.
Garcia, Luis	.279	63	258	39	72	7	4	1	28	20	40	10	8	.349	.342	S	R	6-0	150	12-11-83	2001	Bani, D.R.
Johanning, Ben	.116	26	86	7	10	2	1	2	6	12	40	0	1	.233	.240	L	L	6-3	220	5-2-80	2002	Kissimmee, Fla.
Lester, Anthony	.180	24	50	11	9	0	1	0	3	14	18	2	1	.220	.388	R	R	6-0	180	12-28-81	2002	Tampa, Fla.
Lima, Joseph	.256	63	258	39	66	16	1	8	41	15	67	6	4	.419	.304	R	R	6-1	190	7-16-79	2002	San Diego, Calif.
Lopez, Luis	.207	12	29	2	6	1	0	0	4	3	9	1	0	.241	.324	R	R	6-2	180	1-8-84	2000	Santiago, Veraguas, Panama
McAnulty, Paul	.379	67	235	56	89	29	0	8	51	49	43	7	2	.604	.488	L	R	5-10	220	2-24-81	2002	Oxnard, Calif.
Moore, Mewelde	.197	22	76	7	15	3	3	0	7	8	34	6	0	.316	.291	R	R	6-0	190	7-24-82	2001	Baton Rouge, La.
Moore, Rusty	.157	43	127	20	20	2	0	0	13	25	37	15	1	.173	.304	R	R	6-2	210	10-11-80	2002	Windermere, Fla.
Mora, Ruben	.237	31	114	22	27	5	0	1	13	15	28	4	4	.307	.331	S	R	6-0	150	1-11-82	2000	Sabanitas, Panama
Olson, David	.234	42	137	24	32	6	4	0	15	10	57	11	4	.336	.300	R	R	5-9	150	1-19-82	2000	Caracas, Venez.
Ramirez, Yordany	.179	23	78	8	14	1	0	0	5	3	24	0	2	.192	.244	R	R	6-0	160	7-31-84	2001	Boca Chica, D.R.
Ramos, Peeter	.327	56	202	26	66	10	1	1	25	23	36	12	8	.401	.409	R	R	5-11	150	3-18-82	2001	Caracas, Venez.
Smith, Rashad	.276	66	254	41	70	14	5	0	30	32	45	10	3	.370	.359	L	R	6-4	200	1-20-80	2002	Bolivar, Tenn.

GAMES BY POSITION: C—Falcon 50, Garcia 21, Lester 9, Lopez 11. **1B**—Baez 1, Johanning 15, Lopez 1, McAnulty 55, R. Moore 9. **2B**—Baez 4, Lima 24, Ramos 54. **3B**—Baez 29, Dale 35, Lima 14, R. Moore 1, Ramos1. **SS**—Baez 16, Garcia 62, Ramos 1. **OF**—Antequera 27, Johanning 2, Lester 6, Lima 22, M. Moore 17, R. Moore 24, Mora 31, Olson 39, Ramirez 23, Smith 50.

PITCHING	W	L	ERA	G	GS	CG	SV	IP	H	R	ER	BB	SO	AVG	B	T	HT	WT	DOB	1st Yr	Resides
Beavers, Kevin	4	2	4.13	11	11	0	0	61	71	32	28	14	49	.293	L	L	6-5	190	10-22-79	2002	Irvine, Calif.
Darby, James	2	1	6.75	24	0	0	1	28	24	25	21	29	35	.235	R	R	6-3	180	1-5-84	2002	Camden, Australia
Espinal, Jhovany	3	2	8.87	22	0	0	0	23	31	27	23	23	32	.329	R	R	6-1	170	4-29-84	2001	LaGuna Salada, D.R.
Fernandez, Alfredo	0	3	4.91	6	6	0	0	22	27	23	12	8	10	.287	R	R	6-4	200	9-15-84	2002	Maracaibo, Venez.
Geraldo, Jose	0	1	8.79	14	0	0	0	14	27	19	14	10	5	.402	R	R	6-3	180	9-22-83	2001	Azua, D.R.
Krisch, David	2	3	4.31	32	0	0	16	31	34	18	15	19	32	.278	L	L	6-7	200	5-25-80	2002	El Cajon, Calif.
Laratta, E.J.	2	0	5.68	9	2	0	0	19	25	15	12	9	9	.316	R	R	6-2	190	5-24-80	2002	Englewood, Colo.
Martinez, Hancen	4	3	3.72	14	9	0	0	58	54	32	24	27	61	.246	R	R	6-0	170	6-23-83	2000	La Victoria, D.R.
Montarbo, Adam	1	2	2.04	14	0	0	0	18	16	10	4	10	12	.228	R	R	6-4	220	9-1-80	2002	Morgan Hill, Calif.
Morel, Eudy	0	2	3.24	8	0	0	1	8	9	9	3	2	10	.257	R	R	5-10	160	8-23-79	2000	McAllen, Texas
Oyervidez, Jose	0	4	4.31	32	0	0	3	31	22	22	15	22	58	.198	R	R	6-1	180	2-18-82	2002	McAllen, Texas
Paulino, Johan	0	0	5.68	16	0	0	0	19	20	16	12	22	14	.256	R	R	5-11	150	9-6-82	1999	Sabana Palenque, D.R.
Pena, Luis	1	2	6.84	18	3	0	0	25	36	26	19	8	21	.318	R	R	6-0	170	1-21-81	2001	La Vega, D.R.
Perez, Henry	4	6	4.72	15	15	0	0	74	73	52	39	36	70	.260	R	R	6-3	210	10-27-82	1999	Santo Domingo, D.R.
Ponce, William	1	4	8.47	14	7	0	0	34	45	43	32	33	31	.302	R	R	6-1	190	9-9-84	2002	San Salvador, El Salvador
Thompson, Sean	4	3	3.83	13	11	0	0	56	51	34	24	38	69	.248	L	L	5-11	160	10-13-82	2002	La Junta, Colo.
Thrasher, Jesse	1	5	5.34	21	8	0	0	57	69	59	34	37	38	.296	R	R	6-3	220	12-20-80	1999	St. Joseph, Mo.
Valdes, Carlos	0	1	3.62	21	0	0	0	27	18	13	11	18	22	.202	R	R	6-1	170	3-14-84	2000	Sabana Pulenque, D.R.
Wilson, Brandon	3	0	3.40	17	4	0	1	48	59	27	18	13	38	.307	R	R	6-1	180	2-3-83	2002	Destin, Fla.

ORGANIZATION STATISTICS

SAN FRANCISCO GIANTS

BY JEFF FLETCHER

For the first time in the Brian Sabean-Dusty Baker-Barry Bonds era, the Giants were able to end the cycle of barely missing the playoffs or losing in the first round, but they still came up painfully short of the ultimate goal.

In the previous five years, the Giants had averaged 90 victories but failed to win a postseason series. In 2002, they reached the organization's first World Series since 1989, riding a sizzling September to 95 wins and the wild card, then taking out the Braves and Cardinals in the playoffs.

In a thrilling World Series, though, the Giants lost in seven games to the Angels. They were just eight outs from winning the organization's first championship since 1954, with a 5-0 lead in the seventh inning of Game Six, but the Angels stormed back to win 6-5, and then they won the seventh game, 4-1.

The team trudged home from Anaheim uncertain of its future. Baker, Sabean and Jeff Kent were all potential free agents, with only Sabean considered a lock to return. The Giants also faced the prospect of an aging roster. None of the everyday position players in the World Series were younger than 30, and only two (Rich Aurilia and David Bell) were younger than 34.

Baker got the most out of this group in 2002, though. While just three players—Bonds, Kent and catcher Benito Santiago—were above-average at their positions, the Giants still managed to score the third-most runs in the National League, all while playing in the league's worst hitters' park.

Bonds, as usual, was the guy that made the offense go. Even though he shattered the records for walks (198) and intentional walks (68), he still did enough damage that opponents could hardly be blamed for walking him. Bonds hit .370—winning the first batting title of his career—along with 46 homers, winning an unprecedented fifth MVP award.

Barry Bonds   Jesse Foppert

PLAYERS OF THE YEAR

MAJOR LEAGUE: Barry Bonds, of

How did Bonds follow his magical 2001 season? By shattering the major league records for on-base percentage (.582) and walks (198), and by becoming the oldest first-time batting champion (.370).

MINOR LEAGUE: Jesse Foppert, rhp

Foppert reached Triple-A 12 months after signing with the Giants as a second-round draft pick. He led the minors with 11.7 strikeouts per nine innings by using his mid-90s fastball, slider and splitter.

Bonds also climbed into the elite 600-homer club on Aug. 9, joining Hank Aaron, Babe Ruth and Willie Mays. Bonds finished the year with 613 homers, putting him within range of passing Mays' 660 late in 2003.

Kent got off to a slow start after breaking his wrist in spring training—an injury he said came while washing his truck, but later turned out to be from popping wheelies on his motorcycle outside the team complex in Scottsdale, Ariz. Kent still managed to hit a career-high 37 homers, joining Rogers Hornsby as the only second baseman to have three 30-homer seasons.

Santiago was also a nice story. The 37-year-old catcher made the all-star team, becoming just one of 10 players ever to go 10 years between all-star appearances. He finished the season with the tough job of batting behind Bonds, and he had one of the finest moments of his career when he hit a go-ahead two-run homer after a Bonds intentional walk in Game Four of the NLCS against St. Louis.

The Giants' pitching was the key for them to reach the postseason, but they did it with a staff largely devoid of spectacular individual accomplishments. In fact, they did not have a starter win 15 games, but they had five who won 12 games.

In the minors, a handful of outstanding pitching prospects continued to develop, starting with the fastest-riser of the bunch, righthander Jesse Foppert. He went from the 2001 draft to being the Pacific Coast League's best prospect. Righthanders Jerome Williams and Kurt Ainsworth also spent the season at Triple-A Fresno, readying for a run at spots in the big league rotation in 2003.

Though the system produced some good players, the farm clubs didn't produce too many victories. All four full-season teams—Fresno, Double-A Shreveport, high Class A San Jose and low Class A Hagerstown—had losing records.

ORGANIZATION LEADERS

BATTING

*AVG	Lance Niekro, Shreveport	.310
R	Todd Linden, Fresno/Shreveport	82
H	Deivis Santos, Fresno/Shreveport	152
TB	Todd Linden, Fresno/Shreveport	227
2B	Deivis Santos, Fresno/Shreveport	36
3B	Jamie Athas, San Jose	7
	Carlos Valderrama, Shreveport/San Jose	7
HR	Carlos Valderrama, Shreveport/San Jose	19
RBI	Julian Benevidez, Hagerstown	72
BB	Todd Linden, Fresno/Shreveport	81
SO	Dan Trumble, San Jose	185
SB	Jason Ellison, Fresno/San Jose	25

PITCHING

W	Jeff Clark, Shreveport/San Jose	14
L	Luis Estrella, Fresno	13
	Wes Hutchison, Fresno/Shreveport	13
#ERA	Jeff Clark, Shreveport/San Jose	2.66
G	Troy Brohawn, Fresno	56
CG	Anthony Pannone, Hagerstown	2
	Jeff Clark, Shreveport/San Jose	2
SV	Manny Aybar, Fresno	24
IP	Jeff Clark, Shreveport/San Jose	176
BB	Boof Bonser, Shreveport/San Jose	84
SO	Jesse Foppert, Fresno/Shreveport	183

*Minimum 250 At-Bats #Minimum 75 Innings

SAN FRANCISCO GIANTS

Manager: Dusty Baker

BATTING	AVG	G	AB	R	H	2B	3B	HR	RBI	BB	SO	SB	CS	SLG	OBP	B	T	HT	WT	DOB	1st Yr	Resides
Aurilia, Rich	.257	133	538	76	138	35	2	15	61	37	90	1	2	.413	.305	R	R	6-1	180	9-2-71	1992	Phoenix, Ariz.
Bell, David	.261	154	552	82	144	29	2	20	73	54	80	1	2	.429	.333	R	R	5-10	190	9-14-72	1990	Seattle, Wash.
Benard, Marvin	.276	65	123	16	34	9	2	1	13	7	26	5	1	.407	.321	L	L	5-09	190	1-20-70	1992	Richland, Wash.
Bonds, Barry	.370	143	403	117	149	31	2	46	110	198	47	9	2	.799	.582	L	L	6-2	220	7-24-64	1985	Los Altos Hills, Calif.
Dunston, Shawon	.231	72	147	7	34	5	0	1	9	3	33	1	0	.286	.250	R	R	6-1	180	3-21-63	1982	Fremont, Calif.
Feliz, Pedro	.253	67	146	14	37	4	1	2	13	6	27	0	0	.336	.281	R	R	6-1	200	4-27-77	1994	Azua, D.R.
Goodwin, Tom	.260	78	154	23	40	5	2	1	17	14	25	16	2	.338	.321	L	R	6-1	170	7-27-68	1989	Grapevine, Texas
Hernandez, Livan	.234	37	64	6	15	4	1	0	6	0	9	0	0	.328	.231	R	R	6-2	240	2-20-75	1996	Miami Beach, Fla.
Kent, Jeff	.313	152	623	102	195	42	2	37	108	52	101	5	1	.565	.368	R	R	6-1	210	3-7-68	1989	Foster City, Calif.
Lofton, Kenny	.267	47	180	30	48	10	3	3	9	23	22	7	3	.406	.353	L	L	6-0	180	5-31-67	1988	Tucson, Ariz.
Lunsford, Trey	.667	3	3	0	2	1	0	0	1	0	1	0	0	1.000	.667	R	R	6-1	200	5-25-79	2000	Southaven, Miss.
Martinez, Ramon E.	.271	72	181	26	49	10	2	4	25	14	26	2	0	.414	.335	R	R	6-1	180	10-10-72	1993	Toa Alta, P.R.
Minor, Damon	.237	83	173	21	41	6	0	10	24	24	34	0	0	.445	.333	L	L	6-7	230	1-5-74	1996	Edmond, Okla.
Mueller, Bill	.154	8	13	0	2	0	0	0	1	1	1	0	0	.154	.214	S	R	5-10	180	3-17-71	1993	Maryland Heights, Mo.
2-team (103 Chicago)	.262	111	366	51	96	19	4	7	38	52	42	0	0	.393	.350							
Murray, Calvin	.000	11	12	0	0	0	0	0	0	1	2	0	0	.000	.077	R	R	5-11	180	7-30-71	1993	Spring, Texas
Ransom, Cody	.667	7	3	2	2	0	0	0	1	1	1	0	0	.667	.750	R	R	6-2	190	2-17-76	1998	Chandler, Ariz.
Sanders, Reggie	.250	140	505	75	126	23	6	23	85	47	121	18	6	.455	.324	R	R	6-1	200	12-1-67	1988	Phoenix, Ariz.
Santiago, Benito	.278	126	478	56	133	24	5	16	74	27	73	4	2	.450	.315	R	R	6-1	200	3-9-65	1983	Pembroke Pines, Fla.
Shinjo, Tsuyoshi	.238	118	362	42	86	15	3	9	37	24	46	5	0	.370	.294	R	R	6-1	180	1-28-72	2001	Osaka, Japan
Snow, J.T.	.246	143	422	47	104	26	2	6	53	59	90	0	0	.360	.344	L	L	6-2	200	2-26-68	1989	San Mateo, Calif.
Torcato, Tony	.273	5	11	0	3	1	0	0	0	2	3	0	0	.364	.273	L	R	6-1	190	10-25-79	1998	Woodland, Calif.
Torrealba, Yorvit	.279	53	136	17	38	10	0	2	14	14	20	0	0	.397	.355	R	R	5-11	190	7-19-78	1995	Guarenas, Venez.

PITCHING	W	L	ERA	G	GS	CG	SV	IP	H	R	ER	BB	SO	AVG	B	T	HT	WT	DOB	1st Yr	Resides
Ainsworth, Kurt	1	2	2.10	6	4	0	0	26	22	7	6	12	15	.236	R	R	6-3	190	9-9-78	1999	Baton Rouge, La.
Aybar, Manny	1	0	2.51	15	0	0	0	14	16	6	4	3	11	.271	R	R	6-1	170	5-4-72	1991	Tampa, Fla.
Brohawn, Troy	0	1	6.35	11	0	0	0	6	5	4	4	1	3	.227	L	L	6-1	190	1-14-73	1994	Woolford, Md.
Christiansen, Jason	0	1	5.40	6	0	0	0	5	6	3	3	2	1	.315	R	L	6-5	240	9-21-69	1991	Omaha, Neb.
Eyre, Scott	0	0	1.59	21	0	0	0	11	11	4	2	7	7	.255	L	L	6-1	200	5-30-72	1991	Bradenton, Fla.
Fultz, Aaron	2	2	4.79	43	0	0	0	41	47	22	22	19	31	.293	L	L	6-0	200	9-4-73	1992	Fayette, Ala.
Hernandez, Livan	12	16	4.38	33	33	5	0	216	233	113	105	71	134	.282	R	R	6-2	240	2-20-75	1996	Miami Beach, Fla.
Jensen, Ryan	13	8	4.51	32	30	1	0	172	183	93	86	66	105	.278	R	R	6-0	200	9-17-75	1996	West Valley, Utah
Nathan, Joe	0	0	0.00	4	0	0	0	4	1	0	0	2		.083	R	R	6-4	200	11-22-74	1995	Tempe, Ariz.
Nen, Robb	6	2	2.20	68	0	0	43	74	64	19	18	20	81	.231	R	R	6-5	220	11-28-69	1987	Dove Canyon, Calif.
Ortiz, Russ	14	10	3.61	33	33	2	0	214	191	89	86	94	137	.241	R	R	6-1	200	6-5-74	1995	Gilbert, Ariz.
Rodriguez, Felix	8	6	4.17	71	0	0	0	69	53	33	32	29	58	.212	R	R	6-1	190	9-9-72	1990	Monte Cristi, D.R.
Rueter, Kirk	14	8	3.23	33	33	0	0	204	204	83	73	54	76	.261	L	L	6-2	210	12-1-70	1991	Nashville, Ill.
Schmidt, Jason	13	8	3.45	29	29	2	0	185	148	78	71	73	196	.218	R	R	6-5	185	1-29-73	1991	Longview, Wash.
Witasick, Jay	1	0	2.37	44	0	0	0	68	58	19	18	21	54	.233	R	R	6-4	230	8-28-72	1993	Bel Air, Md.
Worrell, Tim	8	2	2.25	80	0	0	0	72	55	21	18	30	55	.212	R	R	6-4	230	7-5-67	1990	Glendale, Ariz.
Zerbe, Chad	2	0	3.04	50	0	0	0	56	52	22	19	21	26	.247	L	L	6-0	190	4-27-72	1991	Highland, Calif.

FIELDING

Catcher	PCT	G	PO	A	E	DP	PB
Lunsford	.800	3	4	0	1	0	0
Santiago	.995	125	738	54	4	10	7
Torrealba	.993	53	269	20	2	3	0

First Base	PCT	G	PO	A	E	DP
Bell	1.000	2	13	4	0	2
Dunston	1.000	1	6	0	0	0
Kent	1.000	9	55	2	0	7
Martinez	1.000	4	30	3	0	3
Minor	.997	44	310	20	1	29
Snow	.993	135	939	79	7	104

Second Base	PCT	G	PO	A	E	DP
Bell	.943	12	21	29	3	6
Kent	.978	149	293	411	16	113
Martinez	.977	17	17	25	1	6

Third Base	PCT	G	PO	A	E	DP
Bell	.973	139	78	244	9	21
Feliz	.966	44	29	57	3	9
Goodwin	.000	1	0	0	0	0
Martinez	1.000	2	2	0	0	0

Mueller	1.000	3	2	3	0	0

Shortstop	PCT	G	PO	A	E	DP
Aurilia	.980	131	213	334	11	97
Bell	1.000	3	4	7	0	1
Dunston	.000	1	0	0	0	0
Feliz	.000	1	0	0	0	0
Martinez	.950	40	52	82	7	26
Ransom	1.000	3	3	3	0	0

Outfield	PCT	G	PO	A	E	DP
Benard	1.000	38	50	3	0	0
Bonds	.968	135	241	4	8	2
Dunston	1.000	49	47	0	0	0
Feliz	.000	1	0	0	0	0
Goodwin	.990	53	98	0	1	0
Lofton	1.000	45	116	3	0	0
Martinez	1.000	3	8	0	0	0
Murray	.917	10	10	1	1	0
Sanders	.984	137	290	12	5	0
Shinjo	.980	117	286	10	6	3
Torcato	1.000	3	2	0	0	0

LARRY GOREN

Jeff Kent

ORGANIZATION STATISTICS

Vice President, Player Personnel: Dick Tidrow

Class	Farm Team	League	W	L	Pct.	Finish*	Manager	First Yr.
AAA	Fresno (Calif.) Grizzlies	Pacific Coast	57	87	.396	16th (16)	Lenn Sakata	1988
AA	Shreveport (La.) Swamp Dragons	Texas	60	79	.432	7th (8)	Mario Mendoza	1979
High A	San Jose (Calif.) Giants	California	68	72	.486	7th (10)	Bill Hayes	1988
Low A	Hagerstown (Md.) Suns	South Atlantic	63	77	.450	13th (16)	Mike Ramsey	2001
SS A	Salem-Keizer (Ore.) Volcanoes	Northwest	41	35	.539	t-3rd (8)	Fred Stanley	1997
Rookie	Scottsdale (Ariz.) Giants	Arizona	32	23	.582	2nd (7)	Bert Hunter	2000

*Finish in overall standings (No. of teams in league)

FRESNO GRIZZLIES

Class AAA

PACIFIC COAST LEAGUE

BATTING	AVG	G	AB	R	H	2B	3B	HR	RBI	BB	SO	SB	CS	SLG	OBP	B	T	HT	WT	DOB	1st Yr	Resides
Byas, Mike	.200	20	55	5	11	0	2	0	4	5	15	4	1	.273	.267	S	R	6-0	170	4-21-76	1997	Chesterfield, Mo.
Castro, Nelson	.181	28	94	8	17	1	2	2	5	3	20	7	1	.298	.210	S	R	5-10	200	6-4-76	1994	Monte Cristi, D.R.
Clark, Doug	.269	70	212	24	57	9	1	5	19	15	52	3	3	.392	.330	L	R	6-2	200	3-5-76	1998	Springfield, Mass.
Ellison, Jason	.311	49	196	31	61	8	1	3	8	21	28	16	3	.408	.389	R	R	5-10	180	4-4-78	2000	Lewiston, Idaho
Freire, Alejandro	.274	46	146	12	40	7	1	3	7	14	28	0	0	.397	.358	R	R	6-2	180	8-23-74	1992	Caracas, Venez.
Goodwin, Tom	.226	17	62	11	14	3	1	0	7	8	8	3	2	.306	.314	L	R	6-1	170	7-27-68	1989	Grapevine, Texas
Guzman, Edwards	.297	112	390	45	116	22	0	5	55	16	26	1	3	.392	.324	L	R	5-11	200	9-11-76	1996	Naranjito, P.R.
Jordan, Kevin	.229	60	188	13	43	4	1	3	14	8	23	1	0	.309	.267	R	R	6-1	200	10-9-69	1990	Birkdale, Australia
Linden, Todd	.250	29	100	18	25	2	1	3	10	20	35	2	0	.380	.380	S	R	6-2	210	6-30-80	2002	Bremerton, Wash.
Lunsford, Trey	.175	19	57	3	10	0	0	2	9	6	15	0	0	.281	.258	R	R	6-1	200	5-25-79	2000	Southaven, Miss.
Luther, Ryan	.250	5	8	2	2	1	0	0	3	3	3	1	0	.375	.462	R	R	6-0	180	1-21-77	1998	North Bend, Wash.
McGowan, Sean	.246	57	187	12	46	15	2	1	17	5	42	1	1	.364	.272	R	R	6-6	240	5-15-77	1999	Burlington, Mass.
Melo, Juan	.276	135	479	67	132	28	2	16	63	33	93	6	7	.443	.324	S	R	6-3	200	10-11-76	1994	Bani, D.R.
Minor, Damon	.517	9	29	8	15	6	1	0	5	5	5	0	0	.793	.588	L	L	6-7	230	1-5-74	1996	Edmond, Okla.
Nieckula, Aaron	.087	11	23	2	2	0	0	0	1	0	9	1	0	.087	.125	R	R	5-11	200	9-7-76	1998	Stickney, Ill.
Pena, Angel	.262	72	248	27	65	11	2	8	34	15	55	2	2	.419	.301	R	R	5-10	220	2-16-75	1992	San Pedro de Macoris, D.R.
Pernalete, Marco	.265	92	260	29	69	4	1	5	25	13	58	1	1	.346	.297	S	R	6-0	150	10-12-78	1998	Barquisimeto, Venez.
Powell, Dante	.229	17	48	5	11	5	0	0	2	2	16	2	1	.333	.260	R	R	6-2	180	8-25-73	1994	Long Beach, Calif.
Ransom, Cody	.207	135	449	53	93	18	4	13	46	47	151	6	4	.352	.283	R	R	6-2	190	2-17-76	1998	Chandler, Ariz.
Rodriguez, Guillermo	.235	32	115	9	27	5	0	2	8	6	23	0	1	.330	.299	R	R	5-11	215	5-15-78	1996	Barquisimeto, Venez.
Santos, Deivis	.284	23	88	8	25	3	1	3	14	2	14	4	0	.443	.297	L	L	6-1	170	2-9-80	1997	Santo Domingo, D.R.
Servais, Scott	.375	4	8	1	3	0	0	0	1	0	0	0	0	.375	.500	R	R	6-2	210	6-4-67	1989	Castle Rock, Colo.
Shinjo, Tsuyoshi	.000	2	7	0	0	0	0	0	0	0	1	0	0	.000	.125	R	R	6-1	180	1-28-72	2001	Osaka, Japan
Simmons, Brian	.292	91	319	45	93	18	4	11	40	34	76	7	4	.476	.364	S	R	6-2	190	9-4-73	1995	McMurray, Pa.
Torcato, Tony	.290	130	490	64	142	23	3	13	64	29	65	4	6	.429	.330	L	R	6-1	190	10-25-79	1998	Woodland, Calif.
Zuniga, Tony	.240	90	304	22	73	16	1	6	33	18	38	0	4	.359	.287	R	R	6-0	200	1-13-75	1996	Anaheim, Calif.

PITCHING	W	L	ERA	G	GS	CG	SV	IP	H	R	ER	BB	SO	AVG	B	T	HT	WT	DOB	1st Yr	Resides
Ainsworth, Kurt	8	6	3.41	20	19	1	0	116	101	49	44	43	119	.237	R	R	6-3	190	9-9-78	1999	Baton Rouge, La.
Aybar, Manny	1	4	3.75	45	0	0	24	50	46	24	21	18	53	.243	R	R	6-1	170	5-4-72	1991	Tampa, Fla.
Brohawn, Troy	3	3	3.65	56	0	0	1	69	71	31	28	21	55	.261	L	L	6-1	190	1-14-73	1994	Woolford, Md.
Cannon, Jon	1	0	0.00	3	0	0	0	4	3	0	0	5	0	.230	R	L	6-3	200	1-1-75	1996	Los Altos, Calif.
Crabtree, Robbie	1	4	7.91	24	0	0	0	33	38	31	29	14	22	.296	R	R	6-1	170	11-25-72	1996	Bakersfield, Calif.
Estrella, Luis	7	13	4.43	38	20	0	7	144	168	77	71	64	98	.300	R	R	6-1	220	10-7-74	1996	Santa Ana, Calif.
Fernandez, Osvaldo	4	4	4.70	10	9	0	0	59	64	33	31	15	37	.281	R	R	6-2	190	11-4-68	1996	Miami, Fla.
Foppert, Jesse	3	6	3.99	14	14	0	0	79	71	37	35	35	109	.243	R	R	6-6	210	7-10-80	2001	San Rafael, Calif.
Fultz, Aaron	1	3	3.18	17	0	0	4	23	18	8	8	11	22	.222	L	L	6-0	200	9-4-73	1992	Fayette, Ala.
Horgan, Joe	2	2	5.93	27	4	0	0	58	65	38	38	21	37	.286	L	L	6-1	200	6-7-77	1996	Rancho Cordova, Calif.
Hutchison, Wesley	1	4	7.08	17	4	0	0	34	43	28	27	11	27	.296	R	R	6-1	190	5-31-79	2001	Lewiston, Idaho
Jarvis, Matt	3	2	3.03	20	0	0	1	30	31	10	10	10	29	.269	R	L	6-4	180	2-22-72	1991	Albuquerque, N.M.
2-team (23 Tacoma)	5	4	3.34	43	0	0	3	57	57	25	21	20	49	.265							
Nathan, Joe	6	12	5.60	31	25	1	0	146	167	97	91	74	117	.283	R	R	6-4	200	11-22-74	1995	Tempe, Ariz.
Pearson, Jason	0	0	3.75	34	0	0	0	36	35	20	15	16	28	.261	L	L	6-0	190	12-29-75	1998	Freeport, Ill.
2-team (23 Portland)	3	0	2.73	57	0	0	0	66	60	25	20	25	46	.241							
Schmidt, Jason	2	0	3.00	2	2	0	0	12	11	4	4	2	12	.261	R	R	6-5	200	1-29-73	1991	Longview, Wash.
Sparks, Steve	0	0	11.25	3	0	0	0	4	5	5	5	3	3	.277	R	R	6-4	220	3-28-75	1998	Mobile, Ala.
2-team (2 Memphis)	0	0	11.05	5	0	0	0	7	6	9	9	9	5	.222							
Urban, Jeff	5	7	3.41	35	14	0	0	103	114	46	39	36	72	.285	R	L	6-8	210	1-25-77	1998	Alexandria, Ind.
Verplancke, Jeff	5	3	5.78	51	0	0	3	64	60	30	27	25	52	.251	R	R	6-3	200	11-18-77	1999	Ontario, Calif.
Villano, Mike	0	1	12.00	4	0	0	1	3	3	4	4	4	2	.272	R	R	6-0	190	8-10-71	1994	Bay City, Mich.
Williams, Jerome	6	11	3.59	28	28	0	0	161	140	76	64	50	130	.233	R	R	6-3	180	12-4-81	1999	Las Vegas, Nev.
Witasick, Jay	0	0	4.50	2	2	0	0	2	1	1	1	1	2	.142	R	R	6-4	230	8-28-72	1993	Bel Air, Md.
Zerbe, Chad	0	0	0.00	3	3	0	0	10	8	0	0	3	5	.216	L	L	6-0	190	4-27-72	1991	Highland, Calif.

FIELDING

Catcher	PCT	G	PO	A	E	DP	PB
Guzman	.990	36	264	30	3	4	5
Lunsford	.987	19	139	8	2	2	1
Luther	1.000	2	4	0	0	0	0
Nieckula	1.000	6	21	4	0	0	0
Pena	.981	56	372	36	8	8	10
Rodriguez	.989	32	255	12	3	0	5
Servais	1.000	3	11	1	0	0	1

First Base	PCT	G	PO	A	E	DP
Castro	1.000	1	2	0	0	0
Freire	.987	20	146	10	2	13
Guzman	.985	19	125	9	2	9
Jordan	.986	10	68	3	1	5
McGowan	.979	42	303	28	7	22
Melo	1.000	1	1	0	0	1
Minor	.972	9	64	6	2	5

	PCT	G	PO	A	E	DP
Pena	1.000	11	83	7	0	8
Pernalete	1.000	24	146	14	0	18
Santos	.985	23	180	23	3	20

Second Base	PCT	G	PO	A	E	DP
Castro	1.000	1	1	0	0	0
Guzman	.955	13	24	18	2	3
Jordan	.990	27	36	60	1	13
Luther	.750	1	2	1	1	0

	AVG	G	AB	R	H	2B 3B HR RBI
Melo	.991	97	186	244	4	57
Pernalete	.967	21	28	31	2	7

Third Base	PCT	G	PO	A	E	DP
Guzman	.962	25	9	41	2	5
Melo	.947	27	18	36	3	4
Pernalete	.922	23	16	31	4	2
Zuniga	.952	78	40	120	8	11

Shortstop	PCT	G	PO	A	E	DP
Castro	1.000	2	4	2	0	0

	AVG	G	AB	R	H	
Melo	.976	13	13	28	1	6
Pernalete	.000	1	0	0	0	0
Ransom	.973	135	204	347	15	69

Outfield	PCT	G	PO	A	E	DP
Byas	1.000	17	41	3	0	1
Castro	1.000	20	29	3	0	1
Clark	.982	58	108	2	2	0
Ellison	.992	49	115	5	1	1
Freire	1.000	7	13	0	0	0

	PCT	G	PO	A	E	DP
Goodwin	1.000	16	39	0	0	0
Guzman	1.000	10	17	0	0	0
Jordan	1.000	15	18	1	0	0
Linden	1.000	29	50	1	0	0
Luther	1.000	1	2	0	0	0
Pernalete	.000	1	0	0	0	0
Powell	1.000	13	21	0	0	0
Shinjo	1.000	2	5	0	0	0
Simmons	.980	88	189	4	4	2
Torcato	.964	122	212	4	8	0

SHREVEPORT SWAMP DRAGONS — Class AA

TEXAS LEAGUE

BATTING	AVG	G	AB	R	H	2B	3B	HR	RBI	BB	SO	SB	CS	SLG	OBP	B	T	HT	WT	DOB	1st Yr	Resides
Anderson, Keith	.000	2	6	0	0	0	0	0	0	0	3	0	0	.000	.000	R	R	6-1	200	1-6-79	2001	Escondido, Calif.
Carvajal, Jhonny	.279	113	419	58	117	28	5	5	34	37	67	11	4	.406	.343	R	R	5-10	180	7-24-73	1993	Barcelona, Venez.
Castro, Nelson	.223	86	300	35	67	15	4	7	29	11	60	15	9	.370	.269	S	R	5-10	200	6-4-76	1994	Monte Cristi, D.R.
Clark, Doug	.261	44	138	13	36	6	1	2	13	19	35	5	7	.362	.348	L	R	6-2	200	3-5-76	1998	Springfield, Mass.
Flaherty, Tim	.219	76	247	23	54	10	2	6	34	28	81	0	1	.348	.298	R	R	6-4	220	7-11-76	1997	Williamstown, Mass.
Freire, Alejandro	.282	55	177	24	50	9	0	10	32	19	38	0	2	.503	.363	R	R	6-2	180	8-23-74	1992	Caracas, Venez.
Jester, Joe	.279	104	359	52	100	22	2	11	40	29	66	14	5	.437	.335	R	R	5-10	180	7-17-78	1999	Ashdown, Ark.
Linden, Todd	.314	111	392	64	123	26	2	12	52	61	101	9	5	.482	.419	S	R	6-2	210	6-30-80	2002	Bremerton, Wash.
Lunsford, Trey	.281	66	210	26	59	13	0	1	20	29	42	5	2	.357	.379	R	R	6-1	200	5-25-79	2000	Southhaven, Miss.
Luther, Ryan	.278	32	108	10	30	5	0	2	14	11	25	4	0	.380	.350	R	R	6-0	180	1-21-77	1999	North Bend, Wash.
McDowell, Arturo	.181	59	221	18	40	3	1	0	11	15	46	10	5	.204	.246	L	L	6-1	170	9-7-79	1998	Jackson, Miss.
McGowan, Sean	.167	9	30	2	5	2	0	0	1	1	3	0	0	.233	.194	R	R	6-6	240	5-15-77	1999	Burlington, Mass.
Mendoza, Carlos	.244	111	377	44	92	20	2	2	28	68	42	12	9	.324	.361	S	R	6-0	160	11-27-79	1996	Barquisimeto, Venez.
Moreta, Ramon	.260	88	273	34	71	12	3	3	37	20	52	17	16	.359	.312	R	R	5-11	180	9-5-75	1994	La Romana, D.R.
Nieckula, Aaron	.182	14	44	5	8	2	0	0	1	3	13	1	1	.227	.275	R	R	5-11	200	9-7-76	1998	Stickney, Ill.
Niekro, Lance	.310	79	297	33	92	20	1	4	34	7	32	0	2	.424	.327	R	R	6-3	210	1-29-79	2000	Lakeland, Fla.
Pernalete, Marco	.222	15	54	5	12	4	0	1	5	1	8	3	0	.352	.263	S	R	6-0	150	10-12-78	1996	Barquisimeto, Venez.
Rodriguez, Guillermo	.268	13	41	4	11	1	1	1	6	4	10	1	2	.415	.348	R	R	5-11	215	5-15-78	1996	Barquisimeto, Venez.
Santos, Deivis	.312	109	407	54	127	33	5	3	56	18	42	4	4	.440	.349	L	L	6-1	170	2-9-80	1997	Santo Domingo, D.R.
Shabala, Adam	.216	40	148	14	32	8	0	1	16	6	35	3	1	.291	.250	L	R	6-1	190	2-6-78	2000	Streator, Ill.
Valderrama, Carlos	.244	37	135	13	33	3	1	4	15	10	23	4	0	.370	.304	R	R	6-0	180	11-30-77	1995	Maracaibo, Venez.
Walker, Mark	.167	22	72	5	12	2	0	0	8	4	33	0	0	.194	.221	R	R	6-1	190	8-17-78	2000	Miami, Fla.

PITCHING	W	L	ERA	G	GS	CG	SV	IP	H	R	ER	BB	SO	AVG	B	T	HT	WT	DOB	1st Yr	Resides
Anderson, Luke	2	4	2.81	26	0	0	11	32	31	10	10	13	47	.250	R	R	6-5	210	4-9-78	2000	Las Vegas, Nev.
Bonser, Boof	1	2	5.55	5	0	0	0	24	30	15	15	14	23	.315	R	R	6-4	230	10-14-81	2000	Pinellas Park, Fla.
Brown, Elliot	8	4	4.35	25	16	1	0	112	132	65	54	34	37	.305	R	R	6-2	190	6-7-75	1996	Metairie, La.
Cannon, Jon	1	5	4.26	38	0	0	4	63	57	40	30	40	57	.235	R	L	6-3	200	1-1-75	1996	Los Altos, Calif.
Cash, David	5	8	3.05	34	12	0	5	109	94	41	37	39	88	.232	R	R	6-1	180	7-25-79	2001	Modesto, Calif.
Clark, Jeff	2	2	5.05	6	6	1	0	36	45	21	20	2	20	.308	R	R	6-6	240	5-6-80	2000	Ledyard, Conn.
Cox, Ryan	7	9	4.39	27	22	1	0	146	166	81	71	32	72	.288	R	R	6-3	190	12-25-76	1999	Stewardson, Ill.
Cozier, Vance	3	7	5.99	21	8	0	0	68	86	60	45	38	25	.300	R	R	6-6	240	9-26-77	1999	Ajax, Ontario
Diaz, Felix	3	5	2.70	12	12	1	0	60	54	22	18	22	48	.240	R	R	6-1	170	7-27-80	1998	Las Mata de Farfan, D.R.
Esteves, Jake	2	0	5.17	9	2	0	0	16	19	12	9	6	12	.316	R	R	6-1	190	7-31-75	1998	Auburn, Calif.
Foppert, Jesse	3	3	2.79	11	11	1	0	61	44	22	19	21	74	.199	R	R	6-6	210	7-10-80	2001	San Rafael, Calif.
Horgan, Joe	4	3	4.34	10	1	0	0	56	69	35	27	20	35	.305	L	L	6-1	200	6-7-77	1996	Rancho Cordova, Calif.
Hutchison, Wesley	2	9	5.81	22	7	0	3	67	80	50	43	35	35	.295	R	R	6-1	190	5-31-79	2001	Lewiston, Idaho
Jones, Chris	1	7	6.40	36	8	0	0	84	96	71	60	40	57	.286	L	L	6-3	180	8-29-79	1998	Charlotte, N.C.
Sparks, Steve	0	0	12.54	6	0	0	0	9	15	14	13	10	5	.375	R	R	6-4	220	3-28-75	1998	Mobile, Ala.
Uzzell, Todd	0	1	4.73	5	1	0	0	13	12	8	7	10	5	.240	R	R	6-3	200	6-22-78	2000	El Paso, Texas
Vent, Kevin	9	4	3.43	45	2	0	3	81	83	35	31	29	32	.272	R	R	6-0	180	6-1-77	1999	Maumelle, Ark.
Villano, Mike	1	1	7.56	5	0	0	0	8	12	7	7	4	8	.342	R	R	6-0	190	8-10-71	1994	Bay City, Mich.
Walk, Mitch	6	5	2.89	33	17	0	1	125	132	50	40	50	68	.272	L	L	6-2	180	4-7-78	2000	Mattoon, Ill.

FIELDING

Catcher	PCT	G	PO	A	E	DP	PB
Anderson	1.000	2	7	6	0	0	1
Flaherty	.976	37	227	13	6	2	6
Lunsford	.986	63	313	45	5	2	1
Luther	.979	17	87	7	2	0	5
Nieckula	.991	14	97	12	1	0	1
Rodriguez	1.000	7	39	4	0	1	0

First Base	PCT	G	PO	A	E	DP
Carvajal	1.000	1	10	0	0	0
Castro	1.000	4	14	3	0	2
Flaherty	.984	33	288	14	5	28
Freire	.973	9	68	5	2	7
Lunsford	1.000	3	22	4	0	2
Luther	1.000	3	25	1	0	4
McGowan	1.000	3	27	0	0	6
Niekro	1.000	50	418	21	0	39

Second Base	PCT	G	PO	A	E	DP
Santos	.988	39	311	25	4	33
Carvajal	.983	24	53	66	2	17
Jester	.952	88	163	251	21	54
Luther	.750	2	1	2	1	0
Mendoza	.984	26	60	64	2	19
Pernalete	.938	3	6	9	1	2

Third Base	PCT	G	PO	A	E	DP
Carvajal	.927	78	67	148	17	8
Castro	.969	16	14	49	2	3
Mendoza	1.000	12	9	29	0	2
Niekro	.857	27	22	44	11	5
Pernalete	.917	10	10	12	2	1

Shortstop	PCT	G	PO	A	E	DP
Carvajal	.971	8	11	22	1	7

	PCT	G	PO	A	E	DP
Castro	.958	63	100	176	12	36
Mendoza	.949	72	99	215	17	47

Outfield	PCT	G	PO	A	E	DP
Carvajal	.800	3	3	1	1	0
Castro	1.000	3	12	1	0	1
Clark	.974	40	73	2	2	0
Linden	.987	111	222	10	3	1
Luther	1.000	7	21	0	0	0
McDowell	.979	57	134	4	3	0
McGowan	1.000	1	2	0	0	0
Moreta	.988	76	150	11	2	1
Rodriguez	1.000	1	2	0	0	0
Santos	.986	71	133	5	2	0
Shabala	1.000	39	84	3	0	0
Walker	.947	22	50	4	3	2

SAN JOSE GIANTS — High Class A

CALIFORNIA LEAGUE

BATTING	AVG	G	AB	R	H	2B	3B	HR	RBI	BB	SO	SB	CS	SLG	OBP	B	T	HT	WT	DOB	1st Yr	Resides
Athas, Jamie	.251	123	466	65	117	15	7	1	40	48	124	14	6	.320	.328	L	R	6-2	190	10-14-79	2001	Winston-Salem, N.C.

BATTING

BATTING	AVG	G	AB	R	H	2B	3B	HR	RBI	BB	SO	SB	CS	SLG	OBP	B	T	HT	WT	DOB	1st Yr	Resides
Bell, Derek	.158	12	38	6	6	1	0	0	3	6	6	0	0	.184	.273	S	R	6-1	205	9-22-76	2000	Rohnert Park, Calif.
Chavez, Angel	.257	130	471	61	121	20	5	8	62	28	83	21	7	.372	.303	R	R	6-1	180	7-22-81	1999	David Chiriqui, Panama
Cordido, Julio	.239	61	226	32	54	6	0	3	23	17	31	3	1	.305	.294	R	R	6-1	190	7-30-80	1997	Caracas, Venez.
Ellison, Jason	.270	81	322	40	87	13	0	5	40	25	37	9	9	.357	.325	R	R	5-10	180	4-4-78	2000	Lewiston, Idaho
Florence, Branden	.381	5	21	5	8	1	0	1	5	0	3	0	0	.571	.381	R	R	6-0	200	4-3-78	2001	Boise, Idaho
Garrido, Tomas	.000	16	39	2	0	0	0	1	2	7	0	0	0	.000	.049	R	R	6-2	167	8-27-81	1999	Valencia, Venez.
Holst, Micah	.295	117	447	66	132	25	6	7	49	21	71	15	6	.425	.342	R	R	6-2	200	3-5-77	1999	Independence, Mo.
Lunsford, Trey	.255	16	51	7	13	3	0	1	5	3	5	2	0	.373	.321	R	R	6-1	190	5-25-79	2000	Southhaven, Miss.
Luster, Jeremy	.219	49	187	23	41	9	1	3	23	12	40	3	3	.326	.275	S	R	6-4	220	6-10-77	1999	Canton, Ga.
Luther, Ryan	.245	32	94	6	23	3	2	1	8	6	38	2	1	.351	.301	R	R	6-0	185	1-21-77	1999	North Bend, Wash.
Maldonado, Edwin	.226	120	439	39	99	21	3	5	51	13	100	3	8	.321	.251	R	R	6-0	180	1-3-79	2000	Manati, P.R.
McGowan, Sean	.302	55	212	22	64	12	0	4	31	15	34	0	1	.415	.363	R	R	6-6	240	5-15-77	1999	Burlington, Mass.
Nieckula, Aaron	.245	45	147	26	36	7	0	1	18	12	35	3	1	.313	.345	R	R	5-11	200	9-7-76	1998	Stickney, Ill.
Rodriguez, Guillermo	.362	42	152	24	55	15	1	1	20	10	26	2	1	.493	.405	R	R	5-11	215	5-15-78	1996	Barquisimeto, Venez.
Santana, Manny	.273	4	11	1	3	0	0	0	2	2	0	0	0	.273	.385	L	R	6-0	210	8-4-80	1998	Vega Alta, P.R.
Shabala, Adam	.328	73	244	42	80	18	2	7	45	36	64	11	7	.504	.412	L	R	6-2	190	2-6-78	2000	Streator, Ill.
Trumble, Dan	.216	117	412	60	89	21	0	15	53	44	185	8	2	.376	.298	R	R	6-2	215	9-29-79	2000	Nampa, Idaho
Valderrama, Carlos	.314	74	299	65	94	19	6	15	45	34	60	14	5	.569	.384	R	R	6-0	180	11-30-77	1995	Maracaibo, Venez.
Walker, Mark	.121	21	66	4	8	0	0	0	3	11	42	0	1	.121	.263	R	R	6-0	190	8-17-78	2000	Miami, Fla.
Wilfong, Nick	.187	105	353	48	66	19	2	9	46	36	130	8	5	.329	.266	L	R	6-1	190	11-6-78	2000	Wappaello, Mo.
Williams, Jon	.000	2	2	0	0	0	0	0	0	0	1	0	0	.000	.000	L	R	5-10	190	5-18-79	2001	Imperial, Mo.
Wright, Mike	.229	35	109	19	25	5	2	5	16	16	35	0	0	.450	.333	R	R	6-2	210	3-13-76	1999	San Jose, Calif.

PITCHING

PITCHING	W	L	ERA	G	GS	CG	SV	IP	H	R	ER	BB	SO	AVG	B	T	HT	WT	DOB	1st Yr	Resides
Alfano, Jeff	0	1	9.45	6	0	0	0	7	9	8	7	9	3	.310	R	R	6-3	210	8-16-76	1996	Visalia, Calif.
Bonser, Boof	8	6	2.88	23	23	0	0	128	89	44	41	70	139	.194	R	R	6-4	230	10-14-81	2000	Pinellas Park, Fla.
Brous, Dave	2	1	10.80	11	0	0	0	13	12	21	16	17	8	.250	L	L	6-2	190	3-9-80	1999	Crescent City, Calif.
Brown, Elliot	1	2	4.91	6	6	0	0	29	30	19	16	11	13	.260	R	R	6-2	190	6-7-75	1996	Metairie, La.
Clark, Jeff	12	3	2.06	21	21	1	0	140	118	37	32	18	129	.223	R	R	6-6	240	5-6-80	2000	Ledyard, Conn.
Cozier, Vance	3	3	3.90	11	11	0	0	65	72	29	28	22	35	.289	R	R	6-2	200	9-26-77	1999	Ajax, Ontario
Cram, Josh	0	0	3.38	2	0	0	0	3	5	1	1	2	3	.416	R	R	6-2	200	8-22-80	2001	Edmonds, Wash.
Gavelek, Brad	3	3	4.74	46	0	0	1	80	88	49	42	30	56	.285	L	L	6-3	200	3-10-78	2002	Elgin, Ill.
Gomes, Tony	3	2	5.98	16	5	0	0	47	62	34	31	16	41	.317	R	R	6-2	190	9-10-77	1998	Galt, Calif.
Gregg, James	1	2	2.16	5	0	0	0	8	9	7	2	7	1	.250	R	R	6-5	208	11-5-78	2000	De Funiak Springs, Fla.
Gross, Kyle	0	0	6.75	4	0	0	0	5	5	4	4	11	5	.263	R	R	6-4	220	12-11-78	2000	Danville, Calif.
Hannaman, Ryan	0	0	3.00	1	1	0	0	6	3	2	2	3	7	.157	L	L	6-3	205	8-28-81	2000	Mobile, Ala.
Lara, Nelson	5	4	3.29	20	13	0	0	82	64	37	30	45	72	.212	R	R	6-6	215	7-15-78	1995	Santo Domingo, D.R.
Lowry, Noah	6	5	2.15	15	12	0	0	59	38	21	14	20	62	.186	L	L	6-2	190	10-10-80	2001	Las Vegas, Nev.
Markert, Jackson	3	8	5.61	41	0	0	12	59	73	40	37	23	41	.306	R	R	6-6	210	2-9-79	2000	Tulsa, Okla.
Montes, Albert	2	0	2.37	24	0	0	5	30	26	9	8	10	18	.234	R	R	6-2	210	12-11-79	2001	El Paso, Texas
Munter, Scott	0	0	10.38	3	0	0	0	4	12	5	5	4	2	.571	R	R	6-6	240	3-7-80	2001	Omaha, Neb.
Ransom, Troy	0	4	6.36	27	3	0	0	64	85	55	45	19	24	.313	R	R	6-2	190	7-9-78	1999	Chandler, Ariz.
Rigueiro, Rafael	6	11	4.22	25	25	0	0	130	133	66	61	66	87	.264	R	R	6-6	200	5-20-77	2000	Riverside, Calif.
Spiehs, R.D.	6	6	3.66	47	0	0	11	84	86	36	34	32	80	.267	R	R	6-3	210	10-18-79	2001	Grand Island, Neb.
Thomas, John	1	5	6.08	11	11	0	0	40	56	32	27	22	29	.320	L	L	6-2	190	7-24-81	1999	Santa Maria, Calif.
Threets, Erick	0	1	6.67	26	0	0	0	28	23	24	21	28	43	.225	L	L	6-5	240	11-4-81	2000	Livermore, Calif.
Uzzell, Todd	2	2	5.33	7	5	0	0	25	29	17	15	12	15	.276	R	R	6-3	200	6-22-78	2000	El Paso, Texas
Velazquez, Elih	1	2	6.47	35	4	0	1	65	81	55	47	43	61	.304	L	L	6-2	190	6-2-80	1999	San Lorenzo, P.R.
Yacco, Anthony	3	1	3.63	30	0	0	2	40	36	23	16	14	33	.241	R	R	6-3	220	12-2-80	1999	Mahopac, N.Y.

FIELDING

Catcher	PCT	G	PO	A	E	DP	PB
Lunsford	.991	16	104	10	1	0	3
Luther	1.000	12	70	4	0	0	2
Nieckula	.977	43	309	24	8	4	5
Rodriguez	.982	41	299	29	6	1	7
Santana	.950	2	18	1	1	0	0
Williams	.000	1	0	0	0	0	0
Wright	.992	33	209	28	2	1	5

First Base	PCT	G	PO	A	E	DP
Bell	1.000	3	11	0	0	2
Cordido	1.000	9	81	5	0	7
Luster	.992	42	351	24	3	21
Luther	.975	12	73	5	2	7
McGowan	.991	51	437	21	4	40

	PCT	G	PO	A	E	DP
Trumble	.976	31	264	26	7	27

Second Base	PCT	G	PO	A	E	DP
Chavez	.000	1	0	0	0	0
Cordido	.963	23	55	49	4	12
Garrido	1.000	8	5	22	0	1
Maldonado	.980	118	209	319	11	70

Third Base	PCT	G	PO	A	E	DP
Bell	1.000	2	1	5	0	0
Chavez	.928	113	94	242	26	25
Cordido	.949	29	17	76	5	6
Garrido	1.000	2	3	2	0	0
Luther	1.000	1	1	0	0	0

Shortstop	PCT	G	PO	A	E	DP
Athas	.946	120	153	353	29	55

	PCT	G	PO	A	E	DP
Chavez	.989	19	39	53	1	9
Cordido	1.000	1	1	3	0	0
Garrido	.913	6	8	13	2	2

Outfield	PCT	G	PO	A	E	DP
Bell	1.000	5	10	0	0	0
Cordido	.800	3	4	0	1	0
Ellison	.980	79	197	4	4	3
Florence	1.000	5	12	1	0	0
Holst	1.000	110	224	8	0	2
Luther	1.000	4	6	1	0	0
Shabala	.991	70	115	0	1	0
Trumble	.986	47	71	0	1	0
Walker	1.000	21	53	1	0	0
Wilfong	.988	100	153	7	2	3

HAGERSTOWN SUNS — Low Class A

SOUTH ATLANTIC LEAGUE

BATTING	AVG	G	AB	R	H	2B	3B	HR	RBI	BB	SO	SB	CS	SLG	OBP	B	T	HT	WT	DOB	1st Yr	Resides
Alexander, Kevin	.288	97	358	59	103	24	0	4	28	44	65	12	5	.388	.366	R	R	5-10	160	9-15-80	2000	Eugene, Ore.
Anderson, Keith	.288	47	153	20	44	12	0	3	20	15	34	0	1	.425	.349	R	R	6-1	200	1-6-79	2001	Escondido, Calif.
Benavidez, Julian	.265	125	465	58	123	32	2	11	72	49	148	5	2	.413	.339	R	R	6-2	210	4-14-82	2001	Oakland, Calif.
Cabrera, Leonel	.162	37	117	13	19	1	0	0	5	7	15	4	1	.171	.220	R	R	6-1	160	1-10-81	1998	Santo Domingo, D.R.
Carter, Bryan	.242	119	476	62	115	22	2	13	61	36	114	22	9	.378	.319	L	L	6-0	190	2-25-78	2000	Frostproof, Fla.
Cordido, Julio	.260	55	196	24	51	7	1	4	18	18	30	6	3	.367	.326	R	R	6-1	190	7-30-80	1997	Caracas, Venez.
D'Jesus, Francisco	.118	17	51	5	6	3	0	0	9	2	17	0	0	.176	.179	R	R	6-0	190	4-12-81	2000	Santo Domingo, D.R.
Florence, Branden	.303	109	426	63	129	30	3	11	63	31	32	9	7	.465	.354	R	R	6-0	200	4-3-78	2001	Boise, Idaho
Garrido, Tomas	.277	48	141	18	39	3	2	0	13	11	18	2	2	.326	.327	R	R	6-2	167	8-27-81	1999	Valencia, Venez.
Huntingford, Matt	.176	10	34	1	6	1	0	0	0	2	8	0	0	.206	.222	L	L	6-1	170	3-5-79	2001	West Vancouver, B.C.
Knoedler, Justin	.257	86	280	32	72	16	2	5	33	37	56	6	5	.382	.349	R	R	6-2	210	7-17-80	2001	Springfield, Ill.

BATTING	AVG	G	AB	R	H	2B	3B	HR	RBI	BB	SO	SB	CS	SLG	OBP	B	T	HT	WT	DOB	1st Yr	Resides
McDowell, Arturo	.173	54	202	25	35	6	2	2	14	19	54	9	8	.252	.252	L	L	6-1	170	9-7-79	1998	Jackson, Miss.
McMains, Derin	.242	83	330	44	80	11	2	6	32	31	28	14	3	.342	.312	S	R	6-0	180	11-3-79	2001	Little Rock, Ark.
Meyer, Robert	.273	126	447	51	122	24	0	8	37	32	95	6	1	.380	.335	S	R	6-0	190	12-15-78	2001	Berkeley, Calif.
Miranda, Miguel	.263	70	217	25	57	2	1	1	25	17	26	4	1	.295	.316	S	R	6-0	170	6-10-79	2001	Little Rock, Ark.
Turco, Anthony	.311	15	45	5	14	0	0	1	6	6	10	0	0	.378	.392	L	R	5-9	170	10-8-79	2000	Sarasota, Fla.
Von Schell, Tyler	.240	130	483	54	116	16	1	14	69	54	126	3	0	.364	.327	R	R	6-3	210	7-7-79	2001	Goleta, Calif.
Walker, Mark	.204	72	230	28	47	10	1	6	21	37	85	4	3	.335	.330	R	R	6-1	190	8-17-78	2000	Miami, Fla.

PITCHING	W	L	ERA	G	GS	CG	SV	IP	H	R	ER	BB	SO	AVG	B	T	HT	WT	DOB	1st Yr	Resides
Benjamin, Petersen	2	8	5.83	13	13	0	0	59	90	55	38	15	32	.347	R	R	6-4	210	10-28-78	2001	Boca Raton, Fla.
Burres, Brian	5	10	4.75	32	16	0	1	119	114	78	63	53	119	.252	L	L	6-1	170	4-8-81	2001	Clackamas, Ore.
Cram, Josh	1	0	6.20	17	0	0	0	25	36	17	17	11	9	.336	R	R	6-2	200	8-22-80	2001	Edmonds, Wash.
Gregg, James	5	3	5.77	24	0	0	1	34	47	24	22	9	19	.324	R	R	6-5	208	11-5-78	2000	De Funiak Springs, Fla.
Gross, Kyle	2	4	8.22	18	7	0	0	38	35	48	35	54	27	.257	R	R	6-4	220	12-11-78	2000	Danville, Calif.
Guzman, Leiby	6	2	4.35	44	0	0	2	81	95	47	39	27	66	.290	R	R	6-5	160	9-27-75	1994	Hato Del Media Abajo, D.R.
Hannaman, Ryan	7	6	2.80	24	24	1	0	132	129	54	41	46	145	.255	L	L	6-3	205	8-28-81	2000	Mobile, Ala.
Hixson, David	0	2	9.39	5	0	0	0	8	11	10	8	2	5	.323	R	R	6-1	190	9-13-78	2001	Spokane, Wash.
Liriano, Francisco	3	6	3.49	16	16	0	0	80	61	45	31	31	85	.209	L	L	6-2	180	10-26-83	2001	San Cristobal, D.R.
Lopez, Nelson	0	0	27.00	1	0	0	0	1	4	3	3	1	2	.571	R	R	6-2	200	7-28-80	2002	Miami, Fla.
Meaux, Ryan	4	3	2.63	44	0	0	17	55	41	22	16	12	44	.202	R	L	5-11	170	10-5-78	2001	Lamar, Colo.
Miller, Benji	1	1	4.87	12	0	0	1	20	25	11	11	8	17	.308	R	R	6-2	180	5-2-76	1998	Lynchburg, Va.
Montes, Albert	3	2	3.62	28	0	0	3	37	38	19	15	12	35	.256	R	R	6-2	210	12-11-79	2001	El Paso, Texas
Padgett, Daniel	0	1	4.31	27	0	0	3	48	48	31	23	18	41	.265	L	L	6-0	170	1-7-78	2000	Littleton, Colo.
Pannone, Anthony	9	10	3.11	28	28	2	0	168	157	73	58	61	116	.247	R	R	6-3	220	7-7-81	2001	Olympia, Wash.
Pavon, Julio	3	6	3.26	43	8	0	10	116	112	54	42	21	90	.255	R	R	6-2	160	6-14-76	1999	Granada, Nicaragua
Treadway, Brion	5	4	4.39	13	13	0	0	68	57	37	33	28	68	.233	R	R	6-4	200	4-1-79	2000	Oxford, Ohio
Uzzell, Todd	4	7	6.42	15	14	0	0	83	105	67	59	27	42	.315	R	R	6-3	200	6-22-78	2000	El Paso, Texas
Waddell, Jason	0	0	6.75	4	0	0	0	7	6	5	5	1	4	.214	R	L	6-2	180	6-11-81	2001	Riverside, Calif.
Yacco, Anthony	3	2	6.88	18	1	0	0	35	47	28	27	23	26	.335	R	R	6-3	220	12-2-80	1999	Mahopac, N.Y.

FIELDING

Catcher	PCT	G	PO	A	E	DP	PB
Anderson	.978	39	305	55	8	3	5
D'Jesus	1.000	8	61	6	0	0	0
Knoedler	.977	83	559	70	15	2	20
Turco	.963	14	71	8	3	0	8

First Base	PCT	G	PO	A	E	DP
Alexander	1.000	10	76	4	0	4
Cordido	.978	10	80	7	2	4
Von Schell	.991	121	1081	78	10	84

Second Base	PCT	G	PO	A	E	DP
Alexander	.970	43	79	113	6	24
Cabrera	.949	8	15	22	2	2

Third Base	PCT	G	PO	A	E	DP
Alexander	.720	8	9	9	7	1
Anderson	1.000	1	0	1	0	0
Benavidez	.885	118	78	253	43	23
Cordido	1.000	9	8	23	0	1
Garrido	1.000	5	1	6	0	0

Shortstop	PCT	G	PO	A	E	DP
Alexander	.914	14	17	36	5	6
Cabrera	.975	30	42	77	3	13

Cordido	.938	6	10	20	2	4
Garrido	1.000	5	5	10	0	3
McMains	.981	81	153	258	8	44

Garrido	.935	37	48	82	9	11
McMains	.000	1	0	0	0	0
Miranda	.953	69	125	197	16	36

Outfield	PCT	G	PO	A	E	DP
Carter	.971	117	199	5	6	0
Cordido	1.000	2	2	0	0	0
Florence	.970	54	98	0	3	0
Huntingford	1.000	7	13	0	0	0
McDowell	.971	54	96	6	3	1
Meyer	.971	121	189	12	6	0
Walker	.965	72	136	3	5	0

SALEM-KEIZER VOLCANOES — Short-Season A

NORTHWEST LEAGUE

BATTING	AVG	G	AB	R	H	2B	3B	HR	RBI	BB	SO	SB	CS	SLG	OBP	B	T	HT	WT	DOB	1st Yr	Resides
Bell, Derek	.233	31	86	9	20	3	1	2	17	13	20	0	1	.360	.333	S	R	6-1	205	9-22-76	2000	Rohnert Park, Calif.
Buller, Dayton	.200	19	45	5	9	3	0	0	7	10	10	1	1	.267	.345	R	R	6-0	190	6-22-81	2002	Oakhurst, Calif.
Cabrera, Leonel	.242	44	120	18	29	5	1	1	8	8	22	1	3	.325	.295	R	R	6-1	160	1-10-81	1998	Santo Domingo, D.R.
Dryer, Matthew	.253	41	146	21	37	3	1	5	21	14	41	4	0	.390	.335	R	R	6-2	190	11-12-79	2002	Rochester, N.Y.
Holm, Stephen	.172	50	128	15	22	4	0	0	11	15	16	0	0	.203	.255	R	R	6-1	170	10-21-79	2001	Sacramento, Calif.
Hornostaj, Aaron	.429	4	14	4	6	0	0	0	3	3	5	1	0	.429	.529	L	R	6-1	170	5-19-83	2002	Waterloo, Ontario
Ishikawa, Travis	.307	23	88	14	27	2	1	1	17	5	22	1	1	.386	.347	L	L	6-3	190	9-24-83	2002	Federal Way, Wash.
Jernigan, Karl	.287	34	94	14	27	6	0	1	10	6	17	3	1	.383	.330	R	R	6-2	190	4-15-79	2002	Navarre, Fla.
Kelly, Kevin	.100	15	50	6	5	1	0	0	2	7	13	0	0	.120	.211	R	R	6-1	200	3-21-80	2002	Brooklawn, N.J.
Lewis, Fred	.322	58	239	43	77	9	3	1	23	26	58	9	6	.397	.396	L	R	6-2	190	12-9-80	2002	Wiggons, Miss.
Maestrales, Peter	.273	60	165	20	45	9	2	3	19	9	38	4	3	.406	.307	S	R	5-11	180	7-4-79	2001	Delray Beach, Fla.
Ortmeier, Daniel	.292	49	195	32	57	9	1	5	31	18	37	3	0	.426	.352	S	L	6-4	220	5-11-81	2002	Highland Village, Texas
Pinango, Ever	.227	28	22	3	5	0	0	0	5	1	4	0	2	.227	.250	S	R	6-0	150	12-22-81	1999	Guiria Sucre, Venez.
Pinon, Alex	.265	46	117	20	31	6	0	1	11	14	20	2	1	.342	.348	R	R	5-8	170	10-10-78	2001	Miami, Fla.
Santana, Manny	.179	27	67	3	12	4	0	0	6	4	9	0	0	.239	.219	L	R	6-0	210	8-4-80	1998	Vega Alta, P.R.
Sobieraj, Aaron	.283	67	237	28	67	19	4	2	27	28	30	2	2	.422	.358	R	R	6-2	170	5-19-83	2001	Santo Domingo, D.R.
Sosa, Carlos	.500	4	6	4	3	1	0	1	3	5	2	0	1	1.167	.667	L	L	6-2	180	12-30-79	2002	Frederick, Md.
Stone, David	.281	65	199	37	56	3	0	4	21	47	27	4	2	.357	.435	L	R	6-2	180	12-30-79	2002	Frederick, Md.
Turco, Anthony	.132	15	38	2	5	0	0	0	2	3	8	0	0	.132	.214	L	R	5-9	170	10-8-79	2000	Sarasota, Fla.
Wald, Jake	.241	64	228	30	55	7	2	2	24	23	43	2	3	.316	.323	R	R	6-2	180	2-8-81	2002	Alexandria, Va.
Walter, Randy	.287	69	258	26	74	11	4	6	40	20	59	6	3	.430	.342	R	R	6-2	200	4-14-81	2002	Ballantine, Mont.
Williams, Jonny	.286	26	77	13	22	4	0	1	11	11	10	0	1	.377	.409	R	R	5-10	190	5-18-79	2001	Imperial, Mo.
Zuniga, Tony	.231	4	13	1	3	1	0	0	2	4	0	0	0	.308	.421	R	R	6-0	200	1-13-75	1996	Anaheim, Calif.

GAMES BY POSITION: C—Buller 19, Holm 48, Santana 14, Turco 15, Williams 3. **1B**—Bell 23, Dryer 5, Holm 1, Ishikawa 2, Santana 8, Stone 26. **3B**—Cabrera 2, Dryer 33, Hornostaj 1, Kelly 15, Maestrales 7, Pinon 1, Wald 62. **OF**—Cabrera 2, Cleto 3, Jernigan 32, Lewis 53, Maestrales 27, Ortmeier 37, Pinango 20, Stone 33, Walter 64.

PITCHING	W	L	ERA	G	GS	CG	SV	IP	H	R	ER	BB	SO	AVG	B	T	HT	WT	DOB	1st Yr	Resides
Bateman, Jamie	4	3	2.86	19	7	0	2	63	55	31	20	13	51	.228	R	R	6-2	170	5-6-80	2002	Pittsfield, Mass.
Bruso, Greg	4	3	1.99	14	13	0	0	81	58	23	18	17	78	.201	R	R	6-3	190	5-5-80	2002	South Lake Tahoe, Calif.
Correia, Kevin	2	2	4.54	10	8	0	0	38	37	20	19	14	31	.256	R	R	6-3	200	8-24-80	2002	San Diego, Calif.
Cram, Josh	0	1	8.10	16	0	0	0	13	17	12	12	9	13	.309	R	R	6-2	200	8-22-80	2001	Edmonds, Wash.
Garcia, James	1	3	2.08	14	0	0	4	17	9	5	4	6	24	.147	R	R	6-0	210	2-3-80	2002	Torrance, Calif.
Habel, Josh	2	2	6.00	16	7	0	0	48	57	35	32	24	33	.318	L	L	6-1	180	9-10-80	2002	Durango, Iowa

PITCHING	W	L	ERA	G	GS	CG	SV	IP	H	R	ER	BB	SO	AVG	B	T	HT	WT	DOB	1st Yr	Resides
Hensley, Clay	7	0	2.53	15	15	1	0	82	72	31	23	25	84	.235	R	R	5-11	170	8-31-79	2002	Pearland, Texas
Hixson, David	0	0	3.38	3	0	0	0	5	7	3	2	2	3	.350	R	R	6-1	190	9-13-78	2001	Spokane, Wash.
Jefferson, Andrew	2	2	3.81	23	0	0	1	28	27	12	12	8	39	.243	L	L	5-9	180	4-27-80	2002	Normal, Ill.
Lopez, Nelson	0	1	6.23	5	0	0	0	4	3	5	3	6	1	.176	R	R	6-2	200	7-28-80	2002	Miami, Fla.
Matos, Raymond	0	2	4.05	18	0	0	0	27	23	15	12	11	18	.225	L	L	6-1	150	2-23-83	1999	Santo Domingo, D.R.
Mitchell, Ben	2	4	2.16	25	0	0	10	25	14	7	6	17	26	.159	R	R	6-3	200	10-2-79	2002	Scottsdale, Ariz.
Munter, Scott	1	1	6.98	10	4	0	0	30	33	24	23	20	20	.286	R	R	6-6	240	3-7-80	2001	Omaha, Neb.
Nelson, Luke	7	0	1.87	14	0	0	1	43	28	9	9	9	33	.187	R	R	6-2	180	9-28-79	2002	Oconomowoc, Wis.
Palmer, Matt	3	2	1.84	16	9	0	0	54	44	15	11	23	49	.231	R	R	6-2	190	3-21-79	2002	Caruthersville, Mo.
Schmidt, Jeremy	1	1	4.38	9	0	0	0	12	12	7	6	8	13	.255	R	R	6-2	190	11-15-79	2002	Sarasota, Fla.
Serrato, Juan	2	3	7.04	9	0	0	0	15	17	18	12	10	19	.278	R	R	6-2	170	11-4-81	2001	Riverside, Calif.
Waddell, Jason	0	2	5.40	11	2	0	0	20	19	12	12	10	13	.271	R	L	6-2	180	6-11-81	2001	Riverside, Calif.
Woolard, Glenn	3	2	2.96	17	11	0	0	67	51	26	22	32	75	.207	R	R	6-1	200	4-18-81	2002	Lititz, Pa.
Yacco, Anthony	0	1	0.00	2	0	0	0	4	3	3	0	6	4	.166	R	R	6-3	220	12-2-80	1999	Mahopac, N.Y.

SCOTTSDALE GIANTS — Rookie

ARIZONA LEAGUE

BATTING	AVG	G	AB	R	H	2B	3B	HR	RBI	BB	SO	SB	CS	SLG	OBP	B	T	HT	WT	DOB	1st Yr	Resides
Abreu, Johany	.257	33	113	17	29	4	2	0	12	10	24	5	1	.327	.323	S	R	6-0	150	4-3-84	2002	San Cristobal, D.R.
Buller, Dayton	.250	33	112	23	28	5	3	0	15	16	38	2	2	.348	.356	R	R	6-0	190	6-22-81	2002	Oakhurst, Calif.
Ciesluk, Chris	.206	43	141	20	29	7	2	0	17	11	38	6	2	.284	.273	R	R	6-2	210	2-6-83	2001	Taunton, Mass.
Columbus, Jason	.280	42	168	21	47	12	1	4	23	12	40	0	2	.435	.335	R	R	6-6	230	9-27-79	2002	Alamogordo, N.M.
Diaz, Randor	.292	48	185	24	54	3	4	2	22	10	23	6	2	.384	.330	R	R	6-0	180	10-13-82	2000	Santo Domingo, D.R.
Dryer, Matthew	.438	4	16	3	7	1	0	0	5	1	4	1	0	.500	.474	R	R	6-2	190	11-12-79	2002	Rochester, N.Y.
German, Carlos	.209	31	86	16	18	3	1	2	14	13	34	6	0	.337	.324	R	R	6-3	180	3-12-84	2001	San Cristobal, D.R.
Hornostaj, Aaron	.291	53	199	33	58	11	2	1	27	28	43	12	3	.382	.381	L	R	6-1	170	5-19-83	2002	Waterloo, Ontario
Ishikawa, Travis	.279	19	68	10	19	4	2	1	10	7	20	7	0	.441	.364	L	L	6-3	190	9-24-83	2002	Federal Way, Wash.
Martinez, Joan	.063	11	16	2	1	0	0	0	1	1	3	0	0	.063	.118	R	R	6-0	190	5-7-84	2001	Santo Domingo, D.R.
Morillo, Roberto	.288	22	59	14	17	1	1	1	11	8	15	5	1	.390	.380	S	R	6-0	150	7-24-84	2001	Maracaibo, Venez.
Munhall, Brian	.297	46	175	25	52	9	2	0	23	11	25	5	1	.371	.344	R	R	6-0	190	6-17-80	2002	Spokane, Wash.
Paulino, Adalberto	.263	43	175	23	46	7	4	1	18	6	26	7	2	.366	.293	R	R	5-11	150	9-6-82	2000	Nizao, D.R.
Sanchez, Ivan	.195	15	41	5	8	2	0	0	3	2	17	0	0	.244	.233	R	R	6-3	190	3-7-83	2002	San Jose de Ocoa, D.R.
Santana, Henry	.253	47	182	36	46	3	3	2	29	20	39	3	5	.352	.328	S	R	5-11	170	3-12-83	1999	Los Mameyes, D.R.
Sosa, Carlos	.316	54	209	42	66	11	6	5	33	21	52	10	6	.498	.386	L	L	6-1	170	5-19-83	2001	Santo Domingo, D.R.
Turco, Anthony	.364	5	11	3	4	1	1	0	4	4	2	0	1	.636	.563	L	R	5-9	170	10-8-79	2000	Sarasota, Fla.
Williams, Jonny	.313	10	32	9	10	1	2	1	5	2	2	0	0	.563	.563	R	S	5-10	190	5-18-79	2001	Imperial, Mo.

GAMES BY POSITION: C—Buller 9, Martinez 6, Munhall 39, Turco 3, Williams 8. **1B**—Cleto 5, Columbus 32, Diaz 3, Dryer 2, Ishikawa 12, Santana 4. **2B**—Abreu 17, Hornostaj 18, Santana 13. **3B**—Ciesluk 42, Diaz 1, Dryer 1, Hornostaj 2, Santana 14. **SS**—Abreu1, Hornostaj 31,Morillo 2, Santana 15. **OF**—Cleto 48, Diaz 42, Ishikawa 4, Martinez 1, Munhall 1,Paulino 41, Sanchez 14.

PITCHING	W	L	ERA	G	GS	CG	SV	IP	H	R	ER	BB	SO	AVG	B	T	HT	WT	DOB	1st Yr	Resides
Benjamin, Petersen	0	0	0.00	1	0	0	0	2	0	0	0	0	2	.000	R	R	6-4	210	10-2-78	2001	Boca Raton, Fla.
Cain, Matt	0	1	3.72	8	7	0	0	19	13	10	8	11	20	.196	R	R	6-3	180	10-1-84	2002	Collierville, Tenn.
English, Jesse	4	1	2.68	12	12	0	0	47	33	17	14	18	68	.194	L	L	6-3	220	9-13-84	2002	Vista, Calif.
Fernandez, Gilberto	0	2	2.70	7	0	0	1	7	7	2	2	3	4	.269	L	L	6-1	160	5-14-83	2001	San Pedro de Macoris, D.R.
Garcia, James	0	0	0.75	10	0	0	3	12	4	1	1	4	18	.108	R	R	6-0	210	2-3-80	2002	Torrance, Calif.
Garcia, Ruddy	1	2	3.35	15	6	0	0	43	46	27	16	19	32	.272	R	R	6-2	170	8-1-83	2001	Lake Worth, Fla.
Hernandez, Armando	4	3	4.18	18	0	0	0	28	34	20	13	6	29	.285	R	R	6-3	190	11-7-81	2001	Diria, Nicaragua
Hixson, David	1	1	4.26	5	0	0	0	6	8	3	3	0	4	.296	R	R	6-1	190	9-13-78	2001	Spokane, Wash.
Jaquez, Eddi	4	2	4.65	13	13	0	0	62	63	35	32	22	51	.265	R	R	6-1	180	9-2-84	2002	Santo Domingo, D.R.
Lara, Nelson	0	0	0.00	2	0	0	0	4	2	0	0	3	2	.153	R	R	6-6	215	7-15-78	1995	Santo Domingo, D.R.
Magallanes , Fidel	0	0	22.09	4	0	0	0	4	2	9	9	8	5	.153	R	R	6-1	170	4-24-84	2001	Santo Domingo, D.R.
Moreno, Anthony	1	1	3.80	16	1	0	0	24	24	11	10	6	17	.260	R	R	6-1	190	5-4-83	2002	Mesa, Ariz.
Nacar, Leslie	2	1	3.29	18	0	0	0	27	23	12	10	7	25	.221	R	R	6-1	150	7-20-83	1999	Libertad de Baminas, Venez.
Portorreal, Carlos	6	2	3.00	14	14	0	0	72	60	31	24	22	64	.231	R	R	6-2	160	4-28-84	2002	Santo Domingo, D.R.
Ramirez, Rafael	2	5	5.03	13	3	0	0	39	43	36	22	16	25	.279	R	R	6-2	170	1-4-83	2000	San Pedro de Macoris, D.R.
Rondon, Yosy	0	2	5.74	10	0	0	0	16	10	12	10	16	25	.188	L	L	5-10	170	2-3-83	2001	La Romana, D.R.
Schmidt, Jeremy	1	0	0.00	12	0	0	7	13	12	0	0	0	11	.240	R	R	6-2	190	11-15-79	2002	Sarasota, Fla.
Solis, Hairo	1	1	4.68	16	0	0	0	25	36	21	13	7	10	.333	R	R	6-1	170	3-3-84	2001	Las Matas de Farfan, D.R.
St. Amand, Reuben	0	0	3.86	6	0	0	0	7	8	5	3	1	4	.292	R	R	6-4	210	8-4-79	1998	Olympia, Wash.
Stirm, Brian	2	1	4.32	14	0	0	2	17	15	9	8	6	18	.238	R	R	6-6	200	3-13-82	2002	Saratoga, Calif.
Villanueva, Carlos	4	0	0.59	19	0	0	3	30	24	3	2	3	23	.220	S	R	6-2	190	11-28-83	2002	Santo Domingo, D.R.

SEATTLE MARINERS

BY SUSAN WADE

The Seattle Mariners' 2002 season sadly sank in 34 days to baseball's version of "A Streetcar Named Desire."

The defending American League West champions, who equaled a major league record with 116 victories in 2001,  became the AL's Blanche DuBois, depending on the kindness of strangers. While the Mariners squandered the division lead they held from April 10-Aug. 23, the Athletics and Angels cuffed around the competition with the fury of a Stanley Kowalski. And the Mariners' desperate quest for a wild-card berth after a four-game sweep by the Rangers—in which they cheered for Texas to sweep Anaheim while they tried to manhandle Oakland—failed to restore them to their former "Refuse To Lose" glory.

"I don't think teams are in awe of them the way we all were last year," A's third baseman Eric Chavez said at the start of that last series between the rivals. And at the end of it, teammate David Justice remarked, "I'm shocked that I won't see Seattle in the playoffs."

The A's had a 20-game winning streak and the Angels the second-best record after the all-star break, while the Mariners fell on hard times with anemic bats, second-half swoons and haunting transactions that backfired. By the time the Mariners stepped onto the field Sept. 26, they knew they were eliminated from postseason play for the first time since 1999.

Seattle was 22 games above .500 (55-33) before the midway break, but barely better than even afterward.

Center fielder Mike Cameron struggled offensively all season, down 20 points from his career-best average of .267 and finishing with more than 170 strikeouts. Bret Boone came on strong in the second half, cracking the 100-RBI mark, but had a subpar start. Edgar Martinez missed about 2½ months because of a knee injury.

Third baseman Jeff Cirillo, acquired in the offseason at

Ichiro Suzuki   Shin-Soo Choo

PLAYERS OF THE YEAR

MAJOR LEAGUE: Ichiro Suzuki, of

Ichiro didn't quite duplicate his 2001 MVP season in 2002, nor was he the best leadoff man in baseball thanks to Alfonso Soriano's monster season, but the Japanese hit machine still got 208 of them—just one behind Soriano's major league-leading total.

MINOR LEAGUE: Shin-Soo Choo, of

Clint Nageotte led the minors with 214 strikeouts, but his 4.54 can't be overlooked. So the nod goes to Choo, who hit .303-7-57 with 37 steals between Class A San Bernardino and Wisconsin. He also led the organization in walks and played an excellent center field.

David Bell's expense, was a bust at the plate. He came to Seattle as a .311 career hitter but finished at .250. Ruben Sierra, another offseason signee, had 51 RBIs in the first half but only nine more by season's end—along with a strained left quad and hurt wrist. Seattle, idle at the trade deadline, added Jose Offerman from waivers. He contributed little, hitting .232. Sierra and Offerman were let go at season's end.

Righthander James Baldwin, brought in to take departed Aaron Sele's spot in the rotation, was 7-10, 5.28 and out of the rotation by the end of the year. All-star Freddy Garcia—18-6, 3.05 in 2001—fell off to 16-10, 4.40 in 2002.

The Mariners faced a number of changes for 2003, but general manager Pat Gillick, 65, announced soon after the season that he would return. Manager Lou Piniella, however, won't. He begged out of the last year of his contract, so he could look for a managerial job closer to his Tampa home. He eventually signed on with the Devil Rays.

Safeco Field fans did get a look at several young prospects, including pitchers Rafael Soriano, a Double-A callup, and Julio Mateo. Left fielder Chris Snelling lasted eight games before a season-ending injury.

Double-A San Antonio won the Texas League championship, their 43-27 second-half effort marking the second-best turnaround in Texas League history: In the first half, the Missions were 20 games under .500. Short-season Everett, behind Northwest League MVP Ismael Castro and home run and RBI champ Jon Nelson, brought the franchise its first postseason appearance as a Mariners affiliate and the first since 1978. The AquaSox lost three straight to Boise in the championship series.

ORGANIZATION LEADERS

BATTING

*AVG	Luis Figueroa, San Antonio/San Bernardino	.336
R	Shin-Soo Choo, San Bernardino/Wisconsin	83
H	Jose Lopez, San Bernardino	169
TB	John Lindsey, San Bernardino	248
2B	Jose Lopez, San Bernardino	39
3B	Kenny Kelly, Tacoma	10
	Jaime Bubela, San Bernardino	10
HR	John Lindsey, San Bernardino	22
RBI	John Lindsey, San Bernardino	93
BB	Shin-Soo Choo, San Bernardino/Wisconsin	79
SO	Craig Kuzmic, Tacoma/San Antonio	148
SB	Jamal Strong, San Antonio	46

PITCHING

W	Russ Morgan, San Bernardino	13
	Rett Johnson, San Antonio/San Bernardino	13
L	J.J. Putz, Tacoma/San Antonio	14
#ERA	Ryan Ketchner, Tacoma/Wisconsin	2.70
G	Aaron Taylor, San Antonio	61
CG	Ken Cloude, Tacoma	3
	Juan Done, Wisconsin	3
SV	Jared Hoerman, San Bernardino	29
IP	Clint Nageotte, San Bernardino	165
BB	Juan Done, Wisconsin	75
SO	Clint Nageotte, San Bernardino	214

*Minimum 250 At-Bats #Minimum 75 Innings

SEATTLE
MARINERS

Manager: Lou Piniella

BATTING	AVG	G	AB	R	H	2B	3B	HR	RBI	BB	SO	SB	CS	SLG	OBP	B	T	HT	WT	DOB	1st Yr	Resides
Bloomquist, Willie	.455	12	33	11	15	4	0	0	7	5	2	3	1	.576	.526	R	R	5-11	180	11-27-77	1999	Port Orchard, Wash.
Boone, Bret	.278	155	608	88	169	34	3	24	107	53	102	12	5	.462	.339	R	R	5-10	190	4-6-69	1990	Orlando, Fla.
Borders, Pat	.500	4	4	0	2	1	0	0	1	0	1	0	0	.750	.500	R	R	6-2	200	5-14-63	1982	Lake Wales, Fla.
Cameron, Mike	.239	158	545	84	130	26	5	25	80	79	176	31	8	.442	.340	R	R	6-2	190	1-8-73	1991	La Grange, Ga.
Cirillo, Jeff	.249	146	485	51	121	20	0	6	54	31	67	8	4	.328	.301	R	R	6-1	190	9-23-69	1991	Redmond, Wash.
Davis, Ben	.259	80	228	24	59	10	1	7	43	18	58	1	1	.404	.313	S	R	6-4	210	3-10-77	1995	West Chester, Pa.
Gipson, Charles	.236	79	72	22	17	5	2	0	8	9	14	4	0	.361	.329	R	R	6-1	190	12-16-72	1992	Orange, Calif.
Guillen, Carlos	.261	134	475	73	124	24	6	9	56	46	91	4	5	.394	.326	S	R	6-1	200	9-30-75	1993	Maracay, Venez.
Kingsale, Eugene	.667	2	3	0	2	0	0	0	0	0	0	0	0	.667	.667	S	R	6-3	190	8-20-76	1994	Oranjestad, Aruba
Martinez, Edgar	.277	97	328	42	91	23	0	15	59	67	69	1	1	.485	.403	R	R	5-11	210	1-2-63	1983	Kirkland, Wash.
McLemore, Mark	.270	104	337	54	91	17	2	7	41	61	63	18	10	.395	.380	S	R	5-11	200	10-4-64	1982	Southlake, Texas
Offerman, Jose	.234	29	47	9	11	2	1	1	4	4	9	1	1	.383	.294	S	R	6-0	190	11-11-68	1988	Toluca Lake, Calif.
2-team (72 Boston)	.232	101	284	48	66	12	1	5	31	37	38	9	6	.335	.320							
Olerud, John	.300	154	553	85	166	39	0	22	102	98	66	0	0	.490	.403	L	L	6-5	220	8-5-68	1989	Fall City, Wash.
Podsednik, Scott	.200	14	20	2	4	0	0	1	5	4	6	0	0	.350	.320	L	L	6-0	170	3-18-76	1994	West, Texas
Relaford, Desi	.267	112	329	55	88	13	2	6	43	33	51	10	3	.374	.339	S	R	5-9	170	9-16-73	1991	Jacksonville, Fla.
Sierra, Ruben	.270	122	419	47	113	23	0	13	60	31	66	4	0	.418	.319	S	R	6-1	210	10-6-65	1983	Miami, Fla.
Snelling, Chris	.148	8	27	2	4	0	0	1	3	2	4	0	0	.259	.207	L	L	5-10	160	12-3-81	1999	Gorokan, Australia
Suzuki, Ichiro	.321	157	647	111	208	27	8	8	51	68	62	31	15	.425	.388	L	R	5-9	160	10-22-73	2001	Kobe, Japan
Ugueto, Luis	.217	62	23	19	5	0	0	1	1	2	8	8	4	.348	.280	S	R	5-11	170	2-15-79	1996	Maracay, Venez.
Wilson, Dan	.295	115	359	35	106	16	1	6	44	18	81	1	0	.396	.326	R	R	6-3	210	3-25-69	1990	Seattle, Wash.
Wright, Ron	.000	1	3	0	0	0	0	0	0	0	1	0	0	.000	.000	R	R	6-1	230	1-21-76	1994	St. George, Utah

PITCHING	W	L	ERA	G	GS	CG	SV	IP	H	R	ER	BB	SO	AVG	B	T	HT	WT	DOB	1st Yr	Resides
Abbott, Paul	1	3	11.96	7	5	0	0	26	40	36	35	20	22	.350	R	R	6-3	200	9-15-67	1985	Fullerton, Calif.
Baldwin, James	7	10	5.28	30	23	0	0	150	179	95	88	49	88	.298	R	R	6-3	230	7-15-71	1990	Southern Pines, N.C.
Creek, Doug	1	1	4.91	23	0	0	0	18	18	10	10	14	19	.257	L	L	6-0	200	3-1-69	1991	Palm Harbor, Fla.
2-team (29 Tampa Bay)	3	2	5.82	52	0	0	0	56	57	37	36	35	56	.261							
Fitzgerald, Brian	0	0	8.53	6	0	0	0	6	11	8	6	2	3	.343	L	L	5-11	170	12-26-74	1996	Woodbridge, Va.
Franklin, Ryan	7	5	4.02	41	12	0	0	119	117	62	53	22	65	.255	R	R	6-3	160	3-5-73	1993	Spiro, Okla.
Garcia, Freddy	16	10	4.39	34	34	1	0	224	227	110	109	63	181	.259	R	R	6-4	230	6-10-76	1994	Baruta, Venez.
Halama, John	6	5	5.36	31	10	0	0	101	112	45	40	33	70	.280	L	L	6-5	210	2-22-72	1994	Brooklyn, N.Y.
Hasegawa, Shigetoshi	8	3	3.20	53	0	0	1	70	60	26	25	30	39	.238	R	R	5-11	170	8-1-68	1997	Newport Beach, Calif.
Kaye, Justin	0	0	12.00	3	0	0	0	3	6	4	4	1	3	.428	R	R	6-4	180	6-9-76	1995	Fort Lauderdale, Fla.
Mateo, Julio	0	0	4.29	12	0	0	0	21	20	10	10	12	15	.246	R	R	6-0	170	8-2-77	1996	Bani, D.R.
Moyer, Jamie	13	8	3.32	34	34	4	0	231	198	89	85	50	147	.230	L	L	6-0	170	11-18-62	1984	Seattle, Wash.
Nelson, Jeff	3	2	3.94	41	0	0	2	46	36	20	20	27	55	.220	R	R	6-8	230	11-17-66	1984	Issaquah, Wash.
Pineiro, Joel	14	7	3.24	37	28	2	0	194	189	75	70	54	136	.255	R	R	6-1	180	9-25-78	1997	Rio Piedras, P.R.
Rhodes, Arthur	10	4	2.33	66	0	0	2	70	45	18	18	13	81	.186	L	L	6-2	200	10-24-69	1988	Baltimore, Md.
Sasaki, Kazuhiro	4	5	2.52	61	0	0	37	61	44	24	17	20	73	.200	R	R	06-4	220	2-22-68	2001	Yokohama, Japan
Soriano, Rafael	0	3	4.56	10	8	0	1	47	45	25	24	16	32	.243	R	R	6-1	170	12-19-79	1996	San Jose, D.R.
Taylor, Aaron	0	0	9.00	5	0	0	0	5	8	5	5	0	6	.347	R	R	6-5	200	8-20-77	1996	Hahira, Ga.
Valdes, Ismael	2	3	4.93	8	8	1	0	49	59	29	27	11	27	.299	R	R	6-4	220	8-21-73	1991	Victoria, Mexico
2-team (23 Texas)	8	12	4.18	31	31	1	0	196	194	94	91	47	102	.256							
Watson, Mark	1	0	18.00	3	0	0	0	8	8	8	8	4	1	.421	R	L	6-4	230	1-23-74	1996	Dunwoody, Ga.

FIELDING

Catcher	PCT	G	PO	A	E	DP	PB
Borders	1.000	2	2	0	0	0	0
Davis	.998	77	416	23	1	5	5
Ugueto	.000	1	0	0	0	0	0
Wilson	.997	113	692	27	2	4	2

First Base	PCT	G	PO	A	E	DP
Cirillo	1.000	11	32	7	0	2
Davis	1.000	2	8	0	0	0
Offerman	1.000	11	56	8	0	3
Olerud	.996	152	1169	101	5	122
Wilson	1.000	4	17	1	0	0

Second Base	PCT	G	PO	A	E	DP
Bloomquist	1.000	4	5	10	0	1
Boone	.989	153	251	387	7	84
McLemore	1.000	2	2	2	0	0
Offerman	1.000	1	1	2	0	0
Relaford	1.000	11	14	21	0	6
Ugueto	.960	11	10	14	1	3

Third Base	PCT	G	PO	A	E	DP
Cirillo	.973	141	112	217	9	23

	PCT	G	PO	A	E	DP
Gipson	1.000	4	1	1	0	0
McLemore	.909	14	7	13	2	1
Relaford	.957	38	25	41	3	2
Ugueto	1.000	1	0	1	0	0

Shortstop	PCT	G	PO	A	E	DP
Guillen	.966	130	200	304	18	68
McLemore	1.000	1	0	1	0	0
Relaford	.964	40	46	87	5	24
Ugueto	.846	8	1	10	2	4

Outfield	PCT	G	PO	A	E	DP
Bloomquist	1.000	7	12	0	0	0
Cameron	.988	155	415	6	5	0
Gipson	.971	73	65	2	2	1
Kingsale	1.000	2	4	0	0	0
McLemore	.972	88	172	2	5	0
Offerman	1.000	6	8	0	0	0
Podsednik	.938	11	15	0	1	0
Relaford	.957	35	41	3	2	0
Sierra	.979	60	91	1	2	0
Snelling	1.000	8	16	0	0	0
Suzuki	.991	152	333	8	3	0

LARRY GOREN

Mike Cameron

Director, Player Development: Benny Looper

Class	Farm Team	League	W	L	Pct.	Finish*	Manager(s)	First Yr.
AAA	Tacoma (Wash.) Rainiers	Pacific Coast	65	76	.461	13th (16)	Dan Rohn	1995
AA	San Antonio (Texas) Missions	Texas	68	72	.486	+6th (8)	Dave Brundage	2001
High A	San Bernardino (Calif.) Stampede	California	77	63	.550	3rd (10)	Daren Brown	2001
Low A	Wisconsin Timber Rattlers	Midwest	53	86	.381	13th (14)	Gary Thurman	1993
SS A	Everett (Wash.) Aqua Sox	Northwest	44	32	.579	2nd (8)	Omer Munoz/Roger Hansen	1995
Rookie	Peoria (Ariz.) Mariners	Arizona	19	36	.345	7th (7)	Darrin Garner	1988

*Finish in overall standings (No. of teams in league)   +League champion

TACOMA RAINIERS
Class AAA

PACIFIC COAST LEAGUE

BATTING	AVG	G	AB	R	H	2B	3B	HR	RBI	BB	SO	SB	CS	SLG	OBP	B	T	HT	WT	DOB	1st Yr	Resides
Barthol, Blake	.247	56	178	28	44	16	4	3	17	24	44	0	2	.433	.344	R	R	6-0	200	4-7-73	1995	Schnecksville, Pa.
Bloomquist, Willie	.270	104	337	47	91	14	3	6	47	29	44	20	10	.383	.331	R	R	5-11	180	11-27-77	1999	Port Orchard, Wash.
Borders, Pat	.265	92	317	42	84	16	1	12	27	11	47	3	2	.435	.289	R	R	6-2	200	5-14-63	1982	Lake Wales, Fla.
Clark, Jermaine	.266	108	368	47	98	14	4	6	36	62	59	29	14	.375	.370	L	R	5-10	170	9-29-76	1997	Vacaville, Calif.
Connors, Greg	.255	95	325	36	83	27	0	11	54	25	64	0	2	.440	.310	R	R	6-2	180	8-22-74	1996	Smithtown, N.Y.
Gandolfo, Rob	.250	6	16	2	4	0	1	1	3	1	1	0	0	.563	.294	L	R	5-9	178	8-24-77	1999	Dumont, N.J.
Holbert, Aaron	.311	120	399	62	124	24	3	7	42	19	50	17	13	.439	.358	R	R	6-0	160	1-9-73	1990	St. Petersburg, Fla.
Horner, Jim	.300	7	20	5	6	2	0	0	1	0	4	0	0	.400	.364	R	R	6-0	210	11-11-73	1996	Twin Falls, Idaho
Kelly, Kenny	.248	122	391	51	97	13	10	11	53	26	93	11	3	.417	.296	R	R	6-3	180	1-26-79	1997	Plant City, Fla.
Kingsale, Eugene	.261	49	188	25	49	15	3	6	26	15	30	10	3	.468	.317	S	R	6-3	190	8-20-76	1994	Oranjestad, Aruba
Krause, Scott	.294	19	51	5	15	4	0	2	7	4	10	1	0	.490	.368	R	R	6-1	180	8-16-73	1994	Willowick, Ohio
Kuzmic, Craig	.222	63	216	23	48	9	5	6	22	25	68	5	0	.394	.299	S	R	6-0	180	5-2-77	1998	Fountain Valley, Calif.
Menchaca, Eriberto	.118	6	17	2	2	0	0	0	2	1	1	0	0	.118	.167	R	R	6-0	190	2-7-81	2001	Mesa, Ariz.
Minor, Ryan	.229	42	157	15	36	6	1	1	8	12	29	0	0	.299	.297	R	R	6-7	240	1-5-74	1996	Edmond, Okla.
Podsednik, Scott	.279	125	438	63	122	25	6	9	61	43	70	35	13	.425	.347	L	L	6-0	170	3-18-76	1994	West, Texas
Rolison, Nate	.260	80	285	33	74	13	1	8	32	22	95	1	0	.396	.315	L	R	6-6	240	3-27-77	1995	Petal, Miss.
2-team (37 Calgary)	.258	117	411	55	106	20	1	17	53	36	140	1	0	.436	.319							
Thomas, Juan	.263	121	429	47	113	33	2	17	57	43	102	3	1	.469	.340	R	R	6-4	260	4-17-72	1991	Montgomery, Ala.
Ugueto, Luis	.255	12	51	5	13	1	0	0	5	3	13	2	1	.275	.291	S	R	5-11	170	2-15-79	1996	Maracay, Venez.
Weber, Jake	.237	20	59	7	14	1	0	0	3	7	8	3	0	.254	.318	R	R	5-11	180	4-23-78	1995	Wappinger Falls, N.Y.
Wright, Ron	.273	99	359	52	98	20	1	15	57	39	89	0	1	.460	.351	R	R	6-1	230	1-21-76	1994	St. George, Utah

PITCHING	W	L	ERA	G	GS	CG	SV	IP	H	R	ER	BB	SO	AVG	B	T	HT	WT	DOB	1st Yr	Resides
Abbott, Paul	0	1	6.23	2	2	0	0	9	13	10	6	3	8	.342	R	R	6-3	200	9-15-67	1985	Fullerton, Calif.
Atchison, Scott	5	10	4.63	27	21	1	2	124	123	68	64	31	112	.256	R	R	6-2	180	3-29-76	1999	Fort Worth, Texas
Bevel, Bobby	5	2	5.09	31	0	0	1	41	46	25	23	18	37	.283	L	L	5-10	180	10-10-73	1995	West Plains, Mo.
Butler, John	0	0	18.00	1	0	0	0	1	4	2	2	0	2	.571	R	R	6-3	210	8-23-77	2000	Villa Rica, Ga.
Cloude, Ken	9	4	2.33	15	15	3	0	93	73	24	24	20	52	.218	R	R	6-1	200	1-9-75	1994	Baltimore, Md.
Delgado, Oscar	1	8	8.49	3	3	0	0	12	14	11	11	6	8	.318	L	L	5-11	170	4-5-81	1999	Maracay, Venez.
Falkenborg, Brian	4	4	2.74	9	9	0	0	49	51	22	15	13	42	.267	R	R	6-6	190	1-18-78	1996	Redmond, Wash.
Fitzgerald, Brian	2	3	5.59	29	0	0	2	48	57	36	30	23	37	.290	L	L	5-11	170	12-26-74	1996	Woodbridge, Va.
Halama, John	0	1	6.14	2	2	0	0	15	19	11	10	1	9	.322	L	L	6-5	210	2-22-72	1994	Brooklyn, N.Y.
Jarvis, Matt	2	2	3.67	23	0	0	2	27	26	15	11	10	20	.260	R	L	6-4	180	2-22-72	1991	Albuquerque, N.M.
Kaye, Justin	3	7	4.04	47	0	0	6	62	54	32	28	42	65	.240	R	R	6-4	180	6-9-76	1995	Fort Lauderdale, Fla.
Ketchner, Ryan	0	1	4.76	1	1	0	0	6	9	3	3	0	6	.360	L	L	6-1	190	4-19-82	2000	Lantana, Fla.
Lopez, Aquilino	4	4	2.39	34	11	0	5	109	89	33	29	27	103	.221	R	R	6-3	160	4-21-75	1997	Villa Altagracia, D.R.
Martinez, Gustavo	0	1	5.40	1	1	0	0	5	8	4	3	3	3	.380	R	R	5-9	175	11-9-75	1998	Santo Domingo, D.R.
Mateo, Julio	4	2	4.06	20	0	0	6	31	39	15	14	7	23	.317	R	R	6-0	170	8-2-77	1996	Bani, D.R.
Matos, Josue	4	7	5.92	25	25	1	0	135	166	96	89	35	95	.300	R	R	6-4	190	3-15-78	1997	Cabo Rojo, P.R.
Meyer, Jake	0	1	13.50	2	0	0	0	3	4	4	4	6	5	.400	R	R	6-1	190	1-7-75	1997	San Diego, Calif.
Putz, J.J.	2	4	3.83	9	9	0	0	54	51	23	23	21	39	.257	R	R	6-5	220	2-22-77	1999	Trenton, Mich.
Serrano, Wascar	1	3	6.31	41	3	0	5	71	85	53	50	30	56	.296	R	R	6-2	170	6-2-77	1995	Bani, D.R.
Sweeney, Brian	9	5	3.80	30	23	1	2	142	157	67	60	28	113	.274	R	R	6-2	180	6-13-74	1996	Yonkers, N.Y.
Tavarez, David	0	0	9.00	1	0	0	0	1	1	1	1	0	1	.250	R	R	6-3	190	1-13-82	1998	Cerro Alto, D.R.
Ulloa, Enmanuel	4	7	5.96	38	2	0	2	77	91	61	51	29	41	.294	R	R	6-2	170	11-26-78	1997	New York, N.Y.
Watson, Mark	2	0	0.73	6	1	0	2	12	10	2	1	3	8	.212	R	L	6-4	230	1-23-74	1996	Dunwoody, Ga.
Wooten, Greg	4	6	4.91	14	14	1	0	73	88	47	40	16	26	.302	R	R	6-7	210	3-30-74	1996	Vancouver, Wash.

FIELDING

Catcher	PCT	G	PO	A	E	DP	PB
Barthol	.988	54	374	25	5	9	6
Borders	.991	80	536	46	5	9	5
Connors	1.000	3	23	0	0	0	1
Horner	1.000	6	37	7	0	1	0
Kuzmic	.000	1	0	0	0	0	0

First Base	PCT	G	PO	A	E	DP
Borders	1.000	2	7	0	0	0
Connors	.970	9	30	2	1	3
Minor	1.000	3	15	2	0	2
Rolison	.987	41	275	25	4	28
Thomas	.990	56	369	13	4	47
Wright	.989	45	324	26	4	23

Second Base	PCT	G	PO	A	E	DP
Bloomquist	.982	30	54	58	2	13

	PCT	G	PO	A	E	DP
Clark	.981	101	191	228	8	58
Connors	1.000	1	1	2	0	1
Gandolfo	1.000	6	8	13	0	3
Holbert	.957	11	20	24	2	7
Kuzmic	1.000	2	2	3	0	1
Menchaca	1.000	1	1	1	0	0

Third Base	PCT	G	PO	A	E	DP
Bloomquist	.917	25	19	36	5	6
Borders	1.000	3	0	7	0	1
Connors	.915	20	17	26	4	2
Holbert	.667	1	0	2	1	0
Kuzmic	.913	59	33	82	11	5
Minor	.931	40	24	71	7	5

Shortstop	PCT	G	PO	A	E	DP
Bloomquist	.956	19	24	41	3	9
Clark	1.000	8	10	17	0	2
Holbert	.961	106	175	224	16	65
Menchaca	.903	5	17	11	3	5
Ugueto	1.000	12	19	36	0	6

Outfield	PCT	G	PO	A	E	DP
Bloomquist	.970	26	62	3	2	0
Connors	1.000	61	90	3	0	1
Kelly	.972	121	270	11	8	2
Kingsale	1.000	48	94	0	0	0
Krause	1.000	15	34	1	0	0
Podsednik	.985	123	322	2	5	0
Rolison	1.000	29	40	0	0	0
Weber	.968	18	29	1	1	0

TEXAS LEAGUE

BATTING	AVG	G	AB	R	H	2B	3B	HR	RBI	BB	SO	SB	CS	SLG	OBP	B	T	HT	WT	DOB	1st Yr	Resides
Alcala, Juan	.308	3	13	1	4	0	0	0	1	0	1	1	0	.308	.308	R	R	6-2	190	4-15-78	1995	San Pedro de Macoris, D.R.
Barkett, Andy	.249	115	421	55	105	23	2	9	60	55	75	9	9	.378	.339	L	L	6-1	200	9-5-74	1995	Raleigh, N.C.
Brown, Ray	.225	26	89	4	20	4	0	1	6	7	15	0	0	.303	.281	L	R	6-2	200	7-30-72	1994	Redding, Calif.
Carroll, Mark	.120	8	25	0	3	0	0	0	0	5	6	0	0	.120	.267	R	R	6-0	202	10-19-78	1996	Athens, N.Y.
Castellano, John	.263	55	194	15	51	10	0	1	20	10	30	3	3	.330	.295	R	R	5-11	180	9-8-77	1997	Boynton Beach, Fla.
Castillo, Ruben	.218	114	394	40	86	12	4	3	36	16	86	10	7	.292	.251	R	R	6-2	150	8-16-78	1996	San Pedro de Macoris, D.R.
Christianson, Ryan	.253	52	190	20	48	11	0	5	17	16	36	0	2	.389	.317	R	R	6-2	210	4-21-81	1999	Riverside, Calif.
Connors, Greg	.171	14	41	6	7	3	0	0	5	6	10	3	1	.244	.286	R	R	6-2	180	8-22-74	1996	Smithtown, N.Y.
Dobbs, Greg	.365	27	96	13	35	2	0	5	15	9	17	1	3	.542	.425	L	R	6-1	200	7-2-78	2001	Moreno Valley, Calif.
Figueroa, Luis	.339	48	180	25	61	13	0	1	25	24	14	2	1	.428	.417	R	R	6-0	170	3-2-77	1995	Carolina, P.R.
Gandolfo, Rob	.195	75	185	16	36	4	1	0	13	15	25	1	3	.227	.257	L	R	5-9	178	8-24-77	1999	Dumont, N.J.
Horner, Jim	.297	63	209	29	62	18	1	4	30	19	48	1	1	.450	.371	R	R	6-0	210	11-11-73	1996	Twin Falls, Idaho
Krause, Scott	.180	28	89	6	16	3	0	2	6	5	17	2	1	.281	.240	R	R	6-1	180	8-16-73	1994	Willowick, Ohio
Kuzmic, Craig	.206	60	238	34	49	14	2	4	28	43	80	5	2	.332	.332	S	R	6-0	180	5-2-77	1998	Fountain Valley, Calif.
LeBron, Juan	.225	56	204	26	46	12	0	4	21	20	55	3	3	.343	.312	R	R	6-4	190	6-7-77	1995	Arroyo, P.R.
Maynard, Scott	.163	29	92	7	15	5	0	0	6	5	21	0	0	.217	.204	R	R	6-2	210	8-27-77	1995	Laguna Niguel, Calif.
Menchaca, Eriberto	.273	6	22	0	6	0	0	0	2	0	5	0	0	.273	.273	R	R	6-0	190	2-7-81	2001	Mesa, Ariz.
Myers, Adrian	.274	120	449	61	123	27	9	4	49	31	75	16	9	.401	.321	R	R	5-10	170	5-10-75	1996	Bassfield, Miss.
Ndungidi, Ntema	.138	9	29	3	4	0	0	0	1	6	8	1	0	.138	.286	L	R	6-2	190	3-15-79	1997	Montreal, Quebec
Olszta, Eddie	.143	7	14	0	2	0	0	0	2	2	4	0	1	.143	.250	R	R	5-10	180	3-8-79	2001	New Lenox, Ill.
Pecci, Jay	.277	70	271	30	75	10	2	1	25	25	33	9	9	.339	.355	S	R	5-11	180	9-26-76	1998	Novato, Calif.
Perez, Antonio	.258	72	240	30	62	8	2	2	24	11	64	15	9	.333	.312	R	R	5-11	170	1-26-80	1998	Bani, D.R.
Robinson, Bo	.245	116	420	39	103	20	0	3	41	45	51	1	3	.314	.324	R	R	6-2	190	8-21-75	1998	Charlotte, N.C.
Snelling, Chris	.326	23	89	10	29	9	2	1	12	12	11	5	1	.506	.429	L	L	5-10	160	12-3-81	1999	Gorokan, Australia
Strong, Jamal	.278	127	503	63	140	16	5	1	31	62	87	46	16	.336	.366	R	R	5-10	180	8-5-78	2000	Altadena, Calif.

PITCHING	W	L	ERA	G	GS	CG	SV	IP	H	R	ER	BB	SO	AVG	B	T	HT	WT	DOB	1st Yr	Resides
Anderson, Craig	7	7	3.20	27	27	1	0	152	143	61	54	64	94	.253	L	L	6-3	180	10-30-80	1999	Ourimbah, Australia
Bevel, Bobby	1	1	4.20	20	0	0	0	15	13	9	7	3	14	.236	L	L	5-10	180	10-10-73	1995	West Plains, Mo.
Ellison, Jason	1	6	4.07	36	2	0	2	73	80	39	33	33	46	.280	R	R	6-4	180	7-24-75	1996	Buffalo, Texas
Gandolfo, Rob	0	2	6.00	5	0	0	0	9	12	6	6	4	1	1.000	R	R	6-2	210	7-6-79	2000	Aynor, S.C.
Johnson, Rett	10	4	3.62	21	21	1	0	117	107	63	47	53	104	.241	L	R	5-9	178	8-24-77	1999	Dumont, N.J.
Lamber, Justin	1	2	3.24	34	0	0	0	33	35	15	12	15	25	.261	R	L	6-0	210	5-22-76	1997	Hackensack, N.J.
Looper, Aaron	6	1	2.28	57	0	0	0	91	76	33	23	30	73	.229	R	R	6-2	180	9-7-76	1998	Ada, Okla.
Martinez, Gustavo	3	5	3.24	21	14	0	0	97	89	42	35	43	76	.246	R	R	5-9	175	11-9-75	1998	Santo Domingo, D.R.
Mateo, Julio	1	0	0.52	12	0	0	0	17	7	3	1	3	18	.120	R	R	6-0	170	8-2-77	1996	Bani, D.R.
Matos, Josue	1	0	4.91	3	3	0	0	15	15	8	8	6	14	.267	R	R	6-4	190	3-15-78	1997	Cabo Rojo, P.R.
Mears, Chris	6	9	3.14	30	20	1	0	143	138	57	50	38	103	.252	R	R	6-4	190	1-20-78	1996	Victoria, B.C.
Meche, Gil	4	6	6.51	25	13	0	0	65	68	49	47	32	56	.270	R	R	6-3	200	9-8-78	1996	Scott, La.
Navarro, Jason	0	0	3.60	3	0	0	0	5	4	2	2	1	2	.222	L	L	6-4	220	7-5-75	1997	Lilburn, Ga.
Polanco, Elvis	1	1	3.38	4	1	0	0	9	4	3	1	2	5	.310	R	R	6-3	205	3-10-78	1994	Puerto Cabello, Venez.
Putz, J.J.	3	10	3.64	15	15	1	0	84	84	41	34	28	60	.264	R	R	6-5	220	2-22-77	1999	Trenton, Mich.
Simpson, Allan	10	5	3.06	56	0	0	7	82	53	33	28	50	99	.188	R	R	6-4	180	8-26-77	1997	Las Vegas, Nev.
Soriano, Rafael	2	3	2.31	10	8	0	0	47	32	13	12	15	52	.190	R	R	6-1	170	12-19-79	1996	San Jose, D.R.
Taylor, Aaron	4	3	2.34	61	0	0	24	77	51	28	20	34	93	.184	R	R	6-5	200	8-20-77	1996	Hahira, Ga.
Thornton, Matt	1	5	3.63	12	12	0	0	62	52	31	25	29	44	.237	L	L	6-6	220	9-15-76	1998	Allendale, Mich.
Van Dusen, Derrick	1	2	7.20	5	4	0	0	25	31	21	20	12	17	.316	L	L	6-3	182	6-6-81	2000	Fontana, Calif.
Wright, Chris	5	1	1.60	18	0	0	0	34	31	10	6	10	26	.244	R	R	6-2	190	6-6-77	1997	Tampa, Fla.

FIELDING

Catcher	PCT	G	PO	A	E	DP	PB
Alcala	1.000	2	12	3	0	0	2
Carroll	.970	8	59	6	2	1	1
Castellano	1.000	4	25	1	0	0	0
Christianson	.988	45	372	34	5	2	4
Connors	1.000	3	17	2	0	0	0
Horner	.985	55	377	26	6	2	3
Kuzmic	1.000	1	3	0	0	0	0
Maynard	.995	28	192	20	1	6	5

First Base	PCT	G	PO	A	E	DP
Barkett	.984	75	613	54	11	64
Brown	1.000	5	31	4	0	2
Castellano	1.000	1	9	0	0	3
Christianson	1.000	2	9	0	0	1
Connors	.977	4	39	3	1	4
Dobbs	1.000	1	8	0	0	1
Figueroa	1.000	2	5	1	0	2
Robinson	.994	58	474	45	3	53

Second Base	PCT	G	PO	A	E	DP
Gandolfo	.990	24	40	56	1	15
Kuzmic	.943	8	12	21	2	6
Pecci	.980	53	85	162	5	36
Perez	.957	64	97	150	11	34

Third Base	PCT	G	PO	A	E	DP
Castellano	.667	3	0	2	1	0
Connors	.000	1	0	0	0	0
Figueroa	.954	46	27	77	5	5
Gandolfo	.917	10	11	11	2	3
Krause	.667	1	1	1	1	0
Kuzmic	.916	56	36	106	13	11
Menchaca	.500	1	1	1	2	0
Olszta	1.000	2	0	1	0	0
Pecci	1.000	3	4	3	0	0
Robinson	.880	24	9	35	6	5

Shortstop	PCT	G	PO	A	E	DP
Castillo	.951	114	240	343	30	90

	PCT	G	PO	A	E	DP
Gandolfo	.955	5	6	15	1	3
Menchaca	.957	5	10	12	1	5
Pecci	.877	11	28	36	9	9
Perez	.929	10	7	19	2	7

Outfield	PCT	G	PO	A	E	DP
Barkett	.962	13	24	1	1	0
Castellano	.943	28	31	2	2	1
Connors	1.000	2	4	0	0	0
Dobbs	.957	26	44	1	2	1
Gandolfo	1.000	21	27	3	0	0
Krause	.984	27	58	2	1	0
Kuzmic	1.000	4	5	1	0	0
LeBron	.971	55	99	3	3	1
Myers	.973	112	176	6	5	1
Ndungidi	1.000	8	17	0	0	0
Olszta	.000	1	0	0	0	0
Snelling	1.000	23	48	2	0	0
Strong	.980	125	280	13	6	5

CALIFORNIA LEAGUE

BATTING	AVG	G	AB	R	H	2B	3B	HR	RBI	BB	SO	SB	CS	SLG	OBP	B	T	HT	WT	DOB	1st Yr	Resides
Alcala, Juan	.185	28	92	8	17	1	0	1	6	2	23	1	0	.228	.216	R	R	6-2	190	4-15-78	1995	San Pedro de Macoris, D.R.
Bone, Blake	.234	89	286	52	67	18	6	16	50	55	63	0	3	.507	.363	L	R	6-1	200	1-12-79	2000	Southside, Ala.
Bubela, Jaime	.290	118	462	69	134	25	10	7	67	40	129	30	7	.433	.351	L	R	6-1	215	6-6-78	2000	Houston, Texas
Carroll, Mark	.266	72	233	34	62	8	0	4	28	39	60	0	0	.352	.378	R	R	6-0	202	10-19-78	1996	Athens, N.Y.
Castellano, John	.335	63	239	35	80	18	0	3	36	23	25	6	3	.448	.392	R	R	5-11	180	9-8-77	1997	Boynton Beach, Fla.

BATTING	AVG	G	AB	R	H	2B	3B	HR	RBI	BB	SO	SB	CS	SLG	OBP	B	T	HT	WT	DOB	1st Yr	Resides
Castro, Ismael	.150	6	20	4	3	2	0	0	2	1	9	0	1	.250	.261	S	R	5-9	160	8-14-83	1999	Cartagena, Colombia
Choo, Shin-Soo	.308	11	39	14	12	5	1	1	9	9	9	3	0	.564	.460	L	L	5-11	170	7-13-82	2000	Pusan, South Korea
Christianson, Ryan	.282	21	71	12	20	5	1	1	8	4	17	1	0	.423	.346	R	R	6-2	210	4-21-81	1999	Riverside, Calif.
Figueroa, Luis	.341	33	135	26	46	9	0	0	25	11	6	0	0	.407	.392	R	R	6-0	170	3-2-77	1995	Carolina, P.R.
Foley, Steve	.224	21	49	10	11	1	1	1	5	14	12	1	2	.347	.400	R	R	5-9	190	4-6-75	2000	Toronto, Ontario
Freeman, Corey	.281	20	64	7	18	5	0	0	4	1	14	4	0	.359	.303	R	R	5-11	160	10-13-79	1998	Tampa, Fla.
Fulse, Sheldon	.215	108	353	57	76	10	5	4	31	38	117	23	13	.306	.300	S	R	6-1	185	11-10-81	1999	Bartow, Fla.
Gandolfo, Rob	.300	13	30	3	9	1	1	0	4	3	4	1	0	.400	.382	L	R	5-9	178	8-24-77	1999	Dumont, N.J.
Garcia, Cip	.214	24	56	5	12	2	1	0	6	3	12	0	0	.286	.254	R	R	6-0	200	10-23-78	1997	Albuquerque, N.M.
Hernandez, Alexei	.240	79	283	29	68	17	2	4	32	22	57	0	4	.357	.298	R	R	5-10	190	6-20-76	2002	Guatemala City, Guatemala
Hudson, Ben	.348	10	23	5	8	0	0	0	1	6	5	0	0	.348	.483	R	R	6-4	210	11-4-79	2001	Decatur, Ga.
Kunich, Frank	.132	12	38	2	5	0	0	0	5	2	13	1	2	.132	.175	R	R	6-0	190	5-4-79	2002	Rancho Palos Verdes, Calif.
Leone, Justin	.249	98	358	64	89	20	5	18	58	57	98	6	0	.483	.358	R	R	6-1	200	3-9-77	1999	Las Vegas, Nev.
Lindsey, John	.297	127	472	75	140	30	6	22	93	48	109	0	1	.525	.387	R	R	6-3	220	1-30-77	1995	Hattiesburg, Miss.
Lopez, Jose	.324	123	522	82	169	39	5	8	60	27	45	31	13	.464	.360	R	R	6-2	195	11-24-83	2000	Barcelona, Venez.
Martinez, Guillermo	.208	60	207	13	43	6	0	1	16	11	39	1	2	.251	.252	S	R	6-0	150	6-24-80	1997	Maracay, Venez.
Menchaca, Eriberto	.289	11	38	5	11	1	0	0	9	2	10	1	0	.316	.341	R	R	6-0	190	2-7-81	2001	Mesa, Ariz.
Merritt, Tim	.239	57	226	33	54	16	3	0	22	22	43	6	3	.336	.308	R	R	6-0	180	2-7-80	2001	Cantonment, Fla.
Reding, Josh	.160	16	50	4	8	2	0	0	3	3	9	1	1	.200	.208	R	R	6-3	170	3-7-77	1997	Anaheim, Calif.
Williamson, John	.238	123	437	62	104	26	7	7	57	43	103	1	4	.378	.314	S	R	6-1	200	8-23-78	2001	Louisburg, N.C.

PITCHING	W	L	ERA	G	GS	CG	SV	IP	H	R	ER	BB	SO	AVG	B	T	HT	WT	DOB	1st Yr	Resides
Abbott, Paul	0	0	0.00	1	1	0	0	5	3	0	0	2	5	.187	R	R	6-3	200	9-15-67	1985	Fullerton, Calif.
Blackley, Travis	5	9	3.49	21	20	1	0	121	102	52	47	44	152	.226	L	L	6-3	190	11-4-82	2001	Chelienham, Australia
Blood, Justin	1	1	3.91	20	0	0	0	25	18	13	11	24	34	.197	L	L	6-3	210	11-20-79	2001	Swanzey, N.H.
Bott, Glenn	7	7	3.88	30	23	2	0	151	141	70	65	64	142	.246	L	L	6-0	180	9-17-81	2001	Scott, La.
Burton, Tim	4	7	4.11	40	0	0	0	66	65	48	30	15	46	.254	R	R	6-3	240	12-16-76	1999	Stuart, Fla.
Butler, John	0	2	4.50	15	0	0	0	30	26	16	15	12	24	.236	R	R	6-3	210	8-23-77	2000	Villa Rica, Ga.
Grunwald, Erik	2	2	5.40	40	1	0	1	63	77	46	38	18	57	.299	R	R	6-4	235	4-25-77	1999	Riverside, Calif.
Hoerman, Jared	7	4	2.77	54	4	0	29	75	54	31	23	32	97	.201	R	R	6-4	220	4-25-77	1999	Ardmore, Okla.
Johnson, Rett	3	1	3.65	7	7	0	0	37	27	17	15	11	34	.198	L	R	6-2	210	7-6-79	2000	Aynor, S.C.
Lamber, Justin	1	0	2.45	6	0	0	2	11	10	4	3	4	6	.263	R	L	6-0	210	5-22-76	1997	Hackensack, N.J.
Luque, Roger	1	0	3.86	14	0	0	0	16	19	10	7	6	10	.296	L	L	6-1	170	1-8-80	1997	Charallave, Venez.
Martinez, Gustavo	2	3	3.79	16	0	0	2	19	15	11	8	11	14	.205	R	R	5-9	175	11-9-75	1998	Santo Domingo, D.R.
Morgan, Russ	13	6	3.36	36	11	0	0	123	112	58	46	36	107	.241	R	L	6-1	200	11-20-77	2000	New Hartford, N.Y.
Nageotte, Clint	9	6	4.54	29	29	1	0	165	153	101	83	68	214	.240	R	R	6-4	215	10-25-80	1999	Brooklyn, Ohio
Olore, Kevin	10	3	2.73	25	18	0	1	105	89	37	32	41	128	.231	L	R	6-2	200	9-21-78	1999	Southington, Conn.
Patten, Lanny	1	0	7.11	6	0	0	0	6	6	5	5	2	6	.260	R	R	6-3	200	5-30-79	2000	Drayton Valley, Alberta
Perez, Elvis	1	1	2.84	6	6	0	0	25	32	11	8	6	20	.316	R	R	6-4	225	7-4-79	1996	Santo Domingo, D.R.
Polanco, Elvis	2	1	2.54	25	0	0	2	39	33	16	11	22	21	.229	R	R	6-3	205	3-10-78	1994	Puerto Cabello, Venez.
Van Dusen, Derrick	7	6	3.10	20	20	0	0	125	111	46	43	36	118	.236	L	L	6-3	182	6-6-81	2000	Fontana, Calif.
Wiles, Chad	1	4	8.92	29	0	0	0	38	48	39	38	20	30	.301	R	R	6-1	200	5-15-78	2000	Alda, Neb.

FIELDING

Catcher	PCT	G	PO	A	E	DP	PB
Alcala	.995	26	199	20	1	2	12
Carroll	.992	69	657	60	6	4	14
Castellano	.984	28	226	19	4	2	9
Christianson	1.000	18	150	13	0	2	3
Garcia	.969	6	25	6	1	0	2
Hudson	1.000	4	16	0	0	0	1

First Base	PCT	G	PO	A	E	DP
Bone	.983	27	212	17	4	18
Castellano	.995	28	198	16	1	20
Garcia	1.000	3	15	1	0	2
Lindsey	.991	91	712	48	7	56

Second Base	PCT	G	PO	A	E	DP
Castro	1.000	6	8	22	0	5
Figueroa	1.000	4	4	11	0	2
Freeman	.971	11	18	16	1	4
Gandolfo	.938	5	8	7	1	2

	PCT	G	PO	A	E	DP
Lopez	1.000	3	7	10	0	2
Martinez	.960	52	91	125	9	31
Menchaca	1.000	8	18	15	0	4
Merritt	.966	49	78	121	7	27
Reding	.970	8	17	15	1	3

Third Base	PCT	G	PO	A	E	DP
Bone	.818	13	5	13	4	0
Castellano	.714	4	2	3	2	0
Figueroa	.866	25	12	46	9	2
Foley	.000	1	0	0	0	0
Gandolfo	1.000	8	3	10	0	2
Kunich	.500	1	0	2	2	0
Leone	.923	96	59	206	22	23
Martinez	1.000	5	0	6	0	0

Shortstop	PCT	G	PO	A	E	DP
Freeman	1.000	5	4	8	0	2
Leone	.750	1	1	5	2	0

	PCT	G	PO	A	E	DP
Lopez	.936	119	164	293	31	56
Menchaca	.800	2	3	1	1	0
Merritt	.935	9	12	31	3	7
Reding	.929	9	8	31	3	3

Outfield	PCT	G	PO	A	E	DP
Bone	.963	23	25	1	1	0
Bubela	.981	109	202	6	4	1
Choo	1.000	6	8	0	0	0
Foley	.885	16	22	1	3	0
Freeman	.833	5	5	0	1	0
Fulse	.982	106	212	4	4	2
Hernandez	.882	50	59	1	8	0
Kunich	1.000	5	6	1	0	0
Leone	1.000	1	1	0	0	0
Williamson	.973	120	207	8	6	3

ORGANIZATION STATISTICS

WISCONSIN TIMBER RATTLERS — Low Class A

MIDWEST LEAGUE

BATTING	AVG	G	AB	R	H	2B	3B	HR	RBI	BB	SO	SB	CS	SLG	OBP	B	T	HT	WT	DOB	1st Yr	Resides
Amador, Jerry	.145	20	76	7	11	1	0	0	1	3	15	0	0	.158	.188	R	R	6-0	180	1-13-80	1999	Camuy, P.R.
Bastida-Martinez, Evel	.350	11	40	8	14	1	1	0	3	6	5	4	4	.425	.435	L	R	6-0	190	2-28-79	2002	Hialeah, Fla.
Brown, Hunter	.237	44	152	20	36	7	0	5	21	32	33	3	1	.382	.376	R	R	6-2	200	10-24-79	2002	Houston, Texas
Cadena, Alejandro	.264	40	140	14	37	7	0	1	19	12	11	0	0	.336	.335	R	R	5-11	180	3-13-80	2000	Laredo, Texas
Choo, Shin-Soo	.302	119	420	69	127	24	8	6	48	70	98	34	21	.440	.417	L	L	5-11	170	7-13-82	2000	Pusan, South Korea
Cole, John	.256	31	117	14	30	2	2	1	7	11	20	4	1	.333	.320	R	R	5-11	180	11-30-81	2001	Ottawa, Ontario
Collins, Chris	.259	101	374	34	97	24	0	5	44	27	52	0	0	.364	.314	R	R	5-11	180	8-14-81	2001	Phoenix, Ariz.
Cordova, Roman	.200	44	165	20	33	6	0	1	8	6	25	7	5	.255	.246	S	R	6-1	180	9-2-84	2001	Aragua, Venez.
Correa, Antero	.171	26	70	11	12	1	1	0	8	10	22	3	3	.257	.272	R	R	6-2	180	1-3-78	1999	Santo Domingo, D.R.
Dobbs, Greg	.275	86	320	43	88	16	2	10	48	31	50	13	3	.431	.338	L	R	6-1	200	7-2-78	2001	Moreno Valley, Calif.
Ellena, Jeff	.264	48	174	18	46	7	1	2	23	7	48	7	4	.351	.319	R	R	6-0	170	11-3-79	2001	Diamond Bar, Calif.
Floyd, Dan	.265	111	447	41	113	13	1	3	43	15	64	6	11	.321	.296	R	R	5-8	160	1-17-83	2000	South Gilford, Australia
Freeman, Corey	.249	77	253	29	63	16	0	3	19	12	61	5	4	.348	.301	R	R	5-11	160	10-13-79	1998	Tampa, Fla.
Garcia, Cip	.214	45	140	19	30	5	0	3	18	16	30	0	0	.314	.325	R	R	6-0	200	10-23-78	1997	Albuquerque, N.M.
Martinez, Guillermo	.226	38	124	18	28	3	0	0	12	10	17	2	0	.250	.292	S	R	6-0	150	6-24-80	1997	Maracay, Venez.
Menchaca, Eriberto	.206	50	199	21	41	4	2	0	19	13	29	2	2	.246	.256	R	R	6-0	190	2-7-81	2001	Mesa, Ariz.

BATTING	AVG	G	AB	R	H	2B	3B	HR	RBI	BB	SO	SB	CS	SLG	OBP	B	T	HT	WT	DOB	1st Yr	Resides
Merritt, Tim	.188	15	48	3	9	1	0	1	6	5	14	3	0	.271	.281	R	R	6-0	180	2-7-80	2001	Cantonment, Fla.
Monte, Harvey	.123	24	65	5	8	0	0	0	5	16	30	3	5	.123	.296	L	L	5-11	180	10-8-81	2002	Zwyndrecht, Netherlands
Oliveros, Luis	.229	82	280	16	64	11	0	0	20	8	32	1	4	.268	.266	R	R	6-1	180	6-18-83	2000	Guarenas, Venez.
Peless, Sean	.219	108	370	32	81	15	4	12	38	24	111	1	3	.378	.274	L	L	6-5	230	12-24-80	2001	Kirkland, Wash.
Rainey, Jason	.207	34	87	18	18	3	2	1	9	11	31	3	1	.322	.310	L	L	6-0	180	6-11-79	2001	Klondike, Texas
Van Meetren, Jason	.283	80	276	37	78	12	3	6	30	31	59	16	4	.413	.362	R	R	6-3	200	10-4-79	2001	Henderson, Nev.
Villilo, Miguel	.195	77	251	34	49	15	1	0	19	23	76	7	2	.263	.262	S	R	6-1	180	10-10-81	1999	Santo Domingo, D.R.

PITCHING	W	L	ERA	G	GS	CG	SV	IP	H	R	ER	BB	SO	AVG	B	T	HT	WT	DOB	1st Yr	Resides
Acors, Bo	0	1	2.38	13	0	0	3	23	26	6	6	8	23	.302	R	R	5-11	190	9-3-79	2002	Mechanicsville, Va.
Barnes, Pat	1	4	4.91	3	3	0	0	15	15	8	8	7	16	.272	R	L	6-2	180	9-25-79	1998	Jacksonville, Fla.
Corcoran, John	1	0	3.60	15	3	0	1	40	38	20	16	8	19	.256	R	R	6-2	190	9-23-80	2002	Minooka, Ill.
Cortez, Renee	5	8	4.12	17	17	0	0	98	102	62	45	32	67	.264	R	R	6-4	170	12-9-82	2000	Valencia, Venez.
Cullen, Phil	4	7	3.45	17	17	0	0	91	84	40	35	58	95	.246	R	R	6-9	210	12-2-79	2000	Chelan, Wash.
Delgado, Oscar	1	5	5.32	8	8	2	0	46	51	30	27	27	29	.283	L	L	5-11	170	4-5-81	1999	Maracay, Venez.
Done, Juan	9	13	3.94	27	26	3	0	164	130	96	72	75	141	.214	R	R	6-2	220	10-2-80	1999	Miami, Fla.
Fruto, Emiliano	6	6	3.55	33	13	0	1	112	101	57	44	55	99	.238	R	R	6-3	170	6-6-84	2000	Bolivar, Colombia
Head, Daniel	6	6	4.68	35	9	1	3	110	123	73	57	36	81	.285	R	R	6-2	180	10-7-78	2000	Satsuma, Ala.
Kesten, Mike	1	6	2.25	38	0	0	6	44	44	23	11	28	39	.255	S	L	6-2	180	9-22-81	1999	Bellflower, Calif.
Ketchner, Ryan	3	6	2.59	31	12	0	1	111	75	39	32	39	118	.189	L	L	6-1	190	4-19-82	2000	Lantana, Fla.
Patten, Lanny	3	3	3.97	39	0	0	8	48	45	24	21	29	57	.250	R	R	6-1	180	5-30-79	2000	Drayton Valley, Alberta
Perez, Jeffrey	7	2	3.89	38	3	0	4	72	69	35	31	31	62	.250	R	R	6-0	180	11-21-78	2002	Tucson, Ariz.
Rowland-Smith, Ryan	1	2	6.75	12	8	0	0	41	50	39	31	19	38	.289	L	L	6-3	200	1-26-83	2001	Newcastle, Australia
Royce, Ramon	2	11	4.47	34	8	0	2	87	109	57	43	25	52	.307	R	R	6-5	210	9-22-79	2001	Boise, Idaho
Watson, Tanner	2	8	5.36	28	12	1	0	92	89	61	55	54	54	.257	R	R	6-3	190	6-14-82	2000	Arnprior, Ontario
Wear, Gregory	1	1	1.80	3	0	0	0	5	6	2	1	6	5	.285	R	R	6-5	220	7-7-79	2002	Orland Park, Ill.

FIELDING

Catcher	PCT	G	PO	A	E	DP	PB
Cadena	.962	5	22	3	1	0	0
Collins	.980	69	478	50	11	2	16
Garcia	1.000	4	30	0	0	3	
Oliveros	.989	65	485	50	6	3	10

First Base	PCT	G	PO	A	E	DP
Cadena	.984	20	160	21	3	12
Collins	.882	2	14	1	2	2
Garcia	.955	10	77	7	4	6
Oliveros	.984	15	110	13	2	9
Peless	.986	102	796	62	12	53

Second Base	PCT	G	PO	A	E	DP
Bastida-Martinez	1.000	10	18	23	0	5
Cordova	.958	41	70	90	7	15
Ellena	.948	43	93	124	12	24

	PCT	G	PO	A	E	DP	PB
Floyd	.932	22	35	47	6	4	
Martinez	.986	18	29	42	1	7	
Menchaca	1.000	3	4	4	0	0	
Merritt	.935	8	13	16	2	3	

Third Base	PCT	G	PO	A	E	DP
Brown	.952	43	36	83	6	3
Collins	.667	2	1	1	1	0
Dobbs	.902	72	47	164	23	12
Floyd	.836	17	15	31	9	2
Martinez	1.000	1	2	1	0	0
Menchaca	1.000	3	3	8	0	0
Oliveros	1.000	1	1	1	0	0

Shortstop	PCT	G	PO	A	E	DP
Cordova	.857	5	6	6	2	1
Freeman	.931	75	130	196	24	25

Martinez	.816	13	9	22	7	3	
Menchaca	.979	44	71	116	4	25	
Merritt	.939	8	15	16	2	1	

Outfield	PCT	G	PO	A	E	DP
Amador	.972	18	34	1	1	0
Choo	.981	109	204	7	4	1
Cole	.938	17	30	0	2	0
Figueroa	.919	23	33	1	3	0
Floyd	.961	76	137	11	6	1
Garcia	.000	2	0	0	1	0
Monte	1.000	23	47	3	0	2
Rainey	.979	28	45	1	1	0
Van Meetren	.986	71	135	4	2	0
Villilo	.902	67	82	10	10	2

EVERETT AQUASOX — Short-Season A

NORTHWEST LEAGUE

BATTING	AVG	G	AB	R	H	2B	3B	HR	RBI	BB	SO	SB	CS	SLG	OBP	B	T	HT	WT	DOB	1st Yr	Resides
Arroyo, Carlos	.318	62	255	46	81	11	1	0	26	18	31	6	5	.369	.366	L	L	5-11	170	5-30-81	1999	Cartagena, Colombia
Blakeley, Eric	.200	9	15	3	3	0	0	1	2	1	5	1	0	.400	.250	R	R	6-2	180	9-8-79	2002	Greenville, Ohio
Bohn, T.J.	.245	62	212	28	52	10	0	3	20	29	53	7	2	.335	.340	R	R	6-5	200	1-17-80	2002	Otsego, Minn.
Brown, Hunter	.184	15	49	5	9	2	0	2	5	7	13	1	0	.347	.286	R	R	6-2	200	10-24-79	2002	Houston, Texas
Cadena, Alejandro	.237	37	135	13	32	8	0	1	11	7	12	0	0	.319	.300	R	R	5-11	200	3-13-80	2000	Laredo, Texas
Castro, Ismael	.313	66	284	55	89	26	1	9	46	16	41	13	2	.507	.356	S	R	5-9	160	8-14-83	1999	Cartagena, Colombia
Colton, Chris	.231	69	238	30	55	17	3	5	30	35	79	4	2	.391	.335	R	R	6-1	190	9-21-82	2002	Newnan, Ga.
Garciaparra, Michael	.161	9	31	3	5	2	0	0	3	4	15	0	1	.226	.257	R	R	6-1	160	4-2-83	2001	Scottsdale, Ariz.
Hagen, Matt	.289	63	204	40	59	10	1	7	30	35	47	3	1	.451	.408	R	R	6-4	210	1-3-80	2002	Greeley, Colo.
Harrington, Corey	.206	49	165	23	34	11	0	1	17	13	35	3	2	.291	.271	R	R	6-1	190	5-6-80	2002	Lincoln, Neb.
Harris, Gary	.287	69	286	37	82	12	8	6	43	16	63	4	2	.448	.337	L	R	5-10	170	9-9-79	2002	Resaca, Ga.
Henriquez, Hector	.157	17	51	3	8	1	0	0	1	9	0	1	.176	.173	R	R	5-10	170	12-3-81	2002	New York, N.Y.
Hudson, Ben	.056	8	18	1	1	0	0	0	2	2	6	1	0	.056	.150	R	R	6-4	210	11-4-79	2001	Decatur, Ga.
Kunich, Frank	.306	28	85	14	26	5	0	0	5	12	28	1	0	.365	.392	R	R	6-0	190	5-4-79	2002	Rancho Palos Verdes, Calif.
Menchaca, Eriberto	.182	6	22	3	4	0	0	0	3	1	5	0	0	.182	.280	R	R	6-1	190	2-7-81	2001	Mesa, Ariz.
Monte, Harvey	.200	17	45	9	9	1	1	0	3	12	10	1	0	.267	.368	L	L	5-11	180	10-8-81	2002	Zwyndrecht, Netherlands
Nelson, Jon	.234	66	274	37	64	8	0	17	64	14	96	4	1	.449	.289	R	R	6-5	210	1-16-80	2001	Orem, Utah
Rivera, Rene	.242	62	227	29	55	18	1	1	26	16	38	5	2	.344	.314	R	R	5-10	190	7-31-83	2001	Bayamon, P.R.
Woody, Dominic	.226	18	53	3	12	3	0	0	3	3	19	0	2	.283	.293	R	R	6-3	210	8-17-78	1999	Richland, Wash.

GAMES BY POSITION: C—Cadena 1, Hudson 8, Rivera 58, Woody 17. **1B**—Cadena 14, Kunich 2, Nelson 60, Woody 1. **2B**—Castro 64, Garciaparra 2, Henriquez 2, Kunich 8, Menchaca 3. **3B**—Brown 8, Hagen 63, Henriquez 2, Kunich 5, Menchaca 1. **SS**—Blakeley 1, Brown 8, Castro 1, Garciaparra 7, Harrington 49, Henriquez 13, Menchaca 3. **OF**—Arroyo 36, Bohn 53, Colton 64, Harris 64, Kunich 7, Monte 12.

PITCHING	W	L	ERA	G	GS	CG	SV	IP	H	R	ER	BB	SO	AVG	B	T	HT	WT	DOB	1st Yr	Resides
Blood, Justin	0	0	0.00	2	0	0	0	4	1	0	0	0	8	.076	L	L	6-3	210	11-20-79	2001	Swanzey, N.H.
Cate, Troy	1	2	2.00	16	12	1	0	85	62	21	19	11	95	.203	L	L	6-1	200	10-21-80	2002	Temecula, Calif.
Delgado, Oscar	2	2	3.97	10	8	0	0	45	42	22	20	15	41	.248	L	L	5-11	170	4-5-81	1999	Maracay, Venez.
Dorman, Rich	5	6	4.30	15	15	0	0	75	85	53	36	33	68	.281	R	R	6-2	200	9-30-78	2000	Salem, Ore.
Franklin, Ryan	0	0	0.00	1	1	0	0	3	2	1	0	0	1	.200	R	R	6-3	160	3-5-73	1993	Spiro, Okla.
Fulmer, T.A.	1	2	3.24	12	4	0	0	33	35	16	12	9	34	.265	R	R	6-2	200	1-14-80	2002	Charleston, S.C.
Heflin, Theo	5	1	2.43	20	0	0	1	33	25	12	9	21	25	.210	L	L	6-2	170	5-28-81	2000	Topeka, Kan.
Jimenez, Cesar	2	1	2.70	8	0	0	1	20	12	7	6	5	25	.173	L	L	5-11	180	11-12-84	2001	Cunana Sucre, Venez.
Korneev, Oleg	0	3	9.95	5	3	0	0	19	33	21	21	6	7	.383	L	R	6-7	210	5-10-82	2001	Moscow, Russia
Livingston, Bobby	6	5	3.02	15	14	0	0	80	80	33	27	14	76	.254	L	L	6-3	190	9-3-82	2001	Lubbock, Texas
Martinez, Miguel	1	1	3.38	11	0	0	2	16	8	6	6	7	24	.148	L	L	6-2	190	10-22-82	2002	Carolina, P.R.

PITCHING	W	L	ERA	G	GS	CG	SV	IP	H	R	ER	BB	SO	AVG	B	T	HT	WT	DOB	1st Yr	Resides
Morrow, David	0	0	4.00	17	0	0	0	18	19	13	8	19	14	.275	R	R	6-1	200	6-28-81	2002	Sherman, Texas
Nelson, Jeff	0	1	0.00	1	1	0	0	1	1	1	0	0	4	.200	R	R	6-8	230	11-17-66	1984	Issaquah, Wash.
Perez, Elvis	0	0	0.00	1	1	0	0	2	1	0	0	2	1	.166	R	R	6-4	225	7-4-79	1996	Santo Domingo, D.R.
Rivera, Jimmy	2	2	3.98	20	1	0	1	41	45	25	18	18	35	.281	R	R	6-2	180	1-27-80	2000	South Gate, Calif.
Rowland-Smith, Ryan	4	1	2.77	18	6	0	2	62	58	22	19	22	58	.245	L	L	6-3	200	1-26-83	2001	Newcastle, Australia
Sevier, Nathan	3	4	3.03	15	10	0	0	68	67	31	23	20	57	.253	R	R	6-0	200	9-14-79	2002	Salinas, Calif.
Tavarez, David	5	0	3.24	21	0	0	0	33	26	15	12	17	29	.206	R	R	6-3	190	1-13-82	1998	Cerro Alto, D.R.
Thomas, Jared	1	1	2.21	19	0	0	11	20	8	6	5	13	25	.123	L	L	6-3	220	7-28-80	2002	Grand Blanc, Mich.
Viane, David	1	1	6.84	20	0	0	1	25	30	23	19	22	18	.297	R	R	6-1	210	7-15-79	2002	Farmington Hills, Mich.

PEORIA MARINERS — Rookie

ARIZONA LEAGUE

BATTING	AVG	G	AB	R	H	2B	3B	HR	RBI	BB	SO	SB	CS	SLG	OBP	B	T	HT	WT	DOB	1st Yr	Resides
Almanzar, Theiborh	.109	19	55	6	6	0	0	1	6	5	15	0	0	.164	.197	R	R	6-3	210	11-24-82	2002	Bronx, N.Y.
Blakeley, Eric	.242	16	62	8	15	3	1	0	7	4	12	3	1	.323	.294	R	R	6-2	180	9-8-79	2002	Greenville, Ohio
Cole, John	.176	5	17	0	3	1	0	0	2	3	3	0	1	.235	.300	R	R	5-11	180	11-10-81	2001	Ottawa, Ontario
Cordova, Roman	.417	4	12	2	5	0	0	0	0	0	2	0	2	.417	.462	S	R	6-1	180	9-2-84	2001	Aragua, Venez.
Cruz, Elvis	.211	36	133	19	28	5	1	2	17	14	41	6	3	.308	.282	R	R	6-3	180	11-23-83	2001	Santo Domingo, D.R.
Ellison, Josh	.329	39	149	32	49	8	3	0	11	23	21	7	2	.423	.424	R	R	5-10	200	7-24-83	2001	West Palm Beach, Fla.
Figueroa, Luis	.462	3	13	2	6	1	0	1	5	0	0	0	0	.769	.462	R	R	6-0	170	3-2-77	1995	Carolina, P.R.
Garciaparra, Michael	.275	46	160	27	44	8	5	0	20	20	42	13	4	.388	.383	R	R	6-1	160	4-2-83	2001	Scottsdale, Ariz.
Henriquez, Hector	.103	9	29	1	3	1	0	0	1	0	8	0	0	.138	.133	S	R	5-10	170	12-3-81	2002	New York, N.Y.
Hodges, Jarrod	.256	33	121	17	31	6	3	1	20	15	16	8	5	.380	.362	L	L	5-10	170	12-8-82	2000	Ringwood, Australia
Hrynio, Mike	.246	39	134	17	33	8	2	1	15	13	40	2	1	.358	.342	R	R	6-2	190	11-18-82	2001	Mine Hill, N.J.
Imperiali, Francesco	.285	51	186	27	53	7	1	0	26	26	33	6	0	.333	.376	R	R	5-11	180	11-10-83	2000	Rome, Italy
Kroski, Chris	.244	32	82	14	20	5	1	3	19	16	19	1	2	.439	.386	L	R	6-2	220	5-15-82	2002	Clearwater, Fla.
Mateo, Aneudis	.179	12	39	3	7	3	0	0	4	2	7	0	0	.256	.214	R	R	6-0	170	6-11-83	2001	Haina, D.R.
Maynard, Scott	.000	2	2	0	0	0	0	0	0	1	1	0	0	.000	.333	R	R	6-2	210	8-28-77	1995	Laguna Niguel, Calif.
Mazzanti, Giuseppe	.203	34	118	16	24	4	1	3	9	9	40	1	0	.331	.284	R	R	6-2	240	4-5-83	2001	Nettuno, Italy
Olguin, Ruben	.311	48	177	31	55	10	3	4	31	15	40	3	4	.469	.364	L	L	6-2	170	1-5-82	1999	Santo Domingo, D.R.
Olszta, Eddie	.188	32	80	11	15	2	1	0	9	8	38	2	2	.238	.283	R	R	5-10	180	3-8-79	2001	New Lenox, Ill.
Perez, Antonio	.333	6	15	3	5	1	0	1	3	4	2	4	0	.600	.476	R	R	5-11	170	1-26-80	1998	Bani, D.R.
Ware, Matthew	.105	9	19	2	2	0	0	0	0	1	8	0	0	.105	.150	R	R	6-3	200	12-2-82	2002	Malibu, Calif.
Wilson, Michael	.238	41	143	28	34	5	0	4	19	18	52	4	0	.357	.357	R	R	6-2	210	6-29-83	2001	Tulsa, Okla.
Womack, Josh	.269	43	160	20	43	10	5	1	12	13	25	8	1	.413	.337	L	L	6-1	190	1-5-84	2002	San Diego, Calif.
Woody, Dominic	.000	2	5	0	0	0	0	0	0	0	1	0	0	.000	.167	R	R	6-3	210	8-17-78	1999	Richland, Wash.

GAMES BY POSITION: C—Almanzar 18, Kroski 23, Maynard 2, Olszta 27, Woody 1. **1B**—Hrynio 1, Mazzanti 13, Olguin 47. **2B**—Cordova 4, Henriquez 1, Hrynio 1, Imperiali 50, Perez 4. **3B**—Figueroa 2, Hrynio 35, Imperiali 1, Mazzanti 23, **SS**—Cordova 1, Garciaparra 46, Henriquez 8, Hrynio 2, Imperiali 1, Perez 1. **OF**—Cole 3, Cruz 30, Ellison 33, Hodges 27, Mateo 10, Ware 4, Wilson 32, Womack 39.

PITCHING	W	L	ERA	G	GS	CG	SV	IP	H	R	ER	BB	SO	AVG	B	T	HT	WT	DOB	1st Yr	Resides
Acors, Bo	3	1	7.71	5	0	0	0	12	18	11	10	4	16	.360	R	R	5-11	190	9-3-79	2002	Mechanicsville, Va.
Barreras, Rene	0	0	2.11	18	0	0	0	21	21	6	5	16	19	.256	L	L	6-0	180	12-30-79	2002	Miami, Fla.
Bergdall, Kendall	1	0	5.65	6	1	0	0	14	17	11	9	10	16	.283	R	L	6-3	190	11-26-82	2002	Layhoma, Okla.
Bernat, David	0	0	9.53	5	1	0	0	6	5	7	6	7	6	.208	R	R	6-3	180	2-17-84	2002	Miami, Fla.
Cervenka, Dennis	0	1	1.80	3	3	0	0	5	4	5	1	2	2	.190	L	L	6-5	210	10-19-79	2000	La Vernia, Texas
Corcoran, John	0	0	0.82	2	1	0	0	11	6	2	1	0	10	.150	R	R	6-2	190	9-23-80	2002	Minooka, Ill.
Correa, Antero	0	2	12.00	3	1	0	0	6	10	10	8	3	5	.357	R	R	6-2	180	1-3-78	1999	Santo Domingo, D.R.
Cortez, Renee	1	3	3.56	7	5	0	0	43	47	22	17	6	54	.268	R	R	6-4	170	12-9-82	2000	Valencia, Venez.
Espinal, Luis	5	5	3.46	11	9	0	0	65	66	28	25	13	33	.259	R	R	6-1	170	2-20-84	2000	Santo Domingo, D.R.
Forbes, Terry	0	1	4.50	5	2	0	0	14	21	14	7	4	11	.350	L	R	6-3	200	6-27-84	2002	Dartmouth, Nova Scotia
Frye, Randy	1	4	8.29	8	5	0	0	34	50	34	31	15	23	.335	R	R	6-5	210	9-11-83	2002	Lake Orion, Mich.
Graterol, Francisco	1	4	5.88	11	4	0	0	52	86	45	34	8	33	.355	R	R	6-2	160	10-4-83	2001	Valencia, Venez.
Jimenez, Cesar	0	0	3.38	1	0	0	0	3	3	2	1	0	3	.300	L	L	5-11	180	11-12-84	2001	Cunana Sucre, Venez.
Korneev, Oleg	1	2	4.50	3	1	0	0	12	19	9	6	4	12	.365	L	R	6-7	210	5-10-82	2001	Moscow, Russia
Martinez, Miguel	1	4	4.29	6	3	0	0	21	26	10	10	4	20	.317	L	L	6-2	190	10-22-82	2002	Carolina, P.R.
Nisbett, Marshall	1	2	4.30	16	0	0	5	23	26	13	11	9	28	.285	L	R	5-9	170	12-5-79	2002	Tullahoma, Tenn.
Perez, Elvis	0	0	0.00	3	3	0	0	4	1	0	0	0	2	.076	R	R	6-4	225	7-4-79	1996	Santo Domingo, D.R.
Perry, Brandon	3	2	4.47	10	5	0	0	46	52	29	23	18	39	.285	L	L	6-1	180	9-27-84	2002	Graham, N.C.
Ramirez, Luis	0	2	14.94	12	4	0	0	16	30	30	26	22	17	.416	L	L	6-3	170	3-5-82	1999	San Pedro de Macoris, D.R.
Stitt, Brian	0	1	11.25	2	1	0	0	4	9	7	5	1	6	.428	R	R	6-0	180	8-26-82	2002	Wellington, Fla.
Vasquez, Rucki	1	1	4.10	16	0	0	0	26	28	15	12	7	20	.266	L	L	6-4	180	11-21-83	2000	Santo Domingo, D.R.
Wang, Chao	0	2	5.14	13	4	0	0	21	29	19	12	5	7	.315	R	R	6-4	160	3-25-83	2001	Beijing, China
Wear, Gregory	0	2	3.49	15	0	0	2	28	24	12	11	7	23	.228	R	R	6-5	220	7-7-79	2002	Orland Park, Ill.
Wooten, Greg	0	0	0.00	3	3	0	0	6	2	0	0	0	2	.095	R	R	6-7	210	3-30-74	1996	Vancouver, Wash.

BY MARC TOPKIN

The Devil Rays in 2002 lost more games, 106, than they ever had before. But at the end of the long season, they felt they were closer to success than they ever had been before.

"My technical and business training shows me to look at statistics and trends," managing general partner Vince Naimoli said. "We had 40 games where we had the winning or tying run to the plate in the ninth inning, 10 games which we lost after leading with one or two outs in the ninth, 11 walk-off losses, 19 extra-inning games.

"So if you look at it, we're real close. We also saw the evolution of some prospects into everyday major league players, and we have more to go certainly. But if you look at the trends and statistics, we are close. A guy told me once, 'Before you win you've got to be competitive.' So I think we're to the point of being competitive, and we have to turn the next corner."

That would seem to be an optimistic overview after the Rays became the first team since the 1978-79 Blue Jays to lose 100 or more games in consecutive seasons (including a 15-game losing streak) and fired a manager (Hal McRae) for the second time in 18 months.

But the rays of hope come from a combination of reasons—the arrival of prospects such as Carl Crawford and Dewon Brazelton, the development of top minor leaguers such as Rocco Baldelli, and the performance of young players such as Aubrey Huff, Jared Sandberg and Joe Kennedy.

On top of that, the Rays made what team officials say was the most significant announcement since the birth of the franchise by hiring Lou Piniella—a Tampa native and local legend—as manager.

Piniella and team officials were quick to caution that expectations shouldn't be too high in 2003, as it will be

Randy Winn | Rocco Baldelli

PLAYERS OF THE YEAR

MAJOR LEAGUE: Randy Winn, of

Winn led the Devil Rays in eight offensive categories (including hits, runs, doubles, triples, steals and RBIs) and represented the team in the 2002 All-Star Game. His 27 stolen bases also ranked seventh in the American League.

MINOR LEAGUE: Rocco Baldelli, of

A .237 career hitter entering 2002, Baldelli batted a combined .331-19-71 with 25 steals as he shot from Class A to Triple-A. He earned Baseball America's Minor League Player of the Year honors and helped Durham win the International League title.

something of a transition period with a plan to spend money to add key veterans and make a push to be competitive in 2004. Plus, they had to give up their best all-around player, all-star center fielder Randy Winn, to the Mariners as compensation for Piniella, who had a year left on his contract in Seattle.

Piniella, though, will inherit some key pieces, drawing comparisons to the situation he faced in Seattle in 1993.

Crawford, a second-round pick in 1999, was promoted in July and showed the ability to be an impact defensive player with the chance to be a top-of-the-lineup hitter taking advantage of his tremendous speed. Brazelton worked his way from Double-A to Triple-A to the majors and has the makeup and the stuff to stick around a long time.

Huff's season started horribly, as he was unexpectedly demoted to Triple-A at the end of spring training. Then, he was hit in the eye with a ball before Durham's first game and needed surgery. But he came back strong, was promoted to the big leagues May 28, and finished as one of the best hitters in the AL, with a .313 average that would have been in the top 10 if he'd made eight more plate appearances.

Veterans Ben Grieve and Greg Vaughn again had off years. Both are under contract for 2003, so the Rays can only hope they do better.

Baldelli, Baseball America's Minor League Player of the Year after moving gracefully from Class A to Triple-A, is likely to come to spring training with a chance to be the everyday center fielder.

As usual, the Rays had more success at the minor league level, topped by manager Bill Evers leading Triple-A Durham to the International League championship.

ORGANIZATION LEADERS

BATTING

*AVG	Jason Pridie, Hudson Valley/Princeton	.366
R	Jonny Gomes, Bakersfield	102
H	Rocco Baldelli, Durham/Orlando/Bakersfield	158
TB	Jonny Gomes, Bakersfield	256
2B	Jorge Cantu, Orlando	31
3B	Jason Pridie, Hudson Valley/Princeton	10
HR	Jonny Gomes, Bakersfield	30
RBI	Pete LaForest, Durham/Orlando	79
BB	Jonny Gomes, Bakersfield	91
SO	Jonny Gomes, Bakersfield	173
SB	Ryan Freel, Durham	37
	Fernando Cortez, Charleston	37

PITCHING

W	Lance Carter, Durham	12
L	Jim Magrane, Durham/Orlando	11
#ERA	Dewon Brazelton, Durham/Orlando	3.22
G	John Benedetti, Durham	54
	Evan Rust, Orlando/Bakersfield	54
CG	Brandon Backe, Orlando	3
	Mark Malaska, Orlando/Bakersfield	3
SV	Evan Rust, Orlando/Bakersfield	31
IP	Jason Standridge, Durham	173
BB	Neal Frendling, Orlando/Bakersfield	80
SO	Doug Waechter, Orlando/Bakersfield/Charleston	155

*Minimum 250 At-Bats #Minimum 75 Innings

STEVE MOORE

TAMPA BAY DEVIL RAYS

Manger: Hal McRae

2002 Record: 55-106, .342 (5th, AL East)

BATTING	AVG	G	AB	R	H	2B	3B	HR	RBI	BB	SO	SB	CS	SLG	OBP	B	T	HT	WT	DOB	1st Yr	Resides
Abernathy, Brent	.242	117	463	46	112	18	4	2	40	25	46	10	4	.311	.288	R	R	6-0	190	9-23-77	1996	Marietta, Ga.
Conti, Jason	.257	78	222	26	57	15	2	3	21	18	55	4	2	.383	.315	L	R	5-11	180	1-27-75	1996	Phoenix, Ariz.
Cox, Steve	.254	148	560	65	142	30	1	16	72	60	116	5	0	.396	.330	L	L	6-4	220	10-31-74	1992	Strathmore, Calif.
Crawford, Carl	.259	63	259	23	67	11	6	2	30	9	41	9	5	.371	.290	L	L	6-2	210	8-5-81	1999	Houston, Texas
Escalona, Felix	.217	59	157	17	34	8	2	0	9	3	44	7	2	.293	.262	R	R	6-0	190	3-12-79	1996	Puerto Cabello, Venez.
Flaherty, John	.260	76	281	27	73	20	0	4	33	15	50	2	2	.374	.296	R	R	6-1	200	10-21-67	1988	Lutz, Fla.
Gomez, Chris	.265	130	461	51	122	31	3	10	46	21	58	1	3	.410	.305	R	R	6-1	190	6-16-71	1992	Carlsbad, Calif.
Grieve, Ben	.251	136	482	62	121	30	0	19	64	69	121	8	2	.432	.353	L	R	6-4	230	5-4-76	1994	Flower Mound, Texas
Hall, Toby	.258	85	330	37	85	19	1	6	42	17	27	0	1	.376	.293	R	R	6-3	200	10-21-75	1997	Parrish, Fla.
Hoover, Paul	.176	5	17	1	3	0	0	0	2	0	5	0	0	.176	.176	R	R	6-1	210	4-14-76	1997	Steubenville, Ohio
Huff, Aubrey	.313	113	454	67	142	25	0	23	59	37	55	4	1	.520	.364	L	R	6-4	220	12-20-76	1998	Gulfport, Fla.
Johnson, Russ	.216	45	111	15	24	5	0	1	12	16	22	5	2	.288	.320	R	R	5-10	180	2-22-73	1994	Denham Springs, La.
McCarty, Dave	.176	12	34	2	6	0	0	1	2	4	9	0	0	.265	.300	R	L	6-5	210	11-23-69	1991	Menlo Park, Calif.
2-team (13 K.C.)	.136	25	66	5	9	1	0	2	4	6	19	0	0	.242	.230							
Rolls, Damian	.292	21	89	15	26	1	0	6	3	16	2	5	.382	.330	R	R	6-2	200	9-15-77	1996	Tampa, Fla.
Sandberg, Jared	.229	102	358	55	82	21	1	18	54	39	139	3	2	.444	.305	R	R	6-3	180	3-2-78	1996	Seattle, Wash.
Sheets, Andy	.248	41	149	18	37	4	0	4	22	12	41	2	3	.356	.301	R	R	6-2	180	11-19-71	1992	Lafayette, La.
Smith, Bobby	.175	18	63	4	11	2	0	1	6	3	25	0	0	.254	.212	R	R	6-3	190	4-10-74	1992	Oakland, Calif.
Smith, Jason	.200	26	65	9	13	1	2	1	6	2	24	3	0	.323	.224	L	R	6-3	190	7-24-77	1997	Coatopa, Ala.
Tyner, Jason	.214	44	168	17	36	2	1	0	9	7	19	7	1	.238	.249	L	L	6-1	170	4-23-77	1998	Beaumont, Texas
Vaughn, Greg	.163	69	251	28	41	10	2	8	29	41	82	3	2	.315	.286	R	R	6-0	200	7-3-65	1986	Elk Grove, Calif.
Winn, Randy	.298	152	607	87	181	39	9	14	75	55	109	27	8	.461	.360	S	R	6-2	190	6-9-74	1995	Danville, Calif.

PITCHING	W	L	ERA	G	GS	CG	SV	IP	H	R	ER	BB	SO	AVG	B	T	HT	WT	DOB	1st Yr	Resides
Alvarez, Wilson	2	3	5.28	23	10	0	1	75	80	47	44	36	56	.272	L	L	6-1	250	3-24-70	1987	Bradenton, Fla.
Backe, Brandon	0	0	6.92	9	0	0	0	13	15	10	10	7	6	.288	R	R	6-0	180	4-5-78	1998	Texas City, Texas
Brazelton, Dewon	0	1	4.85	2	2	0	0	13	12	7	7	6	5	.279	R	R	6-4	220	6-16-80	2002	Tullahoma, Tenn.
Carter, Lance	2	0	1.33	8	0	0	2	20	15	3	3	5	14	.202	R	R	6-1	190	12-18-74	1994	Bradenton, Fla.
Colome, Jesus	2	7	8.27	32	0	0	0	41	56	41	38	33	33	.341	R	R	6-2	170	12-23-77	1996	San Pedro de Macoris, D.R.
Creek, Doug	2	1	6.27	29	0	0	0	37	39	27	26	21	37	.263	L	L	6-0	200	3-1-69	1991	Palm Harbor, Fla.
De los Santos, Luis	0	3	11.57	3	3	0	0	14	24	19	18	4	7	.387	R	R	6-2	210	11-1-77	1995	San Pedro de Macoris, D.R.
Gardner, Lee	1	1	4.05	12	0	0	0	13	12	11	6	8	8	.235	R	R	6-0	210	1-16-75	1998	Hartland, Mich.
Harper, Travis	5	9	5.46	37	7	0	1	86	101	54	52	27	60	.289	R	R	6-4	190	5-21-76	1997	Riverton, W.Va.
James, Delvin	0	3	6.55	8	6	0	0	34	40	25	25	15	17	.300	R	R	6-4	220	1-3-78	1996	Nacogdoches, Texas
Jimenez, Jason	0	0	5.40	5	0	0	0	7	9	4	4	1	5	.333	R	L	6-2	200	1-10-76	1997	Elk Grove, Calif.
Kennedy, Joe	8	11	4.53	30	30	5	0	197	204	114	99	55	109	.269	R	L	6-4	220	5-24-79	1998	Indian Shores, Fla.
Kent, Steven	0	2	5.65	34	0	0	1	57	67	41	36	38	41	.293	L	L	5-11	170	10-3-78	1999	Killeen, Texas
Martin, Tom	0	0	16.20	2	0	0	0	2	5	3	3	1	1	.500	L	L	6-1	200	5-21-70	1989	Panama City, Fla.
Phelps, Travis	1	2	4.78	26	0	0	0	38	30	20	20	27	36	.222	R	R	6-2	160	7-25-77	1997	Rocky Comfort, Mo.
Rupe, Ryan	5	10	5.60	15	15	2	0	90	83	60	56	25	67	.243	R	R	6-5	230	3-31-75	1998	Houston, Texas
Sosa, Juan	2	7	5.53	31	14	0	0	99	88	63	61	54	48	.235	S	R	6-2	170	4-28-77	1995	San Jose, D.R.
Standridge, Jason	0	0	9.00	1	0	0	0	3	7	3	3	4	1	.500	R	R	6-4	210	11-9-78	1997	Pinson, Ala.
Sturtze, Tanyon	4	18	5.18	33	33	4	0	224	271	141	129	89	137	.302	R	R	6-5	200	10-12-70	1990	St. Petersburg, Fla.
Wilson, Paul	6	12	4.83	30	30	1	0	194	219	113	104	67	111	.287	R	R	6-5	230	3-28-73	1994	Palm City, Fla.
Yan, Esteban	7	8	4.30	55	0	0	19	69	70	35	33	29	53	.259	R	R	6-4	230	6-22-75	1991	San Pedro de Marocos, D.R.
Zambrano, Victor	8	8	5.53	42	11	0	1	114	120	77	70	68	73	.277	R	R	6-0	190	8-6-74	1994	Valencia, Venez.

FIELDING

Catcher	PCT	G	PO	A	E	DP	PB
Flaherty	.992	75	450	33	4	8	7
Hall	.989	83	506	34	6	5	4
Hoover	1.000	4	16	2	0	0	2

First Base	PCT	G	PO	A	E	DP
Cox	.993	110	852	85	7	101
Huff	.987	45	354	21	5	41
McCarty	1.000	9	66	5	0	5
Sandberg	.962	3	23	2	1	4
B. Smith	.981	6	47	6	1	4

Second Base	PCT	G	PO	A	E	DP
Abernathy	.979	116	253	316	12	85
Escalona	.964	25	46	61	4	12
Johnson	.000	1	0	0	0	0
Sheets	.992	26	55	72	1	26
J. Smith	.000	1	0	0	0	0

Third Base	PCT	G	PO	A	E	DP
Escalona	.818	4	1	8	2	1
Huff	.929	14	14	25	3	1
Johnson	.984	27	23	38	1	5

Sandberg	.948	97	83	174	14	19
Sheets	1.000	4	3	10	0	0
B. Smith	.897	10	7	19	3	3
J. Smith	.962	12	7	18	1	3

Shortstop	PCT	G	PO	A	E	DP
Escalona	.945	26	28	58	5	16
Gomez	.980	130	229	356	12	94
Johnson	.000	2	0	0	0	0
Sheets	1.000	11	19	34	0	9
J. Smith	.865	9	15	17	5	4

Outfield	PCT	G	PO	A	E	DP
Conti	.966	74	163	8	6	1
Crawford	.994	63	160	5	1	1
Grieve	.988	118	249	6	3	2
McCarty	1.000	11	20	1	0	0
Rolls	.947	21	53	1	3	1
B. Smith	1.000	2	3	1	0	0
Tyner	.990	42	98	2	1	0
Vaughn	.987	31	75	2	1	0
Winn	.993	146	394	13	3	3

Carl Crawford

FARM SYSTEM

Director, Minor League Operations: Tom Foley

Class	Farm Team	League	W	L	Pct.	Finish*	Manager	First Yr.
AAA	Durham (N.C.) Bulls	International	80	64	.556	+5th (14)	Bill Evers	1998
AA	Orlando (Fla.) Rays	Southern	58	79	.423	10th (10)	Mako Oliveras	1999
High A	Bakersfield (Calif.) Blaze	California	69	72	.489	t-6th (10)	Charlie Montoyo	2001
Low A	Charleston (S.C.) RiverDogs	South Atlantic	60	76	.441	14th (16)	Buddy Biancalana	1997
SS A	Hudson Valley (N.Y.) Renegades	New York-Penn	26	49	.347	14th (14)	David Howard	1996
Rookie	Princeton (W.Va.) Devil Rays	Appalachian	19	49	.279	10th (10)	Edwin Rodriguez	1997

*Finish in overall standings (No. of teams in league)   +League champion

DURHAM BULLS   Class AAA

INTERNATIONAL LEAGUE

BATTING	AVG	G	AB	R	H	2B	3B	HR	RBI	BB	SO	SB	CS	SLG	OBP	B	T	HT	WT	DOB	1st Yr	Resides
Badeaux, Brooks	.250	99	340	45	85	14	2	2	29	28	45	8	2	.321	.316	S	R	5-10	170	10-20-76	1998	Scott, La.
Baldelli, Rocco	.292	23	96	13	28	6	1	3	7	0	23	2	5	.469	.292	R	R	6-4	195	9-25-81	2000	Cumberland, R.I.
Beinbrink, Andy	.375	2	8	1	3	1	0	0	1	0	2	0	0	.500	.375	R	R	6-3	200	9-24-76	1999	San Diego, Calif.
Brown, Emil	.284	116	422	58	120	24	3	12	58	34	81	10	2	.441	.347	R	R	6-2	200	12-29-74	1994	Chicago, Ill.
Brown, Kevin	.150	6	20	4	3	0	0	2	4	2	6	0	0	.450	.227	R	R	6-2	230	4-21-73	1994	Mt. Vernon, Ind.
Caceres, Wilmy	.259	108	347	42	90	6	6	0	20	24	47	16	8	.311	.309	S	R	6-0	160	10-2-73	1997	Moca, D.R.
Crawford, Carl	.297	85	353	59	105	17	9	7	52	20	69	26	8	.456	.335	L	L	6-2	210	8-5-81	1999	Houston, Texas
Fasano, Sal	.257	31	101	11	26	6	0	6	9	12	29	0	1	.495	.385	R	R	6-2	250	8-10-71	1993	Overland Park, Kan.
Figga, Mike	.219	10	32	1	7	1	0	1	3	1	10	0	0	.344	.242	R	R	6-0	200	7-31-70	1990	Tampa, Fla.
Freel, Ryan	.261	119	448	65	117	27	4	8	48	38	51	37	10	.393	.337	R	R	5-10	180	3-8-76	1995	Jacksonville, Fla.
Haad, Yamid	.171	20	70	6	12	1	0	0	5	2	13	0	0	.186	.189	R	R	6-2	210	9-2-77	1994	Cartagena, Colombia
Hall, Toby	.348	22	92	13	32	4	0	2	20	3	10	0	0	.457	.382	R	R	6-3	200	10-21-75	1997	Parrish, Fla.
Hoover, Paul	.220	69	227	27	50	12	3	5	20	18	67	3	3	.366	.285	R	R	6-1	210	4-14-76	1997	Steubenville, Ohio
Huff, Aubrey	.325	32	126	18	41	9	0	3	20	12	13	0	0	.468	.386	L	R	6-4	220	12-20-76	1998	Gulfport, Fla.
Hunter, Brian	.198	28	101	8	20	5	1	3	17	10	22	0	0	.356	.274	R	L	6-0	190	3-4-68	1987	Anaheim, Calif.
Johnson, Russ	.273	10	33	9	9	0	1	2	5	4	5	1	0	.515	.351	R	R	5-10	180	2-22-73	1994	Denham Springs, La.
LaForest, Pete	.258	17	66	7	17	3	0	3	15	3	28	0	1	.439	.290	L	R	6-2	200	1-27-78	1995	Montebello, Quebec
Lennon, Pat	.188	20	69	7	13	1	0	2	15	10	20	1	0	.290	.305	R	R	6-2	200	4-27-68	1986	Whiteville, N.C.
Luke, Matt	.236	29	106	14	25	5	0	1	11	14	28	0	0	.311	.322	L	L	6-5	220	2-26-71	1992	Huntington Beach, Calif.
McCarty, Dave	.325	29	114	25	37	7	1	8	22	14	33	0	1	.614	.398	R	L	6-5	210	11-23-69	1991	Menlo Park, Calif.
Pressley, Josh	.149	16	47	2	7	1	0	0	5	8	6	0	1	.170	.268	L	R	6-6	220	4-2-80	1998	Fort Lauderdale, Fla.
Quatraro, Matt	.198	35	101	12	20	4	1	0	7	5	26	0	0	.257	.248	R	R	6-2	200	11-14-73	1996	East Selkirk, N.Y.
Rolls, Damian	.266	67	244	41	65	6	4	6	35	21	43	15	0	.398	.332	R	R	6-2	200	9-15-77	1996	Tampa, Fla.
Sandberg, Jared	.281	30	114	20	32	9	0	4	21	14	42	1	0	.465	.369	R	R	6-3	180	3-2-78	1996	Seattle, Wash.
Sheets, Andy	.294	98	374	55	110	25	6	14	69	28	72	7	2	.505	.345	R	R	6-2	180	11-19-71	1992	Lafayette, La.
Smith, Jason	.277	54	206	29	57	11	2	4	26	6	41	5	1	.408	.312	L	R	6-3	190	7-24-77	1997	Coatopa, Ala.
Thompson, Andy	.235	77	277	30	65	11	2	7	43	15	51	1	1	.365	.294	R	R	6-3	220	8-28-75	1995	Cottage Grove, Wis.
Tyner, Jason	.291	88	351	59	102	12	4	0	27	34	27	20	7	.348	.362	L	L	6-1	170	4-23-77	1998	Beaumont, Texas

PITCHING	W	L	ERA	G	GS	CG	SV	IP	H	R	ER	BB	SO	AVG	B	T	HT	WT	DOB	1st Yr	Resides
Agosto, Steven	4	4	4.41	15	15	0	0	82	94	52	40	33	69	.288	L	L	5-11	200	9-2-76	1994	Rio Grande, P.R.
Bowers, Cedrick	4	3	3.12	47	0	0	0	69	75	36	24	43	79	.273	R	L	6-2	200	2-10-78	1996	Chiefland, Fla.
Brazelton, Dewon	1	0	0.00	1	1	0	0	5	5	0	0	1	6	.263	R	R	6-4	200	6-16-80	2002	Tullahoma, Tenn.
Carter, Lance	12	2	2.80	33	18	2	1	132	111	43	41	12	90	.229	R	R	6-1	190	12-18-74	1994	Bradenton, Fla.
Chantres, Carlos	4	3	3.93	10	8	0	0	53	54	27	23	18	29	.271	R	R	6-3	190	4-1-76	1994	Miami, Fla.
Colome, Jesus	2	2	2.17	18	0	0	1	29	18	8	7	13	30	.176	R	R	6-2	170	12-23-77	1996	San Pedro de Macoris, D.R.
Croushore, Rich	5	4	3.38	36	3	0	7	64	55	26	24	26	62	.234	R	R	6-4	210	8-7-70	1993	Benton, Ark.
De los Santos, Luis	9	2	2.42	24	16	1	0	115	105	38	31	21	68	.249	R	R	6-2	210	11-1-77	1995	San Pedro de Macoris, D.R.
Dickson, Jason	3	4	5.70	9	9	0	0	47	54	31	30	23	32	.298	L	R	6-0	190	3-30-73	1994	Chandler, Ariz.
Fortunato, Bartolome	1	1	4.15	2	0	0	0	4	6	3	2	2	9	.333	R	R	6-1	170	8-24-74	1996	Santo Domingo, D.R.
Garcia, Gerardo	2	7	6.50	15	15	0	0	64	79	48	46	30	50	.312	R	R	6-0	160	2-13-80	1999	San Nicholas, Mexico
Gardner, Lee	2	1	2.36	45	0	0	25	50	50	14	13	15	52	.261	R	R	6-0	210	1-16-75	1998	Hartland, Mich.
Haines, Talley	4	7	4.52	48	0	0	0	76	84	43	38	24	62	.283	R	R	6-5	200	11-16-76	1998	Cape Girardeau, Mo.
Harper, Travis	1	2	6.98	4	4	0	0	19	31	15	15	3	17	.382	L	R	6-4	190	5-21-76	1997	Riverton, W.Va.
James, Delvin	2	1	3.93	7	7	0	0	34	41	15	15	4	26	.294	R	R	6-4	220	1-3-78	1996	Nacogdoches, Texas
Jimenez, Jason	2	2	2.63	44	0	0	3	51	47	21	15	16	55	.239	L	L	6-2	200	1-10-76	1997	Elk Grove, Calif.
Magrane, Jim	7	8	5.99	20	19	0	0	113	136	81	75	47	53	.305	R	R	6-2	200	7-23-78	1999	Ottumwa, Iowa
Martin, Tom	0	0	0.00	4	0	0	2	3	3	0	0	1	6	.230	L	L	6-1	200	5-21-70	1989	Panama City, Fla.
Phelps, Travis	3	2	4.35	27	0	0	8	31	29	15	15	14	34	.247	R	R	6-2	160	7-25-77	1997	Rocky Comfort, Mo.
Seay, Bobby	0	0	6.00	10	0	0	0	15	15	10	10	2	14	.254	L	L	6-2	200	6-20-78	1996	West Gulfport, Fla.
Standridge, Jason	10	9	3.12	29	29	0	0	173	168	71	60	64	111	.259	R	R	6-4	210	11-9-78	1997	Pinson, Ala.
Wilkins, Marc	2	0	6.23	23	0	0	1	30	36	25	21	9	22	.288	R	R	5-11	210	10-21-70	1992	Palmetto, Fla.
Zambrano, Victor	0	1	1.93	10	0	0	1	14	9	4	3	4	15	.180	R	R	6-0	190	8-6-74	1994	Valencia, Venez.

FIELDING

Catcher	PCT	G	PO	A	E	DP	PB
K. Brown	1.000	3	18	2	0	0	0
Fasano	.984	31	224	17	4	3	0
Figga	.986	9	66	7	1	0	1
Haad	.982	19	149	14	3	4	2
Hall	.993	18	130	7	1	0	3
Hoover	.989	52	313	39	4	4	3
LaForest	.950	13	91	5	5	1	5
Quatraro	.913	6	21	0	2	0	0

First Base	PCT	G	PO	A	E	DP
K. Brown	1.000	1	10	0	0	1
Figga	1.000	1	6	1	0	0
Hoover	.980	8	47	3	1	3
Huff	1.000	25	212	19	0	26
Hunter	1.000	15	129	7	0	19
Luke	1.000	24	186	7	0	22
McCarty	.992	25	220	19	2	25
Pressley	1.000	13	95	9	0	8

	PCT	G	PO	A	E	DP
Quatraro	.984	22	175	12	3	31
Sandberg	.952	2	19	1	1	3
Sheets	1.000	15	116	14	0	19

Second Base	PCT	G	PO	A	E	DP
Badeaux	.976	62	115	171	7	48
Caceres	.971	10	13	20	1	8
Freel	.974	59	115	146	7	45
Sheets	.982	22	51	56	2	20

ORGANIZATION STATISTICS

Third Base

Third Base	PCT	G	PO	A	E	DP
Badeaux	.936	37	26	62	6	7
Beinbrink	1.000	0	0	6	0	0
Caceres	.850	7	6	11	3	0
Hoover	1.000	8	1	20	0	2
Johnson	.903	10	7	21	3	4
Quataro	1.000	1	0	1	0	0
Rolls	.800	5	7	9	4	2
Sandberg	.926	21	13	37	4	3
Sheets	.953	51	50	92	7	13

Smith	.895	7	4	13	2	0

Shortstop	PCT	G	PO	A	E	DP
Badeaux	.000	1	0	0	0	0
Caceres	.957	87	141	277	19	66
Sheets	.983	13	17	42	1	10
Smith	.940	47	69	149	14	43

Outfield	PCT	G	PO	A	E	DP
Badeaux	.000	1	0	0	0	0
Baldelli	1.000	21	43	0	0	0

	PCT	G	PO	A	E	DP
E. Brown	.963	102	223	8	9	1
Crawford	.994	85	170	7	1	0
Freel	1.000	52	89	8	0	0
Hoover	1.000	5	9	1	0	0
Lennon	1.000	4	10	0	0	0
McCarty	1.000	3	5	0	0	0
Rolls	.986	57	129	7	2	4
Thompson	.948	30	50	5	3	2
Tyner	.994	85	154	10	1	4

ORLANDO RAYS — Class AA

SOUTHERN LEAGUE

BATTING

BATTING	AVG	G	AB	R	H	2B	3B	HR	RBI	BB	SO	SB	CS	SLG	OBP	B	T	HT	WT	DOB	1st Yr	Resides
Baldelli, Rocco	.371	17	70	10	26	3	1	2	13	5	11	3	2	.529	.413	R	R	6-4	195	9-25-81	2000	Cumberland, R.I.
Beinbrink, Andy	.282	119	418	56	118	23	1	4	57	55	81	21	10	.371	.367	R	R	6-3	200	9-24-76	1999	San Diego, Calif.
Brewer, Jace	.216	39	153	13	33	5	0	1	16	4	27	2	0	.268	.244	R	R	6-0	190	6-6-79	2000	Norman, Okla.
Cantu, Jorge	.242	131	512	50	124	31	1	3	43	23	74	2	6	.324	.278	R	R	6-1	170	1-30-82	1998	Mission, Mexico
Diaz, Matt	.274	122	449	71	123	28	1	10	50	34	72	31	9	.408	.337	R	R	6-1	200	3-3-78	1999	Lakeland, Fla.
Figga, Mike	.333	10	33	6	11	3	0	1	9	3	7	0	0	.515	.378	R	R	6-0	200	7-31-70	1990	Tampa, Fla.
German, Amado	.267	106	344	55	92	11	4	2	34	39	95	15	15	.340	.343	S	R	6-2	170	3-30-78	1997	San Pedro de Macoris, D.R.
Grummitt, Dan	.251	103	363	54	91	22	1	8	46	35	94	5	3	.383	.333	R	R	6-5	240	6-16-76	1998	Twinsburg, Ohio
Haad, Yamid	.185	29	108	12	20	2	0	3	15	6	23	2	1	.287	.222	R	R	6-2	210	9-2-77	1994	Cartagena, Colombia
Johnson, Russ	.279	12	43	10	12	5	0	0	3	8	7	1	0	.395	.392	R	R	5-10	180	2-22-73	1994	Denham Springs, La.
Kaup, Nathan	.243	85	272	23	66	13	0	2	27	26	46	1	4	.313	.320	R	R	6-3	210	1-11-78	2000	Henderson, Nev.
LaForest, Pete	.270	106	359	57	97	18	1	20	64	60	94	9	6	.493	.374	L	R	6-2	200	1-27-78	1995	Montebello, Quebec
Marconi, Alex	.189	31	95	5	18	4	0	0	12	1	17	1	2	.232	.200	R	R	6-0	180	3-25-78	2000	Cuyahoga Falls, Ohio
Martinez, Greg	.218	28	101	8	22	2	1	0	9	6	15	6	2	.257	.259	S	R	5-10	160	1-27-72	1993	Las Vegas, Nev.
Moore, Frank	.281	96	331	49	93	17	0	2	34	30	62	9	7	.350	.342	L	R	6-2	210	7-2-78	1998	Douglas, Ga.
Neuberger, Scott	.282	118	348	42	98	12	2	5	33	38	58	4	4	.371	.359	R	R	6-3	210	8-14-77	1997	Tallahassee, Fla.
Pressley, Josh	.304	93	342	47	104	19	0	4	45	42	47	5	6	.395	.380	L	R	6-6	220	4-2-80	1998	Fort Lauderdale, Fla.
Rolls, Damian	.429	2	7	1	3	0	1	0	0	1	0	0	1	.714	.500	R	R	6-2	200	9-15-77	1996	Tampa, Fla.
Soler, Ramon	.250	38	144	24	36	7	0	1	12	19	29	14	5	.319	.335	S	R	6-0	170	9-19-77	1997	Elias Pina, D.R.

PITCHING

PITCHING	W	L	ERA	G	GS	CG	SV	IP	H	R	ER	BB	SO	AVG	B	T	HT	WT	DOB	1st Yr	Resides
Agosto, Stevenson	3	1	2.58	7	6	0	0	38	43	19	11	13	28	.281	L	L	5-11	200	9-2-76	1994	Rio Grande, P.R.
Alvarez, Wilson	1	0	1.13	2	2	0	0	8	6	1	1	2	7	.222	L	L	6-1	250	3-24-70	1987	Bradenton, Fla.
Backe, Brandon	4	6	4.68	20	14	3	2	92	91	58	48	37	45	.256	R	R	6-0	180	4-5-78	1998	Texas City, Texas
Brazelton, Dewon	5	9	3.33	26	26	1	0	146	129	69	54	67	109	.241	R	R	6-4	200	6-16-80	2002	Tullahoma, Tenn.
Chantres, Carlos	1	1	3.12	3	0	0	0	9	8	3	3	3	5	.250	R	R	6-3	190	4-1-76	1994	Miami, Fla.
Coward, Chad	9	4	2.98	37	3	0	0	88	82	38	29	33	60	.247	R	R	6-3	170	9-10-78	2000	Siler City, N.C.
Fortunato, Bartolome	3	0	2.10	10	2	0	0	26	16	7	6	11	34	.179	R	R	6-1	170	8-24-74	1996	Santo Domingo, D.R.
Frendling, Neal	5	6	4.50	22	21	0	0	112	107	67	56	65	69	.251	R	R	6-3	200	10-7-79	1999	Dyer, Ind.
Garcia, Gerardo	2	1	2.79	10	4	1	0	39	24	14	12	12	28	.173	R	R	6-0	160	2-13-80	1999	San Nicholas, Mexico
Hines, Carlos	0	0	16.20	3	0	0	0	3	8	9	6	5	3	.400	R	R	6-4	190	9-26-80	1999	Selma, N.C.
James, Delvin	1	2	3.55	3	1	0	0	13	12	7	5	2	13	.235	R	R	6-4	220	1-3-78	1996	Nacogdoches, Texas
Magrane, Jim	0	3	3.09	9	6	1	0	44	35	17	15	22	25	.227	R	R	6-2	200	7-23-78	1999	Ottumwa, Iowa
Malaska, Mark	4	5	3.69	12	11	1	1	71	82	37	29	28	49	.291	L	L	6-3	190	1-17-78	2000	Youngstown, Ohio
McClung, Seth	5	7	5.37	20	19	0	0	114	138	74	68	53	64	.299	R	R	6-6	230	2-7-81	1999	Lewisburg, W.Va.
Minix, Travis	5	7	3.04	38	1	0	0	68	70	31	23	29	49	.267	R	R	6-1	190	8-8-77	1999	Hamlet, Ind.
Ruhl, Nathan	1	4	5.15	40	0	0	19	44	43	30	25	31	38	.248	R	R	6-4	190	7-16-76	1994	Lee's Summit, Mo.
Rust, Evan	3	3	3.70	26	0	0	8	24	30	10	10	14	25	.294	R	R	6-1	200	5-4-78	2000	Ben Lomond, Calif.
Santos, Alex	1	4	8.24	7	5	0	0	32	49	30	29	9	14	.352	R	R	6-1	200	8-9-77	1999	Lake Worth, Fla.
Seay, Bobby	2	0	3.28	15	3	0	0	36	31	16	13	15	24	.236	L	L	6-2	220	6-20-78	1996	West Gulfport, Fla.
Severino, Ronni	0	4	5.09	25	0	0	0	35	40	22	20	23	44	.298	L	L	6-1	190	8-6-75	1996	San Pedro de Macoris, D.R.
Smith, Hans	2	4	4.14	46	0	0	0	54	54	29	25	28	45	.259	L	L	6-9	260	8-3-77	2000	Central Point, Ore.
Sosa, Jorge	0	0	0.00	2	2	0	0	7	4	2	0	1	3	.166	S	R	6-2	170	4-28-77	1995	San Jose, D.R.
Waechter, Doug	1	3	9.00	4	1	0	0	18	27	20	18	13	18	.337	R	R	6-4	200	1-28-81	1999	St. Petersburg, Fla.
White, Matt	1	2	5.56	7	7	0	0	34	33	22	21	19	20	.251	R	R	6-5	230	8-13-78	1996	Largo, Fla.
Wright, Chris	1	3	5.11	19	0	0	0	37	45	26	21	18	15	.294	R	R	6-2	190	6-6-77	1997	Tampa, Fla.

FIELDING

Catcher	PCT	G	PO	A	E	DP	PB
Figga	1.000	10	57	6	0	0	0
Haad	.991	25	183	29	2	0	7
LaForest	.976	79	492	45	13	6	26
Marconi	.973	23	129	15	4	0	7

First Base	PCT	G	PO	A	E	DP
Beinbrink	.800	2	4	0	1	1
Diaz	1.000	1	1	0	0	0
Grummitt	.984	76	637	48	11	57
Kaup	.969	4	31	0	1	4
LaForest	1.000	1	6	1	0	1
Marconi	1.000	1	8	1	0	0
Moore	1.000	2	17	1	0	4
Pressley	.978	54	455	29	11	28

Second Base	PCT	G	PO	A	E	DP
Beinbrink	.971	58	106	159	8	36
Cantu	.846	2	7	4	2	2
Johnson	1.000	2	7	2	0	1
Moore	.929	45	85	112	15	18
Soler	.967	34	82	94	6	15

Third Base	PCT	G	PO	A	E	DP
Beinbrink	.943	59	39	111	9	3
Cantu	.901	33	18	64	9	4
Johnson	.818	5	2	7	2	1
Kaup	.905	40	15	71	9	4
Marconi	1.000	4	1	6	0	1
Moore	.857	4	4	8	2	0

Shortstop	PCT	G	PO	A	E	DP
Beinbrink	1.000	4	8	12	0	1

	PCT	G	PO	A	E	DP
Brewer	.961	37	52	94	6	26
Cantu	.939	95	165	293	30	53
Soler	.818	2	5	4	2	1

Outfield	PCT	G	PO	A	E	DP
Baldelli	.967	16	27	2	1	1
Diaz	.987	113	212	11	3	0
German	.975	104	264	6	7	2
Grummitt	.000	1	0	0	0	0
Johnson	.833	2	5	0	1	0
Kaup	1.000	29	38	1	0	0
Marconi	.000	1	0	0	0	0
Martinez	.981	28	51	2	1	0
Moore	.950	26	34	4	2	1
Neuberger	.988	117	245	11	3	1
Rolls	1.000	1	3	0	0	0

BAKERSFIELD BLAZE — High Class A

CALIFORNIA LEAGUE

BATTING

BATTING	AVG	G	AB	R	H	2B	3B	HR	RBI	BB	SO	SB	CS	SLG	OBP	B	T	HT	WT	DOB	1st Yr	Resides
Baldelli, Rocco	.333	77	312	63	104	19	1	14	51	18	63	21	6	.535	.382	R	R	6-4	195	9-25-81	2000	Cumberland, R.I.

ORGANIZATION STATISTICS

BATTING	AVG	G	AB	R	H	2B	3B	HR	RBI	BB	SO	SB	CS	SLG	OBP	B	T	HT	WT	DOB	1st Yr	Resides
Brewer, Jace	.302	91	378	52	114	17	2	6	44	11	62	8	2	.405	.322	R	R	6-0	190	6-6-79	2000	Norman, Okla.
Candelario, Luis	.226	23	84	10	19	6	0	3	8	3	26	0	1	.405	.253	R	R	6-2	190	8-9-81	1999	San Pedro de Macoris, D.R.
Centeno, Irwin	.291	71	275	41	80	14	4	2	20	27	65	12	4	.393	.357	R	R	6-2	170	6-1-81	1997	Maracay, Venez.
Clark, Aaron	.251	125	446	59	112	26	2	16	77	42	149	11	1	.426	.331	L	L	6-1	190	2-17-79	2001	Ennis, Texas
DeMent, Dan	.264	112	432	58	114	21	3	7	51	34	100	7	4	.375	.319	R	R	5-10	185	6-17-78	2000	Birmingham, Ala.
Eddlemon, Kelly	.260	41	150	20	39	11	0	6	24	11	27	1	0	.453	.315	R	R	6-2	180	8-26-78	2000	Missouri City, Texas
Figga, Mike	.243	10	37	3	9	1	0	1	9	0	0	0	0	.514	.263	R	R	6-0	200	7-31-70	1990	Tampa, Fla.
Gomes, Joey	.227	5	22	1	5	0	0	1	4	0	4	0	0	.364	.227	R	R	6-2	210	11-2-79	2002	Petaluma, Calif.
Gomes, Jonny	.278	134	446	102	124	24	9	30	72	91	173	15	3	.574	.432	R	R	6-1	200	11-22-80	2001	Petaluma, Calif.
Hamilton, Josh	.303	56	211	32	64	14	1	9	44	20	46	10	1	.507	.359	L	L	6-4	220	5-21-81	1999	Parrish, Fla.
Harrison, Vince	.250	32	116	5	29	2	0	2	11	9	28	0	0	.319	.302	R	R	5-11	200	11-29-79	2001	Springdale, Ohio
Isenia, Chairon	.247	68	255	20	63	12	0	1	25	11	45	0	0	.306	.286	R	R	5-11	210	1-23-79	1996	Willemstad, Curacao
Jacobs, John	.196	17	51	3	10	4	0	0	1	2	25	0	1	.275	.226	R	R	6-1	195	11-7-79	1998	Rohnert Park, Calif.
Kaup, Nathan	.236	19	72	5	17	2	1	0	3	5	16	0	0	.292	.291	R	R	6-3	210	11-17-78	2000	Henderson, Nev.
Martin, Brian	.223	112	327	45	73	12	3	9	40	24	87	7	3	.361	.298	R	R	6-2	220	6-14-80	1998	El Centro, Calif.
Massiatte, Danny	.242	68	227	22	55	6	0	3	25	32	54	1	4	.308	.344	R	R	5-11	180	7-25-78	2000	Houston, Texas
Merritt, Graig	.222	14	45	5	10	4	0	1	8	4	15	0	0	.378	.300	R	R	6-1	205	7-2-78	2001	Maple Ridge, B.C.
Perez, Nestor	.252	120	381	40	96	15	0	2	34	33	52	8	6	.307	.309	R	R	5-10	170	11-24-76	1997	Tenerife, Canary Islands
Reece, Eric	.161	21	56	3	9	2	1	1	8	7	18	0	0	.286	.277	L	R	6-3	210	6-16-78	2001	El Dorado Hills, Calif.
Salas, Juan	.323	66	260	32	84	13	0	4	25	9	59	6	3	.419	.349	R	R	6-2	205	11-7-78	1998	Santo Domingo, D.R.
Schuda, Justin	.190	76	242	27	46	11	0	4	25	24	88	0	0	.285	.272	L	R	6-3	217	2-24-81	1999	San Juan Capistrano, Calif.

PITCHING	W	L	ERA	G	GS	CG	SV	IP	H	R	ER	BB	SO	AVG	B	T	HT	WT	DOB	1st Yr	Resides
Aiello, Nick	1	1	5.81	21	0	0	0	26	42	18	17	8	17	.368	L	L	6-2	210	7-31-79	2001	Las Vegas, Nev.
Benedetti, John	6	6	3.87	54	0	0	13	77	74	33	33	21	74	.253	S	R	6-0	188	6-27-78	2000	Palatine, Ill.
Campbell, Jarrett	7	6	4.17	36	7	0	1	82	105	53	38	27	84	.298	R	R	6-3	205	9-8-79	1998	Corpus Christi, Texas
Carbajal, Alex	5	4	3.20	43	1	0	2	76	77	30	27	19	92	.264	L	L	6-2	190	11-6-77	2000	Rosemead, Calif.
Coose, Austin	1	4	7.11	25	0	0	4	32	41	28	25	22	40	.305	R	R	6-2	230	1-27-79	2001	Kokomo, Ind.
Flinn, Chris	0	4	8.64	7	0	0	0	33	52	36	32	17	22	.358	R	R	6-2	195	8-18-80	2001	Levittown, N.Y.
Fortunato, Bartolome	2	4	4.01	25	5	0	0	61	58	31	27	25	85	.251	R	R	6-1	170	8-24-74	1996	Santo Domingo, D.R.
Frendling, Neal	0	3	5.32	4	4	0	0	24	28	15	14	15	21	.294	R	R	6-3	200	10-7-79	1999	Dyer, Ind.
Malaska, Mark	4	4	2.96	15	15	2	0	91	98	48	30	12	94	.263	L	L	6-3	190	1-17-78	2000	Youngstown, Ohio
McClung, Seth	3	2	2.92	7	7	0	0	37	35	16	12	11	48	.243	R	R	6-6	230	2-7-81	1999	Lewisburg, W.Va.
Parker, Josh	0	2	9.00	8	0	0	1	9	18	9	9	6	8	.409	R	R	6-2	220	1-12-81	2001	Calera, Ala.
Peguero, Radhames	3	7	4.55	41	6	0	3	83	94	56	42	38	54	.283	R	R	6-0	180	1-13-79	1996	San Pedro de Macoris, D.R.
Renteria, Juan	2	0	5.55	14	0	0	0	24	25	18	15	11	25	.257	S	R	5-11	190	1-1-80	2000	San Antonio, Texas
Rust, Evan	0	1	2.18	28	0	0	23	33	28	8	8	10	45	.233	R	R	6-1	200	5-4-78	2000	Ben Lomond, Calif.
Santos, Alex	6	4	3.49	19	12	0	0	95	101	53	37	33	105	.259	R	R	6-1	200	8-9-77	1999	Lake Worth, Fla.
Severino, Ronni	0	1	3.97	13	1	0	0	23	14	13	10	17	28	.177	L	L	6-1	190	8-6-75	1996	San Pedro de Macoris, D.R.
Stokes, Brian	10	7	3.26	28	28	1	0	166	156	79	60	57	152	.248	R	R	6-1	200	9-13-79	1999	Chino, Calif.
Switzer, Jon	7	5	4.27	20	20	0	0	103	108	55	49	26	129	.268	L	L	6-3	190	8-13-79	2001	Houston, Texas
Veras, Jose	3	4	5.34	11	11	0	0	59	77	44	35	30	57	.315	R	R	6-5	230	10-20-80	1998	Santo Domingo, D.R.
Waechter, Doug	6	3	2.66	17	17	0	0	108	114	43	32	29	101	.266	R	R	6-4	200	1-28-81	1999	St. Petersburg, Fla.

FIELDING

Catcher	PCT	G	PO	A	E	DP	PB
Figga	.986	7	65	6	1	0	0
Isenia	.981	58	498	32	10	4	14
Massiatte	.989	64	585	55	7	1	10
Merritt	1.000	13	120	9	0	1	6
Reece	1.000	4	18	1	0	0	1

First Base	PCT	G	PO	A	E	DP
Clark	.985	85	604	38	10	52
Eddlemon	.988	10	79	5	1	5
Kaup	.985	15	125	10	2	9
Martin	1.000	1	1	0	0	0
Perez	1.000	1	1	0	0	0
Reece	.969	4	30	1	1	0

	PCT	G	PO	A	E	DP
Schuda	.980	51	354	35	8	27

Second Base	PCT	G	PO	A	E	DP
Centeno	.942	16	31	34	4	5
DeMent	.916	52	79	118	18	22
Eddlemon	.984	16	27	35	1	9
Perez	.981	67	94	167	5	33

Third Base	PCT	G	PO	A	E	DP
DeMent	.813	34	19	42	14	1
Eddlemon	.923	13	10	14	2	3
Harrison	.930	32	22	85	8	11
Salas	.862	65	37	125	26	8

Shortstop	PCT	G	PO	A	E	DP
Brewer	.938	89	104	273	25	50

	PCT	G	PO	A	E	DP
Eddlemon	.800	2	3	5	2	0
Perez	.962	53	64	138	8	21

Outfield	PCT	G	PO	A	E	DP
Baldelli	.975	71	114	5	3	3
Candelario	1.000	11	11	1	0	1
Centeno	.929	54	91	1	7	1
Clark	.968	57	89	3	3	1
DeMent	.895	13	17	0	2	0
Gomes	.961	131	166	8	7	1
Hamilton	1.000	8	13	2	0	1
Jacobs	1.000	16	25	0	0	0
Martin	.981	102	145	12	3	2

CHARLESTON RIVERDOGS — Low Class A
SOUTH ATLANTIC LEAGUE

BATTING	AVG	G	AB	R	H	2B	3B	HR	RBI	BB	SO	SB	CS	SLG	OBP	B	T	HT	WT	DOB	1st Yr	Resides
Bonner, Adam	.261	96	310	44	81	14	0	9	39	37	94	11	6	.394	.344	L	R	6-5	200	3-11-81	2000	Hueytown, Ala.
Candelario, Luis	.207	43	150	17	31	6	1	5	19	6	43	2	2	.360	.252	R	R	6-2	190	8-9-81	1999	San Pedro de Macoris, D.R.
Centeno, Irwin	.263	55	209	37	55	5	4	1	25	27	42	22	5	.340	.351	R	R	6-2	170	6-1-81	1997	Maracay, Venez.
Cortez, Fernando	.267	127	475	60	127	14	5	2	49	41	59	37	16	.331	.327	L	R	6-1	170	8-10-81	2001	San Diego, Calif.
Davis, J.P.	.259	80	259	41	67	8	0	10	41	47	46	4	4	.405	.391	R	R	6-4	220	12-20-78	2001	Russellville, Ark.
De Paula, Luis	.232	125	466	52	108	23	3	4	47	23	100	11	7	.313	.269	R	R	5-11	160	12-11-82	1999	Santo Domingo, D.R.
Dion, Nate	.240	91	304	26	73	5	4	3	18	12	106	6	2	.313	.271	R	R	6-3	170	11-13-81	2000	Yukon, Okla.
Duran, Alexander	.172	19	58	2	10	1	0	1	5	3	12	0	1	.241	.238	R	R	6-1	170	12-7-82	1999	La Sabana, Venez.
Eddlemon, Kelly	.259	23	58	9	15	3	1	5	4	11	1	2		.397	.323	R	R	6-2	180	8-26-78	2000	Missouri City, Texas
Franco, Iker	.259	64	216	28	56	14	2	4	33	14	42	1	1	.398	.309	R	R	6-1	210	5-5-81	1998	Ensenada, Mexico
Gathright, Joey	.264	59	208	30	55	1	0	0	14	21	36	22	7	.269	.360	L	R	5-10	170	4-22-82	2002	La Place, La.
Gonzalez, Edgar	.275	134	447	68	123	28	1	8	62	74	75	21	14	.396	.378	R	R	6-0	170	6-14-78	2000	Chula Vista, Calif.
Harrison, Vince	.210	19	62	11	13	1	0	2	3	5	16	3	0	.323	.290	R	R	5-11	200	11-29-79	2001	Springdale, Ohio
Maduro, Jorge	.258	46	124	12	32	5	0	1	13	8	26	1	0	.323	.324	R	R	6-2	200	3-11-81	1999	Miami, Fla.
Merritt, Graig	.190	63	184	10	35	4	0	0	11	15	32	4	0	.212	.261	R	R	6-1	205	7-2-78	2001	Maple Ridge, B.C.
Nunez, Felix	.368	5	19	2	7	1	0	1	6	1	5	0	0	.579	.400	R	R	6-4	230	8-17-82	1999	San Cristobal, D.R.
Porter, Thomas	.053	10	19	2	1	0	0	0	1	4	14	1	0	.053	.250	R	R	6-2	200	4-28-80	2002	Phoenix, Ariz.
Reece, Eric	.193	65	192	21	37	5	1	2	23	20	46	4	3	.260	.267	L	R	6-3	210	6-16-78	2001	El Dorado Hills, Calif.
Rico, Matt	.220	106	332	42	73	16	1	6	37	32	90	9	6	.328	.295	R	R	6-3	200	10-8-81	2001	Clovis, Calif.

BATTING	AVG	G	AB	R	H	2B	3B	HR	RBI	BB	SO	SB	CS	SLG	OBP	B	T	HT	WT	DOB	1st Yr	Resides
Riley, Ryan	.200	17	45	11	9	1	0	0	3	10	9	1	2	.222	.368	R	R	5-10	180	11-10-78	2001	Seattle, Wash.
St. Clair, Jason	.278	6	18	1	5	1	0	0	1	0	5	0	0	.333	.278	R	R	5-10	170	9-27-82	2001	Phoenix, Ariz.
Wolotka, Brian	.220	58	173	20	38	10	0	3	17	20	72	3	3	.329	.307	L	L	6-5	190	7-7-80	2001	Munster, Ind.

PITCHING	W	L	ERA	G	GS	CG	SV	IP	H	R	ER	BB	SO	AVG	B	T	HT	WT	DOB	1st Yr	Resides
Allen, Brian	0	0	6.75	2	0	0	0	3	5	2	2	1	1	.454	R	R	6-3	180	9-15-79	2002	Cairo, Ga.
Bierbrodt, Nick	0	0	3.60	1	1	0	0	5	5	4	2	2	2	.238	L	L	6-5	190	5-16-78	1996	Tierra Verde, Fla.
Carney, Jake	0	1	10.80	6	0	0	0	7	16	8	8	2	1	.470	R	R	6-2	180	12-25-79	2001	Irving, Texas
Coose, Austin	2	1	0.32	20	0	0	9	28	15	3	1	9	39	.150	R	R	6-2	230	1-27-79	2001	Kokomo, Ind.
Crawford, Chris	5	4	4.57	42	0	0	1	65	70	39	33	28	49	.281	L	L	6-3	210	10-14-77	1999	Marietta, Ga.
Cromer, Jason	1	1	3.63	8	1	0	0	22	29	18	9	6	16	.322	R	L	6-4	220	12-11-80	1999	Des Moines, Iowa
Cromer, Nathan	0	1	5.23	3	3	0	0	10	14	6	6	2	4	.318	L	L	6-4	200	12-11-80	1999	Des Moines, Iowa
Flinn, Chris	8	6	2.31	19	19	2	0	128	103	44	33	41	116	.221	R	R	6-2	195	8-18-80	2001	Levittown, N.Y.
Gaudin, Chad	4	6	2.26	26	17	0	1	119	106	43	30	37	106	.243	R	R	5-11	160	3-24-83	2002	Harahan, La.
Hawk, David	4	7	6.46	32	10	0	0	70	88	69	50	45	42	.315	L	L	6-6	210	6-20-79	1998	Bakersfield, Calif.
Hines, Carlos	1	3	5.21	24	7	0	2	48	54	29	28	15	26	.287	R	R	6-4	190	9-26-80	1999	Selma, N.C.
Lockwood, Brian	4	7	3.32	22	17	0	0	95	97	44	35	30	74	.266	R	R	6-2	170	2-20-81	2001	Torrance, Calif.
Matthews, Jarod	7	9	3.60	24	24	0	0	138	131	67	55	37	115	.254	R	R	6-2	190	11-10-82	2001	Olympia, Wash.
Navaroli, Michael	2	4	5.09	36	0	0	1	53	70	37	30	23	42	.308	R	R	6-3	210	11-17-80	2001	North Palm Beach, Fla.
Parker, Josh	3	7	2.85	45	0	0	15	60	75	29	19	22	64	.302	R	R	6-7	220	1-12-81	2001	Calera, Ala.
Sanders, Shane	0	0	0.00	1	0	0	0	1	0	0	0	0	0	.500	R	R	5-11	190	1-18-80	2002	Cullman, Ala.
Seddon, Chris	6	8	3.62	26	20	0	1	117	93	63	47	68	88	.217	L	L	6-3	170	10-13-83	2001	Santa Clarita, Calif.
Shiery, Shaun	1	2	3.72	22	0	0	0	36	43	19	15	14	31	.298	L	L	6-4	180	12-8-78	2002	Katy, Texas
Vigue, John	6	2	3.49	38	0	0	2	67	68	28	26	20	45	.266	R	R	6-4	170	8-18-78	2001	Seminole, Fla.
Waechter, Doug	3	3	3.47	7	7	0	0	36	39	20	14	16	36	.276	R	R	6-4	200	1-28-81	1999	St. Petersburg, Fla.
White, Matt	3	4	3.15	10	10	0	0	54	48	21	19	15	38	.238	R	R	6-5	230	8-13-78	1996	Largo, Fla.

FIELDING

Catcher	PCT	G	PO	A	E	DP	PB
Franco	.976	42	261	21	7	1	7
Maduro	.959	38	213	21	10	0	11
Merritt	.980	63	403	82	10	4	14
Porter	.976	5	37	4	1	0	5
Reece	.974	10	34	3	1	0	1

First Base	PCT	G	PO	A	E	DP
Davis	.982	66	553	58	11	44
Duran	.500	1	1	0	1	0
Eddlemon	1.000	3	16	1	0	4
Franco	.990	26	195	12	2	20
Maduro	.500	1	1	0	1	0
Nunez	.975	4	36	3	1	3
Porter	.889	2	8	0	1	1
Reece	.983	49	373	36	7	20
Riley	1.000	1	1	1	0	1
Wolotka	1.000	1	3	0	0	0

Second Base	PCT	G	PO	A	E	DP
Centeno	1.000	2	8	2	0	2
Cortez	.968	112	224	327	18	62
De Paula	.900	2	11	7	2	0
Duran	.882	5	6	9	2	2
Eddlemon	.857	6	6	6	2	1
Gonzalez	1.000	1	1	2	0	0
Harrison	1.000	4	4	13	0	1
Riley	.933	6	10	18	2	1
St. Clair	.900	3	3	6	1	1

Third Base	PCT	G	PO	A	E	DP
Cortez	1.000	1	0	1	0	0
Duran	.667	2	1	3	2	0
Eddlemon	.857	2	0	6	1	0
Franco	.000	1	0	0	0	0
Gonzalez	.937	128	71	243	21	13
Harrison	1.000	2	0	5	0	0
Riley	.727	3	2	6	3	1

Shortstop	PCT	G	PO	A	E	DP
Cortez	.983	13	22	36	1	6
De Paula	.932	120	183	348	39	58
Harrison	.000	1	0	0	0	0
Riley	.833	6	8	12	4	3
St. Clair	.857	2	5	7	2	2

Outfield	PCT	G	PO	A	E	DP
Bonner	.969	88	141	14	5	2
Candelario	.885	35	48	6	7	1
Centeno	.976	36	77	3	2	0
Dion	.948	87	140	6	8	0
Eddlemon	1.000	11	5	0	0	0
Gathright	.992	56	120	7	1	2
Harrison	.000	1	0	0	1	0
Reece	.000	1	0	0	0	0
Rico	.958	90	130	8	6	0
Wolotka	.917	31	42	2	4	0

HUDSON VALLEY RENEGADES

Short-season Class A

NEW YORK-PENN LEAGUE

BATTING	AVG	G	AB	R	H	2B	3B	HR	RBI	BB	SO	SB	CS	SLG	OBP	B	T	HT	WT	DOB	1st Yr	Resides
Bankston, Wes	.303	8	33	2	10	1	0	0	1	0	6	1	0	.333	.294	R	R	6-4	200	11-23-83	2002	Plano, Texas
Blount, Pierre	.245	52	143	13	35	4	3	1	9	15	54	1	2	.336	.349	R	R	6-3	200	3-11-81	2001	Redlands, Calif.
Candelario, Luis	.200	10	30	3	6	1	0	1	3	0	7	0	1	.333	.200	R	R	6-2	190	8-9-81	1999	San Pedro de Macoris, D.R.
Cordell, Brent	.211	69	228	25	48	15	1	8	39	23	44	0	0	.390	.303	S	R	6-3	210	5-22-80	2001	Reno, Nev.
Deck, Ronald	.111	7	18	0	2	0	0	0	1	0	4	0	0	.111	.111	R	R	6-3	220	10-24-77	2002	Fort Worth, Texas
Dorsey, Ryan	.000	7	15	0	0	0	0	0	1	13	1	0	0	.000	.063	R	R	6-1	160	8-29-81	1999	Wheaton, Md.
Duncan, Trae	.308	39	159	17	49	13	2	3	25	2	25	0	0	.472	.323	R	R	6-0	220	11-27-80	2001	Baton Rouge, La.
Duran, Alexander	.250	14	28	3	7	0	0	1	3	5	0	1	0	.250	.323	R	R	6-1	170	12-7-82	1999	La Sabana, Venez.
Gomes, Joey	.283	68	276	45	78	14	4	15	48	21	50	4	3	.525	.344	R	R	6-2	210	11-2-79	2002	Petaluma, Calif.
Harrison, Vince	.260	15	50	10	13	2	0	1	2	8	8	1	0	.360	.367	R	R	5-11	200	11-29-79	2001	Springdale, Ohio
Mercedes, Anselmo	.174	39	121	8	21	1	0	0	6	14	25	0	0	.182	.263	R	R	5-11	160	11-16-79	1999	Nizao, D.R.
Nikolic, Adam	.228	71	281	40	64	11	3	2	24	23	58	13	5	.310	.309	L	L	5-9	190	9-16-81	2002	Redondo Beach, Calif.
Nunez, Felix	.228	53	180	21	41	7	2	5	18	5	56	0	1	.372	.263	R	R	6-4	230	8-17-82	1999	San Cristobal, D.R.
O'Brien, Kevin	.246	44	130	9	32	2	0	0	6	5	28	2	1	.262	.272	L	L	6-3	200	6-18-81	2000	St. Petersburg, Fla.
Patterson, Ty	.222	12	27	2	6	0	0	0	0	0	7	0	0	.222	.222	R	R	6-0	170	4-20-81	2002	Eight Mile, Ala.
Porter, Thomas	.143	3	7	0	1	0	0	0	0	1	3	0	0	.143	.250	R	R	6-2	200	4-28-80	2002	Phoenix, Ariz.
Pridie, Jason	.344	8	32	4	11	1	1	1	3	6	6	0	0	.531	.400	L	R	6-1	180	10-9-83	2002	Phoenix, Ariz.
Riggans, Shawn	.263	73	266	34	70	13	0	9	48	32	72	2	2	.414	.343	R	R	6-2	190	7-25-80	2001	Fort Lauderdale, Fla.
Riley, Ryan	.276	75	290	40	80	17	1	2	21	34	47	8	2	.362	.371	R	R	5-10	180	11-10-78	2001	Seattle, Wash.
Robertson, Cedric	.176	40	102	13	18	5	1	3	12	7	35	0	1	.333	.246	R	R	6-2	170	2-11-80	2002	Rowlett, Texas
Rosario, Olmo	.216	13	37	3	8	0	0	0	3	5	11	1	1	.216	.295	R	R	6-1	180	8-24-80	2001	San Cristobal, D.R.
St. Clair, Jason	.261	37	115	13	30	6	2	2	10	7	27	4	2	.400	.306	R	R	5-10	170	9-27-82	2001	Phoenix, Ariz.

GAMES BY POSITION: C—Cordell 69, Deck 6, Porter 3, Riggans 7. **1B**—Duran 1, Nunez 50, O'Brien 36. **2B**—Dorsey 6, Duran 2, Patterson 8, Riley 5, Robertson 1, St. Clair 13. **3B**—Duncan 8, Duran 8, Harrison 15, Riley 6, Rosario 13. **SS**—Blount 1, Mercedes 39, Riley 19, St. Clair 22. **OF**—Bankston 8, Blount 44, Candelario 10, Gomes 68, Nikolic 71, Pridie 7, Robertson 33.

PITCHING	W	L	ERA	G	GS	CG	SV	IP	H	R	ER	BB	SO	AVG	B	T	HT	WT	DOB	1st Yr	Resides
Allen, Brian	1	1	2.55	14	0	0	0	25	25	12	7	9	20	.252	R	R	6-3	180	9-15-79	2002	Cairo, Ga.
Anderson, Julius	3	3	4.43	24	1	0	3	41	57	31	20	11	32	.341	R	R	6-5	180	7-16-79	2000	Grand Bay, Ala.
Autrey, Scott	2	3	3.57	11	11	0	0	58	55	24	23	14	36	.248	R	R	6-2	210	1-26-81	2002	Arlington, Texas
Basilio, Manuel	1	1	3.86	3	3	0	0	14	12	8	6	7	14	.226	R	R	6-2	160	10-20-79	1998	San Pedro de Macoris, D.R.

PITCHING	W	L	ERA	G	GS	CG	SV	IP	H	R	ER	BB	SO	AVG	B	T	HT	WT	DOB	1st Yr	Resides
Beaven, John	0	0	6.62	17	0	0	0	18	15	18	13	24	17	.230	R	R	6-5	210	7-21-80	2002	Carmichael, Calif.
Bulger, Brian	0	4	5.53	12	8	0	0	42	44	28	26	25	38	.273	R	R	6-4	200	12-2-80	2002	Snellville, Ga.
Bustillos, Oscar	0	3	4.79	22	0	0	1	36	33	22	19	16	38	.242	R	R	5-11	180	12-10-79	1999	Culiacan, Mexico
Carney, Jake	2	1	5.48	13	0	0	0	23	33	16	14	9	19	.330	R	R	6-2	180	12-25-79	2001	Irving, Texas
Cromer, Jason	3	6	3.81	15	14	1	0	76	87	45	32	15	53	.288	R	L	6-4	220	12-11-80	1999	Des Moines, Iowa
DeBarr, Nick	1	2	4.24	4	3	0	0	17	18	8	8	2	15	.272	R	R	6-4	220	8-24-83	2002	Pleasanton, Calif.
Dischiavo, John	0	0	4.05	3	0	0	0	7	4	3	3	3	3	.166	R	R	6-4	150	1-1-82	2000	Las Vegas, Nev.
Ellis, Rob	3	5	5.73	15	7	0	0	44	49	40	28	21	39	.273	L	L	6-3	190	1-31-80	2002	Oakland, Calif.
Hammel, Jason	1	5	5.23	13	10	0	1	52	71	41	30	14	38	.314	R	R	6-6	200	9-2-82	2002	Port Orchard, Wash.
Hines, Carlos	2	2	3.96	5	5	0	0	25	28	13	11	7	12	.294	R	R	6-4	190	9-26-80	1999	Selma, N.C.
Keinath, Tim	1	0	3.86	4	0	0	0	7	10	4	3	4	5	.333	R	R	6-5	220	4-13-79	2002	Westbury, N.Y.
Lyon, Nick	2	3	2.16	20	0	0	3	33	26	9	8	9	33	.213	R	R	6-5	190	12-5-78	2002	Monroe, Wash.
Prochaska, Mike	3	6	4.07	15	11	1	1	73	78	43	33	17	77	.271	L	L	6-1	200	5-23-80	2002	Raleigh, N.C.
Sanders, Shane	1	3	3.23	24	0	0	7	31	34	16	11	17	21	.290	R	R	5-11	190	1-18-80	2002	Cullman, Ala.
Vargas, Nelson	0	0	5.23	7	0	0	0	10	16	7	6	3	9	.326	R	R	6-2	190	6-10-79	2002	Guayubin, D.R.
Veras, Jose	0	0	0.00	2	2	0	0	7	2	0	0	5	7	.086	R	R	6-5	230	10-20-80	1998	Santo Domingo, D.R.
Volquez, Bolivar	0	0	5.66	13	0	0	0	21	24	15	13	12	8	.289	R	R	6-3	180	7-3-81	1998	Santo Domingo, D.R.
Yarbrough, Joe	0	1	3.18	6	0	0	0	6	2	2	2	4	5	.105	L	L	6-3	210	4-16-80	2002	Bessemer, Ala.

PRINCETON DEVIL RAYS — Rookie

APPALACHIAN LEAGUE

BATTING	AVG	G	AB	R	H	2B	3B	HR	RBI	BB	SO	SB	CS	SLG	OBP	B	T	HT	WT	DOB	1st Yr	Resides
Arhart, Josh	.300	55	200	25	60	15	0	4	31	13	28	0	1	.435	.344	R	R	6-1	220	9-13-79	2002	Garden Grove, Calif.
Babilonia, Jose	.111	7	18	1	2	0	0	1	3	0	11	0	0	.278	.190	R	R	6-2	190	5-20-81	2002	Arecibo, P.R.
Bankston, Wes	.301	62	246	48	74	10	1	18	57	16	46	2	1	.569	.346	R	R	6-4	200	11-23-83	2002	Plano, Texas
Betemit, Richard	.211	45	142	18	30	0	2	0	10	16	36	5	4	.239	.296	S	R	5-9	160	9-16-82	2001	Santo Domingo, D.R.
Deck, Ronald	.194	11	31	1	6	2	0	0	3	5	8	0	0	.258	.297	R	R	6-3	220	10-24-77	2002	Fort Worth, Texas
Duncan, Trae	.310	29	116	14	36	7	1	1	18	8	12	0	0	.414	.344	R	R	6-0	220	11-27-80	2002	Baton Rouge, La.
Frias, Fernando	.185	36	130	12	24	5	3	2	12	12	60	1	2	.315	.259	R	R	6-1	160	9-27-81	1999	San Pedro de Macoris, D.R.
German, Sandino	.095	11	21	0	2	0	0	0	1	1	2	0	0	.095	.130	R	R	5-11	160	5-7-83	2001	Samana, D.R.
Irvin, Blair	.167	11	36	5	6	1	1	0	1	1	17	2	1	.250	.211	L	R	6-2	170	5-16-83	2002	Marrero, La.
Jaime, Willy	.307	30	101	19	31	4	2	4	13	8	35	4	0	.505	.364	R	R	6-1	160	12-9-82	1999	San Pedro de Macoris, D.R.
Johnson, Elliot	.263	42	152	21	40	10	1	1	13	18	48	14	2	.362	.345	S	R	6-0	160	3-9-84	2002	Thatcher, Ariz.
Martinez, Gabriel	.323	60	217	28	70	17	1	5	26	27	38	1	1	.479	.400	R	R	6-2	160	5-17-83	2002	Sabana Grande, P.R.
Nichols, Thomas	.308	5	13	1	4	0	0	0	0	4	3	1	0	.308	.471	R	R	6-4	190	8-27-83	2001	Fairfield, Calif.
Nunez, Yefrey	.169	24	65	5	11	0	0	0	8	10	17	0	2	.169	.289	S	R	5-11	170	2-19-84	2002	La Romana, D.R.
Paredes, Salvador	.258	55	186	21	48	5	0	0	16	19	56	5	3	.285	.338	R	R	6-1	160	6-16-84	2001	Nagua, D.R.
Pridie, Jason	.368	67	285	60	105	12	9	7	33	19	35	13	9	.547	.410	L	R	6-1	180	10-9-83	2002	Phoenix, Ariz.
Reid, Ivan	.083	14	36	4	3	0	0	0	2	3	11	1	0	.083	.171	L	L	6-1	170	1-26-81	1999	Panama City, Panama
Rosario, Olmo	.200	33	115	13	23	3	2	3	12	8	21	1	0	.339	.268	R	R	6-1	180	8-24-80	2001	San Cristobal, D.R.
Simmons, Coltyn	.363	31	113	12	41	4	2	0	8	5	13	1	1	.434	.395	R	R	6-0	190	12-4-83	2002	Las Vegas, Nev.
Skinner, Steve	.083	4	12	2	1	0	0	0	0	0	3	0	0	.083	.083	R	R	5-9	180	12-10-80	2002	Napa, Calif.
Woodruff, Ernest	.260	39	127	14	33	4	0	4	14	13	31	0	1	.386	.338	R	R	6-4	200	9-23-82	2002	Tuscaloosa, Ala.

GAMES BY POSITION: C—Arhart 23, Deck 11, Simmons 8, Woodruff 35. **1B**—Arhart 13, Martinez 56, Nichols 5, Reid 1 Simmons 3. **2B**—Betemit 35, German 1, Johnson 34, Paredes 2. **3B**—Betemit 2, Duncan 25, German 8, Martinez 5, Paredes 4, Rosario 33. **SS**—Johnson 1, Nunez 23, Paredes 49, Skinner 1. **OF**—Babilonia 7, Bankston 58, Frias 36, Irvin 8, Jaime 20, Martinez 1, Pridie 66, Reid 10, Simmons 14.

PITCHING	W	L	ERA	G	GS	CG	SV	IP	H	R	ER	BB	SO	AVG	B	T	HT	WT	DOB	1st Yr	Resides
Allen, Brian	0	0	4.50	3	0	0	0	4	6	3	2	0	2	.352	R	R	6-3	180	9-15-79	2002	Cairo, Ga.
DeBarr, Nick	3	1	4.71	11	6	0	0	50	60	31	26	12	31	.304	R	R	6-4	220	8-24-83	2002	Pleasanton, Calif.
Farrell, Jarrod	3	3	3.59	12	8	1	0	58	46	34	23	24	34	.220	R	R	6-6	180	1-25-84	2002	Boutte, La.
Garner, Isiah	0	0	3.86	17	0	0	1	21	21	11	9	13	16	.265	L	L	6-6	210	1-8-80	2002	Pine Bluff, Ark.
Guzman, Henry	0	0	13.50	5	0	0	0	4	9	11	6	9	4	.391	L	L	6-4	170	7-25-84	2002	Santo Domingo, D.R.
Hammel, Jason	0	0	0.00	2	0	0	1	5	7	0	0	0	5	.318	R	R	6-6	200	9-2-82	2002	Port Orchard, Wash.
Keinath, Tim	2	1	3.29	17	0	0	1	27	33	14	10	7	23	.277	R	R	6-5	220	4-13-79	2002	Westbury, N.Y.
King, Timothy	2	9	6.20	14	11	0	0	45	59	41	31	27	30	.310	L	L	6-3	200	8-22-83	2001	Deer Park, Texas
Lavergne, Jarrad	0	1	7.80	8	0	0	0	15	22	16	13	15	20	.343	L	L	6-2	200	2-18-83	2002	New Iberia, La.
Lopez, Aleurys	1	3	7.48	15	0	0	2	22	31	21	18	9	19	.340	R	R	6-0	170	2-28-84	2002	Santo Domingo, D.R.
Mann, Brandon	2	5	5.40	10	0	0	0	18	16	17	11	14	15	.250	L	L	6-2	150	5-16-84	2002	Des Moines, Wash.
Miller, Eric	0	3	7.23	8	5	0	0	24	29	21	19	13	18	.308	R	L	6-2	190	7-31-82	2001	Naples, Fla.
Moreno, Adam	0	3	4.33	14	8	0	0	62	68	39	30	22	40	.279	R	R	6-1	180	3-5-84	2002	Fresno, Calif.
Peguero, Tony	0	6	7.45	13	11	0	0	54	80	55	45	13	28	.343	R	R	6-3	180	2-17-81	1999	San Pedro de Macoris, D.R.
Rodriguez, Felix	4	4	5.14	15	8	0	0	49	50	40	28	30	35	.255	R	R	6-0	170	1-1-83	2002	Trujillo Alto, P.R.
Samuel, Dauwill	1	3	7.65	18	0	0	0	20	22	21	17	21	25	.278	R	R	6-2	170	10-29-80	1999	San Pedro de Macoris, D.R.
Sanchez, Juan	1	5	7.59	14	10	0	0	53	67	51	45	26	34	.310	R	R	6-3	210	9-25-82	2001	El Cajun, Calif.
Smith, Cole	3	6	3.48	10	1	0	1	13	17	12		18	15	.209	R	R	6-4	190	10-30-83	2002	Rockwall, Texas
Van Ruiten, Danny	1	0	8.31	14	0	0	0	17	21	19	16	11	12	.287	R	R	6-4	190	9-16-83	2002	Corona, Calif.
Yarbrough, Joe	0	3	7.20	17	0	0	2	20	32	23	16	12	28	.355	L	L	6-3	210	4-16-80	2002	Bessemer, Ala.

TEXAS RANGERS

BY EVAN GRANT

The Rangers got a valuable life lesson in 2002: Those who don't learn from their mistakes are doomed to repeat them.

After mistakenly trying to reload between a last-place finish in 2000 and a last-place finish in 2001, the Rangers were seduced by the same troubled plan. Under a new management team headed by general manager John Hart, the payroll ballooned to nearly $100 million as the Rangers spent wildly on free agents such as Juan Gonzalez and Chan Ho Park and gambled on volatile veterans such as John Rocker and Carl Everett.

What did they have to show for it? Virtually the exact season as 2001. The pitching was by far the worst in the American League's strongest division. The offense was hit-and-miss given that it focused solely on the home run. The free agents were busts, and the gambles didn't pay off. The Rangers ended up with a 72-90 record and their third consecutive last-place finish.

And just as in 2001, somebody paid with his job. In 2001, it was GM Doug Melvin. Two days after the end of the 2002 season, Hart fired manager Jerry Narron; the Rangers replaced him with Buck Showalter.

Despite the poor record, 2002 wasn't a total loss. Shortstop Alex Rodriguez had another MVP-caliber season with 57 home runs and 142 RBIs—the best in the AL in both categories. Rafael Palmeiro had 43 homers, giving him eight consecutive seasons with at least 38 homers; nobody in baseball has ever shown that kind of consistency. As a team, the Rangers pounded out 230 homers, the second-highest total in franchise history.

Perhaps most importantly, there was real evidence that if the Rangers commit to a full-scale rebuilding process, the resources are in place for a successful future. Consider these accomplishments:

■ Second baseman Michael Young, 25, spent his first

Alex Rodriguez

Mark Teixeira

PLAYERS OF THE YEAR

MAJOR LEAGUE: Alex Rodriguez, ss
Rodriguez continued to justify his title as best player in the game—and his $252 million contract—by breaking his own record for homers by a shortstop as he hit 57. That led the majors, as did his 142 RBIs.

MINOR LEAGUE: Mark Teixeira, 3b
An elbow injury meant that Teixeira didn't start his season until June, but that didn't keep the top prospect from hitting .318-19-69 between Class A and Double-A. The 21-year-old showed few flaws.

full year in the majors and emerged as a Gold Glove-caliber fielder. He ranked second to the Mariners' Bret Boone with a .988 fielding percentage, but led all AL second basemen in total chances with 726 (80 more than Boone).

■ Righthander Francisco Cordero, who aged by two years in Birthdate-Gate, showed signs of being the dominant closer the Rangers anticipated when they acquired him from the Tigers after the 1999 season. The oft-injured Cordero had his longest stretch of good health and his longest stretch of effectiveness. From the all-star break until season's end he was 2-0, 0.71 with seven saves in nine chances in 24 games. He held opponents to a .185 average in that stretch.

■ Outfielder Kevin Mench, 24, figured in the AL rookie of the year chase for much of the season before a late swoon knocked him out of the picture.

■ Though he eventually was sent back to the minors, Hank Blalock, at 21, was the youngest player in the majors on an Opening Day roster. Colby Lewis, who figures to be part of the 2003 rotation, also made his debut at 21.

■ The minor league teams were more successful than they had been in a long, long time. The Rangers' top three affiliates all reached the playoffs for only the sixth time in 31 years. Class A Port Charlotte won the Florida State League championship in its final season as a Rangers affiliate. Double-A Tulsa, also in its last season as a Rangers' farm team, took San Antonio to seven games in the Texas League finals. Triple-A Oklahoma capped a furious late-season comeback by reaching the Pacific Coast League playoffs.

The foundation is there. The Rangers now face the choice of learning from their past or repeating it.

ORGANIZATION LEADERS

BATTING
*AVG	Travis Hafner, Oklahoma	.342
R	Ramon Martinez, Charlotte	98
H	Laynce Nix, Charlotte	146
TB	Jason Hart, Oklahoma	244
2B	Jason Jones, Charlotte	33
3B	Jose Morban, Charlotte	12
HR	Jason Hart, Oklahoma	25
RBI	Laynce Nix, Charlotte	110
BB	Jason Jones, Tulsa	87
SO	Kelly Dransfeldt, Oklahoma	133
SB	Ramon Martinez, Charlotte	39

PITCHING
W	C.J. Wilson, Tulsa/Charlotte	11
	Spike Lundberg, Oklahoma/Tulsa	11
L	Kelvin Jimenez, Savannah	10
	David Mead, Savannah	10
#ERA	Ben Kozlowski, Tulsa/Charlotte	2.07
G	Greg Runser, Tulsa	61
CG	Three tied at	2
SV	Greg Runser, Tulsa	25
IP	Spike Lundberg, Oklahoma/Tulsa	164
BB	Travis Hughes, Tulsa	82
SO	Travis Hughes, Tulsa	137

*Minimum 250 At-Bats #Minimum 75 Innings

ORGANIZATION STATISTICS

STEVE MOORE

TEXAS RANGERS

Manager: Jerry Narron

2002 Record: 72-90, .444 (4th, AL West)

BATTING	AVG	G	AB	R	H	2B	3B	HR	RBI	BB	SO	SB	CS	SLG	OBP	B	T	HT	WT	DOB	1st Yr	Resides
Blalock, Hank	.211	49	147	16	31	8	0	3	17	20	43	0	0	.327	.306	L	R	6-1	190	11-21-80	1999	San Diego, Calif.
Catalanotto, Frank	.269	68	212	42	57	16	6	3	23	25	27	9	5	.443	.364	L	R	5-11	190	4-27-74	1992	Southlake, Texas
Everett, Carl	.267	105	374	47	100	16	0	16	62	33	77	2	3	.439	.333	S	R	6-0	210	6-3-71	1990	Brandon, Fla.
Gonzalez, Juan	.282	70	277	38	78	21	1	8	35	17	56	2	0	.451	.324	R	R	6-3	220	10-16-69	1986	Levittown, P.R.
Greene, Todd	.268	42	112	15	30	5	0	10	19	2	23	0	0	.580	.282	R	R	5-10	200	5-8-71	1993	Alpharetta, Ga.
Greer, Rusty	.296	51	199	24	59	9	2	1	17	19	17	1	0	.377	.356	L	L	6-0	190	1-21-69	1990	Colleyville, Texas
Hafner, Travis	.242	23	62	6	15	4	1	1	6	8	15	0	1	.387	.329	L	R	6-3	240	6-3-77	1997	Sykeston, N.D.
Hart, Jason	.267	10	15	2	4	3	0	0	2	7	0	0	.467	.353	R	R	6-4	230	9-5-77	1998	Springfield, Mo.
Haselman, Bill	.246	69	179	16	44	7	0	3	18	11	25	0	0	.335	.297	R	R	6-3	220	5-25-66	1987	New Castle, Wash.
Hollandsworth, Todd	.258	39	132	16	34	6	0	5	19	14	27	1	0	.417	.327	L	L	6-2	210	4-20-73	1991	Castle Rock, Colo.
Kapler, Gabe	.260	72	196	25	51	12	1	0	17	8	30	5	2	.332	.285	R	R	6-2	200	8-31-75	1995	Sherman Oaks, Calif.
Lamb, Mike	.283	115	314	54	89	13	0	9	33	33	48	0	0	.411	.354	L	R	6-1	190	8-9-75	1997	Valinda, Calif.
Ludwick, Ryan	.235	23	81	10	19	6	0	1	9	7	24	2	1	.346	.295	R	L	6-3	200	7-13-78	1999	Las Vegas, Nev.
Mench, Kevin	.260	110	366	52	95	20	2	15	60	31	83	1	1	.448	.327	R	R	6-0	230	1-7-78	1999	Newark, Del.
Murray, Calvin	.169	37	77	16	13	5	1	0	1	6	15	4	0	.260	.238	R	R	5-11	180	7-30-71	1993	Spring, Texas
Ortiz, Hector	.214	7	14	1	3	1	0	1	2	1	1	0	0	.500	.267	R	R	6-0	200	10-14-69	1988	Canovanas, P.R.
Palmeiro, Rafael	.273	155	546	99	149	34	0	43	105	104	94	2	0	.571	.391	L	L	6-0	190	9-24-64	1985	Colleyville, Texas
Perry, Herbert	.276	132	450	64	124	24	1	22	77	34	66	4	2	.480	.333	R	R	6-2	230	9-15-69	1991	Mayo, Fla.
Rivera, Ruben	.209	69	158	17	33	4	0	4	14	17	45	4	2	.310	.302	R	R	6-3	200	11-14-73	1992	La Chorrera, Panama
Rodriguez, Alex	.300	162	624	125	187	27	2	57	142	87	122	9	4	.623	.392	R	R	6-3	210	7-27-75	1994	Miami, Fla.
Rodriguez, Ivan	.314	108	408	67	128	32	2	19	60	25	71	5	4	.542	.353	R	R	5-9	200	11-30-71	1989	Miami, Fla.
Romano, Jason	.204	29	54	8	11	4	0	0	4	4	13	2	0	.278	.254	R	R	6-0	180	6-24-79	1997	Tampa, Fla.
Sadler, Donnie	.100	38	30	6	3	1	0	0	2	3	7	2	2	.133	.229	R	R	5-6	170	6-17-75	1994	Valley Mills, Texas
2-team (35 Kansas City)	.163	73	98	16	16	2	1	0	7	7	19	5	3	.204	.231							
Young, Michael	.262	156	573	77	150	26	8	9	62	41	112	6	7	.382	.308	R	R	6-1	190	10-19-76	1997	Los Angeles, Calif.

PITCHING	W	L	ERA	G	GS	CG	SV	IP	H	R	ER	BB	SO	AVG	B	T	HT	WT	DOB	1st Yr	Resides
Alvarez, Juan	0	4	4.76	52	0	0	0	40	35	22	21	21	30	.241	L	L	6-0	170	8-9-73	1995	Miami, Fla.
Bell, Rob	4	3	6.22	17	15	0	0	94	113	69	65	35	70	.295	R	R	6-5	220	1-17-77	1995	Marlboro, N.Y.
Benoit, Joaquin	4	5	5.31	17	13	0	1	85	91	51	50	58	59	.271	R	R	6-3	200	7-26-77	1996	Santiago, D.R.
Burba, Dave	4	5	5.42	23	18	1	0	111	125	71	67	40	70	.279	R	R	6-4	240	7-7-66	1987	Gilbert, Ariz.
Cordero, Francisco	2	0	1.79	39	0	0	10	45	33	12	9	13	41	.203	R	R	6-2	200	5-11-75	1994	Santo Domingo, D.R.
Davis, Doug	3	5	4.98	10	10	1	0	60	67	36	33	22	28	.290	R	L	6-4	190	9-21-75	1996	Cedar Hill, Texas
Flores, Randy	0	0	4.50	20	0	0	1	12	11	7	6	8	7	.268	L	L	6-0	180	7-31-75	1997	Pico Rivera, Calif.
Garcia, Reynaldo	0	0	31.50	3	0	0	0	2	7	7	7	1	2	.538	R	R	6-2	160	1-3-79	1996	San Joaquin, Venez.
Irabu, Hideki	3	8	5.74	38	2	0	16	47	51	30	30	16	30	.278	R	R	6-4	250	5-5-69	1997	Chiba, Japan
Kolb, Danny	3	6	4.22	34	0	0	1	32	27	17	15	22	20	.226	R	R	6-4	210	3-29-75	1995	Walnut, Ill.
Kozlowski, Ben	0	0	6.30	2	2	0	0	10	11	7	7	11	6	.289	L	L	6-6	220	8-16-80	1999	Seminole, Fla.
Lewis, Colby	1	3	6.29	15	4	0	0	34	42	26	24	26	28	.304	R	R	6-4	230	8-2-79	1999	Bakersfield, Calif.
Miceli, Danny	0	2	8.64	9	0	0	0	8	13	8	8	3	5	.333	R	R	6-0	220	9-9-70	1990	Marlboro, N.Y.
Michalak, Chris	0	2	4.40	13	0	0	0	14	20	7	7	10	5	.338	L	L	6-2	190	1-4-71	1993	Keller, Texas
Myette, Aaron	2	5	10.06	15	12	0	0	48	64	57	54	41	48	.324	R	R	6-4	210	9-26-77	1997	Gig Harbor, Wash.
Nitkowski, C.J.	1	2	1.63	12	0	0	0	14	11	4	4	13	14	.224	L	L	6-3	200	3-9-73	1994	Houston, Texas
Park, Chan Ho	9	8	5.75	25	25	0	0	146	154	95	93	78	121	.273	R	R	6-2	200	6-30-73	1994	Beverly Hills, Calif.
Powell, Jay	3	2	3.44	51	0	0	0	50	50	28	19	24	35	.252	R	R	6-4	220	1-9-72	1993	Madison, Miss.
Reyes, Dennys	4	3	6.38	15	5	0	0	42	55	33	30	21	29	.316	R	L	6-3	240	4-19-77	1994	Higuera de Zaragoza, Mexico
Rocker, John	2	3	6.66	30	0	0	1	24	29	19	18	13	30	.298	L	L	6-4	220	10-17-74	1994	Macon, Ga.
Rodriguez, Rich	3	2	5.40	36	0	0	1	17	14	10	10	11	12	.237	L	L	6-0	200	3-1-63	1984	Duluth, Ga.
Rogers, Kenny	13	8	3.84	33	33	2	0	211	212	101	90	70	107	.261	L	L	6-1	210	11-10-64	1982	Southlake, Texas
Seanez, Rudy	1	3	5.73	33	0	0	0	33	28	25	21	24	40	.229	R	R	5-11	200	10-20-68	1986	El Centro, Calif.
Telford, Anthony	2	1	6.46	20	0	0	1	24	30	18	17	15	19	.315	R	R	6-0	190	3-6-66	1987	Odessa, Fla.
Valdes, Ismael	6	9	3.93	23	23	0	0	147	135	65	64	36	75	.241	R	R	6-4	200	8-21-73	1991	Victoria, Mexico
Van Poppel, Todd	3	2	5.45	50	0	0	1	73	80	44	44	29	85	.274	R	R	6-5	230	12-9-71	1990	Southlake, Texas
Woodard, Steve	0	0	6.62	14	0	0	0	18	20	13	13	8	14	.273	L	R	6-4	210	5-15-75	1994	Hartselle, Ala.

FIELDING

Catcher	PCT	G	PO	A	E	DP	PB
Greene	.989	15	87	7	1	2	2
Haselman	.991	67	310	19	3	0	2
Lamb	1.000	3	10	1	0	0	1
Ortiz	.957	7	22	0	1	0	0
I. Rodriguez	.990	100	632	45	7	6	6

First Base	PCT	G	PO	A	E	DP
Catalanotto	1.000	15	87	5	0	6
Greene	.981	15	92	13	2	11
Greer	1.000	1	8	0	0	0
Hafner	.909	3	7	3	1	0
Hart	1.000	2	2	0	0	0
Kapler	1.000	1	1	0	0	0
Lamb	.987	52	358	28	5	36
Palmeiro	.994	97	739	83	5	83

	PCT	G	PO	A	E	DP
Perry	1.000	12	55	7	0	6

Second Base	PCT	G	PO	A	E	DP
Catalanotto	.986	23	24	47	1	8
Lamb	1.000	1	0	2	0	0
Romano	.947	8	10	8	1	2
Sadler	1.000	2	2	4	0	1
Young	.988	152	298	420	9	97

Third Base	PCT	G	PO	A	E	DP
Blalock	.943	46	28	72	6	7
Lamb	.914	14	12	20	3	0
Perry	.951	112	83	190	14	17
Romano	1.000	1	0	1	0	0
Sadler	1.000	4	2	5	0	0
Young	1.000	4	0	3	0	0

Shortstop	PCT	G	PO	A	E	DP
A. Rodriguez	.987	162	259	472	10	108
Sadler	1.000	12	3	5	0	1
Young	1.000	11	2	10	0	2

Outfield	PCT	G	PO	A	E	DP
Catalanotto	.971	26	34	0	1	0
Everett	.969	83	157	0	5	0
Gonzalez	.992	62	117	9	1	1
Greene	.000	1	0	0	0	0
Greer	.947	26	36	0	2	0
Hart	1.000	1	9	0	0	0
Hollandsworth	1.000	38	64	0	0	0
Kapler	.977	64	119	7	3	0
Lamb	.917	16	11	0	1	0
Ludwick	1.000	22	41	0	0	0

Mench	.990	106	193	7	2	0	Perry	.000	2	0	0	0	0	Romano	1.000	18	32	0	0	0
Murray	1.000	34	69	2	0	1	Rivera	.983	67	167	2	3	1	Sadler	1.000	18	18	1	0	0

Hank Blalock: struggled to .211-3-17 numbers in Texas

Rafael Palmeiro: keeping it up at .270-43-105 for '02

FARM SYSTEM

Director, Player Development: Trey Hillman

Class	Farm Team	League	W	L	Pct.	Finish*	Manager	First Yr.
AAA	Oklahoma RedHawks	Pacific Coast	75	69	.521	t-5th (16)	Bobby Jones	1983
AA	Tulsa (Okla.) Drillers	Texas	72	67	.518	5th (8)	Tim Ireland	1977
High A	Charlotte (Fla.) Rangers	Florida State	84	56	.600	1st (12)	Darryl Kennedy	1987
Low A	Savannah (Ga.) Sand Gnats	South Atlantic	49	89	.355	16th (16)	Paul Carey	1998
Rookie	Pulaski (Va.) Rangers	Appalachian	34	32	.515	6th (10)	Pedro Lopez	1997
Rookie	Port Charlotte (Fla.) Rangers	Gulf Coast	28	32	.467	t-8th (14)	Carlos Subero	1973

*Finish in overall standings (No. of teams in league)

OKLAHOMA REDHAWKS — Class AAA

PACIFIC COAST LEAGUE

BATTING	AVG	G	AB	R	H	2B	3B	HR	RBI	BB	SO	SB	CS	SLG	OBP	B	T	HT	WT	DOB	1st Yr	Resides
Ardoin, Danny	.226	33	106	10	24	5	0	2	11	10	31	0	0	.330	.303	R	R	6-0	220	7-8-74	1995	Ville Platte, La.
2-team (25 Omaha)	.219	58	183	20	40	8	0	5	21	21	56	1	0	.344	.300							
Bierek, Kurt	.205	20	73	8	15	2	1	1	8	7	15	0	0	.301	.280	L	R	6-4	220	9-13-72	1993	Tampa, Fla.
Blalock, Hank	.307	95	387	63	119	32	1	8	62	34	61	2	1	.457	.363	L	R	6-1	190	11-21-80	1999	San Diego, Calif.
Cadiente, Brett	.368	7	19	5	7	2	1	0	5	2	6	1	0	.579	.429	L	L	5-11	180	6-17-77	1999	Mesa, Ariz.
Clark, Jermaine	.298	13	57	13	17	2	1	1	4	7	11	6	2	.421	.375	L	R	5-10	170	9-29-76	1997	Vacaville, Calif.
2-team (108 Tacoma)	.271	121	425	60	115	16	5	7	40	69	70	35	16	.381	.371							
Cole, Eric	.264	66	242	28	64	15	3	3	23	16	54	3	1	.388	.313	R	R	6-0	180	11-15-75	1995	Boulder City, Nev.
Diaz, Edwin	.333	13	54	11	18	5	0	1	7	1	11	2	0	.481	.351	R	R	5-11	170	1-15-75	1993	Vega Alta, P.R.
Dransfeldt, Kelly	.229	140	507	60	116	21	7	13	66	44	133	9	3	.375	.293	R	R	6-2	190	4-16-75	1996	Morris, Ill.
Garcia, Douglas	.000	3	11	0	0	0	0	0	0	0	3	0	0	.000	.000	L	L	6-1	160	4-25-79	1997	Barquisimeto, Venez.
Greene, Todd	.303	39	152	21	46	9	0	6	29	9	27	2	0	.480	.339	R	R	5-10	200	5-8-71	1993	Alpharetta, Ga.
2-team (32 Las Vegas)	.325	71	277	48	90	21	0	17	70	12	48	2	0	.585	.355							
Haas, Chris	.364	11	33	6	12	5	0	1	4	7	8	0	0	.606	.463	L	R	6-1	200	10-15-76	1995	Paducah, Ky.
Hafner, Travis	.342	110	401	79	137	22	1	21	77	79	76	2	1	.559	.463	L	R	6-3	240	6-3-77	1997	Sykeston, N.D.
Hart, Jason	.263	134	514	78	135	32	1	25	83	68	122	1	0	.475	.356	R	R	6-4	230	9-5-77	1998	Springfield, Mo.
Hernandez, Carlos	.171	10	41	2	7	1	0	0	3	0	10	0	0	.195	.171	R	R	5-11	210	5-24-67	1985	Caracas, Venez.
Kapler, Gabe	.471	5	17	6	8	2	0	1	5	3	2	1	0	.765	.550	R	R	6-2	200	8-31-75	1995	Sherman Oaks, Calif.
King, Brad	.308	8	26	7	8	1	0	1	6	4	5	0	0	.462	.438	R	R	6-2	200	12-3-74	1996	Boca Raton, Fla.
Lamb, Mike	.393	6	28	3	11	1	0	0	4	1	4	0	0	.429	.414	L	R	6-1	190	8-9-75	1997	Valinda, Calif.
Ludwick, Ryan	.285	78	305	62	87	27	4	15	52	38	76	2	2	.548	.370	R	L	6-3	200	7-13-78	1999	Las Vegas, Nev.
Meliah, Dave	.247	60	219	31	54	13	2	4	23	17	32	1	2	.379	.307	L	R	6-3	180	3-11-77	1998	Walla Walla, Wash.
Mench, Kevin	.214	26	98	17	21	8	0	6	15	17	33	0	0	.480	.342	R	R	6-0	230	1-7-78	1999	Newark, Del.
Mosquera, Julio	.287	81	272	40	78	14	0	7	32	16	51	14	1	.415	.348	R	R	6-0	190	1-29-72	1991	Dunedin, Fla.
Murray, Calvin	.266	33	139	23	37	7	1	2	14	11	20	4	0	.374	.318	R	R	5-11	180	7-30-71	1993	Spring, Texas
Ortiz, Hector	.207	25	82	3	17	2	0	0	7	11	16	0	1	.232	.298	R	R	6-0	200	10-14-69	1988	Canovanas, P.R.

BATTING	AVG	G	AB	R	H	2B	3B	HR	RBI	BB	SO	SB	CS	SLG	OBP	B	T	HT	WT	DOB	1st Yr	Resides
Perez, Santiago	.333	14	51	6	17	1	1	1	9	7	12	3	2	.451	.417	S	R	6-2	160	12-30-75	1993	Santo Domingo, D.R.
Pickler, Jeff	.299	96	394	62	118	19	0	0	32	54	44	17	8	.348	.384	L	R	5-10	180	1-6-76	1998	Santa Ana, Calif.
Pose, Scott	.202	21	84	5	17	2	1	0	8	10	6	0	2	.250	.287	L	R	5-11	190	2-11-67	1989	Raleigh, N.C.
2-team (23 Las Vegas)	.203	44	158	16	32	5	1	0	14	24	12	5	5	.247	.311							
Rivera, Ruben	.276	27	98	19	27	2	4	7	23	13	23	2	0	.592	.366	R	R	6-3	200	11-14-73	1992	La Chorrera, Panama
Romano, Jason	.270	48	196	28	53	8	1	4	28	19	41	10	3	.383	.329	R	R	6-0	180	6-24-79	1997	Tampa, Fla.
Sadler, Donnie	.233	12	43	7	10	3	1	0	4	6	7	2	1	.349	.340	R	R	5-6	170	6-17-75	1994	Valley Mills, Texas
2-team (5 Omaha)	.266	17	64	13	17	3	1	0	4	8	10	2	3	.344	.365							
Sprague, Ed	.268	106	400	51	107	26	1	10	65	40	92	0	1	.413	.346	R	R	6-2	200	7-25-67	1989	Stockton, Calif.

PITCHING	W	L	ERA	G	GS	CG	SV	IP	H	R	ER	BB	SO	AVG	B	T	HT	WT	DOB	1st Yr	Resides
Alvarez, Juan	0	0	3.63	15	0	0	1	17	19	7	7	9	13	.292	L	L	6-0	170	8-9-73	1995	Miami, Fla.
Bell, Rob	5	0	4.06	12	11	2	0	75	70	36	34	25	55	.247	R	R	6-5	220	1-17-77	1995	Marlboro, N.Y.
Benoit, Joaquin	8	4	3.56	16	16	0	0	99	74	42	39	37	103	.203	R	R	6-3	200	7-26-77	1996	Santiago, D.R.
Cordero, Francisco	0	2	5.84	11	1	0	2	12	15	14	8	7	21	.277	R	R	6-2	195	5-11-75	1994	Santo Domingo, D.R.
Davis, Doug	4	3	4.99	9	9	0	0	61	70	38	34	11	48	.290	L	L	6-4	190	9-21-75	1996	Cedar Hill, Texas
Dickey, R.A.	8	7	4.09	37	19	1	0	154	176	81	70	47	109	.294	R	R	6-3	200	10-29-74	1997	Nashville, Tenn.
Flores, Randy	1	1	5.75	15	0	0	1	20	22	13	13	5	16	.268	L	L	6-0	180	7-31-75	1997	Pico Rivera, Calif.
Garcia, Reynaldo	2	2	2.84	25	0	0	4	32	23	12	10	14	33	.198	R	R	6-3	170	4-15-74	1997	Santo Domingo, D.R.
Gonzalez, Jeremi	6	5	3.33	46	5	0	14	92	86	40	34	39	93	.248	R	R	6-0	220	1-8-75	1992	Maracaibo, Venez.
Graham, Tom	0	0	0.00	2	0	0	0	1	0	0	0	0	3	.000	R	R	6-7	250	1-26-78	2000	Modesto, Calif.
Lewis, Colby	5	6	3.63	20	20	0	0	107	100	49	43	28	99	.245	R	R	6-4	230	8-2-79	1999	Bakersfield, Calif.
Lundberg, Spike	3	4	5.86	13	7	0	0	58	75	41	38	18	34	.311	S	R	6-1	180	5-4-77	1997	San Diego, Calif.
Michalak, Chris	0	0	0.00	1	0	0	0	1	0	0	0	1	.000	L	L	6-2	190	1-4-71	1993	Keller, Texas
Mounce, Tony	0	1	9.00	2	1	0	0	5	10	5	5	1	2	.454	L	L	6-2	170	2-8-75	1994	Kennewick, Wash.
Murray, Dan	5	7	6.24	39	12	0	2	110	132	96	76	51	53	.296	R	R	6-1	190	11-21-73	1995	Garden Grove, Calif.
Myette, Aaron	7	4	3.14	16	16	2	0	106	86	41	37	44	106	.222	R	R	6-4	210	9-26-77	1997	Gig Harbor, Wash.
Nitkowski, C.J.	1	1	1.80	9	0	0	0	10	8	3	2	4	11	.210	L	L	6-3	200	3-9-73	1994	Houston, Texas
Park, Chan Ho	0	1	27.00	1	1	0	0	3	9	9	9	3	3	.500	R	R	6-2	200	6-30-73	1994	Beverly Hills, Calif.
Pena, Jesus	1	6	7.26	29	5	0	2	57	73	48	46	45	57	.310	L	L	6-0	170	3-8-75	1993	Santo Domingo, D.R.
Powell, Jay	2	0	12.38	8	0	0	0	8	14	11	11	3	8	.358	R	R	6-4	220	1-9-72	1993	Madison, Miss.
Ramirez, Erasmo	4	1	1.29	25	0	0	1	21	15	5	3	4	17	.194	L	L	6-0	180	4-29-76	1998	Santa Ana, Calif.
Ramos, Mario	3	8	7.40	34	19	0	0	122	162	107	100	53	75	.321	L	L	5-11	180	10-19-77	1999	Pflugerville, Texas
Regilio, Nick	1	0	10.80	1	1	0	0	5	9	6	6	5	4	.391	R	R	6-2	180	9-4-78	1999	Deltona, Fla.
Rocker, John	1	0	0.00	6	0	0	0	9	4	0	0	2	14	.133	R	L	6-4	220	10-17-74	1994	Macon, Ga.
Rodriguez, Rich	0	0	13.50	3	0	0	0	3	6	4	4	0	1	.428	L	L	6-0	200	3-1-63	1984	Duluth, Ga.
Schmack, Brian	0	4	4.94	29	1	0	1	55	66	35	30	18	45	.306	R	R	6-2	190	12-7-73	1996	Barrington, Ill.
Seanez, Rudy	0	0	4.50	4	0	0	0	4	4	2	2	0	3	.266	R	R	5-11	200	10-20-68	1986	El Centro, Calif.
Telford, Anthony	8	2	3.40	35	0	0	5	50	47	19	19	21	35	.250	R	R	6-0	190	3-6-66	1987	Odessa, Fla.

FIELDING

Catcher	PCT	G	PO	A	E	DP	PB
Ardoin	.984	31	225	19	4	1	8
Greene	.989	23	174	13	2	2	8
Hernandez	1.000	10	73	7	0	1	3
King	1.000	8	64	1	0	0	0
Lamb	.926	4	23	2	2	0	0
Mosquera	.992	51	342	40	3	4	7
Ortiz	.995	25	167	19	1	1	8

First Base	PCT	G	PO	A	E	DP
Bierek	1.000	1	3	0	0	0
Greene	1.000	3	22	2	0	3
Haas	1.000	3	28	1	0	5
Hafner	.993	65	558	28	4	43
Hart	.998	51	464	40	1	41
Meliah	1.000	2	10	0	0	2
Sprague	.995	25	210	10	1	14

Second Base	PCT	G	PO	A	E	DP
Blalock	.967	4	11	18	1	3
Clark	1.000	9	15	24	0	4
Diaz	1.000	7	15	14	0	5
Dransfeldt	1.000	1	0	1	0	0

	PCT	G	PO	A	E	DP
Meliah	.907	11	26	23	5	7
Pickler	.974	85	181	230	11	47
Romano	.987	18	34	44	1	5
Sadler	1.000	5	12	15	0	3
Sprague	.844	9	16	22	7	5

Third Base	PCT	G	PO	A	E	DP
Blalock	.934	91	46	168	15	17
Diaz	.909	2	1	9	1	1
Haas	.955	7	6	15	1	0
Lamb	.000	1	0	0	1	0
Meliah	.889	7	6	10	2	2
Mosquera	.000	1	0	0	0	0
Ortiz	.750	1	1	2	1	0
Perez	1.000	6	5	16	0	0
Pickler	1.000	3	3	3	0	1
Sprague	.878	29	12	53	9	2

Shortstop	PCT	G	PO	A	E	DP
Diaz	.917	4	2	9	1	1
Dransfeldt	.978	139	210	421	14	74
Perez	.667	1	1	1	1	0
Romano	1.000	1	2	4	0	1

Outfield	PCT	G	PO	A	E	DP
Ardoin	.000	1	0	0	0	0
Bierek	1.000	20	43	1	0	0
Cadiente	1.000	7	7	0	0	0
Clark	.941	4	16	0	1	0
Cole	.967	62	82	5	3	3
Garcia	1.000	3	4	0	0	0
Greene	1.000	6	5	0	0	0
Hart	.940	71	106	3	7	1
Kapler	1.000	4	6	3	0	0
Ludwick	.973	78	172	5	5	1
Meliah	.978	26	41	3	1	1
Mench	.965	25	52	3	2	1
Mosquera	1.000	4	5	1	0	0
Murray	1.000	33	88	0	0	0
Perez	.929	8	12	1	1	0
Pickler	.938	9	14	1	1	0
Pose	.978	19	43	1	1	0
Rivera	.955	26	58	6	3	0
Romano	.957	30	85	4	4	0
Sadler	.944	7	16	1	1	1

TULSA DRILLERS   Class AA

TEXAS LEAGUE

BATTING	AVG	G	AB	R	H	2B	3B	HR	RBI	BB	SO	SB	CS	SLG	OBP	B	T	HT	WT	DOB	1st Yr	Resides
Ardoin, Danny	.143	8	21	1	3	0	0	0	4	9	0	0	0	.143	.280	R	R	6-0	220	7-8-74	1995	Ville Platte, La.
Cadiente, Brett	.227	102	300	37	68	14	4	2	19	36	70	12	5	.320	.316	L	L	5-11	180	6-17-77	1999	Mesa, Ariz.
Catalanotto, Frank	.125	4	16	1	2	0	1	0	3	1	1	0	0	.250	.222	L	R	5-11	190	4-27-74	1992	Southlake, Texas
Cole, Eric	.194	47	155	10	30	7	0	3	18	11	41	0	2	.297	.250	R	R	6-0	180	11-15-75	1995	Boulder City, Nev.
Furniss, Eddy	.143	26	84	5	12	3	0	1	7	9	29	0	1	.214	.229	L	L	6-2	200	9-18-75	1998	Nacogdoches, Texas
Gajewski, Matt	.167	14	30	1	5	2	0	0	2	2	6	2	0	.233	.212	S	R	6-2	200	10-8-77	1999	Ashley, Ill.
Garcia, Douglas	.303	45	142	10	43	9	0	1	18	3	32	0	0	.387	.331	L	L	6-1	160	4-25-79	1997	Barquisimeto, Venez.
Greer, Rusty	.412	6	17	4	7	2	0	0	1	5	3	0	0	.529	.545	L	L	6-0	190	1-21-69	1990	Colleyville, Texas
Haas, Chris	.222	60	180	23	40	8	0	10	27	19	63	0	0	.433	.295	L	R	6-1	200	10-15-76	1995	Paducah, Ky.
Jones, Jason	.295	136	471	82	139	33	2	13	75	87	97	12	7	.456	.401	S	R	6-3	210	10-17-76	1999	Marietta, Ga.
Jones, Jeremy	.220	55	132	17	29	4	0	2	8	16	21	1	1	.295	.314	R	R	6-3	190	8-12-77	1998	Raymore, Mo.
King, Brad	.186	15	43	3	8	0	0	1	9	5	0	0	0	.186	.340	R	R	6-2	200	12-3-74	1996	Boca Raton, Fla.
Laird, Gerald	.276	123	442	70	122	21	4	11	67	45	95	8	6	.416	.343	R	R	6-2	190	11-13-79	1999	Garden Grove, Calif.
Maier, T.J.	.228	20	57	14	13	3	0	1	5	15	12	1	0	.333	.389	R	R	6-0	180	2-24-75	1997	Santa Clara, Calif.
Martin, Tyler	.077	4	13	1	1	0	0	1	4	1	3	0	0	.308	.143	S	R	6-2	180	8-31-77	2000	West Melbourne, Fla.

BATTING	AVG	G	AB	R	H	2B	3B	HR	RBI	BB	SO	SB	CS	SLG	OBP	B	T	HT	WT	DOB	1st Yr	Resides
McNally, Sean	.235	66	221	23	52	6	1	8	37	28	66	4	2	.380	.319	R	R	6-4	210	12-14-72	1994	Rye, N.Y.
Meliah, Dave	.257	30	109	14	28	6	0	5	22	4	16	2	2	.450	.281	L	R	6-3	180	3-11-77	1998	Walla Walla, Wash.
Meyer, Drew	.214	4	14	0	3	0	0	0	0	1	5	0	0	.214	.267	L	R	5-10	180	8-29-81	2002	Charleston, S.C.
Moore, Jason	.242	116	417	54	101	21	4	13	69	48	94	3	4	.405	.326	S	R	6-0	180	1-4-78	1999	Miami, Fla.
Mosquera, Julio	.333	2	6	1	2	0	0	0	0	0	1	0	0	.333	.333	R	R	6-0	190	1-29-72	1991	Dunedin, Fla.
Oliver, Brian	.270	97	356	57	96	18	1	3	26	32	54	3	4	.351	.339	L	L	5-10	170	11-7-76	1998	Antioch, Calif.
Ottavinia, Paul	.261	134	522	76	136	31	3	8	60	52	58	15	7	.377	.324	L	L	6-1	190	4-22-73	1994	Drakestown, N.J.
Pickler, Jeff	.167	6	24	2	4	0	0	0	0	2	3	1	0	.167	.231	L	R	5-10	180	1-6-76	1998	Santa Ana, Calif.
Rivera, Ruben	.312	59	205	38	64	17	4	10	43	23	46	4	3	.580	.388	R	R	6-3	200	11-14-73	1992	La Chorrera, Panama
Silvestre, Juan	.146	33	96	6	14	3	0	3	11	9	30	1	0	.271	.219	R	R	5-11	180	1-10-76	1994	San Pedro de Macoris, D.R.
Teixeira, Mark	.316	48	171	31	54	11	3	10	28	25	36	3	2	.591	.415	S	R	6-3	220	4-11-81	2002	Serverna Park, Md.
Vaz, Roberto	.241	24	83	10	20	8	0	2	8	9	15	0	1	.410	.330	L	L	5-9	190	3-15-75	1997	Tuscaloosa, Ala.
Warriax, Brandon	.171	88	263	27	45	7	2	5	18	28	82	3	2	.270	.257	R	R	6-0	160	6-23-79	1997	Maxton, N.C.

PITCHING	W	L	ERA	G	GS	CG	SV	IP	H	R	ER	BB	SO	AVG	B	T	HT	WT	DOB	1st Yr	Resides
Alvarez, Juan	0	0	0.00	2	0	0	0	2	1	0	0	0	0	.142	L	L	6-0	170	8-9-73	1995	Miami, Fla.
Bell, Rob	1	0	0.00	1	1	0	0	8	4	0	0	0	5	.153	R	R	6-5	220	1-17-77	1995	Marlboro, N.Y.
Brink, Jim	7	5	4.94	42	6	0	0	86	102	51	47	21	41	.300	R	R	6-0	180	9-11-76	1998	Stockton, Calif.
Dittfurth, Ryan	1	3	5.66	9	9	0	0	41	42	29	26	23	32	.265	R	R	6-6	200	10-18-79	1998	McKinney, Texas
Figueroa, Carlos	0	2	5.40	11	0	0	0	15	20	10	9	9	10	.317	L	L	6-1	190	10-5-79	1997	Carolina, P.R.
Garcia, Reynaldo	5	1	3.69	18	9	0	0	68	63	36	28	30	54	.246	R	R	6-3	170	4-15-74	1997	Santo Domingo, D.R.
Garcia, Rosman	8	5	3.01	53	0	0	6	75	75	34	25	32	38	.269	R	R	6-2	190	1-3-79	1996	San Joaquin, Venez.
Graham, Tom	1	2	4.36	24	0	0	0	43	47	23	21	13	48	.286	R	R	6-7	250	1-26-78	2000	Modesto, Calif.
Huffaker, Mike	0	0	5.25	16	0	0	0	24	29	18	14	8	17	.305	R	R	6-2	210	8-10-75	1997	Florence, Ala.
Hughes, Travis	9	7	3.52	26	26	1	0	143	139	68	56	82	137	.255	R	R	6-5	230	5-25-78	1998	Beaver City, Neb.
Kolb, Dan	0	1	2.16	5	1	0	0	8	9	2	2	3	4	.290	R	R	6-3	220	3-29-75	1995	Walnut, Ill.
Kozlowski, Ben	4	2	1.90	8	8	0	0	52	28	12	11	22	41	.154	L	L	6-6	220	8-16-80	1999	Seminole, Fla.
Lundberg, Spike	8	5	3.41	16	16	1	0	106	113	43	40	23	60	.278	S	R	6-1	180	5-4-77	1997	San Diego, Calif.
McDill, Allen	1	2	4.97	18	0	0	1	13	15	7	7	4	3	.300	L	L	6-0	170	8-23-71	1992	Arkadelphia, Ark.
Mounce, Tony	5	3	3.90	11	11	0	0	58	59	28	25	15	47	.270	L	L	6-0	170	2-8-75	1994	Kennewick, Wash.
Pena, Jesus	2	3	3.27	17	0	0	0	22	24	9	8	5	15	.282	L	L	6-0	170	3-8-75	1993	Santo Domingo, D.R.
Powell, Jay	0	0	0.00	2	0	0	0	2	0	0	0	1	0	.000	R	R	6-4	220	1-9-72	1993	Madison, Miss.
Ramirez, Erasmo	4	2	3.00	34	0	0	2	54	51	23	18	8	34	.253	L	L	6-0	180	4-29-76	1998	Santa Ana, Calif.
Regilio, Nick	6	8	3.44	19	19	2	0	105	97	46	40	47	59	.244	R	R	6-2	180	9-4-78	1999	Deltona, Fla.
Rocker, John	0	1	13.50	3	0	0	0	3	3	4	4	2	5	.300	R	L	6-4	220	10-17-74	1994	Macon, Ga.
Rodriguez, Rich	0	0	6.75	3	0	0	0	3	4	2	2	2	3	.333	L	L	6-0	190	3-1-63	1984	Duluth, Ga.
Runser, Greg	1	4	3.84	61	0	0	25	61	74	34	26	29	26	.299	R	R	6-1	200	4-5-79	2000	The Woodlands, Texas
Schmack, Brian	1	3	5.79	12	7	0	0	37	45	26	24	7	20	.302	R	R	6-2	190	12-7-73	1996	Barrington, Ill.
Silva, Doug	0	0	19.89	5	0	0	0	6	14	14	14	7	5	.466	R	R	6-3	190	7-8-79	1997	Miranda, Venez.
Stamler, Keith	6	7	4.56	30	21	0	0	134	163	80	68	28	57	.301	R	R	6-2	170	8-20-79	2000	Stockholm, N.J.
Van Dusen, Derrick	1	1	2.25	3	1	0	0	12	14	5	3	3	5	.304	L	L	6-3	182	6-6-81	2000	Fontana, Calif.
2-team (5 San Antonio)	2	3	5.59	8	5	0	0	37	45	26	23	15	22	.312							
Wilson, C.J.	1	0	1.80	5	5	0	0	30	23	6	6	12	17	.211	L	L	6-2	190	11-18-80	2001	Huntington Beach, Calif.
Zimmerman, Jeff	0	0	0.00	3	0	0	0	3	2	0	0	1	3	.200	R	R	6-1	200	8-9-72	1997	Vancouver, B.C.

FIELDING

Catcher	PCT	G	PO	A	E	DP	PB
Ardoin	1.000	6	40	8	0	0	0
Gajewski	1.000	2	5	0	0	0	0
Je. Jones	.982	40	190	30	4	2	4
King	.947	4	15	3	1	0	0
Laird	.988	101	565	72	8	2	9
Mosquera	.800	1	3	1	1	0	0

First Base	PCT	G	PO	A	E	DP
Catalanotto	1.000	2	5	0	0	0
Furniss	1.000	1	1	0	0	0
Haas	.971	14	96	5	3	11
Ja. Jones	.982	121	1145	72	22	93
Je. Jones	1.000	3	8	0	0	0
McNally	1.000	3	7	1	0	0
Ottavinia	1.000	8	61	5	0	5

Second Base	PCT	G	PO	A	E	DP
Catalanotto	1.000	1	1	1	0	0
Haas		6	6	10	0	3
Je. Jones	.000	1	0	0	0	0

	PCT	G	PO	A	E	DP
Maier	.978	18	42	45	2	17
Meliah	.959	11	22	49	3	9
Moore	.969	31	45	78	4	10
Oliver	.972	79	144	239	11	43
Pickler	.933	5	12	16	2	4

Third Base	PCT	G	PO	A	E	DP
Haas	1.000	17	10	33	0	2
King	1.000	6	4	6	0	0
Maier	1.000	1	0	2	0	0
Martin	1.000	2	2	7	0	0
McNally	.921	52	37	79	10	5
Meliah	1.000	1	1	1	0	0
Moore	.944	29	12	39	3	1
Oliver	1.000	2	1	8	0	1
Teixeira	.925	47	46	103	12	11

Shortstop	PCT	G	PO	A	E	DP
Maier	1.000	2	2	1	0	0
Meliah	1.000	2	4	7	0	2
Meyer	.947	4	5	13	1	2

	PCT	G	PO	A	E	DP
Moore	.961	50	76	143	9	33
Oliver	1.000	6	10	16	0	3
Warriax	.948	87	124	281	22	43

Outfield	PCT	G	PO	A	E	DP
Cadiente	.971	96	160	6	5	0
Catalanotto	.000	1	0	0	0	0
Cole	.958	44	62	7	3	0
Gajewski	1.000	4	6	0	0	0
Garcia	.969	37	62	1	2	1
Greer	1.000	3	2	0	0	0
Ja. Jones	1.000	16	26	0	0	0
King	.000	2	0	0	0	0
Laird	1.000	12	12	0	0	0
Meliah	1.000	12	15	1	0	0
Mosquera	1.000	1	1	0	0	0
Oliver	.000	1	0	0	0	0
Ottavinia	.983	127	272	12	5	2
Rivera	.986	59	135	4	2	0
Silvestre	1.000	30	42	0	0	0
Vaz	.880	13	21	1	3	0

ORGANIZATION STATISTICS

CHARLOTTE RANGERS — High Class A

FLORIDA STATE LEAGUE

BATTING	AVG	G	AB	R	H	2B	3B	HR	RBI	BB	SO	SB	CS	SLG	OBP	B	T	HT	WT	DOB	1st Yr	Resides
Acevedo, Inocencio	.238	59	185	28	44	5	1	2	13	9	36	11	3	.308	.278	R	R	5-10	150	6-15-78	1997	Santo Domingo, D.R.
Angell, Rick	.232	98	272	42	63	12	1	2	29	29	69	10	5	.305	.304	R	R	5-9	170	11-24-76	1999	Rhinelander, Wis.
Botts, Jason	.254	116	401	67	102	22	5	9	54	75	99	7	2	.401	.387	S	R	6-6	240	7-26-80	2000	Paso Robles, Calif.
Bourgeois, Jason	.185	9	27	5	5	1	0	0	4	2	4	1	1	.222	.233	S	R	5-9	170	1-4-82	2000	Houston, Texas
Boyd, Patrick	.250	4	12	0	3	1	0	0	3	1	3	0	1	.333	.308	S	R	6-3	200	9-7-78	2002	Palm Harbor, Fla.
Bryan, Jason	.000	2	3	0	0	0	0	0	0	0	3	0	0	.000	.000	R	R	6-2	190	11-18-81	1999	Brooklyn, N.Y.
Dill, Jason	.266	83	271	32	72	17	3	2	38	24	49	2	1	.373	.327	L	L	6-0	190	9-22-78	2001	Punta Gorda, Fla.
Everett, Carl	.500	1	4	1	2	0	1	0	1	0	1	0	0	1.000	.500	S	R	6-0	210	6-3-71	1990	Brandon, Fla.
Gajewski, Matt	.179	9	28	3	5	0	1	0	1	7	10	0	0	.250	.361	S	R	6-2	200	10-8-77	1999	Ashley, Ill.
Garcia, Douglas	.291	50	189	25	55	12	3	5	33	10	31	4	1	.466	.333	L	L	6-1	160	4-25-79	1997	Barquisimeto, Venez.
Jaile, Chris	.176	76	238	19	42	4	2	0	16	27	50	0	0	.210	.259	R	R	6-3	190	2-20-81	1998	Miami, Fla.
Jones, Jeremy	.250	1	4	0	1	0	0	0	1	0	1	0	0	.250	.250	R	R	6-3	190	8-12-77	1998	Raymore, Mo.

BATTING	AVG	G	AB	R	H	2B	3B	HR	RBI	BB	SO	SB	CS	SLG	OBP	B	T	HT	WT	DOB	1st Yr	Resides
Liniak, Cole	.276	33	116	13	32	3	0	2	19	9	15	4	1	.353	.338	R	R	6-1	190	8-23-76	1995	Encinitas, Calif.
Martin, Tyler	.272	115	375	61	102	20	4	16	60	70	70	7	4	.475	.394	S	R	6-2	180	8-31-77	2000	West Melbourne, Fla.
Martinez, Ramon	.305	114	472	98	144	21	8	3	41	32	44	39	15	.403	.353	S	R	5-10	170	2-22-80	1998	San Cristobal, D.R.
Moore, Jason	.150	5	20	2	3	2	0	0	1	1	2	0	0	.250	.190	S	R	6-0	180	1-4-78	1999	Miami, Fla.
Morban, Jose	.260	126	485	75	126	27	12	8	66	46	111	21	9	.414	.326	R	R	6-1	170	12-2-79	1997	Santiago, D.R.
Nix, Laynce	.285	137	512	86	146	27	3	21	110	72	105	17	1	.473	.374	L	L	6-0	190	10-30-80	2000	Midland, Texas
Olivari, Reinaldo	.000	4	8	1	0	0	0	0	0	3	0	0	0	.000	.333	R	R	6-0	140	10-10-80	1997	Maracaibo, Venez.
Pack, Branden	.216	13	37	4	8	3	0	1	9	1	9	0	0	.378	.231	S	R	6-3	210	1-22-79	2000	Salt Lake City, Utah
Rodriguez, Ivan	.333	3	9	1	3	0	0	0	0	0	3	0	0	.333	.333	R	R	5-9	200	11-30-71	1989	Miami, Fla.
Roper, Zach	.250	6	24	1	6	0	0	0	2	2	7	0	0	.250	.333	R	R	6-2	190	9-26-77	2000	Pompano Beach, Fla.
Silvestre, Juan	.000	1	4	1	0	0	0	0	1	1	1	0	0	.000	.200	R	R	5-11	180	1-10-76	1994	San Pedro de Macoris, D.R.
Soules, Ryan	.224	52	174	26	39	9	1	5	30	35	42	2	1	.374	.355	L	R	6-2	190	2-27-76	1997	Seattle, Wash.
Teixeira, Mark	.320	38	150	32	48	10	2	9	41	21	24	2	0	.593	.411	S	R	6-3	220	4-11-81	2002	Serverna Park, Md.
Torres, Frederick	.240	58	183	23	44	11	0	5	22	11	43	0	0	.383	.282	R	R	6-0	160	3-16-80	1997	Santiago, D.R.
Valencia, Vic	.242	80	256	37	62	13	1	8	33	42	68	0	0	.395	.350	R	R	6-2	180	5-30-77	1994	Maracay, Venez.
Vaz, Roberto	.250	2	4	1	1	0	0	1	0	1	1	0	0	.500	.400	L	L	5-9	175	3-15-75	1997	Tuscaloosa, Ala.
Wright, Corey	.191	56	183	25	35	6	2	2	16	23	52	4	0	.279	.294	L	L	5-11	160	11-26-79	1997	La Puente, Calif.

PITCHING	W	L	ERA	G	GS	CG	SV	IP	H	R	ER	BB	SO	AVG	B	T	HT	WT	DOB	1st Yr	Resides
Andrew, Jason	0	0	2.25	1	1	0	0	4	3	1	1	0	3	.200	R	R	6-1	190	1-29-80	2002	Tacoma, Wash.
Barnett, John	3	0	1.44	9	7	0	0	44	21	7	7	8	28	.140	S	R	6-2	190	1-30-81	2002	Fort Meade, Fla.
Benoit, Joaquin	0	0	0.00	1	1	0	0	5	1	0	0	3	5	.058	R	R	6-3	200	7-26-77	1996	Santiago, D.R.
Burke, Erick	7	5	3.35	46	1	0	3	83	79	33	31	28	42	.250	L	L	6-4	230	8-14-77	1999	Houston, Texas
Cavazos, Andy	6	5	3.92	33	10	0	1	83	66	40	36	33	63	.214	R	R	6-3	180	1-5-81	1999	Clute, Texas
Dittfurth, Ryan	3	2	2.45	6	3	0	0	26	11	7	7	7	21	.129	R	R	6-6	200	10-18-79	1998	McKinney, Texas
Echols, Justin	7	5	3.93	46	11	0	4	112	94	57	49	54	117	.224	R	R	6-3	180	10-6-80	1999	Roby, Mo.
Engels, Jackson	1	2	4.36	10	4	0	0	33	33	19	16	13	24	.255	L	L	6-3	200	3-29-79	2001	Sheridan, Wyo.
Figueroa, Carlos	3	1	3.13	15	0	0	0	23	20	12	8	12	16	.227	L	L	6-1	190	10-5-79	1997	Carolina, P.R.
Gardner, Hayden	6	7	3.10	45	5	0	18	93	78	39	32	19	71	.225	R	R	6-2	200	10-7-80	2000	Stafford, Va.
Gilbert, Rich	9	6	5.20	34	16	0	1	109	110	66	63	54	62	.265	L	L	6-2	180	11-14-79	2000	Clyde Park, Mont.
Graham, Tom	4	3	2.87	25	0	0	13	31	24	15	10	7	32	.198	R	R	6-7	250	1-26-78	2000	Modesto, Calif.
Hawkins, Chad	0	4	7.48	9	5	0	1	28	35	28	23	22	12	.299	R	R	6-7	200	7-24-78	2000	Euless, Texas
Huffaker, Mike	1	0	0.00	2	0	0	0	2	3	0	0	0	2	.333	R	R	6-2	210	8-10-75	1997	Florence, Ala.
Kolb, Dan	1	0	1.50	4	0	0	0	6	5	1	1	4	2	.227	R	R	6-4	210	3-29-75	1995	Walnut, Ill.
Kozlowski, Ben	4	4	2.05	21	12	0	0	79	63	31	18	25	76	.218	L	L	6-6	220	8-16-80	1999	Seminole, Fla.
Luna, Brandon	0	0	6.14	7	0	0	0	7	9	5	5	4	2	.321	R	R	6-3	210	6-13-79	2001	Lompoc, Calif.
Moore, Darin	3	4	5.64	45	2	0	0	53	46	48	33	53	37	.225	R	R	6-0	190	12-19-76	1999	Acampo, Calif.
Moreno, Edwin	3	0	0.59	6	6	0	0	31	20	2	2	3	23	.180	R	R	6-1	170	7-30-80	1998	El Mojan, Venez.
Mounce, Tony	3	0	2.06	11	5	0	0	39	32	12	9	11	31	.230	L	L	6-2	190	2-8-75	1994	Kennewick, Wash.
Murray, A.J.	3	3	3.02	19	14	0	2	83	77	31	28	20	68	.242	S	L	6-3	200	3-17-82	2001	Vernal, Utah
Rivard, Reggie	3	0	2.17	15	9	0	1	54	38	14	13	14	36	.192	L	R	6-2	190	3-13-78	2000	Bonnyville, Alberta
Urena, Sixto	0	0	5.40	2	0	0	0	3	4	2	2	2	1	.285	R	R	6-1	180	6-25-79	1997	Santiago, D.R.
Valdez, Domingo	4	3	3.42	26	13	0	2	84	67	36	32	31	67	.218	R	R	6-3	220	6-27-80	1998	Corpus Christi, Texas
Wilson, C.J.	10	2	3.06	26	15	0	1	106	86	48	36	41	76	.215	L	L	6-2	190	11-18-80	2001	Huntington Beach, Calif.
Zimmerman, Jeff	0	0	0.00	2	0	0	0	2	0	0	0	1	2	.000	R	R	6-1	200	8-9-72	1997	Vancouver, B.C.

FIELDING

Catcher	PCT	G	PO	A	E	DP	PB
Jaile	.986	65	388	46	6	3	11
Jones	1.000	1	7	0	0	0	0
Rodriguez	1.000	3	22	2	0	0	0
Torres	.990	34	185	23	2	1	8
Valencia	.994	48	303	26	2	2	9

First Base	PCT	G	PO	A	E	DP
Botts	.971	9	64	4	2	6
Dill	.989	30	255	20	3	23
Gajewski	.968	9	81	10	3	3
Jaile	.971	10	97	3	3	8
Martin	1.000	42	354	16	0	31
Pack	1.000	4	16	1	0	2
Soules	.992	42	347	22	3	30
Torres	.962	5	45	5	2	7
Valencia	.952	4	20	0	1	2

Second Base	PCT	G	PO	A	E	DP
Acevedo	.952	13	27	33	3	6
Bourgeois	.907	8	20	19	4	8
Martin	1.000	28	35	56	0	15
Martinez	.984	100	190	317	8	62
Soules	1.000	3	5	4	0	1

Third Base	PCT	G	PO	A	E	DP
Acevedo	.900	24	8	46	6	9
Angell	.800	4	4	4	2	2
Liniak	.957	33	33	56	4	4
Martin	.921	34	15	55	6	1
Moore	.941	5	1	15	1	0
Olivari	.800	4	2	2	1	0
Roper	.889	5	2	6	1	1
Soules	1.000	1	0	2	0	0
Teixeira	.902	38	26	57	9	5

Shortstop	PCT	G	PO	A	E	DP
Acevedo	.967	10	8	21	1	3
Bourgeois	1.000	1	3	2	0	0
Martinez	.971	13	26	40	2	7
Morban	.943	123	170	389	34	63

Outfield	PCT	G	PO	A	E	DP
Angell	.976	81	160	4	4	0
Botts	.988	86	159	5	2	1
Boyd	1.000	4	3	0	0	0
Bryan	1.000	2	2	0	0	0
Dill	.956	53	87	0	4	0
Everett	1.000	1	3	0	0	0
Garcia	.938	35	45	0	3	0
Martin	1.000	4	1	1	0	0
Nix	.988	124	251	1	3	0
Vaz	1.000	1	3	0	0	0
Wright	.971	55	132	1	4	0

SAVANNAH SAND GNATS — Low Class A

SOUTH ATLANTIC LEAGUE

BATTING	AVG	G	AB	R	H	2B	3B	HR	RBI	BB	SO	SB	CS	SLG	OBP	B	T	HT	WT	DOB	1st Yr	Resides
Bilezikjian, Charlie	.106	35	66	6	7	2	0	1	6	16	31	3	0	.182	.280	R	R	5-11	180	11-12-80	2002	Staten Island, N.Y.
Bourgeois, Jason	.255	127	522	72	133	21	5	8	49	40	66	22	11	.360	.318	S	R	5-9	170	1-4-82	2000	Houston, Texas
Boyd, Patrick	.241	69	257	25	62	15	2	5	30	24	68	8	4	.374	.313	S	R	6-3	200	9-7-78	2002	Palm Harbor, Fla.
Bryan, Jason	.250	1	4	0	1	0	0	0	0	0	1	0	0	.250	.250	R	R	6-2	190	11-18-81	1999	Brooklyn, N.Y.
Bunch, J.C.	.182	5	11	0	2	2	0	0	5	0	6	0	0	.364	.182	R	R	6-1	200	10-19-78	2001	Austin, Texas
Cabrerra, Ulises	.201	87	239	34	48	10	1	1	26	50	86	11	6	.264	.368	R	R	5-10	180	3-26-78	2001	Hawthorne, Calif.
Charles, Julin	.161	8	31	4	5	0	1	0	0	2	11	0	1	.226	.212	R	R	6-1	170	10-31-82	2000	Guaymate, D.R.
Christian, Josh	.194	26	93	5	18	6	1	1	12	3	29	0	0	.312	.242	R	R	6-4	230	3-11-80	2002	Clinton, Miss.
Cruz, Orlando	.230	32	100	7	23	2	0	1	10	7	24	3	3	.280	.300	R	R	6-0	170	10-5-81	1999	Juncos, P.R.
Dill, Jason	.262	24	84	11	22	6	0	1	5	6	14	1	1	.369	.311	L	L	6-1	200	9-22-78	2001	Punta Gorda, Fla.
Eldridge, Rashad	.241	73	228	31	55	7	1	3	23	28	49	4	4	.320	.335	S	R	6-1	180	10-16-81	2000	Macon, Ga.
Gajewski, Matt	.228	19	57	6	13	2	0	0	3	5	15	0	0	.263	.290	S	R	6-2	200	10-8-77	1999	Ashley, Ill.
Gold, Nate	.190	37	142	12	27	7	0	5	14	11	38	0	0	.345	.258	R	R	6-3	220	6-12-80	2002	Centerville, Utah
Gonzalez, Jose	.034	13	29	2	1	0	0	0	0	3	15	0	0	.034	.125	S	R	5-10	140	2-11-81	1998	Cumana, Venez.

BATTING	AVG	G	AB	R	H	2B	3B	HR	RBI	BB	SO	SB	CS	SLG	OBP	B	T	HT	WT	DOB	1st Yr	Resides
Heard, Scott	.213	124	414	40	88	13	1	8	45	67	81	2	1	.307	.325	L	R	6-2	190	9-2-81	2000	San Diego, Calif.
Mercedes, Jose	.115	13	26	3	3	0	0	0	0	5	6	0	0	.115	.258	R	R	5-10	170	3-13-81	1999	La Romana, D.R.
Meyer, Drew	.243	54	214	15	52	5	4	1	24	10	53	7	6	.318	.274	L	R	5-10	180	8-29-81	2002	Charleston, S.C.
Mongeluzzo, Anthony	.216	95	352	51	76	24	1	9	43	38	79	10	6	.366	.308	R	R	6-1	210	11-23-78	2000	Huntington, N.Y.
Mosquera, Julio	.267	5	15	1	4	0	0	0	1	3	4	2	1	.267	.421	R	R	6-0	190	1-29-72	1991	Dunedin, Fla.
O'Riordan, Chris	.273	9	33	6	9	3	0	0	2	7	5	1	1	.364	.400	R	R	5-9	180	1-29-80	2002	La Jolla, Calif.
Olivari, Reinaldo	.286	8	14	2	4	0	0	0	1	3	4	2	0	.286	.444	R	R	6-0	140	10-10-80	1997	Maracaibo, Venez.
Pagan, Felix	.240	30	104	13	25	6	3	1	9	7	25	3	2	.385	.298	R	R	5-11	180	6-12-75	1997	Bayamon, P.R.
Patty, Jason	.138	16	29	2	4	1	0	0	1	2	10	0	0	.172	.188	L	R	5-11	160	7-12-79	2001	El Dorado, Kan.
Ringe, Craig	.083	4	12	2	1	1	0	0	2	2	6	0	0	.167	.353	R	R	5-10	180	3-16-80	2002	Warrensburg, Mo.
Rollins, Antwon	.203	54	148	23	30	10	3	2	17	12	48	3	2	.351	.286	R	R	6-1	190	3-18-80	1998	Alameda, Calif.
Sanchez, Jean	.201	50	134	13	27	5	0	3	18	6	24	2	1	.306	.238	R	R	6-3	170	1-28-79	1996	Lara, Venez.
Shelley, Randall	.231	129	425	65	98	18	4	11	44	77	117	9	8	.369	.368	R	R	6-4	200	1-12-80	2001	Trabuco Canyon, Calif.
Smith, Dustin	.233	63	176	12	41	6	0	0	12	19	38	0	2	.267	.327	R	R	6-2	210	5-8-81	2001	Girard, Kan.
Soules, Ryan	.321	30	106	14	34	10	1	3	22	21	25	0	0	.519	.438	L	R	6-2	190	2-27-76	1997	Seattle, Wash.
Stockton, Brad	.230	90	243	25	56	13	2	1	31	41	69	4	2	.313	.343	L	R	6-0	180	7-28-79	2001	Marietta, Ga.
Stringfellow, Chris	.245	69	229	27	56	8	0	1	15	28	53	9	3	.293	.342	R	R	5-10	170	11-14-80	2002	Vista, Calif.

PITCHING	W	L	ERA	G	GS	CG	SV	IP	H	R	ER	BB	SO	AVG	B	T	HT	WT	DOB	1st Yr	Resides
Abraham, Paul	3	4	3.52	52	0	0	7	69	68	32	27	35	55	.262	R	R	6-1	200	1-10-80	2001	Centreville, Va.
Andrew, Jason	1	0	1.28	11	6	0	0	42	31	7	6	8	30	.203	R	R	6-2	190	1-29-80	2002	Tacoma, Wash.
Barnett, John	0	1	5.00	3	1	0	0	9	12	5	5	2	8	.353	S	R	6-2	190	1-30-81	2002	Fort Meade, Fla.
Bengochea, Kiki	3	4	3.00	12	9	0	0	39	37	18	13	14	36	.251	R	R	6-2	190	12-4-80	2000	Miami, Fla.
Bright, Nathan	2	6	4.79	15	6	0	2	47	49	35	25	16	32	.266	R	R	6-3	180	10-6-79	2001	Byers, Colo.
Corrado, Rob	2	3	4.79	10	5	0	0	36	40	21	19	13	16	.291	R	R	6-6	230	9-13-80	2002	Dayton, Ohio
Cristobal, Luis	0	1	5.06	5	0	0	0	5	5	3	3	3	4	.294	R	R	6-1	170	11-1-77	1998	La Romana, D.R.
Devenney, Nick	0	2	20.86	3	1	0	0	7	13	17	17	9	5	.433	R	R	6-3	240	7-31-80	2001	Denham Springs, La.
Dominguez, Jose	1	3	2.16	16	9	0	1	67	50	23	16	21	70	.209	R	R	6-2	180	8-7-82	2000	Valverde Mao, D.R.
Engels, Jackson	2	1	2.53	15	6	0	2	53	46	25	15	28	39	.228	L	L	6-3	200	3-29-79	2001	Sheridan, Wyo.
Hampton, Royce	0	1	10.80	5	0	0	0	3	7	4	4	3	2	.437	L	L	6-2	170	10-19-82	2001	Lehi, Utah
Herrera, Cesar	0	4	4.85	19	10	0	1	72	79	43	39	25	37	.281	R	R	6-0	170	6-5-81	1999	La Romana, D.R.
Hillaert, Victor	2	6	3.27	32	0	0	1	55	41	30	20	40	65	.206	R	R	6-2	220	11-25-77	1999	Langhorne, Pa.
Jimenez, Kelvin	5	10	3.20	29	16	0	0	121	122	63	43	37	116	.259	R	R	6-2	150	10-27-80	2000	Santo Domingo, D.R.
Keiter, Ben	0	2	5.06	4	2	0	0	16	17	11	9	5	8	.265	R	R	6-3	210	4-23-80	2001	Arvada, Colo.
Luna, Brandon	3	2	4.89	32	0	0	1	42	44	27	23	21	36	.269	R	R	6-5	210	6-13-79	2001	Lompoc, Calif.
Marcano, Luis	2	3	2.93	28	0	0	4	40	36	15	13	12	32	.248	R	R	6-0	170	1-12-81	1998	Cumana, Venez.
Masset, Nick	5	8	4.56	33	16	0	0	120	129	75	61	47	93	.275	R	R	6-4	190	5-17-82	2001	Largo, Fla.
Mead, David	1	10	5.95	28	16	0	1	95	101	76	63	53	81	.268	R	R	6-5	180	3-21-81	1999	Sale Creek, Tenn.
Mounce, Tony	2	0	0.82	4	1	0	1	11	7	1	1	2	16	.179	L	L	6-2	170	2-8-75	1994	Kennewick, Wash.
Murray, A.J.	5	3	2.87	14	8	0	0	63	63	22	20	14	51	.270	S	L	6-3	200	3-17-82	2001	Vernal, Utah
Ramirez, Victor	3	7	4.65	23	13	0	1	81	71	45	42	36	94	.234	R	R	6-1	170	10-25-80	1997	La Romana, D.R.
Rodriguez, Luis	2	1	4.09	9	3	0	0	22	15	10	10	11	17	.194	R	R	6-2	180	7-24-81	1998	Caracas, Venez.
Rowe, Steven	1	2	2.15	11	0	0	0	29	22	7	7	4	29	.203	R	R	6-4	210	7-17-80	2002	Lubbock, Texas
Truselo, Randy	3	3	4.30	18	0	0	0	61	58	33	29	27	25	.254	R	R	6-3	190	1-11-81	2000	New Castle, Del.
Urena, Sixto	0	2	10.13	3	1	0	0	5	8	7	6	6	8	.320	R	R	6-1	180	6-25-79	1997	Santiago, D.R.

FIELDING

Catcher	PCT	G	PO	A	E	DP	PB
Bunch	1.000	2	2	0	0	0	0
Gajewski	1.000	1	4	0	0	0	0
Heard	.989	81	564	51	7	3	11
Mercedes	.966	5	25	3	1	0	2
Mosquera	1.000	2	7	2	0	0	1
Patty	1.000	1	1	0	0	0	0
Sanchez	1.000	13	86	5	0	0	1
Smith	.977	53	344	33	9	4	7

First Base	PCT	G	PO	A	E	DP
Bunch	.923	2	11	1	1	0
Cabrerra	1.000	1	4	0	0	0
Christian	.977	23	192	21	5	12
Dill	1.000	12	80	10	0	11
Gajewski	1.000	2	7	1	0	1
Gold	.989	37	353	20	4	31
Mongeluzzo	.981	26	186	20	4	14
Patty	1.000	1	2	1	0	0
Sanchez	.990	34	186	20	2	12
Smith	.955	3	19	2	1	1
Soules	.995	21	176	21	1	10

Second Base	PCT	G	PO	A	E	DP
Bourgeois	.973	20	41	67	3	8
Cabrerra	.966	56	98	127	8	26
Gonzalez	.907	11	16	23	4	4
Heard	1.000	1	2	2	0	2
Meyer	.989	21	38	51	1	8
Mongeluzzo	1.000	1	2	5	0	1
O'Riordan	.981	9	27	26	1	9
Olivari	.941	7	7	9	1	2
Pagan	1.000	21	31	60	0	10
Patty	1.000	11	4	19	0	1
Soules	1.000	4	6	5	0	2

Third Base	PCT	G	PO	A	E	DP
Cabrerra	.929	17	11	15	2	0
Gajewski	.500	2	0	1	1	0
Mongeluzzo	.000	1	0	0	0	0
Olivari	1.000	1	1	0	0	0
Patty	.000	1	0	0	0	0
Shelley	.932	128	107	274	28	16

Shortstop	PCT	G	PO	A	E	DP
Bourgeois	.920	99	145	268	36	45
Cabrerra	.889	7	8	16	3	1

		G	PO	A	E	DP
Gonzalez	.000	1	0	0	0	0
Meyer	.926	32	45	93	11	19
Ringe	1.000	4	4	9	0	2

Outfield	PCT	G	PO	A	E	DP
Bilezikjian	1.000	29	34	4	0	0
Boyd	.991	59	111	2	1	0
Bryan	1.000	1	3	0	0	0
Cabrerra	1.000	3	1	0	0	0
Charles	.944	8	17	0	1	0
Cruz	.977	32	40	3	1	0
Dill	1.000	12	21	2	0	1
Eldridge	.986	71	140	5	2	1
Gajewski	1.000	6	7	1	0	0
Gonzalez	.000	1	0	0	0	0
Mongeluzzo	.972	61	69	1	2	0
Pagan	1.000	1	3	0	0	0
Patty	1.000	2	1	0	0	0
Rollins	.938	48	74	1	5	0
Sanchez	.000	1	0	0	0	0
Soules	.000	1	0	0	0	0
Stockton	.975	55	78	1	2	0
Stringfellow	.981	68	101	5	2	2

PULASKI RANGERS — Short-season Class A

APPALACHIAN LEAGUE

BATTING	AVG	G	AB	R	H	2B	3B	HR	RBI	BB	SO	SB	CS	SLG	OBP	B	T	HT	WT	DOB	1st Yr	Resides
Baez, Fleming	.163	16	43	6	7	2	0	0	5	10	15	1	1	.209	.315	R	R	6-0	170	6-10-81	1999	Santo Domingo, D.R.
Bilezikjian, Charlie	.227	12	44	9	10	2	0	0	9	11	10	2	1	.273	.375	R	R	5-11	180	11-12-80	2002	Staten Island, N.Y.
Bryan, Jason	.302	14	43	13	13	1	0	3	12	12	14	3	0	.535	.474	R	R	6-2	190	11-18-81	1999	Brooklyn, N.Y.
Bunch, J.C.	.176	5	17	2	3	0	0	0	2	1	7	0	0	.176	.222	R	R	6-1	200	10-19-78	2001	Austin, Texas
Buscher, Gregory	.269	52	182	34	49	11	0	5	26	28	63	1	1	.412	.373	R	R	6-0	200	10-26-82	2001	Jacksonville, Fla.
Carroll, Rich	.260	55	219	33	57	18	1	7	53	17	62	4	3	.447	.311	R	R	6-3	220	12-24-79	2001	Nokomis, Fla.
Charles, Julin	.253	62	241	40	61	12	2	8	44	20	61	18	3	.419	.321	R	R	6-1	170	10-31-82	2000	Guaymate, D.R.
Cruz, Orlando	.273	26	88	15	24	10	0	1	12	5	26	2	0	.420	.326	R	R	6-0	170	10-5-81	1999	Juncos, P.R.
Eldridge, Rashad	.264	17	53	12	14	2	2	2	14	15	6	10	1	.491	.420	S	R	6-1	180	10-16-81	2000	Macon, Ga.

BATTING	AVG	G	AB	R	H	2B	3B	HR	RBI	BB	SO	SB	CS	SLG	OBP	B	T	HT	WT	DOB	1st Yr	Resides
Gold, Nate	.319	30	113	19	36	9	1	5	30	17	20	2	0	.549	.405	R	R	6-3	220	6-12-80	2002	Centerville, Utah
Gonzalez, Jose	.170	27	88	13	15	4	0	1	12	22	22	6	2	.250	.333	S	R	5-10	140	2-11-81	1998	Cumana, Venez.
Guy, Jason	.210	43	124	15	26	5	1	1	10	32	43	11	3	.290	.384	L	L	5-10	170	4-30-82	2001	Fort Myers, Fla.
Hamblen, Chris	.173	46	156	27	27	5	2	5	20	28	33	1	3	.327	.303	S	R	6-1	190	2-17-80	2002	Fort Thomas, Ky.
O'Riordan, Chris	.370	48	173	37	64	16	1	3	24	37	20	14	3	.526	.495	R	R	5-9	180	1-29-80	2002	La Jolla, Calif.
Olivari, Reinaldo	.200	4	10	4	2	0	0	1	3	2	0	1	0	.200	.385	R	R	6-0	140	10-10-80	1997	Maracaibo, Venez.
Richardson, Kevin	.157	24	83	8	13	4	0	1	7	12	32	1	1	.241	.278	R	R	6-3	230	9-12-80	2002	Bellingham, Wash.
Ringe, Craig	.254	64	236	63	60	9	0	1	23	51	55	10	1	.305	.395	R	R	5-10	180	3-16-80	2002	Warrensburg, Mo.
Sulbaran, Orlando	.214	25	84	11	18	3	1	1	11	10	13	4	0	.310	.299	R	R	6-2	160	11-16-81	1998	Maracaibo, Venez.
Volquez, Julio	.254	41	130	20	33	7	0	1	18	8	20	18	1	.331	.338	S	R	5-11	150	7-24-80	1998	San Cristobal, D.R.

GAMES BY POSITION: C—Baez 15, Bunch 1, Hamblen 42, Sulbaran 10, Volquez 1. **1B**—Bunch 3, Carroll 11, Gold 27, Richardson 19, Sulbaran 7. **2B**—Gonzalez 17, O'Riordan 48, Olivari 2, Volquez 1. **3B**—Buscher 52, Gonzalez 8, Olivari 1, Volquez 6. **SS**—Gonzalez 1, Ringe 64, Volquez 2. **OF**—Bilezikjian 12, Bryan 14, Charles 62, Cruz 25, Eldridge 17, Guy 43, Volquez 30.

PITCHING	W	L	ERA	G	GS	CG	SV	IP	H	R	ER	BB	SO	AVG	B	T	HT	WT	DOB	1st Yr	Resides
Andrew, Jason	0	0	1.29	3	0	0	0	7	5	1	1	1	10	.192	R	R	6-1	190	1-29-80	2002	Tacoma, Wash.
Barnett, John	0	0	0.00	1	1	0	0	3	0	0	0	0	1	.000	S	R	6-2	190	1-30-81	2002	Fort Meade, Fla.
Corrado, Rob	2	1	3.86	8	4	0	0	30	32	15	13	9	20	.264	R	R	6-6	230	9-13-80	2002	Dayton, Ohio
Cristobal, Luis	0	0	5.19	3	1	0	1	9	10	5	5	4	4	.294	R	R	6-1	170	11-1-77	1998	La Romana, D.R.
Devenney, Nick	2	5	8.33	21	0	0	0	40	50	38	37	35	39	.306	R	R	6-3	240	7-31-80	2001	Denham Springs, La.
Frydendall, Craig	3	3	4.40	16	7	0	1	43	46	23	21	23	35	.278	L	L	6-4	190	5-25-82	2002	Elkhart, Kan.
Garcia, Benjamin	2	1	5.09	15	0	0	0	23	15	14	13	22	24	.187	R	R	6-2	160	10-16-81	1999	Santo Domingo, D.R.
Herrera, Cesar	3	3	6.24	13	7	0	0	53	77	43	37	20	41	.337	R	R	6-0	170	6-5-81	1999	La Romana, D.R.
Hogan, Gary	1	2	5.04	12	2	0	2	25	33	19	14	6	8	.305	R	R	6-4	200	6-20-81	2002	North Little Rock, Ark.
Kirsten, Joel	2	1	4.29	18	6	0	6	50	55	30	24	12	50	.276	L	L	6-1	180	5-9-81	2002	Reseda, Calif.
Loe, Kameron	4	4	4.47	14	11	0	1	58	64	34	29	17	55	.271	R	R	6-8	220	9-10-81	2002	Chatsworth, Calif.
Meisenheimer, Matt	0	0	20.00	8	0	0	0	9	13	22	20	14	4	.317	R	R	6-3	180	10-1-81	2000	Greenville, Texas
Mendoza, Jorge	0	0	27.00	1	0	0	0	0	1	1	0	0	0	.000	R	R	6-2	180	2-22-82	1999	Quibor, Venez.
Narron, Sam	6	1	3.88	14	9	0	3	70	78	34	30	8	50	.292	L	L	6-7	210	7-12-81	2002	Goldsboro, N.C.
Paustian, Michael	1	2	6.96	12	3	0	0	32	44	26	25	20	21	.330	R	R	6-4	210	3-20-81	2001	Clovis, Calif.
Rowe, Steven	2	1	3.00	5	0	0	1	9	7	4	3	0	12	.205	R	R	6-4	210	7-17-80	2002	Lubbock, Texas
Scheffel, Dustin	4	4	3.98	15	8	0	0	63	55	31	28	27	45	.231	R	R	6-5	200	5-6-81	2002	Cameron Park, Calif.
Thompson, Erik	1	1	3.18	3	3	0	0	17	19	6	6	2	16	.296	R	R	5-11	180	6-23-82	2002	Pensacola, Fla.
Tisdale, Andrew	0	1	11.93	7	4	0	1	14	25	20	19	5	7	.384	R	R	6-0	190	6-9-81	2002	Long Beach, Calif.
Urena, Sixto	0	0	36.00	1	0	0	0	1	6	5	4	1	0	.666	R	R	6-1	180	6-25-79	1997	Santiago, D.R.

PORT CHARLOTTE RANGERS

Rookie

GULF COAST LEAGUE

BATTING	AVG	G	AB	R	H	2B	3B	HR	RBI	BB	SO	SB	CS	SLG	OBP	B	T	HT	WT	DOB	1st Yr	Resides
Agustin, Hugo	.320	41	122	29	39	11	2	5	22	29	40	21	8	.566	.455	R	R	6-1	160	9-4-80	1999	Santo Domingo, D.R.
Baez, Fleming	.000	4	8	0	0	0	0	0	0	0	2	0	0	.000	.000	R	R	6-0	170	6-10-81	1999	Santo Domingo, D.R.
Baez, Lizahio	.233	47	150	21	35	4	0	3	18	14	32	3	3	.320	.299	S	R	6-2	190	11-2-83	2001	San Cristobal, D.R.
Coughlan, Cameron	.291	50	182	36	53	5	0	0	15	35	38	34	7	.319	.406	S	L	5-11	180	8-12-81	2002	Malibu, Calif.
Grayson, Larry	.308	52	182	26	56	14	2	2	28	22	41	7	3	.440	.383	R	R	5-10	180	7-28-82	2002	Orlando, Fla.
Guerra, Alex	.219	55	178	26	39	5	1	1	17	27	38	26	6	.275	.332	S	R	6-1	170	1-22-83	2000	Maturin Monagas, Venez.
Guy, Jason	.316	7	19	1	6	1	0	0	2	4	4	0	1	.368	.435	L	L	5-10	170	4-30-82	2001	Fort Myers, Fla.
Khairy, Masjid	.268	40	127	20	34	3	2	0	12	10	26	10	7	.323	.326	S	R	5-9	160	2-13-81	2001	Compton, Calif.
Kreuzer, Josh	.291	51	165	25	48	13	1	1	28	18	24	2	1	.400	.387	R	R	6-6	240	9-28-82	2002	San Jose, Calif.
Mann, Jason	.178	32	90	9	16	5	1	1	12	15	29	0	2	.289	.299	L	R	6-4	190	7-30-82	2002	Millbrook, Ala.
Mercedes, Jose	.400	5	10	2	4	0	0	0	1	1	1	0	0	.400	.455	R	R	5-10	170	3-13-81	1999	La Romana, D.R.
Pena, Antonio	.187	41	107	20	20	2	1	0	10	12	26	5	3	.224	.298	R	R	5-11	160	9-16-84	2001	Monte Cristi, D.R.
Reames, Joe Don	.231	48	147	18	34	4	3	0	14	16	40	4	0	.299	.311	R	R	5-11	160	9-26-79	2002	Seneca, S.C.
Sandoval, Abigail	.273	51	183	22	50	6	0	0	17	13	30	13	1	.306	.320	R	R	5-11	160	1-23-82	2001	Bolivar, Venez.
Shields, Nick	.250	39	108	11	27	3	0	2	14	19	25	2	2	.333	.359	R	R	6-4	200	5-29-80	2002	Rockford, Ill.
Smith, Justin	.259	22	54	6	14	5	0	1	10	2	7	1	0	.407	.286	S	R	6-5	210	5-20-80	2002	Longwood, Fla.
Vaz, Roberto	.333	1	3	0	1	0	0	0	0	1	0	0	0	.333	.500	L	L	5-9	190	3-15-75	1997	Tuscaloosa, Ala.

GAMES BY POSITION: C—F. Baez 1, Mann 28, Mercedes 2, Shields 25, Smith 16. **1B**—Guerra 2, Kreuzer 50, Sandoval 11, Shields 2. **2B**—Coughlan 32, Guerra 26, Sandoval 7. **3B**—Agustin 24, Guerra 21, Mann 1, Pena 1, Sandoval 14, Smith 5. **SS**—Agustin 14, Guerra 8, Pena 18, Sandoval 25. **OF**—F. Baez 1, L. Baez 32, Coughlan 20, Grayson 47, Guy 6, Khairy 33, Reames 47, Shields 1.

PITCHING	W	L	ERA	G	GS	CG	SV	IP	H	R	ER	BB	SO	AVG	B	T	HT	WT	DOB	1st Yr	Resides
Andrew, Jason	1	0	2.08	2	1	0	0	9	7	2	2	3	10	.241	R	R	6-1	190	1-29-80	2002	Tacoma, Wash.
Cedeno, Jovanny	0	0	0.00	3	1	0	0	5	3	0	0	1	4	.176	R	R	6-0	190	10-25-79	1997	La Romana, D.R.
Espinal, Willy	2	2	3.12	11	2	0	2	35	37	18	12	13	21	.282	R	R	6-2	180	12-8-82	1999	Villa Mella, D.R.
Fernando, Juan	1	1	6.46	11	5	0	0	15	15	12	11	20	5	.250	R	R	6-3	170	10-5-84	2002	San Pedro de Macoris, D.R.
Figueroa, Victor	5	2	1.96	16	4	0	0	55	48	18	12	17	31	.240	R	R	6-0	160	12-24-84	2000	Las Matas de Farfan, D.R.
Garcia, Benjamin	0	1	9.00	2	1	0	0	2	4	3	2	0	2	.400	R	R	6-2	160	10-16-81	1999	Santo Domingo, D.R.
Hampton, Royce	0	3	7.90	4	2	0	0	14	24	15	12	5	11	.375	L	L	6-2	170	10-19-82	2001	Lehi, Utah
Mateo, Carlos	2	5	3.90	18	0	0	1	30	28	15	13	15	21	.245	R	R	6-3	190	6-28-83	2000	Las Matas de Farfan, D.R.
Mendoza, Jorge	0	0	0.00	1	1	0	0	2	2	0	0	0	1	.250	R	R	6-2	180	2-22-82	1999	Quibor, Venez.
Moreno, Edwin	2	2	3.38	9	7	0	0	37	30	18	14	10	23	.212	R	R	6-1	170	7-30-80	1998	El Mojan, Venez.
Moye, Jeffrey	1	1	11.29	5	2	0	0	18	29	23	23	6	12	.353	R	R	6-3	180	8-13-80	2002	Kountz, Texas
Pezely, Franco	0	1	1.17	4	1	0	0	8	2	1	1	1	9	.086	R	L	5-11	190	1-24-80	2002	Riverton, Utah
Rowe, Steve	0	1	3.33	7	1	0	0	24	32	13	9	4	16	.320	R	R	6-4	210	7-17-80	2002	Lubbock, Texas
Schara, Zach	2	2	2.74	5	3	0	0	23	25	9	7	4	16	.284	R	R	6-0	200	10-25-81	2002	Verona, Wis.
Smiley, Gerald	0	2	5.75	12	4	0	1	36	41	26	23	27	26	.284	R	R	6-0	200	10-1-82	2001	Seattle, Wash.
Smith, Julius	3	2	2.44	13	7	0	1	48	43	18	13	17	44	.234	L	L	5-10	180	5-21-83	2002	Lewiston, Idaho
Sullivan, Mark	1	1	4.30	6	0	0	0	15	15	8	7	3	8	.272	R	R	6-1	190	7-25-80	2002	Winchester, Mass.
Thompson, Erik	2	2	2.04	10	5	0	0	40	38	12	9	2	34	.250	R	R	5-11	180	6-23-82	2002	Pensacola, Fla.
Thompson, Justin	0	0	3.00	7	0	0	0	15	19	6	5	1	11	.311	L	L	6-4	210	3-8-73	1991	Spring, Texas
Urena, Sixto	0	1	0.84	3	2	0	0	11	9	2	1	2	7	.236	R	R	6-1	180	6-25-79	1997	Santiago, D.R.
Watts, Joldy	5	3	3.63	14	8	0	0	52	63	34	21	12	25	.302	R	R	6-2	190	6-12-82	2002	St. Anthony, Ind.

TORONTO BLUE JAYS

BY LARRY MILLSON

Despite a second losing season in a row and a record (78-84) that was two games worse than the previous year, the Blue Jays' 2002 season ended on a note of optimism. There was still much work to be done, but the emergence of talented young players left a promise of better things to come.

The Jays were 44-32 after the all-star break. They were 58-51 after Carlos Tosca took over as manager June 3, when second-year skipper Buck Martinez was fired. And at last there seemed to be a sense of continuity building.

Amid rumors he might be moving to the Red Sox, first-year general manager J.P. Ricciardi signed a five-year deal that replaced the three-year agreement he inked in November 2001. And before the season ended, Tosca and his coaches were extended through 2004. The feeling was that under Tosca, the clubhouse atmosphere had improved.

One area that must improve is pitching. That both Chris Carpenter and Luke Prokopec had late-season shoulder surgery added urgency to the need. The Blue Jays used a club-record 24 pitchers in 2002. The team was also young, finishing the year with 15 rookies and using 18 during the season. The club record had been 16 in 1977, the franchise's first season.

Righthander Roy Halladay, who spent the first half of 2001 in the minors to rebuild his pitching mechanics and his mental approach, emerged as the ace of the staff at 19-7, 2.93. Kelvim Escobar, who took over as closer after Billy Koch was traded to the Athletics in the offseason, had 38 saves—24 after the all-star break.

The trade with Oakland netted two promising players, third baseman Eric Hinske and righthander Justin Miller. Hinske, who batted .279-24-84 and was named Baseball America's Rookie of the Year, set club rookie records for

Roy Halladay

Josh Phelps

PLAYERS OF THE YEAR

MAJOR LEAGUE: Roy Halladay, rhp

Halladay made 13 appearances in the Florida State League in 2001 as he tried to get his career back on track, then made an appearance in the All-Star Game a year later. He went 19-7, 2.93 for a team that won 78 games.

MINOR LEAGUE: Josh Phelps, dh/c

A shoulder injury and the emergence of Kevin Cash forced Phelps from behind the plate, but it didn't affect his hitting. He ripped 24 homers in 278 at-bats at Triple-A Syracuse before smacking 15 more after a July promotion to Toronto.

ORGANIZATION STATISTICS

home runs and RBIs, runs scored (99), doubles (38), total bases (272) and walks (77). Miller was 9-5, 5.54 and finished the season in the rotation.

Other rookies who contributed were DH/catcher Josh Phelps, second baseman Orlando Hudson, outfielder Jayson Werth and catcher Kevin Cash. Phelps was called up July 2 and batted .309-15-58 after going .292-24-64 in 70 games at Triple-A Syracuse. Hudson batted .276-4-23 after being promoted in late July.

Righthander Pete Walker, a rookie at 33, was claimed from the Mets May 3 and finished as a mainstay in the rotation, going 10-5, 4.33.

First baseman Carlos Delgado had his franchise-record string of 432 consecutive games ended Aug. 4 because of a strained back that eventually put him on the disabled list. With 33 home runs on the year, he became the franchise leader with 262 for his career.

There were other changes in the organization. The Jays scouting staff was cut back to make it more cost effective, and some long-time members of the organization were let go. Ties also were cut with some long-time minor league staff.

There were also changes in minor league affiliations. A two-year agreement was signed with Double-A New Haven in the Eastern League, three days after the Tennessee Smokies, which had a 23-year association with Toronto, signed on with the Cardinals. A 25-year affiliation with the Rookie-level Medicine Hat also ended. That club was replaced with Pulaski in the Appalachian League.

Righthander Vinny Chulk, who was 13-5, 2.96 at Tennessee, was named the Southern League's outstanding pitcher.

ORGANIZATION LEADERS

BATTING

*AVG	Dominic Rich, Tennessee/Dunedin	.326
R	Rich Thompson, Tennessee	109
H	Dominic Rich, Tennessee/Dunedin	166
TB	Gary Burnham, Syracuse	238
2B	Chad Mottola, Syracuse	35
3B	Alexis Rios, Dunedin	8
	Justin Singleton, Tennessee/Dunedin	8
HR	Josh Phelps, Syracuse	24
RBI	Gary Burnham, Syracuse	88
	Simon Pond, Dunedin	88
BB	Shawn Fagan, Tennessee	102
SO	Jayson Werth, Syracuse	125
SB	Rich Thompson, Tennessee	45

PITCHING

W	Diegomar Markwell, Tennessee	13
	Vinny Chulk, Tennessee	13
L	Peter Bauer, Tennessee	13
#ERA	Francisco Rosario, Dunedin/Charleston	1.94
G	Brian Bowles, Syracuse	59
CG	Peter Bauer, Tennessee	3
SV	John Ogiltree, Dunedin	26
IP	Peter Bauer, Tennessee	177
BB	Diegomar Markwell, Tennessee	60
SO	Dustin McGowan, Charleston	163

*Minimum 250 At-Bats #Minimum 75 Innings

TORONTO
BLUE JAYS

Managers: Buck Martinez, Carlos Tosca

BATTING	AVG	G	AB	R	H	2B	3B	HR	RBI	BB	SO	SB	CS	SLG	OBP	B	T	HT	WT	DOB	1st Yr	Resides
Berg, Dave	.270	109	374	42	101	26	2	4	39	26	57	0	2	.382	.322	R	R	5-11	180	9-3-70	1993	Pembroke Pines, Fla.
Bush, Homer	.231	23	78	9	18	2	0	1	2	2	12	2	0	.295	.268	R	R	5-10	180	11-12-72	1991	Keller, Texas
Cash, Kevin	.143	7	14	1	2	0	0	0	1	4	0	0	0	.143	.200	R	R	6-0	180	12-6-77	1999	Lutz, Fla.
Cruz, Jose	.245	124	466	64	114	26	5	18	70	51	106	7	1	.438	.317	S	R	6-0	210	4-19-74	1995	Houston, Texas
Delgado, Carlos	.277	143	505	103	140	34	2	33	108	102	126	1	0	.549	.406	L	R	6-3	230	6-25-72	1989	Aguadilla, P.R.
Fletcher, Darrin	.220	45	127	8	28	6	0	3	22	4	13	0	0	.339	.239	L	R	6-2	210	10-3-66	1987	Oakwood, Ill.
Hinske, Eric	.279	151	566	99	158	38	2	24	84	77	138	13	1	.481	.365	L	R	6-2	220	8-5-77	1998	Menasha, Wis.
Huckaby, Ken	.245	88	273	29	67	6	1	3	22	9	44	0	0	.308	.270	R	R	6-1	200	1-27-71	1991	Philadelphia, Pa.
Hudson, Orlando	.276	54	192	20	53	10	5	4	23	11	27	0	1	.443	.319	S	R	6-0	180	12-12-77	1998	Darlington, S.C.
Lawrence, Joe	.180	55	150	16	27	4	0	2	15	16	38	2	1	.247	.262	R	R	6-2	190	2-13-77	1996	Lake Charles, La.
Lesher, Brian	.132	24	38	2	5	1	0	0	2	4	15	0	0	.158	.209	R	L	6-5	210	3-5-71	1992	Scottsdale, Ariz.
Lopez, Felipe	.227	85	282	35	64	15	3	8	34	23	90	5	4	.387	.287	S	R	6-0	180	5-12-80	1998	Altmonte Springs, Fla.
Mondesi, Raul	.224	75	299	51	67	16	1	15	45	31	57	9	2	.435	.301	R	R	5-11	230	3-2-71	1988	San Cristobal, D.R.
Phelps, Josh	.309	74	265	41	82	20	1	15	58	19	82	0	0	.562	.362	R	R	6-3	220	5-12-78	1996	Rathdrum, Idaho
Stewart, Shannon	.303	141	577	103	175	38	6	10	45	54	60	14	2	.442	.371	R	R	6-1	210	2-25-74	1992	Miami, Fla.
Swann, Pedro	.083	13	12	3	1	0	0	0	1	1	6	0	0	.083	.154	L	R	6-0	190	10-27-70	1991	Townsend, Del.
Wells, Vernon	.275	159	608	87	167	34	4	23	100	27	85	9	4	.457	.305	R	R	6-1	220	12-8-78	1997	Arlington, Texas
Werth, Jayson	.261	15	46	4	12	2	1	0	6	6	11	1	0	.348	.340	R	R	6-5	210	5-20-79	1997	Chatham, Ill.
Wilson, Tom	.257	96	265	33	68	10	0	8	37	28	79	0	0	.385	.334	R	R	6-3	220	12-19-70	1991	Lake Havasu, Ariz.
Wise, Dewayne	.179	42	112	14	20	4	1	3	13	4	15	5	0	.313	.207	L	L	6-1	180	2-24-78	1997	Chapin, S.C.
Woodward, Chris	.276	90	312	48	86	13	4	13	45	26	72	3	0	.468	.330	R	R	6-0	180	6-27-76	1995	Chino, Calif.

PITCHING	W	L	ERA	G	GS	CG	SV	IP	H	R	ER	BB	SO	AVG	B	T	HT	WT	DOB	1st Yr	Resides
Borbon, Pedro	1	2	4.97	16	0	0	0	13	12	8	7	6	11	.230	L	L	6-1	230	11-15-67	1988	Houston, Texas
Bowles, Brian	2	1	4.05	17	0	0	0	20	13	11	9	14	19	.183	R	R	6-5	220	8-18-76	1995	Manhattan Beach, Calif.
Carpenter, Chris	4	5	5.28	13	13	1	0	73	89	45	43	27	45	.305	R	R	6-6	210	4-27-75	1994	Bedford, N.H.
Cassidy, Scott	1	4	5.73	58	0	0	0	66	52	42	42	32	48	.222	R	R	6-2	170	10-3-75	1998	Clay, N.Y.
Coco, Pasqual	0	1	18.00	2	0	0	0	1	4	2	2	3	0	.571	R	R	6-1	180	9-8-77	1995	Santo Domingo, D.R.
Cooper, Brian	0	1	14.04	2	2	0	0	8	14	13	13	4	3	.400	R	R	6-1	180	8-19-74	1995	Upland, Calif.
Escobar, Kelvim	5	7	4.27	76	0	0	38	78	75	39	37	44	85	.245	R	R	6-1	210	4-11-76	1992	Caracas, Venez.
Eyre, Scott	2	4	4.97	49	3	0	0	63	69	37	35	29	51	.278	L	L	6-1	200	5-30-72	1991	Bradenton, Fla.
File, Bob	0	1	18.90	5	0	0	0	3	8	7	7	2	2	.470	R	R	6-4	210	1-28-77	1998	Morrisville, Pa.
Halladay, Roy	19	7	2.93	34	34	2	0	239	223	93	78	62	168	.244	R	R	6-6	230	5-14-77	1995	Palm Harbor, Fla.
Hendrickson, Mark	3	0	2.45	16	4	0	0	37	25	11	10	12	21	.201	L	L	6-9	230	6-23-74	1998	Mt. Vernon, Wash.
Heredia, Felix	1	2	3.61	53	0	0	0	52	51	29	21	26	31	.257	L	L	6-0	180	6-18-75	1993	Miami, Fla.
Kershner, Jason	0	0	1.69	10	0	0	1	5	5	2	1	4	7	.227	L	L	6-2	160	12-19-76	1995	Scottsdale, Ariz.
Loaiza, Esteban	9	10	5.71	25	25	3	0	151	192	102	96	38	87	.309	R	R	6-3	210	12-31-71	1991	Southlake, Texas
Lyon, Brandon	1	4	6.53	15	10	0	0	62	78	47	45	19	30	.308	R	R	6-1	180	8-10-79	2000	Salt Lake City, Utah
Miller, Justin	9	5	5.54	25	18	0	0	102	103	70	63	66	68	.267	R	R	6-2	200	8-27-77	1997	Torrance, Calif.
Parris, Steve	5	5	5.97	14	14	0	0	75	96	50	50	35	48	.313	R	R	6-0	190	12-17-67	1989	Plainfield, Ill.
Plesac, Dan	1	2	3.38	19	0	0	0	13	11	5	5	6	14	.215	L	L	6-5	210	2-4-62	1983	Valparaiso, Ind.
Politte, Cliff	1	3	3.61	55	0	0	1	57	38	23	23	19	57	.186	R	R	5-11	180	2-27-74	1995	St. Louis, Mo.
Prokopec, Luke	2	9	6.78	22	12	0	0	72	90	57	54	25	41	.302	L	R	5-11	160	2-23-78	1994	Renmark, Australia
Smith, Mike	0	3	6.62	14	6	0	0	35	43	28	26	20	16	.300	R	R	5-11	190	9-19-77	2000	Westwood, Mass.
Thurman, Corey	2	3	4.37	43	1	0	0	68	65	34	33	45	56	.248	R	R	6-1	210	11-5-78	1996	Wake Village, Texas
Walker, Pete	10	5	4.33	37	20	0	1	139	143	72	67	51	80	.269	R	R	6-2	190	4-8-69	1990	Waterford, Conn.
Wiggins, Scott	0	0	3.38	3	0	0	0	3	5	1	1	1	3	.416	L	L	6-3	200	3-24-76	1997	Newport, Ky.

FIELDING

Catcher	PCT	G	PO	A	E	DP	PB
Cash	.968	7	26	4	1	1	2
Fletcher	.995	36	181	12	1	1	0
Huckaby	.989	88	494	31	6	10	13
Wilson	.988	65	318	20	4	4	3

First Base	PCT	G	PO	A	E	DP
Berg	.984	10	61	2	1	5
Delgado	.991	140	1232	95	12	121
Lesher	1.000	12	34	4	0	1
Phelps	1.000	2	9	0	0	1
Wilson	1.000	11	79	2	0	12
Woodward	1.000	3	9	0	0	1

Second Base	PCT	G	PO	A	E	DP
Berg	.966	52	71	126	7	34
Bush	.990	22	38	58	1	12
Hudson	.986	52	117	157	4	49
Lawrence	.967	49	73	131	7	20
Woodward	.917	6	8	14	2	4

Third Base	PCT	G	PO	A	E	DP
Berg	1.000	20	10	35	0	2
Hinske	.946	148	103	245	20	14
Lopez	1.000	2	2	1	0	0
Woodward	1.000	2	2	3	0	0

Shortstop	PCT	G	PO	A	E	DP
Berg	.960	13	23	25	2	8
Lopez	.975	79	112	200	8	51
Woodward	.965	79	131	231	13	63

Outfield	PCT	G	PO	A	E	DP
Berg	1.000	13	20	0	0	0
Cruz	.992	119	255	9	2	2
Lesher	1.000	5	11	0	0	0
Mondesi	.984	62	119	3	2	1
Stewart	.990	99	190	3	2	1
Swann	.000	1	0	0	0	0
Wells	.992	159	381	10	3	1
Werth	1.000	15	33	1	0	0
Wise	1.000	33	79	5	0	3

Carlos Delgado

Eric Hinske: Rookie of the Year tied for team lead with 38 doubles

Vernon Wells: fulfilled promise with 100-RBI season

FARM SYSTEM

Director, Player Development: Dick Scott.

Class	Farm Team	League	W	L	Pct.	Finish*	Manager	First Yr.
AAA	Syracuse (N.Y.) SkyChiefs	International	64	80	.444	10th (14)	Omar Malave	1978
AA	Tennessee Smokies	Southern	69	71	.493	6th (10)	Rocket Wheeler	1980
High A	Dunedin (Fla.) Blue Jays	Florida State	63	72	.467	9th (12)	Marty Pevey	1987
Low A	Charleston (W.Va.) Alley Cats	South Atlantic	61	79	.436	15th (16)	Paul Elliott	2001
SS A	Auburn (N.Y.) Doubledays	New York-Penn	47	29	.618	4th (14)	Dennis Holmberg	2001
Rookie	Medicine Hat (Alberta) Blue Jays	Pioneer	37	38	.493	5th (8)	Rolando Pino	1978

*Finish in overall standings (No. of teams in league)

SYRACUSE SKYCHIEFS   Class AAA

INTERNATIONAL LEAGUE

BATTING	AVG	G	AB	R	H	2B	3B	HR	RBI	BB	SO	SB	CS	SLG	OBP	B	T	HT	WT	DOB	1st Yr	Resides
Burnham, Gary	.281	134	537	70	151	34	1	17	88	53	69	1	2	.443	.363	L	L	5-11	200	10-13-74	1997	South Windsor, Conn.
Cash, Kevin	.220	67	236	27	52	18	0	10	26	25	72	0	1	.424	.299	R	R	6-0	180	12-6-77	1999	Lutz, Fla.
De los Santos, Eddy	.180	22	61	7	11	1	0	0	1	6	13	1	1	.197	.250	R	R	6-2	170	2-24-75	1996	Santo Domingo, D.R.
Fleming, Ryan	.132	16	53	6	7	2	0	0	2	3	3	1	0	.170	.175	L	L	5-11	180	2-11-76	1998	Ashville, Ohio
Hassey, Brad	.286	2	7	0	2	1	0	0	0	0	0	0	0	.429	.286	R	R	5-10	170	11-28-79	2002	Tucson, Ariz.
Huckaby, Ken	.272	21	81	7	22	2	0	0	9	2	15	0	2	.296	.286	R	R	6-1	200	1-27-71	1991	Philadelphia, Pa.
Hudson, Orlando	.305	100	417	63	127	27	3	10	37	35	54	8	5	.456	.363	S	R	6-0	180	12-12-77	1998	Darlington, S.C.
Johnson, Reed	.233	44	159	27	37	8	3	2	10	12	23	1	4	.358	.317	R	R	5-10	180	12-8-76	1999	Temecula, Calif.
Klimek, Josh	.262	118	424	50	111	28	1	8	59	40	69	1	2	.389	.325	L	R	6-1	170	2-2-74	1996	St. Louis, Mo.
Langaigne, Selwyn	.243	73	263	25	64	12	1	5	21	14	61	1	4	.354	.284	L	L	6-0	190	3-22-76	1994	Las Acaias, Venez.
Lawrence, Joe	.167	29	108	13	18	4	1	2	12	14	23	3	0	.278	.262	R	R	6-2	190	2-13-77	1996	Lake Charles, La.
Lesher, Brian	.262	66	248	34	65	13	1	7	28	20	55	6	1	.407	.315	R	L	6-5	210	3-5-71	1992	Scottsdale, Ariz.
Lopez, Felipe	.318	43	173	35	55	11	2	3	16	29	37	13	0	.457	.419	S	R	6-0	180	5-12-80	1998	Altmonte Springs, Fla.
Mottola, Chad	.261	122	476	77	124	35	1	13	67	51	87	12	2	.420	.333	R	R	6-3	220	10-15-71	1992	Casselberry, Fla.
Perez, Jerson	.241	58	203	28	49	7	1	4	15	14	50	2	2	.345	.294	R	R	5-10	180	1-20-76	1996	Lynn, Mass.
Phelps, Josh	.292	70	257	50	75	20	1	24	64	32	83	0	0	.658	.380	R	R	6-3	220	5-12-78	1996	Rathdrum, Idaho
Quiroz, Guillermo	.222	13	45	7	10	4	0	1	6	3	14	0	0	.378	.271	R	R	6-1	200	11-29-81	1999	Maracaibo, Venez.
Swann, Pedro	.277	97	368	52	102	17	4	14	62	37	77	1	3	.459	.353	L	R	6-0	190	10-27-70	1991	Townsend, Del.
Umbria, Jose	.375	5	16	5	6	0	0	0	2	1	4	0	0	.375	.412	R	R	6-2	210	1-20-78	1996	Barquisimeto, Venez.
Werth, Jayson	.257	127	443	65	114	25	2	18	82	67	125	24	7	.445	.354	R	R	6-5	210	5-20-79	1997	Chatham, Ill.
Williams, Glenn	.274	94	339	49	93	18	3	15	47	20	80	2	0	.478	.319	S	R	6-2	190	7-18-77	1994	Wattle Grove, Australia

PITCHING	W	L	ERA	G	GS	CG	SV	IP	H	R	ER	BB	SO	AVG	B	T	HT	WT	DOB	1st Yr	Resides
Abbott, David	0	0	2.84	2	0	0	0	6	9	3	2	0	2	.321	R	R	6-4	230	10-19-77	2000	Tucson, Ariz.
Baker, Chris	4	7	4.33	18	15	2	0	89	94	58	43	29	42	.266	R	R	6-1	200	8-24-77	1999	Valencia, Calif.

PITCHING	W	L	ERA	G	GS	CG	SV	IP	H	R	ER	BB	SO	AVG	B	T	HT	WT	DOB	1st Yr	Resides
Bowles, Brian	4	7	3.36	59	0	0	14	59	46	24	22	32	53	.215	R	R	6-5	220	8-18-76	1995	Manhattan Beach, Calif.
Carpenter, Chris	0	1	4.50	1	1	0	0	6	8	3	3	2	6	.320	R	R	6-6	210	4-27-75	1994	Bedford, N.H.
Casey, Joe	1	1	5.73	18	0	0	1	22	25	14	14	14	8	.297	R	R	6-0	190	1-25-79	1997	Honeybrook, Pa.
Cassidy, Scott	1	0	4.00	3	2	0	0	9	8	4	4	0	4	.242	R	R	6-2	170	10-3-75	1998	Clay, N.Y.
Castellanos, Hugo	0	1	6.35	5	0	0	0	6	3	4	4	2	2	.166	R	R	6-4	200	6-30-80	1996	Nuevo Laredo, Mexico
Chulk, Vinny	1	0	5.79	2	1	0	0	5	6	6	3	6	2	.315	R	R	6-2	180	12-19-78	2000	Miami, Fla.
Coco, Pasqual	4	9	4.98	30	23	1	0	141	145	91	78	57	98	.266	R	R	6-1	180	9-8-77	1995	Santo Domingo, D.R.
Comolli, Mark	0	0	18.00	1	0	0	0	1	3	2	2	1	1	.500	R	R	6-0	190	3-11-79	2001	Millville, Del.
Cooper, Brian	9	9	5.09	27	25	1	0	156	176	98	88	46	71	.288	R	R	6-1	180	8-19-74	1995	Upland, Calif.
Crabtree, Robbie	3	4	4.91	32	0	0	2	51	43	30	28	22	41	.228	R	R	6-1	170	11-25-72	1996	Bakersfield, Calif.
Cumberland, Chris	0	4	3.22	28	0	0	0	36	34	17	13	19	20	.251	R	L	6-1	180	1-15-73	1993	Mandeville, La.
Espina, Rendy	1	0	8.69	27	0	0	0	29	38	31	28	21	27	.306	L	L	6-0	180	5-11-78	1995	Cabimas, Venez.
File, Bob	0	0	5.94	33	0	0	2	36	39	29	24	15	23	.268	R	R	6-4	210	1-28-77	1998	Morrisville, Pa.
Gassner, Dave	1	1	5.40	1	1	0	0	5	7	3	3	2	1	.333	R	L	6-2	190	12-14-78	2001	Hortonville, Wis.
Hamann, Rob	0	0	4.96	7	2	0	0	16	20	12	9	4	6	.312	R	R	6-7	210	12-15-76	1999	Escondido, Calif.
Hendrickson, Mark	7	5	3.52	19	14	0	0	92	90	38	36	22	68	.254	L	L	6-9	230	6-23-74	1998	Mt. Vernon, Wash.
Kingrey, Jarrod	4	1	4.79	26	0	0	1	41	32	23	22	20	28	.213	R	R	6-1	200	8-23-76	1998	Forston, Ga.
Loaiza, Esteban	0	0	2.08	1	1	0	0	4	4	1	1	0	4	.222	R	R	6-3	210	12-31-71	1991	Southlake, Texas
Lyon, Brandon	4	9	5.11	14	14	0	0	76	99	54	43	19	35	.315	R	R	6-1	180	8-10-79	2000	Salt Lake City, Utah
McClellan, Matt	3	2	5.40	12	1	0	0	18	23	11	11	9	20	.306	R	R	6-7	220	8-13-76	1997	Toledo, Ohio
Miller, Justin	3	2	1.61	8	8	0	0	45	34	11	8	16	29	.207	R	R	6-2	200	8-27-77	1997	Torrance, Calif.
Parris, Steve	1	1	1.29	2	2	0	0	14	10	6	2	2	5	.192	R	R	6-0	190	12-17-67	1989	Plainfield, Ill.
Payne, Jerrod	0	0	3.24	6	0	0	0	8	8	3	3	3	7	.222	R	R	5-10	190	8-27-77	2000	Ocala, Fla.
Prokopec, Luke	0	0	0.00	2	0	0	0	2	0	0	0	0	2	.000	L	R	5-11	160	2-23-78	1994	Renmark, Australia
Ratliff, Jon	2	3	3.86	27	0	0	1	37	43	21	16	22	19	.298	R	R	6-5	200	12-22-71	1993	Pittsford, N.Y.
Reimers, Cameron	2	3	4.99	12	10	0	0	49	68	39	27	11	17	.323	R	R	6-5	200	9-15-78	1999	Missoula, Mont.
Ricketts, Chad	1	1	3.24	15	0	0	2	17	15	7	6	7	19	.227	R	R	6-5	250	2-12-75	1995	Thorold, Ontario
Sandoval, Marcos	0	0	0.00	1	0	0	0	1	2	0	0	0	0	.500	R	R	6-1	180	12-29-80	1997	Carabobo, Venez.
Smith, Mike	8	4	3.48	20	20	1	0	122	106	51	47	43	76	.233	R	R	5-11	190	9-19-77	2000	Westwood, Mass.
Valdez, Santo	2	8	8.66	5	4	0	0	18	29	20	17	7	12	.362	R	R	6-1	170	3-30-82	1999	Bani, D.R.
Wiggins, Scott	2	0	2.57	12	0	0	0	14	11	6	4	7	14	.220	L	L	6-3	200	3-24-76	1997	Newport, Ky.
Winchester, Scott	0	2	5.87	23	0	0	1	31	41	23	20	9	19	.315	R	R	6-2	210	4-20-73	1995	Midland, Mich.
2-team (21 Ottawa)	2	4	5.94	44	0	0	2	64	74	47	42	20	41	.285							

FIELDING

Catcher	PCT	G	PO	A	E	DP	PB
Cash	.989	57	315	37	4	6	6
Huckaby	.979	19	134	6	3	2	3
Phelps	.986	34	197	8	3	1	7
Quiroz	.956	9	43	0	2	0	2
Umbria	1.000	5	19	0	0	0	1
Werth	.991	23	105	4	1	1	6

First Base	PCT	G	PO	A	E	DP
Burnham	.992	125	1131	91	10	111
Huckaby	1.000	2	14	3	0	2
Lesher	.990	11	88	7	1	10
Phelps	.984	6	60	1	1	6

Second Base	PCT	G	PO	A	E	DP
Hassey	1.000	2	5	7	0	2
Hudson	.982	98	225	312	10	69
Lawrence	.944	28	45	91	8	23
Perez	.985	7	26	39	1	12
Williams	.980	12	20	28	1	4

Third Base	PCT	G	PO	A	E	DP
Klimek	.932	101	86	201	21	24
Williams	.910	43	23	88	11	6

Shortstop	PCT	G	PO	A	E	DP
De Los Santos	.969	22	33	62	3	13

	PCT	G	PO	A	E	DP
Lopez	.934	43	80	148	16	42
Perez	.968	46	53	131	6	23
Williams	.944	38	40	111	9	22

Outfield	PCT	G	PO	A	E	DP
Fleming	.976	13	40	0	1	0
Johnson	.991	44	111	3	1	1
Langaigne	.968	71	176	7	6	1
Lesher	.955	34	62	2	3	0
Mottola	.946	94	202	8	12	0
Swann	.994	78	151	6	1	0
Werth	.981	102	207	4	4	0

TENNESSEE SMOKIES — Class AA

SOUTHERN LEAGUE

BATTING	AVG	G	AB	R	H	2B	3B	HR	RBI	BB	SO	SB	CS	SLG	OBP	B	T	HT	WT	DOB	1st Yr	Resides
Alvarez, Jimmy	.278	133	497	83	138	32	3	8	69	79	121	20	11	.402	.383	S	R	5-10	160	10-4-79	1996	Santo Domingo, D.R.
Cash, Kevin	.277	55	213	38	59	15	1	8	44	36	44	5	2	.469	.381	R	R	6-0	180	12-6-77	1999	Lutz, Fla.
Chiaffredo, Paul	.194	83	258	38	50	7	2	11	38	13	81	4	0	.364	.253	R	R	6-2	200	5-30-76	1997	Campbell, Calif.
Deschaine, Jim	.225	118	405	59	91	13	0	16	66	51	85	3	3	.375	.313	R	R	6-0	200	9-18-77	1999	Bristol, Conn.
Fagan, Shawn	.268	127	421	71	113	24	0	12	69	102	87	6	3	.411	.411	R	R	5-11	200	3-2-78	2000	Levittown, N.Y.
Fleming, Ryan	.294	62	245	36	72	14	0	4	37	27	26	3	5	.400	.365	L	L	5-11	180	2-11-76	1998	Ashville, Ohio
Gross, Gabe	.238	112	403	57	96	17	5	10	54	53	71	8	2	.380	.333	L	R	6-3	200	10-21-79	2001	Dothan, Ala.
Haltiwanger, Garrick	.218	44	133	21	29	8	1	3	19	18	39	8	2	.361	.312	R	R	6-1	190	3-3-75	1996	Irmo, S.C.
Iorg, Isaac	.200	27	80	12	16	2	1	1	10	9	19	2	1	.288	.289	R	R	6-1	190	6-7-79	2001	Knoxville, Tenn.
James, Kenny	.235	13	34	7	8	0	0	0	2	6	7	2	0	.235	.366	S	R	6-0	190	10-9-76	1995	Ocala, Fla.
Langaigne, Selwyn	.143	6	14	1	2	0	0	0	2	3	5	0	0	.143	.294	L	L	6-0	190	3-22-76	1994	Las Acaias, Venez.
Logan, Matt	.243	104	345	45	84	26	0	3	49	35	63	8	1	.345	.313	L	R	6-3	210	7-22-79	1997	Brampton, Ontario
Martinez, Casey	.500	2	6	3	3	1	0	1	4	0	0	0	0	1.167	.571	R	R	5-11	200	8-31-77	2000	Clearwater, Fla.
Rich, Dominic	.273	38	132	14	36	4	1	1	14	18	23	2	4	.341	.364	L	R	5-10	190	8-22-79	2000	Herndon, Pa.
Rouse, Michael	.260	71	231	35	60	11	0	9	43	29	47	7	6	.424	.342	R	R	5-11	180	4-25-80	2001	San Jose, Calif.
Singleton, Justin	.221	25	77	7	17	1	1	1	10	6	27	0	0	.299	.277	L	R	6-1	190	4-10-79	2001	Sparks, Md.
Solano, Danny	.237	90	249	39	59	11	3	4	37	46	51	7	3	.353	.358	R	R	5-9	150	12-3-75	1997	Santo Domingo, D.R.
Thompson, Rich	.280	135	554	109	155	13	4	2	44	50	86	45	13	.329	.361	L	R	6-3	180	4-23-79	2000	Montrose, Pa.
Umbria, Jose	.210	37	100	5	21	3	0	0	7	7	25	1	1	.240	.275	R	R	6-2	190	1-20-78	1996	Barquisimeto, Venez.
Wise, Dewayne	.297	86	340	59	101	21	4	10	49	29	49	15	8	.471	.350	L	L	6-1	190	2-24-78	1997	Chapin, S.C.

PITCHING	W	L	ERA	G	GS	CG	SV	IP	H	R	ER	BB	SO	AVG	B	T	HT	WT	DOB	1st Yr	Resides
Bauer, Peter	6	13	4.42	28	28	3	0	177	208	103	87	53	93	.295	L	R	6-7	250	11-6-78	2000	Hagerstown, Md.
Carpenter, Chris	0	1	8.20	5	5	0	0	19	26	18	17	8	9	.337	R	R	6-6	210	4-27-75	1994	Bedford, N.H.
Casey, Joe	0	0	6.75	11	0	0	0	13	17	15	10	14	4	.309	R	R	6-0	190	1-25-79	1997	Honeybrook, Pa.
Castellanos, Hugo	3	4	5.23	47	0	0	18	52	46	30	30	28	34	.240	R	R	6-4	200	6-30-80	1996	Nuevo Laredo, Mexico
Chacin, Gustavo	6	5	4.66	35	13	1	1	120	131	73	62	59	68	.282	L	L	5-11	190	12-4-80	1998	Maracaibo, Venez.
Chulk, Vinny	13	5	2.96	25	24	0	1	152	133	55	50	53	108	.236	R	R	6-2	180	12-19-78	2000	Miami, Fla.
Cumberland, Chris	0	1	7.71	9	0	0	1	9	17	8	8	4	5	.386	R	L	6-1	180	1-15-73	1993	Mandeville, La.
Gassner, Dave	1	2	2.49	4	4	0	0	25	22	8	7	7	14	.231	R	L	6-2	190	12-14-78	2001	Hortonville, Wis.

PITCHING	W	L	ERA	G	GS	CG	SV	IP	H	R	ER	BB	SO	AVG	B	T	HT	WT	DOB	1st Yr	Resides
Gracesqui, Frank	4	2	4.64	41	0	0	1	43	40	26	22	34	48	.258	S	L	6-5	210	8-20-79	1998	New York, N.Y.
Hamann, Rob	0	0	2.41	12	0	0	1	19	21	8	5	7	7	.287	R	R	6-7	210	12-15-76	1999	Escondido, Calif.
Kegley, Chuck	1	3	7.88	15	0	0	1	16	18	16	14	15	7	.295	R	R	6-3	200	12-17-79	1999	Orange Park, Fla.
Loaiza, Esteban	2	0	1.88	2	2	0	0	14	10	3	3	1	13	.208	R	R	6-3	210	12-31-71	1991	Southlake, Texas
Markwell, Diegomar	13	9	4.38	28	27	2	1	168	174	95	82	60	101	.267	L	L	6-2	190	8-8-80	1996	Willemstad, Curacao
Orloski, Joe	6	5	5.25	54	0	0	4	60	70	41	35	29	45	.289	R	R	6-3	180	5-17-79	1998	Las Vegas, Nev.
Ozuna, Francisco	2	2	4.63	44	0	0	0	70	73	42	36	19	35	.273	L	L	6-2	180	5-17-81	1997	Santo Domingo, D.R.
Parris, Steve	0	0	3.00	1	1	0	0	6	7	2	2	2	5	.269	R	R	6-0	190	12-17-67	1989	Plainfield, Ill.
Payne, Jerrod	2	0	3.95	21	0	0	0	27	21	16	12	12	12	.207	R	R	5-10	190	8-27-77	2000	Ocala, Fla.
Reimers, Cameron	3	6	5.59	13	11	1	0	68	99	48	42	19	32	.349	R	R	6-5	200	9-15-78	1999	Missoula, Mont.
Spille, Ryan	7	12	5.19	27	25	2	0	160	188	105	92	53	97	.294	L	L	6-3	180	11-11-76	1999	Cincinnati, Ohio
Wiggins, Scott	0	1	0.93	16	0	0	1	19	18	3	2	5	19	.250	L	L	6-3	200	3-24-76	1997	Newport, Ky.

FIELDING

Catcher	PCT	G	PO	A	E	DP	PB
Cash	.987	42	196	31	3	2	7
Chiaffredo	.984	72	386	37	7	5	9
Fagan	1.000	1	5	2	0	0	0
Martinez	.875	1	7	0	1	0	0
Umbria	.978	35	199	19	5	3	3

First Base	PCT	G	PO	A	E	DP
Chiaffredo	1.000	6	47	4	0	2
Deschaine	.000	1	0	0	0	0
Fagan	.982	49	405	29	8	41
Logan	.985	100	865	64	14	89
Umbria	1.000	1	1	0	0	0

Second Base	PCT	G	PO	A	E	DP
Alvarez	.968	112	243	333	19	76

	PCT	G	PO	A	E	DP
Deschaine	.000	1	0	0	0	0
Iorg	.962	12	23	27	2	5
Rich	.920	19	41	51	8	10
Solano	.941	5	6	10	1	1

Third Base	PCT	G	PO	A	E	DP
Cash	.833	1	4	1	1	0
Deschaine	.908	77	47	171	22	10
Fagan	.940	47	28	112	9	16
Iorg	.860	14	7	30	6	3
Logan	1.000	2	0	1	0	0
Solano	.970	16	7	25	1	4

Shortstop	PCT	G	PO	A	E	DP
Deschaine	.936	23	45	72	8	15
Rouse	.944	66	90	197	17	40
Solano	.972	62	103	214	9	43

Outfield	PCT	G	PO	A	E	DP
Deschaine	1.000	3	3	0	0	0
Fagan	.800	3	4	0	1	0
Fleming	.982	59	106	4	2	1
Gross	.991	102	205	14	2	0
Haltiwanger	.943	19	33	0	2	0
James	1.000	11	31	0	0	0
Langaigne	1.000	5	4	0	0	0
Singleton	1.000	24	57	4	0	1
Solano	.500	2	1	0	1	0
Thompson	.992	128	248	9	2	0
Wise	.981	80	196	11	4	2

DUNEDIN BLUE JAYS — High Class A

FLORIDA STATE LEAGUE

BATTING	AVG	G	AB	R	H	2B	3B	HR	RBI	BB	SO	SB	CS	SLG	OBP	B	T	HT	WT	DOB	1st Yr	Resides
Adams, Russ	.231	37	147	23	34	4	2	1	12	18	17	5	2	.306	.321	L	R	6-1	180	8-30-80	2002	Laurinburg, N.C.
Bernhardt, Joe	.235	99	357	38	84	20	1	11	47	27	88	0	3	.389	.293	R	R	6-1	180	9-22-80	1996	San Pedro de Macoris, D.R.
Brosseau, Richard	.188	36	64	13	12	2	0	0	5	15	12	0	0	.219	.350	L	R	5-11	180	9-22-78	2000	Minneapolis, Minn.
Carter, Shannon	.278	123	424	66	118	18	1	5	35	29	68	18	9	.361	.334	L	L	6-0	180	3-23-79	1997	El Reno, Okla.
Davenport, Ron	.227	79	264	26	60	15	3	2	21	18	42	5	4	.330	.282	L	R	6-2	170	2-24-78	1996	Santo Domingo, D.R.
De los Santos, Eddy	.300	3	10	2	3	0	0	0	4	1	2	0	0	.300	.364	R	R	5-11	180	9-19-83	2001	Monte Plata, D.R.
Diaz, Robinzon	.120	10	25	3	3	0	0	0	1	1	4	0	0	.120	.148	R	R	5-11	180	9-19-83	2001	Monte Plata, D.R.
Iorg, Isaac	.250	23	80	8	20	5	0	0	7	5	20	0	0	.313	.302	R	R	6-1	190	6-7-79	2001	Knoxville, Tenn.
Jimenez, Rich	.167	4	12	1	2	0	0	0	2	1	3	0	0	.167	.286	S	R	6-1	170	7-3-80	1997	Santo Domingo, D.R.
Johnson, Jeremy	.303	12	33	4	10	3	0	0	4	3	9	0	0	.394	.378	L	L	6-1	180	5-6-78	2000	Tamms, Ill.
Johnson, Reed	.273	8	33	7	9	3	0	0	6	3	3	0	0	.364	.368	R	R	5-10	180	12-8-76	1999	Temecula, Calif.
Keene, Kurt	.261	108	379	46	99	17	1	1	37	39	39	6	2	.319	.330	R	R	6-0	190	8-22-77	2000	Chattanooga, Tenn.
Martinez, Casey	.083	7	12	1	1	0	0	0	0	2	3	0	0	.083	.267	R	R	5-11	200	8-31-77	2000	Clearwater, Fla.
McEachran, Aaron	.254	90	283	27	72	17	1	0	31	30	58	2	0	.322	.330	L	R	6-0	200	1-28-79	2001	St. Louis Park, Minn.
Perry, Jason	.289	13	45	7	13	3	0	1	5	5	11	0	0	.422	.389	L	R	6-1	190	8-18-80	2002	Jonesboro, Ga.
Pond, Simon	.284	103	401	58	114	25	7	13	88	46	73	2	3	.479	.357	L	R	6-1	190	10-27-76	1994	North Vancouver, B.C.
Quiroz, Guillermo	.260	111	411	50	107	28	1	12	68	35	91	1	0	.421	.330	R	R	6-1	200	11-29-81	1999	Maracaibo, Venez.
Rich, Dominic	.345	95	377	72	130	14	5	8	50	57	49	8	6	.472	.437	L	R	5-10	190	8-22-79	2000	Herndon, Pa.
Rios, Alexis	.305	111	456	60	139	22	8	3	61	27	55	14	6	.408	.344	R	R	6-5	180	2-18-81	1999	Guaynabo, P.R.
Singleton, Justin	.271	101	354	54	96	17	7	3	38	42	91	9	5	.384	.312	R	L	6-1	190	4-10-79	2001	Sparks, Md.
Sisk, Aaron	.222	78	239	32	53	13	3	5	23	36	57	0	3	.364	.327	R	R	6-0	180	9-17-78	2000	Fort Worth, Texas
Tempesta, Nick	.186	18	59	7	11	4	0	0	3	10	10	0	2	.254	.258	R	R	5-10	180	11-20-78	2001	Brockton, Mass.
Umbria, Jose	.388	17	49	3	19	1	0	0	8	9	8	0	1	.408	.483	R	R	6-2	210	1-20-78	1996	Barquisimeto, Venez.
Woodward, Chris	.333	2	6	1	2	0	0	0	0	0	0	0	0	.333	.429	R	R	6-0	180	6-27-76	1995	Chino, Calif.
Zieour, Neesan	.225	57	178	23	40	8	0	0	15	16	29	2	1	.270	.298	R	R	5-11	180	11-2-80	2001	Rocklin, Calif.

PITCHING	W	L	ERA	G	GS	CG	SV	IP	H	R	ER	BB	SO	AVG	B	T	HT	WT	DOB	1st Yr	Resides
Abbott, David	6	5	4.13	17	16	1	0	105	114	54	48	32	49	.280	R	R	6-4	230	10-19-77	2000	Tucson, Ariz.
Bush, David	0	1	2.03	7	0	0	0	13	10	3	3	2	9	.222	R	R	6-2	190	11-9-79	2002	Devon, Pa.
Colson, Jason	2	8	5.44	20	14	0	0	83	83	64	50	53	55	.259	L	R	6-2	220	11-19-78	2001	Weirton, W.Va.
Costello, Ryan	3	5	6.44	26	10	0	1	80	98	63	57	51	63	.307	R	L	6-6	210	7-13-79	2001	Marlton, N.J.
Dean, Aaron	3	7	5.42	28	15	0	1	100	118	63	60	44	82	.291	R	R	6-4	210	4-9-79	1999	Pleasanton, Calif.
File, Bob	0	2	11.12	4	3	0	0	6	13	9	7	3	1	.448	R	R	6-4	210	1-28-77	1998	Morrisville, Pa.
Ford, Matt	9	5	2.37	21	18	0	0	114	100	43	30	42	85	.239	S	L	6-1	170	4-8-81	1999	Tamarac, Fla.
Gassner, Dave	11	6	3.44	23	21	2	0	147	143	64	56	26	104	.254	R	L	6-2	190	12-14-78	2001	Hortonville, Wis.
Glen, William	8	5	4.21	41	5	0	4	94	85	47	44	51	85	.238	R	R	6-1	180	10-30-77	2001	Plainfield, Ind.
Gracesqui, Frank	2	1	2.49	10	0	0	1	22	15	8	6	11	25	.192	S	L	6-5	210	8-20-79	1998	New York, N.Y.
Hamann, Rob	4	5	4.23	23	7	0	0	72	78	44	34	24	37	.272	R	R	6-7	210	12-15-76	1999	Escondido, Calif.
Hecker, Steven	5	0	5.45	19	0	0	0	35	40	25	21	18	21	.283	R	R	6-3	200	11-22-78	2001	Buffalo Grove, Ill.
Hubbel, Travis	0	3	9.47	13	2	0	0	19	13	24	20	29	14	.196	R	R	6-0	190	6-27-79	1998	Welland, Ontario
Loaiza, Esteban	0	0	0.00	2	2	0	0	5	2	0	0	2	2	.125	R	R	6-3	210	12-31-71	1991	Southlake, Texas
Mowday, Chris	1	1	4.32	10	0	0	0	17	17	9	8	10	17	.269	R	R	6-4	210	8-24-81	1997	Strathpine, Australia
Nunley, Derrek	0	3	4.81	39	0	0	0	58	51	37	31	38	51	.230	R	R	6-1	180	9-13-80	1999	Jacksonville, Fla.
Ogilvie, John	5	4	4.01	45	0	0	26	52	50	27	23	31	37	.261	R	R	6-6	220	6-3-78	2001	Mississauga, Ontario
Parris, Steve	0	1	4.41	3	3	0	0	16	19	10	8	1	8	.292	R	R	6-0	190	12-17-67	1989	Plainfield, Ill.
Quick, Ben	1	6	4.91	32	1	0	0	95	114	63	52	31	79	.291	R	R	6-2	180	3-8-79	2001	San Jacinto, Calif.
Rosario, Francisco	3	3	1.29	13	12	0	0	63	33	10	9	25	65	.151	R	R	6-1	180	9-28-80	1999	Del Yuma, D.R.
Sandoval, Marcos	0	1	4.50	3	0	0	0	8	8	4	4	3	4	.266	R	R	6-1	180	12-29-80	1997	Carabobo, Venez.

FIELDING

Catcher	PCT	G	PO	A	E	DP	PB
Diaz	.981	7	46	6	1	0	2
Martinez	1.000	6	24	6	0	0	1
McEachran	.968	25	145	8	5	0	7
Quiroz	.984	93	607	54	11	2	15
Tempesta	.000	1	0	0	0	0	0
Umbria	1.000	13	88	12	0	0	1

First Base	PCT	G	PO	A	E	DP
Bernhardt	.981	84	639	50	13	72
McEachran	.974	29	212	9	6	23
Perry	1.000	6	42	4	0	2
Pond	.996	27	229	17	1	23
Sisk	1.000	2	2	0	0	0

Second Base	PCT	G	PO	A	E	DP
Brosseau	1.000	4	10	9	0	1
Iorg	.971	9	13	20	1	5

	PCT	G	PO	A	E	DP
Keene	.986	29	70	70	2	9
Rich	.977	93	241	277	12	73
Sisk	.950	4	10	9	1	3
Tempesta	1.000	4	4	4	0	1

Third Base	PCT	G	PO	A	E	DP
Bernhardt	1.000	1	0	1	0	0
Brosseau	.906	14	10	19	3	2
Iorg	.933	7	1	13	1	3
Keene	.867	3	5	8	2	2
Pond	.941	67	49	128	11	12
Sisk	.886	45	33	68	13	7
Tempesta	.964	14	7	20	1	0

Shortstop	PCT	G	PO	A	E	DP
Adams	.947	37	55	106	9	16
Brosseau	.957	8	8	14	1	4
De Los Santos	1.000	3	6	10	0	2

	PCT	G	PO	A	E	DP
Keene	.953	76	109	235	17	57
Sisk	.964	18	31	49	3	10
Woodward	1.000	2	1	7	0	1

Outfield	PCT	G	PO	A	E	DP
Brosseau	.000	1	0	0	0	0
Carter	.964	115	209	7	8	0
Davenport	.969	54	91	2	3	0
Jimenez	1.000	2	3	2	0	1
R. Johnson	1.000	8	16	3	0	0
Perry	1.000	3	7	0	0	0
Rios	.967	110	233	2	8	1
Singleton	.986	101	212	4	3	0
Sisk	.947	11	16	2	1	0
Tempesta	1.000	1	1	0	0	0
Zieour	.965	38	55	0	2	0

CHARLESTON ALLEY CATS — Low Class A

SOUTH ATLANTIC LEAGUE

BATTING	AVG	G	AB	R	H	2B	3B	HR	RBI	BB	SO	SB	CS	SLG	OBP	B	T	HT	WT	DOB	1st Yr	Resides
Cosby, Rob	.294	109	419	52	123	20	3	5	59	28	55	2	2	.391	.333	R	R	6-2	200	4-2-81	1999	Rio Piedras, P.R.
Delfino, Lee	.223	113	367	59	82	24	2	3	46	62	76	9	1	.324	.339	R	R	6-0	180	5-21-80	2001	Richmond Hill, Ontario
Durazo, Ernie	.160	15	50	5	8	0	0	0	2	4	21	0	1	.160	.222	L	R	5-9	200	12-6-78	2001	Tucson, Ariz.
Godwin, Tyrell	.281	48	185	31	52	8	5	0	16	20	23	10	2	.378	.364	L	R	6-0	200	7-10-79	2001	Council, N.C.
Jimenez, Rich	.182	15	44	1	8	1	0	0	2	5	15	3	1	.205	.255	S	R	6-1	170	7-3-80	1997	Santo Domingo, D.R.
Johnson, Jeremy	.191	28	89	10	17	4	1	2	14	11	22	0	1	.326	.295	L	L	6-1	180	5-6-78	2000	Tamms, Ill.
Jova, Maikel	.290	118	448	43	130	20	5	5	53	7	70	5	2	.391	.302	R	R	6-0	190	3-5-81	1999	San Jose, Costa Rica
Martinez, Casey	.326	29	92	9	30	3	0	0	13	10	23	0	0	.359	.396	R	R	5-11	200	8-31-77	2000	Clearwater, Fla.
Mayorson, Manuel	.274	133	508	72	139	19	1	0	45	31	29	28	15	.315	.316	R	R	5-10	160	3-10-83	1999	La Romana, D.R.
Medina, Rodney	.286	97	339	52	97	12	7	3	36	33	44	11	10	.389	.354	S	R	6-1	180	10-17-81	1999	Maracaibo, Venez.
Negron, Miguel	.255	118	420	56	107	15	2	5	41	35	77	20	7	.336	.312	L	L	6-2	170	8-22-82	2000	Caguas, P.R.
Snyder, Mike	.286	136	518	67	148	21	4	16	87	76	107	5	2	.434	.378	L	R	6-5	230	2-11-81	1999	Chino Hills, Calif.
Tablado, Raul	.222	103	361	38	80	23	0	2	29	21	98	2	1	.302	.268	R	R	6-2	170	3-3-82	2000	Miami, Fla.
Tempesta, Nick	.280	57	200	29	56	15	1	1	27	12	28	1	4	.380	.336	R	R	5-10	180	11-20-78	2001	Brockton, Mass.
Whittaker, Tim	.308	78	273	31	84	22	1	4	31	25	51	1	1	.440	.373	R	R	6-0	200	1-4-79	2001	Conway, S.C.
Yepez, Jose	.251	76	263	34	66	11	0	5	37	24	31	4	2	.350	.327	R	R	6-0	170	6-19-81	1997	Lara, Venez.
Zieour, Neesan	.303	48	175	32	53	13	3	0	20	22	27	7	6	.411	.408	R	R	5-11	180	11-2-80	2001	Rocklin, Calif.

PITCHING	W	L	ERA	G	GS	CG	SV	IP	H	R	ER	BB	SO	AVG	B	T	HT	WT	DOB	1st Yr	Resides
Chadwick, John	1	5	5.54	19	2	0	1	52	47	35	32	41	38	.250	L	R	6-4	220	5-3-78	2000	Brampton, Ontario
Comolli, Mark	3	3	4.86	15	1	0	2	37	43	25	20	9	36	.288	R	R	6-0	190	3-11-79	2001	Millville, Del.
Esarey, Brad	3	3	5.14	40	0	0	2	49	58	31	28	20	39	.290	L	L	6-3	170	9-20-78	2001	Concord, N.C.
Flores, Neomar	8	10	3.28	27	27	1	0	159	134	65	58	42	120	.226	R	R	6-2	180	3-12-82	1998	Guarenas, Venez.
Fuller, Brendan	3	5	4.24	38	0	0	4	70	59	39	33	51	62	.232	R	R	6-1	200	9-13-80	2001	Clearwater, Fla.
Harper, Jesse	6	5	2.16	21	14	0	1	113	98	38	27	25	97	.235	R	R	6-4	200	11-11-80	2000	Clute, Texas
Hecker, Steven	1	3	3.12	19	0	0	2	40	38	17	14	12	28	.255	R	R	6-3	200	11-22-78	2001	Buffalo Grove, Ill.
Houston, Ryan	2	4	4.25	7	5	0	0	30	31	15	14	9	24	.271	R	R	6-4	190	9-22-79	1999	Pensacola, Fla.
McGowan, Dustin	11	10	4.19	28	28	1	0	148	143	77	69	59	163	.250	R	R	6-3	190	3-24-82	2000	Ludowici, Ga.
Mowday, Chris	2	1	2.67	27	4	0	1	71	51	30	21	25	88	.200	R	R	6-4	210	8-24-81	1997	Strathpine, Australia
Ramirez, Ismael	0	1	4.86	6	1	0	0	17	20	10	9	7	14	.289	R	R	6-2	170	3-3-81	1998	Anzoategui, Venez.
Romero, Felix	0	7	3.98	37	0	0	10	41	46	28	18	13	35	.277	R	R	6-2	160	6-18-80	1997	San Pedro de Macoris, D.R.
Rosario, Francisco	6	1	2.57	13	13	1	0	67	50	22	19	14	78	.205	R	R	6-0	160	9-28-80	1999	Del Yuma, D.R.
Sheffield, Chris	0	0	54.00	3	0	0	0	1	0	4	4	9	2	.000	R	R	6-3	210	12-13-79	2001	Richmond, Texas
Spillman, Jeromie	2	4	4.24	8	0	0	0	17	17	10	8	12	10	.265	L	L	5-11	180	9-24-78	2000	Peoria, Ariz.
Stephenson, Eric	6	12	4.32	23	23	0	0	127	143	80	61	56	70	.290	R	L	6-4	180	9-3-82	2000	Benson, N.C.
Thorpe, Tracy	5	7	4.18	20	19	1	0	103	96	55	48	31	70	.242	R	R	6-4	250	12-15-80	2000	Melbourne, Fla.
Valdez, Santo	5	2	2.95	29	3	0	3	76	67	28	25	20	80	.234	R	R	6-1	170	3-30-82	1999	Bani, D.R.

FIELDING

Catcher	PCT	G	PO	A	E	DP	PB
Martinez	1.000	9	90	9	0	1	4
Whittaker	.988	60	475	35	6	3	4
Yepez	.986	73	540	40	8	3	14

First Base	PCT	G	PO	A	E	DP
Cosby	1.000	5	33	5	0	2
Durazo	.987	8	68	6	1	7
Snyder	.989	127	1003	91	12	82

Second Base	PCT	G	PO	A	E	DP
Delfino	.956	112	189	310	23	61

	PCT	G	PO	A	E	DP
Mayorson	1.000	9	10	16	0	2
Tempesta	.963	27	43	61	4	7

Third Base	PCT	G	PO	A	E	DP
Cosby	.878	44	31	70	14	6
Tablado	.912	74	41	114	15	9
Tempesta	.949	30	22	52	4	6

Shortstop	PCT	G	PO	A	E	DP
Mayorson	.954	125	212	303	25	62
Tablado	.916	21	33	43	7	10

Outfield	PCT	G	PO	A	E	DP
Cosby	.981	43	49	4	1	0
Godwin	.980	47	95	1	2	0
Jimenez	.939	15	30	1	2	0
Johnson	.778	4	7	0	2	0
Jova	.991	116	210	9	2	0
Medina	.966	49	80	5	3	0
Negron	.991	118	212	19	2	4
Tablado	1.000	1	2	3	0	0
Zieour	.978	47	87	3	2	0

AUBURN DOUBLEDAYS — Short-Season A

NEW YORK-PENN LEAGUE

BATTING	AVG	G	AB	R	H	2B	3B	HR	RBI	BB	SO	SB	CS	SLG	OBP	B	T	HT	WT	DOB	1st Yr	Resides
Adams, Russ	.354	30	113	25	40	7	3	0	16	24	11	13	1	.469	.464	L	R	6-1	180	8-30-80	2002	Laurinburg, N.C.
Arnold, Eric	.158	11	19	1	3	0	0	0	1	2	5	0	1	.158	.304	R	R	6-1	190	7-9-80	2002	La Porte, Texas
Blackburn, Alex	.182	22	55	7	10	2	0	0	3	7	9	0	0	.218	.294	R	R	6-1	200	12-30-82	2000	London, Ontario
Dragicevich, Scott	.167	3	12	1	2	0	0	0	0	0	1	0	0	.167	.231	R	R	6-3	200	6-28-80	2002	Westlake, Calif.
Durazo, Ernie	.295	62	200	22	59	14	2	2	31	21	37	0	0	.415	.362	L	R	5-9	200	12-6-78	2001	Tucson, Ariz.

BATTING	AVG	G	AB	R	H	2B	3B	HR	RBI	BB	SO	SB	CS	SLG	OBP	B	T	HT	WT	DOB	1st Yr	Resides
German, Cesar	.194	44	139	21	27	7	0	1	19	16	36	7	0	.266	.296	R	R	6-0	160	6-21-79	1998	San Pedro de Macoris, D.R.
Hassey, Brad	.255	67	251	41	64	20	1	2	25	21	41	6	0	.367	.323	R	R	5-10	170	11-28-79	2002	Tucson, Ariz.
Jimenez, Rich	.247	37	89	11	22	6	1	0	13	5	19	4	2	.337	.299	S	R	6-1	170	7-3-80	1997	Santo Domingo, D.R.
Johnston, Clint	.242	74	264	50	64	10	2	5	41	36	50	0	0	.352	.344	L	L	6-2	210	7-2-77	1998	Nashville, Tenn.
Kimberley, Glynn	.100	20	40	8	4	0	0	1	2	2	15	0	0	.175	.182	R	R	6-4	200	7-30-81	2000	Bayswater, Australia
Owens, Justin	.293	69	242	35	71	11	2	5	31	30	45	13	3	.417	.372	L	L	6-3	190	9-28-79	2002	Myrtle Beach, S.C.
Perez, Jerson	.143	7	28	0	4	0	0	0	2	4	7	1	1	.143	.250	R	R	5-10	180	1-20-76	1996	Lynn, Mass.
Porfirio, A.J.	.221	47	122	17	27	8	0	1	20	18	28	2	0	.311	.322	R	R	6-2	190	12-3-79	2002	Houston, Texas
Richmond, Paul	.245	48	155	18	38	10	1	2	27	20	19	1	3	.361	.333	L	R	6-2	210	5-30-80	2002	Crockett, Texas
Rivera, William	.266	73	290	43	77	7	2	3	35	30	43	5	3	.334	.335	L	R	6-0	150	12-28-81	2000	Caguas, P.R.
Schneider, John	.240	40	125	7	30	8	0	2	11	23	29	0	0	.352	.381	R	R	6-3	220	2-14-80	2002	Lawrenceville, N.J.
Siriveaw, Nom	.294	56	180	26	53	8	6	3	30	24	53	8	3	.456	.385	S	R	6-3	190	12-9-80	2000	Surrey, B.C.
Waugh, Jason	.243	67	255	39	62	14	0	9	38	31	50	5	5	.404	.327	R	R	6-1	190	3-12-80	2002	Bakersfield, Calif.

GAMES BY POSITION: C—Blackburn 22, Richmond 33, Schneider 34. 1B—Durazo 18, Johnston 60, Siriveaw 2. 2B—Arnold 3, Perez 2, Rivera 72. 3B—Arnold 2, Dragicevich 3, German 37, Hassey 21, Siriveaw 17. SS—Adams 30, Hassey 42, Perez 5. OF—Durazo 11, Jimenez 33, Kimberley 14, Owens 63, Porfirio 39, Siriveaw 32, Waugh 66.

PITCHING	W	L	ERA	G	GS	CG	SV	IP	H	R	ER	BB	SO	AVG	B	T	HT	WT	DOB	1st Yr	Resides
Bush, David	1	1	2.82	18	0	0	10	22	13	9	7	7	39	.158	R	R	6-2	210	11-9-79	2002	Devon, Pa.
Cardwell, Brian	2	0	3.71	20	0	0	0	27	24	12	11	22	30	.244	R	R	6-10	210	12-30-80	1999	Jacksonville, Fla.
Comolli, Mark	0	1	1.80	6	0	0	1	10	11	3	2	0	9	.275	R	R	6-0	190	3-11-79	2001	Millville, Del.
DeJong, Jordan	1	0	0.00	2	0	0	0	4	0	0	0	1	3	.000	R	R	6-2	170	4-12-79	2002	Yorba Linda, Calif.
Hanson, D.J.	5	2	1.68	9	9	0	0	48	35	11	9	11	51	.203	R	R	5-11	170	8-7-80	1999	Richland, Wash.
Houston, Ryan	2	2	4.06	7	7	0	0	31	32	15	14	15	19	.266	R	R	6-4	190	9-22-79	1999	Pensacola, Fla.
League, Brandon	7	2	3.15	16	16	0	0	86	80	42	30	23	72	.247	R	R	6-2	180	3-16-83	2001	Honolulu, Hawaii
Maureau, Justin	0	0	1.44	22	0	0	8	44	24	10	7	12	51	.157	R	L	6-1	170	12-17-80	2002	Highlands Ranch, Colo.
Mora, Ramon	2	1	3.15	9	5	0	1	40	42	17	14	16	37	.270	R	L	6-6	190	9-27-82	2001	Monagas, Venez.
Neylan, Chris	0	0	7.84	9	0	0	0	10	11	9	9	5	5	.289	R	R	6-0	170	8-13-80	2000	Tampa, Fla.
Nin, Sandy	4	4	2.92	17	11	0	2	74	61	29	24	11	61	.225	R	R	6-0	170	12-27-80	2000	San Pedro de Macoris, D.R.
Perez, Juan	1	0	3.00	2	0	0	0	6	3	2	2	0	6	.142	R	R	6-4	170	12-27-81	2000	San Pedro de Macoris, D.R.
Perkins, Vince	5	5	3.34	15	15	0	0	73	51	32	27	44	85	.198	L	R	6-5	220	9-27-81	2001	Victoria, B.C.
Peterson, Adam	2	0	2.30	18	0	0	5	31	29	10	8	9	19	.245	R	R	6-3	220	5-18-79	2002	Abrams, Wis.
Pleiness, Chad	8	3	2.42	16	9	0	0	74	48	23	20	32	70	.181	R	R	6-6	230	3-5-80	2002	Scottville, Mich.
Ramirez, Ismael	0	2	7.15	3	3	0	0	11	17	10	9	2	7	.354	R	R	6-2	170	3-3-81	1998	Anzoategui, Venez.
Sandoval, Marcos	2	3	3.48	25	0	0	1	44	40	20	17	20	39	.242	R	R	6-1	180	12-29-80	1997	Carabobo, Venez.
Sheffield, Chris	1	0	9.00	6	0	0	0	6	3	7	6	12	6	.142	R	R	6-3	210	12-13-79	2001	Richmond, Texas
Torres, Andy	4	3	3.43	17	1	0	0	39	36	16	15	15	25	.257	R	R	5-9	160	4-12-78	2002	Bell Gardens, Calif.

MEDICINE HAT BLUE JAYS Rookie

PIONEER LEAGUE

BATTING	AVG	G	AB	R	H	2B	3B	HR	RBI	BB	SO	SB	CS	SLG	OBP	B	T	HT	WT	DOB	1st Yr	Resides
Arnold, Eric	.268	17	56	11	15	2	1	0	1	7	13	2	2	.339	.359	R	R	6-1	190	7-9-80	2002	La Porte, Texas
Ashford, Jon	.000	1	3	0	0	0	0	0	0	0	3	0	0	.000	.000	L	R	6-4	180	8-20-82	2001	Covington, Tenn.
Braun, Randy	.197	20	61	6	12	2	0	1	7	6	14	0	1	.279	.269	L	L	6-4	190	4-19-84	2002	Belton, Mo.
Chourio, Junior	.160	49	119	14	19	2	1	4	11	5	31	2	1	.294	.213	R	R	6-3	170	3-23-83	1999	Maracaibo, Venez.
Corrente, David	.253	33	95	11	24	3	1	4	18	9	22	2	0	.432	.351	R	R	6-3	190	10-13-83	2001	Chatham, Ontario
Cota, Carlo	.271	58	207	21	56	14	2	0	21	23	45	4	0	.357	.346	R	R	5-10	180	9-18-80	2002	Calexico, Calif.
Davis, Morrin	.202	63	193	26	39	5	1	1	18	14	60	7	3	.254	.262	R	R	6-2	190	12-11-82	2000	Tampa, Fla.
Diaz, Robinzon	.297	58	192	29	57	9	0	0	20	13	19	7	4	.344	.345	R	R	5-11	180	9-19-83	2001	Monte Plata, D.R.
Dragicevich, Scott	.303	57	211	30	64	13	2	6	37	23	35	7	4	.469	.376	R	R	6-3	200	6-28-80	2002	Westlake, Calif.
Galloway, Mike	.247	36	93	10	23	4	0	2	7	4	22	1	0	.355	.294	R	R	6-4	240	6-15-80	2002	St. Thomas, Ontario
Kratz, Erik	.275	44	142	20	39	5	0	4	11	6	32	0	1	.394	.318	R	R	6-4	220	6-18-80	2002	Harrisonburg, Va.
Mangioni, Jarad	.257	55	179	23	46	6	0	7	28	19	40	1	0	.408	.330	S	R	5-11	150	6-24-83	2002	Sydney, Australia
Peralta, Juan	.272	71	283	45	77	12	3	4	30	30	38	16	8	.378	.342	R	R	5-11	180	5-9-82	2002	Santiago Rodriguez, D.R.
Perry, Jason	.425	30	106	25	45	6	2	10	36	12	19	0	2	.802	.508	L	R	6-0	200	8-18-80	2002	Jonesboro, Ga.
Rico, Erik	.319	60	163	27	52	14	1	3	29	15	31	3	1	.472	.383	L	L	6-2	190	1-21-80	2002	Miami, Fla.
Salas, Jose	.250	37	76	15	19	1	1	0	6	11	20	3	1	.289	.363	S	R	6-1	190	8-26-81	2002	Caracas, Venez.
Smith, David	.255	43	153	21	39	5	2	2	16	7	31	2	4	.353	.293	L	L	6-1	190	1-12-81	2002	Charleston, W.Va.
Zinsman, Zeph	.244	63	205	22	50	9	0	5	23	28	57	0	0	.361	.335	L	L	6-3	210	12-4-78	2002	Cupertino, Calif.

GAMES BY POSITION: C—Corrente 20, Diaz 31, Kratz 33. 1B—Corrente 3, Diaz 1, Mangioni 2, Perry 18, Zinsman 54. 2B—Arnold 14, Cota 55, Salas 10. 3B—Cota 1, Diaz 2, Dragicevich 53, Mangioni 12, Salas 10. SS—Peralta 71, Salas 7. OF—Braun 16, Chourio 46, Davis 61, Galloway 19, Kratz 1, Mangioni 31, Rico 58, Salas 1, Smith 41.

PITCHING	W	L	ERA	G	GS	CG	SV	IP	H	R	ER	BB	SO	AVG	B	T	HT	WT	DOB	1st Yr	Resides
Berroa, Yesson	2	4	6.84	20	0	0	0	26	32	20	20	16	23	.296	R	R	6-3	180	7-20-83	2000	San Pedro de Macoris, D.R.
Bimeal, Matt	2	1	9.45	16	0	0	1	20	25	23	21	12	22	.294	R	R	6-3	200	8-17-80	1999	Davidsville, Pa.
Buzachero, Bubbie	1	0	3.83	26	0	0	2	40	34	20	17	25	42	.226	R	R	5-11	180	6-13-81	2002	Livingston, Tenn.
DeJong, Jordan	6	1	1.43	33	0	0	16	44	23	10	7	10	62	.149	R	R	6-2	170	4-12-79	2002	Yorba Linda, Calif.
Grant, Brian	1	6	4.59	14	10	0	0	51	70	33	26	14	29	.324	R	R	6-4	190	8-16-84	2002	Goldsboro, N.C.
Mora, Ramon	2	3	5.34	6	6	0	0	32	41	24	19	10	28	.317	R	L	6-6	190	9-27-82	2001	Monagas, Venez.
Neylan, Chris	0	5	9.63	12	6	0	0	38	50	48	41	21	34	.292	R	R	6-0	170	8-13-80	2000	Tampa, Fla.
Perez, Juan	2	3	6.16	13	11	0	0	54	59	41	34	24	42	.292	R	R	6-4	170	12-27-81	2000	San Pedro de Macoris, D.R.
Ramirez, Ismael	4	2	2.98	11	10	0	0	54	51	23	18	14	51	.248	R	R	6-2	170	3-3-81	1998	Anzoategui, Venez.
Roga, Michael	2	3	5.08	24	3	0	1	51	53	39	29	24	76	.248	L	L	5-10	140	3-30-83	1999	Pickering, Ontario
Romero, Davis	3	0	5.19	27	4	0	0	54	44	31	30	29	52	.223	L	L	6-4	170	7-30-83	2002	Cocle, Panama
Savickas, Russell	4	4	3.19	14	10	0	0	54	44	23	19	29	52	.223	R	R	6-4	170	7-30-83	2002	Johnston, R.I.
Seifert, Michael	1	1	9.37	18	0	0	0	16	25	20	17	17	13	.333	L	L	6-0	180	10-5-81	2002	Lancaster, Ohio
Talanoa, Charles	4	3	4.07	15	15	1	0	80	77	42	36	23	91	.254	R	R	6-5	230	12-29-80	2001	El Segundo, Calif.
Torres, Andy	0	0	3.86	6	0	0	0	12	11	6	5	1	13	.229	R	R	5-9	160	4-12-78	2002	Bell Gardens, Calif.
Wesley, John	3	0	1.88	19	0	0	2	29	21	12	6	8	38	.194	R	R	6-6	230	10-14-80	2002	Westbury, N.Y.

2002 In Review 275
League Reports 290

MINOR
LEAGUES

Rochester changes from Orioles after 42-year affiliation

BY WILL LINGO

The biggest news in minor league baseball in 2002 actually happened after the season ended, when the Orioles lost their Triple-A partner in Rochester during the minor leagues' affiliation shuffle.

The change of affiliates happens every two years, as most player-development contracts between major and minor league teams expire. The 2002 edition didn't feature on overwhelming number of changes, but it did include several high-profile moves.

The change in Rochester was the most significant, both in the history of baseball in Rochester and as a statement on the continuing decay of the Orioles farm system.

Rochester is one of the oldest franchises in professional baseball. The city first had a team in 1885 and has been in the International League since 1912.

The Red Wings didn't have a major league affiliate until 1928, when the Cardinals sent players to Rochester. That arrangement continued for 32 years. The Orioles came to town in 1961. That's two affiliates in more than

Dan Mason

100 years of baseball. Rochester's new affiliate will be the Twins, and the Orioles find themselves on the way to Ottawa.

In the 42 years of the Red Wings-Orioles relationship, Rochester had 23 winning seasons, won six Governors' Cup championships, and finished with a 3,068-2,936 (.511) record. But the last league title came in 1997, and the team was abysmal in recent years.

More bothersome to the Red Wings was that the Orioles were warned about the discontent in Rochester and never did anything significant to turn it around.

Red Wings chief executive Naomi Silver told Orioles owner Peter Angelos in July that the Wings would file for free agency, and in September told him they were close to signing with another team. She said he offered minimal resistance. "He said, 'I know how important winning is to you,' " Silver said. "If there is anything we can do, we will do it, but we support you 100 percent.' "

In spite of the long relationships and the strong attachment to the Orioles, the team decided there wasn't enough hope on the horizon with Baltimore.

"Given the poor state of their farm system, it would be two, three or four years before we could expect to win again," Silver said. "We weren't willing to wait."

The Red Wings had been waiting several years for a winner anyway. The situation got worse instead of getting better, and in 2002 the Orioles' top three affiliates combined to finish 109 games below .500. Rochester had the worst record in Triple-A the past two years.

With so few major league teams interested in changing Triple-A affiliations, the Red Wings perhaps didn't have the choices they expected after breaking up with the Orioles. The only other team to inquire about an affiliation was the Expos, and after Silver told them of the

Wings' interest in the Twins, the Expos never visited.

The Expos ended up in Edmonton to replace the Twins, and sources said when Edmonton got down to a choice between the Expos and Orioles, it preferred the Expos even with all the uncertainty surrounding that franchise.

"That the Red Wings would take such drastic measures is astounding," Laura Vecsey wrote in The Washington Post. "That the Orioles could do nothing to preserve this relationship is sad, regrettable, maybe even shameful.

"Pick any of those words, but whatever word you do pick, it only begins to describe a situation within the Orioles organization that no one—not one person—interprets to mean anything except trouble."

Rochester had even used a losing streak as an opportunity to rally the community, with general manager Dan Mason camping out in a bullpen at Frontier Field during the 2002 season until the Red Wings won. Players joined him on some nights, and it became a fun event. But the Red Wings had enough of that kind of fun.

When Jim Mandelaro, who covers the Red Wings for the Democrat and Chronicle newspaper in Rochester, asked fans about the switch to the Twins, most were sad about the end of the Orioles era. But almost everyone supported the move.

"The Baltimore baseball men really lacked sense," said Joe Paris, a fan since 1942. "I don't want Dan Mason to have to sleep in a tent again. With a beautiful wife like his, he has to sleep with (infielder) Brian Roberts?"

ORGANIZATION **STANDINGS**

Cumulative farm club standings for the 30 major league farm systems:

	2002			2001	2000	1999
	W	L	Pct.	Pct.	Pct.	Pct.
Cleveland (6)	408	299	.577	.543	.517	.500
Pittsburgh (6)	399	300	.571	.467	.491	.487
Los Angeles (6)	389	302	.563	.538	.527	.457
Minnesota (6)	368	313	.540	.541	.537	.496
Houston (6)	378	328	.535	.598	.526	.499
New York-AL (6)	365	324	.530	.543	.517	.558
Chicago-NL (6)	366	326	.529	.512	.513	.480
Cincinnati (6)	369	330	.528	.567	.486	.521
Philadelphia (6)	366	331	.525	.504	.568	.523
Kansas City (6)	364	334	.521	.469	.457	.545
San Diego (6)	365	346	.513	.470	.485	.505
Atlanta (6)	350	334	.512	.489	.493	.496
Detroit (6)	355	343	.509	.508	.478	.480
Oakland (6)	354	342	.509	.480	.551	.573
St. Louis (6)	357	345	.509	.423	.472	.442
Texas (6)	342	345	.498	.478	.530	.541
New York-NL (6)	350	356	.496	.524	.509	.516
Florida (6)	338	351	.491	.539	.496	.477
Toronto (6)	341	369	.480	.460	.529	.534
Montreal (6)	329	361	.477	.435	.453	.493
Colorado (6)	336	374	.473	.478	.502	.472
Anaheim (6)	328	367	.472	.499	.426	.486
Seattle (6)	326	366	.471	.560	.577	.483
Chicago-AL (6)	320	367	.466	.495	.483	.520
San Francisco (6)	322	373	.463	.528	.444	.502
Milwaukee (6)	320	372	.462	.496	.495	.442
Arizona (6)	322	388	.454	.477	.466	.483
Boston (6)	314	377	.454	.468	.522	.526
Tampa Bay (6)	312	329	.445	.474	.478	.508
Baltimore (7)	333	434	.434	.445	.481	.453
Number of farm teams in parentheses						

MINOR LEAGUES

Balance In A-Ball

Another significant change coming out of the 2002 affiliation shuffle was the Astros' move away from two low Class A affiliates. Major League Baseball mandated several years ago that all teams were to have one low Class A and one high Class A team, but the Astros and Athletics were exceptions. Then the Astros, who were with Lexington in the South Atlantic League and Michigan in the Midwest League, decided to leave Michigan and sign with Salem in the Carolina League, giving them a high A team.

"Now we'll get back into our normal course of events, where players progress from Rookie ball to Lexington, Lexington to Salem, Salem to (Double-A) Round Rock," farm director Tim Purpura said.

That meant the A's had to leave their California League affiliate in Visalia. They continued their longtime affiliation with Modesto. The prize franchise in low Class A was Kane County, and the A's got the affiliation. "I don't think we could've made a bad decision, but I think we made the right decision," Cougars general manager Jeff Sedivy said. "They wanted to be here. This was the place they targeted, and we really were receptive to that."

While the A's enjoyed the proximity of two teams in the Cal League, Lieppman said the move back to low A will solve at least one dilemma.

"It was great just to have players and instructors going up and down (California) Highway 99," Lieppman said. "It gave so many players an opportunity to get ready for Double-A at a faster speed. The only real downside was that after one year in the league, all the players felt like they belonged in Double-A."

■ In the Eastern League, Trenton exchanged the Red Sox for the Yankees as Portland grabbed the Red Sox affiliation.

While Portland hinted at a possible switch to the Red Sox all summer and then got even more ecstatic before sending in a notice of termination, the Thunder remained mum. Trenton president Joe Finley voiced his frustration over Boston's lack of support and interest in his club in early August, however, basically announcing the end of his team's eight-year run with the Red Sox.

And when the dust settled, the Red Sox ended up in Portland, where the Sea Dogs were so excited they changed their team colors to Red Sox blue and red to celebrate. After the Yankees considered several options, including staying in Norwich, they went to Trenton.

■ The Royals lost their short-season affiliate in Spokane (Northwest), where the Indians signed a two-year contract with the Rangers. That set off a chain reaction that went a little something like this: Pulaski (Appalachian), with the Rangers leaving, signed with the Blue Jays. That left Medicine Hat (Pioneer) free to sign with the Brewers, who left Ogden (Pioneer). Ogden signed with the Dodgers, who had left Great Falls (Pioneer). Great Falls brought in the White Sox, who planned to drop their team in the Arizona League and keep their ties with Bristol in the Appy League.

Both the Rangers and Royals, who had teams in the Gulf Coast League in 2002, will move to the AZL in 2003 with their spring training homes moving. The Royals want another short-season affiliation but had no team to affiliate with.

■ The Texas League's new Frisco franchise ended up as a Rangers affiliate, as expected. Tulsa, which had a player-development contract with the Rangers through 2004, knew Texas would want out with Rangers owner Tom Hicks having controlling interest in the RoughRiders, who move from Shreveport.

The Drillers might have preferred an agreement with the Cardinals, who fielded affiliates in Tulsa at both the

CHANGING PARTNERS

At the end of an even-numbered year comes the chance for major league organizations to change their affiliations with minor league clubs—should either side choose to do so. Here are the changes in affiliation for the 2003 season:

Team (League)	'02 Affiliation	'03 Affiliation
TRIPLE-A		
Edmonton (Pacific Coast)	Twins	Expos
Ottawa (International)	Expos	Orioles
Rochester (International)	Orioles	Twins
DOUBLE-A		
Carolina (Southern)	Rockies	Marlins
*Frisco (Texas)	Giants	Rangers
New Haven (Eastern)	Cardinals	Blue Jays
Norwich (Eastern)	Yankees	Giants
Portland (Eastern)	Marlins	Red Sox
Tennessee (Southern)	Blue Jays	Cardinals
Trenton (Eastern)	Red Sox	Yankees
Tulsa (Texas)	Rangers	Rockies
HIGH CLASS A		
#Palm Beach (Florida State)	Rangers	Cardinals
Potomac (Carolina)	Cardinals	Reds
Salem (Carolina)	Rockies	Astros
Stockton (California)	Reds	Rangers
Visalia (California)	Athletics	Rockies
LOW CLASS A		
Clinton (Midwest)	Expos	Rangers
Greensboro (South Atlantic)	Yankees	Marlins
Kane County (Midwest)	Marlins	Athletics
Michigan (Midwest)	Astros	Yankees
Savannah (South Atlantic)	Rangers	Expos
SHORT-SEASON		
Great Falls (Pioneer)	Dodgers	White Sox
Medicine Hat (Pioneer)	Blue Jays	Brewers
Ogden (Pioneer)	Brewers	Dodgers
Pulaski (Appalachian)	Rangers	Blue Jays
Spokane (Northwest)	Royals	Rangers

*Franchise operated in Shreveport, La., in 2002
#Franchise operated in Port Charlotte, Fla., in 2002

PLAYER OF THE YEAR

Nick Baldelli was excited. He couldn't wait to tell his dad what his older brother had done.

Yet Dan Baldelli couldn't coax it out of Nick, so he went to the source, his oldest son Rocco. Rocco admitted he had gotten a tattoo, and Dan—not a tattoo kind of guy—wasn't pleased.

Rocco pushed down his left sock to reveal a Major League Baseball logo just above his ankle. He got the tattoo during his first instructional league. "I'm not really a tattoo guy, either," Rocco says. "I don't know why I got it. I wasn't really thinking that this was going to be on there for a long time."

His father did. "Now you better get there," Dan told his oldest son, who had just completed his first season of Rookie ball. "You have no business wearing that unless you get there."

Less than two years later, Rocco Baldelli made that branding look more like an act of foreshadowing than a silly, spur-of-the-moment idea. Just 20 years old, Baldelli shot through the Devil Rays farm system from Class A through Double-A to Triple-A in 2002, hitting .331-19-71 with 26 stolen bases to become Baseball America's Minor League Player of the Year.

"That's just an honor," Baldelli said. "Those kind of honors don't come around too often. It's a credit to so many who put in so much time to help me out."

The Devil Rays made the

Rocco Baldelli

Cumberland, R.I., native the sixth overall selection in 2000, but Baldelli was picked more on his athleticism and raw tools than what he had done on the field.

Unlike most minor leaguers, Baldelli hadn't been fed a baseball-only diet since he put down his bottle. He didn't even play baseball for two years, taking time off after sustaining a serious leg injury playing basketball.

Baldelli continued playing as a junior at Bishop Hendricken High—but not just baseball. With no favorite sport, he concentrated on whichever one was in season. Baldelli led his teams to state titles in volleyball, baseball and basketball and became Rhode Island's indoor sprint champion.

Baldelli received scholarship offers in all four sports, including 50 for baseball after he wowed scouts at the 1999 East Coast Showcase in Wilmington, N.C.

"We fell in love with his athletic abilities," says Dan Jennings, Tampa Bay's scouting director at the time. "He showed every tool you want to see. His arm was the only thing that wasn't above-average."

The Devil Rays selected him sixth overall in 2000 and signed him for $2.25 million. Baldelli then reported to Rookie-level Princeton to begin his professional career. He hit .216-3-25 with 56 strikeouts in 232 at-bats. Having never been a year-round player, he wasn't as advanced as some of his new teammates, and he struggled to adjust to playing every day.

"In Princeton, I had a hard time with all parts of the game," he says. "I didn't know how to play the game. Coming out of high school, I'd just come up to the plate and swing as hard as I could every time and try to smoke the ball. I didn't know about hitting mechanics, breaking pitches or reading pitchers."

Baldelli skipped to full-season ball at low Class A Charleston in 2001. After his promotion from Class A Visalia to Double-A Orlando in 2002, the family planned a vacation around visiting him and heading to Disney World. Then Rocco called. He had been promoted to Triple-A Durham after just 17 games. Durham manager Bill Evers wanted Baldelli in his lineup every day as the leadoff man and center fielder as the Bulls chased the International League's Southern Division title (which they eventually captured, along with the league title).

"I didn't expect that at all," Baldelli says. "When I moved up to Orlando, I was excited and figured I'd finish the year there."

The promotion capped a season in which Baldelli had already exceeded the organization's expectations. He says that while he didn't feel pressure to produce from the organization, he knew it was time to show results.

"I wanted to put together a good season," he says. "Numbers don't matter to me, but I felt like I did have to put up good numbers. I couldn't keep coasting and counting on the organization hoping I break out."

If the Devil Rays were waiting and hoping, their patience has paid off. Baldelli exploded, turning his tremendous potential into performance.

–WILL KIMMEY

JEFFREY CAMARATI

MINOR LEAGUES

Double-A and Triple-A level from 1959-76. But St. Louis—making sure it didn't end up back in New Haven—signed on with Tennessee in the Southern League. Tulsa ended up becoming a Rockies affiliate after Colorado and Carolina ended their four-year relationship.

Cardinals Fly South

The first big splash in offseason changes took place when the Rangers, preparing to move their spring training home to Arizona in 2003, sold their Florida State League franchise to the Cardinals.

The Cardinals announced the team would move to Jupiter's Roger Dean Stadium, which also houses the Jupiter Hammerheads.

The Rangers wrapped up 16 years of spring training at Charlotte County Stadium in 2002, with plans to move into a new complex in Surprise, Ariz. The Rangers had an FSL team in Charlotte for each of those 16 years.

Meanwhile in Jupiter, FSL fans will double their pleasure because the complex there will be home to two franchises. The Cardinals, who moved their high Class A affiliate from Potomac back to Florida, had a team in St. Petersburg from 1966-96, but sold the team after the Devil Rays got an expansion franchise.

"The operation of a Florida State League team at our spring training complex will give us added flexibility throughout the year with respect to our minor league operations and will give us rehabilitation opportunities for players at all levels of our organization," Cardinals general manager Walt Jocketty said.

The new team will be identified as Palm Beach in order to avoid confusion. The Jupiter Hammerheads, an affiliate of the Marlins, already play in Roger Dean Stadium, which opened in 1998 as the spring training home of the Cardinals and Expos. The Marlins will move their camp to Jupiter in 2003, and the Expos will take over the Marlins' former home in Melbourne.

The FSL will have about 150 playing dates to get in 140 home games—70 for the Cardinals affiliate and 70 for the Hammerheads.

Where's My Affiliate?

For one weird moment on the eve of spring training, the Marlins had two managers for their Double-A affiliate in Portland, while the Expos had none for their Double-A team in Harrisburg.

Eric Fox had been assigned to manage the 2002 season in Harrisburg. Dave Huppert had a contract to manage in

TEAM OF THE YEAR

The team with the best record in minor league baseball didn't bring home a title in 2002. Consider it a bittersweet ending for a season to remember for the Akron Aeros.

"It was very frustrating, for the players more than anything," Akron manager Brad Komminsk said. "We ran into a good team that  was hot at the time. Harrisburg flat-out beat us in the playoffs. It would have been nice to win the title, but the Mariners ran into the same thing last year."

After Akron won the first two games of the best-of-five series, Harrisburg rolled off three straight wins to eliminate the Aeros in the Eastern League semifinals.

But it's the regular season the Indians organization will remember, and it was Akron's success that made them Baseball America's 2002 Minor League Team of the Year.

In a season when Cleveland committed itself to rebuilding through its farm system, Akron was the showpiece. Akron's 93-48 record was the best in the Eastern League by 14½ games, and the Aeros' .660 winning percentage was the best in the minors. Akron's 3.09 ERA was almost a half-run better than the next best team in the Eastern League, while the Aeros also led the league in runs and slugging percentage.

It was an impressive accomplishment for a team that entered the season with plenty of prospects but few stars. Akron started the season with a number of players who were seen as one-dimensional or with questions that needed to be answered. In most cases, the prospects raised their stock with eye-opening seasons. According to Indians farm director John Farrell, Komminsk's work as manager was one of the big reasons.

"He creates an atmosphere where guys can gain confidence," Farrell said. "Where there is the pressure of every game and every play, he eases that tension."

Komminsk had the comfort of depending on one of the best pitching staffs in the minors. Lefthanders Brian Tallet, Billy Traber and Alex Herrera and righthanders Dave Elder and Jose Colon led a staff that simply dominated the Eastern League. Tallet and Traber fed off a healthy rivalry, as Tallet (10-1, 3.08 at Akron) and Traber (13-2, 2.76) earned callups to Triple-A Buffalo at midseason. Herrera remained in Akron for most of the season, striking out 65 in 61 innings of relief work while posting a 3.00 ERA.

Offensively, Victor Martinez added to his reputation as one of the best-hitting catchers in the minors. The 22-year-old won his second batting title in two years, hitting .336-22-85.

And while Akron didn't bring home an Eastern League title, that didn't mean the end of the season for several Aeros. Six pitchers from the Aeros staff, as well as Martinez and Covelli Crisp, earned promotions to Cleveland. With the Indians' youth movement in high gear, several are expected to compete for major league jobs in 2003.

"This core group, I can't say that they will be the core group for the Indians all together, but there will be players (from this group) who will emerge as the core of the Indians," Farrell said.

–J.J. COOPER

PREVIOUS WINNERS

1993—Harrisburg/Eastern (Expos)	
1994—Wilmington/Carolina (Royals)	
1995—Norfolk/International (Mets)	
1996—Edmonton/Pacific Coast (Athletics)	
1997—West Michigan/Midwest (Tigers)	
1998—Mobile/Southern (Padres)	
1999—Trenton/Eastern (Red Sox)	
2000—Round Rock/Texas (Astros)	
2001—Lake Elsinore/California (Padres)	

Portland. But while Jeffrey Loria was in the midst of unloading the Expos to buy the Marlins, both Fox and Huppert were listed as managers of the Sea Dogs. Then Loria completed his deal and fired Florida's entire minor league staff, including Huppert, so he could bring with him the Expos' minor league staff, including Fox.

"It's very strange," Fox said. "This whole offseason has been so—I don't know the right word for it—uneasy, maybe. I'm going to a new organization, but at least I'll know the staff."

Fox was among more than 50 of Montreal's minor league managers, coaches, coordinators and scouts who jumped to the Marlins. The offers were made in the weeks leading up to Loria's mid-February purchase of the Marlins from John Henry for $158.5 million.

Loria reportedly spiced the offer with a bonus of $5,000 to some of those who switched organizations. Major League Baseball helped by not guaranteeing jobs to any of the Expos' staff members who might have wanted to stay behind after the MLB took over the franchise.

"I had to take this job because it was a guaranteed job," Fox said. "I hadn't heard one thing from Major League Baseball with what they were going to do with the Expos. I couldn't take that chance. You have to take care of yourself sometimes."

The only Expos staffers who turned down Loria's offer and stayed behind were Tim Leiper and Randy St. Claire, the manager and pitching coach at Triple-A Ottawa.

While Fox accepted the offer to manage in Portland, Huppert was unemployed and at home in Zephryhills, Fla., for a few days before he got the Harrisburg job.

Meanwhile, the Florida State League didn't just have a manager swap—it had a full affiliate swap. The Marlins traded affiliations with the Expos, meaning the Jupiter Hammerheads were stocked with Florida prospects, while the Brevard County Manatees had players from Montreal. The switch took place at the end of February, less than a week before minor league spring training was to open.

Franchises On The Move

Albuquerque's new Pacific Coast League team will be called the Isotopes when it returns Triple-A baseball to the city in 2003. The team is moving from Calgary, where the Cannons completed their final season.

The new team name comes from an episode of "The Simpsons," in which the owner of the hometown Springfield Isotopes—so named because of the local nuclear power plant—considers moving the team to Albuquerque. Thanks to a hunger strike by Homer Simpson, the team remains in Springfield.

MANAGER OF THE YEAR

When a guy speaks excitedly about starting out his career in Elizabethton, Tenn., you know he has what it takes to be a minor league manager.

"That was the best place in the world to start," said John Russell, who got his first managerial job in the Appalachian League in 1995 after ending his playing career the season before. "You get all these different types of guys—from Latin America, high schools, other places—and you really get to teach them how to do things right."

Teaching was foremost in Russell's mind as he ascended through the Minnesota Twins organization as a manager. He spent two years in the Florida State League and three in the Eastern League, and he finished his second season at Triple-A Edmonton in the Pacific Coast League in 2002.

After a 60-83 record in his first year in Triple-A, the Trappers surged to an 81-59 record in 2002, second-best in the league. Then they cruised through the playoffs to win Edmonton's fourth PCL title.

"We went through a lot early in the year, with four callups in the first week and one home game in April (thanks to seven lost to cold weather)," Russell said. "But everything started to click in July. It says a lot about the character of the team the way they overcame adversity."

Russell found plenty of good things from his 2001 Edmonton team as well. Even though the record wasn't good, the team produced players like Bobby Kielty who played a role in the 2002 success in Minnesota.

"Last year was a really good developmental year," he said. "But this year's team really wanted to win, and everyone was together on the same goal. And if you can win, it makes development a little easier."

Being able to do both is a rare combination, and it made Russell Baseball America's 2002 Minor League Manager of the Year.

Russell emphasizes teaching because he knows how important it was to him as a player.

Russell was a first-round

John Russell

pick in the June 1982 draft, out of Oklahoma, but he was never more than a journeyman player. He made his major league debut in 1984 and played parts of 10 seasons in the big leagues with the Phillies, Braves and Rangers.

Twins farm director Jim Rantz said Russell has the skills to work with young and veteran players alike. "He is a very good baseball man and a good teacher who has continued to teach at higher levels," Rantz said.

From Russell's point of view, that's nothing special. That's a manager doing his job.

"If you can't teach, you're in trouble," he said. "Once I think I don't need to teach anymore, I need to quit."

—WILL LINGO

PREVIOUS WINNERS

1981—Ed Nottle, Tacoma (Athletics)
1982—Eddie Haas, Richmond (Braves)
1983—Bill Dancy, Reading (Phillies)
1984—Sam Perlozzo, Jackson (Mets)
1985—Jim Lefebvre, Phoenix (Giants)
1986—Brad Fischer, Huntsville (Athletics)
1987—Dave Trembley, Harrisburg (Pirates)
1988—Joe Sparks, Indianapolis (Expos)
1989—Buck Showalter, Albany (Yankees)
1990—Kevin Kennedy, Albuquerque (Dodgers)
1991—Butch Hobson, Pawtucket (Red Sox)
1992—Grady Little, Greenville (Braves)
1993—Terry Francona, Birmingham (White Sox)
1994—Tim Ireland, El Paso (Brewers)
1995—Marc Bombard, Indianapolis (Reds)
1996—Carlos Tosca, Portland (Marlins)
1997—Gary Jones, Edmonton (Athletics)
1998—Terry Kennedy, Iowa (Cubs)
1999—John Mizerock, Wichita (Royals)
2000—Joel Skinner, Buffalo (Indians)
2001—Jackie Moore, Round Rock (Astros)

MINOR LEAGUE ALL-STARS

Selected by Baseball America

Lyle Overbay

Joe Roa

Brad Hawpe

Kirk Saarloos

FIRST TEAM

Pos.	Player, Team (League)	AVG	AB	R	H	2B	3B	HR	RBI	BB	SO	SB
C	Victor Martinez, Akron (Eastern)	.336	443	84	149	40	0	22	85	58	62	3
1B	Lyle Overbay, Tucson (Pacific Coast)	.343	525	83	180	40	0	19	109	42	86	0
2B	Scott Hairston, South Bend (Midwest)/Lancaster (Cal)	.345	473	99	163	46	5	22	98	64	90	10
3B	Mark Teixeira, Charlotte (FSL)/Tulsa (Texas)	.318	321	63	99	21	5	19	69	46	70	5
SS	Jose Reyes, St. Lucie (FSL)/Binghamton (Eastern)	.288	563	104	162	26	19	8	62	46	77	58
OF	Rocco Baldelli, Bakers. (Cal)/Orlando (SL)/Durham (IL)	.331	478	86	158	28	3	19	71	23	97	26
	Robb Quinlan, Salt Lake (Pacific Coast)	.333	528	95	176	31	13	20	112	41	93	8
	Michael Restovich, Edmonton (Pacific Coast)	.286	518	95	148	32	7	29	98	53	151	11
DH	Brad Hawpe, Salem (Carolina)	.347	450	87	156	38	2	22	97	81	84	1

Pos.	Player, Team (League)	W	L	ERA	G	GS	CG	SV	IP	H	BB	SO
SP	Sean Burnett, Lynchburg (Carolina)	13	4	1.80	26	26	2	0	155	118	33	96
	Joe Roa, Scranton/Wilkes-Barre (International)	14	0	1.86	17	17	1	0	111	83	16	74
	Kirk Saarloos, Round Rock (Texas)/New Orleans (PCL)	12	1	1.54	17	15	1	0	95	60	23	101
	Billy Traber, Akron (EL)/Buffalo (IL)	17	5	2.94	27	26	2	0	163	157	32	115
RP	Joe Valentine, Birmingham (Southern)	4	1	1.97	55	0	0	36	59	36	30	63

SECOND TEAM

Pos.	Player, Team (League)	AVG	AB	R	H	2B	3B	HR	RBI	BB	SO	SB
C	Josh Phelps, Syracuse (International)	.292	257	50	75	20	1	24	64	32	83	0
1B	Jason Stokes, Kane County (Midwest)	.341	349	73	119	25	0	27	75	47	96	1
2B	Joe Thurston, Las Vegas (Pacific Coast)	.334	587	106	196	39	13	12	55	25	60	22
3B	Chad Tracy, El Paso (Texas)	.344	514	80	177	39	5	8	74	38	51	2
SS	Brandon Phillips, Harrisburg (EL)/Ottawa (IL)/Buffalo (IL)	.302	503	71	152	31	2	18	67	32	78	14
OF	Lew Ford, New Britain (EL)/Edmonton (PCL)	.318	566	121	180	38	4	20	75	62	68	28
	Dee Haynes, New Haven (Eastern)	.312	504	75	157	29	4	21	98	25	67	3
	Laynce Nix, Charlotte (Florida State)	.285	512	86	146	27	3	21	110	72	105	17
DH	Walter Young, Hickory (South Atlantic)	.333	492	84	164	34	2	25	103	36	102	2

Pos.	Player, Team (League)	W	L	ERA	G	GS	CG	SV	IP	H	BB	SO
SP	Ian Ferguson, Wichita (Texas)/Wilmington (Carolina)	18	3	2.48	28	28	2	0	185	160	37	141
	Ryan Madson, Reading (Eastern)	16	4	3.20	26	26	2	0	171	150	53	132
	Francisco Rosario, Charleston, WV (SAL)/Dunedin (FSL)	9	4	1.94	26	25	1	0	130	83	39	143
	Dontrelle Willis, Kane County (Midwest)/Daytona (FSL)	12	2	1.83	24	24	3	0	158	115	24	128
RP	Franklyn German, Midland (Texas)/Toledo (IL)	2	2	2.53	60	0	0	29	64	43	34	90

Player of the Year: Rocco Baldelli, of, Bakersfield/Orlando/Durham. **Manager of the Year:** John Russell, Edmonton (Pacific Coast).

"In bringing baseball back to Albuquerque, we wanted to bring something that was fun, that was playful, that demonstrated great family entertainment to the fans here," new team owner Ken Young said.

The other obvious choice would have been Dukes, the name of the city's previous team. It comes from the city's nickname, the Duke City, which stems from the city being named for Spain's Duke of Alburquerque.

The modern Albuquerque Dukes joined the PCL in 1972 after 10 seasons in the Texas League and had been affiliated with the Dodgers since 1963. That franchise moved to Portland, Ore., for the 2001 season, and the Dodgers switched their affiliation to Las Vegas.

The city decided to spend $10 million to renovate

Albuquerque Sports Stadium, and Young bought the Cannons to move them to Albuquerque. In addition to a new nickname, the team will be affiliated with the Marlins, not the Dodgers.

The 2002 season was the last for minor league baseball in three other cities. The Texas League's Shreveport Swamp Dragons will become the Frisco RoughRiders, the Columbus RedStixx become the Lake County Captains (based in Eastlake, Ohio) and their South Atlantic League compatriot Macon Braves will move to Rome, Ga.

Another Sally League franchise moved on the eve of the 2002 season. After months of uncertainty surrounding the fate of the Wilmington Waves, the team was sold in March to David Heller, a political consultant from

MINOR LEAGUES

Washington, D.C., and moved to Albany, Ga.

In 2001, their first season as the Dodgers' low Class A affiliate, the Waves drew 135,548 fans in Wilmington and were awash in debt. Attendance was even worse in Albany, however, with 72,025 fans coming out.

Attendance Stays Strong

While strike talk helped drive down attendance at the major league level, the minor leagues had another strong season at the turnstiles, as 38,639,142 fans attended games in 2002, the third-highest total in the 101-year history of the National Association.

The 2001 total of 38.8 million was the second-highest ever, so attendance was down a bit. The record remains 39.8 million in 1949, when there were 448 teams in 59 leagues, compared to the present 176 teams in 15 leagues.

"We were slightly off of last year's, but we were 5½ percent off in April with the bad weather across the country," Minor League Baseball president Mike Moore said. "We had to struggle to get back to the pace from the year before, but we almost made it. I'm pleased with that."

The Pacific Coast League (6.80 million), the International League (6.76 million), the Midwest League (3.37 million) and the New York-Penn League (1.89 million) all set new records. And thanks to new stadiums in Peoria and Cedar Rapids in the MWL and the new Aberdeen franchise in the NY-P, those two leagues set records for their classifications as well.

Sacramento and Memphis finished 1-2 in the attendance race for the third straight season. The River Cats drew 817,317 to Raley Field, while the Redbirds packed 794,550 into AutoZone Park. With 670,167 fans, Round Rock broke the Double-A record for the third straight year, while Brooklyn drew 317,124 to become the first short-season team to top 300,000 fans.

All told, 25 teams set new attendance marks, including Toledo (International), with 547,204 fans in its new ballpark; New Britain (Eastern), with a franchise-best 14 sellouts and 265,484 fans; Midland (Texas), with 272,136; and Charleston, S.C. (South Atlantic) with 242,143.

In addition to the new parks in Peoria and Cedar Rapids, stadiums in Fresno and Toledo provided major boosts for those franchises. A total of 12,792 people watched the Fresno Grizzlies (Pacific Coast) play their first game at their new home, and they finished with 563,079 for the season.

"You're not going to play in too many nicer places than this in the minor leagues," Tacoma third baseman Ryan Minor said. "I'd love to play here every day."

Prior Makes Quick Impression

Mark Prior's stay in the minor leagues was measured in weeks, but he still probably generated more buzz than any other prospect during the 2002 season.

No one knew this better than the West Tenn Diamond Jaxx, the Southern League team where Prior made his professional debut to start 2002. He made just six starts there, but the Diamond Jaxx made him work for his pay, even when he wasn't pitching.

Prior signed 12 dozen baseballs, as well as photographs and copies of a feature article about him that ran in USA Today. The Diamond Jaxx had him wear several different caps during his starts; he signed those and they were sold as game-worn caps. The team also saved baseballs from his starts—including seven from one outing—and had him sign those, selling them as game-used balls.

ALL-STAR FUTURES GAME

DAVID SCHOFIELD

Jose Reyes

Jose Reyes has made a habit of playing better as his competition has gotten tougher. That trend continued in 2002 when Reyes performed on his biggest stage to date—the annual Futures Game.

Before 25,000 fans who came to Milwaukee's Miller Park for the fourth annual game during All-Star Weekend, Reyes snapped a scoreless tie in the third inning with a bases-loaded triple off Rockies righthander Aaron Cook. Reyes' big blow earned him MVP honors and carried the World to a 5-1 victory over the United States, evening the series at two wins apiece.

A top shortstop prospect in the Mets system, Reyes, 19, played three innings at second base for the shortstop-laden World club. His MVP award was another highlight in a season that included a standout performance in high Class A and a promotion to Double-A.

"I definitely think I do better against better players," Reyes said. "On the big occasions, I rise to the occasion. It's all about adjustments, and I make the adjustments that are necessary."

UNITED STATES ROSTER

Pitchers: Brad Baker (Padres), Sean Burnett (Pirates), Aaron Cook (Rockies), Ryan Dittfurth (Rangers), Brett Evert (Braves), Brett Myers (Phillies), Billy Traber (Indians), Adam Wainwright (Braves), Jason Young (Rockies). **Catchers:** John Buck (Astros), Kevin Cash (Blue Jays). **Infielders:** Bill Hall (Brewers), Corey Hart (Brewers), Drew Henson (Yankees), Orlando Hudson (Blue Jays), Lyle Overbay (El Paso), Brandon Phillips (Indians), Jason Stokes (Marlins), Chad Tracy (Diamondbacks). **Outfielders:** Joe Borchard (White Sox), Marlon Byrd (Phillies), Carl Crawford (Devil Rays), Michael Restovich (Twins).

WORLD ROSTER

Pitchers: Ed Almonte (White Sox), Francis Beltran (Cubs), Jorge de la Rosa (Red Sox), Gerardo Garcia (Devil Rays), Franklyn German (Athletics), Francisco Rodriguez (Angels), Ricardo Rodriguez (Dodgers), Seung Song (Red Sox), John Stephens (Orioles). **Catchers:** Justin Huber (Mets), Victor Martinez (Indians). **Infielders:** Angel Berroa (Royals), Miguel Cabrera (Marlins), Hee Seop Choi (Cubs), Victor Diaz (Dodgers), Omar Infante (Tigers), Jose Lopez (Mariners), Justin Morneau (Twins), Jose Reyes (Mets). **Outfielders:** Tony Alvarez (Pirates), Shin-Soo Choo (Mariners), Wily Mo Pena (Reds), Andres Torres (Tigers).

World 5, U.S. 1

WORLD	ab	r	h	bi	USA	ab	r	h	bi
Torres, cf-rf	3	1	2	0	Hudson, 2b	3	0	1	1
Reyes, 2b	2	1	1	3	Byrd, cf	3	0	2	0
Infante, 2b	2	0	1	0	Crawford, lf	3	0	0	0
Martinez, c	2	1	1	1	Borchard, rf	3	0	0	0
Huber, c	2	0	0	0	Overbay, 1b	1	0	0	0
Choi, 1b	2	0	0	0	Stokes, 1b	1	0	0	0
Choo, dh-cf	1	0	0	0	Restovich, dh	2	0	0	0
Morneau, dh-1b	3	0	1	0	Hart, dh	1	0	0	0
Cabrera, 3b	2	0	2	0	Henson, 3b	2	0	0	0
Diaz, 3b	0	0	0	0	Tracy, 3b	0	0	0	0
Alvarez, rf	2	0	0	0	Cash, c	1	0	0	0
Lopez, dh-ss	1	0	0	0	Buck, c	1	0	0	0
Pena, lf	2	1	0	0	Phillips, ss	0	1	0	0
Berroa, ss-dh	3	1	1	0	Hall, ss	1	0	0	0
Totals	**27**	**5**	**9**	**5**	**Totals**	**22**	**1**	**3**	**1**

World						005	000	0—5
USA						001	000	0—1

E—Cash. DP—World 2, U.S. 2. LOB—World 4, U.S. 2. SB—Martinez.

World	ip	h	r	er	bb	so	U.S.	ip	h	r	er	bb	so
Stephens	1	1	0	0	0	1	Young	1	1	0	0	0	2
R. Rodriguez W	1	0	0	0	1	1	Evert	1	1	0	0	0	1
Garcia	1	1	1	1	1	1	Cook L	⅓	3	5	5	1	1
Song	1	0	0	0	0	2	Traber	⅔	2	0	0	0	1
German	1	0	0	0	0	2	Wainwright	1	0	0	0	0	1
Almonte	⅓	1	0	0	0	0	Burnett	1	1	0	0	0	0
de la Rosa	⅔	0	0	0	0	0	Baker	1	0	0	0	1	0
Beltran	⅔	0	0	0	0	2	Myers	½	1	0	0	1	1
F. Rodriguez	⅓	0	0	0	0	1	Dittfurth	½	0	0	0	0	0

HBP—by Cook (Pena). T—2:10.

CLASSIFICATION ALL-STARS

Selected by Baseball America

TRIPLE-A — International League, Pacific Coast League

Pos.	Player, Team (League)	AVG	AB	R	H	2B	3B	HR	RBI	BB	SO	SB
C	Javier Valentin, Edmonton (Pacific Coast)	.286	455	69	130	33	1	21	80	41	96	0
1B	Lyle Overbay, Tucson (Pacific Coast)	.343	525	83	180	40	0	19	109	42	86	0
2B	Joe Thurston, Las Vegas (Pacific Coast)	.334	587	106	196	39	13	12	55	25	60	22
3B	Brandon Larson, Louisville (International)	.340	297	47	101	20	1	25	69	24	70	1
SS	David Lamb, Edmonton (Pacific Coast)	.309	440	72	136	25	3	10	72	45	57	2
OF	Raul Gonzalez, Louisville (International)	.333	432	91	144	27	2	13	69	61	59	9
	Robb Quinlan, Salt Lake (Pacific Coast)	.333	528	95	176	31	13	20	112	41	93	8
	Michael Restovich, Edmonton (Pacific Coast)	.286	518	95	148	32	7	29	98	53	151	11
DH	Josh Phelps, Syracuse (International)	.292	257	50	75	20	1	24	64	32	83	0

Pos.	Player, Team (League)	W	L	ERA	G	GS	CG	SV	IP	H	BB	SO
SP	Trey Hodges, Richmond (International)	15	9	3.19	28	28	1	0	172	158	56	116
	Steve Randolph, Tucson (Pacific Coast)	15	7	3.47	28	27	1	0	163	151	81	129
	Joe Roa, Scranton/Wilkes-Barre (International)	14	0	1.86	17	17	1	0	111	83	16	74
	Jeriome Robertson, New Orleans (Pacific Coast)	12	8	2.55	27	27	2	0	180	160	45	114
RP	Jeff Williams, Las Vegas (Pacific Coast)	6	4	2.60	56	0	0	28	80	80	22	75

Player of the Year: Joe Thurston, Las Vegas (Pacific Coast). **Manager of the Year:** John Russell, Edmonton (Pacific Coast). **Team of the Year:** Edmonton (Pacific Coast).

DOUBLE-A — Eastern League, Southern League, Texas League

Pos.	Player, Team (League)	AVG	AB	R	H	2B	3B	HR	RBI	BB	SO	SB
C	Victor Martinez, Akron (Eastern)	.336	443	84	149	40	0	22	85	58	62	3
1B	John Gall, New Haven (Eastern)	.316	526	82	166	45	3	20	81	38	75	4
2B	Aaron Miles, Birmingham (Southern)	.322	531	67	171	39	1	9	68	40	45	25
3B	Chad Tracy, El Paso (Texas)	.344	514	80	177	39	5	8	74	38	51	2
SS	Brandon Phillips, Harrisburg (Eastern)	.327	245	40	80	13	2	9	35	16	33	6
OF	Tony Alvarez, Altoona (Eastern)	.318	507	79	161	37	1	15	59	27	71	29
	Dee Haynes, New Haven (Eastern)	.312	504	75	157	29	4	21	98	25	67	3
	Henri Stanley, Round Rock (Texas)	.314	456	90	143	36	10	16	72	72	85	14
DH	Travis Chapman, Reading (Eastern)	.301	478	64	144	35	1	15	76	54	77	3

Pos.	Player, Team (League)	W	L	ERA	G	GS	CG	SV	IP	H	BB	SO
SP	Mike Gosling, El Paso (Texas)	14	5	3.13	27	27	2	0	167	149	62	115
	Ryan Madson, Reading (Eastern)	16	4	3.20	26	26	2	0	171	150	53	132
	Kirk Saarloos, Round Rock (Texas)	10	1	1.40	13	13	1	0	83	48	21	82
	Billy Traber, Akron (Eastern)	13	2	2.76	18	17	2	0	108	99	20	82
RP	Joe Valentine, Birmingham (Southern)	4	1	1.97	55	0	0	36	59	36	30	63

Player of the Year: Victor Martinez, Akron (Eastern). **Manager of the Year:** Wally Backman, Birmingham (Southern). **Team of the Year:** Akron (Eastern).

HIGH CLASS A — California League, Carolina League, Florida State League

Pos.	Player, Team (League)	AVG	AB	R	H	2B	3B	HR	RBI	BB	SO	SB
C	Kelly Shoppach, Sarasota (Florida State)	.271	414	54	112	35	1	10	66	59	112	2
1B	Brad Hawpe, Salem (Carolina)	.347	450	87	156	38	2	22	97	81	84	1
2B	Josh Bonifay, Lynchburg (Carolina)	.307	463	83	142	36	1	26	102	63	97	3
3B	Brendan Harris, Daytona (Florida State)	.329	425	82	140	35	6	13	54	43	57	16
SS	Jose Castillo, Lynchburg (Carolina)	.300	503	82	151	25	2	16	81	49	95	27
OF	Rocco Baldelli, Bakersfield (California)	.333	312	63	104	19	1	14	51	18	63	21
	Laynce Nix, Charlotte (Florida State)	.285	512	86	146	27	3	21	110	72	105	17
	Stephen Smitherman, Stockton (California)	.313	482	78	151	36	1	19	99	39	126	17
DH	Corey Hart, High Desert (California)	.288	393	76	113	26	10	22	84	37	101	24

Pos.	Player, Team (League)	W	L	ERA	G	GS	CG	SV	IP	H	BB	SO
SP	Taylor Buchholz, Clearwater (Florida State)	10	6	3.29	23	23	4	0	159	140	51	129
	Sean Burnett, Lynchburg (Carolina)	13	4	1.80	26	26	2	0	155	118	33	96
	Jeff Clark, San Jose (California)	12	3	2.06	21	21	1	0	140	118	18	129
	Bubba Nelson, Myrtle Beach (Carolina)	11	5	1.72	23	23	0	0	136	98	44	105
RP	Beau Kemp, Fort Myers (Florida State)	3	2	0.66	59	0	0	29	68	49	18	49

Player of the Year: Rocco Baldelli, Bakersfield (California). **Manager of the Year:** Jayhawk Owens, Stockton (California). **Team of the Year:** Lynchburg (Carolina).

MINOR LEAGUES

Jason Compton, the team's manager of ticketing and merchandising, put them on eBay. Six game-worn caps brought in from $280-370 each. Seven game-used baseballs sold for $230-310 apiece. Other autographed balls sold for $50-60. And that was just the crest of the wave.

"It was a once-in-a-lifetime thing to have him here, especially in a small market like Jackson, (Tenn.)," Compton said. "Things got so crazy around here the week he made his first start in Chicago, I felt like we should answer the phone, 'Prior Industries.'"

Prior made three starts at Triple-A Iowa before he moved on to Chicago, but the I-Cubs didn't make quite as much of a production out of Prior memorabilia.

"We started working on this in February with the prospect of him being here," Compton said. "We contacted his agent and worked something out. He's a partner in the deal."

The Diamond Jaxx saw a much bigger boost in merchandise sales than they did in attendance. The team had more people in from out of town when Prior pitched, but overall he didn't have a big effect on attendance.

The franchise was also in the news because majority owner David Hersh ended his five-year reign after the season when he sold the club to Altoona Curve (Eastern) owner Bob Lozinak.

"It's been a year of reflection," he said. "It's going to be emotional for me. I'm an emotional person. It's been a child for me in many, many ways. Some days your chil-

LOW CLASS A — Midwest League, South Atlantic League

Pos.	Player, Team (League)	AVG	AB	R	H	2B	3B	HR	RBI	BB	SO	SB
C	Joe Mauer, Quad City (Midwest)	.302	411	58	124	23	1	4	62	61	42	0
1B	Jason Stokes, Kane County (Midwest)	.341	349	73	119	25	0	27	75	47	96	1
2B	Scott Hairston, South Bend (Midwest)	.332	394	79	131	35	4	16	72	58	74	9
3B	Andy Marte, Macon (South Atlantic)	.281	488	69	137	32	4	21	105	41	114	2
SS	John Nelson, Peoria (Midwest)	.274	481	85	132	28	5	16	63	54	123	16
OF	Jason Kubel, Quad City (Midwest)	.321	424	60	136	26	4	17	69	41	48	3
	Todd Self, Michigan (Midwest)	.310	491	81	152	36	5	12	94	65	104	10
	Noochie Varner, Dayton/West Michigan (Midwest)	.306	533	83	163	28	13	10	70	32	121	37
DH	Walter Young, Hickory (South Atlantic)	.333	492	84	164	34	2	25	103	36	102	2

		W	L	ERA	G	GS	CG	SV	IP	H	BB	SO
SP	J.D. Durbin, Quad City (Midwest)	13	4	3.19	27	27	0	0	161	144	51	163
	Macay McBride, Macon (South Atlantic)	12	8	2.12	25	25	2	0	157	119	48	138
	Tyler Johnson, Peoria (Midwest)	15	3	2.00	22	18	0	0	121	96	42	132
	Dontrelle Willis, Kane County (Midwest)	10	2	1.83	19	19	3	0	128	91	21	101
RP	Jared Blasdell, Peoria (Midwest)	6	2	1.37	53	0	0	23	66	34	14	79

Player of the Year: Jason Stokes, Kane County (Midwest). **Manager of the Year:** Tony Beasley, Hickory (South Atlantic). **Team of the Year:** Peoria (Midwest).

SHORT-SEASON CLASS A — New York-Penn League, Northwest League

Pos.	Player, Team (League)	AVG	AB	R	H	2B	3B	HR	RBI	BB	SO	SB
C	Omir Santos, Staten Island (New York-Penn)	.289	232	22	67	10	0	7	44	12	32	2
1B	Kevin Collins, Boise (Northwest)	.342	187	39	64	18	2	13	37	14	52	0
2B	Ismael Castro, Everett (Northwest)	.313	284	55	89	26	1	9	46	16	41	13
3B	Donnie Hood, Boise (Northwest)	.279	172	36	48	13	1	12	42	11	42	2
SS	Kevin Randel, Jamestown (New York-Penn)	.277	253	49	70	11	5	7	27	49	56	13
OF	Ben Francisco, Mahoning Valley (New York-Penn)	.349	235	55	82	23	2	3	23	22	28	22
	Reid Gorecki, New Jersey (New York-Penn)	.281	274	55	77	8	13	8	52	20	57	22
	Curtis Granderson, Oneonta (New York-Penn)	.344	212	45	73	15	4	3	34	20	35	9
DH	Joey Gomes, Hudson Valley (New York-Penn)	.283	276	45	78	14	4	15	48	21	50	4

		W	L	ERA	G	GS	CG	SV	IP	H	BB	SO
SP	Troy Cate, Everett (Northwest)	6	1	2.00	16	12	1	0	85	62	11	95
	Alex Hart, Williamsport (New York-Penn)	7	0	1.85	15	10	0	2	68	52	20	73
	Mike Hinckley, Vermont (New York-Penn)	6	2	1.37	16	16	0	0	92	60	30	66
	Andy Sisco, Boise (Northwest)	7	2	2.43	14	14	0	0	78	51	39	101
RP	Gabe Ribas, Eugene (Northwest)	8	1	1.97	32	1	0	16	50	36	5	66

Player of the Year: Andy Sisco, Boise (Northwest). **Manager of the Year:** Steve McFarland, Boise (Northwest). **Team of the Year:** Boise (Northwest).

ROOKIE — Appalachian League, Arizona League, Gulf Coast League, Pioneer League

Pos.	Player, Team (League)	AVG	AB	R	H	2B	3B	HR	RBI	BB	SO	SB
C	Alex Dvorsky, Provo (Pioneer)	.321	234	48	75	15	0	9	52	47	36	2
1B	Ryan Shealy, Casper (Pioneer)	.368	231	55	85	21	1	19	70	50	52	0
2B	Alberto Callaspo, Provo (Pioneer)	.338	299	70	101	16	10	3	60	17	14	13
3B	Micah Schnurstein, White Sox (Arizona)	.332	205	28	68	26	1	3	48	12	34	1
SS	Hanley Ramirez, Red Sox (Gulf Coast)	.341	164	29	56	11	3	6	26	16	15	8
OF	Wes Bankston, Princeton (Appalachian)	.301	246	48	74	10	1	18	57	18	46	2
	Darren Ciraco, Bristol (Appalachian)	.329	219	47	72	15	0	10	51	27	39	2
	Jason Pridie, Princeton (Appalachian)	.368	285	60	105	12	9	7	33	19	35	13
DH	Prince Fielder, Ogden (Pioneer)	.390	146	35	57	12	0	10	40	37	27	3

Pos.	Player, Team (League)	W	L	ERA	G	GS	CG	SV	IP	H	BB	SO
SP	Ricky Barrett, Elizabethton (Appalachian)	7	1	1.27	12	11	0	0	64	49	25	79
	Anthony Lerew, Danville (Appalachian)	8	3	1.73	14	14	0	0	83	60	25	75
	Elizardo Ramirez, Phillies (Gulf Coast)	7	1	1.10	11	11	2	0	73	44	2	73
	Scott Tyler, Elizabethton (Appalachian)	8	1	2.93	14	13	0	0	68	37	46	92
RP	Jordan DeJong, Medicine Hat (Pioneer)	6	1	1.43	33	0	0	16	44	23	10	62

Player of the Year: Ryan Shealy, Casper (Pioneer). **Manager of the Year:** Woody Huyke, Pirates (Gulf Coast). **Team of the Year:** Great Falls (Pioneer).

MINOR LEAGUES

dren make you happy. Some days your children make you sad. But all days you're proud of your children."

Born Under A Bad Sign?

How bad was 2002 for the Devil Rays organization? So bad that a 106-loss season was the least of their worries. Much more serious were two pitchers in the organization getting shot in separate incidents in June and August.

Nick Bierbrodt, in the words of his doctor, was lucky to be alive after being shot twice in Charleston, S.C. Bierbrodt, 24, was pitching at Class A Charleston as part of his comeback from the severe loss of control in spring training that cost him his spot in the Tampa Bay rotation.

All the baseball plans changed when Bierbrodt was shot around 3 a.m. on June 7 while sitting in a taxicab at a Hardee's restaurant drive-through in Charleston, with Rays minor leaguer John Vigue and a Brandon, Fla., woman.

The man shot Bierbrodt twice with a pistol. The bullets both entered his chest, went through his diaphragm and ended up in his liver, where doctors will leave them. Somehow, the bullets missed his heart and other vital organs and blood vessels.

"For an unfortunate incident, I would say he's an exceptionally lucky individual," said Dr. David Cole of the Medical University of South Carolina. "I don't know how to quantify it, but I would just say the majority of the people that have that situation, with those gunshots to that area, would not have made it to the hospital alive because they would not have been fortunate enough for the bullets to have missed all the major vessels."

Delvin James was also relatively lucky, sustaining only minor left shoulder wounds after being shot several times early Labor Day morning in Raleigh, N.C.

James, a righthander for Triple-A Durham, and a friend were eating at a Waffle House around 3 a.m. when an altercation between two groups of people erupted into gunfire. James and his friend, Monique McNellie, were both shot. "We believe both victims were unintended victims," Raleigh police lieutenant Chris Morgan said.

James, a member of the Rays' inaugural 1996 draft class, made his major league debut in mid-April, but a sore shoulder forced him onto the disabled list after five starts. He had worked his way back from Double-A Orlando to Durham.

James was struck by three or four bullets. Two hit his left shoulder—one passed through, and the other had to be removed by doctors. He was also grazed by a bullet on the neck and possibly the left elbow.

Next to those incidents, another lost season for Rays outfield prospect Josh Hamilton could at least be put in perspective. Hamilton made four appearances on the disabled list before his season ended in July when he tore the rotator cuff in his left (throwing) shoulder.

"It's Murphy's Law with Hamilton," former Devil Rays scouting director Dan Jennings said. "Whatever could happen, has."

The team expected Hamilton, who was hitting .303-9-44 with 10 stolen bases in 211 at-bats for Class A Bakersfield, to be ready for spring training in 2003.

Nobody Makes History

Most minor league teams focus on filling up their stadiums every game. Not the Charleston RiverDogs. They kept Riley Ballpark empty.

Four days after setting a franchise attendance record of 7,885 for Fourth of July fireworks, Charleston set a minor league record of 0 on Nobody Night. Just 12 fans watched Chicago beat Troy in a rain-soaked game on Sept. 17, 1881, in the previous record for smallest crowd.

The idea sounds like one that could have come from the mind of Mike Veeck, one of the team's owners and a Charleston resident. But RiverDogs broadcaster Jim Lucas gets the credit for Nobody Night, though he did dream it up after listening to a speaker talk about the power of opposites at Veeck's November marketing seminar.

"Our primary goal is to sell out games," Lucas said. "What is the opposite? To have absolutely nobody come."

No tickets were sold; the front gates were padlocked. Because a game is official after five innings, the RiverDogs decided to let fans in after that, following a party in Brittle Bank park, just beyond the center-field wall. There were 12 ladders and a cherry picker set up behind the wall so fans could get a sneak peek of the action.

Inside the stadium, all the normal in-game operations still took place. The beer vendors' calls echoed around the empty bleachers. Box-seat wait staff wandered aimlessly for people to serve. Foul balls were left untouched, though ushers raced into the stands to make sure no one was injured. And the promotions all took place as well. T-shirts and candy were fired into the empty seats and two sumo wrestling costumes lay on the field between innings. About 1,800 fans showed up outside. They were waiting at the gate and chanting "Let us in" as the fifth inning came to a close.

Why Can't We Be Friends?

It wouldn't be a year of minor league baseball without a few good brawls and disagreements. Here were the most

Colorado Springs outfielder Jack Cust was the big hitter in the 2002 Triple-A all-star game, as the Pacific Coast League whipped the International League 5-0 July 10 at Louisville's Bricktown Ballpark.

Cust entered the game as the DH in the sixth inning and collected a home run and single and drove in two runs.

The PCL got superb pitching as well with all nine of its hurlers working an inning apiece and limiting the IL stars to five hits.

The PCL struck for three runs in the bottom of the sixth to break a scoreless tie. Robb Quinlan of Salt Lake and Cust had RBIs in the inning.

"It's easy to win when the other team doesn't score," said PCL manager Dan Rohn (Tacoma). "That was the bottom line. All of our guys threw well and we did our best to keep out of the way and let the kids go out and play."

Cust didn't mind not starting.

"It took the pressure off me," said Cust, who socked a 390-foot shot over the left field bullpen in the eighth to finish the scoring. "I was more relaxed not having to go out there at the beginning of the game. I was able to control my adrenaline more, watching from the dugout."

TRIPLE-A ALL-STAR GAME
July 10 at Louisville
Pacific Coast League 5, International League 0

IL	ab	r	h	bi	PCL	ab	r	h	bi
Punto, ss	2	0	0	0	Thurston, 2b	2	0	0	0
Sheets, ss	2	0	0	0	Hill, 2b	1	1	0	0
Gonzalez, rf	3	0	1	0	Ryan, cf	4	1	2	0
Clemente, rf	1	0	0	0	Cuddyer, lf	2	0	0	0
Crawford, lf	4	0	1	0	Quinlan, lf	2	1	1	1
Larson, 3b	2	0	0	0	Overbay, dh	2	0	1	0
Patterson, 3b	1	0	0	0	Cust, dh	2	1	2	2
Crede, dh	2	0	1	0	Wood, 3b	2	0	0	0
Brinkley, dh	2	0	0	0	Blalock, 3b	2	0	0	0
Burnham, 1b	2	0	0	0	Sears, 1b	2	0	0	0
Phillips, c	1	0	1	0	Pelaez, 1b	2	0	0	0
Coste, c-1b	3	0	0	0	Holbert, ss	1	0	0	0
McMillon, lf	2	0	0	0	Berroa, ss	1	0	1	0
Chavez, lf	1	0	0	0	Lopez, M., ss	1	1	1	0
Scutaro, 2b	2	0	1	0	Allen, rf	3	0	0	0
Hudson, 2b	1	0	0	0	Molina, c	2	0	0	0
					Guzman, c	1	0	1	1
Totals	**31**	**0**	**5**	**0**	**Totals**	**32**	**5**	**9**	**4**
International League						000	000	000—0	
Pacific Coast League						000	003	11x—5	

DP—IL 1, PCL 1. LOB—IL 5, PCL 4. 2B—Scutaro, Ryan, Lopez. HR—Cust. SB—Crawford, Berroa.

IL	ip	h	r	er	bb	so	PCL	ip	h	r	er	bb	so
Linton	2	1	0	0	0	3	Myette	1	1	0	0	0	3
Hodges	1	0	0	0	0	0	Robertson	1	0	0	0	0	1
Stephens	2	2	0	0	0	0	Franklin	1	0	0	0	0	0
Ebert L	1	3	3	3	1	1	Walrond	1	2	0	0	0	0
Almonte	1	2	1	1	0	1	Lopez, A.	1	1	0	0	0	1
Gardner	⅔	1	1	1	0	0	Nance W	1	0	0	0	0	0
Zamora	⅓	0	0	0	0	0	Lankford	1	1	0	0	0	0
							Miadich	1	0	0	0	0	1
							Aybar	1	0	0	0	1	3

WP—Myette. T—2:36. A—11,343.

notable ones:

■ A game between Triple-A Columbus and Scranton-Wilkes/Barre–which the Red Barons won in a rout, 19-1—ended up in a fight involving two of the game's top prospects, Brett Myers and Drew Henson.

An exchange of brushback pitches reached a climax as Henson, a 6-foot-5, 222-pound former college football quarterback, charged the 6-foot-4, 215-pound Myers, a former amateur boxer.

"He doesn't intimidate me one bit," Myers said, "because when I hit him and he hit me, we both stopped in our tracks and he had the full momentum. He didn't scare me. You can bring all you want out here, but you're going to hit a linebacker, I'll tell you that.

"If I would have hit him with one of my hands, we'd be in the hospital, both of us, because I'd be in there getting a cast on my hand and he'd be in there for his broken face."

Said Henson: "It's part of baseball. One of our guys almost got hit in the head, and it escalated from there. You guys saw what happened. There's not really a whole lot more to say."

■ For the third year in a row, the Peoria Chiefs topped their previous record for brawling punishment. Midwest League president George Spelius suspended six Chiefs

Brett Myers

and six Quad City River Bandits for their roles in a fight during the Chiefs' 7-6 loss at Quad City on May 10. Both franchises were also fined $2,500.

"Rather than try to identify and determine who was on top of one pile or who was on the bottom of another, we made it a team fine," Spelius said. "There was simply too much going on to single out individuals."

Spelius told the Peoria Journal Star: "This was one of the better ones I've had in my 16 years as president of this league. I'm thoroughly disappointed in both ballclubs. They will be dealt with to the highest degree. I will not tolerate that in this league."

■ The Tulsa Drillers scored five runs in the 13th inning for an 8-4 victory over the Arkansas Travelers, but after the game the talk was about the sour notes coming from the organist at Ray Winder Field in Little Rock.

Tulsa manager Tim Ireland was thrown out in the sixth in a controversy over the stylings of ballpark organist Rich Pharris. Ireland came out to complain about the music, and after a heated argument, crew chief and first-base umpire Casey Moser ejected him.

"We've complained many times," Ireland said. "There's a failure on the institution here to control it, which is embarrassing and unfortunate, and if we'd have lost this game there would have been a stench surrounding that victory by them."

Pharris said he gets carried away but said Tulsa was the only team to consistently complain. "He got thrown out, and I survived and I got the coup," Pharris said of Ireland. "I got to play 'Happy Trails' when he got tossed."

■ Cedar Rapids manager Todd Claus, who earlier in the season staged his own ejection to try to break a losing streak, tackled his team's mascot, Mr. Shucks, after the Kernels swept South Bend.

Mr. Shucks brought out a broom and was prancing around the infield, which Claus took as a sign of disrespect for the Silver Hawks. He put Mr. Shucks in a headlock, wrestled the broom from him and snapped it in half.

"That's everything that we're not about," Claus said. "We preach going about things the right way. It's about professionalism and respect. You don't show anybody up. I don't care who you are. That team fought hard and fought well. To me it's common sense. You treat people the way you want to be treated.

"I asked for the broom. I said, 'Give it to me.' Somehow it became a struggle. I said, 'Give me the broom,' and threw in a few expletives."

DOUBLE-A ALL-STAR GAME

Though the final score of the 12th—and last—Double-A all-star game, July 10 at Norwich's Dodd Memorial Stadium, ended up 11-2 in favor of the American League, the game hinged on one play that could have been the difference between a continued nail-biter and the lopsided result.

With the game tied 2-2 in the bottom of the seventh, righthander Jack Krawczyk (Huntsville) walked leadoff hitter Jorge Sequea (Erie) and allowed a single to Dewayne Wise (Tennessee). With men on first and second and no out, Midland shortstop Marshall McDougall came to the plate.

"I turned to Wally (Backman, the Birmingham manager serving as skipper for the AL) and said, 'You aren't gonna have him bunt, are you?' " said Barons infielder Aaron Miles, who was on deck. "(Backman) said, 'Hell, yeah—I wanna win.' "

McDougall's bunt was a picture-perfect sacrifice to Binghamton first baseman Aaron McNeal. The only problem was, no one was covering first. Everyone was safe, and the play helped open the floodgates on a nine-run AL seventh.

"I'm not gonna be a four-hole (cleanup) guy if I make it (to the majors)," McDougall said, "so I've got to do little things like that."

The seventh also helped clear up a muddled MVP race. As has been the tradition in the Double-A all-star game, three MVPs were awarded, one for each Double-A league. McDougall got the Texas League nod, Sequea the Eastern League and Wise the Southern League.

"That one inning was pretty much the whole game," said Backman. "But it was nice to see a bunch of quality guys go out there and play."

DOUBLE-A ALL-STAR GAME
July 10 at Norwich, Conn.
American League 11, National League 2

NL	ab	r	h	bi	AL	ab	r	h	bi
Medrano, 2b	3	0	1	0	Reese, cf	2	0	1	0
Collins, 2b	2	0	0	0	Wise, cf	2	2	2	1
Stanley, rf	3	0	0	0	Sanchez, ss	2	1	1	0
Linden, rf	1	0	0	0	McDougall, ss	3	1	2	0
Chapman, 3b-dh	3	0	0	0	Phillips, 2b	2	1	1	0
Haynes, lf	1	0	0	0	Miles, 2b	3	1	1	2
Garrett, lf	2	0	0	0	Koonce, dh	4	0	1	1
Tracy, dh-3b	4	1	1	0	Martinez, c	1	0	0	0
Freeman, cf	2	0	1	0	Smith, c	3	1	1	2
Sledge, cf	2	1	2	1	Fernandez, rf	4	0	1	0
Nevers, 1b	2	0	1	0	Ford, lf	4	1	1	1
McNeal, 1b	2	0	1	1	Pressley, 1b	2	0	0	0
Buck, c	2	0	0	0	O'Keefe, 1b	2	1	1	0
Heintz, c	2	0	1	0	Veras, 3b	1	0	0	0
Barmes, ss	4	0	0	0	Sequea, pr-3b	1	2	1	3
Totals	**35**	**2**	**8**	**2**	**Totals**	**36**	**11**	**14**	**11**

National League	000	002	000—	2
American League	100	100	90x—	11

E—Sanchez. DP—AL 1. LOB—AL 8, NL 8. 2B—Sledge, Nevers, McDougall, Miles. 3B—Sledge, Phillips, Smith. HR—Wise, Sanchez, Sequea. SF—Koonce. SB—Fernandez, Ford.

NL	ip	h	r	er	bb	so	AL	ip	h	r	er	bb	so
Madson	1	1	1	1	0	1	Tallet	1	0	0	0	0	0
Villareal	1	0	0	0	1	0	Wood	1	1	0	0	0	2
Janke	1	1	0	0	0	0	Lee	1	0	0	0	0	1
Wayne	1	1	1	1	1	0	Hernandez	1	0	0	0	0	0
Robertson	1	0	0	0	1	1	Ruhl	1	1	0	0	0	1
Sylvester	1	1	0	0	0	1	Valentine	1	4	2	2	1	0
Krawczyk L	⅓	2	5	6	1	2	Padilla W	1	0	0	0	0	2
Spurling	⅓	4	3	3	0	0	Wilson	⅔	1	0	0	0	0
Rivera	1	1	0	0	0	0	Taylor	⅔	0	0	0	0	2
							Runser	⅓	0	0	0	0	1

HBP—by Tallet (Haynes), by Wayne (Martinez), by Robertson (Veras). T—2:50. A—8,009.

MINOR LEAGUE
DEPARTMENT LEADERS
*Full-season teams only

TEAM

WINS
Akron (Eastern) 93
Scranton/Wilkes-Barre (International) 91
Wilmington (Carolina) 89
Stockton (California) 89
Lynchburg (Carolina) 87

LONGEST WINNING STREAK
Pirates (Gulf Coast) 15
Dayton (Midwest) 13
Lynchburg (Carolina) 12
Erie (Eastern) 12
Eugene (Northwest) 12
Auburn (New York-Penn) 12

LOSSES
Frederick (Carolina) 92
Winston-Salem (Carolina) 90
Rochester (International) 89
Erie (Eastern) 89
Arkansas (Texas) 89
Savannah (South Atlantic) 89

LONGEST LOSING STREAK
Yakima (Northwest) 22
Macon (South Atlantic) 14
Winston-Salem (Carolina) 13
Savannah (South Atlantic) 13
Erie (Eastern) 12
Clearwater (Florida State) 12
Rochester (International) 12
Wisconsin (Midwest/1st streak) 12
Wisconsin (Midwest/2nd streak) 12

BATTING AVERAGE*
Salt Lake (Pacific Coast) .... .293
Las Vegas (Pacific Coast) .... .291
Edmonton (Pacific Coast) .... .287
Tucson (Pacific Coast) .... .284
Calgary (Pacific Coast) .... .283

RUNS
Las Vegas (Pacific Coast) 820
Edmonton (Pacific Coast) 820
High Desert (California) 818
Salt Lake (Pacific Coast) 797
Iowa (Pacific Coast) 793

HOME RUNS
Edmonton (Pacific Coast) 202
Iowa (Pacific Coast) 166
Las Vegas (Pacific Coast) 161
High Desert (California) 155
Syracuse (International) 153

Brad Nelson: 116 RBIs, 49 doubles

Joe Thurston: 196 hits

STOLEN BASES
Capital City (South Atlantic) 240
Columbus (South Atlantic) 235
St. Lucie (Florida State) 227
Birmingham (Southern) 220
Binghamton (Eastern) 215

EARNED RUN AVERAGE*
Peoria (Midwest) 2.78
Lynchburg (Carolina) 2.96
Lexington (South Atlantic) 3.03
Akron (Eastern) 3.09
Jacksonville (Southern) 3.10

STRIKEOUTS
Bakersfield (California) 1,281
Modesto (California) 1,269
San Bernardino (California) 1,266
Lake Elsinore (California) 1,227
Charleston, SC (South Atlantic) 1,213

INDIVIDUAL BATTING

BATTING AVERAGE
(Minimum 389 Plate Appearances)
Rick Short, Salt Lake .... .356
Brad Hawpe, Salem .... .347
Scott Hairston, South Bend/Lancaster .... .345
Chad Tracy, El Paso .... .344
Endy Chavez, Ottawa .... .343
Lyle Overbay, Tucson .... .343
Travis Hafner, Oklahoma .... .342
Jason Stokes, Kane County .... .341
Jon Knott, Fort Wayne/Lake Elsinore ...... .339
Victor Martinez, Akron .... .336

RUNS
Lew Ford, Edmonton/New Britain 121
Rich Thompson, Tennessee 109
Tony Miller, Asheville 109
Joe Thurston, Las Vegas 106
Jose Reyes, St. Lucie/Binghamton 104

HITS
Joe Thurston, Las Vegas 196
Lew Ford, Edmonton/New Britain 180
Lyle Overbay, Tucson 180
Chad Tracy, El Paso 177
Robb Quinlan, Salt Lake 176

TOP HITTING STREAKS
Corey Myers, Lancaster 33
Kevin Hooper, Calgary 31
Freddy Sanchez, Trenton 27
Endy Chavez, Ottawa 25
Darren Ciraco, Bristol 25

MOST HITS, ONE GAME
Larry Bigbie, Rochester 6
Brent Butler, Colorado Springs 6
John Castellano, San Bernardino 6
Ray Navarete, Lynchburg 6
Justin Leone, San Bernardino 6

TOTAL BASES
Joe Thurston, Las Vegas 297
Robb Quinlan, Salt Lake 293
Lew Ford, Edmonton/New Britain 286
Scott Hairston, South Bend/Lancaster 285
Mike Ryan, Edmonton 282

EXTRA-BASE HITS
Mike Ryan, Edmonton 73
Scott Hairston, South Bend/Lancaster 73
Brad Nelson, Beloit/High Desert 71
Michael Restovich, Edmonton 68
John Gall, New Haven 68

DOUBLES
Brad Nelson, Beloit/High Desert 49
Scott Hairston, South Bend/Lancaster 46
John Gall, New Haven 45
Jon Knott, Fort Wayne/Lake Elsinore 45
Andy Green, Tucson/Lancaster 44

TRIPLES
Jose Reyes, St. Lucie/Binghamton 19
Chone Figgins, Salt Lake 18
Dave Krynzel, Huntsville/High Desert 15
Donzell McDonald, Omaha 15
Brooks Conrad, Michigan 14
Kory DeHaan, Portland (PCL) 14

HOME RUNS
Ivan Cruz, Memphis 35
Mike Ryan, Edmonton 31
Jorge Soto, Visalia 31
Julio Zuleta, Iowa 31
Jonny Gomes, Bakersfield 30

RUNS BATTED IN
Brad Nelson, Beloit/High Desert 116
Robb Quinlan, Salt Lake 112
Laynce Nix, Charlotte (FSL) 110
Lyle Overbay, Tucson 109
Kevin Witt, Louisville 107

MOST RBIs, ONE GAME
Aaron Fera, Potomac 8
Robb Quinlan, Salt Lake 8
Earl Snyder, Buffalo 8
Garrett Jones, Quad City 8
Doug Gredvig, Bowie 8
Cody McKay, Sacramento 8

STOLEN BASES
Edwin Yan, Winston-Salem 88
Wayne Lydon, Capital City 87
Alex Requena, Kinston 72
Esix Snead, Binghamton 66
Angel Pagan, Capital City/St. Lucie 62

CAUGHT STEALING
Marcus Nettles, Lake Elsinore 26
Mike Spidale, Kannapolis 25
Danny Sandoval, Birmingham 24
Alexis Gomez, Wichita 24
Jose Reyes, St. Lucie/Binghamton 24

HIT BY PITCHES
Mike Campo, Rancho Cucamonga 40
Jonny Gomes, Bakersfield 31
Justin Huber, Capital City/St. Lucie 29
John Lindsey, San Bernardino 25
Bill McCarthy, Myrtle Beach 23
Greg LaRocca, Buffalo 23

WALKS
Graham Koonce, Midland 133
Shawn Fagan, Tennesee 102
Marcus Nettles, Lake Elsinore 101
Hee Seop Choi, Iowa 95
Kevin Youkilis, Augusta/Sarasota/Trenton .. 93

Larry Sutton, Sacramento 93

STRIKEOUTS
Jorge Soto, Visalia 195
Dan Trumble, San Jose 185
Jonny Gomes, Bakersfield 173
Charlton Jimerson, Lexington 168
Tim Lemon, Peoria 165

SACRIFICE FLIES
Robb Quinlan, Salt Lake 15
Stephen Smitherman, Stockton 14
Josh Labandeira, Clinton 12
Rich Paz, Wichita 11
Johnny Peralta, Akron 11
Scott Podsednik, Tacoma 11
Travis Wilson, Richmond 11
Steve Checksfield, Michigan 11

SACRIFICE BUNTS
Luis Rodriguez, New Britain 32
Nestor Perez, Bakersfield 23
Norris Hopper, Wilmington 22
Gary Cates, Delmarva/Bowie 21
Juan Francia, West Michigan 20
Vic Buttler, Hickory 20

SLUGGING PERCENTAGE
Jason Stokes, Kane County .... .645
Scott Hairston, South Bend/Lancaster .... .603
Brad Hawpe, Salem .... .587
Victor Martinez, Akron .... .576
Jonny Gomes, Bakersfield .... .574

ON BASE PERCENTAGE
Travis Hafner, Oklahoma .... .463
Mike Campo, Rancho Cucamonga .... .451
Brad Hawpe, Salem .... .447
Graham Koonce, Midland .... .440
Kevin Youkilis, Augusta/Sarasota/Trenton .... .436

BATTING AVERAGE*
By Position
(Minimum 383 Plate Appearances)
Catchers
Victor Martinez, Akron .... .336
Carlos Mendez, Sacramento .... .324
Chris Heintz, New Haven .... .314
Miguel Olivo, Birmingham .... .306
Joe Mauer, Quad City .... .302

First Basemen
Brad Hawpe, Salem .... .347
Lyle Overbay, Tucson .... .343
Travis Hafner, Oklahoma .... .342
Jason Stokes, Kane County .... .341
Jon Knott, Lake Elsinore/Fort Wayne ...... .339

Second Basemen
Scott Hairston, South Bend/Lancaster .... .345
Joe Thurston, Las Vegas .... .334
Dominic Rich, Tennessee/Dunedin .... .326
Aaron Miles, Birmingham .... .322
Marco Scutaro, Norfolk .... .319

Third Basemen
Chad Tracy, El Paso .... .344

Dan Haren: 194 innings

Brendan Harris, Daytona/West Tenn .... .328
Chris Sexton, Louisville .... .316
Jason Wood, Calgary .... .315
Jason Alfaro, Round Rock .... .314

Shortstops
Jose Lopez, San Bernardino .... .324
Freddy Sanchez, Trenton/Pawtucket .... .318
Aaron Holbert, Tacoma .... .311
David Lamb, Edmonton .... .309
Jose Flores, Sacramento .... .306

Outfielders
Endy Chavez, Ottawa .... .343
Robb Quinlan, Salt Lake .... .333
Raul Gonzalez, Louisville .... .333
Rocco Baldelli, Bakers./Orlando/Durham .... .331
Luke Allen, Las Vegas .... .329

INDIVIDUAL PITCHING

EARNED RUN AVERAGE
(Minimum 115 Innings)
Bubba Nelson, Myrtle Beach 1.72
Sean Burnett, Lynchburg 1.80
Dontrelle Willis, Kane County/Jupiter 1.83
Francisco Rosario, Charleston, WV/Dunedin .. 1.94
Tyler Johnson, Peoria 2.00
Ben Kozlowski, Charlotte (FSL)/Tulsa 2.07
Macay McBride, Macon 2.12
Angel Guzman, Lansing/Daytona 2.19
Nerio Rodriguez, Buffalo/Memphis 2.21
Chad Gaudin, Charleston, SC 2.26

WORST ERA
Justin Gordon, High Desert 7.58
Mario Ramos, Oklahoma 7.40
Nate Tekavec, Erie 7.09
Clint Smith, Erie 6.19
Chris Gissell, Iowa 6.12

WINS
Ian Ferguson, Wilmington/Wichita 18
Billy Traber, Akron/Buffalo 17
Zach Parker, Asheville 16
Ryan Madson, Reading 16
Chad Petty, West Michigan 15
Steve Randolph, Tucson 15
Trey Hodges, Richmond 15
Tyler Johnson, Peoria 15

LOSSES
Heath Phillips, Winston-Salem 16
Yoel Hernandez, Clearwater 16
Kris McWhirter, Winston-Salem/Charlotte (IL) ... 15
Gerrit Simpson, Salem/Asheville 15
Phil Akens, Kane County 15

GAMES
Trever Miller, Louisville 65
Dave Hooten, West Tenn 65
Mike Nicolas, Lake Elsinore 65
Ray Beasley, Richmond 64
Bryan Gaal, Lake Elsinore/Mobile 64

COMPLETE GAMES
Seung Lee, Lakewood/Clearwater/Reading .. 6
Julio De Paula, Norwich 6
Rich Fischer, R. Cucamonga/Arkansas 5
Heath Phillips, Winston-Salem 5
Shane Loux, Toledo 5
Taft Cable, Lakewood 5
Rhett Parrott, Potomac/New Haven 5

SAVES
Joe Valentine, Birmingham 36
Nate Cotton, Dayton 34
Lino Urdaneta, Vero Beach/Jacksonville ... 32
Mike Kobow, West Michigan 31
Evan Rust, Bakersfield/Orlando 31

SHUTOUTS
Rich Fischer, Rancho Cuca./Arkansas 4
Heath Phillips, Winston-Salem 3
Shane Loux, Roledo 3
Daniel Curtis, Greenville/Myrtle Beach 3
Bobby Basham, Dayton 3

INNINGS
Dan Haren, Peoria/Potomac 194

Ian Ferguson, Wilmington/Wichita 185
Andy Van Hekken, Erie/Toledo 183
Chris Waters, Myrtle Beach 183
Taylor Buchholz, Clearwater/Reading 182

WALKS
Mark Phillips, Lake Elsinore 94
Bobby Jenks, Arkansas/Rancho Cucamonga 90
Corwin Malone, Birmingham 89
Colt Griffin, Burlington (MWL)/Wilmington .. 87
Neal Cotts, Modesto 87
John Koronka, Stockton/Chattanooga 87

STRIKEOUTS
Clint Nageotte, San Bernardino 214
Rich Harden, Visalia/Midland 187
Jesse Foppert, Shreveport/Fresno 183
Neal Cotts, Modesto 178
Pedro Liriano, Rancho Cucamonga 176

HITS
Don Wengert, Pawtucket 218
Pete Smart, High Desert 212
Peter Bauer, Tennessee 208
Dennis Springer, Las Vegas 203
Bryan Rekar, Omaha/Colorado Springs 203

STRIKEOUTS/9 INNINGS*
(Starters)
Jesse Foppert, Shreveport/Fresno 11.74
Clint Nageotte, San Bernardino 11.70
Neal Cotts, Modesto 11.64
Travis Blackley, San Bernardino 11.27
Jon Switzer, Bakersfield 11.24

STRIKEOUTS/9 INNINGS*
(Relievers)
Stephen Andrade, Cedar Rapids 15.40
Mike Cox, Capital City/St. Lucie 14.48
Mike Nicolas, Lake Elsinore 14.08
Erick Threets, San Jose 13.66
Joel Barreto, Peoria 13.50

BATTING AVERAGE AGAINST*
(Starters)
Kirk Saarloos, Round Rock/New Orleans .... .175
Francisco Rosario, Charleston, WV/Dunedin .... .180
Andy Boutwell, Dayton/Stockton .... .184
Ben Kozlowski, Charlotte (FSL)/Tulsa ...... .195
Joaquin Benoit, Tulsa/Oklahoma .... .197

BATTING AVERAGE AGAINST*
(Relievers)
Ryan Bukvich, Omaha/Wichita .... .131
Chris Schroder, Clinton/Brevard County .... .144
Mark Corey, St. Lucie/Norfolk .... .147
Jannio Gutierrez, Quad City .... .154
Eric Brown, Lansing/Daytona/WT/Iowa .... .154
Jared Blasdell, Peoria .... .154

MOST STRIKEOUTS IN ONE GAME
Johan Santana, Edmonton 16
Mark Prior, West Tenn 15
Josh Hall, Stockton 15
Mark Malaska, Bakersfield 14
Glen Bott, San Bernardino 14
Cory Stewart, Fort Wayne 14
Chris Flinn, Charleston, SC 14
Darvin Withers, Modesto 14
Travis Blackley, San Bernardino 14
Salomon Torres, Nashville 14
Javier Martinez, Fort Wayne 14
Cory Stewart, Lake Elsinore 14

BALKS
Jason Moates, West Michigan 7
Jon Steitz, Beloit 7
Ben Julianel, Peoria 7
Kevin McDowell, West Michigan 6
Charles Merricks, Asheville 6

INDIVIDUAL FIELDING

MOST ERRORS
Julian Benividez, 3b, Hagerstown 43
Jeff Bannon, ss, Stockton 42
Bill Hall, ss, Indianapolis 41
Jorge Cantu, ss, Orlando 41
Jackson Aquino, ss, Fort Wayne 41
Luis DePaula, ss, Charleston, SC 41

TOM PRIDDY

MINOR LEAGUE BEST TOOLS

Full season leagues only

	International League AAA	Pacific Coast League AAA	Eastern League AA	Southern League AA	Texas League AA	California League A	Carolina League A	Florida State League A	Midwest League A	South Atlantic League A
Best Batting Prospect	Brandon Larson, Louisville	Michael Cuddyer, Edmonton	Victor Martinez, Akron	David Kelton, West Tenn	Chad Tracy, El Paso	Corey Hart, High Desert	Brad Hawpe, Salem	Mark Teixeira, Charlotte	Jason Stokes, Kane County	Victor Diaz, South Georgia
Best Power Prospect	Brandon Larson, Louisville	Julio Zuleta, Iowa	Dee Haynes, New Haven	Wily Mo Pena, Chattanooga	Todd Linden, Shreveport	Jorge Soto, Visalia	Brad Hawpe, Salem	Craig Brazell, St. Lucie	Brad Nelson, Beloit	Walter Young, Hickory
Best Baserunner	Carl Crawford, Durham	Chone Figgins, Salt Lake	Jesus Medrano, Portland	Bernie Castro, Mobile	Jamal Strong, San Antonio	Marcus Nettles, Lake Elsinore	Alex Requena, Kinston	Jose Reyes, St. Lucie	Charlie Frazier, Kane County	Wayne Lydon, Capital City
Fastest Baserunner	Andres Torres, Toledo	Chone Figgins, Salt Lake	Esix Snead, New Haven	Bernie Castro, Mobile	Jamal Strong, San Antonio	Marcus Nettles, Lake Elsinore	Alex Requena, Kinston	Jose Reyes, St. Lucie	Pedro de los Santos, Fort Wayne	Chris Amador, Kannapolis
Best Pitching Prospect	Brett Myers, Scranton/W-B	John Lackey, Salt Lake	Erik Bedard, Bowie	Aaron Cook, Carolina	Kirk Saarloos, Round Rock	Oliver Perez, Lake Elsinore	Sean Burnett, Lynchburg	Jason Arnold, Tampa	Dontrelle Willis, Kane County	John VanBenschoten, Hickory
Best Fastball	Brett Myers, Scranton/W-B	Aaron Myette, Oklahoma	Fernando Rodney, Erie	Francis Beltran, West Tenn	Bobby Jenks, Arkansas	Erick Threets, San Jose	Adam Wainwright, Myrtle Beach	Ben Diggins, Vero Beach	Don Levinski, Clinton	Dustin McGowan, Charleston, W. Va.
Best Breaking Pitch	John Stephens, Rochester	Dennis Tankersley, Portland	Cliff Lee, Harrisburg	Mike Bynum, Mobile	Runelvys Hernandez, Wichita	Jeff Clark, San Jose	Sean Burnett, Lynchburg	Taylor Buchholz, Clearwater	Tyler Johnson, Peoria	Phil Dumatrait, Augusta
Best Control	Joe Roa, Scranton/W-B	Jeriome Robertson, New Orleans	Billy Traber, Akron	Aaron Cook, Carolina	Kirk Saarloos, Round Rock	Jeff Clark, San Jose	Sean Burnett, Lynchburg	Josh Reynolds, St. Lucie	Dontrelle Willis, Kane County	Kris Honel, Kannapolis
Best Reliever	Lee Gardner, Durham	Shane Nance, Las Vegas	Fernando Rodney, Erie	J.J Trujillo, Mobile	Miguel Saladin, Round Rock	Evan Rust, Bakersfield	D.J. Carrasco, Lynchburg	Beau Kemp, Fort Myers	Rusty Tucker, Fort Wayne	Rommie Lewis, Delmarva
Best Defensive Catcher	Brandon Inge, Toldeo	Jose Molina, Salt Lake	Victor Martinez, Akron	Dane Sardinha, Chattanooga	John Buck, Round Rock	Craig Ansman, Lancaster	Humberto Quintero, Winston-Salem	Kelly Shoppach, Sarasota	Joe Mauer, Quad City	Hector Giminez, Lexington
Best Defensive First Baseman	Eric Munson, Toledo	Todd Sears, Edmonton	Carlos Rivera, Altoona	Eric Battersby, Birmingham	Graham Koonce, Midland	Aaron Clark, Bakersfield	Adam LaRoche, Myrtle Beach	Derek Michaelis, Vero Beach	Casey Kotchman, Cedar Rapids	Walter Young, Hickory
Best Defensive Second Baseman	Orlando Hudson, Syracuse	Jesus Medrano, Iowa	Jesus Medrano, Portland	Jason Dellaero, Birmingham	Matt Kata, El Paso	Andy Green, Lancaster	Thomas Lora, Wilmington	Ramon Martinez, Charlotte	Ruben Gotay, Burlington	Jayson Nix, Asheville
Best Defensive Third Baseman	Joe Crede, Charlotte	Hank Blalock, Oklahoma	Wilton Veras, Trenton	Donny Leon, Chattanooga	Luis Terrero, El Paso	Angel Chavez, San Jose	Corey Smith, Kinston	Brendan Harris, Daytona	Dallas McPherson, Cedar Rapids	Andy Marte, Macon
Best Defensive Shortstop	Omar Infante, Toledo	Abraham Nunez, Calgary	Jose Reyes, Binghamton	Jhonny Carvajal, Shreveport	Ruben Castillo, San Antonio	J.J. Hardy, High Desert	Jose Castillo, Lynchburg	Jose Reyes, St. Lucie	John Nelson, Peoria	Ivan Ochoa, Columbus
Best Infield Arm	Omar Infante, Toledo	Angel Berroa, Omaha	Jose Reyes, Binghamton	Jason Dellaero, Birmingham	Ruben Castillo, San Antonio	Jose Lopez, San Bernardino	Jose Castillo, Lynchburg	Jose Reyes, St. Lucie	Tommy Murphy, Cedar Rapids	Victor Diaz, South Georgia
Best Defensive Outfielder	Endy Chavez, Toledo	Luke Allen, Las Vegas	Lew Ford, New Britain	Wilkin Ruan, Jacksonville	Luis Terrero, El Paso	Rocco Baldelli, Bakersfield	Byron Gettis, Wilmington	Brandon Watson, Brevard County	Shin-Soo Choo, Wisconsin	Willy Taveras, Columbus
Best Outfield Arm	Edgard Clemente, Indianapolis	Angel Berroa, Omaha	Keith Reed, Bowie	Alex Fernandez, Birmingham	Luis Terrero, El Paso	Rocco Baldelli, Bakersfield	Skip Schumaker, Potomac	Carlos Rodriguez, Sarasota	Rick Asadoorian, Peoria	Jeremy Harts, Hickory
Most Exciting Player	Carl Crawford, Durham	Angel Berroa, Omaha	Jose Reyes, Binghamton	Bernie Castro, Mobile	Alexis Gomez, Wichita	Jayhawk Owens, Stockton	Jose Castillo, Lynchburg	Jose Reyes, St. Lucie	Jason Stokes, Kane County	Victor Diaz, South Georgia
Best Managerial Prospect	Marc Bombard, Scranton/W-B	John Russell, Edmonton	Howie Freiling, Binghamton	Wally Backman, Birmingham	Jackie Moore, Round Rock		Jeff Garber, Wilmington	Darryl Kennedy, Charlotte	Todd Claus, Cedar Rapids	Tony Tijerina, Capital City

Selected at midseason, 2002, by Baseball America correspondents in consultation with minor league managers

MINOR LEAGUES

FREITAS AWARDS

As a former publisher and president of Baseball America, Dave Chase regularly contributed to the selection of the annual Bob Freitas Awards, presented to franchises that show sustained excellence in the business of minor league baseball.

In fact, Chase helped in the creation of the awards, which were first presented in 1989—shortly after the death of Freitas, a longtime minor league operator, promoter and ambassador. Little did Chase know he would one day be in charge of a team that would win the award.

Shortly after being named president and general manager of the **Memphis Redbirds**, Chase learned the Redbirds were the 2002 Triple-A recipient of the Freitas awards.

"The award is based on more than just attendance," Chase said. "This is an important award to win. It's a milestone the Redbirds have looked forward to. The timing was great."

To be considered for the award, a team must be in existence for at least five years. The Redbirds just completed their five-year anniversary. Since moving into AutoZone Park in 2000, an $80 million downtown gem, the Redbirds have drawn around 900,000 fans a year—second in minor league attendance behind only fellow Pacific Coast League franchise Sacramento.

■ When Frank Burke and his partners—father Daniel and Portland Sea Dogs president and general manager Charlie Eshbach— decided to buy the **Chattanooga Lookouts** in 1995, they had little idea what they were getting into.

 *(Note: CHATTANOOGA LOOKOUTS logo)*

"We sorely underestimated the maintenance with the old stadium," said Burke, referring to the city's antiquated Engel Stadium, which opened in 1930. "It was a lot more expensive to keep that place up and running the way we wanted it to be. It became apparent very quickly that it would be tough to survive there."

Burke and his group wanted to stay in Chattanooga, but it was apparent that a new stadium would be necessary for survival. In November 1998, the Lookouts announced that a new stadium would be built, but only if the community committed to buying 1,800 season tickets and 10 luxury box rentals. It was given 90 days to meet those goals; it got done in 80 days.

The result was a franchise that became a consistent draw at the gate. At BellSouth Park, which opened in 2000, the Lookouts have averaged about 286,000 fans a season—and resulted in the team being selected the 2002 Double-A Freitas winner.

■ The Florida State League is well known for its spring training-groomed facilities, impressive list

of alumni and ever-present evening thunderstorms that are as much a part of game-time preparation as batting practice. The league also has few franchises that annually draw in six figures.

Fort Myers had the league's highest attendance in 2002 at 109,293. Its strong community involvement and an outstanding baseball atmosphere were also factors in the Miracle's selection as the Class A recipient of the Freitas Award—the first FSL team to win in the 14-year history of the award.

■ The **Ogden Raptors** are a repeat Freitas Award winner—sort of. The franchise won the award in

1990, when it was known as the Salt Lake Trappers.

The Trappers, an independently-operated team in the Rookie-level Pioneer League, were forced to leave Salt Lake when a Triple-A team came to town. The Trappers moved to Pocatello, Idaho, in 1993, and relocated to Ogden a year later.

Dave Baggott had served as the Trappers' GM in Salt Lake, but he was out of a job when the city lost the Trappers. A year later, he was hard at work putting together deals with the city of Ogden and the Pioneer League, which had taken over ownership of the Pocatello franchise, to bring the Trappers back to Utah.

In the eight years since, the team has been a consistent winner both on the field and at the gate. Sparkling Lindquist Field—named after Baggott's business partner, John Lindquist—opened in 1997, and in 2002 the Raptors operated at more than 100 percent capacity.

PREVIOUS WINNERS

Triple-A

1989	Columbus (International)
1990	Pawtucket (International)
1991	Buffalo (American Association)
1992	Iowa (American Association)
1993	Richmond (International)
1994	Norfolk (International)
1995	Albuquerque (Pacific Coast)
1996	Indianapolis (American Association)
1997	Rochester (International)
1998	Salt Lake (Pacific Coast)
1999	Louisville (International)
2000	Edmonton (Pacific Coast)
2001	Buffalo (International)

Double-A

1989	El Paso (Texas)
1990	Arkansas (Texas)
1991	Reading (Eastern)
1992	Tulsa (Texas)
1993	Harrisburg (Eastern)
1994	San Antonio (Texas)
1995	Midland (Texas)
1996	Carolina (Southern)
1997	Bowie (Eastern)
1998	Trenton (Eastern)
1999	Portland (Eastern)
2000	Reading (Eastern)
2001	Mobile (Southern)

Class A

1989	Durham (Carolina)
1990	San Jose (California)
1991	Asheville (South Atlantic)
1992	Springfield (Midwest)
1993	South Bend (Midwest)
1994	Kinston (Carolina)
1995	Kane County (Midwest)
1996	Wisconsin (Midwest)
1997	Rancho Cucamonga (California)
1998	West Michigan (Midwest)
1999	Wilmington (Carolina)
2000	Charleston, S.C. (South Atlantic)
2001	Delmarva (South Atlantic)

Short-Season

1989	Eugene (Northwest)
1990	Salt Lake City (Pioneer)
1991	Spokane (Northwest)
1992	Boise (Northwest)
1993	Billings (Pioneer)
1994	Everett (Northwest)
1995	Great Falls (Pioneer)
1996	Bluefield (Appalachian)
1997	Oneonta (New York-Penn)
1998	Hudson Valley (New York-Penn)
1999	Portland (Northwest)
2000	Lowell (New York-Penn)
2001	Salem-Keizer (Northwest)

INTERNATIONAL LEAGUE

BY TIM PEARRELL

The third time turned out to be a cha . . . make that a championship for the Durham Bulls.

The Bulls, making their third appearance in the International League Governors' Cup finals since joining the league in 1998, ended a long title drought by sweeping Buffalo in the best-of-five championship series.

Durham hadn't won a championship since 1967, when it captured the Class A Carolina League crown.

"It's a dream come true," Durham manager Bill Evers said. "I've won at other levels, but Triple-A is a tough situation with all the transactions you have. This is very rewarding."

Evers guided three teams to titles in Class A and Double-A. The only manager Durham has had since it moved to Triple-A had to settle for runner-up finishes in 1998 (to Buffalo) and again in 1999 (to Charlotte).

This time, Durham made sure it would be first and foremost in a series that included an unusual ending to the first game and an unusual hero in Bulls catcher Paul Hoover. The first game was tied 4-4 when it was suspended in the 12th inning because of a thunderstorm. Baseball rules say such a game should be replayed, but IL president Randy Mobley, with the blessings of both managers, decided to resume it at that point.

Durham won the suspended game 6-4 when Emil Brown hit a two-out, two-run homer in the top of the 12th, then won the second game of the playoff doubleheader 8-1 behind a five-hitter from Luis De los Santos. The twinbill was played on Sept. 11, with a pregame ceremony marking the anniversary of the terrorist attacks.

Durham fans got their wish for a sweep when Hoover doubled in a run and starter Gerardo Garcia combined with three relievers on a one-hitter in Game Three. Hoover, who hit .220-5-27 in 69 regular-season games, batted .476 with two homers during the playoffs.

Quick Comeback

The series also included a stirring first-game save by

Paul Hoover helped lead Durham to the league title

Durham pitcher Delvin James, who had been shot nine days earlier in a random wrong-place, wrong-time scenario. The righthander was sitting with a friend in a Raleigh, N.C., Waffle House at 3 a.m. Sept. 2 when police said two groups inside the restaurant had an altercation that escalated into gunfire.

One bullet lodged in James' left shoulder blade. Another entered near his left armpit and exited through his back. A third grazed his left elbow. His friend, Monique McNellie, was hit by a bullet that passed through her kidney and lodged near her spine.

James, a righthander, came off the disabled list and pitched a perfect final inning in Game One, getting a

STANDINGS

Page	EAST	W	L	PCT	GB	Manager	Attendance	Avg.	Last Penn.
211	Scranton/W-B Red Barons (Phillies)	91	53	.632	—	Marc Bombard	466,342	6,580	None
116	Buffalo Bisons (Indians)	87	57	.604	4	Eric Wedge	642,272	9,003	1998
180	Ottawa Lynx (Expos)	80	61	.567	9½	Tim Leiper	191,305	3,037	1995
269	Syracuse SkyChiefs (Blue Jays)	64	80	.444	27	Omar Malave	413,566	6,082	1976
87	Pawtucket Red Sox (Red Sox)	60	84	.417	31	Buddy Bailey	615,540	9,052	1984
79	Rochester Red Wings (Orioles)	55	89	.382	36	Andy Etchebarren	421,494	6,021	1997
Page	**WEST**	**W**	**L**	**PCT**	**GB**	**Manager(s)**	**Attendance**	**Avg.**	**Last Penn.**
131	Toledo Mud Hens (Tigers)	81	63	.563	—	Bruce Fields	567,804	7,707	1967
108	Louisville RiverBats (Reds)	79	65	.549	2	Dave Miley	659,340	9,158	2001
166	Indianapolis Indians (Brewers)	67	76	.469	13½	Ed Romero	571,984	8,056	2000
188	Columbus Clippers (Yankees)	59	83	.415	21	Brian Butterfield/Stump Merrill	490,390	7,006	1996
Page	**SOUTH**	**W**	**L**	**PCT**	**GB**	**Manager**	**Attendance**	**Avg.**	**Last Penn.**
254	Durham Bulls (Devil Rays)	80	64	.556	—	Bill Evers	519,122	7,181	2002
72	Richmond Braves (Braves)	75	67	.528	4	Fredi Gonzalez	452,961	6,565	1994
196	Norfolk Tides (Mets)	70	73	.490	9½	Bobby Floyd	500,192	7,249	1985
94	Charlotte Knights (White Sox)	55	88	.385	24½	Nick Capra	303,321	4,396	1999

GOVERNORS' CUP PLAYOFFS—Semifinals: Durham defeated Toledo 3-0 and Buffalo defeated Scranton/Wilkes-Barre in best-of-5 series. **Finals:** Durham defeated Buffalo 3-0 in best-of-5 series.

NOTE: Team's individual batting and pitching statistics can be found on page indicated in lefthand column.

strikeout to end it.

"I was a couple of inches away from never being able to play again, or not seeing another day," James said. "So it felt wonderful to be able to come out and play well. The man upstairs, he must love me a lot."

Durham, which held off Richmond in the final week of the season to take the Southern Division title, and wild-card Buffalo advanced by sweeping their semifinal series. Durham ended IL West champ Toledo's fairy-tale season thanks to Baseball America Minor League Player of the Year Rocco Baldelli and a 13-inning victory, and Buffalo took out North champ Scranton/Wilkes-Barre in their annual playoff matchup.

Toledo, playing in new digs at Fifth Third Field, won its first pennant since 1968 and made the playoffs for the first time since 1984. The Mud Hens (81-63) enjoyed just their ninth winning season since joining the IL in 1965 and played in front of 27 sellouts. They attracted nearly 550,000 fans and set a franchise record by mid-July.

Scranton (91-53) became just the third club since 1963 to win 90 or more games. But the Red Barons couldn't get past the Bisons in their third straight first-round meeting. Buffalo cemented the sweep by scoring four runs in the ninth inning of Game Three and erasing a 4-1 deficit. Zach Sorensen, Buffalo's No. 9 hitter, went 7-for-12 (.583) with seven RBIs and scored five runs during the series.

Awards Time

Raul Gonzalez, who spent most of the season with Louisville before being traded to the Mets, was named the league's MVP (.333-13-69). Scranton's Joe Roa, who was in two other spring-training camps before being dealt to the Phillies, went 14-0, 1.86 before called up to Philadelphia. He was named the league's most outstanding pitcher.

Durham outfielder Carl Crawford (.297-7-52 with 26 stolen bases) headed a strong cast of prospects and was named rookie of the year and the league's No. 1 prospect.

STAN DENNY

Raul Gonzalez

Scranton's Marc Bombard added another manager-of-the-year award to his resume. He earned that honor twice in the American Association (1992 and 1994).

Indianapolis' Izzy Alcantara claimed the home run title (27) for the second straight season, Ottawa's Endy Chavez (.343) took the batting crown and Louisville's Kevin Witt had the most RBIs (107). Richmond's Trey Hodges, a rookie, was the top winner (15-9), with teammate Doug Linton taking the ERA (2.53) and strikeout (160) titles despite a 9-11 record. Charlotte's Ed Almonte was the top closer with 26 saves.

No individual no-hitters were thrown, but Columbus' Adrian Hernandez, Bob Scanlan and Kevin Lovingier combined on a no-no against Indianapolis.

Jose Canseco, needing 38 homers to reach 500 in the majors, made a hyped-but-brief appearance with Charlotte before retiring.

While several managers hit milestones, Columbus manager Brian Butterfield was reassigned after a 12-25 start. He eventually was replaced by Mr. Clipper, Stump Merrill, who came back for a ninth stint with the club. Louisville's Dave Miley and Pawtucket's Buddy Bailey both went over 1,000 managerial wins.

LEAGUE CHAMPIONS

Last 30 Years

Year	Regular Season*	Pct.	Playoff
1972	Louisville (Red Sox)	.563	Tidewater (Mets)
1973	Charleston (Pirates)	.586	Pawtucket (Red Sox)
1974	Memphis (Expos)	.613	Rochester (Orioles)
1975	Tidewater (Mets)	.607	Tidewater (Mets)
1976	Rochester (Orioles)	.638	Syracuse (Yankees)
1977	Pawtucket (Red Sox)	.571	Charleston (Astros)
1978	Charleston (Astros)	.607	Richmond (Braves)
1979	Columbus (Yankees)	.612	Columbus (Yankees)
1980	Columbus (Yankees)	.593	Columbus (Yankees)
1981	Columbus (Yankees)	.633	Columbus (Yankees)
1982	Richmond (Braves)	.590	Tidewater (Mets)
1983	Columbus (Yankees)	.593	Tidewater (Mets)
1984	Columbus (Yankees)	.590	Pawtucket (Red Sox)
1985	Syracuse (Blue Jays)	.564	Tidewater (Mets)
1986	Richmond (Braves)	.571	Richmond (Braves)
1987	Tidewater (Mets)	.579	Columbus (Yankees)
1988	Tidewater (Mets)	.546	Rochester (Orioles)
	Rochester (Orioles)	.546	
1989	Syracuse (Blue Jays)	.572	Richmond (Braves)
1990	Rochester (Orioles)	.614	Rochester (Orioles)
1991	Columbus (Yankees)	.590	Columbus (Yankees)
1992	Columbus (Yankees)	.660	Columbus (Yankees)
1993	Charlotte (Indians)	.610	Charlotte (Indians)
1994	Richmond (Braves)	.567	Richmond (Braves)
1995	Norfolk (Mets)	.606	Ottawa (Expos)
1996	Columbus (Yankees)	.599	Columbus (Yankees)
1997	Rochester (Orioles)	.589	Rochester (Orioles)
1998	Buffalo (Indians)	.566	Buffalo (Indians)
1999	Columbus (Yankees)	.589	Charlotte (White Sox)
2000	Buffalo (Indians)	.593	Indianapolis (Brewers)
2001	Buffalo (Indians)	.641	Louisville (Reds)
2002	Scranton/W-B (Phillies)	.632	Durham (Devil Rays)

*Best overall record

Affiliation Adjustments

The other major story lines were the uncertainty that continued to loom over Ottawa, and Rochester's divorce from the Baltimore Orioles.

With Ottawa finishing at the bottom of the Triple-A attendance chart for the second straight year, Mobley issued a "use it or lose it" ultimatum to Ottawa fans. The Lynx drew just 191,123—an average of 3,034 in 63 openings—after drawing 205,916 (2,942 average) in 2001.

"While we haven't pursued options in the past, now we are," Mobley said. "We've got a situation here where (owner Ray Pecor) is losing millions of dollars. That's not a good situation for a man or for a league. There needs to be a reason to stay here, and right now that's not being demonstrated."

Mobley said the team would remain in Ottawa for the 2003 season. After that . . . "What more can we do?" Pecor said. "When we first came in here (in 2000), we tried to address all the things people wanted us to address. The weather is awful (in April and May), the Canadian dollar is awful, but we knew that coming in. The economy is not great, I agree, but we've called on all the corporations who will let us in the door. I'm not here to point fingers, but we can't keep going like this."

Unhappy with five straight losing seasons and a lack of prospects in Baltimore's farm system, Rochester ended its 42-year affiliation with the Orioles, instead signing a two-year working agreement with the Minnesota Twins. The Orioles then jumped to Ottawa.

Rochester finished 55-89, the club's worst record in 23 years and its most losses since 1945. Included was a 12-game losing streak that featured a six-night, camp-out-in-the-bullpen-until-we-win promise by Red Wings general manager Dan Mason, as well as an eight-game losing streak to end the season.

2002 INTERNATIONAL LEAGUE STATISTICS

CLUB BATTING

	AVG	G	AB	R	H	2B	3B	HR	BB	SO	SB
Ottawa	.281	141	4697	620	1319	266	38	85	403	759	112
Buffalo	.279	144	4902	684	1367	295	36	107	394	777	78
Louisville	.278	144	4989	699	1387	282	24	133	454	870	57
Toledo	.270	144	4888	665	1319	279	52	119	489	962	94
Scranton/W-B	.269	144	4934	705	1328	277	34	89	471	858	109
Rochester	.269	144	4974	596	1336	239	36	88	380	811	85
Durham	.266	144	4885	681	1298	228	50	105	384	913	153
Syracuse	.264	144	4914	697	1295	287	25	153	478	1014	77
Richmond	.260	142	4719	613	1228	247	17	126	392	954	81
Pawtucket	.259	144	4834	607	1253	237	28	147	440	969	52
Columbus	.258	142	4819	649	1242	273	32	135	388	835	51
Norfolk	.257	143	4751	598	1223	243	32	119	431	934	110
Charlotte	.256	143	4774	572	1221	256	14	131	373	1023	110
Indianapolis	.248	143	4709	526	1170	241	27	93	429	871	92

CLUB PITCHING

	ERA	G	CG	SHO	SV	IP	H	R	ER	BB	SO
Scranton/W-B	3.27	144	7	10	45	1279	1218	535	465	395	878
Buffalo	3.30	144	8	13	43	1269	1209	537	465	387	924
Richmond	3.50	142	4	12	35	1242	1229	562	483	403	950
Ottawa	3.54	141	6	11	41	1215	1134	555	478	415	786
Toledo	3.63	144	11	13	40	1278	1274	587	515	374	884
Norfolk	3.74	143	6	13	30	1249	1296	585	519	382	940
Durham	3.87	143	3	9	49	1274	1305	626	548	425	982
Indianapolis	3.87	143	6	5	42	1254	1241	615	540	415	869
Louisville	4.26	144	2	10	35	1288	1342	671	610	433	1005
Rochester	4.35	144	6	9	22	1268	1370	705	613	413	862
Syracuse	4.50	144	5	3	24	1262	1319	743	631	469	781
Pawtucket	4.62	144	4	6	37	1249	1357	732	641	464	837
Charlotte	4.63	143	4	7	29	1241	1322	700	638	450	875
Columbus	4.69	142	3	4	28	1245	1370	759	649	481	977

CLUB FIELDING

	PCT	PO	A	E	DP		PCT	PO	A	E	DP
Charlotte	.980	3723	1432	103	135	Richmond	.976	3725	1462	130	128
Ottawa	.980	3645	1557	104	147	Durham	.975	3822	1512	136	178
Norfolk	.980	3746	1441	105	117	Pawtucket	.975	3748	1468	133	115
Scranton/W-B	.979	3838	1609	118	162	Toledo	.975	3835	1648	140	144
Louisville	.979	3864	1519	117	132	Indianapolis	.973	3763	1493	144	132
Buffalo	.977	3808	1496	124	142	Syracuse	.972	3786	1574	152	141
Rochester	.976	3805	1394	129	99	Columbus	.970	3736	1384	160	111

INDIVIDUAL BATTING LEADERS
(Minimum 389 Plate Appearances)

	AVG	G	AB	R	H	2B	3B	HR	RBI	BB	SO	SB
Chavez, Endy, Ottawa	.343	103	405	67	139	28	5	4	41	33	37	21
Gonzalez, Raul, Louisville	.333	114	432	91	144	27	2	13	69	61	59	9
Vitiello, Joe, Ottawa	.329	119	431	57	142	34	0	16	82	39	58	1
Monroe, Craig, Toledo	.321	99	358	61	115	30	4	10	49	35	57	7
Scutaro, Marco, Norfolk	.319	97	354	48	113	22	6	7	28	30	61	7
Coste, Chris, Richmond	.318	124	478	59	152	32	1	8	67	34	54	0
Sexton, Chris, Louisville	.316	108	414	79	131	29	5	6	49	42	41	3
Rushford, Jim, Indianapolis	.316	117	405	54	128	33	3	7	68	45	41	0
Crede, Joe, Charlotte	.312	95	359	57	112	21	0	24	65	26	48	0
Clark, Howie, Rochester	.309	108	418	57	129	21	4	7	43	41	28	3

INDIVIDUAL PITCHING LEADERS
(Minimum 115 Innings)

	W	L	ERA	G	GS	CG	SV	IP	H	R	ER	BB	SO
De Los Santos, Luis, Durham	9	2	2.42	24	16	1	0	115	105	38	31	21	68
Linton, Doug, Richmond	9	11	2.53	28	28	1	0	174	167	63	49	26	160
Dawley, Joey, Richmond	9	7	2.63	24	23	1	0	140	113	44	41	36	136
Carter, Lance, Durham	12	2	2.80	33	18	2	1	132	111	43	41	12	90
Stephens, John, Rochester	11	5	3.03	21	21	1	0	143	126	51	48	23	118
Lorraine, Andrew, Indianapolis	7	11	3.05	25	24	2	0	165	157	65	56	42	86
Drew, Tim, Buffalo-Ottawa	14	7	3.08	28	28	2	0	181	173	74	62	47	72
Standridge, Jason, Durham	10	9	3.12	29	29	0	0	173	168	71	60	64	111
Hodges, Trey, Richmond	15	9	3.19	28	28	1	0	172	158	66	61	56	116
Acevedo, Jose, Louisville	12	7	3.20	23	23	0	0	155	146	61	55	34	128

ALL-STAR TEAM

C—Johnny Estrada, Scranton/Wilkes-Barre. **1B**—Joe Vitiello, Ottawa. **2B**—Marco Scutaro, Norfolk. **3B**—Joe Crede, Charlotte. **SS**—Nick Punto, Scranton/Wilkes-Barre. **OF**—Marlon Byrd, Scranton/Wilkes-Barre; Endy Chavez, Ottawa; Raul Gonzalez, Louisville. **DH**—Kevin Witt, Louisville. **Util**—Dave Doster, Scranton/Wilkes-Barre. **SP**—Joe Roa, Scranton/Wilkes-Barre. **RP**—Lee Gardner, Durham.

Most Valuable Player: Raul Gonzalez, Louisville. **Most Valuable Pitcher**: Joe Roa, Scranton/Wilkes-Barre. **Rookie of the Year**: Carl Crawford, Durham. **Manager of the Year**: Marc Bombard, Scranton/Wilkes-Barre.

MINOR LEAGUES

DEPARTMENT LEADERS

BATTING
G	Dave Doster, Scranton/W-B	143
AB	Dave Doster, Scranton/W-B	579
R	Marlon Byrd, Scranton/W-B	103
H	Dave Doster, Scranton/W-B	171
TB	Marlon Byrd, Scranton/W-B	256
XBH	Marlon Byrd, Scranton/W-B	59
2B	Chase Utley, Scranton/W-B	39
3B	Zach Sorensen, Buffalo	12
HR	Israel Alcantara, Indianapolis	27
RBI	Kevin Witt, Louisville	107
SH	Kary Bridges, Columbus	15
	Zach Sorensen, Buffalo	15
SF	Travis Wilson, Richmond	11
BB	Eric Munson, Toledo	77
IBB	Larry Bigbie, Rochester	7
	Johnny Estrada, Scranton/W-B	7
HBP	Greg LaRocca, Buffalo	23
SO	Drew Henson, Columbus	151
SB	Andres Torres, Toledo	42
	Nick Punto, Scranton/W-B	42
CS	Omar Infante, Toledo	15
GIDP	Gary Burnham, Syracuse	19
	Johnny Estrada, Scranton/W-B	19
OB%	Raul Gonzalez, Louisville	.416
SL%	Joe Crede, Charlotte	.571

PITCHING
G	Trever Miller, Louisville	65
GS	Eric Junge, Scranton/W-B	29
	Jason Standridge, Durham	29
CG	Shane Loux, Toledo	5
ShO	Shane Loux, Toledo	3
GF	Brian Bowles, Syracuse	46
SV	Ed Almonte, Charlotte	26
W	Trey Hodges, Richmond	15
L	Jay Spurgeon, Rochester	14
IP	Tim Drew, Buffalo-Ottawa	181
H	Don Wengert, Pawtucket	218
R	Jay Spurgeon, Rochester	104
ER	Jay Spurgeon, Rochester	92
HR	Dan Wheeler, Richmond	23
HB	Luke Hudson, Louisville	16
BB	Carlos Chantres, Durham-Charlotte	67
	Eric Junge, Scranton/W-B	67
SO	Doug Linton, Richmond	160
WP	Jim Magrane, Durham	13
BK	Adrian Hernandez, Columbus	5

FIELDING
C	AVG	Johnny Estrada, Scranton/W-B	.995
	PO	Johnny Estrada, Scranton/W-B	745
	A	Josh Bard, Buffalo	60
	E	Josh Bard, Buffalo	11
	DP	Kevin Cash, Syracuse	6
		Jason Phillips, Norfolk	6
	PB	Luis Rodriguez, Pawtucket	14
1B	AVG	Joe Vitiello, Ottawa	.996
	PO	Eric Munson, Toledo	1159
	A	Gary Burnham, Syracuse	91
	E	Eric Munson, Toledo	12
	DP	J.P. Roberge, Scranton/W-B	120
2B	AVG	Kary Bridges, Columbus	.984
	PO	Orlando Hudson, Syracuse	225
	A	Orlando Hudson, Syracuse	312
	E	Angel Santos, Pawtucket	11
		Craig Wilson, Toledo	11
	DP	Dave Doster, Scranton/W-B	80
3B	AVG	Mike Hessman, Richmond	.941
	PO	Chase Utley, Scranton/W-B	88
	A	Chase Utley, Scranton/W-B	224
	E	Drew Henson, Columbus	35
	DP	Jamey Carroll, Ottawa	26
SS	AVG	Jorge Velandia, Norfolk	.983
	PO	Bill Hall, Indianapolis	207
	A	Omar Infante, Toledo	416
	E	Bill Hall, Indianapolis	41
	DP	Nick Punto, Scranton/W-B	101
OF	AVG	Ozzie Timmons, Richmond	.985
	PO	Damon Hollins, Richmond	308
	A	Juan Rivera, Columbus	14
		Eric Valent, Scranton/W-B	14
	E	Chad Mottola, Syracuse	12
	DP	Ron Calloway, Ottawa	5

PACIFIC COAST LEAGUE

BY COREY BROCK

Some teams win with strong pitching, some with hitting. Other teams rely on strong defense. Great teams often get a mix of all three elements. It doesn't take a rocket scientist to figure how the Edmonton Trappers captured the 2002 Pacific Coast League title. They did it with their bats.

The Trappers bashed a club-record 202 home runs in the regular season in winning 81 games. Just for kicks, Edmonton belted 14 more home runs in the playoffs, eventually defeating Salt Lake in four games for the title.

The Trappers were the top farm team for the Twins in 2002, but there's no chance the team will repeat in 2003. The Trappers signed a player development agreement with the Expos just weeks after the championship, as Minnesota moved to Rochester of the International League.

"To have the kind of season we put together, it wouldn't have been as special if we hadn't won the whole thing," said infielder Casey Blake.

Blake was one of six Edmonton players to hit more than 19 home runs in the regular season as the Trappers led all of minor leagues in home runs. In addition to Blake, Edmonton's potent lineup also included Mike Ryan (31 home runs), Michael Restovich (29), Javier Valentin (21), Todd Sears (20) and Michael Cuddyer (20). No other PCL team could match that power.

Michael Restovich

"The home runs have obviously helped us all year, but we haven't always had to rely upon them to win," said Trappers manager John Russell, Baseball America's Minor League Manager of the Year.

True, but the Trappers hit at least one home run in

Joe Thurston led the minors with 196 hits

each of their eight playoff games. Edmonton started the playoffs by defeating Las Vegas in four games before facing Salt Lake, which beat Oklahoma in three games.

The Trappers blew a 5-3 lead in the first game against Salt Lake—a 7-5 loss—before taking the final three games of the series. Outfielder Lew Ford, who spent most of the season at Double-A New Britain, was the series MVP. He

MINOR LEAGUES

STANDINGS

AMERICAN CONFERENCE

Page	EAST	W	L	PCT	GB	Manager	Attendance	Avg.	Last Penn.
261	*Oklahoma RedHawks (Rangers)	75	69	.521	—	Bobby Jones	432,887	6,274	None
146	New Orleans Zephyrs (Astros)	75	69	.521	—	Chris Maloney	410,183	5,777	2001
218	Nashville Sounds (Pirates)	72	71	.503	2½	Marty Brown	322,059	4,668	None
225	Memphis Redbirds (Cardinals)	71	71	.500	3	Gaylen Pitts	794,550	11,035	2000
Page	CENTRAL	W	L	PCT	GB	Manager(s)	Attendance	Avg.	Last Penn.
58	Salt Lake Stingers (Angels)	78	66	.542	—	Mike Brumley	460,839	6,583	1979
152	Omaha Golden Spikes (Royals)	76	68	.528	2	Bucky Dent	344,718	4,855	None
101	Iowa Cubs (Cubs)	71	73	.493	7	Bruce Kimm/Pat Listach	509,384	7,277	None
124	Colorado Springs Sky Sox (Rockies)	58	86	.403	20	Chris Cron	267,028	3,927	1995

PACIFIC CONFERENCE

Page	WEST	W	L	PCT	GB	Manager	Attendance	Avg.	Last Penn.
173	Edmonton Trappers (Twins)	81	59	.579	—	John Russell	340,387	5,673	2002
232	Portland Beavers (Padres)	72	71	.503	10½	Rick Sweet	454,197	6,779	1994
139	Calgary Cannons (Marlins)	67	71	.486	13	Dean Treanor	182,831	3,517	None
247	Tacoma Rainiers (Mariners)	65	76	.461	16½	Dan Rohn	300,910	4,702	2001
Page	SOUTH	W	L	PCT	GB	Manager	Attendance	Avg.	Last Penn.
159	Las Vegas 51s (Dodgers)	85	59	.590	—	Brad Mills	327,289	4,609	1988
65	Tucson Sidewinders (Diamondbacks)	73	68	.518	10½	Al Pedrique	268,807	3,896	1993
204	Sacramento RiverCats (Athletics)	66	78	.458	19	Bob Geren	817,317	11,512	None
240	Fresno Grizzlies (Giants)	57	87	.396	28	Lenn Sakata	563,079	8,044	None

*Defeated New Orleans 6-2 in one-game playoff for division playoff spot

PLAYOFFS—Semifinals: Edmonton defeated Las Vegas 3-1 and Salt Lake defeated Oklahoma 3-0 in best-of-5 series. **Finals:** Edmonton defeated Salt Lake 3-1 in best-of-5 series.

NOTE: Team's individual batting and pitching statistics can be found on page indicated in lefthand column.

hit .441 in the playoffs with 15 hits in eight games.

For as much attention as Edmonton's bats garnered, the Trappers had a strong pitching staff as well. Scott Randall joined the Trappers in early May from New Britain and went 12-0, 3.35 for Edmonton. Juan Rincon (7-4, 4.78) was strong down the stretch, and closer Kevin Frederick (3-6, 4.58 with 22 saves) closed the door on opponents. But, make no mistake, the 2002 Trappers were mostly about hitting.

More Than Also-Rans

The Trappers might have had the most potent lineup in the PCL, but Salt Lake and Las Vegas weren't too far behind. The Stingers led the league in hitting (.293), with the 51s (.291) not far behind. Both made the playoffs.

Salt Lake's Rick Short won the batting title with a late surge, finishing at .356. Short outlasted Tucson's Lyle Overbay (.343-19-109 in his first crack at Triple-A), but Stingers outfielder Robb Quinlan walked away with the league's MVP and Rookie of the Year awards. Quinlan hit .333-20-112, finishing the year with a league-best 64 extra-base hits. He went 5-for-5 and had eight RBIs in a game against Edmonton May 12.

Las Vegas infielder Joe Thurston earned consideration for MVP honors, hitting .334-12-55 with 22 steals for the 51s. Thurston, the minor league leader with 196 hits, was on pace to be the first league player since Bobby Valentine (1970) to get 200 hits in one season, but the Dodgers recalled him with three games left in the regular season.

Thurston also led the league in runs (106) and total bases (297, which led the minors). Calgary's Kevin Hooper had the PCL's longest hitting streak (31 games).

Though the PCL has always had a reputation as a hitter's league, that's not to say there weren't a handful of strong pitchers in the league.

New Orleans lefthander Jeriome Robertson was named pitcher of the year. The Zephyrs led the league in ERA (3.40) and shutouts (11), led by Robertson's 12-8, 2.55 numbers. Teammate Wayne Franklin (13-9, 3.12) finished third in the ERA race.

There were two no-hitters in the league. Portland's Junior Herndon had a no-hitter in the second game of a May 14 doubleheader against Tacoma. It was the second time in as many seasons that the Rainiers had been no-hit. And Calgary's Jamie Arnold tossed a nine-inning no-hitter on May 25 in a 12-1 victory over Iowa.

But Arnold slipped badly thereafter and was given his release by the Cannons after going 3-8, 7.39 in 16 starts. Tucson's Steve Randolph led the PCL in victories with 15 even though he led the league in walks (81) as well. It was the first time in Randolph's six-year career that he won more than five games in a season.

With a strong finish in the last month of the season, the league set a record for attendance for the third straight year with 6,796,545. The average per-game number was 6,270. Sacramento, didn't quite reach the 900,000 mark in 2002 (817,317) but the RiverCats still out drew Memphis (794,550) for best in the league—and in Minor League Baseball.

Robb Quinlan

Fresno finished third in the league in attendance, averaging 8,044 fans a game at new Grizzlies Stadium. The downtown stadium opened on May 1 to a crowd of 12,792. The Calgary Cannons ranked last in the 16-team league in attendance, averaging just 3,518 fans a game. Of course, it probably didn't help that the Cannons had announced they were moving to Albuquerque, New Mexico for 2003.

Albuquerque was a member of the PCL from 1972-2000 when the team moved to Portland. That team was called the Dukes, which was a finalist for the new team's nickname. However, fans chose 'Isotopes' instead. The somewhat unusual nickname originated in a March 2001 episode of the Fox prime-time cartoon "The Simpsons."

Strange Doings

Consider it another strange twist in a season full of accomplishment and oddities. Just how odd? Consider what Portland faced on May 16. The Beavers, trailing Las Vegas by six runs on the road with two outs in the ninth and nobody on base, rallied for eight runs for a 12-10 win. The PCL's longest game of the season—and the longest in all of professional baseball—occurred Aug. 26 when Oklahoma outlasted Memphis 4-3 in 19 innings.

A 10-minute brawl between Iowa and Salt Lake June 4 resulted in a 35-minute delay, with local police called to the scene after Salt Lake's Brendan Donnelly hit Julio Zuleta with a pitch after Zuleta homered twice. Salt Lake manager Mike Brumley called it "the most violent fight in my 20 years of baseball." A total of four players received suspensions.

Iowa lost manager Bruce Kimm on July 6 after the Cubs fired manager Don Baylor and promoted the Triple-A skipper. The I-Cubs had rookie phenom Mark Prior for all of three games before he joined Chicago. In his first game in Iowa on May 7, Prior struck out 10 and hit two home runs in a 6-1 victory over Tucson. He struck out seven of the first nine batters he faced.

LEAGUE CHAMPIONS

Last 30 Years

Year	Regular Season*	Pct.	Playoff
1972	Albuquerque (Dodgers)	.622	Albuquerque (Dodgers)
1973	Tucson (Athletics)	.583	Spokane (Rangers)
1974	Spokane (Rangers)	.549	Spokane (Rangers)
1975	Hawaii (Padres)	.611	Hawaii (Padres)
1976	Salt Lake City (Angels)	.625	Hawaii (Padres)
1977	Phoenix (Giants)	.579	Phoenix (Giants)
1978	Tacoma (Yankees)	.584	Tacoma (Yankees)#
			Albuquerque (Dodgers)#
1979	Albuquerque (Dodgers)	.581	Salt Lake City (Angels)
1980	Tucson (Astros)	.595	Albuquerque (Dodgers)
1981	Albuquerque (Dodgers)	.712	Albuquerque (Dodgers)
1982	Albuquerque (Dodgers)	.594	Albuquerque (Dodgers)
1983	Albuquerque (Dodgers)	.594	Portland (Phillies)
1984	Hawaii (Pirates)	.621	Edmonton (Angels)
1985	Hawaii (Pirates)	.587	Vancouver (Brewers)
1986	Vancouver (Brewers)	.616	Las Vegas (Padres)
1987	Calgary (Mariners)	.596	Albuquerque (Dodgers)
1988	Albuquerque (Dodgers)	.605	Las Vegas (Padres)
1989	Albuquerque (Dodgers)	.563	Vancouver (White Sox)
1990	Albuquerque (Dodgers)	.641	Albuquerque (Dodgers)
1991	Albuquerque (Dodgers)	.580	Tucson (Astros)
1992	Colo. Springs (Indians)	.596	Colo. Springs (Indians)
1993	Portland (Twins)	.608	Tucson (Astros)
1994	Albuquerque (Dodgers)	.597	Albuquerque (Dodgers)
1995	Tucson (Astros)	.608	Colo. Springs (Rockies)
1996	Edmonton (Athletics)	.592	Edmonton (Athletics)
1997	Phoenix (Giants)	.615	Edmonton (Athletics)
1998	Iowa (Cubs)	.590	New Orleans (Astros)
1999	Vancouver (Athletics)	.592	Vancouver (Athletics)
2000	Salt Lake (Twins)	.629	Memphis (Cardinals)
2001	New Orleans (Astros)	.590	New Orleans (Astros)#
	Tacoma (Mariners)	.590	Tacoma (Mariners)#
2002	Las Vegas (Dodgers)	.590	Edmonton (Twins)

*Best overall record   #Co-champions

2002 PACIFIC COAST LEAGUE STATISTICS

CLUB BATTING

	AVG	G	AB	R	H	2B	3B	HR	BB	SO	SB
Salt Lake	.293	144	5075	797	1489	284	88	142	359	972	127
Las Vegas	.291	144	5018	820	1462	284	47	161	450	1015	63
Edmonton	.287	140	4766	820	1370	278	42	202	458	1021	96
Tucson	.284	141	4869	729	1385	288	40	124	394	1011	77
Calgary	.283	138	4609	681	1304	313	27	119	438	845	113
Colorado Springs	.277	144	4893	725	1356	308	35	142	447	1015	90
Oklahoma	.275	144	5049	754	1387	289	32	140	551	1032	84
Sacramento	.273	144	4941	764	1350	282	19	113	665	886	99
Omaha	.270	144	4874	723	1316	254	43	145	485	922	173
Iowa	.270	144	4812	793	1297	280	30	166	528	993	94
Tacoma	.264	141	4602	597	1215	253	45	121	411	921	140
Nashville	.262	143	4760	662	1246	256	18	110	453	986	117
Portland	.260	143	4719	590	1225	265	34	115	351	945	81
New Orleans	.258	144	4907	617	1268	248	38	102	398	1058	111
Fresno	.257	144	4752	543	1222	218	31	106	338	968	72
Memphis	.247	142	4623	628	1143	250	13	148	459	911	105

CLUB PITCHING

	ERA	G	CG	SHO	SV	IP	H	R	ER	BB	SO
New Orleans	3.40	144	5	11	41	1285	1165	546	485	385	968
Memphis	3.95	142	3	8	38	1233	1274	601	541	396	889
Nashville	4.00	143	10	9	30	1248	1209	608	555	356	1080
Portland	4.04	143	4	9	43	1228	1159	625	551	430	874
Omaha	4.17	144	4	5	38	1268	1289	673	587	510	970
Fresno	4.29	144	2	7	40	1241	1263	649	592	482	1031
Tucson	4.30	141	4	7	36	1232	1279	648	589	415	956
Salt Lake	4.33	144	6	5	31	1275	1357	729	614	438	1066
Tacoma	4.43	141	7	7	35	1202	1278	665	592	371	908
Las Vegas	4.60	144	2	5	47	1288	1497	743	658	433	918
Oklahoma	4.71	144	5	7	33	1297	1375	764	679	494	1062
Iowa	4.87	144	2	4	35	1242	1307	756	672	550	1018
Edmonton	4.95	140	8	3	41	1200	1326	731	660	430	965
Sacramento	5.10	144	0	5	31	1269	1448	815	719	462	977
Calgary	5.34	138	4	6	33	1156	1288	754	686	488	812
Colorado Springs	5.85	144	5	1	36	1245	1521	936	809	545	1007

CLUB FIELDING

	PCT	PO	A	E	DP		PCT	PO	A	E	DP
Nashville	.980	3744	1387	106	132	Tacoma	.977	3605	1184	111	121
Fresno	.979	3722	1372	108	116	Iowa	.977	3727	1489	125	131
Portland	.979	3684	1434	110	119	Oklahoma	.976	3891	1494	132	118
Tucson	.979	3696	1390	110	115	Sacramento	.975	3807	1419	135	129
Calgary	.979	3467	1378	106	122	Las Vegas	.974	3865	1557	144	135
New Orleans	.978	3855	1570	121	149	Salt Lake	.974	3825	1562	144	139
Edmonton	.978	3601	1343	111	126	Omaha	.972	3805	1369	151	159
Memphis	.977	3698	1456	119	157	Colo. Springs	.972	3736	1534	169	156

INDIVIDUAL BATTING LEADERS
(Minimum 389 Plate Appearances)

	AVG	G	AB	R	H	2B	3B	HR	RBI	BB	SO	SB
Short, Rick, Salt Lake	.356	105	410	71	146	29	2	7	68	23	43	3
Overbay, Lyle, Tucson	.343	134	525	83	180	40	0	19	109	42	86	0
Hafner, Travis, Oklahoma	.342	110	401	79	137	22	1	21	77	79	76	2
Thurston, Joe, Las Vegas	.334	136	587	106	196	39	13	12	55	25	60	22
Quinlan, Robb, Salt Lake	.333	136	528	95	176	31	13	20	112	41	93	8
Allen, Luke, Las Vegas	.329	137	501	85	165	28	3	12	78	56	77	4
Mendez, Carlos, Sacramento	.324	103	404	58	131	26	1	12	74	12	52	3
Wood, Jason, Calgary	.315	121	457	78	144	37	2	15	70	38	92	3
Gload, Ross, Colo. Springs	.314	104	442	69	139	28	6	16	71	18	59	9
Barnes, Larry, Salt Lake	.314	114	452	71	142	29	11	20	95	28	90	8

INDIVIDUAL PITCHING LEADERS
(Minimum 115 Innings)

	W	L	ERA	G	GS	CG	SV	IP	H	R	ER	BB	SO
Robertson, Jeriome, New Orleans	12	8	2.55	27	27	2	0	180	160	59	51	45	114
Arroyo, Bronson, Nashville	8	6	2.96	22	21	3	0	143	126	57	47	28	116
Franklin, Wayne, New Orleans	13	9	3.12	29	27	1	0	179	153	68	62	59	141
Ainsworth, Kurt, Fresno	8	6	3.41	20	19	1	0	116	101	49	44	43	119
Calero, Kiko, Omaha	7	7	3.44	20	18	0	0	126	112	52	48	35	109
Randolph, Steve, Tucson	15	7	3.47	28	27	1	0	163	151	70	63	81	129
Condrey, Clay, Portland	10	4	3.50	25	23	0	0	134	128	55	52	40	73
Williams, Jerome, Fresno	6	11	3.59	28	28	0	0	161	140	76	64	50	130
Sweeney, Brian, Tacoma	9	5	3.80	30	23	1	2	142	157	67	60	28	113
Torres, Salomon, Nashville	8	5	3.83	26	24	2	0	162	169	78	69	39	136

ALL-STAR TEAM

C—Javier Valentin, Edmonton. **1B**—Lyle Overbay, Tucson. **2B**—Joe Thurston, Las Vegas. **3B**—Jason Wood, Calgary. **SS**—Aaron Holbert, Tacoma. **OF**—Robb Quinlan, Salt Lake; Michael Restovich, Edmonton; Michael Ryan, Edmonton. **DH**—Ivan Cruz, Memphis. **RHP**—Scott Randall, Edmonton. **LHP**—Jeriome Robertson, New Orleans. **RP**—Jeff Williams, Las Vegas.

Most Valuable Player: Robb Quinlan, Salt Lake. **Most Valuable Pitcher**: Jeriome Robertson, New Orleans. **Rookie of the Year**: Robb Quinlan, Salt Lake. **Manager of the Year**: Brad Mills, Las Vegas.

DEPARTMENT LEADERS

BATTING

G	Kelly Dransfeldt, Oklahoma	140
AB	Joe Thurston, Las Vegas	587
R	Joe Thurston, Las Vegas	106
H	Joe Thurston, Las Vegas	196
TB	Joe Thurston, Las Vegas	297
XBH	Mike Ryan, Edmonton	73
2B	Lyle Overbay, Tucson	40
	Larry Sutton, Sacramento	40
3B	Chone Figgins, Salt Lake	18
HR	Ivan Cruz, Memphis	35
RBI	Robb Quinlan, Salt Lake	112
SH	Cody Ransom, Fresno	12
SF	Robb Quinlan, Salt Lake	15
BB	Hee Seop Choi, Iowa	95
IBB	Colin Porter, New Orleans	8
HBP	Chad Meyers, Sacra.-Memphis	21
SO	Chin-Feng Chen, Las Vegas	160
SB	Chad Meyers, Sacra.-Memphis	43
CS	Jermaine Clark, Tacoma-Okla.	16
GIDP	Ken Harvey, Omaha	22
OB%	Travis Hafner, Oklahoma	.463
SL%	Ivan Cruz, Memphis	.566

PITCHING

G	Matt Whiteside, Colo. Springs	60
GS	Six tied at	28
CG	Three tied at	3
ShO	Three tied at	2
GF	Matt Whiteside, Colo. Springs	49
SV	Jeff Williams, Las Vegas	28
W	Steve Randolph, Tucson	15
L	Tony McKnight, Nashville	14
IP	Jeriome Robertson, New Orleans	181
H	Bryan Rekar, Omaha-Colo. Spr.	203
	Dennis Springer, Las Vegas	203
R	Brad Thomas, Edmonton	112
ER	Chris Gissell, Iowa	105
HR	Junior Herndon, Portland	28
HB	Brad Thomas, Edmonton	17
BB	Steve Randolph, Tucson	81
SO	Wayne Franklin, New Orleans	141
WP	Larry Luebbers, Sacramento	16
BK	Aquilino Lopez, Tacoma	4

FIELDING

C	AVG	Keith McDonald, Memphis	.995
	PO	Raul Chavez, New Orleans	734
	A	Raul Chavez, New Orleans	77
	E	Mike Mahoney, Iowa	12
	DP	Three tied at	9
	PB	Danny Ardoin, Omaha-Oklahoma	11
1B	AVG	Todd Sears, Edmonton	.997
	PO	Hee Seop Choi, Iowa	1074
	A	Lyle Overbay, Tucson	87
	E	Ken Harvey, Omaha	15
	DP	Ivan Cruz, Memphis	129
2B	AVG	Juan Melo, Fresno	.991
	PO	Joe Thurston, Las Vegas	285
	A	Chone Figgins, Salt Lake	380
	E	Chone Figgins, Salt Lake	21
	DP	Chone Figgins, Salt Lake	81
3B	AVG	Mike Coolbaugh, Memphis	.965
	PO	Luis Lopez, Sacramento	87
	A	Luis Lopez, Sacramento	227
	E	Rick Bell, Las Vegas	22
	DP	Jason Wood, Calgary	22
SS	AVG	Kelly Dransfeldt, Oklahoma	.978
	PO	Kelly Dransfeldt, Oklahoma	210
	A	Kelly Dransfeldt, Oklahoma	421
	E	Alfredo Amezaga, Salt Lake	24
	DP	Alfredo Amezaga, Salt Lake	90
OF	AVG	Barry Wesson, New Orleans	.996
	PO	Scott Podsednik, Tacoma	322
	A	Luke Allen, Las Vegas	23
	E	Luke Allen, Las Vegas	9
	DP	Luke Allen, Las Vegas	7

MINOR LEAGUES

EASTERN LEAGUE

BY ANDREW LINKER

The harbinger of what was to become one of the wildest seasons in the Eastern League's 80-year history came in mid-May.

That was when the Yankees decided to shake up their organization and the EL by reassigning Norwich manager Stump Merrill to Triple-A Columbus to replace the struggling Brian Butterfield. Luis Sojo was named to succeed Merrill as the Navigators' manager.

For all of the experience a 1,000-game winner like Merrill brought to running a game, Sojo had none. But in the end, that inexperience did not matter as Sojo—only months removed from a 12-year career in the majors—led Norwich to its first and, ultimately, last EL title as the Yankees' Double-A affiliate.

RODGER WOOD

Luis Sojo

"I won a lot of championships as a player, but my hands were like they had water on them," Sojo said after beating Harrisburg for the title. "I don't know if I will do this again. To manage my first year and win a championship, you don't see it too often."

As Sojo and the Navigators hung on to beat the upstart Senators in five games of the best-of-five finals, the Yankees were making plans to move their Double-A affiliation from Norwich, where they had been since 1995, to Trenton.

The realignment was one of four in the EL, where one-third of the teams changed identities after the season as Portland switched from the Marlins to the Red Sox; New Haven moved from the Cardinals to the Blue Jays; and Norwich, the champions, replaced the Yankees with the Giants.

Norwich's 76-64 record in the regular season was good enough to finish first in the Northern Division, but it trailed those of Akron (93-48) and Harrisburg (79-63) in the South.

In fact, Akron's 93 victories were the most of any team in the minors in 2002 and the most in the EL since

Harrisburg went 94-44 in 1993. That mattered little in the first round of the playoffs, though, as the Senators rallied from an 0-2 deficit in the best-of-five semifinals to stun Akron.

They nearly did the same to Norwich in the finals, too, in a rematch of the 1999 championship series, that ended with Milton Bradley's two-out, two-strike, ninth-inning grand slam.

The Senators reached the playoffs by overtaking the Reading Phillies, who held a commanding five-game lead for the South's final playoff spot with 16 games left to play. The Senators would finally pass the R-Phils with one game left, capping a regular season that started with Altoona's Adrian Burnside, Neal McDade and Chris Spurling combining to no-hit the high-powered Aeros 2-0 on April 23.

Two weeks after the Curve recorded the EL's only no-hitter of 2002, Dee Haynes became the first New Haven player to hit for the cycle.

As for records, there were a few. Some were noteworthy, as Binghamton center fielder Esix Snead stole a franchise-record 66 bases, marking the second straight season in which Snead set a franchise record. A year earlier, Snead had stolen 64 while playing for in the Cardinals' system for New Haven.

Trenton shortstop Freddy Sanchez had the EL's longest hitting streak at 27 games, setting a franchise record. By the time Sanchez was promoted to Triple-A Pawtucket, he had safely reached base in 43 games—four shy of the EL record.

Some records were less flattering. Erie righthander Nate Tekavec surrendered 33 homers, obliterating the previous record of 28 set just two years before by Portland's Scott Comer.

The end of the season also marked the end of Bill Troubh's tenure as league president. Troubh, who replaced the fired John Levenda in 1996, led the league into an era of unprecedented growth.

Under Troubh—who will be succeeded for the 2003 season by his longtime assistant, Joe McEacharn—the league went from 10 to 12 teams as it continued to push its average attendance to 5,000 per game—again, the best average of any league below Triple-A.

STANDINGS

Page	NORTH	W	L	PCT	GB	Manager(s)	Attendance	Avg.	Last Penn.
189	Norwich Navigators (Yankees)	76	64	.543	—	Stump Merrill/Luis Sojo	222,134	3,417	2002
226	New Haven Ravens (Cardinals)	74	65	.532	1½	Mark DeJohn	182,164	2,846	2000
197	Binghamton Mets (Mets)	73	68	.518	3½	Howie Freiling	214,289	3,247	1994
174	New Britain Rock Cats (Twins)	67	72	.482	8½	Stan Cliburn	265,459	4,148	2001
88	Trenton Thunder (Red Sox)	63	77	.450	13	Ron Johnson	408,463	5,835	None
139	Portland Sea Dogs (Marlins)	63	77	.450	13	Eric Fox	382,738	5,713	None

Page	SOUTH	W	L	PCT	GB	Manager(s)	Attendance	Avg.	Last Penn.
117	Akron Aeros (Indians)	93	48	.660	—	Brad Komminsk	400,187	5,973	None
181	Harrisburg Senators (Expos)	79	63	.556	14½	Dave Huppert	266,808	3,924	1999
212	Reading Phillies (Phillies)	76	66	.535	17½	Greg Legg	486,570	7,052	2001
219	Altoona Curve (Pirates)	72	69	.511	21	Dale Sveum	363,871	5,273	None
80	Bowie Baysox (Orioles)	55	85	.393	37½	Dave Cash/Dave Stockstill	341,322	5,019	None
132	Erie SeaWolves (Twins)	52	89	.369	41	Kevin Bradshaw	211,899	3,363	None

PLAYOFFS—Semifinals: Norwich defeated New Haven 3-0 and Harrisburg defeated Akron 3-2 in best-of-5 series. **Finals:** Norwich defeated Harrisburg 3-2 in best-of-5 series.

NOTE: Team's individual batting and pitching statistics can be found on page indicated in lefthand column.

CLUB BATTING

	AVG	G	AB	R	H	2B	3B	HR	BB	SO	SB
New Haven	.278	139	4754	671	1320	281	29	113	409	837	80
Akron	.272	141	4803	734	1305	283	43	150	487	915	95
New Britain	.271	139	4662	651	1262	264	23	104	446	774	96
Altoona	.268	141	4703	642	1261	244	33	115	386	849	99
Binghamton	.262	141	4642	647	1217	239	35	99	485	968	215
Trenton	.262	140	4688	692	1227	262	30	97	505	933	128
Erie	.261	141	4674	602	1220	247	34	112	465	1052	124
Norwich	.257	140	4492	669	1156	249	26	123	499	927	113
Harrisburg	.257	142	4706	676	1211	219	34	120	569	940	68
Bowie	.255	140	4622	565	1178	222	23	79	372	808	149
Reading	.254	142	4724	643	1201	241	25	86	445	922	172
Portland	.252	140	4512	606	1138	255	34	95	437	1068	143

CLUB PITCHING

	ERA	G	CG	SHO	SV	IP	H	R	ER	BB	SO
Akron	3.09	141	4	20	38	1239	1097	492	425	435	1020
Norwich	3.58	140	14	9	32	1193	1143	567	474	384	982
Reading	3.80	142	7	13	36	1247	1211	609	527	440	847
Harrisburg	3.92	142	1	13	33	1247	1226	624	543	438	944
New Haven	3.97	139	8	6	32	1214	1196	536	536	451	913
Binghamton	4.08	141	4	7	38	1226	1176	635	555	505	983
Altoona	4.19	141	5	9	34	1221	1241	618	568	416	894
Portland	4.21	140	10	5	33	1193	1163	661	558	499	879
New Britain	4.30	139	5	4	41	1202	1199	686	575	478	849
Bowie	4.62	140	1	6	26	1206	1308	729	619	487	901
Trenton	4.72	140	6	5	32	1217	1302	741	638	484	1008
Erie	5.29	141	4	2	30	1202	1434	805	707	488	773

CLUB FIELDING

	PCT	PO	A	E	DP		PCT	PO	A	E	DP
Altoona	.978	3663	1420	113	128	New Haven	.972	3641	1509	148	118
Harrisburg	.975	3742	1335	130	118	Erie	.971	3606	1451	151	136
Binghamton	.975	3677	1474	133	130	Bowie	.970	3617	1379	153	103
New Britain	.975	3607	1539	134	121	Trenton	.969	3651	1411	160	122
Akron	.974	3717	1394	136	111	Portland	.969	3578	1457	163	128
Reading	.974	3742	1584	143	144	Norwich	.968	3578	1271	159	100

INDIVIDUAL BATTING LEADERS

(Minimum 383 Plate Appearances)

	AVG	G	AB	R	H	2B	3B	HR	RBI	BB	SO	SB
Martinez, Victor, Akron	.336	121	443	84	149	40	0	22	85	58	62	3
Alvarez, Tony, Altoona	.318	125	507	79	161	37	1	15	59	27	75	3
Gall, John, New Haven	.316	135	526	82	166	45	3	20	81	38	75	4
Heintz, Chris, New Haven	.314	105	373	40	117	29	1	7	45	19	61	1
Haynes, Dee, New Haven	.312	131	504	75	157	29	4	21	98	25	67	3
Ford, Lew, New Britain	.311	93	373	81	116	27	2	15	51	49	47	17
Crisp, Covelli, New Haven-Akron	.310	96	387	70	120	17	1	10	51	39	59	30
Sefcik, Kevin, Altoona	.308	126	467	69	144	32	2	2	51	44	42	12
Perez, Johnny, Erie	.306	94	343	45	105	14	2	3	47	30	51	8
Rivera, Carlos, Altoona	.302	128	494	67	149	28	2	22	84	27	75	1

INDIVIDUAL PITCHING LEADERS

(Minimum 114 Innings)

	W	L	ERA	G	GS	CG	SV	IP	H	R	ER	BB	SO
Borrell, Danny, Norwich	9	4	2.31	21	20	1	0	128	116	44	33	39	91
Wayne, Justin, H'burg-Portland	8	5	3.12	24	24	1	0	141	117	67	49	45	77
Madson, Ryan, Reading	16	4	3.20	26	26	2	0	171	150	68	61	53	132
Bump, Nate, Portland	7	6	3.38	20	20	3	0	128	110	56	48	29	81
Robertson, Nate, Portland	10	9	3.42	27	27	3	0	163	156	77	62	50	109
De Paula, Julio, Norwich	14	6	3.45	27	26	6	0	175	141	74	67	52	152
Kubes, Greg, Reading	13	7	3.46	28	27	0	0	174	177	74	67	45	106
Janke, Cheyenne, New Haven	12	8	3.48	28	23	1	0	150	142	71	58	41	112
Hoard, Brent, New Britain	11	8	3.69	31	26	2	0	161	153	80	66	52	126
Van Hekken, Andy, Erie	4	7	3.83	21	21	1	0	134	138	69	57	34	97

ALL-STAR TEAM

C—Victor Martinez, Akron. **1B**—Carlos Rivera, Altoona. **2B**—Jesus Medrano, Portland. **3B**—Travis Chapman, Reading. **SS**—Jose Reyes, Binghamton. **OF**—Tony Alvarez, Altoona, Lew Ford, New Britain, Cody Ross, Erie. **DH**—John Gall, New Haven. **Util**—Feddy Sanchez, Trenton. **RHP**—Ryan Madson, Reading. **LHP**—Billy Traber, Akron. **RP**—Matt Duff, New Haven.

Most Valuable Player: Victor Martinez, Akron. **Pitcher of the Year:** Ryan Madson, Reading. **Rookie of the Year:** Dee Haynes, New Haven. **Manager of the Year:** Brad Komminsk, Akron.

DEPARTMENT LEADERS

BATTING

G	Nate Espy, Reading	141
AB	Papo Bolivar, New Britain	547
R	Victor Martinez, Akron	84
H	John Gall, New Haven	166
TB	John Gall, New Haven	277
XBH	John Gall, New Haven	68
2B	John Gall, New Haven	45
3B	Tonayne Brown, Trenton	9
HR	Val Pascucci, Harrisburg	27
RBI	Dee Haynes, New Haven	98
SH	Luis Rodriguez, New Britain	32
SF	Johnny Peralta, Akron	11
BB	Val Pascucci, Harrisburg	93
IBB	Travis Chapman, Reading	9
HBP	Travis Chapman, Reading	19
SO	Steve Lomasney, Trenton	133
SB	Esix Snead, Binghamton	66
CS	Three tied at	18
GIDP	John Gall, New Haven	26
OB%	Victor Martinez, Akron	.417
SL%	Corey Richardson, Erie	.857

PITCHING

G	Jason Karnuth, New Haven	58
	Scotty Layfield, New Haven	58
GS	B.R. Cook, New Haven	28
	Isauro Pineda, Trenton	28
CG	Julio DePaula, Norwich	6
ShO	Billy Traber, Akron	2
GF	Scotty Layfield, New Haven	52
SV	Juan Padilla, New Britain	29
W	Ryan Madson, Reading	16
L	Five tied at	13
IP	Julio DePaula, Norwich	175
H	Nate Tekavec, Erie	196
R	Nate Tekavec, Erie	123
ER	Nate Tekavec, Erie	111
HR	Nate Tekavec, Erie	33
HB	Adrian Burnside, Altoona	15
BB	Anastacio Martinez, Trenton	75
SO	Julio DePaula, Norwich	152
WP	Terry Hill, Trenton	16
	Juan Rosario, Bowie	16
BK	John Grabow, Altoona	5

FIELDING

C	AVG	Scott Sandusky, Harrisburg	.997
	PO	Victor Martinez, Akron	770
	A	David Parrish, Norwich	75
	E	David Parrish, Norwich	15
	DP	John Pachot, Altoona	11
	PB	David Parrish, Norwich	19
1B	AVG	Nate Espy, Reading	.994
	PO	Nate Espy, Reading	1214
	A	Justin Morneau, New Britain	96
	E	Adrian Gonzalez, Portland	16
	DP	Nate Espy, Reading	131
2B	AVG	Bo Hart, New Haven	.985
	PO	Jesus Medrano, Portland	220
	A	Jesus Medrano, Portland	282
	E	Josh McKinley, Harrisburg	19
	DP	Jesus Medrano, Portland	72
3B	AVG	Rodney Nye, Binghamton	.965
	PO	Napoleon Calzado, Bowie	133
	A	Scott Hodges, Harrisburg	256
	E	Scott Hodges, Harrisburg	25
	DP	Travis Chapman, Reading	27
SS	AVG	Luis Rodriguez, New Britain	.973
	PO	Luis Rodriguez, New Britain	203
	A	Anderson Machado, Reading	391
	E	Anderson Machado, Reading	28
		Wilson Valdez, Portland	28
	DP	Anderson Machado, Reading	79
OF	AVG	Justin Headley, Trenton	1.000
	PO	Kevin Reese, Norwich	296
	A	Cody Ross, Erie	16
	E	Dee Haynes, New Haven	13
	DP	Keith Reed, Bowie	5

MINOR LEAGUES

SOUTHERN LEAGUE

BY MARK McCARTER

An hour before the season's final game, Birmingham manager Wally Backman was in his clubhouse, thumbing through a stack of money six inches high. It was the bounty collected from his players for their various on-field transgressions, with the proceeds going toward a team party.

"We've already got enough for a steakhouse. But I'm looking for steak and lobster," Backman had said in early August.

To have followed the progress of the Barons in 2002, one might think Backman couldn't have scrounged enough in fines for a Happy Meal, much less some Backman bacchanalia.

Deploying an exciting and devasting style—quickly dubbed "Wally Ball"—the Barons rolled to the Southern League's best record (79-61), then swept defending co-champ Jacksonville in the best-of-five championship series.

Catcher Miguel Olivo, who dazzled scouts with his uncatcher-like speed and 29 regular-season stolen bases, was named MVP of the playoffs, hitting safely in each of the nine postseason games and driving in nine runs. Two days after winning the title, he debuted with the Chicago White Sox and became the 84th man to hit a home run in his first major league at-bat.

Teammate Aaron Miles (.322-9-68) was selected the league's MVP and outfielder Alex Fernandez made it a sweep, winning the MVP award (and the home run derby) at the midsummer league all-star game.

But the Most Valuable Person was Backman, the erstwhile former Mets infielder. He orchestrated the franchise's first pennant since 1993 with an almost anachronistic game—base hits, stolen bases and little power. The Barons led the league in stolen bases (216, some 65 more than any other team) and in batting average—and had the third-fewest homers.

Jacksonville, which bid farewell to 47-year-old Wolfson Park, won 15 of its last 20 games to reign as second-half SL East champ, then eased past Carolina in the playoffs. The Mudcats featured Choo Freeman (.291-12-64), who was anointed the top everyday prospect in the league. Rene Reyes, another Mudcats outfielder, hit for the cycle

at Greenville June 10.

Carolina scissored the relationship with the Rockies after that playoff loss, signing to become a Marlins' affiliate for 2003, while Tennessee divorced the Blue Jays after 23 years and signed with the Cardinals.

Mobile and West Tenn were predicted to be the class of the SL West, but Mobile was riddled by promotions: A half-dozen of its pitchers were promoted to the majors, including No. 1 pitching prospect Jake Peavy. West Tenn was The Mark Prior Show for a while.

The game's most renowned prospect dazzled in his six starts (4-1, 2.60, including a 15-strikeout effort against Chattanooga April 27), then the Diamond Jaxx hid under radar for months before emerging as the second-half champ, albeit a victim to Birmingham in the playoffs.

Chattanooga boasted the league's batting champ for the 12th time in 24 years. This time, it was Brewers castoff Bobby Darula, who batted .325, edging Miles (.322), Jacksonville's Mike Collins and teammate Tom Nevers (both at .313). West Tenn's Dave Kelton tied with Orlando's Pete LaForest for the home run title, with 20, and led the league with 78 RBIs.

Tennessee's Vinny Chulk (13-5, 2.96) led the league in wins and ERA. Though Orlando was not a factor in either half and finished with the fewest wins, it had the season's only no-hitter, as Gerardo Garcia beat Tennessee 2-0 May 22.

Birmingham's Joe Valentine won the Rolaids Minor League Relief Man award, collecting a league-record 37 saves. Maybe the Barons stole their way to a lot of wins. But they closed them out the old-fashioned way.

TYLER BOLDEN

Aaron Miles

STANDINGS: SPLIT SEASON

FIRST HALF

EAST	W	L	PCT	GB
Carolina	40	30	.571	—
Jacksonville	36	33	.522	3½
Tennessee	36	34	.514	4
Orlando	29	39	.426	10
Greenville	28	41	.406	11½

WEST	W	L	PCT	GB
Birmingham	41	29	.586	—
Mobile	37	32	.536	3½
Chattanooga	37	33	.529	4
West Tenn	32	38	.457	9
Huntsville	31	38	.449	9½

SECOND HALF

EAST	W	L	PCT	GB
Jacksonville	41	29	.586	—
Greenville	37	28	.569	1½
Tennessee	33	37	.471	8
Orlando	29	40	.420	11½
Carolina	25	41	.379	14

WEST	W	L	PCT	GB
West Tenn	41	29	.586	—
Mobile	39	31	.557	2
Huntsville	39	31	.557	2
Birmingham	38	32	.543	3
Chattanooga	23	47	.329	18

PLAYOFFS—Semifinals: Birmingham defeated West Tenn 3-2 and Jacksonville defeated Carolina 3-2 in best-of-5 series. **Finals:** Birmingham defeated Jacksonville 3-0 in best-of-5 series.

STANDINGS: OVERALL

Page		W	L	PCT	GB	Manager	Attendance	Avg.	Last Penn.
95	Birmingham Barons (White Sox)	79	61	.564	—	Wally Backman	276,018	4,000	2002
160	Jacksonville Suns (Dodgers)	77	62	.554	1½	Dino Ebel	230,156	3,487	2001
233	Mobile BayBears (Padres)	76	63	.547	2½	Craig Colbert	216,597	3,185	1998
102	West Tenn Diamond Jaxx (Cubs)	73	67	.521	6	Bobby Dickerson	224,698	3,405	2000
167	Huntsville Stars (Brewers)	70	69	.504	8½	Frank Kremblas	206,068	3,170	2001
270	Tennessee Smokies (Blue Jays)	69	71	.493	10	Rocket Wheeler	268,033	3,829	1978
73	Greenville Braves (Braves)	65	69	.485	11	Brian Snitker	214,220	3,150	1997
125	Carolina Mudcats (Rockies)	65	71	.478	12	P.J. Carey	205,812	3,320	1995
109	Chattanooga Lookouts (Reds)	60	80	.429	19	Phillip Wellman	280,692	4,128	1988
255	Orlando Rays (Devil Rays)	58	79	.423	19½	Mako Oliveras	139,489	2,113	1999

NOTE: Team's individual batting and pitching statistics can be found on page indicated in lefthand column.

2002 SOUTHERN LEAGUE STATISTICS

CLUB BATTING

	AVG	G	AB	R	H	2B	3B	HR	BB	SO	SB
Birmingham	.269	140	4564	610	1228	238	26	74	452	866	220
Carolina	.265	136	4691	666	1242	268	28	114	519	975	111
Orlando	.264	137	4492	585	1187	225	14	68	435	859	131
Chattanooga	.262	140	4711	594	1235	243	23	100	485	1038	111
West Tenn	.256	140	4707	596	1203	233	37	89	473	1022	130
Tennessee	.255	140	4737	739	1210	223	26	104	617	956	146
Jacksonville	.252	139	4556	586	1149	211	21	61	585	776	129
Greenville	.249	134	4450	583	1110	225	23	91	539	884	93
Mobile	.245	139	4614	580	1129	226	30	81	511	1006	124
Huntsville	.242	139	4537	598	1097	210	27	96	496	1075	157

CLUB PITCHING

	ERA	G	CG	SHO	SV	IP	H	R	ER	BB	SO
Jacksonville	3.09	139	6	14	38	1236	1072	492	424	533	960
Mobile	3.37	139	2	13	49	1231	1168	552	461	491	1074
Huntsville	3.45	139	4	14	36	1230	1171	568	471	529	1005
West Tenn	3.64	140	1	5	41	1245	1139	577	504	458	1040
Birmingham	3.75	140	1	11	52	1223	1129	605	510	552	928
Greenville	3.77	134	4	7	41	1188	1107	597	498	475	953
Chattanooga	4.13	140	5	4	27	1225	1267	672	562	496	993
Orlando	4.13	137	8	8	50	1192	1208	658	547	553	834
Carolina	4.22	136	6	7	29	1217	1190	701	571	543	914
Tennessee	4.48	140	9	8	30	1237	1339	715	616	482	756

CLUB FIELDING

	PCT	PO	A	E	DP		PCT	PO	A	E	DP
Jacksonville	.978	3707	1452	115	111	Birmingham	.971	3670	1482	156	112
Mobile	.973	3692	1431	142	104	Chattanooga	.971	3675	1466	156	140
Greenville	.973	3565	1447	139	102	Tennessee	.969	3711	1665	172	145
West Tenn	.973	3734	1410	144	105	Orlando	.967	3575	1420	173	105
Huntsville	.971	3689	1560	157	137	Carolina	.962	3652	1683	209	143

INDIVIDUAL BATTING LEADERS
(Minimum 378 Plate Appearances)

	AVG	G	AB	R	H	2B	3B	HR	RBI	BB	SO	SB
Darula, Bobby, Chattanooga	.325	96	323	48	105	17	4	4	36	43	27	10
Miles, Aaron, Birmingham	.322	138	531	67	171	39	1	9	68	40	45	25
Nevers, Tom, Chattanooga	.313	126	444	58	139	26	2	13	77	37	77	9
Collins, Mike, Jacksonville	.313	117	384	40	120	14	1	0	45	44	36	7
Edwards, Mike, Chattanooga	.307	119	424	57	130	19	2	11	60	41	57	9
Olivo, Miguel, Birmingham	.306	106	359	51	110	24	10	6	49	40	66	29
Pressley, Josh, Orlando	.304	93	342	47	104	19	0	4	45	42	47	5
Budzinski, Mark, West Tenn	.297	114	427	68	127	19	6	4	36	51	85	21
Wise, Dewayne, Tennessee	.297	86	340	59	101	21	4	10	49	29	49	15
Reyes, Rene, Carolina	.292	123	455	64	133	33	4	14	54	29	69	10

INDIVIDUAL PITCHING LEADERS
(Minimum 112 Innings)

	W	L	ERA	G	GS	CG	SV	IP	H	R	ER	BB	SO
Chulk, Vinny, Tennessee	13	5	2.96	25	24	0	1	152	133	55	50	53	108
Lee, Derek, Huntsville	5	10	3.04	34	16	0	0	127	138	59	43	45	104
Bruback, Matt, West Tenn	9	7	3.16	28	28	0	0	174	157	70	61	48	158
Pember, David, Huntsville	10	6	3.17	27	27	2	0	156	157	69	55	53	111
Martin, Chandler, Carolina	7	4	3.18	19	19	1	0	113	109	48	40	34	82
Bong, Jung, Greenville	7	8	3.25	27	17	0	2	122	136	59	44	45	107
Cameron, Ryan, Carolina	5	7	3.26	37	15	0	0	119	84	55	43	55	139
Stewart, Paul, Huntsville	12	9	3.28	27	27	2	0	162	147	69	59	42	124
Brazelton, Dewon, Orlando	5	9	3.33	26	26	1	0	146	129	69	54	67	109
Proctor, Scott, Jacksonville	7	9	3.51	26	25	0	0	133	111	63	52	85	131

ALL STAR-TEAM

C—Miguel Olivo, Birmingham. **1B**—David Kelton, West Tenn. **2B**—Aaron Miles, Birmingham. **3B**—Donny Leon, Chattanooga. **SS**—Clint Barmes, Carolina. **OF**—Bobby Darula, Chattanooga; Mike Edwards, Chattanooga; Choo Freeman, Carolina; Dewayne Wise, Tennessee. **DH**—Tom Nevers, Chattanooga. **Util**—Ben Risinger, Mobile. **RHP**—Vinny Chulk, Tennessee. **LHP**—Josh Stewart, Birmingham. **RP**—Joe Valentine, Birmingham.

Most Valuable Player: Aaron Miles, Birmingham. **Most Outstanding Pitcher**: Vinny Chulk, Tennessee. **Best Hustle**: Bernie Castro, Mobile. **Manager of the Year**: Wally Backman, Birmingham.

DEPARTMENT LEADERS

BATTING
G	Aaron Miles, Birmingham	138
AB	Rich Thompson, Tennessee	554
R	Rich Thompson, Tennessee	109
H	Aaron Miles, Birmingham	171
TB	Aaron Miles, Birmingham	239
XBH	David Kelton, West Tenn	54
2B	Aaron Miles, Birmingham	39
3B	Miguel Olivo, Birmingham	10
HR	David Kelton, West Tenn	20
	Pete LaForest, Orlando	20
RBI	David Kelton, West Tenn	79
SH	Shane Victorino, Jacksonville	16
SF	Ryan Hankins, Birmingham	9
BB	Shawn Fagan, Tennessee	102
IBB	Koyie Hill, Jacksonville	11
HBP	Rich Thompson, Tennessee	20
SO	Darron Ingram, Birmingham	140
SB	Bernie Castro, Mobile	53
CS	Danny Sandoval, Birmingham	24
GIDP	Mike Edwards, Chattanooga	19
OB%	Bobby Darula, Chattanooga	.413
SL%	Donny Leon, Chattanooga	.500

PITCHING
G	David Hooten, West Tenn	65
GS	Peter Bauer, Tennessee	28
	Matt Bruback, West Tenn	28
CG	Brandon Backe, Orlando	3
	Peter Bauer, Tennessee	3
ShO	Aaron Cook, Carolina	2
GF	Joe Valentine, Birmingham	48
SV	Joe Valentine, Birmingham	36
W	Vinny Chulk, Tennessee	13
	Diegomar Markwell, Tennessee	13
L	Dennis Ulacia, Birmingham	14
IP	Peter Bauer, Tennessee	177
H	Peter Bauer, Tennessee	208
R	Ryan Spille, Tennessee	105
ER	Ryan Spille, Tennessee	92
HR	Diegomar Markwell, Tennessee	23
HB	Ryan Kibler, Carolina	15
BB	Corwin Malone, Birmingham	89
SO	Matt Bruback, West Tenn	158
WP	Ryan Kibler, Carolina	18
BK	Matt Hampton, Mobile	3
	Ferenc Jongejan, West Tenn	3

FIELDING
C	AVG	Casey Kopitzke, West Tenn	.994
	PO	Koyie Hill, Jacksonville	815
	A	Dane Sardinha, Chattanooga	100
	E	Koyie Hill, Jacksonville	17
	DP	Miguel Oliva, Birmingham	10
	PB	Pete LaForest, Orlando	26
1B	AVG	David Kelton, West Tenn	.990
	PO	David Kelton, West Tenn	965
	A	Hunter Bledsoe, Jacksonville	72
		David Kelton, West Tenn	72
	E	Matt Logan, Tennessee	14
	DP	Matt Logan, Tennessee	89
2B	AVG	Mike Collins, Jacksonville	.988
	PO	Bernie Castro, Mobile	250
	A	Jimmy Alvarez, Tennessee	333
	E	Aaron Miles, Birmingham	26
	DP	Jimmy Alvarez, Tennessee	76
3B	AVG	Brennan King, Jacksonville	.945
	PO	Rusty McNamara, Greenville	84
	A	Garrett Atkins, Carolina	238
	E	Donny Leon, Chattanooga	26
	DP	Garrett Atkins, Carolina	24
SS	AVG	Ranier Olmedo, Chattanooga	.960
	PO	Ranier Olmedo, Chattanooga	195
	A	Clint Barmes, Carolina	359
	E	Clint Barmes, Carolina	33
	DP	Clint Barmes, Carolina	76
OF	AVG	Rich Thompson, Tennessee	.992
	PO	Darren Blakely, Mobile	298
	A	Scott Bikowski, Birmingham	15
	E	Ben Johnson, Mobile	9
	DP	Jackson Melian, WT-Huntsville	4

MINOR LEAGUES

BY TODD TRAUB

In a league known for its sluggers, pitchers held center stage for most of the 2002 Texas League season, right down to the final act.

San Antonio Missions righthander Rafael Soriano's dominant performance in Game Seven lifted the Missions to the Texas League title in a 4-1 victory over Tulsa. Soriano struck out 14 in seven innings, then turned it over to setup man Aaron Looper, who closed it out for his first save as the Missions claimed the four games to three.

The victory capped a tightly-played series in which six games were decided by one run and provided an example of the live arms that dotted the league throughout the year.

League all-star Kirk Saarloos paved the way, posting 10-

LARRY GOREN

Kirk Saarloos

1, 1.40 numbers with Round Rock before he was promoted to Triple-A New Orleans, and eventually to Houston, at the end of the first half. But the league was rife with strong-armed talent, some of it donated from the big leagues, some of it developed on the farm.

"The Texas League has always been a hitter's league," Royals farm director Bob Hegman said. "So it's encouraging to have pitchers go out there and hold teams down."

Hegman's Double-A pitchers at Wichita posted the best team effort with a league best 80-59 record and 3.27 ERA. El Paso lefthander Mike Gosling and righthanded teammate Andrew Good finished one-two in the victories hunt, with Gosling going 14-5, 3.13 and Good finishing at 13-6, 3.54.

Even lowly Arkansas (51-89), the defending champion which narrowly avoided the league futility mark of 90 losses and finished with the league's worst ERA (4.74), got into the pitching act. On May 13 righthanded spot-starter Hatuey Mendoza pitched a nine-inning no-hitter in a 3-0 victory at Tulsa. It was the league's only no-hitter of the year.

"How's that for a spot start?" manager Doug Sisson said.

Offensively, El Paso third baseman Chad Tracy led the league in hitting from wire to wire, finishing with a .344 average after batting above .400 for most of the first half and helping the Diablos to the team batting title with a .282 average. Tracy also finished as the hits leader with 177.

El Paso's Luis Terrero hit for the cycle twice (May 26

and Aug. 24) and San Antonio's Adrian Myers accomplished the feat on July 11.

The Missions' one-run victory in the championship game was a reversal of the club's first-half fortunes, in which San Antonio lost 16 one-run decisions and finished 20 games below .500. The Missions turned it around in the second half, claiming first place in the West Division on July 31 and held on through a four-team race that wasn't decided until the final two weeks.

Tulsa claimed the first-half title in the East with—naturally—pitching and defense. The Drillers won their playoff berth with the lowest batting average in the league. "We made the most with the least," manager Tim Ireland said.

Wichita rolled to the second-half title by 13 games but suffered a three-game sweep by Tulsa in the first round, which ended with a three-hitter by Tulsa starter C.J. Wilson.

The curtain came down on Texas League baseball in Shreveport, which had an affiliate in the league on and off for 40 years. With Fair Grounds Field attendance averaging in the hundreds even in 2001, Texas Rangers owner Tom Hicks purchased an interest in the club and will move it to Frisco, Texas, in 2003.

While most of the teams renewed their player development contracts with their respective organizations, the Giants—affiliated with Shreveport since 1979—signed with Norwich in the Eastern League for 2003. The Rockies signed with Frisco and then swapped affiliations with Tulsa, putting the Rangers' Double-A team closer to home.

"It's tough losing the Giants," league president Tom Kayser said. "They've been in the league for what, 20-some odd years? It's different not having a club in Shreveport. On the other hand, the Frisco thing is going to be phenomenal."

STANDINGS: SPLIT SEASON

FIRST HALF

EAST	W	L	PCT	GB
Tulsa	39	30	.565	—
Wichita	34	35	.493	5
Shreveport	31	38	.449	8
Arkansas	31	39	.443	8½

WEST	W	L	PCT	GB
Round Rock	42	28	.600	—
El Paso	40	28	.588	1
Midland	35	24	.507	6½
San Antonio	25	45	.357	17

SECOND HALF

EAST	W	L	PCT	GB
Wichita	46	24	.657	—
Tulsa	33	37	.471	13
Shreveport	29	41	.414	17
Arkansas	20	50	.286	26

WEST	W	L	PCT	GB
San Antonio	43	27	.614	—
Midland	40	30	.571	3
El Paso	36	34	.514	7
Round Rock	33	37	.471	10

PLAYOFFS—Semifinals: San Antonio defeated Round Rock 3-2 and Tulsa defeated Wichita 3-0 in best-of-5 series. **Finals:** San Antonio defeated Tulsa 4-3 in best-of-5 series.

STANDINGS: OVERALL

Page		W	L	PCT	GB	Manager	Attendance	Avg.	Last Penn.
153	Wichita Wranglers (Royals)	80	59	.576	—	Keith Bodie	142,265	2,189	1999
66	El Paso Diablos (Diamondbacks)	76	62	.551	3½	Chip Hale	234,971	3,455	1994
205	Midland RockHounds (Athletics)	75	64	.540	5	Tony DeFrancesco	276,380	4,006	1975
147	Round Rock Express (Astros)	75	65	.536	5½	Jackie Moore	670,176	9,574	2000
262	Tulsa Drillers (Rangers)	72	67	.518	8	Tim Ireland	306,705	4,578	1998
248	San Antonio Missions (Mariners)	68	72	.486	12½	Dave Brundage	316,983	4,594	2002
241	Shreveport Captains (Giants)	60	79	.432	20	Mario Mendoza	24,560	431	1995
59	Arkansas Travelers (Angels)	51	89	.364	29½	Doug Sisson	192,237	3,004	2001

NOTE: Team's individual batting and pitching statistics can be found on page indicated in lefthand column.

2002 TEXAS LEAGUE STATISTICS

CLUB BATTING

	AVG	G	AB	R	H	2B	3B	HR	BB	SO	SB
El Paso	.282	139	4787	693	1352	278	49	100	420	973	66
Round Rock	.273	140	4722	685	1288	256	41	105	471	895	129
Wichita	.269	139	4653	689	1252	227	36	83	488	757	151
Shreveport	.262	139	4529	540	1186	243	30	75	401	884	118
Midland	.258	141	4714	670	1216	251	31	110	588	1037	79
San Antonio	.253	140	4697	533	1188	224	30	51	449	874	134
Tulsa	.248	140	4592	618	1141	234	29	112	524	994	75
Arkansas	.246	140	4605	566	1134	226	37	88	382	870	161

CLUB PITCHING

	ERA	G	CG	SHO	SV	IP	H	R	ER	BB	SO
Wichita	3.27	139	6	10	34	1226	1102	538	445	486	973
San Antonio	3.43	140	4	18	33	1252	1134	572	477	516	1022
El Paso	3.75	139	9	10	38	1230	1241	613	512	384	992
Round Rock	3.87	140	4	9	37	1229	1187	624	529	464	996
Midland	3.88	141	5	9	43	1239	1241	636	534	504	1018
Tulsa	3.88	140	4	10	34	1215	1260	610	524	437	786
Shreveport	4.28	139	6	7	28	1172	1258	660	557	458	748
Arkansas	4.74	140	14	7	22	1199	1334	741	631	474	749

CLUB FIELDING

	PCT	PO	A	E	DP		PCT	PO	A	E	DP
Round Rock	.974	3687	1357	137	116	El Paso	.971	3690	1490	154	118
Shreveport	.973	3515	1437	140	126	Midland	.971	3717	1491	155	120
Tulsa	.972	3644	1590	149	116	San Antonio	.970	3756	1477	161	148
Wichita	.972	3677	1480	148	157	Arkansas	.969	3596	1555	166	137

INDIVIDUAL BATTING LEADERS
(Minimum 378 Plate Appearances)

	AVG	G	AB	R	H	2B	3B	HR	RBI	BB	SO	SB
Tracy, Chad, El Paso	.344	129	514	80	177	39	5	8	74	38	51	2
Huffman, Royce, Round Rock	.322	132	522	79	168	36	3	12	91	41	70	13
Perry, Chan, Wichita	.316	105	399	59	126	20	2	14	73	29	44	6
Alfaro, Jason, Round Rock	.314	124	455	71	143	36	2	16	74	50	75	11
Linden, Todd, Shreveport	.314	111	392	64	123	26	2	12	52	61	101	9
Stanley, Henri, Round Rock	.314	127	456	90	143	36	10	16	72	72	85	14
Santos, Deivis, Shreveport	.312	109	407	54	127	33	5	3	56	18	42	4
Monahan, Shane, Wichita	.307	97	391	55	120	27	3	10	59	18	53	11
Kata, Matt, El Paso	.298	136	578	95	172	33	9	11	57	37	80	12
Jones, Jason, Tulsa	.295	136	471	82	139	33	2	13	75	87	97	12
Gomez, Alexis, Wichita	.295	114	461	72	136	21	8	14	75	45	84	36

INDIVIDUAL PITCHING LEADERS
(Minimum 112 Innings)

	W	L	ERA	G	GS	CG	SV	IP	H	R	ER	BB	SO
Walk, Mitch, Shreveport	6	5	2.89	33	17	0	1	125	132	50	40	50	68
Rosario, Rodrigo, Round Rock	11	6	3.11	26	23	0	0	130	106	56	45	59	94
Gosling, Mike, El Paso	14	5	3.13	27	27	0	0	167	149	66	58	62	115
Webb, Brandon, El Paso	10	6	3.14	26	25	1	0	152	141	66	53	59	122
Mears, Chris, San Antonio	6	9	3.14	30	20	1	0	143	138	57	50	38	103
Anderson, Craig, San Antonio	7	7	3.20	27	27	1	0	152	143	61	54	64	94
Cervantes, Chris, El Paso	6	4	3.33	33	12	0	0	122	131	56	45	23	89
Rheinecker, John, Midland	7	7	3.38	20	20	1	0	128	137	63	48	24	100
Hughes, Travis, Tulsa	9	7	3.52	26	26	1	0	143	139	68	56	82	137
Good, Andrew, El Paso	13	6	3.55	28	27	2	0	178	170	89	70	26	128

ALL-STAR TEAM

C—John Buck, Round Rock. **1B**—Royce Huffman, Round Rock. **2B**—Matt Kata, El Paso. **3B**—Chad Tracy, El Paso. **SS**—Brian Specht, Arkansas. **OF**—Alexis Gomez, Wichita; Todd Linden, Shreveport; Henri Stanley, Round Rock. **DH**—Graham Koonce, Midland. **Util**—Jason Alfaro, Round Rock. **P**—Craig Anderson, San Antonio; Andrew Good, El Paso; Mike Gosling, El Paso; Runelvys Hernandez, Wichita; Travis Hughes, Tulsa; Rodrigo Rosario, Round Rock; Miguel Saladin, Round Rock; Kirk Saarloos, Round Rock.

Player of the Year: Chad Tracy, El Paso. **Pitcher of the Year**: Kirk Saarloos, Round Rock. **Manager of the Year**: Tim Ireland, Tulsa.

BATTING

G	Graham Koonce, Midland	140
AB	Matt Kata, El Paso	578
R	Matt Kata, El Paso	95
H	Chad Tracy, El Paso	177
TB	Matt Kata, El Paso	256
XBH	Mike O'Keefe, Arkansas	62
	Henri Stanley, Round Rock	62
2B	Chad Tracy, El Paso	39
3B	Kirk Asche, Midland	10
	Henri Stanley, Round Rock	10
HR	Graham Koonce, Midland	24
RBI	Graham Koonce, Midland	94
SH	Jhonny Carvajal, Shreveport	14
SF	Richard Paz, Wichita	11
BB	Graham Koonce, Midland	133
IBB	Graham Koonce, Midland	12
HBP	Tim Olson, El Paso	19
SO	Kirk Asche, Midland	132
SB	Jamal Strong, San Antonio	46
CS	Alexis Gomez, Wichita	24
GIDP	Eric Bruntlett, Round Rock	17
OB%	Graham Koonce, Midland	.440
SL%	Henri Stanley, Round Rock	.542

PITCHING

G	Claudio Galva, Midland	62
GS	Chad Qualls, Round Rock	29
CG	Billy Stokley, Arkansas	4
ShO	Mike Gosling, El Paso	2
GF	Greg Runser, Tulsa	53
SV	Greg Runser, Tulsa	25
W	Mike Gosling, El Paso	14
L	Billy Stokley, Arkansas	14
IP	Andrew Good, El Paso	178
H	Nick Roberts, Round Rock	195
R	Nick Roberts, Round Rock	102
ER	Mike Nannini, Round Rock	91
HR	Andrew Good, El Paso	21
HB	Rodrigo Rosario, Round Rock	19
BB	Travis Hughes, Tulsa	82
SO	Chad Qualls, Round Rock	142
WP	Brandon Webb, El Paso	12
BK	Chad Qualls, Round Rock	4

FIELDING

C	AVG	Robinson Cancel, Midland	.995
	PO	Juan Brito, Wichita	583
	A	Robinson Cancel, Midland	81
	E	Mike Kremblas, Midland	11
	DP	Robinson Cancel, Midland	8
	PB	Robinson Cancel, Midland	15
1B	AVG	Chan Perry, Wichita	.998
	PO	Jason Jones, Tulsa	1145
	A	Jason Jones, Tulsa	72
	E	Jason Jones, Tulsa	22
	DP	Chan Perry, Wichita	98
2B	AVG	Chris Burke, Round Rock	.976
	PO	Brian Harris, Wichita	256
	A	Brian Harris, Wichita	393
	E	Adam Morrissey, Midland	22
	DP	Brian Harris, Wichita	104
3B	AVG	Jason Alfaro, Round Rock	.963
	PO	Jason Alfaro, Round Rock	87
	A	Mike Christensen, Arkansas	263
	E	Chad Tracy, El Paso	25
	DP	Mike Christensen, Arkansas	24
SS	AVG	Ruben Castillo, San Antonio	.951
	PO	Ruben Castillo, San Antonio	240
	A	Ruben Castillo, San Antonio	343
	E	Brian Specht, Arkansas	35
	DP	Ruben Castillo, San Antonio	90
OF	AVG	Mike Lockwood, Midland	.996
	PO	Jamal Strong, San Antonio	280
	A	Elpidio Guzman, Arkansas	15
	E	Alexis Gomez, Wichita	8
		Elpidio Guzman, Arkansas	8
	DP	Jamal Strong, San Antonio	5

MINOR LEAGUES

CALIFORNIA LEAGUE

BY JOSH KLEINBAUM

Rocco Baldelli spent barely half the 2002 season in the California League, yet the Bakersfield Blaze star center fielder left his imprint everywhere.

Baldelli, Tampa Bay's first-round draft pick in 2000, entered the league as a highly-touted prospect who had yet to live up to his potential. His teammate, Josh Hamilton, the No. 1 overall pick in 1999, was expected to provide the excitement. But while Hamilton struggled through injuries for the third year in a row, Baldelli began his amazing rise through Devil Rays system, batting .333-14-51 with 21 steals in 77 games. He finished 36 at-bats shy of qualifying for the Cal League batting title.

LARRY GOREN

Rocco Baldelli

From Bakersfield, he moved to Double-A Orlando and finally to Triple-A Durham—and stung the ball at every level. For his efforts, he was named Baseball America's Minor League Player of the Year.

Baldelli's emergence highlighted an exciting season in the Cal League, one which had a remarkable hit streak, a cycle, a near no-hitter and new team names.

The Mudville Nine abandoned Casey and his bad luck, reverting to its original Stockton Ports name. The change did some good: Stockton ran away with the Northern Division's first-half title, was competitive in the second half and marched through the postseason, sweeping Modesto in the semifinals and topping Lake Elsinore for the title.

After spending the entire 2002 regular season at Class A Dayton, righthander Bobby Basham made his only start in Stockton a memorable one. Basham struck out 13 while allowing five hits and two run in eight innings as Stockton beat Lake Elsinore 6-2 to win its first Cal League title since 1992. Stockton's Stephen Smitherman was the league's playoff MVP after hitting .522 in seven playoff games.

As soon as the season ended, the Cincinnati Reds ended their two-year relationship with Stockton, bolting for the Carolina League. The Ports signed a PDC with the Rangers. Visalia was the only other Cal League team to switch affiliations, signing with the Rockies.

Rancho Cucamonga outfielder Mike Campo set one of the more obscure league records, getting hit by a pitch 40 times. Righthander Pedro Liriano, 10-14 on the season, provided another rare highlight for the Quakes, who finished with a league-worst 52-88 record. Liriano threw six no-hit innings July 30 before allowing a single to Visalia's Jeff Christy. Liriano finished out the one-hitter, the first in Quakes history.

Lancaster became the first team in the minors to lose 40 games in 2002, but then performed a remarkable about-face to win the Southern Division's wild card. A managerial change helped—Steve Scarsone took a leave of absence from the Diamondbacks organization, and former Mariners manager Bill Plummer engineered the turnaround, garnering the league's manager of the year award.

In the process, the JetHawks contributed two of the league's most remarkable individual accomplishments. Infielder Corey Myers, the fourth overall pick in the 1999 draft, resurrected an inconsistent season by hitting safely in 33 consecutive games. The streak began July 22 and ended Aug. 30, in the second-to-last game of the season. Myers missed four games in the middle while suffering from food poisoning. He fell short of the league record by two games.

In the middle of Myers' streak, his teammate and best friend, Andy Green, pulled off an impressive feat of his own. On Aug. 21, Green, a light-hitting second baseman, went 4-for-5 against High Desert, finishing off the cycle with a ninth-inning home run.

San Bernardino, which won the first half in the South, celebrated its playoff appearance by adopting a new name. In an effort to appeal to more than just its metro area, the Stampede changed its name to the Inland Empire 66ers of San Bernardino.

STANDINGS: SPLIT SEASON

FIRST HALF					SECOND HALF				
NORTH	W	L	PCT	GB	**NORTH**	W	L	PCT	GB
Stockton	49	21	.700	—	Modesto	44	26	.629	—
Bakersfield	41	29	.586	8	Stockton	40	30	.571	4
San Jose	37	33	.529	12	Visalia	36	35	.507	8½
Visalia	34	36	.486	15	San Jose	31	39	.443	13
Modesto	34	36	.486	15	Bakersfield	28	43	.394	16½
SOUTH	W	L	PCT	GB	**SOUTH**	W	L	PCT	GB
San Bernardino	37	33	.529	—	Lake Elsinore	42	28	.600	—
High Desert	34	36	.486	3	San Bernardino	40	30	.571	2
Lake Elsinore	33	37	.471	4	Lancaster	40	30	.571	2
Rancho Cuca.	28	42	.400	9	High Desert	26	44	.371	16
Lancaster	23	47	.329	14	Rancho Cuca.	24	46	.343	18

PLAYOFFS—First Round: Modesto defeated Visalia 2-0 and Lake Elsinore defeated Lancaster 2-0 in best-of-3 series. **Semifinals:** Stockton defeated Modesto 3-0 and Lake Elsinore defeated San Bernardino 3-2 in best-of-5 series. **Finals:** Stockton defeated Lake Elsinore 3-1 in best-of-5 series.

STANDINGS: OVERALL

Page		W	L	PCT	GB	Manager(s)	Attendance	Avg.	Last Penn.
110	Stockton Ports (Reds)	89	51	.636	—	Jayhawk Owens	71,333	1,049	2002
205	Modesto A's (Athletics)	78	62	.557	11	Greg Sparks	155,171	2,249	1984
248	San Bernardino Stampede (Mariners)	77	63	.550	12	Daren Brown	222,881	3,230	2000
234	Lake Elsinore Storm (Padres)	75	65	.536	14	George Hendrick	230,957	3,299	2001
206	Visalia Oaks (Athletics)	70	71	.496	19½	Webster Garrison	58,734	864	1978
255	Bakersfield Blaze (Devil Rays)	69	72	.489	20½	Charlie Montoyo	101,377	1,448	1989
241	San Jose Giants (Giants)	68	72	.486	21	Bill Hayes	154,322	2,205	2001
67	Lancaster JetHawks (Diamondbacks)	63	77	.450	26	Steve Scarsone/Bill Plummer	181,007	2,586	None
168	High Desert Mavericks (Brewers)	60	80	.429	29	Mike Caldwell	139,348	2,020	1997
59	Rancho Cucamonga Quakes (Angels)	52	88	.371	37	Bobby Meacham	293,150	4,249	1994

NOTE: Team's individual batting and pitching statistics can be found on page indicated in lefthand column.

CLUB BATTING

	AVG	G	AB	R	H	2B	3B	HR	BB	SO	SB
Lancaster	.273	140	4945	741	1351	257	44	102	455	1133	79
High Desert	.268	140	4866	818	1305	255	55	155	470	1169	182
San Bernardino	.265	140	4783	710	1266	267	54	98	486	1031	118
Bakersfield	.264	141	4825	648	1276	236	27	124	418	1211	107
Stockton	.264	140	4722	760	1245	250	31	134	535	1179	134
Modesto	.264	140	4845	690	1277	263	34	88	567	1032	108
Visalia	.259	141	4804	750	1245	249	32	129	642	1276	121
Rancho Cucamonga	.259	140	4777	662	1235	265	36	96	467	1136	145
Lake Elsinore	.258	140	4835	702	1249	250	44	90	532	1146	206
San Jose	.254	140	4808	663	1221	233	37	92	397	1159	118

CLUB PITCHING

	ERA	G	CG	SHO	SV	IP	H	R	ER	BB	SO
Stockton	3.20	140	5	12	36	1239	1108	541	440	423	1137
Modesto	3.75	140	3	3	36	1248	1203	606	520	496	1269
San Bernardino	3.83	140	4	9	37	1248	1145	634	531	475	1266
Lake Elsinore	3.97	140	0	5	43	1260	1210	677	555	527	1227
Bakersfield	4.00	141	3	8	47	1242	1345	686	552	434	1281
Visalia	4.14	141	4	2	25	1247	1336	714	574	393	1111
San Jose	4.22	140	1	7	32	1242	1246	676	583	555	1007
Rancho Cucamonga	4.97	140	9	9	23	1227	1287	834	678	513	1131
Lancaster	5.00	140	0	6	34	1248	1382	797	693	495	1051
High Desert	6.13	140	0	0	29	1228	1408	979	836	658	992

CLUB FIELDING

	PCT	PO	A	E	DP		PCT	PO	A	E	DP
Modesto	.974	3743	1345	136	104	Stockton	.966	3716	1437	180	86
San Jose	.973	3726	1487	142	117	Visalia	.964	3741	1524	199	100
San Bernardino	.969	3744	1391	166	111	Bakersfield	.963	3727	1431	197	106
Lancaster	.967	3744	1501	179	110	High Desert	.962	3683	1483	205	132
Lake Elsinore	.966	3779	1400	180	98	Rancho Cuca.	.960	3681	1510	219	124

INDIVIDUAL BATTING LEADERS

(Minimum 378 Plate Appearances)

	AVG	G	AB	R	H	2B	3B	HR	RBI	BB	SO	SB
Knott, Jon, Lake Elsinore	.341	93	367	55	125	33	8	8	73	46	68	5
Lopez, Jose, San Bernardino	.324	123	522	82	169	39	5	8	60	27	45	31
Campo, Mike, Rancho Cucamonga	.313	126	450	86	141	35	6	9	53	75	127	18
Smitherman, Stephen, Stockton	.313	128	482	78	151	36	1	19	99	39	126	17
Green, Andy, Lancaster	.309	102	401	74	124	36	4	6	50	60	59	15
Bynum, Freddie, Visalia	.306	135	539	83	165	26	5	3	56	64	116	41
Ansman, Craig, Lancaster	.305	100	374	67	114	21	7	18	55	34	113	3
Brewer, Jace, Bakersfield	.302	91	378	52	114	17	2	6	44	11	62	8
Sellier, Brian, Modesto	.300	116	417	57	125	26	6	5	58	73	82	16
Lindsey, John, San Bernardino	.297	127	472	75	140	30	6	22	93	48	109	0
Schneidmiller, Gary, Visalia	.297	111	381	85	113	17	2	7	53	78	80	6

INDIVIDUAL PITCHING LEADERS

(Minimum 112 Innings)

	W	L	ERA	G	GS	CG	SV	IP	H	R	ER	BB	SO
Clark, Jeff, San Jose	12	3	2.06	21	21	1	0	140	118	37	32	18	129
Bonser, Boof, San Jose	8	6	2.88	23	23	0	0	128	89	44	41	70	139
Van Dusen, Derrick, San Bernardino	7	6	3.10	20	20	0	0	125	111	46	43	36	118
Stokes, Brian, Bakersfield	10	7	3.16	28	28	1	0	166	156	79	60	57	152
McCall, Derell, Modesto	8	5	3.32	25	23	1	0	133	140	54	49	50	82
Morgan, Russ, San Bernardino	13	6	3.36	36	11	0	0	123	112	58	46	36	107
Withers, Darvin, Modesto	7	3	3.46	30	16	1	1	125	116	53	48	33	106
Blackley, Travis, San Bernardino	5	9	3.49	21	20	1	0	121	102	52	47	44	152
Mottl, Ryan, Stockton	13	6	3.50	27	27	2	0	180	169	84	70	39	148
Fischer, Rich, Rancho Cucamonga	7	8	3.50	19	19	5	0	131	118	61	51	29	138

ALL-STAR TEAM

C—Craig Ansman, Lancaster. **1B**—Corey Hart, High Desert. **2B**—Jake Gautreau, Lake Elsinore. **3B**—Brian Barden, Lancaster. **SS**—Jose Lopez, San Bernardino. **OF**—Rocco Baldelli, Bakersfield; Jonny Gomes, Bakersfield; Stephen Smitherman, Stockton. **DH**—Mike Campo, Rancho Cucamonga. **SP**—Jeff Clark, San Jose; Rich Fischer, Rancho Cucamonga; John Koronka, Stockton. **RP**—Evan Rust, Bakersfield.

Most Valuable Player: Rocco Baldelli, Bakersfield. **Pitcher of the Year**: Jeff Clark, San Jose. **Rookie of the Year**: Jose Lopez, San Bernardino. **Manager of the Year**: Bill Plummer, Lancaster.

BATTING

G	Freddie Bynum, Visalia	135
	Jesus Cota, Lancaster	135
AB	Jesus Cota, Lancaster	540
R	Jonny Gomes, Bakersfield	102
H	Jose Lopez, San Bernardino	169
TB	Jonny Gomes, Bakersfield	256
XBH	Jonny Gomes, Bakersfield	63
2B	Jose Lopez, San Bernardino	39
3B	Dave Krynzel, High Desert	12
HR	Jorge Soto, Visalia	31
RBI	Jesus Cota, Lancaster	101
SH	Nestor Perez, Bakersfield	23
SF	Stephen Smitherman, Stockton	14
BB	Marcus Nettles, Lake Elsinore	101
IBB	Jonny Gomes, Bakersfield	6
HBP	Mike Campo, Rancho Cucamonga	40
SO	Jorge Soto, Visalia	195
SB	Marcus Nettles, Lake Elsinore	58
CS	Marcus Nettles, Lake Elsinore	26
GIDP	Jesus Cota, Lancaster	17
	John Lindsey, San Bernardino	17
OB%	Mike Campo, Rancho Cucamonga	.451
SL%	Jonny Gomes, Bakersfield	.574

PITCHING

G	Mike Nicolas, Lake Elsinore	65
GS	Clint Nageotte, San Bernardino	29
	Pete Smart, High Desert	29
CG	Rich Fischer, Rancho Cucamonga	5
ShO	Rich Fischer, Rancho Cucamonga	4
GF	Jared Hoerman, San Bernardino	49
SV	Jared Hoerman, San Bernardino	29
W	Russ Morgan, San Bernardino	13
	Ryan Mottl, Stockton	13
L	Pedro Liriano, Rancho Cucamonga	14
	Brandon O'Neal, Rancho Cucamonga	14
IP	Ryan Mottl, Stockton	180
	Pete Smart, High Desert	180
H	Pete Smart, High Desert	212
R	Justin Gordon, High Desert	128
ER	Justin Gordon, High Desert	107
HR	Jeff Bruksch, Visalia	22
HB	Brandon O'Neal, Rancho Cucamonga	23
BB	Mark Phillips, Lake Elsinore	94
SO	Clint Nageotte, San Bernardino	214
WP	Roberto Maysonet, High Desert	20
	George Perez, High Desert	20
BK	Derell McCall, Modesto	4

FIELDING

C	AVG	Beau Craig, Modesto	.991
	PO	Beau Craig, Modesto	729
	A	Beau Craig, Modesto	77
	E	Brian Foster, High Desert	15
	DP	Beau Craig, Modesto	11
	PB	Jared Abruzzo, Rancho Cuca.	17
		Beau Craig, Modesto	17
1B	AVG	Al Corbeil, Rancho Cuca.	.988
	PO	Al Corbeil, Rancho Cuca.	784
	A	Dan Johnson, Modesto	62
	E	Mitch Gregg, Visalia	13
	DP	Al Corbeil, Rancho Cuca.	70
2B	AVG	Edwin Maldonado, San Jose	.980
	PO	Freddie Bynum, Visalia	288
	A	Freddie Bynum, Visalia	364
	E	Freddie Bynum, Visalia	36
	DP	Freddie Bynum, Visalia	73
3B	AVG	Angel Chavez, San Jose	.928
	PO	Angel Chavez, San Jose	94
	A	Angel Chavez, San Jose	242
	E	Three tied at	26
	DP	Angel Chavez, San Jose	25
SS	AVG	Jamie Athas, San Jose	.946
	PO	Jeff Bannon, Stockton	183
	A	J.T. Stotts, Visalia	398
	E	Jeff Bannon, Stockton	42
	DP	J.J. Hardy, High Desert	57
OF	AVG	Micah Holst, San Jose	1.000
	PO	Jeremy Owens, Lake Elsinore	241
	A	Jeremy Owens, Lake Elsinore	13
	E	Four tied at	8
	DP	Gary Thomas, Modesto	4

MINOR LEAGUES

CAROLINA LEAGUE

BY DAVE UTNIK AND LACY LUSK

After nearly winning a Carolina League triple crown during the 2002 season, Brad Hawpe must wonder what he might have accomplished had he not missed two weeks with tendinitis in his right wrist.

The Salem Avalanche first baseman batted .347-22-97 in 122 games to become the first Salem player to win the league MVP award since Ozzie Olivares in 1977.

"I just try to find a pitch and hit it up the middle," Hawpe said of his philosophy at the plate.

That philosophy earned Hawpe a promotion to Double-A Carolina during the final week of the regular season. Before he left, the 23-year-old slugger dominated the advanced Class A circuit.

"He takes a great path to the ball, and he's starting to hit with his lower half," Avalanche manager Stu Cole said. "With a wide open stance, he can go the other way at times, but he's still mostly a pure hitter."

Hawpe's performance was overshadowed a bit by the collective effort of the Lynchburg Hillcats, who became the second straight wild card team to win the league championship. With a lineup that featured seven all-stars, including league pitcher of the year Sean Burnett and home run champion Josh Bonifay, the Hillcats defeated the Wilmington Blue Rocks and Kinston Indians to capture the 2002 Mills Cup.

Brad Hawpe

The Blue Rocks hosted the Carolina League-California League all-star game, which ended in a tie, and finished the year with the league's best overall record at 89-51. But they lost the Northern Division Championship Series to the Hillcats. Lynchburg also spoiled Kinston's championship hopes. The Indians defeated Myrtle Beach to claim the Southern Division crown and won the first game of the finals before the Hillcats ran off three straight.

A 6-5 victory over the K-Tribe in Game Four of the best-of-5 series gave Lynchburg its fifth league championship since 1978. Left fielder Matt Meath, who joined the team Aug. 26 after spending most of the season at short-season Williamsport, hit .308 and was named the championship series MVP as the Hillcats earned their first title since 1997.

"I've been pretty fortunate," Hillcats manager Pete Mackanin said. "We have some pretty good players here."

The Hillcats finished second behind Wilmington in both halves, tying for the first-half title but losing out on head-to-head record, but they finally overcame the Blue Rocks in the Northern Division playoffs. Closer D.J. Carrasco saved four of Lynchburg's six postseason victories, including the clincher at home against Kinston.

"We were told during spring training that we are going to start trying to win championships at the minor league level," Burnett said. "They're more focused on winning and you can see the results here. It's a fun spot to be in."

There was plenty of fun in Salem, too. In addition to Hawpe's run at the triple crown, the Avalanche took part in a no-hitter. Kip Bouknight, who was part of a perfect game in his rookie season, threw the first no-hitter of his career Aug. 8 at Frederick. Potomac's Aaron Fera had eight RBIs in a game May 3, also against the Keys.

After winning the Carolina League championship in 2001 and staking claim to the MVP in 2002, the Avalanche parted ways with the Rockies organization in September. Salem signed a two-year player development agreement with the Houston Astros, ending an eight-year relationship with the Rockies. The Astros are the fifth major league affiliate in Salem's history dating back to 1968.

The Avalanche weren't the only team to switch affiliations. After he was unable to bring an Expos farm team to Prince William County, Potomac Cannons owner Art Silber agreed to align his club with the Reds for the next two years.

The lure of a major league exhibition game (to christen a new ballpark in 2004) and the success of Cincinnati's minor league clubs were major factors in Silber's decision.

"The Reds were one of the teams that approached us, and they convinced us that they will do things right," Silber said. "Of all the teams on the list, they were the ones that impressed us the most."

STANDINGS: SPLIT SEASON

FIRST HALF

NORTH	W	L	PCT	GB
*Wilmington	47	23	.671	—
Lynchburg	47	23	.671	—
Potomac	24	46	.343	23
Frederick	18	51	.261	28½

SOUTH	W	L	PCT	GB
Myrtle Beach	43	27	.614	—
Salem	39	31	.557	4
Kinston	34	35	.493	8½
Winston-Salem	27	43	.386	16

SECOND HALF

NORTH	W	L	PCT	GB
Wilmington	42	28	.600	—
Lynchburg	40	30	.571	2
Potomac	35	35	.500	7
Frederick	29	41	.414	13

SOUTH	W	L	PCT	GB
Kinston	40	30	.571	—
Myrtle Beach	36	34	.514	4
Salem	35	35	.500	5
Winston-Salem	23	47	.329	17

*Won tie-breaker

PLAYOFFS—Semifinals: Lynchburg defeated Wilmington 2-1 and Kinston defeated Myrtle Beach 2-0 in best-of-3 series. **Final:** Lynchburg defeated Kinston 3-1 in best-of-5 series.

STANDINGS: OVERALL

Page		W	L	PCT	GB	Manager	Attendance	Avg.	Last Penn.
154	Wilmington Blue Rocks (Royals)	89	51	.636	—	Jeff Garber	331,545	4,805	1999
220	Lynchburg Hillcats (Pirates)	87	53	.621	2	Pete Mackanin	127,916	1,881	2002
74	Myrtle Beach Pelicans (Braves)	79	61	.564	10	Randy Ingle	200,463	3,037	2000
118	Kinston Indians (Indians)	74	65	.532	14½	Ted Kubiak	106,472	1,638	1995
126	Salem Avalanche (Rockies)	74	66	.529	15	Stu Cole	196,347	2,931	2001
227	Potomac Cannons (Cardinals)	59	81	.421	30	Joe Cunningham	182,059	2,845	1989
96	Winston-Salem Warthogs (White Sox)	50	90	.357	39	Razor Shines	136,302	2,034	1993
81	Frederick Keys (Orioles)	47	92	.338	41½	Jack Voigt	305,950	4,499	1990

NOTE: Team's individual batting and pitching statistics can be found on page indicated in lefthand column.

CLUB BATTING

	AVG	G	AB	R	H	2B	3B	HR	BB	SO	SB
Lynchburg	.276	140	4776	700	1317	293	25	131	419	849	110
Wilmington	.274	140	4674	691	1281	238	26	58	494	904	108
Salem	.264	140	4774	656	1262	295	34	96	408	929	65
Myrtle Beach	.255	140	4561	555	1161	218	32	66	419	860	136
Kinston	.251	139	4645	598	1168	198	38	99	482	1101	184
Frederick	.251	139	4662	562	1169	193	19	53	411	900	65
Potomac	.248	140	4646	555	1150	204	24	65	450	935	143
Winston-Salem	.243	140	4607	552	1120	193	19	80	420	1002	210

CLUB PITCHING

	ERA	G	CG	SHO	SV	IP	H	R	ER	BB	SO
Lynchburg	2.96	140	3	13	46	1242	1117	520	409	383	1054
Wilmington	3.20	140	0	13	39	1233	1155	519	438	363	960
Myrtle Beach	3.20	140	8	18	37	1213	1098	504	431	392	1010
Kinston	3.61	139	1	11	41	1229	1173	587	493	498	923
Potomac	3.90	140	8	7	29	1220	1248	646	529	431	888
Salem	3.94	140	5	8	39	1240	1260	647	543	467	847
Winston-Salem	4.38	140	6	7	22	1217	1267	686	592	513	810
Frederick	4.75	139	4	6	27	1219	1310	760	644	456	988

CLUB FIELDING

	PCT	PO	A	E	DP		PCT	PO	A	E	DP
Myrtle Beach	.976	3638	1330	121	109	Kinston	.970	3688	1499	158	111
Salem	.974	3723	1582	140	128	Lynchburg	.967	3727	1466	177	130
Wilmington	.973	3699	1475	145	118	Potomac	.967	3659	1496	177	131
Win.-Salem	.972	3651	1595	149	140	Frederick	.964	3657	1392	189	96

INDIVIDUAL BATTING LEADERS

(Minimum 378 Plate Appearances)

	AVG	G	AB	R	H	2B	3B	HR	RBI	BB	SO	SB
Hawpe, Brad, Salem	.347	122	450	87	156	38	2	22	97	81	84	1
Navarrete, Ray, Lynchburg	.318	134	532	75	169	41	2	6	69	38	48	8
Machado, Alejandro, Wilmington	.314	101	325	53	102	9	1	2	29	27	43	20
Gemoll, Justin, Wilmington	.310	93	335	56	104	20	2	1	49	40	55	0
Bonifay, Josh, Lynchburg	.307	126	463	83	142	36	1	26	102	63	97	3
McCarthy, Bill, Myrtle Beach	.305	128	442	52	135	26	4	11	65	38	88	6
Piedra, Jorge, Salem	.301	104	392	64	118	37	12	13	64	37	55	10
Duffy, Chris, Lynchburg	.301	132	539	85	162	27	5	10	52	33	101	22
Tucker, Mamon, Frederick	.300	127	473	62	142	16	4	4	55	33	75	9
Castillo, Jose, Lynchburg	.300	134	503	82	151	25	2	16	80	49	95	27

INDIVIDUAL PITCHING LEADERS

(Minimum 112 Innings)

	W	L	ERA	G	GS	CG	SV	IP	H	R	ER	BB	SO
Nelson, Bubba, Myrtle Beach	11	5	1.72	23	23	0	0	136	98	37	26	44	105
Burnett, Sean, Lynchburg	13	4	1.80	26	26	2	0	155	118	46	31	33	96
Curtis, Daniel, Myrtle Beach	7	7	2.53	17	17	3	0	117	106	37	33	18	99
Parrott, Rhett, Potomac	8	5	2.71	19	19	2	0	113	91	42	34	41	82
Waters, Chris, Myrtle Beach	13	7	2.76	28	28	2	0	183	154	63	56	43	103
Tamayo, Danny, Wilmington	14	4	2.77	23	20	0	0	123	121	48	38	32	108
Jacobsen, Landon, Lynchburg	12	10	2.89	27	27	1	0	162	145	71	52	41	123
Connolly, Mike, Lynchburg	10	3	2.94	29	19	0	0	122	111	46	40	46	100
Mejia, Juan, Potomac	6	7	3.09	23	16	3	0	119	121	50	41	41	49
Buglovsky, Chris, Salem	9	9	3.12	27	27	1	0	165	161	68	57	58	126

ALL-STAR TEAM

C—Ronny Paulino, Lynchburg. **1B**—Brad Hawpe, Salem. **2B**—Josh Bonifay, Lynchburg. **3B**—Justin Gemoll, Lynchburg. **SS**—Jose Castillo, Lynchburg. **OF**—Chris Duffy, Lynchburg; Byron Gettis, Wilmington; Bill McCarthy, Myrtle Beach; Skip Schumaker, Potomac. **DH**—Ray Navarrete, Lynchburg. **Util**—Alejandro Machado, Wilmington. **SP**—Sean Burnett, Lynchburg. **RP**—D.J. Carrasco, Lynchburg.

Most Valuable Player: Brad Hawpe, Salem. **Most Valuable Pitcher**: Sean Burnett, Lynchburg. **Manager of the Year**: Jeff Garber, Wilmington.

DEPARTMENT LEADERS

BATTING

G	Johnny Hernandez, Potomac	139
AB	Cory Sullivan, Salem	560
R	Cory Sullivan, Salem	90
H	Ray Navarrete, Lynchburg	169
TB	Brad Hawpe, Salem	264
XBH	Josh Bonifay, Lynchburg	63
2B	Cory Sullivan, Salem	42
3B	Jorge Piedra, Salem	12
HR	Josh Bonifay, Lynchburg	26
RBI	Josh Bonifay, Lynchburg	102
SH	Norris Hopper, Wilmington	22
SF	Johnny Hernandez, Potomac	9
BB	Brad Hawpe, Salem	81
IBB	Brad Hawpe, Salem	23
HBP	Bill McCarthy, Myrtle Beach	23
SO	Eric Welsh, Winston-Salem	159
SB	Edwin Yan, Winston-Salem	88
CS	Three tied at	19
GIDP	Mamon Tucker, Frederick	19
	Kris Wilken, Frederick	19
OB%	Brad Hawpe, Salem	.447
SL%	Brad Hawpe, Salem	.587

PITCHING

G	D.J. Carrasco, Lynchburg	55
GS	Six tied at	28
CG	Heath Phillips, Winston-Salem	5
ShO	Daniel Curtis, Myrtle Beach	3
	Heath Phillips, Winston-Salem	3
GF	D.J. Carrasco, Lynchburg	44
SV	D.J. Carrasco, Lynchburg	29
W	Kip Bouknight, Salem	14
	Danny Tamayo, Wilmington	14
L	Heath Phillips, Winston-Salem	16
IP	Chris Waters, Myrtle Beach	183
H	Matt Schwager, Frederick	185
R	Matt Schwager, Frederick	124
ER	Matt Schwager, Frederick	100
HR	Scott Dohmann, Salem	22
HB	Chris Waters, Myrtle Beach	24
BB	Wyatt Allen, Winston-Salem	80
SO	Adam Wainwright, Myrtle Beach	167
WP	Ryan Price, Salem	16
BK	Nick Webb, Salem	4

FIELDING

C	AVG	Jean Boscan, Myrtle Beach	.992
	PO	Ron Paulino, Lynchburg	854
	A	Ron Paulino, Lynchburg	88
	E	Ron Paulino, Lynchburg	18
	DP	Tony Arnerich, Wilmington	8
	PB	Heath Wilson, Kinston	18
1B	AVG	Brad Hawpe, Salem	.994
	PO	Brad Hawpe, Salem	1136
	A	Brad Hawpe, Salem	116
	E	Chad Santos, Wilmington	11
	DP	Brad Hawpe, Salem	103
2B	AVG	Richard Lewis, Myrtle Beach	.985
	PO	Edwin Yan, Winston-Salem	270
	A	Edwin Yan, Winston-Salem	381
	E	Edwin Yan, Winston-Salem	29
	DP	Edwin Yan, Winston-Salem	88
3B	AVG	Tommy Nicholson, W-S	.959
	PO	Corey Smith, Kinston	111
	A	Tommy Nicholson, W-S	248
	E	Corey Smith, Kinston	33
	DP	Tommy Nicholson, W-S	30
SS	AVG	Guillermo Reyes, W-S	.957
	PO	Jose Castillo, Lynchburg	245
	A	Jose Castillo, Lynchburg	402
	E	Jose Castillo, Lynchburg	33
		Hector Luna, Kinston	33
	DP	Jose Castillo, Lynchburg	92
OF	AVG	Bill McCarthy, Myrtle Beach	.994
	PO	Chris Morris, Potomac	284
	A	Cory Sullivan, Salem	16
	E	Cory Keylor, Frederick	11
	DP	Cory Sullivan, Salem	4

BY SEAN KERNAN

The Charlotte Rangers made their final season in the Florida State League a memorable one, taking the league championship in a best-of-five series that went the distance before the Lakeland Tigers succumbed in a 6-0 shutout at Henley Field in Lakeland.

Each of the last three games of the series were shutouts. DH Jason Botts and third baseman Cole Liniak each hit home runs to give Charlotte a 3-0 lead by the fourth inning of Game Five.

Rangers pitchers John Connally, Jason Andrew and Rejean Rivard combined for the three-hit shutout. Andrew spun five innings of no-hit ball after he relieved Connally following a nearly two-hour rain delay. It was just Andrew's second appearance for the team. He joined Charlotte late in the season.

"When I went out there to get (Andrew in the eighth inning), I told him, 'Son, that was an outstanding performance,' " said Rangers skipper Darryl Kennedy, who was named the FSL's manager of the year.

Joel Hanrahan

The Rangers' only other FSL title came in 1989. The franchise, which spent 16 years at Charlotte County Stadium, was sold at the end of the regular season to the Cardinals.

St. Louis will move its team to Jupiter's Roger Dean Stadium, sharing the facility with the Marlins affiliate starting in 2003. However, that shouldn't be much of a problem because the Jupiter complex was built to house two major league organizations during spring training. The new team will be known as the Palm Beach Cardinals. It will move to the East Division, enabling Lakeland to move to the West where it will much better situated geographically.

The 2002 season began with a twist as Brevard County and Jupiter switched affiliations. Brevard County became an Expos affiliate and Jupiter became a Marlins team to coincide with moves at the major league level in which former Montreal Expos owner Jeffrey Loria took over control of the Florida Marlins.

Manatees manager Bob Didier didn't last long on the job. He was removed from his position June 1 after an on-field incident with female umpire Ria Cortesio. He was replaced by veteran manager Tony Torchia, who guided the Manatees to the worst record in the league (51-85).

Vero Beach righthander Joel Hanrahan threw not one, but two no-hitters during the 2002 campaign. The 2000 second-round draft choice fired the first no-no April 21, a 5-0 shutout against Jupiter. Two and a half months later, on July 4, Hanrahan tossed six hitless innings in a 5-1 victory over Brevard County that was called early because of rain. Brevard scored a run in the first without a hit.

Daytona's John Webb, Fort Myers' Josmir Romero and Vero Beach's Andrew Brown came close to joining Hanrahan in the 2002 no-hit category. Each hurler spun a one-hitter in shortened seven-inning contests while their clubs were playing doubleheaders. Brevard County escaped the no-hit blues twice: May 12 in a 2-0 loss to Webb and the Cubs, and July 23 in a 3-0 setback to Brown and the Dodgers. Romero had his one-hitter May 20 in a 2-0 win over St. Lucie.

Daytona's Adam Greenberg hit for the cycle in a 17-1 rout of the St. Lucie Mets Aug. 17. Daytona's Jeff Goldbach and Lakeland's Neil Jenkins each hit three home runs in a game. Goldbach smacked three dingers against Jupiter April 8 and Jenkins went deep three times against Vero Beach April 30. Fort Myers' Josh Rabe reached base in 67 consecutive games, during which he had an on-base percentage of .446 and a batting average of .367.

STANDINGS: SPLIT SEASON

FIRST HALF

EAST	W	L	PCT	GB
*Lakeland	40	32	.556	—
St. Lucie	40	32	.556	—
Jupiter	39	32	.549	½
Vero Beach	37	33	.529	2
Daytona	31	41	.431	9
Brevard County	27	45	.375	13

WEST	W	L	PCT	GB
Tampa	42	28	.600	—
Fort Myers	40	32	.556	3
Sarasota	39	33	.542	4
Charlotte	39	33	.542	4
Dunedin	33	38	.465	9½
Clearwater	22	50	.305	21

SECOND HALF

EAST	W	L	PCT	GB
Jupiter	42	25	.627	—
Vero Beach	35	30	.538	6
Daytona	33	32	.508	8
St. Lucie	31	37	.456	11½
Lakeland	29	38	.433	13
Brevard County	23	40	.365	17

WEST	W	L	PCT	GB
Charlotte	45	23	.662	—
Fort Myers	37	30	.552	7½
Clearwater	35	29	.547	8
Dunedin	30	34	.469	13
Tampa	29	34	.460	13½
Sarasota	23	41	.359	20

*Won tie-breaker

PLAYOFFS—Semifinals: Charlotte defeated Tampa 2-0 and Lakeland defeated Jupiter 2-0 in best-of-3 series. **Finals:** Charlotte defeated Lakeland 3-2 in best-of-5 series.

STANDINGS: OVERALL

Page		W	L	PCT	GB	Manager(s)	Attendance	Avg.	Last Penn.
263	Charlotte Rangers (Rangers)	84	56	.600	—	Darryl Kennedy	23,988	369	2002
140	Jupiter Hammerheads (Marlins)	81	57	.587	2	Luis Dorante	103,640	1,502	1991
175	Fort Myers Miracle (Twins)	77	62	.554	6½	Jose Marzan	109,293	1,631	1985
190	Tampa Yankees (Yankees)	71	62	.534	9½	Mitch Seoane	75,061	1,294	2001
160	Vero Beach Dodgers (Dodgers)	72	63	.533	9½	Juan Bustabad	53,088	1,018	1990
198	St. Lucie Mets (Mets)	71	69	.507	13	Ken Oberkfell	78,564	1,139	1998
133	Lakeland Tigers (Tigers)	69	70	.496	14½	Gary Green	21,503	316	1992
103	Daytona Cubs (Cubs)	64	73	.467	18½	Dave Trembley	72,655	1,171	2000
271	Dunedin Blue Jays (Blue Jays)	63	72	.467	18½	Marty Pevey	47,717	734	None
89	Sarasota Red Sox (Red Sox)	62	74	.456	20	Billy Gardner	57,365	991	1963
213	Clearwater Phillies (Phillies)	57	79	.419	25	John Morris/Roly DeArmas	78,459	1,153	1993
182	Brevard County Manatees (Expos)	51	85	.375	31	Bob Didier/Tony Torchia	89,480	1,420	2001

NOTE: Team's individual batting and pitching statistics can be found on page indicated in lefthand column.

CLUB BATTING

	AVG	G	AB	R	H	2B	3B	HR	BB	SO	SB
St. Lucie	.269	140	4702	693	1266	236	41	91	453	885	227
Dunedin	.266	135	4698	632	1251	239	40	65	468	842	72
Daytona	.263	137	4644	682	1221	250	30	107	476	841	154
Charlotte	.257	140	4646	709	1193	227	50	100	554	952	131
Jupiter	.256	138	4689	691	1201	244	45	101	495	914	107
Fort Myers	.255	139	4476	619	1141	210	27	75	464	842	101
Lakeland	.244	139	4558	619	1110	200	33	97	476	1069	175
Tampa	.243	133	4334	581	1055	208	27	74	525	919	64
Vero Beach	.242	135	4398	564	1066	198	36	81	371	985	151
Sarasota	.241	136	4443	529	1071	197	22	56	483	912	88
Brevard County	.241	136	4423	498	1064	181	26	48	397	914	99
Clearwater	.237	136	4498	502	1064	216	36	83	391	864	58

CLUB PITCHING

	ERA	G	CG	SHO	SV	IP	H	R	ER	BB	SO
Charlotte	3.40	140	0	16	47	1224	1025	554	462	471	922
Jupiter	3.41	138	1	11	38	1228	1159	550	465	374	944
Tampa	3.56	133	2	13	30	1149	1081	560	454	434	954
Fort Myers	3.67	139	4	13	43	1193	1178	591	486	463	927
Vero Beach	3.87	135	6	13	38	1166	1089	574	502	434	1009
Brevard County	3.88	136	2	5	23	1174	1142	613	506	449	814
Clearwater	3.93	136	12	11	30	1188	1157	605	519	464	833
Sarasota	3.97	136	2	11	32	1174	1144	617	518	442	836
St. Lucie	3.99	140	6	11	32	1224	1176	660	542	483	943
Lakeland	4.13	139	9	10	32	1206	1125	643	553	529	867
Dunedin	4.25	135	3	10	34	1202	1204	671	568	527	893
Daytona	4.31	137	3	7	26	1198	1223	682	574	483	997

CLUB FIELDING

	PCT	PO	A	E	DP		PCT	PO	A	E	DP
Tampa	.974	3448	1395	131	100	Fort Myers	.970	3580	1446	154	153
Jupiter	.973	3685	1403	141	132	Dunedin	.969	3606	1402	158	128
Charlotte	.972	3672	1480	151	118	Lakeland	.969	3618	1452	162	149
Vero Beach	.971	3498	1332	143	102	St. Lucie	.968	3672	1510	172	120
Brevard County	.971	3522	1404	147	130	Sarasota	.967	3522	1378	168	112
Clearwater	.970	3565	1399	152	118	Daytona	.966	3594	1399	177	121

INDIVIDUAL BATTING LEADERS

(Minimum 378 Plate Appearances)

	AVG	G	AB	R	H	2B	3B	HR	RBI	BB	SO	SB
Rich, Dominic, Dunedin	.345	95	377	72	130	14	5	8	50	57	49	8
McNaughton, Troy, Clearwater	.340	87	324	50	110	20	6	13	45	39	74	2
Harris, Brendan, Daytona	.329	110	425	82	140	35	6	13	54	43	57	16
DuBois, Jason, Daytona	.321	99	361	64	116	25	1	20	85	57	95	6
Martinez, Ramon, Charlotte	.305	114	472	98	144	21	8	3	41	32	44	39
Rios, Alexis, Dunedin	.305	111	456	60	139	22	8	3	61	27	55	14
Smith, Will, Jupiter	.299	133	549	84	164	30	12	14	73	31	75	8
Acuna, Ron, St. Lucie	.298	115	443	67	132	18	5	2	54	38	74	36
Magness, Pat, Jupiter	.292	111	390	73	114	26	1	16	73	79	86	2
Cruz, Enrique, St. Lucie	.291	124	467	69	136	21	2	6	45	32	76	33

INDIVIDUAL PITCHING LEADERS

(Minimum 112 Innings)

	W	L	ERA	G	GS	CG	SV	IP	H	R	ER	BB	SO
Ford, Matt, Dunedin	9	5	2.37	21	18	0	0	114	100	43	30	42	85
Larrison, Preston, Lakeland	10	5	2.39	21	19	3	0	120	86	39	32	45	92
Grace, Bryan, Tampa	8	6	2.86	23	21	0	0	120	101	46	38	61	70
Elliott, Chad, St. Lucie	5	6	2.94	28	13	1	0	110	99	49	36	37	61
Foote, Joe, Fort Myers	12	7	3.11	26	23	2	0	145	141	64	50	35	92
Reynolds, Josh, St. Lucie	11	5	3.13	22	20	1	0	126	123	51	44	26	70
McNutt, Mike, Jupiter	12	8	3.17	27	23	0	2	145	138	66	51	33	102
Holubec, Ken, Fort Myers	5	6	3.22	26	24	1	0	112	93	46	40	44	125
Chipperfield, Calvin, Lakeland	9	10	3.29	27	20	3	0	126	97	57	46	74	114
Buchholz, Taylor, Clearwater	10	6	3.29	23	23	4	0	159	140	66	58	51	129

ALL-STAR TEAM

C—Guillermo Quiroz, Dunedin; Kelly Shoppach, Sarasota. **1B**—Leo Daigle, Lakeland. **2B**—Dominic Rich, Dunedin. **3B**—Brendan Harris, Daytona. **SS**—Jose Reyes, St. Lucie. **OF**—Laynce Nix, Charlotte; Josh Rabe, Fort Myers; Alexis Rios, Dunedin; Will Smith, Jupiter. **DH**—Simon Pond, Dunedin. **Util**—Ramon Martinez, Charlotte. **SP**—Taylor Buchholz, Clearwater; Preston Larrison, Lakeland; Josh Reynolds, St. Lucie; C.J. Wilson, Charlotte. **RP**—Beau Kemp, Fort Myers; Lino Urdaneta, Vero Beach.

Most Valuable Player: Laynce Nix, Charlotte. **Most Valuable Pitcher:** Taylor Buchholz, Clearwater. **Manager of the Year**: Darryl Kennedy, Charlotte. **Coaches of the Year**: Luis Dorante, Jupiter; Jose Marzan, Fort Myers.

DEPARTMENT LEADERS

BATTING

G	Laynce Nix, Charlotte	137
AB	Will Smith, Jupiter	549
R	Ramon Martinez, Charlotte	98
H	Will Smith, Jupiter	164
TB	Will Smith, Jupiter	260
XBH	Will Smith, Jupiter	56
2B	Miguel Cabrera, Jupiter	43
3B	Reggie Abercrombie, Vero Beach	13
HR	Leo Daigle, Lakeland	23
RBI	Laynce Nix, Charlotte	110
SH	Daniel Garcia, St. Lucie	14
SF	Craig Brazell, St. Lucie	10
BB	Pat Magness, Jupiter	79
IBB	Simon Pond, Dundein	11
HBP	Leo Daigle, Lakeland	17
SO	Reggie Abercrombie, Vero Beach	158
SB	Nook Logan, Lakeland	55
CS	Reggie Abercrombie, Vero Beach	17
GIDP	Eric Miller, Brevard County	21
OB%	Dominic Rich, Dunedin	.437
SL%	Jason DuBois, Daytona	.562

PITCHING

G	Beau Kemp, Fort Myers	59
GS	Yoel Hernandez, Clearwater	28
	Aaron Krawiec, Daytona	28
CG	Taylor Buchholz, Clearwater	4
ShO	Taylor Buchholz, Clearwater	2
GF	Mike Flannery, Jupiter	52
SV	Lino Urdaneta, Vero Beach	32
W	Joe Foote, Fort Myers	12
	Mike McNutt, Jupiter	12
L	Yoel Hernandez, Clearwater	16
IP	Yoel Hernandez, Clearwater	170
H	Randy Messenger, Jupiter	178
R	Keith Bucktrot, Clearwater	101
ER	Keith Bucktrot, Clearwater	87
HR	Dave Gassner, Dunedin	17
	Brian Wolfe, Fort Myers	17
HB	Keith Bucktrot, Clearwater	19
BB	Tommy Marx, Lakeland	83
SO	Joel Hanrahan, Vero Beach	139
WP	Paul Viole, St. Lucie	21
BK	Mike Flannery, Jupiter	5

FIELDING

C	AVG	Yoon-Min Kweon, Daytona	.995
	PO	Guillermo Quiroz, Dunedin	607
	A	Rob Bowen, Fort Myers	68
	E	Rob Bowen, Fort Myers	12
	DP	Rob Bowen, Fort Myers	8
		Max St. Pierre, Lakeland	8
	PB	Brad Elwood, Tampa	23
1B	AVG	Mike Dzurilla, Daytona	.994
	PO	Leo Daigle, Lakeland	1046
	A	Leo Daigle, Lakeland	74
	E	Leo Daigle, Lakeland	15
	DP	Leo Daigle, Lakeland	115
2B	AVG	Ramon Martinez, Charlotte	.984
	PO	Dominic Rich, Dunedin	241
	A	Rodney Van Buizen, Vero Beach	322
	E	Sam Bozanich, Tampa	18
	DP	Josh Renick, Fort Myers	76
3B	AVG	Willy Aybar, Vero Beach	.943
	PO	Vince Rooi, Brevard County	77
	A	Vince Rooi, Brevard County	230
	E	Tony Blanco, Sarasota	30
	DP	Juan Richardson, Clearwater	25
SS	AVG	Josh Wilson, Jupiter	.963
	PO	Anderson Hernandez, Lakeland	209
	A	Jose Morban, Charlotte	389
	E	Jose Morban, Charlotte	34
	DP	Anderson Hernandez, Lakeland	88
OF	AVG	Anthony Hensley, Clearwater	.992
	PO	Nook Logan, Lakeland	316
	A	Ron Acuna, St. Lucie	16
	E	Reggie Abercrombie, Vero Beach	11
	DP	Brandon Watson, Brevard County	6

MIDWEST LEAGUE

BY JOE BUSH

In 2000, the Midwest League was a pitcher's circuit; in 2001, it was predominantly a hitter's league. The spotlight returned to the mound in 2002 as the MWL's top two teams in ERA battled for the league title.

Ending a year that didn't feature more than a handful of eye-popping offensive seasons, Peoria, which led the league with a 2.76 team ERA, beat Lansing (second at 3.16) three games to one in the championship series. In an unlikely burst of offensive firepower, the Chiefs rallied from a 10-3, ninth-inning deficit in Game Four for the title, winning 11-10.

ROBERT GURGANUS

Dan Haren

Lansing used four pitchers to try to stop the Chiefs in the top of the inning, but Peoria put together seven hits and three walks in an amazing comeback. Tim Johnson drove in three, while Gabe Johnson had a homer and two RBIs for Peoria.

The Chiefs featured a starting rotation with Tyler Johnson (15-3, 2.00), Dan Haren (7-3, 1.95) and Justin Pope (8-1, 1.38), each of whom was recognized among the MWL's top 20 prospects in a survey of managers. Some of the minors' brightest mound talent shone through on other clubs.

Kane County lefty Dontrelle Willis, acquired by the Marlins from the Cubs just prior to the season, had a breakout year. He pitched enough innings to win the MWL ERA title, before being promoted to Class A Jupiter. Clinton righthander Don Levinski also was one of the league's top pitching prospects, and he, too, became Marlins property when he was involved in a mid-season trade between the Marlins and Montreal Expos. Beloit's Mike Jones, Milwaukee's first-round pick in 2001, delivered on the promise of his fastball and changeup, and improved his breaking ball and changeup. Quad City's J.D. Durbin, in his first full pro season, led the league in strikeouts.

Offensively, three players led the way: Kane County first baseman Jason Stokes, Beloit first baseman Brad Nelson and South Bend second baseman Scott Hairston.

Stokes rebounded from an injury-plagued 2001 season by leading the MWL in batting (.341) and home runs (27), and the minors in slugging percentage (.645). Despite a wrist ailment which forced him to sit for a few games at a time and required season-ending surgery, managers named Stokes the league's MVP and most exciting player.

Stokes and Nelson staged an epic battle one May night in Beloit. They each went 4-for-5; Stokes cracked two doubles and two home runs for six RBIs, while Nelson collected five RBIs with a two-homer night. His solo blast in the ninth ended the 9-8 game.

Nelson nearly won the MWL RBI crown, with 99, despite leaving for the Class A California League in August. Nelson finished the 2002 season with minor league highs of 116 RBIs and 49 doubles.

On July 14, Quad City's Garrett Jones had the best single night of anyone in the league, connecting for four homers and eight RBIs in a rout of Kane County.

Off the field, three clubs switched affiliations after the season. Kane County, which set an attendance mark with 14,392 fans for a game, ended a 10-year relationship with the Marlins and will feature Athletics prospects in 2003. Clinton will be a Rangers affiliate, while the Yankees will replace the Astros in Michigan.

MINOR LEAGUES

2002 MIDWEST LEAGUE STATISTICS

CLUB BATTING

	AVG	G	AB	R	H	2B	3B	HR	BB	SO	SB
Dayton	.261	140	4719	663	1233	252	37	100	421	990	151
Peoria	.261	138	4688	671	1224	256	35	122	465	1075	117
Cedar Rapids	.259	139	4679	698	1212	248	35	78	562	1069	146
Burlington	.259	139	4653	654	1205	244	42	54	546	1005	79
Quad City	.256	136	4548	592	1164	223	19	79	424	824	71
Fort Wayne	.256	137	4615	567	1181	234	28	76	373	989	133
Beloit	.255	139	4687	606	1195	223	26	67	389	883	90
Michigan	.255	140	4598	703	1172	239	44	71	512	944	175
West Michigan	.249	140	4677	634	1165	216	51	48	541	1067	148
Clinton	.248	136	4498	588	1117	226	29	90	427	1059	83
Wisconsin	.244	139	4569	531	1113	194	28	61	399	934	124
Lansing	.242	139	4612	572	1114	237	35	67	408	855	103
Kane County	.239	139	4547	559	1086	190	27	66	506	1090	147
South Bend	.227	139	4593	526	1044	223	29	63	455	1182	90

CLUB PITCHING

	ERA	G	CG	SHO	SV	IP	H	R	ER	BB	SO
Peoria	2.78	138	6	19	36	1227	1075	486	379	350	1100
Lansing	3.16	139	5	10	36	1227	1077	524	431	438	997
Cedar Rapids	3.40	139	2	12	40	1230	1090	563	465	474	1080
West Michigan	3.43	140	5	8	39	1248	1172	571	476	547	1010
Michigan	3.44	140	4	10	43	1218	1117	550	465	387	967
Quad City	3.47	136	3	6	39	1190	1076	540	459	475	1090
Fort Wayne	3.49	137	3	5	40	1202	1188	582	466	318	951
South Bend	3.73	139	9	6	25	1220	1269	650	506	385	928
Dayton	3.74	140	8	10	45	1234	1155	627	513	476	1103
Wisconsin	4.01	139	7	6	29	1200	1157	672	535	537	997
Kane County	4.03	139	5	9	31	1220	1168	653	546	445	952
Clinton	4.17	136	3	6	32	1179	1186	667	546	522	949
Burlington	4.44	139	4	5	29	1210	1233	734	597	484	822
Beloit	4.56	139	2	6	37	1208	1262	745	612	590	1020

CLUB FIELDING

	PCT	PO	A	E	DP		PCT	PO	A	E	DP
Michigan	.973	3653	1490	140	108	South Bend	.964	3661	1466	189	119
Quad City	.970	3571	1407	154	117	W. Michigan	.964	3744	1549	198	134
Kane County	.970	3659	1496	160	109	Fort Wayne	.963	3605	1399	192	100
Cedar Rapids	.969	3690	1387	160	130	Beloit	.963	3623	1485	198	115
Lansing	.967	3680	1587	179	160	Burlington	.961	3629	1496	209	125
Dayton	.965	3701	1461	185	100	Wisconsin	.960	3599	1426	210	90
Peoria	.965	3680	1441	185	111	Clinton	.959	3538	1513	217	126

INDIVIDUAL BATTING LEADERS
(Minimum 378 Plate Appearances)

	AVG	G	AB	R	H	2B	3B	HR	RBI	BB	SO	SB
Stokes, Jason, Kane County	.341	97	349	73	119	25	0	27	75	47	96	1
Hairston, Scott, South Bend	.332	109	394	79	131	35	4	16	72	58	74	9
Kubel, Jason, Quad City	.321	115	424	60	136	26	4	17	69	41	48	3
Boyd, Shaun, Peoria	.313	129	520	91	163	36	5	12	60	54	78	32
Self, Todd, Michigan	.310	134	491	81	152	36	5	12	94	65	104	10
Barfield, Josh, Fort Wayne	.306	129	536	73	164	22	3	8	57	26	105	26
Varner, Noochie, Dayton-W.Mich	.306	132	533	83	163	28	13	10	70	32	121	37
Choo, Shin-Soo, Wisconsin	.302	119	420	69	127	24	8	6	48	70	98	34
Mauer, Joe, Quad City	.302	110	411	58	124	23	1	4	62	61	42	0
Tejeda, Juan, West Michigan	.300	137	524	68	157	34	6	11	106	60	89	5

INDIVIDUAL PITCHING LEADERS
(Minimum 112 Innings)

	W	L	ERA	G	GS	CG	SV	IP	H	R	ER	BB	SO
Willis, Dontrelle, Kane County	10	2	1.83	19	19	3	0	128	91	29	26	21	101
Johnson, Tyler, Peoria	15	3	2.00	22	18	0	0	121	96	35	27	42	132
Yeatman, Matt, Beloit	11	7	2.48	25	25	1	0	127	101	51	35	77	127
Burns, Mike, Michigan	14	9	2.49	28	28	3	0	181	146	59	50	29	126
McDowell, Kevin, West Michigan	11	6	2.60	27	27	0	0	166	156	63	48	64	123
Mitre, Sergio, Lansing	8	10	2.83	27	27	2	0	169	166	72	53	27	96
Gonzalez, Edgar, South Bend	11	8	2.91	23	23	4	0	151	141	66	49	34	110
Levinski, Don, Clinton	12	6	3.02	21	21	1	0	119	92	48	40	55	125
Woods, Jake, Cedar Rapids	10	5	3.05	27	27	1	0	153	128	66	52	54	121
Jones, Mike, Beloit	7	7	3.12	27	27	0	0	139	135	63	48	62	132

ALL-STAR TEAM

C—Joe Mauer, Quad City. **1B**—Jason Stokes, Kane County. **2B**—Scott Hairston, South Bend. **3B**—Edwin Encarnacion, Dayton. **SS**—John Nelson, Peoria. **OF**—Shin-Soo Choo, Wisconsin; Jason Kubel, Quad City; Noochie Varner, Dayton-West Michigan. **DH**—Steve Checksfield, Michigan. **RHP**—Don Levinski, Clinton. **LHP**—Dontrelle Willis, Kane County. **RHRP**—Nate Cotton, Dayton. **LHRP**—Rusty Tucker, Fort Wayne.

Most Valuable Player: Jason Stokes, Kane County. **Prospect of the Year:** Joe Mauer, Quad City. **Manager of the Year:** Todd Claus, Cedar Rapids.

DEPARTMENT LEADERS

BATTING

G	Rick Asadoorian, Peoria	137
	Juan Tejeda, West Michigan	137
AB	Josh Barfield, Fort Wayne	536
R	Three tied at	94
H	Josh Barfield, Fort Wayne	164
TB	Noochie Varner, Dayton-W. Mich.	247
XBH	Ruben Gotay, Burlington	60
2B	Ruben Gotay, Burlington	42
3B	Brooks Conrad, Michigan	14
HR	Jason Stokes, Kane County	27
RBI	Juan Tejeda, West Michigan	106
SH	Juan Francia, West Michigan	20
SF	John Labandeira, Clinton	12
BB	Dallas McPherson, Cedar Rapids	78
IBB	Jason Stokes, Kane County	15
HBP	Michael Sandoval, Quad City	18
SO	Tim Lemon, Peoria	165
SB	Juan Francia, West Michigan	53
CS	Shin-Soo Choo, Wisconsin	21
GIDP	Mike Rabelo, West Michigan	21
OB%	Scott Hairston, South Bend	.426
SL%	Jason Stokes, Kane County	.645

PITCHING

G	John Birtwell, West Michigan	58
GS	Five tied at	28
CG	Bobby Basham, Dayton	4
	Edgar Gonzalez, South Bend	4
ShO	Bobby Basham, Dayton	3
GF	Mike Kobow, West Michigan	50
SV	Nate Cotton, Dayton	34
W	Tyler Johnson, Peoria	15
	Chad Petty, West Michigan	15
L	Phil Akens, Kane County	15
IP	Mike Burns, Michigan	181
H	Phil Akens, Kane County	180
	Ryan Holsten, South Bend	180
R	Mike Stodolka, Burlington	109
ER	Anthony Pluta, Michigan	94
HR	Anthony Pluta, Michigan	18
HB	Ronald Belizario, Kane County	21
BB	Gerry Oakes, Beloit	84
SO	J.D. Durbin, Quad City	163
WP	Jon Steitz, Beloit	29
BK	Three tied at	7

FIELDING

C	AVG	Jeff Mathis, Cedar Rapids	.994
	PO	Mike Rabelo, West Michigan	813
	A	Yadier Molina, Peoria	140
	E	Mike Rabelo, West Michigan	15
	DP	Yadier Molina, Peoria	9
	PB	Winton Zapey, Kane County	19
1B	AVG	Brad Bouras, Lansing	.989
	PO	Clyde Williams, Clinton	1098
	A	Juan Tejeda, West Michigan	84
	E	Clyde Williams, Clinton	26
	DP	Brad Bouras, Lansing	122
2B	AVG	Ruben Gotay, Burlington	.973
	PO	Juan Francia, West Michigan	312
	A	Josh Barfield, Fort Wayne	364
	E	Shaun Boyd, Peoria	40
	DP	Juan Francia, West Michigan	91
3B	AVG	Mike Tucker, Kane County	.921
	PO	Gabe Johnson, Peoria	91
	A	Trevor Mote, Michigan	257
	E	Galindo Gomez, Burlington	40
	DP	Corey Slavik, Lansing	22
SS	AVG	Rex Rundgren, Kane County	.959
	PO	Tommy Murphy, Cedar Rapids	203
	A	John Labandeira, Clinton	392
	E	Jackson Aquino, Fort Wayne	41
	DP	John Labandeira, Clinton	82
OF	AVG	Mike Mallory, Lansing	.992
	PO	Rick Asadoorian, Peoria	352
	A	Rick Asadoorian, Peoria	15
	E	Dominick Ambrosini, Clinton	15
		Jon Guzman, Fort Wayne	15
	DP	Rick Asadoorian, Peoria	5

MINOR LEAGUES

SOUTH ATLANTIC LEAGUE

BY ROB MUELLER

When the South Atlantic League turned out the lights on another season, it also marked the night the lights went out in two Georgia cities.

The 2002 season marked the end of the line for the Macon Braves and Columbus RedStixx, two franchises plagued by poor attendance and inadequate ballparks that ultimately led to their demise. But at least both teams gave their fans something to remember them by.

Armed with several of the Indians' best young pitching prospects, the RedStixx made a valiant run at a championship before falling to the prospect-rich Hickory Crawdads in five games in the Sally League championship series.

The RedStixx, who will become the Lake County (Eastlake, Ohio) Captains in 2003, boasted the top rotation in the league with starters Travis Foley, Dan Denham, J.D. Martin, Mariano Gomez and Jake Dittler. Denham, Martin and Dittler were drafted in the first 51 picks in 2001.

"There are so many things I could say about these kids, but basically, I'm just proud of them," RedStixx pitching coach Steve Lyons said. "They're all committed to developing themselves, not just at getting hitters out, but to have the chance to pitch at a higher level."

Macay McBride

RODGER WOOD

As for Macon, it battled the rival RedStixx to the wire in the race for the Southern Division second-half title before bowing out the final weekend of the regular season.

Though they came up just short in their bid for a playoff spot, the Braves were arguably the most talented club in the Sally League, led by third baseman Andy Marte and an outstanding staff featuring 2001 first-rounder Macay McBride, who won the ERA title and was named the league's top pitcher. After 11 seasons at 79-year old Luther Williams Field, the Braves are moving their Sally League club up Interstate 75 to a new park in Rome, Ga., in 2003.

In Hickory, the Crawdads ran out a lineup of several exceptional Pirates prospects, including league MVP Walter Young and 2001 first-rounder John Van Benschoten, to capture the first title in their 10-year history.

Lakewood BlueClaws righthander Gavin Floyd, the fourth overall pick of the Phillies in 2001 and the league's No. 1-ranked prospect, tossed a no-hitter July 24 against Lexington, but he lost the game 1-0.

The only other no-hitter in the Sally League in 2002 belonged to Francisco Cruceta of the South Georgia Waves, as the righthander tossed a seven-inning gem against the Savannah Sand Gnats April 29. Cruceta later was traded by the Dodgers to Cleveland.

The top hitting performance was by Savannah's Tony Mongeluzzo, who became the first Sally Leaguer since 1988 to hit four homers in a game, April 20 against Asheville. But the glory was short-lived for Mongeluzzo, who was released by the Rangers in July. The only other Sally Leaguer with a three-homer game was Lexington's Ramon German, who did it against Lakewood April 18.

Two players hit for the cycle—Delmarva's Alex Gordon against Greensboro June 28 and Marte against Augusta July 24.

STANDINGS: SPLIT SEASON

FIRST HALF

NORTH	W	L	PCT	GB
Hickory	44	26	.629	—
Lexington	43	27	.614	1
Greensboro	37	33	.529	7
Kannapolis	36	34	.514	8
Hagerstown	34	36	.485	10
Lakewood	33	36	.478	10½
Delmarva	32	38	.457	12
Charleston, W.Va.	25	45	.357	19

SOUTH	W	L	PCT	GB
*Capital City	40	29	.580	—
South Georgia	40	29	.580	—
Asheville	38	31	.551	2
Columbus	38	32	.543	2½
Augusta	34	35	.493	6
Charleston, S.C.	32	37	.464	8
Macon	27	43	.386	13½
Savannah	24	46	.343	16½

SECOND HALF

NORTH	W	L	PCT	GB
Delmarva	44	26	.629	—
Hickory	39	30	.565	4½
Lexington	38	32	.543	6
Greensboro	38	32	.543	6
Lakewood	36	34	.514	8
Charleston, W.Va.	36	34	.514	8
Kannapolis	30	40	.429	14
Hagerstown	29	41	.414	15

SOUTH	W	L	PCT	GB
Columbus	41	28	.594	—
Macon	39	31	.557	2½
Augusta	35	32	.522	5
South Georgia	35	34	.507	6
Capital City	35	35	.500	6½
Charleston, S.C.	28	39	.418	12
Asheville	26	43	.377	15
Savannah	25	43	.368	15½

*Won tie-breaker

PLAYOFFS—Semifinals: Hickory defeated Delmarva 2-0 and Columbus defeated Capital City 2-1 in best-of-3 series. **Finals:** Hickory defeated Columbus 3-2 in best-of-5 series.

STANDINGS: OVERALL

Page		W	L	PCT	GB	Manager	Attendance	Avg.	Last Penn.
221	Hickory Crawdads (Pirates)	83	56	.597	—	Tony Beasley	182,800	2,649	2002
148	Lexington Legends (Astros)	81	59	.579	2½	J.J. Cannon	428,840	6,215	2001
119	Columbus RedStixx (Indians)	79	60	.568	4	Torey Lovullo	52,103	789	None
161	South Georgia Waves (Dodgers)	75	63	.543	7½	Scott Little	72,025	1,059	None
82	Delmarva Shorebirds (Orioles)	76	64	.543	7½	Joe Ferguson	253,171	3,723	2000
199	Capital City Bombers (Mets)	75	64	.540	8	Tony Tijerina	111,349	1,637	1998
191	Greensboro Bats (Yankees)	75	65	.536	8½	Bill Masse	179,393	2,678	1982
90	Augusta GreenJackets (Red Sox)	69	67	.507	12½	Arnie Beyeler	127,314	2,087	1999
213	Lakewood BlueClaws (Phillies)	69	70	.496	14	Jeff Manto	466,474	6,860	None
75	Macon Braves (Braves)	66	74	.471	17½	Lynn Jones	84,001	1,313	None
97	Kannapolis Intimidators (White Sox)	66	74	.471	17½	John Orton	105,873	1,580	None
126	Asheville Tourists (Rockies)	64	74	.464	18½	Joe Mikulik	145,065	2,198	1984
242	Hagerstown Suns (Giants)	63	77	.450	20½	Mike Ramsey	103,188	1,540	None
256	Charleston, S.C., RiverDogs (Devil Rays)	60	76	.441	21½	Buddy Biancalana	242,143	3,669	None
272	Charleston, W.Va., Alley Cats (Blue Jays)	61	79	.436	22½	Paul Elliott	95,187	1,442	1990
264	Savannah Sand Gnats (Rangers)	49	89	.355	33½	Paul Carey	119,223	1,806	1996

NOTE: Team's individual batting and pitching statistics can be found on page indicated in lefthand column.

MINOR LEAGUES

2002 SOUTH ATLANTIC LEAGUE STATISTICS

CLUB BATTING

	AVG	G	AB	R	H	2B	3B	HR	BB	SO	SB
Hickory	.281	139	4645	747	1303	232	26	111	475	954	142
Charleston, W.Va.	.269	140	4751	621	1280	231	35	51	426	797	108
South Georgia	.269	138	4528	632	1216	187	30	67	479	1036	183
Capital City	.267	139	4640	691	1237	219	25	62	485	1038	240
Lexington	.264	140	4749	687	1252	270	26	110	471	1112	171
Macon	.263	140	4608	587	1210	213	41	89	392	896	118
Hagerstown	.253	140	4651	587	1178	220	19	89	448	961	106
Kannapolis	.253	140	4667	563	1180	215	28	50	432	1013	170
Greensboro	.250	140	4677	653	1168	221	30	127	480	1080	119
Asheville	.250	138	4694	639	1172	240	17	105	481	1136	104
Delmarva	.246	140	4576	586	1126	245	31	73	422	1022	121
Lakewood	.245	139	4563	538	1116	212	33	61	440	1026	142
Columbus	.244	139	4483	625	1093	188	33	91	524	1084	235
Charleston, S.C.	.243	136	4328	546	1051	166	23	62	424	981	162
Augusta	.233	136	4368	515	1019	189	24	64	420	1002	74
Savannah	.226	138	4538	529	1025	203	30	66	543	1100	106

CLUB PITCHING

	ERA	G	CG	SHO	SV	IP	H	R	ER	BB	SO
Lexington	3.03	140	1	17	36	1252	1095	517	422	415	1133
South Georgia	3.40	138	5	11	30	1201	1120	582	454	416	936
Lakewood	3.42	139	20	12	28	1216	1138	540	462	384	874
Columbus	3.47	139	1	10	44	1211	1124	585	467	460	1097
Delmarva	3.49	140	5	12	46	1231	1197	575	478	401	983
Hickory	3.51	139	1	8	43	1206	1134	567	470	404	1038
Charleston, S.C.	3.58	136	2	6	32	1163	1170	593	462	433	935
Capital City	3.58	139	1	9	41	1206	1079	593	480	552	1213
Kannapolis	3.62	140	3	10	37	1232	1185	630	495	488	1000
Augusta	3.63	136	1	9	36	1168	1132	578	471	471	1007
Macon	3.68	140	4	13	25	1199	1086	611	491	498	1041
Charleston, W.Va.	3.76	140	4	9	26	1217	1141	609	508	455	1055
Savannah	3.98	138	0	10	22	1220	1179	653	539	496	1010
Greensboro	4.04	140	9	9	38	1229	1263	670	552	547	917
Hagerstown	4.35	140	3	4	39	1213	1258	728	586	460	992
Asheville	4.47	138	3	8	34	1211	1325	715	602	462	1007

CLUB FIELDING

	PCT	PO	A	E	DP		PCT	PO	A	E	DP
Delmarva	.971	3693	1508	156	97	Savannah	.965	3660	1475	184	106
Lakewood	.971	3648	1474	154	119	Macon	.965	3598	1380	179	117
Charl., W.Va.	.970	3651	1389	156	104	Capital City	.965	3619	1514	186	83
Lexington	.969	3757	1596	172	118	Hagerstown	.964	3639	1543	191	100
Hickory	.968	3618	1352	162	107	Columbus	.964	3632	1475	191	110
Augusta	.968	3505	1386	164	116	Asheville	.960	3634	1534	218	122
Kannapolis	.966	3696	1437	179	102	Charl., S.C.	.959	3489	1532	215	100
Greensboro	.965	3686	1570	188	111	S. Georgia	.959	3603	1457	218	106

INDIVIDUAL BATTING LEADERS
(Minimum 378 Plate Appearances)

	AVG	G	AB	R	H	2B	3B	HR	RBI	BB	SO	SB
Diaz, Victor, South Georgia	.350	91	349	64	122	26	2	10	54	29	69	21
Shelton, Chris, Hickory	.340	93	332	72	113	27	2	17	65	47	74	0
Young, Walter, Hickory	.333	132	492	84	164	34	2	25	103	36	102	2
Gretz, Nick, Asheville	.316	104	383	52	121	18	0	5	70	55	72	1
Miller, Greg, Macon	.313	103	361	46	113	14	1	0	34	38	66	17
Mann, Derek, South Georgia	.309	101	350	55	108	13	2	0	36	64	64	17
Whiteman, Tommy, Lexington	.303	90	350	50	106	29	2	10	49	36	66	6
Florence, Branden, Hagerstown	.303	109	426	63	129	30	3	11	63	31	32	9
Acevedo, Anthony, Lexington	.302	116	437	89	132	28	0	12	80	62	89	11
Bautista, Jose, Hickory	.301	129	438	72	132	26	3	14	57	67	104	3

INDIVIDUAL PITCHING LEADERS
(Minimum 112 Innings)

	W	L	ERA	G	GS	CG	SV	IP	H	R	ER	BB	SO
McBride, Macay, Macon	12	8	2.12	25	25	2	0	157	119	49	37	48	138
Harper, Jesse, Charleston, W.Va.	6	5	2.16	21	14	0	1	113	98	38	27	25	97
Gaudin, Chad, Charleston, S.C.	4	6	2.26	26	17	0	1	119	106	43	30	37	106
Flinn, Chris, Charleston, S.C.	8	6	2.31	19	19	2	0	128	103	44	33	41	116
Roberson, Brandon, Lexington	8	5	2.40	23	18	0	0	112	105	34	30	22	115
Peeples, Ross, Capital City	7	7	2.43	20	19	0	1	115	104	49	31	25	98
Oquendo, Ian, Hickory	11	6	2.71	24	22	0	0	140	127	49	42	45	149
Lubisich, Nik, Kannapolis	9	3	2.71	34	13	2	0	123	123	45	37	26	81
Dawson, Layne, Lakewood	7	4	2.76	27	8	3	5	117	102	41	36	21	89

ALL-STAR TEAM

C—Justin Huber, Capital City. **1B**—Walter Young, Hickory. **2B**—Jeff Keppinger, Hickory. **3B**—Andy Marte, Macon. **SS**—Robinson Cano, Greensboro. **OF**—Vic Buttler, Hickory; Jeremy Harts, Hickory; Wayne Lydon, Lexington. **DH**—Chris Shelton, Hickory. **Util**—Victor Diaz, South Georgia; Willy Taveras, Columbus. **RHP**—Kris Honel, Kannapolis. **LHP**—Macay McBride, Macon.

Most Valuable Player: Walter Young, Hickory. **Most Valuable Pitcher**: Macay McBride, Macon. **Outstanding Prospect**: Walter Young, Hickory. **Manager of the Year**: Tony Beasley, Hickory.

DEPARTMENT LEADERS

BATTING

G	Tripper Johnson, Delmarva	136
	Mike Snyder, Charleston, W.Va.	136
AB	Carlos Duran, Macon	533
R	Tony Miller, Asheville	109
H	Walter Young, Hickory	164
TB	Walter Young, Hickory	277
XBH	Walter Young, Hickory	61
2B	Scott Thorman, Macon	38
3B	Carlos Duran, Macon	10
HR	Walter Young, Hickory	25
RBI	Andy Marte, Macon	105
SH	Vic Buttler, Hickory	20
SF	Scott Gillitzer, South Gerogia	9
BB	Tony Miller, Asheville	88
IBB	Ryan Howard, Lakewood	13
HBP	Justin Huber, Capital City	23
SO	Charlton Jimerson, Lexington	168
SB	Wayne Lydon, Capital City	87
CS	Mike Spidale, Kannapolis	25
GIDP	Dan Gonzalez, Lakewood	20
OB%	Chris Shelton, Hickory	.425
SL%	Chris Shelton, Hickory	.587

PITCHING

G	Ryan Meaux, Kannapolis	54
GS	Tim Bittner, Kannapolis	29
CG	Taft Cable, Lakewood	5
	Seung Lee, Lakewood	5
ShO	Four tied at	2
GF	Lee Gronkiewicz, Columbus	48
SV	Lee Gronkiewicz, Columbus	26
W	Zach Parker, Asheville	16
L	Tim Bittner, Kannapolis	13
IP	Taft Cable, Lakewood	177
H	Taft Cable, Lakewood	174
	Zach Parker, Asheville	174
R	Tim Bittner, Kannapolis	98
ER	Tim Bittner, Kannapolis	80
HR	Taft Cable, Lakewood	20
HB	Justin Hampson, Asheville	24
BB	Chris Seddon, Charleston, S.C.	68
SO	Dustin McGowan, Charl., W.Va.	163
WP	Kyle Gross, Hagerstown	17
	David Mead, Savannah	17
BK	Charles Merricks, Asheville	6

FIELDING

C	AVG	Hector Gimenez, Lexington	.993
	PO	Armando Camacaro, Columbus	.713
	A	Dioner Navarro, Greensboro	96
	E	Justin Knoedler, Hagerstown	15
	DP	Armando Camacaro, Columbus	7
		Jose Salas, Macon	7
	PB	Justin Knoedler, Hagerstown	20
1B	AVG	Tyler Von Schell, Hagerstown	.991
	PO	Tyler Von Schell, Hagerstown	1081
	A	Mike Snyder, Charl., W.Va.	91
	E	Sean Swedlow, Columbus	25
	DP	Ryan Howard, Lakewood	97
2B	AVG	Jeff Keppinger, Hickory	.981
	PO	Chris Amador, Kannapolis	239
	A	Jayson Nix, Asheville	351
	E	Jayson Nix, Asheville	36
	DP	Jayson Nix, Asheville	77
3B	AVG	Tripper Johnson, Delmarva	.968
	PO	Tripper Johnson, Delmarva	117
	A	Tripper Johnson, Delmarva	276
	E	Julian Benavidez, Hagerstown	43
	DP	Andy Marte, Macon	25
SS	AVG	Dan Gonzalez, Lakewood	.960
	PO	Ivan Ochoa, Columbus	218
	A	Hector Tena, Asheville	398
	E	Luis DePaula, Charl., S.C.	39
	DP	Dan Gonzalez, Lakewood	88
OF	AVG	Miguel Negron, Charl, W.Va.	.991
	PO	Carlos Duran, Macon	264
	A	Miguel Negron, Charl, W.Va.	19
	E	Gregor Blanco, Macon	13
		Tony Miller, Asheville	13
	DP	Angelo Burrows, Macon	4
		Miguel Negron, Charl, W.Va.	4

MINOR LEAGUES

NEW YORK-PENN LEAGUE

BY WILL KIMMEY AND ADAM RUBIN

Four player transactions created all the buzz around the short-season New York-Penn League in 2002. Two young players on the rise in Scott Kazmir and Hanley Ramirez, both 18, and two more experienced ones on the downslide in Bronson Sardinha and Robinson Cano.

Though it took two months for Kazmir, a high school lefthander selected 15th overall in the June draft, to sign with the Mets for $2.15 million and set foot in the league at Brooklyn, he dominated. He never allowed more than one hit in any of his five outings while registering 34 strikeouts in 18 innings. Facing mostly college-experienced hitters, Kazmir held them to a .089 average.

Ramirez, one of the league's younger everyday players, also didn't get his start in the NY-P until August. After tearing up the Rookie-level Gulf Coast League, the Lowell shortstop quickly proved he belong at the higher level, hitting safely in his first 10 games after the promotion.

Scott Kazmir

"He's the best player in this league, and the best prospect in the Red Sox organization," Lowell manager Mike Boulanger said. "He can do everything. He's got a feel for the game you can't teach. You could put him in Triple-A right now and he'd fit in."

When Kazmir and Ramirez faced each other, the shortstop showed his bat speed by driving a 96 mph fastball off the wall.

Staten Island also called in its own mid-season reinforcements. But rather than promoting up-and-comers from a lower level, the Yankees benefited from two hitters sent down from Class A Greensboro.

Sardinha, a shortstop-turned-outfielder, and Cano, a second baseman, combined to hit .271-26-110 in 816 South Atlantic League at-bats, but were demoted to Staten Island near the end of the season, and many league managers accused New York Yankees owner George Steinbrenner of stacking the roster for a run at a league title.

The duo augmented an already experienced pitching staff that featured 22-year-old righthanders Chien-Ming Wang (6-2, 1.72) and Matt Brumit (22 saves), who dominated the league and fittingly capped Staten Island's title run by combining for a shutout in the clincher.

Wang pitched eight scoreless innings in the 2-0 victory against Oneonta, and Brumit struck out the side in the ninth as the Yankees swept their second straight series and won their second championship in three seasons.

Brumit led the league in saves during the regular season, finishing two shy of the league record. Wang, who missed the entire 2001 season while recovering from right shoulder surgery, signed with the Yankees for a $1.9 million bonus in 2000 and posted the league's second-best ERA at 1.72 this season.

"That guy is awesome," Brumit said. "He may be the best pitcher I've ever seen throwing a baseball."

Vermont lefthander Mike Hinckley led the league in ERA as he went 6-2, 1.37 and won the Kinsella Award as the league's rookie of the year.

Oneonta outfielder Curtis Granderson, the Tigers' third-round draft pick, hit .344-3-34 to earn the league MVP and Stedler awards. The Stedler Award, named for the league's first president, goes to the player with the most major league potential. Granderson finished second in the league in hitting after also ranking second among NCAA Division I batters during the spring at Illinois-Chicago.

In their inaugural season, the Cal Ripken-owned Aberdeen IronBirds finished second in the league in attendance, averaging 6,104 fans per game. Brooklyn, in its second season at scenic KeySpan Park at Coney Island, continued to set the pace, averaging 8,345 and becoming the first short-season team in National Association history to draw more than 300,000 fans in a season. The league's other first-year franchise, Tri-City, averaged 3,013.

With the new franchises and new records, the league itself set a new overall attendance record of 1,890,053—also an all-time record for a short-season league.

STANDINGS

Page	McNAMARA	W	L	PCT	GB	Manager	Attendance	Avg.	Last Penn.
192	Staten Island Yankees (Yankees)	48	26	.649	—	Derek Shelton	181,936	4,917	2002
221	Williamsport Crosscutters (Pirates)	48	28	.632	1	Andy Stewart	82,006	2,216	2001
228	New Jersey Cardinals (Cardinals)	39	37	.513	10	Tommy Shields	129,607	3,518	1994
200	Brooklyn Cyclones (Mets)	38	38	.500	11	Howard Johnson	317,124	8,345	2001
83	Aberdeen IronBirds (Orioles)	31	45	.408	18	Joe Almaraz	231,935	6,104	1983
257	Hudson Valley Renegades (Devil Rays)	26	49	.347	22½	David Howard	162,724	4,282	1999
Page	PINCKNEY	W	L	PCT	GB	Manager	Attendance	Avg.	Last Penn.
272	Auburn Doubledays (Blue Jays)	47	29	.618	—	Dennis Holmberg	62,419	1,643	1998
120	Mahoning Valley Scrappers (Indians)	46	30	.605	1	Chris Bando	160,107	4,327	None
214	Batavia Muckdogs (Phillies)	34	42	.447	13	Ronnie Ortegon	43,494	1,176	1963
142	Jamestown Jammers (Marlins)	32	42	.432	14	Johnny Rodriguez	56,545	1,528	1991
Page	STEDLER	W	L	PCT	GB	Manager	Attendance	Avg.	Last Penn.
135	Oneonta Tigers (Tigers)	47	27	.635	—	Randy Ready	56,602	1,572	1998
90	Lowell Spinners (Red Sox)	34	41	.453	13½	Mike Boulanger	185,000	5,000	None
184	Vermont Expos (Expos)	30	45	.400	17½	Dave Barnett	108,081	3,002	1996
149	Tri-City ValleyCats (Astros)	27	48	.360	20½	Ivan DeJesus	108,454	3,012	1997

PLAYOFFS—Semifinals: Staten Island defeated Williamsport 2-0 and Oneonta defeated Auburn 2-0 in best-of-3 series. **Final:** Staten Island defeated Oneonta 2-0 in best-of-3 series.

NOTE: Team's individual batting and pitching statistics can be found on page indicated in lefthand column.

2002 NEW YORK-PENN LEAGUE STATISTICS

CLUB BATTING

	AVG	G	AB	R	H	2B	3B	HR	BB	SO	SB
Williamsport	.271	76	2605	376	705	129	27	29	225	486	82
Mahoning Valley	.258	76	2527	397	653	119	25	46	282	503	92
Auburn	.255	76	2579	382	657	132	20	36	314	498	65
Jamestown	.254	75	2576	345	655	119	19	42	266	550	64
Oneonta	.254	74	2537	389	645	117	34	31	273	536	65
Staten Island	.249	75	2490	322	619	118	17	32	241	584	61
Brooklyn	.248	77	2605	322	646	101	16	55	198	589	101
Batavia	.247	76	2556	290	632	105	24	30	253	622	115
Aberdeen	.246	76	2521	283	620	104	25	16	239	549	74
New Jersey	.246	77	2477	323	609	112	31	33	210	581	117
Hudson Valley	.245	75	2568	310	630	113	20	53	209	591	38
Lowell	.242	75	2539	337	614	112	15	30	266	590	68
Tri-City	.233	75	2476	284	578	91	16	30	228	523	60
Vermont	.233	75	2511	278	585	93	8	30	232	604	51

CLUB PITCHING

	ERA	G	CG	SHO	SV	IP	H	R	ER	BB	SO
Staten Island	2.57	75	3	12	26	662	543	240	189	185	638
Auburn	3.05	76	0	11	28	681	560	277	231	257	634
New Jersey	3.05	77	3	10	17	663	556	266	225	238	536
Oneonta	3.10	74	0	7	28	665	597	291	229	236	532
Brooklyn	3.40	77	2	8	16	685	658	314	259	233	614
Batavia	3.44	76	1	5	12	686	628	310	262	280	484
Williamsport	3.45	76	1	8	21	678	621	304	260	193	543
Mahoning Valley	3.56	76	0	9	18	668	616	310	264	266	589
Vermont	3.67	75	0	4	18	665	571	355	271	312	594
Aberdeen	4.00	76	2	5	21	667	666	360	296	226	537
Lowell	4.19	75	0	3	16	671	670	384	312	248	551
Hudson Valley	4.29	75	2	0	16	664	723	405	316	248	539
Tri-City	4.35	75	0	6	16	659	650	361	318	258	547
Jamestown	5.36	75	3	3	8	665	789	461	396	256	468

CLUB FIELDING

	PCT	PO	A	E	DP		PCT	PO	A	E	DP
Tri-City	.972	1976	757	80	69	Williamsport	.966	2035	790	99	51
Auburn	.970	2044	816	88	64	Batavia	.964	2058	902	110	75
Aberdeen	.970	2000	795	87	53	Lowell	.962	2012	741	109	56
Staten Island	.968	1986	814	92	50	Jamestown	.961	1996	741	111	61
New Jersey	.968	1989	853	95	54	Oneonta	.960	1996	772	116	70
Brooklyn	.967	2055	911	100	72	Hudson Valley	.959	1991	783	118	58
Mahoning Valley	.967	2003	779	95	48	Vermont	.956	1995	814	129	59

INDIVIDUAL BATTING LEADERS
(Minimum 205 Plate Appearances)

	AVG	G	AB	R	H	2B	3B	HR	RBI	BB	SO	SB
Francisco, Ben, Mahoning Valley	.349	58	235	55	82	23	2	3	23	22	28	22
Granderson, Curtis, Oneonta	.344	52	212	45	73	15	4	3	34	20	35	9
Cortes, Jorge, Williamsport	.328	70	253	38	83	14	4	1	35	44	20	7
Stephenson, Neal, Aberdeen	.310	70	255	30	79	17	6	3	40	13	50	4
Reed, Eric, Jamestown	.308	60	250	35	77	5	1	0	17	17	50	19
Roughton, Jody, Oneonta	.308	54	208	30	64	10	1	3	38	19	43	0
Rohleder, Andy, Jamestown	.308	65	182	29	56	12	4	3	26	28	37	2
Encarnacion, Henry, Vermont	.301	57	209	33	63	9	3	0	26	27	49	15
Durazo, Ernie, Auburn	.295	62	200	22	59	14	2	2	31	21	37	0
Siriveaw, Nom, Auburn	.294	56	180	26	53	8	6	3	30	24	53	8
Hanson, Travis, New Jersey	.294	75	272	31	80	17	5	4	40	12	55	1

INDIVIDUAL PITCHING LEADERS
(Minimum 61 Innings)

	W	L	ERA	G	GS	CG	SV	IP	H	R	ER	BB	SO
Hinckley, Mike, Vermont	6	2	1.37	16	16	0	0	91.2	60	19	14	30	66
Wang, Chien-Ming, Staten Island	6	1	1.72	13	13	0	0	78.1	63	23	15	14	64
Hart, Alex, Williamsport	7	0	1.85	15	10	0	2	68.0	52	15	14	20	73
Bicondoa, Ryan, Staten Island	6	4	1.90	14	14	3	0	85.1	64	25	18	7	94
Ramsey, Keith, Mahoning Valley	6	3	2.04	13	10	0	0	61.2	43	16	14	10	71
Davis, Stockton, Vermont	2	5	2.15	19	2	0	7	71.0	51	23	17	22	81
Marceau, Pierre-Luc, Vermont	5	4	2.31	15	15	0	0	81.2	60	29	21	29	66
Pleiness, Chad, Auburn	8	3	2.42	16	9	0	0	74.1	48	23	20	32	70
Warpinski, Ryan, Jamestown	2	4	2.48	15	5	0	0	76.1	70	31	21	29	61
Isaacson, Charlie, Staten Island	5	3	2.54	14	12	0	0	74.1	57	25	21	21	76

ALL-STAR TEAM

C—Travis Chapman, Williamsport. **1B**—John Santor, New Jersey. **2B**—William Rivera, Auburn. **3B**—Travis Hanson, New Jersey. **SS**—Russ Adams, Auburn. **IF**—Blake Whealy, Brooklyn. **OF**—Jorge Cortes, Williamsport; Ben Francisco, Mahoning Valley; Joey Gomes, Hudson Valley; Curtis Granderson, Oneonta. **DH**—Brad Eldred, Williamsport. **RHP**—Ryan Bicondoa, Staten Island; Chien-Ming Wang, Staten Island. **LHP**—Mike Hinckley, Vermont; Keith Ramsey, Mahoning Valley.

Most Valuable Player: Curtis Granderson, Oneonta. **Manager of the Year**: Randy Ready, Oneonta.

DEPARTMENT LEADERS

BATTING
G	Mike Huggins, Aberdeen	76
AB	Ryan Riley, Hudson Valley	290
	William Rivera, Auburn	290
R	Ben Francisco, Mahoning Valley	55
	Reid Gorecki, New Jersey	55
H	Jorge Cortes, Williamsport	83
TB	Joey Gomes, Hudson Valley	145
XBH	John Santor, New Jersey	38
2B	John Santor, New Jersey	24
3B	Reid Gorecki, New Jersey	13
HR	Joey Gomes, Hudson Valley	15
RBI	John Santor, New Jersey	62
SH	William Rivera, Auburn	10
SF	Brian Wright, Mahoning Valley	9
BB	Kevin Randel, Jamestown	49
IBB	Brad Eldred, Williamsport	4
	Bill Peavey, Mahoning Valley	4
HBP	Alberto Concepcion, Lowell	12
SO	Tim Gilhooly, Aberdeen	79
SB	Joey Vandever, New Jersey	31
CS	Reid Gorecki, New Jersey	11
	Carlos Rodriguez, Batavia	11
GIDP	Chad Chop, Vermont	13
OB%	Jorge Cortes, Williamsport	.426
SL%	John Santor, New Jersey	.565

PITCHING
G	Mathew Brumit, Staten Island	33
GS	Three tied at	16
CG	Ryan Bicondoa, Staten Island	3
ShO	Four tied at	1
GF	Mathew Brumit, Staten Island	31
SV	Mathew Brumit, Staten Island	22
W	Josh Shortslef, Williamsport	10
L	Joey DeLeon, Tri-City	10
IP	Mike Hinckley, Vermont	92
H	Jon Connolly, Oneonta	102
R	Dustin Kupper, Jamestown	54
ER	Dustin Kupper, Jamestown	48
HR	Dustin Kupper, Jamestown	10
HB	Omar Anez, Brooklyn	10
BB	Carlos Cabrera, Batavia	46
SO	Ryan Bicondoa, Staten Island	94
WP	Jason Walker, Vermont	18
BK	Ryan Bicondoa, Staten Island	3
	Mike Hinckley, Vermont	3

FIELDING
C	AVG	Clinton Chauncey, New Jersey	.997
	PO	Brent Cordell, Hudson Valley	447
	A	Brent Cordell, Hudson Valley	79
	E	Three tied at	9
	DP	Brent Cordell, Hudson Valley	7
	PB	Brent Cordell, Hudson Valley	13
1B	AVG	John Santor, New Jersey	.996
	PO	Mike Huggins, Aberdeen	601
	A	Mike Huggins, Aberdeen	53
	E	Rob Cafiero, Batavia	10
		Brad Eldred, Williamsport	10
	DP	Andy Salmela, Tri-City	53
2B	AVG	Manny Del Rosario, Aberdeen	.974
	PO	Jason Conlisk, Vermont	119
		William Rivera, Auburn	119
	A	William Rivera, Auburn	200
	E	William Rivera, Auburn	12
	DP	William Rivera, Auburn	41
3B	AVG	Chris Bass, Williamsport	.932
	PO	Chris Bass, Williamsport	55
	A	Travis Hanson, New Jersey	145
	E	Travis Hanson, New Jersey	14
	DP	Travis Hanson, New Jersey	11
SS	AVG	Corey Ragsdale, Brooklyn	.966
	PO	Carlos Rodriguez, Batavia	122
	A	Corey Ragsdale, Brooklyn	199
	E	Henry Encarnacion, Vermont	26
	DP	Corey Ragsdale, Brooklyn	45
OF	AVG	Andy Rohleder, Jamestown	.992
	PO	Eric Reed, Jamestown	189
	A	Reid Gorecki, New Jersey	13
	E	Three tied at	4
	DP	Reid Gorecki, New Jersey	4

NORTHWEST LEAGUE

BY SUSAN WADE

Boise won its fifth Northwest League title—the first of the post-Kotchman Era. And Everett didn't let a mid-season managerial change slow it down on its way to its first championship series appearance since 1987 and first as a Mariners farm club.

Behind a four-hitter from Micah Hoffpauir and 10-strikeout performance from Luke Hagerty, the Hawks completed a three-game sweep of the AquaSox with an 8-2 victory. They won Games 1 and 2 by 3-2 and 4-3 scores.

Boise's pitching staff, which boasted the best ERA (3.10) among the short-season circuit's eight teams, gave up just seven runs and struck out 30 in three playoff games.

That was especially remarkable, considering Everett wielded some of the toughest bats. Second baseman Ismael Castro, the league MVP, finished first in hits (89), extra-base hits (36), doubles (26) and runs (55).

Luke Hagerty

Meanwhile, first baseman Jon Nelson led the loop with 17 homers and 64 RBIs. Everett also had the top three RBI men with Nelson, Castro and outfielder Gary Harris.

Boise, now a Cubs affiliate, had won championships in 1991, 1993, 1994, and 1995 under manager Tom Kotchman when the club had a player-development contract with the Angels. Kotchman has since moved on to Provo of the Rookie-level Pioneer League.

The Hawks, swept in their last two playoff appearances, tied Spokane and Tri-City with their fifth crown. Under NWL manager of the year Steve McFarland, they posted the best regular-season record in the league at 49-27 and clinched their ninth division title since 1990. Boise is now 101-50 in two seasons as a Cubs affiliate.

Everett barely missed a beat after manager Omer Munoz was fired Aug. 7 for what the Mariners organization called player-development reasons. Roger Hansen, who managed the team in 1996, got help from coaches Andy Bottin and Henry Cotto, and together they guided the AquaSox to a 44-32 record and clinched the West Division pennant on the penultimate night of the season.

Because the Hawks clinched so early, McFarland was able to set his rotation for the playoffs, starting with 6-foot-9 ace Andy Sisco (7-2, 2.43). Sisco, Game 2 starter Carlos Vasquez (5-6, 4.26) and several relievers flew to Seattle while the rest of the team took the 10-hour bus ride.

Sisco, who grew up about 30 miles from Everett in Sammamish, Wash., was named the NWL's top prospect. The second-year pro led the league with 101 strikeouts in 78 innings and boasted the fourth-best ERA—just behind Everett's top pitcher, Troy Cate.

"You look at him and see him throwing four pitches for strikes now, and they will be above-average," said McFarland of the lefthander's future. He was also high on his other high-profile lefty—Hagerty, the league's No. 4 prospect.

"His velocity is so easy and the pitch has such late life that even though he doesn't throw it as hard as Andy, his fastball is a better pitch," McFarland said. "He has a good changeup, which he can also spot well."

Cate was the league's lone pitcher to record a complete-game shutout. He did it in just one hour, 57 minutes Sept. 3 to give the Everett franchise a playoff berth for just the third time in its history.

Eugene rallied from 12½ games behind at mid-season to battle Everett for the West Division title in the last series of the season. The Emerals did it with a 24-6 record in August as they established team standards for consecutive victories—12 overall and 13 at home.

Emeralds reliever Gabe Ribas set a team record for saves (16) and led the league in wins with eight. He also had the most appearances. Tri-City's Jentry Beckstead had 19 saves to lead NWL relievers while Jared Thomas tied an Everett franchise mark for saves with 10.

Spokane, which led the league in attendance, will see a whole new crop of players for at least the next couple of years. The Indians ended their association with the Royals, signing a player-development contract with the Rangers for the 2003 and 2004 seasons. The Rangers' Triple-A affiliate in the Pacific Coast League was in Spokane from 1973 to 1975.

Yakima signed a new five-year lease with Yakima County Stadium, but fans there hope they don't have to endure another losing streak like 2002's. The Bears lost 27 of 28 games in the second half, including 22 in a row from Aug. 1 to Aug. 24. Yakima did have one valuable weapon in outfielder Marland Williams. He led in stolen bases with 51—nearly half of his team's league-leading 113.

STANDINGS

Page	NORTH	W	L	PCT	GB	Manager	Attendance	Avg.	Last Penn.
104	Boise Hawks (Cubs)	49	27	.645	—	Steve McFarland	109,646	2,885	2002
127	Tri-City Dust Devils (Rockies)	40	36	.526	9	Ron Gideon	69,824	1,837	None
155	Spokane Indians (Royals)	29	47	.382	20	Tom Poquette	161,543	4,252	1999
68	Yakima Bears (Diamondbacks)	23	53	.303	26	Mike Aldrete	56,404	1,484	2000

Page	SOUTH	W	L	PCT	GB	Manager(s)	Attendance	Avg.	Last Penn.
250	Everett AquaSox (Mariners)	44	32	.579	—	Omer Munoz/Roger Hansen	110,373	2,983	1985
243	Salem-Keizer Volcanoes (Giants)	41	35	.539	3	Fred Stanley	122,334	3,219	2001
236	Eugene Emeralds (Padres)	41	35	.539	3	Jeff Gardner	123,389	3,335	1980
207	Vancouver Canadians (Athletics)	37	39	.487	7	Orv Franchuk	127,099	3,345	None

PLAYOFFS—Boise defeated Everett 3-0 in best-of-5 championship series.

NOTE: Team's individual batting and pitching statistics can be found on page indicated in lefthand column.

MINOR LEAGUES

2002 NORTHWEST LEAGUE STATISTICS

CLUB BATTING

	AVG	G	AB	R	H	2B	3B	HR	BB	SO	SB
Salem-Keizer	.264	76	2632	368	694	110	20	36	294	511	43
Boise	.259	76	2610	424	676	149	19	77	212	630	102
Everett	.257	76	2649	382	680	145	16	53	244	603	55
Vancouver	.244	76	2508	334	613	122	10	35	299	631	63
Spokane	.241	76	2565	348	618	122	17	28	289	571	94
Eugene	.238	76	2519	353	600	126	16	46	281	669	98
Tri-City	.224	76	2497	288	560	104	11	34	302	583	60
Yakima	.219	76	2496	268	546	90	20	15	227	596	113

CLUB PITCHING

	ERA	G	CG	SHO	SV	IP	H	R	ER	BB	SO
Boise	3.10	76	0	3	21	683	569	306	235	290	648
Salem-Keizer	3.41	76	1	7	18	678	586	313	257	270	627
Everett	3.42	76	1	6	20	685	640	328	260	254	645
Tri-City	3.46	76	0	3	26	687	606	315	264	239	606
Vancouver	3.46	76	0	10	13	665	584	310	256	243	606
Eugene	3.83	76	0	4	21	665	636	358	283	224	631
Yakima	4.05	76	0	2	12	669	662	396	301	331	582
Spokane	4.79	76	0	6	22	673	704	439	358	297	449

CLUB FIELDING

	PCT	PO	A	E	DP		PCT	PO	A	E	DP
Tri-City	.965	2062	810	104	42	Eugene	.961	1994	708	110	52
Salem-Keizer	.965	2033	805	104	60	Yakima	.959	2008	805	119	64
Boise	.964	2048	888	111	67	Spokane	.958	2020	841	125	74
Vancouver	.963	1995	723	104	52	Everett	.956	2055	742	128	53

INDIVIDUAL BATTING LEADERS
(Minimum 205 Plate Appearances)

	AVG	G	AB	R	H	2B	3B	HR	RBI	BB	SO	SB
Collins, Kevin, Boise	.342	52	187	39	64	18	2	13	37	14	52	0
Frend, Tim, Spokane	.326	65	242	36	79	19	2	2	34	33	34	5
Lewis, Freddy, Salem-Keizer	.322	58	239	43	77	9	3	1	23	26	58	9
Arroyo, Carlos, Everett	.318	62	255	46	81	11	1	0	26	18	31	6
Castro, Ismael, Everett	.313	66	284	55	89	26	1	9	46	16	41	13
Hoffpauir, Micah, Boise	.301	60	216	35	65	10	3	10	41	7	35	2
Ortmeier, Dan, Salem-Keizer	.292	49	195	32	57	9	5	1	31	18	37	3
Hagen, Matt, Everett	.289	63	204	40	59	10	1	7	30	35	47	3
Walter, Randy, Salem-Keizer	.287	69	258	26	74	11	4	6	40	20	59	6
Harris, Gary, Everett	.287	69	286	37	82	12	8	6	43	16	63	4

INDIVIDUAL PITCHING LEADERS
(Minimum 61 Innings)

	W	L	ERA	G	GS	CG	SV	IP	H	R	ER	BB	SO
Bruso, Greg, Salem-Keizer	4	3	1.99	14	13	0	0	81	58	23	18	17	78
Cate, Troy, Everett	6	1	2.00	16	12	1	0	85	62	21	19	11	95
Young, Chris, Tri-City	5	5	2.34	17	6	0	0	62	45	20	16	23	47
Sisco, Andy, Boise	7	2	2.43	14	14	0	0	78	51	23	21	39	101
Gonzalez, Enrique, Yakima	3	2	2.45	11	11	0	0	66	53	27	18	23	57
Nolasco, Ricky, Boise	7	2	2.48	15	15	0	0	91	72	32	25	25	92
Hensley, Clay, Salem-Keizer	7	0	2.53	15	15	1	0	82	72	31	23	25	84
Davies, Michael, Tri-City	5	2	2.75	16	9	0	0	69	55	25	21	18	72
Rowland-Smith, Ryan, Everett	4	1	2.77	18	6	0	2	62	58	22	19	22	58
Pauley, David, Eugene	6	1	2.81	15	15	0	0	80	81	32	25	18	62

ALL-STAR TEAM

C—Rene Rivera, Everett. **1B**—Jon Nelson, Everett. **2B**—Ismael Castro, Everett. **3B**—Donnie Hood, Boise. **SS**—Oscar Materano, Tri-City. **OF**—Carlos Arroyo, Everett; Gary Harris, Everett; Freddy Lewis, Salem-Keizer. **DH**—Micah Hoffpauir, Boise. **RHP**—Greg Bruso, Salem-Keizer. **LHP**—Jared Doyle, Yakima; Andy Sisco, Boise. **RHRP**—Gabe Ribas, Eugene. **LHRP**—Billy Keppinger, Spokane; Isaac Pavlik, Tri-City.

Most Valuable Player: Ismael Castro, Everett. **Manager of the Year:** Steve McFarland, Boise.

DEPARTMENT LEADERS

BATTING
G	Three tied at	72
AB	Gary Harris, Everett	286
R	Ismael Castro, Everett	55
H	Ismael Castro, Everett	89
TB	Ismael Castro, Everett	144
XBH	Ismael Castro, Everett	36
2B	Ismael Castro, Everett	26
3B	Gary Harris, Everett	8
	Marland Williams, Yakima	8
HR	Jon Nelson, Everett	17
RBI	Jon Nelson, Everett	64
SH	David Stone, Salem-Keizer	12
SF	Three tied at	6
BB	Doug Bernier, Tri-City	58
IBB	Gary Harris, Everett	3
HBP	Sam Smith, Tri-City	11
	Mel Stocker, Spokane	11
SO	Jon Nelson, Everett	96
SB	Marland Williams, Yakima	51
CS	Mel Stocker, Spokane	12
GIDP	Bernard Stephens, Spokane	8
OB%	David Stone, Salem-Keizer	.435
SL%	Kevin Collins, Boise	.668

PITCHING
G	Gabe Ribas, Eugene	32
GS	Eight tied at	15
CG	Troy Cate, Everett	1
	Clay Hensley, Salem-Keizer	1
ShO	Troy Cate, Everett	1
GF	Gabe Ribas, Eugene	29
SV	Jentry Beckstead, Tri-City	19
W	Gabe Ribas, Eugene	8
L	Three tied at	8
IP	Sergio Lizarraga, Yakima	91
H	Sergio Lizarraga, Yakima	90
R	Rich Dorman, Everett	53
ER	Jonah Bayliss, Spokane	42
HR	Jonah Bayliss, Spokane	9
HB	Greg Atencio, Spokane	10
	Carlos Vasquez, Boise	10
BB	Ira Brown, Spokane	58
SO	Andy Sisco, Boise	101
WP	Rich Dorman, Everett	12
BK	Gabriel Mercedes, Yakima	4

FIELDING
C	AVG	Steven Holm, Salem-Keizer	.991
	PO	Rene Rivera, Everett	489
	A	Rene Rivera, Everett	54
	E	Jacob Guzman, Spokane	8
	DP	Joe Wilkins, Yakima	5
	PB	Sam Montilla, Yakima	13
1B	AVG	Bryan Johnson, Yakima	.994
	PO	Dave Jensen, Spokane	590
	A	Dave Jensen, Spokane	40
	E	Micah Hoffpauir, Boise	8
	DP	Dave Jensen, Spokane	59
2B	AVG	Mark Kiger, Vancouver	.969
	PO	Brian Burgamy, Eugene	131
	A	Robinson Chirinos, Boise	185
	E	Aaron Sobieraj, Salem-Keizer	21
	DP	Robinson Chirinos, Boise	40
3B	AVG	Matt Hagen, Everett	.873
	PO	Bookie Gates, Yakima	43
	A	Matt Hagen, Everett	105
	E	Matt Hagen, Everett	21
		Bookie Gates, Yakima	21
	DP	Matt Hagen, Everett	11
SS	AVG	Jake Wald, Salem-Keizer	.944
	PO	Oscar Materano, Tri-City	114
	A	Oscar Materano, Tri-City	197
	E	Jerry Gil, Yakima	23
		Oscar Materano, Tri-City	23
	DP	Jerry Gil, Yakima	36
OF	AVG	Jeff Salazar, Tri-City	1.000
	PO	Chris Colton, Everett	155
	A	Steve Baker, Eugene	9
	E	Marland Williams, Yakima	10
	DP	Alexis Alexander, Spokane	3
		Jeff Salazar, Tri-City	3

BY WILL KIMMEY

Nick Leyva must have had second thoughts. The former Philadelphia Phillies manager returned to the Rookie-level Appalachian League in 2002 to manage Bristol—25 years after getting his first managerial job with Johnson City. His team started with a dismal 5-14 record.

But Leyva got Bristol back on track, the White Sox went 38-11 the rest of the way to capture the Western Division title and Leyva won manager of the year honors. Bristol then defeated Eastern Division champ Bluefield, which posted the league's best record at 45-23, two games to one to earn its first league title since 1998.

After splitting the first two games, Bluefield rallied to send the clincher into extra innings, but Bristol scored in the bottom of the 10th to prevent the Orioles from repeating as champion.

Bluefield reliever Paul Henry hit left fielder Seth Morris with a pitch to lead off the 10th, and center fielder Anthony Webster, who had six hits in the series, followed with a walk. After failing to get a sacrifice down twice, second baseman Pedro Lopez delivered the game-winning hit, a single to right-center field that scored Morris. Webster hit .352 for the season and looks more and more like a steal as a 15th-rounder from 2001.

Bristol's pitching staff compiled the league's second-best ERA at 3.60, fronted by righthanded starters Rylan Reed (3-0, 2.44), Sean Tracey (5-2, 3.02) and Ruddy Morales (5-0, 3.25).

Danville righthander Anthony Lerew and Elizabethton lefty Ricky Barrett earned honors as co-pitchers of the year. Lerew, an 11th-round pick in 2001, went 8-3, 1.73 to anchor a Danville staff that led the league with a 3.31 ERA. Lerew, 19, ranked second in the league in wins and ERA and fourth in strikeouts.

"He dominated this league unlike any other pitcher," Danville manager Oscar Henriquez said. "He's got great makeup, and I feel he's on the verge of really blossoming into an even better pitcher."

Barrett went 7-1 and his 1.27 ERA was the best in the league. He ranked second behind teammate Scott Tyler

SAMANTHA CRAIG

Wes Bankston

for the strikeout crown.

But as good as the pitching was in 2002, the hitters were an even better class. Bristol led the way, posting a league-leading .287 average. Webster, third baseman Edgar Valera and outfielder Darren Ciraco ranked fourth, fifth and sixth in the league in hitting behind Bluefield's Luis Jimenez, who held down the top spot at .375. Ciraco enjoyed a 23-game hitting streak, but his success must be put in context. He spent 2001 at Class A Kannapolis, batting .255 in 388 at-bats and was sent down to Bristol at the behest of Leyva, who needed another bat in his line-up.

Burlington shortstop Chris De la Cruz also enjoyed a hitting streak of 21 games, which helped him to the league's fourth-best average (.367).

While those numbers were impressive, they don't factor in any of the league's premium batsmen. Princeton outfielder Wes Bankston, the Devil Rays' fourth-round pick out of a Texas high school in June, produced a league-high 18 homers and 57 RBIs while batting .301. "He's a big kid who is going to hit a lot of home runs in this game," Johnson City manager Brian Rupp said. "He not only crushes fastballs and changeups, he can hit any pitch at any time in the count."

Bankston's teammate Jason Pridie, a second-rounder, joined him on the league all-star team. The duo's success especially stood out when compared to the rest of their team. Princeton's staff yielded a league-worst 5.76 ERA as the team sunk to last place with a 19-49 record.

But if you asked anyone about the league's best prospect, it would be a shock not to hear about Danville outfielder Jeff Francoeur. The two-sport high school star turned down a scholarship to play cornerback at Clemson to sign with the Braves for $2.2 million after they used the 23rd overall pick on him in June. League managers voted him the best prospect for his overall athleticism and ability to translate those skills into game action. He hit .327-8-31 in his first 147 pro at-bats, showing no troubles adjusting to wood bats.

While most of these players will head to more advanced leagues in 2003, the ones who return will be greeted by a change in Pulaski. The Rangers ended that affiliation after six years, opting instead for Spokane of the Northwest League. The Blue Jays will come to Pulaski after 25 years with Medicine Hat of the Pioneer League.

STANDINGS

Page	EAST	W	L	PCT	GB	Manager	Attendance	Avg.	Last Penn.
83	Bluefield Orioles (Orioles)	45	23	.662	—	Joe Almaraz	29,462	893	2001
149	Martinsville Astros (Astros)	41	26	.612	3½	Jorge Orta	32,148	1,037	1999
75	Danville Braves (Braves)	37	31	.544	8	Ralph Henriquez	32,981	1,031	None
121	Burlington Indians (Indians)	29	39	.426	16	Rouglas Odor	36,481	1,105	1993
258	Princeton Devil Rays (Devil Rays)	19	49	.279	26	Edwin Rodriguez	29,336	889	1994
Page	WEST	W	L	PCT	GB	Manager	Attendance	Avg.	Last Penn.
97	Bristol Sox (White Sox)	43	25	.632	—	Nick Leyva	21,921	707	2002
176	Elizabethton Twins (Twins)	37	20	.552	5½	Ray Smith	24,959	780	2000
265	Pulaski Rangers (Rangers)	34	32	.515	8	Pedro Lopez	25,492	772	None
229	Johnson City Cardinals (Cardinals)	29	38	.433	13½	Brian Rupp	37,786	1,181	1976
201	Kingsport Mets (Mets)	23	44	.343	19½	Joey Cora	21,911	730	1995

PLAYOFFS—Bristol defeated Bluefield 2-1 in best-of-3 championship series.

NOTE: Team's individual batting and pitching statistics can be found on page indicated in lefthand column.

2002 APPALACHIAN LEAGUE STATISTICS

CLUB BATTING

	AVG	G	AB	R	H	2B	3B	HR	BB	SO	SB
Bristol	.287	68	2382	412	684	119	12	45	273	493	69
Princeton	.275	68	2362	324	650	99	25	50	208	531	51
Martinsville	.273	67	2264	419	618	107	11	29	306	493	100
Bluefield	.268	68	2263	449	606	143	7	75	338	504	80
Elizabethton	.267	67	2243	379	599	110	17	67	225	462	57
Danville	.261	68	2250	341	587	110	17	43	238	527	78
Kingsport	.258	67	2248	295	579	103	16	47	220	512	61
Johnson City	.255	67	2220	345	567	131	25	53	249	575	125
Burlington	.255	68	2367	304	604	93	23	40	236	580	92
Pulaski	.250	66	2127	381	532	120	11	45	339	524	108

CLUB PITCHING

	ERA	G	CG	SHO	SV	IP	H	R	ER	BB	SO
Danville	3.31	68	1	4	21	584	531	284	215	209	584
Bristol	3.60	68	0	6	17	602	544	292	241	271	539
Burlington	4.23	68	0	3	13	608	609	366	286	304	521
Elizabethton	4.24	67	0	5	21	578	537	330	272	286	594
Martinsville	4.32	67	0	4	15	587	573	341	282	295	570
Bluefield	4.47	68	1	1	20	592	608	366	294	275	522
Johnson City	5.04	67	0	1	15	573	646	400	321	235	500
Kingsport	5.21	67	0	1	7	580	648	410	336	235	495
Pulaski	5.31	66	0	2	16	559	638	375	330	226	442
Princeton	5.76	68	1	1	8	586	692	485	375	296	434

CLUB FIELDING

	PCT	PO	A	E	DP		PCT	PO	A	E	DP
Pulaski	.969	1677	678	76	41	Burlington	.958	1824	739	111	64
Bristol	.966	1806	743	89	58	Bluefield	.958	1777	767	111	52
Kingsport	.959	1740	673	102	59	Johnson City	.958	1720	749	108	54
Elizabethton	.959	1733	668	102	45	Martinsville	.958	1761	631	105	47
Danville	.959	1752	634	103	44	Princeton	.944	1757	756	148	71

INDIVIDUAL BATTING LEADERS
(Minimum 184 Plate Appearances)

	AVG	G	AB	R	H	2B	3B	HR	RBI	BB	SO	SB
Jimenez, Luis, Bluefield	.375	51	176	40	66	13	1	8	42	33	33	9
O'Riordan, Chris, Pulaski	.370	48	173	37	64	16	1	3	24	37	20	14
Pridie, Jason, Princeton	.368	67	285	60	105	12	9	7	33	19	35	13
De la Cruz, Chris, Burlington	.367	43	180	33	66	7	6	1	12	17	27	13
Webster, Anthony, Bristol	.352	61	244	58	86	7	3	1	30	38	38	16
Varela, Edgar, Bristol	.330	55	188	30	62	11	1	8	40	13	29	0
Ciraco, Darren, Bristol	.329	56	219	47	72	15	0	10	51	27	39	2
Baldiris, Aaron, Kingsport	.327	58	217	31	71	9	1	3	24	14	24	9
Deeds, Doug, Elizabethton	.325	59	203	48	66	16	1	7	32	41	41	3
Martinez, Gabriel, Princeton	.323	60	217	28	70	17	1	5	26	27	38	1

INDIVIDUAL PITCHING LEADERS
(Minimum 54 Innings)

	W	L	ERA	G	GS	CG	SV	IP	H	R	ER	BB	SO
Barrett, Ricky, Elizabethton	7	1	1.27	12	11	0	0	64	49	15	9	25	79
Lerew, Anthony, Danville	8	3	1.73	14	14	0	0	83	60	23	16	25	75
Nieve, Fernando, Martinsville	4	1	2.39	13	13	0	0	68	46	23	18	27	60
Reed, Rylan, Bristol	3	0	2.44	12	12	0	0	55	38	23	15	37	44
Meyer, Dan, Danville	3	3	2.74	13	13	1	0	66	47	22	20	18	77
Tyler, Scott, Elizabethton	8	1	2.93	14	13	0	0	68	37	23	22	46	92
Tracey, Sean, Bristol	5	2	3.02	13	13	0	0	66	57	27	22	19	50
Escobar, Rodrigo, Martinsville	6	2	3.12	16	10	0	0	78	71	33	27	18	64
Hawksworth, Blake, Johnson City	2	4	3.14	13	12	0	0	66	58	31	23	18	61
Morales, Ruddy, Bristol	5	0	3.25	13	13	0	0	64	60	26	23	21	45

ALL-STAR TEAM

C—Tommy Arko, Bluefield. **1B**—Dusty Gomon, Elizabethton. **2B**—Chris O'Riordan, Pulaski. **3B**—Aaron Baldiris, Kingsport. **SS**—Chris De la Cruz, Burlington. **OF**—Wes Bankston, Princeton; Daren Ciraco, Bristol; Jason Pridie, Princeton. **Util**—Mike McCoy, Johnson City; Anthony Webster, Bristol. **DH**—Luis Jimenez, Bluefield. **RHP**—Anthony Lerew, Danville. **LHP**—Ricky Barrett, Elizabethton. **RP**—Fernando Tadefa, Danville.

Player of the Year: Wes Bankston, Princeton. **Pitchers of the Year**: Ricky Barrett, Elizabethton; Anthony Lerew, Danville. **Manager of the Year**: Nick Leyva, Bristol.

DEPARTMENT LEADERS

BATTING
G	Josh Burrus, Danville	68
AB	Jason Pridie, Princeton	285
R	Craig Ringe, Pulaski	63
H	Jason Pridie, Princeton	105
TB	Jason Pridie, Princeton	156
XBH	Terry Evans, Johnson City	31
	Garrett Guzman, Elizabethton	31
2B	Terry Evans, Johnson City	22
	Carlos Rijo, Bluefield	22
3B	Jason Pridie, Princeton	9
HR	Wes Bankston, Princeton	18
RBI	Wes Bankston, Princeton	57
SH	Pedro Lopez, Bristol	17
SF	Andy Gonzalez, Bristol	7
BB	Robert Done, Bluefield	54
IBB	Anthony Webster, Bristol	3
HBP	Edgar Varela, Bristol	10
SO	Seth Morris, Bristol	73
SB	Matt Lemanczyk, Johnson City	31
CS	Jason Pridie, Princeton	9
GIDP	Darren Ciraco, Bristol	11
OB%	Chris O'Riordan, Pulaski	.495
SL%	Luis Jimenez, Bluefield	.597

PITCHING
G	Jeff Montani, Bluefield	30
	Juan Morales, Johnson City	30
GS	Three tied at	14
CG	Three tied at	1
ShO	James Tiller, Bluefield	1
GF	Jeff Montani, Bluefield	22
SV	Fernando Tadefa, Danville	16
W	Daniel Freeman, Martinsville	9
L	Timothy King, Princeton	9
IP	Anthony Lerew, Danville	83
H	Fausto Carmona, Burlington	89
R	Tony Peguero, Princeton	55
ER	Tony Peguero, Princeton	45
	Juan Sanchez, Princeton	45
HR	Sam Narron, Pulaski	10
HB	Mike Machen, Bluefield	8
BB	Scott Tyler, Elizabethton	46
SO	Scott Tyler, Elizabethton	92
WP	Matthew Haynes, Burlington	11
BK	Brian Miller, Bristol	6

FIELDING
C	AVG	Alonzo Ruelas, Danville	.991
	PO	German Melendez, Martinsville	340
	A	Chris Stewart, Bristol	50
	E	Chris Stewart, Bristol	8
		Ernest Woodruff, Princeton	8
	DP	Chris Stewart, Bristol	4
	PB	Josh Noviskey, Bristol	19
1B	AVG	Zachary Cates, Johnson City	.993
	PO	Gabriel Martinez, Princeton	469
	A	Brandon Bounds, Bristol	40
	E	Johan Camacho, Kingsport	8
	DP	Gabriel Martinez, Princeton	50
2B	AVG	Chris O'Riordan, Pulaski	.983
	PO	Mike Grasso, Danville	99
		Pedro Lopez, Bristol	99
	A	Pedro Lopez, Bristol	160
	E	David Housel, Kingsport	14
		Gabe Veloz, Johnson City	14
	DP	Pedro Lopez, Bristol	29
3B	AVG	Edgar Varela, Bristol	.930
	PO	Josh Burrus, Danville	49
	A	Carlos Rijo, Bluefield	138
	E	Josh Burrus, Danville	24
	DP	Aaron Baldiris, Kingsport	11
SS	AVG	Craig Ringe, Pulaski	.955
	PO	Andy Gonzalez, Bristol	105
	A	Craig Ringe, Pulaski	176
	E	Jonathan Schuerholz, Danville	29
	DP	Salvador Paredes, Princeton	32
OF	AVG	Bjorn Ivy, Bristol	1.000
	PO	Jason Pridie, Princeton	172
	A	Jason Pridie, Princeton	11
	E	Julin Charles, Pulaski	9
	DP	Arturo Rivas, Bluefield	5

PIONEER LEAGUE

BY WILL KIMMEY

The Rookie-level Pioneer League auditioned more than its share of premium talent in 2002, with five first-round draft picks, three top foreign signees and a highly regarded draft-and-follow all making their pro debuts.

Great Falls had the most talent, and not only posted the league's best record by a wide margin but also won four of five playoff games to win the league title. The Dodgers stocked their affiliate with six of their first eight draft picks from 2002, as well as two high profile foreign signees, then watched it go 27-11 to run away with the Northern Division's first-half title.

Dodgers first-round pick James Loney, a sweet-swinging, slick fielding first baseman, and Venezuelan lefthander Jonathan Figueroa ranked as the league's top two prospects. Both were promoted to Class A Vero Beach (where Loney hit .299) and Class A South Georgia (where Figueroa went 5-2, 1.42) for the second half. "That team was loaded when they got there," Provo manager Tom Kotchman said. "Their record said that in the first half, and I'm glad they took away some of their players. They had so many good ones, they couldn't all play at once."

Ryan Shealy

The losses of Loney and Figueroa didn't hamper Great Falls too much. Another pair of Dodgers, shortstop Joel Guzman and lefthander Greg Miller, cracked the top 10 while two more, Jonathan Broxton and Mike Nixon, made the top 20.

While Great Falls, Baseball America's Rookie-level team of the year, and its players rightly garnered much of the attention around the league, Provo also enjoyed a strong season. The Angels, who lost to Great Falls in the final round, were led by their impressive middle infield combo of second baseman Alberto Callaspo and shortstop Eric Aybar. The roommates impressed everyone who saw them play with their style, grace and all-around defensive abilities in the middle infield. Kotchman called them the best double-play combo he'd ever coached, scouted or seen in his 23 years in baseball.

"They're like clones," Kotchman said. "They probably get out of bed in the morning and turn two."

Both switch-hitters are plus runners. The Venezuelan Callaspo has a little better plate discipline while Aybar, a

Dominican , possesses more arm strength. Callaspo, 19, ranked third in the league with a .338 average while Aybar, 18, finished ninth at .326.

But the biggest offensive campaigns were turned in by a trio of slugging first basemen, all of whom were among the league's elder statesmen based on their college experience. Idaho Falls' Paul McAnulty hit .379 to beat out Casper's Ryan Shealy, who hit .368-19-70, for the batting title.

But Shealy, a sixth-round pick out of Florida who earned league player of the year honors, led in homers and RBIs and narrowly missed giving the league a triple crown winner for the second year in a row. Missoula's Jesus Cota turned the trick by hitting .368-16-71 in 2001.

Though he didn't have enough at-bats to qualify for the batting title, Medicine Hat's Jason Perry hit .425-10-36 before the Blue Jays decided to test him more with a promotion to the Florida State League. Like Perry, Loney didn't have enough at-bats to qualify, either, despite his .371 average. Not that league managers minded the 18-year-old's exit. "He can flat-out hit for average and he's very polished," Billings manager Rick Burleson said. "He looks like he's been playing all his life."

Brewers first-rounder Prince Fielder also hit like a veteran before his promotion to Class A Beloit, perhaps because his father, Cecil, is a former major leaguer. The younger Fielder looks, but more importantly, hit like a chip off the old block. He hit an opposite-field homer in his first professional game. The ball traveled over a scoreboard that sits behind Ogden's left-field wall, 335 feet from home plate.

Don't look to Great Falls to be stocked with Dodgers talent again. The Dodgers ended that affiliation and moved to Ogden, while the White Sox took over in Great Falls. The Brewers shifted to Medicine Hat, though that franchise was considering moving to Helena, Mont.

STANDINGS: SPLIT SEASON

FIRST HALF

NORTH	W	L	PCT	GB
Great Falls	27	11	.711	—
Medicine Hat	18	20	.474	9
Billings	15	22	.405	11½
Missoula	15	23	.395	12

SOUTH	W	L	PCT	GB
Provo	21	17	.553	—
Casper	20	18	.526	1
Ogden	18	19	.486	2½
Idaho Falls	17	21	.447	4

SECOND HALF

NORTH	W	L	PCT	GB
Billings	23	15	.605	—
Great Falls	20	17	.541	2½
Missoula	20	18	.526	3
Medicine Hat	19	18	.514	3½

SOUTH	W	L	PCT	GB
Ogden	22	16	.579	—
Provo	17	21	.447	5
Idaho Falls	15	23	.395	7
Casper	15	23	.395	7

PLAYOFFS—Semifinals: Great Falls defeated Billings 2-0 and Provo defeated Ogden 2-1 in best-of-3 series. **Final:** Great Falls defeated Provo 2-1 in best-of-3 series.

STANDINGS: OVERALL

Page		W	L	PCT	GB	Manager	Attendance	Avg.	Last Penn.
162	Great Falls Dodgers (Dodgers)	47	28	.627	—	Dann Bilardello	90,079	2,435	2002
169	Ogden Raptors (Brewers)	40	35	.533	7	Tim Blackwell	126,700	3,334	None
112	Billings Mustangs (Reds)	38	37	.507	9	Rick Burleson	98,345	2,732	2001
61	Provo Angels (Angels)	38	38	.500	9½	Tom Kotchman	55,050	1,573	1981
273	Medicine Hat Blue Jays (Blue Jays)	37	38	.493	10	Rolando Pino	26,285	730	1982
69	Missoula Osprey (Diamondbacks)	35	41	.461	12½	Jack Howell	55,268	1,535	1999
128	Casper Rockies (Rockies)	35	41	.461	12½	Darron Cox	50,573	1,331	1984
237	Idaho Falls Padres (Padres)	32	44	.421	15½	Don Werner	63,192	1,708	2000

NOTE: Team's individual batting and pitching statistics can be found on the page indicated in lefthand column.

2002 PIONEER LEAGUE STATISTICS

CLUB BATTING

	AVG	G	AB	R	H	2B	3B	HR	BB	SO	SB
Provo	.282	76	2642	477	746	136	40	35	320	539	77
Great Falls	.281	75	2573	444	724	134	21	50	291	652	69
Casper	.280	76	2635	461	737	131	37	54	286	576	72
Billings	.278	75	2633	420	733	125	16	60	246	622	88
Ogden	.270	75	2593	446	699	126	23	43	263	555	133
Medicine Hat	.266	75	2537	355	676	112	17	53	232	532	57
Idaho Falls	.258	76	2595	395	670	122	23	33	302	711	100
Missoula	.251	76	2570	397	645	131	25	43	314	628	83

CLUB PITCHING

	ERA	G	CG	SHO	SV	IP	H	R	ER	BB	SO
Billings	3.72	75	1	2	21	662	652	375	274	268	592
Great Falls	3.72	75	0	4	23	655	638	359	271	267	612
Missoula	4.06	76	1	4	16	669	703	404	302	246	615
Medicine Hat	4.83	75	1	5	24	648	668	426	348	269	659
Ogden	4.87	75	0	0	11	661	759	445	358	243	604
Idaho Falls	4.92	75	0	2	22	657	712	502	359	378	617
Casper	4.93	76	0	0	12	661	730	435	362	306	549
Provo	5.10	76	0	1	18	656	768	449	372	277	567

CLUB FIELDING

	PCT	PO	A	E	DP		PCT	PO	A	E	DP
Provo	.960	1968	807	115	72	Ogden	.953	1984	739	135	69
Casper	.958	1982	806	121	54	Billings	.949	1987	805	150	74
Medicine Hat	.958	1945	836	121	69	Missoula	.947	2008	829	158	64
Great Falls	.958	1965	750	119	68	Idaho Falls	.936	1971	830	191	83

INDIVIDUAL BATTING LEADERS

(Minimum 205 Plate Appearances)

	AVG	G	AB	R	H	2B	3B	HR	RBI	BB	SO	SB
McAnulty, Paul, Idaho Falls	.379	67	235	56	89	29	0	8	51	49	43	7
Shealy, Ryan, Casper	.368	69	231	55	85	21	1	19	70	56	52	0
Bergolla, William, Billings	.352	53	210	35	74	9	1	3	29	24	26	16
Callaspo, Alberto, Provo	.338	70	299	70	101	16	10	3	60	17	14	13
Bagley, David, Great Falls	.337	51	175	39	59	7	0	5	31	21	37	2
Crabbe, Callix, Ogden	.328	67	250	55	82	16	4	4	38	29	34	22
Ramos, Peeter, Idaho Falls	.327	56	202	26	66	10	1	1	25	23	36	12
Aybar, Eric, Provo	.326	67	273	64	89	15	6	4	29	21	43	15
Dvorsky, Alex, Provo	.321	65	234	48	75	15	0	9	52	47	36	2
Hendricks, K.J., Casper	.314	64	258	51	81	11	1	1	32	36	24	21

INDIVIDUAL PITCHING LEADERS

(Minimum 61 Innings)

	W	L	ERA	G	GS	CG	SV	IP	H	R	ER	BB	SO
Severino, Cleris, Billings	7	1	0.96	10	10	0	0	66	56	17	7	14	63
Juarez, William, Missoula	6	2	2.43	16	11	1	0	81	85	30	22	12	56
Coffin, Ryan, Missoula	2	5	2.61	22	8	0	3	62	55	25	18	12	54
Whatley, Keith, Missoula	7	2	2.85	22	9	0	0	66	56	25	21	14	75
Gomez, Jose, Billings	2	3	3.06	13	13	0	0	71	52	29	24	23	58
Hernandez, Santos, Casper	8	1	3.50	14	14	0	0	72	65	30	28	32	39
D'Amico, Leonardo, Provo	3	0	3.57	14	14	0	0	63	58	27	25	14	54
Lopez, Arturo, Great Falls	7	3	3.66	15	15	0	0	76	79	44	31	21	72
Hall, Bo, Ogden	2	6	3.82	16	9	0	0	66	53	29	28	21	58
Nelson, Steve, Great Falls	6	5	3.99	14	14	0	0	70	79	39	31	23	44

ALL-STAR TEAM

C—Alex Dvorsky, Provo. **1B**—Ryan Shealy, Casper. **2B**—Alberto Callaspo, Provo. **3B**—Scott Dragicevich, Medicine Hat. **SS**—Erick Aybar, Provo. **OF**—Brain Barre, Casper; Travis Ezi, Great Falls; Mario Mendez, Ogden. **DH**—Paul McAnulty, Idaho Falls. **RHP**—Santos Hernandez, Casper. **LHP**—Arturo Lopez, Great Falls. **RP**—Jordan DeJong, Medicine Hat.

Most Valuable Player: Ryan Shealy, Casper. **Pitcher of the Year**: Cleris Severino, Billings. **Manager of the Year**: Rick Burleson, Billings.

DEPARTMENT LEADERS

BATTING

G	Quan Cosby, Provo	76
AB	Alberto Callaspo, Provo	299
R	Alberto Callaspo, Provo	70
H	Alberto Callaspo, Provo	101
TB	Ryan Shealy, Casper	165
XBH	Ryan Shealy, Casper	41
2B	Paul McAnulty, Idaho Falls	29
3B	Alberto Callaspo, Provo	10
HR	Ryan Shealy, Casper	19
RBI	Ryan Shealy, Casper	70
SH	Five tied at	5
SF	Ryan Shealy, Casper	9
BB	Jeff Stanek, Missoula	68
IBB	Ryan Shealy, Casper	7
HBP	Brandon Simon, Missoula	23
SO	Omar Falcon, Idaho Falls	100
SB	Brandon Simon, Missoula	30
CS	Brandon Simon, Missoula	16
GIDP	Mayobanex Santana, Missoula	13
OB%	Ryan Shealy, Casper	.497
SL%	Ryan Shealy, Casper	.714

PITCHING

G	Jordan DeJong, Medicine Hat	33
GS	Jay Mitchell, Casper	16
CG	Three tied at	1
ShO	O.J. King, Billings	1
	Charles Talanoa, Medicine Hat	1
GF	Jordan DeJong, Medicine Hat	27
SV	Jordan DeJong, Medicine Hat	16
	David Krisch, Idaho Falls	16
W	Santos Hernandez, Casper	8
L	Anthony Reed, Provo	7
	Brian Williams, Provo	7
IP	William Juarez, Missoula	81
H	Kelvin Garcia, Missoula	86
R	Jesse Thrasher, Idaho Falls	59
ER	Ubaldo Jimenez, Casper	45
HR	Chris Neyland, Medicine Hat	12
HB	Brad George, Billings	10
BB	Frankie Keller, Billings	45
SO	Charles Talanoa, Medicine Hat	91
WP	Jesse Thrasher, Idaho Falls	18
BK	Three tied at	3

FIELDING

C	AVG	Steve Booth, Billings	.992
	PO	Mike Nixon, Great Falls	405
	A	Alex Dvorsky, Provo	60
	E	Omar Falcon, Idaho Falls	13
	DP	Five tied at	3
	PB	Angleidy Garcia, Idaho Falls	10
1B	AVG	Ryan Shealy, Casper	.991
	PO	Ryan Shealy, Casper	621
	A	Jeff Stanek, Missoula	47
	E	Paul McAnulty, Idaho Falls	11
	DP	Paul McAnulty, Idaho Falls	55
2B	AVG	Alberto Callaspo, Provo	.972
	PO	Alberto Callaspo, Provo	134
	A	Alberto Callaspo, Provo	207
	E	Callix Crabbe, Ogden	21
	DP	Alberto Callaspo, Provo	53
3B	AVG	Scott Dragicevich, Medicine Hat	.947
	PO	Hector Perozo, Great Falls	35
	A	Scott Dragicevich, Medicine Hat	127
	E	Lachlan Dale, Idaho Falls	23
	DP	Scott Dragicevich, Medicine Hat	12
SS	AVG	Eric Aybar, Provo	.950
	PO	Juan Peralta, Medicine Hat	111
	A	Juan Peralta, Medicine Hat	203
	E	Daniel Mateo, Billings	29
	DP	Eric Aybar, Provo	40
		Juan Peralta, Medicine Hat	40
OF	AVG	Kennard Bibbs, Ogden	1.000
	PO	Quan Cosby, Provo	148
	A	Ricardo Santiago, Missoula	11
	E	Ricardo Santiago, Missoula	12
	DP	Mario Mendez, Ogden	3
		Jason Sugden, Provo	3

ARIZONA LEAGUE

BY ALLAN SIMPSON

The Cubs dominated the Rookie-level Arizona League in 2002, winning the first-half title and sharing the second-half crown with the Giants. But it took an eighth-inning rally in a one-game playoff for the Cubs to officially be crowned champions.

Trailing 1-0 and limited to one hit through seven innings, the Cubs strung together four consecutive one-out hits, including a two-run double by second baseman Francisco Salas and an RBI double by shortstop Jemel Spearman, to pull out a 3-1 win.

Both doubles came off Giants reliever Matt Cain, that club's first-round draft pick. Lefthander Jesse English, the Giants' sixth-round pick, and righthander Leslie Nacar, who was relieved in the eighth by Cain after giving up two singles, had stymied the Cubs, the league's top hitting team, to that point.

Second baseman Matt Creighton and Spearman formed an all-star double-play combination as the Cubs earned a spot in the playoffs by finishing atop the seven-team league in the first half.

Creighton, signed by the Cubs as a free agent from Kansas' tiny Benedictine College, led the league in average (.361), home runs (eight), on-base percentage (.502) and slugging (.598), while Spearman played a steady shortstop and led the league in runs (46) and stolen bases, swiping 29 in 30 attempts.

Jemel Spearman

But the two players earned little support from managers in Baseball America's annual survey of the league's top prospects. In a league where youth rules, Creighton (23) and Spearman (21) were viewed as a couple of graybeards.

Managers preferred the long-range worth of two other Cubs prospects, outfielder Felix Pie and lefthander Justin Jones—both only 17. Pie, the league's No. 1 everyday player, hit .321 and legged out 13 triples; Jones, the No. 1 pitcher, led the league in ERA.

Pie (pronounced PEE-ay) excelled in his first exposure to pro ball. He shared league MVP honors with Creighton and showcased four above-average tools, falling short only on power.

"He was by far the best prospect," Mariners manager Darrin Garner said. "He's got a great idea at the plate and an excellent approach to the game for a 17-year-old. He just needs to mature."

"He needs to learn plate discipline and walk more often," Cubs manager Carmelo Martinez added. "He's only 17, so it will come."

Pie's best tool is his speed. It was most evident as he chased down balls in center field. He got good jumps and covered a lot of ground. He doesn't run the bases all that well yet, but managers say better technique should come with experience.

A small but powerfully-built lefthanded hitter, Pie specialized in driving balls to the alleys and dashing around the bases. He had more than twice as many triples as his closest competitor.

"He doesn't have much power now, but it should come down the road," A's skipper Ruben Escalera said.

Jones, the Cubs' second-round draft pick, led the league with a 1.80 ERA while averaging 11.3 strikeouts per nine innings. Yet managers say the 6-foot-3 Virginia lefthander had only scratched the surface of his ability.

"He's got a great demeanor, a 90-92 mph fastball and can throw his curve at any point in the count," Martinez said. "Down the road, I can see him in the mid-90s. He's got a lot going for him."

Managers also took a liking to White Sox third baseman Micah Schnurstein, a seventh-round pick who set a league record with 26 doubles and also led the circuit in RBIs with 48.

"When he gets a little stronger," White Sox manager Jerry Hairston said, "a lot of the balls he drives to the right-center gap now will go over the fence."

"He's a Scott Rolen-type," added Garner. "He's got good size, good bat speed and will hit and hit with power. He's also a true third baseman. He's got good hands."

Schnurstein's teammate, lefthander Daniel Haigwood, also made an impressive debut, leading the Arizona League with eight wins while finishing second in ERA and strikeouts.

STANDINGS: SPLIT SEASON

FIRST HALF

	W	L	PCT	GB
Cubs	19	9	.679	—
Giants	17	11	.607	2
White Sox	14	14	.500	5
Athletics	13	15	.464	6
Angels	13	15	.464	6
Brewers	12	16	.429	7
Mariners	10	18	.357	9

SECOND HALF

	W	L	PCT	GB
Giants	16	12	.571	—
Cubs	16	12	.571	—
Athletics	15	13	.536	1
Angels	15	13	.536	1
Brewers	14	14	.500	2
White Sox	13	15	.464	3
Mariners	9	19	.321	7

PLAYOFFS—Cubs defeated Giants in one-game playoff.

STANDINGS: OVERALL

Page		Complex Site	W	L	PCT	GB	Manager	Last Penn.
105	Cubs	Mesa	35	21	.625	—	Carmelo Martinez	2002
244	Giants	Scottsdale	33	23	.589	2	Bert Hunter	None
208	Athletics	Phoenix	28	28	.500	7	Ruben Escalera	2001
62	Angels	Mesa	28	28	.500	7	Brian Harper	None
98	White Sox	Phoenix	27	29	.482	8	Jerry Hairston	None
170	Brewers	Phoenix	26	30	.464	9	Carlos Lezcano	1990
251	Mariners	Peoria	19	37	.339	16	Darrin Gamer	2000

NOTE: Teams' individual batting and pitching statistics can be found on page indicated in lefthand column.

DENTON HANNA

MINOR LEAGUES

2002 ARIZONA LEAGUE STATISTICS

CLUB BATTING

	AVG	G	AB	R	H	2B	3B	HR	BB	SO	SB
Cubs	.279	56	1943	316	543	94	35	27	160	406	79
White Sox	.277	56	2011	332	558	130	33	23	172	418	75
Brewers	.272	56	1975	339	538	90	21	15	215	439	62
Giants	.271	56	1988	326	539	85	36	21	183	445	75
Angels	.257	56	1903	255	490	100	22	6	185	494	75
Athletics	.255	56	1931	326	492	76	28	31	225	491	75
Mariners	.252	56	1918	286	483	88	27	22	210	470	68

CLUB PITCHING

	ERA	G	CG	SHO	SV	IP	H	R	ER	BB	SO
Giants	3.57	56	0	1	16	504	467	264	200	178	457
White Sox	3.62	56	1	3	12	505	501	276	203	176	434
Cubs	3.68	56	0	2	23	503	466	264	206	194	455
Angels	4.50	56	0	1	18	496	505	326	248	225	505
Athletics	4.61	56	0	3	11	498	563	351	255	159	451
Mariners	4.94	56	0	1	7	494	601	341	271	165	409
Brewers	5.23	56	0	2	12	494	540	358	287	253	452

CLUB FIELDING

	PCT	PO	A	E	DP		PCT	PO	A	E	DP
Giants	.960	1512	564	87	39	Brewers	.948	1481	580	112	43
Cubs	.958	1510	555	90	53	Mariners	.947	1482	575	114	41
Angels	.953	1487	544	100	36	Athletics	.944	1495	554	122	36
White Sox	.951	1515	570	108	50						

INDIVIDUAL BATTING LEADERS

(Minimum 151 Plate Appearances)

	AVG	G	AB	R	H	2B	3B	HR	RBI	BB	SO	SB
Creighton, Matt, Cubs	.361	50	169	43	61	14	1	8	39	31	27	12
Perez, Luis, Athletics	.339	42	168	33	57	8	4	4	32	16	18	8
Rogers, Nick, Athletics	.337	47	178	33	60	8	6	0	33	31	40	21
Luna, Leonardo, White Sox	.335	50	221	38	74	13	6	1	30	3	13	8
Myers, Mike, White Sox	.333	44	165	34	55	12	3	0	23	24	24	18
Schnurstein, Micah, White Sox	.332	50	205	28	68	26	1	3	48	12	34	1
Ellison, Josh, Mariners	.329	39	149	32	49	8	3	0	11	23	21	7
Pie, Felix, Cubs	.321	55	218	42	70	16	13	4	37	21	47	17
Kendrick, Howard, Angels	.318	42	157	24	50	6	4	0	13	7	11	12
Sosa, Carlos, Giants	.316	54	209	42	66	11	6	5	33	21	52	10

INDIVIDUAL PITCHING LEADERS

(Minimum 45 Innings)

	W	L	ERA	G	GS	CG	SV	IP	H	R	ER	BB	SO
Jones, Justin, Cubs	3	1	1.80	11	11	0	0	50	31	12	10	18	63
Haigwood, Daniel, White Sox	8	4	2.28	14	14	0	0	75	69	31	19	26	74
Corchado, Jose, Athletics	3	1	2.44	14	6	0	1	48	54	23	13	12	38
Garcia, Jairo, Athletics	2	1	2.44	13	8	0	1	59	56	24	16	17	66
Burdette, Jason, Athletics	5	3	2.52	15	8	0	1	61	59	26	17	17	59
English, Jesse, Giants	4	1	2.68	12	12	0	0	47	33	17	14	18	68
McCarthy, Brandon, White Sox	4	4	2.76	14	14	0	0	78	78	40	24	15	79
Portorreal, Carlos, Giants	6	2	3.00	14	14	0	0	72	60	31	24	22	64
Moreno, Abel, Angels	2	3	3.00	13	7	0	0	45	44	27	15	10	47
Espinal, Luis, Mariners	5	5	3.46	11	9	0	0	65	66	28	25	13	33

ALL-STAR TEAM

C—Brian Munhall, Giants. **1B**—Ruben Olguin, Mariners. **2B**—Matt Creighton, Cubs. **3B**—Micah Schnurstein, White Sox. **SS**—Jemel Spearman, Cubs. **OF**—Joshua Ellison, Mariners; Felix Pie, Cubs; Nick Rogers, Athletics; Carlos Sosa, White Sox. **DH**—Luis Perez, Athletics. **RHP**—Carlos Portorreal, Giants. **LHP**—Daniel Haigwood, White Sox. **RHRP**—Daniel Arias, Angels. **LHRP**—Ambiorix Delgadillo, Angels.

Most Valuable Players: Matt Creighton, Cubs; Felix Pie, Cubs. **Manager of the Year:** Carmelo Martinez, Cubs.

BATTING

G	Felix Pie, Cubs	55
	Chris Young, White Sox	55
AB	Leonardo Luna, White Sox	221
R	Jemel Spearman, Cubs	46
H	Leonardo Luna, White Sox	74
TB	Felix Pie, Cubs	124
XBH	Felix Pie, Cubs	33
2B	Micah Schnurstein, White Sox	26
3B	Felix Pie, Cubs	13
HR	Matt Creighton, Cubs	8
RBI	Micah Schnurstein, White Sox	48
SH	Michael Garciaparra, Mariners	6
	Eddie Olszta, Mariners	6
SF	Four tied at	4
BB	Wilber Soto, Angels	34
IBB	Six tied at	2
HBP	Matt Creighton, Cubs	19
SO	Chris Walston, Angels	67
SB	Jemel Spearman, Cubs	29
CS	Wilber Soto, Angels	10
GIDP	Brian Munhall, Giants	8
OB%	Matt Creighton, Cubs	.502
SL%	Matt Creighton, Cubs	.598

PITCHING

G	Daniel Arias, Angels	27
GS	Four tied at	14
CG	Dario Ortiz, White Sox	1
ShO	Dario Ortiz, White Sox	1
GF	Daniel Arias, Angels	26
SV	Daniel Arias, Angels	15
W	Daniel Haigwood, White Sox	8
L	Eight tied at	5
IP	Brandon McCarthy, White Sox	78
H	Francisco Graterol, Mariners	86
R	Anderson Mejia, Cubs	48
ER	Anderson Mejia, Cubs	36
HR	Brandon McCarthy, White Sox	6
	Anibal Reynoso, Athletics	6
HB	Anderson Mejia, Cubs	20
BB	Dario Ortiz, White Sox	32
	Alvaro Martinez Sosa, Brewers	32
SO	Brandon McCarthy, White Sox	79
WP	Candido Santana, Cubs	9
BK	Rafael Ramirez, Giants	5

FIELDING

C	AVG	Brian Munhall, Giants	.994
	PO	Tommy Duenas, Angels	388
	A	Brian Munhall, Giants	42
	E	Tommy Duenas, Angels	10
	DP	Tommy Duenas, Angels	4
	PB	Simon Guhring, Brewers	11
1B	AVG	Tyler Klippenstein, Athletics	.981
	PO	Ruben Olguin, Mariners	378
	A	Ruben Olguin, Mariners	26
	E	Eric Keefner, White Sox	11
		Ruben Olguin, Mariners	11
	DP	Ruben Olguin, Mariners	26
2B	AVG	Leonardo Luna, White Sox	.964
	PO	Guilder Rodriguez, Brewers	99
	A	Francesco Imperiali, Mariners	115
		Guilder Rodriguez, Brewers	115
	E	Guilder Rodriguez, Brewers	14
	DP	Guilder Rodriguez, Brewers	30
3B	AVG	Micah Schnurstein, WS	.941
	PO	Micah Schnurstein, WS	43
	A	Lendon Willis, Brewers	92
	E	Lendon Willis, Brewers	19
	DP	Lendon Willis, Brewers	13
SS	AVG	Jemel Spearman, Cubs	.933
	PO	Jemel Spearman, Cubs	83
	A	Jemel Spearman, Cubs	152
	E	Michael Garciaparra, Mariners	18
	DP	Jemel Spearman, Cubs	39
OF	AVG	Adalberto Paulino, Giants	.975
	PO	Felix Pie, Cubs	112
	A	Jhonny Rivera, White Sox	9
	E	Three tied at	7
	DP	Jhonny Rivera, White Sox	3

MINOR LEAGUES

BY ALLAN SIMPSON

First impressions often can be deceiving at the entry level of professional baseball, but Hanley Ramirez may be the exception. Every manager in the Gulf Coast League's Southern Division was effusive in their praise of the 18-year-old Red Sox shortstop in 2002, saying if ever there was a sure bet to be a future star in the big leagues, Ramirez was it.

"He's the best prospect I've seen in this league in 10 years," said veteran Pirates manager Woody Huyke. "He would have been the No. 1 pick in the draft this year if he had been eligible, no question."

Managers were so enthralled with Ramirez' five-tool ability that they compared him to Alex Rodriguez and Nomar Garciaparra at the same stage of their careers.

"He's awesome," Orioles manager Jesus Alfaro said. "He's tall and thin like A-Rod, and has similar actions. He's got range and arm strength, and is capable of making the spectacular play. And he's an outstanding hitter."

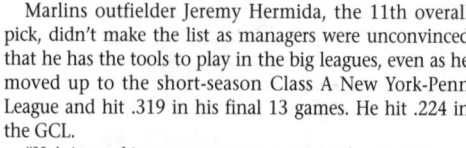

KEN BABBITT

Hanley Ramirez

"He has the gift," Reds manager Edgar Caceres added. "He has great bat speed and should hit for both power and average. There are no holes in his swing."

Ramirez' bat is his best tool. He hit .341 for the Red Sox—second in the league—and outdid himself when he was promoted to the New York-Penn League for the final 19 games. He hit .379 and was also selected that league's No. 1 prospect.

Only three first-round picks from the 2002 draft debuted in the league—compared with eight in 2001—and none made a particularly strong impression on managers as players from Latin America dominated Baseball America's annual survey of the top prospects, claiming the first nine spots. Only one first-rounder, Tigers shortstop Scott Moore, cracked the Top 20—at No. 16.

Marlins outfielder Jeremy Hermida, the 11th overall pick, didn't make the list as managers were unconvinced that he has the tools to play in the big leagues, even as he moved up to the short-season Class A New York-Penn League and hit .319 in his final 13 games. He hit .224 in the GCL.

"He's just a fringe prospect now, more of a scouts' guy," one manager said. "He's got a nice short swing, but he was hitting with wood for the first time and looked lost out there at times. He was adjusting to a lot of things."

The Phillies posted the league's best overall record (39-21) and went on to capture their first-ever Gulf Coast League title, beating the Dodgers two games to one in a best-of-3 final.

After the Dodgers jumped to a 1-0 lead, league ERA leader Elizardo Ramirez pitched a two-hit, 7-0 shutout to square the series and the Phillies rallied the next day to beat the Dodgers 5-3.

Ramirez, the league's No. 6-rated prospect, went 7-1, 1.10 in the regular season while allowing only two walks and striking out 73 in 73 innings. He didn't walk a batter in subduing the Dodgers, who lost in the final for the second straight year.

Outfielder Karl Nonemaker had three hits and first baseman Bryan Hansen drove in two runs in the deciding game as the Phillies, who won the Northern Division title, rallied from a 3-2 deficit with three runs in the seventh.

The Dodgers, the Eastern Division champion, reached the final by beating the Southern Division champion Pirates in a one-game playoff.

For the Pirates' Huyke, who has managed or coached in the GCL every year except one since 1974, it was the first time he'd ever had a team that finished first. At one point during the season, Huyke's team ran off 15 wins in a row—longest in the minors in 2002.

The GCL had the same 14 teams in 2002 as it had a year earlier, but that will not be the case in 2003 as the Rangers and Royals will not field teams. Those clubs are moving their spring training headquarters to Arizona and will operate complex-league clubs in the Arizona League.

STANDINGS

Page	EAST	Complex Site	W	L	PCT	GB	Manager	Last Penn.
163	Dodgers	Vero Beach	33	27	.550	—	Luis Salazar	1990
143	Marlins	Jupiter	31	29	.517	2	Jesus Campos	None
185	Expos	Melbourne	28	32	.467	5	Andy Skeels	1991
76	Braves	Kissimmee	28	32	.467	5	Jim Saul	1964
Page	NORTH	Complex Site	W	L	PCT	GB	Manager	Last Penn.
215	Phillies	Clearwater	39	21	.650	—	Ruben Amaro Sr.	2002
193	Yankees	Tampa	36	24	.600	3	Manny Crespo	2001
135	Tigers	Lakeland	23	37	.383	16	Howard Bushong	None
156	Royals	Baseball City	22	38	.367	17	Lloyd Simmons	1992
Page	WEST	Complex Site	W	L	PCT	GB	Manager	Last Penn.
222	Pirates	Bradenton	37	23	.617	—	Woody Huyke	None
177	Twins	Fort Myers	35	25	.585	2	Rudy Hernandez	None
113	Reds	Sarasota	30	30	.500	7	Edgar Caceras	None
266	Rangers	Port Charlotte	28	32	.467	9	Carlos Subero	2000
91	Red Sox	Fort Myers	26	34	.433	11	John Sanders	None
84	Orioles	Sarasota	24	36	.400	13	Jesus Alfaro	None

PLAYOFFS—Semifinals: Dodgers defeated Pirates in one-game playoff. **Final:** Phillies defeated Dodgers 2-1 in best-of-3 series.

NOTE: Teams' individual batting and pitching statistics can be found on page indicated in lefthand column.

CLUB BATTING

	AVG	G	AB	R	H	2B	3B	HR	BB	SO	SB
Twins	.285	60	2038	330	581	84	21	13	207	320	97
Pirates	.277	60	1903	302	528	93	28	25	216	308	71
Reds	.270	60	1937	293	523	119	13	32	170	403	78
Rangers	.259	60	1835	269	476	81	13	16	238	403	137
Yankees	.259	60	1916	259	497	87	16	14	185	390	29
Phillies	.254	60	1881	265	477	99	13	24	211	380	80
Tigers	.243	60	1916	218	466	71	22	19	165	413	66
Braves	.238	60	1897	235	451	77	18	24	180	397	65
Dodgers	.238	60	1810	268	430	79	11	12	233	314	89
Expos	.231	60	1870	222	432	84	10	19	176	425	39
Marlins	.225	60	1776	240	399	82	19	13	258	430	80
Red Sox	.222	60	1842	246	409	83	18	23	216	461	59
Orioles	.220	60	1811	206	398	66	13	8	193	406	47
Royals	.216	60	1884	205	407	68	7	14	211	440	54

CLUB PITCHING

	ERA	G	CG	SHO	SV	IP	H	R	ER	BB	SO
Phillies	2.44	60	7	13	18	505	380	173	137	139	405
Marlins	2.88	60	3	8	12	498	405	221	159	190	382
Dodgers	2.90	60	0	5	12	490	406	201	158	194	402
Twins	3.25	60	3	1	15	526	452	254	190	249	432
Pirates	3.27	60	2	7	15	501	467	230	182	165	339
Royals	3.49	60	2	5	10	505	511	253	196	183	356
Yankees	3.53	60	1	4	14	503	441	229	197	217	414
Rangers	3.60	60	0	5	9	493	514	253	197	163	337
Tigers	3.68	60	1	5	9	506	515	292	207	233	448
Expos	3.73	60	0	6	15	499	484	256	207	181	347
Orioles	3.87	60	1	4	11	486	467	286	209	244	449
Reds	3.96	60	0	4	14	495	453	293	218	220	381
Braves	4.17	60	1	3	10	503	417	287	233	282	435
Red Sox	4.49	60	2	4	11	497	562	330	248	199	363

CLUB FIELDING

	PCT	PO	A	E	DP		PCT	PO	A	E	DP
Yankees	.972	1508	646	61	58	Expos	.960	1498	587	86	56
Braves	.972	1509	606	61	47	Royals	.959	1516	587	90	55
Phillies	.968	1514	665	73	45	Marlins	.957	1493	629	96	49
Rangers	.966	1479	593	73	55	Reds	.955	1486	628	100	41
Dodgers	.966	1470	643	75	46	Orioles	.953	1457	595	102	58
Twins	.966	1579	672	80	65	Red Sox	.947	1491	606	118	58
Pirates	.961	1503	688	89	57	Tigers	.943	1518	593	127	43

INDIVIDUAL BATTING LEADERS
(Minimum 162 Plate Appearances)

	AVG	G	AB	R	H	2B	3B	HR	RBI	BB	SO	SB
Davis, Rajai, Pirates	.384	58	224	38	86	16	5	4	35	20	25	24
Ramirez, Hanley, Red Sox	.341	45	164	29	56	11	3	6	26	16	15	8
Denorfia, Chris, Reds	.340	57	200	38	68	9	2	0	19	31	23	18
Spataro, Ryan, Twins	.333	53	189	36	63	3	2	0	19	28	34	12
Romero, Alex, Twins	.333	56	186	31	62	13	2	2	42	29	14	16
Espino, Damaso, Reds	.332	58	223	35	74	22	0	0	32	16	30	8
Arbinger, Mike, Pirates	.327	59	214	32	70	11	2	2	46	25	22	4
Brown, Dustin, Red Sox	.321	45	159	28	51	12	2	1	20	23	24	11
Wong, Travis, Reds	.317	52	180	27	57	10	0	10	45	12	23	4
Morales, Jose, Twins	.309	53	175	25	54	7	2	0	28	7	28	3

INDIVIDUAL PITCHING LEADERS
(Minimum 48 Innings)

	W	L	ERA	G	GS	CG	SV	IP	H	R	ER	BB	SO
Ramirez, Elizardo, Phillies	7	1	1.10	11	11	2	0	73	44	18	9	2	73
Mateo, Aneudis, Red Sox	4	3	1.76	11	11	2	0	51	45	14	10	11	45
Peralta, Efigenio, Braves	6	2	1.78	14	5	0	0	56	32	13	11	18	44
Sanchez, Elby, Royals	3	2	1.80	15	5	0	2	50	49	18	10	7	36
Duke, Zach, Pirates	8	1	1.95	11	11	1	0	60	38	15	13	18	48
Figuereo, Victor, Rangers	5	2	1.96	16	4	0	0	55	48	18	12	17	31
Mildren, Paul, Marlins	3	4	1.97	11	10	2	0	59	52	16	13	17	38
Mateo, Manuel, Braves	7	3	1.98	12	8	1	0	68	47	18	15	12	76
German, Rafael, Reds	6	2	2.04	10	10	0	0	53	39	21	12	12	39
Garcia, Anderson, Yankees	4	1	2.30	11	9	1	0	59	43	22	15	22	41

ALL-STAR TEAM

C—Tim Gradoville, Phillies. **1B**—Travis Wong, Reds. **2B**—Jose Morales, Twins. **3B**—Damaso Espino, Reds. **SS**—Hanley Ramirez, Red Sox. **OF**—Mike Arbinger, Pirates; Rajai Davis, Pirates; Alex Romero, Twins. **SP**—Elizardo Ramirez, Phillies. **RP**—Maximo Reyes, Phillies.

Manager of the Year: Woody Huyke, Pirates.

DEPARTMENT LEADERS

BATTING

G	Three tied at	59
AB	Rajai Davis, Pirates	224
R	Javier Guzman, Pirates	42
H	Rajai Davis, Pirates	86
TB	Rajai Davis, Pirates	124
XBH	Rajai Davis, Pirates	25
	Joey Votto, Reds	25
2B	Damaso Espino, Reds	22
3B	Jose Aponte, Marlins	7
HR	Travis Wong, Reds	10
RBI	Mike Arbinger, Pirates	46
SH	Vincent Blue, Tigers	10
SF	Alex Romero, Twins	7
BB	Three tied at	35
IBB	Larry Grayson, Rangers	4
HBP	Luis Bolivar, Reds	11
SO	Devoris Williams, Red Sox	65
SB	Cameron Coughlan, Rangers	34
CS	Four tied at	8
GIDP	J.D. Huether, Twins	11
OB%	Rajai Davis, Pirates	.436
SL%	Hanley Ramirez, Red Sox	.555

PITCHING

G	Aaron Williams, Twins	25
GS	Three tied at	12
CG	Francisco Butto, Phillies	3
ShO	Francisco Butto, Phillies	2
GF	Antonio Batista, Red Sox	21
	Aaron Williams, Twins	21
SV	Maximo Reyes, Phillies	12
W	Zach Duke, Pirates	8
L	Three tied at	7
IP	Elizardo Ramirez, Phillies	73
H	Luis Mendoza, Red Sox	76
R	Matthew Blaney, Red Sox	49
ER	Matthew Blaney, Red Sox	46
HR	Tory Imotichey, Expos	7
HB	Matthew Blaney, Red Sox	10
	Brian Simpson, Braves	10
BB	Chase Wright, Yankees	39
SO	Manuel Mateo, Braves	76
WP	Steve Russell, Braves	16
BK	Jacobo Meque, Orioles	6

FIELDING

C	AVG	Carlos Rosario, Yankees	.992
	PO	Jon DeVries, Red Sox	256
	A	Pedro Andujar, Dodgers	34
	E	Justin Elliott, Twins	9
	DP	Danny Kahr, Expos	7
	PB	Carlos Rosario, Yankees	13
1B	AVG	Bryan Hansen, Phillies	.995
	PO	Josh Kreuzer, Rangers	415
	A	Bryan Hansen, Phillies	34
	E	Three tied at	7
	DP	Josh Kreuzer, Rangers	40
		Tim Thurman, Orioles	40
2B	AVG	Chad Opel, Orioles	.951
	PO	John Smith, Pirates	72
	A	Joaquin Arias, Yankees	118
	E	Jose Gonzalez, Tigers	15
	DP	John Smith, Pirates	27
3B	AVG	Omar Burgos, Twins	.966
	PO	Omar Burgos, Twins	39
	A	Kody Kirkland, Pirates	91
	E	Frederick Bastardo, Marlins	15
	DP	Kody Kirkland, Pirates	15
SS	AVG	Luis Hernandez, Braves	.991
	PO	Andres Blanco, Royals	83
	A	Luis Hernandez, Braves	155
	E	Javier Guzman, Pirates	25
	DP	Andres Blanco, Royals	32
		Angelo Fermin, Twins	21
OF	AVG	Karl Nonemaker, Phillies	1.000
	PO	Miguel Mota, Braves	125
	A	Rogearvin Bernadina, Expos	10
	E	Devoris Williams, Red Sox	7
	DP	Darwinson Salazar, Royals	3

MINOR LEAGUES

DOMINICAN SUMMER
LEAGUE

The Cleveland Indians undertook a massive rebuilding job in 2002, and success was immediate at every level of the farm system—right down to the Latin American summer leagues.

Indians minor league clubs in both the Dominican and Venezuelan summer leagues posted the best overall records in their respective leagues during the regular season. Unlike in Venezuela though, the Indians' DSL club went on to capture the league championship.

Behind manager Felix Fermin, a former big league shortstop, the Indians went 49-19 during the regular season to earn the Cibao Division title by one game. They then went on to beat the Santo Domingo West champion Yankees 2-1 in a best-of-3 semifinal and the San Pedro de Macoris champion Blue Jays 3-0 in a best-of-5 final.

Cleveland's performance was so dominating that it led the 34-team DSL in team batting (.282) and was second in team ERA (2.61). The only Indians player to lead the league in any significant individual category or make the all-star team, however, was lefthander Jairo Gonzalez, who went 10-0 to share the league lead in wins. Gonzalez added another win in the final series.

Outfielder Alfredo Martinez (.285-4-47) and first baseman Roman Ocumarez (.317-4-41) were the team's top run producers during the regular season, but they went just 3-for-23 between them in the championship series against the Blue Jays. Outfielder Gamalier Gabino picked up the slack as he went 8-for-11 with four RBIs in the three-game sweep.

The Dominican Summer League fielded 33 teams from 1999 to 2001, but expanded to 34 in 2002—even as the Devil Rays did not field a team. The Indians had two teams, with their second club also finishing above .500. The Athletics, Braves, Dodgers and Yankees also fielded two clubs.

The league expanded to a fifth division in 2002, with the 13-team Santo Domingo East Division splitting into East and Central sub-divisions.

Marlins third baseman Angelo Guillen won the batting title at .376, but was upstaged by Red Sox second baseman Wilson Reyes. Reyes hit only .256, but he made history by hitting a league-record 22 home runs.

The league played its second all-star game in 2002, with the National League defeating the America League 7-6—squaring the series at a game apiece. Mets center fielder Miguel Garcia was named the game's MVP. Garcia had a single and double, and drove in two runs.

ALL-STAR TEAM: C—Alberto Segura, Brewers. **1B**—Luis Ferrer, Cardinals. **2B**—Wilson Reyes, Red Sox. **3B**—Angelo Guillen, Marlins. **SS**—Eugenio Vancamper, Blue Jays. **OF**—Juan Paulino, Rangers; Edgar Suarez, Giants; Carlos Sanchez, Cubs. **DH**—Hernan Iribarren, Brewers. **LHP**—Jairo Gonzalez, Indians I. **RHP**—Danny Mosquea, Phillies. **RP**—Alberto Arias, Rockies.

Player of the Year: Juan Paulino, Rangers. **Pitcher of the Year:** Jairo Gonzalez, Indians. **Manager of the Year:** Felix Fermin, Indians I.

INDIVIDUAL BATTING LEADERS
(Minimum 150 Plate Appearances)

	AVG	AB	R	H	2B	3B	HR	RBI	SB
Guillen, Angelo, Marlins	.375	251	33	94	16	2	6	42	4
Ramirez, Stivins, White Sox	.352	182	32	64	11	5	1	24	13
Castillo, Luis, Dodgers I/II	.348	227	37	79	15	0	8	47	9

STANDINGS

SANTO DOMINGO EAST/East

	W	L	PCT	GB
Red Sox	41	31	.569	—
Cardinals	36	32	.529	3
Giants	37	35	.514	4
Rockies	34	37	.479	6 ½
Expos	29	40	.420	10 ½
Diamondbacks	30	42	.417	11

SANTO DOMINGO EAST/Central

	W	L	PCT	GB
Phillies	49	22	.690	—
Brewers	48	24	.667	1 ½
Dodgers I	38	33	.535	11
Tigers	34	37	.479	15
Athletics East	31	40	.437	18
Mariners	31	41	.431	18 ½
Yankees II	24	48	.333	25 ½

SANTO DOMINGO WEST

	W	L	PCT	GB
Yankees I	42	28	.600	—
Padres	38	31	.551	3 ½
Indians II	39	33	.542	4
Mets	37	33	.529	5
Dodgers II	34	34	.500	7
Athletics West	34	35	.493	7 ½
Twins	29	40	.420	12 ½
Reds	25	44	.362	16 ½

SAN PEDRO de MACORIS

	W	L	PCT	GB
Blue Jays	46	25	.648	—
Astros	39	32	.549	7
Angels	39	33	.542	7 ½
Cubs	37	34	.521	9
Pirates	36	36	.500	10 ½
Orioles	33	39	.458	13 ½
Rangers	31	40	.437	15
Marlins	25	47	.347	21 ½

CIBAO

	W	L	PCT	GB
Indians	49	19	.721	—
White Sox	47	21	.691	2
Braves II	32	35	.478	16 ½
Braves 1	24	44	.353	25
Royals	17	50	.254	31 ½

PLAYOFFS: Quarterfinals—Phillies defeated Red Sox 1-0 in sudden-death series. **Semifinals**—Blue Jays defeated Phillies 2-1 and Indians defeated Yankees 2-1 in best-of-3 series. **Finals**—Indianss defeated Blue Jays 3-0 in best-of-5 series.

Sanchez, Carlos, Cubs	.347	219	57	76	14	8	6	40	19
Paulino, Juan, Rangers	.343	280	56	**96**	17	3	6	51	11
Suarez, Edgar, Giants	.340	203	54	69	14	2	6	39	5
Cabrera, Eduardo, Phillies	.336	140	30	47	14	2	6	28	4
Cabrera, Melky, Yankees I	.335	218	37	73	19	3	3	29	7
Martinez, Henry, D'backs	.330	200	32	66	11	1	2	22	10
Osoria, Pedro, Mariners	.329	210	40	69	22	2	6	36	8
Ferrer, Luis, Cardinals	.324	259	51	84	18	6	2	57	13
Pineda, Luis, Reds	.322	236	**61**	76	22	2	5	18	26
Mejia, Rainel, Mariners	.321	224	49	72	17	2	1	26	25
Prado, Martin, Braves II	.319	235	36	75	19	3	1	36	14
Arnedo, Rolando, D'backs/Expos	.318	170	23	54	10	6	2	32	12
Ocumarez, Roman, Indians I	.317	230	45	73	17	0	4	41	7
Garamato, Angel, Mariners	.315	232	31	73	7	0	0	24	15
Pimentel, Jose, Indians I	.315	146	35	46	4	3	0	22	6
Puello, Esterlin, Reds	.314	245	38	77	16	0	7	41	7
Valerio, Gregory, Cubs	.314	236	42	74	21	2	7	47	8
Iribarren, Hernan, Brewers	.314	223	35	70	13	2	2	34	7
Santana, Michael, Expos	.313	179	22	56	9	0	1	31	9
Guzman, Randy, Indians I	.311	196	35	61	13	7	4	28	11
Cordova, Luis, Braves I	.310	197	22	61	18	1	5	36	1
Taylor, Marlin, Cardinals	.309	175	36	54	9	2	0	21	22
Tavarez, Junior, Dodgers	.306	235	47	72	10	6	1	24	20
Albizu, Alejandro, Cardinals	.305	177	26	54	8	3	0	23	8
Perez, Angel, Cardinals	.305	223	25	68	8	2	2	32	18
Penalo, Alexander, Red Sox	.304	227	41	69	11	4	2	26	10
Medina, Wilson, Mets	.303	221	40	67	9	3	2	31	20
Jackson, Wispi, Astros	.303	244	46	74	14	2	6	44	8
Arias, Alberdis, Blue Jays	.303	251	40	76	8	8	3	48	17
Diaz, Ricardo, Orioles	.303	165	55	50	6	4	2	25	18

Guerrero, Francisco, Orioles	.303	254	32	77	9	1	1	27	10
Guzman, David, Astros	.302	262	56	79	15	4	7	44	25
Marrun, Alexis, Brewers	.301	259	54	78	8	3	1	28	18
Vancamper, Eugenio, Blue Jays	.301	259	33	78	13	7	1	56	28
Lopez, Nelson, Cubs	.301	153	25	46	6	0	1	18	15
Herrera, Jhonatan, Rockies	.300	230	39	69	10	2	0	22	23
Bonifacio, Emilio, D'backs	.300	227	60	68	9	5	1	15	51
Solano, Solandy, Pirates	.300	200	26	60	8	3	4	29	6
Vargas, Juan, Astros	.300	233	45	70	7	2	1	39	19
Rodriguez, Wilkin, Tigers	.298	225	41	67	5	7	2	14	15
Arias, Yanuell, Indians I	.298	289	54	86	11	**10**	0	31	48
Rodriguez, Manuel, White Sox	.297	158	22	47	9	1	7	28	1
Zorrilla, Johvanny, Athletics West	.295	132	20	39	7	1	1	16	6
Rodriguez, Michael, Braves II	.295	224	32	66	17	1	1	32	2
Alcantara, Gilbert, White Sox	.295	227	33	67	15	3	0	27	11
Eusebio, Juan, Royals	.295	227	26	67	8	0	1	12	13
Brito, Javier, Diamondbacks	.295	207	28	61	11	3	4	38	7
Arias, Angel, White Sox	.294	163	20	48	7	1	1	18	10
Disla, Lisandro, Giants	.291	196	25	57	13	0	1	36	4
Dollis, Rafelito, Orioles	.291	148	23	43	7	1	0	16	7
De la Cruz, Wallys, Marlins	.291	254	32	74	16	3	1	24	9
Jimenez, Gerardo, Blue Jays	.290	241	46	70	9	7	1	35	16
Gonzalez, Fernando, Indians II	.289	242	40	70	16	1	3	35	13
Urdaneta, Marvin, D'backs	.289	149	30	43	6	1	0	12	18
Franco, Jeison, Brewers	.289	249	57	72	6	1	0	37	29
Suarez, Cesar, Yankees II	.289	277	41	80	19	1	2	27	8
Baez, Federico, Mets	.288	212	30	61	13	4	3	23	15
Charles, Larry, Rangers	.288	267	48	77	10	2	2	35	11
Gabino, Gamalier, Indians I	.287	230	46	66	8	3	2	38	9
Herrera, Javier, Athletics East	.286	227	40	65	14	5	5	47	21
Vargas, Candido, Blue Jays	.286	227	56	65	7	7	7	36	40
Rojas, Irwil, Yankees II	.286	168	15	48	7	2	0	18	0
Leal, Pablo, Braves I/II	.286	199	21	57	8	2	1	17	5
Grullon, Nelfri, Padres	.285	235	35	67	7	1	0	24	27
De los Santos, Juse, White Sox	.285	239	36	68	12	5	2	40	6
Martinez, Alfredo, Indians I	.285	267	38	76	23	2	4	47	2
Romero, Luis, Yankees I	.284	215	27	61	7	0	2	27	1
Made, Hector, Yankees I	.283	191	34	54	8	0	0	10	13
Rosario, Robinsom, Braves I	.283	233	44	66	10	8	0	25	15
Bautista, Victor, Braves I/II	.283	138	33	39	3	2	0	6	14
Rosario, Ismael, Red Sox	.283	251	44	71	6	5	3	22	14
Ponce, Arnoldo, Blue Jays	.283	219	54	62	14	6	5	37	14
Mola, Reymis, Red Sox	.283	240	31	68	22	0	7	38	2
Garcia, Miguel, Mets	.282	238	45	67	14	3	1	31	16
Segura, Alberto, Brewers	.282	202	36	57	20	3	1	45	6
Martinez, Andy, Tigers	.282	209	35	59	5	1	0	18	10
Paulino, Daniel, Yankees II	.281	210	21	59	9	4	1	28	3
Bone, Luis Manuel, Indians 1	.281	160	22	45	12	1	5	21	4
Martinez, Ery, Giants	.281	231	46	65	17	0	0	29	8
Petit, Gregorio, Athletics West	.280	218	44	61	11	5	1	21	5
Perez, Randy, Blue Jays	.280	161	27	45	9	3	1	38	9
Mercedes, Jose, Dodgers II	.278	205	29	57	9	1	6	25	4
Gonzalez, Jose, Giants	.277	220	53	61	4	1	0	14	25
Cedeno, Julio Cesar, White Sox	.277	159	27	44	14	1	2	27	7
Mejia, Fausto, Brewers	.276	257	44	71	**24**	1	5	**60**	14
Reyes, Francisco, White Sox	.276	170	35	47	8	3	1	28	11
DeJesus, Henry, Royals	.276	152	14	42	6	0	2	17	5
Pena, Jose, Angels	.276	217	30	60	5	3	1	17	11
Alvarado Ramon, Athletics East	.276	163	19	45	9	3	1	23	4
Mercado, Lorenzo, Giants	.276	174	22	48	7	5	0	33	4
Urena, Juan, Mets	.275	193	27	53	7	0	2	25	4
Lugo, Henry, Mariners	.275	211	41	58	2	4	1	18	11
Garcia, Junior, Indians I	.275	258	48	71	6	3	1	30	38
Robles, Manuel, Red Sox	.275	255	37	70	21	2	6	37	1
Fiss, Juan, Dodgers II	.274	157	19	43	5	1	1	18	6
Garcia, Jose, Phillies	.274	241	41	66	19	3	0	28	10
Sencion, Henry, Padres	.273	183	23	50	2	4	0	9	19
Contreras, Jose, Expos	.273	172	32	47	2	1	0	7	19
Yens, Jose, Giants	.273	220	35	60	15	4	6	44	9
Batista, Jose, Marlins	.273	264	38	72	15	4	1	20	13
Garcia, Carlos, Phillies	.273	128	33	35	1	2	0	11	13
Moya, Leonardo, Red Sox	.273	176	17	48	10	0	5	19	2
Gomez, Wascar, White Sox	.272	250	39	68	15	2	4	28	6
Guzman, Gregorio, Phillies	.271	203	32	55	12	1	0	28	10
Alcantara, Felix, Astros	.271	258	49	70	18	3	7	51	24
Oliva, Jesus, Cardinals	.271	240	60	65	3	3	0	16	**52**
Valdez, Angel, Rockies	.271	207	29	56	2	5	3	26	9
Marte, Luis, Yankees II	.270	137	25	37	1	3	0	10	10
#Reyes, Wilson, Red Sox	.256	254	**61**	65	17	2	**22**	47	13

Statistics in **boldface** indicate league leader
#League leader but non-qualifier

INDIVIDUAL PITCHING LEADERS

(Minimum 50 Innings)

	W	L	ERA	G	SV	IP	H	BB	SO
#Arias, Alberto, Rockies	1	1	0.48	31	**18**	37	24	11	27
Torres, Rony, Phillies	**10**	2	**0.60**	14	1	90	46	16	55
Matos, Aneidys, Indians II	5	3	0.87	22	7	52	38	20	51
Martinez, Hanlet, Indians II	7	1	0.96	13	0	75	58	16	81
Concepcion, Felix, Phillies	8	0	0.98	11	0	64	20	31	84
Pena, Hengely, Tigers	7	1	1.08	15	1	92	64	25	80
Mosquea, Danny O., Phillies	8	2	1.09	14	0	91	42	27	96
Martinez, Ronnie, Astros	6	1	1.17	16	0	84	64	19	91
Sanchez, Irving, Red Sox	5	1	1.31	21	4	62	51	11	39
Reyes, Maiky, Pirates	3	2	1.36	15	0	73	50	20	85
Garcia, Kelvin, Braves I	5	2	1.41	20	1	57	37	17	40
Amador, Jonathan, Indians II	4	5	1.51	14	0	72	33	40	70
Romero, Melvin, Cubs	8	1	1.51	15	2	71	49	13	82
Gonzalez, Jairo, Indians I	**10**	0	1.54	16	0	94	71	22	83
Perez, David, White Sox	3	0	1.57	27	4	57	53	12	49
Lugo, Jorge, Dodgers II	4	2	1.58	11	0	63	51	14	72
Mendoza, Anyelin, Cardinals	6	2	1.64	13	0	66	54	30	43
Arias, Jose, Angels	5	4	1.69	14	0	85	61	22	119
Sanchez, Raymond, Blue Jays	4	1	1.70	15	0	74	41	35	102
Concepcion, Wington, Brewers	5	2	1.71	23	9	58	60	6	35
Peralta, Heriberto, Mets	7	1	1.78	19	0	61	39	28	54
Sanchez, Franklin, Yankees I	4	2	1.79	17	3	50	31	8	57
Ojeda, Alvis, Dodgers I	7	4	1.79	12	0	70	59	22	72
Quiroz, Jimmy, Rockies	6	3	1.82	13	0	59	37	18	64
Bello, Gilbert, White Sox	5	4	1.88	12	0	72	57	26	81
Suarez, Sony, White Sox	7	3	1.88	29	9	96	71	31	78
Requena, Ricardo, Angels	5	5	1.92	13	0	75	53	17	91
Vilorio, Edison, Athletics West	2	3	1.94	11	0	65	49	14	51
Castro, Fabio, White Sox	**10**	2	1.95	25	8	65	37	23	89
Romero, Levi, Astros	4	1	1.96	14	0	73	64	22	53
Sevilla, Wilton, Yankees I	6	1	1.99	11	0	54	48	4	29
Mejia, Santo, Indians I	**10**	4	2.00	16	0	95	91	20	64
Rosario, Adrian, D'backs	3	1	2.05	10	0	57	41	7	57
Rodriguez, Victor, Rockies	3	2	2.12	16	0	64	58	17	38
Hernandez, Danny, Athletics East	8	2	2.16	14	0	83	59	27	75
Mota, Fabio, Cardinals	4	3	2.18	14	0	62	49	33	35
Beltre Casilla, Naldo, Giants	6	1	2.18	14	0	74	68	10	55
Pascual, Juan, Orioles	7	1	2.18	12	0	66	46	24	88
Mola, Heydin, Athletics West	4	2	2.20	12	0	65	55	15	41
Hiraldo, Nelson, Indians I	6	3	2.22	15	0	81	63	10	55
Castillo, Jose, Cardinals	6	4	2.23	19	3	61	52	15	40
Felix, Wilkin, Orioles	5	2	2.25	30	11	52	33	18	55
Brito, Joel, Marlins	4	3	2.27	15	0	79	47	42	**138**
Moscat, Darwin, Yankees II	3	3	2.32	13	0	54	49	15	54
Gonzalez, Emil, D'backs	6	3	2.36	11	0	61	37	32	75
Lorenzo, Luis, Padres	7	3	2.38	14	0	72	60	12	59
Rijo, Kerlin, Marlins	3	2	2.41	20	3	56	40	25	69
Manzueta, Juan, Blue Jays	8	0	2.45	16	2	77	49	24	105
Rosario, Amauris, Mets	3	2	2.47	14	0	69	65	18	76
De la Cruz, Maximo, Phillies	4	2	2.48	11	0	58	43	16	40
Ramos, Kendy, Pirates	1	4	2.50	15	1	68	45	31	82
Garcia, Carlos, Athletics East	3	4	2.56	19	2	53	36	20	43
Tovar, Miguel, Athletics West	4	4	2.57	14	0	74	57	17	45
Perdomo, Apolinar, Pirates	3	3	2.63	14	0	65	61	10	47
Mercedes, Milciades, Indians II	4	6	2.64	13	0	72	64	18	47
Garcia, Abraham, Orioles	5	4	2.65	12	0	75	61	26	73
Severino, Amauris, Braves II	5	2	2.65	11	1	51	51	10	33
Garcia, George, White Sox	5	1	2.66	14	0	68	70	20	47
Garcia, Mariano, Blue Jays	4	1	2.68	16	2	54	37	17	55
Santos, Ivan, Padres	4	3	2.70	12	0	50	43	14	43
Pena, Fabio, Indians I	3	2	2.70	15	1	53	46	22	28
Figueroa, Mallia, Brewers	7	3	2.71	11	0	60	48	26	41
Aguilar, Johneli, Astros	6	4	2.71	16	0	73	60	14	82
De la Cruz, Julian, Dodgers I	1	3	2.72	23	4	50	38	22	37
Aquino, Maiko, Twins	3	6	2.74	11	0	69	58	22	54
De la Rosa, Rafael, Orioles	4	5	2.75	12	0	69	57	25	97
Hernandez, Ramon, White Sox	5	4	2.75	14	0	72	62	22	48
Blanco, Leandro, Royals	2	3	2.81	16	0	58	59	13	31
Velasquez, Reynaldo, Royals	3	4	2.83	16	0	67	63	21	40
Yan, Gilberto, Braves II	3	4	2.84	13	0	70	74	17	57
Cruz, Yonel, Rockies	3	3	2.91	12	0	68	55	23	74
Ventura, Jose, Brewers	6	5	2.92	12	0	65	67	9	41
Made. Luis, Indians II	3	4	2.93	14	0	58	45	30	52
Cruz, Ramon, Mets	6	4	2.95	14	0	76	66	29	56
Cedeno, Jonathan, Brewers	7	1	2.95	9	0	58	63	8	38
Berroa, Juan, Braves I	0	4	2.95	13	0	64	73	16	40
Reina, Jesus, Giants	5	5	2.96	18	0	91	71	35	90
Herrera, Luis, Expos	5	2	2.98	15	1	57	48	22	49
Nova, Wander, Brewers	4	2	3.00	11	0	63	58	23	32

VENEZUELAN SUMMER
LEAGUE

San Felipe won at better than a .700-clip for the third consecutive season while dominating the Venezuelan Summer League's Barquisimeto Division in 2002. But like 2001, the Indians' farm club's season ended in defeat.

Aguirre, a team stocked with Seattle Mariners farmhands, turned the tables on San Felipe by winning two straight games in the league's best-of-3 championship series.

Despite going a combined 130-43 (.751) over the last three seasons, San Felipe has only one title to show for its efforts. After hitting a league-best .252 during the regular season, San Felipe scored just two runs in being eliminated by Aguirre, which dominated the Valencia Division.

League MVP Bladimir Balentien added championship series MVP honors by smacking a two-run homer as Aguirre won the deciding game 3-1. Shortstop Jesus Guzman, who had four hits in the series, delivered a three-run double to lift Aguirre to a 6-1 win in game one.

On the season, Balentien, a center fielder, hit .279 and delivered a league high 10 home runs.

San Felipe had the league's best overall ERA at 1.70. Righthander Edgar Morffe led the league with a 0.71 ERA and also featured the top winner in righthander Daniel Guzman, who went 9-0, 0.95 and tied for the league lead in strikeouts. But Morffe and Guzman, who went 15-1 between them in the regular season, were the losing pitchers in San Felipe's two playoff games.

San Felipe also had the league's top hitter and RBI leader in Jonel Pacheco, who hit .375 while driving in 43 runs.

The VSL held steady at 12 teams in 2002—twice the number from its inaugural season in 1997. But only 18 major league teams provided players to the league, as opposed to 22 in 2001. The league is open to all Spanish-speaking players except those from the Dominican Republic and Puerto Rico.

STANDINGS

BARQUISIMETO	W	L	PCT	GB
San Felipe	42	16	.717	—
Chivacoa	29	28	.508	12 ½
Carora	26	31	.458	15 ½
Cabudare	18	40	.317	24

VALENCIA	W	L	PCT	GB
Aguirre	41	17	.703	—
Cagua	33	26	.558	8 ½
Venoco	32	26	.551	9
Ciudad Alianza	31	29	.517	11
Puerto Cabello	28	29	.492	12 ½
San Joaquin	25	32	.441	15 ½
Mariara	24	36	.400	18
Universidad Carabobo	19	38	.333	21 ½

PLAYOFFS: Aguirre defeated San Felipe 2-0 in best-of-3 series.

AFFILIATIONS: Aguirre (Mariners), Cabudare (Orioles), Cagua (Reds, Twins), Carora (Blue Jays, Cardinals), Chivacoa (Padres, Pirates), Ciudad Alianza (Brewers, Red Sox), Mariara (Phillies), Puerto Cabello (Cubs, Rockies), San Felipe (Indians), San Joaquin (Dodgers, Marlins), Universidad de Carabobo (Mets), Venoco (Astros).

ALL-STAR TEAM: C—Cesar Quintero, Aguirre. **1B**—Mayron Isenia, Ciudad Alianza (Red Sox). **2B**—Victor Bacaloa, Universidad de Carabobo. **3B**—Christian Rodriguez, Venoco. **SS**—Fernando Veracierto, Ciudad Alianza (Red Sox). **OF**—Francisco Caraballo, Venoco; Jose Martinez, Puerto Cabello (Cubs); Pedro Daza, Ciudad Alianza (Red Sox). **DH**—Bladimir Balentien, Aguirre. **SP**—Cesar Jimenez, Aguirre. **RP**—Carlos Bohorquez, Cagua (Reds).

Most Valuable Player: Bladimir Balentien, Aguirre. **Most Outstanding Pitcher:** Cesar Jimenez, Aguirre.

INDIVIDUAL BATTING LEADERS
(Minimum 115 At-Bats)

	AVG	AB	R	H	2B	3B	HR	RBI	SB
Pacheco, Jonel, San Felipe	.375	160	42	60	16	1	3	43	17
Garcia, Winfield, Venoco	.352	142	29	50	8	0	0	17	15
Rodriguez, Christian, Venoco	.342	114	18	39	8	1	2	21	2
Caraballo, Francisco, Venoco	.324	216	33	70	13	2	7	42	4
Canizalez, Jose, San Felipe	.322	146	44	47	11	3	2	21	26
Quintero, Cesar, Aguirre	.319	185	28	59	16	2	6	31	0
Veracierto, Fernando, Ciudad Alianza	.318	170	27	54	6	0	0	28	16
Rivas, Kevin, San Felipe	.309	136	27	42	6	0	0	15	6
Gutierrez, Tonys, Cagua	.307	101	12	31	6	1	1	19	3
Lopez, Mauber, Mariara	.306	209	34	64	8	1	5	34	10
Melendez, Alcides, Cabudare	.303	155	30	47	9	0	6	26	14
Lambis, Alberto, San Joaquin	.302	199	25	60	11	0	0	23	3
Daza, Pedro, Ciudad Alianza	.302	139	26	42	5	3	0	19	7
Garay, Marvin, Chivacoa	.300	180	22	54	11	5	1	18	18
Martinez, Jose, Puerto Cabello	.298	188	33	56	10	5	0	12	22
Benitez, Edixon, Carora	.293	157	17	46	9	1	0	12	8
Alvarez, Wilner, Venoco	.290	176	35	51	9	0	1	19	15
Guzman, Jesus, Aguirre	.280	225	32	63	12	2	4	24	6
Colina, Luis, Carora	.279	104	12	29	1	3	1	4	3
Balentien, Bladimir, Aguirre	.279	197	41	55	13	4	10	39	6
Perez, Randy, Carora	.277	101	18	28	3	0	3	11	4
Chavez, Dirimo, Ciudad Alianza	.277	213	34	59	16	2	2	25	2
Leon, Jose, Ciudad Alianza	.273	139	18	38	12	0	3	20	0
Gamero, Jesus, Universidad	.273	198	24	54	9	0	7	31	9
Rodriguez, Yuber, Carora	.272	206	33	56	17	2	1	22	19
Torres, Fredy, San Felipe	.272	184	24	50	11	1	1	28	5
Perez, Jorge, Cagua	.271	221	34	60	8	1	1	18	2
Bacalao, Victory, Universidad	.269	171	17	46	12	2	0	19	6
Golindano, Jesus, San Joaquin	.267	202	24	54	11	1	2	24	11
Granadillo, Antonio, Carora	.261	134	20	35	9	4	2	15	4
Quesada, Jorge, Aguirre	.261	157	20	41	12	0	1	17	5
Navarro, Odwaldo, Aguirre	.261	119	13	31	4	1	0	9	3
Aristigueta, Darwin, Carora	.260	123	21	32	6	0	3	18	0
Barrios, Cesar, Puerto Cabello	.260	208	27	54	7	3	0	29	12
Rojas, Carlos, Puerto Cabello	.259	201	32	52	10	0	0	14	19
Rodriguez, Jesus, San Joaquin	.259	139	7	36	3	1	0	10	2
Hernandez, Yanko, Cagua	.258	194	20	50	6	6	0	14	1
Torres, Frank, San Joaquin	.257	226	25	58	9	2	2	19	10
Oliveros, Ricky, Universidad	.256	199	26	51	7	0	2	21	4
#Mago, Milwer, Chivacoa	.247	194	25	48	5	1	0	20	33

INDIVIDUAL PITCHING LEADERS
(Minimum 46 Innings)

	W	L	ERA	G	SV	IP	H	BB	SO
Morffe, Edgar, San Felipe	6	1	0.71	13	0	63	32	19	64
Jimenez, Cesar, Aguirre	7	1	0.83	11	0	65	37	12	67
Guzman, Daniel, San Felipe	9	0	0.95	12	0	76	38	11	86
Altuve, Juan, Carora	4	1	0.99	10	0	64	43	25	65
Alvardo, Carlos, San Felipe	4	2	1.04	14	1	61	36	10	57
Martinez, Javier, Cagua	5	1	1.11	11	0	65	43	23	52
Garavito, Jean, Chivacoa	6	3	1.32	14	1	75	50	25	61
Guedez, Willy, Puerto Cabello	6	3	1.37	18	2	66	43	24	44
Sarmiento, Jose, Ciudad Alianza	5	4	1.54	13	0	47	32	19	50
Bravo, Mahler, Mariara	3	5	1.59	12	1	68	53	14	63
Alguera, Winston, Venoco	5	2	1.66	10	0	49	37	12	35
Acosta, Nibaldo, Aguirre	5	3	1.77	12	0	71	53	7	64
Figueroa, Carlos, Aguirre	5	3	1.84	11	0	54	31	14	34
Bohorquez, Carlos, Cagua	1	1	1.85	24	17	34	21	13	50
Blanco, Julio, Ciudad Alianza	4	2	1.88	11	0	53	43	15	43
Alfaro, Gabriel, Carora	4	4	1.93	11	0	61	43	21	49
Salazar, Julio, Venoco	3	2	2.03	12	0	75	65	16	79
Bello, Cibney, Aguirre	7	1	2.04	14	0	71	56	16	77
Rodriguez, Jaime, Chivacoa	2	1	2.09	12	0	60	45	13	36
Pinto, Julio, San Felipe	6	1	2.10	12	1	60	45	3	44
Mendez, Orlin, Cagua	4	3	2.13	10	0	55	42	20	44
Bastardo, Alberto, Cabudare	4	4	2.19	11	0	53	41	12	49
Zarate, Mauro, San Joaquin	4	3	2.25	23	5	48	48	16	39
Benitez, Gabriel, San Joaquin	4	3	2.28	15	0	71	58	20	47
Moncada, Jorge, Venoco	6	2	2.29	11	0	59	46	22	44
Ortega, Joel, Chivacoa	2	3	2.31	16	4	47	39	20	51
Sanchez, Jose, Universidad	2	3	2.37	13	0	57	49	8	60
Brito, Luis, Puerto Cabello	4	3	2.43	18	1	70	59	21	68
Petit, Yusmeiro, Universidad	3	5	2.43	12	0	56	53	16	62
Quijada, Fernando, Mariara	2	3	2.48	11	0	54	50	22	34
Escobar, Carlos, Chivacoa	4	5	2.56	13	1	60	50	27	31

PROSPECTS

BY JOSH BOYD

Following the 2002 season, we decided to put things into perspective by ranking the top prospects by position. We have included only those players who did not exceed their major league rookie eligibility status—130 plate appearances for position players and 50 innings for pitchers.

Ages are as of Oct. 1, 2002. We've also indicated the highest level each player reached this season.

RIGHTHANDED STARTERS

No one expected Jesse Foppert to move all the way to the top of this list prior to the 2002 season, and though he was helped by such pitchers as Mark Prior graduating to the majors, Foppert has frontline stuff. A converted first baseman, he's only been on the mound for a couple years, yet he looks like a veteran with clean mechanics and powerful arm. Foppert gets the slight edge over Gavin Floyd because he's more advanced, but Floyd's ceiling might be higher. Like Foppert, John VanBenschoten made the transition to pitching look easy.

Rank	Player, Team	Age	Highest Level
1.	Jesse Foppert, Giants	22	Triple-A
2.	Gavin Floyd, Phillies	19	Low A
3.	Francisco Rosario, Blue Jays	22	High A
4.	Adam Wainwright, Braves	21	High A
5.	Colby Lewis, Rangers	23	Majors
6.	Taylor Buchholz, Phillies	20	Double-A
7.	Jeremy Bonderman, Tigers	19	High A
8.	Aaron Cook, Rockies	23	Majors
9.	Clint Nageotte, Mariners	21	High A
10.	John VanBenschoten, Pirates	22	Low A
11.	Donald Levinski, Marlins	19	Low A
12.	John Patterson, Diamondbacks	24	Majors
13.	Ben Hendrickson, Brewers	21	Double-A
14.	Mike Jones, Brewers	19	Low A
15.	Dewon Brazelton, Devil Rays	22	Majors
16.	Aaron Heilman, Mets	23	Triple-A
17.	Bobby Jenks, Angels	21	Double-A
18.	Chris Gruler, Reds	19	Low A
19.	Bubba Nelson, Braves	21	High A
20.	Kris Honel, White Sox	19	Low A
21.	Jerome Williams, Giants	20	Triple-A
22.	Rafael Soriano, Mariners	22	Majors
23.	Jimmy Journell, Cardinals	24	Triple-A
24.	Johan Santana, Angels	18	Low A
25.	Jason Arnold, Athletics	23	Double-A

LEFTHANDED STARTERS

It was not a list lacking for talent, but Scott Kazmir's dominant debut in the New York-Penn League boosted him straight to the top. Armed with a 96-mph fastball and nasty hammer, Kazmir moved past Sean Burnett—whom scouts compare favorably to Mark Buehrle—and Francisco Liriano, who consistently operates with upper-90s heat. Dontrelle Willis made tremendous progress after joining the Marlins last spring training in a deal with the Cubs, though the Cubs saw towering southpaw Andy Sisco emerge with overpowering stuff. Injuries to Ty Howington, Erik Bedard, Brandon Claussen and Corwin Malone hurt their stock, while young guns like Jonathan Figueroa, Ben Kozlowski and Macay McBride took advantage to move into the top 10.

Rank	Player, Team	Age	Highest Level
1.	Scott Kazmir, Mets	18	Short-season
2.	Sean Burnett, Pirates	19	High A
3.	Francisco Liriano, Giants	18	Low A
4.	Cliff Lee, Indians	24	Majors
5.	Dontrelle Willis, Marlins	20	High A
6.	Jonathan Figueroa, Dodgers	19	Low A

Jesse Foppert emerged as game's top righthanded prospect

7.	Ben Kozlowski, Rangers	22	Majors
8.	Andy Sisco, Cubs	19	Short-season
9.	Macay McBride, Braves	19	Low A
10.	Joe Saunders, Angels	21	Low A
11.	Erik Bedard, Orioles	23	Double-A
12.	Brandon Claussen, Yankees	23	Triple-A
13.	Mike Gosling, Diamondbacks	22	Double-A
14.	Billy Traber, Indians	23	Triple-A
15.	John Rheinecker, Athletics	23	Double-A
16.	Rob Henkel, Marlins	24	Double-A
17.	Mark Phillips, Padres	20	High A
18.	Phil Dumatrait, Red Sox	21	High A
19.	Neal Cotts, Athletics	22	High A
20.	Jeff Francis, Rockies	21	Low A

RELIEVERS

Francisco Rodriguez made his mark in September and October for the Angels, showcasing some of the nastiest stuff to come along since Mariano Rivera emerged as a dominant postseason force for the Yankees in 1996. While Franklyn German didn't have the same stage as Rodriguez, he's going to be slamming the door for the Tigers with his explosive fastball and splitter soon. Alfredo Gonzalez is the sleeper of the bunch.

Rank	Player, Team	Age	Highest Level
1.	Franklyn German, Tigers	22	Majors
2.	Francisco Rodriguez, Angels	20	Majors
3.	Francis Beltran, Cubs	22	Majors
4.	Duaner Sanchez, Pirates	22	Majors
5.	Alfredo Gonzalez, Dodgers	23	Triple-A
6.	Jeremy Hill, Royals	25	Majors
7.	Zach Day, Expos	24	Majors
8.	Aaron Taylor, Mariners	25	Majors
9.	Rommie Lewis, Orioles	20	Low A
10.	Erick Threets, Giants	20	High A

CATCHERS

Joe Mauer came straight out of high school to lead the catching prospects in 2001, and he solidified his status last season. A well-rounded receiver, Mauer's power is projected to develop into another plus tool as he matures and learns which pitches to drive and lift. Victor Martinez erupted for a monster season in Double-A, where he won his second consecutive batting title. John Buck's 2002 season was a little disappointing after back-to-back seasons in low Class A.

Rank	Player, Team	Age	Highest Level
1.	Joe Mauer, Twins	19	Low A
2.	Victor Martinez, Indians	23	Majors
3.	Jeff Mathis, Angels	19	Low A
4.	Justin Huber, Mets	20	High A
5.	John Buck, Astros	22	Double-A
6.	Kevin Cash, Blue Jays	24	Majors
7.	Miguel Olivo, White Sox	24	Majors
8.	Koyie Hill, Dodgers	23	Double-A
9.	Josh Bard, Indians	24	Majors
10.	Kelly Shoppach, Red Sox	22	High A

FIRST BASEMEN

The class of 2002 produced rookies Carlos Pena and Nick Johnson but the top three bats on this list will require a little more seasoning before jumping to the bigs. Hee Seop Choi, Lyle Overbay and Eric Munson are on the cusp after big Triple-A seasons. Justin Morneau and Casey Kotchman are the top pure hitters in the minors, though Kotchman's debut season was interrupted by wrist injuries. Coming out of high school last June, first-rounder James Loney looked to be much more advanced at the plate than his age would suggest.

Rank	Player, Team	Age	Highest Level
1.	Justin Morneau, Twins	21	Double-A
2.	Casey Kotchman, Angels	19	Low A
3.	Jason Stokes, Marlins	20	Low A
4.	Hee Seop Choi, Cubs	23	Majors
5.	James Loney, Dodgers	18	High A
6.	Adrian Gonzalez, Marlins	20	Double-A
7.	Lyle Overbay, Diamondbacks	25	Majors
8.	Brad Nelson, Brewers	19	High A
9.	Prince Fielder, Brewers	18	Low A
10.	Eric Munson, Tigers	24	Majors

SECOND BASEMEN

With Jeff Kent setting the tone in the majors, teams are looking for more production at second base these days. Not many players at any position provided more than Scott Hairston and Joe Thurston in 2002. Hairston collected an amazing 73 extra-base hits, while Thurston was stopped just shy of the 200-hit plateau. Freddy Sanchez continued to hit for average, and Shaun Boyd rebounded in a repeat of the Midwest League. Robinson Cano is a player who could be on the verge of a breakout with his athleticism and power potential.

Rank	Player, Team	Age	Highest Level
1.	Scott Hairston, Diamondbacks	22	High A
2.	Joe Thurston, Dodgers	23	Majors
3.	Jake Gautreau, Padres	23	High A
4.	Chris Burke, Astros	22	Double-A
5.	Josh Barfield, Padres	19	Low A
6.	Antonio Perez, Mariners	22	Double-A
7.	Freddy Sanchez, Red Sox	24	Majors
8.	Shaun Boyd, Cardinals	21	Low A
9.	Freddie Bynum, Athletics	22	High A
10.	Robinson Cano, Yankees	19	Low A

THIRD BASEMEN

In a year that saw Sean Burroughs and Hank Blalock graduate to the major leagues and struggle, Mark Teixeira maintained a strong reputation. There is a question if Teixeira's arm and Blalock's presence will force him to move elsewhere, but there is no doubt his bat will support him anywhere in the lineup. Miguel Cabrera made the move from shortstop look easy, and the teenager started hitting for corner-infield power, too. While

Andy Marte and Dallas McPherson blossomed at the low Class A level, Drew Henson and Corey Smith struggled to make consistent contact and must show something this season.

Rank	Player, Team	Age	Highest Level
1.	Mark Teixeira, Rangers	22	Double-A
2.	Miguel Cabrera, Marlins	19	High A
3.	Andy Marte, Braves	18	Low A
4.	Dallas McPherson, Angels	22	Low A
5.	Drew Henson, Yankees	22	Majors
6.	David Wright, Mets	19	Low A
7.	Chase Utley, Phillies	23	Double-A
8.	Corey Smith, Indians	20	High A
9.	Chad Tracy, Diamondbacks	22	Double-A
10.	Corey Hart, Brewers	20	Double-A

SHORTSTOPS

As the centerpiece of the Bartolo Colon trade with the Expos, Brandon Phillips got plenty of exposure in 2002. He made the most of his trip to the Futures Game, and his September callup resulted in nightly highlights on "SportsCenter." Mets fans are anxious to see the Futures Game MVP, Jose Reyes, challenge Rey Ordonez for the shortstop job in the spring. Hanley Ramirez emerged as the Red Sox' top prospect, but he'll have to prove himself in a full-season league before he's worthy of all the lofty comparisons being thrown his way. Wilson Betemit and Angel Berroa are at crossroads.

Rank	Player, Team	Age	Highest Level
1.	Brandon Phillips, Indians	21	Majors
2.	Jose Reyes, Mets	19	Double-A
3.	Hanley Ramirez, Red Sox	18	Short-season
4.	B.J. Upton, Devil Rays	17	Did not play
5.	Jose Lopez, Mariners	18	High A
6.	Wilson Betemit, Braves	20	Triple-A
7.	Jose Castillo, Pirates	21	High A
8.	Khalil Greene, Padres	22	High A
9.	J.J. Hardy, Brewers	20	Double-A
10.	Angel Berroa, Royals	24	Majors

OUTFIELDERS

Minor League Player of the Year Rocco Baldelli gets the edge here based on his five-tool potential. His arm is his weakest tool, though it has a chance to be average, while the next four project as plus tools. The Twins are overflowing with outfield talent, and Michael Cuddyer will be a leading candidate for Rookie of the Year. Others including Joe Borchard, Marlon Byrd and Juan Rivera will compete for big league jobs in the spring.

Rank	Player, Team	Age	Highest Level
1.	Rocco Baldelli, Devil Rays	21	Triple-A
2.	Michael Cuddyer, Twins	23	Majors
3.	Michael Restovich, Twins	23	Majors
4.	Joe Borchard, White Sox	23	Majors
5.	Josh Hamilton, Devil Rays	21	High A
6.	Marlon Byrd, Phillies	25	Majors
7.	Laynce Nix, Rangers	21	High A
8.	Juan Rivera, Yankees	25	Majors
9.	Chris Snelling, Mariners	20	Majors
10.	Reggie Abercrombie, Dodgers	21	High A
11.	Nic Jackson, Cubs	23	Double-A
12.	Xavier Nady, Padres	23	Triple-A
13.	Choo Freeman, Rockies	22	Double-A
14.	Alexis Rios, Blue Jays	21	High A
15.	Grady Sizemore, Indians	20	High A
16.	Todd Linden, Giants	22	Triple-A
17.	Felix Pie, Cubs	17	Short-season
18.	Carlos Duran, Braves	19	Low A
19.	Wily Mo Pena, Reds	20	Majors
20.	John-Ford Griffin, Athletics	22	Double-A
21.	Shin-Soo Choo, Mariners	20	High A
22.	Gregor Blanco, Braves	18	Low A
23.	Gabe Gross, Blue Jays	22	Double-A
24.	Bronson Sardinha, Yankees	19	Low A
25.	Luis Terrero, Diamondbacks	22	Double-A

As with most of the prospect lists that appear in Baseball America, the Minor League Top 20 Prospects lists are compiled with long-term major league potential in mind. While we like to see players do well now, what we're really looking for are future major league stars.

These lists do bring a slightly different perspective than the organizational Top 10 Prospects, that begin on page 333. Those lists have more of a scouting angle, while our league lists are based on conversations with league managers. Managers and scouts can often view players differently. Both look at a player's tools, but managers give more weight to what a player does on the field, while scouts look at what a player might eventually do. We think both perspectives are useful, so we give you both even though they don't always agree.

For a player to qualify for a league prospect list, he must have spent at least one-third of the season in a league to qualify. Position players must have one plate appearance per league game. In other words, for a league that plays 140 games, a player is eligible if he has at least 140 plate appearances.

Pitchers must pitch one-third of an inning per league game. Relievers must make at least 20 appearances in a full-season league or 10 appearances in a short-season league.

TRIPLE-A

INTERNATIONAL LEAGUE
1. Carl Crawford, of, Durham (Devil Rays)
2. Brett Myers, rhp, Scranton/Wilkes-Barre (Phillies)
3. Orlando Hudson, 2b, Syracuse (Blue Jays)
4. Marlon Byrd, of, Scranton/Wilkes-Barre (Phillies)
5. Brandon Phillips, ss/2b, Buffalo (Indians)
6. Josh Phelps, dh/c, Syracuse (Blue Jays)
7. Juan Rivera, of, Columbus (Yankees)
8. Joe Borchard, of, Charlotte (White Sox)
9. Eric Munson, 1b, Toledo (Tigers)
10. Joe Crede, 3b, Charlotte (White Sox)
11. Franklyn German, rhp, Toledo (Tigers)
12. Wilson Betemit, ss, Richmond (Braves)
13. Drew Henson, 3b, Columbus (Yankees)
14. Chase Utley, 3b, Scranton/Wilkes-Barre (Phillies)
15. Aaron Heilman, rhp, Norfolk (Mets)
16. Brandon Larson, 3b, Louisville (Reds)
17. Endy Chavez, of, Ottawa (Expos)
18. Willie Harris, 2b, Charlotte (White Sox)
19. Omar Infante, ss, Toledo (Tigers)
20. Josh Bard, c, Buffalo (Indians)

PACIFIC COAST LEAGUE
1. Jesse Foppert, rhp, Fresno (Giants)
2. Michael Cuddyer, 3b-of, Edmonton (Twins)
3. Hank Blalock, 3b, Oklahoma (Rangers)
4. John Lackey, rhp, Salt Lake (Angels)
5. Michael Restovich, of, Edmonton (Twins)
6. Sean Burroughs, 2b/3b, Portland (Padres)
7. Colby Lewis, rhp, Oklahoma (Rangers)
8. Hee Seop Choi, 1b, Iowa (Cubs)
9. Bobby Hill, 2b, Iowa (Cubs)
10. Aaron Cook, rhp, Colorado Springs (Rockies)
11. Travis Hafner, 1b, Oklahoma (Rangers)
12. Francisco Rodriguez, rhp, Salt Lake (Angels)
13. Kurt Ainsworth, rhp, Fresno (Giants)
14. Dennis Tankersley, rhp, Portland (Padres)
15. Lyle Overbay, 1b, Tucson (Diamondbacks)
16. Jerome Williams, rhp, Fresno (Giants)
17. Angel Berroa, ss, Omaha (Royals)
18. Jason Young, rhp, Colorado Springs (Rockies)
19. Brad Lidge, rhp, New Orleans (Astros)
20. Joe Thurston, 2b, Las Vegas (Dodgers)

DOUBLE-A

EASTERN LEAGUE
1. Jose Reyes, ss, Binghamton (Mets)
2. *Brandon Phillips, ss, Harrisburg (Expos)
3. Victor Martinez, c, Akron (Indians)
4. Justin Morneau, 1b, New Britain (Twins)
5. Cliff Lee, lhp, Akron (Indians)
6. Aaron Heilman, rhp, Binghamton (Mets)

Jose Reyes: No. 1 in Eastern League

7. Adrian Gonzalez, 1b, Portland (Marlins)
8. Kevin Youkilis, 3b, Trenton (Red Sox)
9. Erik Bedard, lhp, Bowie (Orioles)
10. Freddy Sanchez, ss, Trenton (Red Sox)
11. Jimmy Journell, rhp, New Haven (Cardinals)
12. Billy Traber, lhp, Akron (Indians)
13. Brian Tallet, lhp, Akron (Indians)
14. Ryan Madson, rhp, Reading (Phillies)
15. Danny Borrell, lhp, Norwich (Yankees)
16. Seung Song, rhp, Harrisburg (Expos)
17. Josh Karp, rhp, Harrisburg (Expos)
18. Julio DePaula, rhp, Norwich (Yankees)
19. Covelli Crisp, of, Akron (Indians)
20. Jesus Medrano, 2b, Portland (Marlins)
    *Since traded to Indians

SOUTHERN LEAGUE
1. Jake Peavy, rhp, Mobile (Padres)
2. Aaron Cook, rhp, Carolina (Rockies)
3. Frank Beltran, rhp, West Tenn (Cubs)
4. Jason Young, rhp, Carolina (Rockies)
5. *Ricardo Rodriguez, rhp, Jacksonville (Dodgers)
6. Miguel Olivo, c, Birmingham (White Sox)
7. Choo Freeman, of, Carolina (Rockies)
8. Vinny Chulk, rhp, Tennessee (Blue Jays)
9. Ben Hendrickson, rhp, Huntsville (Brewers)
10. Dennis Tankersley, rhp, Mobile (Padres)
11. Koyie Hill, c, Jacksonville (Dodgers)
12. Dewon Brazelton, rhp, Orlando (Devil Rays)
13. David Kelton, 1b, West Tenn (Cubs)

14. Corwin Malone, lhp, Birmingham (White Sox)
15. Kevin Cash, c, Tennessee (Blue Jays)
16. Joe Valentine, rhp, Birmingham (White Sox)
17. Jung Bong, lhp, Greenville (Braves)
18. Wily Mo Pena, of, Chattanooga (Reds)
19. Brett Evert, rhp, Greenville (Braves)
20. Steve Colyer, lhp, Jacksonville (Dodgers)
    *Since traded to Indians

TEXAS LEAGUE
1. Mark Teixeira, 3b, Tulsa (Rangers)
2. Jesse Foppert, rhp, Shreveport (Giants)
3. Todd Linden, of, Shreveport (Giants)
4. Rafael Soriano, rhp, San Antonio (Mariners)
5. Francisco Rodriguez, rhp, Arkansas (Angels)
6. Kirk Saarloos, rhp, Round Rock (Astros)
7. Mike Gosling, lhp, El Paso (Diamondbacks)
8. Rich Harden, rhp, Midland (Athletics)
9. Ben Kozlowski, lhp, Tulsa (Rangers)
10. Bobby Jenks, rhp, Arkansas (Angels)
11. Runelvys Hernandez, rhp, Wichita (Royals)
12. *Franklyn German, rhp, Midland (Athletics)
13. Alexis Gomez, of, Wichita (Royals)
14. Chad Tracy, 3b, El Paso (Diamondbacks)
15. Jeremy Hill, rhp, Wichita (Royals)
16. Aaron Taylor, rhp, San Antonio (Mariners)
17. Travis Hughes, rhp, Tulsa (Rangers)
18. John Buck, c, Round Rock (Astros)
19. Jamal Strong, of, San Antonio (Mariners)
20. Gerald Laird, c, Tulsa (Rangers)
    *Since traded to Tigers

HIGH CLASS A

CALIFORNIA LEAGUE
1. Rocco Baldelli, of, Bakersfield (Devil Rays)
2. Oliver Perez, lhp, Lake Elsinore (Padres)
3. Clint Nageotte, rhp, San Bernardino (Mariners)
4. *Jeremy Bonderman, rhp, Modesto (Athletics)
5. Ben Hendrickson, rhp, High Desert (Brewers)
6. Xavier Nady, of, Lake Elsinore (Padres)
7. Boof Bonser, rhp, San Jose (Giants)
8. Jose Lopez, ss, San Bernardino (Mariners)
9. Josh Hamilton, of, Bakersfield (Devil Rays)
10. J.J. Hardy, ss, High Desert (Brewers)
11. Dustin Moseley, rhp, Stockton (Reds)
12. Rich Harden, rhp, Visalia (Athletics)
13. Dave Krynzel, of, High Desert (Brewers)
14. Khalil Greene, ss, Lake Elsinore (Padres)
15. Corey Hart, 3b-1b, High Desert (Brewers)
16. Rich Fischer, rhp, Rancho Cucamonga (Angels)
17. Mark Phillips, lhp, Lake Elsinore (Padres)
18. Bobby Jenks, rhp, Rancho Cucamonga (Angels)
19. Travis Blackley, lhp, San Bernardino (Mariners)
20. Jake Gautreau, 2b, Lake Elsinore (Padres)
    *Since traded to Tigers

CAROLINA LEAGUE

1. Sean Burnett, lhp, Lynchburg (Pirates)
2. Jose Castillo, ss, Lynchburg (Pirates)
3. Adam Wainwright, rhp, Myrtle Beach (Braves)
4. Bubba Nelson, rhp, Myrtle Beach (Braves)
5. Chin-Hui Tsao, rhp, Salem (Rockies)
6. Brad Hawpe, of, Salem (Rockies)
7. Corey Smith, 3b, Kinston (Indians)
8. Dan Haren, rhp, Potomac (Cardinals)
9. Rhett Parrott, rhp, Potomac (Cardinals)
10. Grady Sizemore, of, Kinston (Indians)
11. Fernando Cabrera, rhp, Kinston (Indians)
12. Adam LaRoche, 1b, Myrtle Beach (Braves)
13. Josh Bonifay, 2b/of, Lynchburg (Pirates)
14. Chris Duffy, of, Lynchburg (Pirates)
15. Ryan Church, of, Kinston (Indians)
16. Daniel Curtis, rhp, Myrtle Beach (Braves)
17. Kelly Johnson, ss, Myrtle Beach (Braves)
18. Byron Gettis, of, Wilmington (Royals)
19. Richard Lewis, 2b, Myrtle Beach (Braves)
20. Skip Schumaker, of, Potomac (Cardinals)

FLORIDA STATE LEAGUE

1. Mark Teixeira, 3b, Charlotte (Rangers)
2. Jose Reyes, ss, St. Lucie (Mets)
3. Francisco Rosario, rhp, Dunedin (Blue Jays)
4. Taylor Buchholz, rhp, Clearwater (Phillies)
5. Miguel Cabrera, 3b, Jupiter (Marlins)
6. Laynce Nix, of, Charlotte (Rangers)
7. Alexis Rios, of, Dunedin (Blue Jays)
8. Joel Hanrahan, rhp, Vero Beach (Dodgers)
9. Ben Kozlowski, rhp, Charlotte (Rangers)
10. Reggie Abercrombie, of, Vero Beach (Dodgers)
11. Angel Guzman, rhp, Daytona (Cubs)
12. Andrew Brown, rhp, Vero Beach (Dodgers)
13. Preston Larrison, rhp, Lakeland (Tigers)
14. Rob Henkel, lhp, Jupiter (Marlins)
15. Kelly Shoppach, c, Sarasota (Red Sox)
16. Beau Kemp, rhp, Fort Myers (Twins)
17. Kevin Youkilis, 3b, Sarasota (Red Sox)
18. Ruddy Lugo, rhp, Vero Beach (Dodgers)
19. *Jason Arnold, rhp, Tampa (Yankees)
20. Nook Logan, of, Lakeland (Tigers)
   *Since traded to Athletics

LOW CLASS A

MIDWEST LEAGUE

1. Joe Mauer, c, Quad City (Twins)
2. Jason Stokes, 1b, Kane County (Marlins)
3. Dontrelle Willis, lhp, Kane County (Marlins)
4. *Donald Levinski, rhp, Clinton (Expos)
5. Brad Nelson, 1b, Beloit (Brewers)
6. Casey Kotchman, 1b, Cedar Rapids (Angels)
7. Scott Hairston, 2b, South Bend (White Sox)
8. Shin-Soo Choo, of, Wisconsin (Mariners)
9. Jeff Mathis, c, Cedar Rapids (Angels)
10. Mike Jones, rhp, Beloit (Brewers)
11. J.D. Durbin, rhp, Quad City (Twins)
12. Johan Santana, rhp, Cedar Rapids (Angels)
13. Angel Guzman, rhp, Lansing (Cubs)
14. Dallas McPherson, 3b, Cedar Rapids (Angels)
15. Edwin Encarnacion, 3b, Lansing (Reds)
16. Dan Haren, rhp, Peoria (Cardinals)
17. Shaun Boyd, 2b, Peoria (Cardinals)
18. Justin Pope, rhp, Peoria (Cardinals)
19. Josh Barfield, 2b, Fort Wayne (Padres)
20. Tyler Johnson, lhp, Peoria (Cardinals)
   *Since traded to Marlins

SOUTH ATLANTIC LEAGUE

1. Gavin Floyd, rhp, Lakewood (Phillies)
2. John VanBenschoten, rhp, Hickory (Pirates)
3. Macay McBride, lhp, Macon (Braves)
4. Andy Marte, 3b, Macon (Braves)
5. Francisco Rosario, rhp, Charleston, W.Va. (Blue Jays)
6. Francisco Liriano, lhp, Hagerstown (Giants)
7. Kris Honel, rhp, Kannapolis (White Sox)
8. Francisco Cruceta, rhp, South Georgia (Dodgers)
9. Justin Huber, c, Capital City (Mets)
10. David Wright, 3b, Capital City (Mets)
11. Edwin Jackson, lhp, South Georgia (Dodgers)
12. Carlos Duran, of, Macon (Braves)

Joe Mauer: No. 1 in Midwest League

13. Ryan Hannaman, lhp, Hagerstown (Giants)
14. Scott Thorman, 1b, Macon (Braves)
15. Walter Young, 1b, Hickory (Pirates)
16. Victor Diaz, 3b, South Georgia (Dodgers)
17. Dustin McGowan, rhp, Charleston, W.Va. (Blue Jays)
18. Seung Lee, rhp, Lakewood (Phillies)
19. Travis Foley, rhp, Columbus (Indians)
20. Phil Dumatrait, lhp, Augusta (Red Sox)

SHORT-SEASON CLASS A

NEW YORK-PENN LEAGUE

1. Hanley Ramirez, ss, Lowell (Red Sox)
2. Brandon League, rhp, Auburn (Blue Jays)
3. Mike Hinckley, lhp, Vermont (Expos)
4. Bronson Sardinha, of, Staten Island (Yankees)
5. Russ Adams, ss, Auburn (Blue Jays)
6. Chien-Ming Wang, rhp, Staten Island (Yankees)
7. D.J. Hanson, rhp, Auburn (Blue Jays)
8. Carlos Cabrera, rhp, Batavia (Phillies)
9. Alex Hart, rhp, Williamsport (Pirates)
10. Curtis Granderson, of, Oneonta (Tigers)
11. Robinson Cano, 2b/ss, Staten Island (Yankees)
12. Henry Owens, rhp, Williamsport (Pirates)
13. Darrell Rasner, rhp, Vermont (Expos)
14. Josh Shortslef, lhp, Williamsport (Pirates)
15. Sandy Nin, rhp, Auburn (Blue Jays)
16. Chad Pleiness, rhp, Auburn (Blue Jays)
17. Ben Francisco, of, Mahoning Valley (Indians)
18. Brian Slocum, rhp, Mahoning Valley (Indians)
19. Joey Gomes, of, Hudson Valley (Devil Rays)
20. Roberto Novoa, rhp, Williamsport (Pirates)

NORTHWEST LEAGUE

1. Andy Sisco, lhp, Boise (Cubs)
2. Freddie Lewis, of, Salem-Keizer (Giants)
3. Israel Castro, 2b, Everett (Mariners)
4. Luke Hagerty, lhp, Boise (Cubs)
5. Jae-Kuk Ryu, Boise (Cubs)
6. Ben Fritz, rhp, Vancouver (Athletics)
7. Steve Obenchain, rhp, Vancouver (Athletics)
8. Jerry Gil, ss, Yakima (Diamondbacks)
9. John McCurdy, ss, Vancouver (Athletics)
10. Travis Ishikawa, 1b, Salem-Keizer (Giants)
11. Marland Williams, of, Yakima (Diamondbacks)
12. Kevin Collins, 1b, Boise (Cubs)
13. Dan Ortmeier, of, Salem-Keizer (Giants)
14. Jon Nelson, 1b, Everett (Mariners)
15. Troy Cate, lhp, Everett (Mariners)
16. Ricky Nolasco, rhp, Boise (Cubs)
17. Jared Doyle, lhp, Yakima (Diamondbacks)
18. Brian Stavisky, of, Vancouver (Athletics)
19. Greg Aquino, rhp, Yakima (Diamondbacks)
20. Jason Fransz, of, Boise (Cubs)

ROOKIE ADVANCED

APPALACHIAN LEAGUE

1. Jeff Francoeur, of, Danville (Braves)
2. Wes Bankston, of, Princeton (Devil Rays)
3. Matt Whitney, 3b, Burlington (Indians)

4. Dusty Gomon, 1b, Elizabethton (Twins)
5. Jason Pridie, of, Princeton (Devil Rays)
6. Anthony Lerew, rhp, Danville (Braves)
7. Blake Hawksworth, rhp, Johnson City (Cardinals)
8. Dan Meyer, lhp, Danville (Braves)
9. Scott Tyler, rhp, Elizabethton (Twins)
10. Anthony Webster, of, Bristol (White Sox)
11. Daniel Cabrera, rhp, Bluefield (Orioles)
12. Luis Jiminez, 1b/of, Bluefield (Orioles)
13. Osvaldo Fernandez, ss, Martinsville (Astros)
14. Tommy Arko, c, Bluefield (Orioles)
15. Ricky Barrett, lhp, Elizabethton (Twins)
16. Julian Charles, of, Pulaski (Rangers)
17. Josh Rupe, rhp, Bristol (White Sox)
18. Chris de la Cruz, ss, Burlington (Indians)
19. Pedro Lopez, 2b, Pulaski (Rangers)
20. Chris O'Riordan, 2b, Pulaski (Rangers)

PIONEER LEAGUE

1. James Loney, 1b, Great Falls (Dodgers)
2. Jonathan Figueroa, lhp, Great Falls (Dodgers)
3. Manny Parra, lhp, Ogden (Brewers)
4. Prince Fielder, 1b, Ogden (Brewers)
5. Sergio Santos, ss, Missoula (Diamondbacks)
6. Alberto Callaspo, 2b, Provo (Angels)
7. Joel Guzman, ss, Great Falls (Dodgers)
8. Joe Saunders, lhp, Provo (Angels)
9. Greg Miller, lhp, Great Falls (Dodgers)
10. Dustin Nippert, rhp, Missoula (Diamondbacks)
11. Jonathan Broxton, rhp, Great Falls (Dodgers)
12. Eric Aybar, ss, Provo (Angels)
13. Ching-Lung Lo, rhp, Casper (Rockies)
14. William Bergolla, 2b, Billings (Reds)
15. Mike Nixon, c, Great Falls (Dodgers)
16. Ryan Shealy, 1b, Casper (Rockies)
17. Danny Mateo, ss, Billings (Reds)
18. Ubaldo Jimenez, rhp, Casper (Rockies)
19. Sean Thompson, lhp, Idaho Falls (Padres)
20. Quan Cosby, of, Provo (Angels)

ROOKIE

ARIZONA LEAGUE

1. Felix Pie, of, Cubs
2. Micah Schnurstein, 3b, White Sox
3. Justin Jones, lhp, Cubs
4. Jesse English, lhp, Giants
5. Carlos Sosa, of, Giants
6. Daniel Haigwood, lhp, White Sox
7. Matt Brown, 3b, Angels
8. Travis Ishikawa, 1b, Giants
9. Billy Petrick, rhp, Cubs
10. Ryan Rodriguez, lhp, White Sox
11. Josh Womack, of, Mariners
12. Matt Cain, rhp, Giants
13. Chris Young, of, White Sox
14. Michael Garciaparra, ss, Mariners
15. Matt Creighton, 2b, Cubs
16. Rafael Rodriguez, rhp, Angels
17. Jairo Garcia, rhp, Athletics
18. Steve Moss, of, Brewers
19. Alfredo Francisco, 3b, Cubs
20. Brandon McCarthy, rhp, White Sox

GULF COAST LEAGUE

1. Hanley Ramirez, ss, Red Sox
2. Rudy Guillen, of, Yankees
3. Manuel Mateo, rhp, Braves
4. Leo Nunez, rhp, Pirates
5. Jose Diaz, rhp, Dodgers
6. Elizardo Ramirez, rhp, Phillies
7. Joaquin Arias, 2b, Yankees
8. Alex Romero, of, Twins
9. Luis Hernandez, ss, Braves
10. Brent Clevlen, of, Tigers
11. Javier Guzman, ss, Pirates
12. Victor Prieto, rhp, Marlins
13. Miguel Mota, of, Braves
14. Zach Segovia, rhp, Phillies
15. Joel Zumaya, rhp, Tigers
16. Scott Moore, ss, Tigers
17. Jake Blalock, 3b-of, Phillies
18. Dustin Brown, c-of, Red Sox
19. Zach Duke, lhp, Pirates
20. Brian McCann, c, Braves

TOP 100 PROSPECTS

Through consultation with scouts and player-development people, Baseball America selected its annual list of the game's top 100 minor league prospects in March 2002. The list emphasizes long-range major league potential and considers only players in professional baseball who had not exhausted their major league rookie status entering the 2002 season. The highest level each prospect reached in 2002 is noted.

1.	Josh Beckett, rhp, Marlins	Majors
2.	Mark Prior, rhp, Cubs	Majors
3.	Hank Blalock, 3b, Rangers	Majors
4.	Sean Burroughs, 3b, Padres	Majors
5.	Carlos Pena, 1b, Athletics	Majors
6.	Juan Cruz, rhp, Cubs	Majors
7.	Joe Mauer, c, Twins	A
8.	Wilson Betemit, ss, Braves	Majors
9.	Drew Henson, 3b, Yankees	Majors
10.	Mark Teixeira, 3b, Rangers	AA
11.	Austin Kearns, of, Reds	Majors
12.	Joe Borchard, of, White Sox	Majors
13.	Nick Johnson, 1b, Yankees	Majors
14.	Ryan Anderson, lhp, Mariners	Injured
15.	Angel Berroa, ss, Royals	Majors
16.	Dennis Tankersley, rhp, Padres	Majors
17.	Nick Neugebauer, rhp, Brewers	Majors
18.	Josh Hamilton, of, Devil Rays	A
19.	Jerome Williams, rhp, Giants	AA
20.	Brandon Phillips, ss, Expos	Majors
21.	Justin Morneau, 1b, Twins	AA
22.	Casey Kotchman, 1b, Angels	A
23.	Jon Rauch, rhp, White Sox	Majors
24.	Carlos Hernandez, lhp, Astros	Majors
25.	Ty Howington, lhp, Reds	AA
26.	Marlon Byrd, of, Phillies	Majors
27.	Michael Cuddyer, 3b/of, Twins	Majors
28.	Jake Peavy, rhp, Padres	Majors
29.	Boof Bonser, rhp, Giants	AA
30.	Rafael Soriano, rhp, Mariners	Majors
31.	Adrian Gonzalez, 1b, Marlins	AA
32.	Corwin Malone, lhp, White Sox	AA
33.	Brett Myers, rhp, Phillies	Majors
34.	Jose Reyes, ss, Mets	AA
35.	Kazuhisa Ishii, lhp, Dodgers	Majors
36.	Josh Phelps, c, Blue Jays	Majors
37.	Brandon Claussen, lhp, Yankees	AAA
38.	Miguel Cabrera, ss, Marlins	A
39.	Xavier Nady, 1b, Padres	AAA
40.	Hee Seop Choi, 1b, Cubs	Majors
41.	J.R. House, c, Pirates	AA
42.	Adam Wainwright, rhp, Braves	A
43.	John Buck, c, Astros	AA
44.	Jimmy Journell, rhp, Cardinals	AAA
45.	David Kelton, 3b, Cubs	AA
46.	Chris Snelling, of, Mariners	Majors
47.	Kelly Johnson, ss, Braves	A

Righthander Mark Prior surfaced with the Cubs in 2002 as one of the NL's top rookies

48.	Bobby Hill, 2b, Cubs	Majors
49.	Mario Ramos, lhp, Rangers	AAA
50.	Jimmy Gobble, lhp, Royals	AA
51.	Chris Burke, ss, Astros	AA
52.	Antonio Perez, ss, Mariners	AA
53.	Jason Lane, of, Astros	Majors
54.	Mark Phillips, lhp, Padres	A
55.	Nate Cornejo, rhp, Tigers	Majors
56.	Gavin Floyd, rhp, Phillies	A
57.	Dewon Brazelton, rhp, Devil Rays	Majors
58.	Kurt Ainsworth, rhp, Giants	Majors
59.	Carl Crawford, of, Devil Rays	Majors
60.	Seung Song, rhp, Red Sox	AA
61.	Chin-Hui Tsao, rhp, Rockies	A
62.	Brad Wilkerson, of, Expos	Majors
63.	Mike Restovich, of, Twins	Majors
64.	Chin-Feng Chen, of, Dodgers	Majors
65.	Wily Mo Pena, of, Reds	Majors
66.	Brett Evert, rhp, Braves	AA
67.	Juan Rivera, of, Yankees	Majors
68.	Nic Jackson, of, Cubs	AA
69.	Ricardo Rodriguez, rhp, Dodgers	Majors
70.	Jayson Werth, c, Blue Jays	Majors
71.	Alex Escobar, of, Indians	Injured
72.	Clint Nageotte, rhp, Mariners	A
73.	Corey Smith, 3b, Indians	A
74.	Bobby Jenks, rhp, Angels	AA
75.	Gabe Gross, of, Blue Jays	AA
76.	John-Ford Griffin, of, Yankees	AA
77.	Jake Gautreau, 2b, Padres	A
78.	Aaron Heilman, rhp, Mets	AAA
79.	Kenny Baugh, rhp, Tigers	Injured
80.	Carlos Zambrano, rhp, Cubs	Majors
81.	Orlando Hudson, 2b, Blue Jays	Majors
82.	Colby Lewis, rhp, Rangers	Majors
83.	Tony Torcato, of, Giants	Majors
84.	Mike Jones, rhp, Brewers	A
85.	Adam Johnson, rhp, Twins	AAA
86.	Chris Narveson, lhp, Cardinals	A
87.	Denny Bautista, rhp, Marlins	A
88.	J.D. Martin, rhp, Indians	A

89.	Jon VanBenschoten, rhp, Pirates	A
90.	Erik Bedard, lhp, Orioles	AA
91.	Eric Byrnes, of, Athletics	Majors
92.	Ramon Vazquez, ss, Padres	Majors
93.	Tony Blanco, 3b, Red Sox	A
94.	Joe Crede, 3b, White Sox	Majors
95.	Omar Infante, ss, Tigers	Majors
96.	Matt Belisle, rhp, Braves	AA

Brandon Phillips

97.	Victor Martinez, c, Indians	Majors
98.	Dustin McGowan, rhp, Blue Jays	A
99.	Ryan Dittfurth, rhp, Rangers	AA
100.	Jack Cust, of, Rockies	Majors

Josh Beckett

ANALYSIS BY JOSH BOYD
Player rankings from 2001-02 offseason; Ages as of Oct. 1, 2002

ANAHEIM ANGELS

TOP PROSPECT UPDATE: First baseman Casey Kotchman, the team's first-round draft pick in 2001, was bothered by wrist injuries in his first full season, though he still managed to showcase a pure stroke, advanced plate discipline and Gold Glove-caliber defense.

FADING: It was an impressive year for the Angles Top 10. However, middle infielder Alfredo Amezaga didn't improve upon his impressive 2001 campaign. Now it will be tough

for him to break through with David Eckstein and Adam Kennedy stationed up the middle. Righthander Bobby Jenks took a step back in 2002, going from Double-A to high Class A, but it was more for disciplinary reasons.

EMERGING: Nobody took a bigger step forward in 2002 than righthander Francisco Rodriguez, who became a closer and Angels manager Mike Scioscia's go-to middle reliever in critical situations during the postseason.

TOP 10 PROSPECTS

Player, Pos.	Age	Club (Class)	AVG	AB	R	H	2B	3B	HR	RBI	SB
1. Casey Kotchman, 1b	19	Cedar Rapids (A)	.281	288	42	81	30	1	5	50	2
6. Alfredo Amezaga, ss	24	Anaheim	.538	13	3	7	2	0	0	2	1
		Salt Lake (AAA)	.251	518	77	130	25	7	6	51	23
8. Nathan Haynes, of	23	Salt Lake (AAA)	.283	283	37	80	14	6	2	12	10
		Rancho Cucamonga (A)	.280	50	6	14	0	0	0	2	6
10. Jeff Mathis, c	19	Cedar Rapids (A)	.287	491	75	141	41	3	10	73	7

Player, Pos.	Age	Club (Class)	W	L	ERA	G	SV	IP	H	BB	SO
2. Bobby Jenks, rhp	21	Arkansas (AA)	3	6	4.66	10	0	58	49	44	58
		Rancho Cucamonga (A)	3	5	4.82	11	0	65	50	46	64
3. John Lackey, rhp	23	Anaheim	9	4	3.66	18	0	108	113	33	69
		Salt Lake (AAA)	8	2	2.57	16	0	102	89	28	82
4. Chris Bootcheck, rhp	23	Salt Lake (AAA)	4	3	3.88	9	0	58	64	16	38
		Arkansas (AA)	8	7	4.81	19	0	116	130	35	90
5. Joe Torres, lhp	20	Cedar Rapids (A)	11	8	3.52	25	0	133	125	66	87
7. Francisco Rodriguez, rhp	20	Anaheim	0	0	0.00	5	0	6	3	2	13
		Salt Lake (AAA)	2	3	2.57	27	6	42	30	13	59
		Arkansas (AA)	3	3	1.96	23	9	41	32	15	61
9. Johan Santana, rhp	18	Cedar Rapids (A)	14	8	4.16	27	0	147	133	48	146

Casey Kotchman

STEVE MOORE

ARIZONA DIAMONDBACKS

TOP PROSPECT UPDATE: With outfielder Luis Terrero, it's all about tools. Unfortunately, injuries continue to rob him of the time he needs to refine his raw tools, but he did make slight progress in 2002. Lefthander Mike Gosling and second baseman Scott Hairston had strong seasons, enabling them to jump ahead of Terrero.

FADING: It was just his first season, but 2001 first-rounder Jason Bulger had a disappointing pro debut. A collegiate third baseman originally, Bulger hasn't yet

shown the feel for pitching to go with his arm strength, which may force a move to the bullpen. Catcher Brad Cresse didn't hit with the power that is normally the strength of his game.

EMERGING: Third baseman Chad Tracy flirted with .400 for much of the first half of the season at Double-A El Paso, while righthander John Patterson, who signed for $6.075 million in 1996, finally rediscovered his stuff two years after Tommy John surgery.

Luis Terrero

STEVE MOORE

TOP 10 PROSPECTS

Player, Pos.	Age	Club (Class)	AVG	AB	R	H	2B	3B	HR	RBI	SB
1. Luis Terrero, of	22	El Paso (AA)	.286	360	49	103	20	6	8	54	18
3. Scott Hairston, 2b	22	Lancaster (A)	.405	79	20	32	11	1	6	26	1
		South Bend (A)	.332	394	79	131	35	4	16	72	9
4. Lyle Overbay, 1b	25	Arizona	.100	10	0	1	0	0	0	1	0
		Tucson (AAA)	.343	525	83	180	40	0	19	109	0
6. Jesus Cota, 1b/of	20	Lancaster (A)	.280	540	73	151	33	3	16	101	0
7. Lino Garcia, of	18	South Bend (A)	.185	232	28	43	9	0	4	18	4
		Yakima (A)	.194	62	8	12	2	1	1	6	3
		Missoula (R)	.233	73	15	17	5	0	0	9	4
9. Brad Cresse, c	24	Tucson (AAA)	.270	126	23	34	10	0	2	14	0
		El Paso (AA)	.229	240	25	55	15	0	3	24	1

Player, Pos.	Age	Club (Class)	W	L	ERA	G	SV	IP	H	BB	SO
2. Mike Gosling, lhp	21	El Paso (AA)	14	5	3.13	27	0	167	149	62	115
5. Jose Valverde, rhp	23	Tucson (AAA)	2	4	5.85	49	5	48	45	23	65
8. Jason Bulger, rhp	23	Lancaster (A)	1	1	5.40	2	0	10	11	3	12
		South Bend (A)	4	9	4.94	20	0	95	111	39	84
10. Beltran Perez, rhp	20	El Paso (AA)	3	8	5.47	20	0	97	114	33	77
		Lancaster (A)	3	2	2.51	5	0	32	31	3	30

PROSPECTS

ATLANTA **BRAVES**

TOP PROSPECT UPDATE: Shortstop Wilson Betemit took a step in the wrong direction in 2002. After getting a long look in spring training, he was nicked up and started the season in a terrible slump. His work ethic was also called into question. His tools are still evident, and he spent the year at Triple-A as a 20-year-old.

FADING: Betemit didn't help himself, but his potential is too good for anyone to write him off yet. For the most part, it was an encouraging season for Braves Top 10 pros-

pects, though righthander Brett Evert was demoted after starting the year in Double-A.

EMERGING: The Braves have as many legitimate prospects as any team in the game. Righthander Bubba Nelson continued to show progress at high Class A, displaying command of four pitches to go along with his competitive demeanor. A new wave of prospects surfaced in low Class A, primarily lefthander Macay McBride, 19, and third baseman Andy Marte, 18.

TOP 10 PROSPECTS

Player, Pos.	Age	Club (Class)	AVG	AB	R	H	2B	3B	HR	RBI	SB
1. Wilson Betemit, ss	20	Richmond (AAA)	.245	343	43	84	17	1	8	34	8
3. Kelly Johnson, ss	20	Myrtle Beach (A)	.255	482	62	123	21	5	12	49	12
5. Carlos Duran, of	19	Macon (A)	.270	533	86	144	22	10	7	50	23

Player, Pos.	Age	Club (Class)	W	L	ERA	G	SV	IP	H	BB	SO
2. Adam Wainwright, rhp	21	Myrtle Beach (A)	9	6	3.31	28	0	163	149	66	167
4. Brett Evert, rhp	21	Greenville (AA)	5	8	4.90	16	0	94	94	35	84
		Myrtle Beach (A)	3	5	3.75	10	0	58	53	21	51
6. Matt Belisle, rhp	22	Greenville (AA)	5	9	4.35	26	0	159	162	39	123
7. Zach Miner, rhp	20	Macon (A)	8	9	3.28	29	0	159	143	51	131
8. Gonzalo Lopez, rhp	18	Macon (A)	7	10	3.10	28	0	157	134	51	130
9. Bubba Nelson, rhp	21	Myrtle Beach (A)	11	5	1.72	23	0	136	98	44	105
		GCL Braves (R)	0	0	0.00	3	0	5	1	1	7
10. Jung Bong, lhp	22	Atlanta	0	1	7.50	1	0	6	8	2	4
		Greenville (AA)	7	8	3.25	27	2	122	136	45	107

Wilson Betemit

BALTIMORE **ORIOLES**

TOP PROSPECT UPDATE: Injuries have limited lefthander Rich Stahl to 167 innings in his three full seasons as a pro, including just 10 in 2002. He works in the low 90s when he's right, but his future remains cloudy. Lefthander Erik Bedard's career also is temporarily on hold as he is scheduled to miss the 2003 season with Tommy John surgery.

FADING: Outfielder Keith Reed wasn't protected from the Rule 5 draft after the 2001 season, and nobody took a

chance. He has plenty of athletic ability and untapped power potential still, but hasn't able to put it together for a full season.

EMERGING: Six-foot-6 lefthander Rommie Lewis was labeled as projectable when he was drafted in the fourth round in 2001. His velocity has continued to increase every year since and he notched 25 saves for low Class A Delmarva in 2002.

TOP 10 PROSPECTS

Player, Pos.	Age	Club (Class)	AVG	AB	R	H	2B	3B	HR	RBI	SB
3. Keith Reed, of	23	Bowie (AA)	.246	488	57	120	20	1	15	64	3
5. Ed Rogers, ss	24	Baltimore	.000	3	0	0	0	0	0	0	0
		Bowie (AA)	.261	422	59	110	26	2	11	57	14
7. Tim Raines Jr., of	23	Bowie (AA)	.261	491	66	128	17	4	5	25	33
8. *Willie Harris, 2b	24	White Sox	.233	163	14	38	4	0	2	12	8
		Baltimore	.125	24	3	3	1	0	0	0	0
		Charlotte (AAA)	.283	360	54	102	16	5	5	33	32
10. Bryan Bass, ss	20	Delmarva (A)	.221	457	60	101	20	7	6	59	15

Player, Pos.	Age	Club (Class)	W	L	ERA	G	SV	IP	H	BB	SO
1. Rich Stahl, lhp	21	Delmarva (A)	1	1	5.59	2	0	10	10	5	9
2. Erik Bedard, lhp	23	Bowie (AA)	6	3	1.97	13	0	69	43	30	66
4. Matt Riley, lhp	23	Bowie (AA)	4	10	6.34	22	0	109	136	48	105
6. Sean Douglass, rhp	23	Baltimore	0	5	6.08	15	0	53	58	35	44
		Rochester (AAA)	4	6	4.73	14	0	67	66	35	71
9. John Stephens, rhp	22	Baltimore	2	5	6.09	12	0	65	68	22	56
		Rochester (AAA)	11	5	3.03	21	0	143	126	23	118

*Traded to White Sox

RODGER WOOD

Rich Stahl

BOSTON RED SOX

TOP PROSPECT UPDATE: Righthander Seung Song was traded to the Expos as part of the deal for Cliff Floyd. Song's health was monitored closely throughout the 2002 season by strict pitch counts, but he still threw in the low 90s. His place as the organization's best prospect will be bestowed on Dominican shortstop Hanley Ramirez, 18, named the best prospect in both the Gulf Coast and New York-Penn leagues.

FADING: The 2002 season started with age changes for three of the organization's top 10 prospects—Rene Miniel, Anastacio Martinez and Franklin Francisco—as a result of the crackdown related to the Sept. 11, 2001 terrorist attacks. Francisco was later dealt to the White Sox, while Miniel and Martinez turned in less than inspiring performances.

EMERGING: Third baseman Kevin Youkilis has been an on-base machine since being drafted in the eighth round in 2001. He drew 93 walks against 63 strikeouts and reached Double-A by the end of his first full season.

TOP 10 PROSPECTS

Player, Pos.	Age	Club (Class)	AVG	AB	R	H	2B	3B	HR	RBI	SB
2. Tony Blanco, 3b	20	Sarasota (A)	.221	244	22	54	13	2	6	32	2
6. Freddy Sanchez, ss	24	Boston	.188	16	3	3	0	0	0	2	0
		Pawtucket (AAA)	.301	183	25	55	10	1	4	28	5
		Trenton (AA)	.328	311	60	102	23	1	3	38	19

Player, Pos.	Age	Club (Class)	W	L	ERA	G	SV	IP	H	BB	SO
1. *Seung Song, rhp	22	Harrisburg (AA)	0	0	0.00	1	0	5	5	0	5
		Trenton (AA)	7	7	4.39	21	0	109	106	37	116
3. Rene Miniel, rhp	21	Sarasota (A)	7	10	4.51	26	0	128	125	39	78
4. Manny Delcarmen, rhp	20	Augusta (A)	7	8	4.10	26	0	136	124	56	136
5. Casey Fossum, lhp	24	Boston	5	4	3.46	43	1	107	113	30	101
		Pawtucket (AAA)	0	3	3.96	5	0	25	34	6	28
7. Phil Dumatrait, lhp	21	Sarasota (A)	0	2	3.86	4	0	14	10	15	16
		Augusta (A)	8	5	2.77	22	0	120	109	47	108
8. Josh Thigpen, rhp	20	Augusta (A)	6	6	3.92	25	2	83	76	45	87
9. Anastacio Martinez, rhp	23	Trenton (AA)	5	12	5.31	27	0	139	152	75	127
10. +Franklin Francisco, rhp	23	Trenton (AA)	2	2	5.63	9	0	16	10	16	18
		Winston-Salem (A)	0	4	8.06	6	0	26	31	18	25
		Sarasota (A)	1	5	2.55	16	0	53	33	27	58

*Traded to Montreal   +Traded to White Sox

Seung Song

CHICAGO CUBS

TOP PROSPECT UPDATE: Righthander Mark Prior lived up to the hype and needed only nine minor league starts before joining the Cubs rotation, where he established himself as a future ace.

FADING: Righthanders Ben Christensen and Scott Chiasson saw their 2002 seasons come to an end at the hands of Tommy John surgery. Christensen was already on the comeback trail from shoulder surgery.

EMERGING: Dominican outfielder Felix Pie, 17, showed a full toolbox and won the Rookie-level Arizona League MVP award in his pro debut. Righthander Angel Guzman and 6-foot-9 lefthander Andy Sisco flashed overpowering frontline velocity and could follow the same rapid ascent that carried Juan Cruz and Carlos Zambrano to Wrigley.

TOP 10 PROSPECTS

Player, Pos.	Age	Club (Class)	AVG	AB	R	H	2B	3B	HR	RBI	SB
3. Hee Seop Choi, 1b	23	Cubs	.180	50	6	9	1	0	2	4	0
		Iowa (AAA)	.287	478	94	137	24	3	26	97	3
4. David Kelton, 1b/3b	22	West Tenn (AA)	.261	498	68	130	28	6	20	79	12
5. Bobby Hill, 2b	24	Cubs	.253	190	26	48	7	2	4	20	6
		Iowa (AAA)	.280	354	80	99	23	3	8	39	29
7. Nic Jackson, of	23	West Tenn (AA)	.290	131	18	38	9	1	3	20	8
10. Luis Montanez, ss/2b	20	Daytona (A)	.264	487	69	129	21	5	4	59	14

Player, Pos.	Age	Club (Class)	W	L	ERA	G	SV	IP	H	BB	SO
1. Mark Prior, rhp	22	Cubs	6	6	3.32	19	0	117	98	38	147
		Iowa (AAA)	1	1	1.65	3	0	16	13	8	24
		West Tenn (AA)	4	1	2.60	6	0	35	26	10	55
2. Juan Cruz, rhp	23	Cubs	3	11	3.98	45	1	97	84	59	81
6. Carlos Zambrano, rhp	21	Cubs	4	8	3.66	32	0	108	94	63	93
		Iowa (AAA)	0	0	0.00	3	0	9	2	6	11
8. Ben Christensen, rhp	24	West Tenn (AA)	2	6	6.33	12	0	64	73	35	36
9. Scott Chiasson, rhp	25	Iowa (AAA)	1	4	7.94	27	7	28	34	13	26
		West Tenn (AA)	0	0	3.00	3	0	3	5	1	5

Mark Prior

PROSPECTS

CHICAGO **WHITE SOX**

TOP PROSPECT UPDATE: After suffering a foot injury in spring training 2002, Joe Borhcard got off to a slow start. But he finished the season in Chicago and provided a glimpse of his outstanding power potential by homering in his first trip to the plate.

FADING: Following the 2001 season, the White Sox thought lefty Dennis Ulacia had a chance to develop into the Mark Buehrle mold, but he lacked the consistency and command. Righthander Jon Rauch, Baseball America's 2000 Minor League Player of the Year, bounced back slowly from shoulder problems, which sidelined him most of 2001.

EMERGING: Coming off a solid 2001 debut, outfielder Anthony Webster had to prove himself again in Rookie-ball in 2002. The 15th-rounder turned in another impressive campaign, hitting .352-1-30 with 16 steals for Appy League champion Bristol.

TOP 10 PROSPECTS

Player, Pos.	Age	Club (Class)	AVG	AB	R	H	2B	3B	HR	RBI	SB
1. Joe Borchard, of	23	White Sox	.222	36	5	8	0	0	2	5	0
		Charlotte (AAA)	.272	438	62	119	35	2	20	59	2
		Winston-Salem (A)	.000	3	1	0	0	0	0	0	0
5. Joe Crede, 3b	24	White Sox	.285	200	28	57	10	0	12	35	0
		Charlotte (AAA)	.312	359	57	112	21	0	24	65	0
6. Tim Hummel, ss/2b	23	Charlotte (AAA)	.260	523	55	136	33	0	4	41	6
8. Miguel Olivo, c	24	White Sox	.211	19	2	4	1	0	1	5	0
		Birmingham (AA)	.306	359	51	110	24	10	6	49	29
10. Aaron Rowand, of	25	White Sox	.258	302	41	78	16	2	7	29	0

Player, Pos.	Age	Club (Class)	W	L	ERA	G	SV	IP	H	BB	SO
2. Jon Rauch, rhp	22	White Sox	2	1	6.59	8	0	29	28	14	19
		Charlotte (AAA)	7	8	4.28	19	0	109	91	42	97
3. Corwin Malone, lhp	22	Birmingham (AA)	10	7	4.71	22	0	124	116	89	89
4. *Matt Guerrier, rhp	24	Nashville (AAA)	7	12	4.59	27	0	157	154	47	130
7. Kris Honel, rhp	19	Winston-Salem (A)	0	0	1.69	1	0	5	3	3	8
		Kannapolis (A)	9	8	2.82	26	0	153	128	52	152
9. Dennis Ulacia, lhp	21	Birmingham (AA)	6	14	4.82	28	1	146	173	51	88

*Traded to Pittsburgh

Joe Borchard

CINCINNATI **REDS**

TOP PROSPECT UPDATE: Outfielder Austin Kearns found his way into a crowded Reds outfield, and before a hamstring injury prematurely ended his 2002 rookie season he established himself as a more consistent performer than Adam Dunn or Ken Griffey Jr.

FADING: Catcher Dane Sardinha followed up his .235-9-55 effort in 2001 with another disappointing season. His defense remains light years ahead of his bat. Middle infielder Gookie Dawkins has also been slow to claim a big league job, four years after his major league debut.

EMERGING: Righthander Bobby Basham posted an amazing 9-97 walk-strikeout ratio at Class A Dayton. The 22-year-old then fanned 13 to help Class A Stockton win the California League championship. He throws in the low-90s with a sharp slider and changeup. Third baseman Edwin Encarnacion, 19, solidified his prospect status with a .282-17-73 and 25-steal season in low Class A.

TOP 10 PROSPECTS

Player, Pos.	Age	Club (Class)	AVG	AB	R	H	2B	3B	HR	RBI	SB
1. Austin Kearns, of	22	Cincinnati	.315	372	66	117	24	3	13	56	6
		Louisville (AAA)	.750	4	3	3	2	0	0	2	0
		Chattanooga (AA)	.268	41	10	11	2	0	5	13	1
3. Wily Mo Pena, of	20	Cincinnati	.222	18	1	4	0	0	1	1	0
		Chattanooga (AA)	.255	388	47	99	23	1	11	47	8
6. *Ben Broussard, of	26	Cleveland	.241	112	10	27	4	0	4	9	0
		Buffalo (AAA)	.242	153	30	37	8	0	5	21	0
		Louisville (AAA)	.273	187	31	51	14	1	11	30	4
7. +David Espinosa, 2b	20	Stockton (A)	.245	367	71	90	13	7	7	44	26
8. Gookie Dawkins, ss/2b	23	Cincinnati	.125	48	2	6	2	0	0	0	2
		Louisville (AAA)	.251	167	14	42	5	2	0	8	2
		Chattanooga (AA)	.271	155	21	42	10	1	1	12	5
9. Dane Sardinha, c	23	Chattanooga (AA)	.206	394	34	81	20	0	4	40	0
10. Ranier Olmedo, ss	21	Chattanooga (AA)	.247	478	62	118	21	1	3	30	15

Player, Pos.	Age	Club (Class)	W	L	ERA	G	SV	IP	H	BB	SO
2. Ty Howington, lhp	21	Chattanooga (AA)	1	5	5.12	15	0	65	65	33	51
		Stockton (A)	1	1	3.09	2	0	12	7	4	9
4. Ricardo Aramboles, rhp	20	Chattanooga (AA)	1	0	3.13	4	0	23	22	8	22
5. Dustin Moseley, rhp	20	Chattanooga (AA)	5	6	4.13	13	0	81	91	37	52
		Stockton (A)	6	3	2.74	14	0	89	60	21	80

*Traded to Cleveland   +Traded to Detroit

Austin Kearns

CLEVELAND **INDIANS**

TOP PROSPECT UPDATE: Third baseman Corey Smith's stock suffered slightly after a torrid 2002 start. Pitchers were able to exploit holes in the 20-year-old's swing, while he didn't show the ability to make in-season adjustments. Cleveland was considering moving him to left field. He'll have a tough time fending off middle infielder Brandon Phillips, one of many top prospects acquired by the rebuilding Indians in 2002.

FADING: Outfielder Alex Escobar missed the entire 2002 season after blowing out his knee in spring training. It was the second season in four years that Escobar has missed due to injury, but the Indians were still counting on him to compete for the center field job with Milton Bradley in 2003.

EMERGING: Righthander Jason Davis started 2002 in Class A Kinston, and after a promotion to Akron, he finished the year in the Tribe's rotation where he posted a 1-0, 1.84 mark in three appearances. Righthander Travis Foley upstaged Dan Denham and J.D. Martin in a prospect-laden rotation at Class A Columbus.

TOP 10 PROSPECTS

Player, Pos.	Age	Club (Class)	AVG	AB	R	H	2B	3B	HR	RBI	SB
1. Corey Smith, 3b	20	Kinston (A)	.255	505	71	129	29	2	13	67	7
2. Alex Escobar, of	23	(Injured—Did not play)									
6. Victor Martinez, c	23	Cleveland	.281	32	2	9	1	0	1	5	0
		Akron (AA)	.336	443	84	149	40	0	22	85	3

Player, Pos.	Age	Club (Class)	W	L	ERA	G	SV	IP	H	BB	SO
3. Ryan Drese, rhp	26	Cleveland	10	9	6.55	26	0	137	176	62	102
		Buffalo (AAA)	1	0	1.64	3	0	22	16	4	16
4. Dan Denham, rhp	19	Columbus (A)	9	8	4.76	28	0	125	123	65	109
5. J.D. Martin, rhp	19	Columbus (A)	14	5	3.90	27	0	138	141	46	131
7. David Riske, rhp	25	Cleveland	2	2	5.26	51	1	51	49	35	65
		Buffalo (AAA)	0	1	3.72	9	3	10	6	4	17
		Akron (AA)	0	0	3.00	4	0	6	5	1	10
8. Brian Tallet, lhp	25	Cleveland	1	0	1.50	2	0	12	9	4	5
		Buffalo (AAA)	2	3	3.07	8	0	44	47	16	25
		Akron (AA)	10	1	3.08	18	0	102	93	32	73
9. Billy Traber, lhp	23	Buffalo (AAA)	4	3	3.29	9	0	55	58	12	33
		Akron (AA)	13	2	2.76	18	0	108	99	20	82
10. Alex Herrera, lhp	25	Cleveland	0	0	0.00	5	0	5	3	1	5
		Buffalo (AAA)	0	1	11.57	5	0	7	10	8	5
		Akron (AA)	0	2	3.38	30	5	61	47	30	65

Corey Smith

HAROLD WEST

COLORADO **ROCKIES**

TOP PROSPECT UPDATE: It was the second year in the rehab process for Taiwanese righthander Chin-Hui Tsao and by the second half of the 2002 season, he had regained much of his mid-90s velocity and the abrupt break on his slider.

FADING: Righthander Ryan Kibler led the organization with 14 wins and a 2.15 ERA in 2001, but his command escaped him in 2002 and he's likely to repeat Double-A.

EMERGING: Rated the organization's 27th-best prospect prior to the 2002 season, first baseman/outfielder Brad Hawpe tore up the Class A Carolina League. He made a run at the triple crown before finishing third in home runs (22) and second in RBIs (97), while leading in batting (.347). Ching-Lung Lo was the youngest player in the minors in 2002, pitching all season at age 16.

TOP 10 PROSPECTS

Player, Pos.	Age	Club (Class)	AVG	AB	R	H	2B	3B	HR	RBI	SB
3. Garrett Atkins, 3b	22	Carolina (AA)	.271	510	71	138	27	3	12	61	6
6. Jack Cust, of	23	Colorado	.169	65	8	11	2	0	1	8	0
		Colorado Springs (AAA)	.265	359	74	95	24	0	23	55	6
7. Rene Reyes, 1b	24	Carolina (AA)	.292	455	64	133	33	4	14	54	10
10. Jayson Nix, 2b	20	Asheville (A)	.246	487	73	120	29	2	14	79	14

Player, Pos.	Age	Club (Class)	W	L	ERA	G	SV	IP	H	BB	SO
1. Chin-Hui Tsao, rhp	21	Salem (A)	4	2	2.09	9	0	47	34	12	45
		Tri-City (A)	0	0	0.00	3	0	11	6	2	16
2. Aaron Cook, rhp	23	Colorado	2	1	4.54	9	0	36	41	13	14
		Colorado Springs (AAA)	4	4	3.78	10	0	64	67	18	32
		Carolina (AA)	7	2	1.42	14	0	95	73	19	58
4. Ryan Kibler, rhp	22	Carolina (AA)	7	8	4.91	25	0	143	158	64	59
5. Jason Young, rhp	23	Colorado Springs (AAA)	6	5	4.97	13	0	80	87	38	74
		Carolina (AA)	7	4	2.64	14	0	89	71	30	76
8. Jason Jennings, rhp	24	Colorado	16	8	4.52	32	0	185	201	70	127
9. Ching-Lung Lo, rhp	17	Casper (R)	2	4	3.20	14	0	45	44	22	21

HAROLD WEST

Chin-Hui Tsao

PROSPECTS

DETROIT **TIGERS**

TOP PROSPECT UPDATE: In 19 big league starts, righthander Nate Cornejo is 5-9, 6.12. Though he has been compared to the Dodgers' Kevin Brown because of the heavy movement on his fastball, Cornejo is not overpowering and hasn't been able to find a way to miss bats in the majors.

FADING: Injuries have forced righthander Kenny Baugh, Detroit's first-round pick in 2001, to the sideline for most of his time as a pro. He never pitched in 2002 as shoulder surgery shelved Baugh in spring training.

EMERGING: Righthanded closer Franklyn German, who was acquired from Oakland in a mid-season trade, saved 30 games at three levels in 2002, while striking out 96 in 71 innings. It took just more than two years righthander for Jeremy Johnson to go from high school to Double-A. He compiled 25-6 record along the way, while displaying an advanced feel for pitching as a 20-year-old.

TOP 10 PROSPECTS

Player, Pos.	Age	Club (Class)	AVG	AB	R	H	2B	3B	HR	RBI	SB
2. Omar Infante, ss	20	Detroit	.333	72	4	24	3	0	1	6	0
		Toledo (AAA)	.268	436	49	117	16	8	4	51	19
3. Eric Munson, 1b	24	Detroit	.186	59	3	11	0	0	2	5	0
		Toledo (AAA)	.262	477	77	125	30	4	24	84	1
5. Ramon Santiago, ss	23	Detroit	.243	222	33	54	5	5	4	20	8
		Toledo (AAA)	.429	28	8	12	1	0	2	6	0
		Erie (AA)	.280	75	9	21	0	2	1	7	6
6. Andres Torres, of	24	Detroit	.200	70	7	14	1	1	0	3	2
		Toledo (AAA)	.266	462	80	123	17	8	4	42	42
7. Nook Logan, of	22	Lakeland (A)	.269	506	75	136	14	7	2	26	55
9. Cody Ross, of	21	Erie (AA)	.280	400	73	112	28	3	19	72	16
10. Jack Hannahan, 3b	22	Erie (AA)	.239	226	17	54	12	1	3	20	2
		Lakeland (A)	.272	246	28	67	11	1	6	42	9

Player, Pos.	Age	Club (Class)	W	L	ERA	G	SV	IP	H	BB	SO
1. Nate Cornejo, rhp	23	Detroit	1	5	5.04	9	0	50	63	18	23
		Toledo (AAA)	9	8	4.42	21	0	132	163	31	86
4. Kenny Baugh, rhp	23	(Injured—Did not play)									
8. Andy Van Hekken, lhp	23	Detroit	1	3	3.00	5	0	30	38	6	5
		Toledo (AAA)	5	0	1.82	7	0	49	41	11	19
		Erie (AA)	4	7	3.83	21	0	134	138	34	97

Nate Cornejo

FLORIDA **MARLINS**

TOP PROSPECT UPDATE: Righthander Josh Beckett headed into 2002 as a favorite for Rookie of the Year, but recurring blisters hampered the hard-throwing phenom throughout the season.

FADING: Righthander Denny Bautista didn't arrive until after spring training after encountering problems with his visa in the Dominican Republic. He didn't regain his 2001 form until the near the end of the 2002 season, when his velocity was back into the mid-90s.

EMERGING: First baseman Jason Stokes was healthy long enough to establish himself as one of the top power prospects in the game. He hit .341-27-75 for low Class A Kane County in just 97 games before his season ended with a wrist injury. Lefthander Dontrelle Willis also made a strong impression with his command and location at Kane County, going 10-2, 1.83, before being promoted to high Class A Jupiter.

TOP 10 PROSPECTS

Player, Pos.	Age	Club (Class)	AVG	AB	R	H	2B	3B	HR	RBI	SB
2. Miguel Cabrera, 3b	19	Jupiter (A)	.274	489	77	134	43	1	9	75	10
4. Adrian Gonzalez, 1b	20	Portland (AA)	.266	508	70	135	34	1	17	96	6
6. Abraham Nunez, of	25	Florida	.118	17	2	2	0	0	0	1	0
		Calgary (AAA)	.250	428	68	107	24	5	21	60	31
9. Josh Wilson, ss	21	Portland (AA)	.341	41	5	14	3	0	2	5	0
		Jupiter (A)	.256	398	51	102	17	1	11	50	7

Player, Pos.	Age	Club (Class)	W	L	ERA	G	SV	IP	H	BB	SO
1. Josh Beckett, rhp	22	Florida	6	6	4.10	23	0	108	93	44	113
3. Denny Bautista, rhp	19	Jupiter (A)	4	6	4.99	19	0	88	80	40	79
5. Allen Baxter, rhp	19	Kane County (A)	0	2	3.06	4	0	18	19	8	15
7. *Claudio Vargas, rhp	23	Calgary (AAA)	4	11	6.72	17	0	76	88	35	61
		Harrisburg (AA)	2	4	4.64	8	0	33	38	9	34
8. Blaine Neal, rhp	24	Florida	3	0	2.73	32	0	33	32	14	33
		Calgary (AAA)	3	1	2.90	29	11	31	27	15	26
10. Rob Henkel, lhp	24	Portland (AA)	5	4	3.86	13	0	70	54	27	68
		Jupiter (A)	8	3	2.51	14	0	75	55	22	82

*Traded to Montreal

CLIFF WELCH

Josh Beckett

PROSPECTS

HOUSTON ASTROS

TOP PROSPECT UPDATE: Lefthander Carlos Hernandez returned sooner than expected from the shoulder injury that ended his 2001 season and joined the rotation from the outset of 2002. While he was inconsistent and bothered by nagging injuries, he showed flashes of his nasty stuff though he needs to be more efficient with his pitches.

FADING: Morgan Ensberg won the big league third base job out of spring training, but after hitting 51 home runs

between 2000-2001, he lost his job by the end of May and returned for a second season at Triple-A New Orleans.

EMERGING: Righthander Kirk Saarloos moved into the Double-A rotation in 2002 after spending his first summer in the bullpen and then joined Hernandez in the Astros rotation at midseason, becoming the second player from the Draft Class of '01 to reach the big leagues. Saarloos went 10-1, 1.40 and picked up the Texas League's pitcher of the year honors.

TOP 10 PROSPECTS

Player, Pos.	Age	Club (Class)	AVG	AB	R	H	2B	3B	HR	RBI	SB
2. John Buck, c	22	Round Rock (AA)	.263	448	48	118	29	3	12	89	2
3. Chris Burke, ss/2b	22	Round Rock (AA)	.264	481	66	127	19	8	3	37	16
4. Jason Lane, of	25	Houston	.290	69	12	20	3	1	4	10	1
		New Orleans (AAA)	.272	426	65	116	36	2	15	83	13
7. Morgan Ensberg, 3b	27	Houston	.242	132	14	32	7	2	3	19	2
		New Orleans (AAA)	.288	292	50	84	12	3	7	37	9
10. Tommy Whiteman, ss	23	Round Rock (AA)	.179	56	3	10	2	1	0	5	1
		Lexington (A)	.303	350	50	106	29	2	10	49	6

Player, Pos.	Age	Club (Class)	W	L	ERA	G	SV	IP	H	BB	SO
1. Carlos Hernandez, lhp	22	Houston	7	5	4.38	23	0	111	112	61	93
		New Orleans (AAA)	0	0	0.00	1	0	3	1	1	2
		Round Rock (AA)	0	0	4.15	2	0	9	4	4	10
5. Brad Lidge, rhp	25	Houston	1	0	6.23	6	0	9	12	9	12
		New Orleans (AAA)	5	5	3.39	24	0	112	83	47	110
		Round Rock (AA)	1	1	2.45	5	0	11	9	3	18
6. Anthony Pluta, rhp	19	Michigan (A)	11	13	5.92	28	0	143	155	83	120
8. Rodrigo Rosario, rhp	22	Round Rock (AA)	11	6	3.11	26	0	130	106	59	94
9. Chad Qualls, rhp	24	Round Rock (AA)	6	13	4.36	29	0	163	174	67	142

Carlos Hernandez

KANSAS CITY ROYALS

TOP PROSPECT UPDATE: It was a very disappointing 2002 season for shortstop Angel Berroa, who aged from 22 to 24 before the season. His performance was affected by a knee injury, which limited him to 77 games. On top of that, one of the players the Royals traded for Berroa—Mark Ellis— spurred the A's to the American League West title.

FADING: Outfielder Roscoe Crosby has been unable to get his baseball career off the ground since the Royals signed the 2001 second-rounder for $1.75 million. Crosby also

plays wide receiver for the Clemson football team, had Tommy John surgery in June and missed the 2000 college season.

EMERGING: Righthander Runelvys Hernandez blossomed into the system's top pitching prospect in 2002 and needed just a half season between high Class A Wilmington and Double-A Wichita before settling into the Royals rotation. He showed impressive command of three pitches, including a low-90s fastball and hard breaking ball.

Angel Berroa

TOP 10 PROSPECTS

Player, Pos.	Age	Club (Class)	AVG	AB	R	H	2B	3B	HR	RBI	SB
1. Angel Berroa, ss	24	Kansas City	.227	75	8	17	7	1	0	5	3
		Omaha (AAA)	.215	297	37	64	11	4	8	35	6
5. Roscoe Crosby, of	19	(Injured—Did not play)									
7. Ken Harvey, 1b	24	Omaha (AAA)	.277	488	75	135	30	1	20	75	8
9. Mike Tonis, c	23	GCL Royals (R)	.176	17	2	3	0	0	1	3	0

Player, Pos.	Age	Club (Class)	W	L	ERA	G	SV	IP	H	BB	SO
2. Jimmy Gobble, lhp	21	Wichita (AA)	5	7	3.38	13	0	69	71	19	52
3. Colt Griffin, rhp	20	Wilmington (A)	0	1	3.86	3	0	5	3	5	3
		Burlington (A)	6	6	5.36	19	0	91	75	82	66
4. Mike MacDougal, rhp	25	Kansas City	0	1	5.00	6	0	9	5	7	10
		Omaha (AAA)	3	5	5.60	12	0	53	52	55	30
		Wichita (AA)	1	1	3.06	4	0	18	11	24	14
		Wilmington (A)	0	1	1.08	5	2	8	3	5	10
		GCL Royals (R)	0	0	3.00	1	0	3	3	0	3
6. Miguel Asencio, rhp	22	Kansas City	4	7	5.11	31	0	123	136	64	58
8. Kyle Snyder, rhp	25	Wichita (AA)	2	2	4.21	6	0	26	21	7	18
		Wilmington (A)	0	2	2.98	15	0	48	49	11	48
10. Brad Voyles, rhp	25	Kansas City	0	2	6.51	22	1	28	31	18	26
		Omaha (AAA)	3	4	4.18	26	5	32	29	22	34

PROSPECTS

LOS ANGELES **DODGERS**

TOP PROSPECT UPDATE: The Dodgers sent righthander Ricardo Rodriguez to the Indians along with righty Francisco Cruceta at the 2002 trade deadline for veteran reliever Paul Shuey.

FADING: Hong-Chih Kuo has been lights-out when he's on the mound. Unfortunately, he's been out more often than he's taken the mound. The flame-throwing Taiwanese lefty has accumulated 36 innings since signing for $1.25 million in 1999.

EMERGING: The Dodgers are full of emerging prospects such as Venezuelan lefthander Jonathan Figueroa and righthander Edwin Jackson, who pitched effectively at low Class A South Georgia in their first full seasons. Center fielder Reggie Abercrombie made major strides in 2002, displaying outstanding athletic ability and a rare power-speed combo for Vero Beach. He hit .276-10-56 with 41 steals.

TOP 10 PROSPECTS

Player, Pos.	Age	Club (Class)	AVG	AB	R	H	2B	3B	HR	RBI	SB
2. Chin-Feng Chen, 1b	24	Los Angeles	.000	5	1	0	0	0	0	0	0
		Las Vegas (AAA)	.284	511	90	145	26	4	26	84	1
3. Joel Guzman, ss	17	Great Falls (R)	.252	151	19	38	8	2	3	27	5
		GCL Dodgers (R)	.212	33	4	7	2	0	0	2	1
5. Joe Thurston, 2b	23	Los Angeles	.462	13	1	6	1	0	0	1	0
		Las Vegas (AAA)	.334	587	106	196	39	13	12	55	22
7. Willy Aybar, 3b	19	Vero Beach (A)	.215	372	56	80	18	2	11	65	15
10. *Jorge Nunez, ss	27	Vero Beach (A)	.291	282	42	82	9	4	0	20	27

Player, Pos.	Age	Club (Class)	W	L	ERA	G	SV	IP	H	BB	SO
1. #Ricardo Rodriguez, rhp	22	Cleveland	2	2	5.66	7	0	41	40	18	24
		Buffalo (AAA)	3	1	3.60	4	0	25	26	7	14
		Las Vegas (AAA)	1	0	3.86	2	0	12	13	5	7
		Jacksonville (AA)	5	4	1.99	11	0	68	56	13	44
4. +Ben Diggins, rhp	23	Milwaukee	0	4	8.63	5	0	24	28	18	15
		Huntsville (AA)	2	1	1.91	7	0	38	26	15	34
		Vero Beach (A)	6	10	3.63	20	0	114	103	41	101
6. Hong-Chih Kuo, lhp	21	Vero Beach (A)	0	1	6.75	4	0	8	11	2	8
		GCL Dodgers (R)	0	0	4.50	3	0	6	4	1	9
8. Jose Rojas, rhp	20	Jacksonville (AA)	3	4	4.83	10	0	54	56	30	40
9. Joel Hanrahan, rhp	20	Jacksonville (AA)	1	1	10.64	3	0	11	15	7	10
		Vero Beach (A)	10	6	4.20	25	0	144	129	51	139

*Traded to Montreal   +Traded to Milwaukee   #Traded to Cleveland

Ricardo Rodriguez

MILWAUKEE **BREWERS**

TOP PROSPECT UPDATE: Righthander Nick Neugebauer went on the disabled list after his second big league start in September 2001, and wasn't able to shake the injury bug in 2002.

FADING: The Brewers rushed shortstop Bill Hall to Triple-A after just 41 games at Double-A and he suffered through his worst season in 2002. He made a trip to the Futures Game and was a September callup, but it is unlikely he'll be able to fill Jose Hernandez' shoes in the short term if the incumbent shortstop leaves via free agency. Righthander J.M. Gold, the team's first-round pick in 1998, continues to rebound slowly from injuries. He still hasn't advanced past Class A in five seasons.

EMERGING: Third baseman Corey Hart and first baseman Brad Nelson were two of the minors' most dangerous power hitters in 2002. Ranked as the 15th and 16th prospects in the system before the season, Hart blasted 25 home runs and Nelson led the minors with 116 RBIs.

Nick Neugebauer

TOP 10 PROSPECTS

Player, Pos.	Age	Club (Class)	AVG	AB	R	H	2B	3B	HR	RBI	SB
2. Bill Hall, ss	22	Milwaukee	.194	36	3	7	1	1	1	5	0
		Indianapolis (AAA)	.228	465	35	106	20	1	4	31	17
3. David Krynzel, of	21	Huntsville (AA)	.240	129	13	31	2	3	2	13	13
		High Desert (A)	.268	365	76	98	13	12	11	45	29
5. Cristian Guerrero, of	22	Huntsville (AA)	.223	394	47	88	17	1	8	48	21
7. J.J Hardy, ss	20	Huntsville (AA)	.228	145	14	33	7	0	1	13	1
		High Desert (A)	.293	335	53	98	19	1	6	48	9

Player, Pos.	Age	Club (Class)	W	L	ERA	G	SV	IP	H	BB	SO
1. Nick Neugebauer, rhp	22	Milwaukee	1	7	4.72	12	0	55	56	44	47
		Indianapolis (AAA)	0	3	5.12	5	0	19	20	12	18
4. Mike Jones, rhp	19	Beloit (A)	7	7	3.12	27	0	139	135	62	132
6. Ben Hendrickson, rhp	21	Huntsville (AA)	4	2	2.97	13	0	70	57	33	50
		High Desert (A)	5	5	2.55	14	0	81	61	41	70
8. Jose Mieses, rhp	24	(Injured—Did not pitch)									
9. J.M. Gold, rhp	22	High Desert (A)	1	3	7.63	7	0	31	33	22	33
10. Matt Childers, rhp	23	Milwaukee	0	0	12.00	8	0	9	13	8	6
		Indianapolis (AAA)	0	0	0.00	2	0	4	1	2	4
		Huntsville (AA)	2	5	4.50	35	12	82	103	27	57

PROSPECTS

MINNESOTA TWINS

TOP PROSPECT UPDATE: The first-overall pick in the 2001 draft, Joe Mauer displayed one of the purest strokes in the minors in his first full season. A gifted athlete, Mauer also showcased a strong arm and good actions behind the plate. Scouts expect his power to develop as he turns on balls.

FADING: Righthander Adam Johnson's 2002 season got off to a rocky start when the righthander received negative press for his tirade after he didn't make the big league roster in spring training. Expected to compete for a spot on the Twins staff, he was torched in Triple-A for a .304 batting average.

EMERGING: Righthander J.D. Durbin went 13-4, 3.19 in his first completely healthy season since being drafted in the second round in 2000. The 20-year-old throws in the low-90s with a sharp slider. First baseman Dusty Gomon began to showcase some of the best power potential in the minors by hitting 14 homers at Rookie-level Elizabethton.

TOP 10 PROSPECTS

Player, Pos.	Age	Club (Class)	AVG	AB	R	H	2B	3B	HR	RBI	SB
1. Joe Mauer, c	19	Quad City (A)	.302	411	58	124	23	1	4	62	0
2. Justin Morneau, 1b	21	New Britain (AA)	.298	494	72	147	31	4	16	80	7
3. Michael Cuddyer, of	23	Minnesota	.259	112	12	29	7	0	4	13	2
		Edmonton (AAA)	.309	330	70	102	16	9	20	53	12
4. Michael Restovich, of	23	Minnesota	.308	13	3	4	0	0	1	1	1
		Edmonton (AAA)	.286	518	95	148	32	7	29	98	11
8. Rob Bowen, c	21	Fort Myers (A)	.184	342	52	63	12	1	10	49	1
		Quad City (A)	.190	21	1	4	1	0	0	0	0

Player, Pos.	Age	Club (Class)	W	L	ERA	G	SV	IP	H	BB	SO
5. Adam Johnson, rhp	23	Edmonton (AAA)	13	8	5.47	27	0	151	182	55	112
6. Brad Thomas, lhp	24	Edmonton (AAA)	6	12	5.74	28	0	152	175	54	97
7. Juan Rincon, rhp	23	Minnesota	0	2	6.28	10	0	29	44	9	21
		Edmonton (AAA)	7	4	4.78	19	0	102	111	35	75
9. Matt Kinney, rhp	25	Minnesota	2	7	4.64	14	0	66	78	33	45
		Edmonton (AAA)	2	1	8.89	5	0	27	42	4	21
10. Sandy Tejada, rhp	20	Quad City (A)	9	4	2.76	14	0	91	70	23	78

Joe Mauer

JOHN SPEAR

MONTREAL EXPOS

TOP PROSPECT UPDATE: Following a stellar first half in 2002, middle infielder Brandon Phillips was sent to the Indians as part of a prospect package which included outfielder Grady Sizemore and lefthander Cliff Lee for Bartolo Colon.

FADING: Righthander Donnie Bridges was rated the organization's top prospect after his breakthrough 2000 season, but two years later his stock has spiraled downward. After being dealt to the Marlins in 2002, he was released. Besides, Bridges two other Expos top pitching prospects were traded to Florida during the season. Also making their way to the Marlins were righthander Don Levinski and righthander Justin Wayne.

EMERGING: Lefthander Mike Hinckley led the short-season New York-Penn League with a 1.37 ERA. He has good command of a polished three-pitch arsenal, including a low-90s sinking fastball. Righthander Seung Song, Boston's No. 1 prospect entering the '02 season, was also added to the organization by way of a trade between the Red Sox and Expos.

TOP 10 PROSPECTS

Player, Pos.	Age	Club (Class)	AVG	AB	R	H	2B	3B	HR	RBI	SB
1. *Brandon Phillips, ss	21	Cleveland	.258	31	5	8	3	1	0	4	0
		Buffalo (AAA)	.283	223	30	63	14	0	8	27	8
		Ottawa (AAA)	.257	35	1	9	4	0	1	5	0
		Harrisburg (AA)	.327	245	40	80	13	2	9	35	6
2. Brad Wilkerson, of	25	Montreal	.266	507	92	135	27	8	20	59	7
3. *Grady Sizemore, of	20	Kinston (A)	.343	172	31	59	9	3	3	20	14
		Brevard County (A)	.258	256	37	66	15	4	0	26	9

Player, Pos.	Age	Club (Class)	W	L	ERA	G	SV	IP	H	BB	SO
4. +Donnie Bridges, rhp	23	Portland (AA)	0	4	13.21	6	0	16	29	18	6
		Harrisburg (AA)	4	4	6.14	14	0	63	63	42	49
5. Josh Karp, rhp	22	Harrisburg (AA)	7	5	3.84	16	0	87	83	34	69
		Brevard County (A)	4	1	1.59	7	0	45	31	11	43
6. +Justin Wayne, rhp	23	Florida	2	3	5.32	5	0	24	22	13	16
		Calgary (AAA)	0	1	6.35	2	0	11	8	6	10
		Portland (AA)	3	3	4.85	7	0	43	43	13	30
		Harrisburg (AA)	5	2	2.37	17	0	99	74	32	47
7. Rich Rundles, lhp	21	Brevard County (A)	2	7	4.08	12	0	57	66	16	31
8. Zach Day, rhp	24	Montreal	4	1	3.62	19	1	37	28	15	25
		Ottawa (AAA)	5	6	3.50	17	0	90	77	32	68
9. Luke Lockwood, lhp	21	Brevard County (A)	10	7	3.37	26	0	147	155	38	86
10. Eric Good, lhp	22	(Injured—Did not pitch)									

*Traded to Cleveland   +Traded to Florida

Brandon Phillips

PROSPECTS

NEW YORK METS

TOP PROSPECT UPDATE: Righthander Aaron Heilman pitched his way into contention for a 2003 rotation spot by dealing in the upper levels of the system. The Mets 2001 first-rounder displays an excellent feel for four pitches with above-average command. For all his progress in 2002, Heilman will be hard pressed to keep his place as top prospect in the Mets system as shortstop Jose Reyes enjoyed an outstanding season and lefthander Scott Kazmir, the

team's first-round draft pick, had a sizzling debut.

FADING: Righthander Tyler Yates was looking like a top candidate to solidify the Mets bullpen before Tommy John surgery ended his chances.

EMERGING: Catcher Justin Huber followed up a promising 2001 effort with an even better 2002 in his first full season. The Australian native earned a midseason promotion from low Class A Capital City to high Class A St. Lucie.

TOP 10 PROSPECTS

Player, Pos.	Age	Club (Class)	AVG	AB	R	H	2B	3B	HR	RBI	SB
2. Jose Reyes, ss	19	Binghamton (AA)	.287	275	46	79	16	8	2	24	27
		St. Lucie (A)	.288	288	58	83	10	11	6	38	31
5. David Wright, 3b	19	Capital City (A)	.266	496	85	132	30	2	11	93	21

Player, Pos.	Age	Club (Class)	W	L	ERA	G	SV	IP	H	BB	SO
1. Aaron Heilman, rhp	21	Norfolk (AAA)	2	3	3.28	10	0	49	42	16	35
		Binghamton (AA)	4	4	3.82	17	0	97	85	28	97
3. Pat Strange, rhp	22	Norfolk (AAA)	10	10	3.82	29	0	165	165	59	109
4. Jae Weong Seo, rhp	25	Norfolk (AAA)	6	9	3.99	26	0	129	145	22	87
		Binghamton (AA)	0	0	5.40	1	0	5	5	1	6
6. Satoru Komiyama, rhp	37	Mets	0	3	5.61	25	0	43	53	12	33
		Norfolk (AAA)	3	1	1.42	17	0	44	27	9	43
7. Grant Roberts, rhp	25	Mets	3	1	2.20	34	0	45	43	16	31
		Binghamton (AA)	0	0	0.00	1	0	1	0	0	1
8. Tyler Yates, rhp	25	Norfolk (AAA)	2	2	1.32	24	6	34	29	13	34
9. Jaime Cerda, lhp	23	Mets	0	0	2.45	32	0	26	22	14	21
		Norfolk (AAA)	0	0	0.43	12	1	21	10	7	17
		Binghamton (AA)	5	1	2.27	14	0	32	21	10	33
10. Neal Musser, lhp	22	St. Lucie (A)	2	0	1.42	4	0	19	20	5	12
		Brooklyn (A)	0	0	0.69	4	0	13	7	5	12

Aaron Heilman

RICH ABEL

NEW YORK YANKEES

TOP PROSPECT UPDATE: Third baseman Drew Henson spent his second season at Columbus in 2002, and while he showed prodigious raw power, the holes in his game were exposed by Triple-A pitching. Henson worked with special instructor Don Mattingly in September before heading to the Arizona Fall League for more seasoning.

FADING: Shortstop Erick Almonte has often been described as having similar skills to Derek Jeter, but after failing to hit

in Triple-A in 2002 he was demoted to Double-A Norwich in the second half to work with manager Luis Sojo.

EMERGING: The Yankees were hit hard by injuries in 2002, including lefthanders Brandon Claussen and Sean Henn, but it was another pair of lefties Danny Borrell and Charlie Manning who stepped up. Borrell went 13-5, 2.32 between high Class A Tampa and Norwich, while Manning had a 3.37 ERA at the same two stops.

Drew Henson

TOP 10 PROSPECTS

Player, Pos.	Age	Club (Class)	AVG	AB	R	H	2B	3B	HR	RBI	SB
1. Drew Henson, 3b	22	Yankees	.000	1	1	0	0	0	0	0	0
		Columbus (AAA)	.240	471	68	113	30	4	18	65	2
2. Nick Johnson, 1b	24	Yankees	.243	378	56	92	15	0	15	58	1
		Columbus (AAA)	.091	11	1	1	0	0	0	0	0
4. *John-Ford Griffin, of	22	Midland (AA)	.143	7	0	1	0	0	0	0	0
		Norwich (AA)	.328	67	17	22	3	0	5	10	0
		Tampa (A)	.267	255	32	68	16	1	3	31	1
5. Juan Rivera, of	24	Yankees	.265	83	9	22	5	0	1	6	1
		Columbus (AAA)	.325	264	40	86	21	1	8	47	5
7. Marcus Thames, of	25	Yankees	.231	13	2	3	1	0	1	2	0
		Columbus (AAA)	.207	386	51	80	21	3	13	45	5
8. Erick Almonte, ss	25	Columbus (AAA)	.235	221	25	52	10	1	9	28	2
		Norwich (AA)	.241	187	28	45	7	0	8	33	10
10. Bronson Sardinha, of/ss	19	Greensboro (A)	.263	342	49	90	13	0	12	44	15
		Staten Island (A)	.323	124	25	40	8	0	4	16	4

Player, Pos.	Age	Club (Class)	W	L	ERA	G	SV	IP	H	BB	SO
3. Brandon Claussen, lhp	23	Columbus (AAA)	2	8	3.28	15	0	93	85	46	73
6. Sean Henn, lhp	21	(Injured—Did not pitch)									
9. *Jason Arnold, rhp	23	Midland (AA)	5	1	2.33	10	0	58	42	24	53
		Norwich (AA)	1	2	4.15	3	0	17	17	5	18
		Tampa (A)	7	1	2.48	13	0	80	64	22	83

*Traded to Oakland

PROSPECTS

OAKLAND **ATHLETICS**

TOP PROSPECT UPDATE: After giving up four prospects to acquire first baseman Carlos Pena from Texas in the spring of 2002, the A's quickly ran out of patience with Pena and traded him to the Tigers as part of a three-team deal involving the Yankees. The A's had some concerns about Pena's approach, and decided he didn't fit their blueprint.

FADING: Second baseman Esteban German came off a hot winter ball performance in his native Dominican which prompted GM Billy Beane to tab him as the leading candidate for the A's second base job in 2002. It didn't work out that way, as he spent the majority of the year at Triple-A Sacramento while Mark Ellis staked his claim to the position in Oakland.

EMERGING: Righthander Rich Harden built off of an encouraging 2001 debut and finished 2002 second in the minors with 187 punchouts. He has a wide array of power pitches, including 94-mph heat and a splitter.

TOP 10 PROSPECTS

Player, Pos.	Age	Club (Class)	AVG	AB	R	H	2B	3B	HR	RBI	SB
1. *Carlos Pena, 1b	24	Detroit	.253	273	31	69	13	4	12	36	2
		Oakland	.218	124	12	27	4	0	7	16	0
		Sacramento (AAA)	.240	175	30	42	10	1	10	33	3
2. Eric Byrnes, of	25	Oakland	.245	94	24	23	4	2	3	11	3
		Sacramento (AAA)	.261	119	16	31	7	0	4	16	5
4. Esteban German, 2b	24	Oakland	.200	35	4	7	0	0	0	0	1
		Sacramento (AAA)	.275	458	72	126	16	4	2	43	26
5. Bobby Crosby, ss	22	Midland (AA)	.281	228	31	64	16	0	7	31	9
		Modesto (A)	.307	280	47	86	17	2	2	38	5
6. Mark Ellis, ss/2b	25	Oakland	.272	345	58	94	16	4	6	35	4
		Sacramento (AAA)	.298	84	14	25	10	1	0	5	4
8. Freddie Bynum, 2b	22	Visalia (A)	.306	539	83	165	26	5	3	56	41
10. Chris Tritle, of	20	Modesto (A)	.197	178	20	35	9	0	4	23	3
		Vancouver (A)	.221	190	22	42	10	0	2	13	3

Player, Pos.	Age	Club (Class)	W	L	ERA	G	SV	IP	H	BB	SO
3. Chad Harville, rhp	26	Sacramento (AAA)	1	2	5.40	24	5	30	32	13	26
7. *Jeremy Bonderman, rhp	19	Lakeland (A)	0	1	6.00	2	0	12	11	4	10
		Modesto (A)	9	8	3.61	25	0	145	129	55	160
9. *Franklyn German, rhp	23	Detroit	1	0	0.00	7	1	7	3	2	6
		Toledo (AAA)	1	1	1.59	23	13	23	15	7	31
		Midland (AA)	1	1	3.05	37	16	41	28	27	59

*Traded to Detroit

Carlos Pena

PHILADELPHIA **PHILLIES**

TOP PROSPECT UPDATE: Outfielder Marlon Byrd has averaged 20 home runs, 82 RBIs and 29 steals over the past three years to put himself in position to wrestle the center field job away from Doug Glanville in 2003.

FADING: The Phillies boasted a solid year in 2002, all the way from Byrd at No. 1 to righthander Yoel Hernandez at No. 10, but outfielder Eric Valent didn't make much progress in his second year at Triple-A Scranton/Wilkes-Barre after hitting 20 or more home runs in each of the previous three seasons.

EMERGING: Third baseman Travis Chapman elevated his game by bulking up in the offseason. He hit for power for the first time in his career, connecting for 35 doubles and 15 home runs at Reading. Righthander Ryan Madson also had a breakthrough season in 2002, winning 16 games in Double-A.

TOP 10 PROSPECTS

Player, Pos.	Age	Club (Class)	AVG	AB	R	H	2B	3B	HR	RBI	SB
1. Marlon Byrd, of	25	Philadelphia	.229	35	2	8	2	0	1	1	0
		Scranton/W-B (AAA)	.297	538	103	160	37	7	15	63	15
5. Anderson Machado, ss	21	Reading (AA)	.251	450	71	113	24	3	12	77	40
6. Jorge Padilla, of	23	Reading (AA)	.256	484	71	124	30	2	7	65	32
7. Chase Utley, 2b	23	Reading (AA)	.263	464	73	122	39	1	17	70	8
8. Eric Valent, of	25	Philadelphia	.200	10	1	2	0	0	0	0	0
		Scranton/W-B (AAA)	.251	546	69	137	34	2	9	84	0

Player, Pos.	Age	Club (Class)	W	L	ERA	G	SV	IP	H	BB	SO
2. Brett Myers, rhp	22	Philadelphia	4	5	4.25	12	0	72	73	29	34
		Scranton/W-B (AAA)	9	6	3.59	19	0	128	121	20	97
3. Gavin Floyd, rhp	19	Lakewood (A)	11	10	2.77	27	0	166	119	64	140
4. Taylor Buchholz, rhp	20	Reading (AA)	0	2	7.43	4	0	23	29	6	17
		Clearwater (A)	10	6	3.29	23	0	159	140	51	129
9. Carlos Silva, rhp	23	Philadelphia	5	0	3.21	68	1	84	88	22	41
		Reading (AA)	0	0	0.00	2	1	3	0	0	1
10. Yoel Hernandez, rhp	20	Clearwater (A)	7	16	3.54	28	0	170	176	54	116

Marlon Byrd

PITTSBURGH **PIRATES**

TOP PROSPECT UPDATE: It was a lost season in 2002 for catcher J.R. House, who suffered an offseason abdominal injury, and then had season-ending elbow surgery in September. He isn't expected to play in 2003. There are plenty of candidates to assume the role of No. 1 prospect in the Pirates system like lefthander Sean Burnett, shortstop Jose Castillo and righthander John VanBenschoten. No. 1 overall draft pick Bryan Bullington also could claim that mantra—now that he has signed.

FADING: Righthanders Bobby Bradley and Ryan Vogelsong missed all or most of the 2002 season recovering from Tommy John surgery. Bradley hasn't pitched more than 83 innings in a season since signing with the Pirates as a first-round pick in 1999.

EMERGING: Outfielder Vic Buttler was one of several prospects who emerged on a talent-laden Class A Hickory club. The speedy Buttler hit .285 and stole 30 bases while playing an outstanding center field. First baseman Walter Young mashed to the tune of .333-25-103, but scouts have long-term concerns about his 6-foot-5, 309-pound frame.

TOP 10 PROSPECTS

Player, Pos.	Age	Club (Class)	AVG	AB	R	H	2B	3B	HR	RBI	SB
1. J.R. House, c	22	Altoona (AA)	.264	91	9	24	6	0	2	11	0
		GCL Pirates (R)	.313	16	3	5	2	0	1	2	0
5. Jose Castillo, ss	21	Lynchburg (A)	.300	503	82	151	25	2	16	81	27
6. Tony Alvarez, of	23	Pittsburgh	.308	26	6	8	2	0	1	2	1
		Altoona (AA)	.318	507	79	161	37	1	15	59	29
9. Humberto Cota, c	23	Pittsburgh	.294	17	2	5	1	0	0	0	0
		Nashville (AAA)	.267	404	51	108	27	1	9	54	5

Player, Pos.	Age	Club (Class)	W	L	ERA	G	SV	IP	H	BB	SO
2. John VanBenschoten, rhp	22	Hickory (A)	11	4	2.80	27	0	148	119	62	145
3. Sean Burnett, lhp	20	Lynchburg (A)	13	4	1.80	26	0	155	118	33	96
4. Bobby Bradley, rhp	21	(Injured—Did not pitch)									
7. Ryan Vogelsong, rhp	25	Altoona (AA)	1	5	5.56	8	0	44	47	10	35
		Hickory (A)	1	1	8.04	4	0	16	19	7	20
8. Adrian Burnside, lhp	25	Altoona (AA)	6	9	4.55	32	0	131	120	67	122
10. Chris Young, rhp	23	Hickory (A)	11	9	3.11	26	0	145	127	34	136

J.R. House

ST. LOUIS **CARDINALS**

TOP PROSPECT UPDATE: Injuries bothered righthander Jimmy Journell throughout the 2002 season and prevented him from making his major league debut. Still regarded as the best pitching prospect in the organization, he'll get a long look in 2003.

FADING: Outfielder So Taguchi didn't approach the level the Cardinals expected when they signed the Japanese veteran for $1 million prior to 2002. He spent most of the year in the minors and was released after the season.

EMERGING: Crafty lefthander Tyler Johnson compiled a 15-3, 2.00 record for Midwest League champion Peoria by keeping hitters off balance with outstanding command of his three pitches. Shaun Boyd settled in at second base for the same club and hit .313-12-60 with 32 stolen bases.

Jimmy Journell

TOP 10 PROSPECTS

Player, Pos.	Age	Club (Class)	AVG	AB	R	H	2B	3B	HR	RBI	SB
3. *Luis Garcia, of	23	Akron (AA)	.289	166	24	48	9	0	6	21	1
		New Haven (AA)	.266	308	42	82	16	1	12	37	3
6. So Taguchi, of	33	St. Louis	.400	15	4	6	0	0	0	2	1
		Memphis (AAA)	.247	304	37	75	17	0	5	36	6
		New Haven (AA)	.308	107	21	33	10	0	1	15	3
7. Yadier Molina, c	20	Peoria (A)	.280	393	39	110	20	0	7	50	2
10. Chris Duncan, 1b	21	Peoria (A)	.271	487	58	132	25	4	16	75	5

Player, Pos.	Age	Club (Class)	W	L	ERA	G	SV	IP	H	BB	SO
1. Jimmy Journell, rhp	24	Memphis (AAA)	2	4	3.68	7	0	37	38	18	32
		New Haven (AA)	3	3	2.70	10	0	67	50	18	66
2. Chris Narveson, lhp	20	Peoria (A)	2	1	4.46	9	0	42	49	8	36
		Johnson City (R)	0	2	4.91	6	0	18	23	6	16
4. Josh Pearce, rhp	25	St. Louis	0	0	7.62	3	0	13	20	8	1
		Memphis (AAA)	0	4	7.65	4	0	20	28	3	17
5. Justin Pope, rhp	22	Peoria (A)	8	1	1.38	12	0	78	48	12	72
8. Scotty Layfield, rhp	26	New Haven (AA)	6	4	2.35	58	24	65	54	24	63
9. Dan Haren, rhp	22	Potomac (A)	7	3	1.95	14	0	102	89	12	89
		Peoria (A)	3	6	3.62	14	0	92	90	19	82

*Traded to Cleveland

SAN DIEGO **PADRES**

TOP PROSPECT UPDATE: Third baseman Sean Burroughs brought a .327 career minor league average into his rookie season in 2002. His presence forced a lineup shuffle as Phil Nevin moved across the diamond to first base and Ryan Klesko went to the outfield. But after hitting .221 through May, Burroughs found himself back in Triple-A—playing mostly second base. A shoulder injury affected his hitting and defense.

FADING: Righthander Ben Howard and lefthander Eric Cyr made their major league debuts in 2002, but both ended the season on the disabled list.

EMERGING: Armed with a 96-mph fastball, lefthander Rusty Tucker went 5-1, 1.01 at low Class A Fort Wayne before a second-half promotion to high Class A Lake Elsinore. Tucker combined to fan 83 in 69 innings, while saving 27 games.

TOP 10 PROSPECTS

Player, Pos.	Age	Club (Class)	AVG	AB	R	H	2B	3B	HR	RBI	SB
1. Sean Burroughs, 3b/2b	22	San Diego	.271	192	18	52	5	1	1	11	2
		Portland (AAA)	.302	179	29	54	16	2	2	23	1
4. Xavier Nady, of/dh	23	Portland (AAA)	.283	315	46	89	12	1	10	43	0
		Lake Elsinore (A)	.278	169	41	47	6	3	13	37	2
8. Jake Gautreau, 2b	22	Lake Elsinore (A)	.286	371	43	106	20	1	10	62	2
9. Ramon Vazquez, 2b	25	San Diego	.274	423	50	116	21	5	2	32	7

Player, Pos.	Age	Club (Class)	W	L	ERA	G	SV	IP	H	BB	SO
2. Dennis Tankersley, rhp	23	San Diego	1	4	8.06	17	0	51	59	40	39
		Portland (AAA)	3	4	3.88	9	0	51	43	30	51
		Mobile (AA)	3	3	3.02	10	0	51	47	21	56
3. Jake Peavy, rhp	21	San Diego	6	7	4.52	17	0	98	106	33	90
		Mobile (AA)	4	5	2.80	14	0	80	65	30	89
5. Mark Phillips, lhp	20	Lake Elsinore (A)	10	8	4.19	28	0	148	123	94	156
6. Ben Howard, rhp	23	San Diego	0	1	9.28	3	0	11	13	14	10
		Portland (AAA)	0	4	6.20	11	0	45	47	15	25
		Mobile (AA)	3	1	2.18	6	0	33	26	16	30
7. Eric Cyr, lhp	23	San Diego	0	1	10.50	5	0	6	6	6	4
		Portland (AAA)	0	0	3.14	9	0	14	14	10	11
		Mobile (AA)	4	6	3.24	14	0	72	62	34	65
10. Oliver Perez, lhp	21	San Diego	4	5	3.50	16	0	90	71	48	94
		Mobile (AA)	1	0	1.17	4	0	23	11	16	34
		Lake Elsinore (A)	3	3	1.85	9	0	49	36	24	66

Sean Burroughs

SAN FRANCISCO **GIANTS**

TOP PROSPECT: The Dwight Gooden comparisons waned in 2002 for righthander Jerome Williams. Despite holding his own as a 20-year-old in Triple-A, he didn't show the electric stuff scouts had seen in the past.

FADING: Shortstop Cody Ransom isn't likely to unseat incumbent shortstop Rich Aurilia—not by hitting .207 with 151 strikeouts in his second tour of the Pacific Coast League.

EMERGING: A pair of live-armed lefties, Francisco Liriano and Ryan Hannaman, were impressive in their first look at full-season ball. Liriano overpowered hitters with 97-mph gas, while Hannaman worked in the low-90s with a nasty slider. Liriano's 2002 season was shortened by a sore shoulder, but he struck out 85 in 80 innings. Hannaman rang up 145 in 132 innings.

TOP 10 PROSPECTS

Player, Pos.	Age	Club (Class)	AVG	AB	R	H	2B	3B	HR	RBI	SB
4. Tony Torcato, of	22	San Francisco	.273	11	0	3	1	0	0	0	0
		Fresno (AAA)	.290	490	64	142	23	3	13	64	4
7. Lance Niekro, 3b	23	Shreveport (AA)	.310	297	33	92	20	1	4	34	0
9. Todd Linden, of	22	Fresno (AAA)	.250	100	18	25	2	1	3	10	2
		Shreveport (AA)	.314	392	64	123	26	2	12	52	9
10. Cody Ransom, ss	26	San Francisco	.667	3	2	2	0	0	0	1	0
		Fresno (AAA)	.207	449	53	93	18	4	13	46	6

Player, Pos.	Age	Club (Class)	W	L	ERA	G	SV	IP	H	BB	SO
1. Jerome Williams, rhp	20	Fresno (AAA)	6	11	3.59	28	0	161	140	50	130
2. Boof Bonser, rhp	20	Shreveport (AA)	1	2	5.55	5	0	24	30	14	23
		San Jose (A)	8	6	2.88	23	0	128	89	70	139
3. Kurt Ainsworth, rhp	24	San Francisco	1	2	2.10	6	0	26	22	12	15
		Fresno (AAA)	8	6	3.41	20	0	116	101	43	119
5. *Felix Diaz, rhp	22	Birmingham (AA)	4	0	3.48	7	0	31	25	8	30
		Shreveport (AA)	3	5	2.70	12	0	60	54	23	48
6. Jesse Foppert, rhp	22	Fresno (AAA)	3	6	3.99	14	0	79	75	35	109
		Shreveport (AA)	3	3	2.79	11	0	61	44	21	74
8. Erick Threets, lhp	20	San Jose (A)	0	1	6.67	26	0	28	23	28	43

*Traded to White Sox

Jerome Williams

PROSPECTS

SEATTLE **MARINERS**

TOP PROSPECT UPDATE: Ryan Anderson, once the game's premier lefthanded pitching prospect, sat out the second straight year due to shoulder surgery. The 6-foot-10 left-hander last pitched at Triple-A Tacoma in 2000, when he was 5-8, 3.98 with 146 strikeouts in 108 innings.

FADING: Shortstop Antonio Perez has had difficulty remaining healthy, and when he has been on the field,

he hasn't shown the same ability he did in 2000 when he hit .276-17-63 with 28 steals as one of the youngest players in the high Class A California League.

EMERGING: Shortstop Jose Lopez was the second youngest player in the Cal League in 2002 and represented the Mariners/World Team in the Futures Game in Milwaukee. The 18-year-old hit .324-8-60 with 31 steals.

TOP 10 PROSPECTS

Player, Pos.	Age	Club (Class)	AVG	AB	R	H	2B	3B	HR	RBI	SB
3. Antonio Perez, ss/2b	22	San Antonio (AA)	.258	240	30	62	8	2	2	24	15
		AZL Mariners (R)	.333	15	3	5	1	0	1	3	4
4. Chris Snelling, of	20	Seattle	.148	27	2	4	0	0	1	3	0
		San Antonio (AA)	.326	89	10	29	9	2	1	12	5
7. Shin-Soo Choo, of	20	San Bernardino (A)	.308	39	14	12	5	1	1	9	3
		Wisconsin (A)	.302	420	69	127	24	8	6	48	34
8. Ryan Christianson, c	21	San Antonio (AA)	.253	190	20	48	11	0	5	17	0
		San Bernardino (A)	.282	71	12	20	5	1	1	8	1
9. Jamal Strong, of	24	San Antonio (AA)	.278	503	63	140	16	5	1	31	46

Player, Pos.	Age	Club (Class)	W	L	ERA	G	SV	IP	H	BB	SO
1. Ryan Anderson, lhp	22	(Injured—Did not pitch)									
2. Rafael Soriano, rhp	22	Seattle	0	3	4.56	10	1	47	45	16	32
		San Antonio (AA)	2	3	2.31	10	0	47	32	15	52
5. Clint Nageotte, rhp	21	San Bernardino (A)	9	6	4.54	29	0	165	153	68	214
6. Jeff Heaverlo, rhp	24	(Injured—Did not pitch)									
10. Matt Thornton, lhp	26	San Antonio (AA)	1	5	3.63	12	0	62	52	29	44

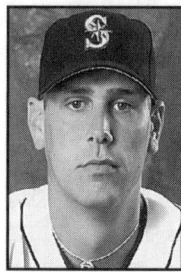

Ryan Anderson

TAMPA BAY **DEVIL RAYS**

TOP PROSPECT UPDATE: It was another trying season for Josh Hamilton, who missed the bulk of the 2001 season with back pain as a result of a car accident in spring training. Back injuries forced him to the sideline again in 2002 before shoulder surgery put an end to his season in July. Shortstop B.J. Upton, the second overall pick in the 2002 draft, will likely ease into the No. 1 ranking among Devil Rays prospects.

FADING: Righthander Matt White spent most of the 2002

season rehabbing his shoulder. It has been six years since the Devil Rays signed him as a loophole free agent, with no return to date on his $10.2 million signing bonus.

EMERGING: Outfielder Jonny Gomes put on a tremendous power show in the high Class A California League. His 30 bombs were the most in the system, though he did whiff an organization-high 173 times. His younger brother, Joey, hit 15 homers to top the short-season New York-Penn League.

Josh Hamilton

TOP 10 PROSPECTS

Player, Pos.	Age	Club (Class)	AVG	AB	R	H	2B	3B	HR	RBI	SB
1. Josh Hamilton, of	21	Bakersfield (A)	.303	211	32	64	14	1	9	44	10
2. Carl Crawford, of	21	Tampa Bay	.259	259	23	67	11	6	2	30	9
		Durham (AAA)	.297	353	59	105	17	9	7	52	26
5. Rocco Baldelli, of	21	Durham (AAA)	.292	96	13	28	6	1	3	7	2
		Orlando (AA)	.371	70	10	26	3	1	2	13	3
		Bakersfield (A)	.333	312	63	104	19	1	4	51	21
8. Jorge Cantu, ss	20	Orlando (AA)	.242	512	50	124	31	1	3	43	2

Player, Pos.	Age	Club (Class)	W	L	ERA	G	SV	IP	H	BB	SO
3. Dewon Brazelton, rhp	22	Tampa Bay	0	1	4.85	2	0	13	12	6	5
		Durham (AAA)	1	0	0.00	1	0	5	5	1	6
		Orlando (AA)	5	9	3.33	26	0	146	129	67	109
4. Jesus Colome, rhp	22	Tampa Bay	2	7	8.27	32	0	41	56	33	33
		Durham (AAA)	2	2	2.17	18	1	29	18	13	30
6. Seth McClung, rhp	21	Orlando (AA)	5	7	5.37	20	0	114	138	53	64
		Bakersfield (A)	3	2	2.92	7	0	37	35	11	48
7. Matt White, rhp	24	Orlando (AA)	1	2	5.56	7	0	34	33	19	20
		Charleston (A)	3	4	3.15	10	0	54	48	15	38
9. Jason Standridge, rhp	23	Tampa Bay	0	0	9.00	1	0	3	7	4	1
		Durham (AAA)	10	9	3.12	29	0	173	168	64	111
10. Delvin James, rhp	24	Tampa Bay	0	3	6.55	8	0	34	40	15	17
		Durham (AAA)	2	1	3.93	7	0	34	41	4	26
		Orlando (AA)	1	2	3.55	3	0	13	12	2	13

TEXAS **RANGERS**

TOP PROSPECT UPDATE: Hank Blalock won the starting third base job with the Rangers in 2002 on the strength of his spring performance. But he had trouble adapting to major league offspeed pitches and was demoted to Triple-A Oklahoma after a brief trial. His power output was affected by a fractured elbow, though he played through the pain.

FADING: The Rangers thought they were acquiring a major league-ready starter in this spring of 2002 when they dealt first baseman Carlos Pena to the A's for lefthander Mario Ramos and three other prospects. After going 16-4 in 2001, Ramos never put it together and was hammered before moving to the Oklahoma bullpen in the second half.

EMERGING: Outfielder Laynce Nix blossomed into one of the organization's top prospects by hitting .285-21-110 to win the Florida State League's MVP award. Lefthander Ben Kozlowski, acquired from the Braves for Andy Pratt before the 2002 season, was a revelation at Double-A Tulsa.

TOP 10 PROSPECTS

Player, Pos.	Age	Club (Class)	AVG	AB	R	H	2B	3B	HR	RBI	SB
1. Hank Blalock, 3b	22	Texas	.211	147	16	31	8	0	3	17	0
		Oklahoma (AAA)	.307	387	63	119	32	1	8	62	2
2. Mark Teixeira, 3b	22	Tulsa (AA)	.316	171	31	54	11	3	10	28	3
		Charlotte (A)	.320	150	32	48	10	2	9	41	2
5. Ryan Ludwick, of	24	Texas	.235	81	10	19	6	0	1	9	2
		Oklahoma (AAA)	.285	305	62	87	27	4	15	52	2
9. Kevin Mench, of	24	Texas	.260	366	52	95	20	2	15	60	1
		Oklahoma (AAA)	.214	98	17	21	8	0	6	15	0
10. Jason Hart, 1b	25	Texas	.267	15	2	4	3	0	0	0	0
		Oklahoma (AAA)	.263	514	78	135	32	1	25	83	1

Player, Pos.	Age	Club (Class)	W	L	ERA	G	SV	IP	H	BB	SO
3. Mario Ramos, lhp	24	Oklahoma (AAA)	3	8	7.40	34	0	122	162	53	75
4. Colby Lewis, rhp	23	Texas	1	3	6.29	15	0	35	42	26	28
		Oklahoma (AAA)	5	6	3.63	20	0	107	100	28	99
6. Ryan Dittfurth, rhp	22	Tulsa (AA)	1	3	5.66	9	0	41	42	23	32
		Charlotte (A)	3	2	2.45	6	0	26	11	7	21
7. Joaquin Benoit, rhp	23	Texas	4	5	5.31	17	1	85	91	58	59
		Oklahoma (AAA)	8	4	3.56	16	0	99	74	37	103
		Charlotte (A)	0	0	0.00	1	0	5	1	3	8
8. Jovanny Cedeno, rhp	22	GCL Rangers (R)	0	0	0.00	3	0	5	3	1	4

Hank Blalock

RODGER WOOD

TORONTO **BLUE JAYS**

TOP PROSPECT UPDATE: After hitting 31 bombs at Double-A Tennessee in 2001, catcher/DH Josh Phelps launched 39 more in 2002—24 in Triple-A and 15 in Toronto. His power surge boosted the Jays down the stretch. His .965 on-base plus slugging percentage (OPS) was second on the team to Carlos Delgado.

FADING: With Phelps, Jayson Werth, Orlando Hudson, Eric Hinske and Kevin Cash making their major league debuts, there weren't many negatives among the organi-zation's top 10 prospects. Outfielder Gabe Gross' production was subpar, though scouts still project him to hit and hit for power. Injuries prevented outfielder Tyrell Godwin from getting his career off the ground.

EMERGING: Dominican righthander Francisco Rosario came out of nowhere with his 96-mph fastball to develop into one of the organization's prized prospects. He fanned 143 in 130 innings between the Jays' two Class A clubs, Charleston and Dunedin.

Josh Phelps

TOP 10 PROSPECTS

Player, Pos.	Age	Club (Class)	AVG	AB	R	H	2B	3B	HR	RBI	SB
1. Josh Phelps, c/dh	24	Toronto	.309	265	41	82	20	1	15	58	0
		Syracuse (AAA)	.292	257	50	75	20	1	24	64	0
2. Gabe Gross, of	22	Tennessee (AA)	.238	403	57	96	17	5	10	54	8
3. Jayson Werth, of/c	23	Toronto	.261	46	4	12	2	1	0	6	1
		Syracuse (AAA)	.257	443	65	114	25	2	18	82	24
5. Orlando Hudson, 2b	24	Toronto	.276	192	20	53	10	5	4	23	0
		Syracuse (AAA)	.305	417	63	127	27	3	10	37	8
6. Eric Hinske, 3b	25	Toronto	.279	566	99	158	38	2	24	84	13
8. Alexis Rios, of	21	Dunedin (A)	.305	456	60	139	22	8	3	61	14
9. Kevin Cash, c	24	Toronto	.200	14	1	2	0	0	0	0	0
		Syracuse (AAA)	.220	236	27	52	18	0	10	26	0
		Tennessee (AA)	.277	213	38	59	15	1	8	44	5
10. Tyrell Godwin, of	23	Charleston (A)	.281	185	31	52	8	5	0	16	10

Player, Pos.	Age	Club (Class)	W	L	ERA	G	SV	IP	H	BB	SO
4. Dustin McGowan, rhp	20	Charleston (A)	11	10	4.19	28	0	149	143	59	163
7. Brandon League, rhp	19	Auburn (A)	7	2	3.15	16	0	86	80	23	72

PROSPECTS

INDEPENDENT
LEAGUES

Indy leagues gaining foothold as 5.25 million fans flock to games

BY J.J. COOPER

A decade after its humble beginnings in 1993, independent baseball continues to establish a solid footing.

The Northern League marked the return of independent leagues with a successful, but modest, 72-game, six-team schedule and the Frontier League staggered to survive its first season in which two franchises folded.

At the time, it wasn't unrealistic to wonder whether independent baseball was a viable undertaking, or a brief passing fad.

Fast forward to today, and independent baseball is once again a solid part of the professional baseball landscape.

Consider that in 2002, six independent leagues drew more than 5.25 million fans. Consider that former independent leaguers making it to the majors, like pitchers

Marty Scott

Jason Simontacchi, Brendan Donnelly and Brandon Puffer did, are no longer a curiosity.

The talent level of independent baseball has improved to such a degree that, faced with an inability to use players from the affiliated minor leagues, Team USA assembled a squad of independent leaguers in October in Mexico and watched as it won a silver medal at the Americas Cup, a qualifying tournament for the 2003 Pan American Games.

The U.S. lost to unbeaten Cuba 6-1 in the championship game. Team USA went only 4-4 in two preliminary rounds and lost three-straight games at one point during round-robin play, but the U.S. rallied in the medal round to beat Nicaragua in the quarterfinals and Panama in the semifinals to earn a spot in the championship game.

It was the second time that Team USA had used independent leaguers for an international tournament. The composition of Team USA gave a pretty good barometer to the distribution of talent in the independent leagues. Half of the 22-player team was composed of Northern Leaguers, including four players from the Northern League champion New Jersey Jackals. The Atlantic League placed five players on the team while the Central League (three) and the Western League (two) were also represented. The team was managed by former St. Paul (Northern) skipper Marty Scott, who moved on to become manager of the Central League's new Fort Worth franchise in 2002.

Stable at the Top

At the top end of the independent league scale, the Northern and Atlantic League have carved out a niche as leagues that draw crowds comprable to Double-A and Triple-A leagues.

The Atlantic League drew 1,859,059 fans for its eight clubs. Long Island continued to be the league's bellwether, as the Ducks drew 437,212. Once again, the Ducks were third in independent baseball in average attendance, as their average of 6,158 fans trailed the Northern League's St. Paul (6,263) and Winnipeg (6,200) franchises.

It was a successful season attendance-wise throughout the Atlantic League, as six teams recorded attendance increases, led by Newark's 35,000 jump and Camden's 33,000 rise in attendance.

The league's biggest problem continued to be its eighth franchise. After the 2001 season, the league promised that the itinerant Lehigh Valley Black Diamonds, who had been without a home stadium for two of the past three seasons, would not have to spend another season on a permanent road trip.

But as bankruptcy proceedings for the team continued to work through the court system, the Atlantic League was forced to operate the team for another season, which meant that the renamed Pennsylvania Road Warriors spent the season on a 126-game road trip.

Not surprisingly, the Road Warriors finished the season with the worst record in the league, and sputtered to the finish, losing 19 of their last 20 games. The team was a second-class citizen of sorts, without its own trainer, without the chance to take extra batting practice or take extra grounders.

At the end of the season, it still wasn't clear if 2002 would be the final season for the bus-bound team or if the team would remain the Road Warriors in 2003.

The Atlantic League wasn't the only team with a permanent road team in 2002, as the Northern League's new Gary franchise also spent the year without a home. The RailCats $45 million stadium was supposed to be ready for the 2002 season, but construction delays meant that the stadium wasn't close to being ready on time. Instead, the Gary team packed up its bus and spent the entire season barnstorming through the Northern League.

Not surprisingly, Gary finished with the worst record

2002 INDEPENDENT LEAGUE ALL-STARS

Selected by Baseball America

Pos.	Player, Club (League)	Avg.	AB	R	H	2B	3B	HR	RBI	SB
C	Francisco Morales, Atlantic City (Atlantic)	.330	430	68	142	25	2	20	85	1
1B	Jose Velasquez, Atlantic City (Atlantic)	.323	465	71	150	31	1	18	94	3
2B	Francisco Matos, Gary (Northern)	.362	304	44	110	19	3	2	40	4
3B	Brent Sachs, Winnipeg (Northern)	.346	364	83	126	29	4	11	60	20
SS	Marc Mirizzi, San Angelo (Central)	.332	368	82	122	26	4	9	56	17
OF	Greg Jacobs, Long Beach (Western)	.382	325	67	124	29	1	18	91	17
OF	Bryan Warner, Lincoln (Northern)	.331	363	56	120	20	2	15	78	15
OF	Phil Willingham, Richmond (Frontier)	.360	364	75	131	19	8	15	86	36
DH	Jimmy Hurst, Newark (Atlantic)	.341	440	87	150	31	1	35	101	10

Pos.	Player, Club (League)	W	L	ERA	G	SV	IP	H	BB	SO
SP	Joel Bennett, New Jersey (Northern)	14	2	2.93	21	0	129	105	40	141
SP	Bobby Madritsch, Winnipeg (Northern)	11	4	2.30	19	0	125	94	36	153
SP	Brian Mazone, Lincoln (Northern)	15	3	2.51	22	0	139	125	27	128
SP	Linc Mikkelsen, Camden (Atlantic)	16	6	3.32	24	0	152	148	31	95
RP	Matt Hammons, Joliet (Northern)	5	2	1.59	44	23	51	36	21	80

PLAYER OF THE YEAR: Bobby Madritsch, lhp, Winnipeg (Northern).

in the NL's Central Division.

It was another successful season at the box office for the Northern League, especially for the more established Central Division. While the Atlantic League has become the most veteran-laden of the independent leagues, with its emphasis on former major league players and other vets, the Northern League continued to have success with its mix of veterans and talented youngsters.

The Northern League is a loose confederation of two largely separate leagues, as the Central and Eastern Divisions do not play each other with the exception of the league's all-star game and a best-of-5 postseason series. It was uncertain, however, whether that alliance would continue beyond 2002.

While the Eastern Division continued to dominate the Northern League championship series, winning for the fourth consecutive year in 2002, it is the Central Division that has better facilities and attendance.

All of the Central Division teams play in ballparks built in the past decade. Only Duluth-Superior failed to average at least 2,300 fans per game, while five of the nine teams drew at least 4,000 per game. The Duluth-Superior franchise, however, was scheduled to move to suburban Kansas City in 2003.

After the season, the two divisions went their separate ways, deciding not to renew their partnership agreement. The Central retained the Northern League name, while the East reverted to being the Northeast League, the name it had used before the partnership agreement began in 1999.

Change is the Only Constant

While the Northern and Atlantic Leagues were relatively stable in 2002, a couple of other leagues went through a large number of changes.

The Texas-Louisiana League picked up a new name and two new teams, as the league added one of the strongest teams from the defunct All-American Association—the Fort Worth Cats—and the Jackson (Miss.) Senators (relocated from Tyler, Texas), then changed its name to the Central League.

The changes appeared to pay off as the Cats became

PLAYER OF THE YEAR

Big league clubs regularly scour independent teams for talent, and occasionally they'll come across a prospect who was overlooked. But they don't usually come across someone as talented as Winnipeg Goldeyes lefthander Bobby Madritsch.

In his second season of independent ball, Madritsch suddenly became one of the hottest prospects in 2002 that the independent leagues had ever seen.

There aren't many lefthanders who can touch 95 mph with their fastball. Finding one in an independent league is practically unheard of.

So it wasn't surprising that scouts lined up to try to sign the 26-year-old lefty, who put up top-notch numbers (11-4, 2.30) and was named Baseball America's 2002 Independent League Player of the Year. After the season, the Seattle Mariners signed him to a contract with its Triple-A Tacoma club and offered an invitation to spring training.

"I get calls every now and then for a player, but it's nothing even close to what Bobby's getting," Goldeyes manager Hal Lanier said as the 2002 season wrapped up. "You know he's that good when you have six or eight organizations at a time calling about him throughout the season, throughout the playoffs."

Lanier, who has been in the Northern League since 1996, said Madritsch is the best prospect he'd ever seen in the league.

Bobby Madritsch

JOHN SPEAR

"A guy I had a few years ago, (Rangers reliever) Jeff Zimmerman, was having a good year," Lanier said. "But clubs were not after Jeff Zimmerman like they are with Bobby Madritsch."

Madritsch started the year 0-3, 5.64 and was sent to the bullpen. Pitching coach Rick Forney said he still believed Madritsch had great talent, but that the lefty needed to gain more confidence. He soon found it and went 11-1 the rest of the way. In August he went 4-0, 0.66 and charged into the playoffs with three dominating starts.

"I think you'd have to give credit to my pitching coach, Rick Forney, and to Bobby Madritsch," Lanier said of the turnaround. "In the end, he's the one who has to do that thing. He really didn't have that many innings under his belt when he came here to the Northern League."

Madritsch grew up in Chicago and attended Point Park (Pa.) College, an NAIA school. He was drafted by the Reds in the sixth round in 1998, but after an impressive debut at Rookie-level Billings, Madritsch had shoulder surgery. He missed most of 1999 and 2000, and then was released by Cincinnati.

In 2001 he played in the independent Western and Texas-Louisiana leagues and joined the Goldeyes prior to the 2002. He helped lead Winnipeg to the Northern League Central Division title.

the best draw in the league, averaging 3,420 fans, while Jackson was in the middle of the league in attendance.

The Frontier League's biggest splash of the season came during its all-star game. A night after Major League Baseball's All-Star Game ended in a controversial tie, the FL announced that it would use a home-run derby to settle any tie at the end of nine innings. In a masterpiece of timing, the game ended in a 4-4 tie. The derby took place and the West defeated the East 2-1. National media immediately picked up the contrast to the MLB game.

It wasn't the only smart move by the FL in 2002. The league moved its Springfield and Canton franchises to Rockford, Ill., and Washington, Pa., and both of the new clubs ranked in the top five in the league in attendance. Thanks in part to the franchise movement, the league topped 750,000 in attendance for the first time in the league's history, as the 12 teams drew 948,343 fans.

Things weren't as rosy in the newly-created Southeastern League. The league got an all-to-quick start when the All-American Association disbanded before the season. With a solid Montgomery, Ala. franchise, which drew 78,069 fans in 2001, looking for a league, a decision was made in April to develop a six-team league that would start play in early June. Without time to find owners for the new franchises before the season began, the Montgomery ownership group decided to foot the bill for the entire league until local owners could be lined up for the other franchises.

In hindsight, the league did not have enough time to get organized and not nearly enough time to promote its teams. Two teams, Americus, Ga., and Ozark, Ala., folded midway through the season.

ATLANTIC LEAGUE

In the five-year history of the Atlantic League, no one has ever had a better year than Newark's Jimmy Hurst's 2002 season.

Hurst became the league's first-ever triple crown winner as he led Newark to the Atlantic League title. Hurst's Newark Bears swept the Bridgeport Bluefish in three games in the championship series.

The Newark designated hitter hit two homers, scored four runs and drove in five in the first two games of the championship series. By Game 3, the Bluefish had given up trying to pitch to Hurst. But when they intentionally walked him twice, the bottom four hitters in the Bears' lineup went 10-for-15, scoring seven runs and driving in eight as Newark clinched the title with a 10-3 victory.

For the playoffs, Hurst was 8-for-19 (.421). It was just a continuation of his dominant regular season, as Hurst hit .341-35-101.

Jimmy Hurst

He won the batting title by nine points, the home run title by 11 homers, and the RBI crown by seven.

Hurst was named the regular season and playoff MVP. Surprisingly, the 30-year-old, who played 13 games with the Detroit Tigers in 1997, was still looking for a job in affiliated baseball when the season ended.

"This league is not a bad league to be in," Hurst said during the season. "But I hear it every day from my teammates, 'Hurst, when are you leaving?' It's all about someone giving me an opportunity."

Newark had earned a spot in the championship series by beating Atlantic City two-games-to-one in the semifinals. Bridgeport edged Camden two-games-to-one in the other semifinal series.

Thanks in part to the weakness of the Pennsylvania Road Warriors, who finished the season with a 34-91 overall record while playing all of their games on the road, parity was prevalent throughout the Atlantic League in 2002. Six of the eight teams finished the season with above-.500 records. Atlantic City, Bridgeport and Camden all finished the season with 71 wins, while sixth-place Long Island was 65-61.

STANDINGS

FIRST HALF

NORTH	W	L	PCT	GB
Bridgeport Bluefish	36	27	.571	—
Long Island Ducks	35	28	.556	1
Nashua Pride	29	34	.460	7
Pennsylvania Road Warriors	17	45	.274	18 ½

SOUTH	W	L	PCT	GB
Somerset Patriots	36	27	.571	—
Newark Bears	36	27	.571	—
Camden Riversharks	34	29	.540	2
Atlantic City Surf	28	34	.452	7 ½

SECOND HALF

NORTH	W	L	PCT	GB
Bridgeport Bluefish	35	28	.556	—
Long Island Ducks	30	33	.476	5
Nashua Pride	25	37	.403	9 ½
Pennsylvania Road Warriors	17	46	.270	18

SOUTH	W	L	PCT	GB
Atlantic City Surf	43	19	.694	—
Camden Riversharks	37	25	.597	6
Newark Bears	33	28	.541	9 ½
Somerset Patriots	29	33	.468	14

PLAYOFFS: Semifinals—Newark defeated Atlantic City 2-1 and Bridgeport defeated Camden 2-1 in best-of-3 series. **Finals**—Newark defeated Bridgeport 3-0 in a best-of-5 series.

MANAGERS: Atlantic City—Mitch Williams. **Bridgeport**—Duffy Dyer. **Camden**—Wayne Krenchicki. **Long Island**—Don McCormack. **Nashua**—Butch Hobson. **Newark**—Marv Foley. **Pennsylvania**—Bert Pena. **Somerset**—Sparky Lyle.

ATTENDANCE: Long Island 437,212; Somerset 358,049; Camden 313,792; Bridgeport 262,015; Newark 208,581; Atlantic City 158,450; Nashua 120,960.

ALL-STAR TEAM: C—Francisco Morales, Long Island. **1B**—Jose Velasquez, Atlantic City. **2B**—Emiliano Escandon, Somerset. **3B**—Aaron Ledesma, Long Island. **SS**—Victor Gutierrez, Atlantic City. **OF**—Desi Wilson, Somerset; Keith Gordon, Atlantic City; Rolo Avila, Bridgeport; Wil Quintana, Pennsylvania/Newark. **DH**—Jimmy Hurst, Newark. **Util**—Edgar Tovar, Newark/Long Island/Nashua. **LHP**—Robert Dodd, Somerset. **RHP**—Linc Mikkelsen, Camden. **RP**—Jimmy Williams, Camden.

Most Valuable Player: Jimmy Hurst, Newark. **Most Valuable Pitcher:** Linc Mikkelsen, Camden. **Manager of the Year:** Wayne Krenchicki, Camden.

INDIVIDUAL BATTING LEADERS
(Minimum 340 Plate Appearances)

	AVG	AB	R	H	2B	3B	HR	RBI	SB
Hurst, Jimmy, Newark	.341	440	87	150	31	1	35	100	10
Morales, Francisco, Long Island	.330	430	68	142	25	2	20	85	1
Wilson, Desi, Somerset	.330	361	47	119	20	1	3	66	7
Velasquez, Jose, AC	.323	465	71	150	31	1	18	94	3
Tovar, Edgar, Nashua/Newark/LI	.321	420	53	135	11	0	3	39	4
Ledesma, Aaron, Long Island	.315	409	55	129	22	1	1	59	9
Avila, Rolo, Bridgeport	.314	477	77	150	26	5	10	58	42
Hall, Justin, Newark/AC	.314	297	44	93	14	7	7	47	10
Quintana, Wil, Penn/Newark	.306	432	62	132	23	0	21	72	10
Gutierrez, Vic, Atlantic City	.300	476	76	143	18	4	9	69	26

INDIVIDUAL PITCHING LEADERS
(Minimum 101 Innings)

	W	L	ERA	G	SV	IP	H	BB	SO
Kester, Tim, Penn	7	7	2.57	30	2	136	141	24	80
Dodd, Robert, Somerset	9	7	2.85	25	0	177	143	51	133
Cornett, Brad, Bridgeport	14	7	3.27	25	0	168	162	36	109
Jensen, Justin, Somerset	8	9	3.29	2	0	139	121	55	100
Mikkelsen, Linc, Camden	16	6	3.32	24	0	152	148	31	95
Osteen, Gavin, Camden	4	10	3.35	21	0	126	130	24	69
Nunez, Maximo, Atlantic City	10	2	3.43	19	0	110	109	24	64
Baptist, Travis, Nashua	8	9	3.63	22	0	117	126	41	72
Mahaffey, Alan, Bridgeport	13	7	3.67	25	0	150	148	62	97
Wolff, Bryan, Bridgeport	4	8	3.67	35	11	105	117	28	84

ATLANTIC CITY

BATTING	AVG	AB	R	H	2B	3B	HR	RBI	SB
Akers, Chad, of-3b	.182	11	0	2	0	0	0	1	0
Ball, Jeff, 3b	.258	194	29	50	9	1	6	21	2
Butt, Gerald, c-of	.182	33	5	6	1	1	0	1	0
Capodieci, Adam, c	.286	28	6	8	0	0	0	5	0
Cochran, Edwin, c	.000	1	0	0	0	0	0	0	0
Deitrick, Jeremy, c	.211	76	7	16	1	0	2	3	0
3-team (13 Penn/24 Long Island)	.219	201	19	44	5	1	4	18	1
Fowler, Maleke, of	.221	217	34	48	10	0	8	23	10

	AVG	AB	R	H	2B	3B	HR	RBI	SB
Gambill, Chad, of	.289	287	44	83	19	0	15	53	4
Goodwin, Joe, c	.289	38	2	11	2	0	0	3	0
Gordon, Keith, of	.293	454	84	133	35	2	20	83	28
Gutierrez, Vic, ss	.300	476	76	143	18	4	9	69	26
Hall, Justin, 2b	.406	101	19	41	7	3	2	18	4
2-team (61 Newark)	.313	297	44	93	14	7	7	47	10
Hamilton, Joe, of	.254	177	37	45	9	3	10	32	5
Hine, Steve, 2b	.286	426	74	122	20	1	6	51	11
Incaviglia, Pete, dh	.295	207	44	61	9	0	12	45	1
Joffrion, Jack, 2b-ss	.150	40	3	6	2	0	1	5	0
Johnson, Ric, of	.374	174	38	65	7	5	2	20	11
2-team (55 Camden)	.295	336	56	99	14	5	3	34	13
LaFlair, Jay, c	.282	117	13	33	3	0	2	13	1
Maddox, Garry, c	.286	182	40	52	9	1	14	44	4
3-team (13 Penn/18 Camden)	.283	283	51	80	13	1	18	54	7
Martinez, Greg, of	.400	20	8	8	0	0	0	4	1
Polanco, Enohel, 3b	.262	168	26	44	7	1	3	21	3
Ramirez, Pito, c	.285	165	31	47	5	0	7	24	3
2-team (38 Newark)	.260	285	50	74	10	0	12	40	5
Rodriguez, Joe, c	.000	7	2	0	0	0	0	0	0
Schmidt, Greg, 3b	.339	59	7	20	3	1	0	3	2
Velasquez, Jose, 1b	.323	465	71	150	31	1	18	94	3

PITCHING	W	L	ERA	G	SV	IP	H	BB	SO
Bedinger, Doug	2	8	6.51	12	0	56	76	18	39
Boker, John	0	2	7.01	7	0	25	28	16	11
Carroll, Dave	4	5	4.29	33	0	115	125	43	69
Censale, Silvio	1	0	8.25	3	0	12	17	5	8
Chapman, Jake	6	3	2.59	50	0	76	79	21	75
Chavez, Anthony	7	1	3.78	10	0	66	75	18	51
Crowell, Jim	8	4	4.17	19	0	108	107	54	95
DeWitt, Scott	0	1	15.43	1	0	2	6	0	1
Hardwick, Bubba	0	2	2.70	7	0	13	22	6	3
Hernandez, Robert	0	0	18.00	2	0	3	3	6	0
2-team (20 Penn)	0	2	8.27	22	0	49	49	31	32
Ludwick, Eric	2	2	6.00	9	0	36	30	34	49
Mallard, Randi	5	3	3.19	50	2	48	44	24	33
Mastrolonardo, Dave	1	0	1.93	20	0	18	16	8	12
Mattson, Craig	3	4	4.50	53	30	52	58	19	47
Nunez, Maximo	10	2	3.43	19	0	110	109	24	64
Richards, Dave	2	1	1.75	8	0	25	24	9	12
Rossiter, Mike	1	0	7.11	11	0	12	20	5	9
Rutherford, Mark	3	3	3.03	51	0	65	55	37	60
Shelby, Anthony	2	4	3.41	36	1	29	27	11	25
2-team (11 Newark)	3	4	3.83	47	2	51	56	18	41
Shumaker, Tony	0	1	6.75	2	0	5	6	8	3
Villegas, Ismael	5	1	2.38	12	1	53	35	17	36
Williams, Brian	8	6	4.00	23	0	141	163	46	105
Williams, Mitch	1	0	3.38	5	0	13	14	4	4

BRIDGEPORT

BATTING	AVG	AB	R	H	2B	3B	HR	RBI	SB
Amado, Jose, 3b-2b	.270	285	39	77	11	1	6	45	3
Anderson, Jeffrey, ss	.250	96	9	24	5	0	1	11	0
Avila, Rolo, of	.314	477	77	150	26	5	10	58	42
Carter, Michael, of	.278	248	33	69	15	1	4	28	0
Devarez, Cesar, c	.319	313	38	100	23	1	4	45	4
Dina, Allen, of	.249	213	30	53	12	0	2	37	10
Dorman, John, ss-2b	.233	172	25	40	6	1	1	14	1
Espada, Angel, 2b-ss	.262	340	48	89	8	0	0	29	28
Hosey, Dwayne, dh-of	.249	370	69	92	22	3	9	42	14
Kingman, Brendan, 3b	.234	325	41	76	17	0	5	36	1
Kuilan, Hector, c	.275	204	21	56	10	0	4	26	0
Lind, Jose, dh	.000	5	1	0	0	0	0	0	0
Marrero, Oreste, 1b	.245	428	78	105	18	2	26	67	6
Martinez, Gabby, ss	.308	133	19	41	2	0	3	22	10
Otanez, Willis, dh	.333	84	15	28	6	1	6	23	0
Rocha, Juan, of	.295	363	58	107	21	3	17	57	2
Rodriguez, Tony, ss	.241	141	10	34	9	0	0	11	0

PITCHING	W	L	ERA	G	SV	IP	H	BB	SO
Ahearne, Pat	5	2	2.17	11	0	74	60	18	48
Cain, Tim	1	3	5.64	8	0	30	27	17	26
Cornett, Brad	14	7	3.27	25	0	167	162	36	109
Davis, Keith	1	1	5.29	15	0	17	21	4	21
Gaskill, Derek	1	2	7.20	7	0	10	11	3	13
2-team (6 Somerset)	1	2	8.16	13	0	14	16	7	20
Guilfoyle, Mike	2	3	2.05	47	16	52	46	20	49
Henthorne, Kevin	3	1	2.08	8	0	43	41	6	25
Imazeki, Masaru	7	4	4.04	30	0	111	104	50	96
Looney, Brian	1	0	0.00	4	0	7	8	1	13
Mahaffey, Alan	13	7	3.67	25	0	149	148	62	97
McCarthy, Greg	4	2	2.77	42	0	52	41	31	63
Perez, Gil	3	9	5.16	25	0	122	140	34	63
Rosenkranz, Terry	2	1	3.92	43	1	57	57	37	50

Sontag, Alan	3	5	5.49	30	2	80	90	26	41
Strong, Joe	7	0	1.04	30	4	34	27	14	35
Wolff, Bryan	4	8	3.67	35	11	105	117	28	84

CAMDEN

BATTING	AVG	AB	R	H	2B	3B	HR	RBI	SB
Azuaje, Jesus, ss	.258	322	48	83	11	0	12	34	13
Collum, Gary, of	.252	115	16	29	4	1	1	9	7
Delgado, Alex, c	.250	372	38	93	18	0	10	46	3
Dubose, Brian, dh	.136	22	3	3	1	0	0	0	0
Eckelman, Alex, 2b	.269	450	51	121	15	3	4	37	5
Fowler, Maleke, of	.260	204	32	53	10	1	2	20	14
2-team (59 Atlantic City)	.240	421	66	101	20	1	10	43	24
Gainey, Bryon, 1b	.231	437	62	101	17	0	25	86	0
Gubanich, Creighton, dh-c	.292	168	21	49	13	0	8	40	0
Johnson, Ric, of	.210	162	18	34	7	0	1	14	2
Lamberg, Joshua, c	.200	80	11	16	7	0	2	10	0
Llanos, Alex, dh-3b	.243	70	7	17	2	0	3	13	2
Maddox, Garry, of	.298	57	7	17	4	0	1	6	2
Maness, Dwight, of	.297	435	73	129	31	3	9	58	32
McDonald, Jason, of	.171	35	3	6	1	0	0	1	2
Nava, Lipso, 3b	.263	388	51	102	19	1	5	38	3
Nunez, Isaias, 1b-of	.233	193	19	45	11	0	2	21	0
2-team (19 Penn)	.229	266	31	61	12	0	5	31	0
Sanchez, Yuri, ss-2b	.234	154	19	36	5	2	5	19	5
Sherlock, Brian, dh-3b	.220	41	9	9	3	0	1	9	0
Strauss, Brad, of	.252	436	73	110	25	7	13	65	11

PITCHING	W	L	ERA	G	SV	IP	H	BB	SO
Carrasco, Troy	4	6	2.83	36	0	82	87	26	51
Daneker, Pat	2	6	6.66	10	0	53	65	31	26
Dougherty, Kevin	9	1	3.46	14	0	78	89	29	43
Flores, Pedro	5	5	3.95	20	0	116	103	62	102
Jones, Calvin	3	2	3.91	35	0	48	44	25	42
Love, Jeff	1	2	4.62	27	0	64	80	6	35
Lowe, Benny	2	2	3.79	14	0	19	19	11	14
Marr, Jason	1	0	3.86	21	1	21	19	13	15
Matthews, Del	10	9	3.98	34	0	147	173	30	107
Mikkelsen, Linc	16	6	3.32	24	0	152	148	31	95
Osteen, Gavin	4	10	3.35	21	0	126	130	24	69
Ricken, Ray	3	1	2.73	5	0	29	19	14	25
Rizzo, Todd	4	3	1.93	56	6	84	54	26	68
Schurman, Ryan	2	0	3.78	5	0	33	34	14	26
Williams, Jimmy	5	1	0.56	48	28	48	39	10	47

LONG ISLAND

BATTING	AVG	AB	R	H	2B	3B	HR	RBI	SB
Almonte, Wady, of	.286	290	43	83	15	1	10	34	4
Baez, Kevin, ss	.236	390	51	92	22	0	5	48	2
Balfe, Ryan, 3b-of	.246	199	18	49	17	0	5	30	0
Caputo, Tom, 3b-2b	.271	140	23	38	5	0	3	14	1
Chamberlain, Wes, dh	.237	114	6	27	7	1	1	16	2
2-team (49 Newark)	.275	313	42	86	18	3	12	66	5
Davies, Justin, of	.275	444	88	122	12	0	0	39	36
Deitrick, Jeremy	.282	71	7	20	3	1	0	9	1
DeLeon, Sandy, c	.209	91	8	19	2	0	0	8	0
3-team (3 Penn/16 Som.)	.205	156	13	32	2	0	0	12	4
Gibbs, Quincy, of	.143	21	3	3	0	1	0	1	1
Gibralter, Dave, of-dh	.266	252	42	67	13	0	14	40	2
Harrison, Adonis, 2b-ss	.286	227	37	65	14	0	2	23	3
Jennings, Doug, 1b	.288	219	47	63	7	2	12	44	6
Ledesma, Aaron, 3b-2b	.315	409	55	129	22	1	1	59	9
Lennon, Pat, dh	.311	222	52	69	12	0	19	61	3
Martin, Norberto, 2b	.231	160	21	37	6	0	2	13	1
Morales, Francisco, c-1b	.330	430	68	142	25	2	20	85	1
Paciorek, Pete, 1b	.212	146	18	31	5	1	3	23	0
Tovar, Edgar, 2b	.246	61	7	15	1	0	0	4	1
Whiten, Mark, of	.266	169	27	45	11	0	7	29	4
Whitmore, Darrell, of	.460	63	19	29	3	1	6	21	2
Williams, P.J., of	.273	205	37	56	4	2	0	19	19

PITCHING	W	L	ERA	G	SV	IP	H	BB	SO
Arnold, Jamie	3	2	2.87	11	0	59	61	22	33
Benz, Jake	4	3	2.88	30	3	34	27	10	31
2-team (11 Nashua)	5	4	4.35	41	3	49	49	19	50
Bullinger, Jim	4	6	3.80	13	0	83	67	28	56
Cumberland, Chris	0	0	8.44	3	0	5	9	5	4
DeSilva, John	3	3	3.62	9	0	55	50	20	39
Falteisek, Steve	3	1	2.15	31	5	37	33	6	41
Frazier, Ron	7	4	5.14	35	0	91	111	22	45
Halla, Ryan	1	0	6.85	26	8	23	26	20	27
Hartmann, Pete	1	0	8.00	16	0	18	25	11	13
Heiserman, Rick	0	1	5.79	26	0	32	41	17	13
Heredia, Julian	3	6	4.11	11	0	61	80	18	56

2-team (18 Nashua)	10	12	4.40	29	0	167	175	53	159
Kessel, Kyle	0	2	10.45	3	0	10	16	13	8
LaRoche, Jeff	0	1	6.35	7	1	17	25	7	6
2-team (17 Penn)	1	7	5.93	24	1	74	105	33	33
Lewis, Richie	0	2	6.10	4	0	20	22	6	18
2-team (5 Newark)	3	2	3.86	9	0	39	33	8	33
Lisio, Joe	0	0	10.13	3	0	2	2	2	0
Meacham, Rusty	9	6	4.42	45	9	97	103	20	72
Mix, Greg	1	0	1.26	4	0	14	7	3	16
Navarro, Jason	0	0	7.43	12	0	13	22	8	7
Ray, Ken	0	0	11.12	4	0	5	10	0	6
Reed, Brandon	6	4	5.42	23	2	78	98	29	60
Ryan, Jason	10	7	5.08	25	0	152	178	39	92
Shumaker, Tony	0	1	6.43	3	0	7	7	8	6
Smith, Hut	4	7	5.72	31	1	83	97	29	51
Snyder, Matt	2	4	4.64	52	1	75	88	29	51
Thompson, Mark	3	3	5.72	7	0	39	54	13	35
Watson, Allen	0	0	0.00	1	0	1	0	0	0

NASHUA

BATTING	AVG	AB	R	H	2B	3B	HR	RBI	SB
Boston, D.J., 1b	.262	61	10	16	0	1	1	6	3
Clark, Phillip, dh-of	.255	47	5	12	3	0	2	11	0
Correa, Miguel, of	.269	160	23	43	7	1	2	14	6
Cuyler, Milt, of	.193	114	18	22	5	1	2	6	4
English, Chris, dh	.000	4	0	0	0	0	0	0	0
Fonville, Chad, 2b-ss	.255	404	75	103	7	0	0	24	16
Glassey, Josh, c	.181	166	11	30	7	0	0	9	1
Howell, Pat, of-2b	.262	355	51	93	9	3	3	32	24
Johnson, Lance, of	.317	205	39	65	22	7	3	33	11
Jones, Bryan, 2b-3b	.219	183	20	40	7	0	1	14	5
Lebron, Francisco, 1b	.284	236	20	67	16	0	8	28	3
Liniak, Cole, 3b-ss	.269	234	35	63	15	1	1	26	5
Malave, Jose, of	.255	196	27	50	4	0	5	30	4
Murray, Glenn, of	.283	322	49	91	22	0	18	67	16
Nicolas, Jose, of	.111	18	1	2	0	0	0	0	0
Pough, Chop, 3b-1b	.256	398	50	102	23	2	20	66	2
Reyes, Jose, c	.223	278	24	62	15	3	6	29	3
Rodriguez, Juan, of-1b	.258	267	26	69	14	1	2	23	7
Staton, T.J., of	.286	220	28	63	7	2	7	47	4
2-team (35 Penn)	.284	342	50	97	11	5	11	63	8
Terhune, Mike, ss	.242	207	25	50	6	3	5	23	7
Tovar, Edgar, ss	.359	117	13	42	8	0	0	13	2
3-team (15 LI/57 Newark)	.321	420	53	135	11	0	3	39	4

PITCHING	W	L	ERA	G	SV	IP	H	BB	SO
Ali, Sam	2	6	5.72	33	0	78	96	24	56
Baptist, Travis	8	9	3.63	22	0	116	126	41	72
Benz, Jake	1	1	7.63	11	0	15	22	9	19
Corbin, Archie	5	8	4.50	47	1	94	91	52	73
Deschenes, Marc	2	2	6.04	19	4	25	22	12	30
Drumheller, Al	7	12	4.76	28	0	151	153	63	140
Enders, Trevor	2	3	4.66	32	0	46	61	7	35
Etler, Todd	0	1	7.71	15	0	14	20	9	10
Heredia, Julian	7	6	4.57	18	0	106	95	35	103
Kelly, Jeff	1	2	5.15	39	1	50	59	21	34
Larose, Steve	0	0	6.75	3	0	4	3	4	0
Miranda, Angel	2	6	2.84	36	5	76	68	39	68
Mitchell, Kelvin	0	2	5.98	36	0	40	49	18	27
Priest, Eddie	0	0	0.00	6	0	10	4	5	8
Reyes, Eddy	1	1	5.50	17	0	18	18	8	10
Rojas, Mel	4	1	3.24	31	13	33	27	12	26
Roper, John	0	1	8.56	4	0	13	19	6	4
Taylor, Tommy	2	1	2.39	12	0	37	35	13	21
Thompson, Chris	2	4	5.95	9	0	42	57	10	32
Welch, Mike	2	1	2.77	8	1	26	22	8	13
Yennaco, Jay	6	4	3.44	37	1	86	79	37	55

NEWARK

BATTING	AVG	AB	R	H	2B	3B	HR	RBI	SB
Bonds Jr., Bobby, of	.169	59	4	10	2	0	0	1	4
Castillo, Alberto, 1b	.240	150	20	36	10	1	1	17	2
Chamberlain, Wes, 1b-of	.296	199	36	59	11	2	11	50	3
Clyburn, Danny, of	.258	66	7	17	6	0	3	9	0
Esposito, Paul, ss-3b	.263	320	42	84	10	1	3	43	7
Goodwin, Curtis, of	.157	51	10	8	0	1	0	2	1
Hage, Tom, 1b-3b	.294	361	53	106	23	1	20	74	4
Hall, Justin, 2b	.265	196	25	52	7	4	5	29	6
Hurst, Jimmy, dh-of	.341	440	87	150	31	1	35	100	10
Joffrion, Jack, ss-2b	.298	235	39	70	12	4	11	35	3
2-team (23 Atlantic City)	.276	275	42	76	14	4	12	40	3
Knight, Marcus, of	.240	167	19	40	4	1	3	15	2
Laflair, Jay, c	.220	127	15	28	3	1	2	16	2

2-team (42 Atlantic City)	.250	244	28	61	6	1	4	29	3
Mathis, Joe, of	.279	419	99	117	19	8	16	56	17
Matullo, Joe, c	.000	3	0	0	0	0	0	0	0
Minor, Ryan, 3b-1b	.304	224	33	68	12	0	8	29	1
Quintana, Wil, of	.309	217	34	67	11	0	10	30	1
2-team (55 Penn)	.306	432	62	132	23	0	21	72	10
Ramirez, Pito, c	.225	120	19	27	5	0	5	16	2
Rexrode, Jackie, 2b	.341	226	29	77	13	0	0	20	16
Torres, Jason, c	.241	187	14	45	10	1	2	21	2
Tovar, Edgar, 3b	.322	242	33	78	2	0	3	22	1
Williams, P.J., of	.269	223	28	60	5	2	2	17	18
2-team (56 Long Island)	.271	428	65	116	9	4	2	36	37

PITCHING	W	L	ERA	G	SV	IP	H	BB	SO
Armstrong, Jack	3	2	4.33	8	0	43	43	8	34
Bair, Denny	4	6	4.63	42	4	58	57	31	48
Batson, Byron	7	8	4.45	23	0	129	140	28	53
Calandriello, Donato	4	5	5.47	17	0	74	86	21	44
Castillo, Alberto	2	2	3.26	28	5	49	37	15	42
Coleman, Billy	0	1	10.50	2	0	6	11	4	2
DeSilva, John	4	1	3.58	8	0	37	31	7	35
2-team (9 Long Island)	7	4	3.61	17	0	92	81	27	74
Dishman, Richard	0	1	27.00	1	0	1	2	1	0
Foster, Kevin	3	1	2.77	8	1	52	37	21	30
2-team (4 Somerset)	4	1	3.28	12	1	71	61	27	39
Gagliano, Steve	5	6	3.19	35	0	87	95	18	66
Greene, Rick	1	3	6.08	21	8	23	34	14	14
Hahn, Steve	0	1	22.09	3	0	3	9	3	1
Kozlowski, Kris	4	1	3.36	40	1	69	56	21	45
Leiter, Mark	7	4	3.78	15	1	95	109	23	70
Lewis, Richie	3	0	1.42	5	0	19	11	2	15
Linares, Ramon	0	1	7.36	3	0	3	4	3	2
Malko, Bryan	0	0	3.68	12	1	14	14	10	9
Manias, Jim	0	1	47.25	1	0	1	5	2	2
Moraga, David	9	3	3.64	17	0	94	89	19	49
Perrucci, Kevin	2	2	5.40	14	0	56	71	19	18
Ponce De Leon, Damon	1	0	5.40	7	0	10	11	6	5
Shelby, Anthony	1	0	4.37	11	1	23	29	7	16
Shumaker, Tony	0	1	5.89	10	0	18	18	14	8
3-team (2 AC/3 LI)	0	3	6.16	15	0	30	31	30	17
Smith, Hut	4	1	3.19	9	1	42	39	9	24
2-team (31 Long Island)	8	8	4.87	40	2	125	136	38	81
Smith, Mike	1	0	1.29	1	0	7	6	2	3
Tabaka, Jeff	2	4	2.70	27	8	30	27	8	30
Weimer, Matt	2	0	5.29	16	0	32	40	11	14

PENNSYLVANIA

BATTING	AVG	AB	R	H	2B	3B	HR	RBI	SB
Burns, Pat, 1b	.274	441	58	121	25	2	8	41	8
Cameron, Stanton, of	.228	123	14	28	3	0	3	12	1
Craig, Benny, of	.220	182	25	40	5	3	9	21	1
Deitrick, Jeremy, c	.148	54	5	8	1	0	2	6	0
DeLeon, Sandy, c	.200	65	5	13	0	0	0	4	4
Figueroa, Carlos, 2b	.240	100	6	24	2	0	0	2	2
Giron, Alijandro, of	.261	203	22	53	5	1	4	20	1
Guzman, Javier, of	.181	94	9	17	3	0	1	1	0
Knight, Marcus, of	.259	112	17	29	4	1	4	19	3
2-team (53 Newark)	.247	279	36	69	8	2	7	34	5
Lush, Zach, c	.074	27	0	2	0	0	0	1	0
Maddox, Garry, of	.250	44	4	11	0	0	3	4	1
Montas, Ricardo, 3b	.281	288	31	81	14	2	3	31	5
Morales, Jorge, of	.236	106	11	25	3	0	0	8	1
Nicolas, Jose, of	.207	121	13	25	5	0	4	8	5
2-team (6 Nashua)	.194	139	14	27	5	0	4	8	5
Nunez, Isaias, of	.219	73	12	16	1	0	3	10	0
Pena, Rodolfo, c	.220	259	20	57	3	0	0	14	1
Pitts, Kevin, of	.268	284	28	76	17	0	5	31	2
Quintana, Wil, of	.302	215	28	65	12	0	11	42	9
Rodriguez, Rafael, 2b	.235	34	2	8	0	0	0	1	0
Sanchez, Wellington, 2b-ss	.280	414	52	116	19	4	5	41	18
Santana, Efrain, c	.205	78	5	16	1	0	2	10	0
Schmidt, Greg, 3b	.280	282	22	79	5	3	2	30	3
2-team (23 Atlantic City)	.290	341	29	99	8	4	2	33	5
Sein, Javier, 1b-dh	.279	258	28	72	17	0	9	47	1
Velazquez, Juan, ss	.251	338	41	85	7	3	2	18	10
Wilder, Paul, of	.071	14	0	1	0	0	0	0	0
Zaragoza, Joel, ss-2b	.177	113	10	20	3	0	1	12	0

PITCHING	W	L	ERA	G	SV	IP	H	BB	SO
Baker, Jason	0	0	0.00	3	0	3	2	2	2
Brack, A.J.	0	2	6.43	13	0	21	25	14	14
Collazo, Rafael	2	7	6.52	27	1	48	61	31	27
Daneker, Pat	2	7	6.21	12	1	58	63	30	32
2-team (10 Camden)	4	13	6.42	22	1	110	128	61	58
Delgado, Reymundo	1	1	4.22	6	0	10	11	8	6

	W	L	ERA	G	SV	IP	H	BB	SO
Hernández, Robert	0	2	7.63	20	0	46	46	25	32
Hurley, Derek	5	11	7.26	33	0	115	173	35	60
Kessel, Kyle	1	4	9.00	7	0	33	55	14	13
2-team (3 Long Island)	1	6	9.35	10	0	43	71	27	21
Kester, Tim	7	7	2.57	30	2	136	141	24	80
LaRoche, Jeff	1	6	5.81	17	0	57	80	26	27
Maldanando, Esteban	1	4	7.27	28	1	64	88	38	26
Mangieri, John	1	4	6.83	20	3	29	31	20	17
Martinez, Romulo	1	0	6.75	12	0	13	16	6	6
Morris, Ryan	0	0	8.10	9	0	16	23	5	8
Navarro, Jason	3	5	3.14	14	1	48	43	11	43
2-team (12 Long Island)	3	5	4.06	26	1	62	65	19	50
Pena, Eduardo	2	2	9.97	15	0	21	39	13	9
Robinson, Dustin	1	2	5.72	17	1	28	37	12	21
Rosa, Cristy	1	7	5.00	13	0	63	84	22	26
Sams, Aaron	3	5	4.13	13	0	76	69	32	55
Smith, Matt	0	4	4.81	24	0	43	48	31	25
Wagner, Hector	0	0	6.75	4	0	9	13	7	2
Wagner, Matt	0	7	3.71	19	2	70	69	22	49
Weimer, Matt	2	2	2.05	13	4	22	24	6	13
2-team (16 Newark)	4	2	3.98	29	4	54	64	17	27
Zallie, Chris	0	2	6.35	7	0	5	7	6	4

SOMERSET

BATTING	AVG	AB	R	H	2B	3B	HR	RBI	SB
Baxter, Duke, ss-3b	.218	211	24	46	9	1	0	13	1
Berblinger, Jeff, 3b	.249	297	41	74	10	2	8	44	31
Cameron, Stanton, of	.318	22	5	7	1	0	1	2	0
2-team (40 Penn)	.241	145	19	35	4	0	4	14	1
DeLeon, Sandy, c	.204	49	4	10	0	0	0	4	4
Diorio, Andrew, of	.323	65	7	21	6	2	0	9	0
Escandon, Emiliano, 2b	.266	448	67	119	23	4	8	68	3
Fennell, Jason, of-c	.290	335	51	97	23	0	5	35	10
Glavine, Mike, 1b	.273	454	64	124	29	0	21	66	2
Hall, Billy, ss-of	.299	331	58	99	14	4	2	25	52
Miller, Orlando, ss	.319	69	15	22	2	2	5	14	1
Mulligan, Sean, c	.277	303	42	84	13	0	8	41	2
Pennyfeather, William, of	.299	435	59	130	27	2	15	76	9
Poe, Charles, of-dh	.281	303	28	85	12	2	11	50	1
Rodarte, Raul, 3b	.169	65	5	11	2	0	0	6	1
Saitta, Rich, ss	.209	43	4	9	3	0	0	1	1
Staton, T.J., of	.279	122	22	34	4	3	4	16	4
Stovall, DaRond, of	.224	196	27	44	5	3	8	15	8
Warner, Michael, of	.343	108	26	37	8	1	2	8	10
Wilson, Desi, of-dh	.329	362	47	119	20	1	3	66	1

PITCHING	W	L	ERA	G	SV	IP	H	BB	SO
Briscoe, John	1	2	4.05	24	4	26	30	8	20
Bullinger, Jim	2	4	3.84	10	0	58	62	20	42
2-team (13 Long Island)	6	10	3.81	23	0	141	129	48	98
Calmus, Lance	4	4	3.34	45	5	59	60	20	38
Corps, Edwin	3	7	5.57	16	0	74	85	33	36
Dace, Derek	0	5	2.89	49	5	37	30	3	20
Davis, Ray	6	4	2.68	13	0	80	64	33	76
Dodd, Robert	9	7	2.85	25	0	176	143	51	133
Foster, Kevin	1	0	4.66	4	0	19	24	6	9
Gaskill, Derek	0	0	10.38	6	0	4	5	4	7
Griffin, Kirk	8	1	2.43	52	1	81	76	18	57
Jensen, Justin	8	9	3.29	23	0	139	121	55	100
Jordan, Ricardo	12	10	4.57	25	0	155	167	57	97
Lane, Brian	0	0	27.00	1	0	1	5	1	0
Luce, Rob	4	2	4.10	38	1	85	90	20	37
Martines, Jason	0	1	2.29	30	6	35	28	10	19
Winston, Darrin	7	4	4.26	46	6	61	71	18	41

CENTRAL LEAGUE

For the first time in more than 50 years, San Angelo has a championship team.

The San Angelo Colts, runners-up in 2001, edged Jackson 1-0 in the deciding Game 5 of the 2002 Central League championship series.

Foye Minton, Carlos Alvarado and Gilbert Landestoy combined for the shutout in the deciding game, while Hector Piemental singled, stole second then scored on a sacrifice fly by Kevin Brown for the only run of the game.

Brown, a .184 hitter during the regular season, had the game-winning home run in Game 4 of the series to go with the game-winning RBI in Game 5 as San Angelo rallied from a two-games-to-one deficit to win the title.

The Colts bullpen led them to the title, as relievers Carlos Alvarado, the playoff MVP, and Gilbert Landestoy dominated the playoffs. In seven playoff games, the left-handed Alvarado struck out 29 in 15 innings while allowing only five hits, two walks and one run. Landestoy saved four of San Angelo's six playoff victories, as he allowed one run and five hits in eight innings, while striking out seven.

Led by player of the year Jorge Alvarez, Alexandria rolled to a 35-13 record in the second half, winning the Eastern Division by an 11-game margin over Jackson. But Jackson turned the tables on Alexandria in the first round of the playoffs, winning 3-1.

Edinburg's Chad Tredaway was named the league's manager of the year for the second consecutive season, as Edinburg had the best overall record in the West.

STANDINGS

FIRST HALF

EAST	W	L	PCT	GB
Jackson Senators	25	22	.532	—
Alexandria Aces	24	23	.511	1
Springfield/Ozark Mountain Ducks	23	25	.479	2 ½
Fort Worth Cats	17	31	.354	8 ½

WEST	W	L	PCT	GB
Rio Grande Valley WhiteWings	27	21	.563	—
Edinburg Roadrunners	27	21	.563	—
Amarillo Dillas	25	23	.521	2
San Angelo Colts	23	25	.479	4

SECOND HALF

EAST	W	L	PCT	GB
Alexandria Aces	35	13	.729	—
Jackson Senators	24	24	.500	11
Springfield/Ozark Mountain Ducks	22	26	.458	13
Fort Worth Cats	19	29	.396	16

WEST	W	L	PCT	GB
San Angelo Colts	27	21	.563	—
Edinburg Roadrunners	27	21	.563	—
Amarillo Dillas	21	27	.438	6
Rio Grande Valley WhiteWings	17	31	.354	10

PLAYOFFS: Semifinals—Jackson defeated Alexandria 3-1 and San Angelo defeated Edinburg 3-1 in best-of-5 series. **Championship**—San Angelo defeated Jackson 3-2 in best-of-5 series.

MANAGERS: Alexandria—Barry Manuel. **Amarillo**—Lonnie Maclin. **Edinburg**—Chad Tredaway. **Fort Worth**—Jim Gentile/Marty Scott. **Jackson**—Dan Shwam. **Rio Grande Valley**—John Harris. **San Angelo**—Steve Maddock. **Springfield/Ozark**—Phil Wilson.

ATTENDANCE: Fort Worth 160,737; Edinburg 140,713; Springfield/Ozark 96,411; San Angelo 93,460; Amarillo 86,361; Jackson 72,536; Alexandria 52,282; Rio Grande Valley 54,281.

ALL-STAR TEAM: C—Jerry Valdez, Alexandria. **1B**—Derek Henderson, Amarillo. **2B**—Robert Hewes, Alexandria. **3B**—John Ballon, Rio Grande Valley. **SS**—Marc Mirizzi, San Angelo. **OF**—Tom Bost, Jackson; Mike Kirkpatrick, San Angelo; Nestor Smith, San Angelo. **DH**—Jorge Alvarez, Alexandria. **LHP**—Matt Vincent, Jackson. **RHP**—Russ Herbert, Jackson. **RP**—Pedro Cervantes, Edinburg.

Player of the Year: Jorge Alvarez, Alexandria. **Rookie of the Year:** Steve Shirley, Edinburg. **Rookie Pitcher of the Year:** James Carroll, Amarillo. **Manager of the Year:** Chad Tredaway, Edinburg.

INDIVIDUAL BATTING LEADERS
(Minimum 259 Plate Appearances)

	AVG	AB	R	H	2B	3B	HR	RBI	SB
Lopez, Manny, Fort Worth	.347	225	45	78	11	2	2	36	4
Kirkpatrick, Mike, San Angelo	.342	365	66	125	19	7	9	71	25
Mirizzi, Marc, San Angelo	.329	368	82	121	26	4	9	56	17
Smith, Nestor, San Angelo	.328	369	73	121	20	9	10	50	37
Hall, Mel, Ft.Worth/Spring.	.325	286	30	93	20	0	0	47	2
Harriman, Preston, Springfield	.317	360	58	114	22	5	3	51	20
Alvarez, Jorge, Alexandria	.316	392	73	124	23	5	23	105	6
Strickland, Greg, Edinburg	.311	312	49	97	21	7	1	40	23
Henderson, Derek, Amarillo	.309	340	62	105	31	1	10	69	9
Hewes, Robert, Alexandria	.307	361	76	111	20	4	9	59	9

INDIVIDUAL PITCHING LEADERS
(Minimum 77 Innings)

	W	L	ERA	G	SV	IP	H	BB	SO
McClain, Jeremy, Jackson	6	3	2.17	16	0	95	67	30	98

INDEPENDENT LEAGUES

	W	L	ERA	G	SV	IP	H	BB	SO
Herbert, Russ, Jackson	11	6	2.62	19	0	134	110	51	110
Perez, Michelandy, San Angelo	7	0	2.85	18	0	88	68	28	79
Vincent, Matt, Jackson	8	7	2.94	19	0	126	104	33	86
Carroll, James, Amarillo	7	4	3.05	33	0	91	84	23	100
Mozley, Brandon, Spring./Edin.	11	5	3.06	21	0	141	126	45	92
Wollscheid, James, Springfield	5	8	3.72	18	0	123	118	59	98
Markray, Thad, Alexandria	11	1	3.81	21	0	102	76	51	103
Smith, Mike, Amarillo	11	9	3.86	24	0	175	178	38	156
Coleman, Billy, Fort Worth	5	5	3.86	19	2	98	79	63	96

ALEXANDRIA

BATTING	AVG	AB	R	H	2B	3B	HR	RBI	SB
Alvarez, Jorge, dh-2b	.316	392	73	124	23	5	23	105	6
DeFeo, Chris, 2b-ss	.200	10	1	2	0	0	0	0	0
Dusan, Joe, 1b	.247	336	52	83	17	2	9	55	7
Ganter, Jason, of	.156	45	5	7	2	0	0	1	0
Goodwin, Keith, dh	.200	10	1	2	1	0	0	1	1
Hewes, Robert, ss-2b	.307	361	76	111	20	4	9	59	9
O'Donnell, Ryan, of	.332	193	42	64	16	0	2	31	10
Pepper, Danny, c	.179	78	10	14	2	0	0	5	0
Ronai, Jason, of	.233	116	13	27	4	2	0	10	10
Rothe, Ryan, of	.282	337	64	95	16	2	1	44	31
Schifano, Tony, 3b-2b	.306	389	58	119	22	0	6	56	30
Townsend, Scott, of	.239	218	34	52	8	0	6	26	1
Valdez, Jerry, of	.285	340	45	97	26	2	6	44	3
White, Eric, 3b-of	.290	200	37	58	14	0	3	34	1
Zabalza, Javier, ss-2b	.256	215	31	55	8	1	0	24	7

PITCHING	W	L	ERA	G	SV	IP	H	BB	SO
Camp, Rusty	3	0	3.55	10	0	33	22	28	28
Craine, Shevin	1	1	6.91	5	0	14	10	16	5
Hebert, Cedric	0	0	0.00	1	0	1	1	1	0
Jenkins, Cortney	5	1	2.87	8	0	37	35	11	33
Johnson, Chad	2	5	3.76	10	0	52	40	28	31
Markray, Thad	11	1	3.81	21	0	101	76	51	103
Massengale, Chad	4	4	4.38	42	1	61	54	22	52
Moody, Jason	1	0	0.54	17	2	16	10	15	14
2-team (13 Rio Grande Valley)	0	2	1.20	30	10	30	22	19	27
Olivera, Manny	9	6	4.10	24	0	138	163	40	82
Rogers, Charlie	0	0	7.36	5	0	7	7	5	5
Ros, Carlos	3	1	5.24	19	0	46	59	24	27
Slanina, Jason	0	1	9.55	10	0	21	30	10	11
Snyder, Ryan	10	9	3.88	35	1	99	106	15	62
Stout, Dan	2	2	1.95	43	18	50	33	12	60
Thomas, Matt	0	1	3.72	7	0	9	3	6	3
2-year (26 Fort Worth)	1	8	3.64	33	4	64	61	31	58
Vael, Rob	7	4	4.51	21	0	121	121	36	105
Vasquez, Tim	1	0	8.22	5	0	7	14	4	1
2-team (9 San Angelo)	1	0	5.54	14	0	26	29	12	12
Winkle, Ken	1	0	3.95	12	0	13	12	10	14

AMARILLO

BATTING	AVG	AB	R	H	2B	3B	HR	RBI	SB
Brack, Josh, ss	.266	320	46	85	16	4	1	46	7
Braddy, Nehemiah, of	.234	128	9	30	7	1	1	17	2
Cullwell, Nathan, 3b-of	.222	297	36	66	8	2	4	40	5
Garland, Tim, of	.293	307	53	90	10	7	2	26	26
Hardge, Mike, 3b-2b	.273	337	61	92	14	5	12	52	34
Henderson, Derek, 1b	.309	340	62	105	31	1	10	69	9
Hughes, Shawn, c	.229	262	35	60	8	3	7	44	1
Ladd, Micah, of-2b	.266	259	42	69	15	2	2	33	9
Lebron, Hector, of	.196	56	6	11	0	1	3	12	0
Nelson, Chris, of	.277	47	14	13	3	2	0	9	4
Pierce, Justin, of	.261	92	12	24	5	0	2	13	2
Rendle, Rob, of	.235	98	15	23	4	5	0	4	1
Rosado, Omar, 3b	.190	42	9	8	4	0	0	4	0
Ross, Clee, of	.192	26	3	5	0	1	0	3	0
Santos, Juan, dh-c	.261	241	39	63	7	2	3	29	1
Swift, Bryan, 2b	.285	221	27	63	7	1	0	19	7
Thomman, Russell, of	.250	100	13	25	8	0	5	15	1

PITCHING	W	L	ERA	G	SV	IP	H	BB	SO
Buchanan, Todd	1	1	7.56	17	0	33	48	14	28
Carroll, James	7	4	3.05	33	0	91	84	23	100
Dutka, Alex	0	2	5.79	10	0	14	18	2	8
Foster, Clifton	0	0	23.14	3	0	2	6	4	1
Litman, Johri	1	2	10.03	11	0	11	20	9	2
Ortiz, Steve	7	12	4.39	23	0	151	159	51	108
Perio, Ian	0	1	9.00	2	0	6	14	6	3
2-team (3 Fort Worth)	0	1	7.27	5	0	8	18	9	4
Seibert, Kevin	6	9	5.05	23	0	133	174	41	92
Smith, Mike	11	9	3.86	24	0	175	178	38	156
Sutton, Kris	6	3	2.64	46	20	61	70	6	35
Trevino, Chris	5	7	4.88	17	0	90	113	41	63

	W	L	ERA	G	SV	IP	H	BB	SO
Valles, Rolando	2	0	4.71	34	0	49	64	10	37

EDINBURG

BATTING	AVG	AB	R	H	2B	3B	HR	RBI	SB
Bartosh, T.J., of	.230	74	15	17	3	0	0	4	2
Garcia, Ismael, 3b-2b	.287	251	29	72	16	1	5	37	1
Gonzalez, Eric, 2b	.282	195	48	55	11	2	3	21	8
Guerrero, Sergio, 2b-ss	.309	94	17	29	6	0	2	12	2
Hamilton, Mike, ss-2b	.207	145	27	30	2	1	0	13	7
Lang, Eddie, of	.221	131	25	29	5	1	1	6	8
Moore, Vince, of	.299	368	63	110	27	1	3	46	15
Murch, Jeremy, of	.299	144	27	43	14	1	5	28	3
2-team (47 Rio Grande Valley)	.304	313	52	95	31	3	8	57	4
Ness, Andrew, c	.175	80	13	14	1	1	3	10	0
Norrell, Troy, c	.196	286	34	56	5	0	8	28	5
Querecuto, Juan, 1b	.284	366	33	104	22	1	7	59	2
Roland, Will, ss-3b	.305	344	44	105	11	1	0	57	8
Shirley, Steve, dh-3b	.301	349	47	105	24	0	8	65	0
Strickland, Greg, of	.311	312	49	97	21	7	1	40	23
Wilson, Mike, of	.255	200	24	51	12	2	0	23	6

PITCHING	W	L	ERA	G	SV	IP	H	BB	SO
Brown, Chris	4	1	3.10	34	0	69	52	37	64
Cervantes, Pedro	3	1	1.52	40	20	53	46	2	78
Chapman, Billy	0	0	18.00	1	0	1	2	0	1
Colvard, Ron	2	1	3.19	30	2	48	45	11	32
Duwe, Josh	1	4	5.27	10	0	27	29	4	35
Fitch, Steve	0	2	10.57	2	0	7	19	3	3
Green, Scott	10	4	4.43	17	0	111	118	47	85
Harris, Ryan	7	6	5.46	19	0	113	141	41	90
Krysa, Jonathan	5	7	4.21	19	0	117	115	38	111
Mozley, Brandon	2	0	2.79	5	0	29	21	8	20
2-team (16 Springfield)	11	5	3.06	21	0	141	126	45	92
Sanders, Frankie	5	6	5.44	14	0	82	89	39	69
Smith, Clint	8	7	5.05	18	0	117	120	44	81
Tijerina, Tano	2	1	3.91	18	0	23	29	13	29
Williams, Randy	5	2	1.20	42	10	52	36	12	77

FORT WORTH

BATTING	AVG	AB	R	H	2B	3B	HR	RBI	SB
Adames, Winter, ss	.210	62	12	13	1	0	0	6	5
Anderson, Sam, c	.216	102	8	22	5	0	0	12	1
Caruso, Joe, 2b	.250	4	1	1	1	0	0	1	0
Davenport, Shane, 1b	.240	129	7	31	7	0	1	14	0
DeGraffenreid, Todd, 3b	.043	23	1	1	1	0	0	2	0
2-team (6 San Angelo)	.111	36	3	4	1	0	0	2	0
DeMarco, Tony, 1b	.259	216	21	56	7	0	3	26	0
Essian, Jim, of	.216	162	29	35	7	1	1	18	16
2-team (51 Springfield)	.247	328	70	81	9	5	2	36	45
Faggett, Ethan, of	.263	133	19	35	3	2	0	16	9
Giuffre, Guy, c	.148	27	7	4	0	0	2	4	0
Greene, Shawn, dh-of	.270	341	50	92	18	0	12	62	1
Gremminger, Jason, c	.279	122	21	34	6	1	3	20	0
Guillen, Jose, 3b-ss	.240	271	39	65	9	1	4	26	30
Hall, Mel, dh	.321	81	13	26	5	0	0	10	0
Hannon, Pat, of	.286	343	50	98	31	1	7	57	3
Jaramillo, Tony, 2b-3b	.275	193	23	53	3	2	0	21	3
Lopez, Manny, of	.347	225	45	78	11	2	2	36	4
Mejias, Erick, 2b	.290	131	24	38	5	6	1	9	10
2-team (51 San Angelo)	.270	304	51	82	11	7	2	31	35
Ortmayer, Andy, c-3b	.236	106	12	25	4	0	1	8	1
Pope, Dwight, of	.167	12	1	2	0	0	1	2	0
Shemwell, Foy, ss-2b	.205	288	34	59	6	1	1	24	1
Taveras, Frank, of	.316	212	37	67	16	3	6	44	2
Taylor, T.D., 3b	.117	60	8	7	0	0	1	6	2
Thomas, Kyle, c	.200	40	7	8	2	0	1	2	0
2-team (1 Jackson)	.186	43	7	8	2	0	1	2	0
Wilkerson, Clint, of	.000	3	0	0	0	0	0	0	0

PITCHING	W	L	ERA	G	SV	IP	H	BB	SO
Coleman, Billy	5	5	3.86	19	2	98	79	63	96
Davidson, Jackie	1	0	8.14	10	1	21	33	3	8
Dobbins, Aaron	1	0	16.62	4	0	4	12	1	1
Guzman, Jose	6	8	4.20	17	0	111	129	27	69
Hahn, Steve	4	6	4.12	30	0	94	99	26	48
Harrington, Matt	2	3	6.84	5	0	25	30	10	24
Heinrichs, Darren	0	0	8.59	5	0	7	8	2	6
Hickey, Mark	0	2	5.92	18	0	24	30	10	16
James, Frank	0	0	7.11	4	0	6	10	3	4
Kimball, Cody	0	0	7.88	7	0	8	11	4	7
Lina, Estivinson	0	2	5.85	13	0	20	21	16	13
Linares, Ramon	0	2	2.89	9	3	9	8	4	11
2-team (28 Jackson)	2	4	3.64	37	6	46	45	15	43
Morgan, Shawn	1	6	6.98	31	0	80	117	41	70

	W	L	ERA	G	SV	IP	H	BB	SO
Onley, Shawn	5	10	4.88	20	0	120	131	44	113
Perio, Ian	0	0	3.38	3	0	2	4	3	1
Powalski, Rick	3	1	3.28	14	4	46	39	13	59
Randel, Matt	4	5	3.05	28	1	65	70	20	75
Ros, Carlos	2	0	6.75	7	0	14	21	7	7
2-team (19 Alexandria)	5	1	5.61	26	0	61	80	31	34
Sanchez, Cade	0	0	11.37	7	0	6	12	4	2
Swinburnson, Tyler	0	2	4.50	10	2	12	12	10	7
Thomas, Matt	1	7	3.62	26	4	54	52	28	52
Urdahl, Tucker	0	0	2.45	2	0	3	3	1	3
Winkle, Ken	1	3	7.58	12	1	19	23	11	12
2-team (12 Alexandria)	2	3	6.06	24	1	32	35	21	26

JACKSON

BATTING	AVG	AB	R	H	2B	3B	HR	RBI	SB
Bost, Tom, of-1b	.304	322	62	98	23	5	14	50	10
Butler, Jeff, 3b	.154	13	1	2	0	0	0	0	0
Capodieci, Adam, c	.133	30	1	4	0	0	0	2	0
Darjean, Eric, of-3b	.341	88	12	30	3	0	0	7	9
Dettman, Matt, 3b	.208	48	5	10	4	0	1	10	0
Gearlds, Aaron, of	.250	4	1	1	0	0	0	0	0
Gonzalez, Carlos, c	.213	61	7	13	2	0	2	5	0
Hawthorne, Kyle, ss	.302	334	56	101	20	4	6	49	7
Lara, Eddie, 2b-1b	.271	85	9	23	3	0	1	9	0
McCall, Gerard, c	.199	261	26	52	8	0	3	31	0
Milliner, Ehren, dh-2b	.118	17	3	2	0	0	1	2	0
Moreno, Juan, of	.296	368	67	109	22	2	6	37	39
Nerei, Yuji, dh-1b	.154	26	2	4	1	0	1	4	0
Osilka, Garret, 2b	.286	322	64	92	16	4	5	35	25
Pimentel, Hector, 3b	.268	220	19	59	12	1	6	30	2
Simmons, Jerry, of	.274	329	45	90	22	10	3	40	14
Singletary, Dan, of	.200	100	14	20	4	0	1	10	6
Sosa, Nick, dh-1b	.227	207	23	47	13	1	5	37	0
Taveras, Frank, 3b	.254	59	10	15	4	0	3	19	2
3-team (22 SA/51 Ft.Worth)	.284	349	58	99	25	4	10	74	4
Thomas, Kyle, c	.000	3	0	0	0	0	0	0	0
Williams, Peanut, 1b-dh	.231	251	31	58	9	1	7	43	5

PITCHING	W	L	ERA	G	SV	IP	H	BB	SO
Canchola, Efren	1	0	7.94	19	0	22	32	9	9
Carroll, Ryan	0	2	5.55	15	0	24	27	14	18
Friske, Parker	10	7	4.27	19	0	130	140	41	73
Hardcastle, J.D.	2	3	6.60	8	0	30	40	21	17
2-team (10 Springfield)	5	7	8.16	18	0	75	101	51	50
Herbert, Russ	11	6	2.62	19	0	134	110	51	110
Linares, Ramon	2	4	3.82	28	3	37	38	11	32
McClain, Jeremy	6	3	2.17	16	0	95	67	30	98
Miyamoto, Eiji	0	0	1.42	5	0	6	9	0	4
Parker, Brandon	1	0	1.64	31	20	33	20	19	54
Patrylo, Ryan	0	0	14.73	3	0	3	7	3	2
Price, Nathan	1	1	1.17	6	0	7	6	6	12
Taniguchi, Koichi	1	3	2.93	14	0	30	33	10	28
Vandergrif, Nick	0	0	1.93	3	0	4	3	1	0
Vincent, Matt	8	7	2.94	19	0	125	104	33	86
Ware, Jeff	8	10	4.08	19	0	132	123	41	99

RIO GRANDE VALLEY

BATTING	AVG	AB	R	H	2B	3B	HR	RBI	SB
Baker, Casey, 2b	.208	96	22	20	8	1	1	6	5
Ballon, John, 3b	.302	344	72	104	20	2	15	74	4
Colameco, Joe, of	.254	350	51	89	23	5	5	45	7
Fox, Brandon, of	.134	67	7	9	0	0	0	4	1
Fuentes, Joel, ss-2b	.293	355	60	104	15	1	0	29	19
Golom, Edmond, 2b	.180	50	6	9	1	0	0	2	0
Hook, Kenny, ss	.234	145	11	34	4	0	0	13	3
Johnson, Ryan, 2b	.250	76	12	19	2	0	0	5	1
Murch, Jeremy, of	.308	169	25	52	17	2	3	29	1
Oropeza, Willie, 1b-c	.304	342	44	104	22	0	11	59	3
Perich, Josh, of	.242	182	22	44	9	0	4	21	0
Ransom, Grant, of	.179	28	1	5	0	0	0	2	0
Ricard, Toby, of-2b	.175	40	6	7	1	0	0	2	0
3-team (13 Spring./38 SA)	.276	243	33	67	9	1	4	23	8
Scott, Charlie, c-1b	.241	320	37	77	18	1	7	44	2
Smith, Brent, of	.145	83	5	12	0	0	0	6	1
Taylor, T.D., 1b-2b	.245	163	20	40	8	0	4	17	1
2-team (19 Fort Worth)	.211	223	28	47	8	0	5	23	3
Van Asselberg, Ricky, dh-1b	.221	271	23	60	13	0	1	35	1
Wilson, Mike, of	.304	135	21	41	9	3	6	25	10
2-team (50 Edinburg)	.275	335	45	92	21	5	6	48	16

PITCHING	W	L	ERA	G	SV	IP	H	BB	SO
Aquino, Julio	1	0	6.35	5	0	5	4	2	4
Brown, Steve	7	8	4.80	24	0	122	137	60	86
Donovan, T.J.	1	3	4.00	7	0	36	36	22	19

	W	L	ERA	G	SV	IP	H	BB	SO
2-team (8 San Angelo)	2	4	5.25	15	0	58	69	31	32
Flanagan, Chris	1	1	3.38	5	0	13	11	3	10
Goure, Sam	9	8	4.08	20	0	132	128	54	100
Guzman, Alex	5	3	1.44	41	18	56	38	10	44
Hampton, Mark	4	3	5.36	7	0	43	55	18	28
Lake, Josh	0	1	4.50	19	0	32	31	22	16
Martinez, Johnny	5	8	6.00	17	0	99	129	34	65
Moody, Jason	1	0	2.03	13	8	13	12	4	13
Mullen, Trey	1	0	7.56	3	0	8	8	12	6
Perez, Julio	1	1	2.75	40	0	52	33	37	50
Rodriguez, Mario	3	2	2.06	8	0	48	50	14	33
Steadham, Ryan	0	1	6.33	18	0	21	21	18	19
2-team (2 San Angelo)	1	1	6.12	20	0	25	26	23	21
Whitworth, Brad	1	4	4.54	25	0	39	45	17	37
Wilcher, Justin	6	7	5.20	24	0	105	127	48	74

SAN ANGELO

BATTING	AVG	AB	R	H	2B	3B	HR	RBI	SB
Baird, Matt, of	.167	60	9	10	2	0	1	5	3
Bollig, Jake, of	.000	3	0	0	0	0	0	0	0
Brown, Kevin, c	.184	147	16	27	3	0	2	12	0
Cairo, Sergio, of	.319	141	16	45	14	0	4	30	1
Campaniello, Ed, dh	.269	104	13	28	4	1	0	11	3
DeGraffenreid, Todd, 3b	.231	13	2	3	0	0	0	0	0
Downing, Brad, of	.182	44	3	8	2	0	1	6	0
James, Tony, 2b	.239	306	47	73	11	3	11	49	10
Jaramillo, Tony, 3b-2b	.198	111	14	22	5	0	0	8	1
2-team (55 Fort Worth)	.247	304	37	75	8	2	0	29	4
Johnson, Ryan, 2b	.143	35	7	5	1	0	0	2	0
2-team (26 Rio Grande Valley)	.216	111	19	24	3	0	0	7	1
Kirkpatrick, Mike, of-1b	.342	365	66	125	19	7	9	71	25
Lara, Eddie, 1b	.310	258	57	80	14	2	11	51	15
2-team (23 Jackson)	.300	343	66	103	17	2	12	60	15
Matos, Malvin, dh-of	.293	164	21	48	11	2	6	31	0
Mejias, Erick, 3b	.254	173	27	44	6	1	1	22	25
Mirizzi, Marc, ss	.332	368	82	122	26	4	9	56	17
Pierce, Justin, dh	.244	45	5	11	3	0	1	8	0
2-team (27 Amarillo)	.255	137	17	35	8	0	3	21	2
Pimentel, Hector, 3b	.278	18	6	5	0	0	0	3	1
2-team (62 Jackson)	.269	238	25	64	12	1	6	33	3
Pope, Dwight, c	.239	109	11	26	6	1	1	14	1
2-team (6 Fort Worth)	.231	121	12	28	6	1	2	16	1
Powell, Paul, 3b-of	.253	158	18	40	9	0	2	22	2
Ricard, Toby, of-2b	.291	148	24	43	7	1	3	17	8
Shindle, Chad, c	.375	16	2	6	0	0	0	3	0
Smith, Bryon, 2b	.091	11	0	1	0	0	0	0	0
Smith, Nestor, of	.328	369	73	121	20	9	10	50	37
Sullivan, Chad, c	.000	3	0	0	0	0	0	0	0
Taveras, Frank, dh-of	.218	78	11	17	5	1	1	11	0
Walker, Keronn, c	.111	18	1	2	1	0	0	2	0
Waller, Garric, of	.000	3	1	0	0	0	0	0	0

PITCHING	W	L	ERA	G	SV	IP	H	BB	SO
Alvarado, Carlos	4	2	3.09	25	0	46	33	22	67
Anderson, Antwoine	8	7	3.97	19	0	111	116	25	59
Baker, Jason	0	1	6.23	4	0	17	16	12	12
Boker, John	0	0	9.00	2	0	10	12	5	9
Donovan, T.J.	1	1	7.25	8	0	22	33	9	13
Duwe, Josh	0	1	5.01	15	0	23	27	7	24
2-team (10 Edinburgh)	1	5	5.15	25	0	50	56	11	59
Hays, Cody	0	0	13.50	2	0	1	2	3	0
Heinrichs, Darren	0	0	6.00	3	0	3	4	0	2
2-team (5 Fort Worth)	0	0	7.84	8	0	10	12	2	8
Landestoy, Gilbert	2	2	2.66	44	22	61	57	21	41
Lina, Estivinson	0	1	5.68	5	0	6	8	3	9
2-team (13 Fort Worth)	0	3	5.81	18	0	26	29	19	22
Martin, Tom	1	3	7.71	4	0	18	28	9	12
Minton, Foye	3	3	1.93	5	0	28	33	4	13
Moore, Eric	3	3	2.63	39	0	48	58	12	34
Moreno, Leo	3	0	2.95	3	0	18	20	6	13
O'Quinn, Mickey	1	1	2.38	7	0	22	26	6	23
Paz, Ivan	0	1	5.73	2	0	11	9	9	1
Perez, Michelandy	7	0	2.85	18	0	88	68	28	79
Perez, Pablo	6	10	4.63	21	0	126	127	48	97
Ramirez, Hector	2	3	5.82	7	0	43	52	13	22
Shirasaka, Katsushi	0	1	18.00	1	0	2	5	4	1
St. Amant, John	8	7	4.15	19	0	99	94	30	80
Steadham, Ryan	1	0	4.91	2	0	3	5	5	2
Trenck, Matthew	0	1	10.80	6	0	6	16	3	5
Vasquez, Tim	0	0	4.42	9	0	18	15	8	11

SPRINGFIELD/OZARK

BATTING	AVG	AB	R	H	2B	3B	HR	RBI	SB
Ayers, Yancey, c	.196	204	22	40	5	1	2	26	0

Beale, Brad, c	.132	38	2	5	1	0	0	6	0
Booker, Steve, of	.158	38	9	6	3	0	0	2	4
Cepeda, Malcolm, dh	.241	79	14	19	2	0	1	6	6
Clark, Jamie, of	.170	47	5	8	3	0	0	5	0
Essian, Jim, of	.277	166	41	46	2	4	1	18	29
Green, Steve, of	.293	140	18	41	8	2	1	19	5
Green, Terence, ss	.286	370	49	106	19	3	3	55	10
Hall, Mel, dh	.324	204	17	66	15	0	0	37	2
2-team (22 Fort Worth)	.323	285	30	92	20	0	0	47	2
Harriman, Preston, 3b	.317	360	58	114	22	5	3	51	20
King, Bryan, 2b-of	.278	115	18	32	6	0	0	5	4
Ortmayer, Andy, c	.244	82	11	20	3	0	2	14	0
2-team (36 Fort Worth)	.239	188	23	45	7	0	3	22	1
Phipps, Tim, of	.215	158	15	34	0	3	1	18	3
Ricard, Toby, of	.309	55	3	17	1	0	1	4	0
Roberts, Damian, 2b	.286	315	51	90	14	0	1	32	9
Schied, Jeremy, 1b	.264	333	34	88	21	1	1	43	6
Thompson, Jason, of	.275	356	55	98	23	5	7	41	3
Valdez, Castulo, c	.167	18	3	3	0	1	0	1	0
Van Allen, Larry, of	.238	101	12	24	6	0	0	9	5
Watchowski, Donnie, 3b-of	.250	40	6	10	1	0	0	8	1

PITCHING	W	L	ERA	G	SV	IP	H	BB	SO
Buchanan, Todd	0	0	3.77	10	1	14	19	1	7
2-team (17 Amarillo)	1	1	6.42	27	1	47	67	15	35
Buschhorn, Bryan	1	1	10.38	15	1	21	27	22	9
Cowling, Ross	3	10	4.39	19	1	80	77	46	56
Dettman, Andy	7	7	4.63	17	0	105	121	42	59
Dill, Matt	4	5	5.12	27	9	58	70	26	36
Eddie, Derek	6	2	3.39	12	1	71	66	20	43
Ellison, Darrin	0	0	5.40	1	0	1	4	2	0
Evans, Brent	1	0	2.72	18	0	36	34	17	23
Goodmann, Joe	1	2	3.77	28	7	43	42	20	41
Hardcastle, J.D.	3	4	9.20	10	0	45	61	30	33
May, Phillip	0	0	6.48	7	0	16	22	4	9
Mozley, Brandon	9	5	3.12	16	0	112	105	37	72
Oelke, Steven	2	2	4.84	11	1	35	44	14	24
Owens, Bert	0	0	4.91	3	0	7	7	5	2
Sanchez, Mike	2	1	5.19	7	0	17	22	7	15
Sanders, Frankie	1	2	6.00	3	0	18	20	9	13
2-team (14 Edinburg)	6	8	5.54	17	0	100	109	48	82
Smith, Brock	0	2	6.50	12	0	18	25	7	9
Wollscheid, James	5	8	3.72	18	0	123	118	59	98

FRONTIER LEAGUE

After he hit .213 in his senior season at Mississippi State in 2001, Phil Willingham figured he was finished with baseball. The Richmond Roosters are glad that Willingham gave the game one more chance.

After much coaxing from his family, Willingham decided in the spring of 2002 to attend a San Diego Padres tryout camp. Willingham didn't impress the Padres enough to earn a contract, but he did catch the eye of Roosters manager Fran Riordan, who offered him a spot on the Frontier League club.

Phil Willingham

Riordan's scouting paid off in a title, as Willingham led the Roosters to their second-straight championship. The center fielder hit .360-15-86 with 36 stolen bases and 75 runs scored to be named the league's MVP and rookie of the year.

Willingham's three-run homer on a full count with two outs in the ninth inning lifted Richmond past Dubois County, 4-3, in the deciding Game 3 of their semifinal playoff series. Richmond then beat Washington three-games-to-one in the championship series.

Over the seven playoff games, Willingham hit .367-3-11. Richmond catcher Jeremiah Klosterman was named the playoff MVP for the second straight season after hitting .400 in the playoffs.

Riordan, who also was the league's all-star first baseman, will have to move on to another league in 2003 if he wants to continue playing, as the league has a 27-year-old age limit.

Willingham will move on as well. The 23-year-old center fielder signed a contract with the Seattle Mariners after the season.

Willingham's year was one of several standout seasons in the FL. With a .405 batting average, Cook County third baseman Pichi Balet broke former major leaguer Morgan Burkhart's league record for batting average, while Washington's Jared Howton (11-3, 1.98) earned the most valuable pitcher award with a dominating season.

As a team, Washington (56-28), in its first year, set a league record for wins in a season.

STANDINGS

EAST	W	L	PCT	GB
Washington Wild Things	56	28	.667	—
Richmond Roosters	53	31	.631	3
Kalamazoo Kings	46	38	.548	10
Canton Coyotes	41	43	.488	15
Chillicothe Paints	35	49	.417	21
Johnstown Johnnies	30	54	.357	26

WEST	W	L	PCT	GB
Dubois County Dragons	52	32	.619	—
Rockford RiverHawks	45	39	.536	7
Cook County Cheetahs	40	44	.476	12
River City Rascals	39	45	.464	13
Gateway Grizzlies	34	50	.405	18
Evansville Otters	33	51	.393	19

PLAYOFFS: Semifinals—Richmond defeated Dubois County 2-1 and Washington defeated Kalamazoo 2-0 in best-of-3 series. **Finals**—Richmond defeated Washington 3-1 in best-of-5 series.

MANAGERS: Canton—Gregg Neuman. **Chillicothe**—Jamie Keefe. **Cook County**—Dana Forsberg. **Dubois County**—Greg Tagert. **Evansville**—Greg Jelks. **Gateway**—Rich Sauget Jr. **Johnstown**—Kirk Taylor. **Kalamazoo**—Woody Sorrell. **Richmond**—Fran Riordan. **River City**—Neil Fiala. **Rockford**—Bob Koopman; **Washington**—Jeff Isom.

ATTENDANCE: River City 162,597; Washington 132,901; Kalamazoo 103,880; Gateway 92,819; Rockford 86,842; Evansville 88,585; Chillicothe 67,452; Cook County 66,214; Richmond 45,322; Dubois County 35,592; Johnstown 35,208; Canton 30,971.

ALL-STAR TEAM: C—Shaun Argento, Washington. **1B**—Fran Riordan, Richmond. **2B**—Ben Fjelland, Rockford. **3B**—Pichi Balet, Cook County. **SS**—Brad Hensler, Washington. **OF**—Phil Willingham, Richmond; Brody Jackson, River City; Adam Olow, Dubois County. **DH**—Joe Gerber, Kalamazoo. **SP**—Jared Howton, Washington. **RP**—Robert Gavin, Washington.

Most Valuable Player—Phil Willingham, Richmond. **Most Valuable Pitcher**—Jared Howton, Washington. **Rookie of the Year**—Phil Willingham, Richmond. **Manager of the Year**—Jeff Isom, Washington. **Organization of the Year:** Washington.

INDIVIDUAL BATTING LEADERS
(Minimum 227 Plate Appearances)

	AVG	AB	R	H	2B	3B	HR	RBI	SB
Balet, Pichi, Cook County	.405	304	56	123	18	2	6	64	0
Willingham, Phil, Richmond	.360	364	75	131	19	8	15	86	36
Argento, Shaun, Washington	.352	290	47	102	20	5	5	62	10
Loggins, Josh, Washington	.347	242	40	84	18	0	5	45	4
Olow, Adam, Dubois County	.345	264	71	91	15	2	10	59	22
Marple, Scott, Richmond	.344	209	33	72	16	0	4	34	7
Fjelland, Ben, Rockford	.344	346	63	119	25	2	9	70	7
Schmitz, John, Cook County	.343	274	59	94	19	1	5	32	12
Leverett, Dave, Richmond	.333	330	60	110	13	1	0	48	12
Fuess, Brian, River City	.331	338	54	112	17	0	9	65	4

INDIVIDUAL PITCHING LEADERS
(Minimum 67 Innings)

	W	L	ERA	G	SV	IP	H	BB	SO
Howton, Jared, Washington	11	3	1.98	17	0	109	86	38	89
Batthauer, Bryan, Rockford	9	4	2.45	17	1	121	111	44	118
Hickman, Ben, Canton	3	4	2.62	23	1	69	68	23	61
Clelland, James, Cook County	7	5	2.80	16	0	113	110	29	88
Baca, Enriques, Richmond	10	4	2.87	18	0	119	111	38	110
Gaines, Jamal, Dubois County	8	2	3.06	17	0	103	103	14	93
Kuiper, David, Dubois County	7	2	3.14	16	0	83	88	21	63
Buck, Pete, Gateway	7	5	3.35	19	0	126	126	35	93
Moenter, Curtis, Richmond	5	3	3.36	16	0	86	79	38	90
Jelovcic, Rich, Richmond	7	5	3.44	20	2	99	115	21	78

CANTON

BATTING	AVG	AB	R	H	2B	3B	HR	RBI	SB
Arroyo, Tim, dh-1b	.217	23	1	5	1	0	1	5	0
Brown, Seth, 3b	.273	271	25	74	6	2	3	35	11
Carroll, Justin, dh	.048	21	3	1	0	0	0	0	0
Clement, Mike, c	.250	12	1	3	0	0	0	2	1
Dorak, Dan, dh	.162	37	6	6	1	0	0	2	1
Driscoll, Jason, of	.231	39	7	9	0	1	0	7	4
Felty, Chad, of	.235	187	28	44	7	1	2	23	18
Forman, Wayne, c	.140	50	1	7	1	0	0	4	0
Friedman, Tim, 2b-3b	.252	111	14	28	4	1	0	19	4
Greenwell, William, 1b-of	.342	111	17	38	10	2	0	21	1
Hendrickson, Justin, 1b	.292	219	32	64	15	1	8	46	6
King, Bryan, 2b	.071	14	0	1	0	0	0	1	0
Larned, Andy, c	.221	226	29	50	11	1	7	29	7
Lindburg, Ryan, P	.133	15	2	2	1	0	0	2	0
Memmert, Gabe, dh-1b	.271	48	10	13	4	0	1	9	0
Morrison, Lee, dh	.263	80	12	21	8	0	1	9	4
2-team (4 Washington)	.245	94	12	23	8	0	1	9	4
Pearl, Matt, of	.233	30	2	7	1	1	0	3	5
Prussing, Ric, of	.232	220	30	51	6	0	0	13	14
Rittenhouse, Adam, 2b	.304	247	34	75	19	0	2	26	10
Simpson, Ernic, dh-of	.188	32	6	6	1	0	0	0	4
Smith, Rod, of-2b	.287	136	25	39	12	1	4	14	13
Thomas, Mark, of	.230	61	10	14	5	0	0	7	9
Vanlderstine, Ben, of	.300	280	34	84	10	3	3	36	14
Vittito, Cooper, ss	.290	276	50	80	5	0	0	22	32

PITCHING	W	L	ERA	G	SV	IP	H	BB	SO
Barbettini, Chris	1	1	1.82	21	6	24	22	14	25
Barnes, Pat	2	1	5.71	6	0	17	16	11	10
Bays, Lenny	0	0	7.36	4	0	7	10	3	4
Bishop, Trevor	5	6	5.92	15	0	65	72	33	49
Buckle, Matt	7	6	3.83	15	0	96	101	22	55
Durkee, Jeremy	2	2	9.11	7	0	26	46	13	22
Forbes, Jeff	1	1	4.15	5	0	8	9	10	7
George, Todd	7	6	4.07	16	0	101	122	25	65
Haupt, John	0	0	0.00	6	0	9	4	0	5
Hickman, Ben	3	4	2.66	23	1	67	67	22	58
Johnson, James	1	0	0.00	7	2	9	4	2	14
Johnson, Jeff	1	0	1.13	5	1	8	3	4	9
Khoury, Josh	0	2	7.04	14	1	15	19	23	12
Kojack, Phil	4	7	3.98	13	0	81	81	27	63
Lindburg, Ryan	0	1	11.45	4	0	11	21	5	8
McMurray, Heath	1	0	0.78	5	0	23	13	10	21
Menke, Craig	1	0	3.60	5	0	5	5	4	8
Mosher, Craig	1	1	5.83	19	1	46	65	22	34
Orr, Ben	0	0	5.93	12	3	13	15	18	20
Rivera, Francisco	0	0	18.00	2	0	2	3	2	0
Rollandini, David	2	4	3.67	27	3	73	59	23	61
Welch, Mike	1	1	1.40	4	0	19	12	10	13

CHILLICOTHE

BATTING	AVG	AB	R	H	2B	3B	HR	RBI	SB
Brown, Justin, 2b-ss	.233	150	23	35	5	0	0	7	1
Cerni, Vincent, 2b	.258	178	17	46	11	1	3	22	2
2-team (9 Washington)	.246	203	19	50	11	1	3	27	3
Edwards, Willie, of	.314	274	47	86	15	2	5	43	7
Elrod, Nick, ss	.293	41	18	12	1	1	1	4	0
Graham, Jess, of	.230	204	25	47	16	1	3	22	0
Guiseppe, John, c	.000	5	1	0	0	0	0	1	0
Gunderson, Jeff, ss	.091	22	4	2	0	0	0	2	0
2-team (13 Kalamazoo)	.132	53	6	7	1	0	0	3	0
Hernandez, Miguel, 3b	.298	168	16	50	12	1	1	21	1
Kinsolving, Darin, 1b	.295	281	62	83	15	3	15	58	1
McCay, Matt, of	.322	326	60	105	15	2	7	50	7
Merkich, Scott, 3b-2b	.267	90	13	24	5	1	0	16	6
Newell, Tim, c	.258	89	9	23	4	0	0	6	0
O'Kelly, Mike, 3b-of	.195	41	2	8	3	0	0	5	0
Patterson, Adam, c	.259	143	20	37	6	1	3	17	0
Rossy, Eric, ss	.235	221	31	52	9	0	5	25	9
See, Andrew, 3b	.230	74	8	17	2	0	1	2	0
Simmons, Michah, of	.179	67	12	12	0	1	1	6	5
Swackhamer, Rusty, dh	.275	200	27	55	15	1	5	41	1
Wallis, Jacob, c	.175	57	7	10	2	0	2	9	0
Warren, Phil, dh-of	.314	242	31	76	12	2	3	41	0

PITCHING	W	L	ERA	G	SV	IP	H	BB	SO
Biddlestone, Jason	3	4	5.80	21	0	71	80	42	76
Blanc, Rick	6	8	4.49	19	0	134	160	42	119
Bogs, Brian	2	2	3.30	50	4	43	45	22	48
Buirley, Kris	2	8	3.56	36	16	43	33	28	50
Flanagan, Chris	2	2	6.26	18	0	27	42	14	26
Goemann, Reed	0	0	0.00	1	0	0	0	1	1

COOK COUNTY

BATTING	AVG	AB	R	H	2B	3B	HR	RBI	SB
Balet, Pichi, 3b	.405	304	56	123	18	2	6	64	0
Berghein, Jeremiah, ss	.371	35	5	13	3	0	1	4	2
Bischofberger, Sean, dh-3b	.290	207	48	60	14	2	12	45	1
Conway, Rob, 2b-3b	.250	252	27	63	18	0	3	38	2
Figueroa, Carlos, 2b	.185	27	2	5	0	0	0	1	0
Firlit, Dan, ss	.261	226	28	59	12	3	3	26	2
Forsberg, Dana, 1b	.571	7	3	4	0	0	1	1	0
Galvan, Ron, c	.219	96	9	21	5	0	3	14	0
Gianfortune, Mario, of	.222	9	1	2	0	1	0	0	2
Gontmaher, Nick, of	.300	260	55	78	19	1	2	23	16
2-team (12 Johnstown)	.293	300	62	88	23	1	2	31	20
Hambelton, Jon, 1b	.281	217	26	61	15	1	6	30	1
Loughrey, Brendan, c	.188	101	13	19	2	0	0	7	2
Luebbert, Garet, 2b	.164	61	8	10	1	1	1	5	2
Pollard, Brandon, of	.218	87	14	19	7	0	1	11	1
Rinne, James, of	.265	272	32	72	11	1	2	41	10
Runnells, T.J., ss	.283	92	14	26	2	0	1	9	4
2-team (11 Evansville)	.260	127	20	33	3	0	1	12	5
Schmitz, John, of	.343	274	59	94	19	1	5	32	12
Stegbauer, Rick, 1b-dh	.302	252	29	76	14	0	1	36	3
Van Horn, Ryan, c	.229	109	17	25	2	0	2	9	1
Wilke, Josh, of	.235	51	10	12	2	1	1	10	0

PITCHING	W	L	ERA	G	SV	IP	H	BB	SO
Barbarossa, Joshua	0	1	0.00	6	2	7	4	8	7
Bircher, Chad	4	4	1.86	30	7	38	30	9	32
Browning, James	0	1	22.50	1	0	2	3	4	1
Chinea, Julio	0	1	1.80	7	0	10	8	3	9
2-team (31 Dubois)	2	3	4.89	38	1	53	63	18	54
Clelland, James	7	5	2.80	16	0	112	110	29	88
David, Toby	2	7	6.28	17	0	81	103	27	49
Etner, Tony	0	3	2.76	4	0	26	23	7	9
Greco, Sam	0	3	6.12	6	0	32	36	17	23
Honda, Tomohiro	4	4	4.96	11	0	65	70	18	56
Houdek, Brian	4	4	3.03	11	0	62	42	33	67
Kerber, Travis	0	1	6.75	4	0	5	6	4	1
Mack, Bobby	3	4	4.88	30	0	55	66	33	46
Marko, Ed	0	0	6.75	1	0	1	2	0	2
Nagasaka, Nideki	0	1	13.50	1	0	4	7	3	2
Nichols, Scott	0	0	45.00	2	0	1	5	0	2
Palmer, Adam	3	3	4.07	32	1	55	68	25	29
Prendes, Alex	2	0	7.36	12	0	11	17	10	11
Regas, Kris	3	0	2.90	10	0	40	38	10	29
Sadowski, Kevin	0	1	7.00	2	0	9	11	8	3
Weel, Mike	0	1	5.74	5	0	15	21	6	10
White, Eric	3	3	3.36	28	3	64	57	34	49
Williams, Grant	3	1	2.70	28	1	40	39	8	36

DUBOIS COUNTY

BATTING	AVG	AB	R	H	2B	3B	HR	RBI	SB
Davis, Matt, of	.400	5	0	2	0	0	0	0	1
Goirilgolzarri, Ray, of	.273	256	53	70	19	1	7	50	21
Huling, Andrew, of	.303	307	61	93	11	1	2	33	29
Kalczynski, Joe, c	.275	200	26	55	10	3	1	38	3
Krance, Max, of-dh	.236	157	20	37	4	0	0	14	3
Landon, Josh, 2b	.266	267	38	71	9	0	1	29	5
Leathers, Todd, dh-3b	.292	106	17	31	10	0	1	17	1
2-team (15 Johnstown)	.289	142	23	41	11	0	1	20	1
Lombardi, Dominick, c	.276	123	18	34	10	0	1	17	0
Olow, Adam, of	.345	264	71	91	15	2	10	59	22
Peerman, Mike, 1b	.300	140	17	42	11	0	1	33	0
Pelfrey, Dennis, 3b	.297	290	60	86	11	4	5	55	38
Riddle, Ron, 2b	.087	23	2	2	0	0	0	1	0
Santangelo, Jason, ss-2b	.207	58	9	12	1	0	1	10	1
Stanley, Aaron, of	.282	163	28	46	6	0	1	20	18
Tranum, Josh, 1b	.330	261	56	86	16	0	9	62	2
Vidal, J.D., ss	.286	301	51	86	18	1	1	28	10

PITCHING	W	L	ERA	G	SV	IP	H	BB	SO
Bennet, Jamie	7	4	3.75	17	0	98	99	29	77
Chinea, Julio	1	3	5.61	31	1	43	55	15	45

(Gostisha, Riley through Swiderski, Chad — top right pitching listing, continuation of Canton)

PITCHING	W	L	ERA	G	SV	IP	H	BB	SO
Gostisha, Riley	1	3	4.78	8	0	43	51	12	18
Graven, Kirk	0	0	7.94	12	0	17	19	18	21
Lehr, George	0	0	6.51	19	1	27	39	18	21
2-team (1 Richmond)	0	0	7.80	20	1	30	44	19	23
McGee, Denny	0	2	13.50	4	0	12	21	9	13
Rahrer, Josh	4	7	4.68	15	0	92	108	35	49
Sampson, Dustin	5	5	5.60	16	0	82	91	40	52
Schiml, Tony	7	5	4.80	22	0	105	134	50	90
See, Andrew	3	3	4.25	19	1	29	30	14	25
Swiderski, Chad	0	0	9.00	3	0	5	10	2	2

INDEPENDENT LEAGUES

PITCHING	W	L	ERA	G	SV	IP	H	BB	SO
Fisher, Cody	9	3	4.80	17	0	95	122	29	75
Fuqua, David	2	2	4.45	39	1	32	39	12	21
Gaines, Jamal	8	2	3.06	17	0	103	103	14	93
Guitron, Ariel	0	0	0.00	1	0	3	2	2	1
Hudspeth, Patrick	0	0	7.50	6	0	6	12	3	4
Kauffman, Matt	0	1	18.00	4	0	4	14	7	4
Kelley, Brent	3	4	5.30	30	5	37	42	26	22
Kuiper, David	7	2	3.14	16	0	83	88	21	63
Lawson, Scott	0	0	9.00	1	0	4	9	1	3
Linde, Joe	3	1	4.47	23	1	46	57	13	30
Livingston, Brett	1	0	4.29	7	0	21	16	10	18
Lopez, Derek	3	4	3.89	24	8	39	43	12	47
Marshall, Gavin	0	1	5.31	12	0	20	27	5	13
Miralles, Rodrigo	1	2	4.21	7	0	25	25	13	17
Tipton, Jeremiah	4	2	4.07	8	0	42	44	12	27
Turner, Jess	3	1	2.41	26	9	33	30	17	41
Williams, Nick	0	0	10.80	3	0	5	7	4	4

EVANSVILLE

BATTING	AVG	AB	R	H	2B	3B	HR	RBI	SB
Belfanti, Matt, of	.255	137	18	35	10	1	0	9	4
Carmona, Luis, ss	.260	100	15	26	5	1	2	14	3
Cash, Condor, 3b	.217	23	3	5	2	0	1	5	0
Champion, Brent, c	.111	9	1	1	0	0	0	0	0
Chatman, Charles, of	.257	35	5	9	2	0	0	3	1
Ciofrone, Paul, of	.229	35	6	8	1	0	1	5	1
Covington, Kevin, of	.262	168	12	44	6	2	0	14	7
Delgado, Gabriel, 2b	.289	291	34	84	10	0	2	30	8
Dorsey, Ryan, ss	.222	63	12	14	2	0	0	5	2
Edwards, John, c-of	.308	234	40	72	21	2	10	45	11
Foreman, Julius, of	.257	74	8	19	1	0	0	3	5
Garza, O.J., of	.310	171	26	53	8	0	1	20	7
Griffin, David, ss-3b	.259	81	8	21	2	0	0	5	2
Hanson, Andrew, of	.304	46	8	14	3	0	1	7	2
Hayden, Wes, of	.299	154	21	46	5	1	4	22	2
Johanning, Ben, dh	.316	98	12	31	7	0	3	13	2
Jones, Tim, dh	.237	38	5	9	1	0	0	5	2
Kaeding, Clint, 3b	.105	19	0	2	0	0	0	1	0
Kane, Jason, 3b	.265	196	23	52	6	1	0	13	8
Luebbert, Garet, ss	.252	155	17	39	4	1	1	15	9
2-team (19 Cook County)	.227	216	25	49	5	2	2	20	11
Maddox, Jeremy, 1b	.222	126	21	28	7	1	5	26	3
Matthews, Mike, 1b	.100	10	0	1	0	0	0	1	0
McDonald, Ryan, dh-1b	.140	86	6	12	2	0	1	4	1
Pirman, Pete, of	.172	29	2	5	1	1	0	5	0
Radwan, Jason, c	.257	70	14	18	3	1	4	13	0
Ready, Alan, c	.185	108	10	20	4	0	1	7	1
Rendle, Rob, of	.185	27	3	5	0	0	0	2	1
Runnells, T.J., 2b	.200	35	6	7	1	0	0	3	1
Shoulders, Jimmy, of	.143	28	3	4	1	0	1	4	0
Steppe, Nicholas, of	.063	16	0	1	0	0	0	0	0
Trujillo, David, 1b	.239	109	17	26	4	1	4	18	2
Walker, Keronn, c	.316	79	17	25	3	0	4	9	2

PITCHING	W	L	ERA	G	SV	IP	H	BB	SO
Ampi, A.J.	0	0	0.00	7	0	11	8	5	8
Boesch, Sean	1	1	6.57	3	0	12	18	5	7
Chmielinski, Ted	0	0	47.25	1	0	1	6	0	1
Faulkner, Steven	2	2	1.57	7	0	28	22	6	25
Fisher, George	3	5	5.17	28	1	62	69	40	63
Forbes, Jeff	0	1	10.13	6	0	16	21	14	14
3-team (5 Canton/5 Wash.)	1	2	7.24	16	0	32	40	33	28
Fry, Nolan	2	8	3.93	12	0	71	80	27	46
Gardner, Paxton	0	0	4.91	4	0	7	12	3	3
Haynes, Brad	0	2	4.97	6	0	29	37	12	13
Hudson, Jeremy	2	2	2.43	20	6	29	21	11	28
Lewis, Brett	4	5	5.10	13	0	72	87	35	44
Little, Aaron	0	0	2.79	4	0	9	13	3	5
McGuire, Rich	0	1	5.87	3	0	15	17	9	10
New, Denny	1	0	2.70	1	0	6	5	4	5
Phalines, Darin	1	1	8.53	5	0	6	11	7	3
Purcell, Brad	5	2	2.50	8	0	54	51	20	28
Richter, B.J.	0	1	7.98	15	2	14	28	8	16
Roe, Terrence	1	5	5.13	37	1	47	57	28	33
Russell, Eddie	0	2	6.88	4	0	17	22	9	23
Stelzner, Nick	1	1	4.60	18	0	43	46	12	39
Stutz, Tony	5	5	4.16	18	3	80	65	44	66
Thomas, Brendon	3	5	4.32	13	0	77	80	28	58
Valenzuela, Daniel	0	2	7.63	6	0	15	22	3	13
Welch, Mark	0	0	2.25	8	0	12	11	13	13

GATEWAY

BATTING	AVG	AB	R	H	2B	3B	HR	RBI	SB
Bolstad, Joe, of	.255	188	15	48	11	1	3	23	1

BATTING	AVG	AB	R	H	2B	3B	HR	RBI	SB
Booker, Steve, of	.154	39	4	6	1	0	0	1	2
Bugger, Mark, 2b	.272	338	40	92	13	2	6	39	5
Clemente, Raphael, of	.210	100	9	21	0	2	0	8	8
Cormell, Eric, or	.000	7	0	0	0	0	0	0	0
Coyne, Tony, ss-3b	.291	275	42	80	18	4	7	23	5
Danzy, Ray, of	.220	50	7	11	2	0	1	3	0
Filson, Gregory, 1b-3b	.308	13	2	4	1	0	0	2	0
Godwin, Cliff, dh	.216	37	4	8	4	0	1	8	0
Haake, Brett, of	.227	66	5	15	4	0	0	6	0
Hanson, Andrew, of	.231	91	9	21	4	0	1	11	0
2-team (19 Evansville)	.255	137	17	35	7	0	2	18	2
Isherwood, Jeremy, of	.250	4	1	1	0	0	0	0	0
Longo, Troy, 1b-dh	.261	283	37	74	13	0	8	41	3
Lopez, Damien, 3b	.250	80	16	20	2	0	1	9	1
Molinari, James, of	.238	122	18	29	6	0	4	14	8
Oetting, Todd, c	.273	44	13	12	3	0	2	8	0
2-team (50 Rockford)	.263	236	34	62	14	0	8	42	2
Perry, Kyle, c	.125	24	0	3	0	0	0	2	1
Rea, Brad, dh-1b	.303	244	33	74	12	0	10	36	0
Santiago, D.J., c	.230	161	12	37	4	0	0	8	1
Schulte, Mark, of	.178	146	10	26	2	0	0	8	3
2-team (27 River City)	.215	214	20	46	5	0	0	12	6
Smith, Brent, of	.172	87	10	15	3	0	1	11	0
Stewart, Josh, 3b-1b	.257	191	23	49	7	0	4	22	3
Talbot, Brandon, c-of	.186	97	13	18	0	2	0	3	0
Tribout, Ryan, of	.152	33	2	5	0	0	0	4	2
Umphres, Chris, of	.111	9	1	1	0	0	0	0	0
Wilson, Kevin, ss	.216	167	17	36	7	1	2	11	4

PITCHING	W	L	ERA	G	SV	IP	H	BB	SO
Anderegg, Jason	4	5	5.26	16	0	65	62	52	45
Buck, Pete	7	5	3.35	19	0	126	126	35	93
Cole, Daniel	0	1	9.00	5	0	9	16	8	4
Dooley, Joe	1	0	4.66	14	9	19	14	11	27
Ellison, Darrin	1	0	2.70	3	0	3	7	5	1
Faigin, Jason	0	0	0.00	1	0	2	1	1	6
Ferretti, Ryan	0	1	14.14	3	0	7	14	4	4
Glassco, Brad	1	2	6.26	9	0	23	28	15	22
Gomez, Carlos	0	0	4.97	9	0	12	13	10	11
Graham, Frank	3	10	5.75	18	0	98	115	43	59
Hensley, John	0	0	9.45	5	0	6	9	5	4
Lee, Tymber	5	9	4.57	17	0	112	139	23	61
Little, Carmen	0	0	6.00	4	0	9	15	5	8
Meyer, Layne	5	7	4.10	17	0	98	84	47	119
Odom, Lance	2	1	4.58	11	2	17	21	5	11
Patterson, Scott	2	2	3.40	13	1	42	33	13	51
Schlenker, Jason	0	3	4.58	23	2	19	23	8	15
Smith, Matt	2	2	1.40	19	8	25	23	12	19
Solano, Travis	1	0	6.43	9	0	14	16	14	9
Urdahl, Tucker	0	0	15.88	4	0	5	13	6	2
Warnecke, Ryan	1	9	9.28	5	0	10	23	6	8
Yost, Kyle	0	1	10.95	5	0	12	20	11	10

JOHNSTOWN

BATTING	AVG	AB	R	H	2B	3B	HR	RBI	SB
Boyle, Jake, of	.500	4	1	2	0	0	0	0	1
Crowley, Ben, of	.282	277	36	78	26	2	5	42	1
Dyer, Matthew, dh	.143	7	0	1	0	0	0	0	0
Ferres, David, 2b	.270	289	47	78	9	4	1	44	20
Filson, Gregory, ss-3b	.283	212	23	60	12	1	0	18	5
2-team (4 Gateway)	.284	225	25	64	13	1	0	20	5
Gontmaher, Nick, of	.250	40	7	10	4	0	0	8	4
Kubachka, John, of	.273	88	11	24	4	0	1	11	1
Law, Jason, of-1b	.268	56	9	15	4	0	1	5	4
Leathers, Todd, dh-of	.278	36	6	10	1	0	0	3	0
Macchi, Brian, dh-of	.250	88	4	22	4	0	0	10	1
Meholick, Brian, ss	.200	5	2	1	0	0	0	1	0
Memmert, Gabe, 1b	.340	153	22	52	10	1	5	29	1
2-team (12 Canton)	.323	201	32	65	14	1	6	38	1
Myler, Jonathan, c	.236	72	4	17	5	0	0	4	1
Passerelle, Matt, c	.208	144	19	30	5	0	0	16	2
Patsilevas, Dan, ss	.000	3	0	0	0	0	0	0	0
Poss, John, 3b	.277	253	26	70	12	0	1	22	0
Schumaker, Shane, 3b	.375	8	2	3	2	0	0	2	1
Sikorski, Mike, of	.111	27	3	3	1	0	0	1	0
Smith, Adonis, ss	.304	56	10	17	8	0	0	7	3
Troncoso, Dan, 3b-2b	.195	123	18	24	3	0	0	7	10
2-team (1 Richmond)	.194	124	18	24	3	0	0	7	10
Tuttle, Jason, of	.299	278	57	83	11	0	1	17	40
Ury, Josh, of	.325	292	34	95	17	2	0	37	7
Van Robays, Charles, c	.315	73	8	23	4	0	0	9	3
Zachry, Drew, of-1b	.310	248	35	77	19	1	5	55	6

PITCHING	W	L	ERA	G	SV	IP	H	BB	SO
Barone, John	1	4	2.53	33	4	46	46	18	33

Name	W	L	ERA	G	SV	IP	H	BB	SO
Chandler, Bobby	2	0	1.31	19	14	20	15	11	23
Foss, Brad	3	7	3.79	23	0	76	72	31	69
Fryman, Jamie	0	0	23.14	2	0	2	7	4	1
Kawecki, Kevin	1	5	6.14	11	0	48	77	14	25
Marshall, Gavin	1	1	5.93	17	1	27	35	7	24
2-team (12 Dubois)	1	2	5.66	29	1	47	62	12	37
Martinez, Chris	8	4	4.09	17	0	105	127	16	73
Matsko, Rick	0	2	6.64	5	0	20	21	13	19
McCall, Dan	0	0	15.43	2	0	4	9	4	4
Molchan, Ryan	0	0	2.77	6	0	13	16	8	10
Nemeth, Peter	4	1	4.88	42	0	66	77	24	63
Parker, Dwayne	0	1	22.09	3	0	3	11	4	3
Rival, Kevin	2	8	7.41	12	0	54	77	34	40
Ruth, Mike	0	3	6.11	7	0	35	49	14	18
Santos, Jesse	0	0	6.55	5	0	11	15	4	11
Steller, Mike	0	3	5.55	5	0	24	34	9	12
Stoner, Simon	2	10	9.09	19	0	65	97	38	46
Velosky, John	0	0	4.50	1	0	4	6	0	3
Wayne, Hawkeye	6	5	4.56	18	0	92	96	44	58

KALAMAZOO

BATTING	AVG	AB	R	H	2B	3B	HR	RBI	SB
Beck, Steven, c	.071	14	0	1	0	0	0	2	0
Brockman, Rob, 3b	.167	24	3	4	1	0	1	3	0
Brown, Trevor, dh	.280	107	14	30	7	0	2	16	0
Carter, Chris, of	.329	255	30	84	11	1	4	26	11
Chinn, Hayden, 3b	.254	138	19	35	8	0	1	15	0
Cook, Josh, dh-1b	.193	83	10	16	4	0	1	12	0
Edwards, Digz, 2b	.271	336	61	91	17	2	5	36	11
Estep, Joe, of	.227	150	16	34	5	1	0	18	2
Frankhouse, Tim, 3b	.208	120	15	25	3	0	1	8	2
Gerber, Joe, 1b	.322	301	57	97	15	2	19	68	1
Gunderson, Jeff, 3b-2b	.161	31	2	5	1	0	0	1	0
Kent, Matthew, c	.263	240	24	63	10	0	5	39	1
Morris, Mark, of	.207	87	15	18	1	2	2	7	4
Peavey, Ryan, of	.173	75	10	13	3	0	2	9	1
Raiburn, Josh, ss	.252	321	54	81	4	0	0	28	12
Scarinci, Michael, dh-2b	.125	24	7	3	0	0	0	0	3
Scott, Kyle, c	.170	53	4	9	0	0	0	4	0
Shaffer, Bret, 3b	.143	7	3	1	0	0	0	1	0
Simmons, Walt, of-c	.253	277	31	70	11	0	7	38	5
Sledd, Aaron, of	.300	223	34	67	15	2	3	39	8

PITCHING	W	L	ERA	G	SV	IP	H	BB	SO
Cavallo, Joey	2	2	5.79	26	2	42	49	11	23
Gillespie, Shawn	1	0	4.78	18	1	37	38	19	27
Gits, Mike	1	2	4.02	23	2	40	47	8	20
Goldwater, Kyle	1	1	11.25	5	0	4	9	1	3
Gunderson, Matt	8	5	3.45	15	0	88	74	41	54
Hayden, Terry	4	5	5.89	13	0	65	91	35	47
Huizinga, Jon	0	0	81.00	1	0	0	1	1	0
Immekus, Jason	0	0	21.21	4	0	4	12	3	2
Kojack, Phil	2	1	1.93	4	0	28	19	7	18
2-team (13 Canton)	6	8	3.46	17	0	109	100	34	81
McGee, Denny	6	1	2.48	11	0	72	66	20	60
2-team (4 Chillicothe)	6	3	4.11	15	0	85	87	29	73
McWatters, David	5	6	3.80	14	0	92	93	23	99
Naplin, Lee	0	1	3.79	12	0	19	20	9	14
Nawrockie, Keith	7	3	1.64	31	5	66	47	13	74
Sheets, Matt	6	6	4.88	18	0	96	117	41	89
Takach, Ryan	0	1	5.46	5	0	31	40	8	22
Walters, Reggie	0	1	6.75	2	0	5	8	1	4
Wiltshire, Greg	2	3	1.82	31	14	39	27	17	32
Wools, Jeff	1	0	2.57	7	0	7	4	9	7

RICHMOND

BATTING	AVG	AB	R	H	2B	3B	HR	RBI	SB
Berry, Denver, c	.364	11	1	4	0	0	0	2	0
Burkhart, Damon, 2b	.288	333	62	96	21	4	5	48	9
Cruz, Raul, of	.231	238	48	55	10	2	10	28	1
Deakins, Jeremiah, of	.339	59	15	20	6	0	3	17	1
Driscoll, Jason, of	.265	196	29	52	6	3	0	24	3
2-team (10 Canton)	.260	235	36	61	6	4	0	31	7
Dunn, Leroy, 2b	.298	57	15	17	5	0	0	9	1
Dyer, Matthew, c	.255	51	10	13	2	0	1	5	0
2-team (2 Johnstown)	.241	58	10	14	2	0	1	5	0
Focht, Eric, of	.000	4	0	0	0	0	0	0	0
Forman, Wayne, c	.000	4	1	0	0	0	0	0	0
2-team (15 Canton)	.130	54	2	7	1	0	0	4	0
Klosterman, Jermiah, c	.293	225	41	66	14	0	2	44	1
Leverett, Dave, 3b	.333	330	60	110	13	1	0	48	12
Marple, Scott, dh-of	.344	209	33	72	16	0	4	34	7
Miller, Drew, of	.356	132	31	47	8	1	2	21	6
Riordan, Fran, 1b	.314	357	67	112	22	0	11	81	17

BATTING	AVG	AB	R	H	2B	3B	HR	RBI	SB
Tavares, John, ss	.233	347	66	81	13	1	5	47	11
Troncoso, Dan, ph	.000	1	0	0	0	0	0	0	0
Voshell, Key, dh-2b	.298	94	13	28	7	1	2	16	6
Willingham, Phil, of	.360	364	75	131	19	8	15	86	36

PITCHING	W	L	ERA	G	SV	IP	H	BB	SO
Baca, Enriques	10	4	2.87	18	0	119	111	38	110
Barbarossa, Joshua	0	0	8.56	6	0	13	18	7	13
2-team (6 Cook County)	0	1	5.66	12	2	20	22	15	20
Boucher, Pat	0	0	6.75	7	0	9	10	6	9
Ellison, Derrick	1	0	1.80	2	0	10	9	5	7
Heaston, Bryan	3	3	3.70	36	11	41	41	31	43
Henry, Mike	2	6	5.12	9	0	51	59	24	46
Hickey, Mark	1	0	2.57	8	0	7	3	3	8
Hudspeth, Patrick	1	0	5.09	15	0	23	29	3	11
2-team (6 Dubois)	1	0	5.59	21	0	29	41	6	15
Jelovcic, Rich	7	5	3.44	20	2	99	115	21	78
Kerins, Mike	2	3	3.99	10	0	38	48	10	22
Kraemer, Mike	2	4	7.26	10	0	39	58	24	41
Lehr, George	0	0	23.14	1	0	2	5	1	2
Moenter, Curtis	5	3	3.36	16	0	85	79	38	90
Needle, Bryan	1	0	4.43	16	1	22	26	14	14
Pahs, Aaron	4	0	2.66	24	1	44	44	25	24
Parker, Jeff	0	0	5.40	7	0	8	6	8	10
Rennaker, Chris	0	0	9.00	9	0	6	9	7	5
Samter, Josh	1	0	4.05	8	0	6	10	2	8
Schweitzer, Matt	8	2	4.29	39	0	50	66	7	55
Sosebee, Chad	2	4	3.40	44	4	47	38	10	34
Spigner, Chris	1	0	3.06	4	0	17	17	14	13
Taylor, Mark	0	0	7.56	7	0	8	14	4	2

RIVER CITY

BATTING	AVG	AB	R	H	2B	3B	HR	RBI	SB
Beckmann, Bryan, 2b-3b	.276	163	30	45	9	0	4	28	5
Boyd, Scott, of	.208	96	11	20	6	0	3	25	1
Bredenkoetter, Jim, 1b-of	.000	1	0	0	0	0	0	0	0
Cotto, Enrique, c	.250	8	1	2	0	0	0	0	0
Fuess, Brian, 3b	.331	338	54	112	17	0	9	65	4
Gordon, Zach, 2b	.188	48	6	9	2	1	0	4	1
Goss, Matt, of	.207	82	9	17	7	0	0	11	5
Haake, Steve, of	.250	12	3	3	1	0	0	1	0
Jackson, Brody, of	.306	310	70	95	19	2	15	44	36
Jager, Corey, c	.259	174	27	45	13	0	3	25	0
Lucas, Kevin, ss	.299	338	54	101	22	2	2	42	19
Molinari, James, 2b-of	.271	181	33	49	13	0	3	21	13
2-team (30 Gateway)	.257	303	51	78	19	0	7	35	21
Piatt, Ben, dh-of	.328	229	34	75	13	0	1	31	4
Schulte, Mark, of	.294	68	10	20	3	0	0	4	3
Shea, Adam, c-1b	.318	211	37	67	11	0	5	30	0
Singer, Matthew, of	.225	169	24	38	8	0	6	21	3
Urban, Joe, 1b	.277	242	32	67	20	2	4	36	1
Zaucha, Chad, of	.281	263	44	74	12	3	7	36	1

PITCHING	W	L	ERA	G	SV	IP	H	BB	SO
Backsmeyer, Justin	4	5	4.15	22	3	65	67	30	70
Bogardus, Ryan	1	1	2.74	10	2	23	22	7	19
Breauchaud, Ed	1	3	1.86	15	1	19	9	4	22
Dobbins, Aaron	0	0	4.96	8	0	16	19	8	16
Hutson, Steve	0	0	27.00	1	0	1	3	2	0
Jackson, Dan	0	0	6.00	4	0	6	3	9	10
Neubauer, Marc	1	0	7.89	15	0	21	22	12	24
Pape, Stace	4	5	3.61	24	2	89	82	29	61
Parton, Troy	1	1	10.57	2	0	7	11	5	3
Pennington, Chad	5	3	5.69	13	1	55	64	28	37
Prater, Drew	2	3	4.04	9	0	49	51	16	26
Prather, Kendall	3	2	4.36	10	0	53	50	21	39
Rhue, Mike	4	1	3.65	7	0	37	35	15	23
Russo, Dennis	2	3	5.40	9	0	46	60	19	19
Shafer, Adam	4	3	2.81	22	0	57	47	24	53
Skyles, Matt	6	8	4.31	16	0	100	113	34	47
Sokoll, Adam	0	1	4.76	27	1	45	52	23	44
Staples, Dave	0	1	54.00	1	0	0	2	2	1
Ulmer, Steve	2	1	5.40	24	3	40	43	25	44
Wehrfritz, Brad	0	0	108.00	1	0	0	2	2	0

ROCKFORD

BATTING	AVG	AB	R	H	2B	3B	HR	RBI	SB
Anderson, Jonathan, ss	.172	58	11	10	1	0	0	4	3
Austin, Richard, of	.300	247	50	74	19	0	11	38	3
Ballard, Brady, 1b-of	.217	184	19	40	8	0	0	15	5
Beck, Steven, c	.048	21	1	1	0	0	0	0	0
2-team (6 Kalamazoo)	.057	35	1	2	0	0	0	2	0
Carmona, Luis, ss	.293	164	24	48	7	0	0	9	6
2-team (29 Evansville)	.280	264	39	74	12	1	2	23	9

	AVG	AB	R	H	2B	3B	HR	RBI	SB
Ciarrachi, Jason, 2b	.111	9	2	1	0	0	0	0	1
Ciarrachi, Kevin, c	.211	19	1	4	1	0	1	3	1
Dettman, Matt, c-1b	.205	127	17	26	8	0	2	16	4
Devine, Rich, of	.227	22	8	5	0	0	0	1	3
Drobiak, Jayson, 1b-3b	.365	178	35	65	15	1	11	43	7
Dufault, Jared, of	.242	149	20	36	7	1	0	10	5
Eden, Carey, 3b	.000	11	0	0	0	0	0	0	0
Fjelland, Ben, 2b-3b	.344	346	63	119	25	2	9	70	7
Garcia, David, c	.200	10	2	2	1	0	0	2	0
Hamilton, Mike, ss	.071	14	3	1	0	0	0	1	4
Heefner, Dan, dh-1b	.185	65	3	12	2	0	0	4	0
Matthews, Bobby, of-c	.303	152	34	46	7	1	1	13	5
Moore, Kevin, of	.233	43	6	10	1	0	1	2	0
Oetting, Todd, c	.260	192	21	50	11	0	6	34	2
Pieczynski, Eddie, c	.200	5	1	1	1	0	0	1	0
Pigott, Anthony, of	.323	322	54	104	13	4	8	57	35
Pomozak, Robert, 3b	.100	20	6	2	1	0	0	2	1
Riera, Zack, c	.338	74	13	25	6	0	0	9	9
Roberts, Dave, of	.273	11	3	3	1	0	0	1	0
Rollins, Antwon, of	.233	90	9	21	8	1	3	16	4
Shorts, Adam, ss-2b	.120	25	4	3	0	0	1	5	1
Sostak, Jim, of	.235	51	9	12	1	0	0	5	3
Vogel, Luke, 1b	.227	22	1	5	0	0	0	0	0
Williams, Justin, 2b-ss	.240	200	20	48	10	0	0	21	7
Wilson, Kevin, 1b	.225	40	2	9	1	1	0	5	0
2-team (49 Gateway)	.217	207	19	45	8	2	2	16	4

PITCHING	W	L	ERA	G	SV	IP	H	BB	SO
Batthauer, Bryan	9	4	2.45	17	1	121	111	44	118
Foster, Cory	1	3	2.59	26	2	41	55	14	43
Hardman, Steven	0	1	5.25	9	0	12	13	6	7
Jackson, Rob	1	0	2.01	20	0	22	14	14	10
Lattimer, Josh	2	1	4.05	27	0	26	33	13	20
Miller, Kevin	4	5	3.76	21	0	91	76	58	72
Montoya, Eric	3	0	5.60	15	2	17	23	14	13
Oksen, Andrew	7	4	4.35	20	0	109	118	48	67
Pearson, Brent	0	0	9.00	7	0	6	9	5	7
Pozza, Chris	0	0	9.00	6	0	3	10	5	1
Saldano, Victor	0	2	2.61	22	2	31	36	5	18
Shelley, Jason	9	5	3.53	18	0	119	98	59	156
Smuin, Shane	1	3	8.44	4	0	21	29	14	11
Takach, Ryan	2	2	4.99	12	0	52	61	11	30
2-team (5 Kalamazoo)	2	3	5.16	17	0	83	101	19	52
Tomsu, Joshua	0	1	8.44	5	0	16	28	10	8
Vaughn, Barton	6	8	3.08	33	10	49	43	18	56

WASHINGTON

BATTING	AVG	AB	R	H	2B	3B	HR	RBI	SB
Argento, Shaun, c-of	.352	290	47	102	20	5	5	62	10
Brock, Les, of	.196	46	11	9	2	0	1	3	3
Buckmiller, Matt, of	.000	4	0	0	0	0	0	0	0
Cash, Condor, of	.214	28	5	6	2	0	0	2	0
2-team (6 Evansville)	.216	51	8	11	4	0	1	7	0
Cerni, Vincent, 3b	.160	25	2	4	0	0	0	5	1
Check, Mike, of-2b	.262	282	61	74	5	1	0	16	34
Clay, Allen, dh-ss	.211	19	4	4	0	0	0	1	1
Coakley, Jay, dh-c	.307	176	29	54	10	2	4	22	3
Copley, Travis, 1b	.294	313	57	92	14	2	6	57	5
Cueruo, Joe, of	.256	281	66	72	13	0	14	57	10
Ehrnsberger, Chad, 3b	.302	291	40	88	14	1	9	54	4
Ellis, Ryan, 2b	.260	242	27	63	6	3	1	29	2
Hensler, Brad, ss	.313	300	60	94	25	4	8	54	15
Kane, Jason, 3b	.390	59	8	23	4	0	0	10	2
2-team (53 Evansville)	.294	255	31	75	10	1	0	23	10
Loggins, Josh, of	.347	242	40	84	18	0	5	45	4
Morrison, Lee, of	.143	14	0	2	0	0	0	0	0
Stone, Casey, of	.269	167	27	45	6	2	0	27	14
Taylor, Anthony, dh-c	.250	96	15	24	3	0	3	14	1
Wright, Ray, of	.238	21	1	5	0	0	0	0	0

PITCHING	W	L	ERA	G	SV	IP	H	BB	SO
Ally, Ben	3	1	2.08	5	0	26	21	4	30
Baber, Matt	8	7	3.63	18	0	111	112	36	74
Bradley, David	11	4	3.55	18	0	114	105	55	94
Cerminaro, David	1	0	2.84	7	0	12	13	2	10
Elkins, Jason	2	0	1.88	23	2	28	20	11	28
Englander, Matt	0	1	6.35	1	0	5	9	3	4
Forbes, Jeff	0	0	4.70	5	0	7	10	9	7
Foreman, Jason	0	0	6.75	6	0	8	9	1	6
Garvin, Robert	2	2	2.30	33	18	47	33	4	59
Giaudrone, Bret	2	2	4.45	17	3	30	29	23	25
Heimbach, Andy	0	1	10.38	4	0	8	15	8	8
Hickman, Jason	6	6	4.62	16	0	89	102	49	66
Howton, Jared	11	3	1.89	17	0	109	86	38	89
Kuklis, Kevin	6	1	4.93	18	0	76	94	20	38

	W	L	ERA	G	SV	IP	H	BB	SO
Putnam, Dylan	2	0	1.04	15	0	17	11	13	16
Sclafani, Anthony	1	0	3.44	11	1	18	16	9	22
Valentin, Dan	1	0	3.46	8	0	13	12	12	8
Wray, Fred	0	0	10.80	12	0	11	18	18	13

NORTHERN LEAGUE

When they had to play on the road in 2002, the New Jersey Jackals were beatable, vulnerable. When they played at home, they were unstoppable.

And because of their invincibility at home, the Jackals claimed the Northern League championship for the second year in a row. New Jersey won 19 of its last 21 regular season home games to wrap up a playoff spot, then won all six home playoff games, including two straight against Winnipeg in the final.

The key was an offense that treated its Yogi Berra Stadium like it was Coors Field East. New Jersey batters hit .315 at home (compared to .270 on the road). At the same time, the Jackals pitching staff allowed opponents to hit only .255 at Yogi Berra Stadium (compared to .278 on the road).

"We don't lose at home," Jackals first baseman Dave Callahan said. "We're comfortable here."

Callahan was named the playoff MVP, largely on the basis of his dramatic, 11th-inning, three-run homer that gave the Jackals a 6-3 win in Game 3 of the final series. The next night, Aaron Myers allowed only two runs in

Geraldo Padua

6⅔ innings while catcher Mikaela Dworken homered and drove in two runs as the Jackals clinched the title with a 5-2 victory.

Dworken also drove in the go-ahead runs in New Jersey's 3-2 victory in Game 2, evening the series after Winnipeg won the opener of the series 3-0.

With a 62-27 record, New Jersey finished with the best record in the East Division.

The title continued the Eastern Division's amazing dominance of the Central Division in head-to-head play. While the Central Division is the older of the two divisions and its teams draw larger crowds than the Eastern Division teams, the victory meant that the East has won all four titles since the Northern League and the Northeast League merged in 1999.

While the Eastern Division won another title, it was a lefthander from the Central Division that drew the most attention during the regular season. Winnipeg lefthander Bobby Madritsch emerged as one of the best pitchers, and best prospects to ever pitch in the Northern League, as he showcased a 95-mph fastball to dominate the Central Division. Madritsch (11-4, 2.30) and righthander Geraldo Padua (12-3, 3.06 ERA) dominated on the mound, while Brent Sachs (.346-11-60) and Pete Rose Jr. (.344-8-53) were second and third in batting in the league, as the Goldeyes won the first and second half titles of the Central Division's North Division.

While Winnipeg finished with the best record in the Central Division, Joliet and Lincoln had to face each other in a one-game playoff for the final spot in the Central Division playoffs. Joliet earned the playoff berth with a 4-0 victory, as leadoff hitter Brian Sprout went 4-for-5 with two home runs while Rich Hyde and Matt Hammons combined for a shutout.

EASTERN DIVISION

STANDINGS

FIRST HALF

NORTH	W	L	PCT	GB
Quebec Les Capitals	29	16	.644	—
Adirondack Lumberjacks	24	21	.533	5
Albany-Colonie Diamond Dogs	21	24	.467	8
Berkshire Black Bears	14	31	.311	15

SOUTH	W	L	PCT	GB
New Jersey Jackals	30	15	.667	—
Elmira Pioneers	25	20	.556	5
Brockton Rox	23	22	.511	7
Allentown Ambassadors	14	31	.311	16

SECOND HALF

NORTH	W	L	PCT	GB
Adirondack Lumberjacks	28	17	.622	—
Albany-Colonie Diamond Dogs	25	19	.568	2 ½
Quebec Les Capitales	23	22	.511	5
Berkshire Black Bears	10	34	.227	17 ½

SOUTH	W	L	PCT	GB
New Jersey Jackals	32	12	.727	—
Elmira Pioneers	29	16	.644	3 ½
Brockton Rox	19	25	.432	13
Allentown Ambassadors	12	33	.267	20 ½

PLAYOFFS: Semifinals—New Jersey defeated Elmira 3-2 and Adirondack defeated Quebec 3-2 in best-of-5 series. **Eastern Finals**—New Jersey defeated Adirondack 3-2 in best-of-5 series. **Northern League Finals:** New Jersey defeated Winnipeg 3-1 in best-of-5 series.

MANAGERS: Adirondack—Kash Beauchamp. **Albany-Colonie**—Mike Marshall. **Allentown**—Ed Ott. **Berkshire**—George Scott. **Brockton**—Ed Nottle. **Elmira**—Mitch Lyden. **New Jersey**—George Tsamis. **Quebec**—Andy McCauley.

ATTENDANCE: Quebec 152,121; Brockton 131,654; New Jersey 104,100; Allentown 80,449; Adirondack 72,183; Elmira 59,116; Berkshire 56,295; Albany-Colonie 53,425.

ALL-STAR TEAM: C—Rafael Pujols, Quebec. **1B**—Vic Davila, Albany-Colonie. **2B**—Pat Scalabrini, Quebec. **3B**—Ryan Kane, New Jersey. **SS**—Chas Terni, New Jersey. **OF**—Billy Brown, New Jersey; Billy Rich, New Jersey; Travis Bailey, New Jersey. **DH**—Lorenzo de la Cruz, Adirondack. **RHP**—Joel Bennett, New Jersey. **LHP**—Chad Ward, Adirondack. **RP**—Mark Cisar, Quebec.

Player of the Year: Lorenzo de la Cruz, Adirondack. **Rookie of the Year:** Pat Scalabrini, Quebec. **Rookie Picher of the Year:** Danny Miller, Adirondack. **Manager of the Year:** George Tsamis, New Jersey.

INDIVIDUAL BATTING LEADERS
(Minimum 243 Plate Appearances)

	AVG	AB	R	H	2B	3B	HR	RBI	SB
De la Cruz, Lorenzo, Adirondack	.367	297	58	109	17	1	15	75	12
Rich, Billy, New Jersey	.342	284	68	97	27	3	8	63	7
Davila, Vic, Albany-Colonie	.329	328	73	108	20	0	20	72	1
Scalabrini, Pat, Quebec	.327	278	54	91	24	0	7	45	19
Diaz, Jorge, Allentown	.322	236	50	76	20	6	0	19	26
Lantigua, Eddie, Quebec	.321	280	47	90	30	2	7	53	2
Bailey, Travis, New Jersey	.321	321	75	103	24	6	16	75	14
Rosario, Carlos, Brockton	.319	254	50	81	13	7	4	23	38
Pujols, Rafael, Quebec	.317	325	58	103	24	1	3	48	3
Brown, Billy, New Jersey	.313	262	48	82	9	5	8	44	14

INDIVIDUAL PITCHING LEADERS
(Minimum 72 Plate Appearances)

	W	L	ERA	G	SV	IP	H	BB	SO
Morse, Bryan, Albany-Colonie	7	5	1.99	21	0	72	71	30	39
Ward, Chad, Adirondack	10	5	2.02	18	0	116	88	24	89
Dunn, Keith, Quebec	11	4	2.81	18	0	119	100	37	82
Keagle, Greg, Elmira	10	9	2.92	19	0	145	101	37	119
Bennett, Joel, New Jersey	14	2	2.93	18	0	129	105	40	141
Brummett, Sean, Elmira	5	3	3.02	19	0	128	116	17	100
Von Haefen, Jason, A-C	7	6	3.06	19	0	115	91	37	101
Andra, Jeff, Elmira	10	7	3.13	19	0	135	124	30	85
Myers, Aaron, New Jersey	11	6	3.28	20	0	140	135	49	87
Lavenia, Mark, A-C	7	6	3.41	16	0	90	95	35	73

ADIRONDACK

BATTING	AVG	AB	R	H	2B	3B	HR	RBI	SB
Brackley, Carlos, of	.000	6	0	0	0	0	0	1	0
Brock, Todd, 3b-2b	.306	144	28	44	10	1	3	23	3
2-team (45 Berkshire)	.272	309	53	84	18	5	8	40	6
Clifton, Rodney, of	.230	139	22	32	12	0	2	16	9
De la Cruz, Lorenzo, dh-of	.367	297	58	109	17	1	15	75	12
Ducey, Rob, of	.245	49	7	12	2	0	0	2	1

	AVG	AB	R	H	2B	3B	HR	RBI	SB
Finnegan, Chris, c-1b	.202	89	9	18	4	1	0	4	1
Guerrero, Sandy, 2b	.265	328	44	87	23	1	8	54	12
Hargreaves, Brad, c	.266	244	31	65	10	1	1	17	7
King, Steven, 1b	.301	279	34	84	20	3	5	46	8
Kobayashi, Mitsuru, ss	.270	330	73	89	11	0	0	23	18
Larkin, Garrett, 3b	.256	293	30	75	11	0	2	28	5
Lebron, Juan, of	.353	102	17	36	7	0	5	20	2
Medina, Junior, of	.255	157	13	40	9	1	1	13	3
Miyake, Chris, 2b	.222	9	1	2	0	0	0	1	0
Oliva, Mike, of	.200	10	3	2	0	0	0	0	0
Shultz, Brian, of	.091	33	3	3	0	0	0	2	0
Silver, Travis, c	.071	14	1	1	0	0	0	1	0
2-team (10 Albany)	.205	44	4	9	1	0	0	2	0
Silvestre, Juan, of	.282	142	22	40	8	0	7	22	3
Tindell, Matt, of	.294	143	24	42	9	2	2	24	8
Tolentino, Juan, dh	.087	23	1	2	0	0	0	4	3
Voltz, Jude, 1b	.333	54	11	18	4	0	2	11	1
Yamauchi, Hiroshi, of	.250	120	22	30	3	0	1	11	10

PITCHING	W	L	ERA	G	SV	IP	H	BB	SO
Cowan, Bobby	6	3	5.69	28	1	80	91	27	34
Greco, Sam	0	0	7.50	3	0	6	8	2	4
Johnson, D.J.	3	3	2.75	42	9	55	51	19	47
Jones, Fontella	1	0	3.90	31	15	30	24	17	38
Jones, Quentin	2	1	4.79	28	1	41	41	30	26
Keelty, Kris	0	0	20.25	5	0	4	13	3	1
Lail, Denny	4	4	5.53	11	0	55	62	21	42
Magri, Joe	2	1	3.28	17	0	49	48	14	26
Mahan, Dallas	1	0	3.86	9	0	9	13	5	9
Miller, Danny	9	5	3.42	26	1	102	91	51	90
Purcell, Trevor	0	0	9.00	2	0	2	4	0	0
Royal, Shannon	2	1	8.44	13	0	21	32	15	15
Santiago, Derek	9	8	4.31	19	0	125	112	57	99
Ward, Chad	10	5	2.02	18	0	116	88	24	89
Zipser, Mike	3	7	3.82	11	0	68	73	24	43

ALBANY-COLONIE

BATTING	AVG	AB	R	H	2B	3B	HR	RBI	SB
Beck, Steven, c	.063	16	1	1	0	0	1	1	0
Bourhill, Scott, 2b-ss	.241	54	7	13	2	0	2	9	0
Brassington, Phil, dh	.000	8	0	0	0	0	0	1	0
Butt, Gerald, c	.272	92	13	25	4	0	1	13	3
Crawford, Todd, 1b	.500	12	1	6	0	0	0	2	0
Cumiskey, Brett, of	.333	6	1	2	0	0	0	0	0
Davila, Vic, 1b-2b	.329	328	73	108	20	0	20	72	1
Espinal, Juan, 3b-1b	.311	90	16	28	9	0	4	22	3
Ewing, Byron, 1b-dh	.176	34	3	6	1	0	1	3	1
Fatur, Brian, 2b-ss	.324	102	17	33	6	0	0	5	5
Figga, Mike, 1b	.000	2	0	0	0	0	0	0	0
Finn, Ryan, dh	.143	7	0	1	0	0	0	0	0
Goldfield, Josh, c	.105	38	3	4	1	0	0	0	0
Hambleton, Jon, 1b	.300	10	2	3	2	0	0	3	0
Hirosawa, Yoshiteru, ss	.143	14	1	2	1	0	0	0	0
Kean, Josh, of	.071	14	1	1	0	0	0	1	0
Matos, Malvin, dh	.219	114	9	25	6	0	3	16	0
Merriman, Terrell, of	.221	113	23	25	3	1	0	9	4
2-team (1 Elmira)	.221	113	23	25	3	1	0	9	4
Pernell, Brandon, of	.241	137	20	33	6	2	2	20	6
Perry, Kyle, c	.172	29	3	5	0	0	0	3	1
Rush, Travis, of	.259	27	4	7	0	1	0	4	0
Scott, Ed, of	.083	12	1	1	0	0	0	0	2
Sepulveda, Carlos, of	.258	159	30	41	13	1	6	27	2
Silver, Travis, c	.267	30	3	8	1	0	0	1	0
Singletary, Dan, of	.281	178	34	50	12	0	6	20	6
Sledd, Aaron, of	.179	78	6	14	3	0	0	10	0
Smith, Ryan, c	.368	38	5	14	2	0	0	4	1
2-team (50 Berkshire)	.249	241	18	60	13	0	0	18	4
Startari, Jason, 3b	.190	158	16	30	4	1	0	13	2
Truitt, Steve, of-1b	.288	299	42	86	20	3	8	51	15
Valdez, Angel, of	.347	121	20	42	6	5	1	13	5
2-team (28 Albany)	.304	181	25	55	7	7	1	19	7
Villacres, Gary, of	.286	63	10	18	3	0	0	5	5
Vilorio, Miguel, ss	.244	225	27	55	8	3	0	18	1
Wiseman, Jeb, c	.110	136	8	15	3	1	3	13	0
Zorrilla, Julio, 2b	.268	224	27	60	11	0	0	18	10

PITCHING	W	L	ERA	G	SV	IP	H	BB	SO
Begg, Chris	3	2	2.53	21	1	53	42	15	39
Berney, Scott	5	6	4.41	14	0	83	107	26	42
Boozer, Thomas	0	0	3.00	2	0	3	5	0	3
Cosgrove, Mike	1	1	1.05	19	4	25	18	6	23
DePriest, Derrick	0	1	3.24	12	1	16	15	8	14
Estes, Eric	5	3	2.81	10	0	64	62	10	63
2-team (6 Elmira)	8	6	3.78	16	0	100	102	16	92
Havens, Chris	0	1	6.30	8	0	10	12	9	7

INDEPENDENT LEAGUES

	W	L	ERA	G	SV	IP	H	BB	SO
Kelley, Chris	1	0	23.63	2	0	2	5	6	2
Lavenia, Mark	7	6	3.41	16	0	89	95	35	73
LeBlanc, Eric	0	2	4.70	8	0	15	22	8	13
Leclair, Aric	2	0	1.67	22	3	32	20	18	45
Marcotte, Trevor	1	2	4.11	21	1	50	48	23	34
Morse, Bryan	7	5	1.99	21	0	72	71	30	39
Philbrick, Frank	0	1	5.88	18	0	26	33	17	15
Ricciardi, Joe	5	2	3.24	29	4	33	28	15	46
Snyder, Bill	1	1	2.70	22	8	33	26	6	27
Valdez, Carlos	1	4	3.99	8	0	47	50	11	59
Von Haefen, Jason	7	6	3.06	19	0	114	91	37	101

ALLENTOWN

BATTING	AVG	AB	R	H	2B	3B	HR	RBI	SB
Bordenick, Ryan, c-1b	.308	325	52	100	29	2	11	68	1
Brackley, Carlos, of	.192	26	4	5	1	0	0	2	0
2-team (3 Adirondack)	.156	32	4	5	1	0	0	3	0
Carter, Josh, of	.214	70	10	15	0	0	0	5	5
Caston, Bernard, of	.193	83	12	16	2	0	0	3	3
Cirone, Joseph, of	.131	61	2	8	4	0	0	6	0
Diaz, Jorge, 2b	.322	236	50	76	20	6	0	19	26
DiPace, Danny, of	.259	27	2	7	1	0	0	3	1
Doakes, Schuyler, of	.317	189	36	60	11	2	0	19	16
Encarnacion, Angelo, c	.200	50	3	10	1	0	0	7	0
Escobar, Gustavo, 3b-ss	.222	279	29	62	9	2	4	33	9
Figga, Mike, c-of	.333	36	4	12	0	0	0	4	0
2-team (1 Albany)	.316	38	4	12	0	0	0	4	0
Hood, Jay, ss	.248	206	27	51	17	0	3	23	2
Johnson, Matt, c	.156	167	15	26	4	0	0	8	0
Katsube, Shin, of	.200	95	9	19	4	0	0	3	3
Kerrigan, Joe, 3b	.341	85	12	29	6	2	0	10	3
2-team (59 Berkshire)	.311	305	42	95	18	4	2	34	10
Kotarski, Justin, of	.346	26	3	9	1	0	0	1	2
Larkin, Stephen, of-1b	.250	320	58	80	26	5	2	53	6
Leday, A.J., 1b-of	.286	105	14	30	8	2	2	22	1
Macko, Tim, 3b	.167	12	0	2	1	0	0	0	0
Maxwell, Keith, 3b	.264	231	29	61	12	0	6	37	1
McDonald, Jason, c	.194	31	2	6	1	0	0	4	0
Motley, Darryl, dh	.161	31	3	5	0	0	2	6	0
Spearman, Vernon, of	.287	94	16	27	1	1	0	10	11
Tehonica, Josh, 1b	.252	206	21	52	16	1	2	21	4
Yagel, Bryan, of	.129	31	4	4	1	0	0	1	2

PITCHING	W	L	ERA	G	SV	IP	H	BB	SO
Acevedo, Adrean	1	3	3.42	30	3	47	49	19	39
Balbuena, Caleb	1	2	4.69	8	0	48	42	24	28
Bauldree, Joe	0	1	12.46	1	0	4	5	2	6
Censale, Silvio	1	1	4.63	2	0	11	14	8	6
Curtiss, Tom	1	2	4.80	25	0	50	59	36	25
Dillinger, John	3	1	2.43	5	0	37	35	10	32
Eagan, David	0	0	12.46	4	0	4	8	4	2
Gannon, Jeff	5	7	5.81	20	1	113	140	60	41
Leonards, Bake	2	9	5.66	21	0	82	102	34	65
Lindley, Ryan	0	1	14.85	4	0	6	15	5	1
Lunney, John	0	6	6.23	15	0	56	72	24	19
Martini, Mike	1	0	6.75	7	0	9	8	9	5
Medina, Carlos	1	3	7.00	4	0	18	32	7	13
Medlock, Chet	5	12	6.12	19	0	110	128	59	73
Meyer, Mike	2	9	5.01	32	7	50	68	20	37
Ramirez, Luis	0	0	8.36	8	0	14	15	8	6
Sexton, Patrick	1	1	8.10	17	0	23	30	7	12
Tehonica, Josh	0	1	6.43	8	0	14	14	12	9
Zallie, Chris	2	5	3.86	11	0	67	70	25	39

BERKSHIRE

BATTING	AVG	AB	R	H	2B	3B	HR	RBI	SB
Aaron, Oginga, 2b	.130	23	1	3	1	0	0	1	0
Allen, Scott, c	.245	98	8	24	4	0	1	7	2
Brock, Todd, ss-2b	.242	165	25	40	8	4	5	17	3
Brown, Larry, of	.212	33	4	7	2	0	0	5	2
Daniels, Jerome, of	.143	91	5	13	2	0	0	3	3
DeMarco, Tony, dh-1b	.208	53	4	11	1	0	1	1	0
Garcia, Jorge, of	.171	76	11	13	5	0	0	3	0
Gonzalez, Ender, 2b-1b	.310	145	20	45	7	0	1	13	8
Goodwin, Curtis, of	.336	152	24	51	7	2	0	13	4
Griffith, Leroy, of	.211	57	4	12	3	0	1	4	1
Kelleher, Pat, of	.100	10	0	1	0	0	0	1	0
2-team (2 Brockton)	.167	12	0	2	0	0	0	1	0
Kerrigan, Joe, 3b-2b	.300	220	30	66	12	2	2	24	7
Maxwell, Keith, 3b	.316	19	2	6	0	0	1	2	0
2-team (61 Allentown)	.268	250	31	67	12	0	7	39	1
Mendoza, Adrian, 1b	.229	144	18	33	4	1	3	16	2
Mercedes, Luis, ss	.152	158	8	24	3	0	0	8	0

BATTING	AVG	AB	R	H	2B	3B	HR	RBI	SB
Moore, Michael, of	.266	177	32	47	10	0	16	40	0
2-team (30 Brockton)	.237	287	41	68	11	1	19	52	2
Nelson, Elvis, of	.200	5	1	1	0	0	0	0	0
Nevins, Ryan, 2b	.189	95	4	18	3	1	0	3	0
Oliva, Mike, of	.229	35	2	8	1	0	0	0	0
2-team (5 Adirondack)	.222	45	5	10	1	0	0	0	0
Perich, Josh, of	.239	92	9	22	5	1	1	13	1
Polanco, Carlos, 2b	.241	83	5	20	1	0	0	3	2
Samboy, Nelson, 2b	.295	44	5	13	5	0	0	5	0
2-team (17 New Jersey)	.355	110	21	39	9	0	0	14	7
Sawyer, Chris, of	.249	185	14	46	9	1	3	16	5
Smith, Ryan, c	.227	203	13	46	11	0	0	14	3
Stovall, DaRond, of	.279	111	17	31	6	3	2	15	3
Valdez, Angel, of	.217	60	5	13	1	2	0	6	2
Valdez, David, 2b	.175	40	3	7	0	1	0	0	0
Varitek, Justin, c	.118	51	4	6	3	0	0	2	0
Vasquez, Chris, of-1b	.300	110	13	33	4	0	4	23	2
2-team (11 Brockton)	.268	153	14	41	6	0	4	26	2
White, Eric, 3b	.173	81	9	14	3	0	1	11	0
Wiseman, Jeb, c	.121	33	0	4	0	0	0	0	0
2-team (13 Albany)	.112	169	8	19	3	1	3	13	0

PITCHING	W	L	ERA	G	SV	IP	H	BB	SO
Akin, Aaron	0	7	5.21	9	0	48	65	27	32
Avery, Paul	0	1	11.05	6	0	14	18	21	7
Bailie, Matt	3	2	2.23	23	0	40	26	15	46
Case, Bob	0	3	6.88	8	0	17	25	11	9
Cotton, Joe	2	3	3.06	25	9	32	25	12	32
Crowther, Jackson	5	7	4.04	18	0	84	94	30	54
Dimma, Doug	0	4	5.83	16	0	54	67	17	28
Gouin, Brian	4	7	4.15	24	1	119	127	38	62
Harrison, James	1	3	4.94	25	1	54	73	35	34
Henderson, Ken	1	4	4.54	13	0	35	35	17	23
Lelless, Alex	0	3	10.05	12	0	28	36	27	14
Linares, Yfrain	0	2	11.37	2	0	6	10	4	2
MacKoul, Greg	3	0	7.28	17	0	29	35	22	16
Mahan, Dallas	4	5	3.75	12	0	69	65	15	34
2-team (9 Adirondack)	5	5	3.76	21	0	79	78	20	43
Minerva, Mike	1	3	4.96	20	0	52	61	21	26
Philbrick, Frank	1	3	6.86	7	0	19	28	12	17
2-team (18 Albany)	1	4	6.31	25	0	45	61	29	32
Rangel, Julio	0	0	4.50	2	0	2	0	3	2
Rogers, Jed	1	0	6.30	4	0	10	10	9	6
Ryburn, Ty	0	1	9.90	8	0	10	14	7	7
Sokol, Trad	1	4	6.86	11	0	39	55	14	16

BROCKTON

BATTING	AVG	AB	R	H	2B	3B	HR	RBI	SB
Beck, Ben, of	.222	18	4	4	1	0	0	2	0
Bustos, Saul, ss	.288	364	52	105	21	2	11	64	13
Caruso, Bryan, c	.000	2	1	0	0	0	0	0	0
Cosbey, Chris, of	.300	340	68	102	20	2	1	34	20
Daubert, John, 3b	.262	336	43	88	15	2	10	53	2
Davis, Mike, 2b-3b	.269	197	31	53	13	2	1	22	10
Figueroa, Carlos, 2b	.000	3	2	0	0	0	0	0	0
Graham, Dan, of	.270	289	50	78	13	3	5	46	14
Hall, Trevor, 1b	.245	192	23	47	5	1	3	23	1
Kelleher, Pat, of	.500	2	0	1	0	0	0	0	0
Landry, Michael, c	.360	50	9	18	1	0	1	8	0
Moore, Michael, of	.191	110	9	21	1	1	3	12	2
Nicholas, Darrell, of	.252	107	14	27	7	0	2	12	2
Rohrmeier, Dan, 1b	.215	65	10	14	2	0	4	9	1
Rosario, Carlos, 2b	.319	254	50	81	13	7	4	23	38
Rosario, Melvin, c	.241	303	40	73	14	3	10	43	9
Sawyer, Chris, of	.200	15	1	3	1	1	0	1	0
2-team (50 Berkshire)	.245	200	15	49	10	2	3	17	5
Shultz, Brian, of	.259	112	19	29	9	1	0	13	0
2-team (13 Adirondack)	.221	145	22	32	9	1	0	15	0
Spoerl, Josh, dh	.207	82	12	17	2	1	3	12	1
Swinton, Jermaine, 1b	.186	70	10	13	3	0	6	17	2
Torres, Mike, dh-2b	.297	118	17	35	5	1	2	21	1
Vasquez, Chris, 1b	.186	43	1	8	2	0	0	3	0

PITCHING	W	L	ERA	G	SV	IP	H	BB	SO
Allen, Rodney	4	3	2.38	9	0	56	49	21	33
Baker, Joey	9	6	4.36	20	0	130	143	22	85
Brand, Cliff	0	0	9.82	1	0	3	7	2	1
Brooks, Conor	2	4	3.63	34	7	44	43	17	44
Cadres, Kevin	1	1	11.68	6	0	12	16	8	9
Fischer, Mike	1	3	5.08	7	0	39	46	15	27
Goodrum, Kevin	1	3	3.97	20	0	45	58	22	33
Hassel, John	1	6	5.80	25	0	45	53	20	30
Hill, Chris	8	7	4.12	19	0	118	115	51	99
Lynn, Kevin	1	5	5.34	29	1	62	91	17	40
Marchesano, Mike	8	7	5.24	19	0	110	123	36	101

	W	L	ERA	G	SV	IP	H	BB	SO
Martin, Scott	1	1	4.29	8	0	21	24	8	15
McCall, Dan	0	0	7.94	3	0	5	7	3	7
Rochford, Duane	3	0	3.98	28	3	43	45	20	43
Siciliano, Jess	1	0	7.16	10	0	16	25	12	12
Sokol, Trad	0	0	14.54	2	0	4	9	8	3
2-team (11 Berkshire)	1	4	7.63	13	0	43	64	22	19
Stelzner, Nick	0	0	5.11	5	0	12	14	7	3
Weymouth, Marty	1	1	6.75	12	3	12	16	10	11

	W	L	ERA	G	SV	IP	H	BB	SO
Humrich, Chris	2	1	4.22	25	1	32	27	18	25
Meady, Todd	0	1	2.70	13	1	13	15	3	12
Myers, Aaron	11	6	3.28	20	0	140	135	49	87
Santucci, Lou	0	0	0.00	1	0	1	1	0	0

ELMIRA

BATTING	AVG	AB	R	H	2B	3B	HR	RBI	SB
Alvarez, Rafael, of	.293	311	60	91	18	5	12	55	4
Baker, Brian, of-dh	.159	88	8	14	3	0	2	7	3
Baker, Casey, 2b	.154	13	1	2	0	0	0	0	1
Bello, Rolando, 2b-ss	.256	129	22	33	6	1	2	15	4
Brostrom, Jeremy, of	.136	44	7	6	1	0	0	1	0
Bush, Ron, 2b	.272	342	52	93	22	4	2	37	8
Coleman, Michael, of	.361	83	20	30	5	0	5	15	1
Garcia, Osmani, 3b	.278	309	30	86	22	1	1	19	3
Hill, Bobby, ss	.253	170	11	43	3	5	1	14	9
Hutchins, Norm, of	.234	256	34	60	10	2	4	29	11
Jones, Brian, c	.284	306	35	87	25	1	11	56	3
King, Cesar, c	.323	62	5	20	3	0	0	5	0
Merriman, Terrell, of	.000	0	0	0	0	0	0	0	0
Pernell, Brandon, of	.278	216	39	60	13	4	8	24	18
2-team (36 Albany)	.263	353	59	93	19	6	10	44	24
Perry, Kyle, c	.000	7	0	0	0	0	0	0	0
2-team (8 Albany)	.139	36	3	5	0	0	0	3	1
Quero, Pedro, 1b	.301	335	45	101	25	4	15	64	8
Smith, Rod, of-2b	.230	165	22	38	9	2	2	14	22
Syfert, Luke, 1b-c	.045	22	2	1	0	0	0	0	1
Terhune, Mike, 2b	.246	61	8	15	3	0	1	4	0
Vasquez, Sandy, 1b-of	.204	108	16	22	6	0	3	20	1

PITCHING	W	L	ERA	G	SV	IP	H	BB	SO
Andra, Jeff	10	7	3.13	19	0	135	124	30	85
Brown, Chris	2	1	3.07	27	1	29	29	11	28
Brummett, Sean	7	5	3.02	19	0	128	116	17	100
Chadwick, John	0	0	0.00	1	0	1	0	1	0
Cook, Bradley	0	0	7.36	4	0	3	6	2	0
Crowther, Jackson	1	1	1.99	3	0	22	17	3	20
2-team (18 Berkshire)	6	8	3.61	21	0	107	111	33	74
Estes, Eric	3	3	5.50	6	0	36	40	6	29
Forbes, Keith	1	1	5.00	7	0	9	12	2	11
2-team (18 Quebec)	3	3	4.68	25	1	32	39	18	36
Griswold, Jordan	0	0	11.05	7	0	7	13	6	3
Iwahara, Kenji	0	0	5.03	14	0	19	23	12	18
Keagle, Greg	10	9	2.92	19	0	144	101	37	119
Perez, Julio	1	0	0.00	26	15	25	14	8	26
Pike, Matthew	7	1	2.01	22	0	40	31	7	39
Sano, Shigeki	3	3	2.75	9	0	59	56	11	25
Stine, Justin	7	5	4.03	16	0	91	81	20	49
Thomas, Donnie	2	0	1.98	33	2	36	29	10	22

NEW JERSEY

BATTING	AVG	AB	R	H	2B	3B	HR	RBI	SB
Bailey, Travis, of	.321	321	75	103	24	6	16	75	14
Brown, Billy, of	.313	262	48	82	9	5	8	44	14
Callahan, Dave, 1b	.265	253	50	67	17	0	9	42	13
Conway, Craig, 2b	.298	258	46	77	10	2	2	30	3
Dworken, Mikaela, c	.330	188	36	62	14	1	11	46	0
Grice, Dan, 2b	.102	49	6	5	1	0	0	5	0
Johannes, Todd, c	.239	188	25	45	7	0	1	16	2
Kane, Ryan, 3b	.298	292	62	87	21	0	12	66	2
Kennedy, David, dh-1b	.262	313	67	82	21	2	6	52	0
Lipari, Jack, of	.215	135	17	29	7	2	1	23	1
Potter, Mike, of	.077	13	1	1	0	0	0	3	1
Rich, Billy, of	.342	284	68	97	27	3	8	63	7
Samboy, Nelson, 2b	.394	66	16	26	4	0	0	9	7
Terni, Chas, ss	.298	332	57	99	34	1	10	63	1
Walker, Andy, dh-1b	.143	7	2	1	0	0	0	1	0

PITCHING	W	L	ERA	G	SV	IP	H	BB	SO
Allan, Scott	1	2	4.67	28	2	34	51	12	27
Bennett, Joel	14	2	2.93	18	0	129	105	40	141
Bertotti, Mike	13	5	3.85	19	0	114	111	46	97
Brack, A.J.	3	1	4.28	17	0	27	32	12	20
Brooks, Jake	1	0	2.78	5	0	22	22	8	15
Callier, Jeremy	6	3	3.46	24	2	75	79	14	41
Chavez, Chris	0	0	0.63	14	3	14	8	4	14
Ennico, Chris	0	2	8.16	5	0	14	23	6	8
Fish, Steve	9	4	6.35	19	0	112	149	27	70
George, Chris	1	0	5.79	7	1	14	17	4	9
Halla, Ryan	1	0	2.79	19	9	19	16	6	20

QUEBEC

BATTING	AVG	AB	R	H	2B	3B	HR	RBI	SB
Bagley, Lee, c	.232	56	10	13	1	0	1	10	0
Cornelius, Brian, of	.297	323	61	96	16	1	11	60	2
Cotton, John, 1b	.307	345	65	106	18	3	12	73	2
DiPrima, Giancarlo, 2b-ss	.000	8	1	0	0	0	0	0	0
Emond, Benoit, of	.287	338	59	97	18	3	0	44	13
Garrison, B.J., of	.282	149	36	42	12	1	4	25	7
Gomez, Rudy, 3b	.290	269	33	78	9	0	2	34	10
Kison, Robbie, ss	.311	283	36	88	14	3	3	42	15
Kofler, Eric, dh-of	.290	255	45	74	19	2	10	39	0
Langlois, Jean Sebastien, of	.111	18	3	2	1	0	1	3	0
Lantigua, Eddie, of-3b	.314	280	47	88	30	2	7	51	2
Lepine, Julien, 2b	.386	57	12	22	5	0	0	5	11
Maldari, Jeff, of	.000	8	1	0	0	0	0	0	0
Marval, Raul, 2b-ss	.239	88	13	21	3	0	0	14	0
Motley, Darryl, dh	.161	31	4	5	4	0	0	5	0
2-team (9 Allentown)	.161	62	7	10	4	0	2	11	0
Myler, Jonathan, c	.000	11	1	0	0	0	0	0	0
Pujols, Rafael, c	.319	326	58	104	24	1	3	49	3
Scalabrini, Pat, 2b-3b	.325	280	54	91	24	0	7	45	19

PITCHING	W	L	ERA	G	SV	IP	H	BB	SO
Blais, Joce	2	2	4.62	21	0	50	58	8	23
Chandler, Bobby	0	0	2.53	11	1	10	13	4	7
Chenard, Christian	4	1	2.96	27	1	54	52	12	42
Cisar, Mark	1	1	0.76	34	19	35	21	12	33
Dunn, Keith	11	4	2.81	18	0	118	100	37	82
Forbes, Keith	2	2	4.56	18	1	23	27	16	25
Hughes, Nial	0	1	18.90	4	0	3	4	13	2
LaPlante, Michel	1	1	5.03	5	0	19	24	4	8
Laplante, Reggie	3	3	7.74	16	0	43	42	51	28
Lavigne, Martin	0	1	12.60	1	0	5	8	6	5
Leach, B.J.	0	2	3.97	12	0	11	13	2	12
Prata, Danny	11	4	4.26	18	0	114	120	31	69
Stanton, Tim	9	6	4.61	20	0	111	124	37	73
Thomas, Joe	9	6	4.37	20	0	134	142	33	77
Tremblay, Andre	4	4	3.35	25	1	45	54	13	28
Yee, Damon	0	0	0.00	1	0	1	1	0	2

CENTRAL DIVISION

STANDINGS

FIRST HALF				
NORTH	W	L	PCT	GB
Winnipeg Goldeyes	28	16	.640	—
Fargo-Moorhead RedHawks	25	19	.568	3
Duluth-Superior Dukes	24	21	.533	4½
Sioux Falls Canaries	18	27	.400	10½
St. Paul Saints	17	27	.386	11
SOUTH	W	L	PCT	GB
Sioux City Explorers	28	16	.636	—
Lincoln Saltdogs	25	20	.556	3½
Joliet Jackhammers	22	23	.489	6½
Schaumburg Flyers	19	24	.442	8½
Gary RailCats	17	28	.380	11½

SECOND HALF				
NORTH	W	L	PCT	GB
Winnipeg Goldeyes	28	17	.622	—
Fargo-Moorhead RedHawks	27	18	.600	1
Sioux Falls Canaries	23	22	.511	5
St. Paul Saints	22	23	.489	6
Duluth-Superior Dukes	12	33	.267	16
SOUTH	W	L	PCT	GB
Joliet Jackhammers	31	15	.674	-
Lincoln Saltdogs	30	16	.652	1
Sioux City Explorers	18	27	.400	12½
Gary RailCats	18	27	.400	12½
Schaumburg Flyers	16	29	.356	14½

PLAYOFFS: Semifinals—Sioux City defeated Joliet 3-0 and Winnipeg defeated Lincoln 3-2 in best-of-5 series. **Finals**—Winnipeg defeated Sioux City 3-1 in best-of-5 series. **Northern League Finals:** New Jersey defeated Winnipeg 3-1 in best-of-5 series.

MANAGERS: Duluth-Superior—Al Gallagher. **Fargo-Moorhead**—Doug Simunic. **Gary**—Joe Calfapietra. **Joliet**—Matt Nokes. **Lincoln**—Les Lancaster. **St. Paul**—Jimmy Johnson. **Schaumburg**—Jim Boynewicz. **Sioux City**—Benny Castillo. **Sioux Falls**—Doc Edwards. **Winnipeg**—Hal Lanier.

INDEPENDENT LEAGUES

ATTENDANCE: Winnipeg 303,786; St. Paul 294,363; Lincoln 247,471; Schaumburg 206,714; Joliet 202,755; Fargo-Moorhead 193,364; Sioux Falls 125,077; Sioux City 109,355; Duluth-Superior 59,254.

ALL-STAR TEAM: C—Kirk Pierce, Fargo-Moorhead. **1B**—Brian Becker, Fargo-Moorhead. **2B**—Francisco Matos, Gary. **3B**—Brent Sachs, Winnipeg. **SS**—Darren Doskocil, Lincoln. **OF**—Bryan Warner, Lincoln; Dustin Delucchi, Lincoln; Harry Berrios, Winnipeg. **DH**—Kevin Roberson, St Paul. **RHP**—Rich Hyde, Joliet. **LHP**—Bobby Madritsch, Winnipeg. **RP**—Matt Hammons, Joliet.

Player of the Year: Bryan Warner, Lincoln. **Rookie of the Year:** Jake Burnham, Sioux Falls. **Rookie Pitcher of the Year:** Dusty Keppen, Schaumburg. **Manager of the Year:** Joe Calfapietra, Gary.

INDIVIDUAL BATTING LEADERS
(Minimum 243 Plate Appearances)

	AVG	AB	R	H	2B	3B	HR	RBI	SB
Matos, Francisco, Gary	.362	304	44	110	19	3	2	40	4
Sachs, Brent, Winnipeg	.346	364	83	126	29	4	11	60	20
Rose Jr., Pete, Winnipeg	.344	209	36	72	17	1	8	53	1
Viera, Jose, Sioux Falls	.337	356	59	120	34	1	18	56	1
Warner, Bryan, Lincoln	.331	363	56	120	20	2	15	78	15
Delucchi, Dustin, Lincoln	.325	329	79	107	28	0	4	40	41
Becker, Brian, Fargo-Moorhead	.325	357	60	116	31	4	11	60	1
Berrios, Harry, Winnipeg	.323	365	83	118	18	1	21	75	3
Murphy, Sean, D-S	.321	349	52	112	31	4	5	55	2
Pierce, Kirk, Fargo-Moorhead	.318	314	56	100	19	1	17	63	1

INDIVIDUAL PITCHING LEADERS
(Minimum 72 Plate Appearances)

	W	L	ERA	G	SV	IP	H	BB	SO
Glick, David, Sioux City	5	3	1.89	11	0	76	59	15	51
Madritsch, Bobby, Winnipeg	11	4	2.30	19	0	125	94	36	153
Fletschock, Justin, F-M	9	3	2.42	17	0	108	111	16	68
Hyde, Rich, Joliet	11	7	2.49	23	0	159	168	19	118
Mazone, Brian, Joliet	15	3	2.51	22	0	140	125	27	128
Silva, Troy, Lincoln	7	1	2.62	17	0	82	65	34	58
Padua, Geraldo, Winnipeg	12	3	3.06	19	0	124	117	36	94
Lontayo, Alex, F-M	8	4	3.12	20	0	130	118	54	106
Whitney, Jake, St. Paul	11	5	3.12	19	0	133	126	26	111
Villalon, Julio, D-S	7	3	3.26	13	0	77	69	17	74

DULUTH-SUPERIOR

BATTING	AVG	AB	R	H	2B	3B	HR	RBI	SB
Estrada, Marco, ss	.237	97	12	23	2	1	0	6	4
2-team (36 Sioux Falls)	.178	213	16	38	4	1	0	7	4
Gibson, Derrick, of	.248	214	28	53	10	0	7	25	6
Jefferson, David, of	.266	263	37	70	13	0	5	30	15
Jones, Terry, of	.217	46	5	10	0	1	0	5	4
LePine, Chris, of	.263	308	39	81	12	1	0	22	4
Maluchnik, Gregg, c-3b	.215	214	11	46	7	0	2	22	3
Morrison, Greg, 1b	.288	365	47	105	16	0	10	61	7
Murphy, Sean, 3b-2b	.321	349	52	112	31	4	5	55	2
Roche, Marlon, dh-of	.287	338	55	97	22	0	8	36	7
Rueber, David, 3b	.246	122	18	30	3	2	0	7	1
Swenson, Leland, ss	.209	297	24	62	7	0	0	24	2
Theoharis, Mike, 3b-2b	.186	70	10	13	2	0	0	6	2
Ullery, Dave, c	.295	95	8	28	3	0	3	9	0
Vinh, Bao, 2b-of	.292	322	36	94	13	5	0	35	10
2-team (7 St. Paul)	.282	347	37	98	13	5	0	36	10
Walker, Jimmy, c	.200	55	4	11	4	0	0	8	0

PITCHING	W	L	ERA	G	SV	IP	H	BB	SO
Bacci, Tony	6	7	3.46	19	0	117	138	38	54
Book, Jeremy	3	9	5.04	15	0	75	105	26	49
Brackeen, Colin	2	0	2.86	11	0	22	29	9	8
Ford, Brian	2	5	3.06	39	3	67	72	19	35
Guess, Scott	3	4	4.11	24	0	70	79	22	50
Lakman, Jason	0	5	4.50	13	2	56	66	16	45
Masterman, Tom	1	2	2.13	7	0	25	25	6	19
Montgomery, Joe	0	6	5.11	21	1	79	93	32	31
O'Donnell, Tony	0	1	6.26	7	0	27	34	10	20
Sigley, Jayson	0	3	4.07	28	1	55	51	18	54
Thompson, Travis	4	8	3.86	29	10	86	87	25	63
Vendela, Chris	0	0	4.05	3	0	6	8	3	3
2-team (7 Fargo-Moorhead)	0	0	5.71	10	1	17	20	10	9
Villalon, Julio	7	3	3.26	13	0	77	69	17	74
Wicklund, Joe	1	0	12.60	6	0	5	5	10	3
Zwirchitz, Andy	2	1	4.15	7	1	30	41	14	23

FARGO-MOORHEAD

BATTING	AVG	AB	R	H	2B	3B	HR	RBI	SB
Becker, Brian, 1b	.325	357	60	116	31	4	11	60	1
Becker, Rich, of	.289	339	54	98	23	2	5	31	4
Figga, Mike, dh	.273	33	2	9	1	0	0	3	0
Gennaro, Brad, of	.186	59	8	11	1	0	1	6	1

Gerald, Ed, of	.216	74	13	16	3	1	6	14	3
2-team (57 Sioux City)	.229	288	43	66	14	3	17	46	12
Hatzell, Eric, c	.182	11	2	2	0	0	0	1	0
Mann, Matt, of	.282	262	35	74	9	4	1	34	6
Mazer, Brad, of	.220	41	6	9	2	0	1	6	0
McCallum, Geoff, ss	.258	267	32	69	11	1	3	32	7
Patton, Josh, 3b	.288	337	54	97	25	2	6	58	10
Pierce, Kirk, c	.318	314	56	100	19	1	17	63	1
Powell, Dante, of	.245	49	8	12	3	1	1	6	8
Rohrmeier, Dan, 1b	.091	22	1	2	1	0	0	1	0
Smith, Demond, of	.300	70	15	21	4	0	1	5	15
Sprout, Brian, ss	.224	67	9	15	2	0	3	10	0
Villalobos, Carlos, 3b	.217	23	1	5	2	0	0	0	0
Ward, Brian, 2b	.285	344	48	98	20	0	7	50	5
Weber, Jon, of	.296	365	69	108	30	3	13	52	11
Williams, Eddie, dh	.299	117	9	35	5	0	1	13	0

PITCHING	W	L	ERA	G	SV	IP	H	BB	SO
Bittiger, Jeff	2	1	2.74	6	0	23	22	13	14
Duffy, John	6	5	4.36	28	0	74	89	35	39
Fletschock, Justin	9	3	2.42	17	0	107	111	16	68
Hooker, Jon	1	3	3.91	25	2	69	52	32	60
Kalinowski, Roger	0	0	4.50	20	0	22	27	10	11
2-team (11 Joliet)	0	1	3.99	31	0	29	36	16	15
Kennedy, Jodie	4	3	4.36	14	0	66	72	29	27
Lontayo, Alex	8	4	3.12	20	0	130	118	54	106
Montgomery, Steve	2	2	1.89	36	19	47	38	17	52
Paull, Kalam	3	3	8.19	8	0	29	45	15	23
Salvevold, Greg	9	5	3.96	19	0	127	140	33	70
Troilo, Joe	1	2	2.73	19	0	33	32	10	18
Vendela, Chris	0	0	6.75	7	1	10	12	7	6
Young, Doug	7	6	2.08	40	2	69	54	22	64

GARY

BATTING	AVG	AB	R	H	2B	3B	HR	RBI	SB
Anderson, John, of-2b	.294	289	38	85	11	1	3	23	16
2-team (91 Sioux Falls)	.298	379	50	113	17	2	3	38	18
Bartolucci, Paul, ss	.175	206	15	36	6	0	0	16	3
Breland, Jason, of	.250	4	0	1	0	0	0	0	0
Carpenter, Bubba, of	.296	189	33	56	12	3	8	29	6
Clark, Jason, of	.245	319	35	78	10	2	2	32	16
De los Santos, Luis, 1b	.279	104	10	29	6	0	3	19	0
Dent, Darrell, dh	.304	23	2	7	0	0	0	0	0
Gomez, Rickey, 2b	.000	7	1	0	0	0	0	0	0
Goodman, Scott, of-1b	.355	62	11	22	3	0	2	11	3
Herrick, Jason, of	.277	94	13	26	9	0	3	14	10
Hill, Bobby, ss	.269	104	13	28	6	0	0	9	6
Jacobson, Kerry, of	.000	9	1	0	0	0	0	0	0
3-team (4 SF/39 St. Paul)	.224	147	17	33	6	1	2	20	4
Lane, Nolan, of	.267	45	7	12	1	0	2	8	0
Malone, Billy, 3b	.262	370	44	97	13	6	3	28	21
Matos, Francisco, 2b	.362	304	44	110	19	3	2	40	4
Pagan, Carlos, c	.289	249	28	72	10	0	10	33	1
Rosario, Carlos, 2b	.260	77	7	20	3	1	1	3	6
Scott, Brad, of	.000	4	0	0	0	0	0	0	0
Swinton, Jermaine, 1b	.248	258	39	64	14	0	15	41	2
Thompson, Phil, of	.220	223	27	49	7	1	6	27	8
Wittmeyer, Kevin, c-of	.188	229	20	43	7	3	2	20	1

PITCHING	W	L	ERA	G	SV	IP	H	BB	SO
Bradford, Josh	2	5	5.05	10	0	46	50	23	26
Demouy, Chris	4	2	2.65	41	1	54	66	19	28
Dimma, Doug	0	0	10.13	4	0	8	15	5	6
Donovan, T.J.	0	1	15.43	1	0	4	6	6	4
Embry, Byron	1	3	3.17	43	1	59	56	28	65
Hardy, Cameron	0	0	0.00	2	0	3	5	1	5
Harrison, Jim	0	0	9.00	5	0	17	25	8	10
Huffaker, Mike	0	1	5.60	13	0	17	23	6	13
Louden, Gary	3	5	5.01	23	0	64	62	42	48
Martin, Larry	0	0	54.00	2	0	1	3	4	2
Mazur, Graham	5	11	4.49	18	0	114	137	43	92
Miller, Benji	6	5	2.61	41	11	51	48	12	33
Montgomery, Joe	1	1	12.86	3	0	7	12	4	5
2-team (21 Duluth-Superior)	6	7	5.73	24	1	86	105	36	36
Paull, Kalam	4	4	8.40	12	0	84	83	34	44
2-team (8 Fargo-Moorhead)	6	7	5.68	20	0	114	128	49	67
Reid, Aaron	0	0	7.32	7	0	19	29	7	10
Riley, Mike	7	9	4.35	20	0	128	141	34	93
Wagner, Matt	0	3	8.35	7	0	32	53	2	20
Webb, Alan	2	6	4.34	18	0	95	107	41	82

JOLIET

BATTING	AVG	AB	R	H	2B	3B	HR	RBI	SB
Allen, Jeff, of	.284	229	18	65	14	1	3	27	3

	AVG	AB	R	H	2B	3B	HR	RBI	SB
Bartolucci, Paul, ss	.196	51	6	10	1	0	0	4	3
2-team (59 Gary)	.179	257	21	46	7	0	0	20	6
Beamon, Trey, of	.240	167	16	40	3	0	4	16	6
Burke, Mark, 1b	.225	102	9	23	7	0	3	16	0
Chance, Tony, of	.258	260	39	67	8	1	9	31	2
DeYoung, Peter, 3b-1b	.239	297	28	71	13	1	2	14	17
Fink, Eddie, of	.292	48	7	14	4	0	3	10	0
Fischer, Rob, of	.292	240	31	70	12	1	4	22	10
Flack, John, 2b-of	.000	7	0	0	0	0	0	0	0
Flores, Ray, 3b-ss	.208	125	9	26	4	0	0	12	2
Henry, Chad, ss-2b	.261	199	15	52	6	1	1	17	3
Kopacz, Derek, of	.257	249	26	64	10	2	4	33	5
2-team (31 Schaumburg)	.272	372	40	101	17	4	5	50	8
Larreal, Roberto, 3b	.200	25	2	5	0	0	0	2	0
2-team (5 Lincoln)	.179	39	4	7	0	0	1	4	0
Nokes, Matt, dh	.280	75	7	21	7	0	0	6	0
Paciorek, Mack, ss	.179	112	3	20	3	0	0	8	2
Quintana, Alberto, 3b-ss	.045	22	0	1	0	0	0	0	0
2-team (28 Schaumburg)	.176	125	7	22	1	0	0	11	0
Sienko, Ryan, c-1b	.329	161	44	53	14	0	18	38	0
Smith, Bubba, 1b	.289	97	20	28	5	0	11	23	0
Snellgrove, Clay, 2b	.227	97	10	22	1	0	1	8	3
Sprout, Brian, 2b	.292	253	50	74	17	3	6	23	11
2-team (Fargo-Moorhead)	.278	320	59	89	19	3	9	33	11
Wilkins, Rick, c-1b	.255	325	44	83	15	0	7	42	2

PITCHING	W	L	ERA	G	SV	IP	H	BB	SO
Faigin, Jason	0	0	16.88	6	0	5	13	7	3
Franklin, Brent	4	2	2.61	44	1	58	49	12	48
Goodrich, Randy	5	5	3.27	21	0	88	95	18	64
Hammons, Matt	5	2	1.59	44	23	51	36	21	80
Horne, Adam	0	1	1.04	12	0	17	13	4	7
Hyde, Rich	11	7	2.49	23	0	159	168	19	118
Johnston, Doug	0	4	4.73	10	0	40	35	9	28
Kalinowski, Roger	0	1	2.45	11	0	7	9	6	4
Lacerenza, Mark	0	0	5.40	2	0	1	2	0	1
Lewis, Rickey	5	9	5.15	22	0	122	149	42	60
Mazone, Brian	15	3	2.51	22	0	139	125	27	128
Orga, Kevin	4	1	3.55	24	0	66	63	28	42
Prater, Drew	1	0	7.82	11	0	12	12	7	12
Rohlfing, Jon	1	1	2.00	20	0	26	14	12	37
Swiatkiewicz, Chris	0	2	11.12	2	0	5	11	4	2
Watson, Greg	2	1	2.45	20	0	22	27	14	17
Weel, Mike	0	0	0.00	1	0	1	1	2	0

LINCOLN

BATTING	AVG	AB	R	H	2B	3B	HR	RBI	SB
Allen, Scott, c	.071	14	0	1	0	0	0	0	0
Bell, Dustin, ph	.000	1	0	0	0	0	0	0	0
Brinkley, Josh, 3b-c	.246	199	18	49	7	2	0	23	7
Britt, Bryan, 1b-of	.210	305	32	64	12	2	14	43	0
Cisneros, Josh, c	.159	44	3	7	2	0	0	3	0
Conner, Michael, of	.091	11	1	1	0	0	0	0	0
De los Santos, Eddy, ss-2b	.270	137	16	37	6	0	0	15	3
Delucchi, Dustin, of	.325	329	79	107	28	0	4	40	41
Doskocil, Darren, ss-2b	.298	366	63	109	15	5	9	61	13
Downing, Lance, 3b-2b	.213	61	6	13	2	0	0	3	1
Driskill, John, 2b-3b	.250	32	2	8	1	0	0	4	0
2-team (9 St. Paul)	.281	57	3	16	2	0	0	6	0
Duross, Gabe, 1b	.297	182	17	54	2	0	3	22	2
Harris, Cory, of	.316	152	27	48	10	2	3	18	9
Hernandez, Alexis, c	.267	221	32	59	10	3	6	38	0
Jernigan, Patrick, c	.077	26	1	2	1	0	0	2	0
Kittelberger, Jimmy, 2b	.277	112	20	31	4	0	1	5	1
Larreal, Limbreth, 3b-ss	.311	132	22	41	4	0	0	14	7
2-team (22 St. Paul)	.272	184	26	50	5	0	0	19	8
Moore, Kevin, 3b-dh	.207	58	5	12	3	0	0	9	2
Munoz, Juan, dh	.341	123	16	42	7	1	1	13	1
Phillips, Dane, c	.000	5	0	0	0	0	0	0	0
Raven, Luis, 1b	.235	51	9	12	2	0	2	5	0
3-team (38 SG/29 Winn.)	.288	340	45	98	26	0	11	56	1
Rodarte, Raul, 3b	.267	30	2	8	1	0	0	3	0
Silvestre, Juan, of	.222	108	16	24	6	0	3	7	0
Umphres, Chris, dh	.171	35	2	6	0	0	0	3	0
Warner, Bryan, of	.331	363	56	120	20	2	15	78	15

PITCHING	W	L	ERA	G	SV	IP	H	BB	SO
Black, Brett	0	5	6.94	9	0	48	70	7	31
Herz, Jason	6	4	3.80	15	0	66	67	15	31
Johnston, Doug	5	1	2.32	8	0	50	46	6	41
2-team (10 Joliet)	5	5	3.39	18	0	90	81	15	69
Kohl, Doug	2	1	2.73	6	0	33	38	12	16
Koutrouba, Tom	5	5	4.66	12	0	77	84	17	47
Lee, Andy	2	3	2.63	35	0	41	47	16	32

		W	L	ERA	G	SV	IP	H	BB	SO
Ochsner, Alan		7	1	2.88	34	2	68	61	16	49
Pageler, Mick		4	1	1.78	30	1	55	43	6	44
Quiros, Jaime		0	0	15.43	4	0	4	10	7	3
Royal, Shannon		0	0	2.16	6	0	8	11	2	7
Schultz, Jeff		1	2	4.76	10	0	17	15	2	15
Sido, Wilson		2	1	4.15	5	0	21	23	11	16
Silva, Troy		1	1	2.62	17	0	82	65	34	58
Sokoll, Adam		0	0	9.00	3	0	3	7	1	2
Strickland, Keith		0	0	1.13	6	0	8	6	3	9
Trapp, Kenny		2	2	3.62	5	0	27	28	8	12
Walters, Cory		6	5	3.72	19	0	116	117	27	80
Weidert, Chris		3	1	1.16	36	22	38	29	4	31
Zipser, Mike		3	3	4.57	7	0	43	41	14	30

ST. PAUL

BATTING	AVG	AB	R	H	2B	3B	HR	RBI	SB
Ashby, Chris, of	.289	187	29	54	10	0	3	20	0
Battle, Howard, 3b	.314	210	25	66	10	0	7	41	0
Buckley, Reagan, c-of	.245	323	43	79	11	5	8	32	5
Cash, Condor, 1b	.333	3	0	1	0	0	0	0	0
Danzy, Ray, of	.111	9	2	1	1	0	0	0	0
2-team (13 Sioux Falls)	.250	48	8	12	4	0	1	2	0
Driskill, John, 2b	.320	25	1	8	1	0	0	2	0
Gomez, Rickey, 2b	.239	138	15	33	4	0	0	4	1
2-team (3 Gary)	.252	131	14	33	4	0	0	4	1
Hill, Jason, 1b	.327	202	25	66	13	0	4	26	7
Hood, Jay, ss	.100	20	1	2	1	0	0	1	0
Jacobson, Kerry, of	.254	122	16	31	6	1	2	20	4
Magdaleno, Ricky, ss-3b	.227	150	19	34	2	0	2	12	2
Marin, Limberth, ss-2b	.173	52	4	9	1	0	0	5	1
Moore, Kevin, of	.211	123	15	26	6	0	3	19	1
2-team (16 Lincoln)	.210	181	20	38	9	0	3	28	3
Nelson, Reggie, 2b-ss	.250	124	17	31	4	1	1	14	9
Nickerson, Brian, 3b-of	.209	91	8	19	2	0	2	11	1
Peterman, Tommy, 1b	.324	213	21	69	12	0	4	21	1
2-team (22 Schaumburg)	.310	297	28	92	15	0	4	32	1
Roberson, Kevin, dh-of	.310	261	56	81	20	0	27	55	0
Ruiz, Ryan, of	.294	177	29	52	8	2	1	13	13
Ruiz, Willy, 2b-ss	.234	94	8	22	4	0	0	5	0
Santana, Osmany, of	.240	154	11	37	7	1	0	13	4
Shallenberger, Joe, ss	.247	97	13	24	5	0	0	7	5
Sullivan, Kevin, c	.116	43	0	5	1	0	0	1	0
Vinh, Bao, dh	.160	25	1	4	0	0	0	1	0
Williams, Keith, of	.258	159	23	41	7	2	5	19	3
Woolf, Jason, ss-2b	.282	39	4	11	0	0	0	3	0

PITCHING	W	L	ERA	G	SV	IP	H	BB	SO
Albin, Scott	5	8	4.25	28	0	91	86	34	69
Bell, Richard	1	1	3.86	8	0	9	9	4	11
Berroa, Oliver	0	1	4.91	4	0	11	11	9	10
Calvert, Klae	5	7	5.49	20	0	114	137	15	83
Crawford, Wesley	2	8	5.13	19	1	86	105	20	53
Cruz, Arian	1	4	2.61	32	3	38	35	12	38
Dickinson, Rodney	3	5	3.41	35	14	37	39	15	39
Eskierka, Ryan	0	0	6.94	7	0	11	14	2	6
Fleetham, Ben	2	1	3.48	12	0	20	21	4	20
2-team (13 Sioux Falls)	4	2	2.76	25	6	32	30	8	33
Friedman, Jody	1	0	6.17	29	0	42	42	14	25
Gawer, Matt	0	0	6.75	1	0	1	2	2	1
Giron, Emiliano	1	4	5.11	8	0	44	45	18	39
Giron, Isabel	5	3	3.45	11	0	62	68	15	51
Goodrum, Kevin	0	0	0.00	2	0	3	2	1	2
Magdaleno, Ricky	1	0	4.82	8	0	9	17	6	9
Martunas, Matthew	0	0	8.10	4	0	3	5	4	3
Meyers, Keith	0	0	13.50	1	0	1	3	1	1
Perez, Miguel	1	3	4.21	9	0	47	54	19	55
Swiatkiewicz, Chris	0	0	3.52	3	0	7	14	1	5
Wheeler, Thomas	0	0	11.57	2	0	2	4	1	1
Whitney, Jake	11	5	3.12	19	0	132	126	26	111

SCHAUMBURG

BATTING	AVG	AB	R	H	2B	3B	HR	RBI	SB
Burke, Mark, 1b	.259	197	32	51	14	0	4	29	3
2-team (31 Joliet)	.247	299	41	74	21	0	7	45	3
Chamberlain, Wes, 1b	.214	42	4	9	2	0	1	5	2
Clifton, Rodney, of	.288	156	32	45	9	2	10	33	6
Deluca, Mario, 2b	.222	9	0	2	0	0	0	0	0
Dour, Craig, 1b	.220	91	13	20	3	0	3	9	1
Dumas, Mike, 2b	.000	14	0	0	0	0	0	0	0
Dunn, Chris, 2b	.222	126	22	28	5	1	1	9	1
Finnegan, Chris, c	.327	104	8	34	3	0	1	11	2
Foley, Steve, of	.282	347	60	98	19	5	7	45	8
Goerdt, Eric, of	.266	143	12	38	5	0	4	12	3

BATTING	AVG	AB	R	H	2B	3B	HR	RBI	SB
Gonzalez, Ender, 2b	.309	136	21	42	8	0	1	13	6
Herrick, Jason, of	.274	219	30	60	10	3	9	43	6
2-team (25 Gary)	.275	313	43	86	19	3	12	57	16
Kopacz, Derek, of	.301	123	14	37	7	2	1	17	3
Leday, A.J., dh	.233	73	6	17	6	0	0	10	1
2-team (10 Winnipeg)	.218	110	12	24	7	0	0	11	1
Marval, Raul, ss-2b	.270	159	14	43	13	0	0	10	0
McDonald, Ashanti, ss-3b	.288	319	42	92	17	2	8	48	5
Melendez, Luis, c	.199	146	17	29	7	0	0	8	0
Peterman, Tommy, 1b	.274	84	7	23	3	0	0	11	0
Powell, Chris, of	.242	120	25	29	3	3	3	20	4
Quintana, Alberto, ss	.204	103	7	21	1	0	0	11	0
Smith, Jeremy, 3b	.267	300	37	80	7	0	3	29	7
Van Horn, Ryan, c	.214	70	13	15	2	2	3	7	0

PITCHING	W	L	ERA	G	SV	IP	H	BB	SO
Capparelli, Richard	0	0	16.88	2	0	2	3	3	3
Chaney, Mike	7	5	5.23	18	0	106	123	35	68
DeHoyos, Gabe	1	1	3.18	18	0	22	19	15	20
Fahrner, Evan	2	5	2.81	49	8	64	51	20	66
Genke, Todd	2	4	6.11	9	0	56	66	19	44
Herbison, Brett	0	5	7.31	6	0	28	40	14	10
John, Tommy	2	4	6.67	32	0	54	70	25	28
Keppen, Dusty	3	4	3.90	35	9	55	60	30	41
Klancnik, Joe	3	2	3.00	8	0	54	49	27	33
Martin, Larry	0	0	7.20	7	0	10	13	12	12
2-team (2 Gary)	0	0	11.45	9	0	11	16	16	14
Mencas, Val	0	1	10.80	15	0	18	31	11	14
Prempas, Lyle	5	6	4.19	22	0	96	83	55	70
Snyder, Bill	1	1	7.71	8	0	7	8	7	5
Swanson, Erick	1	2	4.54	28	0	33	38	23	23
Wagner, Matt	2	6	6.88	10	0	51	64	18	46
2-team (7 Gary)	2	9	7.45	17	0	83	117	20	66
Woodman, Hank	6	5	3.97	20	0	122	118	51	89

SIOUX CITY

BATTING	AVG	AB	R	H	2B	3B	HR	RBI	SB
Byas, Mike, of	.291	320	55	93	9	0	0	21	26
Campaniello, Ed, dh	.248	117	14	29	5	0	2	8	1
Caston, Bernard, of-dh	.284	183	31	52	8	0	3	17	18
Colon, Cris, 3b	.301	362	40	109	22	1	3	62	0
Correa, Dalphie, ss	.227	247	24	56	7	2	0	20	8
Gerald, Ed, of	.234	214	30	50	11	2	11	32	9
Lee, Curt, 2b	.262	317	45	83	9	2	3	26	1
Maluchnik, Gregg, c-1b	.231	26	1	6	0	0	0	4	0
Martin, Jonah, of	.164	73	8	12	4	0	2	7	3
Meggers, Mike, 1b	.132	38	3	5	4	0	0	2	0
Mitchell, Tony, dh-1b	.300	140	18	42	4	0	8	27	2
2-team (37 Sioux Falls)	.309	269	43	83	9	0	17	52	3
Raven, Luis, 1b	.302	149	16	45	16	0	4	25	1
Rodrigues, Rich, c-1b	.211	227	16	48	9	0	6	33	1
Salmela, Andy, 1b	.000	2	0	0	0	0	0	0	0
Santore, Todd, c	.270	148	17	40	3	0	0	21	2
Sawyer, Chris, of	.000	6	0	0	0	0	0	0	0
Theoharis, Mike, ss	.135	52	4	7	1	0	0	4	0
2-team (21 Duluth-Superior)	.164	122	14	20	3	0	0	10	2
Villalobos, Carlos, 1b	.200	15	3	3	1	0	1	4	0
Wilson, Andy, of	.298	346	63	103	18	0	6	35	21
Woodcock, Lance, 3b	.462	13	2	6	0	0	0	1	0

PITCHING	W	L	ERA	G	SV	IP	H	BB	SO
Bermudez, Manny	5	4	2.57	35	8	56	58	9	27
Fauske, Josh	2	1	3.90	19	1	27	27	12	17
George, Chris	2	1	0.66	7	1	27	16	6	24
3-team (11 St. Paul/1 SF)	5	4	3.54	15	0	81	87	24	63
Glick, David	5	3	1.89	11	0	76	59	15	51
Grote, Jason	5	4	4.47	17	0	98	124	21	52
Hooper, Jimmy	3	2	2.60	30	7	52	53	15	52
Horne, Adam	1	0	4.34	8	1	18	19	3	8
2-team (12 Joliet)	1	0	2.75	20	1	36	32	7	15
Luque, Roger	3	2	2.60	9	0	52	45	11	41
McCasland, Ralph	5	7	3.46	23	0	93	96	17	61
McDaniel, Denny	5	4	3.40	30	5	53	53	9	54
McDermott, Toby	0	3	5.54	6	0	26	27	15	12
Romero, Jordan	3	5	5.43	13	0	71	77	29	37
Springston, Adam	3	4	4.42	11	0	55	60	18	25
Stoner, Nat	1	1	2.05	12	0	22	18	5	18
Swiatkiewicz, Chris	3	1	2.57	6	0	42	41	6	29
3-team (2 Joliet/3 St. Paul)	3	3	3.58	11	0	55	66	11	36

SIOUX FALLS

BATTING	AVG	AB	R	H	2B	3B	HR	RBI	SB
Anderson, John, 2b	.311	90	12	28	6	1	0	15	2

BATTING	AVG	AB	R	H	2B	3B	HR	RBI	SB
Beamon, Trey, of	.307	199	29	61	10	0	2	22	8
2-team (44 Joliet)	.276	366	45	101	13	0	6	38	14
Burnham, Jake, of	.275	338	43	93	17	0	20	57	1
Butt, Gerald, c	.244	82	7	20	3	1	0	8	0
Danzy, Ray, of	.282	39	6	11	3	0	1	2	0
Dreher, Doug, 2b-3b	.305	59	10	18	1	0	0	1	0
Encarnacion, Angelo, c	.167	78	5	13	2	0	2	4	1
Estrada, Marco, ss	.129	116	4	15	2	0	0	1	0
Jacobson, Kerry, of	.125	16	0	2	0	0	0	0	0
Krause, Scott, ss	.407	54	14	22	4	1	5	14	0
3-team (60 D-S/4 SC)	.230	291	21	67	9	1	4	34	3
Mitchell, Tony, dh	.318	129	25	41	5	0	9	25	1
Pagan, Felix, 2b	.295	210	35	62	3	0	13	37	7
Pendergrass, Tyrone, of	.255	377	62	96	10	7	12	46	31
Pinkerton, Danny, c	.171	123	14	21	2	1	2	8	0
Rivero, Eddie, of	.248	202	32	50	13	0	13	32	1
Schelhaas, Greg, 1b	.260	335	41	87	13	0	17	49	2
Viera, Jose, 3b	.337	356	59	120	34	1	18	56	1
Villalobos, Carlos, of	.344	61	9	21	4	0	3	11	3
3-team (4 F-M/4 SC)	.293	99	13	29	7	0	4	15	3
Williams, Eddie, dh	.263	19	1	5	1	0	0	1	1
2-team (32 Fargo-Moorhead)	.294	136	10	40	6	0	1	14	1
Woodcock, Lance, ss	.207	208	23	43	5	1	2	13	0
2-team (5 Sioux City)	.222	221	25	49	5	1	2	14	0

PITCHING	W	L	ERA	G	SV	IP	H	BB	SO
Bailie, Matt	2	1	2.12	13	0	17	17	8	20
Bell, Richard	1	2	3.27	22	10	22	20	13	23
2-team (8 St. Paul)	2	3	3.45	30	10	31	29	17	34
Boker, John	0	4	6.10	9	0	41	44	21	17
Coleman, Billy	8	6	4.74	20	0	127	140	24	92
Diaz, Antonio	3	2	5.13	40	3	54	65	20	39
Dimma, Doug	0	0	4.50	3	0	2	1	0	1
2-team (4 Gary)	0	0	9.00	7	0	10	16	5	7
Felkel, Bryan	0	0	3.06	9	0	17	21	5	14
Ferretti, Ryan	0	1	6.35	9	1	17	23	5	5
Fleetham, Ben	2	1	1.50	13	6	12	9	4	13
Fries, Scott	0	1	36.00	3	0	1	6	1	1
Giron, Isabel	0	0	6.75	1	0	6	8	4	1
Gomez, Benito	1	0	9.00	3	0	6	8	2	3
Hessler, Landon	1	2	5.68	14	0	19	20	11	14
Jerue, Tristan	3	3	7.61	12	0	49	68	25	34
Koziara, Matt	5	6	4.19	19	0	109	142	23	60
Lyons, Mike	7	2	3.29	18	0	115	116	24	95
Mathys, Jason	0	1	9.00	3	0	5	11	2	2
McCall, Dan	0	2	4.26	10	0	12	17	6	11
Odom, Lance	0	0	3.38	6	0	10	10	6	8
Renteria, Juan	2	5	3.07	17	0	58	54	23	38
Richter, B.J.	0	0	5.40	1	0	1	3	0	0
Stoner, Nat	2	2	4.91	25	0	25	29	10	18
2-team (12 Sioux City)	3	3	3.59	37	0	47	47	15	36
Tisdale, Marlyn	4	8	4.31	28	1	62	62	16	51

WINNIPEG

BATTING	AVG	AB	R	H	2B	3B	HR	RBI	SB
Berrios, Harry, of-dh	.323	365	83	118	18	1	21	75	3
Boyd, Jared, 2b-ss	.250	164	23	41	1	1	1	13	1
Brown, Bobby, of	.309	272	22	84	7	0	0	31	3
Buckingham, Brock, 2b	.222	9	2	2	0	0	0	2	0
Cassady, Brad, 2b	.000	14	0	0	0	0	0	0	0
Doan, Kory, c	.111	27	4	3	0	0	1	1	0
Franco, Christian, 3b-of	.281	260	30	73	9	0	7	35	1
Hoffer, Kelly, of	.167	12	2	2	1	0	0	0	0
LaManna, Dan, c	.357	14	4	5	2	0	0	2	0
Leday, A.J., dh	.189	37	6	7	1	0	0	1	0
Oakes, Matt, c	.182	11	2	2	1	0	0	1	0
Peterson, Charles, of	.376	186	29	70	15	4	8	41	11
Poulin, Max, ss-2b	.274	274	39	75	11	4	0	23	8
Raven, Luis, 1b	.293	140	20	41	8	0	5	26	0
Robertson, Ryan, c	.277	292	37	81	11	0	2	31	1
Rose Jr., Pete, 1b	.344	209	36	72	17	1	8	53	1
Sachs, Brent, 3b-ss	.346	364	83	126	29	4	11	60	20
Sanchez, Matthew, 2b	.238	105	14	25	6	0	1	10	2
Smith, Ira, of	.309	265	45	82	12	0	9	46	10
Spearman, Vernon, of	.237	135	18	32	2	0	0	13	12

PITCHING	W	L	ERA	G	SV	IP	H	BB	SO
De Jesus, Tony	1	1	4.64	17	0	21	25	14	14
Gross, Rafael	9	4	3.78	17	0	114	123	18	71
Henderson, Ken	0	1	9.00	5	0	5	7	7	5
Little, Jeff	1	1	6.91	10	0	14	19	8	10
Madritsch, Bobby	11	4	2.30	19	0	125	94	36	153
Martin, Scott	5	4	5.80	23	0	85	115	22	45
Mutcheson, Matt	0	0	9.00	2	0	1	1	2	1

INDEPENDENT LEAGUES

Padua, Geraldo	12	3	3.06	19	0	123	117	36	94
Rayborn, Kenny	5	6	3.63	21	0	116	123	31	81
Sherrill, George	3	5	3.07	38	2	41	35	13	61
Smith, Donnie	4	1	1.19	36	8	45	39	14	52
Thomas, Steve	0	0	3.29	16	10	13	12	3	10
Wagner, Denny	3	2	3.29	6	0	38	39	5	28
Webb, Chris	2	1	1.63	36	2	49	42	15	47

SOUTHEASTERN LEAGUE

Southeastern League commissioner James Gamble is straightforward about the mistakes he and his fledgling independent league made in 2002.

The embryonic league was formed way too fast, with too little promotion and too many questions. But after an inaugural season that saw two teams fold and less than expected attendance, simple survival was an accomplishment.

During July it looked unlikely that the SEPBL would make it to its late-August Tournament of Champions. When franchises in Americus, Ga. and Ozark, Ala. went under in mid-July, players throughout the league started to wonder if they would be out on the street.

But the league managed to find some local ownership groups for the remaining teams and distributed players from the folded teams in a dispersal draft.

And with a careful eye on expenses, the league managed to make it to late August's title series, where the Pensacola Pelicans knocked off the Montgomery Wings for the SEPBL title with a 6-3, 11-inning victory.

Pensacola first baseman Jemaine Harrison hit a two-run homer and designated hitter Ryan Satterwhite followed with a solo homer as the Pelicans took a 6-3 lead in the top of the 11th, then held on for the title. Montgomery had a chance to win the game in the 10th, as they loaded the bases with one out against Pelicans' But Pensacola righthander Ted Gebauer induced a double play to squelch the threat.

Gebauer was named the league's player of the year, as he finished the season with an unofficial 2.76 ERA. The league did not keep official statistics.

STANDINGS

	W	L	PCT	GB
Pensacola Pelicans	40	28	.588	—
Baton Rouge River Bats	39	29	.574	1
Montgomery Wings	36	32	.529	4
Selma Cloverleafs	31	35	.470	8
*Americus Arrows	10	17	.370	
#Ozark Patriots	8	23	.258	

*Suspended operations on July 15
#Suspended operations on July 18

PLAYOFFS (Double-elimination tournament): Pensacola 3-1; Montgomery 3-2; Baton Rouge 1-2; Selma 0-2.

WESTERN LEAGUE

After losing in the finals for three straight years, the Chico Heat finally regained the Western League title in 2002.

The Heat, which easily posted the best record in the league and won both halves of the Northern Division race, earned some revenge by knocking off the Long Beach Breakers three-games-to-one in the championship series. It was the Breakers who beat the heavily favored Heat for the title in 2001.

Chico wrapped up the title with a 5-4 victory in Game Four that finished in weird fashion. Long Beach had rallied for a run in the ninth, cutting the lead to 5-3, and had two runners on with one out.

Long Beach's Benny Craig lined a shot to right field that looked like it might be a home run, but Chico right fielder Rick Prieto tracked the ball down near the fence. Greg Jacobs tagged up from third to score, but pinch-runner Reggie Nelson, thinking the ball would drop, had taken off with the crack of the bat. Prieto easily doubled him off of first base to end the game.

Scott Navarro, a Western League all-star, picked up the win for Chico. He also won the championship game in 1997 when Chico won it's only other Western League title. The title was the first for Chico manager Charley Kerfeld, who was named the league's manager of the year.

Chico's title was its last as a WBL member. After the season, Chico and Sonoma County announced that they were leaving the league because of concerns over the long-term viability of the WBL. Both were trying to land California League franchises. Without the two most successful teams, the future of the WBL was in extreme doubt as the league attempted to find additional teams for the 2003 season.

STANDINGS

FIRST HALF

NORTH	W	L	PCT	GB
Chico Heat	25	20	.556	—
Sonoma County Crushers	23	22	.511	2
Yuba-Sutter Gold Sox	22	23	.489	3

SOUTH	W	L	PCT	GB
Yuma Bullfrogs	22	23	.489	—
Solano Steelheads	22	23	.489	—
Long Beach Breakers	21	24	.467	1

SECOND HALF

NORTH	W	L	PCT	GB
Chico Heat	30	15	.667	—
Sonoma County Crushers	26	19	.578	4
Yuba-Sutter Gold Sox	21	24	.467	9

SOUTH	W	L	PCT	GB
Long Beach Breakers	23	22	.511	—
Solano Steelheads	20	25	.444	3
Yuma Bullfrogs	15	30	.333	8

PLAYOFFS: Semifinals—Long Beach defeated Yuma 3-2 and Chico defeated Sonoma County 3-1 in best-of-5 series. Finals—Chico defeated Long Beach 3-1 in a best-of-5 series.

MANAGERS: Chico—Charley Kerfeld. Long Beach—Steve Yeager. Solano—Scott Stover. Sonoma County—Kevin Mitchell. Yuba-Sutter—Tim Gloyd. Yuma—Lonnie Goldberg.

ATTENDANCE: Chico 103,209; Sonoma County 78,218; Solano 62,550; Long Beach 55,897; Yuma 53,024; Yuba-Sutter 40,468.

ALL-STAR TEAM: C—Vic Sanchez, Solano. 1B—John Macalutas, Chico. 2B—Eric Martins, Long Beach. 3B—Henry Calderon, Yuma. SS—Richy Leon, Yuma. OF—Anton French, Sonoma County; Greg Jacobs, Long Beach; Keith Mitchell, Sonoma County. P—Lance Franks, Chico; Jeff Harris, Chico; Scott Navarro, Chico; Jason Olsen, Solano; Tim Scott, Solano.

Player of the Year: Vic Sanchez, Solano. Pitcher of the Year: Jeff Harris, Chico. Manager of the Year: Charley Kerfeld, Chico.

INDIVIDUAL BATTING LEADERS
(Minimum 243 Plate Appearances)

	AVG	AB	R	H	2B	3B	HR	RBI	SB
Jacobs, Greg, Long Beach	.382	325	67	124	29	1	18	91	17
Mitchell, Keith, Sonoma	.363	303	87	110	20	5	20	83	10
French, Anton, Sonoma	.353	303	77	107	15	8	6	53	48
Maier, T.J., Chico	.346	243	62	84	15	1	6	37	11
Howard, Tim, Yuma	.344	337	57	116	17	2	2	62	2
Sanchez, Victor, Solano	.341	270	52	92	13	0	22	72	6
McNabb, Buck, Chico	.335	349	46	117	15	0	5	60	12
Booth, Jeremy, Solano	.327	333	30	109	24	0	7	48	0
Brown, Ray, Chico	.327	211	36	69	8	0	6	48	4
Martins, Eric, Long Beach	.327	352	55	115	14	5	2	48	8

INDIVIDUAL PITCHING LEADERS
(Minimum 72 Innings)

	W	L	ERA	G	SV	IP	H	BB	SO
Olsen, Jason, Solano	8	2	2.77	17	0	107	89	25	109
Harris, Jeff, Chico	9	5	2.85	20	0	136	120	31	109
Stockstill, Jason, Sonoma	6	4	2.90	18	0	115	100	52	84

	W	L	ERA	G	SV	IP	H	BB	SO
Franks, Lance, Chico	11	4	2.98	19	0	127	127	31	96
Navarro, Scott, Chico	10	5	3.20	19	0	132	128	34	77
Alexander, Jordy, Chico/LB	9	3	3.47	16	0	96	101	29	80
Guttormson, Rick, Yuba/Chico	5	10	3.98	18	0	124	143	40	88
Harden, Tony, Yuba-Sutter	6	6	4.20	16	0	96	97	45	63
Buckles, Bucky, Yuba-Sutter	6	5	4.37	20	0	130	156	36	70
Davidson, Tim, Sonoma	12	2	4.39	18	0	113	123	45	82

CHICO

BATTING	AVG	AB	R	H	2B	3B	HR	RBI	SB
Angel, Anthony, 2b-3b	.278	241	38	67	14	2	2	39	2
Brown, Ray, 1b	.327	211	36	69	8	0	6	48	4
Ellis, Kevin, dh-1b	.289	287	39	83	19	0	6	53	3
Fitzpatrick, Eddie, c	.206	160	16	33	5	0	0	20	4
Gennaro, Brad, of	.314	210	54	66	20	2	3	38	5
Goldfield, Joshua, c	.196	46	4	9	1	0	0	4	0
Hindman, Steve, 3b-2b	.195	113	16	22	3	0	3	11	1
Jenkins, Peter, c	.067	15	1	1	0	0	0	0	0
Jones, Jack, ss	.333	102	21	34	4	2	5	26	0
Macalutas, Jon, 1b-3b	.324	336	73	109	18	1	11	65	31
Madsen, Dan, dh	.000	4	0	0	0	0	0	0	0
Maier, T.J., ss-2b	.346	243	62	84	15	1	6	37	11
Mashore, Damon, of	.331	145	34	48	8	1	13	45	4
McNabb, Buck, of	.335	349	46	117	15	0	5	60	12
Mendoza, Miguel, of	.000	2	0	0	0	0	0	0	0
Nicholas, Darrell, of	.250	44	6	11	3	1	0	2	0
Prieto, Chris, of	.167	12	5	2	0	0	1	2	1
Prieto, Rick, of-2b	.313	361	84	113	17	0	4	31	25
Shrum, Allen, c	.202	89	5	18	3	0	0	8	0
Tash, Ryan, 3b	.291	127	11	37	5	0	3	12	2
Zwissig, Zack, c	.211	19	5	4	1	0	1	5	0
2-team (2 Yuba-Sutter)	.238	21	7	5	1	0	1	5	0

PITCHING	W	L	ERA	G	SV	IP	H	BB	SO
Alexander, Jordy	1	1	6.29	5	0	24	38	9	25
Baker, Scott	0	1	20.25	2	0	5	16	6	5
Bland, Nate	0	1	2.30	8	2	15	10	5	17
Borges, Reece	2	3	5.06	16	0	48	62	15	22
Chisnall, Wes	1	0	2.08	15	0	30	29	7	16
Etler, Todd	2	1	5.75	4	0	20	31	9	14
Falbe, Adam	1	0	9.39	5	0	7	10	11	5
Fitzgerald, Danny	0	0	18.00	1	0	1	2	1	2
Franks, Lance	11	4	2.98	19	0	127	127	31	96
Gray, Rusty	3	3	3.79	32	3	42	47	15	36
Guttormson, Rick	2	3	3.69	7	0	46	46	20	40
2-team (11 Yuba-Sutter)	5	10	3.98	18	0	124	143	40	88
Harris, D.J.	0	0	0.00	1	0	2	3	0	3
Harris, Jeff	9	5	2.85	20	0	135	120	31	109
Husted, Brent	4	2	4.95	36	12	36	51	17	28
Kubinski, Tim	0	0	0.00	2	0	5	4	0	3
Marr, Jason	2	1	6.20	17	2	20	19	13	9
Morris, Will	1	0	27.00	1	0	1	3	0	1
Navarro, Scott	10	5	3.20	19	0	132	128	34	77
Ortiz, J.C.	1	2	4.15	29	0	26	28	14	18
Ryan, Jeremy	0	1	6.94	11	0	11	16	12	13
Sierra, Auvin	2	2	6.04	15	0	25	31	10	18
Whitworth, Brad	0	0	0.00	1	0	1	4	0	1

LONG BEACH

BATTING	AVG	AB	R	H	2B	3B	HR	RBI	SB
Anspach, Marc, 1b	.221	136	16	30	6	2	1	14	0
Baderdeen, Kevin, ss-3b	.229	153	26	35	3	2	2	22	5
Betancourt, Tony, c-dh	.252	214	26	54	10	0	2	21	1
Craig, Benny, of	.212	33	7	7	1	0	1	5	0
Hunt, Tim, 3b-2b	.218	55	8	12	0	0	0	4	1
Jacobs, Greg, of	.380	326	67	124	29	1	18	91	17
Lamoure, Luis, 3b-2b	.173	81	12	14	4	0	1	10	1
Lehr, Ryan, 3b	.329	149	20	49	11	0	3	28	2
Martins, Eric, 2b-ss	.327	352	55	115	14	5	2	48	8
Millan, Adan, 1b-c	.280	296	47	83	23	0	5	51	8
Miranda, Jose, of	.231	26	5	6	0	0	1	6	2
Miranda, Tony, of	.305	321	63	98	20	2	7	43	31
Nelson, Reggie, ss	.303	109	22	33	8	0	1	12	5
Perry, Joe, c	.056	18	2	1	0	0	0	0	0
Pini, Ryan, of-1b	.274	212	21	58	18	0	2	31	1
Solano, Ben, 2b	.214	140	27	30	1	0	0	11	1
Teahen, Matt, 3b	.288	59	9	17	1	0	0	9	1
Templeton, Garry, of	.223	103	13	23	3	2	0	8	3
Wiph, Marc, of-dh	.235	115	20	27	8	1	2	16	5
Wright, Corey, of	.362	105	26	38	6	2	0	8	9
Yeager, Steve, c	.209	67	8	14	4	0	0	7	0

PITCHING	W	L	ERA	G	SV	IP	H	BB	SO
Alexander, Jordy	8	2	2.51	11	0	71	63	20	55

	W	L	ERA	G	SV	IP	H	BB	SO
2-team (5 Chico)	9	3	3.47	16	0	96	101	29	80
Carey, Mike	4	6	4.33	11	0	60	75	20	29
Cly, Jason	6	2	4.29	14	0	63	73	13	36
Grebe, Brett	3	1	3.98	34	6	40	41	22	36
Harrington, Matt	0	3	6.68	7	0	32	37	24	25
Hohenstein, Andy	3	1	6.93	20	0	24	30	18	6
Hoyt, Michael	2	5	2.69	37	1	70	65	32	41
Ireland, Eric	4	5	5.75	16	0	97	123	43	67
Isaacson, Joe	0	1	7.50	5	0	6	11	8	7
Leslie, Reggie	1	2	7.91	4	0	19	32	7	10
Linares, Richard	8	5	4.81	18	0	118	142	9	56
Sevier, Nathan	2	0	1.72	4	0	15	11	3	16
Spradlin, Jerry	0	2	5.64	22	8	22	16	12	19
Stevens, Kris	2	2	6.32	28	0	57	69	33	32
Tomita, Wataru	0	2	8.03	6	0	12	21	4	10
Turner, Eric	1	6	5.67	15	0	74	66	41	43
Verplancke, Joe	0	0	14.40	4	0	5	6	10	3
Weathers, Micah	0	0	0.00	1	0	1	0	0	1
Winkle, Ken	0	1	10.38	5	1	4	4	7	0

SOLANO

BATTING	AVG	AB	R	H	2B	3B	HR	RBI	SB
Adams, Ryan, ss	.241	162	19	39	9	0	3	23	3
Booth, Jeremy, 1b	.327	333	30	109	24	0	7	48	0
Bowers, Brent, of	.229	118	18	27	2	1	1	9	15
Caracciolo, Tony, ss	.205	39	6	8	3	1	0	3	0
Ceriani, Matt, c	.290	241	37	70	12	0	7	27	0
Ceriani, Ryan, 2b-ss	.282	71	6	20	2	0	0	10	2
Clements, Jason, 2b-ss	.292	301	53	88	14	9	1	33	31
Gorman, Paul, 3b	.195	77	8	15	3	0	0	3	3
Kolbach, Mike, of	.291	289	33	84	15	1	2	40	4
Landreth, Jason, of	.287	338	63	97	27	2	13	71	28
Marshall, Allen, inf	.107	28	2	3	0	0	0	1	0
Martinez, Eddy, ss	.233	43	8	10	1	0	0	2	3
Martinez, Greg, of	.349	172	42	60	6	0	0	19	23
2-team (35 Sonoma)	.280	161	30	45	6	0	3	18	0
Molidor, David, 3b	.211	38	6	8	1	0	0	2	0
Sanchez, Victor, dh-c	.341	270	52	92	13	0	22	72	6
Sandoval, Jose, 3b-of	.299	261	52	78	14	4	0	33	19
Torres, Paul, dh-1b	.221	86	11	19	3	0	3	18	1
Vaughn, Lateef, of-2b	.233	103	16	24	3	0	0	8	2
Weinheimer, Wayne, dh-1b	.198	81	6	16	3	0	2	7	0

PITCHING	W	L	ERA	G	SV	IP	H	BB	SO
Baker, Scott	0	0	7.41	4	0	17	28	1	18
2-team (2 Chico)	0	1	10.48	6	0	22	44	7	23
Biron, Jeff	0	0	5.40	9	0	11	18	4	7
Brosnan, Jason	5	5	6.10	15	0	90	114	29	53
Davis, Jason	1	3	7.54	5	0	22	28	12	17
Ewen, Clayton	2	3	3.40	9	0	45	48	13	34
Flynt, Will	3	6	5.82	13	0	55	75	15	50
Hollinger, Adrian	2	2	7.65	8	0	20	34	10	11
Kass, Mike	0	0	9.58	6	0	10	18	9	10
McCall, T.J.	0	0	7.45	6	0	9	9	8	5
Nagasaka, Hideki	0	0	4.66	4	0	9	9	5	3
Newman, Eric	1	0	6.17	1	1	11	13	10	14
Olenberger, Kasey	5	2	3.16	35	1	42	44	11	42
Olsen, Jason	8	2	2.77	17	0	107	89	25	109
Orr, Ben	0	0	9.00	4	0	4	6	5	3
Rose, Brian	0	1	3.38	11	0	21	27	8	13
2-team (22 Sonoma)	2	4	4.82	33	3	52	69	18	42
Salcedo, Jose	7	7	6.07	17	0	96	107	44	68
Sanchez, Cade	0	1	19.29	1	0	2	8	2	0
Scott, Tim	6	2	1.48	43	17	48	40	6	60
Stefani, Jason	0	1	40.50	1	0	0	4	1	0
2-team (16 Yuba-Sutter)	0	2	7.32	17	2	19	29	13	22
Stover, C.D.	2	3	3.75	33	0	57	61	21	58
Thompson, Jesse	0	2	6.89	14	0	15	25	10	8
Thompson, John	0	1	4.82	21	0	28	34	12	23
2-team (8 Sonoma)	0	5	7.07	29	0	35	53	19	30
Weinheimer, Wayne	0	0	0.00	1	0	3	0	2	5
Wilkerson, Steven	0	1	7.50	8	0	12	20	11	14
Wright, Shayne	0	4	6.84	9	0	26	34	17	22

SONOMA COUNTY

BATTING	AVG	AB	R	H	2B	3B	HR	RBI	SB
Adames, Winter, ss-2b	.333	24	10	8	2	0	0	1	1
Adolfo, Carlos, of	.284	327	57	93	21	1	15	71	9
Amaya, Pilar, ss-3b	.256	313	39	80	19	1	4	41	2
Briones, Chris, c-1b	.305	220	27	67	12	0	9	52	2
Esposti, Tony, of	.000	2	0	0	0	0	0	0	0
Frank, Nick, 3b-2b	.216	125	18	27	6	0	1	19	2
French, Anton, of	.353	303	77	107	15	8	6	53	48
Goodwin, Curtis, of	.241	87	13	21	4	0	0	9	7

INDEPENDENT LEAGUES

BATTING	AVG	AB	R	H	2B	3B	HR	RBI	SB
Hopgood, Scott, of	.091	11	1	1	0	0	0	0	0
McAffee, Josh, c	.232	155	21	36	11	0	2	17	0
Mitchell, Keith, of	.363	303	87	110	20	5	20	83	10
Molidor, David, 3b-1b	.301	123	24	37	5	0	3	16	0
Muro, Robert, 3b	.236	140	24	33	5	1	2	18	2
Oglesby, Travis, 1b	.265	264	43	70	12	1	12	57	1
Osuna, Ricky, of-ss	.279	341	83	95	17	3	1	33	33
Pridy, Todd, dh	.347	150	28	52	11	0	9	32	0
Vaughn, Lateef, 2b-of	.382	34	14	13	0	1	0	1	4
2-team (32 Solano)	.270	137	30	37	3	1	0	9	6
Vopata, Nate, 2b	.273	275	42	75	9	4	1	34	6

PITCHING	W	L	ERA	G	SV	IP	H	BB	SO
Davidson, Tim	12	2	4.39	18	0	112	123	45	82
Dishman, Glenn	2	1	6.07	9	0	46	56	23	33
Escalante, Jimmy	3	3	3.30	44	14	62	55	25	59
Grant, Brian	3	3	3.50	37	0	54	53	44	38
Harris, Julian	1	2	8.40	13	0	15	19	13	10
Holbrook, Shayne	0	1	11.12	4	0	5	15	4	1
2-team (4 Yuba-Sutter)	0	1	13.06	8	0	10	26	7	2
Hollinger, Adrian	2	3	6.02	19	0	49	66	19	38
2-team (8 Solano)	4	5	6.49	27	0	69	100	29	49
Johnson, Thad	1	1	12.10	8	0	9	21	7	2
Leslie, Reggie	4	5	3.42	12	0	68	69	32	64
2-team (4 Long Beach)	5	7	4.41	16	0	87	101	39	74
McCormick, Terry	0	1	15.43	2	0	2	5	3	1
Moran, George	2	1	6.23	5	0	8	8	6	3
Neboyia, Gabe	9	3	4.76	20	0	123	144	24	74
Newman, Eric	0	2	10.34	4	0	15	19	9	13
2-team (7 Solano)	1	2	8.56	11	1	27	32	19	27
Parker, Dan	1	1	8.37	13	0	23	37	20	17
Pribble, Aaron	1	0	0.00	6	0	7	5	3	3
Rose, Brian	2	1	5.81	23	3	31	42	10	29
Stockstill, Jason	6	4	2.90	18	0	114	100	52	84
Takahashi, Kurt	2	2	5.01	7	0	32	40	17	27
Thompson, John	0	4	15.26	8	0	7	19	7	7
Wells, Zach	0	1	6.75	4	0	6	15	3	1

YUBA-SUTTER

BATTING	AVG	AB	R	H	2B	3B	HR	RBI	SB
Abrams, Grant, 2b-3b	.253	99	9	25	7	1	0	14	2
2-team (9 Yuma)	.238	126	9	30	8	1	0	15	2
Bone, Billy, 2b	.250	116	19	29	7	0	2	14	9
Boyle, Danny, 2b	.333	3	1	1	0	0	0	0	0
Bush, Darren, dh-c	.417	24	9	10	2	0	1	1	1
Ciofrone, Paul, of-1b	.236	165	24	39	7	0	3	22	6
Cook, Josh, 2b-ss	.308	308	57	95	20	1	5	45	8
Cosentino, Tony, c-1b	.283	152	18	43	8	0	5	35	0
Dunaway, Jason, 3b-ss	.222	234	38	52	11	1	4	28	6
Fears, Chris, of	.200	30	5	6	0	0	0	1	2
Forbes, Kevin, of-1b	.316	231	41	73	11	0	4	36	14
Hargrove, Harvey, ss-of	.261	326	53	85	18	3	4	41	14
Leal, Jaeme, dh-1b	.262	107	23	28	5	0	9	24	0
2-team (53 Yuma)	.266	308	53	82	15	3	16	65	0
Lewis, Danny, dh	.329	70	10	23	8	0	0	12	1
Mowry, David, 1b	.222	18	2	4	0	0	0	1	0
Nadeau, Rick, of	.261	329	46	86	18	2	6	53	5
Nystrom, Pete, of	.279	326	51	91	14	0	5	32	5
Paciorek, Pete, 1b	.330	179	30	59	11	0	6	34	1
Rajsich, Kyle, 2b-ss	.412	17	2	7	0	0	1	2	2
Stone, Jon, c	.245	139	21	34	6	1	0	17	2
Tash, Ryan, 3b	.220	100	13	22	5	0	1	8	0
2-team (34 Chico)	.260	227	24	59	10	0	4	20	2
Washburn, Kyle, c-1b	.342	117	21	40	12	0	2	20	1
Zwissig, Zack, of-c	.500	2	2	1	0	0	0	0	0

PITCHING	W	L	ERA	G	SV	IP	H	BB	SO
Abrams, Grant	1	0	7.36	6	0	7	9	7	3
Aragon, Angel	2	2	5.98	10	0	55	76	25	33
Buckles, Bucky	6	5	4.37	20	0	129	156	36	70
Cooper, Eric	1	2	3.43	6	0	21	18	19	8
2-team (23 Yuma)	2	6	5.76	29	1	59	62	37	39
Correa, Dominic	3	3	6.70	29	0	48	60	31	39
Edwards, Bryan	1	1	7.43	11	0	13	18	9	15
Etler, Todd	3	0	4.21	6	0	36	35	11	28
2-team (4 Chico)	5	1	4.76	10	0	56	66	20	42
Foster, Gabe	1	3	5.89	36	14	36	46	15	17
Guttormson, Rick	3	7	4.15	11	0	78	97	20	48
Hall, Courtney	4	4	4.50	12	0	56	60	33	37
Harden, Tony	6	6	4.20	16	0	96	97	45	63
Holbrook, Shayne	0	0	15.43	4	0	4	11	3	1
Khoury, Josh	1	1	10.45	9	1	10	10	15	6
McGurk, Mike	2	6	4.04	32	0	69	84	23	47
Ray, Ken	2	0	2.38	12	3	11	10	3	11
Stefani, Jason	1	0	6.16	16	2	19	25	12	22
Veniard, Jay	2	3	5.34	11	0	55	57	37	40
Wilkerson, Steve	5	3	3.82	29	2	37	36	20	25
2-team (8 Solano)	5	4	4.71	37	2	49	56	31	39

YUMA

BATTING	AVG	AB	R	H	2B	3B	HR	RBI	SB
Abrams, Grant, dh-of	.185	27	0	5	1	0	0	1	0
Brito, Obispo, c	.438	16	1	7	1	0	0	1	0
Calderon, Henry, 3b-2b	.293	369	54	108	27	2	5	54	12
Epke, Brian, c	.228	145	15	33	1	0	0	7	3
Frank, Nick, 2b	.236	106	9	25	1	0	1	9	1
2-team (41 Sonoma)	.225	231	27	52	7	0	2	28	3
Howard, Tim, of	.344	337	57	116	17	2	2	62	2
Howard, Will, of	.237	232	51	55	9	4	0	8	8
Huff, Larry, of-3b	.254	134	20	34	5	0	0	8	7
Kilburg, Joe, 2b-of	.304	355	80	108	23	4	5	54	21
Leal, Jaeme, 1b	.269	201	30	54	10	3	7	41	0
Leon, Richy, ss	.307	329	50	101	19	2	0	32	8
Longmire, Marcel, c-of	.323	319	49	103	29	1	5	68	1
McKinney, Antonio, of	.206	136	20	28	3	1	1	16	7
Soliz, Steve, c	.250	36	3	9	1	0	0	1	0
Tiburcio, Alec, dh	.000	1	0	0	0	0	0	0	0
Todd, Jeremy, 1b-of	.309	298	42	92	20	3	8	48	2
Zamora, Junior, 3b	.319	116	20	37	5	1	3	20	1

PITCHING	W	L	ERA	G	SV	IP	H	BB	SO
Acosta, Cesar	0	0	6.10	12	0	20	20	20	10
Aragon, Angel	1	3	5.03	7	0	48	49	13	27
2-team (10 Yuba-Sutter)	3	5	5.54	17	0	104	125	38	60
Belicic, Adam	0	0	17.18	3	0	3	9	2	1
Blood, Darin	3	2	7.40	10	0	45	52	35	18
Cooper, Eric	1	4	7.04	23	1	38	44	18	31
Crider, J.R.	0	0	7.84	5	0	10	13	18	5
Espinal, Joe	2	2	4.19	9	0	38	44	11	34
Johnson, Craig	6	8	6.73	18	0	101	125	38	69
Martinez, Ramiro	3	3	4.73	12	0	45	40	38	36
Matcuk, Steve	2	1	5.05	27	0	41	49	14	14
Minton, Foye	1	3	7.50	17	2	42	56	19	31
Moore, Brad	3	5	6.46	19	0	71	79	39	57
Perez, Ernesto	0	0	9.35	4	0	8	17	5	0
Pizarro, Melvin	5	5	5.75	21	0	83	99	55	52
Ribaudo, Mike	0	0	18.00	3	0	3	4	8	1
Sexton, Jeff	5	5	2.74	38	11	46	46	15	38
Thomas, Brian	0	2	10.07	11	0	22	34	22	7
Verplancke, Joe	1	1	5.95	15	1	19	21	15	13
2-team (4 Long Beach)	0	1	7.66	19	1	24	27	25	16
Whitesides, Johnny	5	9	5.72	26	0	100	123	33	53

FOREIGN
LEAGUES

Red Devils-Tigers square off again

BY SALO OTERO

The 2002 Mexican League season started with a number of changes: a new league president, a restructured North and South Zone and a two-time defending champion changing playing sites.

MEXICO

But in the end, the same two franchises played for the league championship for the fourth year in a row. The Mexico City Red Devils met the relocated Mexico Tigers (now in Puebla) for the title, with the Reds coming back from a 3-1 best-of-seven series deficit to dethrone the defending champions. The Reds and Tigers are 2-2 in championship series over the last four years.

Raul Gonzalez, a native of Monterrey and an Olympic gold medalist in race walking in the 1984 Olympics in Los Angeles, was named league president, replacing Jose Orozco who returned to private business after two years as president.

The league went back to its familiar North-South division structure, replacing the old North, South and Central Zones. The Red Devils were a member of the North Zone for the first time since 1996.

The other major change had the Tigers moving to Puebla, 100 miles away, because of poor attendance in Mexico City in recent years.

It left Mexico City with one team and put two in Puebla as the Tigers joined the Puebla Parrots. But the Tigers went from averaging 500 fans per game at Mexico City's new Foro Sol Park to 4,000 fans per game in Puebla.

"The response (in Puebla) was tremendous," Tigers' president Chito Rodriguez said. "The fans and local government welcomed us with open arms."

The Tigers and Parrots planned to build a roof over Puebla's Hermanos Serdan Stadium for 2003.

The Tigers started slowly in their new home in their bid to become the first hat-trick champions since the Monterrey Industrials did it from 1947-49. They were 9-23 when Texan Dan Firova, the manager who led them to three league titles in five years, was fired. He was replaced by American Lee Sigman, a former major league scout in Mexico. It was one of seven managerial changes during the season.

New Look For Red Devils

The Red Devils, managed by Dominican Bernie Tatis, cousin of Montreal Expos third baseman Fernando Tatis, won their 13th championship.

Tatis took over the managerial reigns from Tim Johnson, who resigned after leading the Reds to a league title and two appearances in the championship series over the last three years. Johnson resurfaced in Saltillo, which finished one-half game ahead of the Red Devils in the second half North Zone standings.

"It was time for a change. And I joined a great organization in Saltillo," Johnson said. "It was a good fit for me. A beautiful city, great climate and a gorgeous ball park."

Under Tatis, the Red Devils had the best record in the regular season, at 74-36. They finished first in the North in the first half and second in the second half to earn 15 of a possible 16 points. Teams earn points on the basis of their finish in each half.

With a .313 team batting average, the Reds had an offensive juggernaut.

"We have a hitting machine," Tatis said.

"I've been here since 1981 and this is one of the best (Reds teams)," pitching coach Salome Barojas said. "I've seen a lot of good players, but not like this as a conjunto (team)."

Felix Jose

DH Felix Jose, one of four Reds imports with major league experience, led the team with a .383 average, 27 homers and 102 RBIs. He was selected the league MVP. His supporting cast included first baseman Cornelio Garcia (.382), catcher Miguel Ojeda (.352) and outfielder Roberto Kelly (.334).

Jose finished second in the league batting race to Saltillo's Willie Romero, who hit .388. He also went 14-for-31 (.452) in the championship series before being signed by the Arizona Diamondbacks.

The Reds spotted the Tigers a 3-1 lead in the final before rallying to win 9-2, 8-6 and 9-5 with the last two games at Foro Sol before 26,000 fans. Third baseman Ray Martinez hit a three-run homer in game six and a two-run shot in game seven. He was named the series MVP.

"It was a perfect script," Tigers' president Rodriguez said. "A seven-game series and our first and only time to play at Foro Sol during the year. We just didn't win."

League HR Leader Killed

A lot of the Reds' players and other players in the league wore the initials N.B. on their caps in memory of Nelson Barrera, who in 2001 eclipsed the all-time Mexican League home run mark of 453, held by the late Hector Espino.

Barrera, 44, died in a freak accident on July 14, when he was electrocuted on the roof of his home in Campeche when he touched a high voltage electrical cable with a piece of metal.

Barrera, who played 25 seasons—14 of them with the Red Devils—had 455 home runs. He was also the all-time leader in RBIs (1,928), total bases (4,872) and extra-base hits (972).

At the time of his death, Barrera was a player-manager at Campeche. He began the year as a player with the Reds, but missed the first month of the season with knee surgery. He was then traded to Campeche when an opportunity to manage opened.

Nelson Barrera

Union Laguna's Alejandro Ortiz, 41, hit 23 homers on the year to move into third place all-time with 424 homers. He moved within reach of Barrera's mark.

Lefthander Angel Moreno, 45, moved to third all-time in pitching wins with 241. Overall, he was 9-9.

Monterrey's Bubba Smith went 6-for-6 to tie a Mexican League mark held by 29 players.

In a first-time series with Cuba's national team, a Mexican League all-star team swept a three-game series. Mexico won 6-2 in Saltillo, 5-4 in Monterrey and 3-0 in Holguin, Cuba. Only native Mexicans were eligible to play in the series. The Mexican team was managed by Yucatan's Francisco "Paquin" Estrada, who led Culiacan to the Caribbean Series title earlier in the year.

"It shows that our level of play in Mexico is getting better," Tigers president Rodriguez said. "Cuba had 80 percent of its national team and threw its best three pitchers. Mexico won the Caribbean Series and now this."

The all-star series is scheduled to resume in 2003.

STANDINGS

EAST	W	L	PCT	GB
*Mexico City Red Devils	74	36	.673	—
+Saltillo Sarape Makers	66	43	.606	7½
Two Laredos Owls	62	48	.564	12
Monterrey Sultans	60	49	.550	13½
Monclova Steelers	56	54	.509	18
Union Laguna Cotton Pickers	44	65	.404	29½
Reynosa Broncos	43	67	.391	31
Puebla Parrots	38	70	.352	35

WEST	W	L	PCT	GB
*Oaxaca Warriors	62	45	.579	—
+Yucatan Lions	60	47	.561	2
Mexico Tigers	57	49	.538	4½
Veracruz Reds	55	53	.509	7½
Cancun Lobstermen	53	54	.495	9
Campeche Pirates	52	55	.486	10
Tabasco Cattlemen	48	61	.440	15
Cordoba Coffee Growers	37	71	.343	25½

*First-half champion +Second-half champion

PLAYOFFS—Quarterfinals: Mexico City Red Devils defeated Monclova 4-1; Mexico Tigers defeated Yucatan 4-3; Oaxaca defeated Veracruz 4-0; and Two Laredos defeated Saltillo 4-2 in best-of-7 series. **Semifinals:** Mexico City Red Devils defeated Two Laredos 4-3 and Mexico Tigers defeated Oaxaca 4-3 in best-of-7 series. **Finals:** Mexico City Red Devils defeated Mexico Tigers 4-3 in best-of-7 series.

MANAGERS: Campeche—Francisco Chavez, Nelson Barrera, Manuel Cazarin. **Cancun**—Enrique Reyes. **Cordoba**—Julio Cesar Paula, Julian Yan. **Mexico City Red Devils**—Bernie Tatis. **Mexico Tigers**—Dan Firova, Lee Sigman. **Monclova**—Gerardo Sanchez. **Monterrey**—Derek Bryant, Dan Firova. **Oaxaca**—Alfonso Jimenez. **Puebla**—Juan Jose Bellazetin, Marco Antonio Guzman. **Reynosa**—Raul Cano. **Tabasco**—Marco Antonio Guzman; Marco Antonio Vasquez. **Two Laredos**—Juan Francisco Rodriguez. **Saltillo**—Tim Johnson. **Union Laguna**—Francisco Rodriguez, Juan Pacho. **Veracruz**—Luis Mere. **Yucatan**—Paquin Estrada.

REGULAR SEASON ATTENDANCE: Saltillo 564,741; Monterrey 447,401; Yucatan 369,820; Monclova 254,903; Mexico City Red Devils 209,945; Oaxaca 171,944; Cancun 150,085; Mexico Tigers 148,197; Veracruz 131,019; Puebla 122,006; Tabasco 120,392; Union Laguna 120,095; Two Laredos 102,987; Cordoba 98,462; Reynosa 73,858; Campeche 55,277.

INDIVIDUAL BATTING LEADERS
(Minimum 297 Plate Appearances)

	AVG	AB	R	H	2B	3B	HR	RBI	SB
Romero, Willie, Saltillo	.388	363	85	141	29	3	14	77	17
Jose, Felix, Red Devils	.383	324	88	124	21	2	27	102	4
Garcia, Cornelio, Red Devils	.382	395	81	151	19	11	7	54	12
Grijak, Kevin, Union Laguna	.367	308	61	113	21	1	20	69	4
Sherman, Darrell, Monclova	.363	364	73	132	23	3	1	35	25
Connell, Lino, Oaxaca	.356	458	102	163	45	5	8	65	31
Ojeda, Miguel, Red Devils	.352	341	79	120	22	1	19	80	8
Carrillo, Matias, Tigers	.349	364	61	127	18	1	13	71	4
Robles, Oscar, Oaxaca	.348	368	67	128	25	0	9	76	4
Arredondo, Luis, Yucatan	.346	416	62	144	16	5	3	31	21
Orantes, Ramon, Monterrey	.341	343	49	117	16	1	14	61	4
Castro, Arnoldo, Cancun	.341	370	51	126	19	1	10	45	2
Arano, Wilfrido, Laredo	.340	344	53	117	22	0	2	32	3
Kelly, Roberto, Red Devils	.334	314	61	105	16	2	19	80	0
Bojorquez, Victor, Red Devils	.331	302	52	100	13	7	7	45	3
Colina, Roberto, Puebla	.329	392	55	129	18	0	15	54	3

Nunez, Reymond, Laredo	.325	422	71	137	29	1	17	92	2
Rodarte, Raul, Cordoba/Mont.	.324	374	69	121	20	2	16	74	11
Rodriguez, Carlos, UL	.323	433	69	140	20	0	0	37	9
Smith, Bubba, Monterrey	.322	401	77	129	25	0	27	86	2
Jimenez, Eduardo, Saltillo	.321	280	67	90	14	0	29	86	0
Adriana, Sharnol, Cam./Cor.	.317	356	52	113	15	1	18	68	9
Almeida, Shammar, Oaxaca	.316	269	44	85	18	3	14	51	0
Villegas, Fernando, Cancun	.316	269	25	85	15	0	3	23	2
Ramirez, Omar, Veracruz	.316	437	78	138	27	3	11	44	19
Saucedo, Roberto, Laredo	.315	390	68	123	14	0	32	84	5
Smith, Demond, Monterrey	.315	352	74	111	12	2	9	48	41
Ramirez, Gonzalo, Saltillo	.315	276	49	87	14	1	4	31	3
Espinoza, Ramon, Rey./Yuc.	.315	422	64	133	19	4	7	39	11
Quintero, Christian, Oaxaca	.315	394	53	124	21	3	7	53	9
Gonzalez, Jesus, Yuc./Monc.	.314	309	45	97	12	1	7	41	14
Gastelum, Carlos, Puebla/Tigers	.310	371	63	115	15	2	1	29	19
Romero, Marco Antonio, Saltillo	.310	323	54	100	10	0	19	73	4
Mendez, Roberto, Red Devils	.307	290	58	89	18	1	12	53	7
Munoz, Noe, Saltillo	.307	352	61	108	30	0	9	50	0
Iturbe, Pedro, Tigers/Puebla	.307	274	39	84	25	3	8	36	2
Chimelis, Joel, Laredo	.304	392	77	119	19	0	15	66	3
Garcia, Omar, Veracruz	.304	392	59	119	24	2	19	80	1
Valencia, Carlos, Laredo	.302	424	72	128	18	3	12	49	3
Zambrano, Roberto, Laredo	.302	242	54	73	14	1	20	58	1
Hernandez, Julio, Laredo	.301	405	63	122	18	0	3	37	2
Diaz, Edwin, Veracruz	.301	405	72	122	25	2	15	52	10
Mere, Pedro, Veracruz	.301	419	68	126	21	2	13	69	6
Vizcarra, Roberto, Tigers	.301	306	44	92	10	2	5	42	10

(Other Select Players)

	AVG	AB	R	H	2B	3B	HR	RBI	SB
Gil, Eric, Union Laguna	.400	15	7	6	1	0	0	1	0
Pemberton, Rudy, Monclova	.381	215	51	82	18	1	14	53	5
Luke, Matt, Campeche	.370	73	16	27	4	0	4	17	0
Garland, Tim, Reynosa	.357	56	5	20	3	0	0	3	2
Polonia, Luis, Tigers	.354	48	8	17	1	1	0	4	3
Presichi, Cristian, Saltillo	.339	230	53	78	15	1	13	43	15
Figga, Mike, Puebla	.333	21	4	7	0	0	1	5	0
Riggs, Adam, Saltillo	.331	242	42	80	19	1	7	37	10
Barker, Glen, Reynosa	.329	85	17	28	1	4	1	9	3
Miller, Orlando, Tabasco	.328	177	31	58	11	0	12	29	5
Lucca, Lou, Campeche	.326	46	5	15	4	0	1	4	0
Nieves, Melvin, Union Laguna	.315	197	43	62	17	0	14	52	4
Magallanes, Evars, Monterrey	.314	194	24	61	8	0	2	33	2
Castellano, Pedro, Oaxaca	.310	168	29	52	11	0	6	34	1
De los Santos, Luis, Reds/Oaxaca	.307	215	30	66	13	0	5	30	0
Hunter, Brian, Saltillo	.300	30	6	9	3	0	4	11	0
Jennings, Doug, Cor./Tabasco	.296	125	19	37	9	0	4	12	0
Alexander, Manny, Cordoba	.295	217	31	64	10	2	1	21	14
Peterson, Charles, Tab./Cam.	.292	236	31	67	12	0	7	40	3
Prieto, Chris, Oaxaca	.290	252	58	73	18	7	7	51	18
Rojas, Homer, Oaxaca	.290	400	57	116	35	2	11	78	2
Tellez, Alonso, Rey./Yucatan	.284	352	34	100	16	0	11	59	1
Brown, Raymond, Tabasco	.282	149	16	42	4	0	4	20	1
Martin, Norberto, Campeche	.282	117	17	33	3	1	5	21	3
Barron, Tony, Vera./Pueb.	.281	221	28	62	10	0	8	32	0
Velazquez, Guillermo, Salt./Campeche	.279	367	43	91	10	0	15	65	0
Mercedes, Henry, Cordoba	.278	126	26	35	8	0	9	22	0
Garcia, Guillermo, Cord./Tigers	.278	450	66	106	24	0	27	92	0
Estrada, Hector, UL	.274	379	57	104	15	1	13	50	5
Warner, Michael, Yucatan	.270	115	20	31	8	0	1	15	1
Otanez, Willis, Can./Monc.	.270	263	29	71	13	0	12	43	0
O'Sullivan, Patrick, Reynosa	.268	224	30	60	13	1	14	54	2
Whiten, Mark, Tigers	.265	117	14	31	2	0	4	22	1
Phillips, Charles, Yuc./Mont.	.264	197	29	52	13	0	7	22	2
Jones, Chris, Yucatan	.264	144	18	38	6	2	2	23	3
Carpenter, Dalton, Saltillo	.263	80	15	21	5	0	2	10	1
Garcia, Amaury, Campeche	.262	172	29	45	6	2	4	18	8
Carter, Michael, Yucatan	.262	42	4	11	2	0	0	3	1
Candelaria, Ben, Veracruz	.259	143	8	37	9	0	1	15	0
Pearson, Eddie, Tab./Can.	.258	337	40	87	12	0	10	42	0
Fernandez, Daniel, Red Devils	.254	335	56	85	15	4	3	36	14
Cookson, Brent, Reynosa	.250	92	6	23	8	0	2	6	2
Whitmore, Darrell, Tabasco	.250	52	5	13	5	0	0	3	0
Rohrmeier, Daniel, Tabasco	.250	40	3	10	3	0	0	3	0
Barrera, Nelson, Tigers/Camp.	.250	12	1	3	0	0	1	0	0
Benitez, Yamil, Reyn./Camp.	.242	157	14	38	8	1	3	17	0
Newson, Warren, Monterrey	.242	128	24	31	6	0	6	17	3
Fornes, Daniel, Reynosa	.237	354	42	84	16	1	7	41	4
Phillips, Tony, Mexico	.233	30	8	7	0	0	0	2	2
Murray, Glenn, Cam./Yucatan	.231	173	25	40	7	0	8	19	1
Meulens, Hensley, Puebla	.204	137	14	28	3	1	1	24	0
Samuels, Scott, Monterrey	.200	50	4	10	2	0	1	5	1
Barry, Jeff, Tigers	.167	18	1	3	1	0	0	1	0
Sisco, Steve, Saltillo	.164	55	9	9	1	0	2	5	0
Vaz, Roberto, Campeche	.158	19	1	3	0	0	0	3	1

INDIVIDUAL PITCHING LEADERS
(Minimum 88 Innings)

	W	L	ERA	G	SV	IP	H	BB	SO
#Rubio, Miguel, Monterrey	4	2	0.84	54	**32**	65	43	26	80
Hurtado, Edwin, Cancun	9	5	**1.38**	16	1	117	78	27	113
Rodriguez, Salvador, Yucatan	11	5	2.09	21	0	155	146	22	104
Lomeli, Israel, Cancun	7	5	2.45	17	0	92	61	38	83
Mora, Eleazar, Veracruz	**15**	6	2.50	23	0	155	126	32	89
Romero, Alejandro, Monclova	11	6	2.77	22	0	150	145	44	85
Quiroz, Aaron, Saltillo	8	3	2.78	17	0	91	84	19	62
Valdez, Efrain, Cor./Tabasco	9	9	2.83	26	0	156	145	45	94
Delahoya, Javier, Saltillo	11	3	2.84	20	0	133	120	48	97
Ramirez, Roberto, Red Devils	14	2	2.84	20	0	111	132	25	55
Palafox, Juan, Yucatan	10	6	3.05	20	0	139	143	33	73
Dominguez, David, Oaxaca	7	5	3.23	23	0	128	143	39	82
Vega, Obed, Cancun	9	8	3.35	24	1	156	142	41	107
Manrique, Alberto, Rey./Mont.	8	7	3.36	18	1	110	114	34	72
Rios, Jesus, Yuc./Tabasco	9	4	3.37	21	0	120	124	37	72
Elizalde, Carlos, Oaxaca	9	6	3.38	21	0	115	114	44	64
Campos, Francisco, Campeche	8	9	3.45	21	0	133	127	25	**125**
Vargas, Joel, Tabasco	7	10	3.52	22	0	136	139	41	55
Pulido, Carlos, Oaxaca	13	7	3.57	23	0	151	174	27	95
Alvarez, Juan Jesus, UL	7	6	3.65	25	1	136	136	50	74
Loya, Rigoberto, Laredo	6	7	3.75	21	0	103	120	62	58
Alvarez, Octavio, Red Devils	9	3	3.75	22	0	96	90	24	59
Ruiz, Cecilio, Tabasco	6	8	3.76	22	0	122	134	21	68
Moreno, Angel, Veracruz	9	9	3.80	24	0	147	159	39	84
Lopez, Emigdio, Cordoba	10	6	3.80	23	0	147	149	36	73
Alvarez, Antonio, Monclova	4	5	3.97	16	0	91	101	25	33
Diaz, Rafael, Monterrey	8	6	4.00	19	0	117	97	44	78
Atondo, Sergio, Yucatan	5	8	4.05	17	0	93	89	59	81
Gomez, Miguel, Tigers	11	4	4.12	22	0	129	140	36	90
Montemayor, Humberto, Mont.	10	6	4.13	22	0	133	146	29	92
Huerta, Luis, Laredo	10	6	4.23	12	0	113	130	37	54
Olague, Jesus, Pue./Tigers	11	8	4.27	22	0	129	135	41	116
Nunez, Jose, Laredo	9	9	4.37	23	0	154	181	25	93
Huerta, Edgar, Tigers	7	4	4.47	15	2	103	98	56	84
Rivera, Oscar, Yuc./Cam.	7	12	4.53	23	0	149	159	59	97
Bernal, Manuel, Red Devils	12	9	4.55	22	0	142	176	21	76
Garcia, Jose, Puebla	3	8	4.57	16	3	112	139	28	78
Romano, Michael, Saltillo	11	6	4.66	21	0	135	149	59	99
Osuna, Ricardo, Yucatan	7	8	4.71	18	0	92	110	30	46

(Other Select Players)

	W	L	ERA	G	SV	IP	H	BB	SO
Garcia, Michael, Yucatan	1	1	0.96	30	17	37	24	3	52
Rivera, Ben, Mexico	1	1	1.53	44	30	47	41	10	59
Elvira, Narciso, Campeche	5	2	2.11	9	0	64	46	10	73
Bell, Richard, Laredo	2	2	2.41	18	7	19	14	12	13
Preston, George, Reynosa	3	5	2.60	8	0	62	35	50	72
Sinohui, David, Veracruz	3	2	2.61	43	30	52	38	9	44
Alberto, Jose, Monclova	4	2	2.62	42	22	55	41	22	51
Roque, Rafael, Tigers	8	0	2.73	14	0	79	70	27	49
Quiroz, Aaron, Saltillo	8	3	2.78	17	0	91	84	19	62
Ward, Bryan, Union Laguna	5	4	2.86	10	0	66	56	17	33
Kubenka, Jeff, Reynosa	4	4	3.11	13	0	64	51	28	73
Palacios, Vicente, Salt./Cam.	5	1	3.54	34	1	41	35	9	37
Cortes, David, Laredo	3	1	4.18	39	14	47	52	15	50
Lemon, Donald, Campeche	5	5	4.19	13	0	73	79	21	47
Evans, David, Red Devils/Oax.	0	1	4.38	16	8	12	12	9	11
Revenig, Todd, Campeche	1	2	4.50	7	0	8	6	0	8
Wallace, Kent, UL	1	1	4.70	13	6	15	17	2	11
Dorame, Randey, Red Devils	3	2	4.74	22	0	44	70	29	22
Henthorne, Donald, Puebla	2	3	4.95	7	0	36	45	8	16
Silva, Walter, Monterrey	1	2	4.99	21	0	40	36	24	32
Acosta, David, Red Devils	0	0	5.30	11	0	19	18	17	9
Vosberg, Ed, Red Devils	3	4	5.31	12	0	58	73	15	50
Acosta, Aaron, Campeche	0	5	5.84	16	0	62	77	34	41
Flynt, Will, Cancun	2	3	5.86	5	0	28	39	6	15
Hartmann, Peter, UL	3	4	6.37	11	0	59	73	34	45
Sano, Shigeki, Tigers	0	2	6.89	5	0	16	19	10	13

Holguin wins first championship

BY MILTON JAMAIL

After finishing in last place in its division a year earlier, Holguin capped a memorable season in 2002 by winning its first Serie Nacional title.

Holguin won Group D with a 55-35 record, then beat Camaguey and Villa Clara to advance to the finals, where

it defeated Sancti Spiritus four games to two. Sancti Spiritus had upset Pinar del Rio, which set a record for most victories (64) in a 90-game season, in a semifinal matchup.

Holguin, located 500 miles east of Havana, also hosted the Cuban League All-Star Game in March and the first Cuban-Mexican League All-Star Game in May.

Las Tunas' Osmani Urrutia won his second consecutive Serie Nacional batting title, hitting .408. A year earlier, he hit .431. Michel Abreu (Matanzas) led in home runs with 23, and Eduardo Parent (Villa Clara) was tops in stolen bases with 34.

The pitching leaders were Pinar del Rio starters Pedro Luis Lazo (15-5, 3.32) and Jose Contreras (13-4, 1.76), and Sancti Spiritus' Maels Rodriguez (14-3, 2.13), all prominent members of Cuba's famed national team.

Rodriguez worked 165 innings during the Serie Nacional regular season and appeared in 11 of 18 playoff games, tossing 46 innings. He then pitched 43 more innings in the Super Liga—a new post-season event in Cuban baseball. In all, Rodriguez pitched 255 innings, appearing in 45 of a possible 141 games. He saved his best performance for his last game, pitching a no-hitter in the Super Liga playoffs.

The Super Liga de Béisbol was composed of four teams—Occidentales, Orientales, Centrales and Habaneros. The teams played a 30-game schedule in July and August. Cuba's 100 best players were selected to compete for 25 positions on Equipo Cuba—the national

STANDINGS

GROUP A	W	L	PCT	GB
Pinar del Rio	64	26	.711	—
Isla de la Juventud	51	39	.567	13
Matanzas	48	42	.533	16
Metropolitanos	31	59	.344	33

GROUP B	W	L	PCT	GB
Sancti Spiritus	53	37	.589	—
Industriales	49	41	.544	4
Havana	45	45	.500	8
Cienfuegos	33	57	.367	20

GROUP C	W	L	PCT	GB
Villa Clara	54	36	.600	—
Camaguey	44	46	.489	10
Ciego de Avila	42	48	.467	12
Las Tunas	23	67	.256	31

GROUP D	W	L	PCT	GB
Holguin	55	35	.611	—
Santiago de Cuba	54	36	.600	1
Granma	38	52	.422	17
Guantanamo	36	54	.400	19

PLAYOFFS-Quarterfinals: Holguin defeated Camaguey 3-1; Sancti Spiritus defeated Iisa de la Juventud 3-2; Villa Clara defeated Santiago 3-1; and Pinar del Rio defeated Industriales 3-1 in best-of-5 series. **Semifinals:** Holguin defeated Villa Clara 3-2; Sancti Spiritus defeated Pinar del Rio 4-2 in best-of-7 division series. **Final:** Holguin defeated Sancti Spiritus 4-2 in best-of-7 series.

team. In the past, players seeking a position on the national team would practice for a month without playing games.

The change in format was in response to Cuba's withering dominance on the international stage, which culminated with a silver medal in the 2000 Olympics. With many of its stars aging, five of Cuba's all-time best national-team players, all in their mid- to upper-30s, did not play in the Super Liga. They received permission from Cuban sports authorities to play or coach in Japan in 2002.

Third baseman Omar Linares, 34, one of the island

nation's greatest players, became the first non-defecting Cuban to play for a professional team when he joined the Chunichi Dragons of the Japan's Central League.

The early retirements opened positions on Cuba's national team to younger players. The most highly touted of those was Industriales third baseman-outfielder Kendry Morales, 19, playing in his first Serie Nacional. Morales, who was named the top junior baseball player in Latin America in 2001 by the Pan American Baseball Federation, finished his rookie year with a .324 average. He was also third in the league in home runs (21), RBIs (82) and total bases (203.)

Cuba responded with a strong year internationally by winning the inaugural World University Championship in Italy and World Junior Championship in Canada, both in August. Cuban youth national teams also won Pan American titles over the United States in the 14- and 16-year-old age groups.

The Cuban national team also won the Serie de las Americas in Mexico in October, a qualifying event for the 2003 Pan American Games in the Dominican Republic. Also in October, Cuba won the Central American and Caribbean Games in El Salvador. It also hosted the Intercontinental Cup in November.

INDIVIDUAL BATTING LEADERS
(Minimum 243 At-Bats)

	AVG	AB	R	H	2B	3B	HR	RBI
Urrutia, Osmani, Las Tunas	.408	240	35	98	4	1	6	41
Concepcion, Noris, Las Tunas	.402	254	32	102	22	1	7	44
Enriquez, Michel , IJ	.386	329	71	127	29	1	16	58
Cepeda, Frederich, SS	.378	315	57	119	24	4	10	54
Rivera, Luis, IJ	.373	365	73	136	19	3	7	51
Denis, Waldo, Holguin	.366	331	50	121	10	4	9	55
Gomez, Yasser, Industriales	.365	282	52	103	19	3	4	33
Abreu, Michel, Matanzas	.356	320	78	114	22	1	23	82
Acosta, Vaisel, Matanzas	.355	332	45	118	23	1	10	70
Zamora, Andy, Villa Clara	.355	251	49	89	20	2	0	33

INDIVIDUAL PITCHING LEADERS
(Minimum 90 Innings)

	W	L	ERA	G	IP	BB	SO
Contreras, Jose, Pinal del Rio	13	4	1.76	20	143	41	149
Ibar, Jose, Havana	11	3	1.81	17	129	35	142
Coss, Ifreidi, SS	10	3	1.94	26	120	26	87
Rodriguez, Maels, SS	14	3	2.13	24	165	85	219
Marti. Yadel, Industriales	12	3	2.60	30	114	22	66
Vera, Norge, Santiago	13	5	3.08	20	152	40	112
Hernandez, Vladimir, Villa Clara	11	2	3.09	19	125	25	92
Lazo, Pedro, Pinar del Rio	15	5	3.32	23	154	36	129
Miranda, Raidel, Pinar del Rio	11	5	3.85	23	115	54	92
Miguel, Gervasio, IJ	13	3	4.15	21	139	34	51

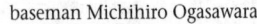
ASIA

'Godzilla'-led Giants take Japan title

BY WAYNE GRACZYK

The Tokyo Yomiuri Giants returned to the top of the Japanese professional baseball world by knocking off the Seibu Lions in an easy four-game sweep in the 2002 Japan Series. Both teams had coasted to pennant victories in their respective leagues under the direction of first-year managers.

JAPAN

Tatsunori Hara guided the Central League Giants to a strong finish with an 11½-game cushion over the defending champion Yakult Swallows. It was Yomiuri's 39th league title and 20th Japan Series victory; the second in three years.

Haruki Ihara piloted Seibu to a 90-win season (in a 140-game schedule) that saw the Lions end up 16½ games ahead of the Osaka Kintetsu Buffaloes and Fukuoka Daiei Hawks. The Lions have now won 14 Pacific League banners since being purchased by the Seibu Railways in 1979.

Giants slugger Hideki Matsui, nicknamed "Godzilla," won Central League most valuable player honors after hitting 50 regular season homers and driving in 107 runs, both league-leading totals. His .334 average left him nine percentage points shy of a triple-crown season, as the batting title was won by Chunichi Dragons outfielder Kosuke Fukudome (.343).

Venezuelan first baseman Alex Cabrera of Seibu was named MVP in the Pacific League after he tied the Japan single-season home run mark of 55 set by Sadaharu Oh of the Yomiuri Giants in 1964 and matched by American Tuffy Rhodes of the Osaka Kintetsu Buffaloes in 2001. Cabrera was also second in the batting race at .336, finishing four points behind Nippon Ham Fighters first

Alex Cabrera

baseman Michihiro Ogasawara.

Besides Cabrera, several other foreign players made big contributions in 2002.

While Rhodes watched Cabrera tie his home run mark, Rhodes did beat out Cabrera for the PL RBI crown with his 117. American righthanders led both leagues in victories: Osaka's Jeremy Powell had 17 wins to lead the Pacific League, while Kevin Hodges of the Yakult Swallows tied with Koji Uehara of Yomiuri to pace the Central loop with 17 victories. Chunichi Dragons' relief ace Eddie Gaillard led the CL with 34 saves.

The leagues split a pair of all-star games in July, with the Central League winning at Tokyo Dome and the Pacific coming back to take the second game at Matsuyama. The PL leads the all-star competition 71-60 with seven ties.

Two Pacific League teams played the first Japan pro baseball games outside of Japan when the Fukuoka Daiei Hawks and Orix BlueWave visited Taiwan for a two-game series in Taipei in May.

Slugger Omar Linares made history as the first player allowed by Cuban baseball officials to join a professional league outside that country, when he joined the Central League's Chunichi Dragons in July. The former Olympian, once the top amateur player in the World, was not in good condition, however, and saw limited action while nursing various injuries.

The Pacific League Nippon Ham Fighters were perhaps Japan's busiest team in 2002. The club announced it would be moving from Tokyo to Sapporo for the 2004 season, then switched major league affiliations from the New York Yankees to the Arizona Diamondbacks. Later in the year, the team survived a beef mislabeling scandal involving Nippon Foods, a subsidiary of its parent company, Nippon Meat Packers. Finally, the Fighters announced the hiring of American Trey Hillman as the team's manager for 2003.

Tokyo Giants fans were disheartened at season's end to learn their hero, Hideki Matsui, would be leaving the team for a crack at the U.S. major leagues, but fans had one last chance to see him play in a Giants' uniform in a series against a team of touring American and National Leaguers during games in Tokyo, Fukuoka, Osaka and Sapporo in November.

CENTRAL LEAGUE STANDINGS

	W	L	T	Pct.	GB
Yomiuri Giants	86	52	2	.623	—
Yakult Swallows	74	62	4	.544	11
Chunichi Dragons	69	66	5	.511	15 ½
Hanshin Tigers	66	70	4	.485	19
Hiroshima Carp	64	72	4	.471	21
Yokohama BayStars	49	86	5	.363	35 ½

INDIVIDUAL BATTING LEADERS
(Minimum 434 Plate Appearances)

	AVG	AB	R	H	2B	3B	HR	RBI	SB
Fukudome, Kosuke, Dragons	.343	542	85	186	42	3	19	65	4
Matsui, Hideki, Giants	.334	500	112	167	27	1	50	107	3
Petagine, Roberto, Swallows	.322	453	90	146	23	1	41	94	0
Iwamura, Akinori, Swallows	.320	510	67	163	32	2	23	71	5
Imaoka, Makoto, Tigers	.317	505	46	160	40	0	15	56	0
Shimizu, Takayuki, Giants	.314	609	92	191	26	5	14	58	12
Maeda, Tomonori, Carp	.308	422	50	130	11	1	20	59	0
Takahashi, Yoshinobu, Giants	.306	409	63	125	18	0	17	53	1
Tatsunami, Kazuyoshi, Dragons	.302	506	62	153	34	2	16	92	4
Ogata, Koichi, Carp	.300	476	77	143	24	0	25	73	4
Furuta, Atsuya, Swallows	.300	420	49	126	24	1	9	60	3
Abe, Shinnosuke, Giants	.298	446	62	133	26	0	18	73	4
Ramirez, Alex, Swallows	.295	539	65	159	25	0	24	92	0
Hiyama, Shinjiro, Tigers	.293	416	51	122	20	2	13	61	7
Miyamoto, Shinya, Swallows	.291	464	53	135	21	1	5	25	6
Ibata, Hirokazu, Dragons	.290	531	67	154	25	1	4	25	6
Arai, Takahiro, Carp	.287	512	63	147	28	2	28	75	1
Nioka, Tomohiro, Giants	.281	398	64	112	21	1	24	67	3
Ishii, Takuro, BayStars	.274	569	78	156	29	2	8	49	19
Kanemoto, Tomoaki, Carp	.274	540	60	148	30	2	29	84	8
Inaba, Atsunori, Swallows	.266	448	59	119	19	3	10	39	3
Rodriguez, Boi, BayStars	.262	451	56	118	24	3	18	60	10
Araki, Masahiro, Dragons	.259	406	43	105	7	1	2	18	16
Arias, George, Tigers	.258	473	64	122	29	1	32	82	3
Taneda, Hitoshi, BayStars	.252	397	47	100	18	0	5	29	5
Eto, Akira, Giants	.242	414	53	100	12	1	18	56	5
Higashide, Akihiro, Carp	.239	377	41	90	7	1	1	17	12
Kimura, Takuya, Carp	.238	412	46	98	18	1	5	27	6
Kataoka, Atsushi, Tigers	.228	425	45	97	17	0	11	46	2
Tanishige, Motonobu, Dragons	.215	446	53	96	21	0	24	78	4

(Remaining U.S. and Latin Players)

	AVG	AB	R	H	2B	3B	HR	RBI	SB
Diaz, Eddy, Carp	.280	353	36	99	16	0	17	51	2
Gomez, Leo, Dragons	.267	247	34	66	10	0	16	43	0
Lopez, Luis, Carp	.245	265	12	65	11	1	5	33	0
Matsumoto, Daniel, Swallows	.250	24	2	6	1	0	0	3	0
White, Derrick, Tigers	.227	220	19	50	10	0	7	21	1
Gulan, Mike, BayStars	.226	248	20	56	16	0	10	34	1
Bullett, Scott, Dragons	.201	149	19	30	8	1	7	15	2
Linares, Omar, Dragons	.174	46	2	8	0	0	1	5	0
Young, Ernie, BayStars	.173	110	15	19	3	0	8	16	0
Crespo, Felipe, Giants	.122	41	4	5	1	0	2	7	0

INDIVIDUAL PITCHING LEADERS
(Minimum 140 Innings)

	W	L	ERA	G	SV	IP	H	BB	SO
Kuwata, Masumi, Giants	12	6	2.22	23	0	158	138	38	108
Kawakami, Kenshin, Dragons	12	6	2.35	27	0	188	170	34	149
Igawa, Kei, Tigers	14	9	2.49	31	1	210	163	53	206
Uehara, Koji, Giants	17	5	2.60	26	0	204	173	23	182
Asakura, Kenta, Dragons	11	11	2.61	31	0	200	193	63	149
Kudo, Kimiyasu, Giants	9	8	2.91	24	0	170	157	26	151
Fujii, Shugo, Swallows	10	9	3.08	28	0	196	167	44	171
Takahashi, Hisanori, Giants	10	4	3.09	24	0	163	143	39	145
Moore, Trey, Dragons	10	11	3.33	27	0	181	165	60	116
Ishikawa, Masanori, Swallows	12	9	3.33	29	0	178	183	29	104
Hodges, Kevin, Swallows	17	8	3.41	32	0	201	183	67	132
Sasaoka, Shinji, Carp	8	9	3.46	25	0	154	167	32	127

Yoshimi, Yuji, BayStars	11	8	3.64	27	1	188	196	47	138
Kuroda, Hiroki, Carp	10	10	3.67	23	0	164	166	34	144
Takahashi, Ken, Carp	9	14	3.84	26	0	173	197	38	142
Hasegawa, Masayuki, Carp	13	10	3.84	30	0	194	212	42	153

(Remaining U.S. and Latin Players)

	W	L	ERA	G	SV	IP	H	BB	SO
Schullstrom, Erik, Carp	0	0	0.00	5	0	5	1	2	6
Almonte, Hector, Giants	0	0	1.50	27	1	24	18	7	18
Gaillard, Eddie, Dragons	1	1	1.52	47	34	47	40	12	27
Valdes, Marc, Tigers	4	3	1.54	42	22	53	40	17	39
Hansell, Greg, Tigers	0	1	1.93	5	0	5	4	1	2
Guzman, Domingo, BayStars	5	5	2.79	19	0	97	85	31	66
Ramirez, Ramon, Carp	0	0	3.00	2	0	3	3	2	3
Bunch, Mel, Dragons	7	7	3.28	17	0	113	112	27	97
Vargas, Martin, Dragons	2	4	3.33	8	0	49	41	21	35
Newman, Alan, Swallows	2	3	3.42	42	0	72	55	30	58
Holt, Chris, BayStars	6	10	3.57	19	0	111	107	11	77
Bowers, Shane, BayStars	4	8	3.77	24	0	131	130	41	90
Wasdin, John, Giants	4	4	4.54	10	0	38	55	9	31
Stanifer, Rob, Carp	0	0	4.74	15	0	19	28	6	15
Turman, Jason, BayStars	0	2	6.16	9	0	19	23	7	13
Carlyle, Buddy, Tigers	0	2	7.53	3	0	14	17	5	13
Beltran, Rigo, Carp	0	1	9.15	25	0	20	23	4	20

PACIFIC LEAGUE STANDINGS

	W	L	T	Pct.	GB
Seibu Lions	90	49	1	.647	—
Osaka Kintetsu Buffaloes	73	65	2	.529	16 ½
Fukuoka Daiei Hawks	73	65	2	.529	16 ½
Chiba Lotte Marines	67	72	1	.482	23
Nippon Ham Fighters	61	76	3	.445	28
Orix BlueWave	50	87	3	.365	39

INDIVIDUAL BATTING LEADERS
(Minimum 434 Plate Appearances)

	AVG	AB	R	H	2B	3B	HR	RBI	SB
Ogasawara, Michihiro, Fighters	.340	486	77	165	27	2	32	81	8
Cabrera, Alex, Lions	.336	447	105	150	23	0	55	115	4
Matsui, Kazuo, Lions	.332	582	119	193	46	6	36	87	33
Tani, Yoshitomo, BlueWave	.326	524	49	171	31	1	5	39	41
Wada, Kazuhiro, Lions	.319	439	64	140	25	2	33	81	5
Ozeki, Tatsuya, Lions	.314	487	59	153	35	1	4	50	15
Valdes, Pedro, Hawks	.303	446	65	135	32	2	21	76	2
Fukuura, Kazuya, Marines	.300	493	48	148	40	0	9	66	2
Nakamura, Norihiro, Buffaloes	.294	511	87	150	27	1	42	115	2
Jojima, Kenji, Hawks	.293	416	60	122	18	0	25	74	8
Kokubo, Hiroki, Hawks	.292	507	89	148	25	0	32	89	8
Omura, Saburo, Marines	.286	441	57	126	33	2	9	43	13
Kaneko, Makoto, Fighters	.285	393	46	112	19	3	6	29	9
Tanaka, Yukio, Fighters	.278	467	57	130	31	4	17	53	0
May, Derrick, Marines	.273	490	57	134	26	1	23	90	2
Takagi, Hiroyuki, Lions	.272	404	52	110	12	1	1	37	11
Rhodes, Tuffy, Buffaloes	.272	534	94	145	31	2	46	117	5
Omura, Naoyuki, Buffaloes	.271	531	65	144	31	4	11	47	1
Isobe, Koichi, Buffaloes	.270	396	44	107	19	1	3	30	6
Yoshioka, Yuji, Buffaloes	.269	520	66	140	40	3	26	72	4
Shibahara, Hiroshi, Hawks	.269	509	73	137	33	2	4	43	5
Obando, Sherman, Fighters	.263	441	49	116	18	1	26	68	3
Matsunaka, Nobuhiko, Hawks	.260	485	75	126	23	1	28	83	1
Iguchi, Tadahiro, Hawks	.259	428	64	111	14	1	18	53	21
Sheldon, Scott, BlueWave	.256	450	65	115	28	1	26	59	4
Hori, Koichi, Marines	.253	387	58	98	21	2	14	36	4
Cromer, D.T., Fighters	.245	478	49	117	27	3	20	54	5
Oshima, Koichi, BlueWave	.230	374	32	86	12	0	1	25	13
Hatsushiba, Kiyoshi, Marines	.223	403	38	90	15	0	17	55	0

(Remaining U.S. and Latin Players)

	AVG	AB	R	H	2B	3B	HR	RBI	SB
Evans, Tom, Lions	.252	242	37	61	14	1	15	45	0
McClain, Scott, Lions	.238	63	6	15	4	0	2	5	0
Wilson, Nigel, Buffaloes	.221	113	14	25	3	0	6	14	0
Burkhart, Morgan, Hawks	.214	126	14	27	1	0	9	18	0
Seguignol, Fernando, BlueWave	.204	280	39	57	8	0	23	47	1
Bolick, Frank, Marines	.204	211	27	43	11	0	6	24	0

INDIVIDUAL PITCHING LEADERS
(Minimum 140 Innings)

	W	L	ERA	G	SV	IP	H	BB	SO
Kaneda, Masahiko, BlueWave	4	9	2.50	23	0	141	135	31	85
Koo, Dae Sung, BlueWave	5	7	2.52	22	0	146	122	47	144
Minchey, Nate, Marines	15	14	2.85	32	0	230	222	43	132
Wakatabe, Kenichi, Hawks	10	8	2.99	26	0	148	152	36	96

Name	W	L	ERA	G	SV	IP	H	BB	SO
Mitsui, Koji, Lions	10	2	3.15	41	0	140	128	34	94
Kanemura, Satoru, Fighters	10	6	3.17	32	0	168	153	53	143
Shoda, Itsuki, Fighters	9	11	3.45	23	0	157	145	37	90
Nishiguchi, Fumiya, Lions	15	10	3.51	29	0	182	166	51	180
Seelbach, Chris, Fighters	8	7	3.60	22	0	140	138	66	75
Yarnall, Ed, BlueWave	6	13	3.61	25	0	164	149	62	120
Iwakuma, Hisashi, Buffaloes	8	7	3.69	23	0	141	132	42	131
Powell, Jeremy, Buffaloes	17	10	3.78	32	0	217	205	41	182
Tanoue, Keizaburo, Hawks	6	9	3.93	26	0	149	154	30	83
Shimizu, Naoyuki, Marines	14	11	4.56	31	0	178	197	57	124
Kato, Kosuke, Marines	11	15	4.58	32	0	159	168	53	148

(Remaining U.S. and Latin Players)

Name	W	L	ERA	G	SV	IP	H	BB	SO
Pedraza, Rod, Hawks	1	2	3.30	34	21	30	36	5	16
Mirabal, Carlos, Fighters	9	6	3.37	18	0	126	111	42	77
Sikorski, Brian, Marines	4	6	3.44	47	2	97	76	20	102
Flury, Pat, Fighters	0	0	3.46	10	0	13	9	5	19
Bergman, Sean, Buffaloes	4	6	5.15	16	0	87	102	26	57
Raggio, Brady, Hawks	6	5	5.44	15	0	83	95	20	49
Johnson, Mike, Buffaloes	1	0	6.65	9	0	22	25	12	8

Samsung earns long-awaited title

BY J.J. COOPER

KOREA

For much of the last decade, the Samsung Lions have been one of the best teams in the Korean Baseball Organization. But until 2002, they hadn't been champions.

Five trips to the Korean Series had ended in failure, but a 17-year drought since the Lions' last title ended in dramatic fashion as Samsung slugged two homers in a four-run bottom-of-the-ninth rally that capped a comeback for a 10-9 win over the LG Twins in the decisive Game 6 of a best-of-seven series.

Lee Seung-Yeop slugged a three-run homer off closer Lee Sang-Hoon, a former member of the Boston Red Sox, to tie the game, and Ma Hae-Young homered off Choi Won-Ho to win it.

It was fitting that Ma hit the game-winning homer, as he dominated the championship series. He homered twice in Game 5, went 4-for-4 with three RBIs in Game 4 and had a run-scoring single in Game 3.

The Korean Series had been postponed until early November because Korean pros were allowed to represent the country in the annual Asian Games—which Korea won in October.

Lee Sang-Hoon

The title capped off a season where the Lions (82-47-4) won 15 straight games late in the season to come-from-behind to catch and pass Kia for the league's best record, earning an automatic spot in the Korean Series.

Their opponent in the Korean Series was a bit of a surprise, as the Twins finished fourth during the regular season, but won their quarterfinal series against third place Hyundai and their semifinal series against second-place Kia.

The Lions earned the title with the league's best offense. Lee Seung-Yeop led the league in home runs with his .323-47-126 season, while Ma was not far behind at .323-33-116. The Lions also had Kim Han-Soo (.311-17-76) and former Toronto Blue Jay Tilson Brito (.283-25-90).

It was not a banner year for North American and Latin hitters in the KBO. SKs Jose Fernandez (.281-45-107) threatened Lee Seung-Yeop for the home run title and Hanhwa's Jay Davis (.287-21-72) had a solid season, but no North American or Latin player cracked the top 10 in batting.

North American and Latin pitchers fared a little better, as Mexican lefthander Narciso Elvira led the league in ERA (13-6, 2.50) while Mark Kiefer (14-10, 3.44) led the league in wins. Both players had lengthy careers in the Milwaukee Brewers organization.

STANDINGS

	W	L	T	Pct.	GB
Samsung Lions	82	47	4	.636	—
Kia Tigers	78	51	4	.605	4
Hyundai Unicorns	70	58	5	.547	11½
LG Twins	66	61	6	.520	15
Doosan Bears	66	65	2	.504	17
SK Wyverns	61	69	3	.469	21½
Hanhwa Eagles	59	69	5	.461	22½
Lotte Giants	35	97	1	.265	48½

PLAYOFFS: Quarterfinals—LG Twins defeated Hyundai 2-0 in best-of-3 series. **Semifinals**—LG Twins defeated Kia 3-2 in best-of-5 series. **Finals**—Samsung defeated LG Twins 4-2 in best-of-7 series.

INDIVIDUAL BATTING LEADERS

	AVG	AB	R	H	HR	RBI	BB	SO
Chang, Seong-Ho, Kia	.343	481	82	165	19	95	86	53
Ma, Hae-Yeong, Samsung	.323	532	92	172	33	116	46	74
Lee, Seung-Yeop, Samsung	.323	511	123	165	47	126	89	109
Shim, Jeong-Soo, Hyundai	.323	502	101	161	46	119	69	114
Kim, Dong-Joo, Doosan	.318	415	63	132	26	79	52	61
Lee, Yeong-Woo, Hanhwa	.315	476	96	150	24	52	73	103
Kim, Han-Soo, Samsung	.311	486	69	151	17	76	35	61
Lee, Chin-Yeoung, SK	.308	419	73	129	13	40	42	57
Jeon, Joon-Ho, Hyundai	.300	420	83	126	3	28	53	51
Lee, Byung-Kyu, LG	.293	389	54	114	12	43	50	57

(Remaining North Americans)

	AVG	AB	R	H	HR	RBI	BB	SO
Herrera, Jose, Lotte	.305	210	23	64	6	20	8	28
Davis, Jay, Hanhwa	.287	404	56	116	21	72	46	97
Brito, Tilson, Samsung	.283	481	89	136	25	90	35	84
Fernandez, Jose, SK	.281	499	81	140	45	107	49	114
Paul, Corey, Hyundai	.280	397	48	111	18	64	35	115
Martinez, Manny, LG	.279	409	59	114	15	69	49	70
Franklin, Micah, Hyundai	.276	152	30	42	14	30	34	52
Woods, Tyrone, Doosan	.256	407	53	104	25	82	50	123
Pemberton, Rudy, Kia	.255	271	28	69	11	48	23	56
Newson, Warren, Kia	.209	115	15	24	7	17	17	38
Hatcher, Chris, Kia	.162	68	6	11	1	5	2	22
Berroa, Geronimo, Lotte	.097	31	1	3	1	3	3	15
Quinlan, Tom, LG	.000	21	0	0	0	0	3	10

INDIVIDUAL PITCHING LEADERS

	W	L	ERA	SV	IP	H	BB	SO
Elvira, Narciso, Samsung	13	6	2.50	0	137	115	52	111
Song, Jin-Woo, Hanhwa	18	7	2.99	0	220	199	54	165
Im, Chang-Yong, Samsung	17	6	3.08	2	204	188	34	160
Rios, Daniel, Kia	14	5	3.14	13	158	140	44	102
Lee, Seung-Ho, SK	6	12	3.15	0	143	120	40	144
Chae, Byung-Ryong, SK	7	9	3.19	11	141	120	44	126
Kiefer, Mark, Kia	19	9	3.34	0	202	172	52	135
Park, Myeong-Hwan, Doosan	14	10	3.44	0	186	173	68	169
Son, Min-Han, Lotte	4	9	3.67	0	142	144	30	82

(Remaining North Americans)

	W	L	ERA	SV	IP	H	BB	SO
Ruffin, Johnny, SK	1	0	2.60	0	17	8	6	18
Hernandez, Fernando, SK	2	0	2.82	6	45	39	11	45
Picota, Lenin, Samsung	6	6	3.51	14	103	115	44	104
Magee, Danny, Lotte	4	5	3.70	0	80	71	48	86
Rath, Gary, Doosan	16	8	3.87	0	202	202	69	154
Cole, Victor, Doosan	12	6	4.01	0	157	152	73	114
Torres, Melquicides, Hyundai	10	11	4.19	0	180	182	64	97
Manzanillo, Ravelo, LG	8	11	4.32	0	162	161	94	122
Magee, Danny, Lotte/SK	6	9	4.70	0	132	127	81	124
Keppen, Jeff, LG	6	4	5.05	0	66	83	33	47
Patrick, Bronswell, Samsung	5	7	5.96	0	77	100	20	45
Parra, Jose, Samsung	3	1	6.00	4	39	48	15	32
Veras, Dario, Hyundai	1	4	7.33	6	23	23	9	19

Defending champs repeat titles

BY JEFFREY WILSON

Maybe it only seemed like they were showing re-runs in Taiwan in 2002. Both league champions in Taiwan's professional leagues repeated as champions.

In the Chinese Professional Baseball League, the

TAIWAN

Brother Elephants were automatic champions by virtue of winning both half-season titles in the regular season. The Elephants then swept the China Trust Whales in four games in a largely meaningless championship series. Righthander Jonathan Hurst pitched a complete game for the win in Game 3.

The first-ever sweep in a championship series in the 13-year history of the CPBL also marked the third-straight championship for the Elephants.

The star of the CPBL regular season was China Trust's Sung Chao-chi, who won the league's first-ever pitching triple crown. He led in ERA (2.13), wins (16) and strikeouts (183), to earn league most valuable player honors.

The only import player in the CPBL to win a post-season award was President Lions pitcher John Burgos, who won a Gold Glove.

In the Taiwan Major League, the regular season champion Taichung Agan won the TML championship series over the Kaohsiung Fala 4 games to 1. Righthander Ned Darley pitched Taichung to the win.

After going a perfect 15-for-15 in save opportunities during the regular season, Darley saved Games 1 and 2. Darley then threw seven shutout innings in a Game 4 start, leading the Agan to a 2-0 victory.

In Game 5, the Agan claimed their second straight TML championship series when Huang Chin-chih and Enrique Quintanilla combined to limit the Fala to four hits in a 7-2 win. Huang had led the TML with 16 wins and a 1.46 ERA.

Former Rockies and Cardinals second baseman Roberto Mejia of Taichung won the batting title (.332) and finished as the runner-up in RBIs and home runs.

A 57 percent attendance increase in the CPBL and Taiwanese native Chin-Feng Chen's debut with the Los Angeles Dodgers continued to boost optimist for the growth of baseball in Taiwan. Chen became the first Taiwanese native to play in the major leagues.

Almost immediately after the conclusion of the 2002 season, Taiwan national sports authorities floated yet another plan for a merger of the CPBL and the Taiwan Major League. The plan would create a new six-team league, tentatively call the Taiwan Professional Baseball League.

TAIWAN MAJOR LEAGUE STANDINGS

	W	L	T	PCT	GB
Taichung Agan	47	24	1	.662	—
Kaohsiung Fala	34	37	1	.479	13
Taipei Gida	31	39	2	.443	15 ½
Chiayi Luka	29	41	2	.414	17 ½

PLAYOFFS: Taichung defeated Kaohsiung 4-1 in best-of-7 series.

INDIVIDUAL BATTING LEADERS
(Minimum 230 Plate Appearances)

	AVG	AB	R	H	2B	3B	HR	RBI	SB
Mejia, Roberto, Taichung	.332	277	46	92	20	0	14	62	20
Hsieh Chia-hsien, Taichung	.321	268	51	86	20	0	19	64	5

Lin Kun-han, Taipei	.307	244	33	75	18	0	2	35	4
Wu Che-tsung, Taichung	.307	218	27	67	12	3	1	33	5
Chen Kuo-liang, Taipei	.302	215	26	65	11	1	1	21	0

(Other Import Players)

	AVG	AB	R	H	2B	3B	HR	RBI	SB
Martinez, Gil, Taipei	.347	121	20	42	5	0	2	14	30
Ozuna, Rafael, Kaohsiung	.280	261	22	73	13	2	3	41	20
Lemonis, Chris, Chiayi	.275	120	20	33	6	0	1	16	4
Gonzalez, Paul, Chiayi	.274	234	31	63	13	1	9	35	1
Fingleson, Gavin, Chiayi	.268	41	5	11	1	0	0	1	0
Buckley, Matt, Chiayi	.206	34	3	7	2	0	0	2	1

INDIVIDUAL PITCHING LEADERS
(Minimum 80 Innings)

	W	L	ERA	G	SV	IP	H	BB	SO
Huang Chin-chih, Taichung	16	2	1.46	24	2	154	129	43	110
Muto, Koji, Taichung	8	3	2.26	15	0	87	84	17	64
Hsu Wen-hsiung, Kaohsiung	6	7	2.78	22	0	123	112	52	86
Vazquez, Lioner, Kaohsiung	7	5	2.88	21	0	128	124	54	101
Liang Ju-hao, Taipei	8	11	2.90	23	0	164	143	43	142

(Other Import Pitchers)

	W	L	ERA	G	SV	IP	H	BB	SO
Darley, Ned, Taichung	2	0	1.13	24	14	32	23	15	30
Williams, Shad, Chiayi	7	4	2.95	18	0	100	102	40	64
Bicknell, Greg, Chiayi	6	11	3.27	29	1	176	170	68	108
Lakman, Jason, Kaohsiung	0	2	3.57	12	4	17	20	7	9
Rodriguez, Frank, Kaohsiung	9	10	3.68	22	0	149	135	61	140
Quintanilla, Juan, Kaohsiung	14	3	3.70	21	1	138	142	32	83
Cepeda, Victor, Taichung	1	1	3.79	7	2	19	22	8	8
Grant, Brian, Kaohsiung	1	3	4.31	14	0	31	33	23	18
Runion, Tony, Kaohsiung	1	1	4.76	12	3	11	15	6	8
Thompson, John, Kaohsiung	2	0	6.92	8	0	13	13	10	7

CPBL STANDINGS

FIRST HALF	W	L	T	PCT	GB
Brother Elephants	25	17	3	.595	—
China Trust Whales	21	21	3	.500	4
Sinon Bulls	21	23	1	.477	5
President Lions	18	24	3	.429	7

SECOND HALF	W	L	T	PCT	GB
Brother Elephants	28	16	1	.636	—
China Trust Whales	24	21	0	.533	4 ½
Sinon Bulls	23	22	0	.511	5 ½
President Lions	14	30	1	.318	14

PLAYOFFS: Brother defeated China Trust 4-0 in best-of-7 series.

INDIVIDUAL BATTING LEADERS
(Minimum 230 Plate Appearances)

	AVG	AB	R	H	2B	3B	HR	RBI	SB
Chen Chien-wie, China Trust	.334	293	52	98	17	1	4	52	4
Huang Chung-yi, Sinon	.326	328	51	107	20	1	15	68	10
Yang Sung-hsien, China Trust	.320	325	52	104	19	4	4	21	16
Wang Chuan-chia, President	.315	260	35	82	14	2	4	30	5
Cheng Chao-hsing, Sinon	.313	291	28	91	11	3	6	53	9

(Other Import Players)

	AVG	AB	R	H	2B	3B	HR	RBI	SB
Anson, Fred, Sinon	.250	12	1	3	0	0	0	1	0

INDIVIDUAL PITCHING LEADERS
(Minimum 90 Innings)

	W	L	ERA	G	SV	IP	H	BB	SO
Sung Chao-chi, China Trust	16	8	2.13	32	0	206	142	62	183
Hurst, Jonathan, Brother	16	8	2.65	30	1	217	193	81	142
Nakayama, Hiroaki, China Trust	12	10	2.80	34	1	176	172	53	117
Martinez, Osvaldo, Sinon	12	12	2.86	41	4	176	159	71	155
Nakagomi, Shin, Brother	15	9	3.26	28	0	190	185	50	123

(Other Import Pitchers)

	W	L	ERA	G	SV	IP	H	BB	SO
Morel, Ramon, Sinon	0	0	1.44	14	7	25	15	14	22
Davenport, Joe, President	6	5	2.99	15	0	87	81	39	31
Burgos, John, President	11	12	3.85	30	0	213	224	62	137
Mota, Daniel, Sinon	0	1	6.23	3	0	4	7	2	3
Arroyo, Luis, President	2	4	6.89	7	0	32	38	27	27
Rivera, Lino, President	0	3	7.08	8	0	34	46	22	18
Morel, Rafael, China Trust	0	1	7.20	1	0	5	5	4	2
Lomeli, Israel, President	0	3	8.56	4	0	13	14	12	9
Serafini, Dan, China Trust	0	2	13.50	2	0	4	10	6	1

Imports lead Rimini to Serie A/1 title

Rimini won the Serie A/1 pennant and went on to beat Nettuno four games to one in the 2002 Italy Series to win their 10th national championship and their third in the last four years.

ITALY

Former big league outfielder Chuck Carr, long time minor league outfielder James Buccheri and Dominican pitcher Martin Sanchez were signed prior to the season as Rimini's three new imports. Carr and Buccheri were expected to bring some speed to the Rimini lineup, and they did just that. The pair combined for 59 stolen bases. Buccheri led the league with 36 thefts.

Carr also topped Rimini and tied for fourth in Serie A/1 with eight homers. Four of those came in the last six games of the regular season, when Rimini caught up with pace-setting Bologna. The two clubs finished with identical records, but Rimini was awarded first place because it won the season series against Bologna, four games to two.

Bologna went with a Japanese import pitcher for the second straight season. Ayahito Shinada (10-4, 2.08) had previously pitched in Japan's Pacific League for the Kintetsu Buffaloes.

Three Australians helped Parma rebound from a sub-.500 season in 2001, but the club failed to make the playoffs for the second straight year. Pitcher Shane Tonkin (10-8, 2.11) and catcher Gavin Edmonson (.247-4-26) formed an all-Aussie battery, while Clint Balgera (.313-6-31) had a solid season as Parma's regular left fielder.

After being relegated to A/2 at the end of the 2001 campaign, Modena was allowed to remain in Serie A/1 when Caserta withdrew from the league. Modena had a respectable season and boasted the league's batting king, Orlando Munoz (.385-3-35). The Venezuelan shortstop overtook Bologna second baseman Davide Dallospedale

(.384-1-30) in the final game of the regular season.
–HARVEY SAHKER

STANDINGS

	W	L	PCT	GB
Rimini	39	15	.722	—
Bologna	39	15	.722	—
Nettuno	37	17	.685	2
Grosseto	35	19	.648	4
Parma	30	24	.556	9
Modena	27	27	.500	12
Anzio	21	32	.396	17 ½
Firenze	20	34	.370	19
Codogno	14	40	.259	25
Paterno	7	46	.132	31 ½

INDIVIDUAL BATTING LEADERS

	AVG	AB	R	H	2B	3B	HR	RBI	SB
Munoz, Orlando, Modena	.385	200	43	77	20	6	3	35	6
Dallospedale, Davide, Bologna	.384	219	52	84	19	1	1	30	14
Tavarez, Ramon, Anzio	.383	162	36	62	15	4	3	38	9
Bautista, Juan, Parma	.371	229	56	85	16	1	10	44	17
Ametler, Jesus, Paterno	.366	172	27	63	16	0	3	20	5
Ramos Gizzi Jairo, Rafael, Grosseto	.363	215	37	78	13	0	7	51	2
Gaiardo, Alessandro, Rimini	.358	162	26	58	9	0	2	39	7
Frignani, Daniele, Bologna	.357	182	41	65	9	4	3	47	7
Liverziani, Claudio, Bologna	.353	190	66	67	18	2	12	61	11
Canate Pacheco, William, Modena	.342	193	43	66	9	5	2	27	18

INDIVIDUAL PITCHING LEADERS

	W	L	ERA	G	SV	IP	H	BB	SO
Vigna, Juan Carlos, Nettuno	9	2	1.21	23	7	97	47	21	107
Ginanneschi, Emiliano, Grosseto	8	4	2.06	22	4	101	86	18	78
Tonkin, Shane, Parma	10	8	2.11	18	0	149	127	48	103
Shinada, Ayahito, Bologna	10	4	2.08	16	0	117	86	22	136
Lanfranco, Otoniel, Nettuno	13	1	2.13	19	0	127	93	53	153
Ventura, Cipriano, Nettuno	8	5	2.26	18	0	123	103	31	113
Newman, Daniel, Bologna	10	2	2.31	19	0	117	83	41	113
Sanchez, Martin, Rimini	9	5	2.46	18	0	146	106	28	155
Cabalisti, Roberto, Rimini	10	3	2.51	20	0	111	91	24	90
Cretis, Rolando, Grosseto	8	3	2.62	18	3	107	109	21	52

Neptunas roll to fourth title in row

Neptunus captured the Dutch Major League pennant and went on to win its fourth consecutive Holland Series. The Rotterdam club was unbeaten in the postseason, sweeping the Hoofddorp Pioniers in the semifinals and HCAW in the finals. It was the first Holland Series sweep since 1991, which also saw Neptunus taking three straight games from HCAW.

HOLLAND

Three Neptunus players ranked among the DML's top four hitters. Outfielder Dirk van t' Klooster won the batting crown with a .376 average. Wim Martinus (.353) and Percy Isenia (.340) finished third and fourth, respectively. It was a remarkable season for Martinus, 39, who had recently returned from a long stint with Neptunus's top farm team.

After shedding their loose, four-year affiliation with the Montreal Expos and reverting to their original nickname, the Amsterdam Pirates got off to a fine start. Maxime Leblanc, the first Frenchman in DML history, blanked Hoofddorp 7-0 on Opening Day. The Pirates endured a difficult season, however, and dropped to the

promotion/relegation pool in midseason.

Dutch clubs won all three of Europe's major club competitions for the second straight season. Neptunus successfully defended its European Cup and Super Cup titles, while Kinheim won its second straight Cup Winners Cup. The Netherlands provided all six finalists in the three competitions.

STANDINGS

PLAYOFF POOL	W	L	T	PCT	GB
Neptunus	38	7	2	.830	—
Kinheim	31	15	1	.670	7 ½
HCAW	29	16	2	.638	9
Hoofddorp Pioniers	21	22	4	.489	16
PSV Eindhoven	20	24	3	.457	17 ½
Hague Tornadoes	20	24	3	.457	17 ½
PROMOTION/RELEGATION POOL	W	L	T	PCT	GB
Sparta/Feyenoord	15	5	0	.750	—
Amsterdam Pirates	12	7	1	.625	2 ½
Almere	12	8	0	.600	3
Oosterhout Twins	10	10	0	.500	5
RCH	6	13	1	.325	6
Alcmaria Victrix	4	16	0	.250	11

WINTER
LEAGUES

Undermanned Mexicans beat odds, Dominicans to win Caribbean title

BY ERIC EDWARDS

It was the usual imbalance of power. On one side of the field stood a Dominican team armed with major league all-stars Vladimir Guerrero (Expos) and Miguel Tejada (Athletics) in the middle of its lineup, and Odalis Perez (Dodgers) at the top of its rotation. Across the way was a Mexican squad with just one major leaguer, out-fielder Jacob Cruz (Tigers).

It was the sword against the stone at the 2002 Caribbean Series—and the Mexicans somehow managed to strike a blow to the temple.

Guerrero and Tejada both made their presence felt in the six-game round-robin tournament, played in Caracas, Venezuela, but it was a little-known catcher from the Mexican Pacific League's Culiacan Tomato Growers who elbowed them both out of the spotlight.

Adan Amezcua, a refugee from the Orioles organization, came to University Stadium with a simple mission: to get the attention of the scores of scouts who would be forced to attend this competition despite a dearth of promising prospects.

By the time the tournament was over, he had achieved far more than that. He had led Culiacan to Mexico's fourth title since joining the Caribbean fray in 1970—and just the second for a country other than the Dominican Republic or Puerto Rico since Venezuela won its last title in 1987.

Amezcua, 27, was already a hero in Culiacan after hitting the home run that won Game Six of the Mexican Pacific League championship series against Mazatlan, propelling Culiacan into the series. His big-hit parade would continue at this bigger venue.

RODGER WOOD

Adan Amezcua

He delivered eight RBIs in the Tomateros' first three games—all victories—and finished the tournament hitting .455 with three homers and nine RBIs. Virtually every hit had a run attached—most of them in key situa-tions—as the Mexicans found myriad ways to win games down the stretch.

"I just came here trying to open some eyes," said Amezcua, who signed with the Padres shortly after the tournament ended. "I still feel like I can play in the major leagues, and I wanted to show I deserve another chance.

"Never did I expect to play this well. But we had something special going with this team. As soon as we rallied for the first win, we had a feeling it could unfold like this."

In Culiacan's opening game against host Magallanes of

WINTER LEAGUES

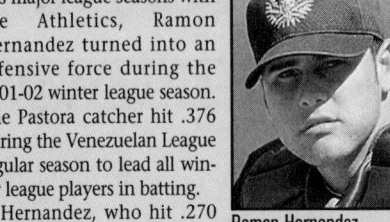

A .252 hitter in three previous major league seasons with the Athletics, Ramon Hernandez turned into an offensive force during the 2001-02 winter league season. The Pastora catcher hit .376 during the Venezuelan League regular season to lead all winter league players in batting.

Ramon Hernandez

Hernandez, who hit .270 and .293 in his two previous Venezuelan League seasons, continued his hot hitting in the postseason. He hit .392 in the circuit's 16-game playoff as Pastora failed to advance, but he was added to the Magallanes roster for the Caribbean Series and led all hitters with a .474 average. Hernandez, 25, hit .388 with 10 homers and 46 RBIs on the season.

For his efforts, Hernandez was selected Baseball America's 2001-02 Winter League Player of the Year. Hernandez went on to hit .233 for the American League West champion A's in 2002.

PREVIOUS WINNERS

1985-1986—Wally Joyner, 1b, Mayaguez (Puerto Rico)	
1986-1987—Vicente Palacios, rhp, Mexicali (Mexican Pacific)	
1987-1988—Jose Nunez, rhp, Escogido (Dominican Republic)	
1988-1989—Phil Stephenson, 1b, Zulia (Venezuela)	
1989-1990—Edgar Martinez, 3b, San Juan (Puerto Rico)	
1990-1991—Henry Rodriguez, of, Licey (Dominican Republic)	
1991-1992—Wilson Alvarez, lhp, Zulia (Venezuela)	
1992-1993—Matias Carrillo, of, Mexicali (Mexican Pacific)	
1993-1994—John Hudek, rhp, Magallanes (Venezuela)	
1994-1995—Carlos Delgado, c, San Juan (Puerto Rico)	
1995-1996—Darryl Brinkley, of, Mexicali (Mexican Pacific)	
1996-1997—Bartolo Colon, rhp, Aguilas (Dominican Republic)	
1997-1998—Jose Hernandez, ss, Mayaguez (Puerto Rico)	
1998-1999—Bob Abreu, of, Caracas (Venezuela)	
1999-2000—Morgan Burkhart, 1b, Navojoa (Mexican Pacific)	
2000-2001—Courtney Duncan, rhp, Caguas (Puerto Rico)	

Venezuela, Amezcua singled home two runs to begin his team's return from a 5-1 deficit. He tied the game with a run-scoring, two-out single in the ninth inning.

An inning later, Cruz won the game with a walk-off home run.

The next night, Amezcua hit a three-run homer that helped stake Culiacan to a 5-2 lead over Licey, the Dominican representative. The Dominicans rallied to tie the game at 5-5, but their defense betrayed them in the seventh inning, leading to two more Mexican runs and a 7-6 victory for Culiacan.

A night later, Amezcua's two-run homer keyed a four-run fifth inning that helped Mexico pull out to an 8-1 lead over the Puerto Rican champion Bayamon Cowboys.

Bayamon staged a late-inning comeback after Mexican starter Pablo Ochoa (Mets) was lifted, pulling to within 9-7 in the final inning. It then put runners at the corners with two out for Eduardo Perez (Cardinals), whose drive through the thin mountain air appeared headed into the bleachers in center field.

Darrell Sherman, a transplanted American who settled in Culiacan, at first believed the ball was headed over the wall. But he tracked it down just before it hit the top of the center-field cushion 385 feet from home plate, preserving the victory for Mexico.

A night later it was Mexico's turn to come from behind, scoring six times in the final two innings to complete a 13-9 victory over Venezuela. In that game, Amezcua made his presence felt again. He hit a solo home run that tied the game at seven in the seventh, after defusing what could have been a big inning in the second by blocking the plate before receiving the throw from center field and tagging Venezuelan baserunner Endy Chavez (Expos).

That victory eliminated both Puerto Rico, which had lost its first three games, and Venezuela, which had lost three of its first four despite collecting 62 hits.

Only the Dominicans had a chance to chase down Culiacan. In order to do so, they would have to win their second head-to-head matchup, then hope their regional rivals from Puerto Rico could knock the Tomato Growers off the next day to force a tiebreaker.

The Mexicans finally ended up on the wrong side of a one-run game against the Dominicans in their rematch, falling 4-3, but rebounded the next day behind ace Rodrigo Lopez (Orioles). He pitched a four-hit shutout to beat Puerto Rico 3-0 and clinch the title for Culiacan—the second in six years under manager Paquin Estrada.

It didn't matter to Estrada that his club was again left to celebrate in a stadium emptied by the early exit of the home team.

"Every year we come to this tournament the underdogs, and each year we set out to prove we belong," Estrada said. "Every year we are determined to show this is

Miguel Tejada

more than just two games between the Dominicans and Puerto Ricans. This club believed in itself from the start.

"The hardest part of being a manager is when you are forced to motivate your team to perform. No such effort was required on my part this year. My guys were hungry from the start, and I believe it was our collective heart, as much as our execution on the field, that carried the day."

Dominican manager Bob Geren, whose Licey team had shown a similar penchant for such enterprises by upsetting Aguilas in the Dominican championship series, felt likewise.

"It's not always the team that looks best on paper that prevails in these short tournaments," Geren said. "The Mexicans were certainly not the most talented team in this competition, but they executed when it mattered most and played fundamentally sound baseball."

One League In, One Out

While it was a stable year in winter baseball's traditional Caribbean lineup, a new four-team circuit emerged in Panama after a 30-year hiatus.

The league was sanctioned by Major League Baseball and accepted into the Caribbean Confederation for a three-year probationary period, but the league elected to suspend operations after just one season.

Panama had winter ball from the 1940s to 1972 and participated in the Caribbean Series from 1949-60, winning in 1952. But most Panamanian prospects were not ready to compete at the same level as other, more experienced winter league players. Import players sent to Panama were also less experienced than those sent to the other Caribbean leagues.

Meanwhile, attempts to stimulate baseball interest in Australia were thwarted—if only temporarily—when the International Baseball League Australia suspended operations in the wake of the Sept. 11 terrorist attacks on New York and Washington.

Citing travel and security concerns in the aftermath of the attacks and the U.S. military response in Afghanistan, the IBLA canceled its season, which was scheduled to begin in November 2001.

"For the last eight weeks we have been working to minimize the impact these events have systemically had on the league," said Glen Partridge, IBLA's general manager for baseball operations. "Given their magnitude we have been forced to consider various fall-back scenarios for this year, and we have been working with (Major League Baseball) to assess the impact of these alternatives. In the end it became clear that none would represent an adequate replacement for the IBLA program. Given this, we are faced with no alternative other than to cancel this year's league."

The IBLA was in its second season as the latest attempt to give Australia a stable professional league. The previous winter, a mix of Australian, American and Asian prospects played in a four-team league. The league planned to return for 2002-03 with four clubs.

DOMINICAN LEAGUE

Aguilas dominated the regular season and first round of playoffs in the Dominican League in 2001-02, but the Licey Tigers turned the tables on the defending Caribbean Series champions with a return trip to the series on the line.

Licey, the most successful team in Caribbean Series history, beat Aguilas four games to three in a best-of-seven final, winning the final two games. But then Licey, winners of 10 Caribbean crowns, finished a disappointing second as the Dominican representative at the Caribbean Series.

The Tigers rode the arm of righthander Felix Rodriguez (Giants) to the Dominican title. Rodriguez had a hand in all four Licey wins, winning three and saving the other. Licey also got a strong effort from shortstop D'Angelo Jimenez (Padres), who led all hitters in the final series with a .464 average and seven RBIs.

LARRY GOREN

Eric Byrnes

Outfielder Eric Byrnes (Athletics) powered Licey in the regular season, winning league MVP honors. He narrowly missed a triple crown, tying for the league lead with 11 homers while finishing second in batting (.345) and RBIs (38). He hit .188 in 25 postseason games with no homers.

Aguilas wasn't able to hold off Licey in the Dominican final, even with a lineup bolstered by major league veterans Tony Batista (Orioles), Raul Mondesi (Blue Jays) and Miguel Tejada (Athletics). The stable of big leaguers joined the team late in the regular season after players like second baseman Bernie Castro (Padres) and third baseman Mendy Lopez lifted Aguilas to the pennant. Castro led the league in hitting (.349) and stolen bases (20), while Lopez finished among the leaders in all triple-crown categories.

Castro also led all players with a .490 average as Aguilas handily won the four-team round-robin. But he hit .188 in the finals as Batista (.296-2-7), Mondesi (.280-

2-6) and Tejada (.429-0-1) played a bigger role.

A number of the island nation's prominent major leaguers also didn't suit up until the end of the regular season. Vladimir Guerrero (Expos) and Alfonso Soriano (Yankees) played for Estrellas in the round-robin but weren't able to push the team into the final.

STANDINGS

REGULAR SEASON	W	L	PCT	GB
Aguilas	30	17	.638	—
Licey Tigers	30	20	.600	1½
Azucareros	26	23	.531	5
Estrellas	26	23	.531	5
Escogido Lions	19	30	.388	12
Pollos	15	33	.313	15½
PLAYOFFS	**W**	**L**	**PCT**	**GB**
Aguilas	13	5	.722	—
Licey Tigers	11	7	.611	2
Estrellas	10	7	.588	2½
Azucareros	1	16	.059	11½

Championship Series: Licey defeated Aguilas 4-3 in best-of-seven final.

INDIVIDUAL BATTING LEADERS
(Minimum 75 At-Bats)

	AVG	AB	R	H	2B	3B	HR	RBI	SB
Franco, Julio, Estrellas	.388	85	15	33	6	0	5	13	1
Castro, Bernie, Aguilas	.349	129	37	45	3	2	1	8	20
Byrnes, Eric, Licey	.345	174	36	60	9	1	11	37	3
Jose, Felix, Estrellas	.336	143	27	48	11	0	11	28	3
Polonia, Luis, Aguilas	.331	148	29	49	11	2	3	27	5
DaVanon, Jeff, Aguilas	.327	104	32	34	7	1	7	23	14
Lopez, Mendy, Aguilas	.323	167	33	54	8	1	10	33	1
Melo, Juan, Azucareros	.310	184	34	57	9	2	7	39	6
Jimenez, D'Angelo, Licey	.310	158	31	49	11	0	0	12	5
Rivera, Roberto, Azucareros	.308	120	16	37	5	0	2	14	2
Garabito, Eddy, Azucareros	.307	179	32	55	14	5	4	19	5
German, Esteban, Azucareros	.305	131	29	40	4	1	0	8	10
Betemit, Wilson, Escogido	.304	135	14	41	8	1	3	19	0
Ozuna, Pablo, Estrellas	.301	133	17	40	6	3	2	12	5
Mateo, Henry, Licey	.297	118	18	35	4	1	2	8	0
Martinez, Felix, Aguilas	.296	98	18	29	6	1	2	17	4
Abad, Andy, Licey	.295	112	16	33	7	0	3	19	1
Encarnacion, Angelo, Pollos	.294	136	15	40	4	0	1	5	2
Pemberton, Rudy, Estrellas	.288	104	15	30	4	0	1	13	0
Mackowiak, Rob, Escogido	.286	119	12	34	7	0	2	15	2
Sosa, Juan, Pollos	.282	110	13	31	6	1	3	10	3
Alcantara, Israel, Licey	.278	176	24	49	9	1	10	34	2
Veras, Wilton, Escogido	.278	158	18	44	7	1	5	18	1
Ensberg, Morgan, Estrellas	.274	164	31	45	7	2	10	32	2
Wilson, Desi, Estrellas	.265	155	13	41	6	0	3	19	2
Guzman, Elpidio, Escogido	.262	84	7	22	1	0	1	6	1
Castillo, Alberto, Aguilas	.258	132	11	34	7	0	0	16	1
Garcia, Guillermo, Aguilas	.256	180	33	46	11	0	8	33	0
Moreta, Ramon, Azucareros	.255	102	7	26	1	0	1	10	2
Pena, Carlos, Licey	.255	157	26	40	12	0	7	30	1
Ortiz, David, Escogido	.250	112	9	28	10	0	3	18	0
Rogers, Ed, Estrellas	.250	100	13	25	7	0	3	16	0
Perez, Santiago, Pollos	.247	85	13	21	5	1	2	9	8
Encarnacion, Mario, Aguilas	.246	134	18	33	9	0	4	16	4
Devarez, Cesar, Estrellas	.244	82	9	20	4	0	2	12	0
Nunez, Abraham, Estrellas	.244	160	28	39	4	3	6	19	4
Brumbaugh, Cliff, Azucareros	.238	101	12	24	4	0	3	16	0
Mateo, Ruben, Escogido	.237	114	14	27	8	1	6	16	0
Mercedes, Henry, Escogido	.237	93	17	22	2	1	4	15	0
Belliard, Ron, Licey	.235	153	21	36	8	1	3	15	0
Rosario, Melvin, Azucareros	.231	78	10	18	4	2	1	5	0
Mercedes, Henry, Estrellas	.226	133	24	30	3	1	6	21	0

INDIVIDUAL PITCHING LEADERS
(Minimum 25 Innings)

	W	L	ERA	G	SV	IP	H	BB	SO
Brea, Leslie, Licey	2	1	1.37	21	1	26	20	9	36
Torres, Mel, Licey	3	0	1.45	20	1	31	26	7	19
Pena, Juan, Aguilas	4	1	1.57	6	0	29	21	13	16
Perez, Odalis, Estrellas	2	2	1.88	8	0	48	31	11	45
#Harville, Chad, Licey	1	1	1.99	22	8	23	26	14	28
Montero, Agustin, Estrellas	2	0	2.13	26	0	38	23	15	34
Benoit, Joaquin, Aguilas	5	0	2.37	10	0	49	37	14	38
Nunez, Vladimir, Licey	4	0	2.48	6	0	33	30	8	30

Player									
Mercedes, Jose, Estrellas	5	2	2.62	11	0	55	54	5	48
Shouse, Brian, Licey	1	0	2.70	25	0	27	25	8	25
Ozuna, Gabriel, Azucareros	2	3	2.76	10	0	46	44	14	42
Heredia, Julian, Estrellas	3	3	2.88	21	1	41	33	10	60
Acevedo, Jose, Aguilas	2	0	3.04	13	0	27	21	8	19
Pichardo, Hipolito, Aguilas	1	0	3.21	9	0	34	29	5	24
Rodriguez, Ricardo, Azu.	4	4	3.27	11	0	44	42	15	32
Santana, Julio, Escogido	3	5	3.32	11	0	60	57	21	39
Coco, Pasqual, Escogido	3	2	3.40	11	0	53	48	12	39
Valdez, Efrain, Pollos	1	3	3.98	10	0	54	56	13	28
Miller, Justin, Aguilas	3	3	3.48	7	0	31	28	10	24
De la Cruz, Fernando, Azu.	3	2	3.49	18	0	28	21	19	11
Martinez, Jose A., Pollos	1	2	3.71	9	0	44	35	19	23
Nunez, Jose, Escogido	1	1	3.72	16	0	36	34	6	26
Soriano, Rafael, Escogido	3	3	3.76	12	0	26	23	8	24
Marte, Damaso, Pollos	**8**	2	3.83	32	0	54	46	25	**65**
Perez, Dario, Licey	4	2	3.86	13	0	68	76	9	35
Roque, Rafael, Licey	1	2	3.96	13	0	39	32	17	32
Padua, Geraldo, Azucareros	4	4	4.13	12	0	52	55	18	32
Jean, Domingo, Estrellas	0	2	4.13	34	2	48	50	15	55
Nunez, Jose, Escogido	1	1	4.19	19	0	39	37	9	29
Estrella, Luis, Licey	4	4	4.25	12	0	36	35	18	15
Hernandez, Fernando, Aguilas	3	1	4.45	8	0	32	31	16	29

Statistics in **bold** indicate league leader.
League leader but non-qualifier

MEXICAN PACIFIC LEAGUE

Righthander Rodrigo Lopez was a revelation in the 2001-02 Mexican Pacific League season. As was his team, the Culiacan Tomato Growers.

The 26-year-old not only fashioned a brilliant winter season, winning 16 games, but he also used it as the stepping stone to a breakout season in the big leagues. Lopez' contract was purchased midway through the winter season by the Orioles, and Lopez went on to become one of the top rookies in the American League in 2002.

The beneficiaries of Lopez' outstanding winter were the Tomato Growers, a surprise winner of the Caribbean Series after finishing dead last in the Mexican Pacific League the previous season.

Lopez had a brief, unsuccessful trial with the Padres in 2000, going 0-3, 7.86. He spent the 2001 season in the minors and became a free agent after the season when the Padres did not re-sign him or protect him on their 40-man roster.

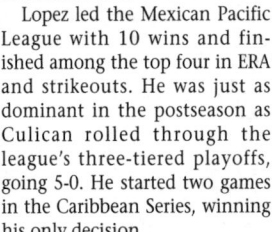

DAVID SEELIG

Rodrigo Lopez

Lopez led the Mexican Pacific League with 10 wins and finished among the top four in ERA and strikeouts. He was just as dominant in the postseason as Culican rolled through the league's three-tiered playoffs, going 5-0. He started two games in the Caribbean Series, winning his only decision.

Overall, Lopez went 16-2, 2.43 with 113 strikeouts in a winter-ball high 141 innings.

Lopez carried the load throughout the playoffs for Culiacan as the team's two biggest bats in the regular season went silent.

Brian Banks, who tied a league record by hitting three grand slams in a 14-day period and led the league with 54 RBIs, hit three homers in a first-round win over Obregon. But he went only 3-for-40 with two RBIs in the next two rounds. Kit Pellow (Royals) also slowed down at the same time. Pellow hit .283 with 16 homers during the regular season and belted four more homers in Culiacan's 4-1 romp over Obregon. But he went 6-for-37 with no homers as Culiacan defeated Hermosillo 4-1 and Mazatlan 4-2 to advance to the Caribbean Series.

Outfielder Darrell Sherman picked up the pieces for

the two sluggers, hitting .359 overall in the playoffs.

—ALLAN SIMPSON

STANDINGS

REGULAR SEASON	W	L	PCT	GB
*Culiacan Tomato Growers	41	27	.603	—
*Los Mochis Sugarcane Growers	38	30	.559	3
Mexicali Eagles	38	30	.559	3
Mazatlan Deer	38	30	.559	3
Hermosillo Orangemen	37	31	.544	4
Obregon Yaquis	29	39	.427	12
Guasave Cottoneers	28	40	.412	13
Navojoa Mayos	23	45	.338	18

*Split-season champions

PLAYOFFS—Quarterfinals: Culiacan defeated Obregon 4-1; Mazatlan defeated Hermosillo 4-3; and Mexicali defeated Los Mochis 4-1 in best-of-seven series. **Semifinals:** Culiacan defeated Hermosillo 4-1 in best-of-seven series; Mazatlan defeated Mexicali 4-3 in best-of-seven series. **Finals:** Culiacan defeated Mazatlan 4-2 in best-of-seven series.

INDIVIDUAL BATTING LEADERS
(Minimum 102 At-Bats)

	AVG	AB	R	H	2B	3B	HR	RBI	SB
Grabowski, Jason, Hermosillo	.318	132	24	42	9	0	7	33	2
LaRocca, Greg, Guasave	.316	155	26	49	14	1	12	32	5
Orantes, Ramon, Los Mochis	**.313**	201	30	63	8	0	11	27	1
Johnson, Rontrez, LM	.311	103	20	32	7	0	6	20	9
Prieto, Chris, Mexicali	.310	126	24	39	8	0	5	14	2
Smith, Demond, Guasave	.305	164	31	50	7	3	12	22	10
Bass, Jayson, Los Mochis	.303	211	46	64	6	1	15	36	11
Samuels, Scott, Mexicali	.303	241	40	73	12	0	12	42	21
Carrillo, Matias, LM	.301	166	29	50	7	0	14	33	0
Rojas, Homar, Obregon	.300	190	23	57	9	0	7	26	2
Salas, Heriberto, Guasave	.296	108	16	32	7	0	1	8	2
Lofton, James, Navojoa	.295	268	46	**79**	14	1	4	18	12
Smith, Bubba, Mexicali	.293	239	41	70	12	0	**19**	50	1
Gload, Ross, Los Mochis	.293	188	27	55	10	0	8	30	2
Cazarin, Manuel, LM	.292	120	12	35	8	0	3	17	1
Garcia, Cornelio, Hermosillo	.291	151	20	44	7	2	1	11	2
Fernandez, Daniel, Mazatlan	.287	209	28	60	6	1	0	12	7
White, Derrick, Mazatlan	.287	108	20	31	6	0	7	22	0
Munoz, Noe, Guasave	.285	207	32	59	13	0	11	34	3
Nelson, Bryant, Hermosillo	.284	169	24	48	10	0	9	23	4
Pellow, Kit, Culiacan	.283	244	45	69	14	0	16	48	1
Sherman, Darrell, Culiacan	.283	230	46	65	14	2	3	24	15
Castro, Arnaldo, Culiacan	.283	106	9	30	1	0	1	9	0
Cruz, Jacob, Mazatlan	.281	203	27	57	**15**	0	9	31	3
Punto, Nick, Culiacan	.279	154	32	43	6	2	2	21	7
Tellez, Alonso, Los Mochis	.279	122	16	34	7	1	10	22	0
Newson, Warren, Herm.	.279	208	36	58	11	0	11	33	7
Brown, Tonayne, Navojoa	.277	260	26	72	10	1	7	25	10
Sisco, Steve, Mazatlan	.275	273	41	75	14	2	7	36	0
Martinez, Ray, Mexicali	.274	219	28	60	12	0	9	25	2
Amezcua, Adan, Culiacan	.273	187	21	51	6	0	5	36	2
Mere, Pedro, Los Mochis	.273	172	28	47	7	2	8	25	2
Morejon, Oswaldo, Guasave	.271	251	32	68	12	2	3	22	2
Garcia, Luis, Obregon	.268	269	23	72	13	2	8	39	7
Velez, Manuel, Obregon	.267	105	12	28	3	1	2	7	0
Hubbard, Trinidad, Herm.	.264	216	35	57	6	1	4	22	**28**
Gastelum, Sergio, Mexicali	.264	239	**51**	63	11	0	4	34	8
Robles, Oscar, Navojoa	.263	133	15	35	2	0	2	13	2
Chevalier, Virgil, Navojoa	.261	253	31	66	8	0	11	28	2
Amezaga, Alfredo, Obregon	.260	246	39	64	9	**5**	0	14	23
Overbay, Lyle, Mazatlan	.260	131	18	34	8	0	4	25	0
Gomez, Heber, Mazatlan	.259	205	23	53	8	0	5	28	3
Grijak, Kevin, Mazatlan	.259	224	29	58	11	2	9	32	0
Canizalez, Juan, Hermosillo	.258	194	23	50	7	0	6	19	0
Sandoval, Jose, Mexicali	.257	218	32	56	7	1	9	21	2
Flores, Miguel, Mazatlan	.254	118	22	30	4	1	6	14	2
Young, Ernie, Mexicali	.253	229	35	58	7	0	15	39	4
Iturbe, Pedro, Guasave	.252	127	16	32	3	1	2	8	1
Guizar, Hector, Guasave	.250	120	14	30	4	0	4	14	1
Munoz, Jose, Culiacan	.246	130	20	32	3	0	2	7	2
Latham, Chris, Culiacan	.245	155	24	38	10	1	6	22	6
Zuniga, Tony, Mexicali	.244	238	43	58	8	0	13	**55**	0
Barnes, Larry, Obregon	.243	148	17	36	6	1	7	17	0
Gil, Benji, Culiacan	.241	116	18	28	7	0	4	18	5
Ojeda, Miguel, Mazatlan	.240	221	26	53	10	2	4	19	0
Banks, Brian, Culiacan	.237	241	38	57	**15**	0	**19**	54	1
Vizcarra, Roberto, Culiacan	.237	232	23	55	12	0	6	26	5

INDIVIDUAL PITCHING LEADERS
(Minimum 34 Innings)

	W	L	ERA	G	SV	IP	H	BB	SO
Perez, Oliver, Culiacan	3	1	0.76	14	0	36	24	14	38
Campos, Francisco, Mazatlan	5	2	1.66	12	0	81	64	20	89
#Revenig, Todd, Mazatlan	1	2	1.67	31	17	32	19	3	19
Valdez, Armando, Hermosillo	4	0	1.96	14	0	41	34	21	24
Ochoa, Pablo, Mazatlan	3	1	2.02	8	0	49	43	21	36
Padilla, Vicente, Culiacan	4	3	2.24	10	0	60	46	9	54
Ayala, Luis, Culiacan	1	1	2.34	31	13	35	25	6	32
Rivera, Oscar, Mazatlan	10	3	2.39	14	0	90	89	26	58
Ortega, Pablo, Mazatlan	4	5	2.40	41	2	45	37	16	25
Lopez, Jose, Los Mochis	8	3	2.48	35	15	40	30	10	41
Lopez, Rodrigo, Culiacan	10	2	2.49	14	0	87	67	31	69
Villarreal, Oscar, Mexicali	6	2	2.55	14	0	71	57	41	79
Reyes, Nahanael, Culiacan	5	3	2.68	15	0	57	46	27	29
Marquez, Isidro, Mexicali	1	3	2.79	36	17	39	31	12	27
Alvarez, Victor, LM	4	1	2.83	11	1	57	52	18	42
Lizarraga, Edgar, LM	1	2	2.95	30	0	37	34	18	30
Jimenez, Isaac, Navojoa	3	3	3.00	16	0	54	52	14	39
Quinones, Enrique, Culiacan	4	4	3.12	13	0	66	59	21	27
De La Hoya, Javier, Herm.	2	3	3.19	10	0	48	38	13	35
Parra, Julio, Navojoa	3	3	3.23	35	3	47	40	28	54
Moreno, Angel, Hermosillo	4	5	3.43	14	0	81	86	17	51
Franklin, Wayne, LM	2	1	3.47	6	0	36	28	10	34
Romero, Alejandro, Mexicali	6	2	3.48	13	0	62	45	13	58
Elvira, Narciso, Hermosillo	4	4	3.57	11	0	63	50	29	76
Rodriguez, Raul, Hermosillo	0	1	3.58	16	1	38	41	8	17
Campillo, Jorge, Culiacan	3	0	3.71	19	0	34	29	11	27
Magee, Danny, Obregon	1	3	3.89	6	0	37	40	12	25
Rodriguez, Salvador, Obregon	1	6	3.90	13	0	83	69	23	62
Armenta, Alejandro, Culiacan	2	0	3.93	12	0	37	30	20	27
Chavez, Carlos, LM	3	4	3.93	30	0	34	24	20	29
Neri, Eduardo, Guasave	4	2	3.98	40	0	43	40	15	53
Bernal, Manuel, Obregon	5	7	3.99	17	0	90	90	28	48
Palafox, Juan, Navojoa	1	2	4.02	12	0	81	87	26	50
Montemayor, Humberto, Obregon	3	4	4.06	14	0	82	78	26	64
Garcia, Gerardo, Guasave	2	4	4.06	15	2	44	48	16	42
Quiroz, Aaron, Navojoa	1	6	4.12	13	0	63	68	24	43
Leyva, Edgar, Guasave	1	6	4.14	13	0	63	69	28	58
Gonzalez, Gilberto, Guasave	4	2	4.17	13	0	73	66	32	62
Aguilar, Hugo, Navojoa	1	5	4.19	14	0	58	52	37	53
Atondo, Sergio, Guasave	4	5	4.45	12	0	61	53	41	56

PUERTO RICAN LEAGUE

The 2001-02 season was a disaster for the Bayamon Cowboys off the field, but a surprisingly successful one on it.

After a .500 record and fourth-place finish during the regular season, the Cowboys caught fire in the postseason and went on to represent the Puerto Rican League in the Caribbean Series.

Through it all, Bayamon attracted little more than 200 fans a game to Juan Ramon Loubriel Stadium—by far the worst support in the six-team league. Even the presence of one-time Puerto Rican star Carlos Baerga in a combined ownership/player role did not change the team's fortunes—at least not at the gate.

Ramon Vazquez

Baerga and his ownership group purchased the struggling franchise late the previous season after it had moved from Arecibo following the 1999-2000 season. A hard sell to begin with, the move to Bayamon was immediately undermined when improvements to Juan Ramon Loubriel Stadium weren't finished on time. The club was forced to play the first five weeks on the road, and finally came home out of contention.

Baerga promised bigger and better promotions in 2001-02, and a better team. The franchise continued to stagnate off the field, but Baerga's presence in the lineup lit a fire. Despite not playing in the big leagues since 1999, Baerga hit .346 in the regular season, second in the

league, and he continued to hit in the playoffs as Bayamon knocked off regular season champion Ponce in the first round and followed by toppling Santurce in a best-of-nine final. Against Santurce, Baerga went 12-for-24. He used his banner winter season as a springboard to returning to the majors in 2002 with the Red Sox.

The Cowboys retooled their pitching staff late in the regular season, and it was clear in the playoffs that the moves paid off. Chris Hammond (Braves) went 3-1 with a 1.93 ERA in four postseason starts and closer Brad Clontz saved four games in the final.

Caguas shortstop Ramon Vasquez led the Puerto Rican League in batting, at .361. His average was a league-best .379 when he learned the Mariners had traded him to the Padres with Tom Lampkin and Brett Tomko for Ben Davis, Wascar Serrano and Alex Arias.

Vazquez edged Ponce outfielder Miguel Correa to win the league's MVP award. Correa, the Lions' fourth outfielder when the season began, led the league with 13 home runs.

Carolina righthander Jon McDonald (Twins) went 4-2 with a league-best 1.72 ERA to earn Puerto Rico's pitcher of the year award.

—ALLAN SIMPSON

STANDINGS

REGULAR SEASON	W	L	PCT	GB
Ponce Lions	31	22	.585	—
Santurce Crabbers	28	25	.528	3
Caguas Criollos	27	25	.519	3½
Bayamon Cowboys	26	26	.500	4½
Carolina Giants	24	29	.453	7
Mayaguez Indians	22	31	.415	9

PLAYOFFS—Semifinals: Bayamon defeated Ponce 4-2; Santurce defeated Caguas 4-2 in best-of-seven series. **Finals:** Bayamon defeated Santurce 5-3 in best-of-nine series.

INDIVIDUAL BATTING LEADERS
(Minimum 81 At-Bats)

	AVG	AB	R	H	2B	3B	HR	RBI	SB
Rodriguez, Victor, Carolina	.393	122	16	48	7	0	1	11	1
Candelaria, Ben, Santurce	.383	107	16	41	7	2	5	22	3
Vazquez, Ramon, Caguas	.361	180	26	65	6	4	4	30	1
Baerga, Carlos, Bayamon	.346	159	30	55	12	2	5	28	4
Chimelis, Joel, Bayamon	.338	154	31	52	8	2	9	30	2
Fox, Andy, Ponce	.330	88	17	29	6	1	0	9	3
Gonzalez, Raul, Bayamon	.328	180	33	59	12	1	7	31	2
Leon, Jose, Bayamon	.320	150	35	48	8	2	9	28	3
Castro, Ramon, Santurce	.318	88	13	28	2	1	8	26	0
Winn, Randy, Santurce	.316	133	22	42	8	0	6	18	4
Figueroa, Luis, Carolina	.315	143	13	45	9	0	1	29	1
Matos, Luis, Caguas	.310	129	26	40	9	1	2	16	4
Feliciano, Jesus, Santurce	.309	97	16	30	8	0	1	11	4
Matos, Julius, Mayaguez	.304	161	20	49	10	2	2	27	1
Podsednik, Scott, Bayamon	.297	118	23	35	4	5	2	11	5
Ledee, Ricky, Bayamon	.295	88	17	26	3	2	5	17	1
Negron, Miguel, Caguas	.294	136	15	40	9	0	4	22	2
Torres, Paul, Mayaguez	.292	120	19	35	9	0	3	15	0
Warner, Michael, Ponce	.291	148	20	43	6	2	1	16	5
Lopez, Luis, Ponce	.288	163	17	47	10	0	1	14	0
Molina, Izzy, Bayamon	.287	101	18	29	1	0	5	18	2
Diaz, Alex, Mayaguez	.281	178	23	50	14	0	3	18	4
Flores, Jose, Santurce	.280	93	12	26	6	0	0	7	5
Correa, Miguel, Ponce	.278	144	32	40	5	0	13	26	4
Figueroa, Luis, Mayaguez	.276	181	21	50	2	0	2	15	11
Rowand, Aaron, Caguas	.274	117	16	32	4	0	5	17	2
Garcia, Omar, Bayamon	.273	139	28	38	12	0	7	36	1
Diaz, Edwin, Santurce	.273	172	30	47	13	0	9	25	3
Nieves, Raul, Caguas	.273	121	25	33	4	0	0	11	1
Villanueva, Hector, Caguas	.266	143	13	38	10	0	1	23	1
Cora, Alex, Caguas	.265	196	38	52	15	0	6	18	5
Powell, Dante, Mayaguez	.265	147	20	39	8	3	3	19	4
Echevarria, Angel, Santurce	.252	131	23	33	5	0	5	21	2
Vaz, Roberto, Ponce	.250	96	6	24	4	3	0	7	1
Espada, Josue, Carolina	.248	157	29	39	7	0	1	7	5
Santos, Angel, Santurce	.248	145	14	36	7	0	0	10	9
LeBron, Juan, Ponce	.248	157	19	39	4	2	11	37	1

	AVG	AB	R	H	2B	3B	HR	RBI	SB
Inglin, Jeff, Ponce	.246	126	20	31	4	1	6	25	0
Munoz, Jose, Mayaguez	.240	196	23	47	5	1	4	18	3
Gotay, Ruben, Carolina	.235	81	7	19	3	4	1	6	0

INDIVIDUAL PITCHING LEADERS
(Minimum 27 Innings)

	W	L	ERA	G	SV	IP	H	BB	SO
McDonald, Jon, Carolina	4	2	**1.72**	11	0	58	49	28	34
Jensen, Ryan, Bayamon	2	2	1.95	8	0	37	32	16	23
Mercado, Hector, Ponce	4	1	2.18	8	0	41	33	13	35
Gonzalez, Dicky, Carolina	2	2	2.22	10	0	57	46	13	36
Coppinger, Rocky, Ponce	5	2	2.25	10	0	56	44	18	54
Johnson, Mike, Ponce	5	1	2.28	11	0	55	47	23	33
Fogg, Josh, Caguas	1	3	2.31	7	0	35	33	13	24
Rivera, Saul, Caguas	1	1	2.33	21	1	27	20	9	20
Irabu, Hideki, Santurce	5	3	2.34	12	0	65	53	17	**61**
Schmack, Brian, Caguas	2	0	2.37	23	4	30	28	7	24
Bones, Ricky, Ponce	2	2	2.55	13	0	53	40	19	35
Cogan, Tony, Mayaguez	3	3	2.58	10	0	52	45	21	28
Agosto, Stevenson, San.	3	3	2.66	15	0	41	31	18	35
Fernandez, Jared, Santurce	1	1	2.68	11	1	40	37	16	31
Romero, J.C. Santurce	**6**	2	3.03	21	4	30	30	12	28
Collazzo, William, Carolina	4	4	3.08	11	0	38	30	11	22
Rodriguez, Jose, Bayamon	**6**	2	3.13	13	0	37	27	17	23
Montalvo, Rafael, Carolina	3	0	3.13	14	0	37	38	9	18
Politte, Cliff, Mayaguez	1	0	3.15	7	0	34	33	11	31
Serrano, Jimmy, Carolina	0	2	3.18	22	**11**	28	17	11	31
Lee, Derek, Mayaguez	3	1	3.27	15	0	33	36	10	14
Padilla, Juan, Caguas	3	1	3.48	21	1	31	36	12	20
Peters, Chris, Caguas	2	3	3.55	10	0	46	48	18	32
Miranda, Angel, Caguas	3	1	3.56	11	0	48	37	15	33
Villegas, Ismael, Caguas	4	5	3.57	13	0	53	50	30	40
Jordan, Ricardo, Bayamon	3	4	3.79	10	0	38	40	16	16
Arroyo, Luis, Bayamon	3	1	3.83	10	0	42	36	16	26
Alvarado, Giancarlos, Ponce	2	2	3.89	12	0	39	25	26	29
Calero, Kiko, Mayaguez	4	4	4.15	11	0	56	39	29	52
Ireland, Eric, Santurce	2	1	4.15	11	0	43	47	14	22

VENEZUELAN LEAGUE

Lara and Oriente were the class of the regular season in the Venezuelan League, but neither club was around at the end as upstart Magallanes surged in postseason play to represent the league in the Caribbean Series.

Magallanes entered the league's 16-game, round-robin playoff with the only sub-.500 record, then raced to a 12-4 mark in the five-team competition and whipped second-place Aragua 5-2 in the best-of-nine championship series. That made Magallanes host team for the Caribbean Series, which was played in Caracas.

Lara and Oriente were shorthanded for the playoffs as righthanders Jeff Farnsworth (Tigers) and Carlos Zambrano (Cubs), who went 1-2 in the league ERA race, were shut down by their parent organizations.

LARRY GOREN

Jeff Farnsworth

Farnsworth was Venezuela's top pitcher after posting a 7-0 record and 1.51 ERA while leading Lara to the Western Division title. In the process, he set a record for most consecutive innings without walking a batter: 53⅓ innings, bettering the record that belonged to Roberto Rodriguez (who played with the Cubs, A's and Padres) with 41 innings in the 1971-72 season.

"I can't believe it," Farnsworth said. "I came to Venezuela to play hard and this is what I want to do to get to the major leagues."

Farnsworth was left off the Mariners' 40-man roster after the 2001 season and was selected by the Tigers in the major league Rule 5 draft in the midst of his record run.

Oriente also lost Zambrano, 20, who was told to stop pitching by the Cubs in mid-December after he had worked in 73 innings, posting a 2.84 ERA. The Indians also clipped the Caribbeans in midstream, pulling the plug on lefthander Alex Herrera (2-1, 2.70, 13 saves), third baseman Luis Gonzalez (.297-5-26) and catcher Victor Martinez (.303-4-14). Those moves crippled Oriente's postseason hopes.

After hitting a league-high .284 during the regular season, Oriente hit just .198 in round-robin play as it dropped 14 of 16 games.

Veteran Aragua first baseman Roberto Zambrano was the overwhelming choice for MVP in Venezuela. He paced the league with 19 home runs, one shy of the record. Caracas outfielder Bobby Abreu (Phillies) hit .402 but didn't have enough plate appearances to qualify for the batting title. His younger brother Dennis (Cubs) also hit .369 for Zulia.

No hitter, however, was as hot as Pastora catcher/first baseman Ramon Hernandez (Athletics), who led the league with a .376 average and .462 on-base percentage. His .461 slugging percentage ranked third, and he added six home runs and 33 RBIs to earn Baseball America's Winter League Player of the Year award.

Hernandez remained hot in the round-robin playoffs, hitting .392 with four homers and 11 RBIs as Pastora was eliminated. He was added to the Magallanes roster for the Caribbean Series and led the event with a .474 average. Overall, Hernandez hit .388 on the winter season.

STANDINGS

EAST	W	L	PCT	GB
Oriente Caribbeans	34	28	.548	—
Magallanes Navigators	30	32	.484	4
La Guaira Sharks	28	34	.452	6
Caracas Lions	24	37	.393	9½
WEST	**W**	**L**	**PCT**	**GB**
Lara Cardinals	39	23	.629	—
Pastora	33	28	.541	5½
Aragua Tigers	33	29	.532	6
Zulia Eagles	26	36	.419	13
PLAYOFFS	**W**	**L**	**PCT**	**GB**
Magallanes Navigators	12	4	.750	—
Aragua Tigers	10	6	.625	2
Lara Cardinals	9	7	.563	3
Pastora	7	9	.438	5
Oriente Caribbeans	2	14	.125	10

Championship Series: Magallanes defeated Aragua 5-2 in best-of-nine final.

INDIVIDUAL BATTING LEADERS
(Minimum 93 At-Bats)

	AVG	AB	R	H	2B	3B	HR	RBI	SB
Abreu, Bob, Caracas	.402	102	29	41	6	0	8	25	6
Hernandez, Ramon, Pastora	**.376**	157	24	59	11	0	6	33	2
Abreu, Dennis, Zulia	.369	130	22	48	7	2	2	14	6
Rodriguez, Liu, Caracas	.361	183	30	66	**19**	0	0	18	4
Munoz, Orlando, Zulia	.358	134	17	48	8	0	1	15	0
Cabrera, Alex, Pastora	.341	132	28	45	10	0	13	27	0
Perez, Robert, Lara	.333	210	35	**70**	13	2	9	32	10
Alfonzo, Eliezer, Oriente	.330	176	33	58	9	2	7	32	0
Cabrera, Raymond, Lara	.329	170	22	56	4	3	3	27	1
Norris, Dax, Caracas	.327	211	25	69	15	1	5	33	0
Perez, Tomas, Oriente	.319	216	32	69	14	2	5	39	3
Acuna, Ronald, Magallanes	.314	153	23	48	12	2	2	26	4
Gonzalez, Wiki, Aragua	.313	131	17	41	7	1	4	24	0
Ryan, Mike, Aragua	.312	202	32	63	14	3	10	29	1
Salazar, Ruben, Aragua	.310	216	29	67	12	0	2	23	2
Ugueto, Luis, Lara	.308	107	17	33	6	2	1	11	6
Urquiola, Carlos, Pastora	.307	140	23	43	3	0	0	9	13
Zambrano, Roberto, Aragua	.306	209	38	64	16	1	**19**	39	0
Sanchez, Alex, La Guaira	.303	132	13	40	6	1	0	15	6
Machado, Robert, Magallanes	.302	192	25	58	9	1	6	34	1
Rivera, Juan, Aragua	.302	172	35	52	6	3	9	17	2
Jones, Chris, La Guaira	.302	192	28	58	10	0	10	28	2
Nicholson, Derek, Magallanes	.301	103	19	31	6	2	4	20	0
Redman, Tike, Oriente	.301	219	**43**	66	8	**5**	2	20	12

	AVG	AB	R	H	2B	3B	HR	RBI	SB
Freel, Ryan, Lara	.301	123	19	37	2	2	1	9	5
Lane, Jason, Caracas	.300	210	31	63	16	1	13	49	1
Cabrera, Miguel, Aragua	.300	180	24	54	11	1	5	18	0
Ramos, Jairo, Caracas	.292	120	10	35	6	1	1	9	0
Soto, Eminson, Pastora	.291	110	17	32	9	1	4	18	0
Chavez, Endy, Magallanes	.289	204	33	59	5	4	1	15	10
Cairo, Miguel, Lara	.288	104	16	30	9	1	2	14	5
Hernandez, Carlos, Mag.	.288	229	27	66	15	2	0	25	7
Cabrera, Jolbert, Zulia	.287	108	18	31	12	0	1	14	0
Jennings, Doug, Lara	.287	167	32	48	10	2	7	21	1
Wakeland, Chris, Oriente	.286	126	25	36	7	1	8	19	0
Alvarez, Tony, Caracas	.286	220	42	63	13	1	5	20	14
Scutaro, Marcos, Pastora	.283	205	33	58	10	1	2	24	4
Delgado, Alex, Lara	.282	103	13	29	3	1	2	15	1
Marquez, Jesus, LaG	.281	121	11	34	7	0	0	18	0
Romero, Wilfredo, Caracas	.274	190	23	52	11	3	4	18	3
Querecuto, Juan, Lara	.274	113	12	31	4	0	4	14	0
Castillo, Jose, Caracas	.273	128	18	35	5	1	3	19	0
Castellano, Pedro, Aragua	.273	187	23	51	8	0	7	36	1
Gibson, Derrick, Aragua	.271	166	26	45	10	1	7	31	5
Isturiz, Cesar, Lara	.271	199	26	54	3	4	0	16	15
Torres, Gabriel, Aragua	.269	93	9	25	6	0	2	14	0
Torrealba, Yorvit, Pastora	.267	161	15	43	9	0	2	17	0
Infante, Omar, Oriente	.265	136	23	36	3	1	1	17	4
Azocar, Oscar, La Guaira	.262	149	11	39	6	0	2	17	1
Olmedo, Rainer, La Guaira	.262	145	18	38	8	2	0	7	3
Bolivar, Papo, Magallanes	.261	157	21	41	9	3	1	30	2
Dillon, Joe, Magallanes	.260	192	32	50	10	1	3	22	4
Sandoval, Danny, Pastora	.256	203	26	52	8	2	0	5	4
Freire, Alejandro, Zulia	.253	221	31	56	12	0	7	24	0
Chavez, Raul, Magallanes	.250	116	7	29	2	0	2	12	0
Machado, Anderson, Zulia	.250	100	14	25	2	1	2	11	2
Gonzalez, Jesus, Zulia	.250	196	19	49	8	1	10	33	2
Paz, Richard, Magallanes	.248	101	19	25	9	2	1	14	1
Langaigne, Selwyn, Lara	.247	146	17	36	4	5	1	14	2
Prieto, Alejandro, Zulia	.245	155	23	38	8	1	4	18	1
Raven, Luis, La Guaira	.245	212	28	52	10	0	10	36	0
Colon, Cris, La Guaira	.244	172	15	42	4	1	2	17	0
Azuaje, Jesus, Lara	.243	206	24	50	8	2	2	26	2
Mendoza, Carlos, Mag.	.243	103	15	25	4	1	1	11	1
Pernalete, Marco, La Guaira	.242	124	17	30	11	1	0	7	3
Valencia, Victor, Zulia	.238	126	11	30	8	0	4	14	0
Freire, Alejandro, Oriente	.237	135	19	32	8	0	5	14	0
Ordaz, Luis, Zulia	.233	206	25	48	9	0	1	19	2

INDIVIDUAL PITCHING LEADERS
(Minimum 31 Innings)

	W	L	ERA	G	SV	IP	H	BB	SO
Carrara, Giovanni, Lara	0	3	1.32	26	15	27	18	2	21
Farnsworth, Jeff, Lara	7	0	1.51	10	0	66	55	5	38
Santana, Johan, Magallanes	2	2	1.57	8	0	46	38	15	43
Marquez, Robert, Oriente	3	2	2.10	28	1	34	33	8	23
Ramirez, Luis, Lara	2	0	2.16	22	0	33	30	7	16
Garcia, Rosman, Aragua	3	1	2.21	10	0	37	38	12	15
Harikkala, Tim, La Guaira	2	1	2.32	17	2	43	31	11	31
Heiserman, Rick, Aragua	3	3	2.51	25	2	32	37	14	15
Linares, Yfrain, Lara	3	1	2.62	22	0	34	26	12	35
Banks, Willie, Oriente	3	3	2.82	8	0	38	35	14	32
Zambrano, Carlos, Oriente	3	0	2.84	12	0	73	61	24	66
Manon, Julio, Pastora	7	2	2.85	11	1	66	60	22	70
Laxton, Brett, Magallanes	5	3	2.91	11	0	59	54	10	36
Lira, Felipe, La Guaira	3	7	3.01	15	0	90	85	14	60
Ahearne, Pat, Lara	3	2	3.05	7	0	41	38	12	23
Simontacchi, Jason, Aragua	3	3	3.06	12	0	68	70	11	43
Stull, Everett, La Guaira	6	4	3.07	15	0	76	60	22	61
Larreal, Guillermo, Pastora	1	1	3.11	5	0	38	32	19	27
Cedeno, Blas, Zulia	1	3	3.25	26	0	36	41	11	35
Murray, Dan, Aragua	2	2	3.34	20	2	57	58	30	38
Rincon, Juan, Lara	1	1	3.34	9	0	35	34	8	33
Kaye, Justin, Lara	4	2	3.34	27	4	32	24	16	36
Driskill, Travis, Caracas	2	3	3.36	14	0	64	53	18	63
Maduro, Calvin, Caracas	1	3	3.47	7	0	36	29	15	22
Cordova, Jorge, Oriente	1	1	3.50	14	0	36	41	13	26
Romero, Josmir, Aragua	1	2	3.58	14	0	38	37	14	25
Andrade, Jancy, Pastora	3	5	3.80	16	0	69	67	28	60
Hurtado, Edwin, Lara	6	5	3.84	13	0	70	72	22	52
Porzio, Mike, Lara	7	3	4.01	12	0	61	58	12	39
DeSilva, John, Zulia	4	1	4.01	8	0	43	45	10	40
Luque, Roger, Caracas	5	4	4.13	15	0	61	70	24	39
Lorraine, Andrew, Magallanes	4	1	4.19	7	0	38	43	7	23
Falteisek, Steve, La Guaira	2	3	4.19	9	0	39	37	9	24
Randolph, Steve, Aragua	5	4	4.43	12	0	65	66	35	50
Chacin, Gustavo, Lara	1	3	4.43	12	0	42	45	17	31
Estrada, Horacio, Pastora	4	5	4.43	14	0	67	69	19	48
Bost, Heath, Oriente	5	1	4.47	11	0	58	64	11	49

ARIZONA FALL LEAGUE
2001

Braves third-base prospect Mike Hessman ended the 2001 Arizona Fall League season in dramatic fashion by blasting a grand slam with two outs in the bottom of the ninth inning to give the Phoenix Desert Dogs a 12-8 win over the Grand Canyon Rafters.

Phoenix trailed 7-1 at one point in the championship, but chipped away at Grand Canyon's lead and ended the comeback by scoring seven runs in the final inning. The usual best-of-three series was replaced by a one-game playoff in 2001.

"We felt we had a chance, even after they got another run in the ninth inning," Phoenix manager Thad Bosley said. "We have battled back all season in games like this."

Lamont Mathews (Dodgers) and Mark Ellis (Athletics) led off the Phoenix ninth with solo homers, setting the stage for Hessman.

"It was awesome," Hessman said. "After we hit the back-to-back home runs to begin the inning, everyone in the dugout had the feeling we were going to do it."

Hessman, who hit .124 with three homers in 89 regular season at-bats, also doubled and scored in the fifth. Outfielder Marlon Byrd (Phillies) had four hits, including two triples, for Grand Canyon, which outhit Phoenix 14-9.

Hank Blalock

The AFL continued to be a showpiece for top major league prospects. Oddly, the two top-rated prospects—Hank Blalock (Rangers) and Drew Henson (Yankees)—played the same position for the same team (Peoria). Blalock hit .344 and hit a league-high 11 home runs, while Henson batted .314 with six homers.

STANDINGS

EAST	W	L	PCT	GB
Phoenix Desert Dogs	25	16	.610	—
Scottsdale Scorpions	22	19	.537	3
Mesa Solar Sox	17	24	.415	8

WEST	W	L	PCT	GB
Grand Canyon Rafters	26	15	.634	—
Peoria Javelinas	21	20	.512	5
Maryvale Saguaros	12	29	.293	14

PLAYOFFS—Phoenix defeated Grand Canyon in one-game playoff.

TOP 10 PROSPECTS: 1. Hank Blalock, 3b, Peoria (Rangers). **2.** Drew Henson, 3b, Peoria (Yankees). **3.** Brandon Phillips, ss, Scottsdale (Expos). **4.** Austin Kearns, of, Grand Canyon (Reds). **5.** Chin-Feng Chen, of, Phoenix (Dodgers). **6.** Marlon Byrd, of, Grand Canyon (Phillies). **7.** Michael Cuddyer, of, Grand Canyon (Twins). **8.** Bobby Jenks, rhp, Peoria (Angels). **9.** Kenny Kelly, of, Peoria (Mariners). **10.** Carl Crawford, of, Maryvale (Devil Rays).

INDIVIDUAL BATTING LEADERS
(Minimum 63 At-Bats)

	AVG	AB	R	H	2B	3B	HR	RBI	SB
Nicholson, Derek, Maryvale	.438	80	11	35	8	0	3	18	0
Hudson, Orlando, Scottsdale	.426	68	16	29	6	5	2	20	8
Ortega, Bill, Phoenix	.387	93	17	36	10	0	2	20	4
Crawford, Carl, Maryvale	.386	70	13	27	3	3	0	3	9
Wilson, Travis, Phoenix	.373	102	20	38	8	1	2	21	0
Kearns, Austin, GC	.371	116	27	43	10	1	4	31	1
Thurston, Joe, Phoenix	.369	111	26	41	6	2	1	14	7
Hill, Jason, Peoria	.364	66	12	24	7	0	2	11	1
Kelly, Kenny, Peoria	.351	111	24	39	7	0	7	21	8
Sanchez, Freddy, GC	.348	115	25	40	4	1	1	16	0
Luster, Jeremy, GC	.348	89	15	31	6	0	1	12	0

WINTER LEAGUES

MICHAEL WALBY

Thames, Marcus, Peoria	.346	81	15	28	4	1	4	20	0
Hill, Bobby, Mesa	.345	113	23	39	3	3	1	10	7
Blalock, Hank, Peoria	.344	122	31	42	8	2	11	36	5
Phillips, Brandon, Scottsdale	.344	93	19	32	10	0	2	16	3
Kelton, Dave, Mesa	.340	100	16	34	5	3	1	16	3
Hermansen, Chad, Maryvale	.337	83	18	28	7	2	5	20	2
Cuddyer, Michael, GC	.336	128	24	43	5	3	4	29	2
Gall, John, Phoenix	.333	69	14	23	8	1	3	18	0
Phelps, Josh, Scottsdale	.333	81	14	27	5	0	1	11	0
Byrd, Marlon, GC	.331	148	34	49	10	0	3	20	2
Dawkins, Travis, GC	.331	136	26	45	7	3	2	13	10
DeHaan, Kory, Peoria	.331	124	32	41	13	1	4	39	9
Requena, Alex, Scottsdale	.252	119	25	30	5	3	2	10	11

INDIVIDUAL PITCHING LEADERS
(Minimum 20 Innings)

	W	L	ERA	G	SV	IP	H	BB	SO
Kane, Kyle, Mesa	0	0	1.80	13	3	20	19	7	24
Gonzalez, Mike, Maryvale	0	1	1.99	9	0	23	15	11	23
Cyr, Eric, Peoria	2	1	2.18	8	0	33	24	12	27
Roberts, Nick, Phoenix	3	1	2.48	12	0	29	21	10	27
Olsen, Kevin, Mesa	0	3	2.57	7	0	21	22	4	22
Jamison, Ryan, Phoenix	3	1	2.73	13	0	26	19	11	25
Harrell, Tim, Phoenix	2	1	2.88	11	1	25	19	9	21
Nunez, Franklin, GC	1	0	2.89	7	0	28	23	14	19
#Ferrari, Anthony, Scottsdale	0	1	3.14	15	8	14	11	6	17
Childers, Matt, Maryvale	1	2	3.19	8	0	31	32	3	19
Blevins, Jeremy, Peoria	2	3	3.27	14	1	22	22	7	23
Izquierdo, Hansel, Mesa	6	1	3.28	13	0	25	23	5	16
Jenks, Bobby, Peoria	1	1	6.97	8	0	31	34	19	49

PANAMA

Winter baseball returned to Panama in 2001-02 after a 30-year hiatus. The new four-team league, sanctioned by Major League Baseball, was accepted into the Caribbean Confederation in 2000 for a three-year probationary period, but there were no plans to send a Panamanian team to the Caribbean Series in the near future.

With about 80 Panamanians under contract to major league organizations, the league was created because most Panamanian prospects are not ready to compete with more experienced winter-league players. Americans and other import players sent to Panama were also less experienced than those sent to the other Caribbean leagues.

DAVID SCHOFIELD

Carlos Lee

Thirteen Panamanians were drafted for each roster, including the likes of big leaguers Carlos Lee (White Sox) and Olmedo Saenz (Athletics), who went 1-2 in the batting race. Each team was allowed 12 imports. All games were played in Estadio National, a new 25,000-seat facility on the outskirts of Panama City.

Carta Vieja clinched the first title by sweeping Cerveza Panamá in a four-game championship series. Carta Vieja pitchers allowed just four runs in the four games. A local product, Bienvenido Cedeño, was the winning pitcher in two of the four games and spun a shutout in Game Three.

Saenz was on pace two-thirds of the way through the season to record the third triple crown season in Panamanian League history, but he slumped at the end. He finished with a league-best .331 average and five homers but had only 20 RBIs. Previous players to turn the trick were American Joe Atkins (.343-8-34) in 1951 and Panamanian Hector Lopez (.387-5-19), who played 12 seasons with the Athletics and Yankees, in 1954.

STANDINGS

	W	L	PCT	GB
Carta Vieja Roneros	24	17	.585	—
Cerveza Panama	22	20	.523	2½
Cerveza Atlas Tiburones	21	21	.500	3½
Azuero Macheteros	16	25	.390	8

Championship Series: Carta Vieja defeated Cerveza Panama 4-0 in best-of-seven final.

INDIVIDUAL BATTING LEADERS
(Minimum 63 At-Bats)

PLAYER, TEAM	AVG	AB	R	H	2B	3B	HR	RBI	SB
Saenz, Olmedo, Mach	.331	133	26	44	10	1	5	20	0
Lee, Carlos N., Mach	.327	113	12	37	6	0	1	12	3
Macias, Jose, CP	.323	155	18	50	5	1	0	16	10
Kelly, Roberto, CP	.303	142	14	43	12	0	3	29	1
Alvarez, Jorge, Mach	.300	140	15	42	5	0	0	16	0
Strong, Jamal, CP	.295	139	32	41	9	0	0	11	13
Seguignol, Fernando, CV	.292	89	8	26	4	0	1	8	0
Rivera, Ruben, CA	.278	126	18	35	10	1	3	17	4
Hankins, Ryan, CV	.267	120	14	32	7	0	0	12	2
Obando, Sherman, CA	.254	71	7	18	2	0	0	7	0
Wathan, Derek, CP	.252	135	18	34	6	1	0	8	7
Dent, Darrell, Mach	.252	103	21	26	1	1	0	2	9
De los Santos, Eddy, Mach	.250	120	15	30	6	0	0	10	0
Mosquera, Julio, CA	.246	114	9	28	5	0	1	12	1
Crisp, Covelli, CV	.235	85	15	20	3	0	2	10	10
Durango, Ariel, Mach	.228	127	13	29	7	1	0	15	2
Diaz, Einar, CV	.225	89	9	20	2	0	0	7	0
Hernandez, Michel, CV	.222	117	10	26	1	0	1	17	4

INDIVIDUAL PITCHING LEADERS
(Minimum 21 Innings)

PITCHER, TEAM	W	L	ERA	SV	IP	H	BB	SO
Pearson, Jason, CP	4	3	0.45	3	40	23	11	40
Kent, Steve, CP	1	2	0.83	0	33	18	13	23
Cortez, Jorge, CP	1	0	0.86	1	21	18	2	18
Felix, Bienvenido, CA	4	3	0.94	0	48	34	18	21
Gomez, Miguel, CV	5	0	1.12	0	40	30	10	23
Hunter, Johnny, CP	2	2	1.15	1	31	22	8	29
Cedeno, Bienvenido, CV	1	1	1.26	0	36	23	6	21
Rangel, Julio, CV	2	2	1.34	1	40	24	17	21
Garcia, Reynaldo, CA	1	1	1.88	0	62	41	28	56
Thompson, Chris, CV	2	2	1.96	4	23	21	6	16
Runser, Greg, CA	1	0	2.12	11	17	8	4	19
Ortiz, Javier, CV	5	3	2.29	0	51	35	21	33
Medina, Rafael, CP	5	2	2.18	0	58	45	27	47
Burgos, Enrique, CP	3	1	2.30	0	43	37	16	44
Picota, Len, Mach	6	1	2.31	0	66	53	30	58
Acosta, Manuel, CV	1	2	2.36	0	27	22	19	19

COLLEGE
BASEBALL

Return to glory
Texas captured its fifth College World Series title in 2002—and first under coach Augie Garrido

Longhorns reach into glorious past by running the table in Omaha

BY JOHN MANUEL

Twenty-seven years after Texas posted a 56-6 record—the best-ever by a College World Series champion—and beat South Carolina in the final, the two teams squared off again in the 2002 CWS championship game.

Texas was victorious again, beating the Gamecocks 12-6, for its fifth national title. The Longhorns ran the table, winning four consecutive games.

But winning the school's latest national title—the previous ones came in 1949-50, 1975 and 1983—was harder than it looked. The Longhorns had to sweat out a trio of one-run victories in pool play, though freshman closer Huston Street brought a veteran's savvy and sizzling stuff that opposing teams found impossible to solve. He saved all four games for Texas to earn tournament Outstanding Player honors.

It wasn't until the final, when they never trailed after scoring three times in the first inning, that the Longhorns opened it up offensively. Reserve outfielder Chris Carmichael hit the game's only home run for the Longhorns, breaking the game open with a three-run blast in the fifth.

South Carolina reached the final by scoring 41 runs in its previous four games, including decisive 12-4 and 10-2 wins over arch-rival Clemson to win its pool. But the Gamecocks were blown out 11-0 by Georgia Tech in its CWS opener

and forced to march through the loser's bracket. By the time they reached the final, they were playing their sixth game to Texas' fourth. The difference showed up quickly as South Carolina ran short on pitching.

The Gamecocks came with one win of becoming the second team under the two-bracket CWS format to battle back from an opening loss to win the national championship.

Balanced Attack

Texas featured a more power-balanced offense in 2002 than recent models, finishing with a school-record 68 home runs—but only after adjusting to the preseason loss of outfielder Ben King, their RBI leader in 2001. The reliance on power was quite a change for coach Augie Garrido, who had won the championship three previous times with Cal State Fullerton.

But even Garrido admitted that coaching in Austin, while aided by plentiful resources, was more difficult because of media scrutiny, lofty tradition and passionate fans with Texas-sized expectations.

"Texas had the most intense program and environment, and my Fullerton teams learned to play in regionals by coming and playing (ex-Texas coach) Cliff

Freshman Huston Street saved four CWS games

(Gustafson) and those great Texas teams in Austin," said Garrido, in his sixth year after taking over for Gustafson, the all-time NCAA Division I leader in wins. "They helped teach us what it took to win a regional. I really, really respect Cliff and what he accomplished."

Despite those obstacles, Garrido had a deep roster that weathered a tough Big 12 Conference season and strong CWS field to claim his fourth title as a coach. He also helped end a Big 12 Conference streak of futility that included an 0-8 record in Omaha since the league's inception in 1997.

"This team was very similar to those Fullerton teams," Garrido added. "It has a lot of speed, which you have to have to defend, particularly at Disch-Falk Field. It has good pitching. And we have added power, which was a factor in today's game."

Experience was another factor. Garrido's fourth Texas team, in 2000, also reached Omaha to end a six-year CWS drought. Nine players from that team were back for 2002, including catcher Ryan Hubele, first baseman Jeff Ontiveros, Carmichael and righthander Ray Clark. Junior-college veterans such as outfielder Dustin Majewski and versatile Brandon Fahey, who settled in at shortstop for the stretch run, helped lend an otherwise young team a veteran air.

"That year (2000) was a minor miracle, when we beat Arizona State in the regional and then got to Omaha," Garrido said. "That has played a key role in getting this team here. We still have players from that team, and they are able to say to the others, 'Whatever we do, whatever work we have to do and whatever we go through together, it's worth it.' "

Justin Simmons: Led nation in wins

The 2002 Longhorns went through plenty. They had to indoctrinate newcomers like righthander Alan Bomer, the erstwhile Iowa State ace who transferred to Austin after the Cyclones dropped baseball. They overcame King's injury, which required Tommy John surgery and deprived Texas of perhaps its most talented player.

Even in Omaha, the 'Horns had injury woes, losing left-hander Brad Halsey, the team's Friday starter down the stretch, to back woes. But pitching depth was a Texas strength, as sophomore lefthander Justin Simmons led the nation with 16 victories—two of them coming in the Series.

The Longhorns had more than enough depth to compensate for their adversity. King's injury opened space for outfielders like Majewski, a junior-college transfer who didn't become an everyday player until March. He finished the season as the team's top hitter (.401-10-50, 20 doubles) and was the outstanding player of both the Big 12 Conference tournament and Texas' regional.

While infielder Omar Quintanilla, the team's top hitter in 2001 as a freshman, sat out a 22-game suspension early in the season, Fahey asserted himself as a steady defender with a solid bat who could play virtually anywhere. Fahey took over at shortstop for the stretch run, with Quintanilla at third.

Carmichael, a seldom-used senior who missed the 2001

Omaha
June 14-22, 2002

STANDINGS

BRACKET ONE	W	L	RF	RA
Texas	3	0	16	13
Stanford	2	2	21	20
Notre Dame	1	2	11	12
Rice	0	2	4	7

Bracket One Final: Texas 6, Stanford 5.

BRACKET TWO	W	L	RF	RA
South Carolina	4	1	41	30
Clemson	2	2	26	39
Georgia Tech	1	2	23	18
Nebraska	0	2	18	21

Bracket Two Finals: South Carolina 12, Clemson 4; South Carolina 10, Clemson 2.
Championship Game: Texas 12, South Carolina 6.

INDIVIDUAL BATTING LEADERS
(Minimum 10 Plate Appearances)

	AVG	AB	R	H	2B	3B	HR	RBI	SB
Jeff Blevins, Nebraska	.625	8	4	5	3	3	0	1	2
Victor Menocal, Ga. Tech	.562	16	6	9	2	0	1	0	1
Jason Perry, Ga. Tech	.545	11	4	6	4	0	0	1	3
Omar Quintanilla, Texas	.471	17	6	8	2	2	1	0	2
Matt Murton, Ga. Tech	.462	13	4	6	2	4	0	0	0
Jed Morris, Nebraska	.444	9	2	4	6	0	0	2	2
Sam Fuld, Stanford	.421	19	6	8	4	0	1	2	0
Jeremy Slayden, Ga. Tech	.417	12	2	5	3	0	0	1	2
Roberto Valiente, Clemson	.400	15	1	6	2	1	0	0	1
Zane Green, Clemson	.389	18	4	7	5	1	0	2	1
Chris Carter, Stanford	.389	18	5	7	2	2	1	1	2

INDIVIDUAL PITCHING LEADERS
(Minimum 5 innings)

	W	L	ERA	G	SV	IP	H	BB	SO
Kyle Bakker, Ga. Tech	1	0	0.00	1	0	8	6	1	9
Ryan McCally, Stanford	0	0	1.29	2	0	7	2	1	3
Huston Street, Texas	0	0	1.42	4	4	6	2	3	5
Philip Perry, Ga. Tech	0	0	1.42	1	0	6	2	1	6
Steven Bondurant, S. Carolina	1	0	2.31	2	0	12	13	4	7
Steven Herce, Rice	0	1	2.35	1	0	8	8	1	8
Justin Simmons, Texas	2	0	2.57	2	0	14	13	4	7
Chris Niesel, Notre Dame	0	0	2.70	1	0	7	5	2	7

ALL-TOURNAMENT TEAM
C—Landon Powell, South Carolina. **1B**—Michael Johnson, Clemson. **2B**—Tim Moss, Texas. **3B**—Omar Quintanilla, Texas. **SS**—Victor Menocal, Georgia Tech. **OF**—Sam Fuld, Stanford; Justin Harris, South Carolina; Dustin Majewski, Texas. **DH**—Steve Stanley, Notre Dame. **P**—Justin Simmons, Texas; Huston Street, Texas.
Most Outstanding Player—Huston Street, rhp, Texas.

CHAMPIONSHIP GAME
Texas 12, South Carolina 6

SOUTH CAROLINA	ab	r	h	bi	TEXAS	ab	r	h	bi
Meyer ss	4	1	1	0	Moss 2b	5	1	2	0
Harris cf	5	0	2	2	Quintanilla 3b	5	2	4	1
Peters 1b	4	1	1	1	Majewski rf	4	3	2	2
Thomas rf	5	0	2	1	Rosenberg rf	0	0	0	0
Dyson dh	4	0	2	1	Ontiveros 1b	4	2	1	0
Gonce lf	2	0	0	0	Fahey ss	3	2	3	2
Bell lf	1	0	0	0	Hubele c	2	0	0	0
Smith ph	1	0	0	0	Carmichael lf	4	1	1	3
Seaton lf	0	0	0	0	Reininger dh	3	1	0	0
Greenwood ph	1	0	0	0	Hollimon ph	1	0	0	0
Buscher 3b	4	0	0	0	Napoleon cf	4	0	1	0
Powell c	4	2	2	0	Ferin pr-cf	0	0	0	0
Melillo 2b	0	2	0	0					
Totals	**35**	**6**	**10**	**5**	**Totals**	**35**	**12**	**13**	**11**

South Carolina	110	000	220— 6
Texas	310	031	04x—12

E—Buscher (13), Powell (8), Melillo (11), Moss (10), Fahey (4). **DP**—Texas 2. **LOB**—South Carolina 9, Texas 10. **2B**—Peters (22), Dyson (15), Powell (17), Quintanilla 2 (15), Majewski (20), Fahey (12), Napoleon (10). **3B**—Majewski (2). **HR**—Carmichael (2). **SB**—Fahey (9). **SF**—Dyson (6), Fahey (4), Hubele (7).

S. Carolina	ip	h	r	er	bb	so	Texas	ip	h	r	er	bb	so
Rawl L (7-2)	3⅓	5	4	3	3	2	Simmons W (16-1)	6⅔	8	4	3	2	4
Spigner	1	2	3	2	1	0	Bomer	⅔	1	2	1	1	1
Wesley	1⅓	2	1	1	2	0	Street SV (14)	1⅔	1	0	0	1	1
Campbell	1⅓	3	4	4	1	1							
Taylor	1	1	0	0	1	1							

HBP—by Simmons 2 (Melillo 2). **Balk**—Rawl. **T**—3:19. **A**—24,089.

season with a broken right wrist, played a pivotal role in the title game. He had started one game since a March series at Missouri but Garrido played a hunch by starting him.

Carmichael made Garrido look good, striking the game's decisive blow in the fifth inning. His three-run homer, making the score 7-2, was just his second of the year but showed the team's newfound commitment to power. Ontiveros, an undrafted senior whose 20 homers in 2002 and 55 in his career set school marks, did most of the damage.

Perhaps the most important development, though, was finding a closer. After trying several hands (including Bomer) at the job, Texas settled on Street, who seemed unfazed by anything, which makes sense considering his athletic pedigree.

His father James was an all-conference pitcher for Texas in the late 1960s, sharing top billing on the staff with future big leaguer Burt Hooton. But he earned more notoriety for leading the Longhorns to a 1970 Cotton Bowl victory that clinched a football national championship.

Street's quarterback qualities drew as many comparisons to his dad as his low-90s fastball and wicked slider. He got all 10 of his regular season saves against Big 12 or Top 25 competition, so he wasn't fazed by what he saw in Omaha.

He sewed up a pair of close wins against Stanford, then got the last five outs of the championship game, including the biggest one. He struck out Gamecocks slugger Yaron Peters, who led the Southeastern Conference in home runs and RBIs, when he was the tying run in the eighth inning. He became the first freshman to win the tournament outstanding player award since Miami's Pat Burrell in 1996.

Street also closed out the 15-year era of the one-game, winner-take-all end of the Series. CBS' contract to broadcast a one-game championship expired in 2002, and ESPN

COLLEGE WORLD SERIES CHAMPIONS: 1947-2002

Year	Champion	Coach	Record	Runner-Up	MVP
1947	California*	Clint Evans	31-10	Yale	None selected
1948	Southern California	Sam Barry	40-12	Yale	None selected
1949	Texas*	Bibb Falk	23-7	Wake Forest	Charles Teague, 2b, Wake Forest
1950	Texas	Bibb Falk	27-6	Washington State	Ray VanCleef, of, Rutgers
1951	Oklahoma*	Jack Baer	19-9	Tennessee	Sid Hatfield, 1b-p, Tennessee
1952	Holy Cross	Jack Berry	21-3	Missouri	Jim O'Neill, p, Holy Cross
1953	Michigan	Ray Fisher	21-9	Texas	J.L. Smith, p, Texas
1954	Missouri	Hi Simmons	22-4	Rollins	Tom Yewcic, c, Michigan State
1955	Wake Forest	Taylor Sanford	29-7	Western Michigan	Tom Borland, p, Oklahoma State
1956	Minnesota	Dick Siebert	33-9	Arizona	Jerry Thomas, p, Minnesota
1957	California*	George Wolfman	35-10	Penn State	Cal Emery, 1b-p, Penn State
1958	Southern California	Rod Dedeaux	35-7	Missouri	Bill Thom, p, Southern California
1959	Oklahoma State	Toby Greene	27-5	Arizona	Jim Dobson, 3b, Oklahoma State
1960	Minnesota	Dick Siebert	34-7	Southern California	John Erickson, 2b, Minnesota
1961	Southern California*	Rod Dedeaux	43-9	Oklahoma State	Littleton Fowler, p, Oklahoma State
1962	Michigan	Don Lund	31-13	Santa Clara	Bob Garibaldi, p, Santa Clara
1963	Southern California	Rod Dedeaux	37-16	Arizona	Bud Hollowell, c, Southern California
1964	Minnesota	Dick Siebert	31-12	Missouri	Joe Ferris, p, Maine
1965	Arizona State	Bobby Winkles	54-8	Ohio State	Sal Bando, 3b, Arizona State
1966	Ohio State	Marty Karow	27-6	Oklahoma State	Steve Arlin, p, Ohio State
1967	Arizona State	Bobby Winkles	53-12	Houston	Ron Davini, c, Arizona State
1968	Southern California*	Rod Dedeaux	45-14	Southern Illinois	Bill Seinsoth, 1b, Southern California
1969	Arizona State	Bobby Winkles	56-11	Tulsa	John Dolinsek, of, Arizona State
1970	Southern California	Rod Dedeaux	51-13	Florida State	Gene Ammann, p, Florida State
1971	Southern California	Rod Dedeaux	53-13	Southern Illinois	Jerry Tabb, 1b, Tulsa
1972	Southern California	Rod Dedeaux	50-13	Arizona State	Russ McQueen, p, Southern California
1973	Southern California*	Rod Dedeaux	51-11	Arizona State	Dave Winfield, of-p, Minnesota
1974	Southern California	Rod Dedeaux	50-20	Miami (Fla.)	George Milke, p, Southern California
1975	Texas	Cliff Gustafson	56-6	South Carolina	Mickey Reichenbach, 1b, Texas
1976	Arizona	Jerry Kindall	56-17	Eastern Michigan	Steve Powers, dh-p, Arizona
1977	Arizona State	Jim Brock	57-12	South Carolina	Bob Horner, 3b, Arizona State
1978	Southern California*	Rod Dedeaux	54-9	Arizona State	Rod Boxberger, p, Southern California
1979	Cal State Fullerton	Augie Garrido	60-14	Arkansas	Tony Hudson, p, Cal State Fullerton
1980	Arizona	Jerry Kindall	45-21	Hawaii	Terry Francona, of, Arizona
1981	Arizona State	Jim Brock	55-13	Oklahoma State	Stan Holmes, of, Arizona State
1982	Miami (Fla.)*	Ron Fraser	57-18	Wichita State	Dan Smith, p, Miami (Fla.)
1983	Texas*	Cliff Gustafson	66-14	Alabama	Calvin Schiraldi, p, Texas
1984	Cal State Fullerton	Augie Garrido	66-20	Texas	John Fishel, of, Cal State Fullerton
1985	Miami (Fla.)*	Ron Fraser	64-16	Texas	Greg Ellena, dh, Miami (Fla.)
1986	Arizona	Jerry Kindall	49-19	Florida State	Mike Senne, of, Arizona
1987	Stanford	Mark Marquess	53-17	Oklahoma State	Paul Carey, of, Stanford
1988	Stanford	Mark Marquess	46-23	Arizona State	Lee Plemel, p, Stanford
1989	Wichita State	Gene Stephenson	68-16	Texas	Greg Brummett, p, Wichita State
1990	Georgia	Steve Webber	52-19	Oklahoma State	Mike Rebhan, p, Georgia
1991	Louisiana State*	Skip Bertman	55-18	Wichita State	Gary Hymel, c, Louisiana State
1992	Pepperdine*	Andy Lopez	48-11	Cal State Fullerton	Phil Nevin, 3b, Cal State Fullerton
1993	Louisiana State	Skip Bertman	53-17	Wichita State	Todd Walker, 2b, Louisiana State
1994	Oklahoma*	Larry Cochell	50-17	Georgia Tech	Chip Glass, of, Oklahoma
1995	Cal State Fullerton*	Augie Garrido	57-9	Southern California	Mark Kotsay, of-p, Cal State Fullerton
1996	Louisiana State*	Skip Bertman	52-15	Miami (Fla.)	Pat Burrell, 3b, Miami
1997	Louisiana State*	Skip Bertman	57-13	Alabama	Brandon Larson, ss, Louisiana State
1998	Southern California	Mike Gillespie	49-17	Arizona State	Wes Rachels, 2b, Southern California
1999	Miami*	Jim Morris	50-13	Florida State	Marshall McDougall, 2b, Florida State
2000	Louisiana State*	Skip Bertman	52-17	Stanford	Trey Hodges, rhp, Louisiana State
2001	Miami*	Jim Morris	53-12	Stanford	Charlton Jimerson, of, Miami
2002	Texas*	Augie Garrido	57-15	South Carolina	Huston Street, rhp, Texas

*Undefeated

PLAYER OF THE YEAR

When Brooks Carey played for the Rookie-level Bluefield Orioles in 1978, he was struck by the athleticism, skills and work ethic of a 17-year-old shortstop.

Cal Ripken stood out on a team that won 19 games. Hall of Famers tend to do that.

Carey didn't have quite the same career and went into coaching, eventually becoming head coach at Key West (Fla.) High. Around 1990, he noticed a Little Leaguer in town who stood out almost as much as Ripken had.

"You could see he was different, this little kid who looks about the same as he does now, but who could really, really play," Carey says. "You could see the talent."

Seven years later, Carey was coaching Khalil Greene for Key West High, the little kid having grown up a bit but still standing out from the crowd. Carey had coaxed Ripken to come to the Keys for a fund-raiser, and had his old friend throw out the first pitch before a Key West game.

"You got any good players?" Ripken asked as he came to the dugout.

"Yeah, the shortstop, Greene," Carey replied. "You should watch him."

About then, Greene slammed a

Khalil Greene: Outstanding senior season

400-foot homer to left field to open the game. By the time Ripken left, Greene had a couple of more hits and a recommendation from the Orioles star, one that wasn't heeded in the 1998 draft.

In fact, no one drafted Khalil Greene out of high school and he lasted until the 14th round as a college junior, facts that seem impossible after his enormous senior season for Clemson. All he did in 2002 was redefine everyone's expectations for him, the way Ripken redefined the shortstop position.

"Nothing Khalil does surprises me anymore," says Clemson coach Jack Leggett, the main benefactor of Greene's gift of a senior season. "Whenever we need a hit, he gets a hit. When we need a play, he makes a play. It's amazing."

Greene went from a 14th-round pick of the Cubs in 2001 to the 13th overall selection, by the Padres, in 2002. His offensive feats, defensive gems and overall dominance made him an easy selection as Baseball America's College Player of the Year.

Greene, whose first name meaning "gift of God" comes from his Baha'i faith, batted .470-27-91, setting a Clemson single-season home runs record in the process. His 34-game hitting streak ended in a rare

0-for-4 performance in a 9-7 victory against Georgia Tech in the College World Series, but Greene made a leaping catch at short that helped save the game for the Tigers.

"We finally got Khalil out for once, and he probably saved the game with his glove," Georgia Tech coach Danny Hall said.

To Greene, that wasn't noteworthy. "I could really care less about a hitting streak," he says. "(The catch) was a big part of the game . . . I've always considered myself as apt defensively as I am at the plate. I think I'm an able defender, and I've been doing that for four years."

Scouts who saw Greene in his first two seasons at Clemson marveled at his savvy and instincts, which helped him step right into the lineup as a freshman. He was emerging as one of the nation's top third basemen and entered his junior year expecting to get drafted.

But for the first time, baseball didn't come easy for Greene. Leggett asked him to switch positions with Jeff Baker, himself a two-time All-American, and Greene moved back to shortstop.

He pressed at the plate, though, slumping to the .260s at midseason before finishing with a flourish at .303-12-52. The Cubs drafted him, but Greene says he didn't seriously consider signing.

"When I was drafted that low, it was going to take something special for me to sign," he says. "I just wanted to come back and have a better year than I had as a junior. I wanted to average 100 hits a year, and I only had 73 last year (after 98 in each of his first two seasons)."

Greene had 129 hits entering the CWS and had three hits in the Tigers' opener, making him just the second player in Division I history to pass 400 hits (Phil Stephenson of Wichita State from 1979-82 is the other).

–JOHN MANUEL

PREVIOUS WINNERS

1981	Mike Sodders, 3b, Arizona State
1982	Jeff Ledbetter, of-lhp, Florida State
1983	Dave Magadan, 1b, Alabama
1984	Oddibe McDowell, of, Arizona State
1985	Pete Incaviglia, of, Oklahoma State
1986	Casey Close, of, Michigan
1987	Robin Ventura, 3b, Oklahoma State
1988	John Olerud, 1b-lhp, Washington State
1989	Ben McDonald, rhp, Louisiana State
1990	Mike Kelly, of, Arizona State
1991	David McCarty, 1b, Stanford
1992	Phil Nevin, 3b, Cal State Fullerton
1993	Brooks Kieschnick, dh-rhp, Texas
1994	Jason Varitek, c, Georgia Tech
1995	Todd Helton, 1b-lhp, Tennessee
1996	Kris Benson, rhp, Clemson
1997	J.D. Drew, of, Florida State
1998	Jeff Austin, rhp, Stanford
1999	Jason Jennings, rhp, Baylor
2000	Mark Teixeira, 3b, Georgia Tech
2001	Mark Prior, rhp, Southern California

THE ROAD TO OMAHA

SUPER-REGIONALS

June 7-9; 16 teams, eight best-of-3 series (Winners advance to College World Series)

REGIONALS

May 31-June 3; 64 teams, 16 double-elimination tournaments (Winners advance to super-regionals)
*Automatic qualifier

NOTRE DAME

■ **Super-Regional Site:** Tallahassee, Fla. (Florida State).
Participants: Notre Dame (47-15) at Florida State (59-12).
(Notre Dame wins 2-1, advances to College World Series).

❑ **Regional Site:** Tallahasse, Fla. (Florida State).
Participants: *No. 1 Florida State (56-12), *No. 2 Central Florida (40-20), No. 3 South Florida (33-27), No. 4 Stetson (42-17).
Champion: Florida State (3-0). **Runner-Up:** South Florida (2-2).
Outstanding Player: Tony Richie, c, Florida State.

❑ **Regional Site:** South Bend, Ind. (Notre Dame).
Participants: No. 1 South Alabama (41-17), *No. 2 Notre Dame (44-15), *No. 3 Ohio State (36-18), *No. 4 Kent State (37-20).
Champion: Notre Dame (3-0). **Runner-Up:** Ohio State (2-2).
Outstanding Player: Steve Sollmann, 2b, Notre Dame.
(Florida State advances to meet Notre Dame in super-regional).

STANFORD

■ **Super Regional Site:** Stanford, Calif. (Stanford).
Participants: Southern California (37-22) at Stanford (43-16).
(Stanford wins 2-0, advances to College World Series).

❑ **Regional Site:** Los Angeles. (Southern California).
Participants: *No. 1 Southern California (34-22), *No. 2 Cal State Northridge (40-15), *No. 3 Maine (40-15), *No. 4 Brigham Young (29-29).
Champion: Southern California (3-0). **Runner-Up:** Brigham Young (2-2).
Outstanding Player: David Jensen, 1b, Brigham Young.

❑ **Regional Site:** Stanford, Calif. (Stanford).
Participants: No. 1 Stanford (42-14), No. 2 Long Beach State (35-21), No. 3 San Jose State (45-15), No. 4 Cal State Fullerton (36-20).
Champion: Stanford (3-0). **Runner-Up:** Long Beach State (2-2).
Outstanding Player: Jeremy Guthrie, rhp, Stanford.
(Southern California advances to meet Stanford in super-regional).

TEXAS

■ **Super Regional Site:** Austin Texas (Texas).
Participants: Houston (43-20) at Texas (51-14).
(Texas wins 2-1, advances to College World Series).

❑ **Regional Site:** Austin, Texas (Texas).
Participants: *No. 1 Texas (48-14), No. 2 Baylor (34-24), *No. 3 Lamar (35-22), *No. 4 Central Connecticut State (34-21).
Champion: Texas (3-0). **Runner-Up:** Baylor (2-2).
Outstanding Player: Dustin Majewski, of, Texas.

❑ **Regional Site:** Tempe, Ariz. (Arizona State).
Participants: No. 1 Houston (44-15), No. 2 Arizona State (35-19), *No. 3 San Diego (38-21), *No. 4 New Mexico State (37-23).
Champion: Houston (3-0). **Runner-Up:** Arizona State (2-2).
Outstanding Player: Keith Whatley, of-dh, Houston.
(Houston advances to meet Texas in super-regional).

RICE

■ **Super Regional Site:** Houston (Rice).
Participants: Louisiana State (4420) at Rice (50-12).
(Rice wins 2-0, advances to College World Series).

❑ **Regional Site:** Baton Rouge, La. (Louisiana State).
Participants: No. 1 Louisiana State (40-19), No. 2 Louisiana-Lafayette (37-21), No. 3 Tulane (35-25), *No. 4 Southern (45-8).
Champion: Louisiana State (4-1). **Runner-Up:** Louisiana-Lafayette (2-2).
Outstanding Player: Jake Tompkins, rhp, Louisiana State.

❑ **Regional Site:** Houston (Rice).

Participants: *No. 1 Rice (47-11), No. 2 Texas Tech (41-18), No. 3 Washington (30-25), *No. 4 Harvard (20-24).
Champion: Rice (3-1). **Runner-Up:** Washington (2-2).
Outstanding Player: Vince Sinisi, 1b, Rice.
(Louisiana State advances to meet Rice in super-regional).

CLEMSON

■ **Super Regional Site:** Clemson, S.C. (Clemson).
Participants: Arkansas (34-26) at Clemson (50-14).
(Clemson wins 2-1, advances to College World Series).

❑ **Regional Site:** Wichita, Kan. (Wichita State).
Participants: *No. 1 Wichita State (46-15), No. 2 Oklahoma (35-25), No. 3 Arkansas (31-26), *No. 4 Oral Roberts (46-17).
Champion: Arkansas (3-0). **Runner-Up:** Oral Roberts (2-2).
Outstanding Player: Nick Pitts, 1b, Arkansas.

❑ **Regional Site:** Clemson, S.C. (Clemson).
Participants: No. 1 Clemson (47-14), *No. 2 East Carolina (41-18), No. 3 Elon (34-21), *No. 4 Georgia Southern (38-23).
Champion: Clemson (3-0). **Runner-Up:** East Carolina (2-2).
Outstanding Player: Khalil Greene, ss, Clemson.
(Arkansas advances to meet Clemson in super-regional).

NEBRASKA

■ **Super Regional Site:** Lincoln, Neb. (Nebraska).
Participants: Ricmond (52-11) at Nebraska (45-18).
(Nebraska wins 2-1, advances to College World Series).

❑ **Regional Site:** Winston-Salem, N.C. (Wake Forest).
Participants: No. 1 Wake Forest (44-11), *No. 2 Richmond (49-10), *No. 3 Navy (22-23), No. 4 George Washington (42-21).
Champion: Richmond (3-1). **Runner-Up:** Wake Forest (3-2).
Outstanding Player: Vito Chiavallotti, 1b, Richmond.

❑ **Regional Site:** Lincoln, Neb. (Nebraska).
Participants: No. 1 Nebraska (42-18), No. 2 Southwest Missouri State (41-19), *No. 3 Marist (40-12), *No. 4 Wisconsin-Milwaukee (36-18).
Champion: Nebraska (3-0). **Runner-Up:** Southwest Missouri State (2-2).
Outstanding Player: Shane Komine, rhp, Nebraska.
(Richmond advances to meet Nebraska in super-regional).

SOUTH CAROLINA

■ **Super Regional Site:** Columbia, S.C. (South Carolina).
Participants: Miami (33-27) at South Carolina (51-15).
(South Carolina wins 2-1, advances to College World Series).

❑ **Regional Site:** Gainesville, Fla. (Florida).
Participants: No. 1 Florida (43-17), No. 2 Florida International (41-18), No. 3 Miami (30-26), *No. 4 Bethune-Cookman (38-20).
Champion: Miami (3-1). **Runner-Up:** Florida (3-2).
Outstanding Player: None selected.

❑ **Regional Site:** Columbia, S.C. (South Carolina).
Participants: No. 1 South Carolina (48-14), No. 2 North Carolina (40-19), No. 3 James Madison (43-14), No. 4 Virginia Commonwealth (38-25).
Champion: South Carolina (3-1). **Runner-Up:** North Carolina (3-2).
Outstanding Player: Yaron Peters, 1b, South Carolina.
(Miami advances to meet South Carolina in super-regional).

GEORGIA TECH

■ **Super Regional Site:** Atlanta, Ga. (Georgia Tech).
Participants: Florida Atlantic (46-19) at Georgia Tech (49-14).
(Georgia Tech wins 2-0, advances to College World Series).

❑ **Regional Site:** Atlanta, Ga. (Georgia Tech).
Participants: No. 1 Georgia Tech (64-14), No. 2 Georgia (30-27), No. 3 Louisville (39-16), No. 4 Coastal Carolina (43-17).
Champion: Georgia Tech (3-0). **Runner-Up:** Georgia (2-2).
Outstanding Player: Victor Menocal, ss-rhp, Georgia Tech.

❑ **Regional Site:** Tuscaloosa, Ala. (Alabama).
Participants: *No. 1 Alabama (48-13), No. 2 Auburn (34-24), No. 3 Florida Atlantic (43-18), *No. 4 Southeast Missouri State (36-18).
Champion: Florida Atlantic (3-1). **Runner-Up:** Alabama (3-2).
Outstanding Player: L.J. Biernbaum, of, Florida Atlantic.
(Florida Atlantic advances to meet Georgia Tech in super-regional).

takes over start-to-finish coverage beginning in 2003.

With the change in broadcast partners comes a change in CWS format. The two separate four-team brackets will now feed into a best-of-three title series that will stretch the tournament to a 12-day affair.

Changes To The Tournament

The eight-team field the 'Horns toppled in Omaha was stout—the only team that could be called a Cinderella was Notre Dame, ranked fifth in the preseason but making its first CWS trip since 1957. It also featured the home team, Nebraska, for the second straight year, and the Huskers set attendance records in each of their two games of the event, with a record 25,581 attending the Sunday session.

All-American outfielder Steve Stanley led Notre Dame to first CWS in 45 years

However, the 64-team regional tournament field was watered down and severely impacted by the aftermath of the Sept. 11, 2001, terrorist attacks on the United States.

The NCAA reacted to the tragedy by mandating reduced air travel for regionals, which affected almost every aspect of the tournament except for the seeding of the top eight teams. With few exceptions, the 64 teams selected were placed in regionals within 400 miles of their campuses—meaning a bus trip instead of a flight. Instead of spreading seeded teams equitably between regionals, the Division I baseball committee was forced to defer to tight geographical constraints. In several cases, teams from the same conference ended up in the same regionals—something that had never previously occurred.

"(The emphasis on geography) makes it harder, definitely," said committee chairman Wally Groff, the athletic director at Texas A&M whose term ended after the 2002 season. "When you are reviewing the brackets, it doesn't make a lot of sense, the weight of some compared to others. It's a less flexible situation than we've had in the past."

The end result of the geography-based changes were unbalanced regionals. The most lopsided example—probably the most difficult regional in NCAA history—happened at Stanford, where the Cardinal overcame a field

that included Big West powers Long Beach State and Cal State Fullerton as well as San Jose State. All four clubs were ranked in the Top 25 at the time and had been to the CWS within the last five seasons.

Stanford, which drew Cal State Fullerton in its first-round game, won that regional and made it four straight trips to Omaha with a super-regional victory the following weekend against Southern California. It was the second time in four years of super-regional play that the two Pacific-10 Conference powers had been forced to play for one Series berth, and USC coach Mike Gillespie was none too pleased about it.

In response to a question about whether the tournament was set up to "knock off as many West Coast teams as possible," Gillespie responded: "I don't think it's even debatable; I think it's a slam dunk. I think it is shameful that the NCAA chose to use the tragedy of Sept. 11 as an excuse for what they did. It's a sham; it's ridiculous. I don't buy it, I didn't buy it when it happened and I don't buy it now, and I don't care who knows about it. It's sickening."

Weak Talent Pool

Overall, the 2002 season was an uninspiring season for college talent. That was thanks to an unusually weak junior class, which saw several top players struggle through difficult years. Rutgers righthander Bobby Brownlie, the consensus top talent at the start of the year, went only 6-6 and slipped to the 21st pick overall in the draft. Clemson third baseman Jeff Baker, the top position talent entering the season, fell to the fourth round.

However, it opened the door for a strong group of seniors to make their mark. Clemson shortstop Khalil Greene was not only the nation's top senior but its top player, earning Baseball America's College Player of the Year award. He

---

RPI RANKINGS

The Ratings Percentage Index (RPI) is a primary tool used by the NCAA in selecting at-large teams for the 64-team Division I regional field. The 2002 rankings reflect a strong year for the Atlantic Coast Conference, with four teams ranked in the top six. The accompanying chart is the final, official 2002 RPI rankings, with records against Division I opponents. Asterisks denote teams that did not get a regional bid; the team's final rank in Baseball America's Top 25 is noted in parentheses. College World Series teams are in boldface.

Team	Record	Team	Record	Team	Record
1. **Clemson** (3)	54-17	17. Louisiana-Lafayette	39-23	34. Coastal Carolina	44-19
2. Florida State (7)	60-14	18. Wichita State (23)	46-17	35. Fla. International	41-20
3. **Texas** (1)	55-15	19. South Alabama	42-19	36. Auburn	34-26
4. **South Carolina** (2)	57-18	20. Georgia	31-27	37. Florida Atlantic (19)	46-21
5. **Georgia Tech** (8)	50-16	21. Long Beach State (21)	39-21	38. South Florida	35-29
6. Wake Forest (12)	47-13	22. **Notre Dame** (6)	49-18	39. SW Missouri State	43-21
7. Houston (10)	48-17	23. Arkansas (25)	31-28	40. Central Florida	41-22
8. **Stanford** (4)	47-18	24. Arizona State (22)	37-21	41. *North Carolina State	32-26
9. Louisiana State (11)	44-22	25. Baylor	34-25	42. Louisville	39-18
10. **Rice** (5)	52-14	26. Cal State Fullerton	36-22	43. *Oklahoma State	37-21
11. Florida (15)	45-19	27. James Madison	44-15	44. Cal State Northridge (18)	41-17
12. Alabama (13)	50-15	28. Texas Tech	41-20	45. *Delaware	34-22
13. North Carolina (17)	42-21	29. Southern California (14)	37-24	46. *Rutgers	35-22
14. **Nebraska** (9)	46-21	30. Stetson	42-19	47. *Texas Christian	30-29
15. Richmond (16)	53-13	31. *Mississippi	37-19	48. *UNC Wilmington	36-21
16. Miami, Fla. (20)	34-29	32. Oklahoma	35-27	49. Elon	34-23
		33. East Carolina	43-20	50. *Mississippi State	33-24

2002 COLLEGE ALL-AMERICA TEAM

Selected by Baseball America

Jeff Baker

Brad Sullivan

Bryan Bullington

Tim Stauffer

Russ Adams

FIRST TEAM

Pos.	Player, Team	YR	Hometown	AVG	AB	R	H	2B	3B	HR	RBI	SB	Drafted/Round
C	Tony Richie, Florida State	So.	Jacksonville	.353	249	59	88	17	2	13	75	1	Not eligible
1B	Yaron Peters, South Carolina	Sr.	Sherman Oaks, Calif.	.377	281	81	106	22	0	29	95	6	Braves (10)
2B	Russ Adams, North Carolina	Jr.	Laurinburg, N.C.	.370	254	75	94	20	3	7	55	45	Blue Jays (1)
3B	Jeff Baker, Clemson	Jr.	Woodbridge, Va.	.325	265	71	86	12	2	25	87	17	Rockies (4)
SS	Khalil Greene, Clemson	Sr.	Key West, Fla.	.470	285	93	134	33	1	27	91	17	Padres (1)
OF	Sam Fuld, Stanford	So.	Durham, N.H.	.375	293	67	110	20	4	8	47	8	Not eligible
OF	Bobby Malek, Michigan State	Jr.	Canton, Mich.	.402	219	66	88	21	3	16	66	16	Mets (4)
OF	Steve Stanley, Notre Dame	Sr.	South Bend, Ind.	.439	271	77	119	17	4	1	36	32	Athletics (2)
DH	Rickie Weeks, Southern	So.	Alta. Springs, Fla.	.495	198	82	98	15	12	20	96	10	Not eligible
UT	Jesse Crain, Houston	Jr.	Louisville, Colo.	.309	262	51	81	13	0	11	47	3	Twins (2)

Pos.	Player, Team	YR	Hometown	W	L	ERA	G	SV	IP	H	BB	SO	Drafted/Round
P	Bryan Bullington, Ball State	Jr.	Madison, Ind.	11	3	2.84	15	0	105	88	18	139	Pirates (1)
P	Jeremy Guthrie, Stanford	Jr.	Ashland, Ore.	13	2	2.51	20	0	158	138	36	136	Indians (1)
P	Tim Stauffer, Richmond	So.	Saratoga Springs, N.Y.	15	3	1.54	20	0	146	110	34	140	Not eligible
P	Brad Sullivan, Houston	So.	Nederland, Texas	13	1	1.82	18	0	129	80	49	157	Not eligible
RP	Royce Ring, San Diego State	Jr.	San Diego	5	1	1.85	36	17	39	29	13	54	White Sox (1)
UT	Jesse Crain, Houston	Jr.	Louisville, Colo.	4	0	0.23	27	10	38	22	10	46	

SECOND TEAM

Pos.	Player, Team	YR	Hometown	AVG	AB	R	H	2B	3B	HR	RBI	SB	Drafted/Round
C	Chris Snyder, Houston	Jr.	Houston	.343	230	59	79	13	0	15	71	8	D'backs (2)
1B	Vince Sinisi, Rice	Fr.	The Woodlands, Texas	.428	271	65	116	22	2	11	80	13	Not eligible
2B	Brian Burgamy, Wichita State	Jr.	Lawton, Okla.	.400	240	68	96	15	3	4	57	24	Padres (9)
3B	Pat Osborn, Florida	Jr.	Bakersfield, Calif.	.414	251	67	104	17	1	17	76	7	Indians (2)
SS	Stephen Drew, Florida State	Fr.	Hahira, Ga.	.402	204	64	82	15	4	16	54	13	Not eligible
OF	Curtis Granderson, Illinois-Chicago	Jr.	Lynwood, Ill.	.483	207	76	100	23	4	9	45	17	Tigers (3)
OF	Darryl Lawhorn, East Carolina	Fr.	Wilmington, N.C.	.416	250	56	104	12	3	19	68	15	Not eligible
OF	Chris Maples, North Carolina	Sr.	Hillsborough, N.C.	.347	274	62	95	24	1	23	79	16	Tigers (6)
DH	John McCurdy, Maryland	Jr.	Crofton, Md.	.443	221	67	98	20	4	19	77	20	Athletics (1)
UT	Ben Fritz, Fresno State	Jr.	San Jose, Calif.	.283	230	47	65	17	0	14	54	0	Athletics (1)

Pos.	Player, Team	YR	Hometown	W	L	ERA	G	SV	IP	H	BB	SO	Drafted/Round
SP	Kyle Bakker, Georgia Tech	So.	Omaha, Neb.	13	2	3.14	19	0	135	132	24	115	Not eligible
SP	Shane Komine, Nebraska	Sr.	Honolulu, Hawaii	10	0	2.33	15	0	96	62	30	115	Athletics (9)
SP	Justin Simmons, Texas	So.	DeSoto, Texas	16	1	2.52	20	0	128	106	39	80	Not eligible
SP	Kyle Sleeth, Wake Forest	So.	Westminster, Colo.	14	0	2.97	18	0	118	115	41	113	Not eligible
RP	Blake Taylor, South Carolina	Sr.	Columbus, Ga.	6	1	2.63	37	21	86	78	44	79	Indians (39)
UT	Ben Fritz, Fresno State	Jr.	San Jose, Calif.	9	5	3.24	16	0	119	99	36	98	

THIRD TEAM

Pos.	Player, Team	YR	Hometown	AVG	AB	R	H	2B	3B	HR	RBI	SB	Drafted/Round
C	Chris Westervelt, Stetson	So.	Batesville, Ark.	.403	236	67	95	17	0	18	46	2	Not eligible
1B	James Jurries, Tulane	Sr.	Lake Jackson, Texas	.400	240	77	96	16	4	20	74	30	Braves (6)
2B	Tim Moss, Texas	So.	Lancaster, Texas	.371	302	73	112	16	7	1	39	40	Not eligible
3B	Ryan Barthelemy, Florida State	Sr.	Miami	.357	297	76	106	24	4	17	94	6	Phillies (10)
SS	Drew Meyer, South Carolina	Jr.	Charleston, S.C.	.359	334	87	120	23	5	6	40	39	Rangers (1)
OF	Joey Gomes, Santa Clara	Jr.	Petaluma, Calif.	.408	238	54	97	31	1	10	51	3	Devil Rays (8)
OF	Adam Greenberg, North Carolina	Jr.	Guilford, Conn.	.337	267	80	90	17	7	17	57	35	Cubs (9)
OF	Brian Wright, North Carolina State	Sr.	Ramseur, N.C.	.418	232	72	97	26	2	14	73	10	Indians (7)
DH	Jed Morris, Nebraska	Jr.	Seabrook, Texas	.382	272	70	104	26	1	23	90	4	Athletics (36)
UT	Wes Whisler, UCLA	Fr.	Noblesville, Ind.	.328	177	33	58	9	0	18	46	2	Not eligible

Pos.	Player, Team	YR	Hometown	W	L	ERA	G	SV	IP	H	BB	SO	Drafted/Round
SP	Abe Alvarez, Long Beach State	So.	Fontana, Calif.	12	3	2.72	17	0	103	94	27	89	Not eligible
SP	Alex Hart, Florida	Jr.	Chambersburg, Pa.	13	3	3.24	17	0	111	81	56	81	Pirates (5)
SP	Philip Humber, Rice	Fr.	Carthage, Texas	11	1	2.77	18	0	111	90	43	130	Not eligible
SP	Wes Littleton, Cal State Fullerton	So.	Oceanside, Calif.	9	4	2.40	19	0	131	116	34	86	Not eligible
RP	David Bush, Wake Forest	Sr.	Devon, Pa.	8	1	1.64	40	13	60	47	10	61	Blue Jays (4)
UT	Wes Whisler, UCLA	Fr.	Noblesville, Ind.	5	2	4.06	18	0	84	94	40	59	

began the season with 13 multi-hit games in his first 16 contests and never really went cold, finishing at .470 with 27 homers and 91 RBIs. He also earned USA Baseball's Golden Spikes Award.

Greene finished on the Division I all-time leader board for hits (second, 403) and doubles (second, 95) and was second in Atlantic Coast Conference history in RBIs (276). He did it all a year after being a 14th-round draft pick of the Cubs; in 2002, the Padres made Greene the 13th pick overall in the first round.

Several other seniors had strong seasons, such as:

■ Notre Dame All-American center fielder Steve Stanley, who hit .439 and ranked just behind Greene in career hits with 385.

■ Gonzaga first baseman Nate Gold, who led the nation in home runs with 33, in the process breaking a West Coast Conference record set in 1999 by San Francisco's Taggert Bozied.

■ All-American Nebraska righthander Shane Komine, who went 10-0 and overcame a back problem to become the Cornhuskers' career wins and strikeouts leader.

COACHING **CAROUSEL**

Division I coaching changes since the end of the 2002 season:

School	Old Coach	New Coach	Previous Position
Arkansas	Norm DeBriyn	Dave Van Horn	Nebraska
Arkansas State	Bill Bethea	Keith Kessinger	Carson-Newman (Tenn.)
Ball State	Rich Maloney	Greg Beals	Assistant (Kent State)
Cal Poly	Ritch Price	Larry Lee	Cuesta, Calif., CC
Cal State Northridge	Mike Batesole	Steve Rousey	Assistant
Central Michigan	Judd Folske	Steve Jaksa	Assistant
Coppin State	Paul Blair	Guy Robertson	Assistant (Towson)
East Carolina	Keith LeClair	Randy Mazey	Assistant (Tennessee)
Evansville	Jim Brownlee	Dave Schrage	Northern Illinois
Fresno State	Bob Bennett	Mike Batesole	Cal State Northridge
Gardner-Webb	Clyde Miller	Rusty Stroupe	Lander, S.C.
Illinois State	Jeff Stewart	Jim Brownlee	Evansville
Kansas	Bobby Randall	Ritch Price	Cal Poly
Liberty	Dave Pastors	Matt Royer	Kutztown (Pa.)
Louisiana Tech	Jeff Richardson	Wade Simoneaux	Assistant (La.-Lafayette)
Marist	John Szefc	Jim Tyrell	Assistant
Michigan	Chris Harrison	Rich Maloney	Ball State
Nebraska	Dave Van Horn	Mike Anderson	Assistant
New Mexico State	Gary Ward	Rocky Ward	Assistant
Northern Illinois	Dave Schrage	Ed Mathey	North Central (Ill.)
Sam Houston State	John Skeeters	Chris Rupp	Rice (assistant)
San Diego State	Jim Dietz	Tony Gwynn	Major league player
Southeastern Louisiana	Greg Marten	Dav Canevari	Assistant (LSU)
Texas-Pan American	Reggie Tredaway	Willie Gawlick	Texas Wesleyan
Troy State	John Mayotte	Bobby Pierce	Alabama-Huntsville
Vanderbilt	Roy Mewbourne	Tim Corbin	Assistant (Clemson)

Changes At The Top

The offseason coach-changing scene was busy, with the biggest moves coming on the West Coast. San Diego State coach Jim Dietz retired after 31 years and was replaced at season's end by former Aztec and future Hall of Famer Tony Gwynn.

Fresno State's Bob Bennett also retired after 34 years, and the Bulldogs found a lower-profile replacement than Gwynn. However, new hire Mike Batesole was coming off a Big West regular-season title in what turned out to be his final season at Cal State Northridge.

A more traumatic coaching change took place at East Carolina, where Keith LeClair was unable to coach the Pirates as the effects of amyotrophic lateral sclerosis (Lou Gehrig's disease) took a debilitating toll. Assistants Kevin McMullen and Tommy Eason ran the team in his stead, leading the team to a Conference USA title in its first year in the conference.

LeClair officially stepped down after the season. He went 212-96 in five seasons and led the Pirates to four consecutive regional appearances. ECU hired Randy Mazey, a former LeClair assistant who had since moved on to Tennessee, to replace LeClair. Mazey retained Eason but didn't keep McMullen.

Long-time Florida Southern coach Chuck Anderson also was forced to step down for health reasons after a long battle with colon and liver cancer.

Dave Van Horn resigned at Nebraska after leading the Cornhuskers to back-to-back appearances in the College World Series and a 214-92 record in five years. He took over at Arkansas, his alma mater, for Norm DiBriyn who retired after 33 years. Assistant Mike Anderson replaced Van Horn at Nebraska.

Gary Ward, who led Oklahoma State to 952 wins from 1978-96 before returning to New Mexico State, his alma mater, in 2000, won the 1,000th game of his NCAA

Gary Ward

Tony Gwynn

Division I coaching career. He went on to lead the Aggies to an unexpected regional bid by winning the Sun Belt Conference tournament as a No. 6 seed.

Following the season though, Ward retired, turning the Aggies coaching reigns back over to his son, Rocky, who previously coached New Mexico State from 1997 to 2000. Rocky had stayed on to serve as an assistant as his father took over the club in 2001 and 2002.

In other major changes, Michigan hired former Ball State coach Rich Maloney; Vanderbilt tabbed former Clemson assistant Tim Corbin to replace the retiring Roy Mewbourne; and Kansas forced Bobby Randall to resign, hiring Cal Poly's Ritch Price as his successor.

In other 2002 news:

■ Louisiana State and Tulane played their April 10 game at the Louisiana Superdome in New Orleans. Though both teams were having subpar seasons at the time, they promoted the game heavily and broke the NCAA attendance record with 27,673 as the paid attendance; 25,101 actually showed up for the Tigers' 9-5 victory.

■ Louisiana State junior third baseman Wally Pontiff, a three-year starter, died unexpectedly of natural causes in July. Pontiff was a 21st-round draft pick of the Oakland A's and had planned to return to LSU for his senior year.

■ Virginia Tech junior center fielder Brad Bauder had a game for the ages by going 8-for-8 in a 35-4 victory against Georgetown. He clubbed five home runs, had 14 RBIs and 23 total bases while hitting for the cycle. Only the six-homer, 16-RBI game by Florida State's Marshall McDougall in 1999 against Maryland qualified as a better day in NCAA history. Dartmouth sophomore outfielder Scott Shirrell also had a historic game, going 5-for-6 with 14 RBIs and three homers in a 25-1 win at Harvard.

■ Howard University announced after the 2002 season that it will discontinue its baseball program.

COACH OF THE YEAR

Augie Garrido acknowledges that his first three seasons as head baseball coach at Texas were difficult. But it was all part of his accepting the challenge of returning the Longhorns to national prominence.

After building the nascent Cal State Fullerton program into a perennial power in two stints over 21 years that culminated in three College World Series championships, Garrido refused to rest on his laurels and moved to Austin after the 1996 season to take over a once-mighty but decaying Texas program.

He knew things might get worse before they got better. But he was ready for anything.

"I have great respect for coach (John) Wooden, and I saw what happened at UCLA after he retired," Garrido said. "It got really ugly. Look at Alabama after Bear Bryant. Look at Texas after Darrell Royal. It could've happened in baseball. That's why I'm here.

"My motivation was I thought I could make a difference, and I was willing to do whatever it took. It's been difficult. I can see why Larry Brown, as great a coach as he is, could not make it work at UCLA."

Garrido eventually made it work at Texas, overcoming his perceived outsider status to win over fans the best way he knew how. He won.

The Longhorns went undefeated during the tournament in winning their fifth CWS title in 2002. In the process, Garrido joined Louisiana

Augie Garrido

State's Skip Bertman (with five) and Southern California's Rod Dedeaux (10) as the only Division I baseball coaches with more than three national championships. He also became the first coach to win one in four different decades (1979, '84, '95 and 2002).

As just reward, Garrido became just the third two-time winner of Baseball America's College Coach of the Year award.

"I said at the time I was hired that I thought I was the right person at the right time," Garrido said. "I think I had a little more staying power because of the three titles.

"Time wouldn't have been given to someone without that background. The first three years were extremely difficult, and I really learned a lot. It does not matter that it was not pleasant. It was about overcoming adversity. Doesn't that sound like a baseball game—like what you have to do to win a baseball game?"

Garrido's Cal State Fullerton teams frequently played the Longhorns under his Texas predecessor, Cliff Gustafson, but that didn't quite prepare Garrido for the environment in Austin when he took over. The Longhorns had been to 18 straight regionals when Gustafson chose to retire in a dispute over summer-camps finances.

Garrido's first Texas team went only 29-22 and 12-15 in the first season of play in the revamped Big 12 Conference. It failed to qualify for regional play. The next season

brought the Longhorns' first losing season since 1956; the 'Horns also fell short of a regional bid in 1999.

Things started to turn a year later as Garrido's fourth team went 46-21 and broke through not just the regional door but made Texas' first CWS appearance since 1993. They came full circle in 2002.

Interestingly, Gustafson remains the all-time Division I wins leader at 1,427, while Garrido now ranks second at 1,380. It's possible he could pass Gustafson sometime during the 2003 season.

The depth, talent and coaching staff that helped produce another national championship for Garrido and the Longhorns may also have cemented Garrido as a Texan.

No amount of "Hook 'Em" hand gestures or renditions of "The Eyes of Texas" could have done what a national championship did.

"It matters to me to be accepted by our fans," Garrido said. "I don't feel I've been treated unfairly. Fans in Texas have passion. I'm part of that and I respect it."

After a CWS championship, it's a good bet they respect him, too.

–JOHN MANUEL

Toman named top assistant

Jim Toman has spent 13 seasons as Ray Tanner's right-hand man. His recruiting and coaching efforts have helped Tanner build South Carolina into a national power. The 2002 team reached the national championship game, and helped earn him the American Baseball Coaches Association/Baseball America Assistant Coach of the Year award.

Jim Toman

"We've been together a long time," Toman said of Tanner. "He's probably ready for me to get out of here and get a head job, honestly."

PREVIOUS WINNERS

1981—Ron Fraser, Miami
1982—Gene Stephenson, Wichita State
1983—Barry Shollenberger, Alabama
1984—Augie Garrido, Cal State Fullerton
1985—Ron Polk, Mississippi State
1986—Skip Bertman, Louisiana State
         Dave Snow, Loyola Marymount
1987—Mark Marquess, Stanford
1988—Jim Brock, Arizona State
1989—Dave Snow, Long Beach State
1990—Steve Webber, Georgia
1991—Jim Hendry, Creighton
1992—Andy Lopez, Pepperdine
1993—Gene Stephenson, Wichita State
1994—Jim Morris, Miami
1995—Rod Delmonico, Tennessee
1996—Skip Bertman, Louisiana State
1997—Jim Wells, Alabama
1998—Pat Murphy, Arizona State
1999—Wayne Graham, Rice
2000—Ray Tanner, South Carolina
2001—Dave Van Horn, Nebraska

FRESHMAN OF THE YEAR

He's not just the Youngest Drew Brother anymore. In 2002, Stephen Drew established his own identity.

Armed with the family's best nickname—call him Dirt—and plenty of ammunition from the Drew gene pool, the Florida State shortstop overcame an early-season injury to become Baseball America's Freshman of the Year.

Drew, 19, led the Seminoles in batting at .402 and was one behind team leader Ryan Barthelemy's 17 home runs. He also had 54 RBIs in 204 at-bats.

His numbers were impressive considering he needed about eight weeks of recovery and rehab after he broke his left foot Feb. 1 running out a triple against Hawaii, but at the end of the year—with the pin still in his foot—he ranked second on the team in homers and stolen bases.

When healthy, the younger brother of J.D. and Tim Drew (who in 1997 became the only brothers to be selected in the first round of the same draft), is one of the fastest Seminoles.

"He's really gotten it done," Seminoles coach Mike Martin said. "He's not been intimidated by any situation he's faced. There have been a lot of outstanding players come in here and make contributions, but not to the extent that he has. Stephen has certainly come up and produced with the game on the line. He's a difference-maker."

It was a strong year for freshmen

in 2002. First baseman Vince Sinisi (.428-11-80) and righthander Philip Humber (11-1, 2.70) of Rice, or outfielder/first baseman Darryl Lawhorn (.416-19-68) of East Carolina would have been solid Freshman of the Year choices in many years.

Drew earned the top freshman award by pushing Florida State to a No. 1 ranking at the close of the regular season. The Seminoles won their last 15 regular season games in the Atlantic Coast Conference, swept through the ACC tournament and took a 25-game winning streak into the super-regional before being upset by Notre Dame.

"It's a great honor to be named Freshman of the Year and I appreciate it, but I would trade any of that to still be playing right now," he said during the College World Series. "I think everybody will work even harder in the offseason and in the fall so we can hopefully get to Omaha next year."

Drew chose to follow in J.D.'s footsteps and play collegiately at Florida State rather than turning pro out of Lowndes County High in Hahira, Ga. The Pirates drafted the youngest Drew in the 11th round of the 2001 draft, but it was hard to turn down a chance to

Stephen Drew

start for the Seminoles.

"Some challenges you're going to have to face someday, so it might as well be now," he said. "When you come to Florida State as a freshman, people actually look up to you because of your brother's name. It's fun, but it's also time to get after it."

Stephen said his older brothers taught him how to play the game, and also toughened him up.

"J.D. taught me how to hit left-handed," he said. "Tim was the one always throwing to us and you didn't get anything right down the middle. He'd come after us."

—JOHN MANUEL

FRESHMAN ALL-AMERICA TEAM

FIRST TEAM

Pos., Player, School	AVG	AB	R	H	2B	3B	HR	RBI	SB
C Devin Ivany, South Florida	.322	230	47	74	11	1	10	56	8
1B Vince Sinisi, Rice	.428	271	65	116	22	2	11	80	13
2B Eric Patterson, Georgia Tech	.346	260	73	90	14	3	3	40	41
3B J.D. Reininger, Texas	.320	203	40	65	19	2	13	51	3
SS Stephen Drew, Florida State	.402	204	64	82	15	4	16	30	13
OF Jeff Frazier, Rutgers	.356	208	45	74	11	0	13	54	4
OF Darryl Lawhorn, East Carolina	.416	250	56	104	12	3	19	68	15
OF Jeremy Slayden, Georgia Tech	.348	256	74	89	15	1	18	66	4
DH Joey Metropoulos, So. California	.358	173	49	62	14	1	13	63	1
UT Wes Whisler, UCLA	.328	177	33	58	9	0	18	46	2

	W	L	ERA	G	SV	IP	H	BB	SO
SP Matt Durkin, San Jose State	11	3	2.75	22	1	98	85	24	85
SP Phil Humber, Rice	11	1	2.77	18	0	111	90	43	130
SP Chris Lambert, Boston College	9	3	2.76	17	0	78	59	51	87
SP Justin Verlander, Old Dominion	7	6	1.90	15	0	114	83	43	137
RP Huston Street, Texas	4	1	0.96	35	14	47	24	9	49
UT Wes Whisler, UCLA	5	2	4.06	18	0	84	94	40	59

SECOND TEAM

C—Chris Iannetta, North Carolina (.333-9-34). **1B**—Kyle Larsen, Washington (.363-5-36). **2B**—J.C. Holt, Louisiana State (.349-3-23). **3B**—Jeff Baisley, South Florida (.358-3-63). **SS**—Dustin Pedroia, Arizona State (.347-1-45). **OF**—Dee Brown, Central Florida (.397-3-56); Jake McClintock, San Diego State (.374-8-58); Seth Smith, Mississippi (.402-4-52). **DH**—Matt Wilkerson, UC Santa Barbara (.311-16-49).

SP—Derek DeCarlo, Florida International (11-0, 3.53); Ryan Gehring, Illinois-Chicago (9-1, 2.80); Grant Johnson, Notre Dame (9-5, 3.46); Scott Lewis, Ohio State (8-2, 2.84). **RP**—Taylor Tankersley, Alabama (8-5, 2.62, 7 SV). **UT**—Tim Layden, Duke (.282-3-36; 4-8, 5.62).

COLLEGE BASEBALL

N C A A
DIVISION I LEADERS

TEAM FIELDING

	G	AVG
South Carolina	75	.975
UNC Wilmington	57	.974
Northwestern State	60	.974
San Jose State	62	.973
Texas	72	.972
Rice	66	.972
Stanford	65	.971
Louisville	57	.971
Clemson	71	.971
South Alabama	61	.971

TEAM BATTING

BATTING AVERAGE	G	AVG
Southern	55	.378
Florida	65	.346
New Mexico	57	.345
Michigan State	57	.344
Delaware State	59	.342
Morehead State	56	.339
North Carolina State	59	.338
Liberty	59	.337
Florida International	61	.337
Bowling Green	54	.335

RUNS SCORED	G	R
Florida State	74	638
Florida	65	633
Southern	55	612
South Carolina	75	584
New Mexico State	62	582
Clemson	71	581
Georgia Tech	68	560
Delaware State	59	555
Nebraska	68	543
Florida International	61	542

DOUBLES	G	2B
Florida State	74	179
South Carolina	75	178
Texas	72	164
Clemson	71	157
Utah	59	154
Alabama	66	154
Nebraska	68	154

TRIPLES	G	3B
College of Charleston	58	42
Southern	55	37
Delaware	57	35
Cal Poly	60	35
Baylor	62	34

HOME RUNS	G	HR
Morehead State	56	127
South Carolina	75	122
Clemson	71	112
Florida	65	111
North Carolina	64	108
Florida International	61	99
Michigan State	57	95
New Mexico State	62	95
Florida Atlantic	67	95
Eastern Michigan	58	93

STOLEN BASES	G	SB	ATT
Coastal Carolina	63	192	222
Bethune-Cookman	61	191	227
Alabama State	50	164	190
Jackson State	51	152	190
Georgia Southern	64	151	195
Oral Roberts	67	145	196
Louisiana-Lafayette	62	145	201
Wichita State	64	139	172
Georgia Tech	68	130	169
North Carolina	64	127	163

TEAM PITCHING

WINNING PERCENTAGE	W	L	PCT
Southern	45	10	.818
Florida State	60	14	.811
Richmond	53	13	.803
Texas	57	15	.792
Rice	52	14	.788
Wake Forest	47	13	.779
Alabama	51	15	.773
Georgia Tech	52	16	.765
Clemson	54	17	.761
South Carolina	57	18	.760

EARNED RUN AVERAGE	G	ERA
Rice	66	2.79

	G	ERA
Texas	72	2.83
Wichita State	64	3.07
Marist	55	3.09
Houston	65	3.20
Illinois-Chicago	55	3.31
Oral Roberts	67	3.33
Coastal Carolina	63	3.40
Louisiana State	66	3.43
The Citadel	57	3.53

INDIVIDUAL BATTING

BATTING AVERAGE
(Minimum 125 At-Bats)

	Yr.	AVG	G	AB	R	H	2B	3B	HR	RBI	BB	SO	SB
Rickie Weeks, Southern	So.	.495	54	198	82	98	15	12	20	96	31	18	10
Curtis Granderson, Ill.-Chicago	Jr.	.483	55	207	76	100	23	4	9	45	32	24	17
Khalil Greene, Clemson	Sr.	.470	71	285	93	134	33	1	27	91	46	22	17
Antoin Gray, Southern	Jr.	.449	54	205	88	92	18	2	19	77	37	27	3
Anthony Bocchino, Marist	Sr.	.444	55	207	65	92	24	9	9	56	34	20	17
John McCurdy, Maryland	Jr.	.443	54	221	67	98	20	4	19	77	18	31	20
Terry Trofholz, Texas Christian	So.	.441	57	213	51	94	10	4	3	40	18	32	22
Steve Stanley, Notre Dame	Sr.	.439	68	271	77	119	17	4	1	36	38	11	32
Joe Wickman, UNLV	Fr.	.437	46	142	37	62	14	1	2	38	28	25	3
Tom Merkle, New York Tech	Sr.	.430	52	186	60	80	6	2	26	80	28	25	8
Vince Sinisi, Rice	Fr.	.428	66	271	65	116	22	2	11	80	31	20	13
Gregg Davies, Towson	Sr.	.428	51	187	59	80	18	6	13	51	37	25	14
Wes Timmons, Beth.-Cookman	Sr.	.425	61	214	79	91	22	1	10	64	45	12	40
Matt Buckmiller, Columbia	Sr.	.424	47	158	56	67	21	0	12	56	35	27	16
Brett Spivey, Charleston	Jr.	.423	57	213	60	90	19	6	8	57	26	28	12
Mike Galloway, Miami (Ohio)	Jr.	.422	59	223	72	94	16	3	15	63	25	26	14
Eddie Kim, James Madison	Jr.	.421	60	235	48	99	24	1	12	74	34	37	9
Casey Long, Rider	Jr.	.419	55	210	51	88	18	4	7	44	21	27	6
Brian Wright, N.C. State	Jr.	.418	.59	232	72	97	26	2	14	75	46	19	10
Justin Owens, Coastal Carolina	Sr.	.417	57	211	60	88	24	2	11	58	29	33	31
Mike Arbinger, Ohio	Sr.	.417	51	192	62	80	15	2	20	57	36	30	4
Darryl Lawhorn, East Carolina	Fr.	.416	64	250	56	104	12	3	19	68	39	45	15
Mark Schramek, UT-San Antonio	Sr.	.416	54	202	63	84	16	2	11	49	23	31	1
Pat Osborn, Florida	Jr.	.414	65	251	67	104	17	1	17	76	37	35	7
Reid Gorecki, Delaware	Jr.	.414	50	198	66	82	13	9	12	50	33	25	34
Mike Gaffney, New York Tech	Jr.	.414	52	191	63	79	12	5	4	39	26	13	14
Mark Teahen, St. Mary's	Jr.	.412	49	194	45	80	15	4	6	36	30	17	7
Adam Bourassa, Wake Forest	Jr.	.412	61	250	71	103	11	4	2	41	35	21	26
Peter Stonard, Alabama	So.	.411	58	236	59	97	22	5	5	42	26	17	18
Dave Jensen, Brigham Young	So.	.411	63	262	58	108	29	0	10	69	33	33	12
David Mann, Central Florida	So.	.410	57	166	50	68	6	1	0	19	40	21	10
Lee Curtis, Charleston	Jr.	.409	56	225	67	92	11	9	15	65	29	31	21
John Vanden Berg, UW-Milwaukee	Sr.	.409	55	186	42	76	16	1	6	57	23	25	5
Joey Gomes, Santa Clara	Sr.	.408	55	238	54	97	31	1	10	51	12	35	3
Pete Pirman, Eastern Illinois	Sr.	.407	51	209	58	85	16	0	10	44	13	21	13
John Rosner, Ill.-Chicago	Sr.	.407	43	150	49	61	14	3	2	43	13	12	14
Fred Lewis, Southern	Jr.	.406	50	165	54	67	12	6	6	40	24	30	14
Jon Peacock, Illinois State	Jr.	.406	52	187	44	76	17	1	9	48	33	28	4
Josh Kean, Siena	Sr.	.406	48	165	41	67	15	3	5	25	15	27	20
Gabe Veloz, New Mexico State	Jr.	.406	61	234	73	95	26	1	15	92	49	48	1
Kelly Knouse, Liberty	Sr.	.405	56	195	55	79	17	4	9	58	31	33	3
Chris McCuiston, Michigan State	Sr.	.404	57	230	59	93	22	0	15	71	16	31	10
Drew Locke, Boston College	Fr.	.404	45	141	34	57	16	0	2	24	11	17	10
Corey Loomis, Bowling Green	Jr.	.404	50	193	61	78	13	4	13	52	22	49	7
Jared Boyd, Md.-Balt. County	Sr.	.404	56	208	58	84	32	3	7	52	30	31	3
Charles D'Elia, Quinnipiac	Sr.	.404	41	156	30	63	17	0	4	40	15	20	0
Marcus Maringola, Liberty	Sr.	.404	58	208	50	84	8	6	8	63	15	20	12
Kennard Jones, Indiana	Jr.	.404	55	228	75	92	14	2	1	33	25	28	22
Mark Kiger, Florida	Sr.	.403	65	258	90	104	12	4	11	55	60	24	11
Brandon Mason, Southern	Fr.	.403	43	144	59	58	5	4	4	46	20	12	14
Stephen Drew, Stetson	So.	.403	61	236	67	95	17	0	18	46	33	34	2
Stephen Drew, Florida State	Fr.	.402	46	204	64	82	15	4	16	54	20	30	13
Bryan Gant, Cal Poly	Sr.	.402	58	241	59	97	11	8	0	38	27	24	20
Seth Smith, Mississippi	Fr.	.402	53	204	36	82	9	2	4	52	22	19	5
Kelly Hunt, Bowling Green	Sr.	.402	54	214	69	86	14	1	22	84	20	14	4
Bob Malek, Michigan State	Jr.	.402	57	219	66	88	21	3	16	66	21	23	16
Jeff Barry, Vermont	Jr.	.401	49	177	50	71	8	5	4	36	28	15	32
Sam Flamont, West. Michigan	Sr.	.401	47	187	44	75	15	6	9	56	22	31	13
Phil Sullinger, Delaware State	Sr.	.401	57	207	71	83	21	3	11	63	21	14	5
Dustin Majewski, Texas	Jr.	.401	64	212	40	85	20	2	10	50	18	43	4
Brian Burgamy, Wichita State	Jr.	.400	63	240	68	96	15	3	4	51	51	30	24
James Jurries, Tulane	So.	.400	63	240	77	96	16	4	20	74	43	43	30
Jason Waugh, St. Mary's	Jr.	.399	48	203	50	81	16	5	14	43	18	21	5
David Castillo, Oral Roberts	So.	.398	67	226	59	90	23	0	14	79	31	24	4

RUNS SCORED

	Yr.	G	R
Khalil Greene, Clemson	Sr.	71	93
Mark Kiger, Florida	Sr.	65	90
Antoin Gray, Southern	Jr.	54	88
Drew Meyer, South Carolina	Jr.	75	87
Rickie Weeks, Southern	So.	54	82
Corey Harrington, New Mex. State	Jr.	61	81
Danny Boyle, Oral Roberts	Sr.	67	81
Yaron Peters, South Carolina	Sr.	72	81
Adam Greenberg, N. Carolina	Jr.	64	80
Wes Timmons, Beth.-Cookman	Sr.	61	79
Chris Walker, Ga. Southern	Sr.	64	79
Bryan Pritz, Richmond	So.	66	78
James Jurries, Tulane	Sr.	63	77
Steve Stanley, Notre Dame	Sr.	68	77

HITS

	Yr.	G	H
Khalil Greene, Clemson	Sr.	71	134
Drew Meyer, South Carolina	Jr.	75	120
Steve Stanley, Notre Dame	Sr.	68	119
Vince Sinisi, Rice	Fr.	66	116
Tim Moss, Texas	So.	72	112
Sam Fuld, Stanford	So.	65	110
Jeff Leise, Nebraska	Jr.	67	109
Dave Jensen, BYU	So.	63	108
Chaz Lytle, Georgia	Jr.	61	108
Ryan Barthelemy, Fla. State	Sr.	71	106
Yaron Peters, South Carolina	Sr.	72	106
Steve Thomas, South Carolina	Sr.	75	105
Darryl Lawhorn, East Carolina	Fr.	64	104
Pat Osborn, Florida	Jr.	65	104
Mark Kiger, Florida	Sr.	65	104
David Reaver, Richmond	Jr.	66	104
Victor Menocal, Ga. Tech	Sr.	67	104
Jed Morris, Nebraska	Jr.	68	104

SLUGGING PERCENTAGE

(Minimum 125 At-Bats)	Yr.	G	PCT
Rickie Weeks, Southern	So.	54	.995
Khalil Greene, Clemson	Sr.	71	.877
Tom Merkle, New York Tech	Sr.	52	.849
Nate Gold, Gonzaga	Sr.	56	.842
Antoin Gray, Southern	Jr.	54	.834
Mike Arbinger, Ohio	Sr.	51	.828
John McCurdy, Maryland	Jr.	54	.828
Brant Colamarino, Pittsburgh	Jr.	53	.802
Brad Eldred, Fla. International	Sr.	61	.798
Bubba Lavender, Morehead State	Sr.	56	.798

TOTAL BASES

	Yr.	G	TB
Khalil Greene, Clemson	Sr.	71	250
Yaron Peters, S. Carolina	Sr.	72	215
Jed Morris, Nebraska	Jr.	68	201
Rickie Weeks, Southern	So.	54	197
Michael Johnson, Clemson	Jr.	71	197
Nate Gold, Gonzaga	Sr.	56	192
Chris Maples, N. Carolina	Sr.	64	190
Ryan Barthelemy, Fla. State	Sr.	71	189
Ryan Shealy, Florida	Sr.	65	186
John McCurdy, Maryland	Jr.	54	183

DOUBLES

	Yr.	G	2B
Khalil Greene, Clemson	Sr.	71	33
Jared Boyd, Md.-Balt. County	Sr.	56	32
Joey Gomes, Santa Clara	Sr.	55	31
Brent Johnson, UNLV	So.	60	30
David Reaver, Richmond	Jr.	66	30
Dave Jensen, Brigham Young	So.	63	29
Adam Tidball, Richmond	So.	61	28
Bryan Zenchyk, Stetson	Sr.	61	28
Brit Pannier, Utah	Sr.	55	26
Brian Wright, N.C. State	Sr.	59	26
Micah Hoffpauir, Lamar	Sr.	60	26
Tom McQuade, Florida State	So.	60	26
Gabe Veloz, New Mexico State	Sr.	61	26
Jose Pabon, Va. Commonwealth	Jr.	65	26
Carlo Cota, San Diego State	Jr.	66	26
Jed Morris, Nebraska	Jr.	68	26
Steve Thomas, S. Carolina	Sr.	75	26

TRIPLES

	Yr.	G	3B
Rickie Weeks, Southern	So.	54	12
Matt Kutler, Brown	So.	49	9
Reid Gorecki, Delaware	Jr.	50	9
Jake Reynolds, Southern Utah	Jr.	54	9
Anthony Bocchino, Marist	Sr.	55	9
Lee Curtis, Charleston	Jr.	56	9
Vern Hatton, SE Mo. State	Sr.	57	9

Gonzaga's Nate Gold: 33 homers

HOME RUNS

	Yr.	G	HR
Nate Gold, Gonzaga	Sr.	56	33
Brad Eldred, Fla. International	Sr.	61	29
Yaron Peters, South Carolina	Sr.	72	29
Khalil Greene, Clemson	Sr.	71	27
Cary Page, Morehead State	Jr.	55	26
Jeff Baker, Clemson	Jr.	68	25
Michael Johnson, Clemson	Jr.	71	25
Bubba Lavender, Morehead State	Sr.	56	24
Ryan Kenning, New Mexico State	Sr.	61	24
Chris Maples, North Carolina	Sr.	64	23
Ryan Shealy, Florida	Sr.	65	23
Vito Chiaravalloti, Richmond	Jr.	66	23
Jed Morris, Nebraska	Jr.	68	23
Kelly Hunt, Bowling Green	Jr.	54	22
Ryan Goleski, Eastern Michigan	So.	58	22
Kevin Matuszek, More. State	Jr.	55	21
Mike Arbinger, Ohio	Sr.	51	20
Tom Merkle, New York Tech	Sr.	52	20
Rickie Weeks, Southern	So.	54	20
Jamie D'Antona, Wake Forest	So.	57	20
Danny Matienzo, Miami	Jr.	62	20
James Jurries, Tulane	Sr.	63	20
Jeff Ontiveros, Texas	Sr.	71	20
Brant Colamarino, Pittsburgh	Jr.	53	19
Antoin Gray, Southern	Jr.	54	19
John McCurdy, Maryland	Jr.	54	19
Steve Booth, San Francisco	Sr.	55	19
Michael Carlin, Miami (Ohio)	Jr.	55	19
Chris Alexander, New Mexico	Jr.	56	19
Mike Bassett, Geo. Washington	Sr.	63	19
Darryl Lawhorn, East Carolina	Fr.	64	19
Matt Craig, Richmond	So.	66	19
Wes Whisler, UCLA	Fr.	48	18
Scott Martin, Delaware State	Jr.	49	18
Adam Berry, UCLA	Sr.	53	18
Brad Rea, Pittsburgh	Sr.	53	18
David Trujillo, UNLV	Sr.	56	18
Mike Johnson, Austin Peay	Sr.	57	18
Matt Hagen, Liberty	Jr.	59	18
Chris Westervelt, Stetson	So.	61	18
Brett Cooley, Houston	Jr.	64	18
Mike Cox, Fla. Atlantic	Jr.	66	18
Jeremy Slayden, Ga. Tech	Fr.	68	18
Trey Dyson, South Carolina	Jr.	75	18

RUNS BATTED IN

	Yr.	G	RBI
Rickie Weeks, Southern	So.	54	96
Ryan Kenning, New Mexico St.	Sr.	61	96
Yaron Peters, South Carolina	Sr.	72	95
Ryan Barthelemy, Fla. State	Sr.	71	94
Gabe Veloz, New Mexico State	Sr.	61	92
Khalil Greene, Clemson	Sr.	71	91
Jed Morris, Nebraska	Jr.	68	90
Jeff Baker, Clemson	Jr.	68	87
Vito Chiaravalloti, Richmond	Jr.	66	86
Kelly Hunt, Bowling Green	Jr.	54	84
Matt Craig, Richmond	So.	66	84
Jamie D'Antona, Wake Forest	So.	57	83
Michael Johnson, Clemson	Jr.	71	81
Ryan Shealy, Florida	Sr.	65	80
Vince Sinisi, Rice	Fr.	66	80

Chris Maples, North Carolina	Sr.	64	79
David Castillo, Oral Roberts	So.	67	79
Chris Alexander, New Mexico	Jr.	56	78
Antoin Gray, Southern	Jr.	54	77
John McCurdy, Maryland	Jr.	54	77
Ryan Johnson, Wake Forest	So.	58	77
Bret Underwood, Delaware State	So.	59	77
Mike Bassett, George Washington	Sr.	63	77
Matt Herring, Ga. Southern	Jr.	63	77
Kevin Matuszek, Morehead State	Jr.	55	76
Nate Gold, Gonzaga	Sr.	56	76
Mike Johnson, Austin Peay	Sr.	57	76
Pat Osborn, Florida	Jr.	65	76
Eric Arnold, Rice	Sr.	66	75
Tony Richie, Florida State	So.	70	75

WALKS

	Yr.	G	BB
Jeremy Brown, Alabama	Sr.	66	69
Mark Kiger, Florida	Sr.	65	60
Shaun Larkin, CS Northridge	Sr.	57	59
Drew Moffitt, Wichita State	So.	61	59
Erik Winegarden, New Mex. State	Sr.	60	58
Danny Boyle, Oral Roberts	Sr.	67	58

STRIKEOUTS

	Yr.	G	SO
Tony Piazza, SW Mo. State	Jr.	63	69
Chad Felty, Coastal Carolina	Sr.	62	68
Matt Womble, Ala.-Birmingham	Jr.	55	68
Nathan Doyle, James Madison	Jr.	59	66
Hal Bisnett, New Mexico State	Jr.	61	66

TOUGHEST TO STRIKE OUT

(Minimum 125 At-Bats)	Yr.	AB	SO	Ratio
Steve Stanley, Notre Dame	Sr.	271	11	24.6
Jason Howarth, Middle Tenn.	Sr.	194	8	24.3
Chad Sterbens, Mississippi	Jr.	229	10	22.9
K.J. Hendricks, UT-Arlington	Jr.	233	11	21.2
Jay Johnson, Xavier	Fr.	175	9	19.4

STOLEN BASES

	Yr.	G	SB	ATT
Ryan McGraw, Coast. Carolina	So.	60	63	70
Bartowski Cowan, Ala. State	So.	50	54	58
Chris Walker, Ga. Southern	Sr.	64	48	54
Russ Adams, North Carolina	Jr.	63	45	57
Micah Simmons, Beth.-Cookman	Sr.	61	43	46
Corey Harrington, New Mex. State	Jr.	61	42	47
Matt Lemanczyk, Sac. Heart	Sr.	47	41	49
Rusty Moore, Beth.-Cook.	Jr.	60	41	49
Eric Patterson, Ga. Tech	Fr.	41	41	50
Ashley Allen, Alabama State	Jr.	47	40	47
Casey Fahy, Delaware	Sr.	56	40	44
Wes Timmons, Beth.-Cook.	So.	61	40	48
Tim Moss, Texas	So.	72	40	49
Jason Tuttle, Elon	Sr.	57	39	46
Drew Meyer, S. Carolina	Jr.	75	39	53
Chris Graziano, Villanova	Jr.	53	38	45
Danny Boyle, Oral Roberts	Sr.	67	38	45
Javy Rodriguez, Miami	Sr.	63	37	48

HIT BY PITCH

	Yr.	G	HBP
Brett Burnham, Connecticut	Jr.	50	32
Chris Nelson, Southern Utah	Sr.	54	29
Nick Blankenship, Texas Tech	Sr.	59	28
Daniel Bruce, Nebraska	Fr.	59	27
Gabe Somarriba, Fla. Atlantic	Sr.	67	27

Southern's Rickie Weeks: 13 triples, 96 RBIs

EARNED RUN AVERAGE
(Minimum 60 Innings)

	Yr.	W	L	ERA	G	GS	CG	SV	IP	H	R	ER	BB	SO
Justin Cerbone, Cent. Conn. State	Sr.	4	1	1.35	17	7	2	0	60	55	23	9	21	47
Steve Obenchain, Evansville	Jr.	3	1	1.38	25	5	1	12	78	53	24	12	23	89
Jeff Stovall, Furman	Sr.	7	2	1.46	23	7	2	0	86	75	22	14	19	56
Matt Hamer, The Citadel	Jr.	9	2	1.51	35	1	0	1	77	77	36	13	15	81
Tim Stauffer, Richmond	So.	15	3	1.54	20	18	13	0	146	110	35	25	34	140
Dave Bush, Wake Forest	Sr.	8	1	1.64	40	0	0	13	60	47	15	11	10	61
John Tetuan, Wichita State	Jr.	10	1	1.72	16	13	2	1	89	62	28	17	31	78
Devin Monds, Northeastern	Fr.	5	2	1.80	11	10	6	1	65	50	17	13	23	53
Von Stertzbach, Central Fla.	Jr.	7	0	1.81	21	1	0	2	65	56	23	13	28	80
Brad Sullivan, Houston	So.	13	1	1.82	18	18	5	0	129	80	32	26	49	157
Justin Verlander, Old Dominion	Fr.	7	6	1.90	15	15	8	0	114	83	34	24	43	137
Ryan Kondratowicz, Marist	Jr.	6	0	1.93	17	5	0	1	65	48	17	14	12	53
Justin Crowder, Rice	Sr.	10	3	2.00	22	13	2	1	121	106	37	27	36	106
Geoff Lefeber, UW-Milwaukee	Jr.	6	1	2.20	16	11	2	0	86	80	34	21	35	53
Jim Carone, Monmouth	Jr.	10	3	2.21	13	13	7	0	98	83	38	24	19	26
Neal Sears, East Carolina	Jr.	9	3	2.23	34	0	0	6	65	54	27	16	16	68
Rene Recio, Oral Roberts	So.	8	5	2.23	15	14	2	0	85	63	28	21	23	106
Joe Wilson, Md.-Balt. County	So.	9	3	2.26	14	13	9	0	92	91	30	23	34	63
John Corcoran, Butler	Sr.	12	3	2.29	16	15	10	0	106	109	36	27	22	76
Shane Komine, Nebraska	Sr.	10	0	2.33	15	13	3	0	97	62	30	25	30	115
Dave Cerminaro, Lehigh	Sr.	9	3	2.34	14	12	9	1	88	82	33	23	14	60
Jesen Merle, Texas	Jr.	3	3	2.35	28	0	0	2	61	42	21	16	12	58
Chris Tracz, Marist	So.	10	3	2.36	15	15	2	0	99	85	37	26	20	78
Ryan Schroyer, Arizona State	So.	4	1	2.37	25	4	0	8	61	50	18	16	35	75
Wes Littleton, CS Fullerton	So.	9	4	2.40	19	18	2	0	131	116	52	35	34	86
Aaron Pullin, UT-Arlington	Jr.	8	1	2.48	19	11	1	1	76	70	32	21	20	46
Jeremy Guthrie, Stanford	Jr.	13	2	2.51	20	20	6	0	158	138	59	44	36	136
Justin Simmons, Texas	So.	16	1	2.52	20	20	4	0	128	106	41	36	39	80
Ryan Bicondoa, Western Ky.	Sr.	11	2	2.55	17	16	5	1	124	106	44	35	23	150
Zach Otte, Indiana	Sr.	7	3	2.56	16	12	5	0	81	77	31	23	31	55
Daniel Hodges, Fla. State	Jr.	4	1	2.56	36	0	0	12	63	68	25	18	10	38
Jared Doyle, James Madison	Jr.	11	3	2.57	17	14	3	0	102	102	36	29	36	92
Bob McCrory, So. Mississippi	So.	7	3	2.57	17	10	2	0	84	77	38	24	32	63
Bryan Williams, Jacksonville	Sr.	6	3	2.58	22	9	5	3	80	59	30	23	36	76
Brad Thomas, Arkansas State	Jr.	5	3	2.58	31	2	1	6	73	58	22	21	28	81
Andy Gros, La.-Lafayette	Jr.	11	4	2.59	24	13	5	2	125	115	50	36	37	111
David Sanders, Wichita State	So.	5	4	2.59	14	14	1	0	73	74	35	21	13	58
Lane Mestepey, LSU	So.	11	5	2.59	19	18	8	0	142	145	57	41	17	74
Nathan Mitchell, Houston	Sr.	5	2	2.62	36	1	0	4	65	43	21	19	14	63
Taylor Tankersley, Alabama	Fr.	8	5	2.62	25	3	0	7	69	55	20	20	20	65
Blake Taylor, South Carolina	Sr.	6	1	2.63	37	4	1	21	86	78	26	25	44	79
O.J. King, Northwestern State	Sr.	8	4	2.63	15	14	5	0	106	105	32	31	35	85

WINS

	Yr.	W	L
Justin Simmons, Texas	So.	16	1
Tim Stauffer, Richmond	So.	15	3
Kyle Sleeth, Wake Forest	So.	14	0
Brad Sullivan, Houston	So.	13	1
Kyle Bakker, Georgia Tech	So.	13	2
Jeremy Guthrie, Stanford	Jr.	13	2
Matt Lynch, Florida State	Jr.	13	2
Alex Hart, Florida	Jr.	13	3
Steven Herce, Rice	Jr.	13	3
Steve Reba, Clemson	Sr.	13	4
Matt Henrie, Clemson	Jr.	13	5
Mike McGirr, Richmond	Jr.	12	1
Scooter Michael, UNC Greensboro	Sr.	12	1
Brandon Smith, SE Mo. State	Sr.	12	2
Abe Alvarez, Long Beach State	Jr.	12	3
John Corcoran, Butler	Sr.	12	3
Roger Lincoln, Stetson	Jr.	12	3
Brad Purcell, SE Mo. State	Sr.	12	3
Michael Rogers, Oral Roberts	Sr.	12	3

LOSSES

	Yr.	W	L
Lee Gwaltney, La. Tech	Sr.	3	12
Duke Acors, Va. Military	Fr.	2	11
Brett Jarrett, Mercer	Sr.	6	11

APPEARANCES

	Yr.	G
Brian Marshall, Va. Commonwealth	So.	41
Joey Livingston, South Florida	Jr.	41
Dave Bush, Wake Forest	Sr.	40
George Huguet, Miami	So.	40
Randy Corn, The Citadel	Sr.	39
Blake Taylor, South Carolina	Sr.	37
Matt Freisleben, UW-Milwaukee	Sr.	37

COMPLETE GAMES

	Yr.	GS	CG
Tim Stauffer, Richmond	So.	18	13
Billy Biggs, West Virginia	Jr.	14	10
John Corcoran, Butler	Sr.	15	10

Stanford's Jeremy Guthrie: 158 innings

	Yr.	G	
Dave Cerminaro, Lehigh	Sr.	12	9
Mike Collar, Maine	So.	13	9
Corey Lawson, Saint Louis	Jr.	13	9
Joe Wilson, Md.-Baltimore County	So.	13	9
Aaron Phillips, Butler	Jr.	13	9
Helpiz Moises, Beth.-Cookman	Sr.	15	9
Shawn Kohn, Washington	Sr.	16	9
Bob Runyon, Fresno State	Sr.	19	9
Adam Jahnsen, Xavier	Sr.	19	9

SAVES

	Yr.	G	SV
Blake Taylor, South Carolina	Sr.	37	21
Royce Ring, San Diego State	Jr.	36	17
James Russell, Villanova	Jr.	22	15
Matt Freisleben, UW-Milwaukee	Sr.	37	15

San Diego State's Royce Ring: 17 saves

	Yr.	G	
Kyle Edens, Baylor	Sr.	35	14
Huston Street, Texas	Fr.	35	14
Randy Corn, The Citadel	Sr.	39	13
Dave Bush, Wake Forest	Sr.	40	13
Andy Wilson, Stetson	Jr.	21	12
Steve Obenchain, Evansville	Jr.	25	12
Chad Cordero, CS Fullerton	So.	33	12
Tim McNab, Fla. Atlantic	Sr.	34	12
Daniel Hodges, Fla. State	Jr.	36	12

INNINGS PITCHED

	Yr.	G	IP
Jeremy Guthrie, Stanford	Jr.	20	158
Tim Stauffer, Richmond	So.	20	146
Bob Runyon, Fresno State	Sr.	20	142
Lane Mestepey, LSU	So.	19	142
Chris Smith, UC Riverside	Jr.	17	136

WALKS

	Yr.	IP	BB
Whit Bryant, Elon	Sr.	86	77
Sean Finnegan, Xavier	So.	84	73
Brian Chapman, Appy State	Fr.	69	71
Bill Murphy, CS Northridge	Jr.	106	69
Anthony Pearson, Jackson State	Jr.	77	67

STRIKEOUTS

	Yr.	IP	SO
Brad Sullivan, Houston	So.	129	157
Ryan Bicondoa, W. Kentucky	Sr.	124	150
Tim Stauffer, Richmond	So.	146	140
Bryan Bullington, Ball State	Jr.	105	139
Whitt Farr, Wm. & Mary	Jr.	120	138
Justin Verlander, Old Dominion	Fr.	114	137
Jeremy Guthrie, Stanford	Jr.	158	136
Joseph Blanton, Kentucky	Jr.	100	133
Phil Humber, Rice	Fr.	111	130
Bill Murphy, CS Northridge	Jr.	106	129
Clay Hensley, Lamar	Sr.	100	127
Robert Swindle, Char. Southern	Fr.	109	127
Chris Smith, UC Riverside	Jr.	136	127
Bobby Sawicki, SW Texas State	So.	118	124
Brett Lewis, Ga. Southern	Jr.	126	122
Bo Pettit, Louisiana State	Jr.	121	121
Michael Rogers, Oral Roberts	Sr.	123	119
Bob Runyon, Fresno State	Sr.	142	119
Ben Crockett, Harvard	Sr.	84	117
Casey Blalock, La. Tech	Sr.	117	116
Shane Komine, Nebraska	Sr.	97	115
Kyle Bakker, Ga. Tech	So.	135	115

STRIKEOUTS/9 INNINGS
(Minimum 50 Innings)

	Yr.	IP	SO	AVG
Chad Pleiness, Cent. Mich.	Sr.	68	100	13.2
Jared Thomas, Oakland	Jr.	71	103	13.1
Ben Crockett, Harvard	Sr.	84	117	12.5
Rich Hill, Michigan	Jr.	76	104	12.3
Joseph Blanton, Kentucky	Jr.	100	133	12.0
Bryan Bullington, Ball State	Jr.	105	139	11.9
Randy Corn, The Citadel	Sr.	59	76	11.6
Clay Hensley, Lamar	Sr.	100	127	11.4
Rene Recio, Oral Roberts	So.	85	106	11.3
Anthony Pearson, Jackson State	Jr.	77	95	11.1
Scott Tolbert, Ga. Southern	So.	66	82	11.1
Von Stertzbach, Central Fla.	Jr.	65	80	11.1
Ryan Schroyer, Ariz. State	So.	61	75	11.1
Stockton Davis, Oral Rob.	Sr.	68	83	11.0
Brad Sullivan, Houston	So.	129	157	11.0

COLLEGE
TOP 25

BATTERS: 10 or more at-bats. **PITCHERS**: 5 or more innings. **Boldface** indicates selected in 2002 draft.

1. TEXAS

Coach: Augie Garrido   Record: 57-15

BATTING	YR	AVG	AB	R	H	2B	3B	HR	RBI	SB
Majewski, Dustin, of	Jr.	.401	212	40	85	20	2	10	50	4
Moss, Tim, 2b	So.	.371	302	73	112	16	7	1	39	40
Crosta, Nic, of	Fr.	.333	30	9	10	1	2	0	5	1
Quintanilla, Omar, 3b	So.	.329	219	41	72	15	3	2	32	8
Reininger, J.D., dh-3b	Fr.	.320	203	40	65	19	2	13	51	3
Carmichael, Chris, of	Sr.	.311	61	11	19	6	2	2	11	0
Fahey, Brandon, of-3b-ss	Jr.	.303	142	29	43	12	0	1	20	9
Ontiveros, Jeff, 1b	Sr.	.302	248	55	75	15	2	20	59	2
Hubele, Ryan, c	Sr.	.288	274	58	79	22	4	5	52	1
Johnston, Seth, inf	Fr.	.267	15	3	4	0	0	0	3	0
Hollimon, Michael, ss	Fr.	.262	210	38	55	8	2	4	37	5
Thigpen, Curtis, c	Fr.	.256	82	18	21	8	0	1	11	2
Napoleon, Kalani, of	Sr.	.251	171	31	43	10	0	2	30	6
Sultemeier, Eric, of	So.	.244	172	34	42	2	3	6	31	11
Ferin, Joe, of	Jr.	.224	58	17	13	2	0	0	8	6
Rosenberg, Matt, of	Sr.	.215	65	9	14	5	0	0	10	2
Neuman, Chris, 1b	So.	.211	19	2	4	2	0	0	5	0

PITCHING		W	L	ERA	G	SV	IP	H	BB	SO
Street, Huston, rhp	Fr.	4	1	0.96	35	14	47	24	9	49
Cody, Buck, lhp	Fr.	0	0	1.64	10	1	11	7	4	10
France, Ryan, rhp	Sr.	1	0	1.69	3	0	5	4	2	5
Espineli, Eugene, lhp	So.	5	0	2.08	17	1	52	49	17	39
Frizzell, Kevin, rhp	Jr.	0	0	2.25	6	0	8	10	2	6
Merle, Jesen, rhp	Jr.	3	3	2.35	28	2	61	42	12	58
Simmons, Justin, rhp	So.	16	1	2.52	20	0	128	106	39	80
Halsey, Brad, lhp	Jr.	7	2	2.74	18	0	99	90	26	82
Jordan, Brantley, lhp	Jr.	1	1	2.96	25	2	24	19	10	28
Clark, Ray, rhp	Jr.	6	4	3.61	15	0	72	66	17	71
McGough, Tim, rhp	So.	1	0	3.93	15	1	34	37	10	22
Bomer, Alan, rhp	Jr.	11	3	3.94	21	2	94	92	21	82
Muegge, Danny, rhp	Jr.	2	0	5.00	8	0	9	12	2	4

2. SOUTH CAROLINA

Coach: Ray Tanner   Record: 57-18

BATTING	YR	AVG	AB	R	H	2B	3B	HR	RBI	SB
Peters, Yaron, 1b	Sr.	.377	281	81	106	22	0	29	95	6
Meyer, Drew, ss	Jr.	.359	334	87	120	23	5	6	40	39
Thomas, Steve, of	Jr.	.355	296	72	105	26	1	13	70	5
Bell, Gary, p-of	Sr.	.333	39	6	13	3	0	2	11	0
Seaton, Tim, p-of	Jr.	.333	15	8	5	0	0	0	0	3
Buscher, Brian, 3b	Jr.	.323	294	56	95	20	6	14	64	1
Greenwood, Jared, c	Fr.	.316	19	5	6	3	0	0	2	1
Gonce, Garris, of	Sr.	.305	279	47	85	14	1	16	55	0
Harris, Justin, of-2b	Jr.	.295	302	49	89	18	2	5	35	11
Powell, Landon, c	So.	.292	274	49	80	17	0	12	53	2
Melillo, Kevin, 2b	Fr.	.280	157	36	44	12	0	3	15	4
Dyson, Trey, dh-1b	Jr.	.268	284	51	76	15	0	18	63	2
Coutlangus, Jon, of	Jr.	.260	131	28	34	4	3	1	11	8
Smith, Demetric, dh-1b	Jr.	.200	20	3	4	1	0	2	9	0
Ross, Jason, of	Fr.	.067	15	3	1	0	0	0	0	0

PITCHING		W	L	ERA	G	SV	IP	H	BB	SO
Campbell, Matt, lhp	Fr.	4	2	2.43	21	0	37	26	31	44
Taylor, Blake, rhp	Sr.	6	1	2.63	37	21	86	78	44	79
Donald, Cliff, rhp	Fr.	0	0	3.12	8	0	9	6	1	12
Evans, Rocky, rhp	Jr.	1	1	3.18	11	0	23	20	10	23
Wilson, Matt, rhp	Sr.	1	0	3.38	6	0	5	3	5	4
Wesley, John, rhp	Jr.	2	0	3.57	11	1	18	13	10	12
Rawl, Aaron, rhp	Fr.	7	2	3.89	28	2	72	84	23	69
Bondurant, Steven, lhp	Jr.	7	4	4.30	21	1	96	96	34	62
Hernandez, Chris, rhp	Jr.	1	1	4.71	13	0	21	24	14	15
Marchbanks, David, lhp	So.	9	4	4.98	19	0	99	109	26	71
Spigner, Chris, rhp	Sr.	7	0	5.08	26	0	80	83	41	82
Adler, Tony, rhp	Jr.	2	0	5.14	8	0	14	12	8	18
Bell, Gary, lhp	Sr.	10	3	5.15	21	0	110	117	46	91

3. CLEMSON

Coach: Jack Leggett   Record: 54-17

BATTING	YR	AVG	AB	R	H	2B	3B	HR	RBI	SB
Greene, Khalil, ss	Sr.	.470	285	93	134	33	1	27	91	17
Johnson, Michael, 1b	Jr.	.384	263	62	101	19	1	25	81	11
Green, Zane, of-dh	So.	.333	87	24	29	7	2	6	20	1
Baker, Jeff, 3b	Jr.	.325	265	71	86	12	2	25	87	17
Frank, Kyle, of	Jr.	.324	284	65	92	18	0	4	43	7
Valiente, Roberto, of	Jr.	.323	127	20	41	7	2	1	19	1
Coder, Chad, of	Jr.	.321	53	18	17	8	0	1	6	3
Miller, Seth, c	Sr.	.310	42	9	13	0	0	0	2	2
Schmidt, Jarrod, of	Jr.	.304	250	46	76	12	1	11	54	7
Triplett, Russell, 2b-dh	So.	.301	146	30	44	6	1	0	18	3
DeMaino, L.J., of	Jr.	.291	127	32	37	3	5	0	15	12
Slevin, David, 2b	Jr.	.284	204	46	58	8	2	0	22	7
Hourigan, Jeff, dh-p	Fr.	.275	149	20	41	9	0	6	22	0
Mahoney, Collin, c	Fr.	.266	94	18	25	6	0	6	21	0
Evans, Garrick, ss	Jr.	.241	29	4	7	2	1	0	9	2
Pyzik, Steve, c	Jr.	.169	118	21	20	7	0	0	11	1

PITCHING		W	L	ERA	G	SV	IP	H	BB	SO
Henrie, Matt, rhp	Jr.	13	5	3.12	21	1	113	112	25	81
Hahn, Jeff, rhp	Fr.	3	0	3.19	23	3	42	46	15	30
Harrelson, Paul, rhp	Jr.	1	1	3.33	24	8	27	20	5	25
Hogan, Patrick, rhp	So.	2	1	3.79	22	4	55	60	11	36
LaMura, B.J., rhp	Jr.	6	2	4.17	19	1	58	45	31	61
Hourigan, Jeff, rhp	Fr.	1	2	4.25	17	3	30	32	9	32
Reba, Steve, rhp	Sr.	13	4	4.39	20	0	113	121	44	82
Childs, Ryan, lhp	Jr.	2	0	4.57	11	1	22	25	5	15
Boozer, Thomas, lhp	Sr.	1	0	5.11	26	3	44	54	9	32
Lumsden, Tyler, lhp	Fr.	4	1	5.28	27	2	58	56	39	63
Jackson, Steven, rhp	So.	6	1	5.37	16	0	64	67	35	55
Schmidt, Jarrod, rhp	Jr.	2	0	9.39	5	0	8	11	7	8

4. STANFORD

Coach: Mark Marquess   Record: 47-18

BATTING	YR	AVG	AB	R	H	2B	3B	HR	RBI	SB
Swope, Tobin, ss	Sr.	.405	37	13	15	4	0	0	5	3
Fuld, Sam, of	So.	.375	293	67	110	20	4	8	47	8
Dragicevich, Scott, ss-3b	Sr.	.350	203	44	71	17	2	5	35	3
Cooper, Jason, dh-of	Jr.	.350	226	45	79	16	2	13	57	1
O'Riordan, Chris, 2b	Jr.	.332	262	59	87	17	1	10	47	7
Garko, Ryan, c-dh	Jr.	.314	239	68	75	18	0	14	55	2
VanZandt, Arik, 1b	So.	.309	165	33	51	6	2	6	26	10
Quentin, Carlos, of	So.	.303	241	55	73	13	4	12	54	11
Carter, Chris, of-1b	Fr.	.299	107	28	32	7	1	8	20	1
Topham, Andy, 3b-ss	So.	.287	216	24	62	11	2	5	42	10
Lucy, Donny, c-1b	Fr.	.282	117	21	33	6	1	3	29	6
Hall, Brian, of-3b	So.	.267	150	34	40	8	2	3	35	14
Ash, Jonny, dh-2b	So.	.250	24	3	6	0	0	0	6	0
Putnam, Danny, of	Fr.	.212	66	12	14	4	2	1	10	2

PITCHING		W	L	ERA	G	SV	IP	H	BB	SO
Rich, Dan, lhp	Sr.	2	2	2.45	20	6	37	30	11	42
Guthrie, Jeremy, rhp	Jr.	13	2	2.51	20	0	158	138	36	136
Naatjes, Darin, rhp	Jr.	4	0	2.53	19	2	21	18	15	25
McCally, Ryan, rhp	Jr.	4	3	3.53	25	7	51	40	22	39
Cunningham, Tim, lhp	Jr.	10	3	4.26	20	0	112	108	47	67
Dyer, Jonny, rhp	Fr.	2	0	4.38	10	0	12	10	3	8
Hudgins, John, rhp	So.	10	1	4.71	19	0	105	106	35	62
O'Hagan, David, rhp	So.	0	0	5.11	9	0	12	16	7	8
Ehrlich, Drew, rhp	So.	0	2	5.45	20	2	40	47	14	40
Willcox, J.D., rhp	Sr.	2	1	6.00	15	0	15	20	9	6
Jecmen, Mark, rhp	Fr.	0	4	8.26	14	0	28	41	14	19

5. RICE

Coach: Wayne Graham   Record: 52-14

BATTING	YR	AVG	AB	R	H	2B	3B	HR	RBI	SB
Sinisi, Vince, 1b	Fr.	.428	271	65	116	22	2	11	80	13
Blackinton, Jeff, c	So.	.364	66	10	24	4	0	0	5	0
Davis, Austin, of	So.	.355	200	48	71	10	1	7	34	1
Kolkhorst, Chris, of	So.	.345	264	62	91	16	1	3	33	8

BATTING	YR	AVG	AB	R	H	2B	3B	HR	RBI	SB
Arnold, Eric, 2b	Sr.	.342	272	60	93	19	4	9	75	7
Porfirio, A.J., of	Sr.	.311	251	45	78	16	2	3	27	8
Janish, Paul, ss	Fr.	.299	197	32	59	14	1	2	30	6
Bubela, Dane, dh-of	Jr.	.285	144	34	41	10	1	7	35	2
Brown, Hunter, 3b	Sr.	.284	208	40	59	18	0	7	35	10
Lorsbach, Mike, of	Sr.	.279	111	24	31	5	1	5	19	2
Ruchti, Justin, c	Jr.	.250	164	23	41	7	1	3	22	1
Cruz, Jose Enrique, dh-ss	So.	.226	199	41	45	6	2	16	36	4

PITCHING		W	L	ERA	G	SV	IP	H	BB	SO
Crowder, Justin, lhp	Sr.	10	3	2.00	22	1	121	106	36	106
Townsend, Wade, rhp	Fr.	2	1	2.28	19	6	51	38	22	51
Humber, Philip, rhp	Fr.	11	1	2.77	18	0	111	90	43	130
Herce, Steven, rhp	Jr.	13	3	2.79	17	0	119	106	23	104
Niemann, Jeff, rhp	Fr.	5	1	3.11	17	0	67	64	27	53
Tribe, Philip, rhp	Sr.	4	4	3.44	23	3	55	48	27	59
Aardsma, David, rhp	So.	7	1	3.47	28	5	60	65	14	53
Bryan, Bobby, rhp	Sr.	0	0	5.40	4	0	5	3	2	9

6. NOTRE DAME

Coach: Paul Mainieri   **Record:** 50-18

BATTING	YR	AVG	AB	R	H	2B	3B	HR	RBI	SB
Stanley, Steve, of	Sr.	.439	271	77	119	17	4	1	36	32
Stavisky, Brian, of-dh	Jr.	.394	193	47	76	14	5	9	57	2
Sollmann, Steve, 2b	So.	.362	213	53	77	8	4	2	47	6
Holba, Mike, dh	Jr.	.360	25	6	9	6	0	0	4	0
Sisko, Zach, inf	Jr.	.333	15	2	5	1	0	0	4	0
Bushey, Andrew, 3b-c	Jr.	.323	226	44	73	19	1	6	59	1
Billmaier, Kris, of	Jr.	.313	230	34	72	8	1	3	41	2
Bok, Matt, of-dh	Jr.	.311	180	33	56	14	2	3	36	3
Edwards, Matt, ss	Fr.	.290	31	3	9	1	0	0	4	1
Sanchez, Javier, ss	So.	.281	231	50	65	7	3	5	29	1
O'Toole, Paul, c-3b	Jr.	.281	217	48	61	12	4	11	50	11
Thaman, Joe, 1b	So.	.272	180	43	49	6	0	6	33	2
Meyer, Ken, dh-1b	Jr.	.268	127	23	34	6	0	2	8	1
Strickroth, Matt, of-1b	Jr.	.240	25	8	6	2	0	1	4	0
Macri, Matt, dh	Fr.	.206	68	10	14	3	0	1	13	1
Weiss, Brent, of-c	Fr.	.200	30	7	6	1	1	2	9	0
Milsom, Geoff, 3b	Fr.	.071	14	1	1	0	0	1	3	0

PITCHING		W	L	ERA	G	SV	IP	H	BB	SO
Duff, Drew, rhp	Sr.	2	0	2.38	9	1	23	25	7	21
Viloria, Brandon, rhp	Jr.	2	1	2.45	16	3	22	16	5	8
Buchmeier, Matt, rhp	So.	0	0	3.09	12	3	12	15	5	18
Gagne, J.P., rhp	Jr.	9	4	3.14	28	6	95	86	16	69
Kalita, Ryan, rhp	Sr.	5	0	3.16	16	0	43	45	14	36
Niesel, Chris, rhp	Fr.	4	0	3.36	14	2	72	68	18	62
Johnson, Grant, rhp	Fr.	9	5	3.46	18	0	101	94	44	86
Vergara, Martin, rhp	Fr.	5	1	3.79	12	0	36	33	17	33
Axford, John, rhp	Fr.	5	2	3.95	17	0	71	59	59	64
Jones, Tyler, rhp	Fr.	1	0	4.00	4	1	9	9	5	5
Bickford, Scott, lhp	Fr.	1	0	4.35	6	1	10	10	1	12
Ogilvie, Peter, rhp	Jr.	7	5	4.65	17	0	79	90	26	58
Laird, Matt, rhp	Jr.	0	0	5.73	12	1	11	14	9	9

7. FLORIDA STATE

Coach: Mike Martin   **Record:** 60-14

BATTING	YR	AVG	AB	R	H	2B	3B	HR	RBI	SB
Drew, Stephen, ss	Fr.	.402	204	64	82	17	4	16	54	13
McQuade, Tony, of	So.	.376	218	63	82	26	4	6	46	6
Barthelemy, Ryan, 3b-1b	Sr.	.357	297	76	106	24	4	17	94	6
Richie, Tony, c	So.	.353	249	59	88	17	2	13	75	1
Rogers, Nick, of	Sr.	.331	257	67	85	22	2	8	69	19
Brown, Jerrod, 1b	Sr.	.327	217	49	71	8	1	4	56	0
Zech, Bryan, 2b	So.	.294	235	58	69	15	0	2	38	10
Futrell, Mike, of-dh	Sr.	.286	220	39	63	15	0	6	28	7
McCaleb, Blair, dh-c	Sr.	.269	182	45	49	14	0	6	49	0
Richmond, Kevin, 2b	Fr.	.267	75	19	20	3	0	0	13	0
Smith, Richie, of	Sr.	.265	185	47	49	9	1	6	30	13
Hart, Chris, 1b	Jr.	.262	42	4	11	3	0	0	6	0
Toole, Scott, ss	Jr.	.232	95	23	22	2	1	0	13	5
Cheesman, Aaron, c	Fr.	.190	42	5	8	2	0	0	7	1
Probst, Jeff, 2b-ss	So.	.188	69	15	13	3	1	0	7	2

PITCHING		W	L	ERA	G	SV	IP	H	BB	SO
Hodges, Daniel, lhp	Jr.	4	1	2.56	36	12	63	68	10	38
Whidden, Chris, rhp	Jr.	0	0	2.93	14	0	15	8	7	11
Peterson, Trent, lhp	So.	4	2	3.35	17	0	51	48	17	46
LaMacchia, Marc, rhp	So.	11	2	3.38	18	0	96	101	21	75
Lynch, Matt, lhp	Jr.	13	2	3.59	20	0	130	132	30	98
Varnes, Blair, rhp	Sr.	10	3	3.98	19	0	106	113	20	77
Davidson, Daniel, lhp	Jr.	6	0	4.33	26	0	44	52	9	43
Lynch, Kevin, rhp	Fr.	4	1	4.64	30	1	33	33	12	27
Miller, Justin, lhp	Fr.	0	0	4.87	17	0	20	21	10	15
Read, Robby, rhp	Jr.	8	1	5.22	19	0	81	81	36	77
Roman, Eric, rhp	Jr.	0	2	7.27	20	9	17	22	8	12

8. GEORGIA TECH

Coach: Danny Hall   **Record:** 52-16

BATTING	YR	AVG	AB	R	H	2B	3B	HR	RBI	SB
Rynders, Wes, of	Sr.	.375	120	28	45	10	2	3	28	11
Menocal, Victor, ss-p	Sr.	.369	282	63	104	20	2	2	49	8
Boggs, Matthew, 3b	Sr.	.363	234	52	85	12	2	1	43	12
Slayden, Jeremy, of	Fr.	.348	256	74	89	15	1	18	66	4
Patterson, Eric, 2b	Fr.	.346	260	73	90	14	3	3	40	41
Murton, Matt, of	So.	.344	250	62	86	16	1	10	58	20
Perry, Jason, 1b-dh	Jr.	.325	237	49	77	17	1	12	60	8
Parker, Tyler, c-dh	Jr.	.310	258	57	80	19	4	11	59	13
Boggs, Brandon, of-dh	Fr.	.305	190	36	58	17	0	0	35	7
Myers, Davis, ss	So.	.294	34	10	10	1	1	0	3	2
Remole, Clifton, 1b	Sr.	.283	152	25	43	3	0	4	34	2
Nickeas, Mike, c	Fr.	.221	95	20	21	3	0	2	18	0
Hall, Jake, inf	Fr.	.207	29	2	6	2	0	0	4	0
Groce, Garrett, of	Fr.	.125	16	5	2	0	1	0	4	2

PITCHING		W	L	ERA	G	SV	IP	H	BB	SO
Menocal, Victor, rhp	Sr.	0	0	1.93	10	2	9	7	3	5
Bakker, Kyle, lhp	So.	13	2	3.14	19	0	135	132	24	115
Kindel, Jeff, lhp	Fr.	1	0	3.52	15	0	15	13	10	13
Perry, Philip, rhp	Jr.	3	0	3.56	17	3	30	22	14	32
Schmidt, Kyle, rhp	Fr.	5	2	3.64	19	0	72	73	31	80
Burks, Brian, rhp	So.	10	7	3.87	25	3	102	114	25	81
Watchko, Jeff, rhp	Jr.	11	1	4.01	29	2	90	94	19	62
Wagner, Nick, rhp	Fr.	0	0	4.24	16	1	17	18	6	12
Goodman, Chris, rhp	Jr.	8	2	4.41	21	0	82	90	16	60
Walker, Aaron, lhp	So.	1	2	5.34	21	0	29	38	8	15
Crews, Jordan, rhp	Fr.	0	0	6.00	8	0	6	10	1	3
Taylor, Drew, rhp	Fr.	0	0	7.71	11	0	9	14	4	5
Andreas, Mike, rhp	Fr.	0	0	13.50	6	0	5	7	4	7

9. NEBRASKA

Coach: Dave Van Horn   **Record:** 47-21

BATTING	YR	AVG	AB	R	H	2B	3B	HR	RBI	SB
Hoffart, Darren, c	Fr.	.400	10	5	4	2	0	0	2	0
Grose, John, c	So.	.384	125	28	48	14	0	4	38	2
Morris, Jed, c-dh	Jr.	.382	272	70	104	26	1	23	90	4
Leise, Jeff, of	Jr.	.371	294	69	109	11	8	12	51	25
Seely, Justin, of	Sr.	.320	203	39	65	19	1	7	37	4
Bolt, Will, 2b-ss	Sr.	.319	238	46	76	18	3	2	29	8
Hopper, Matt, 1b-dh	Jr.	.309	243	52	75	10	2	9	43	3
Blevins, Jeff, 3b-ss	So.	.307	218	44	67	14	1	7	50	8
Bruce, Daniel, of	Fr.	.299	187	53	56	17	1	5	41	5
Anderson, Drew, of	So.	.266	188	36	50	5	1	1	32	8
Eymann, Brandon, 3b-1b	Sr.	.245	155	27	38	6	0	4	33	0
Simokaitis, Joe, ss	Fr.	.236	140	41	33	8	1	0	16	5
Birmingham, Josh, ss	Jr.	.227	44	7	10	2	0	0	11	0
Bonesio, Ryan, 1b	Jr.	.222	27	3	6	1	0	0	3	0
Riddle, Adam, of-dh	Jr.	.217	46	17	10	0	1	0	5	1

PITCHING		W	L	ERA	G	SV	IP	H	BB	SO
Scholten, J.D., rhp	Sr.	0	0	2.08	10	0	13	9	4	10
Komine, Shane, rhp	Sr.	10	0	2.33	15	0	97	62	30	115
Marsden, Aaron, lhp	So.	8	1	2.70	20	0	100	80	40	75
Shirek, Phil, rhp	Fr.	4	2	3.45	18	1	47	45	14	47
Byers, Waylon, lhp	Jr.	1	5	3.45	22	3	29	27	4	24
Hale, Steve, rhp	Jr.	4	2	3.56	25	2	56	59	14	32
Blaesing, Jeff, rhp	Sr.	0	0	4.09	12	1	11	9	7	12
Rodrigue, Jamie, lhp	Jr.	7	3	4.15	17	0	93	107	19	45
Duensing, Brian, lhp	Fr.	6	2	4.73	18	0	78	82	25	60
Sillman, Mike, lhp	So.	1	1	5.12	10	0	19	25	7	17
Burch, Jason, rhp	So.	3	2	5.19	17	1	35	40	14	21
Timm, Dustin, rhp	So.	1	1	5.40	6	0	7	9	2	6
Becker, Jeremy, lhp	Fr.	2	2	5.94	19	3	17	18	5	14

10. HOUSTON

Coach: Rayner Noble   **Record:** 48-17

BATTING	YR	AVG	AB	R	H	2B	3B	HR	RBI	SB
Papavasiliou, Thanos, 1b-dh	So.	.358	123	17	44	8	0	1	20	2
Whatley, Keith, of-p	So.	.356	101	21	36	6	0	1	18	7
Snyder, Chris, c	Jr.	.343	230	59	79	13	0	15	71	8
Cooley, Brett, 1b-dh	Jr.	.339	236	50	80	17	1	18	56	3
Bourn, Michael, of	So.	.327	248	68	81	8	1	1	23	32
Bruce, Cole, 3b	So.	.318	88	20	28	3	1	1	11	2
Mitchell, Sean, of	So.	.306	108	17	33	5	1	1	13	6
Crain, Jesse, ss-p	Jr.	.309	262	51	81	13	0	11	47	3
Musslewhite, Stuart, 2b	Fr.	.299	177	27	53	11	1	1	21	7
Scalise, Anthony, of	Jr.	.284	201	31	57	6	1	1	31	11
Cho, Hyung, 3b	So.	.270	244	33	66	6	1	6	28	4
Lucas, Gabe, of	So.	.264	129	16	34	3	1	1	15	6
Bertillion, Daron, c	Sr.	.263	38	2	10	0	0	0	5	0
Ahrens, Keith, ss	So.	.222	18	3	4	0	0	0	0	0

		AVG	AB	R	H	2B	3B	HR	RBI	SB
Blair, Cameron, 2b	Fr.	.219	32	1	7	0	0	0	5	3

PITCHING		W	L	ERA	G	SV	IP	H	BB	SO
Crain, Jesse, rhp	Jr.	4	0	0.23	27	10	38	22	10	46
Sullivan, Brad, rhp	So.	13	1	1.82	18	0	129	80	49	157
Mitchell, Nathan, rhp	Sr.	5	2	2.62	35	4	61	39	13	59
Wagner, Ryan, rhp	Fr.	2	1	2.66	25	1	44	27	24	65
Zell, Danny, lhp	So.	8	2	2.86	23	0	50	51	14	37
Hooper, Matt, rhp	Sr.	1	1	3.38	20	0	21	25	4	8
Whatley, Keith, lhp	Sr.	8	3	3.96	15	0	61	58	31	38
Flores, Gene, rhp	So.	3	2	4.40	20	0	78	85	24	55
Faught, Austin, lhp	So.	1	3	5.07	23	0	50	58	13	50
Henderson, Brian, lhp	So.	2	0	5.75	21	0	20	20	9	19
Harris, Bryan, rhp	Jr.	0	1	6.75	8	0	5	6	3	3
Gartz, Taylor, lhp	Fr.	0	0	9.00	8	0	12	16	11	7

11. LOUISIANA STATE

Coach: Smoke Laval **Record:** 44-22

BATTING	YR	AVG	AB	R	H	2B	3B	HR	RBI	SB
Barker, Sean, of	Sr.	.382	267	47	102	16	0	8	62	24
Holt, J.C., 2b-ss	Fr.	.349	192	45	67	5	6	3	23	10
Phillips, Chris, c	Jr.	.344	192	30	66	7	0	7	44	0
Pontiff, Wally, 3b	Jr.	.339	248	41	84	20	0	6	46	4
Hill, Aaron, ss-3b	So.	.329	222	46	73	18	2	9	47	10
Gill, Blake, 1b-2b	Fr.	.292	168	29	49	11	2	1	26	2
Heath, Matt, of	Sr.	.290	231	57	67	12	5	10	48	11
Wiethorn, Eric, dh-1b	Jr.	.278	97	17	27	6	0	3	17	0
Scelfo, Rocky, 2b-of	So.	.269	134	29	36	2	1	2	10	3
Raymer, David, of	Sr.	.266	173	40	46	8	0	4	26	5
Zeringue, Jon, of	Fr.	.247	97	10	24	5	0	2	8	1
Hahn, Dustin, of-dh	Fr.	.227	97	13	22	5	2	2	12	0
Columbus, Jason, 1b	Jr.	.224	58	13	13	4	1	2	11	0
Harris, Clay, p-1b	Jr.	.221	68	10	15	3	0	3	12	0
Vargas, Jason, of-p	Jr.	.211	38	9	8	0	1	2	12	0
Welch, Darren, c	Sr.	.118	34	5	4	0	0	1	6	0
Weaver, Dustin, c	So.	.083	12	0	1	0	0	0	0	0

PITCHING		W	L	ERA	G	SV	IP	H	BB	SO
Determann, Jason, lhp	Fr.	1	0	1.29	2	0	7	4	1	3
Vaught, Chad, rhp	Jr.	0	0	1.50	1	0	6	5	1	8
Mestepey, Lane, lhp	So.	11	5	2.59	19	0	142	145	17	74
Tompkins, Jake, rhp	Jr.	7	1	2.68	25	4	87	78	37	96
Pettit, Bo, rhp	Jr.	9	7	3.35	19	0	121	112	57	121
Vargas, Jason, lhp	Jr.	1	1	3.43	13	0	21	18	6	16
Wilson, Brian, rhp	So.	10	5	3.54	23	2	94	112	31	71
Harris, Clay, rhp	Fr.	3	0	4.15	16	0	48	57	5	37
David, Brad, lhp	Jr.	2	1	5.40	19	0	30	41	9	19
Guidroz, Lukas, rhp	Jr.	0	1	5.60	11	0	18	23	6	15
Guidry, Weylin, rhp	Sr.	0	1	10.22	10	1	12	18	8	9

12. WAKE FOREST

Coach: George Greer **Record:** 47-13

BATTING	YR	AVG	AB	R	H	2B	3B	HR	RBI	SB
Bourassa, Adam, of	Jr.	.412	250	71	103	11	4	2	41	26
Johnson, Ryan, dh-of	Jr.	.366	232	56	85	14	4	13	77	1
Blue, Nick, 2b-dh	Jr.	.355	203	60	72	9	0	1	40	21
D'Antona, Jamie, 3b	So.	.336	223	54	75	10	1	20	83	2
Ruziecki, Jeff, 1b	Jr.	.306	222	47	68	13	0	7	34	2
Ingold, Ben, ss	Fr.	.305	203	30	62	16	1	2	29	1
Mathias, Ryder, c	Jr.	.300	110	28	33	5	0	4	30	0
Scioletti, Brad, inf-of	So.	.295	122	29	36	9	0	3	21	2
Ghutzman, Stephen, c	Jr.	.291	175	27	51	16	0	6	39	0
Braun, Ryan, of-p	Jr.	.275	69	18	19	2	0	9	19	1
Hubbard, Ryan, of-2b	Jr.	.274	201	49	55	6	2	7	28	19
LeFaivre, Steve, of	So.	.267	165	34	44	8	1	5	28	0
Riepe, Doug, dh	So.	.000	18	1	0	0	0	0	3	0

PITCHING		W	L	ERA	G	SV	IP	H	BB	SO
Bush, Dave, rhp	Sr.	8	1	1.64	40	13	60	47	10	61
Sleeth, Kyle, rhp	So.	14	0	2.97	18	0	118	115	41	113
Davidson, Daniel, rhp	Fr.	3	0	4.34	15	0	29	30	18	30
Morley, Tim, lhp	Fr.	6	3	4.41	16	0	88	85	39	71
Hanson, Adam, rhp	So.	3	0	4.50	33	2	56	56	19	40
Hill, Seth, lhp	Jr.	3	3	4.86	18	1	74	73	22	53
Braun, Ryan, rhp	Jr.	2	2	5.45	6	0	33	39	14	28
Clayton, Ben, lhp	Jr.	2	1	6.19	4	0	16	24	5	11
Bach, Brian, rhp	Fr.	6	2	6.60	17	0	45	60	20	33
Lewis, Ryan, lhp	Sr.	0	0	8.00	7	0	9	11	8	8
Comer, Brad, rhp	Sr.	0	1	8.31	7	0	13	16	7	12

13. ALABAMA

Coach: Jim Wells **Record:** 51-15

BATTING	YR	AVG	AB	R	H	2B	3B	HR	RBI	SB
Marshall, John, c	Jr.	.429	14	4	6	2	0	0	5	2
Redding, Grant, of	Jr.	.421	76	16	32	9	1	2	18	1
Stonard, Peter, 2b-of	So.	.411	236	59	97	22	5	5	42	18

		AVG	AB	R	H	2B	3B	HR	RBI	SB
Scott, Gabe, of	Fr.	.381	42	9	16	2	0	0	8	0
Hearod, Beau, dh	Jr.	.335	212	39	71	11	1	12	54	3
White, Chad, of	So.	.330	88	14	29	5	0	0	17	0
Garner, Travis, of	Jr.	.323	226	57	73	15	0	6	31	26
Brown, Jeremy, c	Sr.	.320	219	56	70	17	2	11	64	6
McClanahan, Scott, of	Sr.	.297	269	68	80	22	3	14	62	20
Boyd, Brent, 1b-2b	Sr.	.287	237	50	68	18	1	8	51	3
Pavkovich, Adam, ss	So.	.272	213	45	58	14	0	6	31	1
Sosa, Carlos, 3b	Jr.	.269	104	14	28	3	0	1	16	3
Rice, Allen, 3b	Fr.	.247	166	29	41	11	0	0	18	4
Welch, Zac, 1b	Fr.	.229	96	14	22	3	0	1	14	0
Pennington, Spencer, 1b	Fr.	.180	50	4	9	0	0	1	4	0

PITCHING		W	L	ERA	G	SV	IP	H	BB	SO
Reed, Brian, rhp	Jr.	5	0	1.75	27	9	51	43	13	43
Tankersley, Taylor, lhp	Fr.	8	5	2.62	25	7	69	55	20	65
Cormier, Lance, rhp	Sr.	11	3	3.28	17	0	129	135	27	85
Carter, Brent, lhp	Fr.	2	0	3.31	17	2	54	52	10	51
Norris, Jeffrey, lhp	So.	6	1	3.34	14	1	70	74	15	50
Sanders, Shane, rhp	Sr.	8	4	3.87	19	0	93	107	27	58
Woodward, Jared, rhp	So.	6	1	4.52	23	0	66	75	13	57
Mennen, Eric, rhp	Fr.	2	0	4.66	9	2	19	25	5	11
Baker, Josh, rhp	Fr.	3	1	5.93	9	0	30	40	11	22
Brazell, Landon, rhp	So.	0	0	6.75	4	1	7	7	8	4

14. SOUTHERN CALIFORNIA

Coach: Mike Gillespie **Record:** 37-24

BATTING	YR	AVG	AB	R	H	2B	3B	HR	RBI	SB
Concepcion, Alberto, c-3b	Jr.	.363	234	57	85	21	5	11	48	3
Peavey, Bill, 1b	Jr.	.361	216	62	78	17	0	15	71	5
Metropoulos, Joey, dh-3b	Fr.	.352	193	51	68	17	1	13	65	2
Mosich, Nick, inf	Jr.	.352	91	17	32	6	0	2	10	1
Moon, Michael, ss-3b	So.	.336	238	52	80	14	1	8	60	12
Barre, Brian, of	Sr.	.331	242	75	80	16	2	12	43	14
Gordon, David, of	Jr.	.326	89	19	29	5	0	1	22	5
McAndrews, Travis, of	Jr.	.324	136	21	44	4	0	3	28	1
Morales, Michael, of	Jr.	.309	97	22	30	2	2	1	20	11
Bonovich, Matt, c	Sr.	.279	61	6	17	3	0	1	19	0
Brewster, Jon, 3b	So.	.277	119	23	33	5	5	1	8	4
Lunetta, Anthony, 2b	So.	.271	229	41	62	11	0	1	24	6
McCauley, Mark, inf	So.	.267	45	13	12	2	0	0	8	0
Cox, Kris, of	Sr.	.242	91	19	22	3	2	2	11	3
Torres, Rafael, 3b	So.	.206	34	6	7	1	0	0	5	0
Gordon, Spencer, of	So.	.067	15	0	1	0	0	0	3	0

PITCHING		W	L	ERA	G	SV	IP	H	BB	SO
Dizard, Fraser, lhp	So.	0	0	1.50	3	0	6	7	4	5
Reyes, Anthony, rhp	Jr.	4	2	3.44	12	0	65	69	17	49
Bannister, Brett, rhp	Fr.	8	3	3.56	26	0	86	80	32	76
Campos, Cory, rhp	Jr.	3	3	3.84	30	6	68	76	19	69
Rummonds, Josh, lhp	So.	0	1	4.34	14	0	29	29	15	24
Chico, Matt, lhp	Fr.	6	4	5.45	15	0	69	81	47	69
Williams, Jon, rhp	So.	5	2	5.84	29	3	62	84	17	31
Howell, J.P., lhp	Fr.	3	4	6.27	14	0	47	50	35	33
Olson, Jordan, lhp	Jr.	3	2	6.48	19	2	58	78	32	49
Butler, Bret, rhp	Fr.	2	1	8.07	21	0	29	39	13	22
Wentworth, Clayton, rhp	Jr.	0	0	16.20	10	0	8	19	15	13
Clark, Chad, rhp	Jr.	0	2	19.13	10	0	16	31	34	25

15. FLORIDA

Coach: Pat McMahon **Record:** 46-19

BATTING	YR	AVG	AB	R	H	2B	3B	HR	RBI	SB
Mercadante, Joe, c	Jr.	.471	17	5	8	2	0	2	9	0
Osborn, Pat, 3b	Jr.	.414	251	67	104	17	1	17	76	7
Kiger, Mark, ss	Sr.	.403	258	90	104	12	4	11	55	11
Maley, Matt, of	So.	.400	20	7	8	1	0	3	9	0
Shealy, Ryan, 1b	Sr.	.379	261	73	99	14	2	23	80	0
Sobieraj, Aaron, of	Sr.	.354	237	60	84	11	3	8	57	7
Klebonis, David, of	Sr.	.353	85	19	30	5	1	3	24	0
Tucker, Jonathan, 2b-ss	Fr.	.348	92	28	32	4	1	0	10	2
Harrison, Ben, of	So.	.342	161	42	55	14	5	8	38	6
Swackhamer, Wes, of	Fr.	.333	12	3	4	1	0	0	4	1
Goss, Matt, of	Sr.	.321	209	50	67	16	4	6	47	6
Corsaletti, Jeff, of	Fr.	.313	83	19	26	6	1	2	19	1
Davidson, Aaron, 2b	So.	.309	217	58	67	12	2	10	42	19
Garza, Mario, dh	Jr.	.308	182	43	56	13	1	11	41	3
Rose, Brian, c	So.	.281	231	46	65	13	0	7	45	0
Riordan, Jake, of	Jr.	.273	55	19	15	1	1	0	10	3
Smith, C.J., inf	Fr.	.077	13	4	1	0	0	0	1	0

PITCHING		W	L	ERA	G	SV	IP	H	BB	SO
Falkenbach, Connor, rhp	Fr.	0	0	1.40	12	1	19	18	4	12
Hart, Alex, rhp	Jr.	13	3	3.24	17	0	111	81	56	81
Ramsey, Keith, lhp	Sr.	10	3	3.88	19	0	109	92	44	84
Goldfarb, Jamie, lhp	Jr.	2	4	4.00	27	4	45	51	11	31

		W	L	ERA	G	SV	IP	H	BB	SO
Hedgecock, Ben, rhp	Jr.	0	0	4.02	9	0	16	16	0	11
Boss, Tommy, rhp	Fr.	0	1	4.44	18	2	24	29	5	26
Bartelt, David, rhp	Fr.	5	1	4.57	19	2	45	54	8	24
Ramshaw, Jimmy, lhp	Sr.	6	4	4.80	18	1	90	101	39	80
Pete, Mike, lhp	Fr.	4	0	5.40	21	0	48	56	13	34
Coleman, Kevin, rhp	Sr.	2	2	5.40	28	6	32	47	8	26
Foster, Matt, rhp	Jr.	1	1	5.87	5	0	8	10	2	6
Drucker, Scot, rhp	So.	1	0	6.06	13	0	16	18	8	14
Sadowski, Ryan, rhp	Fr.	1	0	8.10	7	0	7	9	5	9

16. RICHMOND

Coach: Ron Atkins — **Record:** 53-13

BATTING	YR	AVG	AB	R	H	2B	3B	HR	RBI	SB
Reaver, David, 3b	So.	.391	266	73	104	30	5	4	54	32
Craig, Matt, ss	So.	.375	248	70	93	22	3	19	84	19
Gula, Mike, 3b	Sr.	.375	16	5	6	0	1	3	7	0
Chiaravalloti, Vito, 1b-of	Jr.	.357	238	69	85	17	1	23	86	3
Pritz, Bryan, of	So.	.345	261	78	90	19	0	8	51	31
Tidball, Adam, c	So.	.339	230	44	78	28	1	11	45	2
Ruscello, Brian, 2b	Fr.	.292	185	24	54	10	3	4	26	4
Dolan, Chris, dh-c	So.	.265	170	29	45	7	3	8	30	1
Board, A.J., of	So.	.260	96	15	25	3	0	1	8	4
Fasano, Jim, 1b	So.	.258	151	17	39	10	0	3	22	0
Cronin, John, of-p	Fr.	.230	152	39	35	1	0	2	13	9
Galligan, Michael, of	Jr.	.200	45	8	9	1	0	2	9	1
LeNoir, Bobby, 2b	So.	.184	76	14	14	1	1	2	12	2
O'Leary, Jim, of	So.	.091	11	1	1	0	0	0	0	0
Klausman, Jarrod, dh	Fr.	.091	11	1	1	1	0	0	1	0
Wilson, Harry, of		.000	28	7	0	0	0	0	1	0

PITCHING	YR	W	L	ERA	G	SV	IP	H	BB	SO
Stauffer, Tim, rhp	So.	15	3	1.54	20	0	146	110	34	140
Martin, Thomas, lhp	So.	8	0	2.98	9	0	54	45	17	55
Givens, Andy, rhp	Jr.	3	3	3.86	17	7	37	32	18	44
McGirr, Mike, rhp	Jr.	12	1	4.06	17	0	109	110	32	85
McLoughlin, Matt, rhp	So.	5	1	4.43	20	3	45	52	17	32
Rice, Tim, lhp	Fr.	5	0	4.77	19	1	55	54	37	53
Bolinski, Jason, rhp	Fr.	3	3	5.72	18	2	57	65	29	41
Duclos, Derek, rhp	Fr.	1	1	6.56	16	1	36	42	21	30
Cronin, John, rhp	Fr.	1	0	8.76	11	4	12	14	11	16

17. NORTH CAROLINA

Coach: Mike Fox — **Record:** 43-21

BATTING	YR	AVG	AB	R	H	2B	3B	HR	RBI	SB
Adams, Russ, ss-2b	Jr.	.370	254	75	94	20	3	7	55	45
Farrell, Sean, of	Jr.	.354	254	66	90	19	1	14	73	10
Maples, Chris, 3b-of	Sr.	.347	274	62	95	24	1	23	79	16
Greenberg, Adam, of	Jr.	.337	267	80	90	17	7	17	57	35
Cleveland, Jeremy, 1b	So.	.333	171	32	57	11	0	10	31	1
Iannetta, Chris, c	So.	.333	165	35	55	7	0	9	34	1
Braun, Ron, dh-c	So.	.307	205	48	63	9	1	13	46	2
Prosser, Chad, 2b-ss	Jr.	.304	227	44	69	11	2	2	33	7
Blake, Ryan, c-1b	Jr.	.299	177	43	53	12	1	7	29	1
Younts, Chase, of	Fr.	.293	41	12	12	2	0	1	9	3
Mangum, Greg, 2b	Fr.	.287	108	12	31	6	1	0	12	2
Adams, Mell, of-p	So.	.284	116	25	33	10	1	4	26	4
Moyer, Wes, of	So.	.200	10	2	2	2	0	0	2	0
Burgess, Mickey, inf	Fr.	.148	27	4	4	1	0	0	2	0

PITCHING	YR	W	L	ERA	G	SV	IP	H	BB	SO
Senatore, Scott, lhp	So.	0	0	2.08	18	1	9	13	6	7
Maples, Chris, rhp	Sr.	0	3	2.45	21	5	22	15	15	25
Brower, Kevin, rhp	So.	3	1	2.82	26	1	38	38	26	29
Manshack, Scott, rhp	So.	7	0	3.70	20	0	66	65	31	60
Harrell, Carter, rhp	Fr.	8	4	3.88	24	1	58	53	25	65
Benson, Whitley, rhp	So.	2	1	3.99	29	3	50	54	21	44
Gross, Michael, rhp	So.	6	4	4.13	32	2	57	48	24	40
Autrey, Scott, rhp	Jr.	5	3	4.42	17	0	98	91	34	87
Bakker, Garry, rhp	Fr.	6	3	4.46	18	0	83	78	44	68
Moore, Daniel, lhp	So.	6	2	6.53	21	0	81	91	36	83
Adams, Mell, rhp	So.	0	0	7.94	8	0	11	15	8	7

18. CAL STATE NORTHRIDGE

Coach: Mike Batesole — **Record:** 41-17

BATTING	YR	AVG	AB	R	H	2B	3B	HR	RBI	SB
Larkin, Shaun, 2b	Sr.	.361	205	58	74	16	1	15	49	3
Haag, Ryan, 3b	So.	.345	168	44	58	18	1	3	27	9
Verbryke, Eric, of	Jr.	.332	226	52	75	14	1	14	54	13
Gorman, Jason, ss	So.	.329	158	40	52	13	2	7	31	4
Allec, Jason, c	Jr.	.320	181	35	58	8	0	8	45	3
Arroyo, Tim, 1b	Jr.	.310	200	39	62	5	0	10	50	0
Nikolic, Jason, of	Jr.	.305	220	37	67	7	2	6	37	17
Robinson, Mel, 2b-ss	Fr.	.283	53	15	15	1	0	0	9	1
Dorn, Tim, 1b-dh	Fr.	.281	114	24	32	4	0	6	20	3
McKenzie, Aaron, of	Jr.	.278	126	25	35	3	0	8	27	0

19. FLORIDA ATLANTIC

(continued top right)

BATTING	YR	AVG	AB	R	H	2B	3B	HR	RBI	SB
Phillips, Dominick, 3b	Jr.	.262	61	11	16	1	0	0	8	2
Simpson, Rudy, of	Jr.	.234	192	39	45	7	3	9	32	6
Voita, John, 3b-dh	Fr.	.221	68	15	15	4	0	2	10	2
Archer, Phillip, c	Sr.	.205	39	5	8	2	0	2	5	0

PITCHING		W	L	ERA	G	SV	IP	H	BB	SO
Murphy, Bill, lhp	Jr.	9	4	3.55	17	1	106	89	69	129
Larson, Matthew, rhp	Jr.	6	2	3.98	17	1	75	90	24	48
Rosales, Leo, rhp	Jr.	3	2	4.05	15	0	27	28	18	20
Davidson, Andy, lhp	Sr.	11	2	4.14	22	1	78	103	19	71
Loe, Kameron, rhp	Jr.	5	3	4.20	18	1	84	90	15	72
Polanco, Phil, rhp	Jr.	3	1	4.41	25	6	35	36	20	38
Robertson, Scott, rhp	Jr.	1	1	5.40	26	2	43	52	19	39
Fortugno, Justin, rhp	So.	2	0	5.97	24	1	29	29	23	35
Cayton, Brett, rhp	Jr.	0	0	7.71	10	0	14	18	13	10
Dorn, Tim, rhp	Fr.	1	1	8.57	7	0	21	24	15	12

19. FLORIDA ATLANTIC

Coach: Kevin Cooney — **Record:** 46-21

BATTING	YR	AVG	AB	R	H	2B	3B	HR	RBI	SB
Gilmore, Marc, c	Jr.	.385	26	6	10	4	0	0	2	0
Pali, Matt, 1b-dh	Jr.	.361	202	37	73	8	0	10	43	2
Biernbaum, L.J., of	Sr.	.350	257	64	90	12	2	16	68	13
Somarriba, Gabe, of	Sr.	.345	235	66	81	13	0	8	50	7
Brown, Rusty, 1b-dh	So.	.343	166	40	57	11	0	11	47	1
Cox, Mike, 3b	Jr.	.331	251	61	83	11	0	18	65	4
Valdes, Mike, dh	Jr.	.329	149	32	49	7	0	5	29	7
Creech, Jeremiah, 2b	Jr.	.328	61	18	20	2	0	1	11	4
Orton, Robert, c	So.	.306	170	30	52	9	0	4	25	1
Fiorentino, Jeff, of	Fr.	.301	309	49	63	10	2	12	53	5
Hutton, Derek, 2b	Fr.	.282	177	38	50	6	0	3	31	10
O'Connor, Shaen, c	Jr.	.263	99	17	26	5	1	2	20	0
deCordova, Andre, dh	Jr.	.259	27	5	7	1	0	2	7	0
Spano, Bobby, ss	Sr.	.250	180	45	45	9	0	0	23	5
Thoms, Andrew, of	Fr.	.250	24	7	6	2	0	2	7	0
Nodes, Eric, of	Fr.	.176	17	12	3	0	0	1	4	1

PITCHING		W	L	ERA	G	SV	IP	H	BB	SO
McNab, Tim, rhp	Sr.	3	2	2.52	34	12	39	50	6	39
Cooney, Jim, lhp	Sr.	2	0	2.67	28	0	34	33	18	35
Callahan, James, lhp	Jr.	0	0	3.00	7	0	6	3	4	5
Core, Danny, rhp	Jr.	8	6	3.72	19	0	106	107	35	87
Della Rocco, Chris, rhp	So.	3	3	4.34	30	0	37	37	19	36
MacLane, Tom, lhp	Jr.	4	2	4.38	22	0	49	49	27	46
Pillsbury, Chris, rhp	So.	10	3	4.60	18	0	106	109	39	85
Eubanks, Greg, rhp	Sr.	3	0	4.70	12	0	15	21	5	12
NeSmith, Travis, lhp	So.	7	2	4.98	18	0	60	72	19	54
Lopez, Nelson, rhp	Sr.	1	1	5.27	19	0	43	51	23	30
O'Brien, Matt, rhp	So.	5	2	5.36	13	0	40	46	11	40
Young, Eddie, rhp	Jr.	0	0	6.35	5	0	6	3	6	7
Ingwell, Brad, lhp	Jr.	0	0	6.94	10	0	12	22	2	12

20. MIAMI (FLA.)

Coach: Jim Morris — **Record:** 34-29

BATTING	YR	AVG	AB	R	H	2B	3B	HR	RBI	SB
Rodriguez, Javy, ss-2b	Sr.	.376	263	57	99	14	2	6	35	37
Howard, Kevin, 3b-ss	Jr.	.363	237	55	86	23	1	12	52	12
Matienzo, Danny, c-dh	Jr.	.335	230	48	77	8	0	20	67	7
Burt, Jim, of-1b	So.	.322	208	42	67	19	0	9	48	4
Giannotti, Richard, of	Fr.	.314	51	16	16	2	1	2	10	1
Safchik, Brad, of	Sr.	.311	193	43	60	17	2	1	40	15
Dryer, Matt, 1b-3b	Sr.	.311	180	39	56	8	1	5	32	7
Figueroa, Danny, of	Fr.	.300	190	37	57	3	1	0	16	16
Figueroa, Paco, 2b-ss	Fr.	.300	130	32	39	5	0	3	20	8
Mannix, Kevin, of	Jr.	.296	162	32	48	11	0	4	21	2
Blanco, Alex, ss-2b	Jr.	.278	18	3	5	0	0	0	1	0
Hooft, Joey, 2b	Fr.	.250	52	10	13	4	0	0	9	2
Dini, Greg, c	Fr.	.247	85	7	21	6	0	1	13	1
Pratt, Haas, 1b-dh	So.	.245	98	15	24	10	0	3	23	1
San Pedro, Erick, c	Fr.	.217	60	7	13	2	0	0	7	0
Barket, Matt, of-dh	Fr.	.194	31	2	6	0	0	1	3	1

PITCHING		W	L	ERA	G	SV	IP	H	BB	SO
Cockroft, J.D., lhp	So.	5	0	2.22	28	0	24	15	10	15
Dixon, Ryan, rhp	Fr.	0	0	3.86	9	1	19	18	10	12
Valdes-Fauli, Shawn, rhp	Fr.	1	1	4.29	31	0	36	41	11	28
Touchet, Dan, rhp	So.	6	2	4.41	21	0	98	101	32	78
Huguet, George, rhp	So.	7	4	4.50	40	8	50	57	17	45
Cohn, Andrew, lhp	So.	0	0	5.27	29	0	14	12	8	8
Bengochea, Kiki, rhp	Jr.	6	7	5.63	18	0	94	105	47	72
Roberson, Troy, rhp	Jr.	2	1	5.71	14	0	52	52	32	49
Prunty, T.J., rhp	So.	5	4	6.07	17	0	76	93	29	44
DeBold, Luke, rhp	Sr.	1	1	6.17	13	1	12	14	3	8
Bongiovanni, Vince, rhp	Fr.	1	4	6.23	14	0	39	43	19	39
Vazquez, Vince, rhp	Jr.	0	2	6.65	21	1	23	30	15	20
Camardese, Brandon, lhp	Fr.	0	3	7.18	13	0	26	40	12	20

21. LONG BEACH STATE

Coach: Mike Weathers **Record:** 39-21

BATTING	YR	AVG	AB	R	H	2B	3B	HR	RBI	SB
Hutting, Tim, 3b	Jr.	.398	103	18	41	2	0	0	14	1
Covarrubias, Nick, of-3b	Sr.	.378	246	56	93	25	1	4	51	4
McAnulty, Paul, of-1b	Jr.	.360	200	50	72	19	2	9	55	6
Reed, Jeremy, of	Jr.	.339	242	59	82	15	3	7	50	19
Varela, Edgar, 3b	Sr.	.333	27	1	9	1	0	0	4	0
Wright, Chris, of	Sr.	.320	225	36	72	14	0	2	34	4
Orlandos, Nick, 2b	Sr.	.318	179	30	57	11	1	2	26	2
Davis, Brad, c	Fr.	.317	183	26	58	6	1	2	20	4
Hofius, Mike, 1b	So.	.314	175	24	55	10	1	2	32	0
Velazco, Steve, of	Fr.	.292	24	7	7	3	0	0	1	3
Genung, Chris, of	Jr.	.280	50	6	14	3	1	1	8	0
Jennings, Todd, c-3b	So.	.277	141	24	39	6	3	3	28	7
Randel, Kevin, ss	Jr.	.274	215	54	59	11	1	8	34	7
Macaluso, Paul, of	So.	.263	57	8	15	1	0	1	10	0
Heether, Adam, 3b	So.	.238	42	5	10	1	0	0	1	0

PITCHING	YR	W	L	ERA	G	SV	IP	H	BB	SO
Muniz, Carlos, rhp	Jr.	3	1	1.52	23	1	24	19	10	26
Demaria, Chris, rhp	Sr.	1	3	2.42	26	5	45	43	5	35
Jamison, Neil, rhp	Fr.	1	1	2.70	22	2	30	28	5	33
Alvarez, Abe, lhp	So.	12	3	2.72	17	0	103	94	27	89
Ashabraner, Bo, rhp	Jr.	0	0	2.79	7	0	10	11	3	7
Beucler, Nate, rhp	Sr.	2	2	3.30	12	1	46	49	8	38
Eisentrager, Dan, rhp	Jr.	10	3	3.95	19	0	96	108	13	73
Weaver, Jered, rhp	Fr.	8	4	4.37	17	0	93	80	32	74
Pace, Joey, rhp	So.	0	0	4.62	15	0	25	31	8	15
Alliston, Josh, rhp	Sr.	2	4	4.63	29	6	47	45	19	46
Baumback, Jeff, rhp	Jr.	0	0	4.91	15	0	18	22	7	16

22. ARIZONA STATE

Coach: Pat Murphy **Record:** 37-21

BATTING	YR	AVG	AB	R	H	2B	3B	HR	RBI	SB
Sheaffer, Jon, of	Sr.	.364	110	31	40	6	1	0	19	8
Ethier, Andre, of	So.	.363	182	38	66	14	3	4	50	1
West, Jeremy, 1b	So.	.356	208	55	74	18	4	13	71	0
Pedroia, Dustin, ss	Fr.	.347	236	51	82	13	2	1	45	5
Garrabrants, Steve, 3b-of	So.	.337	202	55	68	15	7	2	33	16
Garcia, Sergio, 2b	Sr.	.336	113	30	38	4	0	1	14	16
Larish, Jeff, 3b	Fr.	.328	128	31	42	4	3	3	24	0
Wyrick, Dennis, c-3b	Jr.	.315	73	11	23	4	0	0	10	3
Castillo, Cesar, c	Sr.	.287	94	22	27	8	1	1	20	3
Allen, Rodney, of	So.	.278	209	46	58	15	2	6	50	14
McKenna, Ryan, of	So.	.265	83	15	22	3	1	1	15	2
Kartler, Bryce, p-1b	Jr.	.250	16	3	4	3	0	0	4	0
Cadena, Nick, of	Fr.	.239	92	14	22	2	0	6	28	1
Schutt, Doug, of	Sr.	.231	52	15	12	1	1	0	4	7
Kinsler, Ian, ss	So.	.230	61	5	14	2	0	0	9	4
Walsh, Nick, 3b	So.	.219	64	19	14	2	0	0	9	4
Bocchi, Joel, c	Fr.	.214	28	3	6	1	1	0	3	0
Gosewisch, Tuffy, c	Fr.	.128	39	6	5	0	0	0	2	0

PITCHING	YR	W	L	ERA	G	SV	IP	H	BB	SO
Arguello, Carlos, lhp	Jr.	5	1	2.01	14	0	40	38	9	30
Schroyer, Ryan, rhp	So.	4	1	2.37	25	8	61	50	35	75
Sanchez, Miguel, lhp	Fr.	1	0	2.38	3	0	11	9	4	10
Esposito, Mike, rhp	So.	9	6	3.72	17	0	104	109	31	93
McClellan, Robbie, rhp	Jr.	7	6	4.73	21	1	97	94	51	91
Liebeck, Jered, rhp	Jr.	2	1	5.20	14	1	45	53	16	38
Kartler, Bryce, lhp	Jr.	4	4	5.46	19	0	63	55	37	56
Sopko, Mark, rhp	Fr.	2	2	5.56	25	1	34	33	17	26
Klusman, Aaron, rhp	So.	0	0	6.45	15	0	22	28	18	22
Perrault, Josh, rhp	So.	0	0	6.97	9	0	10	20	3	8
Jackson, J.J., rhp	So.	3	0	7.71	14	0	21	22	18	21

23. WICHITA STATE

Coach: Gene Stephenson **Record:** 47-16

BATTING	YR	AVG	AB	R	H	2B	3B	HR	RBI	SB
Burgamy, Brian, 2b	Jr.	.400	240	68	96	15	3	4	57	24
Walter, Randy, of	Jr.	.365	192	55	70	14	2	10	49	30
Hawkins, Dustin, of	Sr.	.356	216	55	77	16	1	6	36	33
Johnson, Mark, of	So.	.343	108	22	37	9	4	3	27	2
Rogers, Don, 3b	So.	.333	27	7	9	3	0	1	11	0
Welch, Tanner, ss	Sr.	.326	181	35	59	6	1	3	33	10
McCarty, Justin, of	Sr.	.314	194	31	61	13	1	5	40	12
Erstad, Bryan, of	So.	.313	16	9	5	0	0	1	5	0
Moffitt, Drew, dh	So.	.312	215	60	67	17	1	16	68	4
Sorensen, Logan, 1b	So.	.305	223	55	68	17	1	11	47	5
McCoola, Nick, ss	Fr.	.304	23	6	7	0	0	1	4	0
Green, Brandon, 3b	So.	.301	216	40	65	14	0	3	34	13
Becker, Kent, c	Sr.	.273	44	8	12	3	0	1	12	0
Owen, Ryan, c	Jr.	.237	118	19	28	6	1	1	17	4
Smarsh, Shawn, 3b	So.	.229	35	13	8	4	0	0	4	1
Bell, Ryan, of	Jr.	.197	66	9	13	3	0	0	3	1
Muich, Joe, c	Fr.	.170	47	7	8	3	0	0	9	0
Wright, Brad, of	Sr.	.158	19	1	3	2	0	0	1	0

PITCHING	YR	W	L	ERA	G	SV	IP	H	BB	SO
Tetuan, John, rhp	Jr.	10	1	1.72	16	1	89	62	31	78
Haines, Steve, rhp	Sr.	1	3	2.28	22	4	28	22	4	18
Maureau, Justin, lhp	Jr.	4	3	2.45	18	3	55	47	9	67
Sanders, David, lhp	So.	5	4	2.59	14	0	73	74	13	58
Jakubov, Mathew, rhp	Fr.	3	1	3.38	11	0	45	42	14	23
Dennison, Mike, rhp	Jr.	4	1	3.43	26	0	42	40	11	35
Peterson, Adam, rhp	Jr.	9	3	3.55	15	0	84	82	23	91
Hottovy, Tommy, lhp	So.	2	0	3.60	22	0	35	38	13	28
Henderson, Trenton, rhp	Jr.	4	0	3.65	20	0	37	38	6	30
Kerbs, Reuben, lhp	Jr.	5	1	4.66	17	0	56	63	12	44

24. SAN JOSE STATE

Coach: Sam Piraro **Record:** 45-17

BATTING	YR	AVG	AB	R	H	2B	3B	HR	RBI	SB
Lopez, Gabe, 2b	Sr.	.369	244	54	90	22	2	4	61	20
Corrick, Nathan, of	Fr.	.353	156	27	55	5	2	1	17	2
Zamora, Hector, 3b-dh	Jr.	.337	202	49	68	17	1	8	57	5
Baker, Bryan, 1b	Jr.	.319	213	50	68	18	0	11	49	1
Frandsen, Kevin, 3b-dh	So.	.317	161	37	51	10	1	7	28	1
Quintero, Dino, of	Sr.	.297	232	59	69	15	2	2	26	9
Shorsher, Adam, c	Sr.	.293	205	41	60	15	0	13	53	5
Bautista, Mark, c	So.	.286	14	3	4	0	0	0	1	0
Kilby, Brad, dh	Fr.	.281	32	7	9	5	0	0	4	0
Becktel, Travis, of	Fr.	.280	218	47	61	9	3	1	37	0
Milton, Kayzell, of	Sr.	.278	18	7	5	0	0	0	4	0
Adams, Ryan, ss	Jr.	.264	216	35	57	9	0	3	43	6
King, Markum, of	Sr.	.262	65	14	17	4	0	1	16	0
Bergstrom, Jordan, of-3b	Jr.	.250	100	22	25	3	0	1	17	1
Contreras, Anthony, ss	Fr.	.250	32	4	8	1	0	0	5	0
Niheu, Scott, dh	So.	.125	16	4	2	0	0	0	1	0

PITCHING	YR	W	L	ERA	G	SV	IP	H	BB	SO
Durkin, Matt, rhp	Fr.	11	3	2.75	22	1	98	85	24	85
Rogelstad, Jeremy, rhp	Sr.	8	5	3.73	20	1	101	105	17	64
Cook, Andy, rhp	Jr.	4	2	3.88	22	1	63	66	14	30
George, Jahseam, lhp	Sr.	9	2	3.93	16	1	101	102	27	68
Malott, Mike, rhp	So.	6	2	4.00	22	4	88	78	32	72
Gemmell, Don, rhp	Sr.	5	2	4.01	22	5	49	41	19	49
Esposito, Frank, lhp	Jr.	1	1	4.15	14	0	22	27	6	14
Minister, Casey, rhp	Jr.	0	0	5.14	10	0	14	15	8	7
Manzo, Mickey, rhp	Jr.	1	0	11.81	5	0	5	7	3	2

25. ARKANSAS

Coach: Norm DeBriyn **Record:** 35-28

BATTING	YR	AVG	AB	R	H	2B	3B	HR	RBI	SB
Bridges, Scott, ss	Fr.	.316	174	34	55	4	2	2	25	13
Wishy, Andrew, of	So.	.314	175	37	55	10	0	4	34	4
Clark, Cody, c	So.	.307	140	29	43	12	0	2	27	0
McConnell, Kirk, of	Fr.	.303	198	42	60	5	8	1	27	7
Goodwin, Clay, 3b	Fr.	.302	116	17	35	6	0	1	22	0
Weatherford, Luke, 2b	Sr.	.300	50	13	15	3	0	1	9	5
Conner, Michael, dh-1b	Sr.	.286	224	52	64	10	2	17	52	10
Toops, Brady, c	Fr.	.284	67	7	19	1	0	0	12	1
Fletcher, Jeff, 3b	Sr.	.281	128	17	36	3	1	2	15	4
Graves, Aaron, c	Sr.	.270	37	8	10	1	0	2	4	0
Pitts, Nick, 1b	Jr.	.267	206	40	55	13	1	4	28	2
Fox, Ryan, of	Jr.	.256	238	43	61	14	0	9	53	5
Hagedorn, Brett, 2b	So.	.255	106	13	27	3	0	1	11	0
Hode, Scott, 2b	Fr.	.242	161	15	39	11	0	1	18	0
Crouse, Cliff, of	Jr.	.228	123	25	28	6	1	4	14	12
Lyles, Tigger, ss	So.	.182	11	2	2	1	0	0	1	0
Woodruff, Patrick, 1b	Jr.	.105	19	2	2	1	0	0	0	0

PITCHING	YR	W	L	ERA	G	SV	IP	H	BB	SO
Woods, Scott, rhp	Sr.	6	2	2.62	17	0	34	39	5	26
Pomeroy, Kyler, rhp	Jr.	1	1	3.60	22	3	25	22	10	15
Richmond, Jonathan, rhp	So.	2	4	3.83	17	0	52	64	13	23
Isaacson, Charlie, rhp	Sr.	7	7	3.99	16	0	90	92	33	53
Gardner, Jarrett, rhp	Jr.	4	4	4.04	24	3	69	69	21	38
Roehl, Scott, rhp	So.	4	1	4.17	21	4	58	53	12	46
Leraris, Justin, rhp	Sr.	1	1	4.29	8	0	21	21	9	14
Merryman, Josh, rhp	Jr.	4	1	4.46	22	1	40	50	7	31
Hogan, Gary, rhp	Jr.	3	6	4.87	22	3	89	110	23	65
Glynn, Josh, rhp	Jr.	2	0	5.36	19	0	44	49	14	30
Brannon, Clint, lhp	Fr.	1	1	5.40	8	0	17	18	9	14
Berry, Layne, lhp	Sr.	0	0	7.96	15	0	26	37	25	23

CONFERENCE
STANDINGS & LEADERS

*Won conference tournament.
Boldface: NCAA regional participant/conference department leader.

#Conference department leader who is a non-qualifier

AMERICA EAST CONFERENCE

	Conference		Overall	
	W	L	W	L
*Maine	16	6	40	17
Vermont	14	8	27	22
Northeastern	11	11	29	22
Stony Brook	11	11	27	24
Binghamton	8	12	17	34
Albany	8	14	20	30
Hartford	8	14	17	29

ALL-CONFERENCE TEAM: C—Luke Carlin, Jr., Northeastern. **1B**—Ryan Cuscovitch, Fr., Hartford. **2B**—Mike Grasso, Jr., Albany. **3B**—Ron Acabbo, So., Hartford. **SS**—Bobby Tewksbary, Fr., Vermont. **OF**—Jeff Barry, Jr., Vermont; Eddie Scott, Sr., Albany; Simon Williams, So., Maine. **DH**—Aaron Izaryk, Fr., Maine. **P**—Mike MacDonald, So., Maine; Mike Collar, So., Maine.
Player of the Year: Jeff Barry, Vermont. **Pitcher of the Year:** Mike MacDonald, Maine. **Rookie of the Year:** Jon Lewis, Stony Brook. **Coach of the Year:** Bill Currier, Vermont.

INDIVIDUAL BATTING LEADERS
(Minimum 125 At-Bats)

	AVG	AB	R	H	2B	3B	HR	RBI	SB
Barry, Jeff, Vermont	.401	177	50	71	8	5	4	36	32
Carlin, Luke, Northeastern	.364	162	46	59	9	1	6	31	17
Williams, Simon, Maine	.363	146	55	53	9	4	8	35	21
Acabbo, Ron, Hartford	.349	146	35	51	20	0	7	39	6
Denorfia, Matt, Hartford	.348	161	30	56	10	1	2	27	3
Grasso, Mike, Albany	.344	183	44	63	6	2	2	30	28
Beck, Ben, Northeastern	.344	163	32	56	16	3	5	35	11
Drapeau, Joe, Maine	.341	214	43	73	18	0	11	61	3
Picard, Alain, Maine	.340	188	46	64	20	0	6	53	14
Scott, Eddie, Albany	.339	171	38	58	9	3	2	27	15
Toms, Jake, Albany	.329	158	34	52	10	0	4	31	5
Tewksbary, Bobby, Vermont	.325	160	37	52	9	2	0	15	6
Carey, Jason, Vermont	.324	170	30	55	13	1	3	24	5
Livulpi, Mike, Maine	.324	170	42	55	13	1	2	25	17
Parker, Cory, Hartford	.323	130	21	42	10	0	4	27	9
Boyer, Jamie, Binghamton	.323	155	28	50	15	2	6	18	1
Cuscovitch, Ryan, Hartford	.323	155	27	50	6	0	5	35	3
#Pena, Omar, Northeastern	.289	194	36	56	15	5	2	27	8

INDIVIDUAL PITCHING LEADERS
(Minimum 50 Innings)

	W	L	ERA	G	SV	IP	H	BB	SO
Monds, Devin, Northeastern	5	2	1.80	11	1	65	50	23	53
Emmerthal, Steve, Albany	6	1	2.38	13	0	57	54	6	42
Kumming, Andy, Vermont	6	2	3.04	19	5	53	46	16	52
Robinson, Brian, Vermont	6	4	3.30	12	0	63	56	41	62
Lewis, Jon, Stony Brook	9	3	3.39	14	0	88	81	33	90
MacDonald, Mike, Maine	7	3	3.44	13	0	86	81	28	74
Roy, Scott, Hartford	4	5	3.64	13	1	64	74	21	64
Eagan, David, Binghamton	5	8	3.69	14	0	83	86	34	68
Sousa, Greg, Binghamton	5	8	3.86	15	0	77	90	31	65
Merchant, Jamie, Vermont	6	4	4.07	14	0	73	83	24	72
Henry, Ken, Northeastern	5	6	4.13	13	1	65	67	23	46
Collar, Mike, Maine	8	4	4.35	15	1	83	79	22	70
Thomson, Jordan, Northeastern	6	4	4.52	10	0	66	78	13	47
Kroft, Adam, Albany	4	6	4.86	14	0	74	83	24	53
#Bissonnette, Justin, Vermont	0	4	5.86	23	6	43	56	13	51

ATLANTIC COAST CONFERENCE

	Conference		Overall	
	W	L	W	L
*Florida State	18	6	60	14
Wake Forest	17	6	47	13
North Carolina	17	7	43	21
Clemson	16	8	54	17
Georgia Tech	14	9	52	16
Virginia	8	16	25	32
North Carolina State	7	17	33	26
Maryland	6	18	34	23
Duke	4	20	24	34

ALL-CONFERENCE TEAM: C—Tony Richie, So., Florida State. **1B**—

Michael Johnson, Jr., Clemson. **2B**—Eric Patterson, Fr., Georgia Tech. **3B**—Ryan Barthelemy, Sr., Florida State. **SS**—Khalil Greene, Sr., Clemson. **OF**—Adam Bourassa, Jr., Wake Forest; Adam Greenberg, Jr., North Carolina; Brian Wright, Sr., North Carolina State. **DH**—Ryan Johnson, Jr., Wake Forest. **Util**—Chris Maples, Sr., North Carolina. **P**—Matt Lynch, Jr., Florida State; Steve Reba, Sr., Clemson; Kyle Sleeth, So., Wake Forest. **RP**—Dave Bush, Sr., Wake Forest.
Player of the Year: Khalil Greene, Clemson. **Rookie of the Year:** Stephen Drew, Florida State. **Coach of the Year:** George Greer, Wake Forest.

INDIVIDUAL BATTING LEADERS
(Minimum 125 At-Bats)

	AVG	AB	R	H	2B	3B	HR	RBI	SB
Greene, Khalil, Clemson	.470	285	93	134	33	1	27	91	17
McCurdy, John, Maryland	.443	221	67	98	20	4	19	77	20
Wright, Brian, NC State	.418	232	72	97	26	2	14	73	10
Bourassa, Adam, Wake Forest	.412	250	71	103	11	4	2	41	26
Drew, Stephen, Florida State	.402	204	64	82	15	4	16	54	13
Johnson, Michael, Clemson	.384	263	62	101	19	1	25	81	11
McQuade, Tony, Florida State	.376	218	63	82	26	4	6	46	6
Hicks, David, NC State	.372	223	30	83	24	0	6	48	0
Street, Dan, Virginia	.371	232	52	86	23	4	12	59	5
Adams, Russ, North Carolina	.370	254	75	94	20	3	7	55	45
Menocal, Victor, Ga Tech	.369	282	63	104	20	2	2	49	8
Swope, Matt, Maryland	.368	220	64	81	20	5	6	55	14
Gaetti, Joe, NC State	.368	182	44	67	10	1	5	39	9
Johnson, Ryan, Wake Forest	.366	232	56	85	14	4	13	77	1
Boggs, Matthew, Ga Tech	.363	234	52	85	12	2	1	43	12
Buffone, Anthony, Maryland	.362	229	53	83	20	2	5	43	2
Stone, David, Virginia	.360	211	53	76	15	0	4	36	26
Whitmer, Daryl, Maryland	.358	204	59	73	11	2	7	37	16
Barthelemy, Ryan, Fla State	.357	297	76	106	24	4	17	94	6
Riley, Justin, NC State	.356	174	31	62	8	1	9	57	1
Blue, Nick, Wake Forest	.355	203	60	72	9	0	1	40	21
Farrell, Sean, North Carolina	.354	254	66	90	19	1	14	73	10
Richie, Tony, Florida State	.353	249	59	88	17	2	13	75	1
Kelly, Kevin, Duke	.350	237	59	83	15	4	9	51	8
Slayden, Jeremy, Georgia Tech	.348	256	74	89	15	1	18	66	4
Maples, Chris, North Carolina	.347	274	62	95	24	1	23	79	16
Patterson, Eric, Georgia Tech	.346	260	73	90	14	3	3	40	41
Patrick, Brian, Duke	.344	212	48	73	17	4	5	52	5
Murton, Matt, Georgia Tech	.344	250	62	86	16	1	10	58	20
Greenberg, Adam, North Carolina	.337	267	80	90	17	7	17	57	35
D'Antona, Jamie, Wake Forest	.336	223	54	75	10	1	20	83	2
Cleveland, Jeremy, North Carolina	.333	171	32	57	11	0	10	31	1
Iannetta, Chris, North Carolina	.333	165	35	55	7	0	9	34	1
Rogers, Nick, Florida State	.331	257	67	85	22	2	8	69	19
Hargrave, Adam, NC State	.330	191	44	63	6	3	1	24	6
Butler, Matt, NC State	.329	146	33	48	13	1	5	26	5
Maxey, Jason, Maryland	.328	186	45	61	17	0	17	60	1
Brown, Jerrod, Florida State	.327	217	49	71	8	1	4	56	0
Orvella, Chad, NC State	.326	221	69	72	9	2	1	34	9
Perry, Jason, Georgia Tech	.325	237	49	77	17	1	12	60	8
Baker, Jeff, Clemson	.325	265	71	86	12	2	25	87	17

INDIVIDUAL PITCHING LEADERS
(Minimum 50 Innings)

	W	L	ERA	G	SV	IP	H	BB	SO
Bush, David, Wake Forest	8	1	1.64	40	13	60	47	10	61
Hodges, Daniel, Florida State	4	1	2.56	36	12	63	68	10	38
Sleeth, Kyle, Wake Forest	14	0	2.97	18	0	118	115	41	113
Henrie, Matt, Clemson	13	5	3.12	21	1	113	112	25	81
Bakker, Kyle, Georgia Tech	13	2	3.14	19	0	135	132	24	115
Kamrath, Jeff, Virginia	7	4	3.28	16	0	96	81	44	67
Peterson, Trent, Florida State	4	2	3.35	17	0	51	48	17	46
LaMacchia, Marc, Florida State	11	2	3.38	18	0	96	101	21	75
Lynch, Matt, Florida State	13	2	3.59	20	0	130	132	30	98
Schmidt, Kyle, Georgia Tech	5	2	3.64	19	0	72	73	31	80
Manshack, Scott, North Carolina	7	0	3.70	20	0	66	65	31	60
Hogan, Patrick, Clemson	2	1	3.79	22	4	55	60	11	36
Burks, Brian, Georgia Tech	10	7	3.87	25	3	102	114	25	81
Harrell, Carter, North Carolina	8	4	3.88	24	1	58	53	25	65
Varnes, Blair, Florida State	10	3	3.98	19	0	106	113	20	77
Benson, Whitley, North Carolina	2	1	3.99	29	3	50	54	21	44
Watchko, Jeff, Georgia Tech	11	1	4.01	29	2	90	94	19	62
Gross, Michael, North Carolina	6	4	4.13	32	2	57	48	24	40
LaMura, B.J., Clemson	6	2	4.17	19	1	58	45	31	61

COLLEGE BASEBALL

Reba, Steve, Clemson	13	4	4.39	20	0	113	121	44	82
Goodman, Chris, Georgia Tech	8	2	4.41	21	0	82	90	16	60
Morley, Tim, Wake Forest	6	3	4.41	16	0	88	85	39	71
Autrey, Scott, North Carolina	5	3	4.42	17	0	98	91	34	87
Bakker, Garry, North Carolina	6	3	4.46	18	0	83	78	44	68
Hanson, Adam, Wake Forest	3	0	4.50	33	2	56	56	19	40
Prochaska, Mike, NC State	5	2	4.65	13	0	72	67	34	46
Hill, Seth, Wake Forest	3	3	4.86	18	1	74	73	22	53
Diluccio, Justin, Duke	5	4	4.91	21	0	59	76	20	34
Burke, Greg, Duke	1	3	5.13	12	1	67	84	11	57
Read, Robby, Florida State	8	1	5.22	19	0	81	81	36	77
Lumsden, Tyler, Clemson	4	1	5.28	27	2	58	56	39	63
Jackson, Steven, Clemson	6	1	5.37	16	0	64	67	35	55
McKee, Derek, NC State	3	4	5.43	10	1	60	70	25	58
DeMarco, Paul, Duke	3	4	5.49	21	3	59	71	30	46
Alleva, Jeff, Duke	5	6	5.60	14	0	72	92	20	49
Layden, Tim, Duke	4	8	5.62	16	1	74	85	38	55
Stuart, Jared, Maryland	5	3	5.64	13	0	67	73	41	67
Caldwell, Daniel, NC State	7	8	5.71	16	0	98	128	31	72

ATLANTIC SUN CONFERENCE

	Conference		Overall	
	W	L	W	L
*Central Florida	23	7	41	22
Florida Atlantic	22	8	46	21
Stetson	19	9	42	19
Troy State	16	14	28	30
Jacksonville	15	15	27	31
Samford	13	17	27	31
Mercer	13	17	22	32
Georgia State	13	17	24	32
Campbell	11	19	22	30
Jacksonville State	9	20	23	31
Belmont	9	20	22	30

ALL-CONFERENCE TEAM: C—Chris Westervelt, So., Stetson. **1B**—Bryan Zenchyk, So., Stetson. **2B**—Andy Wilson, Jr., Stetson. **3B**—Brian Snyder, So., Stetson. **SS**—Mike Myers, Sr., Central Florida. **OF**—Mike Appalucci, Jr., Mercer; L.J. Biernbaum, Sr., Florida Atlantic; Dee Brown, Fr., Central Florida. **DH**—Wade Miller, So., Troy State. **P**—Danny Core, Jr., Florida Atlantic; Chris Pillsbury, So., Florida Atlantic; Eric Wikstrom, So., Troy State. **RP**—Tim McNab, Sr., Florida Atlantic.

Player of the Year: Chris Westervelt, Stetson. **Freshman of the Year:** Dee Brown, Central Florida. **Coach of the Year:** Jay Bergman, Central Florida.

INDIVIDUAL BATTING LEADERS
(Minimum 125 At-Bats)

	AVG	AB	R	H	2B	3B	HR	RBI	SB
Mann, David, Central Fla.	.410	166	50	68	6	1	0	19	10
Westervelt, Chris, Stetson	.403	236	67	95	17	0	18	46	2
Brown, Dee, Central Fla.	.397	214	38	85	13	2	3	56	8
Miller, Wade, Troy State	.393	211	46	83	17	0	10	53	2
Zenchyk, Bryan, Stetson	.383	240	47	92	28	0	11	64	0
Carter, Nic, Campbell	.381	176	40	67	14	3	0	23	32
Snyder, Brian, Stetson	.379	195	69	74	16	1	14	54	7
Wilson, Andy, Stetson	.369	222	54	82	18	0	11	59	4
Phillips, Dustin, Georgia State	.369	206	53	76	9	4	7	35	22
Hanson, Ty, Central Fla.	.364	154	31	56	10	0	0	22	4
Pali, Matt, Fla. Atlantic	.361	202	37	73	8	0	10	43	2
Timpner, Clay, Central Fla.	.361	208	43	75	9	5	5	47	11
Smith, Coby, Troy State	.356	202	48	72	10	1	4	28	25
Walter, Wade, Belmont	.352	159	28	56	7	0	2	19	5
Biernbaum, L.J., Fla. Atlantic	.350	257	64	90	12	2	16	67	12
Reier, Chris, Jacksonville	.347	190	33	66	7	0	0	15	4
Deanda, Sal, Campbell	.347	170	31	59	13	0	0	28	11
Harwell, David, Mercer	.347	173	53	60	14	0	5	31	11
Somarriba, Gabe, Fla. Atlantic	.345	235	66	81	13	0	8	50	7
Miller, Drew, Troy State	.343	201	41	69	12	0	12	47	0
Brown, Rusty, Fla. Atlantic	.343	166	40	57	11	0	11	47	1
Brummett, Josh, Belmont	.342	158	39	54	11	1	8	35	14
Evans, Sae, Samford	.341	182	40	62	10	2	3	27	10
Miller, Adam, Central Fla.	.333	177	36	59	4	1	2	30	4
Evans, Robert, Samford	.332	217	35	72	11	1	9	38	2
Levengood, Kyle, Mercer	.332	205	40	68	11	2	12	53	0
Petit, Ryan, Belmont	.332	187	38	62	18	4	6	40	17
Nover, Phil, Jacksonville	.331	169	27	56	13	1	8	33	1
Rispoli, Tom, Campbell	.331	145	26	48	8	2	0	14	4
#Cox, Mike, Fla. Atlantic	.331	251	61	83	11	0	18	65	4
Laws, Josh, Stetson	.330	221	53	73	13	3	3	30	7
Burroughs, Stephen, Ga. State	.329	155	22	51	7	3	5	31	8
Valdes, Mike, Fla. Atlantic	.329	149	32	49	7	0	5	29	7
Vandiver, Josh, Ga. State	.329	207	34	68	17	3	13	59	1
Cole, Chris, Stetson	.327	165	29	54	9	0	8	43	1
Keelan, Johnny, Campbell	.326	135	26	44	9	0	0	22	6

INDIVIDUAL PITCHING LEADERS
(Minimum 50 Innings)

	W	L	ERA	G	SV	IP	H	BB	SO
Stertzbach, Von, Central Fla.	7	0	1.81	21	2	65	56	28	80
#McNab, Tim, Fla. Atlantic	3	2	2.52	34	12	39	50	6	39
Williams, Bryan, Jacksonville	6	3	2.58	22	3	80	59	36	76
Truty, Darren, Jacksonville	6	4	2.76	18	0	78	63	19	59
Robinson, Ronnie, Ga. State	4	8	3.26	16	0	91	89	31	79
Hall, Bo, Central Fla.	10	0	3.61	17	0	72	69	24	78
Mincks, Lincoln, Central Fla.	7	6	3.64	16	0	89	89	31	55
Core, Danny, Fla. Atlantic	8	6	3.72	19	0	106	107	35	87
Murray, Pat, Campbell	7	6	3.80	22	1	64	73	16	45
Wikstrom, Eric, Troy State	5	4	3.88	13	0	65	82	10	45
Shippey, Steve, JSU	6	6	3.91	17	0	78	92	17	56
Michael, Mark, Central Fla.	7	4	3.93	16	0	89	87	36	91
Lincoln, Roger, Stetson	12	3	3.99	29	4	95	105	22	95
Wassermann, Ehren, Samford	6	3	4.04	25	3	91	98	20	65
Morrison, James, Mercer	6	7	4.24	21	0	98	119	22	77
Strickland, Brett, Georgia State	3	7	4.39	25	6	68	75	27	60
Courson, Ryan, Jacksonville	5	8	4.39	20	0	82	95	19	66
Jones, Brian, Mercer	7	7	4.44	22	0	107	109	39	104
#Wilson, Andy, Stetson	3	1	4.45	21	12	30	24	22	36
Wiley, Mike, Stetson	10	2	4.48	16	0	88	102	38	74
Sullivan, Brian, Stetson	6	4	4.57	18	1	100	114	16	86
Pillsbury, Chris, Fla. Atlantic	10	3	4.60	18	0	106	110	39	85
Jarrett, Brett, Mercer	6	11	4.61	23	1	111	125	40	114
Regas, Kris, Jacksonville	3	9	4.72	17	1	80	90	16	43
Hawkins, David, Georgia State	8	7	4.87	17	0	94	106	26	36
Blackard, Cody, Belmont	5	7	4.93	16	1	77	102	22	52
Nesmith, Travis, Fla. Atlantic	7	2	4.98	18	0	60	72	19	54

ATLANTIC-10 CONFERENCE

	Conference		Overall	
EAST	W	L	W	L
St. Bonaventure	16	7	30	13
Temple	11	13	22	28
Rhode Island	10	14	24	28
St. Joseph's	10	14	16	36
Massachusetts	9	15	21	26
Fordham	6	18	13	36
WEST	W	L	W	L
*Richmond	22	2	53	13
George Washington	17	7	42	23
Xavier	15	8	27	27
Dayton	14	10	32	21
Duquesne	12	12	26	23
La Salle	1	23	10	40

ALL-CONFERENCE TEAM: C—Adam Tidball, So., Richmond. **1B**—Vito Chiaravalloti, Jr., Richmond. **2B**—Eric Greenwell, Jr., Xavier. **3B**—David Reaver, Jr., Richmond. **SS**—Matt Craig, So., Richmond. **OF**—Mike Bassett, Jr., George Washington; Bobby Kingsbury, Jr., Fordham; Bryan Pritz, So., Richmond. **DH**—Alec Moss, So., Xavier. **P**—Mike McGirr, Jr., Richmond; Tim Stauffer, So., Richmond. **RP**—Mike O'Connor, Sr., George Washington.

Player of the Year: Bobby Kingsbury, Fordham. **Pitcher of the Year:** Tim Stauffer, Richmond. **Rookie of the Year:** Jay Johnson, Xavier. **Coach of the Year:** Ron Atkins, Richmond.

INDIVIDUAL BATTING LEADERS
(Minimum 125 At-Bats)

	AVG	AB	R	H	2B	3B	HR	RBI	SB
Reaver, David, Richmond	.391	266	73	104	30	5	4	54	32
Boyle, Tim, Fordham	.389	198	31	77	15	1	2	26	8
Bassett, Mike, GW	.382	241	60	92	19	0	19	77	5
Kingsbury, Bobby, Fordham	.380	179	48	68	20	5	12	43	19
Senez, Aaron, Massachusetts	.377	159	28	60	12	2	6	38	10
Craig, Matt, Richmond	.375	248	70	93	22	3	19	84	19
Boehmer, Andy, Dayton	.372	129	28	48	11	0	1	31	2
Batz, Dan, Rhode Island	.371	194	33	72	14	3	4	31	5
Maropis, Pete, Duquesne	.364	173	36	63	12	1	11	46	8
Ryan, Kevin, St. Bonaventure	.363	146	28	53	10	0	0	33	2
Walls, Mike, St. Joseph's	.359	181	31	65	19	2	6	38	10
Chiaravalloti, Vito, Richmond	.357	238	69	85	17	1	23	86	3
Lyall, Joe, Temple	.355	186	39	66	13	3	1	30	13
Rapacioli, Mike, St. Bonaventure	.353	167	41	59	13	2	9	45	10
Beechem, Tom, Dayton	.349	146	43	51	5	1	5	26	9
Greenwell, Eric, Xavier	.348	207	36	72	10	5	2	30	10
Pritz, Bryan, Richmond	.345	261	78	90	19	0	8	51	31
Godusky, Justin, St. Joseph's	.345	177	33	61	17	2	4	42	1
Krimmel, Matt, GW	.344	221	64	76	23	2	13	65	7
Johnson, Jay, Xavier	.343	175	30	60	8	1	0	22	11
Lee, Gary, Duquesne	.343	137	34	47	14	1	7	30	6

INDIVIDUAL PITCHING LEADERS
(Minimum 50 Innings)

	W	L	ERA	G	SV	IP	H	BB	SO
Stauffer, Tim, Richmond	**15**	3	**1.54**	20	0	146	110	34	**140**
Orenduff, Justin, GW	10	2	1.68	28	1	59	38	19	78
#O'Connor, Mike, GW	4	2	2.06	29	**9**	48	25	26	68
Martin, Thomas, Richmond	8	0	2.98	9	0	54	45	17	55
Pahs, Aaron, Dayton	5	1	3.13	24	4	55	57	13	56
Caron, Mike, Temple	5	2	3.24	18	1	92	106	23	37
Harris, Mike, Rhode Island	5	2	3.34	12	1	65	69	22	46
Popp, Jim, Duquesne	3	3	3.54	10	0	53	56	20	34
Jahnsen, Adam, Xavier	10	7	3.66	20	0	111	105	44	72
Johnson, Kyle, St. Bonaventure	6	1	3.88	12	0	70	65	25	52
Pearce, Dan, Rhode Island	5	8	3.94	15	0	80	79	24	60
Seales, Shawn, Fordham	2	6	3.96	19	1	75	77	38	39
Santos, Jesse, Massachusetts	7	4	4.03	13	0	83	76	37	60
Stamm, Brian, Temple	3	3	4.03	15	0	51	54	28	27
McGirr, Mike, Richmond	12	1	4.06	17	0	109	110	32	85
Bruno, Brandon, Temple	5	7	4.08	19	2	79	84	31	56
Sues, Jarret, Xavier	7	5	4.15	19	0	82	94	19	48
McCollum, Bill, St. Joseph's	5	4	4.18	13	0	60	72	29	36
Solveson, Saul, St. Bonaventure	4	3	4.21	13	0	66	72	20	53
Conden, Greg, GW	11	3	4.22	18	0	96	93	41	69

BIG EAST CONFERENCE

	Conference		Overall	
	W	L	W	L
*Notre Dame	18	8	50	18
Virginia Tech	18	8	33	26
Boston College	15	11	30	25
Rutgers	15	11	35	22
Pittsburgh	14	11	36	16
St. John's	14	12	29	23
Connecticut	13	12	28	22
Villanova	12	13	30	23
Seton Hall	11	15	25	28
West Virginia	9	16	24	26
Georgetown	2	24	9	47

ALL-CONFERENCE TEAM: C—Jeff Mackor, Sr., Boston College. **1B**—Brant Colamarino, Jr., Pittsburgh. **2B**—Marc Tugwell, Jr., Virginia Tech. **3B**—John West, Sr., Virginia Tech. **SS**—Spencer Harris, Jr., Virginia Tech. **OF**—Casey Grimm, Jr., Seton Hall; Neal McCarthy, Sr., Boston College; Steve Stanley, Sr., Notre Dame. **Util**—Charlie Bilezikjian, Sr., St. John's. **P**—Chris Lambert, Fr., Boston College; Isaac Pavlik, Sr., Seton Hall; Joe Saunders, Jr., Virginia Tech.

Player of the Year: Steve Stanley, Notre Dame. **Pitcher of the Year:** Chris Lambert, Boston College. **Rookie of the Year:** Chris Lambert, Boston College. **Coach of the Year:** Peter Hughes, Boston College.

INDIVIDUAL BATTING LEADERS
(Minimum 125 At-Bats)

	AVG	AB	R	H	2B	3B	HR	RBI	SB
Stanley, Steve, Notre Dame	**.439**	271	77	**119**	17	4	1	36	32
Locke, Drew, Boston College	.404	141	34	57	16	0	2	24	10
Stavisky, Brian, Notre Dame	.394	193	47	76	14	**5**	9	57	2
Colamarino, Brant, Pittsburgh	.384	177	58	68	13	2	**19**	58	1
West, John, Virginia Tech	.378	217	46	82	15	0	8	53	12
Soteropoulos, Peter, UConn	.374	190	43	71	11	2	3	46	15
Rea, Brad, Pittsburgh	.369	206	43	76	12	0	18	**66**	1
Kane, Jason, St. John's	.368	193	43	71	22	2	3	32	11
Spamer, Bryan, Pittsburgh	.368	193	41	71	10	1	1	36	10
Hess, Cy, UConn	.366	183	53	67	10	0	11	46	10
Majewski, Val, Rutgers	.364	220	48	80	15	**5**	11	51	8
Grimm, Casey, Seton Hall	.363	157	25	57	9	1	6	38	2
Sollmann, Steve, Notre Dame	.362	213	53	77	8	4	2	47	6
McCarthy, Neal, Boston College	.360	161	49	58	8	0	5	15	7
Frazier, Jeff, Rutgers	.356	208	45	74	11	0	13	54	4
Cafiero, Rob, Villanova	.355	186	45	66	20	0	15	48	3
Blevins, Chad, West Virginia	.352	182	33	64	13	1	1	22	6
Gorrie, Jon, UConn	.348	198	59	69	8	1	1	29	31
Delaney, Jason, Boston College	.348	181	32	63	15	0	2	27	4
Toregas, Wyatt, Virginia Tech	.347	216	38	75	15	4	8	51	0
Bilezikjian, Charlie, St. John's	.347	176	49	61	14	3	11	49	15
Crawford, Todd, Seton Hall	.344	163	33	56	11	1	10	45	3
Tugwell, Marc, Virginia Tech	.342	231	50	79	14	3	5	47	12
Quinn, Bill, Georgetown	.340	191	38	65	14	1	7	35	2
Bauder, Brad, Virginia Tech	.338	228	55	77	21	1	14	60	5
Mannix, Brendan, Villanova	.338	130	30	44	13	0	9	41	3
Leonard, Mike, UConn	.337	187	33	63	16	1	8	40	2
#Trubia, Dan, UConn	.321	187	39	60	15	**5**	3	43	4
#Macchi, Brian, Boston College	.307	212	35	65	**24**	3	5	62	0
#Graziano, Chris, Villanova	.270	189	38	51	9	4	0	20	**38**

INDIVIDUAL PITCHING LEADERS
(Minimum 50 Innings)

	W	L	ERA	G	SV	IP	H	BB	SO
#Russell, James, Villanova	1	3	2.33	22	**15**	27	25	8	35
Lambert, Chris, Boston College	9	3	**2.76**	17	0	78	59	51	87
Pavlik, Isaac, Seton Hall	3	5	2.85	28	8	73	65	24	82
Saunders, Joe, Virginia Tech	9	2	2.86	15	0	98	103	22	**102**
Hiser, P.J., Pittsburgh	6	2	3.01	18	4	75	48	51	87
Gagne, J.P., Notre Dame	9	4	3.14	28	6	95	86	16	69
Niesel, Chris, Notre Dame	4	0	3.36	14	2	72	68	18	62
Wheeler, Tom, Rutgers	9	3	3.40	13	0	90	67	38	67
Slocum, Brian, Villanova	4	2	3.41	12	0	69	58	28	65
Johnson, Grant, Notre Dame	9	5	3.46	18	0	101	94	44	86
Brownlie, Bobby, Rutgers	6	6	3.50	13	0	80	80	19	66
Shepard, Kevin, Boston College	5	3	3.72	13	0	75	59	29	62
Santiago, David, Rutgers	2	2	3.72	12	1	56	64	10	37
Dorsey, Brian, St. John's	7	2	3.80	15	0	71	67	18	46
Ewen, Clayton, West Virginia	6	2	3.81	17	3	76	85	31	76
Wladyka, Jim, St. John's	4	4	3.84	15	0	75	83	27	30
Axford, John, Notre Dame	5	2	3.95	17	0	71	59	59	64
Grzenda, Bob, Villanova	5	5	4.02	13	0	72	76	16	36
Carlson, Jesse, UConn	6	4	4.48	12	0	72	79	32	66
Noonan, Chris, Seton Hall	4	5	4.52	17	0	68	75	35	47
Biggs, Billy, West Virginia	7	7	4.55	16	2	99	98	18	74
Crohan, Tom, Rutgers	4	4	4.61	14	0	68	66	48	58
Ogilvie, Peter, Notre Dame	7	5	4.65	17	0	79	90	26	58
Tucci, Nick, UConn	4	4	4.69	10	0	63	65	20	60
Bush, Jason, Virginia Tech	6	5	4.71	15	0	101	122	22	73
Nippert, Dustin, West Virginia	3	4	4.83	12	0	63	70	27	57
#Sullivan, Mark, Boston College	10	3	5.96	15	0	97	119	30	94

BIG SOUTH CONFERENCE

	Conference		Overall	
	W	L	W	L
*Coastal Carolina	16	5	44	19
Elon	13	8	34	23
Charleston Southern	12	9	25	34
Liberty	11	9	33	24
High Point	9	11	26	31
Winthrop	8	13	29	30
UNC Asheville	7	14	21	30
Radford	7	14	18	31

ALL-CONFERENCE TEAM: C—Randy McGarvey Jr., Sr., Coastal Carolina. **1B**—Justin Owens, Sr., Coastal Carolina. **2B**—Larry Wayne York, Jr., Liberty. **3B**—Matt Hagen, Jr., Liberty. **SS**—Joey Monahan, Jr., Liberty. **OF**—Whit Bryant, Sr., Elon; Marcus Maringola, Sr., Liberty; Ryan McGraw, So., Coastal Carolina. **DH**—Adrian Vanderburg, Jr., Charleston Southern. **P**—Steven Carter, So., Coastal Carolina; Justin Sturge, Jr., Coastal Carolina.

Most Valuable Player: Justin Owens, Sr., Coastal Carolina. **Rookie of the Year:** R.J. Swindle, Charleston Southern. **Coach of the Year:** Gary Gilmore, Coastal Carolina.

INDIVIDUAL BATTING LEADERS
(Minimum 125 At-Bats)

	AVG	AB	R	H	2B	3B	HR	RBI	SB
Owens, Justin, C. Carolina	.417	211	60	88	**24**	2	11	58	31
Knouse, Kelly, Liberty	.405	195	55	79	17	4	9	58	3
Maringola, Marcus, Liberty	.404	208	50	84	8	6	8	63	12
McGraw, Ryan, C. Carolina	.382	233	**72**	**89**	10	1	5	43	**63**
Bryant, Whit, Elon	.380	213	50	81	16	3	9	54	5
York, Larry Wayne, Liberty	.370	216	55	80	17	1	3	37	17
Rembert, Grant, UNCA	.365	167	34	61	7	2	5	40	1
Friedman, Todd, Winthrop	.360	186	43	67	16	1	3	32	5
Monahan, Joey, Liberty	.357	227	61	81	22	3	16	58	25
Keim, Adam, C. Carolina	.352	236	54	83	16	2	16	**66**	17
McGarvey, Randy, C. Carolina	.350	206	39	72	20	1	4	46	7
Miller, Shane, Liberty	.346	127	25	44	12	1	4	26	4
Hodges, Nat, Radford	.345	142	31	49	5	1	1	11	11
Hagen, Matt, Liberty	.344	224	50	77	20	3	**18**	64	11
Ingram, Brian, Elon	.343	207	57	71	14	3	3	47	7
Jones, Brad, Charleston Southern	.341	214	38	73	14	1	9	46	2
Powell, Brandon, C. Carolina	.340	247	59	84	15	6	8	54	26
Cavanaugh, John, High Point	.340	212	50	72	18	2	9	41	17
Haar, Jordan, Charleston South.	.339	183	39	62	16	1	11	30	11
Victor, Israel, UNCA	.338	154	25	52	14	3	3	29	5
#Butler, Keith, Liberty	.310	245	62	76	18	**7**	7	43	18

INDIVIDUAL PITCHING LEADERS
(Minimum 50 Innings)

	W	L	ERA	G	SV	IP	H	BB	SO
Carter, Steven, C. Carolina	**11**	4	**3.01**	18	0	117	119	26	87
Garner, Matt, Elon	7	1	3.19	20	3	96	78	40	92
Reeves, Jeff, Winthrop	3	4	3.20	12	0	65	47	33	71

	W	L	ERA	G	SV	IP	H	BB	SO
Sturge, Justin, Coastal Carolina	6	3	3.20	29	1	79	74	18	72
Donovan, Seamus, Coastal Carolina	9	3	3.26	19	0	102	89	39	64
Fischer, Brian, Coastal Carolina	7	4	3.43	16	0	81	96	26	43
Thurmond, Ben, Winthrop	4	3	3.52	9	0	64	54	21	61
White, David, High Point	3	7	4.03	19	0	80	98	38	71
Plexico, Jeremy, Winthrop	9	5	4.36	23	1	109	126	21	72
Burch, Kevin, High Point	6	7	4.38	16	0	97	113	21	66
Horstman, Steve, Liberty	3	3	4.48	25	1	68	77	40	32
Jones, Jason, Liberty	11	5	4.76	20	0	104	110	27	81
Light, David, Radford	2	3	5.05	12	0	71	88	22	54
Blocker, Tyson, Elon	8	3	5.05	17	1	93	109	23	44
Swindle, Robert, Char. Southern	6	9	5.27	25	1	109	138	19	127
Schuurman, Mark, UNCA	4	6	5.29	15	0	68	80	21	53
Koliscak, Cory, Radford	3	7	5.30	13	0	71	81	22	59
Bryant, Whit, Elon	7	3	5.32	17	1	86	79	77	76
#Chandler, Chris, High Point	3	2	5.54	27	10	39	52	11	29

BIG TEN CONFERENCE

	Conference		Overall	
	W	L	W	L
Minnesota	18	10	32	26
*Ohio State	18	11	38	20
Michigan State	16	12	38	19
Indiana	15	14	35	20
Iowa	15	16	26	29
Northwestern	14	15	26	29
Illinois	14	15	32	19
Michigan	14	17	21	32
Purdue	13	19	24	32
Penn State	11	19	23	30

ALL-CONFERENCE TEAM: C—Patrick Arlis, Jr., Illinois. **1B**—Brad Carlson, Sr., Iowa. **2B**—Luke Appert, Jr., Minnesota. **3B**—Vasili Spanos, Jr., Indiana. **SS**—Scott Welch, Jr., Minnesota. **OF**—Kennard Jones, Jr., Indiana; Bob Malek, Jr., Michigan State; Nick Swisher, Jr., Ohio State. **DH**—Kyle Geswein, Sr., Michigan State. **P**—Chadd Blasko, Jr., Purdue; Andy Dickinson, Sr., Illinois; Scott Lewis, Fr., Ohio State; Nate Smith, Sr., Ohio State; C.J. Woodrow, Jr., Minnesota. **RP**—J.A. Happ, Fr., Northwestern.

Players of the Year: Luke Appert, Minnesota; Kennard Jones, Indiana; Bob Malek, Michigan State. **Pitcher of the Year:** C.J. Woodrow, Minnesota. **Freshman of the Year:** Scott Lewis, Ohio State. **Coach of the Year:** John Anderson, Minnesota.

INDIVIDUAL BATTING LEADERS
(Minimum 125 At-Bats)

	AVG	AB	R	H	2B	3B	HR	RBI	SB
McCuiston, Chris, Michigan State	.404	230	59	93	22	0	15	71	10
Jones, Kennard, Indiana	.404	228	75	92	14	2	1	33	22
Malek, Bob, Michigan State	.402	219	66	88	21	3	16	66	16
Braun, Charlie, Michigan State	.394	188	55	74	7	4	1	32	13
Reohr, Wes, Penn State	.393	191	49	75	11	1	9	38	4
Deeds, Doug, Ohio State	.386	210	66	81	11	1	12	45	5
Spanos, Vasili, Indiana	.385	174	50	67	19	1	16	65	1
Koutnik, Jared, Michigan State	.376	210	52	79	13	3	11	42	6
Koman, Brock, Michigan State	.361	191	46	69	17	0	7	41	9
Appert, Luke, Minnesota	.361	208	55	75	16	1	14	43	9
Snavely, Christian, Ohio State	.360	225	55	81	13	5	10	46	8
Calkins, Mark, Indiana	.357	171	43	61	12	3	3	38	7
DeRenzo, Mike, Penn State	.355	203	52	72	9	3	4	30	5
Swisher, Nick, Ohio State	.348	184	49	64	14	3	10	52	5
Mattiace, Ian, Iowa	.347	193	51	67	17	1	8	38	20
Fazio, Adam, Purdue	.346	205	30	71	6	2	5	34	9
Davidson, Drew, Illinois	.341	173	42	59	11	2	10	26	4
Welch, Scott, Minnesota	.339	192	31	65	10	1	3	33	7
Jansen, Andy, Iowa	.339	192	42	65	12	2	5	31	12
Wright, Chris, Penn State	.337	193	31	65	12	1	6	46	1
Geswein, Kyle, Michigan State	.335	170	45	57	6	1	14	49	3
Hamdan, Gibran, Indiana	.335	173	26	58	12	0	6	38	0
Evans, Nick, Indiana	.333	129	16	43	5	0	1	27	0
Pattee, Ben, Minnesota	.332	205	41	68	11	2	3	43	7
Fox, Jake, Michigan	.331	139	32	46	9	3	11	35	2
Blakeley, Eric, Indiana	.330	218	53	72	12	2	10	60	10
Simmons, Luke, Illinois	.327	165	27	54	10	1	5	39	1
Howard, Scott, Minnesota	.327	205	44	67	14	1	2	28	17
Moreno, James, Michigan State	.327	199	48	65	14	1	4	36	8
Schutzenhofer, Andy, Illinois	.325	169	43	55	11	0	4	32	2
Sokol, Mike, Michigan	.325	157	25	51	11	2	2	25	1
Arlis, Patrick, Illinois	.324	179	37	58	11	1	7	37	14
Wilkins, Joe, Ohio State	.322	183	36	59	12	1	4	45	4
Koerber, Scott, Mich. State	.322	143	27	46	4	0	9	31	4
Rabin, Mike, Ohio State	.319	163	24	52	6	0	0	21	9
#Thousand, Kyle, Iowa	.316	177	32	56	12	8	4	29	12
#Kennedy, Jason, Minnesota	.316	193	61	61	11	3	12	61	27

INDIVIDUAL PITCHING LEADERS
(Minimum 50 Innings)

	W	L	ERA	G	SV	IP	H	BB	SO
James Happ, Northwestern	3	2	2.10	21	4	51	46	24	51
Otte, Zach, Indiana	7	3	2.56	16	0	81	77	31	55
Dickinson, Andy, Illinois	11	2	2.83	18	0	115	111	22	107
Lewis, Scott, Ohio State	8	2	2.84	15	0	92	87	29	91
Bos, Ryan, Northwestern	4	7	2.91	13	0	80	69	30	56
Bates, Nick, Michigan State	9	3	2.97	14	1	88	76	30	100
Blasko, Chadd, Purdue	5	3	2.98	12	0	85	76	21	78
#Smith, Ryan, Indiana	3	2	3.06	26	9	32	30	8	32
Smith, Nate, Ohio State	6	1	3.12	12	0	66	64	17	59
Day, Tim, Michigan State	11	3	3.21	16	0	81	84	13	60
Hill, Rich, Michigan	3	7	3.54	15	0	76	64	38	104
Pruemer, Mitch, Purdue	7	2	3.56	13	0	81	86	15	41
Vitielliss, Nick, Indiana	8	1	3.58	16	0	73	71	37	46
Woodrow, C.J., Minnesota	8	5	3.71	15	0	97	105	13	81
Watson, Mike, Penn State	6	4	3.95	14	1	82	84	38	88
Krogman, Josh, Minnesota	5	4	4.17	13	1	58	66	22	32
Pawelk, Reed, Iowa	4	6	4.20	12	0	81	95	30	62
Korecky, Bobby, Michigan	5	6	4.34	13	1	93	105	26	53
Trzos, Jeff, Michigan	2	5	4.41	12	0	67	81	20	48
Newman, Josh, Ohio State	8	6	4.47	15	0	95	117	32	70
Gill, Pat, Michigan State	6	4	4.50	15	0	100	105	31	72
Ribas, Gabe, Northwestern	6	4	4.53	17	0	89	115	15	94
Gagner, Jay, Minnesota	4	0	4.58	12	0	53	62	29	38
Maliszewski, Chris, Iowa	4	2	4.60	21	1	61	67	12	31
Schara, Zach, Northwestern	5	4	4.62	15	0	74	74	32	59
Molldrem, Craig, Minnesota	5	4	4.67	15	1	81	101	26	56
Gale, Bryan, Michigan State	8	4	4.77	15	0	100	105	31	72
Laratta, E.J., Ohio State	8	4	4.99	16	0	88	106	21	52
Brauer, Jim, Michigan	4	6	5.06	14	0	59	71	16	48
Hollenhorst, Cory, Iowa	2	5	5.24	12	0	57	70	17	30
Tressler, Aaron, Penn State	4	4	6.41	13	1	60	75	32	45

BIG 12 CONFERENCE

	Conference		Overall	
	W	L	W	L
*Texas	19	8	57	15
Nebraska	16	11	47	21
Texas Tech	16	11	42	20
Oklahoma	15	12	35	27
Oklahoma State	13	13	37	21
Baylor	13	13	36	26
Kansas State	13	13	30	25
Texas A&M	13	14	35	24
Missouri	9	16	24	29
Kansas	5	21	22	29

ALL-CONFERENCE TEAM: C—Jed Morris, Jr., Nebraska. **1B**—Mike Huggins, Jr., Baylor. **2B**—Tim Moss, So., Texas. **3B**—Ty Soto, So., Kansas State. **SS**—Gera Alvarez, Sr., Texas Tech. **OF**—Jason Fransz, Jr., Oklahoma; Jeff Leise, Jr., Nebraska; Pat Maloney, Jr., Kansas State; Jon Slack, Jr., Texas Tech. **DH**—Ross Bennett, Jr., Baylor. **P**—Aaron Marsden, So., Nebraska; Justin Simmons, So., Texas; Justin Taylor, Sr., Baylor. **RP**—Steve Rowe, Sr., Texas Tech; Huston Street, Fr., Texas.

Player of the Year: Jed Morris, Nebraska. **Pitcher of the Year:** Justin Simmons, Texas. **Newcomer of the Year:** Aaron Marsden, Nebraska. **Freshman Player of the Year:** J.D. Reininger, Texas. **Freshman Pitcher of the Year:** Huston Street, Texas. **Coach of the Year:** Augie Garrido, Texas.

INDIVIDUAL BATTING LEADERS
(Minimum 125 At-Bats)

	AVG	AB	R	H	2B	3B	HR	RBI	SB
Majewski, Dustin, Texas	.401	212	40	85	20	2	10	50	4
Maloney, Pat, Kansas State	.398	221	66	88	17	2	11	53	7
Grose, John, Nebraska	.384	125	28	48	14	0	4	38	2
Morris, Jed, Nebraska	.382	272	70	104	26	1	23	90	4
Moss, Tim, Texas	.371	302	73	112	16	7	1	39	40
Leise, Jeff, Nebraska	.371	294	69	109	11	8	12	51	25
Soto, Ty, Kansas State	.369	206	44	76	10	0	3	41	2
Jordan, Kevin, Texas Tech	.365	192	44	70	11	4	0	30	13
Durazo, Willie, Texas Tech	.361	227	51	82	14	1	8	53	0
Ehlers, Cody, Missouri	.361	194	45	70	15	1	9	52	2
Bennett, Ross, Baylor	.357	171	32	61	14	2	6	41	3
Fransz, Jason, Oklahoma	.356	236	60	84	18	2	15	56	5
Durbin, Chris, Baylor	.352	244	62	86	25	4	6	46	9
Roughton, Jody, Missouri	.349	212	47	74	18	2	8	60	4
Laskowski, Lee, Missouri	.349	195	39	68	10	2	6	47	7
Williams, Brett, Kansas State	.346	153	27	53	8	1	2	28	2
Tingler, Jayce, Missouri	.346	214	65	74	7	4	0	34	13
Baty, Ryan, Kansas	.341	208	52	71	21	2	6	51	15
Huggins, Mike, Baylor	.338	240	47	81	14	7	10	62	4

BASEBALL AMERICA 2003 ALMANAC • 411

COLLEGE BASEBALL

	AVG	AB	R	H	2B	3B	HR	RBI	SB
Pouk, Justin, Texas A&M	.335	158	26	53	9	0	1	24	2
Webb, Trey, Baylor	.333	267	62	89	16	3	4	33	18
Slack, Jon, Texas Tech	.333	243	76	81	13	0	7	40	29
Monette, Daylon, Okla. State	.333	213	50	71	15	2	7	54	9
Doty, Tim, Kansas State	.330	191	42	63	8	2	8	49	2
Richmond, Paul, Baylor	.329	219	48	72	13	3	6	37	5
Quintanilla, Omar, Texas	.329	219	41	72	15	3	3	32	8
Salazar, Jeff, Oklahoma State	.329	216	64	71	19	7	4	42	23
Alvarez, Gera, Texas Tech	.328	238	46	78	16	2	13	64	20
Castillo, Osmar, Kansas State	.327	220	45	72	16	2	0	32	14
Brown, Jake, Texas Tech	.327	162	20	53	4	0	2	31	0
Cornejo, Eddie, Oklahoma	.325	246	45	80	17	2	0	31	7
Meyer, Rusty, Texas A&M	.321	131	25	42	7	1	4	19	1
Reininger, J.D., Texas	.320	203	40	65	19	2	13	51	3
Seely, Justin, Nebraska	.320	203	39	65	19	1	7	37	4
Wheeler, Kevin, Kansas	.320	169	25	54	14	0	8	42	1
Bolt, Will, Nebraska	.319	238	46	76	18	3	2	29	8
Brown, Nebasett, Okla. State	.318	201	55	64	8	3	5	44	14
Tribble, Matt, Kansas	.318	176	38	56	9	4	6	36	3
Murphy, David, Baylor	.318	173	29	55	10	4	6	38	2
Baldwin, Ryan, Kansas State	.316	171	30	54	8	0	4	40	1
Kitch, Denver, Oklahoma	.315	203	35	64	4	2	5	30	30
Richardson, Ryan, Oklahoma	.315	143	22	45	7	1	8	24	0
Smith, Bryon, Texas Tech	.314	229	51	72	16	0	8	36	1
Hopper, Matt, Nebraska	.309	243	52	75	10	2	9	49	3
Watson, Rob, Oklahoma State	.309	191	57	59	9	2	10	46	7
Blevins, Jeff, Nebraska	.307	218	44	67	14	1	7	50	8
Alexander, Luke, Oklahoma	.305	154	28	47	11	1	8	38	0
Bose, Matt, Oklahoma	.304	227	35	69	18	2	5	40	2
Weiss, Mick, Missouri	.303	188	38	57	15	2	10	53	5
Fahey, Brandon, Texas	.303	142	29	43	12	0	1	20	9
Ontiveros, Jeff, Texas	.302	248	55	75	15	2	20	59	2

INDIVIDUAL PITCHING LEADERS
(Minimum 50 Innings)

	W	L	ERA	G	SV	IP	H	BB	SO
#Street, Huston, Texas	4	1	0.96	35	14	47	24	9	49
Rowe, Steve, Texas Tech	10	2	1.51	26	8	60	50	12	69
Espineli, Eugene, Texas	5	0	2.08	17	1	52	49	17	39
Komine, Shane, Nebraska	10	0	2.33	15	0	97	62	30	115
Merle, Jesen, Texas	3	3	2.35	28	2	61	42	12	58
Simmons, Justin, Texas	16	1	2.52	20	0	128	106	39	80
Pezely, Franco, Kansas State	5	2	2.65	22	4	54	43	23	51
Marsden, Aaron, Nebraska	8	1	2.70	20	0	100	80	40	75
Halsey, Brad, Texas	7	2	2.74	18	0	99	90	26	82
Purcey, David, Oklahoma	5	4	3.35	24	6	75	77	44	84
Melcher, Kevin, Kansas State	5	5	3.39	16	0	82	93	22	54
Edens, Kyle, Baylor	5	6	3.44	35	14	52	43	10	58
Moore, Justin, Texas A&M	5	3	3.48	13	0	93	90	16	55
Parcus, Kyle, Texas A&M	5	5	3.56	16	0	78	82	21	55
Hale, Steve, Nebraska	4	2	3.56	25	2	56	59	14	32
Clark, Ray, Texas	6	4	3.61	15	0	72	66	17	71
Taylor, Justin, Baylor	9	2	3.82	19	0	118	118	30	85
Gooch, Steve, Texas Tech	7	2	3.86	18	0	112	109	21	57
Bomer, Alan, Texas	11	3	3.94	21	2	94	92	21	82
Davis, Jeff, Kansas	5	5	3.99	14	0	95	115	20	56
Olson, Dan, Kansas	4	3	4.00	11	0	70	64	21	49
Reilly, Chris, Oklahoma State	6	3	4.11	14	0	81	81	25	63
Rodrigue, Jamie, Nebraska	7	3	4.15	17	0	93	107	19	45
Baker, Scott, Oklahoma State	6	3	4.23	13	0	77	75	23	47
Farnum, Matt, Texas A&M	6	2	4.28	23	3	55	65	14	51
Buck, Dusty, Texas Tech	8	2	4.30	18	0	73	71	23	41
Roberts, Mark, Oklahoma	7	4	4.32	20	1	94	96	24	78
McCurdy, Nick, Oklahoma State	5	1	4.34	17	0	64	80	22	49
Thorp, Paul, Baylor	4	2	4.38	29	1	62	66	25	59
Meccage, Justin, Oklahoma State	3	0	4.42	21	0	57	55	25	54
Ballouli, Khalid, Texas A&M	6	4	4.44	14	0	73	77	28	59
McAuliff, Jarod, Oklahoma	1	2	4.44	24	2	53	57	20	45
Fouts, Nathan, Texas Tech	8	7	4.62	19	0	101	91	44	76
Warpinski, Ryan, Texas A&M	2	5	4.68	15	1	60	62	24	65
Duensing, Brian, Nebraska	6	2	4.73	18	0	78	82	25	60
Gutierrez, Jonathan, Kansas State	5	0	4.83	13	0	50	42	24	48
White, Steven, Baylor	5	4	4.95	16	0	91	104	48	73

BIG WEST CONFERENCE

	Conference		Overall	
	W	L	W	L
Cal State Northridge	19	5	41	17
Long Beach State	17	7	39	21
Cal Poly	15	9	30	29
Cal State Fullerton	14	10	37	22
UC Irvine	14	10	33	26
UC Riverside	10	14	30	28
UC Santa Barbara	8	16	22	33
Pacific	7	17	26	28
Sacramento State	4	20	22	34

ALL-CONFERENCE TEAM: C—Jason Allec, Jr., Cal State Northridge. **1B**—Brian Haskell, Sr., Cal Poly. **2B**—Shaun Larkin, Sr., Cal State Northridge. **3B**—Ryan Haag, So., Cal State Northridge. **SS**—Jason Gorman, Sr., Cal State Northridge. **OF**—Shane Costa, So., Cal State Fullerton; Jeremy Reed, Jr., Long Beach State; Eric Verbryke, Jr., Cal State Northridge. **DH**—Bryan Gant, Sr., Cal Poly. **Util**—James Stanford, Jr., Pacific. **P**—Abe Alvarez, So., Long Beach State; Wes Littleton, So., Cal State Fullerton; Kevin Correia, Sr., Cal Poly. **RP**—Chad Cordero, So., Cal State Fullerton.

Player of the Year: Eric Verbryke, Cal State Northridge. **Pitcher of the Year:** Abe Alvarez, Long Beach State. **Coach of the Year:** Mike Batesole, Cal State Northridge.

INDIVIDUAL BATTING LEADERS
(Minimum 125 At-Bats)

	AVG	AB	R	H	2B	3B	HR	RBI	SB
Gant, Bryan, Cal Poly	.402	241	59	97	11	8	0	38	20
Horwitz, Jon, UC Irvine	.388	214	42	83	16	0	0	22	10
Seuss, Adam, UC Riverside	.383	240	45	92	22	0	3	50	8
Anderson, Matt, UC Irvine	.381	239	57	91	14	2	3	44	1
Covarrubias, Nick, LBSU	.378	246	56	93	25	1	4	51	4
Fischer, David, CS Fullerton	.368	125	24	46	4	2	5	27	6
Havens, Blair, UC Santa Barbara	.367	147	40	54	12	4	1	22	5
Lake, Cory, Pacific	.367	139	28	51	9	2	1	37	3
Costa, Shane, CS Fullerton	.365	233	55	85	23	6	4	40	14
Wilson, Jake, Cal Poly	.361	238	42	86	19	1	10	51	0
Larkin, Shaun, CS Northridge	.361	205	58	74	15	1	15	49	2
McAnulty, Paul, LBSU	.360	200	50	72	19	2	9	55	6
Haskell, Brian, Cal Poly	.355	169	40	60	14	3	5	38	5
Gilhooly, Tim, Pacific	.348	207	48	72	15	6	0	64	12
Burgos, Richie, CS Fullerton	.346	191	23	66	8	0	3	35	0
Festa, Tony, UC Riverside	.345	206	36	71	6	3	2	35	8
Haag, Ryan, CS Northridge	.343	169	44	58	18	1	3	27	9
Reed, Jeremy, LBSU	.339	242	59	82	15	3	7	50	19
Spilborghs, Ryan, UCSB	.335	219	57	74	9	5	14	59	5
Klemm, Chris, UC Irvine	.335	176	30	59	15	2	1	38	8
Verbryke, Eric, CS Northridge	.332	226	52	75	14	1	14	54	13
Harper, Aaron, Pacific	.332	187	41	62	12	2	2	38	6
Faulkner, Tim, UC Riverside	.330	176	38	58	9	1	4	25	5
Gorman, Jason, CS Northridge	.329	158	40	52	13	2	7	31	4
Escobedo, Aaron, Cal Poly	.328	195	36	64	9	2	1	41	0
Malec, Chris, UC Santa Barbara	.328	229	41	75	17	2	8	60	2
Licht, Dave, UC Santa Barbara	.321	193	42	62	10	2	3	33	8
Allec, Jason, CS Northridge	.320	181	35	58	8	0	8	45	3
Wright, Chris, LBSU	.320	225	36	72	14	0	2	34	4
Fitzgerald, Michael, Pacific	.320	197	41	63	11	0	0	26	7
Orlandos, Nick, LBSU	.318	179	30	57	11	1	2	26	2
Kinsey, Chris, Sacramento State	.318	211	39	67	10	0	16	60	2
#Wahlbrink, Brian, UC Riverside	.307	231	54	71	16	2	2	33	25

INDIVIDUAL PITCHING LEADERS
(Minimum 50 Innings)

	W	L	ERA	G	SV	IP	H	BB	SO
Littleton, Wes, CS Fullerton	9	4	2.40	19	0	131	116	34	86
Alvarez, Abe, LBSU	12	3	2.72	17	0	103	94	27	89
Smith, Chris, UC Riverside	9	8	2.91	17	0	136	130	32	127
Cordero, Chad, CS Fullerton	4	3	2.91	33	12	56	46	20	81
Ingle, Travis, CS Fullerton	3	1	3.17	22	0	54	43	19	42
Stanford, James, Pacific	9	4	3.39	18	0	88	87	24	66
Murphy, Bill, CS Northridge	9	4	3.55	17	1	106	89	69	129
Marzion, Kevin, Sacramento State	4	6	3.65	12	0	79	91	21	44
Koller, Jon, UC Irvine	4	2	3.86	28	2	54	50	17	48
Eisentrager, Dan, LBSU	10	3	3.95	19	0	96	108	13	73
French, Paul, UC Irvine	4	4	3.96	25	2	89	91	32	88
Larson, Matthew, CS Northridge	6	2	3.98	17	1	75	90	24	48
DeJong, Jordan, CS Fullerton	11	3	4.00	21	0	108	101	34	88
Davidson, Andy, CS Northridge	11	2	4.14	22	1	78	103	19	71
Loe, Kameron, CS Northridge	5	3	4.30	18	1	84	90	15	72
Shappi, A.J., UC Riverside	6	5	4.34	17	0	106	121	26	81
Weaver, Jered, LBSU	8	4	4.37	17	0	93	80	32	74
Swanson, Glenn, UC Irvine	8	5	4.44	24	2	97	91	43	82
Tracey, Sean, UC Irvine	8	7	4.47	19	0	107	101	44	96
Jurvakainen, Ryan, Pacific	3	2	4.57	20	5	61	74	6	44
Correia, Kevin, Cal Poly	11	5	4.63	24	0	130	130	39	99
Fitch, Tyler, Cal Poly	7	4	4.75	19	0	108	115	60	47
Groeger, Jeff, Sacramento State	7	8	4.95	20	1	109	116	49	77
Pena, Matthew, Pacific	3	8	5.16	21	1	89	100	41	76
Smith, Brett, UC Irvine	5	2	5.31	16	0	85	91	45	70
Thompson, Sean, UCSB	4	3	5.34	22	1	88	99	30	55
Posthumus, Eric, UCSB	7	1	5.34	18	0	64	73	27	48
Thiessen, David, UC Riverside	6	1	5.42	24	1	76	84	27	78
Vasquez, Matt, UC Santa Barbara	5	10	5.53	19	1	99	112	46	69
Godkin, Jason, Pacific	4	1	5.56	18	0	55	73	20	29
Plouffe, Marshall, Sacramento State	4	7	5.90	17	0	87	104	41	58
Merrell, Darric, CS Fullerton	7	5	6.16	19	0	99	135	30	56
Lozano, Joel, Pacific	4	5	6.42	18	0	76	113	27	42

COLONIAL ATHLETIC ASSOCIATION

AMERICAN	Conference		Overall	
	W	L	W	L
James Madison	15	5	44	16
UNC Wilmington	14	7	36	21
Towson	9	12	23	27
Old Dominion	8	12	26	27
Drexel	5	16	21	34
COLONIAL	W	L	W	L
Delaware	12	7	35	22
George Mason	12	7	28	29
*Virginia Commonwealth	13	8	38	27
William & Mary	12	9	32	26
Hofstra	2	19	12	40

ALL-CONFERENCE TEAM: C—John Schneider, Jr., Delaware. **1B**—Eddie Kim, Jr., James Madison. **2B**—Bryan Gillespie, Sr., Virginia Commonwealth. **3B**—Brent Metheny, Jr., James Madison. **SS**—Kiley Vaughn, Sr., UNC Wilmington. **OF**—Gregg Davies, Sr., Towson; Reid Gorecki, Jr., Delaware; Jamie Hemingway, Jr., UNC Wilmington. **DH**—Bruce Boehm, Sr., Drexel. **P**—Jared Doyle, Jr., James Madison; Whitt Farr, Jr., William & Mary. **RP**—Brian Marshall, So., Virginia Commonwealth.

Player of the Year: Eddie Kim, James Madison. **Rookie of the Year:** Justin Verlander, Old Dominion. **Coach of the Year:** Spanky McFarland, James Madison.

INDIVIDUAL BATTING LEADERS
(Minimum 125 At-Bats)

	AVG	AB	R	H	2B	3B	HR	RBI	SB
Davies, Gregg, Towson	.428	187	59	80	18	6	13	51	14
Kim, Eddie, James Madison	.421	235	48	99	24	1	12	74	9
Gorecki, Reid, Delaware	.414	198	66	82	13	9	12	50	34
Boehm, Bruce, Drexel	.386	153	25	59	22	0	6	49	4
West, Jason, Drexel	.380	158	36	60	12	2	1	29	21
Gillespie, Bryan, VCU	.367	139	31	51	9	3	1	29	15
Hemingway, Jamie, UNC Wilmington	.365	222	49	81	14	1	6	40	21
Costello, Mike, Towson	.360	175	28	63	17	1	6	50	0
Dufner, Kris, Delaware	.350	206	44	72	12	5	7	48	13
Metheny, Brent, James Madison	.349	241	62	84	19	2	4	52	29
Howard, Evan, George Mason	.348	221	42	77	25	2	3	42	12
Brown, Michael, William & Mary	.341	167	32	57	15	2	6	33	4
Cosentino, Ryan, Hofstra	.341	132	19	45	13	0	0	17	2
Jones, Nick, VCU	.340	253	55	86	21	6	2	51	14
Fahy, Casey, Delaware	.338	222	61	75	13	6	0	23	40
Jackson, Joe, VCU	.337	175	33	59	6	2	0	24	11
McKenna, Brian, Towson	.330	197	47	65	16	0	7	30	5
Vaughn, Kiley, UNCW	.329	237	40	78	22	1	2	30	14
Ebaugh, Travis, James Madison	.327	168	46	55	10	2	4	36	7
Kirby, Matt, William & Mary	.326	193	36	63	17	0	4	32	1
Hubbard, Marshall, W&M	.326	218	44	71	15	1	8	42	2
Yocum, Josh, Drexel	.324	139	30	45	11	0	6	32	6
McKenna, David, UNCW	.324	170	41	55	10	1	3	28	12
Taylor, Mike, George Mason	.321	215	38	69	7	0	8	49	7
Jones, Tim, William & Mary	.320	178	26	57	10	3	3	26	5
Donovan, Brock, Delaware	.319	135	30	43	3	3	3	28	0
Palumbo, Jeff, George Mason	.318	223	48	71	12	1	2	40	15
Wakefield, Trey, W&M	.318	220	46	70	14	0	6	36	1
Sollenberger, Brent, ODU	.316	196	40	62	9	3	3	25	8
Shorts, Adam, George Mason	.316	196	43	62	12	0	6	35	26
Lopaze, Danny, VCU	.316	225	44	71	12	0	8	35	3
#Bacon, Scott, Towson	.313	198	49	62	14	1	14	55	2
#Doyle, Nathan, James Madison	.269	201	50	54	8	4	14	51	7
#Pabon, Jose, VCU	.264	250	48	66	26	5	6	41	2

INDIVIDUAL PITCHING LEADERS
(Minimum 50 Innings)

	W	L	ERA	G	SV	IP	H	BB	SO
Verlander, Justin, Old Dominion	7	6	1.90	15	0	114	83	43	137
Doyle, Jared, James Madison	11	3	2.57	17	0	102	102	36	92
Farr, Whitt, William & Mary	9	5	2.77	17	0	120	88	38	138
Bogardus, Ryan, William & Mary	5	2	2.92	17	0	77	73	36	63
Whitaker, Brian, UNCW	7	8	3.00	19	1	117	95	32	83
Marshall, Brian, VCU	6	4	3.08	41	10	79	61	23	92
Meyer, Dan, James Madison	9	2	3.13	17	1	98	93	25	90
Acors, Bo, VCU	8	4	3.51	20	0	103	111	46	93
Murray, Chris, George Mason	7	5	3.57	14	0	93	94	36	52
Rogers, Jason, Delaware	4	4	3.67	16	1	76	79	21	77
Williams, Ryan, Old Dominion	3	7	3.72	13	0	77	84	25	44
Isenberg, Kurt, James Madison	7	4	3.73	13	0	63	67	24	43
Tinkham, Jonathan, Old Dominion	4	4	3.83	27	5	56	69	25	41
Cochran, Chris, James Madison	7	1	3.84	19	2	82	93	20	65
Rambo, Scott, Delaware	7	2	3.86	21	1	51	46	36	39
Gouzd, John, James Madison	7	4	3.92	14	0	78	81	14	60
McDonnell, Matt, UNCW	6	0	4.01	25	1	52	45	21	46

Martin, Davy, VCU	7	8	4.08	20	0	106	109	46	72
Coughlin, Chris, UNCW	5	3	4.16	12	0	63	64	10	55
Gant, Stacen, George Mason	3	3	4.21	16	1	66	73	26	39
Summerlin, Jason, Towson	3	3	4.36	14	1	54	65	12	26
Marshall, Sean, VCU	3	4	4.45	19	1	85	99	26	90
McGuire, Rich, Delaware	5	5	4.64	15	0	83	95	45	51
Glanzmann, Jake, George Mason	5	5	4.74	13	0	82	93	23	51
Sterling, John, George Mason	5	6	4.79	15	0	94	105	30	72
Mullis, Jake, UNCW	6	5	4.83	16	0	91	105	26	50
Burok, James, Old Dominion	5	4	4.85	14	0	82	89	26	68
Boehm, Bruce, Drexel	5	6	4.85	14	0	69	69	24	55
Vincent, Jason, Delaware	6	4	4.89	14	0	96	121	23	49
Higgin, Ryan, Drexel	2	5	5.03	18	0	68	78	15	51

CONFERENCE USA

	Conference		Overall	
	W	L	W	L
Houston	22	7	48	17
Louisville	21	9	39	18
Texas Christian	19	11	30	29
Southern Mississippi	18	11	36	22
Tulane	17	13	36	27
*East Carolina	16	13	43	20
South Florida	16	14	35	29
Saint Louis	11	17	22	30
Cincinnati	11	18	26	29
Memphis	10	20	20	31
Charlotte	9	21	19	35
Alabama-Birmingham	7	23	16	40

ALL-CONFERENCE TEAM: C—Chris Snyder, Jr., Houston. **IF**—Jesse Crain, Jr., Houston; James Jurries, Sr., Tulane; Darryl Lawhorn, Fr., East Carolina; Brad Schutz, Jr., Cincinnati; Allen Winningham, Sr., Southern Mississippi. **OF**—Brett Cooley, Jr., Houston; Jeff Cook, Jr., Southern Mississippi; Mark Jurich, So., Louisville; Terry Trofholz, Jr., Texas Christian. **DH**—Joe List, Sr., Cincinnati. **P**—Nick Bourgeois, Jr., Tulane; Shea Douglas, Jr., Southern Mississippi; Corey Lawson, Jr., Saint Louis; Brad Sullivan, So., Houston. **RP**—Jesse Crain, Jr., Houston.

Player of the Year: James Jurries, Tulane. **Pitcher of the Year:** Brad Sullivan, Houston. **Freshman of the Year:** Darryl Lawhorn, East Carolina. **Coach of the Year:** Lelo Prado, Louisville.

INDIVIDUAL BATTING LEADERS
(Minimum 125 At-Bats)

	AVG	AB	R	H	2B	3B	HR	RBI	SB
Trofholz, Terry, TCU	.441	213	51	94	10	4	3	40	22
Lawhorn, Darryl, E. Carolina	.416	250	56	104	12	3	19	68	15
Jurries, James, Tulane	.400	240	77	96	16	4	20	74	30
Sandel, George, Charlotte	.374	211	47	79	11	3	4	39	7
Brumby, Turner, Tulane	.367	147	23	54	8	0	0	19	8
Winningham, Allen, Southern Miss	.366	183	55	67	19	1	7	34	8
Jurich, Mark, Louisville	.365	203	47	74	15	5	16	60	5
Schutz, Brad, Cincinnati	.362	243	59	88	17	0	8	30	5
Niefer, Justin, Cincinnati	.360	125	20	45	11	0	1	15	3
Baisley, Jeff, South Florida	.358	246	47	88	11	2	3	63	6
Meeks, Chris, TCU	.354	192	42	68	15	4	2	40	6
Snyder, Chris, Houston	.343	230	59	79	13	0	15	71	8
Hamblen, Chris, Cincinnati	.340	209	50	71	14	0	15	43	3
Cooley, Brett, Houston	.339	236	50	80	17	1	18	56	3
Gesell, Andy, Memphis	.338	154	31	52	9	1	5	23	0
Murphy, Ryan, Saint Louis	.337	190	29	64	13	1	4	40	8
Barclay, Mike, South Florida	.336	247	56	83	16	7	10	58	13
Willard, Adam, Charlotte	.336	128	25	43	7	1	2	17	1
Cook, Jeff, So. Miss	.335	245	67	82	11	1	16	63	18
Kaplan, Jon, Tulane	.333	261	60	87	18	0	4	31	30
Israel, Griff, Southern Miss	.330	182	44	60	12	2	5	40	2
Bourn, Michael, Houston	.327	248	68	81	8	1	1	23	32
Lamm, Brad, Charlotte	.325	200	39	65	9	1	2	38	6
Handley, Ronnie, South Florida	.323	130	19	42	7	1	4	33	3
Ivany, Devin, South Florida	.322	230	47	74	11	1	10	56	8
Evans, Kurt, Saint Louis	.321	159	30	51	13	3	1	15	11
Hoffpauir, Jarrett, Southern Miss	.320	197	38	63	17	2	1	32	1
Smith, Jake, Cincinnati	.317	180	33	57	9	0	12	45	1
LaFountain, J.T., Louisville	.316	215	50	68	12	0	4	37	3
Aubrey, Michael, Tulane	.316	209	40	66	15	2	7	52	6
Feldman, Aaron, Tulane	.316	225	57	71	11	2	3	22	23

INDIVIDUAL PITCHING LEADERS
(Minimum 50 Innings)

	W	L	ERA	G	SV	IP	H	BB	SO
#Crain, Jesse, Houston	4	0	0.23	27	10	38	22	10	46
Sullivan, Brad, Houston	13	1	1.82	18	0	129	80	49	157
Sears, Neal, E. Carolina	9	3	2.23	34	6	65	54	16	68
McCrory, Bob, Southern Miss	7	3	2.57	17	0	84	77	32	63
Mitchell, Nathan, Houston	5	2	2.62	36	4	65	43	14	63
Zell, Danny, Houston	8	2	2.86	23	0	50	51	14	37

COLLEGE BASEBALL

Narron, Sam, E. Carolina 8 3 2.98 15 0 97 85 14 65
Douglas, Shea, Southern Miss 10 3 3.14 15 0 100 91 44 108
Bourgeois, Nick, Tulane 10 3 3.27 17 0 116 98 45 114
Lawson, Corey, Saint Louis 8 3 3.29 14 0 101 102 21 66
Jerome, Clayton, TCU 9 5 3.33 16 0 111 94 30 74
Charron, Joey, Tulane 3 4 3.38 29 9 67 65 21 77
Borsa, B.J., Cincinnati 6 9 3.63 17 0 104 106 29 73
Falls, Tony, UAB 3 3 3.78 25 2 52 57 23 43
Penny, Davey, E. Carolina 8 4 3.82 17 0 101 96 28 93
Tisdale, Mike, Louisville 5 1 3.90 11 0 62 61 6 45
Uhl, Jon, South Florida 9 6 3.93 17 0 87 79 36 62
Fernandez, Carlos, Louisville 3 3 3.94 27 4 59 63 16 40
Whatley, Keith, Houston 8 3 3.96 15 0 61 58 31 38
Brinson, Will, E. Carolina 4 3 3.99 19 2 79 73 23 61
Bouldin, Nate, Cincinnati 1 3 3.99 30 6 56 50 14 46
Wehrfritz, Brad, Saint Louis 4 4 4.10 18 0 68 75 29 51
Steht, Nick, Memphis 0 5 4.24 19 0 57 70 43 29
Flores, Gene, Houston 3 2 4.40 20 0 78 85 24 55
Aubrey, Michael, Tulane 8 1 4.45 11 0 61 68 18 36
Shoemaker, Kyle, TCU 7 5 4.55 18 1 97 113 27 51
Stewart, Daniel, Southern Miss 5 5 4.67 15 0 81 90 20 61
Landphair, Matt, Charlotte 1 5 4.70 21 0 52 57 38 50
Markle, Kyle, Cincinnati 6 2 4.74 17 0 57 66 16 29
Newburn, Patrick, TCU 4 4 4.74 16 0 74 84 45 59
Jackson, Zach, Louisville 10 3 4.77 17 0 83 80 24 46
Mandryk, Jason, E. Carolina 7 4 4.82 15 0 65 85 29 45
Ring, Josh, Louisville 8 3 4.95 28 2 67 66 37 71

HORIZON LEAGUE

	Conference		Overall	
	W	L	W	L
Illinois-Chicago	14	5	39	16
*Wisconsin-Milwaukee	15	8	36	20
Youngstown State	11	8	18	26
Butler	11	11	34	23
Cleveland State	11	12	17	35
Wright State	9	14	20	33
Detroit	3	16	15	36

ALL-CONFERENCE TEAM: C—John Vanden Berg, Sr., Wisconsin-Milwaukee. **1B**—Ryan Nance, So., Butler. **2B**—Jeff Steele, Sr., Butler. **3B**—Steve Guden, Sr., Wisconsin-Milwaukee. **SS**—Mike Bruszer, So., Illinois-Chicago. **OF**—Juston Davenport, Sr., Detroit; Curtis Granderson, Jr., Illinois-Chicago; Kendall Schlabach, So., Youngstown State. **DH**—David Carr, Sr., Butler. **Util**—Paul Beck, Jr., Butler; Troy Doering, Jr., Wisconsin-Milwaukee. **P**—John Corcoran, Sr., Butler; Jerry Long, Sr., Cleveland State.
Player of the Year: Curtis Granderson, Illinois-Chicago. **Pitchers of the Year:** John Corcoran, Butler; Jerry Long, Cleveland State. **Newcomer of the Year:** Ryan Gehring, Illinois-Chicago. **Coach of the Year:** Mike Dee, Illinois-Chicago.

INDIVIDUAL BATTING LEADERS
(Minimum 125 At-Bats)

	AVG	AB	R	H	2B	3B	HR	RBI	SB
Granderson, Curtis, UIC	.483	207	76	100	23	4	9	46	17
Vanden Berg, John, UWM	.409	186	42	76	16	1	6	57	5
Rosner, John, UIC	.407	150	49	61	14	3	2	43	14
Davenport, Juston, Detroit	.371	159	31	59	9	1	9	23	14
Schlabach, Kendall, YSU	.367	166	33	61	10	3	1	26	12
Pudlosky, Dave, UWM	.337	166	35	56	13	0	2	41	3
Beck, Paul, Butler	.337	172	31	58	14	1	6	39	0
Tuttle, Chris, Wright State	.333	189	45	63	10	0	0	15	22
Albert, Jeff, Butler	.331	145	24	48	9	0	4	23	2
Shields, Nick, Wright State	.326	181	32	59	17	0	6	44	2
Marks, Tim, Butler	.316	133	16	42	2	1	3	19	2
Mueller, Dale, Butler	.315	203	34	64	7	5	3	32	12
Nance, Ryan, Butler	.315	178	30	56	10	0	10	38	1
Reschke, Charlie, UWM	.312	125	20	39	9	1	2	22	3
Erney, Dominic, Cleveland State	.311	177	23	55	15	0	2	32	1
Hughes, Mike, UIC	.311	167	37	52	17	4	1	30	5
Andrzejak, Tim, Detroit	.311	164	22	51	9	1	2	24	7
Bruszer, Mike, UIC	.305	220	44	67	10	0	1	18	12
Links, Lance, Wright State	.304	181	33	55	12	1	13	49	5

INDIVIDUAL PITCHING LEADERS
(Minimum 50 Innings)

	W	L	ERA	G	SV	IP	H	BB	SO
Lefeber, Geoff, UWM	6	1	2.20	9	0	86	80	35	53
Corcoran, John, Butler	12	3	3.29	16	0	106	109	21	76
Gilliam, Wes, UIC	5	1	2.80	12	0	61	56	17	65
Gehring, Ryan, UIC	9	1	2.80	15	1	87	80	10	71
Phillips, Aaron, Butler	7	4	2.86	15	1	85	84	17	58
Neshek, Pat, Butler	4	6	3.08	13	0	88	96	22	94
Long, Jerry, Cleveland State	6	6	3.34	16	0	108	85	53	106

Banks, Larry, UIC 7 7 3.49 15 0 90 98 14 57
Kleeba, Cory, UWM 3 1 3.60 19 0 50 53 14 26
Oldenburg, Quintin, UWM 9 3 3.86 14 0 82 81 32 68
Astrauckas, Keith, Detroit 3 5 4.02 16 0 63 72 19 34
Brumit, Matt, YSU 4 5 4.15 13 0 61 66 13 60
#Freisleben, Matt, UWM 2 7 4.17 37 15 45 45 10 31
Zizelman, Eric, Cleveland State ... 2 7 4.24 27 7 70 64 27 56
Smart, Jonathan, YSU 3 2 4.25 14 0 49 41 38 35

IVY LEAGUE

	Conference		Overall	
GEHRIG	W	L	W	L
Princeton	13	7	22	23
Pennsylvania	11	9	17	22
Columbia	10	10	22	25
Cornell	6	14	15	30
ROLFE	W	L	W	L
Harvard	13	7	20	26
Brown	13	7	25	24
Dartmouth	9	11	21	20
Yale	5	15	12	27

ALL-CONFERENCE TEAM: C—Greg Metzger, Sr., Brown. **1B**—Mike Mileusnic, Jr., Dartmouth. **2B**—Nick Italiano, Jr., Pennsylvania. **3B**—Ed Lucas, So., Dartmouth. **SS**—Pat Boran, Sr., Princeton. **OF**—Matt Kutler, So., Brown; Erik Rico, Sr., Cornell; Scott Shirrell, So., Dartmouth. **DH**—Trey Hendricks, So., Harvard. **Util**—Andrew McCreery, Jr., Pennsylvania. **P**—Ben Crockett, Sr., Harvard; Jonathan Stern, Sr., Brown. **RP**—Thomas Pauly, So., Princeton.
Player of the Year: Erik Rico, Cornell. **Pitchers of the Year:** Ben Crockett, Harvard; Jonathan Stern, Brown. **Rookie of the Year:** Ross Ohlendorf, Princeton.

INDIVIDUAL BATTING LEADERS
(Minimum 100 At-Bats)

	AVG	AB	R	H	2B	3B	HR	RBI	SB
Buckmiller, Matt, Columbia	.424	158	56	67	21	0	12	56	16
McCreery, Andrew, Pennsylvania	.390	146	35	57	12	1	6	29	6
Johnson, Derek, Columbia	.385	117	20	45	6	1	1	26	0
Rico, Erik, Cornell	.380	150	46	57	10	8	11	42	8
Italiano, Nick, Pennsylvania	.377	138	28	52	9	2	6	33	3
Elkins, Chris, Yale	.374	147	18	55	9	2	1	23	8
Shirrell, Scott, Dartmouth	.369	160	41	59	13	3	6	45	3
Hendricks, Trey, Harvard	.365	148	23	54	13	0	6	29	0
Glass, Steve, Pennsylvania	.363	135	34	49	8	0	2	15	5
Graves, Bryan, Pennsylvania	.358	106	22	38	13	3	4	17	2
Kutler, Matt, Brown	.358	179	38	64	14	9	3	43	6
Livermore, Jorge, Columbia	.337	175	43	59	10	1	0	25	13
Metzger, Greg, Brown	.335	167	33	56	12	0	9	39	3
Lucas, Eddie, Dartmouth	.326	141	26	46	8	2	0	21	7
Eldridge, Ryan, Princeton	.324	139	19	45	7	1	1	26	0
Hess, Billy, Columbia	.320	169	41	54	15	2	0	35	3
Goldblatt, Mike, Pennsylvania	.318	132	24	42	6	2	1	22	8
Boran, Pat, Princeton	.312	154	33	48	7	7	2	33	10
Mager, Matt, Harvard	.311	190	29	59	12	3	2	27	6
Anderson, Michael, Columbia	.309	110	18	34	6	2	0	17	4
Deeb, Robert, Pennsylvania	.309	178	47	55	14	3	4	31	17
Luria, Andrew, Cornell	.308	159	23	49	14	1	6	30	8
Miller, Jon, Princeton	.307	140	22	43	10	0	1	25	1
Mileusnic, Matt, Dartmouth	.307	137	24	42	11	3	4	34	1
Balkan, Adam, Princeton	.305	167	31	51	7	2	1	28	10
#Lynn, Rick, Brown	.296	179	44	53	5	3	4	26	34
#Catsam, Joe, Columbia	.295	132	29	39	11	1	12	42	0

INDIVIDUAL PITCHING LEADERS
(Minimum 40 Innings)

	W	L	ERA	G	SV	IP	H	BB	SO
Pauly, Thomas, Princeton	2	2	1.33	19	8	41	30	15	43
Breslow, Craig, Yale	1	5	2.56	9	0	60	46	29	44
Crockett, Ben, Harvard	6	4	2.79	12	0	84	78	15	117
Ohlendorf, Ross, Princeton	6	3	3.08	10	0	53	53	22	51
Boehle, David, Princeton	1	2	3.15	9	0	40	43	12	27
Stern, Jonathan, Brown	7	4	3.28	11	0	74	70	25	71
Dowling, Patrick, Dartmouth	3	4	3.54	8	0	53	55	15	27
McCreery, Andrew, Pennsylvania	3	4	3.88	8	0	56	59	18	47
McCarthy, Matt, Yale	4	3	3.99	9	0	50	52	18	45
Baysinger, Dan, Cornell	1	5	4.03	8	0	45	67	10	27
Elias, Mike, Yale	2	4	4.18	13	0	56	61	18	28
McKitish, Brian, Columbia	5	4	4.23	10	0	55	64	18	36
Velosky, John, Dartmouth	3	6	4.35	11	1	60	67	17	54
Davidson, Chris, Brown	2	0	4.57	11	0	45	38	25	42
Waldman, Matt, Columbia	4	2	4.58	10	0	55	54	29	31
Grillo, Jamie, Brown	4	2	4.92	8	0	53	71	15	34
Quillian, Ryan, Princeton	2	5	5.06	9	0	48	55	18	35

METRO ATLANTIC CONFERENCE

	Conference		Overall	
	W	L	W	L
*Marist	22	5	41	14
Le Moyne	19	7	30	18
Siena	17	9	28	29
Rider	17	10	33	22
Manhattan	16	11	32	19
Fairfield	12	15	20	30
Iona	10	16	20	28
Niagara	9	17	12	34
Saint Peter's	7	18	12	30
Canisius	3	24	4	38

ALL-CONFERENCE TEAM: C—Jim Buckley, Sr., Siena. **1B**—Chris Gaskin, Fr., Manhattan. **2B**—Kevin Roberts, Jr., Siena. **3B**—Jim Willis, Sr., Marist. **SS**—Travis Garcia, So., Iona. **OF**—Anthony Bocchino, Sr., Marist; Matt Cucurullo, So., Manhattan; Ryan Finn, Sr., Siena. **DH**—Brett Woodcock, Sr., Le Moyne. **Util**—Wendell Anderson, Sr., Manhattan. **P**—Ryan Darcy, Jr., Manhattan; Chris Tracz, So., Marist.

Player of the Year: Anthony Bocchino, Marist. **Pitcher of the Year:** Chris Tracz, Marist. **Rookies of the Year:** Chris Gaskin, Manhattan; Mike Lewis, Le Moyne. **Coach of the Year:** Steve Trimper, Manhattan.

INDIVIDUAL BATTING LEADERS
(Minimum 125 At-Bats)

	AVG	AB	R	H	2B	3B	HR	RBI	SB
Bocchino, Anthony, Marist	.444	207	65	92	24	9	9	56	17
Long, Casey, Rider	.419	210	51	88	18	4	7	44	6
Kean, Josh, Siena	.406	165	41	67	15	3	5	25	20
Anderson, Wendell, Manhattan	.377	167	56	63	14	2	6	42	2
Cucurullo, Matt, Manhattan	.372	180	51	67	9	2	1	36	25
Willis, Jimmy, Marist	.368	185	52	68	17	2	7	44	8
Rich, Scott, Rider	.354	209	37	74	12	1	6	55	11
Rinaldi, Russell, St. Peter's	.346	130	23	45	6	6	4	24	20
Ircandia, Vince, Niagara	.341	176	30	60	8	2	3	27	9
Pesaresi, Erinn, Rider	.340	206	56	70	6	5	7	28	11
Garcia, Travis, Iona	.339	192	36	65	12	0	5	27	5
McGorty, John, Marist	.333	183	45	61	13	0	6	51	7
O'Sullivan, Steve, Marist	.332	223	67	74	12	8	6	34	17
Woodcock, Brett, Le Moyne	.331	166	30	55	8	0	6	29	8
Brooks, Rich, Rider	.330	188	33	62	18	2	5	35	6
Lewandowski, Jesse, St. Peter's	.329	164	32	54	12	0	6	30	16
Cappello, Frank, Manhattan	.329	149	23	49	10	1	0	32	3
Motte, Jason, Iona	.329	143	19	47	11	0	2	32	3
Pineiro, Josh, St. Peter's	.327	156	19	51	5	1	1	17	3
Greco, Josh, Manhattan	.326	193	38	63	14	1	1	36	1
Aquilino, Anthony, Le Moyne	.326	193	42	63	17	0	7	46	12
Cipolla, Tony, Siena	.326	193	45	63	13	0	8	29	6
Gaskin, Chris, Manhattan	.326	187	34	61	12	1	3	37	3
Diaz, Gary, Manhattan	.325	206	43	67	9	1	0	20	10
Novalis, Jon, Fairfield	.321	159	33	51	10	2	3	28	19
Hanan, Blake, Siena	.320	206	43	66	15	0	3	19	20
Bittner, Ryan, Fairfield	.314	185	32	58	14	0	4	35	2
Allen, Tim, Marist	.311	183	38	57	19	2	8	48	2
Harper, Eddie, Le Moyne	.310	213	47	66	16	4	6	36	22
Fortner, Rob, Iona	.307	163	32	50	13	0	4	25	7
#Finn, Ryan, Siena	.297	209	49	62	17	4	13	53	17
#Riley, Kevin, Rider	.293	191	40	56	10	0	11	57	1

INDIVIDUAL PITCHING LEADERS
(Minimum 50 Innings)

	W	L	ERA	G	SV	IP	H	BB	SO
Kondratowicz, Ryan, Marist	6	0	1.93	17	1	65	48	12	53
Tracz, Chris, Marist	10	3	2.36	15	0	99	85	20	78
Ool, Kevin, Marist	10	4	2.77	18	1	91	91	17	85
Parisi, Mike, Manhattan	7	4	2.83	17	3	86	84	28	81
#Homer, Chris, Marist	1	1	3.03	23	11	30	23	7	35
Mattoon, Brian, Le Moyne	6	4	3.04	14	0	95	79	24	86
Pahucki, Dave, Siena	6	4	3.16	18	2	88	81	24	77
Keating, Greg, Iona	5	3	3.48	11	0	54	50	20	40
Gleason, Ken, Manhattan	6	3	3.51	14	2	74	77	29	34
Young, Bob, Rider	5	5	3.54	14	0	84	89	33	75
Darcy, Ryan, Manhattan	5	5	3.71	17	0	107	114	24	79
Copskey, Josh, Siena	3	5	3.79	17	0	81	93	14	42
Lewis, Mike, Le Moyne	5	2	4.11	12	0	66	54	20	59
Bechtel, Chuck, Marist	8	5	4.31	18	0	79	75	34	73
Knoff, Justin, Siena	5	6	4.50	13	0	68	71	20	38
Barlow, Chris, Le Moyne	8	3	4.57	15	0	85	92	17	68
Lambo, Luke, Iona	5	7	4.69	13	0	86	106	21	70
Maisano, Thomas, Fairfield	6	4	4.70	12	0	75	86	18	74
Krines, Dan, Fairfield	5	5	4.89	14	0	96	124	22	63
Berghoff, Joe, Rider	5	1	5.19	14	0	50	60	23	35
Grant, Doug, St. Peter's	5	3	5.24	11	0	67	84	22	57

MID-AMERICAN CONFERENCE

	Conference		Overall	
EAST	W	L	W	L
Bowling Green	18	7	32	22
*Kent State	18	8	37	22
Miami (Ohio)	16	12	31	28
Ohio	14	13	26	25
Akron	8	19	18	33
Buffalo	6	17	16	28
Marshall	7	20	17	35
WEST	W	L	W	L
Eastern Michigan	19	9	30	28
Ball State	17	9	34	23
Central Michigan	14	10	31	25
Western Michigan	12	13	22	25
Northern Illinois	11	14	23	32
Toledo	9	18	18	34

ALL-CONFERENCE TEAM: C—Mitch Maier, So., Toledo. **1B**—Kelly Hunt, Jr., Bowling Green. **2B**—Corey Loomis, Jr., Bowling Green. **3B**—Adam Fox, So., Ohio. **SS**—Nick Elrod, Sr., Bowling Green. **OF**—Mike Arbinger, Sr., Ohio; Sam Flamont, Sr., Western Michigan; Ryan Goleski, So., Eastern Michigan. **DH**—Mike Carlin, Jr., Miami. **Util**—Mike Galloway, Jr., Miami. **P**—Bryan Bullington, Jr., Ball State; Luke Hagerty, Jr., Ball State; Dirk Hayhurst, Jr., Kent State; Chad Pleiness, Sr., Central Michigan. **RP**—Neil Schmitz, So., Bowling Green.

Player of the Year: Kelly Hunt, Bowling Green. **Pitcher of the Year:** Bryan Bullington, Ball State. **Freshman of the Year:** Brian Bixler, Eastern Michigan. **Coach of the Year:** Roger Coryell, Eastern Michigan.

INDIVIDUAL BATTING LEADERS
(Minimum 125 At-Bats)

	AVG	AB	R	H	2B	3B	HR	RBI	SB
Galloway, Mike, Miami	.422	223	72	94	16	3	15	63	14
Arbinger, Mike, Ohio	.417	192	62	80	15	2	20	57	4
Loomis, Corey, BGSU	.404	193	61	78	13	4	13	52	7
Hunt, Kelly, BGSU	.402	214	69	86	14	1	22	84	4
Flamont, Sam, WMU	.401	187	44	75	15	6	9	56	13
Snyder, Brad, Ball State	.389	203	50	79	17	1	13	57	11
Dobson, Sean, Toledo	.387	191	33	74	9	0	2	34	17
Gates, Mike, CMU	.385	182	51	70	16	0	9	62	9
Deckman, Matt, Ball State	.383	209	58	80	11	1	9	43	2
Goleski, Ryan, EMU	.381	218	62	83	17	3	22	70	4
Elrod, Nick, BGSU	.379	177	56	67	16	1	8	40	5
Hudak, Andy, BGSU	.374	171	51	64	15	1	10	57	2
LoCascio, Phil, Kent State	.372	207	53	77	13	2	3	42	1
Fox, Adam, Ohio	.368	201	48	74	14	0	12	59	5
Frankhouse, Tim, WMU	.366	191	36	70	22	0	0	22	2
Newell, Tim, BGSU	.363	204	47	74	19	1	7	44	2
Maier, Mitch, Toledo	.362	221	60	80	16	2	14	43	15
Eckel, Taylor, Toledo	.361	191	41	69	9	0	5	32	4
Dziedziejko, Craig, Marshall	.359	156	31	56	16	0	9	41	2
DeSantis, Clay, Marshall	.359	131	36	47	8	0	10	33	8
Marconi, Rob, No. Illinois	.357	154	38	55	10	4	9	52	4
Brock, John, No. Illinois	.355	169	51	60	9	0	8	24	18
Shockey, Jason, Ohio	.352	165	47	58	15	1	2	33	1
Huber, Eric, Buffalo	.348	158	28	55	12	1	3	26	1
Anglin, Greg, EMU	.345	220	56	76	12	6	14	58	12
Carlin, Michael, Miami	.345	203	56	70	10	3	19	55	3
Crabtree, Ben, Ohio	.344	160	35	55	11	0	6	42	1
Elias, Len, BGSU	.343	201	52	69	15	2	10	57	7
Schroeder, Ben, Ball State	.343	210	62	72	10	2	5	27	14
Danielson, Noel, No. Illinois	.342	193	50	66	16	1	6	36	11
#Colangelo, David, Marshall	.330	209	58	69	15	2	7	35	21

INDIVIDUAL PITCHING LEADERS
(Minimum 50 Innings)

	W	L	ERA	G	SV	IP	H	BB	SO
Bullington, Bryan, Ball State	11	3	2.84	15	0	105	88	18	139
Hagerty, Luke, Ball State	7	4	3.02	15	0	83	71	28	92
#Hlebovy, Gus, Kent State	3	3	3.03	23	11	39	35	16	33
Lowrey, Patrick, Ball State	5	4	3.10	11	0	58	40	17	46
Hayhurst, Dirk, Kent State	8	4	3.29	15	0	93	89	31	94
Pleiness, Chad, CMU	6	3	3.31	11	0	68	52	29	100
Bucklew, Kory, Ball State	3	0	3.52	25	0	54	51	11	43
Lynch, Brian, Ball State	4	3	4.15	16	0	65	71	15	64
Skrukrud, Mark, No. Illinois	6	5	4.36	13	0	89	79	14	74
Garner, Jeff, CMU	4	4	4.45	12	1	59	56	31	60
Mumma, Brad, WMU	5	4	4.55	16	1	61	55	25	69
White, Chris, Kent State	5	3	4.62	13	0	74	83	33	72
Kieninger, Billy, Miami	5	6	4.63	21	2	56	62	22	37
Leonard, Chris, Miami	2	4	4.85	11	0	65	75	26	61
Landis, Shawn, Miami	8	0	4.87	18	2	61	74	19	44
Bayer, Russ, Miami	7	4	4.89	17	0	99	112	29	88

COLLEGE BASEBALL

MID-CONTINENT CONFERENCE

	Conference		Overall	
	W	L	W	L
*Oral Roberts	16	2	48	19
Southern Utah	11	7	18	37
Oakland	9	8	19	35
Valparaiso	7	9	15	32
Western Illinois	6	9	12	39
Chicago State	0	14	5	36

ALL-CONFERENCE TEAM: C—David Castillo, So., Oral Roberts. **1B**—Peter Varon, Jr., Oakland. **2B**—Danny Boyle, Sr., Oral Roberts. **3B**—Joe Rooney, Jr., Western Illinois. **SS**—Doug Bernier, Sr., Oral Roberts. **OF**—Jeff Mandsager, Jr., Valparaiso; Wilton Reynolds, Sr., Oral Roberts; Jeff Wellwood, Sr., Western Illinois. **DH**—Matt Gabrielli, Jr., Oakland. **Util**—James Anderson, Sr., Southern Utah. **P**—James Anderson, Sr., Southern Utah; Rene Recio, So., Oral Roberts; Michael Rogers, Sr., Oral Roberts; Jared Thomas, Jr., Oakland. **RP**—Dallas Martin, Jr., Oral Roberts.

Player of the Year: David Castillo, Oral Roberts. **Pitcher of the Year:** James Anderson, Southern Utah. **Newcomer of the Year:** Jared Thomas, Oakland. **Coach of the Year:** Sunny Golloway, Oral Roberts.

INDIVIDUAL BATTING LEADERS
(Minimum 100 At-Bats)

	AVG	AB	R	H	2B	3B	HR	RBI	SB
Castillo, David, Oral Roberts	.398	226	59	90	23	0	14	79	4
Rooney, Joe, W. Illinois	.358	179	34	64	12	0	12	47	3
Bernier, Doug, Oral Roberts	.351	228	50	80	10	1	0	37	25
Reynolds, Jake, Southern Utah	.349	209	48	73	9	9	3	30	13
DiPonio, Nick, Oakland	.341	185	39	63	9	0	9	32	3
Stewart, Chad, Oral Roberts	.339	192	39	65	13	1	2	35	10
Thornton, Eric, Oral Roberts	.336	217	32	73	20	0	7	52	6
Bertulis, John, West. Illinois	.329	155	28	51	12	0	0	14	5
Newgent, Daniel, Chicago State	.328	131	24	43	9	1	4	24	2
Troy, Nick, W. Illinois	.324	105	14	34	9	0	0	15	6
Boggio, Marc, Valparaiso	.320	181	35	58	17	2	6	23	8
Schrum, Dan, Valparaiso	.314	137	30	43	4	0	13	31	5
Reynolds, Wilton, Oral Roberts	.310	245	65	76	19	2	16	59	12
Young, Kyle, Valparaiso	.306	121	14	37	7	0	1	22	1
Tokarz, Brad, Valparaiso	.305	167	30	51	11	1	3	18	2
Varon, Peter, Oakland	.303	188	45	57	14	1	13	39	0
Crossley, Erik, Oakland	.301	136	28	41	10	1	4	24	6
Kemp, Kelcey, Southern Utah	.301	186	31	56	10	0	1	24	1
Pedersen, Mark, Valparaiso	.300	170	25	51	9	1	2	19	3
Richardson, Billy Joe, ORU	.298	188	40	56	12	1	6	41	4
Nelson, Chris, Southern Utah	.297	182	37	54	10	1	8	39	6
Gabrielli, Matt, Oakland	.294	153	23	45	6	0	5	30	0
Duvall, Ryan, So. Utah	.293	157	33	46	6	3	1	18	4
Jensen, John, Chicago State	.289	128	16	37	7	0	5	25	0
#Boyle, Danny, Oral Roberts	.280	225	81	63	7	1	3	28	38

INDIVIDUAL PITCHING LEADERS
(Minimum 40 Innings)

	W	L	ERA	G	SV	IP	H	BB	SO
Sanderson, Andrew, Oral Roberts	6	2	1.76	28	0	46	29	14	44
Recio, Rene, Oral Roberts	8	5	2.23	15	0	85	63	23	106
#Martin, Dallas, Oral Roberts	0	1	2.50	31	6	40	44	12	45
Rogers, Michael, Oral Roberts	12	3	2.85	19	0	123	94	32	119
Davis, Stockton, Oral Roberts	4	0	3.57	23	1	68	64	30	83
Pickford, Troy, Oral Roberts	5	3	4.43	15	0	45	48	20	53
Humen, David, Oral Roberts	5	2	4.56	15	0	49	55	22	54
Bigley, Dennis, Oral Roberts	7	1	4.67	15	0	62	73	24	50
Thomas, Jared, Oakland	4	4	4.82	16	1	71	63	45	103
Peickert, Sean, Valparaiso	5	2	4.89	10	0	42	44	6	23
Gardner, Chris, Southern Utah	1	3	5.62	21	0	42	54	18	37
Perkins, Shane, Southern Utah	5	8	5.73	15	0	88	113	31	45
Lewis, Brian, W. Illinois	4	7	5.86	17	0	81	95	36	62
Stamper, Jason, Chicago State	1	7	6.15	15	1	53	75	16	26

MID-EASTERN CONFERENCE

	Conference		Overall	
NORTH	W	L	W	L
Delaware State	16	1	40	19
Coppin State	9	7	12	37
Howard	6	12	8	41
Maryland-Eastern Shore	3	14	4	36
SOUTH	W	L	W	L
*Bethune-Cookman	16	2	39	22
Florida A&M	10	8	27	27
North Carolina A&T	6	11	19	39
Norfolk State	3	15	16	34

ALL-CONFERENCE TEAM: C—Chris Branning, So., Florida A&M. **IF**—Scott Holmes, Sr., Florida A&M; Wes Timmons, Sr., Bethune-Cookman; Bret Underwood, So., Delaware State. **OF**—Jason Battle, Sr., North Carolina A&T; Frank Scott, Jr., Florida A&M; Phil Sullinger, Sr., Delaware State. **DH**—Scott Martin, Jr., Delaware State. **P**—Cesar Montes de Oca, Sr., Bethune-Cookman.

Player of the Year: Wes Timmons, Bethune-Cookman. **Rookie of the Year:** Shavon Phillips, Delaware State. **Coach of the Year:** Keith Shumate, North Carolina A&T.

INDIVIDUAL BATTING LEADERS
(Minimum 100 At-Bats)

	AVG	AB	R	H	2B	3B	HR	RBI	SB
Timmons, Wes, B-C	.425	214	79	91	22	1	10	64	40
Sullinger, Phil, Del. State	.401	207	71	83	21	3	11	63	5
Maloney, Kevin, Del. State	.373	217	67	81	15	0	0	36	7
King, Malkum, Del. State	.367	177	66	65	18	3	7	57	10
Underwood, Bret, Del. State	.356	222	62	79	21	1	15	77	7
Battle, Jason, NC A&T	.354	178	41	63	11	3	3	25	15
Martin, Scott, Del. State	.343	181	44	62	13	0	18	68	4
Bones, Jared, Norfolk State	.343	178	39	61	6	5	2	31	12
King, Jeffrey, NC A&T	.342	152	38	52	8	4	4	32	6
Maclin, Charles, Howard	.333	162	33	54	7	4	8	41	20
Williams, Kelly, Del. State	.325	231	67	75	14	1	2	37	14
Ramos, Jose, B-C	.325	194	47	63	11	1	11	57	14
Smith, Adonis, NC A&T	.323	189	40	61	10	1	6	31	16
Goodson, Eugene, Norfolk State	.316	155	28	49	7	1	1	19	2
Linares, Eddy, Del. State	.304	207	40	63	13	4	2	34	7
August, Mike, Del. State	.301	183	46	55	12	0	2	40	3
Goodson, Gregory, Norfolk State	.301	133	26	40	4	1	0	18	3
Geathers, Carlos, NC A&T	.300	170	30	51	12	1	11	47	4
Vazquez, Jose, B-C	.298	178	27	53	3	0	2	29	2
#Simmons, Micah, B-C	.262	195	41	51	4	8	4	28	43

INDIVIDUAL PITCHING LEADERS
(Minimum 40 Innings)

	W	L	ERA	G	SV	IP	H	BB	SO
Moises, Helpiz, B-C	11	3	2.72	15	0	99	78	38	84
Renshaw, Andrew, Norfolk State	4	9	3.35	16	0	91	94	27	67
Montes de Oca, Cesar, B-C	10	3	3.44	17	0	97	97	49	92
Phillips, Shawn, Del. State	9	3	3.63	16	0	92	88	26	68
Brzeczek, Joe, Del. State	9	4	4.46	20	0	73	91	26	50
Scott, Travis, NC A&T	4	7	4.76	21	0	96	109	34	82
Dooley, Jason, B-C	9	6	5.14	18	0	105	124	40	89
Tew, Robert, Norfolk State	3	2	5.16	15	1	45	37	31	32
Gordon, Dave, Del. State	7	4	5.45	16	0	78	94	29	54
Locklear, Joe, NC A&T	5	7	5.68	24	0	78	75	63	85

MISSOURI VALLEY CONFERENCE

	Conference		Overall	
	W	L	W	L
*Wichita State	23	9	47	17
Creighton	21	10	30	24
Southwest Missouri State	19	13	43	21
Southern Illinois	17	15	32	24
Indiana State	16	15	30	27
Northern Iowa	14	18	30	25
Illinois State	12	18	24	30
Evansville	12	20	22	33
Bradley	8	24	18	38

ALL-CONFERENCE TEAM: C—Toby Barnett, Jr., Southern Illinois. **1B**—Jeff Stanek, Sr., Southern Illinois. **2B**—Brian Burgamy, Jr., Wichita State. **3B**—Jason Simon, Sr., Northern Iowa. **SS**—Travis Welsch, Sr., Northern Iowa. **OF**—Dant'e Brinkley, Jr., Southwest Missouri State; Dustin Hawkins, Sr., Wichita State; Andy Rohleder, Sr., Evansville. **DH**—Drew Moffitt, So., Wichita State. **Util**—Shaun Marcum, Southwest Missouri State. **P**—Tom Oldham, So., Creighton; John Tetuan, Jr., Wichita State; Brad Ziegler, Jr., Southwest Missouri State. **RP**—Steve Grasley, So., Creighton; Steve Obenchain, Jr., Evansville.

Player of the Year: Brian Burgamy, Wichita State. **Pitcher of the Year:** John Tetuan, Wichita State. **Newcomer of the Year:** Toby Barnett, Southern Illinois. **Freshman of the Year:** Tony Roth, Creighton. **Coach of the Year:** Jack Dahm, Creighton.

INDIVIDUAL BATTING LEADERS
(Minimum 125 At-Bats)

	AVG	AB	R	H	2B	3B	HR	RBI	SB
Peacock, Jon, Illinois State	.406	187	44	76	17	1	9	48	4
Burgamy, Brian, Wichita State	.400	240	68	96	15	3	4	57	24
Bouris, Brad, Illinois State	.378	156	34	59	13	0	3	28	1
Rohleder, Andy, Evansville	.378	196	50	74	15	1	13	59	15
Ohland, Shane, Bradley	.375	184	33	69	10	2	3	34	13
Welsch, Travis, Northern Iowa	.366	232	54	85	19	0	2	44	16
Walter, Randy, Wichita State	.365	192	55	70	14	2	10	49	30

	AVG	AB	R	H	2B	3B	HR	RBI	SB
Kowzan, Ross, Southern Illinois	.361	158	35	57	10	1	1	24	6
Hawkins, Dustin, Wichita State	.356	216	55	77	16	1	6	36	33
Simon, Jason, Northern Iowa	.356	205	34	73	13	0	5	40	6
Marcum, Shaun, SMS	.354	223	42	79	18	1	5	41	1
Hummel, Roamn, Northern Iowa	.347	150	25	52	11	0	3	29	0
Brinkley, Dant'e, SMS	.345	249	59	86	18	3	6	55	25
Egli, Kevin, Indiana State	.344	195	46	67	14	1	11	44	6
Isenhower, Jeremy, SMS	.340	241	61	82	13	6	5	52	13
Mathis, Greg, SMS	.339	251	58	85	12	3	11	52	14
Hinrichs, Chris, Creighton	.337	205	48	69	12	7	11	49	27
Colvin, Brooks, SMS	.335	188	33	63	8	0	0	28	9
Wilson, Rick, SMS	.333	207	36	69	15	1	1	32	4
Spicer, Todd, Bradley	.332	193	44	64	5	1	0	20	7
Watchowski, Donnie, SMS	.331	163	26	54	10	2	4	30	3
Maurath, Justin, Southern Illinois	.331	145	29	48	8	1	3	24	4
Dvorsky, Alex, Iowa State	.330	197	44	65	22	0	7	49	5
Cantrell, Ryan, Illinois State	.330	197	36	65	17	0	8	37	5
Gardner, Matt, SMS	.328	256	56	84	22	1	7	46	7
Welch, Tanner, Wichita State	.326	181	35	59	6	1	3	33	10
Baker, Jamie, Indiana State	.325	126	27	41	6	1	2	17	14
Stanek, Jeff, Southern Illinois	.322	202	42	65	12	1	7	37	1
Miller, Michael, Indiana State	.320	206	38	66	9	0	1	20	21
Allen, Scott, Creighton	.319	210	42	67	14	3	7	43	15
Reger, Caleb, Indiana State	.317	167	30	53	8	3	6	29	3
Vandever, Joey, Evansville	.315	222	50	70	15	1	2	20	29
Boeve, Adam, Iowa State	.314	169	46	53	7	1	8	33	16
McCarty, Justin, Wichita State	.314	194	31	61	13	1	5	40	12
Moffitt, Drew, Wichita State	.312	215	60	67	17	1	16	68	4
Albano, Anthony, Evansville	.312	199	33	62	9	4	2	29	9
Finigan, P.J., Southern Illinois	.310	210	38	65	12	0	2	34	3

INDIVIDUAL PITCHING LEADERS
(Minimum 50 Innings)

	W	L	ERA	G	SV	IP	H	BB	SO
Obenchain, Steve, Evansville	3	1	1.38	25	12	78	53	23	89
Tetuan, John, Wichita State	10	1	1.72	16	1	89	62	31	78
Thatcher, Joe, Indiana State	4	1	1.73	33	8	52	39	18	46
Maureau, Justin, Wichita State	4	3	2.45	18	3	55	47	9	67
Sanders, David, Wichita State	5	4	2.59	14	0	73	74	13	58
Ziegler, Brad, SMS	7	3	3.03	15	0	95	93	30	95
Arreola, Andrew, Evansville	7	5	3.31	15	0	82	88	30	58
Stetter, Mitch, Indiana State	5	7	3.45	14	0	89	84	38	82
Peterson, Adam, Wichita State	9	3	3.55	15	0	84	82	23	91
Eddie, Derek, SMS	5	1	3.75	16	1	60	70	20	46
Kelchen, Kory, Northern Iowa	3	1	3.77	17	0	60	66	20	31
Alley, Jake, Southern Illinois	6	3	3.86	16	0	86	98	41	81
Oldham, Tom, Creighton	7	3	3.90	15	0	90	107	19	80
Quinlan, Mike, Illinois State	3	4	3.95	12	0	73	78	10	37
Gray, Jeff, SMS	7	2	4.10	15	1	83	84	27	61
Bader, David, SMS	5	4	4.23	18	0	79	78	31	61
Welch, Ryan, Southern Illinois	5	4	4.24	13	1	68	66	27	39
Wear, Greg, Indiana State	6	4	4.32	12	0	73	65	29	48
Kerbs, Reuben, Wichita State	5	1	4.66	17	0	56	63	12	44
Palmer, Matt, SMS	5	3	4.73	15	0	70	71	43	71
Miller, Scott, Iowa State	3	3	4.79	16	1	56	57	35	49
Grasley, Steve, Creighton	4	6	4.87	27	11	61	69	10	56

MOUNTAIN WEST CONFERENCE

	Conference		Overall	
	W	L	W	L
San Diego State	20	10	43	23
Utah	16	14	33	26
*Brigham Young	15	14	31	31
Air Force	14	15	27	28
Nevada-Las Vegas	13	17	30	30
New Mexico	11	19	22	35

ALL-CONFERENCE TEAM: C—Brian Manfred, Sr., San Diego State. 1B—Dave Jensen, So., Brigham Young. 2B—Troy Cairns, Jr., New Mexico. 3B—Bowie Frost, Jr., Air Force. SS—Taber Lee, Jr., San Diego State. OF—Matt Carson, Jr., Brigham Young; Joe Wickman, Fr., Nevada-Las Vegas; Matt Young, Fr., New Mexico. DH—Cameron Coughlan, Jr., Brigham Young. P—Chris Dunwell, Jr., San Diego State; Mitch Maio, Sr., Utah; Rory Shortell, Jr., San Diego State. RP—Royce Ring, Jr., San Diego State.

Players of the Year: Dave Jensen, Brigham Young; Mitch Maio, Utah. Freshman of the Year: Joe Wickman, Nevada-Las Vegas. Coach of the Year: Reed Peters, Air Force.

INDIVIDUAL BATTING LEADERS
(Minimum 125 At-Bats)

	AVG	AB	R	H	2B	3B	HR	RBI	SB
Wickman, Joe, UNLV	.437	142	37	62	14	1	2	38	3
Jensen, Dave, Brigham Young	.412	262	58	108	29	0	10	69	12
Stroud, Todd, New Mexico	.392	158	44	62	14	2	5	26	1
Mader, Josh, New Mexico	.388	209	41	81	8	2	0	39	14

	AVG	AB	R	H	2B	3B	HR	RBI	SB
Young, Matt, New Mexico	.385	213	64	82	4	3	1	24	17
Howes, Adam, Air Force	.379	211	54	80	14	3	3	40	27
Cairns, Troy, New Mexico	.379	243	61	92	11	5	2	57	11
Frost, Bowie, Air Force	.377	199	41	75	22	0	7	44	2
Coughlan, Cameron, BYU	.374	265	76	99	10	7	4	46	33
McLintock, Jade, SDSU	.370	230	51	85	18	4	8	58	1
Castleton, Adam, Utah	.369	195	62	72	14	5	11	52	8
Kasel, Derck, Air Force	.368	163	37	60	16	4	4	39	2
Young, Dusty, New Mexico	.367	240	48	88	25	1	3	51	4
Stephens, Jon, SDSU	.365	241	50	88	10	1	3	40	2
Phifer, Josh, Air Force	.364	195	58	71	20	3	13	69	15
Alexander, Chris, New Mexico	.361	249	61	90	20	2	19	78	2
Westfall, Mike, Utah	.356	225	43	80	18	1	6	44	1
Nielsen, Eric, UNLV	.356	225	46	80	15	1	3	51	2
Lee, Taber, SDSU	.355	245	46	87	15	0	0	46	15
Jackson, Doug, Brigham Young	.348	282	65	98	17	6	5	43	19
Ciaramella, Matt, Utah	.345	226	41	78	17	4	4	37	11
Trujillo, David, UNLV	.345	229	55	79	13	0	18	74	2
Weese, Nate, Utah	.343	242	60	83	8	3	17	60	19
Carson, Matt, Brigham Young	.343	245	54	84	20	4	9	60	10
Cota, Carlo, SDSU	.341	267	57	91	26	5	2	50	9
Gwynn, Anthony, SDSU	.339	248	58	84	9	4	1	36	25
Pannier, Brit, Utah	.329	234	45	77	26	0	6	56	7
#Johnson, Brent, UNLV	.313	259	64	81	30	2	4	42	11

INDIVIDUAL PITCHING LEADERS
(Minimum 50 Innings)

	W	L	ERA	G	SV	IP	H	BB	SO
#Ring, Royce, SDSU	5	1	1.85	36	17	39	29	13	54
Dunwell, Chris, SDSU	8	3	3.92	16	0	96	95	39	89
Maio, Mitch, Utah	9	1	3.98	22	5	93	99	32	94
Shortell, Rory, SDSU	8	7	4.28	18	0	114	110	42	71
Mousser, Jeff, Brigham Young	9	4	4.88	19	1	90	109	38	73
Van, Robbie, UNLV	7	5	5.29	17	0	83	95	41	85
Carque, Joe, SDSU	9	3	5.90	22	0	76	99	29	53
Koegel, Johnny, Air Force	6	6	5.93	18	0	96	132	33	66
Rushton, Cheyenne, Utah	8	6	5.98	19	0	102	139	23	63
Hall, Courtney, UNLV	5	6	6.21	15	0	67	98	29	61
Vermilyea, James, New Mexico	7	9	6.24	18	0	131	164	39	107
Koffman, Scott, Brigham Young	4	4	6.59	16	1	72	83	35	32
Seccombe, David, UNLV	2	2	6.65	21	0	66	93	19	64
Adams, Ryan, Brigham Young	6	5	6.86	18	0	80	112	38	42
Kaercher, Matt, Air Force	7	10	6.93	19	0	110	148	43	80

NORTHEAST CONFERENCE

	Conference		Overall	
	W	L	W	L
Monmouth	23	4	30	21
Maryland-Baltimore County	20	7	32	24
*Central Connecticut State	18	9	34	23
St. Francis (N.Y.)	17	10	22	24
Sacred Heart	14	13	20	27
Mount St. Mary's	10	16	17	35
Quinnipiac	9	18	12	30
Long Island	8	19	11	33
Wagner	8	19	10	39
Fairleigh Dickinson	7	19	9	35

ALL-CONFERENCE TEAM: C—Tim D'Aquila, So., Central Connecticut State. 1B—Jeff Koenig, Sr., Mount St. Mary's. 2B—Charles D'Elia, Sr., Quinnipiac. 3B—Brad Glascock, Jr., Maryland-Baltimore County. SS—Jared Boyd, Sr., Maryland-Baltimore County. OF—Jason Law, Sr., Monmouth; Matt Lemanczyk, Sr., Sacred Heart; Kevin Rival, Sr., Central Connecticut State. DH—Jamie Schilkowski, So., Sacred Heart. P—Jim Carone, Jr., Monmouth; Joe Wilson, So., Maryland-Baltimore County.

Player of the Year: Jared Boyd, Maryland-Baltimore County. Pitcher of the Year: Jim Carone, Monmouth. Rookie of the Year: Phil Rothkugel, Central Connecticut State. Coach of the Year: Dean Ehehalt, Monmouth.

INDIVIDUAL BATTING LEADERS
(Minimum 125 At-Bats)

	AVG	AB	R	H	2B	3B	HR	RBI	SB
Boyd, Jared, UMBC	.404	208	58	84	32	3	7	52	3
D'Elia, Charles, Quinnipiac	.404	156	30	63	17	0	4	40	0
Lemanczyk, Matt, Sacred Heart	.380	184	41	70	9	6	5	28	41
Rothkugel, Phil, CCS	.374	195	43	73	14	0	10	56	1
Davis, Tim, Monmouth	.369	141	34	52	5	1	1	17	12
Schikowski, Jamie, Sacred Heart	.358	159	18	57	19	1	1	40	0
Dick, Chris, Wagner	.353	167	33	59	13	1	10	40	0
Hosgood, Robert, CCS	.350	217	54	76	18	7	3	41	22
Marano, Albert, Quinnipiac	.344	160	27	55	13	1	7	32	2
DiGirolamo, John, Mt. St. Mary's	.343	140	25	48	5	2	1	22	3
Rival, Kevin, CCS	.343	213	41	73	18	1	5	42	4
Iorio, Jason, St. Francis	.342	149	26	51	12	3	1	23	15
D'Aquila, Tim, CCS	.341	211	53	72	14	0	6	47	4

Inserra, Charles, Long Island .... .338 154 20 52 8 4 3 14 3
Geroni, Pat, Fairleigh Dickinson .. .331 157 23 52 8 0 8 38 0
Shuler, John, UMBC .... .330 209 51 69 14 1 3 30 6
Law, Jay, Monmouth .... .330 182 36 60 16 1 9 48 0
Grasso, Paul, Monmouth .... .329 167 27 55 14 2 5 35 3
St. Martine, Mike, Monmouth ...... .325 169 29 55 14 1 2 27 0
McLaughlin, Tom, FDU .... .323 133 30 43 3 2 1 10 11
Guarno, Rick, UMBC .... .323 189 37 61 10 0 0 23 5
Koenig, Lance, Monmouth .... .321 159 43 51 15 0 3 35 12
Nugent, Matt, Fairleigh Dickinson .319 144 27 46 9 2 2 30 5
Macellaro, Nick, CCS .... .318 179 36 57 13 1 1 29 1
Farrison, Khyl, Long Island .... .318 151 31 48 10 1 3 25 15
#Koenig, Jeff, Mt. St. Mary's ...... .315 165 29 52 11 0 16 50 6

INDIVIDUAL PITCHING LEADERS
(Minimum 50 Innings)

	W	L	ERA	G	SV	IP	H	BB	SO
#Kelly, Mike, Monmouth	2	1	0.53	15	9	17	17	3	15
Cerbone, Justin, CCS	4	1	1.35	17	0	60	55	21	47
Carone, Jim, Monmouth	10	3	2.21	13	0	98	83	19	26
Wilson, Joe, UMBC	9	3	2.26	14	0	92	91	34	53
#Pappariella, Lewis, CCS	2	2	2.52	17	9	25	16	7	45
Scott, Dan, Sacred Heart	6	3	3.01	12	0	78	72	19	65
Bailey, Matt, St. Francis	9	3	3.16	18	0	88	99	12	44
Wildasin, Kyle, UMBC	5	2	3.63	27	3	52	45	13	36
Melillo, John, Quinnipiac	4	3	3.71	14	0	70	76	33	63
Hertzler, Barry, CCS	5	5	3.72	13	0	75	81	20	42
Collins, Ryan, Mt. St. Mary's	2	8	4.21	15	0	66	77	18	42
Barrios, Dan, Long Island	4	8	4.48	13	0	78	89	30	62
Esposito, Anthony, St. Francis	4	7	4.58	15	0	77	86	35	59
Palmieri, Andrew, Monmouth	6	3	4.78	15	0	75	79	30	52
Clarke, Jim, CCS	7	6	4.83	15	0	95	111	19	69
Rival, Kevin, CCS	8	4	4.87	15	1	78	82	44	80
Clark, Zach, UMBC	6	5	4.88	16	0	79	103	17	57
Bushor, Eric, Sacred Heart	4	6	4.92	11	0	75	92	17	43
#Santo, Brian, Mt. St. Mary's	5	8	5.79	15	0	78	88	34	85

OHIO VALLEY CONFERENCE

	Conference		Overall	
	W	L	W	L
*Southeast Missouri State	16	5	37	20
Eastern Illinois	12	8	25	26
Austin Peay State	12	9	30	27
Murray State	10	11	20	33
Tennessee Tech	9	11	29	27
Morehead State	9	11	29	27
Eastern Kentucky	9	11	15	40
Tennessee-Martin	4	15	18	33

ALL-CONFERENCE TEAM: C—A.J. Ellis, Jr., Austin Peay. **1B**—Brett McCutchan, Jr., Murray State. **2B**—Jake Allen, Jr., Tennessee Tech. **3B**—Denver Stuckey, Jr., Southeast Missouri. **SS**—Casey Benjamin, Jr., Tennessee Tech. **OF**—Josh Anderson, So., Eastern Kentucky; Vern Hatton, Sr., Southeast Missouri; Pete Pirman, Sr., Eastern Illinois. **DH**—Bret Pignatiello, Jr., Eastern Illinois. **Util**—Neil Sellers, So., Eastern Kentucky. **P**—Brad Purcell, Jr., Southeast Missouri; Mike Weel, Jr., Austin Peay. **RP**—Doug Vincent, Jr., Tennessee Tech.

Player of the Year: Pete Pirman, Eastern Illinois. **Pitcher of the Year:** Brad Purcell, Southeast Missouri. **Rookie of the Year:** Cole Helms, Tennessee Tech. **Coach of the Year:** Mark Hogan, Southeast Missouri.

INDIVIDUAL BATTING LEADERS
(Minimum 125 At-Bats)

	AVG	AB	R	H	2B	3B	HR	RBI	SB
Pirman, Pete, Eastern Illinois	.407	209	58	85	16	0	10	44	13
Lavender, Bubba, Morehead State	.389	203	70	79	11	0	24	69	10
Gilvin, Casey, Morehead State	.383	201	56	77	11	2	8	37	5
Ellis, A.J., Austin Peay	.371	194	37	72	14	1	9	44	0
Hatton, Vern, SEMO	.369	222	58	82	17	9	9	58	11
Anderson, Josh, E. Kentucky	.363	201	54	73	11	3	4	21	30
Duke, Ben, Eastern Illinois	.362	174	40	63	13	3	9	36	4
Allen, Jake, Tennessee Tech	.358	176	51	63	13	4	5	37	12
Page, Cary, Morehead State	.355	200	55	71	10	0	26	71	5
Helms, Cole, Tennessee Tech	.354	246	44	80	17	1	4	44	9
McDonald, Tristen, SEMO	.353	201	43	71	14	0	10	52	2
Matuszek, Kevin, Morehead State	.352	216	68	76	17	1	21	76	1
Stuckey, Denver, SEMO	.349	229	51	80	17	1	5	37	18
Lowe, Nate, Morehead State	.349	126	26	44	4	0	3	42	5
Bonilla, Clemente, SEMO	.347	193	48	67	19	0	1	42	5
Sellers, Neil, Eastern Kentucky	.346	208	40	72	14	1	6	42	5
Benjamin, Casey, Tenn. Tech	.342	196	42	67	10	2	2	32	3
Renaker, Will, Morehead State	.340	203	48	69	13	0	14	44	0
McCutchan, Brett, Murray State ..	.337	169	33	57	14	1	7	39	0
Hughes, David, Austin Peay	.328	201	49	66	20	3	8	41	4
Beech, Travis, Austin Peay	.328	201	38	66	17	1	4	27	16

Hay, Ryan, Tenn. Tech .... .325 191 47 62 12 0 8 46 0
Borowiak, Zach, SEMO .... .324 219 40 71 17 3 4 35 5
Fuller, Ben, Austin Peay .... .324 148 39 48 6 1 4 21 15
Johnson, Michael, Austin Peay .... .322 214 57 69 8 1 18 76 26
Pignatiello, Bret, Eastern Illinois . .321 165 38 53 4 0 14 37 3

INDIVIDUAL PITCHING LEADERS
(Minimum 50 Innings)

	W	L	ERA	G	SV	IP	H	BB	SO
Alvarez, Tim, SEMO	5	1	2.95	16	3	61	48	19	33
Purcell, Brad, SEMO	12	3	3.38	21	0	117	108	38	102
Vincent, Doug, Tennessee Tech.....	10	2	3.40	22	1	79	69	27	74
Weel, Mike, Austin Peay	9	3	3.93	16	0	89	87	27	69
Smith, Brandon, SEMO..................	12	2	4.31	18	1	94	104	34	82
Fuller, Donnie, SEMO....................	3	2	4.56	17	0	53	55	19	46
Buzachero, Bubbie, Tenn. Tech.......	1	5	4.76	8	0	51	72	22	44
Mathews, Tony, Austin Peay...........	6	3	4.82	17	0	84	85	39	60
Frazier, Mark, SEMO......................	3	6	4.86	26	5	54	65	33	60
Perry, Kyle, Murray State	5	5	4.99	15	0	79	90	39	50
Downs, Ben, Tenn. Tech.................	6	5	5.66	19	0	83	79	45	78
Martin, Pete, Eastern Illinois..........	5	4	5.68	13	0	57	69	45	39
Corey, Donnie, Tennessee-Martin......	2	5	6.02	14	0	52	62	33	43
Jackson, David, Tenn. Tech	1	2	6.11	21	1	53	71	25	50
Metz, Scott, Eastern Illinois	3	5	6.14	18	0	81	88	41	50
Pew, Stephen, Austin Peay	5	4	6.17	25	3	58	76	32	52

PACIFIC-10 CONFERENCE

	Conference		Overall	
	W	L	W	L
Southern California	17	7	37	24
Stanford	16	8	47	18
Arizona State	15	9	37	21
Washington	15	9	33	27
California	11	13	29	27
Oregon State	10	14	31	23
UCLA	9	15	26	35
Arizona	9	15	31	24
Washington State	6	18	21	33

ALL-CONFERENCE TEAM: C—John Baker, Jr., California; Alberto Concepcion, Jr., Southern California; Ryan Garko, Jr., Stanford. **1B**—Conor Jackson, So., California; Bill Peavey, Sr., Southern California; Jeremy West, So., Arizona State; Wes Whisler, Fr., UCLA. **2B**—Bookie Gates, Sr., Washington State; Chris O'Riordan, Sr., Stanford. **3B**—Brian Barden, Jr., Oregon State. **SS**—Brad Hassey, Sr., Arizona; Dustin Pedroia, Fr., Arizona State. **OF**—Brian Barre, Sr., Southern California; Tyler Davidson, Jr., Washington; Andre Ethier, So., Arizona State; Sam Fuld, So., Stanford; Carlos Quentin, So., Stanford. **DH**—Joey Metropoulos, Fr., Southern California. **Util**—Jason Cooper, Jr., Stanford. **P**—Jeremy Guthrie, Jr., Stanford; Shawn Kohn, Sr., Washington; Anthony Reyes, Jr., Southern California; Wes Whisler, Fr., UCLA.

Player of the Year: Alberto Concepcion, Southern California. **Pitcher of the Year:** Jeremy Guthrie, Stanford. **Freshman of the Year:** Wes Whisler, UCLA. **Coach of the Year:** Mike Gillespie, Southern California.

INDIVIDUAL BATTING LEADERS
(Minimum 125 At-Bats)

	AVG	AB	R	H	2B	3B	HR	RBI	SB
Baker, John, California	.383	149	34	57	12	1	5	29	0
Jackson, Conor, California	.382	220	43	84	16	2	16	61	7
Fuld, Sam, Stanford	.375	293	67	110	20	4	8	47	8
Hart, Justin, Wash. State	.370	165	37	61	6	1	2	28	5
Francisco, Ben, UCLA	.368	152	42	56	11	1	6	37	20
LaRue, Jeffrey, Wash. State	.367	199	45	73	16	0	10	40	1
Concepcion, Alberto, USC	.363	234	57	85	21	5	11	48	3
Arhart, Josh, UCLA	.363	193	40	70	18	0	7	37	1
Ethier, Andre, Arizona State	.363	182	38	66	14	3	4	50	1
Gates, Bookie, Wash. State	.362	188	29	68	9	3	2	38	14
Peavey, Bill, USC	.361	216	62	78	17	0	15	71	5
West, Jeremy, Arizona State	.356	208	55	74	18	4	13	71	0
Metropoulos, Joey, USC	.352	193	51	68	17	1	13	65	2
Dragicevich, Scott, Stanford	.350	203	44	71	17	2	5	35	3
Cooper, Jason, Stanford	.350	226	45	79	16	2	13	57	1
Barden, Brian, Oregon State	.349	232	47	81	15	1	9	50	3
Pedroia, Dustin, Arizona State	.347	236	51	82	13	2	1	45	5
Reynolds, Tila, Washington	.347	239	45	83	15	5	2	34	19
Grzecka, Casey, UCLA	.346	133	21	46	13	0	2	28	2
Hecker, Evan, Wash. State	.342	190	47	65	19	0	1	25	10
Larsen, Kyle, Washington	.342	190	30	65	11	1	5	37	4
White, Carson, California	.339	227	44	77	15	0	7	32	8
Davidson, Tyler, Washington	.339	251	62	85	18	2	15	51	10
Mathews, Aaron, Oregon State	.338	142	27	48	5	3	2	26	10
Garrabrants, Steve, Arizona State	.337	202	55	68	15	7	2	33	16
Moon, Michael, USC	.336	238	52	80	14	1	8	60	12

	AVG	AB	R	H	2B	3B	HR	RBI	SB
Jarvis, Andy, Oregon State	.335	176	37	59	9	2	11	44	3
O'Riordan, Chris, Stanford	.332	262	59	87	17	1	10	47	7
Barre, Brian, USC	.331	242	**75**	80	16	2	12	43	14
Larish, Jeff, Arizona State	.328	128	31	42	4	3	3	24	0
Whisler, Wes, UCLA	.328	177	33	58	9	0	**18**	46	2
Hardy, John, Arizona	.328	174	36	57	8	1	5	38	5
McAndrews, Travis, USC	.324	136	21	44	4	0	3	28	1
Garthwaite, Jay, Washington	.320	247	49	79	16	3	16	64	8
Isaacson, Greg, Washington	.315	149	32	47	9	1	1	25	11
Hassey, Brad, Arizona	.315	238	50	75	10	2	9	46	15
Garko, Ryan, Stanford	.314	239	68	75	18	0	14	55	2
Hudson, Will, Oregon State	.313	179	44	56	10	2	2	24	4
Averill, Brandon, UCLA	.310	200	28	62	10	0	6	31	1
VanZandt, Arik, Stanford	.309	165	33	51	6	2	6	26	10
Berry, Adam, UCLA	.308	208	47	64	9	0	**18**	50	4
Pietsch, Seth, Oregon State	.307	205	51	63	**24**	6	8	34	2
Falkenborg, Wes, Wash. State	.306	173	27	53	7	0	6	41	1
Nicholson, David, California	.305	220	46	67	7	1	6	23	10
Rasmussen, Ryan, UCLA	.304	230	52	70	8	2	1	22	**20**
St. Clair, Justyn, Arizona	.304	161	39	49	5	3	1	33	8
Mortimer, Steve, Wash. State	.304	138	22	42	8	0	2	27	6
Quentin, Carlos, Stanford	.303	241	55	73	13	4	12	54	11
Hathaway, Aaron, Washington	.303	175	27	53	6	1	4	30	9
Creighton, Tom, Oregon State	.299	201	38	60	7	4	4	36	7
Gastellum, Miguel, Army	.356	132	28	47	6	1	0	22	26
Gonser, Tye, Lafayette	.356	177	40	63	10	1	2	28	14
Alexander, Craig, Lafayette	.352	145	32	51	11	2	4	24	10
Fishman, Eric, Bucknell	.349	172	34	60	14	**6**	6	35	17
Kalkwarf, Kyle, Army	.345	148	20	51	10	0	1	34	7
Novalis, Jesse, Lehigh	.335	176	43	59	9	2	**10**	43	5
Summa, Peter, Holy Cross	.333	123	24	41	5	2	4	19	5
Moll, Jason, Lafayette	.331	118	27	39	4	2	1	25	8
Mack, Jeremy, Lehigh	.327	171	36	56	11	4	5	37	12
Boyd, Jason, Lafayette	.323	167	37	54	**16**	4	2	34	19
Pagan, Justin, Lehigh	.315	181	37	57	8	1	2	31	16
Rosenberg, Adam, Lafayette	.311	148	28	46	5	0	3	17	15
Bucci, Adam, Lafayette	.308	104	16	32	8	0	1	23	1
Tambellini, Matt, Lafayette	.297	118	16	35	8	0	1	21	3
Thoman, Chad, Lehigh	.295	156	26	46	8	0	0	20	12
McEvoy, Matthew, Holy Cross	.287	122	20	35	8	0	1	16	4
Pietrak, Jeff, Lehigh	.285	165	34	47	8	1	6	41	14
Rodgers, Jeff, Lafayette	.284	116	27	33	5	1	0	19	5
Scheetz, Larry, Bucknell	.275	167	26	46	6	2	2	20	2
Cocca, John, Navy	.273	161	29	44	11	1	1	18	**32**
Piccola, Anthony, Lehigh	.273	154	37	42	10	1	1	22	17
Johnson, Dale, Navy	.273	128	11	35	7	0	0	12	2

INDIVIDUAL PITCHING LEADERS
(Minimum 50 Innings)

	W	L	ERA	G	SV	IP	H	BB	SO
Schroyer, Ryan, Arizona State	4	1	2.37	25	8	61	50	35	75
Guthrie, Jeremy, Stanford	**13**	2	2.51	20	0	158	138	36	**136**
Kohn, Shawn, Washington	11	5	3.22	17	0	131	124	23	79
#Sanders, Jared, Oregon State	1	5	3.23	26	**9**	31	30	12	15
Hutchinson, Trevor, California	7	5	3.38	15	0	117	106	34	94
Reyes, Anthony, USC	4	2	3.44	12	0	65	69	17	49
McCally, Ryan, Stanford	4	3	3.53	25	7	51	40	22	39
Bannister, Brett, USC	8	3	3.56	26	0	86	80	32	76
Kline, Ty, Oregon State	6	1	3.68	26	2	51	49	14	29
Brown, Matt, California	5	3	3.70	21	6	73	77	23	55
Esposito, Mike, Arizona State	9	6	3.72	17	0	104	109	31	93
Campos, Cory, USC	6	3	3.84	30	6	68	76	19	69
Whisler, Wes, UCLA	5	2	4.06	18	0	84	94	40	59
Cunningham, Tim, Stanford	10	3	4.26	20	0	112	108	47	67
White, Sean, Washington	7	2	4.28	15	0	95	108	32	56
Kunes, Mike, UCLA	7	4	4.55	27	1	89	97	21	71
Rierson, Sean, Arizona	7	5	4.69	17	0	117	122	26	81
Hudgins, John, Stanford	10	1	4.71	19	0	105	106	35	62
McClellan, Robbie, Arizona State	7	6	4.73	21	1	97	94	51	91
Goodman, Chris, Arizona	5	2	4.86	21	0	54	62	22	31
Cordeiro, Chris, UCLA	2	7	5.00	18	2	77	92	36	47
Montalbo, Brian, California	3	5	5.05	11	0	57	65	23	44
Ingram, Jesse, California	5	2	5.16	29	1	52	53	28	45
McLemore, Mark, Oregon State	3	5	5.17	14	0	63	64	24	48
Little, Joe, Arizona	6	6	5.38	17	0	97	111	29	83
Chico, Matt, USC	6	4	5.45	15	0	69	81	47	69
Kartler, Bryce, Arizona State	4	4	5.46	19	0	63	55	37	56
Copeland, Stephen, Oregon State	5	3	5.49	17	0	97	110	38	41
Rowe, Ben, Oregon State	7	5	5.71	18	0	87	95	38	38
Kaiser, Marc, Arizona	5	4	5.77	16	0	78	96	20	36

INDIVIDUAL PITCHING LEADERS
(Minimum 40 Innings)

	W	L	ERA	G	SV	IP	H	BB	SO
Foster, Matt, Navy	4	1	**2.14**	8	0	42	32	13	34
Cerminaro, Dave, Lehigh	**9**	3	2.34	14	1	88	82	14	**60**
#Farmery, Gregg, Bucknell	4	4	2.48	19	**6**	29	26	13	19
Montano, Mike, Holy Cross	2	5	2.81	11	0	51	47	14	25
Lynch, Jason, Holy Cross	4	2	2.81	10	0	42	45	11	20
Froistad, Andy, Navy	5	2	3.10	12	0	52	53	10	25
Muscalus, Jack, Lehigh	7	3	3.48	12	0	62	60	22	36
McDevitt, Rich, Navy	3	6	3.62	12	0	65	79	12	31
Ward, Marcus, Lafayette	5	3	3.89	12	0	69	67	22	53
Lucey, D.J., Holy Cross	4	4	3.98	12	1	54	53	12	35
Elliott, Brian, Army	5	4	4.08	12	1	68	76	16	38
Saporetti, Joe, Lafayette	6	4	4.11	10	0	57	69	6	33
Magee, Sean, Bucknell	4	4	4.25	15	0	66	79	16	38
Bumgardner, Wes, Army	2	4	4.35	11	0	62	59	18	37
Kashner, Justin, Army	5	2	4.60	10	1	47	56	13	33
Cappello, Dan, Army	3	3	4.83	12	0	41	42	20	32

SOUTHEASTERN CONFERENCE

	Conference		Overall	
EAST	W	L	W	L
South Carolina	21	8	57	18
Florida	20	10	46	19
Georgia	15	15	32	29
Tennessee	12	18	27	28
Vanderbilt	7	21	24	27
Kentucky	6	24	17	36
WEST	W	L	W	L
*Alabama	20	10	51	15
Louisiana State	19	10	44	22
Auburn	15	15	34	26
Mississippi State	14	15	34	24
Arkansas	13	14	35	28
Mississippi	14	16	37	19

ALL-CONFERENCE TEAM: C—Jeremy Brown, Sr., Alabama. **1B**—Yaron Peters, Sr., South Carolina. **2B**—Brent Boyd, Sr., Alabama. **3B**—Pat Osborn, Jr., Florida. **SS**—Drew Meyer, Jr., South Carolina. **OF**—Chaz Lytle, Jr., Georgia; Scott McClanahan, Sr., Alabama; Seth Smith, Fr., Mississippi. **DH**—Trey Dyson, Sr., South Carolina. **P**—Alex Hart, Jr., Florida; Lane Mestepey, So., Louisiana State. **RP**—Blake Taylor, Sr., Louisiana State.

Player of the Year: Yaron Peters, South Carolina. **Freshman of the Year:** Seth Smith, Mississippi. **Coach of the Year:** Jim Wells, Alabama.

INDIVIDUAL BATTING LEADERS
(Minimum 125 At-Bats)

	AVG	AB	R	H	2B	3B	HR	RBI	SB
Osborn, Pat, Florida	.414	251	67	104	17	1	17	76	7
Stonard, Peter, Alabama	.411	236	59	97	22	5	5	42	18
Kiger, Mark, Florida	.403	258	**90**	104	12	4	11	55	11
Smith, Seth, Mississippi	.402	204	36	82	9	2	4	52	5
Lytle, Chaz, Georgia	.387	229	60	108	11	7	3	38	31
Barker, Sean, LSU	.382	267	47	102	16	0	8	62	23
Shealy, Ryan, Florida	.379	261	73	99	14	2	23	80	0
Peters, Yaron, South Carolina	.377	281	81	106	22	0	**29**	**95**	6
Sterbens, Chad, Mississippi	.376	229	38	86	8	1	4	49	7
Leullwitz, Sean, Vanderbilt	.370	208	40	77	16	1	12	51	1
Moran, Javon, Auburn	.365	266	59	97	11	3	3	41	18
Rogers, Drew, Mississippi	.364	165	31	60	11	0	6	34	0

PATRIOT LEAGUE

	Conference		Overall	
	W	L	W	L
*Navy	13	7	23	18
Lehigh	13	7	29	21
Lafayette	12	8	23	22
Army	11	9	22	21
Bucknell	6	14	15	35
Holy Cross	5	15	11	28

ALL-CONFERENCE TEAM: C—Dale Johnson, Jr., Holy Cross. **1B**—Matt Tambellini, Jr., Lafayette. **2B**—Miguel Gastellum, Sr., Army. **3B**—Vince D'Angelis, Sr., Lafayette. **SS**—Larry Scheetz, Sr., Bucknell. **OF**—Eric Fishman, Sr., Bucknell; Tye Gonser, Sr., Lafayette; Josh Holden, Jr., Army. **DH**—Adam Bucci, Fr., Lafayette. **P**—Dave Cerminaro, Sr., Lehigh; Andy Froistad, So., Navy. **RP**—Bryan Koehler, Sr., Navy.

Player of the Year: Vince D'Angelis, Lafayette. **Pitcher of the Year:** Dave Cerminaro, Lehigh. **Rookie of the Year:** Jack Muscalus, Lehigh. **Coach of the Year:** Steve Whitmyer, Navy.

INDIVIDUAL BATTING LEADERS
(Minimum 100 At-Bats)

	AVG	AB	R	H	2B	3B	HR	RBI	SB
Hoffman, Eric, Lehigh	.376	186	**50**	70	13	0	4	31	15
D'Angelis, Vince, Lafayette	.369	157	41	58	10	3	5	**47**	8

Czarniecki, Jordan, Tennessee	.362	199	47	72	20	3	8	46	24
Swann, Adam, Georgia	.361	202	38	73	16	1	12	46	4
Meyer, Drew, South Carolina	.359	334	87	**120**	23	5	6	40	**39**
Broadus, Chris, Vanderbilt	.357	154	24	55	11	0	0	19	6
Thomas, Steve, South Carolina	.355	296	72	105	**26**	1	13	70	5
Huddleston, Bobby, Auburn	.355	203	46	72	21	0	11	50	0
Sobieraj, Aaron, Florida	.354	237	60	84	11	3	8	57	7
Gendron, Steve, Miss. State	.351	239	46	84	14	1	2	48	3
Holt, J.C., LSU	.349	192	45	67	5	6	3	23	10
Phillips, Chris, LSU	.344	192	30	66	7	0	7	44	0
Harrison, Ben, Florida	.342	161	42	55	10	5	8	38	6
Mungle, Jon, Miss. State	.341	179	49	61	11	2	8	36	3
Pontiff, Wally, LSU	.339	248	41	84	20	0	6	46	4
Hearod, Beau, Alabama	.335	212	39	71	11	1	12	54	3
Sevilla, Walter, Tennessee	.330	224	42	74	11	6	1	33	25
Hill, Aaron, LSU	.329	222	46	73	18	2	9	47	10
McClain, Justin, Georgia	.325	163	29	53	11	0	9	32	5
Sternberg, Matt, Tennessee	.325	197	40	64	19	0	4	35	1
Hutchinson, Burney, Miss.	.323	229	55	74	19	3	10	42	5
Buscher, Brian, South Carolina	.323	294	56	95	20	6	14	64	1
Garner, Travis, Alabama	.323	226	57	73	15	0	6	31	26
Swearingen, Jonathan, Miss.	.321	165	44	53	7	1	3	26	13
Nonemaker, Karl, Vanderbilt	.321	212	39	68	11	2	1	29	16
Goss, Matt, Florida	.321	209	50	67	16	4	6	47	6
Brown, Jeremy, Alabama	.320	219	56	70	17	2	11	64	6
Graeter, Spencer, Kentucky	.317	164	34	52	15	1	2	21	7
Long, Casey, Miss. State	.317	202	40	64	8	0	0	30	11
Brinson, Matthew, Miss. State	.316	237	61	75	17	2	14	71	1
Bridges, Scott, Arkansas	.316	174	34	55	4	2	2	25	13
Szabo, Marshall, Georgia	.315	149	27	47	5	1	6	26	4
Wishy, Andrew, Arkansas	.314	175	37	55	10	0	4	34	4
Bibee, Hal, Tennessee	.312	192	24	60	12	0	5	35	3
Lewis, Brent, Miss. State	.312	189	32	59	18	0	3	30	0
Davidson, Aaron, Florida	.309	217	58	67	12	2	10	42	19
Hulett, Tug, Auburn	.308	201	44	62	16	1	0	31	5
Pratt, Trent, Auburn	.308	221	38	68	18	0	8	54	2
Garza, Mario, Florida	.308	182	43	56	13	1	11	41	4
Clark, Cody, Arkansas	.307	140	29	43	12	0	2	27	0
Cavender, Matt, Georgia	.307	189	41	58	9	0	7	33	9
#McConnell, Kirk, Arkansas	.303	198	42	60	5	**8**	1	27	7

INDIVIDUAL PITCHING LEADERS

(Minimum 50 Innings)

	W	L	ERA	G	SV	IP	H	BB	SO
Reed, Brian, Alabama	5	0	**1.75**	27	9	51	43	13	43
Mestepey, Lane, LSU	11	5	2.59	19	0	**142**	145	17	74
Tankersley, Taylor, Alabama	8	5	2.62	25	7	69	55	20	65
Taylor, Blake, South Carolina	6	1	2.63	37	**21**	86	78	44	79
Tompkins, Jake, LSU	7	1	2.68	25	4	87	78	37	96
Hart, Alex, Florida	**13**	3	3.24	17	0	111	81	56	81
Cormier, Lance, Alabama	11	3	3.28	17	0	129	135	27	85
Carter, Brent, Alabama	2	0	3.31	17	2	54	52	10	51
Norris, Jeffrey, Alabama	6	1	3.34	14	1	70	74	15	50
Pettit, Bo, LSU	9	7	3.35	19	0	121	112	57	121
Maholm, Paul, Miss. State	10	3	3.43	14	0	102	103	33	77
Wilson, Brian, LSU	10	5	3.54	23	2	94	112	31	71
Young, Chris, Miss. State	5	2	3.67	24	1	74	64	13	44
Pickens, J.R., Mississippi	7	4	3.74	15	0	91	91	27	76
Richmond, Jonathan, Arkansas	2	4	3.83	17	0	52	64	13	23
Bondurant, Steven, South Carolina	7	4	3.87	21	1	95	92	32	61
Sanders, Shane, Alabama	8	4	3.87	19	0	93	107	27	58
Ramsey, Keith, Florida	10	3	3.88	19	0	109	92	44	84
Rawl, Aaron, South Carolina	7	2	3.89	28	2	72	84	23	69
Isaacson, Charlie, Arkansas	7	7	3.99	16	0	90	92	33	53
Gardner, Jarrett, Arkansas	4	4	4.04	24	3	69	69	21	38
Roehl, Scott, Arkansas	4	1	4.17	21	4	58	53	12	46
Sowers, Jeremy, Vanderbilt	6	5	4.37	15	2	101	104	31	85
Carswell, Jeffrey, Georgia	5	4	4.45	24	4	57	65	21	47
Woods, Matt, Georgia	3	2	4.46	19	1	77	86	24	52
Collums, Joey, Miss. State	3	6	4.58	14	0	59	55	25	56
Blanton, Joseph, Kentucky	5	7	4.59	14	0	100	98	37	**133**
Woodward, Jared, Alabama	6	1	4.66	23	0	66	75	13	57
Terrell, Jeffery, Tennessee	5	8	4.67	25	6	116	125	47	111
Little, Jeff, Vanderbilt	5	6	4.73	15	1	91	97	37	52
Ramshaw, Jimmy, Florida	6	4	4.80	18	1	90	101	39	80
Hahn, Cory, Kentucky	3	8	4.83	18	1	69	82	21	51
Hogan, Gary, Arkansas	3	6	4.87	22	3	89	110	23	65
Speigner, Levale, Auburn	7	6	4.92	20	0	104	118	17	61
Horne, Alan, Mississippi	5	2	4.97	12	0	54	44	34	31
Marchbanks, David, South Carolina	9	4	4.98	19	0	99	109	26	71
Brock, Tanner, Miss. State	7	5	5.04	14	0	80	82	35	54
Montrenes, Pete, Mississippi	8	6	5.04	15	0	86	92	42	70
Riley, Ben, Tennessee	5	3	5.08	15	0	90	98	52	75
Spigner, Chris, South Carolina	7	0	5.08	26	0	80	83	41	82

SOUTHERN CONFERENCE

	Conference W	Conference L	Overall W	Overall L
The Citadel	22	8	31	26
Western Carolina	20	10	33	23
College of Charleston	19	11	36	22
***Georgia Southern**	18	11	39	25
UNC Greensboro	17	11	33	22
Wofford	14	16	26	31
Furman	14	16	26	34
Davidson	13	16	21	29
ETSU State	13	16	21	36
Appalachian State	10	19	16	34
Virginia Military Institute	1	27	10	41

ALL-CONFERENCE TEAM: C—Matt Lauderdale, Jr., Charleston. **1B**—Todd Buchanan, Jr., Western Carolina. **2B**—Jason Sarvis, Jr., UNC Greensboro. **3B**—Lee Curtis, Jr., Charleston. **SS**—Ryan Schade, Sr., Western Carolina. **OF**—Matt Herring, Jr., Georgia Southern; Donovan Minero, Sr., Western Carolina; Brett Spivey, Jr., Charleston. **DH**—Ryan Gordon, So., UNC Greensboro. **P**—Ryan Johnson, Jr., Charleston; Scooter Michael, So., UNC Greensboro. **RP**—Randy Corn, Sr., The Citadel.

Player of the Year: Lee Curtis, Charleston. **Pitcher of the Year:** Randy Corn, The Citadel. **Freshman of the Year:** Matt Lein, Wofford. **Coach of the Year:** Todd Raleigh, Western Carolina.

INDIVIDUAL BATTING LEADERS

(Minimum 125 At-Bats)

	AVG	AB	R	H	2B	3B	HR	RBI	SB
Spivey, Brett, Charleston	**.423**	213	60	90	19	6	8	57	12
Curtis, Lee, Charleston	.409	225	67	**92**	11	**9**	**15**	65	21
Keithley, Kirk, ETSU	.381	194	41	74	14	1	4	31	19
Herring, Matt, Ga. Southern	.380	237	62	90	16	0	14	**77**	14
Lauderdale, Matt, Charleston	.378	185	44	70	19	2	4	43	5
Norman, Derek, Furman	.374	235	57	88	10	3	9	45	6
Beck, Alan, WCU	.374	219	58	82	17	2	10	59	7
Minero, Donovan, WCU	.374	222	48	83	19	0	**15**	62	2
Roper, Todd, WCU	.374	182	40	68	11	1	0	24	8
Caudill, Craig, Furman	.371	175	26	65	7	2	0	16	1
Schade, Ryan, WCU	.367	226	58	83	16	2	7	44	0
Gordon, Ryan, UNCG	.366	172	38	63	12	4	4	44	23
Lein, Matt, Wofford	.362	213	45	77	15	2	6	52	3
Presnell, Ryan, Furman	.357	168	36	60	8	2	4	26	9
Revere, J.R., Ga. Southern	.352	210	42	74	11	4	0	35	22
Frend, Tim, Davidson	.351	194	49	68	15	3	10	45	4
Nix, Stanley, Charleston	.351	154	31	54	14	1	4	42	1
Sarvis, Jason, UNCG	.350	206	49	72	**24**	4	5	41	9
Pittman, Eric, ASU	.348	138	26	48	13	0	4	28	1
Griffin, David, Citadel	.340	159	20	54	15	0	1	23	3
Smith, Derek, ASU	.339	189	29	64	17	2	1	23	2
Buchanan, Todd, WCU	.338	201	47	68	11	2	7	54	3
Anderson, Brett, Charleston	.333	177	42	59	16	2	6	38	5
Hall, Chad, Ga. Southern	.330	218	43	72	7	2	2	41	6
Hill, Clint, Furman	.329	213	44	70	10	2	1	18	14
Spearman, Jemel, Ga. Southern	.328	274	66	90	19	3	3	46	17
Balcom, Jasha, Charleston	.327	211	65	69	12	7	2	27	10
Cross, Brandon, ETSU	.326	187	34	61	9	1	4	31	1
Timanus, Blake, Wofford	.326	132	14	43	5	0	0	18	0
Walker, Chris, Ga. Southern	.324	272	**79**	88	10	4	2	42	**48**

INDIVIDUAL PITCHING LEADERS

(Minimum 50 Innings)

	W	L	ERA	G	SV	IP	H	BB	SO
Corn, Randy, Citadel	1	0	**1.37**	39	**13**	59	33	16	76
Stovall, Jeff, Furman	7	2	1.46	23	0	86	75	19	56
Hamer, Matt, Citadel	9	2	1.51	35	1	77	77	15	81
Metzger, Jay, UNCG	6	6	2.71	25	0	106	96	29	76
Michael, Scooter, UNCG	**12**	1	2.96	27	3	100	93	21	86
Fulmer, T.A., Citadel	6	4	3.11	15	0	90	80	27	96
Jenkins, Raymond, Citadel	5	4	3.12	15	0	84	76	34	83
Rhue, Mike, Charleston	9	4	3.12	18	0	89	11	26	68
Johnson, Ryan, Charleston	11	3	3.14	16	0	100	98	23	55
Rackers, Matt, Charleston	6	2	3.44	16	0	92	103	20	69
Dove, Dennis, Ga. Southern	7	4	3.52	16	0	72	61	36	85
Comstock, Jared, Ga. Southern	6	2	3.52	17	0	69	69	18	53
Josey, Brad, WCU	4	2	3.52	16	1	54	56	20	27
Frend, Tim, Davidson	3	3	3.56	14	2	61	64	16	62
Lehr, George, Wofford	11	6	3.64	36	8	106	104	45	80
Burton, Jared, WCU	7	6	3.76	17	0	103	102	31	105
Lewis, Brett, Ga. Southern	11	6	4.06	21	0	126	123	39	**122**
Wood, Matt, ASU	1	2	4.08	29	8	53	56	15	47
Talbert, Eric, Citadel	6	5	4.08	15	0	82	96	17	52
Cloninger, Chris, UNCG	5	6	4.26	30	3	99	124	23	66
Mastny, Tom, Furman	5	7	4.42	19	0	110	127	29	95

SOUTHLAND CONFERENCE

	Conference		Overall	
	W	L	W	L
Northwestern State	17	10	43	17
La.-Monroe	17	10	29	29
*Lamar	16	11	36	24
Texas-Arlington	15	11	29	29
McNeese State	15	12	30	28
Southwest Texas State	14	13	36	24
Texas-San Antonio	13	14	25	29
Nicholls State	11	15	28	26
Sam Houston State	9	18	21	33
Southeastern Louisiana	7	20	21	33

ALL-CONFERENCE TEAM: C—Ran Prince, Jr., McNeese State. **1B**—Micah Hoffpauir, Sr., Lamar. **2B**—Blake Justice, Jr., Lamar. **3B**—Mark Schramek, Sr., Texas-San Antonio. **SS**—K.J. Hendricks, Jr., Texas-Arlington. **OF**—Philip Gentry, Jr., Texas-San Antonio; Brad Hanson, Sr., Northwestern State; Dan Ortmeier, Jr., Texas-Arlington. **DH**—Anatole Vincent, Jr., Northwestern State. **P**—Clay Hensley, Sr., Lamar; O.J. King, Sr., Northwestern State; Bobby Sawicki, So., Southwest Texas State.

Player of the Year: Mark Schramek, Texas-San Antonio. **Hitter of the Year:** Mark Schramek, Texas-San Antonio. **Pitcher of the Year:** O.J. King, Northwestern State. **Newcomer of the Year:** Ryan Roberts, Texas-Arlington. **Freshman of the Year:** Dooley Prince, McNeese State. **Coach of the Year:** Jim Gilligan, Lamar.

INDIVIDUAL BATTING LEADERS
(Minimum 125 At-Bats)

	AVG	AB	R	H	2B	3B	HR	RBI	SB
Schramek, Mark, UTSA	.416	202	63	84	16	2	11	49	1
Hickman, Chuck, Nicholls State	.396	235	48	93	14	4	8	46	26
Doty, Jerad, La.-Monroe	.385	156	50	60	14	1	6	23	12
Justice, Blake, Lamar	.379	232	66	88	5	2	0	22	28
Gentry, Phil, UTSA	.369	206	34	76	16	0	5	27	9
Hanson, Brad, NW State	.368	204	60	75	14	4	7	46	13
Spencer, Jacob, SW Texas	.367	256	56	94	18	3	13	54	3
Coles, Marc, SW Texas	.362	218	49	79	17	1	12	60	4
Roberts, Ryan, UT-Arlington	.362	213	45	77	21	2	10	60	3
Vincent, Anatole, NW State	.361	205	47	74	13	0	11	60	6
Prince, Ran, McNeese State	.360	225	51	81	20	3	8	47	25
Fontenot, Josh, McNeese State	.355	169	42	60	10	1	2	19	3
Muller, Luke, Nicholls State	.353	167	31	59	10	1	5	36	0
Foster, Jordan, Lamar	.353	173	25	61	14	1	2	42	3
Hendricks, K.J., UT-Arlington	.352	233	63	82	11	3	2	27	33
Lind, Jason, La.-Monroe	.349	169	26	59	8	0	9	30	0
Taylor, Russell, SE Louisiana	.344	215	60	74	12	0	10	41	21
Prince, Dooley, McNeese State	.340	200	48	68	10	6	0	25	19
Bernhardt, Brian, McNeese State	.341	138	38	47	8	2	4	25	3
Ortmeier, Daniel, UT-Arlington	.335	227	52	76	10	7	14	66	12
Hoffpauir, Micah, Lamar	.335	245	54	82	26	1	9	70	10
Krajancic, Anthony, SE Louisiana	.332	217	42	72	17	1	9	50	7
Stanton, Shawn, Lamar	.329	210	53	69	7	3	5	37	12
Phillips, Danny, UTSA	.325	163	30	53	15	3	4	19	4
Menke, Shawn, UT-Arlington	.323	130	26	42	7	0	0	18	3
Estrada, Jaime, La.-Monroe	.322	233	47	75	16	6	9	42	10
Suares, Igacio, SW Texas	.320	197	37	63	14	1	1	20	15
Younk, Mark, SW Texas	.319	185	36	59	11	1	11	54	0
Virtue, Kevin, SW Texas	.319	135	29	43	11	0	1	20	2
Chance, Andy, La.-Monroe	.318	176	37	56	8	3	7	38	4
Hernandez, Mickey, Lamar	.315	222	37	70	11	0	3	37	6
Micheles, Chris, SW Texas	.315	184	32	58	11	0	5	30	0
Wyninger, Blaine, SE Louisiana	.315	130	15	41	1	1	2	11	0
#Eubanks, Tommy, McNeese State	.290	248	46	72	10	4	11	71	6

INDIVIDUAL PITCHING LEADERS
(Minimum 50 Innings)

	W	L	ERA	G	SV	IP	H	BB	SO
Pullin, Aaron, UT-Arlington	8	1	2.48	19	1	76	70	20	46
King, O.J., NW State	8	4	2.63	15	0	106	105	35	85
Johnson, Casey, NW State	11	1	2.70	16	0	87	86	27	64
Hensley, Clay, Lamar	8	6	2.97	20	1	100	87	30	127
Floyd, Jesse, Lamar	8	2	3.11	16	0	93	90	19	89
Snapp, Michael, UT-Arlington	6	8	3.12	34	5	72	69	15	41
Thompson, Ben, Nicholls State	4	5	3.44	12	0	84	81	29	63
Sawicki, Bobby, SW Texas	11	3	3.57	19	3	118	111	12	124
#Munson, Justin, Nicholls State	3	1	3.59	19	5	43	51	4	24
Sanches, Zach, NW State	6	2	3.62	22	2	70	74	13	36
Gray, Josh, Lamar	5	5	3.72	18	1	73	73	17	51
Srp, Mike, UT San Antonio	5	6	3.97	15	0	95	109	28	41
Herrera, Ryan, Sam Houston	4	7	4.12	18	2	83	81	27	54
Dobbins, Aaron, La.-Monroe	6	5	4.18	13	0	67	78	11	30
Carro, Bobby, La.-Monroe	7	3	4.19	27	5	82	85	18	72
Covert, Cory, SW Texas	6	5	4.20	19	4	75	78	14	62

Lobello, Justin, La.-Monroe	4	5	4.23	14	0	87	103	18	48
Slanina, Jason, NW State	7	4	4.31	15	0	100	97	28	59
Trosclair, Steve, SE Louisiana	3	8	4.32	14	0	90	91	48	82
LaStrapes, Seth, McNeese State	3	4	4.42	16	1	73	82	40	46
Makowsky, Carl, NW State	6	5	4.67	20	1	91	99	39	59
McKeller, Laine, McNeese State	4	5	4.72	17	0	82	106	42	68
Begnaud, Rusty, McNeese State	7	4	5.09	17	0	87	94	42	79
Sanders, Scott, UT San Antonio	4	6	5.13	13	0	60	77	21	22

SOUTHWESTERN ATHLETIC CONFERENCE

	Conference		Overall	
EAST	W	L	W	L
Alcorn State	18	14	24	22
Jackson State	15	13	23	28
Alabama State	17	15	23	27
Alabama A&M	13	16	17	26
Mississippi Valley State	10	15	10	42
WEST	**W**	**L**	**W**	**L**
*Southern	27	3	45	10
Texas Southern	21	13	24	28
Arkansas-Pine Bluff	14	16	24	26
Grambling State	14	18	25	28
Prairie View A&M	3	29	3	46

ALL-CONFERENCE TEAM: C—Eric Duff, So., Alabama State. **1B**—Kevin Vital, Jr., Southern. **2B**—Rickie Weeks, So., Southern. **3B**—Byron Tillman, Sr., Alcorn State. **SS**—Bartowski Cowan, Sr., Alabama State. **OF**—Michael Goss, So., Jackson State; Scott Peebles, Sr., Alabama A&M; Kris Peters, Jr., Alcorn State. **DH**—Janone Watts, So., Alcorn State. **P**—Brian Nicholas, Fr., Alabama State; Anthony Pearson, Jr., Jackson State; Josef Rankin, Sr., Southern; Eric Thomas, Sr., Southern.

Player of the Year: Rickie Weeks, Southern. **Outstanding Hitter:** Rickie Weeks, Southern. **Outstanding Pitcher:** Josef Rankin, Southern. **Newcomer of the Year:** Antoin Gray, Southern. **Freshman of the Year:** Brian Nicholas, Alabama State.

INDIVIDUAL BATTING LEADERS
(Minimum 100 At-Bats)

	AVG	AB	R	H	2B	3B	HR	RBI	SB
Weeks, Rickie, Southern	.495	198	82	98	15	12	20	96	10
Gray, Antoin, Southern	.449	205	88	92	18	2	19	77	3
Lewis, Fred, Southern	.406	165	54	67	12	6	6	40	14
Mason, Brandon, Southern	.403	144	59	58	5	4	4	46	14
Goss, Michael, Jackson State	.393	173	40	68	13	4	1	40	19
Herbert, Herman, Texas Southern	.388	134	26	52	18	2	3	37	6
Bell, David, Texas Southern	.386	153	38	59	14	1	12	49	10
Ross, Cleo, Ark.-PB	.384	151	43	58	17	5	4	40	7
Primus, Robert, Southern	.383	120	42	46	12	1	10	47	0
Puebla, Fernando, Southern	.382	186	47	71	11	3	3	55	5
Cooper, James, Grambling	.376	125	40	47	9	4	3	17	6
Burns, Damon, Texas Southern	.373	134	32	50	9	0	6	37	5
Reynolds, Robert, Miss. Valley	.373	153	26	57	8	1	3	23	18
Vital, Kevin, Southern	.362	130	40	47	9	1	9	53	1
Tillman, Byron, Alcorn State	.357	143	35	51	10	5	2	39	6
Campbell, Alberto, Grambling	.345	165	42	57	6	0	12	44	0
Moffat, Joseph, Ala. State	.344	122	26	42	9	3	3	27	12
Banks, Kevin, Ark.-PB	.343	143	44	49	8	6	1	27	2
Dumas, Theo, Southern	.343	102	30	35	12	1	5	28	2
Outlaw, Chris, Jackson State	.341	167	30	57	18	3	1	31	9
Duncan, Trae, Southern	.340	156	37	53	12	2	9	40	1
Felton, Robert, Jackson State	.338	157	31	53	11	3	2	44	23
#Cowan, Bartowski, Ala. State	.328	189	59	62	15	4	3	43	54

INDIVIDUAL PITCHING LEADERS
(Minimum 40 Innings)

	W	L	ERA	G	SV	IP	H	BB	SO
Sims, Aaron, Alabama A&M	3	3	2.36	8	0	42	39	8	30
Bayless, David, Ark.-Pine Pluff	5	4	3.14	11	0	52	42	28	52
Foster, Roy, Grambling	6	5	3.23	15	1	75	77	20	64
Mouton, Daniel, Alcorn State	5	4	3.95	13	1	66	72	19	58
Nicholas, Brian, Alabama State	7	4	4.06	11	0	62	60	30	52
Holley, Heriod, Grambling	5	4	4.15	11	0	52	68	13	34
Thomas, Eric, Southern	7	2	4.16	14	0	63	64	25	41
Rankin, Josef, Southern	8	0	4.30	14	1	52	51	18	61
Young, Clint, Texas Southern	5	3	4.38	16	0	78	94	23	47
Sosstand, Melvin, Texas Southern	5	5	4.42	13	0	75	84	7	42
Poret, Corey, Southern	7	2	4.53	12	0	48	52	7	49
Birmingham, Michael, Ark.-PB	2	5	4.65	8	0	41	43	11	21
Kirk, Joshua, Southern	8	0	4.67	10	0	44	42	13	41
Owens, Lamaric, Alabama State	4	3	5.10	12	0	55	69	24	17
Johnson, Corey, Alcorn State	3	4	5.15	18	4	51	46	49	47
Tolliver, Melvin, Grambling	5	5	5.27	14	1	68	76	42	64
Johnson, William, Jackson State	5	3	5.57	18	4	42	58	19	26
#Pearson, Anthony, Jackson State	4	7	6.22	14	1	77	65	67	95

COLLEGE BASEBALL

SUN BELT CONFERENCE

	Conference		Overall	
	W	L	W	L
South Alabama	17	5	42	19
Louisiana-Lafayette	17	7	39	23
Western Kentucky	14	9	38	20
Florida International	13	11	41	20
New Orleans	12	12	31	28
*New Mexico State	10	14	37	25
Arkansas State	9	14	23	35
Middle Tennessee State	8	16	26	30
Arkansas-Little Rock	5	17	19	35

ALL-CONFERENCE TEAM: C—Tommy Duenas, So., Florida International. **1B**—Brad Eldred, Sr., Florida International. **2B**—Gabe Veloz, Sr., New Mexico State. **3B**—Tanner Townsend, Sr., Western Kentucky. **SS**—Corey Harrington, Sr., New Mexico State. **OF**—Corey Coles, So., Louisiana-Lafayette; Ryan Mulhern, Jr., South Alabama; Justin Sims, Jr., Middle Tennessee State. **DH**—Chris Adams, Fr., New Orleans. **Util**—Josh Archer, Fr., Middle Tennessee State. **P**—Ryan Bicondoa, Jr., Western Kentucky; Andy Gros, Jr., Louisiana-Lafayette. **RP**—Matt Wilhite, Jr., Western Kentucky.

Player of the Year: Brad Eldred, Florida International. **Pitcher of the Year:** Ryan Bicondoa, Western Kentucky. **Newcomer of the Year:** Kevin Kouzmanoff, Arkansas-Little Rock. **Freshman of the Year:** Derek DeCarlo, Florida International. **Coach of the Year:** Joel Murrie, Western Kentucky.

INDIVIDUAL BATTING LEADERS
(Minimum 125 At-Bats)

	AVG	AB	R	H	2B	3B	HR	RBI	SB
Veloz, Gabe, New Mexico State	.406	234	73	95	26	1	15	92	1
Duenas, Tommy, FIU	.387	204	48	79	17	3	12	57	7
Sims, Justin, MTSU	.387	212	47	82	12	2	11	53	11
Winegarden, Erik, NMSU	.383	201	73	77	20	1	15	54	0
Gragg, John, UALR	.372	183	47	68	12	3	4	40	16
Coles, Corey, La.-Lafayette	.368	231	43	85	11	3	6	45	24
Kouzmanoff, Kevin, UALR	.364	195	50	71	15	1	8	59	6
Rayborn, Jansen, South Alabama	.362	199	36	72	16	0	4	41	3
Eldred, Brad, FIU	.358	218	65	78	9	0	29	71	9
Nisbett, Marshall, MTSU	.356	236	49	84	21	1	8	51	15
Ansoleaga, Alex, FIU	.354	195	53	69	9	0	1	27	11
Adams, Chris, New Orleans	.353	156	30	55	10	3	3	38	0
Mulhern, Ryan, South Alabama	.351	225	63	79	18	1	17	64	6
Bustamente, Daniel, FIU	.349	126	23	44	7	1	4	30	1
Townsend, Tanner, Western Ky.	.347	196	58	68	14	2	8	50	18
Archer, Josh, MTSU	.345	200	31	69	8	2	9	34	2
Jaggers, Nate, MTSU	.339	218	44	74	12	2	7	35	2
Touchstone, Josh, USA	.338	216	43	73	15	1	11	40	12
Towns, Antone, Western Ky.	.338	154	27	52	7	2	4	27	2
Hayes, Brad, Arkansas State	.335	197	28	66	18	0	1	31	6
Summerell, Adam, FIU	.335	197	51	66	15	2	10	38	13
Buckingham, Brock, Ark. State	.335	224	53	75	11	1	3	28	2
Licini, David, New Mexico State ...	.333	210	50	70	15	2	4	36	1
Cattell, Ryan, Western Ky.	.333	195	37	65	18	0	10	42	1
Smallwood, Erik, South Alabama	.330	221	55	73	12	1	14	54	12
Gross, Jason, South Alabama	.329	143	19	47	5	0	5	30	4
Huether, J.D., New Orleans	.328	250	45	82	20	3	6	49	0
Suarez, Alejandro, FIU	.326	141	30	46	12	2	3	27	10
Wilkinson, Kurt, N.M. State	.324	213	68	69	18	4	4	34	10
#Harrington, Corey, NMSU	.322	242	81	78	14	2	8	42	42
#Kenning, Ryan, NMSU	.319	229	66	73	15	3	24	96	1
#Bollich, Donnie, New Orleans	.303	185	42	56	5	6	1	18	24

INDIVIDUAL PITCHING LEADERS
(Minimum 50 Innings)

	W	L	ERA	G	SV	IP	H	BB	SO
#Wilhite, Matt, Western Ky.	8	2	2.20	33	7	45	34	12	42
Bicondoa, Ryan, Western Ky.	11	2	2.55	17	1	124	106	23	150
Thomas, Brad, Arkansas State	5	3	2.58	31	6	73	58	28	81
Gros, Andy, La.-Lafayette	11	4	2.59	24	2	125	116	37	111
Gabriel, Justin, La.-Lafayette	10	4	2.87	19	0	132	129	53	111
Lipari, Tom, New Orleans	6	6	3.21	17	0	104	85	38	113
Kling, Brandon, New Orleans	7	5	3.32	19	1	114	95	38	108
Shambough, Kraig, La.-Lafayette	2	1	3.40	24	0	53	46	19	45
Smith, Sam, South Alabama	9	1	3.47	19	0	117	119	37	114
DeCarlo, Derek, FIU	11	0	3.53	15	0	94	94	37	92
Williams, John, MTSU	2	3	3.53	9	0	64	75	31	71
Stander, Mark, New Orleans	4	5	3.78	15	0	88	81	35	81
Hamilton, Ryan, Arkansas State	1	4	4.02	24	0	63	59	31	56
Taylor, Derek, FIU	5	2	4.08	23	2	64	72	18	54
Sanchez, Carlos, FIU	6	0	4.24	26	1	68	61	51	59
Heath, Bert, South Alabama	9	4	4.48	27	2	64	69	24	56
Williams, Jason, NMSU	8	2	4.65	17	0	91	112	22	74
Petty, Jody, Arkansas State	6	5	4.73	17	0	70	76	20	30

Faircloth, J.C., Western Ky.	5	5	4.76	19	0	81	90	31	61
Baluja, Michael, FIU	6	5	4.97	19	0	80	98	28	65
Miller, Brandon, Western Ky.	2	5	5.03	17	1	77	86	23	71
Garretson, Andrew, NMSU	3	1	5.05	23	5	52	66	13	44

WEST COAST CONFERENCE

	Conference		Overall	
COAST	W	L	W	L
Pepperdine	18	12	31	32
Santa Clara	15	14	25	30
St. Mary's	14	15	22	27
Gonzaga	14	16	27	29
WEST	W	L	W	L
*San Diego	18	12	39	23
Portland	16	14	24	30
Loyola Marymount	15	15	22	34
San Francisco	9	21	18	38

ALL-CONFERENCE TEAM: C—Steve Booth, Sr., San Francisco. **1B**—Nate Gold, Sr., Gonzaga. **2B**—Eric Rodland, Jr., Gonzaga; Sean Smith, Fr., Loyola Marymount. **3B**—Mark Teahen, Jr., St. Mary's. **SS**—Billy Lockin, So., Loyola Marymount. **OF**—Joey Gomes, Sr., Santa Clara; Joe Jacobitz, So., San Francisco; Ed Montague, Jr., Pepperdine. **DH**—David Bagley, So., San Diego. **Util**—Tom Caple, Jr., San Diego. **P**—Ricky Barrett, Jr., San Diego; Steve Chamberlain, Sr., Portland; Brent Dayton, Sr., Gonzaga.

Player of the Year: Nate Gold, Gonzaga. **Pitcher of the Year:** Ricky Barrett, San Diego. **Freshman of the Year:** Sean Smith, Loyola Marymount. **Coach of the Year:** Rich Hill, San Diego.

INDIVIDUAL BATTING LEADERS
(Minimum 125 At-Bats)

	AVG	AB	R	H	2B	3B	HR	RBI	SB
Teahean, Mark, St. Mary's	.412	194	45	80	15	4	6	36	7
Gomes, Joey, Santa Clara	.408	238	54	97	31	1	10	51	3
Waugh, Jason, St. Mary's	.399	203	50	81	16	5	14	43	5
Bagley, David, San Diego	.386	202	43	78	15	0	13	56	1
Jacobitz, Joe, San Francisco	.383	222	48	85	10	3	5	44	7
Lockin, Billy, LMU	.371	221	45	82	15	2	1	38	15
Montague, Ed, Pepperdine	.359	195	44	70	19	2	10	31	10
Culpepper, Jeff, Gonzaga	.349	195	42	68	13	2	3	31	3
Hollod, Matt, Portland	.346	185	30	64	13	2	4	39	2
Rodland, Eric, Gonzaga	.345	206	44	71	10	3	6	26	6
LaBarbera, A.J., Santa Clara	.342	237	46	81	8	1	4	35	14
Hess, Sam, Gonzaga	.341	129	19	44	6	0	3	27	0
Zacuto, Kris, LMU	.341	220	48	75	25	2	9	48	2
Allen, Matt, Portland	.337	202	48	68	13	5	9	39	5
Harper, Ty, Pepperdine	.336	250	34	84	10	0	1	40	1
Frazee, Joe, LMU	.335	182	32	61	7	1	0	24	9
Higashi, Jordan, LMU	.335	197	38	66	13	2	0	18	8
Perez, Tony, San Diego	.335	209	47	70	13	4	2	37	6
Gold, Nate, Gonzaga	.333	228	59	76	17	0	33	76	1
Wallace, Jim, Santa Clara	.331	178	38	59	12	0	12	44	1
Brightwell, Cory, Pepperdine	.326	236	53	77	17	3	11	44	2
Houle, Brian, St. Mary's	.325	191	37	62	11	0	9	46	2
Donald, Cy, San Francisco	.325	169	24	55	5	1	0	19	6
Casto, Kory, Portland	.322	205	38	66	12	0	10	46	4
Smith, Sean, LMU	.320	197	36	63	11	1	3	41	6
Caple, Tom, San Diego	.318	217	54	69	11	1	0	30	7
Hahn, Trevor, Portland	.317	167	27	53	10	2	1	15	6
Fukuroku, Royce, San Francisco	.316	158	28	50	9	2	4	33	6
Booth, Steve, San Francisco	.316	215	38	68	13	1	19	65	2
#Assael, S.C., San Diego	.307	202	31	62	10	5	1	38	2
#McCoy, Mike, San Diego	.305	210	56	64	16	3	3	38	26

INDIVIDUAL PITCHING LEADERS
(Minimum 50 Innings)

	W	L	ERA	G	SV	IP	H	BB	SO
Dayton, Brent, Gonzaga	5	4	3.15	14	0	74	88	25	52
Barrack, Jacob, Pepperdine	4	2	3.26	20	3	58	57	21	55
Perez, Tony, San Diego	3	4	3.51	22	7	51	57	20	45
Barrett, Ricky, San Diego	10	2	3.61	19	1	122	125	51	98
Hull, Eric, Portland	2	3	3.64	21	8	59	61	13	61
Chamberlain, Steve, Portland	8	2	4.05	16	0	96	90	41	63
Caple, Tom, San Diego	9	5	4.05	20	3	109	119	35	95
Redmond, John, Santa Clara	6	6	4.33	17	0	96	121	25	43
Travis, Matt, Santa Clara	4	4	4.35	15	0	79	80	26	50
Mills, Derek, Pepperdine	5	3	4.40	23	2	76	92	19	42
Byer, Mike, St. Mary's	7	4	4.73	15	1	103	125	30	59
Diefenderfer, Joe, Santa Clara	4	7	4.77	16	0	104	127	26	70
Wilson, Aaron, San Diego	5	4	4.78	17	0	85	105	38	45
Clelland, Ed, Gonzaga	5	5	4.92	14	1	75	101	32	48
Trochez, Kevin, St. Mary's	5	6	5.05	16	0	103	120	34	72
Boesch, Brandon, Pepperdine	6	5	5.10	18	0	109	142	33	67
Bowden, Eric, St. Mary's	5	6	5.20	15	0	90	109	32	56

Simonitsch, Errol, Gonzaga	3	5	5.44	15	0	81	106	15	66
Abreu, Justin, LMU	5	5	5.76	19	0	70	93	27	31
Dworkis, Eric, Gonzaga	4	6	5.82	17	2	56	62	11	38
Fillinger, Chad, Santa Clara	4	4	5.86	20	3	74	99	22	54
Ramirez, Greg, Pepperdine	5	4	5.91	22	0	78	86	28	72
Kinney, Jeremy, San Francisco	4	4	6.04	21	0	79	101	26	66

WESTERN ATHLETIC CONFERENCE

	Conference		Overall	
	W	L	W	L
*Rice	28	2	52	14
San Jose State	21	9	45	17
Fresno State	19	11	32	27
Nevada	10	20	25	32
Louisiana Tech	7	23	21	37
Hawaii	5	25	16	40

ALL-CONFERENCE TEAM: C—Adam Shorsher, Sr., San Jose State.
1B—Vince Sinisi, Fr., Rice. **2B**—Gabe Lopez, Sr., San Jose State. **3B**—Hunter Brown, Sr., Rice; Casey McGehee, So., Fresno State. **SS**—Paul Janish, Fr., Rice. **OF**—Austin Davis, So., Rice; Chris Kolkhorst, So., Rice; Dino Quintero, Jr., San Jose State. **DH**—Hector Zamora, Jr., San Jose State. **Util**—Ben Fritz, Jr., Fresno State. **P**—Ben Fritz, Jr., Fresno State; Steven Herce, Jr., Rice; Philip Humber, Fr., Rice. **RP**—Derek Brewster, Sr., Louisiana Tech.

Player of the Year: Vince Sinisi, Rice. **Pitcher of the Year:** Ben Fritz, Fresno State. **Freshman of the Year:** Philip Humber, Rice. **Coach of the Year:** Wayne Graham, Rice.

INDIVIDUAL BATTING LEADERS
(Minimum 125 At-Bats)

	AVG	AB	R	H	2B	3B	HR	RBI	SB
Sinisi, Vince, Rice	.428	271	65	116	22	2	11	80	13
Lopez, Gabe, San Jose State	.369	244	54	90	22	2	4	61	20
McGehee, Casey, Fresno State	.367	240	49	88	13	1	8	49	3
Cappuccilli, Tony, Nevada	.357	140	37	50	11	0	10	27	3
Davis, Austin, Rice	.355	200	48	71	10	1	7	34	1
Corrick, Nathan, San Jose State	.353	156	27	55	5	2	1	17	2
Kolkhorst, Chris, Rice	.345	264	62	91	16	1	3	33	8
Gillies, Mike, Nevada	.344	215	52	74	13	0	9	49	2
Arnold, Eric, Rice	.342	272	60	93	19	4	9	75	7
Simmons, Cullen, La. Tech	.341	211	38	72	11	0	6	36	3
Zamora, Hector, San Jose State	.337	202	49	68	17	1	8	57	5
Cook, Brent, Hawaii	.325	206	40	67	7	0	3	27	17
Baker, Bryan, San Jose State	.319	213	50	68	18	0	11	49	1
Frandsen, Kevin, San Jose State	.317	161	37	51	10	1	7	28	1
Tolotti, Jeff, Nevada	.311	148	30	46	6	1	8	26	2
Porfirio, A.J., Rice	.311	251	45	78	16	2	3	27	8
Cauley, Nick, La. Tech	.309	178	24	55	9	0	4	25	0
Hass, Mike, Nevada	.305	187	35	57	16	2	10	41	6
Markel, Craig, Nevada	.304	171	29	52	10	0	4	34	1
Patrick, Chris, Fresno State	.300	240	47	72	13	0	5	32	3
Janish, Paul, Rice	.299	197	32	59	14	1	2	30	6
Quintero, Dino, San Jose State	.297	232	59	69	15	2	2	25	9
McIntyre, JaRell, Nevada	.297	172	22	51	10	1	2	27	11
Laidlaw, Josh, Nevada	.295	149	29	44	11	2	4	21	3
Shorsher, Adam, San Jose State	.293	205	41	60	15	0	13	53	5
Hall, Michael, La. Tech	.290	214	44	62	12	1	9	27	4
Beshears, Scott, Fresno State	.290	145	28	42	9	0	2	12	2
Humphreys, Kyle, La. Tech	.286	206	34	59	12	0	11	45	2
#Cruz, Jose Enrique, Rice	.226	199	41	45	6	2	16	36	4

INDIVIDUAL PITCHING LEADERS
(Minimum 50 Innings)

	W	L	ERA	G	SV	IP	H	BB	SO
Crowder, Justin, Rice	10	3	2.00	22	1	121	106	36	106
Townsend, Wade, Rice	2	1	2.28	19	6	51	38	22	51
Durkin, Matt, San Jose State	11	3	2.75	22	1	98	85	24	85
Humber, Philip, Rice	11	1	2.77	18	0	111	90	43	130
Herce, Steven, Rice	13	3	2.79	17	0	119	106	23	104
Niemann, Jeff, Rice	5	1	3.11	17	0	67	64	27	53
Fritz, Ben, Fresno State	9	5	3.24	16	0	119	99	36	98
Tribe, Philip, Rice	4	4	3.43	23	3	55	48	27	53
Aardsma, David, Rice	7	1	3.47	28	5	60	65	14	53
Rasner, Darrell, Nevada	6	8	3.70	16	0	105	106	49	109
Rogelstad, Jeremy, San Jose State	8	5	3.73	20	1	101	105	17	64
Cook, Andy, San Jose State	4	2	3.88	22	1	63	66	14	30
George, Jahseam, San Jose State	9	2	3.93	16	1	101	102	27	68
Malott, Mike, San Jose State	3	2	4.00	22	4	88	78	32	72
Gwaltney, Lee, Louisiana Tech	3	12	4.05	16	0	107	107	40	113
Pribble, Aaron, Hawaii	2	3	4.08	17	0	64	66	26	52
Blalock, Casey, Louisiana Tech	8	9	4.24	19	0	117	116	24	116

Runyon, Bob, Fresno State	10	8	4.43	20	0	142	147	33	119
Johnson, Bryan, Nevada	5	4	4.64	26	4	54	62	27	39
Kirkendall, Adam, Louisiana Tech	6	5	4.70	18	0	107	104	41	91
Miramontes, Mateo, Nevada	6	8	5.32	18	1	110	135	47	104
Minor, Zach, Fresno State	6	4	5.46	21	0	86	108	26	63
Norris, Craig, Nevada	1	3	5.65	19	2	57	73	13	32
Yamashita, Sean, Hawaii	2	9	5.68	21	1	78	95	24	55

INDEPENDENTS

	Overall	
	W	L
# Birmingham-Southern	32	20
Miami	34	29
NY Tech	27	25
# Lipscomb	24	24
# Texas A&M-Corpus Christi	24	29
Morris Brown	15	35
Texas-Pan American	15	38
Pace	14	36
C.W. Post	11	30
Centenary	15	41
Hawaii-Hilo	10	38

#Provisional Division I in 2002

INDIVIDUAL BATTING LEADERS
(Minimum 100 At-Bats)

	AVG	AB	R	H	2B	3B	HR	RBI	SB
Merkle, Tom, NY Tech	.430	186	60	80	6	6	20	68	8
Gaffney, Mike, NY Tech	.414	191	63	79	12	5	4	39	14
Clay, Anthony, Morris Brown	.381	160	33	61	12	0	3	30	14
Rodriguez, Javy, Miami	.376	263	57	99	14	2	6	35	37
George, Jeremy, Lipscomb	.365	170	35	62	18	1	3	40	1
Howard, Kevin, Miami	.363	237	55	86	23	1	12	52	12
DeLuca, Marc, Pace	.357	112	20	40	7	0	3	23	2
Santana, Roberto, TAMU-CC	.356	208	51	74	17	3	12	52	11
Bohlander, Mike, Pace	.355	172	34	61	10	1	10	39	1
Mincey, Barry, Morris Brown	.355	141	28	50	8	0	3	21	17
Robertson, Connor, BSU	.353	187	48	66	13	2	16	54	8
Goldberg, Brian, NY Tech	.351	194	48	68	18	0	9	64	6
Aguilar, Humberto, TAMU-CC	.351	188	34	66	15	1	15	56	0
Cline, Michael, BSU	.346	107	31	37	6	3	2	17	6
Landin, Jaime, TAMU-CC	.344	163	47	56	4	7	6	27	3
Langford, Shelby, Pace	.342	114	23	39	8	0	1	14	4
Bruner, Michael, TAMU-CC	.342	114	18	39	5	3	1	13	2
Austin, Anthony, Morris Brown	.340	141	36	48	8	1	2	29	17
Grillo, Joe, C.W. Post	.338	154	29	52	16	1	2	22	5
Bogue, Matt, BSU	.336	140	36	47	13	1	2	16	22
Matienzo, Danny, Miami	.335	230	48	77	8	0	20	67	7
Oligo, Kaliko, Hawaii-Hilo	.335	176	20	59	4	2	0	16	4
Goelz, Brian, NY Tech	.328	204	58	67	11	4	6	32	14
Passons, Brian, Lipscomb	.327	159	33	52	9	4	0	14	9
Burt, Jim, Miami	.322	208	42	67	19	0	9	48	4
St. George, Anthony, NY Tech	.320	147	22	47	8	0	6	30	3
Park, Keola, Hawaii-Hilo	.318	170	18	54	11	1	4	25	1
Pease, Adam, BSU	.317	186	46	59	6	4	3	40	21

INDIVIDUAL PITCHING LEADERS
(Minimum 40 Innings)

	W	L	ERA	G	SV	IP	H	BB	SO
Renfro, Jon, BSU	5	2	3.61	15	0	85	85	28	68
Letson, Wes, BSU	3	2	3.94	14	0	48	44	27	53
Durden, Chad, BSU	4	2	4.04	9	0	42	40	14	30
Kurz, Brandon, NY Tech	4	4	4.06	15	1	64	60	23	34
Crew, John, BSU	3	3	4.33	13	0	60	55	14	38
Touchet, Dan, Miami	6	2	4.41	21	0	98	101	32	78
Huguet, George, Miami	7	4	4.50	40	8	50	52	17	45
Good, Logan, Lipscomb	5	3	4.61	11	0	55	59	31	39
Fielder, Jeremiah, Morris Brown	4	4	4.82	9	0	50	64	6	42
Patton, David, Lipscomb	4	6	4.97	14	0	67	68	17	48
Taormina, Rob, NY Tech	5	5	5.01	12	0	56	78	18	38
Hagri, Joe, Pace	4	4	5.20	13	0	73	83	17	44
Nonis, Mark, Centenary	2	7	5.20	20	1	64	81	32	39
Ulutas, Alper, C.W. Post	3	5	5.20	10	0	54	61	36	42
Shields, Clyde, Centenary	1	3	5.27	27	1	68	83	29	42
Griffith, Derek, BSU	3	5	5.43	16	1	60	53	32	68
James, Frank, Texas-Pan Am	6	7	5.44	18	0	99	115	47	69
Van Riper, Robert, Pace	2	3	5.48	11	0	48	48	25	34
Martanovic, Eric, TAMU-CC	6	3	5.50	21	1	93	114	21	49
Karkoulas, Andrew, NY Tech	5	3	5.58	12	1	40	43	27	23
Bengochea, Kiki, Miami	6	7	5.63	18	0	94	105	47	72

Reaching the promised land
Georgia's Columbus State captured the Division II national title in 2002, the school's first

Georgia school claims first crown

Columbus (Ga.) State fought back through the loser's bracket to win its first national baseball championship, capping its comeback with a 5-3 victory against top-ranked Chico State (Calif.) in Montgomery, Ala.

The Cougars (48-15), whose roster included 13 seniors, took five straight games after dropping the opener to

NCAA DIVISION II

Central Missouri State, 7-3. Three wins were come-from-behind victories, and two were walk-off triumphs.

While Jason Burdette went the distance for the victory in the championship game, Columbus State freshman reliever Brian Baker was the tournament most outstanding player. In five appearances, Baker went 3-0, 1.42 with a save.

Kutztown State righthander Glenn Woolard was named the Division II player of the year and Baseball America's Small College Player of the Year.

NCAA DIVISION III

Eastern Connecticut State won an unprecedented fourth NCAA Division III baseball title, defeating Marietta (Ohio) 8-0 in Appleton, Wis. DH Justin Waz went 4-for-5 with three RBIs in the deciding game while Warriors starter Joey Serfass (10-1) pitched a five-hit shutout, striking out six.

It was the only time all season that Marietta (41-9),

which appeared in its ninth championship and lost for the second time in a row, was shut out.

The Warriors latest win surpassed Marietta and Montclair State (N.J.), which both have three CWS titles.

"I never thought we would surpass Marietta," said ECSU coach Bill Holowaty, who won his 1,000th game earlier in the 2002 season and coached in the Series despite dislocating a hip in the CWS opener. "It's humbling. It's great."

Warriors first baseman John Kubachka took home Most Outstanding Player honors. He went 11-for-24 (.458) in the national tournament after batting .130 in regional play.

Holowaty, in his 34th year at Eastern Connecticut State, became only the fourth Division III coach to win 1,000 games. Other coaches to achieve that milestone are Gordie Gillespie (Ripon, Wis.), Don Schaly (Marietta) and Jim Mallon (Southwestern, Texas).

NAIA

Host Lewis-Clark State won its 12th NAIA baseball championship—and third in four years—by defeating Oklahoma City 12-8 in Lewiston, Idaho. The Warriors (41-16) lost to the Stars earlier in the tournament, but Lewis-Clark State came back to defeat Oklahoma City and

FINAL **POLL**	
NCAA Division II	
1. Columbus State (Ga.)	48-15
2. Chico State (Calif.)	55-10
3. Central Missouri State	54-8
4. Delta State (Miss.)	50-8
5. Kennesaw State (Ga.)	46-13
6. Massachusetts-Lowell	35-18
7. Abilene Christian (Texas)	45-14
8. Ashland (Ohio)	48-13
9. Florida Southern	43-16
10. North Florida	39-16

FINAL **POLL**	
NCAA Division III	
1. East. Connecticut State	39-11
2. Marietta (Ohio)	41-9
3. Christopher Newport (Va.)	38-16
4. New Jersey	36-14
5. Rensselaer (N.Y.)	33-11
6. Wooster (Ohio)	38-6
7. Wheaton (Md.)	37-9
8. Lakeland (Wis.)	34-16
9. Concordia (Texas)	35-13
10. Carthage (Wis.)	34-11

finish the tournament 5-1.

Warriors pitcher Andy Torres, a transfer from Arizona State, went 2-0, tallied two shutouts and a save, and was named the tournament's most valuable player.

First baseman Mike Madrid's two-run double in the bottom of the sixth broke a 7-7 tie after the Warriors had blown a 7-0 lead.

Madrid was the catalyst for a seven-run third inning, hitting a bases-loaded single up the middle, scoring a pair of runs to put the Warriors up 3-0. Mark Gallagher and Nick Walker followed with two-RBI hits, but Oklahoma City rallied to tie before Kevin Welch came out of the bullpen to squelch the rally before Torres finished up.

JUNIOR COLLEGES

Central Arizona cruised through the 45th annual NJCAA Division I World Series unbeaten, topping Manatee (Fla.) 18-8 to capture the tournament championship in Grand Junction, Colo.

The Vaqueros (50-17) jumped to an early 5-0 lead and never looked back, eventually winning the game in seven

MARC McCLINTOCK

Andy Torres

innings due to the 10-run mercy rule. A grand slam by freshman right fielder Jay Rodriguez in the seventh ended the game.

Sophomore infielder Gabe Mayorga, who went 2-for-5 with a double in the championship game, was selected the tournament MVP. Mayorga hammered two homers in the semi-finals as Central Arizona hung on to eliminate San Jacinto (Texas), 9-8.

■ Parkland (Ill.) emerged from the loser's bracket to beat Frederick (Md.) twice to win the juco Division II title. The Cobras (55-9) broke open the deciding game early, scoring six run in the first three innings.

■ Richland (Texas) Junior College turned the tables on Gloucester County (N.J.) College, winning 4-2 in the championship game, to capture its first juco Division III title. In 1999 and 2000, Gloucester defeated Richland to win the title.

Tournament MVP Curtis Glover hurled a complete-game six-hitter, striking out 10, for the Thunderducks (40-17). Glover also spun a five-inning one-hitter in Richland's 10-0 win on the opening day of the tournament.

PLAYERS OF THE YEAR

Glenn Woolard

Nick Markakis

Small College: Glenn Woolard, rhp, Kutztown (Pa.)
Woolard had won 14 games in his first two college seasons, then exploded for a 14-2, 2.81 season in 2002, setting school single-season records for wins and strikeouts (148) while carrying the Golden Bears to a conference championship and second straight College World Series berth. The San Francisco Giants drafted Woolard in the 10th round.

Junior College: Nick Markakis, lhp/dh, Young Harris (Ga.) JC
Markakis dominated as a freshman, especially offensively. He hit .455-17-74 while slugging .885, and led the team in almost every offensive category. On the mound, Markakis went 11-3, 4.53, striking out 98 in 91 innings. The 6-foot-2, 185-pounder has been drafted twice, both times by the Cincinnati Reds, most recently in the 2002 (23rd round).

PREVIOUS WINNERS

SMALL COLLEGE

1994—Rick Ladjevich, 3b, Central Missouri State
1995—Tim Jorgensen, ss, Wisconsin-Oshkosh
1996—Dave Townsend, rhp, Delta State (Miss.)
1997—Donnie Thomas, 1b-lhp, Marietta (Ohio)
1998—Keith Hart, 1b, Lubbock Christian (Texas)
1999—Andy Heimbach, rhp, Mount Vernon Nazarene (Ohio)
2000—Jim Kavourias, of, Tampa
2001—Chris Smith, lhp-of, Cumberland (Tenn.)

JUNIOR COLLEGE

1994—Justin Bowles, of, Galveston (Texas)
1995—Brian Conley, ss, Volunteer State (Tenn.)
1996—Derek Baker, 3b, Rancho Santiago (Calif.)
1997—Aaron Akin, rhp, Cowley County (Kan.)
1998—Brian Cole, of, Navarro (Texas)
1999—Kade Johnson, c, Seminole (Okla.)
2000—Brandon Lyon, rhp, Dixie (Utah)
2001—Scott Hairston, 2b, Central Arizona

SMALL COLLEGE ALL-AMERICA TEAM 2002

Selected by Baseball America

Pos., Player, School	Division	Class	AVG	AB	R	H	2B	3B	HR	RBI	SB	Drafted (Round)
C David Harriman, Armstrong Atlantic (Ga.) St.	Division II	Sr.	.412	228	49	94	13	2	14	69	0	Athletics (17)
1B Drew Caravella, Ohio Wesleyan	Division III	Sr.	.534	163	57	87	21	1	16	89	10	Tigers (23)
2B Jason Santangelo, Fort Hays (Kan.) State	Division II	Sr.	.413	208	89	86	18	2	18	68	5	Not drafted
3B Andy Dillard, Delta (Miss.) State	Division II	Jr.	.425	219	60	93	20	2	13	80	5	Not drafted
SS Donny Hood, Kennesaw (Ga.) State	Division II	Sr.	.391	238	72	93	24	3	18	67	10	Cubs (18)
OF Kennard Bibbs, Oklahoma City	NAIA	Sr.	.388	240	69	93	10	2	2	38	56	Brewers (14)
OF Chad Chop, Vanguard (Calif.)	NAIA	Jr.	.395	205	51	81	14	0	15	67	4	Expos (6)
OF Justin Hancock, Florida Southern	Division II	Sr.	.336	223	57	75	12	0	16	64	16	Angels (15)
DH Jose Cortez, Pomona-Pitzer (Calif.)	Division III	Sr.	.510	145	55	74	23	1	16	65	1	Cubs (44)
UT Todd Meyer, Alvernia (Pa.)	Division III	Sr.	.511	178	76	91	17	4	25	107	6	Not drafted

Pos., Player, School	Division	Class	W	L	ERA	G	SV	IP	H	BB	SO	Drafted (Round)
SP Damien Myers, Concordia (N.Y.)	Division II	Sr.	14	1	1.42	16	1	107	84	27	88	Tigers (27)
SP Glenn Woolard, Kutztown (Pa.)	Division II	Jr.	14	2	2.81	18	2	106	87	44	148	Giants (10)
SP Jeff Francis, British Columbia	NAIA	Jr.	7	2	1.93	13	1	75	47	16	101	Rockies (1)
SP Paul Bush, Georgia Southwestern	NAIA	Sr.	13	1	1.63	15	0	110	68	40	152	Braves (24)
RP Anthony Reed, Central Oklahoma	Division II	Sr.	4	1	1.69	24	7	32	16	14	47	Angels FA
UT Todd Meyer, Alvernia (Pa.)	Division III	Sr.	9	0	2.85	11	0	73	48	24	96	

NCAA DIVISION II

WORLD SERIES

Site: Montgomery, Ala.
Participants: Ashland, Ohio (47-11); Chico State, Calif. (52-9); Central Missouri State (48-5); Columbus State, Ga. (43-14); Delta State, Miss. (50-6); Florida Southern (43-14); Kutztown, Pa. (35-22); Massachusetts-Lowell (33-16).
Champion: Columbus State (5-1).
Runner-Up: Chico State (3-1).
Outstanding Player: Brian Baker, rhp, Columbus State.

ALL-AMERICA TEAM

Pos.	Player, School	Yr.	AVG	HR	RBI
C	David Harriman, Armstrong Atlantic State (Ga.) ..	Sr.	.412	14	69
1B	Jeff Renga, Bryant (R.I.)	Jr.	.423	11	65
2B	Jason Santangelo, Fort Hays State (Kan.) .	Sr.	.413	18	68
3B	Andy Dillard, Delta State (Miss.)	Jr.	.425	13	79
SS	Donnie Hood, Kennesaw State (Ga.)	Jr.	.391	18	67
IF	Sam Christensen, Southern Colorado	Sr.	.471	5	66
OF	Ashley Farr, South Carolina-Aiken	So.	.427	13	74
	Heath Mason, Carson-Newman (Tenn.)	Sr.	.402	20	80
	Junior Medina, Stonehill (Mass.)	Sr.	.438	19	60
	Nathan Moore, Ashland (Ohio)	Sr.	.433	10	58
DH	Jason Manwaring, Mansfield (Pa.)	Jr.	.388	23	79

		Yr.	W	L	ERA
SP	Ryan Hartzell, Ashland (Ohio)	Jr.	14	3	3.68
	Jason Herz, Central Missouri State	Sr.	14	0	2.74
	Damien Myers, Concordia (N.Y.)	Sr.	14	1	1.43
	Glenn Woolard, Kutztown (Pa.)	Jr.	14	2	2.81
RP	Adrian Goas, Tampa (17 SV)	Sr.	2	1	1.15

Player of the Year: Heath Mason, Carson-Newman. **Pitcher of the Year:** Glenn Woolard, Kutztown.

NATIONAL LEADERS

BATTING AVERAGE
(Minimum 100 At-Bats)

Player, School	Yr.	AB	H	AVG
Ross Tobin, Colorado Mines	Jr.	163	78	.479
Sam Christensen, So. Colorado	Sr.	223	105	.471
Mike Aviles, Concordia (N.Y.)	Jr.	220	103	.468
Will Carbonara, Incarnate Word (Texas)	Sr.	176	81	.460
Brad Edwards, Metro State (Colo.)	So.	205	94	.459
Juan Matta, Morningside (Iowa)	Sr.	151	68	.450
Rene Barreras, Belmont Abbey (N.C.)	Sr.	212	95	.448
Andrew Newton, Regis (Colo.)	So.	201	90	.448
Bernard Stephens, Virginia State	Sr.	114	51	.447
Tracy Geffre, Southern Arkansas	Jr.	187	83	.444
Mark Salfia, Alderson-Broaddus (W.Va.)	Sr.	107	47	.439
William Gray, Shaw (N.C.)	Jr.	139	61	.439

Department Leaders: Batting

Dept.	Player, School	Yr.	G	Total
R	Jason Santangelo, Fort Hays State (Kan.)	Sr.	57	89
	Craig Ringe, Central Missouri State	Sr.	62	89
H	Sam Christensen, Southern Colorado	Sr.	59	105
TB	Heath Mason, Carson-Newman (Tenn.)	Sr.	58	180
2B	John DiGennaro, Bentley (Mass.)	Sr.	47	27
3B	Rex O'Connor, Coker (S.C.)	Sr.	53	11
	Jerod Fikac, Incarnate Word (Texas)	Jr.	55	11
HR	Jason Manwaring, Mansfield (Pa.)	Jr.	54	23
RBI	Andy Dillard, Delta State (Miss.)	Jr.	56	80
	Heath Mason, Carson-Newman (Tenn.)	Sr.	58	80
SB	Mike Scarinci, Molloy (N.Y.)	Sr.	47	57

EARNED RUN AVERAGE
(Minimum 50 Innings)

Player, School	Yr.	IP	ER	ERA
Ryan Balan, California (Pa.)	Sr.	59	6	0.91
Steve Bray, New Haven (Conn.)	Jr.	67	9	1.20
Mike Peschel, North Dakota State	Jr.	58	9	1.40
Damien Myers, Concordia (N.Y.)	Sr.	107	17	1.43
Jaymie Russ, Belmont Abbey (N.C.)	Jr.	100	16	1.44
Jason Galbraith, Concordia (N.Y.)	Jr.	94	16	1.53
Zach Snyder, Catawba (N.C.)	So.	89	16	1.61
Brad Grieveson, SE Oklahoma	Jr.	93	19	1.84
Greg Bruso, UC Davis	Sr.	93	20	1.94

Department Leaders: Pitching

Dept.	Player, School	Yr.	G	Total
W	Jason Herz, Central Missouri State	Sr.	16	14
	Damien Myers, Concordia (N.Y.)	Sr.	16	14
	Glenn Woolard, Kutztown (Pa.)	Jr.	18	14
	Ryan Hartzell, Ashland (Ohio)	Jr.	20	14
SV	Adrian Goas, Tampa	Sr.	29	17
SO	Glenn Woolard, Kutztown (Pa.)	Jr.	18	148

NCAA DIVISION III

WORLD SERIES

Site: Appleton, Wis.
Participants: Carthage, Wis. (34-9); Christopher Newport, Va. (35-14); College of New Jersey (34-12); Concordia-Texas (35-11); Eastern Connecticut State (35-10); Lakeland, Wis. (33-14-1); Marietta, Ohio (37-7-1); Rensselaer, N.Y. (32-9).
Champion: Eastern Connecticut State (4-1).
Runner-Up: Marietta (4-2).
Outstanding Player: John Kubachka, 1b, Eastern Connecticut State.

ALL-AMERICA TEAM

Pos.	Player, School	Yr.	AVG	HR	RBI
C	Jay Coakley, Marietta (Ohio)	Sr.	.419	14	71
	Jose Cortez, Pomona-Pitzer (Calif.)	Jr.	.500	16	65
1B	Drew Caravella, Ohio Wesleyan	Sr.	.534	16	89
2B	Nick Chaney, Manchester (Ind.)		.440	9	40
3B	Paul Molitor, Wisconsin-Stevens Point	Sr.	.371	13	58
SS	Vinnie Rottino, Wisconsin-LaCrosse	Sr.	.410	15	50
OF	Chris Denorfia, Wheaton (Mass.)	Sr.	.467	7	62
	Brendan Heslin, SUNY-Oneonta	Sr.	.448	10	46
	Eric Swedberg, Worcester State (Mass.)	Sr.	.442	15	63
UT	Todd Meyer, Alvernia (Pa.)	Sr.	.511	25	107
	Travis Teeter, Rensselaer (N.Y.)	Sr.	.401	5	45
DH	Jason Lensmeyer, Carthage (Wis.)	Sr.	.424	13	55

		Yr.	W	L	ERA
SP	Doug Heagan, Ferrum (Va.)	Sr.	11	2	1.33
	Justin Libey, Manchester (Ind.)	Jr.	11	1	2.18
RP	Mike Spavento, Wheaton (Mass.) (19 SV)	Sr.	3	1	1.69
UT	Todd Meyer, Alvernia (Pa.)	Sr.	9	0	2.85

Player of the Year: Drew Caravella, Ohio Wesleyan.

NATIONAL LEADERS

BATTING AVERAGE
(Minimum 100 At-Bats)

Player, School	Yr.	AB	H	AVG
Drew Caravella, Ohio Wesleyan	Sr.	163	87	.534
Todd Meyer, Alvernia (Pa.)	Sr.	178	91	.511
Erik Kratz, Eastern Mennonite (Va.)	Sr.	142	72	.507
Jose Cortez, Pomona-Pitzer (Calif.)	Jr.	154	77	.500
Damion Costantino, Salve Regina (R.I.)	So.	124	60	.484
Joel Brettingen, Macalester (Minn.)	So.	138	66	.478
Brad Mazer, Gustavus Adolphus (Minn.)	Sr.	134	64	.478
Jesse Nelson, Dallas	Sr.	130	62	.477
Justin Taylor, Hendrix (Ark.)	So.	137	65	.474
Justin Evans, Wilmington (Ohio)	Jr.	135	64	.474
Tony Coppola, Simpson (Iowa)	Sr.	136	64	.471
Russ Lorenz, Aurora (Ill.)	Sr.	151	71	.470

Department Leaders: Batting

Dept.	Player, School	Yr.	G	Total
R	Todd Meyer, Alvernia (Pa.)	Sr.	46	76
H	Todd Meyer, Alvernia (Pa.)	Sr.	46	91
TB	Todd Meyer, Alvernia (Pa.)	Sr.	46	191
2B	Pat McSheely, Webster (Mo.)	Sr.	36	25
	Erik Kratz, Eastern Mennonite (Va.)	Sr.	42	25
3B	Matt Diltz, Wilkes (Pa.)	Sr.	42	12
HR	Todd Meyer, Alvernia (Pa.)	Sr.	46	25
RBI	Todd Meyer, Alvernia (Pa.)	Sr.	46	107
SB	James Hymon, Rust (Miss.)	Jr.	41	56

EARNED RUN AVERAGE
(Minimum 40 Innings)

Player, School	Yr.	IP	ER	ERA
Ryan Adams, Southern Maine	Sr.	76	7	0.83
Dave Martin, Tufts	Jr.	53	5	0.85
Josh Paddock, Aurora (Ill.)	Sr.	64	7	0.98
Alex Smith, Pomona-Pitzer (Calif.)	Jr.	45	5	1.00
Mike Kelly, Trinity (Texas)	So.	80	10	1.13
Charlie Ruud, St. Olaf (Minn.)	So.	66	9	1.23
Doug Heagan, Ferrum (Va.)	Sr.	101	15	1.33
Ryan Seyler, Penn State-Behrend	Jr.	66	10	1.36
Jed Musch, Oswego State (N.Y.)	Sr.	46	7	1.37

Department Leaders: Pitching

Dept.	Player, School	Yr.	G	Total
W	Joe Dooley, Guilford (N.C.)	Sr.	20	12
SV	Mike Spavento, Wheaton (Mass.)	Sr.	30	19
SO	Joe Dooley, Guilford (N.C.)	Sr.	20	118

NAIA

Site: Lewiston, Idaho.
Participants: Albertson, Idaho (39-18); Bellevue, Neb. (44-15); Embry-Riddle, Fla. (49-10); Indiana Tech (47-15); Lewis-Clark State, Idaho (36-15); Mayville State, N.D. (32-13); Ohio Dominican (43-11); Oklahoma City (53-13); Olivet Nazarene, Ill. (40-14); Spalding, Ky. (55-21)
Champion: Lewis-Clark State (5-1).
Runner-Up: Oklahoma City (4-2).
Outstanding Player: Andy Torres, rhp, Lewis-Clark State.

ALL-AMERICA TEAM

Pos.	Player, School	Yr.	AVG	HR	RBI
C	Justin Clarey, Mount Vernon Nazarene (Ohio)	Sr.	.411	9	58
	Adam Smith, Embry-Riddle (Fla.)	Jr.	.402	4	25
1B	Luke Vogel, Grand View (Iowa)	Sr.	.432	23	61
2B	Scott Paladichuk, Lambuth (Tenn.)	Sr.	.477	13	64
3B	Rohan Brasher, Lubbock Christian (Texas)	Jr.	.391	21	83
SS	Chris Dunn, William Carey (Miss.)	Sr.	.391	15	48
UT	Joshua Causey, Dallas Baptist	Sr.	.367	24	70
OF	Joe Bolstad, Sioux Falls (S.D.)	Sr.	.463	13	58
	Chad Chop, Vanguard (Calif.)	Jr.	.395	15	67
	Patrick Ranalli, Ohio Dominican	Sr.	.447	9	41
	Rick White, Union (Ky.)	Jr.	.431	23	96

		Yr.	W	L	ERA
SP	Bryan Anderson, Embry-Riddle (Fla.)	Jr.	14	2	3.24
	Paul Bush, Georgia Southwestern State	Sr.	13	1	1.63
	Jeff Francis, British Columbia	Jr.	7	2	1.93
	Andy Torres, Lewis-Clark State (Idaho)	Sr.	10	0	2.68
RP	Jason Elkins, North Georgia College (17 SV)	Sr.	5	3	1.32

Player of the Year: Paul Bush, Georgia Southwestern State

NATIONAL LEADERS

BATTING AVERAGE
(Minimum 100 At-Bats)

Player, School	Yr.	AB	H	AVG
Wes Hayden, Marian (Ind.)	Sr.	171	84	.491
Scott Paladichuk, Lambuth (Tenn.)	Sr.	—	—	.477
Ethan Miller, Northwestern (Iowa)	Jr.	137	65	.474
Joe Barbosa, Park (Mo.)	Jr.	112	53	.473
Nick Miller, Sterling (Neb.)	Jr.	127	60	.472
Joe Bolstad, Sioux Falls (S.D.)	Sr.	142	66	.510
Greg Guzzo, Trinity Christian (Ill.)	Jr.	106	49	.462
Ryan Koerner, Judson (Ill.)	Jr.	143	65	.455
Chris DiBlasi, William Penn (Iowa)	Sr.	145	65	.448
Jason Ellis, Cumberland (Ky.)	Sr.	208	93	.447
Patrick Ranalli, Ohio Dominican	Sr.	191	81	.447
Josh Gillespie, Geneva (Pa.)	Sr.	122	54	.443

Department Leaders: Batting

Dept.	Player, School	Yr.	G	Total
R	Regan Hogestad, Embry-Riddle (Fla.)	Sr.	64	74
H	Jason Ellis, Cumberland (Ky.)	Sr.	63	93
2B	Jason Ellis, Cumberland (Ky.)	Sr.	63	30
3B	Joe Hayden, St. Francis (Ill.)	So.	50	9
HR	Rick White, Union (Ky.)	Jr.	56	23
RBI	Rick White, Union (Ky.)	Jr.	56	96

EARNED RUN AVERAGE
(Minimum 50 Innings)

Player, School	Yr.	IP	ER	ERA
Jeff Hawkins, Auburn-Montgomery	Sr.	93	13	1.26
Jacoby Marshall, Dakota Wesleyan (S.D.)	Sr.	76	11	1.30
Paul Bush, Georgia Southwestern State	Sr.	110	20	1.63
Dave Dostie, Husson (Me.)	Sr.	64	13	1.87
Jeff Francis, British Columbia	Jr.	75	16	1.93
Monte Scott, Peru State (Neb.)	Sr.	86	19	1.98
Rodrigo Miralles, Houston Baptist	Sr.	76	17	2.00
Bryan Heaston, Union (Ky.)	Sr.	83	19	2.05
Brian Morgan, Webber International (Fla.)	Jr.	90	21	2.09
Luis Torrens, St. Thomas (Fla.)	Jr.	70	17	2.20

Department Leaders: Pitching

Dept.	Player, School	Yr.	G	Total
W	Bryan Anderson, Embry-Riddle (Fla.)	Jr.	23	14
SO	Paul Bush, Georgia Southwestern State	Sr.	15	152

JUNIOR COLLEGE

Site: Grand Junction, Colo.
Participants: Central Arizona (45-17); Cowley County, Kan. (43-14); Jefferson, Mo. (42-15); John A. Logan, Ill. (37-19); Lamar, Colo. (57-3); Louisburg, N.C. (49-9); Manatee, Fla. (38-18); Middle Georgia (49-16); San Jacinto-North, Texas (51-9); Wallace State, Ala. (39-10).
Champion: Central Arizona (5-0).
Runner-Up: Manatee (3-2).
Outstanding Player: Gabe Mayorga, 2b, Central Arizona.

ALL-AMERICA TEAM

C—C.J. Medlin, Seminole State (Okla.). **INF**—Ian Bladengroen, Lamar (Colo.); Brian Bowe, New Mexico; Hank Parks, Spartanburg Methodist (S.C.); John Urick, Cowley County (Kan.). **OF**—Larry Grayson, Manatee (Fla.); Jake Manning, Mineral Area (Mo.); Cory Patton, Seward County (Kan.). **DH**—Nick Markakis, Young Harris (Ga.). **P**—Nate Bumstead, Southern Idaho; Michael Gallops, Central Alabama; Rhett James, Pensacola (Fla.).

Player of the Year—Cory Patton, Seward County (Kan.). **Defensive Player of Year**—Eric Baker, Alfred State (N.Y.).

NATIONAL LEADERS

BATTING AVERAGE
(Minimum 100 At-Bats)

Player, School	AB	H	AVG
Brian Bowe, New Mexico	174	94	.540
Matt Wells, Seward County (Kan.)	121	59	.488
Nathan Panther, Muscatine (Iowa)	146	70	.479
Garth McKinney, Walters State (Tenn.)	131	62	.473
Bob Diliberto, Mesa (Ariz.)	169	79	.467
Cory Patton, Seward County (Kan.)	229	106	.463
Stuart Ritchie, Walters State (Tenn.)	158	73	.462
Nate McCall, Central Arizona	149	68	.456
Ben Pulliam, Vernon (Texas)	185	84	.454
Gabe Mayorga, Central Arizona	150	68	.453

Department Leaders: Batting

Dept.	Player, School	G	Total
HR	Cory Patton, Seward County (Kan.)	63	31
RBI	Cory Patton, Seward County (Kan.)	63	119
SB	Ben Duval, Johnson County (Kan.)	42	49

EARNED RUN AVERAGE
(Minimum 50 innings)

Player, School	IP	ER	ERA
Matt Bellon, Hagerstown (Md.)	56	7	1.14
Clint Goocher, San Jacinto (Texas)	96	15	1.41
Nate Bumstead, Southern Idaho	87	15	1.55
Chris Hill, South Suburban (Ill.)	57	11	1.75
Aaron Williams, Alfred State (N.Y.)	68	14	1.84
Eric Ebers, John A. Logan (Ill.)	82	17	1.87
Marcus Davila, Tallahassee (Fla.)	57	12	1.88
Thomas Olejniczak, Jefferson (Mo.)	81	17	1.90

Department Leaders: Pitching

Dept.	Player, School	G	Total
W	Matt Varner, Angelina (Texas)	15	14
SO	Billy Buckner, Young Harris (Ga.)	19	136

Site: Millington, Tenn.
Participants: Brookdale, N.J. (35-13); Frederick, Md. (33-7); Iowa Central (42-15); Jefferson State, Ala. (36-22); Kellogg, Mich. (29-18); Northern Oklahoma-Enid (40-21); Parkland, Ill. (50-8); Pearl River (41-11).
Champion: Parkland (4-1).
Runner-Up: Frederick (3-2).
Outstanding Player: Dan Grant, ss, Parkland.

Site: Batavia, N.Y.
Participants: Columbus State, Ohio (47-15); Dutchess, N.Y. (39-10); Gloucester County, N.J. (46-9); Montgomery, Md. (25-26); Quinsigamond, Mass. (28-9); Richland, Texas (36-17); Ridgewater, Minn. (32-9).
Champion: Richland (4-0).
Runner-Up: Gloucester County (3-2).
Outstanding Player: Curtis Glover, p, Richland.

Site: Fresno.
Participants: Cuesta (42-7); Riverside (42-8); Sacramento (36-12); San Mateo (37-10).
Champion: Riverside (3-0).
Runner-Up: Sacramento (2-2).

COLLEGE BASEBALL

HIGH SCHOOL
BASEBALL

Once-beaten Elkins endures three-way battle to win state, national prep titles

BY ALLAN SIMPSON

From the start of the 2002 high school season, the chase for national supremacy shaped up as an intriguing three-way, cross-country battle. There was one team each from California, Florida and Texas—the powerful Sun Belt states that annually dominate the prep baseball scene and produce far and away the most professional players.

The three teams battled right down to the end of the season. With a national championship at stake, they combined to go a gaudy 95-4. It all came down to who lost, and when—and in the end, who earned the critical final vote as the nation's best team.

Bishop Amat High of La Puente, Calif.; Elkins High of Missouri City, Texas; and Dunedin (Fla.) High started the season ranked 1-2-3 in the Baseball America/National High School Baseball Coaches Association poll.

Jubilant champions
Elkins High captures Texas, national titles

All made excellent cases for a national title throughout the season, but when it was all said and done, Elkins came out on top. Bishop Amat finished second for the second year in a row, while powerful Dunedin dropped to fifth.

Once the Knights moved to No. 1 in the first in-season poll of the year, they never relinquished the spot. Elkins coach Brent Carpenter and his team knew what was at stake as they advanced to the Texas 5-A final four. They had a good idea they were also playing for a national championship.

Two days and two games later, Elkins (35-1) brought home the state title. The national title was ratified a week later when the Knights earned a unanimous No. 1 ranking in the BA/NHSBCA final poll.

"This is really exciting for us—the team, the school and our community," Carpenter said. "We've had a lot of talent come through here, and the kids have been willing to work hard. We've had good assistant coaches. And we've had support from everybody you can name: fans, parents, students, administration. But this group was unique."

■ Elkins High began the season ranked No. 2 behind Bishop Amat. In each of the previous two seasons, Elkins knocked off perennial national power Bellaire High of Houston on its way to the Texas 5-A final four.

Expectations were high for the Knights as they returned first baseman/lefthander James Loney and righthander/outfielder Wardell Starling, two of the nation's best two-way players.

Loney, who went on to become a first-round pick of the Dodgers, threw four no-hitters while hitting .509 with eight homers and 58 RBIs. Starling went unbeaten at 12-0, hit .414 with six homers and was picked in the fourth round by the Pirates.

The Knights got on a roll early and surged to No. 1 when Bishop Amat stumbled out of the blocks. They stayed hot and finished the regular season with an unblemished record.

Though Elkins didn't play a lot of close games in 2002, it responded when adversity did strike. Its only loss came in a playoff game against Lamar High of Houston, but since it was part of a three-game series, it wasn't fatal. The Knights won the other two games of the series to advance.

Carpenter said he was strangely calm before the final against Austin's Bowie High, even though Bowie had reached the semifinals by beating Ronald Reagan High of San Antonio, stopping the Rattlers' 24-game winning streak, and then disposed of traditional power Duncanville High 8-3.

"That's the one that's really hard to describe," he said. "I just felt like we'd win it, and usually in a game like that I've got all kinds of butterflies. With Wardell pitching, I didn't think we'd have to score many runs to win. And I felt like anybody's No. 2 we can get to."

Starling, a righthander, was considered a better prospect than Loney entering the season, before Loney blossomed physically and surpassed him. But Starling turned the final game into his personal showcase.

He threw a five-hitter and went 4-for-4 with three doubles.

He retired the first nine batters and took a no-hitter into the fifth inning, by which time the Knights led 8-0. The final score was 11-4.

■ Bishop Amat High began the season ranked No. 1, and this was supposed to be the Lancers' year. Coach Kenny Kendrena, in fact, was thinking ahead to 2002 when he decided to start seven sophomores two years earlier.

"We knew they were a special group," Kendrena said. "We just thought, it's going to be nice to see how far they can go."

The young Lancers went 26-4 in 2000. A year later, they

PREVIOUS **WINNERS**

Previous No. 1 teams in the year-end Baseball America/National High School Baseball Coaches Association poll:

1992—Westminster Christian HS, Miami
1993—Greenway HS, Phoenix
1994—Sarasota (Fla.) HS
1995—Germantown (Tenn.) HS
1996—Westminster Christian HS, Miami
1997—Jesuit HS, Tampa
1998—Vestavia Hills (Ala.) HS
1999—Lassiter HS, Marietta, Ga.
2000—Gloucester Catholic HS, Gloucester City, N.J.
2001—Seminole (Fla.) HS

finished 27-2, won the National Classic, the nation's most prestigious high school tournament, and won the California Interscholastic Federation Southern Section Division IV championship. They also finished second to unbeaten Seminole (Fla.) High in the BA/NHS-BCA poll. By 2002, they were battle-tested seniors.

"We have a great group of kids, but one thing I've cautioned them about is not striving for perfection," said Kendrena, an All-American pitcher at Cal State Northridge in 1991. "We strive for excellence. You get into trouble trying to be perfect."

The Lancers didn't have any prospective first-round picks, but they boasted five players who signed with Division I colleges, including ace righthander Adam Simon (UCLA).

"Some of the teams we play against actually might have a talent edge," Kendrena said. "Our edge is that we have a group of kids that have been together and they are team-oriented. I'll take this group any day because of the way they go about their business."

The Lancers opened the season with some minor injuries and without a couple of players who were still with the basketball team. They lost two of their first four games and quickly were knocked from their perch as the No. 1 team.

From that point on, the Lancers were perfect. They defended both of their major titles, winning both the CIF Southern Section Division IV title and the National Classic. La Quinta High of Westminster, which went 29-3 overall and was ranked No. 9 nationally, was Bishop Amat's victim in both championship games.

The Lancers beat the Aztecs 6-2 in the National Classic final game. Two months later, the Lancers, who had climbed back to No. 2 nationally, beat La Quinta again, 2-1 in eight innings, in the CIF sectional championship game (California has no state championship).

■ Dunedin (Fla.) High made a compelling case for being one of the top teams in the country in 2001, when it went 25-3. Two of the Falcons losses were to archrival Seminole High, which went undefeated on the field, won the Florida 5-A title, was ranked No. 1 nationally and may have been the best high school team ever.

With almost every position player back in 2002, the Falcons began the season ranked No. 3 behind Bishop Amat and Elkins. They raced out to a 10-0 start—turning the tables on a rebuilding Seminole squad—and moved to second in the year's first in-season poll. The team remained No. 2 as it won 30 straight games entering postseason play.

HIGH SCHOOL TOP 50

Baseball America's final 2002 Top 50, selected in conjunction with the National High School Baseball Coaches Association.

Rank	Team, City	Record	Accomplishment
1	Elkins HS, Missouri City, Texas	35-1	Texas 5-A champion
2	Bishop Amat HS, La Puente, Calif.	28-2	CIF Southern Section IV champion
3	Parkview HS, Lilburn, Ga.	33-4	Georgia 5-A champion
4	Southridge HS, Miami	32-2	Florida 6-A runner-up
5	Dunedin (Fla.) HS	32-1	Lost in playoffs
6	Picayune (Miss.) HS	35-3	Mississippi 4-A champion
7	Clearwater (Fla.) Central Catholic HS	33-1	Florida 2-A champion
8	Mission Bay HS, San Diego	30-4	CIF San Diego Section III champion
9	La Quinta HS, Westminster, Calif.	29-3	CIF Southern Section IV runner-up
10	Gainesville (Ga.) HS	33-3	Georgia 3-A champion
11	Rancho Buena Vista HS, Vista, Calif.	30-4	CIF San Diego Section I champion
12	Wilcox HS, Santa Clara, Calif.	34-3	CIF Central Coast Section I champion
13	Bishop Kenny HS, Jacksonville	28-4	Florida 3-A champion
14	James Madison HS, Vienna, Va.	29-0	Virginia 3-A champion
15	Camarillo (Calif.) HS	30-4	CIF Southern Section I champion
16	Bowie HS, Austin	31-6	Texas 5-A runner-up
17	Fuquay-Varina (N.C.) HS	27-3	North Carolina 4-A champion
18	Covington (Ky.) Catholic HS	39-3	Kentucky champion
19	Northside Christian HS, St. Petersburg, Fla.	33-3	Florida 1-A runner-up
20	Germantown (Tenn.) HS	32-5	Lost in playoffs
21	Ronald Reagan HS, San Antonio	30-5	Lost in playoffs
22	St. Ignatius HS, Cleveland	27-3	Ohio Division I champion
23	Archbishop Mitty HS, San Jose	28-4	Lost in playoffs
24	Apopka (Fla.) HS	30-3	Lost in playoffs
25	Taylorsville (Utah) HS	25-2	Utah 5-A champion
26	Woodinville (Wash.) HS	24-2	Washington 4-A champion
27	Jesuit HS, New Orleans	30-6	Louisiana 5-A champion
28	Union (N.J.) HS	26-3	New Jersey Group 4 champion
29	Clovis (Calif.) HS	27-6	CIF Central Section large school champion
30	Westminster Academy, Fort Lauderdale	30-3	Lost in playoffs
31	Bishop McGuinness HS, Oklahoma City	35-6	Oklahoma 4-A champion
32	Lake Mary (Fla.) HS	24-2	Lost in playoffs
33	Grand Junction (Colo.) Central HS	24-2	Colorado 5-A champion
34	John Curtis HS, New Orleans	34-3	Louisiana 4-A champion
35	Brito Private HS, Miami	31-5	Florida 1-A champion
36	Buchanan HS, Fresno	27-6	CIF Central Section small school runner-up
37	T.C. Roberson HS, Asheville, N.C.	27-2	North Carolina 3-A champion
38	Portage (Mich.) Central HS	35-2	Michigan champion
39	Westwood HS, Austin	32-10	Lost in playoffs
40	Carlsbad (N.M.) HS	24-1	New Mexico 5-A champion
41	Rancho Bernardo HS, San Diego	29-7	CIF San Diego Section I runner-up
42	Canyon del Oro HS, Tucson	27-6	Arizona 5-A champion
43	Pleasure Ridge Park HS, Louisville	29-3	Lost in playoffs
44	Santa Fe HS, Edmond, Okla.	42-8	Oklahoma 6-A runner-up
45	Mount Lebanon (Pa.) HS	22-1	Lost in playoffs
46	Fort Mill (S.C.) HS	29-5	South Carolina 4-A champion
47	Logansport (Ind.) HS	26-4	Lost in playoffs
48	Monroe HS, Bronx, N.Y.	38-4	New York public school champion
49	Lakewood (Calif.) HS	28-6	Lost in playoffs
50	Creighton Prep, Omaha	32-5	Nebraska champion

California (CIF) does not have a state championship

No team in the country had the offensive firepower to match the Falcons, who hit almost .400 as a team. First baseman Brian Dopirak, a second-round pick of the Cubs and one of the nation's premier power hitters, hit .490 with 11 homers and 51 RBIs. Outfielder Steve Doetsch, an eighth-round pick of the Phillies, led Dunedin in hitting with an on-base percentage near .700. Ryan Harvey, a projected first-round pick in 2003, hit .400 with seven homers.

Harvey also doubled as the team's top pitcher. He was one of two pitchers with 10-0 records as the 34-0 Falcons moved to within two games of a perfect season.

But Dunedin got upended, 3-1, in the state 4-A semifinals by unheralded Ridgewood High of New Port Richey as Doetsch lined out to first with two out and the bases loaded in the seventh and last inning. With the loss went Dunedin's hopes for a national title.

Ridgewood's run to glory came to a screeching halt a day after after it beat Dunedin. The Rams lost the title game 13-

0 in five innings to No. 13 Bishop Kenny of Jacksonville.

Clement Wins Homer Duel

The most compelling individual story of the 2002 high school season took place in July, long after the season ended for most teams. Iowa is the lone state to play a summer high school schedule, and the state's top player, Marshalltown High catcher Jeff Clement, entered the season with 59 career home runs. That put him 11 shy of the national record set in 1998 by Drew Henson of Brighton (Mich.), now a prospect in the Yankees organization.

Clement's bid to pass Henson seemed within easy reach, because he had hit 21 homers as a freshman, 21 as a sophomore and 17 as a junior. But the draft presented a complicating factor. As the nation's top catching prospect, the 6-foot-1, 205-pound Clement was a likely early-round pick, and it was possible that he could sign a professional contract before his high school season ended. In the unlikely event that he signed right away, he would have only 13 games to hit his 12 home runs.

"I'll tell you this: If people pitch to him through those 13 games, he has a real shot," Marshalltown coach Steve Hanson said before the season. "However, I would point out that he has 142 career walks . . . and the older he's grown, the faster he's gotten them."

Clement slipped to the 12th round and the Twins, who exerted little pressure on Clement to sign immediately. As he considered a scholarship offer to Southern California, the record was practically his for the taking.

He set it against Mason City High, crushing a Brady Foster 0-1 curveball an estimated 425 feet to right field, hitting the roof of the Mason City bus barn in deep right field and bouncing over for career home run No. 71.

"I've said it so many times because I mean it: I don't play baseball to break records, I play to win," the ever-humble Clement said to a media throng. "I am honored

Jeff Clement

to have the record, sure, but what has been even more fun is that we have won a lot of ball games, and hopefully we will continue to win even more."

Mason City athletic director Dan Delaney said Clement's rocket was only the fourth ball in his 17-year tenure that he could recall hitting the roof of the bus barn. Clement hit three of them.

"I knew it was gone the minute it left my hand," said Foster, a lanky southpaw who greeted Clement at the plate. "I tried to start it over the plate and have it break outside, but when it left it was at his shoulder and was starting to break right over the plate. I knew it was going to go a long way before he even started to swing."

Foster and his teammates all congregated at home to congratulate Clement after his teammates had mobbed him. A prolonged standing ovation and curtain call followed as the crowd of 1,200 roared.

"He hits a home run and damn near sprints around the bases," Foster said. "I don't know Jeff, but I like the way he plays the game and the respect he shows it."

Marshalltown went on to win the Iowa 4-A championship, erasing a 6-2 deficit to beat Kennedy High of Cedar Rapids 9-6 in the final game. Clement was the winning pitcher in the quarterfinal and, pitching on one

PLAYER OF THE YEAR

Unbelievable was how Scott Kazmir described throwing four straight no-hitters as a high school junior. It was also how he described meeting his favorite player, Astros closer Billy Wagner.

Unbelievable also provides an apt description of Kazmir's numbers on the mound in 2002 for Cypress Falls High in Houston. How about going 11-2, 0.37 in 75 innings with 172 strikeouts, 19 walks and 19 hits allowed? That's 38 baserunners all season, to go along with an average of more than 16 strikeouts per seven-inning game.

Stats like those, and a four-pitch repertoire including a 96 mph fastball, plus slider, solid curveball and developing changeup combined to make the 18-year-old lefthander Baseball America's 2002 High School Player of the Year.

Scott Kazmir

His response, if you hadn't guessed it already: "It's an unbelievable honor," Kazmir said. "It was Joe Mauer last year and to even be mentioned with him, I don't know what to think about it."

Winning the award wasn't as perplexing to Kazmir as what happened to him on draft day. A consensus top-five talent, Kazmir's contract demands scared off the Reds, who had been considering him with the No. 3 pick. And when they took Chris Gruler instead, Kazmir started sliding—and worrying—as he listened to the draft's Internet broadcast.

"I thought I was going to go in the top five until 9 in the morning the day of the draft," Kazmir said. "The Reds said they were going with somebody else, and I didn't know what to think because I worked out with them and I pitched pretty good.

"After that, every team that picked, I said that's my new favorite team, and then the next team was my new favorite."

The Mets became Kazmir's final fave, rescuing him at No. 15. Kazmir's high school teammate, righthander Clint Everts, went 10 picks before him to the Expos. Kazmir signed with the Mets for $2.15 million late in the summer and started his professional career with the Mets' short-season Brooklyn affiliate.

Kazmir threw six no-hitters during his high school career, but none as a senior. Two 19-strikeout one-hitters and one with 14 strikeouts were all he could muster.

—WILL KIMMEY

PREVIOUS WINNERS

1992—Preston Wilson, of-rhp, Bamberg-Ehrhardt (S.C.) HS
1993—Trot Nixon, of-lhp, New Hanover HS, Wilmington, N.C.
1994—Doug Million, lhp, Sarasota (Fla.) HS
1995—Ben Davis, c, Malvern (Pa.) Prep
1996—Matt White, rhp, Waynesboro Area (Pa.) HS
1997—Darnell McDonald, of, Cherry Creek HS, Englewood, Colo.
1998—Drew Henson, 3b-rhp, Brighton (Mich.) HS
1999—Josh Hamilton, of-lhp, Athens Drive HS, Raleigh, N.C.
2000—Matt Harrington, rhp, Palmdale (Calif.) HS
2001—Joe Mauer, c, Cretin-Derham Hall, St. Paul, Minn.

State	Class, School/City (Record)
Alabama	6-A: Daphne HS (30-10)
	5-A: Cullman HS (39-10)
	4-A: Childersburg HS (28-5)
	3-A: Dadeville HS (37-8)
	2-A: Gordo HS (30-6)
	1-A: G.W. Long HS, Skipperville (30-7)
Alaska	Douglas HS, Juneau (17-3)
Arizona	5-A: *Canyon del Oro HS, Tucson (27-6)
	4-A: Prescott HS (26-9)
	3-A: Fountain Hills HS (30-3)
	2-A: Bisbee HS (27-6)
	1-A: St. David HS
Arkansas	5-A: Bentonville HS (26-6)
	4-A: Alma HS (21-6)
	3-A: Pulaski Academy, Little Rock (22-5)
	2-A: Parkers Chapel HS, El Dorado (32-4)
	1-A: Fort Smith Christian HS (20-4)
California	No state championship
Colorado	5-A: Central HS, Grand Junction (24-2)
	4-A: Mountain View HS (24-2)
	3-A: Eaton HS (22-3)
	2-A: Wiggins HS (20-2)
Connecticut	LL: Fairfield HS (22-2)
	L: Lyman Hall HS, Wallingford (19-6)
	M: Waterford HS (22-5)
	S: Westbrook HS (19-5)
Delaware	Brandywine HS, Wilmington (19-3)
Florida	6-A: Hialeah HS (24-10)
	5-A: A.C. Mosley HS, Lynnhaven (25-9)
	4-A: *Bishop Kenny HS, Jacksonville (27-4)
	3-A: The Bolles School, Jacksonville (30-4)
	2-A: *Clearwater Central Catholic HS (32-1)
	1-A: *Brito Private HS, Miami (31-5)
Georgia	5-A: *Parkview HS, Lilburn (33-4)
	4-A: Marist School, Atlanta (32-7)
	3-A: *Gainesville HS (33-3)
	2-A: Cartersville HS (33-2)
	1-A: The Walker School, Marietta (30-7)
Hawaii	Mid-Pacific Institute, Honolulu (19-5)
Idaho	5-A: Idaho Falls HS
	4-A: Burley HS
	3-A: Fruitland HS
	2-A: Kendrick HS
Illinois	2-A: Carl Sandburg HS, Orland Park (25-9)
	1-A: Olympia HS, Stanford (38-1)

	Summer: Lyons Township HS, La Grange (23-8)
Indiana	4-A: Munster HS (25-9)
	3-A: Lincoln HS, Vincennes (25-8)
	2-A: Manchester HS, North Manchester (14-16)
	1-A: Blackhawk Christian HS, Fort Wayne (23-6)
Iowa	4-A: Marshalltown HS (37-6)
	3-A: Knoxville HS (37-5)
	2-A: Eagle Grove HS (31-3)
	1-A: Newman Catholic HS, Mason City (40-2)
Kansas	6-A: Olathe East HS (17-8)
	5-A: Arkansas City HS (19-6)
	4-A: Nickerson HS (22-4)
	3-A: Baxter Springs HS (23-2)
	2-A/1-A: Elkhart HS (22-1)
Kentucky	*Covington Catholic HS (40-3)
Louisiana	5-A: *Jesuit HS, New Orleans (30-6)
	4-A: *John Curtis Christian HS, New Orleans (32-3)
	3-A: Parkview Baptist HS, Baton Rouge
	2-A: Christian Life Academy, Baton Rouge
	1-A: Central Catholic HS, Morgan City
	B: Choudrant HS
	C: Stanley HS, Logansport
Maine	A: Sanford HS (17-4)
	B: Maranacook Community HS, Readfield (19-2)
	C: Jay HS (16-5)
	D: North Yarmouth Academy, Yarmouth (14-4)
Maryland	4-A: Gov. Thomas Johnson HS, Frederick (17-10)
	3-A: South Carroll HS, Sykesville (15-9)
	2-A: Atholton HS, Columbia (20-5)
	1-A: Boonsboro HS (19-4)
	Private: Riverdale Baptist HS, Upper Marlboro (34-9)
Massachusetts	I: St. John's Prep, Danvers (19-8)
	II: Hudson HS (22-4)
	III: Nipmuc Regional HS, Upton (21-4)
Michigan	I: *Portage Central HS (35-2)
	II: Jefferson HS, Monroe (32-6)
	III: Blissfield HS (40-4)
	IV: Decatur HS (25-8)
Minnesota	3-A: New Ulm HS (27-3)
	2-A: Lourdes HS, Rochester (30-1)
	1-A: St. Mary's HS, Sleepy Eye (20-8)
Mississippi	5-A: Madison Central HS (32-8)
	4-A: *Picayune Memorial HS, Picayune (35-3)
	3-A: Senatobia HS (26-11)
	2-A: Mooreville HS (36-6)
Missouri	4-A: Liberty HS (23-8)

day's rest, the final. The Bobcats lost in the final game in 2000 and '01.

But first, one more complicating factor. While Clement broke Henson's record and went on to extend the mark to 75, he was actually competing, sort of, with another Iowa player, James Peterson of 3-A Winterset High. Peterson finished his career with 73 homers, though the record book credited him with only 68.

Peterson hit five dingers for Winterset as an eighth-grader, and the National Federation of State High School Associations counts statistics only from grades 9-12. Counting the five extra homers, Peterson actually caught Clement at one point. But he went homerless as Winterset was eliminated from the playoffs on the same night Clement hit Nos. 74 and 75 in a state quarterfinal game against Bettendorf High.

Georgia's Star Power

Two other players also flirted with the national career home run record in 2002, falling just short. Micah Owings of Gainesville (Ga.) High finished with 69 while Kevin Bookout of Stroud (Okla.) High finished with 65.

That means four of the top five home run hitters in high school history completed their careers in 2002.

Owings, drafted in the second round by the Rockies as a pitcher, hit 25 on the season as he helped No. 11 Gainesville defend its Georgia 3-A championship. The Red Elephants beat Loganville High by identical 7-0 scores, as Owings homered in both games and won the title-clinching game on the mound. He improved his record to 12-1 with a 14-strikeout effort. For the year, Owings hit .448 with 69 RBIs; he also struck out 121 in 75 innings while walking just three and posting a 1.03 ERA.

Owings wasn't the only star player to lead a Georgia high school to a second straight state title.

Outfielder Jeff Francoeur, the first-round draft pick of the Braves, led No. 3 Parkview High of Lilburn to a two-game sweep of Lassiter High of Marietta in the 5-A finals. Francoeur won both games with home runs, making himself the winning pitcher both times.

Overall, he homered four times and had two doubles, seven RBIs and 22 total bases as the Panthers defended their state title. The games were played on the same day, meaning Francoeur did all of it in a matter of hours.

In Game One, Francoeur broke a 4-4 tie with a homer in the seventh, giving Parkview a 5-4 victory. Game Two

	3-A: Platte County HS, Platte City (24-3)
	2-A: John Burroughs HS, St. Louis (24-3)
	1-A: Early HS, Morrisville (20-5)
Montana	No high school baseball
Nebraska	Creighton Prep, Omaha (32-5)
Nevada	4-A: Wooster HS (30-9)
	3-A: Bishop Manogue HS, Reno
	2-A: Battle Mountain HS
	1-A: Wells HS
New Hampshire	L: Winnacunnet HS, Hampton (18-4)
	M: Farmington HS
	S: Moultonborough HS (17-5)
	I: Coe-Brown Academy, Northwood (14-7)
New Jersey	IV: *Union HS (26-3)
	III: Toms River South HS
	II: Ridge HS, Basking Ridge
	I: Pennsville Memorial HS, Pennsville (21-6)
	Parochial A: Delbarton HS, Morristown
	Parochial B: Bishop Eustace Prep, Pennsauken (23-8)
New Mexico	5-A: *Carlsbad HS (24-1)
	4-A: Farmington HS (19-6)
	3-A: New Mexico Military Institute, Roswell (21-2)
	2-A/1-A: Jemez Valley HS, Jemez Pueblo (19-4)
New York	A: Clarkstown North HS, New City (27-5)
	B: W.T. Clarke HS, Westbury
	C: Pine Plains HS
	D: Tuckahoe HS, Eastchester
North Carolina	4-A: *Fuquay-Varina HS (27-4)
	3-A: *T.C. Roberson HS, Asheville (27-2)
	2-A: East Rutherford HS, Forest City (24-8)
	1-A: South Stokes HS, Walnut Cove (28-4)
	I: Charlotte Christian HS (30-5)
North Dakota	A: Fargo North HS (22-10)
	B: Cavalier HS (22-5)
Ohio	I: *St. Ignatius HS, Cleveland (27-3)
	II: Tallmadge HS (27-5)
	III: Heath HS (30-2)
	IV: Newark Catholic HS (27-6)
Oklahoma	6-A: Jenks HS (27-12)
	5-A: Chickasha HS (27-15)
	4-A: *Bishop Mcguinness HS, Oklahoma City (35-6)
	3-A: Verdigris HS, Claremore (38-8)
	2-A: Dale HS (34-4)
	A: Silo HS, Durant
	B: Dover HS (30-7)

Oregon	4-A: Southridge HS (21-10)
	3-A: The Dalles HS (25-5)
	2-A/1-A: Umpqua Valley Christian, Roseburg (24-5)
Pennsylvania	3-A: Moon HS, Coraopolis (20-6)
	2-A: Lewistown Area HS (19-5)
	1-A: Greensburg Central Catholic HS (19-2)
Rhode Island	A: South Kingstown HS, Wakefield
	B: Warwick HS
South Carolina	4-A: Fort Mill HS (29-5)
	3-A: Wilson HS, Florence
	2-A: Chapin HS (26-6)
	1-A: Landrum HS (24-4)
South Dakota	No high school baseball
Tennessee	3-A: LaVergne HS (29-7)
	2-A: Lexington HS
	1-A: University HS, Jackson
	II—Father Ryan , Nashville (26-8)
Texas	5-A: *Elkins HS, Missouri City (35-1)
	4-A: Carroll HS, Southlake (31-10)
	3-A: Sinton HS (34-5)
	2-A: Celina HS (33-4)
	1-A: Shiner HS (23-10)
Utah	5-A: *Taylorsville HS (25-2)
	4-A: Timpanogos HS, Orem (21-4)
Vermont	I: Essex HS, Essex Junction (20-1)
	II: Mount Abraham HS, Bristol (18-2)
	III: Enosburg Falls HS
	IV: Whitcomb HS, Bethel
Virginia	3-A: *James Madison HS, Vienna (29-0)
	2-A: Turner Ashby, Bridgewater (22-4)
	1-A: Henry HS (23-3)
Washington	4-A: *Woodinville HS (24-2)
	3-A: North Thurston HS, Lacey (24-0)
	2-A: Ridgefield HS (20-3)
	1-A: Colfax HS (25-1)
	B: De Sales HS, Walla Walla
Washington, D.C.	Wilson HS (18-8)
West Virginia	3-A: Hurricane HS (31-4)
	2-A: Winfield HS (30-6)
	1-A: Moorefield HS (22-7)
Wisconsin	I: Westosha Central HS, Salem
	II: Lutheran HS, Milwaukee (17-7)
	III: Regis HS, Eau Claire (20-5)
Wyoming	No high school baseball

*Ranked in Baseball America/National High School Baseball Coaches Association poll

was tied 3-3 in the sixth when he led off the inning with a homer, but that didn't finish his offensive show. The inning turned out to be a big one for the Panthers, and Francoeur came up again in the same frame—and hit a grand slam to end the scoring in an 11-3 victory.

He pitched in relief in both games, adding his second baseball state title to the two he won in football at Parkview. A top prospect as both a safety and center fielder, Francoeur had signed to play football with Clemson.

On the year, Francoeur hit .487 with 16 homers. A year earlier, he hit .500 with 20 homers for the Georgia 5-A champions.

Hot In Arizona

Like Francoeur, Jason Pridie came about as close as possible to winning a state championship game singlehandedly.

The Prescott (Ariz.) senior tied the Arizona 4-A championship game twice with RBI hits, including once with a double in the seventh inning. He drove in the winning runs with a three-run homer in the ninth and was the winning pitcher, throwing the last three innings in relief after moving from center field. It all produced a 7-5 victory over then-No. 21 Catalina Foothills of Tucson.

Pridie is the brother of Jon Pridie, a righthander in the Twins system, and was a second-round draft pick himself in June.

■ James Madison High of Vienna, Va., was the only team in the BA/NHSBCA top 50 to finish with an unbeaten record. The Warhawks went 29-0 to win the Virginia 3-A title, beating J.R. Tucker High of Richmond 2-1 in the championship game on a last-inning double by No. 9 hitter Joe Lewin.

■ Underdog Hialeah High won its second straight Florida 6-A title, beating No. 4 Southridge High 5-4 in an all-Miami championship game.

Hialeah entered the 2001 championship with eight losses, and 10 in 2002. But both times the Thoroughbreds used Giovany Gonzalez as their starting pitcher. He's now 2-0 in state title games—as a freshman and sophomore.

It was a bitter loss for Southridge (32-2), which had national championship aspirations.

"There is just a feeling of complete emptiness," Southridge athletic director Bob Burnside said. "We came here to leave with the state trophy, not second place. All I can do is tip my hat to Hialeah. They are a great team."

■ Clearwater Central Catholic High shot from 25th to

2002 HIGH SCHOOL ALL-AMERICA TEAM

Selected by Baseball America

*Junior

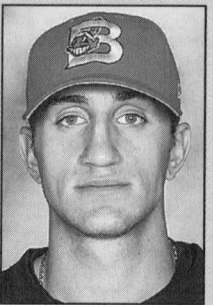

Prince Fielder   Matt Whitney   Lastings Milledge   Zack Greinke

FIRST TEAM

Pos.	Player	School, Hometown	AVG	AB	R	H	2B	3B	HR	RBI	SB	Drafted (Round)
C	Adam Donachie	Timber Creek HS, Orlando	.454	88	41	41	5	1	14	46	14	Royals (2)
1B	Prince Fielder	Eau Gallie HS, Melbourne, Fla.	.524	82	46	44	14	1	11	42	5	Brewers (1)
INF	Micah Schilling	Silliman Institute, Clinton, La.	.489	94	58	46	9	0	16	43	23	Indians (1)
INF	B.J. Upton	Greenbrier Christian HS, Chesapeake, Va.	.641	78	49	50	11	4	11	52	21	Devil Rays (1)
INF	Matt Whitney	Palm Beach Gardens (Fla.) HS	.475	101	38	48	8	3	12	45	7	Indians (1)
OF	Jeff Francoeur	Parkview HS, Lilburn, Ga.	.487	119	51	58	9	1	16	49	21	Braves (1)
OF	*Lastings Milledge	Northside Christian HS, St. Petersburg	.569	109	57	62	7	6	14	71	30	Not eligible
OF	*Delmon Young	Camarillo (Calif.) HS	.542	120	55	65	7	1	17	56	2	Not eligible
DH	Brian Dopirak	Dunedin (Fla.) HS	.490	100	49	49	11	4	11	51	0	Cubs (2)
UT	Zack Greinke	Apopka (Fla.) HS	.495	99	39	49	11	1	10	42	1	Royals (1)
UT	James Loney	Elkins HS, Missouri City, Texas	.509	112	38	57	17	2	8	58	7	Dodgers (1)

Pos.	Player	School, Hometown	W	L	ERA	G	SV	IP	H	BB	SO	Drafted (Round)
P	Clint Everts	Cypress Falls HS, Houston	9	3	1.30	15	0	81	41	28	157	Expos (1)
P	Cole Hamels	Rancho Bernardo HS, San Diego	10	0	0.39	12	1	71	32	23	130	Phillies (1)
P	Kevin Jepsen	Bishop Manogue HS, Sparks, Nev.	9	1	0.84	13	1	58	15	18	116	Angels (2)
P	Scott Kazmir	Cypress Falls HS, Houston	11	2	0.37	14	1	75	19	19	172	Mets (1)
UT	Zack Greinke	Apopka (Fla.) HS	9	2	0.55	12	0	63	22	8	116	
UT	James Loney	Elkins HS, Missouri City, Texas	12	1	1.51	14	0	69	29	40	120	

SECOND TEAM

Pos.	Player	School, Hometown	AVG	AB	R	H	2B	3B	HR	RBI	SB	Drafted (Round)
C	Brian McCann	Duluth (Ga.) HS	.438	64	20	28	3	0	12	27	4	Braves (2)
1B	John Mayberry	Rockhurst HS, Kansas City	.432	74	25	32	5	2	9	29	4	Mariners (1)
INF	Tyler Greene	St. Thomas Aquinas HS, Fort Lauderdale	.525	80	38	42	6	2	6	20	26	Braves (2)
INF	Brandon Jones	Wewahitchka (Fla.) HS	.551	69	20	38	5	3	10	37	14	Royals (6)
INF	Sergio Santos	Mater Dei HS, Santa Ana, Calif.	.388	85	33	33	10	2	8	33	14	D'backs (1)
OF	Brent Clevlen	Westwood HS, Austin	.571	112	49	64	11	1	12	45	6	Tigers (2)
OF	Jason Pridie	Prescott (Ariz.) HS	.550	111	48	61	12	9	13	47	14	Devil Rays (2)
OF	Sean Scobee	Rio Linda (Calif.) HS	.536	71	44	38	10	2	10	48	13	Cubs (5)
DH	Corey Shafer	Choctaw (Okla.) HS	.510	98	37	50	9	2	12	38	3	Orioles (2)
UT	Chance Douglass	Randall HS, Amarillo, Texas	.406	101	55	41	5	2	20	61	5	Astros (12)
UT	Micah Owings	Gainesville (Ga.) HS	.448	105	55	47	22	1	25	69	7	Rockies (2)

Pos.	Player	School, Hometown	W	L	ERA	G	SV	IP	H	BB	SO	Drafted (Round)
P	*Chad Billingsley	Defiance (Ohio) HS	11	0	0.54	17	1	90	35	27	171	Not eligible
P	Allen Ponder	Lee-Scott Academy, Auburn, Ala.	12	0	0.09	12	0	80	22	7	139	Orioles (50)
P	Mark Romanczuk	St. Mark's HS, Wilmington, Del.	10	0	0.64	10	0	66	19	25	146	Devil Rays (5)
P	Zach Segovia	Forney (Texas) HS	9	2	0.82	18	1	77	30	18	150	Phillies (2)
UT	Chance Douglass	Randall HS, Amarillo, Texas	13	1	1.42	17	3	84	47	20	139	
UT	Micah Owings	Gainesville (Ga.) HS	12	1	1.03	13	0	75	41	3	121	

PLAYER OF THE YEAR: Scott Kazmir, lhp, Cypress Falls HS, Houston

11th in the national rankings after winning the Florida 2-A championship, beating Florida Christian of Miami 5-0. CCC finished its season 33-1, with the only loss against Dunedin High in February.

■ Rancho Bernardo High failed to win its fourth straight San Diego Section Division I title, which would have been a record, falling 6-0 to No. 12 Rancho Buena Vista. The Longhorns proved their superiority, beating the Broncos in three of four meetings over the season and ending Rancho Bernardo's five-year conference-championship streak. Lefthander Jesse English was the winning pitcher all three times.

■ Right fielder Chris Walston of El Capitan of Lakeside, Calif., broke the state record for single-season home runs. Walston finished the regular season with 22. Daniel Carte of Hurricane (W.Va.) hit his state-record 51st career home run in a sectional playoff game against Point Pleasant.

■ Phil Clark accepted the head coaching job at nearby Bartlett (Tenn.) High after several successful years at Germantown High, another east Memphis suburb. Clark's last Germantown team (32-5) was upset in the sectionals by Munford High, but still was ranked No. 20. Clark won a national title with an unbeaten Germantown team in 1995.

Team USA 436
Summer College Leagues 442
Youth Leagues 450

AMATEUR
BASEBALL

Cuba dominates international stage as demise of Olympic baseball lurks

BY JOHN MANUEL

The 2002 season was relatively quiet on the field in international baseball, as non-Olympic years tend to be.

But off-the-field issues threatened to make every year a non-Olympic one. The International Olympic Committee, with Belgian national Jacques Rogge replacing Spaniard Juan Antonio Samaranch as president, dropped a bombshell by recommending the removal of baseball from the Olympic program.

An IOC panel passed on its findings in August and suggested dropping baseball, softball and modern pentathlon in favor of rugby and men's and women's golf. Samaranch was the IOC president when baseball became part of the Games as a medal sport in 1992 and later when it made the transition to professional players in 2000, when the United States won the gold medal. Rogge was an avid rugby player and his sister-in-law captains Belgium's golf team.

The recommendation had to be accepted by the IOC's 15-member executive board. If passed, it would move on to the IOC's 127-member general assembly. The meetings were scheduled for Mexico City in November 2002.

The world baseball community reacted swiftly to the threat, as International Baseball Federation president Aldo Notari called an emergency meeting in Montreaux, Switzerland, that brought the game's biggest players to the table. Major League Baseball sent vice president Sandy Alderson and the Players Association sent its international expert, Tony Bernazard.

Japanese League commissioner Hiromori Kawashima and U.S. Olympic Committee president Marty Mankamyer joined USA Baseball CEO Paul Seiler and other members of the sport's international leadership body at the meeting, in which the world's baseball leaders pledged to work together to fight the recommendation.

"We will do whatever we can to ensure that baseball remains in the Olympics," Alderson said. "Baseball is an international and developing sport, and it certainly belongs in the Olympic Games."

IBAF and MLB kept up their efforts leading up to the November deadline, with Alderson and union chief Don Fehr meeting with Rogge in Switzerland in October. They were expected to counter the three "deficiencies" the IOC panel gave for eliminating baseball:

Lelo Prado

■ Global participation with regard for television broadcasts.

■ High-cost baseball-only venues.

■ Conflicting schedule with North American professional baseball, in particular MLB, which precludes the use of major league players in the Olympics.

"We just really need sports to deliver their best athletes," IOC vice president Kevan Gosper of Australia said, "and baseball hasn't been able to deliver."

National Team Reaps Silver

The highest-profile team for USA Baseball in 2002 was its college national team, which represented the U.S. at the first World University Championship in Italy. Not unexpectedly, that tournament resulted in another showdown between the U.S. and Cuba.

Louisville coach Lelo Prado, a Cuban native, served as a assiatant coach for Team USA in 2000, and watched that club win 27 of 31 games, the best performance in USA Baseball history. In 2002, as head coach of the college national team, Prado led his club to a 23-7 record, including victories in the annual Japan Series, a one-loss tour of domestic summer leagues, and a championship at Haarlem Honkbal Week in the Netherlands.

Still, Prado acknowledged that changing one outcome—the gold-medal game of the FISU World University Championship in Italy, a 6-0 loss to Cuba—would have made the summer a lot better.

Team USA won a silver medal at the first world championship for college-aged players, but not the gold thanks to that one loss. It was a successful summer, but it could easily have been better.

"We got beat by a team that was hot," Prado said. "Cuba was very good that day. We had our chances, but we didn't do it. When Cuba scores early on

TEAM USA: COLLEGE 2002

Season Statistics (23-7)

HEAD COACH: Lelo Prado (U. of Louisville)

BATTING	AVG	AB	R	H	2B	3B	HR	RBI	SB	College	Class
Michael Aubrey, 1b	.405	111	25	45	7	2	6	26	0	Tulane	So.
Eric Patterson, 2b-ss	.333	105	17	35	4	1	0	13	17	Georgia Tech	Fr.
Carlos Quentin, of	.313	96	19	30	9	0	3	20	3	Stanford	So.
Conor Jackson, 3b-dh	.312	93	13	29	11	0	1	11	0	California	So.
Aaron Hill, 3b-ss	.277	94	23	26	10	0	3	24	2	Louisiana State	So.
Shane Costa, of	.275	91	17	25	4	1	1	12	1	Cal State Fullerton	So.
Rickie Weeks, 2b-of	.273	99	18	27	2	3	2	14	2	Southern	So.
Mark Jurich, of	.271	59	13	16	1	0	2	11	1	Louisville	So.
Landon Powell, c	.263	95	16	25	4	3	3	17	0	South Carolina	So.
Dustin Pedroia, ss	.208	53	6	11	2	0	0	4	0	Arizona State	Fr.
Sam Fuld, of	.190	105	12	20	3	0	0	13	4	Stanford	So.
Clint Sammons, c	.100	20	0	2	0	0	0	2	0	Georgia	Fr.
Ryan Garko, c	.000	12	2	0	0	0	0	1	0	Stanford	Jr.

PITCHING	W	L	ERA	G	SV	IP	H	BB	SO	College	Class
Chad Cordero	0	1	0.00	13	2	17	8	4	29	Cal State Fullerton	So.
Brad Sullivan	7	0	0.72	7	0	50	27	16	50	Houston	So.
Huston Street	0	0	1.26	13	3	14	8	1	18	Texas	Fr.
Kyle Sleeth	7	1	1.44	8	0	56	36	16	56	Wake Forest	So.
Phil Humber	3	2	1.45	5	0	31	19	17	35	Rice	Fr.
Grant Johnson	2	1	1.80	5	0	20	11	13	25	Notre Dame	Fr.
Abe Alvarez	0	0	1.93	11	0	14	16	1	13	Long Beach State	So.
Kyle Bakker	3	2	2.14	6	0	34	36	4	40	Georgia Tech	So.
Bob Zimmermann	0	0	2.53	12	2	11	4	2	13	SW Missouri State	So.
Wes Littleton	1	0	2.70	13	0	20	14	10	20	Cal State Fullerton	So.

AMATEUR BASEBALL

you, it's a pretty tough team to come back against. They play like the Yankees when they get a lead."

Cuba threw four consecutive shutouts to finish up the Worlds, allowing just four runs overall in the tournament.

The Cubans dealt Team USA ace Kyle Sleeth (14-0 at Wake Forest in the spring) the righthander's first loss since March 2001. The Americans' other loss in the FISU tournament came at the hands of China, a shocking 4-3 defeat in which all of the Chinese runs were unearned.

Those were the twin story lines for Team USA in the summer of 2002—dominant pitching and a constant search for quality defense. That especially was true in Italy, where Prado's club was without shortstop Dustin Pedroia (Arizona State). While the 5-foot-7 Pedroia wasn't an offensive force (.208, four RBIs in 18 games), he steadied the infield defense and was the team's lone true shortstop.

He was injured in the last game of the Honkbal tournament, leading Prado to push second baseman Eric Patterson (Georgia Tech) to shortstop and bring in Rickie Weeks (Southern) to second base from left field. Patterson struggled at times in his new role but showed that with more strength, he could handle the position in the future. Weeks also proved to pro scouts—many of whom consider him the top college prospect for the 2003 draft—that he has the range, arm and feet for second base.

"No question, we didn't field like we needed do," Prado said. "We were lucky with Pedroia down that it only cost us in the one game against China. The left side of our infield was a concern."

First baseman Michael Aubrey had an all-star summer, leading the team in the triple crown categories at .406-6-26 and turning it up when the team needed it most. He homered in the first three games in Italy and generally carried the offense all summer.

No American pitcher had a bad summer, as the pitching staff set a record for the national-team program with a 1.48 ERA, breaking a mark set by the 2000 club's staff that featured Mark Prior, Kirk Saarloos, Dewon Brazelton and Josh Karp. "That group was special, especially with Prior, but we had more quality arms this year," said Prado, who served as pitching coach for part of the 2000 summer. "We were not worried about putting anyone out there, and you could take your pick of closer."

Sleeth and righty Brad Sullivan (Houston) set the tempo from the front of the rotation, while freshmen righties Philip Humber (Rice) and Grant Johnson (Notre Dame) also flashed power arms. The back of the bullpen was nearly impregnable—righties Chad Cordero (Cal State Fullerton), Huston Street (Texas) and Bob Zimmermann (Southwest

WORLD JUNIOR CHAMPIONSHIP

Sherbrooke, Quebec
August 1-11, 2002

POOL-PLAY STANDINGS

POOL A	W	L	RF	RA
Cuba	4	1	52	18
Taiwan	4	1	62	37
Canada	4	1	69	37
Panama	2	3	43	49
The Netherlands	1	4	31	56
Italy	0	5	15	75

POOL B	W	L	RF	RA
United States	5	0	68	28
Venezuela	4	1	58	32
Korea	3	2	48	40
Australia	2	3	58	31
Brazil	1	4	46	64
Spain	0	5	12	95

SEMI-FINALS: Taiwan 4, United States 3; Cuba 8, Canada 4. **GOLD-MEDAL GAME:** Cuba 9, Taiwan 6. **BRONZE-MEDAL GAME:** United States 12, Canada 3.

FINAL STANDINGS: 1. Cuba. 2. Taiwan. 3. United States. 4. Canada. 5. Australia. 6. Korea. 7. Venezuela. 8. Panama. 9. Brazil. 10. The Netherlands. 11. Italy. 12. Spain.

ALL-TOURNAMNENT TEAM: C—Michael Sadler, Australia. 1B—Ian Stewart, United States. 2B—Vicente Cafaro, Venezuela. 3B—Yuliesky Gourriel, Cuba. SS—Shawn Bowman, Canada. OF—Adam Loewen, Canada; Lastings Milledge, United States; Eliu Torres, Cuba. DH—Delmon Young, United States. RHP—Juan Linares, Cuba; Wei-Yin Chen, Taiwan.
Most Valuable Player: Delmon Young, United States.

INDIVIDUAL BATTING LEADERS
(Minimum 25 Plate Appearances)

	AVG	AB	R	H	2B	3B	HR	RBI	SB
Tyler Williams, Canada	.571	28	12	16	1	1	2	11	3
Kenny Berkenbosch, Neth.	.571	21	5	12	4	1	0	7	0
Adam Loewen, Canada	.542	24	12	13	3	1	1	10	0
Delmon Young, USA	.513	39	18	20	1	0	9	18	3
Allen Craig, USA	.485	33	11	16	3	0	2	10	0
Chin-Ming Chen, Taiwan	.485	33	11	16	4	0	3	12	0
Chin-Lung Hu, Taiwan	.474	38	11	18	5	2	4	12	1
Eliu Torres, Cuba	.469	32	11	15	1	1	0	7	1
Adam Pelley, Australia	.462	26	11	12	3	1	0	7	2
Joo-Hwan Na, Korea	.452	31	12	14	4	0	1	10	2
Ian Stewart, USA	.448	29	8	13	1	0	3	8	0
Lastings Milledge, USA	.419	31	12	13	2	0	5	14	1
Chao-Kuan Wu, Taiwan	.419	31	10	13	1	0	3	7	0
Ernesto Molinet, Cuba	.419	31	11	13	1	0	1	6	2
Ryan Hastie, Australia	.417	24	5	10	2	0	1	9	0
Leonardo Zileri, Italy	.417	24	5	10	1	0	2	9	1
Bart Gabriels, Neth.	.409	22	4	9	2	0	0	1	1
Steve Bell-Irving, Canada	.409	22	8	9	4	0	0	3	0
Juan Linares, Cuba	.407	27	9	11	2	0	4	13	0
Chien-Yu Kuo, Taiwan	.406	32	10	13	3	0	4	10	0
Joo-Ho Kim, Korea	.400	25	4	10	2	0	0	4	0
Shawn Bowman, Canada	.395	38	9	15	4	0	4	17	1

INDIVIDUAL PITCHING LEADERS
(Minimum 8 Innings)

	W	L	ERA	G	SV	IP	H	BB	SO
Woo-Seok Ko, Korea	1	0	1.93	4	0	9	12	3	9
Justin Fletcher, Australia	1	0	2.03	3	0	13	9	9	3
Adam Bright, Australia	1	1	2.53	2	0	11	9	8	10
Chad Billingsley, USA	2	0	2.70	3	0	10	7	7	18
Ian Kennedy, USA	1	0	2.77	2	0	13	9	5	20
Liuben Morales, Cuba	2	0	2.81	5	1	16	21	1	14
Wei-Yin Chen, Taiwan	2	0	2.96	5	0	24	20	5	25
Juan Linares, Cuba	2	0	3.07	3	0	15	9	5	18
Simon Ramos, Venezuela	2	0	3.29	3	0	14	9	0	11
Jeff Allison, USA	1	1	3.86	2	0	14	11	4	17

TEAM USA
Tournament Statistics

BATTING	AVG	AB	R	H	2B	3B	HR	RBI	SB
Delmon Young, of	.513	39	18	20	1	0	9	18	3
Allen Craig, ss	.485	33	11	16	3	0	2	10	0
Ian Stewart, 1b	.448	29	8	13	2	0	3	8	0
Tyler Bullock, dh-1b	.444	18	7	8	3	0	3	4	0
Lastings Milledge, of	.419	31	12	13	3	0	5	15	2
Jarrod Saltalamacchia, c	.391	23	9	9	2	0	1	11	0
Philip Stringer, 2b-3b	.385	26	10	10	1	0	2	4	1
Chris Lubanski, of	.382	34	10	13	3	1	3	10	3
Justin Tordi, 3b-2b	.371	35	10	13	6	0	1	9	0
David Uribes, inf	.308	13	3	4	0	0	0	4	2
Michael Rogers, of-dh	.238	21	5	5	2	0	1	2	1
Brian Opdyke, c	.200	5	1	1	1	0	0	1	0

PITCHING	W	L	ERA	G	SV	IP	H	BB	SO
Austin Creps	0	0	0.00	2	0	3	3	1	4
Chris Lubanski	0	0	0.00	1	0	2	2	0	3
Delmon Young	0	0	0.00	1	0	1	1	0	2
Chad Billingsley	3	0	2.45	3	0	11	7	7	19
Jeff Allison	1	1	2.57	2	0	14	11	4	17
Ian Kennedy	1	0	2.77	2	0	13	9	5	20
Tyler Bullock	0	0	3.00	2	1	3	2	1	6
Chuck Tiffany	1	0	3.60	3	0	5	3	1	16
Michael Rogers	1	0	4.50	2	0	8	4	5	12
Tim Gustafson	0	0	9.00	3	1	5	7	1	8
Justin Tordi	0	0	18.00	2	0	2	5	1	0

WORLD UNIVERSITY CHAMPIONSHIP

Messina, Italy
August 2-11, 2002

POOL-PLAY STANDINGS

POOL A	W	L	RF	RA
United States	3	1	38	7
Italy	3	1	18	14
Korea	2	2	23	23
China	2	2	13	13
Canada	0	4	7	42

POOL B	W	L	RF	RA
Cuba	4	0	29	4
Japan	3	1	25	2
Taiwan	2	2	17	14
Czech Republic	1	3	5	30
France	0	4	6	32

SEMI-FINALS: United States 2, Japan 1; Cuba 2, Taiwan 0. **GOLD-MEDAL GAME:** Cuba 6, United States 0. **BRONZE-MEDAL GAME:** Japan 5, Taiwan 0.

FINAL STANDINGS: 1. Cuba. 2. United States. 3. Japan. 4. Taiwan. 5. Korea. 6. Italy. 7. China. 8. Czech Republic. 9. Canada. 10. France.

ALL-TOURNAMENT TEAM: C—Ren Min, China. 1B—Michael Aubrey, United States. 2B—David Dallospedale, Italy. 3B—Kao Wei, Taiwan. SS—Takashi Toritani, Japan. OF—Shane Costa, United States; Jeong Ho Seo, Korea; Leslie Anderson, Cuba. DH—Pedro J. Rodriguez, Cuba. RHP—Brad Sullivan, United States. LHP—Tsuyoshi Wada, Japan.
Most Valuable Player—Orelvis Avila, Cuba

TEAM USA
Tournament Statistics

BATTING	AVG	AB	R	H	2B	3B	HR	RBI	SB
Michael Aubrey, 1b/dh	.400	30	10	12	4	2	3	7	0
Aaron Hill, 3b	.400	25	8	10	4	0	3	10	1
Rickie Weeks, 2b	.370	27	7	10	0	1	1	4	0
Shane Costa, of	.348	23	4	8	0	0	0	4	0
Mark Jurich, of	.333	15	5	5	1	0	1	7	1
Conor Jackson, 1b/3b	.318	22	2	7	3	0	0	5	0
Eric Patterson, ss	.286	28	5	8	1	1	0	3	3
Sam Fuld, of	.269	26	5	7	1	0	0	3	1
Landon Powell, c	.227	22	2	5	1	1	0	3	0
Carlos Quentin, of	.227	22	4	5	4	0	0	2	0
Ryan Garko, c	.000	5	2	0	0	0	0	1	0
Huston Street, p	.000	1	0	0	0	0	0	0	0

PITCHING	W	L	ERA	G	SV	IP	H	BB	SO
Brad Sullivan	2	0	0.00	2	0	14	7	5	13
Philip Humber	1	0	0.00	1	0	6	3	6	8
Chad Cordero	0	0	0.00	3	1	5	1	1	6
Bob Zimmermann	0	0	0.00	2	0	2	0	1	2
Abe Alvarez	0	0	0.00	2	0	2	1	0	1
Kyle Bakker	0	1	1.35	1	0	7	11	0	5
Kyle Sleeth	1	1	1.50	2	0	12	9	4	13
Grant Johnson	0	0	1.69	1	0	5	3	7	7
Wes Littleton	0	0	3.00	1	0	6.0	3	4	0
Huston Street	0	0	3.38	3	0	3	3	1	3

Missouri State) combined to give up seven runs (five earned) in more than 42 innings.

"We did everything we thought we could do except win the gold medal," Prado said. "In a one-game championship setup, anything can happen."

The Pro Side

USA Baseball assembled another professional team in 2002, this time a group of independent leaguers who represented the U.S. at the America Series, a Pan American Games qualifying tournament in Mexico in October. The club, managed by indy league manager Marty Scott (Fort Worth/Central League), needed only to finish in the top nine at the 12-team Americas Series, in order to qualify the United States for the 2003 Pan American Games in the Dominican Republic.

Scott's team accomplished that goal by going 4-1 in the preliminary round-robin phase. It lost all three games in the next phase, which determined seedings for the medal round. But as a No. 7 seed the U.S. defeated Nicaragua and Panama to reach the gold-medal game, where it lost to unbeaten Cuba, 6-1. Righthander Maels Rodriguez pitched a five-hitter and struck out 13 to stymie the U.S., which went 6-5 overall. Cuba went 10-0.

Team USA hit only .238 overall, with part-time outfielder Dave Callahan from the Northern League's New Jersey Jackals leading the squad at .368. Even though he was the loser in the gold-medal game, righthander Tim Kester (2-1, 2.45) from the Atlantic League's Pennsylvania Road Warriors was the U.S. team's best pitcher.

The biggest news of the tournament focused on the defection of Cuban ace righthander Jose Contreras. A seven-year veteran of the island's powerful national team, Contreras—who turned 31 on Dec. 12—had a lifetime record of 117-50, 2.82 in Cuban league play. In 2002, he won 13 of 17 decisions with a league-best 1.76 ERA.

A 6-foot-4, 224-pound righthander with a 93-mph fastball and a darting forkball, Contreras is best known for the eight shutout innings he pitched against the Orioles during a nationally televised exhibition game in Havana in 1999. In that game, Contreras allowed just two hits and struck out 10, including Albert Belle twice.

The U.S. chose not to send a team to the major international competition of the year, the Intercontinental Cup, played in Cuba in November.

A year earlier, in November 2001, USA Baseball assembled a relatively strong professional team—using players

PATTY ORTIN

Jose Contreras

It was a big year in 2002 for the Golden Spikes Award, which USA Baseball presents annually to the nation's top amateur player. The 25th anniversary of the award was celebrated with an all-time Golden Spikes team.

Clemson senior shortstop Khalil Greene lapped the competition. He became the first Clemson player to win the award, which is sponsored by the Major League Baseball Players Association.

Khalil Greene

Greene, a native of Key West, Fla., set numerous Tigers and Atlantic Coast Conference records in his senior season. He led the Tigers to a third-place finish at the College World Series by hitting .470 with a school-record 27 homers and 91 RBIs. The Tigers' everyday shortstop became just the second NCAA player to collect 400 hits, as he finished with 403, and broke the NCAA career doubles' record with his 95th against South Carolina on June 21. He also started 269 consecutive games at Clemson, and had a 34-game hitting streak down the stretch.

"I wanted to go out and play every game as hard as I could this season, with it being my last year in college," said Greene, whom the Padres drafted 13th overall in June. "To be able to look back on the year and know that I was named the best amateur player as the Golden Spikes Award winner, it's just a very special honor."

–JOHN MANUEL

PREVIOUS **WINNERS**

1981—Mike Sodders, 3b, Arizona State	
1982—Jeff Ledbetter, of-lhp, Florida State	
1983—Dave Magadan, 1b, Alabama	
1984—Oddibe McDowell, of, Arizona State	
1985—Pete Incaviglia, of, Oklahoma State	
1986—Casey Close, of, Michigan	
1987—Robin Ventura, 3b, Oklahoma State	
1988—John Olerud, 1b-lhp, Washington State	
1989—Ben McDonald, rhp, Louisiana State	
1990—Mike Kelly, of, Arizona State	
1991—David McCarty, 1b, Stanford	
1992—Phil Nevin, 3b, Cal State Fullerton	
1993—Brooks Kieschnick, dh-rhp, Texas	
1994—Jason Varitek, c, Georgia Tech	
1995—Todd Helton, 1b-lhp, Tennessee	
1996—Kris Benson, rhp, Clemson	
1997—J.D. Drew, of, Florida State	
1998—Jeff Austin, rhp, Stanford	
1999—Jason Jennings, rhp, Baylor	
2000—Kip Bouknight, rhp, South Carolina	
2001—Mark Prior, rhp, Southern California	

from affiliated minor league clubs—for the 34th World Cup in Taiwan. The team, managed by Terry Francona, featured prospects such as second baseman Orlando Hudson (Blue Jays), outfielder Carl Crawford (Devil Rays) and outfielder Joe Borchard (White Sox), but relied mostly on lower-profile pitchers.

The team performed well, reaching the championship game before losing to Cuba 5-3 and settling for the silver medal. It was Cuba's seventh straight title and the 23rd time it has won the World Cup since 1952.

Bronze Extends Juniors' Streak

Cuba also exhibited its international supremacy at the junior (18-and-under) level by winning the 2002 World Junior Championship in Sherbrooke, Quebec. It beat Taiwan in the final, 9-6.

Taiwan upset Team USA in the semifinals, but the U.S. extended its World Junior medal streak to 20 when it overcame a one-run deficit with 10 runs in the eighth inning to beat Canada 12-3 in the bronze-medal match.

Canada scored twice in the top of eighth to take a 3-2 lead as Orioles' unsigned first-round pick Adam Loewen hit an RBI triple and scored on a single by Mets' draft pick Shawn Bowman. The U.S. quickly answered back, sending 14 players to the plate in the bottom of the inning, with home runs from outfielders Delmon Young (Camarillo, Calif.) and Chris Lubanski (Schwenksville, Pa.) the highlights.

Team USA's bid for a gold medal fell short when Taiwan upset the Americans, the only undefeated team in pool play, 4-3 in the semifinals. Taiwan defeated ace

SUMMER PLAYER OF THE YEAR

Sophomore righthander Brad Sullivan had a tough act to follow when he went 13-1 with a 1.82 ERA for Houston, handed national champion Texas its last loss of the 2002 college season and earned first-team All-America honors. But he may have outdone himself with Team USA during the summer.

The 6-foot Sullivan went 7-0 with a 0.72 ERA, just missing Dewon Brazelton's Team USA record for lowest ERA. He beat Japan twice to help the Americans win the two nations' annual series in five games, then beat the Japanese again to clinch a medal for Team USA in the World University Championship in Italy. In the process, he became the latest Team USA player to earn recognition as Baseball America's summer league Player of the Year.

Using a 90-92 mph fastball, plus slider and improved curveball and changeup, he allowed just 27 hits in 50 innings, striking out 50 and walking 15. Sullivan even outperfomed Wake Forest righthander Kyle Sleeth, the top-rated college pitcher for the 2003 draft.

"It's hard to say if I could have done any better than that," Sullivan said matter-of-factly. "I had help from the defense, and the camaraderie on the team and with the other pitchers was great. I was always getting pointers."

The 6-foot-5 Sleeth went 7-1 with a 1.44 ERA, his lone loss coming in the gold medal game of the inaugural World University

Brad Sullivan

championship. Sullivan, also a projected first-rounder, thought his stuff compared favorably to Sleeth's.

"My slider might be a tad better, but his fastball is a tad better," Sullivan said. "He's got that leverage because of his height (6-foot-5), but we both throw similar other pitches, so in a lot of ways we're kind of carbon copies of each other."

Sullivan saved his best for last when he beat powerful Japan in the semifinals in Italy. He compared the experience to beating Texas in an NCAA regional game.

"In the super-regional, there were 8,000 fans rooting against me," he said. "Just playing in that game was something I wanted to do so bad—our team was on the brink of the College World Series, and I had to produce.

"In the semifinal in Italy, it was a little different as far as the fans go. But I knew if I won, we were guaranteed a medal. I wanted the ball in that situation and wanted to get the ball to Kyle."

Unfortunately, Sleeth faltered against Cuba, losing 6-0.

Sullivan never faltered, and that gave him the edge on Sleeth in his selection as Baseball America's Summer Player of the Year.

—JOHN MANUEL

PREVIOUS WINNERS

1984	Will Clark, 1b, Team USA
	Rafael Palmeiro, of, Hutchinson (Jayhawk)
1985	Jeff King, 3b, Team USA
	Bob Zupcic, of, Liberal (Jayhawk)
1986	Jack Armstrong, rhp, Wareham (Cape Cod)
	Mike Harkey, rhp, Fairbanks (Alaska)
1987	Cris Carpenter, rhp, Team USA
1988	Robin Ventura, 3b, Team USA
	Ty Griffin, 2b, Team USA
1989	John Olerud, 1b-lhp, Palouse Empire (Alaska)
1990	Calvin Murray, of, Anchorage Bucs (Alaska)
1991	Chris Roberts, of, Team USA
1992	Jeffrey Hammonds, of, Team USA
1993	Geoff Jenkins, of, Team USA
1994	Steve Carver, 1b, Anch. Glacier Pilots (Alaska)
1995	Travis Lee, 1b, Team USA
1996	Seth Greisinger, rhp, Team USA
1997	Pat Burrell, 3b, Team USA
1998	Bobby Kielty, of, Bourne (Cape Cod)
1999	Xavier Nady, 3b, Team USA
2000	Mark Teixeira, 3b, Team USA
2001	Bobby Brownlie, rhp, Team USA

SUMMER LEAGUE ALL-AMERICA TEAM

Selected by Baseball America

FIRST TEAM

Player	Club/League	College	AVG	AB	H	HR	RBI	SB
C Landon Powell	Team USA	South Carolina	.263	95	25	3	17	0
1B Michael Aubrey	Team USA	Tulane	.405	111	45	6	26	0
2B Eric Patterson	Team USA	Georgia Tech	.333	105	35	0	13	17
3B Brian Snyder	Cotuit (Cape Cod)	Stetson	.294	153	45	4	21	15
SS Brian Bixler	Delaware (Great Lakes)	Eastern Michigan	.389	144	56	4	19	7
OF Carlos Quentin	Team USA	Stanford	.313	96	30	3	20	3
OF Peter Stonard	Cotuit (Cape Cod)	Alabama	.348	161	56	2	27	18
OF Mike Wagner	North Adams (New England)	Washington	.342	146	50	5	22	13
DH Wes Whisler	Yar.-Dennis (Cape Cod)	UCLA	.309	123	38	6	16	1

Player	Club/League	College	W	L	ERA	IP	H	BB	SO
SP David Purcey	Anch. Glacier Pilots	Oklahoma	2	1	1.08	50	22	26	69
SP Kyle Sleeth	Team USA	Wake Forest	7	1	1.44	56	36	16	56
SP Brad Sullivan	Team USA	Houston	7	0	0.72	50	27	15	50
SP Jered Weaver	Anchorage Bucs	Long Beach State	5	1	1.11	65	35	21	73
RP David Aardsma	Falmouth (Cape Cod)	Rice	3	0	0.68	27	7	5	45
RP Chad Cordero	Team USA	Cal State Fullerton	0	1	0.00	17	8	4	29

SECOND TEAM

C—Chris Westervelt, New Market/Valley (Stetson). **1B**—Matt Anderson, Alexandria/Northwoods (UC Irvine). **2B**—Joe Honce, Covington/Valley (West Virginia Wesleyan). **3B**—Dusty Bensko, Springfield/Central Illinois (Illinois). **SS**—Blake Gill, Mat-Su, Goldpanners/Alaska (Louisiana State). **OF**—Adam Bourassa, Yarmouth-Dennis/Cape Cod (Wake Forest); Jeff Frazier, Danbury/New England (Rutgers); Mike Reese, Wilson/Coastal Plain (Rollins, Fla.). **DH**—Eric Rodland, Athletes In Action/Alaska (Gonzaga). **SP**—Chris Coughlin, Wilmington/Coastal Plain (UNC Wilmington); Aaron Marsden, Brainerd/Northwoods (Nebraska); Brian Rogers, Orleans/Cape Cod (Georgia Southern); Tim Stauffer, Chatham/Cape Cod (Richmond). **RP**—Ryan Schroyer, Goldpanners/Alaska (Arizona State); Huston Street, Team USA (Texas).

YOUTH PLAYER OF THE YEAR

Delmon Young was just five years old when his older brother Dmitri was drafted out of Rio Mesa High in Oxnard, Calif., by the Cardinals with the fourth overall pick in 1991. He was too young to remember, or understand the significance of it at the time. But 11 years later Delmon entered his senior season at Camarillo (Calif.) High with scouts raving about him the same way they were about Dmitri.

Coming off a torrid 2002 season in which he earned All-America honors and set a Team USA junior national team home run record, Delmon Young was selected Baseball America's first Youth Player of the Year.

After hitting .542-17-56 during the spring at Camarillo High, Young had an even more productive summer. He launched three key home runs in helping his team to the championship at USA

Delmon Young: Top youth player

Baseball's Tournament of Stars in Joplin, Mo. From there, he continued to show a knack for delivering the big hits by leading Team USA to a bronze medal at the World Junior Championship in Sherbrooke, Quebec, something that can be attributed to his maturity, according to U.S. coach Edgar Soto.

"He plays like a player much older than he is. He played the game the way it is supposed to be played," said Soto, the coach at Pima (Ariz.) Community College. "Every at-bat is a quality at-

bat. A lot of younger players give away a lot of at-bats, but he doesn't give an inch."

Young finished the summer with a team-high 16 homers and 49 RBIs, while tying Lastings Milledge with a .474 average.

"He has incredible power," Soto said. "I haven't seen anything like it. I have been with Team USA for three years and he's on another level and he was the youngest player there."

While Delmon spends a lot of time talking about the game with his big league brother, he also puts in a lot of hard work on his own.

"With Dmitri, we mostly talk about staying focused," Young said. "If it's too hot, if you're hurt, but not injured, or if you're tired, you still have to give it your all. You have the rest of the day to recover. Just suck it up for those three hours."

When Young isn't talking shop with Dmitri or running sprints or spending time in the cage working on his hitting, he spends a lot of time studying the swing mechanics of major leaguers like Alex Rodriguez, Manny Ramirez and Larry Walker.

"I try to take things from all of them and put them into my swing," Young said. "Change a little here and a little there. They are all balanced and I have a leg kick like them. I look at when they get ready and how they attack the ball."

–JOSH BOYD

righthander Jeff Allison (Peabody, Mass.), the top-ranked high school pitcher for the 2003 draft, while an American offense that hit .406 and scored in double digits in almost every game in the tournament was held in check by three Taiwan pitchers.

In the gold-medal game, tournament MVP Juan Linares slugged two home runs for Cuba and outfielder Ronnier Mustelier added another as the Cubans claimed their 10th championship since 1984 but their first since 1997. The Cubans finished the 12-nation tournament with a 7-1 record, losing only to host Canada in a pool-play game.

No player dominated the 18-and-under competition more than Young, a top prospect for the 2003 draft. He was named the event's MVP after slamming nine home runs in eight games. He also hit .513 with 18 RBIs. His nine homers shattered the previous Team USA tournament record of three.

Young, a rising senior at Camarillo (Calif.) High, was joined on the all-tournament team by first baseman Ian Stewart (Huntington Beach, Calif.) and outfielder Lastings Milledge (St. Petersburg, Fla.). Loewen, the fourth overall pick in the 2002 draft (as a pitcher), was one of two Canadian players named to the all-tournament team. He went 11-for-15 with 10 walks, but did not pitch in the tournament at the request of the Orioles.

The American squad was selected from players who participated in the Tournament of Stars in Joplin, Mo., in June. The talent-laden team included several players who are expected to be first-round picks in 2003, including Milledge and Young.

Team USA played 29 games on the summer. It played a series of exhibition games around the Joplin area before the team reconvened in Canada for two weeks prior to the start of the World Championship. Overall, Team USA went 25-4.

Youth Settles For Silver

Cuba continued its dominance on the international stage in 2002 by beating Team USA 3-1 at the COPABE Pan American Youth championship in Venezuela in September. The 16-and-under competition served as a qualifier for the 2003 World Youth Championship, with the top three teams advancing.

Team USA, the two-time defending World youth champion, had its 26-game international winning streak snapped during the tournament by losing twice. The silver medal was the youth program's fourth medal in five years of international competition.

Shortstop/righthander Matt Bush (San Diego) was the top player for Team USA, hitting .385 while working a team-high 14 innings.

SUMMER LEAGUES

BY JOHN MANUEL

Cotuit started the 2002 Cape Cod League season getting all the fanfare. That happens when a team sets a league record with 12 consecutive victories to open the season.

But in the end, all the attention was directed at Wareham, which eliminated Cotuit in the semifinals and swept rival Orleans in the league's best-of-three championship series to become the first team to repeat as Cape Cod champions since Yarmouth-Dennis in 1989-90.

In the deciding game against Orleans, Wareham rallied from a 2-1 deficit going into the ninth against Orleans closer Whitley Benson (North Carolina), who had 11 saves and a 1.37 ERA during the regular season. The Gatemen had two outs and none on before four consecutive batters reached safely, resulting in a 3-2 win.

Matt Kutler (Brown), one of just six regulars to hit .300 or better during the regular season, delivered the game-winning hit, a shot off the left-center field wall. Kutler had eight RBIs in five playoff games.

The Cape, considered the nation's premier summer collegiate league, made plenty of history during the 2002 season. Cotuit, under first-year head coach Garrett Quinn (St. Thomas, Fla.), got things rolling with its record winning streak. Win No. 12 came on a combined no-hitter by lefthander Joe Little (Arizona) and relievers Jarred Stuart (Maryland), Kevin Ool (Marist) and Josh Banks (Florida International) in a 9-1 victory against Chatham.

Another Cotuit milestone came July 23 in a 6-3 victory against Hyannis, as catcher Steven Ghutzman (a transfer from Wake Forest to Nevada-Las Vegas) homered from both sides of the plate. That had not happened in the Cape League during its wood bat era. Ghutzman provided two of 12 homers hit that day, another league record.

Other Cape notables:

■ Orleans righthander Brian Rogers (Georgia Southern) was selected the league's pitcher of the year after he didn't allow an earned run in his first 32 innings en route to a 4-0, 0.40 season.

■ Yarmouth-Dennis charged into the playoffs behind the league's No. 1 prospect, first baseman/lefthander Wes Whisler (UCLA). The sweet-swinging two-way talent focused almost solely on hitting and had a streak of nine consecutive hits (breaking a league mark set in 1979), homering four times in his first 56 at-bats and finishing up at .309-6-16.

Wes Whisler: Cape Cod's No. 1 prospect

Goldpanners had beaten the Pilots for the NBC title. They also did so in 1972 and 1976.

Shortstop Blake Gill (Louisiana State) earned the tournament MVP award by going 4-for-4 in the championship game and 11-for-27 overall as the Goldpanners went 7-1 in the 48-team NBC field.

The Goldpanners and Glacier Pilots tied for the Alaska League regular-season crown, but the Pilots upended the Panners in the league's season-ending tournament.

It was a year of repeat champions in some of the nation's other traditional summer leagues:

■ New Jersey won its second consecutive Atlantic Collegiate League title and third in four years by defeating the Metro Cadets 4-1 in a one-game playoff. Colts reliever Steve Bucchignano (Kean, N.J.) earned a save in the title game for the second straight year.

■ Arlington continued its domination of the Clark Griffith League and the All-American Amateur Baseball Association. The Senators won the CGL for the fifth consecutive season, tying the regular-season mark for victories while becoming the third team since 1993 to win both halves of the regular season. Arlington then returned to Johnstown, Pa., and won its fourth AAABA title in five years behind tournament MVP Wyatt Toregas (Virginia Tech), who went 14-for-23 in the tournament with 13 RBIs in six games.

■ Northern Ohio won its third consecutive Great Lakes League championship under coach Guido Aspeitia, beating Columbus 6-3 in the tournament title game.

■ Newport successfully defended its New England Collegiate League crown, sweeping Keene, which had the league's top regular-season record, in a best-of-three final. The Gulls won the clincher 3-2 on an eighth-inning home run by first baseman Vito Chiaravalloti (Richmond), the playoff MVP.

Cheff Is Chief At NBC

Lewis-Clark State (Idaho) coach Ed Cheff, who won his 12th national championship at the NAIA level in June, won another national title two months later with the Alaska Goldpanners. Cheff took over the reigns of the storied Fairbanks-based club in 2002 and led it to a record sixth National Baseball Congress World Series championship, and first since 1980.

Blake Gill

The Goldpanners defeated their arch rivals, the Anchorage Glacier Pilots, 8-3 in the final at Wichita's Lawrence-Dumont Stadium. It marked the third time the

C O L L E G E
SUMMER LEAGUES

NCAA-CERTIFIED

ATLANTIC COLLEGIATE LEAGUE

WOLFF	W	L	PCT	GB
Quakertown Blazers	30	10	.750	—
Delaware Valley Gulls	23	17	.575	7
Jersey Pilots	14	26	.350	16
Scranton Red Soxx	12	28	.300	18

KAISER	W	L	PCT	GB
New Jersey Colts	26	14	.650	—
Metro New York Cadets	20	20	.500	6
Long Island Collegians	19	21	.475	7
New York Generals	16	24	.400	10

PLAYOFFS: Semifinals—New Jersey defeated Delaware Valley and Metro New York defeated Quakertown in one-game series. **Finals**—New Jersey defeated Metro New York on one-game series.

TOP 10 PROSPECTS: 1. Matt Powell, rhp, Quakertown (Temple). **2.** Tommy Boss, rhp, New Jersey (Florida). **3.** Joe Martinez, rhp, Jersey (Boston College). **4.** Dan McKenna, rhp, Delaware Valley (Rutgers-Camden). **5.** Sean Kramer, lhp, New York (Iona). **6.** Carl Loadenthal, of, Quakertown (Rider). **7.** Wes Swackhamer, of, New Jersey (Florida). **8.** Rich Graham, inf, Long Island (Stony Brook). **9.** P.J. Antoniato, inf, Metro New York (Briarcliffe, N.Y., JC). **10.** Steve Echevarria, of, New Jersey (Brookdale, N.J., CC).
Most Valuable Player: Carl Loadenthal, Quakertown (Rider). **Outstanding Pitcher:** Matt Powell, Quakertown (Temple).

INDIVIDUAL BATTING LEADERS
(Minimum 100 Plate Appearances)

	AVG	AB	R	H	2B	3B	HR	RBI	SB
Echevarria, Steve, NJ	.387	119	27	46	5	2	1	29	19
Loadenthal, Carl, Quakertown	.381	139	37	53	10	9	2	25	18
Antoniato, P.J., Metro NY	.357	143	17	51	9	1	0	10	6
Long, Casey, Quakertown	.314	140	30	44	9	2	4	32	3
Goldblatt, Mike, Del. Valley	.314	121	20	38	8	0	0	16	7
O'Brien, Kevin, New York	.313	99	19	31	4	0	0	16	3
Badger, Greg, NJ	.312	109	23	34	1	0	0	15	23
Jones, Kyle, Quakertown	.312	138	27	43	12	0	5	26	0
Cruz, Carlos, Metro NY	.312	93	13	29	4	0	0	16	11
Stezenko, John, Quakertown	.306	147	26	45	7	1	0	13	16
Novalis, Jesse, Quakertown	.303	132	26	40	12	0	4	32	4
Volosin, Jon, Metro NY	.303	119	20	36	4	0	0	9	12
Sandora, Rob, Long Island	.300	110	13	33	4	1	0	12	1
Moffie, Nate, Del. Valley	.295	132	24	39	5	1	2	25	17
Ziolkowski, Bobby, LI	.295	112	11	33	5	1	1	19	2

INDIVIDUAL PITCHING LEADERS
(Minimum 30 innings)

	W	L	ERA	G	SV	IP	H	BB	SO
Rambo, Scott, Del. Valley	3	1	1.15	9	0	39	29	10	35
Powell, Matt, Quakertown	6	0	1.44	12	1	50	25	12	41
Kennedy, Ryan, NJ	3	2	1.47	9	0	37	26	9	24
Grass, Nick, Long Island	6	1	1.57	10	1	52	39	23	43
Haack, Keith, Metro NY	4	4	1.67	8	0	54	41	13	49
Palmieri, Andrew, NJ	3	1	1.72	11	0	37	22	11	22
Paolillo, Andrew, Metro NY	3	3	1.97	7	0	50	43	16	43
Gentekos, Dan, Del. Valley	5	1	2.39	9	0	38	40	9	22
Lane, Josh, New Jersey	5	1	2.53	11	1	43	33	10	33
McKitish, Biran, Quakertown	7	0	2.57	10	0	35	23	10	29

CAPE COD LEAGUE

EAST	W	L	T	PCT	PTS
Orleans Cardinals	29	13	2	.682	60
Yarmouth-Dennis Red Sox	21	20	3	.511	45
Brewster Whitecaps	20	20	4	.500	44
Harwich Mariners	21	23	0	.477	42
Chatham A's	19	23	2	.455	40

WEST	W	L	T		PTS
Cotuit Kettleers	23	16	6	.580	51
Wareham Gatemen	23	21	0	.523	46
Falmouth Commodores	20	21	3	.489	43
Bourne Braves	16	24	4	.409	36
Hyannis Mets	15	26	3	.375	33

PLAYOFFS—Semifinals: Wareham defeated Cotuit 2-1 and Orleans defeated Yarmouth-Dennis 2-1 in best-of-3 series. **Final:** Wareham defeated Orleans 2-0 in best-of-3 series.

Tim Stauffer: No. 2-ranked prospect on Cape Cod

ALL-STAR TEAM: C—Ryan Hanigan, Orleans (Rollins, Fla.). **1B**—Wes Whisler, Yarmouth-Dennis (UCLA). **2B**—Chris Snavely, Harwich (Ohio State). **3B**—Brian Snyder, Cotuit (Stetson). **SS**—Trey Webb, Bourne (Baylor). **IF**—Brett Cooley, Yarmouth-Dennis (Houston). **OF**—Adam Bourassa, Yarmouth-Dennis (Wake Forest); Anthony Gwynn, Brewster (San Diego State); David Murphy, Wareham (Baylor); Danny Putnam, Hyannis (Stanford); Peter Stonard, Cotuit (Alabama). **DH**—Vasili Spanos, Falmouth (Indiana). **SP**—Brian Rogers, Orleans (Georgia Southern); David Sanders, Wareham (Wichita State); Taylor Tankersley, Brewster (Alabama). **RP**—David Aardsma, Falmouth (Rice); Zane Carlson, Chatham (Baylor); Shaun Marcum, Harwich (Southwest Missouri State).
Most Valuable Player: Peter Stonard, Cotuit. **Outstanding Pitcher:** Brian Rogers, Orleans.
TOP 20 PROSPECTS: 1. Wes Whisler, 1b, Yarmouth-Dennis (UCLA). **2.** Tim Stauffer, rhp, Chatham (Richmond). **3.** Matt Murton, of, Wareham (Georgia Tech). **4.** David Aardsma, rhp, Falmouth (Rice). **5.** Matt Brown, rhp, Bourne (California). **6.** Ben Harrison, of, Hyannis (Florida). **7.** Chris Ray, rhp, Bourne (William & Mary). **8.** Brian Snyder, 3b, Cotuit (Stetson). **9.** Peter Stonard, 2b-of, Cotuit (Alabama). **10.** Jeremy Sowers, lhp, Wareham (Vanderbilt). **11.** Lee Mitchell, 3b, Cotuit (Georgia). **12.** Anthony Gwynn, of, Brewster (San Diego State). **13.** Rodney Allen, of, Orleans (Arizona State). **14.** Jeremy Slayden, of, Falmouth (Georgia Tech). **15.** Scott Baker, rhp, Orleans (Oklahoma State). **16.** Frazer Dizard, rhp, Chatham (Southern California). **17.** Nick Touchstone, lhp, Wareham (Okaloosa-Walton, Fla., JC). **18.** Robbie Van, lhp, Orleans (Nevada-Las Vegas). **19.** Gary Bakker, rhp, Cotuit (North Carolina). **20.** Daniel Moore, lhp, Chatham (North Carolina).

INDIVIDUAL BATTING LEADERS
(Minimum 118 Plate Appearances)

	AVG	AB	R	H	2B	3B	HR	RBI	SB
Stonard, Pete, Cotuit	.348	161	23	56	3	1	2	27	18
Bourassa, Adam, Y-D	.323	155	21	50	3	1	0	8	18
Tingler, Jayce, Brewster	.311	151	32	47	6	0	0	12	12
Whisler, Wes, Y-D	.309	123	19	38	7	0	6	16	1
Murphy, David, Wareham	.304	158	17	48	10	2	1	18	7
Kutler, Matt, Wareham	.301	143	12	43	9	1	2	15	1
Harrison, Ben, Hyannis	.295	122	16	36	6	1	3	12	10
Coffey, David, Orleans	.295	139	20	41	4	0	6	20	7

WALSH

AMATEUR BASEBALL

	AVG	AB	R	H	2B	3B	HR	RBI	SB
Snyder, Brian, Cotuit	.294	153	19	45	9	0	4	21	15
Hanigan, Ryan, Orleans	.292	120	13	35	3	1	0	8	7

INDIVIDUAL PITCHING LEADERS
(Minimum 35 Innings)

	W	L	ERA	G	SV	IP	H	BB	SO
Rogers, Brian, Orleans	4	0	0.40	8	0	45	22	7	53
Sanders, David, Wareham	4	3	0.73	9	1	62	36	8	51
Van, Robbie, Y-D/Orleans	3	2	1.01	19	3	36	19	14	48
Hudgins, John, Y-D	3	1	1.03	10	3	35	16	15	45
Brown, Matt, Bourne	3	3	1.20	8	0	52	36	11	59
Hahn, Cory, Hyannis	3	3	1.30	11	0	55	35	26	53
Misch, Pat, Falmouth	3	3	1.34	8	0	54	32	15	57
Tankersley, Taylor, Brewster	6	1	1.41	9	0	51	44	15	45
Elia, Frank, Orleans	1	0	1.51	12	0	36	24	16	21
Sowers, Jeremy, Wareham	5	4	1.52	9	0	65	49	12	56

BOURNE

BATTING	AVG	AB	R	H	2B	3B	HR	RBI	SB
Bubela, Dane, of	.240	121	10	29	8	1	1	10	0
Castillo, David, c	.197	117	9	23	8	0	0	11	1
Cliburn, Dustin, 1b	.159	126	13	20	5	0	0	2	1
Dorr, Jayme, 2b	.220	41	2	9	0	0	1	3	0
2-team (5 Wareham)	.245	53	4	13	1	0	1	3	1
Frank, Kyle, of	.188	112	12	21	5	0	0	10	2
Italiano, Nick, 2b	.247	89	6	22	2	0	0	3	1
Layden, Tim, of-p	.333	6	0	2	0	0	0	1	0
Lipman, Brian, of-3b	.127	142	4	18	2	0	2	15	0
Lombardi, Michael, c	.178	45	3	8	2	0	0	3	0
2-team (10 Hyannis)	.191	68	6	13	4	0	0	5	0
McEvoy, Matt, of	.136	22	1	3	0	0	0	1	0
Morgan, Ryan, 3b	.167	138	16	23	5	0	2	11	2
Paganetti, Billy, 1b-of	.116	69	1	8	2	0	0	6	0
Picard, Alain, c	.118	17	2	2	2	0	0	0	0
Smithlin, Zachary, of	.216	125	8	27	3	0	0	5	5
Tolbert, Matt, 2b	.125	56	2	7	3	0	0	1	0
Webb, Trey, ss	.222	185	17	41	9	0	0	6	6

PITCHING	W	L	ERA	G	SV	IP	H	BB	SO
Alleva, Jeff	1	1	1.17	13	0	31	23	9	16
Brown, Matt	3	3	1.20	8	0	52	36	11	59
Darcy, Ryan	2	1	3.96	14	1	36	40	11	34
Durkin, Matt	1	3	4.13	6	0	33	26	20	38
Howell, J.P.	0	2	3.16	7	0	26	24	15	25
Laganiere, Rich	0	0	27.00	1	0	0	1	2	0
Layden, Tim	0	0	0.00	1	0	1	0	2	0
Malott, Mike	2	2	3.64	10	0	30	33	11	22
Morgan, Ryan	0	1	3.68	6	0	7	12	5	8
Ray, Chris	2	1	1.93	20	10	28	15	5	38
Rowe, Ben	1	4	3.23	15	1	47	53	11	35
Schmidt, Kyle	1	4	3.48	7	0	41	26	24	41
Theodorakos, Jared	1	3	3.09	6	0	32	25	15	35
Thorp, Paul	1	0	0.00	2	0	15	10	2	10
Toffey, John	0	1	6.35	11	0	17	17	8	9

BREWSTER

BATTING	AVG	AB	R	H	2B	3B	HR	RBI	SB
Aviles, Mike, ss	.168	101	12	17	2	1	1	4	1
Burrill, Brady, c	.257	109	9	28	5	0	0	14	0
Davis, Brad, c	.159	82	7	13	1	0	0	3	0
Dickerson, Chris, of	.132	76	6	10	1	1	1	9	2
Gwynn, Anthony, of	.291	165	20	48	5	1	0	14	11
Macaluso, Paul, of	.241	83	10	20	5	1	0	10	1
Maloney, Pat, 1b-of	.204	152	15	31	7	2	3	22	4
Obrey, Kainoa, dh-3b	.244	135	11	33	3	0	2	16	0
Scioletti, Brad, 2b	.193	88	11	17	1	2	1	7	1
3-team (Orl 1, 3 Y-D)	.196	102	11	20	1	2	1	7	1
Tingler, Jayce, of	.311	151	32	47	6	0	0	12	12
Tugwell, Marc, 2b-ss	.188	101	10	19	2	0	1	8	0
Wakefield, Trey, 3b	.222	135	14	30	4	0	3	16	0
Wennersten, Lucas, dh-1b	.212	66	5	14	4	0	0	5	0

PITCHING	W	L	ERA	G	SV	IP	H	BB	SO
Borsa, B.J.	1	0	5.63	0	3	8	9	2	7
Collar, Mike	1	2	4.32	14	0	25	32	9	26
Gale, Bryan	2	1	1.82	16	2	25	19	8	24
Hill, Seth	1	1	2.36	8	0	27	21	7	20
Huguet, George	0	3	2.08	18	11	22	12	10	18
James, Justin	1	1	4.33	11	0	35	36	10	21
Jones, Brian	0	0	2.78	11	2	23	20	9	21
Kamrach, Jeff	2	5	3.78	10	0	64	57	26	50
McGirr, Mike	0	0	2.25	2	0	4	5	0	4
Roberts, Mark	0	1	1.93	2	0	14	10	3	13
Sawicki, Bobby	2	4	3.96	9	0	50	53	10	25
Tankersley, Taylor	6	1	1.41	9	0	51	44	15	45
White, Sean	4	1	2.14	7	0	46	38	14	38

CHATHAM

BATTING	AVG	AB	R	H	2B	3B	HR	RBI	SB
Cleveland, Jeremy, 1b	.250	164	14	41	9	0	2	12	0
D'Antona, Jamie, 3b	.235	153	19	36	8	0	5	19	0
Hanan, Blake, 2b	.176	68	5	12	1	0	0	3	1
Himes, Ben, of	.192	26	0	5	0	0	0	3	0
Hubbard, Ryan, of	.000	3	1	0	0	0	0	0	1
Ianetta, Chris, c-dh	.222	108	7	24	3	0	2	9	0
Johnson, Ryan, of	.200	120	15	24	6	1	3	10	1
Layden, Tim, of-p	.159	82	4	13	3	0	1	6	1
2-team (4 Bourne)	.170	88	4	15	3	0	1	7	1
LeFaivre, Steve, of	.229	140	16	32	5	0	5	14	2
Moon, Michael, 2b-3b	.263	152	21	40	11	2	2	14	4
Morton, Colt, c-dh	.187	123	12	23	5	0	6	18	0
Orvella, Chad, ss	.173	156	12	27	4	0	0	4	4
Udvarhelyi, Travis, of	.140	50	3	7	1	0	0	1	0
Williams, Simon, of	.184	87	8	16	3	0	1	9	4

PITCHING	W	L	ERA	G	SV	IP	H	BB	SO
Carlson, Zane	2	2	3.13	23	12	23	16	11	36
Condon, Greg	1	2	4.91	9	0	22	27	12	21
Dizard, Frazer	2	1	1.59	6	0	28	24	14	37
Everson, Eric	0	0	4.10	15	1	26	19	18	29
Gramolini, Dennis	0	0	4.50	2	0	3	0	6	7
Hindman, Scott	2	1	3.21	5	0	14	9	9	12
McDonald, Mike	1	2	5.14	4	0	21	23	7	20
Moore, Daniel	2	5	3.50	10	0	54	45	21	51
Pauly, Thomas	4	0	3.26	14	0	47	36	11	47
Shea, Chris	0	0	7.36	2	0	4	4	5	7
Stauffer, Tim	3	2	2.59	9	0	63	50	17	67
Trolia, Aaron	1	5	3.95	9	0	41	39	31	34
Yates, Adam	3	2	2.85	21	2	41	35	12	39

COTUIT

BATTING	AVG	AB	R	H	2B	3B	HR	RBI	SB
Anderson, Brian, of	.245	49	10	12	3	0	3	7	1
Braun, Ryan, of	.318	66	16	21	1	1	2	6	1
DiLiberto, Bobby, 3b	.000	13	0	0	0	0	0	0	0
Ghutzman, Stephen, c-of	.256	121	15	31	3	1	4	17	1
Giarratano, Anthony, ss	.187	150	16	28	5	0	0	10	5
Haar, Jordan, of	.200	5	1	1	0	0	0	0	1
Higashi, John, c	.235	17	3	4	0	0	0	0	1
Ingram, Brian, 2b	.261	142	32	37	1	5	0	19	14
Lytle, Chaz, or	.259	27	5	7	1	0	0	2	3
McQuade, Tony, of	.204	98	12	20	5	1	0	7	3
Mitchell, Lee, 3b-dh	.244	127	16	31	4	1	6	23	1
Nielsen, Eric, of	.118	17	0	2	1	0	0	1	0
Pyzik, Steve, c	.158	57	6	9	1	0	0	4	0
Quintanilla, Omar, 3b-2b	.268	82	12	22	2	0	1	8	2
Richie, Tony, dh-of	.235	51	4	12	4	0	0	6	0
Snyder, Brian, 3b-of	.294	153	19	45	9	0	4	21	15
Stonard, Pete, of-2b	.348	161	23	56	3	1	2	27	18
Zenchyk, Bryan, 1b	.160	144	11	23	5	0	2	15	1

PITCHING	W	L	ERA	G	SV	IP	H	BB	SO
Bakker, Garry	4	1	3.61	7	0	42	37	13	36
Banks, Josh	4	1	2.05	9	0	44	35	14	48
Braun, Ryan	2	2	1.53	8	0	29	18	16	32
Espineli, Eugene	0	0	0.89	11	1	20	10	6	15
Hanson, Adam	1	1	1.82	21	7	35	27	14	36
Jordan, Brantley	0	2	10.50	5	0	12	21	7	8
LaMacchia, Marc	3	0	1.29	7	0	28	18	12	30
Little, Joe	2	4	4.37	7	0	35	31	15	35
Ool, Kevin	1	0	2.90	22	3	40	37	9	33
Pillsbury, Chris	1	5	2.64	8	0	44	38	13	41
Stetter, Mitch	1	0	1.53	6	1	18	7	7	17
Stuart, Jarred	0	0	0.00	4	0	4	1	1	3
Touchet, Dan	4	2	3.35	8	0	46	49	9	27

FALMOUTH

BATTING	AVG	AB	R	H	2B	3B	HR	RBI	SB
Davis, Austin, of	.138	29	2	4	1	0	0	2	0
DeMartino, Joe, of	.167	6	1	1	0	0	0	1	0
Eastman, Colin, ph	.000	1	0	0	0	0	0	0	0
Erstad, Bryan, of	.042	24	2	1	0	0	0	0	0
Frisella, Sal, of-dh	.248	137	19	34	4	1	1	21	6
Isenberg, Kurt, p-dh	.042	24	1	1	0	0	0	0	0
Ivany, Devin, c-of	.176	91	10	16	2	3	0	6	2
Kaplan, Jon, of	.272	173	34	47	7	0	5	13	21
Kehoe, Joe, ss	.091	22	1	2	1	0	0	0	0
Mahoney, Collin, c	.198	86	14	17	3	0	6	14	0
Puebla, Fernando, ss	.231	147	18	34	3	0	0	8	0
Schindewolf, Eric, 2b	.270	137	15	37	7	0	0	13	6
Sinisi, Vince, of-1b	.212	154	14	33	6	0	0	11	11
Slayden, Jeremy, of	.275	69	7	19	4	0	3	10	0

	AVG	AB	R	H	2B	3B	HR	RBI	SB
Spanos, Vasili, 1b-3b	.270	174	20	47	11	2	7	33	1
Thurmond, Ben, p-dh	.000	13	0	0	0	0	0	0	0
Vasquez, Alberto, c	.200	5	2	1	0	0	0	0	0
Wilson, Andy, 3b	.247	146	24	36	6	0	4	21	1

PITCHING	W	L	ERA	G	SV	IP	H	BB	SO
Aardsma, David	3	0	0.68	18	7	27	7	5	45
Elfeldt, Matt	0	2	3.57	13	0	18	13	16	18
Farrell, Jim	0	1	18.00	1	0	1	3	1	1
2-team (2 Harwich)	0	1	27.00	3	0	2	4	2	3
Finch, Brian	3	1	3.48	12	0	41	36	14	41
Gale, Chris	1	1	6.23	2	0	13	17	2	6
Isenberg, Kurt	0	1	3.03	14	0	36	36	9	32
Jackson, Steve	0	1	3.77	7	0	29	31	13	15
Lumsden, Tyler	1	1	9.00	5	0	16	21	11	10
Martin, Thomas	2	3	2.87	7	0	38	29	18	31
Misch, Pat	3	3	1.34	8	0	54	32	15	57
Niesel, Chris	3	1	3.42	4	0	24	18	7	25
Thurmond, Ben	0	1	9.00	1	0	4	5	3	5
Tracz, Chris	5	3	2.12	9	0	59	49	14	43
Varner, Matt	0	0	5.14	6	0	7	7	2	4
Vergara, Martin	0	0	4.30	9	0	15	11	20	12
Wilson, Andy	0	2	2.57	5	0	7	6	3	5

HARWICH

BATTING	AVG	AB	R	H	2B	3B	HR	RBI	SB
Akers, Chuck, of	.232	112	16	26	1	0	0	8	11
Bergeron, Jabe, dh	.164	55	2	9	1	0	0	4	0
Brinkley, Dant'e, of	.184	141	16	26	3	2	0	14	11
Festa, Ryan, 2b-3b	.258	124	18	32	6	0	0	9	2
Goleski, Ryan, of	.270	126	14	34	6	2	4	18	5
Johnson, Dale, c	.246	61	3	15	1	0	0	8	3
Kaye, John, of-1b	.147	68	5	10	0	0	2	5	0
Kitch, Denver, ss-2b	.113	53	4	6	0	0	0	1	5
Maier, Mitch, c-of	.253	146	21	37	7	2	0	14	2
Marcum, Shaun, ss-2b	.208	77	7	16	4	0	1	9	0
McCann, Brad	.210	138	13	29	5	0	3	12	3
Nicolas, Cesar, 1b	.209	134	14	28	5	0	3	12	1
Snavely, Chris, 2b-of	.264	144	20	38	6	1	4	17	7
Tucker, Jonathan, ss-2b	.230	87	9	20	3	0	0	7	11

PITCHING	W	L	ERA	G	SV	IP	H	BB	SO
Baldwin, Andy	0	2	3.86	19	1	33	27	20	35
Bass, Adam	0	0	4.26	4	1	13	10	5	13
Bechtel, Chuck	0	2	5.40	2	0	10	8	9	12
Burch, Jason	0	1	3.86	10	0	23	20	5	18
Clark, Zach	0	1	3.00	3	0	12	6	4	10
Cline, Zac	2	2	3.00	13	0	30	33	13	32
Harrelson, Paul	1	0	1.38	12	2	13	10	5	10
Holmes, Greg	0	0	2.45	1	0	4	1	3	4
Maki, Pete	0	0	3.00	1	0	3	2	0	1
Marcum, Shaun	4	1	1.48	16	10	24	14	4	31
Newman, Josh	3	5	3.86	9	0	49	48	19	35
Niemann, Jeff	1	2	2.05	5	0	31	25	12	30
Saunders, Tim	0	0	4.50	2	0	2	1	1	0
Schwartz, Josh	2	4	4.23	11	0	28	29	16	22
Weinmunson, Mark	2	3	1.64	8	0	55	31	13	46
Williams, John	2	0	2.31	4	0	12	7	5	10
Wilson, Joe	0	0	36.00	2	0	1	6	1	1
Ziegler, Brad	4	2	2.14	9	0	55	39	5	53

HYANNIS

BATTING	AVG	AB	R	H	2B	3B	HR	RBI	SB
Fox, Adam, 3b	.225	151	18	34	10	0	4	16	4
Garcia, Travis, ss	.148	115	8	17	1	0	1	10	1
Garko, Ryan, c-dh	.300	50	3	15	4	0	1	6	2
Garza, Mario, dh	.217	69	7	15	5	0	1	7	0
Green, Brandon, 2b	.214	117	18	25	5	1	0	11	3
Griffin, Mike, of-3b	.285	130	8	37	6	0	0	9	6
Harrison, Ben, of	.295	122	16	36	6	1	3	12	10
Horwitz, Brian, of	.148	54	4	8	1	0	0	4	0
Lombardi, Michael, c	.217	23	3	5	2	0	0	2	0
Lucy, Donny, c	.159	107	7	17	2	1	1	6	5
Niefer, Justin, of	.198	96	4	19	3	0	0	6	3
Pena, Omar, 2b-ss	.148	54	2	8	0	0	1	3	0
Putnam, Danny, of	.289	128	20	37	13	0	3	8	3
Silva, Mike, dh	.000	5	0	0	0	0	0	0	0
Sorensen, Logan, 1b	.196	153	11	30	4	0	2	9	5

PITCHING	W	L	ERA	G	SV	IP	H	BB	SO
Axford, John	0	3	7.17	12	1	21	21	30	25
Bass, Adam	0	1	2.70	7	0	13	12	6	9
2-team (4 Harwich)	0	1	3.46	11	1	26	22	11	22
Dixon, Ryan	0	0	4.76	5	0	6	5	5	1
Hahn, Cory	3	3	1.30	11	0	55	35	26	53
Hawk, Shane	0	0	6.19	15	1	16	20	10	17
Hedgecock, Ben	2	1	2.57	14	0	35	40	10	33
Jecmen, Mark	0	1	4.30	7	0	15	20	12	17
Kandybowicz, Tom	0	1	12.00	3	0	6	7	6	4
Oldham, Tom	2	6	5.14	8	0	42	51	11	41
Peterson, Trent	3	1	1.59	8	0	51	36	13	49
Rauch, Brian	1	1	4.50	2	0	12	11	6	8
Trussell, Mike	0	0	1.84	6	1	15	12	2	13
Walker, Sean	2	8	2.80	15	6	35	27	14	34
Watts, Joey	2	4	5.12	7	0	39	48	10	28
Wilson, Brian	1	1	2.00	3	0	18	12	13	18

ORLEANS

BATTING	AVG	AB	R	H	2B	3B	HR	RBI	SB
Allen, Rod, of	.254	142	19	36	1	1	2	15	19
Boggs, Brandon, of	.228	101	16	23	7	1	2	16	7
Coffey, David, of-dh	.295	139	20	41	4	0	6	20	7
Garrabrants, Steve, 2b	.178	152	19	27	4	1	3	20	15
Hanigan, Ryan, c-dh	.292	120	13	35	3	1	0	8	7
Jackson, Doug, of	.189	122	13	23	4	1	0	10	6
Lemke, Tim, 3b	.300	10	2	3	0	0	1	3	0
Leslie, Myron, 3b-ss	.248	149	16	37	6	1	2	14	9
Lewis, Brent, 1b-3b	.253	91	10	23	6	0	1	12	4
Maniscalco, Matt, ss	.184	141	17	26	2	1	1	4	13
Norman, Derek, c-dh	.115	26	0	3	1	0	0	1	0
Rapacioli, Mike, 3b	.215	135	13	29	9	0	2	13	1
Scioletti, Brad, 3b	.286	7	0	2	0	0	0	0	0
Wolfe, Joey, c-dh	.272	92	12	25	5	0	1	8	0

PITCHING	W	L	ERA	G	SV	IP	H	BB	SO
Baker, Scott	3	1	1.61	9	0	56	38	8	52
Benson, Whitley	1	0	1.37	20	11	26	13	9	29
Del Prete, Anthony	1	1	5.40	9	3	10	6	3	5
Elia, Frank	1	0	1.51	12	0	36	24	16	21
Metzger, Jason	2	2	2.27	7	0	32	31	15	20
Murray, Chris	2	2	2.63	13	2	24	21	10	20
Ottman, Justin	0	0	7.71	3	0	5	6	3	5
Rogers, Brian	4	0	0.40	8	0	45	22	7	53
Smith, Brett	2	1	5.46	10	1	28	30	12	27
Talbert, Eric	4	1	0.96	9	0	28	17	5	25
Van, Robbie	3	2	1.42	14	2	25	14	11	32
2-team (5 Yarmouth-Dennis)	3	2	1.01	9	3	36	19	14	48
Weaver, Joe	2	3	3.48	15	1	34	29	10	18
White, Steven	4	0	1.60	9	0	45	27	17	40

WAREHAM

BATTING	AVG	AB	R	H	2B	3B	HR	RBI	SB
Dorr, Jayme, 2b	.333	12	2	4	1	0	0	0	1
Douillard, Jon, c	.127	71	1	9	0	0	0	2	0
Durbin, Chris, of	.180	161	17	29	3	0	2	8	5
Ford, Josh, 1b	.206	160	9	33	6	0	0	11	5
Graeter, Spencer, 2b	.167	54	8	9	2	0	0	1	2
Johnson, Mark, of-1b	.250	16	4	4	0	0	1	0	1
Kutler, Matt, of	.301	143	12	43	9	1	2	15	1
Mattox, Jay, of	.042	24	1	1	0	0	0	1	0
Moss, Ty, 3b-dh	.255	98	11	25	3	1	1	7	9
Murphy, David, of	.304	158	17	48	10	2	1	18	7
Murton, Matt, dh	.400	55	9	22	6	1	0	8	5
Nickeas, Mike, c-dh	.204	108	13	22	3	0	2	15	1
Pontiff, Wally, 3b	.250	44	6	11	1	0	0	1	0
Rogelstad, Matt, ss-3b	.235	170	17	40	8	1	0	13	5
Soto, Ty, 3b-dh	.226	106	8	24	1	0	0	9	0
Suarez, Ignacio, ss-2b	.182	55	6	10	0	0	0	6	4

PITCHING	W	L	ERA	G	SV	IP	H	BB	SO
Burks, Brian	0	2	4.26	19	11	19	23	5	20
Cunningham, Tim	0	3	3.00	4	1	6	2	6	5
Douillard, Jon	0	0	0.00	1	0	3	0	1	3
Guyette, Kevin	5	1	2.05	9	0	53	41	17	41
Parcus, Kyle	3	1	1.34	21	2	34	27	19	37
Parisi, Mike	0	0	0.00	2	0	2	1	0	2
Ramsey, Robert	0	0	5.40	7	0	7	7	8	5
Ransom, Robert	1	3	2.22	10	1	28	23	5	32
Sanders, David	4	3	0.73	9	1	62	36	8	51
Shortell, Rory	1	1	0.87	8	0	31	28	13	30
Sowers, Jeremy	5	4	1.52	9	0	65	49	12	56
Taylor, Trey	3	3	3.13	8	0	46	45	19	34
Touchstone, Nic	1	3	1.69	6	0	32	21	24	33

YARMOUTH-DENNIS

BATTING	AVG	AB	R	H	2B	3B	HR	RBI	SB
Bourassa, Adam	.323	155	21	50	3	1	0	8	18
Bourn, Michael	.287	129	22	37	3	1	0	3	23
Carter, Chris	.233	90	13	21	4	1	2	8	4
Cooley, Brett	.255	137	24	35	9	1	7	27	2
Coultas, Ryan	.206	102	7	21	3	0	0	6	4
Duncan, Jake	.167	72	8	12	3	0	5	16	0
Fox, Jake	.258	128	9	33	10	1	0	18	2

AMATEUR BASEBALL

Fry, Matt	.231	26	2	6	2	0	0	1	1
Gendron, Steve	.241	54	4	13	0	1	0	5	1
Kungl, Jake	.211	123	15	26	6	0	0	10	1
Leahy, Ryan	.125	8	1	1	0	0	0	0	0
Malec, Chris	.250	40	3	10	1	0	0	6	1
McIntyre, Nick	.235	136	15	32	2	0	0	15	3
Roach, Sean	.143	7	0	1	0	0	0	0	0
Scioletti, Brad	.143	7	0	1	0	0	0	0	0
Slone, John	.000	5	0	0	0	0	0	0	0
Sollmann, Steve	.143	112	10	16	3	1	0	8	3
Whisler, Wes	.309	123	19	38	7	0	6	16	1

PITCHING	W	L	ERA	G	SV	IP	H	BB	SO
Brauer, Jim	3	3	1.77	9	0	56	48	18	63
Campbell, Ryan	2	1	1.99	12	0	32	24	12	48
Coultas, Ryan	0	0	3.00	3	0	3	1	1	4
Farnum, Matt	4	3	2.74	9	0	49	45	18	48
Goodman, Chris	0	0	2.61	6	0	21	16	7	17
Hordon, Marc	0	0	2.03	9	0	13	14	11	12
Hudgins, John	3	1	1.03	10	3	35	16	15	45
Letz, Kevin	0	0	0.00	1	0	1	0	2	0
Marchbanks, David	0	1	3.12	6	0	26	18	14	18
Merrell, Darric	2	4	3.92	10	0	44	36	20	42
Mock, Garrett	1	0	1.46	3	0	12	9	1	13
Morley, Tim	0	3	3.28	9	1	25	17	14	22
Rogers, Michael	5	1	1.82	9	0	40	25	17	37
Van, Robbie	0	0	0.00	5	1	10	5	3	16
Vermilyea, Jamie	1	3	1.63	15	4	28	25	8	35
Whisler, Wes	0	0	0.00	1	1	24	14	6	29

CENTRAL ILLINOIS COLLEGIATE LEAGUE

EAST	W	L	PCT	GB
Danville Dans	24	24	.500	—
Decatur Blues	20	27	.426	3 ½
Twin City Stars	16	31	.340	7 ½

WEST	W	L	PCT	GB
Bluff City Bombers	28	20	.583	—
Springfield Rifles	28	20	.583	—
Quincy Gems	27	21	.563	1

POSTSEASON TOURNAMENT: Decatur 3-0, Bluff City 2-2, Springfield 1-2, Danville 0-2.

Co-Most Valuable Players: Wayne Astrauskas, Bluff City (Quincy, Ill.); Drew Anderson, Quincy (Ohio State). **Co-Outstanding Pitchers:** Jason Horvath, Springfield (IU-PU Fort Wayne); Brian Keating, Bluff City (Southwest Missouri State).

TOP 10 PROSPECTS: 1. Dustin Bensko, 1b/3b, Springfield (Illinois). **2.** Brandon Cashman, of, Decatur (Illinois). **3.** Brock Till, rhp, Springfield (Bradley). **4.** Logan Hughes, of, Springfield (Missouri-St. Louis). **5.** Anthony Tomey, rhp, Springfield (Eastern Michigan). **6.** Drew Anderson, 2b, Quincy (Ohio State). **7.** J. C. Holt, 2b/of, Danville (Louisiana State). **8.** Kyle Bloom, lhp, Springfield (Illinois State). **9.** Anthony Cupps, rhp, Danville (Mississippi). **10.** P.J. Finigan, ss, Springfield (Southern Illinois).

INDIVIDUAL BATTING LEADERS
(Minimum 100 Plate Appearances)

	AVG	AB	R	H	2B	3B	HR	RBI	SB
Anderson, Drew, Quincy	.352	145	21	51	8	4	2	17	16
Holt, J.C., Danville	.343	102	22	35	8	3	0	8	11
Hughes, Logan, Spring.	.325	157	28	51	13	1	4	21	10
Bensko, Dustin, Spring.	.324	142	27	46	5	1	6	19	5
Beer, Travis, Twin City	.313	134	19	42	10	0	2	24	2
Astrauskas, Wayne, BC	.303	175	25	53	13	0	6	30	0
Paras, Mike, Danville	.299	134	24	40	2	1	0	9	10
Mowery, Kyle, Springfield	.296	115	17	34	10	1	5	20	1
Nowak, Chris, Twin City	.287	136	13	39	5	0	0	18	2
Hutting, Tim, Danville	.286	147	19	42	7	0	0	20	7
Finigan, P.J., Spring.	.279	154	15	43	8	0	0	15	6
Strebin, Kirk, Danville	.279	165	22	46	11	0	2	15	19
Cashman, Brandon, Decatur	.276	174	29	48	12	0	5	23	12
Redding, Grant, BC	.273	128	31	35	9	0	2	19	18
Frederickson, Trevor, TC	.268	112	14	30	5	0	3	17	1

INDIVIDUAL PITCHING LEADERS
(Minimum 36 innings)

	W	L	ERA	G	SV	IP	H	BB	SO
Horvath, Jason, Spring.	6	2	1.38	14	5	65	39	14	50
Keating, Brian, Bluff City	7	1	1.58	10	0	63	39	22	56
Pals, Jordan, Decatur	5	3	1.77	10	0	71	57	19	45
Henderson, Brian, Quincy	5	2	1.92	8	0	52	41	12	48
Phillips, Aaron, Quincy	5	2	1.93	9	0	61	45	16	39
Tomey, Anthony, Spring.	5	3	2.02	11	0	80	48	37	71
Biale, Tony, Danville	2	2	2.04	8	1	40	33	18	45
Troyer, David, Danville	2	2	2.16	8	0	42	46	12	38

Ofat, Chris, Decatur	3	2	2.31	13	0	62	51	27	51
Dixon, Jake, Quincy	4	1	2.35	8	0	46	43	13	28

COASTAL PLAIN LEAGUE

NORTH	W	L	PCT	GB
+Outer Banks Daredevils	28	21	.571	—
Peninsula Pilots	27	23	.540	1 ½
Petersburg Generals	25	26	.490	4
*Edenton Steamers	24	25	.490	4

SOUTH	W	L	PCT	GB
+*Wilmington Sharks	31	17	.646	—
Florence Redwolves	27	21	.562	4
Fayetteville Swampdogs	24	27	.471	8 ½
Wilson Tobs	16	34	.320	16

WEST	W	L	PCT	GB
+*Gastonia Grizzlies	28	21	.571	—
Durham Americans	24	25	.490	4
Thomasville Hi-Toms	23	24	.489	4
Asheboro Copperheads	19	32	.373	10

* First-half champion   + Second-half champion

POSTSEASON TOURNAMENT: Outer Banks (4-1) defeated Petersburg (4-1) in championship game of eight-team tournament.

Most Valuable Player: Mike Reese, Wilson (Rollins, Fla.). **Pitcher of the Year:** Jaymie Russ, Gastonia (Belmont Abbey, N.C.).

TOP 10 PROSPECTS: 1. Justin Verlander, rhp, Wilson (Old Dominion). **2.** Mike Reese, of, Wilson (Rollins, Fla.). **3.** Chris Coughlin, rhp, Wilmington (UNC Wilmington). **4.** Josh Archer, 1b, Florence (Middle Tennessee State). **5.** Thomas Berkery, c, Edenton (Mississippi State). **6.** Jaymie Russ, rhp, Gastonia (Belmont Abbey, N.C.). **7.** Tug Hulett, 3b, Peninsula (Auburn). **8.** Tim Turner, lhp, Wilson (East Tennessee State). **9.** Justin Sturge, rhp, Fayetteville (Coastal Carolina). **10.** Marshall Hubbard, of, Outer Banks (William & Mary).

INDIVIDUAL BATTING LEADERS
(Minimum 100 Plate Appearances)

	AVG	AB	R	H	2B	3B	HR	RBI	SB
Reese, Mike, Wilson	.350	137	19	48	7	0	2	22	22
Hulett, Tug, Peninsula	.336	143	28	48	4	0	0	9	29
Cooper, Chad, Fayette.	.333	192	34	64	6	2	1	18	16
Palumbo, Jeff, OB	.332	193	38	64	5	0	0	16	11
Jones, Nick, Durham	.331	145	17	48	11	1	0	20	4
Buffone, Anthony, OB	.303	178	28	54	7	0	4	40	4
Whitmer, Daryl, Asheboro	.303	89	17	27	8	2	0	4	11
Hubbard, Marshall, OB	.299	157	27	47	15	0	4	27	4
Dutton, J.D., Durham	.298	168	27	50	12	3	5	37	3
Moyer, Wes, Outer Banks	.292	120	23	35	3	0	4	20	1
Powell, Brandon, Florence	.291	189	34	55	8	0	4	18	14
Archer, Josh, Florence	.288	170	26	49	11	0	4	27	2
Rucci, Michael, Outer Banks	.286	189	28	54	13	0	2	27	0
Snapp, Kevin, Peninsula	.286	175	28	50	4	2	2	25	14
Waldron, Matt, Gastonia	.284	176	30	50	6	1	1	21	5

INDIVIDUAL PITCHING LEADERS
(Minimum 35 innings)

	W	L	ERA	G	SV	IP	H	BB	SO
Coughlin, Chris, Wilmington	8	1	0.92	10	0	69	40	12	63
Buck, Mike, Wilmington	3	1	1.05	25	13	26	15	7	30
Goyen, Matt, Wilmington	4	1	1.10	12	0	65	31	28	72
Stephens, Brett, Petersburg	6	3	1.13	9	0	64	37	19	54
Cook, Steven, Gastonia	5	2	1.18	11	0	69	52	22	58
Turner, Tim, Wilson	3	4	1.22	10	0	66	44	25	95
Russ, Jaymie, Gastonia	9	1	1.23	11	1	66	38	29	90
Rawl, Aaron, Wilmington	4	1	1.25	8	0	36	29	6	32
McLaughlin, Joey, Petersburg	3	4	1.55	16	5	41	25	16	49
Cribb, Josh, Florence	6	2	1.73	12	0	78	60	16	83

GREAT LAKES LEAGUE

	W	L	PCT	GB
Northern Ohio Baseball	30	10	.750	—
Columbus All-Americans	29	11	.711	1
Delaware Cows	24	16	.600	6
Youngstown Express	23	17	.575	7
Stark County Terriers	21	19	.525	9
Lima Locos	18	22	.450	12
Southern Ohio Baseball	18	22	.450	12
Pittsburgh Pandas	17	23	.425	13
Murrysville Mighty Eagles	16	24	.400	14
Grand Lake Mariners	13	27	.325	17
Michigan Lake Area Rams	11	29	.275	19

POSTSEASON TOURNAMENT: Northern Ohio (4-0) defeated Columbus (3-1) in championship game.

ALL-STAR TEAM: C—Pat O'Brien, Columbus (Kent State), P.J. Pilittere, Northern Ohio (Cal State Fullerton). 1B—Nick Walsh, Youngstown (Arizona State). 2B—Billy Hess, Columbus (Columbia). 3B—Chase Odenreider, Youngstown (Nebraska). SS—Brian Bixler, Delaware (Eastern Michigan); Kevin Estrada, Northern Ohio (Pepperdine); Brad Schutz, Youngstown (Cincinnati). OF—Josh Anderson, Stark County (Eastern Kentucky); Dave Barkholz, Stark County (Bowling Green); Jason Carey, Lima (Vermont); Dan Greisbaum, Michigan (Central Michigan). DH—Andrew McCreery, Lima (Pennsylvania). UT—Cole Hilt, Northern Ohio (UC Riverside). P—Eric Bowden, Northern Ohio (St. Mary's); Chris Cordeiro, Northern Ohio (UCLA); Rhett Gulledge, Northern Ohio (McNeese State); Dan Horvath, Northern Ohio (Central Michigan); Adam Kirkendall, Grand Lake (Louisiana Tech); Brian Lynch, Stark County (Ball State); Doug Vincent, Columbus (Tennessee Tech).

Most Valuable Player: Andrew McCreery, Lima. **Outstanding Pitcher:** Dan Horvath, Northern Ohio.

TOP 10 PROSPECTS: 1. Brian Bixler, ss, Delaware (Eastern Michigan). **2.** Chris Cordiero, rhp, Northern Ohio (UCLA). **3.** Josh Anderson, of, Stark County (Eastern Kentucky). **4.** Chase Odenreider, 3b, Youngstown (Nebraska). **5.** Dan Horvath, rhp, Northern Ohio (Central Michigan). **6.** Kevin Estrada, ss, Northern Ohio (Pepperdine). **7.** Matt Davis, rhp, Lima (Ohio State). **8.** Brad Schutz, ss, Youngstown (Cincinnati). **9.** Caleb Brock, c, Delaware (Kentucky). **10.** Adam Kirkendall, lhp, Grand Lake (Louisiana Tech).

INDIVIDUAL BATTING LEADERS
(Minimum 100 Plate Appearances)

	AVG	AB	R	H	2B	3B	HR	RBI	SB
McCreery, Andrew, Lima	.426	94	16	40	6	1	5	26	6
Carey, Jason, Lima	.423	123	27	52	11	1	6	19	8
Anderson, Josh, SC	.398	123	15	49	5	2	1	11	8
Bixler, Brian, Delaware	.389	144	32	56	9	5	4	13	7
Hess, Billy, Columbus	.378	119	26	45	8	0	1	24	5
Griesbaum, Dan, MLA	.355	121	16	43	10	0	1	20	5
Hunton, Bart, Delaware	.354	113	22	40	7	0	5	20	2
Schutz, Brad, Youngstown	.344	128	28	44	8	2	1	22	5
Barkholz, Dave, SC	.343	143	20	49	7	1	1	17	8
Brock, Caleb, Delaware	.339	112	22	38	7	0	1	16	6
Kowalchuk, T.J., Murrysville	.339	115	21	39	4	1	2	19	3
Odenreider, Chase, Young.	.338	133	20	45	17	0	1	45	6
Hall, Chris, Grand Lake	.337	86	8	29	2	2	3	19	4
Walsh, Nick, Youngstown	.337	104	40	35	4	1	0	19	27
Whitman, Brad, Youngstown	.337	95	18	32	4	1	1	19	2
Statzer, Nate, Pittsburgh	.333	102	12	34	3	1	0	9	5
Pease, Adam, Delaware	.331	139	23	46	7	1	0	12	24
Estrada, Kevin, Northern Ohio	.329	149	30	49	7	1	2	15	15

INDIVIDUAL PITCHING LEADERS
(Minimum 35 innings)

	W	L	ERA	G	SV	IP	H	BB	SO
Horvath, Dan, Northern Ohio	4	2	0.57	11	4	47	33	12	49
Bowden, Eric, Northern Ohio	6	1	0.78	8	0	46	36	7	38
Lynch, Brian, SC	5	0	0.86	8	0	49	37	5	35
Kirkendall, Adam, GL	2	2	0.94	8	0	58	39	15	63
Day, Tim, Columbus	3	1	1.47	6	0	37	26	12	21
Cordeiro, Chris, No. Ohio	5	0	1.47	13	1	43	32	6	34
Vincent, Doug, Columbus	6	1	1.50	9	0	36	30	12	39
Michael, Scooter, Columbus	5	1	1.58	7	0	40	34	6	26
Sharpless, Josh, Pitt	3	3	1.79	11	1	60	40	25	67

NEW ENGLAND COLLEGIATE LEAGUE

WEST	W	L	PCT	GB
Danbury Westerners	25	16	.610	—
North Adams Steeplecats	23	19	.548	2½
Torrington Twisters	22	20	.524	3½
Manchester Silkworms	16	26	.381	9½

NORTH	W	L	PCT	GB
Keene Swamp Bats	31	11	.738	—
Concord Quarry Dogs	24	17	.585	6½
Mill City All-Americans	24	18	.571	7
Sanford Mainers	15	27	.357	16

SOUTH	W	L	PCT	GB
Newport Gulls	25	17	.595	—
Middletown Giants	23	19	.548	2
Riverpoint Royals	13	29	.310	12
Thread City Tides	10	32	.238	15

PLAYOFFS: Quarterfinals—Keene defeated Torrington 2-1, Danbury defeated Middletown 2-0, Mill City defeated Concord 2-1 and Newport defeated North Adams 2-1 in best-of-3 series. **Semifinals**—Newport defeated Danbury 2-0 and Keene defeated Mill City 2-1 in best-of-3 series. **Final**—Newport defeated Keene 2-0 in best-of-3 series.

ALL-STAR TEAM: C—A.J. Zickgraf, Newport (Georgia Southern). **1B**—Trey Hendricks, Keene (Harvard). **2B**—Rafael Lara, Newport (Miami-Dade CC). **3B**—Rocky Baker, Keene (Georgia Southern). **SS**—Josh DiScipio, Concord

(Boston College). **OF**—Jeff Frazier, Danbury (Rutgers); Eddie Harper, Newport (LeMoyne); Mike Wagner, North Adams (Washington). **DH**—Clint Eury, Danbury (Penn State). **P**—David Austen, Keene (South Florida); Chris Homer, North Adams (Marist); Grant Reynolds, Concord (Kennesaw State, Ga.).

Most Valuable Player: Mike Wagner, of, North Adams

TOP 10 PROSPECTS: 1. Chris Lambert, rhp, Concord (Boston College). **2.** Jeff Frazier, of, Danbury (Rutgers). **3.** Mike Wagner, of, North Adams (Washington). **4.** Grant Reynolds, rhp, Concord (Kennesaw State, Ga.). **5.** Justin Orenduff, rhp, Keene (George Washington). **6.** Chris Homer, rhp, North Adams (Marist). **7.** Trey Hendricks, 1b, Keene (Harvard). **8.** David Austen, rhp, Keene (South Florida). **9.** Brian Harrison, rhp, Keene (Georgia Southern). **10.** Jason Motte, c, Sanford (Iona).

INDIVIDUAL BATTING LEADERS
(Minimum 100 Plate Appearances)

	AVG	AB	R	H	2B	3B	HR	RBI	SB
DiScipio, Josh, Concord	.351	94	13	33	4	1	1	7	12
Wagner, Mike, NA	.342	146	39	50	12	4	5	22	13
Hendricks, Trey, Keene	.327	147	21	48	7	0	7	25	1
Frazier, Jeff, Danbury	.325	151	26	49	7	0	7	23	18
Harper, Eddie, Newport	.320	122	14	39	8	0	0	16	17
Baker, Rocky, Keene	.310	155	28	48	11	1	3	16	16
Lara, Rafael, Newport	.308	120	19	37	6	0	0	14	22
Zickgraf, A.J., Newport	.306	85	10	26	8	0	0	8	1
Baisley, Jeff, Danbury	.298	151	23	45	6	0	0	18	7
Laskowski, Lee, Danbury	.297	101	9	30	7	0	1	19	1
Green, Zane, Manchester	.297	91	19	27	6	1	2	14	2
Barry, Jeff, Keene	.293	133	24	39	7	0	3	18	6
Mason, Brandon, Concord	.293	123	14	36	3	0	0	17	6
LaRoche, Andy, Keene	.290	100	20	29	4	1	2	13	2

INDIVIDUAL PITCHING LEADERS
(Minimum 35 innings)

	W	L	ERA	G	SV	IP	H	BB	SO
Reynolds, Grant, Concord	6	1	0.46	10	0	59	35	11	66
Hahn, Jeff, Keene	5	1	1.00	6	0	45	35	13	26
Sonnanstine, Andy, Sanford	1	1	1.19	10	0	38	24	10	44
Frederick, Dan, Mill City	4	3	1.33	9	0	54	31	13	46
Weagle, Matt, Mill City	1	2	1.38	8	2	52	42	9	48
Lambert, Chris, Concord	3	2	1.55	9	0	46	28	28	72
Maisano, Thomas, Danbury	4	1	1.57	7	0	46	31	7	45
Dowling, Patrick, Concord	4	2	1.65	11	0	49	39	14	28
Monds, Devin, Mill City	3	2	1.77	8	0	56	51	19	38
Bergeron, Michael, Newport	6	2	1.84	10	0	49	38	16	51

NEW YORK COLLEGIATE LEAGUE

WEST	W	L	PCT	GB
Wellsville Nitros	26	15	.634	—
Hornell Dodgers	24	18	.571	2½
Wayne County Raptors	20	22	.476	6½
Geneva Lakers	18	23	.439	8
Cortland Apples	16	22	.421	8½

EAST	W	L	PCT	GB
Schenectady Mohawks	30	12	.714	—
Mohawk Valley RedLegs	26	16	.619	4
Rome Indians	18	22	.450	11
Plattsburgh Thunder	15	27	.357	15
Watertown Wizards	13	29	.310	17

PLAYOFFS: Semifinals—Hornell defeated Wellsville 2-0 and Schenectady defeated Mohawk Valley 2-0 in best-of-3 series. **Final**—Hornell defeated Schenectady 2-1 in best-of-3 series.

Most Valuable Player: Shaen O'Conner, Mohawk Valley. **Pitcher of the Year:** Erin Jones, Schenectady. **Coach of the Year:** Dave Fields, Schenectady.

INDIVIDUAL BATTING LEADERS
(Minimum 100 Plate Appearances)

	AVG	AB	R	H	2B	3B	HR	RBI	SB
Casanova, Adrian, Mo. Valley	.369	103	12	38	5	0	0	15	0
Friedrich, Jake, Wellsville	.354	124	24	40	3	1	1	18	6
O'Conner, Shaen, Mo. Valley	.339	109	23	37	6	0	9	27	4
Sullivan, Jason, Mo. Valley	.336	119	18	40	8	0	0	16	5
Shimer, Nick, Schnectady	.333	141	15	47	7	0	1	29	1
Thoms, Andrew, Mo. Valley	.324	105	22	34	6	1	1	14	3
Holt, Josh, Geneva	.320	125	19	40	3	0	1	14	1
Accardo, Jeremy, Wellsville	.317	101	15	32	8	0	1	14	7
Knell, Kory, Hornell	.315	127	24	40	4	5	2	18	4
Hayes, Lance, Wayne County	.314	121	24	38	6	1	1	15	18
Pecchia, Mike, Wayne County	.313	115	18	36	9	1	0	23	1
Pali, Matt, Mohawk Valley	.312	125	22	39	8	1	3	24	4
Ledbetter, Matt, Hornell	.311	135	17	42	7	3	0	11	2
Meacham, Eric, Watertown	.308	107	12	33	0	0	0	15	2
Schmid, Tony, Wellsville	.299	107	20	32	6	0	0	13	8

AMATEUR BASEBALL

INDIVIDUAL PITCHING LEADERS
(Minimum 35 innings)

	W	L	ERA	G	SV	IP	H	BB	SO
Jones, Erin, Schnectady	7	0	0.48	8	0	57	36	8	53
Blevins, Eric, Hornell	5	1	1.01	9	0	53	33	10	36
Forgione, Brian, Schenectady	4	1	1.45	7	0	50	30	15	31
Huotari, Chase, Rome	3	0	1.77	5	0	36	25	10	34
Haggerty, Jake, Mo. Valley	3	2	1.80	6	0	40	32	10	29
Merchant, Jamie, Plattsburgh	2	4	1.93	8	0	51	38	26	65
McKinney, Dustin, Geneva	3	1	2.08	5	0	35	22	10	24
Poell, Justin, Schenectady	3	1	2.11	12	1	38	28	12	26
Wyatt, Blake, Rome	5	2	2.25	8	0	48	40	8	49
Shone, Jason, Watertown	4	5	2.33	11	0	66	44	22	66

NORTHWOODS LEAGUE

NORTH	W	L	PCT	GB
*+Brainerd Mighty Gulls	39	25	.609	—
St. Cloud River Bats	34	30	.531	5
Mankato Moondogs	33	31	.516	6
Alexandria Beetles	28	36	.438	11

SOUTH	W	L	PCT	GB
+Waterloo Bucks	34	30	.531	—
Wisconsin Woodchucks	32	31	.508	1.5
*Rochester Honkers	31	32	.492	2.5
Madison Mallards	24	40	.375	10

* First-half champion   + Second-half champion

PLAYOFFS: Semifinals—Brainerd defeated St. Cloud 2-0 and Waterloo defeated Rochester 2-1 in best-of-3 series. **Final**—Waterloo defeated Brainerd 2-0 in best-of-3 series.

ALL-STAR TEAM: C—John Purdom, Brainerd (Indiana State); Jason Jaramillo, St. Cloud (Oklahoma State). **1B**—Matt Anderson, Alexandria (UC Irvine). **2B**—Jeff Cammann, Waterloo (Neosho County, Kan., CC). **3B**—Wes Long, St. Cloud (Alabama-Huntsville). **SS**—Kyle Haines, Waterloo (Olney Central, Ill., CC). **IF**—Ben Pattee, Mankato (Minnesota). **OF**—Steve Adams, Brainerd (Northwestern State); Adam Boeve, Waterloo (Northern Iowa); Drew Davidson, Waterloo (Illinois); Joe Gaetti, St. Cloud (North Carolina State); Andrew Wishy, Mankato (Arkansas). **DH**—Ryan Finan, Brainerd (Hutchinson, Kan., CC). **RHP**—Dustin Baud, Brainerd (Bossier Parish, La., CC); Marc Craigmile, Alexandria (Southwest, Minn., State); Connor Falkenbach, Rochester (Florida); Chris Goodman, Brainerd (Arizona); Steve Grasley, Wisconsin (Creighton); Nathan Hochgesang, Rochester (Golden West, Calif., JC); Cory Hollenhorst, Alexandria (Iowa); Danny Muegge, Waterloo (Texas); Jeff Spicer, Mankato (Lynn, Fla.). **LHP**—B.J. Brandenberger, Wisconsin (Texas-Arlington); Aaron Marsden, Brainerd (Nebraska); Adam Rowe, Wisconsin (Mt. Vernon Nazarene, Ohio).

Most Valuable Player: John Purdom, Brainerd.

TOP 10 PROSPECTS: 1. Aaron Marsden, lhp, Brainerd (Nebraska). **2.** Connor Falkenbach, rhp, Rochester (Florida). **3.** Matt Anderson, 1b, Alexandria (UC Irvine). **4.** Andre Ethier, of, Rochester (Arizona State). **5.** Andrew Wishy, of, Mankato (Arkansas). **6.** Jason Jaramillo, c, St. Cloud (Oklahoma State). **7.** John Purdom, c/1b, Brainerd (Indiana State). **8.** Steve Grasley, rhp, Wisconsin (Creighton). **9.** Mark Sopko, rhp, Madison (Arizona State). **10.** B.J. Brandenberger, lhp, Wisconsin (Texas-Arlington).

INDIVIDUAL BATTING LEADERS
(Minimum 150 Plate Appearances)

	AVG	AB	R	H	2B	3B	HR	RBI	SB
Pattee, Ben, Mankato	.351	202	41	71	10	0	2	30	17
Wishy, Andrew, Mankato	.347	199	35	69	14	3	3	36	10
Anderson, Matt, Alexandria	.342	193	32	66	9	2	3	36	6
Finan, Ryan, Brainerd	.341	167	31	57	10	0	1	21	7
Cammann, Jeff, Waterloo	.319	216	39	69	10	0	0	22	23
Tierce, Evan, Wisconsin	.314	153	19	48	11	0	0	8	15
Edwards, Madison, Madison	.311	212	24	66	11	1	0	17	6
Howard, Josh, Alexandria	.309	162	33	50	1	0	0	12	15
Martinez, Jaime, Madison	.300	180	19	54	8	1	2	28	1
Babineaux, Charlie, Madison	.295	183	23	54	11	0	3	19	5
Long, Wes, St. Cloud	.286	245	30	70	10	0	0	21	24
Davidson, Drew, Waterloo	.285	193	29	55	12	5	2	41	16
Purdom, John, Brainerd	.284	218	34	62	11	2	6	51	4
Smith, Jake, St. Cloud	.281	171	27	48	12	0	4	26	1
Kinsey, Chris, St. Cloud	.280	232	30	65	17	0	5	38	2

INDIVIDUAL PITCHING LEADERS
(Minimum 51 Innings)

	W	L	ERA	G	SV	IP	H	BB	SO
Marsden, Aaron, Brainerd	7	1	1.60	8	0	62	35	16	48
Falkenbach, Connor, Rochester	5	3	1.67	12	1	76	58	17	85
Muegge, Danny, Waterloo	5	3	2.04	8	0	57	46	13	41
Rowe, Adam, Wisconsin	8	3	2.11	12	0	73	61	27	53
Goodman, Chris, Brainerd	6	1	2.16	11	0	67	61	14	51
Craigmile, Mark, Alexandria	4	3	2.17	11	0	75	54	30	61

Hamilton, Ryan, Brainerd	5	2	2.47	15	0	62	52	19	57
Beck, Bryan, Brainerd	4	5	2.47	9	0	58	59	10	40
Brandenberger, B.J., Wisconsin	6	3	2.48	11	0	69	52	20	66
Seger, J.D., St. Cloud	5	1	2.49	15	0	65	55	22	31

SHENANDOAH VALLEY LEAGUE

NORTH	W	L	PCT	GB
Winchester Royals	21	19	.525	—
New Market Rebels	20	20	.500	1
Front Royal Cardinals	16	24	.400	5
Luray Wranglers	15	25	.375	6

SOUTH	W	L	PCT	GB
Covington Lumberjacks	26	14	.650	—
Harrisonburg Turks	25	15	.625	1
Staunton Braves	20	20	.500	6
Waynesboro Generals	17	23	.425	9

PLAYOFFS: Semifinals—New Market defeated Winchester 3-1 and Covington defeated Harrisonburg 3-1 in best-of-5 series. **Finals**—New Market defeated Covington 3-1 in best-of-5 series.

ALL-STAR TEAM: C—Chris Westervelt, New Market (Stetson). **1B**—Chris Alexander, New Market (New Mexico). **2B**—Joe Honce, Covington (West Virginia Wesleyan). **SS**—Tommy Manzella, Waynesboro (Tulane). **3B**—Kevin Matuszek, Covington (Morehead State). **OF**—Alan Beck, Waynesboro (Western Carolina); Brent Metheny, Harrisonburg (James Madison); Kevin White, New Market (Presbyterian, S.C.). **DH**—Justin Morgan, Luray (Troy State). **UT**—Adam Pavkovich, Waynesboro (Alabama). **SP**—Taylor Cobb, Staunton (Central Florida), Carlos Guevara, Covington (Louisiana-Lafayette). E.J. Shanks, Harrisonburg (Oklahoma City). **RP**—Logan Kensing, Harrisonburg (Texas A&M), Grant Smith, Winchester (George Mason).

Most Valuable Player: Joe Honce, Covington.

TOP 10 PROSPECTS: 1. E.J. Shanks, rhp, Harrisonburg (Oklahoma City). **2.** Chris Westervelt, c, New Market (Stetson). **3.** Logan Kensing, rhp, Harrisonburg (Texas A&M). **4.** Taylor Cobb, rhp, Staunton (Central Florida). **5.** Taylor Cobb, rhp, Staunton (Central Florida). **6.** Elvys Quezada, rhp, Winchester (Seton Hall). **7.** John Hardy, ss, Harrisonburg (Arizona). **8.** Jason Martinez, lhp, Harrisonburg (Mesa State, Colo.). **9.** Clayton Hamilton, rhp, Winchester (Penn State). **10.** Carlos Guevara, rhp, Covington (St. Mary's, Texas).

INDIVIDUAL BATTING LEADERS
(Minimum 100 At-Bats)

	AVG	AB	R	H	2B	3B	HR	RBI	SB
Morgan, Justin, Luray	.342	120	15	41	6	0	3	19	0
Westervelt, Chris, New Market	.336	140	20	47	13	0	2	28	3
Beck, Alan, Waynesboro	.331	130	22	43	7	0	2	22	1
Houston, Matt, Harrisonburg	.315	124	16	39	4	0	1	10	2
Manzella, Tommy, Waynesboro	.313	147	22	46	5	0	0	9	9
Pahuta, Tim, Winchester	.310	155	20	48	13	0	2	38	0
Pavkovich, Adam, Waynesboro	.310	100	21	31	4	0	2	14	1
Rice, Davis, New Market	.307	101	15	31	4	0	0	9	4
Metheny, Brent, Harrisonburg	.304	158	24	48	10	1	4	24	17
Honce, Joe, Covington	.303	188	41	57	8	1	2	21	20
Sittauer, Ryan, Harrisonburg	.303	109	13	33	6	0	2	18	1
Richmond, Kevin, Winchester	.303	119	21	36	7	1	1	10	5
Alexander, Chris, NM	.301	163	20	49	8	0	2	24	0
White, Kevin, NM	.301	173	25	52	10	1	10	36	2
Matuszek, Kevin, Covington	.289	159	28	46	10	1	2	37	2

INDIVIDUAL PITCHING LEADERS

	W	L	ERA	G	SV	IP	H	BB	SO
Cobb, Taylor, Staunton	4	1	1.06	8	0	42	22	21	48
Guevara, Carlos, Covington	3	1	1.30	18	6	48	33	9	68
Coles, Corey, Covington	5	0	1.30	7	0	48	39	7	61
Shanks, E.J., Harrisonburg	4	1	1.30	7	0	48	40	2	68
Lubrano, Paul, Harrisonburg	3	1	1.81	10	1	50	39	19	55
Hamilton, Clay, Winchester	4	1	1.81	8	0	50	36	19	56
Camardese, Brandon, Staunton	4	2	1.93	7	0	42	33	15	46
Dagenhart, Jeff, New Market	6	2	1.94	14	2	51	31	18	73
Hendley, Blake, Harrisonburg	3	5	2.01	9	0	63	42	19	61
Harden, Steve, Covington	3	1	2.20	16	1	49	43	13	59

NON-AFFILIATED LEAGUES

ALASKA LEAGUE

	W	L	PCT	GB	Overall W	Overall L
Fairbanks Goldpanners	22	13	.629	—	38	19
Anchorage Glacier Pilots	22	13	.629	—	39	21
Anchorage Bucs	20	15	.571	2	25	24
Kenai Peninsula Oilers	15	20	.429	7	20	28
Athletes In Action-Alaska	14	21	.400	8	24	27
Mat-Su Miners	12	23	.343	10	19	30

ALL-STAR TEAM: C—Sean Flynn, Bucs (Texas-Pan American). 1B—Andy Schutzenhofer, Oilers (Illinois). 2B—Eric Rodlund, Athletes In Action (Gonzaga). 3B—Tim Petru, Athletes In Action (Texas A&M). SS—Preston Griffin, Oilers (UCLA). OF—Tony Perez, Goldpanners (San Diego); Scott Robinson, Goldpanners (Rancho Bernardo HS, San Diego); Terry Trofholz, Bucs (Texas Christian). DH—Dennis Bigley, Glacier Pilots (Oral Roberts). UT—Joe Diefenderfer, Bucs (Santa Clara). P—Zak Basch, Goldpanners (Hofstra); David Purcey, Glacier Pilots (Oklahoma); Derek Roper, Athletes In Action (Missouri); Sean Timmons, Goldpanners; Sean Warlop, Glacier Pilots (San Diego); Jered Weaver, Bucs (Long Beach State).

TOP 10 PROSPECTS: 1. David Purcey, lhp, Anchorage Glacier Pilots (Oklahoma). 2. Jered Weaver, rhp, Anchorage Bucs (Long Beach State). 3. Ryan Schroyer, rhp, Alaska Goldpanners (Arizona State). 4. Marc Kaiser, rhp, Alaska Goldpanners (Arizona). 5. Paul Janish, ss/rhp, Kenai Peninsula Oilers (Rice). 6. Blake Gill, 2b-ss, Mat-su Miners (Louisiana State). 7. Chad Corona, 3b, Alaska Goldpanners (San Diego State). 8. Drew Anderson, of, Anchorage Glacier Pilots (Nebraska). 9. Dennis Bigley, rhp/inf, Anchorage Glacier Pilots (Oral Roberts). 10. Eric Rodland, 2b-ss, Athletes in Action (Gonzaga).

INDIVIDUAL BATTING LEADERS
(Minimum 100 Plate Appearances)

	AVG	AB	R	H	2B	3B	HR	RBI	SB
Rodland, Eric, AIA	.423	168	25	71	7	5	1	18	20
Gill, Blake, Mat-Su	.336	116	15	39	7	2	1	8	4
Swope, Tobin, Mat-Su	.330	97	9	32	8	0	0	9	5
Robinson, Scott, Fairbanks	.324	139	8	45	9	0	2	25	4
Trofoltz, Terry, Bucs	.323	127	19	41	3	1	0	14	8
Schutzenhofer, Andy, Kenai	.312	138	23	43	13	1	1	22	9
Pratt, Haas, Glacier Pilots	.311	119	12	37	4	0	4	17	1
Burt, Jim, AIA	.310	116	12	36	1	2	2	16	3
Anderson, Drew, Gl. Pilots	.306	98	15	30	2	3	3	20	2
Marks, Tim, AIA	.289	121	15	35	7	0	0	6	2
Griffin, Preston, Kenai	.288	125	19	36	8	0	0	12	2
Harper, Jerin, Bucs	.286	105	13	30	5	0	0	6	0
Diefenderfer, Joe, Bucs	.283	120	14	34	3	2	0	17	2
Rogers, Grant, Fairbanks	.282	117	17	33	2	0	1	10	2
Wahlbrink, Brian, Oilers	.274	124	15	34	5	3	1	5	9
Deevers, Robby, AIA	.273	154	27	42	9	1	2	12	9
Underwood, Daniel, Kenai	.271	97	14	26	3	0	1	6	6
Flynn, Sean, Bucs	.271	133	12	36	8	0	1	20	1

INDIVIDUAL PITCHING LEADERS
(Minimum 35 innings)

	W	L	ERA	G	SV	IP	H	BB	SO
Basch, Zak, Fairbanks	4	1	0.76	13	2	35	19	10	33
Roper, Derek, AIA	5	2	0.87	9	1	62	47	14	45
Purcey, David, Glacier Pilots	2	1	1.13	9	1	48	21	26	66
Huddy, Kyle, Mat-Su	3	0	1.21	9	2	37	22	21	37
Weaver, Jered, Bucs	4	1	1.25	10	0	58	35	19	61
Warlop, Sean, Glacier Pilots	4	1	1.32	9	0	61	40	19	35
Timmons, Sean, Fairbanks	5	0	1.38	7	0	52	45	5	40
Moat, Mike, Fairbanks	5	2	1.57	9	0	57	41	19	38
Mentkowski, Ryan, Pilots	2	1	1.70	8	0	48	40	2	29
Lincoln, Roger, Kenai	3	4	1.78	7	0	51	43	18	32
McCally, Ryan, Bucs	4	1	1.84	7	0	49	41	7	37
Kerbs, Reuben, Gl. Pilots	4	1	2.09	7	0	39	35	15	28
Abreu, Justin, Mat-Su	3	2	2.20	9	0	61	51	11	31
Johnson, Bryan, Bucs	2	2	2.45	16	4	51	42	15	48
Kaiser, Marc, Fairbanks	4	2	2.47	7	1	47	44	20	44
Perry, Kyle, Mat-Su	3	3	2.68	8	0	47	40	19	43

CLARK GRIFFITH LEAGUE

	W	L	PCT	GB
*+Arlington Senators	32	10	.762	—
Bethesda Big Train	27	14	.659	4 ½
Vienna Mustangs	20	19	.513	10 ½
Silver Spring-Takoma Thunderbolts	20	20	.500	11
Fauquier Gators	16	25	.390	15 ½
Baltimore Pride	16	25	.390	15 ½
Reston Hawks	15	24	.384	15 ½
Germantown Black Rox	15	25	.375	16

* First-half champion   + Second-half champion
PLAYOFFS: None.

INDIVIDUAL BATTING LEADERS
(Minimum 100 Plate Appearances)

	AVG	AB	R	H	2B	3B	HR	RBI	SB
Stanton, Chris, Vienna	.386	153	34	59	10	1	0	14	19
Lucas, Ed, Germantown	.346	133	29	46	8	1	1	10	7
Hughes, David, Bethesda	.339	121	13	41	6	1	0	7	7
Butia, Mike, Arlington	.333	123	23	41	5	1	3	25	3
Keeton, Ben, Germantown	.329	161	23	53	5	2	0	15	11
Hutton, Derek, Bethesda	.327	107	16	35	8	3	0	9	5
Toregas, Wyatt, Arlington	.320	128	18	41	9	1	0	20	4
Tucker, Derrick, Fauquier	.319	94	9	30	2	0	0	16	5
Luina, Miguel, Vienna	.316	152	20	48	10	4	1	29	9
Blair, Cameron, Arlington	.316	95	25	30	4	0	0	14	9
Weir, Garrett, SS-T	.311	103	16	32	5	2	0	9	11
Underwood, Bret, SS-T	.310	142	21	44	10	1	3	33	2
Bennett, Stacy, Arlington	.309	94	20	29	6	0	1	17	2
Cafe, Sadry, Fauquier	.294	119	17	35	10	2	1	12	9
Howell, Kris, SS-T	.293	140	22	41	7	1	1	17	5

INDIVIDUAL PITCHING LEADERS
(Minimum 35 innings)

	W	L	ERA	G	SV	IP	H	BB	SO
Binda, Byron, Bethesda	6	0	1.16	11	1	54	37	16	52
Foster, Matt, Bethesda	4	2	1.43	7	0	50	39	10	38
Hlebovy, Gus, Bethesda	6	2	1.45	13	2	50	31	11	38
Meredith, Clay, Arlington	4	2	1.64	9	0	55	34	14	52
Johnson, Steve, Baltimore	2	2	1.76	8	1	41	34	11	31
Payne, Kenny, Reston	3	4	1.80	8	0	65	68	16	35
Strayhorne, Jimmy, Germ.	2	1	1.98	7	0	50	34	16	31
Glanzmann, Jake, Arlington	5	0	2.09	9	0	60	48	20	41
Dunham, Todd, Germantown	4	3	3.25	10	0	60	40	36	44
St. Germain, Risley, Arlington	4	1	2.32	7	0	50	37	13	47

JAYHAWK LEAGUE

	W	L	PCT	GB	Overall W	L
Hays Larks	20	6	.769	—	21	9
El Dorado Broncos	13	8	.619	4½	18	9
Liberal Beejays	13	9	.591	5	17	11
Nevada Griffons	10	12	.455	8	14	16
Topeka Capitols	7	14	.333	10½	10	18
Elkhart Dusters	6	20	.231	14	7	23

INDIVIDUAL BATTING LEADERS
(Minimum 55 Plate Appearances)

	AVG	AB	R	H	2B	3B	HR	RBI	SB
Ehlers, Cody, Hays	.337	101	18	34	7	0	4	18	0
Preston, Daryl, Liberal	.325	83	12	27	7	0	3	18	1
Martin, Scott, Liberal	.322	90	17	29	4	0	4	15	2
Chance, Andy, Liberal	.313	99	16	31	2	3	1	18	5
Blasi, Nick, El Dorado	.309	94	17	29	4	0	1	12	5
Patrick, Chris, Liberal	.303	76	14	23	3	0	2	8	2
Thornton, Rory, Hays	.298	94	20	28	3	1	2	9	8
D'Antonio, Brad, Elkhart	.296	81	14	24	5	1	1	3	10
Moeller, Brian, Hays	.292	89	17	26	7	0	0	11	10
Julo, Chris, Hays	.286	77	13	22	5	0	3	13	1
Allen, John, Topeka	.284	81	13	23	4	1	2	17	5
Gilbert, Gary, Nevada	.279	86	9	24	1	0	0	7	0
Witt, Paul, Hays	.277	94	13	26	2	0	1	10	9
Wilson, Kyle, Topeka	.270	74	12	20	3	1	1	11	1
Cox, Adam, Hays	.270	89	17	24	8	0	1	8	0

INDIVIDUAL PITCHING LEADERS
(Minimum 20 Innings)

	W	L	ERA	G	SV	IP	H	BB	SO
Blair, Buddy, Liberal	4	1	0.82	7	0	44	23	12	45
Clancy, Shawn, El Dorado	3	0	0.85	5	0	32	20	7	20
Ehling, Andrew, El Dorado	2	0	1.01	5	0	27	24	7	19
Carson, Murray, Elkhart	2	2	1.57	5	0	29	21	17	25
Broshuis, Garrett, Liberal	5	0	1.74	5	0	31	18	2	35
Wendte, Travis, Hays	3	1	1.74	7	0	31	27	15	25
Hebert, Robbie, El Dorado	1	0	2.05	5	0	26	21	13	21
Hottovy, Tommy, Hays	3	0	2.17	6	0	37	34	12	23
Weems, Ryan, Topeka	0	0	2.18	5	0	21	16	5	16
Uhlmansiek, Steve, Liberal	4	0	2.32	5	0	31	29	20	20

YOUTH BASEBALL

BY ALLAN SIMPSON

Louisville's Valley Sports became the first U.S. team since 1998 and only the fifth in the last 18 years to win the Little League (11-12) World Series, as it beat defending champion Japan 1-0 in the 2002 championship game. The game was seen by more than 40,000 fans and a national television audience.

Five-foot-7, 175-pound ace Aaron Alvey dominated Japan with a three-hitter and 11 strikeouts in a battle of unbeaten teams. Alvey also pro-duced the game's only run with a long first-inning home run.

"It was 68 mph down the middle," Alvey said. "It was belt-high, so it was going to get crushed."

Alvey's dominating perfor-mance continued a brilliant showing by the Louisville pitch-ing staff, which allowed only four runs in six games. Alvey himself set three tournament

Zach Osborne

records. He had 44 strikeouts, eight more than the previ-ous record; 20 consecutive scoreless innings, eight more than the previous best; and 12 consecutive hitless innings, which tied the record set in 1993 by Little League legend Sean Burroughs of Long Beach, Calif., now a member of the San Diego Padres.

In one of the greatest Little League games ever, an 11-inning, 2-1 Louisville win over Fort Worth, Texas, in the first round of bracket play, Alvey worked nine hitless innings, striking out 19. His counterpart, Fort Worth left-hander Walker Kelly, struck out 21 while allowing two hits. Both pitchers had no-hitters through the regulation six innings. Little League rules prohibit pitchers from working more than nine innings in a game, so the two pitchers exited with 40 strikeouts between them. In all, there were 49 strikeouts in the game.

Zach Osborne, Louisville's other two-way star, led off the 11th with a home run and Alvey followed with another to open a 2-0 lead. Osborne, who pitched a scoreless 10th inning, earned the win. He then came back two days later to beat Worcester, Mass., 4-0 on two hits in the U.S. cham-pionship game against Japan a day later.

Overall, Osborne was 3-0 and allowed no runs in 13 innings while striking out 27. At the plate, he led the tournament with 10 hits and was one of five players, including Alvey, to hit three home runs.

Louisville went a perfect 24-0 on its way to the title, outscoring its opponents in district, state, regional and World Series play 106-10. It became the first American team since Toms River, N.J., to win the title. Japan, which allowed only two runs in six tournament games, had won two of the previous three World Series.

Visalia continues U.S. streak

Visalia, Calif., leaned heavily on its two best players throughout the Cal Ripken (12 and under) World Series, but in the end it was a team effort that propelled the team to the series title.

Visalia dominated Korea in a 6-1 victory in the cham-

pionship game, led by cleanup hitter Ross Hebert, who pitched two scoreless innings to pick up a save and hit a home run in the first to stake Visalia to a lead it would never give up. Hebert led his team in innings and had three home runs in the tournament, tying him for the team lead with outfielder David Palacios. Palacios, who was named the outstanding United States player in the tournament, had 12 RBIs and a 1.105 slugging percent-age. He also pitched in three games.

Visalia's win was the third straight year that a U.S. team won the Cal Ripken series, which is a division of Babe Ruth Baseball.

■ Hazel Dell of Vancouver, Wash., won the Babe Ruth 13-year-old World Series in 2001 and repeated as 14-year-old champions by defeating Tri-Valley, Calif., 3-0 on a two-hitter by Jackson Evans—his second two-hit win of the tournament.

■ Mobile, Ala., failed in its bid to win a record third consecutive Babe Ruth 16-18 World Series title as it fell 3-2 in the championship game to Weimar, Texas. Texas A&M-bound righthander B.J. Boening, a 14th-round draft pick of the Astros in June, scattered eight hits and struck out eight to beat Mobile.

■ El Segundo, Calif., completed a rain-delayed 6-1 win over Tallahassee, Fla., and then pounded four home runs in a 17-11 victory over Beaverton, Ore., to win the Babe Ruth 13-15 World Series. Jeff Nisen homered in both games for El Segundo and went 15-for-21 overall, while tournament MVP Sean McNally had five hits on the final day. El Segundo won all six games it played.

Dual champions

The powerful East Cobb baseball program from Marietta, Ga., added to its bulging trophy case by win-ning four more national titles in 2002.

The 16-year-old East Cobb Astros stood out, winning 19 straight games to capture two major national titles in a 20-day span. They went 10-0, beating the Bloomfield Hills (Mich.) Wolves 18-0 in the final, to win the 24-team Continental Amateur Baseball Association (CABA) World Series, played at East Cobb's own new $9.8 million com-plex in Marietta. The Astros then went 9-0, beating the Arlington (Texas) Wizards 4-1 in the final, to win the 48-team Amateur Athletic Union (AAU) Junior Olympics national title in Knoxville, Tenn. East Cobb's victory in the Junior Olympics marked the sixth time in the last seven years that it won the gold medal. It fin-ished second in 2000.

TOP-RANKED YOUTH TEAMS		
2002		
Compiled by USA Sports Rankings		
12	Tucson Wildcats (64-7)	
13	Houston Raiders (71-9)	
14	Houston Banditos (105-8)	
15	Central Arkansas Sox (45-3)	
16	East Cobb, Ga., Astros (60-7)	
18	Florida Bombers (50-2)	

"This was the best team we've ever had," said Astros manager Guerry Baldwin, who was instrumental in build-ing the East Cobb program into a national power.

East Cobb's 13-year-old Astros also won the AAU 13-year-old national title and the East Cobb Trojans won the U.S. Specialty Sports Association (USSSA) 15-year-old World Series. East Cobb's 14-year-old Eagles finished sec-ond at the USSSA 14 World Series.

AMATEUR/YOUTH CHAMPIONS 2002

TEAM USA

COLLEGE TEAM	Site	Champion	Runner-up
FISU World University	Messina, Italy	Cuba	United States

JUNIOR TEAM (18-and-under)	Site	Champion	Runner-up
World Junior Championship	Sherbrooke, Quebec	Cuba	Chinese Taipei

YOUTH TEAM (16-and-under)	Site	Champion	Runner-up
COPABE Pam Am AA Champ.	Barquisimeto, Venez.	Cuba	United States
USA Junior Olympics—East	Jupiter, Fla.	Orlando Scorpions	Apopka, Fla.
USA Junior Olympics—West	Tucson, Ariz.	Subia, Ariz.	Dallas Yankees

ALL-AMERICAN AMATEUR BASEBALL ASSOCIATION (AAABA)

Event	Site	Champion	Runner-up
World Series (21 &under)	Johnstown, Pa.	Arlington (Va.) Senators	New Orleans

AMATEUR ATHLETIC UNION (AAU)

Event	Site	Champion	Runner-up
9 & Under	Orlando	San Diego Stars-North	Orlando Xplosion
10 & Under (60-foot)	Des Moines	Tampa Heat	Iowa Sting
10 & Under (65-foot)	Knoxville	Florida Xtreme	Carolina Angels
11 & Under	Orlando	Sandy Plains (Ga.) Wildcats	Richmond Braves-National
12 & Under	Burnsville, Minn.	Orlando Blast	Team Texas
13 & Under (90-foot)	Sarasota, Fla.	Greensboro, N.C.	St. Petersburg Stingers
13 & Under (80-foot)	Tulsa	East Cobb (Ga.) Astros	Tulsa Lookouts
14 & Under (90-foot)	Norman, Okla.	Florida Hitmen	Southern California Rebels
15 & Under	Kingsport, Tenn.	Northern California Baseball	West Bay (Calif.) Titans
Junior Olympics/16 & u	Orlando	East Cobb (Ga.) Astros	Arlington (Texas) Wizards
17 & Under	Orlando	Dulin's (Tenn.) Dodgers	Knoxville Thunder
18 & Under	Fort Myers, Fla.	Dulin's (Tenn.) Dodgers	Shoetiques Baseball

AMERICAN AMATEUR BASEBALL CONGRESS (AABC)

Event	Site	Champion	Runner-up
Roberto Clemente (8 & u)	McDonough, Ga.	McDonough (Ga.) Braves	Puerto Rico
Willie Mays (10 & u)	Calano, P.R.	Ponce, P.R.	Rockford, Ill.
Pee Wee Reese (12 & u)	Toa Baja, P.R.	Gresham Park, Ga.	Tulsa
Sandy Koufax (14 & u)	Jersey City, N.J.	Memphis	Monrovia, Calif.
Mickey Mantle (16 & u)	McKinney, Texas	Dallas Knights	Orange County, Calif.
Connie Mack (18 & u)	Farmington, N.M.	Long Beach Cardinals	Bill Hood (La.) Broncos
Stan Musial (open)	Battle Creek, Mich.	Northwest Houston Wildcats	Easton (Mass.) Huskies

AMERICAN LEGION BASEBALL

Event	Site	Champion	Runner-up
World Series (19 & u)	Danville, Va.	West Point, Miss.	Excelsior, Minn.

BABE RUTH BASEBALL

Event	Site	Champion	Runner-up
Cal Ripken (10 & under)	Bakersfield, Calif.	Jacksonville, Fla.	Willamette Valley, Ore.
Cal Ripken (11-12)	Mattoon, Ill.	Visalia, Calif.	Korea
13	Abbeville, La.	Levittown, Pa.	Nord Lakeshore, La.
14	Clifton Park, N.Y.	Vancouver, Wash.	Tri-Valley, Calif.
13-15	Connersville, Ind.	El Segundo, Calif.	Beaverton, Ore.
16	Russellville, Ark.	Nederland, Texas	Lakeville, Minn.
16-18	Stamford, Conn.	Weimar (Texas) Rattlers	Mobile (Ala.) Rawdogs

CONTINENTAL AMATEUR BASEBALL ASSOCIATION (CABA)

Event	Site	Champion	Runner-up
9 & under	Charles City, Iowa	Omaha Pacesetters	Cedar Rapids (Iowa) Cougars
10 & under	Aurelia, Iowa	Omaha Pacesetters	Mansfield, Ohio
11 & under	Marion, Ohio	Norris, Tenn.	North Royalton, Ohio
12 & under	Omaha	Oklahoma City Indians	Omaha Pacesetters
13 & under	Broken Arrow, Okla.	Kansas City, Kan.	Sao Paulo, Brazil
14 & under	Dublin, Ohio	Washington State Cannons	Upper Deck (Ill.) Cougars
15 & under	Crystal Lake, Ill.	Dallas	Woodbury, Minn.
16 & under	Marietta, Ga.	East Cobb (Ga.) Astros	Bloomfield Hills (Mich.) Wolves
High school age	Euclid, Ohio	Bergen Beach, N.Y.	Kansas City, Mo.
18 & under	Homestead, Fla.	Palos, Ill.	Cincinnati

DIXIE BASEBALL

Event	Site	Champion	Runner-up
Dixie Youth (9-10) Majors WS	Pascagoula, Miss.	North Gwinnett, Ga.	Bartow, Fla.
Dixie Youth (12 & u)	Pascagoula, Miss.	Nacogdoches, Texas	Hattiesburg, Miss.
Dixie 13	Covington, Ga.	Longview, Texas	Dentsville, S.C.
Dixie Boys (13-14)	Euless, Texas	Columbia County, Ga.	Bossier City, La.
Dixie Pre-Majors (15-16)	Guntersville, Ala.	Laurel/Jones County, Miss.	Monroe, La.
Dixie Majors (15-18)	Monroe, La.	Monroe, La.	Marshall, Texas

DIZZY DEAN BASEBALL

Event	Site	Champion	Runner-up
Minor League (9-10)	Huffman, Ala.	Madison, Miss.	Grenada, Miss.
Freshman (11-12)	Pace, Fla.	Grenada, Miss.	Northport, Ala.
Sophomore (13-14)	Southaven, Miss.	Pace, Fla.	Maryland Athletics
Junior (15-16)	Southaven, Miss.	Maryland	Boynton, Ga.
Senior (17-18)	Southaven, Miss.	Lufkin, Texas	Tri-Cities, Tenn.
High school	Starkville, Miss.	Dallas, Ga.	Suniton, Ala.

HAP DUMONT BASEBALL/National Baseball Congress

Event	Site	Champion	Runner-up
8 & under	Kansas City, Mo.	North Kansas City Canes	Lawrence, Kan.
10 & under	Roswell, Ga.	West Cobb (Ga.) Warriors	Collierville (Minn.) Rebels
11 & under	Oklahoma City	Wichita Diamondbacks	Houston Mudbugs
12 & under	Greenville, Ind.	Fredrick (Okla.) Greyhounds	Memphis Travelers
13 & under	Casper, Wyo.	Topeka Gorillas	Redmond (Wash.) Rockets
14 & under	Brainerd, Minn.	Omaha Patriots	Wichita Cardinals
15 & under	Harrison, Ark.	Kansas City Players	Baton Rouge Outlaws
16 & under	Nashville, Tenn.	Tennessee Athletics	Wichita Jets
18 & under	Bartlesville, Okla.	Wichita Sluggers	Dallas Express

LITTLE LEAGUE BASEBALL

Event	Site	Champion	Runner-up
Little League (11-12)	Williamsport, Pa.	Louisville, Ky.	Sendai, Japan
Junior League (13-14)	Taylor, Mich.	Cartersville, Ga.	Panama City, Panama
Senior League (15-16)	Kissimmee, Fla.	Curacao	East Boynton Beach, Fla.
Big League (17-18)	Easley, S.C.	Puerto Rico	Hughesville, Md.

NATIONAL AMATEUR BASEBALL FEDERATION (NABF)

Event	Site	Champion	Runner-up
Rookie (10 & u)	Baltimore	Baltimore Buzz	Cincinnati Storm
Freshman (12 & u)	Hopkinsville, Ky.	Howard County (Md.) Raiders	Ohio Flames
Sophomore (14 & u)	Joplin, Mo.	New York Giants	Frederick (Md.) Hustles
Junior (16 & u)	Northville, Mich.	Maryland Orioles	Indiana Bulls
High School (17 & u)	Millington, Tenn.	Dulin's (Tenn.) Dodgers	Apopka (Fla.) Baseball
Senior (18 & u)	Welland, Ontario	Columbus (Ohio) Cobras	Jackson (Miss.) 96ers
College (22 & u)	Dayton, Ohio	Cincinnati Stars	Ohio Warhawks
Major (open)	Louisville	Spingfield (Ohio) Giants	Evansville (Ind.) Outlaws

PERFECT GAME/BASEBALL AMERICA WORLD WOOD BAT ASSOCIATION

Event	Site	Champion	Runner-up
Summer Championship	Marietta, Ga.	Florida Bombers	Ohio Warhawks
Fall Championship	Jupiter, Fla.	Baseball America	South Bay (Calif.) Sharks
Underclassmen Championship	Fort Myers, Fla.	East Cobb (Ga.) Astros	Florida Yard Dogs

PONY BASEBALL

Event	Site	Champion	Runner-up
Mustang (9-10)	Irving, Texas	Levittown, P.R.	Santa Clarita, Calif.
Bronco (11-12)	Monterey, Calif.	Agoura, Calif.	Taipei, Taiwan
Pony (13-14)	Washington, Pa.	Norwalk, Calif.	Levittown, P.R.
Colt (15-16)	Lafayette, Ind.	Santa Clara, Calif.	Bayamon, P.R.
Palomino (17-18)	Santa Clara, Calif.	Santa Clara (Calif.) Red Sox	Orange County (Calif.) Renegades

REVIVING BASEBALL IN INNER CITIES (RBI)

Event	Site	Champion	Runner-up
Junior (13-15)	Chicago	Atlanta	Los Angeles
Senior (16-18)	Chicago	Los Angeles	Cincinnati

TRIPLE CROWN BASEBALL

Event	Site	Champion	Runner-up
9 & under	Steamboat Springs, Colo.	Orange County (Calif.) Aztecs	Dallas (Texas) Sports
10 & under	Steamboat Springs, Colo.	Flower Mound (Texas) Rattlers	Miami Mudcats
11 & under	Steamboat Springs, Colo.	Spanish Fork (Utah) Mariners	O'Keiki (Calif.) Mustangs
12 & under	Steamboat Springs, Colo.	Tucson Wildcats	Fort Collins (Colo.) Lugnuts
13 & under	Steamboat Springs, Colo.	So Cal Bombers	Dallas Tigers
14 & under	Steamboat Springs, Colo.	Seattle Stars	Palm Desert (Calif.) Tigers
15 & under	Steamboat Springs, Colo.	Ann Arbor (Mich.) Braves	Riverside (Calif.) Falcons
16 & under	Steamboat Springs, Colo.	Oakland (Minn.) Bulldogs	Inland Valley (Calif.) Stealth
18 & under	Steamboat Springs, Colo.	Hillcrest (Utah) Huskies	Kansas City Generals

U.S. AMATEUR BASEBALL ASSOCIATION (USABA)

Event	Site	Champion	Runner-up
11 & under	Gig Harbor, Wash.	Seattle Stars	Everett (Wash.) Bulldogs
12 & under	Gig Harbor, Wash.	Washington Cobras	Bainbridge (Wash.) Hawks
14 & under	Pasco, Wash.	Portland (Ore.) Ravens	Yakima Valley, Wash.
15 & under	Albany, Ore.	Kennewick (Wash.) Dirt Dogs	Fresno
16 & under	Richland, Wash.	Pasco (Wash.) Bulldogs	Kennewick (Wash.) Dirt Dogs
18 & under	Carson City, Nev.	Sumner (Wash.) Triple Play	Arlington (Texas) Apatche Reds

U.S. SPECIALTY SPORTS ASSOCIATION (USSSA)

Event	Site	Champion	Runner-up
9 & under/Majors	Sulphur, La.	Oklahoma City Mets	Georgia Seminoles
10 & under/Majors	Henderson, Nev.	Alabama Rockets	Murrieta (Calif.) Muddogs
11 & under/Majors	Houston	San Diego Stallions	Texas Thunder
12 & under/Majors	Omaha	Florida Diamond Kings	Puerto Rico
13 & under/Majors	High Point, N.C.	Houston Raiders	Beaver Valley, Pa.
14 & under/Majors (80-foot)	Houston	Houston Banditos	San Antonio Wildcats
14 & Under/Majors (90-foot)	Lynchburg, Tenn.	Sandy Plains (Ga.) Wildcats	East Cobb (Ga.) Eagles
15 & under/Majors	Winter Haven, Fla.	East Cobb (Ga.) Trojans	St. Louis Mustangs
16 & under/Majors	Oklahoma City	Kansas Sluggers	Inland (Calif.) Terrors
17 & Under/Majors	Bourbonnais, Ill.	Orland (Ill.) Magic	Michigan Cobras
18 & under/Majors	Jupiter, Fla.	Savannah (Ga.) Chain	Connecticut Bombers

BASEBALL FOR THE AGES

Like a fine wine, Baseball America's annual Baseball For The Ages winners just continue to get better.

Six age-group selections in 2002 were repeat winners, including 16-year-old Delmon Young, Baseball America's inaugural Youth Player of the Year. He was the pick of his age group in 1999 as a 13-year-old and a year later at 14.

Four of the other five repeat winners also won in 2001, while Austin Jackson, 15, is back after a three-year absence. He was our winner in 1999 as a 12-year-old.

In each case, the youth baseball cutoff date of Aug. 1 is used to establish a player's age.

12 ZACH OSBORNE, ss/rhp, Louisville

You'd be hard-pressed to find an amateur team at any level that got more attention than Louisville's Valley Sports Little League team in 2002. The team tore through the Little League World Series, completing an unbeaten season. Leading the way was Osborne, who with Aaron Alvey took the Louisville team through the tournament with a 24-0 record as it swept to local, district, state, national and overall titles. Osborne's highlights included a tournament-best 10 hits and three home runs; a two-hit, 11-strikeout shutout over Worcester, Mass., in the U.S. championship game (he also drove in the game's first run in a 4-0 win); an overall record of 3-0, 0.00 with 27 strikeouts in 13 innings in the tournament; and strong defense at shortstop from the team's first game.

13 RYAN STILL, ss/rhp, Houston

Thirteen is the most difficult age to gauge youth talent as pitchers are forced to step up to 54- or 60-foot mounds, and hitters are challenged by knocking balls out of high school-sized fields. None made a smoother transition to the larger dimensions as easily as the 5-foot-7, 145-pound Still, our 12-year-old winner in 2001. The switch-hitting Still earned MVP honors at the USSSA World Series in his age group for the third straight year as his team, the Houston Raiders (71-9), won the USSSA title for the third year in a row. In 77 games for the nation's No. 1-ranked 13-year-old team, Still hit .527 with 124 runs and 58 extra-base hits, including 11 home runs. He went 10-3, 1.99 with 12 saves and 106 strikeouts in 84 innings when called on to pitch. His fastball has been clocked at 84 mph.

14 JUSTIN UPTON, ss, Chesapeake, Va.

How do you upstage your brother if you're three years younger and he was the second overall pick in the 2002 draft? Go out to the Area Code Games in California and stand head and shoulders above the older competition. That's exactly what Upton did in 2002, displaying outstanding defensive skills and an overall game that's more advanced than older brother B.J.'s at the same age. But the Area Codes weren't the only stage where the younger Upton showcased his skills. He also went 11-for-20 with nine extra-base hits in eight games for a predominantly 14-year-old squad that finished fifth out of 56 teams at USA Baseball's 16-and-under Junior Olympics in Jupiter, Fla.; participated in the 16-and-under national

Justin Upton

youth team trials; and hit better than .500 for the runner-up team at the Triple Crown World Series in Colorado. And he hit .385-4-26 in the spring as a freshman at Chesapeake's Hickory High.

15 AUSTIN JACKSON, of, Denton, Texas

After being named the nation's top 12-year-old in 1999, Jackson didn't pursue baseball as vigorously as his other passion, basketball. But baseball moved to the forefront again in 2002 as Jackson hit .452 as a freshman at Denton Ryan High before helping the Dallas Panthers to a third-place finish at Team USA's Junior Olympics in Tucson. Over the summer, he hit more than .600 and struck out just three times. As a result of that performance, he was selected to play for Team USA at the COPABE Youth (16-and-under) championship—a qualifying event for the 2003

Austin Jackson

World Youth Championship—in Venezuela. Despite being one of the team's younger players, his .440 average was second-best on the team.

16 DELMON YOUNG, of/rhp, Camarillo, Calif.

After hitting .542-17-56 and becoming one of only two juniors on Baseball America's 2002 High School All-America team in the spring, Young went on a rampage during the summer. Young starring for Team USA's junior national team. He shattered the World Junior Championship record with nine home runs in 39 at-bats, earning him tournament MVP honors. Young went on to hit 16 home runs overall for Team USA while leading the squad in the triple crown categories (.474-16-49).

17 B.J. UPTON, ss, Devil Rays

Before the Devil Rays snagged him with the second overall pick in the 2002 draft, Upton capped off his second straight All-America season at Greenbrier Christian Academy in Chesapeake, Va. Upton, whose brother Justin was the top 14-year-old, hit .641-11-52 with 21 stolen bases as a senior. He also batted .633-13-44 with 43 steals as a junior. Upton was signed to a $4.6 million contract—the largest in the 2002 draft—with Tampa Bay in September, meaning he won't make his pro debut until 2003.

18 SCOTT KAZMIR, lhp, Mets

Kazmir was a clear choice as Baseball America's 2002 High School Player of the Year award after posting an 11-2, 0.37 record with 172 strikeouts in 75 innings, with just 19 walks and 19 hits allowed as a senior at Cypress Falls High in Houston. A consensus top-five talent in the 2002 draft, rumors about Kazmir's contract demands caused him to slide until the Mets picked him at No. 15. After inking a $2.15 million deal, the 6-foot southpaw made his debut in the college-dominated New York-Penn League. He actually topped his unearthly high school strikeout ratio (16 K/9 IP) by striking out 34 in 18 innings (17 K/9) for short-season Brooklyn. Kazmir, whose fastball consistently travels up to 96 mph, allowed five hits and seven walks while going 0-1, 0.50 in his five pro starts.

WINNERS AGES 19-25

| 19. JOSE REYES, ss, New York Mets |
| 20. ROCCO BALDELLI, of, Tampa Bay Devil Rays |
| 21. MARK PRIOR, rhp, Chicago Cubs |
| 22. ALBERT PUJOLS, of/3b, St. Louis Cardinals |
| 23. MARK BUEHRLE, lhp, Chicago White Sox |
| 24. ALFONSO SORIANO, 2b, New York Yankees |
| 25. PAT BURRELL, of, Philadelphia Phillies |

AMATEUR BASEBALL

DRAFT

First-round bonuses take downturn as MLB, union wrestle with changes

BY JIM CALLIS

For a change, the biggest news involving the first-year player draft didn't concern which prospects were taken by which teams. The most significant developments in 2002 were the curbing of first-round bonus inflation, and a temporary change of draft rules that would have encouraged teams to cherish ability more than signability—had an agreement between the owners and players not unraveled.

After Baseball America started tracking bonuses in 1989, the average first-round bonus always rose from one year to the next. Increases of 25 percent or more were commonplace. Inflation slowed to an annual average of 10 percent in 1999-2001, then hit the wall in 2002.

The 27 first-rounders who had signed by November received an average of $2.05 million, down 5.2 percent from the 2001 average of $2.163 million. Just nine first-rounders got that much in 2002, including the top seven picks who had signed. If and when Adam Loewen (No. 4, Orioles) and Bobby Brownlie (No. 21, Cubs) agree to terms, they're still unlikely to raise the 2002 average past 2001's.

Rampant inflation wasn't about to return in the near future, had a significant alteration to draft rules taken hold. While talk of a worldwide draft and other extensive changes to the process were tabled when the owners and players narrowly averted a strike by agreeing to a Basic Agreement on Aug. 30, the sides did agree to adjust the rules.

To create a more open market for its major league constituents, the union sought the elimination of draft-pick compensation for the loss of top free agents. In return, the union gave teams a hammer it could use against future first-round selections.

Starting in 2003, teams that failed to sign a first-round pick would have gotten a bonus choice following the corresponding selection in the next year's draft. In other words, if a club didn't sign the No. 3 overall pick, it would have recouped a choice between the third and fourth selections a year later.

Under existing rules, a team that is unable to sign its first-round pick receives only a sandwich pick between the first and second rounds, which often falls somewhere between 35th and 40th picks overall. Sandy Alderson, Major League Baseball's executive vice president of baseball operations, said the intent of the new rule was to equalize the leverage between the team and the draftee.

However, the owners and the union couldn't agree on what they agreed upon when the Basic Agreement was being finalized in

Pittsburgh selected Ball State's Bryan Bullington with No. 1 pick

writing. Both sides agreed to revert to the old rules—at least temporarily.

A joint committee of MLB representatives, union officials and possibly owners were scheduled to revisit the shelved rules changes and also continue to work toward the formation of a worldwide draft. The owners and players agreed to the concept in mid-July, and the number of rounds probably will be shortened from the current 50 to somewhere between 20 and 38. Among other hurdles to be cleared are determining the eligible age of players from other nations; devising a registration process so teams won't be able to stash players and sign them as free agents after the draft; and possibly placing the system of club-run academies in foreign countries under MLB's watch.

The committee also was expected to consider allowing teams to trade picks, which has been forbidden since the draft started in 1965. The teams preferred allowing picks to be dealt only before the draft, while the union proposed that unsigned draftees and signees with less than a year under contract also be tradeable.

Bullington Goes No. 1

The Pirates owned the No. 1 pick in the 2002 draft. Their decision went down to the wire.

BONUS ESCALATION

For the first time since at least 1989, first-round bonuses decreased in 2002. Here's the year-by-year, first-round average with the resulting annual increase (decrease). The 2002 figures include signings through October.

Year	Average Bonus	Increase
1989	$176,000	—
1990	$246,000	39.7%
1991	$355,000	44.3%
1992	$482,000	35.8%
1993	$611,000	26.8%
1994	$790,000	29.3%
1995	$913,000	15.6%
1996*	$924,000	1.2%
1997	$1,326,000	43.5%
1998	$1,638,000	23.5%
1999	$1,810,000	10.5%
2000	$1,873,000	3.5%
2001	$2,163,000	15.5%
2002	$2,050,214	-5.2%

*Average doesn't include four loophole free agents who didn't sign with the teams that drafted them.

Five days before the two-day draft began on June 4, the Pirates whittled their list of candidates down to three: Ball State righthander Bullington, Virginia high school shortstop B.J. Upton and Canadian prep lefthander Loewen.

Bullington, tabbed as a future first-round pick since his freshman year, pushed his velocity to a consistent 92-94 mph and refined a hard slider as a junior. He went 11-3, 2.84 with a 139-18 strikeout-walk ratio in 105 innings to capture his second straight Mid-American Conference pitcher of the year award.

While he didn't pitch well in his final start for Ball State, he eased those concerns with an impressive workout performance in front of Pittsburgh general manager Dave Littlefield and scouting director Ed Creech. It also didn't hurt that Bullington was a collegian, the preference of Pirates owner Kevin McClatchy.

Bullington was the Pirates' man. They made courtesy calls to the teams picking directly behind them, the Devil Rays and Reds, to let them know of their intent.

The next step was to contact Bullington's advisers at IMG to discuss bonus parameters before the draft. (While this technically violates MLB rules, virtually every team does this while MLB looks the other way.) Several sources confirm that the Pirates floated a $4 million deal—the figure he ultimately agreed to Oct. 30.

When IMG declined and countered with $6 million—an increase rather than a decrease from the $5.15 million Minnesota high school catcher Joe Mauer received from the Twins as the No. 1 overall pick in 2001—all of a sudden the Pirates' plans weren't so concrete any longer.

Pittsburgh made offers to Upton and Loewen, but were rebuffed in both cases. The Pirates also sounded out Texas high school lefthander Scott Kazmir, though they didn't regard him as highly as some other teams did and didn't mention a specific dollar figure. That led them back to Bullington.

On the afternoon of June 3, they decided to take him and let negotiations unfold as they may.

All of this made for some anxious waiting on the part of Bullington, who didn't know for sure that he would go first until he heard his name called on MLB's Internet broadcast of the draft.

"I heard it when everyone else did," Bullington said from his home in Fishers, Ind., where a group of 25 family members and friends celebrated his selection. "I had heard I was in their top three for the last couple of days, but that was it."

Littlefield said that when the time came for a final decision, it came down to the fact that Bullington was the best player on Pittsburgh's draft board. While the Pirates see tremendous upside, Littlefield also cautioned that Bullington isn't the second coming of Mark Prior, the first college pitcher drafted in 2001. After going No. 2 to the Cubs, Prior started all of nine minor league games in 2002 before being whisked to Wrigley Field.

The last time the Pirates had the No. 1 overall pick was in 1996, when they also selected a college pitcher. Kris Benson was hyped nearly as much as Prior is these days, but he didn't reach Pittsburgh until 1999 and has 30 victories in six professional seasons.

"I think one of the downsides for Prior doing well is that expectations are raised for the next college pitcher in the draft," Littlefield said. "We won't be swayed by how we handle things. We'll just try to manage the expectations and inform people that Mark Prior is a very unique guy."

Lengthy Negotiations For Top Picks

Before managing any expectations, Pittsburgh had to get Bullington under contract. He didn't sign by the time classes enrolled at Ball State in the fall, though he kept his options open by sitting out the fall semester. Bullington's camp reportedly was seeking $5.2 million, just more than Mauer's bonus, while the Pirates were holding firm at $3.5 million.

"We keep making progress, though it's slow, but I don't think it's anything out of the ordinary when compared to the pace of negotiations with other high draft picks in recent years throughout the industry," Littlefield said when negotiations were at a standstill.

"In the end, the Pirates made an aggressive push to reward Bryan for his talents and his draft position by increasing the total value of the deal and adjusting the payment schedule," said Casey Close, Bullington's agent.

Only twice had the No. 1 overall pick in the June draft not signed. Danny Goodwin spurned the White Sox in 1971 and went No. 1 again in 1975 to the Angels. In 1983, the Twins lost out on Tim Belcher, who went No. 1

No. 2 pick B.J. Upton signed draft's largest bonus ($4.6 million)

CLIFF WELCH

in the January 1984 draft to the Yankees. The longest holdout by a No. 1 pick who eventually signed came in 1997, when Matt Anderson didn't come to terms with the Tigers until Dec. 27.

Upton, the top position player available, went No. 2 overall to the Devil Rays. He, too, had yet to make his pro debut because he didn't sign until Sept. 11.

Like Dewon Brazelton did after Tampa Bay selected him third overall in 2001, Upton balked at the Rays' first offers because they contained relatively little up-front money. The club started with a $4.1 million bonus, but it would be spread over five years (as allowed by MLB rules because Upton, also a football star, is a two-sport athlete) and included just $100,000 payable upon signing.

Upton eventually agreed to $4.6 million over five years, with $250,000 payable immediately. The overall figure was the third largest bonus ever given to a player signing with the club that drafted him. No other player in the 2002 draft received more than $3 million as of October.

The Reds had no such trouble with the No. 3 pick. Cincinnati officials were evenly split on Kazmir and California prep righthander Chris Gruler, both of whom had bullpen sessions at Cinergy Field the weekend prior to the draft. Word quickly spread that Gruler's workout was lackluster while Kazmir's was spectacular. The assumption was that Cincinnati would go with Kazmir, who along with North Carolina high school righty Jason Neighborgall had one of the two best pure arms in the draft.

But the Reds never talked money with Kazmir, apparently using him to leverage Gruler into signing for a club-record $2.5 million bonus, an agreement announced shortly after teams finished drafting on June 4. That was little more than half of the $4.8 million Brazelton received as the No. 3 pick in the 2001 draft, which had more blue-chip talent than the 2002 crop. It was a good deal for

MAJOR LEAGUE CONTRACTS

Two more players were signed to major league contracts in 2002. Such contracts require players to be placed immediately on the selecting team's 40-man roster. The 2002 signings increased the number of major league contracts to 19 since Bo Jackson agreed to a major league deal with the Royals in 1986 as a condition of his being pried away from a promising NFL career. Here's the full list, including the bonus the player received as well as the amount he was guaranteed in major league salaries and roster bonuses.

Year	Club (Round)	Player, Pos.	Bonus	Guar. Amount
1986	Royals (4)	Bo Jackson, of	$100,000	$1,066,000
1989	Orioles (1)	Ben McDonald, rhp	350,000	824,000
	Blue Jays (3)	John Olerud, 1b	575,000	800,000
1990	Athletics (1)	*Todd Van Poppel, rhp	500,000	1,200,000
1993	Mariners (1)	*Alex Rodriguez, ss	1,000,000	1,300,000
1998	Phillies (1)	Pat Burrell, 1b-of	3,150,000	8,000,000
	Cardinals (1)	J.D. Drew, of	3,000,000	7,000,000
		Chad Hutchinson, rhp	2,300,000	3,400,000
1999	Marlins (1)	*Josh Beckett, rhp	3,625,000	7,000,000
	Tigers (1)	Eric Munson, c	3,500,000	6,750,000
2000	Reds (1)	*David Espinosa, ss	None	2,950,000
	Reds (2)	Dane Sardinha, c	None	1,950,000
	Padres (2)	Xavier Nady, 3b	1,100,000	2,850,000
	Devil Rays (5)	Jace Brewer, ss	450,000	1,200,000
2001	Cubs (1)	Mark Prior, rhp	4,000,000	10,500,000
	Devil Rays (1)	Dewon Brazelton, rhp	4,200,000	4,800,000
	Rangers (1)	Mark Teixeira, 3b	4,500,000	9,500,000
2002	Indians (1)	Jeremy Guthrie, rhp	3,000,000	4,000,000
	Rockies (4)	Jeff Baker, 3b	200,000	2,000,000

* High school signee   # Secondary phase

Gruler, who would have gotten less had the Reds not taken him and he had fallen to the seventh or eighth pick.

Loewen, the No. 4 overall selection by the Orioles, began classes at Chipola (Fla.) Junior College on Aug. 30. The first first-rounder to opt for a junior college since the draft-and-follow era began when the old January draft was phased out in 1986, he won't be eligible to sign until the spring of 2003. Baltimore has retained his rights and can sign him between the end of Chipola's season and a week before the 2003 draft begins.

"I'm really disappointed that this didn't work out with the Orioles," Loewen said. "Right now, I look forward to starting my college education, continuing to develop as a player and grow as a person. I love baseball. It's still a dream of mine to one day play professionally."

Loewen and the Orioles never came close to an agreement. Baltimore initially offered $2 million, while Loewen and adviser Michael Moye sought $4.8 million—a 14 percent increase from the $4.2 million bonus that Gavin Floyd, the No. 4 overall pick in 2001, got from the Phillies. The Orioles eventually came up to $2.5 million, matching what Gruler and No. 5 choice Clint Everts (Expos) received, while the Loewen camp came down to $3.9 million.

Loewen, the highest draft pick ever from Canada, originally committed to Arizona State but chose to attend a juco so he wouldn't have to wait until 2005 to enter pro ball. Chipola coach Jeff Johnson said he planned to use Loewen as both a pitcher and an outfielder. Loewen also had first-round potential as a hitter and was named the top prospect at the 2002 World Junior Championship in Quebec as an outfielder.

The Signability Factor

For the most part, teams went after ability and didn't let signability dictate their first-round selections. After Bullington, the rest of the top 10 unfolded mostly as expected, though Kazmir's name was notably absent.

Indians righthander Jeremy Guthrie was the 22nd pick overall

DRAFT

Kazmir was believed to want a bonus in the $3.5 million range, and after the Reds passed there were few teams with early picks who had the desire and the resources to spend more than MLB-recommended slot money on their first-round pick. The first team that might have done so was the Rangers at No. 10, but they instead went with the top player remaining on their draft board—South Carolina shortstop Drew Meyer, who signed quickly for $1.875 million.

The next obvious possible destination for Kazmir was the Mets, who pounced on him at No. 15. He was a prep teammate of Everts, and they made Houston's Cypress Falls the fourth high school ever to produce two first-round picks in a single draft.

"If he's the best player there, you have to be prepared to select him," Mets director of amateur scouting Jack Bowen said. "We're just as happy as could be that he was there for us to select."

Kazmir was a bit puzzled as to why he lasted so long but wasn't chagrined.

"There are a lot of rumors going around, like I wanted $100 million or whatever," Kazmir said. "I don't know what it is. I'm just happy I'm with the Mets."

Kazmir settled for far less than $100 million, agreeing to a $2.15 million deal on Aug. 2.

Two of the best college pitchers available also slid because of signability concerns. Brownlie was considered the top overall prospect in the 2002 draft class before he came down with biceps tendinitis and didn't pitch well for Rutgers down the stretch. He went 21st overall to the Cubs and remained unsigned in October.

"We knew he had a chance to get to us a couple of weeks ago," said Cubs scouting director John Stockstill, who had Brownlie near the top of his team's draft board. "It seems signability played a big part with a lot of clubs. We started to realize it was a possibility. We've checked it out and there's nothing serious with his arm."

Stanford's Jeremy Guthrie, who like Brownlie is advised by Scott Boras, went one pick later to the Indians. Guthrie became the 18th player in draft history to receive a major league contract, signing a four-year, $4 million deal on Oct. 3. His $3 million bonus trailed only Upton's among 2002 draftees.

Other Boras-advised players weren't as fortunate as Brownlie and Guthrie. Jeff Baker, the Clemson third baseman at one point considered the top college position player in the draft, went in the fourth round to the Rockies. Neighborgall went to the Red Sox in the seventh round, and several others plummeted even further.

"It was interesting to see where some of the Boras guys fell," one scouting director said. "They really tumbled. The feeling I got from a lot of our scouts was that those guys didn't show the ability of a premium guy, and it's not worth going through the battle. His guys didn't separate themselves."

Baker and Colorado finalized a four-year major league contract in October. Baker received a guaranteed $2 million, including $200,000 in signing bonuses. Neighborgall decided to attend Georgia Tech rather than sign with Boston.

Signability also was a factor for two of the better athletes in the 2002 crop. Georgia high school outfielder Jeff Francoeur, an all-America defensive back with a Clemson football scholarship in hand, faxed teams two days before the draft to notify them of a $4 million asking price.

When the Braves, picking 23rd, made a predraft offer

Lefthanders Adam Loewen (Orioles, fourth overall), left, and Jeff Francis (Rockies, ninth) became Canada's two highest picks ever

below that, they were told a team selecting later in the draft had agreed to that amount. That club reportedly was the Red Sox, but Atlanta, which likes to stockpile homestate players, decided to take Francoeur anyway. He signed for $2.2 million on July 9.

Missouri high school outfielder John Mayberry Jr., the son of former Astros first-round pick and Royals all-star John Mayberry, was considered by at least two clubs picking in the top 10. But he also committed to Stanford and told clubs he wanted $3 million. The Mariners took him 28th overall and offered him more than slot money, but couldn't lure him away from the Cardinal.

"We made him a good offer, higher than the people around him," said Roger Jongewaard, the Mariners vice president of scouting and player development. "But we knew we would have to come in a little higher."

As of October, Mayberry was the only first-rounder from the 2002 draft who conclusively won't sign. Seattle hadn't failed to land a first-rounder since 1989, when righthander Scott Burrell opted to play college basketball at Connecticut.

Requisite Draft Tidbits

■ Mayberry was one of three first-round picks whose fathers were major league all-stars. Florida high school first baseman Prince Fielder's (No. 7, Brewers) dad Cecil led the American League in homers twice and in RBIs three times during the 1990s. Ohio State outfielder Nick Swisher's (No. 16, Athletics) father Steve was a White Sox first-rounder in 1973.

■ There were several other draftees with significant baseball relatives. The Braves took two on the draft's first day: North Carolina high school catcher/righthander Kris

DRAFT '02 TOP 100 PICKS

Signing bonuses do not include scholarships, incentive bonus plans or salaries from a major league contract.
*Highest level of professional baseball attained   #Signed major league contract   +College Senior

Rank Team. Player, Pos.	School	Hometown	Bonus	Birthdate	B-T	Ht.	Wt.	AVG	AB	H	HR	RBI	SB	*2002 Assignment
2. Devil Rays. B.J. Upton, ss	Greenbrier Christian Acad.	Chesapeake, Va.	$4,600,000	8-21-84	R-R	6-2	170	.641	78	50	11	52	21	Did not play
7. Brewers. Prince Fielder, 1b	Eau Gallie HS	Melbourne, Fla.	2,400,000	5-9-84	L-R	5-11	250	.524	82	43	10	41	5	Beloit (A)
8. Tigers. Scott Moore, ss	Cypress HS	Cypress, Calif.	2,300,000	11-17-83	L-R	6-2	170	.329	76	25	11	25	4	GCL Tigers ®
10. Rangers. Drew Meyer, ss	U. of South Carolina	Charleston, S.C.	1,875,000	8-29-81	L-R	5-11	183	.359	334	120	6	40	39	Tulsa (AA)
11. Marlins. Jeremy Hermida, of	Wheeler HS	Marietta, Ga.	2,012,500	1-30-84	L-R	6-3	180	.485	68	33	7	25	9	Jamestown (A)
13. +Padres. Khalil Greene, ss	Clemson U.	Key West, Fla.	1,500,000	10-21-79	R-R	5-10	190	.470	285	134	27	91	17	Lake Elsinore (A)
14. Blue Jays. Russ Adams, 2b	U. of North Carolina	Laurinburg, N.C.	1,785,000	8-30-80	L-R	6-1	170	.370	254	94	7	55	45	Dunedin (A)
16. Athletics. Nick Swisher, 1b/of	Ohio State U.	Parkersburg, W.Va.	1,780,000	11-25-80	B-L	6-0	200	.348	184	64	10	58	5	Visalia (A)
20. Twins. Denard Span, of	Tampa Catholic HS	Tampa	1,700,000	2-27-84	L-L	6-1	175	.490	98	48	0	22	24	Did not play
23. Braves. Jeff Francoeur, of	Parkview HS	Lilburn, Ga.	2,200,000	1-8-84	R-R	6-4	205	.487	119	58	16	49	21	Danville (R)
26. Athletics. John McCurdy, ss	U. of Maryland	Crofton, Md.	1,375,000	4-17-81	R-R	6-2	195	.443	221	98	19	77	20	Missoula (R)
27. D'backs. Sergio Santos, ss	Mater Dei HS	Hacienda Heights, Calif.	1,400,000	7-4-83	R-R	6-3	190	.388	85	33	8	33	14	Missoula (R)
28. Mariners. John Mayberry, 1b	Rockhurst HS	Kansas City, Mo.	Did not sign	12-21-83	R-R	6-4	195	.432	74	32	9	29	4	Did not play
33. Indians. Matt Whitney, 3b	Palm Beach Gardens HS	Palm Beach Gardens, Fla.	1,125,000	2-13-84	R-R	6-4	190	.475	101	48	12	45	7	Columbus (A)
35. +Athletics. Jeremy Brown, c	U. of Alabama	Hueytown, Ala.	350,000	10-25-79	R-R	5-10	210	.320	219	70	11	64	6	Visalia (A)
39. Athletics. Mark Teahen, 3b	St. Mary's (Calif.) College	Yucaipa, Calif.	725,000	9-6-81	L-R	6-3	205	.412	194	80	15	36	7	Modesto (A)
40. +Reds. Mark Schramek, 3b	U. of Texas-San Antonio	San Antonio	Did not sign	6-2-80	L-R	6-0	220	.416	202	84	11	49	1	Did not play
41. Indians. Micah Schilling, 2b	Silliman Institute	Clinton, La.	915,000	12-27-82	L-R	6-0	185	.489	94	46	16	43	23	Burlington (R)
43. Devil Rays. Jason Pridie, of	Prescott HS	Prescott, Ariz.	892,500	10-9-83	L-L	6-1	180	.550	111	61	13	47	14	Hudson Valley (A)
44. Reds. Joey Votto, c	Richview Collegiate HS	Toronto	600,000	9-10-83	L-R	6-3	205	No high school team						GCL Reds (R)
45. Orioles. Corey Shafer, of	Choctaw HS	Choctaw, Okla.	800,000	12-17-82	L-L	6-3	210	.510	98	50	12	38	3	Did not play
47. Royals. Adam Donachie, c	Timber Creek HS	Orlando	800,000	3-13-84	R-R	6-2	180	.454	88	41	14	46	16	GCL Royals (R)
48. Brewers. Josh Murray, ss	Jesuit HS	Tampa	825,000	8-12-84	R-R	6-2	185	.384	112	43	3	25	14	Ogden (R)
49. Tigers. Brent Clevlen, of	Westwood HS	Cedar Park, Texas	805,000	10-27-83	R-R	6-2	185	.571	112	64	12	45	6	GCL Tigers (R)
52. Marlins. Robert Andino, ss	Southridge HS	Miami	750,000	4-25-84	R-R	5-11	175	.355	107	38	4	32	26	Jamestown (A)
54. Padres. Michael Johnson, 1b	Clemson U.	Georgetown, S.C.	Did not sign	6-25-80	L-L	6-4	220	.384	263	101	25	81	11	Did not play
56. Cubs. Brian Dopirak, 1b	Dunedin HS	Dunedin, Fla.	740,000	12-20-83	R-R	6-4	225	.490	100	49	11	51	0	AZL Cubs (R)
59. White Sox. Jeremy Reed, of	Long Beach State U.	La Verne, Calif.	650,000	6-15-81	L-L	6-0	185	.339	242	82	7	50	19	Kannapolis (A)
64. Braves. Brian McCann, c	Duluth HS	Duluth, Ga.	750,000	2-20-84	L-R	6-3	190	.438	64	28	12	27	4	GCL Braves (R)
65. Braves. Tyler Greene, ss	St. Thomas Aquinas HS	Fort Lauderdale, Fla.	Did not sign	8-17-83	R-R	6-2	175	.525	80	42	6	38	20	Did not play
66. Giants. Fred Lewis, of	Southern U.	Wiggins, Miss.	595,000	12-9-80	L-R	6-2	190	.392	158	62	5	38	14	Salem-Keizer (A)
67. +Athletics. Steve Stanley, of	U. of Notre Dame	South Bend, Ind.	200,000	12-23-79	L-L	5-7	155	.439	271	119	1	36	32	Modesto (A)
68. D'backs. Chris Snyder, c	U. of Houston	Houston	567,000	2-12-81	R-R	6-4	225	.343	230	79	15	71	8	Lancaster (A)
69. Mariners. Josh Womack, of	Crawford HS	San Diego	550,000	1-5-84	B-R	6-1	185	.519	77	40	5	19	22	AZL Mariners (R)
72. Indians. Pat Osborn, 3b	U. of Florida	Bakersfield, Calif.	647,500	2-27-81	B-R	6-3	210	.414	251	104	17	76	7	Mahoning Valley (A)
73. Pirates. Taber Lee, ss	San Diego State U.	Ventura, Calif.	525,000	10-18-80	B-R	6-0	180	.355	245	87	0	47	14	Did not play
74. Devil Rays. Elijah Dukes, of	Hillsborough HS	Tampa	500,000	6-26-84	R-R	6-2	223	.458	72	33	4	24	27	Did not play
76. Orioles. Val Majewski, of	Rutgers U.	Freehold, N.J.	400,000	6-19-81	L-L	6-3	200	.364	220	80	11	51	8	Delmarva (A)
77. Expos. Larry Broadway, 1b	Duke U.	Wellington, Fla.	450,000	12-17-80	L-L	6-4	225	.323	220	71	8	53	3	Vermont (A)
78. Royals. David Jensen, 1b	Brigham Young U.	Henderson, Nev.	472,500	12-16-79	L-R	6-3	215	.411	263	108	10	69	13	Spokane (A)
80. Tigers. Curtis Granderson, of	U. of Illinois-Chicago	Lynwood, Ill.	469,000	3-16-81	L-R	6-1	185	.483	207	100	9	45	17	Oneonta (A)
82. Indians. Jason Cooper, of	Stanford U.	La Verne, Calif.	472,500	12-6-80	L-R	6-2	215	.350	226	79	13	57	1	Columbus (A)
85. Padres. Kennard Jones, of	Indiana U.	Beltsville, Md.	465,000	9-8-81	L-L	5-11	180	.404	228	92	1	33	22	Fort Wayne (A)
88. Red Sox. Scott White, 3b	Walton HS	Kennesaw, Ga.	825,000	10-18-83	R-R	6-3	195	.533	90	48	12	50	1	Did not play
89. Phillies. Kiel Fisher, 3b	Poly HS	Riverside, Calif.	450,000	9-29-83	L-R	6-4	190	.412	74	34	11	34	2	GCL Phillies (R)
91. D'backs. Mike Nixon, c	Sunnyslope HS	Phoenix	950,000	8-17-83	R-R	6-2	210	.543	92	50	4	31	31	Great Falls (R)
96. Cubs. Matt Craig, ss	U. of Richmond	Dallas	399,000	4-16-81	B-R	6-2	198	.375	248	71	19	62	12	Boise (A)
97. Giants. Dan Ortmeier, of	U. of Texas-Arlington	Highland Village, Texas	450,000	5-11-81	B-L	6-4	220	.341	208	71	13	62	12	Salem-Keizer (A)
100. Mariners. Eddy Martinez-Esteve, of	Westminster Christian HS	Miami	Did not sign	7-14-83	R-R	6-2	194	.549	82	45	11	40	24	Did not play

DRAFT '02 TOP 100 PICKS

Signing bonuses do not include scholarships, incentive bonus plans or salaries from a major league contract.
*Highest level of professional baseball attained   #Signed major league contract

Rank. Team, Player, Pos.	School	Hometown	Bonus	Birthdate	B-T	Ht.	Wt.	W-L	ERA	IP	H	BB	SO	*2002 Assignment
1. Pirates, Bryan Bullington, rhp	Ball State U.	Madison, Ind.	$4,000,000	9-30-80	R-R	6-5	212	11-3	2.84	105	88	18	139	Did not play
3. Reds, Chris Gruler, rhp	Liberty HS	Brentwood, Calif.	2,500,000	9-11-83	R-R	6-3	200	4-3	1.49	66	32	26	135	Dayton (A)
4. Orioles, Adam Loewen, lhp	Fraser Valley Christian HS	Surrey, B.C.	Did not sign	4-9-84	L-L	6-6	210	No high school team						Did not play
5. Expos, Clint Everts, rhp	Cypress Falls HS	Houston	2,500,000	8-10-84	R-R	6-2	170	9-3	1.30	81	41	28	157	Did not play
6. Royals, Zack Greinke, rhp	Apopka HS	Orlando	2,475,000	10-21-83	R-R	6-2	185	9-2	0.55	63	22	8	116	Wilmington (A)
9. Rockies, Jeff Francis, lhp	U. of British Columbia	Vancouver, B.C.	1,850,000	1-8-81	L-L	6-5	195	7-2	1.93	75	47	16	101	Asheville (A)
12. Angels, Joe Saunders, lhp	Virginia Tech	Springfield, Va.	1,825,000	6-16-81	L-L	6-3	195	9-2	2.86	98	103	22	102	Cedar Rapids (A)
15. Mets, Scott Kazmir, lhp	Cypress Falls HS	Houston	2,150,000	1-24-84	L-L	6-0	170	11-2	0.37	75	19	19	172	Brooklyn (A)
17. Phillies, Cole Hamels, lhp	Rancho Bernardo HS	San Diego	2,000,000	12-27-83	L-L	6-2	185	5-1	0.39	71	32	23	130	Did not play
18. White Sox, Royce Ring, lhp	San Diego State U.	San Diego	1,600,000	12-21-80	L-L	6-0	215	5-1	1.83	39	29	13	55	Winston-Salem (A)
21. Cubs, Bobby Brownlie, rhp	Rutgers U.	Edison, N.J.	Did not sign	10-5-80	R-R	6-1	195	6-6	3.50	80	80	19	66	Did not play
22. #Indians, Jeremy Guthrie, rhp	Stanford U.	Ashland, Ore.	3,000,000	4-8-79	R-R	6-1	195	13-2	2.51	158	138	36	136	Did not play
24. Athletics, Joseph Blanton, rhp	U. of Kentucky	Brownsville, Ky.	1,400,000	12-11-80	R-R	6-2	210	5-7	4.59	100	98	37	133	Modesto (A)
25. Giants, Matt Cain, rhp	Houston HS	Germantown, Tenn.	1,375,000	10-1-84	R-R	6-3	185	7-3	1.02	62	28	23	83	AZL Giants (R)
29. Astros, Derick Grigsby, rhp	Northeast Texas CC	Marshall, Texas	1,125,000	6-30-82	R-R	6-0	200	3-7	3.68	63	47	27	91	Did not play
30. Athletics, Ben Fritz, rhp	Fresno State U.	San Jose	1,200,000	3-29-81	R-R	6-4	220	9-5	3.24	119	99	36	98	Visalia (A)
31. Dodgers, Greg Miller, lhp	Esperanza HS	Yorba Linda, Calif.	1,200,000	11-3-84	L-L	6-5	190	9-4	1.50	84	56	29	137	Great Falls (R)
32. Cubs, Luke Hagerty, lhp	Ball State U.	Defiance, Ohio	1,150,000	4-1-81	R-L	6-7	225	7-4	3.02	83	71	29	92	Boise (A)
34. Braves, Dan Meyer, lhp	James Madison U.	Mickleton, N.J.	1,000,000	7-3-81	R-L	6-3	190	9-2	3.13	102	102	36	92	Danville (R)
36. Cubs, Chadd Blasko, rhp	Purdue U.	Mishawaka, Ind.	1,050,000	3-9-81	R-R	6-5	200	5-3	2.98	85	76	21	78	Boise (A)
37. Athletics, Steve Obenchain, rhp	U. of Evansville	Henderson, Ky.	750,000	7-29-81	R-R	6-3	200	3-1	1.38	78	53	23	89	Visalia (A)
38. Cubs, Matt Clanton, rhp	Orange Coast (Calif.) JC	Huntington Beach, Calif.	875,000	4-16-81	R-R	6-2	210	6-3	2.26	84	48	39	108	Boise (A)
42. Pirates, Blair Johnson, rhp	Washburn HS	Topeka, Kan.	885,000	3-25-84	R-R	6-4	195	6-1	0.76	46	25	12	80	GCL Pirates (R)
46. Expos, Darrell Rasner, rhp	U. of Nevada	Carson City, Nev.	800,000	1-13-81	R-R	6-2	210	6-8	3.70	105	106	49	109	Vermont (A)
50. Rockies, Micah Owings, rhp	Gainesville HS	Gainesville, Ga.	Did not sign	9-28-82	R-R	6-3	205	12-1	1.03	75	41	3	121	Did not play
51. Dodgers, Zach Hammes, rhp	City HS	Iowa City, Iowa	750,000	5-15-84	R-R	6-6	220	No high school team						GCL Dodgers (R)
53. Angels, Kevin Jepsen, rhp	Bishop Manogue HS	Sparks, Nev.	745,000	7-26-84	R-R	6-2	210	9-1	0.84	58	47	18	116	AZL Angels (R)
55. +Blue Jays, David Bush, rhp	Wake Forest U.	Devon, Pa.	450,000	11-9-79	R-R	6-1	210	8-1	1.64	60	47	10	61	Dunedin (A)
57. Red Sox, Jon Lester, lhp	Bellarmine Prep	Tacoma, Wash.	1,000,000	1-7-84	L-L	6-4	220	4-2	1.50	42	19	12	86	GCL Red Sox (R)
58. Phillies, Zach Segovia, rhp	Forney HS	Forney, Texas	712,500	4-11-83	R-R	6-1	220	9-2	0.82	77	30	18	150	GCL Phillies (R)
60. Dodgers, Jonathan Broxton, rhp	Burke County HS	Waynesboro, Ga.	685,000	6-16-84	R-R	6-4	240	9-2	1.21	74	40	20	134	Great Falls (R)
61. Twins, Jesse Crain, rhp	U. of Houston	Louisville, Colo.	650,000	7-5-81	R-R	6-2	200	4-0	0.23	38	22	10	46	Quad City (A)
62. Cubs, Justin Jones, lhp	Kellam HS	Virginia Beach, Va.	625,000	9-25-84	L-L	6-4	185	7-5	3.38	117	106	34	94	Boise (A)
63. Indians, Brian Slocum, rhp	Villanova U.	Eastchester, N.Y.	625,000	3-27-81	R-R	6-3	195	6-1	3.41	69	58	28	65	Mahoning Valley (A)
70. Astros, Mitch Talbot, rhp	Canyon View HS	Cedar City, Utah	550,000	10-17-83	R-R	6-1	170	2-4	3.09	45	36	10	57	GCL Astros (R)
71. Yankees, Brandon Weeden, rhp	Santa Fe HS	Edmond, Okla.	565,000	10-14-83	R-R	6-3	215	2-4	1.39	77	30	18	86	GCL Yankees (R)
75. Reds, Kyle Edens, rhp	Baylor U.	San Antonio, Texas	Did not sign	1-25-80	R-R	5-10	200	5-6	3.44	52	43	15	58	Did not play
79. Brewers, Eric Thomas, rhp	U. of South Alabama	Orange, Mass.	470,000	3-24-81	R-R	6-8	225	2-4	5.50	36	29	22	117	Ogden (R)
81. +Rockies, Ben Crockett, rhp	Harvard U.	Topsfield, Mass.	345,000	12-19-79	R-R	6-3	200	6-4	2.79	84	78	15	70	Tri-City (A)
83. +Marlins, Trevor Hutchinson, rhp	U. of California	San Diego	Did not sign	10-8-79	R-R	6-5	220	7-5	3.38	78	78	18	94	Did not play
84. Angels, Kyle Pawelczyk, lhp	Chipola (Fla.) JC	Elkins, W. Va.	465,000	11-18-81	L-L	6-0	175	6-1	2.14	117	106	39	67	Cedar Rapids (A)
86. Blue Jays, Justin Maureau, lhp	Wichita State U.	Highlands Ranch, Colo.	455,000	12-17-80	R-R	6-5	215	4-3	2.45	55	44	9	79	Auburn (A)
87. Tigers, Matt Petrick, rhp	Kennesaw State (Ga.) U.	Kathleen, Ga.	440,000	6-11-81	R-R	6-0	180	11-1	2.85	58	47	33	84	Oneonta (A)
90. White Sox, Josh Rupe, rhp	Louisburg (N.C.) JC	Chesapeake, Va.	440,000	8-18-82	R-R	6-5	210	7-2	3.88	58	64	34	128	Bristol (R)
92. Twins, Mark Sauls, rhp	Bay HS	Panama City, Fla.	Did not sign	8-8-84	R-R	6-3	190	12-2	0.94	67	33	12	97	Did not play
93. Cubs, Billy Petrick, rhp	Morris HS	Morris, Ill.	459,500	4-29-84	R-R	6-6	190	5-0	1.01	101	68	22	128	AZL Cubs (R)
94. Indians, Daniel Cevette, lhp	Elkland HS	Elkland, Pa.	400,000	10-19-83	L-L	6-4	190	9-4	3.55	106	89	69	129	Burlington (A)
95. Braves, Charlie Morton, rhp	Joel Barlow HS	Redding, Conn.	415,000	11-12-83	R-R	6-5	195	11-3	0.40	35	9	36	84	GCL Braves (R)
98. Athletics, Bill Murphy, lhp	Cal State Northridge	Riverside, Calif.	410,000	5-9-81	L-L	6-0	190	9-4	2.57	106	89	69	129	Vancouver (A)
99. D'backs, Jared Doyle, lhp	James Madison U.	Wilmington, N.C.	390,000	1-30-81	L-L	6-2	195	11-3	3.55	102	102	36	92	Yakima (A)

Harvey (fifth round), the son of former all-star closer Bryan; and Auburn infielder Jon Schuerholz (eighth), the son of Atlanta general manager John. The Phillies took California high school corner infielder Jake Blalock in the fifth round and hope he'll blossom like his brother Hank, a 1999 third-rounder who has become one of the best hitting prospects in the game. Five clubs selected the sons of their major league managers: California high school righty Bryan Tracy (21st), son of Dodgers manager Jim; Florida prep outfielder Shawn Williams (35th), son of Astros manager Jimy; Cal Poly righty Greg Bochy (36th), son of Padres manager Bruce; Westark (Ark.) CC shortstop Toby Gardenhire (38th), son of Twins manager Ron; and Kishwaukee (Ill.) JC second baseman Anthony Manuel (48th), son of White Sox manager Jerry.

■ One of the more intriguing first-round picks was lefthander Cole Hamels, a teammate of Jake Blalock's at Rancho Bernardo High in San Diego. As a high school sophomore, Hamels broke the humerus bone in his arm while pitching in a game and missed all of 2001. Unlike Tom Browning, Dave Dravecky and Tony Saunders, whose careers were all but ended when they suffered the same injury while pitching, Hamels apparently hurt his arm before taking the mound while playing football in the street. He returned in 2002 to show command of three quality pitches, and at least one club rated him as

BOB LIBBY

Clint Everts, left, and Scott Kazmir were the highest picks ever from the same school

the top pitcher available in the draft. While most teams' doctors cleared Hamels physically before the draft, several clubs passed him over for players with less risky medical backgrounds. The Phillies took him 17th overall and signed him for $2 million.

■ No one topped Sean Henn's $1.7 million bonus from the Yankees, a draft-and-follow record established in 2001, but four junior college players selected in 2001 received seven-figure bonuses on the eve of the 2002 draft. American River (Calif.) JC lefthander Manny Parra, considered the top draft-and-follow prospect, got $1.55 million from the Brewers, who took him in the 26th round a

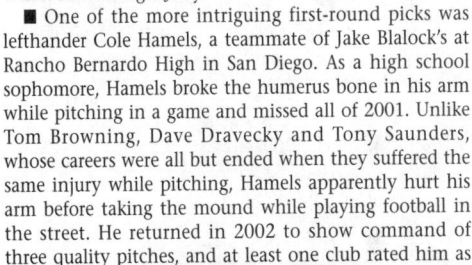

NO. 1 PICKS, 1965-2002

Year	Club, Player, Pos.	School	Hometown	Highest Level (G#)	2002 Team	Bonus
1965	A's. Rick Monday, of	Arizona State U.	Santa Monica, Calif.	Majors (1,996)	Out of Baseball	$104,000
1966	Mets. Steve Chilcott, c	Antelope Valley HS	Lancaster, Calif.	Triple-A (2)	Out of Baseball	75,000
1967	Yankees. Ron Blomberg, 1b	Druid Hills HS	Atlanta	Majors (461)	Out of Baseball	75,000
1968	Mets. Tim Foli, ss	Notre Dame HS	Sherman Oaks, Calif.	Majors (1,696)	Out of Baseball	75,000
1969	Senators. Jeff Burroughs, of	Wilson HS	Long Beach, Calif.	Majors (1,689)	Out of Baseball	88,000
1970	Padres. Mike Ivie, c	Walker HS	Decatur, Ga.	Majors (857)	Out of Baseball	80,000
1971	White Sox. Danny Goodwin, c	Central HS	Peoria, Ill.	Majors (252)	Out of Baseball	DNS
1972	Padres. Dave Roberts, 3b	U. of Oregon	Corvallis, Ore.	Majors (709)	Out of Baseball	60,000
1973	Rangers. David Clyde, lhp	Westchester, HS	Houston	Majors (84)	Out of Baseball	125,000
1974	Padres. Bill Almon, ss	Brown U.	Warwick, R.I.	Majors (1,236)	Out of Baseball	90,000
1975	Angels. Danny Goodwin, c	Southern U.	Peoria, Ill.	Majors (252)	Out of Baseball	125,000
1976	Astros. Floyd Bannister, lhp	Arizona State U.	Seattle	Majors (431)	Out of Baseball	100,000
1977	White Sox. Harold Baines, of	St. Michaels HS	St. Michaels, Md.	Majors (2,830)	Out of Baseball	40,000
1978	Braves. Bob Horner, 3b	Arizona State U.	Glendale, Ariz.	Majors (1,020)	Out of Baseball	175,000
1979	Mariners. Al Chambers, of	Harris HS	Harrisburg, Pa.	Majors (57)	Out of Baseball	60,000
1980	Mets. Darryl Strawberry, of	Crenshaw HS	Los Angeles	Majors (1,583)	Out of Baseball	152,500
1981	Mariners. Mike Moore, rhp	Oral Roberts U.	Eakly, Okla.	Majors (450)	Out of Baseball	100,000
1982	Cubs. Shawon Dunston, ss	Jefferson HS	New York	Majors (1,750)	Giants	100,000
1983	Twins. Tim Belcher, rhp	Mt. Vernon Naz. Coll.	Sparta, Ohio	Majors (362)	Out of Baseball	DNS
1984	Mets. Shawn Abner, of	Mechanicsburg HS	Mechanicsburg, Pa.	Majors (392)	Out of Baseball	150,000
1985	Brewers. B.J. Surhoff, c	U. of North Carolina	Rye, N.Y.	Majors (2,029)	Braves	150,000
1986	Pirates. Jeff King, 3b	U. of Arkansas	Colorado Springs	Majors (1,201)	Out of Baseball	160,000
1987	Mariners. Ken Griffey Jr., of	Moeller HS	Cincinnati	Majors (1,871)	Reds	169,000
1988	Padres. Andy Benes, rhp	U. of Evansville	Evansville, Ind.	Majors (403)	Cardinals	235,000
1989	Orioles. Ben McDonald, rhp	Louisiana State U.	Denham Springs, La.	Majors (211)	Out of Baseball	*350,000
1990	Braves. Chipper Jones, ss	The Bolles School	Jacksonville	Majors (1,252)	Braves	275,000
1991	Yankees. Brien Taylor, lhp	East Carteret HS	Beaufort, N.C.	Double-A (27)	Out of Baseball	1,550,000
1992	Astros. Phil Nevin, 3b	Cal State Fullerton	Placentia, Calif.	Majors (779)	Padres	700,000
1993	Mariners. Alex Rodriguez, ss	West. Christian HS	Miami	Majors (1,114)	Rangers	*1,000,000
1994	Mets. Paul Wilson, rhp	Florida State U.	Orlando, Fla.	Majors (104)	Devil Rays	1,550,000
1995	Angels. Darin Erstad, of	U. of Nebraska	Jamestown, N.D.	Majors (935)	Angels	1,575,000
1996	Pirates. Kris Benson, rhp	Clemson U.	Kennesaw, Ga.	Majors (88)	Pirates	2,000,000
1997	Tigers. Matt Anderson, rhp	Rice U.	Louisville, Ky.	Majors (222)	Tigers	2,505,000
1998	Phillies. Pat Burrell, 3b	U. of Miami	Boulder Creek, Calif.	Majors (423)	Phillies	*3,150,000
1999	Devil Rays. Josh Hamilton, of	Athens Drive HS	Raleigh, N.C.	Double-A (23)	Devil Rays (A)	3,960,000
2000	Marlins. Adrian Gonzalez, 1b	Eastside HS	Chula Vista, Calif.	Double-A (138)	Marlins (AA)	3,000,000
2001	Twins. Joe Mauer, c	Cretin-Derham Hall	St. Paul, Minn.	Class A (110)	Twins (A)	5,150,000
2002	Pirates. Bryan Bullington, rhp	Ball State U.	Fishers, Ind.	Has not played	———	4,000,000

*Received major league contract with guaranteed incentives   #No. of games at that level   DNS—Did not sign

year earlier. The Cardinals, who didn't start drafting until the last pick in the third round in 2002, got a first-round-caliber talent in Bellevue (Wash.) CC righthander Blake Hawksworth (28th round in 2001) for $1.475 million. Sacramento CC righthander Sean Smith (16th round) received $1.1 million from the Indians, while Connors State (Okla.) JC righty Humberto Sanchez (31st round) signed for approximately $1 million with the Tigers.

■ While teams stuck closely to the commissioner's office mandate to pay bonuses according to slot in the first five rounds, no such rules apparently existed in the later rounds. In the 11th round, University of Miami righthander Kiki Bengochea, who projected as a possible first-rounder before a subpar junior year, was paid $550,000—comparable to late second-round money. In the 21st round, Washington high school first baseman Travis Ishikawa was given a bonus of $955,000 by the Giants. "We obviously had him much higher on our draft board," Giants GM Brian Sabean said. "He's very accomplished in a lot of ways, offensively and defensively. He's got a chance to hit for average and power at (first base) and be a well above-average fielder."

■ For the second year in a row, a third baseman selected by Oakland died weeks after being drafted. Shortly

Wally Pontiff

after the A's completed the signing of every one of its picks in the first 16 rounds—including all seven first-round selections—the A's learned of the death of Louisiana State third baseman Wally Pontiff, their 21st-round pick. Pontiff died at his parents' home in Metairie, La., on July 24, of what was determined to be a heart abnormality. A year earlier, Washington high school third baseman Mark Hilde, a

32nd-round pick, was killed when a vehicle driven by Padres former first-rounder Gerik Baxter crashed near Indio, Calif.

■ The Reds, who usually operate on as tight a draft budget as any club, still hadn't signed four of their picks from the first five rounds by October. Texas-San Antonio third baseman Mark Schramek, selected with a supplemental first-round pick Cincinnati received for failing to sign 2001 first-rounder Jeremy Sowers, got so frustrated with the Reds that he looked to Japan. Cincinnati's first offer was $150,000, roughly one-fifth of what Schramek's draft slot should have commanded, so he went overseas to try out for Japan's Orix Blue Wave. The Blue Wave offered him a nine-year contract with a $40,000 signing bonus, but Schramek declined and returned to the United States. Third-rounder Kyle Edens, fourth-rounder Camilo Vazquez and fifth-rounder Kevin Howard also had not signed, though there was a strong likelihood that some or all may do so after Nov. 1, when Cincinnati's new fiscal year begins.

■ Texas A&M, which didn't even advance to the 64-team NCAA regional field, had the most players drafted of any college, 11. Texas, the College World Series champion and the Aggies' chief rival, had eight. At the high school level, Durango High of Las Vegas and Xaverian High of Brooklyn had five players drafted each. Both schools were ranked in Baseball America's preseason national poll but had disappointing years and were not in the final top 50.

UNSIGNED PICKS

A list of the players selected in the first 12 rounds of the 2002 draft who didn't sign, and the college they're attending. Players denoted with an asterisk are collegians who are returning to the same school. Teams control the rights to players attending junior college and may sign them next spring between the completion of their junior college season and the start of the closed period (one week before the draft).

FIRST ROUND
4. Orioles. Adam Loewen, lhp	Chipola (Fla.) JC
21. Cubs. Bobby Brownlie, rhp	Not in school
28. Mariners. John Mayberry Jr., 1b	Stanford

FIRST-ROUND SUPPLEMENTAL
40. Reds. Mark Schramek, 3b	Eligibility expired

SECOND ROUND
50. Rockies. Micah Owings, rhp	Georgia Tech
54. Padres. Michael Johnson, 1b	*Clemson
65. Braves. Tyler Greene, ss	Georgia Tech

THIRD ROUND
75. Reds. Kyle Edens, rhp	Eligibility expired
83. Marlins. Trevor Hutchinson, rhp	Eligibility expired
92. Twins. Mark Sauls, rhp	Florida State
100. Mariners. Eddy Martinez-Esteve, of	Florida State

FOURTH ROUND
103. Pirates. Wardell Starling, rhp-of	Odessa (Texas) JC
105. Reds. Camilo Vasquez, lhp	Not in school

FIFTH ROUND
134. Devil Rays. Mark Romanczuk, lhp	Stanford
135. Reds. Kevin Howard, 3b	Not in school
139. Brewers. Jarrad Page, of	UCLA
143. Marlins. Nick Hundley, c	Arizona
152. Twins. Clete Thomas, of	Auburn
153. Cubs. Shawn Scobee, of	Cal State Fullerton
155. Braves. Kris Harvey, c-rhp	Clemson
161. Astros. Pat Misch, lhp	*Western Michigan
162. Cardinals. Josh Bell, c	Auburn

SIXTH ROUND
164. Devil Rays. Cesar Ramos, lhp	
168. Royals. Brandon Jones, 3b	Tallahassee (Fla.) CC
178. Red Sox. Barrett Browning, lhp	Middle Georgia JC
180. White Sox. Chris Getz, ss	Wake Forest

SEVENTH ROUND
204. Angels. Jeff Leise, of	*Nebraska
205. Padres. Matt Lynch, lhp	*Florida State
208. Red Sox. Jason Neighborgall, rhp	Georgia Tech
215. Braves. Patrick Clayton, rhp	Clemson
217. Giants. Michael Musgrove, rhp	Central Florida CC
221. Astros. Scott Robinson, 1b/of	Palomar (Calif.) JC

EIGHTH ROUND
227. Expos. Friedel Pinkston, rhp	Chipola (Fla.) JC
229. Brewers. Steve Kahn, rhp	Loyola Marymount
239. Phillies. Steve Doetsch, of	Indian River (Fla.) CC
242. Twins. Adam Lind, of	South Alabama
249. Diamondbacks. Ryan Mahoney, c	South Carolina

NINTH ROUND
254. Devil Rays. Chris Leroux, c	Winthrop
262. Rangers. Steve Herce, rhp	*Rice
267. Mets. Christian Colonel, ss	Texas Tech
271. Dodgers. Denver Kitch, ss	*Oklahoma
275. Braves. Nick Starnes, rhp	UNC Greensboro

10th ROUND
287. Expos. Justin Azze, lhp	Hawaii
309. Diamondbacks. Mike Pierce, c	Fresno CC
311. Astros. Brad Chester, rhp	Louisiana Tech

11th ROUND
316. Orioles. Mark McCormick, rhp	Baylor
318. Royals. Kainoa Obrey, 3b	*Brigham Young
319. Brewers. Brian Hernandez, c	Duke
329. Phillies. T.J. Beam, rhp	*Mississippi
331. Dodgers. James McDonald, 1b	Golden West (Calif.) JC
332. Twins. Evan Meek, rhp	Midland (Texas) JC

12th ROUND
358. Red Sox. Dustin Majewski, of	*Texas
360. White Sox. Jayson Ruhlman, lhp	Central Michigan
362. Twins. Jeff Clement, c	Southern California
367. Giants. Kellen Ludwig, rhp	*Chipola (Fla.) JC

DRAFT 2002

CLUB-BY-CLUB SELECTIONS

■ Order of selection indicated in parentheses
■ **Boldface** indicates player signed

ANAHEIM (12)

■ **SCOUTING DIRECTOR:** Donnie Rowland.

1. **Joe Saunders, lhp, Virginia Tech.**
2. **Kevin Jepsen, rhp, Bishop Manogue HS, Sparks, Nev.**
3. **Kyle Pawelczyk, lhp, Chipola (Fla.) JC.**
4. **Jordan Renz, of, Tulsa Union HS, Broken Arrow, Okla.**
5. **Javy Rodriguez, ss, U. of Miami (Fla.).**
6. **Chris Walston, 1b, El Capitan HS, Lakeside, Calif.**
7. Jeff Leise, of, U. of Nebraska.
8. **James Holcomb, rhp, U. of Nevada.**
9. **Caleb Maher, of, Ceres (Calif.) HS.**
10. **Howard Kendrick, 2b, St John's River (Fla.) CC.**
11. **Aaron Peel, of, Seminole (Texas) HS.**
12. **Ryan Kenning, of, New Mexico State U.**
13. **Osvaldo Lugo, rhp, Florida International U.**
14. **Ronnie Ray, rhp, Pacific (Mo.) HS.**
15. **Justin Hancock, 3b, Florida Southern College.**
16. **Thomas Duenas, c, Florida International U.**
17. Tony Mandel, rhp, Chipola (Fla.) JC.
18. **Nick Touchstone, lhp, Okaloosa-Walton (Fla.) JC.**
19. **Mike Perdomo, c, Broward (Fla.) CC.**
20. Ryan Broderick, of, Palm Desert HS, Rancho Mirage, Calif.
21. **Matt McCarthy, lhp, Yale U.**
22. **Scott Hindman, lhp, Princeton U.**
23. Andrew Slorp, rhp, Bellarmine Prep, Morgan Hill, Calif.
24. Brett Martinez, c, Redlands (Calif.) East Valley HS.
25. Michel Simard, rhp, St. Petersburg (Fla.) JC.
26. **Alex Dvorsky, c, U. of Northern Iowa.**
27. **Bryan Williams, rhp, Jacksonville U.**
28. **Jake Mathis, 3b, U. of Alabama-Huntsville.**
29. Ryan Rote, rhp, Kishwaukee (Ill.) JC.
30. **Jeffrey Marquez, rhp, Broward (Fla.) CC.**
31. Ross Lewis, rhp-of, Central Florida CC.
32. Chris Hunter, rhp, Utah Valley State JC.
33. Chris Roque, rhp, Broward (Fla.) CC.
34. Jeremy King, lhp, Itawamba (Miss.) JC.
35. **Jason Sugden, of, Harrisburg, Pa.**
36. Matthew Byrd, c, Hunt HS, Kenly, N.C.
37. Trevor Weedon, c, Nordhoff HS, Ojai, Calif.
38. Buck Shaw, rhp, Wagoner (Okla.) HS.
39. Taylor McIntyre, lhp, Edmond Santa Fe HS, Oklahoma City.
40. Adam Rodgers, c, Grayson County (Texas) CC.
41. Jason Cox, 1b, Lamar (Colo.) CC.
42. Brad Beaman, of, Northglenn HS, Thornton, Colo.
43. Steven Delabar, rhp, Volunteer State (Tenn.) CC.
44. Wayne Hedden, rhp, Hillsborough (Fla.) CC.
45. Shawn McGill, c, South Kingstown HS, Wakefield, R.I.
46. Brock Keffer, rhp, Illinois Valley CC.
47. Karl Gelinas, rhp, Edourard Montpetit (Quebec) College.
48. Robert Wilson, c, St. Petersburg (Fla.) CC.
49. Jason Corbett, rhp, Palm Harbor (Fla.) University HS.
50. Cody Dickens, rhp, Forbush HS, East Bend, N.C.

ARIZONA (27)

■ **SCOUTING DIRECTOR:** Mike Rizzo.

1. **Sergio Santos, ss, Mater Dei HS, Hacienda Heights, Calif.**
2. **Chris Snyder, c, U. of Houston.**
3. **Jared Doyle, lhp, James Madison U.**
4. **Lance Cormier, rhp, U. of Alabama.**
5. **Mark Rosen, lhp, Salisbury (Conn.) Prep.**
6. **Brian Barden, 3b, Oregon State U.**
7. **Matt Henrie, rhp, Clemson U.**
8. Ryan Mahoney, c, Carmel HS, Patterson, N.Y.
9. **Klent Corley, rhp, Grand Canyon U.**
10. Mike Pierce, c, Clovis (Calif.) HS.
11. **Nebasset Brown, 2b, Oklahoma State U.**
12. **Mitch Douglas, lhp, Augusta State (Ga.) U.**
13. **Adam Haley, ss, U. of Louisville.**
14. **Jay Garthwaite, of, U. of Washington.**
15. **Dustin Nippert, rhp, West Virginia U.**
16. **Bryan Johnson, 1b, U. of Washington.**
17. **Donnie Saba, of, U. of Utah.**
18. **Matthew Morgan, ss, Lewis-Clark State (Idaho) College.**
19. **Sam Smith, rhp, U. of South Alabama.**
20. **Jeffrey Stanek, 1b, Southern Illinois U.**
21. **Dan Callahan, of, Tufts (Mass.) U.**

22. Kenneth Parker, 1b, Henry Foss HS, Tacoma.
23. **Jared Bonnell, rhp, U. of Nevada-Las Vegas.**
24. **Matt Incinelli, rhp, U. of North Florida.**
25. **Bookie Gates, 2b, Washington State U.**
26. **Wes Gilliam, lhp, U. of Illinois-Chicago.**
27. **Joshua Kranawetter, rhp, Polk (Fla.) CC.**
28. **Sean Luellwitz, 1b-c, Vanderbilt U.**
29. Mike Buss, rhp, Wellington (Fla.) Community HS.
30. Anthony Isabella, cf, Chemeketa (Ore.) CC.
31. Clint Goocher, lhp, San Jacinto (Texas) JC.
32. T.J. Large, rhp, Chipola (Fla.) JC.
33. Donta Warfield, ss, Riverview HS, Sarasota, Fla.
34. Jesus Albino, rhp, Northwest Mississippi CC.
35. Jake Hanen, of, Scottsdale (Ariz.) CC.
36. Nicholas Richardson, c, Elgin (Ill.) CC.
37. Kirk Gross, rhp, San Ramon Valley HS, Danville, Calif.
38. Matt Falk, rhp, Dana Hills HS, San Juan Capistrano, Calif.
39. **Grady Symonds, c, U. of Hawaii.**
40. **Billy Biggs, rhp, West Virginia U.**
41. **Keith Whatley, lhp, U. of Houston.**
42. Michael Ridgway, lhp, Tacoma (Wash.) CC.
43. Kris Krise, rhp, Crescenta Valley HS, La Crescenta, Calif.
44. Conor Lalor, rhp, Houston HS, Germantown, Tenn.
45. Jon Crosby, rhp, Christian Brothers HS, Germantown, Tenn.
46. Ryan Gloger, lhp, U. of South Florida.
47. **Robert Ferns, rhp, Darton (Ga.) CC.**
48. Ronald Lowe, lhp, Ridgewood HS, New Port Richey, Fla.
49. Matthew Raguse, rhp, St. Louis CC-Forest Park.
50. Kyle Reynolds, ss, Second Baptist HS, Houston.

ATLANTA (23)

■ **SCOUTING DIRECTOR:** Roy Clark.

1. **Jeff Francoeur, of, Parkview HS, Lilburn, Ga.**
1. **Dan Meyer, lhp, James Madison U.** (Supplemental pick—34th—for loss of Type A free agent Steve Karsay).
2. **Brian McCann, c, Duluth (Ga.) HS.**
2. Tyler Greene, ss, St. Thomas Aquinas HS, Plantation, Fla. (Choice from Yankees—65th—for loss of Karsay).
3. **Charlie Morton, rhp, Joel Barlow HS, Redding, Conn.**
4. **Steve Russell, rhp, Cimarron Memorial HS, Las Vegas.**
5. Kris Harvey, c, Bandys HS, Catawba, N.C.
6. **James Jurries, 1b, Tulane U.**
7. Patrick Clayton, rhp, Walton HS, Marietta, Ga.
8. **Jon Schuerholz, ss, Auburn U.**
9. Nick Starnes, rhp, Graham HS, Haw River, N.C.
10. **Yaron Peters, 1b, U. of South Carolina.**
11. **Mike Grasso, 2b, U. of Albany.**
12. **Wes Timmons, ss, Bethune-Cookman College.**
13. **Daniel Mead, lhp, Manatee (Fla.) JC.**
14. **Michael Reiss, rhp, Seminole State (Okla.) CC.**
15. J.P. Lowen, c, Lassiter HS, Marietta, Ga.
16. **Mike Mueller, rhp, Auburn U.**
17. **Brad David, lhp, Louisiana State U.**
18. **Joshua Adams, lhp, Franklin (Ind.) College.**
19. **Fernando Tadefa, lhp, St. Mary's (Texas) U.**
20. **Chuck James, lhp, Chattahoochee Valley (Ala.) CC.**
21. **Aaron Parker, rhp, Sonoma State (Calif.) U.**
22. Trey Shields, rhp, Bay HS, Panama City, Fla.
23. Tim Cunningham, lhp, Stanford U.
24. **Paul Bush, rhp, Georgia Southwestern College.**
25. **Steven Reiss, rhp, Seminole State (Okla.) CC.**
26. Chris Maher, rhp, Pensacola (Fla.) JC.
27. Travis Stanton, rhp, Lake City (Fla.) CC.
28. Devin Anderson, lhp, West Orange HS, Ocoee, Fla.
29. Mark Wagner, c, Mayfair HS, Lakewood, Calif.
30. Cooper Osteen, ss, Indian River (Fla.) CC.
31. Brandon Nall, rhp, George C. Wallace (Ala.) CC.
32. Darrell Qualls, ss, Middleburg (Fla.) HS.
33. Jacob Eckley, lhp, Burke HS, Omaha.
34. Ryan Patterson, of, Texarkana (Texas) CC.
35. Kenneth Brock, lhp, Lane (Ore.) CC.
36. Abraham Vargas, rhp, Bay City (Texas) HS.
37. Matt Dale, rhp, Walton HS, Marietta, Ga.
38. Jeffrey Timmons, c, Manatee (Fla.) CC.
39. Brett Young, 1b, Gloucester County (N.J.) CC.
40. Kevin Kotch, c, Middlesex (N.J.) HS.
41. David Hayes, rhp, American Heritage HS, Sunrise, Fla.
42. Ryan Paul, lhp, Moorpark (Calif.) HS.
43. Ken Livesley, rhp, Cosumnes River (Calif.) CC.
44. Chris Tyndall, rhp, Armstrong (Ill.) HS.
45. Daniel Collins, lhp, Indian River (Fla.) CC.
46. Brandon Judge, rhp, Santa Margarita HS, Rancho Santa Margarita, Calif.
47. **Rick Aguilar, lhp, Cypress (Calif.) JC.**
48. Christopher Widing, lhp, East Paulding HS, Dallas, Ga.
49. Christopher Dunbar, of, La Conner HS, Camana Island, Wash.

50. Matt Handley, lhp, Greater Atlanta Christian HS, Duluth, Ga.

BALTIMORE (4)

■ SCOUTING DIRECTOR: Tony DeMacio.
1. Adam Loewen, lhp, Fraser Valley Christian HS, Surrey, B.C.
2. **Corey Shafer, of, Choctaw (Okla.) HS.**
3. **Val Majewski, of, Rutgers U.**
4. **Tim Gilhooly, of, U. of the Pacific.**
5. **Hayden Penn, rhp, Santana HS, Santee, Calif.**
6. **John Maine, rhp, UNC Charlotte.**
7. **Paul Henry, rhp, Ball State U.**
8. **Ryan Hubele, c, U. of Texas.**
9. **Trevor Caughey, lhp, Cuesta (Calif.) JC.**
10. **Matt Bolander, rhp, Pendleton Heights HS, Anderson, Ind.**
11. Mark McCormick, rhp, Clear Creek HS, Clear Lake Shores, Texas.
12. **Brandon Fahey, 3b, U. of Texas.**
13. **Mike Huggins, 1b, Baylor U.**
14. **Matthew Rohr, lhp, Cal State San Bernardino.**
15. **Matthew Howerton, of, Riverdale HS, Fort Myers, Fla.**
16. **Gera Alvarez, ss, Texas Tech.**
17. **Neal Stephenson, of, Texas A&M U.**
18. **Carl Makowsky, rhp, Northwestern State U.**
19. **Mike Patitucci, lhp, Oklahoma State U.**
20. **George Cox, c, U. of Central Florida.**
21. **Gregg Davies, of, Towson U.**
22. **Zach Sutton, rhp, U. of Central Florida.**
23. **Jason Cierlik, lhp, Minnesota State U.-Mankato.**
24. Ryan Soehlig, 3b, U. of North Florida.
25. **Tim Thurman, 1b, Cal Poly Pomona.**
26. **Erik Smallwood, of, U. of South Alabama.**
27. Antoan Richardson, of, Palm Beach (Fla.) JC.
28. **Zach Davis, rhp, J.A. Fair HS, Little Rock, Ark.**
29. **Edward Colbert, of, Catonsville (Md.) CC.**
30. **Melvin Spencer, rhp, U. of South Alabama.**
31. **Justin Nash, rhp, Penn State U.**
32. **Whitney Robinson-Pierce, c, Cuesta (Calif.) JC.**
33. **Ryan Childs, rhp, Clemson U.**
34. **Levi Robinson, ss, Texas Christian U.**
35. **Nick McCurdy, rhp, Oklahoma State U.**
36. Jordan Compton, lhp, Haysi (Va.) HS.
37. Russell Petrick, lhp, Bellevue (Wash.) CC.
38. Alex Muszynski, 1b, Alpena (Mich.) HS.
39. Henry Lozado, rhp, Adolfina Irizarry de Puig HS, Toa Baja, P.R.
40. Steven Guerra, rhp, Paso Robles (Calif.) HS.
41. Charles White, c, Overlea HS, Baltimore.
42. Barry Roe, rhp, Heath (Okla.) HS.
43. Randy Youtsey, 2b, Coolidge (Ariz.) HS.
44. Bradford Wiggins, cf, Arlington Heights HS, Fort Worth.
45. **James Cooney, lhp, Florida Atlantic U.**
46. David Mittelberger, lhp, Righetti HS, Santa Maria, Calif.
47. Andre Psaradelis, cf, Bellevue (Wash.) CC.
48. **Mark Wahl, c, U. of Dayton.**
49. Gabe Somarriba, cf, Florida Atlantic U.
50. Allen Ponder, rhp, Lee-Scott Academy, Auburn, Ala.

BOSTON (16)

■ SCOUTING DIRECTOR: David Chadd.
1. (Choice to Athletics as compensation for Type A free agent Johnny Damon.)
2. **Jon Lester, lhp, Bellarmine Prep, Puyallup, Wash.**
3. **Scott White, 3b, Walton HS, Marietta, Ga.**
4. **Chris Smith, rhp, UC Riverside.**
5. **Chad Spann, ss, Southland Academy, Buena Vista, Ga.**
6. Barrett Browning, lhp, Wayne County HS, Jesup, Ga.
7. Jason Neighborgall, rhp, Riverside HS, Durham, N.C.
8. **Brandon Moss, ss, Loganville HS, Monroe, Ga.**
9. **Tyler Pelland, lhp, Mount Abraham HS, Bristol, Vt.**
10. **Greg Stone, ss, Bacone (Okla.) College.**
11. **Mike Goss, of, Jackson State U.**
12. Dustin Majewski, of, U. of Texas.
13. Stoney Stone, rhp, Ruston (La.) HS.
14. **John Priola, rhp, Faulkner (Ala.) U.**
15. **Ian Cronkhite, of, Westmoore HS, Oklahoma City.**
16. **Peter Ciofrone, ss, Smithtown HS, Nesconset, N.Y.**
17. **Arian Alcala, 3b, St. Thomas (Fla.) U.**
18. **Brandon Smith, rhp, Southeast Missouri State U.**
19. **Tom MacLane, lhp, Florida Atlantic U.**
20. **Luis Villarreal, lhp, Northwood (Texas) U.**
21. **Alberto Concepcion, c, U. of Southern California.**
22. John Anderson, rhp, Arkansas State U.
23. **David Pahucki, rhp, Siena College.**
24. **Pat Boran, ss, Princeton U.**
25. **Jim Buckley, c, Siena College.**
26. Adam Davis, rhp, Metter HS, Pulaski, Ga.

27. Michael Armstrong, rf, Chabot (Calif.) JC.
28. **Mike Barclay, of, U. of South Florida.**
29. Matt Clarkson, c, Broken Arrow (Okla.) HS.
30. Jonathan Williams, rhp, Opelika (Ala.) HS.
31. Steve Boggs, of, San Diego HS.
32. Brock Hunton, rhp, Dublin Coffman HS, Dublin, Ohio.
33. Luke Taylor, rhp, Lowndes HS, Valdosta, Ga.
34. Mitchell Woolf, rhp, Madison HS, Rexburg, Idaho.
35. **Jose Vaquedano, rhp, Vernon Regional (Texas) JC.**
36. Don Powers, rhp, Shawnee (Okla.) HS.
37. Ricky Romero, lhp, Roosevelt HS, Los Angeles.
38. Koley Kolberg, rhp, Navarro (Texas) JC.
39. Tyler Jacobson, rhp, Auburn River HS, Sumner, Wash.
40. Dustin Roddy, c, Northeast Texas JC.
41. Matthew Inouye, c, Mid-Pacific HS, Honolulu.
42. Rosalino Valenzuela, rhp, Marcos de Niza HS, Guadalupe, Ariz.
43. Lance Schartz, c, Garden City (Kan.) CC.
44. David Baker, c, Rogers HS, Puyallup, Wash.
45. Brian Bannister, rhp, U. of Southern California.
46. West Harris, lhp, Lone Oak HS, Paducah, Ky.
47. **Anthony Bianucci, of, Daytona Beach (Fla.) CC.**
48. Sergio Roman, c, Allen County (Kan.) CC.
49. Robert Caruso, 1b, Chaminade-Madonna Prep, Pembroke Pines, Fla.
50. Seth Dhaenens, ss, Mountain Pointe HS, Chandler, Ariz.

CHICAGO/NL (21)

■ SCOUTING DIRECTOR: John Stockstill.
1. Bobby Brownlie, rhp, Rutgers U.
1. **Luke Hagerty, lhp, Ball State U.** (Supplemental pick—32nd—for loss of Type A free agent David Weathers).
1. **Chadd Blasko, rhp, Purdue U.** (Supplemental pick—36th—for loss of Type A free agent Rondell White).
1. **Matt Clanton, rhp, Orange Coast (Calif.) JC** (Supplemental pick—38th—for loss of Type A free agent Todd Van Poppel).
2. **Brian Dopirak, 1b, Dunedin (Fla.) HS** (Choice from Mets—56th—for loss of Weathers).
2. **Justin Jones, lhp, Kellam HS, Virginia Beach.**
3. **Billy Petrick, rhp, Morris (Ill.) HS.**
3. **Matt Craig, ss, U. of Richmond** (Choice from Yankees—96th—for loss of White).
4. **Rich Hill, lhp, U. of Michigan** (Choice from Rangers—112th—for loss of Van Poppel).
4. **Alan Rick, c, Palatka (Fla.) HS.**
5. Shawn Scobee, of, Rio Linda (Calif.) HS.
6. **Chris Walker, of, Georgia Southern U.**
7. **Joey Monahan, ss, Liberty U.**
8. **Jason Fransz, of, U. of Oklahoma.**
9. **Adam Greenberg, of, U. of North Carolina.**
10. **Keith Butler, of, Liberty U.**
11. **Chris Miller, c, UC Irvine.**
12. **Jason Wylie, rhp, U. of Utah.**
13. **Micah Hoffpauir, of, Lamar U.**
14. Rocky Cherry, rhp, U. of Oklahoma.
15. **C.J. Medlin, c, Seminole State (Okla.) JC.**
16. **Jemel Spearman, ss, Georgia Southern U.**
17. Forrest Beverly, lhp, Conway (S.C.) HS.
18. **Donnie Hood, ss, Kennesaw State (Ga.) U.**
19. **Rick Atlee, rhp, Lamar U.**
20. **Matthew Hines, rhp, Olivet Nazarene (Ill.) U.**
21. **Paul O'Toole, c, U. of Notre Dame.**
22. Taylor Teagarden, c, Creekview HS, Carrollton, Texas.
23. **Steve O'Sullivan, ss, Marist College.**
24. Ben Thurmond, rhp, Winthrop U.
25. Bear Bay, rhp, Angelina (Texas) JC.
26. Jeff Jacobsen, rhp, Durango HS, Las Vegas.
27. **Travis Welsch, ss-2b, U. of Northern Iowa.**
28. Evan Seibly, lhp, Los Angeles Pierce JC.
29. Brett Lewis, rhp, Georgia Southern U.
30. Kyle Emmons, ss, Chaparral HS, Scottsdale, Ariz.
31. Kurt Steele, rhp/ss, Crescent Valley HS, Corvallis, Ore.
32. Jose Rios, ss, Pablo Gonzalez Bendecia HS, Barranquitas, P.R.
33. Adam Harvey, c, Celina (Texas) HS.
34. Grant Staniszewski, c, Marquette HS, Chesterfield, Mo.
35. Anthony McLin, c, McLaurin HS, Florence, Miss.
36. Kalen Gibson, rhp, Webster HS, Slaughters, Ky.
37. Kyle Dubois, rhp, Manatee (Fla.) JC.
38. **Randy Wells, c, Southwestern Illinois JC.**
39. Daniel DeSouza, of, Xaverian HS, Brooklyn.
40. Collin Walker, rhp, Minooka HS, Channahon, Ill.
41. Mark Holliman, rhp, Germantown (Tenn.) HS.
42. Geoff Orr, ss, Carl Sandburg HS, Orland Park, Ill.
43. Cory Anderson, rhp, Chaparral HS, Scottsdale, Ariz.
44. Jose Cortez, c, Pomona-Pitzer (Calif.) College.
45. Chris Ericksen, lhp, Joliet Catholic Academy, Joliet, Ill.
46. Patrick McIntyre, c, Walla Walla (Wash.) JC.

DRAFT

47. Josh Morgan, c, Thomasville (Ala.) HS.
48. Clemon Bailey, of, Southern HS, Durham, N.C.
49. Gary Kerschke, rhp, Bartlett HS, Hanover Park, Ill.
50. Brian Kayser, 1b, Bartlesville (Okla.) HS.

CHICAGO/AL (18)

■ SCOUTING DIRECTOR: Doug Laumann.
1. **Royce Ring, lhp, San Diego State U.**
2. **Jeremy Reed, of, Long Beach State U.**
3. **Josh Rupe, rhp, Louisburg (N.C.) JC.**
4. **Ryan Rodriguez, lhp, Keller (Texas) HS.**
5. **B.J. LaMura, rhp, Clemson U.**
6. Chris Getz, ss, Grosse Pointe (Mich.) South HS.
7. **Micah Schnurstein, 3b, Basic HS, Henderson, Nev.**
8. **Sean Tracey, rhp, UC Irvine.**
9. **Todd Deininger, rhp, Texas A&M U.**
10. **Orionny Lopez, rhp, Forest Hill HS, West Palm Beach, Fla.**
11. **Matt Herring, 1b-of, Georgia Southern U.**
12. Jayson Ruhlman, lhp, L'Anse Creuse North HS, Macomb, Mich.
13. **Demetrius Banks, lhp, Chattahoochee Valley (Ala.) CC.**
14. Christian Madson, rhp, Bloomingdale HS, Valrico, Fla.
15. **Adam Larson, rhp, Middle Tennessee State U.**
16. **Daniel Haigwood, lhp, Midland HS, Batesville, Ark.**
17. **Brandon McCarthy, rhp, Lamar (Colo.) CC.**
18. **Shane Scoville, c, U. of South Alabama.**
19. Paul Keck, c, Granada HS, Pleasanton, Calif.
20. Boone Logan, lhp, Sandra Day O'Connor HS, Helotes, Texas.
21. **Seth Morris, of, U. of Kentucky.**
22. **Eric Keefner, 1b, Mesa (Ariz.) CC.**
23. David Beasley, lhp, Cooper City (Fla.) HS
24. **Thomas Brice, 1b-of, Faulkner State (Ala.) JC.**
25. Jay Marshall, lhp, Jefferson (Mo.) JC.
26. Kris Dufner, ss, U. of Delaware.
27. **Michael Bohlander, lhp, Pace U.**
28. Hector Ambriz, rhp, Valencia HS, Placentia, Calif.
29. Neil Giesler, 3b, Jasper (Ind.) HS.
30. **Jacob Nowlen, rhp, U. of Arkansas-Monticello.**
31. **Edgar Varela, 3b, Long Beach State U.**
32. **Rick Hummel, rhp, U. of Indianapolis.**
33. Tony Sipp, lhp, Okaloosa-Walton (Fla.) CC.
34. Brandon Durden, lhp, Cook (Ga.) HS.
35. Eric Everly, lhp, Seagoville (Texas) HS.
36. Jason Pilkington, lhp, Central Arizona JC.
37. **Jamin Hutchinson, rhp, Fayetteville (Ark.) HS.**
38. D.J. Wabick, of, Stagg HS, Palos Park, Ill.
39. Gabriel Casanova, 2b, Coral Park HS, Miami.
40. Dennis Pawelek, rhp, Snow (Utah) JC.
41. Daniel Barone, rhp, Monterey Peninsula (Calif.) JC.
42. Ian Ganzer, rhp, Wellington (Fla.) Community HS.
43. Matthew Sibigtroth, ss, Kishwaukee (Ill.) JC.
44. Ramon Castro, 2b-ss, George Washington HS, Manhattan.
45. Jorge Mico, c, Hialeah (Fla.) HS.
46. Jeremy Paul, c, Trinity International (Ill.) U.
47. Tim Grogan, ss, Covington (Ky.) Catholic HS.
48. Anthony Manuel, 2b, Kishwaukee (Ill.) JC.
49. Fernando Hernandez, rhp, Miami Southwest HS.
50. **Matt Payne, rhp, U. of California.**

CINCINNATI (3)

■ SCOUTING DIRECTOR: Kasey McKeon.
1. **Chris Gruler, rhp, Liberty Union HS, Brentwood, Calif.**
1. Mark Schramek, 3b, U. of Texas-San Antonio (Supplemental pick—40th—for failure to sign 2001 first-round pick Jeremy Sowers).
2. **Joey Votto, c, Richview Collegiate Institute, Toronto.**
3. **Kyle Edens, rhp, Baylor U.**
4. **Camilo Vazquez, lhp, Hialeah (Fla.) HS.**
5. **Kevin Howard, 3b, U. of Miami (Fla.).**
6. **Walter Olmstead, 1b, Texas Christian U.**
7. **Corey Wachman, rhp, Valdosta State (Ga.) U.**
8. **O.J. King, rhp, Northwestern State (La.) U.**
9. **Steve Booth, c, U. of San Francisco.**
10. **Frankie Keller, lhp, Abilene (Texas) Christian U.**
11. **Mike Bassett, of, George Washington U.**
12. **Don Gemmell, rhp, San Jose State U.**
13. Jose Enrique Cruz, ss, Rice U.
14. **Joe Curran, lhp, Fort Hays State (Kan.) U.**
15. Glenn Kamis, rhp, Elgin (Ill.) CC.
16. **Jonathan George, rhp, Camden Catholic HS, Pennsauken, N.J.**
17. Trey Lavender, c, Pelham (Ala.) HS.
18. Zach McCormack, lhp, Sacramento CC.
19. **Christopher Denorfia, of, Wheaton (Mass.) College.**
20. Tyler Coon, lhp, Silverado HS, Las Vegas, Nev.
21. Mike Causey, rhp, Moorpark (Calif.) JC.
22. Matt Luca, rhp, Ball HS, Galveston, Texas.
23. Nick Markakis, lhp, Young Harris (Ga.) JC.

24. **Jarrod Schmidt, c-rhp, Clemson U.**
25. **Robert Mosby, 1b, Northeastern Oklahoma A&M JC.**
26. Chris Dunn, ss, Chaparral HS, Parker, Colo.
27. Juan Velazquez, rhp, Montgomery HS, San Diego.
28. Jay Tust, 2b, Stadium HS, Tacoma.
29. **Richard Correll, ss, Limestone (S.C.) College.**
30. **Justin Knoff, rhp, Siena College.**
31. **Mayque Quintero, rhp, Sonoma County/Western League.**
32. Gerald Smith, of, Thomas Jefferson HS, Tampa
33. Bart Braun, lhp, Diablo Valley (Calif.) JC.
34. Cody McAllister, rhp, Snohomish (Wash.) HS
35. Stantrel Smith, of, Towers HS, Decatur, Ga.
36. **Matt Krimmel, 3b, George Washington U.**
37. **Shawn Aichele, rhp, Western Hills HS, Cincinnati.**
38. Hardy Hutto, rhp, Garden City (Kan.) CC.
39. Calvin Medlock, rhp, Westbury HS, Houston.
40. **Chris Bell, rhp, Miami Dade North JC.**
41. Marcus Townsend, of, U. of Texas-Brownsville.
42. Danny Kelly, ss, Durango HS, Las Vegas, Nev.
43. Derek Hawk, rhp, Mendocino (Calif.) CC.
44. Jason Baca, rhp, Sweeny (Texas) HS.
45. Dennis Leduc, rhp, Cuesta (Calif.) JC.
46. **Troy Cairns, ss, U. of New Mexico.**
47. Michael Bryant, rhp, Sam Rayburn HS, Pasadena, Texas.
48. **Travis Wong, 1b, Texas A&M U.**
49. **William Dennis, of, Incarnate Word (Texas) U.** (contract voided)
50. Ben Himes, of, Texas A&M U.

CLEVELAND (22)

■ SCOUTING DIRECTOR: John Mirabelli.
1. Jeremy Guthrie, rhp, Stanford U.
1. **Matt Whitney, 3b, Palm Beach Gardens (Fla.) HS** (Supplemental pick—33rd—for loss of Type A free agent Juan Gonzalez).
1. **Micah Schilling, 2b, Silliman Institute, Clinton, La.** (Supplemental pick—41st—for failure to sign 2001 first-round pick Alan Horne).
2. **Brian Slocum, rhp, Villanova U.**
2. **Pat Osborn, 3b, U. of Florida** (Supplemental pick—72nd—as compensation for Type B free agent Marty Cordova).
3. **Jason Cooper, of, Stanford U.** (Choice from Rangers—82nd—for loss of Gonzalez).
3. **Daniel Cevette, lhp, Elkland (Pa.) HS.**
4. **Fernando Pacheco, 1b, Montgomery HS, San Ysidro, Calif.**
5. **Ben Francisco, of, UCLA.**
6. **Michael Hernandez, lhp, Fresno State U.**
7. **Brian Wright, of, North Carolina State U.**
8. **Blake Allen, lhp, Union (Tenn.) U.**
9. **Shaun Larkin, 2b, Cal State Northridge.**
10. **Keith Ramsey, lhp, U. of Florida.**
11. **Bill Peavey, 1b, U. of Southern California.**
12. **Chad Longworth, of, J.J. Kelly HS, Wise, Va.**
13. Reid Santos, lhp, Saddleback (Calif.) CC.
14. Mike Mitchell, rhp, St. Charles (Mo.) JC.
15. **Nathan Panther, of, Muscatine (Iowa) CC.**
16. **Omar Casillas, c, Ana J. Candelas HS, Cidra, P.R.**
17. Jeff Ostrander, lhp, Patrick Henry HS, Montpelier, Va.
18. **Jahseam George, lhp, San Jose State U.**
19. Curt Mendoza, of, Redlands (Calif.) HS.
20. **Chris White, lhp, Kent State U.**
21. Zeke Parraz, ss, CC of Southern Nevada.
22. **Clayton McCullough, c, East Carolina U.**
23. Aaron Tennyson, lhp, Milan (Mich.) HS.
24. Dan Donaldson, lhp, Memorial HS, Houston.
25. Nicholas Pesco, rhp, Cosumnes River (Calif.) JC.
26. Jose Cardona, lhp, American Military Academy, Guaynabo, P.R.
27. Derek Dunne, rhp, Sullivan (Mo.) HS.
28. Tim Sabo, rhp, Don Bosco Prep, Suffern, N.Y.
29. Ruben Flores, rhp, Riverside HS, El Paso.
30. **Daniel Eisentrager, rhp, Long Beach State U.**
31. **Jeff Davis, rhp, U. of Kansas.**
32. **Shea Douglas, lhp, U. of Southern Mississippi.**
33. Jensen Lewis, rhp, Anderson HS, Cincinnati.
34. Chris Williams, c, Marcus HS, Flower Mound, Texas.
35. Kevin Hawkins, rhp, Embry-Riddle (Fla.) Aeronautical College.
36. Aaron Braithwaite, of, Indian River (Fla.) CC.
37. Luis DeJesus, ss, New Mexico JC.
38. John Moran, ss, Southaven (Miss.) HS.
39. **Blake Taylor, rhp, U. of South Carolina.**
40. Shea McFeely, ss, Federal Way (Wash.) HS.
41. Andrew Knight, lhp, Maize (Kan.) HS.
42. Chris Rosario, of, Pine Ridge HS, Deltona, Fla.
43. Matt Paz, rhp, Long Beach State U.
44. Richard Wells, 3b, Glendale (Calif.) JC.
45. Truan Mehl, of, Hutchinson (Kan.) CC.
46. **Aaron Davidson, 2b, U. of Florida.**
47. Jimmy Mayer, ss, Somerset (Pa.) Area HS.

48. Bryce Kartler, lhp, Arizona State U.
49. Daniel Lindner, rhp, Potomac State (W.Va.) JC.
50. Ricardo Concepcion, of, Petra Corretser HS, Manati, P.R.

COLORADO (9)

■ **SCOUTING DIRECTOR:** Bill Schmidt.
1. **Jeff Francis, lhp, U. of British Columbia.**
2. Micah Owings, rhp, Gainesville (Ga.) HS.
3. **Ben Crockett, rhp, Harvard U.**
4. **Jeff Baker, 3b, Clemson U.**
5. **Neil Wilson, c, Vero Beach (Fla.) HS.**
5. **Doug Johnson, rhp, Bryant (R.I.) College** (Choice from Rangers—142nd—as compensation for Type B free agent Jay Powell).
6. **Sean Barker, of, Louisiana State U.**
7. **Ryan Spilborghs, of, UC Santa Barbara.**
8. **Jeff Salazar, of, Oklahoma State U.**
9. **John Tetuan, rhp, Wichita State U.**
10. **Isaac Pavlik, lhp, Seton Hall U.**
11. **Ryan Shealy, 1b, U. of Florida.**
12. **Mike Esposito, rhp, Arizona State U.**
13. **Brian Barre, of, U. of Southern California.**
14. **Bernard Gonzalez, of, Florida International U.**
15. **Andy Bushey, c-3b, U. of Notre Dame.**
16. Brad Corley, of, Pleasure Ridge Park HS, Louisville.
17. **Steven Ponder, rhp, Texas A&M U.**
18. **Chris Young, rhp, Mississippi State U.**
19. **Duke Sardinha, 3b, Pepperdine U.**
20. **Dan Street, 3b, U. of Virginia.**
21. **Steve Reba, rhp, Clemson U.**
22. **Pete Montrenes, rhp, U. of Mississippi.**
23. **Carson White, 2b, U. of California.**
24. **Mitsuru Sakamoto, of, Arizona Western JC.**
25. **Rock Mills, c, Pepperdine U.**
26. **K.J. Hendricks, ss, U. of Texas-Arlington.**
27. Lance Beus, lhp, Cochise County (Ariz.) CC.
28. Jose Lado, lhp, Delgado (La.) JC.
29. **Richard Cartier, rhp, Cuesta (Calif.) JC.**
30. Aaron Gamboa, ss, Bakersfield (Calif.) JC.
31. Daniel Lonsberry, rhp, Northeast Texas CC.
32. Derek Patterson, lhp, Evangel Christian Academy, Keithville, La.
33. **Mike Watson, rhp, Penn State U.**
34. Ryan Mattheus, rhp, Galt (Calif.) Union HS.
35. Robert Madsen, rhp, McLennan (Texas) CC.
36. Clayton Trenary, of, Crystal River (Fla.) HS.
37. Victor Alvarez, ss, Chipola (Fla.) JC.
38. Stephen Sutton, ss, Texarkana (Texas) CC.
39. **Tomas Santiago, rhp, Pikeville (Ky.) College.**
40. Matthew Albidrez-Garza, rhp, Washington Union HS, Fresno.
41. John DeFendis, of, Xaverian HS, Brooklyn.
42. **Jason Dooley, rhp, Bethune-Cookman College.**
43. Justin Hoyman, rhp, Brevard (Fla.) CC.
44. Ryan Earnest, rhp, Hardaway HS, Columbus, Ga.
45. Tyler Littlehales, of, Boulder (Colo.) HS.
46. Joshua Merino, rhp, Kirkwood (Mo.) CC.
47. John Brownell, rhp, Butler County (Kan.) CC.
48. Jim Popp, rhp, Duquesne U.
49. Jared Theodorakos, lhp, Baylor U.
50. Andrew York, c, JC. of the Siskiyous (Calif.).

DETROIT (8)

■ **SCOUTING DIRECTOR:** Greg Smith.
1. **Scott Moore, ss, Cypress HS, Long Beach, Calif.**
2. **Brent Clevlen, of, Westwood HS, Cedar Park, Texas.**
3. **Curtis Granderson, of, U. of Illinois-Chicago.**
3. **Matt Pender, rhp, Kennesaw State (Ga.) U.** (Choice from Mets—87th—as compensation for Type B free agent Roger Cedeno).
4. **Robbie Sovie, of, Stratford Academy, Macon, Ga.**
5. **Bo Flowers, of, Walter Lutheran HS, Maywood, Ill.**
6. **Chris Maples, rhp, U. of North Carolina.**
7. **Wilton Reynolds, rhp, Oral Roberts U.**
8. **Troy Pickford, rhp, Oral Roberts U.**
9. **Marcos Hernandez, rhp, Juan Ponce de Leon HS, San Juan, P.R.**
10. **Luke Carlin, c, Northeastern U.**
11. **Joel Zumaya, rhp, Bonita Vista HS, Chula Vista, Calif.**
12. **Corey Hamman, lhp, Montclair State (N.J.) U.**
13. Anthony Reyes, rhp, U. of Southern California.
14. **Jason Graham, rhp, U. of Central Florida.**
15. **Jesse Carlson, lhp, U. of Connecticut.**
16. **Michael Smith, lhp, Valdosta State (Ga.) U.**
17. **Rob Watson, ss, Oklahoma State U.**
18. Jacob Coash, lhp, Canyon HS, Saugus, Calif.
19. **Rafael Mendez, c, Notre Dame HS, Caguas P.R.**
20. **Jason Kennedy, of, U. of Minnesota.**
21. **Corey Loomis, 2b, Bowling Green U.**

22. Cameron McGuire, c, South Grand Prairie (Texas) HS.
23. **Drew Caravella, 1b, Ohio Wesleyan U.**
24. **Jody Roughton, 3b, U. of Missouri.**
25. Daniel Nelson, ss, Crenshaw HS, Los Angeles
26. **Billy Kieninger, rhp, Miami (Ohio) U.**
27. **Damian Myers, lhp, Concordia (N.Y.) College.**
28. **Everett Hancock, lhp, UNC Greensboro.**
29. Miguel Donate, 1b, Morell HS, Vega Alta, P.R.
30. **David Garcia, ss, Santa Ana (Calif.) JC.**
31. Chris McCuiston, of, Michigan State U.
32. Douglas Webb, rhp, Newbury Park (Calif.) HS.
33. Jose Rodriguez, c, Cypress (Calif.) JC.
34. **Jason Allec, c, Cal State Northridge.**
35. Brandon McCormick, rhp, W.W. King Academy, Batesburg, S.C.
36. **Chris Steinborn, lhp, Lakeland (Ohio) CC.**
37. Ronald Baron, rhp, Blinn (Texas) JC.
38. **Edward Romprey, ss, Bellevue (Neb.) College.**
39. **Kevin McDonald, c, U. of Maryland.**
40. Matthew Taylor, lhp, Antioch (Tenn.) HS.
41. **Edgar Ortiz, 1b, Compton (Calif.) CC.**
42. Travis Simmons, 3b, Cleveland (Tenn.) HS.
43. Corey McCoy, of, Pine Bluff (Ark.) HS.
44. Sean Richardson, c, Palomar (Calif.) JC.

FLORIDA (11)

■ **SCOUTING DIRECTOR:** Stan Meek.
1. **Jeremy Hermida, of, Wheeler HS, Marietta, Ga.**
2. **Robert Andino, ss, Southridge HS, Miami.**
3. Trevor Hutchinson, rhp, U. of California.
4. **Josh Johnson, rhp, Jenks HS, Tulsa.**
5. Nick Hundley, c, Lake Washington HS, Redmond, Wash.
6. **Scott Olson, lhp, Crystal Lake (Ill.) South HS.**
7. **Xavier Arroyo, of, Antilles HS, Fort Buchanan, P.R.**
8. **Ryan Warpinski, rhp, Texas A&M U.**
9. **Eric Reed, of, Texas A&M U.**
10. **Robert Word, 1b, U. of Virginia.**
11. **Patrick Arlis, c, U. of Illinois.**
12. **Jimmy deMontel, rhp, Bellevue (Neb.) College.**
13. **Kevin Randel, ss, Long Beach State U.**
14. **Travis Chick, rhp, Whitehouse (Texas) HS.**
15. **Tom Merkle, 3b, New York Tech.**
16. Chris Goodman, rhp, Georgia Tech.
17. **Evan Greusel, rhp, U. of Oklahoma.**
18. **Ross Wolf, rhp, Wabash Valley (Ill.) CC.**
19. **Jordan Baker, of, Zane Trace HS, Chillicothe, Ohio.**
20. **Jason Iehl, rhp, Downers Grove (Ill.) North HS.**
21. Waylon Byers, lhp, U. of Nebraska.
22. **Shaun O'Connor, rhp, Pasco Hernando (Fla.) CC.**
23. **Carl Primus, rhp, Southern U.**
24. **Andy Rohleder, of, U. of Evansville**
25. **Eric Ordorica, 2b, Azusa Pacific (Calif.) U.**
26. Brae Wright, lhp, Southaven (Miss.) HS.
27. **Casey Blalock, rhp, Louisiana Tech.**
28. Aaron Gabriel, rhp, Lake City HS, Coeur d'Alene, Idaho.
29. **Chris Gabriel, rhp, Chaffey (Calif.) JC.**
30. Kurt Koehler, rhp, Pinole Valley HS, Pinole, Calif.
31. **Kyle Eazor, lhp, Chandler-Gilbert (Ariz.) CC.**
32. **Daniel Olson, rhp, U. of Kansas.** (contract voided)
33. **Joseph Apotheker, of, Barry (Fla.) U.**
34. Kyle Dickson, rhp, Granada HS, Livermore, Calif.
35. Greg Goetz, lhp, Newport HS, Bellevue, Wash.
36. Neil Warchol, rhp, St. Laurence HS, Burbank, Ill.
37. Ryan Anderson, lhp, St. Petersburg (Fla.) JC.
38. Patrick Connelly, lhp, Cowley County (Kan.) CC.
39. Matthew Miller, of, Modesto (Calif.) JC.
40. Bradley Pahs, c, Triton (Ill.) JC.
41. Robert Johnson, c, Saddleback (Calif.) JC.
42. Zachary Lerch, rhp, Muscatine (Iowa) CC.
43. Tyler Williams, c, North Delta (B.C.) SS.
44. Timothy Wood, rhp, Pima (Ariz.) CC.
45. Shany Carle, rhp, U. of Quebec.
46. Nicholas Ewen, of, Triton (Ill.) JC.
47. Jacob Manning, of, Mineral Area (Mo.) JC.
48. Matthew Hayes, lhp, Parkland (Ill.) JC.
49. Michael Gaffney, ss, New York Tech.
50. Dustin Hughes, c, Northgate HS, Walnut Creek, Calif.

HOUSTON (29)

■ **SCOUTING DIRECTOR:** David Lakey.
1. **Derick Grisby, rhp, Northeast Texas CC.**
2. **Mitch Talbot, rhp, Canyon View HS, Cedar City, Utah.**
3. **Rory Shortell, rhp, San Diego State U.**
4. **Mark McLemore, lhp, Oregon State U.**
5. Pat Misch, lhp, Western Michigan U.

6. J.P. Duran, rhp, St. Mary's (Texas) U.
7. Scott Robinson, 1b-of, Rancho Bernardo HS, San Diego.
8. Bill Westhoff, rhp, U. of Dallas.
9. Andy Topham, ss, Stanford U.
10. Brad Chester, rhp, Panola (Texas) JC.
11. Jason Reuss, of, U. of Nevada-Las Vegas.
12. Chance Douglass, rhp, Randall HS, Amarillo, Texas.
13. Nick Covarrubias, of, Long Beach State U.
14. B.J. Boening, rhp, Yoakum HS, Portland, Texas.
15. Jeff Mackor, c, Boston College.
16. Jared Gothreaux, rhp, McNeese State U.
17. Daniel Freeman, rhp, Texarkana (Texas) CC.
18. Brent Long, rhp, Brevard (N.C.) College.
19. Aaron Heitzman, lhp, Minnesota State U.-Mankato.
20. Justin Glover, of, Grant HS, Portland, Ore.
21. Ivan Naccarata, 2b, Chipola (Fla.) JC.
22. Sam Fischer, rhp, U. of Dayton.
23. Jesse Harrington, ss, Concordia (Ore.) U.
24. Nick Tisone, rhp, Mandeville HS, Covington, La.
25. Ethien Santana, of, Colegio Bautista, Carolina, P.R.
26. Randy McGarvey, c, Coastal Carolina U.
27. Shawn Burris, lhp, Poteet HS, Mesquite, Texas.
28. Kevin Davidson, c, Rollins (Fla.) College.
29. Sean Kramer, rhp, Hill (Texas) JC.
30. Ladd Hall, rhp, Eastern Arizona JC.
31. Andrew Salmela, 1b, Augustana (S.D.) College.
32. Tyson Olson, of, Dixie (Utah) JC.
33. Pat Peavey, 3b, U. of Santa Clara.
34. Mike Lorsbach, of, Rice U.
35. Shawn Williams, of, Clearwater (Fla.) Central Catholic HS.
36. Adam Seuss, of, UC Riverside.
37. Dustin Hawkins, of, Wichita State U.
38. Ryan Larson, 3b, UC San Diego.
39. Nicholas Stavinoha, of, San Jacinto (Texas) JC.
40. Adam Yesalusky, lhp, Minersville (Pa.) Area HS.
41. Scott Feldman, rhp, JC of San Mateo (Calif.).
42. Chase Medford, lhp-of, Richland (Texas) HS.
43. Freddie Thon, 1b, Baldwin HS, Guaynabo, P.R.
44. William Mac-Holmes, rhp, Northwest HS, Omaha, Neb.
45. Ryan McKeller, rhp, McLennan (Texas) CC.
46. Eric Brock, rhp, Santa Margarita HS, Laguna Niguel, Calif.
47. Raymar Diaz, of, Laredo (Texas) CC.
48. Kyle Thompson, rhp, Palomar (Calif.) CC.

KANSAS CITY (6)

■ SCOUTING DIRECTOR: Deric Ladnier.
1. Zack Greinke, rhp, Apopka HS, Orlando.
2. Adam Donachie, c, Timber Creek HS, Orlando.
3. David Jensen, 1b, Brigham Young U.
4. Danny Christensen, lhp, Xaverian HS, Brooklyn.
5. Don Murphy, ss, Orange Coast (Calif.) JC.
6. Brandon Jones, ss, Wewahitchka (Fla.) HS.
7. Jonah Bayliss, rhp, Trinity (Conn.) College.
8. Kenard Springer, 3b, Nettleton (Miss.) HS.
9. Matt Tupman, c, U. of Massachusetts-Lowell.
10. Greg Atencio, rhp, Lamar (Colo.) CC.
11. Kainoa Obrey, 3b, Brigham Young U.
12. Adam Keim, ss, Coastal Carolina U.
13. Rusty Meyer, c, Texas A&M U.
14. Steven Chamberlain, rhp, U. of Portland.
15. Micah Kaaihue, 1b, Iolani HS, Honolulu.
16. Eric Ackerman, lhp, U. of Pittsburgh.
17. Jason Bartz, rhp, U. of South Florida. (contract voided)
18. Donnie Poles, of, Pitt (N.C.) CC.
19. Alex Crooks, 1b, Sierra Vista HS, Azusa, Calif.
20. Nate Zettler, rhp, Union (Ky.) College.
21. Steve Mena, 3b, South Miami HS, Miami.
22. Nick Bates, rhp, Michigan State U.
23. Tim Frend, of, Davidson College.
24. Michael Aguilar, rhp, Franklin HS, Portland, Ore.
25. Carlos Caballero, of, Ines Maria Mendoza HS, Cabo Rojo, P.R.
26. J.J. Brown, of, Vicksburg (Miss.) HS.
27. Michael Hernandez, of, Xaverian HS, Brooklyn, N.Y.
28. Robert Grana, c, CC of Southern Nevada.
29. Michael Honce, rhp, Bridgeport (W.Va.) HS.
30. Clinton Johnson, rhp, Murrah HS, Jackson, Miss.
31. Matthew Castillo, of, Mesa (Ariz.) CC.
32. Leon Stephens, of, Virginia State U.
33. Cesar Carrillo, rhp, Mount Carmel (Ill.) HS.
34. Eric Lonnquist, ss, Minnesota State U.-Mankato.
35. Tyler Kimmons, rhp, Mandeville (La.) HS.
36. Chris Turner, c, El Dorado (Ark.) HS.
37. Jason Ward, rhp, Utah Valley State JC.
38. Justin Taylor, rhp, Baylor U.

Zack Greinke was selected by Kansas City, sixth overall

39. Eric Hullinger, rhp, Kishwaukee (Ill.) JC.
40. Vince Berry, of, Triton (Ill.) JC.
41. Drew Endicott, rhp, U. of Missouri.
42. Odell Cosby, of, Paris (Ky.) HS.
43. David Nelson, lhp, North Carolina A&T U.
44. Bryan McCaulley, rhp, San Jacinto (Calif.) JC.
45. Andrew Scholl, of-1b, Lamar (Colo.) CC.
46. Devan Ewell, of, Osborne HS, Manassas, Va.
47. Ty Wallace, c, Newman Smith HS, Carrollton, Texas.
48. Lenny Bays, rhp, Northern Kentucky U. (contract voided)
49. Luis Rivera, ss, Carvin School, Carolina, P.R.
50. Matt Hobbs, lhp, U. of Missouri.

LOS ANGELES (19)

■ SCOUTING DIRECTOR: Logan White.
1. James Loney, 1b, Elkins HS, Missouri City, Texas.
1. Greg Miller, lhp, Esperanza HS, Yorba Linda, Calif. (Supplemental pick—31st—for loss of Type A free agent Chan Ho Park).
2. Zach Hammes, rhp, Iowa City HS, Iowa City, Iowa (Choice from Rangers—51st—for loss of Park).
2. Jonathan Broxton, rhp, Burke County HS, Waynesboro, Ga.
3. Mike Nixon, c, Sunnyslope HS, Phoenix.
4. Delwyn Young, 2b, Santa Barbara (Calif.) CC.
5. Mike Megrew, lhp, Chariho Regional HS, Hope Valley, R.I.
6. Marshall Looney, lhp, La Pine (Ore.) HS.
7. David Bagley, 3b, U. of San Diego.
8. Jamaal Hamilton, lhp, Monterey HS, Lubbock, Texas.
9. Denver Kitch, ss, U. of Oklahoma.
10. Ryan Williams, rhp, Old Dominion U.
11. James McDonald, 1b, Poly HS, Long Beach, Calif.
12. Ryan Owen, c, Wichita State U.
13. Julio LaSalle, rhp, Palm Beach Atlantic (Fla.) College.
14. Karl Mejlholm, rhp, Dover Bay HS, Nanaimo, B.C.
15. Eric Stults, lhp, Bethel (Ind.) College.
16. Sambu Ndungidi, of, St. Georges HS, Montreal.
17. Russell Martin, 2b, Chipola (Fla.) JC.
18. Curtis Hudson, c, Yuba City (Calif.) HS.
19. Michael White, lhp, St. Petersburg (Fla.) JC.
20. Andrew Walker, rhp, Cowley County (Kan.) CC.
21. Ryan Tracy, rhp, Claremont (Calif.) HS.
22. Brett Wayne, ss, St. Mary's (Calif.) College.
23. Josh Bartusick, 1b, Fountain Valley (Calif.) HS.
24. Derry Jackson, of, Jesuit HS, Portland, Ore.
25. Alvin Hayes, rhp, Alabama Southern CC.
26. Jarod Plummer, rhp, South Garland (Texas) HS.
27. Mike Potoczny, rhp, North Marion HS, Farmington, W. Va.
28. Robert Ray, rhp, Lufkin (Texas) HS.
29. Dominique Laurin, ss-2b, Eastern Oklahoma State JC.
30. Edward Roberts, rhp, Key West (Fla.) HS.

31. **Ross Hawley, rhp, Kansas State U.**
32. Richard Robnett, of, Santa Barbara (Calif.) CC.
33. Eddie Baeza, rhp, Poly HS, Sun Valley, Calif.
34. Douglas Mathis, rhp, Show Low (Ariz.) HS.
35. Matt Long, rhp, Granville (Ohio) HS.
36. **Bryan Goelz, of, New York Tech.**
37. Jon Riggleman, 3b, Hillsborough (Fla.) CC.
38. Danny Forrer, lhp, Jefferson Davis HS, Montgomery, Ala.
39. Luke Hochevar, rhp, Fowler (Col.) HS.
40. Eric Wolfe, 1b, York Mills HS, Willowdale, Ontario.
41. Ryan Lennerton, Eastern Oklahoma State JC.
42. Nathan Warrick, of, Belton (Texas) HS.
43. **David Parker, rhp, Eastern Oklahoma State CC.**
44. James Bailie, c, Kodiak (Alaska) HS.
45. Justin Estrada, ss, Tampa Jesuit HS, Tampa.
46. **Mickey Jordan, of, Armstrong Atlantic State (Ga.) U.**
47. Chad Bailey, lhp, North Idaho JC.
48. Andre Trahan, of, Yuba (Calif.) CC.
49. Jeffrey Cristy, c, Southeast HS, Lincoln, Neb.
50. Jason Farrand, c, Conway (S.C.) HS.

MILWAUKEE (7)

■ **SCOUTING DIRECTOR:** Jack Zduriencik.
1. **Prince Fielder, 1b, Eau Gallie HS, Melbourne, Fla.**
2. **Josh Murray, ss, Jesuit HS, Tampa.**
3. **Eric Thomas, rhp, U. of South Alabama.**
4. **Nic Carter, of, Campbell U.**
5. Jarrad Page, ss, San Leandro (Calif.) HS.
6. **Khalid Ballouli, rhp, Texas A&M U.**
7. **Tom Wilhelmsen, rhp, Tucson Magnet HS, Tucson.**
8. Steve Kahn, rhp, Servite HS, Anaheim, Calif.
9. **Edwin Walker, lhp, Highland HS, San Antonio.**
10. **Jeremy Frost, c, U. of Central Florida.**
11. Brian Hernandez, c, John I. Leonard HS, Boynton Beach, Fla.
12. **Callix Crabbe, 2b, Manatee (Fla.) CC.**
13. Tila Reynolds, ss, U. of Washington.
14. **Kennard Bibbs, of, Oklahoma City U.**
15. Justin Barnes, rhp, Manatee (Fla.) CC.
16. Dana Eveland, lhp, Hill (Texas) JC.
17. Adam Mannon, rhp, Hamilton HS, Chandler, Ariz.
18. Steven White, rhp, Baylor U.
19. **Bo Hall, rhp, U. of Central Florida.**
20. **Tyler Shepple, rhp, U. of Washington.**
21. **Josh Alliston, rhp, Long Beach State U.**
22. **Lenden Willis, 3b, Motlow State (Tenn.) CC.**
23. **Keith Bohanan, 3b, Oklahoma City U.**
24. **Arturo Bravo, c, Montgomery HS, San Ysidro, Calif.**
25. **John Vanden Berg, c, U. of Wisconsin-Milwaukee.**
26. **Craig Breslow, lhp, Yale U.**
27. **Dallas Bates, of, Chandler (Ariz.) HS.**
28. **Eric Thomas, rhp, Southern U.**
29. **Steve Moss, of, Notre Dame HS, Sherman Oaks, Calif.**
30. **Justin Gabriel, lhp, U of. Louisiana-Lafayette.**
31. **Jason Baker, rhp, George Washington U.**
32. Simon Beresford, rhp, Tyler (Texas) JC.
33. **Jeff Housman, lhp, Cal State Fullerton.**
34. Tim Dillard, c, Itawamba (Miss.) CC.
35. Emmanuel Cividanes, of, Colegio San Antonio, San Juan, P.R.
36. Daniel Carter, rhp, Tallahassee (Fla.) CC.
37. Stephen Bryant, c, Warren Central HS, Indianapolis.
38. David Hancox, rhp, Pasco Hernando (Fla.) CC.
39. Juan Herrera, lhp, Arizona Western JC.
40. Hunter Pence, of, Texarkana (Texas) CC.
41. Jonathan Shapland, of, St. Petersburg (Fla.) JC.
42. Neil Avery, of, Dartmouth HS, North Dartmouth, Mass.

MINNESOTA (20)

■ **SCOUTING DIRECTOR:** Mike Radcliff.
1. **Denard Span, of, Tampa Catholic HS.**
2. **Jesse Crain, rhp, U. of Houston.**
3. Mark Sauls, rhp, Bay HS, Panama City, Fla.
4. **Alex Merricks, lhp, Oxnard (Calif.) HS.**
5. Clete Thomas, of, Mosley HS, Lynn Haven, Fla.
6. **Pat Neshek, rhp, Butler U.**
7. **Ricky Barrett, lhp, U. of San Diego.**
8. Adam Lind, 1b, Highland HS, Anderson, Ind.
9. **Doug Deeds, of, Ohio State U.**
10. **Kyle Phillips, c, El Capitan HS, Lakeside, Calif.**
11. Evan Meek, rhp, Inglemoor HS, Bothell, Wash.
12. Jeff Clement, c, Marshalltown (Iowa) HS.
13. Bo Pettit, rhp, Louisiana State U.
14. Garrett Mock, rhp, Grayson County (Texas) CC.
15. **Adam Harben, rhp, Westark (Ark.) CC.**
16. **KC Jones, rhp, Eatonville (Wash.) HS.**

17. Adam Hawes, rhp, St. Theresa's Catholic HS, Victoria Harbour, Ontario.
18. **Javier Lopez, of, Galveston (Texas) JC.**
19. Adam Daniels, lhp, North Vancouver, B.C.
20. Ryan Schreppel, lhp, Lincoln HS, Stockton, Calif.
21. **T.J. Prunty, rhp, U. of Miami (Fla.).**
22. **Justin Sims, of, Middle Tennessee State U.**
23. **Dan Matienzo, c, U. of Miami (Fla.).**
24. Joshua Petersen, 1b, Jupiter (Fla.) HS.
25. **Justin Keeling, lhp, California Lutheran U.**
26. Jared Johnson, rhp, Cimarron Memorial HS, Las Vegas.
27. **Ronald Perodin, of, El Camino (Calif.) CC.**
28. Hasan Rasheed, of, Whites Creek HS, Nashville, Tenn.
29. James Avery, rhp, Central Collegiate HS, Moose Jaw, Sask.
30. Roberto Martinez, rhp, St. Petersburg (Fla.) CC.
31. Terry Killion, rhp, Bowie HS, Austin, Texas.
32. Jonathon Koch, rhp, Lake City (Fla.) CC.
33. Thomas Ferrara, rhp, Brevard (Fla.) CC.
34. Christian Castorri, rhp, Thomas County Central HS, Thomasville, Ga.
35. **Tarrence Patterson, of, Bartow HS, Lakeland, Fla.**
36. **John Cahill, rhp, Lakewood (Calif.) HS.**
37. Michael Costantino, 3b, Somerset (Mass.) HS.
38. Toby Gardenhire, ss, Westark (Ark.) CC.
39. Brandon Doddo, c, Cooper City (Fla.) HS.
40. Rodney Story, lhp, Gulf Coast (Fla.) CC.
41. Chris Brown, 2b, Cooper City (Fla.) HS.
42. Kyle Geiger, c, Rend Lake (Ill.) JC.
43. Jacob Jean, lhp, Cosumnes River (Calif.) CC.
44. Chris Beatty, ss, Kokomo (Ind.) HS.
45. John Stocco, rhp, Academy of Holy Angels HS, Richfield, Minn.
46. Wayne Renfrow, rhp, Kellam HS, Virginia Beach, Va.
47. Brandon Carlton, lhp, Bay HS, Panama City, Fla.
48. Brandon Cohen, of, River Dell HS, Oradell, N.J.
49. **Brock Peterson, 3b, West HS, Chehalis, Wash.**
50. Michael Ballard, lhp, Ocean Lakes HS, Virginia Beach, Va.

MONTREAL (5)

■ **SCOUTING DIRECTOR:** Dana Brown.
1. **Clint Everts, rhp, Cypress Falls HS, Houston.**
2. **Darrell Rasner, rhp, U. of Nevada.**
3. **Larry Broadway, 1b, Duke U.**
4. **Jon Felfoldi, lhp, Glendale (Calif.) CC.**
5. **Anthony Pearson, rhp, Jackson State U.**
6. **Chad Chop, 1b, Vanguard (Calif.) U.**
7. **Mike O'Connor, lhp, George Washington U.**
8. Friedel Pinkston, rhp, Hart County HS, Hartwell, Ga.
9. **Chris Barlow, rhp, Le Moyne College.**
10. Justin Azze, lhp, Orange Coast (Calif.) JC.
11. **Jason Bergmann, rhp, Rutgers U.**
12. **Danny Rueckel, rhp, Furman U.**
13. **Brett Nyquist, lhp, College of St. Scholastica (Minn.).**
14. **Erik Fiedler, rhp, San Diego State U.**
15. **Isaiah Wright, rhp, Dover (Del.) HS.**
16. **Brian Ellerson, rhp, Montclair State (N.J.) U.**
17. **Jason Conlisk, ss, Fordham U.**
18. **Anthony Brown, of, George Washington U.**
19. **Franklyn Jimenez, 2b, Muscatine (Iowa) CC.**
20. **Tim Sweeney, ss, Rutgers U.**
21. **Stockton Davis, rhp, Oral Roberts U.**
22. Marcus Davis, rhp, Luray (Va.) HS.
23. **Nathan Weese, of, U. of Utah.**
24. **Matt Swope, of, U. of Maryland.**
25. **Adrian Urquhart, of, Alabama State U.**
26. **Maurice Cobb, of, Rocky Mount (N.C.) HS.**
27. Matt Bonovich, c, U. of Southern California.
28. Tony Irvin, rhp, Hillsborough (Fla.) CC.
29. Tim Hudnall, 1b, Lake Michigan JC.
30. Robert Rohrbaugh, lhp, Littlestown (Pa.) Area HS.
31. Ruben Kerbs, lhp, Wichita State U.
32. Cam O'Donnell, rhp, Middle Georgia JC.
33. Andrew Wells, lhp, St. Stephens-St. Agnes HS, Alexandria, Va.
34. Jack Lyons, lhp, Maret HS, Washington, D.C.
35. Sean White, rhp, U. of Washington.
36. Jeffrey Miller, 1b, Pine Grove (Pa.) Area HS.
37. Jarvis Hicks, rhp, South Florida CC.
38. Nicholas Ponomarenko, rhp, Cuesta (Calif.) JC.
39. Jonathan Hunton, rhp, Miami-Dade CC North.
40. Bryan Coffey, rhp, Culpepper HS, Rixeyville, Va.
41. Michael Romeo, 3b, Lindenhurst (N.Y.) HS.
42. Randy Dicken, rhp, Allegany (Md.) CC.
43. Brody Taylor, rhp, Louisburg (N.C.) CC.
44. Michael Gibbs, rhp, Roxborough HS, Philadelphia.
45. Jon Link, rhp, Chantilly (Va.) CC.
46. Marc Nunez, rhp, Countryside HS, St. Petersburg, Fla.
47. Ronald Ball, rhp, John F Kennedy HS, Buena Park, Calif.

48. Ken Beck, rhp, U. of. Maryland.
49. James Treece, rhp, Orange Coast (Calif.) CC.
50. Joe Gregory, rhp, Western HS, Davie, Fla.

NEW YORK/AL (24)

■ **SCOUTING DIRECTOR:** Lin Garrett.
1. (Choice to Athletics as compensation for Type A free agent Jason Giambi).
2. (Choice to Braves as compensation for Type A free agent Steve Karsay).
2. **Brandon Weeden, rhp-ss, Santa Fe HS, Edmond, Okla.** (Choice from Cardinals—71st—as compensation for Type B free agent Tino Martinez).
3. (Choice to Cubs as compensation for Type A free agent Rondell White).
4. **Alan Bomer, rhp, U. of Texas.**
5. **Matt Carson, of, Brigham Young U.**
6. **Brandon Harmsen, rhp, Grand Rapids (Mich.) JC.**
7. **Ross Michelsen, 1b, Lamar (Texas) HS.**
8. **Brad Halsey, lhp, U. of Texas.**
9. **Eric Verbryke, of, Cal State Northridge.**
10. **Gary Bell, lhp, U. of South Carolina.**
11. **Scott McClanahan, of, U. of Alabama.**
12. **Matt Mamula, 1b, Point Loma Nazarene (Calif.) College.**
13. **Blake Blase, 1b, Jefferson (Mo.) JC.**
14. **Ray Clark, rhp, U. of Texas.**
15. **Philip Tribe, rhp, Rice U.**
16. **Jared Koutnik, ss, Michigan State U.**
17. **Gabe Lopez, 2b, San Jose State U.**
18. **Luis Robles, c, Riverside (Calif.) CC.**
19. **Jon Sheaffer, of, Arizona State U.**
20. **Ben King, lhp, U. of Texas.**
21. **Hector Zamora, 3b, San Jose State U.**
22. Skyler Fulton, of, Skagit Valley (Wash.) JC.
23. **Eric Hacker, rhp, Duncanville (Texas) HS.**
24. Dane de la Rosa, rhp, Riverside (Calif.) CC.
25. **Joshua Neitz, rhp, Saint Leo (Fla.) College.**
26. Philip Coke, lhp, San Joaquin Delta (Calif.) JC.
27. Mike Knox, rhp, Jesuit College Prep, Dallas.
28. **Nathan Kopp, lhp, Wright State U.**
29. **Charlie Isaacson, rhp, U. of Arkansas.**
30. Kyle Marlatt, rhp, San Jacinto (Texas) JC.
31. **Paul Thorp, rhp, Baylor U.**
32. **Justin Meccage, rhp, Oklahoma State U.**
33. David Smith, lhp, Parkland (Ill.) JC.
34. **Nathan Bowden, ss, U. of North Alabama.**
35. Michael Brown, rhp, Owasso (Okla.) HS.
36. **Doug Boone, c, Ball State U.**
37. Richard Cowan, rhp, Navarro (Texas) JC.
38. Justin Keadle, rhp, Cypress (Calif.) JC.
39. Randy Gattis, rhp, Mesquite HS, Dallas.
40. **Joseph DiFranco, rhp, St. Thomas (Fla.) U.**
41. **Mike Miehls, c, Tennessee Tech.**
42. Matthew Goodson, rhp, Galveston (Texas) JC.
43. Jason Maes, lhp, Folsom HS, Elk Grove, Calif.
44. **Matthew Brumit, rhp, Youngstown State U.**
45. Matthew Yost, 1b, Elk City (Okla.) HS.
46. **Jared Treadway, of, College of Wooster (Ohio).**
47. Ryan Jennings, rhp, James Monroe HS, Lindside, W.Va.
48. Billy Carnline, rhp, New Caney (Texas) HS.
49. Levi Dartt, lhp, Denton (Texas) HS.
50. Arthur Christal, of, Ennis (Texas) HS.

NEW YORK/NL (15)

■ **SCOUTING DIRECTOR:** Jack Bowen.
1. **Scott Kazmir, lhp, Cypress Falls HS, Houston.**
2. (Choice to Cubs as compensation for Type A free agent David Weathers).
3. (Choice to Tigers as compensation for Type B free agent Roger Cedeno).
4. **Bob Malek, of, Michigan State U.**
5. **Jon Slack, of, Texas Tech.**
6. **Adam Elliott, rhp, Clayton Valley HS, Concord, Calif.**
7. **Jim Anderson, c, UC Riverside.**
8. **Tyler Davidson, of, U. of Washington.**
9. Christian Colonel, ss, JC of Southern Idaho.
10. **Matt Lindstrom, rhp, Ricks (Idaho) JC.**
11. **Kelvin Garay, lhp, Santa Cruz HS, Trujillo Alta, P.R.**
12. **Shawn Bowman, 3b, Dr. Charles Best SS, Coquitlam, B.C.**
13. **Blake Whealy, 2b, U. of Evansville.**
14. **Jeff Brewer, rhp, U. of British Columbia.**
15. Elvys Quezada, rhp, Seton Hall U.
16. **Zachary Clements, c, Christian Brothers (Tenn.) U.**
17. **Laron Wilson, of, Longwood (Va.) College.**
18. **Ivan Maldonado, rhp, Indian Hills (Iowa) CC.**
19. **Bryan King, rhp, Mesa State (Colo.) College.**
20. **Will Hudson, ss, Oregon State U.**
21. Brendan Winn, of, Brevard (Fla.) CC.
22. **Tim McNab, rhp, Florida Atlantic U.**
23. **Rashad Parker, of, UCLA.**

24. **Robert Paulk, rhp, North Florida JC.**
25. Nathan Kiser, 1b, Lebanon (Va.) HS.
26. Kyle Cullinan, 3b, Fullerton (Calif.) JC.
27. Ricky Steik, rhp, John F. Kennedy HS, La Palma, Calif.
28. Chris Munn, rhp, St. Thomas Aquinas HS, Fort Lauderdale.
29. Timothy Didjurgis, rhp, Pima (Ariz.) JC.
30. Chris Robinson, c, Lord Dorchester SS, Dorchester, Ontario.
31. Marcos Cabral, ss-2b, Southwest Miami HS, Miami.
32. Todd Dulaney, 2b, Wabash Valley (Ill.) JC.
33. Tim Jones, of, Morristown (N.J.) HS.
34. **Chase Lambin, ss, U. of Louisiana-Lafayette.**
35. John Findley, rhp, Nettleton HS, Jonesboro, Ark.
36. Joey Huskins, c, Fountain Valley (Calif.) HS.
37. Billy Weitzman, rhp, Briarcliffe (N.Y.) JC.
38. Derek Antelo, rhp, Broward (Fla.) JC.
39. Dewayne Carver, rhp, Daytona Beach (Fla.) CC.
40. Jonathan Malo, ss, Montmorency (Quebec) College.
41. Steven Romero, rhp, South Hills HS, Walnut, Calif.
42. Ryan DiPietro, lhp, Berlin HS, Kensington, Conn.
43. Jeremy Brown, of, Sylvan Hills HS, Sherwood, Ark.
44. Ian Bladergroen, 1b, Lamar (Colo.) CC.
45. Brian Rabbitt, rhp, Brookdale (N.J.) CC.
46. Doug Fink, rhp, Southington (Conn.) HS.
47. Troy Roberson, rhp, U. of Miami (Fla.).
48. Alfred Profeet, c, Delaware Tech & CC.
49. Esteban Lopez, c, Chandler (Ariz.) HS.
50. Jack Spradlin, lhp, Eastlake HS, Chula Vista, Calif.

OAKLAND (26)

■ **SCOUTING DIRECTOR:** Eric Kubota.
1. **Nick Swisher, 1b-of, Ohio State U.** (Choice from Red Sox—16th—as compensation for Type A free agent Johnny Damon).
1. **Joseph Blanton, rhp, U. of Kentucky** (Choice from Yankees—24th—as compensation for Type A free agent Jason Giambi).
1. **John McCurdy, ss, U. of Maryland.**
1. **Ben Fritz, rhp, Fresno State U.** (Choice from Cardinals—30th—as compensation for Type A free agent Jason Isringhausen).
1. **Jeremy Brown, c, U. of Alabama** (Supplemental pick—35th—for loss of Giambi).
1. **Steve Obenchain, rhp, U. of Evansville** (Supplemental pick—37th—for loss of Isringhausen).
1. **Mark Teahen, 3b, St. Mary's (Calif.) College** (Supplemental pick—39th—for loss of Damon).
2. **Steve Stanley, of, U. of Notre Dame.**
3. **Bill Murphy, lhp, Cal State Northridge.**
4. **John Baker, c, U. of California.**
5. **Mark Kiger, ss, U. of Florida.**
6. **Brian Stavisky, of, U. of Notre Dame.**
7. **Brant Colamarino, 1b, U. of Pittsburgh.**
8. **Jared Burton, rhp, Western Carolina U.**
9. **Shane Komine, rhp, U. of Nebraska.**
10. **J.R. Pickens, rhp, U. of Mississippi.**
11. **Justin Crowder, lhp, Rice U.**
12. **Kirk Nordness, of, Armstrong Atlantic State (Ga.) U.**
13. **Tyler Klippenstein, 3b, U. of Lethbridge (Alberta).**
14. **Brad Knox, rhp, Central Arizona JC.**
15. **Chris Dunwell, rhp, San Diego State U.**
16. **Lloyd Turner, 2b, Kennesaw (Ga.) State U.**
17. **David Harriman, c, Armstrong Atlantic State (Ga.) U.**
18. **Jose Corchado, rhp, Hilberto Domenech, Isabela, P.R.**
19. Dusty Barnard, rhp, Moore (Okla.) HS.
20. Trevor Crowe, ss, Westview HS, Portland, Ore.
21. Wally Pontiff, 3b, Louisiana State U.
22. **Shawn Kohn, rhp, U. of Washington.**
23. **Chris Shank, rhp, Franklin Pierce (N.H.) College.**
24. **Daniel Gibbons, of, Central Michigan U.**
25. **Steve Schilsky, rhp, Illinois Wesleyan U.**
26. **Ty Bubalo, c, Beaverton (Ore.) HS.**
27. Gregory Dupas, rhp, Arlington HS, Riverside, Calif.
28. **Andy Dickinson, lhp, U. of Illinois.**
29. **Daniel Barnett, rhp, Salt Lake (Utah) CC.**
30. Brian Rodgers, of, Berkmar HS, Lilburn, Ga.
31. Brad Ziegler, rhp, Southwest Missouri State U.
32. Justin Towles, c, Crosby (Texas) HS.
33. Nate Nelson, 1b, Holy Name Central Catholic HS, Worcester, Mass.
34. Rene Quintana, ss, Patria la Torres HS, San Sebastien, P.R.
35. Robby Jacobson, c, Durango HS, Las Vegas, Nev.
36. **Jed Morris, c, U. of Nebraska.**
37. Mark Rodrigues, rhp, Los Medanos (Calif.) JC.
38. Jason Williams, rhp, Cactus Shadows HS, Cave Creek, Ariz.
39. Joel Evans, rhp, Columbia Basin (Wash.) CC.
40. Jon Papelbon, rhp, Mississippi State U.
41. Don Sutton, 1b, Durango HS, Las Vegas, Nev.
42. Joe Ryan, rhp, Assumption HS, Davenport, Iowa.

43. Curtis White, lhp, U. of Oklahoma.
44. Ty Taubenheim, rhp, Edmonds (Wash.) CC
45. Matthew Elfeldt, rhp, Boston College.

PHILADELPHIA (17)

■ SCOUTING DIRECTOR: Marti Wolever.
1. **Cole Hamels, lhp, Rancho Bernardo HS, San Diego.**
2. **Zach Segovia, rhp, Forney (Texas) HS.**
3. **Kiel Fisher, 3b-of, Riverside Poly (Calif.) HS.**
4. **Nick Bourgeois, lhp, Tulane U.**
5. **Jake Blalock, 3b, Rancho Bernardo HS, San Diego.**
6. **Lee Gwaltney, rhp, Louisiana Tech.**
7. **Robby Read, rhp, Florida State U.**
8. Steven Doetsch, of, Dunedin (Fla.) HS.
9. **Rob Harrand, rhp, San Diego State U.**
10. **Ryan Barthelemy, 1b, Florida State U.**
11. T.J. Beam, rhp, U. of Mississippi.
12. **Trent Pratt, c, Auburn U.**
13. **Brian Manfred, c, San Diego State U.**
14. **Darin Naatjes, rhp, Stanford U.**
15. **Victor Menocal, ss, Georgia Tech.**
16. **Leslie Bramasco, ss, Long Beach CC.**
17. **Scott Mathieson, rhp, Aldergrove (B.C.) SS.**
18. **Chad Oliva, c, Jacksonville U.**
19. **Bobby Korecky, rhp, U. of Michigan.**
20. **Karl Nonemaker, of, Vanderbilt U.**
21. Brett McMillan, 3b, Ponderosa HS, Shingle Springs, Calif.
22. Brad McCann, 3b, Gulf Coast (Fla.) CC.
23. Jason Fletcher, rhp, Indian River (Fla.) CC.
24. **Whit Bryant, lhp, Elon (N.C.) College.**
25. **Zach Minor, rhp, Fresno State U.**
26. **Erik Winegarden, c, New Mexico State U.**
27. **Brad Busbin, rhp, U. of Central Florida.**
28. **Derek Brewster, rhp, Louisiana Tech.**
29. **Adam Steen, rhp, Minnesota State U.-Mankato.**
30. **Ryan Wardinsky, ss, Texas A&M U.**
31. **Jeremy Isenhower, 2b, Southwest Missouri State U.**
32. **Rob Cafiero, 1b, Villanova U.**
33. **Jeremy Rogelstad, rhp, San Jose State U.**
34. **Beau Richardson, lhp, Tulane U.**
35. **Joshua Paddock, rhp, Aurora (Ill.) U.**
36. Keahi Rawlins, rhp, Molokai HS, Kaunakakai, Hawaii.
37. **Tim Gradoville, c, Creighton U.**
38. Corey Carter, of, West Point (Miss.) HS.
39. Daniel Lewis, rhp, Folsom (Calif.) HS.
40. Brandon Joseph, of, A.J. Dimond HS, Anchorage, Alaska.
41. McCay Green, rhp, Edgewater HS, Orlando.
42. Clay Dirks, lhp, Hernando (Miss.) HS.
43. Byron Cragg, rhp, Galena HS, Reno.
44. Jacob Habsieger, lhp, Festus (Mo.) HS.
45. Sam Lecure, rhp, Helias HS, Centertown, Mo.
46. Dusty Ryan, c, Golden Valley HS, Merced, Calif.
47. Ryan Greaves, rhp, Benton Central HS, Otterbein, Ind.
48. Dennis Winn, ss, Bowling Green, Ky.

PITTSBURGH (1)

■ SCOUTING DIRECTOR: Ed Creech.
1. **Bryan Bullington, rhp, Ball State U.**
2. **Blair Johnson, rhp, Washburn HS, Topeka, Kan.**
3. **Taber Lee, ss, San Diego State U.**
4. Wardell Starling, rhp, Elkins HS, Missouri City, Texas.
5. **Alex Hart, rhp, U. of Florida.**
6. **Brad Eldred, 1b, Florida International U.**
7. **Matt Capps, rhp, Alexander HS, Douglasville, Ga.**
8. **Bobby Kingsbury, of, Fordham U.**
9. **Joseph Hicks, of, Forest Brook HS, Houston.**
10. **David Davidson, lhp, Denis Morris HS, Thorold, Ontario.**
11. **Anthony Bocchino, of, Marist College.**
12. **Brian Holliday, lhp, Moon Area HS, Moon Township, Pa.**
13. Chris Cunningham, c, U. of Arizona.
14. **John Smith, 2b, Middle Georgia JC.**
15. **Jonathan Schneider, rhp, Liberty U.**
16. **John Hummel, lhp, Schaumburg (Ill.) HS.**
17. **Chris DeMaria, rhp, Long Beach State U.**
18. Jeff Watchko, rhp, Georgia Tech.
19. Herbert Andres, rhp, W.J. Mouat HS, Abbotsford, B.C.
20. **Russ Bayer, lhp, Miami (Ohio) U.**
21. **Chris Holt, rhp, Flagler (Fla.) College.**
22. Paul Harp, rhp, Middle Georgia JC.
23. **Dean Devine, 3b-2b, U. of South Dakota.**
24. **Sam Christensen, lhp, U. of Southern Colorado.**
25. Matthew Cundiff, rhp, Cooper City (Fla.) HS.
26. Calvin Beamon, of, Smoky Hill HS, Aurora, Colo.
27. Gene Filyaw, ss, Jasper (Texas) HS.

28. Anthony Stevens, ss, South Doyle HS, Knoxville.
29. Francis Poni, c, Los Angeles Harbor JC.
30. Chris Toneguzzi, rhp, Markville SS, Thunder Bay, Ontario.
31. William Webster, c, Moon Valley HS, Phoenix.
32. Angel Colon, of, San Vicente de Paul HS, Toa Baja, P.R.
33. **Nyger Morgan, of, Walla Walla (Wash.) CC.**
34. Adam Howard, rhp, Ooltewah (Tenn.) HS.
35. Eric King, 2b, Los Medanos (Calif.) JC.
36. Ryan Aldridge, rhp, Wayne County HS, Jesup, Ga.
37. Tony Snow, rhp, Cascade HS, Everett, Wash.
38. Phillip Stillwell, rhp, North Florida JC.
39. Chase Moore, of, St. Mary's College HS, Albany, Calif.
40. Matt Maropis, ss, Franklin Regional HS, Murrysville, Pa.
41. Rollie Gibson, lhp, Buchanan HS, Fresno.
42. **Chaz Lytle, of, U. of Georgia.**
43. Michael Hicks, lhp, St. Stephens HS, Hickory, N.C.

ST. LOUIS (30)

■ SCOUTING DIRECTOR: Marty Maier.
1. (Choice to Athletics as compensation for Type A free agent Jason Isringhausen).
2. (Choice to Yankees as compensation for Type B free agent Tino Martinez).
3. **Calvin Hayes, ss, East Rowan HS, Salisbury, N.C.**
4. **Kyle Boyer, ss, Dixie (Utah) JC.**
5. Josh Bell, c, North Side HS, Jackson, Tenn.
6. **Cody Haerther, 3b, Chaminade Prep, Chatsworth, Calif.**
7. **David Williamson, lhp, U. of Massachusetts-Lowell.**
8. **Tyler Parker, c, Georgia Tech.**
9. **Travis Hanson, ss, U. of Portland.**
10. **Matt Lemanczyk, of, Sacred Heart (Conn.) U.**
11. **David Brockman, rhp, Grand Canyon U.**
12. **Bob Runyon, rhp, Fresno State U.**
13. **Reid Gorecki, of, U. of Delaware.**
14. **Joe Van Gorder, lhp, West Virginia U.**
15. **Daylon Monette, of, Oklahoma State U.**
16. **Bradley Thompson, rhp, Dixie (Utah) JC.**
17. Chad Clark, rhp, U. of Southern California.
18. **Scott Schweitzer, lhp, Kentucky Wesleyan College.**
19. Ryan Mulhern, of, U. of South Alabama.
20. **Hal Chafey, lhp, Francis Marion (S.C.) U.**
21. **Gabe Veloz, 2b, New Mexico State U.**
22. **Andy Davidson, rhp, Cal State Northridge.**
23. **Richard Scalamandre, rhp, Dominican (N.Y.) College.**
24. **Kevin Coleman, rhp, U. of Florida.**
25. **Kyle McClellan, rhp, Hazelwood West HS, Hazlewood, Mo.**
26. **Mitch Maio, rhp, U. of Utah.**
27. Matt Elliott, rhp, Basic HS, Henderson, Nev.
28. **Melvin Falu, 2b, Southern Arkansas U.**
29. **Wes Jaillet, rhp, St. Louis U.**
30. **Zach Cates, 1b, Oklahoma State U.**
31. **Garris Gonce, rhp, U. of South Carolina.**
32. Sean Kasmar, ss, Las Vegas (Nev.) HS.
33. **Joshua Bridges, c, Martin Methodist (Tenn.) College.**
34. **Mike McCoy, 2b, U. of San Diego.**
35. Julian Williams, of, Long Beach (Calif.) CC.
36. **James Mondesir, rhp, Dominican (N.Y.) College.**
37. **Tyler Durham, 2b, Northwestern State (La.) U.**
38. Matt Varner, rhp, Angelina (Texas) JC.
39. **Jeff Tolotti, of, U. of Nevada.**
40. **Brian Flynn, rhp, St. Thomas Aquinas (N.Y.) College.**
41. **Jonathan Estes, rhp, Freed-Hardeman (Tenn.) College.**
42. Kevin Estrada, ss, Pepperdine U.
43. **Joey Vandever, rhp, U. of Evansville.**
44. **Brock Jacobsen, of, Dixie (Utah) JC.**
45. Sean Clark, rhp, Chaminade Prep, Chatsworth, Calif.
46. **Jason Galbraith, lhp, Concordia (N.Y.) College.**
47. Chris Gibson 1b-of, Bellevue East HS, Bellevue, Neb.
48. Philip Perry, rhp, Georgia Tech.
49. David Denson, lhp, Valhalla HS, El Cajon, Calif.
50. John Powell, rhp, McGehee HS, Tillar, Ark.

SAN DIEGO (13)

■ SCOUTING DIRECTOR: Bill Gayton.
1. **Khalil Greene, ss, Clemson U.**
2. **Michael Johnson, 1b, Clemson U.**
3. **Kennard Jones, of, U. of Indiana.**
4. **Aaron Coonrod, rhp, John A. Logan (Ill.) JC**
5. **Sean Thompson, rhp, Thunder Ridge HS, Denver.**
6. **Adam Shorsher, c, San Jose State U.**
7. Matt Lynch, lhp, Florida State U.
8. **Luke Steidlmayer, rhp, UC Davis.**
9. **Brian Burgamy, 2b, Wichita State U.**
10. **L.J. Biernbaum, of, Florida Atlantic U.**
11. **Brandon Wilson, rhp, Okaloosa-Walton (Fla.) JC.**

12. Paul McAnulty, 1b, Long Beach State U.
13. Lance Pendleton, rhp, Kingwood (Texas) HS.
14. **Gabe Ribas, rhp, Northwestern U.**
15. **Rolando Agosto, ss, Union (Tenn.) U.**
16. **Kevin Beavers, lhp, Pepperdine U.**
17. **Rashad Smith, of, Lambuth (Tenn.) U.**
18. Michael Gallaway, lhp, Grayson County (Texas) CC.
19. Spencer Grogan, lhp, Okaloosa-Walton (Fla.) CC
20. George Kottaras, c, Connors State (Okla.) JC.
21. Andy LaRoche, ss, Grayson County (Texas) CC.
22. **David Krisch, lhp, Cal Poly Pomona.**
23. **Rusty Moore, of, Bethune-Cookman College.**
24. **Adam Montarbo, rhp-3b, Chico State (Calif.) U.**
25. Chuck Bechtel, rhp, Marist U.
26. **E.J. Laratta, rhp, Ohio State U.**
27. **Brian Whitaker, rhp, UNC Wilmington.**
28. **Mike Richardson, of-c, Sonoma State (Calif.) U.**
29. **Steve Baker, of, Liberty U.**
30. Danny Delao, lhp, Fresno CC.
31. Jared Wells, rhp, Tyler (Texas) JC.
32. Jesse Estrada, rhp, Socorro HS, El Paso, Texas.
33. Bo Banach, 3b, Lakewood (Calif.) HS.
34. Bill Silvestri, rhp, Dixie (Utah) JC.
35. Drew Macias, of, Chaffey (Calif.) JC.
36. **Greg Bochy, rhp, Cal Poly.**
37. Corey Hall, rhp, Seminole (Okla.) JC.
38. Brendan Katin, c, Okaloosa-Walton (Fla.) JC.
39. Scott Lonergan, rhp, Poway (Calif.) HS.
40. Daniel Fitch, c, Mt. Carmel HS, San Diego.
41. Ryan Werner, c, San Diego CC.
42. Brian Wahlbrink, of, UC Riverside.
43. Jason Catala, of, Margarita Janer HS, Guaynabo, P.R.
44. Marcus Barriger, rhp, Kaskaskia (Ill.) CC.
45. Chad Etheridge, of, Columbia State (Tenn.) CC.
46. Craig Bartosh, of, Grayson County (Texas) CC.
47. Stephen Nam, 1b-2b, Mississauga, Ontario
48. Matthew Morizio, rhp-ss, Waltham (Mass.) HS.
49. John Parscal, lhp, Northglenn HS, Denver.
50. Chris Regan, 1b-of, Earl Wooster HS, Reno, Nev.

SAN FRANCISCO (25)

■ SCOUTING DIRECTOR: Dick Tidrow.
1. **Matt Cain, rhp, Houston HS, Germantown, Tenn.**
2. **Freddie Lewis, of, Southern U.**
3. **Dan Ortmeier, of, U. of Texas-Arlington.**
4. **Kevin Correia, rhp, Cal Poly.**
5. **Kevin Kelly, ss, Duke U.**
6. **Jesse English, lhp, Rancho Buena Vista, Vista, Calif.**
7. Michael Musgrave, rhp, Forest HS, Ocala, Fla.
8. **Clay Hensley, rhp, Lamar U.**
9. **Randy Walter, of, Wichita State U.**
10. **Glenn Woolard, rhp, Kutztown (Pa.) U.**
11. **Jake Wald, ss, George Washington U.**
12. Kellen Ludwig, rhp, Chipola (Fla.) JC.
13. **Aaron Sobieraj, 3b, U. of Florida.**
14. **Josh Habel, lhp, U. of Northern Iowa.**
15. **Matt Dryer, 1b, U. of Miami.**
16. **Greg Bruso, rhp, UC Davis.**
17. **Luke Nelson, rhp, Southern Illinois U.**
18. **Bryan Millikan, rhp, Black Hills HS, Olympia, Wash.**
19. David Timm, lhp, Seminole (Fla.) CC.
20. **Ben Mitchell, rhp, Grand Canyon U.**
21. **Travis Ishikawa, 1b-of, Federal Way (Wash.) HS.**
22. **Nelson Lopez, rhp, Florida Atlantic U.**
23. Neil Walton, ss, Santa Cruz (Calif.) HS.
24. Jay Knowlton, ss, Lewis-Clark State (Idaho) College.
25. Justin Gee, rhp, Sarasota (Fla.) HS.
26. Sean Rierson, rhp, U. of Arizona.
27. Ryan McGovern, lhp, W.J. Mouat HS, Abbotsford, B.C.
28. Philip Tapley, rhp, Greenbrier HS, Evans, Ga.
29. Alex Hinshaw, lhp, Chaffey (Calif.) JC.
30. Matt Somnis, rhp, Lassen (Calif.) HS.
31. **Matt Palmer, rhp, Southwest Missouri State U.**
32. **Joe Bateman, rhp, Massachusetts College of Liberal Arts.**
33. Brett Cooley, 1b-of, U. of Houston.
34. Phil Monte, lhp, Cosumnes River (Calif.) JC.
35. Ryan Stevenson, rhp, Chabot (Calif.) JC.
36. **David Stone, of, U. of Virginia.**
37. Chris Sweet, rhp, U. of Virginia.
38. Randal Hodge, lhp, Pearl-Cohn HS, Nashville.
39. **Anthony Moreno, rhp, South Mountain (Ariz.) CC.**
40. Mike Redford, rhp, Woodland HS, Sacramento
41. Danny Muegge, rhp, U. of Texas.
42. **Andrew Jefferson, lhp, Southwest Missouri State U.**
43. Jason Chavez, rhp, Mineral Area (Mo.) JC.

44. Tim Torres, ss, Diablo Valley (Calif.) JC.
45. Matthew Berezay, of, Sierra HS, Manteca, Calif.
46. Matt Ircandia, lhp, Semiahmoo HS, Surrey, B.C.
47. Scott Dodge, of, Cuesta (Calif.) JC.
48. Dante Brinkley, of, Southwest Missouri State U.
49. Zach Borowiak, ss, Southeast Missouri State U.
50. Robert Davis, c, Greenbrier HS, Evans, Ga.

SEATTLE (28)

■ SCOUTING DIRECTOR: Frank Mattox.
1. John Mayberry Jr., of, Rockhurst HS, Kansas City, Mo.
2. **Josh Womack, of, Crawford HS, San Diego.**
3. Eddy Martinez-Esteve, of, Westminster Christian HS, Miami.
4. **Randy Frye, rhp, Lake Orion (Mich.) HS.**
5. **Kendall Bergdall, lhp, Cimarron HS, Layhoma, Okla.**
6. **Troy Cate, lhp, Ricks (Idaho) JC.**
7. **Evel Bastida-Martinez, 2b, Miami.**
8. **Brandon Perry, lhp, Graham (N.C.) HS.**
9. **Terry Forbes, rhp, Auburn Drive HS, Halifax, N.S.**
10. **Brian Stitt, rhp, Indian River (Fla.) CC.**
11. **Jared Thomas, lhp, Oakland (Mich.) U.**
12. **Matt Hagen, 3b, Liberty U.**
13. **T.A. Fulmer, rhp, The Citadel.**
14. **Theiborh Almanzar, c, Bronx (N.Y.) CC.**
15. Gaby Sanchez, 3b, Brito Private HS, Miami.
16. Ryan Leaist, rhp, Montreat (N.C.) College.
17. **Corey Harrington, ss, New Mexico State U.**
18. **Gary Harris, of, Georgia College.**
19. **Chris Kroski, c, St. Petersburg (Fla.) CC.**
20. **David Viane, rhp, Oakland (Mich.) U.**
21. **Eric Blakeley, 2b, U. of Indiana.**
22. **Hunter Brown, 3b, Rice U.**
23. Travis Buck, ss, Richland (Wash.) HS.
24. Johnnie Bassham, lhp, Grayson County (Texas) CC.
25. Cory Vanderhook, c, Edison HS, Fountain Valley, Calif.
26. **David Bernat, rhp, South Miami HS, Miami.**
27. Royce Dickerson, of, Central HS, Kalamazoo, Mich.
28. **Vance Hall, lhp, Allderdice HS, Pittsburgh.**
29. Michael Nesbitt, of, Los Angeles Pierce JC.
30. **T.J. Bohn, of, Bellevue (Neb.) College.**
31. Clayton Stewart, rhp, San Jacinto (Texas) JC.
32. Dane Awana, lhp, Waianae (Hawaii) HS.
33. Kyle Patrick, rhp, Apopka (Fla.) HS.
34. Brady Burrill, c, Michigan State U.
35. Patrick Pfeiffer, rhp, Brentwood School, Los Angeles
36. Jermaine Smith, ss, King HS, Tampa
37. Brad Rose, rhp, Walters State (Tenn.) JC.
38. Deandre Green, of, Encinal HS, Alameda, Calif.
39. Bryan Lahair, of, St. Petersburg (Fla.) JC.
40. Josh Cooper, rhp, South HS, Pueblo, Colo.
41. Andrew Edwards, rhp, Florida International U.
42. Brandon Jones, 1b, Grayson County (Texas) CC.
43. Adam Pernasilici, of-1b, St. Anne HS, Tecumseh, Ontario.
44. Omar Borges, of, Brito Private HS, Miami.
45. Ray Lockhart, of, Compton (Calif.) HS.
46. Roberto Mena, 2b, Pedro Falu HS, Rio Grande, P.R.
47. Jason Godin, rhp, North Stafford HS, Stafford, Va.
48. Cardoza Tucker, rhp, Bullard HS, Fresno.
49. Aaron Ruchti, c, San Jacinto (Texas) JC.
50. Oliver Arias, rhp, CC of Rhode Island.

TAMPA BAY (2)

■ SCOUTING DIRECTOR: Dan Jennings.
1. **B.J. Upton, ss, Greenbrier Christian Academy, Chesapeake, Va.**
2. **Jason Pridie, of, Prescott (Ariz.) HS.**
3. **Elijah Dukes, of, Hillsborough HS, Tampa**
4. **Wes Bankston, of, Plano East HS, Plano, Texas**
5. Mark Romanczuk, lhp, St. Mark's HS, Newark, Del.
6. Cesar Ramos, lhp, El Rancho HS, Pico Rivera, Calif.
7. **Scott Autrey, rhp, U. of North Carolina.**
8. **Joey Gomes, of, U. of Santa Clara.**
9. Chris Leroux, c, St. Joseph's SS, Mississauga, Ontario.
10. **Jason Hammel, rhp, Treasure Valley (Ore.) JC**
11. **Adam Moreno, rhp, Fresno (Calif.) HS.**
12. **Blair Irvin, of, Patterson (La.) HS.**
13. Matt Harrington, rhp, Long Beach/Western League.
14. **Nicholas DeBarr, rhp, Lassen (Calif.) JC.**
15. Mike Pelfrey, rhp, Wichita Heights HS, Wichita.
16. **Mike Prochaska, lhp, North Carolina State U.**
17. **Ernest Woodruff, c, Gulf Coast (Fla.) CC.**
18. **Romelio Lopez, rhp, Conroe (Texas) HS.**
19. **Cole Smith, rhp, Rockwall (Texas) HS.**
20. **Jarred Farrell, rhp, Hahnville HS, Boutte, La.**
21. Chris Garcia, rhp, Xaverian HS, Brooklyn, N.Y.

22. Travis Ingle, rhp, Cal State Fullerton.
23. Jacoby Ellsbury, of, Madras (Ore.) HS.
24. Adam Nikolic, of, Cal State Northridge.
25. Brian Bulger, rhp, Georgia College.
26. Jarrad LaVergne, lhp, Westgate HS, New Iberia, La.
27. Brandon Mann, lhp, Mt. Rainier HS, Des Moines, Wash.
28. Adam Olerio, rhp, North Kingston (R.I.) HS.
29. Michael McGowan, rhp, Navarro (Texas) JC.
30. Mike Geddes, rhp, Jenison (Mich.) HS.
31. Isiah Garner, lhp, U. of Arkansas-Pine Bluff.
32. Rodney Keener, lhp, Minden (La.) HS.
33. Coltyn Simmons, c, Durango HS, Las Vegas.
34. John-Austin Emmons, of, Wharton County (Texas) JC.
35. Luke Cosmos, rhp, McAteer HS, San Francisco.
36. Dionisio Muyco, c, Richland (Wash.) HS.
37. Shane Shelley, ss, Belle Chasse (La.) HS.
38. Matthew Cobb, lhp, Shelton State (Ala.) CC.
39. Brandon Rousseve, ss, Holy Cross HS, New Orleans.
40. Justin Hopes, rhp, Jeanerette (La.) HS.
41. Daron Roberts, c, Cosumnes River (Calif.) JC.
42. Brandon Federici, lhp, Riverview HS, Oakmont, Pa.
43. Steve Skinner, 2b, Santa Rosa (Calif.) JC.
44. Rolando Quinonez, c, San Juan, P.R.
45. Justin Standridge, rhp, Clay Chalkville HS, Pinson, Ala.
46. Rejino Gonzalez, lhp, CC of Southern Nevada.
47. Adam Dalby, c, Daingerfield HS, Hughes Spring, Texas.
48. Jason Urquidez, rhp, Central Arizona JC.
49. Shane Sanders, rhp, U. of Alabama.
50. Bryan Banks, rhp, St. Petersburg (Fla.) JC.

TEXAS (10)

■ **SCOUTING DIRECTOR:** Grady Fuson.
1. Drew Meyer, ss, U. of South Carolina.
2. (Choice to Dodgers as compensation for Type A free agent Chan Ho Park).
3. (Choice to Indians as compensation for Type A free agent Juan Gonzalez).
4. (Choice to Cubs as compensation for Type A free agent Todd Van Poppel).
5. (Choice to Rockies as compensation for Type B free agent Jay Powell).
6. John Barnett, rhp, Florida Southern College.
7. Andrew Tisdale, rhp, Chapman (Calif.) College.
8. Chris O'Riordan, 2b, Stanford U.
9. Steven Herce, rhp, Rice U.
10. Nate Gold, 1b, Gonzaga U.
11. Kiki Bengochea, rhp, U. of Miami.
12. Erik Thompson, rhp, Pensacola (Fla.) JC.
13. Chris Hamblen, c, U. of Cincinnati.
14. Charlie Bilezikjian, of, St. John's U.
15. Sam Narron, lhp, East Carolina U.
16. Josh Kreuzer, 1b, West Valley (Calif.) JC.
17. Chris Wilson, 3b, Redlands (Calif.) HS.
18. Cameron Coughlan, 2b, Brigham Young U.

North Carolina infielder Russ Adams was Toronto's top pick

19. Jesus Maldonado, rhp, Manuel Negron HS, Humacao, P.R.
20. Kameron Loe, rhp, Cal State Northridge.
21. Jason Mann, c, Central Alabama CC.
22. Robert Andrews, of, Rancho Buena Vista HS, Vista, Calif.
23. Craig Ringe, ss, Central Missouri State U.
24. Chad Decker, lhp, Valley View HS, Moreno Valley, Calif.
25. Joel Kirsten, lhp, Los Angeles Pierce JC.
26. Julius Smith, lhp, Lewiston (Idaho) HS.
27. John McCarthy, of, St. Rita HS, Palos Park, Ill.
28. Jake Tompkins, rhp, Louisiana State U.
29. Nick Shields, c, Wright State U.
30. Rob Corrado, rhp, U. of Kentucky.
31. Michael Tamulionis, rhp, St. John's U.
32. Gary Hogan, rhp, U. of Arkansas.
33. Larry Grayson, of, Manatee (Fla.) CC.
34. Charles Fletcher, of, North Springs HS, Atlanta.
35. Ken Pokryfke, lhp, Wilmot Union HS, Wilmot, Wis.
36. Frans Meyer, 3b, Northridge HS, Layton, Utah.
37. Dion McDaniel, rhp, Hales Franciscan HS, Chicago.
38. Robert Wachman, rhp, Middle Georgia JC.
39. Paul Sandoval, rhp-3b, Trabuco Hills HS, Mission Viejo, Calif.
40. Jared Gaston, ss-of, Cleveland (Tenn.) HS.
41. Andy Myette, rhp, Kwantlen (B.C.) JC.
42. Jesse Chavez, rhp, Riverside (Calif.) CC.
43. Ronald Harris, c, George Washington HS, Denver.
44. Ryan Mieszala, of, Greenway HS, Glendale, Ariz.
45. Tom Zimmerman, rhp, Whitnall HS, Milwaukee.
46. Josh Hernandez, c-3b, Los Lunas (N.M.) HS.
47. Paul Oseguera, lhp, La Costa Canyon HS, Carlsbad, Calif.
48. Steven Friend, ss-of, Kishwaukee (Ill.) JC.
49. Brad Burkhead, of, Northwest Mississippi CC.
50. Will Peterson, of, Valdosta (Ga.) HS.

TORONTO (14)

■ **SCOUTING DIRECTOR:** Chris Buckley.
1. Russ Adams, ss, U. of North Carolina.
2. David Bush, rhp, Wake Forest U.
3. Justin Maureau, lhp, Wichita State U.
4. Adam Peterson, rhp, Wichita State U.
5. Chad Pleiness, rhp, Central Michigan U.
6. Jason Perry, of, Georgia Tech.
7. Brian Grant, rhp, C.B. Aycock HS, Goldsboro, N.C.
8. Chris Leonard, lhp, Miami (Ohio) U.
9. Russell Savickas, rhp, Johnston (R.I.) HS.
10. Eric Arnold, 2b, Rice U.
11. Jason Waugh, of, St. Mary's (Calif.) College.
12. Michael Roga, rhp, Armstrong Atlantic State U.
13. John Schneider, c, U. of Delaware.
14. Mike Galloway, 1b-of, Miami (Ohio) U.
15. David Smith, of, West Virginia State College.
16. Aric Van Gaalen, lhp, Harry Ainlay HS, Edmonton.
17. Randy Braun, of, Belton (Mo.) HS.
18. Jordan DeJong, rhp, Cal State Fullerton.
19. Brad Hassey, ss, U. of Arizona.
20. Jesus Carnevale, Fernando Chavez HS, Arecibo. P.R.
21. Melvin Burkhalter, 1b, Seminole (Fla.) CC.
22. Eric Rico, of, Cornell U.
23. Bubbie Buzachero, rhp, Tennessee Tech.
24. Matt Farnum, rhp, Texas A&M U.
25. Zeph Zinsman, 1b, Lewis-Clark State (Idaho) College.
26. Dewan Day, rhp, Southern U.
27. Jared Odom, rhp, Vero Beach (Fla.) HS.
28. Paul Richmond, c, Baylor U.
29. Erik Kratz, c, Eastern Mennonite (Va.) U.
30. A.J. Porfirio, of, Rice U.
31. Jeff Terrell, lhp, U. of Tennessee.
32. Michael Seifert, lhp, Rend Lake (Ill.) JC.
33. Carlo Cota, 2b, San Diego State U.
34. Justin Owens, of, Coastal Carolina U.
35. Andy Torres, rhp, Lewis-Clark State (Idaho) U.
36. Scott Dragicevich, ss, Stanford U.
37. Ross Swisher, lhp, Hudson's Bay HS, Vancouver, Wash.
38. Bryan Hansen, lhp, Fontana (Calif.) HS.
39. Nick Thomas, rhp, Sacramento CC.
40. Danny Anderson, of, San Joaquin Delta (Calif.) JC.
41. Adam Carr, rhp, San Lorenzo (Calif.) HS.
42. Dirk Kleinmann, lhp, King (Tenn.) College.
43. Chris Nicoll, rhp, Righetti HS, Santa Maria, Calif.
44. Ben Harrison, lhp, Colleyville Heritage HS, Colleyville, Texas.
45. Brandon Bailey, c-of, Sacramento CC.
46. Justin Tordi, ss, Dr. Phillips HS, Orlando.
47. Tim Maloney, of, Kansas State U.
48. Andrew Butera, c, Bishop Moore HS, Orlando.
49. James Jewell, of, Roosevelt HS, Gary, Ind.
50. J. Brent Cox, rhp, Bay City (Texas) HS.

APPENDIX
OBITS/INDEX

OBITUARIES
NOVEMBER 2001-OCTOBER 2002

Fritz Ackley, a longtime minor league righthander who also appeared in five games with the White Sox over two seasons, died May 22 in Duluth, Minn. He was 65. Ackley went 1-0, 4.19 for Chicago in 1963 and '64.

Bill Adair, who had a 41-year career as a player, manager, coach and scout, died June 17 in Bay Minette, Ala. He was 89. Adair probably was best known as a minor league manager, at which he went 1,611-1,305 in 21 seasons. A longtime employee of the Braves, he was Hank Aaron's first minor league manager at Eau Claire (Northern) in 1952.

Bob Barr, a righthander for the Brooklyn Dodgers in 1935, died Aug. 1 in Dover, New Hampshire. He was 94. Barr pitched in two games for the Dodgers, but then was shipped back to the minors after he was blamed for a teammate's misconduct.

Nelson Barrera, the career leader in home runs and RBIs in the Mexican League, died of electrocution while repairing the roof of his home in Campeche, Mexico. He was 44. The ballpark in Campeche is named after Barrera, who played 25 full seasons—14 with the Mexico City Reds—and had 455 career homers, eclipsing the late Hector Espino's record by two. He played in nine games in 2002 before retiring after a knee injury. Barrera also managed in the Mexican League, leading Oaxaca to the 1998 championship and also guiding his hometown Campeche squad.

Joe Bauldree, a righthander for Allentown of the independent Northern League and a former Braves farmhand, died in his sleep on the afternoon of May 29 in Allentown, Pa. He was 25. Bauldree was 7-3, 4.22 in his four years in the Braves system. He then spent the 1999 season with Massachusetts in the Northern League East (2-2, 1.58), the 2000 campaign with New Jersey in the Atlantic League (2-6, 3.82) and 2001 with Camden in the Atlantic League (0-0, 6.06) and Allentown (2-2, 5.82).

Bo Belinsky, the 1960s lefthander famed for being a playboy as much as a pitcher, died Nov. 23, 2001, in Las Vegas. He was 64. The quintessential flash in the pan, Belinsky went 5-0 and no-hit the Orioles in his first month in the big leagues, with the Los Angeles Angels in 1962. But he finished 10-11 that year, led the American League with 122 walks and went on to a 28-51, 4.10 record in eight big league seasons with the Angels (1962-64), Phillies (1965-66), Astros (1967), Pirates (1969) and Reds (1970).

Joe Black, the former Brooklyn Dodgers and Negro Leagues righthander, died of prostate cancer May 17 in Scottsdale, Ariz. He was 78. Black gradually improved during his career with the Baltimore Elite Giants from 1943-50, and was signed by the Dodgers just as he hit his prime years. Overall he went 30-12, 3.91 in six major league seasons with the Dodgers (1952-55), Reds (1955-56) and Washington Senators (1957). Black also had a significant career after baseball, as an executive with Greyhound Lines Inc.

Jimmy Bloodworth, an infielder on the 1950 Philadelphia Phillies Whiz team, died Aug. 17 in Apalachicola, Fla. He was 85. Bloodworth was a career .248 hitter and a solid second baseman in the majors for 11 seasons from 1937-51. His best offensive year was in 1939, when he hit .289-11-70 in 318 at-bats for the Senators. He led American League second basemen in fielding during three seasons in the early 1940s.

Hank Boney, a righthander who appeared in three games for the 1927 New York Giants, died June 12 in Lake Worth, Fla. He was 98. Boney pitched four innings for New York, giving up one earned run.

Charlie Brewster, a former major league shortstop and a standout minor leaguer for many years, died Oct. 1 in

Alma, Ga. He was 84. In the majors, he batted .221-0-14 in 69 games with the Reds (1943), Phillies (1943), Cubs (1944) and Indians (1946).

Mace Brown, a former all-star Pirates righthander, died March 24 in Greensboro, N.C. He was 92. Brown pitched the last three innings of the 1938 All-Star Game for the National League, and led the league that year with 51 appearances. He also led the American League in appearances in 1943, with the Red Sox. He gave up Gabby Hartnett's famous Homer in the Gloamin' during the '38 pennant race, and overall went 76-57, 3.46 in 10 major league seasons with the Pirates (1935-41), Brooklyn Dodgers (1941) and Red Sox (1942-43, 1946).

Jack Buck, the legendary broadcaster for the Cardinals and of many other sports events, died June 18 in St. Louis. He was 77. Because of the extensive reach of KMOX radio and the television networks, most every sports fan has a set of Buck memories, though his résumé is fairly simple. The common thread is the Cardinals, for whom he broadcast games for nearly half a century, since 1954. Even before that, his minor league broadcasting experience was with Cardinals farm teams in Columbus, Ohio, and Rochester, N.Y. Just as well known for his football work, Buck shared the Monday Night Football radio booth with Hank Stram for 16 seasons, and also did baseball nationally in both media. He won the Hall of Fame's Ford Frick Award in 1987 and a lifetime-achievement Emmy in 2000.

Jack Buck

Don Carlsen, a former major leaguer, died in Denver on Sept. 22. He was 75. Carlsen was a righthander for the Chicago Cubs in 1948 and the Pittsburgh Pirates in 1951-52. He went 2-4, 6.00 in 54 innings in the majors. After retiring from baseball, Carlsen also was a founding member of the Colorado Baseball Boosters Club, which helped spearhead the drive to bring major league baseball to Denver.

Joe Cascarella, a righthander who pitched for four major league teams in five seasons, died May 22 in Baltimore. He was 94. Cascarella went 27-48, 4.84 for the Philadelphia Athletics (1934-35), Red Sox (1935-36), Washington Senators (1936-37) and Reds (1937-38).

Harry Chiti, a catcher for four major league teams, died Jan. 31 in Haines City, Fla. He was 69. Chiti batted .238-41-179 in 10 big league seasons with the Cubs (1950-52, 1955-56), Kansas City Athletics (1958-60), Tigers (1960-61) and Mets (1962). He gained notoriety near the end of his career for being traded for himself. The Indians sent him to the Mets in 1962 for a player to be named, who turned out to be Chiti.

Gene Cook, longtime general manager for Toledo (International), died Feb. 15 in Toledo. He was 70. As GM of the Mud Hens from 1978-99, and as a Toledo city councilman from 1965-95, Cook was an important force behind Fifth Third Field, which opened in 2002. Cook also was a three-sport star at the University of Toledo in the mid-1950s and later played semipro football, though he never played professional baseball.

Pete Coscarart, an all-star Brooklyn Dodgers second baseman who later became a crusader for pension and licensing money for players who retired before 1947, died of an aortic aneurysm July 24 in Escondido, Calif. He was 89. A standout fielder, Coscarart batted .243-28-269 in nine major league seasons with the Dodgers (1938-41) and Pirates (1942-46). He was a National League all-star in 1940.

Al Cowens, the runner-up to Rod Carew in 1977 American League MVP voting, died of a heart attack March 11 in Downey, Calif. He was 50. Cowens, a mainstay on Royals teams that won three straight AL West titles from 1976-78, batted .270-108-717 in 13 major league seasons with Kansas City (1974-79), the California Angels (1980), the Tigers (1980-81) and Mariners (1982-86).

Frank Crosetti, the longtime Yankees shortstop, died Feb. 11 in Stockton, Calif., of complications from a fall in January. He was 91. Crosetti played in the majors for 17 years, all with the Yankees. He played in seven World Series, and appeared in 15 more during a 20-year run as the Yankees' third-base coach. A two-time all-star, Crosetti led the American League in stolen bases with 27 in 1938, and led AL shortstops in fielding percentage the next year. Overall, he batted .245-98-649 in 1,683 major league games.

Mike Darr, an outfielder for the Padres, was killed in a one-vehicle crash Feb. 15 in Phoenix. He was 25. Darr was killed when the SUV he was driving rolled on Loop 101 in Phoenix, about five miles from the Padres' training complex. Darr's friend, former Phillies farmhand Duane Johnson, also was killed. Padres pitcher Ben Howard, also in the vehicle, escaped injury. Darr hit .273-5-67 in 542 at-bats for San Diego.

STEVE MOORE
Mike Darr

Bob Davids, founder of the Society for American Baseball Research, died Feb. 10 in Washington, D.C. He was 75. After 20 years as a freelance baseball writer and researcher, Davids gathered about 30 like-minded people at a meeting in Cooperstown on Aug. 10, 1971. They drew up a set of bylaws for what became SABR. Thirty years later, the organization, with its headquarters in Cleveland, has more than 6,000 members.

Bob Davis, a righthander who played for the Kansas City Athletics in 1958 and 1960, died Dec. 22, 2001, in New York. He was 68. An 11-8, 2.17 season for Little Rock (Southern Association) got Davis to the big leagues for eight games in '58, and he returned two years later for 21 more. He went 0-4, 5.71 in the majors.

Red Davis, a longtime minor league infielder and manager who also had a brief big league career as a third baseman, died April 26 in Laurel, Miss. He was 86. Davis' major league career consisted of 21 games for the 1941 New York Giants, during which he batted .214-0-5.

Mel Deutsch, a righthander who appeared in three games for the 1946 Red Sox, died Nov. 18, 2001, in Austin. He was 86. Deutsch pitched six innings in the majors, giving up four earned runs without any decisions. He reached Boston after four minor league seasons in which his highest ERA was 2.88.

Paul Erickson, a Cubs righthander for most of the 1940s, died April 5 in Fond du Lac, Wis. He was 86. Erickson went 37-48, 3.86 in eight years in the big leagues, nearly all with Chicago from 1941-48. He also appeared in four games for the Phillies and two for the New York Giants in '48. He also made four relief appearances in the 1945 World Series, which the Cubs lost to the Tigers in seven games.

Ralph Erickson, the oldest living former major leaguer at the time of his death, died June 27 in Chandler, Ariz. He turned 100 two days before he died. Erickson, a lefthander, pitched in one game for the Pirates in 1929 and seven more in 1930. He went 1-0, 8.40 in 15 innings.

Bill Faul, a righthander for three major league teams, died Feb. 21 in Cincinnati. He was 61. Faul went 12-16, 4.72 in six big league seasons with the Tigers (1962-64), Cubs (1965-66) and Giants (1970).

Earl Francis, a 1960s-era Pirates righthander, died July 3 in Pittsburgh. He was 66. Francis went 16-23, 3.77 in the big leagues, appearing with Pittsburgh from 1960-64 and with the Cardinals for two games in '65.

Jerry Gambardella, a sophomore first baseman at Hofstra, died Nov. 14, 2001, after collapsing during a game of touch football with other Pride players. He was 19.

Rob Garibaldi, an outfielder at Santa Rosa Junior College, Southern California and Sonoma State, died Oct. 2 in an apparent suicide in Petaluma, Calif. He was 24. Garibaldi had a stellar high school career and continued his success at Santa Rosa before moving on to Southern California.

Paul Giel, a former major league righthander and long-time athletic director at the University of Minnesota, died May 22 in Minneapolis, after collapsing in his car on the way home from a Twins-Rangers game. He was 69. Also a star football player at Minnesota, and runner-up to Notre Dame's Johnny Lattner in the 1953 Heisman Trophy voting, Giel went 11-9, 5.39 with the New York and San Francisco Giants (1954-55, 1958), the Pirates (1959-60), Twins (1961) and Kansas City Athletics (1961).

Bob Gillespie, a righthander for three major league teams, died Nov. 4, 2001 in Winston-Salem, N.C. He was 82. Gillespie went 5-13, 5.07 in 58 big league games with the Tigers (1944), White Sox (1947-48) and Red Sox (1950).

Roy Gillespie, former president of the youth baseball organization PONY Baseball, died Feb. 5 in Washington, Pa., of complications from a ruptured aneurysm. He was 73. Gillespie joined PONY Baseball as assistant to the president in 1958, became commissioner in 1964 and president in 1980, and retired in 1995. He served as a consultant and corporate secretary for the organization until his death.

Pete Gray, the famed one-armed outfielder for the St. Louis Browns, died June 30 in Scranton, Pa. He was 87. Gray, who lost his right arm in a childhood accident, batted .218-0-13 in 77 games for the Browns in 1945, his only major league experience. Still, Gray was a real baseball player and not just another Eddie Gaedel-like Browns publicity stunt. Gray, whose real name was Peter Wyshner, played eight seasons of professional ball from 1938-49.

Steve Gromek, one of the heroes of the Indians' last World Series championship in 1948, died March 12 in Clinton Township, Mich. He was 82. Gromek, a righthander, won Game Four, 2-1 as he and the Boston Braves' Johnny Sain each pitched a complete game. Overall, Gromek went 123-108, 3.41 in 17 major league seasons with the Indians (1941-53) and Tigers (1953-57).

Warren Hacker, a former righthander for the Cubs and three other major league teams, died May 22 in Lenzburg, Ill. He was 77. Hacker went 62-89, 4.21 in 12 big league seasons with the Cubs (1948-56), Reds (1957), Phillies (1957-58) and White Sox (1961). He was a dominant pitcher in 1952, when he went 15-9, 2.58 and led the National League in opponents' batting average (.212) and opponents' on-base percentage (.247).

Roger Hanners, manager of the Chillicothe Paints of the independent Frontier League from 1994-2000, died of a heart attack Jan. 24 in Chillicothe, Ohio. He was 70. Hanners also spent four years in the Yankees system, playing with Hall of Famers Mickey Mantle and Roger Maris.

Andy Hansen, a righthanded reliever for the New York Giants and the Phillies in the 1940s and '50s, died Feb. 2 in Lake Worth, Fla. He was 77. Hansen went 23-30, 4.22 in a nine-season big league career with New York (1944-45, 1947-50) and Philadelphia (1951-53).

Mel Harder, one of the best pitchers in Cleveland Indians history, died Oct. 20 in Chardon, Ohio. He was 93.

APPENDIX

Harder won 223 games in a 20-year career for the Indians. He put together his best season in 1934, as he went 20-12, 2.61 while leading the league with six shutouts. Harder won 10 or more games for 11 straight seasons from 1930-40, and he was named to the American League all-star team four times. He retired after the 1947 season. The Indians retired his number, 18, in 1990.

Mickey Haslin, an infielder for three major league teams, died March 7 in Wilkes-Barre, Pa. He was 91. Haslin batted .272-9-109 in six big league seasons with the Phillies (1933-36), Boston Braves (1936) and New York Giants (1937-38).

Raymond Hayworth, Ty Cobb's last living teammate, died Sept. 25 in Salisbury, N.C. He was 98. A catcher, Hayworth was a 17-year major leaguer who led the American League in fielding percentage in 1936. Hayworth hit .265 with five homers and 238 RBIs in 699 games in his career. He also worked as a minor league manager and director of player personnel for the Cubs and Braves.

John Hoffman, a catcher who appeared briefly for the Astros in 1964 and '65, died Dec. 27, 2001, in Seattle. He was 58. Hoffman went 3-for-21 with an RBI in the majors and played in the minors from 1963-69.

Willis Hudlin, who spent the bulk of his career with the Indians and gave up Babe Ruth's 500th homer on Aug. 11, 1929, died Aug. 5 in Little Rock. He was 96. His sidearm sinker helped him reach the seventh-most wins (157) and third-most losses (151) in Cleveland history. In 1940, he became one of nine players since 1900 to play for four teams in one season—the Indians, Washington Senators, St. Louis Browns and New York Giants.

Pancho Ito, a former public-relations director for Japan's Pacific League, a radio and television personality and an important link between baseball in Japan and America, died July 4 in Tokyo. He was 68.

Jack Jenkins, a righthander who had cups of coffee in the majors with the Washington Senators and the Dodgers, died June 18 in Tampa. He was 59. Jenkins appeared in seven games with Washington from 1962-63, then resurfaced for one game with Los Angeles in '69. He went 0-3, 4.73.

Irv Kaze, the original publicist for the Los Angeles Angels, died June 29 in Glendale, Calif. He was 75. Kaze worked for the Angels from 1961-65 after working for the Hollywood Stars (Pacific Coast) and the Pirates.

Darryl Kile, the Cardinals righthander and one of the big leagues' top pitchers in recent years, died of heart failure June 22 in his Chicago hotel room. He was 33. Kile was found hours before the start of an afternoon game against the Cubs, which was subsequently postponed. For more information on Kile's death, see the Major League and National League year-in-review stories.

Ron Kline, a 17-year major leaguer as a starter and reliever, died June 22 in Callery, Pa. He was 70. Overall, he went 114-144, 3.75 with the Pirates (1952, 1955-59, 1968-69), Cardinals (1960), Los Angeles Angels (1961), Tigers (1961-62), Senators (1963-66), Twins (1967), Giants (1969), Red Sox (1969) and Braves (1970).

Ray Knoblauch, a legendary high school coach in Bellaire, Texas, and the father of Royals outfielder Chuck Knoblauch, died of Alzheimer's disease March 18 in Houston. He was 74. Knoblauch compiled a 598-225 record as head coach at Bellaire High in suburban Houston during a 25-year career that included four state championships and three runner-up finishes.

Kazuhiko Kondo, a former star outfielder/first baseman for Japan's Taiyo Whales, died June 10 in Meguro, Japan. He was 66. A nine-time all-star in Japan's Central League, Kondo was the runner-up for the league batting title four times without ever winning one. Kondo played 16 seasons (1958-73), all but the last for the Whales, and finished in the league's top 10 in hitting nine times.

Izzy Leon, a standout pitcher in Cuba and Venezuela who later reached the big leagues for 14 games, died July 25 in Miami. He was 91. Leon, a Cuban native, went 0-4, 5.35 in his only time in the big league with the 1945 Phillies. After, he played in the U.S. minors and had seasons of 20 and 17 wins.

Johnny Lucadello, a former St. Louis Browns infielder, died Oct. 30, 2001, in San Antonio. He was 82. Lucadello batted .264-5-60 in six big league seasons, playing all but 12 games of his career with the Browns from 1938-41 and in 1946. The other 12 games were with the Yankees in '47.

Hal Marnie, a former Phillies second baseman, died Jan. 7 in Philadelphia. He was 83. Marnie batted .221-0-15 in 96 big league games, all with the Phillies from 1940-42.

Ned Martin, longtime broadcaster of Red Sox games, died July 23 at the Raleigh/Durham, N.C., airport, shortly after returning from ceremonies honoring Ted Williams the day before at Fenway Park. Martin was 79. Martin broadcast the Red Sox on radio and television from 1961 until his retirement in 1992, after beginning his career in 1956 with Charleston (American Association).

Kohei Matsuda, owner of the Hiroshima Carp of the Japanese Central League, died of stomach cancer July 10 in Tokyo. He was 80. Matsuda also was president of Toyo Kogyo, the company that developed the first rotary engine for motor vehicles and now is the Mazda Motors Corporation.

Lee Maye, an outfielder for five major league teams from 1959-71, died July 17 in Riverside, Calif. He was 67. Maye, not to be confused with first baseman Lee May (their careers overlapped), batted .274-94-419 in 13 big league seasons with the Milwaukee Braves (1959-65), Astros (1965-66), Indians (1967-69), Washington Senators (1969-70) and White Sox (1970-71).

Tom McBride, an outfielder for the Red Sox and Washington Senators in the 1940s, died Dec. 26, 2001, in Wichita Falls, Texas. He was 87. McBride hit .275-2-141 in six major league seasons with Boston (1943-47) and Washington (1947-48).

Mel McGaha, former manager of the Indians and Kansas City Athletics, died Feb. 3 in Tulsa. He was 75. McGaha joined the Indians as a coach in 1961 and managed in '62. He managed the A's for most of 1963 and part of '64 before returning to the minors as a manager and joining the Astros as a coach. He went 123-173 as a major league manager.

Jim McKee, who pitched for the Pirates in 1972-73, died Sept. 14 in Pickaway County, Ohio, in a car accident. He was 55. McKee pitched five innings for the Pirates in 1972 and 27 for them in 1973. He retired after the 1974 season.

Bob Meccage, pitching coach at Trinity (Texas) University, was found dead in his hotel room May 17, while the team was in Round Rock, Texas, for an NCAA Division III regional. He was 45.

Frank Messer, former broadcaster of White Sox, Orioles and Yankees games, died Nov. 13, 2001, in Deerfield Beach, Fla. He was 76. Messer probably was best known for his television and radio work with the Yankees, over the last 16 seasons of his career before his retirement in 1984. He emceed Yankees old-timers' day for many years after that.

Briggs Miles, a former owner and general manager of the Winston-Salem franchise in the Carolina League, died April 21 in Winston-Salem, N.C. He was 75. Miles was involved with the franchise from the late 1960s until the late 1970s.

Bill Mueller, a former major league outfielder, died Oct. 24, 2001, in Glenview, Ill. He was 80. Mueller, who began his minor league career as a pitcher, played for the White Sox in 1942 and '45, batting .149-0-5 in 39 big league games.

Joe Murray, a lefthander who appeared in eight games for the 1950 Philadelphia Athletics, died Oct. 19, 2001, in San Clemente, Calif. He was 80. Murray earned a callup to the A's with a 20-14, 2.94 season with West Palm Beach (Florida International). He went 0-3, 5.70 in Philadelphia, making two starts and six relief appearances.

Dick O'Connell, a former Red Sox general manager, died Aug. 18 in Lexington, Mass. He was 87. O'Connell joined the Red Sox in 1949 and became executive vice president and GM in 1965. The Red Sox won at least 83 games while under his leadership as GM from 1965-77, and they went to the World Series in 1967 and 1975. Boston also led the AL in attendance for five of those years. He was inducted into the Red Sox hall of fame in 1997.

Sam Page, a righthander who appeared in four games for the 1939 Philadelphia Athletics, died May 29 in Greenville, S.C. He was 86. Page went 0-3, 6.95 for the A's, starting in three of his four outings in the same year he led the Eastern League with 49 appearances for Williamsport.

Wally Pontiff, the regular third baseman at Louisiana State, was found dead by family members July 24 in his parents' home in Metairie, La. He was 21. Pontiff played three seasons at LSU and was a team captain and spokesman. A popular player with fans and teammates, he was trying to decide whether to return to LSU for his senior season or sign with the Athletics, who selected him in the 21st round of the June 2002 draft.

Eddie Popowski, a player, manager and coach in the Red Sox organization for 65 years, died Dec. 4 in Sayreville, N.J. He was 88. Best known as a major league coach for the Red Sox' World Series teams in 1967 and 1975, Popowski joined the organization as a second baseman in 1937 after a stint with the House of David barnstorming team. His 10-year playing career peaked with one season in the American Association, and he became a player-manager in the low minors after that. Popowski's teams finished first 14 times in his 21 seasons as a minor league manager. He also was twice interim manager of the big league team, going 5-4 in 1969 and 1-0 in 1973.

Darrell Porter, who played 17 years in the major leagues, died in Kansas City on Aug. 5. He was 50. Porter was found dead near his car in a park in a Kansas City suburb. A medical examiner said Porter had a level of cocaine in his system, and while he did not die of an overdose, it was determined to be the cause of death. The 1982 World Series MVP for the Cardinals, Porter battled substance abuse throughout his career. He hit .247-188-826 overall with the Brewers (1971-76), Royals (1977-80), Cardinals (1981-85) and Rangers (1986-87).

Darrell Porter

Willie Powell, the Braves' area scout for Alabama, Georgia and North Florida, died Jan. 31 in Prattville, Ala. He was 49. Powell, who was based in Pensacola, Fla., was the brother of former Twins and Blue Jays outfielder Hosken Powell.

Tom Purcell, a successful coach at Division III North Central (Ill.), died of a heart attack Oct. 29, 2001, in Joliet, Ill. He was 49. Purcell was head coach at North Central for 13 seasons, ending in 1993.

Steve Rachunok, a righthander who appeared in two games for the 1940 Brooklyn Dodgers, died May 11 in Corona, Calif. He was 85. Rachunok made a start and a relief appearance for the Dodgers, going 0-1, 4.50 in 10 innings.

Minnie Rojas, a righthander who led the American League in saves in 1967 before his career was cut short when he was paralyzed in an auto accident, died of complications from pneumonia March 24 in Los Angeles. He was 63. Rojas played three seasons in the majors with the California Angels from 1966-68, before the accident paralyzed him from the neck down. He had 27 saves in '67, and also went 12-9, 2.52. Overall, he was 23-16, 3.00.

John Roseboro, a major league catcher who played from 1957-70 mostly with the Dodgers, died Aug. 16 in Los Angeles. He was 69. A lefthanded hitter, he had a lifetime average of .249 in 14 seasons with the Dodgers, Twins and Washington Senators. He was a member of the NL all-star team in 1958, '61 and '62 and the AL team in 1969. Roseboro ended his playing career with Washington in 1970 and coached for the Senators in 1971 and the California Angels from 1972-74. He was a Dodgers minor league batting instructor in 1977-78, and a minor league catching instructor in 1987.

Steve Roser, a righthander for the Yankees and Boston Braves, died Feb. 8 in Utica, N.Y. He was 84. Roser went 6-5, 4.04 in three major league seasons with New York (1944-46) and Boston (1946).

Ben Sankey, a Pirates shortstop from 1929-31, died Oct. 14, 2001, in Washington, Ga. He was 94. Sankey hit .213-0-14 in 72 games with Pittsburgh, his only major league team.

Ted Sepkowski, a former utilityman for the Indians and Yankees, died March 8 in Severna Park, Md. He was 78. Sepkowski batted .231-0-1 in 19 major league games, spread across three years with Cleveland (1942, 1946-47) and New York (1947).

Spec Shea, an American League all-star as a Yankees rookie in 1947, died July 19 in New Haven, Conn. He was 81. Shea went 14-5, 3.07 for the '47 Yankees, leading the AL in winning percentage (.734) and average against (.200). He was equally successful in that year's World Series, going 2-0 in three starts as the Yankees beat the Brooklyn Dodgers in seven games. Overall, Shea went 56-46, 3.80 in eight major league seasons with the Yankees (1947-49, 1951) and Washington Senators (1952-55).

Willie Simms, a leadoff hitter on the 1942 Negro League champion Kansas City Monarchs, died on May 20, 2002 in Perris, Calif. He was 93. Simms played for three teams during a career that stretched from 1934-1943.

Al Silvera, a 1950s bonus baby who had a brief career as an outfielder with the Reds, died July 24 in Los Angeles. He was 66. Under existing bonus rules, Silvera opened his professional career in the big leagues, and batted .143-0-2 in just 13 games in 1955. After making just a pinch-running appearance the next year, he finally went to the minors and played through 1958.

Enos Slaughter, a Hall of Fame outfielder who spent most of his career with the Cardinals, died Aug. 12 in Durham, N.C. Known mostly for his hustle, Slaughter was instantly famous after his "mad dash" in the 1946 World Series, scoring from first base on Harry Walker's base hit in the eighth inning of Game Seven. He hit .300-169-1,304 in 19 seasons with the Cardinals (1938-53), Yankees (1954-55, 56-59), Kansas City Athletics (1955-56) and Milwaukee Braves (1959).

Al Smith, a two-time all-star as a major league outfielder/third baseman from 1953-64, died Jan. 3 in Hammond, Ind. He was 73. Smith led the American League with 123 runs in 1955, when he made his first all-star game with the Indians. He was an all-star again in 1960 with the White Sox. He played in the 1954 and '59 World Series, going a combined 8-for-34 with a home run. Overall, Smith batted .272-164-676 with the Indians (1953-57, 1964), White Sox (1858-62), Orioles (1963) and Red Sox (1964).

Clay Smith, a former major league righthander, died March 5 in Cambridge, Kan. He was 87. Smith appeared in four games for the 1938 Indians and 14 more for the 1940 Tigers, going 1-1, 5.49 for his major league career. Despite that short tenure, he appeared in a World Series, working four innings in relief in Game Four in 1940, allowing one run in a 5-2 loss to the Reds.

Hank Soar, best known as a longtime American League umpire but a man who had significant careers before and after that, died Dec. 24, 2001, in Pawtucket, R.I. He was 87.

Soar was an AL umpire from 1950-75, working five World Series (he was at first base for Don Larsen's perfect game in 1956) and three All-Star Games. He became the league's umpiring supervisor for several years after '75. Soar also was a significant pro football player with the New York Giants from 1938-46, playing in five NFL championship games.

Steve Souchock, an outfielder/first baseman who played for the Yankees, White Sox and Tigers, died July 28, in Westland, Mich. He was 83. Souchock broke into the majors with the Yankees in 1946 and made it back to New York in 1948. He was traded to the White Sox for the 1949 season and then to the Tigers. He finished with a .255 lifetime batting average and had 50 home runs in 473 major league games.

Jim Spencer, a former American League all-star first baseman, died of a heart attack Feb. 10 in Fort Lauderdale. He was 54. Spencer won two Gold Gloves and led AL first basemen in fielding percentage four times. He played in the 1973 All-Star Game while with the Rangers, and appeared in the postseason three times. He went 2-for-12 for the Yankees in the 1978 World Series, which New York won in six games over the Dodgers. Overall, Spencer batted .250-146-599 in 15 major league seasons with the California Angels (1968-73), Rangers (1973-75), White Sox (1976-77), Yankees (1978-81) and Athletics (1981-82).

Red Steiner, a catcher for the Indians and Red Sox in 1945, died Nov. 16, 2001, in Gardena, Calif. He was 86. Steiner batted .190-0-6 in 38 big league games, then became one of the players banned for jumping to the Mexican League the next year.

Ernie Stewart, a former American League umpire, died Nov. 15 in Oceanside, Calif. He was 92. Stewart served as an AL umpire from 1941-45, after a three-week playing career as an outfielder for Portland (Pacific Coast) in 1934.

Tom Sunkel, a lefthander for three major league teams and a longtime minor league player and manager, died April 6 in Paris, Ill. He was 89. Sunkel went 9-15, 4.53 in six big league seasons with the Cardinals (1937, 1939), New York Giants (1941-43) and Brooklyn Dodgers (1944).

Karl Swanson, the oldest living former major leaguer at the time of his death, died April 3 in Rock Island, Ill. He was 101. Swanson, a second baseman, played for the White Sox for 22 games in 1928 and two more in '29, batting .138-0-6. He had a much more distinguished minor league career, leading the Mississippi Valley League in stolen bases three times and batting more than .300 four times in 13 years.

Fred Taylor, a hall of fame Ohio State basketball coach, died Jan. 6 in Columbus. He was 77. Taylor played in 22 big league games for the Washington Senators from 1950-52, going 9-for-47 with four RBIs. His Ohio State basketball teams won the 1960 national championship and advanced to the Final Four three other times.

Jack Tighe, who spent the better part of 60 years in the game, mostly as a manager, died Aug. 1 in Pompano Beach, Fla. He was 88. In 1942, Tighe was a coach with the Tigers. He became a scout for Detroit in 1954 and then was named the Tigers manager from 1957-58. He guided the team to a 78-76 record and fourth-place finish in 1957, then was fired after the team got off to a 21-28 start in '58.

Jim Toomey, longtime assistant general manager and public-relations director for the Cardinals, died of brain cancer March 24 in St. Louis. He was 84. Toomey spent 38 years in the Cardinals front office before retiring in 1987. He stayed on as a consultant to the team until 1994, and as an official scorer through 2000. The Busch Stadium press box is named for him.

Gary Vitto, senior director and special assistant to Tigers president John McHale Jr., died of cancer Dec. 9, 2001, in Detroit. He was 59. Vitto joined the Tigers as an assistant general manager in 1992, and was senior director of corporate sales from 1995-98.

Jim Warfield, longtime trainer for the Indians, died July 16 in Cleveland, a day after suffering a brain hemorrhage at Jacobs Field. He was 60. Warfield had been the Indians' trainer for 32 years.

Wes Westrum, who was probably best known as a New York Giants catcher but also was a manager, coach and scout, died May 28 in Clearbrook, Minn. He was 79. Westrum batted .217-96-315 in an 11-year major league career, all with the Giants from 1947-57. He holds the unusual distinction of being named to the All-Star Game twice (in 1952 and '53), but never appearing in the game. Westrum later managed the Mets from the middle of the 1965 season until late in 1967, and the San Francisco Giants from mid-1974 through '76.

Bill Wickert, former president of the California League and briefly a minor league first baseman, died May 11 in Kerrville, Texas. He was 78. Wickert helped run the Pirates' complex in Bradenton, Fla., beginning in 1970, and was elected Cal League president in 1976, succeeding Eddie Mulligan. He served until 1981.

Whitey Wietelmann, a former Boston Braves middle infielder and longtime Padres employee, died at his home in San Diego on March 26. He was 83. Wietelmann batted .232-7-122 in nine big league seasons from 1939-47, almost all with the Braves. He played 48 games for the Pirates in '47. After his major league career, Wietelmann became a fixture in San Diego baseball, playing and coaching for the city's Pacific Coast League team and coaching for the big league Padres from their inception in 1969. He served the Padres in a variety of capacities until his retirement after the 1993 season.

Del Wilber, a former major league catcher and coach, died July 18 in St. Petersburg, Fla. He was 83. Wilber batted .242-19-115 in eight big league seasons with the Cardinals (1946-49), Phillies (1951-52) and Red Sox (1952-54). He also coached in the big leagues for the White Sox (1955-56), Washington Senators (1970) and Rangers (1973).

Hoyt Wilhelm, a Hall of Fame knuckleball righthander, died Aug. 24 in Sarasota, Fla. He was 80. Wilhelm was one of the most durable pitchers in history, retiring days shy of his 49th birthday with a 143-122, 2.52 record and 227 saves. His 1,070 career games remained the most in history until passed by one in 1998 by Dennis Eckersley, who was then passed by Jesse Orosco the following year. Wilhelm also played for the Cardinals, Indians, California Angels, Atlanta Braves, Cubs, White Sox and Los Angeles Dodgers. Later he served as a coach with the Yankees.

Ellis Williams, a former minor leaguer and big league scout, died Sept. 3 in Colton, Calif. He was 55. Williams, who died after complications following surgery, was an area scout for the Tigers.

Ted Williams died July 5 in Crystal River, Fla. He was 83. The last man to hit .400—his 6-for-8 doubleheader on the last day of the season in 1941, which raised his average from .3996 to .406 is the stuff of legend—Williams was known for his irascibility, his keen knowledge of the strike zone, a pair of eyes that helped him become John Glenn's wingman in the Navy during World War II, and the unfortunate events surrounding his death. For more on Williams, see the Major League year-in-review story.

Bob Wren, the head coach during Ohio University's baseball glory days, died June 11 in Athens, Ohio. He was 81. The Bobcats' winningest coach, Wren went 464-160-4 in 24 seasons (1949-72). His teams never had a losing season, won 11 Mid-American Conference titles and went 2-2 in the 1970 College World Series, including a win over No. 1-ranked Southern California.

Ray Yochim, a righthander who appeared in four games for the Cardinals and the brother of Pirates senior advisor Lenny Yochim, died Jan. 26 in New Orleans. He was 79. Yochim pitched once for the Cards in 1948 and three times in '49, going 0-0, 10.80 in 3⅓ innings overall.

INDEX GENERAL INFORMATION

A

Alaska League 448
All-America Team
  College 396
  High School 434
  Summer Amateur 440
All-Star Game
  Major League 20
  Futures Game 281
  Triple-A 284
  Double-A 285
All-Star Team
  Independent Leagues 349
  Major Leagues 10
  Minor League/Classification 282
  Minor League/Overall 280
  Winter Leagues 381
American League
  Best Tools 37
  Club Batting, Pitching Statistics 40
  Composite Box Scores, AL Playoffs 41
  Department Leaders 38
  Postseason Awards 40
  Standings 33
  Year-by-Year Champions 32
  Year-by-Year Leaders: Batting 34
  Year-by-Year Leaders: Pitching 36
Appalachian League
  Club Batting, Pitching Statistics 317
  Department Leaders 317
  Standings 316
Arizona Fall League 387
Arizona League
  Club Batting, Pitching Statistics 321
  Department Leaders 321
  Standings 320
Atlantic Collegiate League 443
Atlantic League 351

B

Baseball For The Ages 453
Best Tools Surveys
  American League 37
  Minor Leagues 288
  National League 49

C

California League
  Club Batting, Pitching Statistics 303
  Department Leaders 303
  Standings 302
Cape Cod League 443
Caribbean Series 381
Carolina League
  Club Batting, Pitching Statistics 305
  Department Leaders 305
  Standings 304
Central Illinois League 446
Central League 354
Clark Griffith League 449
Coastal Plain League 446
Collective Bargaining Agreement 8
College Baseball
  All-America Team 396
  Coach of Year 398
  College World Series 391
  Conference Statistics 408
  Freshman of Year 399
  Junior College 427
  NAIA 427
  National Leaders 400
  NCAA Division II 426
  NCAA Division III 426
  NCAA Regionals/Super-Regionals 394
  Player of Year 393
  Statistics, Top 25 403
  Year-by-Year Champions 392
Cuban League 374

D

Debuts, Major League 2002 24
Dominican Summer League 324
Dominican Winter League 383
Draft, First-Year Player
  Bonus Escalations 455
  Club-by-Club Selections 463
  Major League Contracts 457
  Top 100 Picks 459
  Unsigned Picks 462

E

Eastern League
  Club Batting, Pitching Statistics 297
  Department Leaders 297
  Standings 296
Executive of Year, Major League 18

F

Florida State League
  Club Batting, Pitching Statistics 307
  Department Leaders 307
  Standings 306
Freitas Awards 289
Frontier League 357

G

Golden Spikes Award 439
Great Lakes League 446
Gulf Coast League
  Club Batting, Pitching Statistics 323
  Department Leaders 323
  Standings 322

H

Hall of Fame Inductions 23
High School
  All-America Team 434
  Player of Year 431
  State Champions 432
  Top 50 430
  Year-by-Year National Champions 429
Holland League (Dutch) 379

I

International League
  Club Batting, Pitching Statistics 292
  Department Leaders 292
  League Champions 291
  Standings 290
Italian League 379

J

Japanese League 375
Jayhawk League 449
Junior College 427

K

Korea Baseball Organization 377

M

Manager of Year, Major League 18
Manager of Year, Minor League 279
Managerial Changes, Major Leagues 19
Mexican League 372
Mexican Pacific League 384
Midwest League
  Club Batting, Pitching Statistics 309
  Department Leaders 309
  Standings 308
Minor Leagues
  All-Star Team 280
  Best Tools 288
  Classification All-Stars 282
  Department Leaders 286
  Double-A All-Star Game 285
  Freitas Awards 289
  Futures Game 281
  Manager of Year 279
  Organization Standings 275
  Player of Year 277
  Team of Year 278
  Triple-A All-Star Game 284

N

National League
  Best Tools 49
  Club Batting, Pitching Statistics 52
  Composite Box Scores, NL Playoffs 53
  Department Leaders 50
  Postseason Awards 52
  Standings 45
  Year-by-Year Champions 44
  Year-by-Year Leaders: Batting 46
  Year-by-Year Leaders: Pitching 48
New England Collegiate League 447
New York Collegiate League 447
New York-Penn League
  Club Batting, Pitching Statistics 313
  Department Leaders 313
  Standings 312
Northern League 361
Northwest League
  Club Batting, Pitching Statistics 315
  Department Leaders 315
  Standings 314
Northwoods League 448

O

Obituaries 474
Organization of the Year 14
Organization Standings 275
Organization Top 10 Prospects 333

P

Pacific Coast League
  Club Batting, Pitching Statistics 295
  Department Leaders 295
  League Champions 294
  Standings 293
Panamanian League 388
Pioneer League
  Club Batting, Pitching Statistics 319
  Department Leaders 319
  Standings 318
Player of Year
  College 393
  High School 431
  Independent 350
  Major League 6
  Minor League 277
  Summer Amateur 440
  Winter Leagues 382
  Youth 441
Prospect Rankings
  Organization Top 10 Prospects 333
  Prospect Position Rankings 328
  Top 20 Prospects, by League 330
  Top 100 Prospects 332
Puerto Rican League 385

R

Rookie of Year, Major League 16

S

Shenandoah Valley League 448
South Atlantic League
  Club Batting, Pitching Statistics 311
  Department Leaders 311
  Standings 310
Southern League
  Club Batting, Pitching Statistics 299
  Department Leaders 299
  Standings 298
Southeastern League 368
Summer Amateur
  All-America Team 440
  Champions 451
  Player of the Year 440

T

Taiwanese Leagues 378
Team USA 436
Texas League
  Club Batting, Pitching Statistics 301
  Department Leaders 301
  Standings 300
Top 100 Prospects 332
Top 20 Prospects, by League 330

V

Venezuelan Summer League 326
Venezuelan Winter League 386

W

Western League 368
World Junior Championship 438
World Series
  Box Scores 29
  Year-by-Year Champions 26

Y

Youth Baseball
  National Champions 451
  Top Youth Teams 450
  Player of Year 441

APPENDIX

INDEX MAJOR & MINOR LEAGUE CLUBS

AMERICAN LEAGUE
Anaheim 56
Baltimore 77
Boston 85
Chicago 92
Cleveland 114
Detroit 129
Kansas City 150
Minnesota 171
New York 186
Oakland 202
Seattle 245
Tampa Bay 252
Texas 259
Toronto 267

NATIONAL LEAGUE
Arizona 63
Atlanta 70
Chicago 99
Cincinnati 106
Colorado 122
Florida 137
Houston 144
Los Angeles 157
Milwaukee 164
Montreal 178
New York 194
Philadelphia 209
Pittsburgh 216
St. Louis 223
San Diego 230
San Francisco 238

INTERNATIONAL LEAGUE
Buffalo 116
Charlotte 94
Columbus 188
Durham 254
Indianapolis 166
Louisville 108
Norfolk 196
Ottawa 180
Pawtucket 87
Richmond 72
Rochester 79
Scranton/Wilkes-Barre 211
Syracuse 269
Toledo 131

PACIFIC COAST LEAGUE
Calgary 139
Colorado Springs 124
Edmonton 173
Fresno 240
Iowa 101
Las Vegas 159
Memphis 225
Nashville 218
New Orleans 146
Oklahoma 261
Omaha 152
Portland 232
Sacramento 204
Salt Lake 58
Tacoma 247
Tucson 65

EASTERN LEAGUE
Akron 117
Altoona 219
Binghamton 197
Bowie 80
Erie 132
Harrisburg 181
New Britain 174
New Haven 226
Norwich 189
Portland 139
Reading 212
Trenton 88

SOUTHERN LEAGUE
Birmingham 95
Carolina 125
Chattanooga 109
Greenville 73
Huntsville 167
Jacksonville 160
Mobile 233
Orlando 255
Tennessee 270
West Tenn 102

TEXAS LEAGUE
Arkansas 59
El Paso 66
Midland 205
Round Rock 147
San Antonio 248
Shreveport 241
Tulsa 262
Wichita 153

CALIFORNIA LEAGUE
Bakersfield 255
High Desert 168
Lake Elsinore 234
Lancaster 67
Modesto 206
Rancho Cucamonga 59
San Bernardino 248
San Jose 241
Stockton 110
Visalia 207

CAROLINA LEAGUE
Frederick 81
Kinston 118
Lynchburg 220
Myrtle Beach 74
Potomac 227
Salem 126
Wilmington 154
Winston-Salem 96

FLORIDA STATE LEAGUE
Brevard County 182
Charlotte 263
Clearwater 213
Daytona 103
Dunedin 271
Fort Myers 175
Jupiter 140
Lakeland 133
St. Lucie 198
Sarasota 89
Tampa 190
Vero Beach 160

MIDWEST LEAGUE
Beloit 168
Burlington 154
Cedar Rapids 60
Clinton 183
Dayton 111
Fort Wayne 235
Kane County 141
Lansing 103
Michigan 147
Peoria 228
Quad City 176
South Bend 67
West Michigan 134
Wisconsin 249

SOUTH ATLANTIC LEAGUE
Asheville 126
Augusta 90
Capital City 199
Charleston, S.C. 256
Charleston, W.Va. 272
Columbus 119
Delmarva 82

Greensboro 191
Hagerstown 242
Hickory 221
Kannapolis 97
Lakewood 213
Lexington 148
Macon 75
Savannah 264
South Georgia 161

NEW YORK-PENN LEAGUE
Aberdeen 83
Auburn 272
Batavia 214
Brooklyn 200
Hudson Valley 257
Jamestown 142
Lowell 90
Mahoning Valley 120
New Jersey 228
Oneonta 135
Staten Island 192
Tri-City 149
Vermont 184
Williamsport 221

NORTHWEST LEAGUE
Boise 104
Eugene 236
Everett 250
Salem-Keizer 243
Spokane 155
Tri-City 127
Vancouver 207
Yakima 68

APPALACHIAN LEAGUE
Bluefield 83
Bristol 97
Burlington 121
Danville 75
Elizabethton 176
Johnson City 229
Kingsport 201
Martinsville 149
Princeton 258
Pulaski 265

PIONEER LEAGUE
Billings 112
Casper 128
Great Falls 162
Idaho Falls 237
Medicine Hat 273
Missoula 69
Ogden 169
Provo 61

ARIZONA LEAGUE
Angels 62
Athletics 208
Brewers 170
Cubs 105
Giants 244
Mariners 251
White Sox 98

GULF COAST LEAGUE
Braves 76
Dodgers 163
Expos 185
Marlins 143
Orioles 84
Phillies 215
Pirates 222
Rangers 266
Red Sox 91
Reds 113
Royals 156
Tigers 135
Twins 177
Yankees 193

APPENDIX